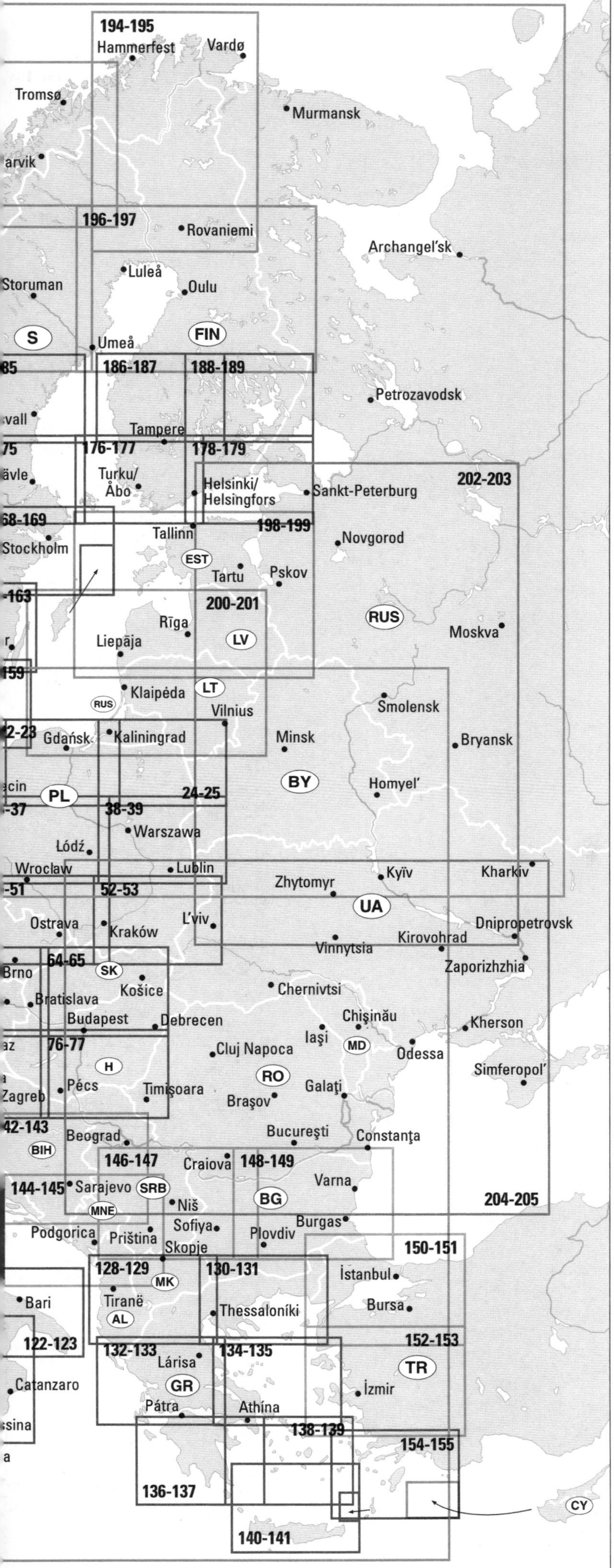

KEY TO MAPS
QUADRO D'UNIONE
MAPA ÍNDICE
TABLEAU D'ASSEMBLAGE
KARTENÜBERSICHT

Scale-Scala-Escala
Échelle-Maßstab
1 : 8 000 000

1 cm = 80 km **1 inch = 126.26 miles**

0 100 200 300 400 500 km
0 50 100 150 200 250 300 miles

Scale-Scala-Escala
Échelle-Maßstab
1 : 3 000 000

1 cm = 30 km **1 inch = 47.35 miles**

0 50 100 150 200 km
0 25 50 75 100 miles

Scale-Scala-Escala
Échelle-Maßstab
1 : 1 500 000
(Is. Canarias, Madeira, Açores 1 : 2 000 000)

1 cm = 15 km **1 inch = 23.67 miles**

0 25 50 75 100 km
0 20 40 60 miles

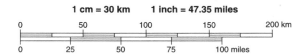

Scale-Scala-Escala
Échelle-Maßstab
1 : 1 000 000

1 cm = 10 km **1 inch = 15.78 miles**

0 10 20 30 40 50 60 km
0 5 10 15 20 25 30 35 miles

Scale-Scala-Escala
Échelle-Maßstab
1 : 800 000

1 cm = 8 km **1 inch = 12.63 miles**

0 10 20 30 40 50 km
0 5 10 15 20 25 30 miles

LOCAL FORM FORMA LOCALE FORMA LOCAL FORME LOCALE LOKALFORM		GB	I	E	F	D
A	**Österreich**	Austria	Austria	Austria	Autriche	Österreich
AL	**Shqipëria**	Albania	Albania	Albania	Albanie	Albanien
AND	**Andorra, Andorre**	Andorra	Andorra	Andorra	Andorre	Andorra
B	**België, Belgique**	Belgium	Belgio	Bélgica	Belgique	Belgien
BG	**Bălgarija**	Bulgaria	Bulgaria	Bulgaria	Bulgarie	Bulgarien
BIH	**Bosna i Hercegovina**	Bosnia and Herzegovina	Bosnia ed Erzegovina	Bosnia-Herzegovina	Bosnie-Herzégovine	Bosnien-Herzegowina
BY	**Belarus'**	Belarus	Bielorussia	Bielorrusia	Biélorussie	Weißrußland
CH	**Schweiz, Suisse, Svizzera**	Switzerland	Svizzera	Suiza	Suisse	Schweiz
CY	**Kýpros, Kıbrıs**	Cyprus	Cipro	Chipre	Chypre	Zypern
CZ	**Česká Republika**	Czech Republic	Repubblica Ceca	República Checa	République Tchèque	Tschechische Republik
D	**Deutschland**	Germany	Germania	Alemania	Allemagne	Deutschland
DK	**Danmark**	Denmark	Danimarca	Dinamarca	Danemark	Dänemark
E	**España**	Spain	Spagna	España	Espagne	Spanien
EST	**Eesti**	Estonia	Estonia	Estonia	Estonie	Estland
F	**France**	France	Francia	Francia	France	Frankreich
FIN	**Suomi, Finland**	Finland	Finlandia	Finlandia	Finlande	Finnland
FL	**Fürstentum Liechtenstein**	Liechtenstein	Liechtenstein	Liechtenstein	Liechtenstein	Liechtenstein
FR	***Føroyar, Færøerne***	*Faeroe Islands*	*Isole Fær Øer*	*Islas Feroe*	*Îles Féroé*	*Färöer*
GB	**Great Britain**	Great Britain	Gran Bretagna	Gran Bretaña	Grande-Bretagne	Grossbritannien
GBG	***Guernsey, Guernesey***	*Guernsey*	*Guernsey*	*Guernesey*	*Guernesey*	*Guernsey*
GBJ	***Jersey***	*Jersey*	*Jersey*	*Jersey*	*Jersey*	*Jersey*
GBM	***Isle of Man, Mona***	*Isle of Man*	*Isola di Man*	*Isla de Man*	*Île de Man*	*Insel Man*
GBZ	***Gibraltar***	*Gibraltar*	*Gibilterra*	*Gibraltar*	*Gibraltar*	*Gibraltar*
GR	**Hellas**	Greece	Grecia	Grecia	Grèce	Griechenland
H	**Magyarország**	Hungary	Ungheria	Hungría	Hongrie	Ungarn
HR	**Hrvatska**	Croatia	Croazia	Croacia	Croatie	Kroatien
I	**Italia**	Italy	Italia	Italia	Italie	Italien
IRL	**Ireland**	Ireland	Irlanda	Irlanda	Irlande	Irland
IS	**Ísland**	Iceland	Islanda	Islandia	Islande	Island
L	**Lëtzebuerg, Luxembourg**	Luxembourg	Lussemburgo	Luxemburgo	Luxembourg	Luxemburg
LT	**Lietuva**	Lithuania	Lituania	Lituania	Lituanie	Litauen
LV	**Latvija**	Latvia	Lettonia	Letonia	Lettonie	Lettland
M	**Malta**	Malta	Malta	Malta	Malte	Malta
MC	**Principauté de Monaco**	Monaco	Monaco	Mónaco	Monaco	Monaco
MD	**Moldova**	Moldova	Moldova	Moldavia	Moldavie	Moldau
MK	**Makedonija**	Macedonia	Macedonia	Macedonia	Macédoine	Makedonien
MNE	**Crna Gora**	Montenegro	Montenegro	Montenegro	Montenegro	Montenegro
N	**Norge**	Norway	Norvegia	Noruega	Norvège	Norwegen
NIR	***Northern Ireland***	*Northern Ireland*	*Irlanda del Nord*	*Irlanda del Norte*	*Irlande du Nord*	*Nordirland*
NL	**Nederland**	Netherlands	Paesi Bassi	Países Bajos	Pays-Bas	Niederlande
P	**Portugal**	Portugal	Portogallo	Portugal	Portugal	Portugal
PL	**Polska**	Poland	Polonia	Polonia	Pologne	Polen
RO	**România**	Romania	Romania	Rumanía	Roumanie	Rumänien
RSM	**San Marino**	San Marino	San Marino	San Marino	Saint-Marin	San Marino
RUS	**Rossija**	Russia	Russia	Rusia	Russie	Rußland
S	**Sverige**	Sweden	Svezia	Suecia	Suède	Schweden
SK	**Slovensko**	Slovakia	Slovacchia	Eslovaquia	Slovaquie	Slowakei
SLO	**Slovenija**	Slovenia	Slovenia	Eslovenía	Slovénie	Slowenien
SRB	**Srbija**	Serbia	Serbia	Serbia	Serbie	Serbien
TR	**Türkiye Cumhuriyeti**	Turkey	Turchia	Turquia	Turquie	Türkei
UA	**Ukraïna**	Ukraine	Ucraina	Ucrania	Ukraine	Ukraine
V	**Città del Vaticano**	Vatican City	Città del Vaticano	Ciudad del Vaticano	Cité du Vatican	Vatikanstadt

ROAD ATLAS
ATLANTE STRADALE
ATLAS DE CARRETERAS
ATLAS ROUTIER
STRASSENATLAS

EUROPE
EUROPA

Contents

II-III Legend
IV-V Northern Europe 1: 8 000 000 scale
VI-VII Southern Europe 1: 8 000 000 scale
VIII-1 Driver information
2-205 **Road atlas**
206-253 City and urban routes
254-304 Index of names

Sommario

II-III Legenda
IV-V Europa settentrionale 1: 8 000 000
VI-VII Europa meridionale 1: 8 000 000
VIII-1 Informazioni utili
2-205 **Atlante stradale**
206-253 Città e aree urbane
254-304 Indice dei nomi

Sumario

II-III Leyenda
IV-V Europa norte 1: 8 000 000
VI-VII Europa sur 1: 8 000 000
VIII-1 Direcciones útiles
2-205 **Atlas de carreteras**
206-253 Ciudades y áreas urbanas
254-304 Índice de topónimos

Sommaire

II-III Légende
IV-V Europe nord 1: 8 000 000
VI-VII Europe sud 1: 8 000 000
VIII-1 Informations utiles
2-205 **Atlas routier**
206-253 Villes et aires urbaines
254-304 Index des noms

Inhaltsverzeichnis

II-III Zeichenerklärung
IV-V Nördliche Europa 1: 8 000 000
VI-VII Südliche Europa 1: 8 000 000
VIII-1 Nützliche Auskünfte
2-205 **Straßenatlas**
206-253 Städte und Zufahrten
254-304 Namenverzeichnis

GB Legend	I Legenda
Toll-free motorway, dual carriageway	Autostrada senza pedaggio a doppia carreggiata
Toll-free motorway, single carriageway	Autostrada senza pedaggio a singola carreggiata
Toll motorway, dual carriageway	Autostrada a pedaggio a doppia carreggiata
Toll motorway, single carriageway	Autostrada a pedaggio a singola carreggiata
Interchange; restricted interchange; service area	Svincolo; svincolo con limitazione; area di servizio
Motorway under construction (opening year)	Autostrada in costruzione (anno di apertura)
Motorway in tunnel	Autostrada in galleria
Number of motorway; european road; national road; regional or local road	Numero di autostrada; itinerario europeo; strada nazionale; strada regionale o locale
National road, dual carriageway	Strada nazionale a doppia carreggiata
National road, single carriageway	Strada nazionale a singola carreggiata
Regional road, dual carriageway	Strada regionale a doppia carreggiata
Regional road, single carriageway	Strada regionale a singola carreggiata
Local road, dual carriageway	Strada locale a doppia carreggiata
Local road, single carriageway	Strada locale a singola carreggiata
Secondary road	Strada secondaria
Road under construction (opening year)	Strada in costruzione (anno di apertura)
Road in tunnel	Strada in galleria
Motorway distances in kilometres (miles in United Kingdom and Ireland)	Distanze in chilometri (miglia nel Regno Unito e Irlanda) sulle autostrade
Road distances in kilometres (miles in United Kingdom and Ireland)	Distanze in chilometri (miglia nel Regno Unito e Irlanda) sulle strade
Gradient 14% and over; gradient 6%–13%	Pendenza maggiore del 14%; pendenza dal 6% al 13%
Panoramic routes	Percorsi panoramici
Pass with height and winter closure	Passo di montagna, quota e periodo di chiusura invernale
Toll point	Barriera di pedaggio
Railway and tunnel	Ferrovia e tunnel ferroviario
Ferry route (with car transportation) and destination	Linea di traghetto (con trasporto auto) e destinazione
Transport of cars by rail	Trasporto auto per ferrovia
National park, natural reserve	Parco nazionale, riserva naturale
International boundaries	Confini internazionali
Disputed boundary; internal boundary	Confine in contestazione; confine interno
International airport	Aeroporto internazionale
Religious building; Castle, fortress	Edificio religioso; Castello, fortezza
Isolated monument	Monumento isolato
Ruins, archaeological area; wall	Rovine, area archeologica; vallo, muraglia
Cave; natural curiosity	Grotta; curiosità naturale
Panoramic view	Punto panoramico
Other curiosities (botanical garden, zoo, amusement park etc.)	Altre curiosità (giardino botanico, zoo, parco divertimenti ecc.)
Town or place of great tourist interest	Città o luogo di grande interesse turistico
Interesting town or place	Città o luogo interessante
Other tourist town or place	Altra città o luogo turistico
Ski resort, mountain tourist resort	Stazione sciistica o di turismo montano
Area covered and page number of more detailed maps in this atlas	Area e numero di pagina delle mappe di dettaglio presenti nell'atlante

	Ⓔ Leyenda	Ⓕ Légende	Ⓓ Zeichenerklärung
	Autopista de doble vía sin peaje	Autoroute sans péage à chaussées séparées	Zweibahnige Autobahn ohne Gebühr
	Autopista de una vía sin peaje	Autoroute sans péage à chaussée unique	Einbahnige Autobahn ohne Gebühr
	Autopista de doble vía de peaje	Autoroute à péage et chaussées séparées	Zweibahnige Autobahn mit Gebühr
	Autopista de una vía de peaje	Autoroute à péage et chaussée unique	Einbahnige Autobahn mit Gebühr
12 13 S	Acceso; acceso parcial; estación de servicio	Échangeur; échangeur partiel; aire de service	Anschlussstelle; Autobahnein- und/oder -ausfahrt; Tankstelle
2009	Autopista en construcción (año de apertura)	Autoroute en construction (année d'ouverture)	Autobahn in Bau (Fertigstellungsjahr)
	Túnel en autopista	Tunnel autoroutier	Autobahntunnel
A11 E50 N13 D951	Número de autopista; carretera europea; carretera nacional; carretera regional o local	Numéro d'autoroute; route européenne; route nationale; route régionale ou locale	Straßennummer: Autobahn; Europastraße; Nationalstraße; Regional- oder Lokalstraße
	Carretera nacional de doble vía	Route nationale à chaussées séparées	Zweibahnige Nationalstraße
	Carretera nacional de vía unica	Route nationale à chaussée unique	Einbahnige Nationalstraße
	Carretera regional de doble vía	Route régionale à chaussées séparées	Zweibahnige Regionalstraße
	Carretera regional de vía unica	Route régionale à chaussée unique	Einbahnige Regionalstraße
	Carretera local de doble vía	Route locale à chaussées séparées	Zweibahnige Lokalstraße
	Carretera local de vía unica	Route locale à chaussée unique	Einbahnige Lokalstraße
	Carretera secundaria	Route secondaire	Nebenstraße
2009	Carretera en construcción (año de apertura)	Route en construction (année d'ouverture)	Straße in Bau (Fertigstellungsjahr)
	Túnel en carretera	Tunnel routier	Straßentunnel
63	Distancias en kilómetros (millas en Gran Bretaña e Irlanda) en autopista	Distances autoroutières en kilomètres (miles en Royaume-Uni et Irlande)	Autobahnentfernungen in Kilometern (Meilen in Großbritannien und Irland)
23	Distancias en kilómetros (millas en Gran Bretaña e Irlanda) en carretera	Distances routières en kilomètres (miles en Royaume-Uni et Irlande)	Straßenentfernungen in Kilometern (Meilen in Großbritannien und Irland)
	Pendientes superiores al 14%; pendientes entre 6%–13%	Pente 14% et outre; pente 6%–13%	Steigungen über 14%; Steigungen 6%–13%
	Rutas panorámicas	Routes panoramiques	Aussichtsstraßen
Col d'Izoard 2360 10-6	Puerto de montaña con altura y cierre invernal	Col avec altitude et fermeture en hiver	Pass mit Höhe und Wintersperre
	Peaje	Barrière de péage	Gebührenstelle
	Ferrocarril y túnel	Chemin de fer et tunnel	Eisenbahn und Tunnel
Bastia	Línea marítima (con transporte de coches) y destino	Ligne de navigation (bac pour voitures) et destination	Schiffahrtslinie (Autofähre) und Ziel
	Transporte de coches por ferrocarril	Transport de voitures par chemin de fer	Autoverladung per Bahn
	Parque nacional, reserva natural	Parc national, réserve naturelle	Nationalpark, Naturschutzgebiet
	Límites internacionales	Frontières internationales	Staatsgrenzen
	Frontera en disputa; límite interno	Frontière en contestation; frontière intérieure	Strittige Grenze; Verwaltungsgrenze
	Aeropuerto internacional	Aéroport international	Internationaler Flughafen
	Edificio religioso; Castillo, fortaleza	Édifice religieux; Château, château-fort	Religiösgebäude; Schloss, Festung
	Monumento aislado	Monument isolé	Alleinstehendes Denkmal
	Ruinas, zona arqueológica; muralla	Ruines, site archéologique; vallum, muraille	Ruinen, archäologisches Ausgrabungsgebiet; Wall, Mauer
	Cueva; paraje de interés natural	Grotte; curiosité naturelle	Höhle; Natursehenswürdigkeit
	Vista panorámica	Vue panoramique	Rundblick
★	Otras curiosidades (jardín botánico, zoo, parque de atracciones etc.)	Autres curiosités (jardin botanique, zoo, parc d'attractions etc.)	Andere Sehenswürdigkeiten (Botanischer Garten, Zoo, Freizeitpark usw.)
LONDON	Ciudad o lugar de gran interés turístico	Localité ou site de grand intérêt touristique	Ortschaft oder Platz von großem touristischen Interesse
RAVENNA	Ciudad o lugar interesante	Localité ou site remarquable	Sehenswerte Ortschaft oder Platz
MONTPELLIER	Otra ciudad o lugar turístico	Autre localité ou site touristique	Andere touristischen Ortschaft oder Platz
Zermatt	Estación de esquí, localidad turística de montaña	Station de ski, localité touristique de montagne	Skistation, Touristenort in den Bergen
216	Área geográfica cubierta y número de página de otros mapas más detallados en este atlas	Zone couverte et numéro de page pour des cartes plus détaillées dans cet atlas	Abgedecktes Gebiet und Seitennummer von ausführlicheren Karten in diesem Atlas

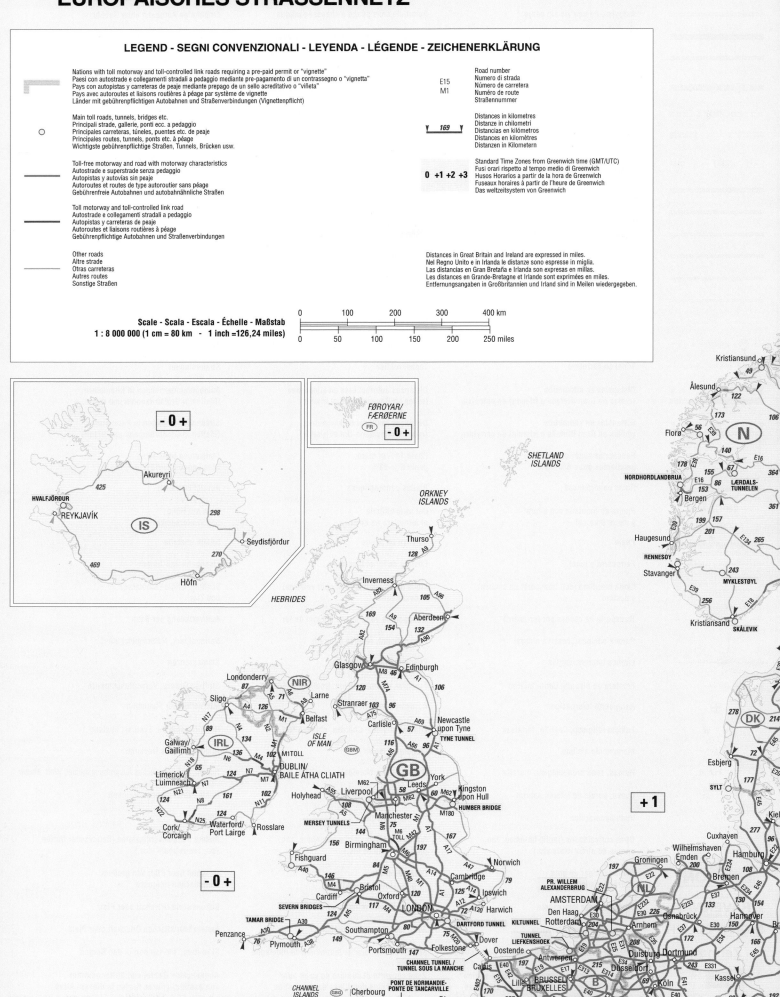

EUROPEAN ROAD NETWORK   RETE STRADALE EUROPEA
RED EUROPEA DE CARRETERAS   RÉSEAU ROUTIER EUROPÉEN
EUROPÄISCHES STRASSENNETZ

LEGEND - SEGNI CONVENZIONALI - LEYENDA - LÉGENDE - ZEICHENERKLÄRUNG

Nations with toll motorway and toll-controlled link roads requiring a pre-paid permit or "vignette"
Paesi con autostrade e collegamenti stradali a pedaggio mediante pre-pagamento di un contrassegno o "vignetta"
Pays con autopistas y carreteras de peaje mediante prepago de un sello acreditativo o "viñeta"
Pays avec autoroutes et liaisons routières à péage par système de vignette
Länder mit gebührenpflichtigen Autobahnen und Straßenverbindungen (Vignettenpflicht)

Main toll roads, tunnels, bridges etc.
Principali strade, gallerie, ponti ecc. a pedaggio
Principales carreteras, túneles, puentes etc. de peaje
Principales routes, tunnels, ponts etc. à péage
Wichtigste gebührenpflichtige Straßen, Tunnels, Brücken usw.

Toll-free motorway and road with motorway characteristics
Autostrade e superstrade senza pedaggio
Autopistas y autovías sin peaje
Autoroutes et routes de type autoroutier sans péage
Gebührenfreie Autobahnen und autobahnähnliche Straßen

Toll motorway and toll-controlled link road
Autostrade e collegamenti stradali a pedaggio
Autopistas y carreteras de peaje
Autoroutes et liaisons routières à péage
Gebührenpflichtige Autobahnen und Straßenverbindungen

Other roads
Altre strade
Otras carreteras
Autres routes
Sonstige Straßen

E15
M1

Road number
Numero di strada
Número de carretera
Numéro de route
Straßennummer

169

Distances in kilometres
Distanze in chilometri
Distancias en kilómetros
Distances en kilomètres
Distanzen in Kilometern

0 +1 +2 +3

Standard Time Zones from Greenwich time (GMT/UTC)
Fusi orari rispetto al tempo medio di Greenwich
Husos Horarios a partir de la hora de Greenwich
Fuseaux horaires à partir de l'heure de Greenwich
Das weltzeitsystem von Greenwich

Distances in Great Britain and Ireland are expressed in miles.
Nel Regno Unito e in Irlanda le distanze sono espresse in miglia.
Las distancias en Gran Bretaña e Irlanda son expresas en millas.
Les distances en Grande-Bretagne et Irlande sont exprimées en miles.
Entfernungsangaben in Großbritannien und Irland sind in Meilen wiedergegeben.

Scale - Scala - Escala - Échelle - Maßstab
1 : 8 000 000 (1 cm = 80 km - 1 inch =126,24 miles)

0 100 200 300 400 km
0 50 100 150 200 250 miles

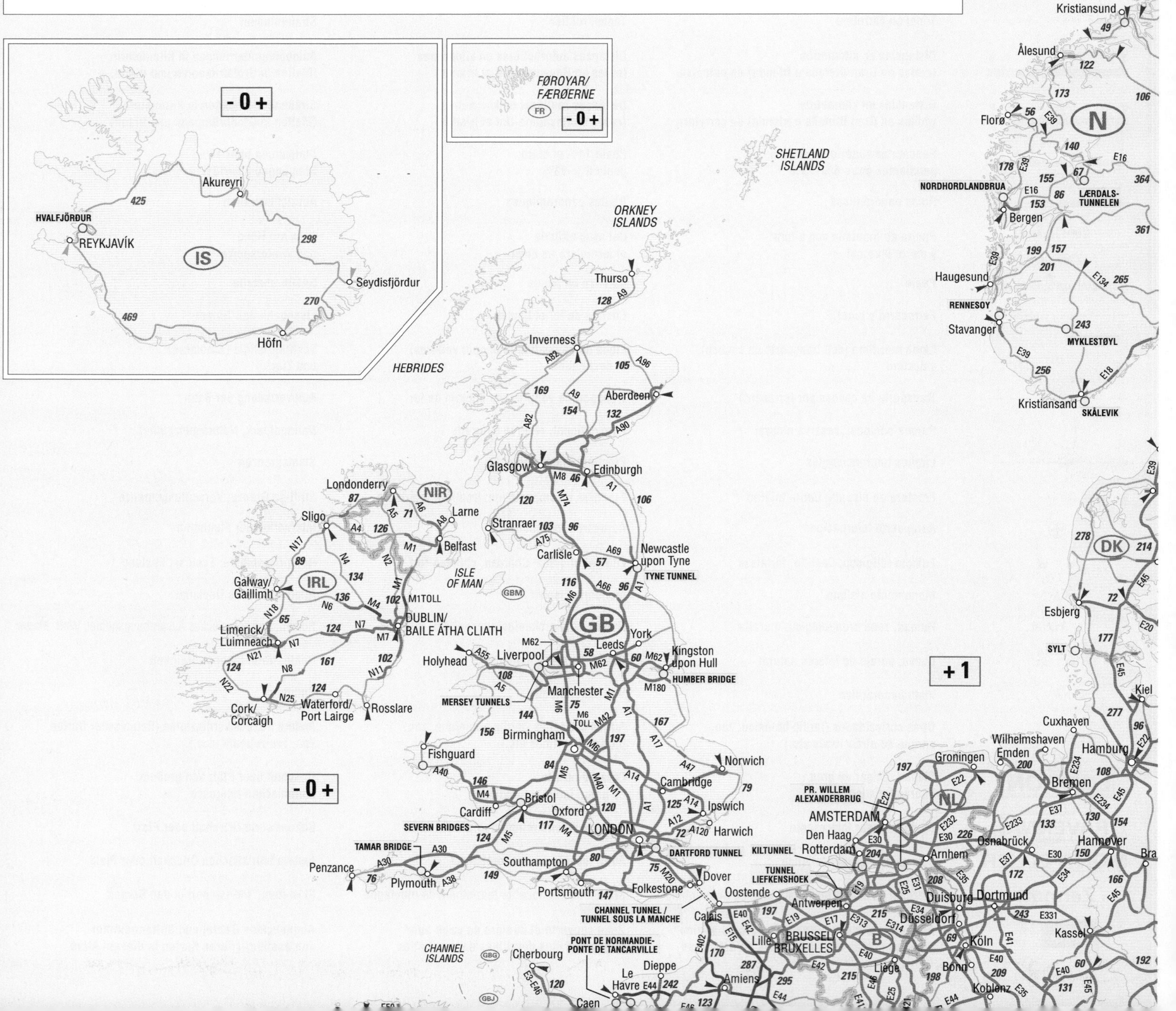

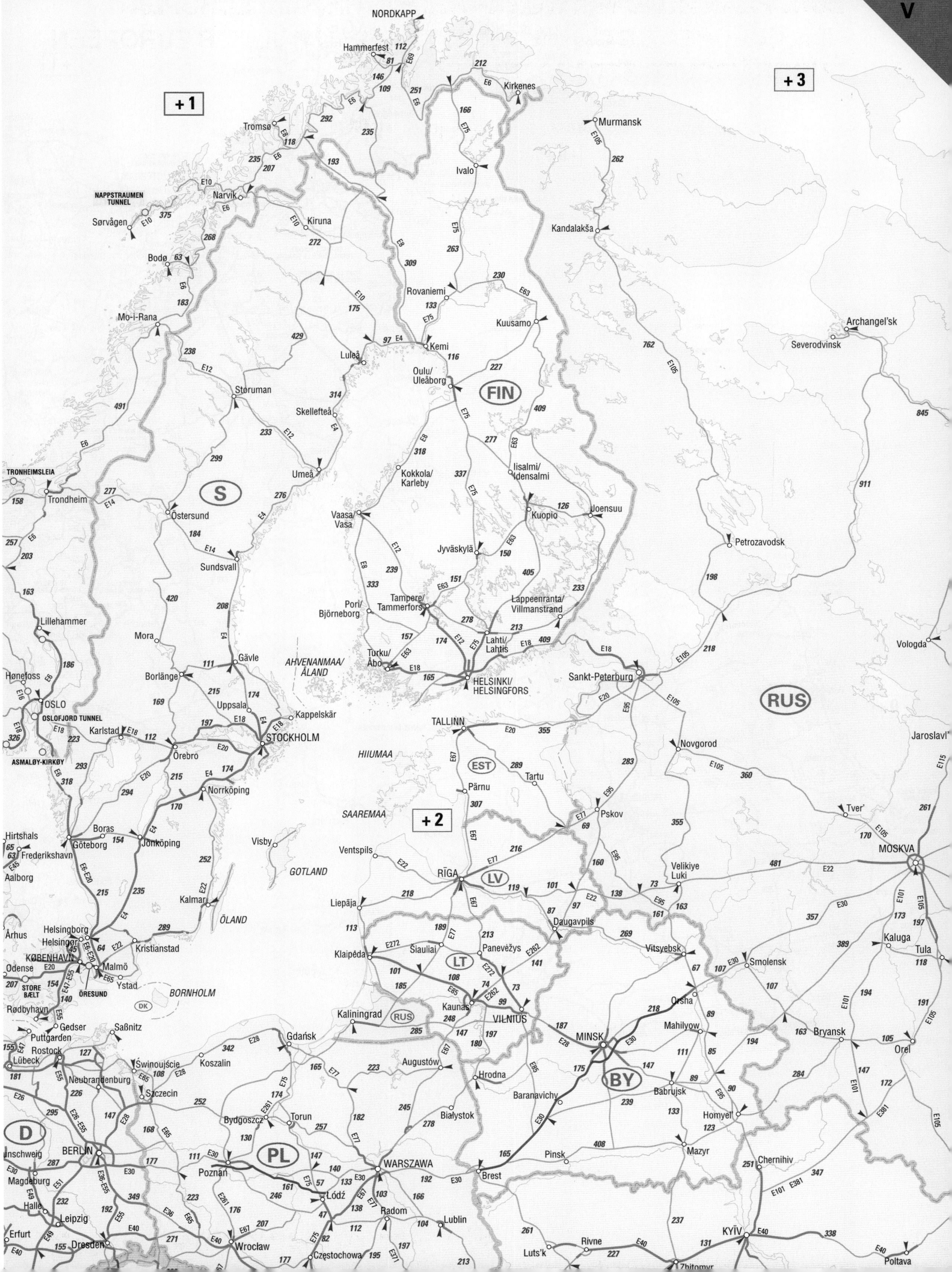

NORDKAPP
Hammerfest
Kirkenes
Murmansk
+3
+1
Tromsø
Ivalo
NAPPSTRAUMEN TUNNEL
Narvik
Sørvågen
Kiruna
Kandalakša
Bodø
Rovaniemi
Kuusamo
Mo-i-Rana
Kemi
Archangel'sk
Severodvinsk
Luleå
Oulu/ Uleåborg
Storuman
FIN
Skellefteå
Umeå
Iisalmi/ Idensalmi
Kokkola/ Karleby
TRONHEIMSLEIA
S
Trondheim
Östersund
Vaasa/ Vasa
Kuopio
Joensuu
Petrozavodsk
Jyväskylä
Sundsvall
Tampere/ Tammerfors
Pori/ Björneborg
Lappeenranta/ Villmanstrand
Lillehammer
Mora
Lahti/ Lahtis
Vologda
Gävle
Turku/ Åbo
AHVENANMAA/ ÅLAND
Borlänge
HELSINKI/ HELSINGFORS
Sankt-Peterburg
Hønefoss
OSLO
Uppsala
Kappelskär
RUS
OSLOFJORD TUNNEL
TALLINN
Karlstad
STOCKHOLM
ASMALØY-KIRKØY
Örebro
HIIUMAA
Novgorod
Jaroslavl'
EST
Tartu
Norrköping
Pärnu
Pskov
SAAREMAA
+2
Tver'
Hirtshals
Göteborg
Boras
Jönköping
Frederikshavn
Visby
Ventspils
MOSKVA
Aalborg
GOTLAND
RĪGA
LV
Velikiye Luki
Kalmar
Liepāja
ÖLAND
Daugavpils
Helsingborg
Helsingør
Århus
Kristianstad
Klaipėda
Šiauliai
Panevėžys
Kaluga
Tula
KØBENHAVN
Malmö
Vitsyebsk
Smolensk
Odense
LT
STORE BÆLT
ØRESUND
Ystad
BORNHOLM
DK
Orsha
Rødbyhavn
Kaunas
Gedser
Kaliningrad
RUS
VILNIUS
Mahilyow
Puttgarden
Saßnitz
Gdańsk
MINSK
Bryansk
Rostock
Orel
Lübeck
Świnoujście
Koszalin
Augustów
Hrodna
Neubrandenburg
BY
Szczecin
Babrujsk
Baranavichy
Homyel'
D
Bydgoszcz
Torun
Białystok
PL
Mazyr
Pinsk
unschweig
BERLIN
Chernihiv
Poznań
WARSZAWA
Brest
Magdeburg
Łódź
Halle
Leipzig
Radom
Lublin
Erfurt
Dresden
Wrocław
Częstochowa
Luts'k
Rivne
KYÏV
Poltava
Zhitomyr

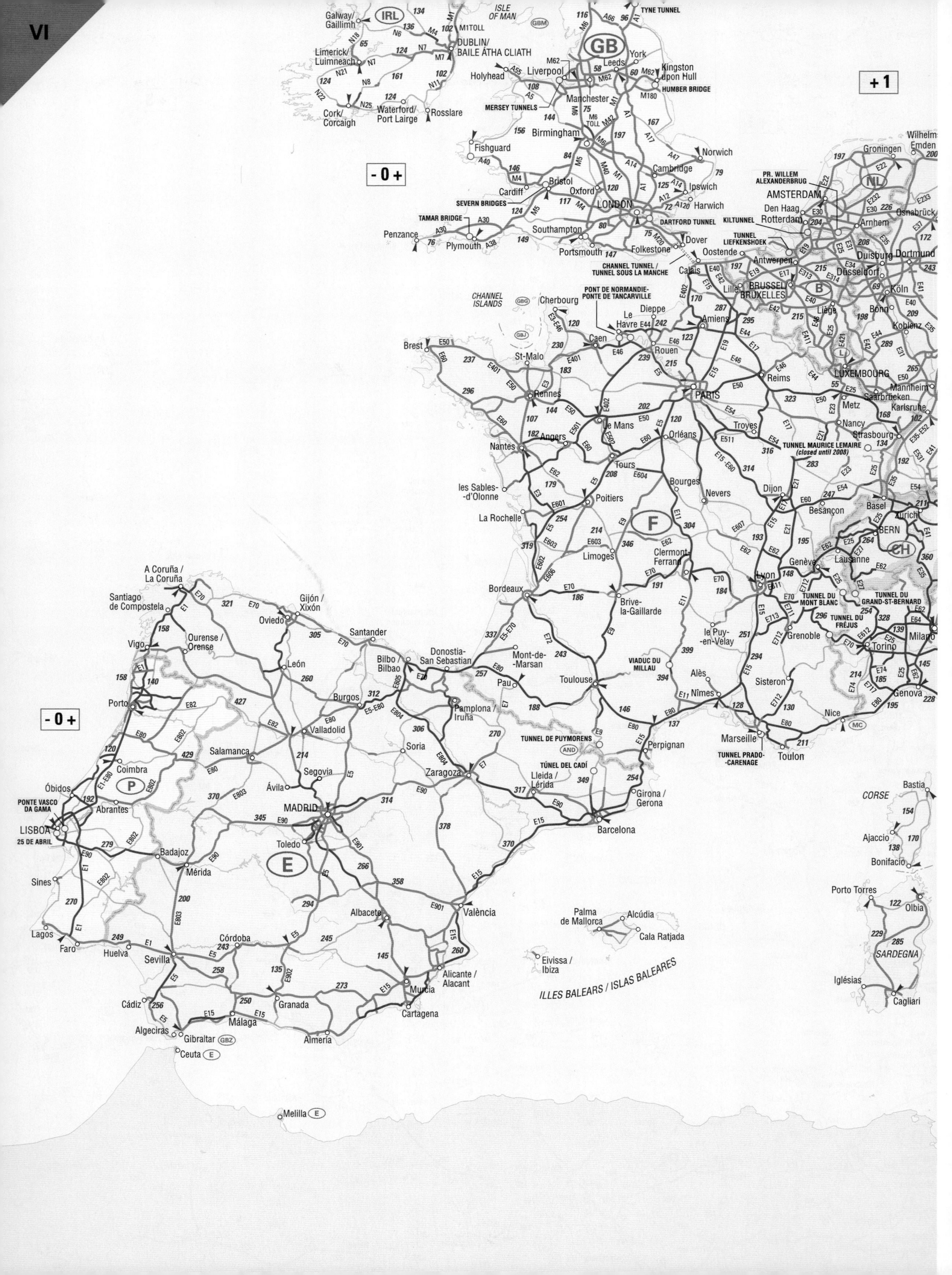

IRL
GB
GBM
ISLE OF MAN
TYNE TUNNEL
Galway/ Gaillimh
Limerick/ Luimneach
DUBLIN/ BAILE ÁTHA CLIATH
Cork/ Corcaigh
Waterford/ Port Lairge
Rosslare
Holyhead
Liverpool
Leeds
York
Kingston upon Hull
HUMBER BRIDGE
Manchester
MERSEY TUNNELS
Birmingham
Norwich
Fishguard
Cambridge
Ipswich
Harwich
Cardiff
Bristol
Oxford
LONDON
SEVERN BRIDGES
TAMAR BRIDGE
DARTFORD TUNNEL
Penzance
Plymouth
Southampton
Portsmouth
Dover
Folkestone
+1
- 0 +
Wilhelm
Emden
Groningen
PR. WILLEM ALEXANDERBRUG
AMSTERDAM
NL
Den Haag
Rotterdam
KILTUNNEL
Arnhem
Osnabrück
TUNNEL LIEFKENSHOEK
Oostende
Antwerpen
Duisburg
Dortmund
Düsseldorf
CHANNEL TUNNEL / TUNNEL SOUS LA MANCHE
Calais
Lille
BRUSSEL/ BRUXELLES
B
Köln
Liège
Bonn
Koblenz
CHANNEL ISLANDS
GBG
GBJ
Cherbourg
PONT DE NORMANDIE- PONTE DE TANCARVILLE
Dieppe
Le Havre
Amiens
Caen
Rouen
Brest
St-Malo
LUXEMBOURG
L
Reims
PARIS
Mannheim
Saarbrücken
Karlsruhe
Metz
Rennes
Le Mans
Nancy
Strasbourg
Troyes
Angers
Nantes
Orléans
TUNNEL MAURICE LEMAIRE (closed until 2008)
Tours
Bourges
Nevers
Dijon
les Sables- -d'Olonne
Poitiers
Basel
Zürich
Besançon
La Rochelle
F
BERN
CH
Limoges
Clermont- Ferrand
Genève
Lausanne
Bordeaux
Lyon
TUNNEL DU MONT BLANC
TUNNEL DU GRAND-ST-BERNARD
Brive- la-Gaillarde
TUNNEL DU FRÉJUS
Grenoble
le Puy- -en-Velay
Torino
Milano
Mont-de- Marsan
VIADUC DU MILLAU
Pau
Toulouse
Alès
Nîmes
Sisteron
Genova
Nice
MC
Marseille
Toulon
TUNNEL PRADO- CARENAGE
TUNNEL DE PUYMORENS
AND
Perpignan
TÚNEL DEL CADÍ
Lleida / Lérida
Girona / Gerona
Barcelona
A Coruña / La Coruña
Santiago de Compostela
Gijón / Xixón
Oviedo
Santander
Ourense / Orense
Vigo
León
Bilbo / Bilbao
Donostia- San Sebastian
Burgos
Pamplona / Iruña
Porto
Valladolid
Soria
Salamanca
Zaragoza
Coimbra
P
Segovia
Ávila
Óbidos
PONTE VASCO DA GAMA
Abrantes
MADRID
LISBOA
25 DE ABRIL
Toledo
Badajoz
Mérida
E
Sines
València
Albacete
Lagos
Faro
Huelva
Córdoba
Sevilla
Alicante / Alacant
Murcia
Cartagena
Granada
Cádiz
Málaga
Almería
Algeciras
Gibraltar
GBZ
Ceuta
Melilla
Palma de Mallorca
Alcúdia
Cala Ratjada
Eivissa / Ibiza
ILLES BALEARS / ISLAS BALEARES
CORSE
Bastia
Ajaccio
Bonifacio
Porto Torres
Olbia
SARDEGNA
Iglésias
Cagliari

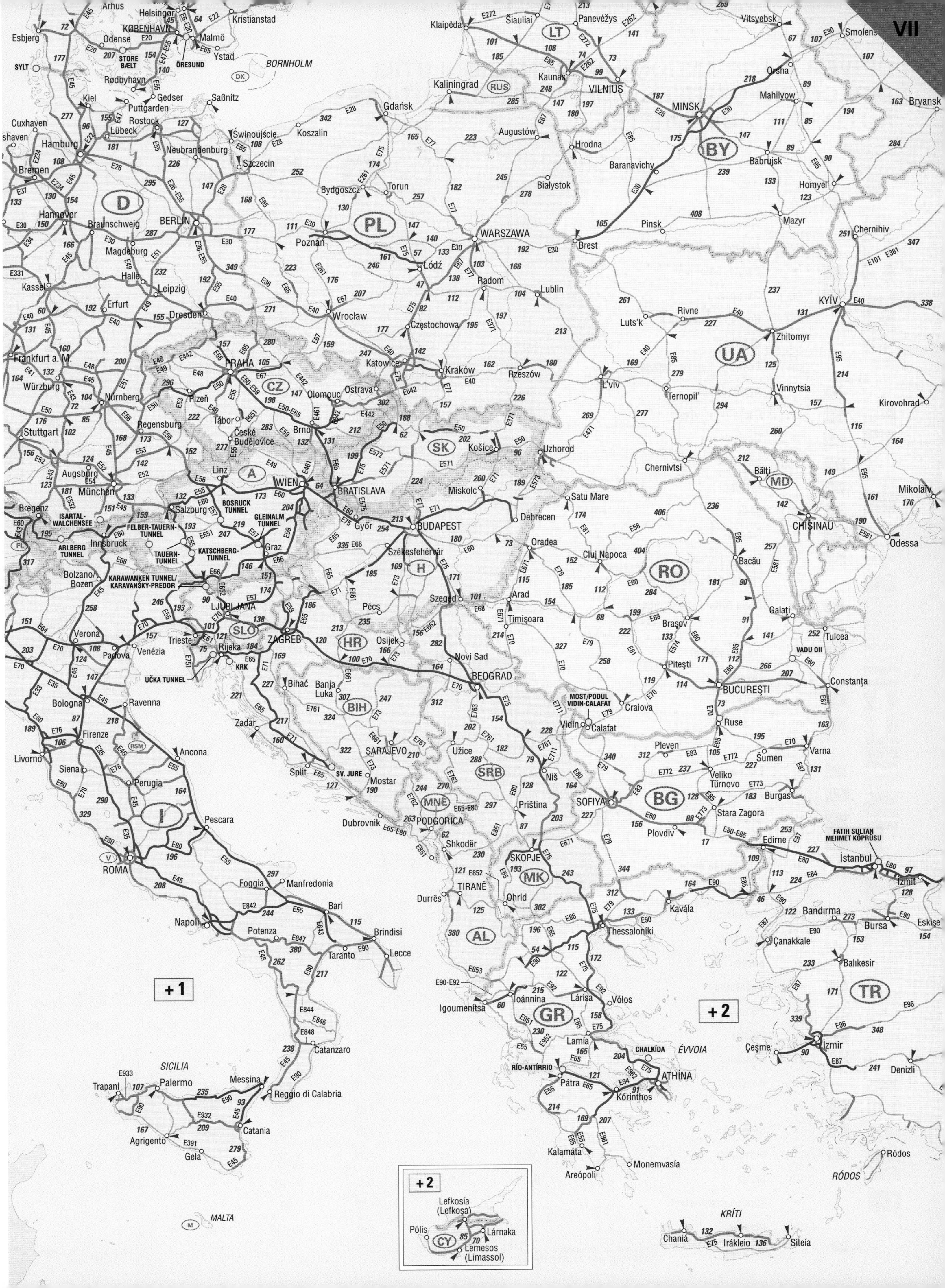

Århus
Helsingør
København
Kristianstad
Esbjerg
Odense
Malmö
Store Bælt
Øresund
Ystad
Bornholm
Sylt
Rødbyhavn
Gedser
Saßnitz
Kiel
Puttgarden
Rostock
Cuxhaven
Lübeck
Świnoujście
Koszalin
Gdańsk
Hamburg
Neubrandenburg
Szczecin
Bremen
Hannover
Braunschweig
Berlin
Magdeburg
Halle
Leipzig
Kassel
Erfurt
Dresden
Frankfurt a. M.
Würzburg
Nürnberg
Stuttgart
Regensburg
Augsburg
München
Bregenz
Isartal-Walchensee
Arlberg Tunnel
Innsbruck
Felber-Tauern-Tunnel
Tauern-Tunnel
Katschberg-Tunnel
Bosruck Tunnel
Gleinalm Tunnel
Salzburg
Linz
Wien
Graz
Bolzano/Bozen
Karawanken Tunnel/Karavanško-Predor
Ljubljana
Trieste
Rijeka
Krk
Učka Tunnel
Zagreb
Verona
Padova
Venézia
Bologna
Ravenna
Firenze
Livorno
Siena
Ancona
Perugia
Pescara
Roma
Foggia
Manfredonia
Bari
Napoli
Potenza
Taranto
Brindisi
Lecce
Catanzaro
Reggio di Calabria
Messina
Palermo
Trapani
Sicilia
Catania
Agrigento
Gela
Malta
Praha
Plzeň
Tábor
České Budějovice
Brno
Olomouc
Ostrava
Bratislava
Győr
Budapest
Székesfehérvár
Pécs
Szeged
Miskolc
Košice
Debrecen
Uzhorod
Poznań
Bydgoszcz
Torun
Łódź
Warszawa
Radom
Lublin
Wrocław
Częstochowa
Katowice
Kraków
Rzeszów
Kaliningrad
Klaipėda
Šiauliai
Panevėžys
Kaunas
Vilnius
Augustów
Hrodna
Białystok
Brest
Minsk
Vitsyebsk
Orsha
Smolensk
Mahilyow
Babrujsk
Baranavichy
Pinsk
Mazyr
Homyel'
Bryansk
Chernihiv
Kyïv
Zhitomyr
Rivne
Luts'k
L'viv
Ternopil'
Vinnytsia
Kirovohrad
Chernivtsi
Bălţi
Chişinău
Mikolaiv
Odessa
Satu Mare
Oradea
Cluj Napoca
Bacău
Arad
Timişoara
Braşov
Piteşti
Galaţi
Tulcea
Vadu Oii
Constanţa
Bucureşti
Craiova
Most/Podul Vidin-Calafat
Vidin
Calafat
Ruse
Pleven
Šumen
Varna
Veliko Tŭrnovo
Burgas
Sofiya
Stara Zagora
Plovdiv
Edirne
Fatih Sultan Mehmet Köprüsu
İstanbul
İzmit
Bandırma
Bursa
Eskişehir
Çanakkale
Balıkesir
İzmir
Çeşme
Denizli
Ródos
Novi Sad
Beograd
Osijek
Bihać
Banja Luka
Zadar
Split
Sv. Jure
Sarajevo
Mostar
Dubrovnik
Užice
Niš
Priština
Podgorica
Shkodër
Tiranë
Durrës
Skopje
Ohrid
Thessaloníki
Kavála
Igoumenítsa
Ioánnina
Lárisa
Vólos
Lamía
Chalkída
Évvoia
Río-Antírrio
Pátra
Athína
Kórinthos
Kalamáta
Monemvasía
Areópoli
Kríti
Chaniá
Irákleio
Siteía
Lefkosía (Lefkoşa)
Pólis
Lárnaka
Lemesos (Limassol)
D
PL
CZ
A
SK
H
SLO
HR
BIH
SRB
MNE
MK
AL
GR
BG
RO
MD
UA
BY
LT
RUS
DK
FL
RSM
V
M
I
CY
TR
+1
+2

DRIVER INFORMATION - INFORMAZIONI UTILI
DIRECCIONES ÚTILES - INFORMATIONS UTILES
NÜTZLICHE AUSKÜNFTE

EU	A	Österreich	A, C	0043	112	130	100	50	0,5 ‰	✓
	AL	Shqipëria	B, C, D/E	00355	129	-	80	40	0,0 ‰	-
	AND	Andorra, Andorre	A, C	00376	110; 116	-	90	50	0,5 ‰	-
EU	B	België, Belgique	A, C	0032	112	120	90-120	50	0,5 ‰	-
EU	BG	Bălgarija	A, C, D/E	00359	166; 150	130	90	50	0,5 ‰	-
	BIH	Bosna i Hercegovina	A, C, D/E	00387	92; 94	100	80	50	0,5 ‰	-
	BY	Belarus'	B, C, D/E	00375	02; 03	110	90	60	0,0 ‰	-
	CH	Schweiz, Suisse, Svizzera	A, C	0041	117; 144	120	80-120	50	0,5 ‰	-
EU	CY	Kýpros, Kıbrıs	[a] A, C, E/D	00357	112	100	80	50	0,5 ‰	-
EU	CZ	Česká Republika	A, C	00420	155	130	90	50	0,0 ‰	[b] ✓
EU	D	Deutschland	A, C	0049	110	130	100	50	0,5 ‰	✓
EU	DK	Danmark	A, C	0045	112	130	80	50	0,5 ‰	✓
EU	E	España	A, C	0034	112	120	90-120	50	0,5 ‰	-
EU	EST	Eesti	A/B, C	00372	112	110	90-110	50	0,0 ‰	✓
EU	F	France	A, C	0033	17; 112	130	90-110	50	0,5 ‰	✓
EU	FIN	Suomi, Finland	A, C	00358	112	120	80-100	50	0,5 ‰	✓
	FL	Fürstentum Liechtenstein	A, C	00423	117; 144	-	80	50	0,8 ‰	-
EU	GB	Great Britain and N. Ireland	A, C	0044	999; 112	112 (70 mph)	96 (60 mph)	48 (30 mph)	0,8 ‰	-
EU	GR	Hellas	A, C	0030	100; 112	120	90-110	50	0,5 ‰	-
EU	H	Magyarország	A, C	0036	104	130	90-100	50	0,0 ‰	✓
	HR	Hrvatska	A, C	00385	94; 92	130	80-90	50	0,0 ‰	✓
EU	I	Italia	A, C	0039	112; 118	130	90-110	50	0,5 ‰	✓
EU	IRL	Ireland	A, C	00353	112	120	100	50	0,8 ‰	-
	IS	Ísland	A, C	00354	112	-	80-90	50	0,5 ‰	✓
EU	L	Lëtzebuerg, Luxembourg	A, C	00352	112	130	90	50	0,8 ‰	-
EU	LT	Lietuva	A, C	00370	112	110	90	50	0,0 ‰	✓
EU	LV	Latvija	A/B, C	00371	112	110	90	50	0,5 ‰	✓
EU	M	Malta	A, C	00356	191; 196	-	80	50	0,8 ‰	-
	MC	Principauté de Monaco	A, C	00377	17; 931 530 15	-	50	50	0,5 ‰	-
	MD	Moldova	B, C, D	00373	902; 903	-	90	40	0,0 ‰	-
	MK	Makedonija	A, C, D	00389	192; 194	120	80	50	0,5 ‰	✓
	MNE	Crna Gora	A, C, D	00381	92; 94	-	80	40	0,5 ‰	✓
	N	Norge	A, C	0047	112; 113	100	80	50	0,2 ‰	✓
EU	NL	Nederland	A, C	0031	112	120	80-100	50	0,5 ‰	-
EU	P	Portugal	A, C	00351	112	120	90-100	50	0,5 ‰	-
EU	PL	Polska	A, C	0048	112; 999	130	90-100	50	0,2 ‰	[b] ✓
EU	RO	România	A/B, C, D/E	0040	112; 955	120	90	50	0,0 ‰	-
	RUS	Rossija	B, C, D/E	007	02; 03	110	90	60	0,0 ‰	✓
EU	S	Sverige	A, C	0046	112	110	70-90	50	0,2 ‰	✓
EU	SK	Slovensko	A, C	00421	112	130	90	60	0,0 ‰	[b] ✓
EU	SLO	Slovenija	A, C	00386	112	130	90-100	50	0,5 ‰	✓
	SRB	Srbija	[a] A, C, D	00381	92; 94	120	80-100	60	0,5 ‰	✓
	TR	Türkiye Cumhuriyeti	A, C, D	0090	155; 112	120	90	50	0,5 ‰	-
	UA	Ukraïna	B, C, D	0038	02; 03	130	90-110	60	0,0 ‰	-

EU

[a] Green cards are not accepted in Northern Cyprus and Kosovo (Serbia)

[b] in winter

+1	*Euro* (€)	0810 101 818	www.austria.info/
+1	*Lek* (ALL)	4 258 323	www.albaniantourism.com/
+1	*Euro* (€)	827 117	www.andorra.ad/
+1	*Euro* (€)	25 040 390	www.visitbelgium.com/
+2	*Lev* (BGN)	29 335 845	www.bulgariatravel.org/
+1	*Konvertibilna Marka* (BAM)	33 252 924	www.bhtourism.ba/
+2	*Belarus Rouble* (BYR)	172 269 971	www.belarus-misc.org/
+1	*Schweizer Franken* (CHF)	432 105 500	www.myswitzerland.com/
+2	*Cyprus Pound* (CYP)	22 691 100	www.visitcyprus.org.cy/
+1	*Koruna Česká* (CZK)	221 580 111	www.czechtourism.com/
+1	*Euro* (€)	(0)69 751 903	www.germany-tourism.de/
+1	*Danske Krone* (DKK)	32 889 923	www.visitdenmark.com/
+1	*Euro* (€)	913 433 500	www.spain.info/
+2	*Kroon* (EEK)	645 7777	www.visitestonia.com/
+1	*Euro* (€)	(0)142 967 000	other.franceguide.com/
+2	*Euro* (€)	(0)106 058 000	www.visitfinland.com/
+1	*Schweizer Franken* (CHF)	2 396 300	www.tourismus.li/
0	*Pound Sterling* (GBP)	020 8846 9000	www.visitbritain.com/
+2	*Euro* (€)	2 108 707 000	www.gnto.gr/
+1	*Forint* (HUF)	1 4388080	www.hungary.com/
+1	*Kuna* (HRK)	1 469 9333	www.croatia.hr/
+1	*Euro* (€)	06 49711	www.enit.it/
0	*Euro* (€)	1850230330	www.ireland.ie/
0	*Íslensk Króna* (ISK)	5 355 500	www.visiticeland.com/
+1	*Euro* (€)	42 82821	www.ont.lu/
+2	*Litas* (LTL)	52 629 660	www.travel.lt/
+2	*Lats* (LVL)	67 224 664	www.latviatourism.lv/
+1	*Maltese Lira* (MTL)	22915000	www.visitmalta.com/
+1	*Euro* (€)	92166166	www.visitmonaco.com/
+2	*Leu* (MDL)	22 227 620	www.turism.md/
+1	*Denar* (MKD)	fax: (0)23 075 333	www.exploringmacedonia.com/
+1	*Euro* (€)	812 351 558	www.visit-montenegro.com/
+1	*Norsk Krone* (NOK)	24144600	www.visitnorway.com/
+1	*Euro* (€)	(0)703 705 705	www.holland.com/
0	*Euro* (€)	848391818	www.visitportugal.com/
+1	*Złoty* (PLN)	22 63 01 736	www.poland.travel/
+2	*Leu* (ROL)	0 213 149 957	www.romaniatourism.com/
[c] +3	*Russian Rouble* (RUB)	095 207 7117	www.russiatourism.ru/
+1	*Svensk Krona* (SEK)	620 150 10	www.visitsweden.com/
+1	*Slovenská Koruna* (SKK)	48 41 36146	www.slovakiatourism.sk/
+1	*Euro* (€)	13 064 775	www.slovenia.info/
+1	*Srpski Dinar* (RSD)	0 113 230 566	www.serbia-tourism.org/
+2	*Türk Lirası* (TRL)	3 122 128 300	www.tourismturkey.org/
+2	*Hrivna* (UAH)	(202)2 232 228	www.traveltoukraine.org/

[c] *Moskva*

Key to table
Legenda
Leyenda
Légende
Zeichenerklärung

Required driver's papers
Documenti di guida richiesti
Documentos requeridos para conducir
Papiers de conduire requis
Erforderliche Fahrzeugpapiere

A Driver's licence
Patente di guida
Carné de conducir
Permis de conduire
Führerschein

B International driver's licence
Patente di guida internazionale
Carné de conducir internacional
Permis international de conduire
Internationaler Führerschein

C Log-book
Carta di circolazione
Carné de circulación
Permis de circulation
Kraftfahrzeugschein

D Green card
Carta verde
Carta verde
Carte verte
Grüne Versicherungskarte

E Special insurance
Assicurazione speciale
Seguro especial
Assurance spéciale
Spezialversicherung

International code
Prefisso internazionale
Prefijo telefónico internacional
Indicatif international
Internationale Vorwahl

Emergency numbers
Numeri d'emergenza
Números de emergencia
Numéros d'urgence
Notrufnummern

Tourist office numbers
Numeri degli uffici turistici
Números de las oficinas de turismo
Numéros des bureaux de tourisme
Touristenämternummern

Tourist office websites
Siti web degli uffici turistici
Sitios web de las oficinas de turismo
Sites web des bureaux de tourisme
Touristenämterwebsites

(km/h)
Speed limit on motorway
Limite di velocità in autostrada
Límite de velocidad en autopista
Limite de vitesse sur l'autoroute
Höchstgeschwindigkeit auf der Autobahn

(km/h)
Speed limit outside the towns
Limite di velocità su strade extraurbane
Límite de velocidad en carreteras extraurbanas
Höchstgeschwindigkeit außerhalb der Städte
Limite de vitesse sur les routes extra-urbaines

(km/h)
Speed limit in towns
Limite di velocità nei centri abitati
Límite de velocidad en ciudades
Limite de vitesse dans les villes
Höchstgeschwindigkeit innerhalb der Städte

Maximum permitted alcohol level
Tasso alcolemico massimo tollerato
Límite alcohólico màximo consentido
Taux d'alcoolémie maximum admis
Höchsterlaubte Blutalkoholgehalt

Lights on during the day
Obbligo luci accese di giorno
Encender los faros durante el dia
Feux allumés obligatoires de jour
Licht-Pflicht am Tag

Time zone from Greenwich
Fuso orario da Greenwich
Huso horario de Greenwich
Fuseaux horaires de Greenwich
Zeitzone gegenüber Greenwich

Local currency
Valuta locale
Divisa local
Devise locale
Lokalwährung

Note: the table is indicative; it is advisable to check the information before leaving.
Nota: la tabella è indicativa; si consiglia di verificare le informazioni prima della partenza.
Nota: el prospecto es indicativo; se aconseja verificar las informaciones antes de partir.
Nota: le tableau est indicatif; il est conseillé de vérifier les renseignements avant de partir.
Notiz: die Informationen sind als Hinweis gedacht; es empfiehlt sich, die Auskünfte vor der Abfahrt zu überprüfen.

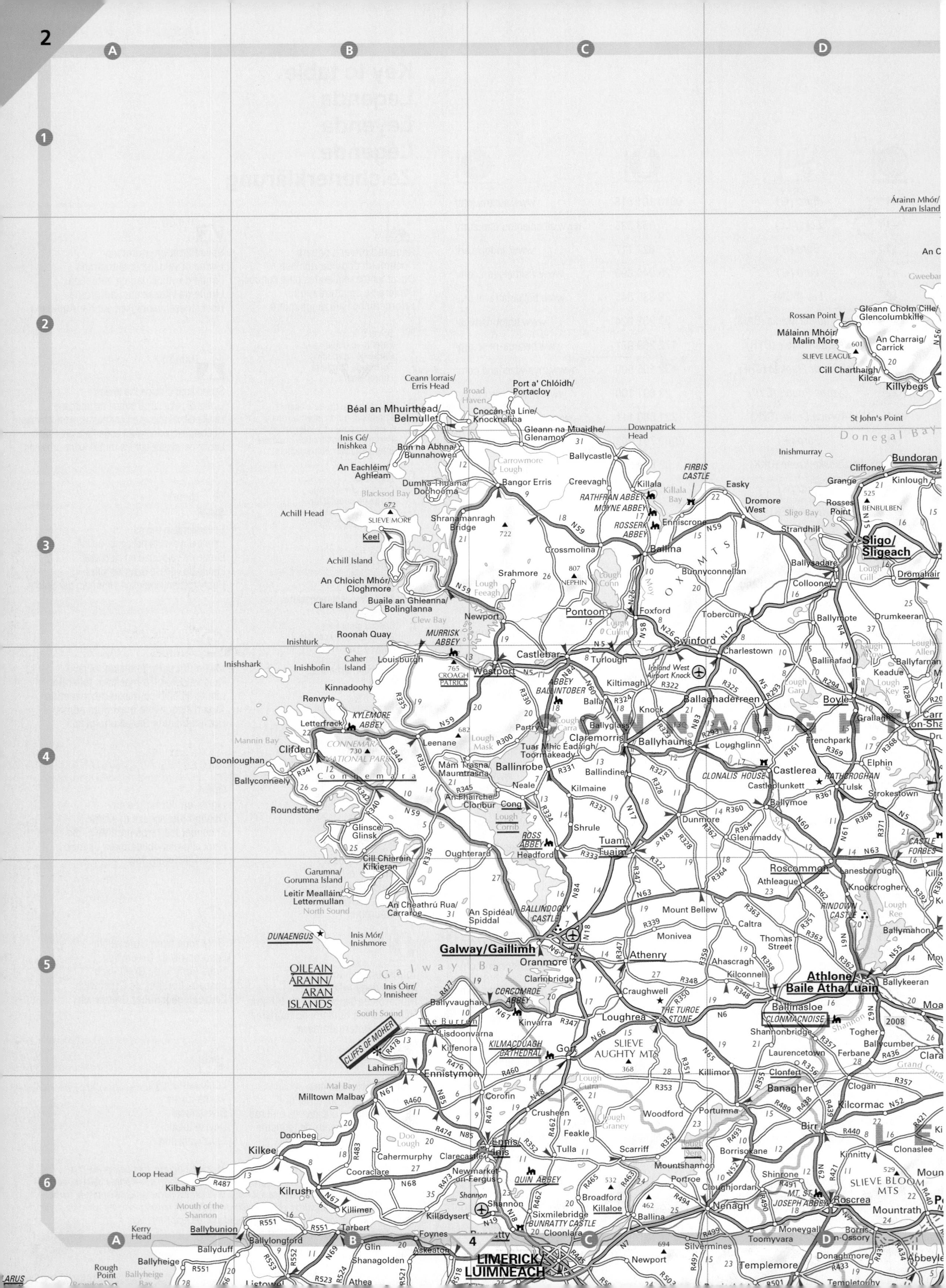
A
B
C
D
1
2
3
4
5
6
Árainn Mhór/
Aran Island
Rossan Point
Gleann Cholm Cille/
Glencolumbkille
Málainn Mhóir/
Malin More
601
SLIEVE LEAGUE
An Charraig/
Carrick
Cill Charthaigh/
Kilcar
Killybegs
St John's Point
Donegal Bay
Ceann Iorrais/
Erris Head
Broad Haven
Port a' Chlóidh/
Portacloy
Béal an Mhuirthead/
Belmullet
Cnocán na Líne/
Knocknalina
Gleann na Muaidhe/
Glenamoy
Downpatrick
Head
Inis Gé/
Inishkea
Bun na Abhna/
Bunnahowen
Ballycastle
Carrowmore
Lough
An Eachléim/
Aghleam
Dumha Thuama/
Doohoma
Bangor Erris
Creevagh
Killala
Killala Bay
FIRBIS
CASTLE
Easky
Inishmurray
Bundoran
Cliffoney
Grange
Kinlough
Blacksod Bay
672
SLIEVE MORE
Achill Head
Keel
Shranamanragh
Bridge
722
RATHFRAN ABBEY
MOYNE ABBEY
ROSSERK
ABBEY
Enniscrone
Dromore
West
Rosses
Point
525
BENBULBEN
Sligo Bay
Strandhill
Sligo/
Sligeach
Achill Island
Crossmolina
Ballina
Ballysadare
Lough Gill
Dromahair
An Chloich Mhór/
Cloghmore
Srahmore
807
NEPHIN
Lough
Conn
OX MTS
Bunnyconnellan
Collooney
Lough
Feeagh
Clare Island
Buaile an Ghleanna/
Bolinglanna
Clew Bay
Newport
Pontoon
Foxford
Tobercurry
Ballymote
Drumkeeran
Roonah Quay
MURRISK
ABBEY
Lough Cullin
Inishturk
Castlebar
Turlough
Swinford
Charlestown
Inishshark
Inishbofin
Caher
Island
Louisburgh
765
CROAGH
PATRICK
Westport
Ireland West
Airport Knock
Ballinafad
Lough Arrow
Ballyfarnan
Lough Allen
Kinnadoohy
ABBEY
BALLINTOBER
Kiltimagh
Keadue
Lough Key
Renvyle
Balla
Ballaghaderreen
Boyle
KYLEMORE
ABBEY
Letterfrack
682
Lough Carra
Partry
Ballyglass
Knock
Grallagh
CONNAUGHT
Carrick-on-Shannon
Mannin Bay
Clifden
CONNEMARA
NATIONAL PARK
730
Leenane
Lough
Mask
Tuar Mhic Éadaigh/
Toormakeady
Claremorris
Ballyhaunis
Loughglinn
Frenchpark
Elphin
Doonloughan
Connemara
Máam Trasna/
Maumtrasna
Ballinrobe
Ballindine
CLONALIS HOUSE
Castlerea
RATHCROGHAN
Ballyconneely
Neale
Kilmaine
Castleplunkett
Tulsk
Strokestown
An Fhairche/
Clonbur
Cong
Lough Corrib
Ballymoe
Roundstone
Glinsce/
Glinsk
Shrule
Dunmore
Glenamaddy
ROSS
ABBEY
Headford
Tuam/
Tuaim
Cill Chiaráin/
Kilkieran
Oughterard
CASTLE
FORBES
Roscommon
Lanesborough
Killashee
Garumna/
Gorumna Island
Leitir Mealláin/
Lettermullan
North Sound
Athleague
Knockcroghery
An Cheathrú Rua/
Carraroe
An Spidéal/
Spiddal
BALLINDOOLY
CASTLE
Mount Bellew
RINDOWN
CASTLE
Lough Ree
Caltra
DUNAENGUS
Inis Mór/
Inishmore
Monivea
Thomas
Street
Ballymahon
Galway/Gaillimh
Oranmore
Athenry
Ahascragh
OILEAIN
ARANN/
ARAN
ISLANDS
Galway Bay
Clarinbridge
Kilconnell
Athlone/
Baile Átha Luain
Ballykeeran
Inis Oírr/
Inisheer
Craughwell
Ballinasloe
South Sound
Ballyvaughan
CORCOMROE
ABBEY
THE TUROE
STONE
CLONMACNOISE
2008
Moate
The Burren
Kinvarra
Loughrea
Shannonbridge
Togher
CLIFFS OF MOHER
Lisdoonvarna
Kilfenora
KILMACDUAGH
CATHEDRAL
Gort
SLIEVE
AUGHTY MTS
368
Laurencetown
Ferbane
Ballycumber
Clara
Lahinch
Ennistymon
Killimor
Clonfert
Grand Canal
Mal Bay
Lough Cutra
Banagher
Clogh
Milltown Malbay
Corofin
Woodford
Portumna
Kilcormac
Crusheen
Lough Graney
Doonbeg
Doo Lough
Feakle
Birr
Kilkee
Cahermurphy
Ennis/
Inis
Tulla
Scarriff
Borrisokane
Kinnitty
Clonaslee
Cooraclare
Lough Derg
Mountshannon
Loop Head
Kilbaha
Newmarket-
on-Fergus
QUIN ABBEY
532
Portroe
Shinrone
529
SLIEVE BLOOM
MTS
Kilrush
Cloughjordan
MT. ST.
JOSEPH ABBEY
Roscrea
Mouth of the
Shannon
Killimer
Shannon
Broadford
Killaloe
462
Nenagh
Mountrath
Killadysert
Sixmilebridge
BUNRATTY CASTLE
Ballina
Kerry
Head
Ballybunion
Tarbert
Cloonlara
Moneygall
Borris-in-Ossory
Ballylongford
Foynes
Bunratty
Newport
Silvermines
Toomyvarra
Ballyduff
Glin
Askeaton
4
694
Donaghmore
Ballyheige
Shanagolden
LIMERICK/
LUIMNEACH
Templemore
Abbeyleix
Rough
Point
Ballyheige
Bay
Listowel
Athea
Templetuohy
N59
N5
N17
N26
N58
N84
N60
N83
N63
N61
N4
N15
N6
N18
N65
N66
N67
N85
N68
N69
N62
N52
N7
N19
N55
R335
R330
R300
R336
R344
R341
R342
R340
R345
R334
R331
R332
R333
R324
R322
R323
R327
R328
R325
R293
R294
R284
R361
R369
R367
R360
R362
R364
R368
R371
R347
R339
R348
R350
R356
R357
R359
R363
R392
R477
R478
R476
R460
R474
R483
R487
R473
R462
R352
R351
R353
R461
R465
R463
R494
R493
R490
R491
R421
R440
R438
R439
R489
R436
R445
R497
R498
R499
R503
R501
R433
R434
R435
R551
R552
R553
R523
R524
R521
R518
LARUS

NORTHERN IRELAND
ULSTER
NIR
IRL
GBM
IRISH SEA
NORTH CHANNEL
Jura
Islay
Port Askaig
Portnahaven
Port Ellen
Laggan Bay
Coul Point
Gigha
Campbeltown
Mull of Kintyre
Rathlin Island
Toraigh/ Tory Island
Tory Sound
Cnoc Fola/ Bloody Foreland
Horn Head
Dunfanaghy
Downings
Machair Loiscthe/ Rosepenna
Carraig Airt/ Carrickart
Malin Head
Inishtrahull Sound
Ballyhillin
Dunaff
Clonmany
Malin
Culdaff
Carndonagh
Portsalon
INISHOWEN
Lough Swilly
Buncrana
Moville
Stroove
Inishowen Head
Donegal
Errigal
Doe Castle
Cresslough
Croithlí/ Crolly
Glenveagh National Park
Milford
Lochán Liath/ Dunglow
Kilmacrenan
Rathmullan/ Rathmullen
Carrowkeel
Lough Foyle
Rathmelton
Muff
Grianan of Aileach
Carrigans
City of Derry
Eglinton
Letterkenny
Glenties
Ardara
LONDONDERRY (DERRY)
Limavady
St Johnston
Portstewart
Portrush
Bushmills
White Park Bay
Ballycastle
Coleraine
Armoy
Ballymoney
Dungiven
Claudy
Ballybofey
Stranorlar
Lifford
Strabane
Lough Eske
Dunkineely
Mount Charles
Donegal / Dún na nGall
Ballintra
Lough Derg
SPERRIN MTS
Dunloy
Carnlough
Maghera
Portglenone
Newtownstewart
Ballyshannon
Belleek
Pettigo
Kesh
Lower Lough Erne
Rosscor
Omagh
Magherafelt
Bellaghy
Broughshane
Ballymena
Ballygalley Head
Larne
Island Magee
Moneymore
Kilderss
Randalstown
Ballyronan
Antrim
Seskinore
Irvinestown
Cookstown
Belfast International
Ballyclare
Whitehead
Carrickfergus
Manorhamilton
Belcoo
Enniskillen
Lough Neagh
Crumlin
Newtownabbey
Holywood
Bangor
Donaghadee
Blacklion
Fivemiletown
Augher
Ballygawley
Dungannon
Moy
BELFAST
Dunmurry
Lisburn
Newtownards
Dowra
Maguiresbridge
Aughnacloy
Lurgan
Craigavon
IRON MTS
Swanlinbar
Upper Lough Erne
Emyvale
Armagh
Portadown
Hillsborough
Carryduff
Comber
Ballywalter
Greyabbey
Newtown Butler
Rosslea
Tynan
Tandragee
Gilford
Dromore
Ballygowan
Saintfield
Kircubbin
Monaghan
Clones
Markethill
Banbridge
Ballinahinch
Killyleagh
Keady
Belturbet
Butler's Bridge
Newbliss
Poyntzpass
Loughbrickland
Cavan/An Cabhán
Cootehill
Rockcorry
Ballybay
Newtownhamilton
Rathfriland
Portaferry
Strangford
Castleblayney
Newry
Castlewellan
Clough
Downpatrick
Hilltown
Mourne Mts
Newcastle
Ardglass
St John's Point
Crossmaglen
Warrenpoint
Rostrevor
Carlingford
Kilkeel
Annalong
Greencastle
Longford
Granard
Bailieborough
Carrickmacross
Dundalk / Dún Dealgan
Dundalk Bay
Castlebellingham
Kingscourt
Virginia
Ballyjamesduff
Oldcastle
Lough Ramor
Drumconrath
Ardee
Dunleer
Dunany Point
Kells
Old Mellifont Abbey
Slane
Monasterboice
Termonfeckin
Mullingar
Navan / An Uaimh
Newgrange
Drogheda/ Droichead Átha
Trim
Tara
Duleek
Gormanston Castle
Balbriggan
Skerries
Kinnegad
Tullamore
Durrow Abbey
Edenderry
Enfield
Rush
Lambay
Maynooth
Swords
Malahide
St Doulagh's Church
Portmarnock
Howth
Castletown House
Lucan
Celbridge
Clondalkin
Portarlington
Monasterevin
Newbridge/ Droichead Nua
Kildare
Naas/ An Nás
Tallaght
DUBLIN / BAILE ÁTHA CLIATH
Dún Laoghaire
Dalkey
Blessington
Bray/Bré
Powerscourt House
Greystones
Athy
Rath of Mullamast
Portlaoise
Troon
Stranraer
Portpatrick
Fleetwood
Douglas
Liverpool
Holyhead
Isle of Man
Port Erin
Anglesey

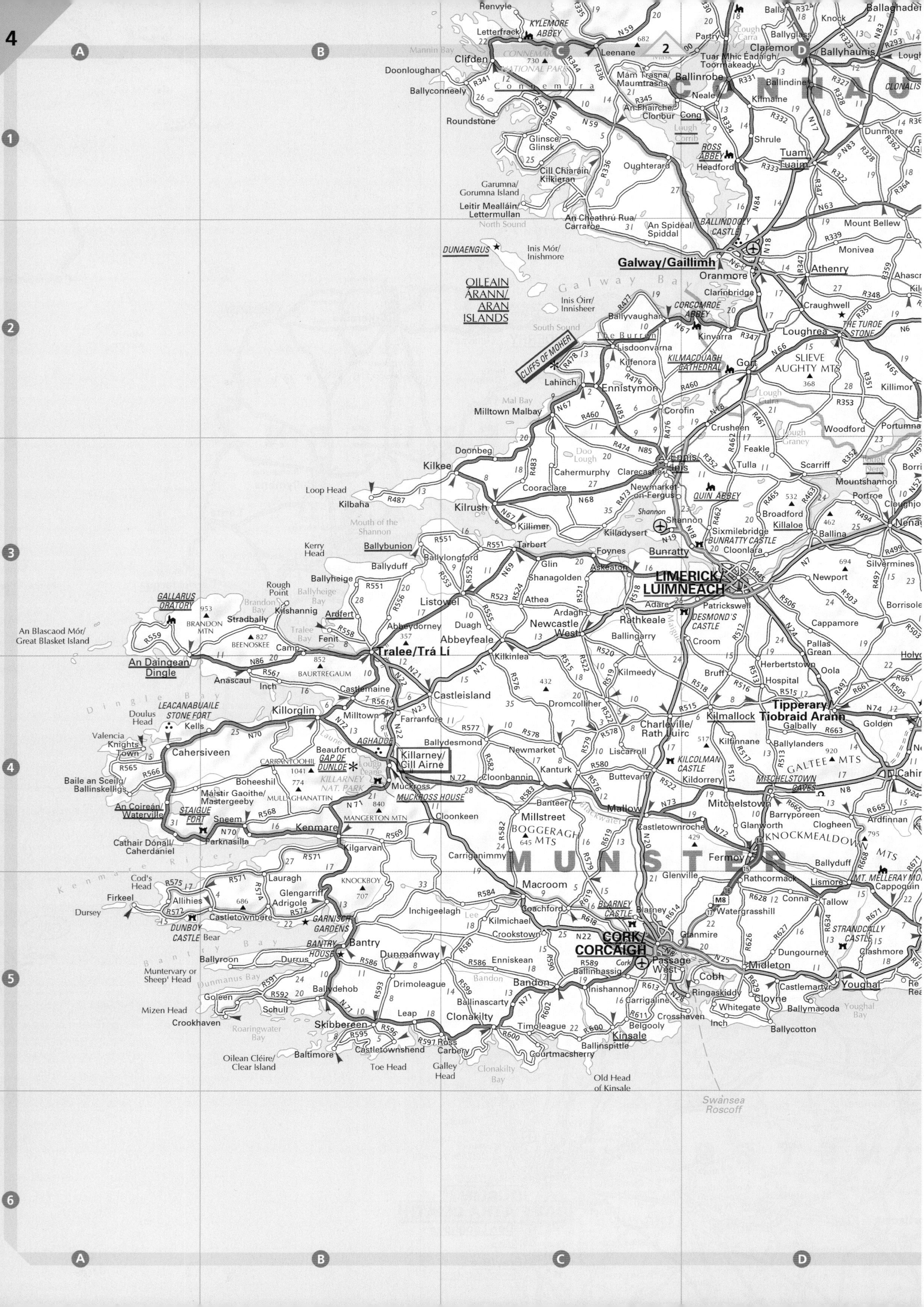

A
B
C
D
1
2
3
4
5
6
2
CONNAUGHT
MUNSTER
Renvyle
Letterfrack
KYLEMORE ABBEY
Clifden
Leenane
Partry
Ballinrobe
Claremorris
Ballyhaunis
Ballaghaderreen
Knock
Ballyglass
Doonloughan
Ballyconneely
Connemara
CONNEMARA NATIONAL PARK
Máimeacha Trasna/Maumtrasna
Tuar Mhic Éadaigh/Toormakeady
Neale
Cong
An Fhairche/Clonbur
Kilmaine
Ballindine
Roundstone
Glinsce/Glinsk
Lough Corrib
ROSS ABBEY
Headford
Shrule
Tuam/Tuaim
Dunmore
Cill Chiaráin/Kilkieran
Oughterard
Garumna/Gorumna Island
Leitir Mealláin/Lettermullan
North Sound
An Cheathrú Rua/Carraroe
An Spidéal/Spiddal
BALLINDOOLY CASTLE
Mount Bellew
Monivea
DUNAENGUS
Inis Mór/Inishmore
Galway/Gaillimh
Oranmore
Athenry
OILEAIN ÁRANN/ARAN ISLANDS
Galway Bay
Inis Oírr/Inisheer
Clarinbridge
Craughwell
CORCOMROE ABBEY
Ballyvaughan
South Sound
Kinvarra
Loughrea
THE TUROE STONE
The Burren
Lisdoonvarna
Kilfenora
CLIFFS OF MOHER
KILMACDUAGH CATHEDRAL
Gort
SLIEVE AUGHTY MTS
Killimor
Lahinch
Ennistymon
Mal Bay
Milltown Malbay
Corofin
Lough Cutra
Crusheen
Woodford
Portumna
Doonbeg
Doo Lough
Ennis/Inis
Feakle
Tulla
Scarriff
Kilkee
Cahermurphy
Clarecastle
Mountshannon
Loop Head
Cooraclare
QUIN ABBEY
Newmarket-on-Fergus
Portroe
Kilbaha
Kilrush
Broadford
Killaloe
Killimer
Shannon
Sixmilebridge
Ballina
Mouth of the Shannon
Killadysert
BUNRATTY CASTLE
Kerry Head
Ballybunion
Tarbert
Ballylongford
Glin
Foynes
Bunratty
Cloonlara
Ballyduff
Shanagolden
Askeaton
LIMERICK/LUIMNEACH
Newport
Silvermines
Ballyheigue
Rough Point
Ballyheigue Bay
Listowel
Athea
Adare
Patrickswell
GALLARUS ORATORY
BRANDON MTN
Brandon Bay
Kilshannig
Ardfert
Ardagh
Newcastle West
Rathkeale
DESMOND'S CASTLE
Cappamore
Borrisoleigh
An Blascaod Mór/Great Blasket Island
Stradbally
BEENOSKEE
Tralee Bay
Fenit
Abbeydorney
Duagh
Abbeyfeale
Ballingarry
Croom
Pallas Grean
Camp
Tralee/Trá Lí
Kilkinlea
An Daingean/Dingle
BAURTREGAUM
Anascaul
Inch
Kilmeedy
Herbertstown
Oola
Bruff
Hospital
Dingle Bay
Castlemaine
Castleisland
Dromcolliher
LEACANABUAILE STONE FORT
Tipperary/Tiobraid Árann
Doulus Head
Kells
Killorglin
Milltown
Farranfore
Charleville/Rath Luirc
Kilmallock
Galbally
Golden
Valencia
Knights Town
AGHADOE
Ballydesmond
Kilfinnane
Ballylanders
Cahersiveen
Beaufort
GAP OF DUNLOE
Killarney/Cill Airne
Newmarket
Liscarroll
KILCOLMAN CASTLE
GALTEE MTS
Cahir
CARRANTOOHIL
KILLARNEY NAT. PARK
Lough Leane
Cloonbannin
Kanturk
Buttevant
Kildorrery
MITCHELSTOWN CAVES
Baile an Sceilg/Ballinskelligs
Boheeshil
Muckross
Máistir Gaoithe/Mastergeeby
MULLAGHANATTIN
MUCKROSS HOUSE
Banteer
Mallow
Mitchelstown
An Coireán/Waterville
STAIGUE FORT
Sneem
Kenmare
MANGERTON MTN
Cloonkeen
Millstreet
Blackwater
Castletownroche
Barryporeen
Clogheen
Ardfinnan
Cathair Dónall/Caherdaniel
Parknasilla
Kilgarvan
BOGGERAGH MTS
Glanworth
KNOCKMEALDOWN MTS
Kenmare River
Carriganimmy
Fermoy
Ballyduff
Cod's Head
Lauragh
KNOCKBOY
Glenville
Rathcormack
Lismore
MT. MELLERAY MON.
Cappoquin
Firkeel
Allihies
Glengarriff
Adrigole
Macroom
Watergrasshill
Conna
Tallow
Dursey
Castletownbere
GARNISCH GARDENS
Inchigeelagh
Coachford
BLARNEY CASTLE
Blarney
DUNBOY CASTLE
Bear
Kilmichael
Crookstown
Glanmire
STRANCALLY CASTLE
Bantry Bay
Bantry
BANTRY HOUSE
Dunmanway
CORK/CORCAIGH
Passage West
Dungourney
Clashmore
Ballyroon
Durrus
Enniskean
Ballinhassig
Cork
Midleton
Muntervary or Sheep' Head
Dunmanus Bay
Ballydehob
Drimoleague
Bandon
Inishannon
Cobh
Castlemartyr
Youghal
Goleen
Schull
Ballinascarty
Carrigaline
Ringaskiddy
Cloyne
Whitegate
Mizen Head
Crookhaven
Leap
Clonakilty
Crosshaven
Ballymacoda
Youghal Bay
Roaringwater Bay
Skibbereen
Timoleague
Belgooly
Inch
Kinsale
Ballycotton
Oilean Cléire/Clear Island
Baltimore
Castletownshend
Rosscarbery
Courtmacsherry
Ballinspittle
Toe Head
Galley Head
Clonakilty Bay
Old Head of Kinsale
Swansea
Roscoff

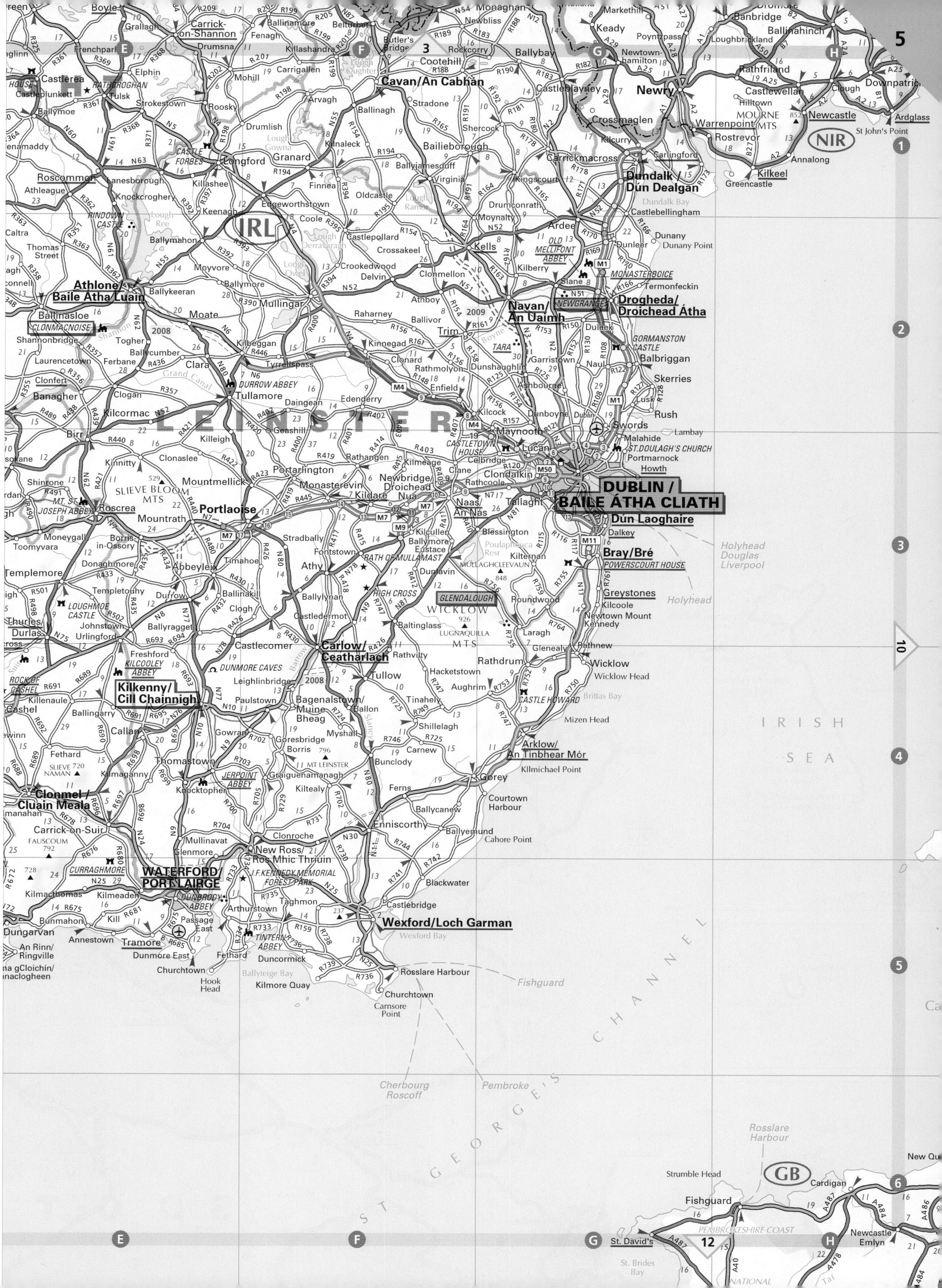
IRL
NIR
GB
LEINSTER
IRISH SEA
ST GEORGE'S CHANNEL
DUBLIN / BAILE ÁTHA CLIATH
Dún Laoghaire
Dalkey
Bray/Bré
Greystones
Howth
Malahide
Swords
Portmarnock
Lambay
Rush
Skerries
Balbriggan
Drogheda/ Droichead Átha
Termonfeckin
Dundalk / Dún Dealgan
Dundalk Bay
Castlebellingham
Carlingford
Newry
Banbridge
Ballynahinch
Downpatrick
Newcastle
Ardglass
Kilkeel
Annalong
Rostrevor
Warrenpoint
Crossmaglen
Castleblayney
Carrickmacross
Monaghan
Keady
Markethill
MOURNE MTS
St John's Point
Cavan/An Cabhán
Cootehill
Ballybay
Bailieborough
Kingscourt
Virginia
Kells
Navan/ An Uaimh
Slane
NEWGRANGE
MONASTERBOICE
OLD MELLIFONT ABBEY
Ardee
Trim
TARA
Dunshaughlin
Ashbourne
Maynooth
Lucan
Celbridge
CASTLETOWN HOUSE
Clondalkin
Tallaght
Naas/ An Nás
Newbridge/ Droichead Nua
Kildare
Monasterevin
Portarlington
Edenderry
Enfield
Kinnegad
Mullingar
Athlone/ Baile Átha Luain
CLONMACNOISE
Moate
Kilbeggan
Tullamore
DURROW ABBEY
Clara
Birr
Banagher
Roscommon
Longford
Granard
Edgeworthstown
Ballymahon
Castlerea
Strokestown
Carrick-on-Shannon
Boyle
Mohill
Ballinamore
Belturbet
Portlaoise
Mountmellick
Mountrath
SLIEVE BLOOM MTS
Roscrea
MT ST JOSEPH ABBEY
Abbeyleix
Athy
Stradbally
RATH OF MULLAMAST
Blessington
Poulaphouca Resr
POWERSCOUNT HOUSE
Enniskerry
Roundwood
GLENDALOUGH
WICKLOW MTS
LUGNAQUILLA
Laragh
Rathdrum
Wicklow
Wicklow Head
Brittas Bay
CASTLE HOWARD
Arklow/ An Tinbhear Mór
Mizen Head
Kilmichael Point
Gorey
Courtown Harbour
Carlow/ Ceatharlach
Tullow
Baltinglass
Castledermot
HIGH CROSS
Kilkenny/ Cill Chainnigh
KILCOOLEY ABBEY
DUNMORE CAVES
Castlecomer
Bagenalstown/ Muine Bheag
Borris
MT LEINSTER
Bunclody
Ferns
Enniscorthy
Thomastown
JERPOINT ABBEY
New Ross/ Ros Mhic Thriúin
J.F.KENNEDY MEMORIAL FOREST PARK
Wexford/Loch Garman
Wexford Bay
Rosslare Harbour
Carnsore Point
Kilmore Quay
TINTERN ABBEY
Hook Head
WATERFORD/ PORT LÁIRGE
CURRAGHMORE
Tramore
Dunmore East
Dungarvan
Clonmel / Cluain Meala
Carrick-on-Suir
Callan
Cashel
ROCK OF CASHEL
Thurles
Templemore
Holyhead
Douglas
Liverpool
Fishguard
Pembroke
Cherbourg
Roscoff
Rosslare Harbour
Strumble Head
Cardigan
Newcastle Emlyn
St. David's
St. Brides Bay
PEMBROKESHIRE COAST
E
F
G
H
1
2
3
4
5
6
10
12

A
B
C
D
1
2
3
4
5
6
Rudha Rhobhanais/
Butt of Lewis
Port Nis/
Port of Ness
Isle of
Lewis
A857
16
A858
12
A857
Steornabhagh/
Stornoway
A866
Loch
Langavat
16
Scarp
THE WESTERN ISLES
17
A859
Taransay
Tairbeart/
Tarbert
Pabbay
Berneray
Scalpay
Harris
Renish Point
Sound of Harris
A865
A867
Loch nam Madadh/
Lochmaddy
Uibhist a Tuath/
North Uist
Beinn na Faoghla/
Benbecula
Ardivachar Point
A865
Uibhist a Deas/
South Uist
Loch Baghasdail/
Lochboisdale
Eriskay
A888
Bagh a Chaisteil/
Castlebay
Oban
Sound of Barra
The Little Minch
Waternish
Point
Loch
Snizort
Uig
A855
35
A87
Neist Point
Dunvegan
A850
22
16
Sound of Raasay
Rona
A863
Portree
9
A87
Inner
Sound
Raasay
23
Isle of
Skye
Crowlin
Scalpay
1009
927
BLAVEN
17
10
A87
Kyle of Lochalsh
5
Canna
Soay
Sound of Canna
Rum
A851
17
Armadale
Sound of Sleat
Loch Hourn
Loch Nevis
Mallaig
Sound of Rum
Eigg
Muck
19
Loch Morar
Sound of Arisaig
HEBRIDES
Barraigh/
Barra
A888
Bagh a Chaisteil/
Castlebay
Lochboisdale
Mingulay
Oban
Sound of Barra
Erisk
Castlebay
Lochboisdale
Coll
Arinagour
Tiree
Scarinish
Ardmore Point
Tobermory
INNER
A848
Sound of Mull
Loch Tuath
Loch Na Keal
A861
A830
14
33
Loch Shiel
A884
A861
Lochaline
Isle of
Mull
A849
Iona
Fionnphort
Loch Scridain
8
The Minch
Cape Wrath
Kinlochbervie
A838
20
31
Scourie
Eddrachillis
Bay
24
A894
Loch
More
Loch
Meadie
Altna
38
Lochinver
A837
11
Enard
Bay
8
A837
A838
Loch
Shin
20
A835
Ullapool
19
A837
8
A839
12
A837
Longa
Gairloch
15
A832
Fionn
Loch
29
A832
Loch
Maree
A832
A835
12
32
Loch Torridon
Loch a'
Bhraoin
19
19
Kinlochewe
Loch
Fannich
Loch
Glass
A896
34
Loch
Damh
9
Achnasheen
A832
16
A896
19
A890
GB
A835
13
A834
A862
A9
Dingwall
Muir of Ord
Fortros
Loch Kishorn
A890
15
NORTH WEST HIGHLANDS
1150
SGURR NA LAPAICH
A87
Loch
Mullardoch
Cannich
A831
12
16
A862
Inverness
A833
13
16
Drumnadrochit
A82
13
33
Loch
Cluaine
Invermoriston
A887
16
Loch
Ness
Toma
Loch Quoich
13
A87
13
Fort Augustus
Invergarry
Loch
Lochy
Loch Arkaig
15
A82
Spey
Newtonmore
A86
12
1128
Loch Eil
11
8
Spean Bridge
Fort William
Nevis
Range
30
A86
A889
24
16
1343
BEN NEVIS
Loch
Treig
Loch
Ericht
15
1145
CARN
Kinlochleven
Glencoe
Ballachulish
A82
Loch Linnhe
31
38
A828
Glencoe
Loch
Laidon
Loch
Garry
A9
29
Loch Ericht
Loch
Rannoch
Blair Ath
SCOT
GRAMPIAN MOU

E
F
G
H
1
2
3
4
5
6
ORKNEY ISLANDS
Westray
Westray Firth
The North Sound
North Ronaldsay
Fair Isle
Rousay
Sanday
Eday
Stronsay Firth
Stronsay
Mainland
Stromness
Shapinsay
Lerwick
Kirkwall
Rora Head
Hoy
Scapa Flow
Aberdeen
Flotta
Burray
Copinsay
St Margaret's Hope
South Ronaldsay
A966
A986
A964
A960
A961
Pentland Firth
Durness
Bettyhill
Tongue
A838
A836
Melvich
Reay
Scrabster
Thurso
Gills
John o'Groats
Loch Loyal
Loch Calder
Loch Naver
A897
A9
A99
A882
Sinclair's Bay
Noss Head
Wick
Dunbeath
Helmsdale
Lairg
A839
Golspie
Bonar Bridge
A949
Dornoch
Dornoch Firth
Tain
Alness
Invergordon
Cromarty
A832
Moray Firth
SHETLAND ISLANDS
Herma Ness
Unst
Haroldswick
Yell
Gutcher
Uyeasound
The Faither
Isbister
Yell Sound
West Sandwick
Tresta
Fetlar
Hillswick
A970
A968
Rams Ness
Booth of Toft
Burravoe
St Magnus Bay
Muckle Roe
Brae
Lunna Ness
Papa Stour
Vidlin
Sandness
Whalsay
Symbister
A971
Heglibister
Foula
Mainland
GB
Scalloway
Lerwick
Seyðisfjörður
Tórshavn
Bergen
West Burra
Bressay
Fladdabister
Aberdeen
Kirkwall
Tolob
Sumburgh Head
Lossiemouth
Spey Bay
Nairn
A96
Forres
Elgin
Buckie
A942
Cullen
A98
Banff
A941
A940
A939
Daviot
Rothes
A95
Fraserburgh
Keith
A97
Aberlour
Aberchirder
A981
A90
Loch of Strathberg
Dufftown
Turriff
840 BEN RINNES
Carrbridge
A938
Grantown-on-Spey
Dulnain Bridge
Huntly
A920
A947
A950
A948
A952
Peterhead
Aviemore
Tomintoul
Insch
CAIRNGORM MOUNTAINS
CAIRNGORMS NATIONAL PARK
Lecht
A944
Oldmeldrum
Ellon
A975
Alford
Inverurie
1309 BEN MACDHUI
Don
Kirkwall
Aberdeen
Dyce
Lerwick
A93
Braemar
Ballater
Aboyne
A980
Banchory
ABERDEEN
Glenshee
996 BROAD CAIRN
9
MOUNT BATTOCK 779
A957
A924
Stonehaven

Tiree
Scarinish
Ardmore Point
Tobermory
Fort William
Nevis Range
1343 BEN NEVIS
Lochaline
Glencoe
Kinlochleven
Ballachulish
Loch Tuath
Loch Na Keal
Isle of Mull
Iona
Fionnphort
Loch Scridain
INNER HEBRIDES
Loch Linnhe
Loch Laidon
Loch Rannoch
GRAMPIAN
SC
Oban
1074 BEN DORAIN
Tyndrum
Firth of Lorne
Loch Awe
Crianlarich
Killin
Lochearnhead
Kilmelford
Colonsay
Scalasaig
Gulf of Corryvreckan
Ford
Inveraray
LOCH LOMOND AND THE TROSSACHS NATIONAL PARK
Loch Katrine
983 BEN VORLICH
Loch Earn
Callander
Kilmartin
Lochgilphead
Loch Fyne
Loch Eck
L. Long
Loch Lomond
Sound of Jura
Jura
Port Askaig
Coul Point
Islay
Portnahaven
Laggan Bay
Port Ellen
Helensburgh
Stirling
Carron Resr
Colintraive
Dunoon
Tarbert
Greenock
Dumbarton
Rothesay
Firth of Clyde
Kilsyth
Gigha
Largs
Johnstone
Glasgow
Paisley
GLASGOW
Lochranza
Beith
Dalry
East Kilbride
Motherwell
Hamilton
Kilbrannan Sound
Brodick
Arran
Ardrossan
Kilwinning
Stewarton
Irvine
Kilmarnock
Strathaven
Whiting Bay
Troon
Galston
Campbeltown
Rathlin Island
White Park Bay
Prestwick
Ayr
Mauchline
Auchinleck
Cumnock
Douglas
Larne
Mull of Kintyre
Dunure
Turnberry
Maybole
NORTH CHANNEL
Girvan
Sanquhar
Loch Doon
GALLOWAY FOREST PARK
Ballantrae
Troon
Thornhill
Cairnryan
Loch Ryan
New Galloway
Stranraer
Portpatrick
Newton Stewart
Fleetwood
Wigtown
Gatehouse of Fleet
Castle Douglas
Dalbeattie
Dumfries
Loch Ken
Luce Bay
Drummore
Port William
Sorbie
Whithorn
Kirkcudbright
Douglas Liverpool
Mull of Galloway
Burrow Head
Solway Firth
IRISH SEA
Maryport
Workington
Cockermouth
St Bees Head
Egremont
Keswick
Seatoller
Point of Ayre
GBM
Ramsey
Isle of Man
Peel
Stroove
Inishowen Head
Portrush
Portstewart
Coleraine
Bushmills
Ballycastle
Armoy
Ballymoney
Dunloy
NIR
NORTHERN IRELAND
Maghera
Portglenone
Carnlough
Broughshane
Ballymena
Bellaghy
Magherafelt
Ballygalley Head
Larne
Randalstown
Ballyronan
Island Magee
Cookstown
Antrim
Ballyclare
Belfast International
Whitehead
Lough Neagh
Crumlin
Carrickfergus
Newtownabbey
Holywood
Bangor
BELFAST
Donaghadee
Dunmurry
Lisburn
Lurgan
Newtownards
Craigavon
Portadown
Carryduff
Comber
Ballywalter
Hillsborough
Ballygowan
Greyabbey
Gilford
Dromore
Saintfield
Banbridge
Kircubbin
Ballynahinch
Killyleagh
Loughbrickland
Portaferry
Rathfriland
Strangford
Castlewellan
Clough
Downpatrick
Newry
Hilltown
MOURNE MTS
852
Newcastle
Ardglass
Warrenpoint
St John's Point
Rostrevor
Carlingford
Annalong
Kilkeel
Greencastle
Dundalk / Dún Dealgan
Dundalk Bay
Castlebellingham
Dunany
A B C D
1 2 3 4 5 6
6
10

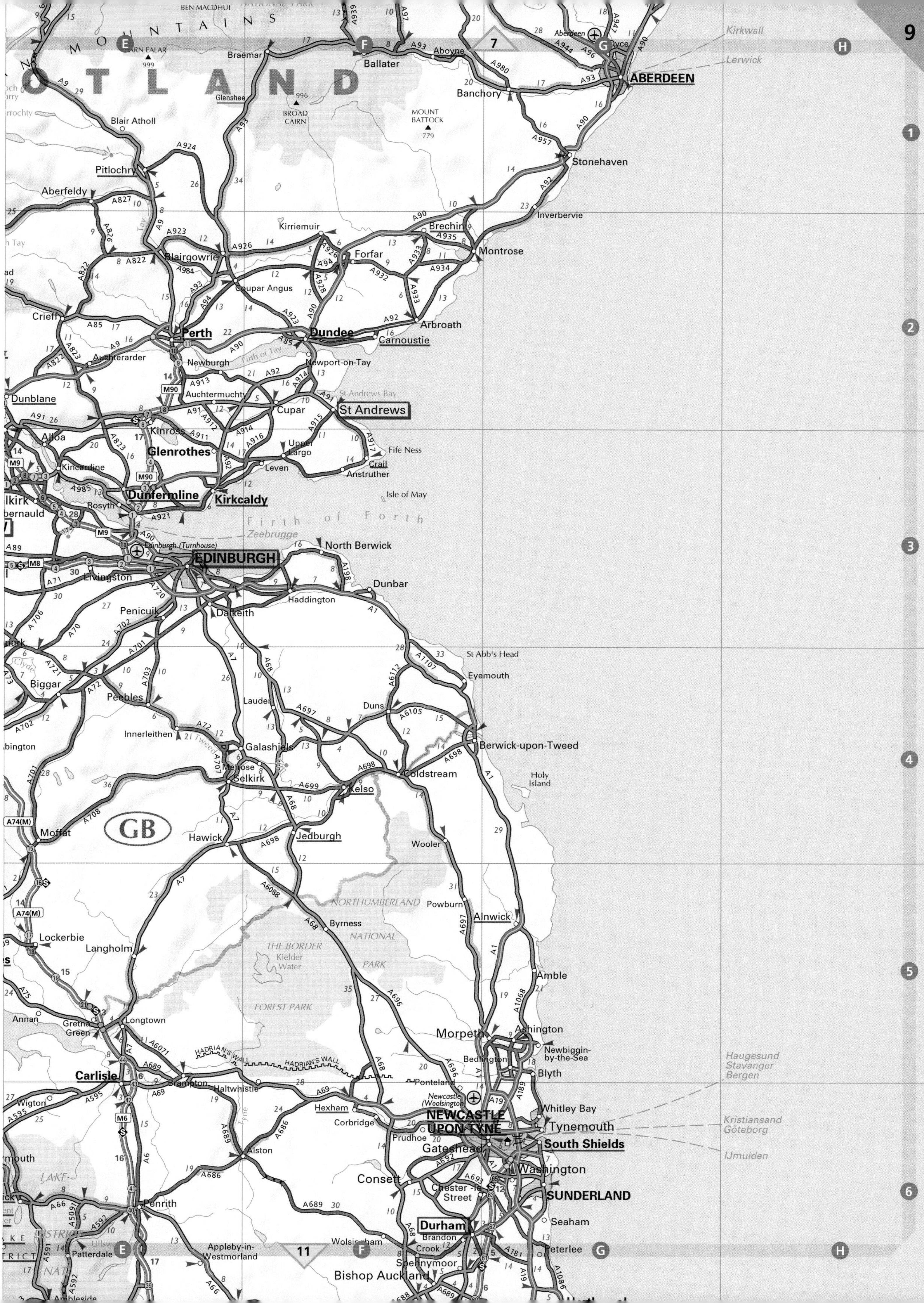
SCOTLAND
MOUNTAINS
ABERDEEN
Kirkwall
Lerwick
Braemar
Ballater
Aboyne
Banchory
Stonehaven
Inverbervie
Blair Atholl
Pitlochry
Aberfeldy
Kirriemuir
Brechin
Montrose
Blairgowrie
Forfar
Coupar Angus
Crieff
Perth
Dundee
Arbroath
Carnoustie
Auchterarder
Newburgh
Newport-on-Tay
Firth of Tay
Dunblane
Auchtermuchty
Cupar
St Andrews
St Andrews Bay
Alloa
Kinross
Glenrothes
Upper Largo
Fife Ness
Kincardine
Leven
Crail
Anstruther
Dunfermline
Kirkcaldy
Isle of May
Rosyth
Firth of Forth
Zeebrugge
Edinburgh (Turnhouse)
EDINBURGH
North Berwick
Livingston
Dunbar
Haddington
Penicuik
Dalkeith
St Abb's Head
Eyemouth
Biggar
Peebles
Lauder
Duns
Innerleithen
Galashiels
Berwick-upon-Tweed
Melrose
Selkirk
Coldstream
Kelso
Holy Island
GB
Moffat
Hawick
Jedburgh
Wooler
NORTHUMBERLAND NATIONAL PARK
Powburn
Alnwick
Byrness
Lockerbie
Langholm
THE BORDER FOREST PARK
Kielder Water
Amble
Annan
Gretna Green
Longtown
Morpeth
Ashington
Newbiggin-by-the-Sea
HADRIAN'S WALL
Bedlington
Blyth
Carlisle
Brampton
Haltwhistle
Ponteland
Haugesund
Stavanger
Bergen
Wigton
Hexham
Newcastle (Woolsington)
Whitley Bay
Corbridge
NEWCASTLE UPON TYNE
Tynemouth
Kristiansand
Göteborg
Prudhoe
Gateshead
South Shields
IJmuiden
Alston
Washington
Consett
Chester-le-Street
SUNDERLAND
Penrith
Seaham
Durham
Brandon
Crook
Peterlee
Appleby-in-Westmorland
Wolsingham
Patterdale
Spennymoor
Bishop Auckland
Ambleside

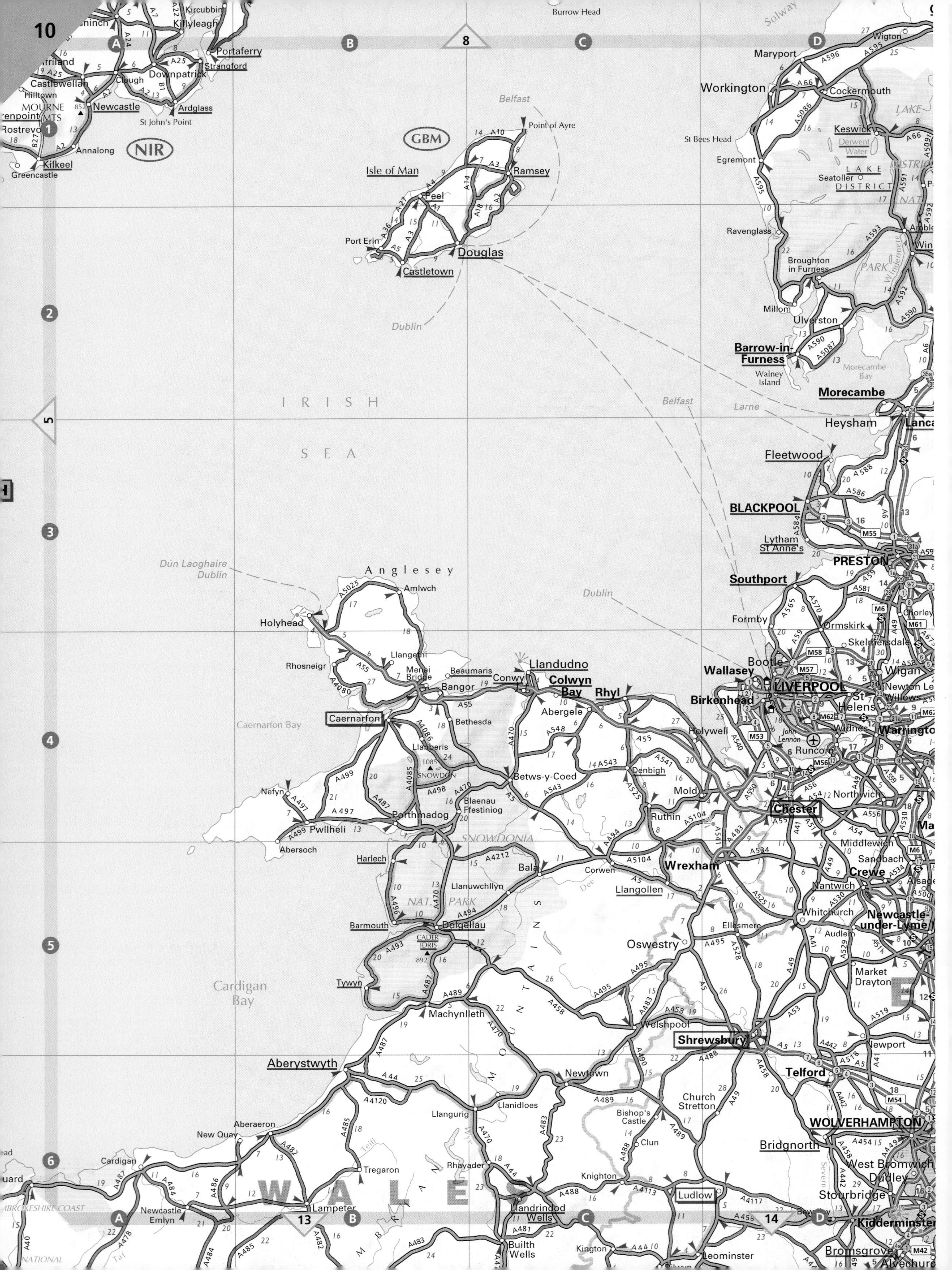

Kircubbin
Killyleagh
Portaferry
Strangford
Downpatrick
Clough
Castlewellan
Hilltown
MOURNE MTS
Newcastle
Ardglass
St John's Point
Annalong
NIR
Kilkeel
Greencastle
Burrow Head
Solway
8
B
C
D
A
Maryport
Wigton
Workington
Cockermouth
Keswick
Derwent Water
St Bees Head
Egremont
Seatoller
LAKE DISTRICT
NAT. PARK
Ravenglass
Broughton in Furness
Windermere
Millom
Ulverston
Barrow-in-Furness
Walney Island
Morecambe Bay
Morecambe
Heysham
Belfast
GBM
Point of Ayre
Isle of Man
Ramsey
Peel
Port Erin
Douglas
Castletown
Dublin
IRISH SEA
5
Belfast
Larne
Fleetwood
BLACKPOOL
Lytham St Anne's
PRESTON
Southport
Dublin
Dún Laoghaire Dublin
Anglesey
Amlwch
Holyhead
Rhosneigr
Llangefni
Menai Bridge
Beaumaris
Bangor
Llandudno
Conwy
Colwyn Bay
Rhyl
Abergele
Caernarfon
Caernarfon Bay
Bethesda
Llanberis
1085 SNOWDON
Betws-y-Coed
Denbigh
Holywell
Formby
Ormskirk
Skelmersdale
Chorley
Bootle
Wallasey
LIVERPOOL
Birkenhead
St Helens
Wigan
Newton Le Willows
Widnes
John Lennon
Runcorn
Warrington
Nefyn
Pwllheli
Abersoch
Porthmadog
Blaenau Ffestiniog
Mold
Ruthin
Chester
Northwich
Middlewich
Sandbach
Crewe
Alsager
Nantwich
Harlech
SNOWDONIA
Bala
Llanuwchllyn
Corwen
Wrexham
Llangollen
Dee
NAT. PARK
Barmouth
Dolgellau
CADER IDRIS 892
Ellesmere
Whitchurch
Audlem
Newcastle-under-Lyme
Oswestry
Market Drayton
Cardigan Bay
Tywyn
Machynlleth
Welshpool
Shrewsbury
Newport
Telford
CAMBRIAN MOUNTAINS
Aberystwyth
Newtown
Llanidloes
Llangurig
Church Stretton
Bishop's Castle
Clun
WOLVERHAMPTON
Bridgnorth
West Bromwich
Dudley
Stourbridge
Aberaeron
New Quay
Teifi
Tregaron
Rhayader
Wye
Cardigan
Newcastle Emlyn
Lampeter
WALES
Knighton
Ludlow
Severn
Llandrindod Wells
Builth Wells
Kington
Leominster
Kidderminster
Bromsgrove
Alvechurch
PEMBROKESHIRE COAST NATIONAL PARK
13
14

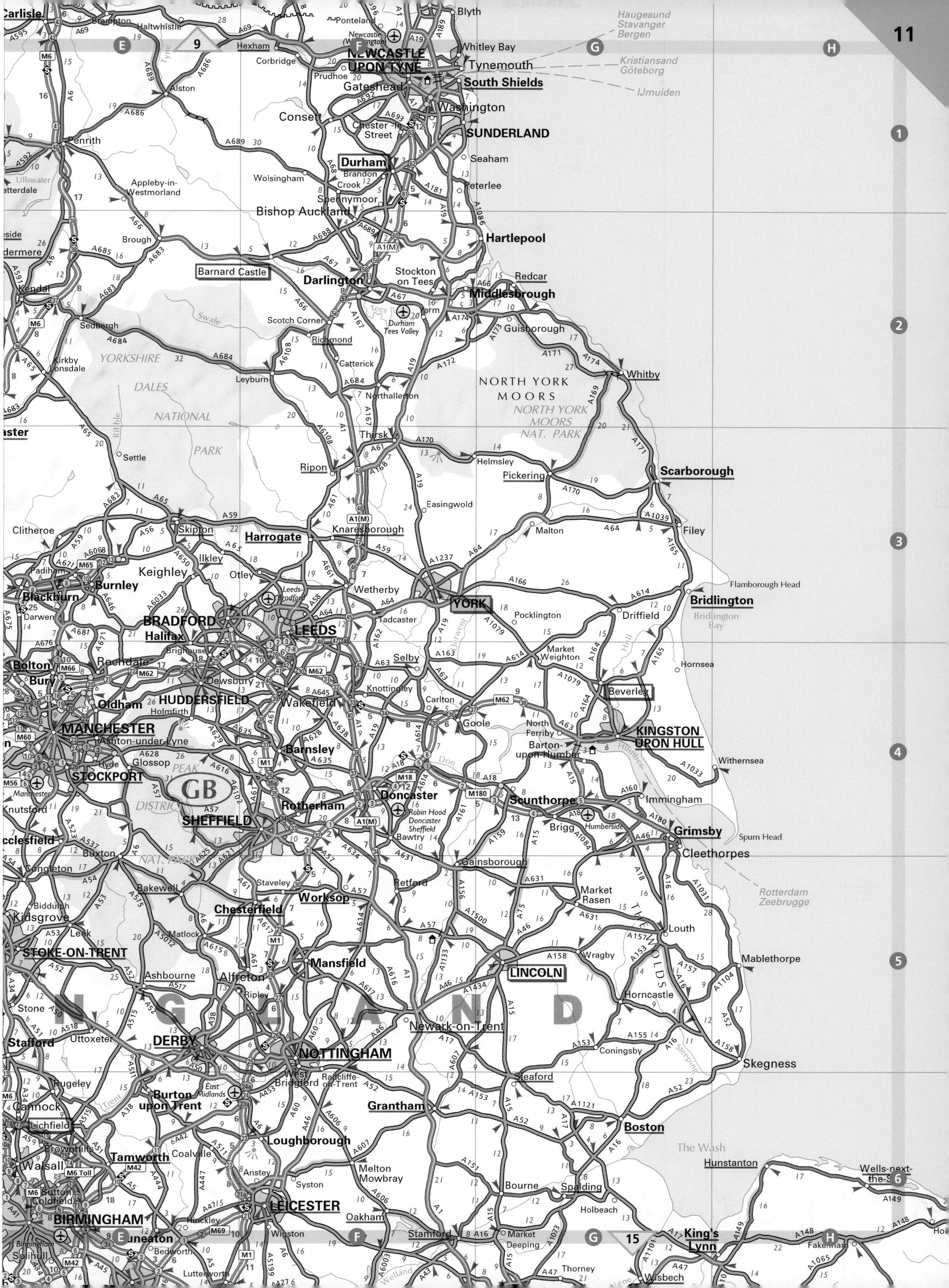
Carlisle
Brampton
Haltwhistle
Hexham
Corbridge
Ponteland
Blyth
Newcastle (Woolsington)
Whitley Bay
NEWCASTLE UPON TYNE
Tynemouth
Prudhoe
Gateshead
South Shields
Haugesund
Stavanger
Bergen
Kristiansand
Göteborg
IJmuiden
Washington
Consett
Chester -le- Street
SUNDERLAND
Alston
Penrith
Durham
Seaham
Ullswater
Patterdale
Appleby-in-Westmorland
Wolsingham
Brandon
Crook
Spennymoor
Peterlee
Bishop Auckland
Hartlepool
Brough
Barnard Castle
Darlington
Stockton on Tees
Redcar
Middlesbrough
Kendal
Sedbergh
Scotch Corner
Durham Tees Valley
Yarm
Guisborough
Richmond
Catterick
Whitby
Kirkby Lonsdale
YORKSHIRE
DALES
NATIONAL
PARK
Leyburn
Northallerton
NORTH YORK MOORS
NORTH YORK MOORS NAT. PARK
Thirsk
Settle
Helmsley
Pickering
Ripon
Scarborough
Easingwold
Malton
Filey
Clitheroe
Skipton
Harrogate
Knaresborough
Keighley
Ilkley
Otley
Burnley
Padiham
Leeds-Bradford
Wetherby
YORK
Flamborough Head
Bridlington
Bridlington Bay
Blackburn
Darwen
BRADFORD
Halifax
LEEDS
Tadcaster
Pocklington
Driffield
Bolton
Bury
Rochdale
Brighouse
Dewsbury
Selby
Market Weighton
Hornsea
Beverley
Oldham
HUDDERSFIELD
Wakefield
Knottingley
Holmfirth
Carlton
Goole
MANCHESTER
Ashton-under-Lyne
Barnsley
North Ferriby
KINGSTON UPON HULL
Barton-upon-Humber
Withernsea
Glossop
Hyde
STOCKPORT
PEAK
GB
DISTRICT
Doncaster
Scunthorpe
Immingham
Manchester
Knutsford
Rotherham
Robin Hood Doncaster Sheffield
Brigg
Humberside
Grimsby
SHEFFIELD
Bawtry
Cleethorpes
Spurn Head
Macclesfield
Buxton
NAT. PARK
Gainsborough
Market Rasen
Rotterdam
Zeebrugge
Congleton
Bakewell
Staveley
Worksop
Retford
Biddulph
Chesterfield
Kidsgrove
Leek
Matlock
Louth
THE WOLDS
STOKE-ON-TRENT
Mansfield
Wragby
LINCOLN
Mablethorpe
Ashbourne
Alfreton
Ripley
Stone
E N G L A N D
Horncastle
Newark-on-Trent
Stafford
Uttoxeter
DERBY
NOTTINGHAM
Coningsby
Skegness
Rugeley
Burton upon Trent
East Midlands
West Bridgford
Radcliffe-on-Trent
Sleaford
Cannock
Grantham
Boston
Lichfield
Brownhills
Loughborough
The Wash
Walsall
Tamworth
Coalville
Hunstanton
Sutton Coldfield
Anstey
Melton Mowbray
Syston
Bourne
Spalding
Wells-next-the-Sea
BIRMINGHAM
LEICESTER
Oakham
Holbeach
Hinckley
Nuneaton
Wigston
Stamford
Market Deeping
King's Lynn
Fakenham
Solihull
Bedworth
Lutterworth
Thorney
Wisbech
Welland

A
B
5
C
D
1
2
3
4
5
6
Rosslare Harbour
Strumble Head
Fishguard
Cardigan
St. David's
PEMBROKESHIRE COAST
NATIONAL
PARK
St. Brides Bay
Rosslare Harbour
Haverfordwest
Milford Haven
Dale
Narberth
St C
Pembroke Dock
Pembroke
Pendine
Tenby
Caldey
Carmarthen Bay
Kid
Worms Head
Port Ey
Cork/Corcaigh
B R I S T O
Lundy
Hartland Point
Barnstaple or Bideford Bay
Northam
Hartland
Bideford
Great Torrington
Bude
Holsworthy
Tamar
Padstow
Camelford
Launceston
Ok
Wadebridge
Newquay
Bodmin
BODMIN MOOR
Colliford Lake
Fowey
Tavy
DARTM
Callington
Tavistock
Liskeard
Yelverton
St Ives
St Austell
Lostwithiel
Hayle
Camborne
Redruth
Truro
Fowey
St Just
Land's End
Penzance
Mounts Bay
Penryn
Helston
Falmouth
St Mawes
Falmouth Bay
Lizard
Lizard Point
Looe
Saltash
Torpoint
PLYMOUTH
Buckfastleig
Ivybridge
Bigbury Bay
Roscoff Santander
Salcombe
ISLES OF SCILLY
Tresco
Bryher
St Martin's
St Mary's
St Agnes
A487
A40
A478
A477
A4139
A39
A361
A388
A386
A3072
A3079
A395
A30
A389
A3059
A392
A3075
A391
A390
A38
A393
A394
A3083
A3078
A3071
A379

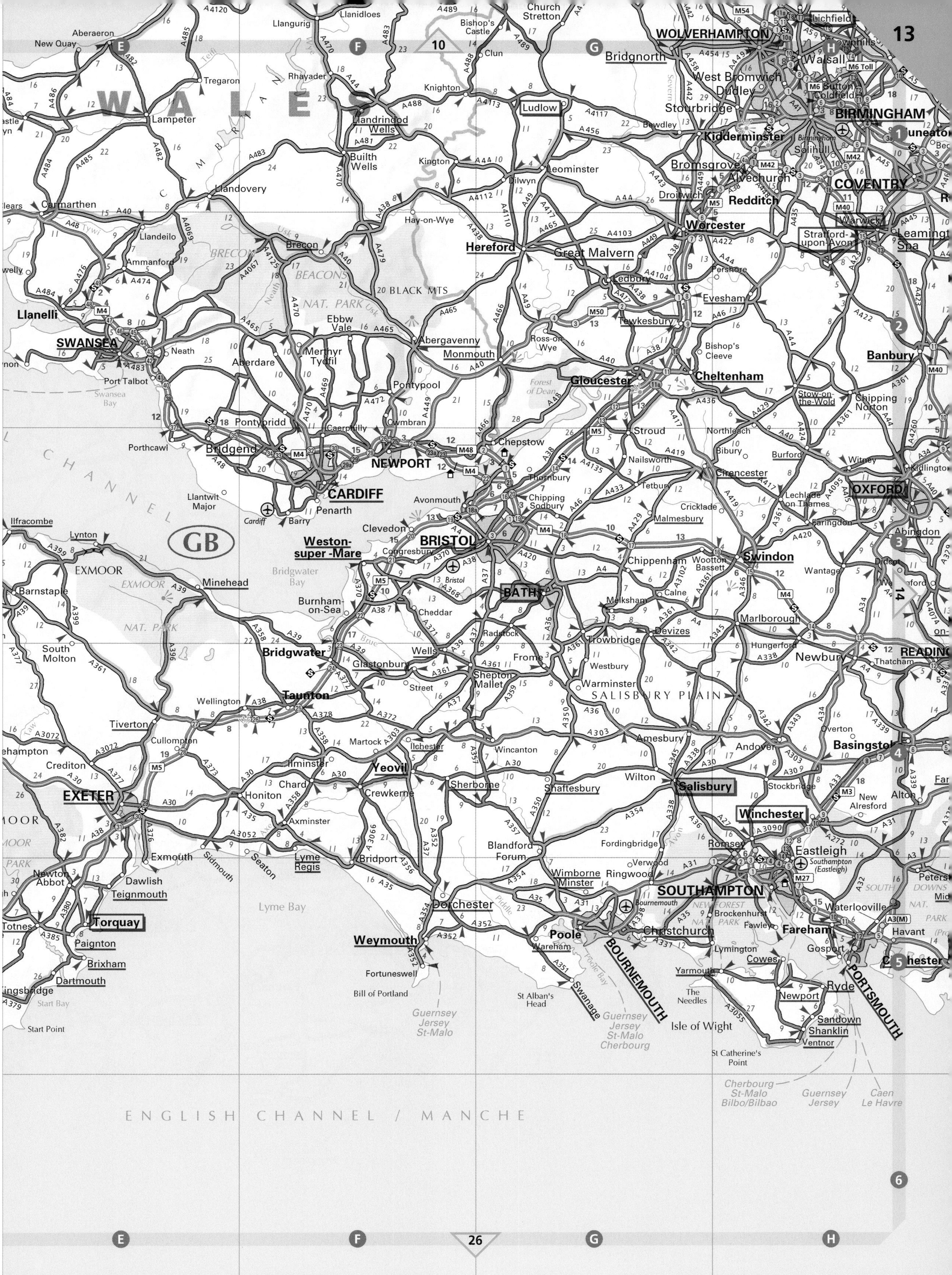
WALES
CAMBRIAN
Aberaeron
New Quay
Llangurig
Llanidloes
Bishop's Castle
Church Stretton
Clun
WOLVERHAMPTON
Lichfield
Brownhills
Walsall
Bridgnorth
West Bromwich
Dudley
Sutton Coldfield
Stourbridge
BIRMINGHAM
Nuneaton
Tregaron
Rhayader
Knighton
Ludlow
Lampeter
Llandrindod Wells
Builth Wells
Kington
Bewdley
Kidderminster
Solihull
Bromsgrove
Alvechurch
Leominster
Dilwyn
Droitwich
Redditch
COVENTRY
Carmarthen
Llandovery
Hay-on-Wye
Worcester
Warwick
Stratford-upon-Avon
Leamington Spa
Llandeilo
Ammanford
Brecon
BRECON BEACONS NAT. PARK
BLACK MTS
Hereford
Great Malvern
Pershore
Ledbury
Evesham
Llanelli
SWANSEA
Neath
Aberdare
Merthyr Tydfil
Ebbw Vale
Abergavenny
Monmouth
Ross-on-Wye
Tewkesbury
Bishop's Cleeve
Cheltenham
Gloucester
Banbury
Port Talbot
Swansea Bay
Pontypool
Forest of Dean
Stow-on-the-Wold
Chipping Norton
Pontypridd
Caerphilly
Cwmbran
Chepstow
Stroud
Northleach
Porthcawl
Bridgend
NEWPORT
Nailsworth
Bibury
Burford
Witney
Kidlington
Thornbury
Tetbury
Cirencester
Lechlade on Thames
OXFORD
CHANNEL
Llantwit Major
CARDIFF
Penarth
Barry
Avonmouth
Chipping Sodbury
Cricklade
Malmesbury
Faringdon
Ilfracombe
Lynton
GB
Clevedon
Weston-super-Mare
BRISTOL
Congresbury
Abingdon
Wootton Bassett
Swindon
Chippenham
Wantage
Didcot
Wallingford
EXMOOR
EXMOOR NAT. PARK
Minehead
Bridgwater Bay
Barnstaple
Burnham-on-Sea
BATH
Melksham
Calne
Cheddar
Marlborough
Radstock
Trowbridge
Devizes
Hungerford
Newbury
Thatcham
READING
South Molton
Bridgwater
Wells
Frome
Westbury
Glastonbury
Street
Shepton Mallet
Warminster
SALISBURY PLAIN
Taunton
Wellington
Tiverton
Cullompton
Martock
Ilchester
Wincanton
Amesbury
Andover
Overton
Basingstoke
Crediton
Ilminster
Yeovil
Chard
Crewkerne
Sherborne
Shaftesbury
Wilton
Salisbury
Stockbridge
Alton
New Alresford
EXETER
Honiton
Axminster
Winchester
Eastleigh
Romsey
Blandford Forum
Fordingbridge
Exmouth
Sidmouth
Seaton
Lyme Regis
Bridport
Verwood
Ringwood
Southampton (Eastleigh)
Newton Abbot
Dawlish
Teignmouth
Lyme Bay
Dorchester
Wimborne Minster
SOUTHAMPTON
NEW FOREST NAT. PARK
Brockenhurst
Fawley
Waterlooville
Torquay
Totnes
Paignton
Brixham
Weymouth
Poole
Christchurch
BOURNEMOUTH
Fareham
Havant
Wareham
Lymington
Cowes
Gosport
PORTSMOUTH
Dartmouth
Kingsbridge
Fortuneswell
Bill of Portland
Swanage
St Alban's Head
Yarmouth
The Needles
Newport
Ryde
Sandown
Shanklin
Ventnor
Isle of Wight
Start Bay
Start Point
Guernsey Jersey St-Malo
Guernsey Jersey St-Malo Cherbourg
St Catherine's Point
Cherbourg St-Malo Bilbo/Bilbao
Guernsey Jersey
Caen Le Havre
ENGLISH CHANNEL / MANCHE
SOUTH DOWNS NAT. PARK
10
14
26
E
F
G
H

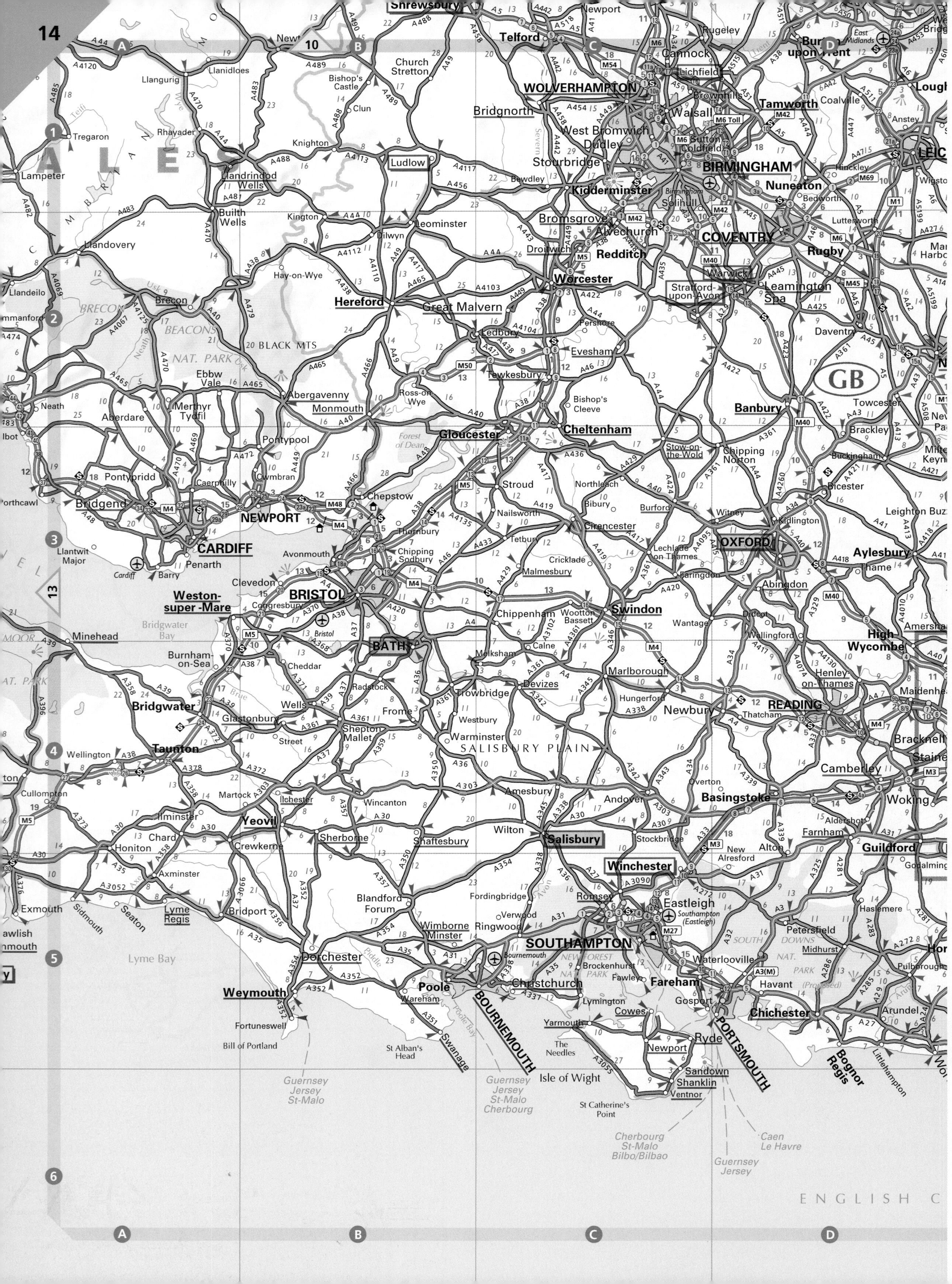
A
B
C
D
1
2
3
4
5
6
10
13
WALES
CAMBRIAN
BRECON BEACONS NAT. PARK
BLACK MTS
Shrewsbury
Telford
Newport
Rugeley
Cannock
Lichfield
Burton upon Trent
East Midlands
WOLVERHAMPTON
Bridgnorth
Walsall
Brownhills
Tamworth
Coalville
West Bromwich
Dudley
Sutton Coldfield
Stourbridge
BIRMINGHAM
Birmingham
Solihull
Kidderminster
Bewdley
Nuneaton
Hinckley
Bedworth
Bromsgrove
Alvechurch
Redditch
Droitwich
COVENTRY
Rugby
Lutterworth
Warwick
Leamington Spa
Stratford-upon-Avon
Worcester
Pershore
Evesham
Daventry
Llanidloes
Llangurig
Rhayader
Tregaron
Lampeter
Church Stretton
Bishop's Castle
Clun
Knighton
Ludlow
Llandrindod Wells
Builth Wells
Kington
Leominster
Dilwyn
Llandovery
Hay-on-Wye
Hereford
Great Malvern
Ledbury
Tewkesbury
Llandeilo
Brecon
Ebbw Vale
Abergavenny
Monmouth
Ross-on-Wye
Forest of Dean
Gloucester
Cheltenham
Bishop's Cleeve
Neath
Aberdare
Merthyr Tydfil
Pontypool
Cwmbran
Pontypridd
Caerphilly
Bridgend
Porthcawl
NEWPORT
Chepstow
CARDIFF
Cardiff
Penarth
Barry
Llantwit Major
Thornbury
Chipping Sodbury
Avonmouth
Clevedon
BRISTOL
Bristol
Weston-super-Mare
Congresbury
Stroud
Nailsworth
Tetbury
Cirencester
Northleach
Bibury
Burford
Stow-on-the-Wold
Chipping Norton
Banbury
Towcester
Brackley
Buckingham
Bicester
Witney
Kidlington
OXFORD
Lechlade on Thames
Faringdon
Abingdon
Thame
Aylesbury
Leighton Buzzard
Malmesbury
Cricklade
Swindon
Wootton Bassett
Chippenham
Calne
Melksham
Devizes
Marlborough
Wantage
Didcot
Wallingford
Henley-on-Thames
High Wycombe
Amersham
Maidenhead
READING
Thatcham
Newbury
Hungerford
Bracknell
Camberley
Woking
Guildford
Farnham
Aldershot
Basingstoke
Overton
Andover
Alton
New Alresford
Winchester
Stockbridge
Godalming
Haslemere
Petersfield
Midhurst
Pulborough
Arundel
Littlehampton
Bognor Regis
Chichester
Havant
Waterlooville
Fareham
Gosport
PORTSMOUTH
Eastleigh
Southampton (Eastleigh)
Romsey
SOUTHAMPTON
NEW FOREST NAT. PARK
Brockenhurst
Fawley
Lymington
Yarmouth
The Needles
Cowes
Newport
Ryde
Sandown
Shanklin
Ventnor
St Catherine's Point
Isle of Wight
Christchurch
BOURNEMOUTH
Bournemouth
Ringwood
Verwood
Fordingbridge
Salisbury
Wilton
Amesbury
SALISBURY PLAIN
Warminster
Westbury
Trowbridge
Frome
Radstock
BATH
Minehead
Bridgwater Bay
Burnham-on-Sea
Cheddar
Wells
Shepton Mallet
Glastonbury
Street
Bridgwater
Taunton
Wellington
Cullompton
Ilminster
Chard
Honiton
Axminster
Martock
Ilchester
Yeovil
Crewkerne
Sherborne
Wincanton
Shaftesbury
Blandford Forum
Wimborne Minster
Poole
Wareham
Swanage
St Alban's Head
Dorchester
Weymouth
Fortuneswell
Bill of Portland
Bridport
Lyme Regis
Lyme Bay
Seaton
Sidmouth
Exmouth
Dawlish
Teignmouth
Guernsey Jersey St-Malo
Guernsey Jersey St-Malo Cherbourg
Cherbourg St-Malo Bilbo/Bilbao
Guernsey Jersey
Caen Le Havre
ENGLISH CHANNEL
GB
M4
M5
M6
M6 Toll
M40
M42
M50
M54
M69
M3
M27
M1
M45
M48
A3(M)

Skegness
Sleaford
Grantham
Boston
The Wash
Hunstanton
Wells-next-the-Sea
Sheringham
Cromer
Holt
Fakenham
North Walsham
Aylsham
King's Lynn
Melton Mowbray
Oakham
Stamford
Bourne
Spalding
Holbeach
Market Deeping
Peterborough
Thorney
Wisbech
March
Downham Market
Swaffham
Dereham
Watton
Wymondham
Attleborough
NORWICH
Caister-on-Sea
Great Yarmouth
THE BROADS
Lowestoft
Bungay
Beccles
Diss
Thetford
Mildenhall
Ely
Littleport
Chatteris
Corby
Oundle
Kettering
Wellingborough
Rushden
NORTHAMPTON
Huntingdon
St Ives
St Neots
Bedford
Cambridge
Burwell
Newmarket
Bury St Edmunds
Stowmarket
Halesworth
Southwold
Framlingham
Wickham Market
Aldeburgh
Woodbridge
Orford Ness
Hollesley Bay
IPSWICH
Felixstowe
Harwich
The Naze
Hadleigh
Sudbury
Haverhill
Saffron Walden
Royston
Biggleswade
Shefford
Baldock
Letchworth
Hitchin
Luton
Dunstable
Stevenage
Harpenden
Hemel Hempstead
Welwyn Garden City
Hertford
Ware
Bishop's Stortford
Stansted
Great Dunmow
Braintree
Halstead
Colchester
Clacton-on-Sea
Esbjerg
Hoek van Holland
St Albans
Hatfield
Harlow
Watford
Beaconsfield
Slough
Witham
Maldon
Blackwater
Chelmsford
Brentwood
Billericay
Burnham-on-Crouch
Rayleigh
Basildon
Foulness Island
Southend-on-Sea
Canvey Island
LONDON
Heathrow
London City
Thames
Dartford
Tilbury
Gravesend
Croydon
Orpington
Leatherhead
Dorking
Reigate
Sheerness
Rochester
Chatham
Sittingbourne
Whitstable
Herne Bay
Margate
North Foreland
Kent International
Broadstairs
Ramsgate
Sandwich
Deal
Canterbury
Sevenoaks
Maidstone
Gatwick
Crawley
Edenbridge
Tonbridge
East Grinstead
Tunbridge Wells
Haywards Heath
Crowborough
Uckfield
Heathfield
Ashford
Tenterden
Hythe
Dymchurch
Folkestone
Dover
New Romney
Lydd
Dungeness
Rye
Battle
Hastings
Bexhill
Hailsham
Pevensey
Eastbourne
Beachy Head
Seaford
Newhaven
Lewes
BRIGHTON
Dieppe
Le Havre
CHANNEL / MANCHE
Strait of Dover / Pas de Calais
CHANNEL TUNNEL / TUNNEL SOUS LA MANCHE
Oostende
Calais
Blériot-Plage
Gravelines
Dunkerque Ouest
Dunkerque
Malo-les-Bains
De Panne
Oostduinkerke
Koksijde-Bad
Middelkerke
Westende-B
Veurne
Furnes
Bergues
Bourbourg
Loon Plage
Cap Gris Nez
Wissant
Framzelle
Marquise
Guînes
Ardres
Audruicq
Nordausques
Wormhout
Wimereux
Boulogne-sur-Mer
Le Portel
Pont-de-Briques
Colembert
Licques
Quercamps
St-Omer
Cassel
Steenvoorde
Woesten
Poperinge
Hardelot-Plage
Desvres
Lumbres
Samer
Météren
Bailleul
11
28
29
226
E
F
G
H
1
2
3
4
5
6

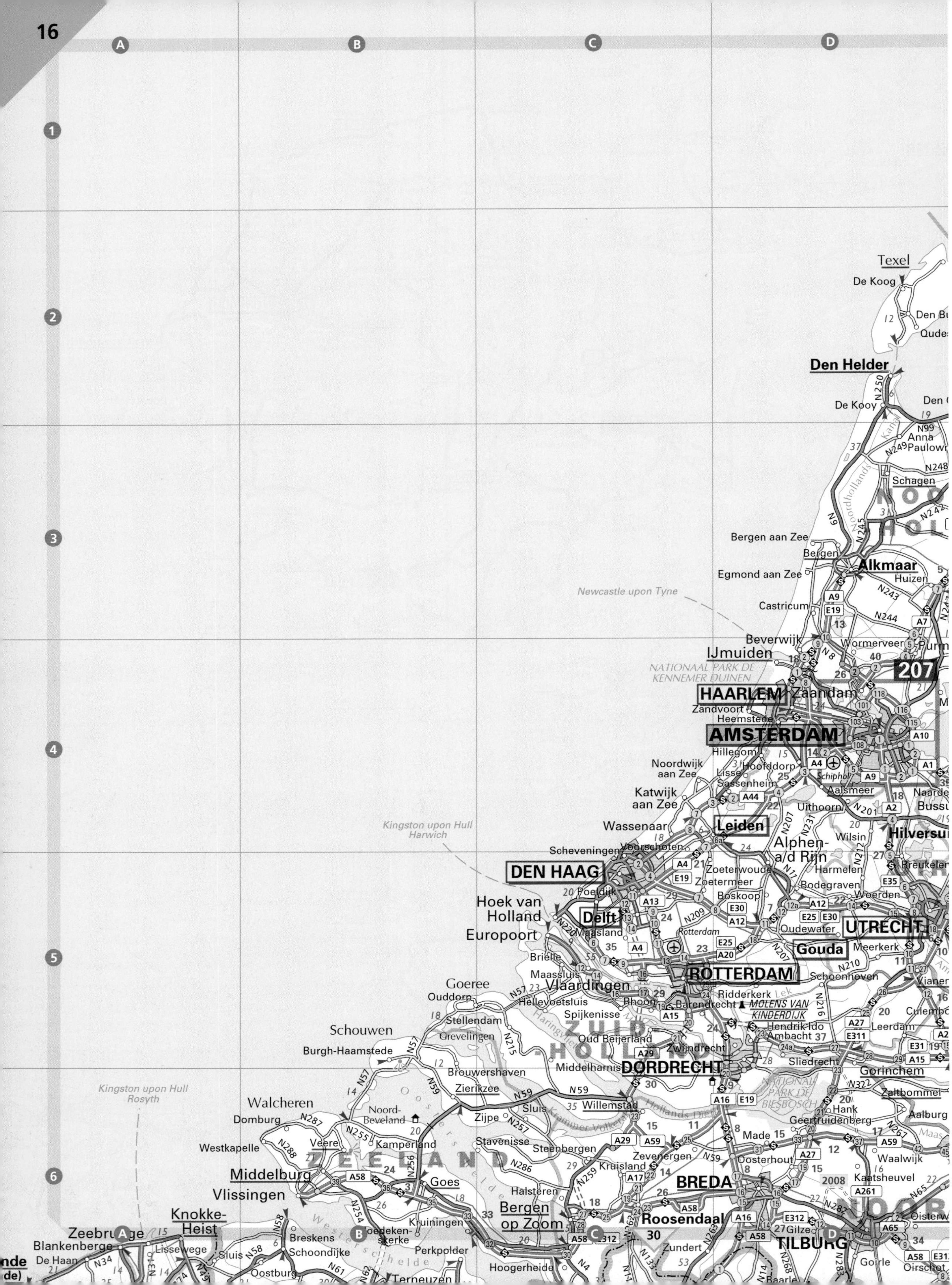

A
B
C
D
1
2
3
4
5
6
Texel
De Koog
Den Helder
De Kooy
Anna Paulowna
Schagen
Bergen aan Zee
Bergen
Alkmaar
Egmond aan Zee
Heiloo
Castricum
Beverwijk
IJmuiden
NATIONAAL PARK DE KENNEMER DUINEN
Newcastle upon Tyne
HAARLEM
Zaandam
Zandvoort
Heemstede
AMSTERDAM
207
Wormerveer
Hillegom
Hoofddorp
Schiphol
Aalsmeer
Noordwijk aan Zee
Lisse
Sassenheim
Katwijk aan Zee
Uithoorn
Wassenaar
Leiden
Alphen-a/d Rijn
Wilsin
Hilversum
Scheveningen
Voorschoten
DEN HAAG
Zoeterwoude
Zoetermeer
Harmelen
Bodegraven
Woerden
Boskoop
Hoek van Holland
Delft
Poeldijk
Maasland
Europoort
Rotterdam
Oudewater
UTRECHT
Gouda
Meerkerk
Brielle
Maassluis
Vlaardingen
ROTTERDAM
Schoonhoven
Vianen
Goeree
Ouddorp
Hellevoetsluis
Rhoon
Barendrecht
Ridderkerk
MOLENS VAN KINDERDIJK
Spijkenisse
Stellendam
Schouwen
Burgh-Haamstede
Grevelingen
ZUID HOLLAND
Oud Beijerland
Zwijndrecht
Hendrik Ido Ambacht
Leerdam
Culemborg
Middelharnis
DORDRECHT
Sliedrecht
Gorinchem
Brouwershaven
Zierikzee
NATIONAAL PARK DE BIESBOSCH
Zaltbommel
Kingston upon Hull Rosyth
Kingston upon Hull Harwich
Walcheren
Domburg
Noord-Beveland
Willemstad
Hollands Diep
Sluis
Zijpe
Geertruidenberg
Aalburg
Westkapelle
Veere
Kamperland
Stavenisse
Steenbergen
Zevenbergen
Made
Oosterhout
Waalwijk
ZEELAND
Kruisland
Kaatsheuvel
Middelburg
Goes
BREDA
Vlissingen
Halsteren
Knokke-Heist
Bergen op Zoom
Roosendaal
Kruiningen
Zeebrugge
Blankenberge
De Haan
Lissewege
Breskens
Schoondijke
Hoedekenskerke
Perkpolder
Westerschelde
Oostburg
Terneuzen
Hoogerheide
Zundert
TILBURG
Gilze
Goirle
Oirschot
Baarle
Oisterwijk
NOORD

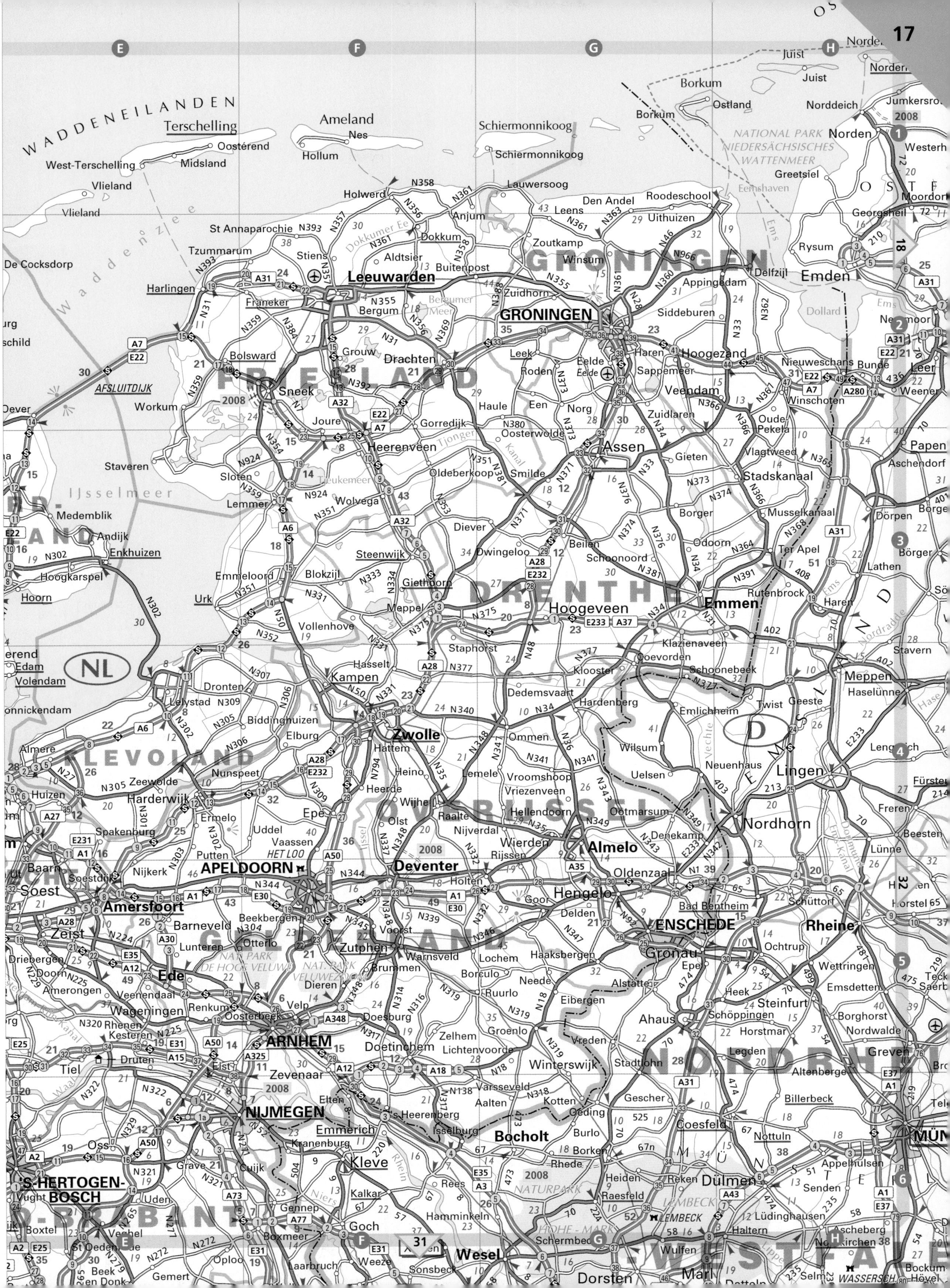
WADDENEILANDEN
Terschelling
West-Terschelling
Oosterend
Midsland
Vlieland
Ameland
Nes
Hollum
Schiermonnikoog
Borkum
Juist
Norden
Norddeich
Ostland
NATIONAL PARK NIEDERSÄCHSISCHES WATTENMEER
Greetsiel
Emden
Delfzijl
Leeuwarden
GRONINGEN
Harlingen
Franeker
Dokkum
Holwerd
Lauwersoog
Zoutkamp
Uithuizen
Appingedam
Hoogezand
Drachten
Bolsward
Sneek
Heerenveen
Joure
Workum
Stavoren
Lemmer
Wolvega
Assen
Veendam
Winschoten
Stadskanaal
Emmen
Hoogeveen
Meppel
Steenwijk
Giethoorn
Emmeloord
Urk
Kampen
Zwolle
Dronten
Lelystad
Almere
Harderwijk
Ermelo
Amersfoort
APELDOORN
Deventer
Zutphen
Hengelo
Almelo
ENSCHEDE
Oldenzaal
Gronau
Nordhorn
Lingen
Meppen
Rheine
Ede
ARNHEM
NIJMEGEN
'S-HERTOGEN-BOSCH
Kleve
Emmerich
Bocholt
Coesfeld
Dülmen
Wesel
MÜN
FRIESLAND
DRENTHE
FLEVOLAND
OVERIJSSEL
GELDERLAND
NL
D
Afsluitdijk
IJsselmeer
Waddenzee
31

Utersum
Wyk
Amrum
FRIESISCHE
Wittdün
Langeness
Hooge
Pellworm
INSELN
NATIONALPARK
SCHLESWIG-
HOLSTEINISCHES
WATTENMEER
Westerhever
St Peter -Ording
Helgoland
Deutsche Bucht
Scharhörn
NATIONALPARK
NIEDERSÄCHSISCHES
WATTENMEER
Neuwerk
Duhnen
Cuxh
Altenwalde
OSTFRIESISCHE INSELN
Juist
Norderney
Baltrum
Langeoog
Spiekeroog
Wangerooge
Borkum
Ostland
Norddeich
Jumkersrott
Dornum
Bensersiel
Esens
Carolinensiel
Minsen
Kirchen
Hooksiel
Norden
Westerholt
Ogenbargen
Wittmund
Jever
Langwarden
Midlum
Dorum
Langen
Greetsiel
OSTFRIESLAND
NATIONAL PARK
NIEDERSÄCHSISCHES
WATTENMEER
Eemshaven
Roodeschool
Den Andel
Leens
Uithuizen
Zoutkamp
Moordorf
Georgsheil
Aurich
Neuer Weg
Wilhelmshaven
Eckwarden
Blexen
BREMERHAVEN
Nordenham
Sande
Rysum
Emden
Delfzijl
GRONINGEN
Appingedam
Siddeburen
Wiesmoor
Ems-Jade Kanal
Friedeburg
Zetel
Varel
Jadebusen
Stotel
Beverstedt
Rodenkirchen
Timmel
Neuenburg
Dollard
Neermoor
Remels
Hesel
Spohle
Jade
Sandstedt
Hagen
Brake
Fehnter Kanal
Haren
Hoogezand
Sappemeer
Eelde
Roden
Nieuweschans
Bunde
Leer
Loga
Weener
Westerstede
Apen
Wiefelstede
Hahn
Rastede
Uthlede
Veendam
Winschoten
AMMERLAND
Elsfleth
Schwanewede
Zuidlaren
Oude-Pekela
Barssel
Bad Zwischenahn
Berne
Lesum
Assen
Gieten
Vlagtweed
Papenburg
Aschendorf
Strücklingen
Edewecht
OLDENBURG
Stadskanaal
Sedelsberg
Küsten-Kanal
Friesoythe
Wardenburg
Bösel
BREMEN
Delmenhorst
Ganderkesee
Borger
Musselkanaal
Dörpen
Börgermoor
Esterwegen
NL
Beilen
Odoorn
Lorup
Vrees
Ter Apel
Schoonoord
Börger
Lathen
Peheim
Garrel
Grossenkneten
Brinkum
Rutenbrock
DRENTHE
Emmen
Hoogeveen
Haren
Sögel
Werlte
Lindern
Ahlhorn
Wildeshausen
Harpstedt
Syke
Wachtum
Cloppenburg
Emstek
Visbek
Bassum
Klazienaveen
Coevorden
Schoonebeek
Stavern
Lastrup
Elsten
Goldenstedt
Twistringen
Kloosters
Meppen
Haselünne
Löningen
Bakum
Engeln
Hardenberg
Emlichheim
Twist
Geeste
Herzlake
Essen
Vechta
Ehrenburg
Asendorf
Schwaförden
Quakenbrück
Lohne
Cornau
Barnstorf
Wisum
Lengerich
Dinklage
Sulingen
Uelsen
Neuenhaus
Lingen
Bersenbrück
Holdorf
Diepholz
Barver
Barenburg
NIEDERSACHSEN
EMSLAND
NATURPARK WILDESHAUSER GEEST
NATURPARK NÖRDL.
Ems
Hunte
Weser
Hase
Vechte
Soeste
Nordradde
A B C D
1 2 3 4 5 6
17
32

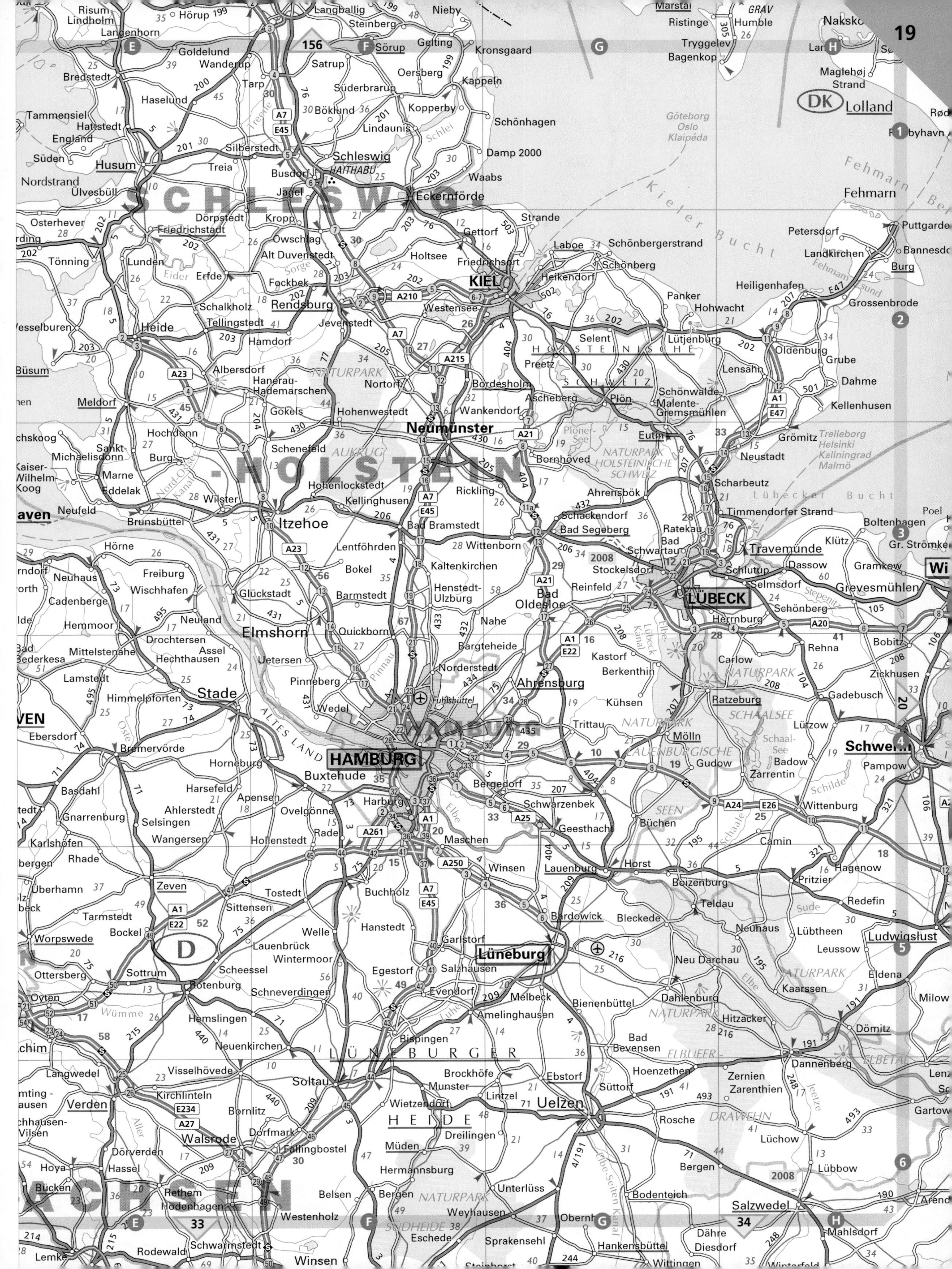
SCHLESWIG-HOLSTEIN
NIEDERSACHSEN
DK
Lolland
D
Risum-Lindholm
Langenhorn
Hörup
Langballig
Nieby
Marstal
Ristinge
Humble
Tryggelev
Bagenkop
Nakskov
Maglehøj Strand
Rødbyhavn
Goldelund
Wanderup
Sörup
Gelting
Kronsgaard
Steinberg
Satrup
Oersberg
Kappeln
Bredstedt
Tarp
Süderbrarup
Haselund
Böklund
Kopperby
Schönhagen
Tammensiel
Hattstedt
England
Lindaunis
Schlei
Treene
Göteborg
Oslo
Klaipėda
Süden
Husum
Silberstedt
Schleswig
HAITHABU
Damp 2000
Nordstrand
Ülvesbüll
Treia
Busdorf
Jagel
Waabs
Eckernförde
Fehmarn
Fehmarnbelt
Kieler Bucht
Osterhever
Dörpstedt
Kropp
Strande
Puttgarden
Petersdorf
Bannesdorf
Friedrichstadt
Owschlag
Gettorf
Laboe
Schönbergerstrand
Landkirchen
Burg
Tönning
Lunden
Alt Duvenstedt
Holtsee
Friedrichsort
Schönberg
Fehmarnsund
Eider
Erfde
Sorge
Fockbek
KIEL
Heikendorf
Heiligenhafen
Grossenbrode
Rendsburg
Schalkholz
Westensee
Panker
Hohwacht
Wesselburen
Heide
Tellingstedt
Jevenstedt
Selent
Lütjenburg
Oldenburg
Hamdorf
Büsum
Albersdorf
Hanerau-Hademarschen
Nortorf
NATURPARK
HOLSTEINISCHE SCHWEIZ
Preetz
Bordesholm
Ascheberg
Lensahn
Grube
Dahme
Schönwalde
Malente-Gremsmühlen
Kellenhusen
Meldorf
Gokels
Hohenwestedt
Wankendorf
Plön
Plöner See
Neumünster
Eutin
Grömitz
Hochdonn
Schenefeld
AUKRUG
Trelleborg
Helsinki
Kaliningrad
Malmö
Sankt-Michaelisdonn
Burg
Bornhöved
Neustadt
Marne
Kaiser-Wilhelm-Koog
Nord-Ostsee-Kanal
Eddelak
Hohenlockstedt
Rickling
Ahrensbök
Scharbeutz
Lübecker Bucht
Wilster
Kellinghusen
Neufeld
Cuxhaven
Brunsbüttel
Itzehoe
Bad Bramstedt
Schackendorf
Bad Segeberg
Timmendorfer Strand
Ratekau
Poel
Boltenhagen
Klütz
Gr. Strömkendorf
Hörne
Lentföhrden
Wittenborn
Bad Schwartau
Travemünde
Freiburg
Kaltenkirchen
Stockelsdorf
Schlutup
Dassow
Gramkow
Wismar
Neuhaus
Wischhafen
Bokel
Henstedt-Ulzburg
Bad Oldesloe
Reinfeld
Selmsdorf
Grevesmühlen
Cadenberge
Glückstadt
Barmstedt
LÜBECK
Stepenitz
Schönberg
Hemmoor
Neuland
Nahe
Herrnburg
Elmshorn
Quickborn
Rehna
Bobitz
Drochtersen
Assel
Bargteheide
Kastorf
Carlow
Bad Bederkesa
Mittelstenahe
Hechthausen
Uetersen
Lübeck Kanal
Elbe
Berkenthin
Zickhusen
Norderstedt
Lamstedt
Pinneberg
Pinnau
Ahrensburg
Ratzeburg
Gadebusch
Stade
Himmelpforten
Fuhlsbüttel
Wedel
Kühsen
SCHAALSEE
ALTES LAND
Trittau
Lützow
Oste
Ebersdorf
Bremervörde
HAMBURG
Schaal-See
Mölln
Schwerin
Horneburg
Buxtehude
LAUENBURGISCHE SEEN
Gudow
Badow
Pampow
Basdahl
Harsefeld
Bergedorf
Zarrentin
Schilde
Apensen
Harburg
Schwarzenbek
Wittenburg
Gnarrenburg
Ahlerstedt
Ovelgönne
Selsingen
Rade
Geesthacht
Büchen
Wangersen
Hollenstedt
Maschen
Karlshöfen
Camin
Rhade
Horst
Hagenow
Winsen
Lauenburg
Boizenburg
Pritzier
Zeven
Uberhamn
Tostedt
Buchholz
Teldau
Redefin
Sittensen
Sude
Tarmstedt
Bardowick
Bleckede
Bockel
Welle
Hanstedt
Neuhaus
Lübtheen
Worpswede
Lauenbrück
Garlstorf
Ludwigslust
Wintermoor
Lüneburg
Neu Darchau
Leussow
Scheessel
Egestorf
Salzhausen
Ottersberg
Sottrum
Eldena
Rotenburg
Schneverdingen
Evendorf
Karrsen
Oyten
Melbeck
Dahlenburg
Wümme
Bienenbüttel
Milow
Hemslingen
Amelinghausen
Hitzacker
Dömitz
Achim
Neuenkirchen
Bispingen
Bad Bevensen
ELBUFER
LÜNEBURGER HEIDE
Dannenberg
ELBETAL
Langwedel
Visselhövede
Soltau
Brockhöfe
Ebstorf
Hoenzethen
Zernien
Zarenthien
Jeetze
Munster
Süttorf
Lenzen
Kirchlinteln
Verden
Wietzendorf
Linzel
Uelzen
Rosche
DRAWEHN
Gartow
Etelsen
Bornlitz
Achim-Baden
Aller
Walsrode
Dorfmark
Dreilingen
Lüchow
Dörverden
Fallingbostel
Müden
Hoya
Hassel
Hermannsburg
Elbe-Seitenkanal
Bergen
Lübbow
Bücken
Rethem
Belsen
Unterlüss
Bodenteich
Salzwedel
Arendsee
Hodenhagen
Westenholz
Weyhausen
Obernholz
SÜDHEIDE
Eschede
Sprakensehl
Dähre
Mahlsdorf
Diesdorf
Schwarmstedt
Rodewald
Lemke
Winsen
Hankensbüttel
Wittingen
Steinhorst
Winterfeld

Stokkemarke
Guldborg
Alslev
FANEFJORD
Møns Klint
Bandholm
Sakskøbing
Stubbekøbing
Søllested
Toreby
Ørbelev
157
Hesnæs
Maribo
KRENKERUP
Strand
Nykøbing
Lolland
Holeby
Falster
Rødby
Frejlev
Væggerløse
Rødbyhavn
Øster Ulslev
Nysted
Marielyst
ÅLHOLM SLOT
Marrebæk
Gedesby
DK
Fehmarn Belt
Fehmarn
Gedser
NATIONALPARK VORPOMMERSCHE BODDENLANDSCHAFT
Kap Arkona
Putgarten
Dranske
Altenkirchen
Wiek
Glowe
Puttgarden
Bannesdorf
Burg
Fehmarnsund
Grossenbrode
Trelleborg
Tallinn
Hanko/Hangö
Helsinki/Helsingfors
Kotka
Liepāja
Kaliningrad
Darsser Ort
Hiddensee
NATURPARK Grosser Jasmunder Bodden
Sagard
Schaprode
Kluis
Prerow
Zingst
Gingst
Bergen
Neu Mukran
Klausdorf
Grube
Wustrow
Barth
Gross Mohrdorf
Rambin
Binz
Dahme
Mecklenburger Bucht
Stralsund
Samtens
Putbus
Dierhagen
Saaler Bodden
Graal-Müritz
Löbnitz
Garz
RÜGEN
Kellenhusen
Ribnitz-Damgarten
Steinhagen
Zudar
Kühlungsborn
Nienhagen
Warnemünde
Richtenberg
Greifswalder Bodden
Rerik
Bad Doberan
Krummendorf
Rövershagen
Abtshagen
Reinberg
Franzburg
Marlow
Lubmin
Pepelow
Brodestorf
Bad Sülze
Tribsees
Grimmen
Greifswald
Poel
Kröpelin
ROSTOCK
Sanitz
Kemnitz
Boltenhagen
Kirchdorf
Neubukow
Satow
Tessin
Glewitz
Poggendorf
Klütz
Gr. Strömkendorf
Recknitz
Trebel
Loitz
Gramkow
Wismar
Zusow
D
Gnoien
Züssow
Grevesmühlen
Schwaan
Laage
Peene
Toitz
Neukloster
Weitendorf
Jördenstorf
Dargun
Demmin
Jarmen
Gützkow
Bobitz
Bützow
Ziethen
Rehna
Qualitz
MECKLENBURG-
Thürkow
Warin
Güstrow
Neukalen
Tollense
Zickhusen
Bad Kleinen
Prüzen
Kummerower-See
Klempenow
Gadebusch
Brüel
Teterow
Malchin
Golchen
Sarnow
Sternberg
Malchiner See
Tützpatz
Lohmen
Reuterstadt Stavenhagen
Schwanbeck
Krakow am See
Ziddorf
Schweriner See
SCHLITZ
Altentreptow
Boldekow
Schwerin
Dahmen
Kittendorf
Neddemin
Pampow
MECKLENBURGISCHE
Friedland
Mestlin
VORPOMMERN
Schilde
Crivitz
Goldberg
Wittenburg
Zölkow
Kl. Plasten
Rothemühl
Herzberg
Karow
Marihn
Schönbeck
Elde
Severin
Waren
Lollense See
Neubrandenburg
Hagenow
Lübz
Malchow
Penzlin
Klink
Klein Vielen
Burg Stargard
Parchim
Plau
Woldegk
Redefin
Plauer See
Müritz See
Neustadt-Glewe
Dambeck
Tannenhof
Röbel
MÜRITZ-NATIONALPARK
MECKLENBURGISCHE SEENPLATTE
NATURPARK FELDBERGER SEEN
Ludwigslust
Marnitz
Möllenbeck
Neustrelitz
Grabow
Meyenburg
Fürstenwerder
Zierzow
Wredenhagen
MÜRITZ-NATIONLP.
Eldena
Freyenstein
Feldberg
Carwitz
Putlitz
Wesenberg
LANDSCHAFT
Boitzenburg
Milow
Mirow
Wustrow
Beenz
Karstädt
Reetz
Lychen
Dömitz
Hassleben
PRIGNITZ
Pritzwalk
Ravensbrück
NATURPARK UCKERMÄRKISCHE SEEN
Mittenwalde
ELBETAL
Lenzen
Wittstock
Fürstenberg
Perleberg
Schnackenburg
Herzsprung
Gramzow
Templin
Milmersdorf
Tüchen
Gartow
Fretzdorf
Rheinsberg
Menz
Schönebeck
Dannenwalde
Wittenberge
Neu Schrepkow
BIOSPHÄRENRESERVAT
Köpernitz
Grosswoltersdorf
Friedrichswalde
Aland
Bad Wilsnack
Katerbow
Gransee
Lübbow
Gumtow
Dosse
Ledge
Kyritz
Zehdenick
Havel
Alt Ruppin
Lindow
Joachimsthal
Arendsee
Seehausen
Glöwen
Breddin
Neuruppin
JAGDSHL HUBERTUSSTOCK
Wusterhausen
BRANDENBURG
Gross Schönebeck
Mahlsdorf
Werben
Herzberg
Lückstedt
Neustadt
Bückwitz
Rüthnick
Löwenberg
Havelberg
Osterburg
Sommerfeld
Liebenwalde
Sandau
Fehrbellin

Dueodde
E
F
159
G
H
1
2
3
4
5
6
Trelleborg
GSSTUHL
NATIONALPARK JASMUND
Sankt-Peterburg
Klaipėda
Rønne
Sassnitz
Mukran
Rügen
JAGDSCHL. GRANITZ
Sellin
Göhren
BIOSPHÄRENRESERVAT SÜDOST RÜGEN
Thiessow
Peenemünde
Freest
Zinnowitz
Ystad
København
Rønne
Wolgast
Koserow
Usedom
NATURPARK USEDOM
Bansin
Heringsdorf
Lassan
Ahlbeck
Murchin
Świnoujście
Usedom
Zirchow
Anklam
Międzyzdroje
Wisełka
Dziwnów
Dziwnówek
Wolin
Pobierowo
Rewal
Niechorze
Mrzeżyno
Dźwirzyno
Kołobrzeg
Ustronie Morskie
Sarbinowo
Mielno
Jezioro Jamno
Łazy
Darłów
Dąbki
Sia
Kukinia
Będzino
Koszalin
Dygowo
Błotnica
Parsęta
Trzebiatów
Kamień Pomorski
Cerkwica
Gościno
Karlino
Biesiekierz
Niedalino
Radew
Białogard
Nartkowo
Rymań
Brojce
Kołczewo
WOLIŃSKI PARK NARODOWY
Rzewnowo
Świerzno
Gryfice
Mechowo
Rzesznikowo
Podwilcze
Powalice
Sławoborze
Byszyno
Weldk
Tych
Stare Dęb
Wicimice
Karsibór
Wolin
Parłówko
Golczewo
Stettiner Haff
Zalew Szczeciński
Płoty
Rusinowo
Świdwin
Nw. Ludzicko
Kołacz
Ducherow
Ueckermünde
UECKERMÜNDER HEIDE
Altwarp
Nowe Warpno
Jarszewko
Przybiernów
Błotno
Resko
Starogard
Połczyn-Zdrój
Eggesin
Rieth
Zielonczyn
Babigoszcz
Radowo Wielkie
Słonowice
DRAWSKI PARK KRAJOBRAZOWY
ZACHODNIOPOMORS
Heinrichsruh
Ahlbeck
Trzebież
Stepnica
Nowogard
Łobez
Łabędzie
Ostrowice
Torgelow
Hintersee
PUSZCZA WKRZAŃSKA
Katy
Stallberg
Grünhof
Święta
Jenikowo
Dobra
Zarańsko
Cieszyno
POJEZIERZE
Pasewalk
Tanowo
Police
Goleniów
PUSZCZA GOLENIOWSKA
Nastazin
Węgorzyno
Drawsko Pomorskie
Złocieniec
Czaplin
Strasburg
Buk
Jezioro Dąbie
Maszewo
Chociwel
IŃSKI PARK KRAJOBR.
Jezioro Lubie
Linken
Lubieszyn
SZCZECIN
Löcknitz
Przemocze
Łęczyca
Ińsko
Konotop
Göritz
Grambow
Dąbie
Brüssow
Dobrzany
Ciemnik
Pomellen
Morzyczyn
Stargard-Szczeciński
Mirosławiec
PL
Schmölln
Kołbaskowo
SZCZECIŃSKI PARK KRAJOBRAZOWY
Kołbacz
Penkum
Stare Czarnowo
Jezioro Miedwie
Suchań
Recz
Kalisz Pomorski
Bronikowo
Zollchow
NATIONALPARK
Gartz
Gryfino
Warnice
Bedgoszcz
Kolin
Piasecznik
Drawno
Gramzow
Casekow
UNTERES ODERTAL
Nowe Czarnowo
Dolice
Choszczno
Suliszewo
Tuczno
Passow
Kunow
Lubiatowo
Widuchowa
Pyrzyce
Zatom
DRAWIEŃSKI PARK NARODOWY
Greiffenberg
Ognica
Banie
Płotno
Krzęcin
Łasko
Człopa
Schwedt
Piaseczno
Jesionowo
Breń
Radęcin
Angermünde
Krajnik Gorny
Trzcińsko Zdrój
Pełczyce
Sowiniec
Bierzwnik
Lipiany
Otanów
Rów
Barlinek
Dobiegniew
Stare Osieczno
Chojna
CEDYŃSKI PARK KRAJOBRAZOWY
STOLPE
KLOSTER CHORIN
35
Myślibórz
BARLINECKO GORZOWSKI PARK KRAJOBR.
Dańków
36
Oderberg
Cedynia
Trzcinna
Strzelce Krajeńskie
Długie
Krzyż Wlkp.
Wieleń
Rosk
Witnica
A20
A11
E28
A6
E28
E65
E28/E65
22

A
B
C
D
1
2
3
4
5
6
NADMORSKI PARK KRAJOBRAZOWY
SŁOWIŃSKI PARK NARODOWY
Białogóra
Karwia
Jastrzębia
Władysławowo
Wierzchucino
Łeba
Ulinia
Krokowa
Swarzewo
Choczewo
Puck
Mierzyno
Celbowo
Jezioro Gardno
Jezioro Łebsko
Kluki
Steknica
Żelazna
Wielka Piaśnica
Rowy
Wicko
Smołdzino
Zamostne
Bolszewo
Reda
Ustka
Objazda
Gąbino
Żelkowo
Główczyce
Wejherowo
Rumia
Jarosławiec
Jezioro Wicko
Nowa Wieś Lęborska
Lębork
Godętowo
Wicie
Lubuczewo
Damno
TRÓJMIEJSKI PARK KRAJOBRAZOWY
Postomino
Słupsk
Osowo Lęborskie
Drozdowo
Mianowice
Koleczkowo
Darłówko
Kanin
Rędzikowo
Łebno
Chwaszczyno
Wieprza
Staniewice
Lupawa
Oskowo
Dąbki
Darłowo
Warszkowo
Dębnica Kaszubska
Czarna Dąbrówka
Miszewo
Rębiechowo
Bukowo Morskie
Sławno
Słupia
KASZUBSKI
Przodkowo
Sierakowice
Kartuzy
Łazy
Malechowo
Korzybie
Budowo
Rokity
Żukowo
Kolbudy Górne
Ostrowiec
Barcino
Suchorze
Unichowo
DOLINA SŁUPI
Mielno
Jasień
Klukowa Huta
Egiertowo
Jezioro Jamno
Niemica
Kępice
Kołczygłowy
Sulęczyno
Będzino
Laski
Pomysk Wielki
WIEŻYCA
Koszalin
Sianów
Krąg
Borzysław
Bytów
Półczno
Nowa Karczma
Trzepowo
Mzdowo
Łubno
Korne
Biesiekierz
Jacinki
Tuchomie
Udorpie
Kościerzyna
Mostowo
Polanów
Dretyń
POMORSKIE
Skarszewy
Niedalino
Radew
Studzienice
Lipusz
Rosnowo
Piaszczyna
Białogard
Wdzydze
Starogard Gdański
Głodowa
Drzewiany
Miastko
Lipnica
Dziemiany
Byszyno
Wełdkowo
WDZYDZKI PARK KRAJDZRAZ.
ZABORSKI PARK KRAJOBRAZOWY
Jezioro Wdzydze
Bobolice
Upiłka
Wiele
Zblewo
Tychowo
Bytonia
Borzechowo
Nw. Łudzicko
Stare Dębno
Biały Bór
Koczała
Zielona Chocina
Brusy
Osowo Leśne
Wierzchowo
Brzezie
Parsęta
Grzmiąca
Konarzyny
Swornegacie
Męcikal
Czarna Woda
Ocypel
Kołacz
Przechlewo
BORY
Wda
Połczyn Zdrój
Gwda Wielka
Rzeczenica
Rytel
Czersk
Osieczna
Barwice
PARK NAR. BORY TUCHOLSKIE
Brda
DRAWSKI PARK KRAJOBRAZOWY
Charzykowy
Legbąd
Śliwice
Luby
Szczecinek
POJEZIERZE DRAWSKIE
Chojnice
TUCHOLSKIE
TUCHOLSKI PARK KRAJOBR.
Ostrowice
Czarne
Człuchów
Silno
TUCHOLSKI PARK KRAJOBRAZOWY
Jelenino
Tleń
Osie
Zarańsko
Lotyn
Barkowo
Zamarte
Tuchola
Cieszyno
Łubowo
Jezioro Pile
Borne Sulinowo
Czaplinek
Debrzno
Kamień Krajeński
Lniano
Drawsko Pomorskie
Złocieniec
Okonek
Lędyczek
Pamiętowo
Ostrowite
Machliny
Lipka
Gostycyn
Bisław
Laskowice
Jezioro Lubie
Podgaje
Radawnica
Lutowo
Sępólno Krajeńskie
Obodowo
PL
Iłowiec
Jastrowie
Sośnica
Byszki
Górzna
Mąkowarsko
Tuszyny
Sypniewo
KUJAWSKO-POMORSKIE
Mirosławiec
Złotów
Więcbork
Łowinek
Kłębowiec
Szwecja
Koronowo
Pruszcz
Chełmno
Zbrachlin
Kalisz Pomorski
Bronikowo
Płytnica
Krajenka
Rudna
Wierzchucin Królewski
WIŚLANY
Wałcz
Łobżenica
Dobrcz
Skórka
Mrocza
Tryszczyn
Unisław
Tuczno
Gostomia
Wysoka
Kosztowo
Sadki
Ślesin
Rusinowo
Szydłowo
Piła
Wyrzysk
Nakło nad Notecią
Wybcz
DRAWIEŃSKI PARK NARODOWY
Śmiłowo
Ostromecko
Człopa
Paterek
BYDGOSZCZ
Trzcianka
Noteć
Studzienki
Drawno
Ujście
Smogulec
Rynarzewo
Brzoza
Solec Kujawski
Stare Osieczno
Szamocin
Szubin
Kcynia
Siedlisko
Chodzież
Margonin
Łabiszyn
Sarbia
Gołańcz
Krzyż Wlkp.
Wieleń
Rosko
Czarnków
Budzyń
Pawłowo Żońskie
Morakowo
Murczyn
Gniewkowo
36
21

Zelenogradsk
Svetlogorsk
Primor'ye
Zalivnoye
Kashirskoye
Kaliningrad
Yantarnyy
Kruglovo
Primorsk
KALININGRAD
КАЛИНИНГРАД
Svetlyy
Baltiysk
Gvardeysk
Pregolya
Komsomol'sk
Ushakovo
Ladushkin
Chekhovo
RUS
Prokhladnaya
Juzhnyj
Tishino
Druzhba
Pyatidorozhnoye
Kaliningradskiy Zaliv
Mamonovo
Kornevo
Gvardeiskoye
Dolgorukovo
Domnovo
Pravdinsk
Bagrationovsk
Bogatovo
Shirokoye
Karlskrona
Rostock
Travemünde
Nynäshamn
Jastarnia
Zatoka Pucka
Hel
Zatoka Gdańska
GDYNIA
Sopot
GDAŃSK
PARK KRAJOBR. MIERZEJA WIŚLANA
Nowa Karczma
Krynica Morska
Zalew Wiślany
Frombork
Braniewo
Żelazna Góra
Głębock
Lipowina
Lelkowo
Górowo Iławeckie
Sępopol
Mikoszewo
Sztutowo
Sobieszewo
Stegna
Tolkmicko
Pogrodzie
Płoskinia
Pluty
Bartoszyce
Łyna
Pruszcz Gdański
Kiezmark
PARK KRAJOBR. WYSOCZYZNY ELBLĄSKIEJ
Pakosze
Pieniężno
Korsze
Trutnowy
Łęgowo
Nowy Dwór Gdański
Milejewo
Pasłęka
Babiak
Galiny
Ostaszewo
Młynary
Nowica
STOCZEK KLASZTORNY
Wozławki
ELBLĄG
Orneta
Lidzbark Warmiński
Bisztynek
Nowy Staw
Wisła
Nogat
Tczew
Jegłownik
Godkowo
Lubomino
Krosno
Pasłęk
WARMIŃSKO
Lutry
Swarożyn
Malbork
Str. Pole
Zwierzno
Miłakowo
Radostowo
Kalnik
Wilczkowo
Dobre Miasto
Jeziorany
Subkowy
Szropy
Rychliki
Rudno
Piekło
Myślice
Małdyty
Morąg
Kalisty
Gradki
Tuławki
Sztum
Dzierzgoń
Pelplin
Czernin
Balewo
Przezmark
Spręcowo
Biskupiec
Barczewo
Stary Dzierzgoń
Zalewo
Zawroty
Kromerowo
Gniew
Gurcz
Mikołajki Pomorskie
Jerzwałd
Śliwa
Łukta
OLSZTYN
Skórcz
Brachlewo
Jezioro Jeziorak
Miłomłyn
Gietrzwałd
Dźwierzuty
Mała Karczma
Prabuty
Susz
Siemiany
PARK KRAJOBR. POJEZIERZA IŁAWSKIEGO
Ostróda
Osiek
Kwidzyn
MAZURY
Mańki
Pasym
Stawiguda
Frednowy
Warlubie
Nowe
Gardeja
Szymbark
Kisielice
Lipowo
Rychnowo
Olsztynek
Butryny
Dzierzki
Iława
Pietrzwałd
DYLEWSKA GÓRA
Zgniłocha
Pawłowo
Jedwabno
Dusocin
Lasin
Lubawa
Marwałd
Frygnowo
Grunwald
Rączki
Zimna Woda
Dolna Grupa
Biskupiec
Nowe Miasto Lubawskie
Dąbrówno
Nidzica
Wielbark
Grudziądz
Okonin
Jabłonowo Pomorskie
BRODNICKI PARK KRAJOBR.
Kurzętnik
Rybno
Wierzbowo
Muszaki
Świecie
Paparzyn
Radzyń Chełmiński
Brzozie Lubawskie
Uzdowo
WELSKI PARK KRAJOBR.
Janowo
Stolno
Płużnica
Grzybno
Kozłowo
Chorzele
Wąbrzeźno
Papowo Biskupie
Niedźwiedź
Brodnica
Lidzbark
Działdowo
Załęże
Małowidz
GÓRZNIEŃSKO-LIDZBARSKI PARK KRAJOBR.
Bielczyny
Orzechowo
Wrocki
Górzno
Kuklin
Krzynowłoga Mała
Chełmża
Lipnica
Zieluń
Mława
Łubianka
Kowalewo Pomorskie
Okalewo
Lubowidz
Rzęgnowo
Drążdżewo
Mchowo
Łysomice
Golub Dobrzyń
Rypin
Żuromin
Grudusk
Radomin
Grębocin
Szreńsk
Przasnysz
Dobrzejewice
Zbójno
Karniszyn
Szulmierz
Wola Wierzbowska
TORUŃ
Bieżuń
Mdzewo
Czernikowo
Karlewo
Radzanów
Ciechanów
Aleksandrów Kujawski
Ciechocinek
Kikół
Grodzeń
Skępe
Rościszewo
Strzegowo
Ościsłowo
Sierpc

KALININGRAD
KALININGRAD
КАЛИНИНГРАД
Zelenogradsk
Kashirskoye
Zalivnoye
Krasnoye
Bol'shakovo
Zhilino
Instruch
Ul'janovo
Uzlovoye
Dobrovol'sk
Vesnovo
Kaliningrad
Poles
Kalinovka
Petino
Krasnyy Bor
Visokoye
Lipovka
Kruglovo
Talpaki
Chernyakhovsk
Черняховск
Nesterov
Svetlyy
Gvardeysk
Pregolya
Znamensk
Podgornoye
Gusev
Гусев
Chkalovo
Komsomol'sk
Ushakovo
RUS
Novobobruysk
Svoboda
Chekhovo
Prokhladnaya
Juzhnyj
Tishino
Druzhba
Lava
Dubrava
Angrapa
Mozyr'
Luzhki
Kornevo
Gvardeiskoye
Pravdinsk
Ozersk
Dolgorukovo
Domnovo
Krasnosel'e
Zheleznodorozhnyj
Zaozernoye
Bagrationovsk
Shirokoye
Krylovo
PUSZCZA ROMINCKA
Żelazna Góra
Bogatovo
Głębock
Olownik
Gołdap
Błąka
Dzietrzychowo
Michałkowo
Perly
PUSZCZY ROMINCKIEJ PARK KRAJOBRAZOWY
Lelkowo
Górowo Iławeckie
Budry
Banie Mazurskie
Sępopol
Łyna
Pluty
Filipów
Puszcza
Bartoszyce
Barciany
Srokowo
Węgorzewo
PUSZCZA BORECKA
Pieniężno
Korsze
Kowale Oleckie
Jezioro Mamry
Pozedrze
Babiak
STOCZEK KLASZTORNY
Galiny
Czerwony Dwór
Cichy
Garbno
Sztynort
Orneta
Wozławki
Gałwany
Kętrzyn
Gryzy
Lidzbark Warmiński
Bisztynek
Giżycko
Olecko
Lubomino
Reszel
Wronki
WARMIŃSKO-MAZURSKIE
Kąp
Wielic
Cimochy
Lutry
Święta Lipka
Sterławki Wielkie
Jezioro Niegocin
Wydminy
Gąski
Radostowo
Ryn
Ridzewo
Jez. Łaśmiady
Wilczkowo
Dobre Miasto
Jeziorany
Straduny
Szestno
Kalinowo
Gradki
Tuławki
Mrągowo
Spręcowo
Biskupiec
Tałty
Orzysz
Ełk
Barczewo
Sorkwity
Mikołajki
Jezioro Śniardwy
Klusy
Nowa Wieś Ełcka
Wiśniewo Ełckie
Łukta
Kromerowo
Kobułty
MAZURSKI PARK KRAJOBRAZOWY
Piecki
OLSZTYN
Jezioro Roś
Prostki
Gietrzwałd
Dźwierzuty
Babięta
Ukta
Ruciane-Nida
Drygały
Grajewo
Mańki
Pasym
Pisz
Biała Piska
Ruda
Stawiguda
PUSZCZA PISKA
Wiartel
Szczuczyn
Butryny
Spychowo
Jezioro Nidzkie
Lachowo
Olsztynek
Zgniłocha
Dzierzki
Szczytno
Karwica
Wąsosz
Pawłowo
Jedwabno
Turośl
Grabowskie
Frygnowo
Rozogi
PL
Radziłów
Grunwald
Rączki
Zieleniec Duży
Kolno
Dąbrówno
Zimna Woda
Stawiski
Przytuły
Myszyniec
Dęby
Łyse
Korzeniste
Nidzica
Wielbark
Mały Płock
Jedwabne
Wierzbowo
Muszaki
PUSZCZA MYSZYNIECKA
Uzdowo
Kisielnica
Strękowa Góra
Janowo
Krukowo
Omulew
Kozłowo
Chorzele
Brodowe Łąka
Kadzidło
Rozoga
Nowogród
Działdowo
Wizna
Załęże
Baranowo
Dylewo
Łomża
Narew
Małowidz
Miastkowo
Kuklin
Krzynowłoga Mała
Jednorożec
Rutki-Kossaki
Mława
Dróżdżewo
Nowa Wieś
Gać
Mężenin
Rzęgnowo
Ostrołęka
Grudusk
Mchowo
Krasnosielc
Zamość
Zambrów
Szreńsk
Sypniewo
Przasnysz
Tyszki-Nadbory
Szulmierz
Zamość
Młynarze
Szumowo
Mdzewo
Wola Wierzbowska
Krzyżewo
Radzanów
Różan
Goworowo
Zaręby-Warchoły
Dąbrowa Kościelna
Ciechanów
Opinogóra Górna
Maków Mazowiecki
Strzegowo
Ościłowo
Ostrów Mazowiecka
Czyżew-Osada
Stary Szelków
200
38
E77
E28
E67
A229
A192
A191
A190
A216
A195
A196
A197
A198
A194
A193
P510
P512
P514
P516
P508
P517
P5
1
2
3
4
5
6
A
B
C
D
23
216
240
203
156

Griškabūdis
Višakio Rūda
Piliuona
Elektrenai
E85
201
Kazlu-Rūda
Kudirkos Naumiestis
Pilviškiai
Vilunai
Trakai
Lentvaris
Vilnius
TRAKU ISTORINIS NACIONALINIS PARKAS
Prienai
Jieznas
Aukštadvaris
Vilkaviškis
Kybartai
Igliauka
Birštonas
Rūdiškės
Marijampolė
Onuškis
Baltoji Voke
Jaši
Mikalavas
Pirčiupiai
Valkininkai
LT
Gražiškiai
Vishtytis
Girgantai
Kalvarija
Alytus
Daugai
Babriškes
Simnas
Krosna
Wiżajny
Meškasalis
Niadingė
Byenyakoni
Rutka-Tartak
Senoji Varena
Varena
Eišiškės
Lazdijai
Seriaji
Szypliszki
Merkine
Jeleniewo
Wojtokiemie
Nemunas
Merkys
DZŪKIJOS NACIONALINIS PARKAS
Radun'
Krasnopol
Sejny
Poćkuny
Veisiejai
Leipalingis
Randamonys
ČEPKELIU REZ.
Suwałki
WIGIERSKI PARK NARODOWY
Jez Wigry
Druskininkai
Zelwa
Kapčiamiestis
Fracki
Zabalats'
Matyli
Raczki
Rospuda
PUSZCZA
Serwy
Rudawka
Parechcha
Byershty
Khadziloni
Myto
Novyy Dvor
Vasilishki
Augustów
AUGUSTOWSKA
Sajenek
Sapotskin
Hozha
Astryna
203
Netta Pierwsza
Kurianka
Ratsichy
Azyory
Lipsk
HRODNA
ГРОДНА
Rajgród
Sztabin
Dąbrowa Białostocka
Shchuchin
Zhaludok
Nyoman
Bagny
Nowy Dwór
Skidal'
Razhanka
Orlya
BIEBRZAŃSKI PARK
Dębowo
Sidra
Suchowola
Kuźnica
Kvasowka
BY
Jedeszki
Nowowola
Sokolany
Indura
Lunna
Ruda Yavarskaya
Goniądz
Osowiec
Korycin
Janów
Struha
Masty
Kazlowshc
Sokółka
Vowpa
Pyaski
Jasionówka
Mońki
Popiołówka
Czarna Białostocka
PUSZCZA
Alyekshytsy
Ros'
Dzyarechyn
Krasnasyel'ski
Krasne Folwarczne
Krynki
KRAJOBRAZOWY
Gugny
Knyszyn
Czarna Białostocka
PUSZCZY KNYSZYŃSKIEJ
Vial. Berestavica
Vawkavysk
Zyel'va
Zel'vyenskaye vadaskhovishcha
Zal'vyan'ka
Wasilków
Supraśl
KNYSZYŃSKA
Jurowce
Tykocin
Żółtki
Królowy Most
Bobrowniki
Pahranichny
Karalin
Choroszcz
BIAŁYSTOK
Grabówka
Gródek
Svislach
Padarosk
Michałowo
Jałówka
NARWIAŃSKI PARK NARODOWY
Zabłudów
Porazava
Dashkavichy
Roszki-Wodźki
Łapy
Sokoły
Trześcianka
Juszkowy Gród
Ruzhany
Suraż
Doktorce
Narew
Ryboły
Wysokie Mazowieckie
Poświętne
Narewka
Klejniki
PUSZCZA
Topczewo
Wyszki
Nowosady
BIAŁOWIESKI PARK NARODOWY
Naraw
Nowe Piekuty
Bielsk Podlaski
Hajnówka
Białowieża
NATS. PARK
39
Brańsk
Zbucz
Vadaskhovishch Syalyets
Kharava
PODLASKIE

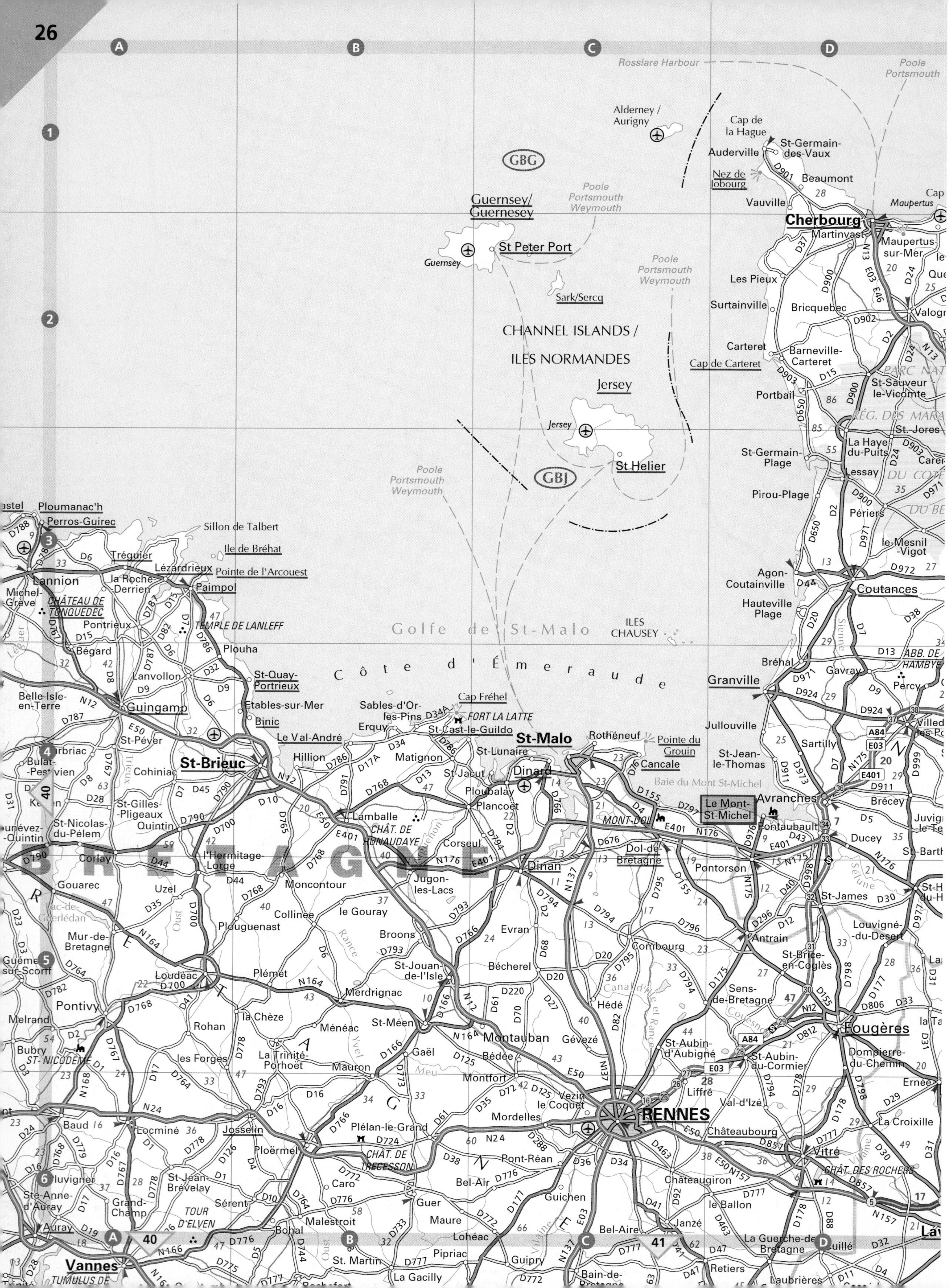

Rosslare Harbour
Poole Portsmouth
Alderney / Aurigny
Cap de la Hague
Auderville
St-Germain-des-Vaux
Nez de Jobourg
Beaumont
Vauville
Cherbourg
Martinvast
Maupertus
Maupertus-sur-Mer
GBG
Guernsey/Guernesey
St Peter Port
Guernsey
Poole Portsmouth Weymouth
Sark/Sercq
Les Pieux
Surtainville
Bricquebec
Valognes
CHANNEL ISLANDS /
ILES NORMANDES
Carteret
Barneville-Carteret
Cap de Carteret
Jersey
Portbail
St-Sauveur-le-Vicomte
PARC NAT
RÉG. DES MARA
La Haye-du-Puits
St.-Jores
St-Germain-Plage
Lessay
Pirou-Plage
Périers
St Helier
GBJ
Poole Portsmouth Weymouth
le-Mesnil-Vigot
Agon-Coutainville
Coutances
Hauteville Plage
ILES CHAUSEY
Golfe de St-Malo
Côte d'Émeraude
Bréhal
Gavray
ABB. DE HAMBYE
Granville
Percy
Jullouville
Sartilly
Villedieu-les-Poêles
St-Jean-le-Thomas
Ploumanac'h
Perros-Guirec
Sillon de Talbert
Ile de Bréhat
Tréguier
Lézardrieux
Pointe de l'Arcouest
Lannion
la Roche-Derrien
Paimpol
Michel-Grève
CHÂTEAU DE TONQUEDEC
TEMPLE DE LANLEFF
Pontrieux
Bégard
Plouha
Lanvollon
St-Quay-Portrieux
Belle-Isle-en-Terre
Guingamp
Etables-sur-Mer
Binic
Cap Fréhel
FORT LA LATTE
Sables-d'Or-les-Pins
Erquy
St-Cast-le-Guildo
St-Malo
Rothéneuf
Pointe du Grouin
Cancale
Le Val-André
St-Péver
St-Brieuc
Hillion
Matignon
St-Lunaire
Dinard
St-Jacut
Ploubalay
Plancoët
Baie du Mont St-Michel
Le Mont-St-Michel
Avranches
Brécey
Pontaubault
Ducey
Juvigny-le-Tertre
Bulat-Pestivien
Cohiniac
St-Gilles-Pligeaux
Quintin
St-Nicolas-du-Pélem
Lamballe
CHÂT. DE HUNAUDAYE
Corseul
MONT-DOL
Dol-de-Bretagne
Pontorson
St-Barthélemy
St-Hilaire-du-Harcouët
Corlay
l'Hermitage-Lorge
BRETAGNE
Jugon-les-Lacs
Dinan
St-James
Gouarec
Uzel
Moncontour
Lac-de-Guerlédan
Collinée
le Gouray
Evran
Mur-de-Bretagne
Plouguenast
Broons
Combourg
Antrain
Louvigné-du-Désert
St-Brice-en-Coglès
Guémené-sur-Scorff
Loudéac
Plémet
St-Jouan-de-l'Isle
Bécherel
Canal d'Ille et Rance
Hédé
Sens-de-Bretagne
Pontivy
Merdrignac
Melrand
Rohan
la Chèze
Ménéac
St-Méen
Montauban
Gévezé
St-Aubin-d'Aubigné
St-Aubin-du-Cormier
Fougères
Bubry
ST-NICODÈME
les Forges
La Trinité-Porhoët
Gaël
Bédée
Dompierre-du-Chemin
Mauron
Montfort
Liffré
Ernée
Vezin-le-Coquet
RENNES
Val-d'Izé
Baud
Locminé
Josselin
Plélan-le-Grand
Mordelles
Châteaubourg
La Croixille
Ploërmel
CHÂT. DE TRECESSON
Pont-Réan
Vitré
CHÂT. DES ROCHERS
Pluvigner
St-Jean-Brévelay
Caro
Bel-Air
Châteaugiron
Ste-Anne-d'Auray
Grand-Champ
Sérent
Guichen
le Ballon
Guer
TOUR D'ELVEN
Malestroit
Maure
Janzé
Auray
Bohal
Lohéac
Bel-Aire
La Guerche-de-Bretagne
Cuillé
Vannes
TUMULUS DE
St. Martin
Pipriac
Guipry
Bain-de-Bretagne
Retiers
Laval
La Gacilly
Laubrières

ENGLISH CHANNEL/
MANCHE
BASSE-NORMANDIE
Baie de la Seine
Côte du Calvados
Côte Fleurie
Newhaven
Portsmouth
Pointe de Barfleur
Barfleur
St-Pierre-l'Eglise
St-Vaast-la-Hougue
Quinéville
Montebourg
Ste-Mère-Eglise
Ste-Marie-du-Mont
Grandcamp-Maisy
Isigny-sur-Mer
Vierville
St-Laurent
Port-en-Bessin
MEMORIAL DU OMAHA BEACH
Arromanches-les-Bains
Courseulles-sur-Mer
St-Aubin-sur-Mer
Luc-sur-Mer
CHÂTEAU DE FONTAINE HENRY
Bayeux
Moon-sur-Elle
ABB. DE MONDAYE
Balleroy
St-Lô
Riva-Bella
Ouistreham
Cabourg
Houlgate
Dives-sur-Mer
Villers
Deauville
Trouville
Honfleur
Villerville
Pont l'Evêque
Beuzeville
St-Maclou
POINTE DE LA ROQUE
LE HAVRE
Cap de la Hève
Octeville
Cauville
Montivilliers
Harfleur
Etretat
Cap d'Antifer
FALAISE D'AVAL
Yport
Fécamp
BAILLEUL
Goderville
St-Pierre-en Port
Veulettes-sur-Mer
Cany-Barville
St-Valery-en-Caux
Veules-les-Roses
Fontaine-le-Dun
Bacqueville-en-Caux
Doudeville
Fauville
Yerville
Yvetot
Bolbec
Lillebonne
Tancarville
Caudebec-en-Caux
St-Wandrille
Barentin
Pavilly
Duclair
Jumièges
Bourneville
Sotteville-Les Rouen
Bosgouet
Pont-Audemer
Bourg-Achard
Bourgtheroulde-Infreville
Elbeuf
ABB. DE BONPORT
CHÂT. DU CHAMP DU BATAILLE
Louviers
Le Neubourg
Brionne
Lieurey
Cormeilles
Lisieux
Cambremer
Dozulé
Troarn
CAEN
ST CLAIR
Caumont
Torigni-sur-Vire
Tessy-sur-Vire
Villers-Bocage
Aunay-sur-Odon
Laize-la-Ville
Moult
Airan
Crevecoeur en-Auge
Thibérville
Bernay
Beaumont-le-Roger
Beaumesnil
Broglie
Orbec
Livarot
St-Pierre-sur-Dives
Thury-Harcourt
Clécy
Vire
Vassy
St-Sever
Gouvets
St-Pois
Falaise
Condé-sur-Noireau
Tinchebray
Sourdeval
Mortain
ROCHE D'OETRE
Taillebois
Flers
Putanges-Pont-Ecrepin
Vimoutiers
Courteilles
Trun
Landepéreuse
La Neuve-Lyre
Evreux
Conches-en-Ouche
Monnai
Gauville
Argentan
Fromental
Briouze
Barenton
Domfront
Le Teilleul
HARAS DU PIN
Exmes
Le Pin-au-Haras
Nonant-le-Pin
Gacé
Rugles
Damville
Ste-Gauburge-Ste-Colombe
L'Aigle
Breteuil
La Ferté-Macé
Rânes
Bagnoles-de-l'Orne
PARC NATUREL RÉGIONAL
Mortrée
CHÂT. D'O
Sées
Le Merlerault
Moulins-la-Marche
Verneuil-sur-Avre
Nonancourt
Carrouges
Couterne
Couptrain
Lassay
Gorron
Ambrières
Pré-en-Pail
MONT DES AVALOIRS
Courtomer
Bazoches-sur-Hoëne
La Ferté-Vidame
Brézolles
Blévy
Javron
Alençon
Mortagne-au-Perche
Longny-au-Perche
Senonches
Digny
Châteauneuf-en-Thymerais
Mayenne
Chailland
Villaines-la-Juhel
NORMANDIE-MAINE
PARC NATUREL RÉGIONAL DU PERCHE
Bais
Assé-le-Boisne
La Hutte
Mamers
Bellême
Rémalard
MANOIR DE COURBOYER
La Loupe
Courville
Champrond-en-Gâtine
CHÂT. DU ROCHER
Montsûrs
Evron
Fresnay-sur-Sarthe
Beaumont-sur-Sarthe
Courgains
St.-Cosme-en-Vairais
Nogent-le-Rotrou
Chassant
Illiers-Combray
Thivars
Argentré
Sillé-le-Guillaume
Ste-Suzanne
Vaiges
Conlie
Ballon
Bonnétable
Luigny
E
F
G
H
1
2
3
4
5
6
28
42

Haywards Heath
Crowborough
Ashford
Deal
Uckfield
Heathfield
Lewes
BRIGHTON
Worthing
Littlehampton
Battle
Rye
Hythe
Dymchurch
New Romney
Dover
Folkestone
GB
Hailsham
Lydd
Dungeness
Newhaven
Seaford
Eastbourne
Bexhill
Hastings
Pevensey
Beachy Head
Dieppe Le Havre
CHANNEL TUNNEL/ TUNNEL SOUS LA MANCHE
Strait of Dover/
Pas de Calais
Blériot-Plage
Cap Gris Nez
Wissant
Framzelle
Marquise
Guînes
Wimereux
Robertingue
Boulogne-sur-Mer
Colembert
Le Portel
Pont-de-Briques
Hardelot-Plage
Desvres
Samer
ENGLISH CHANNEL/
MANCHE
Le Touquet-Paris-Plage
Etaples
Hucqueliers
Hénoville
Montreuil
Berck-Plage
Fort-Mahon-Plage
ABBAYE DE VALLOIRES
Hesdin
Vron
Rue
Le Crotoy
Crécy-en-Ponthieu
Nouvion
Auxi-le-Château
Sailly Flibeaucourt
St-Valery-sur-Somme
Newhaven
Newhaven Portsmouth
Ault
Le Tréport
Mesnil-Val
Eu
Abbeville
St-Riquier
Bernaville
Canaples
St-Ouen
Veulettes-sur-Mer
St-Valery-en-Caux
Varengeville-sur-Mer
Dieppe
St-Pierre-en Port
Veules-les-Roses
Cany-Barville
MANOIR D'ANGO
Bellengreville
Gamaches
Blangy-sur-Bresle
Oisemont
Etretat
Yport
Fécamp
Fontaine-le-Dun
Cap d'Antifer
FALAISE D'AVAL
Airaines
Londinières
Bacqueville-en-Caux
BAILLEUL
Goderville
Doudeville
HAUTE-
Osmoy-St-Valery
Foucarmont
Picquigny
Molliens
Hornoy
Cauville
Octeville
Fauville
Yerville
Bellencombre
Neufchâtel-en-Bray
Montivilliers
Harfleur
Tôtes
St-Saëns
Aumale
Poix
Bolbec
Yvetot
LE HAVRE
Tancarville
Lillebonne
Pavilly
Clères
Les Hayons
Bosc-Mesnil
Conty
POINTE DE LA ROQUE
Honfleur
Trouville
Caudebec-en-Caux
St-Wandrille
Barentin
Sommery
Buchy
Formerie
Grandvilliers
PARC ZOOL.
Duclair
Forges-les-Eaux
Beuzeville
St-Maclou
St-Samson-la-Poterie
Marseille-en-Beauvaisis
Crevecoeur
Pont-l'Evêque
Bourneville
Jumièges
Sotteville Les Rouen
ROUEN
Pont-Audemer
Bosgouet
Boos
la Haye
la-Feuille
Bourg-Achard
Gournay-en-Bray
Crillon
Froissy
Cormeilles
Bourgtheroulde-Infreville
Oissel
ABB. DE FONTAINE GUÉRARD
Lyons-la-Forêt
Cambremer
Lieurey
St-Germer-de-Fly
Beauvais
Lisieux
Brionne
Elbeuf
ABB. DE BONPORT
Pont-de-l'Arche
Fleury
Morgny
Ecouis
Etrepagny
Thiberville
CHÂT. DU CHAMP DU BATAILLE
Louviers
Le Vaudreuil
Auneuil
Bresles
Clermont
Bernay
Les Andelys
les-Thilliers en-Vexin
Gisors
Livarot
Orbec
Le Neubourg
Vironvay
Gaillon
Noailles
Mouy
NORMANDIE
Beaumont-le-Roger
Tourny
Broglie
Courteilles
Magny-en-Vexin
Lierville
Arronville
Méru
Vernon
Marines
St-Leu-d'Esserent

Kingston upon Hull
Rosyth
Ramsgate
Middelburg
Vlissingen
Goes
Knokke-Heist
Zeebrugge
Blankenberge
Lissewege
Sluis
Breskens
Schoondijke
Hoedekenskerke
Kruiningen
Perkpolder
Hoogerheide
Oostende (Ostende)
De Haan
Oostburg
Terneuzen
Middelkerke-Bad
Westende-Bad
Oostduinkerke
Koksijde-Bad
De Panne
Damme
BRUGGE (BRUGES)
Maldegem
Axel
Hulst
Dunkerque Ouest
Dunkerque
Malo-les-Bains
Nieuwpoort
Gistel
Eeklo
ANTWERPEN (ANVERS)
Gravelines
Loon Plage
Veurne (Furnes)
Zelzate
St-Niklaas (St-Nicolas)
Bergues
Bourbourg
Diksmuide
Torhout
Aalter
VLAANDEREN
Looberghe
Lokeren
Audruicq
Klerken
Roeselare (Roulers)
GENT (Gand)
OOIDONK
Nordausques
Wormhout
Woesten
Tielt
Deinze
Dendermonde (Termonde)
Watten
Poperinge
Ingelmunster
Willebroek
Cassel
Izegem
Wetteren
St-Omer
Steenvoorde
Ieper (Ypres)
Waregem
Aalst (Alost)
Méteren
Marke
Kortrijk (Courtrai)
Oudenaarde (Audenarde)
Lumbres
Hazebrouck
Bailleul
Menen
Halluin
Aire-sur-la-Lys
Nieppe
Ninove
BRUSSEL / BRUXELLES
Thérouanne
St. Hilaire Cottes
Merville
Armentières
Tourcoing
Brakel
Cuhom
Rely
Roubaix
Ronse (Renaix)
GAASBEEK
Fléchin
Lillers
Estaires
Lomme
Mons En Baroeul
Celles
Geraardsbergen
Gooik
Fruges
LILLE
Villeneuve D'Ascq
Lessines
Huizingen
Halle
Béthune
La Bassée
Seclin
Lesquin
Enghien
Waterloo
DE-CALAIS
Noeux
Tournai (Doornik)
Leuze
Ath
ATTRE
Anvin
Carvin
Houdain
Orchies
Beloeil
Braine-le-Comte
CHÂTEAU FÉODAL D'OLHAIN
Lens
Soignies
St-Pol-sur-Ternoise
Hénin-Beaumont
St-Amand-les-Eaux
Péruwelz
Nivelles
PARC NATUREL RÉG. DU NORD - PAS DE CALAIS PLAINE DE LA SCARPE ET DE L'ESCAUT
Casteau
ROEULX
Seneffe
Frévent
Avesnes-le-Comte
Douai
La Louvière
Arras
Fresnes
Crespin
Saint-Ghislain
Mons (Bergen)
MARIEMONT
Beaumetz
Denain
Onnaing
Tilloy-Lès-Mofflaines
Aniche
Valenciennes
Binche
Gosselies
Pas-en-Artois
Hordain
Bavay
Givry
CHARLEROI
Doullens
Ecoust-St-Mein
Thuin
GROTTES DE NAOURS
Marieux
Bucquoy
Marquion
Le Quesnoy
Jeumont
Acheux-en-Amiénois
Bapaume
Cambrai
Solesmes
Hautmont
Maubeuge
Englefontaine
Beaumont
Contay
Hédauville
ABB. DE VAUCELLES
PARC NATUREL RÉGIONAL DE L'AVESNOIS
Walcourt
Albert
Caudry
Landrecies
Cerfontaine
Serain
Le Cateau-Cambrésis
Avesnes-sur-Helpe
Philippeville
AMIENS
Bray-sur-Somme
Corbie
Villers-Bretonneux
Longueau
Le Catelet
Péronne
Bohain-en-Vermandois
Roisel
Le Nouvion-en-Thiérache
Fourmies
Chimay
Couvin
Lesdins
St-Quentin
Chigny
La Capelle
Moreuil
Bouchair
Guise
Hirson
Sourdon
Ham
Nesle
Ribemont
Étréaupont
Rocroi
Breteuil
Roye
le-Hérie-la-Vieville
Vervins
la-Ferté-Chevresis
Sains
Voulpaix
Montdidier
Rumigny
Auvillers-les-Forges
Cuvilly
Lassigny
Tergnier
La Fère
Crécy-sur-Serre
Marle
Brunehamel
PICARDIE
St-Just-en-Chaussée
Noyon
Chauny
St-Gobain
Montcornet
Rozoy
Aubigny-les-Pothées
Charleville-Mézières
Ressons
ABB. D'OURSCAMPS
Liesse
Dizy-le-Gros
Signy-l'Abbaye
Estrées-St-Denis
Ribécourt
Bléranourt
Coucy-le-Château-Auffrique
Laon
Sissonne
Seraincourt
Compiègne
Nizy-le-Comte
Novion-Porcien
Arsy
Vic-sur-Aisne
Château-Porcien
CAVERNE DU DRAGON
Verberie
FORÊT DE COMPIÈGNE
Pierrefonds
Vailly
Bourg-et-Comin
Corbeny
Asfeld
Rethel
Senlis
Soissons
Braine
Neufchâtel-sur-Aisne
Attigny
Canal de St-Quentin
Canal de l'Oise à l'Aisne
Canal des Ardennes
Canal du Nord
Somme
Oise
Escaut (Schelde)
Dender
Westerschelde

30
43
44

Holland
Europoort
Delft
Maasland
Rotterdam
ROTTERDAM
Gouda
Oudewater
Brielle
Maassluis
Vlaardingen
Goeree
Ouddorp
Hellevoetsluis
Spijkenisse
Rhoon
Barendrecht
Ridderkerk
MOLENS VAN KINDERDIJK
Hendrik-Ido-Ambacht
Stellendam
Grevelingen
Schouwen
Burgh-Haamstede
ZUID-HOLLAND
Oud Beijerland
Zwijndrecht
Middelharnis
DORDRECHT
Sliedrecht
Brouwershaven
Zierikzee
Kingston upon Hull
Rosyth
Walcheren
Domburg
Noord-Beveland
Zijpe
Sluis
Willemstad
NATIONAAL PARK DE BIESBOSCH
Geertruidenberg
Westkapelle
Veere
Kamperland
Stavenisse
Steenbergen
Zevenbergen
Made
Oosterhout
ZEELAND
Middelburg
Vlissingen
Goes
Kruisland
BREDA
Halsteren
Bergen op Zoom
Roosendaal
Knokke-Heist
Zeebrugge
Blankenberge
Breskens
Schoondijke
Hoedekenskerke
Kruiningen
Perkpolder
Hoogerheide
Zundert
TILBURG
Gilze
Oostende (Ostende)
De Haan
Lissewege
Sluis
Oostburg
Terneuzen
Baarle-Nassau
Hoogstraten
Middelkerke-Bad
Westende-Bad
BRUGGE (BRUGES)
Damme
Maldegem
Axel
Hulst
Wuustwezel
Brecht
Nieuwpoort
Gistel
Brasschaat
Veurne (Furnes)
Eeklo
Zelzate
ANTWERPEN (ANVERS)
Schilde
Turnhout
Oostmalle
Torhout
Diksmuide
VLAANDEREN
St-Niklaas (St-Nicolas)
Zandhoven
Deurne
Oeijenbraak
Kasterlee
Klerken
Aalter
Lokeren
Temse
Roeselare (Roulers)
GENT (Gand)
OOIDONK
Dendermonde (Termonde)
Herentals
Mol
Tielt
Deinze
Boom
Lier
Olen
Geel
Poperinge
Ingelmunster
Willebroek
Izegem
Wetteren
Mechelen (Malines)
Westerlo
Ieper (Ypres)
Waregem
Aalst (Alost)
BRUSSEL
Herselt
AVERBODE
Menen
Halluin
Marke
Kortrijk (Courtrai)
Oudenaarde (Audenarde)
Aarschot
Nieppe
Ninove
BRUSSEL / BRUXELLES
National
Kortenberg
Diest
HORST
Armentières
Brakel
Tourcoing
Roubaix
Leuven (Louvain)
Heverlee
Rummen
Lomme
Mons-en-Barœul
Villeneuve-d'Ascq
Ronse (Renaix)
Celles
Geraardsbergen
GAASBEEK
Gooik
Tervuren
Overijse
Tienen (Tirlemont)
Zoutleeuw
LILLE
Lessines
Huizingen
Halle
BEERSEL
Enghien
Waterloo
St.-Truiden (St.-Trond)
Seclin
Lesquin
Tournai (Doornik)
Leuze
Ath
ATTRE
Wavre (Waver)
Carvin
Jodoigne
Belœil
Braine-le-Comte
Soignies
Marilles
Orchies
St-Amand-les-Eaux
Péruwelz
Hannut
Waremme
Hénin-Beaumont
PARC NATUREL RÉGIONAL NORD - PAS DE CALAIS PLAINE DE LA SCARPE ET DE L'ESCAUT
Casteau
ROEULX
Seneffe
Nivelles
Genappe
VILLERS
Gembloux
Perwez
Eghezée
Douai
Fresnes
Crespin
Onnaing
Saint-Ghislain
La Louvière
MARIEMONT
Fleurus
Meux
Aniche
Denain
Valenciennes
Mons (Bergen)
Binche
Gosselies
Spy
Hordain
Bavay
CHARLEROI
Châtelet
Namur (Namen)
Andenne
Écoust-St-Mein
Givry
Thuin
Fosses
Wépion
Marquion
Le Quesnoy
Solesmes
Jeumont
Maubeuge
Profondeville
Modave
Cambrai
Hautmont
Mettet
Yvoir
Courrière
Havelange
WALLONIE
Englefontaine
Beaumont
ABB. DE VAUCELLES
Landrecies
PARC NATUREL RÉGIONAL DE L'AVESNOIS
Florennes
Bouvignes
Caudry
Walcourt
Dinant
Ciney
Serain
Le Cateau-Cambrésis
Avesnes-sur-Helpe
Cerfontaine
Hastière-Lavaux
Philippeville
Anseremme
Le Catelet
Waulsort
Marche-en-Famenne
Péronne
Bohain-en-Vermandois
Givet
Rochefort
Roisel
Le Nouvion-en-Thiérache
Fourmies
Chimay
Beauraing
Han-sur-Lesse
Lesdins
Couvin
Vonêche
Wellin
St-Quentin
Guise
Chigny
La Capelle
Hargnies
Etréaupont
Hirson
Fumay
St-Hubert
Ribemont
le-Hérie-la-Viéville
Revin
Gedinne
Ham
Canal de St-Quentin
la-Ferté-Chevresis
Sains
Voulpaix
Vervins
ROCHES DE LAIFOUR
Monthermé
F
B
16
44
215

UTRECHT
Zeist
Barneveld
Meerkerk
Doorn
Amerongen
Vianen
Culemborg
Leerdam
Gorinchem
Zaltbommel
Aalburg
Waalwijk
Kaatsheuvel
Tiel
Druten
Ede
Lunteren
Otterlo
Veenendaal
Wageningen
Rhenen
Kesteren
Renkum
Oosterbeek
ARNHEM
Velp
Dieren
Zutphen
Voorst
Warnsveld
Doesburg
Doetinchem
Zevenaar
Elst
Elten
NIJMEGEN
Emmerich
's-Heerenberg
Kranenburg
Kleve
Kalkar
Goch
Gennep
Boxmeer
Cuijk
Grave
Oss
'S-HERTOGENBOSCH
Vught
Uden
Veghel
Oisterwijk
Boxtel
St Oedenrode
Goirle
Oirschot
Best
Beek en Donk
Gemert
Helmond
EINDHOVEN
Veldhoven
Geldrop
Hilvarenbeek
Reusel
Arendonk
Valkenswaard
Heeze
Asten
Someren
Deurne
Venray
Oploo
Horst
Arcen
Venlo
Tegelen
Maasbree
Meijel
Weert
Roermond
Nettetal
Swalmen
Elmpt
Niederkrüchten
Lommel
Bocholt
Kinrooi
Bree
Hechtel
Meeuwen
Neeroeteren
Maaseik
Beringen
Houthalen
Zolder
Lummen
Hasselt
Genk
Maasmechelen
As
Zonhoven
Opglabbeek
Molenheide
Tongeren (Tongres)
MAASTRICHT
Valkenburg
Heerlen
Kerkrade
Sittard
Geleen
Brunssum
Beek
AACHEN
Eschweiler
Stolberg
Düren
Jülich
Heinsberg
Geilenkirchen
Erkelenz
MÖNCHENGLADBACH
Rheydt
Viersen
Dülken
Süchteln
KREFELD
Kempen
DUISBURG
Moers
Kamp Lintfort
Rheinberg
Geldern
Kevelaer
Straelen
Kerken
Weeze
Xanten
Wesel
Sonsbeck
Alpen
Rees
Hamminkeln
Bocholt
Isselburg
Aalten
Winterswijk
Groenlo
Zelhem
Lichtenvoorde
Varsseveld
Borculo
Ruurlo
Neede
Eibergen
Haaksbergen
ENSCHEDE
Gronau
Epe
Alstätte
Ahaus
Vreden
Stadtlohn
Heek
Steinfurt
Schöppingen
Horstmar
Legden
Gescher
Coesfeld
Billerbeck
Nottuln
Borken
Rhede
Heiden
Reken
Dülmen
Raesfeld
Lembeck
Schermbeck
Dorsten
Haltern
Marl
Datteln
Recklinghausen
Waltrop
Lünen
Dinslaken
Gladbeck
Bottrop
Gelsenkirchen
Herne
Castrop-Rauxel
Oberhausen
ESSEN
BOCHUM
Mülheim
Hattingen
Witten
Wetter
Kettwig
Velbert
Hagen
Ratingen
Mettmann
Schwelm
WUPPERTAL
DÜSSELDORF
Neuss
Benrath
Hilden
SOLINGEN
Remscheid
Radevormwald
Lüdenscheid
Halver
Wermelskirchen
Wipperfürth
Langenfeld
Opladen
Monheim
Grevenbroich
Dormagen
Rommerskirchen
Bedburg
Bergheim
LEVERKUSEN
Bergisch Gladbach
Bensberg
Gummersbach
Engelskirchen
Overath
Frechen
Kerpen
KÖLN
Brühl
Erftstadt
Wesseling
Siegburg
Troisdorf
BONN
Beuel
Hennef
Königswinter
Bad Godesberg
Euskirchen
Zülpich
Nideggen
Mechernich
Bad Münstereifel
Rheinbach
Bad Neuenahr
Ahrweiler
Altenahr
Remagen
Sinzig
Bad Breisig
Linz
Bad Hönningen
Neuwied
Andernach
Koblenz
Lahnstein
Mayen
Mendig
Maria Laach
Nürburg
Adenau
Kelberg
Gerolstein
Hillesheim
Blankenheim
Dahlem
Stadtkyll
Prüm
Daun
Ulmen
Kaisersesch
Cochem
Boppard
Hollerath
Schleiden
Gemünd
Simmerath
Monschau
Eupen
Verviers
Spa
Theux
Malmedy
Stavelot
St Vith
Bütgenbach
Losheim
Amel
Vielsalm
Houffalize
Bastogne
Clervaux
LIÈGE (LUIK)
Seraing
Herstal
Visé
Barchon
Battice
Limbourg
Remouchamps
Hamoir
Durbuy
La Roche-en-Ardenne
Hotton
Dochamps
Nadrin
Champlon
Trois-Ponts
Wemperhaardt
Pronsfeld
Waxweiler
Dasburg
Manderscheid
NL
D
NORDRHEIN-WESTFALEN
RHEINLAND-PFALZ
NOORD-BRABANT
LIMBURG
GELDERLAND
MÜNSTERLAND
NATURPARK

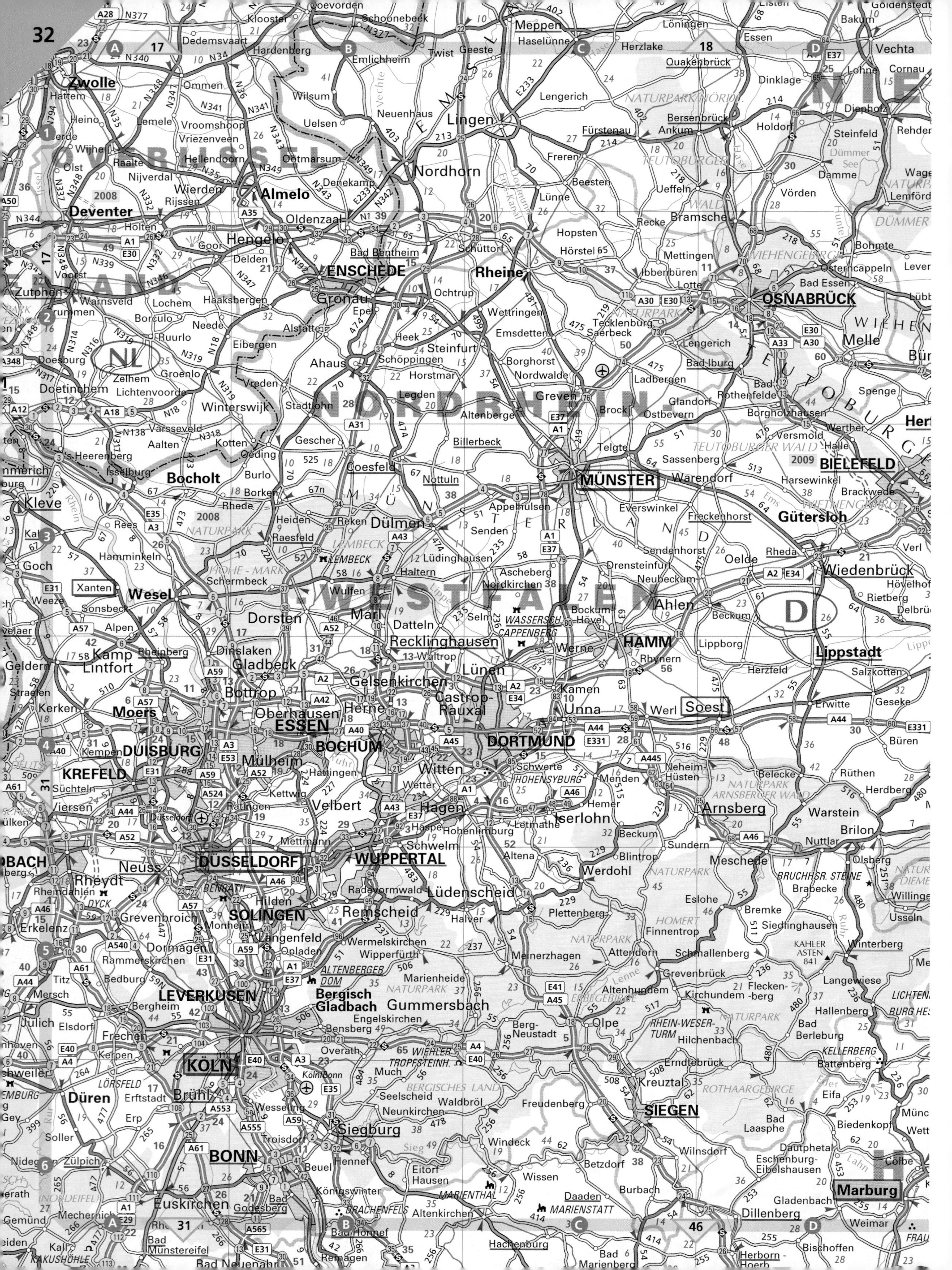
OVERIJSSEL
NL
NORDRHEIN-WESTFALEN
D
MÜNSTERLAND
EMSLAND
Zwolle
Hattem
Heino
Wijhe
Olst
Raalte
Nijverdal
Deventer
Holten
Rijssen
Wierden
Almelo
Hellendoorn
Vriezenveen
Vroomshoop
Ommen
Dedemsvaart
Hardenberg
Coevorden
Schoonebeek
Emlichheim
Wilsum
Uelsen
Neuenhaus
Ootmarsum
Denekamp
Nordhorn
Oldenzaal
Hengelo
Goor
Delden
Enschede
Gronau
Bad Bentheim
Schüttorf
Rheine
Lingen
Meppen
Haselünne
Twist
Geeste
Löningen
Herzlake
Quakenbrück
Essen
Bakum
Vechta
Lohne
Cornau
Dinklage
Diepholz
Rehden
Holdorf
Steinfeld
Dümmer See
Damme
Vörden
Lemförde
Lengerich
Bersenbrück
Ankum
Fürstenau
Freren
Beesten
Lünne
Uffeln
Bramsche
Recke
Hopsten
Hörstel
Mettingen
Ibbenbüren
Lotte
Osnabrück
Bohmte
Ostercappeln
Bad Essen
Melle
Tecklenburg
Saerbeck
Emsdetten
Wettringen
Ochtrup
Steinfurt
Borghorst
Nordwalde
Greven
Ladbergen
Lengerich
Bad Iburg
Bad Rothenfelde
Glandorf
Borgholzhausen
Versmold
Halle
Werther
Spenge
Bielefeld
Brackwede
Harsewinkel
Gütersloh
Wiedenbrück
Rheda
Verl
Oelde
Warendorf
Sassenberg
Freckenhorst
Everswinkel
Telgte
Ostbevern
Münster
Altenberge
Billerbeck
Nottuln
Coesfeld
Legden
Horstmar
Schöppingen
Heek
Epe
Ahaus
Stadtlohn
Vreden
Gescher
Alstätte
Haaksbergen
Neede
Eibergen
Borculo
Ruurlo
Lochem
Zutphen
Warnsveld
Vorden
Doesburg
Doetinchem
Zelhem
Groenlo
Lichtenvoorde
Winterswijk
Aalten
Varsseveld
's-Heerenberg
Isselburg
Emmerich
Kleve
Bocholt
Rhede
Borken
Burlo
Oeding
Heiden
Reken
Raesfeld
Dülmen
Appelhülsen
Senden
Lüdinghausen
Ascheberg
Nordkirchen
Drensteinfurt
Sendenhorst
Neubeckum
Beckum
Ahlen
Hamm
Lippborg
Lippstadt
Herzfeld
Rietberg
Hövelhof
Delbrück
Rees
Hamminkeln
Wesel
Xanten
Goch
Kalkar
Weeze
Sonsbeck
Alpen
Schermbeck
Dorsten
Haltern
Wulfen
Marl
Datteln
Selm
Bockum-Hövel
Werne
Recklinghausen
Waltrop
Lünen
Kamp Lintfort
Rheinberg
Dinslaken
Gladbeck
Bottrop
Gelsenkirchen
Castrop-Rauxel
Kamen
Unna
Werl
Soest
Erwitte
Geseke
Salzkotten
Büren
Rüthen
Warstein
Belecke
Brilon
Geldern
Straelen
Kerken
Moers
Oberhausen
Essen
Herne
Bochum
Dortmund
Duisburg
Kempen
Krefeld
Mülheim
Hattingen
Witten
Schwerte
Hohensyburg
Menden
Neheim-Hüsten
Arnsberg
Sundern
Meschede
Olsberg
Süchteln
Viersen
Düsseldorf
Ratingen
Kettwig
Velbert
Wetter
Hagen
Hohenlimburg
Letmathe
Iserlohn
Hemer
Beckum
Balve
Mönchengladbach
Rheydt
Rheindahlen
Neuss
Mettmann
Wuppertal
Schwelm
Haspe
Altena
Werdohl
Plettenberg
Lüdenscheid
Radevormwald
Hilden
Solingen
Remscheid
Erkelenz
Grevenbroich
Monheim
Langenfeld
Wermelskirchen
Wipperfürth
Halver
Meinerzhagen
Attendorn
Finnentrop
Eslohe
Bremke
Schmallenberg
Siedlinghausen
Winterberg
Kahler Asten 841
Dormagen
Rommerskirchen
Leverkusen
Opladen
Bergisch Gladbach
Gummersbach
Marienheide
Grevenbrück
Altenhundem
Kirchhundem
Lennestadt
Olpe
Langewiese
Hallenberg
Bad Berleburg
Jülich
Titz
Bedburg
Bergheim
Elsdorf
Frechen
Kerpen
Köln
Bensberg
Overath
Engelskirchen
Berg-Neustadt
Hilchenbach
Erndtebrück
Kreuztal
Siegen
Düren
Brühl
Erftstadt
Wesseling
Much
Seelscheid
Neunkirchen
Waldbröl
Freudenberg
Siegburg
Troisdorf
Bonn
Beuel
Hennef
Eitorf
Hausen
Windeck
Wissen
Betzdorf
Burbach
Wilnsdorf
Bad Laasphe
Biedenkopf
Dautphetal
Eschenburg-Eibelshausen
Dillenberg
Gladenbach
Marburg
Zülpich
Euskirchen
Mechernich
Königswinter
Bad Godesberg
Bad Honnef
Altenkirchen
Hachenburg
Daaden
Bad Münstereifel
Remagen
Herborn
Bischoffen
Weimar

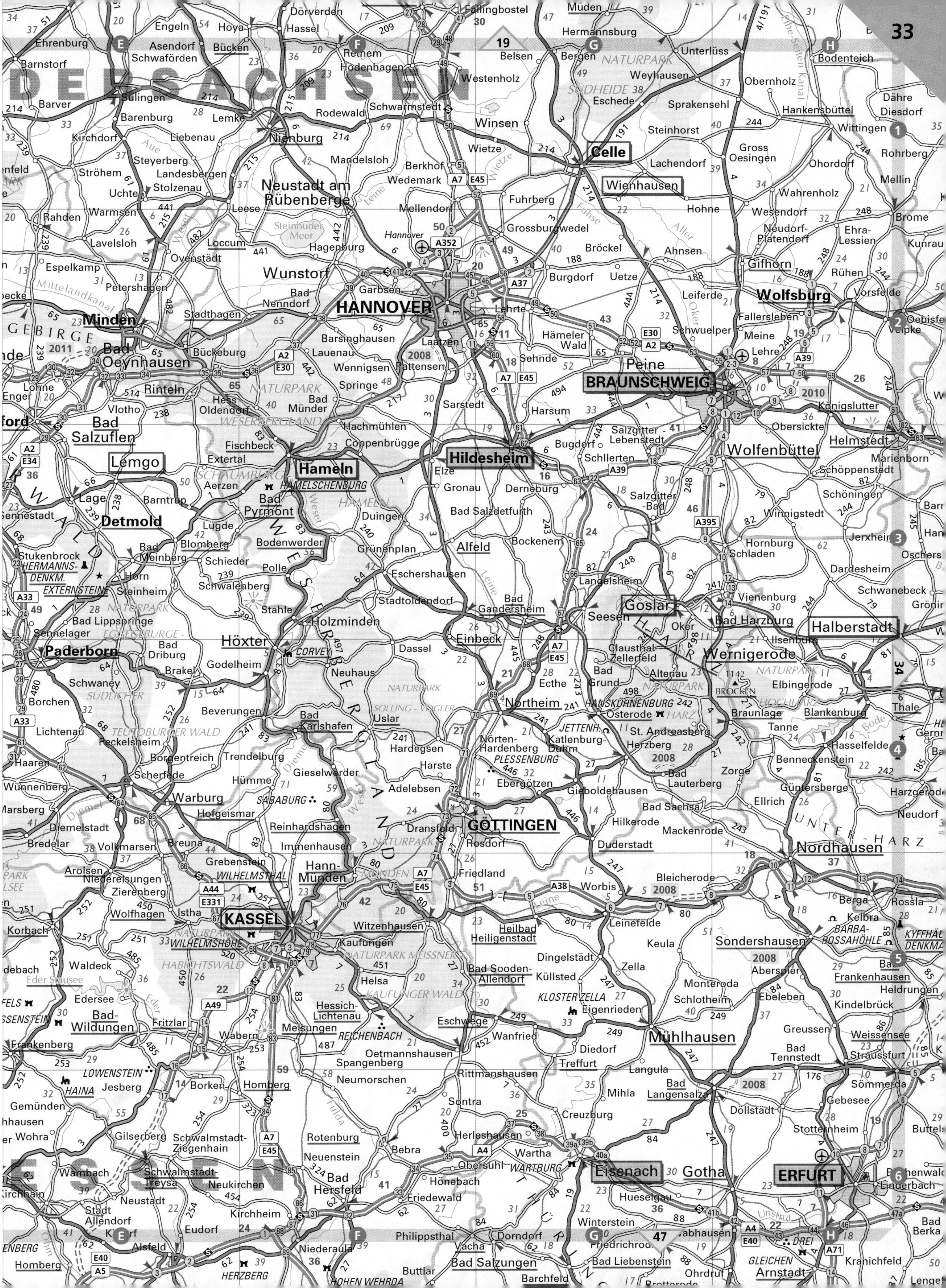
NIEDERSACHSEN
HESSEN
THÜRINGEN
Dörverden
Fallingbostel
Muden
Hermannsburg
Engeln
Hoya
Hassel
Ehrenburg
Asendorf
Schwaförden
Bücken
Rethem
Hodenhagen
Belsen
Bergen
Unterlüss
Bodenteich
Barnstorf
Westenholz
Weyhausen
Obernholz
Sulingen
Schwarmstedt
Eschede
Sprakensehl
Hankensbüttel
Dähre
Diesdorf
Barver
Barenburg
Lemke
Rodewald
Winsen
Steinhorst
Wittingen
Kirchdorf
Liebenau
Nienburg
Celle
Gross Oesingen
Rohrberg
Steyerberg
Mandelsloh
Berkhof
Wietze
Lachendorf
Ohrdorf
Ströhem
Landesbergen
Wedemark
Wienhausen
Mellin
Uchte
Stolzenau
Neustadt am Rübenberge
Fuhrberg
Wahrenholz
Rahden
Warmsen
Leese
Mellendorf
Hohne
Wesendorf
Brome
Lavelsloh
Loccum
Steinhuder Meer
Hannover
Grossburgwedel
Neudorf-Platendorf
Ehra-Lessien
Kunrau
Espelkamp
Ovenstädt
Hagenburg
Bröckel
Ahnsen
Gifhorn
Rühen
Petershagen
Wunstorf
Burgdorf
Uetze
Mittellandkanal
Bad Nenndorf
Garbsen
HANNOVER
Leiferde
Wolfsburg
Vorsfelde
Minden
Stadthagen
Lehrte
Fallersleben
Oebisfelde
Velpke
GEBIRGE
Barsinghausen
Hämeler Wald
Schwuelper
Meine
Bad Oeynhausen
Bückeburg
Lauenau
Laatzen
Lehre
Wennigsen
Pattensen
Sehnde
Peine
Löhne
Rinteln
Springe
Enger
BRAUNSCHWEIG
Vlotho
Hess. Oldendorf
Bad Münder
Sarstedt
Königslutter
Herford
Bad Salzuflen
WESERBERGLAND
Hachmühlen
Harsum
Obersickte
Helmstedt
Coppenbrügge
Salzgitter-Lebenstedt
Marienborn
Lemgo
Fischbeck
Extertal
Hameln
Hildesheim
Bugdorf
Schlierten
Wolfenbüttel
Aerzen
SCHAUMBURG
HÄMELSCHENBURG
Elze
Schöppenstedt
Lage
Barntrup
Bad Pyrmont
Gronau
Derneburg
Salzgitter-Bad
Schöningen
Sennestadt
Detmold
Lügde
Duingen
Bad Salzdetfurth
Winnigstedt
Blomberg
Bodenwerder
Grünenplan
Alfeld
Bockenem
Hornburg
Schladen
Jerxheim
Stukenbrock
HERMANNS-DENKM.
Bad Meinberg
Schieder
Polle
Oschersleben
Horn
Schwalenberg
Eschershausen
Langelsheim
Dardesheim
EXTERNSTEINE
Steinheim
Stadtoldendorf
Bad Gandersheim
Vienenburg
Schwanebeck
Gröningen
NATURPARK
EGGEGEBIRGE
Bad Lippspringe
Stahle
Holzminden
Seesen
Goslar
Oker
Bad Harzburg
Halberstadt
Sennelager
Paderborn
Bad Driburg
Höxter
CORVEY
Dassel
Einbeck
Clausthal-Zellerfeld
Ilsenburg
Wernigerode
Godelheim
Brakel
Neuhaus
Bad Grund
Altenau
Elbingerode
Schwaney
Ecthe
Brocken
Borchen
SÜDLICHER
Beverungen
SOLLING-VOGLER
Northeim
HANSKÜHNENBURG
Osterode
Braunlage
Blankenburg
Thale
Lichtenau
Bad Karlshafen
Uslar
JETTENH.
Tanne
Gernrode
Peckelsheim
TEUTOBURGER WALD
Hardegsen
Nörten-Hardenberg
Katlenburg-Duhm
St. Andreasberg
Herzberg
Hasselfelde
Haaren
Borgentreich
Trendelburg
Harste
PLESSENBURG
Benneckenstein
Scherfede
Gieselwerder
Ebergötzen
Bad Lauterberg
Zorge
Wünnenberg
Hümme
Adelebsen
Gieboldehausen
Güntersberge
Harzgerode
Marsberg
Warburg
Hofgeismar
SABABURG
Bad Sachsa
Ellrich
Diemelstadt
Reinhardshagen
Dransfeld
GÖTTINGEN
Hilkerode
Mackenrode
Neudorf
Bredelar
Volkmarsen
Breuna
Immenhausen
Rosdorf
Duderstadt
UNTER-HARZ
Arolsen
Grebenstein
Hann-Münden
Friedland
Nordhausen
Niederelsungen
Zierenberg
WILHELMSTHAL
Worbis
Bleicherode
Korbach
Wolfhagen
Istha
KASSEL
Witzenhausen
Heilbad Heiligenstadt
Leinefelde
Berga
Rossla
Kaufungen
Keula
Sondershausen
Kelbra
BARBA-ROSSAHÖHLE
KYFFHÄUSER-DENKMAL
WILHELMSHÖHE
HABICHTSWALD
NATURPARK MEISSNER
Dingelstädt
Bad Sooden-Allendorf
Küllstedt
Zella
Abersprier
Frankenhausen
Waldeck
Eder Stausee
Helsa
KAUFUNGER WALD
Monteroda
Heldrungen
Edersee
Hessich-Lichtenau
KLOSTER ZELLA
Schlotheim
Ebeleben
Kindelbrück
Bad Wildungen
Fritzlar
Melsungen
Eschwege
Eigenrieden
Greussen
Wabern
REICHENBACH
Wanfried
Mühlhausen
Weissensee
Frankenberg
Oetmannshausen
Diedorf
Bad Tennstedt
Straussfurt
LOWENSTEIN
Spangenberg
Treffurt
Langula
HAINA
Jesberg
Borken
Homberg
Neumorschen
Rittmanshausen
Mihla
Bad Langensalza
Sömmerda
Gemünden
Sontra
Creuzburg
Döllstädt
Gebesee
Wohra
Gilserberg
Schwalmstadt-Ziegenhain
Rotenburg
Herleshausen
Stotternheim
Buttelstedt
Bebra
Wartha
Wambach
Schwalmstadt-Treysa
Neuenstein
Obersuhl
WARTBURG
Eisenach
Gotha
ERFURT
Neukirchen
Bad Hersfeld
Hönebach
Linderbach
Kirchhain
Neustadt
Friedewald
Hueselgau
Stadt Allendorf
Kirchheim
Winterstein
Eudorf
Philippsthal
Dorndorf
Friedrichroda
Bad Berka
Alsfeld
Niederaula
Vacha
Bad Liebenstein
DREI GLEICHEN
Kranichfeld
Homberg
HERZBERG
Buttlar
Bad Salzungen
Barchfeld
Ohrdruf
Arnstadt
HOHEN WEHRDA

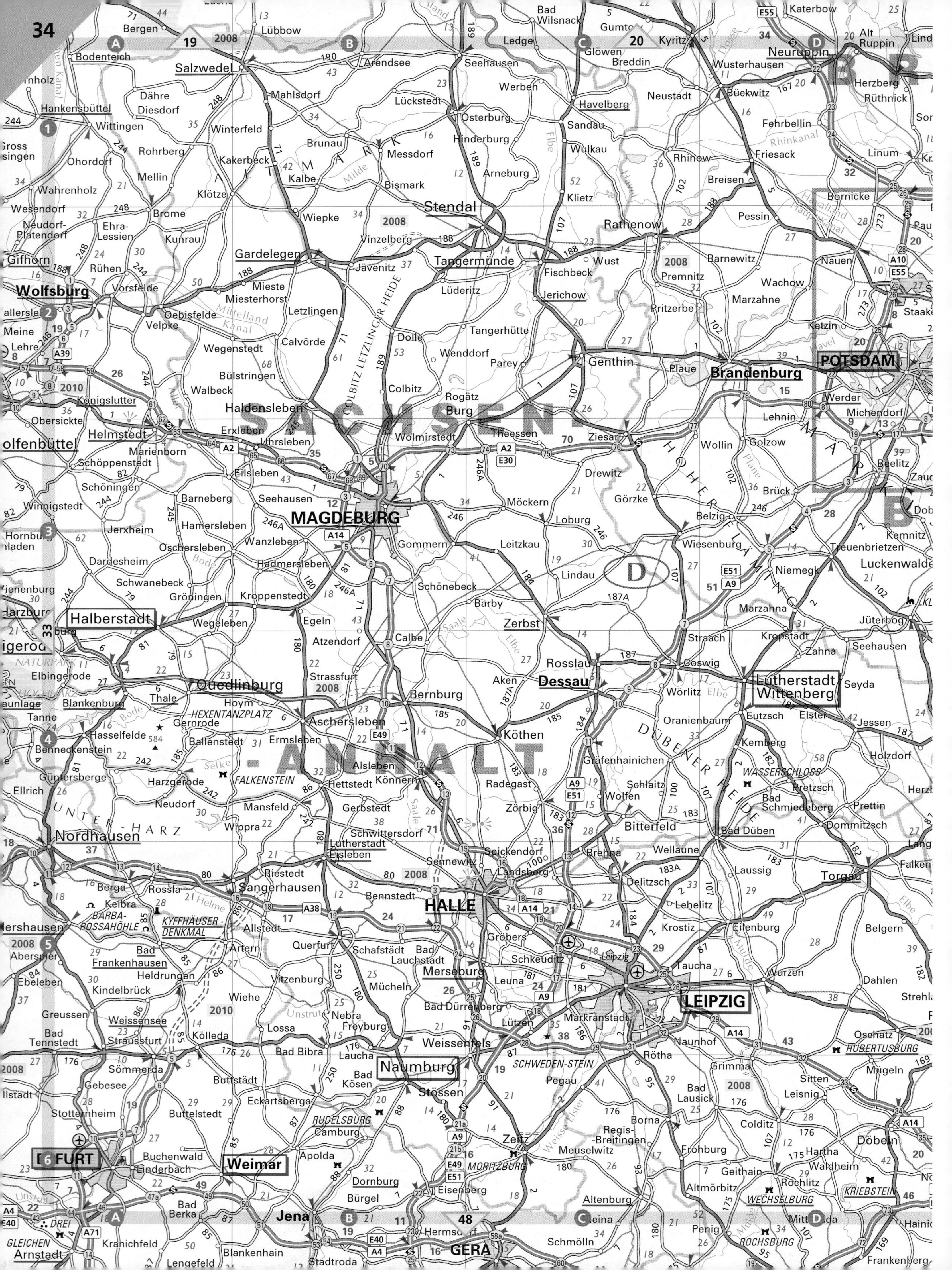
SACHSEN-ANHALT
ALTMARK
COLBITZ LETZLINGER HEIDE
HOHER FLÄMING
DÜBENER HEIDE
UNTER-HARZ
MAGDEBURG
HALLE
LEIPZIG
POTSDAM
Stendal
Salzwedel
Gardelegen
Tangermünde
Wolfsburg
Helmstedt
Haldensleben
Burg
Genthin
Brandenburg
Rathenow
Neuruppin
Nauen
Werder
Beelitz
Halberstadt
Quedlinburg
Aschersleben
Bernburg
Köthen
Dessau
Rosslau
Zerbst
Lutherstadt Wittenberg
Jüterbog
Luckenwalde
Bitterfeld
Delitzsch
Torgau
Eilenburg
Wurzen
Grimma
Döbeln
Lutherstadt Eisleben
Sangerhausen
Nordhausen
Merseburg
Weissenfels
Naumburg
Zeitz
Altenburg
Weimar
Erfurt
Jena
Gera
Arnstadt
Sömmerda
Bad Frankenhausen
Oschersleben
Schönebeck
Staßfurt
Wernigerode
HEXENTANZPLATZ
FALKENSTEIN
KYFFHÄUSER-DENKMAL
BARBAROSSAHÖHLE
RUDELSBURG
MORITZBURG
SCHWEDEN-STEIN
HUBERTUSBURG
WASSERSCHLOSS
KRIEBSTEIN
WECHSELBURG
ROCHSBURG
Mittelland Kanal
Elbe
Saale
Havel
Mulde
Weisse Elster
Unstrut

Gransee
Zehdenick
Joachimsthal
JAGDSHL HUBERTUSSTOCK
SCHORFHEIDE
Angermünde
STOLPE
Krajnik Gorny
Chojna
Trzcińsko Zdrój
Rów
Lipiany
Jesionowo
Pełczyce
Sowinie
Piaseczno
Gross Schönebeck
Löwenberg
KLOSTER CHORIN
Oderberg
Cedynia
CEDYŃSKI PARK KRAJOBRAZOWY
Myślibórz
Barlinek
BARLINECKO GORZOWSKI PARK KRAJOBR.
Trzcinna
Danków
Strzelce Krajeńskie
Liebenwalde
NATURPARK
Eberswalde
Finow
Osinów
Moryń
Witnica
Warnice
Łubianka
Oranienburg
Wandlitz
BARNIM
Bad Freienwalde
Siekierki
Smolnica
Mieszkowice
Tarnów
Kłodawa
Różanki
Biesenthal
Wollenberg
Schönwalde
Bernau
Wriezen
Barnówko
Baczyna
Santok
Dębno
Birkenwerder
Stolpe
Tiefensee
NATURPARK MÄRKISCHE SCHWEIZ
ODERBRUCH
Boleszkowice
Witnica
Bogdaniec
Gorzów Wielkopolski
Nowe Polichno
Tegel
Werneuchen
Prötzel
Reichenberg
Sarbinowo
PARK KRAJOBR. UJŚCIE WARTY
Bolemin
BERLIN
Lindenberg
Altlandsberg
Strausberg
Marxwalde
Letschin
Kostrzyn
Krzeszyce
Skwierzyna
Spandau
Buckow
Manschnow
Kostrzyn-Kietz
Słońsk
Vogelsdorf
Müncheberg
Seelow
Tempelhof
Herzfelde
Rüdersdorf
Jahnsfelde
Górzyca
Trzebów
Lubniewice
Köpenick
Heinersdorf
Podelzig
Ośno Lubuskie
Sulęcin
Modlęcin
Drewitz
Grossbeeren
Mahlow
Schönefeld
Grünheide
Fürstenwalde
Lebus
Lisów
Pieski
Blankenfelde
Genshagen
Spreenhagen
Petershagen
Frankfurt (Oder)
Słubice
PUSZCZA
Rzepin
Łagówek
Łagów
Jacobsdorf
Mittenwalde
Königs Wusterhausen
Friedersdorf
Streitberg
Bad Saarow-Pieskow
Biegen
Świecko
Torzym
Pożrzadło
Nunsdorf
Storkow
Scharmützelsee
Brieskow-Finkenheerd
RZEPIŃSKA
Wilkowo
Świebodzin
Trebbin
Zossen
Töpchin
Selchow
Müllrose
Sądów
Debrznica
BIOSPHÄRENRESERVAT SPREEWALD
NATURPARK SCHLAUBETAL
Cybinka
LUBUSKIE
Klausdorf
Teupitz
Beeskow
Dammendorf
Eisenhüttenstadt
Węgrzynice
Bytnica
Skąpe
Neuhof
Egsdorf
Märkisch Buchholz
Alt Schadow
Friedland
Korczyców
Stülpe
Neu Lübbenau
Trebatsch
Osiecznica
NIZINA
Radnica
Brody
KLOSTER ZINNA
Baruth
HEIDE
Treppeln
Neuzelle
Maszewo
Krosno Odrzańskie
Petkus
Chlebowo
Lieberose
Golssen
Lübben
Biebersdorf
Lamsfeld
Guben
Lesniów Wielki
Czerwieńsk
Gubin
Bobrowice
Zielona Góra
SPREEWALD
Dahme
Duben
Straupitz
Świdnica
PL
Lübbenau
Luckau
Peitz
Burg
Brandis
Wüstermarke
Vetschau
Cottbus
Krzystkowice
Mirocin Średni
Brody
Gahro
Calau
SCHL BRANITZ
Lubsko
Zasieki
Jasień
Nowogród Bobrzański
Schlieben
Forst
Kożuchów
Dabern
Münchhausen
Ogrosen
Bronice
Bronkow
Tuplice
Bieniów
Nowe Miasteczko
Doberlug Kirchhain
Drebkau
Lipinki Łużyckie
Olszyna
Finsterwalde
Lieskau
Trzebiel
Żary
Żagań
Gross-Räschen
Spremberg
Döbern
Łęknica
Mielno
Szprotawa
Bönitz
Bad Liebenwerda
Staupitz
Tschernitz
Bad Muskau
Senftenberg
Schwarze Pumpe
Lauchhammer
Weisswasser
Przewóz
Iłowa
Rudawica
Leszno Górne
Mühlberg
Elsterwerda
Ruhland
Gröditz
Riegel
Hoyerswerda
MUSKAUER FORST
HEIDE
Gozdnica
BORY
Ławszowa
Uhyst
Kreba-Neudorf
Ruszów
DOLNOŚLĄSKIE
Ortrand
Bernsdorf
Wittichenau
Rietschen
Riesa
Lieske
Jagodzin
Golnice
Kliczków
Thiendorf
Königswartha
Mücka
Mikow
Rothenburg
Węgliniec
Seerhausen
Grossenhain
Kamenz
Niesky
Bolesławiec
SACHSEN
OBERLAUSITZ
Radeburg
SCHLOSS MORITZBURG
Königsbrück
Kodersdorf
Pieńsk
Pulsnitz
Zebrzydowa
Meissen
Moritzburg
Weissenberg
Żarska Wieś
Nowogrodziec
Coswig
Bautzen
Görlitz
Zgorzelec
Chmielno
Radebeul
Radeberg
Bischofswerda
Reichenbach
Gradówek
Lubań
Lwówek
DRESDEN
Neukirch
Löbau
Olszyna
Oppach
Płóczki
Kesselsdorf
Stolpen
LAUSITZER BERGLAND
Zawidów
Pławna
Neustadt
Herrnhut
Tharandt
Heidenau
Ostritz
Leśna
Sucha
Gryfów Śląski
Freital
Pirna
Ebersbach
Freiberg
Höckendorf
FESTUNG KÖNIGSTEIN
Bad Schandau
Sebnitz
Neugersdorf
Rumburk
Niederoderwitz
Habartice
Nové Město
Seifhennersdorf
A4
E40
A13
E36
E55
A15
E30
A12
A10
A11
E28
A18
E65
2008
2009
212
49
21
36

Krzęcin
Breń
Radęcin
Bierzwnik
Sowini
21
Trzcianka
Ujście
Noteć
Studzienki
Smogulec
Szamocin
22
Kcynia
Szubin
Rynarzew
Stare Osieczno
Dobiegniew
Danków
Siedlisko
Chodzież
Margonin
Gołańcz
Strzelce Krajeńskie
Długie
Krzyż Wlkp.
Wieleń
Rosko
Czarnków
Sarbia
Budzyń
Pawłowo Żońskie
Morakowo
Łubianka
Kleśno
Drezdenko
Chełst
Krucz
Lubasz
Przybychowo
Wągrowiec
Damasławek
Żnin
Różanki
Santok
Gorzów Wielkopolski
Noteć
Klempicz
Połajewo
Janowiec Wielkopolski
PUSZCZA NOTECKA
Rzecin
Piotrowo
Ludomy
Rogoźno
Mieścisko
Goszczanowo
Nowe Polichno
Wronki
Dąbrówka Leśna
SIERAKOWSKI PARK KRAJOBR.
Sowia Góra
Wróblewo
Oborniki
Skoki
Charbowo
Ostroróg
Uchorowo
Kłecko
Modliszewko
Sieraków
Międzychód
Szamotuły
Kiszkowo
Skwierzyna
Lutomek
Otorowo
Pamiątkowo
Przytoczna
Gorzyń
Kwilcz
Murowana Goślina
PARK KRAJOBR. PUSZCZA ZIELONKA
Gniezno
Lubniewice
PSZCZEWSKI PARK KRAJOBR.
POJEZIERZE
Łowyń
Pniewy
Młodasko
Tarnowo Podgórne
Pobiedziska
Łubowo
Modlęcin
Pszczew
Duszniki
POZNAŃ
Czerniejewo
Pieski
Międzyrzecz
Lwówek
Przeźmierowo
Swarzędz
Kostrzyn
Żydowo
Łagówek
Lutol Suchy
Trzciel
POZNAŃSKIE
Niepruszewo
Wrześnią
Łagów
Buk
Luboń
Brzeźno
Nowy Tomyśl
Dąbrówka Wielkopolska
Opalenica
Wilkowo
Świebodzin
Zbąszynek
Bukowiec
Stęszew
Puszczykowo
Kórnik
Środa Wielkopolska
WIELKOPOLSKIE
Szczaniec
Zbąszyń
Grodzisk Wielkopolski
Granowo
Mosina
Rogalin
Koszuty
Miłosław
Brudzewo
WIELKOPOLSKI PARK NARODOWY
Chobienice
Jabłonna
Głuchowo
Grójec
Pyzdry
Skąpe
Babimost
Czempiń
Zaniemyśl
Rakoniewice
Wolsztyn
Nowe Miasto nad Wartą
Brody
WIELKOPOLSKA
Kościan
Śrem
Prosna
Sulechów
Wielichowo
Chrzan
Kargowa
PARK KRAJOBR. IM. DEZYDEREGO CHŁAPOWSKIEGO
Czacz
PL
Świętno
Czerwieńsk
Zawada
Mochy
Śmigiel
Jerka
Dolsk
Jarocin
Zabór
Zielona Góra
Lubiń
Kotlin
Świdnica
PRZEMĘCKI PARK KRAJOBR.
Krzywiń
Kunowo
Borek Wielkopolski
Konotop
Osieczna
Gostyń
Piaski
Sława
Tarnów Jez.
Leszno
Dobrzyca
Mirocin Średni
Nowa Sól
Wschowa
Rydzyna
Pogorzela
Nowogród Bobrzański
Koźmin
Siedlisko
Poniec
Pepowo
Bytom Odrzański
Krobia
Wolenice
Kożuchów
Raszków
Nowe Miasteczko
Szlichtyngowa
Bojanowo
Zmysłowo
Dłoń
Kobylin
Krotoszyn
Głogów
Wroniniec
Jutrosin
WZGÓRZA DALKOWSKIE
Odra
Góra
Miejska Górka
Daniszyn
Żagań
Szprotawa
Kłobuczyn
Sarnowa
Rawicz
Dubin
Sulmierzyce
Zduny
Luboszyce
Barycz
Wąsosz
Odolanów
Rudawica
Leszno Górne
Przemków
Polkowice
Chobienia
Radziądz
Dąbki
PARK KRAJOBR. DOLINA BARYCZY
Milicz
BORY
Rudna
Białawy Wielkie
Sułów
Ławszowa
Szklary Górne
Mleczno
Wińsko
Krzelów
Żmigród
Cieszyn
DOLNOŚLĄSKIE
Chocianów
Lubin
Ścinawa
Piotrkowice
Skoroszów
Goszcz
Międzybórz
Golnice
Kliczków
Pełczyn
Strupina
Prusice
Twardogóra
Żabice
Wołów
Komorowo
Drołtowice
Bolesławiec
Karczowiska
Prochowice
Mojęcice
Oborniki Śląskie
Zawonia
Syców
Chojnów
Warta Bolesławiecka
Lubiąż
Brzeg Dolny
Trzebnica
Dobroszyce
Zebrzydowa
Legnica
Wilczków
Środa Śląska
Borowa
Dziadowa Kłoda
Oleśnica
Nowogrodziec
Grodziec
Widawa
Chmielno
Złotoryja
Błonie
Żerniki
Długołęka
Bierutów
Gradówek
Legnickie Pole
Cesarzowice
Rakoszyce
Olszyna
Lwówek Śląski
WROCŁAW
Namysłów
Pławna
Kostomłoty
Kąty Wrocławskie
Wleń
Jawor
Luboradz
50
Jelcz-Laskowice
Gryfów Śląski
Świerzawa
Lusina
Bielany Wrocł.
Biskupice Oławskie
GÓRY KACZAWSKIE
Stara Kraśnica
Gniechowice
Pasiecznik
Jelenia
Wojcieszów
Strzegom

TORUŃ
Grębocin
Radomin
Zbójno
Brzoza
Solec Kujawski
Dobrzejewice
Karniszyn
Bieżuń
Radzanów
Łabiszyn
Czernikowo
Karlewo
Rościszewo
Strzegowo
Aleksandrów Kujawski
Ciechocinek
Kikół
Grodzeń
Skępe
Sierpc
Koziebrody
Gniewkowo
Barcin
Złotniki Kujawskie
Nieszawa
Lipno
Jeżewo
Raciąż
Wenecja
Pakość
Służewo
Raciążek
Mochowo
Tłuchowo
Drobin
Inowrocław
Bobrowniki
Łochocin
Lelice
Zakrzewo
Ujma Duża
Szpetal Górny
Dyblin
Brudzeń Duży
Bielsk
Góra
Płońsk
Dąbrowa
Tupadły
Bądkowo
Kruszwica
WŁOCŁAWEK
Dobrzyń nad Wisłą
Sikórz
Goślice
Staroźreby
Mogilno
Radziejów
Brześć Kujawski
Ciółkowo
Strzelno
Witowo
GOSTYNIŃSKO - WŁOCŁAWSKI PARK KRAJOBRAZOWY
Nowy Duninów
PŁOCK
Bulkowo
Kowal
Radziwie
Słupno
Wójcin
Lubraniec
Piotrków Kujawski
Choceń
Łąck
Cieśle
Bodzanów
Skulsk
Anastazewo
Witkowo
Izbica Kujawska
Chodecz
Lubień Kujawski
Gostynin
Gąbin
Wisła
Słubice
Wyszogród
Ostrowite
Powidz
Kleczew
Sompolno
Dobrosołowo
Ślesin
Babiak
Przedecz
Sanniki
Kamion
Strzałkowo
Słupca
Kazimierz Biskupi
Luboniek
Strzelce
Oporów
Pacyna
Kiernozia
Janów
Maliniec
Wrząca Wielka
Krośniewice
Kutno
Żychlin
Sochaczew
Golina
Kłodawa
Konin
Święte
Koło
Kościelec
Ląd
Drzewce
Daszyna
Plecka Dąbrowa
Zdunу
Aleksandrów
Zagórów
Szetlewek
Grabów
Młogoszyn
Łowicz
Arkadia
Wyszyna
Łukom
Tuliszków
Dąbie
Łęczyca
Bielawy
Bolimów
Tum
Piątek
Nieborów
BOLIMOWSKI PARK KRAJOBR.
Rychwał
Gizałki
Turek
Uniejów
Powodów II
Ozorków
Głowno
Skierniewice
Stary Gostków
Stryków
Byczki
Pleszew
Janków
Stawiszyn
Ceków Kolonia
Tokary
Dobra
Dąbrowa
Krępa
Poddębice
Zgierz
Brzeziny
Kurzeszyn
Jeżów
Brzezie
Głuchów
Porczyny
Aleksandrów Łódzki
Gołuchów
Bratków Dolny
Lutomiersk
ŁÓDŹ
Koluszki
Głuchów
KALISZ
Chlewo
Kwiatkowice
Konstantynów Łódzki
Andrespol
Radwanca
Górzno
Opatówek
Jezioro Jeziorsko
Warta
Wola Rakowa
Kurowice
Budziszewice
Nowe Skalmierzyce
Rossoszyca
Szadek
Pabianice
Rokiciny
Błaszki
Rzgów
Ujazd
Rzeczyca
Ostrów Wielkopolski
Godziesze Wielkie
Zduńska Wola
Tuszyn
Wróblew
Męka
Łask
Będków
Inowłódz
Przygodzice
Sieradz
Tomaszów Mazowiecki
Brzeziny
Rowy
Mikstat
Brąszewice
Buczek
Wadlew
Wolbórz
Czajków
Zapole
Zelów
Treście Rzadowe
Antonin
Grabów nad Prosną
Burzenin
Rogoźno
Szydłów
Bronisławów
Jezioro Sulejowskie
PARK KRAJOBR. MIĘDZYRZECZA WARTY I WIDAWKI
Widawa
Sobki
Rasy
Mzurki
Piotrków Trybunalski
Januszewice
Złoczew
Ostrzeszów
Lututów
Bełchatów
Podklasztorze
Sulejów
Kluki
Wyszanów
Wielgie
Paradyż
Wieruszów
Sokolniki
Rusiec
Szczerców
Rozprza
Czarnożyły
Chorzyna
Żarnów
Kępno
Raduczyce
Osjaków
Łękawa
Radoszewice
Czastary
Trzepnica
Stara
Mroczeń
Opatów
Sieniec
Gorzkowice
Laski
Bolesławiec
Wieluń
Krzeczów
Sulmierzyce
Kamieńsk
Ręczno
Gomunice
Łubnice
Skomlin
Pątnów
Bogumiłowice
Ruda Maleniecka
Rychtal
Kostów
ZAŁĘCZAŃSKI PARK KRAJOBR.
Pajęczno
Kodrab
Byczyna
Działoszyn
Nowa Brzeźnica
Strzelce Małe
Przedbórz Chalupy
Fałków
Komorzno
Radoszyce
Radomsko
Domaszowice
Popów
Kobiele Wlk.
Wołczyn
Praszka
Gorzów Śląski
Rudniki
Zawady
Ważne Młyny
Folwarki
Dobromierz
Wólka
PRZEDBORSKI PARK KRAJOBR.
Świerczów
Kluczbork
Krzepice
Miedźno
Kruszyna
Gidle
Silnica
Oleszno
POMORSKIE
WIELKOPOLSKIE
ŁÓDZKIE
KUJAWY

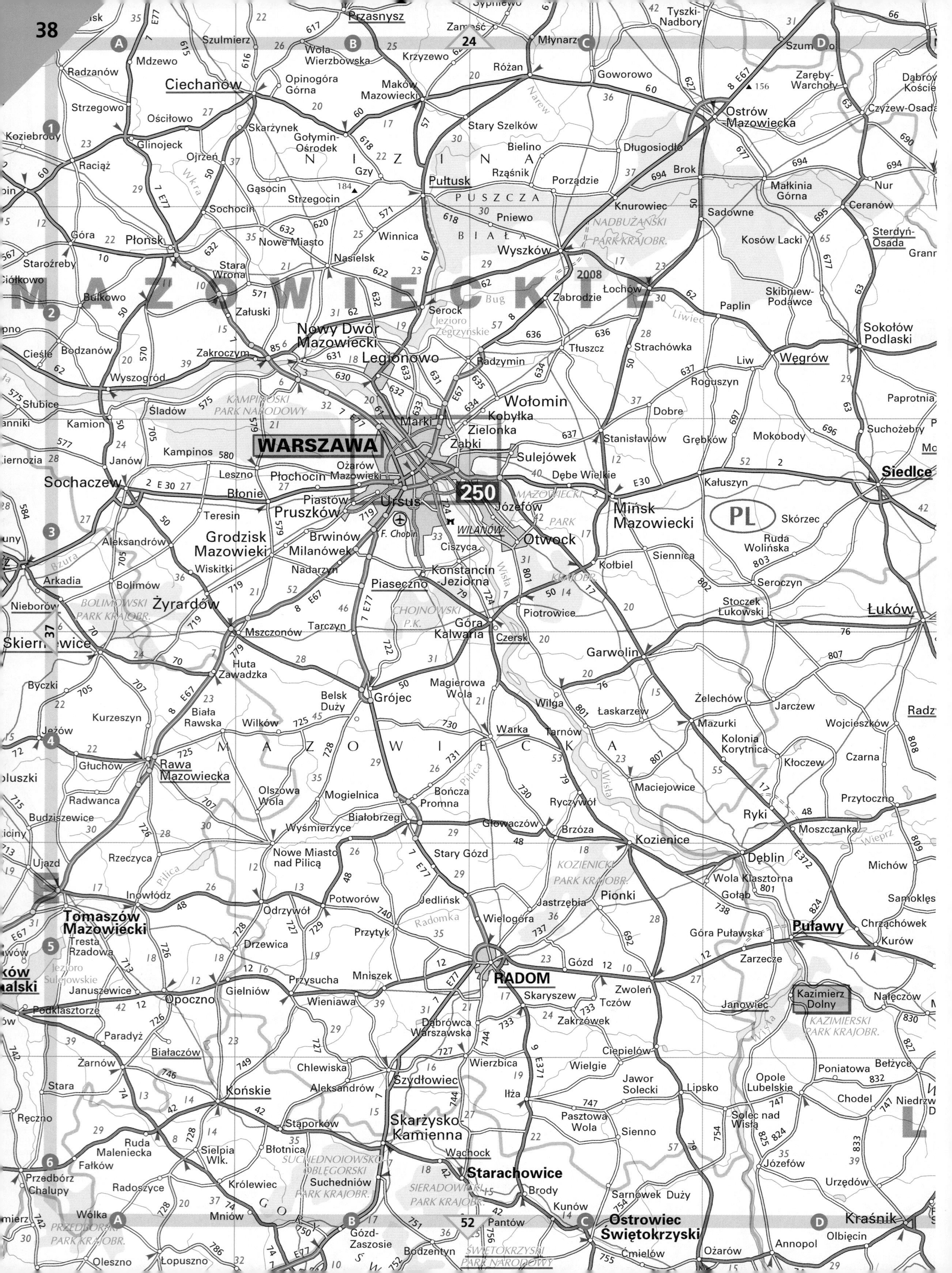

Przasnysz
Szulmierz
Mdzewo
Wola Wierzbowska
Krzyżewo
Zamość
Różan
Młynarze
Tyszki-Nadbory
Szumowo
Radzanów
Ciechanów
Opinogóra Górna
Maków Mazowiecki
Goworowo
Ostrów Mazowiecka
Zaręby-Warchoły
Dąbrówka Kościelna
Strzegowo
Ościłowo
Skarżynek
Gołymin-Ośrodek
Stary Szelków
Bielino
Długosiodło
Czyżew-Osada
Koziebrody
Glinojeck
Ojrzeń
Raciąż
N I Z I N A
Gzy
Pułtusk
Rząśnik
Porządzie
Brok
Małkinia Górna
Nur
Gąsocin
Strzegocin
PUSZCZA
Knurowiec
Sadowne
Ceranów
Sochocin
Pniewo
NADBUŻAŃSKI PARK KRAJOBR.
Góra
Płońsk
Nowe Miasto
Winnica
BIAŁA
Wyszków
Kosów Lacki
Sterdyń-Osada
Staroźreby
Stara Wrona
Nasielsk
Łochów
Ciółkowo
MAZOWIECKIE
Bulkowo
Załuski
Zabrodzie
Skibniew-Podawce
Paplin
Serock
Jezioro Zegrzyńskie
Bug
Liwiec
Nowy Dwór Mazowiecki
Sokołów Podlaski
Cieśle
Bodzanów
Zakroczym
Legionowo
Radzymin
Tłuszcz
Strachówka
Liw
Węgrów
Wyszogród
Roguszyn
Słubice
KAMPINOSKI PARK NARODOWY
Wołomin
Kobyłka
Dobre
Paprotnia
Śladów
Kamion
Marki
Zielonka
Stanisławów
Grębków
Mokobody
Suchożebry
WARSZAWA
Ząbki
Kampinos
Sulejówek
Janów
Leszno
Ożarów Mazowiecki
Dębe Wielkie
Siedlce
Sochaczew
Płochocin
Błonie
Piastów
Ursus
Kałuszyn
Pruszków
Józefów
Mińsk Mazowiecki
PL
Teresin
F. Chopin
WILANÓW
MAZOWIECKI PARK KRAJOBR.
Skórzec
Grodzisk Mazowiecki
Brwinów
Milanówek
Otwock
Aleksandrów
Ciszyca
Ruda Wolińska
Bzura
Wiskitki
Nadarzyn
Konstancin-Jeziorna
Kołbiel
Siennica
Arkadia
Bolimów
Piaseczno
Seroczyn
Nieborów
BOLIMOWSKI PARK KRAJOBR.
Żyrardów
CHOJNOWSKI P.K.
Piotrowice
Stoczek Łukowski
Łuków
Skierniewice
Mszczonów
Tarczyn
Góra Kalwaria
Czersk
Garwolin
Huta Zawadzka
Byczki
Belsk Duży
Grójec
Magierowa Wola
Wilga
Żelechów
Jarczew
Biała Rawska
Kurzeszyn
Wilków
Łaskarzew
Mazurki
Wojcieszków
Radzyń
Jeżów
Warka
Tarnów
Kolonia Korytnica
Głuchów
Rawa Mazowiecka
MAZOWIECKA
Kłoczew
Czarna
Koluszki
Olszowa Wola
Mogielnica
Bończa
Promna
Pilica
Wisła
Maciejowice
Ryczywół
Ryki
Przytoczno
Radwanca
Budziszewice
Białobrzegi
Głowaczów
Brzóza
Moszczanka
Wieprz
Lubochnia
Wyśmierzyce
Stary Gózd
Kozienice
Ujazd
Rzeczyca
Nowe Miasto nad Pilicą
KOZIENICKI PARK KRAJOBR.
Dęblin
Michów
Wola Klasztorna
Inowłódz
Potworów
Jedlińsk
Jastrzębia
Pionki
Gołąb
Samoklęski
Tomaszów Mazowiecki
Odrzywół
Radomka
Wielogóra
Chrząchówek
Przytyk
Góra Puławska
Puławy
Tresta Rzadowa
Drzewica
Kurów
Jezioro Sulejowskie
Zarzecze
Gózd
Piotrków Trybunalski
Przysucha
Mniszek
RADOM
Zwoleń
Januszewice
Opoczno
Gielniów
Skaryszew
Tczów
Kazimierz Dolny
Nałęczów
Podklasztorze
Wieniawa
Janowiec
Zakrzówek
Paradyż
Dąbrówka Warszawska
KAZIMIERSKI PARK KRAJOBR.
Białaczów
Ciepielów
Żarnów
Chlewiska
Wierzbica
Wielgie
Poniatowa
Bełżyce
Opole Lubelskie
Jawor Solecki
Stara
Końskie
Aleksandrów
Szydłowiec
Iłża
Lipsko
Chodel
Niedrzwica
Ręczno
Stąporków
Skarżysko-Kamienna
Pasztowa Wola
Solec nad Wisłą
Sienno
Ruda Maleniecka
Sielpia Wlk.
Błotnica
SUCHEDNIOWSKO-OBLĘGORSKI PARK KRAJOBR.
Wąchock
Józefów
Fałków
Przedbórz
Chałupy
Radoszyce
Królewiec
Suchedniów
SIERADOWICKI PARK KRAJOBR.
Starachowice
Brody
Urzędów
Sarnówek Duży
Wólka
Mniów
Kunów
Ostrowiec Świętokrzyski
Kraśnik
PRZEDBORSKI PARK KRAJOBR.
Gózd-Zaszosie
Pantów
Annopol
Olbięcin
Oleszno
Łopuszno
Bodzentyn
ŚWIĘTOKRZYSKI PARK NARODOWY
Ćmielów
Ożarów

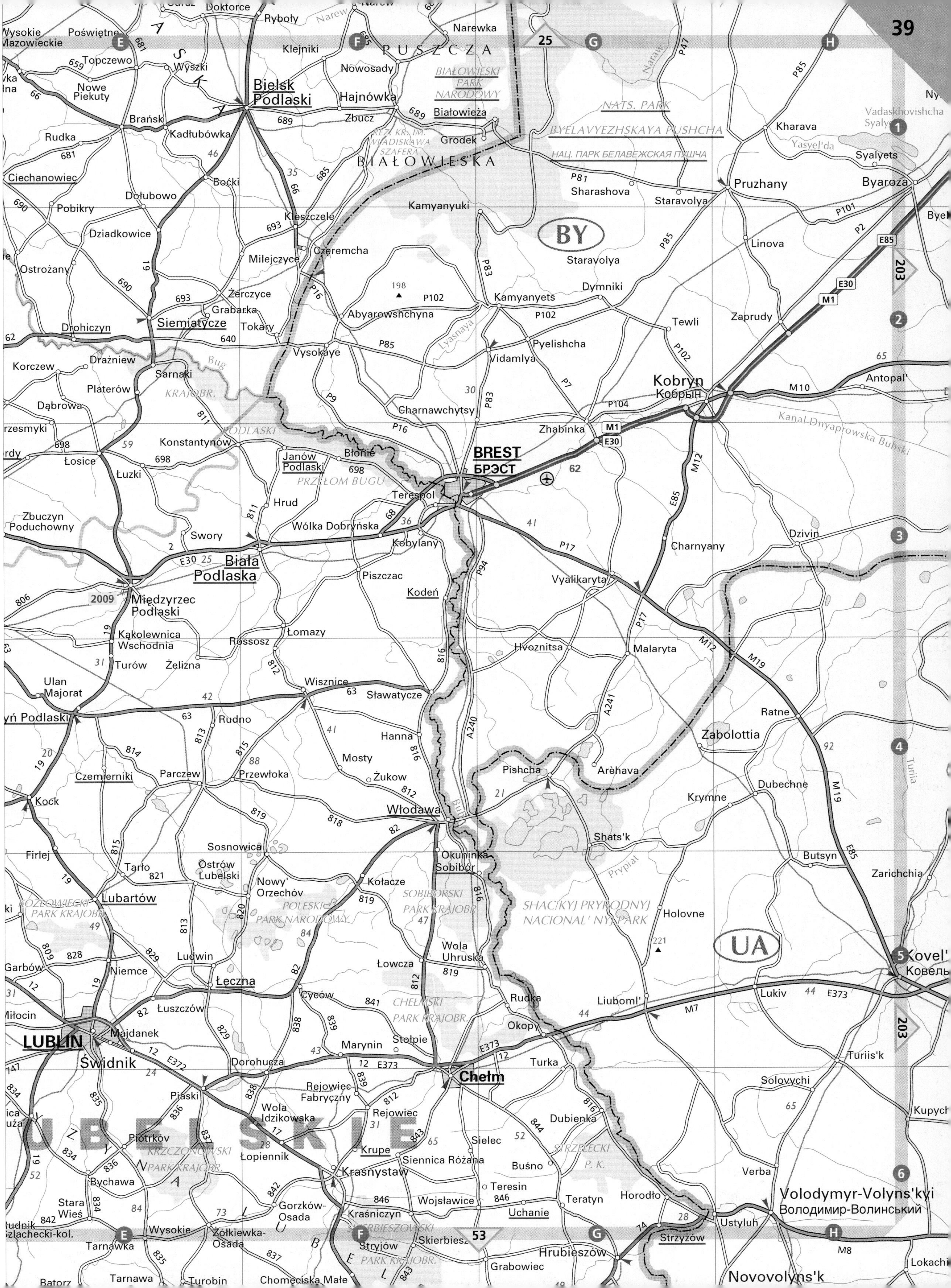
Wysokie Mazowieckie
Poświętne
Doktorce
Ryboły
Narewka
PUSZCZA
BIAŁOWIESKA
Topczewo
Wyszki
Bielsk Podlaski
Klejniki
Nowosady
Hajnówka
BIAŁOWIESKI PARK NARODOWY
Białowieża
Nowe Piekuty
Brańsk
Kadłubówka
Zbucz
Grodek
NATS. PARK
BYELAVYEZHSKAYA PUSHCHA
НАЦ. ПАРК БЕЛАВЕЖСКАЯ ПУШЧА
Rudka
Ciechanowiec
Boćki
Dołubowo
Pobikry
Dziadkowice
Kleszczele
Czeremcha
Milejczyce
Ostrożany
Żerczyce
Grabarka
Tokary
Siemiatycze
Drohiczyn
Kamyanyuki
Sharashova
Staravolya
Pruzhany
Byaroza
Vadaskhovishcha Syalyets
Kharava
Yasyel'da
Syalyets
BY
Linova
Dymniki
Kamyanyets
Abyarowshchyna
Tewli
Zaprudy
Vysokaye
Vidamlya
Pyelishcha
Korczew
Drażniew
Sarnaki
Platerów
KRAJOBR.
Bug
Lyasnaya
Kobryn
Кобрын
Antopal'
Kanal Dnyaprowska Buhski
Charnawchytsy
Zhabinka
Dąbrowa
Konstantynów
PODLASKI
Łosice
Łuzki
Janów Podlaski
Błonie
PRZEŁOM BUGU
BREST
БРЭСТ
Terespol
Hrud
Wólka Dobryńska
Kobylany
Zbuczyn Poduchowny
Swory
Biała Podlaska
Charnyany
Dzivin
Piszczac
Koden
Vyalikaryta
Międzyrzec Podlaski
Kąkolewnica Wschodnia
Rossosz
Łomazy
Hvoznitsa
Malaryta
Turów
Żelizna
Ulan Majorat
Wisznice
Sławatycze
Radzyń Podlaski
Rudno
Ratne
Zabolottia
Hanna
Mosty
Żukow
Pishcha
Arèhava
Czemierniki
Parczew
Przewłoka
Włodawa
Krymne
Dubechne
Kock
Sosnowica
Shats'k
Firlej
Tarło
Ostrów Lubelski
Nowy Orzechów
Kołacze
Okuninka
Sobibór
Butsyn
Zarichchia
KOZŁOWIECKI PARK KRAJOBR.
Lubartów
POLESKI PARK NARODOWY
SOBIBORSKI PARK KRAJOBR.
SHACKYJ PRYRODNYJ NACIONAL' NYJ PARK
Prypiat
Holovne
Ludwin
Wola Uhruska
UA
Kovel'
Ковель
Garbów
Niemce
Łowcza
Łęczna
Cyców
Rudka
Liuboml'
Lukiv
Milocin
Łuszczów
CHEŁMSKI PARK KRAJOBR.
Okopy
LUBLIN
Majdanek
Marynin
Stołpie
Świdnik
Dorohucza
Chełm
Turka
Turiis'k
Piaski
Rejowiec Fabryczny
Solovychi
Wola Idzikowska
Rejowiec
Dubienka
Kupych
LUBELSKIE
Piotrków
KRZCZONOWSKI PARK KRAJOBR.
Łopiennik
Krupe
Sielec
Siennica Różana
STRZELECKI P. K.
Bychawa
Krasnystaw
Busno
Verba
Teresin
Stara Wieś
Gorzków-Osada
Kraśniczyn
Wojsławice
Uchanie
Teratyn
Horodło
Volodymyr-Volyns'kyi
Володимир-Волинський
Rudnik Szlachecki-kol.
Wysokie
Żółkiewka-Osada
Skierbieszów
SKIERBIESZOWSKI PARK KRAJOBR.
Strzyżów
Ustyluh
Tarnawka
Stryjów
Hrubieszów
Grabowiec
Lokachi
Batorz
Tarnawa
Turobin
Chomęciska Małe
Novovolyns'k

A
B
C
D
1
2
3
4
5
6
Cork/Corcaigh
Rosslare Harbour
Plymouth
Ile de Batz
Roscoff
St-Pol-de-Léon
Carantec
Brignogan-Plage
Guissény
Plouguerneau
L'Aber-Wrac'h
Ploudalmézeau
Lampaul
Ile d'Ouessant
Lampaul-Plouarzel
Ile de Molène
Ile de Beniguet
Le Conquet
Pointe de St-Mathieu
St-Renan
BREST
Guipavas
Plabennec
Lannilis
le Folgoët
Lesneven
Goulven
Plouescat
Château de Kerjean
Landivisiau
Landerneau
Guimiliau
St-Thégonnec
Morlaix
Plougastel-Daoulas
Daoulas
Camaret-sur-Mer
Pointe de Penhir
Crozon
Morgat
Landévennec
Le Faou
Sizun
Parc Naturel Régional d'Armorique
Monts d'Arrée
Roc Trévezel
Montagne St-Michel
Tál ar Groaz
Menez Hom
Pentrez-Plage
Châteaulin
Ste-Anne-la-Palud
Ile de Sein
Pointe du Van
Pointe du Raz
Audierne
Tréboul
Douarnenez
Pont-Croix
Locronan
Landudec
Plozévet
Baie d'Audierne
Chapelle de Languidou
Quimper
Quimper-Pluguffan
Briec
Roche du Feu
Pleyben
Châteauneuf-du-Faou
Montagnes Noires
Gourin
Coray
Scaër
Rosporden
N.-D. de Kerdevot
Vire Court
Plonéour Lanvern
Pont-l'Abbé
St-Guénolé
Pointe de Penmarch
Guilvinec
Loctudy
Bénodet
Fouesnant
Beg-Meil
Concarneau
Pont-Aven
Port-Manec'h
Iles de Glénan
Le Faouët
St-Fiacre
Bannalec
Quimperlé
Clohars-Carnoët
Le Pouldu
Lorient
Larmor
Groix
Ile de Groix
Port-Luis
Plouay
Pont-Scorff
Hennebont
Merlevenez
Belz
Kernascléden
Ste-Barbe
Guémené-sur-Scorff
Plouray
Carhaix-Plouguer
Huelgoat
Berrien
Scrignac
Loqueffret
Callac
Plouigneau
Plougonven
Roche de Kiriou
Lanmeur
Plougasnou
Primel-Trégastel
Locquirec
Plestin-les Grèves
Plouaret
St Michel-en-Grève
Lannion
Château de Tonquédec
Trébeurden
Trégastel
Ploumanac'h
Perros-Guirec
Tréguier
Lézardrieux
la Roche-Derrien
Pontrieux
Bégard
Lanvollon
Belle-Isle-en-Terre
Guingamp
Bourbriac
Bulat-Pestivien
Kerien
St-Péver
Cohiniac
St-Gilles-Pligeaux
Quintin
St-Nicolas-du-Pélem
Plounévez-Quintin
Rostrenen
Corlay
Gouarec
Uzel
Lac-de-Guerlédan
Mur-de-Bretagne
Loudéac
Pontivy
Melrand
Bubry
St-Nicodème
Baud
Locminé
Pluvigner
Ste-Anne-d'Auray
Grand-Champ
Auray
Vannes
Menec
Carnac
La Trinité
Tumulus de Gavrinis
Locmariaquer
Port-Navalo
St-Pierre-Quiberon
Quiberon
Sarzeau
Chât. de Suscinio
Pointe des Poulains
Sauzon
Grotte de l'Apothicairerie
Le Palais
Bangor
Belle-Ile
Locmaria
Ile de Houat
Ile de Hoedic
Piriac-sur-Mer
Guérande
Le Croisic
Pointe du Croisic
Batz-sur-Mer
Korrigans
Côte d'Amour
BRETAGNE

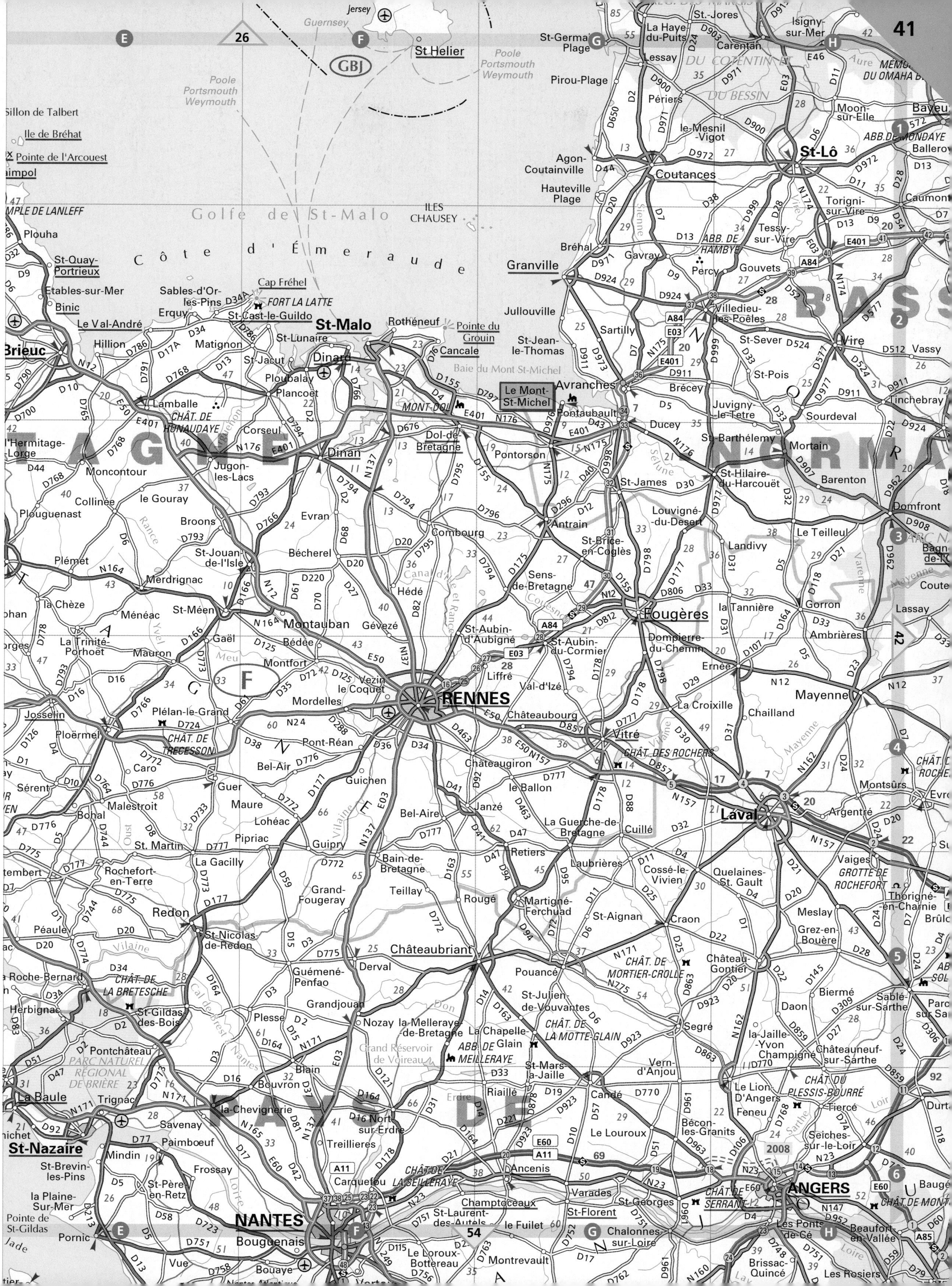

Jersey
Guernsey
St Helier
GBJ
Poole Portsmouth Weymouth
Golfe de St-Malo
Côte d'Émeraude
ILES CHAUSEY
Ile de Bréhat
Pointe de l'Arcouest
Plouha
St-Quay-Portrieux
Etables-sur-Mer
Binic
Le Val-André
Sables-d'Or-les-Pins
Cap Fréhel
FORT LA LATTE
Erquy
St-Cast-le-Guildo
St-Malo
Rothéneuf
Pointe du Grouin
Cancale
Dinard
St-Lunaire
Matignon
Hillion
Lamballe
CHÂT. DE HUNAUDAYE
Ploubalay
Plancoët
Corseul
Baie du Mont St-Michel
Le Mont-St-Michel
MONT-DOL
Dol-de-Bretagne
Pontorson
Pontaubault
Avranches
Granville
Jullouville
St-Jean-le-Thomas
Bréhal
Hauteville Plage
Agon-Coutainville
Coutances
Pirou-Plage
St-Germain-Plage
Lessay
La Haye-du-Puits
St.-Jores
Carentan
Isigny-sur-Mer
Périers
le-Mesnil-Vigot
St-Lô
Moon-sur-Elle
Bayeux
ABB.DE MONDAYE
Balleroy
Torigni-sur-Vire
Caumont
Tessy-sur-Vire
ABB. DE HAMBYE
Percy
Gavray
Gouvets
Villedieu-les-Poêles
Sartilly
St-Sever
Vire
Vassy
St-Pois
Brécey
Tinchebray
Juvigny-le-Tetre
Sourdeval
Ducey
St-Barthélemy
Mortain
St-Hilaire-du-Harcouët
Barenton
St-James
Louvigné-du-Desert
Domfront
Le Teilleul
Landivy
St-Brice-en-Coglès
Antrain
Sens-de-Bretagne
Fougères
la Tannière
Gorron
Lassay
Ambrières
Dompierre-du-Chemin
Ernée
Mayenne
Chailland
La Croixille
Vitré
CHÂT. DES ROCHERS
Laval
Montsûrs
Argentré
Vaiges
GROTTE DE ROCHEFORT
Thorigné-en-Charnie
Meslay
Grez-en-Bouère
Sablé-sur-Sarthe
Château-Gontier
Biermé
Daon
la-Jaille-Yvon
Champigné
Châteauneuf-sur-Sarthe
CHÂT. DU PLESSIS-BOURRÉ
Le Lion-D'Angers
Feneu
Tiercé
Seiches-sur-le-Loir
Angers
Baugé
CHÂT. DE MONT
Les Ponts-de-Cé
Beaufort-en-Vallée
Brissac-Quincé
Les Rosiers
Jugon-les-Lacs
Dinan
Moncontour
Collinée
le Gouray
Plouguenast
Broons
Evran
Combourg
Bécherel
St-Jouan-de-l'Isle
Plémet
Merdrignac
Hédé
la Chèze
Ménéac
St-Méen
Montauban
Gévezé
St-Aubin-d'Aubigné
St-Aubin-du-Cormier
La Trinité-Porhoët
Gaël
Mauron
Bédée
Montfort
Liffré
Val-d'Izé
Vezin le Coquet
Mordelles
RENNES
Châteaubourg
Josselin
Plélan-le-Grand
CHÂT. DE TRECESSON
Ploërmel
Pont-Réan
Bel-Air
Guichen
Châteaugiron
le Ballon
Caro
Guer
Maure
Lohéac
Sérent
Malestroit
Bohal
Janzé
Bel-Aire
La Guerche-de-Bretagne
Cuillé
St. Martin
Pipriac
Guipry
Retiers
La Gacilly
Bain-de-Bretagne
Rochefort-en-Terre
Grand-Fougeray
Teillay
Rougé
Martigné-Ferchaud
Laubrières
Cossé-le-Vivien
Quelaines-St. Gault
Redon
St-Nicolas-de-Redon
Péaule
St-Aignan
Craon
Châteaubriant
Derval
Guémené-Penfao
Pouancé
CHÂT. DE MORTIER-CROLLE
La Roche-Bernard
CHÂT. DE LA BRETESCHE
St-Gildas-des-Bois
Herbignac
Grandjouan
Nozay
la-Melleraye-de-Bretagne
St-Julien-de-Vouvantes
La Chapelle-Glain
CHÂT. DE LA MOTTE-GLAIN
Segré
Plessé
ABB. DE MEILLERAYE
Grand Réservoir de Voireau
Pontchâteau
PARC NATUREL RÉGIONAL DE BRIÈRE
Blain
St-Mars-la-Jaille
Vern-d'Anjou
Riaillé
Candé
La Baule
Trignac
Bouvron
la-Chevignerie
St-Nazaire
Savenay
Nort-sur-Erdre
Le Louroux
Bécon-les-Granits
Mindin
Paimboeuf
Treillieres
St-Brevin-les-Pins
Frossay
Carquefou
CHÂT. DE LA SEILLERAYE
Ancenis
Varades
St-Georges
CHÂT. DE SERRANT
St-Père-en-Retz
la Plaine-Sur-Mer
Pointe de St-Gildas
Pornic
Champtoceaux
St-Laurent-des-Autels
le Fuilet
St-Florent
Chalonnes-sur-Loire
NANTES
Bouguenais
Bouaye
Vue
Le Loroux-Bottereau
Montrevault
PAYS DE
BASSE
NORMANDIE
BRETAGNE

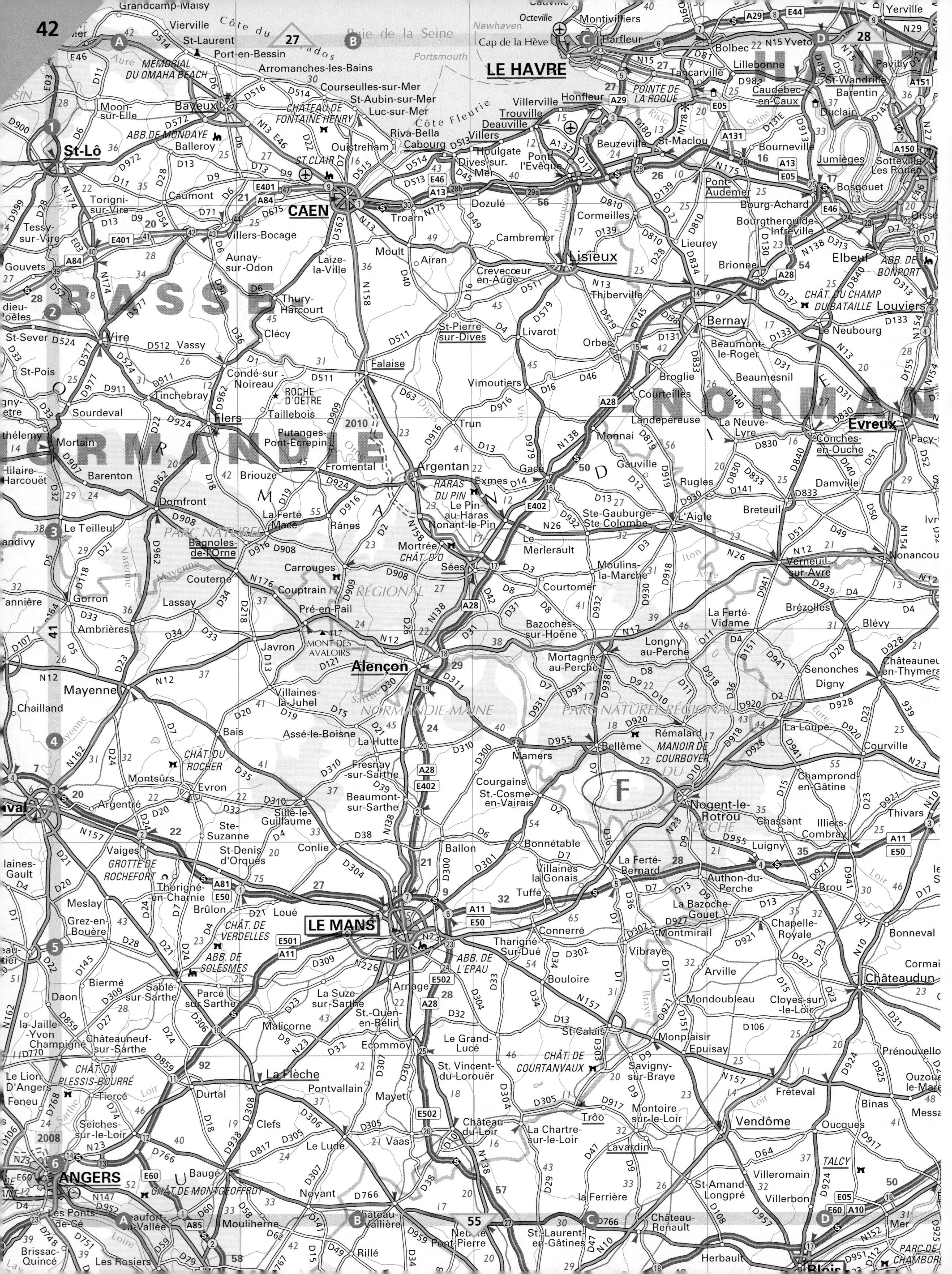
Grandcamp-Maisy
Vierville
St-Laurent
Port-en-Bessin
Côte du Calvados
Baie de la Seine
MÉMORIAL DU OMAHA BEACH
Arromanches-les-Bains
Courseulles-sur-Mer
St-Aubin-sur-Mer
Luc-sur-Mer
CHÂTEAU DE FONTAINE HENRY
Newhaven
Portsmouth
Octeville
Montivilliers
Cap de la Hève
Harfleur
LE HAVRE
Bolbec
Yvetot
Yerville
Lillebonne
Tancarville
POINTE DE LA ROQUE
Caudebec-en-Caux
St-Wandrille
Barentin
Duclair
Jumièges
Sotteville-lès-Rouen
Bourneville
Côte Fleurie
Villerville
Honfleur
Trouville
Deauville
Villers
Cabourg
Houlgate
Dives-sur-Mer
Pont-l'Évêque
Beuzeville
St-Maclou
Pont-Audemer
Bourg-Achard
Bosgouet
Bourgtheroulde-Infreville
Elbeuf
ABB. DE BONPORT
Moon-sur-Elle
Bayeux
ABB. DE MONDAYE
Balleroy
Riva-Bella
Ouistreham
ST CLAIR
St-Lô
Torigni-sur-Vire
Caumont
CAEN
Troarn
Dozulé
Cormeilles
Tessy-sur-Vire
Villers-Bocage
Aunay-sur-Odon
Moult
Airan
Cambremer
Lisieux
Lieurey
Brionne
Gouvets
Laize-la-Ville
Crevecœur en-Auge
Thiberville
CHÂT. DU CHAMP DU BATAILLE
Louviers
BASSE-NORMANDIE
HAUTE-NORMANDIE
Thury-Harcourt
St-Pierre-sur-Dives
Livarot
Orbec
Bernay
Le Neubourg
Beaumont-le-Roger
St-Sever
Vire
Vassy
Clécy
Falaise
Broglie
Beaumesnil
St-Pois
Condé-sur-Noireau
ROCHE D'OETRE
Vimoutiers
Courteilles
Tinchebray
Sourdeval
Flers
Taillebois
Trun
Landepéreuse
La Neuve-Lyre
Conches-en-Ouche
Évreux
Pacy-s
Mortain
Putanges-Pont-Ecrepin
Monnai
Gauville
Hilaire-Harcouët
Barenton
Briouze
Fromental
Argentan
HARAS DU PIN
Exmes
Gacé
Rugles
Damville
Domfront
La Ferté-Macé
Rânes
Le Pin-au-Haras
Nonant-le-Pin
Ste-Gauburge-Ste-Colombe
L'Aigle
Breteuil
Le Teilleul
PARC NATUREL RÉGIONAL
Bagnoles-de-l'Orne
Mortrée
CHÂT. D'O
Le Merlerault
Carrouges
Sées
Moulins-la-Marche
Verneuil-sur-Avre
Nonancourt
Couterne
Couptrain
Courtomer
Gorron
Lassay
Pré-en-Pail
Bazoches-sur-Hoëne
La Ferté-Vidame
Brézolles
Blévy
Ambrières
MONT DES AVALOIRS
Javron
Longny-au-Perche
Châteauneuf-en-Thymerais
Alençon
Mortagne-au-Perche
Senonches
Digny
Mayenne
Chailland
Villaines-la-Juhel
NORMANDIE-MAINE
PARC NATUREL RÉGIONAL DU PERCHE
Bais
Assé-le-Boisne
La Hutte
Mamers
Bellême
Rémalard
MANOIR DE COURBOYER
La Loupe
Courville
CHÂT. DU ROCHER
Montsûrs
Evron
Fresnay-sur-Sarthe
Courgains
St.-Cosme-en-Vairais
Nogent-le-Rotrou
Champrond-en-Gâtine
Thivars
Argentré
Sillé-le-Guillaume
Beaumont-sur-Sarthe
Chassant
Illiers-Combray
Ste-Suzanne
Vaiges
St-Denis-d'Orques
Conlie
Ballon
Bonnétable
Luigny
GROTTE DE ROCHEFORT
Thorigné-en-Charnie
Villaines-la-Gonais
La Ferté-Bernard
Authon-du-Perche
Brou
Meslay
Brûlon
Loué
Tuffé
La Bazoche-Gouet
CHÂT. DE VERDELLES
LE MANS
Connerré
Montmirail
Chapelle-Royale
Bonneval
Grez-en-Bouère
ABB. DE SOLESMES
ABB. DE L'EPAU
Thorigné-sur-Dué
Vibraye
Arville
Châteaudun
Bierné
Sablé-sur-Sarthe
Parcé-sur-Sarthe
La Suze-sur-Sarthe
Arnage
Bouloire
Mondoubleau
Cloyes-sur-le-Loir
Daon
St.-Ouen-en-Belin
St-Calais
Monplaisir
Épuisay
la-Jaille-Yvon
Champigné
Châteauneuf-sur-Sarthe
Malicorne
Ecommoy
Le Grand-Lucé
Prénouvellon
CHÂT. DU PLESSIS-BOURRÉ
La Flèche
St. Vincent-du-Lorouër
CHÂT. DE COURTANVAUX
Savigny-sur-Braye
Le Lion-d'Angers
Tiercé
Feneu
Durtal
Pontvallain
Mayet
Fréteval
Ouzouer-le-Marché
Seiches-sur-le-Loir
Clefs
Trôo
Montoire-sur-le-Loir
Vendôme
Binas
Oucques
Messas
Château-du-Loir
La Chartre-sur-le-Loir
Vaas
Le Lude
Lavardin
TALCY
ANGERS
Baugé
CHÂT. DE MONTGEOFFROY
Noyant
Villeromain
Villerbon
St-Amand-Longpré
la Ferrière
Les Ponts-de-Cé
Beaufort-en-Vallée
Mouliherne
Château-la-Vallière
Château-Renault
Mer
Brissac-Quincé
Les Rosiers
Rillé
Neuillé-Pont-Pierre
St.-Laurent-en-Gâtines
Herbault
Blois
PARC DE CHAMBORD

Bellencombre
Neufchâtel-en-Bray
Longueau
Corbie
Villers-Bretonneux
Péronne
Tôtes
St-Saëns
Aumale
Poix
Les Hayons
Bosc-Mesnil
Clères
Sommery
Buchy
Conty
Essertaux
Moreuil
Sourdon
Formerie
Grandvilliers
Forges-les-Eaux
St-Samson-la-Poterie
Marseille-en-Beauvaisis
Crevecoeur
Breteuil
Montdidier
Roye
Nesle
Ham
Bouchair
St-Quentin
ROUEN
Boos
ABB. DE FONTAINE GUÉRARD
la-Feuille
la Haye
Lyons-la-Forêt
Gournay-en-Bray
Crillon
Froissy
Cuvilly
Lassigny
Noyon
Tergnier
La Fère
Chauny
St-Gobain
ABB. D'OURSCAMPS
Ribécourt
Blérancourt
Coucy-le-Château-Auffrique
St-Germer-de-Fly
Beauvais
Essuilles
St-Just-en-Chaussée
Ressons
Pont-de-l'Arche
Fleury
Morgny
Ecouis
Etrepagny
Le Vaudreuil
Les Andelys
les-Thilliers-en-Vexin
Gisors
Auneuil
Bresles
Clermont
Estrées-St-Denis
Compiègne
Noailles
Mouy
Arsy
Vironvay
Gaillon
Tourny
Lierville
Méru
Verberie
Vic-sur-Aisne
Pierrefonds
Soissons
FORÊT DE COMPIÈGNE
Vernon
Magny-en-Vexin
Arronville
Creil
St-Leu-d'Esserent
Chantilly
Senlis
ABB. DE LA VICTOIRE
ABB. DE LIEU-RESTAURE
Braine
Marines
L'Isle-Adam
ABB. DE ROYAUMONT
Luzarches
Crépy-en-Valois
Longpont
Bonnières
Rosny Sur Seine
Chaufour-lès-Bonnières
Auvers-s-Oise
ABB. DE CHAALIS
Villers-Cotterêts
Grand-Rozoy
Fismes
Mantes-la-Jolie
Meulan
Pontoise
Surviliers
Ermenonville
Betz
La Ferté-Milon
Neuilly-St-Front
Nanteuil-le-Haudouin
Fère-en-Tardenois
CHÂTEAU DE FÈRE
Epône
Flins
Orgeval
Bourget
Charles de Gaulle
Dammartin-en-Goële
Anet
PARC ZOOL.
St-Germain
St-Denis
Lizy
Bonnesvalyn
Houdan
Montfort-l'Amaury
Pontchartrain
L'Agiot
Elancourt
Meaux
Montreuil-aux-Lions
Château-Thierry
Dreux
PARIS
Lagny
Couilly
Charly
Trappes
DISNEYLAND
Crécy
Jouarre
La Ferté-sous-Jouarre
Versailles
Dampierre
Chevreuse
Coutevroult
Nogent-le-Roi
FORÊT DE RAMBOUILLET
Rambouillet
Palaiseau
Orly
Rebais
Maintenon
Limours
Janvry
Champlan
Tournan
Coulommiers
Montmirail
Champaubert
Epernon
Brie-Comte-Robert
Fontenay-Trésigny
CHÂT. DU VIVIER
Evry
Rozay-en-Brie
La Ferté-Gaucher
Chartres
Ablis
Arpajon
Guignes
CHÂT. DE LA GRANGE-BLENEAU
Vaudoy en Brie
Dourdan
Corbeil-Essonnes
Mormant
Courtacon
Esternay
Sézanne
Auneau
Allainville
VAUX-LE VICOMTE
Villiers-St-Georges
Voise
Étampes
Morigny Champigny
Melun
Nangis
Villenauxe-la-Grande
Provins
CHÂT. DE FARCHEVILLE
Allonnes
FORÊT DE FONTAINEBLEAU
Barbizon
GORGES D'APREMONT
Fontainebleau
Méréville
Angerville
Dontilly
Nogent-sur-Seine
Romilly-sur-Seine
Voves
Malesherbes
Ury
Montereau-Faut-Yonne
Moret-sur-Loing
Bray-sur-Seine
Allaines
Janville
Toury
La Belle Etoile
Pithiviers
Nemours
Voulx
Grange-le-Bocage
Marigny-le-Châtel
Puiseaux
Souppes-sur-Loing
Pont-sur-Yonne
Marcilly-le-Hayer
Artenay
Neuville-aux-Bois
Château-Landon
Chéroy
Patay
CHÂT. DE CHEVILLY
Beaune-la-Rolande
Dordives
Ferrières
Sens
Villeneuve-l'Archevêque
Estissac
Loury
Bellegarde
Cerisiers
Aix-en-Othe
ORLÉANS
Ladon
Montargis
Courtenay
Villeneuve-sur-Yonne
Meung-sur-Loire
Olivet
Mardié
Chailley-Turny
Cléry
Jargeau
Germigny-des-Prés
Châteauneuf-sur-Loire
Lorris
Châteaurenard
Douchy
Joigny
Precy Sur Vrin
Migennes
Ervy-le-Châtel
St-Benoît-sur-Loire
Montereau
St-Florentin
La Ferté-St-Aubin
Sully-sur-Loire
Châtillon-
Charny
Flogny-la-Chapelle
PICARDIE
ÎLE-DE-FRANCE

DE L'AVESNOIS
St-Quentin
Le Catelet
Bohain-en-Vermandois
Le Nouvion-en-Thiérache
Fourmies
Chimay
Givet
Rochefort
Roisel
Lesdins
La Capelle
Couvin
Beauraing
Han-sur-Lesse
Chigny
Guise
Hirson
Vonêche
Hargnies
Wellin
Etréaupont
Fumay
Gedinne
St-Hubert
Ham
Ribemont
le-Hérie-la Vieville
Voulpaix
Vervins
Rocroi
Revin
ROCHES DE LAIFOUR
Monthermé
la-Ferté-Chevresis
Sains
Rumigny
Auvillers-les-Forges
Vresse
Paliseul
Tergnier
La Fère
Crécy-sur-Serre
Marle
Brunehamel
Château-Regnault
ROCHE AUX 7 VILLAGES
Rochehaut
Bertrix
Noyon
Chauny
St-Gobain
Montcornet
Rozoy
Aubigny-les-Pothées
Charleville-Mézières
Gespunsart
Cugnon-sur-Semois
Senseruth
Neufchâteau
Bouillon
Herbeumont
Coucy-le-Château-Auffrique
Laon
Liesse
Dizy-le-Gros
Signy-l'Abbaye
Sissonne
Seraincourt
Flize
Sedan
Nizy-le-Comte
Château-Porcien
Novion-Porcien
Poix-Terron
Chémery-sur-Bar
Douzy
Florenville
Carignan
ABBAYE D'ORVAL
Vic-sur-Aisne
CAVERNE DU DRAGON
Corbeny
Asfeld
Canal des Ardennes
Rethel
Mouzon
Fromy
Soissons
Vailly
Bourg-et-Comin
Neufchâtel-sur-Aisne
Attigny
Le Chesne
Braine
Stenay
Longpont
Montmédy
Grand-Rozoy
Fismes
Bourgogne
Juniville
Machault
Mazagran
Vouziers
Buzancy
Louppy-sur-Loison
Neuilly-St-Front
CHÂTEAU DE FÈRE
Fère-en-Tardenois
Gneux
REIMS
St-Martin-l'Heureux
Sommepy-Tahure
Monthois
Grandpré
Bantheville
Dun
Vrigny
Sivry-sur-Meuse
Ville-en-Tardenois
Aubérive
Séchault
Damvillers
Châtillon-sur-Marne
Verzy
Sept-Saulx
Charpentry
Ville-devant-Chaumont
Varennes-en-Argonne
Château-Thierry
Dormans
Champillon
Suippes
Neuvilly-en-Argonne
Bras-sur-Meuse
FORT DU DOUAUMONT
Charly
Condé-en-Brie
Épernay
Ay
Ste-Menehould
Verdun
Clermont-en-Argonne
CHAMPAGNE-ARDENNE
Rebais
Montmirail
Champaubert
Montmort
Vertus
Etoges
l'Epine
Châlons-en-Champagne
Auve
Triaucourt-en-Argonne
Dieue-sur-Meuse
Lavoye
Souilly
Fresnes-en-Woëvre
La Ferté-Gaucher
Givry-en-Argonne
Beausite
Heippes
Troyon
Ecury
SACRÉE
Laheycourt
Chaumont-sur-Aire
Pierrefitte-sur-Aire
Esternay
Fère-Champenoise
Nettancourt
Fontaine-sur-Coole
Raival
Sézanne
Villiers-St-Georges
Connantre
Sommesous
Pargny-sur-Saulx
Revigny-sur-Ornain
Fains Le Sources
St-Mihiel
Villenauxe-la-Grande
Sompuis
Mailly-le-Camp
Vitry-le-François
Thiéblemont-Farémont
Sermaize-les-Bains
VOIE
Rumont
Bar-le-Duc
Provins
Anglure
Salon
ABB. DES TROIS FONTAINES
Commercy
Sauvaux
Nogent-sur-Seine
Romilly-sur-Seine
Arcis-sur-Aube
Hallignicourt
St-Dizier
Ancerville
Stainville
Ligny-en-Barrois
Méry
Void
La Belle Etoile
Lac du Der-Chantecoq
Tréveray
Marigny-le-Châtel
Marcilly-le-Hayer
Montier-en-Der
Wassy
Lesmont
Houdelaincourt
Delouze-Rosières
Troyes
Piney
Brienne-le-Château
Saudron
Joinville
Gondrecourt
PARC NAT. RÉGIONAL DE LA FORÊT D'ORIENT
Soulaines-Dhuys
Poissons
Villeneuve-l'Archevêque
Estissac
Lac du Temple
Lac d'Orient
Maison-Neuve
Doulevant-le-Château
Germay
Domrémy-la-Pucelle
Greux
Aix-en-Othe
Lusigny
Bouilly
Thors
Doulaincourt
Neufchâteau
Vendeuvre
Bar-sur-Aube
Vignory
Chailley-Turny
Crésantignes
Colombey-les-Deux-Églises
St-Blin
Andelot
Bologne
Ervy-le-Châtel
Bar-sur-Seine
Juzennecourt
Rimaucourt
St-Florentin
Chaource
Essoyes
Chaumont
St-Thiébault
Bourmont
Flogny-la-Chapelle
Pontigny
Les Riceys
Esnouveaux
Clefmont
Bulgnéville
Contrexéville

RHEINLAND
PFALZ
SAARLAND
LORRAINE
ALSACE
EIFEL
HUNSRÜCK
LUXEMBOURG
Trier
METZ
NANCY
SAARBRÜCKEN
STRASBOURG
Kaiserslautern
Bad Kreuznach
Idar-Oberstein
Neunkirchen
Homburg
Zweibrücken
Pirmasens
Saarlouis
Völklingen
Forbach
Sarreguemines
St-Avold
Thionville
Esch-sur-Alzette
Longwy
Arlon (Aarlen)
Bastogne (Bastenaken)
Ettelbruck
Echternach
Bitburg
Wittlich
Cochem
Mayen
Andernach
Boppard
Bernkastel-Kues
Traben-Trarbach
Saarburg
Merzig
St Wendel
Pont-à-Mousson
Toul
Lunéville
Sarrebourg
Saverne
Haguenau
Offenburg
Kehl
St-Dié
Vittel
Mirecourt
Château-Salins
Dieuze
Molsheim
Obernai
Erstein
DEUTSCH-LUXEMBURGISCHER NATURPARK
PFÄLZERWALD
PARC NATUREL RÉGIONAL DES VOSGES DU NORD
PARC NAT. RÉG. DE LORRAINE
Canal de la Marne au Rhin
31
58
59
46

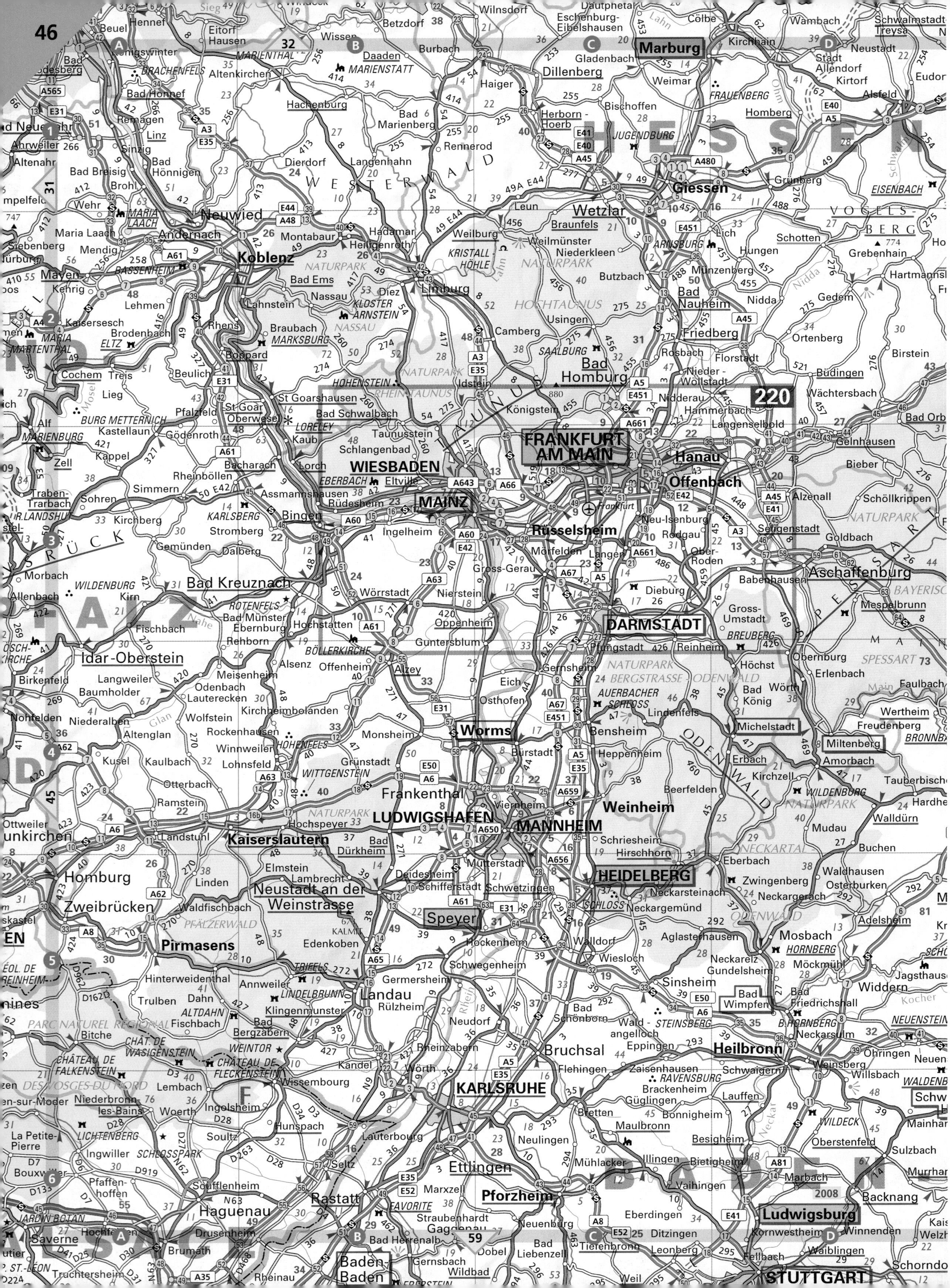

Marburg
HESSEN
Giessen
Wetzlar
Limburg
Koblenz
Neuwied
Andernach
Bad Ems
Boppard
WESTERWALD
Dillenburg
Herborn
Bad Homburg
Friedberg
Bad Nauheim
WIESBADEN
MAINZ
FRANKFURT AM MAIN
Hanau
Offenbach
Rüsselsheim
Aschaffenburg
DARMSTADT
Bad Kreuznach
Idar-Oberstein
PFALZ
Alzey
Worms
Bensheim
Michelstadt
Miltenberg
ODENWALD
Frankenthal
LUDWIGSHAFEN
MANNHEIM
Weinheim
HEIDELBERG
Kaiserslautern
Homburg
Zweibrücken
Pirmasens
Neustadt an der Weinstrasse
Bad Dürkheim
Speyer
Landau
Sinsheim
Heilbronn
Bruchsal
KARLSRUHE
Ettlingen
Pforzheim
Rastatt
Baden-Baden
Haguenau
Saverne
Wissembourg
Ludwigsburg
STUTTGART
Backnang
Mosbach
BADEN-
220
32
59

Eisenach
Gotha
ERFURT
Weimar
Apolda
Jena
Bad Hersfeld
Friedewald
Hönebach
Obersuhl
WARTBURG
Kirchheim
Niederaula
Philippsthal
Vacha
Dorndorf
Bad Salzungen
Winterstein
Friedrichroda
Bad Liebenstein
Schwabhausen
Arnstadt
Kranichfeld
Bad Berka
Blankenhain
Stadtroda
Kahla
LEUCHTENBURG
HERZBERG
HOHEN WEHRDA
Buttlar
Barchfeld
Brotterode
Ohrdruf
GLEICHEN
DREI
Lengefeld
Schlitz
Burghaun
Geisa
Geblar
Weilar
Dermbach
Breitungen
Stadtilm
Teichel
Hünfeld
Schmalkalden
Oberhof
Zella-Mehlis
PAULINZELLA
Bad Blankenburg
Langenorla
Neustadt
Lauterbach
NATURPARK
Tann
Wasungen
Ilmenau
Rudolstadt
HESSISCHE RHÖN
GR BEERBERG
Königsee
Pössneck
Kaltennordheim
Gehren
Schwarzburg
Hohenwarte Talsperre
Fulda
Hilders
Meiningen
Suhl
Saalfeld
MILSEBURG
SCHL. FASANERIE
WASSERKUPPE
Fladungen
Grossbreitenbach
FEENGROTTEN
Ziegenrück
Leutenberg
Steinau
Henneberg
Schleusingen
Themar
Neuhaus
Probstzella
Bleiloch Talsperre
Döllbach
Gersfeld
Ostheim
Eussenhausen
Mellrichstadt
Hildburghausen
Ludwigsstadt
Wurzbach
Lobenstein
Schlüchtern
Bischofsheim
STEINSBURG
Eisfeld
Rudolphstein
HESSISCHER SPESSART
SCHWARZENFELS
BAYERISCHE RHÖN
Bad Neustadt
Heustreu
D
Rottenbach
Steinbach
Sonneberg
Nordhalben
Berg
Bad Brückenau
SALZBURG
Streufdorf
Bad Rodach
Neustadt
Lichtenberg
Münnerstadt
Bad Königshofen
Hedburg
Coburg
Stockheim
Naila
Burgjoss
Obersinn
Hasslach
VESTE ROSENBERG
Selbitz
Burgsinn
Rieneck
Hammelburg
Bad Kissingen
Stadtlauringen
Mitwitz
Wallenfels
Kronach
Losau
FRANKENWALD
TRIMBURG
BETTENBURG
Hofheim
Pfaffendorf
Marktzeuln
Markleugast
Poppenhausen
Gemünden
Gaushach
Schweinfurt
HASSBERGE
Ebern
BANZ
Lichtenfels
Stadtsteinach
Burgkunstadt
Kupferberg
Kirchenlamitz
Lohr
Büchold
Arnstein
Hassfurt
Kirchlauter
Staffelstein
Vierzehnheiligen
PLASSENBURG
Gefrees
Karlstadt
Werneck
Knetzgau
Weismain
Kulmbach
Himmelkron
Bad Berneck
FICHTELGEBIRGE
Neustadt
Grettstadt
Ebelsbach
Zapfendorf
Thurnau
Bischofsgrün
Birkenfeld
Hausen
Eltmann
Schesslitz
FELSENGARTEN
Warmensteinach
Marktheidenfeld
Escherndorf
Gerolzhofen
Breitengüssbach
Hallstadt
WÜRGAU
Hollfeld
EREMITAGE
Veitshöchheim
Volkach
Ebrach
Bamberg
FRÄNKISCHE SCHWEIZ
Bayreuth
Weidenberg
WÜRZBURG
Dettelbach
Burgebrach
Waischenfeld
Kemnath
Höchberg
Wiesentheid
Prichsenstadt
Hirschaid
BINGHÖHLE
Streitberg
SOPHIENHÖHLE
Kist
Kitzingen
Geiselwind
Schlüsselfeld
Wachenroth
Ebermannstadt
Muggendorf
Creussen
Gerchsheim
Iphofen
Pommersfelden
Behringersmühle
SPEINSHART
WEISSENSTEIN
Gössweinstein
TEUFELSHÖHLE
Kirchenthumbach
Eschenbach
Höchstadt
Pottenstein
Ochsenfurt
Marktbreit
STEIGERWALD
Forchheim
Weidensees
Pegnitz
Euerhausen
Markt Bibart
Scheinfeld
WELDENSTEINER
Gräfenberg
Grafenwöhr
Auerbach
Königshofen
Aub
Gollhofen
SPIELBG
Neustadt an der Aisch
Herzogenaurach
Erlangen
Plech
Neuhaus
Boxberg
Röttingen
Bierberchren
Uffenheim
Forth
Velden
Mönlas
Bad Windsheim
Emskirchen
Heroldsberg
MAXIMILIANS-GROTTE
R.ROTHENBURG
Vilseck
Bad Mergentheim
Weikersheim
Creglingen
HOHENECK
Langenzenn
Markt Erlbach
Fürth
Lauf
Hersbruck
Hahnbach
HERRGOTTS KIRCHE
Rothenburg ob der Tauber
Burgbernheim
NÜRNBERG
Sulzbach-Rosenberg
Dörzbach
Ammersricht
Riedbach
FRANKENHÖHE
Grosshabersdorf
Stein
Alfeld
Illschwang
Amberg
Künzelsau
Blaufelden
Lehrberg
Heilsbronn
Feucht
Altdorf
Langenburg
Gerabronn
Ansbach
Schwabach
Lauterhofen
Kupferzell
Wörnitz
Berg bei Neumarkt
Kastl
Kirchberg
Aurach
Windsbach
Abenberg
KÖNIG-OTTO-HÖHLE
Burgoberbach
Roth
Allersberg
Neumarkt
Hohenburg
Ilshofen
Crailsheim
Merkendorf
Wolframs-Eschenbach
Schmidmühlen
Feuchtwangen
Freystadt
Velburg
Schopfloch
Bechhofen
Spalt
Hilpoltstein
Deining
Burglengenfeld
COMBURG
Gunzenhausen
Mühlhausen
Obersontheim
Dinkelsbühl
Pleinfeld
Heideck
Dasswang
Parsberg
Gaildorf
Thalmässing
Berching
Rosenberg
ST. MARIA
Wassertrüdingen
Weissenburg
Ellingen
Greding
Sulzbach
Ellenberg
ALTMÜHLTAL
Beilngries
Gschwend
Ellwangen
Oettingen
Dietfurt
Hemau
Abtsgmünd
Treuchtlingen
Rothenstein
Kinding
Nittendorf
Wasseralfingen
Wallerstein
Riedenburg
SCHLOSS PRUNN
Mutlangen
Aalen
Nördlingen
Wemding
Pappenheim
Solnhofen
Denkendorf
Bad Abbach
THÜRINGER WALD
FRANKENWALD
FRÄNKISCHE ALB
33
34
60
61

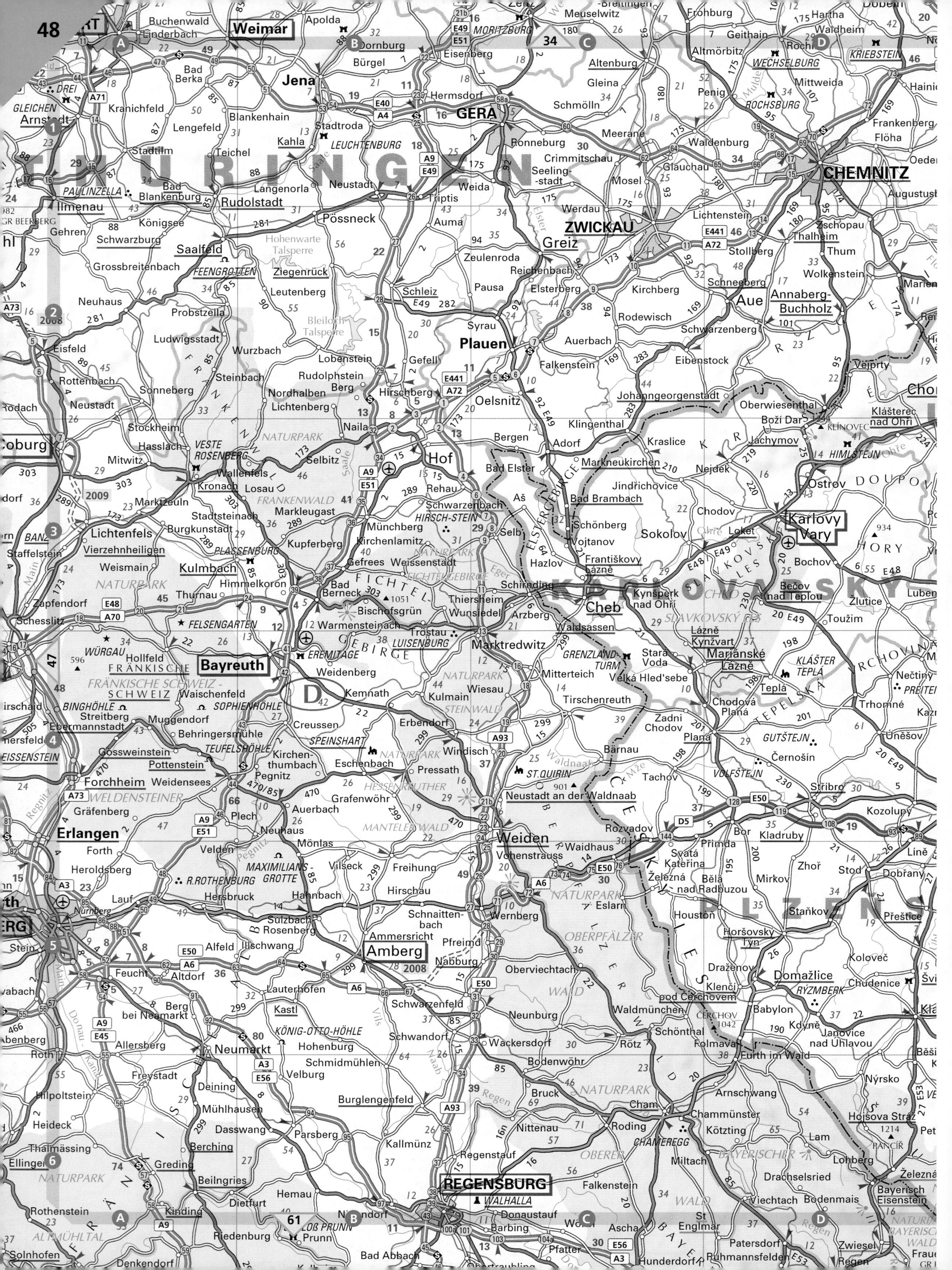
THÜRINGEN
Weimar
Buchenwald
Linderbach
Apolda
Dornburg
Bürgel
Eisenberg
MORITZBURG
Meuselwitz
Frohburg
Geithain
Hartha
Waldheim
Döbeln
Rochlitz
WECHSELBURG
KRIEBSTEIN
Altmörbitz
Altenburg
Gleina
Mittweida
Penig
ROCHSBURG
Hainichen
Bad Berka
Jena
Hermsdorf
GERA
Schmölln
Frankenberg
Flöha
Arnstadt
GLEICHEN
DREI
Kranichfeld
Lengefeld
Blankenhain
Stadtroda
Kahla
LEUCHTENBURG
Ronneburg
Meerane
Waldenburg
CHEMNITZ
Stadtilm
Teichel
Crimmitschau
Seeling-stadt
Glauchau
Mosel
Oederan
PAULINZELLA
Bad Blankenburg
Langenorla
Neustadt
Triptis
Weida
Ilmenau
Rudolstadt
Werdau
ZWICKAU
Lichtenstein
Augustusburg
Zschopau
Königsee
Pössneck
Auma
Gehren
Schwarzburg
Hohenwarte Talsperre
Saalfeld
Zeulenroda
Greiz
Thalheim
Thum
Stollberg
Grossbreitenbach
FEENGROTTEN
Ziegenrück
Reichenbach
Wolkenstein
Leutenberg
Schleiz
Pausa
Elsterberg
Kirchberg
Schneeberg
Aue
Annaberg-Buchholz
Neuhaus
Probstzella
Bleiloch Talsperre
Syrau
Rodewisch
Schwarzenberg
Ludwigsstadt
Wurzbach
Plauen
Auerbach
Eisfeld
Lobenstein
Gefell
Falkenstein
Eibenstock
Vejprty
Rottenbach
Steinbach
Rudolphstein
Oelsnitz
Sonneberg
Nordhalben
Berg
Hirschberg
Johanngeorgenstadt
Chomutov
Rodach
Neustadt
Lichtenberg
Oberwiesenthal
Boží Dar
Klášterec nad Ohří
Stockheim
Naila
Klingenthal
Coburg
Hasslach
VESTE ROSENBERG
NATURPARK
Bergen
Kraslice
Jáchymov
KLÍNOVEC
Adorf
Hof
Selbitz
HIMLŠTEJN
Mitwitz
Wallenfels
Bad Elster
Markneukirchen
Nejdek
Kronach
Losau
Rehau
Jindřichovice
Ostrov
DOUPOV
Marktzeuln
FRANKENWALD
Markleugast
Schwarzenbach
Aš
Bad Brambach
Chodov
Stadtsteinach
HIRSCH-STEIN
Burgkunstadt
Münchberg
Schönberg
Sokolov
Loket
Karlovy Vary
Lichtenfels
Kupferberg
Kirchenlamitz
Selb
Vojtanov
HORY
BANZ
Vierzehnheiligen
Staffelstein
PLASSENBURG
Gefrees
Weissenstadt
Hazlov
Františkovy Lázně
Bochov
Weismain
Kulmbach
FICHTELGEBIRGE
Himmelkoron
Thurnau
Bad Berneck
FICHTEL
Schirnding
KARLOVARSKÝ
Kynšperk nad Ohří
Bečov nad Teplou
Zapfendorf
Thiersheim
Cheb
Žlutice
Bischofsgrün
Wunsiedel
Arzberg
Toužim
Schesslitz
FELSENGARTEN
Warmensteinach
Tröstau
Waldsassen
SLAVKOVSKÝ LES
LUISENBURG
Lázně Kynžvart
WÜRGAU
Hollfeld
Bayreuth
EREMITAGE
GEBIRGE
Marktredwitz
GRENZLAND-TURM
Stará Voda
Mariánské Lázně
KLÁŠTER TEPLÁ
FRÄNKISCHE
Weidenberg
Mitterteich
Velká Hled'sebe
Nečtiny
FRÄNKISCHE SCHWEIZ - SCHWEIZ
Waischenfeld
Kemnath
Wiesau
Teplá
PREITENSTEIN
BINGHÖHLE
SOPHIENHÖHLE
Kulmain
STEINWALD
Tirschenreuth
Chodová Planá
Trhomné
Streitberg
Ebermannstadt
Muggendorf
Creussen
Erbendorf
Zadní Chodov
Behringersmühle
SPEINSHART
Planá
GUTŠTEJN
Úněšov
Gossweinstein
TEUFELSHÖHLE
Kirchen-thumbach
Windisch
Bärnau
Pottenstein
Eschenbach
Pressath
ST. QUIRIN
Černošín
Forchheim
Weidensee
Pegnitz
HESSENREUTHER
Tachov
VOLFŠTEJN
WELDENSTEINER
Grafenwöhr
Neustadt an der Waldnaab
Stříbro
Gräfenberg
Plech
Auerbach
Kozolupy
Erlangen
Neuhaus
MANTELER WALD
Weiden
Rozvadov
Bor
Kladruby
Forth
Velden
Mönlas
Waidhaus
Přimda
Líně
Heroldsberg
MAXIMILIANS-GROTTE
Vilseck
Freihung
Vohenstrauss
Svatá Kateřina
Zhoř
Stod
Dobřany
R. ROTHENBURG
Železná
Bělá nad Radbuzou
Mirkov
Lauf
Hersbruck
Hahnbach
Hirschau
NATURPARK
Eslarn
Nürnberg
Schnaittenbach
Wernberg
Houstoň
Staňkov
Přeštice
Sulzbach-Rosenberg
Ammersricht
OBERPFÄLZER
Horšovský Týn
Stein
Alfeld
Illschwang
Pfreimd
Amberg
Nabburg
Draženov
Koloveč
Feucht
Altdorf
Oberviechtach
Domažlice
Švihov
Lauterhofen
Klenčí pod Čerchovem
RÝZMBERK
Chudenice
Schwarzenfeld
WALD
Berg bei Neumarkt
Kastl
Neunburg
Waldmünchen
Babylon
ČERCHOV
Kdyně
Janovice nad Úhlavou
Schwabach
KÖNIG-OTTO-HÖHLE
Hohenburg
Schwandorf
Wackersdorf
Rötz
Schönthal
Folmava
Allersberg
Neumarkt
Schmidmühlen
Bodenwöhr
Furth im Wald
Běšiny
Roth
Freystadt
Velburg
Nýrsko
Hilpoltstein
Deining
Bruck
NATURPARK
Arnschwang
Mühlhausen
Burglengenfeld
Cham
Heideck
Dasswang
Parsberg
Nittenau
Roding
Chammünster
Hojsova Stráž
Kötzting
Lam
PANCÍŘ
Thalmässing
Berching
Kallmünz
CHAMEREGG
Greding
Regenstauf
OBERER BAYERISCHER
Lohberg
Ellingen
NATURPARK
Beilngries
Miltach
Drachselsried
Železná Ruda
REGENSBURG
Falkenstein
Dietfurt
Hemau
WALHALLA
Viechtach
Bodenmais
Bayerisch Eisenstein
Rothenstein
Kinding
Nittendorf
Donaustauf
Wörth
St Englmar
ALTMÜHLTAL
Riedenburg
LOß PRUNN
Prunn
Barbing
Ascha
NATURPARK BAYERISCHER WALD
Solnhofen
Denkendorf
Bad Abbach
Pfatter
Patersdorf
Ruhmannsfelden
Zwiesel
Hunderdorf
Regen
Frauenau
2008
2009
D

DRESDEN
Radebeul
Radeberg
Bischofswerda
Bautzen
Görlitz
Zgorzelec
Reichenbach
Löbau
Lubań
Gradówek
Olszyna
Pławna
Neukirch
Oppach
Kesselsdorf
Stolpen
Neustadt
Herrnhut
Zawidów
Tharandt
Freital
Heidenau
Pirna
Ebersbach
Ostritz
Lésna
Sucha
Gryfów Śląski
Freiberg
Höckendorf
Dippoldiswalde
Festung Königstein
Bad Schandau
Sebnitz
Neugersdorf
Niederoderwitz
Habartice
Nové Město pod Smrkem
Jelenia Góra
Brand-Erbisdorf
Königstein
Schmilka
Rumburk
Krásná Lípa
Seifhennersdorf
Zittau
Frýdlant
Mirsk
Pasiecznik
Świeradów-Zdrój
Rybnica
Glashütte
Bad Gottleuba
Hřensko
Varnsdorf
Hrádek nad Nisou
Sieniawka
Bogatynia
Hejnice
Piechowice
Frauenstein
Mittelsaida
Lauenstein
Česká Kamenice
Chrastava
Szklarska Poręba
Sobieszów
Jakuszyce
Altenberg
Zinnwald-Georgenfeld
Děčín
Benešov nad Ploučnicí
Liberec
Harrachov
Cínovec
Nový Bor
Cvikov
Jablonné v Podještědí
Desná
Jablonec nad Jizerou
Tanvald
Špindlerův Mlýn
Olbernhau
Dubí
Hrob
Vrabinec
Velké Březno
Zákupy
Ještěd
Jablonec nad Nisou
Mimoň
Teplice
Ústí nad Labem
Česká Lípa
Zahrádky
Hodkovice nad Mohelkou
Frýdštejn
Železný Brod
Litvínov
Lom
Červený Hrádek u Jirkova
Duchcov
Úštěk
Kravaře
Jestřebí
Doksy
Dolní Krupá
Hrubý Rohozec
Turnov
Semily
Jilemnice
Vrchlabí
Hora Svatého Šebestiána
Bílina
Milešovka
Litoměřice
Střední Hoří
Starý Bernštejn
Bezděz
Mnichovo Hradiště
Valdštejn
Jirkov
Most
Lovosice
Terezín
Hrádek
Polepy
Dubá
Bělá pod Bezdězem
Příšovice
Studenec
Hostinné
Chomutov
Třebenice
Roudnice nad Labem
Štětí
Kokořín
Sláviń
Valečov
Trosky
Humprecht
Kumburk
Nová Paka
Údlice
Kozly
Hazmburk
Kosmonosy
Mladá Boleslav
Kost
Sobotka
Jičín
Dvůr Králové nad Labem
Kadaň
Havraň
Libochovice
Mšeno
Kokořín
Liběchov
Stránov
Úlibice
Lázně Bělohrad
Louny
Budyně nad Ohří
Peruc
Slapanice
Mělník
Libáň
Domousnice
Královéhradecký
Žatec
Postoloprty
Zlonice
Černuc
Benátky nad Jizerou
Jabkenice
Kopidlno
Milovice u Hořic
Hořice
Holedeč
Dolní Ročov
Panenský Týnec
Velvary
Kralupy nad Vltavou
Veltrusy
Byšice
Neratovice
Křinec
Činěves
Slavhostice
Smidary
Podbořany
Slaný
Kostelec nad Labem
Vlkava
Nový Bydžov
Řevničov
Brandýsek
Okoř
Lysá nad Labem
Městec Králové
Nechanice
Krupá
Švermov
Kladno
Roztoky
Brandýs nad Labem
Stará Boleslav
Nymburk
Hrádek
Bílenec
Nové Strašecí
Lidice
PRAHA
Zdiby
Čelákovice
Starý Vestec
Poděbrady
Chlumec nad Cidlinou
Rakovník
Ruzyně
Jeneč
Kyšice
Sadská
Jesenice
Úvaly
Žďár
Hubenov
Křivoklát
Unhošť
Český Brod
Týnec nad Labem
Pardubice
Chyňava
Uhříněves
Šember
Kostelec nad Černými lesy
Kolín
Kačina
Kralovice
Týřov
Leontýnský zámek
Průhonice
Nupaky
Přelouč
Plasy
Krašov
Beroun
Radotín
Zbraslav
Říčany
Sedlec
Heřmanův Městec
Kozojedy
Křivoklátsko
Karlštejn
Dobřichovice
Davle
Mnichovice
Vysoká
Kutná Hora
Čáslav
Zdice
Koněpruské jeskyně
Mníšek pod Brdy
Jílové u Prahy
Pyšely
Uhlířské Janovice
Sion
Lichnice
Chotětín
Žebrák
Kaceřov
Radnice
Třemošná
Břasy
Hostomice
Štěchovice
Sázava
Žleby
Hořovice
Středočeský
Konopiště
Český Šternberk
Zbraslavice
Golčův Jeníkov
Oheb
Vilémov
PLZEŇ
Mýto
Jince
Dobříš
Nový Knín
Neveklov
Benešov
Kalná
Kácov
Habry
Rokycany
Starý Plzenec
Mirošov
Tok
Příbram
Úd. nádrž Slapy
Strúhařov
Zruč nad Sázavou
Ledeč nad Sázavou
Chotěboř
Kozel
Spálené Poříčí
Vysoká u Příbramě
Svatá Hora
Obory
Červený Hrádek
Bystřice
Vlašim
Světlá nad Sázavou
Česká Bělá
Milín
Kamýk nad Vltavou
Sedlčany
Jankov
Blovice
Seč
Rožmitál pod Třemšínem
Maková Hora
Krásná Hora nad Vltavou
Vysoký Chlumec
Votice
Čechtice
Lipnice nad Sázavou
Havlíčkův Brod
Nové Mitrovice
Březnice
Orlík nad Vltavou
Petrovice
Zvěřinek
Sedlec-Prčice
Šelmberk
Růžkovy Lhotice
Senožaty
Košetice
Humpolec
Zelená Hora
Nepomuk
Mirovice
Vodní nádrž Orlík
Mladá Vožice
Červená Řečice
Želiv
Štoky
Potenštejn
Kasejovice
Lnáře
Orlík nad Vltavou
Jistebnice
Chýnovská J.
Pacov
Větrný Jeníkov
Blatná
Sepekov
Plánice
Zvíkov
Milevsko
Opařany
Tábor
Kozí Hrádek
Chýnov
Kámen
Vyskytná
Pelhřimov
Jihlava
Nalžovské Hory
Velký Bor
Sedlice
Horažďovice
Červená
Příběnice
Bernartice
Malšice
Sezimovo Ústí
Horní Cerekev
Velký Beranov
Rabí
Prácheň
Katovice
Putim
Písek
Záhoří
Albrechtice nad Vltavou
Bechyně
Planá nad Lužnicí
Mnich
Kamenice nad Lipou
Batelov
Kostelec
Sušice
Strakonice
Putim
Soběslav
Červená Lhota
Třešť
Stonařov
Brtnice
Kašperk
Drahonice
Myšenec
Protivín
Týn nad Vltavou
Veselí nad Lužnicí
Kardašova Řečice
Počátky
Žirovnice
Javořice
Roštejn
Třeštín
Nalžovské Hory
Kašperské Hory
Volyně
Temelín
Studená
Štamberk
Řásná
Ruda
Rejštejn
Dobrš
Helfenburk
Vodňany
Sv. Barbora
Jindřichův Hradec
Strmilov
Telč
Želetava
Srní
Stachy
Vlachovo Březí
Bavorov
Vysoký Hrádek
Nová Říše
Modrava
Vimperk
Hluboká nad Vltavou
Lomnice nad Lužnicí
Kunžak
Budeč
Kvilda
Husinec
Netolice
Lásenice
Markvarec
Dačice
Moravské Budějovice
CZ
PL
Elbsandsteingebirge
Lausitzer Bergland
Jizerské Hory
Krkonoše
Lužické Hory
Ústecký
Středočeský
Vysočina
Jihočeský
Šumava

Chmielno
Grodziec
Złotoryja
Legnickie Pole
Błonie
Żerniki
Wrocław
Długołęka
Lwówek Śląski
Cesarzowice
Rakoszyce
Bierutów
Pławna
Kostomłoty
Kąty Wrocławskie
Namysłów
Wleń
Świerzawa
Jawor
Luboradz
Jelcz-Laskowice
Biskupice Oławskie
Gryfów Śląski
Stara Kraśnica
Lusina
Bielany Wrocł.
Mirsk
Pasiecznik
Jelenia Góra
Wojcieszów
Strzegom
Gniechowice
Rogalice
Świeradów-Zdrój
Rybnica
Kaczorów
Dobromierz
Żarów
Wierzbice
Oława
Piechowice
Bolków
Sobótka
Stary Ślęszów
Lubsza
Szklarska Poręba
Cieplice Śląskie-Zdrój
Marciszów
Świebodzice
Jordanów Śląski
Brzeg
Jakuszyce
Sobieszów
Kowary
Kamienna Góra
Książ
Marcinowice
Świdnica
Ludów Polski
Harrachov
Karkonoski Park Nar.
Wałbrzych
Wiry
Łagiewniki
Jablonec nad Jizerou
Krzeszów
Karpacz
Śnieżka
Grodno
Strzelin
Przylesie
Tanvald
Krkonoše
Bogushów-Gorce
Jedlina-Zdrój
Pieszyce
Dzierżoniów
Kolnica
Lewin Brzeski
Lubawka
Špindlerův Mlýn
Pec pod Sněžkou
Královec
Głuszyca
Niemcza
Grodków
Witostowice
Góry Sowie
Bielawa
Sowa
Henryków
Wojtowice
Sarby
Vrchlabí
Janské Lázně
Mladé Buky
Mieroszów
Teplice nad Metují
Świerki
Wolibórz
Ząbkowice Śląskie
Ziębice
Jaszów
Niemodlin
Jaczowice
Semily
Jilemnice
Trutnov
Chvaleč
Broumov
Nowa Ruda
Słupiec
Kamieniec Ząbkowicki
Pakosławice
Sidzina
Tułowice
Studenec
Hostinné
Radków
Police nad Metují
Bardo
Jezioro Otmuchowskie
Nysa
Korfantów
Kumburk
Nová Paka
Kocbeře
Úpice
Hronov
Wambierzyce
Park Narodowy Gór Stołowych
Złoty Stok
Jičín
Dvůr Králové nad Labem
Červený Kostelec
Kudowa-Zdrój
Paczków
Otmuchów
Pogórze
Piorunkowice
Úlibice
Lázně Bělohrad
Česká Skalice
Náchod
Szczytna
Kłodzko
Przełęk
Biała
Kuks
Hořice
Jaroměř
Nové Město nad Metují
Duszniki-Zdrój
Polanica-Zdrój
Javorník
Vidnava
Prudník
Kopidlno
Milovice u Hořic
Josefov
Góry Orlické
Deštné
Gorzanów
Bystrzyca Kłodzka
Lądek-Zdrój
Żulová
Łąka Prudnicka
Slavhostice
Smidary
Opočno
Dobruška
Stronie Śląskie
Mikulovice
Trzebina
Nový Bydžov
Nechanice
Hradec Králové
Třebechovice pod Orebem
Velká Deštná
Na Špičáku
Głuchołazy
Jindřichov
Hrádek
Góry Bystrzyckie
Iglicźna
Bolesławów
Na Pomezí
Zlaté Hory
Osoblaha
Chlumec nad Cidlinou
Solnice
Rychnov nad Kněžnou
Międzygórze
Lipová-lázně
Jeseník
Głubczyce
Týniště nad Orlicí
Rokytnice
Krajobr.
Ramzova-Petříkov
Hrubý Jeseník
Heřmanovice
Vamberk
Międzylesie
Staré Město pod Sněžníkem
Červenohorské sedlo
Bělá pod Pradědem
Město Albrechtice
Kostelec nad Orlicí
Litice
Žamberk
Jablonné nad Orlicí
Králíky
Loučná nad Desnou
Praděd
Vrbno pod Pradědem
Krnov
Labem
Holice
Pardubice
České Libchavy
Lanšperk
Hanušovice
CHKO Jeseníky
Karlova Studánka
Kačina
Přelouč
Pardubický
Choceň
Červená Voda
Velké Losiny
Dašice
Letohrad
Sobotín
Bruntál
Horní Benešov
Heřmanův Městec
Chrudim
Svatý Mikuláš
Ústí nad Orlicí
Bukovice
Rabštejn
Hrochův Týnec
Vysoké Mýto
Česká Třebová
Štíty
Šumperk
Rýmařov
Litultovice
Čáslav
Lichnice
Stradov
Slatiňany
Chrast
Luže
Lanškroun
Bludov
Moravs
Železné Hory
Ležáky
Košumberk
Litomyšl
Třebovice
Zábřeh
Sovinec
Dvorce
Žleby
Seč
CHKO Železné Hory
Oheb
Trhová Kamenice
Skuteč
Rychmburk
Proseč
Hoštejn
Šumvald
Dětřichov nad Bystřicí
Budišov nad Budišovkou
Vilémov
Staré Město
Mohelnice
Úsov
Habry
Krouna
Svitavy
Dlouhá Loučka
Moravský Beroun
Hlinsko
Svratka
Polička
Moravská Třebová
Uničov
Horní Loděnice
Chotěboř
Ždírec nad Doubravou
Karlštejn
Hradec nad Svitavou
Křenov
Mladečské jeskyně
Litovel
Jakubčov nad Odrou
Světlá nad Sázavou
Česká Bělá
Devět skal
Sněžné
Starkov
Cimburk
Šternberk
Město Libavá
Sv. Anna
Žďárské vrchy
Bystré
Brněnec
Plankenburk
Jevíčko
Slavětín
Zoo Svatý Kopeček
Potštát
Havlíčkův Brod
Přibyslav
Jimramov
Nové Město na Moravě
Javoříčko
Olomouc
Velký Újezd
Letovice
Velké Opatovice
Konice
Drahanovice
Olešnice
Olomoucký
Štoky
Žďár nad Sázavou
J. Blanických rytířů
CZ
Kostelec na Hané
Lipník nad Bečvou
Bystřice nad Pernštejnem
Helfštýn
Polná
Bohdalov
Boskovice
Prostějov
Přerov
Větrný Jeníkov
Ostrov nad Oslavou
Bobrová
Kunštát
Protivanov
Dub nad Moravou
Tovačov
Bystřice pod Hostýnem
Vysočina
Pernštejn
Sloup
Jihlava
Nedvědice
Černá Hora
Sloupsko-šošůvské jeskyně
Křižanov
Olší
Blansko
Kojetín
Velký Beranov
Měřín
Macocha
Velké Meziříčí
Kateřinská
Kostelec
Řikonín
Tišnov
Jedovnice
Ivanovice na Hané
Holešov
Bátelov
Brtnice
Velká Bíteš
Nový Hrad
Hulín
Třešť
Stonařov
Trnava
Kuřim
Ochozská jesk.
Vyškov
Kroměříž
Čechtín
Ochoz u Brna
Tlumačov
Roštejn
Střeliště
Třebíč
Rapotice
Morkovice-Slížany
Zdounky
Zlín
Telč
Náměšť nad Oslavou
Brno
Slavkov u Brna
Otrokovice
Malenovice
Nová Říše
Želetava
Hrotovice
Rosice
Brankovice
Chřiby
Velehrad
Babylon
Jaroměřice nad Rokytnou
Ivančice
Bučovice
Koryčany
Buchlov
Staré Město
Budeč
Moravské Budějovice
Dukovany
Dolní Kounice
Pracký kopec
Cimburk
Luhačovice
Rouchovany
Moravský
Ivančický viadukt
Židlochovice
Žarošice
Uherské Hradiště

Łubnice
Skomlin
Pątnów
Pajęczno
Bogumiłowice
Kodrąb
Kostów
Byczyna
Działoszyn
ZAŁĘCZAŃSKI PARK KRAJOBR.
Nowa Brzeźnica
Strzelce Małe
Chałupy
Radomsko
Kobiele Wlk.
Folwarki
Praszka
Rudniki
Popów
Zawady
Ważne Młyny
Domaszowice
Wołczyn
Gorzów Śląski
Dobromierz
PRZEDBORSKI PARK KRAJOBR.
Wólka
Świerczów
Kluczbork
Krzepice
Miedźno
Kruszyna
Gidle
Silnica
Maluszyn
Kluczewsko
Radłów
Bodzanowice
Łobodno
Witkowice
Kurzelów
Włoszczowa
PARK KRAJOBR.
Pokój
Jasienie
Olesno
Przystajń
Kłobuck
Święta Anna
Chudoba
Zagwiździe
Panki
Wręczyca Wielka
Mstów
Bierdzany
Szumirad
STOBRAWSKIE
Kup
Jełowa
Sieraków
JASNA GÓRA
CZĘSTOCHOWA
Koniecpol
Secemin
Mikolin
Dobrzeń Wielki
Jezioro Turawskie
Kadłub Turawski
Ciasna
Blachownia
Olsztyn
Janów
Turawa
Dobrodzień
Herby
NAD DOLNĄ
Poczesna
Poraj
Lelów
Starzyny
Nagłowice
Zawada
Chlewice
Jędrzejów
OPOLE
Ozimek
Pawonków
LISWARTA
PARK
Staromieście
Goleniowy
Dąbrowa
Kolonowskie
Lubliniec
Boronów
Koszęcin
Koziegłowy
Żarki
Mirów
Kotowice
Wilków
Szczekociny
Sędziszów
PL
Przywory
Izbicko
Zawadzkie
Woźniki
Prószków
Kalety
Sośnice
Myszków
Pradła
Kroczyce
Strzelce Opolskie
Tworóg
Miasteczko Śląskie
Poręba
Zawiercie
Pilica
Wodzisław
Gogolin
Góra Świętej Anny
Wielowieś
Krapkowice
Toszek
Tarnowskie Góry
Siewierz
Ogrodzieniec
Smoleń
Żarnowiec
Żywocice
Zdzieszowice
Pyskowice
Piekary Śląskie
ORLICH GNIAZD
Wolbrom
Dębina
Leśnica
DĄBROWA GÓRNICZA
Miechów
Kędzierzyn-Koźle
Ujazd
BYTOM
Będzin
Klucze
Maków
Racławice
ZABRZE
Czeladź
Sławków
Większyce
CHORZÓW
Rabsztyn
OJCOWSKI PARK NARODOWY
GLIWICE
SOSNOWIEC
Mysłowice
Pieskowa Skała
Skała
Słomniki
Klisino
KATOWICE
Olkusz
Pawłowiczki
Kotlarnia
Sośnicowice
Polska Cerekiew
Knurów
Jaworzno
Lgota
Ojców
Widoma
Kuźnia Raciborska
Rudy
Ochojec
Mikołów
Trzebinia
P. K. DOLINKI KRAKOWSKIE
Boguchwałów
Szonowice
Orzesze
Czerwionka-Leszczyny
Nędza
TYCHY
Chrzanów
Krzeszowice
Zabierzów
Rudnik
LUBOWITZ
Łaziska Górne
Balice
Racibórz
RYBNIK
Chełmek
Libiąż
KRAKÓW
Nowa Cerekwia
Kietrz
Rydułtowy
Żory
Babice
RUDNIAŃSKI P. K.
Kryspinów
Tyniec
Pszów
Oświęcim
Wiechowice
Tworków
Wodzisław Śląski
Zator
Skawina
Wieliczka
Pszczyna
Brzeszcze
Olza
Kobeřice
Brzeźnica
Opava
Kravaře
Hlučín
Jastrzębie-Zdrój
Strumień
Łąka
Czechowice-Dziedzice
Gierałtowice
Głogoczów
Dobczyce
Bohumín
Jezioro Goczałkowickie
Kęty
Wadowice
Sułkowice
Hradec nad Moravicí
Karviná
Kalwaria Zebrzydowska
Myślenice
Andrychów
Kozy
Jasienica
PARK KRAJOBR.
Stróża
Těškovice
OSTRAVA
Grodziec
VIKŠTEJN
Skoczów
BIELSKO-BIAŁA
BESKIDU MAŁEGO
Międzybrodzie Bialskie
Sucha Beskidzka
Maków Podhalański
Pcim
Kasinka Wielka
Tokarnia
Vítkov
Bílovec
Havířov
Český Těšín
Lubień
Studénka
Ustroń
Rybarzowice
Petřvald
Cieszyn
PARK KRAJOBR.
Szczyrk
Fulnek
Třinec
Żywiec
Zawoja
PARK NAR. BABIOGÓRSKI
Jordanów
Skomielna Biała
Odry
Příbor
Frýdek-Místek
Oldřichovice
Wisła
BESKIDU ŚLĄSKIEGO
Jeleśnia
Rabka
Kunín
HUKVALDY
Istebna
Korbielów
Spytkowice
Nový Jičín
Kopřivnice
Frýdlant nad Ostravicí
LYSÁ HORA
Morávka
Jablunkov
Milówka
Zubrzyca Górna
Hranice
ŠTRAMBERK
ŻYWIECKI PARK KRAJOBR.
Podwilk
Frenštát pod Radhoštěm
CHKO BESKYDY
Oravská Polhora
Jabłonka
Nowy Targ
Valašské Meziříčí
Pustevny
Svrčinovec
Skalité
CHKO HORNÁ ORAVA
vodná nádrž Orava
Glinka
Čadca
Rabča
Chyżne
Czarny Dunajec
Rožnov pod Radhoštěm
Bílá
Krásno nad Kysucou
Námestovo
Rakova
Breza
Suchá Hora
ZUBŘÍČ
Bystřička
Turzovka
Ratiboř
Velké Karlovice
VEĽKÝ JAVORNÍK
CHKO
Nová Bystrica
Oravská Lesná
Lokca
Trstená
Chochołów
Stará Bystrica
Vsetín
Makov
Ústí
Halenkov
KYSUCE
Nižná
Zakopane
Poronin
Kysucké Nové Mesto
SK
Oravský Podzámok
Zuberec
TATRZAŃSKI PARK NARODOWY
JASENNÁ
Valašská Polanka
Terchová
Zázriva
MÚZEUM ORAVSKEJ DEDINY
Vizovice
Vrátna
Bytča
Žilina
Varín
NÁRODNÝ PARK MALÁ FATRA
Dolný Kubín
Kvačany
Liptovské Matiašovce
Podbanské
Štrbské Pleso
KRIVÁŇ
TATRANSKÝ NÁRODNÝ PARK
Horní Lideč
POVAŽSKÝ HRAD
Dohňany
SÚĽOVSKÉ SKALY
Kraľovany
vodná nádrž Liptovská Mara
Liptovský Mikuláš
Valašské Klobouky
LEDNICA
Červený Kameň
Púchov
Rajecké Teplice
Turany
LIKAVSKÝ HRAD
Slavičín
LIPOVÁ
Považská Bystrica
Rajec
Martin
Sučany
Ružomberok
Demänová
VAŽECKÁ JASKYŇA
Bojkovice
Brumov
Beluša
SKALABINA
Vlkolinec
DEMÄNOVSKÁ

Ruda Maleniecka
Fałków
Sielpia Wlk.
Błotnica
SUCHEDNOIOWSKO-OBLĘGORSKI PARK KRAJOBR.
Wąchock
Starachowice
38
Józefów
Przedbórz
Chalupy
Radoszyce
Suchedniów
Brody
Sarnówek Duży
Kobiele Wlk.
Dobromierz
Wólka
Mniów
Kunów
Pantów
Ostrowiec Świętokrzyski
PRZEDBORSKI PARK KRAJOBR.
Gózd-Zaszosie
Bodzentyn
ŚWIĘTOKRZYSKI PARK NARODOWY
Ćmielów
Ożarów
Annopol
Oleszno
Łopuszno
Promnik
KIELCE
Bidziny
Zawichost
Maluszyn
Kluczewsko
Krasocin
JASKINIA RAJ
Górno
Nowa Słupia
Opatów
Borów
Kurzelów
Włoszczowa
Małogoszcz
Daleszyce
Zdziechów
Chęciny
Borków
Łagów
Bąćkowice
Lipnik
ŚWIĘTOKRZYSKIE
Błogoszów
Tokarnia
Morawica
Iwaniska
Ocieseki
Ujazd
Antoniów
Secemin
Sobków
Sandomierz
Starzyny
Nagłowice
Mnichów
Włoszczowice
Piotrkowice
Raków
Klimontów
Gorzyce
Lelów
Chlewice
Życiny
Bogoria
Jędrzejów
Kije
Chmielnik
Mostki
Koprzywnica
Wilków
Goleniowy
Wolica
Szydłów
Kurozwęki
Łoniów
Tarnobrzeg
Szczekociny
Sędziszów
Staszów
Osiek
Przyszów
Pradła
Kroczyce
Pińczów
Kargów
Baranów Sandomierski
Wodzisław
Michałów
Busko-Zdrój
Bojanów
Pilica
Żarnowiec
Stopnica
Połaniec
Nowa Dęba
Smoleń
Wędchadłów
Beszowa
Tuszów Narodowy
Majdan Królewski
PUSZCZA SANDOMIERSKA
Książ Wielki
JAWOR SOLECKI NADNIDZIAŃSKI P.K.
Solec-Zdrój
Słupia
Wolbrom
Działoszyce
Miechów
Maków
Wiślica
Mielec
Cmolas
Skalbmierz
Szczucin
Racławice
Nowy Korczyn
Przyłęk Dukielska
Kolbuszowa
Rabsztyn
OJCOWSKI PARK NARODOWY
Kazimierza Wielka
Zgórsko
Pieskowa Skała
Skała
Słomniki
Klimontów
Opatowiec
Łęg
Wygoda
Bzemień
Muniaczkowice
Smęgorzów
Radomyśl Wielki
P.K. DOLINKI KRAKOWSKIE
Ojców
Widoma
Bobin
Dąbrowa Tarnowska
PODKARPACKIE
Pustków
Krzeszowice
Proszowice
Koszyce
Biskupice Radłowskie
Żabno
Brzeźnica
Sędziszów Małopolski
Zabierzów
Nowe Brzesko
Lisia Góra
Wesoła
Balice
Igołomia
Szczurowa
Dębica
A4
PUSZCZA NIEPOŁOMICKA
Rudy-Rysie
Pogórska Wola
Ropczyce
KRAKÓW
Niepołomice
Mokrzyska
TARNÓW
Pilzno
Kryspinów
Tyniec
Bochnia
Brzesko
Łęki Górne
Czudec
Skawina
Wieliczka
Dębno
Wojnicz
Bielowy
Brzeźnica
Nowy Wiśnicz
WIŚNICKO-LIPNICKI P.K.
Tuchów
Joniny
Strzyżów
Wiśniowa
Gdów
Głogoczów
Dobczyce
Jurków
Zakliczyn
Brzostek
Godowa
Wadowice
MAŁOPOLSKIE
Łapanów
Muchówka
Czchów
Gromnik
PARK KRAJOBR. PASMA BRZANKI
Frysztak
CZARNORZECKO-STRZYŻOWSKI P.K.
Kalwaria Zebrzydowska
Sułkowice
Myślenice
CIĘŻKOWICKO-ROŻNOWSKI P.K.
Ciężkowice
Jasienica Rosielna
Stróża
Wiśniowa
Laskowa
Rożnów
Zborowice
Biecz
Jasło
Korczyna
Maków Podhalański
Pcim
Tokarnia
Kasinka Wielka
Łososina Dolna
Gródek nad Dunajcem
Libusza
Potok
Krosno
Lubień
Dobra
Tymbark
Bilsko
Korzenna
Zagórzany
Limanowa
Wielogłowy
Wilczyska
Bednarka
Miejsce Piastowe
Jordanów
Skomielna Biała
Mszana Dolna
Przyszowa
Grybów
Gorlice
Nowy Żmigród
Iwonicz-Zdrój
Rymanów
Spytkowice
Rabka
Kamienica
Stary Sącz
Nowy Sącz
Ropa
Iwla
Dukla
GORCZAŃSKI PARK NARODOWY
Zabrzeż
Łabowa
Uście Gorlickie
MAGURSKI PARK NARODOWY
Zubrzyca Górna
Podwilk
POPRADZKI PARK KRAJOBR.
Berest
Tylawa
Jabłonka
Nowy Targ
Dębno
Krościenko nad Dunajcem
Rytro
Huta
Konieczna
Daliow
Łopuszna
Szczawnica
Piwniczna
Krynica
Wysowa
Przełęcz Dukielska
VOJENSKÉ PRÍRODNÉ
Chyżne
Czarny Dunajec
PIENIŃSKI PARK NARODOWY
Czorsztyn
Żegiestów-Zdrój
Muszynka
Niżna Polianka
Suchá Hora
Bukowina Tatrzańska
Kamienka
ČERVENÝ KLÁŠTOR
Muszyna
Zborov
Krajná Pol'ana
Trstená
Chochołów
Poronin
SPIŠSKÁ MAGURA
Hniezdne
Stará L'ubovňa
Bardejovské Kúpele
Malcov
Svidník
Medzilaborce
Zakopane
Bardejov
Havaj
Nižná
Łysa Polana
sedlo Pod Príslopom
Podolínec
L'ubotín
Livov
ČERGOV
Zuberec
TATRZAŃSKI PARK NARODOWY
Tatranská Kotlina
Jakubany
KAMENICHÝ HRAD
SK
Stropkov
MÚZEUM ORAVSKEJ DEDINY
Kriváň
Gerlachovský štít
BELIANSKA JASKYŇA
Spišská Belá
Hertník
Marhaň
Ol'ka
TATRANSKÝ NÁRODNÝ PARK
STRÁŽKY
Brezovica
Lipany
Raslavice
Kručov
vodná nádrž Vel'ká Domaša
Liptovské Matiašovce
Podbanské
Štrbské Pleso
PREŠOVSKÝ
Tatranská Lomnica
Kežmarok
Sabinov
Giraltovce
Liptovský Mikuláš
Starý Smokovec
ŠARIŠSKÝ HRAD
E50
65
Poprad
Dušovce
Mala Domaša
Košar
Spišskýý Štvrtok
Levoča
Vel'ký Šariš
Kapušany
Šalgovík
VAŽECKÁ
Štrba
Hranovnica
Prešov
Zlatá

Kraśnik
Bychawa
Krasnystaw
Siennica Różana
Łopiennik
Buśno
Teresin
Wojsławice
Uchanie
Teratyn
Horodło
Ustyluh
Stara Wieś
Rudnik Szlachecki-kol.
Gorzków-Osada
Kraśniczyn
Skierbieszów
Stryjów
Wysokie
Żółkiewka-Osada
Tarnawka
Hrubieszów
Strzyżów
Grabowiec
Novovolyns'k
Нововолинськ
Batorz
Tarnawa Duża
Turobin
Chomęciska Małe
Zamość
Miączyn
Terebiń
Gródki
Modliborzyce
Bodaczów
Kotlice
Zhovtneve
Zaklików
Janów Lubelski
Szczebrzeszyn
Łabunie
Ivanychi
Lipa
Frampol
Lipsko
Przewale
Dolhobyczów
PARK KRAJOBR. LASY JANOWSKIE
Zwierzyniec
Wólka Łabuńska
Witków
Panasówka
ROZTOCZAŃSKI PARK NARODOWY
Wożuczyn
Stalowa Wola
Kąty
PUSZCZA
Tarnawatka
Łaszczów
Nowosiółki
Variazh
Biłgoraj
KRASNOBRODZKI P. K.
Sokal'
Nisko
Zarzecze
Nowy Majdan
Józefów
Tomaszów Lubelski
Ulhówek
Chervonohrad
Червоноград
Ulanów
SOLSKA
Aleksandrów
Belz
Hirnyk
Nowosielec
Rudnik
PARK KRAJOBR.
Bełżec
Uhniv
Stany
Krzeszów
PL
Narol
Tarnogród
PUSZCZY SOLSKIEJ
Sosnivka
Jeżowe
Naklik
Dąbrówka
Wola Obszańska
Płazów
Hrebenne
Velyki Mosty
Kamień
Nowa Sarzyna
POŁUDNIOWOROZTOCZAŃSKI P. K.
Richky
Rava-Rus'ka
Raniżów
Cewków
Dachnów
Cieszanów
Leżajsk
Radruż
Dobrosyn
Sokołów Małopolski
Oleszyce
Lubaczów
Maheriv
Głogów Małopolski
Sieniawa
Mołodycz
Tryńcza
Budomierz
Nemyriv
Zhovkva
Zapałów
Sople
Łańcut
Wiązownica
Laszki
Starychi
Kulykiv
Przeworsk
Jarosław
Buczyna
Krakovets'
RZESZÓW
Kidałowice
Yavoriv
Novoiavorivs'ke
L'VIV
Львів
Kańczuga
Dunkowice
Tyczyn
Radymno
Ivano-Frankove
Stary Borek
Hyżne
Rokietnica
Pruchnik
Vynnyky
Błażowa
Szklary
Bachórz
Żurawica
Mostys'ka
Horodok
Skniyliv
Dynów
Babice
Medyka
Sudova Vyshnia
Krasiczyn
Przemyśl
UA
Vel. Liubin'
Blizne
PARK KRAJOBR. POGÓRZA PRZEMYSKIEGO
Schirets'
Nozdrzec
Bircza
Rudky
Komarno
Brzozów
Peremozhne
Nyzhankovychi
Vel. Horozhanka
Vybranivka
Grabownica Starzeńska
Mrzygłód
Huwniki
Mykolaïv
Kuźmina
Dnister
Kolodruby
Zarszyn
Dobromyl'
Novyi Rozdil
Sanok
Khyriv
Sambir
Самбір
Dubliany
Rozdil
Załuż
PARK KRAJOBR. GÓR SŁONNYCH
Krościenko
Zagórz
Uherce Mineralne
Lesko
Staryi Sambir
Medenychi
Bukowsko
Drohobych
Дрогобич
Ustrzyki Dolne
Hoczew
Szczawne
J. Solińskie
Strilky
Czarna Górna
Myczków
Boryslav
Борислав
Truskavets'
Трускавець
Stryi
Стрий
Komańcza
Sakowczyk
BIESZCZADY
CIŚNIAŃSKO WETLIŃSKI PARK KRAJOBR.
PARK KRAJOBR. San
Limna
Morshyn
Palota
Cisna
Dołżyca
DOLINY SANU
NATS. PARK
Stuposiany
Turka
Verch. Syn'ovydne
Wetlina
KARPATY
BIESZCZADZKI PARK NARODOWY
SKOLIVS'KI
Bolekhiv
Svetlice
NÁRODNÝ
Ustrzyki Górne
Borynia
Skole
Hostovice
Wołosate
Broshniv-Osada
Hrubov
PARK
Nová Sedlica
BESKYDY
Dolyna
Zubné
Zboj
POLONINY
UZHANS'KYI
Rozhniativ
Koškovce
Stakčín
Uzhok
Uzhots'kyi Pereval
Vyhoda
Snina
Ruská Volová
Ulič
NATS. PARK
Udavské

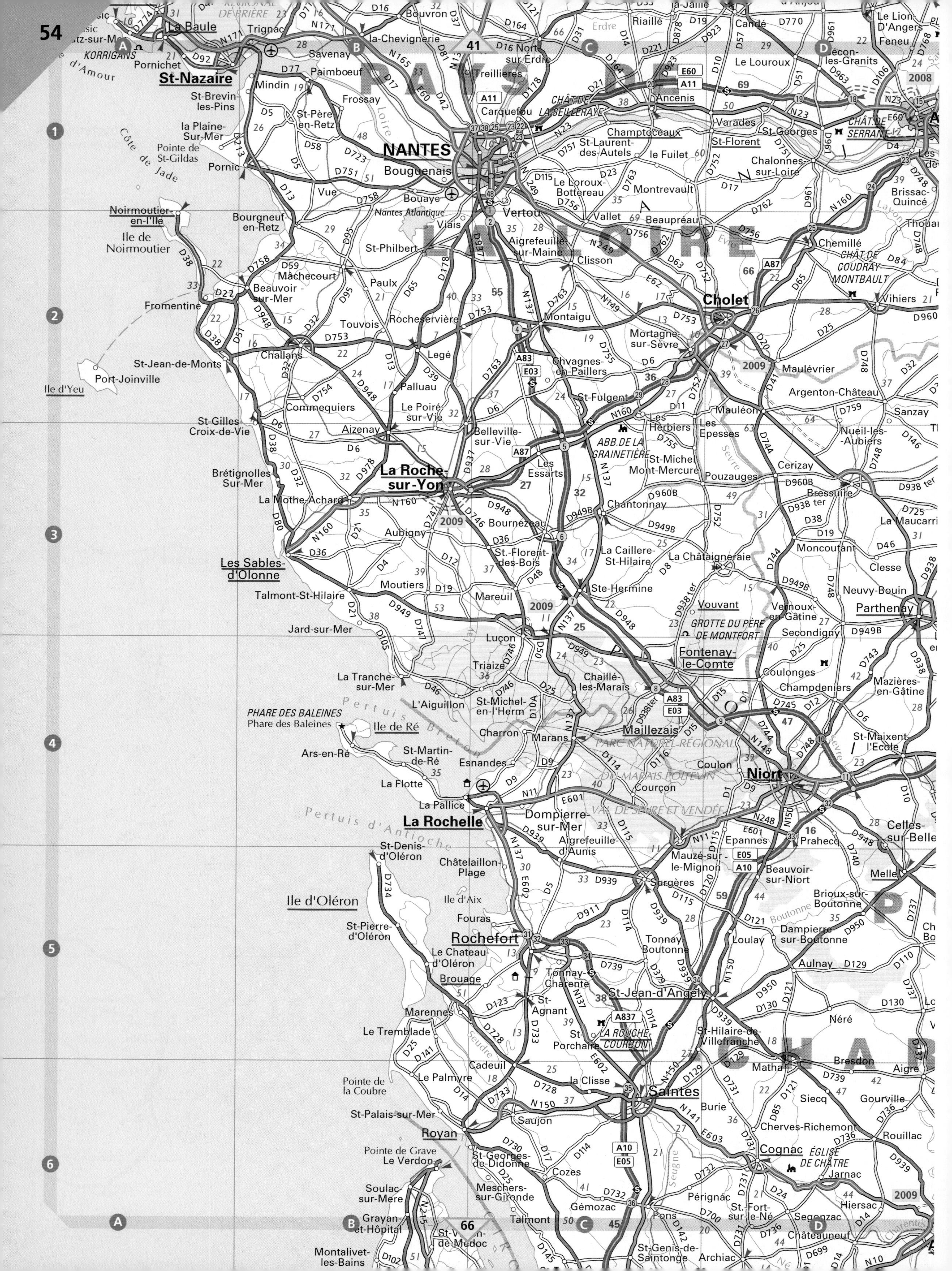
La Baule
Trignac
Bouvron
Riaillé
Candé
Le Lion-d'Angers
Feneu
Pornichet
St-Nazaire
Savenay
la-Chevignerie
Nort-sur-Erdre
Le Louroux
Bécon-les-Granits
KORRIGANS
Côte d'Amour
Mindin
Paimboeuf
Treillières
Ancenis
St-Brevin-les-Pins
Frossay
Carquefou
CHÂT. DE LA SEILLERAYE
Varades
St-Georges
CHÂT. DE SERRANT
PAYS DE LA LOIRE
la Plaine-Sur-Mer
St-Père-en-Retz
Loire
Champtoceaux
St-Florent
Pointe de St-Gildas
Côte de Jade
NANTES
St-Laurent-des-Autels
le Fuilet
Chalonnes-sur-Loire
Pornic
Bouguenais
Le Loroux-Bottereau
Montrevault
Brissac-Quincé
Vue
Bouaye
Nantes Atlantique
Noirmoutier-en-l'Ile
Bourgneuf-en-Retz
Vertou
Vallet
Beaupréau
Thouars
Viais
Ile de Noirmoutier
St-Philbert
Aigrefeuille-sur-Maine
Clisson
Chemillé
CHÂT. DE COUDRAY-MONTBAULT
Machecourt
Paulx
Beauvoir-sur-Mer
Fromentine
Cholet
Vihiers
Montaigu
Rocheservière
Touvois
Mortagne-sur-Sèvre
Challans
Legé
Maulévrier
St-Jean-de-Monts
Chavagnes-en-Paillers
Port-Joinville
Ile d'Yeu
Palluau
St-Fulgent
Argenton-Château
Commequiers
Le Poiré-sur-Vie
Les Herbiers
Mauléon
Sanzay
St-Gilles-Croix-de-Vie
Aizenay
Belleville-sur-Vie
Les Epesses
Nueil-les-Aubiers
ABB. DE LA GRAINETIÈRE
St-Michel-Mont-Mercure
Brétignolles-Sur-Mer
La Roche-sur-Yon
Les Essarts
Pouzauges
Cerizay
Bressuire
La Mothe Achard
Chantonnay
La Maucarrière
Aubigny
Bournezeau
Moncoutant
Les Sables-d'Olonne
St.-Florent-des-Bois
La Caillere-St-Hilaire
La Châtaigneraie
Clessé
Moutiers
Ste-Hermine
Neuvy-Bouin
Talmont-St-Hilaire
Mareuil
Vouvant
Vernoux-en-Gâtine
Parthenay
GROTTE DU PÈRE DE MONTFORT
Secondigny
Jard-sur-Mer
Luçon
Fontenay-le-Comte
Triaize
Chaillé-les-Marais
Coulonges
La Tranche-sur-Mer
Champdeniers
Mazières-en-Gâtine
L'Aiguillon
St-Michel-en-l'Herm
PHARE DES BALEINES
Phare des Baleines
Ile de Ré
Pertuis Breton
Maillezais
Charron
Marans
PARC NATUREL RÉGIONAL DU MARAIS POITEVIN
St-Maixent-l'Ecole
Ars-en-Ré
St-Martin-de-Ré
Esnandes
Coulon
Niort
La Flotte
Courçon
La Pallice
Dompierre-sur-Mer
VAL DE SÈVRE ET VENDÉE
La Rochelle
Pertuis d'Antioche
Aigrefeuille-d'Aunis
Mauzé-sur-le-Mignon
Epannes
Prahecq
Celles-sur-Belle
St-Denis-d'Oléron
Châtelaillon-Plage
Beauvoir-sur-Niort
Melle
Surgères
Ile d'Oléron
Ile d'Aix
Brioux-sur-Boutonne
Fouras
St-Pierre-d'Oléron
Loulay
Dampierre-sur-Boutonne
Rochefort
Tonnay-Boutonne
Le Chateau-d'Oléron
Aulnay
Brouage
Tonnay-Charente
St-Jean-d'Angély
Marennes
St-Agnant
Néré
La Tremblade
LA ROCHE COURBON
St-Hilaire-de-Villefranche
St-Porchaire
Matha
Bresdon
Aigre
Cadeuil
Le Palmyre
Pointe de la Coubre
la Clisse
Saintes
Siecq
Gourville
Burie
St-Palais-sur-Mer
Saujon
Cherves-Richemont
Rouillac
Royan
Pointe de Grave
Le Verdon
St-Georges-de-Didonne
Cognac
ÉGLISE DE CHÂTRE
Jarnac
Cozes
Soulac-sur-Mer
Meschers-sur-Gironde
Pérignac
Gémozac
St.-Fort-sur-le-Né
Hiersac
Grayan-et-Hôpital
Talmont
Pons
Segonzac
St-Vivien-de-Médoc
Châteauneuf
Montalivet-les-Bains
St-Genis-de-Saintonge
Archiac
A
B
C
D
1
2
3
4
5
6
41
66

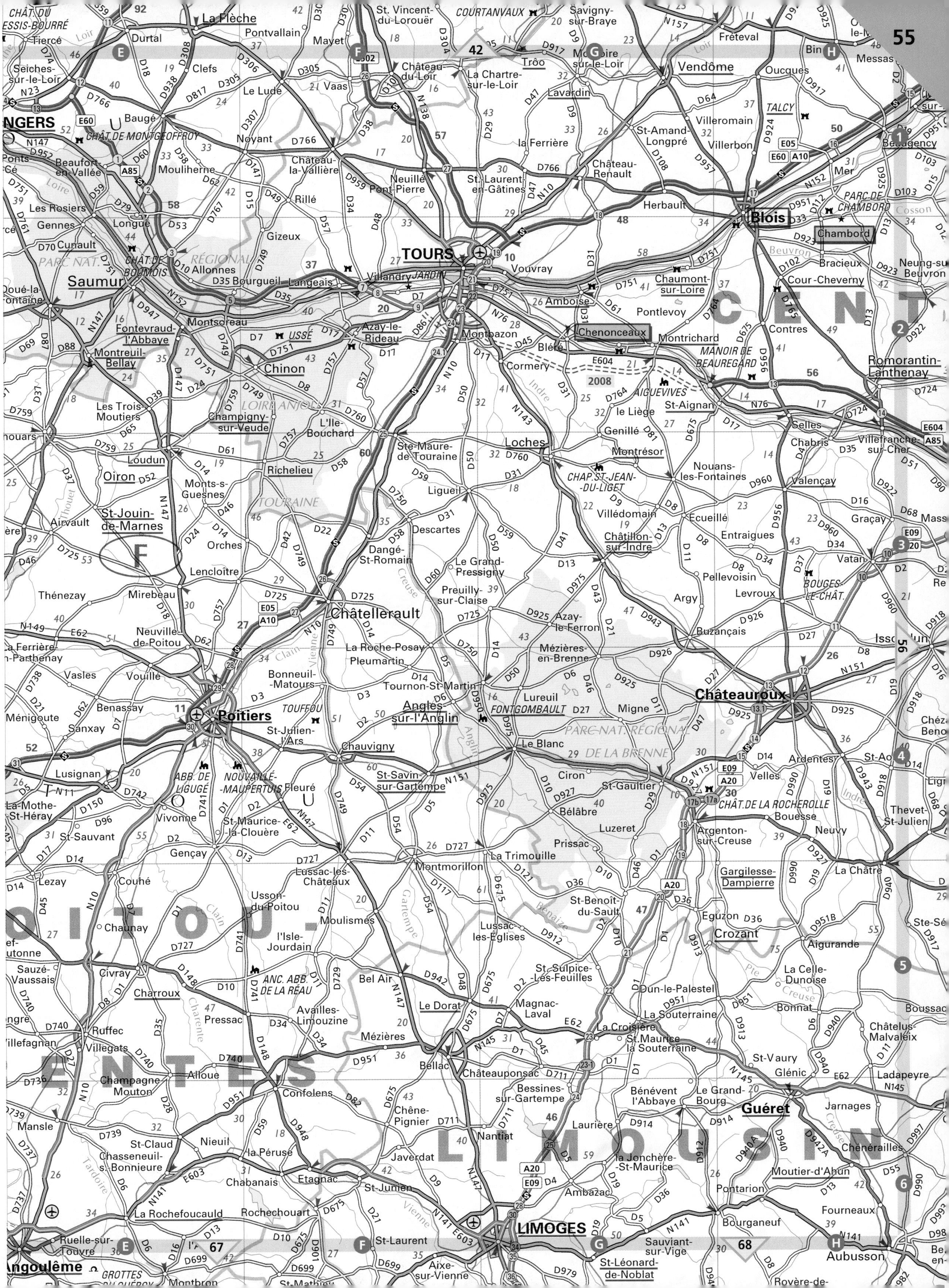

La Flèche
Pontvallain
Mayet
St. Vincent-du-Lorouër
COURTANVAUX
Savigny-sur-Braye
Fréteval
Durtal
Tiercé
Seiches-sur-le-Loir
Clefs
Le Lude
Vaas
Château-du-Loir
La Chartre-sur-le-Loir
Trôo
Montoire-sur-le-Loir
Lavardin
Vendôme
Oucques
Messas
TALCY
Villeromain
Villerbon
St-Amand-Longpré
la Ferrière
Beaugency
Mer
Baugé
ANGERS
CHÂT. DE MONTGEOFFROY
Noyant
Château-la-Vallière
Neuillé Pont-Pierre
St-Laurent-en-Gâtines
Château-Renault
Herbault
Blois
PARC DE CHAMBORD
Chambord
Beaufort-en-Vallée
Mouliherne
Rillé
Les Rosiers
Gennes
Longué
Gizeux
Cunault
PARC NAT. RÉGIONAL
CHÂT. DE BOUMOIS
Allonnes
Bourgueil
Langeais
Villandry JARDIN
TOURS
Vouvray
Chaumont-sur-Loire
Bracieux
Cour-Cheverny
Neung-sur-Beuvron
Saumur
Doué-la-Fontaine
Montsoreau
Fontevraud-l'Abbaye
Montreuil-Bellay
USSÉ
Azay-le-Rideau
Montbazon
Amboise
Pontlevoy
Chenonceaux
Bléré
Montrichard
Contres
Romorantin-Lanthenay
Chinon
Cormery
MANOIR DE BEAUREGARD
AIGUEVIVES
St-Aignan
Selles
LOIRE ANJOU TOURAINE
Les Trois-Moutiers
Champigny-sur-Veude
L'Ile-Bouchard
le Liège
Genillé
Chabris
Villefranche-sur-Cher
Loudun
Richelieu
Ste-Maure-de-Touraine
Loches
Montrésor
Oiron
Monts-s-Guesnes
Ligueil
CHAP. ST-JEAN-DU-LIGET
Nouans-les-Fontaines
Valençay
Airvault
St-Jouin-de-Marnes
Descartes
Villédomain
Ecueillé
Graçay
Orches
Dangé-St-Romain
Le Grand-Pressigny
Châtillon-sur-Indre
Entraigues
Vatan
Lencloître
Pellevoisin
BOUGES-LE-CHÂT.
Thénezay
Mirebeau
Preuilly-sur-Claise
Argy
Levroux
Châtellerault
Azay-le-Ferron
Buzançais
Neuville-de-Poitou
La Roche-Posay
Pleumartin
Mézières-en-Brenne
La Ferrière-en-Parthenay
Vasles
Vouillé
Bonneuil-Matours
Tournon-St-Martin
Châteauroux
Ménigoute
Benassay
Poitiers
TOUFFOU
Angles-sur-l'Anglin
FONTGOMBAULT
Lureuil
Migne
Sanxay
St-Julien-l'Ars
PARC NAT. RÉGIONAL DE LA BRENNE
Le Blanc
Chauvigny
Lusignan
ABB. DE LIGUGÉ
NOUVAILLÉ-MAUPERTUIS
Fleuré
St-Savin-sur-Gartempe
Ciron
St-Gaultier
Ardentes
Velles
La-Mothe-St-Héray
Vivonne
St-Maurice-la-Clouère
Bélâbre
CHÂT. DE LA ROCHEROLLE
Bouesse
Thevet-St-Julien
St-Sauvant
Gençay
Luzeret
Argenton-sur-Creuse
Neuvy
Prissac
La Trimouille
Montmorillon
Lussac-les-Châteaux
La Châtre
Lezay
Couhé
Gargilesse-Dampierre
Usson-du-Poitou
St-Benoît-du-Sault
Eguzon
Chaunay
Moulismes
Lussac-les-Eglises
Crozant
Aigurande
L'Isle-Jourdain
POITOU-CHARENTES
Sauzé-Vaussais
Civray
ANC. ABB. DE LA RÉAU
Bel Air
St-Sulpice-Les-Feuilles
La Celle-Dunoise
Charroux
Dun-le-Palestel
Availles-Limouzine
Le Dorat
Magnac-Laval
La Souterraine
Bonnat
Boussac
Pressac
La Croisière
St.Maurice la Souterraine
Châtelus-Malvaleix
Ruffec
Mézières
Villefagnan
Villegats
Alloue
Bellac
Châteauponsac
St-Vaury
Glénic
Ladapeyre
Champagne Mouton
Confolens
Bessines-sur-Gartempe
Bénévent l'Abbaye
Le Grand-Bourg
Guéret
Jarnages
Mansle
Chêne-Pignier
Nantiat
Laurière
St-Claud
Nieuil
la Péruse
LIMOUSIN
la Jonchère-St-Maurice
Chénérailles
Chasseneuil-s.-Bonnieure
Javerdat
Moutier-d'Ahun
Chabanais
Etagnac
St-Junien
Ambazac
Pontarion
La Rochefoucauld
Rochechouart
LIMOGES
Bourganeuf
Fourneaux
Ruelle-sur-Touvre
St-Laurent
Sauviant-sur-Vige
Aubusson
Angoulême
GROTTES
Montbron
St-Mathieu
Aixe-sur-Vienne
St-Léonard-de-Noblat
Rovère-de-

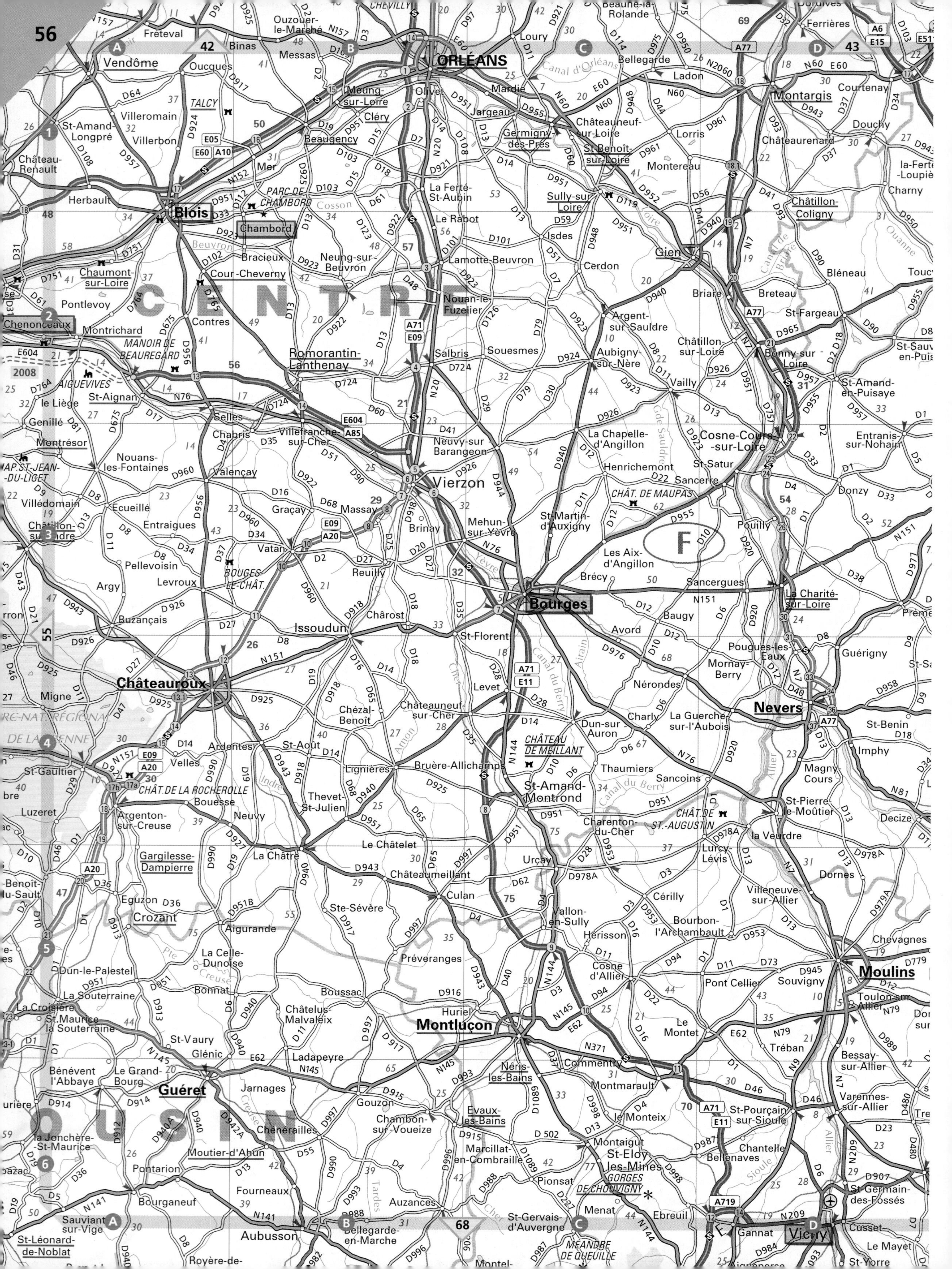
42
43
55
68
A
B
C
D
1
2
3
4
5
6
CENTRE
LIMOUSIN
F
Fréteval
Vendôme
Binas
Ouzouer-le-Marché
Messas
Oucques
Orléans
Loury
Beaune-la-Rolande
Bellegarde
Ladon
Montargis
Ferrières
Courtenay
Douchy
Châteaurenard
la-Ferté-Loupière
Charny
Châtillon-Coligny
Bléneau
Toucy
Meung-sur-Loire
Olivet
Mardié
Canal d'Orléans
Cléry
Jargeau
Châteauneuf-sur-Loire
Germigny-des-Prés
St-Benoît-sur-Loire
Lorris
Montereau
TALCY
Villeromain
St-Amand-Longpré
Villerbon
Beaugency
Château-Renault
Mer
Herbault
Blois
PARC DE CHAMBORD
Chambord
Cosson
La Ferté-St-Aubin
Le Rabot
Sully-sur-Loire
Isdes
Gien
Briare
Breteau
Chaumont-sur-Loire
Bracieux
Beuvron
Cour-Cheverny
Neung-sur-Beuvron
Lamotte-Beuvron
Cerdon
Pontlevoy
Contres
Nouan-le-Fuzelier
Argent-sur-Sauldre
Chenonceaux
Montrichard
MANOIR DE BEAUREGARD
Romorantin-Lanthenay
Salbris
Souesmes
Aubigny-sur-Nère
Châtillon-sur-Loire
Bonny-sur-Loire
St-Fargeau
St-Sauveur-en-Puisaye
AIGUEVIVES
St-Aignan
le Liège
Genillé
Montrésor
Selles
Chabris
Villefranche-sur-Cher
Vailly
St-Amand-en-Puisaye
Entrains-sur-Nohain
CHAP. ST-JEAN-DU-LIGET
Nouans-les-Fontaines
Valençay
Neuvy-sur-Barangeon
La Chapelle-d'Angillon
Henrichemont
Cosne-Cours-sur-Loire
St-Satur
Sancerre
Gde Sauldre
Villedomain
Ecueillé
Graçay
Massay
Vierzon
CHÂT. DE MAUPAS
Donzy
Châtillon-sur-Indre
Entraigues
Brinay
Mehun-sur-Yèvre
St-Martin-d'Auxigny
Pouilly
Pellevoisin
Vatan
Reuilly
Les Aix-d'Angillon
Argy
Levroux
BOUGES-LE-CHÂT.
Brécy
Sancergues
La Charité-sur-Loire
Buzançais
Issoudun
Chârost
St-Florent
Bourges
Avord
Baugy
Prémery
Pougues-les-Eaux
Guérigny
Mornay-Berry
Nérondes
Châteauroux
Mignе
PARC NAT. RÉGIONAL DE LA BRENNE
Levet
Canal du Berry
Chézal-Benoît
Châteauneuf-sur-Cher
Charly
La Guerche-sur-l'Aubois
Nevers
St-Benin
Dun-sur-Auron
Imphy
St-Gaultier
Ardentes
St-Août
CHÂTEAU DE MEILLANT
Velles
Lignières
Bruère-Allichamps
Thaumiers
Sancoins
Magny-Cours
CHÂT. DE LA ROCHEROLLE
Bouesse
Thevet-St-Julien
St-Amand-Montrond
St-Pierre-le-Moûtier
Decize
Luzeret
Argenton-sur-Creuse
Neuvy
CHÂT. DE ST.-AUGUSTIN
Charenton-du-Cher
la Veurdre
Gargilesse-Dampierre
La Châtre
Le Châtelet
Lurcy-Lévis
Urçay
Dornes
St-Benoît-du-Sault
Châteaumeillant
Eguzon
Culan
Cérilly
Villeneuve-sur-Allier
Crozant
Ste-Sévère
Aigurande
Vallon-en-Sully
Hérisson
Bourbon-l'Archambault
Chevagnes
La Celle-Dunoise
Dun-le-Palestel
Préveranges
Cosne-d'Allier
Pont Cellier
Souvigny
Moulins
La Souterraine
Bonnat
Boussac
Toulon-sur-Allier
La Croisière
St.Maurice la Souterraine
Châtelus-Malvaleix
Huriel
Montluçon
Le Montet
Tréban
St-Vaury
Glénic
Ladapeyre
Commentry
Bessay-sur-Allier
Bénévent l'Abbaye
Le Grand-Bourg
Guéret
Jarnages
Néris-les-Bains
Montmarault
Gouzon
Evaux-les-Bains
le Monteix
St-Pourçain-sur-Sioule
Varennes-sur-Allier
la Jonchère-St-Maurice
Chénérailles
Chambon-sur-Voueize
Montaigut
Moutier-d'Ahun
Marcillat-en-Combraille
St-Eloy-les-Mines
Chantelle
Bellenaves
Pontarion
Fourneaux
Pionsat
GORGES DE CHOUVIGNY
St-Germain-des-Fossés
Bourganeuf
Auzances
Menat
Ebreuil
Sauviant-sur-Vige
Aubusson
Bellegarde-en-Marche
St-Gervais-d'Auvergne
Gannat
Vichy
Cusset
St-Léonard-de-Noblat
MÉANDRE DE QUEUILLE
Le Mayet
St-Yorre
Royère-de-
Montel-
Sioule
Allier
Cher
Indre
Creuse
Tardes
Loire
Yèvre
Arnon
Airain
Canal de Briare
Ouanne
Pte Creuse
2008
A6
E15
A10
E60
E05
A71
E09
A20
A85
E604
E11
A77
N7
A719
A2
N151
N76
N144
N145
N141
N79
N371
E62
N60
N2060
N209
N152

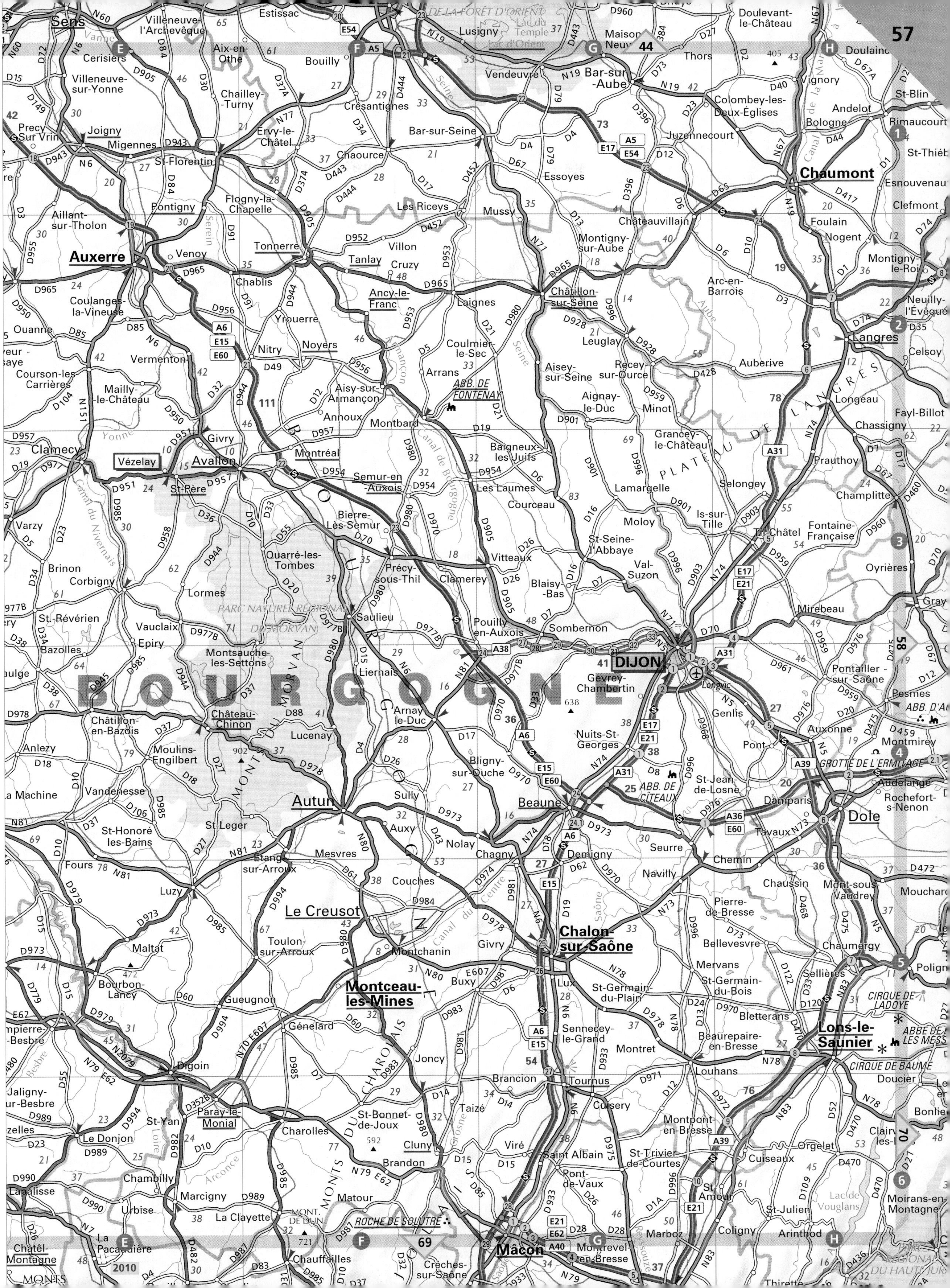
BOURGOGNE
PARC NATUREL RÉGIONAL DU MORVAN
MONTS DU MORVAN
PLATEAU DE LANGRES
MONTS DU CHAROLAIS
Sens
Villeneuve-l'Archevêque
Estissac
Lusigny
Lac du Temple
Lac d'Orient
Doulevant-le-Château
Maison Neuve
Cerisiers
Aix-en-Othe
Bouilly
Vendeuvre
Bar-sur-Aube
Thors
Doulaincourt
Villeneuve-sur-Yonne
Chailley-Turny
Crésantignes
Colombey-les-Deux-Églises
Vignory
St-Blin
Andelot
Precy Sur Vrin
Joigny
Migennes
St-Florentin
Ervy-le-Châtel
Bar-sur-Seine
Juzennecourt
Bologne
Rimaucourt
St-Thiébault
Chaource
Essoyes
Chaumont
Esnouveaux
Aillant-sur-Tholon
Pontigny
Flogny-la-Chapelle
Les Riceys
Mussy
Châteauvillain
Foulain
Clefmont
Auxerre
Venoy
Tonnerre
Villon
Tanlay
Cruzy
Montigny-sur-Aube
Nogent
Montigny-le-Roi
Chablis
Ancy-le-Franc
Laignes
Châtillon-sur-Seine
Arc-en-Barrois
Neuilly-l'Évêque
Coulanges-la-Vineuse
Ouanne
Yrouerre
Langres
Celsoy
Courson-les-Carrières
Vermenton
Nitry
Noyers
Coulmier-le-Sec
Leuglay
Recey-sur-Ource
Auberive
Mailly-le-Château
Aisy-sur-Armançon
Arrans
ABB. DE FONTENAY
Aisey-sur-Seine
Aignay-le-Duc
Minot
Longeau
Fayl-Billot
Annoux
Montbard
Chassigny
Clamecy
Givry
Vézelay
Avallon
Montréal
Baigneux-les-Juifs
Grancey-le-Château
Prauthoy
St-Père
Semur-en-Auxois
Les Laumes
Lamargelle
Selongey
Champlitte
Courceau
Varzy
Bierre-Lès-Semur
Moloy
Is-sur-Tille
Til-Châtel
Fontaine-Française
Quarré-les-Tombes
St-Seine-l'Abbaye
Vitteaux
Val-Suzon
Brinon
Corbigny
Précy-sous-Thil
Clamerey
Blaisy-Bas
Oyrières
Lormes
Saulieu
Pouilly-en-Auxois
Sombernon
Mirebeau
Gray
St.-Révérien
Vauclaix
Epiry
Bazolles
Montsauche-les-Settons
Liernais
DIJON
Gevrey-Chambertin
Longvic
Pontailler-sur-Saône
Pesmes
ABB. D'ACEY
Château-Chinon
Châtillon-en-Bazois
Arnay-le-Duc
Genlis
Auxonne
Montmirey
Anlezy
Moulins-Engilbert
Lucenay
Nuits-St-Georges
Bligny-sur-Ouche
GROTTE DE L'ERMITAGE
ABB. DE CÎTEAUX
St-Jean-de-Losne
Pont
Audelange
La Machine
Vandenesse
Sully
Rochefort-s-Nenon
Autun
Beaune
Damparis
Dole
St-Honoré les-Bains
St-Leger
Auxy
Nolay
Tavaux
Seurre
Chagny
Demigny
Étang-sur-Arroux
Mesvres
Couches
Chemin
Fours
Navilly
Chaussin
Mont-sous-Vaudrey
Mouchard
Luzy
Pierre-de-Bresse
Le Creusot
Chalon-sur-Saône
Bellevesvre
Maltat
Toulon-sur-Arroux
Montchanin
Givry
Chaumergy
Mervans
Bourbon-Lancy
Montceau-les-Mines
Buxy
St-Germain-du-Plain
St-Germain-du-Bois
Sellières
Poligny
CIRQUE DE LADOYE
Gueugnon
Génelard
Sennecey-le-Grand
Bletterans
Beaurepaire-en-Bresse
Lons-le-Saunier
ABBE DE BAUME LES MESS
Dompierre-sur-Besbre
Joncy
Montret
Louhans
Digoin
Brancion
Tournus
CIRQUE DE BAUME
Jaligny-sur-Besbre
Taizé
Cuisery
Doucier
Paray-le-Monial
St-Yan
Montpont-en-Bresse
Bonlieu
Le Donjon
Charolles
St-Bonnet-de-Joux
Cluny
Clairvaux-les-Lacs
Viré
Saint Albain
St-Trivier-de-Courtes
Cuiseaux
Orgelet
Brandon
Chambilly
Pont-de-Vaux
St-Amour
Lapalisse
Marcigny
Matour
Urbise
Lac de Vouglans
Moirans-en-Montagne
La Clayette
St-Julien
MONT. DE DUN
ROCHE DE SOLUTRÉ
La Pacaudière
Coligny
Arinthod
Marboz
Mâcon
Montrevel-en-Bresse
Châtel-Montagne
Chauffailles
Crèches-sur-Saône
PARC RÉGIONAL DU HAUT-JURA
Thirette
2010
Canal de Bourgogne
Canal du Nivernais
Canal du Centre
Seine
Aube
Yonne
Loire
Saône
Armançon
Serein
Vanne
Arconce
Besbre
Grosne
Reyssouze
A5
A6
A31
A36
A38
A39
A40
E15
E17
E21
E54
E60
E62
N6
N7
N19
N67
N70
N71
N73
N74
N78
N79
N80
N81
N83
44
58
69
70

Tréveray
Ugny-sur-Meuse
NANCY
Arracourt
Lagarde
Sarrebourg
Phalsbourg
Houdelaincourt
Vaucouleurs
Neuves-Maisons
St-Nicolas-de-Port
Dombasle
Emberménil
Héming
Saudron
Delouze-Rosières
Pont-St-Vincent
Flavigny-sur-Moselle
Lunéville
Abreschviller
Dabo
Joinville
Gondrecourt
Colombey-les-Belles
Blâmont
Poissons
Germay
Greux
Vézelise
St-Clément
Cirey
Wangenbourg
Domrémy-la-Pucelle
Haroué
Gerbéviller
Bayon
Badonviller
Col du Donon
Doulaincourt
SION
Neufchâteau
Baccarat
Vignory
Magnières
St-Blin
Charmes
Raon-l'Etape
Schirmeck
Andelot
Rouvres-en-Xaintois
Moriville
Col du Hantz
Bologne
Rimaucourt
Châtenois
Sandaucourt
Poussay
Rambervillers
Senones
Le Hohwald
Mirecourt
Vroville
Jeanménil
Col de Saales
St-Thiébault
Bourmont
Nomexy
Saales
St-Dié
Chaumont
Bulgnéville
Vittel
Dompaire
Urbeis
Esnouvenaux
Contrexéville
Begnécourt
Brouvelieures
Ste-Marie-aux-Mines
Clefmont
Dombrot-le-Sec
Ville-sur-Illon
Épinal
Bruyères
Col de Ste-Marie
Foulain
Anould
Fraize
Nogent
Lamarche
Darney
Dinozé
Corcieux
Col du Bonhomme
Riquewihr
Montigny-le-Roi
Hennezel
Arches
Jarménil
Granges-sur-Vologne
Lapoutroie
Monthureux-sur-Saône
Xertigny
PARC NAT. RÉGIONAL
Orbey
Kaysersberg
Neuilly-l'Évêque
Bourbonne-les-Bains
Fresnes
Bains-les-Bains
Remiremont
St-Amé
Gérardmer
Col de la Schlucht
Les Trois-Epis
Hohrodberg
Langres
Plombières-les-Bains
Col de la Grosse Pierre
Turckheim
Celsoy
Corre
Vauvillers
HOHNECK
Munster
Cornimont
La Bresse
Laferté
St-Loup-sur-Semouse
Col du Mont de Fourche
Saulxures
DES BALLONS
Longeau
Jussey
Senoncourt
Rupt
Le Markstein
Rouffach
Fayl-Billot
Fougerolles
Bussang
Col de Bussang
Guebwiller
Chassigny
Gevigney-et-Mercey
Amance
Le Thillot
Conflans-sur-Lanterne
Luxeuil-les-Bains
Faucogney-et-la-Mer
St Maurice-sur-Moselle
Soultz
Prauthoy
Faverney
Col du Ballon d'Alsace
Combeaufontaine
Flagy
Mélisey
Cernay
Champlitte
Larret
Port-sur-Saône
Saulx
N.-D.-DES VOSGES DU-HAUT
Giromagny
Masevaux
Thann
Sausheim
Fontaine-Française
Theuley
Vaite
Pomoy
Lure
Ronchamp
Rougemont
Noidans-le-Ferroux
Vesoul
MULHOUSE
Dampierre-sur-Salon
GROTTE DE LA BAUME
Magny-Jobert
Belfort
Oyrières
ABB. DE LA CHARITÉ
Villersexel
Héricourt
Dannemarie
ST.-MORAND
Sierentz
Altkirch
Mirebeau
Gray
Fretigney-et-Velloreille
Esprels
Montbéliard
Sochaux
Hirsingue
Velleclaire
Rougemont
Delle
Basel/Mulhouse
Choye
Gy
Rioz
L'Isle-sur-le-Doubs
Courtelevant
Pontailler-sur-Saône
Oiselay-et-Grachaux
Audincourt
Valentigney
Ferrette
Mathay
Pesmes
Marnay
FORT DE CHAILLUZ
Clerval
Porrentruy
ABB. D'ACEY
Recologne
Audeux
Marchaux
Baume-les-Dames
Pont-de-Roide
Auxonne
Montmirey
École-Valentine
Chevenez
VORBOURG
Laufen
Delémont
BESANÇON
Aïssey
Sancey-le-Grand
St-Ursanne
GROTTE DE L'ERMITAGE
Vaucluse
St-Hippolyte
Audelange
Dampierre
Goumois
GORGES DE PICHOUX
VAL MOUTIER
Damparis
Rochefort-s-Nenon
Étalans
Maîche
Saignelégier
Moutier
NOTRE DAME DE CONSOLATION
Dole
Tavaux
Quingey
Valdahon
Tramelan
FRANCHE-COMTÉ
Tavannes
Sonceboz
TAUBENLOCHSCHLUCHT
Ornans
Montgesoye
Nods
Le Russey
St-Imier
Grenchen
Fuans
Biel/Bienne
Chaussin
Mont-sous-Vaudrey
Amancey
Mouthier
les-Fins
Villers-le-Lac
La Chaux-de-Fonds
Mouchard
Pagnoz
SOURCE DE LA LOUE
Morteau
TWANN-SCHLUCHT
SOURCE DU LISON
St-Gorgon-Main
MT CHAUMONT
Vue des Alpes
LE CHASSERAL
Büren
Salins-les-Bains
Levier
Le Locle
La Neuveville
Lyss
Arbois
Montbenoît
Neuchâtel
Chaumergy
CIRQUE DU FER À CHEVAL
Pontarlier
Aarberg
NEUCHÂTEL
Sellières
Poligny
Travers
Boudry
Ins
GORGIER
Kerzers
Frasne
La Cluse-et-Mijoux
Verrières-de-Joux
Couvet
CIRQUE DE LADOYE
Nozeroy
Fleurier
CHENAUX
Murten
Ardon
Malbuisson
Ste-Croix
Estavayer-le-Lac
Laupen
BERN
Lons-le-Saunier
ABBE DE BAUME LES MESSIEURS
Champagnole
Jougne
Avenches
Köniz
Belp
CHAMPVENT
Grandson
Cerniébaud
Metabief
Payerne
CIRQUE DE BAUME
Doucier
Mouthe
MONT D'OR
Dudingen
Les Planches-en-Montagne
Chaux-Neuve
Vallorbe
Orbe
Yverdon-les-Bains
Fribourg
ABB. DE HAUTERIVE
PONT DE PÉROLLES
Bonlieu
VAUD
Le Mouret
BURGISTEIN
Thun
Clairvaux-les-Lacs
Orgelet
St-Laurent-en Grandvaux
Le Sentier
Pompaples
ST. BARTHÉLEMY
Moudon
Romont
Cossonay
Echallens
La Roche
Schwarzsee
FRIBOURG

Pforzheim
Rastatt
Haguenau
Baden-Baden
Ludwigsburg
STUTTGART
Esslingen
STRASBOURG
Kehl
Sindelfingen
Böblingen
Offenburg
Freudenstadt
Tübingen
Reutlingen
Lahr
Rottweil
Balingen
Hechingen
Sigmaringen
Villingen
Schwenningen
FREIBURG IM BREISGAU
Donaueschingen
Tuttlingen
Singen
Radolfzell
Konstanz
Friedrichshafen
Überlingen
Schaffhausen
Winterthur
Frauenfeld
St.Gallen
Bregenz
Lindau
ZÜRICH
Baden
Aarau
Olten
Lörrach
Rheinfelden
Waldshut
Luzern
Zug
Schwyz
Glarus
Altdorf
Vaduz
Feldkirch
Sélestat
Colmar
Breisach
Mulhouse
SCHWARZWALD
WÜRTTEMBERG
SCHWÄBISCHE
SCHWYZ
GLARUS
OBWALDEN
URI
CH
D
FL
Bodensee
253

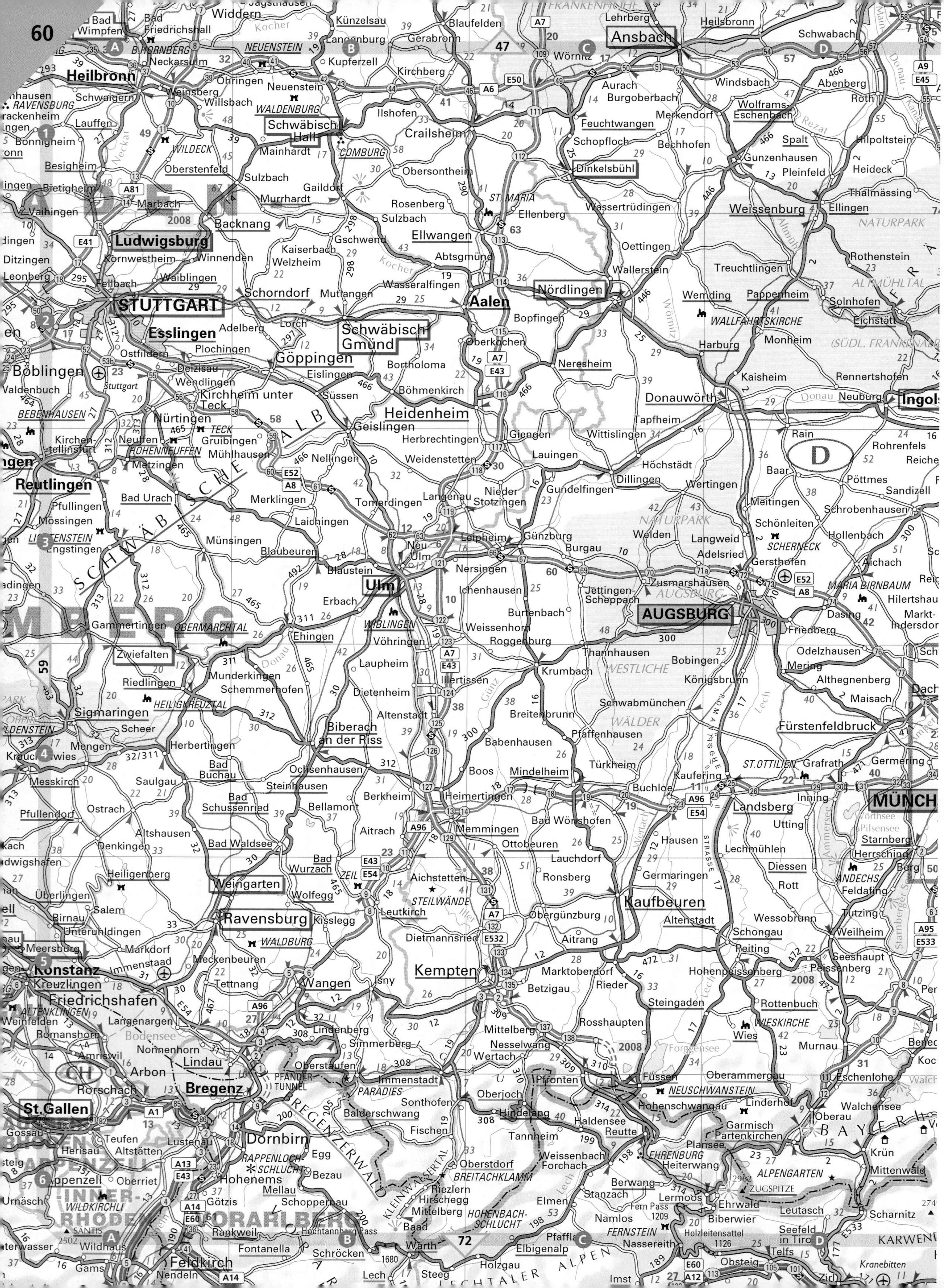
Bad Wimpfen
Bad Friedrichshall
Widdern
Künzelsau
Blaufelden
Lehrberg
Heilsbronn
Schwabach
B. HORNBERG
NEUENSTEIN
Langenburg
Gerabronn
47
Wörnitz
Ansbach
Heilbronn
Neckarsulm
Kupferzell
Kirchberg
Windsbach
Abenberg
Roth
Öhringen
Neuenstein
Aurach
Burgoberbach
Schwaigern
Weinsberg
Willsbach
WALDENBURG
Ilshofen
RAVENSBURG
Wolframs-Eschenbach
Merkendorf
Lauffen
Schwäbisch Hall
Crailsheim
Feuchtwangen
Bönnigheim
WILDECK
Mainhardt
COMBURG
Schopfloch
Bechhofen
Spalt
Hilpoltstein
Gunzenhausen
Besigheim
Oberstenfeld
Sulzbach
Obersontheim
Dinkelsbühl
Pleinfeld
Heideck
Bietigheim
Gaildorf
Thalmässing
Marbach
Murrhardt
ST. MARIA
Rosenberg
Ellenberg
Wassertrüdingen
Weissenburg
Ellingen
Vaihingen
Backnang
Sulzbach
NATURPARK
Ludwigsburg
Gschwend
Ellwangen
Oettingen
Rothenstein
Ditzingen
Kornwestheim
Winnenden
Kaiserbach
Welzheim
Abtsgmünd
Treuchtlingen
ALTMÜHLTAL
Leonberg
Fellbach
Waiblingen
Wallerstein
Wasseralfingen
Schorndorf
Mutlangen
Nördlingen
Wemding
Pappenheim
Solnhofen
STUTTGART
Aalen
Bopfingen
WALLFAHRTSKIRCHE
Eichstätt
Adelberg
Lorch
Schwäbisch Gmünd
Esslingen
Oberkochen
Harburg
Monheim
(SÜDL. FRANKENALB)
Ostfildern
Plochingen
Göppingen
Böblingen
Deizisau
Wendlingen
Eislingen
Bortholoma
Neresheim
Kaisheim
Rennertshofen
Waldenbuch
Kirchheim unter Teck
Süssen
Böhmenkirch
Donauwörth
Donau
Neuburg
Ingolstadt
BEBENHAUSEN
Nürtingen
TECK
Heidenheim
Tapfheim
Kirchentellinsfurt
Neuffen
Geislingen
Herbrechtingen
Giengen
Wittislingen
Rain
Rohrenfels
HOHENNEUFFEN
Gruibingen
Mühlhausen
SCHWÄBISCHE ALB
Nellingen
Weidenstetten
Lauingen
D
Metzingen
Reutlingen
Höchstädt
Baar
Pöttmes
Sandizell
Dillingen
Wertingen
Nieder Stotzingen
Gundelfingen
Langenau
Pfullingen
Bad Urach
Merklingen
Tomerdingen
Meitingen
Schrobenhausen
Mössingen
NATURPARK
Schönleiten
Laichingen
Welden
Hollenbach
Langweid
LICHTENSTEIN
Engstingen
Münsingen
Leipheim
Günzburg
SCHERNECK
Blaubeuren
Neu-Ulm
Burgau
Adelsried
Aichach
Gersthofen
Blaustein
Ulm
Nersingen
Zusmarshausen
MARIA BIRNBAUM
Ichenhausen
Jettingen-Scheppach
Erbach
AUGSBURG
Hilertshausen
Dasing
Markt-Indersdorf
Burtenbach
Gammertingen
OBERMARCHTAL
WIBLINGEN
Weissenhorn
Friedberg
Ehingen
Vöhringen
Roggenburg
Thannhausen
Odelzhausen
Zwiefalten
Bobingen
Mering
Laupheim
Krumbach
WESTLICHE
Königsbrunn
Munderkingen
Illertissen
Althegnenberg
Riedlingen
Schemmerhofen
Maisach
Dietenheim
Schwabmünchen
Sigmaringen
HEILIGKREUZTAL
Altenstadt
Breitenbrunn
WÄLDER
Scheer
Biberach an der Riss
Pfaffenhausen
Fürstenfeldbruck
Mengen
Herbertingen
Babenhausen
Krauchenwies
Türkheim
ST. OTTILIEN
Grafrath
Germering
Messkirch
Bad Buchau
Saulgau
Ochsenhausen
Boos
Mindelheim
Kaufering
Steinhausen
Berkheim
Heimertingen
Buchloe
Inning
MÜNCHEN
Pfullendorf
Ostrach
Bad Schussenried
Bellamont
Landsberg
Wörthsee
Pilsensee
Utting
Altshausen
Aitrach
Memmingen
Bad Wörishofen
Denkingen
Bad Waldsee
Ottobeuren
Hausen
Lechmühlen
Starnberg
Herrsching
Bad Wurzach
ZEIL
Lauchdorf
Heiligenberg
Aichstetten
Ronsberg
Germaringen
Diessen
ANDECHS
Berg
Weingarten
Wolfegg
STEILWÄNDE
Rott
Feldafing
Überlingen
Salem
Leutkirch
Obergünzburg
Kaufbeuren
Tutzing
Birnau
Ravensburg
Kisslegg
Altenstadt
Wessobrunn
Unteruhldingen
WALDBURG
Dietmannsried
Aitrang
Schongau
Weilheim
Meersburg
Markdorf
Peiting
Seeshaupt
Konstanz
Meckenbeuren
Immenstaad
Kempten
Marktoberdorf
Hohenpeissenberg
Peissenberg
Kreuzlingen
Tettnang
Wangen
Isny
Betzigau
Rieder
Friedrichshafen
ALTENKLINGEN
Weinfelden
Langenargen
Steingaden
Rottenbuch
Romanshorn
Bodensee
Lindenberg
Mittelberg
Rosshaupten
WIESKIRCHE
Wies
Amriswil
Nonnenhorn
Simmerberg
Nesselwang
Murnau
Forggensee
Lindau
Wertach
CH
Arbon
Oberstaufen
PFÄNDER-TUNNEL
Füssen
Oberammergau
Eschenlohe
Rorschach
Bregenz
PARADIES
Immenstadt
Pfronten
NEUSCHWANSTEIN
St. Gallen
Sonthofen
Oberjoch
Hohenschwangau
Linderhof
Walchensee
BREGENZERWALD
Balderschwang
Hindelang
Haldensee
Oberau
Gossau
Teufen
Dornbirn
Fischen
Tannheim
Reutte
Garmisch Partenkirchen
BAYERISCHE
Herisau
Altstätten
Lustenau
Plansee
Krün
RAPPENLOCH-SCHLUCHT
Egg
Weissenbach
EHRENBURG
Forchach
Heiterwang
Obersdorf
ALPENGARTEN
Mittenwald
Appenzell
Oberriet
Hohenems
Bezau
BREITACHKLAMM
Berwang
ZUGSPITZE
Mellau
KLEINWALSERTAL
Riezlern
Stanzach
Lermoos
Ehrwald
Urnäsch
Götzis
Schoppernau
Hirschegg
Elmen
Fern Pass
WILDKIRCHLI
Mittelberg
HOHENBACH-SCHLUCHT
Namlos
Biberwier
Leutasch
Scharnitz
SÄNTIS
Rankweil
VORARLBERG
Hochtannberg Pass
Baad
Pfafflar
FERNSTEIN
Holzleitensattel
Seefeld in Tirol
Wildhaus
Fontanella
Schröcken
Warth
72
Elbigenalp
Nassereith
Telfs
KARWENDEL
Gams
Feldkirch
Nendeln
Lech
Steeg
Holzgau
LECHTALER ALPEN
Imst
Obsteig
Zirl
Kranebitten

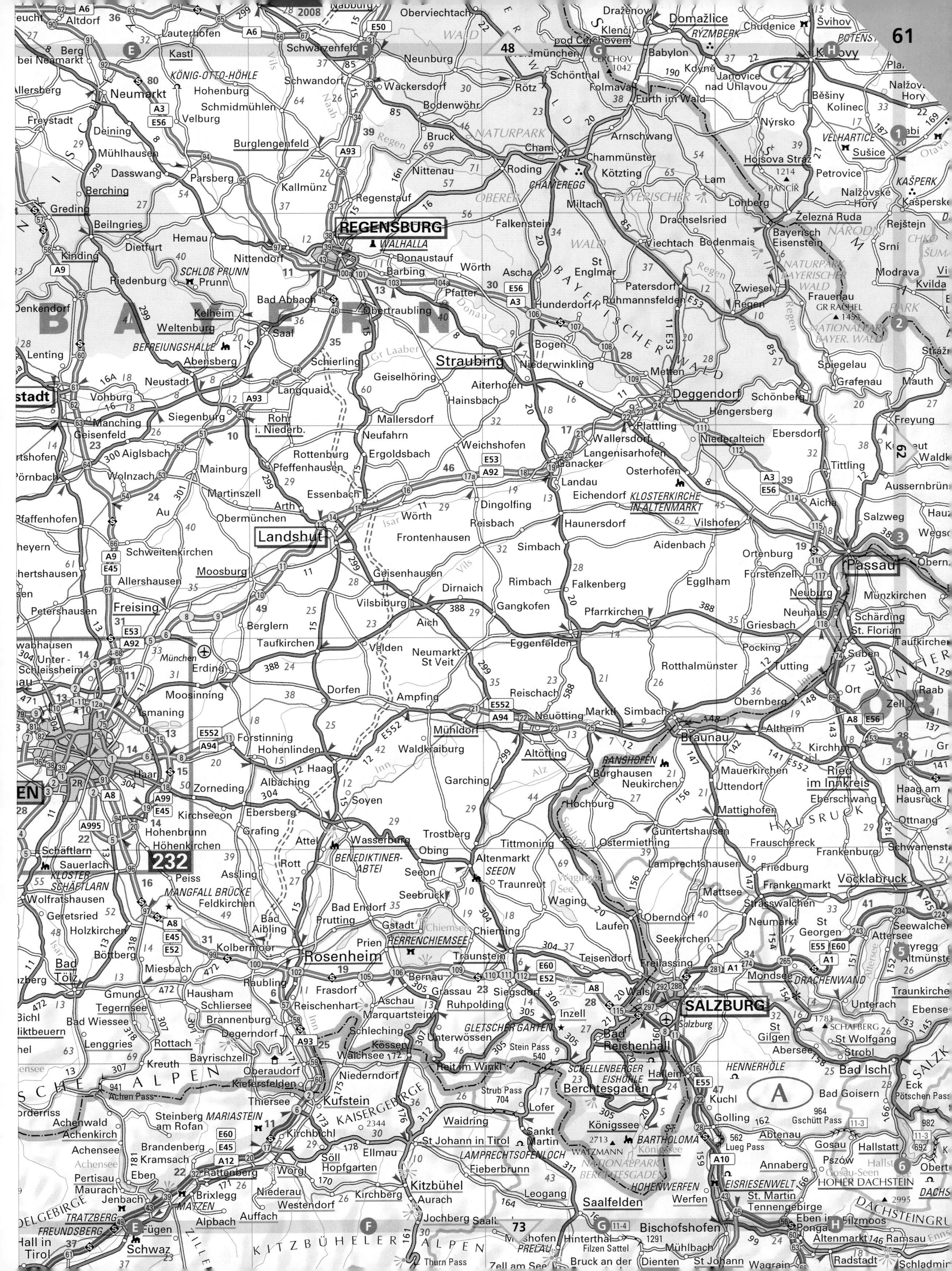
Altdorf
Lauterhofen
Nabburg
Oberviechtach
Domažlice
Klenčí pod Čerchovem
Chudenice
Švihov
Berg bei Neumarkt
Kastl
Schwarzenfeld
Neunburg
Waldmünchen
Babylon
Kdyně
Klatovy
Neumarkt
KÖNIG-OTTO-HÖHLE
Hohenburg
Schwandorf
Wackersdorf
Schönthal
ČERCHOV 1042
Janovice nad Úhlavou
Nalžovy Hory
Schmidmühlen
Rötz
Folmava
Furth im Wald
Běšiny
Kolinec
Freystadt
Velburg
Bodenwöhr
Nýrsko
Deining
Burglengenfeld
Bruck
NATURPARK
Arnschwang
VELHARTICE
Žihobce
Mühlhausen
Regen
Cham
Chammünster
Hojsova Stráž
Sušice
Dasswang
Parsberg
Nittenau
Roding
Kötzting
Lam
PANČÍŘ 1214
Petrovice
Berching
Kallmünz
CHAMEREGG
Miltach
Nalžovské Hory
KAŠPERK
Kašperské Hory
Greding
Regenstauf
OBERER
BAYERISCHER
Lohberg
Beilngries
REGENSBURG
Falkenstein
Drachselsried
Železná Ruda
Rejštejn
Hemau
WALHALLA
Bayerisch Eisenstein
Viechtach
Bodenmais
NÁRODNÍ
Kinding
Dietfurt
Nittendorf
Donaustauf
WALD
St Englmar
Srní
Barbing
Wörth
Ascha
Modrava
Kvilda
SCHLOß PRUNN
Prunn
Riedenburg
Patersdorf
NATURPARK BAYERISCHER WALD
Zwiesel
Pfatter
Ruhmannsfelden
Frauenau
Regen
GR RACHEL 1453
Denkendorf
Bad Abbach
Hunderdorf
Obertraubling
BAYERN
Kelheim
Weltenburg
Saal
NATIONALPARK BAYER. WALD
Donau
BEFREIUNGSHALLE
Bogen
Lenting
Abensberg
Schierling
Gr Laaber
Straubing
Niederwinkling
Spiegelau
Neustadt
Geiselhöring
Aiterhofen
Metten
Grafenau
Mauth
Ingolstadt
Vohburg
Langquaid
Hainsbach
Deggendorf
Schönberg
Manching
Siegenburg
Rohr i. Niederb.
Mallersdorf
Hengersberg
Freyung
Geisenfeld
Plattling
Aiglsbach
Neufahrn
Wallersdorf
Niederalteich
Ebersdorf
Rottenburg
Ergoldsbach
Weichshofen
Langenisarhofen
Mainburg
Pfeffenhausen
Ganacker
Osterhofen
Tittling
Wolnzach
Landau
Pörnbach
Martinszell
Essenbach
Dingolfing
Eichendorf
KLOSTERKIRCHE IN ALTENMARKT
Aicha
Au
Arth
Wörth
Reisbach
Haunersdorf
Vilshofen
Salzweg
Pfaffenhofen
Obermünchen
Frontenhausen
Landshut
Aidenbach
Simbach
Weitenkirchen
Ortenburg
Passau
Moosburg
Geisenhausen
Fürstenzell
Rimbach
Falkenberg
Egglham
Allershausen
Dirnaich
Neuburg
Münzkirchen
Freising
Petershausen
Vilsbiburg
Gangkofen
Pfarrkirchen
Neuhaus
Schärding
Berglern
Aich
Griesbach
St. Florian
Taufkirchen
Eggenfelden
Pocking
Velden
Neumarkt-St Veit
München
Erding
Rotthalmünster
Tutting
Suben
Unter-Schleissheim
Dorfen
Reischach
Ort
Moosinning
Ampfing
Obernberg
Raab
Ismaning
Neuötting
Marktl
Simbach
Mühldorf
Braunau
Altheim
Forstinning
Hohenlinden
Waldkraiburg
Altötting
Kirchheim
Haag
Burghausen
RANSHOFEN
Neukirchen
Mauerkirchen
Ried im Innkreis
Haar
Zorneding
Albaching
Garching
Uttendorf
Haag am Hausruck
Soyen
Hochburg
Eberschwang
Ebersberg
Mattighofen
Kirchseeon
Ottnang
Grafing
Hohenbrunn
Attel
Wasserburg
Trostberg
Tittmoning
Guntertshausen
Höhenkirchen
Obing
Ostermiething
Frauschereck
Frankenburg
Schäftlarn
Altenmarkt
Lamprechtshausen
Sauerlach
Rott
Assling
BENEDIKTINER-ABTEI
SEEON
Friedburg
KLOSTER SCHÄFTLARN
Peiss
Seeon
Traunreut
Waging
Vöcklabruck
MANGFALL BRÜCKE
Frankenmarkt
Wolfratshausen
Feldkirchen
Seebruck
Mattsee
Geretsried
Bad Endorf
Strasswalchen
Bad Aibling
Prutting
Gstadt
Chiemsee
Chieming
Laufen
Oberndorf
Neumarkt
St Georgen
Seewalchen
Holzkirchen
Attersee
Kolbermoor
Prien
HERRENCHIEMSEE
Seekirchen
Böttberg
Rosenheim
Traunstein
Teisendorf
Freilassing
Bad Tölz
Miesbach
Raubling
Bernau
Grassau
Siegsdorf
Wals
Mondsee
DRACHENWAND
Gmund
Frasdorf
Aschau
Hausham
Tegernsee
Schliersee
Reischenhart
Ruhpolding
Inzell
SALZBURG
Salzburg
Unterach
Traunkirchen
Ebensee
Bad Wiessee
Brannenburg
Marquartstein
GLETSCHER GARTEN
St Gilgen
SCHAFBERG 1783
St Wolfgang
Degerndorf
Schleching
Unterwössen
Stein Pass 540
Bad Reichenhall
Lenggries
Rottach
Kössen
Strobl
Abersee
Kreuth
Bayrischzell
Oberaudorf
Walchsee
Reit im Winkl
SCHELLENBERGER EISHÖHLE
Hallein
HENNERHÖLE
Bad Ischl
Niederndorf
Kiefersfelden
Berchtesgaden
Strub Pass 704
Achen Pass 941
ALPEN
Thiersee
Kufstein
KAISERGEBIRGE
Lofer
Kuchl
Bad Goisern
Steinberg am Rofan
MARIASTEIN
Königssee
Sankt Martin
Golling
Gschütt Pass 964
Achenwald
Achenkirch
Kirchbichl
Waidring
St. BARTHOLOMÄ
Abtenau
Achensee
Brandenberg
Kramsach
St Johann in Tirol
LAMPRECHTSOFENLOCH
WATZMANN 2713
Lueg Pass 562
Gosau
Hallstatt
Söll
Hopfgarten
Ellmau
NATIONALPARK BERCHTESGADEN
Pertisau
Eben
Rattenberg
Wörgl
Fieberbrunn
Annaberg
Gosau-Seen
Obertraun
Maurach
Jenbach
Brixlegg
Niederau
Westendorf
Kitzbühel
Aurach
HOHENWERFEN
EISRIESENWELT
HOHER DACHSTEIN
St. Martin
TRATZBERG
MATZEN
Kirchberg
Leogang
Saalfelden
Werfen
Tennengebirge
DACHSTEIN 2995
FREUNDSBERG
Fügen
Alpbach
Auffach
Jochberg
Saalbach
Bischofshofen
Eben im Pongau
Filzmoos
Hall in Tirol
Schwaz
KITZBÜHELER ALPEN
Maishofen
PRELAU
Hinterthal
Filzen Sattel 1291
Mühlbach
Altenmarkt
Ramsau
Thurn Pass
Zell am See
Bruck an der
Dienten
St Johann
Wagrain
Radstadt
Schladming
CZ
A
232
48
62
73

Nepomuk
Potenštejn
Kasejovice
Lnáře
Mirovice
Orlík nad Vltavou
Jistebnice
Mladá Vožice
Červená Řečice
Želiv
Větrný Jeníkov
Klatovy
Blatná
Zvíkov
Milevsko
Sepekov
Tábor
Chýnovská J.
Pacov
Vyskytná
Pelhřimov
Jihlava
Plánice
Nalžovské Hory
Velký Bor
Sedlice
Horažďovice
Červená
Opařany
Příběnice
Kozí Hrádek
Chýnov
Kámen
Běšiny
Kolinec
Nýrsko
Rabí
Prácheň
Putim
Písek
Záhoří
Bernartice
Malšice
Sezimovo Ústí
Planá nad Lužnicí
Černovice
Horní Cerekev
Kostelec
Velhartice
Sušice
Katovice
Strakonice
Albrechtice nad Vltavou
Bechyně
Mnich
Kamenice nad Lipou
Batelov
Petrovice
Kašperk
Putim
Myšenec
Soběslav
Červená Lhota
Počátky
Třešť
Javořice
Roštejn
Nalžovské Hory
Kašperské Hory
Drahonice
Protivín
Temelín
Týn nad Vltavou
Veselí nad Lužnicí
Kardašova Řečice
Žirovnice
Studená
Štamberk
Řásná
Železná Ruda
Rejštejn
Dobrš
Volyně
Helfenburk
Vodňany
Sv. Barbora
Jindřichův Hradec
Telč
Bayerisch Eisenstein
Srní
Stachy
Vlachovo Březí
Bavorov
Vysoký Hrádek
Strmilov
Nová Říše
Nationalpark Bayerischer Wald
Šumava
Modrava
Vimperk
Husinec
Hluboká nad Vltavou
Ševětín
Lomnice nad Lužnicí
Kunžak
Markvarec
Budeč
Frauenau
Kvilda
Netolice
Lásenice
Dačice
Gr. Rachel
Borová Lada
Prachatice
Holašovice
Lišov
Třeboň
Nová Bystřice
Landštejn
Regen
Horní Vltavice
Hus
České Budějovice
Chlum u Třeboně
Grametten
Slavonice
Stážný
Lenora
Smědeč
Trocnov
Hrachoviště
Blanský les
Spiegelau
Volary
Křemže
Suchdol nad Lužnicí
Eisgarn
Rancířov
Dobersberg
Grafenau
Mauth
Kleť
Zlatá Koruna
Kamenný Újezd
Borovany
Trhové Sviny
Heidenreichstein
Raabs an der Thaya
Schönberg
Philippsreut
Kájov
Velešín
Halámky
Neunagelberg
Waidhofen an der Thaya
Freyung
Želnava
Horní Planá
Český Krumlov
Žumberk
Nové Hrady
Schrems
Vitis
Ebersdorf
Kumreut
Waldkirchen
Černá v Pošumaví
Vodní nádrž Lipno
Kaplice
Benešov nad Černou
České Velenice
Gross-Siegharts
Tittling
Klaffer
Rožmberk nad Vltavou
Gmünd
Schwarzenau
Aussernbrünst
Aicha
Aigen
Frymburk
Lipno nad Vltavou
Dolní Dvořiště
Novohradské hory
Weitra
Allentsteig
Göpfritz
Salzweg
Hauzenberg
Schlägl
Wullowitz
St. Martin
Grossglobnitz
Greillenstein
Neupölla
Wegscheid
Gross-Pertholz
Jagenbach
Stift Zwettl
Altenburg
Passau
Obernzell
Rohrbach
Haslach
Studánky
Vyšší Brod
Karlstift
Gross-Gerungs
Zwettl
Ottenstein
Neuburg
Weigetschlag
Sandl
Liebenau
Rastenfeld
Münzkirchen
Engelhartszell
Pürnstein
Freistadt
Rosenhof
Rappottenstein
Waldviertel
Neuhaus
Schärding
Altenfelden
Neufelden
Bad Leonfelden
St Oswald
Gföhl
St. Florian
Taufkirchen
Waxenberg
Zwettl an der Rodl
Weitersfelden
Arbesbach
Lichtenau i.w.
Haibach ob der Donau
Mühlviertel
Unterweissenbach
Schönbach
Albrechtsburg
Suben
Innviertel
Aschach
Kefermarkt
Kronegg
Ottenschlag
Krems
Weissenkirchen
Peuerbach
Schaumberg
Ottensheim
Gallneukirchen
Hagenberg
Königswiesen
Gross-Pertenschlag
Ort
Raab
Oberösterreich
Pregarten
Dürnstein
Zell
Wilhering
Eferding
Mönchdorf
Laimbach
Spitz
Altheim
Schlüssberg
Alkoven
Linz
Aggstein
Göttweig
Pöggstall
Aggsbach-Markt
Aggsbach-Dorf
Grieskirchen
Bad Schallerbach
Mauthausen
Häusling
Ried im Innkreis
Traun
Asten
Perg
Burg Klam
Maria Taferl
Haag am Hausruck
Haid
Enns
Grein
Persenbeug
Pöchlarn
Melk
St Pölten
Eberschwang
Gaspoltshofen
Ansfelden
Markt St Florian
Ybbs an der Donau
Loosdorf
Hausruck
Ottnang
Wels
Neuhofen an der Krems
St Valentin
Strengberg
Schallaburg
Lambach
St Leonhard
Frankenburg
Schwanenstadt
Achleiten
Haag
Aschbach Markt
Amstetten
Mank
Obergrafendorf
Kremsmünster
Salaberg
Wieselburg
Vöcklabruck
Attnang-Puchheim
Sierning
Steyr
Seitenstetten Markt
Euratsfeld
Purgstall
Texing
Bad Hall
Randegg
Vorchdorf
Grünburg
Christkindl
Plankenstein
Traisen
Laakirchen
Pettenbach
Sonntagberg
Scheibbs
Kirchberg an der Pielach
St Georgen
Seewalchen
Attersee
Weyregg
Schlierbach
Ternberg
Waidhofen an der Ybbs
Gresten
Gmunden
Altmünster
Kirchdorf an der Krems
Losenstein
Nixhöhle
Scharnstein
Steyr-Durchbruch
Gaflenz
Ybbsitz
Gaming
Wastl am Wald
Türnitz
Drachenwand
Traunsee
Micheldorf
Frauenstein
Grossraming
Opponitz
Ochsattel
Traunkirchen
Grünau
Klaus an der Pyhrnbahn
Weyer-Markt
Lunz
Annaberg
Unterach
Ebensee
Point
Seehof
Gr. Ötscher
Tobiasl
Schafberg
Salzkammergut
Habernau
Hollestein
St Wolfgang
Strobl
St. Pankraz
Sengsengebirge
Göstling
Mariazell
Terz
Lahnsattel
Abersee
Offensee
Almsee
Gr Priel
Totes Gebirge
Mending
Altenmarkt
Bad Ischl
Windischgarsten
Piessling Urspr.
Polfau
Gusswerk
Nasswald
Eck
Pötschen Pass
Altaussee
Gössl
Hinterstoder
Hengst Pass
Spital am Pyhrn
St Gallen
Gallenstein
Naturschutz-Gebiet
Weichselboden
Brandhof
Bad Goisern
Bärenalm
Mürzsteg
Gschütt Pass
Grundlsee
Pyhrn Pass
Bosruck Tunnel
Buchauer Sattel
Kraushöhle
Wildalpen
Gschöder
Niederalpl Pass
Neuberg an der Mürz
Gosau
Bad Aussee
Friedstein
Liezen
Lainbach
Hieflau
Hallstatt
Koppensattel
Bad Mitterndorf
Seewiesen
Mürzzuschlag
Gosau-Seen
Hallstätter See
Obertraun
Tauplitz
Admont
Gesäuse
Hochschwab
Aflenz Kurort
Au
Langenwang
Hoher Dachstein
Dachsteinhöhlen
Pürgg
Trautenfels
Stainach
Rottenmann
Eisenerz
Präbichl Pass
Krieglach
Gröbming
Irdning
Eisenerzer Alpen
Thörl
Ob. Kindberg
Dachsteingruppe
Eben im Pongau
Filzmoos
Öblarn
Donnersbach
Trieben
Schober Pass
Vordernberg
Kindberg
Altenmarkt
Ramsau
Hohentauern
Kalwang
Kapfenberg
Radstadt
Rottenmanner Tauern
Kammerstein
Trofaiach
Schladming
Leoben

CZ
SK
H
BRNO
WIEN
BRATISLAVA
GYŐR
Prostějov
Přerov
Kroměříž
Zlín
Vyškov
Blansko
Třebíč
Znojmo
Hodonín
Břeclav
Mikulov
Kyjov
Uherské Hradiště
Uherský Brod
Veselí nad Moravou
Slavkov u Brna
Tišnov
Kuřim
Velká Bíteš
Ivančice
Rosice
Moravský Krumlov
Hustopeče
Pohořelice
Moravské Budějovice
Jaroměřice nad Rokytnou
Náměšť nad Oslavou
Boskovice
Holešov
Hulín
Kojetín
Otrokovice
Bystřice pod Hostýnem
Luhačovice
Staré Město
Kunovice
Bzenec
Strážnice
Skalica
Holíč
Senica
Myjava
Kúty
Malacky
Stupava
Pezinok
Trnava
Hlohovec
Piešťany
Senec
Sereď
Galanta
Šaľa
Dunajská Streda
Šamorín
Mosonmagyaróvár
Hegyeshalom
Kapuvár
Csorna
Sopron
Fertőd
Eisenstadt
Neusiedl am See
Wiener Neustadt
Baden
Mödling
Schwechat
Hainburg
Bad Deutsch Altenburg
Kittsee
Parndorf
Bruck an der Leitha
Gänserndorf
Mistelbach
Hollabrunn
Stockerau
Korneuburg
Tulln
Klosterneuburg
Poysdorf
Laa an der Thaya
Retz
Eggenburg
Horn
Herzogenburg
Neulengbach
Pressbaum
Perchtoldsdorf
Neunkirchen
Gloggnitz
Semmering
Mattersburg
Oberpullendorf
WEINVIERTEL
NIEDERÖSTERREICH
JIHOMORAVSKÝ
ZLÍNSKÝ
TRNAVSKÝ
BRATISLAVSKÝ
GYŐR-MOSON-SOPRON
BÍLÉ KARPATY
MALÉ KARPATY
CHKO PÁLAVA
Neusiedler See
D1
D2
E50
E65
E58
E75
E60
E59
E49
E461
E571
A1
A2
A3
A4
A6
A21
A22
M1
M15
251
214
50
75
2008

CZ
SK
Frenštát pod Radhoštěm
Valašské Meziříčí
Pustevny
Rožnov pod Radhoštěm
Bystřička
Velké Karlovice
Vsetín
Ústí
Halenkov
Holešov
Hostýn
Zubříč
Ratiboř
Lukov
Jasenná
Fryšták
Zlín
Vizovice
Valašská Polanka
Horní Lideč
Lípa
Valašské Klobouky
Malenovice
Lednica
Červený Kameň
Púchov
Dohňany
Považský hrad
Lipová
Slavičín
Uherské Hradiště
Uherský Brod
Bojkovice
Brumov-Bylnice
Bánov
Luhačovice
Beluša
Pruské
Považská Bystrica
Nemšová
Dubnica nad Váhom
Trenčianske Teplice
Stary Hrozenkov
Strání
Trenčín
Trenčianska Turná
Trenčianske Bohuslavice
Moravské Lieskové
Nové Mesto nad Váhom
Hrad Beckov
Stará Turá
Čachtice
Bánovce nad Bebravou
Uhrovec
Uhrovský hrad
Svinná
Prašice
Topoľčiansky hrad
Partizánske
Piešťany
Banka
Topoľčany
Vrbové
Drahovce
Radošina
Ludanice
Veľké Ripňany
Kovarce
Bošany
Veľké Uherce
Hlohovec
Nové Sady
Bučany
Rišňovce
Čakajovce
Gýmeš
Sereď
Šoporňa
Sládkovičovo
Galanta
Šaľa
Nitra
Cabaj-Čápor
Vráble
Branč
Trnovec nad Váhom
Kráľov Brod
Jatov
Tvrdošovce
Šurany
Dunajská Streda
Neded
Nové Zámky
Dvory nad Žitavou
Gabčíkovo
Veľký Meder
Kolárovo
Bajč
Hurbanovo
Balvany
Kameničná
Zlatná na Ostrove
Komárno
Medveďov
Vámosszabadi
Gönyü
Komárom
Almásfüzitő
Szőny
Ács
Bábolna
Bana
Nagyigmánd
Kocs
Tata
Tatabánya
Győr
Nyúl
Pér
Mezőörs
Pannonhalma
Ravazd
Ászár
Kisbér
Ete
Dad
Bokod
Bakonypéterd
Bakonyszombathely
Bakonysárkány
Gic
Veszprémvarsány
Oroszlány
Környe
Vértesszőlős
Héreg
Tarján
Bajna
Gyermely
Nyergesújfalu
Neszmély
Tokod
Dorog
Piliscsaba
Pilisvörösvár
Zsámbék
Páty
Budakeszi
Budaörs
Bicske
Biatorbágy
Falcsút
Érd
Esztergom
Sturovo
Helemba
Mužla
Moča
Svätý Peter
Gbelce
Pribeta
Svodín
Bíňa
Kolta
Želiezovce
Tekovské Lužany
Šarovce
Demandice
Dudince
Maňa
Kalná nad Hronom
Levice
Tlmače
Žemberovce
Tesárske Mlyňany
Bátovce
Zlaté Moravce
Nová Baňa
Hrušov
Skýcov
Žarnovica
Revište
Malá Lehota
Banská Štiavnica
Svätý Anton
Krupina
Hostianske Nemce
Bzovík
Senohrad
Plešovce
Dobrá Niva
Zvolen
Vígľaš
Detva
Hriňová
Podkriváň
Kriváň
Mýtna
Látky
Kokava nad Rimavicou
Málinec
Hrachovo
Poltár
Divínsky hrad
Horný Tisovník
Kalinovo
Halič
Lučenec
Fiľakovo
Brusník
Dolná Strehová
Pôtor
Modrý Kameň
Veľký Krtíš
Drienovo
Čebovce
Plášťovce
Vinica
Kolárе
Šahy
Drégelypalánk
Nagyoroszi
Parassapuszta
Kemence
Vámosmikola
Nagy-Hideg-hegy
Letkés
Salka
Szob
Szent István Templom
Börzsöny
Rétság
Szendehely
Verőce
Nagymaros
Visegrád
Vác
Naszály
Galgaguta
Penc
Acsa
Becske
Bercel
Balassagyarmat
Szécsény
Nagylóc
Mohora
Cserhát-Surány
Alsótold
Mátraverebély
Pásztó
Szurdokpüspöki
Jobbágyi
Vanyarc
Szirák
Galgagyörk
Váchartyán
Kálló
Verseg
Aszód
Hatvan
Hort
Galgamácsa
Veresegyház
Dunakeszi
Szada
Gödöllő
Göd
Szentendre
Pomáz
Tahitótfalu
Pilis
Budapest
Ferihegyi repülőtér
Gyömrő
Isaszeg
Jászfényszaru
Tura
Jászberény
Sülysáp
Tápiószecső
Nagykáta
Salgótarján
Karancslapujtő
Endrefalva
Kishartyán
Zagyvapálfalva
Bátonyterenye
Litke
Radzovce
Večelkov
Mátraszentimre
Gyöngyöspata
Lőrinci
Čadca
Skalité
Krásno nad Kysucou
Rakova
Turzovka
Makov
Bílá
Vyrčinovec
Veľký Javorník
Nové Mesto Kysucké
Bytča
Žilina
Súľovské skaly
Rajecké Teplice
Rajec
Vrútky
Martin
Varín
Terchová
Vrátna
Zázrivá
Stará Bystrica
Nová Bystrica
Oravská Lesná
Oravský Podzámok
Dolný Kubín
Kraľovany
Turany
Sučany
Ružomberok
Likavský hrad
Vlkolínec
Lazisko
Demänová
Liptovský Mikuláš
Liptovské Matiašovce
Podbanské
Kvačany
Zuberec
Múzeum Oravskej dediny
Nižná
Trstená
Zakopane
Chochołów
Sucha Hora
Chyžne
Czarny Dunajec
Jabłonka
Nowy Targ
Rabča
Oravská Polhora
Námestovo
Breza
Lokca
Gorna
Podwilk
Demänovská jaskyňa slobody
Jasná
Nižná Boca
Važecká jaskyňa
Skalabiňa
Príbovce
Blatnica
Kláštor pod Znievom
Zniev
Fačkov
Čičmany
Zliechov
Valaská Belá
Nitrianske Pravno
Nitrianske Rudno
Bojnice
Prievidza
Handlová
Nováky
Oslany
Turčianske Teplice
Vyšná Revúca
Liptovská Osada
Donovaly
Korytnica-Kúpele
Srdiečko
Polomka
Bystrianska jaskyňa
Podbrezová
Brezno
Čierny Balog
Lom nad Rimavicou
Staré Hory
Slovenská Ľupča
Harmanec
Ulanka
Horná Štubňa
Harmanecký priesm
Harmanecká jaskyňa
Banská Bystrica
Poniky
Čerín
Sliač
Kremnica
Žiar nad Hronom
Šášov
Ráztočno
Vtáčnik
Veľká Fatra
Malá Fatra
Nízke Tatry
Tatranský národný park
Kysuce
Štiavnické vrchy
Tribeč
Ponitrie
Krupinská planina
Cserhát
Nógrád
Komárom-Esztergom
Banská Bystrica
Nitriansky
Trenčiansky
Žilinský
Javorníky
Beskydy
Biele Karpaty
Strážovské vrchy
Gerecse
Pilis
Budai
Gödöllői dombság
Romtemplom
Sikenica
Hron
Váh
Ipeľ
Dunaj
Žitava
Nitra
Ferihegyi repülőtér
D1
E50
E75
E77
E571
E58
E60
E71
R1
M1
M3
2008
51
63
76
216
A
B
C
D
1
2
3
4
5
6

Dunajec
Dębno
Krościenko nad Dunajcem
Rytro
Piwniczna
Huta
Krynica
Wysowa
Konieczna
Przełęcz Dukielska
VOJENSKÉ PRÍRODNÉ MÚZEUM
Łopuszna
PIENIŃSKI PARK NARODOWY
Czorsztyn
Szczawnica
Żegiestów-Zdrój
Muszynka
Nižná Polianka
Krajná Poľana
Komańcza
PL
Bukowina Tatrzańska
Kamienka
ČERVENÝ KLÁŠTOR
Hniezdne
Stará L'ubovňa
Muszyna
Bardejovské Kúpele
Zborov
Svidník
Medzilaborce
CIŚNIAŃSKO WETLIŃSKI PARK KRAJOBR.
Palota
Poronin
SPIŠSKÁ MAGURA
Malcov
ČERGOV
Bardejov
Havaj
VÝCHODNÉ KARPATY
Podolínec
L'ubotín
Livov
Tatranská Kotlina
Jakubany
KAMENICHÝ HRAD
Hertník
Marhaň
Stropkov
sedlo Pod Príslopom
BELIANSKA JASKYŇA
Spišská Belá
Lipany
Oľka
Svetlice
Hostovice
GERLACHOVSKÝ ŠTÍT 2663
STRÁŽKY
Brezovica
Raslavice
Kručov
vodná nádrž Veľká Domaša
NÁRODNÝ PARK
Tatranská Lomnica
Kežmarok
PREŠOVSKÝ
Sabinov
Giraltovce
Hrubov
Zubné
Starý Smokovec
VRCHY
ŠARIŠSKÝ HRAD
Hanušovce
Mala Domaša
Košarovce
Koškovce
Stakčín
Poprad
Spišský Štvrtok
Levoča
Veľký Šariš
Kapušany
Snina
Udavské
Ruská Volová
Štrba
Hranovnica
Šalgovík
Zlatá Baňa
Prešov
Spišské Podhradie
SPIŠSKÝ HRAD
Široké
Sol
Vranov nad Topľou
Humenné
Liptovská Teplička
Spišská Nová Ves
Krompachy
Kendice
Strážske
Vernárske Sedlo
NÁRODNÝ PARK SLOVENSKÝ RAJ
Hornád
Margecany
Podhorod'
Jovsa
vodná nádrž Zemplínska Šírava
Markušovce
Sedlo Besník
SLOVENSKÝ RAJ
Nálepkovo
Gelnica
Veľký Folkmar
Herľany
Banské
Tibava
DOBŠINSKÁ L'ADOVÁ JASKYŇA
Hnilec
Prakovce
Michalovce
Sobrance
Červená Skala
KOŠICKÝ
Mníšek nad Hnilcom
Bidovce
Sečovce
Dargovský priesmyk
Vyšné Nemecké
Smolník
Medzev
Jasov
KOŠICE
Palín
Trhovište
Uzhorod
Ужгород
Muráň
Nižná Slaná
Gemerská Poloma
Vojčice
Revúca
Betliar
Rožňava
JASOVSKÁ JASKYŇA
Trebišov
Budkovce
Tisovec
RUDOHORIE
Štítnik
KRÁSNA HORKA
Moldava nad Bodvou
Šaca
Zemplínska Teplica
Vojany
Jelšava
Čečejovce
NAGY MILLIC
SLOVENSKÝ KRAS
GOMBASECKÁ JASKYŇA
Turňa nad Bodvou
Seňa
Veľké Kapušany
Ratková
Rybník
Hnúšt'a
Komjáti
Hidasnémeti
Zemplínske Jastrabie
Veľké Raškovce
Ondava
AGGTELEKI NEMZETI PARK
Bódva
Chop
Rimavská Baňa
Plešivec
JASKYŇA DOMICA
Jósvafő
Krasznokvajda
Pálháza
Mikóháza
Kráľovský Chlmec
Gemerská Ves
BARADLA
Szemere
Gönc
Szephalom
Slovenské Nové Mesto
Zsurk
Tornal'a
Aggtelek
Szalonna
Rakaca
Vilmány
Sátoraljaújhely
Záhony
Ragály
Gadna
Novajidrány
Regéc
Óhuta
Tuzsér
Mándok
Rimavská Sobota
Szendrő
BORSOD-
Baktakék
Vizsoly
Erdőhorváti
Pácin
Ricse
Sárospatak
Felsőnyárád
Szendrőlád
Lak
CSERHÁT
Encs
Tolcsva
Kelemér
Putnok
Edelény
Csobád
Abaújszántó
Cigánd
Nagyhomok
Döge
Kisvárda
Jesenské
Bánréve
Vadna
Ziliz
Hernád
Bodrog
Hodejov
Kazincbarcika
ABAÚJ-
Tállya
Aprohomok
Tiszacsermely
Dombrád
Tiszatelek
Szabolcsbáka
Sajószentpéter
Szikszó
Boldva
Megyaszó
Mád
Gávavencsellő
SZABOLCS
Ózd
Bodrogkeresztúr
Nagyhalász
Ilk
Arló
Csernely
DIÓSGYŐR
Szerencs
Rakamaz
Ibrány
Demecser
Vásárosnamény
Domaháza
Dédestapolcsány
Felsőzsolca
Tokaj
Buj
Berkesz
Borsodnádasd
ZEMPLÉN
Kemecse
Nyírmada
Zabar
Lillafüred
Szilvásvárad
MISKOLC
Prügy
Kótaj
Virányos
Székely
Salgótarján
Tarnalelesz
Bélapátfalva
BÜKKI NEMZETI PARK
ISTÁLLÓS-KŐ
Miskolctapolca
Alsózsolca
Tiszalúc
Tiszalök
Baktalórántháza
Vaja
Nyírtura
Nyírtelek
Mátraterenye
Szúcs
Mályi
Répáshuta
Tiszadob
Nagycserkesz
SZATMÁR
Őr
Ivád
Pétervására
Nyékládháza
NYÍREGYHÁZA
Ófehértó
Mátraverebély
Szarvaskő
Felsőtárkány
Emőd
Tiszavasvári
Máriapócs
Recsk
Vatta
Tiszaújváros
Nagykálló
Parád
Sirok
Eger
Bükkábrány
Bogács
Polgár
Hajdúnánás
Kálmánháza
Kállósemjén
Nyírbátor
Galyatető
Verpelét
Andornaktálya
Mezőnyárád
Újfehértó
Nyírbogát
Terem
KÉKES
MÁTRA
Mezőkövesd
Gelej
Mezőcsát
Hajdúdorog
BEREG
Balkány
Kékestető
Kerecsend
Mezőkeresztes
Folyás
Keleti-főcsatorna
Bököny
Encsencs
HEVES
Gyöngyös
Árokto
Téglás
Nyírlugos
Detk
Kápolna
Füzesabony
Egerlövő
Borsodiánka
Hajdúvid
Nyíradony
Nyírbéltek
Kál
Dormánd
Tiszacsege
Hajdúhadház
Besenyőtelek
Tiszabábolna
Cserepes
Hajdúböszörmény
Penészlek
Atkár
Nagyfüged
Tarnaméra
HORTOBÁGYI NEMZETI PARK
Nyíracsád
Telekháza
Balmazújváros
Józsa
Hajdúsámson
Boconád
Poroszló
Tiszafüred
Jászárokszállás
Tenk
Tisza-tó
Egyek
Ohat
HAJDÚ-
Nyírábrány
Tarnaörs
Vámospércs
Heves
Kömlő
Tiszanána
Kócsújfalu
Hortobágy
Jászszentandrás
Nagyhegyes
DEBRECEN
Jászapáti
Tarnaszentmiklós
Tiszaszőlős
Ebes
Újléta
Tiszaörs
Nagyiván
Hajdúszoboszló
Jászkohalma
Kisköre
Jásztelek
Pély
Abádszalók
BIHAR
Bánk
Bagamér
Jászkisér
Tiszabura
Kunmadaras
Nádudvar
Sáránd
Tiszasüly
Tiszaroff
Hajdúszovát
Hosszúpályi
Létavértes
Zagyva
Karcag
Kaba
Derecske
Sácueni
Dallowa
PARK KRAJOBR.
Bukowina
Hajdúdorog
Tiszaújváros
E50
E58
E71
E79
E371
E571
E573
D1
M3
M30
M35
M6
2008
2009
52
77
204
E
F
G
H
1
2
3
4
5
6

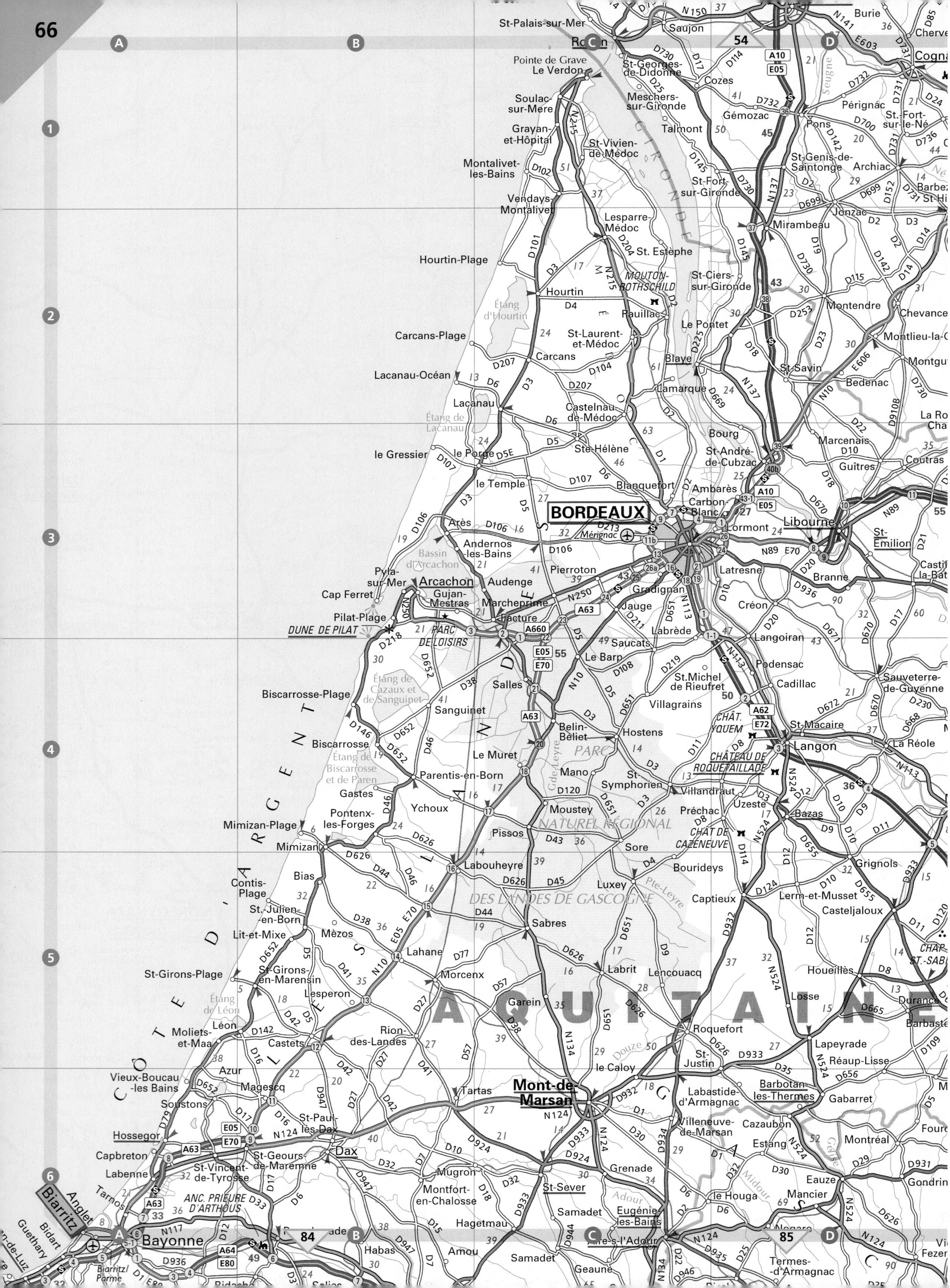
A
B
C
D
1
2
3
4
5
6
54
84
85
St-Palais-sur-Mer
Royan
Saujon
Burie
Cherves
Cognac
Pointe de Grave
Le Verdon
St-Georges-de-Didonne
Cozes
Meschers-sur-Gironde
Soulac-sur-Mere
Talmont
Gémozac
Pérignac
St.-Fort-sur-le-Né
Pons
Grayan-et-Hôpital
St-Vivien-de-Médoc
GIRONDE
St-Genis-de-Saintonge
Archiac
Montalivet-les-Bains
St-Fort-sur-Gironde
Barbezieux
Vendays-Montalivet
Jonzac
Lesparre-Médoc
Mirambeau
St. Estèphe
Hourtin-Plage
MOUTON-ROTHSCHILD
St-Ciers-sur-Gironde
Hourtin
Étang d'Hourtin
Pauillac
Montendre
Chevanceaux
Le Pontet
Carcans-Plage
St-Laurent-et-Médoc
Montlieu-la-Garde
Carcans
Blaye
Montguyon
Lacanau-Océan
St-Savin
Bedenac
Lamarque
Lacanau
Castelnau-de-Médoc
Étang de Lacanau
Bourg
La Roche-Chalais
St-André-de-Cubzac
Marcenais
le Gressier
le Porge
Ste-Hélène
Guîtres
Coutras
le Temple
Blanquefort
Ambarès
Carbon-Blanc
BORDEAUX
Mérignac
Lormont
Libourne
Arès
St-Émilion
Andernos-les-Bains
Bassin d'Arcachon
Pyla-sur-Mer
Arcachon
Audenge
Pierroton
Latresne
Branne
Castillon-la-Bataille
Cap Ferret
Gujan-Mestras
Marcheprime
Gradignan
Créon
Pilat-Plage
Facture
Jauge
DUNE DE PILAT
PARC DE LOISIRS
Labrède
Langoiran
Saucats
Le Barp
Podensac
Étang de Cazaux et de Sanguinet
Salles
St.Michel de Rieufret
Cadillac
Sauveterre-de-Guyenne
Biscarrosse-Plage
Villagrains
Sanguinet
CHÂT. YQUEM
St-Macaire
Belin-Béliet
Hostens
Langon
La Réole
Biscarrosse
Étang de Biscarrosse et de Paren
Le Muret
PARC
CHÂTEAU DE ROQUETAILLADE
Parentis-en-Born
Mano
St-Symphorien
Villandraut
Gastes
Ychoux
Moustey
Préchac
Uzeste
Bazas
Pontenx-les-Forges
NATUREL RÉGIONAL
Mimizan-Plage
CHÂT DE CAZENEUVE
Mimizan
Pissos
Sore
Bourideys
Grignols
Bias
Labouheyre
Luxey
Captieux
Lerm-et-Musset
Contis-Plage
DES LANDES DE GASCOGNE
Casteljaloux
St.-Julien-en-Born
Mèzos
Sabres
Lit-et-Mixe
Lahane
CHAP. ST.-SABIN
Morcenx
Labrit
Lencouacq
Houeillès
St-Girons-Plage
St-Girons-en-Marensin
Lesperon
Étang de Léon
Garein
Losse
AQUITAINE
Durance
Barbaste
Léon
Moliets-et-Maa
Castets
Rion-des-Landes
Roquefort
Lapeyrade
Réaup-Lisse
Azur
le Caloy
St-Justin
Vieux-Boucau-les Bains
Magescq
Tartas
Mont-de-Marsan
Labastide-d'Armagnac
Barbotan-les-Thermes
Gabarret
Soustons
Villeneuve-de-Marsan
Cazaubon
Hossegor
St-Paul-lès-Dax
Montréal
Capbreton
Dax
Estang
St-Geours-de-Maremne
Labenne
St-Vincent-de-Tyrosse
Mugron
Grenade
Eauze
Gondrin
Montfort-en-Chalosse
St-Sever
Le Houga
Mancier
Tarnos
ANC. PRIEURE D'ARTHOUS
Anglet
Biarritz
Samadet
Eugénie-les-Bains
Hagetmau
Nogaro
Bidart
Guethary
Bayonne
Amou
Aire-s-l'Adour
Habas
Termes-d'Armagnac
Fezensac
St-Jean-de-Luz
Biarritz/Parme
Geaune
Samadet
Adour
Douze
Midour
Gelise
Seugne
Leyre
Pte-Leyre
Gde-Leyre
CÔTE D'ARGENT
LANDES
A10
E05
A63
A660
E70
A62
E72
A64
E80
N10
N89
N124
N134
N137
E606
E603
N141
N150
N113
N524
N117
N215
N250

LIMOUSIN
LIMOGES
Angoulême
Périgueux
Bergerac
Brive-la-Gaillarde
Tulle
Cahors
Agen
Montauban
Villeneuve-sur-Lot
Marmande
Sarlat-la-Canéda
Figeac
Villefranche-de-Rouergue
Siecq
Gourville
Mansle
St-Claud
Nieuil
Chasseneuil-s-Bonnieure
la Péruse
Chabanais
Etagnac
St-Junien
Javerdat
Nantiat
Laurière
la Jonchère-St-Maurice
Ambazac
Pontarion
Bourganeuf
ÉGLISE DE CHÂTRE
Jarnac
Hiersac
Segonzac
Châteauneuf
Ruelle-sur-Touvre
La Rochefoucauld
Rochechouart
l'Arbre
St-Laurent
Sauviant-sur-Vige
St-Léonard-de-Noblat
GROTTES DU QUEROY
Montbron
St-Mathieu
Aixe-sur-Vienne
Solignac
Peyrat-le-Château
Royère-Vassivière
Jurignac
Marthon
Pluviers
Châlus
Nexon
CHÂTEAU DE CHALUSSET
la Croix Ferrée
Gentioux
Dignac
Grassac
Pierre-Buffière
Eymoutiers
Nedde
Blanzac
Édon
Nontron
Villebois-Lavalette
Mareuil
St-Pardoux-la-Rivière
La Coquille
St-Germain
MONT GARGAN
Millevaches
PLATEAU
Montmoreau-St-Cybard
Brossac
Verteillac
Gout-Rossignol
PUYGUILHEM
St-Yrieix-la-Perche
Chamberet
Masseret
Bugeat
Aubeterre-sur-Dronne
Chalais
Brantôme
Thiviers
Treignac
Lestards
Ribérac
BOURDEILLES
Lisle
Négrondes
Excideuil
Lanouaille
Lubersac
Uzerche
SUC-AU-MAY
St-Aulaye
CHÂT.-L'ÉVÊQUE
Savignac-les-Eglises
Cherveix-Cubas
Arnac-Pompadour
Juillac
Seilhac
Échourgnac
St-Astier
CHÂTEAU DE HAUTEFORT
Objat
La Corrèze
Egletons
Neuvic
Montpon-Ménestérol
Mussidan
PUY D'YSSANDON
Dorzenac
Gimel-les-Cascades
Niversac
St-Pierre-de-Chignac
Thenon
Terrasson-la-Villedieu
Villefranche-de-Lonchat
Vergt
GROTTE DE ROUFFIGNAC
Montignac
GROTTE DE LASCAUX
Larche
GROTTES DE LAMOUROUX
Beynat
St-Mamest
Clermont-de-Beauregarde
CRO-MAGNON
Collonges-la-Rouge
St-Privat
Ste-Foy-la-Grande
GRAND ROC
Les Eyzies-de-Tayac
Cressensac
Turenne
Argentat
Le Bugue
Salignac-Eyvigues
TOURS DE MERLE
Pellegrue
MIN. DE MALFOURAT
Lalinde
St-Cyprien
Beynac-et-Cazenac
Martel
Vayrac
Beaulieu-sur-Dordogne
Flaugeac
Bouniagues
Duras
Beaumont
Siorac-en-Périgord
Souillac
Carennac
Laroquebrou
Monségur
Arnac
Eymet
Issigeac
La Roque-Gageac
Lacave
GOUFFRE DE PADIRAC
Bretenoux
Plaisance
Belvès
Domme
CASTELNAU
Miramont-de-Guyenne
Castillonnès
GROTTES DE COUGNAC
Payrac
Alvignac
St-Céré
Sousceyrac
Lauzun
Monpazier
Gourdon
Rocamadour
Seyches
Villeréal
Villefranche-du-Périgord
Gramat
Cayrols
Laugratte
CHÂTEAU DE BIRON
Salviac
Latronquière
Lacapelle-Marival
Cancon
Tombebœuf
CHÂTEAU DE BONAGUIL
Cazals
Frayssinet
Monflanquin
Teysset
Labastide-Murat
Tonneins
Castelmoron
Ste-Livrade-sur-Lot
Fumel
Catus
Livernon
Maurs
Puy-l'Evêque
Rostassac
GROTTE DU PECH-MERLE
Capdenac-Gare
Aiguillon
Tournon-d'Agenais
Sauzet
Laroque-des-Arcs
St-Géry
Cabrerets
Laugnac
Decazeville
Port-Ste-Marie
St-Cirq-Lapopie
Cajarc
Montaigu-de-Quercy
Villesèque
Peyrusse-le-Roc
Vianne
Limogne-en-Quercy
Villeneuve
Lavardac
Beauville
Montcuq
Montbazens
Nérac
Calignac
Lauzerte
Castelnau-Montratier
Memer
Rignac
Fourquet
Laplume
Montpezat-de-Quercy
Astaffort
Valence
Molières
Caylus
Parisot
Rieupeyroux
Condom
Moissac
Lafrançaise
Caussade
St-Antonin-Noble-Val
Najac
Baraqueville
La Salvetat
Castelsarrasin
Motricoux
Laguépie
Naucelle
FLARAN
Valence-sur-Baïse
Lectoure
Lavit
Cordes
Bruniquel
St-Clar
Beaumont-de-Lomagne
Larroque
Cassagnes-Bégonhès
Fleurance
Tanus
Carmaux
Gimat
Montfort
Castelnau-
55
106

56
70
Guéret
Gouzon
Chénérailles
Chambon-sur-Voueize
Evaux-les-Bains
le Monteix
St-Pourçain-sur-Sioule
Varennes-sur-Allier
Montaigut
St-Eloy-les-Mines
Chantelle
Bellenaves
Marcillat-en-Combraille
Moutier-d'Ahun
Pontarion
Bourganeuf
Fourneaux
Auzances
Pionsat
GORGES DE CHOUVIGNY
Menat
Ebreuil
Gannat
Vichy
Cusset
St-Germain-des-Fossés
Sauviant-sur-Vige
St-Léonard-de-Noblat
Aubusson
Bellegarde-en-Marche
St-Gervais-d'Auvergne
MEANDRE DE QUEUILLE
Aigueperse
Le Mayet
St-Yorre
Randan
Ferrières-sur-Sichon
Peyrat-le-Château
Royère-de-Vassivière
Felletin
St-Bard
Montel-de-Gelat
Combronde
Lac de Vassivière
Gentioux
Crocq
LA CHARTREUSE DE PORT-ST-MARIE
Manzat
Thuret
Eymoutiers
Nedde
Bunleix
PLATEAU DE MILLEVACHES
Pontaumur
Châtelguyon
CHÂTEAU DE TOURNOEL
Riom
Ennezat
Maringues
Puy-Guillaume
Giat
Pontgibaud
Volvic
Col des Goules
Aulnat
PUY DE MONT
Herment
Sauvagnat
PUY DE DÔME
MONTS DÔME
Lezoux
Thiers
MONT GARGAN
Chamberet
Millevaches
La Courtine
Eygurande
Royat
Col de la Moreno
CLERMONT-FERRAND
Pont-de-Dore
Noirétable
Masseret
Bugeat
Treignac
Bourg-Lastic
Laqueuille
Ceyrat
Courpière
Billom
SUC-AU-MAY
Lestards
Meymac
Ussel
GORGE D'AVÈZE
Col de Guéry
Col de la Ventouse
Col de la Croix Morand
Uzerche
La Bourboule
Le Mont-Doré
AUVERGNE
St-Nectaire
Vic-le-Comte
Olliergues
Seilhac
CHÂTEAU DE VENTADOUR
Tauves
PUY DE SANCY
Chambon-sur-Lac
Champeix
CHÂT. DE BURON
Sugères
La Corrèze
Egletons
Lanobre
GROTTES DE JONAS
Besse-en-Chandesse
Issoire
St-Amant-Roche-Savine
Tulle
Neuvic
Bort-les-Orgues
MONTS DORE
Sauxillanges
Col des Fourches
Ambert
Gimel-les-Cascades
PARC NATUREL RÉGIONAL DES VOLCANS D'AUVERGNE
MONTS DU CÉZALLIER
Condat
St-Germain-Lembron
Brassac-Jumeaux
St-Germain-l'Herm
PARC NATUREL RÉGIONAL DU LIVRADOIS FOREZ
Col des Pradeaux
Lempdes
GORGES DE L'ALAGNON
Auzon
Arlanc
Beynat
Mauriac
Riom-ès-Montagnes
Lorlanges
Blesle
Champagnac-le-Vieux
Apchon
Argentat
St-Privat
MASSIF CENTRAL
Massiac
Brioude
La Chaise-Dieu
Allanche
Pleaux
TOURS DE MERLE
Salers
Dienne
Pas de Peyrol
PUY MARY
Paulhaguet
la-Chapelle-Laurent
Beaulieu-sur-Dordogne
Vayrac
St-Cernin
Murat
Col de la Fageole
Lavoûte-Chilhac
Bretenoux
CASTELNAU
Laroquebrou
PLOMB DU CANTAL
MONTS DU CANTAL
Roffiac
Langeac
St-Paulien
Vorey
CHÂT. DE LAVOÛTE-POLIGNAC
St-Céré
Sousceyrac
Aurillac
Vic-sur-Cère
ROCHER DES PENDUS
St-Flour
Loudes
Le Puy-en-Velay
Tagenac
CHÂTEAU D'ALLEUZE
MTS DE LA MARGERIDE
Pinols
Cayrols
Latronquière
Lacapelle-Marival
Prunet
Raulach
Pierrefort
Neuvéglise
Saugues
Monistrol-d'Allier
Mur-de-Barrez
Chaudes-Aigues
Maurs
PUY DE L'ARBRE
Brommat
Lacalm
Jaubrun
Fournels
Esplantas
Figeac
Capdenac-Gare
Montsalvy
Cassuéjouls
MONTS D'AUBRAC
St-Chély-d'Apcher
Chanaleilles
Arlempdes
Entraygues-sur-Truyère
GORGES DU LOT
Laguiole
St-Alban
Grandrieu
Decazeville
Conques
Malbouzon
Aumont-Aubrac
Pradelles
Cajarc
Nasbinals
la Panouse
Langogne
Peyrusse-le-Roc
Villeneuve
Estaing
Aubrac
St-Amans
Châteauneuf-de-Randon
Montbazens
Marcillac-Vallon
Espalion
St-Chély-d'Aubrac
St-Côme-d'Olt
Lachamp
Bozouls
TROU DE BOZOULS
MAILHEBIAU
Marvejols
Rignac
Villefranche-de-Rouergue
CAUSSE DU COMTAL
St-Geniez-d'Olt
La Bastide-Puylaurent
St-Laurent-les-Bains
Mende
La Canourgue
Rieupeyroux
Rodez
Laissac
Bagnols-les-Bains
La Salvetat
Baraqueville
CAUSSE DE SAUVETERRE
la Primaube
Ste-Enimie
PARC MT LOZERE
Villefort
Sévérac-le-Château
Ségur
Pont-de-Salars
Laguépie
Naucelle
PARC NATUREL
Le Pont-de-Montvert
La Malène
Bois-du-Four
POINT SUBLIME
CASTELBOUC
Florac
Cassagnes-Bégonhès
GORGES DU TARN
Génolhac
106
107
Salles-Curan
St-Beauzély
Tanus
Le Rozier
CAUSSE MÉJEAN
AVEN ARMAND
Carmaux
la Selve
Barre-des-Cévennes
Meyrueis
Villefranche-
VIADUC DU
MONTPELLIER
GROTTE DE
63
67
35

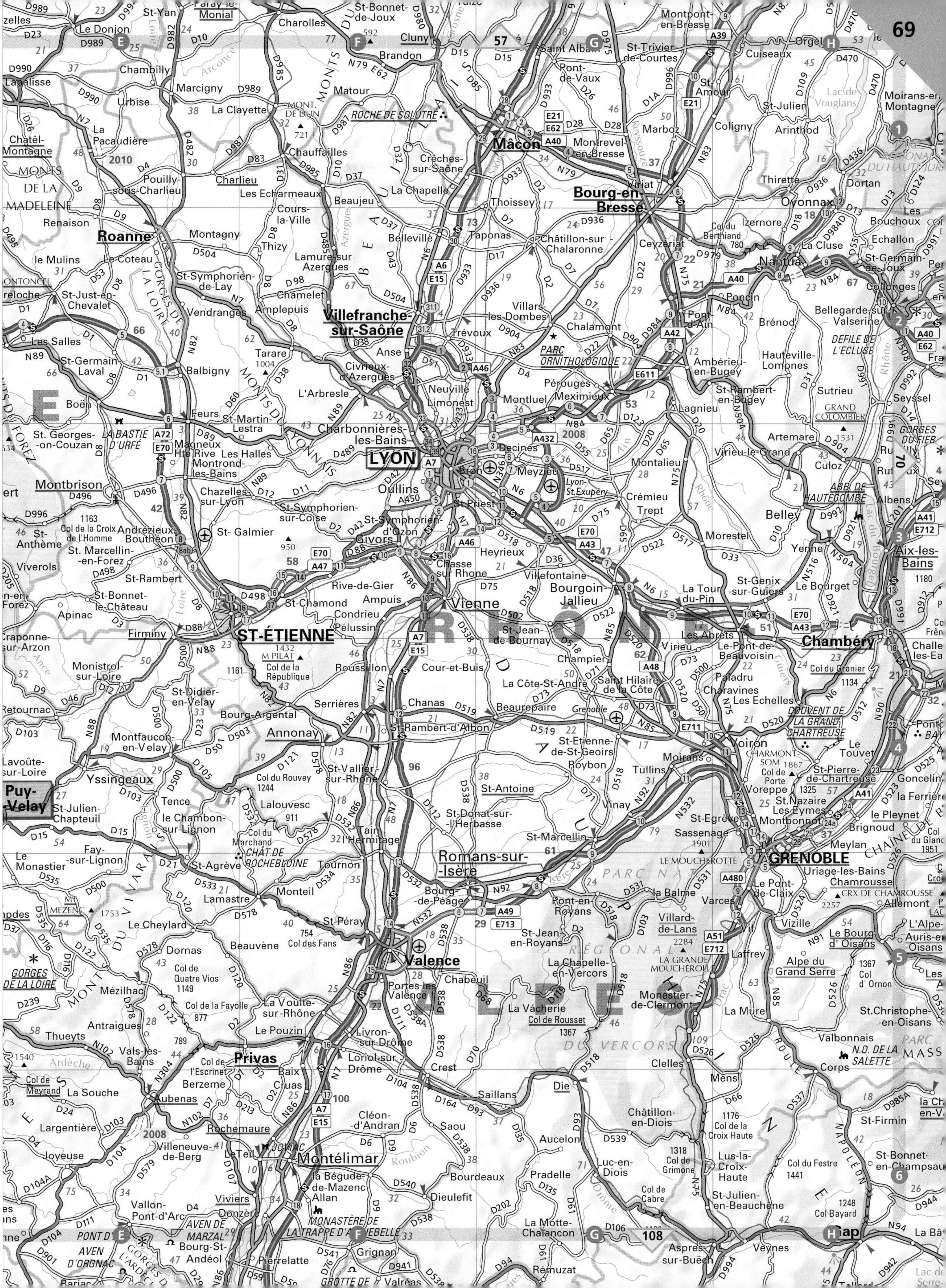
Le Donjon
St-Yan
Paray-le-Monial
Charolles
St-Bonnet-de-Joux
Cluny
Brandon
Montpont-en-Bresse
Saint Albain
St-Trivier-de-Courtes
Cuiseaux
Orgelet
Lapalisse
Chambilly
Marcigny
Urbise
La Clayette
Matour
MONTS DU MACONNAIS
ROCHE DE SOLUTRÉ
Pont-de-Vaux
St-Amour
St-Julien
Lac de Vouglans
Moirans-en-Montagne
La Pacaudière
Chatel-Montagne
MONTS DE LA MADELEINE
Pouilly-sous-Charlieu
Charlieu
Chauffailles
Crêches-sur-Saône
Mâcon
Montrevel-en-Bresse
Marboz
Coligny
Arinthod
Thirette
Dortan
Les Echarmeaux
Beaujeu
La Chapelle
Thoissey
Bourg-en-Bresse
Viriat
Oyonnax
Renaison
Roanne
Montagny
Cours-la-Ville
Thizy
Belleville
Taponas
Châtillon-sur-Chalaronne
Ceyzériat
Izernore
Col du Berthiand 780
Nantua
La Cluse
Echallon
le Mulins
Le Coteau
GORGES DE LA LOIRE
Lamure-sur-Azergues
St-Symphorien-de-Lay
St-Just-en-Chevalet
Chamelet
Amplepuis
Villars-les-Dombes
Poncin
St-Germain-de-Joux
Collonges
Bellegarde-sur-Valserine
Vendranges
Villefranche-sur-Saône
Trévoux
Chalamont
Pont-d'Ain
Brénod
Les Salles
St-Germain-Laval
Balbigny
Tarare
MONTS DU LYONNAIS
Anse
PARC ORNITHOLOGIQUE
Ambérieu-en-Bugey
Hauteville-Lompnes
DEFILE DE L'ECLUSE
Civrieux-d'Azergues
Neuville
Limonest
Pérouges
Meximieux
Montluel
St-Rambert-en-Bugey
Sutrieu
Seyssel
GRAND COLOMBIER
Boën
Feurs
L'Arbresle
St-Martin-Lestra
Lagnieu
LA BASTIE D'URFÉ
St. Georges-on-Couzan
Magneux Hte Rive
Montrond-les-Bains
Les Halles
Charbonnières-les-Bains
LYON
Décines
Bron
Meyzieu
Lyon-St.Exupéry
Montalieu
Virieu-le-Grand
Artemare
Culoz
GORGES DU FIER
Montbrison
Chazelles-sur-Lyon
Oullins
St-Priest
Crémieu
Trept
ABB. DE HAUTECOMBE
Belley
Albens
Col de la Croix de l'Homme 1163
St-Anthème
Andrézieux-Bouthéon
St-Galmier
St-Symphorien-sur-Coise
St-Symphorien-d'Ozon
Givors
Heyrieux
Morestel
Yenne
Aix-les-Bains
St. Marcellin-en-Forez
Viverols
St-Rambert
Chasse sur Rhone
Rive-de-Gier
Villefontaine
Bourgoin-Jallieu
La Tour du-Pin
St-Genix-sur-Guiers
Le Bourget
St-Bonnet-le-Château
Apinac
St-Chamond
Ampuis
Vienne
Condrieu
Pélussin
Firminy
ST-ÉTIENNE
RHÔNE
St-Jean-de-Bournay
Les Abrets
Virieu
Le-Pont-de-Beauvoisin
Chambéry
Craponne-sur-Arzon
M PILAT 1432
Col de la République 1161
Champier
Monistrol-sur-Loire
Roussillon
Cour-et-Buis
La Côte-St-André
Saint Hilaire de la Côte
Col du Granier 1134
Paladru
Charavines
Les Echelles
St-Didier-en-Velay
Bourg-Argental
Serrières
Chanas
Beaurepaire
COUVENT DE LA GRAND CHARTREUSE
Retournac
Montfaucon-en-Velay
Annonay
St-Rambert-d'Albon
St-Etienne-de-St-Geoirs
Voiron
Le Touvet
Lavoûte-sur-Loire
Yssingeaux
St-Vallier-sur-Rhône
Col du Rouvey 1244
Roybon
Tullins
Moirans
CHARMONT-SOM 1867
Col de Porte 1325
St-Pierre-de-Chartreuse
Goncelin
Puy-Velay
St-Julien-Chapteuil
Tence
Le Chambon-sur-Lignon
Lalouvesc 911
St-Antoine
St-Donat-sur-l'Herbasse
Vinay
Voreppe
St.Nazaire Les Eymes
Montbonnot
Le Pleynet
Fay-sur-Lignon
Col du Marchand
CHÂT DE ROCHEBLOINE
Tain-l'Hermitage
St-Marcellin
St-Egrève
Sassenage
LE MOUCHEROTTE 1901
GRENOBLE
Meylan
Brignoud
Le Monastier
St-Agrève
Tournon
Romans-sur-Isère
PARC NAT
Uriage-les-Bains
Chamrousse
CRX DE CHAMROUSSE 2257
MT MEZENC 1753
Lamastre
Monteil
Bourg-de-Péage
Pont-en-Royans
la Balme
Varces
Le Pont-de-Claix
Allemont
Le Cheylard
St-Péray
Col des Fans 754
St-Jean-en-Royans
Villard-de-Lans 2284
Vif
Vizille
L'Alpe-d'Huez
Le Bourg-d'Oisans
Auris-en-Oisans
GORGES DE LA LOIRE
Dornas
Beauvène
Valence
Chabeuil
La Chapelle-en-Vercors
LA GRANDE MOUCHEROLLE
Laffrey
Alpe du Grand Serre
Col d' Ornon 1367
Col de Quatre Vios 1149
Mézilhac
Portes les Valence
La Vâcherie
Col de Rousset 1367
Monestier-de-Clermont
La Mure
St.Christophe-en-Oisans
Antraigues
Col de la Fayolle 877
La Voulte-sur-Rhône
Le Pouzin
Livron-sur-Drôme
Crest
DU VERCORS
Valbonnais
N.D. DE LA SALETTE
Corps
Thueyts
Vals-les-Bains
Col de l'Escrinet
Privas
Baix
Cruas
Loriol-sur-Drôme
Saillans
Die
Clelles
Mens
Col de Meyrand
La Souche
Aubenas
Berzeme
Châtillon-en-Diois
Col de la Croix Haute 1176
St-Firmin
Largentière
Rochemaure
Cléon-d'Andran
Saou
Aucelon
Joyeuse
Villeneuve-de-Berg
Le Teil
Montélimar
Col de Grimone 1318
Lus-la-Croix-Haute
Col du Festre 1441
St-Bonnet-en-Champsaur
la Bégude-de-Mazenc
Bourdeaux
Luc-en-Diois
Pradelle
Col de Cabre
Allan
Dieulefit
St-Julien-en-Beauchêne
Col Bayard 1248
Vallon-Pont-d'Arc
AVEN DE MARZAL
Viviers
Donzère
MONASTÈRE DE LA TRAPPE D'AIGUEBELLE
La Motte-Chalancon
PONT D'ARC
AVEN D'ORGNAC
Bourg-St-Andéol
Grignan
Pierrelatte
Aspres-sur-Buëch
Veynes
Gap
Rémuzat
GROTTE DE
Valréas
NAPOLEON
PARC RÉGIONAL DU VERCORS

58
108
109
CH
F
VAUD
FRIBOURG
BERNER
VALAIS
VALLE D'AOSTA
PIEMONTE
GENÈVE
LAUSANNE
TORINO
Doucier
Les Planches-en-Montagne
Chaux-Neuve
Vallorbe
Orbe
Yverdon-les-Bains
Fribourg
PONT DE PÉROLLES
ABB. DE HAUTERIVE
Le Mouret
BURGISTEIN
Thun
Bonlieu
Clairvaux-les-Lacs
Orgelet
St-Laurent-en Grandvaux
Le Sentier
Pompaples
ST. BARTHÉLEMY
Moudon
Romont
la Roche
Schwarzsee
Gwatt
L'Isle
Cossonay
CHÂTEAU DE VUFFLENS
CHARRIÈRES
Echallens
Oron-la-Ville
Bulle
Boltigen
Jaun
Faulen
Lac de Vouglans
Moirans-en-Montagne
Morez
St.George
Morges
Châtel-St-Denis
Gruyères
Jaunpass
SIMMENTAL
NIESEN
Frutigen
St-Julien
Arinthod
St-Claude
Lézat
La Cure
Les Rousses
St-Cergue
Rolle
Lac Léman
Les Avants
Château d'Oex
Sannenmöser
Zweisimmen
Mijoux
PARC NATUREL RÉGIONAL DU HAUT-JURA
Divonne-les-Bains
Nyon
Yvoire
Amphion
Evian
Vevey
Montreux
CHILLON
Saanen
Gstaad
Adelboden
Thirette
Dortan
Col de la Faucille
Gex
ROCHERS DE NAYE
Col des Mosses
Lenk
Kandersteg
Oyonnax
Les Bouchoux
MONT COLOMBY DE GEX
Versoix
Douvaine
Thonon-les-Bains
St-Gingolph
Le Bouveret
Leysin
Col du Pillon
WILDSTRUBEL
Nantua
La Cluse
Echallon
St-Germain-de-Joux
Peron
LES VOIRONS
Abondance
Aigle
Les Diablerets
Leukerbad
Col de la Croix
WILDHORN
Montana
Collonges
St-Julien-en-Genevois
Annemasse
Boëge
Le Biot
Châtel
Pas de Morgins
Morgins
Monthey
Villars
LES DIABLERETS
Crans
Leuk
Bellegarde-sur-Valserine
Brénod
MT CHÉRY
St-Jeoire
Mieussy
Morzine
St-Maurice
Bex
Sion
Sierre
St-Luc
DEFILE DE L'ECLUSE
Reignier
MT SALÈVE
Avoriaz
Champéry
PYRAMIDES
Hauteville-Lompnes
Frangy
Cruseilles
Bonneville
Les Gets
Taninges
Samoëns
Haute-Nendaz
Sutrieu
Roche-sur-Foron
Col de la Colombière
Cluses
Sixt-Fer-à-Cheval
LA BÂTIAZ
Martigny
Verbier
Zinal
GRAND COLOMBIER
Seyssel
CHÂTEAU DE THORENS-GLIÈRES
Vallorcine
Col de la Forclaz
Evolène
Les Haudères
Dixence
Val d'Hérens
Val de Bagnes
Val d'Entremont
Artemare
GORGES DU FIER
Rumilly
Annecy
Veyrier
Flaine
MT BUET
Argentière
Trient
Col des Montets
Champex
Orsières
Arolla
WEISSHORN
Culoz
Ruffieux
Sevrier
Menthon
Thônes
Sallanches
LE BRÉVENT
Fionnay
Mauvoisin
DENT BLANCHE
ABB. DE HAUTECOMBE
Seynod
Talloires
La Clusaz
Le Fayet
Chamonix-Mont-Blanc
GRAND COMBIN
Albens
St-Jorioz
Duingt
Col des Aravis
CHAÎNE DES ARAVIS
Megève
St-Gervais-les-Bains
Les Houches
TUNNEL DU MONT-BLANC
Col du Grand-St-Bernard
MATTERHORN/ MONTE CERVINO
Belley
Col de Leschaux
MT CHARVIN
Marlens
Flumet
Breuil-Cervinia
Aix-les-Bains
Doussard
Les Contamines-Montjoie
MONT BLANC
Entrèves
TUNNEL DU GRAND-ST-BERNARD
Bionaz
Oyace
Valtournenche
Yenne
Faverges
Les Saisies
Ugine
Courmayeur
Échevennoz
Valpelline
Antey St. André
Antagnod
Le Bourget
Le Pont
Le Châtelard
Beaufort-sur-Doron
Cormet de Roselend
Pré St-Didier
Morgex
Aosta/Aoste
Genix
Guiers
Col de Plainpalais
Albertville
COFLANS
Arêches-Beaufort
Ayas
Col du Frêne
St-Pierre-d'Albigny
LANCE-BRANLETTE
La Thuile
Col du Petit St-Bernard
Nus
Châtillon
St-Vincent
Fénis
Chambéry
Challes-les-Eaux
LE GRAND ARC
Bourg-St-Maurice
Valle d'Aosta
Pila
USSEL
Verrès
Col du Granier
Montmélian
Aiguebelle
St. Marcel
Aime
Valgrisenche
Cogne
Champorcher
Les Echelles
La Rochette
Les Arcs
Rhêmes N.D.
Valsavaranche
LILLAZ
Issogne
COUVENT DE LA GRANDE CHARTREUSE
Pontcharra
BAYARD
Moûtiers
La Plagne
GRANDE SASSIÈRE
PARCO NAZIONALE DEL GRAN PARADISO
Le Touvet
Valmorel
Bozel
Colle del Nivolet
Pont
Col de la Madeleine
Allevard
Tignes
Val d'Isère
GRAN PARADISO
Campiglia Soana
CHAMROUSSE
St-Pierre-de-Chartreuse
Goncelin
La Chambre
Meribel-les-Allues
Courchevel
Val-Claret
ROCHER DE BELLEVARDE
Noasca
Ronco Canavese
Col de Porte
St.Nazaire
Les Eymes
La Ferrière
Pralognan-la-Vanoise
Col de l'Iseran
Ceresole Reale
Montbonnot
le Pleynet
CHAÎNE DE BELLEDONNE
St-Jean-de-Maurienne
Val Thorens
Les Menuires
PARC NATIONAL DE LA VANOISE
MASSIF DE LA VANOISE
Bonneval-sur-Arc
Forno Alpi Graie
Locana
Pont Canavese
Brignoud
Bessans
Chialamberto
Cuorgnè
Meylan
GRENOBLE
Col du Glandon
St. Jean-d'Arves
CIAMARELLA
Ala di Stura
Castellamonte
Ozegna
Uriage-les-Bains
Col de la Croix de Fer
Albier Montrond
St-Michel-de-Maurienne
Lanslebourg-Mont-Cenis
Col du Mont Cenis
Ceres
Balme
Rivarolo Canavese
Le Pont-de-Claix
CRX DE CHAMROUSSE
PIC DU LAC BLANC
Valloire
Le Freney
Modane
ABB. DI NOVALESA
Usseglio
Lanzo Torinese
Feletto
Allemont
CIME DES TORCHES
Col du Télégraphe
Valfréjus
TUNNEL DE FRÉJUS
ST. PIERRE D'EXTRAVACHE
Viù
Saletta
Ciriè
Sandro Pertini
Volpiano
Vizille
Le Bourg d'Oisans
L'Alpe-d'Huez
Auris-en-Oisans
Col du Galibier
La Grave
Susa
Bussoleno
Niquidetto
Caselle
Alpe du Grand Serre
Col d'Ornon
Les Deux-Alpes
Col du Lautaret
MT THABOR
Bardonècchia
Condove
Avigliana
Venaria Reale
Leinì
FORTE
St.Christophe-en-Oisans
La Bérarde
Le Monêtier-les-Bains
Sauze d'Oulx
SACRA DI SAN MICHELE
Settimo Torinese
SUPERGA
Valbonnais
PARC NATIONAL DES ÉCRINS
MASSIF DES ÉCRINS
S. Sicario
Colle di Sestriere
Fenestrelle
Rivoli
Collegno
N.D. DE LA SALETTE
Corps
MT PELVOUX
Les Salles-les Alpes
Chantemerle
Col de Montgenèvre
Sestriere
Perosa Argentina
Orbassano
Ailefroide
Briançon
Claviere
Montgenèvre
Cesana Torinese
Perrero
Piossasco
Stupinigi
Moncalieri
Chieri
la Chapelle-en-Valgaudemar
Vallouise
Villar Perosa
Prali
Pinerolo
Airasca
Carignano
Santena
St-Firmin
L'Argentière-la-Bessée
Col d'Izoard
Bobbio Pellice
Torre Pellice
Poirino
La Roche-de-Rame
Aiguilles
Abriès
Col du Festre
St-Bonnet-en-Champsaur
SOUMT. DROUVET
Arvieux
Château-Queyras
L'Echalp
Cavour
Villafranca Piemonte
Carmagnola
Orcières
Mt-Dauphin
Bagnolo Piemonte
Col Bayard
Gap
St-Clément-sur-Durance
Ceillac
St-Véran
Crissolo
Barge
Moretta
Racconigi
Sommariva del Bosco
La Bâtie-Neuve
Guillestre
DU QUEYRAS
BELVEDERE DU CIRQUE
Paesana
ABB. DI STAFFARDA
Chorges

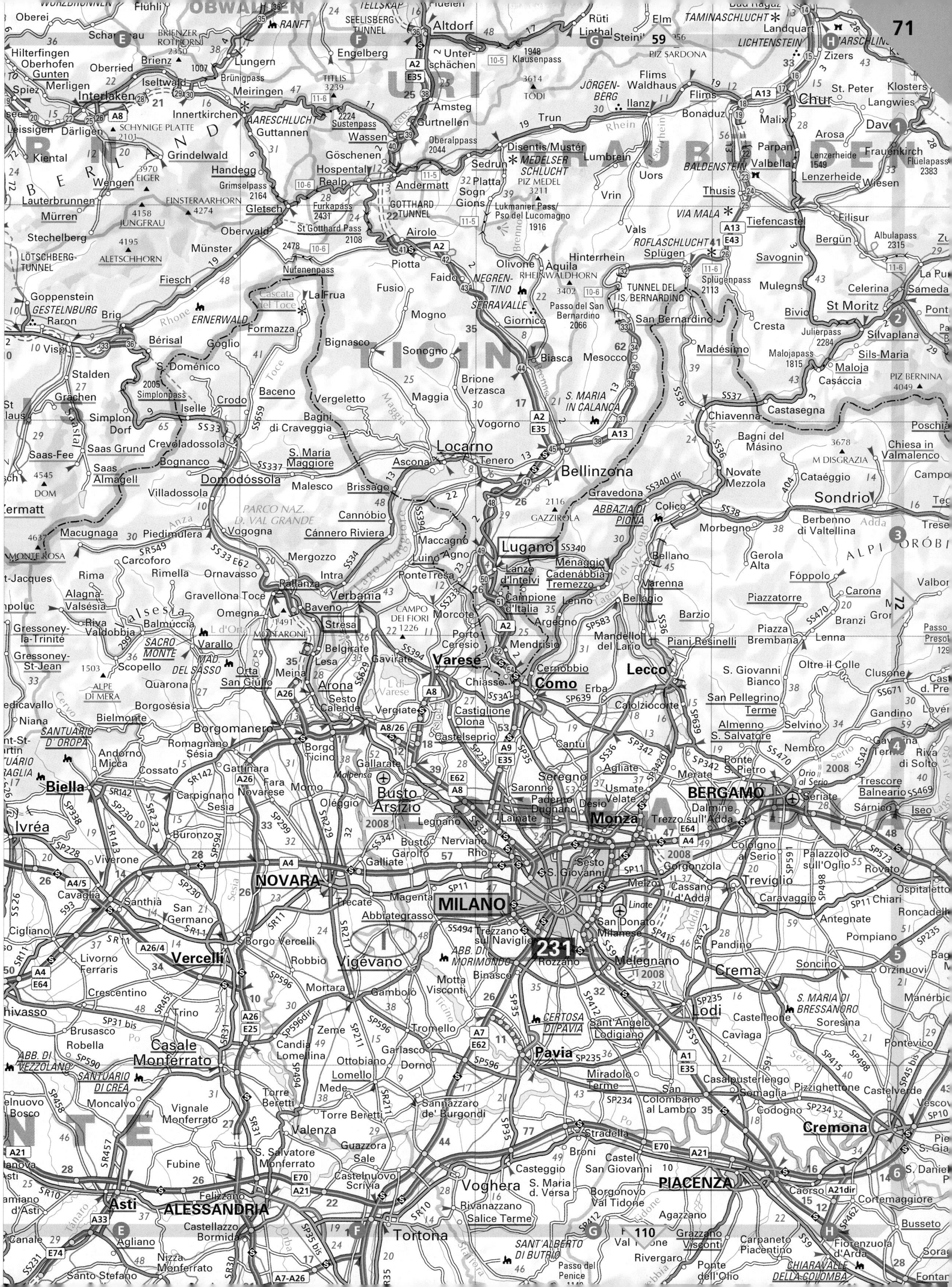

OBWALDEN
TELLSKAP
RANFT
SEELISBERG TUNNEL
Altdorf
Rüti
Linthal
Elm
TAMINASCHLUCHT
Landquart
LICHTENSTEIN
Zizers
59
PIZ SARDONA
Oberei
Flühli
Brienzer Rothorn 2350
Engelberg
Unterschächen
Klausenpass 1948
Hilterfingen
Oberhofen
Gunten
Oberried
Brienz
Lungern
Brünigpass
Titlis 3239
Tödi 3614
Jörgenberg
Flims Waldhaus
Flims
Chur
St. Peter
Klosters
Langwies
Spiez
Merligen
Interlaken
Iseltwald
Meiringen
Innertkirchen
Amsteg
Trun
Ilanz
Bonaduz
Malix
Arosa
Leissigen
Därligen
Schynige Platte 2101
Aareschlucht
Guttannen
Sustenpass 2224
Gurtnellen
Wassen
Oberalppass 2044
Disentis/Mustér
Rhein
Parpan
Valbella
Lenzerheide 1549
Frauenkirch
Flüelapass 2383
Kiental
Grindelwald
Göschenen
Sedrun
Medelser Schlucht
Lumbrein
Baldenstein
Lenzerheide
Wiesen
Handegg
Hospental
Realp
Andermatt
Platta
Piz Medel 3211
Uors
Thusis
Eiger 3970
Wengen
Grimselpass 2164
Sogn Gions
Vrin
Lauterbrunnen
Finsteraarhorn 4274
Gletsch
Furkapass 2431
Gotthard Tunnel
Lukmanier Pass/ Pso del Lucomagno 1916
Via Mala
Tiefencastel
Filisur
Mürren
Jungfrau 4158
Oberwald
St Gotthard Pass 2108
Vals
Roflaschlucht
Splügen
Bergün
Albulapass 2315
Stechelberg
Aletschhorn 4195
Münster
Airolo
Hinterrhein
Savognin
Lötschberg-Tunnel
Nufenenpass 2478
Piotta
Olivone
Àquila
Rheinwaldhorn 3402
Splügenpass 2113
Mulegns
Celerina
Samedan
La Punt
Fiesch
Faido
Negrentino
Tunnel del S. Bernardino
St Moritz
Goppenstein
Gestelnburg
Raron
Cascata del Toce
La Frua
Fusio
Serravalle
Passo del San Bernardino 2066
San Bernardino
Bivio
Pontresina
Brig
Rhone
Ernerwald
Mogno
Giornico
Cresta
Julierpass 2284
Silvaplana
Visp
Bérisal
Formazza
Bignasco
Sils-Maria
Goglio
TICINO
Sonogno
Biasca
Mesocco
Madésimo
Maloja
Malojapass 1815
Casàccia
Piz Bernina 4049
Stalden
S. Doménico
Brione Verzasca
Grächen
Simplonpass 2005
Crodo
Baceno
Maggia
S. Maria in Calanca
Chiavenna
Castasegna
Poschiavo
Simplon Dorf
Iselle
Vergeletto
Bagni di Craveggia
Vogorno
Bagni del Másino
Chiesa in Valmalenco
Saas-Fee
Saas Grund
Crevoladossola
Locarno
Ascona
Tenero
Bellinzona
Monte Disgrazia 3678
Saas Almagell
Bognanco
Domodóssola
S. María Maggiore
Malesco
Brissago
Novate Mezzola
Cataéggio
Campo
Dom 4545
Villadossola
Gravedona
Colico
Sondrio
Zermatt
Parco Naz. d. Val Grande
Cannóbio
Gazzirola 2116
Abbazia di Piona
Berbenno di Valtellina
Macugnaga
Piedimulera
Vogogna
Cánnero Riviera
Morbegno
Adda
Monte Rosa 4637
Maccagno
Agno
Lugano
Alpi Oróbie
Mergozzo
Luino
Menaggio
Bellano
Gerola Alta
Carcoforo
Rimella
Ornavasso
Intra
Ponte Tresa
Lanzo d'Intelvi
Cadenábbia
Tremezzo
Varenna
Fóppolo
Carona
Rima
Pallanza
Verbania
Campione d'Italia
Lenno
Bellágio
Piazzatorre
Alagna Valsésia
Gravellona Toce
Baveno
Campo dei Fiori 1226
Morcote
Barzio
Branzi
Valsesia
Omegna
Stresa
Mottarone 1491
L. d'Orta
Argegno
Mandello del Lario
Gressoney-la-Trinité
Riva Valdobbia
Balmúccia
Porto Ceresio
Mendrisio
Piazza Brembana
Lenna
Sacro Monte
Varallo
Belgirate
Piani Resinelli
Gressoney-St-Jean
Scopello
Mad. del Sasso
Orta San Giúlio
Lesa
Gavirate
Varese
Cernobbio
Lecco
Oltre il Colle
Clusone
Alpe di Mera 1503
Quarona
Meina
Arona
L. di Varese
Chiasso
Como
Erba
S. Giovanni Bianco
Sesto Calende
Vergiate
Castiglione Olona
Calolziocorte
San Pellegrino Terme
Gandino
Niana
Borgosésia
Bielmonte
Santuario d'Oropa
Borgomanero
Castelseprio
Almenno S. Salvatore
Selvino
Andorno Micca
Romagnano Sésia
Borgo Ticino
Gallarate
Cantù
Nembro
Riva di Solto
Cossato
Gattinara
Fara Novarese
Malpensa
Seregno
Agliate
Merate
Ponte S. Pietro
Trescore Balneario
Biella
Carpignano Sesia
Momo
Busto Arsizio
Saronno
Paderno Dugnano
Desio
Usmate Velate
BERGAMO
Orio al Serio
Seriate
Sárnico
Iseo
Ivréa
Buronzo
Oléggio
Legnano
Lainate
Monza
Dalmine
Trezzo sull'Adda
Busto Garolfo
Nerviano
Rho
Cologno al Serio
Palazzolo sull'Oglio
Rovato
Viverone
Galliate
Sesto S. Giovanni
Gorgonzola
Cavaglià
NOVARA
Melzo
Cassano d'Adda
Treviglio
Ospitaletto
Santhià
Magenta
Trecate
MILANO
Linate
Caravaggio
Chiari
San Germano
Abbiategrasso
Trezzano sul Naviglio
San Donato Milanese
Antegnate
Roncadelle
Cigliano
Borgo Vercelli
Pandino
Pompiano
Livorno Ferraris
Vercelli
Robbio
Vigevano
Abb. di Morimondo
Rozzano
Melegnano
Crema
Soncino
Orzinuovi
Crescentino
Mortara
Gambolò
Motta Visconti
Binasco
S. Maria di Bressanoro
Manérbio
Chivasso
Trino
Zeme
Tromello
Certosa di Pavia
Sant'Angelo Lodigiano
Lodi
Castelleone
Soresina
Brusasco
Robbiano
Po
Candia Lomellina
Garlasco
Pavia
Caviaga
Pontevico
Abb. di Vezzolano
Casale Monferrato
Santuario di Crea
Ottobiano
Lomello
Dorno
Miradolo Terme
Casalpusterlengo
Mede
San Colombano al Lambro
Somaglia
Pizzighettone
Castelverde
Moncalvo
Torre Beretti
Sannazzaro de' Burgondi
Codogno
Vescovato
Vignale Monferrato
Valenza
Stradella
Cremona
Guazzora
Sale
Broni
Castel San Giovanni
S. Salvatore Monferrato
Fubine
Casteggio
Asti
Felizzano
ALESSANDRIA
Castelnuovo Scrivia
Voghera
S. Maria d. Versa
Borgonovo Val Tidone
PIACENZA
Caorso
Cortemaggiore
Castellazzo Bormida
Tortona
Rivanazzano
Salice Terme
Agazzano
Busseto
Agliano
Canale
Nizza Monferrato
Sant'Alberto di Butrio
Val Tidone
Grazzano Visconti
Carpaneto Piacentino
Fiorenzuola d'Arda
Santo Stefano
Passo del Penice
Rivergaro
Ponte dell'Olio
Chiaravalle della Colomba
Fontanellato
LOMBARDIA
PIEMONTE
GRAUBÜNDEN
URI
BERNER OBERLAND

VORARLBERG
Götzis
Schoppernau
Hirschegg
Mittelberg
HOHENBACH-SCHLUCHT
Elmen
Stanzach
Lermoos
Ehrwald
Leutasch
Scharnitz
KARWENDELGEBIRGE
Rankweil
Hochtannberg Pass
Warth
Pfafflar
Elbigenalp
Namlos
Fern Pass
Biberwier
Holzleitensattel
Seefeld in Tirol
Telfs
Hall in Tirol
Fontanella
Schröcken
Holzgau
LECHTALER ALPEN
FERNSTEIN
Nassereith
Obsteig
Zirl
Kranebitten
Feldkirch
Nendeln
Lech
Steeg
Imst
Silz
Stams
Kühtai
Volders
Buchs
Schaan
Vaduz
FL
Bludenz
Klösterle
Dalaas
Zürs
Flexen Pass
Stuben
Langen
Pettneu am A.
Flirsch
PERJEN-TUNNEL
PETERSBURG
INNSBRUCK
Igls
PATSCHERKOFEL
Patsch
Balzers
ARLBERG TUNNEL
St Anton
St Christoph
Arlberg Pass
Landeck
Arzl
Wenns
Jerzens
Ried
Oetz
Gries in Sellrain
EUROPA-BRÜCKE
Lanersbach
MONTAFON
Brand
Lünersee
Schruns
Kappl
See
WIESBERG
Kauns
Umhausen
STUIBENFALL
Lüsens
Mieders
Schönberg
Matrei am Brenner
Maienfeld
Bad Ragaz
St Gallenkirch
Ischgl
Sinsen
TRISANNA-BRÜCKE
Fiss
BERNEK
PITZTAL
ÖTZTAL
STUBAIER ALPEN
Fulpmes
Neustift
Obernberg am Brenner
Steinach
Landquart
LICHTENSTEIN
MARSCHLINS
Grüsch
Schiers
Gaschurn
Partenen
Valzul
Serfaus
Ried
Sankt Leonhard
Längenfeld
Huben
Egg
Gschnitz
Ranalt
Gries-am-Brenner
Zizers
Küblis
Gargellen
Galtür
PAZNAUNTAL
Tösens
Spiss
Am See
Mittelberg
Bielerhöhe
FLUCHTHORN
Samnaun
Pfunds
KAJETANS-BRÜCKE
Sölden
Brenner Pass/Passo del Brennero
Monbiel
St. Peter
Klosters
Martina/Martinsbruck
Nauders
ÖTZTALER ALPEN
Timmelsjoch/Passo del Rombo
Colle Isarco/Gossensass
Chur
Langwies
Davos
Arosa
PIZ BUIN
Scuol
Guarda
Ramosch
Reschen Pass/Passo di Résia
WILDSPITZE
Obergurgl
Vent
Passo di Monte Giovo/Jaufen Pass
Vipiteno/Sterzing
Fundres/Pfunders
Parpan
Lenzerheide
Frauenkirch
Flüelapass
Valbella
Lenzerheide
Wiesen
Susch
Ardez
Tarasp
Lago di Résia/Reschensee
Curon Venosta/Graun im Vinschgau
San Valentino a.Muta/Sankt Valentin a. d. Haide
Moso in Passiria/Moos in Passeier
San Leonardo in P./Sankt Leonhard in P.
Riobianco/Weissenbach
Passo di Pennes
GRAUBÜNDEN
Zernez
Ofen Pass/Pass dal Fuorn
ABB. DI M. MARIA/KLOST. MARIENBERG
Málles Venosta/Mals im Vinschgau
Varna (Vahrn)
Tiefencastel
Filisur
NATIONAL PARK
Brail
Tubre/Taufers
Sluderno/Schluderns
Madonna di Senales/Unserfrau
ALTO ADIGE
SARNTALER ALPEN
Bergün
Albulapass
Zuoz
Tschierv
MUNT LA SCHERA TUNNEL
Müstair
Silandro/Schlanders
Naturno/Naturns
Tirolo/Tirol
Merano/Meran
Savognin
CH
La Punt
Livigno
Umbrailpass
Passo d'Eira
PARCO
Láces
Adige/Etsch
Avelengo/Hafling
Lana
Sarentino/Sarnthein
Chiusa/Klausen
Selva di Val Gardena/Wolkenstein
Mulegns
Celerina
Samedan
Pontresina
Trafoi
NAZIONALE
S. Pancrázio
Avigna
Ortisei/St Ulrich
Bivio
St Moritz
Julierpass
Silvaplana
Passo del Bernina
Passo di Foscagno
Bagni di Bormio
Passo dello Stelvio/Stilfser Joch
Solda/Sulden
Passo delle Palade
BOLZANO/BOZEN
Renon/Ritten
S.ta Cristina/St Christina
Maloja
Malojapass
Sils-Maria
Forcola di Livigno
Bórmio
DELLO STELVIO
Appiano/Eppan
Siusi/Seis
Passo di Sella
Casáccia
PIZ BERNINA
La Rösa
Santa Caterina Valfurva
Bagni di Rabbi
Santa Gertrude/Sankt Gertraud
Fondo
Nova Levante/Welschnofen
Canazei
Castasegna
Sóndalo
Passo di Gávia
Pejo
Gógolo
Cles
Revò
Passo di Costalunga
Vigo di Fassa
Poschiavo
Grósio
Dimaro
Malé
Passo della Mendola
Carezza al Lago/Karersee
Moena
Bagni del Másino
M DISGRAZIA
Chiesa in Valmalenco
Brúsio
Madonna di Tirano
Ponte di Legno
Passo del Tonale
Vermiglio
Dermulo
Ora/Auer
Predazzo
Novate Mezzola
Cataéggio
Campocológno
Campo Carlo Magno
Folgarida
Egna/Neumarkt
Bellamonte
Sondrio
Teglio
Tirano
Oglio
Bédole
Lago di Tovel
Cavalese
Berbenno di Valtellina
Adda
Tresenda
Aprica
Édolo
CASCATA DI NARDIS
Madonna di Campiglio
Fai d. Paganella
Mezzolombardo
Sover
San Martino di Castrozza
ALPI ORÓBIE
Passo dell' Aprica
ADAMELLO
CIMA BRENTA
Andalo
San Michele all' Adige
Caoria
Gerola Alta
Malonno
Saviore dell'Adamello
Pinzolo
Molveno
Lavis
Baselga di Pinè
CIMA D'ASTA
Fóppolo
Passo del Vivione
TRENTINO
Carona
Valbondione
Pontarso
Piazzatorre
Mola
Gromo
Schilpário
PARCO NAZIONALE DELLE INCISIONI RUPESTRI
Tione di Trento
Vezzano
Trento
Pérgine Valsugana
Roncegno
Castello Tesino
Branzi
Capo di Ponte
Ponte Arche
Comano Terme
M. Bondone
Vetriolo Terme
Borgo Valsugana
Piazza Brembana
Lenna
Passo della Presolana
Dezzo
Lardaro
Levico Terme
Fonzaso
Oltre il Colle
Boário Terme
Breno
Pieve di Bono
Lavarone
Passo di Vèzzena
Arsiè
S. Giovanni Bianco
Clusone
Castione d. Presolana
Condino
Riva del Garda
Arco
Primolano
Pellegrino Terme
Darfo
Passo di Croce Domini
Storo
Bezzecca
ALTOPIANO DEI
Gandino
Lovére
Limone sul Garda
Torbole
Mori
Folgaria
Rovereto
Roana
Selvino
Bagolino
Asiago
SETTE COMUNI
Nembro
Gaverina Terme
Pisogne
Cóllio
Lago d'Idro
Pian delle Fugazze
Arsiero
Orio al Serio
Riva di Solto
Bóvegno
Anfo
Magasa
Malcesine
Ràossi
Piovene-Rocchette
Bassano del Grappa
Monte Isola
Trescore Balneario
Avio
Seriate
Sárnico
Iseo
Vestone
Idro
Gargnano
M BALDO
Ala
Passo Xon
Marόstica
Gardone Val Trómpia
Toscolano Maderno
Berenzone
MONTI LESSINI
Thiene
Lumezzane
Gardone Riviera
Recoaro Terme
Schio
Breganze
Palazzolo sull'Oglio
Rovato
Concesio
Bosco Chiesanuova
Malo
Sandrigo
Treviglio
Gavardo
Salò
Torri del Benaco
S.Anna di Alfaedo
Valdagno
Dueville
Cittadella
Ospitaletto
BRÉSCIA
Garda
S. Andrea
Bolca
Caravaggio
Chiari
Manerba del Garda
Bardolino
Negrar
Chiampo
Roncadelle
Sirmione
Lazise
Grezzana
VICENZA
Antegnate
Pompiano
Bagnolo Mella
Lonato
Desenzano del Garda
Peschiera del Garda
Bussolengo
Tregnago
Arzignano
Piazzola sul Brenta
Soncino
Orzinuovi
Ghedi
Montichiari
VERONA
Montecchio Maggiore
Soave
San Martino d. Battaglia
San Martino Buon Albergo
S. MARIA DI BRESSANORO
Manèrbio
Castiglione d. Stiviere
Villafranca Veronese
Barbarano Vicentino
Grisignano di Zocco
Castelleone
Leno
Carpenédolo
S. Giovanni Lupatoto
San Bonifácio
Lonigo
PADOVA
Soresina
Isorella
Medole
Váleggio s Mincio
Villafranca di Verona
Buttapietra
Albaredo d'Adige
Sossano
Abano Terme
Montegrotto Terme
Gottolengo
Castel Goffredo
Góito
Isola d. Scala
Noventa Vicentina
COLLI EUGANEI
Gambara
Cologna
I
2008

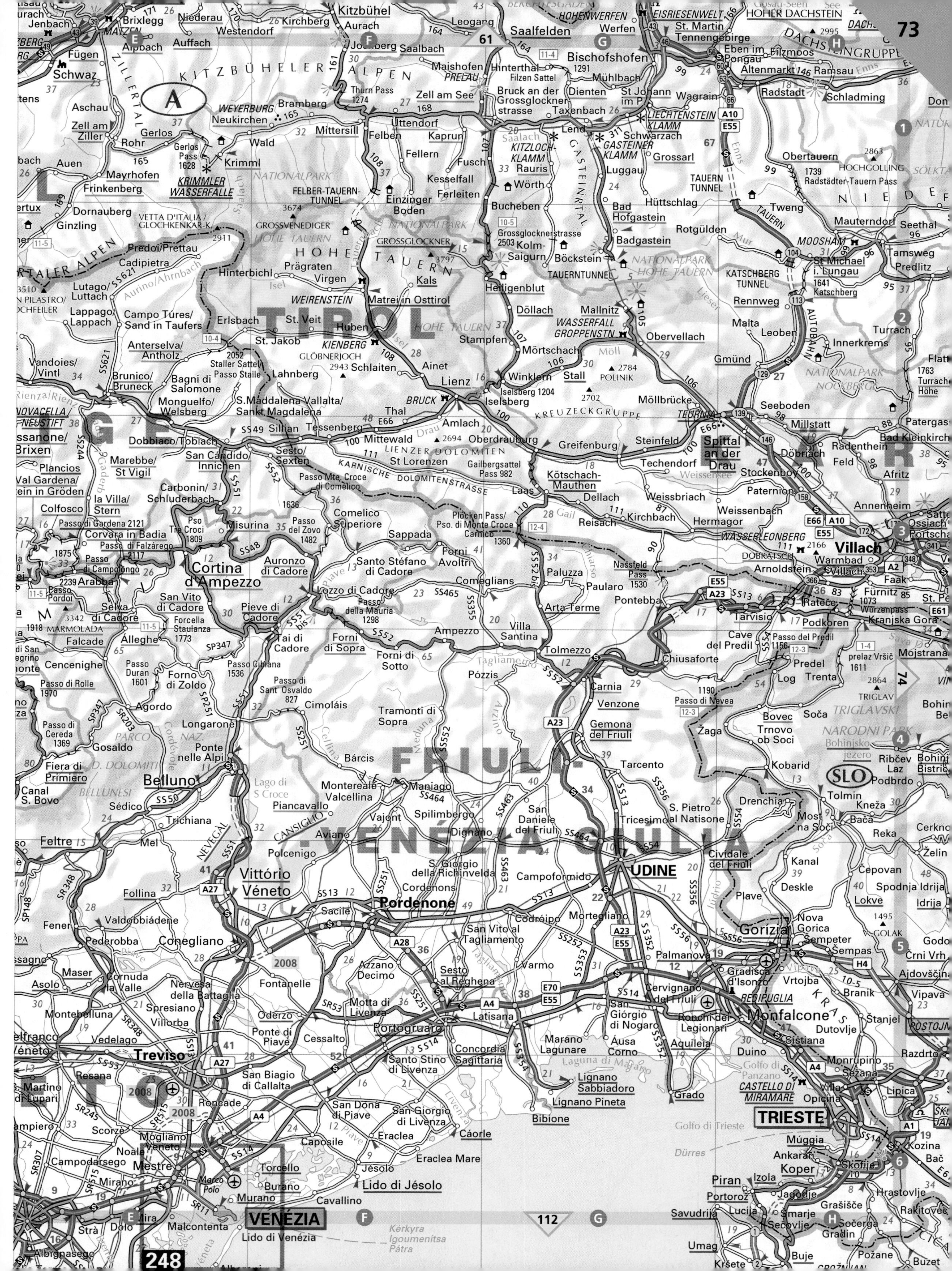
A
TIROL
FRIULI-VENÉZIA GIULIA
SLO
KITZBÜHELER ALPEN
HOHE TAUERN
NATIONALPARK HOHE TAUERN
ZILLERTAL
GASTEINERTAL
KREUZECKGRUPPE
LIENZER DOLOMITEN
KARNISCHE DOLOMITENSTRASSE
Kitzbühel
Jenbach
Brixlegg
Schwaz
Fügen
Alpbach
Auffach
Niederau
Westendorf
Kirchberg
Aurach
Jochberg
Saalbach
Leogang
Saalfelden
Maishofen
Zell am See
Thurn Pass 1274
Mittersill
Bramberg
Neukirchen
Krimml
KRIMMLER WASSERFÄLLE
Gerlos
Gerlos Pass 1628
Zell am Ziller
Mayrhofen
Finkenberg
Dornauberg
Ginzling
Uttendorf
Kaprun
Fusch
Kesselfall
Ferleiten
FELBER-TAUERN-TUNNEL
Einzinger Boden
GROSSVENEDIGER 3674
GROSSGLOCKNER 3797
Prägraten
Virgen
Matrei in Osttirol
Kals
Heiligenblut
Döllach
Huben
Lienz
Bischofshofen
Werfen
HOHENWERFEN
EISRIESENWELT
St. Martin
Tennengebirge
Eben im Pongau
Filzmoos
Altenmarkt
Radstadt
Schladming
Wagrain
St Johann im Pongau
Schwarzach
Taxenbach
Bruck an der Grossglocknerstrasse
Dienten
Mühlbach
Lend
LIECHTENSTEINKLAMM
KITZLOCHKLAMM
GASTEINER KLAMM
Rauris
Wörth
Bucheben
Grossarl
Luggau
Hüttschlag
Bad Hofgastein
Badgastein
Böckstein
TAUERNTUNNEL
Kolm-Saigurn
Obertauern
TAUERN TUNNEL
Tweng
Mauterndorf
MOOSHAM
Tamsweg
St. Michael i. Lungau
KATSCHBERG TUNNEL
Rennweg
Malta
Leoben
Gmünd
Mallnitz
Obervellach
WASSERFALL GROPPENSTN
Stall
Winklern
Iselsberg
Möllbrücke
Spittal an der Drau
Millstatt
Seeboden
Radenthein
Döbriach
Afritz
Stockenboy
Paternion
Weissenbach
Greifenburg
Steinfeld
Techendorf
Weissbriach
Kirchbach
Hermagor
Oberdrauburg
Kötschach-Mauthen
Dellach
Reisach
Villach
Warmbad Villach
Arnoldstein
Faak
Nassfeld Pass 1530
Plöcken Pass
Predoi/Prettau
Hinterbichl
Lutago/Luttach
Campo Túres/Sand in Taufers
Erlsbach
St. Veit
St. Jakob
Anterselva/Antholz
Brunico/Bruneck
Bagni di Salomone
Monguelfo/Welsberg
S.Mãddalena Vallalta/Sankt Magdalena
Sillian
Tessenberg
Thal
Amlach
Dobbiaco/Toblach
San Cándido/Innichen
Sesto/Sexten
Marebbe/St Vigil
Bressanone/Brixen
Val Gardena
Colfosco
Corvara in Badia
Carbonin/Schluderbach
Misurina
Cortina d'Ampezzo
Arabba
Passo Pordoi
Selva di Cadore
San Vito di Cadore
Pieve di Cadore
Auronzo di Cadore
Santo Stéfano di Cadore
Sappada
Comelico Superiore
Forni Avoltri
Comeglians
Paluzza
Paularo
Arta Terme
Pontebba
Tarvisio
Villa Santina
Tolmezzo
Ampezzo
Forni di Sopra
Forni di Sotto
Tai di Cadore
Álleghe
Falcade
Cencenighe
Agordo
Forno di Zoldo
Longarone
Ponte nelle Alpi
Belluno
Sédico
Trichiana
Feltre
Mel
Gosaldo
Fiera di Primiero
Canal S. Bovo
Cimoláis
Tramonti di Sopra
Bárcis
Maniago
Montereale Valcellina
Piancavallo
Aviano
Spilimbergo
San Daniele del Friuli
Gemona del Friuli
Venzone
Carnia
Chiusaforte
Tarcento
Tricesimo
S. Pietro al Natisone
Cividale del Friuli
UDINE
Campoformido
Codróipo
Pordenone
Sacile
Cordenons
Vittório Véneto
Conegliano
Valdobbiádene
Follina
Pederobba
Asolo
Maser
Montebelluna
Treviso
Oderzo
Motta di Livenza
Portogruaro
Latisana
Palmanova
Cervignano del Friuli
Aquileia
Grado
Lignano Sabbiadoro
Lignano Pineta
Bibione
Cáorle
Eraclea
Jésolo
Lido di Jésolo
San Donà di Piave
Mestre
Mira
Dolo
Stra
Torcello
Burano
Murano
VENÉZIA
Lido di Venézia
Cavallino
Gorizia
Nova Gorica
Monfalcone
Duino
Sistiana
TRIESTE
Múggia
Koper
Izola
Piran
Portorož
Lucija
Umag
Savudrija
Sežana
Opicina
Lipica
Kozina
Kranjska Gora
Podkoren
Rateče
Bovec
Kobarid
Tolmin
Most na Soči
Kanal
Plave
Vipava
Ajdovščina
Bled
TRIGLAV 2864
Drenchia
Golfo di Trieste

62
73
113

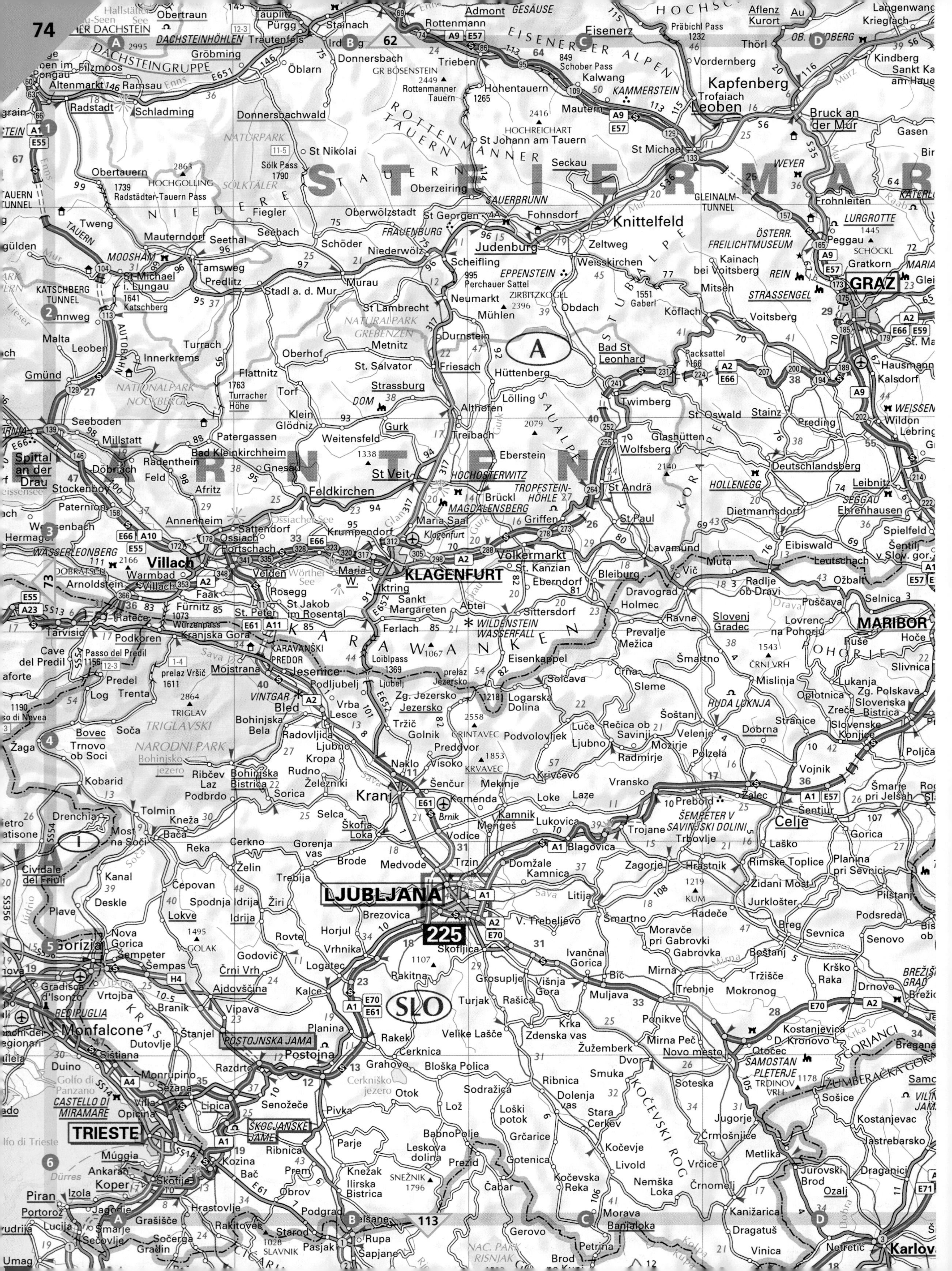
STEIERMARK
KÄRNTEN
A
SLO
I
DACHSTEINGRUPPE
NIEDERE TAUERN
ROTTENMANNER TAUERN
EISENERZER ALPEN
HOCHSCHWAB
SAUALPE
STUBALPE
KORALPE
POHORJE
KARAWANKEN
KOČEVSKI ROG
GORJANCI
KRAS
Hallstätter See
Obertraun
Tauplitz
Pürgg
Stainach
Admont
GESÄUSE
Aflenz Kurort
Au
Langenwang
Krieglach
HOHER DACHSTEIN
DACHSTEINHÖHLEN
Trautenfels
Irdning
Rottenmann
Eisenerz
Präbichl Pass 1232
Thörl
OB. VEITSBERG
Gröbming
Donnersbach
Trieben
Schober Pass 849
Vordernberg
Kindberg
Sankt Katharein am Hauenstein
Filzmoos
Öblarn
GR BÖSENSTEIN 2449
Rottenmanner Tauern 1265
Hohentauern
Kalwang
Kapfenberg
Altenmarkt
Ramsau
Trofaiach
KAMMERSTEIN
Leoben
Radstadt
Schladming
Donnersbachwald
Mautern
HOCHREICHART 2416
Bruck an der Mur
Gasen
St Johann am Tauern
NATURPARK SÖLKTÄLER
St Nikolai
Sölk Pass 1790
St Michael
WEYER
HOCHGOLLING 2863
Obertauern
Radstädter-Tauern Pass 1739
Seckau
Oberzeiring
SAUERBRUNN
GLEINALM-TUNNEL
Frohnleiten
TAUERN TUNNEL
Fiegler
Oberwölzstadt
St Georgen
Fohnsdorf
Knittelfeld
LURGROTTE 1445
Tweng
Seebach
FRAUENBURG
Judenburg
Zeltweg
ÖSTERR. FREILICHTMUSEUM
Peggau
SCHÖCKL
Mauterndorf
Seethal
Schöder
Niederwölz
Weisskirchen
Kainach bei Voitsberg
Gratkorn
MOOSHAM
Tamsweg
Scheifling
EPPENSTEIN
REIN
GRAZ
St Michael i. Lungau
Predlitz
Murau
Perchauer Sattel 995
Mitsch
KATSCHBERG TUNNEL
Katschberg 1641
Stadl a. d. Mur
St Lambrecht
Neumarkt
ZIRBITZKOGEL 2396
Gaberl 1551
Köflach
STRASSENGEL
Rennweg
Mühlen
Obdach
Voitsberg
NATURALPARK GREBENZEN
Durnstein
Bad St Leonhard
Malta
Leoben
Turrach
Metnitz
Packsattel 1166
Kalsdorf
Innerkrems
Oberhof
Friesach
Hausmannstätten
Gmünd
NATIONALPARK NOCKBERGE
Flattnitz
St. Salvator
Hüttenberg
Turracher Höhe 1763
Torf
Strassburg
Lölling
DOM
Twimberg
Stainz
WEISSENEGG
Seeboden
Klein Glödniz
Althofen
St. Oswald
Preding
Wildon
Lebring
Millstatt
Patergassen
Gurk
Treibach
Glashütten
Wolfsberg
Weitensfeld
Spittal an der Drau
Radenthein
Bad Kleinkirchheim
Eberstein
Deutschlandsberg
Döbriach
Feld
Gnesau
St Veit
HOCHOSTERWITZ
Leibnitz
Stockenboi
Afritz
Feldkirchen
Brückl
TROPFSTEIN-HÖHLE
St Andrä
HOLLENEGG
SEGGAU
Ehrenhausen
Paternion
MAGDALENSBERG
Dietmannsdorf
Annenheim
Sattendorf
Maria Saal
Griffen
St Paul
Spielfeld
Weissenbach
Ossiacher See
Krumpendorf
Klagenfurt
Eibiswald
Šentilj v Slov. gor.
Hermagor
Ossiach
Lavamünd
Muta
Leutschach
WASSERLEONBERG
Villach
Pörtschach
Völkermarkt
DOBRATSCH 2166
Warmbad Villach
Velden
Wörther See
Maria Wörth
KLAGENFURT
St. Kanzian
Bleiburg
Vič
Radlje ob Dravi
Ožbalt
Arnoldstein
Faak
Rosegg
Viktring
Eberndorf
Dravograd
Selnica
Fürnitz
St Jakob im Rosental
Sankt Margareten
Abtei
Sittersdorf
Holmec
Puščava
Rateče
Wurzenpass 1073
St. Peter
Ferlach
WILDENSTEIN WASSERFALL
Ravne
Slovenj Gradec
Lovrenc na Pohorju
MARIBOR
Tarvisio
Podkoren
Kranjska Gora
Prevalje
Mežica
Ruše
Hoče
Cave del Predil
Passo del Predil 1156
KARAVANŠKI PREDOR
Loiblpass 1369
Eisenkappel
Šmartno
ČRNI VRH 1543
Slivnica
Predel
prelaz Vršič 1611
Mojstrana
Jesenice
prelaz Jezersko
Solčava
Črna
Sleme
Mislinja
Lukanja
Zg. Polskava
Log
Trenta
Podljubelj
Ljubelj
Zg. Jezersko
Jezersko
Logarska Dolina
HUDA LUKNJA
Oplotnica
Slovenska Bistrica
VINTGAR
Bled
TRIGLAV 2864
Lesce
Vrba
Tržič
GRINTAVEC 2558
Šoštanj
Zreče
Stranice
Slovenske Konjice
Bovec
Soča
TRIGLAVSKI NARODNI PARK
Bohinjska Bela
Radovljica
Golnik
Podvolovljek
Luče
Rečica ob Savinji
Velenje
Dobrna
Žaga
Trnovo ob Soči
Bohinjsko jezero
Ljubno
Kropa
Preddvor
KRVAVEC 1853
Mozirje
Polzela
Poljčane
Kobarid
Ribčev Laz
Bohinjska Bistrica
Rudno
Naklo
Visoko
Radmirje
Vojnik
Podbrdo
Sorica
Železniki
Kranj
Šenčur
Mekinje
Kričevo
Vransko
Prebold
Žalec
Šmarje pri Jelšah
Drenchia
Tolmin
Kneža
Selca
Škofja Loka
Komenda
Brnik
Loke
Laze
ŠEMPETER V SAVINJSKI DOLINI
Šentjur
Celje
Most na Soči
Bača
Kamnik
Lukovica
Trojane
Trbovlje
Gorica
Reka
Cerkno
Gorenja vas
Vodice
Menges
Blagovica
Laško
Cividale del Friuli
Kanal
Želin
Brode
Medvode
Trzin
Domžale
Kamnica
Zagorje
Hrastnik
Rimske Toplice
Planina pri Sevnici
Trebija
Čepovan
Spodnja Idrija
Žiri
LJUBLJANA
Litija
KUM 1219
Zidani Most
Deskle
Lokve
Idrija
Brezovica
Šmartno
Radeče
Jurklošter
Pilštanj
Plave
V. Trebeljevo
Moravče pri Gabrovki
Podsreda
Nova Gorica
Gorizia
Šempeter
Šempas
GOLAK 1495
Horjul
Rovte
Vrhnika
Škofljica
Ivančna Gorica
Gabrovka
Breg
Sevnica
Boštanj
Senovo
Godovič
Črni Vrh
Logatec
Rakitna
Grosuplje
Višnja Gora
Bič
Mirna
Tržišče
Krško
Raka
BREŽICE GRAD
Gradisca d'Isonzo
Vrtojba
Ajdovščina
Kalce
Turjak
Rašica
Muljava
Trebnje
Mokronog
Drnovo
Brežice
REDIPUGLIA
Branik
Vipava
Monfalcone
Štanjel
Dutovlje
Planina
Velike Lašče
Krka
Zdenska vas
Ponikve
Mirna Peč
Kostanjevica
D. Kronovo
Bregana
Sistiana
POSTOJNSKA JAMA
Rakek
Cerknica
Postojna
Žužemberk
Novo mesto
Otočec
SAMOSTAN PLETERJE
Duino
Monrupino
Sežana
Razdrto
Grahovo
Bloška Polica
Cerkniško jezero
Otok
Sodražica
Ribnica
Smuka
Dvor
Soteska
TRDINOV VRH 1178
ŽUMBERAČKA GORA
Golfo di Panzano
CASTELLO DI MIRAMARE
Opicina
Lipica
Senožeče
Pivka
Lož
Loški potok
Dolenja vas
Stara Cerkev
Jugorje
Sošice
TRIESTE
ŠKOCJANSKE JAME
Ribnica
Parje
Babno Polje
Grčarice
Kočevje
Črmošnjice
Kostanjevac
Jastrebarsko
Golfo di Trieste
Muggia
Kozina
Leskova dolina
Prezid
Gotenica
Livold
Vrčice
Metlika
Ankaran
Koper
Škofije
Bač
Prem
Knežak
Ilirska Bistrica
SNEŽNIK 1796
Kočevska Reka
Nemška Loka
Črnomelj
Jurovski Brod
Ozalj
Draganić
Piran
Izola
Obrov
Podgrad
Čabar
Portorož
Jagodje
Hrastovlje
Kanižarica
Lucija
Grašišče
Šmarje
Sečovlje
Sočerga
Gradin
Rakitovec
Starod
Pasjak
SLAVNIK 1028
Jelšane
Rupa
Sapjane
Gerovo
NAC. PARK RISNJAK
Morava
Banjaloka
Petrina
Brod na Kupi
Dragatuš
Vinica
Netretić
Karlovac
Umag

PRETUL
WARTENSTEIN
Aspang Markt
Weppersdorf
Horitschon
Markt St Martin
Nagycenk
Pетőháza
Fertőszentmiklós
Rábatamási
Merges
Árpás
Móricháza
THOMASBERG
1099 Alpl Pass
1372 Plaffen Sattel
Mönichkirchen
Bad Schönau
Kirchschlag
Oberpullendorf
Csapod
Mihályi
Szil
Gyarmat
Tét
Bakonypéterd
63
FESTENBURG
KRUMBACH
Ratten-Unterdorf
Friedberg
Steinberg
Lövő
Beled
Páli
Szany
Rába
Marcal
Lutzmannsburg
Vág
Gic
Bernstein
Lockenhaus
Répcelak
Takácsi
Vorau
Pinkafeld
Rattersdorf
Kőszeg
Simaság
Kenyeri
Csót
Papateszér
NATURPARK PÖLLAUER
Bad Tatzmannsdorf
Bük
Acsád
Pósfa
Kemenesmagasi
Uraiújfalu
Mezőlak
Újmajor
704 KÖRIS-HEGY
Pöllau
Hartberg
SCHLAINING
Rechnitz
Vönöck
Nagygyimót
Anger
NEUBERG
Oberwart
Vassurány
Vát
Nyárád
Pápa
Tapolcafő
Schachendorf
Gencsapáti
Celldömölk
Nemesszalók
Bakonybél
Unterbergen
Torony
Sárvár
Kup
Akli
Kaindorf
BURGENLAND
Grosspetersdorf
SZOMBATHELY
Gérce
Bakonyjákó
Farkasgyepű
HERBERSTEIN
Hirnsdorf
HÖBERMAYER-HOFEN
Kohfidisch
VAS
VESZPRÉM
TROST
FEISTRITZ
Stegersbach
Pornóapáti
Balogunyom
Káld
Bakonygyepes
Herend
Burgau
Ják
Hosszú-Pereszteg
Duka
Jánosháza
Városlőd
KALSDORF
St Michael
Rum
Devecser
Ajka
Úrkút
Gaas
Nagykölked
Rábahidvég
Kám
Ukk
Pusztamiske
VESZPRÉM
Güssing
Moschendorf
KESZTHELYI HEGYSÉG
BAKONY
KAB-HEGY 600
Fürstenfeld
Strem
Vasvár
Batyk
Nagyvázsony
Totvázsony
Studenzen
Riegersburg
Körmend
Sümeg
Rábafüzes
Csákánydoroszló
Hegyhátsál
Zalabér
H
Kapolcs
Mencshely
Heiligenkreuz
Gasztony
Aszófő
Feldbach
Teglaszin
Egervár
Zalaszentgrót
Jennersdorf
Kirchbach
Fehring
Doiber
Pókaszepetk
Balatonakali
Gnas
Kondorfa
Bagod
Zalaszántó
Tapolca
Zánka
Bad Gleichenberg
Martinje
Őriszentpéter
Zalaegerszeg
Révfülöp
Balatonföldvár
Trössing
Kuzma
Hodoš
Zalalövő
Kehidakustány
414 SZENT GYÖRGY-HEGY
Balatonszemes
Waltsberg
Šalovci
Badacsonytomaj
Sulzbach
Pertoča
Mačkovci
Bajánsenye
TV-TORONY
Hévíz
Balatonederics
Balatonlelle
Gosdorf
Cankova
Moščanci
Magyarszombatfa
Zalaksáni
Szigliget
Balatonboglár
Mureck
Bad Radkersburg
Martjanci
Szilvágy
Zalaapáti
Keszthely
Balatongyörök
Fonyód
Visz
Trate
Gornja Radgona
Krajna
Bak
Fenékpuszta
Balatonbereny
Karád
Pórszombat
Pacsa
VALCUM
Balatonkeresztúr
Pesnica pri Mariboru
Benedikt v Slov. gor.
Radenci
Murska Sobota
Zalabaksa
Dobrovnik
ZALA
Nova
Zalaszabar
Lengyeltóti
Lipovci
Rédics
Mumor
Vadépuszta
Vučja vas
Beltinci
Odranci
Lenti
Hahót
Holládi
Nikla
Veržej
Črenšovci
Dolga vas
Szentliszló
Garabonc
Sávoly
Jazvina-puszta
Sv. Jurij
Lendava
Kányavár
Zalaszentbalázs
Zalakaros
Somogyvár
Lenart v Slovenskih goricah
Cerkvenjak
Boreci
Razkrižje
Lovászi
Marcali
Maribor
Ljutomer
Sv. Martin
Pince
Zalakomár
Korpavár
Mesztegnyő
Osztopán
Mernye
Destrnik
Štrigova
Mursko Središće
Borsfa
Orehova vas
Rače
Dornava
Savci
Becsehely
Nagykanizsa
Tapsony
Szenyér
Somogyjad
Kaposfüred
Kidričevo
Ptuj
V.Nedelja
Ormož
Belica
Letenye
Vése
Böhönye
Juta
Moškanjci
Zavrč
Čakovec
Goričan
Inke
Nagybajom
Pragersko
Markovci
Središće ob Dravi
Hodošan
Iharosberény
SOMOGY
Kaposvár
Ptujska Gora
Dravinja
Podlehnik
Vratno
Nedelišće
Mala Subotica
Prelog
Dubrava
Murakeresztúr
Segesd
Varaždin
Somogyszob
Nagypuszta
Gruškovje
Žetale
Maruševec
Drava
Legrad
Trakošćan
Csurgó
Rogatec
Macelj
Ivanec
Ludbreg
Mike
Kadarkút
Đelekovec
Nagyatád
Lábod
Bősz
Lepoglava
1061 IVANŠĆICA
Novi Marof
Bednja
Varaždinske Toplice
Peteranec
Berzence
Krapina
Gola
Kivadár
Szentlászló
Bolde
VELIKI TABOR
Koprivnica
Reka
Ždala
Görgeteg
Lad
643 KALNIK
HR
Krapinske Toplice
Budiščina
Vukovec
Háromfa
Somogyapáti
Kumrovec
Zlatar Bistrica
Konjščina
Glogovac
Novigrad Podravski
Homokszentgyörgy
Leopovina
Csokonyavisonta
Zabok
Breznica
Rinya
Szigetvár
Marija Bistrica
Bedenica
Zrinski Topolovac
Hampovica
Virje
Đurđevac
Babócsa
Kisdobsza
Klanjec
Komin
Križevci
Kloštar Podravski
Somogytarnóca
Hobol
V. Trgovišće
Zelina
Sveti Ivan Žabno
Rovišće
Čurlovac
Barcs
Darány
MEDVEDNICA
Laz Stubički
BILOGORA
Pitomača
Stari Gradac
Terezino Polje
Drava Fok
252
1035
Zaprešić
Kašina
Sesvete
Vrbovec
Bjelovar
Sandrovac
Lakócsa
ZAGREB
Prikraj
Dubrava
MOSLAVAČKA GORA
Severin
Špišić Bukovica
Lukač
Virovitica
Sellye
Dugo Selo
Lupoglav
Narta
Bulinac
Topolovica
Kapinci
Stupnik
Botinec
Pleso Velika Gorica
Kloštar Ivanić
Ivanska
Vel. Grđevac
Suhopolje
Novi Senkovac
Klinča Sela
Rugvica
Ivanić Grad
Čazma
Berek
Grubišno Polje
Lončarica
Velika Dapčevica
Pivnica
Čađavica
Starjak
Ježevo
Veliki Zdenci
Miokovićevo
Slatina
Milanovac
Buševec
Oborovo
Križ
Popovac
Hercegovac
Donja-Vrijeska
N. Bukovica
Sikleuš
Gorica
Kravarsko
Podgarić
489
Končanica
Gornja-
Voćin
Čeralije
Jamnička
Pisarovina
Lekenik
Mahovo
Potok
Popovača
Garešnica
Daruvar
Novo Zvečevo
Slatinski Drenovac
Orahovica
Gradec
Prokupski
Pokupsko
Žažina
Stružec
Kupa
Sava
Ilova
Ujanik
Badljevina
Gaj
Sirač
Španovica
Kamanski Vučiak
953 PAPUK
PAPUK
Velika
Kutina
142

TATABÁNYA
Mezőörs
Ete
Ászár
Dad
Kisbér
Bokod
Környe
Oroszlány
Bakonypéterd
Bakonyszombathely
Bakonysárkány
Gic
Veszprémvarsány
Lázi
Csót
Pápateszér
Újmajor
Cseszneк
Szápár
Bakonycsernye
704 KÖRIS-HEGY
Dudar
Zirc
Olaszfalu
Bakonybél
Akli
Farkasgyepű
Eplény
Herend
Városlőd
Úrkút
VESZPRÉM
KAB-HEGY 600
Tótvázsony
Mencshely
Aszófő
Balatonakali
Zánka
Balatonfüred
Tihany
Siófok
Zamárdi
Balatonföldvár
Balatonszemes
Balatonlelle
Balaton
Balatonalmádi
Alsóörs
Csopak
Balatonfűzfő
Balatonkenese
Polgárdi
Litér
Berhida
Pétfürdő
Várpalota
SZÉKESFEHÉRVÁR
Csór
Moha
Pátka
Söréd
Mór
CSÓKAKŐI - VÁR
Csákvár
Lovasberény
Óbarok
Bicske
Biatorbágy
Falcsút
Tárnok
Zsámbék
Páty
Budakeszi
Budaörs
ROMTEMPLOM
Érd
Halásztelek
Szigetszentmiklós
Dunaharaszti
Taksony
Ócsa
Martonvásár
Százhalombatta
Velence
Gárdony
Borgond
Puszta-Szabolcs
Seregélyes
Aba
Szabadegyháza
Perkáta
Sárkeresztúr
Soponya
Káloz
Lepsény
Enying
Kisláng
Mezőfalva
Sárbogárd
Dég
Tóház
Újtelep
Lajoskomárom
Ságvár
Mezőszilas
Fancs
Alap
Előszállás
Simontornya
Cece
Ozora
Magyarkeszi
Pusztaszemes
Visz
Tab
Karád
Iregszemcse
Lengyeltóti
Vadépuszta
Andocs
Tamási
Pincehely
Nagykónyi
Sárszentlőrinc
Jazvina-puszta
Somogyacsa
Gyönk
Szakcs
Igal
Lápafő
Kocsola
Szakály
Kölesd
Osztopán
Mernye
Raksi
Felsőleperd
Gyulaj
Hőgyész
Medina
Murga
Kaposfüred
Juta
Kurd
Döbrököz
Tevel
Zomba
Nagybajom
Kaposvár
Baté
Dombóvár
Bonyhád
Nagypuszta
Gödre
Sásd
Szászvár
Hidas
Kárász
Kadarkút
Bőszénfa
Oroszló
Komló
MECSEK
Szentlászló
Boldogasszonyfa
Hetvehely
Mánfa
Pécsvárad
Lad
Somogyapáti
Bükkösd
PÉCS
Erzsébet
Szigetvár
Szentlőrinc
Pellérd
Lánycsók
Hobol
Királyegyháza
Baksa
Szederkény
Bóly
Szalánta
Újpetre
Darány
Lakócsa
Drava Fok
Magyarmecske
Túrony
Villány
Páprád
Siklós
Sellye
Vajszló
Harkány
Magyarboly
Kapinci
Kémes
Moslavina
Drávaszabolcs
Novi Senkovac
Donji Miholjac
Čađavica
Slatina
Milanovac
Karašica
HR
N. Bukovica
Mikleuš
Čačinci
Voćin
Čeralije
Zdenci
Slatinski Drenovac
Orahovica
953 PAPUK
Feričanci
Našice
Koška
Budimci
Martinci Čepinski
Čepin
Osijek
Tenja
Bijelo Brdo
Dalj
Erdut
Ernestinovo
Bizovac
Klokočevci
Beničanci
Valpovo
Belišće
Petlovac
Črnkovci
Drava
Darda
Bilje
Josipovac
Jagodnjak
Lug
KOPAČKI RIT
Kozarac
Kneževi Vinogradi
Beli Manastir
Kneževo
Zmajevac
Batina
Udvar
Mohács
Nagybaracska
Dunaszekcső
Bátmonostor
Bátaszék
Baja
Vaskút
Bácsbokod
Bácsborsód
Gara
Katymár
Hercegszántó
Bački Breg
Kolut
Bezdan
Gakovo
Sombor
Сомбор
Kljajićevo
Prigrevica
Apatin
Svilojevo
Stapar
Sonta
Srpski Miletić
Bogojevo
Karavukovo
Odžaci
Оџаци
Ridjica
Stanišić
Aleksa Šantić
Svetozar Miletić
Čonoplja
Bajmok
Subotica
Суботица
Mala Bosna
Kelebija
Bikovo
Mišićevo
Žednik
Stara Moravica
Bački Sokolac
Bačka Topola
Bajša
Njegoš.
Sivac
Mali Iđoš
Lipar
Feketić
Crvenka
Kruščić
Kula
Vrbas
Ruski Krstur
Despotovo
Savino Selo
Ravno Selo
Veliki Kanal
Tompa
Tataháza
Bácsalmás
Mélykút
Felsőszentiván
Csávoly
Sükösd
Jánoshalma
Nemesnádudvar
Kisszállás
Pusztamérges
Kunfehértó
Zsana
Gárgyán
Kiskunhalas
Császártöltés
Imrehegy
Kecel
Hajós
Dusnok
Fadd
Tolna
Szedres
Szekszárd
Várdomb
Kalocsa
Bátya
Szakmár
Kiskunmajsa
Pirtó
Tázlár
Szank
Soltvadkert
Jászszentlászló
Bócsa
Kiskőrös
Dunapataj
Dunaszentbenedek
Paks
Nagydorog
Dumaköllöd
Németkér
Harta
Akasztó
Páhi
Fischerbócsa
Bugac
Kiskunfélegyháza
Jakabszállás
Orgovány
Izsák
Fülöpszállás
Solt
Dunatetétlen
Dunaföldvár
Dunavecse
Szalkszentmárton
Dunaújváros
Rácalmás
Kunszentmiklós
Kunadacs
Lajosmizse
Kerekegyháza
Szabadszállás
Ágasegyháza
KECSKE
Nagy
Hantháza
Kunpeszér
Tatárszentgyörgy
Örkény
Szittyóúrbő
Apaj
Dömsöd
Adony
Lórév
Bankháza
Kiskunlacháza
Ráckeve
Ercsi
Delegyháza
Bugyi
Sári
Dabas
Újhartyán
Albertirsa
Dánszentmiklós
Cegléd
Pilis
Monor
Káva
Tápiószele
Tápiószőlő
Úllő
Gyömrő
Ferihegyi repülőtér
Sülysap
Tápiószentmárton
Tápiószecső
Nagykáta
Isaszeg
Gödöllő
GÖDÖLLŐI-DOMBSÁG
Jászfényszaru
Jászberény
BUDAPEST
FEJÉR
PEST
VESZPRÉM
TOLNA
BARANYA
BÁCS-KISKUN
SOMOGY
PANNONHALMA
H
216
142
75
64
2008
2009
NEMZETI PARK
KISKUNSÁGI
Duna
Sárviz
Sió
Kapos
Dunav
M1
M0
M5
M6
M7
M9
E60
E66
E71
E73
E75
E662
A22

Jászapáti
Jászkőhalma
Jásztelek
Jászkisér
Tarnaszentmiklós
Kisköre
Pély
Tiszaszőlős
Tiszaörs
Abádszalók
Nagyiván
NEMZETI
PARK
65
Tiszabura
Tiszaroff
Tiszasüly
Kunmadaras
Karcag
Kunhegyes
Jászladány
Kőtelek
Bánhalma
Újszász
JÁSZ-NAGYKUN
Besenyszög
Fegyvernek
Kenderes
Dobapuszta
SZOLNOK
Kisújszállás
Abony
Szolnok
Törökszentmiklós
Kuncsorba
Túrkeve
Szandaszőlős
Kengyel
Tószeg
Rákóczifalva
Jászkarajenő
Tiszajenő
Martfű
Mezőhék
Mezőtúr
Kocsér
Tiszaföldvár
Cibakháza
Tiszakécske
Öcsöd
Endrőd
Gyomaendrőd
SZARVASI ARBORETUM
Lakitelek
Békésszentandrás
Szarvas
Örménykút
Csárdaszállás
Cserkeszőlő
Kunszentmárton
Csabacsüd
Kardos
Mezőberény
Murony
Csépa
Kondoros
Bokros
Csereköböny
Kajánújfalu
Kétsoproni
Csongrád
Fábiánsebestyén
Nagyszénás
Gátér
Felgyő
Szentes
Gádoros
Csorvás
BÉKÉS
Békéscsaba
Csanytelek
Szegvár
Nagymágocs
Újkígyós
Kétegyháza
Lapistó
Orosháza
Csanádapáca
Baks
Mindszent
Székkutas
Vilmajor
Medgyesháza
Ópusztaszer
Kardoskút
Magyarbánhegyes
Kistelek
CSONGRÁD
Mártély
Kaszaper
Lőkösháza
Tótkomlós
Kunágota
Dóc
Balástya
Hódmezővásárhely
Nagyér
Mezőkovácsháza
Sándorfalva
Dombegyház
Földeák
Makó-Rákos
Pitvaros
Mezőhegyes
Battonya
Algyő
Maroslele
Kiskundorozsma
SZEGED
Csanádpalota
Mako
Nagylak
Nădlac
Pecica
Röszke
Deszk
Kiszombor
Apátfalva
Horgoš
Djala
Cheglevici
Cenad
Sânnicolau Mare
Beba Veche
Banatsko Aranđelovo
Dudeştii Vechi
Periam
Kanjiža
Novi Kneževac
Velebit
Vălcani
Pesac
Variaş
Teremia Mare
Lovrin
Sanad
Crna Bara
Čoka
Comloşu Mare
Mokrin
Senta
Grabaţ
Nakovo
Tornjoš
Idjoš
Kikinda
Кикинда
Jimbolia
Utrine
Ada
Padej
SRB
Mol
Novi Kozarci
Novo Miloševo
Srpska Crnja
Cenei
Milesevo
Bačko Petrovo Selo
Ban. Topola
Nova Crnja
Hetin
Ulivar
Bečej
Бечеј
Novi Bečej
Bašaid
Banatsko Karadjordjevo
Srp. Itebej
Otelec
Kumane
Srbobran
Bačko Gradište
Melenci
Žitište
Jaša Tomić
Čurug
Zrenjanin
Krajišnik
Širig
Stari Begej
Begejski Kanal
Foeni
Cruceni
Giera
Giulvăz
Peciu Nou
Can. Bega
Şag
Jebel
Liebling
Tormac
Voiteg
Gătaia
Berini
Vermeş
Fârliug
Berzovia
Ezeriş
Măureni
Bocşa
Bocşa Vasiovei
Deta
Bârzava
DEBRECEN
Nagyhegyes
Ebes
Újléta
Hajdúszoboszló
Bánk
Almaer
BIHAR
Sáránd
Nádudvar
Hosszúpályi
Hajdúszovát
Létavértes
Sácueni
Kaba
Derecske
Püspökladány
Pocsaj
Báránd
Földes
Hencida
Roşiori
Barcău
Sărretudvari
Berettyóújfalu
Berettyó
Nagykereki
Sălard
Bucsa
Biharnagybajom
Nagyrábé
Berettyószentmárton
Bakonszeg
Biharia
Ecsegfalva
Kertészsziget
Darvas
Furta
Mezősas
Biharkeresztes
Ártánd
Borş
Tileagd
Füzesgyarmat
ORADEA
Oşorhei
Berek
Faluszigeti
Komádi
Livada de Bihor
Sânmartin
Băile Felix
Dévaványa
Szeghalom
Csökmő
Leş
Újiráz
Körösladány
Zsadány
Sebes-Körös
Vésztő
Okány
Nagygyanté
Ceica
Miersig
Köröstarcsa
Musasău de Tinca
Tarhos
Salonta
Tulca
Sarkadkeresztúr
Tinca
Békés
Sarkad
Belfir
Doboz
Ciumeghiu
Batăr
Városerdő
Gyula
Berechiu
Zerind
Mişca
Craiova
Vărşand
Şepreuş
Pilu
Cermei
Elek
Socodor
Chişineu Criş
Beliu
Sintea Mare
Nădab
Cintei
Ineu
Şimand
Bocsig
Zărand
Seleuş
ARAD
Curtici
Şilindia
Sântana
Buteni
Târnova
Zimandu Nou
Mâsca
Şiria
Nadăş
HOGHIS
Horia
Covăsinţ
Arad
Vladimirescu
Păuliş
Radna
Bârzava
Felnac
Lipova
Vinga
Zăbrani
Ususău
Şagu
Şiştarovăţ
Zăbalt
Vinga
Fibiş
Bogda
Cuveşdia
Orţişoara
Gelu
Satchinez
Pişchia
RO
Brestovăţ
Bethausen
Biled
Giarmata
Lucareţ
Balinţ
Becicherecu Mic
Timişoara
Recaş
Topolovăţu Mare
Cărpiniş
Belinţ
Remetea Mare
Săcălaz
TIMIŞOARA
TIMIŞ
Lugoj
Hitiaş
Buziaş
Mureş
Timiş
Beregsău
Bega
Hortobágy-Berettyó
Tisza
Körös
Zagyva
Fehér-tó
M5
E75
E60
E573
E79
E671
E68
E70
E
F
G
H
2009
143
204
1
2
3
4
5
6

RÍAS
Punta Candelaria
Cedeira
SAN ANDRÉS
Cabo Prior
Valdoviño
Ferrol
Cabo Prioriño
Xubia
CASTILLO DE MOECHE
San Sadurniño
Murgados
Neda
Fene
CAST. DE NARAIO
Illas Sisargas
Cabo San Adrián
Malpica de Bergantiños
Punta del Roncudo
A CORUÑA/
LA CORUÑA
Ría de Betanzos
Ares
Cabanas
MONASTERIO DE CAAVEIRO
Pontedeume
Miño
CAST. DE ANDRADE
Laxe
Ponteceso
Cabo Vilán
Camariñas
CASTRO DE BORNEIRO
Arteixo
Oleiros
Sada
Bergondo
Muxía
CEREIXO
DOLMEN DE DOMBATE
Baio
San Roque
Carballo
Laracha
Cambre
Guisamo
Betanzos
As Pontes de García Rodríguez
Puentes de García Rodríguez
Cabo Touriñán
Vimianzo
Zás
Silva
Carral
Monfero
Embalse de Eume
Coirós
Irixoa
Pedreira
Cerceda
Fisterra/
Finisterre
Cee
Corcubión
Ézaro
Brandomil
Mesón do Vento
Cabo Fisterra
Ponte Oliveras
Santa Comba
Bembirre
Ordes
Curtis
Lourdes
Trazo
Lanzá
Guitiriz
Pino do Val
A Baña
Carnota
Embalse Barrié de la Maza
Outes
Negreira
Portomouro
Oroso
Ru
Teixeiro
Baamonde
STA. MARIA DE MEZONZO
SOBRADO DOS MONXES
Sobrado
Begonte
Muros
Ría de Muros
Santiago de Compostela
Sigüeiro
Labacolla
Pastor
Rabade
Punta Carreiros
Noia/
Noya
STA. MARIA DE CONXO
Santiago
O Pino
Arzúa
Friol
Porto do Son
CASTRO DE BAROÑA
Padrón
Teo
Ramallosa
Fontedias
Toques
Lugo
El Picato
660
Pobra do Caramiñal/
Puebla del Caramiñal
Boiro
Enfesta/
Pontecesures
Ponte Ulla
Melide
Oleiros
Rianxo
Catoira
Embalse de Portodemouros
Palas de Rei
Cabo Corrubedo
Vilagarcía de Arousa
PAZO DE OCA
A Estrada
Cruces
Santa Uxía de Ribeira
Illa de Arousa
Cuntis
Guntín
Punta de Couso
Vilanova de Arousa
Caldas de Reis
Silleda
Agolada
Monterroso
GALICIA
Ría de Arousa
Illa de Sálvora
O Grove
Cambados
A Lagoa /
Campo Lameiro
Antas de Ulla
Narón
Portomarín
A Toxa
Lalín
Taboada
PARQUE NACIONAL
Forcarei
Rodeiro
Paradela
O Convento
Poio
Soutelo
Dozón /
Castro
Illa de Ons
DAS ILLAS
Sanxenxo
Combarro
Cerdedo
1012
Pontevedra
Alto de Santo Domingo
725
SIERRA DO FARO
Embalse de Belesar
Chantada
MONASTERIO DE RIBAS DO MIÑO
Escairón
RÍAS BAIXAS
Ría de Pontevedra
Marín
Ponte-Caldelas
Beariz
STA. MARIA DA REAL
La Barrela
ATLÁNTICAS
Hío
Moaña
CAST. DE SOUTOMAIOR
SIERRA DO SUIDO
Piñor
Cea
Illas Cíes
Cangas
Avión
O Carballiño
Maside
Embalse dos Peares
Pantón
VIGO
Redondela
Berducido
MONASTERIO DE SAN CLODIO
Ría de Vigo
Leiro
Punxin
Cambeo
Monforte de Lemos
Mondariz-Balneario
Os Peares
Panxón
Nigrán
Areas
Mondariz
Sober
Cabo Silleiro
Baiona
Ramallosa
Ponteareas
Porriño
Ribadavia
OURENSE/
ORENSE
Parada del Sil
Embalse de San Esteban
SANTO ESTEVO
Arrabal/
Oia
Vilameán
A Cañiza
Cartelle
MONASTERIO DE SANTO ESTEVO
Castro Caldelas
Puerto de A
Cortegada
Esgos
Valença do Minho
Tui
Salvaterra de Miño
Ramirás
A Merca
Maceda
890
A Guarda/
La Guardia
Monção
Melgaço
São Gregório
Padrenda
Xunqueira de Espadanedo
950
Puerto de Alto do Rodicio
Paredes
A Pobra de Trives
MTE. DE STA. TEGRA
Vila Nova de Cerveira
Celanova
Allariz
Xunqueira de Ambía
Embalse de Chandrexa
Caminha
Lanhelas
Extremo
1778
MANZANEDA
Moledo
Paredes de Coura
Portela
Verea
Sandias
Vila Praia de Âncora
SERRA DA PENEDA
1416
Vilar de Barrio
SERRA DE QU
Afife
VIANA DO CASTELO
Arcos de Valdevez
Bande
Entrimo
Xinzo de Limia/
Ginzo de Limia
Villariño de Conso
STA. LUZIA
Soajo
Muiños
Trasmiras
Laza
Viana do Castelo
Ponte de Lima
Lindoso
Lobios
Puerto Estivadas
849
Campobecerros
Darque
Deão
Ponte da Barca
PARQUE NACIONAL DA PENEDA-GERÊS
Cualedro
Portela do Home
Baltar
A Gudiña
Castelo do Neiva
Balugães
Randín
SERRA DO GERÊS
Verín
Covide
Barragem de Paradela
Montalegre
Ríos
Esposende
Feitos
N. S. D'ABADIA
Vila Verde
Caldelas
Gerês
Paradela
Barragem de Venda Nova
Cavado
Gralhos
Oímbra
Vilardevós
Barcelos
TIBÃES
BOM JESUS DO MONTE
Amares
Louredo
Barragem do Alto Rabagão
N. SENHORA DA AZINHEIRA
Vila Verde da Raia
Estela
Braga
Venda Nova
80

E
F
G
H
1
2
3
4
5
6
ALTA
COSTA VERDE
ASTURIAS
E
Cabo Ortegal
Punta da Estaca de Bares
Cariño
Cabo de Bares
Vicedo
Ortigueira
Portocelo
Xove
Mañón
Viveiro
Cervo
Cabo Burela
Ourol
Burela
Embalse de la Ribeira
Cangas
720
La Gañadoira
Ferreira
Muras
Foz
XISTRAL 1036
Alfoz
San Cosme/ Barreiros
SIERRA DE LA CARBA
Cabo Cebes
Tapia de Casariego
Cabreiros
Mondoñedo
Ribadeo
La Caridad
Castropol
Abadín
Lourenzá
N634 E70
590 Puerto de la Xesta
Trabada
Vegadeo
Jarrio
Navia
POBLADO CELTICO
Coaña
Luarca
Cabo Busto
Cadavedo
Cabo Vidio
Cabo de Peñas
Villalba Alta
A Pontenova
Taramundi
Boal
Canero
Cudillero
El Pito
Salinas
Lluanco/Luanco
Rábade
Cospeito
Pastoriza
Castrillón
Brieves
Soto del Barco
Avilés
Candás
Castro de Rei
575 Marco de Alvare
Embalse de Doiras
Illano
MINAS DE ORO (ROMANAS)
MONASTERIO DEL CRISTO
Pravia
GIJÓN XIXÓN
Meira
Santa Eulalia de Oscos
La Espina
CUEVA DE CANDAMO
Nubledo
Pesoz
Grandas de Salime
Tineo
Salas
Cornellana
Candamo
Pol
Texeiro
SIERRA DE RAÑADOIRO
Berducedo
Pola de Allande
Soto de los Infantes
Grado
Posada
A Fonsagrada
La Florida
S.M. DE NARANCO
Lugones
Castroverde
960 Alto de Cerrado
OVIEDO
El Berrón
Pola de Siero
Baleira
Cangas del Narcea
Belmonte
Trubia
CORDILLERA
Embalse de Grandas de Salime
Aguasmestas
Santa Eulalia
Llangréu/ Langreo
Cecos
S. PEDRO DE TEVERGA
Caranga
Puerto Campo de Arbol 794
A Pobra de Navia
Venta Nueva
Mieres
Sotrondio/ San Martín del Rey Aurelio
Baralla
BOSQUE DE MUNIELLOS
Valladas
HERMO
Pola de Somiedo
La Plaza/ Teverga
Riosa
Pola de Lena
MONASTERIO DE SAMOS
Becerreá
PARQUE NAT. DE SOMIEDO
La Pola (Lena)
Triacastela
As Nogais
1989 MIRAVALLES
Puerto Leitariegos 1525
1486 Puerto Somiedo
1587 Puerto de Ventana
STA. CRISTINA DE LENA
Cabañaquinta
Samos
SIERRA DE ANCARES
Degaña
Campomanes
Pino
Pereda de Ancares
Villablino
Piedrafita de Babia
Felecho
O Incio
1109 Puerto Pedrafita do Cebreiro
Palacios del Sil
PARQUE NAT. DEL VALLE DE S. EMILIANO
1270 Puerto de Piedrafita de Babia
San Emiliano
Puerto de Pajares 1379
Cebreiro
A Pobra de Brollón/ Puebla del Brollón
Balboa
Vega de Espinareda
Fabero
Páramo del Sil
Sena de Luna
Murias de Paredes
Villamanín/ de la Tercia
Cármenes
Puerto San Isidro
Vega de Valcarce
SIERRA DE GISTREO
1616 Seara
Folgoso
Barjas
Trabadelo
Toreno
Embalse de Barrios de Luna
2111
Fasgar
Mirantes
Valporquero de Torío
SIERRA DO COUREL
Villafranca del Bierzo
Noceda
Igüeña
Riello
La Pola de Gordón
Vegacervera
Quiroga
Cacabelos
Embalse de Bárcena
Robles de la Valcueva
Ribas de Sil
Toral de los Vados
Embalse del Omañas
Magdalena
La Robla
Camponaraya
Bembibre
Embalse de Villameca
Embalse de Selga-Ordás
La Vecilla
San Miguel de las Dueñas
Rioseco de Tapia
A Rúa
Priaranza del Bierzo
Ponferrada
Torre del Bierzo
Quintana del Castillo
Cuadros
O Barco de Valdeorras
LAS MÉDULAS
Riego de Ambrós
Garrafe de Torío
Puente de Domingo Flórez
Ríofrio
Manzaneda
Cardelleda de Valdeorras
1230 Puerto del Manzanal
MONTES DE LEÓN
S. Andrés del Rabanedo
O Bolo
Embalse de Prada
Rodrigatos de la Obispalia
Carrizo
Villaquilambre
Vegas del Condado
1052 Alto de Covelo
Santa Colomba de Somoza
La Virgen del Camino
Astorga
Benavites
Villadangos del Páramo
León
A Veiga
Pobladura de la Sierra
Hospital de Orbigo
Onzonilla
Gradefes
PEÑA TREVINCA 2142
Viana do Bolo
La Baña
SIERRA DE LA CABRERA
Porto
Encinedo
Truchas
Destriana
Santa María del Páramo
Mansilla de las Mulas
S. MIGUEL DE ESCALADA
Portilla de la Canda 1262
Ribadelago
Lago de Sanabria
Morla
La Bañeza
Santas Martas
Mezquita
Puebla de Sanabria
Cebrones del Rio
Castromil
1360 Portilla del Padornelo
Castrocontrigo
Villamañán
81
Palacios de Sanabria
Donado
Ayoó de Vidriales
Castrocalbón
82
Matallana de Torío
Bercinos del Real Camino
Landedo
Calabor
La Antigua
Valencia de Don Juan
Gordaliza del Pino
Sahagún
NATURAL
N634
N640
N632
N120
NVI
A6
A8
AP66
AP71
E70
AS12
AS217
AS216
AS225
AS227
AS213
AS28
LU540
LU541
LU546
LU636
LU633
LU634
CL623
CL626
CL631
CL621
CL622
N536
N630
N621
N601
N625
A231
C622
N525
LE133
A52
OU533

Illas Cíes
Cangas
Moaña
CAST. DE SOUTOMAIOR
VIGO
Ría de Vigo
Redondela
Berducido
Avión
O Carballiño
Leiro
Mondariz-Balneario
Mondariz
Panxón
Nigrán
Cabo Silleiro
Baiona
Ramallosa
O Porriño
Areas
Ponteareas
Ribadavia
A Cañiza
Cortegada
Arrabal/Oia
Vilameán
Salvaterra de Miño
Valença do Minho
Tui
Monção
Melgaço
São Gregório
Padrenda
Ramirás
Celanova
A Guarda/La Guardia
MTE. DE STA. TEGRA
Caminha
Vila Nova de Cerveira
Lanhelas
Moledo
Vila Praia de Âncora
Afife
Paredes de Coura
Portela
Extremo
SERRA DA PENEDA
Arcos de Valdevez
Soajo
Entrimo
Bande
Lobios
Muiños
VIANA DO CASTELO
STA. LUZIA
Viana do Castelo
Darque
Ponte de Lima
Ponte da Barca
Lindoso
Portela do Home
PARQUE NACIONAL DA PENEDA-GERÊS
SERRA DO GERÊS
Deão
Balugães
Castelo do Neiva
Covide
Barragem de Paradela
Paradela
Feitos
Esposende
Vila Verde
Caldelas
N. S. D'ABADIA
Gerês
Barragem de Venda Nova
Ofir
Barcelos
TIBÃES
BOM JESUS DO MONTE
Braga
Caniçada
Louredo
Barragem do Alto Rabagão
Estela
Venda Nova
BRAGA
Póvoa de Lanhoso
Póvoa de Varzim
Rio Mau
Vila do Conde
BAGUNTE
Vila Nova de Famalicão
Guimarães
SERRA DO BARROSO
Arco de Baúlhe
Fafe
Lavra
Nespereira
Ribeira de Pena
Porto
Perafita
Moreira
Santo Tirso
Paços de Ferreira
Felgueiras
Celorico de Basto
Mondim de Basto
N. SENHORA DA GRAÇA
Matosinhos
Maia
Alfena
Caldas de Vizela
Lixa
PORTO
Ermesinde
Valongo
Lousada
Paredes
Amarante
Vila Nova de Gaia
Gondomar
Penafiel
Francelos
Aguda
Granja
Vila Real
PANOIAS
Entre Ambos-os-Rios
Espinho
Lourosa
Baião
Sabrosa
Esmoriz
Cinfães
Mesão Frio
Penaguião
Castelo de Paiva
Resende
Peso da Régua
Pinhão
SANTA MARIA MAYOR
SERRA DO MARÃO
Santa Maria da Feira
Lamego
SÃO PEDRO DE BALSEMÃO
Furadouro
São João da Madeira
N. SENHORA DOS REMÉDIOS
Ovar
Oliveira de Azeméis
Arouca
Rossas
Tabuaço
Válega
Bestida
Vale de Cambra
NOSSA SENHORA DE TAUDE
SERRA DA GRALHEIRA
Tarouca
Torreira
Estarreja
DUNAS DE SÃO JACINTO
Murtosa
Castro Daire
São Jacinto
Praia da Barra
Costa Nova do Prado
Angeja
Albergaria-a-Velha
Sever
São João da Serra
Moimenta da Beira
Barragem de Vilar
Aveiro
Ílhavo
Vagos
Lamas do Vouga
Trofa
Oliveira de Frades
São Pedro do Sul
VISEU
Vila Nova de Paiva
AVEIRO
Vouzela
Lordosa
Sátão
Praia de Mira
Águeda
Oiã
Alcofra
Aguiar da Beira
Mira
Mamarrosa
Oliveira do Bairro
Bolfiar
SERRA DO CARAMULO
Caramulo
Viseu
Penalva do Castelo
Boialvo
Anadia
Praia da Tocha
Curia
Mealhada
Mangualde
Fornos de Algodres
Cantanhede
Tocha
Luso
Tondela
Canas de Senhorim
Nelas
Celorico da Beira
Murtinheira
Arazede
Buçaco
Mortágua
Santa Comba Dão
Rojão Grande
Carregal do Sal
Rio Torto
Cabo Mondego
SÃO MARCOS
Seixo
Figueira da Foz
Tábua
Oliveira do Hospital
Gouveia
PARQUE NATURAL DA SERRA DA ESTRELA
Montemor-o-Velho
Penacova
Gândara
Seia
Leirosa
Lavos
COIMBRA
Condeixa
São Martinho
SÃO PEDRO
Vendas de
Manteigas
Guarda
COSTA VERDE
86
87

78
79
82
88
E
F
G
H
OURENSE/ ORENSE
Monforte de Lemos
Quiroga
A Rúa
O Barco de Valdeorras
Ponferrada
Bembibre
Astorga
La Bañeza
Benavente
Puebla de Sanabria
Verín
Chaves
Vila Verde da Raia
Bragança
Mirandela
Macedo de Cavaleiros
Vimioso
Miranda do Douro
Mogadouro
Alcañices
Fonfría
Zamora
Torre de Moncorvo
Vila Nova de Foz Côa
Freixo de Espada à Cinta
Figueira de Castelo Rodrigo
Pinhel
Lumbrales
Vitigudino
Ledesma
SALAMANCA
Santa Marta de Tormes
Vilar Formoso
Fuentes de Oñoro
Almeida
Xinzo de Limia/ Ginzo de Limia
Allariz
A Gudiña
Viana do Bolo
Manzaneda
Ribas de Sil
Villafranca del Bierzo
Cacabelos
Toreno
Vega de Espinareda
Santa Colomba de Somoza
Rionegro del Puente
Camarzana de Tera
Tábara
Gallegos del Río
Muelas del Pan
Bermillo de Sayago
Fermoselle
Aldeadávila de la Ribera
Vinhais
Valpaços
Murça
Alijó
Carrazeda de Ansiães
Vila Flor
Alfândega da Fé
MONTES DE LEÓN
SIERRA DE LA CABRERA
SIERRA DE LA CULEBRA
SERRA DE QUEIXA
SIERRA DO COUREL
SERRA DA NOGUEIRA
SERRA DE BORNES
MONTES
PARQUE NATURAL DE MONTEZINHO
PARQUE NATURAL ARRIBES DEL DUERO Y ÁGUEDA
Lago de Sanabria
Embalse de Cernadilla
Embalse de Ricobayo
Embalse de Almendra
Embalse de Saucelle
Embalse de Aldeadavila
Barragem do Picote
PEÑA TREVINCA 2142
MANZANEDA 1778
LAS MÉDULAS
MONASTERIO DE SANTO ESTEVO
MONASTERIO DE MORERUELA
SAN PEDRO DE LA NAVE
RUINAS CASTROTORAFE
CASTELO RODRIGO
PARQUE ARQUEOLÓGICO DO VALE DO CÔA
CASTILLO BUEN AMOR
BRAGANÇA
VILA REAL
GUARDA
E
C
A52
N525
N120
N122
N630
E82
E80
IP4
A6
A62
A25

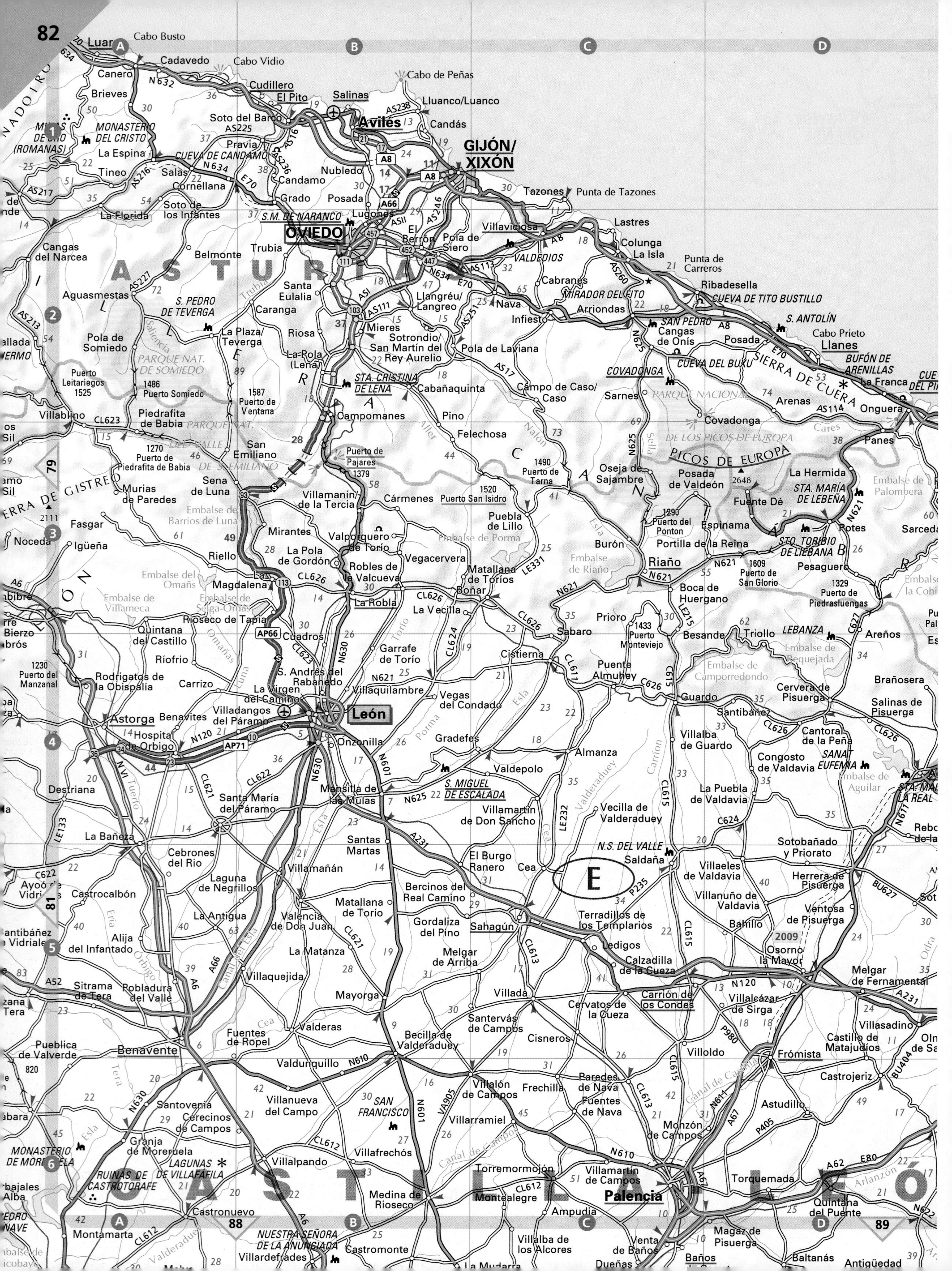
A
B
C
D
1
2
3
4
5
6
Luarca
Cabo Busto
Cadavedo
Cabo Vidio
Canero
Cudillero
El Pito
Brieves
Salinas
Cabo de Peñas
Lluanco/Luanco
Soto del Barco
Avilés
Candás
MINAS DE ORO (ROMANAS)
MONASTERIO DEL CRISTO
Pravia
GIJÓN/ XIXÓN
La Espina
CUEVA DE CANDAMO
Tineo
Salas
Nubledo
Candamo
Cornellana
Grado
Posada
Tazones
Punta de Tazones
Soto de los Infantes
La Florida
S.M. DE NARANCO
Lugones
OVIEDO
El Berrón
Pola de Siero
Villaviciosa
Lastres
Colunga
La Isla
Cangas del Narcea
Belmonte
Trubia
VALDEDIOS
Punta de Carreros
ASTURIAS
Santa Eulalia
Cabranes
Ribadesella
Aguasmestas
Caranga
S. PEDRO DE TEVERGA
Llangréu/ Langreo
Nava
MIRADOR DEL FITO
CUEVA DE TITO BUSTILLO
Infiesto
Arriondas
S. ANTOLÍN
SAN PEDRO
Cangas de Onís
Cabo Prieto
Pola de Somiedo
La Plaza/ Teverga
Riosa
Mieres
Sotrondio/ San Martín del Rey Aurelio
Pola de Laviana
Posada
Llanes
BUFÓN DE ARENILLAS
PARQUE NAT. DE SOMIEDO
La Pola (Lena)
CUEVA DEL BUXU
SIERRA DE CUERA
COVADONGA
La Franca
Puerto Leitariegos 1525
1486 Puerto Somiedo
1587 Puerto de Ventana
STA. CRISTINA DE LENA
Cabañaquinta
Campo de Caso/ Caso
Sarnes
PARQUE NACIONAL
Arenas
Onguera
Villablino
Piedrafita de Babia
PARQUE NAT. DEL VALLE DE S. EMILIANO
Campomanes
Pino
Covadonga
Felechosa
DE LOS PICOS DE EUROPA
Panes
San Emiliano
Puerto de Pajares 1379
PICOS DE EUROPA
1270 Puerto de Piedrafita de Babia
1490 Puerto de Tarna
Oseja de Sajambre
Posada de Valdeón
2648
La Hermida
Embalse de Palombera
Sena de Luna
Murias de Paredes
Villamanín/ de la Tercia
Cármenes
1520 Puerto San Isidro
STA. MARÍA DE LEBEÑA
Fuente Dé
SIERRA DE GISTREDO
2111
Embalse de Barrios de Luna
Puebla de Lillo
1290 Puerto del Pontón
Potes
Sarceda
Fasgar
Mirantes
Valporquero de Torío
Embalse de Porma
Espinama
Noceda
Igüeña
Riello
La Pola de Gordón
Burón
Portilla de la Reina
STO. TORIBIO DE LIÉBANA
Vegacervera
Embalse de Riaño
Riaño
Embalse del Omañas
Magdalena
Robles de la Valcueva
Matallana de Torío
1609 Puerto de San Glorio
Pesaguero
Embalse de Villameca
Embalse de Selga-Ordás
Boñar
Boca de Huergano
1329 Puerto de Piedrasluengas
La Robla
La Vecilla
Quintana del Castillo
Rioseco de Tapia
Cuadros
Prioro
1433 Puerto Monteviejo
Triollo
LEBANZA
Areños
Sabaro
Besande
Embalse de Requejada
Ríofrio
Garrafe de Torío
Cistierna
Puente Almuhey
Embalse de Camporredondo
1230 Puerto del Manzanal
Rodrigatos de la Obispalía
Carrizo
S. Andrés del Rabanedo
Villaquilambre
Cervera de Pisuerga
Brañosera
La Virgen del Camino
Vegas del Condado
Guardo
Salinas de Pisuerga
Astorga
Benavites
Villadangos del Páramo
León
Santibáñez
Villalba de Guardo
Cantoral de la Peña
Hospital de Orbigo
Onzonilla
Gradefes
Almanza
Congosto de Valdavia
SANTA EUFEMIA
Embalse de Aguilar
Valdepolo
Destriana
Mansilla de las Mulas
S. MIGUEL DE ESCALADA
Vecilla de Valderaduey
La Puebla de Valdavia
STA. MARÍA LA REAL
Santa María del Páramo
Villamartín de Don Sancho
La Bañeza
Santas Martas
Sotobañado y Priorato
Cebrones del Rio
N.S. DEL VALLE
El Burgo Ranero
Cea
Saldaña
Villaeles de Valdavia
Herrera de Pisuerga
Ayoó de Vidriales
Villamañán
Laguna de Negrillos
E
Castrocalbón
Bercinos del Real Camino
Villanuño de Valdavia
Matallana de Torío
Terradillos de los Templarios
Ventosa de Pisuerga
La Antigua
Valencia de Don Juan
Gordaliza del Pino
Sahagún
Bahillo
Alija del Infantado
2009
Osorno la Mayor
Santibáñez de Vidriales
Ledigos
La Matanza
Melgar de Arriba
Calzadilla de la Cueza
Melgar de Fernamental
Sitrama de Tera
Pobladura del Valle
Villaquejida
Mayorga
Villada
Carrión de los Condes
Villalcázar de Sirga
Cervatos de la Cueza
Santervás de Campos
Villasadino
Benavente
Fuentes de Ropel
Valderas
Becilla de Valderaduey
Cisneros
Castillo de Matajudíos
Pueblica de Valverde
Valdunquillo
Frómista
Villoldo
Villalón de Campos
Frechilla
Paredes de Nava
Castrojeriz
Santovenia
Villanueva del Campo
SAN FRANCISCO
Fuentes de Nava
Astudillo
Cerecinos de Campos
Villarramiel
Monzón de Campos
Granja de Moreruela
MONASTERIO DE MORERUELA
Villafrechós
LAGUNAS DE VILLAFÁFILA
Villalpando
Torremormojón
Villamartín de Campos
RUINAS DE CASTROTORAFE
Medina de Rioseco
Montealegre
Palencia
Torquemada
Quintana del Puente
Castronuevo
Ampudia
Montamarta
NUESTRA SEÑORA DE LA ANUNCIADA
Villalba de los Alcores
Venta de Baños
Magaz de Pisuerga
Castromonte
Villardefrades
Baños
Baltanás
Antigüedad
Dueñas
La Mudarra
CASTILLA Y LEÓN
LEÓN
CANTABRIA
79
81
88
89
A8
A66
AP66
AP71
A6
A52
A62
A67
A231
N632
N634
N630
N120
N621
N625
N601
N610
E70
E80

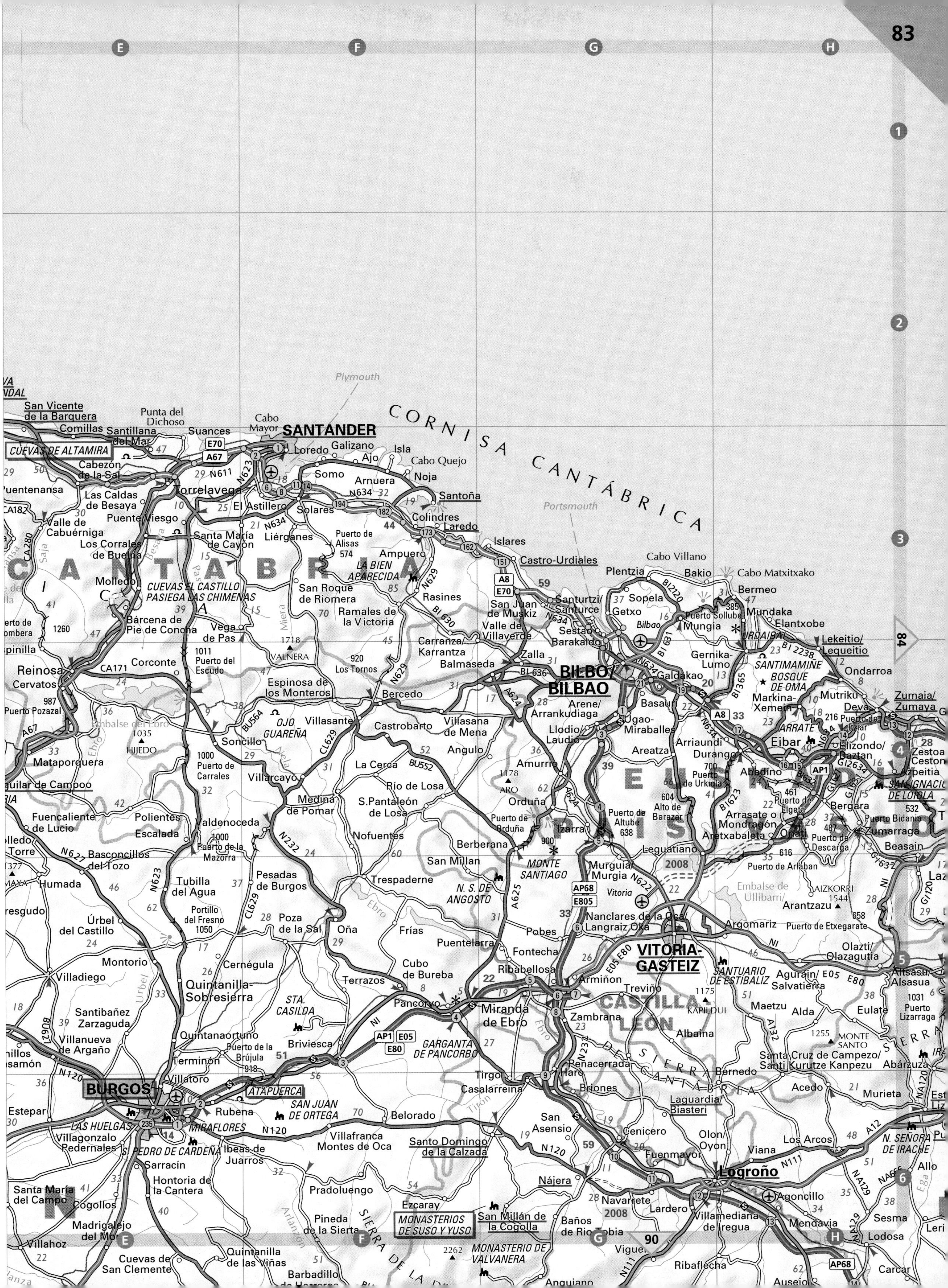
E
F
G
H
1
2
3
4
5
6
84
90
CORNISA CANTÁBRICA
Plymouth
Portsmouth
CANTABRIA
EUSKADI
PAIS VASCO
CASTILLA Y LEÓN
SANTANDER
BILBO/ BILBAO
VITORIA-GASTEIZ
BURGOS
Logroño
San Vicente de la Barquera
Comillas
Santillana del Mar
Punta del Dichoso
Suances
Cabo Mayor
Loredo
Galizano
Ajo
Isla
Cabo Quejo
Noja
Somo
Arnuera
Santoña
CUEVAS DE ALTAMIRA
Cabezón de la Sal
Puentenansa
Torrelavega
Las Caldas de Besaya
El Astillero
Solares
Colindres
Laredo
Puente Viesgo
Valle de Cabuérniga
Santa María de Cayón
Liérganes
Puerto de Alisas 574
Ampuero
Islares
Castro-Urdiales
Los Corrales de Buelna
LA BIEN APARECIDA
Molledo
CUEVAS EL CASTILLO
PASIEGA LAS CHIMENEAS
San Roque de Riomera
Rasines
Bárcena de Pie de Concha
Vega de Pas
Ramales de la Victoria
1718 VALNERA
1260
Reinosa
Cervatos
Corconte
1011 Puerto del Escudo
920 Los Tornos
Carranza/ Karrantza
Balmaseda
Espinosa de los Monteros
Bercedo
987 Puerto Pozazal
Embalse del Ebro
1035 HIJEDO
OJO GUAREÑA
Villasante
Castrobarto
Villasana de Mena
Soncillo
Mataporquera
1000 Puerto de Carrales
Villarcayo
La Cerca
Angulo
Río de Losa
Medina de Pomar
S.Pantaleón de Losa
Aguilar de Campoo
Fuencaliente de Lucio
Polientes
Escalada
Valdenoceda
1000 Puerto de la Mazorra
Nofuentes
Basconcillos del Tozo
Humada
Tubilla del Agua
Pesadas de Burgos
Trespaderne
San Millan
Berberana
N. S. DE ANGOSTO
Portillo del Fresno 1050
Úrbel del Castillo
Poza de la Sal
Oña
Frías
Puentelarra
Montorio
Cernégula
Cubo de Bureba
Villadiego
Quintanilla-Sobresierra
Terrazos
Pancorvo
STA. CASILDA
Santibañez Zarzaguda
Villanueva de Argaño
Quintanaortuno
Puerto de la Brújula 918
Briviesca
Terminón
GARGANTA DE PANCORBO
Villatoro
ATAPUERCA
Rubena
SAN JUAN DE ORTEGA
LAS HUELGAS
MIRAFLORES
Estepar
Belorado
Villagonzalo Pedernales
S. PEDRO DE CARDEÑA
Ibeas de Juarros
Villafranca Montes de Oca
Santo Domingo de la Calzada
Sarracín
Hontoria de la Cantera
Pradoluengo
Santa María del Campo
Cogollos
Madrigalejo del Monte
Villahoz
Cuevas de San Clemente
Quintanilla de las Viñas
Pineda de la Sierra
Ezcaray
MONASTERIOS DE SUSO Y YUSO
San Millán de la Cogolla
Barbadillo
SIERRA DE LA DEMANDA
2262
MONASTERIO DE VALVANERA
Anguiano
Plentzia
Cabo Villano
Bakio
Cabo Matxitxako
Bermeo
Sopela
Getxo
Santurtzi/ Santurce
San Juan de Muskiz
Valle de Villaverde
Sestao
Barakaldo
Mundaka
Puerto Sollube
Mungia
Elantxobe
URDAIBAI
Lekeitio/ Lequeitio
Zalla
Gernika-Lumo
SANTIMAMIÑE
Ondarroa
BOSQUE DE OMA
Galdakao
Basauri
Arene/ Arrankudiaga
Markina-Xemein
Mutriku
Deva
Zumaia/ Zumaya
Llodio/ Laudio
Ugao-Miraballes
ARRATE
Areatza
Arriaundi
Durango
Eibar
Elizondo/ Baztan
Zestoa
Cestona
Amurrio
700 Puerto de Urkiola
Abadiño
Azpeitia
SAN IGNACIO DE LOIOLA
1178 ARO
Orduña
604 Alto de Barazar
461 Puerto de Elgeta
Bergara
Puerto de Orduña
Puerto de Altube 638
Arrasate o Mondragón
Oñati
487 Puerto de Descarga
Puerto Bidania
Zumarraga
Izarra
Aretxabaleta
Beasain
900 MONTE SANTIAGO
Legutiano
2008
Puerto de Arlaban
Murguía/ Murgia
Vitoria
Embalse de Ullibarri
AIZKORRI 1544
Arantzazu
Nanclares de la Oca/ Langraiz Oka
Argomariz
Puerto de Etxegarate
Pobes
Olazti/ Olazagutia
Fontecha
Altsasu/ Alsasua
SANTUARIO DE ESTIBALIZ
Agurain/ Salvatierra
Ribabellosa
Armiñon
Treviño
1175 KAPILDUI
Maetzu
Alda
Eulate
1031 Puerto Lizarraga
Miranda de Ebro
Zambrana
Albaina
1255 MONTE SANTO
Santa Cruz de Campezo/ Santi Kurutze Kanpezu
Abárzuza
SIERRA DE CANTABRIA
Tirgo
Haro
Peñacerrada
Bernedo
Casalarreina
Briones
Acedo
Murieta
Laguardia/ Biasteri
San Asensio
Cenicero
Olon/ Oyon
Los Arcos
N. SEÑORA DE IRACHE
Fuenmayor
Viana
Allo
Nájera
Navarrete
Lardero
Agoncillo
Sesma
Baños de Rio Tobia
Villamediana de Iregua
Mendavia
Lodosa
Ribaflecha
Carcar
E70
A67
A8
E80
AP1
E05
AP68
E805
N120
N623
N611
N634
N629
N232
N622
N627
N111
A12
A624
A625
CL629
BU552
BU564
BI 630
BI 631
BI 636
CA171
CA182

Golfe de Gascogne / Bizkaiko Golkoa / Golfo de Vizcaya
CÔTE D'ARGENT
DONOSTIA-SAN SEBASTIÁN
Biarritz
Anglet
Bayonne
Dax
Hossegor
Capbreton
Labenne
Tarnos
Vieux-Boucau-les Bains
Soustons
Moliets-et-Maa
Léon
Castets
Azur
Magescq
St-Paul-lès-Dax
St-Vincent-de-Tyrosse
St-Geours-de-Maremne
Lesperon
St-Girons-en-Marensin
Girons-Plage
Lahane
Morcenx
Rion-des-Landes
Tartas
Mugron
Montfort-en-Chalosse
Hagetmau
Amou
Habas
Peyrehorade
Bidache
Salies-de-Béarn
Orthez
Sault-de-Navailles
Sauveterre-de-Béarn
Lacq
Artix
Navarrenx
Mauléon-Licharre
Oloron-Ste-Marie
Aramits
Arudy
Louvie-Juzon
Bedous
Accous
Laruns
Eaux-Chaudes
Urdos
Lescun
Tardets-Sorholus
Larrau
St-Palais
Larceveau-Arros-Cibits
St-Jean-Pied-de-Port
St-Etienne-de-Baigorry
Hasparren
Cambo-les-Bains
Itxassou
Ustaritz
Espelette
Ainhoa
Ascain
St Jean-de-Luz
Ciboure
Hendaye
Guethary
Bidart
Hondarribia/Fuenterrabia
Errenteria/Renteria
Pasaia
Irun
Hernani
Tolosa
Zarautz
Getaria
Zumaia/Zumaya
Deva
Mutriku
Ondarroa
Lekeitio/Lequeitio
Bermeo
Mundaka
Elantxobe
Cabo Matxitxako
Eibar
Elizondo/Baztan
Azpeitia
Zestoa/Cestona
Lasarte-Oria
Villabona
Bergara
Oñati
Zumarraga
Beasain
Lazkao
Alsasua
Altsasu
Olazti/Olazagutia
Echarri/Etxarri
Lekunberri
Leitza
Goizueta
Lesaka
Vera de Bidasoa
San Esteban
Almandoz
Elizondo
Irurita
Erratzu
Les Aldudes
Luzaide/Valcarlos
Roncesvalles
Auritz/Burguete
Zubiri
Erro
Ochagavía/Otsagi
Isaba/Izaba
Roncal/Erronkari
Ansó
Hecho
Canfranc
Candanchú
Villanúa
Jaca
Sabiñánigo
Biescas
Sallent de Gállego
PAMPLONA/IRUÑA
Burlada
Huarte
Villava
Berriozar
Mutilva
Noain/Elorz
Aoiz/Agoitz
Urroz
Lumbier/Irunberri
Yesa/Esa
Javier/Xabier
Sangüesa/Zangoza
Aibar
Monreal/Elo
Estella/Lizarra
Puente la Reina/Gares
Campanas/Kanpaneta
Tafalla
Olite
Ujué
Lerga
San Martín de Unx
Barásoain
Artajona
Larraga
Lerín
Miranda
Lodosa
Sesma
Mendavia
Viana
Los Arcos
Allo
Carcar
Peralta
Marcilla
Caparroso
Carcastillo
Santacara
San Adrián
Calahorra
Arnedo
Autol
Rincón de Soto
Alfaro
Corella
Cintruénigo
Fitero
Tudela
Cascante
Ribaforada
Tarazona
Agreda
Cortes
Borja
Gallur
Tauste
Ejea de los Caballeros
Sádaba
Castilliscar
Uncastillo
Luesia
Biel
Fuencalderas
Agüero
Riglos
Ayerbe
Luna
Ardisa
Erla
Sierra de Luna
Plasencia del Monte
Tormos
Huesca
Nueno
Igriés
Arguis
Nocito
Sos del Rey Católico
Puente la Reina de Jaca
Berdún
Sigües
Valtierra
Arguedas
Pinsoro
Valareña
Logroño
Agoncillo
NAVARRA
NAFARROA
E

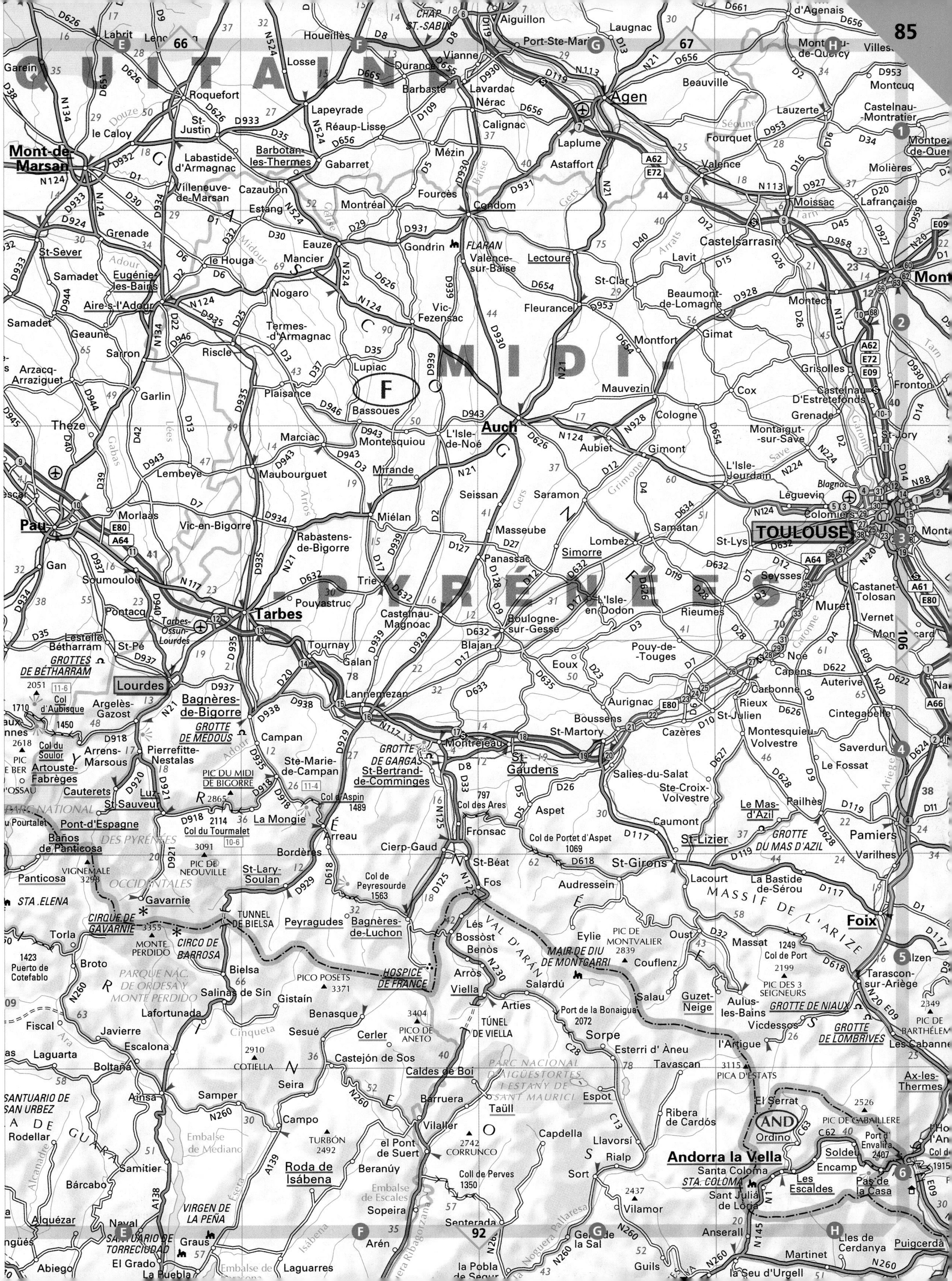

AQUITAINE
MIDI-PYRÉNÉES
Mont-de-Marsan
Agen
Auch
Tarbes
Pau
Lourdes
TOULOUSE
Montauban
Foix
Andorra la Vella
Labrit
Houeillès
Aiguillon
Port-Ste-Marie
Laugnac
Roquefort
St-Justin
Lapeyrade
Réaup-Lisse
Barbotan-les-Thermes
Gabarret
Mézin
Nérac
Lavardac
Barbaste
Vianne
Durance
Losse
Calignac
Laplume
Astaffort
Beauville
Lauzerte
Castelnau-Montratier
Montcuq
Fourquet
Valence
Molières
Moissac
Lafrançaise
Castelsarrasin
Lavit
Beaumont-de-Lomagne
Montech
Grisolles
Fronton
Castelnau-D'Estretefonds
Grenade
Montaigut-sur-Save
St-Jory
Léguevin
Colomiers
Blagnac
St-Lys
Seysses
Muret
Castanet-Tolosan
Vernet
Noé
Capens
Carbonne
Rieux
Auterive
Cintegabelle
Saverdun
Pamiers
Varilhes
Villeneuve-de-Marsan
Cazaubon
Estang
Montréal
Fourcès
Condom
Labastide-d'Armagnac
Le Caloy
Grenade
St-Sever
Samadet
Eugénie-les-Bains
Aire-s-l'Adour
Le Houga
Eauze
Mancier
Gondrin
Valence-sur-Baïse
Lectoure
St-Clar
Fleurance
Nogaro
Termes-d'Armagnac
Riscle
Geaune
Sarron
Vic-Fezensac
Montfort
Gimat
Mauvezin
Cologne
Cox
Arzacq-Arraziguet
Garlin
Plaisance
Lupiac
Bassoues
Marciac
Montesquiou
L'Isle-de-Noé
Aubiet
Gimont
L'Isle-Jourdain
Thèze
Lembeye
Maubourguet
Mirande
Seissan
Saramon
Samatan
Lombez
Simorre
Morlaas
Vic-en-Bigorre
Miélan
Rabastens-de-Bigorre
Masseube
Panassac
Gan
Soumoulou
Trie
Pouyastruc
L'Isle-en-Dodon
Rieumes
Pontacq
Castelnau-Magnoac
Boulogne-sur-Gesse
Lestelle-Bétharram
St-Pé
Tournay
Galan
Blajan
Pouy-de-Touges
Eoux
Lannemezan
Aurignac
Boussens
St-Martory
Cazères
St-Julien
Montesquieu-Volvestre
Le Fossat
Argelès-Gazost
Bagnères-de-Bigorre
Campan
Montréjeau
St-Gaudens
Salies-du-Salat
Ste-Croix-Volvestre
Arrens-Marsous
Pierrefitte-Nestalas
Ste-Marie-de-Campan
St-Bertrand-de-Comminges
Aspet
Le Mas-d'Azil
Rimont
Cauterets
Luz-St-Sauveur
La Mongie
Arreau
Cierp-Gaud
Fronsac
St-Béat
St-Girons
St-Lizier
Caumont
Lacourt
La Bastide-de-Sérou
Pont-d'Espagne
Baños de Panticosa
Bordères
St-Lary-Soulan
Fos
Audressein
Massat
Tarascon-sur-Ariège
Gavarnie
Peyragudes
Bagnères-de-Luchon
Lés
Bossòst
Benòs
Eylie
Oust
Torla
Broto
Bielsa
Salinas de Sín
Gistaín
Arròs
Viella
Salardú
Arties
Salau
Guzet-Neige
Aulus-les-Bains
Vicdessos
Lafortunada
Benasque
Sorpe
Esterri d'Àneu
L'Artigue
Fiscal
Javierre
Escalona
Sesué
Cerler
Castejón de Sos
Tavascan
Laguarta
Boltaña
Seira
Caldes de Boi
Espot
Ainsa
Samper
Barruera
Taüll
El Serrat
Ordino
Campo
Vilaller
Capdella
Llavorsí
Ribera de Cardós
Rodellar
Samitier
El Pont de Suert
Rialp
Encamp
Soldeu
Bárcabo
Roda de Isábena
Beranúy
Sort
Santa Coloma
Sant Julià de Lòria
Les Escaldes
Pas de la Casa
Alquézar
Sopeira
Vilamor
Naval
Graus
Senterada
Gerri de la Sal
Anserall
Llés de Cerdanya
Puigcerdà
Abiego
El Grado
La Puebla
Arén
Laguarres
La Pobla de Segur
Guils
Martinet
La Seu d'Urgell
GROTTES DE BÉTHARRAM
GROTTE DE MÉDOUS
GROTTE DE GARGAS
GROTTE DU MAS D'AZIL
GROTTE DE NIAUX
GROTTE DE LOMBRIVES
FLARAN
PIC DU MIDI DE BIGORRE
Col du Tourmalet
Col d'Aspin
Col des Ares
Col de Portet d'Aspet
Col de Peyresourde
Col de Port
Col d'Aubisque
Col du Soulor
PARC NATIONAL DES PYRÉNÉES OCCIDENTALES
CIRQUE DE GAVARNIE
CIRCO DE BARROSA
MONTE PERDIDO
VIGNEMALE
PIC DE NEOUVILLE
TUNNEL DE BIELSA
HOSPICE DE FRANCE
PICO POSETS
PICO DE ANETO
TÚNEL DE VIELLA
VAL D'ARÁN
MAIR DE DIU DE MONTGARRI
PIC DE MONTVALIER
PIC DES 3 SEIGNEURS
MASSIF DE L'ARIZE
PARQUE NAC. DE ORDESA Y MONTE PERDIDO
PARC NACIONAL D'AIGÜESTORTES I ESTANY DE SANT MAURICI
Port de la Bonaigua
PICA D'ESTATS
PIC DE CABAILLERE
Port d'Envalira
COTIELLA
TURBÓN
CORRUNCO
Coll de Perves
SANTUARIO DE SAN URBEZ
VIRGEN DE LA PEÑA
SANTUARIO DE TORRECIUDAD
Embalse de Mediano
Embalse de Escales
AND
F
66
67
92
106

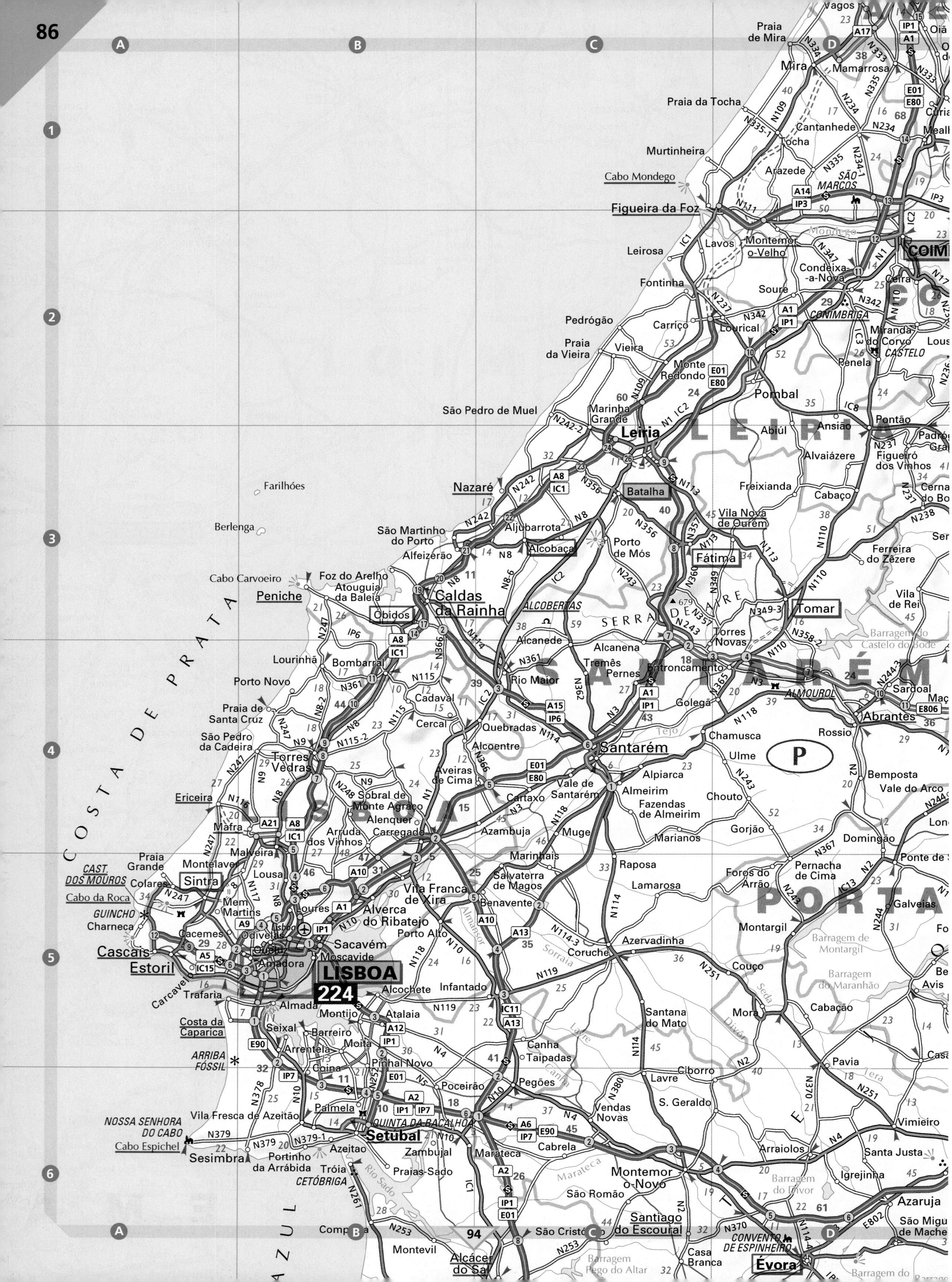
Vagos
Praia de Mira
Mira
Mamarrosa
Praia da Tocha
Cantanhede
Tocha
Murtinheira
Arazede
SÃO MARCOS
Cabo Mondego
Figueira da Foz
Lavos
Montemor-o-Velho
Mondego
Leirosa
Condeixa-a-Nova
COIMBRA
Ceira
Fontinha
Soure
CONIMBRIGA
Pedrógão
Carriço
Louriçal
Praia da Vieira
Vieira
Miranda do Corvo
CASTELO
Penela
Monte Redondo
Pombal
São Pedro de Muel
Marinha Grande
Leiria
LEIRIA
Abiúl
Ansião
Pontão
Alvaiázere
Figueiró dos Vinhos
Nazaré
Batalha
Freixianda
Cabaço
Farilhões
Vila Nova de Ourém
Berlenga
São Martinho do Porto
Aljubarrota
Alcobaça
Porto de Mós
Fátima
Ferreira do Zêzere
Alfeizerão
Cabo Carvoeiro
Foz do Arelho
Atouguia da Baleia
Peniche
Caldas da Rainha
Óbidos
ALCOBERTAS
SERRA DE AIRE
Tomar
Vila de Rei
Torres Novas
Barragem do Castelo do Bode
Alcanede
Alcanena
Lourinhã
Bombarral
Tremês
Pernes
Entroncamento
Rio Maior
SANTARÉM
ALMOUROL
Sardoal
Abrantes
Porto Novo
Cadaval
Golegã
Rossio
Praia de Santa Cruz
Cercal
Quebradas
Chamusca
São Pedro da Cadeira
Torres Vedras
Alcoentre
Santarém
Ulme
Aveiras de Cima
Vale de Santarém
Alpiarca
Bemposta
Vale do Arco
Ericeira
Sobral de Monte Agraço
Cartaxo
Almeirim
Fazendas de Almeirim
Chouto
Alenquer
LISBOA
Mafra
Arruda dos Vinhos
Carregado
Azambuja
Muge
Gorjão
Marianos
Domingão
Malveira
Marinhais
COSTA DE PRATA
Praia Grande
Montelavar
Pernacha de Cima
Ponte de Sor
Lousa
Raposa
Foros do Arrão
CAST. DOS MOUROS
Sintra
Colares
Salvaterra de Magos
Vila Franca de Xira
Lamarosa
PORTALEGRE
Cabo da Roca
Mem Martins
Loures
Alverca do Ribatejo
Benavente
Galveias
GUINCHO
Charneca
Odivelas
Porto Alto
Montargil
Cacemes
Queluz
Sacavém
Moscavide
Azervadinha
Coruche
Barragem de Montargil
Cascais
Estoril
Amadora
Sorraia
Couço
Barragem do Maranhão
Avis
LISBOA 224
Alcochete
Infantado
Carcavelos
Trafaria
Almada
Montijo
Atalaia
Cabação
Costa da Caparica
Seixal
Barreiro
Santana do Mato
Mora
ARRIBA FÓSSIL
Arrentela
Moita
Canha
Taipadas
Coina
Pinhal Novo
Ciborro
Pavia
Poceirão
Pegões
Lavre
NOSSA SENHORA DO CABO
Vila Fresca de Azeitão
Palmela
QUINTA DA BACALHOA
Vendas Novas
S. Geraldo
Vimieiro
Cabo Espichel
Setúbal
Zambujal
Cabrela
Arraiolos
Santa Justa
Sesimbra
Portinho da Arrábida
Azeitão
Marateca
Tróia
CETÓBRIGA
Praias-Sado
Montemor-o-Novo
Barragem do Divor
Igrejinha
Rio Sado
São Romão
Azaruja
Comporta
Montevil
Alcácer do Sal
São Cristóvão
Santiago do Escoural
CONVENTO DE ESPINHEIRO
São Miguel de Machede
Barragem Pego do Altar
Casa Branca
Évora
COSTA AZUL
94

Águeda
Alcofra
Viseu
Lordosa
Sátão
Aguiar da Beira
Marialva
de Alva
La Fregeneda
DUERO
80
81
Figueira de Castelo Rodrigo
CASTELO RODRIGO
Lumbrales
Bolfiar
Caramulo
Boialvo
SERRA DO CARAMULO
1074
Anadia
Penalva do Castelo
Trancoso
Mangualde
Dão
Tondela
Canas de Senhorim
Nelas
Fornos de Algodres
Celorico da Beira
Pinhel
Freixedas
S.Felices de los Gallegos
Villavieja
Luso
Mortágua
Buçaco
Santa Comba Dão
Rojão Grande
Carregal do Sal
Mondego
Rio Torto
Seixo
Villar de Ciervo
Almeida
Castillejo de Martín Viejo
Tábua
Oliveira do Hospital
Gândara
Penacova
Gouveia
PARQUE NATURAL
Guarda
Pinzio
Vilar Formoso
Fuentes de Oñoro
Sancti-Spíritus
Seia
Manteigas
DA SERRA
SERRA DA ESTRÊLA
GUARDA
São Martinho
SÃO PEDRO
Vendas de Galizes
Vide
Vila Fernando
Cerdeira
2009
Ciudad Rodrigo
Arganil
MALHAO
1993
POÇO DO INFERNO
Belmonte
Pega
Gois
Cepos
DA ESTRÊLA
Covilhã
Caria
Aldeia da Ponte
El Bodón
Morasverdes
1418
Santo Estevão
Sabugal
Alfaites
Fuenteguinaldo
Embalse de Águeda
Barragem de Santa Luzia
Tortosendo
Silvares
Castanheira de Pera
Pampilhosa da Serra
Capinha
Aldeia do Bispo
Robleda
Barragem do Sobugal
Zêzere
Fundão
Penamacor
Valverde del Fresno
Villasrubias
Robledillo de Gata
Orvalho
SERRA DA GUARDUNHA
Alpedrinha
1492
SIERRA DE GATA
Barragem do Cabril
Orca
São Vicente da Beira
Foz Giraldo
Oleiros
Hoyos
São Miguel de Acha
Medelim
Pinofranqueado
Sertã
CASTELO BRANCO
Lardosa
Barragem da Idanha
Monsanto
Cilleros
Villanueva de la Sierra
Sarzedas
Alcafores
Termas de Monfortinho
Pozuelo de Zarzón
Ahigal
Proença-a-Nova
Sobreira Formosa
Idanha-a-Nova
Moraleja
Montehermoso
Moitas
Castelo Branco
Ocreza
Zebreira
Ladoeiro
Ponsul
Coria
Chão de Codes
Perdigão
Segura
Zarza la Mayor
Pesqueza
Alagón
Carcaboso
Fratel
Vila Velha de Ródão
Monforte da Beira
Galisteo
Belver
PORTAS DE RODÃO
Montalvão
Cedillo
Tejo
Tajo
Rosmaninhal
Piedras Albas
Ceclavín
Torrejoncillo
Riolobos
MONASTERIO DEL PALANCAR
Gavião
Santiago de Alcántara
PUENTE ROMANO
Acehuche
Nisa
Carbajo
Alcántara
Embalse de Alcántara
Portezuelo
Cañaveral
Puerto de los Castaños
Mirabel
Tolosa
Barragem da Póvoa
Mata de Alcántara
Garrovillas
Serradilla
Alpalhão
Sor
PARQUE NATURAL
Membrío
Brozas
Navas del Madroño
Hinojal
Talaván
Monte da Pedra
Castelo de Vide
Marvão
Sever
Salorino
Salor
Santiago del Campo
Crato
LEGRE
DE SERRA
Valencia de Alcántara
Herreruela
E
Monroy
Portalegre
1025
Arroyo de la Luz
Casar de Cáceres
Alter do Chão
DE S. MAMEDE
SERRA DE SÃO MAMEDE
San Vicente de Alcántara
Aliseda
624
Malpartida de Cáceres
Cáceres
VIRGEN DE LA MONTAÑA
PIEDRABUENA
SIERRA DE SAN PEDRO
Cabeço de Vide
La Codosera
Alburquerque
Valdesalor
Sierra de Fuentes
Torrequemada
Fronteira
Arronches
Embalse de la Peña de Águila
Puerto del Clavín
425
La Cumbre
Monforte
Sousel
Puebla de Obando
MAYORALGO
Aldea del Cano
Torremocha
Veiros
Santo Aleixo
Santa Eulália
Campo Maior
Villar del Rey
Bótoa
Torre de Sta. María
Barragem do Caia
Estremoz
La Roca de la Sierra
Cordobilla de Lácara
Santa Cruz de la Sierra
Montánchez
Alcuéscar
Almoharín
Evora Monte
Borba
ACUEDUCTO DE AMOREIRA
Elvas
La Nava de Santiago
Badajoz
Pueblonuevo del Guadiana
EXTREMADURA
Aljucén
Conquista del Guadiana
Miajadas
Vila Viçosa
Alandroal
Villafranco del Guadiana
Talavera la Real
95
Montijo
La Garrovilla
Puebla de la Calzada
San Pedro de Mérida
Santa Amalia
88
96

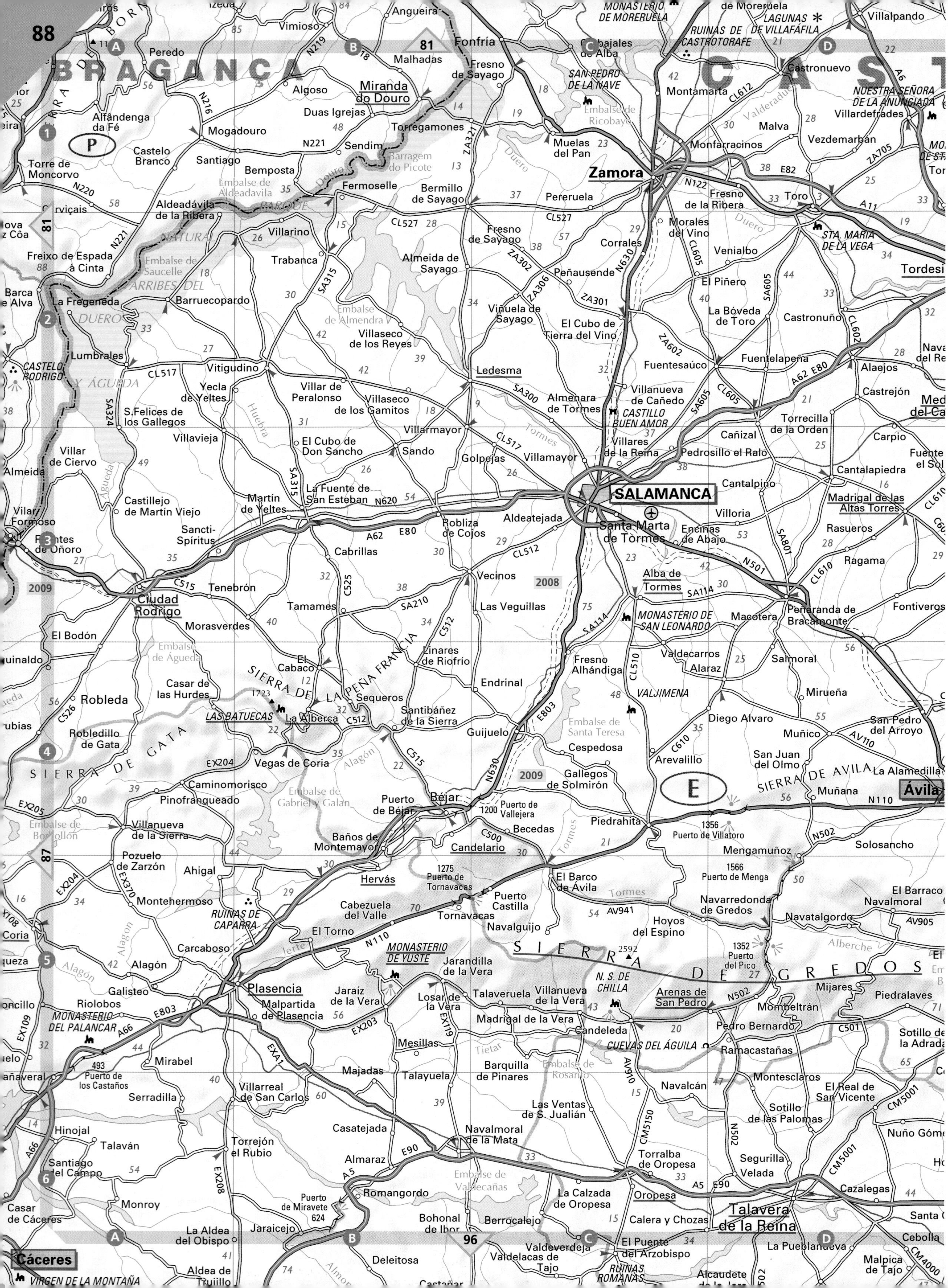

BRAGANÇA
CAST
P
E
81
87
96
2009
2008
Peredo
Vimioso
Angueira
Fonfría
Carbajales de Alba
MONASTERIO DE MORERUELA
RUINAS DE CASTROTORAFE
LAGUNAS DE VILLAFÁFILA
Villalpando
Castronuevo
Malhadas
Fresno de Sayago
SAN PEDRO DE LA NAVE
Montamarta
NUESTRA SEÑORA DE LA ANUNCIADA
Villardefrades
Algoso
Miranda do Douro
Embalse de Ricobayo
Malva
Alfândenga da Fé
Duas Igrejas
Torregamones
Muelas del Pan
Monfarracinos
Vezdemarbán
Mogadouro
Sendim
Barragem do Picote
Castelo Branco
Santiago
Zamora
Torre de Moncorvo
Bemposta
Fresno de la Ribera
Toro
Fermoselle
Bermillo de Sayago
Pereruela
Embalse de Aldeadávila
Aldeadávila de la Ribera
PARQUE
Morales del Vino
STA. MARIA DE LA VEGA
Tordesi
Freixo de Espada à Cinta
Villarino
Fresno de Sayago
Corrales
Venialbo
Trabanca
Almeida de Sayago
Peñausende
Embalse de Saucelle
NATURAL
ARRIBES DEL
DUERO
El Piñero
Barca d'Alva
La Fregeneda
Barruecopardo
Viñuela de Sayago
Embalse de Almendra
La Bóveda de Toro
Castronuño
El Cubo de Tierra del Vino
Villaseco de los Reyes
Lumbrales
CASTELO RODRIGO
Vitigudino
Ledesma
Fuentesaúco
Fuentelapeña
Alaejos
Y ÁGUEDA
Yecla de Yeltes
Villar de Peralonso
Villaseco de los Gamitos
Almenara de Tormes
Villanueva de Cañedo
CASTILLO BUEN AMOR
Castrejón
S.Felices de los Gallegos
Villarmayor
Torrecilla de la Orden
Villavieja
El Cubo de Don Sancho
Sando
Villares de la Reina
Cañizal
Pedrosillo el Ralo
Carpio
Villar de Ciervo
Golpejas
Villamayor
Almeida
Cantalapiedra
Cantalpino
La Fuente de San Esteban
SALAMANCA
Madrigal de las Altas Torres
Castillejo de Martín Viejo
Martín de Yeltes
Vilar Formoso
Fuentes de Oñoro
Sancti-Spíritus
Robliza de Cojos
Aldeatejada
Santa Marta de Tormes
Encinas de Abajo
Villoria
Rasueros
Cabrillas
Vecinos
Ragama
Tenebrón
Ciudad Rodrigo
Tamames
Alba de Tormes
Las Veguillas
MONASTERIO DE SAN LEONARDO
Macotera
Peñaranda de Bracamonte
Fontiveros
Morasverdes
El Bodón
Embalse de Águeda
Linares de Riofrío
Fresno Alhándiga
Valdecarros
Alaraz
Salmoral
El Cabaco
SIERRA DE LA PEÑA FRANCIA
Casar de las Hurdes
Endrinal
VALJIMENA
Mirueña
Robleda
Sequeros
LAS BATUECAS
La Alberca
Santibáñez de la Sierra
Embalse de Santa Teresa
Diego Alvaro
San Pedro del Arroyo
Robledillo de Gata
Guijuelo
Muñico
Cespedosa
SIERRA DE GATA
Vegas de Coria
Arevalillo
San Juan del Olmo
La Alamedilla
Caminomorisco
Gallegos de Solmirón
SIERRA DE AVILA
Pinofranqueado
Embalse de Gabriel y Galán
Puerto de Béjar
Béjar
Puerto de Vallejera
Piedrahita
Muñana
Ávila
Embalse de Borbollón
Villanueva de la Sierra
Becedas
Puerto de Villatoro
Baños de Montemayor
Candelario
Mengamuñoz
Solosancho
Pozuelo de Zarzón
Ahigal
Hervás
Puerto de Tornavacas
El Barco de Ávila
Puerto de Menga
Montehermoso
RUINAS DE CAPARRA
Cabezuela del Valle
Puerto Castilla
Tornavacas
Navarredonda de Gredos
El Barraco
Navalmoral
Navalguijo
Hoyos del Espino
Navatalgordo
Coria
El Torno
Carcaboso
MONASTERIO DE YUSTE
Puerto del Pico
SIERRA DE GREDOS
Alagón
Jarandilla de la Vera
N. S. DE CHILLA
Galisteo
Plasencia
Jaraíz de la Vera
Losar de la Vera
Talaveruela
Villanueva de la Vera
Arenas de San Pedro
Mijares
Piedralaves
Riolobos
Malpartida de Plasencia
Mombeltrán
MONASTERIO DEL PALANCAR
Madrigal de la Vera
Candeleda
Pedro Bernardo
Sotillo de la Adrada
Mesillas
CUEVAS DEL ÁGUILA
Ramacastañas
Puerto de los Castaños
Mirabel
Majadas
Talayuela
Barquilla de Pinares
Embalse de Rosarito
Montesclaros
Serradilla
Villarreal de San Carlos
Navalcán
El Real de San Vicente
Sotillo de las Palomas
Las Ventas de S. Julián
Hinojal
Talaván
Casatejada
Navalmoral de la Mata
Nuño Gómez
Torrejón el Rubio
Santiago del Campo
Almaraz
Torralba de Oropesa
Segurilla
Velada
Embalse de Valdecañas
La Calzada de Oropesa
Cazalegas
Casar de Cáceres
Monroy
Puerto de Miravete
Romangordo
Oropesa
Talavera de la Reina
Bohonal de Ibor
Berrocalejo
Calera y Chozas
Santa
La Aldea del Obispo
Jaraicejo
El Puente del Arzobispo
Cebolla
Cáceres
Deleitosa
Valdeverdeja
Valdelacasas de Tajo
La Pueblanueva
Malpica de Tajo
Aldea de Trujillo
VIRGEN DE LA MONTAÑA
RUINAS ROMANAS
Alcaudete

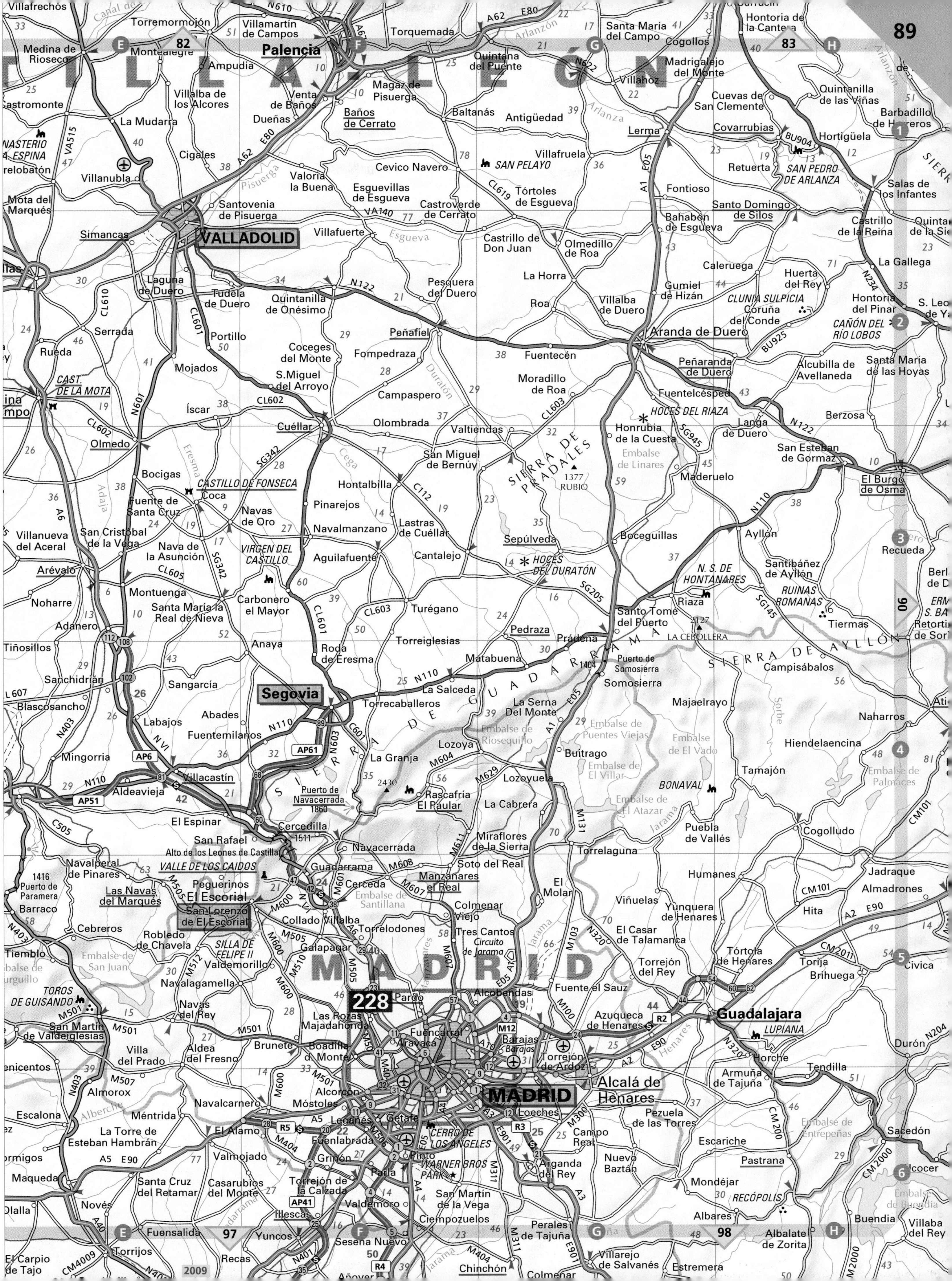
CASTILLA Y LEÓN
Villafrechós
Torremormojón
Villamartín de Campos
Palencia
Torquemada
Santa María del Campo
Cogollos
Hontoria de la Cantera
Medina de Rioseco
Montealegre
Ampudia
Quintana del Puente
Madrigalejo del Monte
Villahoz
Castromonte
Villalba de los Alcores
Venta de Baños
Magaz de Pisuerga
Baños de Cerrato
Cuevas de San Clemente
Quintanilla de las Viñas
Barbadillo de Herreros
La Mudarra
Dueñas
Baltanás
Antigüedad
Lerma
Covarrubias
Hortigüela
MONASTERIO LA ESPINA
Cigales
Villafruela
Retuerta
SAN PEDRO DE ARLANZA
Villanubla
Valoria la Buena
Cevico Navero
SAN PELAYO
Tórtoles de Esgueva
Fontioso
Salas de los Infantes
Mota del Marqués
Esguevillas de Esgueva
Castroverde de Cerrato
Santovenia de Pisuerga
Santo Domingo de Silos
Bahabón de Esgueva
Castrillo de la Reina
Simancas
VALLADOLID
Villafuerte
Castrillo de Don Juan
Olmedillo de Roa
La Gallega
Caleruega
Huerta del Rey
Laguna de Duero
Tudela de Duero
Quintanilla de Onésimo
Pesquera del Duero
La Horra
Gumiel de Hizán
CLUNIA SULPICIA
Coruña del Conde
Hontoria del Pinar
Roa
Villalba de Duero
CAÑÓN DEL RÍO LOBOS
Serrada
Portillo
Peñafiel
Aranda de Duero
Rueda
Coceges del Monte
Fompedraza
Fuentecén
Peñaranda de Duero
Alcubilla de Avellaneda
Santa María de las Hoyas
Mojados
S.Miguel del Arroyo
Moradillo de Roa
CAST. DE LA MOTA
Campaspero
Fuentelcéspes
HOCES DEL RIAZA
Íscar
Olombrada
Valtiendas
Honrubia de la Cuesta
Langa de Duero
Berzosa
Cuéllar
Olmedo
San Miguel de Bernúy
SIERRA DE PRADALES
Embalse de Linares
San Esteban de Gormaz
Bocigas
Hontalbilla
1377 RUBIO
Maderuelo
El Burgo de Osma
CASTILLO DE FONSECA
Coca
Fuente de Santa Cruz
Pinarejos
Navas de Oro
Lastras de Cuéllar
Villanueva del Aceral
San Cristóbal de la Vega
Navalmanzano
Sepúlveda
Boceguillas
Ayllón
Recueda
Nava de la Asunción
VIRGEN DEL CASTILLO
Aguilafuente
Cantalejo
HOCES DEL DURATÓN
N. S. DE HONTANARES
Santibáñez de Ayllón
Arévalo
Montuenga
RUINAS ROMANAS
Noharre
Carbonero el Mayor
Turégano
Riaza
Santa María la Real de Nieva
Santo Tomé del Puerto
Tiermas
Adanero
Pedraza
Tiñosillos
Anaya
Roda de Eresma
Torreiglesias
Prádena
LA CEBOLLERA
SIERRA DE AYLLÓN
Matabuena
Puerto de Somosierra
Campisábalos
Sanchidrián
Sangarcía
Somosierra
Segovia
La Salceda
Blascosancho
Abades
Torrecaballeros
La Serna Del Monte
Majaelrayo
Labajos
SIERRA DE GUADARRAMA
Embalse de Riosequillo
Embalse de Puentes Viejas
Embalse de El Vado
Naharros
Fuentemilanos
Lozoya
Buitrago
Hiendelaencina
Mingorria
La Granja
Embalse de El Villar
Tamajón
Villacastín
Aldeavieja
Puerto de Navacerrada 1860
Rascafría
El Paular
Lozoyuela
BONAVAL
Embalse de Palmaces
La Cabrera
Embalse de El Atazar
El Espinar
Cercedilla
Puebla de Vallés
Cogolludo
San Rafael
Alto de los Leones de Castilla
Navacerrada
Miraflores de la Sierra
Torrelaguna
Navalperal de Pinares
1416 Puerto de Paramera
VALLE DE LOS CAIDOS
Guadarrama
Soto del Real
Humanes
Jadraque
Las Navas del Marqués
Peguerinos
Cerceda
Manzanares el Real
El Molar
Almadrones
El Escorial
San Lorenzo de El Escorial
Embalse de Santillana
Viñuelas
Yunquera de Henares
Hita
Barraco
Colmenar Viejo
Collado Villalba
Cebreros
Robledo de Chavela
Torrelodones
Tres Cantos
Circuito de Jarama
El Casar de Talamanca
Tiemblo
Embalse de San Juan
SILLA DE FELIPE II
Galapagar
Tórtola de Henares
Torija
Valdemorillo
MADRID
Torrejón del Rey
Brihuega
Cívica
TOROS DE GUISANDO
Navalagamella
Fuente el Sauz
Navas del Rey
Pardo
Alcobendas
Azuqueca de Henares
Guadalajara
San Martín de Valdeiglesias
LUPIANA
Las Rozas
Majadahonda
Fuencarral
Barajas
Aravaca
Torrejón de Ardoz
Durón
Villa del Prado
Aldea del Fresno
Brunete
Boadilla d. Monte
Horche
Almorox
Alcorcón
MADRID
Alcalá de Henares
Armuña de Tajuña
Tendilla
Navalcarnero
Móstoles
Escalona
Méntrida
Leganés
Getafe
Loeches
Pezuela de las Torres
Embalse de Entrepeñas
La Torre de Esteban Hambrán
El Álamo
CERRO DE LOS ÁNGELES
Campo Real
Sacedón
Fuenlabrada
Escariche
Griñón
Pinto
Arganda del Rey
Nuevo Baztán
Pastrana
Maqueda
Valmojado
WARNER BROS PARK
Alcocer
Santa Cruz del Retamar
Casarubios del Monte
Torrejón de la Calzada
Parla
Mondéjar
Embalse de Buendía
Novés
Valdemoro
San Martín de la Vega
RECÓPOLIS
Illescas
Ciempozuelos
Albares
Buendía
Fuensalida
Yuncos
Perales de Tajuña
Albalate de Zorita
Villaba del Rey
Torrijos
Seseña Nuevo
Recas
Villarejo de Salvanés
El Carpio de Tajo
Añover
Chinchón
Colmenar
Estremera
2009
82
83
90
97
98
228

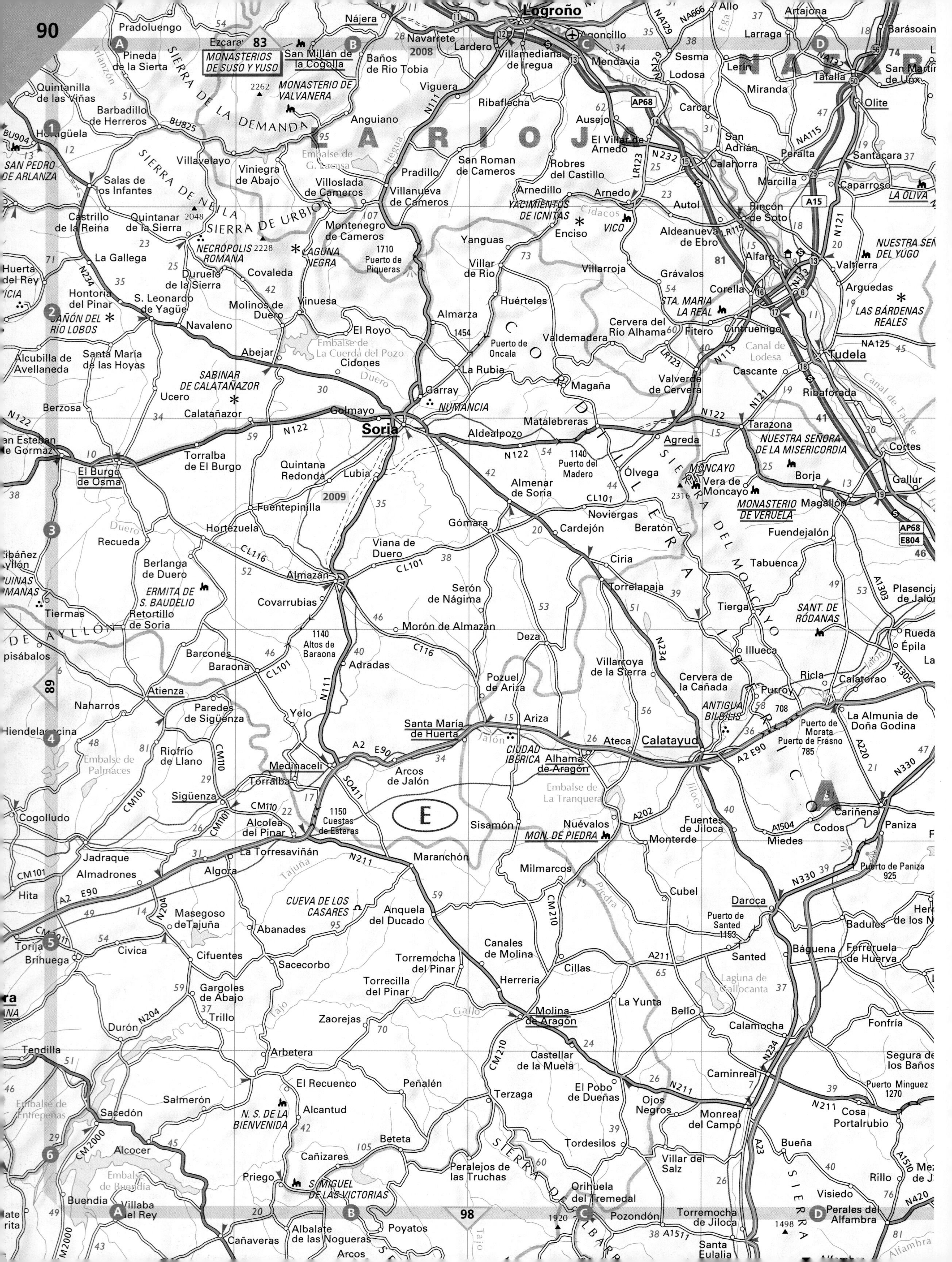
Logroño
Nájera
Pradoluengo
Ezcaray
83
MONASTERIOS DE SUSO Y YUSO
San Millán de la Cogolla
Navarrete
Lardero
Villamediana de Iregua
Agoncillo
Mendavia
Allo
Artajona
Barásoain
Larraga
Sesma
Lodosa
Lerín
Tafalla
San Martín de Unx
Olite
Miranda
Carcar
San Adrián
Peralta
Santacara
Marcilla
Caparroso
LA OLIVA
Pineda de la Sierra
Baños de Rio Tobia
Viguera
Ribaflecha
Ausejo
Quintanilla de las Viñas
Barbadillo de Herreros
SIERRA DE LA DEMANDA
MONASTERIO DE VALVANERA
Anguiano
Hortigüela
LA RIOJA
El Villar de Arnedo
Calahorra
SAN PEDRO DE ARLANZA
Villavelayo
Viniegra de Abajo
Embalse de G. Lacasa
San Roman de Cameros
Robres del Castillo
Salas de los Infantes
SIERRA DE NEILA
Pradillo
Villoslada de Cameros
Villanueva de Cameros
Arnedillo
Arnedo
Autol
Rincón de Soto
Castrillo de la Reina
Quintanar de la Sierra
SIERRA DE URBION
Montenegro de Cameros
YACIMIENTOS DE ICNITAS
VICO
Enciso
Aldeanueva de Ebro
Alfaro
NUESTRA SEÑORA DEL YUGO
Valtierra
La Gallega
NECRÓPOLIS ROMANA
LAGUNA NEGRA
Puerto de Piqueras
Yanguas
Villar de Río
Villarroja
Grávalos
Arguedas
Huerta del Rey
Hontoria del Pinar
S. Leonardo de Yagüe
Duruelo de la Sierra
Covaleda
Molinos de Duero
Vinuesa
Huérteles
Corella
STA. MARÍA LA REAL
LAS BÁRDENAS REALES
CAÑÓN DEL RÍO LOBOS
Navaleno
El Royo
Almarza
Puerto de Oncala
Valdemadera
Cervera del Río Alhama
Fitero
Cintruénigo
Tudela
Canal de Lodesa
Alcubilla de Avellaneda
Santa María de las Hoyas
Abejar
Embalse de La Cuerda del Pozo
Cidones
La Rubia
Magaña
Cascante
SABINAR DE CALATAÑAZOR
Garray
NUMANCIA
Valverde de Cervera
Ribaforada
Berzosa
Ucero
Calatañazor
Golmayo
Soria
Aldealpozo
Matalebreras
Tarazona
San Esteban de Gormaz
Agreda
NUESTRA SEÑORA DE LA MISERICORDIA
Cortes
El Burgo de Osma
Torralba de El Burgo
Quintana Redonda
Lubia
Almenar de Soria
Puerto del Madero
Ólvega
MONCAYO
Vera de Moncayo
Borja
Gallur
Fuentepinilla
Noviercas
MONASTERIO DE VERUELA
Magallón
Hortezuela
Gómara
Cardejón
Beratón
Fuendejalón
Recueda
Viana de Duero
Ciria
Tabuenca
Berlanga de Duero
Almazán
Torrelapaja
Plasencia de Jalón
ERMITA DE S. BAUDELIO
Serón de Nágima
Tierga
SANT. DE RÓDANAS
Tiermas
Covarrubias
Retortillo de Soria
Morón de Almazán
Deza
Rueda
Épila
SIERRA DE AYLLÓN
Altos de Baraona
Illueca
Barcones
Baraona
Adradas
Villarroya de la Sierra
Cervera de la Cañada
Ricla
Calatorao
Atienza
Naharros
Paredes de Sigüenza
Yelo
Pozuel de Ariza
Purroy
ANTIGUA BILBILIS
La Almunia de Doña Godina
Hiendelaencina
Riofrío de Llano
Santa María de Huerta
Ariza
Ateca
Calatayud
Puerto de Morata
Puerto de Frasno
Embalse de Palmaces
Medinaceli
Torralba
Arcos de Jalón
CIUDAD IBERICA
Alhama de Aragón
Embalse de La Tranquera
Sigüenza
Cariñena
Cogolludo
Alcolea del Pinar
Cuestas de Esteras
E
Sisamón
Nuévalos
MON. DE PIEDRA
Fuentes de Jiloca
Codos
Paniza
Miedes
Monterde
Jadraque
La Torresaviñán
Maranchón
Puerto de Paniza
Almadrones
Algora
Milmarcos
Hita
Masegoso de Tajuña
CUEVA DE LOS CASARES
Anquela del Ducado
Cubel
Daroca
Abanades
Puerto de Santed
Badules
Torija
Brihuega
Civica
Cifuentes
Sacecorbo
Canales de Molina
Torremocha del Pinar
Santed
Báguena
Ferreruela de Huerva
Herrería
Cillas
Laguna de Gallocanta
Gargoles de Abajo
Torrecilla del Pinar
Trillo
Durón
Zaorejas
Molina de Aragón
La Yunta
Bello
Calamocha
Fonfría
Tendilla
Arbetera
Castellar de la Muela
Segura de los Baños
Caminreal
El Recuenco
Peñalén
El Pobo de Dueñas
Puerto Minguez
Embalse de Entrepeñas
Salmerón
N. S. DE LA BIENVENIDA
Terzaga
Ojos Negros
Monreal del Campo
Cosa
Portalrubio
Sacedón
Alcantud
Alcocer
Beteta
Cañizares
SIERRA DE ALBARRACÍN
Tordesilos
Bueña
Embalse de Buendía
Priego
S. MIGUEL DE LAS VICTORIAS
Peralejos de las Truchas
Orihuela del Tremedal
Villar del Salz
Rillo
Visiedo
Buendía
Villaba del Rey
98
Pozondón
Torremocha de Jiloca
Perales del Alfambra
Albalate de las Nogueras
Poyatos
Cañaveras
Arcos
Santa Eulalia
Alfambra
SIERRA DEL MONCAYO
CORDILLERA IBÉRICA
NAVARRA
ARAGÓN
2008
2009

Lumbier/ Irunberri
Monasterio de Leyre
Nabaskoze
Burgui/Burgi
Ansó
Hecho
TÚNEL DE SOMPORT
Candanchú
Canfranc
Villanúa
PIC DU MIDI D'OSSAU
Fabrèges
Cauterets
Luz-St-Sauveur
DE BIGORRE
Sallent de Gállego
Col du Pourtalet
Pont-d'Espagne
Baños de Panticosa
PARC NATIONAL DES PYRÉNÉES OCCIDENTALES
Col du Tourmalet
PIC DE NEOUVILLE
Arreau
Bordères
St-Lary-Soulan
Col de Peyresourde
Aibar
Sangüesa/ Zangoza
Javier/ Xabier
S. SALVADOR DE LEYRE
Sigües
Embalse de Yesa
Berdún
Ujué
Sos del Rey Católico
PEÑA
Saqués
Panticosa
VIGNEMALE
STA. ELENA
Gavarnie
CIRQUE DE GAVARNIE
CIRCO DE BARROSA
TUNNEL DE BIELSA
Peyragudes
Bagnères-de-Luchon
Puente la Reina de Jaca
SIERRA DE LA PEÑA
Jaca
Santa Cruz de la Serós
Biescas
Torla
MONTE PERDIDO
Puerto de Santa Barbara
Puerto de Oroel
S. JUAN DE LA PEÑA
Sabiñánigo
Puerto de Cotefablo
Broto
PARQUE NAC. DE ORDESA Y MONTE PERDIDO
Bielsa
PICO POSETS
HOSP DE FRA
Carcastillo
CRUZ
Castilliscar
Uncastillo
S. DOMINGO
Biel
Bernués
Salinas de Sín
Gistaín
Luesia
Agüero
Fiscal
Lafortunada
Benasque
Sádaba
Fuencalderas
LOS MALLOS
Riglos
Embalse de La Nava
CAST. DE LOARRE
Molino de Villobas
Laguarta
Javierre
Escalona
Cinqueta
Sesué
Cerler
Boltaña
COTIELLA
Castejón de Sos
Pinsoro
Puerto de Monrepós
Arguís
Aínsa
Samper
Seira
Valareña
Ayerbe
Embalse de Arguis
Nocito
SANTUARIO DE SAN URBEZ
Campo
Luna
Nueno
SIERRA DE GUARA
Rodellar
TURBÓN
Ejea de los Caballeros
NUESTRA SEÑORA DE MONLORA
Ardisa
Plasencia del Monte
Embalse de Mediano
el Pont de Suert
Igriés
Samitier
Roda de Isábena
Beranúy
Erla
Sierra de Luna
Embalse de la Sotonera
Bárcabo
Embalse de Escales
Tormos
Huesca
Liesa
Ibieca
Alquézar
VIRGEN DE LA PEÑA
Sopeira
Gurrea de Gállego
Almudévar
Naval
Tauste
Castejón de Valdejasa
Albero Alto
Angüés
SANTUARIO DE TORRECIUDAD
Graus
Arén
Abiego
El Grado
Embalse de Barasona
Laguarres
Tardienta
Novales
La Puebla de Castro
Remolinos
Pertusa
Estada
Benabarre
Zuera
MONASTERIO DE PUEYO
Barbastro
Purroy de Solana
Puente de Montañana
Alagón
Grañén
Sesa
Huerto
Embalse de Canelles
Villanueva de Gállego
San Mateo de Gállego
Robres
Selgua
Azanúy
Puerto de Àger
CARTUJA DE AULA DEI
Leciñena
Alcubierre
Lalueza
El Tormillo
Monzón
Baells
SALDUBA
Utebo
Montañana
Perdiguera
Lanaja
Sariñena
Pomar
Pantà de Santa Anna
de Jalón
Zaragoza
Muela
SIERRA DE ALCUBIERRE
Castelflorite
Binéfar
Tamarite de Litera
les Avellanes
ZARAGOZA
Farlete
Pallaruelo de Monegros
Villanueva de Sigena
Albalate de Cinca
Alfarràs
Altorricón
COVA DELS VILARS
Cadrete
LOS GALACHOS
Alfajarín
El Burgo de Ebro
Monegrillo
Castejón de Monegros
MONASTERIO DE SIGENA
Ontiñena
Canal de Zaidín
Almenar
Botorrita
YACIMIENTO DE BOTORRITA
Osera de Ebro
Balaguer
Muel
Embalse de Mezalocha
Fuentes de Ebro
La Almolda
Ballobar
Almacelles
Torrefarrera
Bellcaire d'Urgell
Valmadrid
Villanueva de Huerva
ARAGON
Pina de Ebro
Zaidín
CASTELL DE GIMENELLS
Raimat
Vilanova de la Barca
Bell-lloc d'Urgell
Quinto
Gelsa
Bujaraloz
Lérida/ Lleida
Alcarràs
Fraga
Mollerussa
Candasnos
Embalse de las Torcas
Belchite
CIUDAD ROMANA
Soses
Alfés
Azuara
ACROPOLIS IBERICA
Azaila
Torrente de Cinca
CASTILLO DE MEQUINENZA
Serós
Castelldans
Embalse de Moneva
Escatrón
MONASTERIO DE RUEDA
Embalse de Mequinenza
COVA DEL COGUL
l'Albagés
Lécera
La Puebla de Híjar
Mequinenza
Maials
Moyuela
L'Albi
Loscos
Híjar
Samper de Calanda
Chiprana
Caspe
Granadella
Bellaguarda
Albalate del Arzobispo
MAUSOLEO DE FABARA
Fayón
Pantà de Riba-roja
La Bisbal de Falset
Embalse de Caspe II
Muniesa
Nonaspe
MONTSANT
Ulldemolins
Ariño
Flix
Embalse de Cueva Foradada
Maella
Ascó
CARTOIXA D'ESCALDEI
Cornudella de Montsant
La Hoz de la Vieja
Vivel del Río Martín
Alcañiz
La Pobla de Massaluca
Vinebre
Garcia
Batea
Andorra
CUEVA DE LA VAL DEL CHARCO DEL AGUA AMARGA
Corbera d'Ebre
Pradell
Falset
Castelserás
Móra d'Ebre
ESCORNALBOU
Los Olmos
Montalbán
Utrillas
Calanda
Valdeltormo
Calaceite
Gandesa
Miravet
Móra la Nova
Mont-roig del Camp
Alcorisa
La Canada de Verich
La Fresneda
POBLADO IBERICO
Escucha
Molinos
Ejulve
Mas de las Matas
Arnes
Prat de Compte
Benifallet
Rasquera
Cambrils
Vandellós
Valderrobres
CUEVA DE LAS GRADERAS
Castellote
MARE DE DÉU DE LA BALMA
Xerta
MORRAL DE CABRAFEIXET
Miami Platja
L'Hospitalet de l'Infant
Aliaga
Embalse de Santolea
Monroyo
L'ESPINA
Embalse de Pena
Cap de Terme
Calafat
84
85
92
99
91

SANTUARIO DE SAN URBEZ
Aínsa
Samper
Seira
N260
85
Barruera
Espot
PICA D'ESTATS
El Serrat
AND
PIC DE CAS
Campo
Vilaller
Capdella
Ribera de Cardós
Ordino
Rodellar
Embalse de Mediano
TURBÓN 2492
2742 CORRUNCO
Llavorsí
Rialp
el Pont de Suert
Andorra la Vella
Santa Coloma
STA. COLOMA
Encamp
Les Escaldes
Sant Julià de Lòria
Roda de Isábena
Beranúy
Coll de Perves 1350
Sort
Samitier
Bárcabo
Embalse de Escales
Sopeira
Senterada
Vilamor
Ibieca
Liesa
VIRGEN DE LA PEÑA
Alquézar
Naval
Angües
SANTUARIO DE TORRECIUDAD
Graus
El Grado
Arén
Gerri de la Sal
Anserall
Guils
Martinet
Abiego
La Puebla de Castro
Embalse de Barasona
Laguarres
la Pobla de Segur
la Seu d'Urgell
Novales
Pertusa
Adrall
PARC NAT.
Bellver Cerdanya
Estada
Benabarre
Pantà de Talarn
SERRA DE BOUMORT
2567
SERRA DEL CADÍ
DEL CADÍ-MOIXERÓ
MONASTERIO DE PUEYO
Barbastro
Purroy de Solana
Puente de Montañana
Tremp
Organyà
Huerto
Embalse de Canelles
Pantà de Terradets
Bóixols
Tuixén
Gósol
Selgua
Azanúy
1677
Cellers/ Castell de Mur
Isona
Coll de Nargó
Alinyà
Sariñena
El Tormillo
Monzón
Baells
Puerto de Ager 912
SERRA DEL MONTSEC
Coll de Comiols 1102
Pantà d'Oliana
Coll de Jou 1470
Pomar
Tamarite de Litera
Pantà de Santa Anna
Pantà de Camarasa
Montargull/ Artesa de Segre
Pantà de Rialb
Oliana
Odèn
Sant Llorenç de Morunys
M. D. DE QUERALT
Castelflorite
Binéfar
les Avellanes
STA. M. DE BELLPUIG DE LES AVELLANES
Berga
Villanueva de Sigena
Albalate de Cinca
Alfarràs
Altorricón
COVA DELS VILARS
Artesa de Segre
Segre
Ponts
Solsona
Gironella
MONASTERIO DE SIGENA
Ontiñena
Almenar
Camarasa
Cubells
Sanaüja
St. Susanna
Nevès
Puig-reig
Balaguer
Cardona
Almacelles
Ballobar
N
Torrefarrera
Bellcaire d'Urgell
Agramunt
CATALU
Tora
M. D. DE PINÓS
Balsareny
Zaidín
CASTELL DE GIMENELLS
Raimat
Vilanova de la Barca
Guissona
E
Súria
Candasnos
Lérida/ Lleida
Bell-lloc d'Urgell
Alcarràs
Fraga
Mollerussa
Sant Joan de Vilatorrada
Calaf
Bellpuig
Tàrrega
Cervera
Manresa
Torrente de Cinca
Soses
Alfés
Belianes
CATALU
CASTILLO DE MEQUINENZA
Embalse de Mequinenza
Serós
COVA DEL COGUL
Castelldans
les Borges Blanques
Guimerà
Port del Bruc 620
Mequinenza
l'Albagés
Santa Coloma de Queralt
Igualada
Monistrol de Montserrat
VALLBONA DE LES MONGES
MONTSERRAT
Maials
Vinaixa
Solivella
Santa Margarida de Montbui
Caspe
L'Albi
Capellades
Esparreguera
Terrassa
la Granadella
Bellaguarda
l'Espluga de Francolí
Sarral
Olesa de Montserrat
MAUSOLEO DE FÁBARA
Fayón
Pantà de Riba-roja
La Bisbal de Falset
POBLET
Montblanc
Esblada
Sant Martí Sarroca
Sant Sadurní d'Anoia
Nonaspe
Ulldemolins
MONTSANT
Flix
Puerto de Lilla
el Pla de Santa Maria
SANTES CREUS
Gelida
Maella
Ascó
Cornudella de Montsant
Vila-rodona
Vilafranca del Penedès
Sant Cugat Sesgarrigues
La Pobla de Massaluca
Batea
Vinebre
CARTOIXA D'ESCALDE
Alcover
Valls
S. Feliu de Llobregat
Garcia
Alforja
Nules
Sant Boi de Llobregat
DEL CHARCO MARGA
Corbera d'Ebre
Falset
Pradell
ARC DE BERA
OLÈRDOLA
Viladecans
Móra d'Ebre
Reus
Constantí
PONT DEL DIABLE
S. Pere de Ribes
Calaceite
Gandesa
Móra la Nova
ESCORNALBOU
Castelldefels
Valdeltormo
Miravet
Mont-roig del Camp
La Canonja
El Vendrell
La Fresneda
POBLADO IBÉRICO
Vila-seca
Altafulla
Creixell
Calafell
Vilanova i la Geltrú
Sitges
Garraf
Arnes
Prat de Compte
Rasquera
Cambrils
Tamarit
Torredembarra
Valderrobres
Benifallet
Vandellós
Salou
Tarragona
Miami Platja
Xerta
MORRAL DE CABRAFEIXET
L'Hospitalet de l'Infant
TORRE DELS ESCIPIONS
1181
L'ESPINA
Embalse de Pena
EL PORT
PORT AVENTURA
Cap de Terme
Calafat
COSTA DA
El Perelló
Arroya Tastavins
Roquetes
Tortosa
L'Ametlla de Mar
Mas de Barberans
Santa Bàrbara
Golf de Sant Jordi
L'Ampolla
MONESTIR
L'Aldea
Amposta
ABRIC D'ERMITES
Cava
PARC NATURAL
Riomar
la Sénia
San Rafael del Río
St. Jaume d'Enveja
Cap de Tortosa
St. Carles de la Ràpita
Port del Alfacs
DEL DELTA DE L' EBRE
Ulldecona
Traiguera
Les Cases d'Alcanar
La Jana
Alcanar
Platja del Trabucador
Càlig
Salzadella
Vinaròs
Magdalena de Polpis
Benicarló
Peñíscola/ Peníscola
CASTELL DE XIVERT
A
B
C
D
91
99

Ax-les-Thermes
Pailhères
Usson-les-Bains
Maury
Salses-le-Château
Port-Leucate
Port-Barcarès
St-Laurent-de-la-Salanque
Sournia
Rivesaltes
Baixas
PERPIGNAN
106
F
l'Hospitalet-l'Andorre
Col de Puymorens
Puyvalador
Formiguères
PIC CARLIT
BELVÉDÈRE
Col de la Quillane
Font-Romeu
Olette
Prades
ST.-MICHEL-DE-CUXA
Villefranche-de-Conflent
Vinça
Millas
Thuir
Canet-Plage
Vernet-les-Bains
Prunet-et-Belpuig
St-Cyprien-Plage
Elne
Puigcerdà
Llívia
Mont-Louis
Saillagouse
Bourg-Madame
ST.-MARTIN-DU-CANIGOU
PIC DU CANIGOU
Le Boulou
Argelès-Plage
Amélie-les-Bains
Argelès-sur-Mer
Collioure
Valter 2000
SANTUARI DE NÚRIA
Prats-de-Mollo-la-Preste
Arles-sur-Tech
Céret
Le Perthus
Port-Vendres
Cap Béar
Banyuls-sur-Mer
Cap l'Abeille
Cerbère
Cap Cerbère
Portbou
Colera
Llançà
Alp
Collada de Toses
La Molina
TÚNEL DEL CADÍ
ESPOT ESQUÍ
Setcases
Col d'Ares
Planoles
Ribes de Freser
SANT QUIRZE DE COLERA
la Jonquera
Maçanet de Cabrenys
Capmany
Camprodón
Sant Pau de Seguries
Darnius
el Llobregat
la Pobla de Lillet
Sant Joan de les Abadesses
QUERMANÇO
el Port de la Selva
SANT PERE DE RODES
Cap de Creus
Ripoll
Vallfogona de Ripollès
Castellfollit de la Roca
Montagut
Figueres/Figueras
Castelló d'Empúries
Borredà
Coll de Coubet
Besalú
Navata
Roses/Rosas
Cadaqués
Mostesquiu
Olot
Santa Pau
Esponellà
Empúriabrava
Cap Norfeu
Sant Agustí de Lluçanes
Sant Quirze de Besora
ZONA VOLCÀNICA DE LA GARROTXA
Sant Pere Pescador
Torelló
Bas
Banyoles/Bañolas
EMPÚRIES
Golf de Roses
Prats de Lluçanès
Sant Hipòlit de Voltregà
Manlleu
les Planes d'Hostoles
Viladamat
L'Escala
Olost
Pantà de Sau
M. D. DE LA SALUT
Amer
Flaçà
CASTELL DE MONTGRÍ
L'Estartit
Avinyó
Vic
Pantà de Susqueda
Anglès
Salt
Gerona/Girona
POBLADO IBERICO
Torroella de Montgrí
Malla
Osor
la Bisbal d'Empordà
Pals
Tona
Sant Hilari Sacalm
Girona
Cassà de la Selva
Begur
Moià
Palafrugell
Aiguablava
Centelles
Arbúcies
Sta. Coloma de Farners
Mont-Ras
Llafranc
Castellterçol
ST. MIQUEL DEL FAI
SERRA DEL MONTSENY
Sils
Caldes de Malavella
Llagostera
Calonge
Calella de Palafrugell
Montseny
Maçanet de la Selva
Castell D'Aro
Antoni de Calonge
Palamós
Sant Feliu de Codines
La Garriga
Hostalric
Sta.Cristina d'Aro
Platja d'Aro
S'Agaró
Caldes de Montbui
Sant Celoni
SANT GRAU
Sant Feliu de Guíxols
Cardedeu
Tordera
Granollers
Sabadell
la Roca del Vallès
Blanes
Lloret de Mar
Tossa de Mar
Canyet de Mar
Mollet del Vallès
Santa Susanna
Pineda de Mar
Calella
Sant Pol de Mar
Canet de Mar
Arenys de Mar
Caldes d'Estrac
Sta. Coloma de G.
Mataró
Vilassar de Mar
Premià de Mar
El Masnou
Montgat
Badalona
Molins de Rei
BARCELONA
l'Hospitalet de Llobregat
el Prat de Llobregat
Barcelona
209
Génova
Civitavécchia
COSTA BRAVA
URADA
Palma de Mallorca
Eivissa/Ibiza
Maó/Mahón-Menorca
E
F
G
H
1
2
3
4
5
6

A
B
C
D
1
2
3
4
5
6
NOSSA SENHORA DO CABO
Cabo Espichel
Sesimbra
Vila Fresca de Azeitão
Azeitão
Palmela
Setúbal
QUINTA DA BACALHÔA
Portinho da Arrábida
Tróia
CETÓBRIGA
Zambujal
Praias-Sado
Rio Sado
Poceirão
Pegões
Lavre
Vendas Novas
S. Geraldo
Marateca
Cabrela
Montemor-o-Novo
Arraiolos
São Romão
Santiago do Escoural
Barragem do Divor
CONVENTO DE ESPINHEIRO
Évora
Casa Branca
Comporta
Montevil
São Cristóvão
Alcácer do Sal
Barragem Pego do Altar
COSTA AZUL
NOSSA SENHORA DA CONCEIÇÃO
Alcáçovas
Xarrama
Torrão
Aguiar
São Man
Viana do Alentejo
Melides
Lagoa de Santo André
Grândola
São Romão
SETÚBAL
SERRA DE GRÂNDOLA
Vila Nova de S. André
São Francisco da Serra
Santo André
Barragem de Vale de Gaio
Alvito
Barragem do Alvito
Cabo de Sines
Sines
Santiago do Cacém
MIRÓBRIGA
São Bartolomeu da Serra
Azinheira dos Barros
Santa Margarida do Sado
Odivelas
Barragem de Odivelas
RUÍNAS ROMANAS
Vidigu
SERRA
Abela
Porto Covo
Ermidas-Aldeia
Ferreira do Alentejo
Cuba
Matos
São Matias
Pedrógão
São Domingos
Alvalade
Beringel
Barragem de Campilhas
Cercal
Ervidel
Santa Vitória
Beja
Baleizão
Vila Nova de Milfontes
Derreada
Bicos
Torre Vã
Barragem do Roxo
Aljustrel
Trindade
Salvada
Almograve
São Luis
Santa Luzia
Carregueiro
Albernoa
Serpa
Mira
Odemira
BEJA
Garvão
Barragem do Monte da Rocha
Telheiro
Zambujeira do Mar
Entradas
Vale de Açor
Santa Iria
Milharadas
São Martinho das Amoreiras
Ourique
CASTRO DA COLA
Castro Verde
Algodor
Odeceixe
São Teotónio
Barragem de Santa Clara
São Marcos da Ataboeira
Alcaria Ruiva
Vale do Po
Santa Clara-a-Velha
Aldeias das Neves
Rogil
Praia de Monte Clérigo
Nave Redonda
Santana da Serra
São João dos Caldeireiros
Aljezur
Corte Zorrinha
Semblana
Mértola
Arrifana
Gomes Aires
SERRA DE MONCHIQUE
Almodôvar
São Miguel do Pinheiro
Alfambras
FÓIA 902
Monchique
Marmelete
São Pedro de Solis
São Bartolomeu
Espírito Santo
Santa de Ca
Carrapateira
Bordeira
Barragem da Bravura
São Marcos da Serra
Dogueno
Caldas de Monchique
Barragem do Funcho
São Barnabé
Corte Figueira
SERRA DO CALDEIRÃO
578
Vascão
Castelejo
Bensafrim
Barragem de Arade
Arade
Ameixial
Martim Longo
Gióes
Santa Marta
NUES DE PI
Vila do Bispo
Mexilhoeira Grande
Silves
São Bartolomeu de Messines
Cachopo
Pereiro
Alcout
Cabo São Vicente
Salema
Lagos
Portimão
Messines de Baixo
Vale da Rosa
Ponta de Sagres
Sagres
Burgau
Alvor
Vau
PONTA DA PIEDADE
Lagoa
Salir
Peralva
Barragem de Odeleite
S. Silvestre de Guzmán
Carvoeiro
PONTAL
Paderne
Querença
Barranco do Velho
ALGARVE
Armação de Pera
Albufeira
Alportel
São Brás de Alportel
Odeleite
Guadiana
Vilamoura
Loulé
Portos dos Fusos
Quarteira
Almancil
MILREU
Estói
Castro Marim
Ayamor
Vale de Lobos
Faro
Moncarapacho
Tavira
Monte Gordo
Vila Real de Santo António
RÍA FORMOSA
Olhão
Fuzeta
Cabo de Santa Maria
FARO
P
É

Sousel
Veiros
Vimieiro
Santa Justa
Estremoz
Igrejinha
Évora Monte
Azaruja
São Miguel de Machede
Borba
Vila Viçosa
Santo Aleixo
Santa Eulália
Barragem do Caia
Elvas
ACUEDUCTO DE AMOREIRA
Badajoz
Villar del Rey
Puebla de Obando
La Roca de la Sierra
Cordobilla de Lácara
Alcuéscar
La Nava de Santiago
Pueblonuevo del Guadiana
Talavera la Real
Villafranco del Guadiana
Montijo
La Garrovilla
Aljucén
Conquista del Guadiana
San Pedro de Mérida
Puebla de la Calzada
Calamonte
Mérida
Lobón
Arroyo de San Serván
Medellín
EXTREM
Alandroal
Barragem do Monte Novo
Barragem da Vigia
Redondo
Terena
ÉVORA
Pias
Montoito
Vendinha
Barragem d'Alqueva
Olivenza
S.Benito de la Contienda
Valverde de Leganés
La Albuera
Cortes de Peleas
Solana de los Barros
Torremejía
Zarza de Alange
Alange
Guareña
Oliva de Mérida
Monte do Trigo
Reguengos de Monsaraz
S. PEDRO
Monsaraz
Cheles
LOS ARCOS
Almendral
Alconchel
Táliga
Nogales
Santa Marta
Aceuchal
Almendralejo
Villalba de los Barros
Palomas
Embalse de Alange
Portel
Campo
Mourão
Barcarrota
Salvatierra de los Barros
Puebla de la Reina
Villanueva del Fresno
Higuera de Vargas
Villafranca de los Barros
MENDRO
Alqueva
Granja
Fuente del Maestre
Valle de Matamoros
Valle de la Serena
Hornachos
Ribera del Fresno
Retamal de Llerena
Póvoa
Zahinos
Burguillos del Cerro
Feria
Zafra
Los Santos de Maimona
Jerez de los Caballeros
Valencia de Mombuey
Oliva de la Frontera
Hinojosa del Valle
Moura
Amareleja
Santo Amador
Puerto de Sto Domingo 570
E
Llera
Brinches
Pias
Safara
Sobral da Adiça
Barrancos
Encinasola
Fregenal de la Sierra
Valencia del Ventoso
Usagre
Valencia de las Torres
Villagarcia de la Torre
Manguilla
Bienvenida
Fuente de Cantos
Santo Aleixo da Restauração
Rosal de la Frontera
Vila Nova de São Bento
Vila Verde de Ficalho
Vales Mortos
Higuera la Real
Cumbres de S. Bartolomé
Segura de León
Puerto de la Loba
CIUDAD ROMANA
Llerena
Berlanga
Montemolín
Casas de Reina
SIERRA PELADA
Aroche
Cumbres Mayores
Fuentes de León
MON. DE TENTUDÍA
Monesterio
Pallarés
Fuente del Arco
Paymogo
Santa Bárbara
Cortegana
La Nava
Cañaveral de León
SIERRA DE TUDIA
Mina de São Domingos
SIERRA DE ARACENA
Almonaster la Real
Jabugo
PARQUE NATURAL
Puebla del Maestre
Puerto de las Marismas
CUEVAS DE SANTIAGO
Guadalcanal
San Telmo
Aracena
Cala
Embalse de Aracena
El Real de la Jara
Puebla de Guzmán
Cabezas Rubias
El Cerro de Andévalo
CUEVA DE LAS MARAVILLAS
Santa Olalla del Cala
Embalse de El Pintado
Alanís
Villanueva de las Cruces
VIRGEN DE LA PEÑA
Tharsis
Calañas
Minas de Riotinto
La Granada de Rio Tinto
Y PICOS DE AROCHE
Almadén de la Plata
Cazalla de la Sierra
Alosno
Villanueva de los Castillejos
Zalamea la Real
Nerva
El Ronquillo
El Pedroso
San Bartolomé de la Torre
Embalse del Piedras
El Madroño
Valverde del Camino
El Castillo de las Guardas
Embalse de la Minilla
Berrocal
Embalse de Cala
Villablanca
Gibraleón
Beas
Tumbalejo
El Garrobo
Venta El Alto
Castilblanco de los Arroyos
MULBA
Villanueva del Río y Minas
Cartaya
Trigueros
Aljaraque
Lepe
El Rompido
Burguillos
Villaverde del Río
Cantillana
Alcolea del Río
Aznalcóllar
Huelva
La Antilla
San Juan del Puerto
Niebla
La Palma del Condado
Villaba del Alcor
Manzanilla
Gerena
Guillena
Alcalá del Río
Brenes
Tocina
Lora del Río
El Portil
Moguer
Bonares
Olivares
ITALICA
La Rinconada
ARVA
Guadajoz
Palos de la Frontera
Punta Umbría
MONASTERIO DE LA RABIDA
Rociana del Condado
Bollullos Par del Condado
Sanlúcar la Mayor
Santiponce
La Algaba
S. ISIDORO DEL CAMPO
Camas
NECRÓPOLIS ROMANA
La Campana
Almonte
Pilas
Bollullos de la Mitación
SEVILLA
El Viso del Alcor
Carmona
Hinojos
NUESTRA SEÑORA DEL ROCÍO
Villamanrique de la Condesa
Mairena del Aljarafe
Alcalá de Guadaira
Mairena del Alcor
Mazagón
El Rocío
Coria del Río
La Puebla del Río
Dos Hermanas
MARCHENILLA
MARISMAS
ASPERILLO 103
Isla Mayor
Paradas
Marchena
GUADALQUIVIR
87
96
101
102

EXTREMADURA
E
Santiago del Campo
Almaraz
Romangordo
Puerto de Miravete 624
Embalse de Valdecañas
La Calzada de Oropesa
Oropesa
Segurilla
Velada
Talavera de la Reina
Casar de Cáceres
Monroy
La Aldea del Obispo
Jaraicejo
Bohonal de Ibor
Berrocalejo
Calera y Chozas
Cáceres
VIRGEN DE LA MONTAÑA
Aldea de Trujillo
Deleitosa
Valdeverdeja
Valdelacas de Tajo
El Puente del Arzobispo
RUINAS ROMANAS
Embalse de Azután
La Pueblanueva
Alcaudete de la Jara
Ipartida Cáceres
Castañar de Ibor
Villar del Pedroso
Valdesalor
Sierra de Fuentes
Torrecillas de la Tiesa
Retamosa
Carrascalejo
La Estrella
Belvis de la Jara
San Martín de Pusa
Puerto del Clavín 425
Torrequemada
Aldeacentenera
Navalvillar de Ibor
La Nava de Ricomalillo
La Cumbre
Trujillo
MAYORALGO
Aldea del Cano
Torremocha
Madroñera
Puerto de San Vicente
Los Navalucillos
Torre de Sta. María
Puerto de Santa Cruz
Garciaz
SIERRA DE GUADALUPE
1602
Guadalupe
Sevilleja de la Jara
Puerto de San Vicente 807
Robledo del Buey
MALAMONA
Cordobilla de Lácara
Montánchez
Santa Cruz de la Sierra
Conquista de la Sierra
MONASTERIO DE GUADALUPE
Alía
Alcuéscar
Almoharín
Zorita
Logrosán
Puerto Llano 836
Anchuras
Los Alares
Nava Santiago
Villamesias
Aljucén
Conquista del Guadiana
Miajadas
Valdeazores
Valdecaballeros
Castilblanco
Bohonal
San Pedro de Mérida
Santa Amalia
Madrigalejo
Villar de Rena
Embalse de García de Sola
Embalse de Cíjara
Horcajo de los Montes
SIERRA DE
Mérida
Medellín
Acedera
Navalvillar de Pela
Villarta de los Montes
Herrera del Duque
Fuenlabrada de los Montes
Zarza de Alange
Don Benito
Villanueva de la Serena
Casas de Don Pedro
Talarrubias
Embalse de Orellana
Navalpino
Alcoba de los Montes
Alange
Guareña
La Haba
La Coronada
Embalse de Zújar
Puebla de Alcocer
GARGANTA DE RETAMA
969
Oliva de Mérida
Campanario
Sancti-Spiritus
Siruela
Puebla de Don Rodrigo
Arroba de los Montes
Palomas
Embalse de Alange
Agudo
Puebla de la Reina
Quintana de la Serena
Embalse de la Serena
El Gato
Retama
Valle de la Serena
Castuera
Peñalsordo
Saceruela
Ribera del Fresno
Hornachos
Benquerencia de la Serena
Retamal de Llerena
Higuera de la Serena
Zalamea de la Serena
Helechal
Cabeza del Buey
Zarza-Capilla
Chillón
Almadén
Abenójar
Campillo de Llerena
Monterrubio de la Serena
SIERRA DEL PEDROSO
Guadalmez
Almadenojos
Fontanosas
Usagre
Valencia de las Torres
Alhamillo
Valdeazogues
Manguilla
Peraleda del Zaucejo
Belalcázar
Santa Eufemia
SIERRA DE ALCUDIA
Bienvenida
Almodóvar del Campo
Berlanga
Los Blázquez
Hinojosa del Duque
San Benito
Brazatortas
Llerena
Granja de Torrehermosa
El Viso
El Guijo
1106
PLAZA DEL JUDIO
Casas de Reina
Azuaga
La Granjuela
Dos Torres
Puerto de Niefla 902
Fuente del Arco
Fuente Obejuna
Villanueva del Duque
Alcaracejos
Pedroche
Torrecampo
Peñarroya-Pueblonuevo
Puerto de Valderrepiso 860
CUEVAS DE SANTIAGO
Malcocinado
Argallón
Belmez
Pozoblanco
Conquista
CUEVAS DE PEÑA ESCRITA
Guadalcanal
El Alcornocal
Villanueva de Córdoba
Fuencaliente
1323
Embalse de El Pintado
Valdeinfierno
SIERRA DE LOS SANTOS
Villanueva del Rey
727 Puerto Espiel
Torrubia
896
Alanís
PARQUE NATURAL
S. Nicolás del Puerto
Espiel
Villaharta
Azuel
Cazalla de la Sierra
Embalse de Puente Nuevo
Embalse de Bembézar
Cardeña
Villaviciosa
Obejo
PARQUE NATURAL
Las Navas de la Concepción
El Pedroso
Constantina
PARQUE NATURAL SIERRA DE HORNACHUELOS
PARQUE NATURAL SIERRA DE CARDEÑA Y MONTORO
SIERRA NORTE
Cerro Muriano
Adamuz
VIRGEN DE LA CABEZA
MULBA
La Puebla de los Infantes
Hornachuelos
Embalse de la Breña
MEDINA AZAHARA
SANTO DOMINGO
Montoro
Marmolejo
Villanueva del Río y Minas
ALMENARA
Cantillana
Alcolea del Río
El Priorato
Posadas
Almodóvar del Río
CÓRDOBA
El Carpio
Pedro Abad
Andújar
87
88
95
102
A5
E90
N521
A66
E803
N630
EX206
EX208
EX102
EX335
EX2
E90
A5
N430
N502
EX103
EX104
EX346
EX336
EX115
EX322
EX111
EX202
N432
A422
A449
A430
A423
A433
A447
SE163
A432
A455
A436
A431
A3075
A421
N420
A420
CO510
C424
CM411
CM4100
CM4171
N502
Almonte
Guadiana
Zújar
Matachel
Bembézar
Cuzna
Guadalbarbo
Guadalmez
Yeguas
Esteras

Hormigos
Maqueda
Cazalegas
Santa Cruz del Retamar
Casarubios del Monte
Torrejón de la Calzada
Griñón
Valmojado
Parla
Pinto
WARNER BROS PARK
Arganda del Rey
Nuevo Baztán
Mondéjar
ECÓPOLIS
Santa Olalla
Novés
Illescas
Valdemoro
San Martín de la Vega
Ciempozuelos
Albares
Albalate de Zorita
Cebolla
Fuensalida
Yuncos
Seseña Nuevo
Perales de Tajuña
Malpica de Tajo
El Carpio de Tajo
Torrijos
Recas
Chinchón
Villarejo de Salvanés
Estremera
Bartolomé de las Abiertas
Escalonilla
La Puebla de Montalbán
Bargas
VILLALUENGA
Añover de Tajo
Colmenar de Oreja
Aranjuez
Mocejón
Fuentidueña de Tajo
Belinchón
Barajas de Melo
Toledo
STA. MARÍA DE MELQUE
Los Navalmorales
MONTALBÁN
GUADAMUR
CASTILLO DE SAN SERVANDO
Ocaña
Villarrubia de Santiago
Villasequilla
Huerta de Valdecarábanos
Santa Cruz de la Zarza
Tarancón
Nambroca
Villamuelas
MONREAL
Dosbarrios
Argés
Polán
Gálvez
Villatobas
Carrascosa del Campo
UCLÉS
Navahermosa
Menasalbas
Pulgar
Sonseca
A Guarda/La Guardia
Fuente de Pedro Naharro
Saelices
Cuerva
Mora
Cabezamesada
Horcajo de Santiago
SEGÓBRIGA
Navas de Estena
Las Ventas con Peña Aguilera
Orgaz
Tembleque
Romeral
Corral de Almaguer
Laguna de Hito
Retuerta del Bullaque
MORA
Lillo
Marjalija
VIRGEN DE LA MUELA
Villarejo de Fuentes
Los Yébenes
Turleque
Villamayor de Santiago
El Molinillo
Villacañas
La Puebla de Almoradiel
Villanueva de Alcardete
Fuentelespino de Haro
Embalse de Torre de Abraham
GUADALERZAS
Quintanar de la Orden
Los Hinojosos
Villaescusa de Haro
Pedrera
Consuegra
Madridejos
Miguel Esteban
Urda
MOLINOS
Villafranca de los Caballeros
El Toboso
Mota del Cuervo
Belmonte
El Robledo
Cortijos de Abajo
MONTES DE TOLEDO
CASTILLA-LA MANCHA
SIERRA DE LA CALDERINA
CHORITO
ERMITA DE VILLAJOS
Herencia
CRISTO DEL ESPÍRITU-SANTO
Puerto Lápice
Alcázar de San Juan
VIRGEN DE CRIPTANA
Campo de Criptana
El Pedernoso
Las Pedroñeras
Puerto de los Majales
Fuente el Fresno
Villarrubia de los Ojos
Porzuna
Embalse de Gasset
Malagón
Villarta de San Juan
Pedro Muñoz
Las Mesas
MIRAFLORES
Fernancaballero
PARQUE NACIONAL DE LAS TABLAS DE DAIMIEL
Vega de los Árboles
Luciana
Piedrabuena
CALATRAVA LA VIEJA
El Minguillo
Cinco Casas
Socuéllamos
Ciudad Real
Carrión de Calatrava
Daimiel
Villarrobledo
NUESTRA SEÑORA DE ARCOS
HERRERA
Torralba
Argamasilla de Alba
Tomelloso
Cabezarados
Miguelturra
Caracuel de Calatrava
Manzanares
CASTILLO DE PEÑARROYA
Almagro
Bolaños de Calatrava
Membrilla
Embalse de Peñarroya
Argamasilla de Calatrava
Granátula de Calatrava
La Solana
Ruidera
Sotuélamos
Aldea del Rey
Moral de Calatrava
San Carlos del Valle
Munera
Puertollano
Alhambra
Lagunas de Ruidera
CUEVA DE MONTESINOS
Ossa de Montiel
El Bonillo
La Calzada de Calatrava
CONVENTO DE CALATRAVA
Valdepeñas
Carrizosas
SALVATIERRA
SIERRA MESTANZA
Embalse de Montoro
Salinas de Pinilla
El Ballestero
Mestanza
La Alameda
Santa Cruz de Mudela
Alcubillas
Villanueva de los Infantes
Villahermosa
CASTILLO DE MUDELA
NUESTRA SEÑORA DE LA ANTIGUA
Viveros
Solana del Pino
Torrenueva
Cózar
Montiel
Villanueva de la Fuente
Viso del Marqués
Almedina
Robledo
San Lorenzo de Calatrava
Torre de Juan Abad
Albaladejo
N. S. DE CORTÉS
Almuradiel
Castellar de Santiago
Puebla del Príncipe
Alcaraz
Peñascosa
Colonia Selladores
DESPEÑAPERROS
MONTIZÓN
Villamanrique
Villapalacios
Reolid
Vianos
Embalse de Jandúla
El Centenillo
Aldeaquemada
SIERRA DE ALCARAZ
Paterna del Madera
Santa Elena
Embalse de Guadalmena
Venta de los Santos
Génave
CHORROS DEL MUNDO
Riópar
Bogarra
Embalse del Rumblar
La Carolina
Puente de Génave
Vilches
Chiclana de Segura
Baños de la Encina
Guarromán
Santisteban del Puerto
La Puerta de Segura
Siles
CUEVA DE LOS CHORROS
Molinicos
Arquillinos
Castellar
Beas de Segura
Orcera
Navas de San Juan
Sorihuela
Segura
Yeste
Bailén
Tajo
Tajuña
Jarama
Algodor
Cedrón
Riánsares
Cigüela
Záncara
Guadiana
Bullaque
Azuer
Jabalón
Fresnedas
Córcoles
Guadalmena
Guadalimar
Guarrizas
Guadalén
Pinto
89
98
103
2009

Pastrana
Alcocer
Beteta
Tordesilos
Cañizares
Priego
S. MIGUEL DE LAS VICTORIAS
SIERRA DE ALBARRACÍN
Villar del Salz
Albares
Buendia
Villaba del Rey
Orihuela del Tremedal
Pozondón
Torremocha de Jiloca
Albalate de Zorita
Albalate de las Nogueras
Poyatos
Cañaveras
Estremera
Arcos de la Sierra
NACIMIENTO DEL RIO CUERVO
La Noguera
Santa Eulalia
Villarquemado
Gascueña
SERRANÍA DE CUENCA
MONTES UNIVERSALES
La Peraleja
Torrecilla
Tragacete
Cella
Albarracín
Gea de Albarracín
Belinchón
Barajas de Melo
Huete
Bonilla
Villar de Domingo García
Villalba de la Sierra
Una
Huélamo
CUEVAS DE ALBARRACÍN
Tarancón
Caracenilla
Sotos
LA CIUDAD ENCANTADA
Terriente
Carrascosa del Campo
UCLÉS
Chillarón de Cuenca
Embalse de la Toba
Embalse del Arquillo de San Blas
Naharros
Valdecabras
Villastar
Fuente de Pedro Naharro
Saelices
Palomares del Campo
Puerto de Cabrejas 1150
Villar de Olalla
Cuenca
Toril
CUEVAS DE LA TAJADA
Villel
Horcajo de Santiago
SEGÓBRIGA
Valdemoro Sierra
Laguna del Marquesado
LAS TORCAS
Laguna de Hito
Altarejos
Arcas
Montalbo
Cañete
Villarejo de Fuentes
Villares del Saz
Fuentes
Salvacañete
La Torre Baixa
Ademuz
Villamayor de Santiago
San Lorenzo de la Parrilla
RUINAS ROMANAS
Puerto de Tórdiga 1200
Puerto de Rocho 1150
Algarra
VALENCIA
Villanueva de Alcardete
Fuentelespino de Haro
Cervera del Llano
Olivares de Júcar
Valeria
Carboneras de Guadazaón
Fuentelespino de Moya
Santa Cruz de Moya
Los Hinojonos
Villalgordo del Marquesado
La Hinojosa
Arguisuelas
ABRIGO DE LA PEÑA DEL ESCRITO
Landete
Villaescusa de Haro
La Almarcha
Valverde de Júcar
Solera del Gabaldón
Almodóvar del Pinar
Embalse de Villora
Mota del Cuervo
Belmonte
Embalse de Alarcón
Honrubia
Olmedilla de Alarcón
Cardenete
Talayuelas
Titaguas
Garaballa
El Pedernoso
El Cañavate
Las Pedroñeras
La Alberca de Záncara
Cañadajuncosa
Campillo de Altobuey
Mira
Enguídanos
Sinarcas
Las Mesas
Alarcón
Motilla del Palancar
SAN AGUSTÍN
Camporrobles
Embalse de Contreras
Embalse de Benagéber
Villar de Cantos
San Clemente
La Torre
Embalse de Loriguilla
Socuéllamos
Casas de Fernando Alonso
Sisante
Minglanilla
Villargordo del Cabriel
N. S. DEL REMEDIO
Villarrobledo
VIRGEN DE LA CABEZA
Casas de Benítez
Villanueva de la Jara
Iniesta
Villalpardo
Utiel
Chera
Minaya
Quintanar del Rey
Villarta
HOCES DEL CABRIEL
Venta del Moro
Requena
Ledaña
Villamalea
Los Isidros
Moharras
La Roda
Tarazona de la Mancha
Cenizzate
Villatoya
La Portera
Mijares
Sotuélamos
Santa Marta
Fuentealbilla
Casas-Ibáñez
Mahora
Alborea
Montilleja
Munera
Ossa de Montiel
El Bonillo
La Gineta
Villar del Pozo
Abengibre
Alcalá del Júcar
Valdeganga
Villa de Ves
Embalse de Embarcaderos
Lezuza
Barrax
Jorquera
Cofrentes
Casas de Juan Núñez
Cortes de Pallás
CUEVA DE DON JUAN
Carcelén
Jarafuel
El Ballestero
Albacete
La Felipa
Alatoz
Muela de Cortes
Balazote
Teresa de Confrentes
CUEVA DE LA ARAÑA
Viveros
Aguas Nuevas
Chinchilla de Monte-Aragón
Hoya-Gonzalo
CUEVA DE LA VIEJA
Ayora
San Pedro
Robledo
El Salobral
Higueruela
Las Fuentes
Pozuelo
N. S. DE CORTÉS
Alpera
CUEVA DEL REY MORO
SIERRA DE ALCARAZ
Alcaraz
Peñascosa
Pozo-Cañada
Pétrola
Bonete
Corral Rubio
CERRO DE LOS SANTOS
Almansa
Navalón
Vianos
Peñas de San Pedro
Pozohondo
Las Anorias
Paterna del Madera
Alcadozo
La Higuera
Montealegre del Castillo
La Font de la Figuera
Bogarra
Fuente Álamo
CUEVA DE MONTE ARABÍ
Moixent
Riópar
CHORROS EL MUNDO
SANT. DE LA ENCARNACIÓN
Ayna
Liétor
Ontur
Tobarra
Caudete
Fontanars dels Alforins
CUEVA DE LOS CHORROS
Molinicos
Elche de la Sierra
Embalse de Talave
Benejama/Beneixama
Hellín
Yecla
Yeste
Isso
89
90
97
104

Bueña
Utrillas
Montalbán
Olmos
Calanda
Calaceite
Gandesa
Valdeltormo
Mezquita de Jarque
Escucha
Ejulve
Molinos
Alcorisa
91
La Cañada de Verich
La Fresneda
Rillo
Visiedo
Perales del Alfambra
Aliaga
CUEVA DE LAS GRADERAS
Castellote
Mas de las Matas
MARE DE DÉU DE LA BALMA
Valderrobres
Arnes
Prat de Compte
Benifallet
Xerta
MORRAL DE CABRAFEIXET
SIERRA PALOMERA
Alfambra
Camarillas
Aguilar del Alfambra
Villarluengo
Embalse de Santolea
Sorita
Monroyo
Embalse de Pena
Peñarroya de Tastavins
1181
L'ESPINA
EL PORT
El Perelló
Tortosa
Peralejos
Villarroga de los Pinares
Olocau del Rey
Cañada de Benatanduz
Forcall
Puerto Torre Miró 1250
Castell de Cabres
Mas de Barberans
Roquetes
Santa Bàrbara
L'Ampolla
Allepuz
Cantavieja
Morella
MORELLA LA VELLA
MONESTIR DE BENIFASSÀ
Amposta
L'Aldea
Corbalán
Vallivana
ABRIC D'ERMITES
la Sénia
Cava
Teruel
SIERRA DE CAMARENA
SIERRA DE GÚDAR
La Iglesuela del Cid
SIERRA DEL MAESTRAZGO
San Rafael del Río
St. Carles de la Ràpita
St. Jaume d'Enveja
Alcalá de la Selva
Ares del Maestre/ Ares del Maestrat
La Vallivana
Xert
Traiguera
Ulldecona
Port del Alfacs
DEL DELTA DE
NUESTRA SEÑORA DE LA VEGA
Villafranca del Cid/ Vilafranca del Maestrat
COVA REMÍGIA
Sant Mateu
La Jana
Les Cases d'Alcanar
Alcanar
1242 Puerto de Escandón
La Puebla de Valverde
Mosqueruela
Càlig
Platja de Trabucador
Mora de Rubielos
Linares de Mora
Benassal
COVA DELS CAVALLS
la Salzadella
Vinaròs
Embalse de los Toranes
Puertomingalvo
Albocácer/ Albocàsser
Santa Magdalena de Polpis
Benicarló
92
Camarena de la Sierra
Rubielos de Mora
ST. JOAN DE PENYAGOLOSA
Chodos/ Xodos
les Coves de Vinromà
Peñíscola/ Peñíscola
E
Sarrión
Atzeneta del Maestrat
CASTELL DE XIVERT
Albentosa
Olba
Lucena del Cid/ Llucena
Vilanova d'Alcolea
Alcalá de Chivert/ Alcalá de Xivert
Cabo de Irta
Manzanera
Castillo de Villamalefa
La Pelechaneta/ Pelejaneta
Torreblanca
Alcocèber/ Alcossebre
Montanejos
Useras/ les Useres
Barracas
Embalse Alcora
Cabanes
Torrenostra
Alpuente
Vilafamés
la Pobla Tornesa
Espadilla
Alcora/ l'Alcora
Oropesa del Mar/ Orpesa
La Yesa
Fuentes de Ayódar
Embalse María Cristina
Borriol
Benicasim/ Benicàssim
Bejís
Viver
Jérica
Onda
Andilla
Castellón de la Plana/ Castelló de la Plana
LA CUEVA SANTA
Alcublas
Villarreal/ la Vila Real
Segorbe
Artana
Almazora/ Almassora
COSTA DEL AZAHAR
Villar del Arzobispo
Altura
la Vall d'Uixó
Nules
Burriana/ Borriana
Casinos
Gátova
GRUTA DE SANT JOSEP
Moncofa
Almenara
VALÈNCIA
CARTOIXA DE PORTA COELI
Pedralba
Serra
Els Columbrets
Llíria
CONVENT DEL SANCTI SPIRITUS
El Grau
la Pobla de Vallbona
Bétera
Sagunto/Sagunt
Cheste
Riba-roja de Túria
Puig
Puçol
Chiva
Massamagrell
Burjassot
Buñol
Paterna
Mislata
Alboraya/Alboraia
Alaquàs
Torrent
VALÈNCIA
Alfafar
Golfo de València
Turís/ Torís
Catarroja
Montroy/ Montroi
Picassent
El Saler
Silla
247
Eivissa/Ibiza
Palma de Mallorca
Palermo
Maó/Mahón-Menorca
Benifaió
el Palmar
Alginet
Sollana
Carlet
L'Alcúdia
El Perelló
Puerta de Levante
Algemesí
Sueca
Alberic
Alzira
Cullera
Carcaixent
Castelló de la Ribera
Favara
La Pobla Llarga
LA MURTA
Tavernes de la Valldigna
Xàtiva
Xeraco
Alcúdia de Crespins
l'Olleria
Xeresa
Grao/el Grau
Benigànim
MONESTIR DE S. JERONI
Gandia
Palma de Mallorca
Sant Antoni de Portmany
Eivissa/Ibiza
Ontinyent
Rótova
Albaida
Terrateig
Oliva
Puerto de Albaida 600
Muro de Alcoy/ Muro del Comtat
105
Bañeres de Mariola
Benimarfull
Pego
Ondara
Dénia
Cocentaina
Les Rotes
A7
AP7
E15
N340
N332
N234
A23
N420
N211
N232
N238
CV50
CV35
CV15
CV10
CV125
CV129
CV133
CV190
CV18
CV230
CV245
CV500
CV60
CV610
CV700
T340
C12
C42
E901

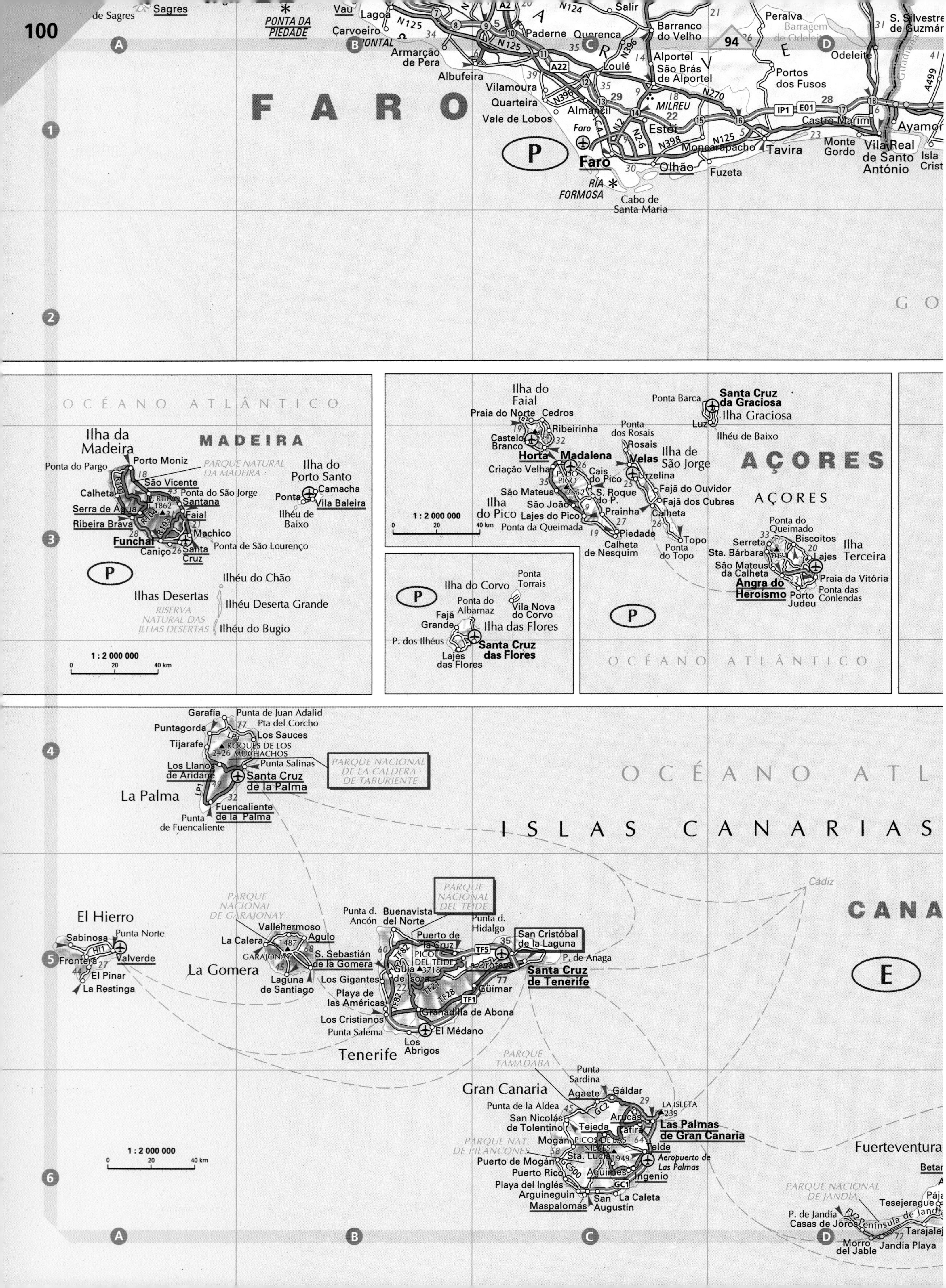
FARO
Sagres
de Sagres
PONTA DA PIEDADE
Lagoa
Carvoeiro
Armação de Pera
Albufeira
Vilamoura
Quarteira
Vale de Lobos
Paderne
Querença
Salir
Barranco do Velho
Loulé
Alportel
São Brás de Alportel
Almancil
MILREU
Estói
Faro
Olhão
Moncarapacho
Fuzeta
Tavira
RÍA FORMOSA
Cabo de Santa Maria
Peralva
Barragem de Odeleite
Odeleite
Portos dos Fusos
Castro Marim
Monte Gordo
Vila Real de Santo António
S. Silvestre de Guzmán
Ayamonte
Isla Cristina
P
OCÉANO ATLÂNTICO
MADEIRA
Ilha da Madeira
Ponta do Pargo
Porto Moniz
PARQUE NATURAL DA MADEIRA
São Vicente
Ponta do São Jorge
Santana
Calheta
Serra de Água
Ribeira Brava
Faial
Machico
Funchal
Caniço
Santa Cruz
Ponta de São Lourenço
Ilha do Porto Santo
Camacha
Ponta
Vila Baleira
Ilhéu de Baixo
Ilhéu do Chão
Ilhas Desertas
Ilhéu Deserta Grande
RISERVA NATURAL DAS ILHAS DESERTAS
Ilhéu do Bugio
1 : 2 000 000
0 20 40 km
Ilha do Faial
Praia do Norte
Cedros
Castelo Branco
Ribeirinha
Horta
Madalena
Criação Velha
PICO
São Mateus
São João
Ilha do Pico
Lajes do Pico
Ponta da Queimada
Cais do Pico
S. Roque do P.
Prainha
Piedade
Calheta de Nesquim
Ponta dos Rosais
Rosais
Velas
Urzelina
Ilha de São Jorge
Fajã do Ouvidor
Fajã dos Cubres
Calheta
Topo
Ponta do Topo
Ponta Barca
Santa Cruz da Graciosa
Ilha Graciosa
Luz
Ilhéu de Baixo
AÇORES
Ponta do Queimado
Serreta
Biscoitos
Sta. Bárbara
Lajes
Ilha Terceira
São Mateus da Calheta
Angra do Heroísmo
Praia da Vitória
Porto Judeu
Ponta das Contendas
Ilha do Corvo
Ponta Torrais
Ponta do Albarnaz
Vila Nova do Corvo
Fajã Grande
Ilha das Flores
P. dos Ilhéus
Santa Cruz das Flores
Lajes das Flores
ISLAS CANARIAS
Garafía
Punta de Juan Adalid
Pta del Corcho
Puntagorda
Los Sauces
Tijarafe
ROQUES DE LOS MUCHACHOS
Los Llanos de Aridane
Punta Salinas
Santa Cruz de la Palma
PARQUE NACIONAL DE LA CALDERA DE TABURIENTE
La Palma
Fuencaliente de la Palma
Punta de Fuencaliente
El Hierro
Sabinosa
Punta Norte
Frontera
Valverde
El Pinar
La Restinga
PARQUE NACIONAL DE GARAJONAY
Vallehermoso
Agulo
La Calera
S. Sebastián de la Gomera
La Gomera
Laguna de Santiago
PARQUE NACIONAL DEL TEIDE
Punta d. Ancón
Buenavista del Norte
Punta d. Hidalgo
Puerto de la Cruz
San Cristóbal de la Laguna
P. de Anaga
PICO DEL TEIDE
La Orotava
Santa Cruz de Tenerife
Los Gigantes
Guía de Isora
Güimar
Playa de las Américas
Granadilla de Abona
Los Cristianos
Punta Salema
El Médano
Los Abrigos
Tenerife
Cádiz
CANA
E
PARQUE TAMADABA
Punta Sardina
Gran Canaria
Agaete
Gáldar
LA ISLETA
Punta de la Aldea
San Nicolás de Tolentino
Arucas
Tejeda
Tafira
Las Palmas de Gran Canaria
PARQUE NAT. DE PILANCONES
Mogán
PICOS DE LAS NIEVES
Telde
Puerto de Mogán
Sta. Lucía
Aeropuerto de Las Palmas
Puerto Rico
Agüimes
Ingenio
Playa del Inglés
Arguineguín
San Augustín
La Caleta
Maspalomas
Fuerteventura
PARQUE NACIONAL DE JANDÍA
Tesejerague
P. de Jandía
Casas de Jorós
Península de Jandía
Tarajalejo
Morro del Jable
Jandía Playa
1 : 2 000 000
0 20 40 km

San Bartolomé de la Torre
Embalse del Piedras
Valverde del Camino
El Madroño
Berrocal
95
El Castillo de las Guardas
Ronquillo
Embalse de Cala
El Pedroso
Villablanca
Gibraleón
Beas
Tumbalejo
Trigueros
El Garrobo
Venta El Alto
Castilblanco de los Arroyos
MULBA
Villanueva del Río y Minas
Cartaya
Lepe
Aljaraque
El Rompido
La Palma del Condado
Aznalcóllar
Burguillos
Villaverde del Río
Cantillana
Alcolea del Río
Tocina
La Antilla
Huelva
San Juan del Puerto
Niebla
Bonares
Villalba del Alcor
Manzanilla
Gerena
Guillena
Alcalá del Río
La Rinconada
Brenes
Guadajoz
ARVA
Lora del Río
El Portil
Moguer
Palos de la Frontera
Rociana del Condado
Bollullos Par del Condado
Olivares
Sanlúcar la Mayor
ITALICA
Santiponce
La Algaba
NECRÓPOLIS ROMANA
La Campana
Punta Umbria
MONASTERIO DE LA RÁBIDA
Almonte
Pilas
Bollullos de la Mitación
S. ISIDORO DEL CAMPO
Camas
Carmona
SEVILLA
Mairena del Aljarafe
Hinojos
Villamanrique de la Condesa
Coria del Río
La Puebla del Río
El Viso del Alcor
Alcalá de Guadaira
Mairena del Alcor
Dos Hermanas
MARCHENILLA
Mazagón
NUESTRA SEÑORA DEL ROCÍO
El Rocío
MARISMAS DEL GUADALQUIVIR
COSTA DE LA LUZ
GOLFO DE CÁDIZ
ASPERILLO 103
Isla Mayor
Paradas
Marchena
Matalascañas
TORRE DE LA HIGUERA
Los Palacios y Villafranca
Utrera
Arahal
Los Molares
PARQUE NACIONAL DE DOÑANA
La Señuela
Trajano
El Palmar de Troya
Embalse de la Torre del Águila
Morón de la Frontera
Mosteiros
Lagoa Azul
Ponta da Agulha
Capelas
Ponta Delgada
Ribeira Grande
Maia
Fenais da Ajuda
Pta. da Ribeira
Lagoa
Vila Franca do Campo
Furnas
Nordeste
Povoação
Pta. da Madrugada
Ilha de São Miguel
AÇORES
Ilha de Santa Maria
Anjos
Baía do São Lourenço
Almagreira
Vila do Porto
Maia
Ponta do Castelo
Lebrija
Las Cabezas de San Juan
El Coronil
AGUZADERA
La Encinilla y El Rubio
Montellano
COTE
Coripe
Punta de Malandar
Bonanza
Trebujena
Sanlúcar de Barrameda
El Cuervo
Chipiona
Santa Cruz de la Palma
Santa Cruz de Tenerife
Las Palmas de Gran Canaria
Espera
Bornos
Villamartín
Puertoserrano
JEREZ DE LA FRONTERA
Arcos de la Frontera
Jédula
Embalse de Bornos
Algodonales
Zahara
El Castor
Olvera
Rota
LA CARTUJA
MELGAREJO
La Barca de la Florida
Prado del Rey
El Bosque
Embalse de Zahara-El Gastor
ACINIPO
El Puerto de Santa María
Bahía de Cádiz
Embalse de Guadalcacín
SIERRA DE GRAZALEMA
CÁDIZ
El Torno
Algar
Grazalema
Puerto Real
Ubrique
San José del Valle
Benaoján
Ronda
FÁTIMA
San Fernando
BERROQUEJO
Embalse de Los Hurones
CUEVA DE LA PILETA
Chiclana de la Frontera
Medina-Sidonia
Paterna de Rivera
Cortes de la Frontera
SERRANÍA DE RONDA
ÁNTICO
Barrosa
Sancti Petri
La Sauceda
Algatocín
Igualeja
Alcalá de los Gazules
Gaucín
Roche
Embalse de Barbate
PARQUE NATURAL DE LOS ALCORNOCALES
Sierra Bermeja
Cabo Roche
Conil de la Frontera
Benalup
Jimena de la Frontera
Casares
San Pedro de Alcántara
Vejer de la Frontera
CUEVA DEL TAJO DE LAS FIGURAS
Castellar de la Frontera
Manilva
Estepona
Guadalmina
RIAS
Cabo de Trafalgar
Los Caños de Meca
Barbate
CASTILLO DE LA DUQUESA
Punta de Chullera
Almoraima
PARQUE NATURAL DEL ARCHIPIÉLAGO CHINIJO
Isla Alegranza
Alegranza
Roque d. Este
Montaña Clara
Isla Graciosa
Zahara de los Atunes
BAELO CLAUDIA
Tahivilla
Taraguilla
San Roque
Torreguadiaro
Punta Mala
Los Barrios
Punta Camarinal
PARQUE NACIONAL DE TIMANFAYA
Lanzarote
La Caleta
Orzola
Haría
Tinajo
Yaiza
Uga
Teguise
Playa Blanca
Pto. d. Carmen
Aeropuerto de Arrecife
Arrecife
P. de la Tiñosa
P. d. Papagayo
Algeciras
North Front
La Línea de la Concepción
Gibraltar
GBZ
Tarifa
Punta de Europa
Punta de la Tarifa
Estrecho de Gibraltar
Bahía de Algeciras
Corralejo
Lobos
El Cotillo
Lajares
PARQUE NATURAL DEL ISLOTE DE LOBOS
Tindaya
La Oliva
PARQUE NATURAL DE CORRALEJO
Casillas d. Ángel
Puerto Lajas
Puerto del Rosario
Aeropuerto de Fuerteventura
Tuineje
Pozo Negro
Gran Tarajal
Sète
Benzú
Pointe Leona
Punta de Almina
Cap Spartel
TANGER
MA
Ksar-es-Seghir
Fnideq
Ceuta
Melloussa
Riffien
Briech
Alboran Sea

Constantina
PARQUE NATURAL
SIERRA NORTE
SIERRA DE HORNACHUELOS
96
Cerro Muriano
Adamuz
PARQUE NATURAL SIERRA DE CARDEÑA Y MONTORO
VIRGEN DE LA CABEZA
MULBA
La Puebla de los Infantes
Hornachuelos
Embalse de la Breña
MEDINA AZAHARA
SANTO DOMINGO
Montoro
Marmolejo
Villanueva del Río y Minas
ALMENARA
Alcolea del Río
El Priorato
Posadas
Almodóvar del Río
CÓRDOBA
El Carpio
Pedro Abad
Villa del Río
Lopera
Arjonilla
Cantillana
Tocina
ARVA
Peñaflor
Palma del Río
Guadalcázar
Brenes
Lora del Río
Fuente Palmera
Bujalance
Guadajoz
Torres Cabrera
Arjona
NECRÓPOLIS ROMANA
La Campana
La Carlota
Porcuna
Carmona
La Luisiana
Fernán Núñez
Santiago de Calatrava
Mairena del Alcor
Écija
MONCLOVA
La Rambla
Espejo
Castro del Río
Fuentes de Andalucía
Izcar
Torredonjimeno
Santaella
Montilla
Paradas
La Lantejuela
Aguilar de la Frontera
Nueva-Carteya
Baena
Embalse de Valdomojón
Marchena
Doña Mencía
Arahal
Los Ojuelos
El Rubio
Marinaleda
Monturque
Luque
Alcaudete
Molares
La Puebla de Cazalla
Puente Genil
Cabra
CUEVA DE LOS MURCIÉLAGOS
Castillo de Locubín
Herrera
Osuna
Estepa
Embalse de Cordobilla
Lucena
Carcabuey
Morón de la Frontera
Casariche
ARACELI
Priego de Córdoba
Almendinilla
El Coronil
Pedrera
Rute
Alcalá la Real
LA MOTA
COTE
SIERRA DE LOS CABALLOS
Alameda
Cuevas de San Marcos
Algarinejo
Martín de la Jara
La Roda de Andalucía
El Saucejo
El Tejar
Embalse de Iznájar
Iznájar
Coripe
Sierra de Yeguas
Villanueva de Algaidas
Montefrío
Puertoserrano
Campillos
Mollina
Villanueva de Tapia
Pruna
CUEVA DE MENGA
Íllora
Algodonales
Almargen
Huétor Tájar
Olvera
Cañete la Real
Embalse del Guadalhorce
El Castor
Alcalá del Valle
Antequera
Archidona
Loja
Salar
Moraleda de Zafayona
Pinos Puente
El Bosque
Embalse de Zahara
Cuevas del Becerro
Valle de Abdalajís
1369
EL TORCAL
Villanueva del Trabuco
Castillo de Tajarja
Granada
ACINIPO
Embalse del Conde de Guadalhorce
GARGANTA DEL CHORRO
Puerto de las Pedrizas 780
Grazalema
GRAZALEMA
Arriate
Ardales
Ronda
Elburgo/Burgelu
Ventas de Zefarraya
Alhama de Granada
Ventas de Huelma
FÁTIMA
Benaoján
2009
Casabermeja
CUEVA DE LA PILETA
Casarabonela
Álora
Periana
Arenas del Rey
Puerto del Suspiro del Moro 860
SERRANÍA DE RONDA
Yunquera
Pizarra
Colmenar
Almogía
2065
Jayena
Algatocín
Alozaina
Canillas del Aceituno
Puerto del León 960
Embalse de los Bermejales
Gaucín
Igualeja
1918
Tolox
LA CONCEPCIÓN
SIERRA DE ALMIJARA
Sierra Bermeja
Coín
Cártama
MÁLAGA
MAXIMILIANA
Albuñuelas
Embalse de la Concepción
Alhaurín el Grande
Málaga
El Palo
Vélez-Málaga
Cómpeta
Ojén
Alhaurín de la Torre
San Pedro de Alcántara
EL RETIRO
Rincón de la Victoria
Torrox
Otivar
Casares
Marbella
Mijas
Torremolinos
La Cala del Moral
Torre del Mar
CUEVA DE NERJA
Ensenada de Málaga
Manilva
Guadalmina
Puerto Banús
Elviria
Arroyo de la Miel-Benalmádena Costa
Torre
Nerja
Almuñécar
Estepona
Bahía de Marbella
Calahonda-Chaparral
Fuengirola
Benalmádena
Punta de Torrox
BALCON DE EUROPA
2008
CASTILLO DE LA DUQUESA
Melilla
Salobreña
Punta de Chullera
Torreguadiaro
COSTA DEL SOL
Punta Mala
Línea de Concepción
Gibraltar GBZ
de Europa
de Almina
n Sea
A
B
C
D
1
2
3
4
5
6
ANDALUCÍA
101

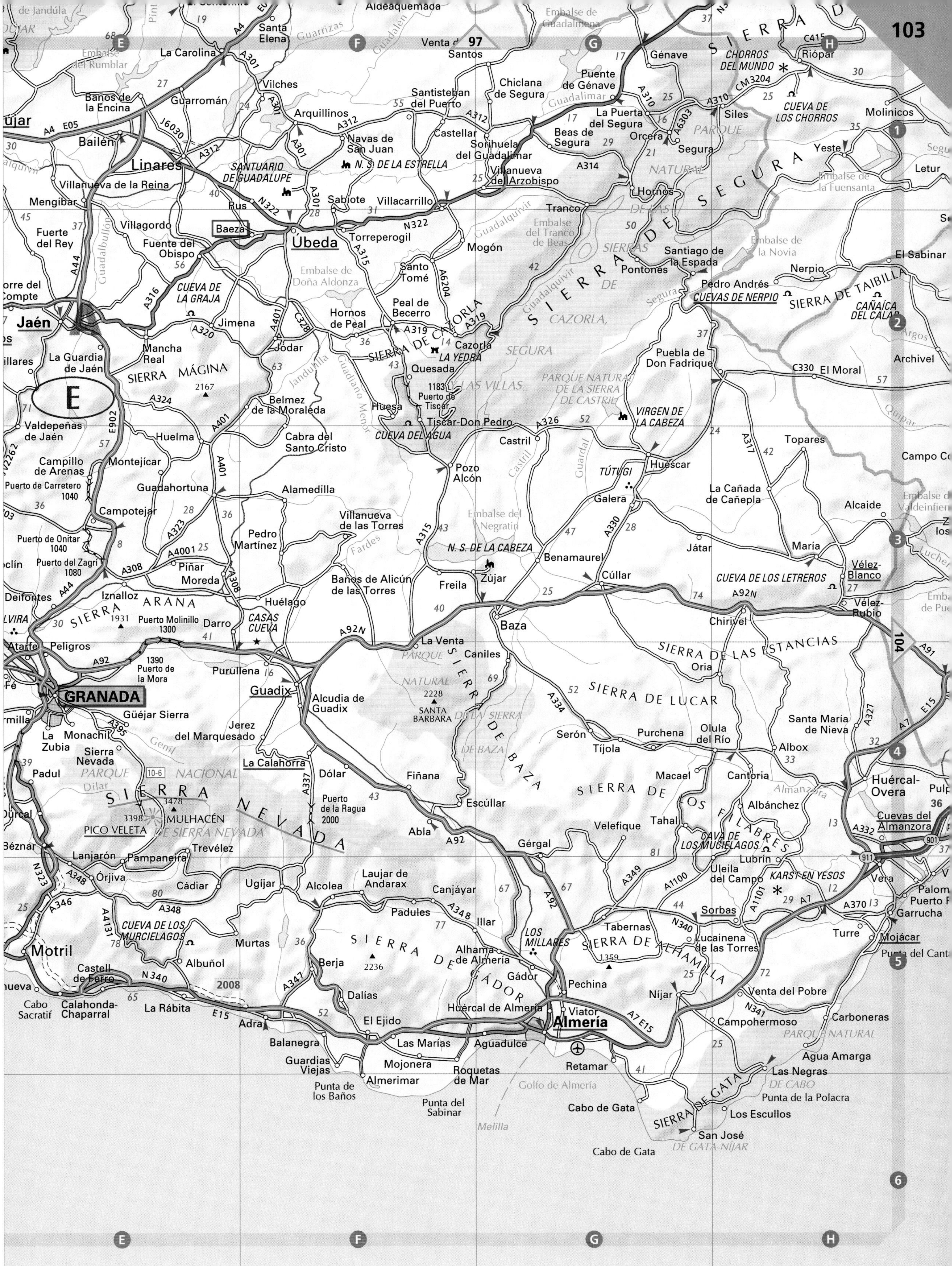
E
F
G
H
97
104
1
2
3
4
5
6
La Carolina
Santa Elena
Aldeaquemada
Venta de Santos
Génave
Chorros del Mundo
Riópar
Vilches
Baños de la Encina
Guarromán
Arquillinos
Santisteban del Puerto
Chiclana de Segura
Puente de Génave
La Puerta del Segura
Siles
Cueva de los Chorros
Molinicos
Bailén
Linares
Navas de San Juan
Castellar
Sorihuela del Guadalimar
Beas de Segura
Orcera
Segura
Yeste
Santuario de Guadalupe
N. S. de la Estrella
Villanueva del Arzobispo
Hornos
Letur
Villanueva de la Reina
Mengíbar
Rus
Sabiote
Villacarrillo
Tranco
Embalse de la Fuensanta
Fuerte del Rey
Villagordo
Baeza
Úbeda
Torreperogil
Embalse del Tranco de Beas
Fuente del Obispo
Mogón
Santiago de la Espada
Embalse de la Novia
El Sabinar
Pontones
Nerpio
Santo Tomé
Embalse de Doña Aldonza
Cueva de la Graja
Pedro Andrés
Cuevas de Nerpio
Sierra de Taibilla
Cañaíca del Calar
Jaén
Jimena
Hornos de Peal
Peal de Becerro
Sierra de Cazorla
Cazorla
La Yedra
Quesada
Mancha Real
Jódar
Sierra de Segura
Sierra de Cazorla, Segura y Las Villas
Parque Natural
Puebla de Don Fadrique
Archivel
El Moral
La Guardia de Jaén
Sierra Mágina
2167
1183 Puerto de Tíscar
Parque Natural de la Sierra de Castril
E
Belmez de la Moraleda
Huesa
Tíscar-Don Pedro
Virgen de la Cabeza
Valdepeñas de Jaén
Cueva del Agua
Castril
Huelma
Cabra del Santo Cristo
Topares
Pozo Alcón
Huéscar
Campo Coy
Campillo de Arenas
Montejícar
Puerto de Carretero 1040
Guadahortuna
Alamedilla
Túgui
Galera
La Cañada de Cañepla
Alcaide
Campotejar
Villanueva de las Torres
Embalse del Negratín
Puerto de Onitar 1040
Pedro Martínez
N. S. de la Cabeza
Játar
María
Puerto del Zagrí 1080
Píñar
Moreda
Benamaurel
Vélez-Blanco
Baños de Alicún de las Torres
Freila
Zújar
Cúllar
Cueva de los Letreros
Deifontes
Iznalloz
Sierra Arana
Huélago
Vélez-Rubio
1931
Puerto Molinillo 1300
Darro
Casas Cueva
Baza
Chirivel
Atarfe
Peligros
La Venta
Caniles
Sierra de las Estancias
1390 Puerto de la Mora
Purullena
Oria
Granada
Guadix
Alcudia de Guadix
2228 Santa Barbara
Parque Natural de la Sierra de Baza
Sierra de Lucar
Güéjar Sierra
La Zubia
Monachil
Jerez del Marquesado
Serón
Tíjola
Purchena
Olula del Río
Santa María de Nieva
Albox
Sierra Nevada
Padul
La Calahorra
Dólar
Fiñana
Macael
Cantoria
Huércal-Overa
Parque Nacional
Puerto de la Ragua 2000
Escúllar
Sierra de los Filabres
Albánchez
3478 Mulhacén
3398
Pico Veleta
Dúrcal
Abla
Velefique
Tahal
Cuevas del Almanzora
Béznar
Trevélez
Gérgal
Cava de los Murciélagos
Lubrín
Lanjarón
Pampaneira
Órjiva
Uleila del Campo
Karst en Yesos
Vera
Cádiar
Ugíjar
Alcolea
Laujar de Andarax
Canjáyar
Palomares
Puerto Rey
Garrucha
Padules
Sorbas
Cueva de los Murciélagos
Illar
Tabernas
Sierra de Alhamilla
1359
Turre
Mojácar
Murtas
Sierra de Gádor
2236
Los Millares
Lucainena de las Torres
Punta del Cantal
Motril
Albuñol
Berja
Alhama de Almería
Castell de Ferro
Gádor
Pechina
Níjar
Venta del Pobre
2008
Dalías
Cabo Sacratif
Calahonda-Chaparral
La Rábita
Huércal de Almería
Viator
Almería
Campohermoso
Carboneras
Adra
El Ejido
Balanegra
Las Marías
Aguadulce
Parque Natural de Cabo de Gata-Níjar
Guardias Viejas
Mojonera
Roquetas de Mar
Retamar
Agua Amarga
Las Negras
Almerimar
Golfo de Almería
Punta de la Polacra
Punta de los Baños
Punta del Sabinar
Cabo de Gata
Sierra de Gata
Los Escullos
Melilla
San José

98
103
Paterna del Madera
Alcadozo
Bogarra
Riópar
Ayna
Liétor
SANT. DE LA ENCARNACIÓN
La Higuera
Fuente Álamo
Montealegre del Castillo
CUEVA DE MONTE ARABÍ
La Font la Figuera
Moixent
Fontanars dels Alforins
Caudete
Benejama/ Beneixama
Bocairent
CUEVA DE LOS CHORROS
Siles
Molinicos
Elche de la Sierra
Tobarra
Ontur
Albatana
Hellín
Isso
Yeste
Letur
CUEVAS DE MINATEDA
CUEVA DE PELICIEGO
Yecla
Villena
Biar
Onil
Minateda-Horca
Ferez
Agramón
Jumilla
Raspay
Salinas
Sax
Castalla
Socovos
Casas del Puerto
Elda
SIERRA DE MAIGMÓ
Embalse de la Novia
El Sabinar
MONASTERIO DE STA. ANA
Pinoso/ el Pinós
Petrer
Nerpio
Moratalla
Monóvar/ Monòver
Agost
SIERRA DE TAIBILLA
CAÑAICA DEL CALAR
Calasparra
Embalse de Alfonso XIII
E
l'Alguenya
Novelda
San Vicente del Raspeig
Cieza
CAÑÓN DE LOS ALMADENES
Abarán
Blanca
SIERRA DE LA PILA
el Fondó dels Frares
Aspe
Archivel
Caravaca
Cehegín
El Moral
EL PALMERAL
Ojós
Villanueva del Río Segura
Abanilla
Crevillente/ Crevillent
Elche/ Elx
La Almudena
Bullas
Archena
Lorqui
Fortuna
L'ALCÚDIA (ILICE)
Topares
Mula
Ceutí
Molina de Segura
Cabezo de Torres
Callosa de Segura
Santa Pola
Campo Coy
Pliego
Albudeite
Alguazas
Las Torres de Cotillas
Orihuela
Dolores
La Marina
Cañada Cañepla
La Paca
Zarzadilla de Totana
MON. DE LOS JERÓNIMOS
Santomera
Almoradí
Guardamar del Segura
Alcaide
SIERRA DE ESPUÑA
Beniel
Bigastro
Rojales
Zarcilla de los Ramons
MURCIA
María
Librilla
Alcantarilla
La Mata
Alhama de Murcia
Sangonera la Verde
FUENSANTA
San Miguel de Salinas
Vélez-Blanco
Torrevieja
CUEVA DE LOS LETREROS
Aledo
Vélez-Rubio
Totana
Corvera
Sucina
Pilar de la Horadada
Dehesa de Campoamor
Balsicas
San Pedro del Pinatar
LAS ESTANCIAS
Lorca
Paretón
La Campana
Fuente Álamo de Murcia
Albujón
Torre-Pacheco
San Javier
Santiago de la Ribera
FÉLIX
Puerto Lumbreras
SIERRA DE LA ALMENARA
Las Palas
La Palma
Los Alcázares
Isla Grosa
Mar Menor
EL RAMONETE
Santa María de Nieva
TALAYÓN
Cuesta Blanca de Arriba
Los Urrutias
Albox
Mazarrón
MONASTERIO DE S.GINÉS DE LA JARA
La Manga del Mar Menor
Puerto de Mazarrón
ISLAS HORMIGAS
Cantoria
Huércal-Overa
CASTILLO DE S. JUAN
Puntas de Calnegre
Golfo de Mazarrón
La Azohía
CARTAGENA
La Unión
Cabo de Palos
Pulpí
Cope
Cabo Cope
Escombreras
Portman
Albánchez
Cuevas del Almanzora
Águilas
Cabo Negrete
San Juan de los Terreros
Lubrín
Vera
Villaricos
KARST EN YESOS
Palomares
Puerto Rey
Garrucha
Turre
Mojácar
Punta del Cantal
Venta del Pobre
Campohermoso
Carboneras
PARQUE NATURAL
Agua Amarga
Las Negras
Punta de la Polacra
Los Escullos
Eivissa/ Ibiza
Portinatx
Sant Miquel de Balansat
Sant Joan de Llabritja
Cap Nunó
Sant Vicent de sa Cala
Sant Antoni de Portmany
es Figueral
ES FORNÁS
Tagomago
Sa Conillera
Cala Tarida
Platja des Canar
Sant José/Sant Josep
Sant Rafel
Santa Eulalia del Río/ Santa Eulària des Riu
Cala Vadella
ES PEIX
SA TALAIA
Es Vedrá
COVA SANTA
Es Cubells
Eivissa / Ibiza
Cap Llentrisca
El Canal
Punta de ses Portes
s'Espalmador
s'Espardell
BALEARS / BALEARES
Punta de sa Pedrera
Sa Savina
Sant Francesc de Formentera
Formentera
Sant Ferran de Ses Roquetes
Pilar de la Mola
Cap de Barbaria
Punta de Sa Creu
LA MOLA
Punta Roja
Banyalbufar
Estellenchs
sa Dragonera
GALATZÓ
CASTELL DE BELLVER
Andraitx
es Port d'Andraitx
Calvià
Cap de sa Mola
Peguera
Santa Ponça
Magalluf
Cap de Cala Figuera

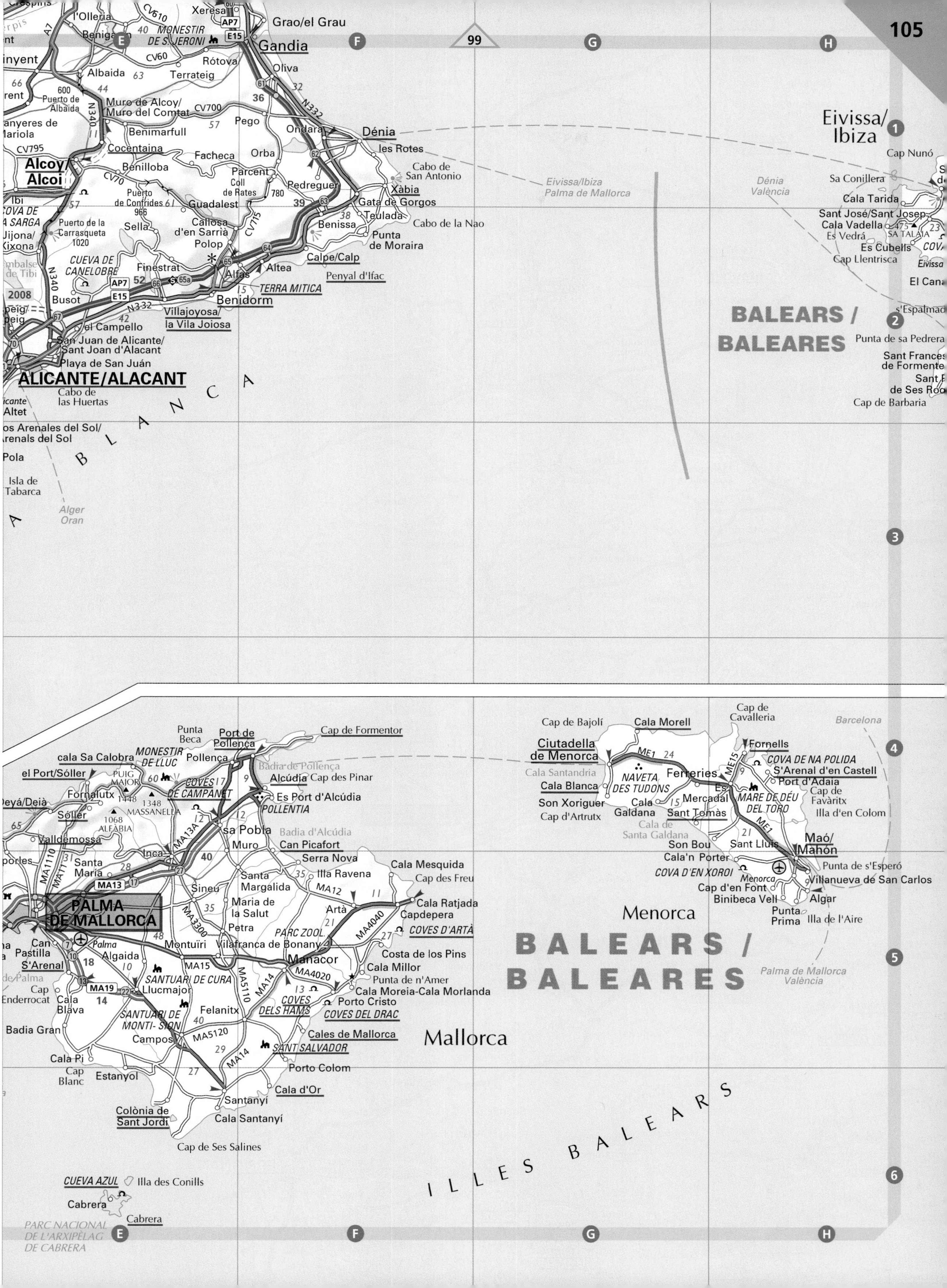
Gandia
Dénia
Xàbia
Benidorm
Alcoy/Alcoi
ALICANTE/ALACANT
Eivissa/Ibiza
BALEARS / BALEARES
PALMA DE MALLORCA
Mallorca
Menorca
Ciutadella de Menorca
Maó/Mahón
Manacor
Alcúdia
Pollença
Sóller
Llucmajor
Campos
Santanyí
Felanitx
Cabrera
ILLES BALEARS
COSTA BLANCA
Cap de Formentor
Cap de Ses Salines
Eivissa/Ibiza Palma de Mallorca
Dénia València
Palma de Mallorca València
Barcelona
Alger Oran

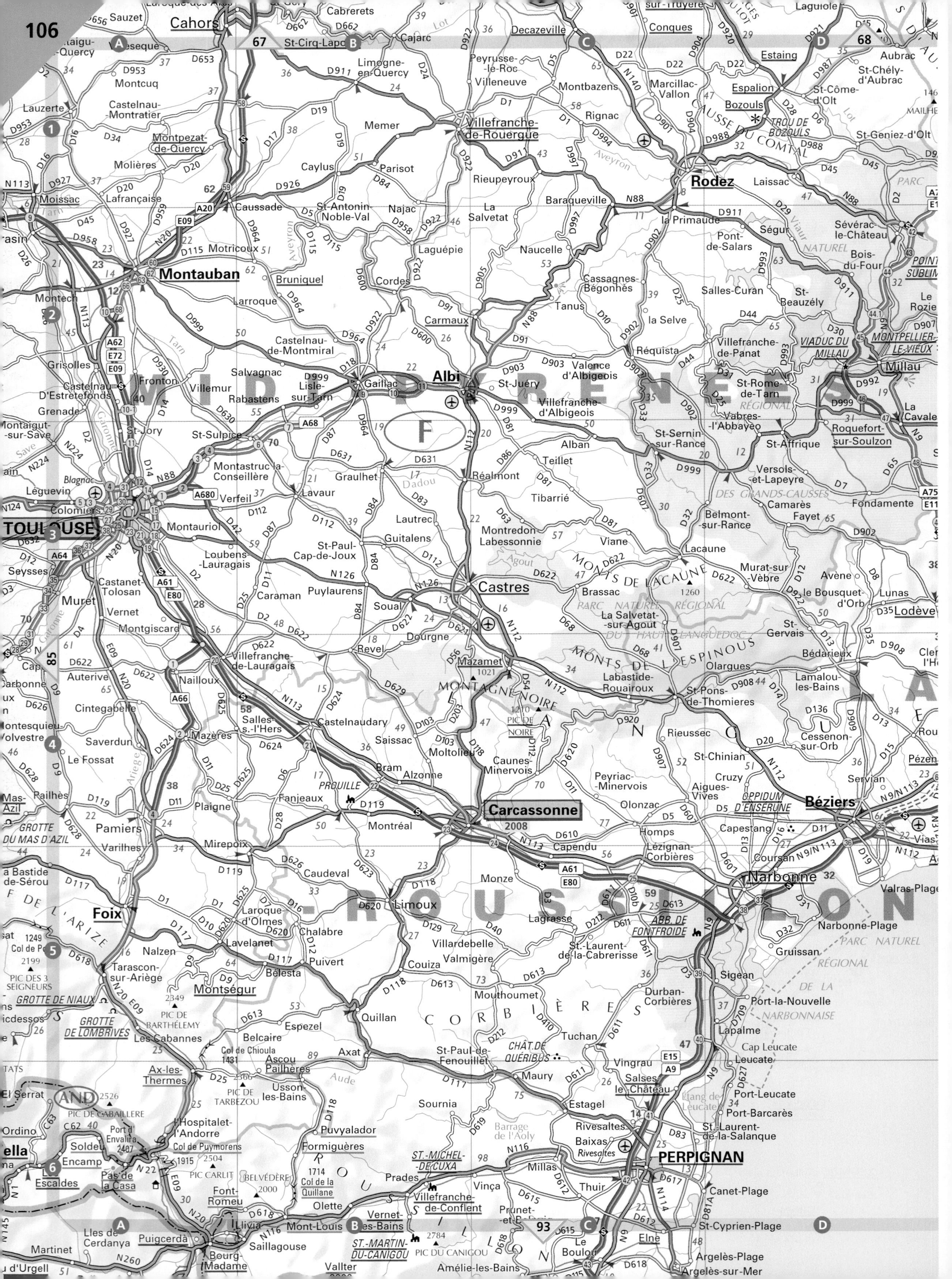

MIDI-PYRÉNÉES
LANGUEDOC-ROUSSILLON
F
Cahors
Cabrerets
Decazeville
Conques
Laguiole
Aubrac
St-Cirq-Lapopie
Cajarc
Limogne-en-Quercy
Peyrusse-le-Roc
Villeneuve
Montbazens
Marcillac-Vallon
Estaing
Espalion
Bozouls
Trou de Bozouls
St-Chély-d'Aubrac
St-Côme-d'Olt
Causse du Comtal
St-Geniez-d'Olt
Montcuq
Lauzerte
Castelnau-Montratier
Montpezat-de-Quercy
Molières
Memer
Villefranche-de-Rouergue
Rignac
Caylus
Parisot
Rieupeyroux
Rodez
Laissac
Moissac
Lafrançaise
Caussade
St-Antonin-Noble-Val
Najac
La Salvetat
Baraqueville
la Primaube
Sévérac-le-Château
Ségur
Pont-de-Salars
Montauban
Motricoux
Bruniquel
Laguépie
Naucelle
Bois-du-Four
Point Sublime
Montech
Larroque
Cordes
Cassagnes-Bégonhès
Tanus
Salles-Curan
St-Beauzély
le Rozier
la Selve
Carmaux
Castelnau-de-Montmiral
Réquista
Villefranche-de-Panat
Viaduc du Millau
Montpellier-le-Vieux
Millau
Grisolles
Fronton
Salvagnac
Villemur
Rabastens
Lisle-sur-Tarn
Gaillac
Albi
St-Juéry
Valence d'Albigeois
Villefranche d'Albigeois
St-Rome-de-Tarn
Vabres-l'Abbaye
Roquefort-sur-Soulzon
La Cavalerie
Castelnau-d'Estretefonds
Grenade
Montaigut-sur-Save
St-Jory
St-Sulpice
Alban
St-Sernin-sur-Rance
St-Affrique
Montastruc-la-Conseillère
Graulhet
Réalmont
Teillet
Versols-et-Lapeyre
Blagnac
Léguevin
Colomiers
Toulouse
Verfeil
Lavaur
Tibarrié
Camarès
Fondamente
Montauriol
Lautrec
Montredon-Labessonnie
Viane
Belmont-sur-Rance
Fayet
Des Grands-Causses
Parc Naturel Régional
Seysses
Loubens-Lauragais
St-Paul-Cap-de-Joux
Guitalens
Lacaune
Murat-sur-Vèbre
Avène
Castanet-Tolosan
Caraman
Puylaurens
Castres
Monts de Lacaune
Brassac
le Bousquet-d'Orb
Lunas
Lodève
Muret
Vernet
Soual
La Salvetat-sur-Agout
Montgiscard
Dourgne
Revel
Du Haut Languedoc
St-Gervais
Villefranche-de-Lauragais
Mazamet
Monts de l'Espinouse
Bédarieux
Auterive
Nailloux
Montagne Noire
Labastide-Rouairoux
Olargues
St-Pons-de-Thomieres
Lamalou-les-Bains
Cintegabelle
Pic de Noire
Salles-s.-l'Hers
Castelnaudary
Saissac
Moltolieu
Cessenon-sur-Orb
Montesquieu-Volvestre
Saverdun
Mazères
Rieussec
St-Chinian
Le Fossat
Caunes-Minervois
Peyriac-Minervois
Cruzy
Servian
Pézenas
Bram
Alzonne
Prouille
Aigues-Vives
Oppidum d'Ensérune
Béziers
Pailhès
Fanjeaux
Carcassonne
Olonzac
Mas-d'Azil
Grotte du Mas d'Azil
Plaigne
Montréal
Homps
Capestang
Pamiers
Varilhes
Mirepoix
Capendu
Lézignan-Corbières
Coursan
Vias
La Bastide-de-Sérou
Caudeval
Monze
Narbonne
Valras-Plage
Foix
Laroque-d'Olmes
Limoux
Lagrasse
Abb. de Fontfroide
Narbonne-Plage
Chalabre
Lavelanet
Villardebelle
St.-Laurent-de-la-Cabrerisse
Gruissan
Nalzen
Puivert
Valmigère
Sigean
Tarascon-sur-Ariège
Bélesta
Couiza
Pic des 3 Seigneurs
Montségur
Mouthoumet
Durban-Corbières
Port-la-Nouvelle
Grotte de Niaux
Narbonnaise
Grotte de Lombrives
Pic de Barthélemy
Espezel
Quillan
Corbières
Lapalme
Les Cabannes
Belcaire
Tuchan
Col de Chioula
Ascou Pailhères
Axat
St-Paul-de-Fenouillet
Chât. de Quéribus
Cap Leucate
Leucate
Ax-les-Thermes
Vingrau
Maury
Salses-le-Château
Port-Leucate
El Serrat
AND
Pic de Tarbezou
Usson-les-Bains
Sournia
Estagel
Étang de Leucate
Port-Barcarès
Ordino
Pic de Caballiere
Port d'Envalira
L'Hospitalet-l'Andorre
Puyvalador
Barrage de l'Aoly
Rivesaltes
St. Laurent-de-la-Salanque
Soldeu
Encamp
Col de Puymorens
Formiguères
Baixas
Perpignan
Escaldes
Pas de la Casa
Pic Carlit
St.-Michel-de-Cuxa
Millas
Belvédère
Col de la Quillane
Prades
Vinça
Thuir
Canet-Plage
Font-Romeu
Villefranche-de-Conflent
Olette
Prunet-et-Belpuig
Llivia
Mont-Louis
Vernet-les-Bains
St-Cyprien-Plage
Lles de Cerdanya
Puigcerdà
Saillagouse
St.-Martin-du-Canigou
Pic du Canigou
Le Boulou
Elne
Martinet
Bourg-Madame
Valter
Argelès-Plage
Argelès-sur-Mer
Amélie-les-Bains
La Seu d'Urgell
A
B
C
D
1
2
3
4
5
6
67
68
85
93

Valence
Privas
Aubenas
Montélimar
Mende
Marvejols
Langogne
Pradelles
Châteauneuf-de-Randon
Bagnols-les-Bains
Villefort
Florac
Meyrueis
Le Vigan
Ganges
Alès
Anduze
St-Jean-du-Gard
Les Vans
Joyeuse
Largentière
Vallon-Pont-d'Arc
Bourg-St-Andéol
Pierrelatte
Bollène
Pont-St-Esprit
Bagnols-sur-Cèze
Orange
Nyons
Valréas
Vaison-la-Romaine
Carpentras
Avignon
Uzès
Remoulins
Nîmes
Sommières
Lunel
MONTPELLIER
Sète
Agde
Aigues-Mortes
La Grande-Motte
Le Grau-du-Roi
Stes-Maries-de-la-Mer
Arles
Beaucaire
Tarascon
St-Rémy-de-Provence
Cavaillon
Salon-de-Provence
Istres
Martigues
Aix-en-Provence
MARSEILLE
Cassis
La Ciotat
Crest
Dieulefit
Grignan
Sorgues
L'Isle-sur-la-Sorgue
Apt
GOLFE DU LION
CAUSSE DE SAUVETERRE
CAUSSE MÉJEAN
GORGES DU TARN
MONTS DE VAUCLUSE
CHAÎNE DES ALPILLES
PARC NATUREL RÉGIONAL DE CAMARGUE
PONT DU GARD
LES CALANQUES
CHÂTEAU D'IF
E
F
G
H
1
2
3
4
5
6
69
108

PROVENCE-ALPES-CÔTE D'AZUR
Privas
Aubenas
Le Pouzin
Livron-sur-Drôme
Loriol-sur-Drôme
Crest
Die
Saillans
La Vacherie
Col de Rousset
DU VERCORS
Clelles
Mens
La Mure
St.Christophe-en-Oisans
La Bérarde
Valbonnais
N.D. DE LA SALETTE
Corps
PARC NATIONAL DES ÉCRINS
MASSIF DES ÉCRINS
MT PELVOUX
Ailefroide
La Chapelle-en-Valgaudemar
Vallouise
L'Argentière-la-Bessée
St-Firmin
St-Bonnet-en-Champsaur
SOUMT. DROUVET
Orcières
St-Clément-sur-Durance
Baix
Cruas
Berzeme
Rochemaure
Villeneuve-de-Berg
Le Teil
Cléon-d'Andran
Saou
Montélimar
la Bégude-de-Mazenc
Allan
Aucelon
Bourdeaux
Dieulefit
Pradelle
Luc-en-Diois
Châtillon-en-Diois
Col de la Croix Haute
Col de Grimone
Lus-la-Croix-Haute
Col du Festre
St-Julien-en-Beauchêne
Col de Cabre
Col Bayard
ROUTE NAPOLÉON
Gap
La Bâtie-Neuve
Chorges
Embrun
Vallon-Pont-d'Arc
Viviers
Donzère
AVEN DE MARZAL
Bourg-St-Andéol
MONASTÈRE DE LA TRAPPE D'AIGUEBELLE
GORGES DE L'ARDÈCHE
Pierrelatte
Grignan
GROTTE DE ROCHECOURBIÈRE
Valréas
La Motte-Chalancon
Rémuzat
Aspres-sur-Buëch
Veynes
Serres
Rosans
Tallard
Lac de Serre-Ponçon
Savines-le-Lac
St-Vincent-les-Forts
Le Lauzet-Ubaye
BARRY
Bollène
Pont-St-Esprit
Nyons
Ste.- Jalle
St-Auban-sur-l'Ouvèze
Buis-les-Baronnies
Vaison-la-Romaine
Laborel
Laragne-Montéglin
Monêtier-Allemont
La Motte-du-Caire
Selonnet
ANC. BATTERIE
Seyne
Col de Maure
Uvernet-Fours
Col d'Allos
Bagnols-sur-Cèze
Orange
Violès
Malaucène
MT. VENTOUX
Montbrun-les-Bains
Séderon
Curel
Noyers-sur-Jabron
Sisteron
Authon
GROTTE DE ST-VINCENT
Barles
Le Vernet
Col du Labouret
Allos
Roquemaure
Châteauneuf-du-Pape
Beaumes-de-Venise
Carpentras
Sorgues
Villeneuve
GORGES DE LA NESQUE
Sault
MONTAGNE DE LURE
N.-D. DE LURE
Thoard
La Javie
Colmars
Beauvezer
Avignon
Pernes-les-Fontaines
MONTS DE VAUCLUSE
St-Etienne-les-Orgues
Château-Arnoux
CHEVAL BLANC
ABB. DE ST.-ROMAN
Fontaine-de-Vaucluse
St-Saturnin-lès-Apt
Banon
Peyruis
PRIEURÉ GANAGOBIE
Forcalquier
Digne-les-Bains
Tarascon
Noves
L'Isle-sur-la-Sorgue
Gordes
Roussillon
Mézel
La Colle St. Michel
St-André-les-Alpes
St-Rémy-de-Provence
LES ANTIQUES
Cavaillon
Plan d'Orgon
Apt
Reillanne
La Brillanne
Bras-d'Asse
Oraison
Voix
CHAÎNE DES ALPILLES
Les Baux-de-Provence
Fontvieille
Orgon
Bonnieux
FORT DE BUOUX
MONTAGNE DU LUBERON
Manosque
Valensole
Moustiers-Ste-Marie
Barrême
St. Julien-du-Verdon
Senez
Col des Leques
Arles
Sénas
St-Martin-de-Crau
Eyguières
SILVACANE
Cadenet
Ste-Tulle
Riez
Gorges du Verdon
Castellane
Salon-de-Provence
Pertuis
Gréoux-les-Bains
Vinon-sur-Verdon
Lac de Ste-Croix
Col de l'Illoire
Corniche Sublime
La Palud-sur-Verdon
Mas Thibert
Miramas
St-Chamas
Lambesc
Peyrolles
Meyrargues
Rians
Montmeyan
Comps-sur-Artuby
La Bastide
Istres
Berre-l'Etang
ST. BLAISE
Rognac
Aix-en-Provence
Vauvenargues
Varages
Tavernes
Aups
Ampus
Montferrat
Fayence
Fos-sur-Mer
Salin-de-Giraud
Port-St-Louis-du-Rhône
Port-de-Bouc
Martigues
Marignane
Marseille/Provence
Gardanne
Trets
St-Maximin-la-Ste-Baume
Barjols
Cotignac
Sillans-la-Cascade
Salernes
Draguignan
Bagnols-en-Forêt
Carro
Cap Couronne
Carry-le-Rouet
CHÂTEAU D'IF
MARSEILLE
Peypin
Allauch
Auriol
Aubagne
Gémenos
ST PILON
Nans-les-Pins
Tourves
Brignoles
La Roquebrussanne
Signes
Carcès
Lorgues
ABB. DU THORONET
Les Arcs
Le Muy
Vidauban
Le Luc
Besse-sur-Issole
NOTRE-DAME DE LA ROQUETTE
Fréjus
Puget-sur-Argens
St-Aygulf
Cap Croisette
LES CALANQUES
Cassis
Ile de Riou
La Ciotat
Les Lecques
Bandol
Sanary-sur-Mer
Six-Fours-les-Plages
Le Beausset
MT CAUME
MT FARON
Puget-Ville
Cuers
Solliès-Pont
La Garde-Freinet
Ste-Maxime
Grimaud
Port-Grimaud
Beauvallon
Cogolin
St-Tropez
MASSIF DES MAURES
Ile des Embiez
La Seyne
TOULON
Carqueiranne
Cap Cépet
Cap Sicié
N.-D. DU MAI
Hyères
La Capte
Bormes-les-Mimosas
Le Lavandou
Aiguebelle
Cavalière
Rayol
Cavalaire-sur-Mer
La Croix-Valmer
Cap Camarat
Giens
Cap Bénat
Porquerolles
Ile de Porquerolles
Port-Cros
Ile de Port-Cros
Ile du Levant
PARC NATIONAL DE PORT-CROS
ILES D'HYÈRES
Oran Alger Tunis Annaba Bejaia Skikda
Ajaccio Propriano Porto Tórres
Porto-Vecchio Bastia L'Ile-Rousse Calvi
Ajaccio Porto Tórres
Bastia
69
107
230
A B C D
1 2 3 4 5 6

TORINO
Collegno
Rivoli
Moncalieri
Chieri
SUPERGA
Settimo Torinese
Casale Monferrato
Robella
PIEMONTE
Pinerolo
Perosa Argentina
Piossasco
Orbassano
Stupinigi
Airasca
Carignano
Santena
Poirino
Villanova d'Asti
Asti
ALESSANDRIA
Moncalvo
Vignale Monferrato
Castelnuovo Don Bosco
Fubine
Felizzano
Valenza
Carmagnola
Villafranca Piemonte
S. Damiano d'Asti
Canale
Sommariva del Bosco
Racconigi
Moretta
Saluzzo
Savigliano
Bra
Alba
Cherasco
Grinzane Cavour
Nizza Monferrato
Castellazzo Bormida
Agliano
Santo Stefano Belbo
Canelli
Cassine
Acqui Terme
Ovada
Rocchetta Belbo
Cortemilia
Roccaverano
Molare
Mornese
Rossiglione
Campo Ligure
Pian Castagna
Sassello
Piana Crixia
Murazzano
Dogliani
Carrù
Fossano
Centallo
Costigliole Saluzzo
Busca
Verzuolo
Brossasco
Frassino
Sampéyre
Stroppo
Acceglio
S. Damiano Macra
Dronero
Caraglio
Cuneo
Boves
Peveragno
Borgo San Dalmazzo
Mondovì
Morozzo
Ceva
Priero
Millesimo
Carcare
Cairo Montenotte
Pontinvrea
Varazze
Celle Ligure
Albissola Marina
Savona
Vado Ligure
Spotorno
Noli
Finale Ligure
Pietra Ligure
Loano
Ceriale
Albenga
Alássio
Laiguéglia
Diano Marina
Imperia
Sanremo
Taggia
Ospedaletti
Bordighera
Ventimíglia
Menton
Roquebrune-Cap-Martin
Monte-Carlo
Monaco
MC
NICE
Cagnes-sur-Mer
Villeneuve-Loubet
Antibes
Juan-les-Pins
Cap d'Antibes
Golfe-Juan
Cannes
Îles de Lérins
La Napoule-Plage
Théoule
Le Trayas
Miramar
Agay
Anthéor
Mandelieu
Mougins
Grasse
Vence
St-Paul
Carros
Levens
L'Escarène
Sospel
Breil-sur-Roya
Saorge
Tende
Limone Piemonte
Valdieri
Terme di Valdieri
Demonte
Vinádio
Bagni di Vinadio
Argentera
Castelmagno
Monterosso Grana
Isola
Isola 2000
St-Étienne-de-Tinée
Auron
St-Sauveur-sur-Tinée
St-Martin-Vésubie
Roquebillière
Lantosque
Valberg
Beuil
Guillaumes
Puget-Théniers
Entrevaux
Villars-sur-Var
Jausiers
Barcelonnette
Larche
Guillestre
Vars
Mt-Dauphin
Briançon
Cesana Torinese
Claviere
Montgenèvre
Sestriere
Fenestrelle
Perrero
Villar Perosa
Prali
Bobbio Pellice
Torre Pellice
Cavour
Bagnolo Piemonte
Barge
Paesana
Crissolo
Casteldelfino
Pontechianale
Château-Queyras
Abriès
Aiguilles
Arvieux
Ceillac
St-Véran
Garéssio
Ormea
Pieve di Teco
Triora
Montalto Ligure
Badalucco
Pigna
Dolceácqua
Calizzano
Bossea
Viozene
Frabosa Soprana
Chiusa di Pesio
Pamparato
RIVIERA DI PONENTE
COTE D'AZUR
L'Ile-Rousse
Ajaccio
Calvi
Bastia
E
F
G
H
70
71
110

Vigevano
Mortara
Motta Visconti
Binasco
Rozzano
Melegnano
Crema
Soncino
Orzinuovi
Mella
Ghedi
Trino
Casale Monferrato
Zeme
Candia Lomellina
Tromello
Garlasco
Dorno
Ottobiano
Lomello
Mede
Torre Beretti
Sannazzaro de' Burgondi
CERTOSA DI PAVIA
Sant'Angelo Lodigiano
Pavia
Miradolo Terme
San Colombano al Lambro
Lodi
Castelleone
S. MARIA DI BRESSANORO
Soresina
Caviaga
Casalpusterlengo
Somaglia
Codogno
Pizzighettone
Castelverde
Manèrbio
Leno
Pontevico
Carpenedolo
Isorella
Gottolengo
Gambara
Vescovato
Cremona
Canneto sull'Oglio
Pieve S. Giacomo
Piádena
S. Daniele Po
S. Giovanni in Croce
Vignale Monferrato
Valenza
Torre Beretti
Guazzora
Sale
Fubine
S. Salvatore Monferrato
Castelnuovo Scrivia
Stradella
Broni
Castel San Giovanni
Casteggio
Voghera
S. Maria d. Versa
Borgonovo Val Tidone
PIACENZA
Caorso
Cortemaggiore
Roccabianca
Felizzano
ALESSANDRIA
Castellazzo Bormida
Tortona
Rivanazzano
Salice Terme
Agazzano
Pianello Val Tidone
Grazzano Visconti
Rivergaro
Carpaneto Piacentino
Fiorenzuola d'Arda
Busseto
Casalmaggiore
Sissa
Soragna
Nizza Monferrato
Cassine
Canelli
SANT'ALBERTO DI BUTRIO
Passo del Penice 1149
Varzi
Garbagna
Novi Ligure
Borghetto di Borbera
S. Sebastiano Curone
Caldirola
Bóbbio
Travo
Ponte dell'Olio
CHIARAVALLE DELLA COLOMBA
Castell'Arquato
Lugagnano Val d'Arda
VELLEIA
Fontanellato
Fidenza
Salsomaggiore Terme
Noceto
PARMA
Acqui Terme
Gavi
Castelletto d'Orba
Ovada
Arquata Scrivia
CAST. DORIA
Molare
Mornese
Rossiglione
Ronco Scrivia
Busalla
Campo Ligure
Pian Castagna
Sassello
Montaldo di Cosola
Carrega Ligure
Ottone
Corte Brugnatella
Farini
Bore
Parmense Pellegrino
Tabiano Bagni
Sant'Andrea Bagni
Collécchio
Monticelli Terme
Varsi
Ferriere
Bardi
Varano de' Melegari
Fornovo di Taro
Pilastro
CASTELLO DI TORRECHIARA
Langhirano
San Polo d'Enza
Torríglia
Montebruno
M. MAGGIORASCA 1799
Ponteceno di Sopra
LIGURIA
EMILIA
Pontedecimo
Col del Giovo 516
Pontinvrea
Passo della Scoffera 674
S. Stefano d'Aveto
Bedonia
Borgo Val di Taro
Passo della Cisa 1039
CASTELLO DI CANOSSA
Voltri
Pegli
Arenzano
Varazze
Cristoforo Colombo
GÉNOVA
Nervi
Camogli
Rapallo
Santa Margherita Ligure
SAN FRUTTUOSO
Portofino
ABB. DI BORZONE
Passo di Bocco 956
Passo di Cento Croci 1055
Berceto
Casina
Celle Ligure
Albissola Marina
Savona
Vado Ligure
Spotorno
Noli
Finale Ligure
BASILICA DEI FIESCHI
Chiavari
Lavagna
Cavi
Sestri Levante
Passo del Bracco 613
Varese Ligure
Pontremoli
Córniglio
Mónchio d. Corti
PIETRA BISMANTOVA
Castelnovo ne' Monti
Busana
Zeri
Mulazzo
Bagnone
Licciana Nardi
Passo di Pradarena
M. CUSNA 2121
Passo del Cerreto
Barcelona
Tùnis
Valletta
Porto Tórres
Ólbia
Árbatax
Palermo
RIVIERA DI PONENTE
RIVIERA DI LEVANTE
Monéglia
Brugnato
Bonassola
Lévanto
Monterosso al Mare
Vernazza
Riomaggiore
PARCO NAZ. D. CINQUE TERRE
LA SPÉZIA
Portovenere
Lerici
Aulla
Fivizzano
Capodiponte
SAN PELLEGRINO IN ALPE
Sarzana
ALPI APUANE
Piazza al Serchio
Castelnuovo di Garfagnana
Carrara
Barga
Fornaci di Barga
Marina di Carrara
Massa
Marina di Massa
Culaccio
GROTTA DEL VENTO
Seravezza
Pietrasanta
Pescaglia
Forte dei Marmi
Marina di Pietrasanta
Camaiore
Lido di Camaiore
Viaréggio
Lucca
Torre del Lago Puccini
Lago di Massaciuccoli
Migliarino
San Giuliano
Gombo
PISA
CERTOSA DI PISA
Marina di Pisa
Cáscina
Galileo Galilei
Tirrénia
LIVORNO
Collesalvetti
Casciana Terme
GOLFO DI GÉNOVA
Ísola di Gorgona
P. N. DELL'ARCIP. TOSCANO
Capráia
Quercianella
Castiglioncello
Rosignano Solvay
Cágliari
Cécina
109
114
71

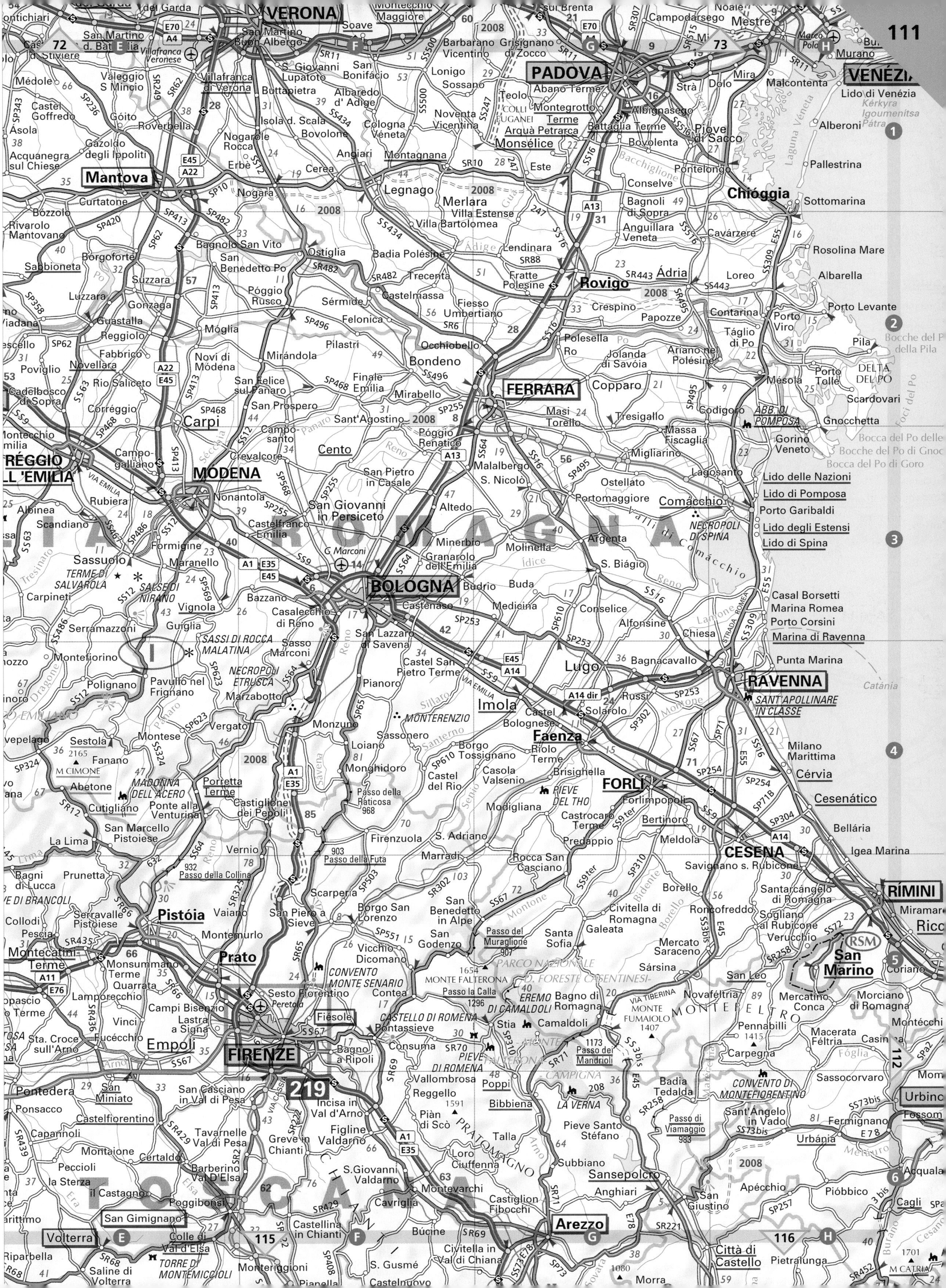
VERONA
PADOVA
VENÉZIA
Mestre
Mantova
Legnago
Monsélice
Chióggia
Rovigo
Ádria
Ostiglia
Sabbioneta
Guastalla
Mirándola
Bondeno
FERRARA
Copparo
Carpi
RÉGGIO NELL'EMILIA
MODENA
Cento
Comácchio
Lido delle Nazioni
Lido di Pomposa
Porto Garibaldi
Lido degli Estensi
Lido di Spina
DELTA DEL PO
ABB. DI POMPOSA
EMILIA ROMAGNA
Sassuolo
Maranello
BOLOGNA
Budrio
Argenta
Medicina
Lugo
Imola
Faenza
RAVENNA
SANT'APOLLINARE IN CLASSE
Marina di Ravenna
Punta Marina
Cérvia
Cesenático
Bellária
Igea Marina
FORLÌ
CESENA
RÍMINI
San Marino
RSM
Pistóia
Prato
Montecatini-Terme
Empoli
FIRENZE
Fiésole
Arezzo
Sansepolcro
Città di Castello
San Gimignano
Volterra
Urbino
TOSCANA
219
115
116
112
72
73
E
F
G
H
1
2
3
4
5
6

Mestre
Marco Polo
Torcello
Burano
Murano
Jésolo
Eraclea Mare
Lido di Jésolo
Cavallino
73
VENÉZIA
Lido di Venézia
Malcontenta
Mira
Dolo
Strà
Mirano
Albignasego
Battaglia Terme
Piove di Sacco
Bovolenta
248
Alberoni
Kérkyra
Igoumenítsa
Pátra
Laguna Veneta
Pallestrina
Pontelongo
Bacchiglione
Conselve
Chióggia
Sottomarina
Bagnoli di Sopra
Anguillara Veneta
Cavárzere
Rosolina Mare
Ádria
Loreo
Albarella
Rovigo
Crespino
Papozze
Contarina
Porto Viro
Porto Levante
Táglio di Po
Pila
Bocche del Po della Pila
Ariano nel Polésine
Jolanda di Savóia
Copparo
Porto Tolle
DELTA DEL PO
Mésola
Scardovari
Codigoro
ABB. DI POMPOSA
Gnocchetta
Tresigallo
Massa Fiscaglia
Gorino Veneto
Bocca del Po delle Tolle
Bocche del Po di Gnocca
Bocca del Po di Goro
Migliarino
Lagosanto
Ostellato
Lido delle Nazioni
Lido di Pomposa
Porto Garibaldi
Comácchio
NECROPOLI DI SPINA
Lido degli Estensi
Lido di Spina
Argenta
Valli di Comácchio
S. Biágio
111
Reno
Casal Borsetti
Marina Romea
Porto Corsini
Marina di Ravenna
Alfonsine
Chiesa
Punta Marina
Catánia
Bagnacavallo
RAVENNA
SANT'APOLLINARE IN CLASSE
Russi
Solarolo
Milano Marittima
Cérvia
FORLÌ
Forlimpopoli
Cesenático
Bertinoro
Meldola
Bellária
I
CESENA
Igea Marina
Savignano s. Rubicone
Santarcángelo di Romagna
RÍMINI
Borello
Roncofreddo
Civitella di Romagna
Galeata
Sogliano al Rubicone
Miramare
Riccione
Verucchio
Mercato Saraceno
RSM
San Marino
Cattolica
Gabicce Mare
Sársina
Coriano
San Leo
Pésaro
Novafeltria
Mercatino Conca
Morciano di Romagna
MONTEFELTRO
MONTE FUMAIOLO
1407
Pennabilli
1415
Montécchio
Macerata Féltria
Casinina
Fano
Madonna del Ponte
Montelabbate
Carpegna
Torretta di Fano
Foglia
CONVENTO DI MONTEFIORENTINO
Sassocorvaro
Mombaroccio
VIA FLAMINIA
Marotta
Badia Tedalda
Urbino
Passo di Viamaggio
983
Sant'Angelo in Vado
Fermignano
Fossombrone
Mondolfo
Senigállia
Urbánia
Metauro
Corinaldo
Marzocca
Falconara Marittima
Sansepolcro
Anghiari
2008
Apécchio
Acqualagna
San Lorenzo in Campo
Ostra
Chiaravalle
ANCONA
San Giustino
Piobbico
Cagli
Pergola
Belvedere Ostrense
Ancona Falconara
SANTA MARIA DI PORTONOVO
BADIA DI SAN PIETRO
Città di Castello
Arcévia
116
Serra de'Conti
Jesi
Santa Maria Nuova
Osimo
Sirolo
Numana
Pietralunga
1701
M CATRIA
MONASTERO DI FONTE AVELLANA
Serra S.Quirico
Cupramontana
Sassoferrato
Castelfidardo
Morra
1080
Zadar
Split
Igoumenítsa
Durrës
Pátra
Çeşme
Ankaran
Koper
Škofije
Piran
Izola
Portorož
Jagodje
Hrastovlje
Lucija
Savudrija
Grašišće
Šmarje
Sečovlje
Sočerga
Gradin
Umag
Buje
Požane
Kršete
GROŽNJAN
Livade
Istarske Toplice
Mirna
Vižinada
Novigrad
Motovun
Karojba
Pazin
Poreč
Baderna
Gračišće
Vrsar
Limski kanal
Žminj
Kanfanar
Petehi
Rovinj
Svetvinčenat
Crveni Otok
Barban
Bale
Vodnjan
NAC. PARK
Brijuni
Galižana
Loborika
Pula
Medulin
Premantura
Rt Kamenjak
A
B
C
D

Bač
Prem
Knežak
Ilirska Bistrica
SNEŽNIK 1796
Čabar
Kočevska Reka
Nemška loka
Črnomelj
Jurovski Brod
Draganići
Ozalj
A1
E71
E65
Gorica Jamnička
Kravarsko
Obrov
Podgrad
Jelšane
Morava
Banjaloka
74
SLO
Kanižarica
Pisarovina
Starod
Rupa
Pasjak
Šapjane
SLAVNIK 1028
Gerovo
Dragatuš
Šišljavić
Gradec Prokupski
Pokupsko
Petrina
Brod na Kupi
Vinica
Netretić
Karlovac
Kupa
Kolpa
NAC. PARK RISNJAK
1528 RISNJAK
GORSKI KOTAR
Klana
Skrad
Kupjak
Moravice
Bosanci
Duga Resa
Zagorje
Skakavac
Rječina
ISTARIJA
UČKA TUNNEL
Matulji
Viškovo
Delnice
Lokve
Bosiljevo
Tušilović
Graberje
Opatija
RIJEKA
E61
A7
E65
A6
Vrbovsko
Generalski Stol
Krnjak
Gvozd
Bović
Glina
Vranja
1396
UČKA
Lovran
Bakar
Kraljevica
Mrkopalj
Perjasica
Korana
Vojnić
PETROVA GORA
Topusko
Ravno Rašće
Maja
Boljun
Bakarski z.
Mošćenička Draga
Črišnjeva
1533 BIJELOLASICA
Jasenak
Ogulin
A1
Tounj
Veljun
Obljaj
Dragotina
Mošćenice
Brseč
Omišalj
Voz
2008
Oštarije
Mrežnica
Primišlje
Maljevac
Brezovo Polje
Kršan
Riječki zaljev
Njivice
Rijeka
Crikvenica
Mosune
Josipdol
Velika Kladuša
Bosanska Bojna
Plomin
Brestova
Porozina
Šilo
Selce
VELIKA KAPELA
Drežnica
Modruš
Mala Kladuša
Zborište
Labin
Rabac
Beli
Malinska
Sv. Vid
Vrbnik
Novi Vinodolski
Klenovica
Plaški
Jezero
Slunj
Vejinac
Stupnica
Varoška Rijeka
Valbiska
Krk
Punat
Jezerane
MALA KAPELA
Brinje
Saborsko
Rakovica
Krakača
BIH
Mrazovac
Koromačno
Rt Ubac
Cres
Pernat
Baška
Senj
Žuta Lokva
HR
Cazin
Jezerski
Otoka
Plavnik
Krk
Prvić
Sv. Juraj
NAC. PARK PLITVIČKA JEZERA
Plitvička jezera
Poljanak
Drežnik-Grad
Ostrožac
LUBENICE
Sv Grgur
Kompolje
Otočac
Plitvice
Izačić
Vransko jez.
Kvarner
Goli
Lukovo
Gusić jezero
Zalužnica
Prijeboj
Brekovica
Bosans
Korčula Dubrovnik Split
Cres
Vrana
Lopar
Starigrad
Devčići
Babin Potok
Ličko Lešće
Plitvički Ljeskovac
Bihać
SOKOLAC
Gudavac
Zeča
Belej
Kampor
Rab
Rab
Lipovo Polje
KRBAVA
Vrelo
Ripač
Osor
588
Barbat
Lun
Jablanac
Čanak
Korenica
Dubovsko
Unije
Nerezine
Punta Križa
Štirovača
Bakovac
Perušić
Bunić
Bjelopolje
Kruge
142
Orašac
Bokinić
Vranjak
Klanac
Pećane
Vrtoče
Ćunski
Lošinj
Stara Novalja
Gradina
Lički Osik
Susak
Mali Lošinj
Veli Lošinj
Novalja
Cesarica
Stara vrata 927
Baške Oštarije
Gospić
Jadova
Jošan
Udbina
Donji Lapac
Kulen Vakuf
Karlobag
Šimuni
Brušane
Mogorić
Gornji Lapac
Doljani
Ilovik
Škrda
Maun
Lukovo Šugarje
Medak
Lika
Gornja Ploča
Ondić
Maunski kanal
Olib
Pag
Tribanj Kruščica
Donja Suvaja
Silba
Gorica
Pag
NAC. PARK PAKLENICA
1758
Bruvno
Gornji srb
Premuda
Virsko more
VAGANSKI VRH
MANITA PEĆ
Sveti Rok
Deringaj
Starigrad Paklenica
Miletići
Gračac
Kupirovo
Škarda
Vir
Ist
Privlaka
Rovanjska
Mali Alan Prolaz 1045
CEROVAČKE ŠPILJE
Otrić
Molat
Petrčane
Nin
Posedarje
Maslenica
Obrovac
Kaštel Žegarski
Sestrunj
Poličnik
Novigrad
Zrmanja
Ancona
Božava
Ugljan
Murvica
Zadar
Ervenik
Ugljan
Donji Zemunik
Medvida
Preko
ASSERIA
Benkovac
Bruška
Rodaljice
Padjene
Brbinj
Iž
Sukošan
Raducić
Knin
Srednji kanal
Zadarski kanal
Kakma
Zaglav
Vrana
A1
Kistanje
Oklaj
Dugi Otok
Sali
Pašman
Pašman
Biograd
Bribirske Mostine
Bribir
1148 V. PROMINA
Pakoštane
Tkon
Vransko jezero
NAC. PARK KRKA
Krka
Širitovci
Kornat
Žut
Murter
Pirovac
Skradin
Visovačko jezero
Drniš
Stari Grad
NAC. PARK KORNATI
Tisno
Prukljansko jezero
SKRADINSKI BUK
Murter
Vodice
Lozovac
Lavsa
Šibenik
Kakan
Zablaće
Vrpolje
Sitno
Kurba Vela
Zlarin
Brodarica
Žirje
Split
117
Primošten
Prapatnica
Bristivica
Rogoznica
E65
Seget

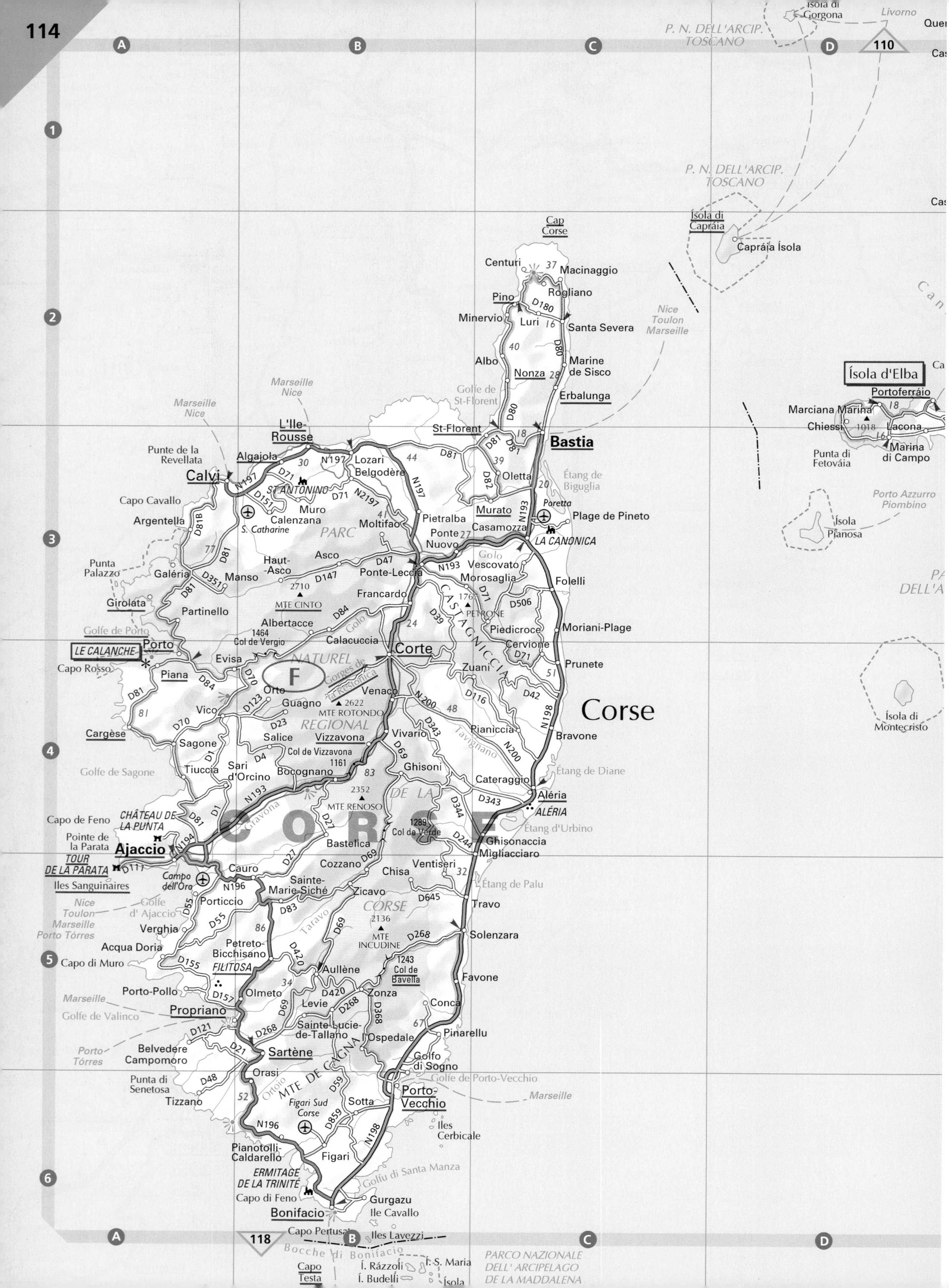
A
B
C
D
110
1
2
3
4
5
6
118
Ísola di Gorgona
Livorno
P. N. DELL'ARCIP. TOSCANO
Ísola di Capráia
Capráia Ísola
Cap Corse
Centuri
Macinaggio
Rogliano
Pino
Luri
Minervio
Santa Severa
Nice Toulon Marseille
Albo
Nonza
Marine de Sisco
Erbalunga
Golfe de St-Florent
St-Florent
Bastia
Oletta
Étang de Biguglia
Ísola d'Elba
Portoferráio
Marciana Marina
Chiessi
Lacona
Marina di Campo
Punta di Fetováia
Porto Azzurro Piombino
Ísola Pianosa
Marseille Nice
L'Ile-Rousse
Algajola
Punte de la Revellata
Calvi
Lozari
Belgodère
ST ANTONINO
Capo Cavallo
Argentella
Calenzana
Muro
S. Catharine
Pietralba
Murato
Poretta
Plage de Pineto
Casamozza
LA CANONICA
Moltifao
Ponte Nuovo
PARC
Punta Palazzo
Galéria
Manso
Haut-Asco
Asco
Ponte-Leccia
Vescovato
Morosaglia
Folelli
Girolata
Partinello
MTE CINTO
Francardo
CASTAGNICCIA
PETRONE
Piedicroce
Moriani-Plage
Golfe de Porto
Albertacce
Col de Vergio
Calacuccia
Cervione
LE CALANCHE
Porto
Capo Rosso
Evisa
NATUREL
Corte
Zuani
Prunete
Piana
Gorges de la Restonica
F
Orto
Venaco
Guagno
MTE ROTONDO
Corse
Vico
REGIONAL
Pianiccia
Cargèse
Sagone
Salice
Vizzavona
Vivario
Bravone
Col de Vizzavona
Tavignano
Golfe de Sagone
Tiuccia
Sari d'Orcino
Bocognano
Ghisoni
Cateraggio
Étang de Diane
Aléria
ALÉRIA
MTE RENOSO
DE LA
CORSE
Capo de Feno
CHÂTEAU DE LA PUNTA
Col de Verde
Étang d'Urbino
Pointe de la Parata
Ajaccio
Bastelica
Ghisonaccia
Migliacciaro
TOUR DE LA PARATA
Cauro
Cozzano
Ventiseri
Campo dell'Oro
Chisa
Iles Sanguinaires
Sainte-Marie-Siché
Zicavo
Étang de Palu
Nice Toulon Marseille Porto Tórres
Golfe d' Ajaccio
Porticcio
Travo
Verghia
MTE INCUDINE
Solenzara
Acqua Doria
Petreto-Bicchisano
Capo di Muro
FILITOSA
Col de Bavella
Aullène
Favone
Porto-Pollo
Olmeto
Zonza
Marseille
Golfe de Valinco
Propriano
Levie
Conca
Sainte-Lucie-de-Tallano
L'Ospedale
Pinarellu
Porto Tórres
Belvedere Campomoro
Sartène
Golfo di Sogno
Orasi
MTE DE CAGNA
Golfe de Porto-Vecchio
Punta di Senetosa
Porto-Vecchio
Marseille
Tizzano
Figari Sud Corse
Sotta
Iles Cerbicale
Pianotolli-Caldarello
Figari
ERMITAGE DE LA TRINITÉ
Golfu di Santa Manza
Capo di Feno
Gurgazu
Bonifacio
Ile Cavallo
Capo Pertusato
Iles Lavezzi
Bocche di Bonifacio
Capo Testa
Í. Rázzoli
Í. Budelli
I. S. Maria
PARCO NAZIONALE DELL' ARCIPELAGO DE LA MADDALENA
Ísola di Montecristo

TOSCANA
COLLINE METALLIFERE
LE CRETE
UMBRIA
LAZIO
I
Volterra
San Gimignano
Poggibonsi
Colle di Val d'Elsa
Siena
Arezzo
Castellina in Chianti
Cavriglia
Montevarchi
Castiglion Fibocchi
Anghiari
Città di Castello
Rosignano Marittimo
Rosignano Solvay
Castiglioncello
Riparbella
Saline di Volterra
Cécina
Casino di Terra
Pomarance
Bibbiona
Forte di Bibbiona
Larderello
MUSEO DELLA GEOTERMIA
TORRE DI MONTEMICCIOLI
Monteriggioni
Pianella
Pievescola
S. Gusmè
Castelnuovo Berardenga
Civitella in Val di Chiana
Bucine
Castiglion Fiorentino
Morra
Bolgheri
Castagneto Carducci
Marina di Castagneto-Donorático
Canneto
Castelnuovo di Val di Cecina
Monterotondo Marittimo
ABBAZIA DI S. GALGANO
Monticiano
Monteroni d'Arbia
Murlo
Asciano
Monte San Savino
Lucignano
Sinalunga
Foiano di Chiana
Cortona
Petrelle
Umbertide
Mercatale
Passignano sul Trasimeno
Magione
Lago Trasimeno
Castiglione del Lago
PERÚG
San Vincenzo
Suvereto
Massa Marittima
Campiglia Marittima
TOMBE ETRUSCHE
Populónia
Piombino
Follónica
Golfo di Follónica
Sassofortino
Montemassi
Roccastrada
Ribolla
Cura Nuova
Civitella Paganico
Montalcino
ABBAZIA DI MONTE OLIVETO MAGGIORE
Buonconvento
Torrita di Siena
Pienza
Montepulciano
San Quírico d'Orcia
Bagno Vignoni
ABBAZIA DI SANT'ANTIMO
Chianciano Terme
NECROPOLI ETRUSCA
Chiusi
Corciano
Mugnano
Panicale
S. Martino dei Colli
Tavernelle
Città della Pieve
Montegabbione
Marsciano
San Venanzo
Ficulle
Castiglione d'Orcia
Sarteano
Cetona
Abbadia San Salvatore
MT AMIATA
Arcidosso
Santafiora
Castel del Piano
Páganico
Sticciano Scalo
Cinigiano
Campagnático
Gavorrano
Vetulónia
NECROPOLI ETRUSCHE
ROSELLE
Punta Ala
Pian d' Alma
Castiglione della Pescáia
Grosseto
Marina di Grosseto
Arcille
Roccalbegna
Castell'Azzara
San Casciano dei Bagni
Acquapendente
San Lorenzo Nuovo
Orvieto
Todi
Acquasparta
Sta. Pestituta
I. Palmaiola
I. Cerboli
Cavo
Rio Marina
VOLTERRAIO
Porto Azzurro
Capolíveri
Punta dei Ripalti
Pianosa
Ólbia
Scansano
Magliano in Toscana
Pereta
Saturnia
TERME DI SATURNIA
Sorano
Pitigliano
Manciano
S. BRUZIO
Marina di Alberese
TORRE DELL'UCCELLINA
PARCO NAZIONALE ARCIPELAGO TOSCANO
Formiche di Grosseto
Talamone
Golfo di Talamone
Marsiliana
Fornace
Farnese
Valentano
Latera
Lago di Bolsena
Bolsena
TOMBE ETRUSCHE
Bagnoregio
Civita
Montefiascone
Amélia
CASTRO
Capodimonte
Marta
FERENTO
Bomarzo
Orbetello
SPACCO DELLA REGINA
Capalbio
Porto Santo Stéfano
Monte Argentário
COSA
Ansedónia
Porto Ércole
Ísola del Gíglio
Giglio Porto
Ísola di Giannutri
VULCI
Canino
Abbadia
Arlena di Castro
BAGNI DI VITERBO
Tuscánia
Viterbo
Soriano nel Cimino
MONTE CIMINO
MONTI CIMINI
Lago di Vico
Vignanello
Civita Castellana
Orte
Montalto di Castro
Il Casalone
NORCHIA
Vetralla
Blera
Ronciglione
Capranica
Sutri
FALERII NOVI
Nepi
Riva dei Tarquini
Tarquinia
TARQUINIA
Tarquínia Lido
PORTO CLEMENTINO
NECROPOLI ETRUSCA
SAN GIOVENALE
Tolfa
Vejano
MONTI SABATINI
Rignano Flaminio
Vicarello
Trevignano Romano
Lago di Bracciano
Lago di Martignano
Civitavécchia
TERME TAURINE
BAGNI DI STIGLIANO
Bracciano
Anguillara Sabazia
Cerveteri
VEIO
Settebagni
MADONNA DI BRACCIANO
Santa Marinella
Capo Linaro
Santa Severa
Ladispoli
Città del Vaticano
Fregene
Leonardo da Vinci
Fiumicino
OSTIA
Lido di Óstia
Lido di Castel Fusano
Castel Porziano
Pomézia
Tor Vaiánica
Marina di Ardea
Ólbia
Árbatax
Cágliari
Palermo
Tùnis
Barcelona
E
F
G
H
111
116

Piobbico
Cagli
Pergola
Chiaravalle
ANCONA
Ancona Falconara
SANTA MARIA DI PORTONOVO
BADIA DI SAN PIETRO
Belvedere Ostrense
Jesi
Sirolo
Numana
Città di Castello
Pietralunga
M. CATRIA
MONASTERO DI FONTE AVELLANA
Arcévia
Serra S.Quirico
Santa Maria Nuova
Osimo
Cupramontana
Sassoferrato
GROTTE DI FRASASSI
MARCHE
Filottrano
Castelfidardo
Loreto
Porto Recanati
Schéggia
Recanati
Gúbbio
Fabriano
San Vittore delle Chiuse
Cingoli
HELVIA RECINA
Villa Potenza
Potenza Picena
Porto Potenza Picena
Civitanova Marche
Umbertide
Branca
Colcerasa
S.CLAUDIO AL CH.
S. MARIA DI RAMBONA
Macerata
Mercatale
Scritto
Gualdo Tadino
Matelica
San Severino Marche
Castiglione del Lago
Passignano sul Trasimeno
Sforzacosta
SANTA MARIA A PIE DI CHIENTI
Porto Sant'Elpidio
Castelraimondo
Tolentino
Corridonia
Magione
Valfábbrica
Terme S. Lucia
ABBADIA DI FIASTRA
Lido di Fermo
PERÚGIA
Pióraco
S.Elpidio a Mare
Porto San Giorgio
Corciano
Nocera Umbra
Camerino
Caldarola
Bastia
Montegiorgio
Fermo
Mugnano
Assisi
SAN GIUSTO
Marina Palmense
S. Martino dei Colli
EREMO DELLE CARCERI
Muccia
S. Ginesio
Monterubbiano
Pedaso
Torgiano
Colfiorito
Servigliano
Campofilone
Spello
Sarnano
Cannara
Carassai
Cupra Marittima
Deruta
PARCO
Amandola
Ripatransone
Bevagna
MONTI SIBILLINI
Grottammare
Marsciano
Gualdo Cattáneo
Foligno
Nera
NAZIONALE
Comunanza
Montalto delle Marche
San Benedetto del Tronto
Montefalco
Visso
Offida
Trevi
ABBAZIA DI S. EUTIZIO
Áscoli Piceno
Porto d'Áscoli
TEMPIO D.CLITUNNO
MONTI MARTANI
FONTI DEL CLITUNNO
Martinsicuro
Triponzo
MONTE VETTORE
Alba Adriatica
Norcia
Arquata del Tronto
Nereto
Tortoreto Lido
UMBRIA
Todi
Spoleto
Lago di Corbara
Civitella del Tronto
Tortoreto
Giulianova
Cascia
Acquasanta Terme
Tronto
Acquasparta
SAN PIETRO IN VALLE
MADONNA DELLA NEVE
S. MARIA DI PROPEZZANO
Sta. Restituta
CARSULAE
Sambucheto
Bellante
Téramo
Roseto degli Abruzzi
SAN GEMINI FONTE
Rúscio
Accumoli
Amatrice
MONTI DELLA LAGA
San Gemini
Villa Vomano
Pineto
Amélia
TERNI
Leonessa
Montorio al Vomano
S. CLEMENTE AL VOMANO
Narni
CASCATE DELLE MARMORE
Piediluco
Posta
Lago di Campotosto
Silvi Marina
Orte
MONTE TERMINILLO
L. Lungo
Borbona
Lodonero
Montereale
Prati di Tivo
S. MARIA DI RONZANO
Atri
Città Sant'Angelo
Soriano nel Cimino
CONVENTO LA FORESTA
Terminillo
Passo d. Capannelle
GRAN SASSO D'ITALIA
S. GIOVANNI AL MAVONE
Isola del Gran Sasso d'Italia
Montesilvano Marina
Itieli
Contigliano
Cittaducale
CORNO GRANDE
Penne
Spoltore
PESCARA
Vignanello
Magliano Sabina
CONVENTO DI FONTE COLOMBO
Rieti
Antrodoco
Pizzoli
AMITERNUM
Assergi
Loreto Aprutino
Moscufo
Civita Castellana
Sella di Corno
PARCO NAZ. DEL GRAN SASSO E MONTI DELLA LAGA
MONTI SABINI
L'Aquila
Barisciano
Villa S.Lucia degli Abruzzi
Cepagatti
Chieti
FALERII NOVI
Rocca Sinibalda
Nepi
Rignano Flaminio
Lago di Turano
Fiamignano
S. Paolo di di Peltuino
Navelli
Torre de' Passeri
Bucchianico
Trevignano Romano
ABBAZIA DI FARFA
Castel di Tora
Lago del Salto
Pescorocchiano
Casamáina
Capestrano
S. MARIA ARABONA
LUCUS FERONIAE
Borgorose
Rocca di Cambio
Bominaco
Scafa
S. CLEMENTE A CASAURIA
Lanciano
Castelnuovo di Porto
Lago di Martignano
Orvinio
MONTE VELINO
Rocca di Mezzo
Ovindoli
ABRUZZO
Ortona
Guardiagrele
S.MARIA IN VALLE PORCLANETA
Magliano dei Marsi
Castelvecchio Subequo
Popoli
PARCO NAZIONALE DELLA MAIELLA
Palombara Sabina
Carsoli
Passo San Leonardo
Casoli
VEIO
Monterotondo
Tagliacozzo
Celano
Settebagni
ROMA
Guidonia
Arsoli
ALBA FUCENS
Forca Caruso
Sulmona
Città del Vaticano
Vicovaro
Sambuci
Avezzano
Pescina
MONTAGNA DELLA MAIELLA
Tivoli
Cerreto Laziale
S. Benedetto dei Marsi
Pacentro
Cansano
Lama dei Peligni
Subiaco
Capistrello
Luco dei Marsi
Lago di Scanno
Palena
JUVANUM
Lago di Bomba
VILLA ADRIANA
San Vito Romano
Civitella Roveto
Rocca Pia
Arcinazzo Romano
MONTI SIMBRUINI
Scanno
Quadri
Palestrina
Altipiani di Arcinazzo
PARCO NAZ. D'ABRUZZO LAZIO E MOLISE
Pescocostanzo
Genazzano
Balsorano
Passo del Diavolo
Roccaraso
Piglio
MONTI ERNICI
Pescasseroli
MONTE MARSICANO
Capracotta
OSTIA
Ciampino
Frascati
Valmontone
Fiuggi
Guarcino
Opi
Villetta Barrea
Castel Porziano
Albano Laziale
Lago Albano
Lariano
Lago di Nemi
Artena
Anagni
Alatri
ABBAZIA DI TRISULTI
Forca d'Acero
Lago di Barrea
Castel di Sangro
Genzano di Roma
Colleferro
Veroli
Sora
MONTI DELLA META
Alfedena
LAZIO
Pomézia
Velletri
Segni
Ferentino
Alvito
Tor Vaiánica
Cori
Carpineto Romano
ABBAZIA DI CASAMARI
Isola del Liri
Forlì del Sannio
Ardea
Cisterna di Latina
Frosinone
Aprilia
Norma
Supino
Atina
ABBAZIA DI S. VINCENZO
Marina di Ardea
NINFA
Sermoneta
Cardito
Isernia
Lavinio Lido di Enea
MONTI LEPINI
Ceccano
Ceprano
Giuliano di Roma
Sant'Elia Fiumerapido
Sezze
Nettuno
Castro
Aquino
ABBAZIA DI MONTECASSINO

Kurba Vela
Žirje
Zlarin
Brodarica
Primošten
Prapatnica
Bristvica
Split
Rogoznica
Seget
Kaštel Stari
Marina
Trogir
Okrug
Rt Ploča
Splitski kanal
HR
Drvenik
Maslinica
Rogač
Šolta
Stomorska
Jabuka
Svetac
Komiža
Vis
Viški kanal
Korčula
MODRA ŠPILJA
Biševo
Palagruža
Marina
Ortona
San Vito Chietino
SAN GIOVANNI IN VENERE
Torino di Sangro Marina
Torino di Sangro
Punta di Penna
Casalbordino
Vasto
Marina di Vasto
Cupello
Atessa
Gissi
MONTI DEI FRENTANI
San Salvo
Térmoli
Montenero di Bisáccia
Campomarino
Marina di Chiéuti
Guglionesi
MADONNA DI CANNETO
Montefalcone nel Sannio
Castelmauro
Guardialfiera
Agnone
Trivento
Larino
S.Martino in Pensilis
Serracapriola
Ururi
RUDERI ROMANI
Lucito
Limosano
Casacalenda
Santa Croce di Magliano
Bonefro
Colletorto
Petrella Tifernina
Casalciprano
Sant'Elia a Pianisi
Carlantino
Lago di Occhito
Castelnuovo della Dáunia
Campobasso
San Paolo di Civitate
Torremaggiore
San Severo
Apricena
Lésina
Lago di Lésina
Lido di Torre Mileto
Rodi Gargánico
Lago di Varano
Péschici
Vieste
Vico del Gargano
Carpino
Sannicandro Gargánico
Cagnano Varano
PROMONTORIO DEL GARGANO
PARCO NAZIONALE DEL GARGANO
Pugnochiuso
Baia delle Zagare
Mattinata
San Marco in Lamis
San Giovanni Rotondo
Monte Sant'Angelo
Manfredónia
SANTA MARIA DI SIPONTO
SAN LEONARDO
Golfo di
Í Pianosa
Í. Capráia
Í. S. Dómino
ÍSOLE TRÉMITI
Í. S. Nicola
A14
E55
E65
SS16
SS89
SS272

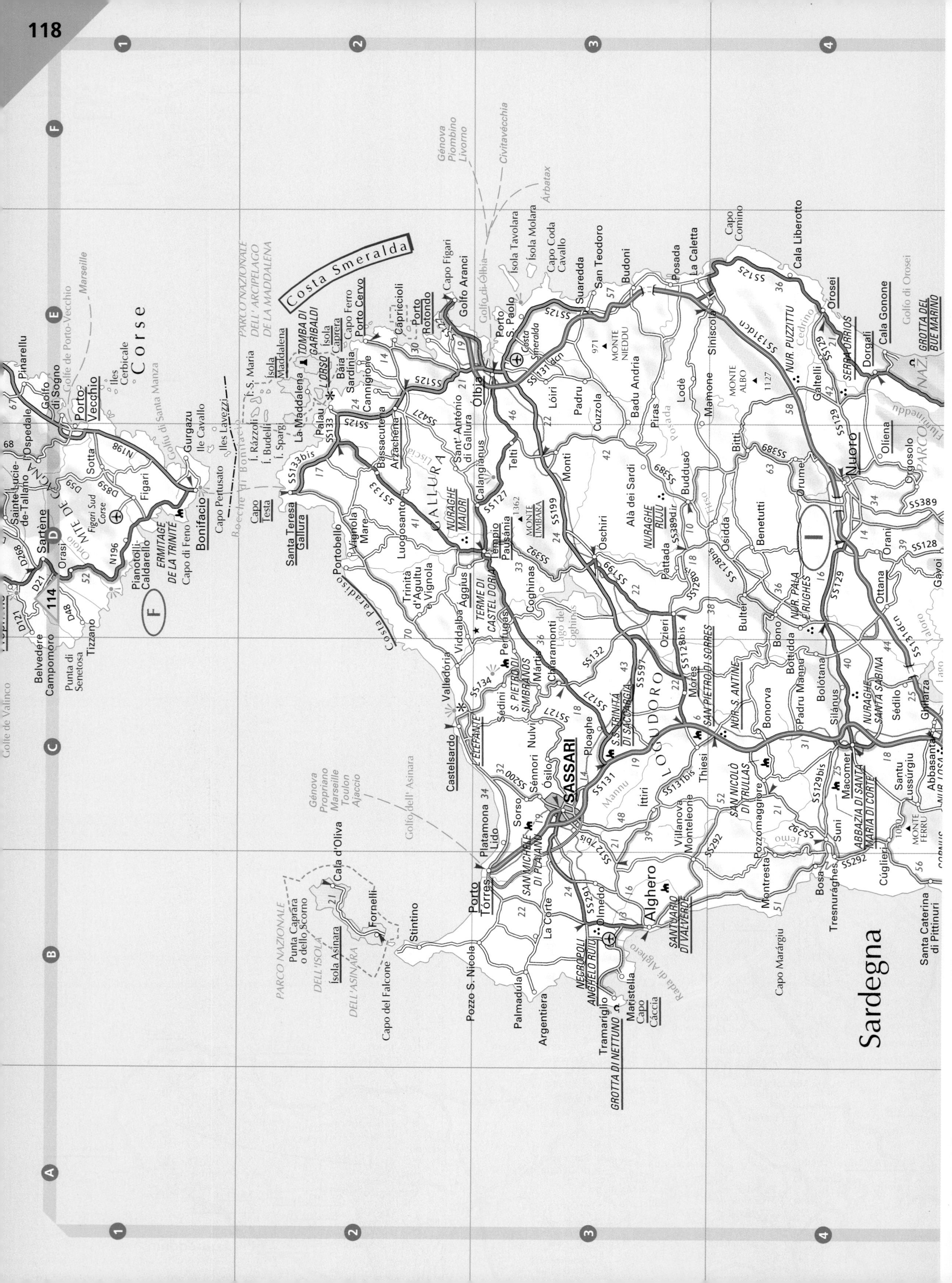

Costa Smeralda
Corse
Sardegna
SASSARI
Nuoro
Olbia
Alghero
Porto Torres
Tempio Pausània
Bonifacio
Porto-Vecchio
Sartène
La Maddalena
Palau
Santa Teresa Gallura
Castelsardo
Stintino
Ozieri
Macomer
Bosa
Siniscola
Orosei
Dorgali
Cala Gonone
Posada
La Caletta
Budoni
San Teodoro
Golfo Aranci
Porto Cervo
Porto Rotondo
Arzachena
Calangianus
Luogosanto
Bono
Bonorva
Thiesi
Ploaghe
Sorso
Sènnori
Ìttiri
Pozzomaggiore
Sìndia
Suni
Cùglieri
Ottana
Orani
Oliena
Orgosolo
Gavoi
Fonni
Golfo dell' Asinara
Ìsola Asinara
PARCO NAZIONALE DELL' ÌSOLA DELL' ASINARA
PARCO NAZIONALE DELL' ARCIPELAGO DE LA MADDALENA
Capo Testa
Capo Càccia
GROTTA DI NETTUNO
GALLURA
LOGUDORO
Golfo di Orosei
Bocche di Bonifacio
Golfe de Valinco
Génova Piombino Livorno
Civitavécchia
Árbatax
Génova Propriano Marseille Toulon Ajaccio
Marseille

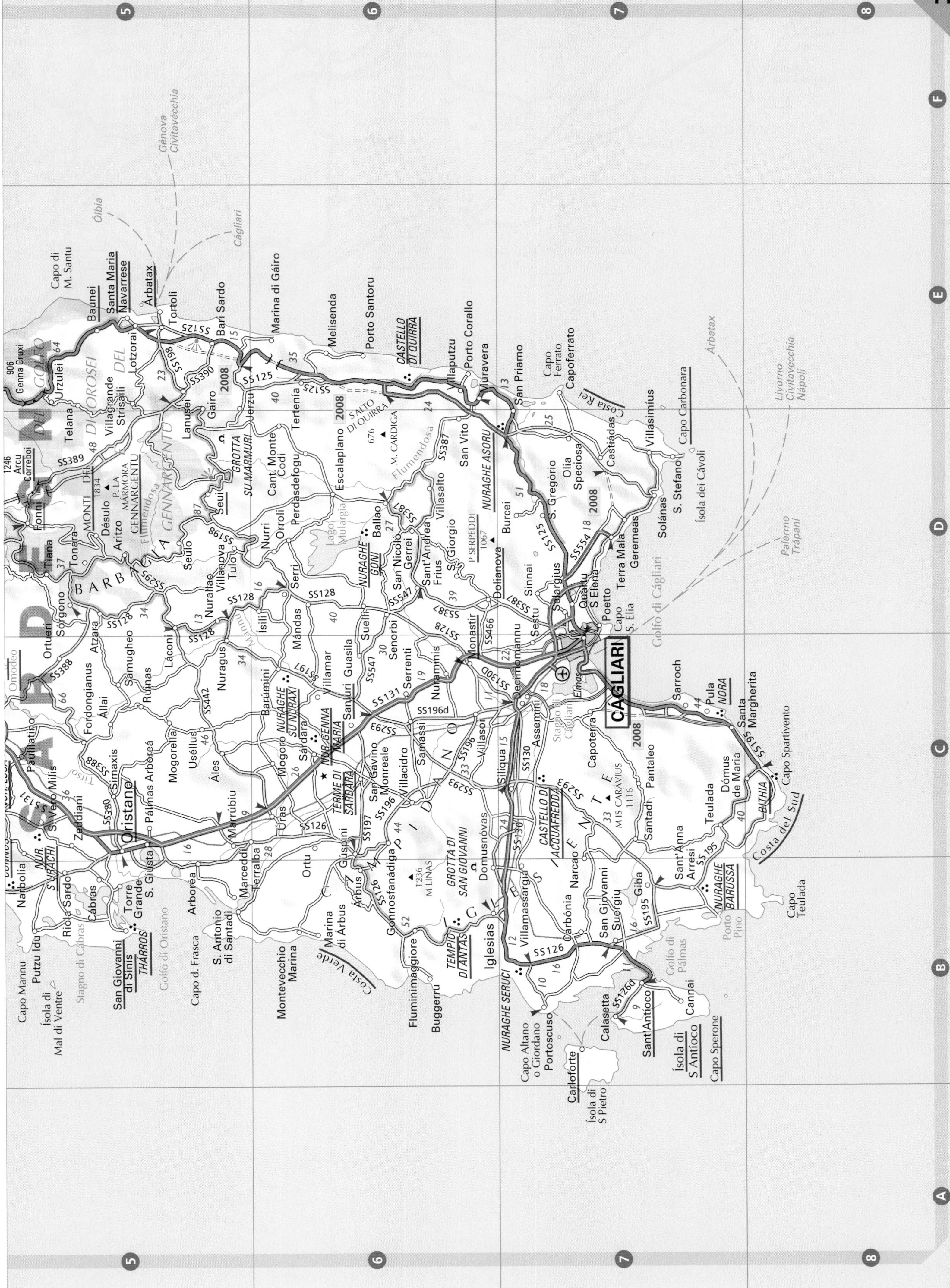
5
6
7
8
A
B
C
D
E
F
SARDEGNA
CÁGLIARI
Oristano
Iglesias
Carbónia
Golfo di Cágliari
Golfo di Oristano
Golfo di Pálmas
Golfo di Orosei
Costa Verde
Costa del Sud
Costa Rei
Stagno di Cábras
Stagno di Cágliari
Ísola di S Pietro
Ísola di S Antíoco
Ísola di Mal di Ventre
Ísola dei Cávoli
Carloforte
Calasetta
Sant'Antíoco
Cannai
Capo Sperone
Portoscuso
Capo Altano o Giordano
Buggerru
Fluminimaggiore
Arbus
Guspini
Gonnosfanadiga
Villacidro
San Gavino Monreale
Sanluri
Sardara
Mogoro
Uras
Marrùbiu
Terralba
Arborea
Marceddì
S. Antonio di Santadi
Capo d. Frasca
San Giovanni di Sinis
Cábras
Riola Sardo
Putzu Idu
Capo Mannu
Narbolia
Zeddiani
Simaxis
Pálmas Arborea
S. Giusta
Torre Grande
Villasor
Decimomannu
Assemini
Elmas
Quartu S Elena
Selargius
Poetto
Capo S. Elia
Sarroch
Pula
Santa Margherita
Capo Spartivento
Dómus de Maria
Teulada
Capo Teulada
Sant'Anna Arresi
Giba
San Giovanni Suergiu
Villamassargia
Domusnovas
Narcao
Santadi
Villaperuccio
Capoterra
Pantaleo
Siliqua
Monastir
Sestu
Sinnai
Dolianova
Burcei
San Vito
Muravera
Villaputzu
Porto Corallo
San Priamo
Capo Ferrato
Capoferrato
Castiádas
Villasimíus
Capo Carbonara
Solánas
S. Stefano
Olia Speciosa
S. Gregório
Terra Mala
Geremeas
Villasalto
Ballao
Armungia
San Nicolò Gerrei
Sant'Andrea Frius
S. Giorgio
Senorbì
Suelli
Guasila
Mandas
Ísili
Serri
Nurri
Orroli
Escalaplano
Perdasdefogu
Tertenia
Jerzu
Gairo
Lanusei
Tortolì
Árbatax
Bari Sardo
Lotzorai
Baunei
Santa Maria Navarrese
Capo di M. Santu
Urzulei
Villagrande Strisáili
Telana
Fonni
Désulo
Aritzo
Tonara
Tiana
Sórgono
Atzara
Ortueri
Samugheo
Láconi
Nuraghe
Nurallao
Villanova Tulo
Seulo
Seui
Sadali
Nuragus
Genoni
Barúmini
Villamar
Usellus
Áles
Mogorella
Ruinas
Allai
Fordongianus
Paulilatino
Villanova Truschedu
Marina di Gáiro
Melisenda
Porto Santoru
Cant. Monte Codi
Capo Sandalo
Montevecchio Marina
Marina di Árbus
Samassi
Serrenti
Nuraminis
Furtei
Villanovafranca
Serramanna
BARBAGIA
GENNARGENTU
MONTI DEL GENNARGENTU
P. LA MÁRMORA 1834
M. LINAS 1236
P. SERPEDDI 1067
M. CARDIGA 676
M.IS CARÁVIUS 1116
Arcu Correboi 1246
Genna Cruxi 906
Lago Mulargia
Flumendosa
Tirso
CAMPIDANO
SULCIS
IGLESIENTE
THARROS
NORA
BITHIA
NURAGHE BARUSSA
NURAGHE SERUCI
TEMPIO DI ANTAS
GROTTA DI SAN GIOVANNI
CASTELLO DI ACQUAFREDDA
TERME DI SARDARA
NUR. GENNA MARIA
NURAGHE SU NURAXI
NURAGHE GONI
NURAGHE ASORU
CASTELLO DI QUIRRA
GROTTA SU MARMURI
S. ALTO DI QUIRRA
NUR. S'URACHI
Omodeo
SS131
SS130
SS126
SS125
SS128
SS195
SS196
SS197
SS293
SS387
SS554
SS547
SS198
SS389
SS390
SS388
SS442
SS466
2008
Olbia
Génova
Civitavécchia
Cágliari
Livorno
Nápoli
Palermo
Trápani

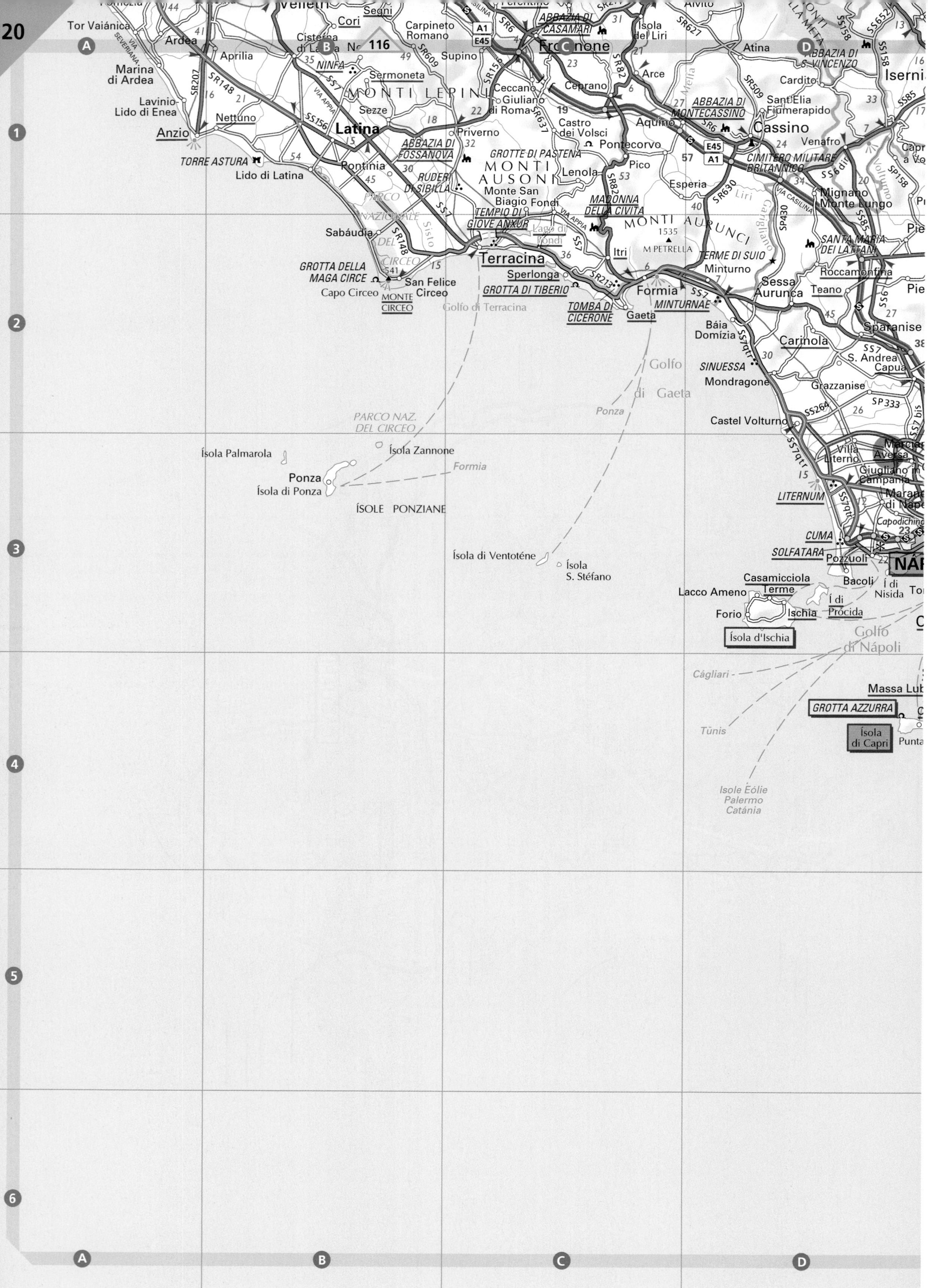
116
Tor Vaiánica
Ardea
Marina di Ardea
Aprilia
Lavinio-Lido di Enea
Nettuno
Anzio
TORRE ASTURA
Lido di Latina
Cori
Segni
Carpineto Romano
Supino
NINFA
Sermoneta
MONTI LEPINI
Sezze
Latina
Pontinia
Priverno
ABBAZIA DI FOSSANOVA
RUDERI DI SIBILLA
PARCO NAZIONALE DEL CIRCEO
Sabáudia
GROTTA DELLA MAGA CIRCE
San Felice Circeo
Capo Circeo
MONTE CIRCEO
Golfo di Terracina
Terracina
TEMPIO DI GIOVE ANXUR
Lago di Fondi
Monte San Biagio
Fondi
MONTI AUSONI
GROTTE DI PASTENA
Ceccano
Giuliano di Roma
ABBAZIA DI CASAMARI
Ceprano
Castro dei Volsci
Pontecorvo
Lenola
MADONNA DELLA CIVITA
Pico
Esperia
Isola del Liri
Arce
Aquino
ABBAZIA DI MONTECASSINO
Cassino
Atina
ABBAZIA DI S. VINCENZO
Cardito
Sant'Elia Fiumerapido
Venafro
CIMITERO MILITARE BRITANNICO
Mignano Monte Lungo
SANTA MARIA DEI LATTANI
Roccamonfina
Teano
Sessa Aurunca
MONTI AURUNCI
M PETRELLA
1535
Itri
TERME DI SUIO
Minturno
Sperlonga
GROTTA DI TIBERIO
TOMBA DI CICERONE
Gaeta
Formia
MINTURNAE
Báia Domízia
Carinola
SINUESSA
Mondragone
Golfo di Gaeta
Ponza
S. Andrea
Capua
Grazzanise
Sparanise
Castel Volturno
Villa Literno
Aversa
Giugliano in Campania
LITERNUM
CUMA
SOLFATARA
Pozzuoli
Bacoli
Í di Nisida
Casamicciola Terme
Lacco Ameno
Forio
Ischia
Í di Prócida
Ísola d'Ischia
Golfo di Nápoli
Cágliari
Tūnis
Isole Eólie Palermo Catánia
Massa Lubrense
GROTTA AZZURRA
Ísola di Capri
PARCO NAZ. DEL CIRCEO
Ísola Palmarola
Ísola Zannone
Formia
Ponza
Ísola di Ponza
ÍSOLE PONZIANE
Ísola di Ventoténe
Ísola S. Stéfano
A
B
C
D
1
2
3
4
5
6

MOLISE
Campobasso
Benevento
Caserta
Avellino
SALERNO
FOGGIA
Lucera
San Severo
Manfredónia
Golfo di Manfredónia
Cerignola
Canosa di Púglia
Andria
Potenza
Melfi
Venosa
Nocera
Cava de' Tirreni
Amalfi
Positano
Sorrento
Castellammare di Stábia
Torre Annunziata
Pompei
Vesúvio
Ercolano
Nola
Acerra
Casoria
Pomigliano d'Arco
Maddaloni
Santa Maria Cápua Vetere
Limatola
Telese Terme
Guardia Sanframondi
Alife
Piedimonte Matese
Lago del Matese
MONTI DEL MATESE
SAEPINUM
Sepino
Bojano
Frosolone
Carpinone
Pescolanciano
Limosano
Petrella Tifernina
Jelsi
Riccia
Gambatesa
Castelvetere in Val Fortore
Colle Sannita
Basilice
San Bartolomeo in Galdo
Roseto Valfortore
Faeto
Troia
Orsara di Púglia
Castelfranco in Miscano
San Marco dei Cavoti
Buonalbergo
Ariano Irpino
Savignano Irpino
Bovino
Deliceto
Sant'Agata di Púglia
Accadia
Candela
Ascoli Satriano
Stornara
Orta Nova
Castelluccio dei Sauri
HERDONIAE
Lago di Capacciotti
Lavello
Minervino Murge
CASTEL DEL MONTE
Spinazzola
Rapolla
Rionero in Vúlture
VULTURE
Atella
Palazzo San Gervasio
Genzano di Lucánia
Forenza
Acerenza
Oppido Lucano
Pietragalla
Vaglio Basilicata
Tolve
Tricárico
Grassano
Albano di Lucánia
Passo Croce di Scrivano
Pignola
Tito
Picerno
Vietri di Potenza
Ruoti
Avigliano
Bella
Muro Lucano
San Fele
Pescopagano
Sant'Andrea di Conza
Calitri
Aquilonia
Monteverde
Lacedonia
Leonessa
Vallata
Bisaccia
Flumeri
Grottaminarda
Apice
Andretta
Lioni
Guardia Lombardi
Gesualdo
Paternopoli
Taurasi
Atripalda
Montella
Calabritto
M CERVIALTO 1809
MONTI PICENTINI
PARCO REG.
Acerno
Giffoni
Montecorvino Rovella
Éboli
Battipáglia
Campagna
Contursi Terme
BAGNI CONTURSI
Colliano
Laviano
S. Gregorio Magno
Auletta
Sicignano d. Alburni
M ALBURNO 1742
GROTTA DI PERTOSA
Altavilla Silentina
Spineta Nuova
Golfo di Salerno
Palermo Messina Catánia Valletta
PENISOLA SORRENTINA
Punta Campanella
Praiano
Vico Equense
Gragnano
Ravello
Maiori
Vietri sul Mare
Paestum
PAESTUM
Agropoli
Capaccio
Albanella
Roccadáspide
Controne
Castel San Lorenzo
Ogliastro Cilento
Prignano Cilento
Castellabate
Punta Licosa
Perdifumo
Montecorice
Acciaroli
Vallo di Lucania
Casal Velino
Ceraso
Ascea-Velia
Pisciotta
Palinuro
GROTTA AZZURRA
Capo Palinuro
Marina di Camerota
Golfo di Policastro
San Giovanni a Piro
Celle di Bulgheria
Policastro Bussentino
Sapri
Torre Orsaia
Alfano
Rofrano
Sanza
VALLO DI DIANO
PARCO NAZIONALE DEL CILENTO E
M CERVATI 1899
Laurino
Piaggine
Teggiano
Sala Consilina
San Rufo
Padula
Brienza
Abriola
Anzi
Calvello
Marsico Nuovo
Marsico Vetere
PARCO NAZ. DELL' APPENNINO LUCANO
Viggiano
GRUMENTUM
Lago di Pietra del Pertusillo
Moliterno
Montesano sulla Marcellana
VAL D'AGRI
Casalbuono
Lagonegro
LAGONEGRESE
M SIRINO 2005
Rivello
Lauria
Maratea
Tortora
Praia a Mare
Papasidero
Scalea
Cirella
Í. di Cirella
Diamante
Castelsaraceno
S. Chirico Raparo
Roccanova
Missanello
Corleto Perticara
Laurenzana
Accettura
S. Mauro Forte
Chiaromonte
Senise
Latronico
Episcopia
Castelluccio Sup.
Viggianello
Terranova di Pollino
PARCO NAZIONALE DEL POLLINO
SERRA DOLCEDORMA 2267
Mormanno
Morano Cálabro
Castrovillari
Orsomarso
Verbicaro
Lungro
Altomonte
S. Agata di Esaro
San Sosti
Buonvicino
Trinitápoli
Margherita di Savoia
San Ferdinando di Púglia
SALINE
Lupara
Zapponeta
Lido di Rivoli
Onoranza
SAN LEONARDO
SANTA MARIA DI SIPONTO
Pasta Monte Granata
San Marco in Lamis
San Giovanni Rotondo
Monte Sant'Angelo
Mattinata
CANNE
Torremaggiore
Castelnuovo Monterotaro
Castelnuovo della Dáunia
Motta Montecorvino
Volturara Appula
Carlantino
Lago di Occhito
Sant'Elia a Pianisi
Bonefro
Santa Croce di Magliano
Casacalenda
Vinchiaturo
Santa Croce del Sannio
Morcone
Pontelandolfo
Amorosi
Caiazzo
Frasso
Sant'Agata de' Goti
Montesarchio
Cervinara
SANTUARIO DI MONTE VERGINE
Baiano
Cicciano
Monteforte Irpino
Ottaviano
Sarno
Forino
Serino
Mercato S. Severino
S. Giorgio del Sannio
Giardinetto
Savoia

A
B
C
D
117
124
121
1
2
3
4
5
6
San Severo
Santa Croce di Magliano
Torremaggiore
Castelnuovo Monterotaro
Carlantino
Lago di Occhito
Volturara Appula
Motta Montecorvino
Castelnuovo della Daunia
Lucera
Gambatesa
San Marco in Lamis
San Giovanni Rotondo
Monte Sant'Angelo
Mattinata
Baia delle Zagare
Pasta Monte Granata
SANTA MARIA DI SIPONTO
Manfredónia
SAN LEONARDO
Golfo di Manfredónia
Candelaro
Onoranza
Lido di Rivoli
Zapponeta
Cervaro
FOGGIA
SALINE
Margherita di Savoia
Trinitápoli
Lupara
Castelvetere in Val Fortore
Colle Sannita
Basilice
San Bartolomeo in Galdo
Roseto Valfortore
Faeto
Troia
Giardinetto
Celone
Castellúccio dei Sáuri
Orta Nova
San Ferdinando di Púglia
Barletta
Trani
Biscéglie
Molfetta
Giovinazzo
San Marco dei Cavoti
Castelfranco in Miscano
Orsara di Púglia
HERDONIAE
Stornara
Cerignola
CANNE
Canosa di Púglia
Andria
Corato
DOLMEN DI CHIANCA
IL PULO
Buonalbergo
Savignano Irpino
Bovino
Deliceto
Ascoli Satriano
Sant'Agata di Púglia
Ariano Irpino
Accadia
Lago di Capacciotti
Ófanto
Candela
CASTEL DEL MONTE
Minervino Murge
PARCO NAZ. DELL'ALTA MURGIA
Ruvo di Púglia
Terlizzi
Bitonto
Palese
Modugno
Bitetto
Palo del Colle
Apice
Grottaminarda
Flumeri
Vallata
Leonessa
Lavello
Lacedonia
S. Giorgio del Sannio
Gesualdo
Bisaccia
Monteverde
Melfi
Taurasi
Guardia Lombardi
Aquilonia
Rapolla
Venosa
Spinazzola
Mariotto
Sannicandro di Bari
Acquaviva delle Fonti
Paternopoli
Andretta
VULTURE
Rionero in Vúlture
Ripacandida
Palazzo San Gervasio
Atripalda
Avellino
Lioni
Calitri
Forenza
Genzano di Lucánia
Cassano delle Murge
Montella
Calabritto
Sant'Andrea di Conza
Pescopagano
Atella
Acerenza
Gravina in Púglia
Altamura
PARCO REG. MONTI PICENTINI
M CERVIALTO
San Fele
Bella
Brádano
Santéramo in Colle
Laviano
Muro Lucano
Avigliano
Oppido Lucano
Irsina
Acerno
Colliano
Pietragalla
Gravina di Picciano
SALERNO
BAGNI CONTURSI
Ruoti
Tolve
Vaglio Basilicata
Montecorvino Rovella
S. Gregorio Magno
Contursi Terme
Campagna
Éboli
Picerno
Potenza
Tricárico
Matera
Battipáglia
Vietri di Potenza
Pignola
Passo Croce di Scrivano
Grassano
Lago di S. Giuliano
Miglionico
Altavilla Silentina
Sicignano d. Alburni
M ALBURNO
Tito
Auletta
GROTTA DI PERTOSA
Albano di Lucánia
Garaguso
Ginosa
Montescaglioso
BASILICATA
Abriola
Anzi
Accettura
Pomarico
Controne
Albanella
Roccadáspide
Brienza
Calvello
Laurenzana
S. Mauro Forte
Ferrandina
Paestum
PAESTUM
Capaccio
Castel San Lorenzo
San Rufo
PARCO DELL' APPENNINO LUCANO
Marsico Nuovo
Marsico Vetere
Sala Consilina
Corleto Perticara
Stigliano
Craco
Pisticci
TAVOLE PALATINE
Bernalda
Agropoli
Ogliastro Cilento
Teggiano
Padula
Piaggine
Viggiano
Peschiera
Montalbano Jonico
Prignano Cilento
Laurino
PARCO NAZIONALE DEL CILENTO E VALLO DI DIANO
M CERVATI
Montesano sulla Marcellana
GRUMENTUM
Missanello
Castellabate
Perdifumo
Vallo di Lucania
Lago di Pietra del Pertusillo
Roccanova
SANTA MARIA D'ANGLONA
Lido di Scanzano
Scanzano Jónico
ERACLEA
Policoro
Montecorice
Casal Velino
Ceraso
Rofrano
Sanza
VAL D'AGRI
Moliterno
Sant'Arcangelo
Acciaroli
Ascea-Velia
Pisciotta
Alfano
Torre Orsaia
Casalbuono
Castelsaraceno
S. Chírico Raparo
Valsinni
Celle di Bulgheria
Policastro Bussentino
Lagonegro
LAGONEGRESE
M SIRINO
Senise
Chiaromonte
Rotondella
Palinuro
GROTTA AZZURRA
Capo Palinuro
Sapri
Rivello
Lauria
Latronico
Episcopia
Noépoli
Rocca Imperiale
Montegiordano Marina
San Giovanni a Piro
Marina di Camerota
Golfo di Policastro
Maratea
Castelluccio Sup.
Viggianello
PARCO NAZIONALE DEL POLLINO
Cersosimo
Oriolo
Terranova di Pollino
Roseto Capo Spúlico
Amendolara
Capo Spúlico
Tortora
Alessandria del Carretto
Praia a Mare
Mormanno
SERRA DOLCEDORME
Cerchiara di Calabria
Villaplana
Marina di Amendolara
Papasidero
Trebisacce
Morano Cálabro
Scalea
Orsomarso
Castrovillari
Villapiana Scalo
Verbicaro
Lungro
Cassano allo Ionio
Cirella
Í. di Cirella
Sibari
SYBARIS COPIA
Golfo di Corigliano
Buonvicino
Altomonte
Diamante
S. Agata di Esaro
San Sosti
Spezzano Albanese
Marina di Schiavonea

E
F
G
H
1
2
3
4
5
6
Kérkyra
Durrës
Igoumenítsa
Pátra
Dubrovnik
BARI
Mola di Bari
Capurso
Rutigliano
Polignano a Mare
Monópoli
Casamássima
Conversano
Turi
GROTTE DI CASTELLANA
Castellana Grotte
Savelletri
Putignano
GROTTA DI PUTIGNANO
Gioia del Colle
Torre Canne
Fasano
Rosa Marina
Villanova
Alberobello
Noci
Locorotondo
Cisternino
Ostuni
Torre S. Sabina
Pátra
Kérkyra
Vlorë
Igoumenítsa
Çeşme
Bríndisi - Casale
Brindisi
Martina Franca
Ceglie Messápica
San Vito dei Normanni
Móttola
Palagianello
Massafra
Crispiano
San Michele Salentino
GROTTA S. GIOVANNI
Villa Castelli
Latiano
Mesagne
Palagiano
Statte
Grottaglie
Francavilla Fontana
Torre S. Gennaro
TÁRANTO
San Pietro Vernotico
Oria
Torre Santa Susanna
Casalabate
Carosino
Marina di Ginosa
Ísole Coradi o Cheradi
San Giorgio Iónico
Sava
San Pancrazio Salentino
San Dónaci
Squinzano
Surbo
METAPONTIUM
Capo San Vito
Leporano
Lizzano
Manduria
San Cataldo
Campi Salentina
Torricella
Lido di Metaponto
2009
Veglie
LECCE
Lido Silvana
Avetrana
Monteroni di Lecce
Rocca Vecchia
Cavallino
Campomarino
Porto Cesareo
Copertino
Calimera
Sant'Andrea
Martano
Galatina
Nardò
Otranto
Galatone
Capo d'Otranto
Máglie
Minervino di Lecce
Gallípoli
Parábita
Santa Cesarea Terme
Casarano
Ruffano
GOLFO DI TÁRANTO
Taviano
GROTTA ZINZULUSA
Taurisano
Ugento
Tricase
AUSENTUM
Presicce
Corsano
Gagliano del Capo
Marina di Léuca
Capo S Maria di Léuca
SALENTO
VIA APPIA
VIA APPIA ANTICA

TÁRANTO
Matera
Potenza
SALERNO
Cosenza
Rossano
Castrovillari
Páola
GOLFO DI TÁRANTO
Golfo di Corigliano
Golfo di Policastro
BASILICATA
SILA GRANDE
SILA GRECA
PARCO NAZIONALE DEL POLLINO
PARCO NAZIONALE DEL CILENTO E VALLO DI DIANO
PARCO NAZ. DELL' APPENNINO LUCANO VAL D'AGRI LAGONEGRESE
Martina Franca
Massafra
Statte
Crispiano
San Giorgio Iónico
Leporano
Capo San Vito
Ísole Coradi o Cheradi
Palagianello
Móttola
Palagiano
Castellaneta
Laterza
Ginosa
Montescaglioso
Marina di Ginosa
METAPONTUM
Lido di Metaponto
Bernalda
TAVOLE PALATINE
Pomarico
Miglionico
Ferrandina
Pisticci
Craco
Stigliano
Grassano
Garaguso
Salandra
Tricárico
Albano di Lucania
Accettura
San Mauro Forte
Tolve
Vaglio Basilicata
Pietragalla
Pignola
Anzi
Abriola
Calvello
Laurenzana
Corleto Perticara
Marsico Nuovo
Marsico Vetere
Viggiano
GRUMENTUM
Tito
Brienza
Sala Consilina
Padula
Montesano sulla Marcellana
Casalbuono
Lagonegro
Lauria
Rivello
Maratea
Sapri
Policastro Bussentino
Torre Orsaia
San Giovanni a Piro
Marina di Camerota
Palinuro
Capo Palinuro
GROTTA AZZURRA
Pisciotta
Ascea-Velia
Casal Velino
Acciaroli
Agropoli
PAESTUM
Paestum
Capaccio
Castellabate
Punta Licosa
Montecorice
Battipaglia
Éboli
Campagna
Contursi Terme
BAGNI CONTURSI
Sicignano d. Alburni
Controne
Teggiano
Sanza
Rofrano
Celle di Bulgheria
Laurino
Vallo di Lucania
Ceraso
GROTTA DI PERTOSA
Policoro
ERACLEA
Scanzano Jónico
Lido di Scanzano
Montalbano Jonico
Tursi
SANTA MARIA D'ANGLONA
Valsinni
Rotondella
Rocca Imperiale
Montegiordano Marina
Roseto Capo Spúlico
Capo Spúlico
Amendolara
Marina di Amendolara
Trebisacce
Villapiana Scalo
Sibari
SYBARIS-COPIA
Cassano allo Ionio
Corigliano Calabro
Marina di Schiavonea
Capo Trionto
Mirto
Crosia
Cariati
Torretta
Ciró Marina
Ciró
Punta Alice
TEMPIO DI APOLLO ALÉO
Torre Melissa
CASTELLO ARAGONESE
Strongoli
Pallagório
Casabona
San Giovanni in Fiore
Savelli
Campana
Crucoli
Mandatoríccio
Longobucco
Cropalati
Acri
Bisignano
ABBAZIA DELLA SAMBUCINA
Luzzi
Tarsia
Spezzano Albanese
San Demetrio Corone
Rende
Montalto Uffugo
Guárdia Piemontese
Fuscaldo
Cetraro
Belvedere Marittimo
Diamante
Scalea
Praia a Mare
Tortora
Mormanno
Morano Cálabro
Orsomarso
Verbicaro
Lungro
Altomonte
San Sosti
S. Agata di Esaro
Fagnano Castello
San Marco Argentano
Cerchiara di Calabria
Villapiana
Alessandria del Carretto
Oriolo
Nocara
Cersosimo
Noépoli
Terranova di Pollino
SERRA DOLCEDORME 2267
San Lúcido
Fiumefreddo Bruzio
Camigliatello
Lorica
Celico
Aprigliano
M. BOTTE DONATO 1925
M. SIRINO 2005
M. CERVATI 1899
M. ALBURNO 1742

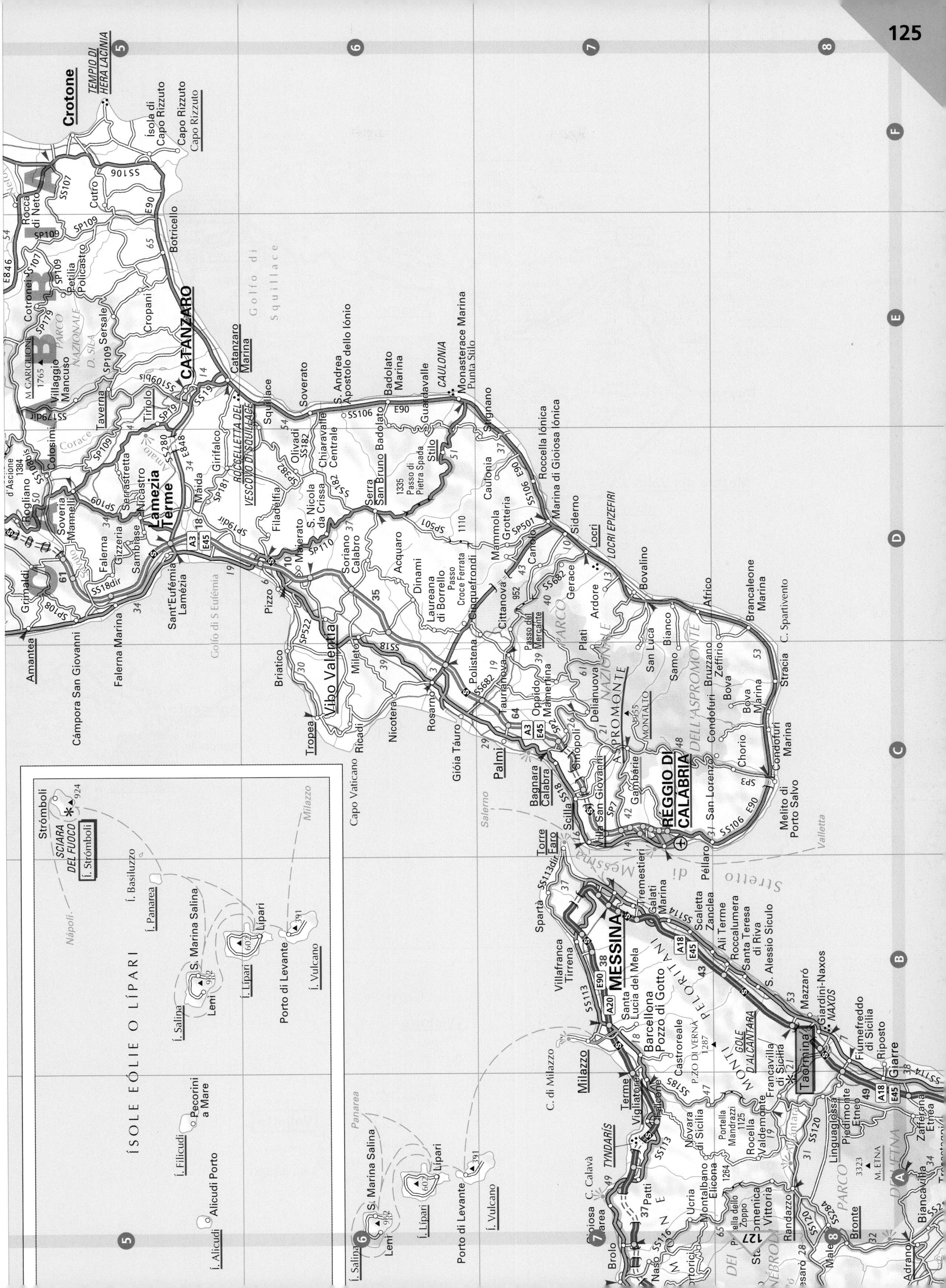
Crotone
TEMPIO DI HERA LACINIA
Ísola di Capo Rizzuto
Capo Rizzuto
Cutro
Rocca di Neto
Botricello
Petilia Policastro
Cotronei
Cropani
Sersale
Villaggio Mancuso
CATANZARO
Catanzaro Marina
Golfo di Squillace
Tiriolo
Taverna
Colosimi
Rogliano
Soveria Mannelli
Lamezia Terme
Nicastro
Serrastretta
Girifalco
Maida
ROCCELLETTA DEL VESCOVO DI SQUILLACE
Squillace
Soverato
Olivadi
Chiaravalle Centrale
S. Andrea Apostolo dello Ionio
Badolato Marina
Guardavalle
CAULONIA
Monasterace Marina
Punta Stilo
Stignano
Stilo
Serra San Bruno
Filadelfia
S. Nicola da Crissa
Caulonia
Roccella Iónica
Marina di Gioiosa Iónica
Siderno
Locri
LOCRI EPIZEFIRI
Grotteria
Mammola
Gerace
Bovalino
Ardore
Platì
Bianco
San Luca
Samo
Africo
Brancaleone Marina
C. Spartivento
Stracia
Bruzzano Zeffirio
Bova
Bova Marina
Condofuri
Condofuri Marina
Chorio
Melito di Porto Salvo
San Lorenzo
REGGIO DI CALÁBRIA
Gambárie
MONTALTO
ASPROMONTE
PARCO NAZIONALE DELL'ASPROMONTE
Delianuova
Sinopoli
Villa San Giovanni
Scilla
Bagnara Calabra
Palmi
Gióia Táuro
Rosarno
Taurianova
Cittanova
Polistena
Oppido Mamertina
Passo del Mercante
Cinquefrondi
Laureana di Borrello
Dinami
Acquaro
Soriano Calabro
Vibo Valentia
Mileto
Nicotera
Tropea
Ricadi
Capo Vaticano
Briatico
Pizzo
Sant'Eufémia Lamézia
Golfo di S Eufémia
Falerna Marina
Falerna
Gizzeria
Sambiase
Cámpora San Giovanni
Amantea
Grimaldi
Torre Faro
Stretto di Messina
MESSINA
Tremestieri
Scaletta Zanclea
Alì Terme
Roccalumera
Santa Teresa di Riva
S. Alessio Siculo
Spartà
Villafranca Tirrena
Santa Lucia del Mela
Barcellona Pozzo di Gotto
Castroreale
MONTI PELORITANI
Milazzo
C. di Milazzo
Terme Vigliatore
Falcone
TYNDARÍS
Patti
C. Calavà
Gioiosa Marea
Brolo
Novara di Sicilia
Montalbano Elicona
Francavilla di Sicilia
GOLE D'ALCANTARA
Taormina
Giardini-Naxos
NAXOS
Mazzarò
Fiumefreddo di Sicilia
Riposto
Giarre
Piedimonte Etneo
Linguaglossa
Randazzo
Bronte
Adrano
Biancavilla
Zafferana Etnea
M. ETNA
PARCO DELL'ETNA
ÍSOLE EÓLIE O LÍPARI
Strómboli
SCIARA DEL FUOCO
Í. Strómboli
Í. Basiluzzo
Í. Panarea
S. Marina Salina
Í. Salina
Leni
Í. Lípari
Lípari
Porto di Levante
Í. Vulcano
Pecorini a Mare
Í. Filicudi
Alicudi Porto
Í. Alicudi

A
B
C
D
1
2
3
4
5
6
Tùnis
Valéncia
Cágliari
Ústica
Génova
Civitavécchia
Nápoli
Salerno
Ísola delle Fémmine
Ísola delle Fémmine
Capo Gallo
Mondello
Golfo di Palermo
600
MONTE PELLEGRINO
P. Ráisi
Falcone-Borsellino
Cinisi
Capaci
PALERMO
San Vito lo Capo
Capo S. Vito
Torre dell'Impiso
Scopello
Golfo di Castellammare
Castelluzzo
Custonaci
Cágliari
Erice
Castellammare del Golfo
Balestrate
SAN MARTINO DELLE SCALE
C. Zafferano
SOLUNTO
Bagheria
Í. Maréttimo
686
Maréttimo
Í. di Lévanzo
Levanzo
ÍSOLE ÉGADI
Favignana
Í. Favignana
Trápani
Paceco
Valderice
Buseto Palizzolo
Partinico
Monreale
Misilmeri
San Giuseppe Jato
Piana degli Albanesi
Marineo
Términi Imerese
Trabia
Cáccamo
Birgi
MOZIA
Í. dello Stagnone
Ballio Zaffarana
SEGESTA
Calatafimi
Alcamo
Camporeale
San Cipirello
MADONNA DEL ROSARIO
Buonfornello
Cerda
Montemaggiore Belsito
Villafrati
Mezzojuso
1613
R BUSAMBRA
Corleone
Campofelice di Fitalia
Bivio Manganaro
Roccapalumba
Alia
Caltavu
Balio Chitarra
Salemi
Gibellina
Santa Ninfa
RUDERI DI GIBELLINA
Marsala
Tùnis
Pantelleria
Casale
Partanna
Campofiorito
Lercara Friddi
Lago della Trinità
Santa Margherita di Bélice
Bisacquino
Prizzi
Petrosino
Castelvetrano
Sambuca di Sicília
Chiusa Sclàfani
Palazzo Adriano
Filaga
Mazara del Vallo
Bivona
Borgo Callea
Campobello di Mazara
ROCCHE DI CUSA
Menfi
Lago Aráncio
S. Carlo
Cammarata
Granitola Torretta
SELINUNTE
C. Granítola
Marinella
Caltabellotta
Búrgio
Santo Stéfano Quisquina
SAN CALOGERO
Alessándria della Rocca
Mussomeli
C. S. Marco
Sciacca
Ribera
Cianciana
San Biágio Plátani
Casteltérmini
Serradifalco
Cattolica Eraclea
Milena
ERACLEA MINOA
Raffadali
Aragona
Racalmuto
Montallegro
Siciliana
Agrigento
Porto Empedocle
VALLE DEI TEMPLI
Naro
Campobello di Licata
CASTELLO DI MONTECHIARO
Palma di Montechiaro
Sicilia
Linosa
Lampedusa
Trápani
Pantelleria
836
Tracino
M.GNA GRANDE
Ísola di Pantelleria
I
Ísola di Linosa
Linosa
Porto Empedocle
ÍSOLE PELÁGIE
I
Ísola di Lampione
Porto Empedocle
Lampedusa
Ísola di Lampedusa
Gozo
Victoria
Mgarr
M
Génova
Pozzallo
Salerno
Réggio di Calábria
Catánia
Mellieha
Sliema
Valletta
Mosta
Rabat
Vittoriosa
Dingli
Luqa
Birzebbuga
Zurrieq
Malta
A29
A29dir
A19
E90
E931
E933
SS113
SS115
SS118
SS121
SS186
SS187
SS188

E
F
G
H
125
Ísola di Ústica
Palermo
Í. Lípari
Lípari
602
Porto di Levante
391
Í. Vulcano
Salerno
1
2
3
4
5
6
C. di Milazzo
Milazzo
Villafranca Tirrena
Spartà
Torre Faro
Bagnara Calabra
Scilla
Villa San Giovanni
MESSINA
Tremestieri
Galati Marina
REGGIO CALABRIA
Pèllaro
San Lorenzo
Melito di Porto Salvo
Stretto di Messina
Gioiosa Marea
C. Calavà
TYNDARÍS
Terme Vigliatore
Falcone
Santa Lucia del Mela
Barcellona Pozzo di Gotto
Capo d'Orlando
Brolo
Patti
Sant'Ágata di Militello
Acquedolci
Marina di Caronía
Caronía
Naso
Tortorici
Ucria
Montalbano Elicona
Novara di Sicilia
Castroreale
P.ZO DI VERNA
1287
MONTI PELORITANI
Scaletta Zanclea
Ali Terme
Roccalumera
Santa Teresa di Riva
S. Alessio Siculo
Cefalù
Santo Stefano di Camastra
SANTUARIO DI GIBILMANNA
Collesano
Castelbuono
Tusa
Mistretta
San Fratello
PARCO DEI NÉBRODI
M. SORO
1847
Portella Femmina Morta
1524
F. di Cutò
Portella dello Zoppo
1264
Portella Mandrazzi
1125
Sta. Domenica Vittoria
Rocella Valdemonte
Francavilla di Sicilia
GOLE D'ALCANTARA
Randazzo
Taormina
Mazzaró
Giardini-Naxos
NAXOS
PZO CARBONARA
1979
PARCO DELLE MADONIE
San Mauro Castelverde
1107
Colle del Contrasto
Capizzi
Lago d'Áncipa
Cesarò
Castellana Sicula
1147
Portella Madonnuzza
Gangi
Cerami
Maletto
Linguaglossa
Piedimonte Etneo
PARCO DELL'ETNA
M. ETNA
3323
Bronte
Fiumefreddo di Sicilia
Riposto
Giarre
Petralia Soprana
Nicosia
Pancallo
Troina
Gagliano Castelferrato
Lago di Pozzillo
Alimena
Villadoro
Vallelunga Pratameno
Marianopoli
Villapriolo
Leonforte
Agira
Regalbuto
Adrano
Biancavilla
Zafferana Etnea
Trecastagni
Acireale
Aci Catena
Aci Trezza
ISOLE DEI CICLOPI
Aci Castello
Santa Caterina Villarmosa
Villarosa
Calascibetta
Nissoria
Assoro
Centúripe
Catenanuova
Paternò
Nicolosi
Belpasso
Enna
San Cataldo
SABBUCINA
Caltanissetta
Valguarnera Caropepe
Raddusa
Castel di Iúdica
Misterbianco
CATÁNIA
Nápoli
Salerno
Marina di Ravenna
Valletta
Fontana Rossa
Pietraperzia
MORGANTINA
Aidone
Piazza Armerina
Barrafranca
Ramacca
PIANA DI CATÁNIA
Golfo di Catánia
VILLA ROMANA DEL CASALE
Mirabella Imbáccari
Palagonia
Délia
Sommatino
Riesi
Mazzarino
S. Michele di Ganzaria
Scordia
Militello in Val di Catania
Lentini
Agnone Bagni
Ravanusa
Lago d. Disueri
Caltagirone
Grammichele
Mineo
Carlentini
Francofonte
C. S. Croce
Augusta
MEGARA HYBLAEA
Golfo di Augusta
Penisola Magnisi
Butera
Niscemi
Licodia Eubea
Pedagaggi
Melilli
Priolo Gargallo
Vizzini
Buccheri
Sortino
NECROPOLI DI PANTALICA
Ferla
Licata
CASTELLO DI FALCONARA
Gela
Mazzarrone
Monterosso Almo
Giarratana
Palazzolo Acreide
AKRAI
Floridia
CASTELLO EURIALO
SIRACUSA
C. S. Panagía
Canicattini Bagni
Acate
Villa Cancellieri
Chiaramonti Gulfi
MONTI IBLEI
Capo Murro di Porco
Cassibile
2009
Vittoria
Cómiso
Ragusa
NOTO ANTICA
Noto
Avola
Scoglitti
Santa Croce Camerina
Modica
CAVA D'ISPICA
Rosolini
ELORO
Marina di Ragusa
Scicli
Íspica
I. Vendicari
Roselle Módica
Marzamemi
Donnalucata
Pozzallo
Pachino
Capo Pássero
Portopalo di Capo Pássero
P. d. Formiche
Capo d. Correnti
Valletta
A18
A19
A20
E45
E90
E931
E932

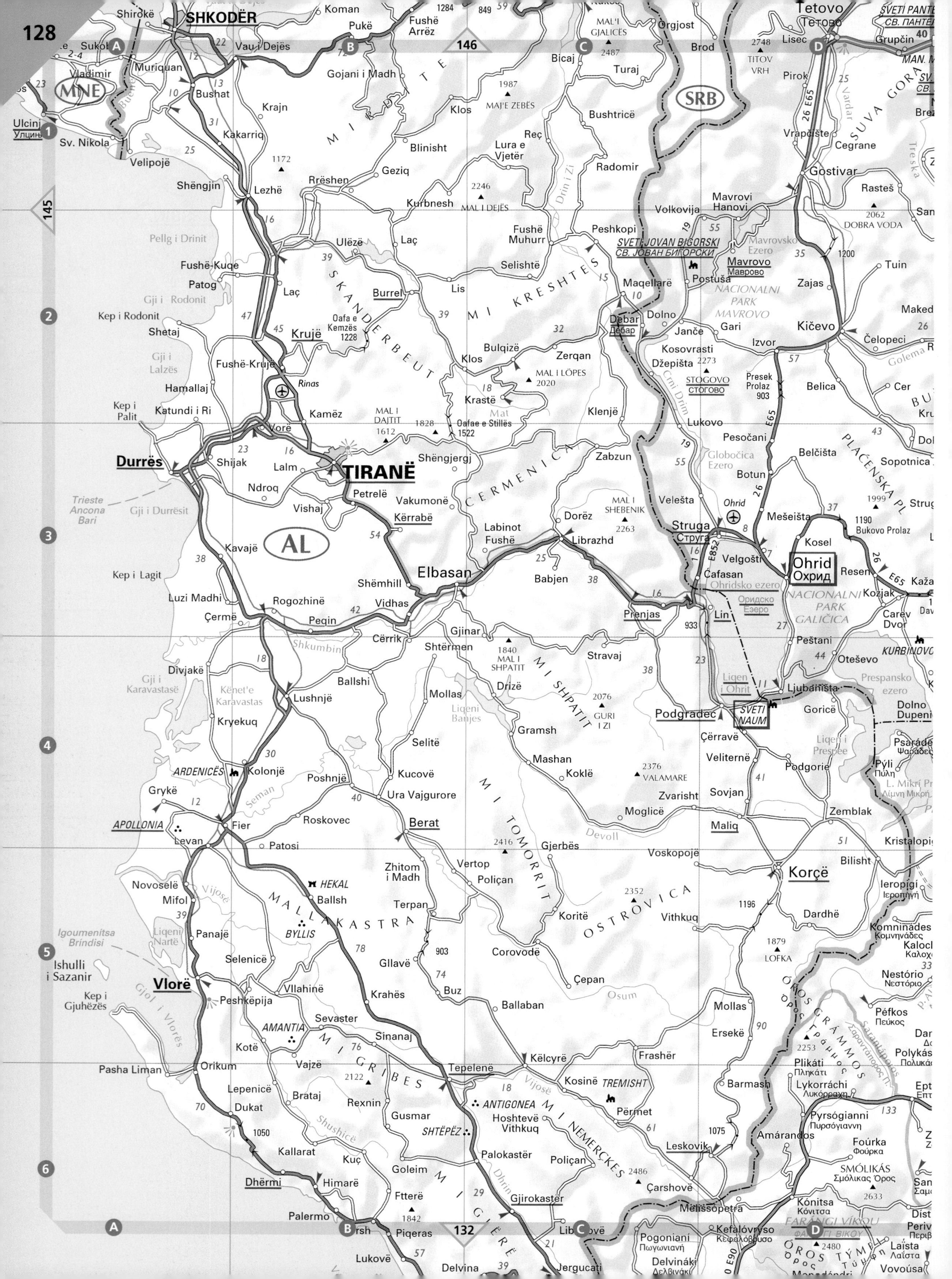

Shirokë
SHKODËR
Koman
Pukë
Fushë Arrëz
1284
849
MAL'I GJALICËS
2487
Orgjost
Tetovo
Тетово
SVETI PANTE
СВ. ПАНТЕ
Sukobi
Vau i Dejës
146
Brod
Lisec
2748
TITOV VRH
Grupčin
MAN.
Vladimir
MNE
Muriquan
Bushat
Gojani i Madh
Bicaj
Turaj
SRB
Pirok
Ulcinj
Улцињ
Sv. Nikola
Krajn
Kakarriq
1987
MAJ'E ZEBËS
Klos
Bushtricë
Vrapčište
Cegrane
SUVA GORA
Velipojë
1172
Blinisht
Reç
Lura e Vjetër
Radomir
Gostivar
Shëngjin
Lezhë
Rrëshen
Geziq
MIRDITE
2246
MAL I DEJËS
Kurbnesh
Drin i Zi
Volkovija
Mavrovi Hanovi
Rasteš
2062
DOBRA VODA
145
Pellg i Drinit
Ulëzë
Laç
Fushë Muhurr
Peshkopi
SVETI JOVAN BIGORSKI
СВ. ЈОВАН БИГОРСКИ
Mavrovsko Ezero
1200
Tuin
Fushë-Kuqe
Patog
Selishtë
Mavrovo
Маврово
Postuša
Zajas
Gji i Rodonit
Laç
Burrel
Lis
MI KRESHTES
Maqellarë
NACIONALNI PARK MAVROVO
Kep i Rodonit
Shetaj
Krujë
Qafa e Kemzës 1228
SKANDERBEUT
Debar
Дебар
Dolno
Janče
Gari
Kičevo
Čelopeci
Makedonski
Gji i Lalzës
Fushë-Krujë
Bulqizë
Zerqan
Kosovrasti
Džepišta
2273
STOGOVO
СТОГОВО
Izvor
Golema
Hamallaj
Rinas
Klos
MAL I LOPËS 2020
Presek Prolaz 903
Belica
Cer
Kep i Palit
Katundi i Ri
Kamëz
MAL I DAJTIT 1612
1828
Qafae e Stillës 1522
Krastë
Mat
Klenjë
Crni Drim
Lukovo
Kru
Vorë
Shëngjergj
Zabzun
Pesočani
Globočica Ezero
Belčišta
PLAĆENSKA PL
Dol
Durrës
Shijak
Lalm
TIRANË
CERMENICA
Sopotnica
Trieste Ancona Bari
Gji i Durrësit
Ndroq
Petrelë
Vakumonë
MAL I SHEBENIK 2263
Velešta
Botun
Ohrid
1999
Strug
Vishaj
Kërrabë
Dorëz
Mešeišta
1190 Bukovo Prolaz
AL
Kavajë
Labinot Fushë
Librazhd
Struga
Струга
Kosel
Elbasan
Babjen
Velgošti
Ohrid
Охрид
Resen
Kaža
Kep i Lagit
Shëmhill
Čafasan
Ohridsko ezero
Оридско Езеро
NACIONALNI PARK GALIČICA
Kozjak
Luzi Madhi
Rogozhinë
Vidhas
Prenjas
Carev Dvor
Dav
Çermë
Peqin
Lin
Gjinar
933
Shkumbin
Cërrik
1840 MAL I SHPATIT
Peštani
KURBINOVO
Divjakë
Shtërmen
Stravaj
Otešovo
Gji i Karavastasë
Kënet'e Karavastas
Ballshi
Mollas
Drizë
MI SHPATIT
Liqen i Ohrit
Ljubaništa
Prespansko ezero
Lushnjë
Liqeni Banjes
2076 GURI I ZI
Podgradec
SVETI NAUM
Goricë
Dolno Dupeni
Kryekuq
Gramsh
Čërravë
Psarádes
Ψαράδες
Selitë
Mashan
Koklë
2376 VALAMARE
Veliternë
Liqen i Prespes
Podgorie
Pýli
Πύλη
ARDENICËS
Kolonjë
Poshnjë
Kucovë
L. Mikrí Pr
Λίμνη Μικρή
Grykë
Seman
Ura Vajgurore
Zvarisht
Sovjan
Roskovec
MI TOMORRIT
Moglicë
Zemblak
APOLLONIA
Fier
Berat
Maliq
Levan
Patosi
2416
Gjerbës
Devoll
Kristalopi
Voskopojë
Bilisht
Zhitom i Madh
Vertop
Novoselë
Poliçan
Korçë
Ieropigi
Ιεροπηγή
Mifol
HEKAL
Ballsh
Terpan
2352
OSTROVICA
1196
Vjosë
MALLAKASTRA
Koritë
Vithkuq
Dardhë
Igoumenítsa Brindisi
Panajë
Liqeni Nartë
BYLLIS
Komninádes
Κομνηνάδες
1879 LOFKA
Kaloch
Καλοχ
Ishulli i Sazanir
Selenicë
Gllavë
903
Corovodë
Vlorë
74
Çepan
Nestório
Νεστόριο
Kep i Gjuhëzës
Peshkëpija
Vllahinë
Krahës
Buz
Osum
Ballaban
Mollas
Péfkos
Πεύκος
Gjol i Vlorës
AMANTIA
Sevaster
Sinanaj
Ersekë
ÓROS GRÁMMOS
Όρος Γράμμος
Dar
Polykás
Πολυκάσ
Kotë
MI GRIBES
2253
Pasha Liman
Orikum
Vajzë
2122
Tepelenë
Këlcyrë
Frashër
Plikáti
Πληκάτι
Lepenicë
Brataj
Reхnin
Kosinë
TREMISHT
Barmash
Lykorráchi
Λυκόρραχη
Ept
Dukat
ANTIGONEA
MI NEMERÇKES
Përmet
Pyrsógianni
Πυρσόγιαννη
Gusmar
Hoshtevë
Vithkuq
Shushicë
1050
SHTËPËZ
1075
Amárandos
Fourka
Φούρκα
Kallarat
Kuç
Palokastër
Poliçan
Leskovik
SMÓLIKAS
Σμόλικας Όρος
San
Goleim
Dhrin
2486
Çarshovë
2633
Dhërmi
Himarë
Fterë
Gjirokastër
MI GJERE
Melissópetra
Kónitsa
Κόνιτσα
Dist
1842
Palermo
FARÁNGI VÍKOU
ΦΑΡΑΓΓΙ ΒΙΚΟΥ
Periv
Περιβ
Borsh
Piqeras
132
Libohovë
Kefalóvryso
Κεφαλόβρυσο
Pogoniani
Πωγωνιανή
2480
Laísta
Λαΐστα
Lukovë
Delvina
Jergucat
Delvináki
Δελβινάκι
E90
ÓROS TÝMFI
Vovoúsa

SKOPJE
СКОПЈЕ
243
Probištip
Pantelej
Istibanja
Kalimansko ezero
Delčevo
147
G. Konjare
KATLANOVSKA BANJA
Stanjevci
Bučište
MAN. PANTELEJ
Obleševo
Kočani
Vinica
Razlovci
Polena
Krupnik
Katlanovo
Dračevo
Markova Sušica
MARKOV MANASTIR
МАРКОВ МАН.
VENAC
Gorobinci
Sveti Nikole
Krupište
Крупиште
Zrnovci
Obozna Prolaz
Mitrašinci
Kresna
Kadrifakovo
Krivi Dol
Radanje
Turtel
Laki
Pehčevo
Milino
Džumajlija
Bregalnica
Štip
Штип
PLAČKOVICA
Šipkovica
Alil Abasi
Stojmirovo
Berovo
JAKUPICA
Aldinci
Veles
Велес
MK
BG
SOLUNSKA GLAVA
Dragoevo
Radoviš
Mikrevo
Belica
Nežilovo
KONEČKA PL
Lakavica
Ezero Turisko
OGRAŽDEN
Igralište
Modrište
Teovo
Viničani
Dedino
Dobrošinci
Lebnika
Dragov Doll
Izvor
Gradsko
Donji Lipovik
Hamzali
Levunovo
Devic
Rosoman
Stobi
Стоби
Krivolak
Dunjica
Konče
Suševo
Uši
Negotino
VUČJAK
GRADEŠKA PL
Strumica
Novo Selo
Zlatarevo
Stepanci
Kavadarci
Dabilja
Petrich
Петрич
Ropotovo
Mukos Prolaz
Vozarci
Raec
Moklište
Demir Kapija
Bansko
Kolešino
Kosturino
Udovo
MAN. TRESKOVEC
Prisad
Ezero Tikveš
Valandovo
ÓROS KERKÍNI
Όρος Κερκίνη
Vyróneia
RAZBOJNA DUPKA
Prilep
Прилеп
Pletvar Prolaz
Miravci
Barovo
Platanákia
Πλατανάκια
Rodópoli
Ροδόπολη
Krivogaštani
DREN
ORLE
Pološko
VITAČEVO
Bohula
Smokvica
Dojransko ezero
Mouriés
Μουριές
Limni Kerkini
Alinci
Dunje
Crna
Konopiste
Sermenin
Novi Dojran
Kerkíni
Κερκίνη
Bučin
Topolčani
Rasimbegov
KOŽUF
Limni Doïráni
Kentrikó
Κεντρικό
Murgaševo
Vitolište
Mrežičko
Konsko
Bogdanci
Stari Dojran
Drosáto
Δροσάτο
Negorci
Bogorodica
Plagiá
Πλαγιά
Váthi
Βάθη
Ágios Márkos
Άγιος Μάρκος
Kanatlarci
SELEČKA PL
MARIOVO
Majdan
Gevgelija
Évzonoi
Εύζωνοι
Chérso
Χέρσο
Srpci
Budakovo
Skra
Σκρα
Fanós
Φανός
Efkarpía
Ευκαρπία
Makovo
Gradešnika
Nótia
Νότια
KROÚSIA ÓRI
Κρούσια όρη
Kilkís
Κιλκίς
Kogila
Foústani
Φούστανη
Polýkastro
Πολύκαστρο
Vafiochóri
Βαφιοχώρι
Kukurečani
Bitola
Битола
Voreinó
Βορεινό
Axioúpoli
Αξιούπολη
P. Gynaikókastro
Π. Γυναικόκαστρο
Koronoúda
Κορωνούδα
Novaci
Budmirici
Prómachoi
Πρόμαχοι
Kristóni
Κριστώνη
Loutrá Aridaías
Λουτρά Αριδαίας
Exaplátanos
Εξαπλάτανος
Gouménissa
Γουμένισσα
130
HERACLEA
ХЕРАКЛЕА
Skočivir
Aridaía
Αριδαία
PELISTER
NAC. PARK PELISTER
Sarakinoí
Σαρακηνοί
Polykárpi
Πολυκάρπι
KENTRIKI MAKEDONIA
Kampánis
Καμπάνης
Mikrókampos
Μικρόκαμπος
Pénte Vrýses
Πέντε Βρύσες
Medžitlija
Bač
Filyriá
Φιλυριά
BABA
Velušina
KAÏMAKCHALÁN
Καϊμακτσαλάν
Ápsalos
Άψαλος
Aravissós
Αραβησσός
Ag. Pétros
Άγ. Πέτρος
Ássiros
Άσσηρος
Níki
Νίκη
Skopós
Σκοπός
Ag. Athanásios
Αγ. Αθανάσιος
Kalí
Καλή
Giannitsá
Γιαννιτσά
Próchoma
Πρόχωμα
Drymós
Δρυμός
Ágios Germanos
Άγιος Γερμανός
Kélla
Κέλλα
Ágras
Άγρα
Édessa
Έδεσσα
PELLA
ΠΕΛΛΑ
Koufália
Κουφάλια
Géfyra
Γέφυρα
Laginá
Pisodéri
Πισοδέρι
Flórina
Φλώρινα
Vévi
Βεύη
Árnissa
Άρνισσα
Rizári
Ριζάριο
Skýdra
Σκύδρα
Karyótissa
Καρυώτισσα
Chalkidóna
Χαλκηδόνα
Diavatá
Διαβατά
Lití
Λητή
Lagýna
Λαγυνά
L. Vegorítida
Λ. Βεγορίτιδα
GR
L. Petrón
Λ. Πετρών
Pisodéri Pass
Ag. Panteleímonas
Άγ. Παντελεήμονας
Krýa Vrýsi
Κρύα Βρύση
Ag. Athanásios
Άγ. Αθανάσιος
Ionia
THESSALONÍKI
ΘΕΣΣΑΛΟΝΙΚΗ
Trígono
Τρίγωνο
Polypótamo
Πολυπόταμο
Xynó Nveró
Ξυνό Νερό
Drosopigí
Δροσοπηγή
Amýntaio
Αμύνταιο
Pýrgoi
Πύργοι
Lefkádia
Λευκάδια
Kýmina
Κύμινα
Pýrgos
Πύργος
Kalamariá
Καλαμαριά
Kótas
Κώτας
VÉRNON Ó.
Βέρνον Όρος
Aetós
Αετός
Alexándreia
Αλεξάνδρεια
Vyssineá
Βυσσινέα
Anárgyroi
Ανάργυροι
Náousa
Νάουσα
Stavrós
Σταυρός
Tríkala
Τρίκαλα
Peristerá
Gávros
Γάβρος
Toichío
Τοιχίο
Léchovo
Λέχοβο
Filótas
Φιλώτας
Séli
Σέλι
VÉRMIO ÓROS
Βέρμιο Όρος
Makrochóri
Μακροχώρι
K. Thessaloníkis
Κόλπος Θεσσαλονίκης
Thérmi
Θέρμη
L. Kastoriás
Λ. Καστοριάς
L. Cheimadítida
Λ. Χειμαδίτιδα
Kastoriá
Καστοριά
Komniná
Κομνηνά
Anatolikó
Ανατολικό
Véroia
Βέροια
Aigínio
Αιγίνιο
Agía Triáda
Αγ. Τριάδα
Peraía
Περαία
Souroti
Σουρωτή
Dispíli
Δισπηλιό
Mavrochóri
Μαυροχώρι
Ptolemaïda
Πτολεμαΐδα
Káto Vérmio
Κάτω Βέρμιο
Vergína
Βεργίνα
Melíki
Μελίκη
Néa Michanióna
Νέα Μηχανιώνα
Korisós
Κορησός
Charavgí
Χαραυγή
Georgianoí
Γεωργιανοί
PALATITSA
ΠΑΛΑΤΙΤΣΑ
Kolindrós
Κολινδρός
Methóni
Μεθώνη
Órmos
Όρμος
Epanomí
Επανομή
Anarráchi
Ανάρραχη
Kaslania Pass
Kastaniá
Καστανιά
Ryákia
Ρυάκια
Akr. Epanomís
Ακρ. Επανομής
DYTIKI MAKEDONIA
Árgos Orestikó
Άργος Ορεστικό
Vogatsikó
Βογατσικό
SINIA TSIKON
Pontokómi
Ποντοκώμη
Liverá
Λιβερά
Tetrálofo
Τετράλοφο
Exochí
Εξοχή
Kítros
Κίτρος
PIDNA
Akr. Acheráda
Ακρ. Αχεράδα
Néa Kallikráteia
Νέα Καλλικράτεια
Skalochóri
Σκαλοχώρι
Kíla
Drépano
Δρέπανο
Rizómata
Ριζώματα
Moschopótamos
Μοσχοπόταμος
PIERIA
Korinós
Κορινός
Néa Moudaniá
Erátyra
Εράτυρα
Kozáni
Κοζάνη
L. Aliákmona
Λ. Αλιάκμονα
Petraná
Πετρανά
Ritíni
Ρητίνη
Kateríni
Κατερίνη
Paralía
Παραλία
Neápoli
Neápoli
Kalonéri
Καλονέρι
Vathýlakkos
Βαθύλακκος
Velventós
Βελβεντός
Foteiná
Φωτεινά
Iráklelo-Kríti
Tínos
Mýkonos
Páros
Thira-Santoríni
Mýrina-Límnos
Skiáthos
Mytilíni-Lésvos
Alexandroúpoli
Siátista
Σιάτιστα
Pétra
Πέτρα
Omalí
Ομαλή
Tsotíli
Τσοτύλι
Vrontoú
Βροντού
DÍON
ΔΙΟΝ
Limín Litochórou
Λιμήν Λιτοχώρου
Avgerinós
Αυγερινός
Kivotós
Κιβωτός
VOÚRINOS Ó.
Βούρινος Όρος
Aianí
Αιανή
Sérvia
Σέρβια
Agios Dimítrios
Αγ. Δημήτριος
ÁG. DIONÝSIOS
Άγ. Διονύσιος
Pentálofos
Πεντάλοφος
Vatólakkos
Βατόλακκος
Váris
Βάρης
Rýmnio
Ρύμνιο
Polýrracho
Πολύρραχο
Livádi
Λιβάδι
Litóchoro
Λιτόχωρο
Leptokaryá
Λεπτοκαρυά
Kalirráchi
Καλιρράχη
Grevená
Γρεβενά
Knídi
Κνίδι
Itéa
Ιτέα
Tranóvalto
Τρανόβαλτο
Metaxás
Μεταξάς
ÓROS ÓLYMPOS
ΟΡΟΣ ΌΛΥΜΠΟΣ
Paralía Skotínas
Παραλία Σκοτίνας
Platamónas
Πλαταμώνας
Dolíchi
Δολίχη
Kallithéa
Καλλιθέα
Eleftherochóri
Ελευθεροχώρι
Panagía
Παναγία
Eláti
Ελάτη
KAMVOÚNIA
Karyá
Καρυά
ÓLYMPOS
Όλυμπος
Akrotírio Platamón
Ακρ. Πλαταμών
133
Melíssi
Μελίσσι
Karperó
Καρπερό
Paliouriá
Παλιουριά
Deskáti
Δεσκάτη
Kranéa Elassónas
Κρανέα Ελασσόνας
Elassóna
Ελασσόνα
KÁTO ÓLYMPOS
Κάτω Όλυμπος
Rapsáni
Ραψάνη
TÉMPI
ΤΕΜΠΗ
Stómio
Στόμιο
AVGÓ
Αυγό
PÍNDOS
Kipoureío
Κηπουρείο
Ánoixi
Kefalóvryso
Κεφαλόβρυσο
Tsaritsani
Gónnoi
Ampelákia
Kókkino Neró
Κόκκινο Νερό

147
133
134
129
A
B
C
D
1
2
3
4
5
6
MK
GR
BLAGOEVGRAD
SMOL
ANATOL
KENTRIKÍ
MAKEDONIA
CHALKIDIKÍ
Χαλκιδική
Razlog
Gradevo
1140
Predel Pateka
Simitli
Симитли
Banya
Баня
Bansko
Банско
Medeni Poljani
Goit Kamăk
GOLYAMA SYUTKYA
Mikhalkovo
Михалково
GOLYAMA PERSENK
Chepelare
Чепеларе
Polena
Krupnik
Dobrinishte
Добринище
NARODEN
PARK
Mesta
1938
BESLET
Sŭrnitsa
Devin
Девин
Beden
Shiroka Lŭka
Широка лъка
Obozna Prolaz
1300
Mitrašinci
Laki
Kresna
2914
VIHREN
Vihren
Вихрен
PIRIN
ПИРИН
Breznica
Borino
Nastan
868
Pehčevo
Stojmirovo
Berovo
Kovachevica
Ковачевица
Dospat
Доспат
2191
GOLYAN PEREL
Smol
Plosky
Ognjanovo
Satovcha
Chavdar
Mikrevo
Sandanski
Сандански
Gotse Delchev
Гоце Делчев
Dŭbnitsa
Hadzhidimovo
1812
KAINCHAL
Mogilica
Ezero Turisko
OGRAŽDEN
Igralište
Pirin
ROŽENSKI MANASTIR
РОЖЕНСКИ МАН.
1380 Popski Preslop
Koprivlen
Mesta
Dobrošinci
1744
Lebnica
Levunovo
Melnik
Мелник
Petrovo
Linden
Exochí
Εξοχή
Potamoí
Ποταμοί
Skalotí
Σκαλωτή
Dipótamos
Διπόταμος
Hamzali
Suševo
Marikostinovo
Katuntsi
Lefkógeia
Λευκόγεια
Sidiróneros
Σιδηρόνερο
Novo Selo
Zlatarevo
2212
ALİ BUTÜŞ
Katáfyto
Κατάφυτο
Vólakas
Βώλακας
Leiva
Λειβα
Dabilja
Petrich
Петрич
Kulata
Livaderó
Λιβαδερό
Bansko
Kolešino
Kosturino
Promachónas
Προμαχώνας
Áno Vrontoú
Άνω Βροντού
Káto Nevrokópi
Κάτω Νευροκόπι
2194
Paranésti
Παρανέστι
Achladochóri
Αχλαδοχώρι
Káto Vrontoú
Κάτω Βροντού
FALAKRÓN ÓROS
Φαλακρό Όρος
p. Nestos
Νέστος Π.
ÓROS KERKÍNI
Όρος Κερκίνη
N. Petritsi
Ν.Πετρίτσι
Laïliás
Λαϊλιάς
Vathýlakkos
Βαθύλακκος
Makryplágio
Μακρυπλάγιο
Pteléa
Πτελέα
Valandovo
Vyróneia
Βυρώνεια
Sidirókastro
Σιδηρόκαστρο
Petroussa
Πετρούσσα
Dráma
Δράμα
Lekáni
Λεκάνη
Platanákia
Πλατανάκια
Rodópoli
Ροδόπολη
Oreiní
Ορεινή
Nikifóros
Νικηφόρος
Dojransko ezero
Pontisméno
Ποντισμένο
MENOÍKIO ÓROS
Μενοίκιο Όρος
Mikrópoli
Μικρόπολη
Prosotsáni
Προσοτσάνη
Choristí
Χωριστή
Limniá
Λιμνιά
Mouries
Μουριές
Limni Kerkínis
Λίμνη Κερκίνη
Palaiókastro
Παλαιόκαστρο
Irákleia
Ηράκλεια
Kallithéa
Καλλιθέα
Doxáto
Δοξάτο
Platam
Novi Dojran
Kerkini
Κερκίνη
Ágio Pnévma
Άγιο Πνεύμα
Mavroléfki
Μαυρολεύκη
Kalampáki
Καλαμπάκι
Gravo
Bogdanci
Kentrikó
Κεντρικό
1179
Skotoússa
Σκοτούσσα
Alistráti
Αλιστράτη
FILIPPOI
ΦΙΛΙΠΠΟΙ
Krinídes
Κρηνίδες
Néa Karváli
Νέα Καρβάλη
Bogorodica
Star Dojran
Drosáto
Δροσάτο
Plagiá
Πλαγιά
Váthi
Βάθη
Ágios Márkos
Άγιος Μάρκος
Cheimarros
Χείμαρρος
Sérres
Σέρρες
Néa Zíchni
Νέα Ζίχνη
Amygdaleónas
Αμυγδαλεώνας
Chérso
Χέρσο
Strymonikó
Στρυμονικό
K. Kamíla
Κ. Καμήλα
Gázoros
Γάζωρος
Stat. Angístis
Σταθμ. Αγγίστης
Polistilo
Efkarpía
Ευκαρπία
Skoútari
Σκούταρι
Pethelinós
Πεθελινός
Próti
Πρώτη
PANGAÍO Ó.
Παγγαίο Όρος
Nikísiani
Νικήσιανη
Kavála
Καβάλα
Kilkís
Κιλκίς
Kalókastro
Καλόκαστρο
Anthí
Ανθή
p. Strymónas
Στρυμόνας Π.
Draviskos
Δραβήσκος
1956
Akrovoúni
Ακροβούνι
Eleftheroúpoli
Ελευθερούπολη
Kólpos Kavála
Κόλπος Καβάλα
Vafiochóri
Βαφιοχώρι
Vérgi
Βέργη
Terpní
Τερπνή
Rodolívos
Ροδολίβος
P. Gynaikókastro
Π. Γυναικόκαστρο
Koronoúda
Κορωνούδα
Lachanás
Λαχανάς
Achinós
Αχινός
Mavrothálassa
Μαυροθάλασσα
Avlí
Αυλή
Néa Péramos
Νέα Πέραμος
Kristóni
Κριστώνη
Xylópoli
Ξυλόπολη
Nigríta
Νιγρίτα
Podochóri
Ποδοχώρι
Foliá
Φωλεά
VERTÍSKOS Ó.
Βερτίσκος Όρος
Choumnikó
Χουμνικό
Ívira
Ίβηρα
AMFÍPOLI
Αμφίπολη
Galipsós
Γαληψός
Órmos Prínou
Όρμος Πρίνου
Dorkáda
Δορκάδα
Kampánis
Καμπάνης
Mikrokampos
Μικρόκαμπος
Pente Vrýses
Πέντε Βρύσες
Óssa
Όσσα
1107
Sochós
Σοχός
Skepastó
Σκεπαστό
Stefaniná
Στεφανινά
Akropótamos
Ακροπόταμος
Pétros
Πέτρος
Ássiros
Άσσηρος
Néa Kerdýllia
Νέα Κερδύλλια
Próchoma
Πρόχωμα
Filadélfi
Φιλαδέλφιο
Aréthousa
Αρέθουσα
Kariani
Καριανή
Loutrá Eleftherón
Λουτρά Ελευθερών
Skála Kallirachis
Σκάλα Καλλιράχης
p. Gallikós
Γαλλικός Π.
Drymós
Δρυμός
Lagkadás
Λαγκαδάς
Askós
Ασκός
Aretí
Αρετή
Akrogiáli
Ακρογιάλι
Koufália
Κουφάλια
Gefýra
Γέφυρα
Lagina
Loutrá Lagkadá
Λουτρά Λαγκαδά
Megáli Vólvi
Μεγάλη Βόλβη
Asprovalta
Ασπρόβαλτα
Limen
Λιμεν
Lití
Λητή
Diavatá
Διαβατά
Profítis
Προφήτης
Limni Vólvi
Λίμνη Βόλβη
Stavrós
Σταυρός
Strymonikós Kólpos
Στρυμονικός Κόλπος
Ikidóna
Ag. Athanásios
Αγ. Αθανάσιος
Lagyná
Λαγυνά
L. Koronia
Λίμνη Κορώνεια
Loutrá Vólvis
Λουτρά Βόλβης
Apollonía
Απολλωνία
Rentína
Ρεντίνα
Ionia
Lagkadíkia
Λαγκαδίκια
Néa Mádytos
Νέα Μάδυτος
Olympiáda
Ολυμπιάδα
Mýrina-Límnos
Kýmina
Κύμινα
Pýrgos
Πύργος
THESSALONÍKI
ΘΕΣΣΑΛΟΝΙΚΗ
Gerakarou
Γερακαρού
Varvára
Βαρβάρα
Akr. Marmári
Ακρ. Μαρμάρι
Kalamariá
Καλαμαριά
Melissourgós
Μελισσουργός
Stanós
Στανός
Stratonikí
Στρατονίκη
Trikala
Τρίκαλα
p. Axiós
Αξιός Π.
Peristerá
Περιστέρα
Zagklivéri
Ζαγκλιβέρι
Stágeira
Στάγειρα
Stratóni
Στρατώνι
K. Thessaloníkis
Κόλπος Θεσσαλονίκης
Thérmi
Θέρμη
Livádi
Λιβάδι
Saná
Σανά
Arnaía
Αρναία
Palaiochóri
Παλαιοχώρι
Akrotírio Arápis
Ακρ. Αράπης
Aiginio
Αιγίνιο
Vasiliká
Βασιλικά
Galátista
Γαλάτιστα
Ág. Prodromos
Άγ. Πρόδρομος
1165
Kólpos Ierissoú
Κόλπος Ιερισσού
Agia Triáda
Αγ. Τριάδα
Peraia
Περαία
Souroti
Σουρωτή
1020
Cholomóntas Monopati
Meg. Panagía
Μεγ. Παναγία
Ierissós
Ιερισσός
MONÍ CHILIANDARÍOU
Μ. ΧΙΛΙΑΝΔΑΡΙΟΥ
Néa Michanióna
Νέα Μηχανιώνα
Ág. Antónios
Άγιος Αντώνιος
Polýgyros
Πολύγυρος
Néa Róda
Νέα Ρόδα
Kolindrós
Κολινδρός
Methóni
Μεθώνη
Órmos
Όρμος
Vrástama
Βράσταμα
Trypití
Τρυπητή
MONÍ VATOPEDÍOU
Μ. ΒΑΤΟΠΕΔΙΟΥ
Epanomí
Επανομή
Pyrgadíkia
Πυργαδίκια
ÁGION ÓROS
ΑΓΙΟΝ ΟΡΟΣ
Akr. Epanomís
Ακρ. Επανομής
Petrálona
Πετράλωνα
Elaiochória
Ελαιοχώρια
Metagkítsi
Μεταγκίτσιο
Amoliani
Ν. Αμολιανή
Ouranoúpoli
Ουρανούπολη
Karyés
Καρυές
Kítros
Κίτρος
Akr. Acherάda
Ακρ. Αχεράδα
PIDNA
Néa Kallikráteia
Νέα Καλλικράτεια
Néa Tríglia
Νέα Τρίγλια
ÓLYNTHOS
ΟΛΥΝΘΟΣ
Gerakiní
Γερακινή
Singitikós
MONÍ IVÍRON
Μ. ΙΒΗΡΩΝ
Dáfni
Δάφνη
Néa Plágia
Νέα Πλάγια
Nikítas
Νικήτη
Órmos Panagías
Όρμος Παναγίας
MONÍ SÍMONOS PÉTRAS
Μ. ΣΙΜΩΝΟΣ ΠΕΤΡΑΣ
Korinós
Κορινός
Iráklelo-Kríti
Tínos
Mýkonos
Páros
Thíra-Santoríni
Mýrina-Límnos
Skíathos
Mytilíni-Lésvos
Alexandroúpoli
Néa Moudaniá
Νέα Μουδανιά
Metamórfosi
Μεταμόρφωση
Vourvouroú
Βουρβουρού
Kólpos
MONÍ AG. DIONYSÍOU
Μ. ΑΓ. ΔΙΟΝΥΣΙΟΥ
2033
ÁTHOS
Άθως
Paralía
Παραλία
Néa Poteídaia
Νέα Ποτείδαια
SITHONÍA
ΣΙΘΩΝΙΑ
Sárti
Σάρτη
Akr. Pínnes
Ακρ. Πίννες
DÍON
ΔΙΟΝ
Néa Fókaia
Νέα Φώκαια
Néos Marmarás
Νέος Μαρμαράς
Akr. Rigás
Ακρ. Ρηγάς
Limín Litochórou
Λιμήν Λιτοχώρου
Akr. Pýrgos
Ακρ. Πύργος
Sáni
Σανή
Áfytos
Άφυτος
Pórto Karrás
Πόρτο Καρράς
Sykiá
Συκιά
Kólpos Kassándras
Κόλπος Κασσάνδρας
Akr. Ádolo
Ακρ. Άδολο
Kólpos Agíou Órous
Κόλπος Αγίου Όρους
Kassándreia
Κασσάνδρεια
Kallithéa
Καλλιθέα
Skíathos
Kryopigí
Κρυοπηγή
Litóchoro
Λιτόχωρο
Leptokaryá
Λεπτοκαρυά
Síviri
Σίβηρη
Chaniótis
Χανιώτης
Toróni
Τορώνη
Kalamítsi
Καλαμίτσι
OLYMPOS
KASSÁNDRA
ΚΑΣΣΑΝΔΡΑ
Koufós
Κουφός
Paralía Skotínas
Παραλία Σκοτίνας
Kalándra
Καλάνδρα
Paliouri
Παλιούρι
Platamónas
Πλαταμώνας
Akr. Poseídio
Ακρ. Ποσείδιο
Poseídio
Ποσείδιο
N. Skióni
Ν. Σκιώνη
Ág. Nikólaos
Άγιος Νικόλαος
Akr. Paliouri
Ακρ. Παλιούριο
Akr. Drépano
Ακρ. Δρέπανο
1587
Karyá
Καρυά
ÓLYMPOS
Όλυμπος
Akrotírio Platamón
Ακρ. Πλαταμών
Thermaïkós
Θερμαϊκός
Skíathos
Rapsáni
Ραψάνη
TÉMPI
ΤΕΜΠΗ
Stómio
Στόμιο
Gónnoi
Kókkino Neró
E75
E79
E90
Mýrina-Límnos

Komuniga
Pchelarovo
Most
Tănkovo
Petrotá
Петрота
Dikaia
Δίκαια
Kastaniés
Καστανιές
Dabovets
Monastir
PRESPA
2000
PRESPA
BG
148
E
F
G
H
CHUKATA
GORATA
Kŭrdzhali
Кърджали
Borislavtsi
Pláti
Πλάτη
Rízia
Ρίζια
Kómara
Κόμαρα
Fylákio
Φυλάκιο
Néa Výssa
Νέα Βύσσα
Kavýli
Καβύλη
Váltos
Βάλτος
Orestiáda
Ορεστιάδα
Progled
Yazovir Kŭrdzhali
Yazovir Studen Kladenec
Oreshari
Yazovir Ivaylovgrad
Huhla
Pamporovo
Пампорово
Oryahovec
KŬRDZHALI
Arda
Popsko
Cherni rid
Ivaylovgrad
Ardino
Kobilyane
Momchilgrad
Момчилград
Perunika
Belopolci
Zóni
Ζώνη
Ládi
Λάδη
Ampelákia
Αμπελάκια
Thoúrio
Θούριο
Máni
Μάνη
Elçili
Vlahovo
Byal Izvor
Dzhebel
Metaxádes
Μεταξάδες
Didymóteicho
Διδυμότειχο
Srednogortsi
Madan
Pripek
Zvezdel
Krumovgrad
Byala R.
Smiljan
Rudozem
Mavrokklísi
Μαυροκκλήσι
Podkova
Tokačka
Goljamo Kamenjane
Mikró Déreio
Μικρό Δέρειο
Protokklísi
Πρωτοκκλήσι
Lávara
Λάβαρα
Starcevo
Koritata
Zlatograd
Dobromirtsi
Zavoya
Chorbadzhijsko
Roússa
Ρούσσα
Mándra
Μάνδρα
Sidiró
Σιδηρώ
Kavakli
1755
TSÍNGA
Mega Dére
Μέγα Δέρειο
Melívoia
Μελίβοια
Médousa
Μέδουσα
Orgáni
Οργάνη
A. Drosiní
Κάτω Δροσίνη
Giannoúli
Γιαννούλη
EDİR
Meriç
Echínos
Εχίνος
Nymfaía
Νυμφαία
Souflí
Σουφλί
Kurtbey
Sátres
Σάτρες
1482
1065
SÍLO
Smínthi
Σμίνθη
ANATOLIKÍ MAKEDONÍA
ANATOLIKÍ RODÓPI
ΑΝΑΤΟΛΙΚΗ ΡΟΔΟΠΗ
Lykófos
Λυκόφως
Küplü
Dafnónas
Δαφνώνας
Plagiá
Πλαγιά
Pessáni
Πεσσάνη
Kimméria
Κιμμέρια
Íasmos
Ίασμος
Sóstis
Σώστης
Komotiní
Κομοτηνή
Fillýra
Φιλλύρα
Soúnio
Σούνιο
Sultanköy
İbriktepe
Néa Sánta
Νέα Σάντα
Thymariá
Θυμαριά
Komniná
Κομνηνά
Xánthi
Ξάνθη
E90
Áratos
Άρατος
Aisými
Αισύμη
Paşayiğit
Vafaïka
Βαφαΐκα
Dialampí
Διαλαμπή
Kósmio
Κόσμιο
Sápes
Σάπες
Kírki
Κίρκη
Parádeisos
Παράδεισος
Amvrosía
Αμβροσία
L. Vistonída
Λ. Βιστονίδα
Koutsó
Κουτσό
Méga Doukáto
Μέγα Δουκάτο
Ipsala
Kesar
Mélissa
Μέλισσα
Pórpi
Πόρπη
Vénna
Βέννα
Féres
Φέρες
Esatçe
Pezoúla
Πεζούλα
Lágos
Λάγος
Xylagani
Ξυλαγανή
Mési
Μέση
Ímeros
Ίμερος
Mésti
Μέστη
Ávas
Άβας
Loutrós
Λουτρός
Chrysoúpoli
Χρυσούπολη
Ávdira
Άβδηρα
Fanári
Φανάρι
ÁVDIRA
ΑΒΔΗΡΑ
Maróneia
Μαρώνεια
TR
Chrysochóri
Χρυσοχώρι
Ág. Charálampos
Αγ. Χαράλαμπος
Mesimvría
Μεσημβρία
Mákri
Μάκρη
Alexandroúpoli
Αλεξανδρούπολη
Monastiráki
Μοναστηράκι
Yeni Karpuzlu
Dasochóri
Δασοχώρι
Keramotí
Κεραμωτή
THRÁKI
Orhanıye
Gala Gölü
Çeltikköy
Mýrina-Límnos
Kamariótissa-Samothráki
Thessaloníki
Akr. Koén
Kamariótissa-Samothráki
Enez
Yenice
Hasköy
Thásos
Θάσος
Makryámmos
Μακρύαμμος
Erikli
Panagía
Παναγία
Potamiá
Ποταμιά
Abdürrahim
Sultanıca
Prínos
Πρίνος
1046
Theológos
Θεολόγος
Thásos
Ν. Θάσος
150
Saroz Körf
Alykí
Αλυκή
Akrotírio Stavrós
Ακρ. Σταυρός
ALYKÍ
Kefálas
Κεφάλας
Alexandroúpoli
Kavála
Palaiópoli
Παλαιόπολη
Thermá
Θερμά
1600
Kamariótissa
Καμαριώτισσα
Samothráki
Σαμοθράκη
Lákkoma
Λάκκωμα
Akrotírio Kípos
Ακρ. Κήπος
Tayfur
Karainebeyli
YARIMADASI
Samothráki
Ν. Σαμοθράκη
Mýrina-Límnos
Büyük Kemikli Burun
GELİBOLU
Yolağzı
Ulgardereköyü
GELİBOLU
LİMNAE
YARIMADASİ
Eceabat
Kilitbahir
Gökçeada
Kaleköy
Kabaltepe
MİLLİ PARKI
İmroz
Çan
Behramlı
Aydıncık
Kepez
Alçitepe
Abide
Uğurlutepe
Ayagalip
İlyasbaba Burun
MEGÍSTIS LÁVRAS
Alexandroúpoli
Kamariótissa-Samothráki
Kavála
Akrotírio Pláka
Ακρ. Πλάκα
Límnos
Ν. Λήμνος
Kumkale
ACHILLEUM
Intepe
Tevfikiye
Yeniköy
TRUVA
Pláka
Πλάκα
Akr. Moúrtzeflos
Ακρ. Μούρτζεφλος
430
Dáfni
Δάφνη
IFAÍSTIA
ΗΦΑΙΣΤΙΑ
Kumburun
GION
ROS
Kontopoúli
Κοντοπούλι
Káspakas
Κάσπακας
Livadochóri
Λιβαδοχώρι
Bozcaada
Geyikli
Pazarkö
Moúdros
Μούδρος
Kamínia
Καμίνια
Bozca Adasi
Ezine
Mýrina
Μύρινα
Kontiás
Κοντιάς
Fisíni
Φισίνη
Thessaloníki
Rafina
Dalyan
ALEXANDRIA TROAS
NEANDRIA
319
Skandáli
Σκανδάλι
Akr. Agía Eirínis
Ακρ. Αγ. Ειρήνης
Sígri-Lésvos
Mytilíni-Lésvos
Ág Efstrátios
İzmir
135
Tavaklı
Kösedere
672
Ayvacık
Tuzla

Dhërmi
Himarë
Fterë
29
Gjirokastë
1842
128
Çarshovë
Melissopetra
Zmolikas Oros
2633
Samarina
Σαμαρίνα
51
A
B
C
D
Palermo
Borsh
Piqeras
Libohovë
Kónitsa
Κόνιτσα
FARÁNGI VÍKOU
ΦΑΡΑΓΓΙ ΒΙΚΟΥ
Dístrato Δίστρατο
Perivóli
Περιβόλι
43
Pogonianí
Πωγωνιανή
Kefalóvryso
Κεφαλόβρυσο
2480
ÓROS TÝMFI
Όρος Τύμφη
Laísta
Λαΐστα
AVGÓ
Αβγό
2177
PÍNDOS
Πίνδος
57
Lukovë
Delvina
39
21
Jergucati
Delvináki
Δελβινάκι
Monodéndri
Μονοδένδρι
Vovoúsa
Βοβούσα
Vlorë
Ancona
Bari
Venézia
Bríndisi
Kep
Kefali
PHÖNIKE
570
10
Ktísmata
Κτίσματα
28
20 E90
Kalpáki
Καλπάκι
ZAGÓRIA
Ζαγόρια
Flampourári
Φλαμπουράρι
Krani
Κραν
Vóreio Stenó Kérkyras
Βόρειο Στενό Κέρκυρας
N. Ereíkousa
N. Ερεικούσσα
Saranda
Finiq
34
Kakavi
Doliianá
Δολιανά
22
36
52
L. Pigón
Λ. Πηγών
AL
E853
N. Óthonoi
N. Οθωνοί
Akr. Ag. Aikateríni
Ακρ. Αγ. Αικατερίνης
Pilake
Kokloí
Κοκλιοί
Votonósi
Βοτονόσι
68
21
Livadhja
Asfáka
Ασφάκα
Kamínia
Καμινιά
Métsovo
Μέτσοβο
N. Mathráki
N. Μαθράκι
Sidári
Σιδάρι
Róda
Ρόδα
54
Tsamantás
Τσαμαντάς
Aetópetra
Αετόπετρα
Zítsa
Pérama
Πέραμα
PERISTÉRI
Λάκμος Όρος
2295
(Περιστέρι)
Avliótes
Αυλιώτες
Karousádes
Καρουσάδες
906
Kassiópi
Κασσιόπη
BUTHROTUM
Butrint
Afiónas
Αφιώνας
36
Soulópoulo
Σουλόπουλο
Klimátia
Κλιμάτια
Mázia
Μάζια
Shkalle
Ýpsos
Ύψος
Nisáki
Νησάκι
Ágios Nikólaos
Άγ. Νικόλαος
ÍPEIROS
Palaiokastrítsa
Παλαιοκαστρίτσα
Gouviá
Γουβιά
25
Konispol
E90
Grammeno
Γραμμένο
Ioánnina
Ιωάννινα
Liapádes
Λιαπάδες
Sagiáda
Σαγιάδα
Keramitsa
Κεραμίτσα
E92
Koúrenta
Κούρεντα
31
Kontokáli
Κοντοκάλι
Kérkyra
Κέρκυρα
Filiátes
Φιλιάτες
Vrosína
Βροσίνα
60
Mouzakaíoi
Μουζακαίοι
Serviané
Σερβιανά
Prámanta
Πράμαντα
TZOU
2469
Pélekas
Πέλεκας
80
Dodóni
Δωδώνη
5 E951
Kalétzi
Καλέντζι
ATHAMANICÁ ÓRI
Αθαμανικά Όρη
Ágios Górdios
Άγ. Γόρδιος
Mpenítses
Μπενίτσες
Parapótamos
Παραπόταμος
24
1974
TÓMAROS
Τόμαρος
Agnánta
Αγνάντα
Igoumenítsa
Ηγουμενίτσα
Thesprotía
Ménina
Μένινα
Petoúsi
Πετούσι
Kérkyra
N. Κέρκυρα
Moraïtika
Μωραΐτικα
Akr. Lefkímis
Ακρ. Λευκίμμης
Paramythiá
Παραμυθιά
Pérdika
Πέρδικα
Ág. Matthaios
Άγ. Ματθαίος
49
Plataria
Πλαταριά
68
Dafnotí
Δαφνωτή
Palaioch
Παλαιοχ
Lefkími
Λευκίμμη
Sývota
Σύβοτα
Karvounári
Καρβουνάρι
Tsangário
Τσαγγάριο
Dervíziana
Δερβίζιανα
Térovo
Τέροβο
89
Argyrádes
Αργυράδες
50
18
72
Kleisoúra
Κλεισούρα
Kávos
Κάβος
Pérdika
Πέρδικα
Kartéri
Καρτέρι
Margaríti
Μαργαρίτι
Glykí
Γλυκή
Palaiochóri
Παλαιοχώρι
Pitsiána
Πιτσιάνα
30
Akr. Asprókavos
Ακρ. Ασπρόκαβος
Mórfi
Μόρφι
Kerasóna
Κεράσωνα
p. Loúros
Λούρος π.
54
NEKROMANTEÍO
ΝΕΚΡΟΜΑΝΤΕΙΟ
ÉFYRAS
ΕΦΥΡΑ
Ammótopos
Αμμότοπος
Párga
Πάργα
E55
Melátes
Μελάτες
Vrysoúla
Βρυσούλα
Lákka
Λάκκα
Mesopótamo
Μεσοπόταμο
Kanalláki
Καναλλάκι
Filippiáda
Φιλιππιάδα
VLACHERNÁ
Βλαχέρνα
Gaios
Γάιος
28
18
Stefáni
Στεφάνη
14
Paxoí
N. Παξοί
Loúros
Árta
Άρτα
5 E951
KASSOPI
ΚΑΣΣΩΠΗ
40
21
Antípaxoi
N. Αντίπαξοι
Kastrosykiá
Ακρ. Καστροσυκιάς
Archángelos
Αρχάγγελος
Psathotópi
Ψαθοτόπι
Kompóti
Κομπότι
Vígla
Βίγλα
Menídi
Μενίδ
Salaóra
Σαλαώρα
Komméno
Κομμένο
NIKÓPOLI
ΝΙΚΟΠΟΛΗ
IÓNIOI
NISOI
23
Agía Triáda
Αγ. Τριάδα
Amvrakikós Kólpos
Αμβρακικός Κόλπος
Sámi-Kefalloniá
Pátra
Préveza
Πρέβεζα
Vónitsa
Βόνιτσα
Mpoúkka
Μπούκκα
Spárto
Σπάρτο
44
42 E55/E952
58
Ág. Nikólaos
Άγ. Νικόλαος
Lefkáda
Λευκάδα
L. Voulkariá
Λ. Βουλκαριά
Monastiráki
Μοναστηράκι
Loutráki
Λουτράκι
Ágios Nikítas
Άγ. Νικήτας
Karyá
Καρυά
Pálairos
Πάλαιρος
Katoúna
Κατούνα
92
L. Amvrakía
Λίμνη Αμβρακία
Lefkáda
N. Λευκάδα
Nydrí
Νυδρί
1141
60
Fyteíe
Φυτείε
Mýtikas
Μύτικας
Aetós
Αετός
Ágios Pétros
Άγ. Πέτρος
Vlychó
Βλυχό
Kérkyra
Igoumenítsa
Paxoí
Póros
Πόρος
Kálamos
N. Κάλαμος
Mpampíni
Μπαμπίνη
Vasilikí
Βασιλική
Meganísi
N. Μεγανήσι
Akr. Doukáto
Ακρ. Δουκάτο
Arkoúdi
N. Αρκούδι
Kastós
N. Καστός
Astako
Αστακό
Akr. Mélissa
Ακρ. Μέλισσα
Átokos
N. Άτοκος
Echinádes Nísoi
Εχινάδες Νήσοι
POLI
ΠΟΛΗ
Fiskárdo
Φισκάρδο
Kióni
Κιόνι
Petalás
N. Πεταλάς
Plat
Πλατ
Stavrós
Σταυρός
Itháki
N. Ιθάκη
Ásos
Άσος
Itháki
Ιθάκη
Akrotírio Athéras
Ακρωτήριο Αθέρας
Athéras
Αθέρας
Venézia
Ancona
Bari
Bríndisi
Kérkyra
Igoumenítsa
Ag. Efimía
Αγ. Ευφημία
Oxeía
N. Οξεία
Kardakáta
Καρδακάτα
MELISSÁNI
ΜΕΛΙΣΣΑΝΗ
Sámi
Σάμη
Argostóli
Lixoúri
Ληξούρι
25
Kefalloniá
N. Κεφαλλονιά
20
Póros
Πόρος
ÓROS AÍNOS
1628
ETHN. D. AÍNOS
Argostóli
Αργοστόλι
22
Kyllíni
Zákynthos
Loutrá Ko
Λουτρ
Skála
Σκάλα
Markópoulo
Μαρκόπουλο
29
Akrotírio Moúnta
Ακρ. Μούντα
Pátra
Kyllíni
1
2
3
4
5
6

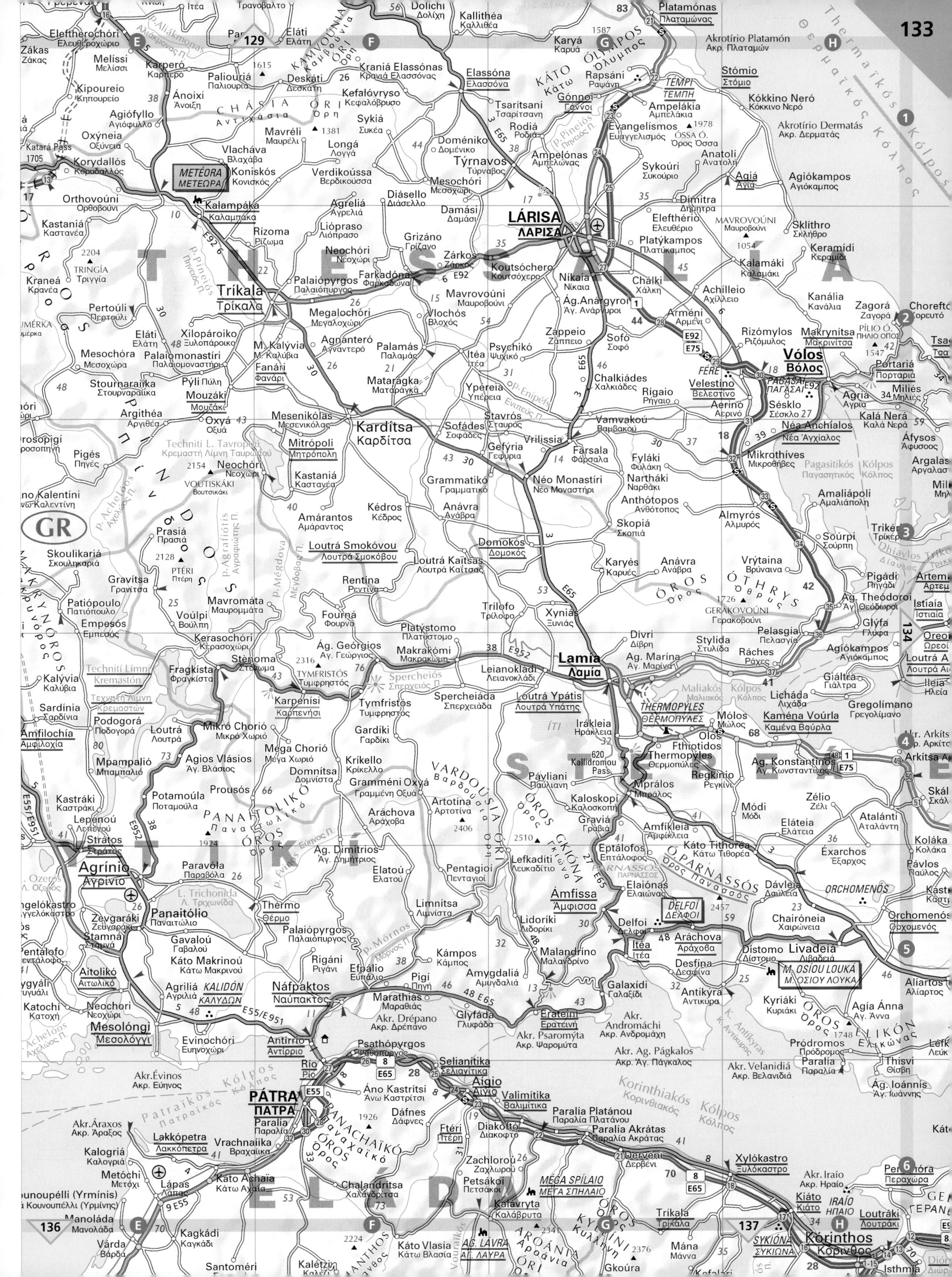

THESSALÍA
STEREÁ ELLÁDA
GR
LÁRISA
ΛΑΡΙΣΑ
Vólos
Βόλος
Lamía
Λαμία
Tríkala
Τρίκαλα
Kardítsa
Καρδίτσα
Agrínio
Αγρίνιο
PÁTRA
ΠΑΤΡΑ
Kórinthos
Κόρινθος
Livadeiá
Λιβαδειά
Ámfissa
Άμφισσα
Karpenísi
Καρπενήσι
Náfpaktos
Ναύπακτος
Mesolóngi
Μεσολόγγι
Delfoí
Δελφοί
Elassóna
Ελασσόνα
Týrnavos
Τύρναβος
Kalampáka
Καλαμπάκα
METÉORA
ΜΕΤΕΩΡΑ
DELFOÍ
ΔΕΛΦΟΙ
M. OSÍOU LOUKÁ
Μ. ΟΣΙΟΥ ΛΟΥΚΑ
THERMOPYLES
ΘΕΡΜΟΠΥΛΕΣ
ÓLYMPOS
ÓSSA Ó.
ÓROS ÓTHRYS
Ó. PARNASSÓS
VARDOÚSIA ÓRI
PANAITOLIKÓ ÓROS
PANACHAÏKÓ ÓROS
GKIÓNA
ELIKÓN
KYLÍNI
AROÁNIA ÓRI
Thermaïkós Kólpos
Θερμαϊκός Κόλπος
Pagasitikós Kólpos
Παγασητικός Κόλπος
Maliakós Kólpos
Μαλιακός Κόλπος
Korinthiakós Kólpos
Κορινθιακός Κόλπος
Patraïkós Kólpos
Πατραϊκός Κόλπος
Technití L. Tavropoú
L. Trichonída
Λ. Τριχωνίδα
Technití Límni Kremastón
Τεχνητή Λίμνη Κρεμαστών
Platamónas
Πλαταμώνας
Karyá
Καρυά
Rapsáni
Ραψάνη
TÉMPI
ΤΕΜΠΗ
Stómio
Στόμιο
Agiá
Αγιά
Velestíno
Βελεστίνο
Fársala
Φάρσαλα
Domokós
Δομοκός
Almyrós
Αλμυρός
Stylída
Στυλίδα
Kaména Voúrla
Καμένα Βούρλα
Itéa
Ιτέα
Galaxídi
Γαλαξίδι
Aígio
Αίγιο
Río
Ρίο
Antírrio
Αντίρριο
Xylókastro
Ξυλόκαστρο
Kalávryta
Καλάβρυτα
MÉGA SPÍLAIO
ΜΕΓΑ ΣΠΗΛΑΙΟ
AG. LÁVRA
ΑΓ. ΛΑΥΡΑ
Loutrá Ypátis
Λουτρά Υπάτης
Loutrá Smokóvou
Λουτρά Σμοκόβου
ORCHOMENÓS
Orchomenós
Αταλάντη
Atalánti
Arkítsa
Chairóneia
Dístomo
Aráchova
Αράχωβα
Thérmo
Θέρμο
Panaitólio
Stános
Amfilochía
Αμφιλοχία
Stratos
Στράτος
Kalidón
ΚΑΛΥΔΩΝ
Lakkópetra
Λακκόπετρα
SYKIÓNA
ΣΥΚΙΩΝΑ
Kiáto
Κιάτο
Loutráki
Λουτράκι
Isthmia
E65
E75
E92
E952
E55/E951
E55
129
136
137
134

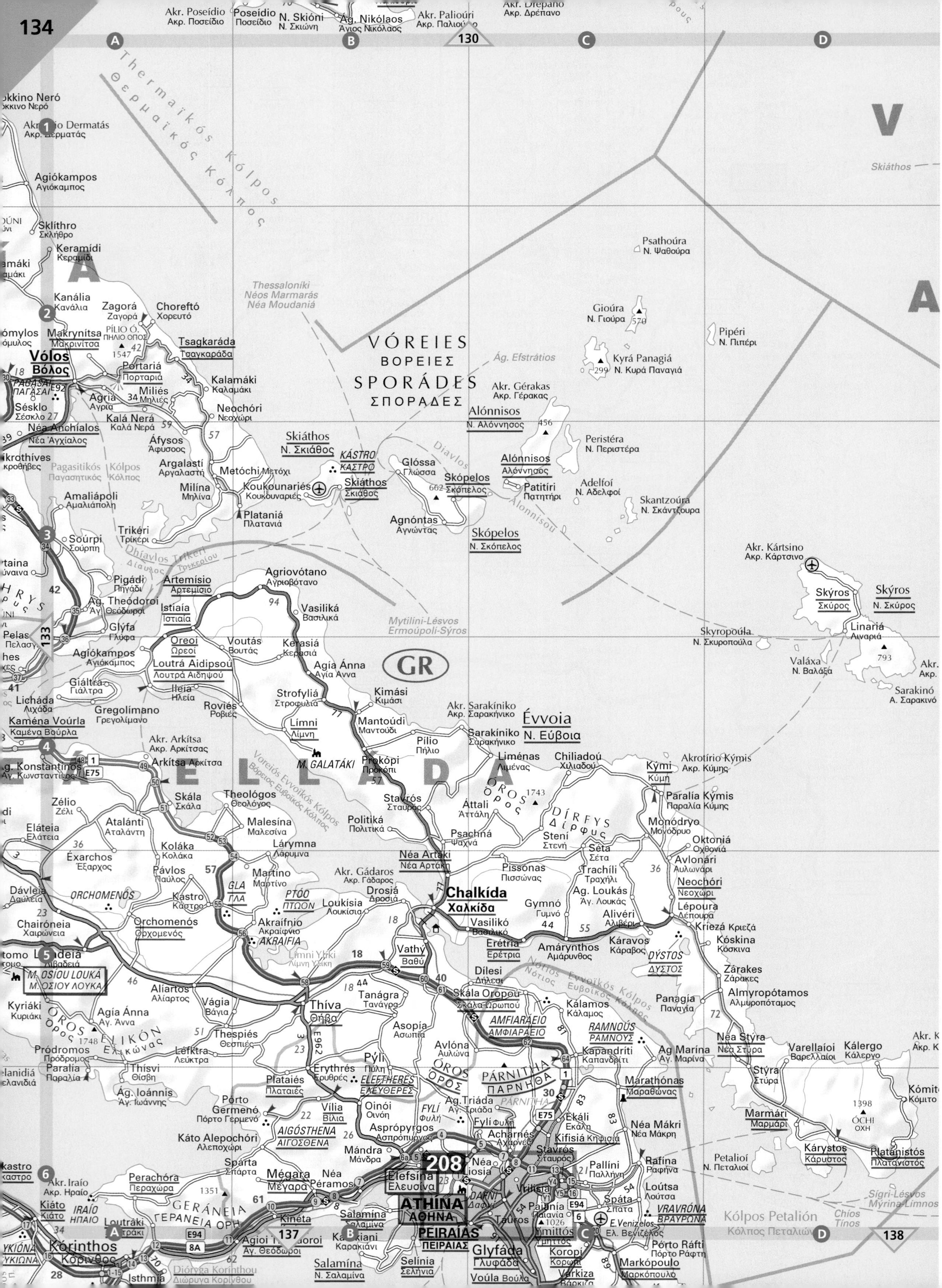
Akr. Poseídio
Ακρ. Ποσείδιο
Poseídio
Ποσείδιο
N. Skióni
Ν. Σκιώνη
Ag. Nikólaos
Άγιος Νικόλαος
Akr. Palioúri
Akr. Drépano
Ακρ. Δρέπανο
A
B
130
C
D
Thermaïkós Kólpos
Θερμαϊκός Κόλπος
V
Skiáthos
Akr. Dermatás
Ακρ. Δερματάς
Agiókampos
Αγιόκαμπος
Sklíthro
Σκλήθρο
Keramídi
Κεραμίδι
Psathoúra
Ν. Ψαθούρα
Thessaloníki
Néos Marmarás
Néa Moudaniá
Kanália
Καναλία
Zagorá
Ζαγορά
Choreftó
Χορευτό
Gioúra
Ν. Γιούρα
570
Pipéri
Ν. Πιπέρι
Makrynítsa
Μακρινίτσα
PÍLIO Ó.
ΠΗΛΙΟ ΟΡΟΣ
1547
Tsagkaráda
Τσαγκαράδα
VÓREIES
ΒΟΡΕΙΕΣ
SPORÁDES
ΣΠΟΡΑΔΕΣ
Ág. Efstrátios
Kyrá Panagiá
Ν. Κυρά Παναγιά
299
Vólos
Βόλος
Portariá
Πορταριά
Kalamáki
Καλαμάκι
Akr. Gérakas
Ακρ. Γέρακας
PAGASAÍ
ΠΑΓΑΣΑΙ
Agria
Αγριά
Miliés
Μηλιές
Neochóri
Νεοχώρι
Alónnisos
Ν. Αλόννησος
456
Sésklo
Σέσκλο
Kalá Nerá
Καλά Νερά
Néa Anchíalos
Νέα Αγχίαλος
Áfysos
Άφυσσος
Skiáthos
Ν. Σκιάθος
Peristéra
Ν. Περιστέρα
Pagasitikós Kólpos
Παγασητικός Κόλπος
Argalastí
Αργαλαστή
Metóchi
Μετόχι
KÁSTRO
ΚΑΣΤΡΟ
Glóssa
Γλώσσα
Diavlos
Alónnisos
Αλόννησος
Skópelos
Σκόπελος
662
Patitíri
Πατητήρι
Adelfoí
Ν. Αδελφοί
Milína
Μηλίνα
Koukounariés
Κουκουναριές
Skiáthos
Σκιάθος
Amaliápoli
Αμαλιάπολη
Platania
Πλατανιά
Skantzoúra
Ν. Σκάντζουρα
Agnóntas
Αγνώντας
Skópelos
Ν. Σκόπελος
Alonnisou
Soúrpi
Σούρπη
Trikéri
Τρικέρι
Dhíavlos Trikeri
Δίαυλος Τρικερίου
Akr. Kártsino
Ακρ. Κάρτσινο
Agriovótano
Αγριοβότανο
Pigádi
Πηγάδι
Artemísio
Αρτεμίσιο
Ag. Theodoroi
Άγ. Θεόδωροι
Istiaía
Ιστιαία
Vasiliká
Βασιλικά
Skýros
Σκύρος
Skýros
Ν. Σκύρος
133
Glýfa
Γλύφα
Mytilíni-Lésvos
Ermoúpoli-Sýros
Linariá
Λιναριά
Skyropoúla
Ν. Σκυροπούλα
Pelas
Oreoí
Ωρεοί
Voutás
Βουτάς
Kerasiá
Κερασιά
793
Agiókampos
Αγιόκαμπος
Loutrá Aidipsoú
Λουτρά Αιδηψού
Agía Ánna
Αγία Άννα
GR
Valáxa
Ν. Βαλάξα
Giáltra
Γιάλτρα
Ileía
Ηλεία
Strofyliá
Στροφυλιά
Kimási
Κιμάσι
Sarakinó
Α. Σαρακινό
Licháda
Λιχάδα
Gregolímano
Γρεγολίμανο
Roviés
Ροβιές
Akr. Sarakíniko
Ακρ. Σαρακίνικο
Kaména Voúrla
Καμένα Βούρλα
Límni
Λίμνη
Mantoúdi
Μαντούδι
Sarakíniko
Σαρακίνικο
Évvoia
Ν. Εύβοια
Pílio
Πήλιο
Akr. Arkítsa
Ακρ. Αρκίτσα
Ag. Konstantínos
Άγ. Κωνσταντίνος
Arkítsa
Αρκίτσα
M. GALATÁKI
Prokópi
Προκόπι
Liménas
Λιμένας
Chiliadoú
Χιλιαδού
Kými
Κύμη
Akrotírio Kýmis
Ακρ. Κύμης
ELLADA
Vóreios Evvoïkós Kólpos
Βόρειος Ευβοϊκός Κόλπος
ÓROS
1743
Zélio
Ζέλι
Skála
Σκάλα
Theológos
Θεολόγος
Stavrós
Σταυρός
Áttali
Άτταλη
Paralía Kýmis
Παραλία Κύμης
DÍRFYS
Δίρφυς
Eláteia
Ελάτεια
Atalánti
Αταλάντη
Malesína
Μαλεσίνα
Politiká
Πολιτικά
Monódryo
Μονόδρυο
Psachná
Ψαχνά
Stení
Στενή
Oktoniá
Οχθονιά
Koláka
Κολάκα
Lárymna
Λάρυμνα
Séta
Σέτα
Avlonári
Αυλωνάρι
Éxarchos
Έξαρχος
Néa Artáki
Νέα Αρτάκη
Pissónas
Πισσώνας
Pávlos
Παύλος
Martíno
Μαρτίνο
Akr. Gádaros
Ακρ. Γάδαρος
Trachíli
Τραχήλι
Neochóri
Νεοχώρι
Dávleia
Δαύλεια
ORCHOMENÓS
GLA
ΓΛΑ
PTÓO
ΠΤΩΟΝ
Kástro
Κάστρο
Drosiá
Δροσιά
Chalkída
Χαλκίδα
Ag. Loukás
Άγ. Λουκάς
Lépoura
Λέπουρα
Loukísia
Λουκίσια
Gymnó
Γυμνό
Aliveri
Αλιβέρι
Kriezá
Κριεζά
Chairóneia
Χαιρώνεια
Orchomenós
Ορχομενός
Akraífnio
Ακραίφνιο
AKRAIFIA
Vasilikó
Βασιλικό
Eretría
Ερέτρια
Amárynthos
Αμάρυνθος
Káravos
Κάραβος
Kóskina
Κόσκινα
Livadeia
Λιβαδειά
Límni Ylíki
Λίμνη Υλίκη
Vathý
Βαθύ
DÝSTOS
ΔΥΣΤΟΣ
M. OSIOU LOUKÁ
Μ. ΟΣΙΟΥ ΛΟΥΚΑ
Dílesi
Δήλεσι
Nótios Evvoïkós Kólpos
Νότιος Ευβοϊκός Κόλπος
Zárakes
Ζάρακες
Aliartos
Αλίαρτος
Vágia
Βάγια
Thíva
Θήβα
Tanágra
Τανάγρα
Skála Oropoú
Σκάλα Ωρωπού
Kálamos
Κάλαμος
Panagía
Παναγία
Almyropótamos
Αλμυροπόταμος
Kyriáki
Κυριάκι
Agía Ánna
Αγ. Άννα
ÓROS ELIKÓN
Όρος Ελικώνας
1748
AMFIARÁEIO
ΑΜΦΙΑΡΑΕΙΟ
Asopía
Ασωπία
RAMNOÚS
ΡΑΜΝΟΥΣ
Thespiés
Θεσπιές
Avlóna
Αυλώνα
Nea Stýra
Νέα Στύρα
Varellaíoi
Βαρελλαίοι
Kálergo
Κάλεργο
Pródromos
Πρόδρομος
Léfktra
Λεύκτρα
Kapandríti
Καπανδρίτι
Ag Marína
Αγ. Μαρίνα
Paralía
Παραλία
Thísvi
Θίσβη
Erythrés
Ερυθρές
Pýli
Πύλη
ÓROS
PÁRNITHA
ΠΑΡΝΗΘΑ
Stýra
Στύρα
ELEFTHERES
ΕΛΕΥΘΕΡΕΣ
Plataiés
Πλαταιές
Marathónas
Μαραθώνας
Ág. Ioánnis
Άγ. Ιωάννης
Pórto Germenó
Πόρτο Γερμενό
Vília
Βίλια
Oinói
Οινόη
FYLÍ
ΦΥΛΗ
Ag. Triáda
Αγ. Τριάδα
Fylí
Φυλή
Ekáli
Εκάλη
1398
ÓCHI
ΟΧΗ
Kómito
Κόμιτο
Marmári
Μαρμάρι
AIGÓSTHENA
ΑΙΓΟΣΘΕΝΑ
Asprópyrgos
Ασπρόπυργος
Acharnés
Αχαρνές
Kifisiá
Κηφισιά
Néa Mákri
Νέα Μάκρη
Káto Alepochóri
Αλεποχώρι
Mándra
Μάνδρα
Stavrós
Σταυρός
Kastro
Kastro
Spárta
Σπάρτα
Pallíni
Παλλήνη
Rafína
Ραφήνα
Kárystos
Κάρυστος
Platanistós
Πλατανιστός
208
Néa Iosia
Akr. Iraío
Ακρ. Ηραίο
Perachóra
Περαχώρα
Mégara
Μέγαρα
Néa Péramos
Elefsína
Ελευσίνα
Vrilíssia
Loútsa
Λούτσα
Petalioí
Ν. Πεταλιοί
1351
GERÁNEIA
ΓΕΡΑΝΕΙΑ ΟΡΗ
61
ATHÍNA
ΑΘΗΝΑ
DAFNÍ
Paianía
Παιανία
1026
Spáta
Σπάτα
VRAVRÓNA
ΒΡΑΥΡΩΝΑ
Sigri-Lésvos
Mýrina-Límnos
Chíos
Tínos
Kiáto
Κιάτο
IRAÍO
ΗΡΑΙΟ
Loutráki
Kinéta
Κινέτα
Salamína
Σαλαμίνα
Tavros
E. Venizelos
Ελ. Βενιζέλος
Kólpos Petalión
Κόλπος Πεταλιών
137
138
Kórinthos
Κόρινθος
Agioi Theodoroi
Άγ. Θεόδωροι
Kakiani
Καρακιάνι
PEIRAIÁS
ΠΕΙΡΑΙΑΣ
Glyfáda
Γλυφάδα
Ymittós
Koropí
Κορωπί
Pórto Ráfti
Πόρτο Ράφτη
Isthmia
Dióryga Korinthou
Διώρυγα Κορίνθου
Salamína
Ν. Σαλαμίνα
Selínia
Σελήνια
Voúla
Βούλα
Várkiza
Βάρκιζα
Markópoulo
Μαρκόπουλο

Skandáli
Σκανδάλι
Akr. Agía Eirínis
Ακρ. Αγ. Ειρήνης
E
131
F
G
150
H
ALEXANDRIA TROAS
NEANDRIA
Mýrina-Límnos
Kösedere
Tavaklı
672
Ayvacık
776 DİKİLİ TEPE
ANTANDROS
Küçükkuyu
Ahmetçe
Tuzla
Tamis
Kurobası
ASSOS
Gülpınar
Behramkale
Bademli
Baba Burun
POLYMEDIUM
Edremit Körfezi
PASSANDRA
Alibey Adasi
ÓREIO
IGAÍO
Akr. Kalamáki
Ακρ. Καλαμάκι
Mytilíni-Lésvos
Skiáthos
Thessaloníki
Mýrina-Límnos
Ágios Efstrátios
Ág. Efstrátios
Άγ. Ευστράτιος
298
Ágios Efstrátios
Ν. Άγ. Ευστράτιος
Akrotírio Trypití
Ακρ. Τρυπητή
Akr. Skamniá
Ακρ. Σκαμνιά
Sykaminéa
Συκαμινέα
Míthymna
Μήθυμνα
Pétra
Πέτρα
Stýpsi
Στύψη
Mantamádos
Μανταμάδος
Ayvalık
ŞEYTAN SOFRASI
Altınova
ÁNTISSA
Fília
Φίλια
Agía Paraskeví
Αγ. Παρασκευή
Mystegná
Μιστεγνά
Antissa
Άντισσα
Kalloní
Καλλονή
Thermí
Πύργοι Θέρμης
Mýrina-Límnos
Sígri
Σίγρι
Vatoúsa
Βατούσσα
MEL
Eresós
Ερεσός
Parákoila
Παράκοιλα
Kólpos Kallonís
Κόλπος Καλλονής
Kerameía
Κεραμεία
Mytilíni
Μυτιλήνη
Akr. Sígri
Ακρ.Σιγρίου
Vasiliká
Βασιλικά
Rafína
Skála Eresoú
Σκάλα Ερεσού
Skála
Σκάλα
Agiásos
Αγιάσος
968
CAR
Polychnítos
Πολιχνίτος
Ampelikó
Αμπελικό
Skópelos
Σκόπελος
Loutrá
Λουτρά
Krátigos
Κράτηνος
Vaterá
Βατερά
Lésvos
Ν. Λέσβος
Plomári
Πλωμάρι
Vólos
Chíos
Peiraías
Aslan Burun
PHOK.
Kara Burun
152
Mytilíni-Lésvos
Lithári
Λιθάρι
Hasseki
Karaburun
Parlak
1212
AK DAĞ
Psará
Ν. Ψαρά
531
Psará
Ψαρά
Antípsara
Ν. Αντίψαρα
Agiásmata
Αγιάσματα
Kampiá
Καμπιά
1297
Mármaro
Μάρμαρο
Küçükbahçe
Mordoğan
Kardámyla
Καρδάμυλα
Melaniós
Μελανιός
Oinoússes
Ν. Οινούσσες
Volissós
Βολισσός
Lagkáda
Λαγκάδα
Vrontádos
Βροντάδος
Balıklıova
TR
Chíos
Χίος
Ildır
Chíos
Ν. Χίος
NÉA MONÍ
ΝΕΑ ΜΟΝΗ
Çeşme
Uzunkuyu
Alaçatı
Thymianá
Θυμιανά
Kallimasiá
Καλλιμασιά
Pasá Limáni
Πασά Λιμάνι
Vessa
Βέσσα
Armólia
Αρμόλια
Mestá
Μεστά
Kalamotí
Καλαμωτή
Pyrgío
Πυργίο
Kómi
Κώμη
Emporeiós
Εμπορειός
Koraka Burun
Akr. Mástichо
Ακρ. Μάστιχο
Ancona
Brindisi
Rafína
Mýkonos
Peiraías
Sámos
Karlóvasi
Kafiréas
Καφηρέας
Akr. Kampanós
Kalivári
Καλυβάρι
Ándros
Ν. Άνδρος
Gávrio
Γαύριο
Mpatsí
Μπατσί
Apoíkia
Αποίκια
995
Tínos
Ándros
Άνδρος
Palaiópoli
Παλαιόπολη
Órmos
Όρμος
Kórthi
139
Akr. Fanári
Ακρ. Φανάρι
Ag. Kyrikos
Ikaría
Ν. Ικαρία
Évdilos
Εύδηλος
Thérma
Θέρμα
Foúrnoi
Ν. Φούρνοι

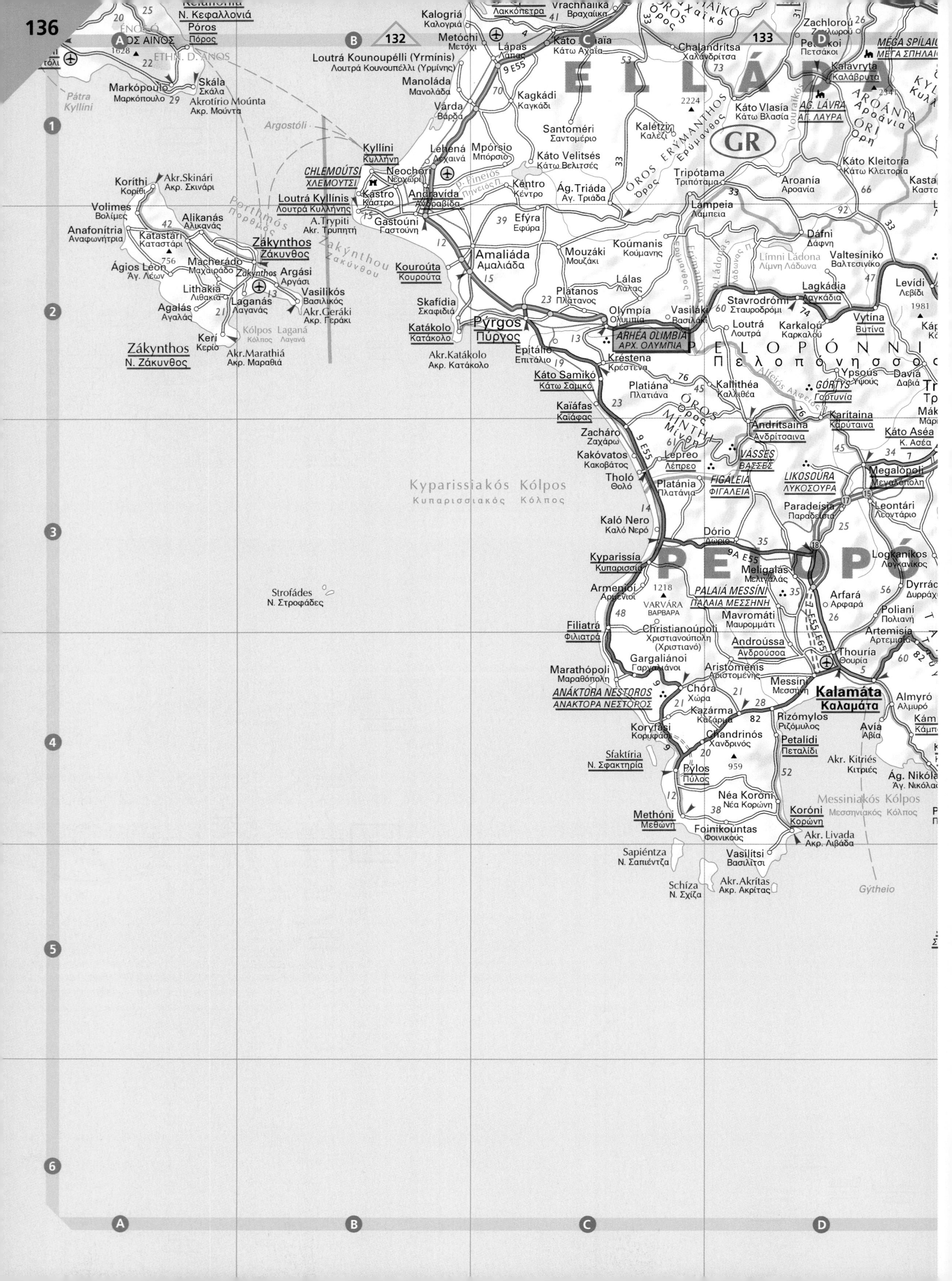
132
133
ELLÁDA
GR
PELOPÓNNI
Πελοπόννησος
PELOPÓ
N. Κεφαλλονιά
Póros
Πόρος
ΟΣ ΑΙΝΟΣ
ETHN. D. AÍNOS
Markópoulo
Μαρκόπουλο
Skála
Σκάλα
Akrotírio Moúnta
Ακρ. Μούντα
Pátra
Kyllíni
Argostóli
Kalogriá
Καλογριά
Metóchi
Μετόχι
Lápas
Λάπας
Káto Achaïa
Κάτω Αχαΐα
Loutrá Kounoupélli (Yrmínis)
Λουτρά Κουνουπέλλι (Υρμίνης)
Manoláda
Μανολάδα
Várda
Βάρδα
Kagkádi
Καγκάδι
Lehená
Λεχαινά
Mpórsio
Μπόρσιο
Kyllíni
Κυλλήνη
CHLEMOÚTSI
ΧΛΕΜΟΥΤΣΙ
Neochóri
Νεοχώρι
Kástro
Κάστρο
Loutrá Kyllínis
Λουτρά Κυλλήνης
Andravída
Ανδραβίδα
A.Trypiti
Ακρ. Τρυπητή
Gastoúni
Γαστούνη
Vrachnaíika
Βραχναίικα
Lakkópetra
Λακκόπετρα
Chalandrítsa
Χαλανδρίτσα
Zachloroú
Pteri
Petsákoi
Πετσάκοι
Kalávryta
Καλάβρυτα
MÉGA SPÍLAIO
ΜΕΓΑ ΣΠΗΛΑΙΟ
AG. LÁVRA
ΑΓ. ΛΑΥΡΑ
Káto Vlasía
Κάτω Βλασία
AROÁNIA
Αροάνια
ÓRI
Όρη
Santoméri
Σαντομέριο
Kalétzi
Καλέτζι
ÓROS ERÝMANTHOS
Όρος Ερύμανθος
Káto Velitsés
Κάτω Βελιτσές
Kéntro
Κέντρο
Ág. Triáda
Αγ. Τριάδα
Tripótama
Τριπόταμα
Aroanía
Αροανία
Káto Kleitoría
Κάτω Κλειτορία
Lámpeia
Λάμπεια
Efýra
Εφύρα
Dáfni
Δάφνη
Valtesiníko
Βαλτεσινίκο
Límni Ládona
Λίμνη Λάδωνα
Koúmanis
Κούμανης
Mouzáki
Μουζάκι
Amaliáda
Αμαλιάδα
Kouroúta
Κουρούτα
Lálas
Λάλας
Plátanos
Πλάτανος
Skafídia
Σκαφιδιά
Pýrgos
Πύργος
Katákolo
Κατάκολο
Akr.Katákolo
Ακρ. Κατάκολο
Olympía
Ολυμπία
Vasiláki
Βασιλάκι
ARHÉA OLIMBÍA
ΑΡΧ. ΟΛΥΜΠΙΑ
Stavrodrómi
Σταυροδρόμι
Lagkádia
Λαγκάδια
Levídi
Λεβίδι
Vytína
Βυτίνα
Loutrá
Λουτρά
Karkaloú
Καρκαλού
Epitálio
Επιτάλιο
Kréstena
Κρέστενα
Káto Samikó
Κάτω Σαμικό
Platiána
Πλατιάνα
Kallithéa
Καλλιθέα
Ypsoús
Υψούς
Davía
Δαβιά
GÓRTYS
Γορτυνία
Kaïáfas
Καϊάφας
ÓROS MÍNTHI
Όρος Μίνθη
Andrítsaina
Ανδρίτσαινα
Karítaina
Καρύταινα
Káto Aséa
Κ. Ασέα
Zacháro
Ζαχάρω
Kakóvatos
Κακόβατος
Lepreo
Λέπρεο
VÁSSES
ΒΑΣΣΕΣ
Tholó
Θολό
Plátania
Πλατάνια
FIGÁLEIA
ΦΙΓΑΛΕΙΑ
LIKOSOÚRA
ΛΥΚΟΣΟΥΡΑ
Megalópoli
Μεγαλόπολη
Kyparissiakós Kólpos
Κυπαρισσιακός Κόλπος
Kaló Nero
Καλό Νερό
Paradeísia
Παραδείσια
Leontári
Λεοντάριο
Dório
Δώριο
Kyparissía
Κυπαρισσία
Meligalás
Μελιγαλάς
Logkaníkos
Λογκανίκος
Strofádes
Ν. Στροφάδες
Armeniói
Αρμενιοί
VARVÁRA
ΒΑΡΒΑΡΑ
PALAIÁ MESSÍNI
ΠΑΛΑΙΑ ΜΕΣΣΗΝΗ
Arfará
Αρφαρά
Dyrrác
Δυρράχ
Mavromáti
Μαυρομμάτι
Poliani
Πολιανή
Filiatrá
Φιλιατρά
Christianoúpoli
Χριστιανούπολη
(Χριστιανό)
Artemisía
Αρτεμισία
Androússa
Ανδρούσα
Thouría
Θουρία
Gargaliánoi
Γαργαλιάνοι
Marathópoli
Μαραθόπολη
Aristoménis
Αριστομένης
ANÁKTORA NESTOROS
ΑΝΑΚΤΟΡΑ ΝΕΣΤΟΡΟΣ
Chóra
Χώρα
Messíni
Μεσσήνη
Kalamáta
Καλαμάτα
Almyró
Αλμυρό
Kazárma
Καζάρμα
Rizómylos
Ριζόμυλος
Koryfási
Κορυφάσι
Chandrinós
Χανδρινός
Petalídi
Πεταλίδι
Avía
Αβία
Sfaktíria
Ν. Σφακτηρία
Pýlos
Πύλος
Akr. Kitriés
Κιτριές
Ág. Nikóla
Άγ. Νικόλα
Messiniakós Kólpos
Μεσσηνιακός Κόλπος
Néa Koróni
Νέα Κορώνη
Methóni
Μεθώνη
Koróni
Κορώνη
Foinikoúntas
Φοινικούντας
Akr. Livada
Ακρ. Λιβάδα
Sapiéntza
Ν. Σαπιέντζα
Vasilítsi
Βασιλίτσι
Schíza
Ν. Σχίζα
Akr. Akrítas
Ακρ. Ακρίτας
Gýtheio
Koríthi
Κορίθι
Akr.Skinári
Ακρ. Σκινάρι
Volimes
Βολίμες
Anafonítria
Αναφωνήτρια
Alikanás
Αλικανάς
Katastári
Καταστάρι
Porthmós Zakýnthou
Πορθμός Ζακύνθου
Zákynthos
Ζάκυνθος
Ágios Léon
Άγ. Λέων
Mácherádo
Μαχαιράδο
Argási
Αργάσι
Lithakiá
Λιθακιά
Vasilikós
Βασιλικός
Laganás
Λαγανάς
Akr.Geráki
Ακρ. Γεράκι
Agalás
Αγαλάς
Kerí
Κερίο
Kólpos Laganá
Κόλπος Λαγανά
Akr.Marathiá
Ακρ. Μαραθιά
Zákynthos
Ν. Ζάκυνθος
A
B
C
D
1
2
3
4
5
6

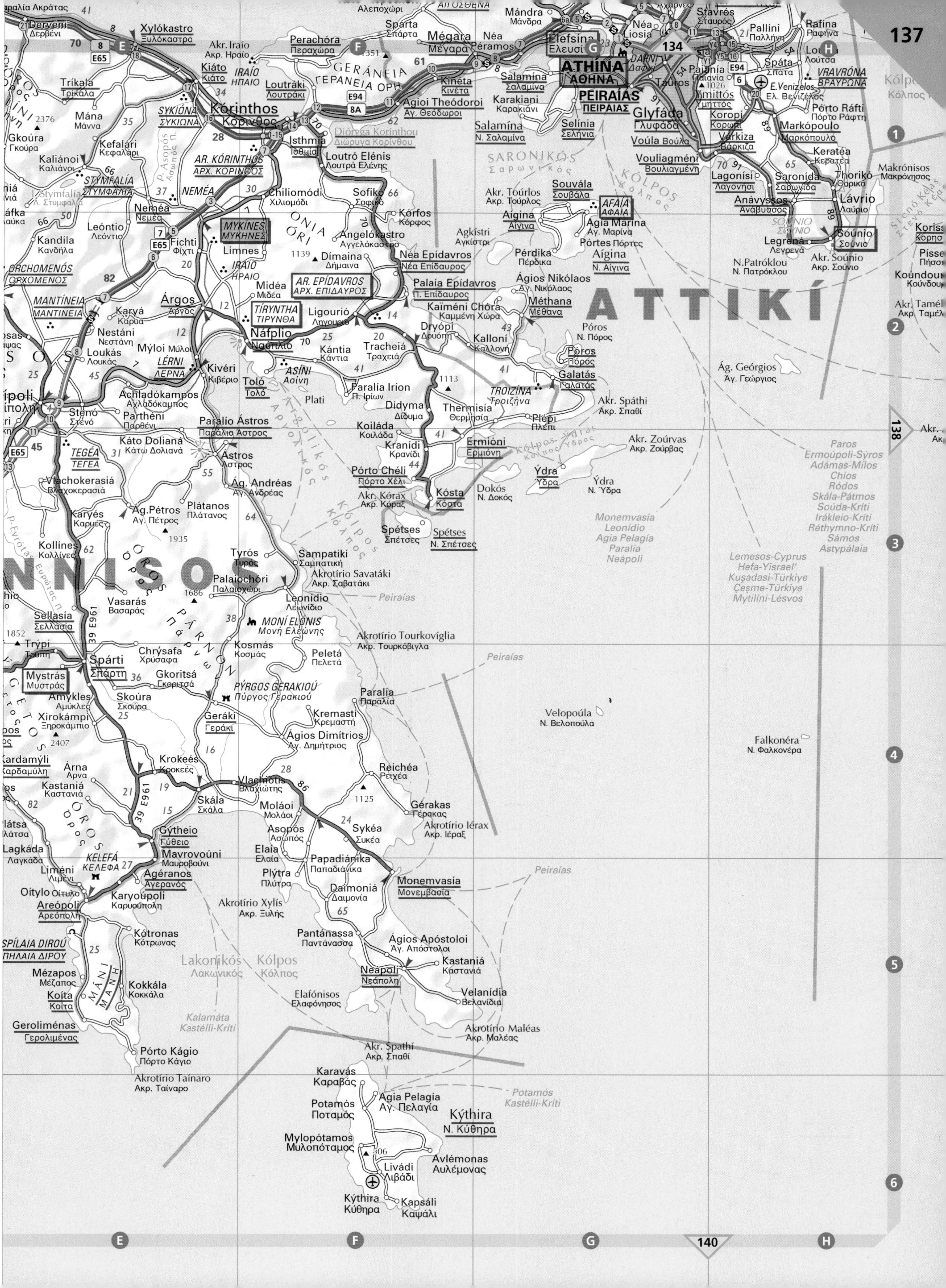
Dervéni
Δερβένι
Xylókastro
Ξυλόκαστρο
Akr. Iraío
Ακρ. Ηραίο
Perachóra
Περαχώρα
Spárta
Σπάρτα
Mégara
Μέγαρα
Néa Péramos
Mándra
Μάνδρα
Elefsína
Ελευσίνα
Néa Liosia
Stavrós
Σταυρός
Pallíni
Παλλήνη
Rafína
Ραφήνα
Kiáto
Κιάτο
IRAÍO
ΗΡΑΙΟ
GERÁNEIA
ΓΕΡΑΝΕΙΑ ΟΡΗ
Loutráki
Λουτράκι
Kinéta
Κινέτα
Salamína
Σαλαμίνα
ATHÍNA
ΑΘΗΝΑ
PEIRAIÁS
ΠΕΙΡΑΙΑΣ
Daría
Dafní
Taúros
Paianía
Παιανία
Spáta
Σπάτα
Loútsa
Λούτσα
VRAVRÓNA
ΒΡΑΥΡΩΝΑ
Kólpos
Κόλπος
Tríkala
Τρίκαλα
Mána
Μάννα
Kórinthos
Κόρινθος
SYKIÓNA
ΣΥΚΙΩΝΑ
Agioi Theódoroi
Άγ. Θεόδωροι
Karakiani
Καρακιάνι
Ymittós
Υμηττός
E.Venizelos
Ελ. Βενιζέλος
Pórto Ráfti
Πόρτο Ράφτη
Gkoúra
Γκούρα
Kefalári
Κεφαλάρι
Isthmia
Ισθμία
Diórvga Korínthou
Διώρυγα Κορίνθου
Salamína
Ν. Σαλαμίνα
Selínia
Σελήνια
Glyfáda
Γλυφάδα
Koropí
Κορωπί
Markópoulo
Μαρκόπουλο
Kalianoi
Καλιάνοι
STYMFALÍA
ΣΤΥΜΦΑΛΙΑ
AR. KÓRINTHOS
ΑΡΧ. ΚΟΡΙΝΘΟΣ
Loutró Elénis
Λουτρά Ελένης
Voúla
Βούλα
Várkiza
Βάρκιζα
Keratéa
Κερατέα
SARONIKÓS
Σαρωνικός
KÓLPOS
Κόλπος
Vouliagméni
Βουλιαγμένη
Lagonísi
Λαγονήσι
Saronída
Σαρωνίδα
Thorikó
Θορικό
Makrónisos
Μακρόνησος
Lávrio
Λαύριο
Stymfalía
Λ. Στυμφαλία
NEMÉA
Chiliomódi
Χιλιομόδι
Sofikó
Σοφικό
Akr. Toúrlos
Ακρ. Τούρλος
Souvála
Σουβάλα
AFAÍA
ΑΦΑΙΑ
Anávyssos
Ανάβυσσος
Neméa
Νεμέα
Kórfos
Κόρφος
Aígina
Αίγινα
Agía Marína
Αγ. Μαρίνα
SOÚNIO
ΣΟΥΝΙΟ
Soúnio
Σούνιο
Leóntio
Λεόντιο
Kandíla
Κανδήλα
Fichti
Φίχτι
MYKÍNES
ΜΥΚΗΝΕΣ
Límnes
Angelókastro
Αγγελόκαστρο
Agkístri
Αγκίστρι
Pórtes
Πόρτες
Legrená
Λεγρενά
Dímaina
Δήμαινα
Néa Epídavros
Νέα Επίδαυρος
Pérdika
Πέρδικα
Aígina
Ν. Αίγινα
N.Patróklou
Ν. Πατρόκλου
Akr. Soúnio
Ακρ. Σούνιο
ORCHOMENÓS
ΟΡΧΟΜΕΝΟΣ
IRAÍO
ΗΡΑΙΟ
Midéa
Μιδέα
AR. EPÍDAVROS
ΑΡΧ. ΕΠΙΔΑΥΡΟΣ
Palaía Epídavros
Π. Επίδαυρος
Ágios Nikólaos
Αγ. Νικόλαος
Méthana
Μέθανα
MANTÍNEIA
ΜΑΝΤΙΝΕΙΑ
Karyá
Καρυά
Árgos
Άργος
TÍRYNTHA
ΤΙΡΥΝΘΑ
Ligourió
Λυγουριό
Kaiméni Chóra
Καμμένη Χώρα
ATTIKÍ
Nestáni
Νεστάνη
Náfplio
Ναύπλιο
Drymós
Δρυόπη
Kalloní
Καλλονή
Póros
Ν. Πόρος
Lukás
Λουκάς
Mýloi
Μύλοι
Kántia
Κάντια
Tracheiá
Τραχειά
Póros
Πόρος
Ág. Geórgios
Άγ. Γεώργιος
LÉRNI
ΛΕΡΝΑ
Kivéri
Κιβέριο
ASÍNI
Ασίνη
Toló
Τολό
Paralía Iríon
Π. Ιρίων
TROIZÍNA
Τροιζήνα
Galatás
Γαλατάς
Achladókampos
Αχλαδόκαμπος
Plati
Dídyma
Δίδυμα
Thermisía
Θερμησία
Plépi
Πλέπι
Akr. Spáthi
Ακρ. Σπαθί
Parthéni
Παρθένι
Paralío Ástros
Παράλιο Άστρος
Koiláda
Κοιλάδα
Stenó
Στενό
Kranídi
Κρανίδι
Ermióni
Ερμιόνη
Kólpos Ýdras
Κόλπος Ύδρας
Akr. Zoúrvas
Ακρ. Ζούρβας
Káto Doliána
Κάτω Δολιανά
TEGÉA
ΤΕΓΕΑ
Ástros
Άστρος
Pórto Chéli
Πόρτο Χέλι
Ýdra
Ύδρα
Ýdra
Ν. Ύδρα
Vlachokerasiá
Βλαχοκερασιά
Ág. Andréas
Αγ. Ανδρέας
Akr. Kórax
Ακρ. Κόρας
Kósta
Κόστα
Dokós
Ν. Δοκός
Paros
Ermoúpoli-Sýros
Adámas-Mílos
Chíos
Ródos
Skála-Pátmos
Soúda-Kríti
Irákleio-Kríti
Réthymno-Kríti
Sámos
Astypálaia
Karyés
Καρυές
Ag.Pétros
Αγ. Πέτρος
Plátanos
Πλάτανος
Spétses
Σπέτσες
Spétses
Ν. Σπέτσες
Monemvasía
Leonídio
Agia Pelagia
Paralía
Neápoli
Kollínes
Κολλίνες
Tyrós
Τυρός
Sampatikí
Σαμπατική
Lemesos-Cyprus
Hefa-Yisrael'
Kuşadasi-Türkiye
Çeşme-Türkiye
Mytilíni-Lésvos
NNISOS
ÓROS
Palaiochóri
Παλαιοχώρι
Akrotírio Savatáki
Ακρ. Σαβατάκι
Vasarás
Βασαράς
PÁRNON
Leonídio
Λεωνίδιο
Peiraías
Sellasía
Σελλασία
MONÍ ELONIS
Μονή Ελώνης
Trýpi
Chrýsafa
Χρύσαφα
Kosmás
Κοσμάς
Akrotírio Tourkovíglia
Ακρ. Τουρκοβίγλα
Spárti
Σπάρτη
Peletá
Πελετά
Mystrás
Μυστράς
Gkoritsá
Γκοριτσά
PÝRGOS GERAKIOÚ
Πύργος Γερακιού
Amýkles
Αμύκλες
Skoúra
Σκούρα
Paralía
Παραλία
Xirokámpi
Ξηροκάμπι
Geráki
Γεράκι
Kremasti
Κρεμαστή
Velopoúla
Ν. Βελοπούλα
Ágios Dimítrios
Αγ. Δημήτριος
Falkonéra
Ν. Φαλκονέρα
Kardamýli
Καρδαμύλη
Árna
Άρνα
Krokeés
Κροκεές
Reichéa
Ρειχέα
Kastaniá
Καστανιά
Vlachiótis
Βλαχιώτης
Skála
Σκάλα
Moláoi
Μολάοι
Gérakas
Γέρακας
Akrotírio Iérax
Ακρ. Ιέραξ
Asopós
Ασωπός
Sykéa
Συκέα
Gýtheio
Γύθειο
Lagkáda
Λαγκάδα
Elaía
Ελαία
KELEFÁ
ΚΕΛΕΦΑ
Mavrovoúni
Μαυροβούνι
Papadiánika
Παπαδιάνικα
Liméni
Λιμένι
Agéranos
Αγερανός
Plýtra
Πλύτρα
Monemvasía
Μονεμβασία
Oítylo
Οίτυλο
Karyoúpoli
Καρυούπολη
Daimoniá
Δαιμονία
Areópoli
Αρεόπολη
Akrotírio Xylís
Ακρ. Ξυλής
SPÍLAIA DIROÚ
ΣΠΗΛΑΙΑ ΔΙΡΟΥ
Kótronas
Κότρωνας
Pantánassa
Παντάνασσα
Ágios Apóstoloi
Άγ. Απόστολοι
Lakonikós Kólpos
Λακωνικός Κόλπος
Mézapos
Μέζαπος
Neápoli
Νεάπολη
Kastaniá
Καστανιά
Kokkála
Κοκκάλα
MÁNI
ΜΑΝΗ
Koíta
Κοίτα
Elafónisos
Ελαφόνησος
Velanídia
Βελανίδια
Gerolimménas
Γερολιμένας
Kalamáta
Kastélli-Kríti
Akrotírio Maléas
Ακρ. Μαλέας
Pórto Kágio
Πόρτο Κάγιο
Akr. Spathí
Ακρ. Σπαθί
Akrotírio Taínaro
Ακρ. Ταίναρο
Karavás
Καραβάς
Potamós
Kastélli-Kríti
Agia Pelagía
Αγ. Πελαγία
Potamós
Ποταμός
Kýthira
Ν. Κύθηρα
Mylopótamos
Μυλοπόταμος
Livádi
Λιβάδι
Avlémonas
Αυλέμονας
Kýthira
Κύθηρα
Kapsáli
Καψάλι
Korissía
Pisses
Koúndouros
Akr. Tamélos
138
E
F
G
H
140
1
2
3
4
5
6

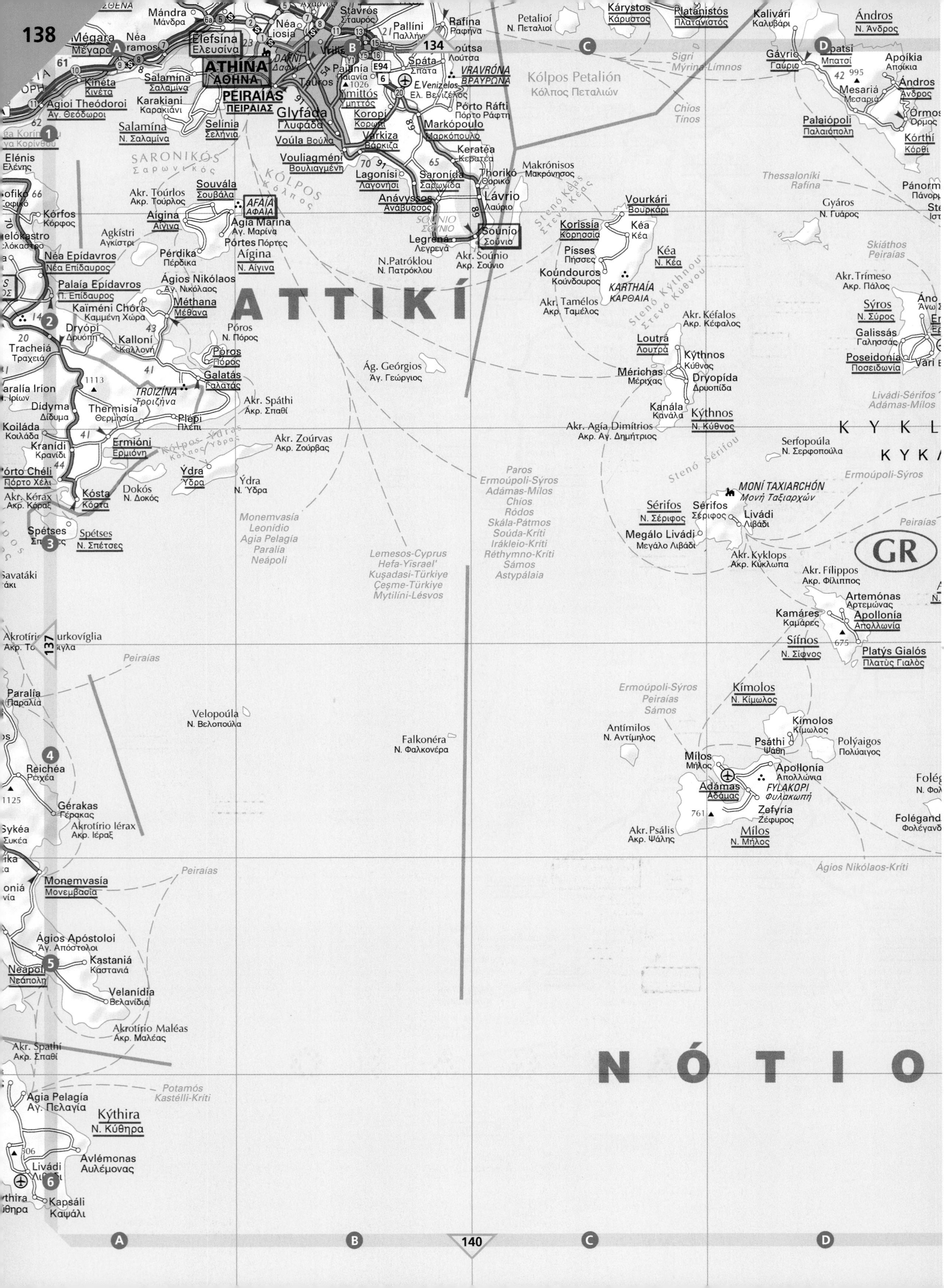
ATTIKÍ
NÓTIO
KYKL
GR
Mándra
Μάνδρα
Mégara
Μέγαρα
Elefsína
Ελευσίνα
ATHÍNA
ΑΘΗΝΑ
PEIRAIÁS
ΠΕΙΡΑΙΑΣ
Néa Liosia
Stavrós
Σταυρός
Pallíni
Παλλήνη
Rafína
Ραφήνα
Petalioí
Ν. Πεταλιοί
Kárystos
Κάρυστος
Platanistós
Πλατανιστός
Kalivári
Καλυβάρι
Ándros
Ν. Άνδρος
Kíneta
Κινέτα
Salamína
Σαλαμίνα
Agioi Theódoroi
Αγ. Θεόδωροι
Karakiani
Καρακιάνι
Selínia
Σελήνια
N. Σαλαμίνα
Glyfáda
Γλυφάδα
Voúla
Βούλα
Vouliagméni
Βουλιαγμένη
Ymittós
Υμηττός
Koropí
Κορωπί
Vári
Várkiza
Βάρκιζα
Spáta
Σπάτα
Paiania
Παιανία
Loútsa
Λούτσα
VRAVRÓNA
ΒΡΑΥΡΩΝΑ
E.Venizelos
Ελ. Βενιζέλος
Pórto Ráfti
Πόρτο Ράφτη
Markópoulo
Μαρκόπουλο
Keratéa
Κερατέα
Kólpos Petalión
Κόλπος Πεταλιών
Sigri
Mýrina-Límnos
Chíos
Tínos
Gávrio
Γαύριο
Batsí
Μπατσί
Apoíkia
Αποίκια
Mesariá
Μεσαριά
Ándros
Άνδρος
Órmos
Όρμος
Palaiópoli
Παλαιόπολη
Kórthi
Κόρθι
SARONIKÓS
Σαρωνικός
KÓLPOS
Κόλπος
Elénis
Ελένης
Sofikó
Σοφικό
Kórfos
Κόρφος
Akr. Toúrlos
Ακρ. Τούρλος
Souvála
Σουβάλα
AFAÍA
ΑΦΑΙΑ
Aígina
Αίγινα
Agía Marína
Αγ. Μαρίνα
Pórtes
Πόρτες
Agkístri
Αγκίστρι
Pérdika
Πέρδικα
Aígina
Ν. Αίγινα
Lagonísi
Λαγονήσι
Saronída
Σαρωνίδα
Anávyssos
Ανάβυσσος
Thorikó
Θορικό
Lávrio
Λαύριο
Makrónisos
Μακρόνησος
SOÚNIO
Legrená
Λεγρενά
Soúnio
Σούνιο
Akr. Soúnio
Ακρ. Σούνιο
N.Patróklou
Ν. Πατρόκλου
Thessaloníki
Rafína
Pánormos
Gyáros
Ν. Γυάρος
Vourkári
Βουρκάρι
Korissía
Κορησσία
Kéa
Κέα
Pisses
Πήσσες
Kéa
Ν. Κέα
Koúndouros
Κούνδουρος
KARTHAÍA
ΚΑΡΘΑΙΑ
Akr. Tamélos
Ακρ. Ταμέλος
Stenó Kéas
Στενό Κέας
Stenó Kýthnou
Στενό Κύθνου
Skiáthos
Peiraías
Akr. Trímeso
Ακρ. Πάλος
Sýros
Ν. Σύρος
Galissás
Γαλησσάς
Poseidonía
Ποσειδωνία
Vári
Neókastro
Néa Epídavros
Νέα Επίδαυρος
Palaía Epídavros
Π. Επίδαυρος
Ágios Nikólaos
Αγ. Νικόλαος
Kaïméni Chóra
Καμμένη Χώρα
Méthana
Μέθανα
Dryópi
Δρυόπη
Kalloní
Καλλονή
Póros
Ν. Πόρος
Póros
Πόρος
Galatás
Γαλατάς
TROIZÍNA
Τροιζήνα
Tracheiá
Τραχειά
Paralía Irion
Didyma
Δίδυμα
Thermisía
Θερμησία
Plépi
Πλέπι
Koiláda
Κοιλάδα
Kranídi
Κρανίδι
Ermióni
Ερμιόνη
Kólpos Ýdras
Κόλπος Ύδρας
Pórto Chéli
Πόρτο Χέλι
Akr. Kórax
Ακρ. Κόραξ
Kósta
Κόστα
Dokós
Ν. Δοκός
Ýdra
Ύδρα
Ýdra
Ν. Ύδρα
Spétses
Ν. Σπέτσες
Akr. Spáthi
Ακρ. Σπαθί
Ág. Geórgios
Άγ. Γεώργιος
Akr. Zoúrvas
Ακρ. Ζούρβας
Akr. Kéfalos
Ακρ. Κέφαλος
Loutrá
Λουτρά
Kýthnos
Κύθνος
Mérichas
Μέριχας
Dryopída
Δρυοπίδα
Kanála
Κανάλα
Kýthnos
Ν. Κύθνος
Akr. Agía Dimítrios
Ακρ. Αγ. Δημήτριος
Livádi-Sérifos
Adámas-Mílos
Serfopoúla
Ν. Σερφοπούλα
Stenó Sérifou
MONÍ TAXIARCHÓN
Μονή Ταξιαρχών
Sérifos
Ν. Σέριφος
Sérifos
Σέριφος
Livádi
Λιβάδι
Megálo Livádi
Μεγάλο Λιβάδι
Akr. Kyklops
Ακρ. Κύκλωπα
Ermoúpoli-Sýros
Peiraías
Monemvasía
Leonídio
Agia Pelagía
Paralía
Neápoli
Paros
Ermoúpoli-Sýros
Adámas-Mílos
Chíos
Ródos
Skála-Pátmos
Soúda-Kríti
Irákleio-Kríti
Réthymno-Kríti
Sámos
Astypálaia
Lemesos-Cyprus
Hefa-Yisrael'
Kuşadasi-Türkiye
Çeşme-Türkiye
Mytilíni-Lésvos
Savatáki
Akr. Fílippos
Ακρ. Φίλιππος
Artemónas
Αρτεμώνας
Kamáres
Καμάρες
Apollonía
Απολλωνία
Sífnos
Ν. Σίφνος
Platýs Gialós
Πλατύς Γιαλός
Akrotírio Kourkovíglia
Peiraías
Paralía
Παραλία
Velopoúla
Ν. Βελοπούλα
Falkonéra
Ν. Φαλκονέρα
Ermoúpoli-Sýros
Peiraías
Sámos
Kímolos
Ν. Κίμωλος
Kímolos
Κίμωλος
Antímilos
Ν. Αντίμηλος
Psáthi
Ψάθη
Polýaigos
Πολύαιγος
Mílos
Μήλος
Apollonía
Απολλώνια
Adámas
Αδάμας
FYLAKOPI
Φυλακωπή
Zefyría
Ζεφύρια
Akr. Psális
Ακρ. Ψάλης
Mílos
Ν. Μήλος
Folégandros
Φολέγανδρος
Reichéa
Ρειχέα
Gérakas
Γέρακας
Akrotírio Iérax
Ακρ. Ιέραξ
Sykéa
Συκέα
Monemvasía
Μονεμβασία
Peiraías
Ágios Nikólaos-Kríti
Ágios Apóstoloi
Άγ. Απόστολοι
Kastaniá
Καστανιά
Neápoli
Νεάπολη
Velanídia
Βελανίδια
Akrotírio Maléas
Ακρ. Μαλέας
Akr. Spathí
Ακρ. Σπαθί
Potamós
Kastélli-Kríti
Agia Pelagía
Αγ. Πελαγία
Kýthira
Ν. Κύθηρα
Avlémonas
Αυλέμονας
Livádi
Kapsáli
Καψάλι
134
137
140
A
B
C
D
1
2
3
4
5
6

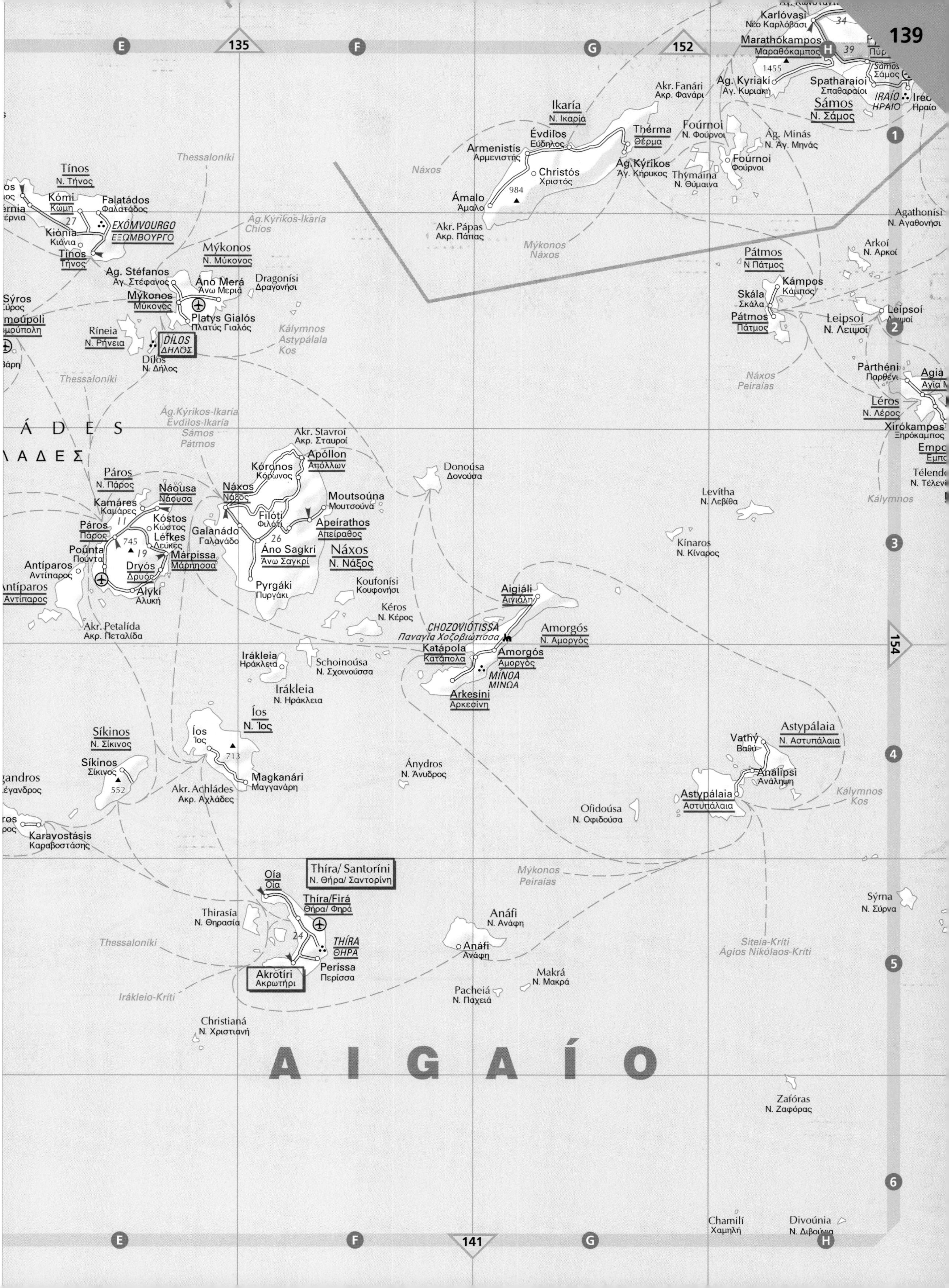

135
152
154
141
E
F
G
H
1
2
3
4
5
6
Karlóvasi
Νεο Καρλόβασι
Marathókampos
Μαραθόκαμπος
1455
Ag. Kyriakí
Αγ. Κυριακή
Spatharaíoi
Σπαθαραίοι
IRAÍO
ΗΡΑΙΟ
Sámos
Ν. Σάμος
Akr. Fanári
Ακρ. Φανάρι
Ikaría
Ν. Ικαρία
Évdilos
Εύδηλος
Thérma
Θέρμα
Foúrnoi
Ν. Φούρνοι
Ág. Minás
Ν. Άγ. Μηνάς
Armenistís
Αρμενιστής
Christós
Χριστός
Ag. Kýrikos
Άγ. Κήρυκος
Thýmaina
Ν. Θύμαινα
Foúrnoi
Φούρνοι
984
Ámalo
Άμαλο
Akr. Pápas
Ακρ. Πάπας
Náxos
Thessaloníki
Tínos
Ν. Τήνος
Kómi
Κώμη
Falatádos
Φαλατάδος
27
EXÓMVOURGO
ΕΞΩΜΒΟΥΡΓΟ
Kiónia
Κιόνια
Tínos
Τήνος
Ág. Kýrikos-Ikaría
Chíos
Mýkonos
Ν. Μύκονος
Ag. Stéfanos
Αγ. Στέφανος
Áno Merá
Άνω Μεριά
Dragonísi
Δραγονήσι
Mýkonos
Μύκονος
Platys Gialós
Πλατύς Γιαλός
Sýros
Rineia
Ν. Ρήνεια
DÍLOS
ΔΗΛΟΣ
Dílos
Ν. Δήλος
Kálymnos
Astypálaia
Kos
Mýkonos
Náxos
Agathonísi
Ν. Αγαθονήσι
Arkoí
Ν. Αρκοί
Pátmos
Ν. Πάτμος
Kámpos
Κάμπος
Skála
Σκάλα
Pátmos
Πάτμος
Leipsoí
Ν. Λειψοί
Leipsoí
Náxos
Peiraías
Parthéni
Παρθένι
Agia
Léros
Ν. Λέρος
Xirókampos
Ξηρόκαμπος
Télendos
Kálymnos
Thessaloníki
Ág. Kýrikos-Ikaría
Évdilos-Ikaría
Sámos
Pátmos
ÁDES
ΛΑΔΕΣ
Akr. Stavroí
Ακρ. Σταυροί
Apóllon
Απόλλων
Kóronos
Κόρωνος
Páros
Ν. Πάρος
Náousa
Νάουσα
Náxos
Νάξος
Moutsoúna
Μουτσούνα
Donoúsa
Δονούσα
Kamáres
Καμάρες
Kóstos
Κώστος
Filóti
Φιλότι
26
Apeírathos
Απείραθος
11
Páros
Πάρος
Léfkes
Λεύκες
Galanádo
Γαλανάδο
745
19
Poúnta
Πούντα
Márpissa
Μάρπισσα
Áno Sagkrí
Άνω Σαγκρί
Náxos
Ν. Νάξος
Levítha
Ν. Λεβίθα
Kínaros
Ν. Κίναρος
Antíparos
Αντίπαρος
Dryós
Δρυός
Antíparos
Ν. Αντίπαρος
Alykí
Αλυκή
Pyrgáki
Πυργάκι
Koufonísi
Κουφονήσι
Aigiáli
Αιγιάλη
Kéros
Ν. Κέρος
Akr. Petalída
Ακρ. Πεταλίδα
CHOZOVIÓTISSA
Panagía Χοζοβιώτισσα
Amorgós
Ν. Αμοργός
Katápola
Κατάπολα
Amorgós
Αμοργός
Irákleia
Ηράκλεια
Schoinoúsa
Ν. Σχοινούσα
MÍNOA
ΜΙΝΩΑ
Arkesíni
Αρκεσίνη
Irákleia
Ν. Ηράκλεια
Íos
Ν. Ίος
Síkinos
Ν. Σίκινος
Íos
Ίος
713
Astypálaia
Ν. Αστυπάλαια
Vathý
Βαθύ
Síkinos
Σίκινος
Magkanári
Μαγκανάρι
Ánydros
Ν. Άνυδρος
Análipsi
Ανάληψη
552
Akr. Achládes
Ακρ. Αχλάδες
Astypálaia
Αστυπάλαια
Kálymnos
Kos
Ofidoúsa
Ν. Οφιδούσα
Karavostásis
Καραβοστάσης
Thíra/ Santoríni
Ν. Θήρα/ Σαντορίνη
Oía
Οία
Mýkonos
Peiraías
Thíra/Firá
Θήρα/ Φηρά
Sýrna
Ν. Σύρνα
Thirasía
Ν. Θηρασία
Anáfi
Ν. Ανάφη
Thessaloníki
24
THÍRA
ΘΗΡΑ
Anáfi
Ανάφη
Siteía-Kríti
Ágios Nikólaos-Kríti
Akrotíri
Ακρωτήρι
Perissa
Περίσσα
Makrá
Ν. Μακρά
Pacheiá
Ν. Παχειά
Irákleio-Kríti
Christianá
Ν. Χριστιανή
AIGAÍO
Zafóras
Ν. Ζαφόρας
Chamilí
Χαμηλή
Divoúnia
Ν. Διβούνια

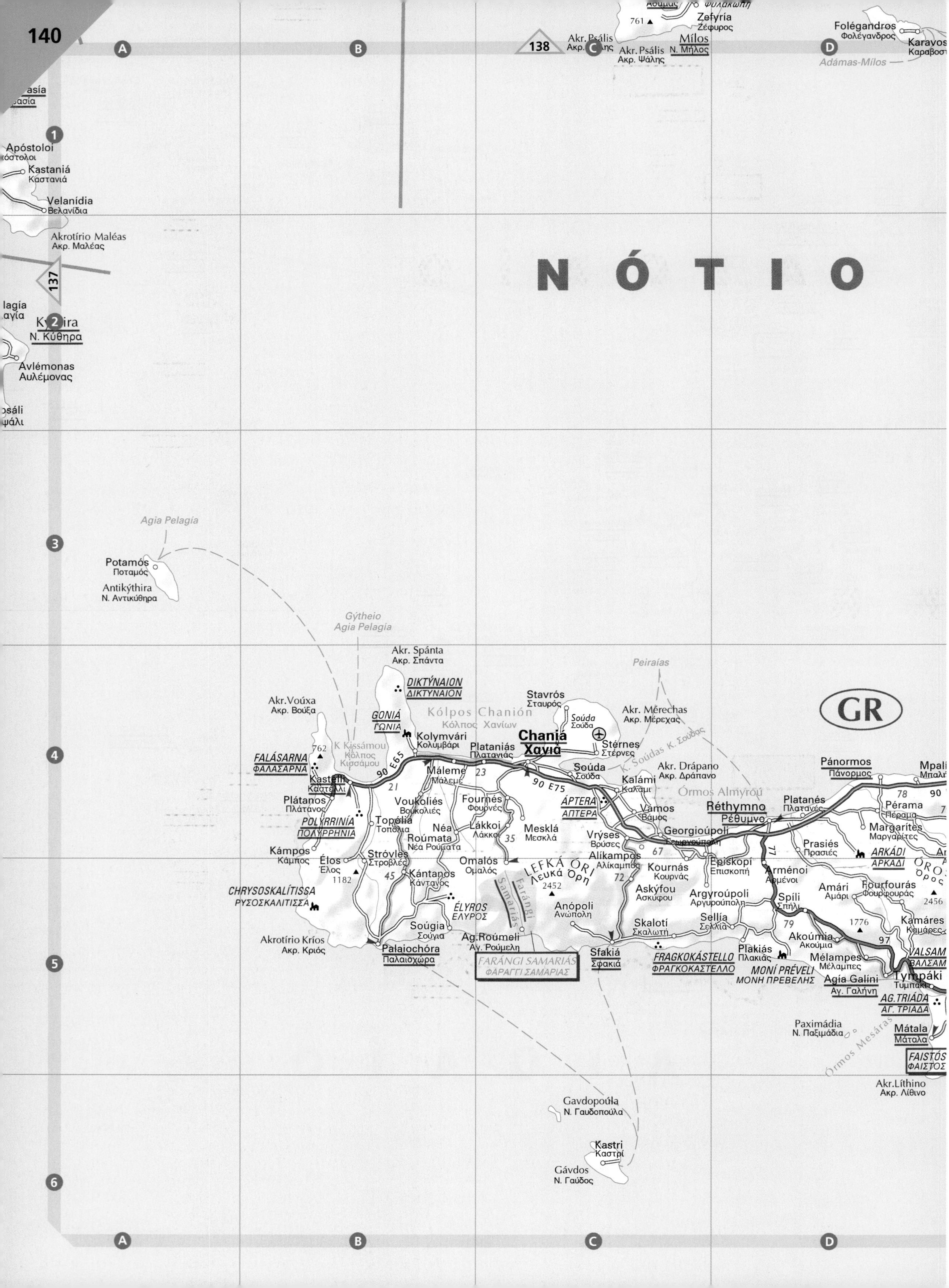

A
B
C
D
138
Akr. Psális
Akr. Psális
Ακρ. Ψάλης
Mílos
Ν. Μήλος
761
Zefyría
Ζέφυρος
Folégandros
Φολέγανδρος
Karavos
Adámas-Mílos
1
Apóstoloi
Kastaniá
Καστανιά
Velanídia
Βελανίδια
Akrotírio Maléas
Ακρ. Μαλέας
137
2
Kythira
Ν. Κύθηρα
Avlémonas
Αυλέμονας
NÓTIO
3
Agia Pelagía
Potamós
Ποταμός
Antikýthira
Ν. Αντικύθηρα
Gýtheio
Agia Pelagía
Akr. Spánta
Ακρ. Σπάντα
DIKTÝNAION
ΔΙΚΤΥΝΑΙΟΝ
GONIÁ
ΓΩΝΙΑ
Kólpos Chanión
Κόλπος Χανίων
Stavrós
Σταυρός
Soúda
Σούδα
Akr. Mérechas
Ακρ. Μέρεχας
Peiraías
GR
4
Akr.Voúxa
Ακρ. Βούξα
762
K Kissámou
Κόλπος Κισσάμου
FALÁSARNA
ΦΑΛΑΣΑΡΝΑ
Kastélli
Καστέλλι
Kolymvári
Κολυμβάρι
Plataniás
Πλατανιάς
Chaniá
Χανιά
Stérnes
Στέρνες
K. Soúdas
Κ. Σούδας
Akr. Drápano
Ακρ. Δράπανο
Pánormos
Πάνορμος
Mpali
90 E65
Máleme
Μάλεμε
23
90 E75
Soúda
Σούδα
Kalámi
Καλάμι
Órmos Almyroú
Platanés
Πλατανές
Réthymno
Ρέθυμνο
78
Pérama
Πέραμα
90
Plátanos
Πλάτανος
21
Voukoliés
Βουκολιές
Fournés
Φουρνές
ÁPTERA
ΑΠΤΕΡΑ
Vámos
Βάμος
Margarítes
Μαργαρίτες
POLYRRINÍA
ΠΟΛΥΡΡΗΝΙΑ
Topólia
Τοπόλια
Néa Roúmata
Νέα Ρούματα
Lákkoi
Λάκκοι
35
Mesklá
Μεσκλά
Vrýses
Βρύσες
Georgioúpoli
Γεωργιούπολη
Prasiés
Πρασιές
Kámpos
Κάμπος
Élos
Έλος
Strovlés
Στροβλές
Omalós
Ομαλός
LEFKÁ ÓRI
Λευκά Όρη
Alíkampos
Αλίκαμπος
67
Episkopí
Επισκοπή
77
ARKÁDI
ΑΡΚΑΔΙ
1182
45
Kántanos
Κάντανος
Faráñgi Samariás
2452
72
Kournás
Κουρνάς
Arménoi
Αρμένοι
CHRYSOSKALÍTISSA
ΧΡΥΣΟΣΚΑΛΙΤΙΣΣΑ
ÉLYROS
ΕΛΥΡΟΣ
Anópoli
Ανώπολη
Askýfou
Ασκύφου
Argyroúpoli
Αργυρούπολη
Spíli
Σπήλι
Amári
Αμάρι
Fourfourás
Φουρφουράς
2456
5
Akrotírio Kríos
Ακρ. Κριός
Soúgia
Σούγια
Ag.Roúmeli
Αγ. Ρούμελη
Skaloti
Σκαλωτή
Sellía
Σελλία
1776
79
Kamáres
Καμάρες
Palaiochóra
Παλαιοχώρα
FARÁNGI SAMARIÁS
ΦΑΡΑΓΓΙ ΣΑΜΑΡΙΑΣ
Sfakiá
Σφακιά
FRAGKOKÁSTELLO
ΦΡΑΓΚΟΚΑΣΤΕΛΛΟ
Plakiás
Πλακιάς
Akoúmia
Ακούμια
97
MONÍ PRÉVELI
ΜΟΝΗ ΠΡΕΒΕΛΗΣ
Mélampes
Μέλαμπες
Agía Galíni
Αγ. Γαλήνη
Tympáki
Τυμπάκι
AG. TRIÁDA
ΑΓ. ΤΡΙΑΔΑ
Paximádia
Ν. Παξιμάδια
Órmos Mesáras
Mátala
Μάταλα
FAISTÓS
ΦΑΙΣΤΟΣ
Akr.Líthino
Ακρ. Λίθινο
Gavdopoúla
Ν. Γαυδοπούλα
Kastri
Καστρί
Gávdos
Ν. Γαύδος
6

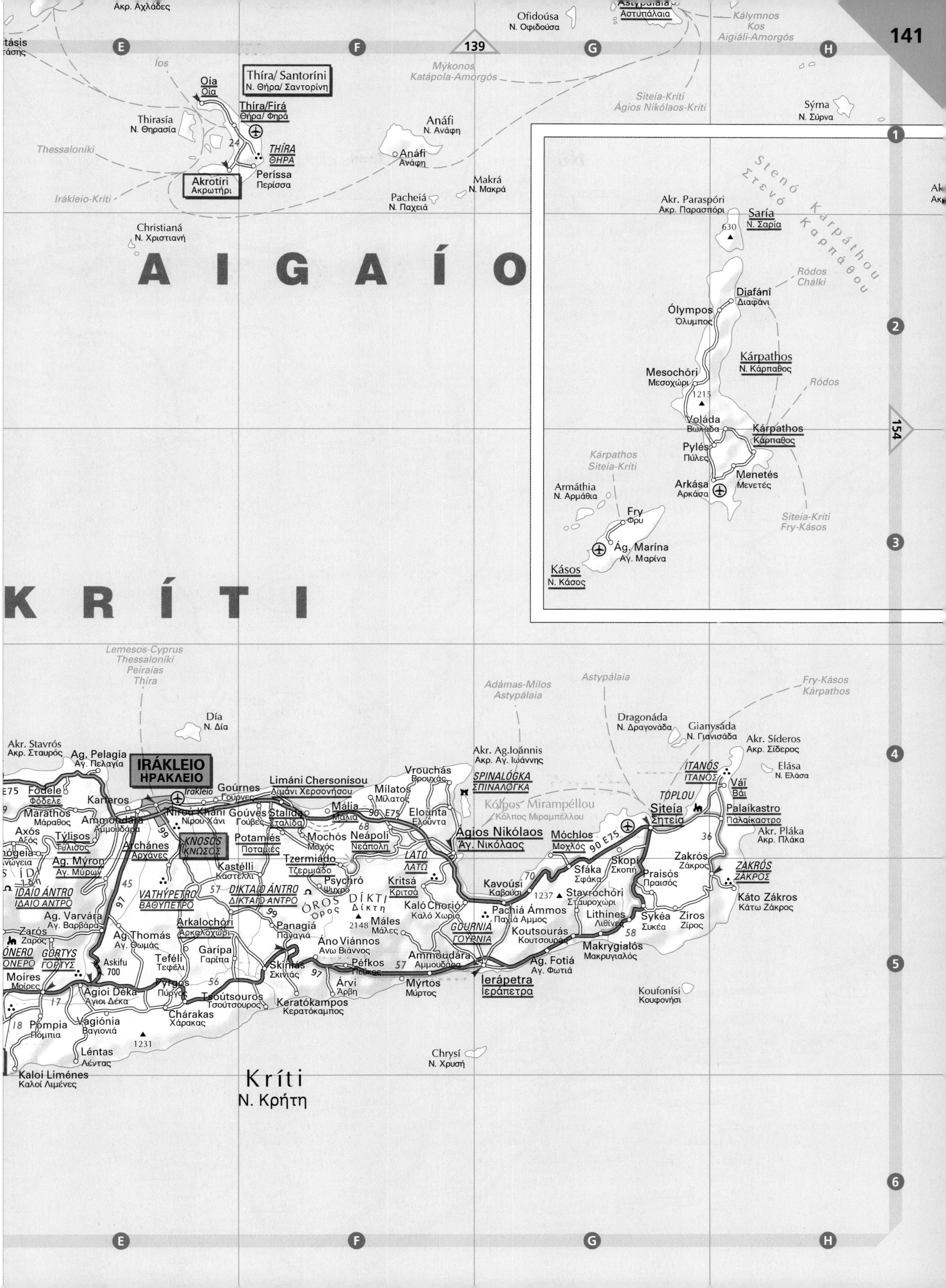
Akr. Achládes
Akr. Αχλάδες
Ofidoúsa
N. Οφιδούσα
Astypálaia
Αστυπάλαια
Kálymnos
Kos
Aigiáli-Amorgós
139
Íos
Thíra/ Santoríni
N. Θήρα/ Σαντορίνη
Oía
Οία
Mýkonos
Katápola-Amorgós
Siteía-Kríti
Ágios Nikólaos-Kríti
Sýrna
N. Σύρνα
Thirasía
N. Θηρασία
Thíra/Firá
Θήρα/ Φηρά
Anáfi
N. Ανάφη
THÍRA
ΘΗΡΑ
Thessaloníki
Anáfi
Ανάφη
Akrotíri
Ακρωτήρι
Perissa
Περίσσα
Makrá
N. Μακρά
Pacheiá
N. Παχειά
Irákleio-Kríti
Christianá
N. Χριστιανή
AIGAÍO
Steno Karpáthou
Στενό Καρπάθου
Akr. Paraspóri
Akr. Παρασπόρι
Saría
N. Σαρία
630
Ródos
Chálki
Diafáni
Διαφάνι
Ólympos
Όλυμπος
Kárpathos
N. Κάρπαθος
Mesochóri
Μεσοχώρι
1215
Ródos
Voláda
Βωλάδα
Kárpathos
Κάρπαθος
Pylés
Πύλες
Kárpathos
Siteía-Kríti
Menetés
Μενετές
Arkása
Αρκάσα
Armáthia
N. Αρμάθια
Fry
Φρυ
Siteía-Kríti
Fry-Kásos
Ág. Marína
Αγ. Μαρίνα
Kásos
N. Κάσος
154
KRÍTI
Lemesos-Cyprus
Thessaloníki
Peiraias
Thíra
Adámas-Mílos
Astypálaia
Astypálaia
Fry-Kásos
Kárpathos
Día
N. Δία
Dragonáda
N. Δραγονάδα
Gianysáda
N. Γιανισάδα
Akr. Síderos
Akr. Σίδερος
Akr. Stavrós
Akr. Σταυρός
Ag. Pelagía
Αγ. Πελαγία
IRÁKLEIO
ΗΡΑΚΛΕΙΟ
Akr. Ag.Ioánnis
Akr. Αγ. Ιωάννης
Elása
N. Ελάσα
Vrouchás
Βρουχάς
SPINALÓGKA
ΣΠΙΝΑΛΟΓΚΑ
ITANÓS
ΙΤΑΝΟΣ
Fodele
Φόδελε
Karteros
Irakleio
Goúrnes
Γούρνες
Limáni Chersonísou
Λιμάνι Χερσονήσου
Mílatos
Μίλατος
Kólpos Mirampéllou
Κόλπος Μιραμπέλλου
TÓPLOU
Siteía
Σητεία
Vái
Βάι
Márathos
Μάραθος
Ammoudára
Αμμουδάρα
Nirou Khani
Νίρου Χάνι
Goúves
Γούβες
Stalída
Σταλίδα
Mália
Μάλια
Elounta
Ελούντα
Palaíkastro
Παλαίκαστρο
Axós
Αξός
Týlisos
Τύλισος
Archánes
Αρχάνες
KNOSÓS
ΚΝΩΣΟΣ
Potamiés
Ποταμιές
Mochós
Μοχός
Neápoli
Νεάπολη
Ágios Nikólaos
Άγ. Νικόλαος
Móchlos
Μοχλός
Akr. Pláka
Akr. Πλάκα
Ag. Mýron
Αγ. Μύρων
Tzermiádo
Τζερμιάδο
LATÓ
ΛΑΤΩ
Zakrós
Ζάκρος
ZAKRÓS
ΖΑΚΡΟΣ
Kastélli
Καστέλλι
Psychró
Ψυχρό
Kritsá
Κριτσά
Sfáka
Σφάκα
Skopí
Σκοπή
Praisós
Πραισός
IDAÍO ÁNTRO
ΙΔΑΙΟ ΑΝΤΡΟ
VATHÝPETRO
ΒΑΘΥΠΕΤΡΟ
DIKTAÍO ÁNTRO
ΔΙΚΤΑΙΟ ΑΝΤΡΟ
ÓROS DÍKTI
Όρος Δίκτη
Kavoúsi
Καβούσι
Stavrochóri
Σταυροχώρι
Káto Zákros
Κάτω Ζάκρος
Kaló Chorió
Καλό Χωριό
Pachiá Ámmos
Παχιά Άμμος
Ag. Varvára
Αγ. Βαρβάρα
Arkalochóri
Αρκαλοχώρι
Panagiá
Παναγιά
2148
Máles
Μάλες
GOURNIÁ
ΓΟΥΡΝΙΑ
Lithínes
Λιθίνες
Sykéa
Συκέα
Zíros
Ζίρος
Zarós
Ζαρός
Ag.Thomás
Αγ. Θωμάς
Áno Viánnos
Άνω Βιάννος
Koutsourás
Κουτσουράς
Makrygialós
Μακρυγιαλός
GÓRTYS
ΓΟΡΤΥΣ
Askifu
700
Teféli
Τεφέλι
Garípa
Γαρίπα
Skiniás
Σκινιάς
Péfkos
Πεύκος
Ammoudára
Αμμουδάρα
Ag. Fotiá
Αγ. Φωτιά
Moíres
Μοίρες
Agioi Déka
Άγιοι Δέκα
Pýrgos
Πύργος
Árvi
Άρβη
Mýrtos
Μύρτος
Ierápetra
Ιεράπετρα
Koufonísi
Κουφονήσι
Tsoútsouros
Τσούτσουρος
Keratókampos
Κερατόκαμπος
Chárakas
Χάρακας
Pompia
Πόμπια
Vagiónia
Βαγιονιά
1231
Léntas
Λέντας
Chrysí
N. Χρυσή
Kaloí Liménes
Καλοί Λιμένες
Kríti
N. Κρήτη
E
F
G
H
1
2
3
4
5
6

Oborovo
Popovac
Hercegovac
Podgarić
Končanica
Donja-
Vrijeska
Gornja-
N. Bukovica
Mikleuš
Čačinci
Valpovo
Beničanci
Bizovac
Mahovo
Potok
Popovača
Garešnica
Daruvar
Voćin
Ćeralije
Zdenci
Klokočevci
75
Žažina
Pokupsko
Stružec
Kutina
Uljanik
Badljevina
Gaj
Sirač
Španovica
Novo Zvečevo
Kamanski Vučiak
Slatinski Drenovac
Orahovica
PAPUK
Feričanci
Đurđenovac
Koška
Našice
Budimci
Martinci Čepinski
Sisak
Petrinja
Mošćenica
Gušće
Poljana
Pakrac
Velika
Vetovo
Kutjevo
Podgorač
Graberje
Glina
Kut
Blinja
Sunja
Lipovljani
Lipik
PSUNJ
Kamenska
Ferovac
Vukojevica
Potnjani
Topusko
Ravno Rašće
Vlaković
Maja
Dodoši
Novska
Rajić
HR
Požega
Jakšić
Ruševo
Breznica Đak.
Đakovo
Viškovci
Slovinci
Brestovac
Cernik
Jasenovac
Okučani
Nova Gradiška
Pleternica
Kondrić
Budrovci
Obljaj
Dragotina
Prevršac
Miočinovići
Stubal
Hrvatska Kostajnica
Živaja
DILJ
Vrpolje
Brezovo Polje
ZRINSKA GORA
Dubica
Nova Kapela
Batrina
Lužani
St. Slatnik
Sibinj
Podvinje
Garčin
D. Andrijevci
Velika Kopanica
Bosanska Bojna
Mala Kladuša
Bosanska Kostajnica
Bosanska Dubica
Draksenić
Stara Gradiška
Slavonski Brod
Zborište
Divuša
PROSARA
Bosanska Gradiška
Bosanski Brod
D. Stupnica
Knežica
Vrbaška
Gornji Podgradci
Razboj
MOTAJICA
N. Selo
Bosanski Šamac
Varoška Rijeka
Dvor
Blagaj Japra
Srbac
Velika Brusnica
Novi Grad
Odžak
Krakača
Bosanski Novi
KOZARA
Nova Topola
Crkvina
Mrazovac
Brezičani
Mrakovica
Nožičko
Derventa
Polje
Garavac
Cazin
Jezerski
Prijedor
NACIONALNI PARK KOZARA
Modriča
Otoka
Kozarac
Podnovlje
Čarakovo
Ivanjska
Laktaši
Milosavci
Modran
Pelagić
BOSANSKA
Klašnice
Lišnja
Kotorsko
Gradačac
Brekovica
Bosanska Krupa
Omarska
Prnjavor
Osinja
Budimić Japra
Oštra Luka
Vučkovci
Gudavac
KRAJINA
MANASTIR STERN
Ripač
Kamengrad
Stratinska
Jošavka
SVINJAR
Dubovsko
Sanski Most
DABARSKA SPILJA
Vrbanja
Dubrava
Kulaši
Doboj
Klokotnica
Lušci Palanka
Kola
Banja Luka
Čelinac
UZLOMAC
Šnjegotina Gornja
Gračanica
Kruge
Krnjeuša
SPILJA HRUSTOVAČA
Jagare
Makljenovac
Orašac
CRNI VRH
Vrhpolje
Dobrinja
Krupa na Vrbasu
Kotor Varoš
Klupe
Teslić
Jelah
OZREN
Vrtoče
Kamičak
Ribnik
Bosanski Petrovac
Krasulje
MANASTIR OZREN
Kulen Vakuf
Jesenovac
Velagići
Bočac
Maslovare
BORJA PLANINA
Maglaj
Lukavac
Donji Lapac
Kolunić
Ključ
Čađavica
MANJAČA
Gornji Lapac
Doljani
Oštrelj
KLEKOVAČA
Baljvine
Skender Vakuf
OLAUŠ
Blatnica
OSJEČENICA
Unac
Una
Mrkonjić-Grad
KANJON UGAR
BIH
Žepče
Zavidovići
Donja Suvaja
Podrašnica
Vozuća
TITOVA SPILJA
Drvar
Bruvno
Gornji srb
Donji Koričani
Begov Han
Ribnica
113
Protići
Jezero
VLAŠIĆ
Jajce
Nemila
Kupirovo
Poljice
Mliniště
Šipovo
Vrandu k
BOSNA KLANAC
Rijeka
CEROVAČKE ŠPILJE
Otrić
Resanovci
JADOVNIK
Rore
Mujdžić
Vinac
Turbe
Travnik
Zenica
Crkvice
Čuniš
Kaštel Žegarski
Bosansko Grahovo
Vagan
VITOROG
Todorići
Komar Prolaz
Novi Travnik
Kakanj
Vareš
BIJAMBARSKA PEĆINA
Zrmanja
Ervenik
ŠATOR
Medena Selišta
Donji Vakuf
Dubravica
Kaonik
Lašva
Ivančići
Padjene
Strmica
Crni Lug
STARETINA
Busovača
Kraljeva Sutjeska
Raducić
Knin
Glamoč
Bugojno
Srednje
DINARA
Polača
Kazanci
Carevac
CINCAR
Kupres
RADUŠA
Fojnica
Breza
Kistanje
Kijevo
Čelebić
Uskopolje
Visoko
Podlugovi
Oklaj
PROMINA
Semizovac
Bribir
Vrlika
Ilijaš
Jošanica
Širitovci
LIVANJSKO POLJE
Priluka
Kiseljak
Vogošća
NAC. PARK KRKA
Podosoje
Prijelaz Makljen
SARAJEVO
Skradin
Visovačko jezero
Drniš
Miočić
Maljkovo
Livno
Šuica
Rumboci
Prozor-Rama
TREBEVIĆ
SVILAJA
Peručko jezero
Gornji Ravno
Hadžići
Ilidža
SKRADINSKI BUK
Lozovac
Planjane
Guber
Jezero Šćit
Tarčin
Krupac
Kijevo
Hrvace
Srđevići
LJUBUŠA
Pazarić
Vrpolje
Ramljane
Obrovac
Tomislavgrad
Bradina
BJELAŠNICA
Sitno
Muć
KONJ
Prisoje
Jablaničko Jezero
Daljani
Trnovo
Brodarica
Kladnjice
Sinj
Kolo
Ostrožac
Konjic
TRESKAVICA
Korušce
Gizdavac
Brnaze
Turjaci
Buško Jezero
Lipa
Podborje
Jablanica
Prapatnica
SALONA
Dugopolje
Kamensko
Trilj
Aržano
PLOČNO
ČVRSNICA
Rogoznica
Bristvica
Lukšić
Kaštel Stari
Klis
Solin
Bisko
Budimir
Svib
Petrovići
PRENJ
Borci
VISOČICA
Seget
Marina
Trogir
Okrug
Čiovo
ŠPLIT
Stobreč
MOSOR
Ugljane
Cista Velika
Blato
Cista Provo
Gornja Grabovica
Čičevo
Kalinovik
Rt Ploča
Zadar
Splitski kanal
Jesenice
KANJON CETINE
Šestanovac
Imotski
Posušje
ČABULJA
NERETVA KANJON
Jasenjani
Krupac
Drvenik
Dugi Rat
Omiš
Zadvarje
Gorica
Kočerin
Potoci
Ulog
Maslinica
Rogač
Sutivan
Supetar
Brački kanal
Mimice
Zagvozd
Vinjani
Runović
Grude
Lištica
ZELENGORA
Rijeka Ancona
Šolta
Stomorska
Pučišća
Donja Brela
Baška Voda
Slivno
Drinovci
Široki Brijeg
Mostar
Vrapčići
VELEŽ
CRVANJ
Milna
Nerežišća
Povlja
NAC. PARK BIOKOVO
BIOKOVO
Pridvorci
Brač
Bol
Sumartin
Makarska
Kozica
Klobuk
Hamzići
Gnojnice
Plužine
Brbinj
Tučepi
Vitina
Blagaj
Nevesinje
Fojnica
Hvarski kanal
Podgora
Duge Njive
Ravča
Vrgorac
Orahovlje
Čitluk
Buna
VRELO BUNE
BJELAŠNICA
Vira
Stari Grad
Vrboska
Igrane
Živogošće
Drvenik
Ljubuški
Medugorje
Žitomislići
Rijeka
Hvar
Jelsa
Poljica
Hvar
Sućuraj
Mali Prolog
Počitelj
Domanovići
Tabaja
Gacko
Viški kanal
Zaostrog
Čapljina
Radimlja
Šćedro
Vela Luka
Gradac
HUTOVO BLATO
Kula Norinska
Dračevo
144
Korčula
Komiža
Vis
Korčulanski kanal
MOGORJELO
Gabela
Stolac
Bjeljani
Korita
Vis
Korčula
Lovište
Pelješac
Ploče
Metković
Mramor
Pocrnje
Fatnica
A
B
C
D
1
2
3
4
5
6

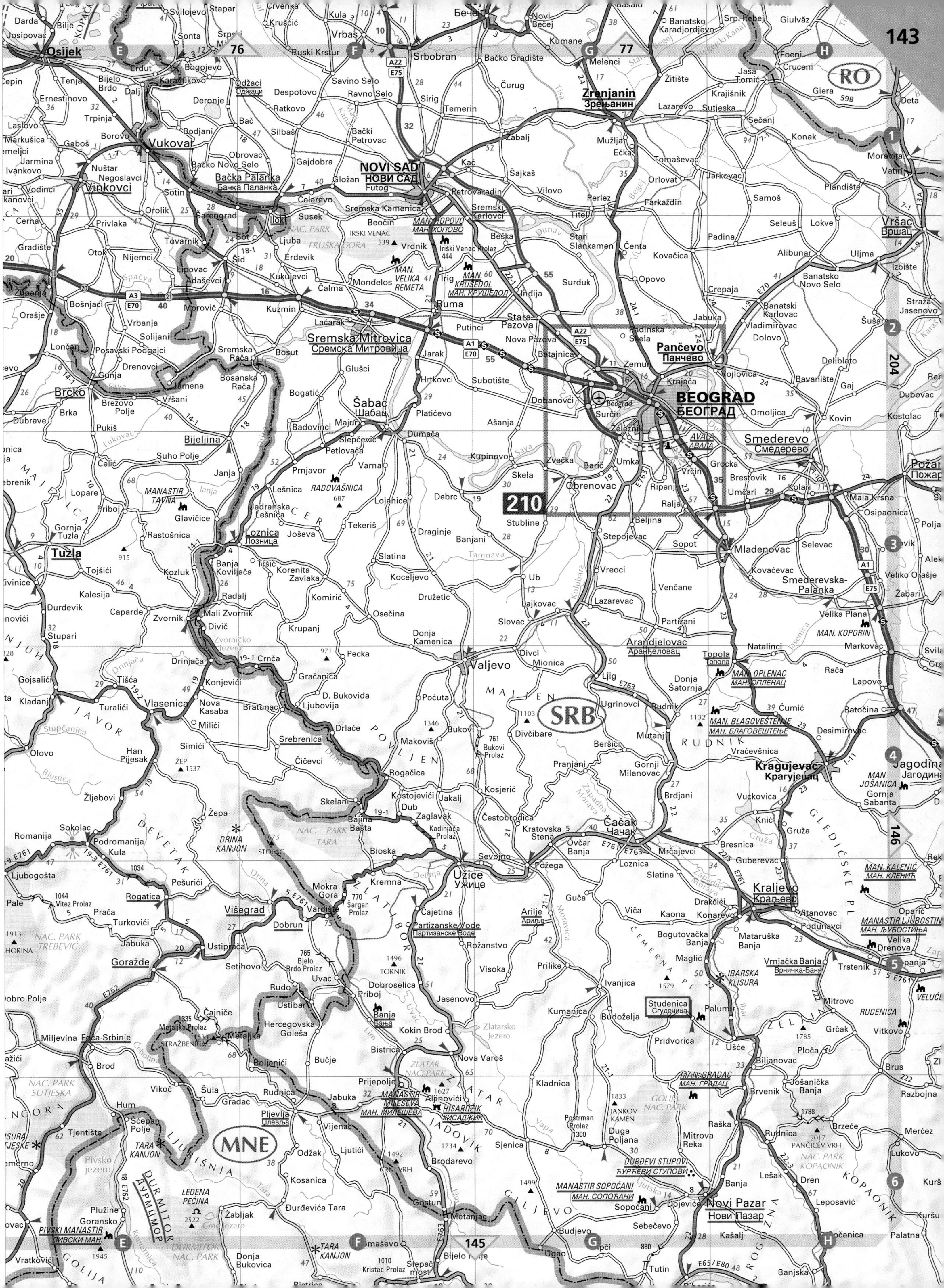
Osijek
Vukovar
Vinkovci
NOVI SAD
НОВИ САД
Zrenjanin
Зрењанин
Bačka Palanka
Бачка Паланка
Sremska Mitrovica
Сремска Митровица
Šabac
Шабац
BEOGRAD
БЕОГРАД
Pančevo
Панчево
Smederevo
Смедерево
Vršac
Вршац
Požarevac
Пожаревац
Brčko
Bijeljina
Tuzla
Loznica
Лозница
Zvornik
Valjevo
Mladenovac
Arandjelovac
Аранђеловац
Topola
Топола
Kragujevac
Крагујевац
Jagodina
Јагодина
Smederevska-Palanka
Čačak
Чачак
Užice
Ужице
Kraljevo
Краљево
Arilje
Ариље
Vrnjačka Banja
Врњачка-Бања
Novi Pazar
Нови Пазар
Priboj
Prijepolje
Pljevlja
Пљевља
Višegrad
Rogatica
Goražde
Foča-Srbinje
Srebrenica
Vlasenica
Studenica
Студеница
SRB
MNE
RO
MALJEN
RUDNIK
ZLATIBOR
JAVOR
DEVETAK
ZLATAR
JADOVIK
GOLIJA
KOPAONIK
ŽELJIN
GLEDIĆSKE PL.
ČEMERNA PL.
DURMITOR
ДУРМИТОР
LJUBIŠNJA
NAC. PARK FRUŠKA GORA
NAC. PARK TARA
NAC. PARK SUTJESKA
NAC. PARK KOPAONIK
DRINA KANJON
TARA KANJON
IBARSKA KLISURA
76
77
145
146
204
210
A1
E70
E75
E761
E763
A3
A22

A
B
C
D
142
1
2
3
4
5
6
HR
BIH
Kazanci
Čelebić
Carevac
Kupres
Bugojno
Fojnica
Visoko
Breza
Podlugovi
Ilijaš
Semizovac
Jošanica
Vogošća
Kiseljak
SARAJEVO
Ilidža
Hadžići
Tarčin
Pazarić
Bradina
Krupac
Kijevo
Pale
Trebević
Romanija
Sokolac
Podromanija
Kula
Ljubogošta
Vitez Prolaz
Prača
Turkovići
Rogat
Jabuka
Goražde
Žljebovi
NAC. PARK TREBEVIĆ
JAHORINA
Trnovo
Dobro Polje
Miljevina
Foča-Srbinje
Brod
Jažići
Kalinovik
Ulog
NAC. PARK SUTJESKA
ZELENGORA
KLISURA SUTJESKE
Tjentište
Hum
Šćepan Polje
Čemerno
Fojnica
Gacko
Avtovac
PIVSKI MANASTIR
Pivsko jezero
Plužine
Goransko
Vratkovići
GOLIJA
NJEGOŠ
Krstac
Živa Sec Sedlo Prolaz
Rastovac
Krupačko jezero
Velimlje
Kuside
Podbožur
Straševina
Slano jezero
Osječenica
Grahovo
Vilusi
Mosko
Lastva
Konjsko
Grab
ORJEN
Han
Risan
Dobra
Perast
Kotor
Котор
Kamenari
Lepetane
Tivat
Zelenika
Herceg Novi
Igalo
Radovići
Radanovići
LOVĆEN NAC. PARK
Boka Kotorska
Budva
Будва
Sveti Stefan
Свети Стефан
Vrbanje
Dubravka
Čilipi
Gruda
Cavtat
Mlini
Dubac
Lokrum
Dubrovnik
Trebinje
Ljubovo
Lug
Dobromani
Orahov Do
Zavala
Ravno
Veličani
VJETRENICA
Bileća
Bilećko jezero
Plana
Gradac
Ljubinje
VIDUŠA
Fatnica
Korita
Bijeljani
Berkovići
BJELAŠNICA
Tabaja
Nevesinje
Plužine
Pridvorci
VELEŽ
CRVANI
Krupac
Jasenjani
Potoci
Vrapčići
Čičevo
Borci
PRENJ
VISOČICA
TRESKAVICA
BJELAŠNICA
Konjic
Ostrožac
Jablanica
Jablaničko jezero
Daljani
Prozor-Rama
Jezero Šćit
Rumboci
Uskoplje
Prijelaz Makljen
RADUŠA
Šuica
Gornji Ravno
LJUBUŠA
Tomislavgrad
Prisoje
Kolo
Lipa
Podborje
Buško Jezero
Livno
Guber
Srdevići
CINCAR
LIVANJSKO POLJE
Priluka
Peručko jezero
Maljkovo
Podosoje
SVILAJA
Hrvace
Obrovac
Ramljane
Sinj
Muć
Kladnjice
Gizdavac
Brnaze
Turjaci
Trilj
Kamensko
Dugopolje
Bisko
SALONA
Klis
Solin
Kaštel Stari
Okrug
Čiovo
SPLIT
Stobreč
Jesenice
MOSOR
Ugljane
Budimir
Aržano
Cista Velika
Svib
Cista Provo
Blato
KANJON CETINE
Dugi Rat
Omiš
Zadvarje
Šestanovac
Imotski
Gorica
Posušje
Vinjani
Zagvozd
Runović
Slivno
Grude
Kočerin
Lištica
Široki Brijeg
Mostar
ČVRSNICA
Gornja Grabovica
ČABULJA
NERETVA KANJON
PLOČNO
Petrovići
Mimice
Donja Brela
Baška Voda
NAC. PARK BIOKOVO
BIOKOVO
Makarska
Tučepi
Podgora
Igrane
Živogošće
Drvenik
Zaostrog
Gradac
Kozica
Drinovci
Klobuk
Hamzići
Vitina
Čitluk
Orahovlje
Ljubuški
Mali Prolog
Vrgorac
Ravča
Duge Njive
Plina Jezero
Čapljina
Međugorje
Počitelj
Domanovići
Radimlja
Stolac
Pocrnje
Mramor
Cerovica
Hutovo
Neum
Gabela
Metković
Kula Norinska
Opuzen
Ploče
MEGORJELO
Blagaj
Buna
VRELO BUNE
Žitomislići
Gnojnice
Brijesta
Doli
Ston
Slano
Trsteno
Orašac
Šipan
Lopud
Olipa
Sobra
Korita
Mljet
MLJET NAC. PARC
Polače
Govedjari
Mljetski Kanal
Janjina
Pelješac
Trpanj
Orebić
Lovište
Korčula
Lumbarda
Čara
Blato
Vela Luka
Ubli
Lastovski Kanal
Lastovo
Sušac
Kopište
Korčulanski kanal
Ščedro
Sućuraj
Hvar
Jelsa
Poljica
Vrboska
Stari Grad
Vira
Hvarski kanal
Brač
Bol
Sumartin
Povlja
Pučišća
Nerežišća
Milna
Supetar
Sutivan
Bračkí kanal
Stomorska
Rogač
Brbinj
Rijeka
Vis
Bari
Palagruža
E65
E73
E761
E762
E80
E71

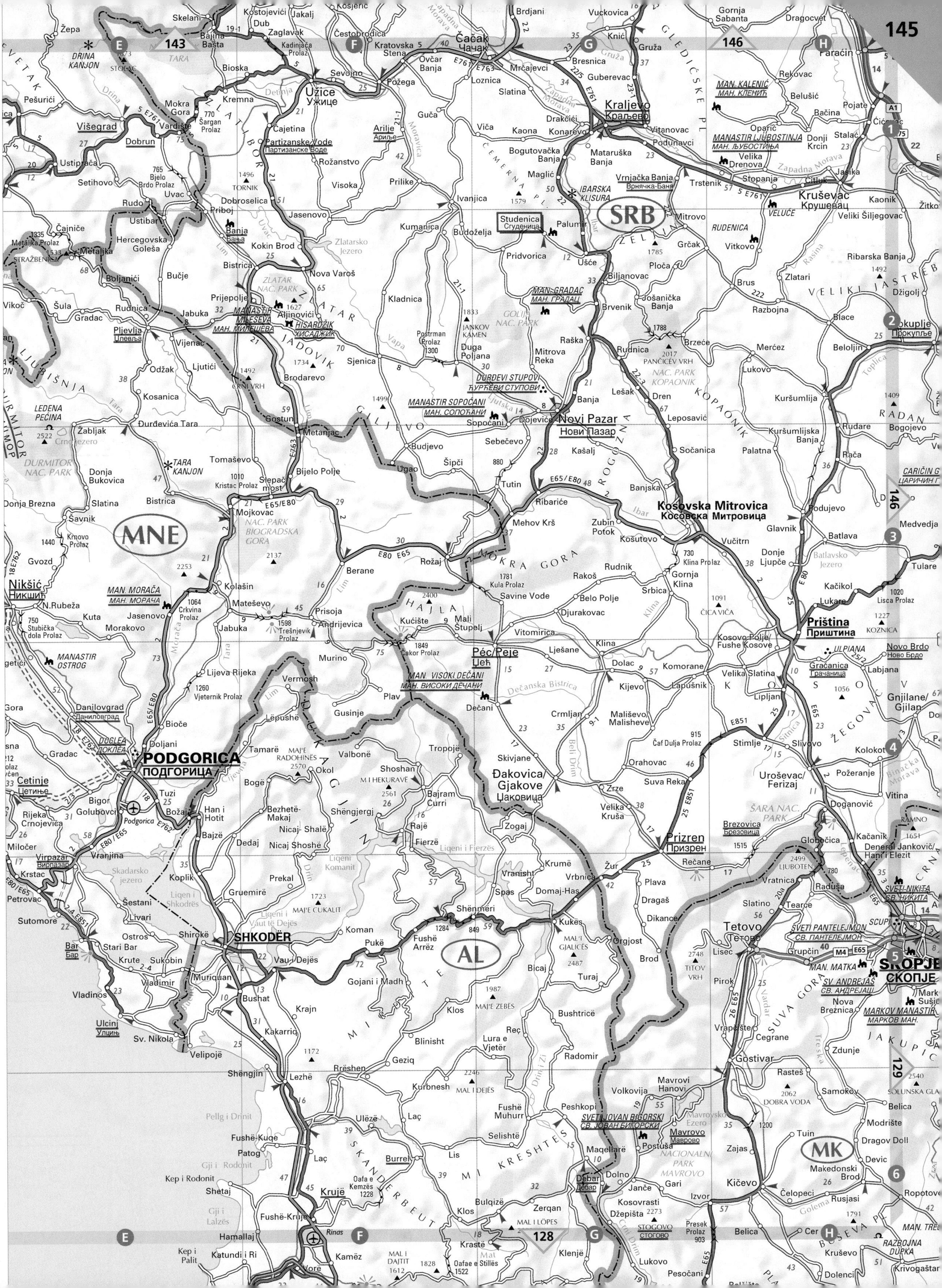

143
146
E
F
G
H
1
2
3
4
5
6
Žepa
Skelani
Kostojevići
Jakalj
Kosjerić
Brdjani
Vuckovica
Gornja Sabanta
Dragocvet
DRINA KANJON
Bajina Bašta
Dub
Zaglavak
Kadinjača Prolaz
Čestobrodica
Kratovska Stena
Čačak
Чачак
Bresnica
Knić
Gruža
Paraćin
TARA
STOLAC
Bioska
Sevojno
Ovčar Banja
Mrčajevci
Guberevac
GLEDIĆSKE PL.
Rekovac
Pešurići
Kremna
Užice
Ужице
Požega
Loznica
Slatina
MAN. KALENIĆ
МАН. КЛЕНИЋ
Belušić
Mokra Gora
ZLATIBOR
Drina
Kraljevo
Краљево
Bačina
Pojate
Višegrad
Vardište
Šargan Prolaz
Cajetina
Arilje
Ариље
Guča
Viča
Drakčići
Vitanovac
Oparić
Ćićevac
Dobrun
Kaona
Konarevo
MANASTIR LJUBOSTINJA
МАН. ЉУБОСТИЊА
Stalać
Donji Krcin
Partizanske Vode
Партизанске Воде
Bogutovačka Banja
Mataruška Banja
Podunavci
Velika Drenova
Ustiprača
Rožanstvo
Moravica
Zapadna Morava
Setihovo
Bjelo Brdo Prolaz
TORNIK
Visoka
Prilike
Maglić
Vrnjačka Banja
Врњачка Бања
Trstenik
Stopanja
Čitluk
Jasika
Kruševac
Крушевац
Kaonik
Žitko
Uvac
ČEMERNA PL.
IBARSKA KLISURA
Rudo
Dobroselica
Jasenovo
Ivanjica
VELUĆE
Veliki Šiljegovac
Ustibar
Priboj
SRB
Mitrovo
Čajniče
Banja
Бања
Kumanica
Studenica
Студеница
Palumir
RUDENICA
Metaljka Prolaz
Metaljka
Hercegovska Goleša
Kokin Brod
Zlatarsko Jezero
Budoželja
Ibar
Vitkovo
STRAŽBENICA
Pridvorica
Ušće
Grčak
Ribarska Banja
Bistrica
Nova Varoš
ŽELIN
Ploča
Rasina
Boljanići
Bučje
ZLATAR NAC. PARK
Biljanovac
Zlatari
VELIKI JASTREBAC
Džigolj
Prijepolje
Kladnica
Jošanička Banja
Brus
Vikoč
Šula
Rudnica
MANASTIR MILEŠEVA
МАН. МИЛЕШЕВА
Aljinovići
HISARDŽIK
ХИСАДЖИК
ZLATAR
JANKOV KAMEN
GOLIJA NAC. PARK
MAN. GRADAC
МАН. ГРАДАЦ
Brvenik
Razbojna
Gradac
Jabuka
JADOVIK
Blace
Prokuplje
Прокупље
Pljevlja
Пљевља
Vijenac
Postrman Prolaz
Duga Poljana
Raška
Rudnica
PANČIĆEV VRH
Brzeće
Merćez
Beloljin
LJUBIŠNJA
Odžak
Ljutići
CRNI VRH
Sjenica
Brodarevo
Vapa
Mitrova Reka
NAC. PARK KOPAONIK
Dren
Lukovo
Toplica
Kosanica
ĐURĐEVI STUPOVI
ЂУРЂЕВИ СТУПОВИ
Banja
Lešak
KOPAONIK
Kuršumlija
LEDENA PEĆINA
MANASTIR SOPOĆANI
МАН. СОПОЋАНИ
Tara
GILJEVO
Sopoćani
Dojeviće
Novi Pazar
Нови Пазар
Leposavić
RADAN
Žabljak
Crno Jezero
Đurđevića Tara
Gostun
Metanjac
Rudare
Bogojevo
DURMITOR NAC. PARK
Tomaševo
Budjevo
Sebečevo
Kašalj
Sočanica
Kuršumlijska Banja
Palatna
Rača
Donja Bukovica
TARA KANJON
Kristac Prolaz
Slepač most
Bijelo Polje
Ugao
Šipći
ROGOZNA
Banjska
CARIČIN G
ЦАРИЧИН Г
Donja Brezna
Slatina
Bistrica
Mojkovac
Tutin
Ribariće
Kosovska Mitrovica
Косовска Митровица
Podujevo
Šavnik
NAC. PARK BIOGRADSKA GORA
Mehov Krš
Zubin Potok
Glavnik
Medvedja
Krnovo Prolaz
MNE
Kosutovo
Vučitrn
Batlava
Gvozd
Berane
Rožaj
MOKRA GORA
Klina Prolaz
Donje Ljupče
Batlavsko Jezero
Tulare
Nikšić
Никшић
Kolašin
Rudnik
Gornja Klina
Kačikol
MAN. MORAČA
МАН. МОРАЧА
Crkvina Prolaz
Mateševo
Kula Prolaz
Savine Vode
Rakoš
Belo Polje
Srbica
Lukare
Lisca Prolaz
N.Rubeža
Kuta
Jasenovo
HAJLA
Prisoja
Mali Štupelj
Djurakovac
Klina
ČIČA VIČA
Priština
Приштина
KOZNICA
Stubička dola Prolaz
Morakovo
Jabuka
Trešnjevik Prolaz
Andrijevica
Kućište
Vitomirica
Kosovo Polje/ Fushë Kosove
ULPIANA
Novo Brdo
Ново Брдо
MANASTIR OSTROG
Čakor Prolaz
Murino
Peć/Peje
Пећ
Ljesane
Dolac
Komorane
Gračanica
Грачаница
Labjana
Lijeva Rijeka
Vjeternik Prolaz
Vermosh
MAN. VISOKI DEČANI
МАН. ВИСОКИ ДЕЧАНИ
Plav
Dečanska Bistrica
Kijevo
Lapušnik
Velika Slatina
KOSOVO
Lipljan
Gnjilane/ Gjilan
Gora
Danilovgrad
Даниловград
Lëpushë
Gusinje
Dečani
Crmljan
Mališevo/ Malisheve
ŽEGOVAC
Bioče
PROKLETIJE
Tropojë
Čaf Dulja Prolaz
Štimlje
Slivovo
Kolokot
DOCLEA
ДОКЛЕА
Doljani
Tamarë
MAJ'E RADOHINËS
Valbonë
Skivjane
Orahovac
Uroševac/ Ferizaj
Požeranje
Binačka Morava
Gradac
PODGORICA
ПОДГОРИЦА
Okol
Shoshan
MAJ I HEKURAVË
Đakovica/ Gjakove
Ђаковица
Suva Reka
Cetinje
Цетиње
Tuzi
Bogë
Bajram Curri
Zrze
Vitina
Bigor
Golubovci
Podgorica
Božaj
Han i Hotit
Bezhetë- Makaj
Shëngjergj
Zogaj
Velika Kruša
ŠARA NAC. PARK
Doganović
Rijeka Crnojevića
Nicaj- Shalë
Rajë
Brezovica
Брезовица
RAMNO
Miločer
Bajzë
Dedaj
Nicaj Shoshë
Fierzë
Prizren
Призрен
Kačanik
Deneral Janković/ Hani i Elezit
Virpazar
Вирпазар
Vranjina
Liqeni i Fierzës
Globočica
Liqeni Komanit
Krumë
Žur
Rečane
LJUBOTEN
Krstac
Skadarsko jezero
Koplik
Vranisht
Vrbnica
Plava
Vratnica
Raduša
SVETI NIKITA
СВ. НИКИТА
Petrovac
Prekal
Domaj-Has
Dragaš
Slatino
Tearce
Liqen i Shkodrës
Šestani
Gruemirë
Spas
Dikance
Tetovo
Тетово
SCUPI
Sutomore
Livari
MAJ'E CUKALIT
Liqeni i Vaut të Dejës
Shënmëri
Kukës
SVETI PANTELEJMON
СВ. ПАНТЕЛЕЈМОН
Ostros
Shirokë
Koman
Fushë Arrëz
MAL'I GJALICËS
Orgjost
Lisec
Grupčin
Bar
Бар
Stari Bar
SHKODËR
Pukë
AL
TITOV VRH
Skopje
Скопје
Krute
Sukobin
Vau i Dejës
Brod
MAN. MATKA
Vladimir
Muriquan
Gojani i Madh
Bicaj
Turaj
Pirok
SV. ANDREJAŠ
СВ. АНДРЕЈАШ
Marko Sušica
Vladinos
Bushat
MAJ'E ZEBËS
Nova Breznica
MARKOV MANASTIR
МАРКОВ МАН.
Ulcinj
Улцињ
Krajn
MI RDITE
Klos
Bushtricë
SUVA GORA
Vardar
JAKUPICA
Sv. Nikola
Kakarriq
Blinisht
Reç
Lura e Vjetër
Vrapčište
Cegrane
Velipojë
Radomir
Zdunje
Geziq
Gostivar
Rasteš
Shëngjin
Rrëshen
Drini i Zi
Lezhë
Kurbnesh
MAL I DEJËS
Volkovija
Mavrovi Hanovi
DOBRA VODA
Samokov
SOLUNSKA GLAVA
Belica
Pellg i Drinit
Ulëzë
Fushë Muhurr
Peshkopi
SVETI JOVAN BIGORSKI
СВ. ЈОВАН БИГОРСКИ
Mavrovsko Ezero
Modrište
Laç
Selishtë
Mavrovo
Маврово
Crvivci
Fushë-Kuqe
SKANDERBEUT
MI KRESHTES
Postuša
NACIONALNI PARK MAVROVO
Zajas
Tuin
Dragov Doll
Patog
Burrel
Lis
Maqellarë
MK
Gji i Rodonit
Debar
Дебар
Dolno
Gari
Kičevo
Makedonski Brod
Devic
Kep i Rodonit
Shetaj
Krujë
Qafa e Kemzës
Janče
Izvor
Čelopeci
Rusjasi
Ropotovo
Gji i Lalzës
Fushë-Krujë
Klos
Bulqizë
Zerqan
Kosovrasti
Džepišta
STOGOVO
СТОГОВО
Presek Prolaz
Golema
BUŠEVA PL.
Rinas
MAL I LOPËS
Hamallaj
Belica
Cer
MAN. TRE
Kep i Palit
Katundi i Ri
Krastë
Klenjë
Lukovo
Kruševo
RAZBOJNA DUPKA
Vorë
Kamëz
MAL I DAJTIT
Qafa e Stillës
Pesočani
Dolenci
Krivogaštani
128
129

143
Obrenovac
Ripanj
Umčari
Kolari
Mala Krsna
Salakovac
Rabrovo
Debrc
Ralja
Osipaonica
Batuša
Makce
Turija
Brodica
ŠOMRDA
Svinjita
Stubline
Stepojevac
Sopot
Mladenovac
Selevac
Lozovik
Kučevo
RAJKOVA PEĆINA
Donji Milanovac
Mosna
Draginje
Banjani
Tamnava
Aleksandrovac
Topolnica
Slatina
Vreoci
Kovačevac
Smederevska-Palanka
Veliko Orašje
Melnica
CEREMOSNJA
MAN. VRA
Koceljevo
Ub
Venčane
Žabari
Petrovac
Majdanpek
Družetic
Lazarevac
V. Laole
Rudna Glava
Klok
Osečina
Lajkovac
Velika Plana
Miloševa Kula
Slovac
Partizani
MAN. KOPORIN
Jasikovo
Plavr
Donja Kamenica
Arandjelovac
Аранђеловац
Krepoljin
Tanda
Natalinci
Markovac
Pecka
Valjevo
Divci
Mionica
Topola
Топола
Svilajnac
MANASTIR GORNJAK
Luk
Grabovac
Žagubica
STOL
Ljig
MAN. OPLENAC
МАН. ОПЛЕНАЦ
Rača
Krupaja
Krivelj
Kovilda
Donja Šatornja
Lapovo
Resava
BELJANICA
Počuta
MALJEN
Ugrinovci
Rudnik
Čumić
Batočina
MAN. MANASIJA
МАН. МАНАСИЈА
Bor
Bukovi
MAN. BLAGOVEŠTENJE
МАН. БЛАГОВЕШТЕЊЕ
Despotovac
RESAVSKA PEĆINA
Brestovačka Banja
Divčibare
Mutanj
Desimirovac
Velika Morava
RAVANIČKA PEĆINA
РАВАНИЧКА ПЕЋИНА
Brestovac
Rgotina
Makoviš
Bukovi Prolaz
POVLJEN
RUDNIK
Vraćevšnica
Ravna Reka
ZLOTSKA PEĆINA
Zlot
Beršići
Rogačica
Pranjani
Gornji Milanovac
Kragujevac
Крагујевац
Jagodina
Јагодина
Šarbanova
Kostojevići
Jakalj
Kosjerić
Brdjani
MAN. JOŠANICA
Gornja Sabanta
MAN. RAVANICA
МАН. РАВАНИЦА
Podgorac
Selište
Gamzig
Dub
Zaglavak
Zapadna Morava
Vuckovica
Dragocvet
Ćuprija
SVETA PETKA
Bajina Bašta
Čestobrodica
Čačak
Чачак
Knić
Bogovina
Planinica
Kadinjača Prolaz
Kratovska Stena
Gruža
GLEDIĆSKE PL
Izvor
Straža
BOGOVINSKA PEĆINA
Bioska
Ovčar Banja
Bresnica
Paraćin
Stolice Prolaz
Boljevac
Lukovo
Vra
Kremna
Sevojno
Mrčajevci
Guberevac
Rekovac
Lasovo
Užice
Ужице
Požega
Loznica
Slatina
MAN. KALENIĆ
МАН. КЛЕНИЋ
Belušić
SRB
Rtanj
Rujište
ZLATIBOR
Šargan Prolaz
Kraljevo
Краљево
Bačina
Pojate
Bu
Cajetina
Arilje
Ариље
Guča
Viča
Kaona
Drakčići
Konarevo
Vitanovac
Oparić
Stalać
Ćićevac
Blendija
Partizanske Vode
Партизанске Воде
Podunavci
MANASTIR LJUBOSTINJA
МАН. ЉУБОСТИЊА
Donji Krcin
Moravica
Rožanstvo
Bogutovačka Banja
Mataruška Banja
Velika Drenova
Bovan
Soko Banja
Соко Бања
Bulino
TORNIK
Prilike
Maglić
ČEMERNA PL
Vrnjačka Banja
Врњачка-Бања
Zapadna Morava
Jasika
OZREN
DEVICA
Visoka
Ivanjica
IBARSKA KLISURA
Trstenik
Stopanja
Čitluk
Aleksinac
Dobroselica
Priboj
Kruševac
Крушевац
Kaonik
Žitkovac
Jasenovo
VELUĆE
Veliki Šiljegovac
Latinac
Studenica
Студеница
Mitrovo
RUDENICA
Kumanica
Palumir
Bučoželja
Kokin Brod
Zlatarsko Jezero
Vitkovo
Grčak
Gornja Toponica
Svrljig
Bistrica
Pridvorica
Ušće
Ribarska Banja
Nova Varoš
ZLATAR NAC. PARK
Ploča
Zlatari
VELIKI JASTREBAC
Sićevo
Prijepolje
Biljanovac
Brus
Džigolj
MAN. GRADAC
МАН. ГРАДАЦ
Josanička Banja
Kladnica
MANASTIR MILEŠEVA
МАН. МИЛЕШЕВА
Aljinovići
HISARDŽIK
ХИСАРЏИК
ZLATAR
Brvenik
GOLIJA NAC. PARK
Razbojna
Merošina
Niš
Ниш
Niška Banja
Нишка Бања
Blace
Prokuplje
Прокупље
JANKOV KAMEN
Postrman Prolaz
Raška
Rudnica
Brzeće
Merćez
Beloljin
Gadžin Han
JADOVIK
Sjenica
Duga Poljana
Mitrova Reka
PANČIĆEV VRH
NAC. PARK KOPAONIK
Doljevac
Brodarevo
CRNI VRH
DJURDJEVI STUPOVI
ЂУРЂЕВИ СТУПОВИ
Lukovo
Toplica
Žitoradja
Južna Morava
Lešak
Dren
Kuršumlija
Brestovac
Pečenjevce
MANASTIR SOPOĆANI
МАН. СОПОЋАНИ
Banja
KOPAONIK
RADAN
Žitni Potok
Lipovica
Gostun
GILJEVO
Sopoćani
Dojeviće
Novi Pazar
Нови Пазар
Leposavić
Zlata
Orašac
Metanjac
Sebečevo
Rudare
Bogojevo
Leskovac
Лесковац
Tomaševo
Budjevo
Kašalj
ROGOZNA
Kuršumlijska Banja
Vujanovo
Bojnik
Bijelo Polje
Ugao
Šipči
Sočanica
Palatna
Rača
Kristac Prolaz
Slepač most
Tutin
CARIČIN GRAD
ЦАРИЧИН ГРАД
Bošnjace
Mojkovac
NAC. PARK BIOGRADSKA GORA
Ribariće
Banjska
Kosovska Mitrovica
Косовска Митровица
Lebane
Dobri Do
Podujevo
Oraovica
Mehov Krš
Zubin Potok
Ibar
Glavnik
Medvedja
Vina
Jablanica
Veternica
Predejane
MNE
Berane
Rožaj
Košutovo
Vučitrn
Batlava
Batlavsko Jezero
Sijarinska Banja
Tulare
Vladičin Han
Kolašin
MOKRA GORA
Rudnik
Klina Prolaz
Donje Ljupče
Kula Prolaz
Rakoš
Gornja Klina
Kačikol
Golemo Selo
Mateševo
HAJLA
Savine Vode
Belo Polje
Srbica
Lukare
Lisca Prolaz
KUKAVICA
Prisoja
Jabuka
Trešnjevik Prolaz
Andrijevica
Kućište
Mali Štupelj
Djurakovac
ČIČA VIČA
Priština
Приштина
KOZNICA
Trstena
Lepenica
Vitomirica
Kosovo Polje/ Fushe Kosove
Ajnovce
Drenovac
Čakor Prolaz
Peć/Peje
Пећ
Ljušane
Klina
ULPIANA
Novo Brdo
Ново Брдо
MARKOVO KALE
Priboj
Korbe
Lijeva Rijeka
Murino
Dolac
Komorane
Velika Slatina
Gračanica
Грачаница
Labjana
Vranje
Врање
Vermosh
MAN. VISOKI DEČANI
МАН. ВИСОКИ ДЕЧАНИ
Kijevo
Lapušnik
KOSOVO
Vranjska Banja
Врањска-Бања
Zeternik Prolaz
Plav
Dečanska Bistrica
Lipljan
Gnjilane/ Gjilan
Vel. Trnovac
Gusinje
Dečani
Crmljan
Mališevo/ Malisheve
Ristovac
Lëpushe
Beli Drim
Bujanovac
Dobrčane
ŽEGOVAC
Stimlje
Slivovo
Sitnica
Klenike
Tamarë
RICA
Valbonë
Tropojë
MAJ'E RADOHINËS
Čaf Dulja Prolaz
Skivjane
Kolokot
Orahovac
Uroševac/ Ferizaj
Požeranje
Binačka Morava
Prohor Pčinjski
Preševo
Bogë
Okol
Shoshan
MI HEKURAVË
Đakovica/ Gjakove
Ђаковица
Suva Reka
Zrze
Šurlane
Vitina
Pelince
Han i Hotit
Bezhetë-Makaj
Bajram Curri
Shëngjergj
Velika Kruša
ŠARA NAC. PARK
Doganović
Strezovce
MANASTIR STARO NAGORIČANE
МАН. СТАРО НАГОРИЧАНЕ
Nicaj- Shalë
Nicaj Shoshë
Rajë
Zogaj
Prizren
Призрен
Brezovica
Брезовица
Globočica
Kačanik
RAMNO
Sopot
243
Bajzë
Dedaj
Fierzë
Liqeni Komanit
Liqeni i Fierzës
Krumë
Žur
Rečane
LJUBOTEN
General Janković/ Hani i Elezit
CRNA GORA
Kumanovo
Куманово
Tabanovce
Makreš
Stracin
Prekal
Vranisht
Vrbnica
Plava
Vratnica
Raduša
SVETI NIKITA
СВ. НИКИТА
MAN. MATEJČE
Mlado Nagoričane
Stracin Prolaz
Gruemirë
MAJ'E CUKALIT
AL
Spas
Domaj-Has
Dragaš
Tearce
Aračinovo
Beljakovci
Orašac
Pezovo
Liqeni i Vau-te Dejës
Shënmëri
Slatino
Dikance
SKOPJE
SCUPI
Pčinja
SHKODËR
Koman
Fushë Arrëz
Kukës
Orgjost
Tetovo
Тетово
SVETI PANTELEJMON
СВ. ПАНТЕЛЕЈМОН
Pukë
GJALICËS
Lisec
Brod
Grupčin
G. Konjare
Vau i Dejës
Bicaj
TITOV
MAN. MATKA
KATLANOVSKA BANJA
Stanjev
128
145
A1
E75
E65
E80
E761
E763
E851
M1
M3
M4

204
MEHEDINŢI
DOLJ
OLT
CRAIOVA
RO
Vidin
Видин
Calafat
VIDIN
Lom
Лом
Oryakhovo
Оряхово
MONTANA
Montana
Монтана
VRATSA
Vratsa
Враца
PLEVEN
Pleven
Плевен
Lovech
Ловеч
148
SOFIYA
СОФИЯ
SOFIYSKA
OBLAST
244
BG
PERNIK
Pernik
Перник
KYUSTENDIL
Kyustendil
Кюстендил
PAZARDZHIK
Pazardzhik
Пазарджик
Blagoevgrad
Благоевград
Zaječar
Зајечар
Pirot
Пирот
Negotin
Knjaževac
Dimitrovgrad
Botevgrad
Ботевград
Samokov
Самоков
Dupnitsa
Дупница
Caracal
Corabia
Balş
Băileşti
Bechet
Teteven
Тетевен
Troyan
Троян
Panagyurishte
Панагюрище
Velingrad
Велинград
Razlog
Bansko
Банско
Simitli
Симитли
MK
129
130
STARA PLANINA
CHIPROVSKA PL.
ZLATISHKO-TETEVENSKA PL.
GOLEMA PL.
RILA
NARODEN PARK
RILSKI MAN.
РИЛСКИ МАН.
MUSALA
МУСАЛА
2925
VITOSHA
N.P. VITOSHA
ВИТОША
Dunărea
Lacul Bistreţ
Iskŭr
Ogosta
Danube
E79
E80
E83
E772
E871
A1
A2

RO
BG
OLT
TELEORMAN
GIURGIU
RUSE
RAZGRAD
PLEVEN
VELIKO TŬRNOVO
TŬRGOVISHTE
LOVECH
GABROVO
STARA ZAGORA
SLIVEN
PLOVDIV
PAZARDZHIK
KHASKOVO
204
147
130
131
2009
Brebeni
Şerbăneşti
Balaci
Barza
Gumeşti
Slăveşti
Teleorman
Blejeşti
Trivatea-Moşteni
Videle
Dobroteşti
Necşeşti
Vârtoapele
Perii Broşteni
Olteni
Văleni
Didesti
Brebina
Botoroaga
Orbeasca
Drăgăneşti-Vlaşca
Ghimpaţi
Naipu
Adunaţii-Copăceni
Călugăreni
Vidra
Vărăşti
Budeşti
Luica
Herăşti
Şoldr
Curcani
Ulmeni
Hotarele
Căscioarele
Comana
Mihai Bravu
Prundu
Greaca
Olteniţa
Tutrakan
Schitu
Vlaşin
Băneasa
Daia
Toporu
Izvoarele
Vitănesti
Alexandria
Buzescu
Peretu
Drăgăneşti de Vede
Lăceni
Mihăeşti
Roşiori de Vede
Drăgăneşti-Olt
Dăneasa
Brâncoveni
Bălăneşti
Teslui
Caracal
Radomiru
Deveselu
Băbiciu
Crăngeni
Redea
Celaru
Vlădila
Studina
Amărăştii de Sus
Daneţi
Beciu
Plopii Slăviteşti
Călmăţuiu
Putineiu
Bogdana
Furculeşti
Smârdioasa
Putineiu
Vieru
Slobozia
Giurgiu
Marten
Ryakhovo
Staro Selo
Belica
Slivo Pole
Biserci
Sevar
Slobozia Mândra
Vişina Veche
Izbiceni
Ocolna
Vădastra
Crângu
Piatra
Traian
Conţeşti
Pietroşani
Vedea
Fântânele
Bujoru
Corabia
Gârcov
Turnu Măgurele
Dăbuleni
Ianca
Grojdibodu
Zimnicea
Chervena Voda
Tetovo
Kubrat
Novo Selo
Belovec
Kamenovo
Vetovo
Pisanets
Topchii
Kichenitsa
Senovo
RUSE
РУСЕ
Pirgovo
Mechka
IVANOVO MANASTIR
ИВАНОВО МАН.
Batin
Dve Mogili
Kacelovo
Khlebarovo
Osenets
Balkanski
Razgrad
Разград
Sadina
Oryakhovo
Gigen
Гиген
Dăbovan
Somovit
Cerkovitsa
Baykal
Nikopol
Belene
Svishtov
Novgrad
Vardim
Tsarevets
Obretenik
Selanovtsi
Krushovene
Brest
Gulyantsi
Galovo
Bregare
Komarevo
Debovo
Dekov
Stezherovo
Tsenovo
Volovo
Baniska
Krepcha
Blagoevo
Asenovo
Hadzhidimitrovo
Dragomirovo
Borovo
Opaka
Trapish
Stavertsi
Orehovica
Trăstenik
Staroselci
Podem
Koilovtsi
Dolna Mitropoliya
Gorna Mitropoliya
Dolna Mitropolia
Slavyanovo
Bacova mahala
Bŭlgarene
Gorna Studena
Alekovo
Pavel
Byala
Polsko Kosovo
Koprivets
Car Asen
Popovo
Chudomir
Knezha
Brenica
Pelovo
Yasen
Obnova
Totleben
Kozar Belene
Maslarevo
Polski Trŭmbesh
Lom
Cherkovna
Kamen
Voditsa
Svetlen
Pogoritsa
Aprilovo
Glava
PLEVEN
ПЛЕВЕН
Grivitsa
Dolni Dŭbnik
Pordim
Levski
Karaisen
Obedinenie
Sushitsa
Letnitsa
Gradishte
NICOPOLIS AD ISTRUM
НИКОПОЛИС
Petko Karavelov
Dragomirovo
Stražica
Tŭrgovishki Pateka
Prolaz
Telish
Breslovec
Sadovets
Aleksandrovo
Pavlikeni
Polikrayshte
Arbanasi
Арбанаси
Džul'unica
Antonovo
Beglezh
Dojrenci
Bjala Cherkva
Stambolovo
Gorna Oryakhovitsa
Kesarevo
Kamburovo
Omurtag
Mengish
Zelena morava
Devetaki
Suhindol
Samovodene
Lyaskovets
Lukovit
Aglen
Lovech
Ловеч
Kăkrina
Kramolin
Vishovgrad
PREOBRAZHENSKI MAN.
ПРЕОБРАЖЕНСКИ МАН.
Dermantsi
Orlyane
Dobromirka
Balvan
Veliko Tŭrnovo
Велико Търново
Dedinci
LISA PL
Ticha
Roman
Zlatna Panega
Ugŭrchin
Prelon
Petko Slaveykov
Debelets
Stevrek
Toros
Sokolovo
Sevlievo
Севлиево
Dryanovo
Дряново
Kilifarevo
Bebrovo
Bŭlgarski Izvor
Ablanitsa
Bŭlgarene
Sennik
KOTLENSKA PLANINA
Kotlenski Pateka
Kotel
Котел
Yablanitsa
GLOZHENSKI MANASTIR
Mikre
Staro selo
Yavorets
Vranilovci
Elena
Елена
Shilkovci
Vŭglevtsi
Stara Reka
Zeravna
Жеравна
Glozhene
Dzhurovo
Borima
Dobrodan
Bariyevo
Debnevo
Tryavna
Трявна
Gradets
Teteven
Тетевен
Osikovitsa
Velchevo
Gabrovo
Габрово
Bozhenci
Боженци
Voneshta voda
Republik Pateka
Tvŭrdishki Pateka
CHUMERNA
Vratnik Pateka
Rakovo
Troyan
Троян
Oresak
TROYANSKI MANASTIR
ТРОЯНСКИ МАН.
Novo Selo
Stokite
Shipchenski Prokhod
Шипченски проход
ELENO TVARDISHKA PL
Shipkovo
Sliven
Сливен
SINITE KAMŬNI
Lăga
Balkanec
Troyanski Pateka
TREVENSKA PL
Shivatsevo
Etropole
Етрополе
Zlatishki Pateka
Ribaritsa
ZLATISHKO-TETEVENSKA PL.
VEZHEN
ВЕЖЕН
BALKAN
BOTEV
Shipka
Шипка
Radunci
Tvŭrditsa
Binkos
Gurkovo
KALOFERSKA PL
SHIPCHENSKI MAN.
Kazanlŭk
Казанлък
Dăbovo
Banya
Zlati voyvoda
Silvenski bani
Силвенски бани
Rosino
Kŭrnare
Karlovo
Карлово
Tŭzha
Vetren
Muglizh
Korten
Nikolaevo
Kermen
Zlatitsa
Anton
Pirdop
Klisura
Sopot
Kalofer
Pavel Banya
Yagoda
Nova Zagora
Нова Загора
Dolno Kamartsi
ROSOVA DOLINA
РОСОВА ДОЛИНА
BOGDAN
Koprivshtitsa
Копривщица
Banya
Баня
Svežen
BRATAN
Tundzha
Podslon
Gŭlŭbintsi
Petrich
Hisariya
Хисаря
Gorno Novo Selo
STARA ZAGORA
СТАРА ЗАГОРА
Pŭstrovo
Strelcha
Стрелча
Starosel
Babek
Mlekarevo
Polbrene
Oborishte
Panagyurishte
Панагюрище
Krasnovo
Černičevo
Zhitnica
Kaloyanovo
Dolna Mahala
Strelci
Săedinenie
Rakitnica
Sharnevo
Novoseletz
Popintsi
Brezovo
Bratya Daskolovi
Sredno gradishte
Radnevo
Bădeshte
Skalitsa
Lesichovo
Elšica
Dragomir
Lyuben
Dolno Levski
Rakovski
Раковски
Sredets
Ljubenovo
Polski Gradets
Svetlina
Goljam Man.
Kalugerovo
Săedinenie
Stroevo
Kalekovets
Stryama
Trud
Chirpan
Чирпан
Venets
Obruchishte
Mŭdrets
Kostenets
Костенец
Bjal izvor
Merichleri
Gŭlŭbovo
Гълъбово
Glavan
Topolovgrad
Septemvri
Pazardzhik
Пазарджик
Caracovo
Belozem
Popovitsa
Vasil Levski
Bŭlgarska Polyana
Belovo
Goljamo Belovo
Lozen
Varvara
Novi Krichim
PLOVDIV
ПЛОВДИВ
Sadovo
Садово
Pŭrvomay
Dimitrovgrad
Димитровград
Simeonovgrad
Cherepovo
Dervishka mogila
Bolyartsi
Debŭr
Filevo
Dŭlbok Izvor
Branica
Draginovo
Dorkovo
Peshtera
Пещера
Krichim
Кричим
Perushtica
Перущица
Asenovgrad
Асеновград
Lenovo
Bagarin
Kharmanli
Velingrad
Велинград
Sveti Konstantin
Bracigovo
Брацигово
Yazovir Batak
Bachkovo
Бачково
BACHKOVSKI MANASTIR
БАЧКОВСКИ МАН.
Mineralni Bani
Khaskovo
Хасково
Podkrepa
Ivanovo
Lyubimets
Lefka
Rakitovo
Ракитово
Narechenski Bani
Нареченски бани
Yazovir Trakiec
Konush
Lozen
Malko Gradishte
Svilengrad
Свиленград
Kapit Andr
Graševo
Batak
Батак
Topolovo
Novakovo
Karamanci
Goljam izvor
Lŭki
Khrojna
Panichkovo
GOLYAMA SYUTKYA
Mikhalkovo
Михалково
GOLYAMA PERSENK
Komuniga
Tenkovo
Most
Vărbovo
Petrota
Πετρωτά
Dikaia
Δίκαια
Pláti
Πλάτη
Dabovets
Poljani
Pobit Kamăk
Zabardo
Chepelare
Чепеларе
Monastir
CHUKATA
Rani list
GORATA
Dunav
Dunărea
Yantra
Osŭm
Vit
Iskŭr
Stryama
Maritsa
Sazliyka
Chernil Lom
Stara reka

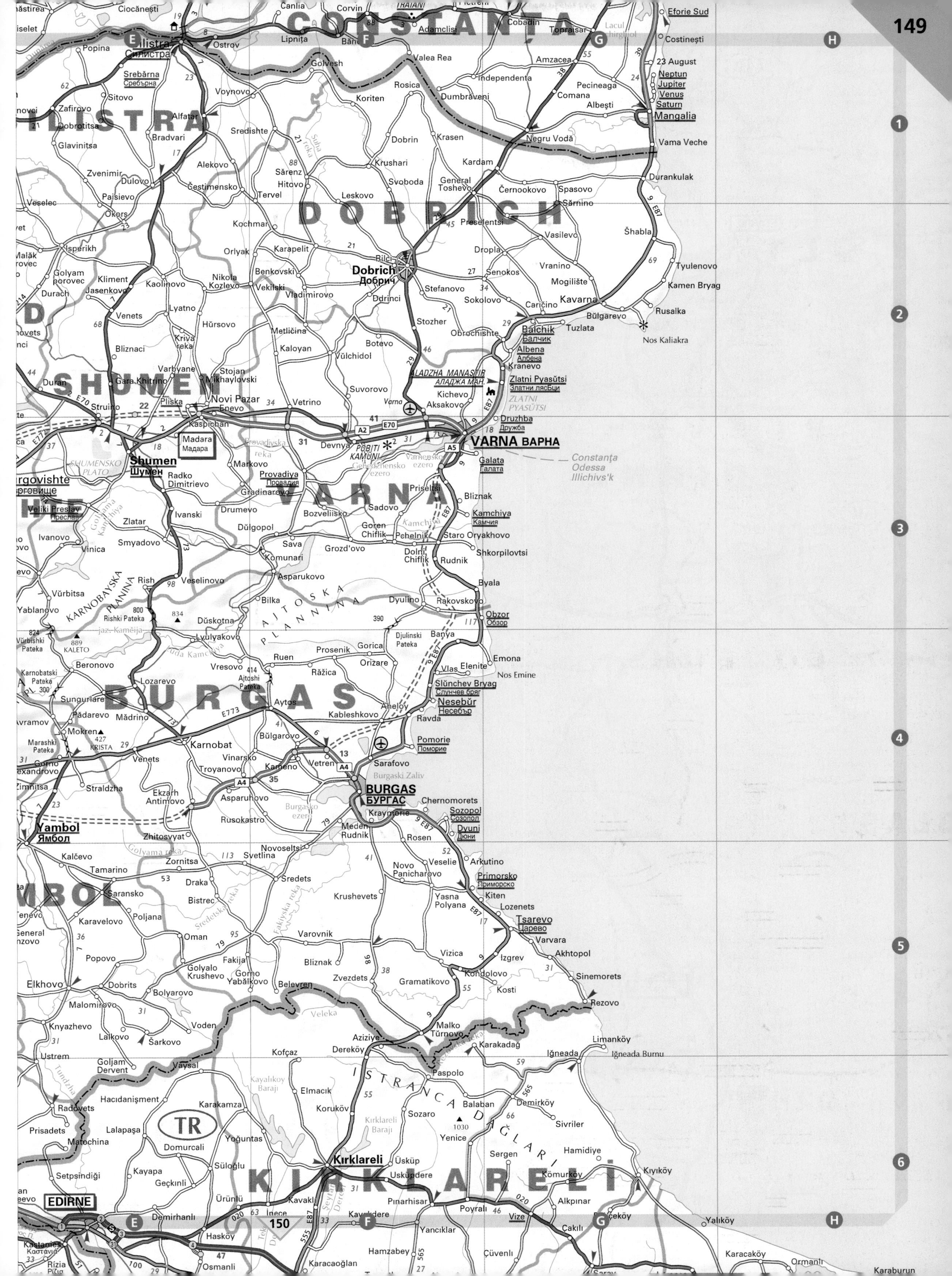
CONSTANȚA
Eforie Sud
Costinești
23 August
Neptun
Jupiter
Venus
Saturn
Mangalia
Vama Veche
Negru Vodă
Amzacea
Independenta
Pecineaga
Comana
Albești
Dumbrăveni
Cobadin
Topraisar
Adamclisi
Băneasa
Lipnița
Ostrov
Silistra
Силистра
Srebărna
Сребърна
Sitovo
Popina
Zafirovo
Dobrotitsa
Glavinitsa
Alfatar
Bradvari
SILISTRA
Voynovo
Golvesh
Valea Rea
Rosica
Koriten
Sredishte
Dobrin
Krasen
Kardam
Krushari
General Toshevo
Svoboda
Durankulak
Sărnino
Spasovo
Černookovo
Preselentsi
Alekovo
Dulovo
Zvenimir
Paisievo
Okorsh
Čestimensko
Sărenz
Hitovo
Tervel
Leskovo
DOBRICH
Šhabla
Vasilevo
Kochmar
Orlyak
Karapelit
Rilci
Dobrich
Добрич
Dropla
Vranino
Tyulenovo
Kamen Bryag
Senokos
Mogilište
Kavarna
Sokolovo
Stefanovo
Dorinci
Stozher
Kaolinovo
Nikola Kozlevo
Benkovski
Vekilski
Vladimirovo
Isperikh
Kliment
Golyam porovec
Jasenkovo
Durach
Venets
Lyatno
Hursovo
Metličina
Kaloyan
Vulchidol
Botevo
Obrochishte
Caričino
Bulgarevo
Rusalka
Tuzlata
Balchik
Балчик
Albena
Албена
Kranevo
Nos Kaliakra
Bliznaci
Kriva reka
Varbyane
Stojan Mikhaylovski
Suvorovo
Aladzha Manastir
Аладжа Ман.
Zlatni Pyasŭtsi
Златни пясъци
Kichevo
Aksakovo
Varna
SHUMEN
Duran
Gara Khitrino
Struino
Pliska
Novi Pazar
Enevo
Vetrino
Kaspichan
Madara
Мадара
Druzhba
Дружба
VARNA ВАРНА
Devnya
Pobiti Kamŭni
Provadiyska reka
Beloslav
Varnensko ezero
Galata
Галата
Constanța
Odessa
Illichivs'k
Shumen
Шумен
Shumensko Plato
Targovishte
Търговище
Markovo
Radko Dimitrievo
Provadiya
Провадия
Gradinarovo
Priseltsi
Bliznak
Veliki Preslav
Преслав
Ivanski
Drumevo
VARNA
Bozveliisko
Sadovo
Kamchiya
Камчия
Zlatar
Dŭlgopol
Goren Chiflik
Pchelnik
Staro Oryakhovo
Ivanovo
Smyadovo
Vinica
Sava
Grozd'ovo
Dolni Chiflik
Shkorpilovtsi
Rudnik
Komunari
Asparukovo
Byala
Rish
Veselinovo
Vŭrbitsa
KARNOBAYSKA PLANINA
Yablanovo
Bilka
Dyulino
Rakovsko
Obzor
Обзор
Rishki Pateka
Dŭskotna
AJTOSKA PLANINA
Vŭrbishki Pateka
KALETO
jaz. Kamčija
Lyulyakovo
Djulinski Pateka
Banya
Luda Kamchiya
Prosenik
Gorica
Emona
Nos Emine
Ruen
Vresovo
Ajtoshi Pateka
Rŭzhica
Orizare
Vlas
Elenite
Slŭnchev Bryag
Слънчев бряг
Beronovo
Karnobatski Pateka
Lozarevo
BURGAS
Sungurlare
Aytos
Nesebŭr
Несебър
Ravda
Aheloy
Pădarevo
Mădrino
Kableshkovo
Avramov
Mokren
KRISTA
Karnobat
Bŭlgarovo
Pomorie
Поморие
Marashki Pateka
Venets
Vinarsko
Vetren
Sarafovo
Burgaski Zaliv
Gorno Aleksandrovo
Troyanovo
Kameno
Zimnitsa
Straldzha
Ekzarh Antimovo
Asparuhovo
BURGAS
БУРГАС
Chernomorets
Sozopol
Созопол
Burgasko ezero
Kraymorie
Dyuni
Дюни
Yambol
Ямбол
Rusokastro
Meden Rudnik
Rosen
Zhitosvyat
Golyama reka
Kalčevo
Novoseltsi
Svetlina
Zornitsa
Tamarino
Arkutino
Veselie
Novo Panicharovo
Primorsko
Приморско
Sredets
Draka
Kiten
Lozenets
Saransko
Bistrec
Krushevets
Yasna Polyana
Tsarevo
Царево
Varvara
Akhtopol
Poljana
Karavelovo
Sredetska reka
Fakiyska reka
Varovnik
Vizica
Izgrev
Oman
Popovo
Fakija
Bliznak
Golyalo Krushevo
Gorno Yabalkovo
Zvezdets
Gramatikovo
Kondolovo
Sinemorets
Kosti
Elkhovo
Dobrits
Bolyarovo
Belevren
Rezovo
Malomirovo
Veleka
Voden
Knyazhevo
Lalkovo
Šarkovo
Malko Tŭrnovo
Aziziye
Dereköy
Karakadağ
Limanköy
İğneada
İğneada Burnu
Ustrem
Goljam Dervent
Vaysal
Kofçaz
ISTRANCA DAĞLARI
Paspolo
Tundzha
Kayalıkoy Barajı
Elmacık
Hacıdanişment
Radovets
Karakamza
TR
Koruköy
Balaban
Demirköy
Sozaro
Sivriler
Prisadets
Lalapaşa
Kırklareli Barajı
Yenice
Matochina
Yoğuntas
Domurcali
Sergen
Hamidiye
Setpsindiği
Kayapa
Süloglu
Kırklareli
Üsküp
Kıyıköy
Geçkinli
Uskupdere
Kömürköy
KIRKLARELİ
EDIRNE
Ürünlü
Kavaklı
Pınarhisar
Alkpınar
Demirhanlı
Inece
Kavaklıdere
Poyralı
Vize
Çeköy
Yalıköy
Hasköy
Yancıklar
Çakılı
Kastanies
Καστανιές
Hamzabey
Çüvenli
Karacaköy
Ormanlı
Rizia
Osmanli
Karacaoğlan
Karaburun
Saray
150

149
BG
GR
EDIRNE
Kırklareli
KIRKLARELİ
İSTRANCA DAĞLARI
EDİRNE
TEKİRDAĞ
ÇANAKKALE
MARMARA DEN
Saroz Körfezi
Erdek Körfezi
Bandırma Körfezi
KURU DAĞI
GANOS DAĞI
KOCAKTRAN DAĞ
Elkhovo
Dobrits
Bolyarovo
Belevren
Gramatikovo
Kosti
Rezovo
Goljam Man.
Malomirovo
Knyazhevo
Lalkovo
Šarkovo
Voden
Malko Türnovo
Aziziye
Dereköy
Karakadağ
Limanköy
İğneada
İğneada Burnu
Glavan
Topolovgrad
Ustrem
Goljam Dervent
Vaysal
Kofçaz
Paspolo
Bŭlgarska Polyana
Cherepovo
Dervishka mogila
Radovets
Hacıdanişment
Kayalıkoy Barajı
Elmacık
Karakamza
Koruköy
Kırklareli Barajı
Sozaro
Balaban
Demirköy
Sivriler
Yenice
Prisadets
Lalapaşa
Yoğuntas
Matochina
Domurcali
Lefka
Süloğlu
Üsküp
Sergen
Hamidiye
Setpsindiği
Kayapa
Geçkinli
Üsküpdere
Kömurköy
Kıyıköy
Kapitan Andreevo
Svilengrad
Свиленград
Ürünlü
Kavaklı
Pınarhisar
Poyralı
Vize
Alkpınar
Bahçeköy
Yalıköy
Demirhanlı
İnece
Kavakdere
Yancıklar
Çakılı
Petrota
Πετρωτά
Dabovets
Dikaia
Δίκαια
Kastanies
Καστανιές
Pláti
Πλάτη
Rízia
Ρίζια
Hasköy
Teke Deresi
Hamzabey
Çüvenli
Saray
Karacaköy
Osmanli
Karacaoğlan
Turgutbey
Ahmetbey
Istranca
Karamandere
Kómara
Κόμαρα
Fylákio
Φυλάκιο
Néa Vyssa
Νέα Βύσσα
Kavýli
Καβύλη
Váltos
Βάλτος
Orestiáda
Ορεστιάδα
Havsa
Kuleli
Azath
Çukurköi
Lüleburgaz
Büyükyoncalı
Hulha
Ivaylovgrad
Zóni
Ζώνη
Ládi
Λάδη
Ampelákia
Αμπελάκια
Thoúrio
Θούριο
Máni
Μάνη
Elçili
Babaeski
Alpullu
Evrensekiz
Beyazköy
Gümüşpınar
Hallaçli
Cerkezköy
Kabakca
Subaşi
Akalar
Kırcaşalih
Metaxades
Μεταξάδες
Didymóteicho
Διδυμότειχο
Hamitli
Pehlivanköy
Mandira
Büyükkarıştıran
Vakiflar
Ulaş
Sinekli
Çatalca
Mavrokklisi
Μαυροκκλήσι
Protokklisi
Πρωτοκκλήσι
Mikró Dérelo
Μικρό Δέρειο
Lávara
Λάβαρα
Uzunköprü
Sipahi
Hayrabolu
Dambaslar
Muratli
Çorlu
Silivri
Roússa
Ρούσσα
Mandra
Μάνδρα
Kavakli
Çöpköy
Çeneköy
Sarılar
Seymen
Méga Dére
Μέγα Δέρειο
Sidiró
Σιδηρώ
Giannoúli
Γιαννούλη
Meriç
Soufli
Σουφλί
Kavacık
Süleymaniye
Hamidiye
Karakagür
Banarli
Kayı
Gümüşsuyu
Sultanköy
Yeniçiftlik
Marmaraereğlisi
Kurtbey
Kozyürük
Bıvıkali
Pessáni
Πεσσάνη
Lykofos
Λυκόφως
Küplü
Alıç
Hacısungur
Liman Burun
Tekirdağ
NAPLES
Şahin
Genereli
Karaidemir Barajı
İnecik
Barbaros
Sultanköy
İbriktepe
Aisými
Αισύμη
Thymariá
Θυμαριά
Pasayiğit
İbrice
Kumbağ
Malkara
Ballı
Yeniköy
İpsala
Esatçe
Keşan
Kadıköy Barajı
Balabancik
Uçmakdere
Loutrós
Λουτρός
Féres
Φέρες
Monastiráki
Μοναστηράκι
Alexandroúpoli
Αλεξανδρούπολη
Gaziköy
Yeni Karpuzlu
Bahçeköy
Ishakı
MİLLİ PARKI
Marmara Adasi
Orhanıye
Gala Gölü
Gölcük
Mürefte
Marmara
Çeltikköy
Kadıköy
Kocaaeli
Kocaçeşme
Şarköy
Kocaburgaz
Sahinburgaz
Enez
Yenice
Hasköy
Kavak
Türkeli
Türkeli Adasi
İlhan
Karşıyaka
Kurşunlu
Erikli
İbrikbaba
Abdürrahim
Sultanıca
Koruköy
İstanbul
Kara Burun
Paşalimani Adasi
Ocaklar
KYZIKOS
Yenice
PLAKI
Bolayır
Aksaz
Erdek
Edincik
Bandırma
Gölecik
Ocaklı
Karabiga
Gelibolu
Kemer
Bozlar
Şevketiye
Çakırlı
Denizkent
Kuşcenneti
Tayfur
Çardak
Güreci
Belıklıçeşme
Gülec
Sinekçi
Buğdayli
KUŞCENNETİ MİLLİ PARKI
Aksakal
o Kipos
Karainebeyli
Lapseki
Bayırköy
Sariköy
Gölyaka
Kuş Gölü
Büyük Kemikli Burun
Yolağzı
Bakacak
Biga
Ulgardereköyü
Umurbey
Umurbey Çayı
Beycayırı
Gurçeşme
Armutlu
Hasanbey
Şevketiye
Ergili
GELİBOLU YARIMADASI
LIMNAE
Eceabat
Kilitbahir
Balcılar
Yakacık Dere
Emese
Gönen
PEMANINOS
Manyas
Gökçeada
Kaleköy
Kabaltepe
MİLLİ PARKI
CREMASTE
Dondurma
Bostandere
Nacıvelioba
Aşağıinova
Darıca
Göbel
Söve
İmroz
Behramlı
Çanakkale
KARA DAĞ
Maltepe
Susu
Aydıncık
Alçitepe
Kepez
Ortaca
Kirazlı
Kumarlar
Çan
Ortaoba
Kocapınar
Ayagalip
Abide
Navruz
Çakır
Orhanlar
Yeşilova
Sultan
İlyasbaba Burun
Intepe
Etili
Denizgören
Hcıkasım
Gönen Brj.
Ilıca
Ömerköy
Kumkale
ACHILLEUM
Muratlar
Yenice
Danişment
Şamlı
Tevfikiye
Kuşçayır
Zeybekçayırı
Örencik
Hamdibey
Pazarköy
Yeniköy
Kayalar
Alancık
TRUVA
Yeniköy
Yiğitler
SCEPSIS
Küçük Menderes
Karaköy
Gönen Çayı
Kalkım
Kepsut
Kumburun
Kırıklar
Çakallar
Balya
Bozcaada
Pazarköy
Bayramiç
Geyikli
Evciler
Armutcuk
BALIKESİR
Bozca Adasi
Ezine
KEBRENE
Serhat
KAZ DAĞI
Akbaş
Ergama
Nusret
Dalyan
ALEXANDRIA TROAS
NEANDRIA
Zeytinli
Osmanlar
Gükçeyazı
Çağış
Baharlar
Edremit
İvrindi
Ertuğrul
Tavaklı
DİKİLİ TEPE
Altınoluk
Akcay
152
İSTIRA
Yağlılar
Pamukça
Kösedere
İzmir
Ayvacık
ANTANDROS
Ören
Havran
ADRAMITTIUM THEBE
Duztarla
Minnetler
Konakpınar
Tuzla
Ahmetçe
Küçükkuyu
Burhaniye
Korucu
Kayapa
Karacalar
BABAKÖY

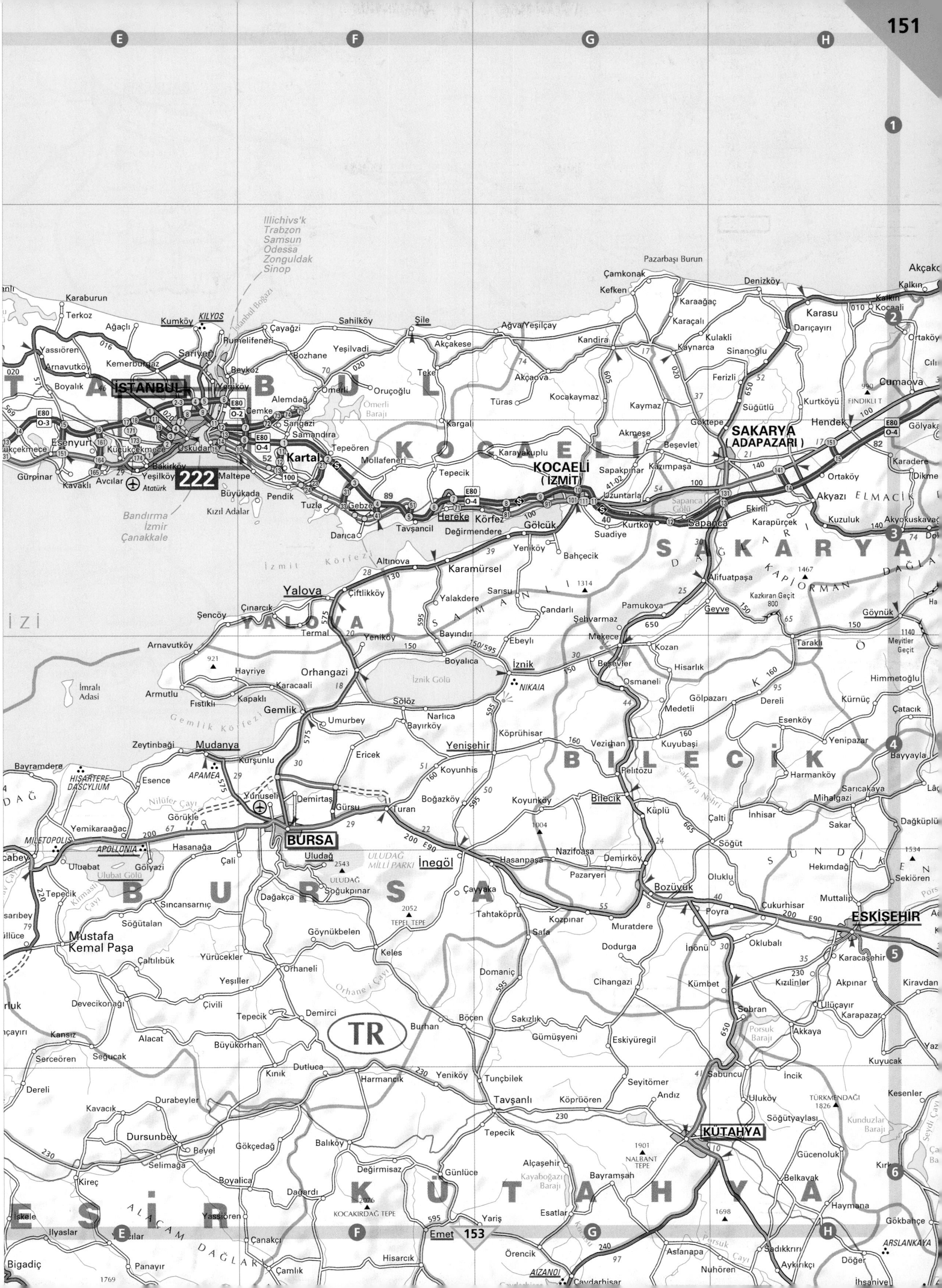
E
F
G
H
1
2
3
4
5
6
Illichivs'k
Trabzon
Samsun
Odessa
Zonguldak
Sinop
İstanbul Boğazı
Pazarbaşı Burun
Akçakoca
Çamkonak
Kefken
Denizköy
Kalkın
Karaburun
Terkoz
Ağaçlı
Kumköy
KILYOS
Çayağzi
Sahilköy
Şile
Ağva/Yeşilçay
Karaağaç
Karasu
Kocaali
Karaçalı
Darıçayırı
Ortaköy
Yassıören
Rumelifeneri
Sarıyer
Yeşilvadi
Bozhane
Akçakese
Kandira
Kulakli
Kaynarca
Sinanoğlu
Arnavutköy
Kemerburgaz
Beykoz
Teke
Akçaova
Ferizli
Cumaova
Boyalık
İSTANBUL
Yeniköy
Alemdağ
Ömerli
Oruçoğlu
Türas
Kocakaymaz
Kaymaz
Söğütlü
Kurtköyü
FINDIKLI T
Ömerli Barajı
Cemke
Sangazi
Samandıra
Kargalı
Göktepe
Hendek
Gölyaka
Esenyurt
Küçükçekmece
Büyükçekmece
Üsküdar
Kartal
Tepeören
Mollafeneri
Akmeşe
SAKARYA
(ADAPAZARI)
Karayakuplu
Beşevlet
KOCAELİ
Karadere
Gürpinar
Kavaklı
Avcılar
Bakırköy
Yeşilköy
Atatürk
222
Maltepe
Tepecik
Sapakpınar
(İZMİT)
Kazımpaşa
Ortaköy
Dikme
Büyükada
Pendik
Uzuntarla
Akyazı
ELMACIK
Kızıl Adalar
Tuzla
Gebze
Hereke
Körfez
Sapanca Gölü
Ekinli
Bandırma
İzmir
Çanakkale
Darıca
Tavşancil
Değirmendere
Gölcük
Kurtköy
Sapanca
Karapürçek
Kuzuluk
Akyokuskavağı
Suadiye
Yeniköy
Bahçecik
SAKARYA
İzmit Körfezi
Altınova
Karamürsel
DAĞI
KAPIORMAN DAĞLARI
Alifuatpaşa
Yalova
Çiftlikköy
Sarısu
Yalakdere
SAMANLI
Kazkıran Geçit
Pamukova
Geyve
Çınarcık
Çandarlı
Göynük
Şencöy
YALOVA
Termal
Şehvarmaz
Yeniköy
Bayındır
Ebeylı
Mekece
Arnavutköy
Hayriye
Boyalıca
İznik
Kozan
Tarakli
Meyitler Geçit
Beşevler
Hisarlık
İmralı Adası
Orhangazi
İznik Gölü
NİKAIA
Osmaneli
Himmetoğlu
Armutlu
Fıstıklı
Karacaali
Kapaklı
Gemlik
Sölöz
Gölpazarı
Dereli
Kürnüç
Medetli
Çatacık
Gemlik Körfezi
Umurbey
Narlıca
Bayırköy
Esenköy
Köprühisar
Zeytinbağı
Mudanya
Yenişehir
Vezirhan
Kuyubaşi
Yenipazar
Kurşunlu
Ericek
BİLECİK
Bayyayla
Bayramdere
HISARTEPE
DASCYLIUM
Esence
APAMEA
Koyunhisar
Pelitozu
Harmanköy
Sarıcakaya
Nilüfer Çayı
Yunuseli
Demirtaş
Boğazköy
Koyunköy
Bilecik
Mihalgazi
Görükle
Gürsu
Turan
Küplü
Sakarya Nehri
İnhisar
Çalti
Sakar
Dağküplü
Yemikaraağaç
MILETOPOLIS
BURSA
Nazifoaşa
Söğüt
APOLLONIA
Hasanağa
Uludağ
ULUDAĞ MİLLİ PARKI
İnegöl
Hasanpaşa
Demirköy
SÜNDİKEN
Uluabat
Gölyazi
Çali
ULUDAĞ
Pazaryeri
Oluklu
Hekimdağ
Sekiören
Ulubat Gölü
Tepecik
Soğukpınar
Bozüyük
BURSA
Dağakça
Çayyaka
Muttalip
Kirmastı Çayı
Sıncansarnıç
Tahtaköprü
Poyra
Çukurhisar
ESKİŞEHİR
TEPEL TEPE
Kozpınar
Muratdere
Söğütalan
Safa
Mustafa Kemal Paşa
Göynükbelen
Oklubalı
İnönü
Dodurga
Karacaşehir
Keles
Çaltılıbük
Yürücekler
Orhaneli
Domaniç
Kızılinler
Akpınar
Kiravdan
Yeşiller
Orhaneli Çayı
Cihangazi
Kümbet
Devecikonağı
Çivili
Ulüçayır
Karapazar
Tepecik
Demirci
Sobran
TR
Alacat
Burhan
Böçen
Sakızlık
Porsuk Barajı
Akkaya
Kansız
Gümüşyeni
Eskiyüregil
Büyükorhan
Serceören
Seğucak
Kuyucak
Dutluca
Kınık
Harmancık
Yeniköy
Tunçbilek
Sabuncu
İncik
Dereli
Seyitömer
Andız
Durabeyler
Tavşanlı
Köprüören
Uluköy
TÜRKMENDAĞI
Kesenler
Kavacık
Söğütyaylası
Kunduzlar Barajı
Tepecik
KÜTAHYA
Dursunbey
Beyel
Gökçedağ
Balıköy
NALBANT TEPE
Gücenoluk
Selimağa
Değirmisaz
Günlüce
Alçaşehir
Bayramşah
Kayaboğazı Barajı
Kireç
Boyalıca
Belkavak
Dağardı
KÜTAHYA
KOCAKIRDAĞ TEPE
Haymana
İskele
Yassıören
Esatlar
Yariş
Gökbahçe
Ilyaslar
Emet
153
ALAÇAM DAĞLARI
Çanakçı
Örencik
Aslanapa
Porsuk Çayı
Sadıkkırı
ARSLANKAYA
Bigadiç
Panayır
Hisarcık
Nuhören
Aykırıkçı
Döğer
Çamlık
AIZANOI
Çavdarhisar
İhsaniye
BALIKESİR
İZMİT

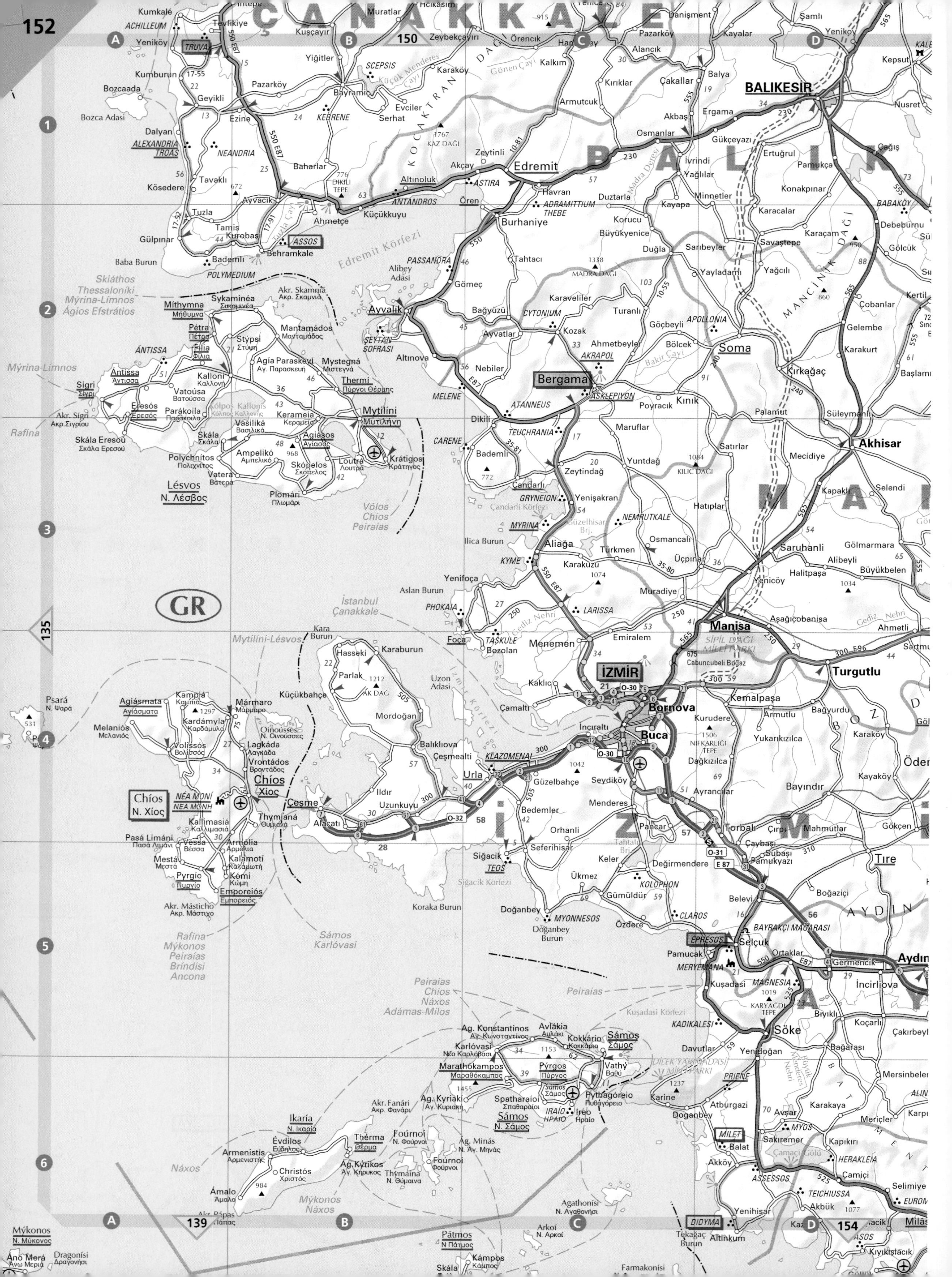
ÇANAKKALE
BALIKESİR
MANİSA
İZMİR
AYDIN
GR
150
135
139
154
A
B
C
D
1
2
3
4
5
6
Kumkale
ACHILLEUM
Tevfikiye
TRUVA
Yeniköy
Kumburun
Bozcaada
Bozca Adasi
Geyikli
Ezine
Dalyan
ALEXANDRIA TROAS
NEANDRIA
Tavaklı
Kösedere
Ayvacık
Tuzla
Tamis
Kurobası
Gülpınar
Baba Burun
Bademli
POLYMEDIUM
ASSOS
Behramkale
Ahmetçe
Küçükkuyu
Muratlar
Kuşçayır
Yiğitler
Pazarköy
SCEPSIS
Bayramiç
Karaköy
Evciler
Serhat
KEBRENE
Baharlar
Zeybekçayırı
Örencık
Kalkım
Altınoluk
ANTANDROS
Akçay
ASTIRA
Zeytinli
Edremit
Havran
Ören
Burhaniye
KAZ DAĞI
KOCAKTRAN DAĞI
Gönen Çayı
Küçük Menderes Çayı
Edremit Körfezi
PASSANDRA
Alibey Adası
Ayvalık
ŞEYTAN SOFRASI
Altınova
Gömeç
Tahtacı
Bağyüzü
Ayvatlar
CYTONIUM
Kozak
Karaveliler
Nebiler
Bergama
ASKLEPIYON
AKRAPOL
MELENE
ATANNEUS
Dikili
CARENE
Bademli
TEUCHRANIA
Çandarlı
GRYNEION
Çandarlı Körfezi
MYRINA
Güzelhisar Brj.
Yenişakran
Aliağa
KYME
Ilica Burun
Yenifoça
Aslan Burun
PHOKAIA
Foça
TAŞKULE
Bozolan
Menemen
LARISSA
Gediz Nehri
Danişment
Pazarköy
Alancık
Kırıklar
Çakallar
Balya
Armutcuk
Akbaş
Ergama
Osmanlar
Gükçeyazı
İvrindi
Yağlılar
Minnetler
Duztarla
Kayapa
Korucu
Büyükyenice
Duğla
Sarıbeyler
Yayladamı
Madra Deresi
MADRA DAĞI
ADRAMITTIUM THEBE
Turanlı
Göçbeyli
APOLLONIA
Ahmetbeyler
Bölcek
Soma
Bakır Çayı
Kınık
Poyracık
Maruflar
Satırlar
Yuntdağ
KILIÇ DAĞI
Zeytindağ
NEMRUTKALE
Hatıplar
Osmancalı
Türkmen
Karakuzu
Üçpınar
Muradiye
Manisa
SİPİL DAĞI MİLLİ PARKI
Emiralem
Cabuncubeli Boğaz
Şamlı
Yeniköy
Kayalar
BALIKESİR
Kepsut
Nusret
Çağış
Ertuğrul
Pamukça
Konakpınar
BABAKÖY
Karacalar
Debeburnu
Savaştepe
Karaçam
Gölcük
Yağcılı
MANCINIK DAĞI
Çobanlar
Kertil
Gelembe
Karakurt
Kırkağaç
Başlamı
Palamut
Süleymanlı
Akhisar
Mecidiye
Kapaklı
Selendi
Saruhanli
Gölmarmara
Alibeyli
Halitpaşa
Büyükbelen
Yeniçöy
Aşağıçobanisa
Ahmetli
Turgutlu
Sartmu
Kemalpaşa
Armutlu
Bağyurdu
BOZ DAĞ
Kurudere
NİFKARLIĞI TEPE
Yukarıkızılca
Karaköy
Ödemiş
Dağkızılca
Kayaköy
Bayındır
Ayrancılar
Torbalı
Çırpı
Mahmutlar
Gökçen
Çaybaşı
Subaşı
Pamukyazı
Tire
Boğaziçi
Belevi
BAYRAKÇI MAĞARASI
Selçuk
EPHESOS
Pamucak
MERYEMANA
Ortaklar
Germencik
Aydın
İncirliova
Kuşadası
MAGNESIA
KARYAĞDI TEPE
Kuşadası Körfezi
KADIKALESİ
Söke
Bıyıklı
Koçarlı
Çakırbeyli
Davutlar
Yenidoğan
Bağarası
DİLEK YARIMADASI MİLLİ PARKI
Büyük Menderes Nehri
PRIENE
Karine
Atburgazi
Mersinbeleni
Doğanbey
Avşar
MYOS
Karakaya
Meriçler
MILET
Balat
Sakiremer
Kapıkırı
Çamiçi Gölü
HERAKLEIA
Akköy
ASSESSOS
Çamiçi
TEICHIUSSA
Akbük
Selimiye
EUROMOS
Yenihisar
DIDYMA
Altınkum
Tekağaç Burun
Kazıklı
Milas
IASOS
Kıyıkışlacık
İZMİR
Bornova
Buca
İnciraltı
Kaklıç
Çamaltı
Seydiköy
Güzelbahçe
Menderes
Bedemler
Orhanli
Seferihisar
Pancar
Değirmendere
Keler
Tahtalı Brj.
Sığacık
TEOS
Sığacık Körfezi
Ükmez
KOLOPHON
Gümüldür
CLAROS
Özdere
Doğanbey
MYONNESOS
Doğanbey Burun
Koraka Burun
Karaburun
Hasseki
Parlak
AK DAĞ
Küçükbahçe
Mordoğan
Uzon Adasi
İzmir Körfezi
Balıklıova
Çeşmealti
KLAZOMENAI
Urla
Ildır
Uzunkuyu
Çeşme
Alaçatı
Kara Burun
Akr. Skamniá
Μýthymna
Sykaminéa
Pétra
Stýpsi
Filia
ÁNTISSA
Ántissa
Mantamádos
Agia Paraskeví
Mystegná
Thermí
Kalloní
Vatoúsa
Sígri
Eresós
Parákoila
Kólpos Kallonís
Kerameia
Mytilíni
Akr. Sígri
Skála Eresoú
Skála
Vasiliká
Agiásos
Ampelikó
Skópelos
Loutrá
Krátigos
Polychnitos
Vatera
Lésvos
N. Λέσβος
Plomári
Skiáthos
Thessaloníki
Mýrina-Límnos
Ágios Efstrátios
Mýrina-Límnos
Rafína
Vólos
Chíos
Peiraías
İstanbul
Çanakkale
Mytilíni-Lésvos
Psará
N. Ψαρά
Kampiá
Agiásmata
Mármaro
Kardámyla
Melaniós
Oinoússes
N. Οινούσσες
Volissós
Lagkáda
Vrontádos
Chíos
N. Χίος
NÉA MONÍ
Thymianá
Kallimasiá
Pasá Limáni
Vessa
Armólia
Kalamotí
Mestá
Pyrgío
Kómi
Emporeiós
Akr. Mástichó
Rafína
Mýkonos
Peiraías
Bríndisi
Ancona
Sámos
Karlóvasi
Peiraías
Chíos
Náxos
Adámas-Mílos
Ag. Konstantínos
Avlákia
Kokkário
Sámos
Karlóvasi
Vathý
Marathókampos
Pýrgos
Ag. Kyriakí
Spatharaíoi
Pythagóreio
Sámos
N. Σάμος
IRAÍO
Ireo
Akr. Fanári
Ikaría
N. Ικαρία
Évdilos
Thérma
Fournoi
N. Φούρνοι
Ag. Minás
N. Ag. Μηνάς
Armenistis
Ag. Kýrikos
Christós
Thymaina
N. Θύμαινα
Fournoi
Náxos
Ámalo
Mýkonos
Náxos
Akr. Pápas
Agathonísi
N. Αγαθονήσι
Arkoí
N. Αρκοί
Pátmos
N. Πάτμος
Kámpos
Skála
Farmakonísi
Mýkonos
N. Μύκονος
Áno Merá
Dragonísi

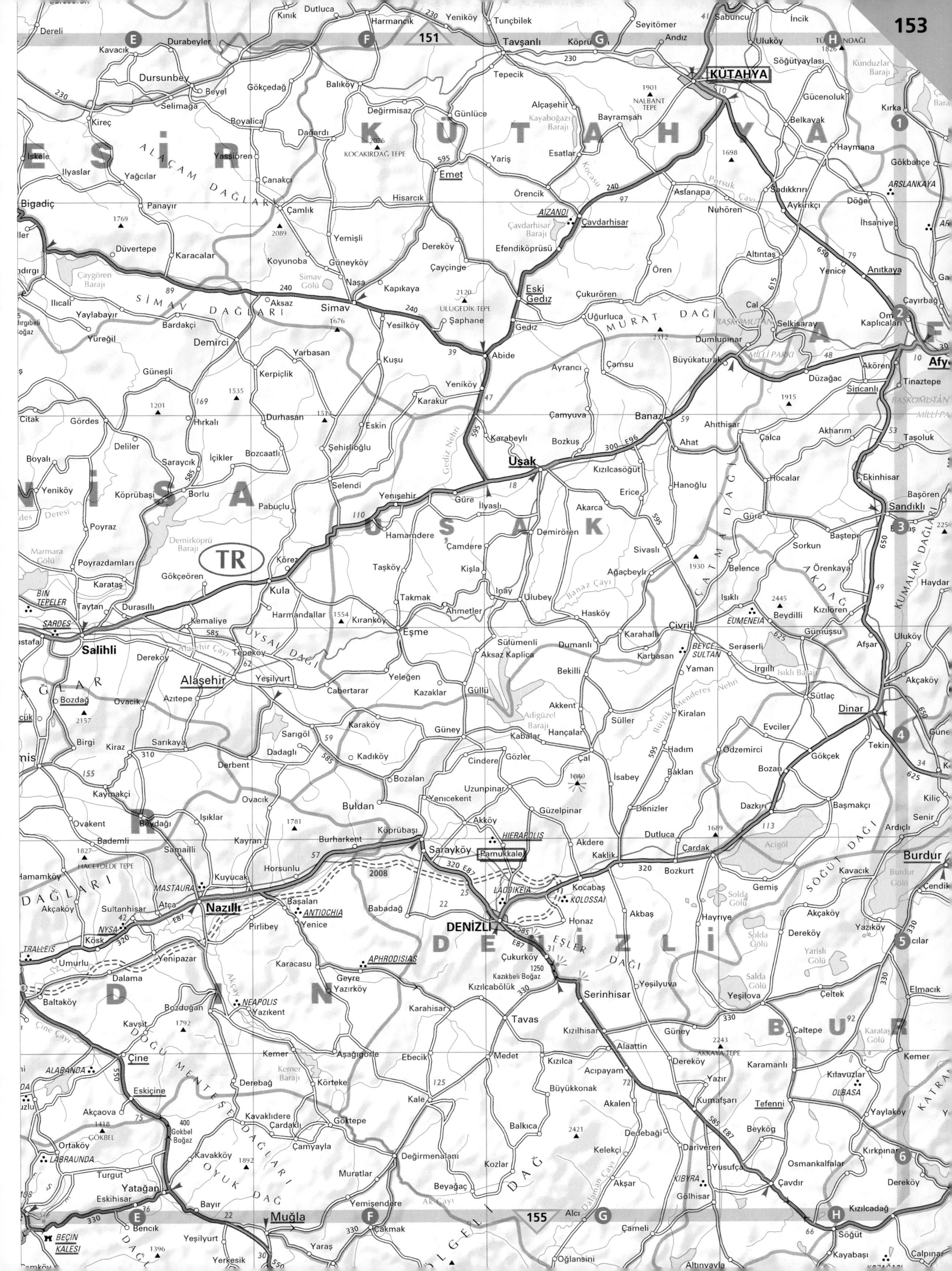

E
F
G
H
151
155
KÜTAHYA
MANİSA
UŞAK
DENİZLİ
AYDIN
BURDUR
TR
Kınık
Dutluca
Harmancık
Yeniköy
Tunçbilek
Seyitömer
Sabuncu
İncik
Dereli
Kavacık
Durabeyler
Tavşanlı
Köprü
Andız
Uluköy
Söğütyaylası
Kunduzlar Barajı
Dursunbey
Beyel
Gökçedağ
Balıköy
Tepecik
KÜTAHYA
Gücenoluk
Kırka
Selimağa
Değirmisaz
Günlüce
Alçaşehir
1901 NALBANT TEPE
Kayaboğazı Barajı
Bayramşah
Belkavak
Kireç
Boyalıca
Dağardı
2076 KOCAKIRDAĞ TEPE
1698
Haymana
İskele
ALAÇAM DAĞLARI
Yassıören
Yariş
Esatlar
Kocasu
Gökbahçe
İlyaslar
Yağcılar
Emet
Porsuk Çayı
ARSLANKAYA
Çanakçı
Örencik
Aslanapa
Sadıkkırı
Bigadiç
Panayır
Çamlık
Hisarcık
AİZANOİ
Çavdarhisar
Nuhören
Aykırıkçı
Döğer
1769
2089
Yemişli
Çavdarhisar Barajı
İhsaniye
Düvertepe
Karacalar
Dereköy
Efendiköprüsü
Altıntaş
Yenice
Anıtkaya
Çaygören Barajı
Koyunoba
Güneyköy
Çayçinge
Ören
Simav Gölü
Naşa
Kapıkaya
Eski Gediz
Çukurören
Cal
Ilıcalı
Aksaz
Simav
2120 ULUGEDİK TEPE
Şaphane
Uğurluca
MURAT DAĞI
BAŞKOMUTAN
Selkisaray
Çayırbağ
Kaplıcaları
Yaylabayır
SİMAV DAĞLARI
Bardakçı
1676
Yeşilköy
Gediz
2312
Dumlupınar
Yüreğil
Demirci
Abide
MİLLİ PARKI
Büyükaturak
Akören
Afyon
Yarbasan
Kuşu
Ayrancı
Çamsu
Düzağaç
Tinaztepe
Güneşli
Kerpiçlik
Yeniköy
Sincanlı
1535
Karakur
1915
1201
Durhasan
1514
Çamyuva
Banaz
Ahıthisar
Citak
Gördes
Hırkalı
Eskin
Karabeylı
Bozkuş
Ahat
Akharım
Çalca
Taşoluk
Deliler
Şehirlioğlu
Boyalı
Saraycık
İçikler
Bozcaatlı
Uşak
Kızılcasöğüt
Hocalar
Ekinhisar
Selendi
Gediz Nehri
Yeniköy
Köprübaşı
Borlu
Pabuçlu
Yenişehir
Güre
İlyaslı
Erice
Hanoğlu
Başören
Akarca
Sandıklı
Poyraz
Demirköprü Barajı
Hamamdere
Çamdere
Demirören
Güre
Baştepe
Marmara Gölü
Poyrazdamları
Körez
Taşköy
Kışla
Sivaslı
1930
Belence
Sorkun
Örenkaya
Haydar
Gökçeören
Ağaçbeyli
AKDAĞ
KUMALAR DAĞLARI
Karataş
Kula
İnay
Ulubey
Banaz Çayı
ÇATMA DAĞI
Isıklı
2445
BİN TEPELER
Taytan
Durasıllı
Takmak
Ahmetler
Hasköy
Beydilli
Kızılören
Harmandallar
1554
Kıranköy
EUMENEIA
SARDES
Kemaliye
Eşme
Karahallı
Çivril
Gümüşsu
Uluköy
Salihli
UYSAL DAĞI
Sülümenli
Dumanlı
BEYCE SULTAN
Seraserli
Afşar
Dereköy
Tepeköy
Alaşehir Çayı
Aksaz Kaplıca
Karbasan
Yaman
Irgıllı
Işıklı Barajı
Alaşehir
Yeşilyurt
Yeleğen
Bekilli
Akçaköy
Bozdağ
Ovacık
Azıtepe
Cabertarar
Kazaklar
Güllü
Büyük Menderes Nehri
Sütlaç
Dinar
2157
Akkent
Kiralan
Adıgüzel Barajı
Süller
Evciler
Sarıgöl
Karaköy
Güney
Hançalar
Kabalar
Birgi
Kiraz
Sarıkaya
Dadaglı
Kadıköy
Gözler
Çal
Hadım
Ödzemirci
Gökçek
Tekin
Derbent
Cindere
İsabey
Baklan
Bozan
Kaymakçi
Ovacık
Bozalan
Uzunpınar
1840
Yenicekent
Buldan
Güzelpınar
Denizler
Dazkırı
Başmakçı
Kiliç
Işıklar
Akköy
1781
1689
Senir
Ovakent
Beydağı
Köprübaşı
Burharkent
HIERAPOLIS
Dutluca
Ardıçlı
Bademli
Sarayköy
Pamukkale
Akdere
Çardak
SÖĞÜT DAĞI
Acıgöl
1827 HACETDEDE TEPE
Samailli
Kayran
Burdur
Horsunlu
Kaklik
Bozkurt
Burdur Gölü
Hamamköy
MASTAURA
Kuyucak
2008
Kocabaş
Kavacık
Çendik
LAODIKEIA
KOLOSSAI
Solda Gölü
Gemiş
Akçaköy
Sultanhisar
Atça
Nazilli
Başalan
ANTIOCHIA
Babadağ
Akbaş
Hayrıye
Akçaköy
NYSA
Pirlibey
Honaz
Yazıköy
Kösk
Yenice
DENİZLİ
Dereköy
TRALLEIS
EŞLER DAĞI
Yarislı Gölü
Umurlu
Yenipazar
Karacasu
APHRODISIAS
Çukurköy
Salda Gölü
Dalama
Geyre
1250 Kazıkbeli Boğaz
Yeşilyuva
Yazırköy
Kızılcabölük
Serinhisar
Yeşilova
Çeltek
Elmacık
Baltaköy
Bozdoğan
NEAPOLIS
Yazıkent
Karahisar
Tavas
Kavşit
1792
Kızılhisar
Güney
Çaltepe
Karataş Gölü
DOĞU MENTEŞE DAĞLARI
Alaattin
2243 AKKAYA TEPE
Çine Çayı
Çine
Kemer
Aşağıgörle
Ebecik
Medet
Kızılca
Dereköy
Karamanlı
Kemer
ALABANDA
Kemer Barajı
Acıpayam
Yazır
Kılavuzlar
Derebağ
Körteke
Büyükkonak
OLBASA
Eskiçine
Kale
Akalen
Kumafşarı
Tefenni
Akçaova
1418 GÖKBEL
400 Gokbel Boğaz
Kavaklıdere
Çardaklı
Göktepe
Balkıca
2421
Yaylaköy
KATRANCI
Ortaköy
Çamyayla
Dedebağı
Beyköy
LABRAUNDA
Kavakköy
1892
Değirmenalanı
Kelekçi
Dariveren
Kırkpınar
Turgut
Kozlar
Yusufça
Osmankalfalar
YÜK DAĞ
Muratlar
Dalaman Çayı
Akşar
KİBYRA
Dereköy
Yatağan
Beyağaç
Gölhisar
Çavdır
Eskihisar
Yemişendere
Ak Çayı
Kızılcadağ
GÖLGELİ DAĞ
Alcı
Muğla
Bencık
Bayır
Çakmak
Çameli
Söğüt
BEÇİN KALESİ
Yeşilyurt
1396
Yaraş
Oğlansini
Kayabaşı
Yerkesik
Altınyayla
Çalpınar
E87
E96
585
595
230
240
320
330
650
625

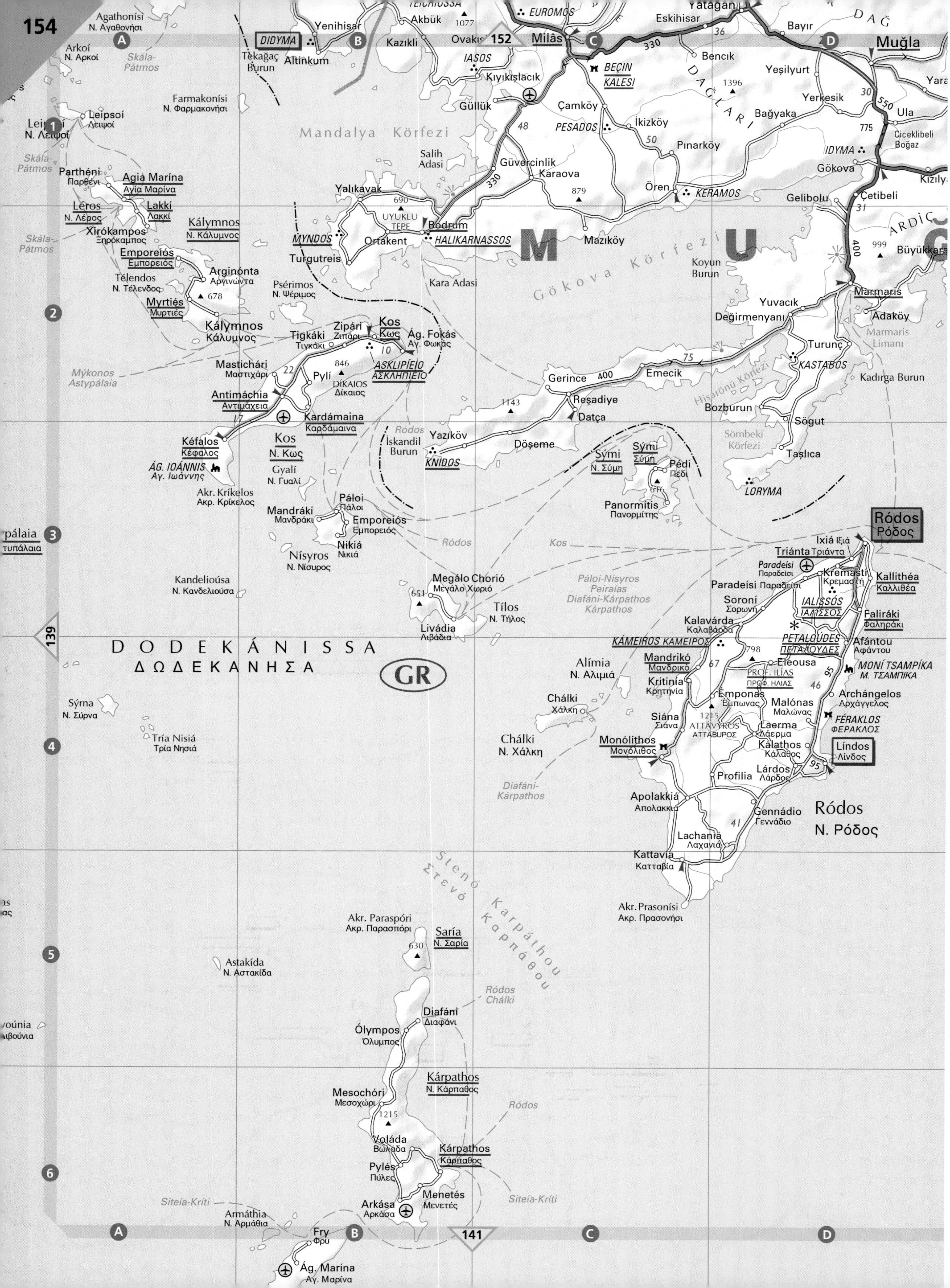
Agathonísi
N. Αγαθονήσι
Arkoí
N. Αρκοί
Skála-Pátmos
DIDYMA
Tekağaç Burun
Altınkum
Yenihisar
Akbük
1077
Kazıklı
Ovakışla
152
Milâs
Eskihisar
Yatağan
Bayır
Muğla
DAĞ
EUROMOS
IASOS
Kıyıkışlacık
BEÇİN KALESİ
Bencık
330
36
Yeşilyurt
Yara
1396
DAĞLARI
Farmakonísi
N. Φαρμακονήσι
Leipsoí
Λειψοί
Leipsoí
N. Λειψοί
Güllük
Çamköy
Yerkesik
30
550
Ula
Bağyaka
775
PESADOS
İkizköy
48
50
Pınarköy
Çiceklibeli Boğaz
IDYMA
Mandalya Körfezi
Salih Adasi
Güvercinlik
Karaova
Gökova
Kızılya
Skála-Pátmos
Parthéni
Παρθένι
Agia Marína
Αγία Μαρίνα
Léros
N. Λέρος
Lakkí
Λακκί
Yalıkavak
690
UYUKLU TEPE
Bodrum
879
Ören
KERAMOS
Gelibolu
Çetibeli
31
Kálymnos
N. Κάλυμνος
Xirókampos
Ξηρόκαμπος
Skála-Pátmos
MYNDOS
Ortakent
HALIKARNASSOS
Turgutreis
MUĞ
Mazıköy
ARDIÇ
400
999
Büyükkara
Emporeiós
Εμπορειός
Arginónta
Αργινώντα
Télendos
N. Τέλενδος
678
Myrtiés
Μυρτιές
Psérimos
N. Ψέριμος
Kara Adasi
Gökova Körfezi
Koyun Burun
Marmaris
Adaköy
Marmaris Limanı
Yuvacık
Değirmenyanı
Kálymnos
Κάλυμνος
Zipári
Ζιπάρι
Kos
Κως
Tigkáki
Τιγκάκι
Ág. Fokás
Αγ. Φωκάς
10
Turunç
KASTABOS
75
Mýkonos
Astypálaia
Mastichári
Μαστιχάρι
22
846
Pylí
DÍKAIOS
Δίκαιος
ASKLIPÍEIO
ΑΣΚΛΗΠΙΕΙΟ
Gerince
400
Emecik
Hisarönü Körfezi
Kadırga Burun
Antimáchia
Αντιμάχεια
17
Kardámaina
Καρδάμαινα
1143
Reşadiye
Datça
Bozburun
Sögut
Kéfalos
Κέφαλος
Kos
N. Κως
ÁG. IOANNIS
Αγ. Ιωάννης
Ródos
İskandil Burun
Yazıköv
KNIDOS
Döşeme
Sými
N. Σύμη
Sými
Σύμη
Pédi
Πέδι
Sömbeki Körfezi
Taşlıca
Gyalí
N. Γυαλί
Akr. Kríkelos
Ακρ. Κρίκελος
Mandráki
Μανδράκι
Páloi
Πάλοι
Emporeiós
Εμπορειός
616
Panormítis
Πανορμίτης
LORYMA
Ródos
Ρόδος
Astypálaia
Ródos
Kos
Nikiá
Νικιά
Nísyros
N. Νίσυρος
Ixiá
Ιξιά
Triánta
Τριάντα
Paradeísi
Παραδείσι
Kandelioúsa
N. Κανδελιούσα
Megálo Chorió
Μεγάλο Χωριό
651
Tílos
N. Τήλος
Livádia
Λιβάδια
Páloi-Nísyros
Peiraias
Diafáni-Kárpathos
Kárpathos
Kremastí
Κρεμαστή
Kallithéa
Καλλιθέα
Paradeísi
Παραδείσι
Sorōní
Σορωνή
IALISSÓS
ΙΑΛΥΣΟΣ
Faliráki
Φαληράκι
Kalavárda
Καλαβάρδα
PETALOÚDES
ΠΕΤΑΛΟΥΔΕΣ
Afántou
Αφάντου
139
DODEKÁNISSA
ΔΩΔΕΚΑΝΗΣΑ
GR
KÁMEIROS ΚΑΜΕΙΡΟΣ
798
Alímia
N. Αλιμιά
Mandrikó
Μανδρικό
67
Eleousa
PROF. ILIAS
ΠΡΟΦ. ΗΛΙΑΣ
MONÍ TSAMPÍKA
Μ. ΤΣΑΜΠΙΚΑ
95
46
Kritinía
Κρητηνία
Émponas
Έμπωνας
Archángelos
Αρχάγγελος
Chálki
Χάλκη
Síana
Σιάνα
1215
Malónas
Μαλώνας
FÉRAKLOS
ΦΕΡΑΚΛΟΣ
ATTÁVYROS
ΑΤΤΑΒΥΡΟΣ
Laerma
Λάερμα
Sýrna
N. Σύρνα
Tría Nisiá
Τρία Νησιά
Chálki
N. Χάλκη
Monólithos
Μονόλιθος
Kálathos
Κάλαθος
Líndos
Λίνδος
95
Profilia
Lárdos
Λάρδος
Diafáni-Kárpathos
Apolakkiá
Απολακκιά
Gennádio
Γεννάδιο
Ródos
N. Ρόδος
41
Lachaniá
Λαχανιά
Kattavía
Καττάβια
Stenó Kárpathou
Στενό Καρπάθου
Akr. Prasonísi
Ακρ. Πρασονήσι
Akr. Paraspóri
Ακρ. Παρασπόρι
Saría
N. Σαρία
630
Astakída
N. Αστακίδα
Ródos
Chálki
Diafáni
Διαφάνι
Ólympos
Όλυμπος
Kárpathos
N. Κάρπαθος
Mesochóri
Μεσοχώρι
Ródos
1215
Voláda
Βωλάδα
Kárpathos
Κάρπαθος
Pylés
Πύλες
Siteía-Kríti
Siteía-Kríti
Menetés
Μενετές
Arkása
Αρκάσα
Armáthia
N. Αρμάθια
Fry
Φρυ
141
Ág. Marína
Αγ. Μαρίνα
A
B
C
D
1
2
3
4
5
6

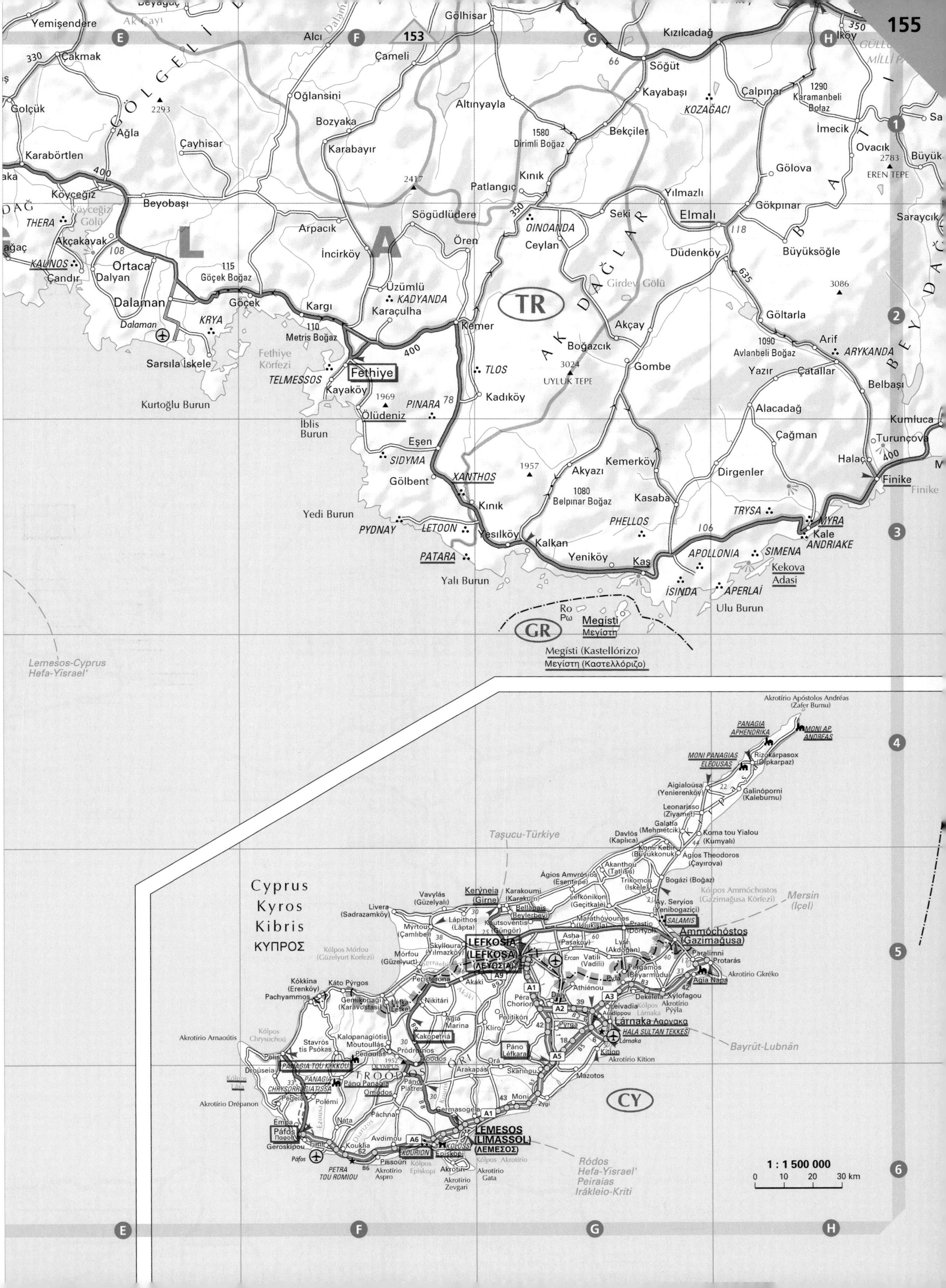
Fethiye
Fethiye Körfezi
Dalaman
Ortaca
Köyceğiz
Elmalı
Kaş
Finike
Kemer
Kınık
Kalkan
Ölüdeniz
TR
GR
Megísti
Μεγίστη
Megísti (Kastellórizo)
Μεγίστη (Καστελλόριζο)
Lemesos-Cyprus
Hefa-Yisrael'
Cyprus
Kyros
Kibris
ΚΥΠΡΟΣ
LEFKOSIA (LEFKOŞA) (ΛΕΥΚΩΣΙΑ)
LEMESOS (LIMASSOL) (ΛΕΜΕΣΟΣ)
Lárnaka
Ammóchostos (Gazimağusa)
Kerýneia (Girne)
Páfos
Agia Napa
CY
Taşucu-Türkiye
Mersin (İçel)
Bayrūt-Lubnān
Ródos
Hefa-Yisrael'
Peiraías
Irákleio-Kríti
1 : 1 500 000
0 10 20 30 km

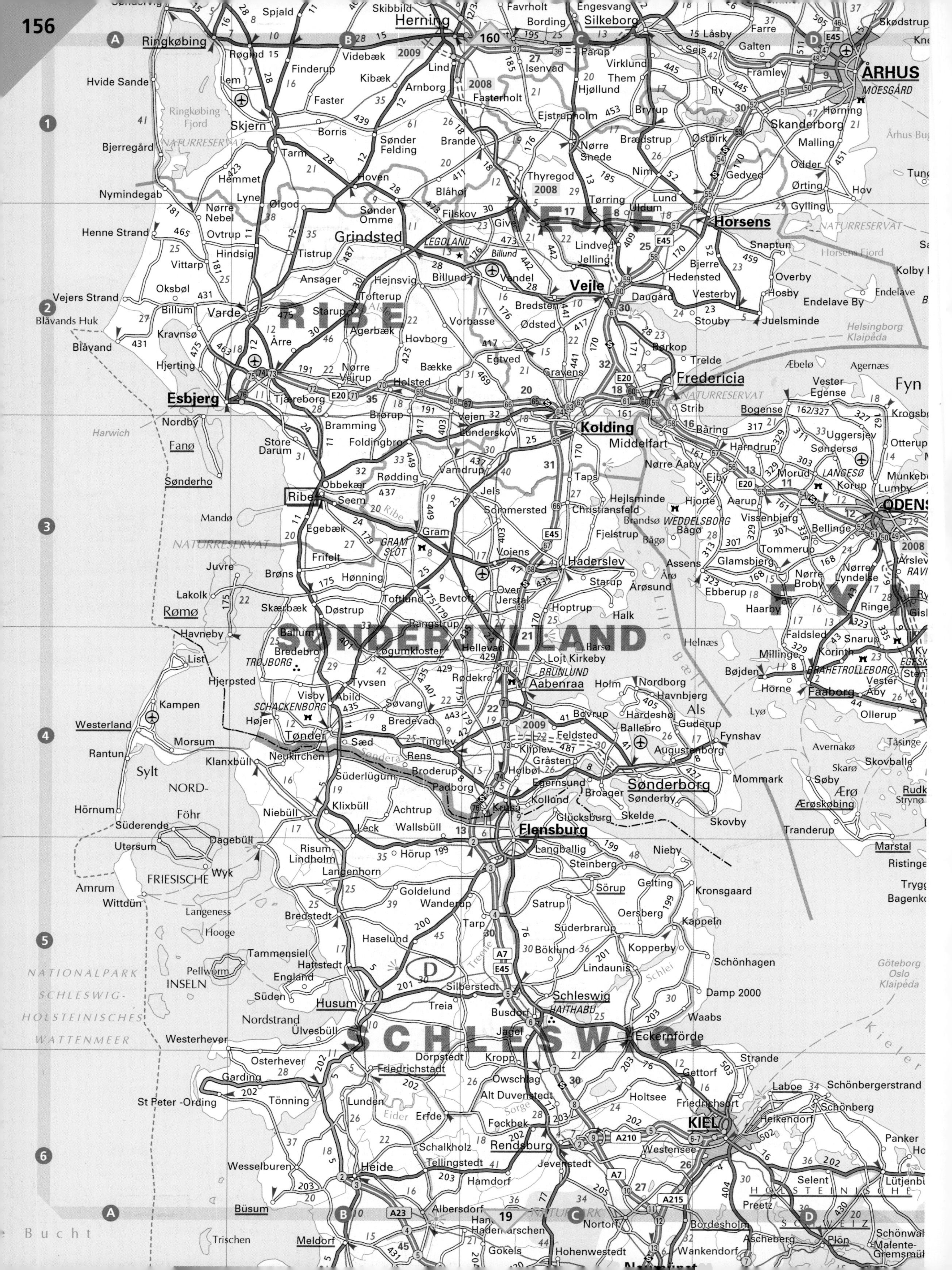
Ringkøbing
Herning
Silkeborg
Århus
Moesgård
Skødstrup
Spjald
Skibbild
Favrholt
Engesvang
Bording
Farre
Galten
Låsby
Sejs
Videbæk
Lind
Parup
Isenvad
Virklund
Them
Framley
Røgind
Lem
Hvide Sande
Finderup
Kibæk
Arnborg
Fasterholt
Hjøllund
Ry
Faster
Bryrup
Ejstrupholm
Hørning
Skanderborg
Ringkøbing Fjord
Skjern
Borris
Sønder Felding
Brande
Nørre Snede
Brædstrup
Østbirk
Malling
Århus Bugt
Bjerregård
Naturreservat
Tarm
Hoven
Thyregod
Nim
Gedved
Odder
Hemmet
Lyne
Blåhøj
Tørring
Lund
Ørting
Hov
Nymindegab
Ølgod
Sønder Omme
Filskov
Give
Uldum
Gylling
Nørre Nebel
Horsens
Henne Strand
Ovtrup
Grindsted
Legoland
Billund
Lindved
Snaptun
Hindsig
Tistrup
Jelling
Horsens Fjord
Vittarp
Kolby
Ansager
Hejnsvig
Vandel
Bjerre
Hedensted
Oksbøl
Vejle
Overby
Vejers Strand
Billum
Varde
Tofterup
Daugård
Vesterby
Hosby
Endelave
Endelave By
Blåvands Huk
Starup
Ribe
Vorbasse
Bredsten
Stouby
Juelsminde
Kravnsø
Agerbæk
Ødsted
Helsingborg
Klaipėda
Blåvand
Årre
Hovborg
Børkop
Egtved
Trelde
Hjerting
Nørre Vejrup
Bække
Gravens
Fredericia
Æbelø
Agernæs
Holsted
Vester Egense
Fyn
Esbjerg
Tjæreborg
Bogense
Krogsbølle
Brørup
Vejen
Strib
Nordby
Bramming
Lunderskov
Kolding
Båring
Uggerslev
Harwich
Store Darum
Foldingbro
Middelfart
Harndrup
Søndersø
Otterup
Fanø
Vamdrup
Nørre Aaby
Morud
Langesø
Munkebo
Sønderho
Rødding
Taps
Ejby
Korup
Lumby
Obbekær
Jels
Hejlsminde
Hjorte
Aarup
Odense
Seem
Sommersted
Christiansfeld
Mandø
Egebæk
Gram
Gram Slot
Brandsø
Weddelsborg
Vissenbjerg
Bellinge
Båg
Fjelstrup
Bågø
Tommerup
Frifelt
Vojens
Haderslev
Assens
Glamsbjerg
Årslev
Juvre
Brøns
Hønning
Starup
Årø
Nørre Lyndelse
Nørre Broby
Lakolk
Toftlund
Bevtoft
Over Jerstal
Årøsund
Ebberup
Rømø
Skærbæk
Døstrup
Hoptrup
Haarby
Ringe
Rangstrup
Halk
Lille Bælt
Sønderjylland
Havneby
Ballum
Bredebro
Løgumkloster
Hellevad
Barsø
Helnæs
Faldsled
Snarup
List
Trøjborg
Lojt Kirkeby
Millinge
Korinth
Brunlund
Bøjden
Brahetrolleborg
Egeskov
Rødekro
Hjerpsted
Tyvsen
Aabenraa
Holm
Nordborg
Vester Åby
Kampen
Visby
Abild
Havnbjerg
Horne
Faaborg
Schackenborg
Søvang
Als
Hardeshøj
Lyø
Westerland
Højer
Bredevad
Bovrup
Guderup
Ollerup
Tønder
Tinglev
Ballebro
Fynshav
Morsum
Sæd
Feldsted
Augustenborg
Tåsinge
Rantum
Rens
Kliplev
Avernakø
Klanxbüll
Neukirchen
Søndera
Gråsten
Skovballe
Sylt
Broderup
Holbøl
Skarø
Nord-
Süderlügum
Egernsund
Sønderborg
Mommark
Søby
Rudkøbing
Padborg
Broager
Sønderby
Ærø
Strynø
Hörnum
Klixbüll
Kollund
Ærøskøbing
Föhr
Niebüll
Achtrup
Kruså
Skelde
Glücksburg
Süderende
Leck
Wallsbüll
Flensburg
Skovby
Tranderup
Dagebüll
Utersum
Risum-Lindholm
Hörup
Langballig
Nieby
Marstal
Steinberg
Ristinge
Friesische
Wyk
Amrum
Langenhorn
Gelting
Sörup
Kronsgaard
Bagenkop
Goldelund
Wittdün
Wanderup
Satrup
Langeness
Bredstedt
Oersberg
Hooge
Tarp
Süderbrarup
Kappeln
Haselund
Kopperby
Tammensiel
Hattstedt
Böklund
Schönhagen
Göteborg
Oslo
Klaipėda
Nationalpark
Pellworm
D
Lindaunis
Schlei
Schleswig-
Inseln
England
Silberstedt
Schleswig
Damp 2000
Süden
Holsteinisches
Husum
Treia
Haithabu
Busdorf
Nordstrand
Waabs
Wattenmeer
Ülvesbüll
Westerhever
Jagel
Eckernförde
Kieler
Schleswig
Osterhever
Dörpstedt
Kropp
Strande
Friedrichstadt
Gettorf
Garding
Owschlag
Laboe
Schönbergerstrand
Alt Duvenstedt
Tönning
Holtsee
Schönberg
St Peter -Ording
Friedrichsort
Lunden
Sorge
Heikendorf
Eider
Erfde
Kiel
Fockbek
Panker
Schalkholz
Rendsburg
Westensee
Wesselburen
Heide
Tellingstedt
Jevenstedt
Selent
Lütjenburg
Hamdorf
Holsteinische Schweiz
Büsum
Albersdorf
Preetz
Bordesholm
Trischen
Hanerau-Hademarschen
Nortorf
Schönwalde
Meldorf
Gokels
Hohenwestedt
Wankendorf
Ascheberg
Plön
Malente-Gremsmühlen
Bucht
160
19

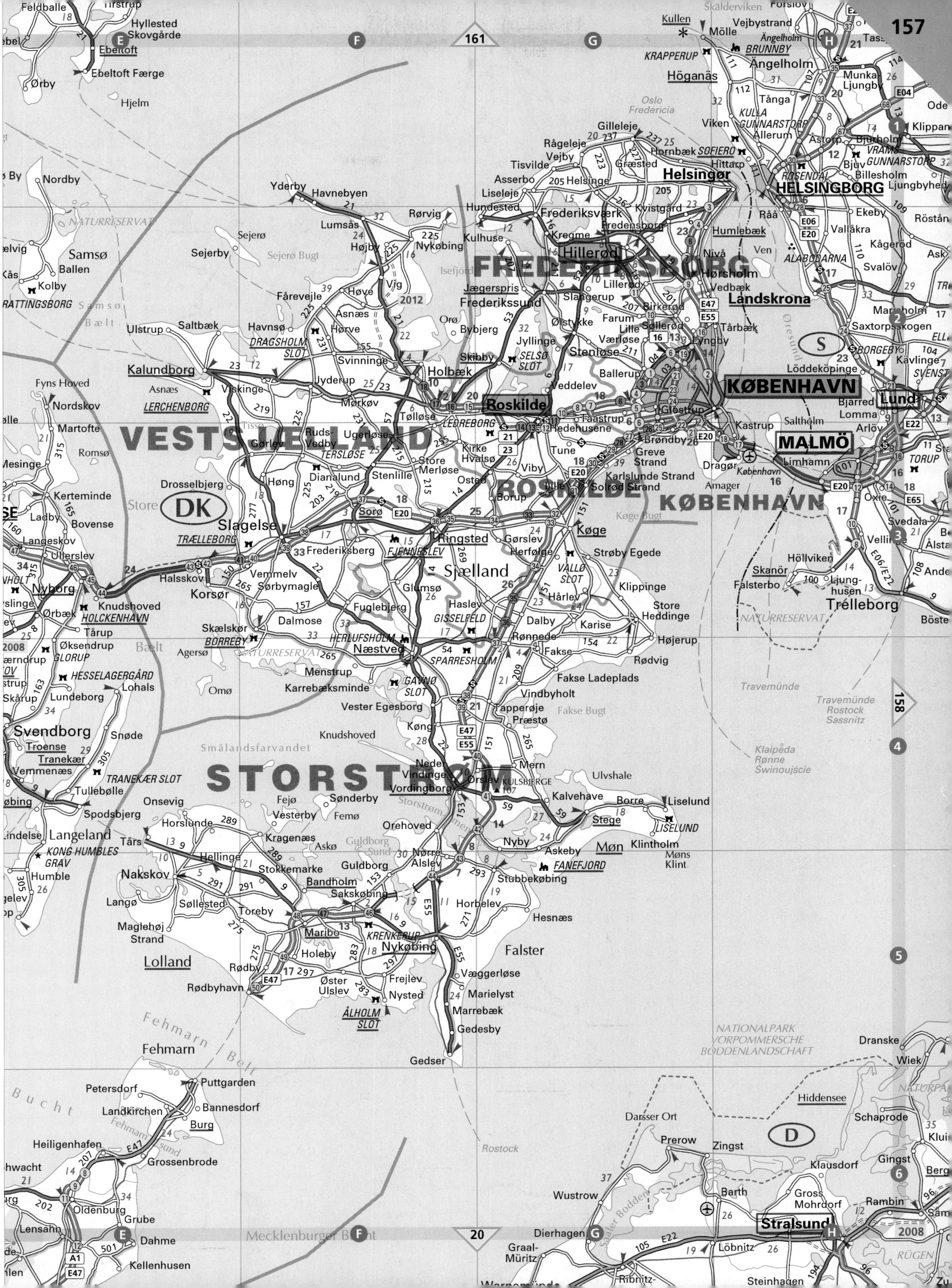
161
20
158
Feldballe
Hyllested Skovgårde
Ebeltoft
Ebeltoft Færge
Ørby
Hjelm
Nordby
Samsø
Ballen
Kolby
RATTINGSBORG
Samsø Bælt
NATURRESERVAT
Yderby
Havnebyen
Lumsås
Rørvig
Sejerø
Sejerby
Sejerø Bugt
Højby
Nykøbing
Isefjord
Vig
Fårevejle
Høve
Asnæs
Hørve
Havnsø
Saltbæk
Ulstrup
DRAGSHOLM SLOT
Svinninge
Kalundborg
Asnæs
LERCHENBORG
Viskinge
Jyderup
Holbæk
Mørkøv
Tølløse
Fyns Hoved
Nordskov
Martofte
Romsø
Mesinge
Kerteminde
Ladby
Bovense
Langeskov
Ullerslev
Nyborg
Ørbæk
Knudshoved
HOLCKENHAVN
Tårup
Øksendrup
GLORUP
HESSELAGERGÅRD
Lohals
Lundeborg
Skårup
Svendborg
Troense
Tranekær
Snøde
Vemmenæs
TRANEKÆR SLOT
Tullebølle
Spodsbjerg
Langeland
KONG HUMBLES GRAV
Humble
VESTSJÆLLAND
Ruds-Vedby
Ugerløse
Gørlev
TERSLØSE
Høng
Dianalund
Stenlille
Drosselbjerg
Store Bælt
DK
Slagelse
TRÆLLEBORG
Sorø
Frederiksberg
Ringsted
FJENNESLEV
Halsskov
Korsør
Vemmelv
Sørbymagle
Glumsø
Sjælland
Skælskør
BORREBY
Agersø
Dalmose
Fuglebjerg
Næstved
HERLUFSHOLM
Menstrup
Karrebæksminde
GAVNØ SLOT
Omø
Vester Egesborg
Knudshoved
Smålandsfarvandet
Kong
STORSTRØM
Neder Vindinge
Vordingborg
Ørslev
KULSBJERGE
Fejø
Sønderby
Femø
Vesterby
Onsevig
Horslunde
Kragenæs
Askø
Orehoved
Tårs
Hellinge
Nakskov
Stokkemarke
Guldborg Sund
Guldborg
Bandholm
Sakskøbing
Langø
Søllested
Toreby
Maglehøj Strand
Maribo
KRENKERUP
Holeby
Nykøbing
Lolland
Rødby
Rødbyhavn
Øster Ulslev
Frejlev
Nysted
ÅLHOLM SLOT
Falster
Væggerløse
Marielyst
Marrebæk
Gedesby
Gedser
Horbelev
Hesnæs
Stubbekøbing
Nørre Alslev
FANEFJORD
Nyby
Askeby
Møn
Klintholm
Møns Klint
Stege
Kalvehave
Borre
Liselund
LISELUND
Ulvshale
Fehmarn Belt
Fehmarn
Petersdorf
Puttgarden
Bannesdorf
Landkirchen
Burg
Heiligenhafen
Fehmarnsund
Großenbrode
Oldenburg
Grube
Lensahn
Dahme
Kellenhusen
Mecklenburger Bucht
Rostock
Kullen
Mölle
Vejbystrand
Ängelholm
BRUNNBY
KRAPPERUP
Höganäs
Munka-Ljungby
Tånga
KULLA GUNNARSTORP
Viken
Allerum
Åstorp
Bjuv
Klippan
Billesholm
Ljungbyhed
VRAMS GUNNARSTORP
SOFIERO
Hittarp
ROSENDAL
HELSINGBORG
Råå
Ekeby
Vallåkra
Kågeröd
Svalöv
Röstånga
Ven
ALABODARNA
Landskrona
Marieholm
Saxtorpsskogen
Gilleleje
Rågeleje
Vejby
Tisvilde
Asserbo
Liseleje
Hundested
Hornbæk
Græsted
Helsinge
Helsingør
Kvistgård
Frederiksværk
Fredensborg
Kregme
Kulhuse
Humlebæk
Hillerød
FREDERIKSBORG
Nivå
Hørsholm
Vedbæk
Lillerød
Jægerspris
Frederikssund
Slangerup
Birkerød
Ølstykke
Farum
Søllerød
Tårbæk
Lille Værløse
Lyngby
Stenløse
Jyllinge
Bybjerg
Orø
Skibby
SELSØ SLOT
Ballerup
Veddelev
Roskilde
LEDREBORG
Glostrup
Fåastrup
Hedehusene
KØBENHAVN
Kastrup
Saltholm
Brøndby
Tune
Greve Strand
Kirke Hvalsø
Store Merløse
Viby
Osted
Karlslunde Strand
Solrød Strand
Dragør
Amager
ROSKILDE
Borup
KØBENHAVN
Køge Bugt
Køge
Gørslev
Herfølge
Strøby Egede
VALLØ SLOT
Klippinge
Hårlev
Store Heddinge
Hasley
GISSELFELD
Dalby
Karise
Rønnede
Fakse
Højerup
SPARRESHOLM
Rødvig
Fakse Ladeplads
Vindbyholt
Fakse Bugt
Tappernøje
Præstø
Mern
Øresund
S
BORGEBY
Kävlinge
Löddeköpinge
SVENSTORP
Lund
Bjarred
Lomma
Arlöv
MALMÖ
Limhamn
TORUP
Oxie
Svedala
Vellinge
Höllviken
Skanör
Falsterbo
Ljunghusen
Trelleborg
Ålstad
Anderslöv
Böste
NATURRESERVAT
Travemünde
Travemünde Rostock Sassnitz
Klaipėda Rønne Świnoujście
Oslo Fredericia
NATIONALPARK VORPOMMERSCHE BODDENLANDSCHAFT
Dranske
Wiek
Hiddensee
Schaprode
D
Darsser Ort
Prerow
Zingst
Gingst
Klausdorf
Wustrow
Barth
Gross Mohrdorf
Rambin
Stralsund
Dierhagen
Löbnitz
Graal-Müritz
Ribnitz-
Steinhagen
RÜGEN

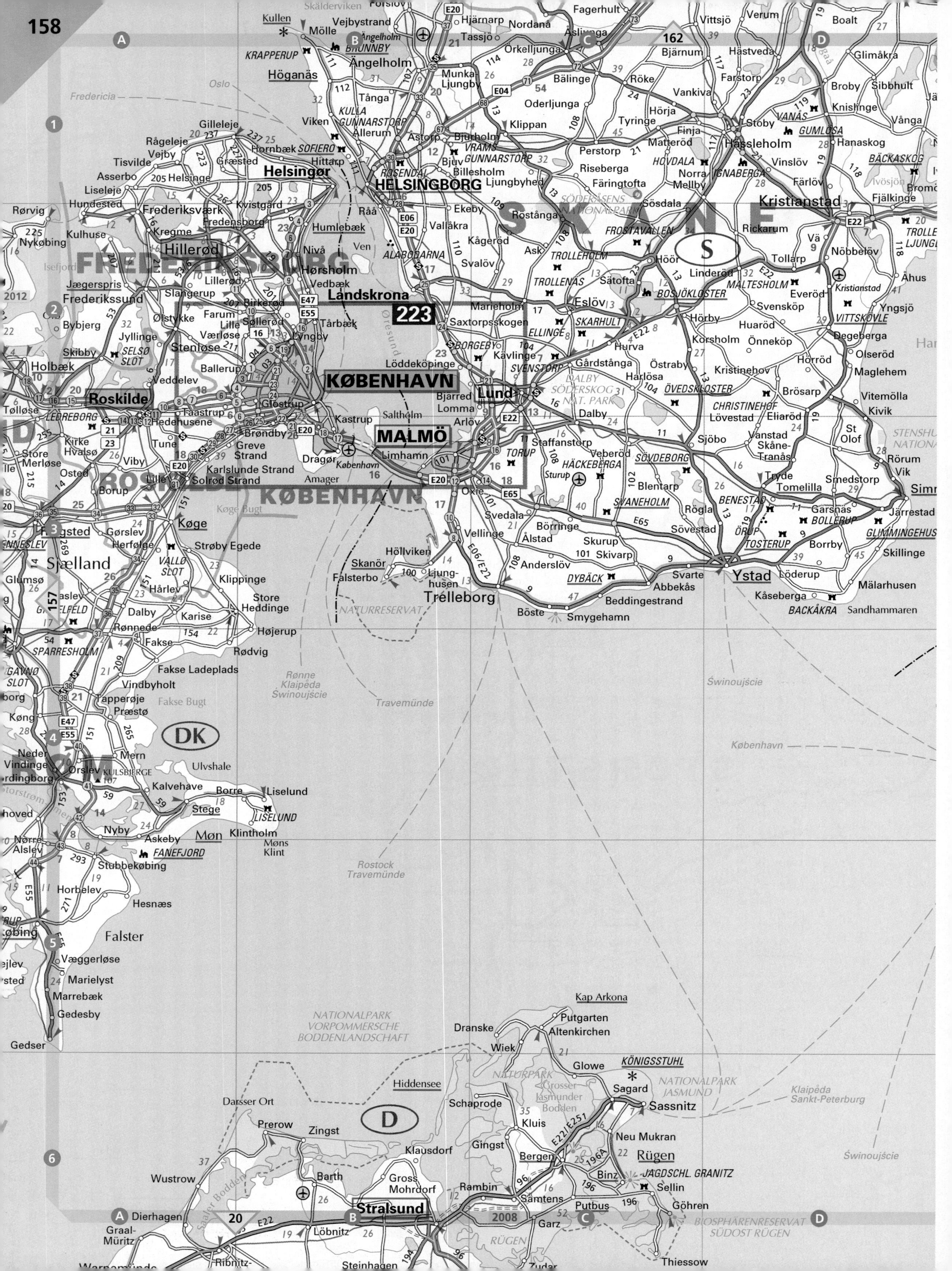
Kullen
Mölle
Vejbystrand
Hjärnarp
Nordanå
Fagerhult
Åsljunga
Vittsjö
Verum
Boalt
Ängelholm
BRUNNBY
Tassjö
Örkelljunga
Bjärnum
Hästveda
Glimåkra
KRAPPERUP
Ängelholm
Höganäs
Munka-Ljungby
Bälinge
Röke
Farstorp
Broby
Sibbhult
Oslo
Fredericia
Tånga
Vankiva
Oderljunga
Hörja
Knislinge
KULLA GUNNARSTORP
Viken
Klippan
Tyringe
VANÅS
Stoby
Vånga
Gilleleje
Allerum
Åstorp
Bjurholm
Finja
GUMLÖSA
Hässleholm
Hanaskog
Rågeleje
Vejby
Hornbæk
SOFIERO
VRAMS GUNNARSTORP
Perstorp
Matteröd
HOVDALA
Vinslöv
BÄCKASKOG
Tisvilde
Græsted
Hittarp
Bjuv
Riseberga
Norra Mellby
IGNABERGA
Asserbo
Helsinge
Helsingør
ROSENDAL
Billesholm
Färlöv
Ivösjön
Liseleje
HELSINGBORG
Ljungbyhed
Färingtofta
Hundested
Frederiksværk
Kvistgård
Råå
Ekeby
SÖDERÅSENS NATIONALPARK
Sösdala
Kristianstad
Fjälkinge
Rørvig
Fredensborg
Röstånga
SKÅNE
Nykøbing
Kulhuse
Kregme
Humlebæk
Vallåkra
FROSTAVALLEN
Rickarum
TROLLE LJUNGBY
Hillerød
Nivå
Ven
ALABODARNA
Kågeröd
Ask
TROLLEHOLM
Höör
Vä
Nöbbelöv
Isefjord
FREDERIKSBORG
Hørsholm
Svalöv
Tollarp
Linderöd
Lillerød
Vedbæk
Sätofta
TROLLENÄS
MALTESHOLM
Åhus
Jægerspris
Slangerup
Landskrona
BOSJÖKLOSTER
Everöd
Frederikssund
Birkerød
Marieholm
Eslöv
Svensköp
Yngsjö
Bybjerg
Ølstykke
Farum
Søllerød
Tårbæk
Öresund
Saxtorpsskogen
SKARHULT
Hörby
VITTSKÖVLE
Jyllinge
Værløse
Lyngby
ELLINGE
Huaröd
Degeberga
SELSØ SLOT
Skibby
Stenløse
BORGEBY
Kävlinge
Hurva
Korsholm
Önneköp
Olseröd
Holbæk
Ballerup
Löddeköpinge
SVENSTORP
Gårdstånga
Östraby
Hörröd
Maglehem
KØBENHAVN
Harlösa
Kristinehov
Veddelev
Lund
DALBY SÖDERSKOG NAT. PARK
ÖVEDSKLOSTER
Brösarp
Roskilde
Bjärred
Vitemölla
Tølløse
LEDREBORG
Faastrup
Glostrup
Saltholm
Lomma
CHRISTINEHOF
Lövestad
Eliaröd
Kivik
Hedehusene
Kastrup
Dalby
St Olof
Kirke Hvalsø
Tune
Brøndby
Arlöv
Vanstad
Skåne-Tranås
STENSHUVUD NATIONALPARK
Store Merløse
Greve Strand
MALMÖ
Staffanstorp
Sjöbo
Rörum
Viby
Dragør
København
Limhamn
TORUP
Veberöd
HÄCKEBERGA
SÖVDEBORG
Vik
Osted
Lille
Karlslunde Strand
Solrød Strand
Amager
Sturup
Tryde
Smedstorp
ROSKILDE
KØBENHAVN
Oxie
Blentarp
Tomelilla
Simrishamn
Borup
Køge Bugt
Svedala
SVANEHOLM
BENESTAD
Rögla
Gärsnäs
Järrestad
Ringsted
Gørslev
Køge
Börringe
BOLLERUP
Herfølge
Strøby Egede
Vellinge
Ålstad
Skurup
Sövestad
ÖRUP
TOSTERUP
Borrby
GLIMMINGEHUS
Sjælland
VALLØ SLOT
Höllviken
Skivarp
Skillinge
Glumsø
Klippinge
Skanör
Falsterbo
Ljunghusen
Anderslöv
Svarte
Ystad
Löderup
Haslev
Hårlev
Store Heddinge
DYBÄCK
Abbekås
Kåseberga
Mälarhusen
Dalby
Karise
Trelleborg
NATURRESERVAT
Beddingestrand
BACKÅKRA
Sandhammaren
Rønnede
Höjerup
Böste
Smygehamn
Fakse
SPARRESHOLM
Rødvig
GAVNØ SLOT
Fakse Ladeplads
Rønne
Klaipėda
Świnoujście
Vindbyholt
Travemünde
Tappernøje
Fakse Bugt
Præstø
DK
København
Mern
Vindinge
Ørslev
KULSBJERGE
Ulvshale
Vordingborg
Kalvehave
Borre
Liselund
LISELUND
Stege
Nyby
Askeby
Møn
Klintholm
Nørre Alslev
FANEFJORD
Møns Klint
Stubbekøbing
Rostock
Travemünde
Horbelev
Hesnæs
Falster
Væggerløse
Marielyst
Marrebæk
Gedesby
Gedser
Kap Arkona
Putgarten
NATIONALPARK VORPOMMERSCHE BODDENLANDSCHAFT
Dranske
Altenkirchen
Wiek
KÖNIGSSTUHL
Glowe
NATURPARK
Grosser Jasmunder Bodden
NATIONALPARK JASMUND
Klaipėda
Sankt-Peterburg
Hiddensee
Sagard
Darsser Ort
Schaprode
Sassnitz
Kluis
Prerow
D
Zingst
Neu Mukran
Klausdorf
Gingst
Bergen
Rügen
Świnoujście
Wustrow
Barth
Gross Mohrdorf
Binz
JAGDSCHL. GRANITZ
Rambin
Sellin
Samtens
Dierhagen
Stralsund
Putbus
Göhren
Graal-Müritz
Löbnitz
RÜGEN
Garz
BIOSPHÄRENRESERVAT SÜDOST RÜGEN
Ribnitz-
Steinhagen
Thiessow

BLEKINGE
Kyrkhult
Vilshult
Hallabro
Ringamåla
Bökemåla
Olofström
Svängsta
Asarum
Rödby
Bräkne-Hoby
Mörrum
Pukavik
Karlshamn
Sonekulla
Ronneby
Kallinge
Hjortsberga
Tving
Nättraby
Listerby
Karlskrona
Kuggeboda
Tjurkö
Drottningskär
Rödeby
Lyckeby
Sälleryd
Jämjöslätt
Torhamn
Flyme
163
Bidalite
Brömsebro
Kristianopel
Bergkvara
GETTLINGE
Degerhamn
Segerstad
Mellstaby
Grönhögen
Ottenby
Näsby
LÅNGE JAN
Ölands södra udde
Norje
Pukaviksbukten
Sölvesborg
Mjällby
Nogersund
Liepāja
Klaipėda
Utlängan
Gdynia
Hammerodde
Christiansø
Sandvig
HAMMERSHUS
Allinge
Tejn
Bornholm
DK
BORNHOLM
Gudhjem
Hasle
Klemensker
Østerlars
Svaneke
Nyker
Østermarie
Rønne
Nylars
Aakirkeby
Arnager
Neksø
Pedersker
Snogebæk
Dueodde
Helsinki
Jezioro Gardno
Rowy
PL
Ustka
Objazda
Gabino
Jarosławiec
Jezioro Wicko
Wicie
Postomino
Słupsk
Drozdowo
Kanin
Darłówko
Wieprza
Dąbki
Darłowo
Staniewice
Warszkowo
Sławno
Morskie
2008
Korzybie
Łazy
Malechowo
E
F
G
H
1
2
3
4
5
6
22

A
B
C
D
1
2
3
4
5
6
FÆRØERNE
FØROYAR
FÆRØERNE /
FØROYAR
FR
1 : 1 000 000
0
10
20 km
Kalsoy
Kunoy
Viðoy
Viðareiði
Tjørnuvík
Eiði
882
Gjógv
Fugloy
Eysturoy
Oyndartfjørður
Streymoy
Fuglafjørður
Mykines
Vestmanna
722
Hvalvík
Leirvík
Klaksvík
Svínoy
Vágar
Sørvágur
Borðoy
Toftir
Seyðisfjörður
Lerwick
Bergen
Hanstholm
Tórshavn
Nólsoy
Kirkjubøur
Skopun
Sandoy
Sandur
479
Skálavík
Skúvoy
Suðuroyarfjørður
Hvalba
Tvøroyri
Fámjin
Suðuroy
Vágur
Sumba
Egersund
Bergen
Tórshavn
Seyðisfjörður
Larvik
Kristiansand
Skallerup Kit
Lønstrup
Løkken
BØRGLUMKLOSTER
Saltum
Blokhus
Brønders
Pandrup
Jammerbugten
Rødhus Klit
Tranum
Strand
Kås
Aabybro
Lild
Strand
Torup
Strand
Vigsø
Bugt
Hanstholm
Ræhr
NATURRESERVAT
NATURRES.
Frøstrup
Slettestrand
Ryå
Klitmøller
Nors
Korsø
Fjerritslev
Vangså
Østerild
Skinnerup
Øsløs
Skerping
Brovst
Aalborg
Lindholm
Attrup
Aggersund
AALBORG
Nørre Vorupør
Sjørring
Amtoft
Thisted
Feggeklit
Løgstør
Nibe
Frejev
Stenbjerg
Snedsted
Sebbersund
Svenstrup
Sønder
Dråby
Bislev
Limfjorden
NORDJYLLA
Ranum
Vegger
Lyngby
Vilsund
VITSKØL
KLOSTER
Solbjerg
Bedsted
Koldby
Tødsø
Hornum
Sørup
Agger
Fur
Trend
Suldrup
Vestervig
Hurup
Karby
Vils
Nykøbing
Strandby
Thyborøn
Ør. Hvidbjerg
Mors
Selde
Glyngøre
Aars
BORREMOSE
Rold
Arden
Roslev
Farsø
Harre
Nørager
Nissum
Bredning
Hvidbjerg
Hvalpsund
Harboøre
SPØTTRUP
Rødding
Sundsøre
Gedsted
Aalestrup
Tambohuse
Oddesund
HESSEL
Løvns
Bredning
Hove
Sønder
Balling
Ulbjerg
Øls
Mariage
Lemvig
KRABBESHOLM
Hobro
Ferring
Humlum
Lihme
Skive
Møldrup
FYRKAT
Venø
Bugt
Lindum
Fjaltring
Rom By
Struer
Højslev
Stby
LYNDERUPGÅRD
Skals
Vinderup
STUBBERGÅRD
VIBORG
Torsminde
Bækmarksbro
KALKGRUBER
Foulum
TJELE
Råsted
Linde
Sevel
Mønsted
Hammershøj
Nissum Fjord
Skave
Bjergby
Sjørup
Ørum
Vemb
Hagebro
Birgittelyst
Viborg
Ålum
Fjand Gårde
Bur
Storå
Holstebro
Haderup
Grønhøj
Langå
Husby
Idom
Tvis
Bjerringbro
Vedersø Klit
Ulfborg
Karup
Rødkærsbro
Ulstrup
Gudenå
Frederiks
Houlbjerg
Sønderby
Ørnhøj
Avlum
Simmelkær
Kjellerup
Ans
Hadsten
Kryle
Hee
Vildbjerg
Ilskov
Vinderslev
Fårvang
RINGKØBING
Hinnerup
Søndervig
Sunds
Gjern
Spjald
Skibbild
Favrholt
Engesvang
Hammel
Herning
Bording
Silkeborg
Farre
Ringkøbing
Ikast
Låsby
Galten
Røgind
Videbæk
Pårup
Sejs
Framlev
Lind
Virklund
Isenvad
Them
Hvide Sande
Lem
Finderup
Kibæk
Arnborg
Hjøllund
Ry
Faster
Fasterholt
Ringkøbing
Fjord
Skjern
Ejstrupholm
Bryrup
Mossø
Skander
Borris
Sønder
Felding
Brande
Nørre
Brædstrup
Østbirk
Bjerregård
NATURRESERVAT
156

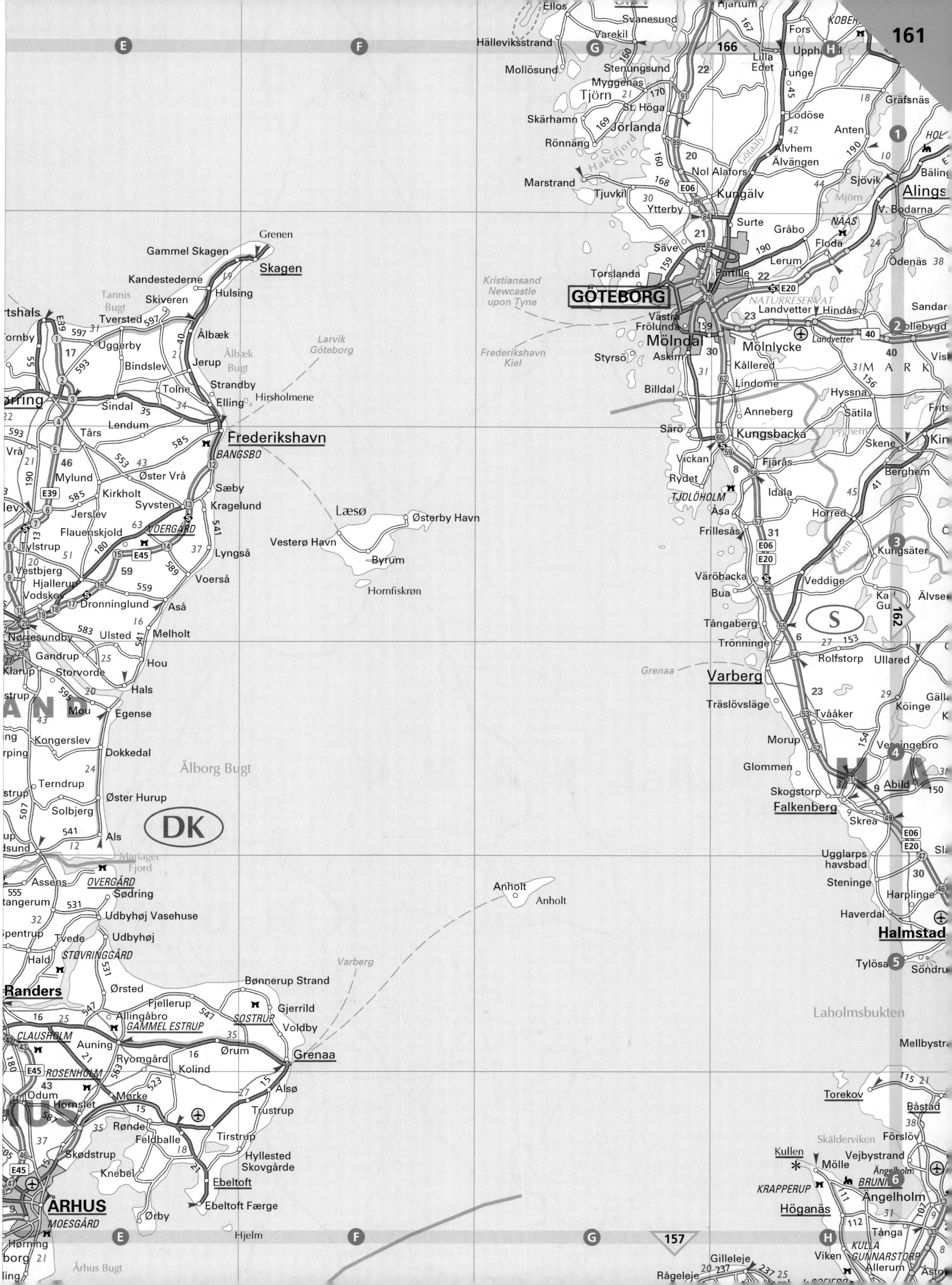
E
F
G
H
166
157
162
Ellos
Svanesund
Hjartum
Fors
Hälleviksstrand
Varekil
Upphärad
Lilla Edet
Mollösund
Stenungsund
Tunge
Myggenäs
Tjörn
St. Höga
Gräfsnäs
Skärhamn
Jörlanda
Lödöse
Anten
Rönnäng
Alvhem
Älvängen
Hakefjord
Göta älv
Nol
Alafors
Sjövik
Marstrand
Tjuvkil
Kungälv
Mjörn
Alingsås
Ytterby
Surte
V. Bodarna
Gråbo
NÄÄS
Säve
Floda
Ödenäs
Lerum
Torslanda
Partille
Kristiansand
Newcastle upon Tyne
GÖTEBORG
E20
NATURRESERVAT
Hindås
Landvetter
Sandared
Västra Frölunda
Mölndal
Mölnlycke
Landvetter
Bollebygd
Frederikshavn
Kiel
Styrsö
Askim
Kållered
M A R K
Lindome
Billdal
Hyssna
Anneberg
Sätila
Lygnern
Särö
Kungsbacka
Skene
Kinna
Vickan
Fjärås
Rydet
Berghem
TJOLÖHOLM
Idala
Åsa
Horred
Frillesås
E06
E20
Kungsäter
Viskan
Väröbacka
Veddige
Bua
Älvsered
Tångaberg
S
Trönninge
Rolfstorp
Ullared
Grenaa
Varberg
Träslövsläge
Tvååker
Köinge
Gällared
Morup
Vessigebro
Glommen
Abild
Skogstorp
Falkenberg
Skrea
Ugglarps havsbad
Steninge
Harplinge
Haverdal
Halmstad
Tylösand
Söndrum
Laholmsbukten
Mellbystrand
Torekov
Båstad
Skälderviken
Förslöv
Kullen
Vejbystrand
Mölle
Ängelholm
KRAPPERUP
BRUNNBY
Höganäs
Tånga
KULLA GUNNARSTORP
Viken
Allerum
Åstorp
Gilleleje
Rågeleje
Grenen
Gammel Skagen
Skagen
Kandestederne
Hulsing
Tannis Bugt
Skiveren
Hirtshals
Tversted
Uggerby
Ålbæk
Ålbæk Bugt
Larvik
Göteborg
Bindslev
Jerup
Tolne
Strandby
Hjørring
Sindal
Elling
Hirsholmene
Lendum
Tårs
Frederikshavn
BANGSBO
Mylund
Øster Vrå
Vrå
Kirkholt
Sæby
Syvsten
Kragelund
Jerslev
Læsø
Østerby Havn
Flauenskjold
VOERGÅRD
Vesterø Havn
Byrum
Tylstrup
Lyngså
Vestbjerg
Hjallerup
Voerså
Vodskov
Hornfiskrøn
Dronninglund
Aså
Ulsted
Melholt
Nørresundby
Gandrup
Hou
Klarup
Storvorde
Hals
Egense
Mou
Kongerslev
Dokkedal
Ålborg Bugt
Terndrup
Øster Hurup
Solbjerg
DK
Als
Mariager Fjord
Assens
OVERGÅRD
Sødring
Udbyhøj Vasehuse
Tvede
Udbyhøj
Hald
STØVRINGGÅRD
Randers
Ørsted
Bønnerup Strand
Varberg
Anholt
Anholt
Fjellerup
Gjerrild
Allingåbro
SOSTRUP
Voldby
CLAUSHOLM
GAMMEL ESTRUP
Auning
Ryomgård
Ørum
Grenaa
ROSENHOLM
Kolind
Odum
Hornslet
Mørke
Alsø
Trustrup
Rønde
Tirstrup
Feldballe
Skødstrup
Hyllested Skovgårde
Knebel
Ebeltoft
ÅRHUS
Ebeltoft Færge
MOESGÅRD
Ørby
Hjelm
Hørning
Århus Bugt

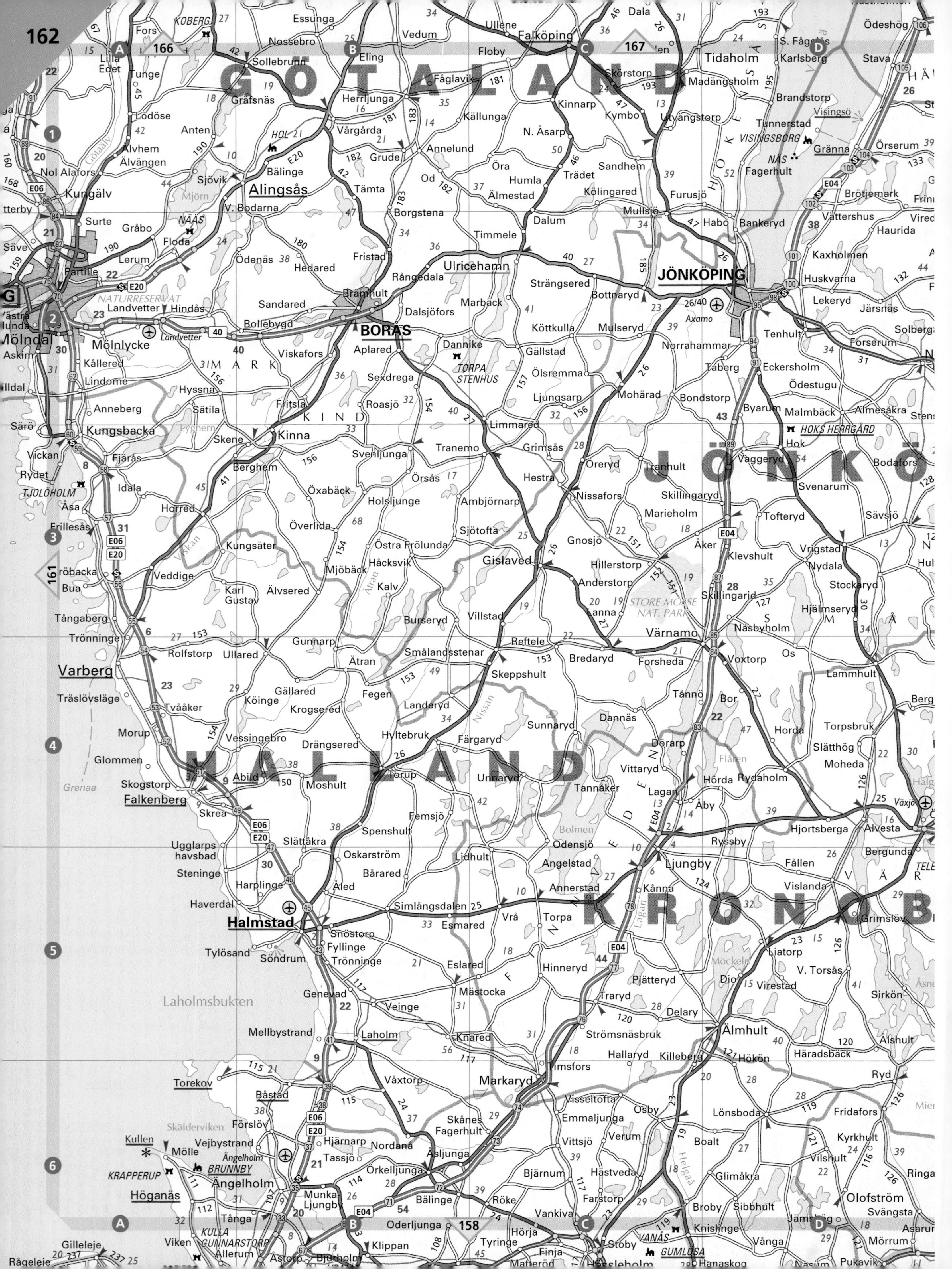
GÖTALAND
HALLAND
JÖNKÖ
KRONOB
166
167
161
158
Lilla Edet
Fors
Essunga
Nossebro
Vedum
Ullene
Falköping
Dala
Ödeshög
Tidaholm
S. Fågelås
Karlsberg
Stava
Floby
Eling
Sollebrunn
Tunge
Fåglavik
Skörstorp
Madängsholm
Gräfsnäs
Herrljunga
Kinnarp
Kymbo
Brandstorp
Visingsö
Lödöse
Anten
Vårgårda
Källunga
Utvängstorp
Tunnerstad
VISINGSBORG
Gränna
NÄS
Örserum
Älvhem
Älvängen
HOL
Grude
Annelund
N. Åsarp
Sandhem
Fagerhult
Nol Alafors
Bälinge
Öra
Humla
Trädet
Sjövik
Alingsås
Tämta
Od
Älmestad
Kölingared
Furusjö
Brötjemark
Kungälv
V. Bodarna
Borgstena
Mullsjö
Habo
Bankeryd
Vättershus
Surte
NÄÄS
Dalum
Haurida
Gråbo
Floda
Timmele
Kaxholmen
Säve
Lerum
Ödenäs
Hedared
Fristad
Ulricehamn
Huskvarna
Partille
Rångedala
JÖNKÖPING
Strängsered
Bottnaryd
Lekeryd
Järsnäs
Västra Frölunda
NATURRESERVAT
Landvetter
Hindås
Sandared
Brämhult
Marbäck
Dalsjöfors
Axamo
Mölndal
Bollebygd
BORÅS
Köttkulla
Mulseryd
Tenhult
Solberga
Askim
Mölnlycke
Landvetter
Viskafors
Aplared
Dannike
Gällstad
Norrahammar
Forserum
Kållered
MARK
TORPA STENHUS
Taberg
Eckersholm
Lindome
Sexdrega
Ölsremma
Ödestugu
Hyssna
Mohärad
Bondstorp
Anneberg
Sätila
Fritsla
Roasjö
Ljungsarp
Byarum
Malmbäck
Almesåkra
KIND
Limmared
HOKS HERRGÅRD
Särö
Kungsbacka
Skene
Kinna
Grimsås
Hok
Vickan
Fjärås
Svenljunga
Tranemo
Öreryd
Tranhult
Vaggeryd
Bodafors
Rydet
Berghem
Örsås
Hestra
TJOLÖHOLM
Idala
Öxabäck
Nissafors
Svenarum
Åsa
Horred
Holsljunge
Ambjörnarp
Skillingaryd
Frillesås
Överlida
Marieholm
Tofteryd
Sävsjö
Sjötofta
Kungsäter
Östra Frölunda
Gnosjö
Åker
Vrigstad
Håcksvik
Gislaved
Klevshult
Nydala
Fröbacka
Mjöbäck
Hillerstorp
Veddige
Bua
Kalv
Älvsered
Karl Gustav
Anderstorp
Stockaryd
STORE MOSSE NAT. PARK
Skillingarid
Hjälmseryd
Lanna
Tångaberg
Burseryd
Villstad
Näsbyholm
SMÅLAND
Trönninge
Gunnarp
Reftele
Värnamo
Rolfstorp
Ullared
Smålandsstenar
Bredaryd
Forsheda
Voxtorp
Os
Varberg
Ätran
Skeppshult
Lammhult
Gällared
Tånnö
Träslövsläge
Köinge
Fegen
Bor
Tvååker
Krogsered
Landeryd
Berg
Dannäs
Nissan
Horda
Torpsbruk
Morup
Vessingebro
Sunnaryd
Hyltebruk
Färgaryd
Dörarp
Slätthög
Glommen
Drängsered
Moheda
Grenaa
Torup
Vittaryd
Flåren
Skogstorp
Abild
Moshult
Unnaryd
Tannåker
Hörda
Rydaholm
Falkenberg
Lagan
Växjö
Skrea
Femsjö
Åby
Hjortsberga
Alvesta
Bolmen
Spenshult
Slättåkra
Odensjö
Ryssby
Bergunda
Ugglarps havsbad
Oskarström
Ljungby
Fållen
Lidhult
Angelstad
Steninge
Bårared
Vislanda
Harplinge
Kånna
Annerstad
Åled
VÄRENDS
Haverdal
Simlångsdalen
Vrå
Halmstad
Snöstorp
Esmared
Torpa
Grimslöv
Fyllinge
Liatorp
Tylösand
Söndrum
Trönninge
V. Torsås
Eslared
Hinneryd
Möckeln
Dio
Virestad
Genevad
Mästocka
Pjätteryd
Sirkön
Laholmsbukten
Veinge
Traryd
Delary
Mellbystrand
Laholm
Knäred
Strömsnäsbruk
Älmhult
Alshult
Hallaryd
Killeberg
Hökön
Häradsbäck
Torekov
Timsfors
Våxtorp
Markaryd
Ryd
Båstad
Visseltofta
Skäldervike
Förslöv
Skånes Fagerhult
Emmaljunga
Osby
Lönsboda
Fridafors
Kullen
Vejbystrand
Hjärnarp
Nordanå
Vittsjö
Verum
Boalt
Kyrkhult
Mölle
Ängelholm
Tassjö
Åsljunga
Vilshult
BRUNNBY
KRAPPERUP
Örkelljunga
Bjärnum
Hästveda
Helgeå
Glimåkra
Ringa
Ängelholm
Höganäs
Munka-Ljungby
Bälinge
Röke
Farstorp
Broby
Sibbhult
Olofström
Tånga
Vankiva
Svängsta
Oderljunga
Knislinge
Jämshög
Asarum
KULLA GUNNARSTORP
Hörja
VANÅS
Vånga
Gilleleje
Viken
Klippan
Tyringe
Finja
Stoby
GUMLÖSA
Mörrum
Rågeleje
Allerum
Åstorp
Bjuvholm
Matteröd
Hässleholm
Hanaskog
Pukavik

Ekeby
Svaneholm
Roster
Strålsnäs
Bestorp
Valdemarsvik
Trehörna
Boxholm
Brokind
Nora
Tryserum
Gryt
Lavedeen
Sommen
Ulrika
Rimforsa
Kättilstad
Falerum
Fågelvik
Somvik
Rosendal
Broddebo
Skedshult
Tranås
Gripenberg
Blåvik
Malexander
Örsebo
Oppeby
Björkefors
Edsbruk
Östra Ed
Säby
Hestra
Sommen
Kisa
Åsunden
Dalhem
Överum
Ripenberg
Lofta
Sundhultsbrunn
Tidersrum
Hycklinge
Björnsholm
Loftahammar
Asby
Horn
Marbäck
Liden
N. Vi
Odensvi
Gamleby
Kälvik
Aneby
Tjust
Almvik
Askeryd
Österbymo
Gullringen
Höghult
Blackstad
Västervik
Hisby
Ydrefors
Rydsnäs
Anneberg
Svinhult
Norra Kvills Nat. Park
Södra Vi
Gladhammar
Gunnebo
Skurugata
Eksjö
Hult
Vimmerby
Frödinge
Ankarsrum
Västrum
Bruzaholm
Totebo
Helgerum
Hjorted
Mariannelund
Storebro
Blankaholm
Tuna
Bellö
Mellby
Karlstorp
Silverdalen
Mörtfors
Björkö
Ekenässjön
Vena
Visby
Hultsfred
Stenbo
Paulisiström
N.Sandsjö
Holsbybrunn
Krokstorp
Misterhult
Vetlanda
Kvillsfors
Järnforsen
Landsbro
Skirö
Målilla
Kristdala
Fårbo
Figeholm
Nabbelund
Ölands norra udde
Jönköping
Nye
Kalmar
Fröderyd
Virserum
Mörlunda
Stensjö
Björnhult
Byxelkrok
Grankullavik
Korsberga
Saltvik
Lemnhult
Bockara
Oskarshamn
Böda
Döderhult
Byrum
Blå Jungfrun Nationalpark
Berga
Asa
Ramkvilla
Hultanäs
Fågelfors
Emån
Åseda
Fagerhult
Högsby
Finsjö
Påskallavik
Löttorp-Högby
Norrhult
Emsfors
Tolg
Böcksholm
Notteback
Mjösebo
Ruda
Fliseryd
Källa
Braås
Grönskåra
Allgunnen
Sandvik
Rottne
Dädesjö
Långemåla
Älghult
Mönsterås
Kalmarsund
Kråksmåla
Gårdsby
Lenhovda
Sävsjöström
Blomstermåla
Föra
Alböke
Alstermo
Alsterbro
Ålem
Timmernabben
Öland
Djäby
Herråkra
Fröseke
Måleras
Strömsrum
Löt
Furuby
Häggemåla
Köpingsvik
Växjö
Kosta
Gullaskruv
Bäckebo
Kåremo
Solliden
Borgholm
Bergdala
Hälleberga
Flerahopp
Kapelludden
Hovmantorp
Orrefors
Rockneby
Kristvallabrunn
Läckeby
Rälla
Gärdslösa
Lessebo
Eriksmåla
Boda glasbruk
Nybro
Linsdal
Långlöt
Ingelstad
Rottnen
Ismantorp
Nöbbele
Johansfors
Örsjö
Trekanten
Glömminge
Algutsrum
Jät
Linneryd
Klackeberga
Gråborg
Väckelsång
Emmaboda
Ljungbyholm
Skogsby
Färjestaden
Korrö
Lindås
Oskar
Tvärskog
Vassmolösa
Karlevistenen
Gårdby
Hagby
Rävemåla
Påryd
Resmo
Stora Alvaret
Tingsryd
Urshult
Vissefjärda
Halltorp
Mörbylånga
Möre
Konga
Dångebo
Bårbyborg
Alby
Djuramåla
Gullabo
Söderåkra
Kastlösa
Skärlöv
Holmsjö
Torsås
Eringsboda
Hallabro
Bergkvara
Bidalite
Ronnebyån
Gettlinge
Segerstad
Blekinge
Flymen
Degerhamn
Bökemåla
Tving
Brömsebro
Mellstaby
Rödby
Kallinge
Sälleryd
Grönhögen
Bräkne-Hoby
Hjortsberga
Rödeby
Kristianopel
Ottenby
Näsby
Nättraby
Ronneby
Listerby
Lyckeby
Jämjöslätt
Långe Jan
Ölands södra udde
Karlshamn
Karlskrona
168
159
E22

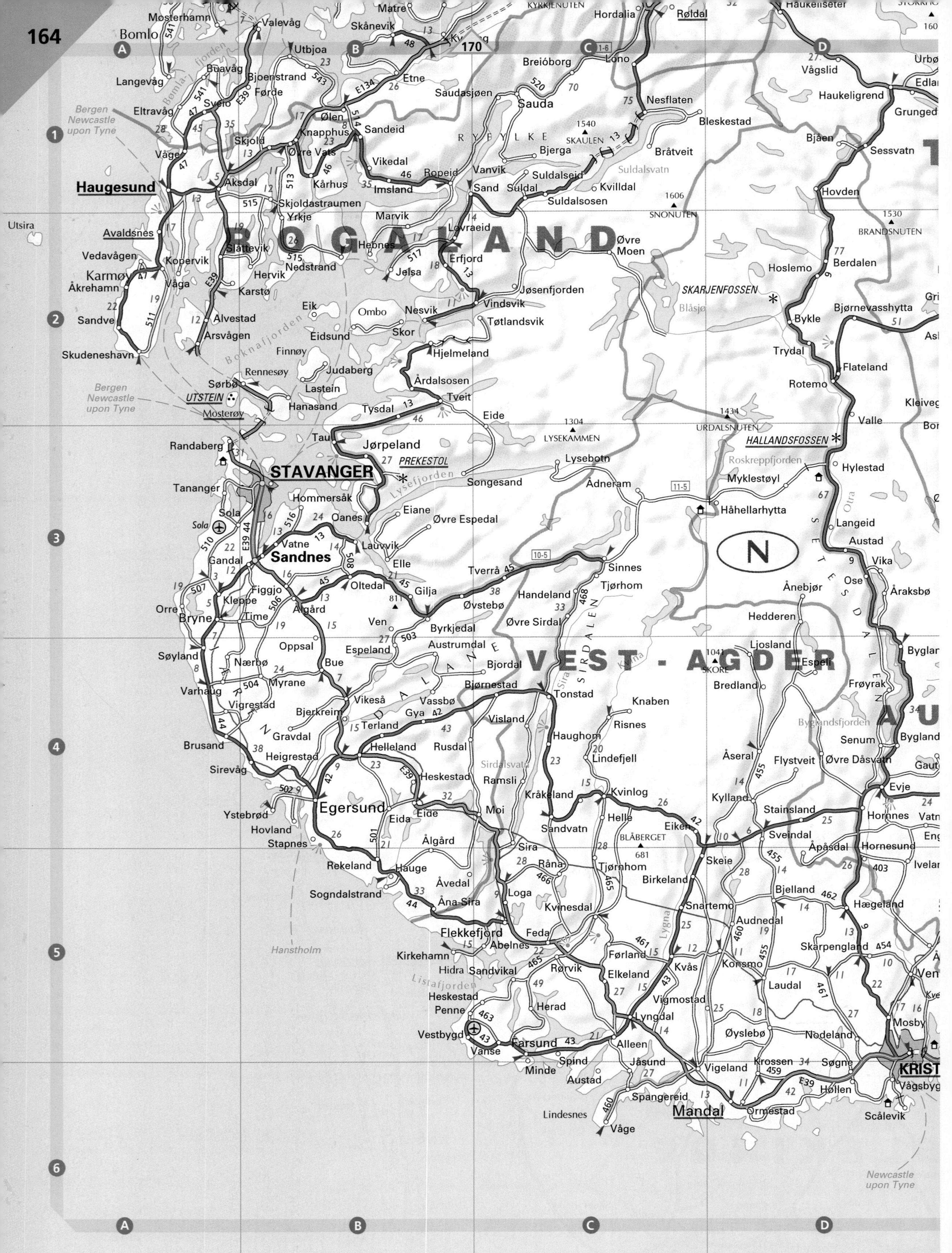

A
B
C
D
1
2
3
4
5
6
170
Bomlo
Mosterhamn
Valevåg
Matre
Skånevik
Kvinnherad
Hordalia
Røldal
Haukeliseter
Utbjoa
Etne
Breióborg
Lono
Vågslid
Urbø
Edland
Langevåg
Buavåg
Bjoenstrand
Førde
Saudasjøen
Sauda
Nesflaten
Haukeligrend
Grungedal
Bergen Newcastle upon Tyne
Eltravåg
Sveio
Ølen
Sandeid
Bleskestad
Knapphus
RYFYLKE
SKAULEN
1540
Bjerga
Bråtveit
Bjåen
Sessvatn
Skjold
Vikedal
Øvre Vats
Vanvik
Suldalseid
Suldalsvatn
Våge
Aksdal
Kårhus
Ropeid
Imsland
Sand
Suldal
Kvilldal
Hovden
Haugesund
Skjoldastraumen
Suldalsosen
1606
SNONUTEN
1530
BRANDSNUTEN
Utsira
Yrkje
Marvik
Løvraeid
Avaldsnes
ROGALAND
Sletteviik
Hebnes
Øvre Moen
Vedavågen
Kopervik
Nedstrand
Jelsa
Erfjord
Hoslemo
Berdalen
Karmøy
Åkrehamn
Hervik
Våga
Karstø
Josenfjorden
SKARJENFOSSEN
Vindsvik
Eik
Ombo
Nesvik
Blåsjø
Bjørnevasshytta
Sandve
Alvestad
Tøtlandsvik
Bykle
Eidsund
Skor
Arsvågen
Skudeneshavn
Finnøy
Hjelmeland
Trydal
Boknafjorden
Rennesøy
Judaberg
Flateland
Sørbø
Lastein
Årdalsosen
Rotemo
UTSTEIN
Mosterøy
Hanasand
Tveit
Tysdal
Eide
Valle
1304
LYSEKAMMEN
1434
URDALSNUTEN
Randaberg
Tau
Jørpeland
HALLANDSFOSSEN
PREKESTOL
Lysebotn
Roskreppfjorden
STAVANGER
Lysefjorden
Songesand
Ådneram
Myklestøyl
Hylestad
Tananger
Hommersåk
11-5
Sola
Oanes
Eiane
Øvre Espedal
Håhellarhytta
Langeid
Austad
Vatne
Lauvvik
Sandnes
10-5
Sinnes
Vika
Gandal
Elle
Tverrå
Ose
Tjørhom
Åraksbø
Figgjo
Olteda
Gilja
Handeland
Ånebjør
Kleppe
Ålgård
Øvstebø
Orre
Bryne
Time
811
Ven
Øvre Sirdal
Hedderen
Byrkjedal
Oppsal
Austrumdal
Espeland
Ljosland
Søyland
Bue
VEST-AGDER
1041
SKORE
Espeli
Byglandsfjorden
Nærbø
Bjordal
Bredland
Frøyrak
Varhaug
Myrane
Bjørnestad
Tonstad
Vigrestad
Vikeså
Vassbø
Knaben
Bjerkreim
Gya
Visland
Terland
Risnes
Gravdal
Haughom
Senum
Bygland
Brusand
Helleland
Rusdal
Sirdalsvatn
Lindefjell
Åseral
Flystveit
Øvre Dåsvatn
Heigrestad
Sirevåg
Heskestad
Ramsli
Kvinlog
Kylland
Evje
Egersund
Kråkeland
Stainsland
Hornnes
Ystebrød
Eida
Eide
Moi
Helle
Eiken
Sveindal
Hovland
Sandvatn
BLÅBERGET
681
Ǻpåsdal
Hornesund
Stapnes
Ålgård
Sira
Skeie
Rekeland
Hauge
Råna
Tjørnhom
Birkeland
Bjelland
Hægeland
Åvedal
Loga
Snartemo
Sogndalstrand
Åna-Sira
Kvinesdal
Audnedal
Flekkefjord
Feda
Skarpengland
Hanstholm
Kirkehamn
Abelnes
Førland
Kvås
Konsmo
Hidra
Sandvikal
Rørvik
Elkeland
Laudal
Listafjorden
Heskestad
Vigmostad
Penne
Herad
Lyngdal
Mosby
Vestbygd
Farsund
Øyslebø
Nodeland
Alleen
Vanse
Spind
Jåsund
Krossen
Søgne
Minde
Vigeland
Austad
Høllen
Vågsbygd
Spangereid
Lindesnes
Mandal
Ormestad
Scålevik
Våge
Newcastle upon Tyne
Otra
SETESDALEN
SIRDALEN
JÆREN
DALANE

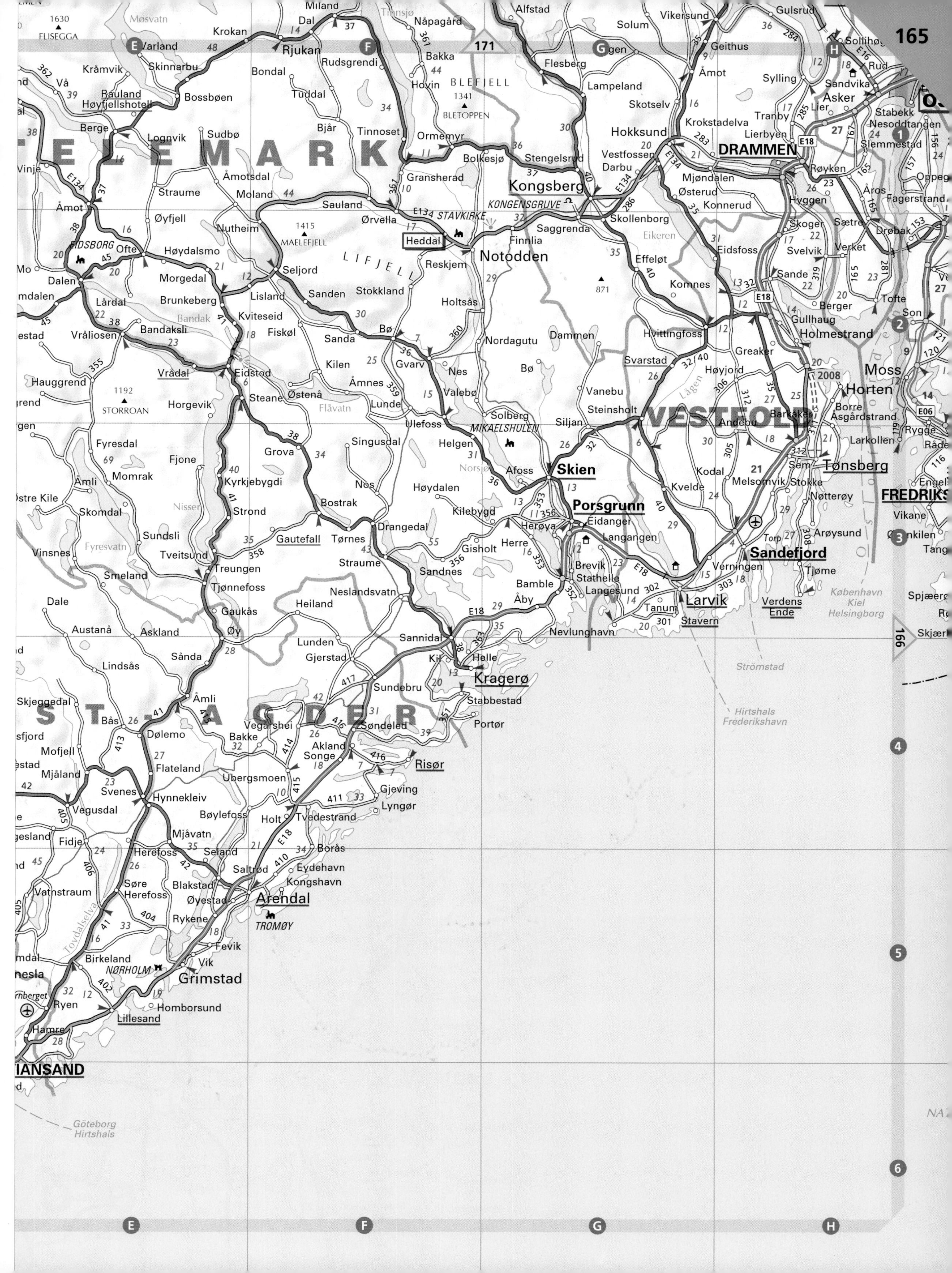
171
166
TELEMARK
VESTFOLD
ST. AGDER
E
F
G
H
1
2
3
4
5
6
1630
FLISEGGA
Møsvatn
Miland
Dal
Tinnsjø
Nåpagård
Alfstad
Solum
Vikersund
Gulsrud
Krokan
Varland
Rjukan
Rudsgrendi
Bakka
Geithus
Sollihøg
Rud
Kråmvik
Skinnarbu
Bondal
Hovin
BLEFJELL
Flesberg
Åmot
Sylling
Sandvika
Vå
Rauland
Høyfjellshotell
Bossbøen
Tuddal
1341
BLETOPPEN
Lampeland
Skotselv
Asker
Lier
Stabekk
Nesoddtangen
Berge
Bjår
Tinnoset
Krokstadelva
Tranby
Lognvik
Sudbø
Ormemyr
Hokksund
Lierbyen
Slemmestad
Bolkesjø
Stengelsrud
Vestfossen
Darbu
DRAMMEN
Vinje
Åmotsdal
Gransherad
Kongsberg
Mjøndalen
Røyken
Oppeg
Straume
Moland
Sauland
Østerud
Åros
Åmot
KONGENSGRUVE
Konnerud
Hyggen
Fagerstrand
Øyfjell
Ørvella
1415
MAELEFJELL
STAVKIRKE
Skollenborg
Skoger
Sætre
Nutheim
Heddal
Saggrenda
Drøbak
EIDSBORG
Ofte
Høydalsmo
Finnlia
Eikeren
Svelvik
Verket
LIFJELL
Notodden
Eidsfoss
Mo
Dalen
Seljord
Reskjem
Effeløt
Sande
mdalen
Morgedal
Lårdal
Brunkeberg
Lisland
Sanden
Stokkland
Holtsås
871
Komnes
Berger
Tofte
Gullhaug
Son
Bandak
Kviteseid
Holmestrand
estad
Vråliosen
Bandaksli
Fiskøl
Sanda
Bø
Nordagutu
Dammen
Hvittingfoss
Greaker
Kilen
Gvarv
Nes
Bø
Svarstad
Høyjord
Moss
Hauggrend
Vrådal
Eidstod
Åmnes
Valebø
Vanebu
2008
Horten
1192
STORROAN
Horgevik
Steane
Østenå
Flåvatn
Lunde
Solberg
Steinsholt
Barkåker
Borre
Åsgårdstrand
Ulefoss
MIKAELSHULEN
Siljan
Andebu
Rygge
Fyresdal
Singusdal
Helgen
Larkollen
Råde
Grova
Fjone
Momrak
Norsjø
Afoss
Skien
Kodal
Tønsberg
Åmli
Kyrkjebygdi
Nos
Høydalen
Melsomvik
Stokke
Engel
FREDRIKS
Østre Kile
Skomdal
Nisser
Strond
Bostrak
Kilebygd
Porsgrunn
Kvelde
Nøtterøy
Vikane
Drangedal
Herøya
Eidanger
Arøysund
Sundsli
Gautefall
Tørnes
Langangen
Torp
Vinsnes
Fyresvatn
Tveitsund
Straume
Gisholt
Herre
Brevik
Stathelle
Sandefjord
Vernngen
Treungen
Sandnes
Tjøme
Smeland
Tjønnefoss
Neslandsvatn
Bamble
Langesund
København
Kiel
Helsingborg
Verdens Ende
Spjærøy
Dale
Heiland
Gaukås
Åby
Tanum
Larvik
Stavern
Austanå
Askland
Øy
Lunden
Sannidal
Nevlunghavn
Skjærhalden
Sånda
Gjerstad
Kil
Helle
Lindsås
Kragerø
Strömstad
Sundebru
Skjeggedal
Åmli
Stabbestad
Bås
Vegårshei
Søndeled
Portør
Hirtshals
Frederikshavn
sfjord
Dølemo
Bakke
Akland
Songe
Mofjell
Risør
estad
Mjåland
Flateland
Ubergsmoen
Gjeving
Svenes
Hynnekleiv
Lyngør
Vegusdal
Bøylefoss
Holt
Tvedestrand
Fidje
Mjåvatn
Herefoss
Seland
Borås
Saltrød
Eydehavn
Kongshavn
Søre Herefoss
Blakstad
Vatnstraum
Øyestad
Arendal
Rykene
TROMØY
Tovdalselva
Fevik
Birkeland
NØRHOLM
Vik
Grimstad
Ryen
Homborsund
Lillesand
Hamre
IANSAND
Göteborg
Hirtshals

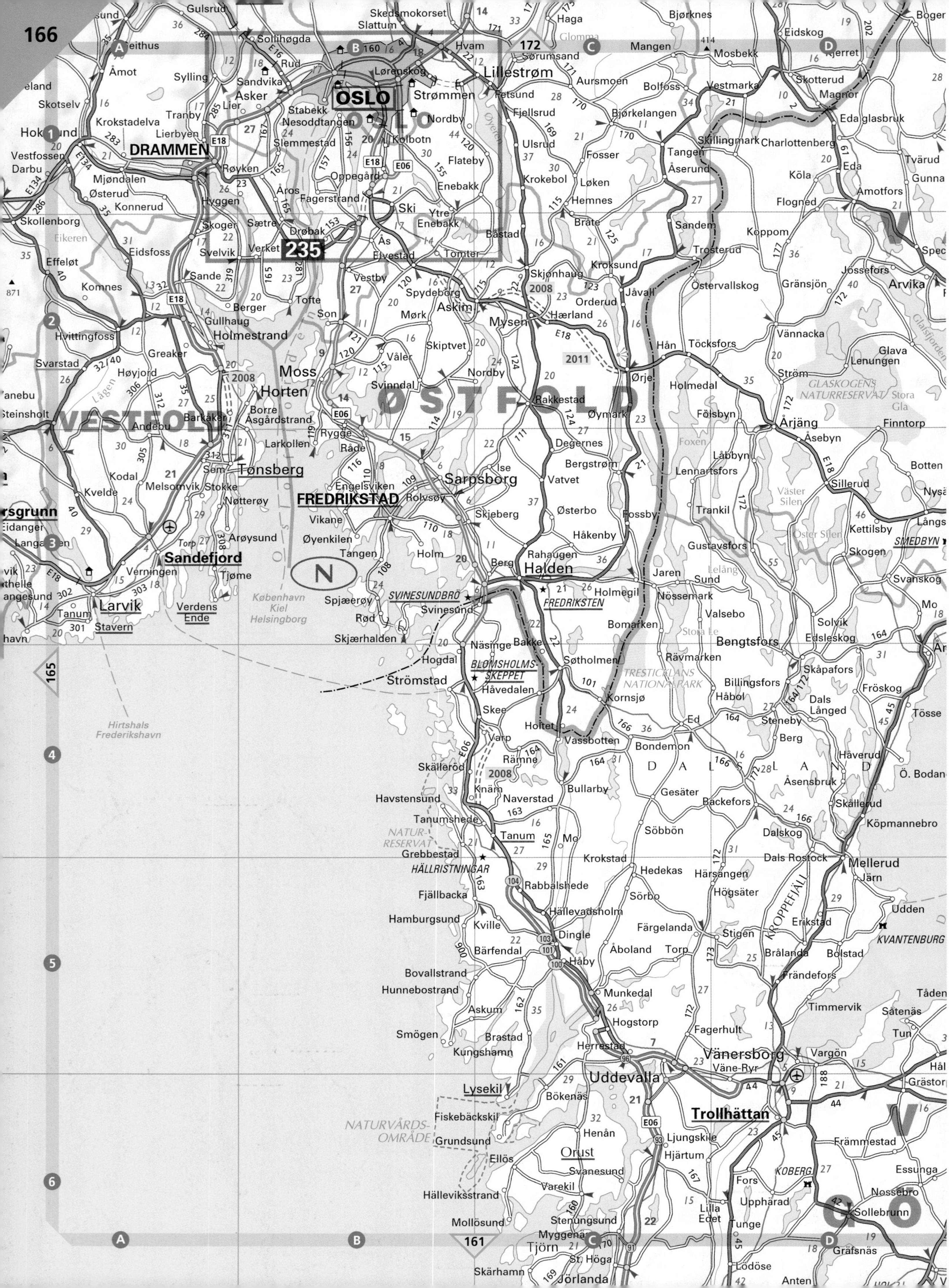

OSLO
DRAMMEN
ØSTFOLD
VESTFOLD
DALSLAND
Lillestrøm
Skedsmokorset
Slattum
Hvam
Gulsrud
Sollihøgda
Heithus
Åmot
Sylling
Rud
Sandvika
Asker
Lier
Lørenskog
Strømmen
Fetsund
Sørumsand
Aursmoen
Haga
Glomma
Mangen
Bjørknes
Mosbekk
Eidskog
Kjerret
Vestmarka
Skotterud
Magnor
Bolfoss
Bjørkelangen
Fjellsrud
Eda glasbruk
Charlottenberg
Skillingmark
Tangen
Åserund
Tvärud
Gunna
Eda
Köla
Åmotfors
Flogned
Ulsrud
Fosser
Krokebol
Løken
Hemnes
Brate
Båstad
Sandem
Koppom
Trosterud
Kroksund
Jåvall
Jössefors
Arvika
Gränsjön
Östervallskog
Skjønhaug
Orderud
Hærland
Mysen
Askim
Spydeberg
Tomter
Elvestad
Ås
Ski
Ytre Enebakk
Enebakk
Flateby
Kolbotn
Oppegård
Nordby
Nesoddtangen
Stabekk
Slemmestad
Røyken
Åros
Fagerstrand
Drøbak
Hyggen
Sætre
Skoger
Svelvik
Verket
Sande
Berger
Vestby
Tofte
Son
Mørk
Kråkstadelva
Tranby
Lierbyen
Hokksund
Vestfossen
Darbu
Mjøndalen
Østerud
Konnerud
Skollenborg
Eikeren
Eidsfoss
Effeløt
Komnes
Hvittingfoss
Holmestrand
Gullhaug
Greaker
Svarstad
Høyjord
Moss
Horten
Borre
Åsgårdstrand
Barkåker
Andebu
Kodal
Kvelde
Melsomvik
Stokke
Nøtterøy
Tønsberg
Sem
Larkollen
Rygge
Råde
Engelsviken
Rolvsøy
Sarpsborg
FREDRIKSTAD
Vikane
Øyenkilen
Tangen
Holm
Skipvet
Våler
Svinndal
Nordby
Rakkestad
Øymark
Degernes
Bergstrøm
Vatvet
Ise
Skjeberg
Østerbo
Håkenby
Rahaugen
Halden
Berg
Fossby
Ørje
Hån
Töcksfors
Holmedal
Vännacka
Glava
Lenungen
Ström
GLASKOGENS NATURRESERVAT
Stora Gla
Årjäng
Finntorp
Åsebyn
Fölsbyn
Foxen
Låbbyn
Lennartsfors
Sillerud
Botten
Nysä
Väster Silen
Öster Silen
Tranekil
Kettilsby
Långs
Skogen
SMEDBYN
Gustavsfors
Lelång
Jaren
Sund
Svanskog
Nössemark
Holmegil
FREDRIKSTEN
Valsebo
Bomarken
Stora Le
Bengtsfors
Solvik
Edsleskog
Mo
Porsgrunn
Eidanger
Langangen
Sandefjord
Torp
Arøysund
Verningen
Tjøme
Larvik
Tanum
Stavern
Verdens Ende
Helgeroa
København
Kiel
Helsingborg
Spjærøy
Rød
Skjærhalden
SVINESUNDBRO
Svinesund
Näsinge
Bakke
Hogdal
Strömstad
BLOMSHOLMS-SKEPPET
Søtholmen
Håvedalen
Rävmarken
TRESTICKLANS NATIONALPARK
Billingsfors
Skåpafors
Fröskog
Håbol
Kornsjø
Dals Långed
Steneby
Tösse
Skee
Holtet
Vassbotten
Ed
Bondemon
Berg
Håverud
Ö. Bodane
Åsensbruk
Skällerud
Varp
Rämne
Skälleröd
Bullarby
Gesäter
Bäckefors
Knäm
Naverstad
Havstensund
Tanumshede
NATURRESERVAT
Tanum
Mo
Söbbön
Dalskog
Köpmannebro
Grebbestad
HÄLLRISTNINGAR
Krokstad
Dals Rostock
Mellerud
Järn
Hedekas
Härsängen
Rabbalshede
Fjällbacka
Högsäter
Sörbo
Hällevadsholm
KROPPEFJÄLL
Udden
Hamburgsund
Kville
Färgelanda
Stigen
Erikstad
KVANTENBURG
Dingle
Bärfendal
Åboland
Torp
Brålanda
Bolstad
Håby
Bovallstrand
Frändefors
Hunnebostrand
Munkedal
Tåden
Askum
Timmervik
Sätenäs
Hogstorp
Smögen
Brastad
Fagerhult
Tun
Kungshamn
Herrestad
Vänersborg
Vargön
Väne-Ryr
Hål
Lysekil
Uddevalla
Grästorp
Bökenäs
Fiskebäckskil
Trollhättan
NATURVÅRDSOMRÅDE
Grundsund
Henån
Ljungskile
Främmestad
Orust
Hjärtum
Ellös
Svanesund
Essunga
Fors
KOBERG
Varekil
Nossebro
Upphärad
Hälleviksstrand
Lilla Edet
Sollebrunn
Stenungsund
Tunge
Mollösund
Myggenäs
Tjörn
St. Höga
Gräfsnäs
Skärhamn
Jörlanda
Lödöse
Anten
Hirtshals
Frederikshavn
Oyeren
Lågen
Glafsfjorden

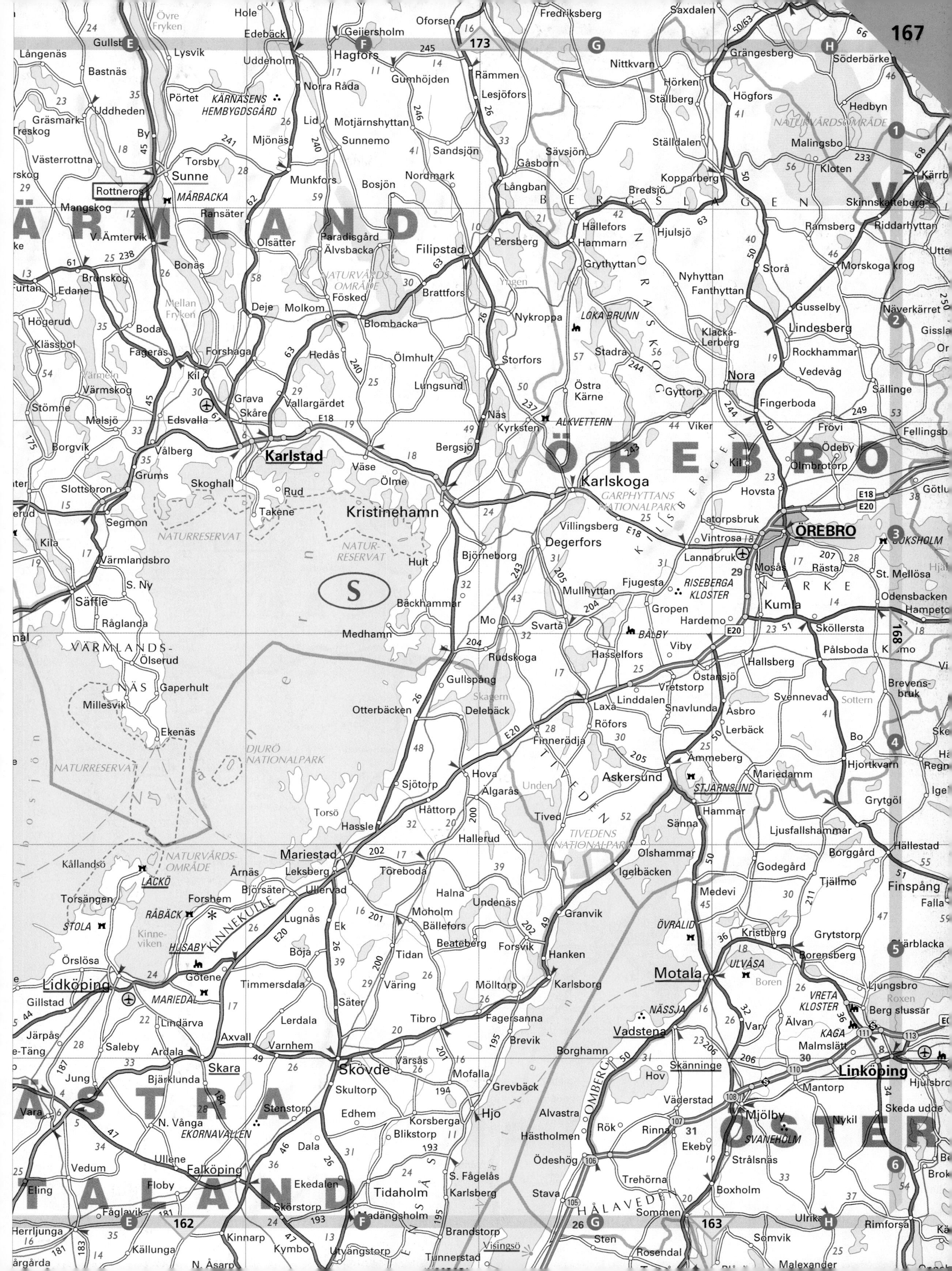
Övre Fryken
Hole
Edebäck
Geijersholm
Oforsen
Fredriksberg
Saxdalen
Gullsby
Lysvik
Uddeholm
Hagfors
Rämmen
Nittkvarn
Grängesberg
Söderbärke
Långenäs
Bastnäs
Norra Råda
Gumhöjden
Lesjöfors
Hörken
Ställberg
Högfors
Hedbyn
Pörtet
KÄRNÅSENS HEMBYGDSGÅRD
Uddheden
Gräsmark
Treskog
By
Lid
Motjärnshyttan
NATURVÅRDSOMRÅDE
Mjönäs
Sunnemo
Sandsjön
Sävsjön
Ställdalen
Malingsbo
Västerrottna
Torsby
Sunne
Munkfors
Nordmark
Gåsborn
Kopparberg
Kloten
Kärrbo
Rottneros
MÅRBACKA
Bosjön
Långban
Bredsjö
Mangskog
Ransäter
BERGSLAGEN
Skinnskatteberg
VÄRMLAND
Persberg
Hällefors
Hjulsjö
Ramsberg
Riddarhyttan
V. Ämtervik
Olsätter
Paradisgård
Älvsbacka
Filipstad
Hammarn
Utter
Bonäs
Grythyttan
Storå
Morskoga krog
Furtan
Edane
Brunskog
NATURVÅRDSOMRÅDE
Fösked
Brattfors
Ygen
Nyhyttan
Fanthyttan
Mellan Fryken
Deje
Molkom
Blombacka
Nykroppa
LOKA BRUNN
NORASKOG
Klacka-Lerberg
Gusselby
Näverkärret
Högerud
Boda
Lindesberg
Gissla
Klässbol
Fagerås
Forshaga
Hedås
Ölmhult
Storfors
Stadra
Rockhammar
Vedevåg
Kil
Värmeln
Värmskog
Grava
Vallargärdet
Lungsund
Östra Kärne
Nora
Gyttorp
Sällinge
Stömne
Malsjö
Edsvalla
Skåre
Näs
Kyrksten
ALKVETTERN
Fingerboda
Viker
Frövi
Fellingsbo
Borgvik
Vålberg
Karlstad
Väse
Bergsjö
ÖREBRO
Ödeby
Ölmbrotorp
Grums
Skoghall
Ölme
Karlskoga
Kil
Hovsta
Slottsbron
Rud
GARPHYTTANS NATIONALPARK
Götlunda
Takene
Kristinehamn
Villingsberg
Latorpsbruk
Segmon
NATURRESERVAT
Degerfors
KILSBERGEN
Vintrosa
ÖREBRO
BOKSHOLM
Kila
NATURRESERVAT
Hult
Björneborg
Lannabruk
Mosås
Rästa
St. Mellösa
Värmlandsbro
Fjugesta
RISEBERGA KLOSTER
Odensbacken
S. Ny
Mullhyttan
NÄRKE
Säffle
Bäckhammar
Gropen
Kumla
Hampetorp
Råglanda
Mo
Svartå
BÅLBY
Hardemo
Sköllersta
Medhamn
VÄRMLANDS-NÄS
Rudskoga
Hasselfors
Viby
Pålsboda
Kilsmo
Ölserud
Gullspång
Östansjö
Hallsberg
Vretstorp
Gaperhult
Skagern
Linddalen
Millesvik
Otterbäcken
Delebäck
Laxå
Snavlunda
Svennevad
Brevens-bruk
Sottern
Åsbro
Röfors
Lerbäck
Ekenäs
Finnerödja
Bo
DJURÖ NATIONALPARK
Ämmeberg
Hjortkvarn
NATURRESERVAT
TIVEDEN
Askersund
Mariedamm
Regna
Hova
Sjötorp
Älgarås
Unden
STJÄRNSUND
Grytgöl
Torsö
Håttorp
Tived
Hammar
Hassle
Sänna
Ljusfallshammar
Hallerud
TIVEDENS NATIONALPARK
Hällestad
Mariestad
Olshammar
Borggård
Kållandsö
NATURVÅRDSOMRÅDE
Töreboda
Årnäs
Leksberg
Igelbäcken
Godegård
LÄCKÖ
Björsäter
Ullervad
Tjällmo
Finspång
Torsängen
Forshem
Halna
Medevi
Falla
Undenäs
RÅBÄCK
KINNEKULLE
Lugnås
Moholm
Granvik
ÖVRALID
Grytstorp
STOLA
Bällefors
Ek
Kinne-viken
Beateberg
Forsvik
Kristberg
Ärblacka
HUSABY
Böja
Tidan
Hanken
ULVÅSA
Borensberg
Örslösa
Götene
Motala
Boren
Lidköping
Timmersdala
Väring
Mölltorp
Karlsborg
Ljungsbro
Roxen
Gillstad
MARIEDAL
VRETA KLOSTER
NÄSSJA
Berg slussar
Lindärva
Säter
Tibro
Fagersanna
Vadstena
Varv
Älvan
Järpås
Lerdala
Brevik
KAGA
Malmslätt
Saleby
Axvall
Varnhem
e-Täng
Ardala
Borghamn
Linköping
Jung
Skara
Skövde
Värsås
Mofalla
Hov
Skänninge
Bjärklunda
Skultorp
Grevbäck
Mantorp
Hjulsbro
VÄSTRA
Väderstad
Vara
Stenstorp
N. Vånga
EKORNAVALLEN
Edhem
Korsberga
Hjo
Alvastra
OMBERG
Mjölby
Skeda udde
Rök
Rinna
Nykil
SVANEHOLM
ÖSTER
Blikstorp
Hästholmen
Vedum
Ullene
Dala
Ekeby
Strålsnäs
Falköping
Ödeshög
Eling
Floby
Ekedalen
S. Fågelås
Trehörna
Boxholm
Broknäs
GÖTALAND
Tidaholm
Karlsberg
Stava
HÅLAVEDEN
Fåglavik
Skörstorp
Madängsholm
Sommen
Ulrika
Rimforsa
Herrljunga
Kinnarp
Brandstorp
Sten
Somvik
Källunga
Kymbo
Utvängstorp
Tunnerstad
Visingsö
Rosendal
Malexander
Årgårda
N. Åsarp
VÄTTERN
VÄNERN
E18
E20
162
163
168
173

174
VÄSTMANLAND
SÖDERMANLAND
ÖSTERGÖTLAND
UPPSALA
STOCKHOLM
ÖREBRO
VÄSTERÅS
NORRKÖPING
Avesta
Krylbo
Folkärna
Bäsinge
Tärnsjö
Ekedal
Harbo
Vendel
2008
Morkarla
Söderbärke
Norberg
Vansjö
Hede
Runhällen
Huddunge
Läby
Skyttorp
SALSTA
Vad
Fagersta
Nykrogen
Karbenning
Broddbo
Saladamm
Roteberg
Björklinge
GAMLA GRÄNOME
Hedbyn
Västansfors
Ängelsberg
Västerfärnebo
Östfora
Storvreta
NATURVÅRDSOMRÅDE
Malingsbo
Sala
Heby
Morgongåva
Jumkil
Bälinge
Gävsta
Kloten
Kärrbo
Virsbo
Salbohed
Kila
Vittinge
Järlåsa
Gamla Uppsala
Almunge
Skinnskatteberg
Virsbo bruk
Sätra brunn
Ransta
Altuna
Åland
Brunna
Sävja
LINNÉS HAMMARBY
Ramsberg
Riddarhyttan
Gunnilbo
Tärna
Fjärdhundra
Österunda
Hagby
MORA STENAR
Sunnersta
Färna
Ramnäs
Romfartuna
Västeråker
VIK
Knivsta
Husby
Långhundra
Uttersberg
Frösthult
Skokloster
Storå
Morskoga krog
Solmyra
Surahammar
Skultuna
Härkeberga
Örsundsbro
Arlanda
Hed
Tillberga
Bred
Litslena
EKOLSUND
VENNGARN
Märsta
Gusselby
Näverkärret
Lillhärad
Hökåsen
Sigtuna
Lindesberg
Hallstahammar
ANUNDSHÖGEN
Hummelsta
Enköping
Gisslarbo
Kolsva
Odensvi
Grillby
STENINGE
Rockhammar
Orsta
Hässlö
Boglösa
Bålsta
ROSERSBERG
NORRSUND
Vedevåg
Kolbäck
GÄDDEHOLM
Vallentuna
Nora
STRÖMSHOLM
Barkarö
Köping
Sällinge
ÄNGSÖ
Upplands Väsby
TIDÖ
NATURRESERVAT
Fingerboda
Kvicksund
Veckholm
Bro
Aspö
Frövi
Fellingsbro
Valskog
SUNDBYHOLM
Fogdö
GRÖNSÖ
Kungsängen
Ödeby
Kungsör
Torshälla
FIHOLM
TYNNELSÖ
Överselö
Ölmbrotorp
KUNGSHÅLLET
YTTERSELÖ
MÄLSÅKER
Munsö
Arboga
Härad
Adelsö
Sundbyberg
Hovsta
Götlunda
Eskilstuna
Strängnäs
Skogstorp
Stallarholmen
Stenhamra
Solna
Lista
Ekerö
Johannes
TORESUND
Alberga
ST.SUNDBY
GÖKSHOLM
Hällsta
Ärla
Länna
Mariefred
Ekeby
STUREHOV
Mosås
Rästa
Bälgviken
Nähulta
Spånga
Åkers styckebruk
Södertälje
Huddinge
NÄRKE
St. Mellösa
Hjälmaren
Odensbacken
Hampetorp
JULITA
Hälleforsnäs
Dunker
Tumba
Tullinge
Kumla
Äsköping
Nykvarn
Västerhaninge
167
Sköllersta
Läppe
Malmköping
Laxne
Pershagen
Pålsboda
Kilsmo
Gryt
Järna
Tungelsta
Hallsberg
Vingåker
Bie
STENHAMMAR
Sparreholm
Björnlunda
Mölnbo
Västerby
Brevens-bruk
Flen
Gnesta
Svennevad
Sottern
Marsjö
Kantorp
Sorunda
Åsbro
Katrineholm
St.Malm
Ärdala
Båven
Tisnaren
Torsåker
Ösmo
Skedevi
Ripsa
TULLGARN
Bo
ERIKSBERG
Bettna
Husbygård
Aspa
Ludgo
Vagnhärad
Solsa
Nynäs
Hävla
Hjortkvarn
Regna
Strångsjö
Broby
Yngaren
Lästringe
Trosa
Mariedamm
Ändebol
Vrena
Råby-Rönö
Igelfors
Rejmyre
Björkvik
Tystberga
Krabbfjärden
Torö
Grytgöl
Stigtomta
Svärta
Ljusfallshammar
Simonstorp
Oxbakken
Hällestad
Lotorp
Hälgö
Borggård
Jönåker
Nyköping
Godegård
KOLMÅRDEN
Risinge
Tjällmo
Finspång
Strömsfors
Oxelösund
Falla
Glan
Åby
Krokek
Kvarsebo
NATURRESERVAT
Svärtinge
Bråviken
RINGSTAD
ÅLLONÖ
Tunaberg
Kristberg
Grytstorp
Skärblacka
Kungsängen
Östra Husby
Nävekvarn
Borensberg
LÖVSTAD
ULVÅSA
Kuddby
Boren
Norsholm
VIKBOLANDET
Jonsberg
VRETA KLOSTER
Ljungsbro
Tingstad
Roxen
Göta Kanal
Berg slussar
Söderköping
Arkösund
Varv
Älvan
V. Husby
KAGA
Skönberga
STEGEBORG
Malmslätt
Linghem
Rönö
Ö. Ryd
Örtomta
Linköping
VÅRDSBERG
Mantorp
Hjulsbro
Lagnö
Kulefall
Börrum
Björsäter
Ringarum
S:t Anna
Mjölby
Skeda udde
Nykil
Yxnerum
Tyrislöt
SVANEHÖLM
Gusum
Röster
Stralsnäs
Bestorp
Valdemarsvik
Brokind
Nora
Åtvidaberg
Gryt
Tryserum
Ulrika
Rimforsa
163
Kättilstad
Valerum
FÅGELVIK
Somvik
Broddebo
Malexander
Skedshult

Herräng
Storby
Grisslehamn
Maarianhamina/
Mariehamn
Lumparland
Seglinge
Långnäs
Överö
Husö
175
E
F
G
H
176
Lemland
Flaka
Degerby
Hastersboda
Turku
Föglö
Herröskatan
Hellsö
Kökar
Karlby
1
2
3
4
5
6
Stensunda
Hallstavik
Edebo
Häverö
Edeby
Ålandshav
ROSLAGEN
Bladåker
Faringe
Skebobruk
Älmsta-Väddö
Turku
Kappelskär
Stockholm
Visby
Helsinki
FIN
Rörvik
Knutby
Söderby-Karl
Edsbro
Björkö
Erken
Rånäs
Roslags-Bro
Vätö
Skeppsmyra
EKEBYHOLM
Gräddö
Rimbo
FINSTA
Norrtälje
Maarianhamina
Bottniska viken/
Gottröra
Närtuna
Husby-Sjuhundra
PENNINGBY
Kappelskär
Turku
Furusund
Frösunda
Bergshamra
Blidö
Pohjanlahti
Karby
Brottby
Roslags-Kulla
ÄNGSÖ NATIONALPARK
Ö. Lagnö
Ljustero
Ljusterö
Täby
Maarianhamina
Åkersberga
Tranvik
Möja
Vaxholm
Oskar-Fredriksborg
Värmdö
Kalsvik
Överby
Tallinn
Helsinki
Sankt-Peterburg
Lidingö
Gustavsberg
Värmdölandet
Nacka
Saltsjöbaden
Stavsnäs
Runmarö
Tyresö
Brevik
Vendelsö
Dyvik
245
Nämdö
TYRESTA NATIONALPARK
Dalarö
Solbacken
NATURRESERVAT
Ornö
Muskö
NATURRESERVAT
Utö
Gdańsk
Visby
Ventspils
Fårö
Langhammars
Lauter
Holmudden
Hallshuk
Ar
Fårö
Nynäshamn
Maarianhamina
Hangvar
Kappelshamn
Bunge
Fårösund
Lickershamn
Lärbro
Lummelunda
LUMMELUNDAGROTTORNA
Kyllaj
Tingstäde
Slite
Boge
Visby
Bro
Bäl
Oskarshamn
Åminne
Högklint
Gothem
Barlingbo
Dalhem
Burs
Gnisvärd
S
Romakloster
Anga
Eskelhem
Isums
Kräklingbo
Ala
Katthammarsvik
Västergarn
Hejde
TORSBURGEN
Herrvik
Buttle
Klintehamn
Ansarve
Fröjel
Lojsta
Ljugarn
L. Karlsö
Lye
Stånga
Burs
St. Karlsö
DJAUVIK
Sproge
När
Hemse
Gotland
Hablingbo
Ronehamn
Havdhem
Näs
Kattlunds
GOTLAND
Burgsvik
Vamlingbo
Faludden
Sallmunds
Sundre
Hoburgen

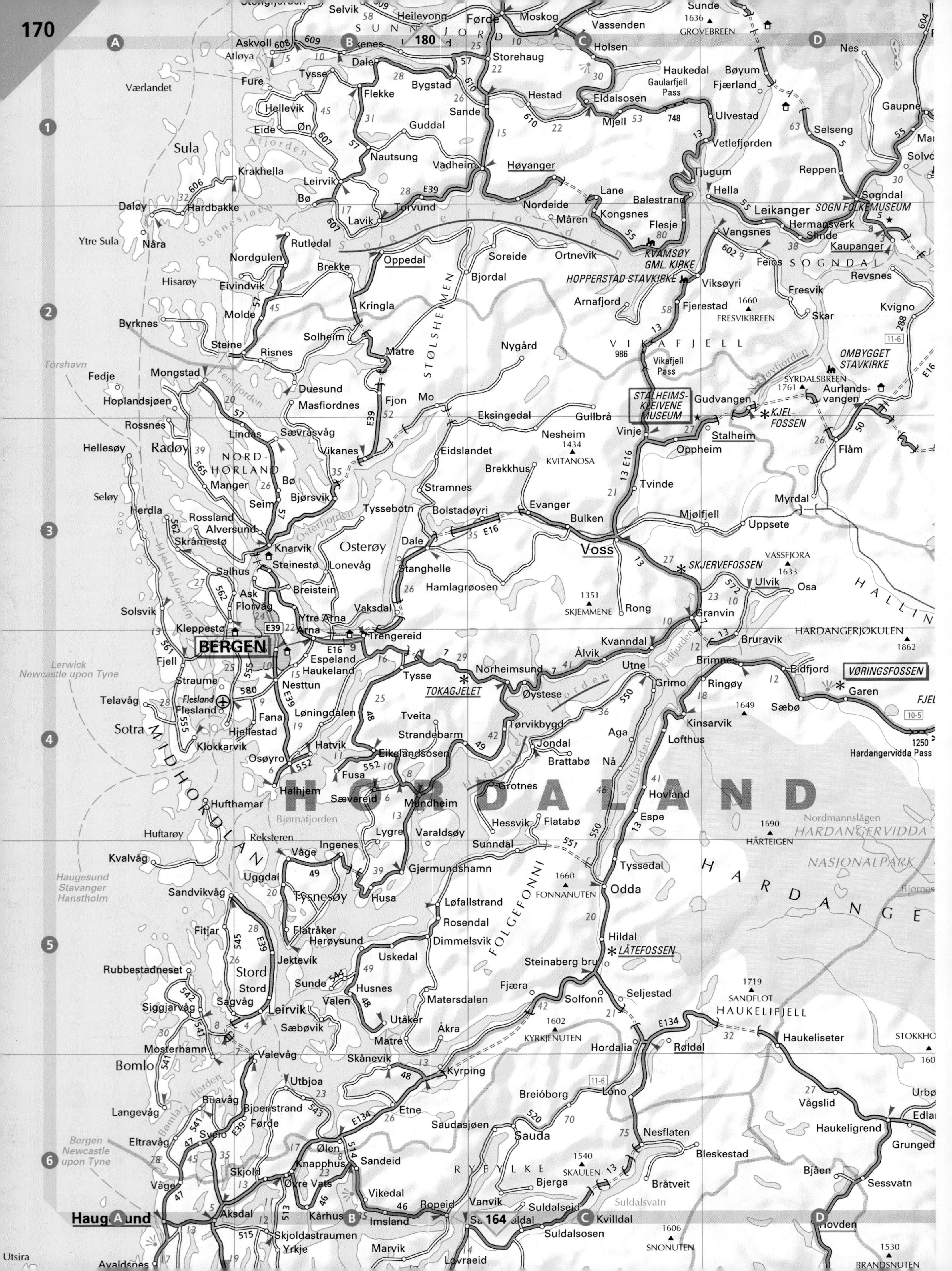
A
B
C
D
1
2
3
4
5
6
180
164
HORDALAND
SUNNFJORD
SOGNDAL
VIKAFJELL
STØLSHEIMEN
NORDHORLAND
MIDHORDLAND
FOLGEFONNI
RYFYLKE
HARDANGER
HALLING
HAUKELIFJELL
HARDANGERVIDDA
NASJONALPARK
Sognefjorden
Fensfjorden
Osterfjorden
Hjeltefjorden
Hardangerfjorden
Bjørnafjorden
Eidfjorden
Sørfjorden
Nærøyfjorden
Aifjorden
Sognesjøen
Bømlafjorden
Suldalsvatn
Selvik
Heilevong
Førde
Moskog
Vassenden
Sunde
1636
GROVEBREEN
Askvoll
Atløya
Dale
Storehaug
Holsen
Nes
Værlandet
Fure
Tysse
Flekke
Bygstad
Haukedal
Gaularfjell Pass
Bøyum
Fjærland
Hellevik
Eide
Øn
Guddal
Sande
Hestad
Eldalsosen
Mjell
748
Ulvestad
Gaupne
Sula
Nautsung
Vadheim
Høyanger
Vetlefjorden
Selseng
Krakhella
Leirvik
Tjugum
Reppen
Solvorn
Daløy
Hardbakke
Bø
Torvund
Lavik
Nordeide
Lane
Balestrand
Hella
Leikanger
Sogndal
SOGN FOLKEMUSEUM
Ytre Sula
Nåra
Måren
Kongsnes
Flesje
Hermansverk
Slinde
Kaupanger
Rutledal
Oppedal
Soreide
Ortnevik
KVAMSØY GML. KIRKE
Vangsnes
Feios
Nordgulen
Brekke
Bjordal
HOPPERSTAD STAVKIRKE
Viksøyri
Revsnes
Hisarøy
Eivindvik
Fresvik
Kringla
Arnafjord
Fjerestad
1660
FRESVIKBREEN
Skar
Kvigno
Byrknes
Molde
Solheim
Steine
Risnes
Matre
Nygård
986
Vikafjell Pass
OMBYGGET STAVKIRKE
Tórshavn
Fedje
Mongstad
Duesund
SYRDALSBREEN
1761
Aurlandsvangen
Hoplandsjøen
Masfiordnes
Fjon
Mo
STALHEIMS-KLEIVENE MUSEUM
Gudvangen
KJELFOSSEN
Rossnes
Lindås
Sævråsvåg
Eksingedal
Gullbrå
Nesheim
Vinje
Stalheim
Oppheim
Flåm
Hellesøy
Radøy
Vikanes
Eidslandet
1434
KVITANOSA
Brekkhus
Manger
Bø
Stramnes
Tvinde
Myrdal
Seløy
Seim
Bjørsvik
Tyssebotn
Bolstadøyri
Evanger
Bulken
Mjølfjell
Uppsete
Herdla
Rossland
Alversund
Skråmestø
Knarvik
Osterøy
Dale
Voss
SKJERVEFOSSEN
VASSFJORA
1633
Steinestø
Lonevåg
Stanghelle
Salhus
Breistein
Hamlagrøosen
Ulvik
Osa
Solsvik
Ask
Florvåg
1351
SKJEMMENE
Rong
Granvin
Kleppestø
Vaksdal
Ytre Arna
Arna
Trengereid
Kvanndal
Bruravik
HARDANGERJØKULEN
1862
BERGEN
Fjell
Espeland
Haukeland
Tysse
Norheimsund
Ålvik
Utne
Brimnes
Eidfjord
VØRINGSFOSSEN
Lerwick
Newcastle upon Tyne
Straume
Nesttun
TOKAGJELET
Øystese
Grimo
Ringøy
Garen
Telavåg
Flesland
Fana
Løningdalen
Tveita
Tørvikbygd
Kinsarvik
1649
Sæbø
Sotra
Hjellestad
Strandebarm
Aga
Lofthus
1250
Hardangervidda Pass
Klokkarvik
Hatvik
Eikelandsosen
Jondal
Osøyro
Brattabø
Nå
Fusa
Halhjem
Grotnes
Hovland
Sævareid
Mundheim
Hufthamar
Espe
Nordmannslågen
Hessvik
Flatabø
Huftarøy
Reksteren
Lygre
Varaldsøy
1690
HÅRTEIGEN
Ingenes
Sunndal
Kvalvåg
Våge
Tyssedal
Haugesund
Stavanger
Hanstholm
Uggdal
Gjermundshamn
1660
FONNANUTEN
Odda
Sandvikvåg
Tysnesøy
Husa
Løfallstrand
Fitjar
Flatråker
Rosendal
Herøysund
Dimmelsvik
Hildal
LÅTEFOSSEN
Jektevik
Uskedal
Rubbestadneset
Stord
Steinaberg bru
Sunde
Husnes
Fjæra
Seljestad
1719
SANDFLOT
Siggjarvåg
Sagvåg
Leirvik
Valen
Matersdalen
Solfonn
Sæbøvik
Utåker
1602
KYRKJENUTEN
Åkra
Matre
E134
Røldal
Mosterhamn
Haukeliseter
STOKKHO
Valevåg
Hordalia
Bomlo
Skånevik
Kyrping
Utbjoa
Lono
Breióborg
Urbø
Vågslid
Langevåg
Buavåg
Bjoenstrand
Etne
Førde
Haukeligrend
Edlan
Saudasjøen
Sauda
Nesflaten
Bergen
Newcastle
upon Tyne
Eltravåg
Svelo
Grunged
Ølen
Bleskestad
1540
SKAULEN
Skjold
Knapphus
Sandeid
Bjerga
Bjåen
Våge
Øvre Vats
Bråtveit
Sessvatn
Vikedal
Ropeid
Vanvik
Suldalseid
Haugesund
Aksdal
Kårhus
Imsland
Sand
Kvilldal
Hovden
Skjoldastraumen
Suldalsosen
1606
SNONUTEN
Utsira
Yrkje
Marvik
1530
BRANDSNUTEN
Avaldsnes
Lovraeid
E39
E16
E134
11-6
10-5

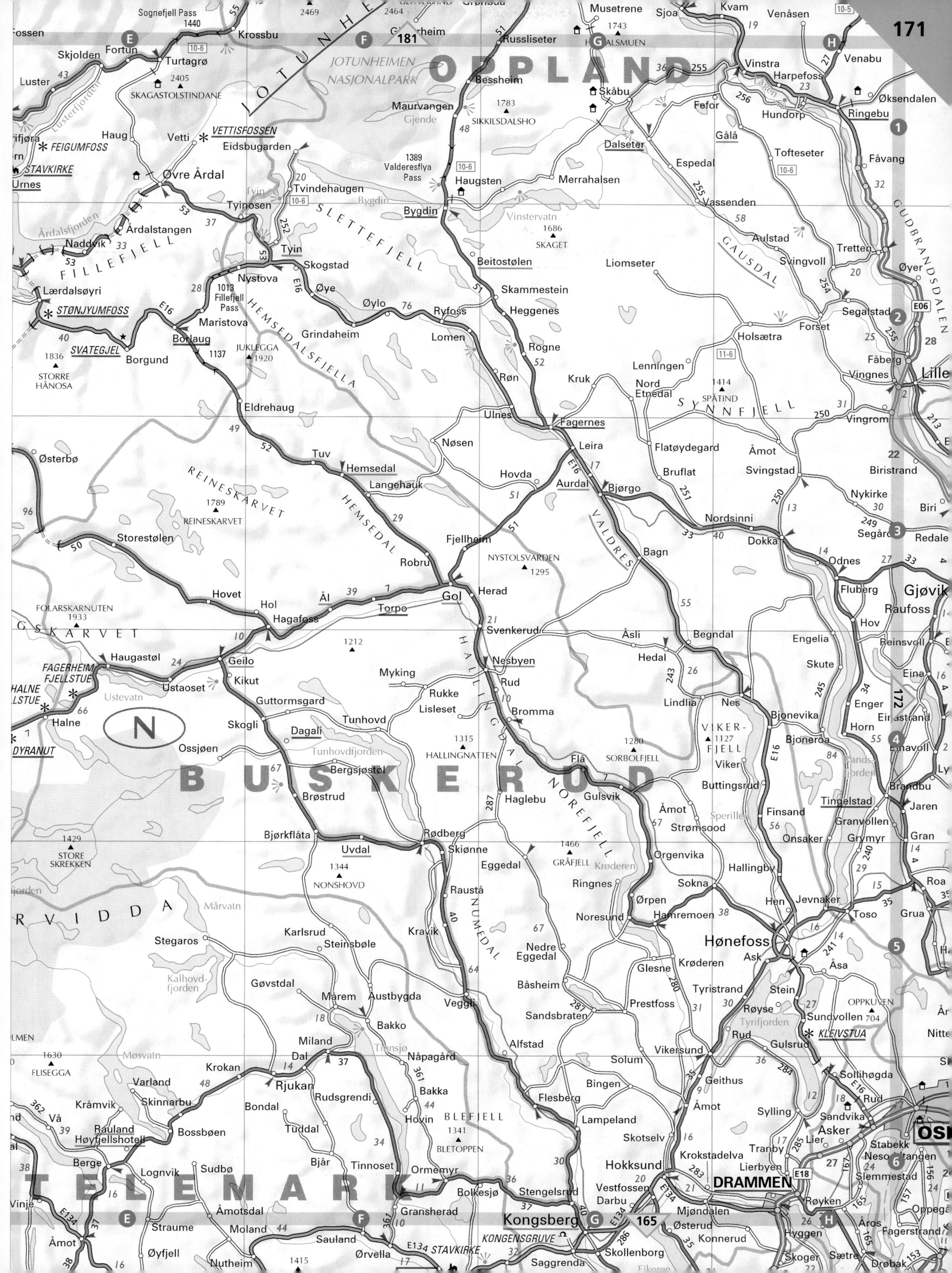
OPPLAND
BUSKERUD
TELEMARK
JOTUNHEIMEN NASJONALPARK
JOTUNHEIMEN
Sognefjell Pass 1440
Krossbu
Fortun
Skjolden
Turtagrø
Luster
Lusterfjorden
2405
SKAGASTOLSTINDANE
Haug
Vetti
VETTISFOSSEN
Eidsbugarden
FEIGUMFOSS
STAVKIRKE
Urnes
Øvre Årdal
Tyin
Tvindehaugen
Tyinosen
Årdalsfjorden
Årdalstangen
Naddvik
FILLEFJELL
Lærdalsøyri
STØNJYUMFOSS
SVATEGJEL
Borgund
1836
STORRE HÅNOSA
Nystova
1013 Fillefjell Pass
Maristova
Borlaug
1137
JUKLEGGA 1920
Skogstad
Øye
Øylo
Grindaheim
HEMSEDALSFJELLA
SLETTEFJELL
Bygdin
Gjende
Maurvangen
1783 SIKKILSDALSHO
1389 Valderesflya Pass
Haugsten
Merrahalsen
Vinstervatn
1686 SKAGET
Beitostølen
Skammestein
Heggenes
Ryfoss
Lomen
Rogne
Røn
Russliseter
Bessheim
Gjendesheim
Musetrene
1743
Sjoa
Kvam
Venåsen
HALSMUEN
Skåbu
Vinstra
Harpefoss
Venabu
Øksendalen
Ringebu
Fefor
Hundorp
Dalseter
Gålå
Espedal
Tofteseter
Fåvang
Vassenden
GAUSDAL
Aulstad
Svingvoll
Tretten
GUDBRANDSDALEN
Øyer
Liomseter
Segalstad
Forset
Holsætra
Fåberg
Vingnes
Lille
Lenningen
Kruk
Nord Etnedal
1414 SPÅTIND
SYNNFJELL
Vingrom
Eldrehaug
Ulnes
Fagernes
Leira
Nøsen
Flatøydegard
Åmot
Biristrand
Østerbø
REINESKARVET
1789 REINESKARVET
Tuv
Hemsedal
Langehauk
Hovda
Aurdal
Bjørgo
Bruflat
Svingstad
Nykirke
Biri
HEMSEDAL
VALDRES
Nordsinni
Segård
Redale
Storestølen
Fjellheim
Dokka
Robru
NYSTOLSVARDEN 1295
Bagn
Odnes
Fluberg
Gjøvik
Raufoss
Hov
Hovet
Hol
Ål
Gol
Herad
Torpo
FOLARSKARNUTEN 1933
Hagafoss
Svenkerud
Åsli
Begndal
Engelia
Reinsvoll
HALLINGDAL
1212
Haugastøl
Geilo
Nesbyen
Hedal
Skute
FAGERHEIM FJELLSTUE
Ustaoset
Kikut
Myking
Rud
Eina
HALNE FJELLSTUE
Ustevatn
Halne
Guttormsgard
Rukke
Lisleset
Lindlia
Nes
Enger
Einastrand
Bromma
Tunhovd
Skogli
Dagali
Bjonevika
Horn
DYRANUT
Ossjøen
1315 HALLINGNATTEN
1280 SORBOLFJELL
VIKER-FJELL 1127
Bjoneroa
Einavoll
Tunhovdfjorden
Bergsjøstøl
Flå
Viker
Randsfjorden
Brandbu
NOREFJELL
Brøstrud
Haglebu
Gulsvik
Buttingsrud
Tingelstad
Jaren
Åmot
Sperillen
Finsand
Granvollen
1429 STORE SKREKKEN
Bjørkflåta
Uvdal
Rødberg
Strømsood
Onsaker
Grymyr
Gran
1344 NONSHOVD
Skiønne
Eggedal
1466 GRÅFJELL
Krøderen
Orgenvika
Hallingby
Roa
HARDANGERVIDDA
Mårvatn
Rauståa
NUMEDAL
Ringnes
Sokna
Ørpen
Noresund
Hamremoen
Hen
Jevnaker
Toso
Grua
Stegaros
Karlsrud
Steinsbøle
Kravik
Nedre Eggedal
Hønefoss
Ask
Åsa
Kalhovd-fjorden
Gøvstdal
Glesne
Krøderen
Båsheim
Tyristrand
Stein
Mårem
Austbygda
Veggli
Prestfoss
Sandsbraten
Røyse
Sundvollen
OPPKUVEN 704
Tyrifjorden
KLEIVSTUA
Bakko
Alfstad
Rud
Gulsrud
Møsvatn
Miland
Dal
Tinnsjø
Nåpagård
Vikersund
Solum
Sollihøgda
1630 FLISEGGA
Krokan
Varland
Rjukan
Bakka
Geithus
Bingen
Flesberg
Kråmvik
Skinnarbu
Bondal
Rudsgrendi
Hovin
BLEFJELL
1341 BLETOPPEN
Åmot
Sylling
Sandvika
Asker
Lampeland
Rauland Høyfjellshotell
Bossbøen
Tuddal
Skotselv
Lier
Stabekk
Neso
Stangen
Berge
Lognvik
Sudbø
Bjår
Tinnoset
Ormemyr
Hokksund
Krokstadelva
Tranby
Lierbyen
Slemmestad
DRAMMEN
Vinje
Bolkesjø
Stengelsrud
Vestfossen
Darbu
Mjøndalen
Røyken
Oppegå
Åmotsdal
Gransherad
Kongsberg
Østerud
Åros
Straume
Moland
Sauland
Konnerud
Hyggen
Fagerstrand
Åmot
Øyfjell
Ørvella
STAVKIRKE
KONGENSGRUVE
Skollenborg
Skoger
Sætre
Drøbak
Nutheim
1415
Saggrenda
181
165
172

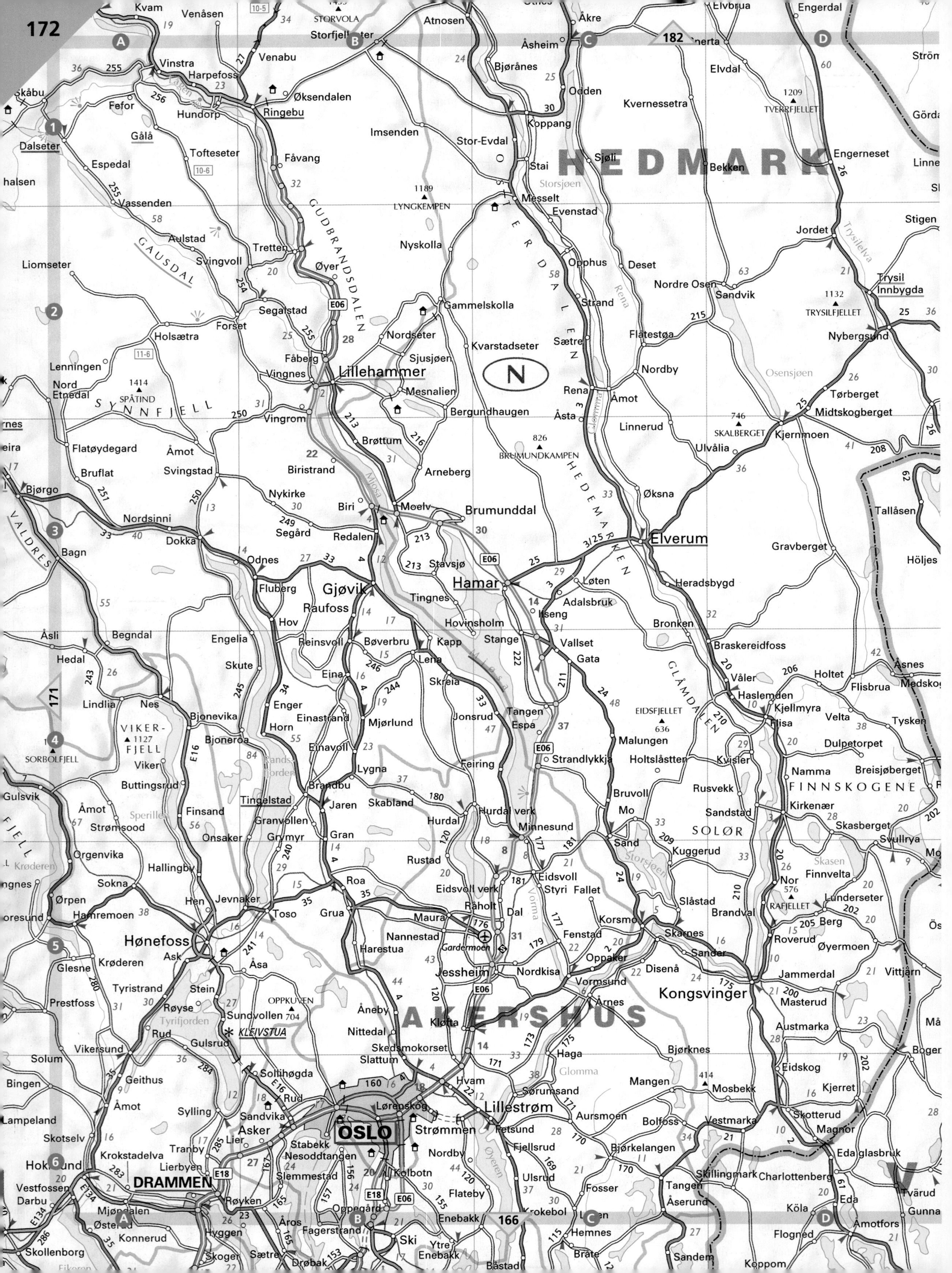
HEDMARK
AKERSHUS
OSLO
GUDBRANDSDALEN
ØSTERDALEN
HEDEMARKEN
GLÅMDALEN
GAUSDAL
VALDRES
SYNNFJELL
VIKER-FJELL
FINNSKOGENE
SOLØR
Kvam
Venåsen
STORVOLA
Storfjellseter
Atnosen
Åkre
Elvbrua
Engerdal
Åsheim
Vinstra
Harpefoss
Venabu
Bjøråneset
Elvdal
Skåbu
Fefor
Hundorp
Ringebu
Øksendalen
Odden
Kvernessetra
TVERRFJELLET
Koppang
Dalseter
Gålå
Imsenden
Stor-Evdal
Tofteseter
Fåvang
Sjøli
Stai
Bekken
Engerneset
Espedal
Storsjøen
Vassenden
LYNGKEMPEN
Messelt
Evenstad
Stigen
Aulstad
Tretten
Nyskolla
Jordet
Liomseter
Svingvoll
Øyer
Opphus
Deset
Nordre Osen
Sandvik
Trysil
Innbygda
Strand
Rena
Gammelskolla
Segalstad
TRYSILFJELLET
Forset
Holsætra
Nordseter
Flåtestøa
Nybergsund
Sætre
Fåberg
Kvarstadseter
Sjusjøen
Lenningen
Lillehammer
Nordby
Osensjøen
Nord Etnedal
Vingnes
SPÅTIND
Mesnalien
Tørberget
Åmot
Midtskogberget
Vingrom
Bergundhaugen
Åsta
SKALBERGET
Kjernmoen
Linnerud
Flatøydegard
Åmot
Brøttum
BRUMUNDKAMPEN
Ulvålia
Bruflat
Svingstad
Biristrand
Arneberg
Tallåsen
Bjørgo
Nykirke
Øksna
Biri
Moelv
Brumunddal
Nordsinni
Segård
Redalen
Elverum
Dokka
Gravberget
Bagn
Odnes
Stavsjø
Höljes
Hamar
Løten
Heradsbygd
Fluberg
Gjøvik
Tingnes
Raufoss
Adalsbruk
Ilseng
Hov
Hovinsholm
Bronken
Åsli
Begndal
Engelia
Reinsvoll
Bøverbru
Kapp
Stange
Vallset
Braskereidfoss
Hedal
Skute
Lena
Gata
Åsnes
Holtet
Eina
Skreia
Våler
Flisbrua
Medskog
Lindlia
Nes
Enger
Haslemoen
Kjellmyra
Bjonevika
Einastrand
Jonsrud
Tangen
EIDSFJELLET
Velta
Tysken
Horn
Mjørlund
Espa
Flisa
SORBOLFJELL
Bjoneroa
Malungen
Dulpetorpet
Einavoll
Randsfjorden
Strandlykkja
Holtslåsttere
Kvisler
Viker
Lygna
Feiring
Namma
Breisjøberget
Buttingsrud
Brandbu
Rusvekk
Gulsvik
Tingelstad
Jaren
Skabland
Bruvoll
Kirkenær
Åmot
Finsand
Sperillen
Hurdal
Hurdal verk
Mo
Sandstad
Skasberget
Strømsood
Granvollen
Minnesund
Svullrya
Onsaker
Grymyr
Gran
Sand
Kuggerud
Orgenvika
Krøderen
Rustad
Skasen
Hallingby
Eidsvoll
Nor
Finnvelta
Sokna
Roa
Eidsvoll verk
Styri
Fallet
RAFJELLET
Lunderseter
Ørpen
Jevnaker
Råholt
Slåstad
Brandval
Hen
Toso
Grua
Hamremoen
Dal
Maura
Korsmo
Berg
Skarnes
Roverud
Hønefoss
Nannestad
Fenstad
Gardermoen
Sander
Øyermoen
Harestua
Oppaker
Ask
Glesne
Krøderen
Åsa
Jessheim
Nordkisa
Disenå
Vittjärn
Jammerdal
Tyristrand
Stein
Vormsund
Kongsvinger
OPPKUVEN
Masterud
Prestfoss
Røyse
Sundvollen
Åneby
Årnes
Tyrifjorden
KLEIVSTUA
Nittedal
Kløfta
Austmarka
Rud
Gulsrud
Vikersund
Skedsmokorset
Haga
Boger
Solum
Slattum
Bjørknes
Eidskog
Geithus
Sollihøgda
Hvam
Glomma
Bingen
Mangen
Mosbekk
Åmot
Rud
Sørumsand
Kjerret
Sylling
Sandvika
Lørenskog
Lillestrøm
Aursmoen
Lampeland
Asker
Strømmen
Bolfoss
Skotterud
Vestmarka
Magnor
Skotselv
Lier
Stabekk
Fetsund
Tranby
Nesoddtangen
Fjellsrud
Krokstadelva
Nordby
Bjørkelangen
Eda glasbruk
Hokksund
Lierbyen
Slemmestad
Kolbotn
Øyeren
Ulsrud
Skillingmark
Charlottenberg
DRAMMEN
Vestfossen
Tangen
Tvärud
Darbu
Røyken
Fosser
Åserund
Eda
Mjøndalen
Flateby
Køla
Østerud
Oppegård
Åros
Enebakk
Krokebol
Gunna
Konnerud
Hyggen
Fagerstrand
Hemnes
Åmotfors
Ski
Ytre Enebakk
Flogned
Skollenborg
Skoger
Sætre
Drøbak
Bråte
Sandem
Koppom
Båstad
182
171
166

DALARNA
VÄRMLAND
BERGSLAGEN
Snössvallen
Lovnasvallen
Sunnanå
Östansjö
Fågelsjö
Olingsjövallen
Rullbo
183
Heden
Östomsjön
Haftorsbygget
NJUPESKÄRS VATTENFALL
Mörkret
Särna
FULUFJÄLLETS NATIONALPARK
FULUFJÄLLET
HAMRA NATIONALPARK
Sidertjärn
Los
Lillhaga
Karlsberg
Tandsjöborg
Hamra
Västbacka
Sandsjö
Björkberg
Öjung
Mossiberg
Ulvsjön
Trängsletsjön
Kristineberg
Noppikoski
Tackåsen
Lobonäs
Voxnan
Sörsjön
Bunkris
Flögåsen
Kräckelbäcken
Kvarnberg
Ljørdalen
Trängslet
Bössbo
Untorp
Rosentorp
Ejheden
Överbo
Grundforsen
Fulunäs
Vervnäs
Lövnäs
Åsen
Brunnsberg
Ämådalen
Korsåsen
Voxna
Østby
Støa
Ringnäs
Rot
Österdalälven
Älvdalen
Tallhed
Gubbmyran
Sälen
Västermyckeläng
Heden
Skattungbyn
Furudal
Dalfors
Plassen
Orrliden
Dysbodarna
Evertsberg
Östanvik
Amungen
Rundfloen
Rörbäcksnäs
Vanån
Våmhus
Orsa
Slättberg
Norrboda
Lutnes
Transtrand
Risberg
Oxberg
Orsasjön
Dalbyn
Långflon
Mångsbodarna
Tennänget
Bonäs
Vattnäs
Gulleråsen
Västerdalälven
Norra Löten
Mora
Boda
Mårtsviken
Torgåsmon
Venjan
Acksi
Vika
Färnäs
Norra Finnskoga
Tisjön
Nusnäs
Garsås
Vikarbyn
Nedre Gärdsjö
Ljugaren
Limedsforsen
Venjansjön
Sollerön
Kärrbackstrand
Gesunda
Siljan
Rättvik
Söderås
174
Övertäng
Tandö
Öje
Johannisholm
Björka
Tällberg
Finnbo
Klarabro
Sysslebäck
Ytterboda
Envik
Siljansnäs
Alvik
Bjursås
Bograngen
Letten
Gävunda
Malungsfors
Gammalsälen
Brintbodarna
Leksand
Skallskog
Sågmyra
Ransby
Malung
Grycksbo
KLARÄLVDALEN
Kindsjön
Utsjö
Insjön
Likenäs
Rexbo
Bjurberget
KÖLARNA
Yttermalung
Djura
Gagnef
Falun
Mörbacka
Hedby
Djurås
Sifferbo
Hjällstad
Dala-Järna
Ambjörby
Vansbro
Nordanholen
Lisskogsbrändan
Dala-Floda
Bäsna
Ornäs
Nyskoga
Appelbo
Kristinefors
Ö Näsberg
Nås
Björbo
Mockfjärd
Borlänge
Stöllet
Granåbron
Eldforsen
Skansbacken
TIOMILASKOGEN
Avradsberg
Orsala
Floda
Naglarby
Röjdåfors
Halvarsgårdarna
Vitsand
Vakern
Tuna Hästberg
Mora
Åstrand
Kroktorp
Lindesnäs
Skenshyttan
Överbyn
Vägsjöfors
Lövsjön
Rämshyttan
Uvanå
Tyngsjö
Nyhammar
Källarbo
Laxtjärn
Grangärde
Vikmans
Kollerud
Myren
Ingevallsbo
Lekvattnet
Rådom
Håvberget
Kvarnberget
Sunnansjö
Gräsberg
Oleby
Ekshärad
Håksberg
Råda
Gustavfors
Tyfors
Hån
Norhyttan
Västman
Åsmansbo
Torsby
Ludvika
Blötberget
Övre Fryken
Hole
Fredriksberg
Saxdalen
Smedjebacken
Edebäck
Geijersholm
Oforsen
Gullsby
Hagfors
Grängesberg
Söderbärke
Lysvik
Uddeholm
Nittkvarn
Långenäs
Rämmen
Gumhöjden
Hörken
Vad
Bastnäs
Norra Råda
Ställberg
Högfors
Pörtet
KÄRNÄSENS HEMBYGDSGÅRD
Lesjöfors
Hedbyn
Uddheden
NATURVÅRDSOMRÅDE
Gräsmark
Treskog
Lid
Motjärnshyttan
By
Mjönäs
Sunnemo
Sandsjön
Sävsjön
Ställdalen
Malingsbo
Västerrottna
Torsby
Gåsborn
Kloten
Sunne
Munkfors
Nordmark
167
Bredsjö
Kopparberg
Kärrb
Rottneros
MÅRBACKA
Mangskog
Ransäter
Hällefors
Hjulsjö
Skinnskatteberg
Ramsberg
Riddarhyttan

184
173
167
GÄVLEBO
DALARNA
HAMRA NATIONALPARK
BERGSLAGEN
NATURVÅRDSOMRÅDE
FÄRNEBOFJ. NATION
HÄLSINGSKOGEN
KLOSTER
Sunnanå
Östansjö
Olingsjövallen
Fågelsjö
Rullbo
Los
Korskrogen
Nore
Ljusdal
Hybo
Delsbo
Lillbo
Färila
Stocksbo
Järvsö
Stråsjö
Sidertjärn
Lillhaga
Karlsberg
Tandsjöborg
Hamra
Västbacka
Sandsjö
Björkberg
Öjung
Harsa
Hamre
Karsjö
Mossiberg
Ulvsjön
Trängsletsjön
Lobonäs
Fluren
Långbo
Vallsta
Nordsjö
Arbrå
Noppikoski
Tackåsen
Voxnan
Flögåsen
Kräckelbäcken
Bunkris
Kvarnberg
Lottefors
Trängslet
Bössbo
Untorp
Rosentorp
Ejheden
Överbo
Edsbyn
Bollnäs
Ovanåker
Alfta
Glössb
Ämådalen
Korsåsen
Voxna
Åsen
Brunnsberg
Rot
Österdalälven
Älvdalen
Tallhed
Annefors
Hällbo
Kilafors
Västermyckeläng
Heden
Skattungbyn
Furudal
Dalfors
Flytåsen
Evertsberg
Våmhus
Östanvik
Amungen
Skålsjön
Oxberg
Risberg
Orsa
Slättberg
Norrboda
Flätsbo
Orsasjön
Dalbyn
Holmsveden
Tennänget
Bonäs
Gruvberget
Vattnäs
Gulleråsen
Svabensverk
Lingbo
Mora
Katrineberg
Venjan
Acksi
Vika
Färnäs
Boda
Bingsjö
Lamborn
Åmot
Nusnäs
Garsås
Vikarbyn
Ljugaren
Venjansjön
Sollerön
Nedre Gärdsjö
Svartnäs
Vallsbo
Gesunda
Rättvik
Söderås
Siljan
Ockelbo
Öje
Johannisholm
Björka
Tällberg
Övertänger
Finnbo
Jädraås
Ytterboda
Vintjärn
Linghed
Enviken
Siljansnäs
Malungsfors
Gävunda
Alvik
Bjursås
Svärdsjö
Kungsberg
Brintbodarna
Leksand
Toftbyn
Järbo
Malung
Skallskog
Sågmyra
Grycksbo
Utsjö
Insjön
Lumsheden
Stocksbo
Sundborn
Rexbo
Yttermalung
Djura
Gagnef
Falun
Hosjö
Sandv
Storvik
Hedby
Djurås
Sifferbo
Dala-Järna
Hofors
Vansbro
Nordanholen
Runn
Ängelsfors
Skogsbrändan
Dala-Floda
Västerdalälven
Bäsna
Vika
Äppelbo
Ornäs
Torsåker
Näsberg
Granåbron
Nås
Björbo
Mockfjärd
Borlänge
Långshyttan
Hästbo
Eldforsen
Skansbacken
Floda
Naglarby
Lövåsen
Avradsberg
Orsala
Halvarsgårdarna
Stjärnsund
Mora
Dala-Husby
Fäggeby
Bastfal
Vakern
Tuna Hästberg
Skenshyttan
Säter
Kroktorp
Lindesnäs
Lövsjön
Rämshyttan
Uvanå
Tyngsjö
Nyhammar
Källarbo
Garpenberg
Laxtjärn
Grangärde
Vikmanshyttan
Hedemora
Horndal
Österfä
Ingevallsbo
Kvarnberget
Håvberget
Gräsberg
Sunnansjö
Håksberg
Tyfors
Hån
Norhyttan
Väsman
Åsmansbo
Norn
Fors
By
Gustavfors
Ingolsbenning
Ludvika
Blötberget
Smedjebacken
Folkärna
Fredriksberg
Saxdalen
Avesta
Oforsen
Krylbo
Bäsinge
Geijersholm
Dalälven
Grängesberg
Söderbärke
Norberg
Hagfors
Vansjö
Gumhöjden
Rämmen
Nittkvarn
Vad
Hede
Norra Råda
Hörken
Fagersta
Nykrogen
Lesjöfors
Ställberg
Högfors
Hedbyn
Karbenning
Broddbo
Västansfors
Mårnshyttan
Ängelsberg
Västerfärnebo
Sunnemo
Sandsjön
Sävsjön
Ställdalen
Malingsbo
Ämänningen
Sala
Gåsborn
Kloten
Virsbo
Salbohed
Kila
Nordmark
Bosjön
Långban
Bredsjö
Kopparberg
Kärrbo
Sätra brunn
Skinnskatteberg
Virsbo bruk
Ranstad
Hällefors
Hjulsjö
Ramsberg
Riddarhyttan
Gunnilbo
Ramnäs

185
168
169
176
Hålsjö
Norra Dellen
Södra Dellen
Edsta
Strömsbruk
Välsta
Näsviken
Sånna
Sörforsa
Hudiksvall
Arnön
NATURRESERVAT
Hornslandet
Hölick
Iggesund
Nianfors
Njutånger
Agön
Enånger
Lindefallet
Långvind
Norrala
Mo
Söderhamn
Bergvik
Söderala
Sandarne
Ljusne
Vallvik
Skog
Axmarby
Norrsundet
Bergby
Hamrångefjärden
Trödje
Hille
Utvalnäs
Gävlebukten
Kögbo
Valbo
GÄVLE
Furuvik
Skutskär
Gårdskär
Forsbacka
Hästbo
Storsjön
Älvkarleby
Fågelsundet
Årsunda
Marma
Karlholmsbruk
Hållnäs
Ångskär
Öregrundsgrepen
Skärplinge
Finnböle
Österlövsta
Västland
Hedesunda
Lövstabruk
Forsmark
Tolfta
Tierp
Söderfors
Öregrund
Gräsö
Norrboda
Söderboda
Bjurön
Kavaröskaten
Gysinge
Valö
Norrskedika
Östhammar
Horsskog
Örbyhus
ÖRBYHUS
Börstil
Harg
Tuskö
Ellan
Singö
Kerstimbo
Hökhuvud
Östervåla
Månkarbo
Österbybruk
Gimo
Hargshamn
Tärnsjö
Vendel
2008
Ekedal
Harbo
Morkarla
Herräng
Grisslehamn
Tämnaren
Läby
Skyttorp
SALSTA
Sanda
Alunda
Hallstavik
Huddunge
Stensunda
Runhällen
Roteberg
Skoby
Häverö
Edeby
Edebo
Björklinge
GAMLA GRÄNOME
Bladåker
Östfora
Faringe
Älmsta-Väddö
Storvreta
Skebobruk
Jumkil
Bälinge
Morgongåva
Heby
Gåvsta
Knutby
Rörvik
Vittinge
Järlåsa
Gamla Uppsala
Almunge
Söderby-Karl
UPPSALA
Edsbro
Åland
Brunna
LINNÉS HAMMARBY
Rånäs
Erken
Roslags-Bro
Vätö
Skeppsmyra
Gräddö
Tärna
Altuna
Hagby
Sävja
MORA STENAR
EKEBYHOLM
Färdhundra
Österunda
Sunnersta
Bottniska viken/
Pohjanlahti
Södra Kvarken
Ålandshav
ROSLAGEN
UPPSALA
GÄSTRIKLAND
UPPLAND
AHV
Ahver
BOLSTAHOLM
Bovik
Storby
Eckerö
Torp
Hamn
Gottb
Maarianha
Marieh
FIN
E
F
G
H
1
2
3
4
5
6

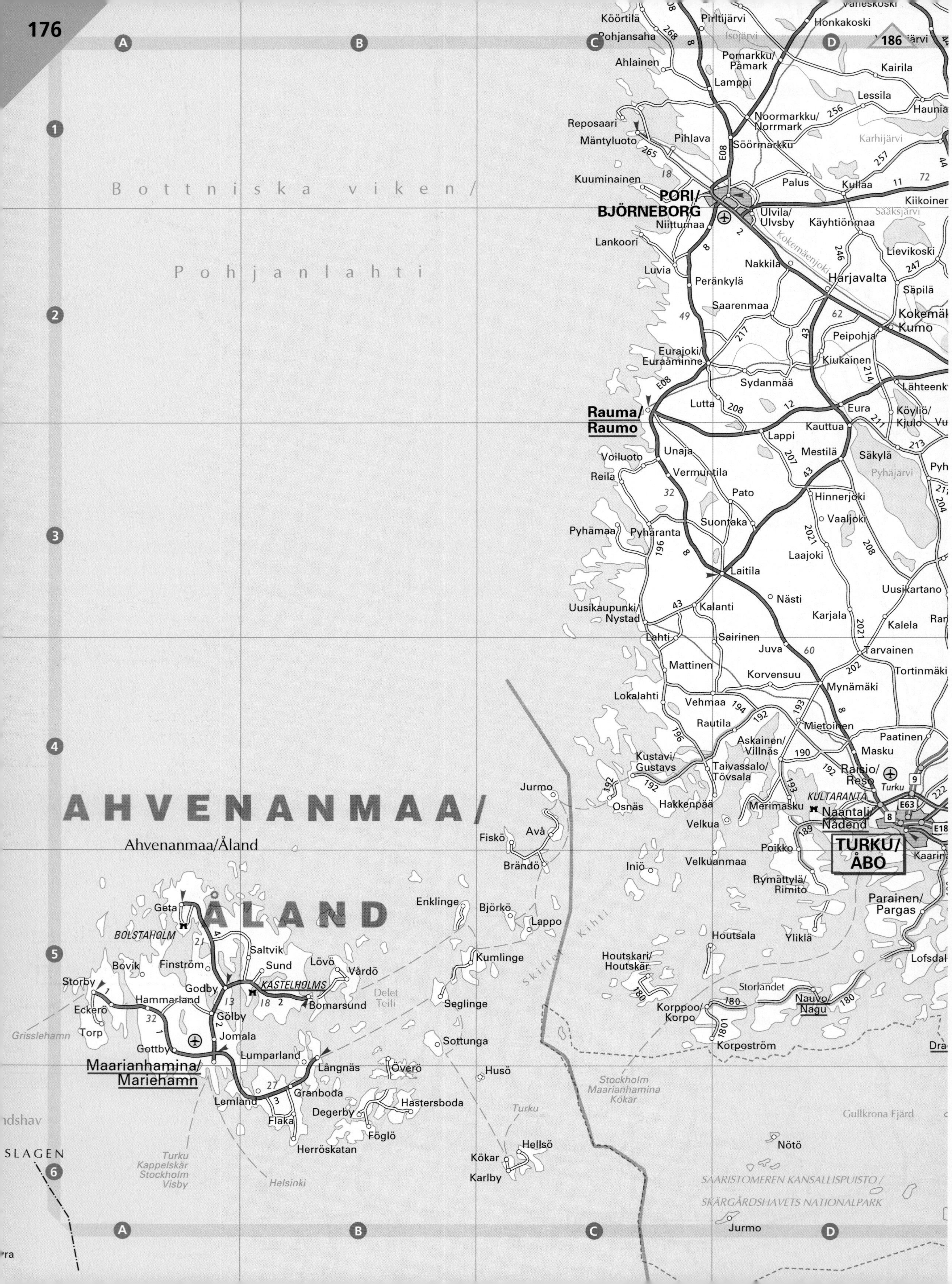
186
A
B
C
D
1
2
3
4
5
6
Bottniska viken/
Pohjanlahti
AHVENANMAA/
Ahvenanmaa/Åland
ÅLAND
Köörtilä
Pohjansaha
Ahlainen
Pirltijärvi
Isojärvi
Pomarkku/
Påmark
Lamppi
Honkakoski
Kairila
Lessila
Haunia
Reposaari
Mäntyluoto
Pihlava
Noormarkku/
Norrmark
Söörmarkku
Karhijärvi
Kuuminainen
PORI/
BJÖRNEBORG
Niittumaa
Ulvila/
Ulvsby
Palus
Kullaa
Kiikoinen
Sääksjärvi
Käyhtiönmaa
Lankoori
Kokemäenjoki
Lievikoski
Nakkila
Luvia
Peränkylä
Harjavalta
Säpilä
Saarenmaa
Kokemäki
Kumo
Peipohja
Eurajoki/
Euraäminne
Kiukainen
Sydanmää
Lähteenkylä
Rauma/
Raumo
Lutta
Eura
Köyliö/
Kjulo
Kauttua
Lappi
Unaja
Mestilä
Säkylä
Voiluoto
Vermuntila
Reila
Pyhäjärvi
Pato
Hinnerjoki
Suontaka
Vaaljoki
Pyhämaa
Pyhäranta
Laajoki
Laitila
Nästi
Uusikartano
Uusikaupunki/
Nystad
Kalanti
Karjala
Kalela
Lahti
Sairinen
Juva
Tarvainen
Mattinen
Korvensuu
Tortinmäki
Lokalahti
Mynämäki
Vehmaa
Rautila
Mietoinen
Paatinen
Askainen/
Villnäs
Masku
Kustavi/
Gustavs
Taivassalo/
Tövsala
Raisio/
Reso
Turku
Jurmo
Osnäs
Hakkenpää
KULTARANTA
Merimasku
Naantali/
Nådend
Velkua
Fiskö
Avå
Poikko
TURKU/
ÅBO
Kaarina
Brändö
Iniö
Velkuanmaa
Rymättylä/
Rimito
Enklinge
Björkö
Lappo
Parainen/
Pargas
Geta
BOLSTAHOLM
Skiftet Kihti
Houtsala
Yliklä
Saltvik
Kumlinge
Houtskari/
Houtskär
Lofsdal
Bovik
Finström
Sund
Lövö
Vårdö
Storby
KASTELHOLMS
Delet
Teili
Storlandet
Godby
Hammarland
Bomarsund
Seglinge
Korppoo/
Korpo
Nauvo/
Nagu
Eckerö
Gölby
Grisslehamn
Torp
Jomala
Sottunga
Korpoström
Gottby
Lumparland
Maarianhamina/
Mariehamn
Långnäs
Överö
Husö
Stockholm
Maarianhamina
Kökar
Lemland
Granboda
Hastersboda
Degerby
Turku
Gullkrona Fjärd
Flaka
Föglö
Herröskatan
Hellsö
Nötö
SLAGEN
Turku
Kappelskär
Stockholm
Visby
Kökar
Karlby
Helsinki
SAARISTOMEREN KANSALLISPUISTO /
SKÄRGÅRDSHAVETS NATIONALPARK
Jurmo

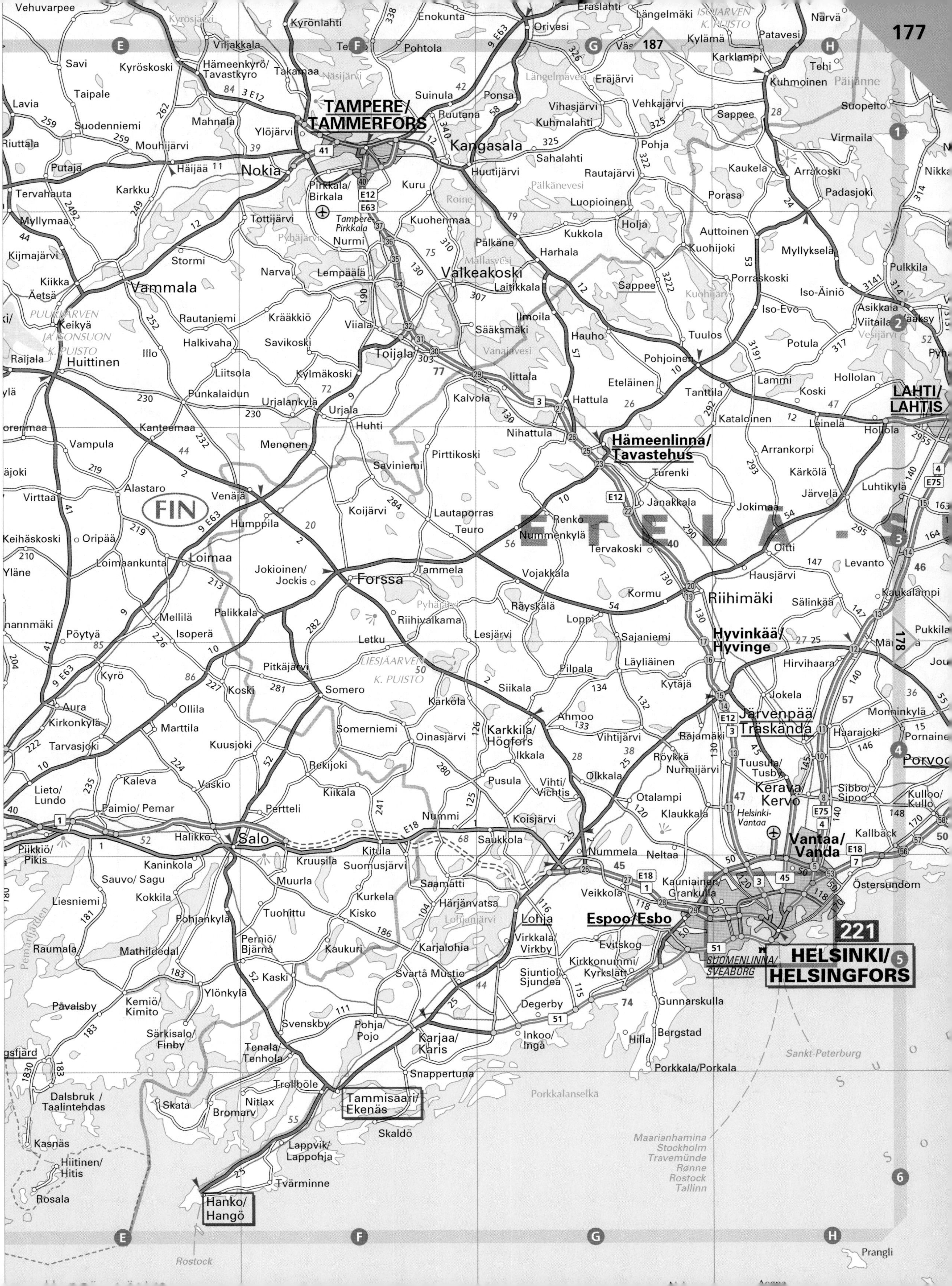
Vehuvarpee
Kyrösjärvi
Kyrönlahti
Enokunta
Eräslahti
Längelmäki
ISOJÄRVEN K. PUISTO
Närvä
Orivesi
Viljakkala
Pohtola
187
Kylämä
Patavesi
Savi
Kyröskoski
Hämeenkyrö/ Tavastkyro
Takamaa
Näsijärvi
Längelmävesi
Eräjärvi
Karklampi
Tehi
Kuhmoinen
Päijänne
Lavia
Taipale
Suinula
Ponsa
TAMPERE/ TAMMERFORS
Ruutana
Vihasjärvi
Kuhmalahti
Vehkajärvi
Sappee
Suopelto
Suodenniemi
Mahnala
Ylöjärvi
Riuttala
Mouhijärvi
Kangasala
Sahalahti
Pohja
Virmaila
Putaja
Häijää
Nokia
Huutijärvi
Rautajärvi
Kaukela
Arrakoski
Nikka
Tervahauta
Karkku
Pirkkala/ Birkala
Kuru
Pälkänevesi
Porasa
Padasjoki
Roine
Luopioinen
Myllymaa
Tottijärvi
Tampere Pirkkala
Kuohenmaa
Holja
Auttoinen
Kijmajärvi
Pyhäjärvi
Nurmi
Kukkola
Kuohijoki
Myllykselä
Stormi
Pälkäne
Harhala
Mallasvesi
Pulkkila
Kiikka
Äetsä
Narva
Lempäälä
Valkeakoski
Laitikkala
Sappee
Porraskoski
Vammala
Kuohijärvi
Iso-Äiniö
PUURIJÄRVEN JA ISONSUON K. PUISTO
Keikyä
Rautaniemi
Krääkkiö
Viiala
Ilmoila
Iso-Evo
Asikkala
Viitaila
Vääksy
Halkivaha
Savikoski
Sääksmäki
Hauho
Tuulos
Potula
Vesijärvi
Raijala
Huittinen
Illo
Toijala
Vanajavesi
Pohjoinen
Liitsola
Kylmäkoski
Lammi
Hollolan
Punkalaidun
Iittala
Eteläinen
Tanttila
Koski
LAHTI/ LAHTIS
Urjalankylä
Kalvola
Hattula
Kataloinen
Leinelä
Urjala
Hollola
Kanteemaa
Huhti
Nihattula
Hämeenlinna/ Tavastehus
Vampula
Menonen
Pirttikoski
Arrankorpi
Saviniemi
Turenki
Kärkölä
Äjoki
Alastaro
Venäjä
Luhtikylä
Virttaa
FIN
Janakkala
Järvelä
Koijärvi
Lautaporras
Jokimaa
Humppila
Renko
Teuro
ETELÄ-S
Keihäskoski
Oripää
Nummenkylä
Tervakoski
Oitti
Loimaankunta
Loimaa
Levanto
Yläne
Jokioinen/ Jockis
Forssa
Tammela
Vojakkala
Hausjärvi
Kaukalampi
Mellilä
Palikkala
Pyhäjärvi
Räyskälä
Kormu
Riihimäki
Sälinkää
Pukkila
nannmäki
Isoperä
Riihivalkama
Loppi
Pöytyä
Letku
Lesjärvi
Sajaniemi
Hyvinkää/ Hyvinge
178
Mäntsälä
LIESJÄRVEN K. PUISTO
Pitkäjärvi
Läyliäinen
Hirvihaara
Jou
Kyrö
Pilpala
Kytäjä
Koski
Somero
Siikala
Jokela
Aura
Ollila
Kärkölä
Ahmoo
Järvenpää/ Träskända
Monninkylä
Kirkonkylä
Marttila
Somerniemi
Oinasjärvi
Karkkila/ Högfors
Vihtijärvi
Rajamäki
Haarajoki
Pornainen
Tarvasjoki
Kuusjoki
Ikkala
Röykkä
Nurmijärvi
Tuusula/ Tusby
Porvoo
Rekijoki
Olkkala
Kaleva
Vaskio
Pusula
Kerava/ Kervo
Sibbo/ Sipoo
Kulloo/ Kullo
Lieto/ Lundo
Kiikala
Vihti/ Vichtis
Otalampi
Paimio/ Pemar
Pertteli
Nummi
Klaukkala
Helsinki-Vantaa
Koisjärvi
Kallbäck
Piikkiö/ Pikis
Halikko
Salo
Saukkola
Vantaa/ Vanda
Kitula
Nummela
Neltaa
Kaninkola
Kruusila
Suomusjärvi
Östersundom
Sauvo/ Sagu
Muurla
Saamatti
Veikkola
Kauniainen/ Grankulla
Kokkila
Kurkela
Härjänvatsa
Liesniemi
Tuohittu
Kisko
Lohjanjärvi
Lohja
Espoo/Esbo
Pohjankylä
Raumala
Perniö/ Bjärnå
Kaukuri
Karjalohja
Virkkala/ Virkby
Evitskog
221
Mathildedal
Pemarfjärden
Kirkkonummi/ Kyrkslätt
SUOMENLINNA/ SVEABORG
HELSINKI/ HELSINGFORS
Kaski
Svartå
Mustio
Siuntio/ Sjundeå
Ylönkylä
Påvalsby
Kemiö/ Kimito
Degerby
Gunnarskulla
Svenskby
Pohja/ Pojo
Särkisalo/ Finby
Karjaa/ Karis
Inkoo/ Ingå
Hilla
Bergstad
Tenala/ Tenhola
Sankt-Peterburg
Snappertuna
Porkkala/Porkala
Trollböle
Porkkalanselkä
Dalsbruk / Taalintehdas
Skata
Nitlax
Bromarv
Tammisaari/ Ekenäs
Skaldö
Kasnäs
Lappvik/ Lappohja
Maarianhamina
Stockholm
Travemünde
Rønne
Rostock
Tallinn
Hiitinen/ Hitis
Tvärminne
Rosala
Hanko/ Hangö
Rostock
Prangli
E
F
G
H
FIN

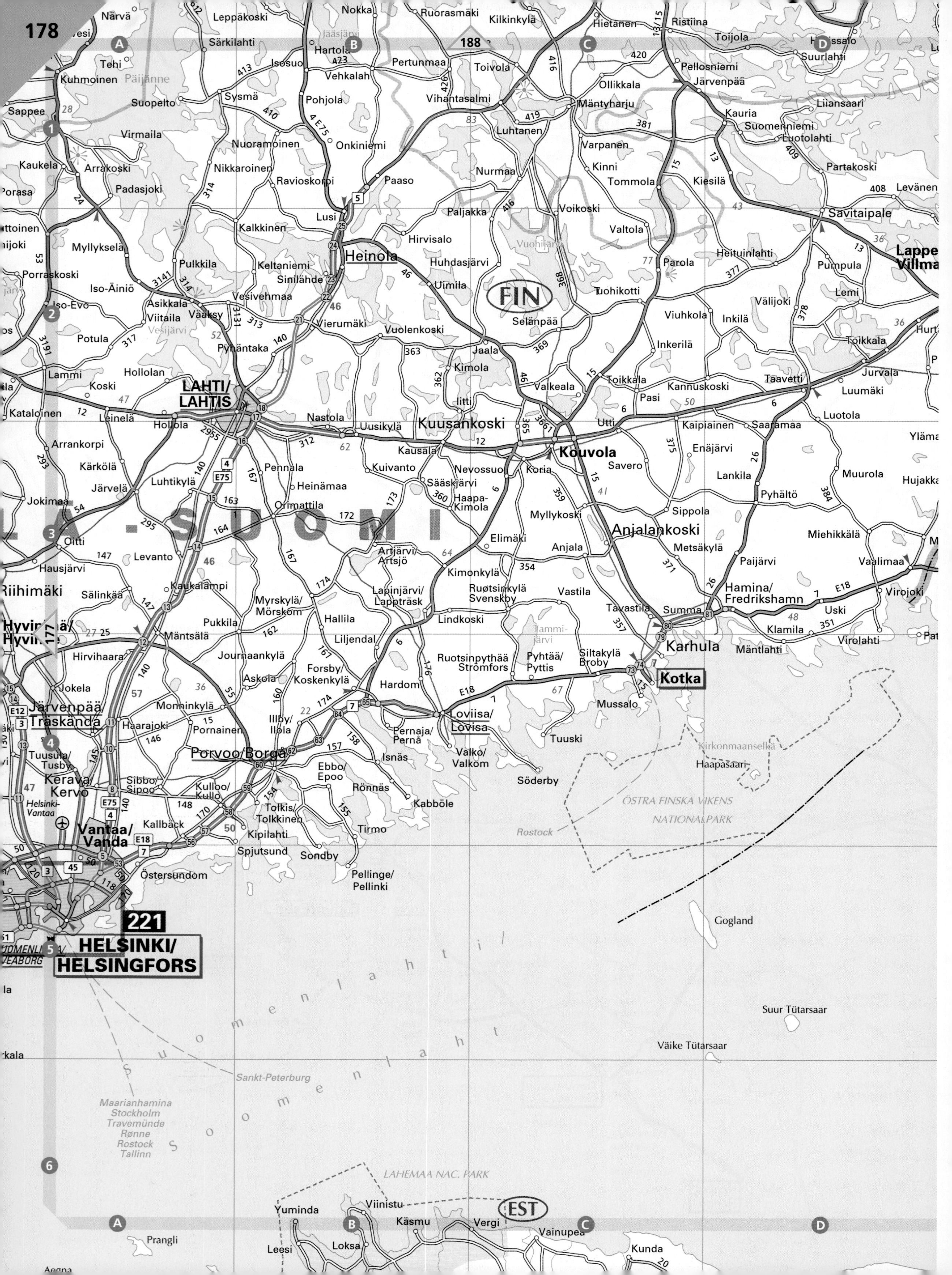

Narvä
Leppäkoski
Nokka
Ruorasmäki
Kilkinkylä
Hietanen
Ristiina
Toijola
Suurlahti
Särkilahti
Hartola
Jääsjärvi
188
Tehi
Kuhmoinen
Päijänne
Isosuo
Vehkalahti
Pertunmaa
Toivola
Pellosniemi
Järvenpää
Ollikkala
Sysmä
Pohjola
Vihantasalmi
Mäntyharju
Liiansaari
Sappee
Suopelto
Kauria
Suomenniemi
Luotolahti
Virmaila
Onkiniemi
Luhtanen
Varpanen
Nuoramoinen
Kaukela
Arrakoski
Nikkaroinen
Nurmaa
Kinni
Tommola
Kiesilä
Partakoski
Padasjoki
Ravioskorpi
Paaso
Levänen
Porasa
Voikoski
Savitaipale
Lusi
Paljakka
Valtola
Kalkkinen
Hirvisalo
Myllykselä
Heinola
Vuohijärvi
Heituinlahti
Lappee
Villma
Porraskoski
Pulkkila
Keltaniemi
Huhdasjärvi
Parola
Pumpula
Sinilähde
Uimila
Iso-Äiniö
FIN
Tuohikotti
Lemi
Vesivehmaa
Välijoki
Iso-Evo
Asikkala
Viuhkola
Inkilä
Viitaila
Vääksy
Vierumäki
Selänpää
Vesijärvi
Potula
Vuolenkoski
Pyhäntaka
Jaala
Inkerilä
Toikkala
Lammi
Kimola
Hollolan
Koski
LAHTI/
LAHTIS
Toikkala
Kannuskoski
Taavetti
Jurvala
Valkeala
Pasi
Luumäki
Iitti
Kataloinen
Leinelä
Hollola
Nastola
Uusikylä
Kuusankoski
Utti
Kaipiainen
Saaramaa
Luotola
Ylämaa
Arrankorpi
Kausala
Kouvola
Enäjärvi
Kärkölä
Pennala
Kuivanto
Nevossuo
Koria
Savero
Muurola
Hujakka
Luhtikylä
Heinämaa
Sääskjärvi
Haapa-Kimola
Lankila
Järvelä
E75
Pyhältö
Jokimaa
Orimattila
Myllykoski
Sippola
LA - SUOMI
Anjalankoski
Miehikkälä
Oitti
Elimäki
Anjala
Metsäkylä
Hausjärvi
Levanto
Artjärvi/
Artsjö
Kimonkylä
Paijärvi
Vaalimaa
Riihimäki
Sälinkää
Kaukalampi
Lapinjärvi/
Lappträsk
Ruotsinkylä
Svenskby
Vastila
Hamina/
Fredrikshamn
Virojoki
Myrskylä/
Mörskom
Tavastila
Summa
Uski
Hyvinkää/
Hyvinge
177
Pukkila
Mäntsälä
Hallila
Lindkoski
Tammijärvi
Klamila
Liljendal
Karhula
Virolahti
Hirvihaara
Journaankylä
Ruotsinpyhtää
Strömfors
Pyhtää/
Pyttis
Siltakylä
Broby
Mäntlahti
Askola
Forsby/
Koskenkylä
Kotka
Jokela
Hardom
Järvenpää
Träskända
Monninkylä
Loviisa/
Lovisa
Mussalo
Haarajoki
Pornainen
Illby/
Ilola
Pernaja/
Pernå
Tuuski
Tuusula/
Tusby
Porvoo/Borgå
Isnäs
Valko/
Valkom
Kirkonmaanselkä
Haapasaari
Kerava/
Kervo
Sibbo/
Sipoo
Ebbo/
Epoo
Söderby
Kulloo/
Kullo
Rönnäs
Helsinki-
Vantaa
Tolkis/
Tolkkinen
Kabböle
ÖSTRA FINSKA VIKENS
NATIONALPARK
Vantaa/
Vanda
Kallbäck
Kipilahti
Tirmo
Rostock
Spjutsund
Sondby
Östersundom
Pellinge/
Pellinki
Gogland
221
HELSINKI/
HELSINGFORS
Suomenlahti
Suur Tütarsaar
Väike Tütarsaar
Sankt-Peterburg
Maarianhamina
Stockholm
Travemünde
Rønne
Rostock
Tallinn
LAHEMAA NAC. PARK
Yuminda
Viinistu
EST
Käsmu
Vergi
Vainupea
Prangli
Leesi
Loksa
Kunda

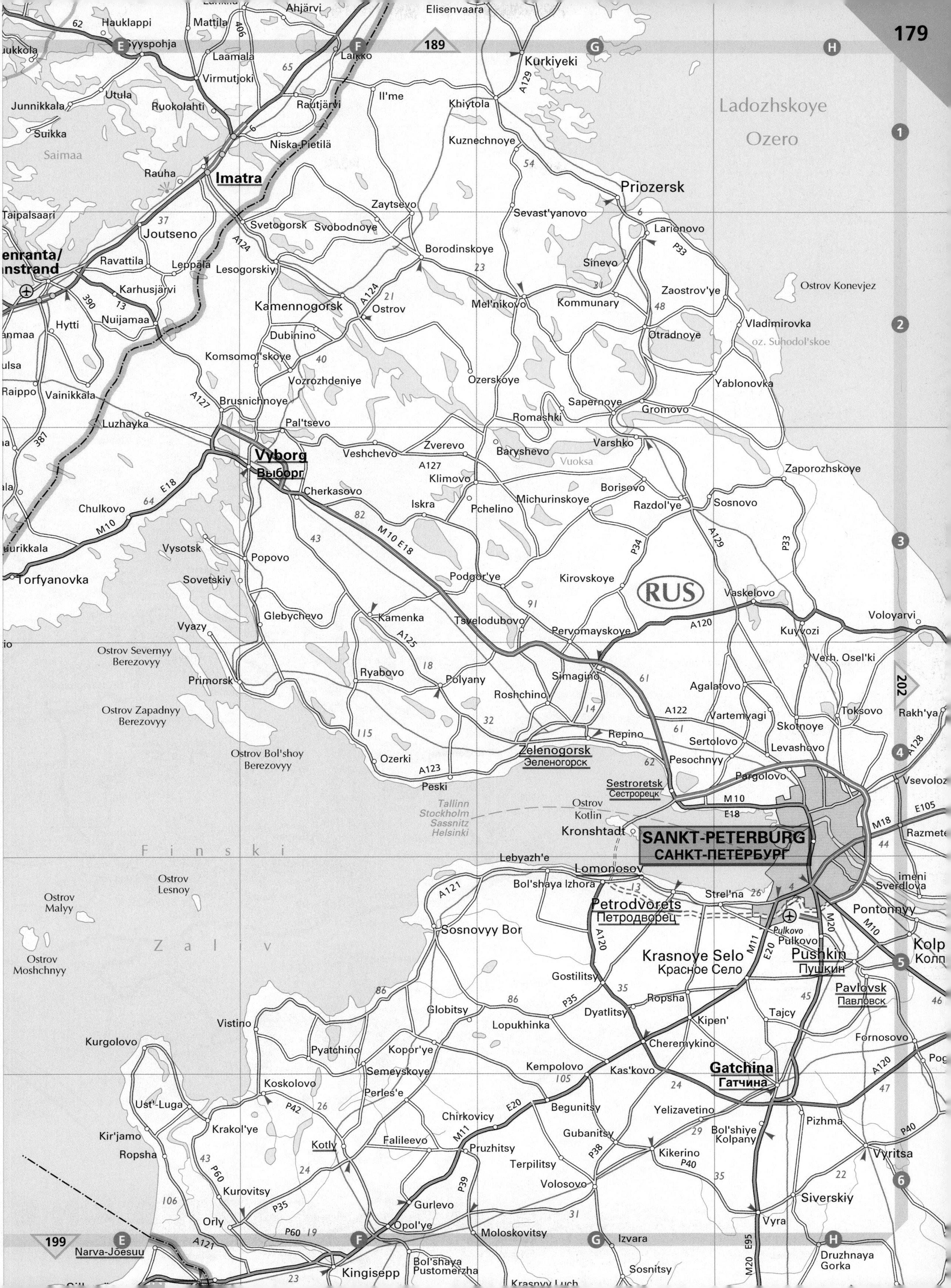
189
199
202
E
F
G
H
1
2
3
4
5
6
Ahjärvi
Elisenvaara
Hauklappi
Mattila
Syyspohja
Laamala
Lalkko
Kurkiyeki
Virmutjoki
Utula
Junnikkala
Ruokolahti
Rautjärvi
Il'me
Khiytola
Suikka
Saimaa
Niska-Pietilä
Kuznechnoye
Ladozhskoye
Ozero
Rauha
Imatra
Priozersk
Taipalsaari
Zaytsevo
Sevast'yanovo
Joutseno
Svetogorsk
Svobodnoye
Larionovo
Ravattila
Leppälä
Lesogorskiy
Borodinskoye
Sinevo
Karhusjärvi
Zaostrov'ye
Ostrov Konevjez
Kamennogorsk
Ostrov
Mel'nikovo
Kommunary
Hytti
Nuijamaa
Vladimirovka
Dubinino
Otradnoye
oz. Suhodol'skoe
Komsomol'skoye
Vozrozhdeniye
Ozerskoye
Yablonovka
Raippo
Vainikkala
Brusnichnoye
Sapernoye
Gromovo
Luzhayka
Pal'tsevo
Romashki
Vyborg
Выборг
Veshchevo
Zverevo
Baryshevo
Varshko
Vuoksa
Zaporozhskoye
Klimovo
Cherkasovo
Borisovo
Chulkovo
Iskra
Pchelino
Michurinskoye
Razdol'ye
Sosnovo
Vysotsk
Popovo
Torfyanovka
Podgor'ye
Kirovskoye
RUS
Sovetskiy
Vaskelovo
Glebychevo
Kamenka
Tsvelodubovo
Voloyarvi
Vyazy
Pervomayskoye
Kuyvozi
Ostrov Severnyy Berezovyy
Verh. Osel'ki
Primorsk
Ryabovo
Polyany
Simagino
Roshchino
Agalatovo
Ostrov Zapadnyy Berezovyy
Vartemyagi
Toksovo
Rakh'ya
Skotnoye
Repino
Sertolovo
Zelenogorsk
Зеленогорск
Levashovo
Ostrov Bol'shoy Berezovyy
Ozerki
Pesochnyy
Pargolovo
Peski
Sestroretsk
Сестрорецк
Vsevoloz
Tallinn
Stockholm
Sassnitz
Helsinki
Ostrov Kotlin
Kronshtadt
SANKT-PETERBURG
САНКТ-ПЕТЕРБУРГ
Razmete
Finski
Lebyazh'e
Lomonosov
Ostrov Lesnoy
imeni Sverdlova
Ostrov Malyy
Bol'shaya Izhora
Strel'na
Petrodvorets
Петродворец
Pontonnyy
Pulkovo
Sosnovyy Bor
Kolp
Колп
Zaliv
Ostrov Moshchnyy
Krasnoye Selo
Красное Село
Pushkin
Пушкин
Gostilitsy
Pavlovsk
Павловск
Ropsha
Globitsy
Dyatlitsy
Tajcy
Vistino
Lopukhinka
Kipen'
Kurgolovo
Cheremykino
Fornosovo
Pyatchino
Kopor'ye
Kempolovo
Gatchina
Гатчина
Semeyskoye
Kas'kovo
Koskolovo
Perles'e
Ust'-Luga
Begunitsy
Yelizavetino
Chirkovicy
Pizhma
Krakol'ye
Kir'jamo
Bol'shiye Kolpany
Gubanitsy
Falileevo
Ropsha
Kotly
Pruzhitsy
Kikerino
Vyritsa
Terpilitsy
Kurovitsy
Volosovo
Siverskiy
Gurlevo
Orly
Opol'ye
Vyra
Moloskovitsy
Narva-Joesuu
Izvara
Druzhnaya Gorka
Kingisepp
Bol'shaya Pustomerzha
Sosnitsy
Krasnyy Luch
E18
E20
E95
E105
M10
M11
M18
M20
A120
A121
A122
A123
A124
A125
A127
A128
A129
P33
P34
P35
P38
P39
P40
P42
P60

A
B
C
D
1
2
3
4
5
6
NORDØYANE
Haroy
Løvik
Småge
Gossen
Myklebust
Sundsbø
Nogva
Austnes
Otrøy
Midsund
Kjerstad
Roald
Skjelten
Hildre
Ørsnes
Fiksdal
Brattvåg
Vatne
Tomrefjord
Søvik
Valderöy
Ålesund
Skodje
Langevåg
Spjelkavik
Digernes
Sjøholt
Runde
Brandal
Magerholm
Ørskog
Kvalsvik
Hareid
Sulesund
Solevåg
Ikornnes
Aursnes
Nerlandsøy
SØRØYANE
Ulsteinvik
Fosnavåg
Hareidlandet
Festøy
Sykkylven
Fausa
Storfjorden
Gurskøy
Vartdal
Årsnes
Eiksund
Rjånes
Hjørundfjorden
Drottninghaug
Velle
Stranda
Honningsvåg
Ervik
Larsnes
Årvik
1463
KOLÅSTIND
Storestandal
Overåneset
Borgund
Åram
Ørsta
Sæbø
Leknes
Fursest
STADLANDET
Koparnes
Lauvstad
BÅTMUSEUM
Volda
Vatne
Øye
Herdal
Leikanger
Fiska
Vik
Folkestad
Viddal
Selje
KLOSTERRUINER
Syvde
Dale
Bjørke
SØSTREFOSS
Raudeberg
Åheim
Austefjord
Hellesylt
Vågsøy
Steinsvik
Botnen
Geirangerfjorden
Sunnylvsfjorden
Måløy
Bjørkedal
Kalvatn
Trygge-stad
Lyngvoll
HELLERISTNINGER
Bryggia
Maurstad
Kjølsdal
Oldeide
Stårheim
Navelsaker
Grodås
SVORMUSEET
Davik
Nordfjord
Hjelle
Bremangerlandt
NORDFJORD
Bortnen
Isane
Nordfjordeid
Nor
Hornindalsvatn
Hornindal
Leirgulen
Frøysjøen
Lote
Skrede
Lunde
Frøya
Smørhamn
Kalvåg
Ålfoten
Hestenesøyri
Stryn
Loen
Anda
Innvik
1670
GJEGNALUNDSBREEN
GRAVHAUG
Howden
Midtgulen
Svelgen
Sandane
Olden
Damba
Myklebust
Staume
Utvik
Grøndal
Gimmestad
1717
CECILIEKRUNA
Årebrot
Hyen
Haukå
Skorpa
Hjorteset
Brein
Byrkjelo
Gorv
Giengedal
NONSFOSSEN
Reksta
Florø
Eidiet
1572
JOSTEDALSBREEN
Eikefjørd
Nes
Askrova
Storebru
SOGN OG
Birksdal
Stavang
Gjerde
Vevring
Hove
Aksla
Skei
Klakegg
JOSTEDALSBREEN
NASJONALPARK
Svanøy
Førdefjorden
Naustdal
Ålhus
Årdal
Stavfjorden
Erdal
Stongfjorden
Berg
Lunde
Selvik
Heilevong
Førde
Moskog
Sunde
SUNNFJORD
1636
GROVEBREEN
Vassenden
Askvoll
Atløya
Eikenes
Laukeland
Holsen
FJORDANE
Nes
Storehaug
Dale
Haukedal
Bøyum
Værlandet
Fure
Tysse
170
Bygstad
Gaularfjell Pass
Fjærland
Flekke
Hestad
Eldalsosen
Hellevik
Sande
Gaupne
E39

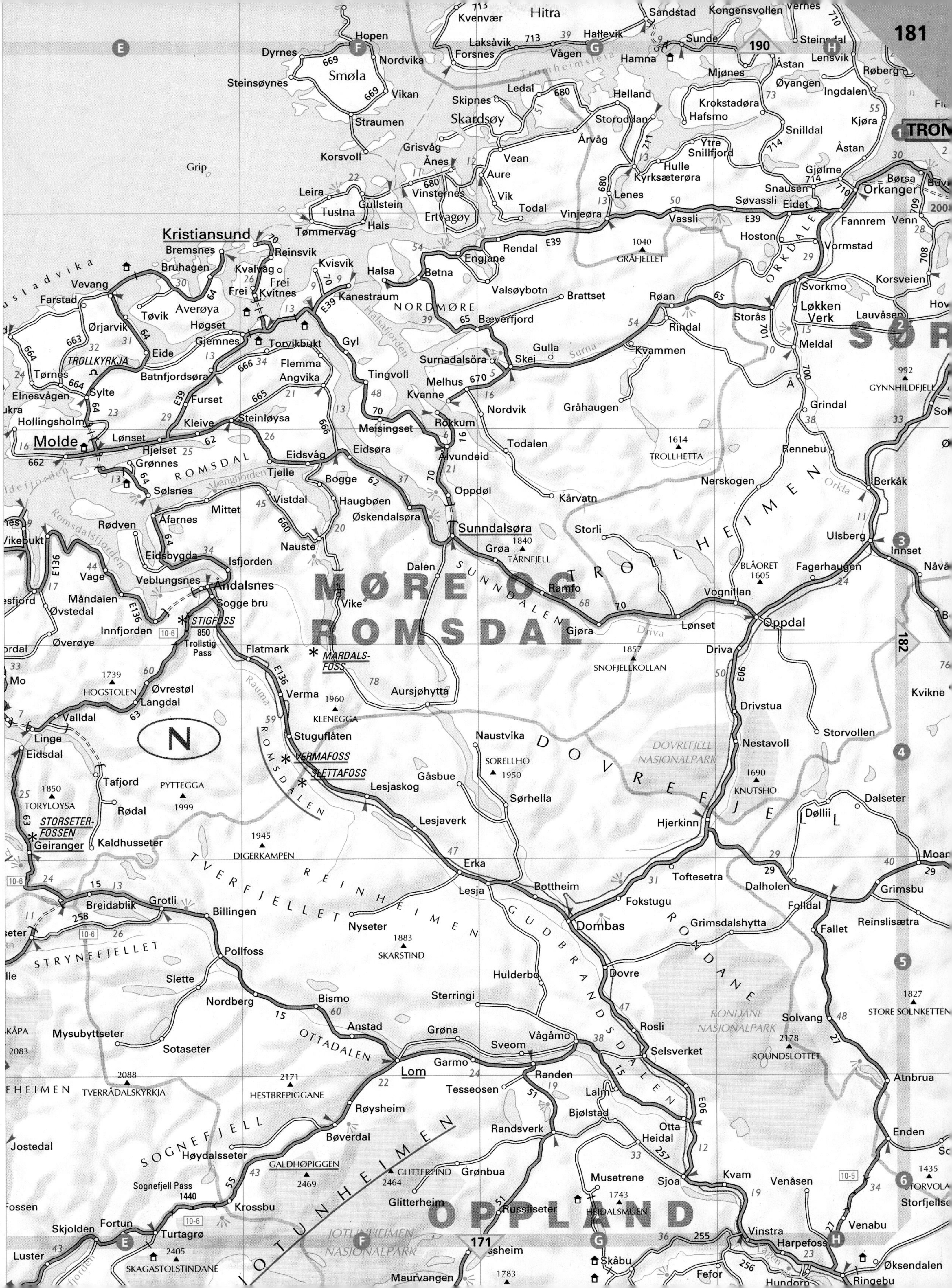
MØRE OG
ROMSDAL
OPPLAND
Hitra
Smøla
Averøya
Tustna
Ertvågøy
Skardsøy
NORDMØRE
ROMSDAL
TROLLHEIMEN
SUNNDALEN
DOVREFJELL
DOVREFJELL NASJONALPARK
RONDANE
RONDANE NASJONALPARK
GUDBRANDSDALEN
REINHEIMEN
TVERFJELLET
ROMSDALEN
OTTADALEN
STRYNEFJELLET
SOGNEFJELL
JOTUNHEIMEN
JOTUNHEIMEN NASJONALPARK
ORKDALEN
Trondheimsleia
Halsafjorden
Romsdalsfjorden
Langfjorden
Driva
Rauma
Orkla
Surna
Kristiansund
Molde
Åndalsnes
Sunndalsøra
Oppdal
Orkanger
Dombas
Lom
Otta
Kvenvær
Sandstad
Kongensvollen
Hopen
Dyrnes
Nordvika
Laksåvik
Hallevik
Forsnes
Vågen
Hamna
Sunde
Steinsdal
Lensvik
Røberg
Åstan
Mjønes
Øyangen
Ingdalen
Steinsøynes
Vikan
Ledal
Helland
Skipnes
Krokstadøra
Hafsmo
Storoddan
Kjøra
Straumen
Snilldal
Grisvåg
Årvåg
Ytre Snillfjord
Åstan
Korsvoll
Ånes
Vean
Hulle
Kyrksæterøra
Grip
Aure
Gjølme
Børsa
Leira
Vinsternes
Vik
Lenes
Snausen
Gullstein
Todal
Vinjeøra
Søvassli
Eidet
Hals
Vassli
Fannrem
Venn
Tømmervåg
Hoston
Vormstad
Bremsnes
Reinsvik
Rendal
Engjane
GRÅFJELLET
Bruhagen
Kvalvåg
Kvisvik
Halsa
Betna
Korsveien
Vevang
Frei
Kvitnes
Valsøybotn
Brattset
Svorkmo
Farstad
Kanestraum
Røan
Løkken Verk
Lauvåsen
Tøvik
Høgset
Bæverfjord
Storås
Rindal
Gjemnes
Torvikbukt
Gyl
Meldal
Eide
Ørjarvik
TROLLKYRKJA
Gulla
Kvammen
Batnfjordsøra
Flemma
Angvika
Tingvoll
Surnadalsöra
Skei
Tørnes
Sylte
Melhus
Kvanne
Nordvik
Elnesvågen
Furset
Grindal
Hollingsholm
Steinløysa
Kleive
Meisingset
Røkkum
Gråhaugen
GYNNHILDFJELL
Lønset
Hjelset
Alvundeid
Todalen
TROLLHETTA
Rennebu
Grønnes
Eidsvåg
Eidsøra
Tjelle
Bogge
Oppdøl
Nerskogen
Berkåk
Sølsnes
Vistdal
Haugbøen
Kårvatn
Mittet
Øskendalsøra
Åfarnes
Rødven
Storli
Ulsberg
Nauste
Grøa
TÅRNFJELL
Innset
Vikebukt
Eidsbygda
Isfjorden
Dalen
Vage
Veblungsnes
Fagerhaugen
BLÅORET
Måndalen
Sogge bru
Ramfo
Vike
Vognillan
Øvstedal
STIGFOSS
Trollstig Pass
Lønset
Innfjorden
Gjøra
Øverøye
Flatmark
MARDALS-FOSS
SNOFJELLKOLLAN
Driva
Mo
HOGSTOLEN
Øvrestøl
Langdal
Verma
KLENEGGA
Aursjøhytta
Kvikne
Valldal
Drivstua
Stuguflåten
Naustvika
Linge
Storvollen
Eidsdal
VERMAFOSS
SORELLHO
Nestavoll
SLETTAFOSS
Tafjord
Gåsbue
KNUTSHO
PYTTEGGA
Lesjaskog
Sørhella
Dalseter
TORYLOYSA
Rødal
Døllii
STORSETER-FOSSEN
Lesjaverk
Hjerkinn
Geiranger
Kaldhusseter
DIGERKAMPEN
Moan
Erka
Toftesetra
Dalholen
Grimsbu
Breidablik
Grotli
Lesja
Bottheim
Folldal
Fokstugu
Billingen
Nyseter
Fallet
Reinslisætra
Grimsdalshytta
SKARSTIND
Pollfoss
Dovre
Hulderbo
Slette
STORE SOLNKETTEN
Nordberg
Bismo
Sterringi
Anstad
Rosli
Solvang
Mysubyttseter
Grøna
Vågåmo
Sveom
Sotaseter
ROUNDSLOTTET
Selsverket
Garmo
Randen
Atnbrua
TVERRÅDALSKYRKJA
HESTBREPIGGANE
Tesseosen
Lalm
Røysheim
Bjølstad
Jostedal
Randsverk
Heidal
Enden
Bøverdal
Høydalsseter
GALDHØPIGGEN
GLITTERTIND
Grønbua
Musetrene
Kvam
Venåsen
Sognefjell Pass
Sjoa
Storfjellse
Krossbu
Glitterheim
HEIDALSMUEN
Russliseter
Venabu
Fossen
Vinstra
Harpefoss
Skjolden
Fortun
Turtagrø
Luster
SKAGASTOLSTINDANE
Skåbu
Øksendalen
Maurvangen
Fefor
Hundorp
Ringebu

SØR-TRØNDELAG
TRONDHEIM
Kongensvollen
Rissa
Seter
Frosta
Hammer
Markabygd
Sul
Sunde
Steinsdal
Vanvikan
Åsen
Trættlia
190
Mjønes
Åstan
Lensvik
Røberg
Rørvik
Haugan
Skatval
Okkelberg
Sulåmo
1249
KJOLHAUGEN
Feren
Helland
Krokstadøra
Hafsmo
Øyangen
Ingdalen
Trolla
Flakk
Stjørdal
Leirfall
STJØRDALEN
Nyvollen
Storoddan
Kjøra
Snilldal
Malvik
Hell
Hegra
Flornes
Vaernes
E14
Ytre
Snillfjord
Hulle
Kyrksæterøra
Åstan
Gjølme
Snausen
Børsa
Buvika
Orkanger
Brå
Heimdal
Hommelvik
Ytterås
Kirkeby
Meråker
Kopperå
Elvran
Bakken
Espås
Øvre Jervan
Øyan
Lenes
Søvassli
Eidet
Vassli
2008
Melhus
Klæbu
Selbusjøen
Tømra
Storlien
Fannrem
Venn
Hoston
1040
GRÅFJELLET
Vormstad
ORKDALEN
Kvål
Brøttem
Okstad
Fuglem
Rotvoll
Storvallen
Ler
Selbu
Korsveien
Svorkmo
Røan
Rindal
Storås
Løkken Verk
Lauvåsen
Hovin
Lundamo
REINSFJELL
941
Kråklivollen
Vikvarvet
Öras
1441
FONGEN
Kvammen
Meldal
Støren
Rognes
Hilmo
Essandsjøen
Aunet
Ås
Kirkvollen
992
GYNNHILDFJELL
Trøyen
Almås
1766
SYLARNA
Grindal
Soknedal
GAULDALEN
Singsås
Nesjøen
augen
1614
TROLLHETTA
Rennebu
Økdal
Budal
Haltdalen
Stuguvollmoen
1321
BLÅSTOTEN
Storsjøn
Nerskogen
Orkla
Berkåk
Ålen
Renbygda
Stugudal
TROLLHEIMEN
Enmo
N
Vårhus
Jensåsvoll
Unsholtet
Reitan
Ulsberg
Innset
Kjerrengvoll
Meiåvollen
Storelvavoll
BLÅORET
1605
Fagerhaugen
Nåvårdalen
Rugldalen
1332
FORELSHOGNA
Myrmoen
Vognillan
Glåmos
Lønset
Oppdal
Børlia
Aursunden
Brekken
Vauldalen
Driva
181
Såtåhaugvoll
Hitterdal
Steinsåsen
SNOFJELLKOLLAN
Røros
Feragen
Fjällnäs
Kvikne
Smedås
Os
Drivstua
Yset
Storvollen
DOVREFJELL
NASJONALPARK
Nestavoll
Vingelen
Tolga
Narjordet
Nytrøa
1543
GRAHOGDA
Hodalen
Søndervika
1690
KNUTSHO
Dalseter
Døllii
DOVREFJELL
Narbuvollen
MONTRØEN
Hjerkinn
Fåset
Hodal
FEMUNDSMARKA
NASJONALPARK
Glomma
Tynset
Kvitten
Hodøl
Seter
Toftesetra
Dalholen
Moan
Brydal
Jonasvollen
Fokstugu
Grimsbu
Folldal
Tylldal
Holøydal
Spekedalssetra
Grimsdalshytta
Fallet
Reinslisætra
Gjelten
Alvdal
1604
ELGEPIGGEN
Brenna
Elgå
Finnstad
Femunden
Dovre
RONDANE
Storlægda
Sømådal
Røstvollen
Grövelsjön
1827
STORE SOLNKETTEN
Brua
Barkald
Sørvollen
Valdalen
RONDANE
NASJONALPARK
Solvang
GUTULIA
NASJONALPARK
Rosli
2178
RONDSLOTTET
Unset
Fiskevollen
Selsverket
Granvika
Sømåseter
Atnbrua
Øvre Rendal
Sølnsjøen
RENDALEN
Femundsenden
Galten
Drevsjø
Flötningen
Hanestad
Otta
Heidal
Enden
Rydland
Lillebo
Sollia
Nygarden
Musetre
Sjoa
Kvam
1435
STORVOLA
Otnes
Elvbrua
Engerdal
1743
BIDALSMUEN
Venåsen
Atnosen
Åkre
Storfjellseter
Venabu
Åsheim
Snerta
Vinstra
Harpefoss
172
Bjøråne
Elvdal
Strömsund
Skåbu
Fefor
Øksendalen
Odden
Kvernessetra
1209
TVERRFJELLET
Hundorp
Ringebu

JÄMTLAND
HÄRJEDALEN
Sandvika
Sundet
Sulviken
Olden
Finnsäter
Vallrun
Storholmsjö
Föllinge
Gåxsjö
Storrensjön
Kallsjön
Rönnöfors
Enarsvedjan
Lillholmsjö
Raftsjöhöjden
Silkås
Skalstugan
Saxvallen
Smedjeviken
Vassnäs
Djupsjö
Valla
Landögssjön
Hammerdal
Ede
Medstugan
Häggsjöbränna
Berge
Landön
Munkflohögen
Huså
Nordhallen
Kall
Naxås
Lundsjön
Edefors
912
Bodsjöedet
1420
ÅRESKUTAN
Tulleråsen
TÄNNFORSEN
Sta
Bonäset
Västbacken
Änge
Norderåsen
Duved
Åre
Näldsjön
Bleckåsen
Alsen
Böle
Häggenås
Storhögen
Ånn
Gevsjön
Såbole
Järpen
Nälden
Enafors
Trångsviken
Vaplan
Aspås
Handöl
Trillevallen
Undersåker
Mörsil
Mattmar
Ytterån
Krokom
Lit
Gränningen
1463
ÅSAHÖGARNA
Nordbottnen
Arversund
Dvärsätt
Bye
Fjäl
Ottsjö
Håckren
Nybyn
Mårdsund
Storsjön
Ås
Indalsälven
Ottsjön
Hammarnäs
1554
BUNNERFJÄLLEN
Vålådalen
Fångåmon
1159
VÄSTERFJÄLLET
Hallen
FRÖSÖ
Östersund
Ope
Stugun
Eriksberg
VÅLÅDALENS NATURRESERVAT
NORDERÖ
Höge
Marieby
Bom
ANARISFJÄLLEN
1423
Häggsåsen
Månsåsen
Orrviken
Brunflo
Rissna
1250
STORFJÄLLET
Myrviken
Fåker
Väster-Arådalen
1371
HUNDSHÖGEN
Tandsbyn
Pilgrimstad
Holmsjö
1796
HELAGSFJÄLLET
Hackås
Gällö
Ljungdalen
Kövra
Tunvågen
Revsund
Näkten
Torsborg
Galåbodarna
Vigge
Bodsjö
Stavre
Lundberget
Storsjö
Hoverberg
Nor
Storsjön
Ljungan
Flåsjön
Börtnan
Svenstavik
Skucku
Hunge
1056
Bingsta
Mittådalen
RUVALLEN
Rörön
Bräcke
Bruksvallarna
Messlingen
Källberget
Tossåsen
Flon
Skålan
Särvsjön
1169
SÄRVFJÄLLET
Löningsberg
Åsen
1347
Åsarna
Gillhov
Kåvenvallen
ANÅFJÄLLET
Ocksjön
Funäsdalen
Rönnigsåsen
Lännässjön
Digerberget
Nästeln
Näsvallen
Ovansjö
Lossnen
Klövsjö
Handsjö
Byberget
Ljusnan
Alby
Långå
Fjällgården
Tännäs
Norr Hede
Vemdalen
Röjan
Rätan
Överturingen
Hedeviken
Holmsjön
Kolbenshån
Björnrike
1009
Ytterturingen
Kölsillre
Östavall
Risåsvallen
Nederhögen
Viken
SÅNFJÄLLETS NATIONALPARK
Havern
Sörtjärn
Malsjöbodarna
Orten
Brändåsen
Rannsundet
1277
SÅNFJÄLLET
Vemhån
Torrflonäs
Mellansjö
Högvålen
Överhogdal
TÖFSINGDALENS NATIONALPARK
Rånddalen
Minne
Sörvattnet
Slagavallen
Randsjö
Linsell
Ramsjö
1204
STORSÄTERN
Knätten
Klutsjön
Strådalen
Lofsdalen
Linkvarnen
Glissjöberg
Ytterhogdal
Glöte
Remmet
Flor
Storsätern
Lofssjön
Mosätt
Sänna
1196
Överberg
Andåsen
Sundsjö
Foskros
NIPFJÄLLETS NATIONALPARK
Härjån
Svegssjön
Älvros
Sveg
Ytterberg
Kolsätter
Finneby
1102
Strömmen
Vänsjö
Brånden
Bodarsjön
Ångersjö
Kårböle
1131
STÄDJAN
Härjåsjön
Laforsen
Grötholen
Foskvallen
Idre
Öjvasslan
Lillhärdal
Olingdal
Drosbacken
Älvros
Snössvallen
Lövnäsvallen
Sunnanå
Fågelsjö
Korsk
Östansjö
Heden
Olingsjövallen
Rullbo
Haftorsbygget
HAMRA NATIONALPARK
Los
Lillsilltret
NJUPESKÄRS VATTENFALL
Östomsjön
Sidertjärn
Lillhaga
Mörkret
Särna
Tandsjöborg
Karlsberg
FULUFJÄLLET
191
173
184
E14
S

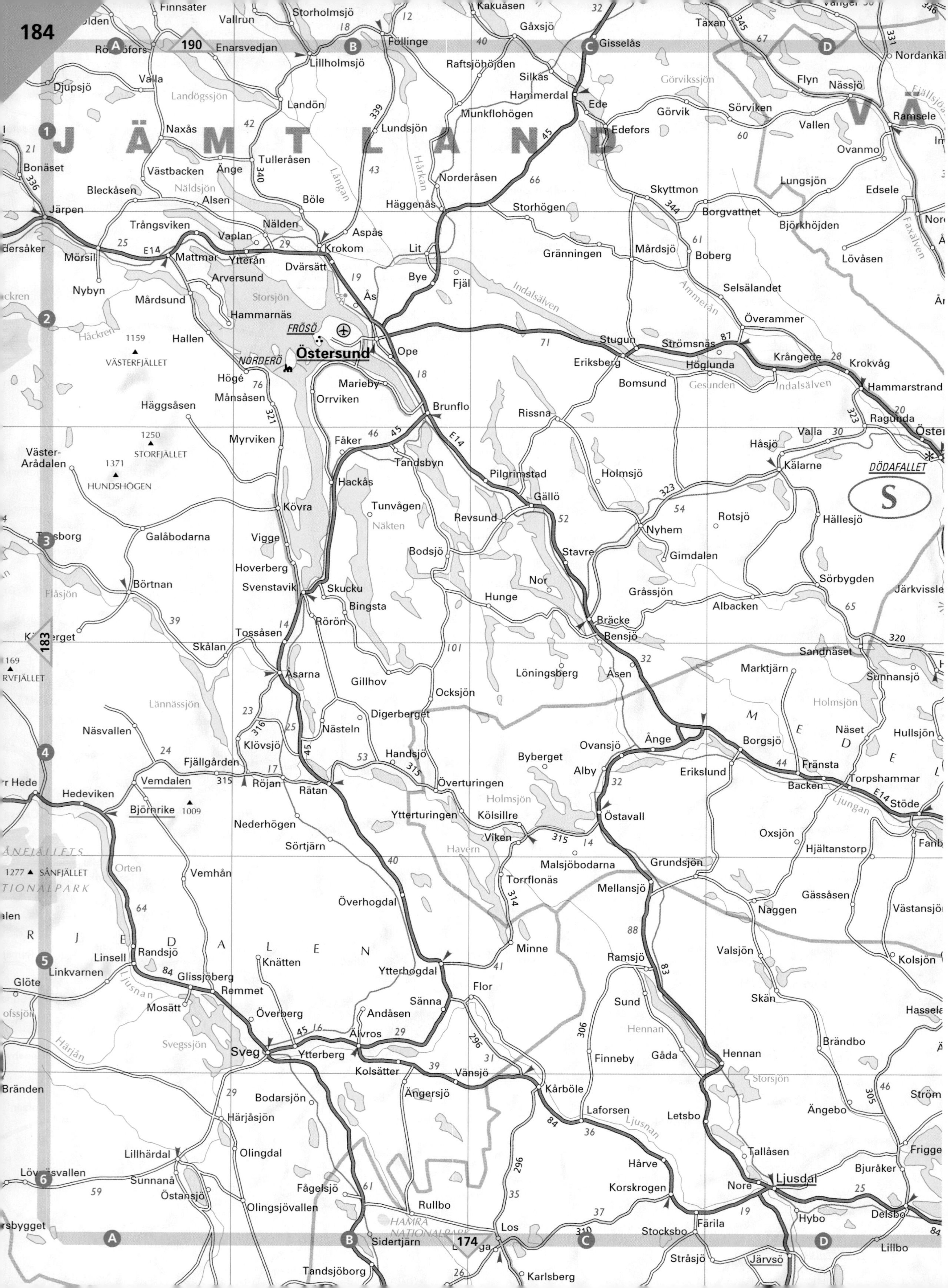
JÄMTLAND
190
183
174
Finnsater
Vallrun
Storholmsjö
Kakuåsen
Gåxsjö
Täxan
Röjdåfors
Enarsvedjan
Föllinge
Gisselås
Lillholmsjö
Raftsjöhöjden
Silkås
Hammerdal
Nordankäl
Flyn
Nässjö
Djupsjö
Valla
Landögssjön
Landön
Görviksjön
Ede
Edefors
Görvik
Sörviken
Ramsele
Vallen
Munkflohögen
Lundsjön
Naxås
Ovanmo
Bonäset
Tulleråsen
Västbacken
Änge
Långan
Härkan
Norderåsen
Lungsjön
Edsele
Bleckåsen
Näldsjön
Alsen
Böle
Häggenås
Skyttmon
Storhögen
Borgvattnet
Björkhöjden
Järpen
Trångsviken
Nälden
Aspås
Vaplan
Krokom
Lit
Gränningen
Mårdsjö
Boberg
Lövåsen
Faxälven
Mörsil
Mattmar
Ytterån
Dvärsätt
Arversund
Bye
Fjäl
Nybyn
Mårdsund
Storsjön
Ås
Indalsälven
Ammerån
Selsälandet
Hammarnäs
Överammer
Håckren
1159
VÄSTERFJÄLLET
Hallen
FRÖSÖ
Östersund
NORDERÖ
Ope
Stugun
Strömsnäs
Eriksberg
Höglunda
Gesunden
Krångede
Krokvåg
Hammarstrand
Högé
Månsåsen
Marieby
Orrviken
Bomsund
Häggsåsen
Brunflo
Rissna
Ragunda
Valla
Håsjö
Kälarne
DÖDAFALLET
1250
STORFJÄLLET
Myrviken
Fåker
Tandsbyn
Väster-Arådalen
1371
HUNDSHÖGEN
Hackås
Pilgrimstad
Holmsjö
Gällö
Kövra
Tunvågen
Näkten
Revsund
Rotsjö
Hällesjö
Nyhem
Galåbodarna
Vigge
Bodsjö
Stavre
Gimdalen
Hoverberg
Nor
Sörbygden
Järkvissle
Börtnan
Svenstavik
Skucku
Hunge
Gråssjön
Albacken
Flåsjön
Bingsta
Bräcke
Bensjö
Rörön
Tossåsen
Skålan
Sandnäset
RVFJÄLLET
Åsarna
Gillhov
Löningsberg
Åsen
Marktjärn
Sunnansjö
Holmsjön
Ocksjön
Lännässjön
Digerberget
Näsvallen
Nästeln
Ånge
Ovansjö
Borgsjö
Näset
Hullsjön
Klövsjö
Handsjö
Byberget
Alby
Fjällgården
Erikslund
Fränsta
Torpshammar
Hede
Vemdalen
Röjan
Rätan
Överturingen
Backen
Stöde
Hedeviken
Björnrike
1009
Holmsjön
Ljungan
Nederhögen
Ytterturingen
Kölsillre
Östavall
Viken
Oxsjön
Fanb
Sörtjärn
Havern
Hjältanstorp
Malsjöbodarna
Grundsjön
ÅNEFJÄLLETS NATIONALPARK
Orten
1277 SÅNFJÄLLET
Vemhån
Torrflonäs
Mellansjö
Gässåsen
Överhogdal
Naggen
Västansjö
HÄRJEDALEN
Minne
Randsjö
Linsell
Knätten
Ramsjö
Valsjön
Kolsjön
Linkvarnen
Ytterhogdal
Glissjöberg
Glöte
Remmet
Flor
Ljusnan
Sund
Skån
Mosätt
Sänna
Andåsen
Hasselå
Överberg
Hennan
Älvros
Brändbo
Svegssjön
Härjån
Sveg
Ytterberg
Finneby
Gåda
Hennan
Kolsätter
Vänsjö
Storsjön
Bränden
Ängersjö
Kårböle
Ängebo
Ström
Bodarsjön
Laforsen
Letsbo
Härjåsjön
Lillhärdal
Olingdal
Tallåsen
Frigge
Lövåsvallen
Sunnanå
Hårve
Bjuråker
Östansjö
Fågelsjö
Korskrogen
Nore
Ljusdal
Olingsjövallen
Rullbo
Färila
Hybo
Delsbo
HAMRA NATIONALPARK
Los
Stocksbo
Sidertjärn
Lillbo
Tandsjöborg
Stråsjö
Järvsö
Karlsberg
A
B
C
D
1
2
3
4
5
6
E14
45
84
83
321
323
339
340
336
344
345
315
316
296
305
306
314
320
331

VÄSTERNORRLAND
Å N G E R M A N L A N D
M E D E L P A D
H Ö G A K U S T E N
B o t t n i s k a v i k e n /
P o h j a n l a h t i
Sundsvallsbukten
SKULESKOGENS NATIONALPARK
NATURRESERVAT
E
F
G
H
1
2
3
4
5
6
191
175
E04
Junsele
Kläppsjö
Åbosjö
Storborgaren
Trehörningsjö
Storfall
Örsbäck
Holmsjö
Gålborget
Hemling
Baggård
Hörnefors
Ängersjö
Långviksmon
Gårelehöjden
Myckelgensjö
Seltjärn
Olofsfors
Nordmaling
Hädanberg
Flärke
Lögdeå
Rundvik
Storsjön
Björna
Nyland
Håleforsen
Grundtjärn
Skalmsiö
Kubbe
Svedje
Ore
Leding
Omsjö
Björnsjö
Ava
Perstorp
Kråkan
Gideå
Hällvattnet
Näsåker
Bredbyn
Mellansel
Gottne
Fors
Saluböle
Aspeå
Gidböle
Långron
Järnäsklubb
Skorped
Norrtannflo
Byvattnet
Mosjö
Täfteå
Degerfjärden
Grundsunda
Moliden
Resele
Billsta
Västerhus
Arnäs
Husum
Selsjön
Ållsjön
Sidensjö
Överhörnäs
Örnsköldsvik
Banafjäl
Mo
Forsmo
Björksjön
Västersel
Ed
Sånga
Nätra
Fjällskog
Bjästa
Långsele
Gålsjö bruk
Köpmanholmen
Österforse
Sollefteå
Multrå
Ångermanälven
Överlännäs
Helgum
Boteå
Magdbäcken
Styrnäs
Graninge
Hällsjö
Dockstа
Sandslån
Ullånger
Västansjö
Nyland
Salsåker
Mjällom
Bispgården
Bollstabruk
Bjärtrå
Östergraninge
Lungvik
Kramfors
Herrskog
Nordingrå
Lunde
Klockestrand
Boda
Bonhamn
SANDÖ BRO
Laxsjön
Ramvik
HÖGAKUSTENBRON
Viksjö
Högsjö
Sillre
Utansjö
Nordanå
Klärke
Liland
Hemsö
Liden
Ålandsbro
Backen
Bredsjön
Holm
Indalsälven
Härnösand
Östloning
Ljustorp
Stigsjö
Indal
Åsäng
Antjärn
Stavreviken
Bye
Härnön
Nyland
Midlanda
Bergeforsen
Söråker
Barsviken
Gåltjärn
Kovland
Timrå
Tynderö
Huljen
Nedansjö
Sundsvall
Åstön
Alnön
Vattjom
Svartvik
Matfors
Tunbyn
Attmar
Kvissleby
Lucksta
Njurundabommen
Njurunda
Junibodsand
Svedje
Nyrå
Brämön
Västan
Galtström
Malungen
Grängsjö
Gnarp
Alvsund
Sörfjärden
Älgered
Jättendal
Bergsjö
Harmånger
Fönebo
Vattlång
Stocka
Ilsbo
Norra Dellen
Strömsbruk
Hälsjö
Edsta
Välsta
Södra Dellen
Näsviken
Sånna
Hudiksvall
Sörforsa
Arnön

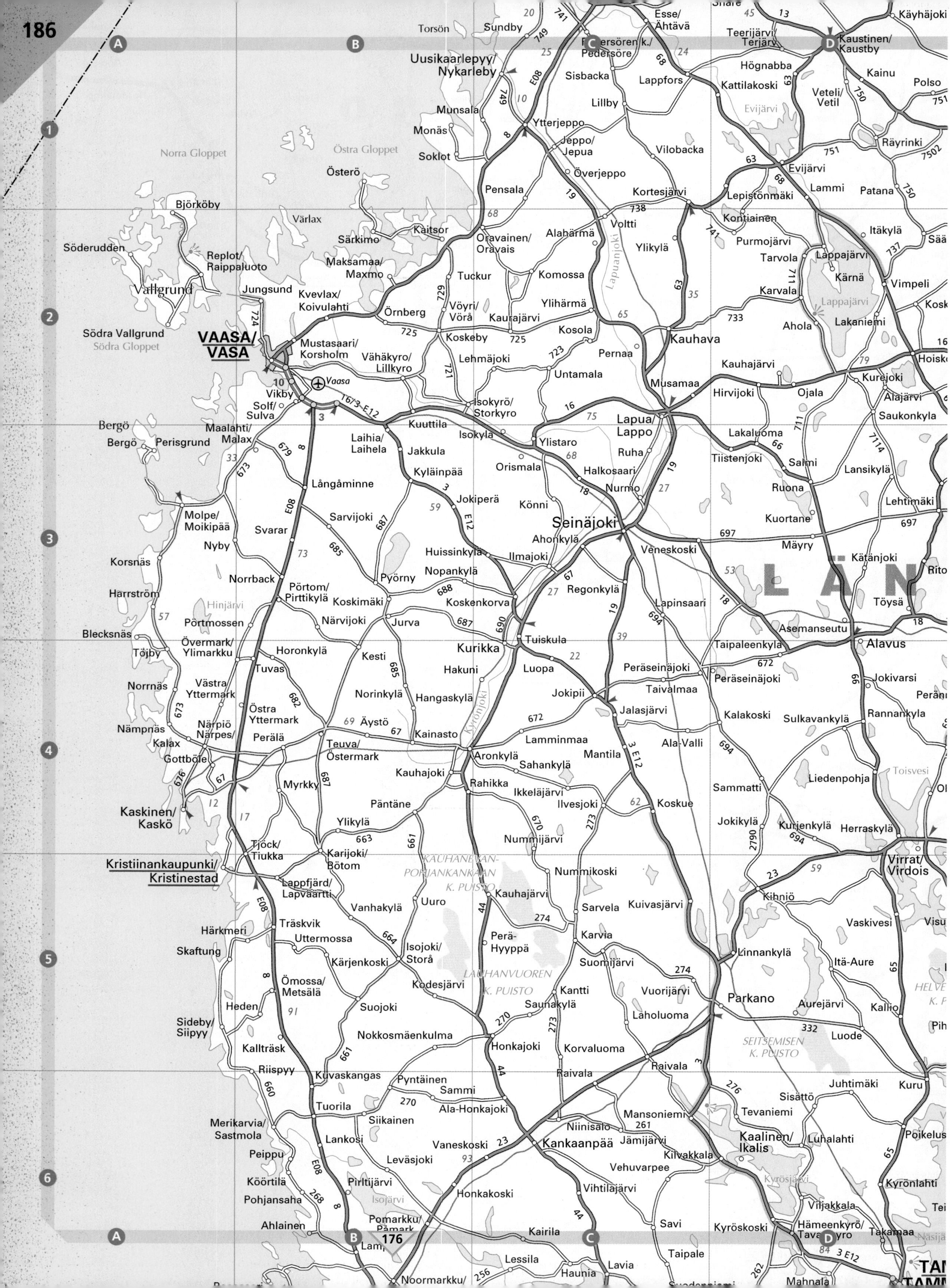
Torsön
Sundby
Esse/
Ähtävä
Teerijärvi/
Terjärv
Kaustinen/
Kaustby
Käyhäjoki
Pedersören k./
Pedersöre
Uusikaarlepyy/
Nykarleby
Sisbacka
Lappfors
Högnabba
Kattilakoski
Kainu
Polso
Veteli/
Vetil
Lillby
Evijärvi
Munsala
Ytterjeppo
Monäs
Jeppo/
Jepua
Vilobacka
Räyrinki
Norra Gloppet
Östra Gloppet
Soklot
Överjeppo
Evijärvi
Lammi
Patana
Österö
Pensala
Kortesjärvi
Lepistönmäki
Björköby
Värlax
Voltti
Kontiainen
Itäkylä
Söderudden
Kaitsor
Särkimo
Oravainen/
Oravais
Alahärmä
Ylikylä
Purmojärvi
Replot/
Raippaluoto
Tarvola
Lappajärvi
Maksamaa/
Maxmo
Tuckur
Komossa
Lapuanjoki
Kärnä
Vallgrund
Jungsund
Kvevlax/
Koivulahti
Karvala
Vimpeli
Örnberg
Vöyri/
Vörå
Ylihärmä
Lappajärvi
Kaurajärvi
Ahola
Lakaniemi
Södra Vallgrund
Södra Gloppet
VAASA/
VASA
Mustasaari/
Korsholm
Koskeby
Kosola
Kauhava
Vähäkyro/
Lillkyro
Lehmäjoki
Pernaa
Kauhajärvi
Hoisko
Untamala
Vaasa
Musamaa
Hirvijoki
Ojala
Kurejoki
Vikby
Isokyrö/
Storkyro
Alajärvi
Solf/
Sulva
Lapua/
Lappo
Saukonkylä
Kuuttila
Isokyla
Bergö
Maalahti/
Malax
Laihia/
Laihela
Jakkula
Ylistaro
Ruha
Lakaluoma
Perisgrund
Tiistenjoki
Kyläinpää
Orismala
Halkosaari
Salmi
Lansikylä
Långåminne
Nurmo
Ruona
Jokiperä
Könni
Lehtimäki
Molpe/
Moikipää
Sarvijoki
Seinäjoki
Kuortane
Svarar
Ahonkylä
Nyby
Veneskoski
Mäyry
Huissinkylä
Ilmajoki
Kätänjoki
Korsnäs
Nopankylä
Pyörny
Norrback
Pörtom/
Pirttikylä
Regonkylä
Harrström
Koskimäki
Koskenkorva
Hinjärvi
Lapinsaari
Töysä
Pörtmossen
Närvijoki
Jurva
Asemanseutu
Blecksnäs
Övermark/
Ylimarkku
Tuiskula
Alavus
Töjby
Horonkylä
Kurikka
Taipaleenkylä
Kesti
Tuvas
Hakuni
Luopa
Peräseinäjoki
Norrnäs
Peräseinäjoki
Jokivarsi
Västra
Yttermark
Norinkylä
Hangaskylä
Jokipii
Taivalmaa
Östra
Yttermark
Kyrönjoki
Jalasjärvi
Kalakoski
Sulkavankylä
Rannankylä
Närpiö
Närpes
Äystö
Nämpnäs
Perälä
Kainasto
Lamminmaa
Ala-Valli
Kalax
Teuva/
Östermark
Aronkylä
Mantila
Gottböle
Sahankylä
Kauhajoki
Toisvesi
Myrkky
Rahikka
Liedenpohja
Ikkelajärvi
Sammatti
Ilvesjoki
Koskue
Kaskinen/
Kaskö
Päntäne
Jokikylä
Kurjenkylä
Herraskylä
Ylikylä
Nummijärvi
Tjöck/
Tiukka
Karijoki/
Bötom
Kristiinankaupunki/
Kristinestad
KAUHANEVAN-
POHJANKANKAAN
K. PUISTO
Nummikoski
Virrat/
Virdois
Lappfjärd/
Lapväärtti
Kihniö
Vanhakylä
Uuro
Kauhajärvi
Sarvela
Kuivasjärvi
Härkmeri
Träskvik
Vaskivesi
Uttermossa
Perä-
Hyyppä
Karvia
Skaftung
Isojoki/
Storå
Kärjenkoski
Linnankylä
Suomijärvi
Itä-Aure
Ömossa/
Metsälä
LAUHANVUOREN
K. PUISTO
Kodesjärvi
Kantti
Vuorijärvi
Heden
Suojoki
Saunakylä
Parkano
Aurejärvi
Kallio
Sideby/
Siipyy
Laholuoma
Nokkosmäenkulma
Luode
Honkajoki
SEITSEMISEN
K. PUISTO
Kallträsk
Korvaluoma
Raivala
Riispyy
Kuvaskangas
Raivala
Juhtimäki
Kuru
Pyntäinen
Sammi
Sisättö
Ala-Honkajoki
Tevaniemi
Tuorila
Mansoniemi
Siikainen
Merikarvia/
Sastmola
Niinisalo
Lankosi
Vaneskoski
Kankaanpää
Jämijärvi
Kaalinen/
Ikalis
Luhalahti
Poikelus
Peippu
Kilvakkala
Leväsjoki
Vehuvarpee
Köörtilä
Pirltijärvi
Kyrösjärvi
Vihtilajärvi
Kyrönlahti
Pohjansaha
Isojärvi
Honkakoski
Viljakkala
Ahlainen
Pomarkku/
Påmark
Savi
Kyröskoski
Hämeenkyrö/
Tavastkyro
Takamaa
Kairila
Lessila
Lavia
Taipale
Haunia
Noormarkku/
Mahnala
176
LÄN

196
177
178
188
FIN
SI-SUOMI
JYVÄSKYLÄ
Hanhisalo
Lestijärvi
Kangasvieri
Muurasjärvi
Sulkavanperä
Alvajärvi
Elämäjärvi
Rönnynkylä
Haapamäki
Koivujärvi
Petäjäkylä
Sulkava
Lampaanjärvi
Laukkala
Lapinl
Leppälahti
Yli-Lesti
Kanala
Halsua
Kangaskylä
Ylikylä
Urpila
Pihtipudas
Kärväskylä
Sulkavanjärvi
Korppinen
Saarela
Pielavesi
Heinämäki
Onkivesi
Tossavanlahti
Jylhä
Ahkiola
Kinnula
Linnanperä
Kolima
Salamajärvi
Kivikangas
Muhola
Myllyaho
Löytänä
Pajuskylä
Maaninka
Säviä
Oksakoski
SALAMAJÄRVEN K. PUISTO
Kotvala
Viitajärvi
Pahkamäki
Keitele
Puralankylä
Permo
Risupera
Taimoniemi
Kärnä
Nilakka
Taipale
Kurolanlahti
Leppäselkä
Kivijärvi
Keihärinkoski
Kymönkoski
Hallapuro
Möttönen
Lahdenperä
Kivijärvi
Viitasaari
Jokijärvi
Talluskylä
Poranem
Naposenaho
Tiironkylä
Lokakylä
Huopanankoski
Hamula
Äyskoski
Suovanlahti
Niinivesi
Pirttimäki
Itä-Kartt
Kyyjärvi
Mustikkaperä
Piispala
Jurvansalo
Haarala
Möksy
Kyyjärvi
Ratipera
Vuorilahti
Vesanto
Vesamäki
Tervo
Karttula
Pihkainmä
Kimінki
Oinoskylä
Kannonkoski
Niinilahti
Ahveninen
Syvänn
Kortekylä
Keisala
Alamaa
PYHÄ-HÄKIN K. PUISTO
Keitele
Virmasvesi
Humppi
Maso
Närhilä
Saikari
Virmaanpää
Laasala
Karstula
Salmenniemi
Särkisalo
Soini
Vehkaperä
Vahanka
Kalmari
Häkkilä
Kerkonkoski
Vaajasalmi
Suokonmäki
Kangasaho
Konginkangas
Istunmäki
Haapakylä
Iisvesi
Kukko
Raitaperä
Pääjärvi
Pyyrinlahti
Kivisalmi
Rautalampi
Pyhäjärvi
Taipale
Saarijärvi
Linna
Sumiainem
Konnevesi
Konnevesi
Kolu
Parantala
Hoikhankylä
Ahtärinranta
Vehu
Pylkönmäki
Äänekoski
Katumäki
Mahlu
Honkola
Suolahti
Tankolampi
Lannevesi
Ähtärinjärvi
Väätäiskylä
Kukko
Kärkäälä
Suonte
Äijälä
Nikaranperä
Säkinmäki
Myhinpää
Ähtäri/Etseri
Uurainen
Kangashäkki
Myllymäki
Hokusukoski
Kuusaa
Kynsivessi
Piippaharju
Liperonmäki
Mäkkilkylä
Sahrajärvi
Kyynämöinen
Vehniä
Laukaa
Liesjärvi
Hankasalmi
Paltanen
Höytiä
Tikkaksoki
Paanala
Valkeajärvi
Multia
Ristilä
Naarajärvi
Vertaala
Leppävesi
Killinkoski
Salmenkylä
Pihlajaveden as.
Lihjamo
Kuivasmäki
Palokka
Lievestuore
Niemisjärvi
Neuvola
Kintaus
Vesanka
Vaajakoski
Kylmämäki
Itämen
Haapamäki
Keuruu
Petäjävesi
Kotala
Kairahta
Kankainen
Nykälä
Pöllākkä
Piesalankylä
Isolahti
Oravasaari
Riiho
Pohjoislahti
Häppälä
Säynätsalo
Synsiö
Tikkala
Muurame
Kutemajärvi
Pohjaslahti
Keurusselkä
Toivakka
Haarajoki
Pohosky
Kolho
Mäkikylä
Viisarimäki
Häkkiskylä
Vitalahti
Kouhi
Kangasniemi
Innala
Koskenpää
Vuojalahti
Korpilahti
Tarjannevesi
Rutalahti
Mänttä
Vilppula
Mustalahti
Mustajärvi
Haavisto
Läsänk
Leivonmäki
Hokka
Ahveninen
Kivisuo
Ruovesi
Holiseva
Jämsänkoski
Juokslahti
Korespohja
Puula
Kälä
Vanhamäki
Savenaho
Ruhala
Väärinmaja
Suinula
Jäminkipohja
Jämsä
Tammijärvi
Kitula
Tammilahti
Halli
Alhojärvi
Vaheri
Murole
Tyry
Luhanka
Tuukkala
Joutsa
Eväjärvi
Suontee
Juupajoki
Hassi
Kaanaa
Porvola
Judinsalo
Vuorenkylä
Hirvensalmi
Hirsilä
Länkipohja
Harjunsalmi
Eräslahti
Längelmäki
ISOJÄRVEN K. PUISTO
Närvä
Nokka
Ruorasmäki
Kilkinky
Leppäkoski
Enokunta
Orivesi
Patavesi
Kylämä
Västillä
Särkilahti
Jääsjärvi
Pohtola
Karklampi
Hartola
Pertunmaa
Toivola
Tehi
Isosuo
Eräjärvi
Kuhmoinen
Päijänne
Suinula
Ponsa
Vihasjärvi
Vehkajärvi
Suopelto
Sysmä
Pohjola
Vihantasalmi
Ruutana
Sappee
TAMPERE/

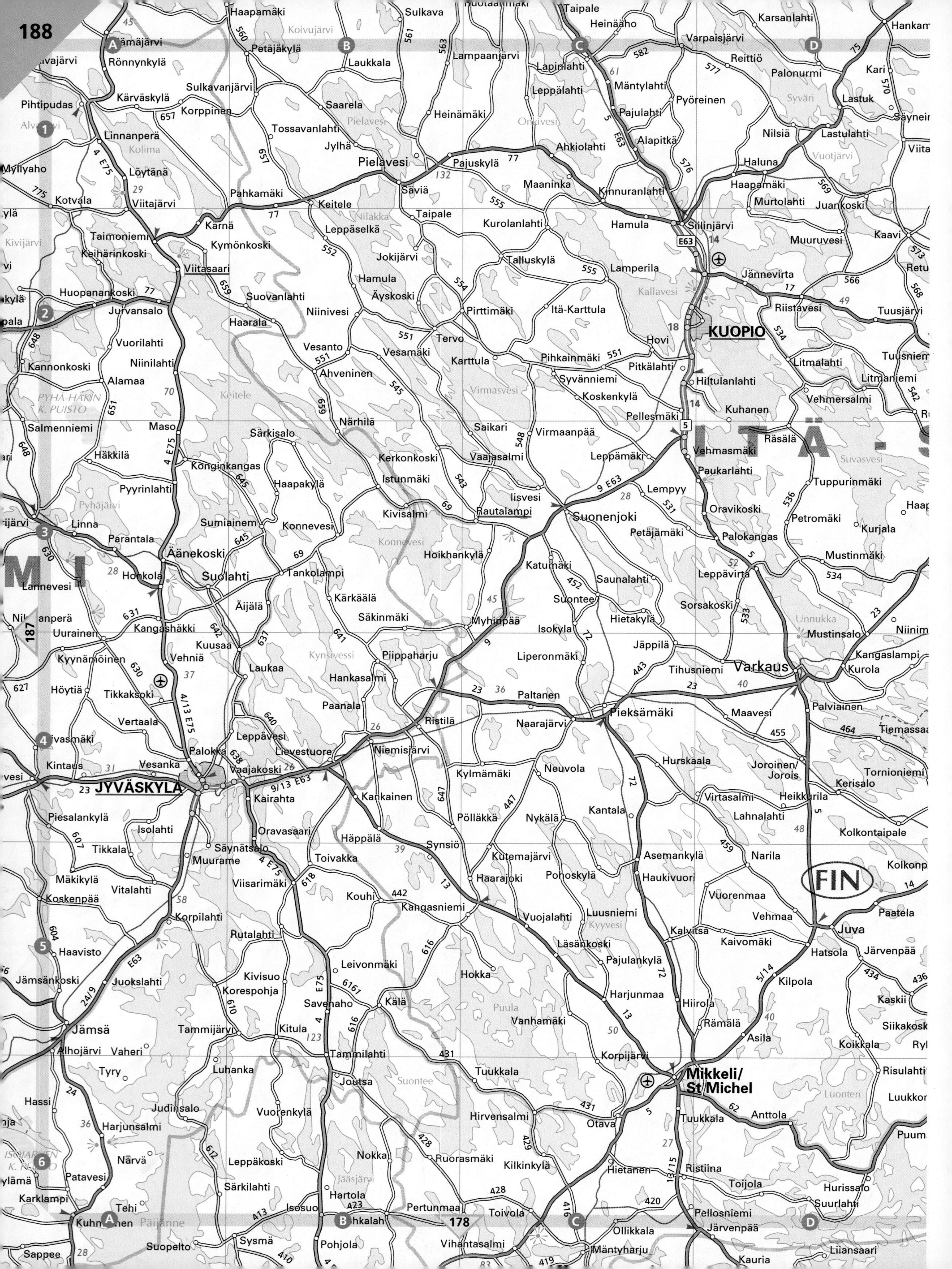
Haapamäki
Sulkava
Taipale
Heinäaho
Karsanlahti
Hankam
Koivujärvi
Ämäjärvi
Petäjäkylä
Varpaisjärvi
Rönnynkylä
Laukkala
Lampaanjärvi
Lapinlahti
Reittiö
Palonurmi
Kari
Mäntylahti
Pyöreinen
Leppälahti
Syväri
Lastuk
Pihtipudas
Kärväskylä
Sulkavanjärvi
Saarela
Korppinen
Heinämäki
Pajulahti
Säynei
Alvajärvi
Pielavesi
Onkivesi
Nilsiä
Lastulahti
Tossavanlahti
Alapitkä
Linnanperä
Kolima
Jylhä
Ahkiolahti
Vuotjärvi
Viita
Myllyaho
Löytänä
Pielavesi
Pajuskylä
Haluna
Haapamäki
Maaninka
Kinnuranlahti
Kotvala
Viitajärvi
Pahkamäki
Säviä
Murtolahti
Juankoski
Keitele
Nilakka
Taipale
Kurolanlahti
Hamula
Siilinjärvi
Karnä
Taimoniemi
Leppäselkä
Muuruvesi
Kaavi
Kivijärvi
Kymönkoski
Keihärinkoski
Jokijärvi
Talluskylä
Viitasaari
Lamperila
Jännevirta
Retu
Hamula
Äyskoski
Kallavesi
Huopanankoski
Suovanlahti
Riistavesi
Tuusjärvi
Jurvansalo
Niinivesi
Pirttimäki
Itä-Karttula
Haarala
KUOPIO
Vesanto
Tervo
Hovi
Vuorilahti
Vesamäki
Niinilahti
Karttula
Pihkainmäki
Pitkälahti
Litmalahti
Tuusniemi
Kannonkoski
Ahveninen
Syvänniemi
Hiltulanlahti
Alamaa
Koskenkylä
Litmaniemi
Virmasvesi
Vehmersalmi
PYHÄ-HÄKIN K. PUISTO
Keitele
Pellesmäki
Kuhanen
Salmenniemi
Maso
Närhilä
Saikari
Virmaanpää
Särkisalo
ITÄ-S
Vehmasmäki
Räsälä
Häkkilä
Kerkonkoski
Vaajasalmi
Leppämäki
Suvasvesi
Konginkangas
Paukarlahti
Haapakylä
Istunmäki
Tuppurinmäki
Pyyrinlahti
Iisvesi
Lempyy
Pyhäjärvi
Rautalampi
Suonenjoki
Oravikoski
Haap
Linna
Kivisalmi
Petromäki
Sumiainem
Konnevesi
Petäjämäki
Kurjala
Parantala
Konnevesi
Palokangas
Hoikhankylä
Äänekoski
Katumäki
Mustinmäki
Leppävirta
MI
Honkola
Suolahti
Tankolampi
Lannevesi
Saunalahti
Kärkäälä
Suontee
Äijälä
Sorsakoski
Nilkanperä
Säkinmäki
Myhinpää
Hietakylä
Unnukka
Uurainen
Kangashäkki
Isokylä
Mustinsalo
Niinim
Kuusaa
Jäppilä
Kynsivessi
Vehniä
Laukaa
Piippaharju
Liperonmäki
Kangaslampi
Kyynämöinen
Tihusniemi
Varkaus
Kurola
Höytiä
Hankasalmi
Tikkakoski
Paltanen
Paanala
Palviainen
Vertaala
Ristilä
Pieksämäki
Naarajärvi
Maavesi
Tiemassaa
Leppävesi
Vasmäki
Lievestuore
Niemisjärvi
Palokka
Hurskaala
Kintaus
Vesanka
Neuvola
Joroinen/Joros
Tornioniemi
Vaajakoski
Kylmämäki
Kerisalo
JYVÄSKYLÄ
Kairahta
Kankainen
Virtasalmi
Heikkurila
Kantala
Piesalankylä
Pöllökkä
Nykälä
Lahnalahti
Isolahti
Oravasaari
Kolkontaipale
Häppälä
Säynätsalo
Synsiö
Tikkala
Muurame
Kutemajärvi
Asemankylä
Narila
Toivakka
Kolkonp
Mäkikylä
Viisarimäki
Haarajoki
Pohoskylä
Haukivuori
FIN
Vitalahti
Kouhi
Kangasniemi
Vuorenmaa
Koskenpää
Luusniemi
Kyyvesi
Vehmaa
Paatela
Korpilahti
Vuojalahti
Juva
Rutalahti
Kalvitsa
Kaivomäki
Läsänkoski
Hatsola
Järvenpää
Haavisto
Leivonmäki
Pajulankylä
Jämsänkoski
Hokka
Kilpola
Juokslahti
Kivisuo
Korespohja
Harjunmaa
Kaskii
Savenaho
Kälä
Puula
Hiirola
Vanhamäki
Siikakosk
Jämsä
Tammijärvi
Kitula
Rämälä
Alhojärvi
Vaheri
Asila
Koikkala
Ryl
Tammilahti
Korpijärvi
Tyry
Luhanka
Tuukkala
Mikkeli/St Michel
Risulahti
Joutsa
Suontee
Luonteri
Luukkor
Hassi
Judinsalo
Vuorenkylä
Hirvensalmi
Otava
Tuukkala
Anttola
Harjunsalmi
Puum
Nokka
Ruorasmäki
Kilkinkylä
Närvä
Leppäkoski
Hietanen
Ristiina
ISOJÄRVEN K. PUISTO
Patavesi
Toijola
Särkilahti
Jääsjärvi
Hurissalo
Karklampi
Hartola
Suurlahti
Tehi
Pertunmaa
Toivola
Pellosniemi
Kuhmoinen
Päijänne
Ihkalahti
Järvenpää
Ollikkala
Sysmä
Suopelto
Pohjola
Vihantasalmi
Mäntyharju
Liiansaari
Sappee
Kauria
187
178

Luosta
Vaikko
197
E
Petäjävaara
Juuka
Pielinen
F
Vuonislahti
Välivaara
Kontiovaara
G
PATVINSUONI K. PUISTO
Pihlajavaara
H
Nunnanlahti
Piispa
Koli
Sokovaara
Jaakonvaara
Naarva
Polvela
Losomäki
Timovaara
Ahmovaara
Kelvä
KOLIN K. PUISTO
Kuora
Kontiovaara
Hattuvaara
Kajoo
Martonvaara
Harivaara
Herajoki
Ukkola
Kivilahti
Käenkoski
Koitere
Korentovaara
Niemijärvi
Ukonvaara
Romppala
Tyrjänsaari
Sammakkovaara
Ruvasiahtio
Ahverinen
Uimaharju
Huhus
Lehtovaara
Sivakkavaara
Mekrijärvi
Luikonlahti
Hukkala
Polvijärvi
Varparanta
Luhtapohja
Putkela
Nuorajärvi
Maarianvaara
Höytiäinen
Eno
Sonkaja
Möhkö
Kontiolahti
Sarvinki
Ilomantsi/ Ilomants
Kuuksenvaara
Horsmanaho
Kokonvaara
Jakokoski
Paakkila
Sotkuma
Revonkylä
PETKELJÄRVEN K. PUISTO
Uuro
Mönni
Outokumpu
Viinijärvi
Marjovaara
Patrikka
Juojärvi
Lehmo
Selkie
Kuusjärvi
Viinijärvi
Kontkala
Joensuu
Kovero
Mutalahti
Ylämylly
Heinävaara
SUOMI
Reijola
Eimisjärvi
Tuupovaara
Palokki
Kiihtelysvaara
Juojärvi
Ristinkylä
Liperi
Pyhäselkä
Suurmäki
Pyhäselkä
Hammaslahti
Lamminkylä
Huhtilampi
Öllölä
Tolvoyarvi
Sarvikumpu
Karvio
Leppälahti
Tutjunniemi
Uskali
Hoilola
Kypäräjärvi
Sintsi
Viesimo
Rummukkala
Heinävesi
Tikkala
Saarivaara
RUS
Latvalampi
Oravisalo
Onkamo
Rääkkylä
Saario
Vihtari
Kerma
Sappu
Tohmajärvi
Värtsilä
Koivumäki
Karpasolo
Rasivaara
Malkkila
Säimen
Orivesi
Uusi-Värtsilä
Niirala
Vyartsilya
Pölläkkä
Haapasalmi
Leipämäki
Muljula
Tolosenmäki
Viljolahti
Heinoniemi
Soanlahti
Savonranta
Kitee
Puhos
Puykkola
Ozero Yanis'yarvi
Korkeakangas
Ahvensalmi
Hannivirta
Kokkolahti
Raykonkoski
Kirkkolakhti
Suystamo
Oravi
Villala
LINNANSAAREN K. PUISTO
Enonkoski
Lutojärvi
Juurikka
Yakkima
Alalampi
Haukivesi
Simanala
Tasapää
Ruskeala
Alattu
Rantasalmi
Juvola
Rasti
Kaalamo
Ylä-Kuona
Makkola
Aittolahti
Valkeavaara
Ryuttyu
Varparanta
Pyhäjärvi
Parkumäki
Kerimäki
Lyaskelya
Rinkilä
Kesälahti
Anttola
Purujärvi
Kallislahti
Puruvesi
Khelyulya
Uukuniemen kk.
Pihlajalahti
Kulennoinen
Savonlinna/ Nyslott
Sortavala
Сортавала
Impilakhti
Hiukkajoki
Uukuniemi
Kommerniemi
Punkaharju
Tarnala
Saari
Sulkava
Sikopkh'ya
Khaapalampi
Rauhaniemi
Putikko
Pihlajavesi
Akonpohja
Heikkurila
Käärmelahti
Kiviapaja
Oppola
Kaartilankoski
Särkisalmi
Rayvio
Lohikoski
Vuoriniemi
Parikkala
Lakhdenpokh'ya
Ostrov Valaam
Kietävälä
Ikhala
Särkilahti
Joukio
Auvila
Lamminkyulya
Valkiamäki
Simpelejärvi
Lumivaara
Ladozhskoye Ozero
Pohja-Lankila
Simpele
Elisenvaara
Ahjärvi
Hauklappi
Mattila
Luukkola
Syyspohja
Laikko
Laamala
Kurkiyeki
179
Virmutjoki
Utula
Junnikkala
Ruokolahti
Rautjärvi
Il'me
Khiytola
1
2
3
4
5
6

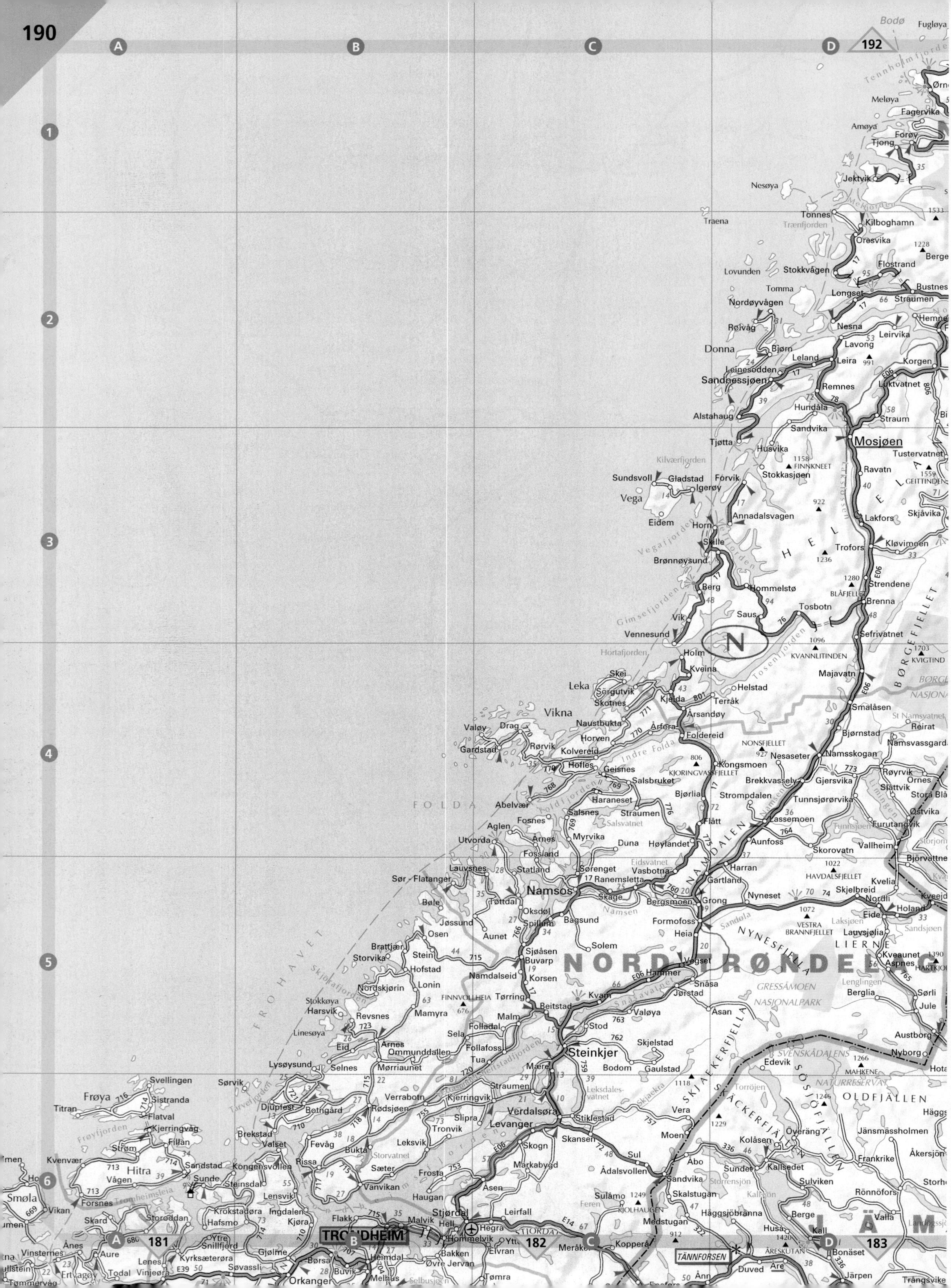
A
B
C
D
192
Bodø
Fugløya
Tennholmfjorden
Ørnes
Meløya
Fagervika
Amøya
Forøy
Tjong
Jektvik
Nesøya
Tonnes
Traena
Trænfjorden
Kilboghamn
Oresvika
Berge
Lovunden
Stokkvågen
Flostrand
Tomma
Longset
Bustnes
Straumen
Nordøyvågen
Nesna
Hemnes
Rølvåg
Leirvika
Donna
Bjørn
Lavong
Leland
Leira
Leinesodden
Korgen
Sandnessjøen
Remnes
Luktvatnet
Hundåla
Alstahaug
Straum
Sandvika
Tjøtta
Mosjøen
Husvika
Tustervatnet
Kilværfjorden
FINNKNEET
Ravatn
Sundsvoll
Gladstad
Forvik
Stokkasjøen
GEITTINDEN
Igerøy
Vega
Lakfors
Skjåvika
Annadalsvagen
Eidem
Horn
Vegafjorden
Skille
Trofors
Kløvimoen
Brønnøysund
H E L G E L A N D
Strendene
BLÅFJELLET
Berg
Hommelstø
Brenna
Gimsefjorden
Saus
Tosbotn
Vik
Vennesund
N
Sefrivatnet
Hortafjorden
Holm
KVANNLITINDEN
KVIGTIND
Kveina
BØRGEFJELLET
Majavatn
Tosenfjorden
Helstad
Leka
Skei
Sörgutvik
Kjelda
Terråk
Skotnes
Vikna
Årsandøy
Smalåsen
Naustbukta
St Namsvatnet
Valøy
Drag
Årfora
Reirat
Bjørnstad
Rørvik
Horven
Foldereid
Gardstad
Kolvereid
NONSFJELLET
Namsvassgarda
Nesaseter
Namsskogan
Hofles
KJORINGVASSFJELLET
Kongsmoen
Geisnes
Røyrvik
Salsbruket
Brekkvasselv
Gjersvika
Ornes
Slåttvik
Indre Folda
Bjørlia
Strompdalen
Stora Blå
Tunnsjørørvika
FOLDA
Abelvær
Haraneset
Østvika
Salsnes
Straumen
Lassemoen
Fosnes
Salsvatnet
Furutangvik
Aglen
Flått
Funnsjøen
Myrvika
NAMDALEN
Vallheim
Utvorda
Arnes
Duna
Høylandet
Aunfoss
Skorovatn
Fossland
Bjørvattnet
Lauvsnes
Statland
Eidsvatnet
Harran
HAVDALSFJELLET
Sørenget
Vasbotna
Kvelia
Sør-Flatanger
Ranemsletta
Gartland
Skjelbreid
Namsos
Skage
Bergsmoen
Nyneset
Nordli
Kveejd
Løttdal
Grong
Holand
Bøle
Oksdøl
Eide
Namsen
Formofoss
VESTRA BRANNFJELLET
Laksjøen
Jøssund
Spillum
Bagsund
Sandola
Lauvsjølia
Sandsjøen
Osen
Aunet
Heia
NYNESFJELLA
LIERNE
Solem
Brattjær
Kveaunet
Stein
Storvika
Sjøåsen
Aspnes
HARTKJØLEN
Buvarp
Vegset
Hofstad
Namdalseid
Hammer
NORD-TRØNDELAG
Lenglingen
Korsen
GRESSÅMOEN NASJONALPARK
Snåsa
Berglia
Nordskjørin
Lonin
Sørli
FINNVOLLHEIA
Tørring
Kvam
Jørstad
Snåsavatnet
Jule
Stokkøya
Harsvik
Beitstad
Mamyra
Revsnes
Malm
Asan
Valøya
Linesøya
Folladal
Stod
Sela
Austborg
Arnes
Eid
Ommunddallen
Follafoss
Skjelstad
Tua
Steinkjer
Nyborg
Lysøysund
Selnes
Mørriaunet
Bodom
Gaulstad
SVENSKÅDALENS
MAHKENE
Hota
Mære
Edevik
Sørvik
Svellingen
NATURRESERVAT
Frøya
Sistranda
Straumen
Leksdalsvatnet
Torröjen
Titran
Verrabotn
Kjerringvik
OLDFJÄLLEN
Djupfest
Rødsjøen
Verdalsøra
SKJÆKERFJELLA
SÖCKERFJÄLLEN
Häggs
Flatval
Botngård
Slipra
Stiklestad
Vera
Frøyfjorden
Kjerringvåg
Tronvik
Levanger
Jänsmässholmen
Fillan
Brekstad
Valset
Fevåg
Leksvik
Skansen
Moen
Överäng
Strøm
Bukta
Storvatnet
Åkersjön
Kvenvær
Hitra
Sandstad
Kongensvollen
Skogn
Kolåsen
Frankrike
Rissa
Sæter
Markabygd
Sul
Vågen
Sunde
Frosta
Ådalsvollen
Åbo
Sunder
Kallsedet
Smøla
Steinsdal
Vanvikan
Åsen
Sandvika
Sulviken
Storh
Forsnes
Lensvik
Trondheimsleia
Storsjön
Vikan
Haugan
Sulåmo
Skalstugan
Rönnöfors
Feren
KJOLHAUGEN
Kallsjön
Skard
Storøddan
Krokstadøra
Ingdalen
Stjørdal
Leirfall
Häggsjöbränna
Berge
Valla
Hafsmo
Flakk
Malvik
Hegra
Medstugan
JÄM
Kjøra
Hell
Hommelvik
Husa
Kall
Ånes
Aure
181
Ytre Snillfjord
TRONDHEIM
Ytteren
182
Meråker
Kopperå
ÅRESKUTAN
Bonäset
183
Vinsternes
Kyrksæterøra
Gjølme
Bakken
Elvran
TÄNNFORSEN
Todal
Vinjeøra
Lenes
Søvassli
Børsa
Buvik
Heimdal
Øvre Jervan
Duved
Åre
Järpen
Tømra
Ertvågøy
Orkanger
Melhus
Selbusjøen
Ånn
Trångsvike
Tømmervåg
FROHAVET
Skjørafjorden
Beitstadfjorden
Trondheimsfjorden
STJØRDAL

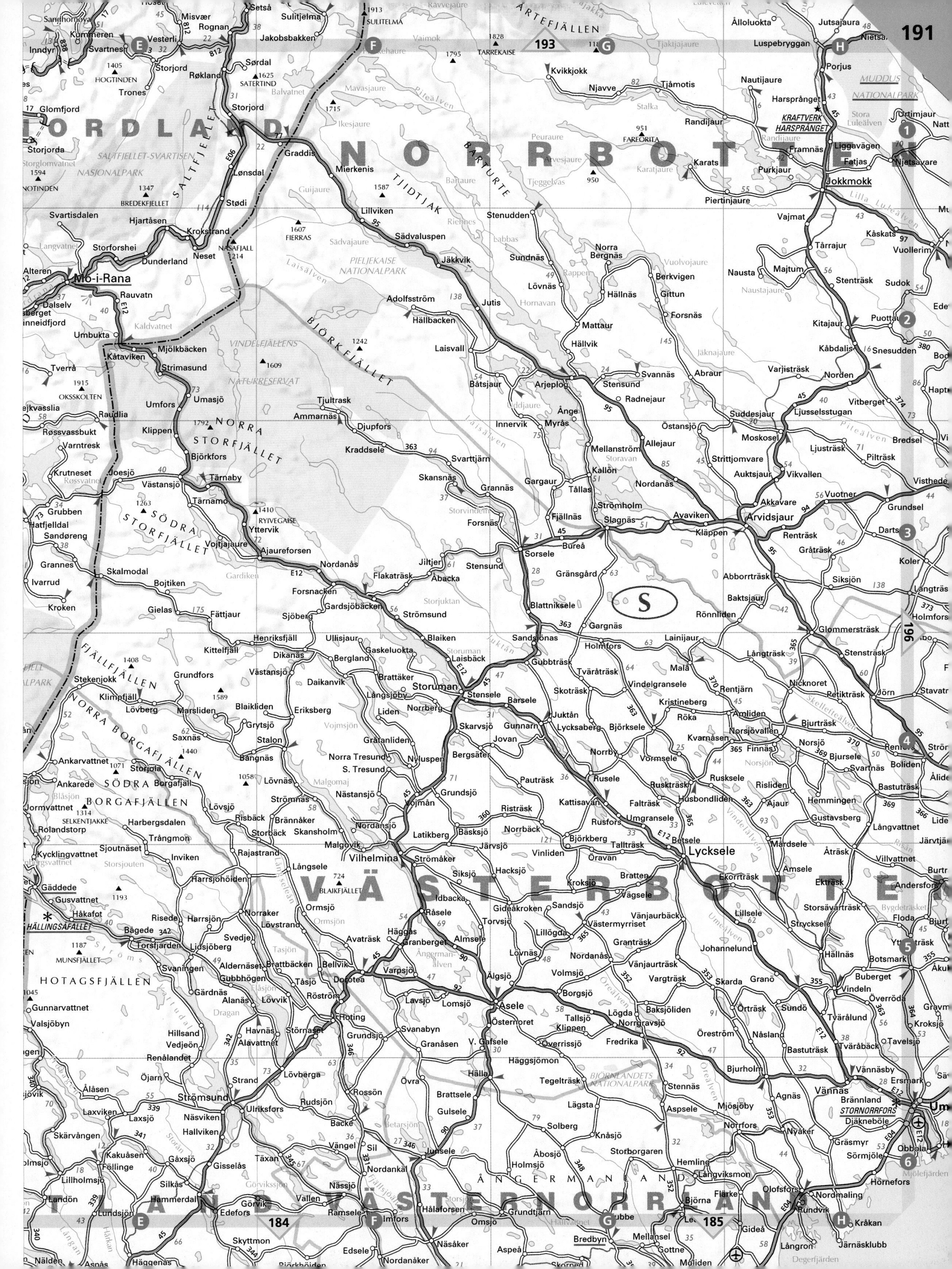
NORRBOTTEN
VÄSTERBOTTEN
VÄSTERNORRLAND
NORDLAND
SALTFJELLET
SALTFJELLET-SVARTISEN NASJONALPARK
PIELJEKAISE NATIONALPARK
MUDDUS NATIONALPARK
BJÖRNLANDETS NATIONALPARK
VINDELFJÄLLENS NATURRESERVAT
ARTEFJÄLLEN
BARTURTE
TJIDTJAK
BJÖRKFJÄLLET
NORRA STORFJÄLLET
SÖDRA STORFJÄLLET
FJÄLLFJÄLLEN
NORRA BORGAFJÄLLEN
SÖDRA BORGAFJÄLLEN
HOTAGSFJÄLLEN
ÅNGERMANLAND
KRAFTVERK HARSPRÅNGET
HÄLLINGSÅFALLET
STORNORRFORS
193
196
184
185
Sulitjelma
Jakobsbakken
Rognan
Misvær
Vesterli
Kummeren
Svartnes
Inndyr
Sørdal
Røkland
Storjord
Trones
Glomfjord
Storjorda
Lønsdal
Stødi
Graddis
Mierkenis
Lillviken
Sädvaluspen
Jäkkvik
Kvikkjokk
Njavve
Tjåmotis
Nautijaure
Harsprånget
Porjus
Randijaur
Framnäs
Liggavägen
Fatjas
Purkjaur
Karats
Jokkmokk
Piertinjaure
Vajmat
Tårrajur
Kåskats
Vuollerim
Nausta
Majtum
Stenträsk
Sudok
Kitajaur
Puottau
Kåbdalis
Snesudden
Svartisdalen
Hjartåsen
Krokstrand
Neset
Storforshei
Dunderland
Mo-i-Rana
Rauvatn
Dalselv
Umbukta
Kåtaviken
Mjölkbäcken
Strimasund
Umasjö
Umfors
Tverrå
Raudlia
Røssvassbukt
Klippen
Varntresk
Krutneset
Joesjö
Västansjö
Tärnaby
Björkfors
Tärnamo
Grubben
Hattfjelldal
Sandøreng
Yttervik
Vojtjajaure
Ajaureforsen
Grannes
Skalmodal
Ivarrud
Kroken
Bojtiken
Gielas
Fättjaur
Henriksfjäll
Kittelfjäll
Stekenjokk
Klimpfjäll
Lövberg
Marsliden
Grundfors
Saxnäs
Ankarvattnet
Ankarede
Storjola
Borgafjäll
Jormvattnet
Rolandstorp
Kycklingvattnet
Gäddede
Gusvattnet
Håkafot
Bågede
Torsfjärden
Harbergsdalen
Trångmon
Sjoutnäset
Inviken
Harrsjöhöiden
Risede
Harrsjön
Lidsjöberg
Svaningen
Gärdnäs
Gunnarvattnet
Valsjöbyn
Hillsand
Vedjeön
Renålandet
Öjarn
Ålåsen
Strömsund
Laxviken
Laxsjö
Skärvången
Kakuåsen
Föllinge
Lillholmsjö
Landön
Lundsjön
Hammerdal
Gåxsjö
Gisselås
Edefors
Skyttmon
Häggenås
Nälden
Adolfsström
Hällbacken
Laisvall
Jutis
Tjultrask
Ammarnäs
Djupfors
Kraddsele
Svarttjärn
Skansnäs
Grannäs
Forsnäs
Sorsele
Jiltjer
Stensund
Abacka
Nordanås
Flakaträsk
Forsnacken
Gardsjöbäcken
Strömsund
Sjöberg
Blaiken
Ullisjaur
Dikanäs
Gaskeluokta
Bergland
Västansjö
Daikanvik
Brattåker
Storuman
Stensele
Långsjöby
Liden
Norrberg
Eriksberg
Blaikliden
Grytsjö
Stalon
Bångnäs
Lövnäs
Strömnäs
Risbäck
Storbäck
Brännåker
Skansholm
Nordansjö
Malgovik
Vilhelmina
Rajastrand
Långsele
Norraker
Lövstrand
Svedje
Aldernäset
Gubbhögen
Alanäs
Havnäs
Alavattnet
Brattbäcken
Bellvik
Dorotea
Tåsjö
Avaträsk
Häggås
Granberget
Ormsjö
Lövvik
Röström
Hoting
Störnäset
Grundsjö
Lövberga
Rossön
Ulriksfors
Näsviken
Hallviken
Rudsjön
Backe
Vängel
Sil
Täxan
Nordankäl
Silkås
Görvik
Vallen
Nässjö
Ramsele
Imfors
Edsele
Näsåker
Nordanåker
Stenudden
Sundnäs
Lövnäs
Norra Bergnäs
Berkvigen
Hällnäs
Gittun
Forsnäs
Mattaur
Hällvik
Arjeplog
Båtsjaur
Stensund
Svannäs
Radnejaur
Ånge
Myrås
Innervik
Mellanström
Allejaur
Kallön
Tållas
Gargaur
Nordanås
Strömholm
Fjällnäs
Slagnäs
Avaviken
Klappen
Arvidsjaur
Bureå
Gränsgård
Blattnikséle
Gargnäs
Sandsjönäs
Holmfors
Lainijaur
Gubbträsk
Tväråträsk
Malå
Skoträsk
Vindelgransele
Rentjärn
Barsele
Juktån
Gunnarn
Lycksaberg
Björksele
Skarvsjö
Jovan
Bergsäter
Norra Tresund
S. Tresund
Nyluspen
Pauträsk
Ruselε
Grundsjö
Nästansjö
Vojmån
Risträsk
Bäsksjö
Norrbäck
Latikberg
Järvsjö
Vinliden
Björkberg
Tallträsk
Örarvan
Strömåker
Siksjö
Hacksjö
Idbacka
Råsele
Gideåkroken
Sandsjö
Torvsjö
Lillögda
Västermyrriset
Almsele
Lövnäs
Älgsjö
Varpsjö
Lavsjö
Lomsjö
Åsele
Österноret
Svanabyn
Granåsen
V. Gafsele
Överrissjö
Häggsjömon
Hälla
Övra
Brattsele
Gulsele
Junsele
Solberg
Holmsjö
Åbosjö
Knåsjö
Storborgaren
Ågsjö
Tegelträsk
Lägsta
Stennäs
Aspsele
Mjösjöby
Fredrika
Lögda
Norrgravsjö
Klippen
Tallsjö
Borgsjö
Baksjöliden
Volmsjö
Nordanås
Vänjaurträsk
Granträsk
Vänjaurbäck
Vargträsk
Skarda
Kattisavan
Falträsk
Umgransele
Rusfors
Betsele
Lycksele
Bratten
Krokśjö
Vägsele
Ekorrträsk
Lillsele
Johannelund
Norrby
Vormsele
Kristineberg
Röka
Kvarnåsen
Amliden
Norsjövallen
Finnäs
Norsjö
Bjursele
Ruskträsk
Husbondliden
Ruskele
Ajaur
Risliden
Mårdsele
Amsele
Åträsk
Hemmingen
Gustavsberg
Långvattnet
Ekträsk
Storsävarträsk
Strycksele
Hällnäs
Botsmark
Granö
Vindeln
Buberget
Överrödå
Sundö
Örträsk
Tväråbäck
Tvärålund
Nåsland
Öreström
Bastuträsk
Bjurholm
Agnäs
Vännäs
Vännäsby
Brännland
Norrfors
Nyåker
Djäkneböle
Gräsmyr
Sörmjöle
Obbola
Hemling
Långviksmon
Björna
Olofsfors
Nordmaling
Rundvik
Hörnefors
Kråkan
Järnäsklubb
Långron
Gideå
Bredbyn
Mellansel
Gottne
Moliden
Aspeå
Omsjö
Hålaforsen
Grundtjärn
Flärke
Gubbe
Suddesjaur
Ljusselstugan
Östansjö
Moskosel
Strittjomvare
Auktsjaur
Vikvallen
Akkavare
Vuotner
Grundsel
Renträsk
Gråträsk
Darts
Koler
Abborrträsk
Siksjön
Baktsjaur
Rönnliden
Glommersträsk
Långträsk
Stensträsk
Petikträsk
Nicknoret
Jörn
Bjurträsk
Renfors
Boliden
Svartnäs
Bastuträsk
Varjisträsk
Abraur
Norden
Vitberget
Ljusträsk
Pilträsk
Bredsel
Vistheden
Lidsjöberg
Ersmark
Umeå

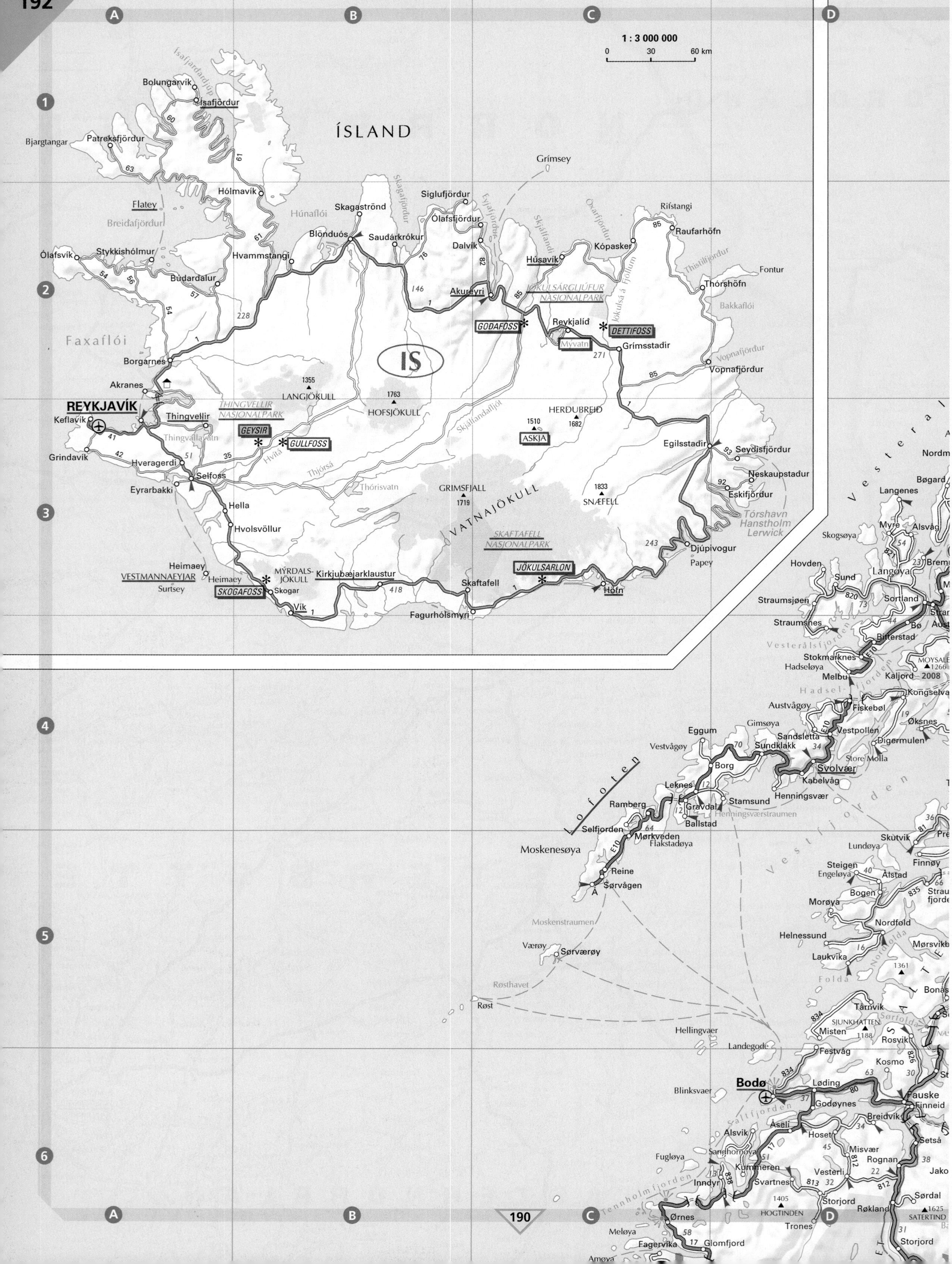
A
B
C
D
1
2
3
4
5
6
1 : 3 000 000
0 30 60 km
ÍSLAND
IS
Ísafjarðardjúp
Bolungarvík
Ísafjördur
Bjargtangar
Patreksfjördur
Hólmavík
Flatey
Breiðafjörður
Húnaflói
Skagaströnd
Skagafjörður
Siglufjördur
Ólafsfjördur
Dalvík
Eyjafjörður
Skjálfandi
Öxarfjörður
Grímsey
Rifstangi
Raufarhöfn
Kópasker
Húsavík
Thistilfjörður
Fontur
Thórshöfn
Bakkaflói
Blönduós
Saudárkrókur
Ólafsvík
Stykkishólmur
Hvammstangi
Búdardalur
Akureyri
JÖKULSÁRGLJÚFUR NASJONALPARK
Jökulsá á Fjöllum
GODAFOSS
Reykjalíd
Mývatn
DETTIFOSS
Grímsstadir
Vopnafjörður
Vopnafjördur
Faxaflói
Borgarnes
Akranes
REYKJAVÍK
Keflavík
Grindavík
Hveragerdi
Selfoss
Eyrarbakki
THINGVELLIR NASJONALPARK
Thingvellir
Thingvallavatn
GEYSIR
GULLFOSS
Hvítá
Thjórsá
Thórisvatn
LANGJÖKULL
1355
1763
HOFSJÖKULL
Skjálfandafljót
HERÐUBREIÐ
1682
1510
ASKJA
Egilsstadir
Seydisfjördur
Neskaupstaður
Eskifjördur
GRIMSFJALL
1719
1833
SNÆFELL
VATNAJÖKULL
Tórshavn
Hanstholm
Lerwick
Hella
Hvolsvöllur
SKAFTAFELL NASJONALPARK
Djúpivogur
Papey
Heimaey
VESTMANNAEYJAR
Surtsey
MÝRDALS-JÖKULL
SKOGAFOSS
Skogar
Kirkjubæjarklaustur
Skaftafell
JÖKULSARLON
Höfn
Vík
Fagurhólsmýri
60
63
61
54
56
57
228
1
146
76
82
85
271
35
41
42
51
92
93
243
418
Vesterålen
Nordm
Bøgard
Langenes
Myre
Alsvåg
Skogsøya
Hovden
Sund
Langøya
Brem
Straumsjøen
Sortland
Straumsnes
Bø
Bitterstad
Vesterålsfjorden
Stokmarknes
Hadseløya
MOYSALEN
1266
2008
Melbu
Kaljord
Hadselfjorden
Kongselva
Austvågøy
Fiskebøl
Øksnes
Gimsøya
Eggum
Sandsletta
Vestpollen
Vestvågøy
Sundklakk
Digermulen
Store Molla
Borg
Svolvær
Kabelvåg
Lofoten
Leknes
Stamsund
Henningsvær
Ramberg
Gravdal
Henningsværstraumen
Ballstad
Vestfjorden
Selfjorden
Mørkveden
Flakstadøya
Moskenesøya
Reine
Å
Sørvågen
Skutvik
Lundøya
Finnøy
Steigen
Engeløya
Ålstad
Bogen
Straumfjorde
Morøya
Moskenstraumen
Nordfold
Helnessund
Mørsvikb
Værøy
Sørværøy
Laukvika
Folda
1361
Røsthavet
Bonås
Røst
Tårnvik
Sørfolda
SJUNKHATTEN
1188
Misten
Rosvik
Hellingvaer
Landegode
Festvåg
Kosmo
Bodø
Løding
Blinksvaer
Fauske
Finneid
Saltfjorden
Godøynes
Breidvik
Alsvik
Åseli
Hoset
Setså
Misvær
Fugløya
Sandhornøya
Rognan
Kjemmeren
Vesterli
Jako
Svartnes
Inndyr
Sørdal
Tennholmfjorden
1405
HOGTINDEN
Storjord
Røkland
SATERTIND
1625
Ørnes
Trones
Meløya
Fagervika
Glomfjord
Storjord
Amøya
E10
70
34
12
64
40
835
16
834
826
63
30
80
37
45
812
22
38
838
813
32
31
58
17
820
73
44
23
19
36
81
66
54
821

E
F
G
H
1
2
3
4
5
6
194
195
191
196
TROMS
N
FIN
S
LAPPLAND
Silda
Loppa
Stjernøya
Nuvsvåg
Hummelvik
Øksfjord
Myrnes
Sletta
Sør-Tverrfjord
Segelvik
BERGSFJORD-HALVØYA
Isnestoften
Arøya
Laukvik
Talvik
Langfjord
Alta
Alteidet
Burfjord
HALDDE
HELLERISTN
Hombukt
Spildra
Haukøya
Kvænangen
Valanhamn
Skorpa
Oksfjordhamn
Storsnes
Badderen
Karvik
Navit
Kvænangsbotn
Storslett
RIEPPE
Potka
Sappen
Bilto
MOLLIJUS
Bidjovagge
Suolovuo
Mieron
Oaivos
Stuorajavre
NATURRESERVAT
Fugløva
Årviksand
Arnøy
Nymo
Laukøy
Lauksundskaret
Skjervøy
Kågen
Flåten
Nakkesletta
Vanna
Kristoffervalen
Nordkvaløya
Grøtøy
Helgøya
Rebbenesøya
Mikkelvika
Skåningbukt
Sandøya
Skarsfjord
Hansnes
Ringvassøy
Stakkvik
Reinøy
Nord-Lenangen
Uløya
Vengsøy
Nordhella
LYNGS-FJELLAN
Hamnes
Sørkjosen
Djupvik
Futrikelv
Tromvik
Rekvik
Vasstrand
TROMSØ
Kroken
Breivikeidet
Oldervik
Koppangen
Svensby
Olderdalen
Trollvik
Hillesøy
Kvaløy
Skarmunken
Lyngseidet
Jøvik
Odden
Laukvik
Vikran
Fagernes
Mefjordvær
Bø
Fjordgård
Bakkejord
Sørbotn
JIEKKEVARE
Furuflaten
Straumsnes
Sætra
Kårvikhamn
Rossfjord
Målsnes
Kantornes
Oteren
Skibotn
Brennfjell
Gryllefjord
Gibostad
Mestervik
Balsfjord
Slettmo
Olteren
Storfjord
Rovjok
Andenes
Bleik
Senja
Kaldfarnes
Silsand
Finnsnes
Storsteinnes
Helligskogen
SKIBOTNDALEN
HALTI
REISA NASJONALPARK
Stave
Skarstein
Flakkstadvågen
ÅNDERDALEN
Selfjorden
Gjøvik
Vaggsvik
Sørreisa
Olsborg
BLÅTINDAN
Heia
Nordkjosbotn
Govddajavre
Perskogen
SAANA
Kilpisjärvi
Myre
Sjursvika
Stonglandseidet
Buktamo
Moen
Bardufoss
Vingstad
Åse
Risøyhamn
Dyrøya
Tangen
Andselv
Maukdal
Øverbygd
ROSTAFJELLET
Lille Rostavatn
PÅLSTAN
Saananmaja
VIRDNITSIELGI
Grøtavær
Mikkelbostad
Sandsøy
Kåstneshamn
HJERTTIND
Elverum
Holt
Tverrelvmo
Peera
TSAIBMA
Grytøya
Klåpen
Høgstadgård
Kummavuopio
Devdisjavre
Buksnes
Elgsnes
Andørja
Sjøvegan
Setermoen
ROPI
Harstad
Ibestad
Sørvik
Lavangnes
Brandvoll
Bjørkåsen
Frihetsli
Saarikoski
TARJU
Børkenes
Rolla
Tennevol
ØSTERDALEN
Råstojaure
Brattli
NJUNES
Mybotn
Grovfjord
Rensa
Fossbakken
Innset
Hyttegrend
ØVRE DIVIDAL NASJONALPARK
Ropinsalmi
Flesnes
Refnes
Gausvik
SKITTENDAL-STINDEN
Gratangen
Sørmo
Altevatnet
RÅSTO
Hinnøya
Øse
ISTIND
Bjerkvik
VADVETJÅKKA NATIONALPARK
Kiepanjaure
Kelottijärvi
Markkina
Ulvika
Bogen
Karesuvanto
Kanstad
Narvik
Leirvik
Skogvatnet
Gævdnja-jävrre
Leinavatnet
TSÅKTSO
Tavvaätno
Luspa
Karesuando
Kuttan
Tjeldøya
Tjeldnes
Nygård
Riksgränsen
Björkliden
TUOPTETJÅKKAH
Pulsujärvi
Lødingen
Ankenesstrand
Bleisfjord
Stordalen
Torneträsk
Laimoluokta
Närvä
Kjeldebotn
Håkvika
Grindjorda
NJULLA
Abisko
Kattuvuoma
Rinøya
Kjeeringvika
Ballangen
Kaisepakte
ABISKO NATIONALPARK
Järämä
Jårkastaka
Idivuoma
Tjalme
Forsa
Rånvassbotn
Latteluokta
Suijavaara
Bognes
Skarberget
STORSTEINFJELLET
Torneträsk
Bergfors
Saivom
Tranøya
Kjøpsvik
Fjellbu
Apparjaure
Vuolle Alesjaure
Vittangijärvi
Övre Soppero
Ulvsvåg
Drag
Ájluokta
Rautasjaure
Lannavaara
Nedre Soppero
Rautas
Innhavet
BJORNTOPPEN
Sitasjaure
Kåbtåjaure
VISTASVAGGE
Krokvik
Kurravaara
Tømmernes
Upmas
KEBNEKAISE
Åresjåkk
Jukkasjärvi
Sitasjaurestugorna
Nikkaluokta
Laukuluspa
Kiruna
Sappisaasi
Parkalompolo
Kråkmo
Autajaure
Paittasjärvi
Alttajärvi
Lainio
Vivungi
KÅRSATJÅKKA
Kaitumjaure
Kaalasjärvi
Vittangi
Oksajärvi
Akkajaure
Ritsem
KALLAKTJÅKKÅ
Teusajaure
Tjuoltajaure
Svappavaara
Kuoksu
STORA SJÖFALLETS NATIONALPARK
Sjisjka
Kurkkio
Kaitumälven
Kalixälven
AKKAVARE
Kobbelveid
Sollohaure
Suorva
Killinge
Parakka
Nujaure
Fjällåsen
Masugnsbyn
Junosuando
Neitisuanto
Puoltikasvaara
Skaulo
STORA SJÖFALLET
Vietas
Satihaure
Kirjaluokta
Harrå
Vettasjärvi
Kääntöjärvi
SAREKTJÅKKÅ
PADJELANTA NATIONALPARK
Vastenjaure
Saltoluokta
Saittarova
Ruokto
Tjautjas
Aluokta
Karmas
Lina älv
Nilivaara
Talinen
Virihaure
Alajaure
SAREKS NATIONALPARK
Sitojaure
Malmberget
Koskullskulle
BLÅMANNSISEN
PÅRTEFJÄLLEN
Rapajåkka
Stora Lulevatten
Markitta
Granhult
Sulitjelma
SULITELMA
Råvvejaure
Ålloluokta
Gällivare
Dokkas
Nytorp
Ekorrbäck
Jutsajaure
Leipojärvi
Ullatti
Kainulasjärvi
Vaimok
TARREKAISE
Tjaktjajaure
Luspebryggan
Nietsak
DUNDRET
Ripats
Pieskehaure
Porjus
Kvikkjokk
Njavve
Tjåmotis
Nautijaure
MUDDUS NATIONALPARK
Palohuornas
Satter
Lahnajärvi
Mavasjaure
Harsprånget
KRAFTVERK HARSPRÅNGET
Stalka
Stora Luleälven
Urtimjaur
Nattavaara
Kilvo
Randijaur
Sarvisvaara
Skröven
Ängesan
Ikesjaure

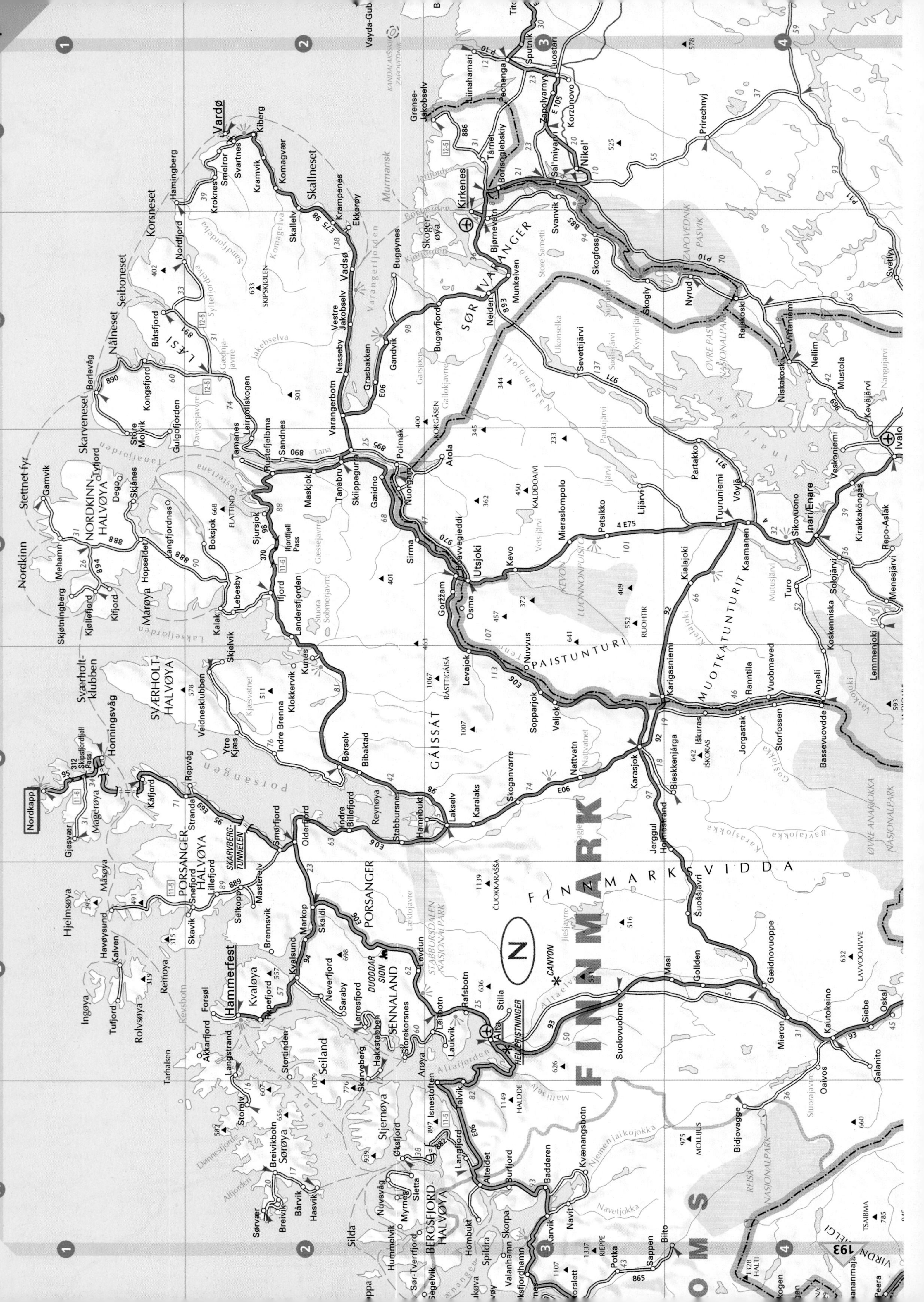
Nordkapp
Gjesvær
Magerøya
Honningsvåg
Skipsfjordfjell Pass
Kåfjord
Repvåg
Stranda
PORSANGER-HALVØYA
SKARVBERG-TUNNELEN
Smørfjord
Hjelmsøya
Måsøya
Havøysund
Snefjord
Lillefjord
Masterelv
Selkopp
Skavik
Ingøya
Tufjord
Kalven
Rolvsøya
Reinøya
Revsbotn
Hammerfest
Forsøl
Kvaløya
Rypefjord
Kvalsund
Brennsvik
Markop
Skaidi
PORSANGER
Neverfjord
Saraby
Lerresfjord
SENNALAND
DUODDAR SION
Levdun
STABBURSDALEN NASJONALPARK
Akkarfjord
Langstrand
Stortinden
Seiland
Hakkstabben
Storekorsnes
Skarveberg
Tarhalsen
Storelv
Sørøya
Breivikbotn
Sørvær
Breivik
Bårvik
Hasvik
Stjernøya
Øksfjord
Isnestoften
Talvik
Langfjord
Alteidet
Burfjord
Badderen
Kvænangsbotn
Nuvsvåg
Mymes
Sletta
Silda
BERGSFJORD-HALVØYA
Hummelvik
Hombukt
Spildra
Skorpa
Karvik
Navit
Valanhamn
Bilto
Sappen
Potka
Altafjorden
Alta
Leirbotn
Laukvik
Rafsbotn
Stilla
HELLERISTNINGER
CANYON
FINNMARK
Suolovuobme
Masi
Gollen
Gæidnovuoppe
Mieron
Kautokeino
Siebe
Oskal
Galanito
Oaivos
Bidjovagge
REISA NASJONALPARK
Navetjokka
Njemenjaikojokka
FINNMARKSVIDDA
Šuoššjavri
Jerggul
Hoimestrand
Karasjok
Bieskkenjárga
Iškuras
Jorgastak
Storfossen
Bassevuovdde
ØVRE ANARJOKKA NASJONALPARK
Bavtajokka
Karasjokka
Nattvatn
Skoganvarre
Karalaks
Lakselv
Hamnbukt
Stabbursnes
Reynøya
Indre Billefjord
Olderfjord
Børselv
Bibaktad
GÁISSÁT
Sopparjok
Valjok
Levajok
Nuvvus
PAISTUNTURI
Karigasniemi
MUOTKATUNTURIT
Ranntila
Vuobmaved
Angeli
Lemmenjoki
Koskenniska
Turo
Kaamanen
Kielajoki
Sikovuono
Inari/Enare
Kirakkakongas
Repo-Aslak
Menesjärvi
Solojärvi
Veskoniemi
Ivalo
Kevajärvi
Mustola
Nellim
Virtaniemi
Niskakoski
Rajakoski
ØVRE PASVIK NASJONALPARK
Partakko
Vöyjä
Tuuruniemi
Lijärvi
Petsikko
Mieraslompolo
Kevo
Utsjoki
Osma
Gorzzam
Sirma
Nuorgam
Polmak
Arola
Gæidno
Skippagurra
Tanabru
Maskjok
Sjursjok
Ifjord
Ifjordfjell Pass
Landersfjorden
Kunes
Klokkervik
Indre Brenna
Ytre Kjæs
Veidnesklubben
SVÆRHOLT-HALVØYA
Sværholt-klubben
Skjelvik
Kalak
Lebesby
Laksefjorden
Kjøllefjord
Skjøtningberg
Kifjord
Mehamn
Nordkinn
Gamvik
Stettnet fyr
NORDKINN-HALVØYA
Dego
Skjånes
Hopseidet
Langfjordnes
Boksjok
Tyfjord
Tanafjorden
Skarveneset
Store Molvik
Gulgofjorden
Kongsfjord
Berlevåg
Nålneset
Båtsfjord
LASI
Seiboneset
Nordfjord
Korsneset
Hamningberg
Kroknes
Smelror
Svartnes
Vardø
Kiberg
Kramvik
Komagvær
Skallneset
Skallelv
Krampenes
Ekkerøy
Vadsø
Vestre Jakobselv
Nesseby
Varangerbotn
Tamanes
Leirpollskogen
Rustefjelbma
Sandnes
Grasbakken
Gandvik
Bugøyfjord
Bugøynes
Varangerfjorden
Murmansk
SØR VARANGER
Neiden
Munkelven
Skogerøya
Kirkenes
Bjørnevatn
Svanvik
Skogfoss
Skogly
Nyrud
PASVIK
Jarfjorden
Grense-Jakobselv
Tårnet
Borisoglebskiy
Sal'miyarvi
Nikel'
Korzunovo
Zapolyarnyy
Pechenga
Liinahamari
Sputnik
Luostari
Prirechnyj
Svetlyy
Vayda-Guba
193

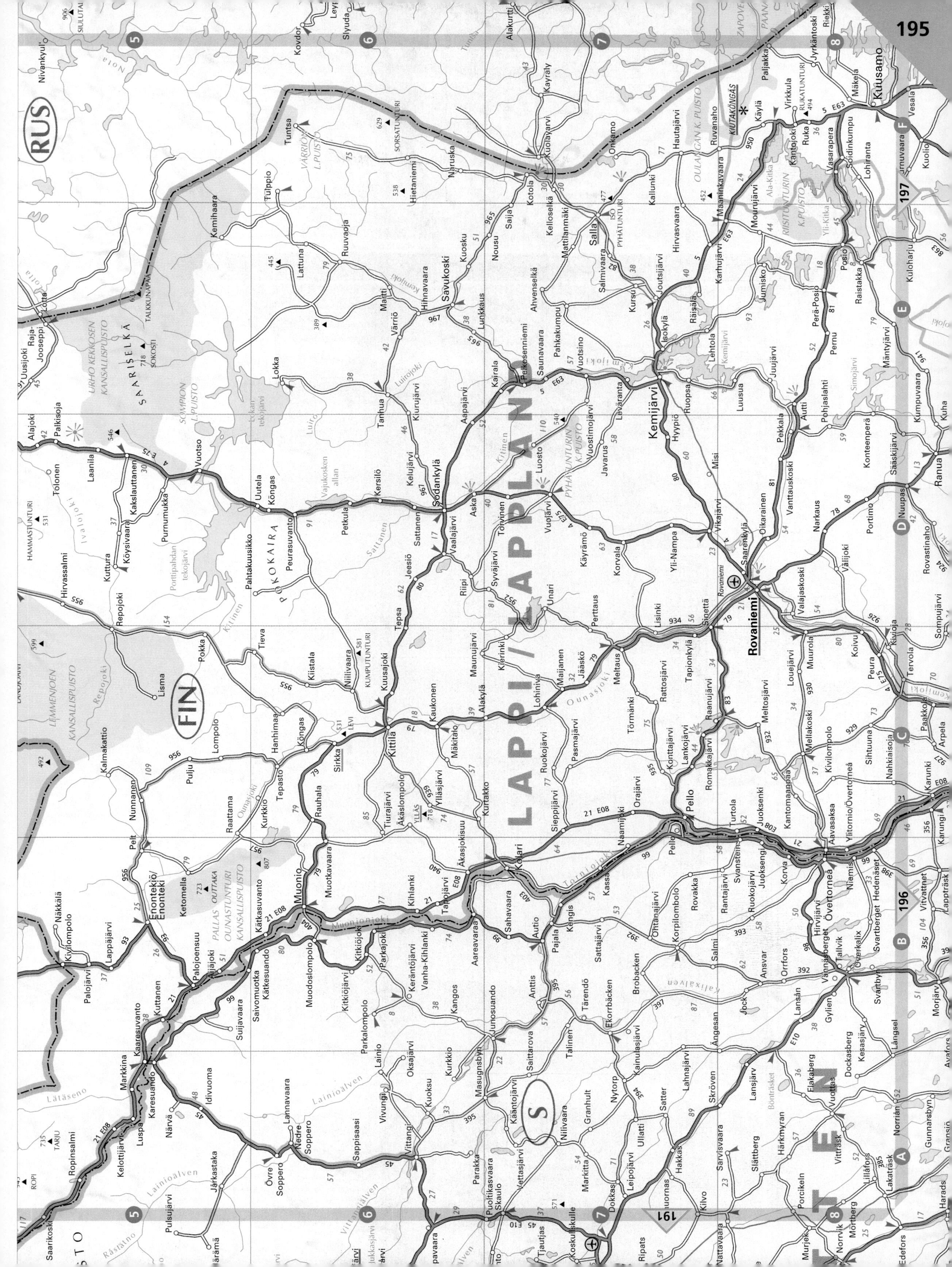
RUS
FIN
S
LAPPI / LAPPLAND
Rovaniemi
Kemijärvi
Sodankylä
Kittilä
Muonio
Pello
Kolari
Salla
Savukoski
Kuusamo
Posio
Ranua
Tervola
Ylitornio/Övertorneå
Övertorneå
Pajala
Enontekiö/Enonteki
Karesuando
Vittangi
Sirkka
Levi
Äkäslompolo
Ylläs
Luosto
Pelkosenniemi
Saarenkylä
Sinettä
Kiutaköngäs
Urho Kekkosen kansallispuisto
Pallas Ounastunturi kansallispuisto
Lemmenjoen kansallispuisto
Pyhätunturin k.puisto
Oulangan k. puisto
Riisitunturin k.puisto
Sompion l.puisto
Värriön l.puisto
Pokokaira
Saariselkä
Lokan tekojärvi
Porttipahdan tekojärvi
Kemijoki
Ounasjoki
Tornionjoki
Muonionjoki
Lainioälven
Kalixälven
E8
E10
E63
E75
191
196
197

193
195
191
186
187
A
B
C
D
1
2
3
4
5
6
820
DUNDRET
MUDDUS NATIONALPARK
Stora Luleälven
Jokkmokk
Lilla Luleälven
Liggavägen
Fatjas
Njetsavare
Murjek
Porcikeln
Kaskats
Vuollerim
Norrvik
Mörtberg
Lillåfors
Lakaträsk
Edefors
Sudok
Stenträsk
Vuottaure
Snesudden
Bodträskfors
Harads
Svartlå
Gransjö
Gunnarsbyn
Norrån
Vitträsk
Vuottas
Hapträsk
Vitberget
Vittjärv
Boden
Ängesbyn
Sävast
Unbyn
Persön
Gammelstaden
Luleå
Rutvik
Pålsträsk
Alvik
Klöverträsk
Antnäs
Ersnäs
Måttsund
Sandön
Germandön
Kallfjärden
Rosvik
Norrfjärden
Öjebyn
Piteå
Bergsviken
Roknäs
Lillpite
Önusberg
Långträsk
Holmfors
Koler
Sikfors
Storsund
Dartsel
Grundsel
Älvsbyn
Vistheden
Piltträsk
Bredsel
Vidsel
Brännberg
Ö.Tväråsel
Piteälven
Vuotner
Siksjön
Grönbo
Stensträsk
Hemmingsmark
Jävre
Fällfors
Ålund
Åbyälven
Kinnbäck
Selet
Stavaträsk
Jörn
Retikträsk
Lillkågeträsk
Åbyn
Drängsmark
Byske
Strömfors
Kusmark
Renfors
Boliden
Bjursele
Svartnäs
Kåge
Ostvik
Åliden
Klintfors
Bastuträsk
Skellefteå
Skelleftestrand
Skelleftehamn
Orviken
Rönnskär
Skelleftebukten
Bureå
Medle
Langviken
Liden
Långvattnet
Järvtjärn
Burvik
Övre Bäck
Bjuröklubb
Lappvattnet
Burträsk
Villvattnet
Andersfors
Lövånger
KYRKSTAD
Bygdeträsk
Vebomark
Bjurfors
Floda
Bygdsiljum
Ytteräträsk
Ånäset
Skäran
Gumboda
Botsmark
Åkullsjön
Robertsfors
Sikeå
Buberget
Vindeln
Överrödå
Gravmark
V. Sjulsmark
Kroksjö
Tavelsjö
Tväråbäck
Tvärålund
Bullmark
Bygdeå
Ratan
Vännäsby
Ersmark
Sävar
Brännland
STORNORRFORS
Djäkneböle
Umeå
Ostnäs
Holmön
Skeppsvik
Ängesön
Holmsund
Obbola
Gräsmyr
Sörmjöle
Hörnefors
Västra Kvarken
Mjölefjärden
Kråkan
Järnäsklubb
Norra Gloppet
Östra Gloppet
Björköby
Värlax
Dokkas
Leipojärvi
Ullatti
Nytorp
Ekorrbäcken
Kainulasjärvi
Brobacken
Satter
Palohuornas
Hakkas
Kilvo
Nattavaara
Sarvisvaara
Slättberg
Härkmyran
Skröven
Lahnajärvi
Ängesan
Lansjärv
Bönträsket
Flakaberg
Gylien
Dockasberg
Kesasjärvi
Svartbyn
Långsel
Morjärv
Avafors
Niemisel
Skogså
Töre
Råneå
Jämtön
Påläng
Nyborg
Bergön
Rånön
Gunnarsfjärden
Harufjärden
Kalix
Karlsborg
Sangis
Haparanda
Nikkala
Seskarön
Pukkofjärden
HAPARANDA SKÄRGÅRDS NATIONALPARK
Borielsbyn
Lappträsk
Korpikå
Vitvattnet
Karungi
Tornio/Torneå
KUKKOLANKOSKI
Kalixälven
Jock
Salmi
Ansvar
Orrfors
Lansån
Vännäsberget
Tallvik
Överkalix
Svartberget
Hedenäset
Hirvijärvi
Övertorneå
Niemis
Ohtanajärvi
Korpilombolo
Rovakka
Rantajärvi
Svanstein
Ruokojärvi
Juoksengi
Korva
Kassa
Naamijoki
Pello
Turtola
Juoksenki
Kantomaanpää
Aavasaksa
Ylitornio/Övertorneå
Mellakoski
Kivilompolo
Sihtuuna
Nahkiaisoja
Karunki
Arpela
Paakkola
Kemijoki
Maula
Liedakkala
Keminmaa
Kemi
Ajos
Hepola
Simo
PERÄMEREN KANSALLISPUISTO
Törmänki
Meltaus
Konttajärvi
Lankojärvi
Romakkajärvi
Raanujärvi
Rattosjärvi
Tapionkylä
Meltosjärvi
Louejärvi
Muurola
Koivu
Peura
Tervola
Kivioja
Sompujärvi
Taininiemi
Huhtala
Yli-Kärppä
Korvala
Lisinki
Yli-Nampa
Sinettä
Rovaniemi
Vikajärvi
Misi
Saarenkylä
Oikarainen
Vanttauskoski
Valajaskoski
Narkaus
Välijoki
Portimo
Nuupas
Rovastinaho
Simojoki
Ranua
Valajanaapa
Asmunt
Harjula
Oijärvi
Hyry
Kuivaniemi
Yli-Olhava
Tannila
Ohlava
Yli-Ii
Haapala
Iijoki
Ii
Jakkukylä
Alakylä
Kaarela
Haukipudas
Kiiminki
Jääli
Hailuoto
Marjaniemi
Hailuoto/Karlö
OULU/ULEÅBORG
Madekoski
Oulunsalo
Oulu
Kempele
Laukka
Lumijoenselkä
Luodonselkä
Varjakka
Karinkanta
Liminka/Limingo
Soso
Muhos
Siikajoki
Keskikylä
Lumijoki
Ala-Temmes
Tyrnävä
Temmes
Raahe/Brahestad
Revonlahti
Pattijoki
Ruukki
Jokikylä
Tuomioja
Paavola
Kärsämä
Kylmälä
Haapajoki
Kopsa
Rantsila
Rankinen
Vihanti
Isokylä
Alpua
Pyhäjoki
Kopisto
Lampinsaari
Liminkakylä
Yppäri
Korvenkylä
Karhukangas
Terskanperä
Vasankari
Merijärvi
Oulainen
Mehtäkylä
Pirnespera
Latva
Pulkkila
Kalajoki
Mieluskylä
Leskelä
Tynkä
Alavieska
Rytkynkylä
Haapavesi
Himankakylä
Pahkala
Kangas
Ylivieska
Kantokylä
Rautio
Raudaskylä
Alajoki
Porkkala
Lohtaja/Lochteå
Himanka
Hillilä
Huhtapuhto
Suotuperä
Kärsämäki
Märsylä
Kannus
Eskola
Nivala
Maliskylä
Kuusaa
Marinkainen
Sievi
Jokikylä
Ojakylä
Vuolle
Aittoperä
Parkkila
Kokkola/Karleby
Oksava
Parkkima
Oja
Kälviä/Kelviå
Kiiskilä
Haapajärvi
Kuona
Pyhäsalmi
Holm
Luoto/Larsmo
Aivo/Oivu
Nedervetil/Alaveteli
Toholampi
Pietarsaari/Jakobstad
Kruunupyy/Kronoby
Ullava
Korpi
Reisjärvi
Kalaja
Pitäjänmäki
Pirttiniemi
Torsön
Esse/Ähtävä
Teerijärvi/Terjärv
Sykäräinen
Lestijärvi
Muurasjärvi
Alvajärvi
Elämäjärvi
Uusikaarlepyy/Nykarleby
Pedersöre
Sisbacka
Kaustinen/Kaustby
Kainu
Yli-Lesti
Kärväs
Lillby
Lappfors
Veteli/Vetil
Halsua
Kangaskylä
Kinnula
Pihtipudas
Munsala
Monäs
Ytterjeppo
Räyrinki
Salamajärvi
Muhola
Evijärvi
Kortesjärvi
Lammi
Oksakoski
Permo
SALAMAJÄRVEN K.PUISTO
Oravainen/Oravais
Kaitsor
Voltti
Viitasaari
Bottniska viken/
Pohjanlahti
E04
E08
E10
E12
E75

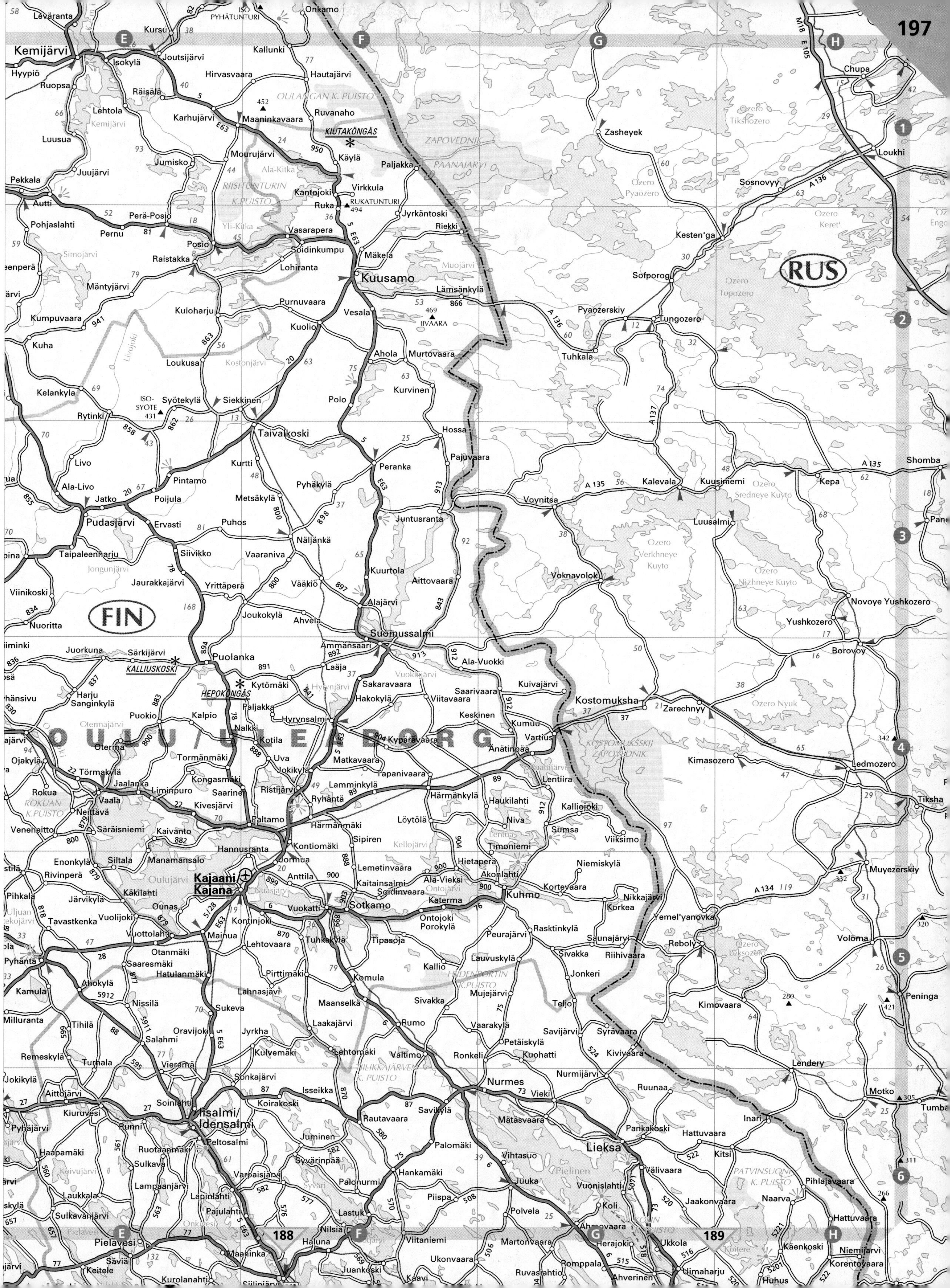
Leväranta
Kemijärvi
Isokylä
Joutsijärvi
Kursu
ISO PYHÄTUNTURI
Onkamo
Kallunki
Hautajärvi
Hyypiö
Ruopsa
Hirvasvaara
Räisälä
OULANGAN K. PUISTO
Lehtola
Kemijärvi
Karhujärvi
Maaninkavaara
Ruvanaho
KIUTAKÖNGÄS
Luusua
ZAPOVEDNIK
Jumisko
Mourujärvi
Käylä
Paljakka
PAANAJARVI
Juujärvi
Ala-Kitka
Pekkala
RIISITUNTURIN K.PUISTO
Kantojoki
Virkkula
Autti
Ruka
RUKATUNTURI
Pohjaslahti
Perä-Posio
Jyrkäntoski
Pernu
Yli-Kitka
Riekki
Vasarapera
Posio
Simojärvi
Soidinkumpu
Mäkelä
Raistakka
Lohiranta
Muojärvi
Kuusamo
Mäntyjärvi
Lämsänkylä
Kuloharju
Purnuvaara
Vesala
IIVAARA
Kumpuvaara
Kuolio
Kuha
Livojoki
Loukusa
Kostonjärvi
Ahola
Murtovaara
Kurvinen
Kelankylä
ISO-SYÖTE
Syötekylä
Siekkinen
Polo
Rytinki
Taivalkoski
Hossa
Pajuvaara
Livo
Kurtti
Peranka
Ala-Livo
Pintamo
Pyhäkylä
Jatko
Poijula
Metsäkylä
Juntusranta
Pudasjärvi
Ervasti
Puhos
Näljänkä
Taipaleenharju
Siivikko
Vaaraniva
Jongunjärvi
Kuurtola
Jaurakkajärvi
Yrittäperä
Vääkiö
Aittovaara
Viinikoski
Alajärvi
FIN
Joukokylä
Ahvela
Nuoritta
Suomussalmi
Ämmänsaari
Juorkuna
Särkijärvi
Puolanka
Laaja
Ala-Vuokki
KALLIUSKOSKI
Kytömäki
Vuokkijärvi
Sakaravaara
Saarivaara
Kuivajärvi
HEPOKONGAS
Hyrynjärvi
Hakokylä
Viitavaara
Harju
Sanginkylä
Paljakka
Puokio
Kalpio
Hyrynsalmi
Keskinen
Kumuu
Otermanjärvi
OULU/ULEÅBORG
Nalkki
Kotila
Kypärävaara
Vartius
Oterma
Änätinpää
Ojakylä
Uva
Törmänmäki
Matkavaara
Törmäkylä
Jokikylä
Tapanivaara
Kongasmäki
Lamminkylä
Lentiira
Jaalanka
Liminpuro
Saarinen
Ristijärvi
Rokua
Vaala
Ryhäntä
Härmänkylä
ROKUAN K.PUISTO
Neittävä
Kivesjärvi
Haukilahti
Kalliojoki
Paltamo
Löytölä
Niva
Veneheitto
Säräisniemi
Kaivanto
Härmänmäki
Sumsa
Lentua
Viiksimo
Sipiren
Kontiomäki
Timoniemi
Hannusranta
Kellojärvi
Enonkylä
Siltala
Manamansalo
Jormua
Hietaperä
Niemiskylä
Rivinperä
Oulujärvi
Kajaani
Kajana
Lemetinvaara
Ala-Vieksi
Akonlahti
Anttila
Kaitainsalmi
Pihkala
Käkilahti
Soidinvaara
Ontojärvi
Kortevaara
Nikkajärvi
Järvikylä
Nuasjärvi
Kuhmo
Ounas
Vuokatti
Sotkamo
Katerma
Korkea
Uljuan tekojärvi
Tavastkenka
Vuolijoki
Kontinjoki
Ontojoki
Porokylä
Rasktinkylä
Vuottolahti
Mainua
Tuhkakylä
Tipasoja
Peurajärvi
Saunajärvi
Otanmäki
Lehtovaara
Sivakka
Riihivaara
Pyhäntä
Saaresmäki
Lauvuskylä
Hatulanmäki
Pirttimäki
Kallio
Jonkeri
HIIDENPORTIN K.PUISTO
Kamula
Ahokylä
Komula
Lahnasjärvi
Mujejärvi
Nissilä
Sivakka
Teljo
Milluranta
Sukeva
Maanselkä
Tihilä
Oravijoki
Laakajärvi
Rumo
Vaarakylä
Salahmi
Jyrkha
Savijärvi
Syrävaara
Remeskylä
Petäiskylä
Kulvemäki
Lehtomäki
Valtimo
Ronkeli
Kuohatti
Kivivaara
Turhala
Vieremä
HIIDENPORTIN... K.PUISTO
Nurmijärvi
Jokikylä
Sonkajärvi
Nurmes
Aittojärvi
Isseikka
Vieki
Ruunaa
Soinlahti
Koirakoski
Kiuruvesi
Iisalmi
Idensalmi
Rautavaara
Savikylä
Mätäsvaara
Pyhäjärvi
Runni
Peltosalmi
Juminen
Palomäki
Lieksa
Pankakoski
Hattuvaara
Haapamäki
Ruotaanmäki
Syvärinpää
Vihtasuo
Kitsi
Sulkava
Keivujärvi
Varpaisjärvi
Hankamäki
Pielinen
Välivaara
PATVINSUON K. PUISTO
Lampaanjärvi
Syväri
Palonurmi
Juuka
Vuonislahti
Koli
Laukkala
Lapinlahti
Piispa
Jaakonvaara
Pihlajavaara
Sulkavanjärvi
Pajulahti
Lastuk
Polvela
Naarva
Onkivesi
Hattuvaara
Pielavesi
188
Nilsiä
KOLIN PUISTO
189
Ahmovaara
Käenkoski
Pielavesi
Maaninka
Haluna
Viitaniemi
Martonvaara
Herajoki
Ukkola
Koitere
Niemijärvi
Säviä
Keitele
Juankoski
Ukonvaara
Kurolanahti
Siilinjärvi
Kaavi
Ruvaslahti
Romppala
Uimaharju
Ahveninen
Huhus
Korentovaara
Zasheyek
Ozero Tikshozero
Chupa
Loukhi
Sosnovyy
Ozero Pyaozero
Ozero Keret'
Kesten'ga
RUS
Sofporog
Ozero Topozero
Pyaozerskiy
Tungozero
Tuhkala
Shomba
Kepa
Kalevala
Kuusiniemi
Ozero Sredneye Kuyto
Voynitsa
Luusalmi
Ozero Verkhneye Kuyto
Voknavolok
Ozero Nizhneye Kuyto
Novoye Yushkozero
Yushkozero
Borovoy
Kostomuksha
Zarechnyy
Ozero Nyuk
KOSTOMUKSSKIJ ZAPOVEDNIK
Kimasozero
Ledmozero
Tiksha
Muyezerskiy
Yemel'yanovka
Reboly
Voloma
Ozero Leksozero
Peninga
Kimovaara
Lendery
Motko
Inari
Tumba

A
B
C
D
176
177
169
200
246
239
1
2
3
4
5
6
FIN
LT
Herröskkatan
Kökar
Jurmo
SKÄARGÅRDSHAVETS NATIONALPARK
SAARISTOMEREN KANSALLISPUISTO
Hitis/
Hiitinen
Rosala
Hangö/
Ha
Lappvik/
Lappohja
Helsinki
Hangö västra
fjärd
Rostock
Stockholm
Rostock
Naissaar
Aegna
Rohu
TALLINN
Keila-Joa
Paldiski
Saue
Keila
Vasalemma
Nova
Kirikküla
Hageri
Riisipere
Hara
Valgeristi
Turba
Varbola
Vormsi
Norbi
Risti
Hiiumaa
Kärdla
Haapsalu
Rohuküla
Märjamaa
Koluvere
Napi
Luidja
Ristna
Heltermaa
Suuremõisa
Käina
Kassari
Martna
Vana-Vigala
Järvakan
Puise
MATSALU
NAT. PARK
Lihula
Kirbla
Kivi-
Vigala
Väinameri
Emmaste
Muhu
Liiva
Kuivastu
Virtsu
Karuse
Kõima
Pärnu-
Jaagup
Koonga
Leisi
Orissaare
Metsküla
Tagaranna
Undva
Vohma
Pamma
Pöide
Kalli
Varbla
Audru
Pärnu
Mustjala
Kurevere
VILSANDI
NATIONAL PARK
Kihelkonna
Kaarma
Kõljala
Sandla
Saaremaa
Murru
Lao
Kogula
Karala
Kipi
Kuressaare
Võiske
Siare
Kihnu
Salme
Lõmala
RIIA LAHT
Häädemeeste
Jamaja
Mäebe
Mässa
Sääre
Ainaži
Ruhnu
Salacgrīva
Holmudden
Fårö
Irbeni väin/
Irves šaurums
Kolka
Mazirbe
SLITERE
REZERVĀTS
Ezermuiža
RĪGAS JŪRAS
LĪCIS
Tūja
Laži
Dundaga
Roja
Ance
Nynäshamn
Ventspils
Pope
Valdemārpils
Nogale
Mērsrags
Skulte
Saulkrasti
Ciruli
Lilaste
Ugāle
Talsi
Nurmulža
Leči
Spare
Usma
Engure
Piltene
Stende
Garkalne
Kandava
RĪGA
Sarnate
Renda
Kupli
Ragaciems
Kāpas
Sabile
Tukums
Jūrmala
Edole
Kabile
Zemīte
Rīga
Labrags
Alsunga
Kuldīga
Vāne
Kalnciems
Ķekava
Pavilosta
Basi
Zante
Olaine
Baldo
Lutrini
Remte
Jaunpils
Pikšas
Lankas
Broceni
Dobele
Jelgava
Garoza
Iecava
Ziemupe
Aizpute
Skrunda
Saldus
Gluda
Medze
Mazilmaja
Durbe
Jauniniumuiža
Ezernijeki
Code
Kursiši
Pujjas
Bauska
Rostock
Karlshamn
Liepāja
Grobina
Krote
Embute
Auce
Bene
Eleja
PILSRUNDALE
Vajnede
Ruba
Ukri
Žagari
Priekule
Ezere
Naujoji
Akmanė
Kiburi
Gramzda
Mažeikiai
Joniškis
Bernati
Viekšniai
Pašvitinys
Skuodas
Ylakiai
Akmyanė
Venta
Lunkuva
Barstyčiai
Papile
Rucava
Seda
Gruzdžiai
Pape
Varduva
Tryškiai
Salantai
Kuršėnai
Pakruojis
Darbėnai
Telšiai
Šiauliai

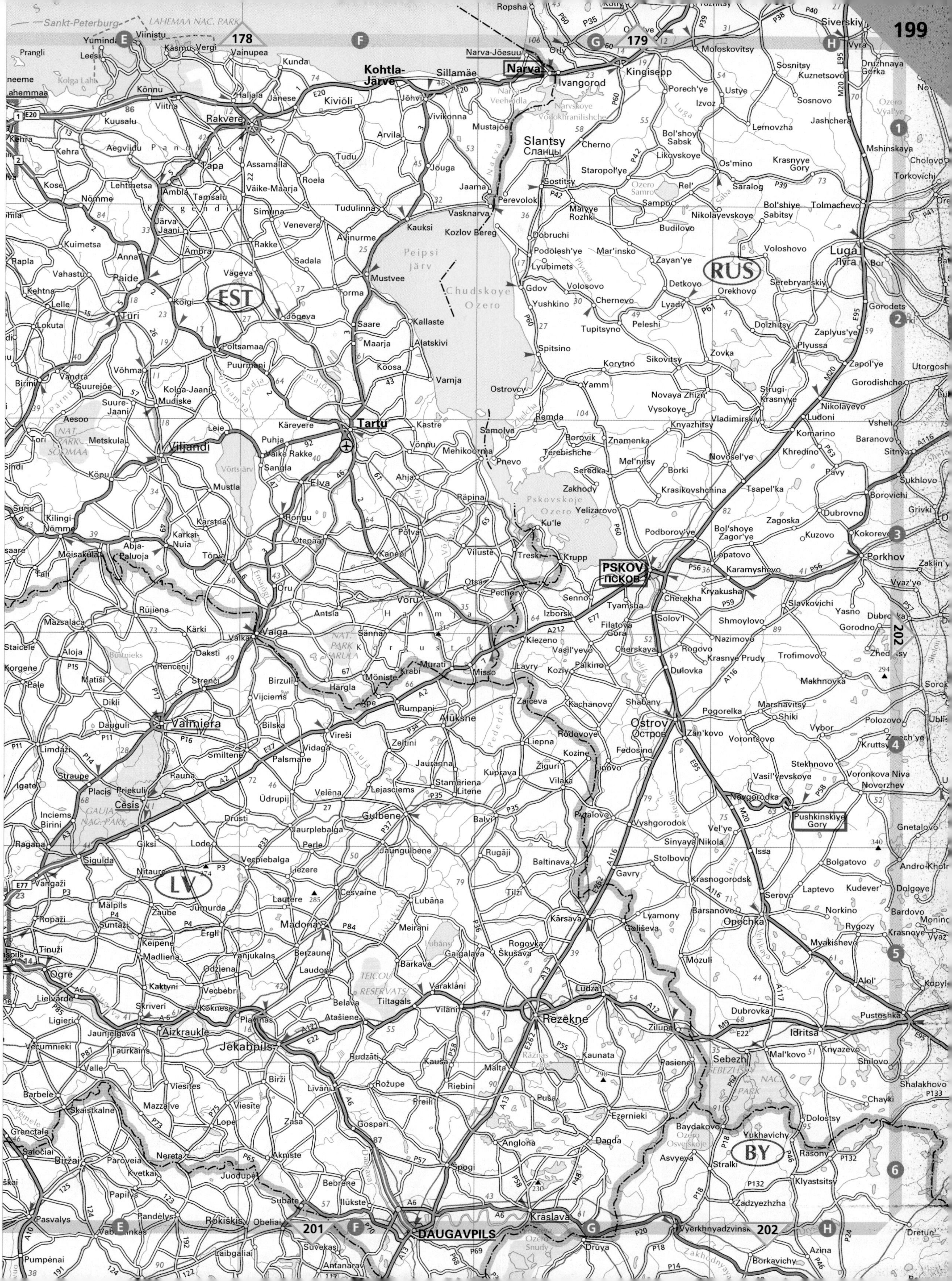

Sankt-Peterburg
LAHEMAA NAC. PARK
178
179
Ropsha
Siverskiy
Vyra
Yuminda
Viinistu
Prangli
Leesi
Kolga Laht
Lahemmaa
Käsmu
Vergi
Vainupea
Kunda
Kohtla-Järve
Sillamäe
Narva-Jõesuu
Narva
Ivangorod
Kingisepp
Moloskovitsy
Druzhnaya Gorka
Haljala
Könnu
Viitna
Rakvere
Kiviõli
Jõhvi
Vivikonna
Mustajõe
Narvskoye Vodokhranilishche
Porech'ye
Ustye
Izvoz
Sosnitsy
Kuznetsovo
Sosnovo
Lemovzha
Jashchera
Kuusalu
Kehra
Aegviidu
Pandivere
Tapa
Assamalla
Tudu
Arvila
Jõuga
Slantsy
Сланцы
Cherno
Bol'shoy Sabsk
Likovskoye
Os'mino
Krasnyye Gory
Mshinskaya
Cholovo
Torkovichi
Kose
Lehtmetsa
Ambla
Tamsalu
Väike-Maarja
Roela
Jaama
Perevolok
Gostitsy
Staropol'ye
Ozero Samro
Sampo
Rel'
Saralog
Nõmme
Korgendik
Simuna
Tudulinna
Vasknarva
Malyye Rozhki
Nikolayevskoye
Bol'shiye Sabitsy
Tolmachevo
Järva-Jaani
Venevere
Avinurme
Kauksi
Kozlov Bereg
Dobruchi
Budilovo
Rapla
Kuimetsa
Anna
Ämbra
Rakke
Peipsi Järv
Podolesh'ye
Mar'insko
Zayan'ye
Voloshovo
Luga
Луга
Bor
Vahastu
Paide
Vägeva
Sadala
Mustvee
Lyubimets
RUS
Kehtna
Lelle
EST
Kõrgi
Torma
Chudskoye Ozero
Gdov
Volosovo
Detkovo
Orekhovo
Serebryanskiy
Yushkino
Chernevo
Lyady
Gorodets
Lokuta
Türi
Jõgeva
Kallaste
Tupitsyno
Peleshi
Dolzhitsy
Zaplyus'ye
Saare
Maarja
Alatskivi
Spitsino
Plyussa
Vändra
Võhma
Põltsamaa
Puurmani
Koosa
Varnja
Korytno
Sikovitsy
Zovka
Zapol'ye
Utorgosh
Birini
Suurejõe
Kolga-Jaani
Mudiske
Ostrovcy
Yamm
Strugi-Krasnyye
Gorodishche
Suure-Jaani
Novaya Zhizn'
Vysokoye
Nikolayevo
Aesoo
NAT. PARK SOOMAA
Kärevere
Tartu
Kastre
Remda
Vladimirskiy
Ludoni
Vsheli
Tori
Metskula
Leie
Puhja
Väike Rakke
Samolva
Borovik
Znamenka
Knyazhitsy
Komarino
Baranovo
Viljandi
Võrtsjärv
Sangla
Võnnu
Mehikoorma
Pnevo
Terebishche
Novosel'ye
Khredino
Sitnya
Sindi
Köpu
Mustla
Elva
Ahja
Seredka
Mel'nitsy
Borki
Pavy
Sukhlovo
Zakhody
Krasikovshchina
Tsapel'ka
Borovichi
Räpina
Pskovskoye Ozero
Yelizarovo
Dubrovno
Grivki
Surju
Kilingi-Nõmme
Kärstna
Rõngu
Põlva
Ku'le
Podborov'ye
Bol'shoye Zagor'ye
Zagoska
Kuzovo
Kokorevo
Karksi-Nuia
Abja-Paluoja
Mõisaküla
Otepää
Kanepi
Viluste
Treski
Krupp
PSKOV
ПСКОВ
Lopatovo
Karamyshevo
Porkhov
Zaklin'ye
Tali
Tõrva
Oru
Otsa
Pechory
Senno
Cherekha
Kryakusha
Vyaz'ye
Võru
Izborsk
Tyamsha
Slavkovichi
Rüjiena
Antsla
Haanja
Filatova Gora
Solov'i
Shmoylovo
Yasno
Mazsalaca
Kärki
Valga
Valka
Sänna
NAT. PARK KARULA
Kõrgustik
Klezeno
Nazimovo
Gorodno
Staicele
Aloja
Burtnieks
Dakstī
Rencēni
Vasil'yevo
Cherskaya
Rogovo
Krasnyye Prudy
Trofimovo
Korgene
Matīši
Strenči
Birzuli
Mõniste
Krabi
Murati
Misso
Lavry
Kozly
Palkino
Dulovka
Makhnovka
Pale
Vijciems
Hargla
Ape
Zaiceva
Kachanovo
Shabany
Pogorelka
Marshavitsy
Shiki
Polozovo
Dikli
Valmiera
Rumpani
Alūksne
Ostrov
Остров
Zan'kovo
Vybor
Dauguli
Bilska
Vireši
Zeltini
Liepna
Rodovoye
Fedosino
Vorontsovo
Kruttsy
Limdaži
Smiltene
Vidaga
Palsmane
Gauja
Jaunanna
Kozine
Žiguri
Linovo
Stekhnovo
Straupe
Rauna
Kuprava
Vilaka
Vasil'yevskoye
Voronkova Niva
Novorzhev
Igate
Placis
Priekuli
Cēsis
Velēna
Lejasciems
Stameriena
Litene
Novgorodka
Pushkinskiye Gory
Inciems
Birini
GAUJA NAC. PARK
Ūdrupij
Gulbene
Balvi
Pytalovo
Vyshgorodok
Vel'ye
Gnetalovo
Ragana
Drusti
Jaurplebalga
Sinyaya
Nikola
Issa
Giksi
Lode
Perle
Jaungulbene
Rugāji
Stolbovo
Bolgatovo
Sigulda
Nitaure
Vecpiebalga
Liezere
Baltinava
Gavry
Andro-Kholm
Vangaži
LV
Cesvaine
Tilži
Krasnogorodsk
Laptevo
Kudever'
Dolgove
Lautere
Lubāna
Serovo
Mālpils
Jūmurda
Zaube
Kārsava
Lyamony
Barsanovo
Opochka
Norkino
Bardovo
Ropaži
Suntaži
Ērgli
Madona
Meirāni
Goliševa
Rygozy
Krasnoye
Keipene
Lubāns
Gaigalava
Šķilbēni
Rogovka
Myakishevo
Tinuži
Madliena
Jaunjukalns
Berzaune
Barkava
Mozuli
Ogre
Odziena
Laudona
TEICU RESERVATS
Kaktyni
Vecbebri
Varaklāni
Tiltagals
Ludza
Alol'
Kopyl
Lielvārde
Skrīveri
Koknese
Belava
Pļaviņas
Atašiene
Viļāni
Rēzekne
Zilupe
Dubrovka
Pustoshka
Ligieri
Jaunjelgava
Aizkraukle
Idritsa
Vecumnieki
Taurkains
Jēkabpils
Rudzāti
Kauša
Riebini
Malta
Kaunata
Rāznas Ezers
Pasiene
Sebezh
Mal'kovo
Knyazevo
Shilovo
Valle
Birži
Līvāni
Rožupe
Preiļi
Puša
SEBEZHSKIY NAC. PARK
Shalakhovo
Barbele
Viesītes
Chayki
Skaistkalne
Mazzalve
Viesite
Ezernieki
Dolostsy
Lope
Zasa
Gospari
Baydakovo
Ozero Osveyskoye
Yukhavichy
Grenctale
Saločiai
Biržai
Paroveia
Nereta
Akniste
Anglona
Dagda
Asvyeya
Stralki
BY
Rasony
Kvetkai
Juodupė
Spogi
Klyastsitsy
Papilys
Bebrene
Zadzyezhzha
Pasvalys
Pandėlys
Subate
Ilūkste
Krāslava
Vabalninkas
Rokiškis
Obeliai
201
DAUGAVPILS
Vyerkhnyadzvinsk
202
Dretun'
Pumpėnai
Laibgaliai
Suvekas
Antanarav
Druya
Ozero Snudy
Borkavichy
Azina
Zakhodnyaya
E20
E77
E22
E95
E262
M20
M9
A2
A3
A6
A12
A13
A116
A117
A212
P39
P42
P56
P59
P61
P63

A
B
C
D
198
163
1
2
3
4
5
6
23
24
S
GOTLAND
Gotland
Visby
Högklint
Gnisvärd
Eskelhem
Klintehamn
Fröjel
L. Karlsö
St. Karlsö
DJAUVIK
Sproge
Hemse
Hablingbo
Havdhem
Ronehamn
Burgsvik
Faludden
Sallmunds
Sundre
Hoburgen
Barlingbo
Roma
Isums
Ala
Hejde
Buttle
TORSBURGEN
Lojsta
Lye
Burs
Ljugarn
Katthammarsvik
Gothem
Bro
Bäl
Slite
Tingstäde
Lärbro
Kyllaj
Kappelshamn
Hallshuk
Lickershamn
LUMMELUNDAGROTTORNA
Lauter
Fårö
Fårösund
Holmudden
Nynäshamn
Maarianhamina
Oskarshamn
Ölands norra udde
Grankullavik
Byxelkrok
Böda
Löttorp-Hög
Mäebe
Mässa
Sääre
Irbeni väin
Irves Šaurums
Mazirbe
Laži
Ance
Nynäshamn
Ventspils
Pope
Ugāle
Spāre
Usma
Leči
Piltene
Sarnate
Kapas
Renda
Ēdole
Labrags
Alsunga
Kuldīga
Pavilosta
Basi
Lankas
Ziemupe
Aizpute
Skrunda
Medze
Durbe
Mazilmaja
Liepāja
Grobiņa
Krote
Embūte
Vajnede
Priekule
Gramzda
Rostock
Karlshamn
Kiburi
Bernati
Skuodas
Ylakiai
Rucava
Barstyčiai
Mosėdis
Varduva
Seda
Pape
Salantai
Darbėnai
Palanga
Plungė
Kretinga
Kartena
Kuliai
Rietavas
Karlshamn
Fredericia
København
Sassnitz
Kiel
KLAIPĖDA
Gargždai
A1
E85
A13
KURŠIU NERIJOS
NACIONALINIS PARKAS
Veiviržėnai
Kvėdarna
Priekulė
Švėkšna
Saugos
Kintai
Vainutas
Neringa
Neringa-Nida
Ventė
Šilutė
Kuršiu Nerija
Kuršiu marios
Rusnė
Žemaičių Naumiestis
Juknaičiai
Katyčiai
Morskoye
Mysovka
Rybachiy
Kurshskiy Zaliv
Kurshskaya Kosa
Timiryazevo
Pagegiai
Sovetsk
Neman
Slavsk
Matrosovo
NAC. P. KURSHSKAYA KOSA
RUS
Gromovo
Bol'shakovo
Kalinovka
Svetlogorsk
Pionerskiy
Zelenogradsk
Kashirskoye
Zalivnoye
Polessk
Yantarnyy
Kaliningrad
KALININGRAD
КАЛИНИНГРАД
Primorsk
Chernyakhovsk
Черняховск
Baltiysk
Svetlyy
Gvardeysk
Znamensk
Ushakovo
Svoboda
Yuzhnyy
Chekhovo
Tishino
Gvardeiskoye
Domnovo
Pravdinsk
Luzhki
Mamonovo
Bagrationovsk
Zhelenodorozhnyy
Krylovo
Shirokoye
Kaliningradskiy Zaliv
Zalew Wiślany
Karlskrona
Nynäshamn
Rostock
Travemünde
PL
NADMORSKI PARK KRAJOBRAZOWY
Władysławowo
Łeba
Krokowa
Wielka Piaśnica
Puck
Zatoka Pucka
Hel
Żelazno
Wicko
Kluki
Główczyce
Wejherowo
Rumia
Lębork
GDYNIA
Sopot
Zatoka Gdańska
Nowa Karczma
PARK KRAJOBR. MIERZEJA WIŚLANA
Damno
Objazda
Łebno
Chwaszczyno
Osowo Lęborskie
Lupawa
Czarna Dąbrówka
Dębnica Kaszubska
Kartuzy
GDAŃSK
Żukowo
Kolbudy
Górne
Pruszcz Gdański
Sierakowice
Suchorze
Stegna
Pogrodzie
Frombork
Braniewo
Lelkowo
Górowo Iławeckie
Pieniężno
Bartoszyce
Galiny
Węgorzewo
Garbno
Kętrzyn
Giżycko
Nowy Dwór Gdański
Nowica
ELBLĄG
Łęgowo
Nowa Karczma
Pomysk Mały
Bytów
Lubno
Ornęta
Lidzbark
Bisztynek
Godkowo
STOCZEK KLASZTORNY
E28
E77
A229
A196
A197
A194
A195
A192
A193
A191
A190
A216
A186
P512
P514
P508
P515
P513
P516
A11
A10
A9
P112
P108
P124
E272
E28
E77

RĪGAS JŪRAS LĪCIS
Ruhnu
Ainaži
Mazsalaca
Staicele
Aloja
Salacgrīva
Korgene
Matīši
Pāle
Kārki
Valka
Valga
Dakstī
Rencēni
Strenči
Birzuli
Vijciems
Hargla
Mõniste
Krabi
Misso
Murati
Ape
Rumpani
Aluksne
Zaiceva
Dikli
Valmiera
Dauguli
Bilska
Vireši
Zeltini
Tūja
Limdaži
Smiltene
Palsmane
Vidaga
Jauranna
Kuprava
Žiguri
Vilaka
Straupe
Rauna
Stameriena
Litene
Igate
Placis
Priekuli
Cēsis
Lejasciems
Velēna
Skulte
Inciems
Birini
GAUJAS NAC. PARK
Ūdrupij
Gulbene
Balvi
Saulkrasti
Drusti
Jaurplebalga
Lode
LV
Perle
Rugāji
Lilaste
Ragana
Giksi
Jaunguibene
Sigulda
Nitaure
Vecpiebalga
Liezere
Baltinava
Kolka
Ezermuiža
Roja
Valdemārpils
Nogale
Mērsrags
Talsi
Nurmulža
Engure
Kandava
Sabile
Kabile
Vāne
Kupli
Tukums
Ragaciems
Jūrmala
RĪGA
Zemīte
Zante
Lutrini
Jaunpils
Remte
Broceni
Saldus
Dobele
Jelgava
Kalnciems
Pikšas
Olaine
Kekava
Baldone
Salaspils
Ogre
Tinuži
Vangaži
Garkalne
Ropaži
Mālpils
Suntaži
Zaube
Jumurda
Lautere
Cesvaine
Lubāna
Tilži
Kārsav
Madona
Meirani
Ergli
Keipene
Madliena
Jaunjukalns
Berzaune
Gaigalava
Šķušava
Rogo
Odziena
Laudona
Barkava
Kaktyni
Vecbebri
Teicou Reservats
Varakļāni
Tiltagals
Lielvarde
Ligieri
Skriveri
Koknese
Plavinas
Belava
Atašiene
Viļāni
Rezekn
Jaunjelgava
Aizkraukle
Jēkabpils
Garoza
Iecava
Vecumnieki
Taurkains
Valle
Rudzāti
Kauša
Malta
Gluda
Ezernijeki
Pujjas
Kursiši
Bene
Eleja
Bauska
Code
Barbele
Skaistkalne
Viesites
Birži
Livāni
Rožupe
Riebini
Preili
Puša
Mazzalve
Viesite
Lope
Zasa
Gospari
Auce
Ukri
Žagari
PILSRUNDĀLE
Grenctale
Saločiai
Nereta
Akniste
Anglona
Ezere
Ruba
Mažeikiai
Naujoji Akmenė
Viekšniai
Akmyane
Joniškis
Biržai
Vaškai
Paroveja
Kvetkai
Juodupė
Bebrene
Špogi
Papilys
Pašvitinys
Venta
Papilė
Lunkuva
Pasvalys
Pandėlys
Rokiškis
Obeliai
Subate
Ilūkste
Kraslava
Daugavpils
Gruzdžiai
Tryšiai
Vabalninkas
Kuršėnai
Telšiai
Siauliai
Pakruojis
Pumpenai
Laibgaliai
Suvekas
Antanarav
Turmantas
Braslaw
Bubiai
Diarvialiai
Alksniupiai
Kupiškis
Dusetos
Zarasai
Radviliškis
Panevėžys
Subačius
Viešintos
Svedasai
Užpaliai
Diagučiai
Visaginas
Užventis
Vaiguva
Šeduva
Sibabravas
Baisogala
Naumestis
Troškūnai
Kiaunoriai
Raguva
Anykščiai
Utena
Dūkštas
Opsa
Varniai
Kelmė
Kriakėnava
Laukuva
Kražiai
Tytuvėnai
Šiluva
Grinkiškis
Ramygala
Kovarskas
AUKŠTAITIJOS NACIONALINIS PARKAS
Ignalina
Vidzy
Kaltinėnai
Kaz'yany
Upyna
Šilale
Skaudvilė
Raseiniai
Krakės
Dotnuva
LT
Taujėnai
Alanta
Kaltanėnai
Varapayeva
Dunil
Biatigala
Šėta
Ukmerge
Želva
Molėtai
Švenčionėliai
Adutiškis
Pastavy
Batakiai
Paupys
Ariogala
Kėdainiai
Bukonys
Inturkė
Švenčionys
Lyntupy
Tauragė
Eržvilkas
Šimkaičiai
Čekiškė
Giedraičiai
Narach
Smalininkai
Vandžiogala
Jonava
Liukoniai
Širvintos
Pabradė
Myadzyel
Jurbarkas
Gelgaudiškis
Vilkija
Pabiarže
Svir
Maišiogala
Nemenčinė
Šakiai
Zapyškis
KAUNAS
Kaišiadorys
Žiežmariai
Bezdonys
Varnany
Lyuban'
Kasts
Krasnoznamensk
Pobedino
Griškabūdis
Kazlų Rūda
Piliuona
Vievis
Dūkštos
Hyervyaty
Uzlovoye
Kudirkos Naumiestis
Vilūnai
Lentvaris
VILNIUS
Astravyets
BY
Vesnovo
Dobrovol'sk
Pilviškiai
Prienai
TRAKAI ISTORINIS NACIONALINIS PARKAS
Vilnius
Smarhon'
Vilyey
Nesterov
Vilkaviškis
Kybartai
Igliauka
Birštonas
Jieznas
Aukštadvaris
Trakai
Medininkai
Zhuprany
Gusev
Гусев
Marijampolė
Rūdiškės
Turgeliai
Ashmyany
Kreva
Maladzyechna
Молодечна
Vishtytis
Gražiškiai
Kalvarija
Alytus
Daugai
Valkininkai
Pirčiupiai
Jašiūnai
Hal'shany
Girgantai
Wiżajny
Krosna
Simnas
Babriškės
Šalčininkai
Harodz'ki
Ozersk
Niadinge
Senoji Varena
Varena
Byenyakoni
Vishnyeva
Gołdap
Szypliszki
Lazdijai
Seirijai
Eišiškės
Dieveniškės
Valozhyn
Psarshai
Filipów
Merkinė
DZŪKIJOS NACIONALINIS PARKAS
Varanava
Yuratsishki
Kowale Oleckie
Suwałki
Veisiejai
Leipalingis
Radun'
Lipnishki
Ivyanyets
Cichy
Żelwa
Druskininkai
Matyli
Lida
Iwye
PUSZCZA ROMINCKA

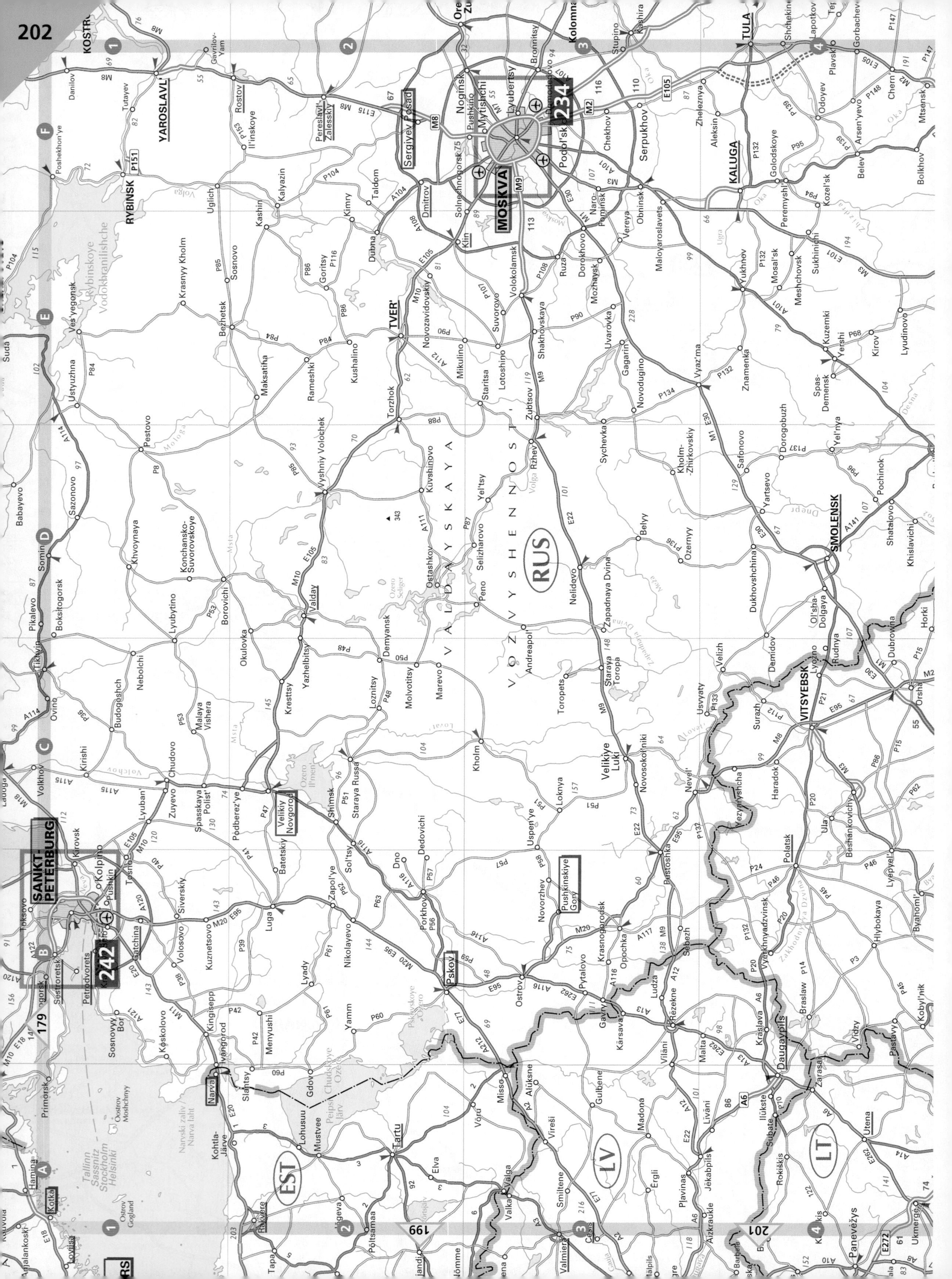

MOSKVA
SANKT-PETERBURG
YAROSLAVL'
RYBINSK
TVER'
KALUGA
TULA
SMOLENSK
VITSYEBSK
Velikiy Novgorod
Pskov
Tartu
Narva
Daugavpils
Panevėžys
Valga
RUS
EST
LV
LT
VALDAYSKAYA
VOZVYSHENNOST'
242
234
179
199
201

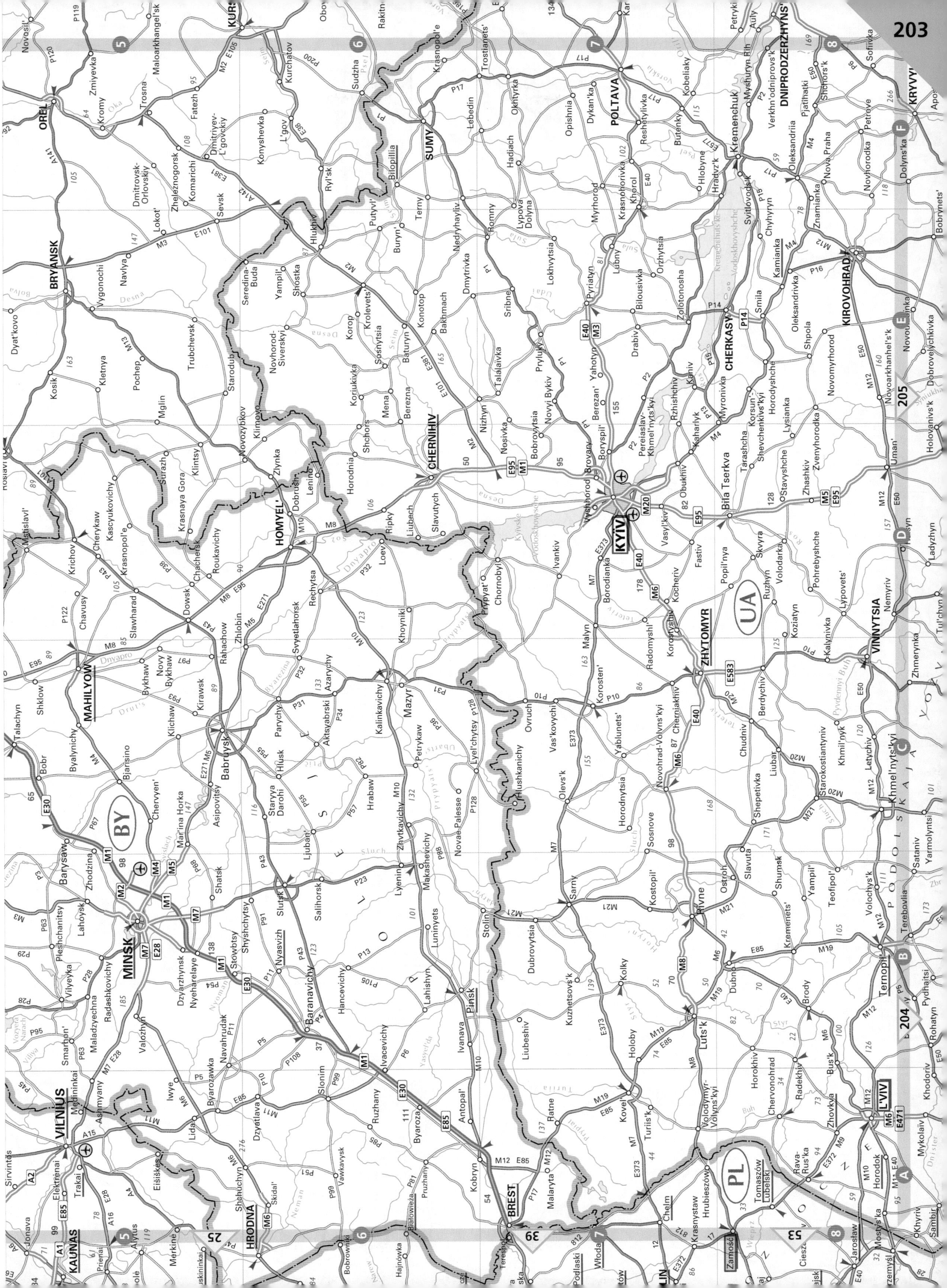
BY
UA
PL
KYIV
MINSK
VILNIUS
KAUNAS
HRODNA
BREST
HOMYEL'
MAHILYOW
BRYANSK
OREL
SUMY
POLTAVA
CHERNIHIV
ZHYTOMYR
VINNYTSIA
CHERKASY
KIROVOHRAD
KREMENCHUK
DNIPRODZERZHYNS'K
L'VIV
Rivne
Luts'k
Ternopil'
Khmel'nyts'kyi
Bila Tserkva
Pinsk
Babruysk
Mazyr
POLESSE
PODOL'SKAJA VOZV.
204
205
25
39
53

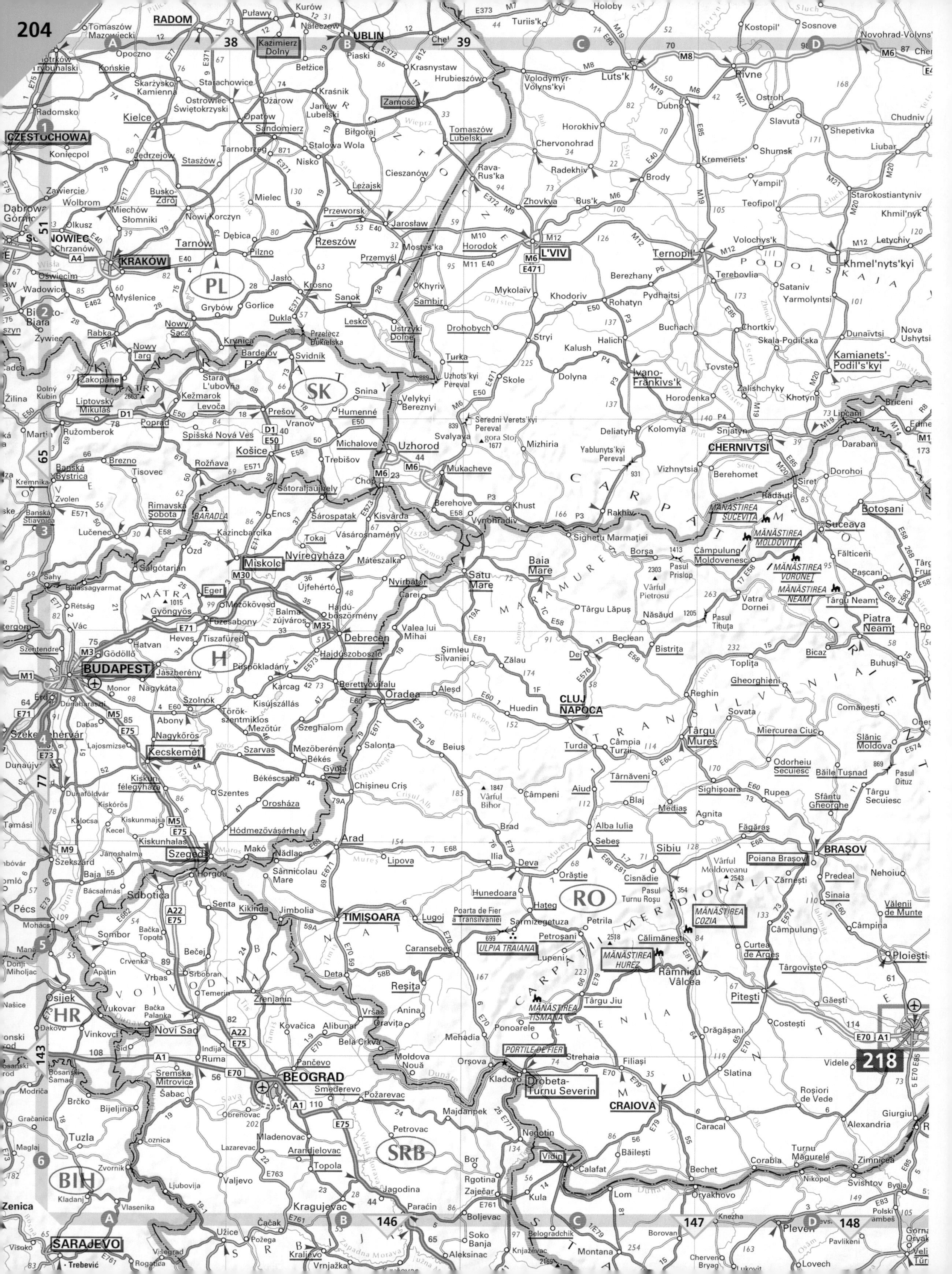
38
39
51
65
77
143
146
147
148
218
PL
SK
H
RO
HR
SRB
BIH
RADOM
Puławy
Kazimierz Dolny
LUBLIN
Chełm
Kurów
Nałęczów
Turiis'k
Holoby
Kostopil'
Sosnove
Novohrad-Volyns'kyi
Tomaszów Mazowiecki
Opoczno
Piotrków Trybunalski
Końskie
Skarżysko-Kamienna
Starachowice
Piaski
Bełżice
Krasnystaw
Hrubieszów
Volodymyr-Volyns'kyi
Luts'k
Rivne
Ostroh
Radomsko
Kielce
Ostrowiec Świętokrzyski
Ożarow
Opatów
Kraśnik
Janów Lubelski
Zamość
Dubno
Chudniv
Slavuta
Shepetivka
Horokhiv
CZĘSTOCHOWA
Koniecpol
Sandomierz
Tarnobrzeg
Stalowa Wola
Biłgoraj
Tomaszów Lubelski
Chervonohrad
Shumsk
Liubar
Kremenets'
Jędrzejów
Staszów
Nisko
Cieszanów
Rava-Rus'ka
Radekhiv
Brody
Yampil'
Starokostiantyniv
Zawiercie
Wolbrom
Busko-Zdrój
Mielec
Leżajsk
Zhovkva
Bus'k
Teofipol'
Khmil'nyk
Dąbrowa Górnicza
Miechów
Słomniki
Nowy Korczyn
Przeworsk
Jarosław
Olkusz
Sosnowiec
Chrzanów
KRAKÓW
Tarnów
Dębica
Rzeszów
Pilzno
Przemyśl
Mostys'ka
Horodok
L'VIV
Ternopil'
Volochys'k
Letychiv
Khmel'nyts'kyi
Oświęcim
Wadowice
Myślenice
Jasło
Krosno
Sanok
Khyriv
Sambir
Mykolaïv
Khodoriv
Rohatyn
Berezhany
Pydhaitsi
Terebovlia
Sataniv
Yarmolyntsi
Bielsko-Biała
Żywiec
Grybów
Gorlice
Nowy Sącz
Dukla
Lesko
Ustrzyki Dolne
Drohobych
Stryi
Halich
Buchach
Chortkiv
Dunaïvtsi
Nova Ushytsi
Rabka
Nowy Targ
Krynica
Przełęcz Dukielska
Bardejov
Svidník
Turka
Kalush
Skala-Podil's'ka
Kamianets'-Podil's'kyi
Zakopane
Stara L'ubovňa
Uzhots'kyi Pereval
Skole
Dolyna
Ivano-Frankivs'k
Tovste
Zalishchyky
Khotyn
Žilina
Dolný Kubín
Liptovský Mikuláš
Kežmarok
Levoča
Poprad
Prešov
Snina
Velykyi Bereznyi
Humenné
Horodenka
Briceni
Lipcani
Ružomberok
Spišská Nová Ves
Vranov
Seredni Verets'kyi Pereval
Svalyava
gora Stoj
Mizhiria
Deliatyn
Kolomyia
Sniatyn
Edineț
Banská Bystrica
Brezno
Rožňava
Košice
Michalovce
Uzhorod
Yablunyts'kyi Pereval
CHERNIVTSI
Darabani
Kremnica
Zvolen
Tisovec
Trebišov
Chop
Mukacheve
Vizhnytsia
Berehomet
Dorohoi
Siret
Rimavská Sobota
Sátoraljaújhely
Berehove
Khust
Rakhiv
Rădăuți
Banská Štiavnica
Lučenec
Baradla
Encs
Sárospatak
Kisvárda
Vynohradiv
Mânăstirea Sucevița
Botoșani
Kazincbarcika
Tokaj
Vásárosnamény
Sighetu Marmației
Mânăstirea Moldovița
Suceava
Ózd
Miskolc
Nyíregyháza
Mátészalka
Borșa
Câmpulung Moldovenesc
Fălticeni
Salgótarján
Satu Mare
Baia Mare
Pasul Prislop
Mânăstirea Voroneț
Pașcani
Balassagyarmat
Eger
Újfehértó
Nyírbátor
Carei
Vârful Pietrosu
Mânăstirea Neamț
Târgu Neamț
Rétság
Gyöngyös
Mezőkövesd
Hajdúböszörmény
Târgu Lăpuș
Vatra Dornei
Vác
Füzesabony
Balmazújváros
Valea lui Mihai
Năsăud
Pasul Tihuța
Piatra Neamț
Hatvan
Heves
Tiszafüred
Debrecen
Beclean
Bistrița
Szentendre
Gödöllő
Hajdúszoboszló
Șimleu Silvaniei
Zalău
Dej
Toplița
Bicaz
Buhuși
BUDAPEST
Jászberény
Püspökladány
Gheorghieni
Monor
Nagykáta
Karcag
Berettyóújfalu
Aleșd
Huedin
Reghin
Érd
Szolnok
Törökszentmiklós
Kisújszállás
Oradea
CLUJ NAPOCA
Comănești
Dabas
Abony
Mezőtúr
Szeghalom
Sovata
Onești
Székesfehérvár
Lajosmizse
Nagykőrös
Salonta
Beiuș
Turda
Câmpia Turzii
Târgu Mureș
Miercurea Ciuc
Slănic Moldova
Kecskemét
Szarvas
Mezőberény
Békés
Odorheiu Secuiesc
Băile Tușnad
Pasul Oituz
Dunaújváros
Kiskunfélegyháza
Békéscsaba
Gyula
Chișineu Criș
Vârful Bihor
Câmpeni
Aiud
Târnăveni
Sighișoara
Rupea
Sfântu Gheorghe
Târgu Secuiesc
Dunaföldvár
Kiskőrös
Szentes
Orosháza
Blaj
Mediaș
Agnita
Tamási
Kalocsa
Kecel
Kiskunmajsa
Hódmezővásárhely
Brad
Alba Iulia
Făgăraș
Kiskunhalas
Szeged
Makó
Nădlac
Arad
Lipova
Ilia
Deva
Sebeș
Sibiu
Poiana Brașov
BRAȘOV
Jánoshalma
Szekszárd
Baja
Horgoš
Sânnicolau Mare
Orăștie
Cisnădie
Vârful Moldoveanu
Zărnești
Predeal
Nehoiu
Bácsalmás
Subotica
Hunedoara
Pasul Turnu Roșu
Sinaia
Vălenii de Munte
Pécs
Mohács
Senta
Kikinda
Jimbolia
TIMIȘOARA
Lugoj
Poarta de Fier a Transilvaniei
Hațeg
Sarmizegetusa
Petrila
Mânăstirea Cozia
Câmpulung
Câmpina
Sombor
Bačka Topola
Petroșani
Călimănești
Ulpia Traiana
Caransebeș
Lupeni
Mânăstirea Hurez
Curtea de Argeș
Ploiești
Târgoviște
Crvenka
Bečej
Apatin
Vrbas
Srbobran
Deta
Reșița
Râmnicu Vâlcea
Temerin
Zrenjanin
Vršac
Oravița
Anina
Pitești
Găești
Osijek
Vukovar
Bačka Palanka
Novi Sad
Kovačica
Alibunar
Târgu Jiu
Mânăstirea Tismana
Costești
Đakovo
Vinkovci
Indija
Bela Crkva
Mehadia
Ponoarele
Drăgășani
Šid
Ruma
Pančevo
Moldova Nouă
Orșova
Portile de Fier
Strehaia
Filiași
Slatina
Videle
Bosanski Šamac
Sremska Mitrovica
Šabac
BEOGRAD
Smederevo
Požarevac
Kladovo
Drobeta-Turnu Severin
CRAIOVA
Roșiori de Vede
Modriča
Brčko
Bijeljina
Obrenovac
Majdanpek
Caracal
Alexandria
Giurgiu
Gračanica
Tuzla
Loznica
Mladenovac
Petrovac
Negotin
Băilești
Turnu Măgurele
Zimnicea
Lazarevac
Aranđelovac
Bor
Vidin
Calafat
Corabia
Bechet
Zvornik
Valjevo
Topola
Rgotina
Zaječar
Kula
Nikopol
Svishtov
Byala
Ljubovija
Jagodina
Lom
Oryakhovo
Zenica
Kladanj
Vlasenika
Kragujevac
Paraćin
Boljevac
Knezha
Pleven
Polski Trambesh
Čačak
Užice
Požega
Soko Banja
Belogradchik
Borovan
Pavlikeni
SARAJEVO
Trebević
Višegrad
Rogatica
Kraljevo
Vrnjačka
Aleksinac
Knjaževac
Montana
Cherven Bryag
Lovech
Visoko

203
149
UA
MD
BG
Radomyshl'
Korostyshiv
ZHYTOMYR
Fastiv
Vasyl'kiv
Obukhiv
Bila Tserkva
Popil'nya
Berdychiv
Ruzhyn
Skvyra
Volodarka
Koziatyn
Pohrebyshche
Kalynivka
Lypovets'
VINNYTSIA
Nemyriv
Zhmerynka
Haisyn
Ladyzhyn
Tul'chyn
Dzhuryn
Trostianets'
Bershad'
Mohyliv-Podilis'kyi
Yampil'
Kalynivka
Pereiaslav-Khmel'nyts'kyi
Kaniv
Kaharlyk
Myronivka
CHERKASY
Smila
Korsun'-Shevchenkivs'kyi
Tarashcha
Horodyshche
Stavyshche
Lysianka
Zhashkiv
Zvenyhorodka
Shpola
Kamianka
Oleksandrivka
Novomyrhorod
KIROVOHRAD
Uman'
Novoarkhanhel's'k
Novoukraïnka
Holovanivs'k
Dobrovelychkivka
Ul'yanovka
Pervomais'k
Kryve Ozero
Ol'hopil'
Balta
Kotovs'k
Anan'iv
Troïts'ke
Oleksandrivka
Domanivka
Yuzhnoukrains'k
Voznesens'k
Veselynove
Shyryayeve
Frunzivka
Zhovten'
Berezivka
Chervonoznamianka
Radisne
Rozdil'na
ODESSA
Illichivs'k
Zatoka
Bilhorod Dnistrovs'kyi
Tarutyne
Sarata
Artsyz
Tatarbunary
Suvorove
Kyliia
Vylkove
Izmaïl
Reni
Bolhrad
Drabiv
Bilousivka
Zolotonosha
Orzhytsia
Khorol
Reshetylivka
Butenky
Kobeliaky
Hlobyne
Hradyz'k
Kremenchuk
Svitlovods'k
Chyhyryn
Myshuryn Rih
Verkhn'odniprovs'k
DNIPRODZERZHYNS'K
Oleksandriia
Znamianka
Nova Praha
Pjatihatki
Shchors'k
Novhorodka
Petrove
Sofiivka
Dolyns'ka
KRYVYI RIH
Bobrynets'
Kazanka
Apostolove
Novovorontsovka
Shyroke
Novyi Buh
Elanets'
Vossijatskoye
Ivanivka
Bereznehuvate
Bashtanka
Snihurivka
Voskresens'ke
Nova Odessa
MYKOLAÏV
KHERSON
Hola Prystan'
Ochakiv
Tsiurupyns'k
Beryslav
Kakhovka
Nova Kakhovka
Krasnopalivka
Lozova
Pereshchepyne
Novomoskovs'k
Pavlograd
Petrykivka
Auly
DNIPROPETROVS'K
Vasyl'kivka
Rozdory
Novomykolaïvka
Pokrov
ZAPORIZHZHIA
Tomakivka
Marhanets'
Orikhiv
Nikopol'
Vasylivka
Tokmak
Kamianka-Dniprovs'ka
Dniprorudne
Verkhnii Rohachyk
Velyka Lepetykha
Vesele
Melitopol'
Nyzhni Sirohozy
Kyryliv
Chkalove
Askaniia-Nova
Heniches'k
Kalanchak
Armyansk
Krasnoperekops'k
Skadovs'k
Dzhankoï
Voïnka
Razdol'e
Pervomais'ke
Krasnohvardiis'ke
Sterehushche
Oktiabrs'ke
Bilohirsk
Chornomors'ke
Saky
mys Tarhankut
Myrnyi
Yevpatoria
SIMFEROPOL'
Mikolaivka
Bakhchysarai
Alushta
SEVASTOPOL'
mys Hersonesski
Alupka
Yalta
mys Saryzh
K R Y M S ' K Y I
P I V O S T R I V
Korbu
Soroca
Camenca
Florești
Ribnița
Bălți
Orhei
Dubăsari
Grigoriopol
Călărași
CHIȘINĂU
Ungheni
Tiraspol
Tighina
Hâncești
Căușani
VERHNI TRAJANOV VAL
Cimișlia
Comrat
Ceadâr-Lunga
Cahul
Vulcănești
IAȘI
Huși
Vaslui
Bacău
Bârlad
Adjud
Tecuci
Focșani
GALAȚI
Brăila
Isaccea
Tulcea
Sulina
Murighiol
Râmnicu Sărat
Buzău
Babadag
Însurăței
Mizil
Hârșova
Istria
HISTRIA
Urziceni
Slobozia
Cernavodă
Mamaia
Medgidia
CONSTANȚA
VALUL-LUI TRAIAN
Eforie
BUCUREȘTI
Budești
Călărași
ADAMCLISI
Negru Vodă
Silistra
Oltenița
Mangalia
Tutrakan
Alfatar
Tervel
General Toshevo
Dulovo
Shabla
Nos Kaliakra
Kavarna
Balchik
Dobrich
Zlatni Pyasătsi
Razgrad
Novi Pazar
Shumen
MADARA
Provadiya
VARNA
Popovo
Tŭrgovishte
Veliki Preslav
Rudnik
Obzor
Kotlenski Pateka
Slŭnchev Bryag
Nesebŭr
Aytos
DELTA DUNĂRII
Varna
Batumi
Varna İstanbul
Odessa Illichivs'k
ČERNO MORE
Cide
Kurucașile
Azdavay
Amasra
Inebolu
DOBROGEA
MOLDAVA

CITY AND URBAN ROUTES
CITTÀ E AREE URBANE
CIUDADES Y ÁREAS URBANAS
VILLES ET AIRES URBAINES
STÄDTE UND ZUFAHRTEN

● City plans / Piante di città / Planos de ciudades / Plans de villes / Stadtpläne

□ Urban route maps / Aree urbane / Áreas urbanas / Aires urbaines / Stadtdurchfahrtspläne

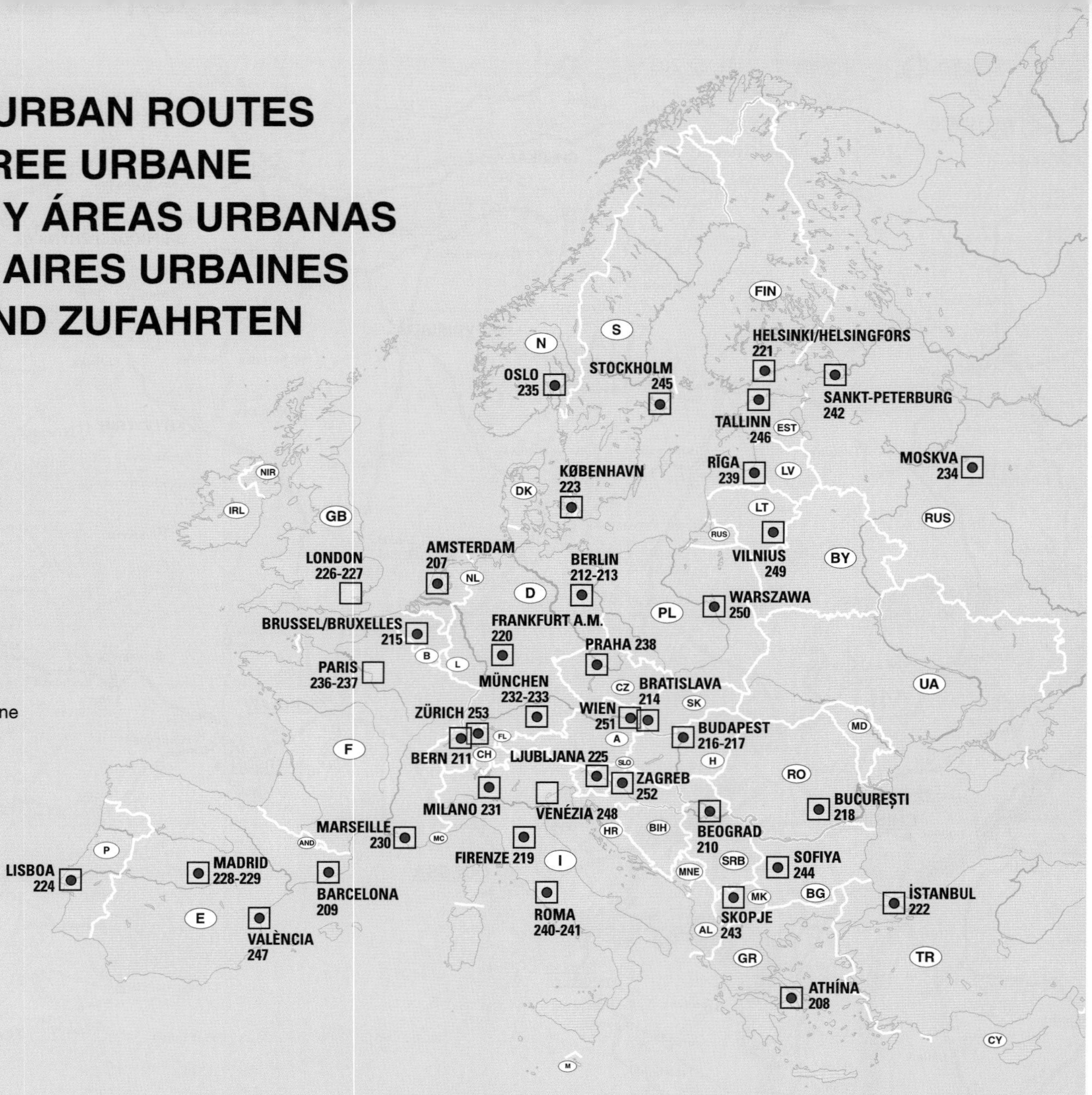

	GB Legend	I Legenda	E Leyenda	F Légende	D Zeichenerklärung
	Built-up area	Caseggiati	Zona edificada	Zones bâties	Bebauung
	Building of interest	Edificio d'interesse	Edificio relevante	Édifice remarquable	Bemerkenswertes Gebäude
6	Motorway, access points, service area	Autostrada, caselli, stazione di servizio	Autopista, accesos, estación de servicio	Autoroute, accès, aire de service	Autobahn, Anschlüsse, Tankstelle
	Road with motorway characteristics	Superstrada	Autovía	Route-express	Autobahnähnliche Schnellstraße
	Through road	Strada di attraversamento	Travesía	Route de traversée	Hauptdurchfahrtsstraße
	Other road	Altra strada	Otra carretera	Autre route	Sonstige Straße
A9 N202	Numbering of motorway and national roads	Numeri di autostrada e strade nazionali	Números de autopista y carreteras nacionales	Numéros d'autoroute et routes nationales	Autobahnnummer, Staatsstraßennummer
	Road in tunnel	Galleria stradale	Túnel en carretera	Tunnel routier	Straßentunnel
2009	Motorway and road under construction (opening year)	Autostrada e strada in costruzione (anno di apertura)	Autopista y carretera en construcción (año de apertura)	Autoroute et route en construction (année d'ouverture)	Autobahn und straße in Bau (Fertigstellungsjahr)
Utrecht	Destination	Direzione	Direccion	Direction	Richtung
	Railway and station	Ferrovia e stazione	Ferrocarril y estacion	Chemin de fer et gare	Eisenbahn und Bahnhöf
	Garden and park; cemeteries	Giardino e parco; cimiteri	Jardin y parque; cementerios	Jardin et parc; cimetières	Gärten und Park; Friedhöfe
P	Hospital; Parking	Ospedale; Parcheggio	Hospital; Aparcamiento	Hôpital; Parking	Krankenhaus; Parkplatz
	Camping site	Campeggio	Cámping	Camping	Campingplatz
	Vehicle ferry route	Trasporto auto su traghetto	Transbordador de automóviles	Bac pour autos	Autofähre
	Panoramic view	Punto panoramico	Vista panorámica	Vue panoramique	Aussichtspunkt
M	Underground railway station	Fermata della metropolitana	Estación del metro	Station de métro	U-Bahnhöfe
i	Tourist information	Ufficio informazioni	Información turística	Informations touristiques	Touristische Auskünfte
	Pedestrian area	Area pedonali	Área peatonales	Zone réservé aux piétons	Fußgängerzone

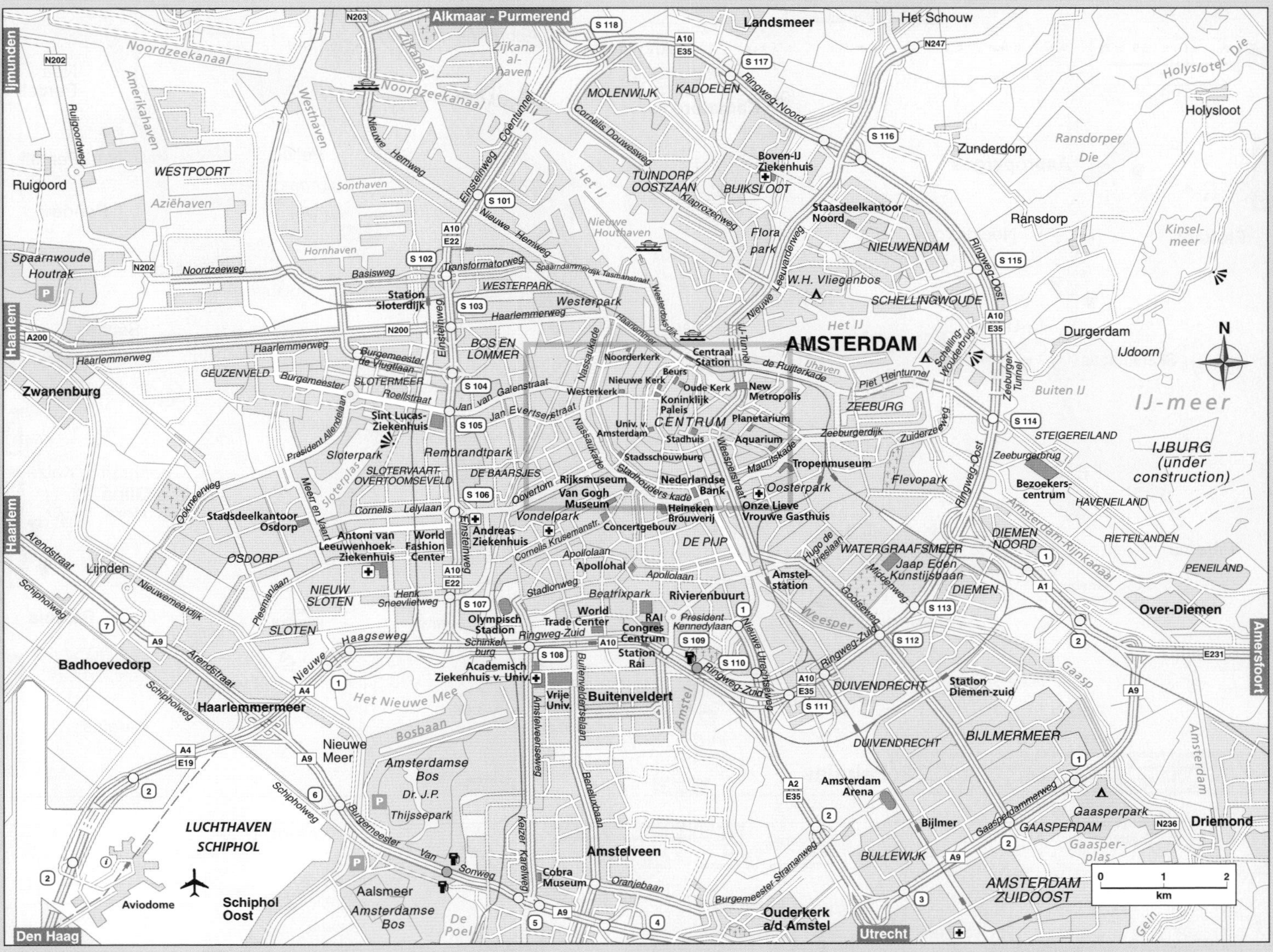
Alkmaar - Purmerend
Landsmeer
Het Schouw
IJmuiden
Noordzeekanaal
Zijkanaal
Zijkana al-haven
MOLENWIJK
KADOELEN
Ringweg-Noord
Holysloot
Amerikahaven
Westhaven
Coentunnel
Cornelis Douweswег
Zunderdorp
Ransdorper Die
Ruigoord
WESTPOORT
Sonthaven
Aziëhaven
Het IJ
TUINDORP OOSTZAAN
BUIKSLOOT
Boven-IJ Ziekenhuis
Staasdeelkantoor Noord
Ransdorp
Spaarnwoude Houtrak
Hornhaven
Nieuwe Houthaven
Flora park
NIEUWENDAM
Kinsel-meer
Noordzeeweg
Basisweg
Transformatorweg
WESTERPARK
Station Sloterdijk
Westerpark
W.H. Vliegenbos
SCHELLINGWOUDE
Haarlemmerweg
Haarlem
Durgerdam
IJdoorn
AMSTERDAM
Het IJ
BOS EN LOMMER
Centraal Station
Burgemeester de Vlugtlaan
GEUZENVELD
SLOTERMEER
Noorderkerk
Beurs
Oude Kerk
New Metropolis
Nieuwe Kerk
Westerkerk
Koninklijk Paleis
Piet Heintunnel
Zwanenburg
Sint Lucas-Ziekenhuis
Jan van Galenstraat
Jan Evertsenstraat
Univ. v. Amsterdam
CENTRUM
Planetarium
ZEEBURG
Buiten IJ
IJ-meer
Stadhuis
Aquarium
STEIGEREILAND
Sloterpark
Rembrandtpark
Stadsschouwburg
Mauritskade
Tropenmuseum
IJBURG (under construction)
SLOTERVAART-OVERTOOMSEVELD
DE BAARSJES
Rijksmuseum
Nederlandse Bank
Flevopark
Bezoekers-centrum
Van Gogh Museum
Heineken Brouwerij
Oosterpark
Onze Lieve Vrouwe Gasthuis
HAVENEILAND
Stadsdeelkantoor Osdorp
Vondelpark
Andreas Ziekenhuis
Concertgebouw
DE PIJP
WATERGRAAFSMEER
DIEMEN NOORD
RIETEILANDEN
Antoni van Leeuwenhoek-Ziekenhuis
World Fashion Center
Apollolaan
Apollohal
Jaap Eden Kunstijsbaan
DIEMEN
PENEILAND
OSDORP
Lijnden
NIEUW SLOTEN
Beatrixpark
Rivierenbuurt
Amstel-station
Over-Diemen
Olympisch Stadion
World Trade Center
RAI
President Kennedylaan
SLOTEN
Ringweg-Zuid
Congres Centrum
Station Rai
Badhoevedorp
Academisch Ziekenhuis v. Univ.
Vrije Univ.
Buitenveldert
Ringweg-Zuid
DUIVENDRECHT
Station Diemen-zuid
Haarlemmermeer
Het Nieuwe Meer
Bosbaan
Amstel
DUIVENDRECHT
BIJLMERMEER
Amersfoort
Nieuwe Meer
Amsterdamse Bos
Dr. J.P. Thijssepark
Amsterdam Arena
Gaasperpark
GAASPERDAM
Driemond
LUCHTHAVEN SCHIPHOL
Bijlmer
Amstelveen
Cobra Museum
Oranjebaan
BULLEWIJK
AMSTERDAM ZUIDOOST
Aviodome
Schiphol Oost
Aalsmeer
Amsterdamse Bos
De Poel
Ouderkerk a/d Amstel
Den Haag
Utrecht
N
0 1 2 km

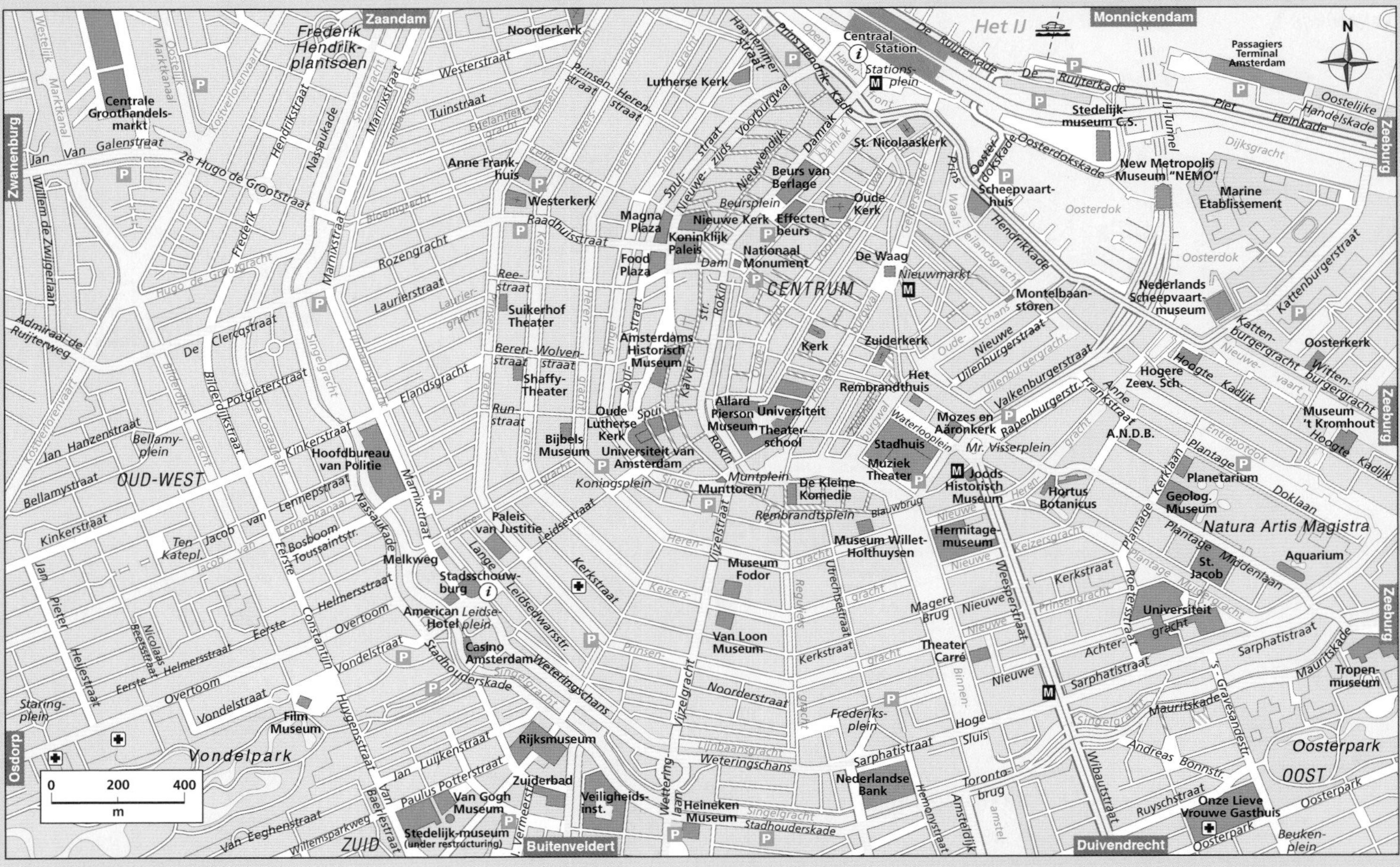
Zaandam
Monnickendam
Frederik Hendrik-plantsoen
Noorderkerk
Centraal Station
Het IJ
Passagiers Terminal Amsterdam
Westerstraat
Lutherse Kerk
Stations-plein
De Ruijterkade
Oostelijke Handelskade
Centrale Groothandels-markt
Tuinstraat
Piet Heinkade
Zeeburg
Stedelijk museum C.S.
Zwanenburg
Jan Van Galenstraat
St. Nicolaaskerk
Oosterdokskade
New Metropolis Museum "NEMO"
Ze Hugo de Grootstraat
Anne Frank-huis
Beurs van Berlage
Scheepvaart-huis
Marine Etablissement
Westerkerk
Magna Plaza
Nieuwe Kerk
Effecten-beurs
Oude Kerk
Oosterdok
Koninklijk Paleis
Nationaal Monument
De Waag
Rozengracht
Food Plaza
Dam
CENTRUM
Nieuwmarkt
Nederlands Scheepvaart-museum
Kattenburgerstraat
Suikerhof Theater
Montelbaan-storen
Admiraal de Ruijterweg
De Clercqstraat
Kerk
Zuiderkerk
Oosterkerk
Amsterdams Historisch Museum
Hogere Zeev. Sch.
Shaffy-Theater
Het Rembrandthuis
Potgieterstraat
Elandsgracht
Allard Pierson Museum
Universiteit Theater-school
Mozes en Aäronkerk
Museum 't Kromhout
Jan Hanzenstraat
Oude Lutherse Kerk
Bijbels Museum
Universiteit van Amsterdam
Mr. Visserplein
A.N.D.B.
Kinkerstraat
Hoofdbureau van Politie
Stadhuis
Muziek Theater
Joods Historisch Museum
Planetarium
OUD-WEST
Koningsplein
Muntplein
Munttoren
De Kleine Komedie
Hortus Botanicus
Geolog. Museum
Bellamystraat
Rembrandtsplein
Natura Artis Magistra
Paleis van Justitie
Museum Willet-Holthuysen
Hermitage-museum
Aquarium
Melkweg
Museum Fodor
St. Jacob
Stadsschouw-burg
Leidseplein
American Hotel
Magere Brug
Universiteit
Casino Amsterdam
Van Loon Museum
Theater Carré
Sarphatistraat
Tropen-museum
Overtoom
Vondelstraat
Film Museum
Frederiks-plein
Mauritskade
Rijksmuseum
Vondelpark
Oosterpark
Zuiderbad
Veiligheids-inst.
Nederlandsche Bank
OOST
Van Gogh Museum
Heineken Museum
Stadhouderskade
Onze Lieve Vrouwe Gasthuis
Stedelijk-museum (under restructuring)
ZUID
Osdorp
Buitenveldert
Duivendrecht
Beuken-plein
0 200 400 m
N

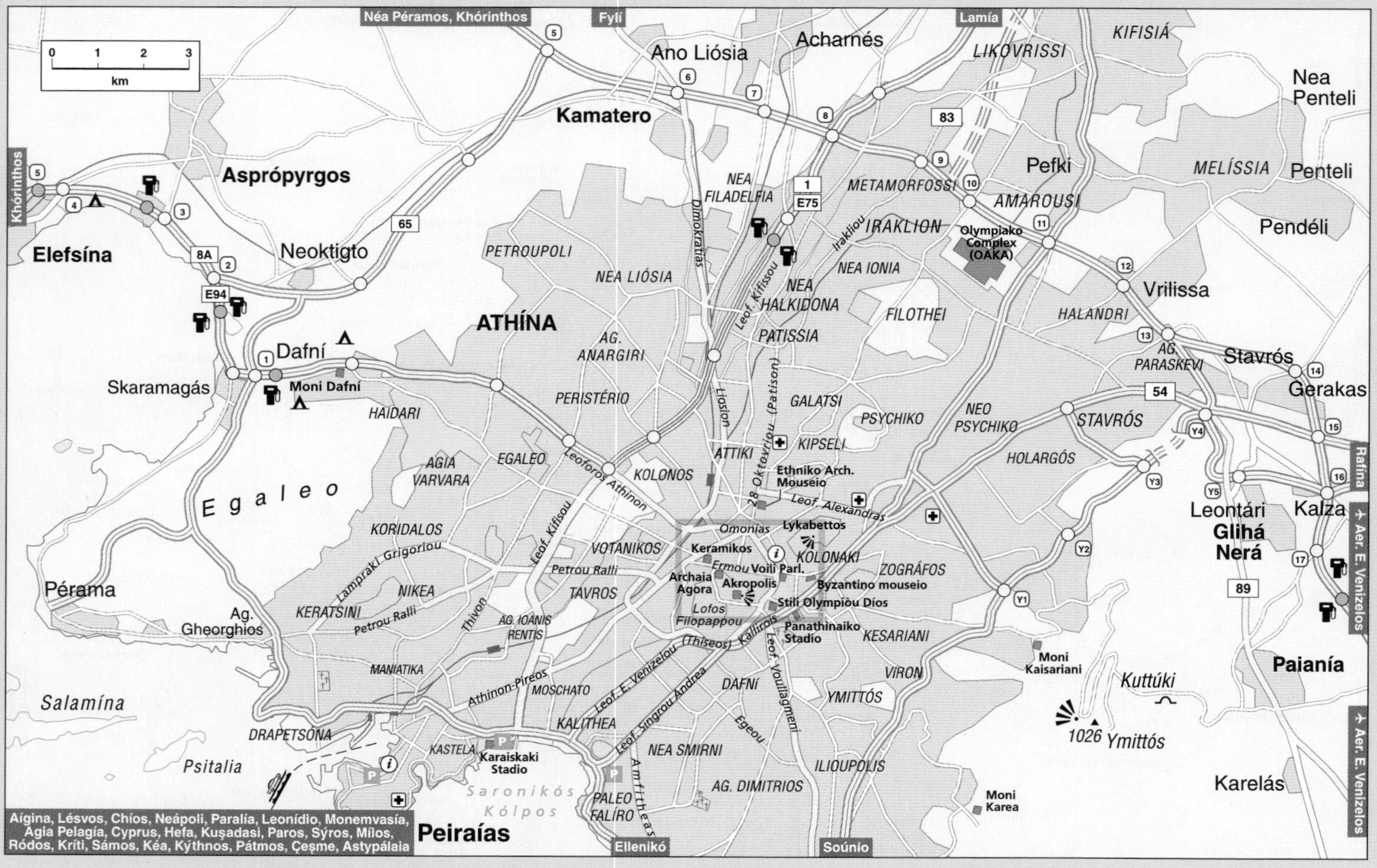

Néa Péramos, Khórinthos
Fylí
Lamía
0 1 2 3
km
Ano Liósia
Acharnés
LIKOVRISSI
KIFISIÁ
Nea Penteli
Kamatero
83
Pefki
MELÍSSIA
Penteli
Khórinthos
Asprópyrgos
NEA FILADELFIA
E75
METAMORFOSSI
AMAROUSI
65
IRAKLION
Olympiako Complex (OAKA)
Pendéli
Elefsína
8A
Neoktigto
PETROUPOLI
NEA LIÓSIA
Dimokratías
Leof. Kifissou
NEA HALKIDONA
NEA IONIA
Vrilissa
E94
ATHÍNA
FILOTHEI
HALANDRI
Dafní
AG. ANARGIRI
PATISSIA
AG. PARASKEVI
Stavrós
Skaramagás
Moni Dafní
HAIDARI
PERISTÉRIO
Liosion
28 Oktovriou (Patison)
GALATSI
PSYCHIKO
NEO PSYCHIKO
STAVRÓS
54
Gerakas
AGIA VARVARA
EGALEO
ATTIKI
KIPSELI
HOLARGÓS
Rafína
Egaleo
Leoforos Athinon
KOLONOS
Ethniko Arch. Mouseio
Leof. Alexandras
KORIDALOS
Omonias
Lykabettos
Leontári
Kalza
Glihá Nerá
Aer. E. Venizelos
Pérama
Lamprakí Grigoriou
Leof. Kifisou
VOTANIKOS
Keramikos
Ermou
Voili Parl.
KOLONAKI
ZOGRÁFOS
Petrou Ralli
Archaia Agora
Akropolis
Byzantino mouseio
89
NIKEA
TAVROS
Lofos Filopappou
Stili Olympiou Dios
Ag. Gheorghios
KERATSINI
Petrou Ralli
Thivon
AG. IOANIS RENTIS
Thiseos
Kallirois
Panathinaiko Stadio
KESARIANI
MANIATIKA
Leof. E. Venizelou
Leof. Vouliagmeni
VIRON
Moni Kaisariani
Paianía
Salamína
Athinon-Pireos
MOSCHATO
DAFNI
YMITTÓS
Kuttúki
Leof. Singrou Andrea
Egeou
KALITHEA
1026 Ymittós
DRAPETSÓNA
Psitalia
KASTELA
Karaiskaki Stadio
NEA SMIRNI
ILIOUPOLIS
Karelás
Saronikós Kólpos
AG. DIMITRIOS
Amfitheas
PALEO FALÍRO
Moni Karea
Aígina, Lésvos, Chíos, Neápoli, Paralía, Leonídio, Monemvasía, Agia Pelagía, Cyprus, Hefa, Kuşadasi, Paros, Sýros, Mílos, Ródos, Kríti, Sámos, Kéa, Kýthnos, Pátmos, Çeşme, Astypálaia
Peiraías
Ellenikó
Soúnio

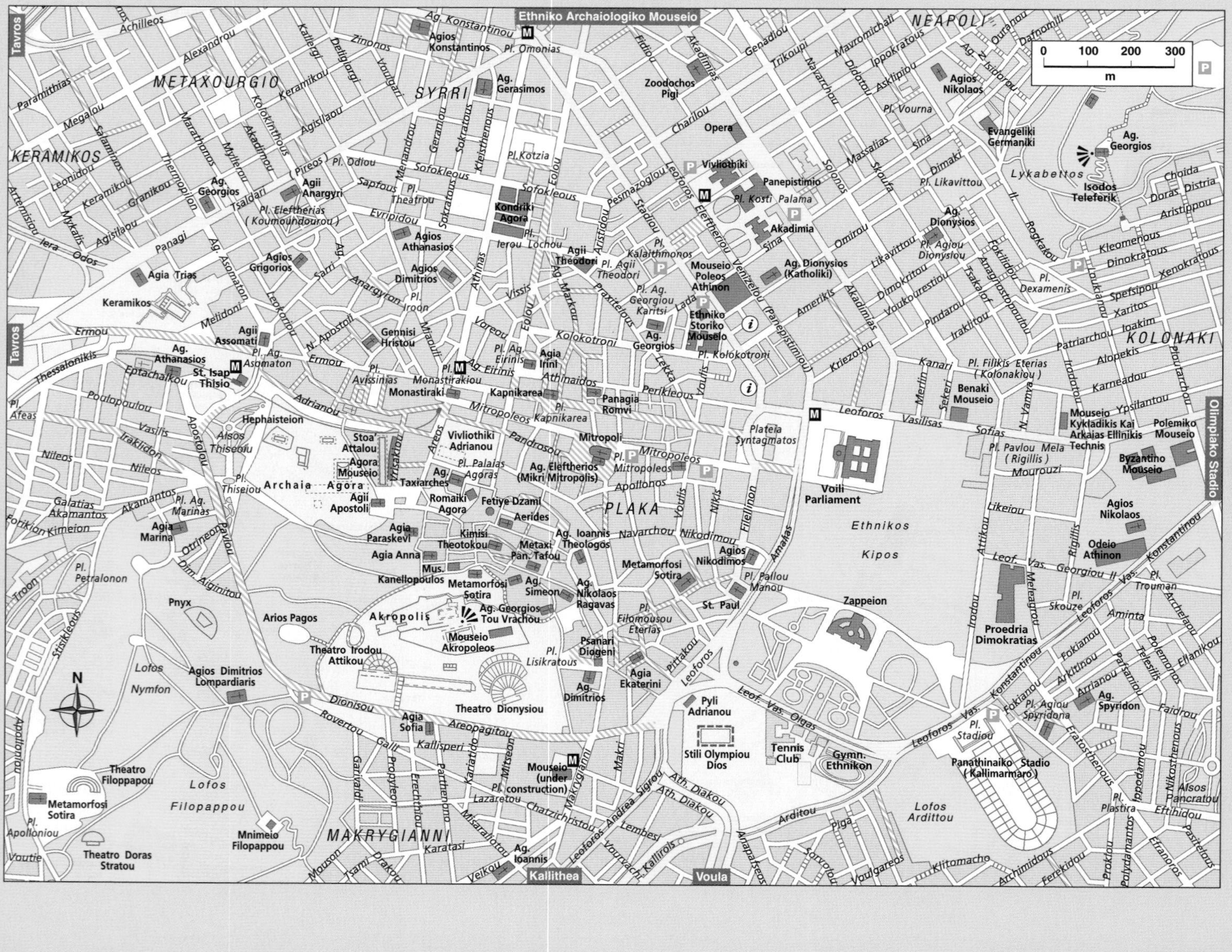

Ethniko Archaiologiko Mouseio
Tavros
Achilleos
Ag. Konstantinou
Agios Konstantinos
Pl. Omonias
NEAPOLI
0 100 200 300
m
METAXOURGIO
SYRRI
Ag. Gerasimos
Zoodochos Pigi
Agios Nikolaos
KERAMIKOS
Opera
Evangeliki Germaniki
Ag. Georgios
Pl. Kotzia
Vivliothiki
Panepistimio
Lykabettos
Isodos Teleferik
Ag. Georgios
Agii Anargyri
Pl. Eleftherias (Koumoundourou)
Pl. Theatrou
Kondriki Agora
Pl. Kosti Palama
Akadimia
Pl. Likavittou
Ag. Dionysios
Agios Athanasios
Agios Grigorios
Agia Trias
Agii Theodori
Pl. Agii Theodori
Mouseio Poleos Athinon
Ag. Dionysios (Katholiki)
Pl. Agiou Dionysiou
Pl. Dexamenis
Agios Dimitrios
Keramikos
Pl. Ag. Georgiou Karitsi
Ag. Georgios
Ethniko Storiko Mouseio
Gennisi Hristou
Agii Assomati
Pl. Ag. Assomaton
Ag. Athanasios
St. Isap Thisio
Pl. Ag. Eirinis
Agia Irini
Pl. Kolokotroni
KOLONAKI
Monastiraki
Pl. Monastirakiou
Kapnikarea
Panagia Romvi
Pl. Filikis Eterias (Kolonakiou)
Benaki Mouseio
Hephaisteion
Mitropoleos
Pl. Kapnikarea
Plateia Syntagmatos
Leoforos Vasilisas Sofias
Mouseio Kykladikis Kai Arkaias Ellinikis Techis
Polemiko Mouseio
Byzantino Mouseio
Olimpiako Stadio
Stoa Attalou
Agora Mouseio
Vivliothiki Adrianou
Pl. Palaias Agoras
Mitropoli
Pl. Mitropoleos
Pl. Pavlou Mela (Rigillis)
Archaia Agora
Pl. Thiseiou
Ag. Taxiarches
Ag. Eleftherios (Mikri Mitropolis)
Voili Parliament
Agii Apostoli
Romaiki Agora
Fetiye Dzami
PLAKA
Aerides
Agios Nikolaos
Pl. Ag. Marinas
Agia Marina
Agia Paraskevi
Kimisi Theotokou
Metaxi Pan. Tafou
Ag. Ioannis Theologos
Ethnikos Kipos
Odeio Athinon
Agia Anna
Agios Nikodimos
Pl. Petralonon
Mus.
Kanellopoulos
Metamorfosi Sotira
Metamorfosi Sotira
Pl. Pallou Manou
Pnyx
Ag. Georgios Tou Vrachou
Ag. Simeon
Ag. Nikolaos Ragavas
St. Paul
Zappeion
Proedria Dimokratias
Arios Pagos
Akropolis
Pl. Filomousou Eterias
Mouseio Akropoleos
Theatro Irodou Attikou
Psanari Diogeni
Lofos Nymfon
Agios Dimitrios Lompardiaris
Pl. Lisikratous
Agia Ekaterini
Ag. Dimitrios
Pyli Adrianou
Ag. Spyridon
Theatro Dionysiou
Agia Sofia
Pl. Ag. Spyridona
Pl. Stadiou
Stili Olympiou Dios
Tennis Club
Gymn. Ethnikon
Panathinaiko Stadio (Kallimarmaro)
Theatro Filoppappou
Lofos Filopappou
Mouseio (under construction)
Metamorfosi Sotira
Pl. Apolloniou
Mnimeio Filopappou
Lofos Ardittou
Pl. Plastira
MAKRYGIANNI
Ag. Ioannis
Theatro Doras Stratou
Kallithea
Voula
N

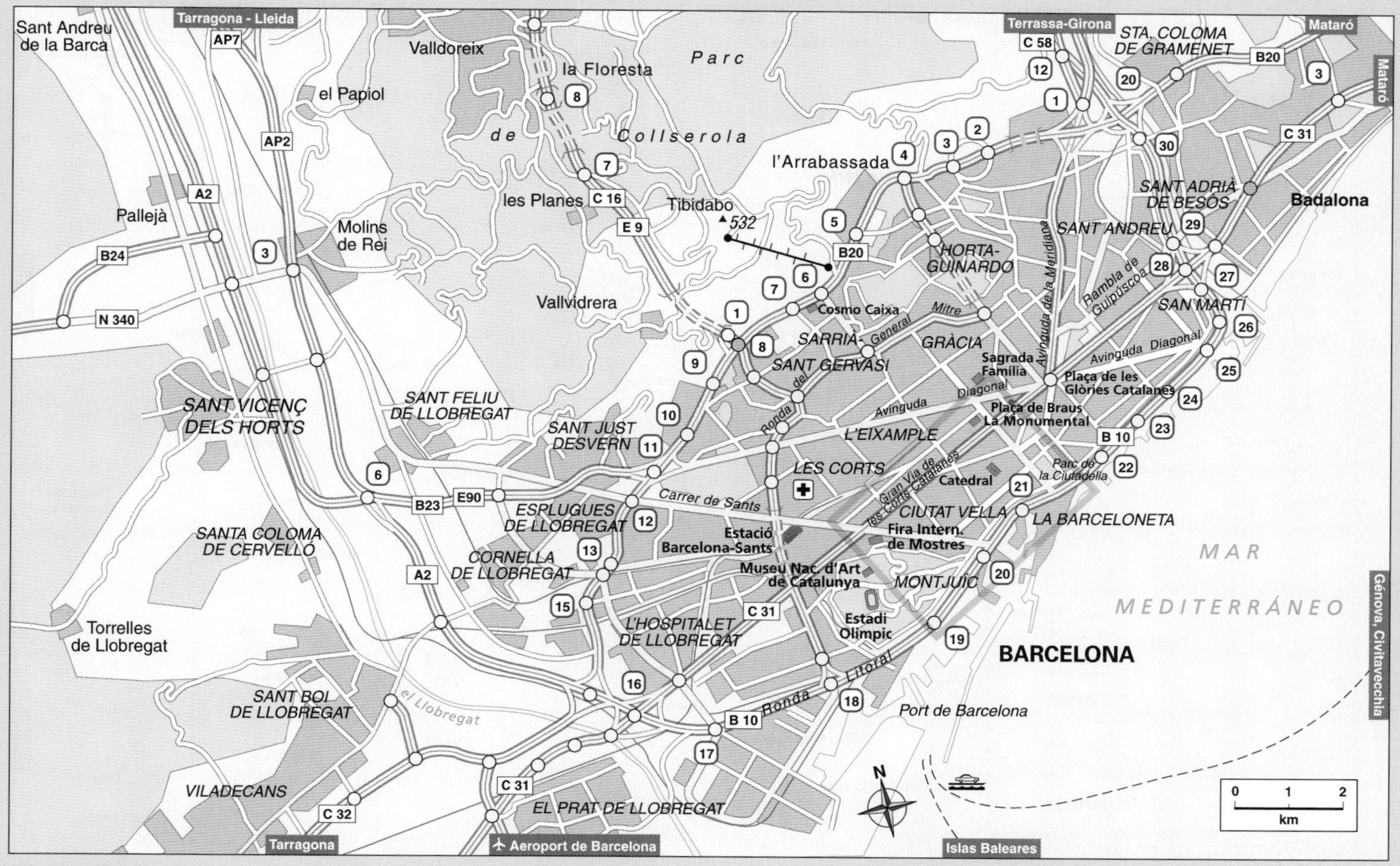
Tarragona - Lleida
Terrassa-Girona
Mataró
Sant Andreu de la Barca
Valldoreix
la Floresta
Parc de Collserola
el Papiol
STA. COLOMA DE GRAMENET
l'Arrabassada
Tibidabo
532
Pallejà
Molins de Rei
les Planes
SANT ADRIÀ DE BESÒS
Badalona
SANT ANDREU
HORTA-GUINARDÓ
Vallvidrera
Cosmo Caixa
SARRIÀ-SANT GERVASI
GRÀCIA
Sagrada Família
Plaça de les Glòries Catalanes
Avinguda Diagonal
Plaça de Braus La Monumental
SANT VICENÇ DELS HORTS
SANT FELIU DE LLOBREGAT
SANT JUST DESVERN
L'EIXAMPLE
LES CORTS
Carrer de Sants
Catedral
CIUTAT VELLA
LA BARCELONETA
Parc de la Ciutadella
ESPLUGUES DE LLOBREGAT
SANTA COLOMA DE CERVELLÓ
Estació Barcelona-Sants
Fira Intern. de Mostres
CORNELLÀ DE LLOBREGAT
Museu Nac. d'Art de Catalunya
MONTJUÏC
MAR MEDITERRÁNEO
Torrelles de Llobregat
L'HOSPITALET DE LLOBREGAT
Estadi Olímpic
BARCELONA
Génova, Civitavecchia
SANT BOI DE LLOBREGAT
el Llobregat
Ronda Litoral
Port de Barcelona
VILADECANS
EL PRAT DE LLOBREGAT
Tarragona
Aeroport de Barcelona
Islas Baleares
0 1 2 km
N

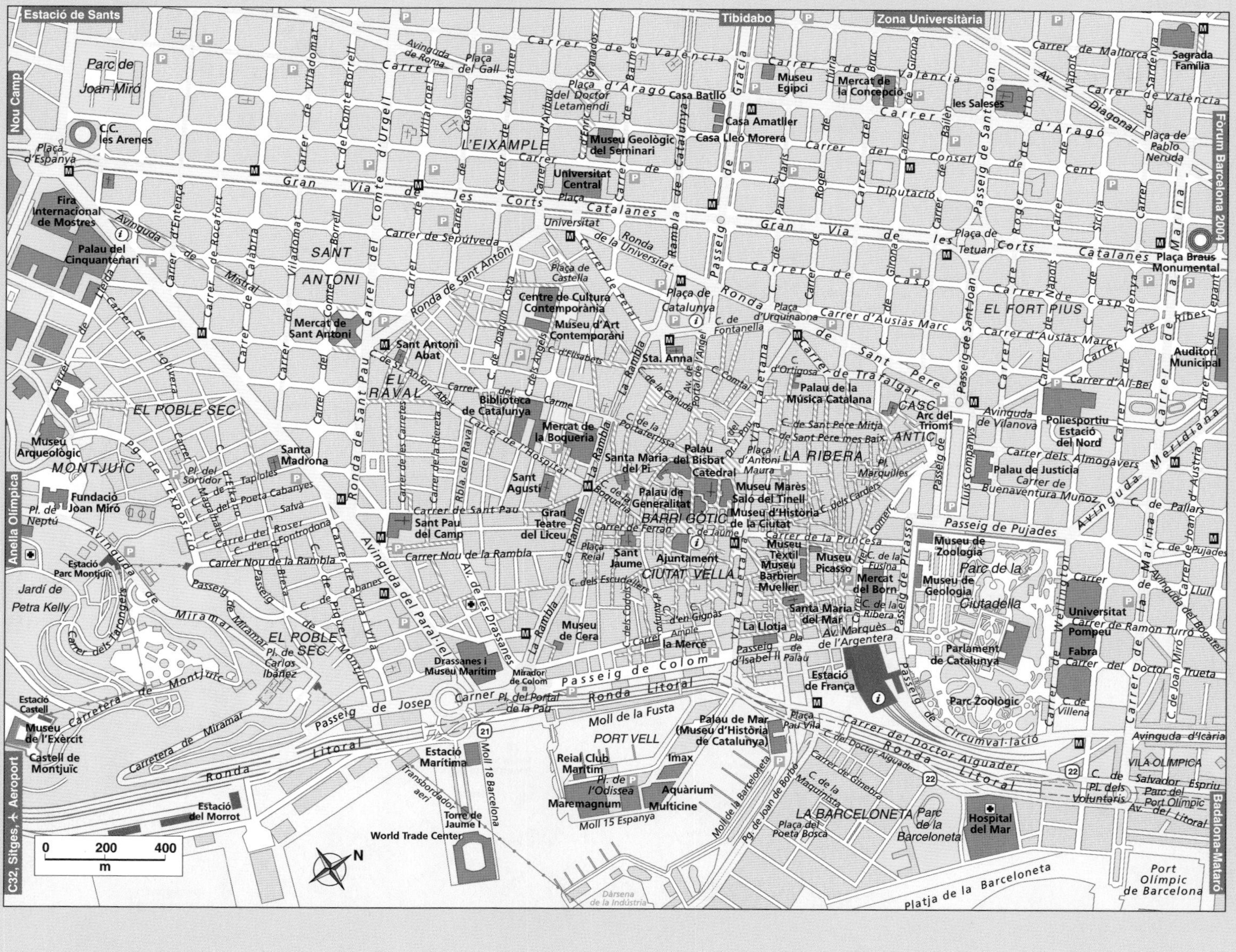
Estació de Sants
Tibidabo
Zona Universitària
Nou Camp
Fòrum Barcelona 2004
Anella Olímpica
C32, Sitges, Aeroport
Badalona-Mataró
Parc de Joan Miró
C.C. les Arenes
Plaça d'Espanya
Fira Internacional de Mostres
Palau del Cinquantenari
Museu Egipci
Mercat de la Concepció
Casa Batlló
Casa Amatller
Casa Lleó Morera
Museu Geològic del Seminari
Universitat Central
L'EIXAMPLE
Gran Via de les Corts Catalanes
Sagrada Família
Plaça de Pablo Neruda
Plaça Braus Monumental
SANT ANTONI
Mercat de Sant Antoni
Centre de Cultura Contemporània
Museu d'Art Contemporani
Plaça de Catalunya
EL FORT PIUS
Auditori Municipal
Sant Antoni Abat
Sta. Anna
EL RAVAL
Palau de la Música Catalana
EL POBLE SEC
Biblioteca de Catalunya
Mercat de la Boqueria
Arc del Triomf
Poliesportiu Estació del Nord
Museu Arqueològic
Santa Madrona
Santa Maria del Pi
Palau del Bisbat
Catedral
LA RIBERA
Palau de Justícia
MONTJUÏC
Fundació Joan Miró
Sant Agustí
Museu Marès
Saló del Tinell
Palau de la Generalitat
BARRI GÒTIC
Museu d'Història de la Ciutat
Sant Pau del Camp
Gran Teatre del Liceu
Passeig de Pujades
Museu de Zoologia
Estació Parc Montjuïc
Jardí de Petra Kelly
Sant Jaume
Ajuntament
CIUTAT VELLA
Museu Tèxtil
Museu Barbier Mueller
Museu Picasso
Mercat del Born
Parc de la Ciutadella
Museu de Geologia
Universitat Pompeu Fabra
EL POBLE SEC
Museu de Cera
Santa Maria del Mar
La Llotja
la Mercè
Parlament de Catalunya
Drassanes i Museu Marítim
Mirador de Colom
Passeig de Colom
Estació de França
Parc Zoològic
Estació Castell
Museu de l'Exèrcit
Castell de Montjuïc
Moll de la Fusta
PORT VELL
Palau de Mar (Museu d'Història de Catalunya)
Carrer del Doctor Aiguader
Vila Olímpica
Estació Marítima
Reial Club Marítim
Imax
Aquàrium
Maremagnum
Multicine
Moll 15 Espanya
Torre de Jaume I
World Trade Center
Moll 18 Barcelona
Estació del Morrot
LA BARCELONETA
Parc de la Barceloneta
Hospital del Mar
Port Olímpic de Barcelona
Platja de la Barceloneta
Dàrsena de la Indústria
0 200 400 m
N

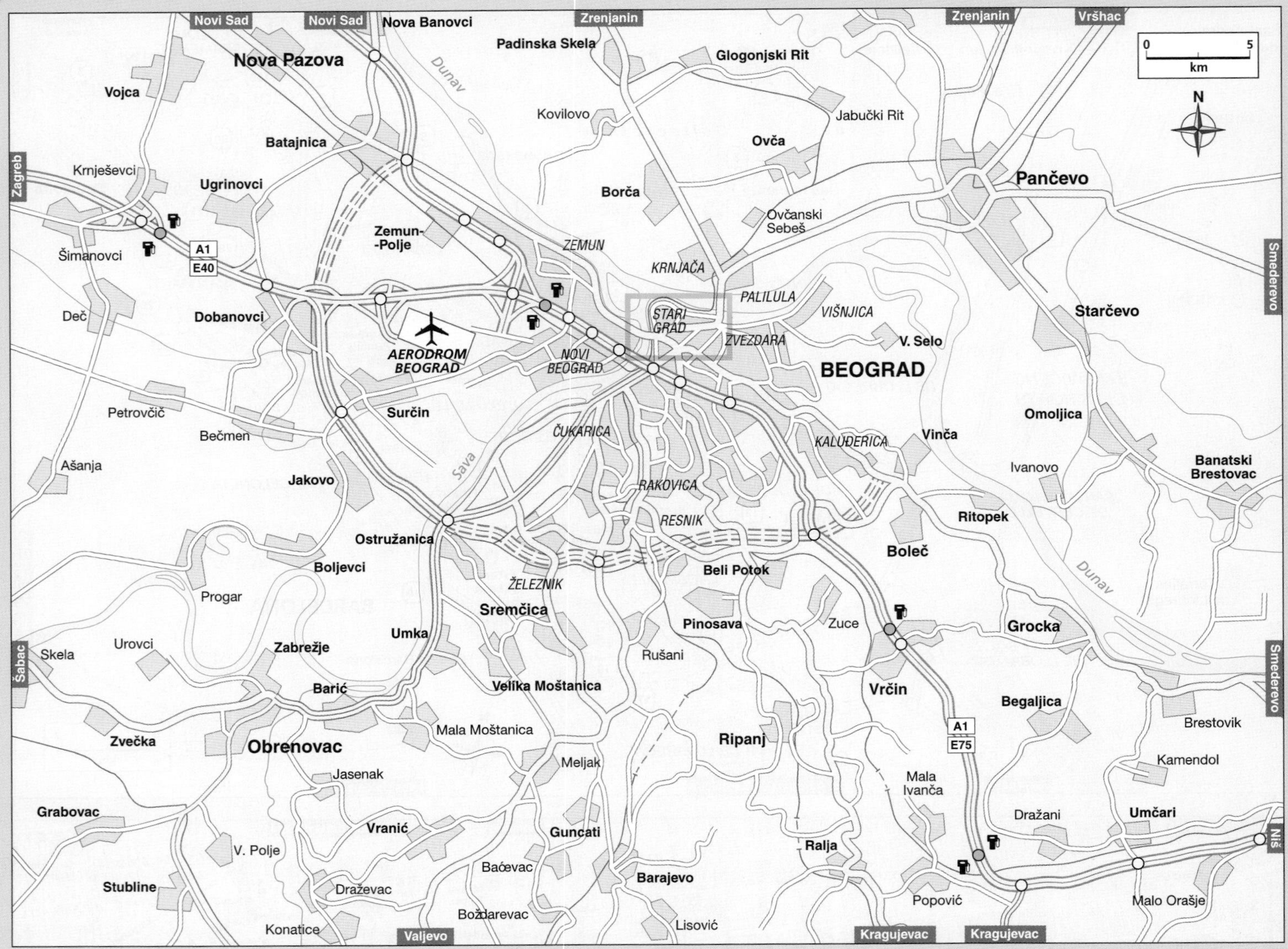
Novi Sad
Novi Sad
Nova Banovci
Zrenjanin
Zrenjanin
Vršhac
0
5
km
N
Padinska Skela
Nova Pazova
Glogonjski Rit
Dunav
Vojca
Kovilovo
Jabučki Rit
Batajnica
Ovča
Zagreb
Krnješevci
Pančevo
Ugrinovci
Borča
Ovčanski Sebeš
Šimanovci
A1
E40
Zemun--Polje
ZEMUN
KRNJAČA
Smederevo
PALILULA
Deč
Dobanovci
STARI GRAD
VIŠNJICA
Starčevo
ZVEZDARA
V. Selo
AERODROM BEOGRAD
NOVI BEOGRAD
BEOGRAD
Petrovčič
Surčin
Omoljica
Bečmen
ČUKARICA
Vinča
KALUĐERICA
Sava
Ašanja
Ivanovo
Banatski Brestovac
Jakovo
RAKOVICA
Ritopek
RESNIK
Ostružanica
Boleč
Boljevci
Beli Potok
Dunav
ŽELEZNIK
Progar
Sremčica
Pinosava
Zuce
Grocka
Umka
Šabac
Skela
Urovci
Zabrežje
Rušani
Smederevo
Barič
Velika Moštanica
Vrčin
Begaljica
A1
E75
Brestovik
Zvečka
Mala Moštanica
Ripanj
Obrenovac
Meljak
Kamendol
Jasenak
Mala Ivanča
Grabovac
Dražani
Umčari
Vranić
Guncati
Niš
V. Polje
Ralja
Baćevac
Stubline
Draževac
Barajevo
Popović
Malo Orašje
Boždarevac
Konatice
Lisović
Valjevo
Kragujevac
Kragujevac

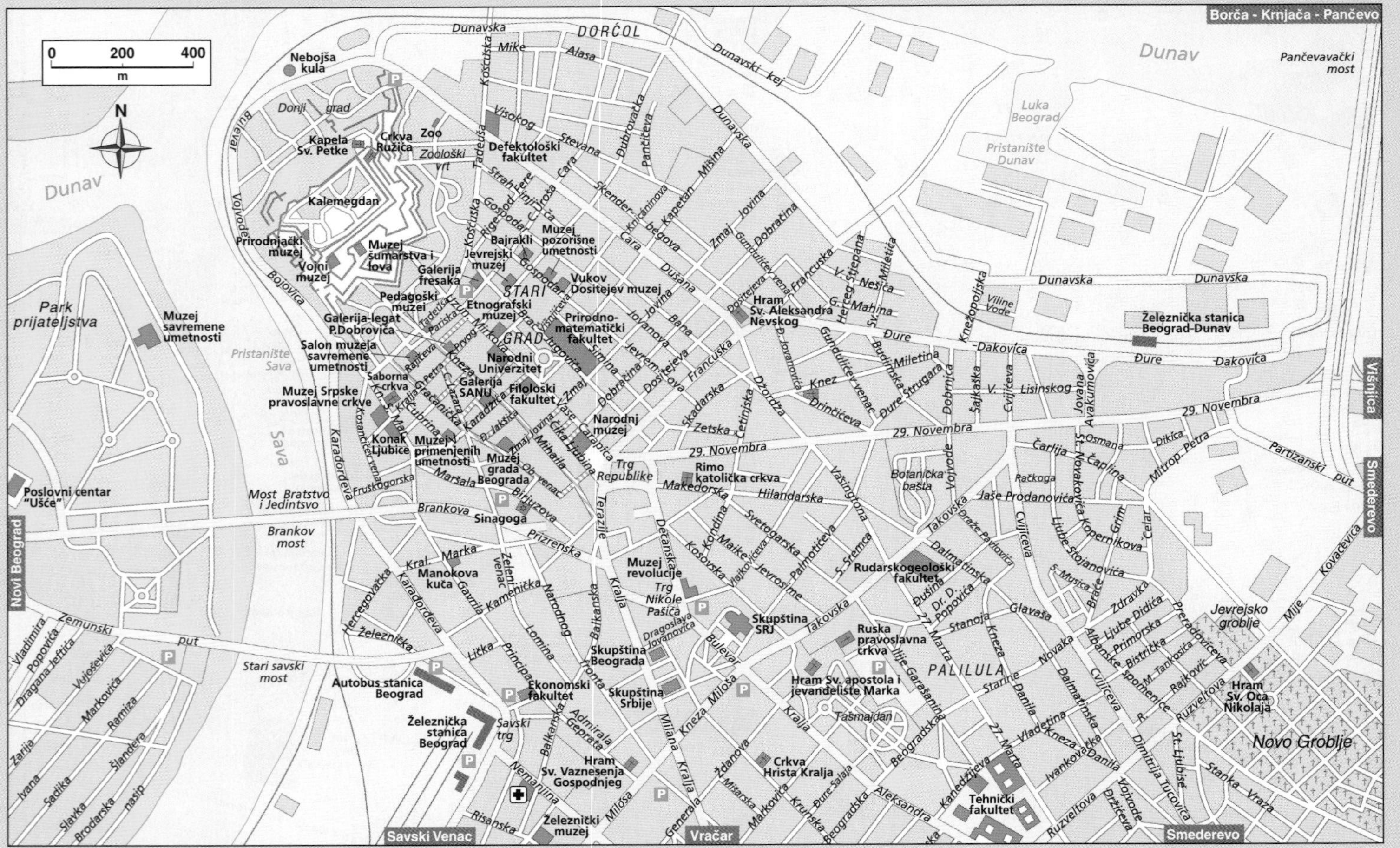
Borča - Krnjača - Pančevo
Dunavska
DORĆOL
0
200
400
m
Nebojša kula
Dunav
Pančevavački most
Dunavski kej
Luka Beograd
Pristanište Dunav
N
Donji grad
Zoo
Crkva Ružica
Kapela Sv. Petke
Zoološki vrt
Defektološki fakultet
Dunav
Kalemegdan
Muzej pozorišne umetnosti
Prirodnjački muzej
Muzej šumarstva i lova
Bajrakli
Jevrejski muzej
Vojni muzej
Galerija fresaka
Vukov Dositejev muzej
Dunavska
Dunavska
Pedagoški muzej
STARI
Hram Sv. Aleksandra Nevskog
Park prijateljstva
Muzej savremene umetnosti
Galerija-legat P.Dobrovića
Etnografski muzej
Prirodno-matematički fakultet
Železnička stanica Beograd-Dunav
Salon muzeja savremene umetnosti
GRAD
Pristanište Sava
Narodni Univerzitet
Muzej Srpske pravoslavne crkve
Galerija SANU
Filološki fakultet
Saborna crkva
Sava
Narodni muzej
29. Novembra
29. Novembra
Konak Ljubice
Muzej primenjenih umetnosti
Muzej grada Beograda
Trg Republike
Rimo katolička crkva
Botanička bašta
Poslovni centar "Ušće"
Most Bratstva i Jedintsvo
Brankova
Sinagoga
Brankov most
Novi Beograd
Manokova kuća
Muzej revolucije
Rudarskogeološki fakultet
Trg Nikole Pašića
Skupština SRJ
Ruska pravoslavna crkva
Jevrejsko groblje
Skupština Beograda
PALILULA
Stari savski most
Autobus stanica Beograd
Ekonomski fakultet
Skupština Srbije
Hram Sv. apostola i jevanđeliste Marka
Hram Sv. Oca Nikolaja
Železnička stanica Beograd
Savski trg
Tašmajdan
Novo Groblje
Hram Sv. Vaznesenja Gospodnjeg
Crkva Hrista Kralja
Tehnički fakultet
Železnički muzej
Savski Venac
Vračar
Smederevo
Višnjica
Smederevo

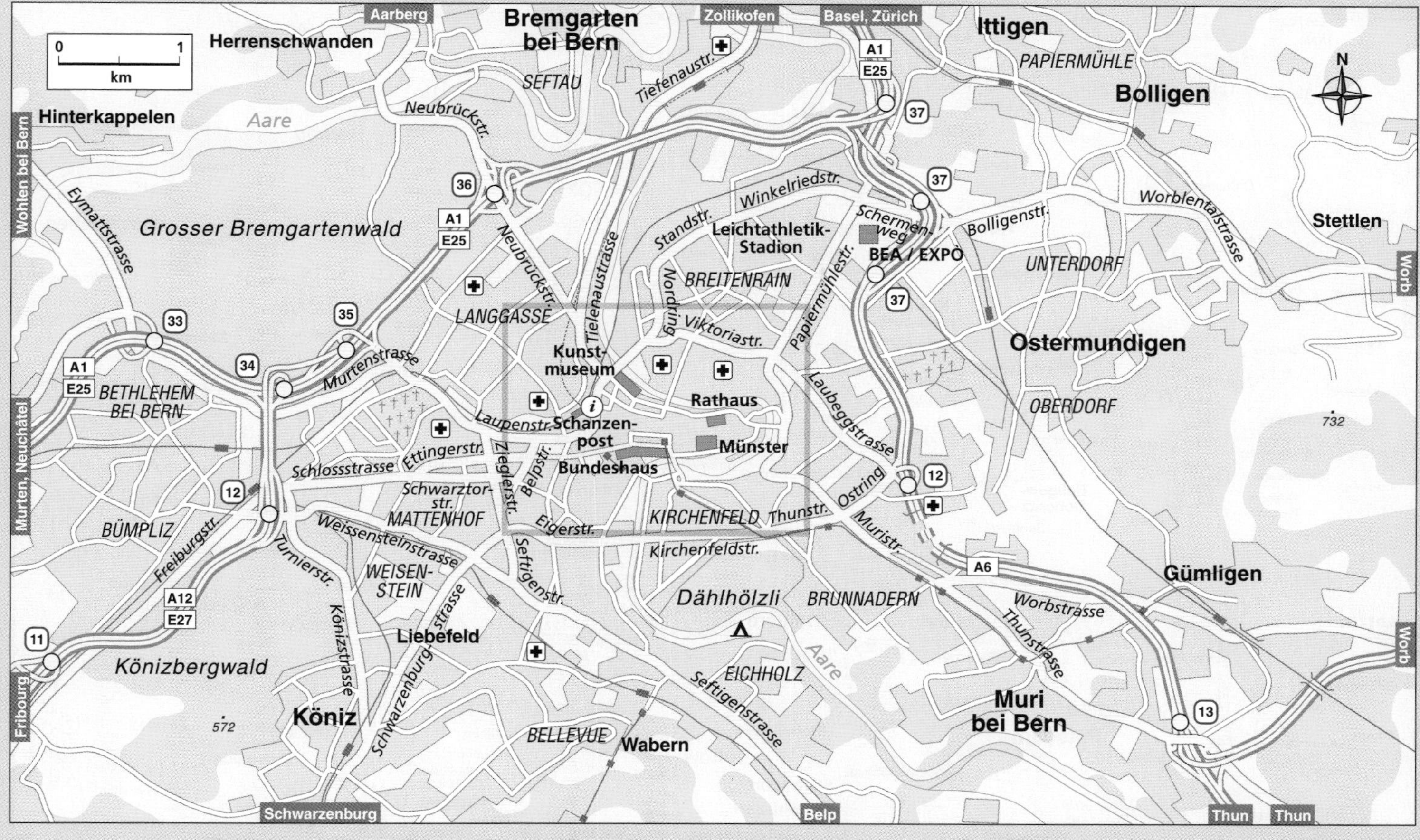
Aarberg
Zollikofen
Basel, Zürich
Bremgarten bei Bern
Ittigen
Herrenschwanden
0 1 km
PAPIERMÜHLE
SEFTAU
Bolligen
Hinterkappelen
Aare
Neubrückstr.
Tiefenaustr.
Wohlen bei Bern
Eymattstrasse
Grosser Bremgartenwald
Winkelriedstr.
Standstr.
Leichtathletik-Stadion
Schermenweg
BEA / EXPO
Bolligenstr.
Worblentalstrasse
Stettlen
UNTERDORF
Worb
Neubrückstr.
Tiefenaustrasse
Nordring
BREITENRAIN
Papiermühlestr.
LANGGASSE
Viktoriastr.
Ostermundigen
BETHLEHEM BEI BERN
Murtenstrasse
Kunstmuseum
Rathaus
Laubeggstrasse
OBERDORF
Murten, Neuchâtel
Laupenstr.
Schanzenpost
Münster
732
Schlossstrasse
Ettingerstr.
Bundeshaus
Schwarztorstr.
MATTENHOF
Ziegelstr.
Belpstr.
Eigerstr.
KIRCHENFELD
Thunstr.
Ostring
Muristr.
BÜMPLIZ
Freiburgstr.
Weissensteinstrasse
WEISENSTEIN
Turnierstr.
Seftigenstr.
Kirchenfeldstr.
Dählhölzli
BRUNNADERN
Gümligen
Worbstrasse
Thunstrasse
Worb
Köniz
Liebefeld
Schwarzenburgstrasse
Könizstrasse
Könizbergwald
EICHHOLZ
Aare
Seftigenstrasse
Muri bei Bern
Fribourg
572
BELLEVUE
Wabern
Schwarzenburg
Belp
Thun
Thun
A1
E25
A6
A12
E27
11
12
13
33
34
35
36
37

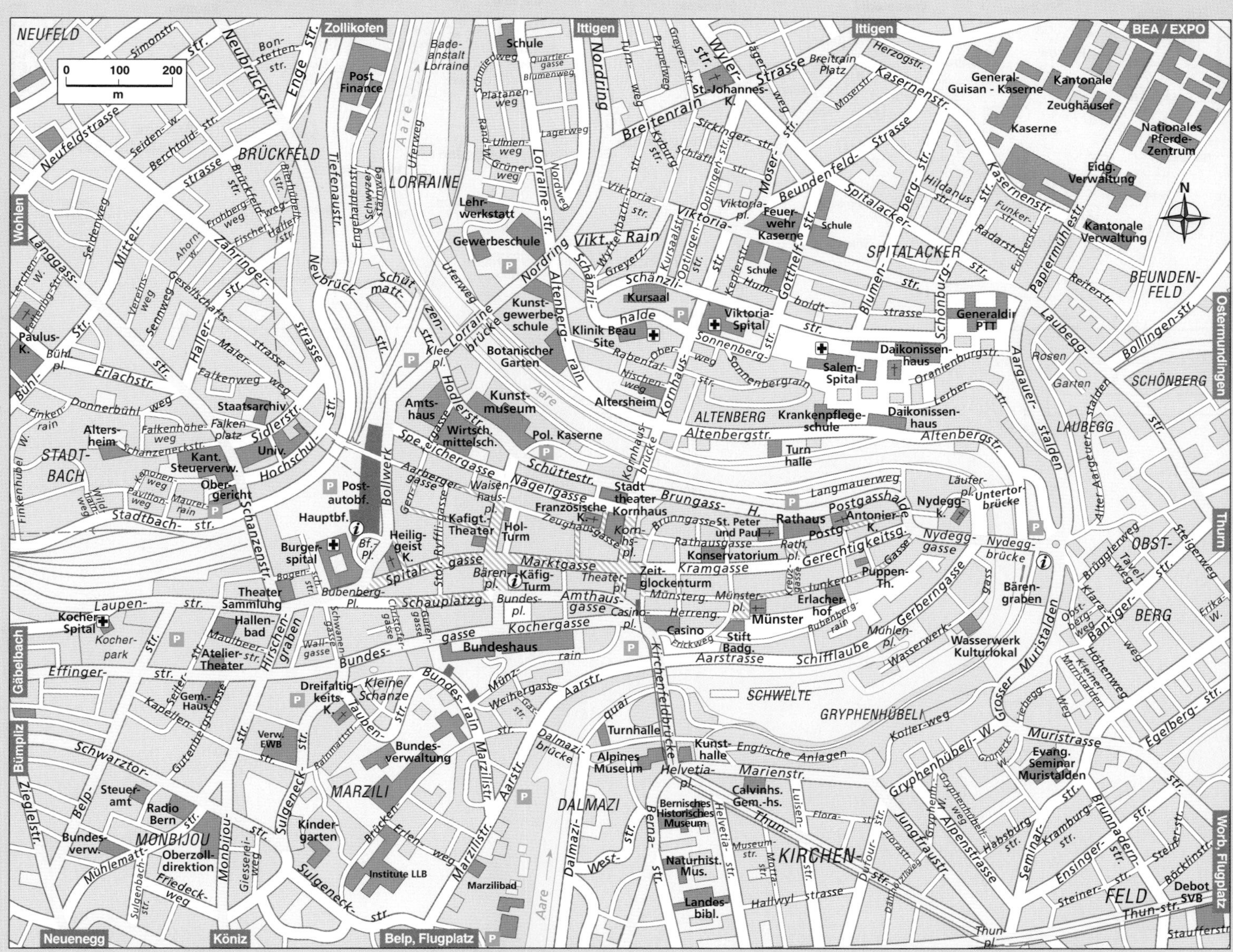
NEUFELD
Zollikofen
Ittigen
Ittigen
BEA / EXPO
0 100 200 m
Neubrückstr.
Engestr.
Bonstettenstr.
Simonstr.
Post Finance
Bade-anstalt Lorraine
Schule
Nordring
Wylerstr.
St.-Johannes-K.
Breitrain Platz
Herzogstr.
Kasernenstr.
General-Guisan - Kaserne
Kantonale Zeughäuser
Kaserne
Nationales Pferde-Zentrum
Neufeldstrasse
BRÜCKFELD
LORRAINE
Aare
Uferweg
Breitenrain
Beundenfeldstrasse
Eidg. Verwaltung
Lehrwerkstatt
Gewerbeschule
Viktoriastr.
Viktoriapl.
Feuerwehr Kaserne
Schule
Spitalackerstr.
SPITALACKER
Kasernenstr.
Kantonale Verwaltung
Papiermühlestr.
BEUNDENFELD
Wohlen
Langgassstr.
Mittelstr.
Zähringerstr.
Neubrückstrasse
Lorrainebrücke
Kunstgewerbeschule
Schänzlistr.
Kursaal
Viktoria-Spital
Schule
Generaldir PTT
Ostermundingen
Paulus-K.
Bühlpl.
Erlachstr.
Hallerstrasse
Falkenweg
Botanischer Garten
Klinik Beau Site
Rabental
Sonnenbergstr.
Salem-Spital
Daikonissenhaus
Oranienburgstr.
Laubeggstr.
SCHÖNBERG
Donnerbühlweg
Staatsarchiv
Falkenplatz
Amtshaus
Kunstmuseum
Hodlerstr.
Altersheim
Kornhausstr.
Krankenpflegeschule
Daikonissenhaus
Aargauerstalden
LAUBEGG
STADTBACH
Altersheim
Univ.
Hochschulstr.
Kant. Steuerverw.
Obergericht
Wirtsch. mittelsch.
Pol. Kaserne
ALTENBERG
Altenbergstr.
Turnhalle
Speichergasse
Schüttestr.
Nägeligasse
Stadttheater
Kornhaus
Brunngasse
Langmauerweg
Nydeggk.
Untertorbrücke
Thurn
Postautobf.
Hauptbf.
Bollwerk
Aarbergergasse
Waisenhauspl.
Französische K.
Kornhauspl.
St. Peter und Paul
Rathaus
Postgasse
Antonier-K.
Postg.
Gerechtigkeitsg.
Nydegggasse
Nydeggbrücke
OBST-BERG
Stadtbachstr.
Burgerspital
Bf.-Pl.
Kafigt. Theater
Holl.-Turm
Heiliggeist K.
Spitalgasse
Marktgasse
Käfigturm
Bärenpl.
Zeitglockenturm
Kramgasse
Konservatorium
Puppen-Th.
Junkerngasse
Bärengraben
Laupenstr.
Schanzenstr.
Theater Sammlung
Bubenbergpl.
Schauplatzg.
Amthausgasse
Casinopl.
Münsterg.
Herreng.
Münsterpl.
Erlacherhof
Münster
Bubenbergrain
Kocher Spital
Kocherpark
Hallenbad
Atelier-Theater
Hirschengraben
Bundesgasse
Kochergasse
Bundeshaus
Casino
Stift Badg.
Mühlenpl.
Gerberngasse
Wasserwerk Kulturlokal
BERG
Bantigerstr.
Gäbelbach
Effingerstr.
Dreifaltigkeits-K.
Kleine Schanze
Bundesrain
Aarstr.
Aarstrasse
Schifflaube
Wasserweg
SCHWELTE
Grosser Muristalden
Kapellenstr.
Gem.-Haus
Verw. EWB
Turnhalle
Kirchenfeldbrücke
GRYPHENHÜBELI
Kollerweg
Egelbergstr.
Bümpliz
Schwarztorstr.
Bundesverwaltung
Dalmazibrücke
Alpines Museum
Kunsthalle
Helvetiapl.
Englische Anlagen
Marienstr.
Muristrasse
Evang. Seminar Muristalden
Ziegelstr.
Steueramt
Radio Bern
MARZILI
DALMAZI
Calvinhs. Gem.-hs.
Bernisches Historisches Museum
Gryphenhübeliweg
Jungfraustr.
Alpenstrasse
Brunnadernstr.
Bundesverw.
MONBIJOU
Oberzolldirektion
Kindergarten
Sulgeneckstr.
Mühlemattstr.
Friedeckweg
Institute LLB
Marzilibad
Aare
Dalmaziweg
Bernastr.
Naturhist. Mus.
Landesbibl.
KIRCHENFELD
Hallwylstrasse
Thunstr.
FELD
Debot SVB
Stauffacherstr.
Worb, Flugplatz
Neuenegg
Köniz
Belp, Flugplatz

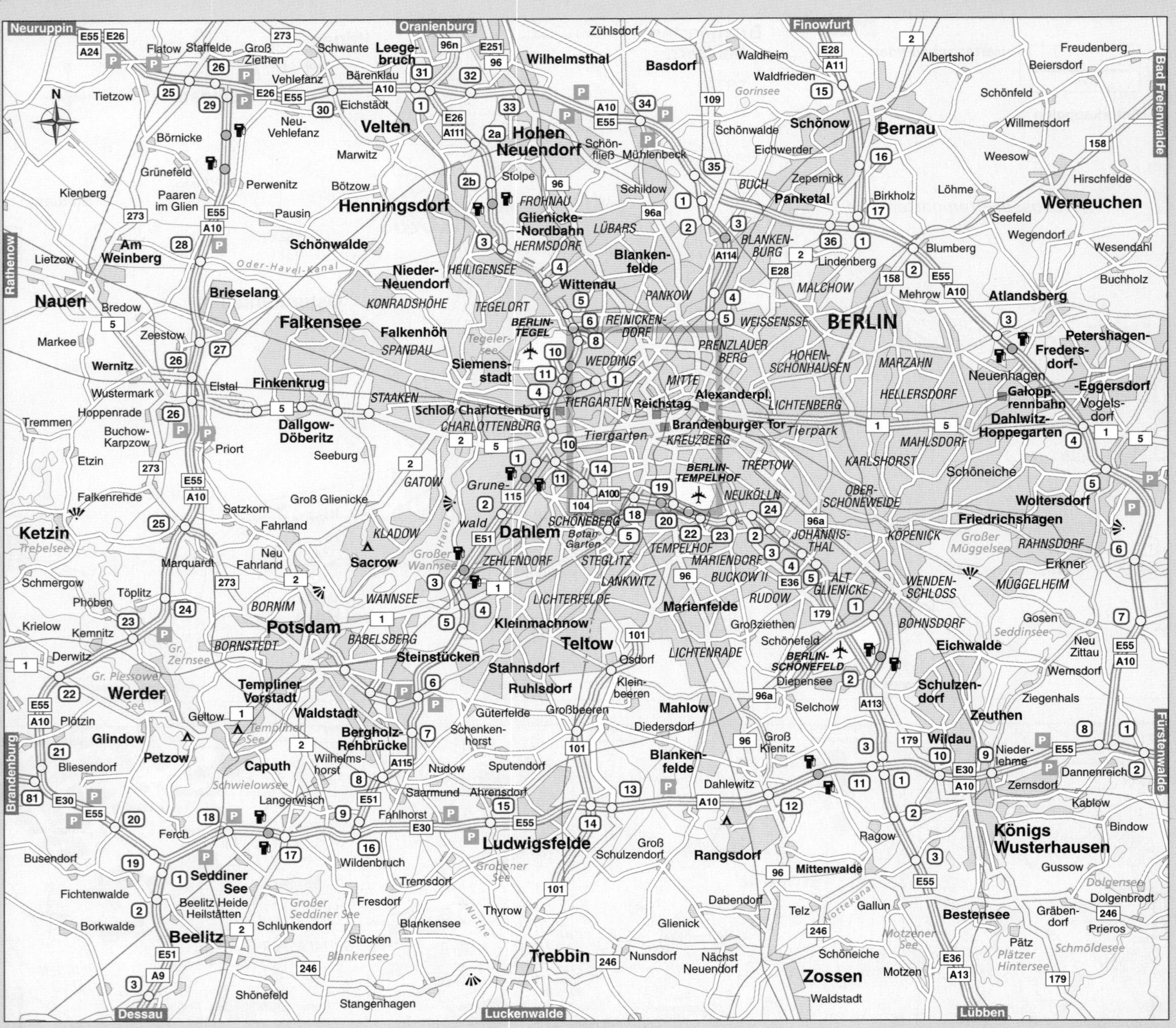
Neuruppin
Oranienburg
Finowfurt
Bad Freienwalde
Rathenow
Brandenburg
Fürstenwalde
Dessau
Luckenwalde
Lübben
N
Flatow
Staffelde
Groß Ziethen
Schwante
Leegebruch
Zühlsdorf
Wilhelmsthal
Basdorf
Waldheim
Waldfrieden
Albertshof
Freudenberg
Beiersdorf
Tietzow
Vehlefanz
Bärenklau
Eichstädt
Neu-Vehlefanz
Velten
Hohen Neuendorf
Schönfließ
Mühlenbeck
Gorinsee
Schönow
Bernau
Schönfeld
Willmersdorf
Börnicke
Grünefeld
Marwitz
Schönwalde
Eichwerder
Weesow
Hirschfelde
Kienberg
Paaren im Glien
Perwenitz
Bötzow
Pausin
Henningsdorf
Stolpe
FROHNAU
Glienicke-Nordbahn
HERMSDORF
LÜBARS
Schildow
BUCH
Zepernick
Panketal
Birkholz
Löhme
Werneuchen
Seefeld
Wegendorf
Wesendahl
Am Weinberg
Schönwalde
Oder-Havel-Kanal
Nieder-Neuendorf
HEILIGENSEE
Wittenau
Blankenfelde
BLANKENBURG
Lindenberg
Blumberg
Lietzow
Nauen
Bredow
Brieselang
KONRADSHÖHE
TEGELORT
PANKOW
MALCHOW
Mehrow
Atlandsberg
Buchholz
Falkensee
Falkenhöh
SPANDAU
BERLIN-TEGEL
Tegeler See
REINICKENDORF
WEISSENSEE
BERLIN
Petershagen-Fredersdorf-
Markee
Zeestow
Wernitz
Siemensstadt
WEDDING
PRENZLAUER BERG
HOHENSCHÖNHAUSEN
MARZAHN
Neuenhagen
-Eggersdorf
Wustermark
Elstal
Finkenkrug
STAAKEN
MITTE
Alexanderpl.
LICHTENBERG
HELLERSDORF
Galopprennbahn
Vogelsdorf
Tremmen
Hoppenrade
Buchow-Karpzow
Dallgow-Döberitz
Schloß Charlottenburg
TIERGARTEN
Reichstag
Brandenburger Tor
CHARLOTTENBURG
Tiergarten
KREUZBERG
Tierpark
MAHLSDORF
Dahlwitz-Hoppegarten
Etzin
Priort
Seeburg
GATOW
Grunewald
BERLIN-TEMPELHOF
TREPTOW
KARLSHORST
Schöneiche
Falkenrehde
Satzkorn
Groß Glienicke
NEUKÖLLN
OBER-SCHÖNEWEIDE
Woltersdorf
Ketzin
Trebelsee
Fahrland
KLADOW
Havel
Dahlem
Botan. Garten
SCHÖNEBERG
TEMPELHOF
JOHANNISTHAL
KÖPENICK
Friedrichshagen
Großer Müggelsee
RAHNSDORF
Marquardt
Neu Fahrland
Sacrow
Großer Wannsee
ZEHLENDORF
STEGLITZ
MARIENDORF
Erkner
Schmergow
Phöben
Töplitz
BORNIM
WANNSEE
LICHTERFELDE
LANKWITZ
BUCKOW II
ALT GLIENICKE
WENDENSCHLOSS
MÜGGELHEIM
Krielow
Kemnitz
Potsdam
Kleinmachnow
Marienfelde
RUDOW
Großziethen
BOHNSDORF
Gosen
Derwitz
Gr. Zernsee
BORNSTEDT
BABELSBERG
Teltow
Schönefeld
BERLIN-SCHÖNEFELD
Eichwalde
Seddinsee
Neu Zittau
Wernsdorf
Gr. Plessower See
Werder
Steinstücken
Stahnsdorf
Osdorf
LICHTENRADE
Diepensee
Schulzendorf
Templiner Vorstadt
Waldstadt
Ruhlsdorf
Kleinbeeren
Mahlow
Selchow
Ziegenhals
Zeuthen
Plötzin
Geltow
Templiner See
Güterfelde
Großbeeren
Diedersdorf
Glindow
Petzow
Bergholz-Rehbrücke
Schenkenhorst
Groß Kienitz
Wildau
Niederlehme
Bliesendorf
Caputh
Wilhelmshorst
Nudow
Sputendorf
Blankenfelde
Dahlewitz
Dannenreich
Schwielowsee
Langerwisch
Saarmund
Ahrensdorf
Zernsdorf
Kablow
Fahlhorst
Ferch
Bindow
Busendorf
Ludwigsfelde
Groß Schulzendorf
Rangsdorf
Ragow
Königs Wusterhausen
Gussow
Seddiner See
Wildenbruch
Großer Seddiner See
Tremsdorf
Mittenwalde
Dolgensee
Dolgenbrodt
Fichtenwalde
Beelitz Heide
Heilstätten
Fresdorf
Thyrow
Dabendorf
Telz
Gallun
Nottekanal
Bestensee
Gräbendorf
Prieros
Borkwalde
Beelitz
Schlunkendorf
Blankensee
Glienick
Motzener See
Pätz
Plätzer Hintersee
Schmöldesee
Stücken
Nuthe
Trebbin
Nunsdorf
Nächst Neuendorf
Schöneiche
Zossen
Motzen
Shönefeld
Stangenhagen
Waldstadt

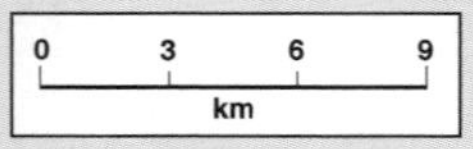
0
3
6
9
km

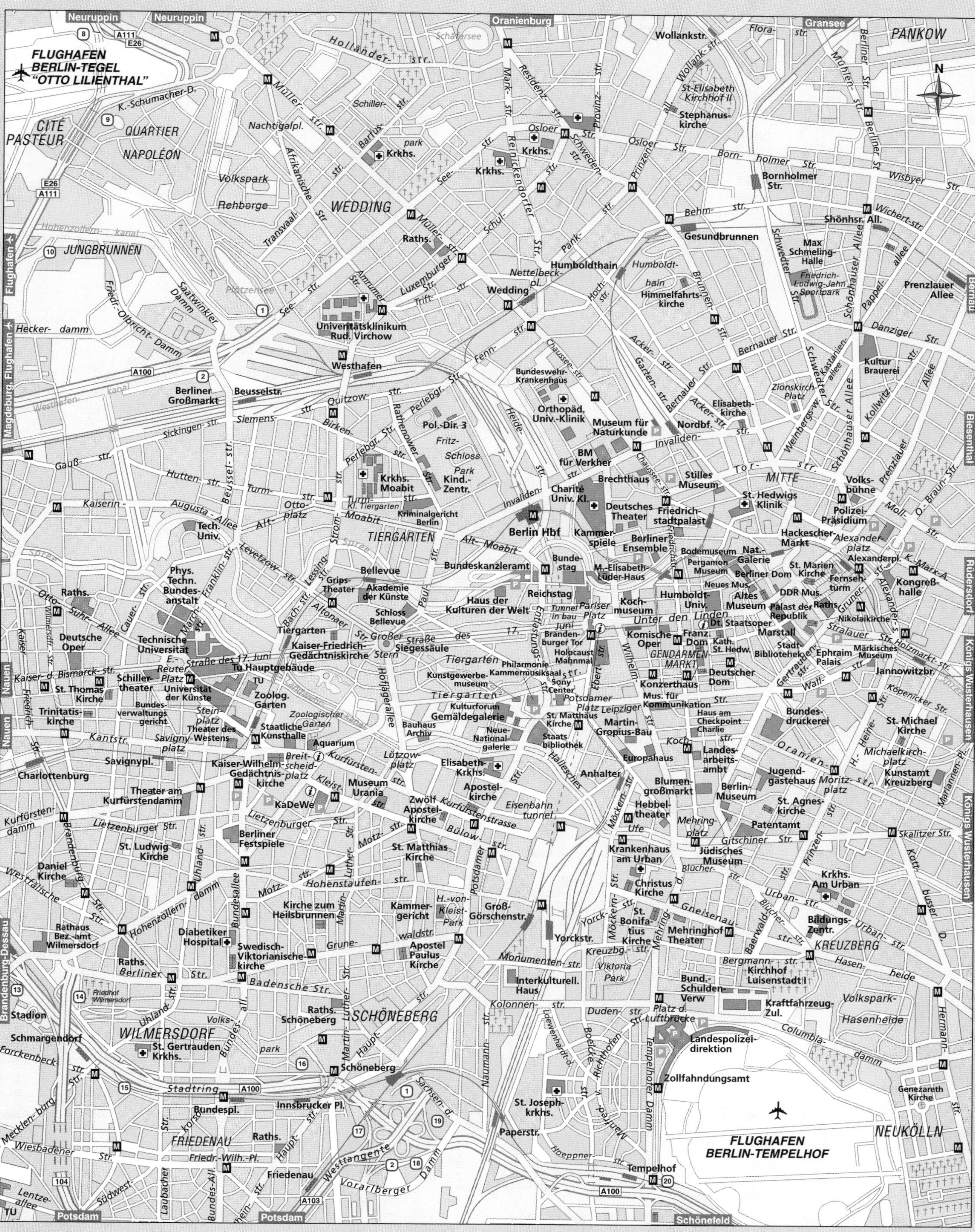
Neuruppin
Neuruppin
Oranienburg
Gransee
PANKOW
FLUGHAFEN
BERLIN-TEGEL
"OTTO LILIENTHAL"
A111
E26
Schäfersee
Holländer-str.
Wollankstr.
Flora-str.
Berliner Str.
Mühlen-str.
Müller-str.
Schiller-park
K.-Schumacher-D.
CITÉ PASTEUR
QUARTIER NAPOLÉON
Nachtigalpl.
Barfus-str.
Krkhs.
Osloer Str.
Schweden-str.
Residenz-str.
Provinz-str.
St.-Elisabeth Kirchhof II
Stephanus-kirche
Born-holmer Str.
Wisbyer Str.
Bornholmer Str.
Volkspark Rehberge
Afrikanische Str.
See-str.
Reinickendorfer Str.
WEDDING
Transvaal-str.
Hohenzollern-kanal
JUNGBRUNNEN
Flughafen
Raths.
Schul-str.
Pank-str.
Behm-str.
Gesundbrunnen
Schönhsr. Allee
Wichert-str.
Max Schmeling-Halle
Friedrich-Ludwig-Jahn Sportpark
Humboldthain
Humboldt-hain
Himmelfahrts-kirche
Brunnen-str.
Nettelbeck-pl.
Wedding
Luxemburger Str.
Amrumer Str.
Plötzensee
Saatwinkler Damm
Friedr.-Olbricht-Damm
Hecker-damm
Universitätsklinikum Rud. Virchow
Westhafen
Fenn-str.
Chaussee-str.
Acker-str.
Bernauer Str.
Schwedter Str.
Pappel-allee
Danziger Str.
Kultur Brauerei
Prenzlauer Allee
Bernau
Magdeburg, Flughafen
A100
Westhafen-kanal
Berliner Großmarkt
Beusselstr.
Quitzow-str.
Perlebgr. Str.
Rathenower Str.
Bundeswehr-Krankenhaus
Orthopäd. Univ.-Klinik
Zionskirch-Platz
Elisabeth-kirche
Kastanien-allee
Kollwitz-str.
Sickingen-str.
Siemens-str.
Birken-str.
Pol.-Dir. 3
Fritz-Schloss Park
Heide-str.
Museum für Naturkunde
Nordbf.
Invaliden-str.
Weinbergs-w.
Blesenthal
Gauß-str.
Hutten-str.
Turm-str.
Krkhs. Moabit
Kind.-Zentr.
BM für Verkehr
Brechthaus
Stilles Museum
Tor-str.
MITTE
Volks-bühne
Kaiserin-Augusta-Allee
Otto-platz
Kl. Tiergarten
Kriminalgericht Berlin
Charité Univ. Kl.
Deutsches Theater
St. Hedwigs Klinik
Polizei-Präsidium
Tech. Univ.
Alt-Moabit
TIERGARTEN
Berlin Hbf
Kammer-spiele
Friedrich-stadtpalast
Hackescher Markt
Alexander-platz
Levetzow-str.
Bellevue
Bundeskanzleramt
Bunde-stag
Berliner Ensemble
M.-Elisabeth-Lüder-Haus
Bodemuseum
Pergamon Museum
Nat. Galerie
Berliner Dom
St. Marien Kirche
Fernseh-turm
Alexanderpl.
Kongreß-halle
Rüdersdorf
Phys. Techn. Bundes-anstalt
Raths.
Grips-Theater
Akademie der Künste
Schloss Bellevue
Haus der Kulturen der Welt
Reichstag
Pariser Platz
Koch-museum
Humboldt-Univ.
Neues Mus.
Altes Museum
DDR Mus.
Palast der Republik
Raths.
Nikolaikirche
Deutsche Oper
Technische Universität
Tiergarten
Kaiser-Friedrich-Gedächtniskirche
Siegessäule
Straße des 17. Juni
Unter den Linden
Branden-burger Tor
Komische Oper
Franz. Dom
Kath. St. Hedw.
Dt. Staatsoper
Marstall
Stadt-bibliothek
Ephraim Palais
Märkisches Museum
Jannowitzbr.
Königs Wusterhausen
Nauen
Kaiser-d.-Bismarck-str.
St. Thomas Kirche
Schiller-theater
Ernst-Reuter-Platz
Universität der Künste
TU Hauptgebäude
TU
Philharmonie
Kammermusiksaal
Holocaust Mahnmal
Sony Center
GENDARMEN-MARKT
Konzerthaus
Deutscher Dom
Trinitatis-kirche
Bundes-verwaltungs-gericht
Theater des Westens
Zoolog. Garten
Zoologischer Garten
Kunstgewerbe-museum
Kulturforum
Gemäldegalerie
Potsdamer Platz
Leipziger Platz
Mus. für Kommunikation
Haus am Checkpoint Charlie
Bundes-druckerei
St. Michael Kirche
Kantstr.
Savigny-platz
Staatliche Kunsthalle
Aquarium
Bauhaus Archiv
Neue National-galerie
St. Matthäus Kirche
Staats bibliothek
Martin-Gropius-Bau
Landes-arbeits-amt
Michaelkirch-platz
Savignypl.
Charlottenburg
Kaiser-Wilhelm-Gedächtnis-kirche
Breit-scheid-platz
Lützow-platz
Elisabeth-Krkhs.
Europahaus
Jugend-gästehaus
Moritz-platz
Kunstamt Kreuzberg
Theater am Kurfürstendamm
KaDeWe
Museum Urania
Apostel-kirche
Anhalter
Blumen-großmarkt
Berlin-Museum
St. Agnes-kirche
Kurfürsten-damm
Lietzenburger Str.
Zwölf Apostel-kirche
Kurfürstenstrasse
Eisenbahn tunnel
Hebbel-theater
Mehring-platz
Patentamt
Berliner Festspiele
St. Ludwig Kirche
Bülow-str.
St. Matthias Kirche
Möckern-str.
Ufe
Krankenhaus am Urban
Gitschiner Str.
Jüdisches Museum
Skalitzer Str.
Daniel Kirche
Westfälische Str.
Hohenzollern-damm
Hohenstaufen-str.
Kirche zum Heilsbrunnen
Kammer-gericht
H.-von-Kleist-Park
Groß-Görschenstr.
Christus Kirche
Krkhs. Am Urban
Blücher-str.
Urban-str.
Bildungs-Zentr.
Rathaus Bez.-amt Wilmersdorf
Diabetiker Hospital
Swedisch-Viktorianische-kirche
Apostel Paulus Kirche
Yorckstr.
St. Bonifa-tius Kirche
Mehringhof Theater
KREUZBERG
Gneisenau-str.
Raths.
Berliner Str.
Monumenten-str.
Kreuzbg.
Viktoria Park
Bergmann-str.
Kirchhof Luisenstadt I
Hasen-heide
Brandenburg-Dessau
Friedhof Wilmersdorf
Badensche Str.
Interkulturell. Haus
Bund.-Schulden-Verw
Kraftfahrzeug-Zul.
Volkspark-Hasenheide
Stadion
Schmargendorf
WILMERSDORF
Raths. Schöneberg
SCHÖNEBERG
Kolonnen-str.
Duden-str.
Platz d. Luftbrücke
Columbia-damm
Forckenbeck-str.
St. Gertrauden Krkhs.
Volks-park
Schöneberg
Landespolizei-direktion
Hermann-str.
Stadtring
Innsbrucker Pl.
Bundespl.
Zollfahndungsamt
St. Joseph-krkhs.
Genezareth Kirche
Mecklen-burg
FRIEDENAU
Raths.
Sachsen-d.
Paperstr.
Tempelhofer Damm
Manfred-v.-Richthofen-str.
FLUGHAFEN BERLIN-TEMPELHOF
NEUKÖLLN
Wiesbadener Str.
Friedr.-Wilh.-Pl.
Friedenau
Westtangente
Vorarlberger Damm
Hoeppner-str.
Tempelhof
Südwest-korso
Lentze-allee
TU
Potsdam
Potsdam
A103
A100
Schönefeld

0 400 800
m

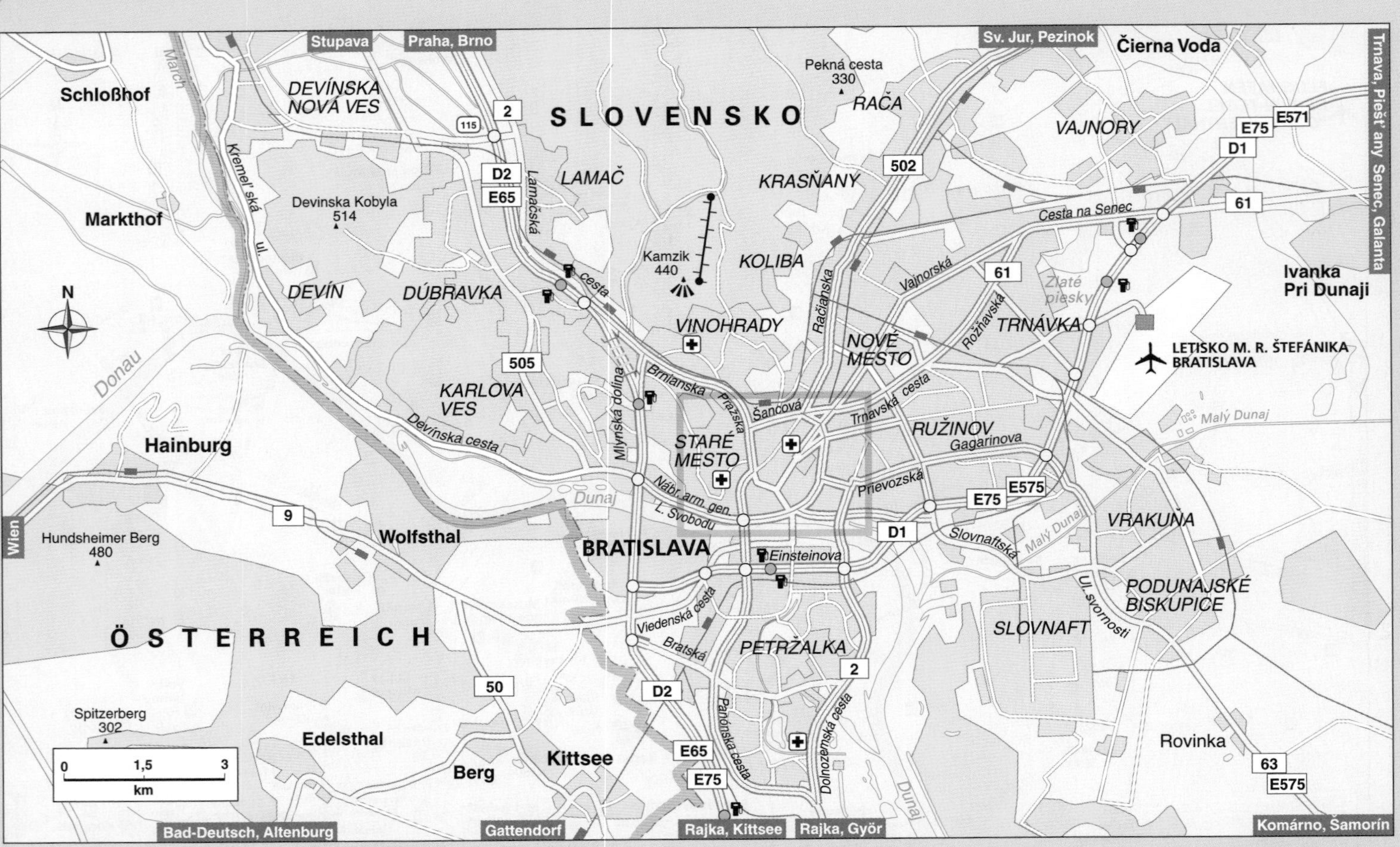
Stupava
Praha, Brno
Sv. Jur, Pezinok
Čierna Voda
Trnava, Piešťany Senec, Galanta
Schloßhof
DEVÍNSKA NOVÁ VES
SLOVENSKO
Pekná cesta 330
RAČA
VAJNORY
E75
E571
D1
502
Kremeľ ská ul.
Devinska Kobyla 514
Markthof
D2
E65
Lamačská
LAMAČ
KRASŇANY
Kamzík 440
KOLIBA
Cesta na Senec
61
Ivanka Pri Dunaji
N
DEVÍN
DÚBRAVKA
cesta
VINOHRADY
Račianska
Vajnorská
Rožňavská
Zlaté piesky
TRNÁVKA
LETISKO M. R. ŠTEFÁNIKA BRATISLAVA
Donau
505
KARLOVA VES
Mlynská dolina
Brnianska
Pražská
NOVÉ MESTO
Šancová
Trnavská cesta
RUŽINOV
Gagarinova
Malý Dunaj
Hainburg
Devínska cesta
STARÉ MESTO
Prievozská
E75
E575
VRAKUŇA
Dunaj
Nábr. arm. gen. L. Svobodu
D1
Slovnaftská
Malý Dunaj
Wien
Hundsheimer Berg 480
9
Wolfsthal
BRATISLAVA
Einsteinova
PODUNAJSKÉ BISKUPICE
Ul. svornosti
Viedenská cesta
SLOVNAFT
ÖSTERREICH
Bratislavská
PETRŽALKA
2
50
D2
Spitzerberg 302
Edelsthal
Panónska cesta
Dolnozemská cesta
Dunaj
Rovinka
63
E575
0 1,5 3 km
Berg
Kittsee
E65
E75
Bad-Deutsch, Altenburg
Gattendorf
Rajka, Kittsee
Rajka, Györ
Komárno, Šamorín

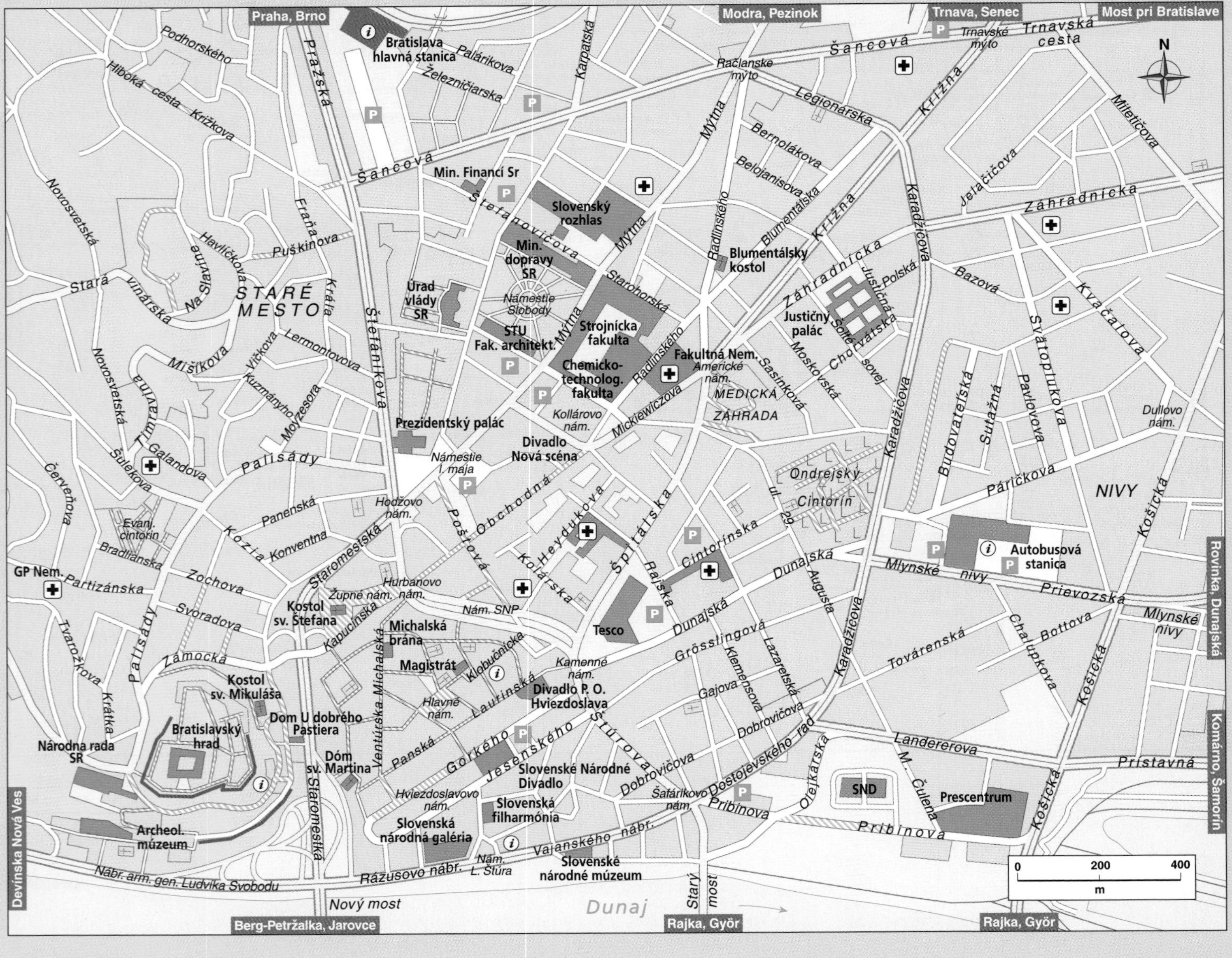
Praha, Brno
Modra, Pezinok
Trnava, Senec
Most pri Bratislave
Bratislava hlavná stanica
Palárikova
Železničiarska
Karpatská
Račianske mýto
Trnavské mýto
Trnavská cesta
Šancová
N
Podhorského
Hlboká cesta
Križkova
Pražská
Legionárska
Krížna
Mýtna
Bernolákova
Miletičova
Šancová
Min. Financí Sr
Belojanisova
Štefanovičova
Slovenský rozhlas
Jelačičova
Záhradnícka
Novosvetská
Fraňa Kráľa
Puškinova
Havlíčkova
Na Slavíne
Min. dopravy SR
Radlinského
Blumentálska
Blumentálsky kostol
Krížna
Karadžičova
Stará vinárska
STARÉ MESTO
Úrad vlády SR
Námestie Slobody
Starohorská
Záhradnícka
Justičná
Polská
Bazová
Kvačalova
Justičný palác
Šoltésovej
Chorvátska
Strojnícka fakulta
STU Fak. architekt.
Mýtna
Fakultná Nem.
Americké nám.
Chemicko-technolog. fakulta
Radlinského
Sasinkova
Moskovská
Svätoplukova
Mišíkova
Vlčkova
Lermontovova
Kuzmányho
Moyzesova
Štefánikova
Timravina
Kollárovo nám.
Mickiewiczova
MEDICKÁ ZÁHRADA
Budovateľská
Sutážná
Pavlovova
Dullovo nám.
Prezidentský palác
Divadlo Nová scéna
Šulekova
Galandova
Palisády
Námestie 1. maja
Ondrejský Cintorín
ul. 29. augusta
Páričkova
NIVY
Košická
Červeňova
Paneská
Hodžovo nám.
Obchodná
Evanj. cintorín
Kozia
Konventná
Poštová
Heydukova
Špitálska
Cintorínska
Autobusová stanica
Bradlianska
Staromestská
Kolárska
Rajská
Dunajská
Mlynské nivy
Prievozská
GP Nem.
Partizánska
Zochova
Župné nám.
Hurbanovo nám.
Kostol sv. Štefana
Nám. SNP
Tesco
Svoradova
Kapucínska
Michalská brána
Mlynské nivy
Tvarožkova
Zámocká
Palisády
Grösslingová
Chalupkova
Bottova
Košická
Magistrát
Klobučnícka
Kamenné nám.
Klemensova
Lazaretská
Továrenská
Kostol sv. Mikuláša
Ventúrska
Michalská
Laurinská
Divadlo P. O. Hviezdoslava
Gajova
Karadžičova
Krátka
Dom U dobrého Pastiera
Hlavné nám.
Dobrovičova
Národna rada SR
Bratislavský hrad
Dóm sv. Martina
Panská
Gorkého
Jesenského
Štúrova
Dostojevského rad
Landererova
Prístavná
Slovenské Národné Divadlo
Dobrovičova
Olejkárska
M. Čulena
SND
Prescentrum
Devínska Nová Ves
Hviezdoslavovo nám.
Šafárikovo nám.
Pribinova
Slovenská filharmónia
Archeol. múzeum
Staromestská
Slovenská národná galéria
Vajanského nábr.
Pribinova
Nábr. arm. gen. Ludvika Svobodu
Rázusovo nábr.
Nám. L. Štúra
Slovenské národné múzeum
Starý most
0 200 400 m
Nový most
Dunaj
Rovinka, Dunajská
Komárno, Šamorín
Berg-Petržalka, Jarovce
Rajka, Györ
Rajka, Györ

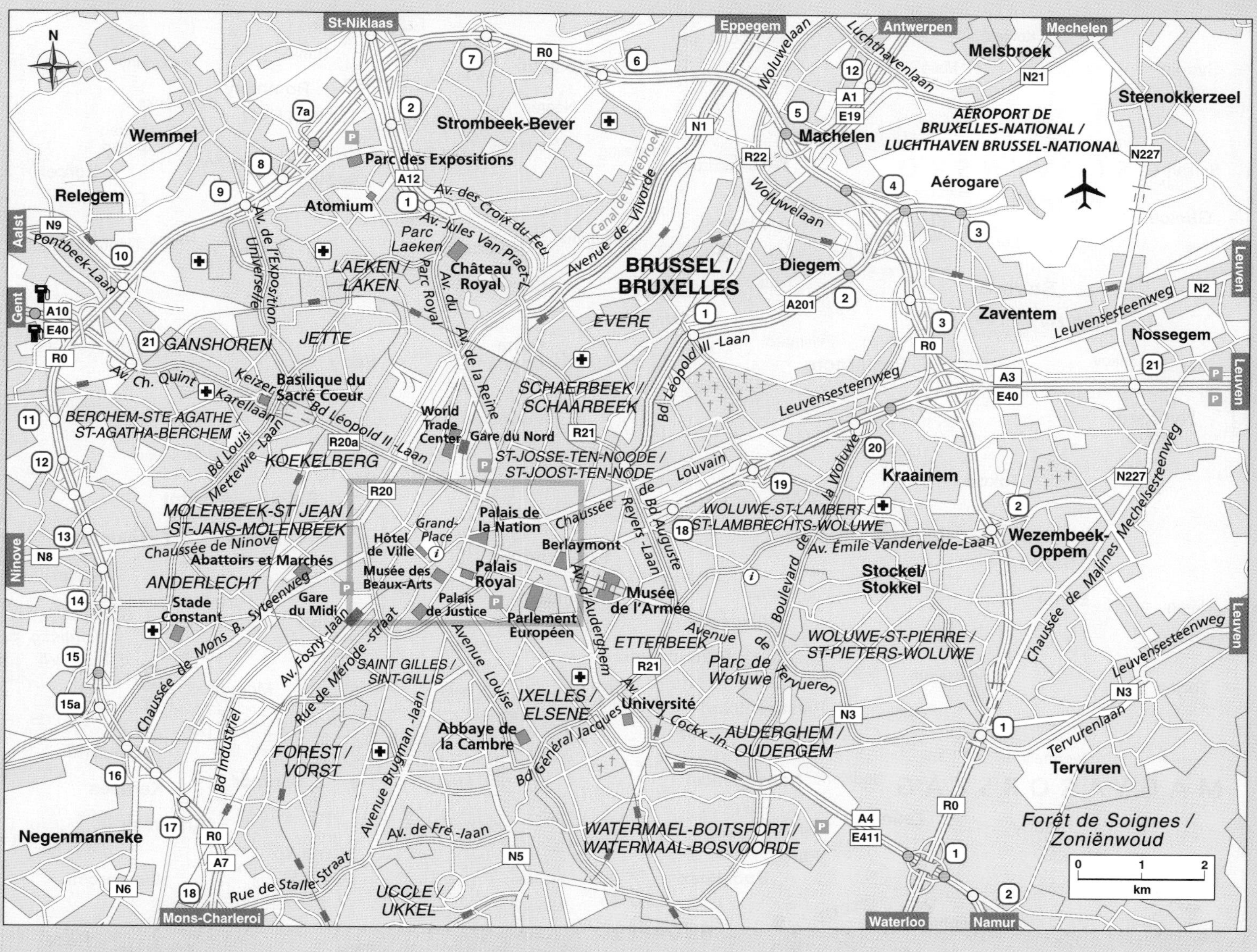
St-Niklaas
Eppegem
Antwerpen
Mechelen
Melsbroek
Steenokkerzeel
AÉROPORT DE BRUXELLES-NATIONAL / LUCHTHAVEN BRUSSEL-NATIONAL
Aérogare
Machelen
Strombeek-Bever
Wemmel
Parc des Expositions
Relegem
Atomium
Parc Laeken
Château Royal
LAEKEN / LAKEN
Aalst
Gent
GANSHOREN
JETTE
BRUSSEL / BRUXELLES
Diegem
EVERE
Zaventem
Nossegem
Leuven
Basilique du Sacré Coeur
BERCHEM-STE AGATHE / ST-AGATHA-BERCHEM
KOEKELBERG
World Trade Center
Gare du Nord
SCHAERBEEK / SCHAARBEEK
ST-JOSSE-TEN-NOODE / ST-JOOST-TEN-NODE
Kraainem
MOLENBEEK-ST JEAN / ST-JANS-MOLENBEEK
Grand-Place
Hôtel de Ville
Palais de la Nation
Berlaymont
WOLUWE-ST-LAMBERT / ST-LAMBRECHTS-WOLUWE
Wezembeek-Oppem
Ninove
Abattoirs et Marchés
ANDERLECHT
Musée des Beaux-Arts
Palais Royal
Musée de l'Armée
Stockel/ Stokkel
Stade Constant
Gare du Midi
Palais de Justice
Parlement Européen
ETTERBEEK
WOLUWE-ST-PIERRE / ST-PIETERS-WOLUWE
SAINT GILLES / SINT-GILLIS
Parc de Woluwe
IXELLES / ELSENE
Université
Abbaye de la Cambre
FOREST / VORST
AUDERGHEM / OUDERGEM
Tervuren
Forêt de Soignes / Zoniënwoud
WATERMAEL-BOITSFORT / WATERMAAL-BOSVOORDE
Negenmanneke
UCCLE / UKKEL
Mons-Charleroi
Waterloo
Namur
0 1 2 km

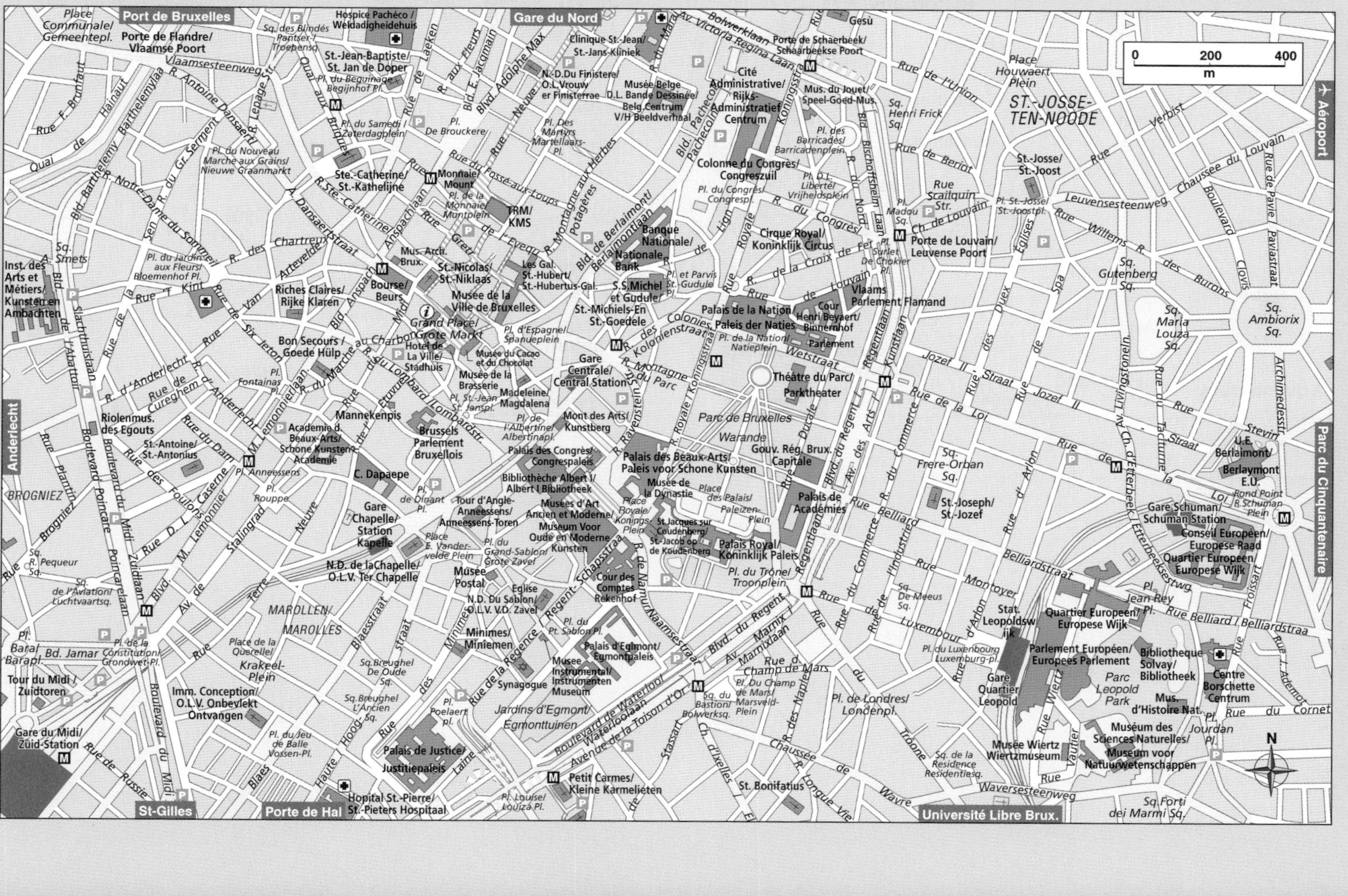
Port de Bruxelles
Gare du Nord
Aéroport
Anderlecht
Parc du Cinquantenaire
ST.-JOSSE-TEN-NOODE
0 200 400 m
Porte de Flandre/ Vlaamse Poort
St.-Jean-Baptiste/ St. Jan de Doper
Cité Administrative/ Rijks-Administratief Centrum
Colonne du Congrès/ Congreszuil
Ste.-Catherine/ St.-Kathelijne
Monnaie/ Munt
Banque Nationale/ Nationale Bank
Cirque Royal/ Koninklijk Circus
Porte de Louvain/ Leuvense Poort
Bourse/ Beurs
St.-Nicolas/ St.-Niklaas
S.S.Michel et Gudule/ St.-Michiels-En St.-Goedele
Palais de la Nation/ Paleis der Naties
Vlaams Parlement Flamand
Grand Place/ Grote Markt
Hôtel de La Ville/ Stadhuis
Gare Centrale/ Central Station
Théâtre du Parc/ Parktheater
Parc de Bruxelles/ Warande
Mannekenpis
Palais des Beaux-Arts/ Paleis voor Schone Kunsten
Palais des Académies
Gare Schuman/ Schuman Station
Berlaymont E.U.
Conseil Européen/ Europese Raad
Gare Chapelle/ Station Kapelle
Palais Royal/ Koninklijk Paleis
MAROLLEN/ MAROLLES
Quartier Européen/ Europese Wijk
Parlement Européen/ Europees Parlement
Gare Quartier Leopold
Parc Leopold Park
Palais de Justice/ Justitiepaleis
Jardins d'Egmont/ Egmonttuinen
Gare du Midi/ Zuid-Station
Hopital St.-Pierre/ St.-Pieters Hospitaal
Musée Wiertz/ Wiertzmuseum
Museum des Sciences Naturelles/ Museum voor Natuurwetenschappen
St-Gilles
Porte de Hal
Université Libre Brux.

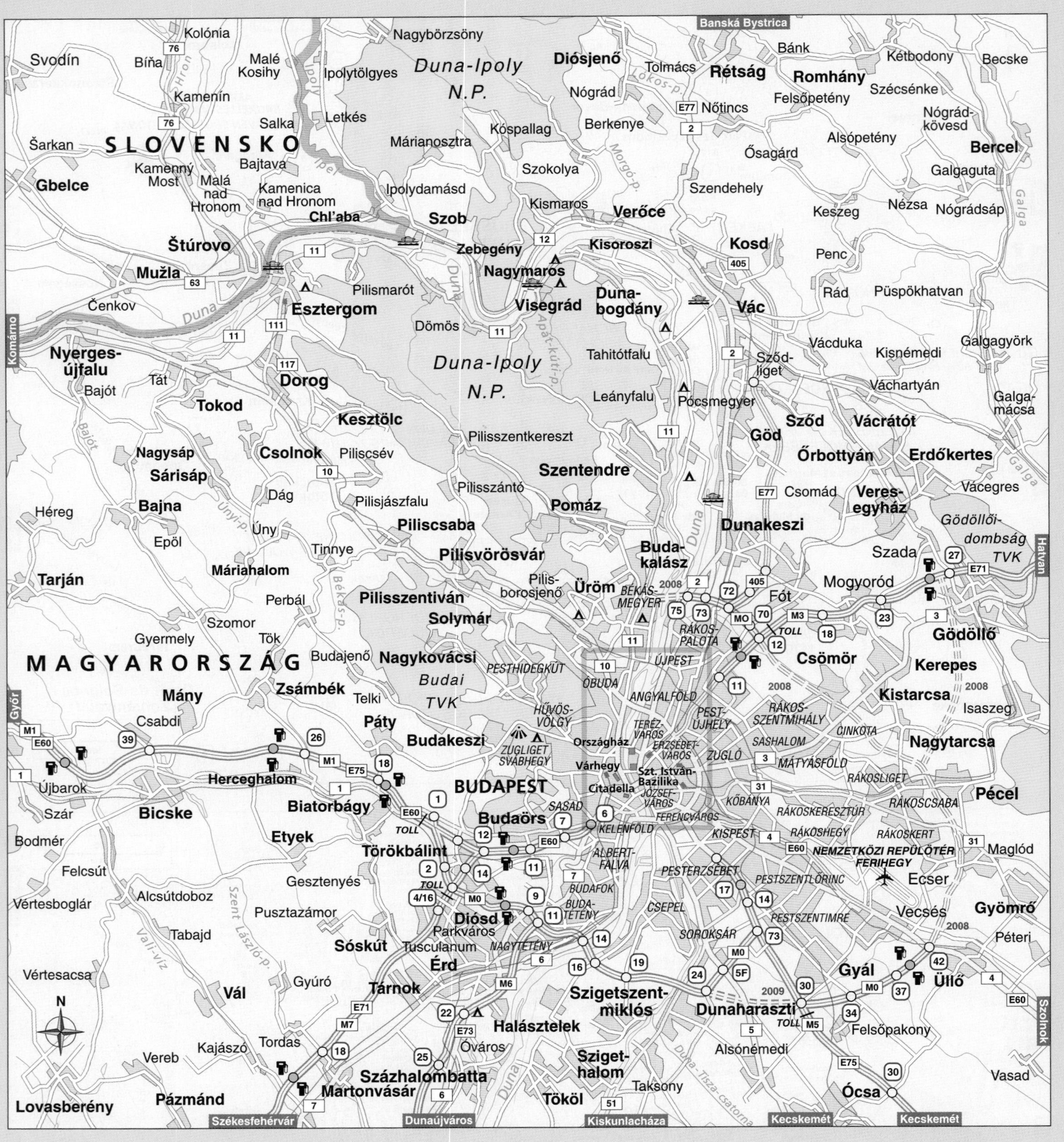
Banská Bystrica
Kolónia
Svodín
Bíňa
Malé Kosihy
Ipolytölgyes
Nagybörzsöny
Duna-Ipoly N.P.
Diósjenő
Tolmács
Rétság
Bánk
Romhány
Kétbodony
Becske
Kamenín
Letkés
Nógrád
Nőtincs
Felsőpetény
Szécsénke
Nógrád-kövesd
Šarkan
SLOVENSKO
Salka
Kóspallag
Berkenye
Márianosztra
Alsópetény
Ősagárd
Bercel
Kamenný Most
Malá nad Hronom
Bajtava
Kamenica nad Hronom
Ipolydamásd
Szokolya
Szendehely
Galgaguta
Gbelce
Chľaba
Szob
Kismaros
Verőce
Keszeg
Nézsa
Nógrádsáp
Štúrovo
Zebegény
Kisoroszi
Kosd
Penc
Mužla
Nagymaros
Pilismarót
Esztergom
Visegrád
Duna-bogdány
Vác
Rád
Püspökhatvan
Čenkov
Dömös
Komárno
Nyerges-újfalu
Tahitótfalu
Vácduka
Sződ-liget
Kisnémedi
Galgagyörk
Bajót
Tát
Dorog
Duna-Ipoly N.P.
Leányfalu
Pócsmegyer
Váchartyán
Galga-mácsa
Tokod
Kesztölc
Sződ
Vácrátót
Göd
Pilisszentkereszt
Nagysáp
Csolnok
Piliscsév
Szentendre
Őrbottyán
Erdőkertes
Sárisáp
Pilisszántó
Csomád
Veres-egyház
Vácegres
Héreg
Bajna
Dág
Pilisjászfalu
Pomáz
Dunakeszi
Gödöllői-dombság TVK
Úny
Piliscsaba
Epöl
Tinnye
Pilisvörösvár
Buda-kalász
Szada
Hatvan
Tarján
Máriahalom
Pilis-borosjenő
Üröm
Mogyoród
Perbál
Pilisszentiván
BÉKÁS-MEGYER
Fót
Szomor
Solymár
RÁKOS-PALOTA
Gödöllő
Gyermely
Tök
TOLL
MAGYARORSZÁG
Budajenő
Nagykovácsi
PESTHIDEGKÚT
ÚJPEST
Csömör
Kerepes
Budai TVK
ÓBUDA
Zsámbék
Mány
Telki
ANGYALFÖLD
Kistarcsa
Győr
Csabdi
Páty
HŰVÖS-VÖLGY
PEST-ÚJHELY
RÁKOS-SZENTMIHÁLY
Isaszeg
TERÉZ-VÁROS
CINKOTA
Budakeszi
ZUGLIGET
SVÁBHEGY
Országház
ERZSÉBET-VÁROS
SASHALOM
Nagytarcsa
Herceghalom
Várhegy
ZUGLÓ
MÁTYÁSFÖLD
Újbarok
BUDAPEST
Szt. István-Bazilika
RÁKOSLIGET
Szár
Bicske
Biatorbágy
Citadella
JÓZSEF-VÁROS
KŐBÁNYA
RÁKOSCSABA
Pécel
SASAD
FERENCVÁROS
RÁKOSKERESZTÚR
Bodmér
Etyek
Budaörs
KELENFÖLD
KISPEST
RÁKOSHEGY
RÁKOSKERT
Maglód
Törökbálint
ALBERT-FALVA
NEMZETKÖZI REPÜLŐTÉR FERIHEGY
Felcsút
PESTERZSÉBET
PESTSZENTLŐRINC
Ecser
Gesztenyés
BUDAFOK
Vértesboglár
Alcsútdoboz
Diósd
BUDA-TÉTÉNY
CSEPEL
Vecsés
Gyömrő
Pusztazámor
Parkváros
PESTSZENTIMRE
Tabajd
Szent László-p.
Sóskút
Tusculanum
NAGYTÉTÉNY
SOROKSÁR
Péteri
Vértesacsa
Érd
Gyál
Üllő
Gyúró
Tárnok
Szigetszent-miklós
Dunaharaszti
Vál
Halásztelek
Felsőpakony
Szolnok
Tordas
Óváros
Alsónémedi
Kajászó
Vereb
Százhalombatta
Sziget-halom
Vasad
Martonvásár
Taksony
Ócsa
Lovasberény
Pázmánd
Tököl
Székesfehérvár
Dunaújváros
Kiskunlacháza
Kecskemét
Kecskemét
N

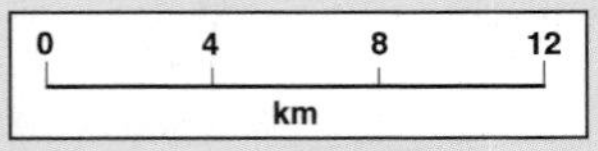
0
4
8
12
km

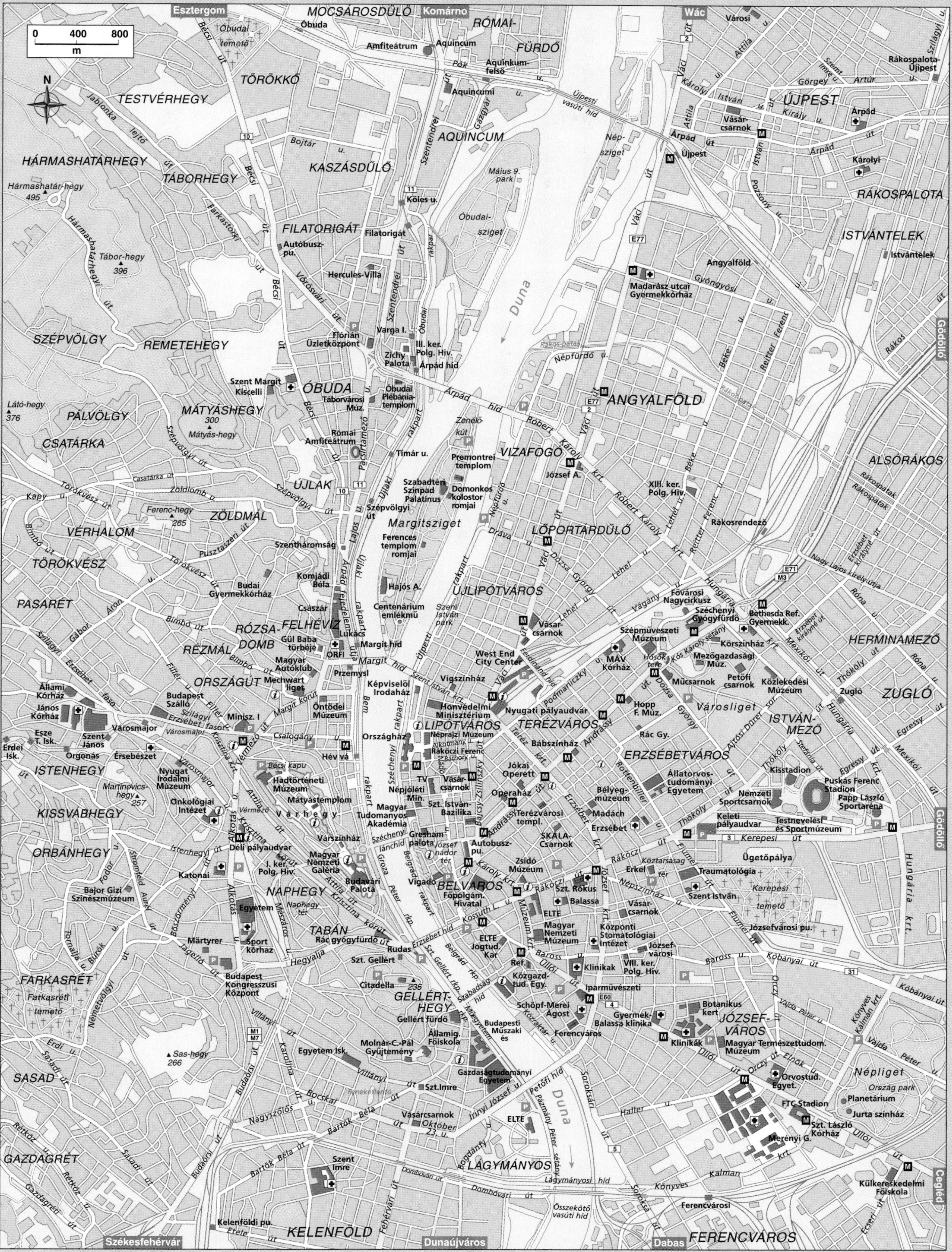
0 400 800
m
N
Esztergom
Komárno
Wác
Gödöllő
Cegléd
Székesfehérvár
Dunaújváros
Dabas
MOCSÁROSDŰLŐ
Óbuda
RÓMAI-FÜRDŐ
Aquincum
Amfiteátrum
Aquinkum-felső
TÖRÖKKŐ
TESTVÉRHEGY
ÚJPEST
Rákospalota-Újpest
Árpád
Újpest
Károlyi
AQUINCUM
KASZÁSDŰLŐ
HÁRMASHATÁRHEGY
TÁBORHEGY
Hármashatár-hegy 495
Köles u.
Május 9. park
Óbudai-sziget
RÁKOSPALOTA
FILATORIGÁT
Filatorigát
Autóbusz-pu.
Tábor-hegy 396
ISTVÁNTELEK
Istvántelek
Angyalföld
Hercules-Villa
Madarász utcai Gyermekkórház
Duna
SZÉPVÖLGY
REMETEHEGY
Flórián Üzletközpont
Varga I.
III. ker. Polg. Hiv.
Zichy Palota
Árpád híd
Népfürdő u.
Szent Margit Kiscelli
ÓBUDA
Táborvárosi Múz.
Óbudai Plébánia-templom
ANGYALFÖLD
Látó-hegy 376
PÁLVÖLGY
MÁTYÁSHEGY
Mátyás-hegy 300
CSATÁRKA
Római Amfiteátrum
Zenélő kút
Timár u.
Premontrei templom
VIZAFOGÓ
József A.
ALSÓRÁKOS
ÚJLAK
Szabadtéri Színpad Palatinus
Domonkos kolostor romjai
XIII. ker. Polg. Hiv.
Szépvölgyi út
Ferenc-hegy 265
ZÖLDMÁL
Margitsziget
LŐPORTÁRDŰLŐ
Rákosrendező
VÉRHALOM
Szentháromság
Ferences templom romjai
TÖRÖKVÉSZ
Komjádi Béla
Budai Gyermekkórház
Hajós A.
ÚJLIPÓTVÁROS
PASARÉT
Császár
Centenárium emlékmű
Szent István park
Fővárosi Nagycirkusz
Széchenyi Gyógyfürdő
Bethesda Ref. Gyermekk.
RÓZSA-DOMB
FELHÉVÍZ
Vásár-csarnok
Gül Baba türbéje
Lukács
Margit híd
Szépművészeti Múzeum
Körszínház
HERMINAMEZŐ
REZMÁL
ORFI
West End City Center
MÁV Kórház
Hősök tere
Mezőgazdasági Múz.
Magyar Autóklub
ORSZÁGÚT
Mechwart liget
Przemysl
Képviselői Irodaház
Vígszínház
Műcsarnok
Petőfi csarnok
Közlekedési Múzeum
Zugló
ZUGLÓ
Állami Kórház
János Kórház
Budapest Szálló
Öntödei Múzeum
Honvédelmi Minisztérium
Nyugati pályaudvar
Hopp F. Múz.
Városliget
Minisz. I
LIPÓTVÁROS
TERÉZVÁROS
ISTVÁN-MEZŐ
Városmajor
Esze T. Isk.
Szent János
Erdei Isk.
Orgonás
Érsebészet
Országház
Néprajzi Múzeum
Rákóczi Ferenc
Bábszínház
Rác Gy.
ERZSÉBETVÁROS
Hév vá
ISTENHEGY
Nyugat Irodalmi Múzeum
Hadtörténeti Múzeum
Jókai Operett
Állatorvos-tudományi Egyetem
Kisstadion
Puskás Ferenc Stadion
Papp László Sportaréna
Mártinovics-hegy 257
Mátyástemplom
TV
Népjóléti Min.
Vásár-csarnok
Operaház
Bélyeg-múzeum
Nemzeti Sportcsarnok
KISSVÁBHEGY
Onkológiai Intézet
Várhegy
Magyar Tudományos Akadémia
Szt. István-Bazilika
Terézvárosi templ.
Madách
Keleti pályaudvar
Testnevelési és Sportmúzeum
Kerepesi út
ORBÁNHEGY
Déli pályaudvar
Várszínház
Gresham palota
SKÁLA-Csarnok
Erzsébet
Ügetőpálya
Katonai
I. ker. Polg. Hiv.
Magyar Nemzeti Galéria
Autóbusz-pu.
Zsidó Múzeum
Erkel
Traumatológia
Bajor Gizi Színészmúzeum
NAPHEGY
Budavári Palota
Vigadó
BELVÁROS
Főpolgám. Hivatal
Szt. Rókus
Balassa
Szent István
Kerepesi temető
Egyetem
ELTE
Vásár-csarnok
TABÁN
Rác gyógyfürdő
Magyar Nemzeti Múzeum
Központi Stomatológiai Intézet
Józsefvárosi pu.
Mártyrer
Sport kórház
Rudas
ELTE Jogtud. Kar
József-városi
Szt. Gellért
Ref.
Klinikak
VIII. ker. Polg. Hiv.
Kőbányai út
FARKASRÉT
Budapest Kongresszusi Központ
Citadella 235
Közgazd. tud. Egy.
Iparművészeti
Farkasréti temető
GELLÉRT-HEGY
Schöpf-Merei Ágost
Botanikus kert
Gellért fürdő
Budapesti Műszaki és
Gyermek-Balassa klinika
JÓZSEF-VÁROS
Államig. Főiskola
Ferencváros
Klinikák
Magyar Természettudom. Múzeum
Sas-hegy 266
Egyetem Isk.
Molnár-C.-Pál Gyűjtemény
Népliget
SASAD
Gazdaságtudományi Egyetem
Orvostud. Egyet.
Ország park
Planetárium
Szt.Imre
Petőfi híd
FTC Stadion
Jurta színház
Vásárcsarnok
Szt. László Kórház
ELTE
Duna
Merényi G.
GAZDAGRÉT
Szent Imre
LÁGYMÁNYOS
Lágymányosi híd
Könyves Kálmán
Külkereskedelmi Főiskola
Összekötő vasúti híd
Ferencvárosi
Kelenföldi pu.
KELENFÖLD
FERENCVÁROS

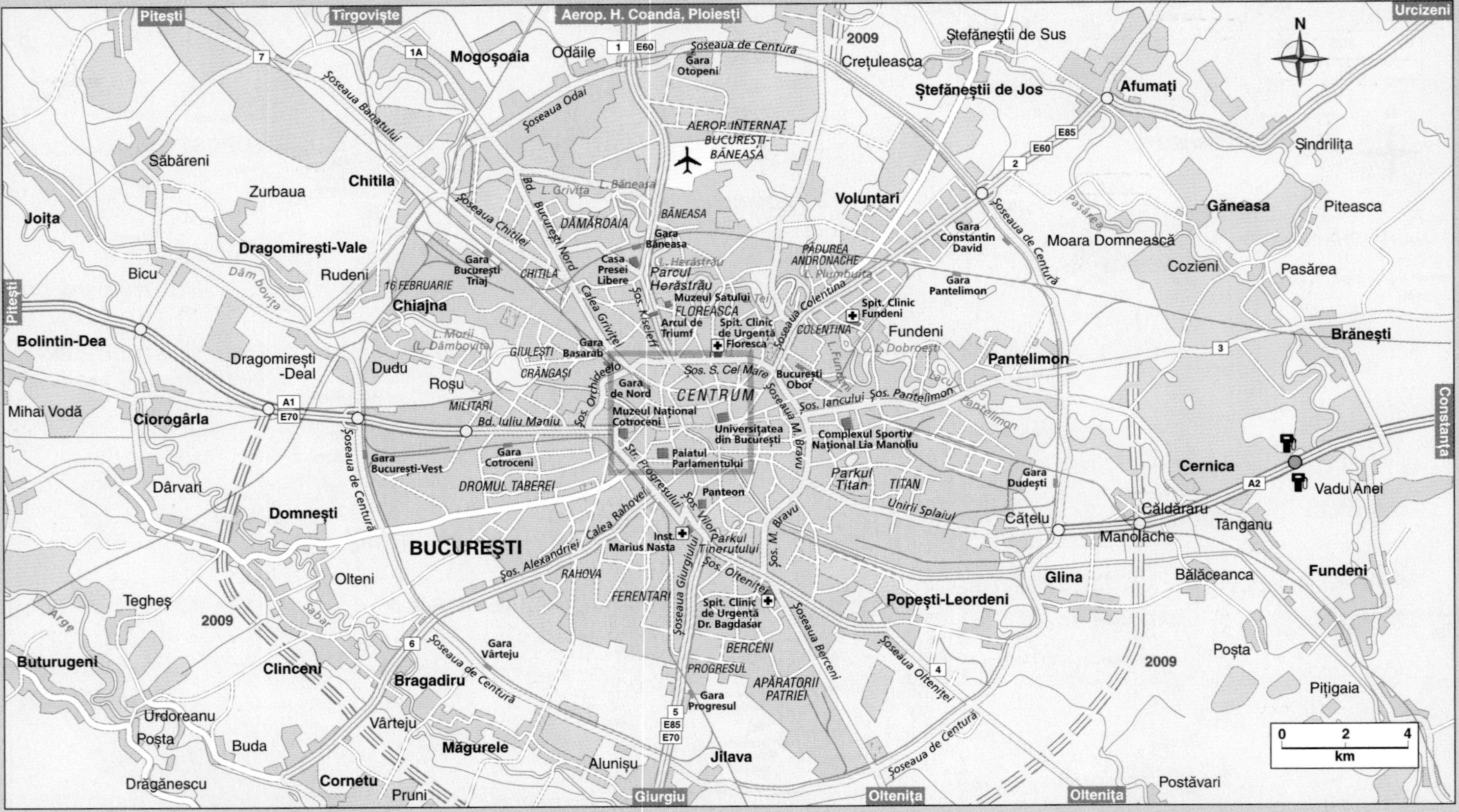

Piteşti
Tîrgovişte
Aerop. H. Coandă, Ploieşti
Urcizeni
N
Mogoşoaia
Odăile
Şoseaua de Centura
2009
Ştefăneştii de Sus
Creţuleasca
Gara Otopeni
Ştefăneştii de Jos
Afumaţi
Şoseaua Odai
Şoseaua Banatului
AEROP. INTERNAŢ. BUCUREŞTI-BĂNEASA
Şindrilita
Săbăreni
Zurbaua
Chitila
Voluntari
Găneasa
Piteasca
Joiţa
Şoseaua Chitilei
Băneasa
Gara Băneasa
Gara Constantin David
Moara Domnească
Dragomireşti-Vale
Dămăroaia
Bd. Bucureşti Nord
Casa Presei Libere
Pădurea Andronache
Cozieni
Pasărea
Bicu
Rudeni
Gara Bucureşti Triaj
Chitila
Parcul Herăstrău
L. Herăstrău
L. Plumbuita
Gara Pantelimon
Dâmboviţa
16 Februarie
Muzeul Satului
Floreasca
Colentina
Spit. Clinic Fundeni
Chiajna
Arcul de Triumf
Spit. Clinic de Urgenţă Floreasca
Fundeni
Brăneşti
Bolintin-Dea
L. Morii
L. Dâmboviţa
Gara Basarab
Giuleşti
L. Dobroieşti
Dragomireşti-Deal
Dudu
Crângaşi
Şos. S. Cel Mare
Bucureşti Obor
Pantelimon
Roşu
Gara de Nord
CENTRUM
Şos. Iancului
Şos. Pantelimon
Militari
Muzeul Naţional Cotroceni
Bd. Iuliu Maniu
Universitatea din Bucureşti
Complexul Sportiv Naţional Lia Manoliu
Mihai Vodă
Ciorogârla
A1
E70
Şos. Orhideelor
Şoseaua de Centura
Gara Bucureşti-Vest
Gara Cotroceni
Palatul Parlamentului
Constanţa
Dârvari
Dromul Taberei
Str. Progresului
Parkul Titan
Titan
Gara Dudeşti
Cernica
Panteon
Unirii Splaiul
A2
Vadu Anei
Domneşti
Calea Rahovei
Căţelu
Căldăraru
Inst. Marius Nasta
Parkul Tineretului
Manolache
Tânganu
BUCUREŞTI
Şos. Alexandriei
Glina
Bălăceanca
Fundeni
Olteni
Rahova
Şos. Olteniţei
Teghes
Ferentari
Spit. Clinic de Urgenţă Dr. Bagdasar
Popeşti-Leordeni
2009
Berceni
Şoseaua Berceni
Gara Vârteju
Şoseaua Olteniţei
2009
Poşta
Buturugeni
Clinceni
Progresul
Bragadiru
Aparătorii Patriei
Piţigaia
Şoseaua de Centura
Gara Progresul
E85
E70
Urdoreanu
Vârteju
Poşta
Buda
Măgurele
Aluniş
Jilava
Şoseaua de Centura
0 2 4
km
Drăgănescu
Cornetu
Pruni
Giurgiu
Olteniţa
Olteniţa
Postăvari

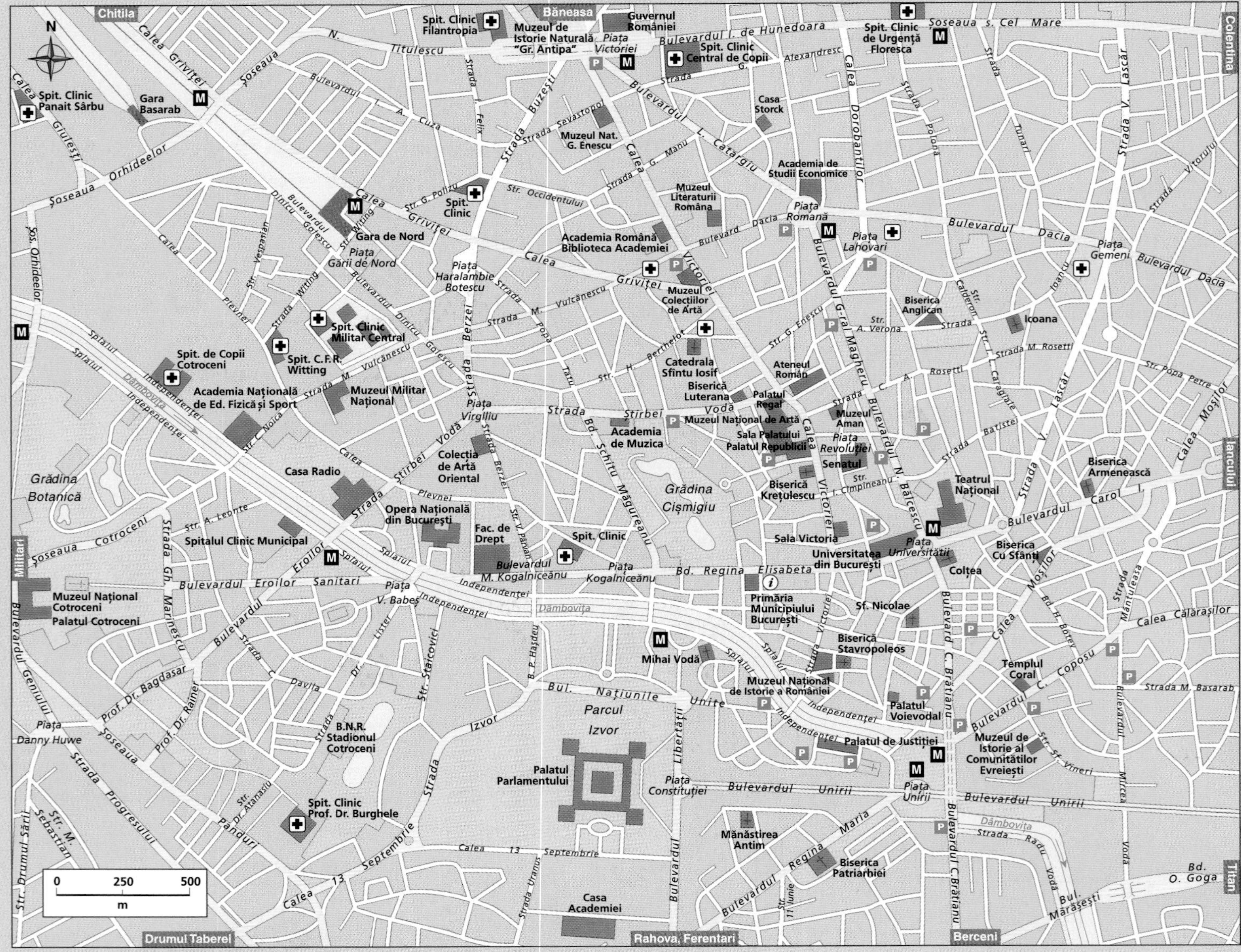

Chitila
Băneasa
Colentina
N
Spit. Clinic Filantropia
Muzeul de Istorie Naturală "Gr. Antipa"
Piaţa Victoriei
Guvernul României
Spit. Clinic Central de Copii
Spit. Clinic de Urgenţă Floreasca
Bulevardul I. de Hunedoara
Şoseaua S. Cel Mare
Calea Griviţei
Spit. Clinic Panait Sârbu
Gara Basarab
Bulevardul L. Catargiu
Casa Storck
Calea Dorobanţilor
Muzeul Nat. G. Enescu
Academia de Studii Economice
Şoseaua Orhideelor
Gara de Nord
Piaţa Gării de Nord
Spit. Clinic
Muzeul Literaturii Române
Piaţa Romană
Piaţa Lahovari
Bulevardul Dacia
Academia Română Biblioteca Academiei
Piaţa Gemeni
Piaţa Haralambie Botescu
Calea Victoriei
Muzeul Colecţiilor de Artă
Biserica Anglican
Icoana
Spit. Clinic Militar Central
Spit. C.F.R. Witting
Spit. de Copii Cotroceni
Catedrala Sfîntu Iosif
Ateneul Român
Academia Naţională de Ed. Fizică şi Sport
Muzeul Militar Naţional
Biserica Luterana
Palatul Regal
Piaţa Virgiliu
Strada Ştirbei Vodă
Muzeul Naţional de Artă
Muzeul Aman
Academia de Muzica
Sala Palatului
Palatul Republicii
Piaţa Revoluţiei
Senatul
Colecţia de Artă Oriental
Biserica Armenească
Casa Radio
Grădina Botanică
Grădina Cişmigiu
Biserica Kreţulescu
Teatrul Naţional
Opera Naţională din Bucureşti
Fac. de Drept
Spit. Clinic
Sala Victoria
Universitatea din Bucureşti
Piaţa Universităţii
Bulevardul Carol I
Spitalul Clinic Municipal
Biserica Cu Sfânti
Şoseaua Cotroceni
Piaţa V. Babeş
Bulevardul M. Kogălniceanu
Piaţa Kogălniceanu
Bd. Regina Elisabeta
Colţea
Muzeul Naţional Cotroceni
Palatul Cotroceni
Bulevardul Eroilor
Splaiul Independenţei
Dâmboviţa
Primăria Municipiului Bucureşti
Sf. Nicolae
Militari
Biserica Stavropoleos
Calea Călăraşilor
Mihai Vodă
Templul Coral
Muzeul Naţional de Istorie a României
Bul. Naţiunile Unite
Palatul Voievodal
Strada M. Basarab
Parcul Izvor
B.N.R. Stadionul Cotroceni
Palatul de Justiţiei
Muzeul de Istorie al Comunităţilor Evreieşti
Piaţa Danny Huwe
Palatul Parlamentului
Piaţa Constituţiei
Bulevardul Unirii
Piaţa Unirii
Spit. Clinic Prof. Dr. Burghele
Strada Progresului
Mănăstirea Antim
Biserica Patriarhiei
Calea 13 Septembrie
Bd. O. Goga
Titan
Bul. Mărăşeşti
0 250 500
m
Casa Academiei
Drumul Taberei
Rahova, Ferentari
Berceni

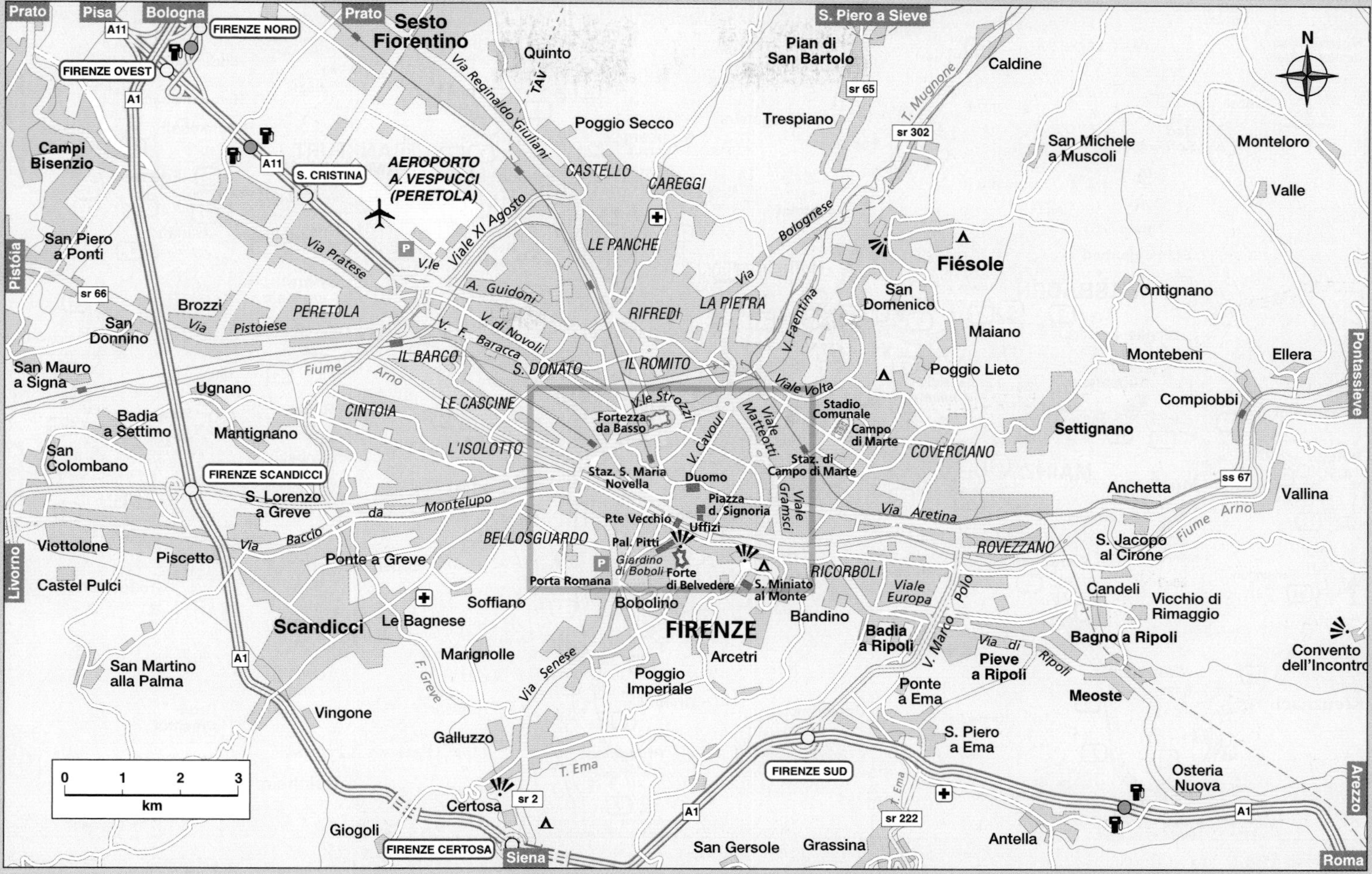
Prato
Pisa
Bologna
FIRENZE NORD
FIRENZE OVEST
A11
A1
Sesto Fiorentino
Quinto
Via Reginaldo Giuliani
TAV
S. Piero a Sieve
Pian di San Bartolo
Caldine
sr 65
Trespiano
sr 302
T. Mugnone
Poggio Secco
Campi Bisenzio
S. CRISTINA
AEROPORTO A. VESPUCCI (PERETOLA)
CASTELLO
CAREGGI
San Michele a Muscoli
Monteloro
Valle
San Piero a Ponti
Pistóia
Viale XI Agosto
V.le
Via Pratese
LE PANCHE
Bolognese
Via
Fiésole
sr 66
A. Guidoni
San Domenico
Ontignano
Brozzi
Via
Pistoiese
PERETOLA
V. F. Baracca
V. di Novoli
RIFREDI
LA PIETRA
V. Faentina
Maiano
San Donnino
IL BARCO
S. DONATO
IL ROMITO
Montebeni
Ellera
San Mauro a Signa
Fiume Arno
Poggio Lieto
Pontassieve
Ugnano
V.le Strozzi
Viale Volta
Stadio Comunale
Compiobbi
Badia a Settimo
CINTOIA
LE CASCINE
Fortezza da Basso
V. Cavour
Viale Matteotti
Campo di Marte
Settignano
Mantignano
L'ISOLOTTO
COVERCIANO
San Colombano
Staz. S. Maria Novella
Duomo
Staz. di Campo di Marte
ss 67
FIRENZE SCANDICCI
Anchetta
Vallina
S. Lorenzo a Greve
Montelupo
Piazza d. Signoria
Viale Gramsci
Via Aretina
Fiume Arno
da
P.te Vecchio
Uffizi
Baccio
Via
BELLOSGUARDO
Pal. Pitti
ROVEZZANO
S. Jacopo al Cirone
Viottolone
Piscetto
Ponte a Greve
Giardino di Boboli
Forte di Belvedere
RICORBOLI
Viale Europa
Livorno
Castel Pulci
Porta Romana
S. Miniato al Monte
Polo
Candeli
Vicchio di Rimaggio
Soffiano
Bobolino
Bandino
Scandicci
Le Bagnese
FIRENZE
Badia a Ripoli
V. Marco
Via di Ripoli
Bagno a Ripoli
Convento dell'Incontro
Marignolle
Arcetri
Pieve a Ripoli
San Martino alla Palma
Via Senese
F. Greve
Poggio Imperiale
Ponte a Ema
Meoste
Vingone
S. Piero a Ema
Galluzzo
T. Ema
FIRENZE SUD
Osteria Nuova
Arezzo
0 1 2 3 km
Certosa
sr 2
T. Ema
A1
sr 222
Giogoli
FIRENZE CERTOSA
Siena
San Gersole
Grassina
Antella
Roma
N

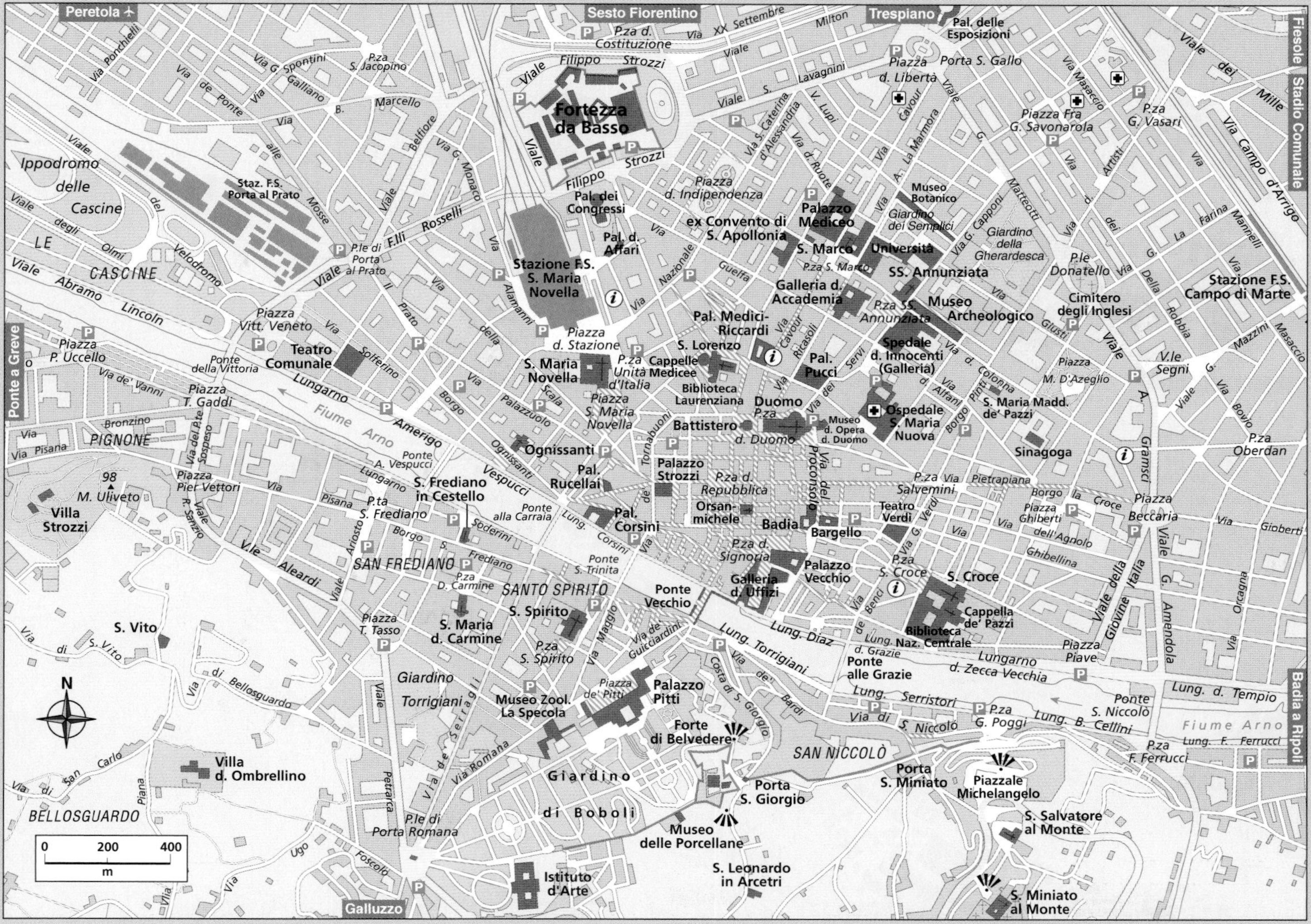
Peretola
Sesto Fiorentino
Trespiano
Pal. delle Esposizioni
Fiesole
Stadio Comunale
P.za d. Costituzione
Via XX Settembre
Milton
Viale Filippo Strozzi
Via Ponchielli
Via G. Spontini
Galliano
P.za S. Jacopino
Via de Ponte
Marcello
Piazza d. Libertà
Porta S. Gallo
Viale S. Lavagnini
Via Masaccio
Viale dei Mille
Fortezza da Basso
Via S. Caterina d'Alessandria
V. Lupi
Cavour
Piazza Fra G. Savonarola
P.za G. Vasari
Via Campo d'Arrigo
Ippodromo delle Cascine
Staz. F.S. Porta al Prato
Via G. Monaco
Belfiore
Viale Filippo Strozzi
Via d. Ruote
Via A. La Marmora
Museo Botanico
Matteotti
Viale degli Olmi
Piazza d. Indipendenza
Pal. dei Congressi
Palazzo Medici
Giardino dei Semplici
Via G. Capponi
Giardino della Gherardesca
La Farina
Mannelli
LE CASCINE
Velodromo
P.le di Porta al Prato
Via F.lli Rosselli
Pal. d. Affari
ex Convento di S. Apollonia
S. Marco
Università
Viale Abramo Lincoln
Stazione F.S. S. Maria Novella
Nazionale
Guelfa
P.za S. Marco
SS. Annunziata
P.le Donatello
Stazione F.S. Campo di Marte
Galleria d. Accademia
Museo Archeologico
Cimitero degli Inglesi
Piazza Vitt. Veneto
Alamanni
P.za SS. Annunziata
Pal. Medici-Riccardi
Piazza d. Stazione
Via Cavour
Ricasoli
Spedale d. Innocenti (Galleria)
Piazza P. Uccello
Teatro Comunale
Solferino
S. Lorenzo
Giusti
Ponte a Greve
Ponte della Vittoria
S. Maria Novella
P.za Unità d'Italia
Cappelle Medicee
Pal. Pucci
Via d. Colonna
Piazza M. D'Azeglio
V.le Segni
Via de' Vanni
Lungarno
Piazza S. Maria Novella
Biblioteca Laurenziana
Servi
Via Alfani
S. Maria Madd. de' Pazzi
Piazza T. Gaddi
Fiume Arno
Amerigo
Borgo
Palazzuolo
Duomo
Museo d. Opera d. Duomo
Ospedale S. Maria Nuova
Bronzino
PIGNONE
Battistero
P.za d. Duomo
Borgo Pinti
Via Pisana
Ponte A. Vespucci
Ognissanti
Proconsolo
Sinagoga
P.za Oberdan
Gramsci
Lungarno
Vespucci
Pal. Rucellai
Palazzo Strozzi
P.za d. Repubblica
P.za Salvemini
Pietrapiana
Piazza Pier Vettori
S. Frediano in Cestello
Teatro Verdi
Piazza Beccaria
Gioberti
M. Uliveto
Villa Strozzi
P.ta S. Frediano
Ponte alla Carraia
Pal. Corsini
Orsanmichele
Badia
Bargello
Piazza Ghiberti
dell'Agnolo
Soderini
Ghibellina
Tornabuoni
P.za d. Signoria
Palazzo Vecchio
P.za S. Croce
S. Croce
V.le Aleardi
SAN FREDIANO
Ponte S. Trinita
Galleria d. Uffizi
Cappella de' Pazzi
Viale della Giovine Italia
Via G. Amendola
Orcagna
P.za D. Carmine
SANTO SPIRITO
Ponte Vecchio
Lung. Diaz
Biblioteca Naz. Centrale
S. Vito
Piazza T. Tasso
S. Maria d. Carmine
S. Spirito
Via Maggio
Via de' Guicciardini
Lung. Torrigiani
Lungarno d. Zecca Vecchia
Piazza Piave
P.za S. Spirito
Ponte alle Grazie
Via di Bellosguardo
Giardino Torrigiani
Museo Zool. La Specola
Piazza de' Pitti
Palazzo Pitti
Costa di S. Giorgio
Lung. Serristori
Ponte S. Niccolò
Lung. d. Tempio
Via de' Serragli
Via Romana
Forte di Belvedere
Via di S. Niccolò
P.za G. Poggi
Lung. B. Cellini
Fiume Arno
Lung. F. Ferrucci
P.za F. Ferrucci
Badia a Ripoli
SAN NICCOLÒ
Villa d. Ombrellino
Giardino di Boboli
Porta S. Miniato
Piazzale Michelangelo
Porta S. Giorgio
S. Salvatore al Monte
BELLOSGUARDO
P.le di Porta Romana
Museo delle Porcellane
0 200 400 m
Istituto d'Arte
S. Leonardo in Arcetri
S. Miniato al Monte
Galluzzo
Foscolo
Ugo
N

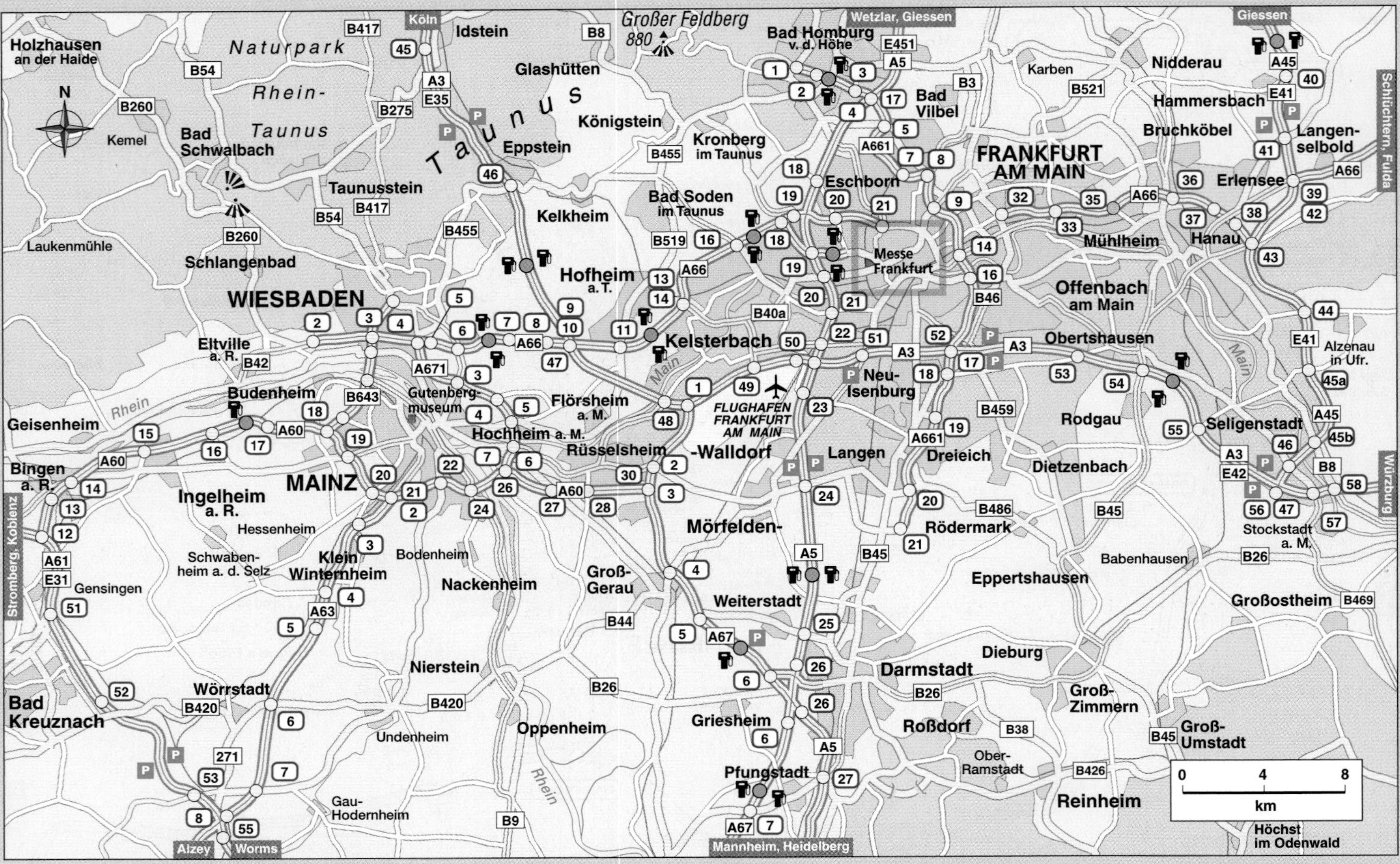

Köln
Wetzlar, Giessen
Giessen
Schlüchtern, Fulda
Würzburg
Stromberg, Koblenz
Alzey
Worms
Mannheim, Heidelberg
Holzhausen an der Haide
Naturpark
Rhein-
Taunus
Taunus
Großer Feldberg 880
Idstein
Glashütten
Königstein
Eppstein
Kemel
Bad Schwalbach
Taunusstein
Laukenmühle
Schlangenbad
Kelkheim
Kronberg im Taunus
Bad Homburg v. d. Höhe
Bad Vilbel
Karben
Nidderau
Hammersbach
Bruchköbel
Langenselbold
Erlensee
Hanau
Mühlheim
FRANKFURT AM MAIN
Eschborn
Bad Soden im Taunus
Messe Frankfurt
Offenbach am Main
Obertshausen
Alzenau in Ufr.
Hofheim a. T.
WIESBADEN
Eltville a. R.
Kelsterbach
Main
Rhein
Budenheim
Gutenberg-museum
Flörsheim a. M.
Hochheim a. M.
Rüsselsheim
FLUGHAFEN FRANKFURT AM MAIN
Neu-Isenburg
Rodgau
Seligenstadt
Geisenheim
Bingen a. R.
MAINZ
Ingelheim a. R.
Hessenheim
Mörfelden-Walldorf
Langen
Dreieich
Dietzenbach
Rödermark
Stockstadt a. M.
Babenhausen
Schwabenheim a. d. Selz
Gensingen
Klein Winternheim
Bodenheim
Nackenheim
Groß-Gerau
Weiterstadt
Eppertshausen
Großostheim
Dieburg
Darmstadt
Nierstein
Wörrstadt
Bad Kreuznach
Groß-Zimmern
Griesheim
Roßdorf
Groß-Umstadt
Oppenheim
Undenheim
Ober-Ramstadt
Pfungstadt
Reinheim
Gau-Hodernheim
Höchst im Odenwald
0 4 8 km

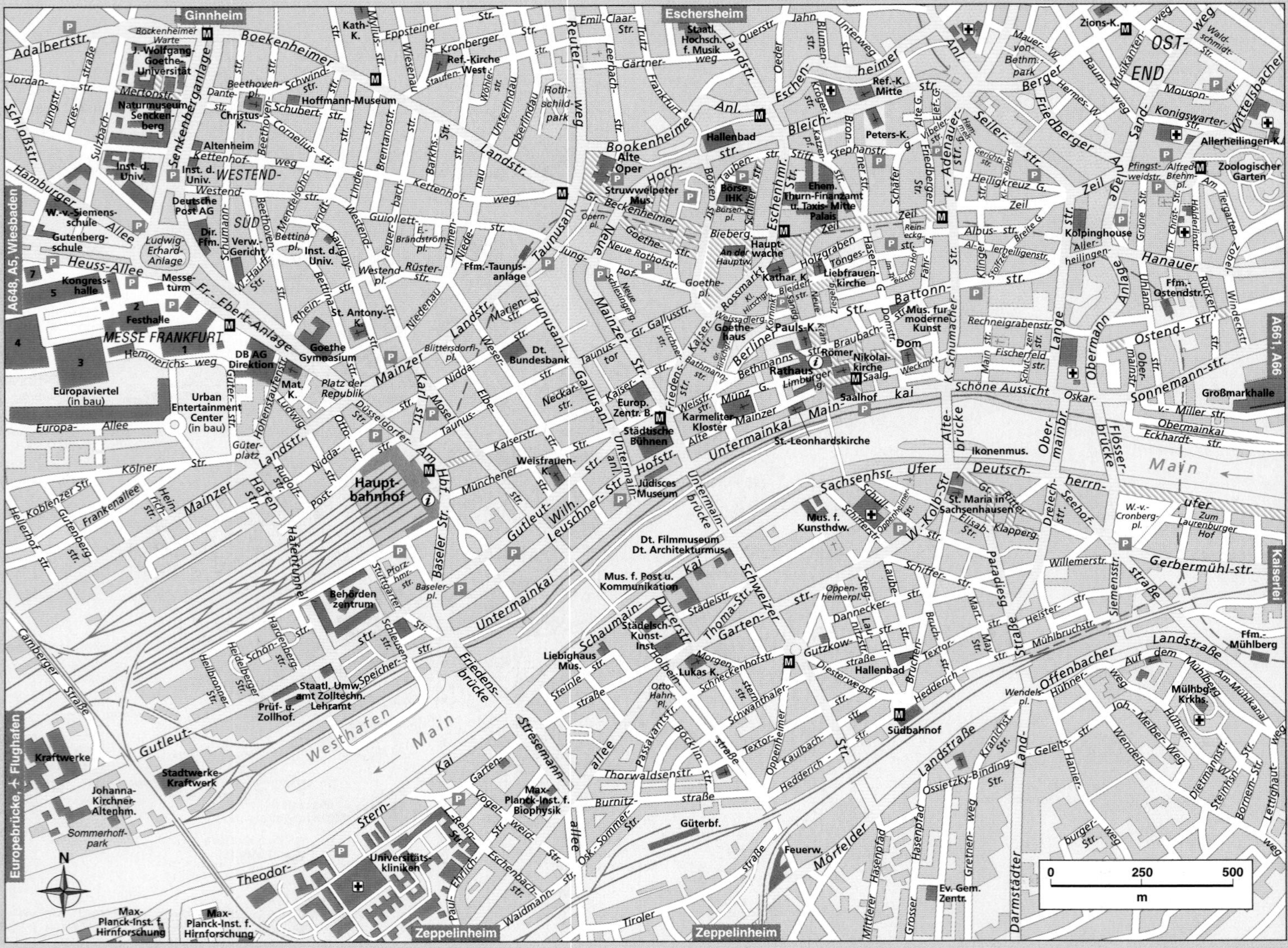

Ginnheim
Eschersheim
A648, A5, Wiesbaden
A661, A66
Kaiserlei
Europabrücke, Flughafen
Zeppelinheim
Zeppelinheim
Bockenheimer Warte
J.-Wolfgang-Goethe-Universität
Naturmuseum Senckenberg
Senckenberganlage
Altenheim
Inst. d. Univ.
WESTEND-SÜD
Deutsche Post AG
W.-v.-Siemens-schule
Gutenberg-schule
Ludwig-Erhard-Anlage
Heuss-Allee
Kongress-halle
Messe-turm
Festhalle
MESSE FRANKFURT
Europaviertel (in bau)
Urban Entertainment Center (in bau)
Hoffmann-Museum
Ref.-Kirche West
Rothschild-park
Hallenbad
Alte Oper
Struwwelpeter Mus.
Börse IHK
Thurn-Finanzamt u. Taxis-Palais
Zeil
Staatl. Hochsch. f. Musik
Ref.-K. Mitte
Peters-K.
OST-END
Allerheiligen-K.
Zoologischer Garten
Kolpinghouse
Ffm.-Ostendstr.
Großmarkthalle
Ffm.-Taunus-anlage
Goethe Gymnasium
DB AG Direktion
Dt. Bundesbank
Goethe-haus
Hauptwache
Liebfrauen-kirche
Pauls-K.
Rathaus Römer
Nikolai-kirche
Dom
Mus. für moderne Kunst
Saalhof
Europ. Zentr. B.
Städtische Bühnen
Karmeliter Kloster
St.-Leonhardskirche
Platz der Republik
Hauptbahnhof
Jüdisches Museum
Weisfrauen-K.
Ikonenmus.
Alte brücke
Main
St. Maria in Sachsenhausen
Mus. f. Kunsthdw.
Dt. Filmmuseum
Dt. Architekturmus.
Mus. f. Post u. Kommunikation
Städelsch. Kunst-Inst.
Liebighaus Mus.
Behörden zentrum
Staatl. Umw. amt Zolltechn. Lehramt
Prüf- u. Zollhof.
Westhafen
Kraftwerke
Stadtwerke-Kraftwerk
Johanna-Kirchner-Altenhm.
Sommerhoff-park
Lukas K.
Hallenbad
Südbahnof
Ffm.-Mühlberg
Mühlberg Krkhs.
Max-Planck-Inst. f. Biophysik
Universitäts-kliniken
Max-Planck-Inst. f. Hirnforschung
Max-Planck-Inst. f. Hirnforschung
Güterbf.
Feuerw.
Ev. Gem. Zentr.
0 250 500 m

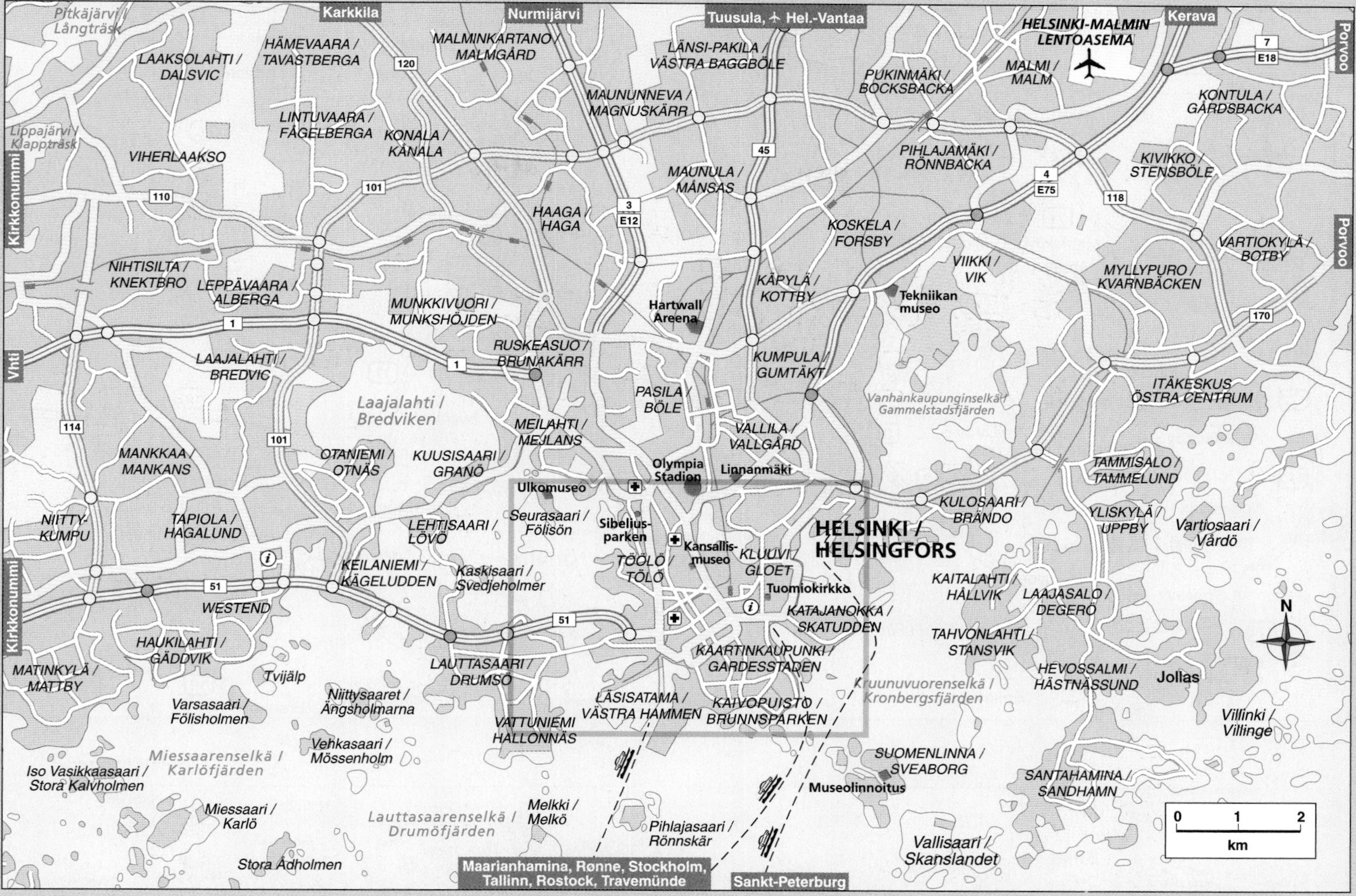
Karkkila
Nurmijärvi
Tuusula, Hel.-Vantaa
HELSINKI-MALMIN LENTOASEMA
Kerava
Porvoo
Pitkäjärvi / Långträsk
LAAKSOLAHTI / DALSVIC
HÄMEVAARA / TAVASTBERGA
MALMINKARTANO / MALMGÅRD
LÄNSI-PAKILA / VÄSTRA BAGGBÖLE
PUKINMÄKI / BOCKSBACKA
MALMI / MALM
KONTULA / GÅRDSBACKA
Lippajärvi / Klappträsk
LINTUVAARA / FÅGELBERGA
KONALA / KÅNALA
MAUNUNNEVA / MAGNUSKÄRR
PIHLAJAMÄKI / RÖNNBACKA
KIVIKKO / STENSBÖLE
VIHERLAAKSO
MAUNULA / MÅNSAS
Kirkkonummi
HAAGA / HAGA
KOSKELA / FORSBY
VARTIOKYLÄ / BOTBY
NIHTISILTA / KNEKTBRO
LEPPÄVAARA / ALBERGA
MUNKKIVUORI / MUNKSHÖJDEN
VIIKKI / VIK
MYLLYPURO / KVARNBÄCKEN
Hartwall Areena
KÄPYLÄ / KOTTBY
Tekniikan museo
RUSKEASUO / BRUNAKÄRR
LAAJALAHTI / BREDVIC
KUMPULA / GUMTÄKT
Vihti
Laajalahti / Bredviken
PASILA / BÖLE
Vanhankaupunginselkä / Gammelstadsfjärden
ITÄKESKUS / ÖSTRA CENTRUM
MEILAHTI / MEJLANS
VALLILA / VALLGÅRD
MANKKAA / MANKANS
OTANIEMI / OTNÄS
KUUSISAARI / GRANÖ
Olympia Stadion
Linnanmäki
TAMMISALO / TAMMELUND
Ulkomuseo
KULOSAARI / BRÄNDÖ
NIITTY-KUMPU
TAPIOLA / HAGALUND
Seurasaari / Fölisön
Sibelius-parken
LEHTISAARI / LÖVÖ
Kansallis-museo
HELSINKI / HELSINGFORS
YLISKYLÄ / UPPBY
Vartiosaari / Vårdö
KEILANIEMI / KÄGELUDDEN
Kaskisaari / Svedjeholmer
TÖÖLÖ / TÖLÖ
KLUUVI / GLOET
Tuomiokirkko
KAITALAHTI / HÅLLVIK
LAAJASALO / DEGERÖ
WESTEND
KATAJANOKKA / SKATUDDEN
HAUKILAHTI / GÄDDVIK
LAUTTASAARI / DRUMSÖ
KAARTINKAUPUNKI / GARDESSTADEN
TAHVONLAHTI / STANSVIK
MATINKYLÄ / MATTBY
Tvijälp
Kruunuvuorenselkä / Kronbergsfjärden
HEVOSSALMI / HÄSTNÄSSUND
Jollas
Varsasaari / Fölisholmen
Niittysaaret / Ängsholmarna
LÄSISATAMA / VÄSTRA HAMNEN
KAIVOPUISTO / BRUNNSPARKEN
VATTUNIEMI / HALLONNÄS
Villinki / Villinge
Miessaarenselkä / Karlöfjärden
Vehkasaari / Mössenholm
SUOMENLINNA / SVEABORG
Iso Vasikkaasaari / Stora Kalvholmen
Museolinnoitus
SANTAHAMINA / SANDHAMN
Miessaari / Karlö
Lauttasaarenselkä / Drumöfjärden
Melkki / Melkö
Pihlajasaari / Rönnskär
Vallisaari / Skanslandet
Stora Ådholmen
Maarianhamina, Rønne, Stockholm, Tallinn, Rostock, Travemünde
Sankt-Peterburg
0 1 2
km
N

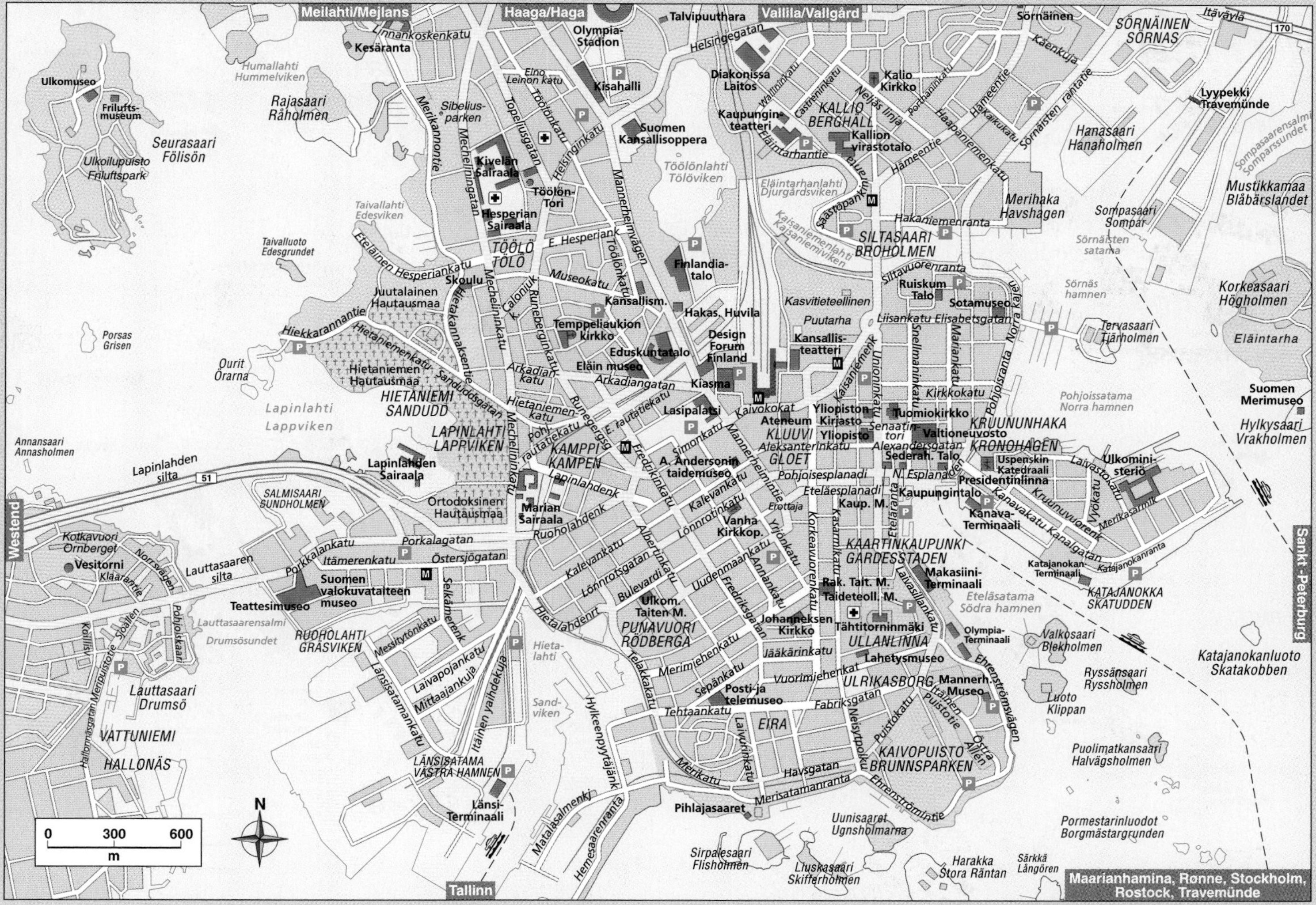
Meilahti/Mejlans
Haaga/Haga
Talvipuutharа
Vallila/Vallgård
Sörnäinen
Itäväylä
SÖRNÄINEN SÖRNÄS
Linnankoskenkatu
Olympia-Stadion
Kesäranta
Humallahti / Hummelviken
Ulkomuseo
Friluftsmuseum
Kisahalli
Diakonissa Laitos
Kallio Kirkko
Lyypekki Travemünde
Rajasaari / Råholmen
Sibelius-parken
Suomen Kansallisooppera
Kaupungin-teatteri
KALLIO BERGHÅLL
Kallion virastotalo
Seurasaari / Fölisön
Hanasaari / Hanaholmen
Ulkoilupuisto / Friluftspark
Kivelän Sairaala
Töölönlahti / Tölöviken
Töölön-Tori
Eläintarhanlahti / Djurgårdsviken
Mustikkamaa / Blåbärslandet
Merihaka / Havshagen
Hesperian Sairaala
Sompasaari / Sompar
SILTASAARI / BROHOLMEN
Taivalluoto / Edesgrundet
TÖÖLÖ TÖLÖ
Finlandia-talo
Sörnäisten satama
Skoulu
Juutalainen Hautausmaa
Ruiskum. Talo
Korkeasaari / Högholmen
Kansallism.
Hakas. Huvila
Kasvitieteellinen
Sotamuseo
Temppeliaukion kirkko
Puutarha
Tervasaari / Tjärholmen
Porsas / Grisen
Design Forum Finland
Kansallis-teatteri
Eläintarha
Eduskuntatalo
Eläin museo
Hietaniemen Hautausmaa
Ourit / Örarna
Kiasma
Kirkkokatu
Pohjoissatama / Norra hamnen
Suomen Merimuseo
HIETANIEMI SANDUDD
Lasipalatsi
Ateneum
Yliopiston Kirjasto
Tuomiokirkko
Lapinlahti / Lappviken
Yliopisto
Senaatin tori
Valtioneuvosto
KRUUNUNHAKA KRONOHAGEN
Hylkysaari / Vrakholmen
LAPINLAHTI LAPPVIKEN
KLUUVI GLOET
Sederh. Talo
Uspenskin Katedraali
Annansaari / Annasholmen
KAMPPI KAMPEN
A. Andersonin taidemuseo
Presidentinlinna
Ulkoministeriö
Lapinlahden Sairaala
Kaupungintalo
Lapinlahden silta
Kaup. M.
Kanava-Terminaali
SALMISAARI / BUNDHOLMEN
Ortodoksinen Hautausmaa
Westend
Marian Sairaala
Vanha Kirkkop.
Kotkavuori / Örnberget
Porkalagatan
Katajanokan Terminaali
Vesitorni
Itämerenkatu
Östersjögatan
KAARTINKAUPUNKI GARDESSTADEN
Lauttasaaren silta
Suomen valokuvataiteen museo
Makasiini-Terminaali
Teattesimuseo
Rak. Talt. M.
Taideteoll. M.
KATAJANOKKA SKATUDDEN
Ulkom. Taiten M.
Eteläsatama / Södra hamnen
RUOHOLAHTI GRÄSVIKEN
PUNAVUORI RÖDBERGA
Johanneksen Kirkko
Tähtitorninmäki
Olympia-Terminaali
Valkosaari / Blekholmen
ULLANLINNA
Katajanokanluoto / Skatakobben
Lahetysmuseo
Ryssänsaari / Ryssholmen
ULRIKASBORG
Mannerh. Museo
Lauttasaari / Drumsö
Posti-ja telemuseo
Luoto / Klippan
VATTUNIEMI HALLONÄS
EIRA
KAIVOPUISTO BRUNNSPARKEN
Puolimatkansaari / Halvägsholmen
LÄNSISATAMA VÄSTRA HAMNEN
Länsi-Terminaali
Pihlajasaaret
Uunisaaret / Ugnsholmarna
Pormestarinluodot / Borgmästargrunden
Sirpalesaari / Flisholmen
Liuskasaari / Skifferholmen
Harakka / Stora Räntan
Särkkä / Långören
Tallinn
Maarianhamina, Rønne, Stockholm, Rostock, Travemünde
Sankt-Peterburg
0 300 600
m
N

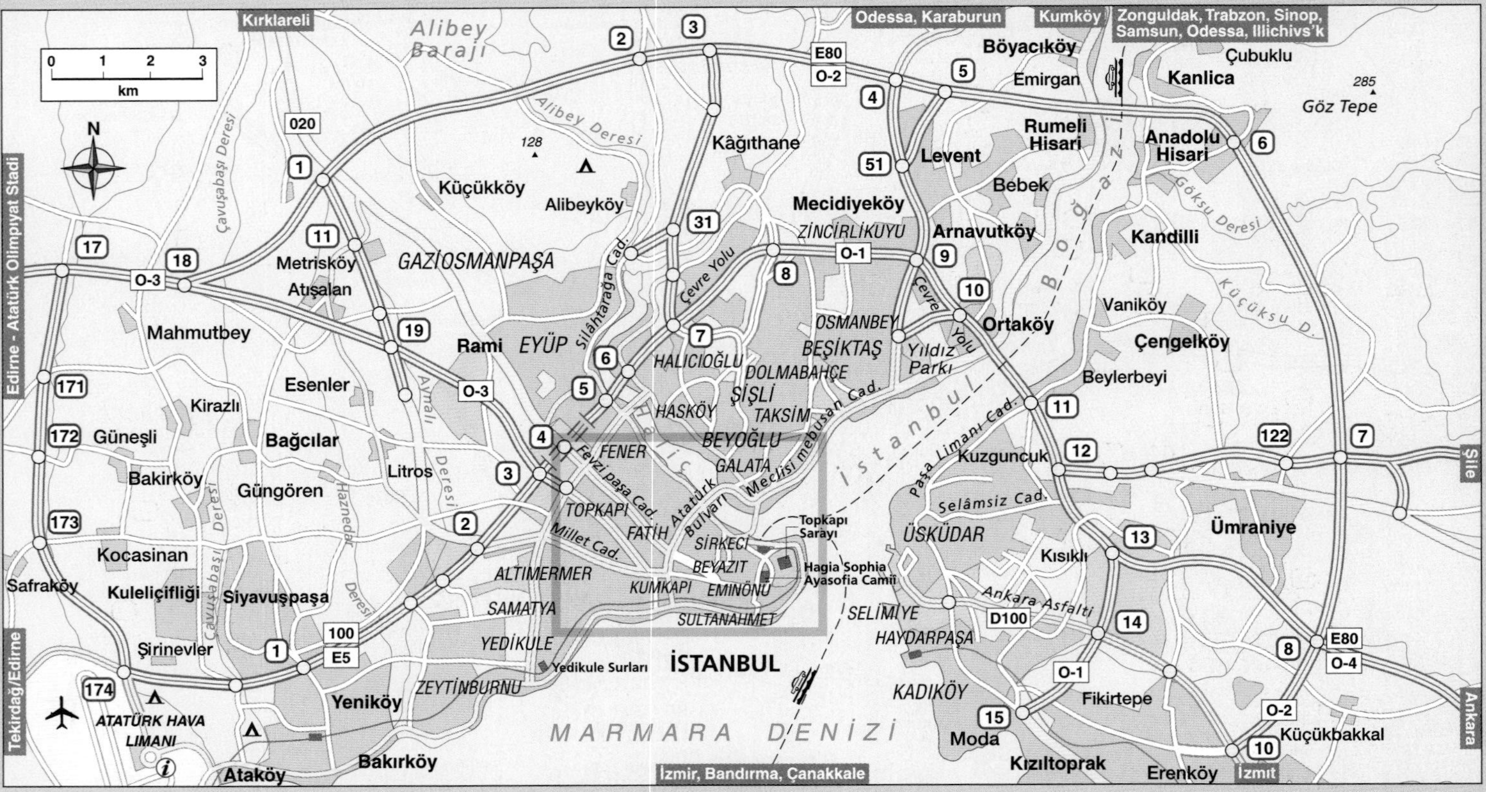
Kırklareli
Odessa, Karaburun
Kumköy
Zonguldak, Trabzon, Sinop, Samsun, Odessa, Illichivs'k
Alibey Barajı
Alibey Deresi
0 1 2 3
km
N
Böyacıköy
Emirgan
Kanlıca
Çubuklu
285
Göz Tepe
Kâğıthane
Küçükköy
Alibeyköy
128
Rumeli Hisari
Anadolu Hisari
Levent
Bebek
Mecidiyeköy
ZİNCİRLİKUYU
Arnavutköy
Kandilli
Göksu Deresi
Metrisköy
Atışalan
GAZİOSMANPAŞA
Mahmutbey
Rami
EYÜP
Silahtarağa Cad.
Çevre Yolu
HALICIOĞLU
OSMANBEY
BEŞİKTAŞ
DOLMABAHÇE
Yıldız Parkı
Ortaköy
Vaniköy
Küçüksu D.
Çengelköy
Beylerbeyi
Esenler
Kirazlı
HASKÖY
ŞİŞLİ
TAKSİM
Meclisi mebusan Cad.
İstanbul
Boğaz
Güneşli
Bağcılar
Bakirköy
Güngören
Litros
FENER
BEYOĞLU
GALATA
Fevzi paşa Cad.
TOPKAPI
FATİH
Atatürk Bulvari
Millet Cad.
SİRKECİ
BEYAZIT
EMİNÖNÜ
KUMKAPI
SULTANAHMET
Topkapı Sarayı
Hagia Sophia
Ayasofia Camii
Paşa Limanı Cad.
Kuzguncuk
Selâmsiz Cad.
ÜSKÜDAR
Kısıklı
Ümraniye
Şile
Kocasinan
Safraköy
Kuleliçifliği
Siyavuşpaşa
ALTIMERMER
SAMATYA
YEDİKULE
Yedikule Surları
ZEYTİNBURNU
Şirinevler
Yeniköy
İSTANBUL
Ankara Asfaltı
SELİMİYE
HAYDARPAŞA
KADIKÖY
Fikirtepe
Moda
Kızıltoprak
Erenköy
Küçükbakkal
ATATÜRK HAVA LIMANI
Ataköy
Bakırköy
MARMARA DENİZİ
İzmir, Bandırma, Çanakkale
İzmit
Ankara
Edirne - Atatürk Olimpiyat Stadi
Tekirdağ/Edirne
E80
O-2
O-1
O-3
O-4
E5
D100
020
100
171
172
173
174

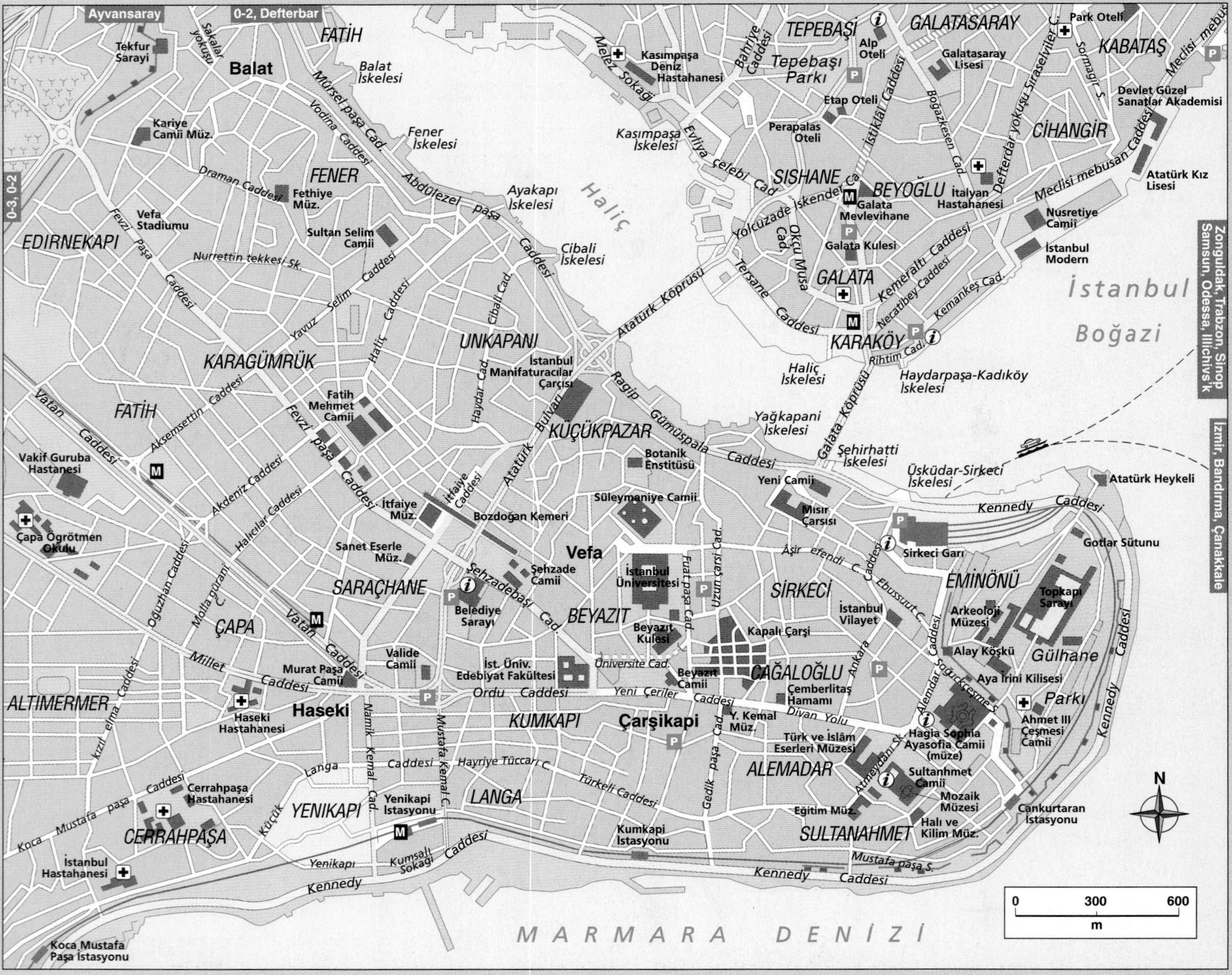
Ayvansaray
0-2, Defterbar
Tekfur Sarayı
Sakalar yokuşu
Balat
FATİH
Balat İskelesi
Mürsel paşa Cad.
Vodina Caddesi
Kariye Camii Müz.
Fener İskelesi
Draman Caddesi
FENER
Fethiye Müz.
Abdülezel paşa Caddesi
Ayakapı İskelesi
Haliç
Vefa Stadiumu
EDİRNEKAPI
Fevzi Paşa Caddesi
Nurrettin tekkesi Sk.
Sultan Selim Camii
Cibali İskelesi
Yavuz Selim Caddesi
Haliç Cad.
Cibali Cad.
UNKAPANI
KARAGÜMRÜK
İstanbul Manifaturacılar Çarçısı
Fatih Mehmet Camii
Vatan Caddesi
FATİH
Aksemsettin Caddesi
Vakif Guruba Hastanesi
Akdeniz Caddesi
Halıcılar Caddesi
Haydar Cad.
Atatürk Bulvari
KÜÇÜKPAZAR
Ragip Gümüşpala Caddesi
Botanik Enstitüsü
İtfaiye Müz.
İtfaiye Caddesi
Bozdoğan Kemeri
Süleymaniye Camii
Çapa Öğrötmen Okulu
Sanet Eserle Müz.
Vefa
Şehzade Camii
Şehzadebaşı Cad.
SARAÇHANE
Belediye Sarayı
İstanbul Üniversitesi
Fuat paşa Cad.
Uzun çarşı Cad.
BEYAZIT
Beyazıt Kulesi
Oğuzhan Caddesi
Molla gürani C.
ÇAPA
Valide Camii
İst. Üniv. Edebiyat Fakültesi
Üniversite Cad.
Murat Paşa Camii
Millet Caddesi
Ordu Caddesi
ALTIMERMER
Haseki Hastahanesi
Haseki
Namik Kemal Cad.
Mustafa Kemal C.
KUMKAPI
Yeni Çeriler Caddesi
Kızıl elma Caddesi
Caddesi
Hayriye Tüccarı C.
Türkeli Caddesi
Langa
Cerrahpaşa Hastahanesi
Koca Mustafa paşa Caddesi
Küçük
YENİKAPI
Yenikapı İstasyonu
LANGA
CERRAHPAŞA
Kumkapı İstasyonu
İstanbul Hastahanesi
Yenikapı
Kumsalı Sokaği
Caddesi
Kennedy
Koca Mustafa Paşa İstasyonu
MARMARA DENİZİ
0 300 600
m
N
Kasımpaşa Deniz Hastahanesi
Melez Sokaği
Kasımpaşa İskelesi
Evliya çelebi Cad.
Bahriye Caddesi
TEPEBAŞİ
Alp Oteli
Tepebaşı Parkı
GALATASARAY
Galatasaray Lisesi
Park Oteli
KABATAŞ
Sormagir S.
Meclisi mebusan
Etap Oteli
Perapalas Oteli
İstiklâl Caddesi
Boğazkesen Cad.
Defterdar yokuşu
Siraselviler C.
Devlet Güzel Sanatlar Akademisi
CİHANGİR
Meclisi mebusan Caddesi
Atatürk Kız Lisesi
ŞİŞHANE
Yolcuzade İskender Ca.
BEYOĞLU
Galata Mevlevihane
İtalyan Hastahanesi
Nusretiye Camii
İstanbul Modern
Galata Kulesi
Okçu Musa Cad.
GALATA
Kemeraltı Caddesi
Necatibey Caddesi
Kemankeş Cad.
Tersane Caddesi
Atatürk Köprüsü
KARAKÖY
Rıhtım Cad.
İstanbul Boğazi
Haliç İskelesi
Haydarpaşa-Kadıköy İskelesi
Galata Köprüsü
Yağkapani İskelesi
Şehirhatti İskelesi
Üsküdar-Sirkeci İskelesi
Atatürk Heykeli
Yeni Camii
Mısır Çarşısı
Kennedy Caddesi
Gotlar Sütunu
Aşir efendi C.
Ebusuut C.
Sirkeci Garı
EMİNÖNÜ
SİRKECİ
İstanbul Vilayet
Topkapı Sarayı
Arkeoloji Müzesi
Kapalı Çarşi
Ankara Cad.
Alemdar Caddesi
Alay Köşkü
Gülhane Parkı
Soğukçeşme S.
Beyazıt Camii
ÇAĞALOĞLU
Çemberlitaş Hamamı
Aya İrini Kilisesi
Divan Yolu
Y. Kemal Müz.
ÇARŞIKAPI
Ahmet III Çeşmesi Camii
Kennedy Caddesi
Türk ve İslâm Eserleri Müzesi
Hagia Sophia Ayasofia Camii (müze)
Alemdarı Sk.
ALEMADAR
Gedik paşa Cad.
Atmeydanı Sk.
Sultanhmet Camii
Eğitim Müz.
Mozaik Müzesi
Cankurtaran İstasyonu
SULTANAHMET
Halı ve Kilim Müz.
Mustafa paşa S.
Kennedy Caddesi
0-3, 0-2
Zonguldak, Trabzon, Sinop, Samsun, Odessa, Illichivs'k
İzmir, Bandırma, Çanakkale

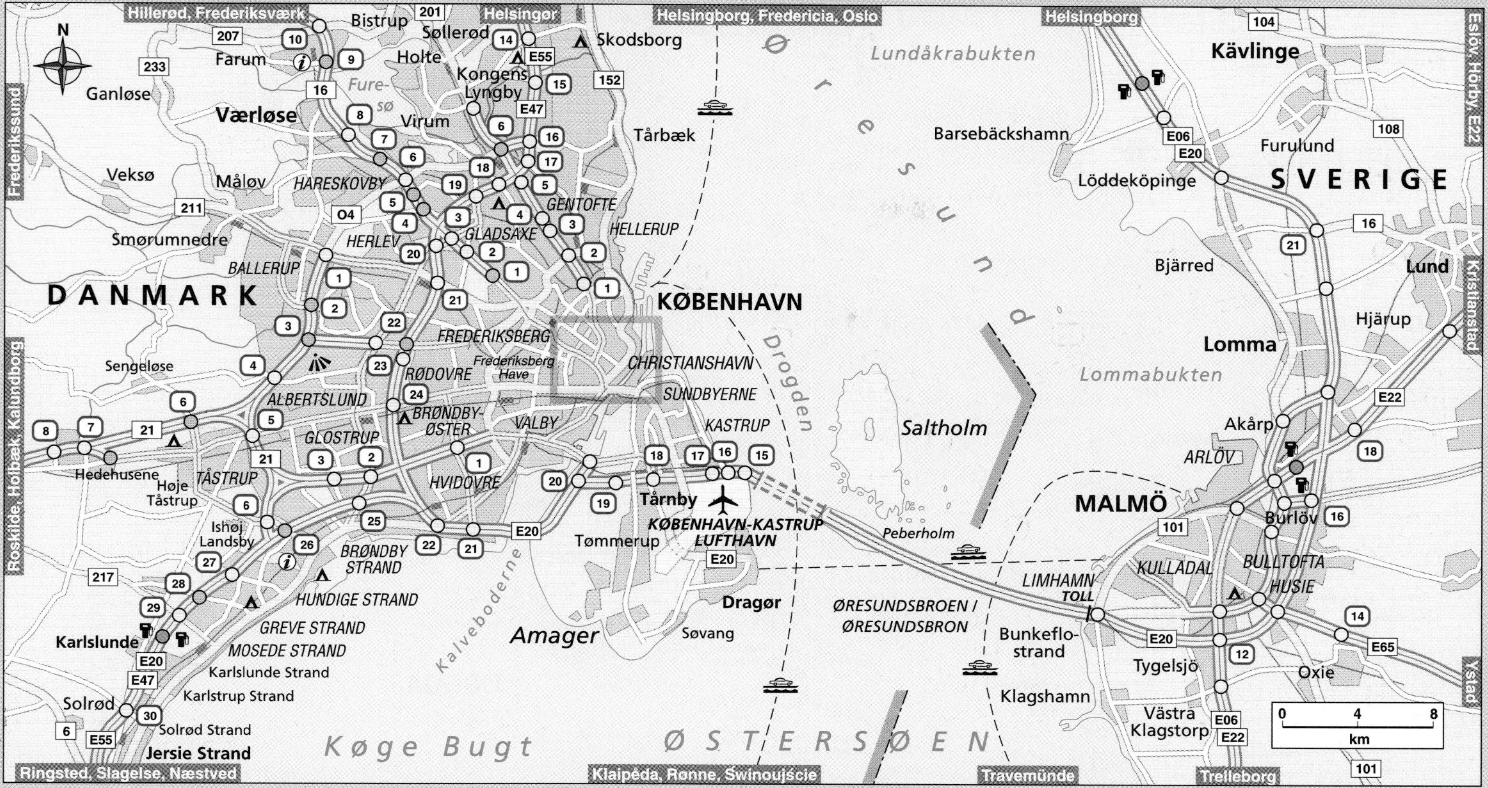
Hillerød, Frederiksværk
Helsingør
Helsingborg, Fredericia, Oslo
Helsingborg
Eslöv, Hörby, E22
Frederikssund
Roskilde, Holbæk, Kalundborg
Kristianstad
Ystad
Ringsted, Slagelse, Næstved
Klaipėda, Rønne, Świnoujście
Travemünde
Trelleborg
Bistrup
Søllerød
Skodsborg
Farum
Holte
Kongens Lyngby
Ganløse
Fure-sø
Værløse
Virum
Tårbæk
Veksø
Måløv
HARESKOVBY
GENTOFTE
HELLERUP
Smørumnedre
HERLEV
GLADSAXE
BALLERUP
DANMARK
KØBENHAVN
FREDERIKSBERG
Frederiksberg Have
CHRISTIANSHAVN
Sengeløse
RØDOVRE
ALBERTSLUND
SUNDBYERNE
BRØNDBY-ØSTER
VALBY
KASTRUP
GLOSTRUP
Hedehusene
Høje Tåstrup
TÅSTRUP
HVIDOVRE
Tårnby
KØBENHAVN-KASTRUP LUFTHAVN
Ishøj Landsby
Tømmerup
BRØNDBY STRAND
HUNDIGE STRAND
GREVE STRAND
MOSEDE STRAND
Karlslunde
Karlslunde Strand
Karlstrup Strand
Solrød
Solrød Strand
Jersie Strand
Køge Bugt
Kalveboderne
Amager
Dragør
Søvang
Drogden
Øresund
Lundåkrabukten
Saltholm
Peberholm
ØRESUNDSBROEN / ØRESUNDSBRON
ØSTERSØEN
Barsebäckshamn
Kävlinge
Furulund
Löddeköpinge
SVERIGE
Bjärred
Lund
Hjärup
Lomma
Lommabukten
Akårp
ARLÖV
Burlöv
MALMÖ
KULLADAL
BULLTOFTA
HUSIE
LIMHAMN
TOLL
Bunkeflo-strand
Tygelsjö
Oxie
Klagshamn
Västra Klagstorp
0 4 8
km

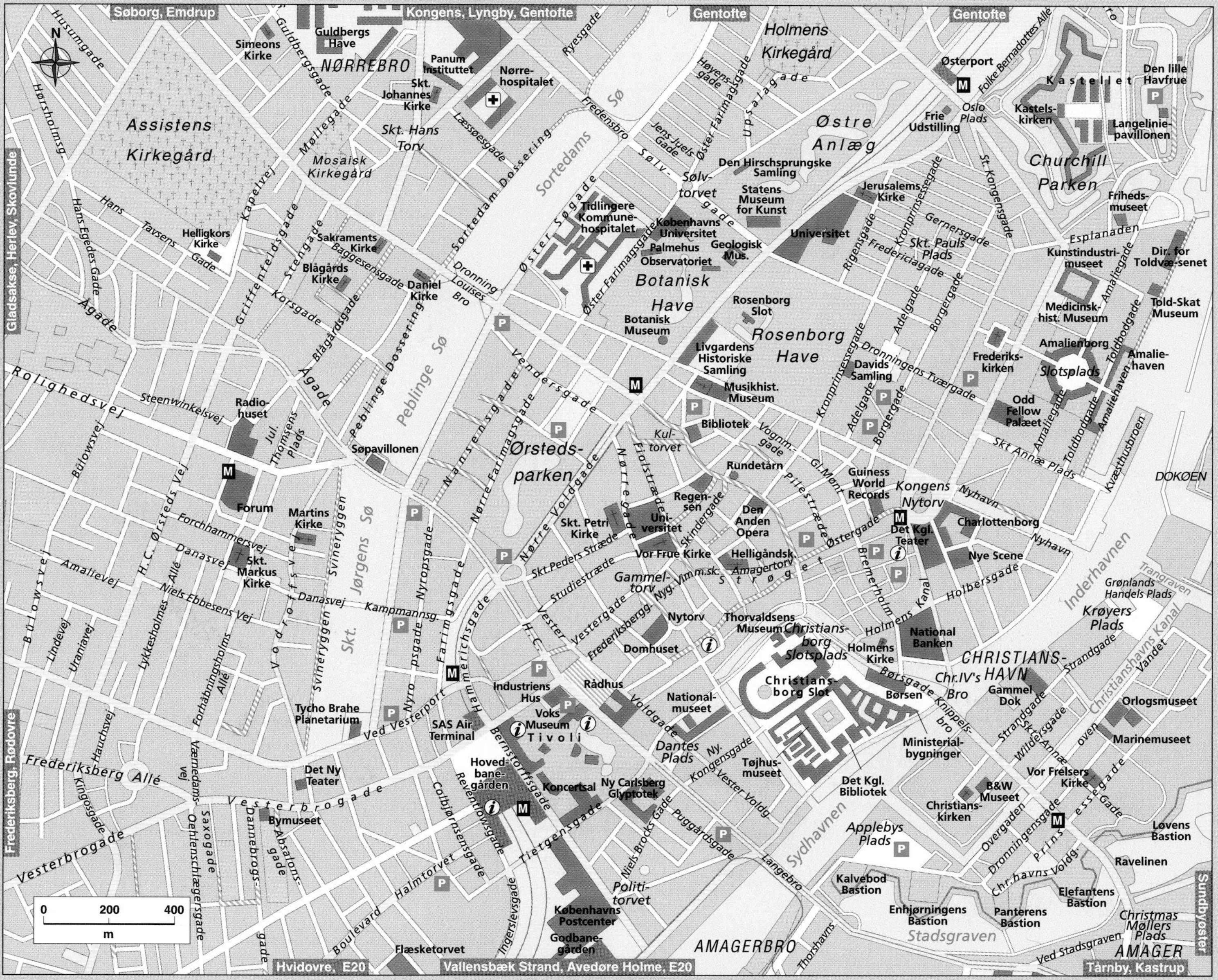
Søborg, Emdrup
Kongens, Lyngby, Gentofte
Gentofte
Gentofte
Gladsakse, Herlev, Skovlunde
Frederiksberg, Rødovre
Hvidovre, E20
Vallensbæk Strand, Avedøre Holme, E20
Tårnby, Kastrup
Sundbyøster
Husumgade
Hørsholmsg.
Simeons Kirke
Guldbergsgade
Guldbergs Have
NØRREBRO
Panum Instituttet
Nørre-hospitalet
Skt. Johannes Kirke
Skt. Hans Torv
Ryesgade
Fredensbro
Sortedams Sø
Holmens Kirkegård
Østerport
Folke Bernadottes Allé
Kastellet
Den lille Havfrue
Kastels-kirken
Oslo Plads
Frie Udstilling
Langelinie-pavillonen
Assistens Kirkegård
Møllegade
Mosaisk Kirkegård
Læssøesgade
Øster Farimagsgade
Jens Juels Gade
Upsalagade
Østre Anlæg
Sølvgade
Den Hirschsprungske Samling
Sølv-torvet
Statens Museum for Kunst
Churchill Parken
Jerusalems Kirke
Kronprinsessegade
St. Kongensgade
Gernersgade
Friheds-museet
Hans Tavsens Gade
Helligkors Kirke
Kapelvej
Sakraments Kirke
Baggesensgade
Tidligere Kommune-hospitalet
Københavns Universitet
Palmehus
Observatoriet
Geologisk Mus.
Universitet
Rigensgade
Fredericiagade
Skt. Pauls Plads
Esplanaden
Kunstindustri-museet
Dir. for Toldvæ-senet
Hans Egedes Gade
Griffenfeldsgade
Stengade
Blågårds Kirke
Daniel Kirke
Dronning Louises Bro
Sortedam Dosseringen
Øster Søgade
Botanisk Have
Botanisk Museum
Rosenborg Slot
Adelgade
Borgergade
Amaliegade
Told-Skat Museum
Ågade
Korsgade
Blågårdsgade
Peblinge Dosseringen
Peblinge Sø
Vendersgade
Rosenborg Have
Davids Samling
Dronningens Tværgade
Medicinsk-hist. Museum
Amalienborg
Frederiks-kirken
Slotsplads
Amalie-haven
Toldbodgade
Rolighedsvej
Steenwinkelsvej
Radio-huset
Jul. Thomsens Plads
Livgardens Historiske Samling
Musikhist. Museum
Bibliotek
Odd Fellow Palæet
Skt Annæ Plads
Kvæsthusbroen
DOKØEN
Bülowsvej
Søpavillonen
Ørsteds-parken
Nansensgade
Nørre Farimagsgade
Nørre Voldgade
Kul-torvet
Vognmagergade
Rundetårn
Gl. Mønt
Pilestræde
Guiness World Records
Kongens Nytorv
Nyhavn
Forum
H.C. Ørsteds Vej
Martins Kirke
Svineryggen
Skt. Jørgens Sø
Skt. Petri Kirke
Regen-sen
Uni-versitet
Den Anden Opera
Østergade
Det Kgl. Teater
Charlottenborg
Forchhammersvej
Skt. Markus Kirke
Danasvej
Vodroffsvej
Nyropsgade
Skt. Pedersstræde
Skindergade
Vor Frue Kirke
Helligåndsk.
Amagertorv
Strøget
Bremerholm
Nye Scene
Holbergsgade
Inderhavnen
Trangraven
Grønlands Handels Plads
Amalievej
Niels Ebbesens Vej
Kampmannsg.
Studiestræde
Gammel-torv
Nyg.
Vimm.sk.
Krøyers Plads
Bülowsvej
Lindevej
Uranivej
Lykkesholms Allé
Forhåbningsholms Allé
Farimagsgade
Vestergade
Nytorv
Frederiksbergg.
Thorvaldsens Museum
Christians-borg Slotsplads
Holmens Kanal
National Banken
CHRISTIANS-HAVN
Christianshavns Kanal
Strandgade
Vandet
H.C. Andersens Boulevard
Hammerichsgade
Domhuset
Holmens Kirke
Christians-borg Slot
Børsgade
Børsen
Chr.IV's Bro
Gammel Dok
Orlogsmuseet
Industriens Hus
Rådhus
Voldgade
National-museet
Knippelsbro
Ministerial-bygninger
Wildersgade
Sankt Annæ Gade
Overgaden oven Vandet
Marinemuseet
Tycho Brahe Planetarium
Ved Vesterport
SAS Air Terminal
Voks Museum
Tivoli
Dantes Plads
Ny Kongensgade
Tøjhus-museet
Vor Frelsers Kirke
Hauchsvej
Frederiksberg Allé
Det Ny Teater
Værnedamsvej
Hoved-bane-gården
Bernstorffsgade
Koncertsal
Ny Carlsberg Glyptotek
Ny Vester Voldg.
Det Kgl. Bibliotek
B&W Museet
Christians-kirken
Kingosgade
Vesterbrogade
Oehlenschlægersgade
Saxogade
Dannebrogsgade
Absalonsgade
Bymuseet
Colbjørnsensgade
Reventlowsgade
Tietgensgade
Niels Brocks Gade
Puggårdsgade
Sydhavnen
Langebro
Applebys Plads
Overgaden
Dronningensgade
Prinsessegade
Løvens Bastion
Halmtorvet
Ingerslevsgade
Politi-torvet
Chr. havns Volde
Ravelinen
Elefantens Bastion
Kalvebod Bastion
Enhjørningens Bastion
Panterens Bastion
Stadsgraven
Christmas Møllers Plads
Ved Stadsgraven
AMAGER
Boulevard
Flæsketorvet
Københavns Postcenter
Godbane-gården
AMAGERBRO
Thorshavns
0 200 400
m

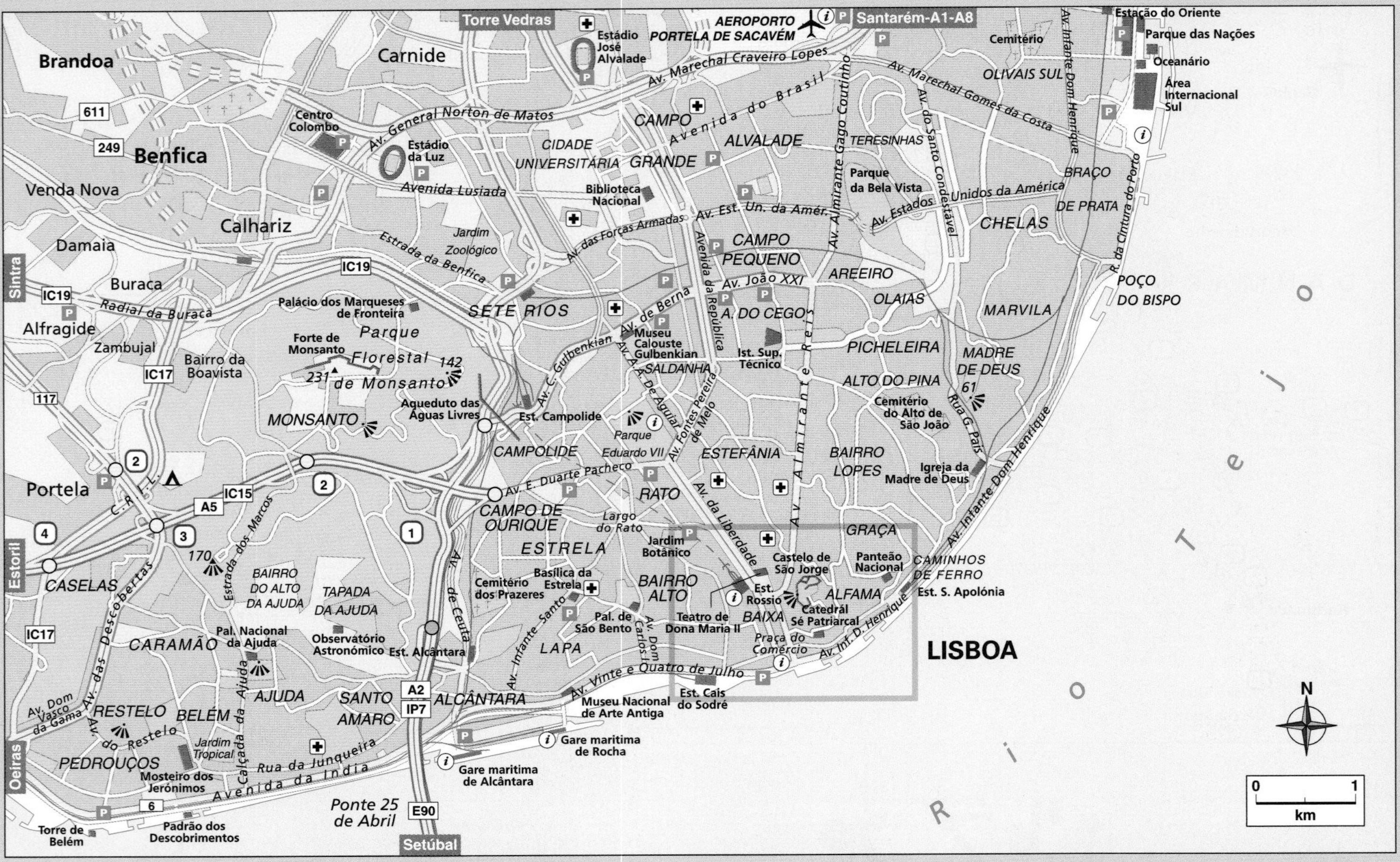

Torre Vedras
Estádio José Alvalade
AEROPORTO PORTELA DE SACAVÉM
Santarém-A1-A8
Estação do Oriente
Parque das Nações
Oceanário
Área Internacional Sul
Cemitério
OLIVAIS SUL
Brandoa
Carnide
Av. Marechal Craveiro Lopes
Av. Marechal Gomes da Costa
Av. Infante Dom Henrique
611
249
Benfica
Centro Colombo
Estádio da Luz
Av. General Norton de Matos
CIDADE UNIVERSITÁRIA
CAMPO GRANDE
Avenida do Brasil
ALVALADE
TERESINHAS
Av. Almirante Gago Coutinho
Av. do Santo Condestável
Parque da Bela Vista
BRAÇO DE PRATA
Venda Nova
Avenida Lusíada
Biblioteca Nacional
Av. Est. Un. da Amér.
Av. Estados Unidos da América
CHELAS
Calhariz
Damaia
Jardim Zoológico
Estrada da Benfica
Av. das Forças Armadas
CAMPO PEQUENO
Avenida da República
R. da Cintura do Porto
Sintra
IC19
Buraca
Radial da Buraca
Palácio dos Marqueses de Fronteira
SETE RIOS
Av. João XXI
AREEIRO
OLAIAS
MARVILA
POÇO DO BISPO
Alfragide
Zambujal
Forte de Monsanto
Parque Florestal de Monsanto
142
231
Av. de Berna
Museu Calouste Gulbenkian
A. DO CEGO
Ist. Sup. Técnico
PICHELEIRA
MADRE DE DEUS
Bairro da Boavista
IC17
117
SALDANHA
Av. C. Gulbenkian
ALTO DO PINA
61
Cemitério do Alto de São João
MONSANTO
Aqueduto das Águas Livres
Est. Campolide
Parque Eduardo VII
Av. Fontes Pereira de Melo
Rua G. Pais
CAMPOLIDE
ESTEFÂNIA
BAIRRO LOPES
Igreja da Madre de Deus
Portela
C.R.I.L.
Av. E. Duarte Pacheco
RATO
IC15
A5
Av. Almirante Reis
Av. Infante D. Henrique
CAMPO DE OURIQUE
Largo do Rato
GRAÇA
Estrada dos Marcos
1
2
3
4
170
Jardim Botânico
Castelo de São Jorge
Panteão Nacional
CAMINHOS DE FERRO
Av. da Liberdade
ESTRELA
Estoril
CASELAS
Av. das Descobertas
BAIRRO DO ALTO DA AJUDA
TAPADA DA AJUDA
Cemitério dos Prazeres
Basílica da Estrela
BAIRRO ALTO
Est. Rossio
ALFAMA
Est. S. Apolónia
Catedral Sé Patriarcal
BAIXA
Av. de Ceuta
Av. Infante Santo
Pal. de São Bento
Teatro de Dona Maria II
Praça do Comércio
Av. Inf. D. Henrique
LISBOA
IC17
CARAMÃO
Pal. Nacional da Ajuda
Observatório Astronómico
Est. Alcântara
LAPA
Av. Dom Carlos I
Av. Vinte e Quatro de Julho
AJUDA
Calçada da Ajuda
Av. Dom Vasco da Gama
RESTELO
BELÉM
SANTO AMARO
ALCÂNTARA
A2
IP7
Museu Nacional de Arte Antiga
Est. Cais do Sodré
Av. do Restelo
Jardim Tropical
PEDROUÇOS
Rua da Junqueira
Gare maritima de Rocha
Gare maritima de Alcântara
Oeiras
Mosteiro dos Jerónimos
Avenida da Índia
6
Torre de Belém
Padrão dos Descobrimentos
Ponte 25 de Abril
E90
Setúbal
Rio Tejo
N
0
1
km

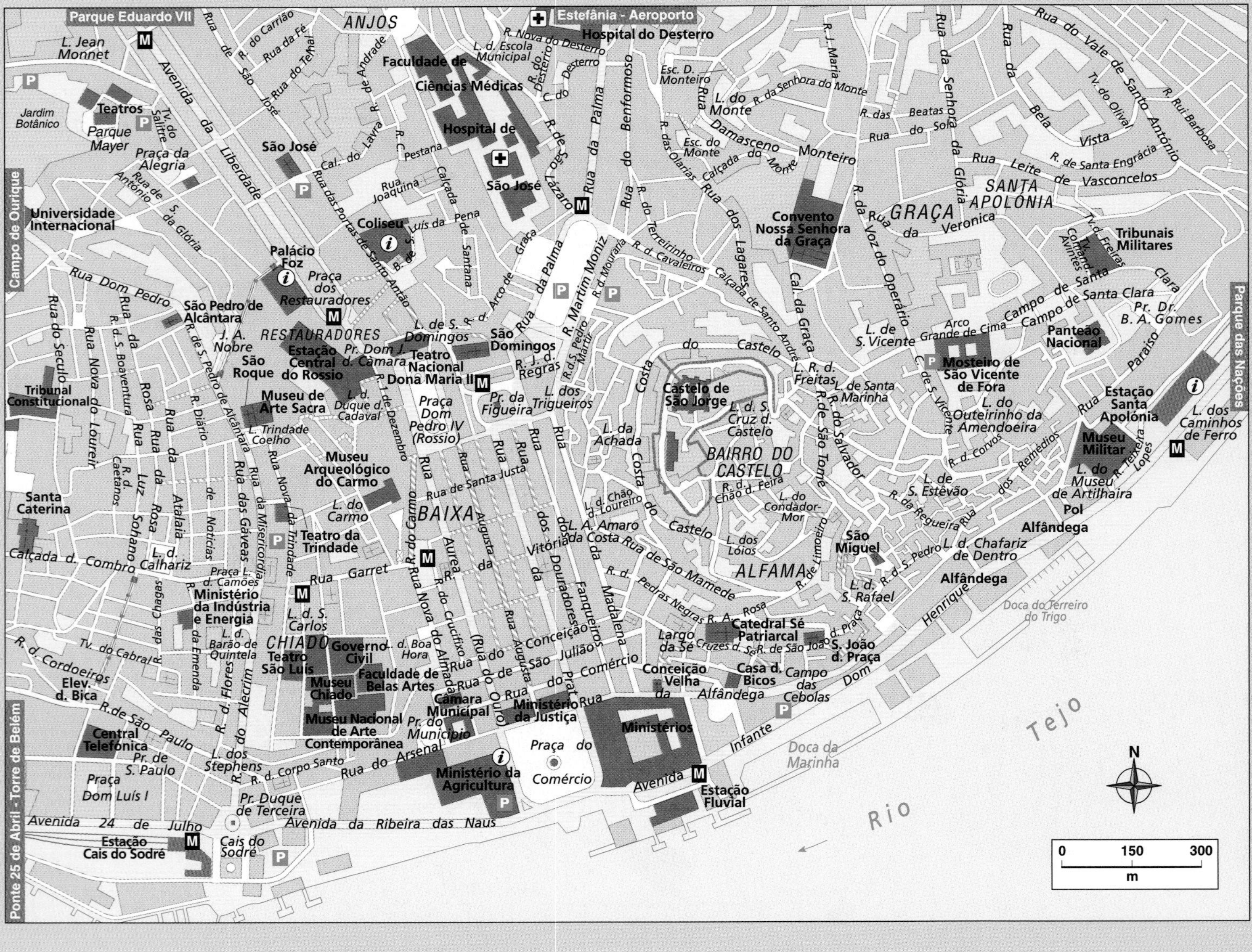

Parque Eduardo VII
Estefânia - Aeroporto
ANJOS
Hospital do Desterro
L. Jean Monnet
Avenida da Liberdade
R. do Carrião
Rua da Fé
Rua do Telhal
R. Nova do Desterro
L. d. Escola Municipal
Faculdade de Ciências Médicas
Hospital de São José
Rua do Benformoso
Rua da Palma
Esc. D. Monteiro
L. do Monte
Rua Damasceno Monteiro
R. da Senhora do Monte
R. J. Maria
Rua da Senhora da Glória
Rua do Vale de Santo António
Tv. do Olival
R. Rui Barbosa
Rua da Bela Vista
Jardim Botânico
Teatros
Parque Mayer
Tv. do Salitre
Praça da Alegria
Rua de São José
Cal. do Lavra
R. C. Pestana
Rua Joaquina
Calçada de Santana
R. de São Lázaro
R. das Olarias
Esc. do Monte
Calçada do Monte
Rua dos Lagares
R. das Beatas
Rua do Sol
Rua Leite de Vasconcelos
R. de Santa Engrácia
SANTA APOLÓNIA
São José
Rua de S. António
Rua de S. da Glória
Rua das Portas de Santo Antão
Coliseu
Luís da B. de S.
Rua da Pena
Campo de Ourique
Universidade Internacional
Palácio Foz
Praça dos Restauradores
R. do Arco da Graça
Rua Martim Moniz
R. d. Mouraria
R. do Terreirinho
R. d. Cavaleiros
Calçada de Santo André
Convento Nossa Senhora da Graça
Cal. da Graça
R. da Voz do Operário
GRAÇA
Rua da Veronica
Tribunais Militares
Tv. d. Freiras
Campo de Santa Clara
Pr. Dr. B. A. Gomes
Parque das Nações
Rua Dom Pedro
São Pedro de Alcântara
RESTAURADORES
L. de S. Domingos
São Domingos
Rua do Século
Rua Nova do Loureiro
R. d. S. Boaventura
R. de S. Pedro de Alcântara
J. A. Nobre
São Roque
Estação Central do Rossio
Pr. Dom J. d. Câmara
Teatro Nacional Dona Maria II
R. J. d. Regras
R. d. S. Pedro Mártir
Costa do Castelo
Castelo de São Jorge
L. R. d. Freitas
L. de Santa Marinha
L. de S. Vicente
Arco Grande de Cima
Mosteiro de São Vicente de Fora
Panteão Nacional
Paraíso
Estação Santa Apolónia
L. dos Caminhos de Ferro
Tribunal Constitucional
Rua da Rosa
R. Diário
Museu de Arte Sacra
L. Trindade Coelho
L. d. Duque d. Cadaval
R. 1 de Dezembro
Praça Dom Pedro IV (Rossio)
Pr. da Figueira
L. dos Trigueiros
L. da Achada
L. d. S. Cruz d. Castelo
R. de São Tomé
R. do Salvador
C. de S. Vicente
L. do Outeirinho da Amendoeira
R. d. Corvos
R. dos Remédios
Museu Militar
R. Teixeira Lopes
L. do Museu de Artilhaira
R. d. Caetanos
Rua da Luz Soriano
Rua da Atalaia
Rua das Gáveas
Rua Nova da Trindade
Museu Arqueológico do Carmo
Rua de Santa Justa
BAIRRO DO CASTELO
R. d. Chão d. Feira
Santa Catarina
L. do Carmo
BAIXA
Rua do Carmo
Rua Áurea
Rua Augusta
Rua dos Douradores
Rua dos Fanqueiros
Rua da Madalena
Rua da Vitória
L. d. Chão d. Loureiro
L. A. Amaro da Costa
Rua do Castelo
L. do Condador-Mor
L. de S. Estêvão
R. da Regueira
Pol
Alfândega
Calçada do Combro
L. d. Calhariz
Rua das Chagas
Rua da Misericórdia
Teatro da Trindade
Rua Garret
Rua Nova do Almada
R. do Crucifixo
Rua de São Mamede
R. d. Pedras Negras
L. dos Loios
ALFAMA
R. de Limoeiro
São Miguel
L. d. S. Rafael
L. d. Chafariz de Dentro
R. d. S. Pedro
Praça L. d. Camões
Ministério da Indústria e Energia
L. d. S. Carlos
CHIADO
Governo Civil
L. d. Boa Hora
Rua da Conceição
Rua de São Julião
Rua do Comércio
Largo da Sé
R. A. Rosa
Cruzes d. Sé
R. de São João da Praça
Catedral Sé Patriarcal
S. João d. Praça
Henrique
Doca do Terreiro do Trigo
Tv. do Cabral
L. d. Barão de Quintela
R. d. Emenda
Teatro São Luis
Faculdade de Belas Artes
Conceição Velha
Rua da Alfândega
Casa d. Bicos
Campo das Cebolas
Dom
R. d. Cordoeiros
Elev. d. Bica
Museu Chiado
Museu Nacional de Arte Contemporânea
Câmara Municipal
Pr. do Município
Ministério da Justiça
Rua do Ouro
Rua da Prata
Ministérios
Infante
Doca da Marinha
Tejo
Central Telefónica
R. de São Paulo
R. d. Flores
R. do Alecrim
L. dos Stephens
Pr. de S. Paulo
R. d. Corpo Santo
Rua do Arsenal
Ministério da Agricultura
Praça do Comércio
Avenida
Estação Fluvial
Praça Dom Luís I
Pr. Duque de Terceira
Avenida 24 de Julho
Avenida da Ribeira das Naus
Rio
Ponte 25 de Abril - Torre de Belém
Estação Cais do Sodré
Cais do Sodré
N
0
150
300
m

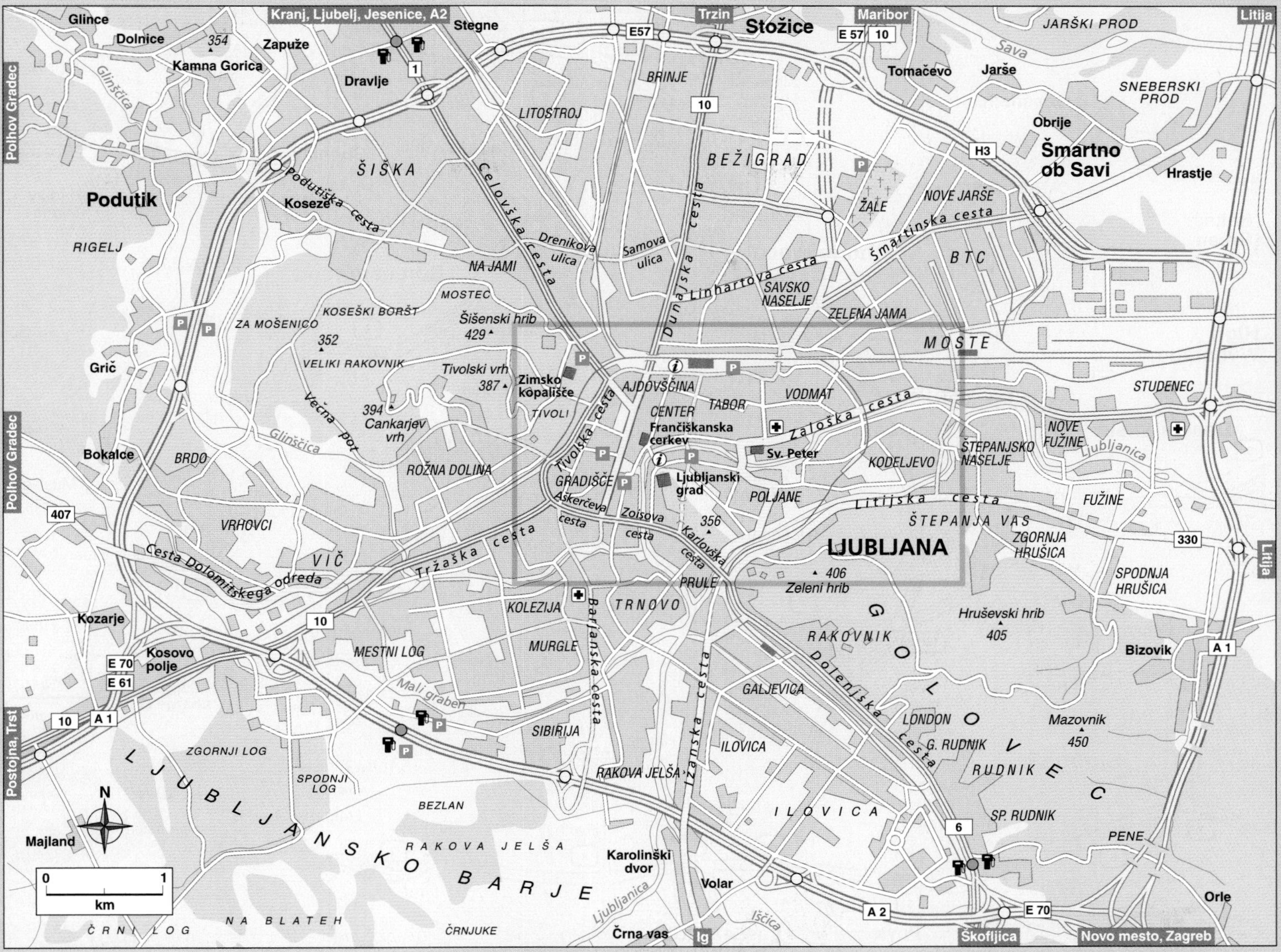
Kranj, Ljubelj, Jesenice, A2
Trzin
Maribor
Litija
Stožice
Glince
Dolnice
Kamna Gorica
Zapuže
Stegne
Dravlje
Polhov Gradec
E57
E 57
10
1
H3
JARŠKI PROD
Sava
Tomačevo
Jarše
SNEBERSKI PROD
Obrije
Šmartno ob Savi
Hrastje
BRINJE
LITOSTROJ
BEŽIGRAD
ŠIŠKA
Podutiška cesta
Koseze
Podutik
RIGELJ
Celovška cesta
Dunajska cesta
Drenikova ulica
Samova ulica
ŽALE
NOVE JARŠE
Šmartinska cesta
BTC
NA JAMI
MOSTEC
Linhartova cesta
SAVSKO NASELJE
KOSEŠKI BORŠT
ZA MOŠENICO
Šišenski hrib 429
352
ZELENA JAMA
MOSTE
VELIKI RAKOVNIK
Tivolski vrh 387
Zimsko kopališče
AJDOVŠČINA
TABOR
VODMAT
STUDENEC
Grič
Večna pot
394 Cankarjev vrh
TIVOLI
Tivolska cesta
CENTER
Frančiškanska cerkev
Zaloška cesta
FUŽINE
Glinščica
Bokalce
BRDO
ROŽNA DOLINA
Sv. Peter
KODELJEVO
ŠTEPANJSKO NASELJE
Ljubljanica
GRADIŠČE
Ljubljanski grad
POLJANE
Aškerčeva cesta
Litijska cesta
FUŽINE
407
VRHOVCI
Zoisova cesta
356
Karlovška cesta
ŠTEPANJA VAS
ZGORNJA HRUŠICA
330
Cesta Dolomitskega odreda
VIČ
Tržaška cesta
LJUBLJANA
406 Zeleni hrib
SPODNJA HRUŠICA
PRULE
Kozarje
10
KOLEZIJA
Barjanska cesta
TRNOVO
RAKOVNIK
GOLOVEC
Hruševski hrib 405
Kosovo polje
E 70
E 61
MESTNI LOG
MURGLE
Dolenjska cesta
Bizovik
A 1
Mali graben
GALJEVICA
Ižanska cesta
Postojna, Trst
10
A 1
SIBIRIJA
LONDON
G. RUDNIK
Mazovnik 450
ZGORNJI LOG
ILOVICA
RUDNIK
SPODNJI LOG
RAKOVA JELŠA
LJUBLJANSKO BARJE
BEZLAN
ILOVICA
SP. RUDNIK
6
N
Majland
PENE
RAKOVA JELŠA
Karolinški dvor
0
1
km
Volar
Orle
Ljubljanica
A 2
E 70
Iščica
ČRNI LOG
NA BLATEH
ČRNJUKE
Črna vas
Ig
Škofljica
Novo mesto, Zagreb

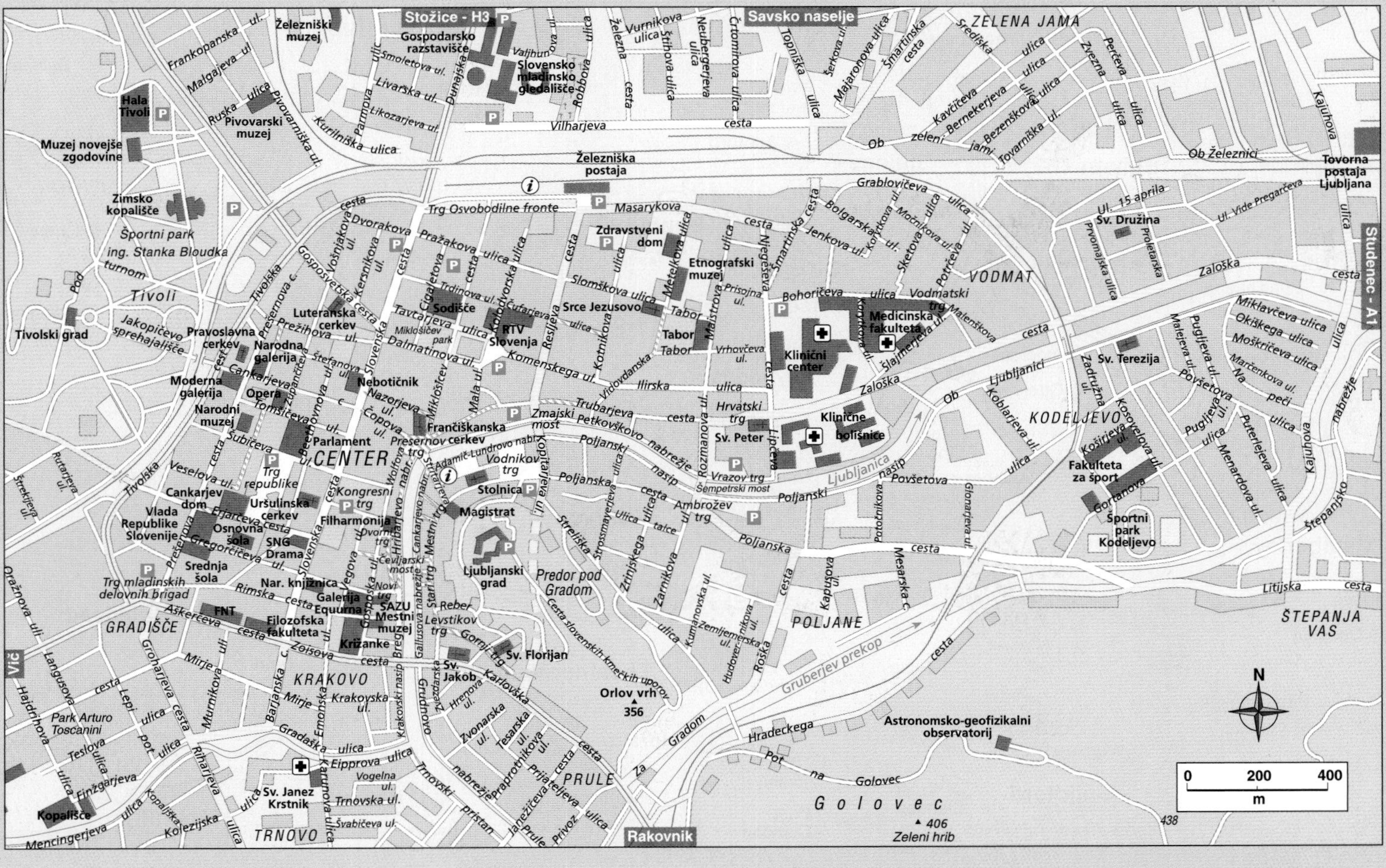
Stožice - H3
Savsko naselje
ZELENA JAMA
Železniški muzej
Frankopanska ul.
Gospodarsko razstavišče
Slovensko mladinsko gledališče
Vurnikova ulica
Neubergerjeva ulica
Črtomirova ulica
Topniška ulica
Šmartinska cesta
Hala Tivoli
Pivovarniška ulica
Pivovarski muzej
Muzej novejše zgodovine
Vilharjeva cesta
Ob železnici
Tovorna postaja Ljubljana
Železniška postaja
Masarykova
Trg Osvobodilne fronte
Zimsko kopališče
Športni park ing. Stanka Bloudka
Tivoli
Grablovičeva ulica
Ul. 15 aprila
Sv. Družina
Ul. Vide Pregarčeva
Zdravstveni dom
Etnografski muzej
VODMAT
Zaloška
Studenec - A1
Tivolski grad
Jakopičevo sprehajališče
Luteranska cerkev
Pravoslavna cerkev
Sodišče
RTV Slovenija
Srce Jezusovo
Tabor
Medicinska fakulteta
Vodmatski trg
Klinični center
Moderna galerija
Narodna galerija
Nebotičnik
Komenskega ul.
Sv. Terezija
Opera
Narodni muzej
Parlament
Frančiškanska cerkev
Zmajski most
Trubarjeva
Petkovškovo nabrežje
Hrvatski trg
Kliničnе bolnišnice
Sv. Peter
Zaloška
Ljubljanica
Ob Ljubljanici
KODELJEVO
CENTER
Trg republike
Vodnikov trg
Stolnica
Magistrat
Šempetrski most
Vrazov trg
Povšetova
Fakulteta za šport
Cankarjev dom
Uršulinska cerkev
Kongresni trg
Vlada Republike Slovenije
Osnovna šola
SNG Drama
Filharmonija
Športni park Kodeljevo
Srednja šola
Trg mladinskih delovnih brigad
Nar. knjižnica
Ljubljanski grad
Predor pod Gradom
Poljanska
Mesarska c.
Litijska cesta
Galerija Equurna
FNT
SAZU
Filozofska fakulteta
Mestni muzej
Križanke
Levstikov trg
POLJANE
ŠTEPANJA VAS
GRADIŠČE
Sv. Florijan
Sv. Jakob
KRAKOVO
Gruberjev prekop
Orlov vrh 356
Park Arturo Toscanini
Astronomsko-geofizikalni observatorij
Hradeckega
Pot na Golovec
Sv. Janez Krstnik
PRULE
Golovec
406 Zeleni hrib
0
200
400
m
Kopališče
Vič
TRNOVO
Rakovnik
N

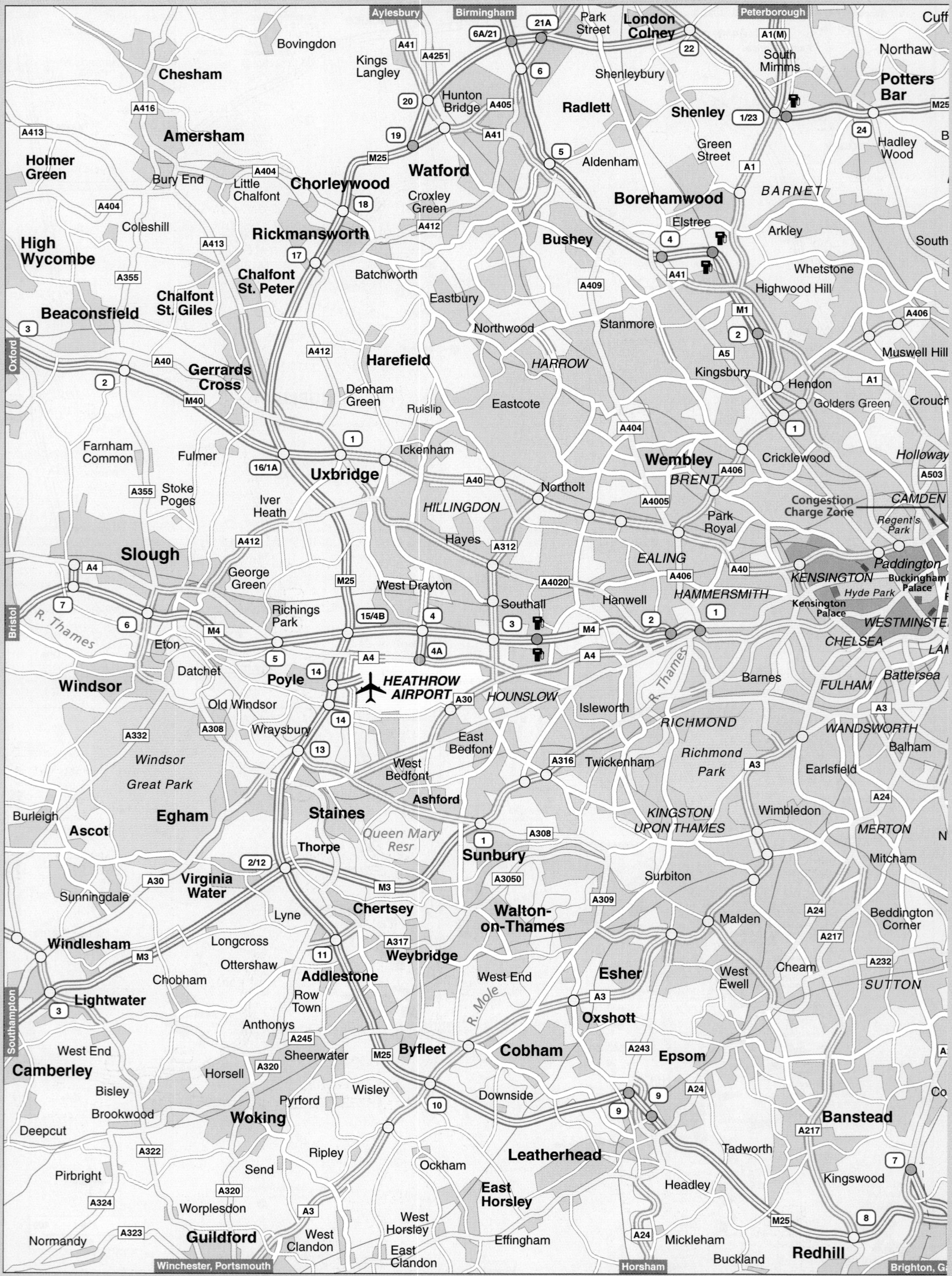

Aylesbury
Birmingham
Peterborough
Park Street
London Colney
21A
6A/21
A1(M)
Cuff
Northaw
South Mimms
22
Bovingdon
A41
Kings Langley
A4251
6
Shenleybury
Potters Bar
Chesham
20
Hunton Bridge
A405
Radlett
Shenley
1/23
M25
A416
24
Hadley Wood
A413
Amersham
19
A41
5
Green Street
Holmer Green
M25
Aldenham
A1
A404
Watford
Bury End
Little Chalfont
Chorleywood
BARNET
A404
18
Croxley Green
Borehamwood
Coleshill
Elstree
A412
Arkley
High Wycombe
A413
Rickmansworth
4
Bushey
South
17
Whetstone
A355
Chalfont St. Peter
Batchworth
A41
A409
Highwood Hill
Chalfont St. Giles
Eastbury
M1
Beaconsfield
A406
3
Northwood
Stanmore
2
Oxford
A412
Harefield
HARROW
A5
Muswell Hill
A40
Gerrards Cross
Kingsbury
2
Hendon
A1
Denham Green
Golders Green
Crouch
M40
Ruislip
Eastcote
A404
1
1
Farnham Common
Ickenham
Cricklewood
Fulmer
Wembley
Holloway
16/1A
Uxbridge
A40
BRENT
A406
A503
Northolt
A355
Stoke Poges
Iver Heath
HILLINGDON
A4005
Congestion Charge Zone
CAMDEN
Park Royal
Regent's Park
Hayes
A412
A312
Slough
EALING
A4
A40
Paddington
George Green
A406
A4020
KENSINGTON
Buckingham Palace
M25
West Drayton
Hyde Park
Hanwell
HAMMERSMITH
Kensington Palace
Southall
7
Richings Park
15/4B
4
1
R. Thames
3
2
WESTMINSTER
6
M4
M4
Bristol
Eton
CHELSEA
A4
4A
A4
5
Datchet
14
Barnes
Battersea
Poyle
HEATHROW AIRPORT
Windsor
FULHAM
A30
HOUNSLOW
Isleworth
R. Thames
Old Windsor
A3
14
RICHMOND
A332
A308
Wraysbury
WANDSWORTH
East Bedfont
13
Balham
Windsor
West Bedfont
A316
Twickenham
Richmond Park
A3
Earlsfield
Great Park
Ashford
A24
Burleigh
Egham
Staines
KINGSTON UPON THAMES
Wimbledon
Ascot
Queen Mary Resr
1
A308
MERTON
Thorpe
Sunbury
2/12
Mitcham
Virginia Water
A30
M3
A3050
Surbiton
Sunningdale
A309
Walton-on-Thames
Lyne
Chertsey
A24
Beddington Corner
Malden
Windlesham
Longcross
A317
A217
M3
11
Weybridge
Ottershaw
A232
Addlestone
West End
Esher
West Ewell
Cheam
Chobham
SUTTON
Lightwater
Row Town
A3
R. Mole
3
Oxshott
Southampton
Anthonys
A245
West End
A243
Camberley
M25
Byfleet
Cobham
Epsom
Sheerwater
A320
Horsell
Bisley
Wisley
A24
Pyrford
9
Downside
10
Banstead
Brookwood
9
Woking
Deepcut
A217
Tadworth
A322
Ripley
Leatherhead
7
Send
Ockham
Pirbright
Kingswood
A320
Headley
East Horsley
A324
Worplesdon
A3
M25
8
West Horsley
West Clandon
A323
Guildford
A24
Normandy
Effingham
Mickleham
East Clandon
Buckland
Redhill
Winchester, Portsmouth
Horsham
Brighton

Cambridge
Cuffley
Cheshunt
Epping Upland
Cambridge
Epping
North Weald Bassett
High Ongar
A414
Loves Green
Ipswich
N
Toot Hill
Chipping Ongar
Goff's Oak
Churchgate
Waltham Cross
Waltham Abbey
R. Lea
M25
25
26
27/6
Kelvedon Hatch
0 2 4 6 km
0 1 2 3 miles
Botany Bay
M11
Theydon Bois
Doddinghurst
A10
High Beach
Navestock Side
A128
Ingatestone
ENFIELD
Mountnessing
King George V Resr
Loughton
Abridge
Lambourne End
Brentwood
A12
5
Coxtie Green
Billericay
outhgate
Chigwell
Bournebridge
Abbotts
M25
A129
Palmers Green
Edmonton
Chingford
Havering-atte-Bower
Harold Hill
A1023
A128
Little Burstead
Woodford
Barkingside
28
Tottenham
A12
Little Warley
Ingrave
Hill
WALTHAM FOREST
4
REDBRIDGE
Great Warley
A503
A127
Southend-on-Sea
HARINGEY
Walthamstow
A12
Ilford
Romford
ouch End
R. Lea
Cranham
29
Basildon
Wanstead
HAVERING
Stamford Hill
Leyton
A116
BARKING
Upminster
North Ockendon
way
A10
A406
Bulphan
A503
DAGENHAM
A128
ISLINGTON
West Ham
Rainham
Southend-on-Sea
HACKNEY
A13
NEWHAM
A1306
Holborn
TOWER HAMLETS
A12
Wennington
South Ockendon
British Museum
Tower of London
Canning Town
Creekmouth
Aveley
Stanford le Hope
CITY
A13
CITY AIRPORT
A2016
A13
Houses of Parliament
Tower Bridge
A1020
30
SOUTHWARK
Chadwell St. Mary
R. Thames
31
Grays
A1089
LAMBETH
Walworth
GREENWICH
Woolwich
A2
Erith
West Thurrock
East Wickham
Purfleet
A202
New Cross
Greenwich Park
Kidbrooke
A206
Brixton
BEXLEY
1A
Tilbury
A23
A20
A2
Bexleyheath
A206
LEWISHAM
Eltham
Dartford
1B
Swanscombe
Tulse Hill
North Cray
A205
Gravesend
Sydenham
Mottingham
Joyden's Wood
Sidcup
A223
A20
Hawley
Hook
2
Hextable
Sutton at Hone
Penge
Canterbury, Ramsgate, Dover
Norbury
Swanley
M25
A2
Widmore
3/1
A225
Dean Bottom
Meopham Station
A23
South Norwood
BROMLEY
A224
Southborough
Luddensdown
Orpington
Hartley
A232
A232
Farningham
Meopham
Shirley
Chelsfield
M20
CROYDON
R. Darent
Eynsford
New Ash Green
A20
4
Ash
New Addington
A21
A225
A227
Downe
West Kingsdown
Romney Street
Purley
Selsdon
Stansted
Shoreham
Fickleshole
Halstead
Folkestone, Dover
A23
Cudham
Otford
2
3
A22
Farleigh
Biggin Hill
M25
Kemsing
Heaverham
Leybourne
Coulsdon
A20
M26
2A
Knockholt
West Malling
Warlingham
Tatsfield
5
Longford
Seal
A25
Borough Green
Chaldon
A225
M25
A21
A228
Woldingham
Westerham
Sevenoaks
Mereworth
Caterham
7/8
Hosey Hill
Plaxtol
6
Limpsfield
Under River
M23
Godstone
Ide Hill
Oxted
Shipbourne
A26
on, Gatwick Airport
Hastings

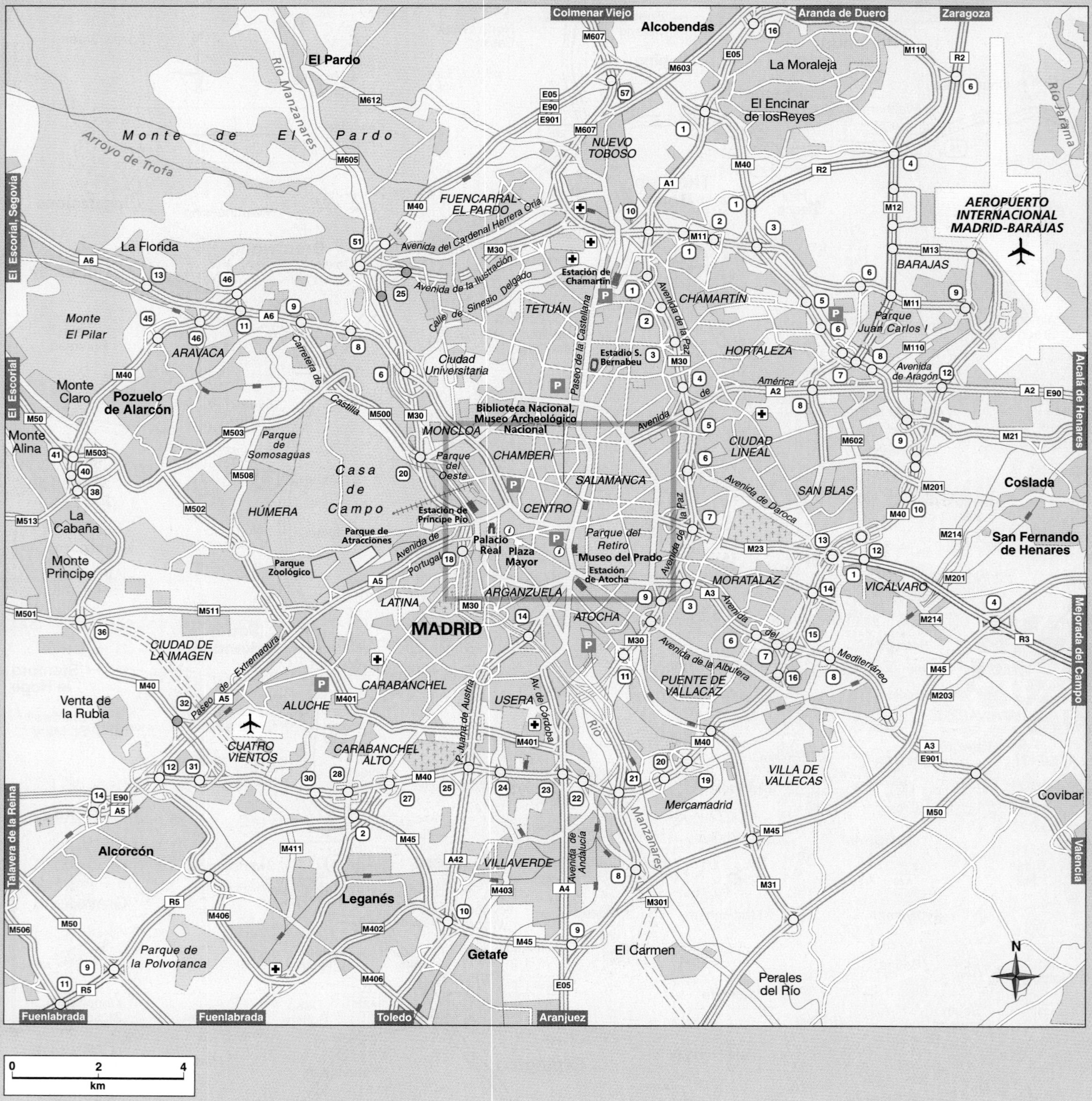

Colmenar Viejo
Alcobendas
Aranda de Duero
Zaragoza
El Pardo
La Moraleja
El Encinar de losReyes
Monte de El Pardo
Arroyo de Trofa
Río Manzanares
Río Jarama
NUEVO TOBOSO
FUENCARRAL-EL PARDO
AEROPUERTO INTERNACIONAL MADRID-BARAJAS
BARAJAS
Avenida del Cardenal Herrera Oria
Avenida de la Ilustración
Calle de Sinesio Delgado
Estación de Chamartín
CHAMARTÍN
Avenida de la Paz
La Florida
Monte El Pilar
ARAVACA
TETUÁN
Parque Juan Carlos I
HORTALEZA
Estadio S. Bernabeu
Paseo de la Castellana
Ciudad Universitaria
Carretera de Castilla
Avenida de América
Avenida de Aragón
Monte Claro
Pozuelo de Alarcón
Monte Alina
Biblioteca Nacional, Museo Archeológico Nacional
MONCLOA
CIUDAD LINEAL
Parque de Somosaguas
Parque del Oeste
CHAMBERÍ
SALAMANCA
Casa de Campo
SAN BLAS
Coslada
La Cabaña
HÚMERA
Estación de Príncipe Pío
CENTRO
Avenida de Daroca
Parque de Atracciones
Palacio Real
Plaza Mayor
Parque del Retiro
Museo del Prado
San Fernando de Henares
Monte Principe
Parque Zoológico
Avenida de Portugal
Estación de Atocha
ARGANZUELA
MORATALAZ
VICÁLVARO
LATINA
ATOCHA
MADRID
Avenida del Mediterráneo
CIUDAD DE LA IMAGEN
Paseo de Extremadura
Avenida de la Albufera
CARABANCHEL
PUENTE DE VALLACAZ
Venta de la Rubia
ALUCHE
USERA
Av. de Córdoba
P. Juana de Austria
CUATRO VIENTOS
CARABANCHEL ALTO
Río Manzanares
VILLA DE VALLECAS
Covibar
Mercamadrid
Alcorcón
VILLAVERDE
Avenida de Andalucía
Leganés
Parque de la Polvoranca
Getafe
El Carmen
Perales del Río
El Escorial, Segovia
El Escorial
Alcalá de Henares
Mejorada del Campo
Talavera de la Reina
Valencia
Fuenlabrada
Fuenlabrada
Toledo
Aranjuez
N
0
2
4
km

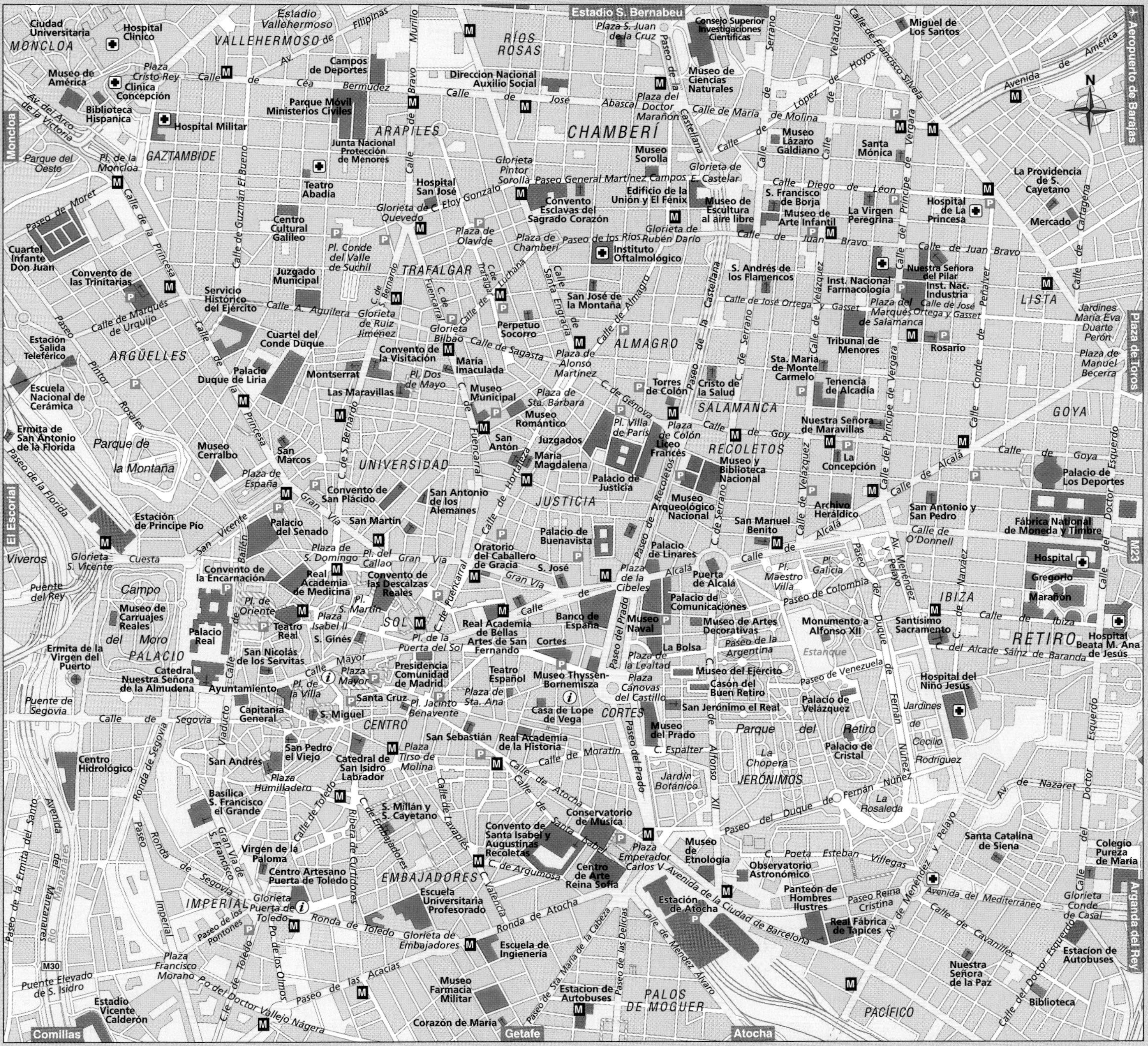
Estadio S. Bernabeu
Aeropuerto de Barajas
Plaza de Toros
M23
Arganda del Rey
Atocha
Getafe
Comillas
El Escorial
Moncloa
Ciudad Universitaria
Hospital Clínico
MONCLOA
Estadio Vallehermoso
VALLEHERMOSO
Ríos Rosas
Consejo Superior Investigaciones Científicas
Miguel de Los Santos
Museo de América
Plaza Cristo Rey
Clínica Concepción
Biblioteca Hispanica
Campos de Deportes
Dirección Nacional Auxilio Social
Parque Móvil Ministerios Civiles
Museo de Ciencias Naturales
Plaza del Doctor Marañón
Hospital Militar
Junta Nacional Protección de Menores
ARAPILES
CHAMBERÍ
Museo Lázaro Galdiano
Santa Mónica
Parque del Oeste
Pl. de la Moncloa
GAZTAMBIDE
Museo Sorolla
Glorieta de E. Castelar
La Providencia de S. Cayetano
Teatro Abadía
Glorieta Pintor Sorolla
Hospital San José
Convento Esclavas del Sagrado Corazón
Edificio de la Unión y El Fénix
Museo de Escultura al aire libre
S. Francisco de Borja
Museo de Arte Infantil
La Virgen Peregrina
Hospital de La Princesa
Mercado
Cuartel Infante Don Juan
Centro Cultural Galileo
Glorieta de Quevedo
Plaza de Olavide
Plaza de Chamberí
Instituto Oftalmológico
Glorieta de Rubén Darío
Convento de las Trinitarias
Juzgado Municipal
Pl. Conde del Valle de Suchil
TRAFALGAR
S. Andrés de los Flamencos
Inst. Nacional Farmacología
Nuestra Señora del Pilar
Inst. Nac. Industria
LISTA
Servicio Histórico del Ejército
Glorieta de Ruiz Jiménez
Glorieta Bilbao
Perpetuo Socorro
San José de la Montaña
Plaza del Marqués de Salamanca
Jardines María Eva Duarte Perón
Estación Salida Teleférico
Cuartel del Conde Duque
ARGÜELLES
Convento de la Visitación
María Inmaculada
Plaza de Alonso Martínez
ALMAGRO
Tribunal de Menores
Rosario
Plaza de Manuel Becerra
Escuela Nacional de Cerámica
Palacio Duque de Liria
Montserrat
Las Maravillas
Pl. Dos de Mayo
Museo Municipal
Plaza de Sta. Bárbara
Torres de Colón
Cristo de la Salud
Sta. María de Monte Carmelo
Tenencia de Alcadía
SALAMANCA
GOYA
Ermita de San Antonio de la Florida
Parque de la Montaña
Museo Cerralbo
San Marcos
Museo Romántico
San Antón
Juzgados
María Magdalena
Pl. Villa de París
Plaza de Colón
Liceo Francés
RECOLETOS
Nuestra Señora de Maravillas
La Concepción
Palacio de Los Deportes
UNIVERSIDAD
Plaza de España
Convento de San Plácido
San Antonio de los Alemanes
Palacio de Justicia
JUSTICIA
Museo y Biblioteca Nacional
Museo Arqueológico Nacional
Archivo Heráldico
San Antonio y San Pedro
Fábrica Nacional de Moneda y Timbre
Estación de Principe Pío
Palacio del Senado
San Martín
Palacio de Buenavista
San Manuel Benito
Viveros
Glorieta S. Vicente
Plaza de S. Domingo
Pl. del Callao
Oratorio del Caballero de Gracia
Palacio de Linares
Pl. Galicia
Hospital Gregorio Marañón
Puente del Rey
Campo del Moro
Convento de la Encarnación
Real Academia de Medicina
Convento de las Descalzas Reales
S. José
Plaza de la Cibeles
Puerta de Alcalá
Pl. Maestro Villa
Museo de Carruajes Reales
Pl. de Oriente
Pl. S. Martín
Palacio de Comunicaciones
IBIZA
Palacio Real
Teatro Real
Plaza Isabel II
SOL
Real Academia de Bellas Artes de San Fernando
Banco de España
Museo Naval
Museo de Artes Decorativas
Monumento a Alfonso XII
Santísimo Sacramento
Hospital Beata M. Ana de Jesús
RETIRO
PALACIO
S. Ginés
Pl. de la Puerta del Sol
Cortes
La Bolsa
Plaza de la Argentina
Estanque
Ermita de la Virgen del Puerto
San Nicolás de los Servitas
Presidencia Comunidad de Madrid
Teatro Español
Museo Thyssen-Bornemisza
Plaza de la Lealtad
Museo del Ejército
Catedral Nuestra Señora de la Almudena
Ayuntamiento
Plaza Mayor
Pl. de la Villa
Santa Cruz
Pl. Jacinto Benavente
Plaza de Sta. Ana
Plaza Cánovas del Castillo
Casón del Buen Retiro
Palacio de Velázquez
Hospital del Niño Jesús
Puente de Segovia
Capitanía General
S. Miguel
CENTRO
Casa de Lope de Vega
CORTES
San Jerónimo el Real
Museo del Prado
Parque del Retiro
Jardines de Cecilio Rodríguez
Centro Hidrológico
San Pedro el Viejo
San Sebastián
Real Academia de la Historia
Palacio de Cristal
San Andrés
Catedral de San Isidro Labrador
Plaza Tirso de Molina
C. Espalter
La Chopera
Plaza Humilladero
Jardín Botánico
JERÓNIMOS
Basílica S. Francisco el Grande
S. Millán y S. Cayetano
La Rosaleda
Conservatorio de Música
Convento de Santa Isabel y Augustinas Recoletas
Plaza Emperador Carlos V
Museo de Etnología
Observatorio Astronómico
Santa Catalina de Siena
Colegio Pureza de María
Virgen de la Paloma
Centro Artesano Puerta de Toledo
Centro de Arte Reina Sofía
EMBAJADORES
Escuela Universitaria Profesorado
Estación de Atocha
Panteón de Hombres Ilustres
Glorieta Conde de Casal
IMPERIAL
Glorieta Puerta de Toledo
Real Fábrica de Tapices
Estación de Autobuses
Nuestra Señora de la Paz
Plaza Francisco Morano
Glorieta de Embajadores
Escuela de Ingeniería
Puente Elevado de S. Isidro
Museo Farmacia Militar
Estacion de Autobuses
PALOS DE MOGUER
Biblioteca
PACÍFICO
Estadio Vicente Calderón
Corazón de María
M30
Río Manzanares
Calle de Bravo Murillo
Paseo de la Castellana
Calle de Serrano
Calle de Velázquez
Calle de Alcalá
Gran Vía
Calle Mayor
Calle de Atocha
Paseo del Prado
Paseo de Recoletos
Calle de la Princesa
Calle de Fuencarral
Calle de Génova
Calle de Goya
Calle de Segovia
Ronda de Segovia
Ronda de Toledo
Ronda de Atocha
Avenida de la Ciudad de Barcelona
Calle del Doctor Esquerdo
Avenida de América
N

0 200 400
m

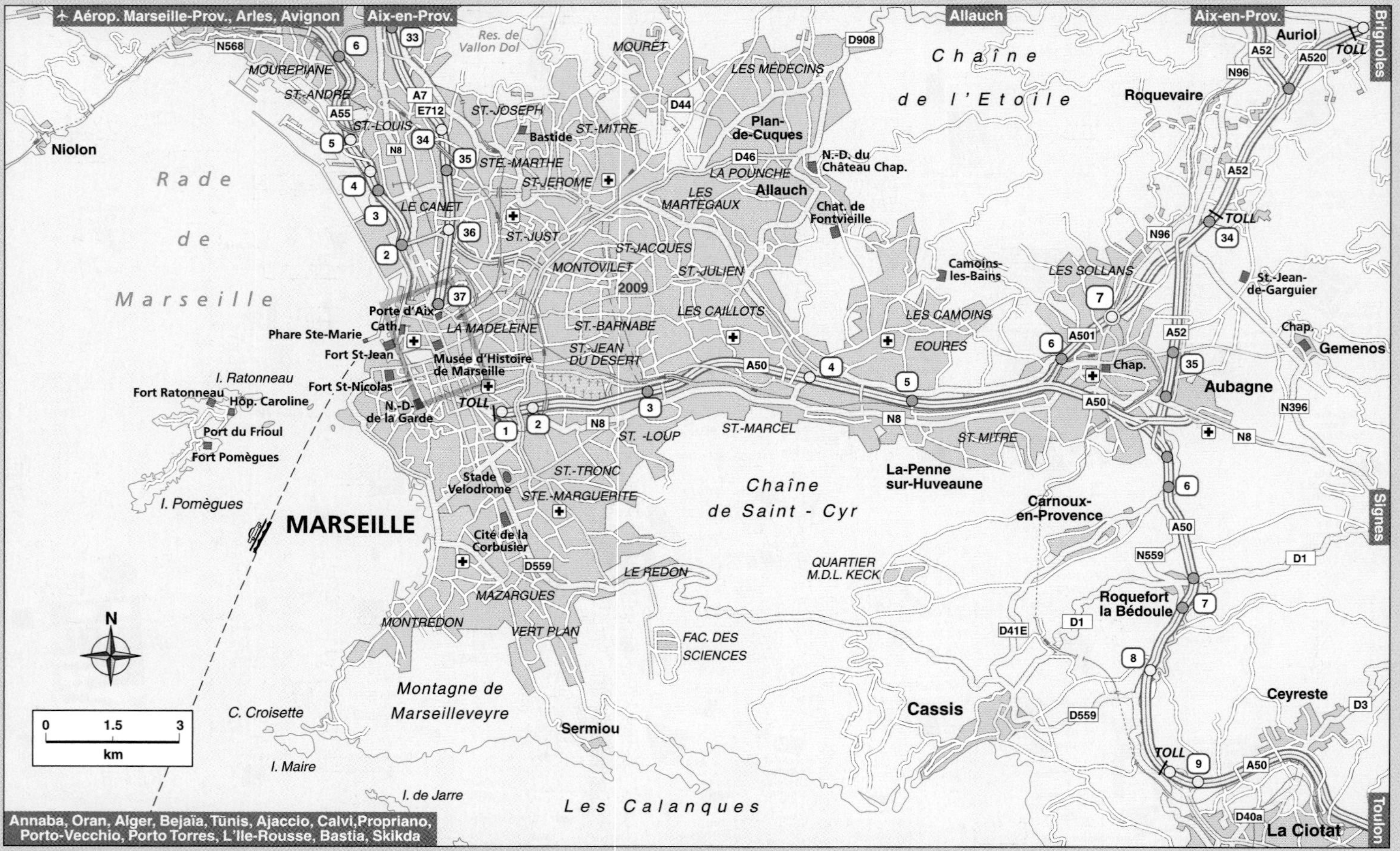

Aérop. Marseille-Prov., Arles, Avignon
Aix-en-Prov.
Allauch
Aix-en-Prov.
Brignoles
Signes
Toulon
Chaîne de l'Etoile
Rade de Marseille
Niolon
Mourepiane
St.-André
St.-Louis
St.-Joseph
Bastide
St.-Mitre
Ste.-Marthe
St.-Jérome
Le Canet
St.-Just
Res. de Vallon Dol
Mouret
Les Médecins
Plan-de-Cuques
N.-D. du Château Chap.
La Pounche
Allauch
Les Martegaux
Chat. de Fontvieille
St.-Jacques
Montolivet
St.-Julien
2009
Les Caillots
Camoins-les-Bains
Les Camoins
Eoures
Les Sollans
Auriol
Roquevaire
St.-Jean-de-Garguier
Chap.
Gemenos
Aubagne
Porte d'Aix
Cath.
La Madeleine
St.-Barnabe
Phare Ste-Marie
Fort St-Jean
Musée d'Histoire de Marseille
St.-Jean du Desert
I. Ratonneau
Fort Ratonneau
Hôp. Caroline
Fort St-Nicolas
N.-D. de la Garde
TOLL
Port du Frioul
Fort Pomègues
St.-Loup
St.-Marcel
St. Mitre
Stade Velodrome
St.-Tronc
Ste.-Marguerite
I. Pomègues
MARSEILLE
Chaîne de Saint-Cyr
La Penne sur-Huveaune
Carnoux-en-Provence
Cité de la Corbusier
Le Redon
Quartier M.D.L. Keck
Mazargues
Montredon
Vert Plan
Fac. des Sciences
Roquefort la Bédoule
Montagne de Marseilleveyre
Sermiou
Cassis
Ceyreste
C. Croisette
I. Maire
I. de Jarre
Les Calanques
La Ciotat
N
0 1.5 3 km
Annaba, Oran, Alger, Bejaïa, Tunis, Ajaccio, Calvi, Propriano, Porto-Vecchio, Porto Torres, L'Ile-Rousse, Bastia, Skikda
N568
A55
A7
E712
N8
D908
D44
D46
A50
A52
A520
N96
N396
A501
N559
D559
D1
D41E
D3
D40a

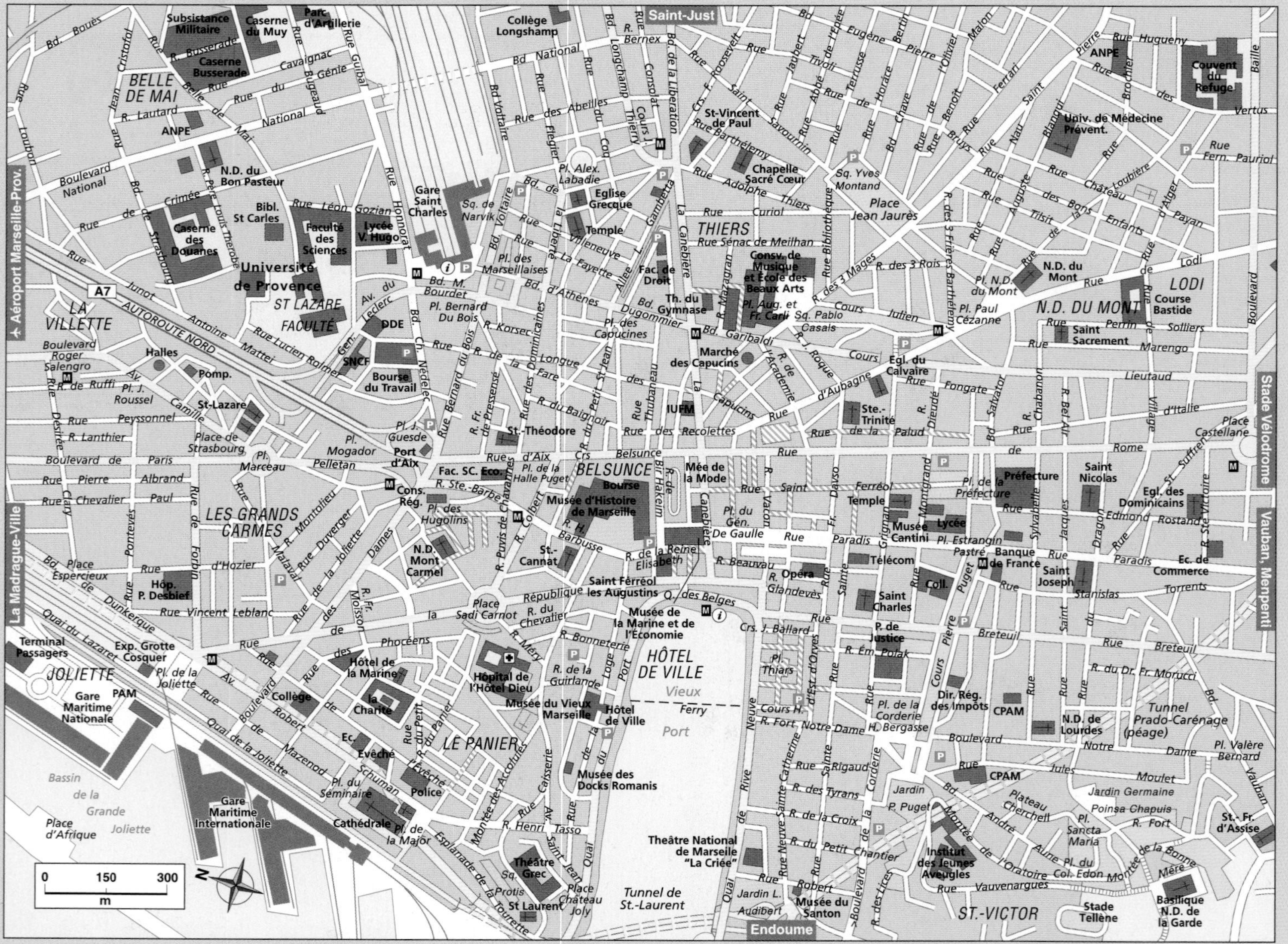

Saint-Just
Aéroport Marseille-Prov.
La Madrague-Ville
Stade Vélodrome
Vauban, Menpenti
Endoume
Subsistance Militaire
Caserne du Muy
Parc d'Artillerie
Caserne Busserade
Collège Longshamp
Belle de Mai
ANPE
N.D. du Bon Pasteur
Bibl. St Carles
Caserne des Douanes
Faculté des Sciences
Lycée V. Hugo
Université de Provence
St Lazare
Faculté
Gare Saint Charles
Sq. de Narvik
St-Vincent de Paul
Chapelle Sacré Cœur
Eglise Grecque
Temple
Sq. Yves Montand
Place Jean Jaurès
Thiers
Rue Sénac de Meilhan
Consv. de Musique et École des Beaux Arts
Fac. de Droit
Th. du Gymnase
Pl. Aug. et Fr. Cari
Sq. Pablo Casals
Marché des Capucins
Univ. de Médecine Prevent.
Couvent du Refuge
N.D. du Mont
Lodi
Course Bastide
Saint Sacrement
N.D. du Mont
Pl. Paul Cézanne
Egl. du Calvaire
La Villette
Halles
Pomp.
DDE
SNCF
Bourse du Travail
St-Lazare
Place de Strasbourg
Pl. Marceau
St-Théodore
IUFM
Ste.-Trinité
Port d'Aix
Fac. SC. Eco.
Cons. Rég.
Belsunce
Bourse
Musée d'Histoire de Marseille
Mée de la Mode
Temple
Musée Cantini
Lycée
Préfecture
Saint Nicolas
Egl. des Dominicains
Place Castellane
Les Grands Carmes
N.D. Mont Carmel
St.-Cannat
Hôp. P. Desbief
Saint Ferréol les Augustins
Télécom
Opéra
Saint Charles
Coll.
Banque de France
Saint Joseph
Ec. de Commerce
Terminal Passagers
Exp. Grotte Cosquer
Joliette
Gare Maritime Nationale
PAM
Collège
Hôtel de la Marine
Hôpital de l'Hôtel Dieu
La Charité
Musée de la Marine et de l'Économie
Hôtel de Ville
Vieux Port
Ferry
P. de Justice
Dir. Rég. des Impôts
CPAM
N.D. de Lourdes
Tunnel Prado-Carénage (péage)
Musée du Vieux Marseille
Hôtel de Ville
Ec.
Evêché
Le Panier
Police
Musée des Docks Romanis
CPAM
Bassin de la Grande Joliette
Gare Maritime Internationale
Cathédrale
Place d'Afrique
Théâtre Grec
St Laurent
Théatre National de Marseille "La Criée"
Tunnel de St.-Laurent
Jardin L. Audibert
Musée du Santon
Institut des Jeunes Aveugles
St.-Victor
Stade Tellène
Basilique N.D. de la Garde
St.-Fr. d'Assise
A7
Autoroute Nord
0 150 300 m
N

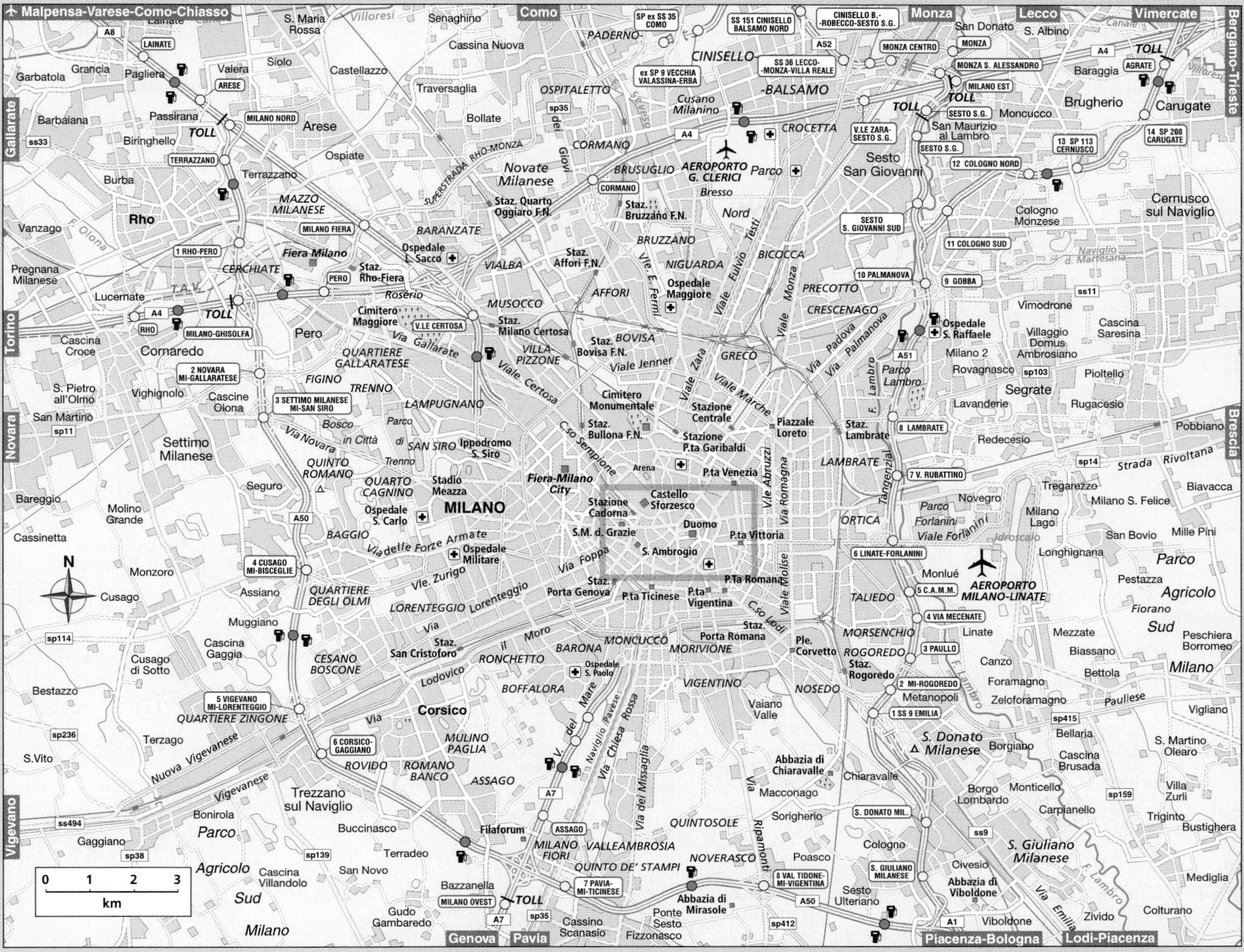
Malpensa-Varese-Como-Chiasso
Como
Monza
Lecco
Vimercate
Bergamo-Trieste
Gallarate
Torino
Novara
Vigevano
Brescia
Genova
Pavia
Piacenza-Bologna
Lodi-Piacenza
Rho
Arese
Bollate
Senaghino
Cassina Nuova
Cinisello-Balsamo
Cusano Milanino
Aeroporto G. Clerici
Bresso
Sesto San Giovanni
Monza
San Donato
Brugherio
Carugate
Cernusco sul Naviglio
Cologno Monzese
Novate Milanese
Pero
Cornaredo
Settimo Milanese
Fiera Milano
Staz. Rho-Fiera
Cimitero Maggiore
Cimitero Monumentale
Stazione Centrale
Stazione P.ta Garibaldi
Piazzale Loreto
Staz. Lambrate
Segrate
Ospedale S. Raffaele
Milano 2
Ippodromo S. Siro
Stadio Meazza
MILANO
Fiera-Milano City
Castello Sforzesco
Stazione Cadorna
Duomo
S.M. d. Grazie
S. Ambrogio
P.ta Venezia
P.ta Vittoria
P.ta Romana
P.ta Ticinese
Staz. Porta Genova
Staz. S. Cristoforo
Porta Romana
Ple. Corvetto
Staz. Rogoredo
Aeroporto Milano-Linate
Parco Forlanini
Idroscalo
Parco Agricolo Sud Milano
Corsico
Trezzano sul Naviglio
Buccinasco
Assago
Rozzano
Filaforum
Milano Fiori
Abbazia di Chiaravalle
Abbazia di Mirasole
S. Donato Milanese
S. Giuliano Milanese
Abbazia di Viboldone
Sesto Ulteriano
Ospedale S. Paolo
Ospedale Militare
Ospedale S. Carlo
TOLL
0 1 2 3 km

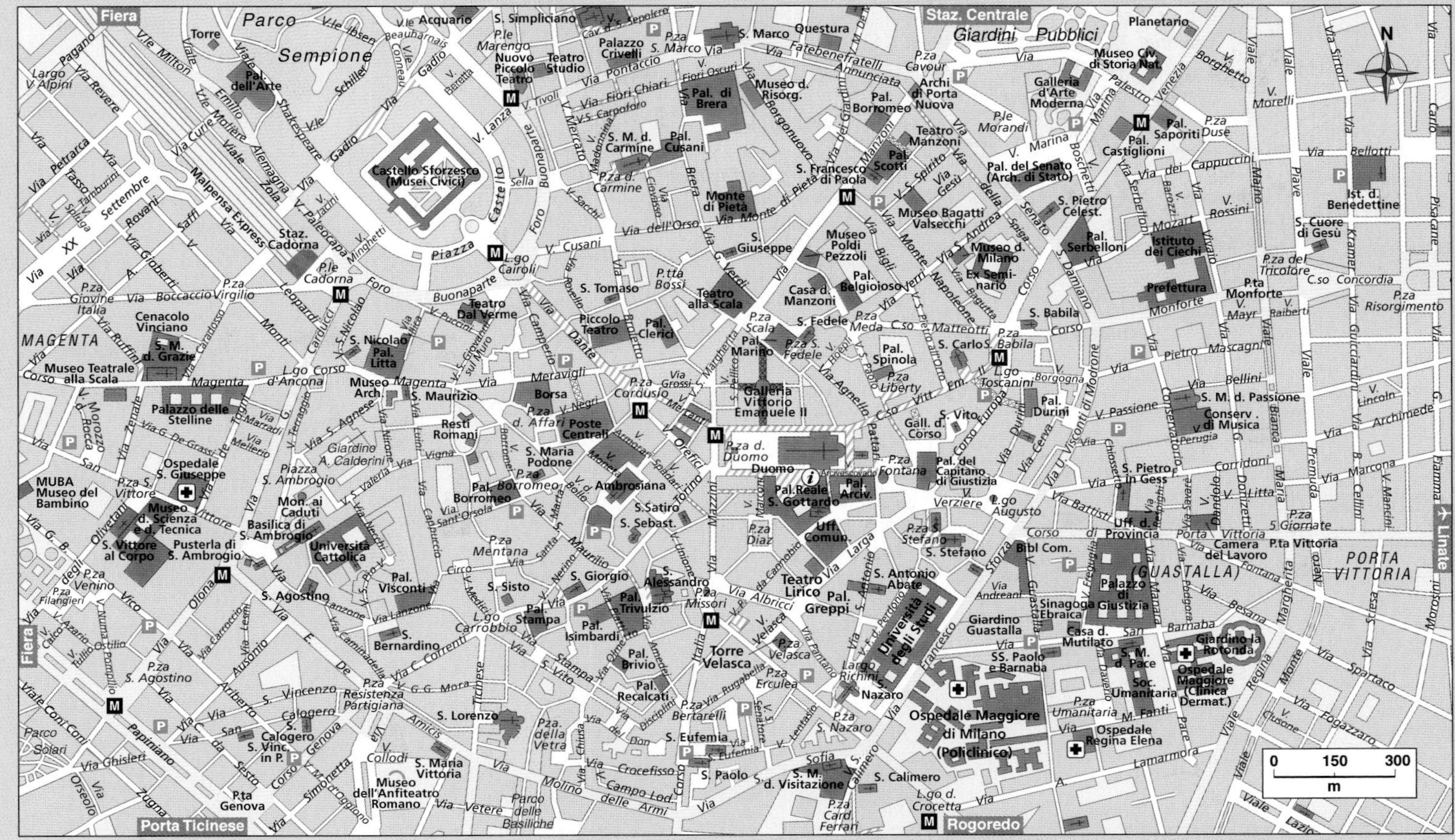
Fiera
Staz. Centrale
Linate
Porta Ticinese
Rogoredo
Parco Sempione
Giardini Pubblici
Pal. dell'Arte
Castello Sforzesco (Musei Civici)
Staz. Cadorna
Cenacolo Vinciano
S. M. d. Grazie
Museo Teatrale alla Scala
Palazzo delle Stelline
Ospedale S. Giuseppe
MUBA Museo del Bambino
Museo d. Scienza e d. Tecnica
S. Vittore al Corpo
Pusterla di S. Ambrogio
Basilica di S. Ambrogio
Università Cattolica
Pal. di Brera
Museo d. Risorg.
Teatro alla Scala
Galleria Vittorio Emanuele II
P.za d. Duomo
Duomo
Pal. Reale
Ambrosiana
S. Satiro
Borsa
Teatro Dal Verme
Piccolo Teatro
Museo Poldi Pezzoli
Museo Bagatti Valsecchi
Galleria d'Arte Moderna
Museo Civ. di Storia Nat.
Planetario
Pal. del Senato (Arch. di Stato)
Istituto dei Ciechi
Prefettura
Torre Velasca
Università degli Studi
Ospedale Maggiore di Milano (Policlinico)
Palazzo di Giustizia
Sinagoga Ebraica
Giardino Guastalla
S. Lorenzo
S. Eustorgio
Museo dell'Anfiteatro Romano
0 150 300 m

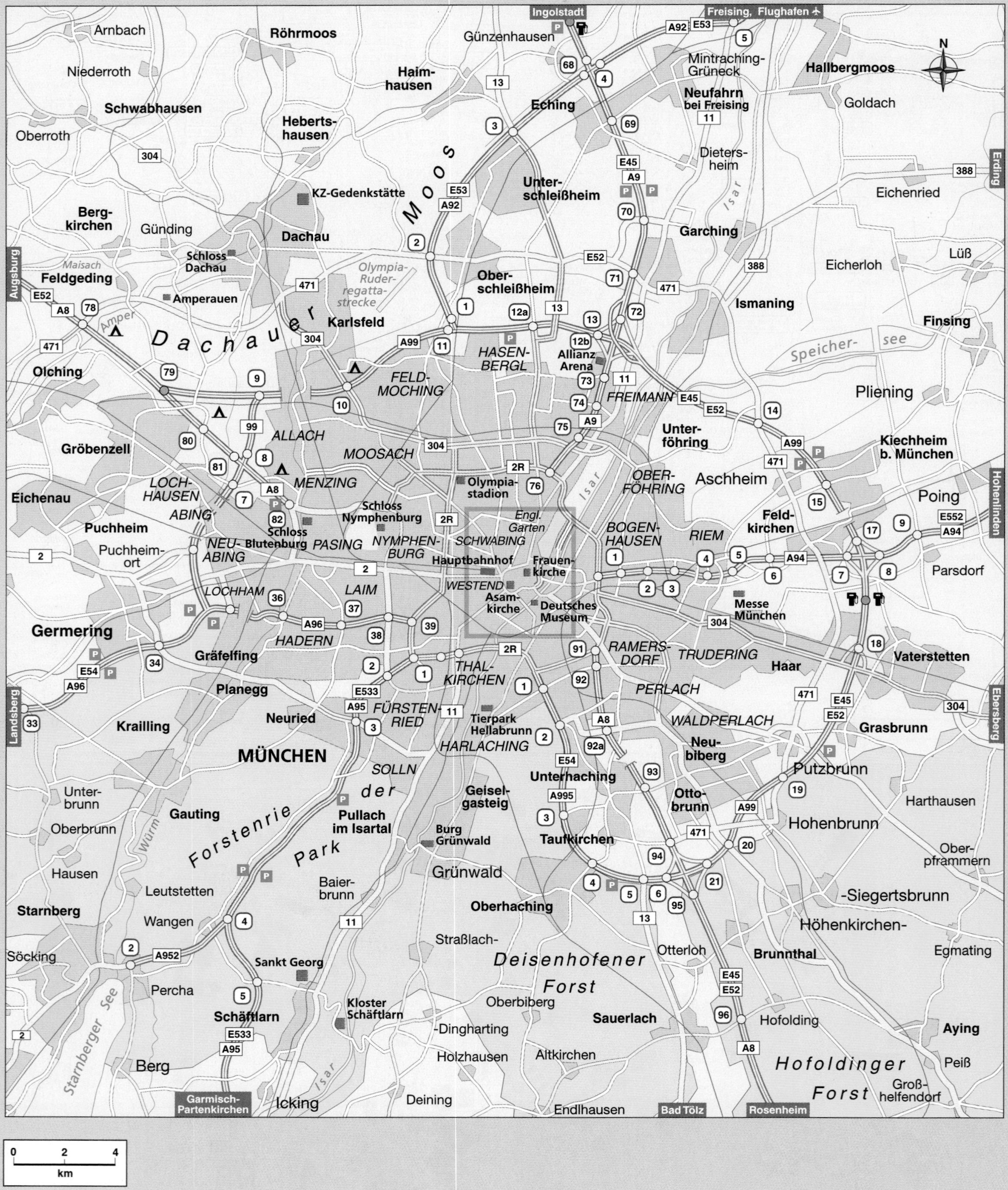
Ingolstadt
Freising, Flughafen
Arnbach
Röhrmoos
Günzenhausen
Niederroth
Haim-
hausen
Mintraching-
Grüneck
Hallbergmoos
Eching
Neufahrn
bei Freising
Goldach
Schwabhausen
Heberts-
hausen
Oberroth
Dieters-
heim
Erding
Unter-
schleißheim
Eichenried
KZ-Gedenkstätte
Moos
Berg-
kirchen
Günding
Dachau
Garching
Augsburg
Schloss
Dachau
Maisach
Feldgeding
Olympia-
Ruder-
regatta-
strecke
Ober-
schleißheim
Lüß
Eicherloh
Ismaning
Amperauen
Amper
Karlsfeld
Finsing
Dachauer
HASEN-
BERGL
Allianz
Arena
Speicher-
see
Olching
FELD-
MOCHING
FREIMANN
Pliening
Gröbenzell
ALLACH
Unter-
föhring
Kiechheim
b. München
MOOSACH
LOCH-
HAUSEN
MENZING
Olympia-
stadion
OBER-
FÖHRING
Aschheim
Hohenlinden
Eichenau
Poing
ABING
Schloss
Nymphenburg
Engl.
Garten
Feld-
kirchen
Puchheim
Schloss
Blutenburg
PASING
NYMPHEN-
BURG
SCHWABING
BOGEN-
HAUSEN
RIEM
Puchheim-
ort
NEU-
ABING
Hauptbahnhof
Frauen-
kirche
Parsdorf
LOCHHAM
LAIM
WESTEND
Asam-
kirche
Deutsches
Museum
Messe
München
Germering
HADERN
RAMERS-
DORF
TRUDERING
Gräfelfing
THAL-
KIRCHEN
Haar
Vaterstetten
Planegg
PERLACH
FÜRSTEN-
RIED
Tierpark
Hellabrunn
WALDPERLACH
Ebersberg
Landsberg
Krailling
Neuried
Grasbrunn
HARLACHING
Neu-
biberg
MÜNCHEN
SOLLN
Unterhaching
Putzbrunn
Unter-
brunn
der
Geisel-
gasteig
Otto-
brunn
Harthausen
Gauting
Pullach
im Isartal
Oberbrunn
Forstenrie
Burg
Grünwald
Taufkirchen
Hohenbrunn
Würm
Park
Ober-
pframmern
Hausen
Grünwald
Leutstetten
Baier-
brunn
-Siegertsbrunn
Starnberg
Oberhaching
Wangen
Höhenkirchen-
Straßlach-
Söcking
Sankt Georg
Deisenhofener
Otterloh
Brunnthal
Egmating
Percha
Forst
Schäftlarn
Kloster
Schäftlarn
Oberbiberg
Sauerlach
Hofolding
Aying
-Dingharting
Starnberger See
Berg
Holzhausen
Altkirchen
Hofoldinger
Peiß
Isar
Forst
Groß-
helfendorf
Icking
Deining
Endlhausen
Garmisch-
Partenkirchen
Bad Tölz
Rosenheim
0
2
4
km

Felmoching, Oberschleißheim, A92
A9, A99, Garching, Flughafen Munchen
Dachau
Menzing, Moosach
Pasing-A8
Sending-A95-A96
Thalkirchen
Harlaching
A995, Grünwald
A8, A995, Unterhaching
Perlach Neubiberg
Haar
A94, Feldkirchen
A94
2R
SCHWABING
SCHWABING-WEST
MAX-VORSTADT
ALT-STADT
LEHEL
LUDWIGS-VORSTADT
ISAR-VORSTADT
AU-
-HAIDHAUSEN
Englischer Garten
Kleinhesseloher See
Neues Seehaus
Isarring
St. Sylvester
Wedekindplatz
Kaiserplatz
St. Ursula K.
Hohenzollernpl.
Kurfürsten Pl.
Habsburgerplatz
Nikolaiplatz
Leopoldpark
Josephspl.
St. Joseph
Alter Nördlicher Friedhof
Akademie der Bildenden Künste
Siegestor
Chinesischer Turm
Monopteros
St. Barbara-Kirche
Fachhochschule
St. Benno-K.
Ferdinand-Miller-Platz
Technische Universität
Universität
Neue Pinakothek
Sammlung Brandhorst (in bau)
Alte Pinakothek
Pinakothek der Moderne
Geschwister-Scholl-Pl.
Prof.-Huber-Pl.
Ludwig-Maximilians-Universität
Ludwigskirche
Bayerische Staatsbibliothek
Hauptstaatsarchiv
Stiglmaierplatz
Lenbachhaus
Glyptothek
Königsplatz
Propyläen
Staatliche Antikensammlung
Staatliche Hochschule für Musik
Basilika St. Bonifaz
Karolinenplatz
Obelisk
Staatliche Graphische Sammlung
Amerikahaus
Bayerischer Rundfunk
Augustinerkeller
Bahnpostamt
Siemens Mus.
Leuchtenberg Palais
Odeonsplatz
Wittelsbacherpl.
Prinz-Carl-Palais
Staatsgalerie für Moderne Kunst
Haus der Kunst
Neue Sammlung
Prähistorische Staatssammlung
Bayerisches Nationalmuseum
Monacensiasammlung
Schackgalerie
Friedensengel
Europaplatz
Villa Stuck
St. George
Hofgarten
Theatinerkirche
Feldherrnhalle
Sammlung Ägyptischer Kunst
Residenz
Neue Staatskanzlei
St.-Anna Kloster
St.-Anna
Theater im Marstall
Nationaltheater
Regierung v. Oberbayern
Alter Botanischer Garten
Maximiliansplatz
Justizpalast
Hauptbahnhof
Lenbachpl.
Bürgersaal.
Promenadeplatz
M.-Joseph-Platz
Bahnhofpl.
Karlspl.
Karlstor
St. Michael
Frauenkirche
Frauenplatz
Neues Rathaus
Alter Hof
Hofbräuhaus
Altes Rathaus
Marienpl.
St. Peter
Hl. Geist
Viktualienmarkt
Isartor
St. Anna Damenstifsk.
Deutsches Theater
St. Pauls-Platz
St. Pauls-K.
Georg-Hirth-Platz
Med. Physiolog. Institut
Augenklinik
Poliklinik
Anatomie
Pharmazie
Chirurgische Klinik
Asamkirche
Hist. Stadtmuseum
Sendlinger Tor
St.-Jakobs-Platz
St. Jakob-K.
Beethovenplatz
Klinikum der Universität München
St. Matthäus-Kirche
Marionetten-Theater
Theresienwiese (Oktoberfest)
Kaiser-Ludwig-Platz
Zahnklinik
Esperantoplatz
Freie Ev. Kirche
Goetheplatz
Frauenklinik
Alter Südlicher Friedhof
Mod. Theater
Theater im Fraunhofer
Gärtnerplatz
Herz-Jesu-Kloster
Jüdisches Mus.
Europäisches Patentamt
Deutsches Museum
Museumsinsel
Forum der Technik
IMAX
Müllersches Volksbad
Muffathalle
Alpines Museum
Praterinsel
St. Lucas-K.
Völkerkunde-Museum
Maximilianeum
Maximiliansbrücke
Klinikum rechts der Isar
Gasteig Kulturzentrum
St. Johannes-K.
Preysingplatz
St. Johann-Baptist
Johannisplatz
Bordeauxplatz
Rosenheimer Pl.
Weißenburger Platz
St. Maximilian-K.
Kapuzinerplatz
Neuer Südlicher Friedhof
St. Antonius-Kapuzinerkloster
Frühlingsanlagen
Mariahilfkirche
Regerplatz
Simon-Knoll-Platz
St. Wolfgangs-K.
St.-Wolfgangs-Platz
Tassiloplatz
Ostfriedhof
Isar
Eisbach
Schwabinger Bach
Am Hirschanger
Maximilian-anlagen
Schwere-Reiter-Str.
Leopoldstr.
Ludwigstr.
Dachauer Str.
Nymphenburger Str.
Arnulfstr.
Landsberger Str.
Bayerstr.
Schwanthalerstr.
Lindwurmstr.
Sonnenstr.
Prinzregentenstr.
Maximilianstr.
Zweibrückenstr.
Rosenheimer Str.
Wittelsbacherstr.
Ismaninger Str.
Einsteinstr.
N

0 200 400
m

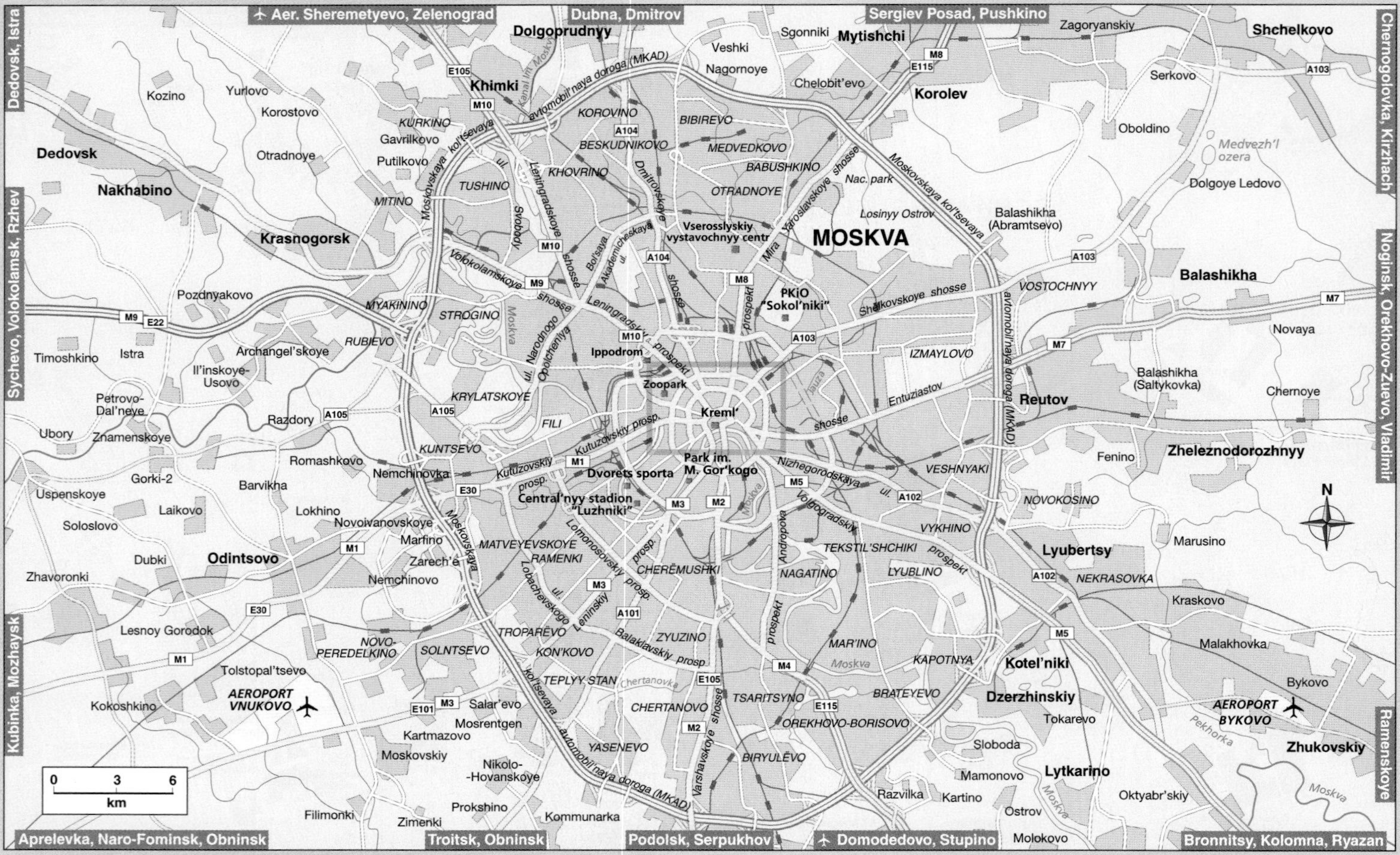

Aer. Sheremetyevo, Zelenograd
Dubna, Dmitrov
Sergiev Posad, Pushkino
Chernogolovka, Kirzhach
Noginsk, Orekhovo-Zuevo, Vladimir
Ramenskoye
Bronnitsy, Kolomna, Ryazan
Domodedovo, Stupino
Podolsk, Serpukhov
Troitsk, Obninsk
Aprelevka, Naro-Fominsk, Obninsk
Kubinka, Mozhaysk
Sychevo, Volokolamsk, Rzhev
Dedovsk, Istra
Dolgoprudnyy
Veshki
Sgonniki
Mytishchi
Zagoryanskiy
Shchelkovo
Nagornoye
Chelobit'evo
Korolev
Serkovo
Oboldino
Medvezh'I ozera
Dolgoye Ledovo
Khimki
Kozino
Yurlovo
Korostovo
KURKINO
Gavrilkovo
Putilkovo
Otradnoye
Dedovsk
Nakhabino
MITINO
TUSHINO
KHOVRINO
KOROVINO
BIBIREVO
BESKUDNIKOVO
MEDVEDKOVO
BABUSHKINO
OTRADNOYE
Nac. park
Losinyy Ostrov
Balashikha (Abramtsevo)
Krasnogorsk
Vserosslyskiy vystavochnyy centr
MOSKVA
PKiO "Sokol'niki"
Balashikha
VOSTOCHNYY
Pozdnyakovo
MYAKININO
STROGINO
RUBLEVO
Timoshkino
Istra
Archangel'skoye
Il'inskoye-Usovo
Petrovo-Dal'neye
Ippodrom
Zoopark
Kreml'
IZMAYLOVO
Novaya
Balashikha (Saltykovka)
Chernoye
Reutov
KRYLATSKOYE
Razdory
Ubory
Znamenskoye
FILI
KUNTSEVO
Romashkovo
Nemchinovka
Dvorets sporta
Park im. M. Gor'kogo
Central'nyy stadion "Luzhniki"
VESHNYAKI
Fenino
Zheleznodorozhnyy
NOVOKOSINO
Gorki-2
Barvikha
Uspenskoye
Laikovo
Lokhino
Novoivanovskoye
Soloslovo
Marfino
Zarech'e
MATVEYEVSKOYE
RAMENKI
CHEREMUSHKI
TEKSTIL'SHCHIKI
VYKHINO
LYUBLINO
NAGATINO
Lyubertsy
Marusino
NEKRASOVKA
Dubki
Odintsovo
Zhavoronki
Nemchinovo
Kraskovo
Lesnoy Gorodok
NOVO-PEREDELKINO
SOLNTSEVO
TROPAREVO
KON'KOVO
ZYUZINO
MAR'INO
Malakhovka
Tolstopal'tsevo
AEROPORT VNUKOVO
TEPLYY STAN
KAPOTNYA
Kotel'niki
Bykovo
BRATEYEVO
Dzerzhinskiy
AEROPORT BYKOVO
Kokoshkino
Salar'evo
CHERTANOVO
TSARITSYNO
OREKHOVO-BORISOVO
Tokarevo
Kartmazovo
Mosrentgen
YASENEVO
Sloboda
Zhukovskiy
Moskovskiy
Nikolo-Hovanskoye
BIRYULEVO
Mamonovo
Lytkarino
Prokshino
Razvilka
Kartino
Oktyabr'skiy
Filimonki
Zimenki
Kommunarka
Ostrov
Molokovo
Moskva
Pekhorka
0 3 6 km
N

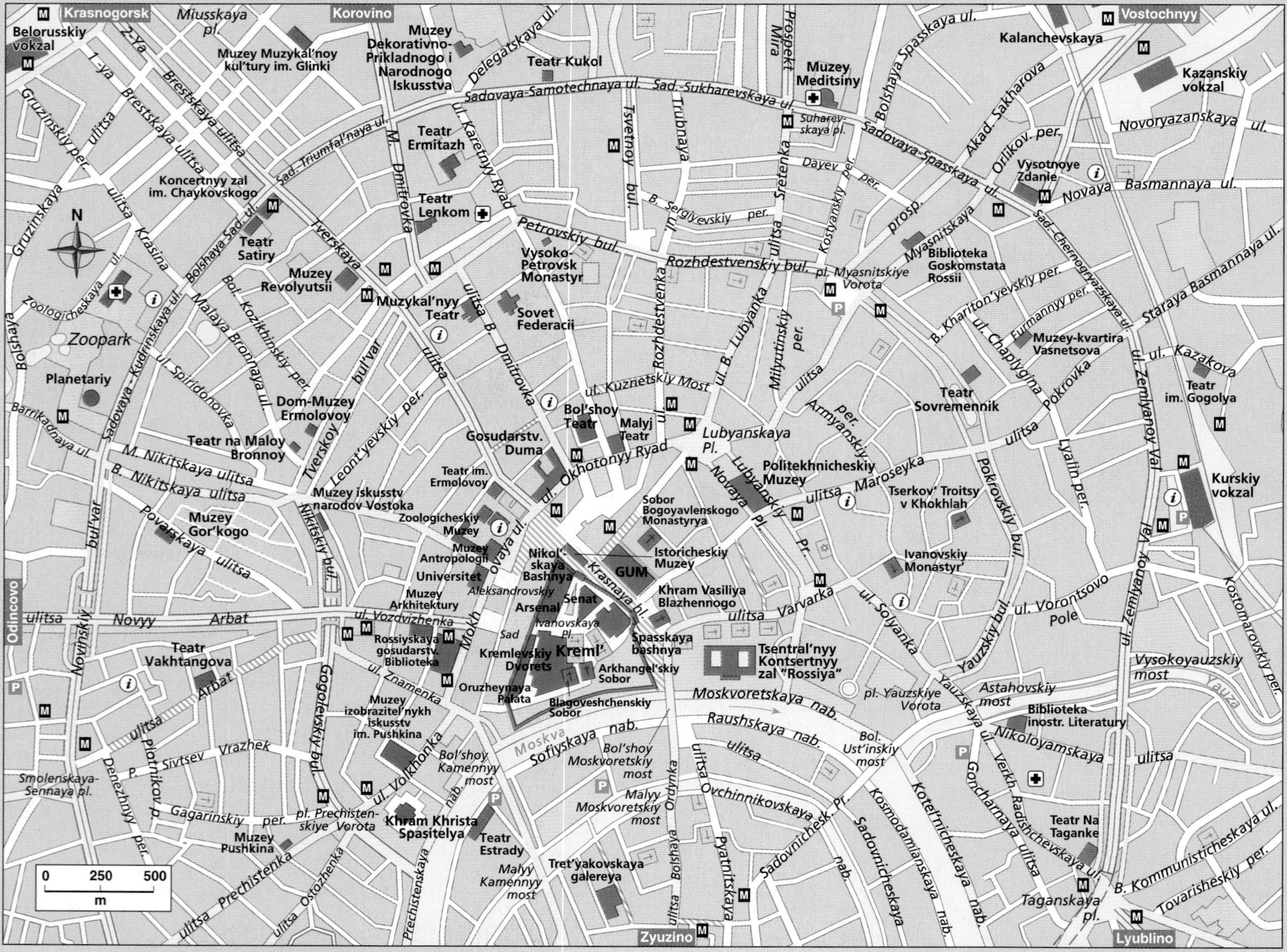

Krasnogorsk
Korovino
Vostochnyy
Belorusskiy vokzal
Miusskaya pl.
Muzey Muzykal'noy kul'tury im. Glinki
Muzey Dekorativno-Prikladnogo i Narodnogo Iskusstva
Teatr Kukol
Prospekt Mira
Muzey Meditsiny
Kalanchevskaya
Kazanskiy vokzal
Sadovaya-Samotechnaya ul.
Sad. Sukharevskaya ul.
Suharevskaya pl.
Novoryazanskaya ul.
Teatr Ermitazh
Vysotnoye Zdanie
Novaya Basmannaya ul.
Koncertnyy zal im. Chaykovskogo
Teatr Lenkom
Teatr Satiry
Muzey Revolyutsii
Vysoko-Petrovsk Monastyr
Rozhdestvenskiy bul.
pl. Myasnitskiye Vorota
Biblioteka Goskomstata Rossii
Staraya Basmannaya ul.
Muzykal'nyy Teatr
Sovet Federacii
Zoopark
Planetariy
Muzey-kvartira Vasnetsova
Dom-Muzey Ermolovoy
ul. Kuznetskiy Most
Teatr Sovremennik
Teatr im. Gogolya
Teatr na Maloy Bronnoy
Bol'shoy Teatr
Malyj Teatr
Gosudarstv. Duma
Lubyanskaya Pl.
Politekhnicheskiy Muzey
Tserkov' Troitsy v Khokhlah
Kurskiy vokzal
Teatr im. Ermolovoy
Muzey iskusstv narodov Vostoka
Muzey Gor'kogo
Zoologicheskiy Muzey
Sobor Bogoyavlenskogo Monastyrya
Muzey Antropologii
Universitet
Nikol'skaya Bashnya
GUM
Istoricheskiy Muzey
Ivanovskiy Monastyr'
Aleksandrovskiy Sad
Muzey Arkhitektury
Arsenal
Senat
Khram Vasiliya Blazhennogo
ulitsa Novyy Arbat
Rossiyskaya gosudarstv. Biblioteka
Kremlevskiy Dvorets
Kreml'
Ivanovskaya Pl.
Spasskaya bashnya
Tsentral'nyy Kontsertnyy zal "Rossiya"
Teatr Vakhtangova
Arbat
Oruzheynaya Palata
Arkhangel'skiy Sobor
Blagoveshchenskiy Sobor
Vysokoyauzskiy most
Muzey izobrazitel'nykh iskusstv im. Pushkina
Moskvoretskaya nab.
Raushskaya nab.
pl. Yauzskiye Vorota
Astakhovskiy most
Biblioteka inostr. Literatury
Smolenskaya-Sennaya pl.
Bol'shoy Kamennyy most
Bol'shoy Moskvoretskiy most
Sofiyskaya nab.
Bol. Ust'inskiy most
Nikoloyamskaya ulitsa
Khram Khrista Spasitelya
pl. Prechistenskiye Vorota
Malyy Moskvoretskiy most
Teatr Estrady
Teatr Na Taganke
Muzey Pushkina
Malyy Kamennyy most
Tret'yakovskaya galereya
Taganskaya pl.
B. Kommunisticheskaya ul.
Tovarishchskiy per.
Zyuzino
Lyublino
Odincovo
0 250 500 m
N

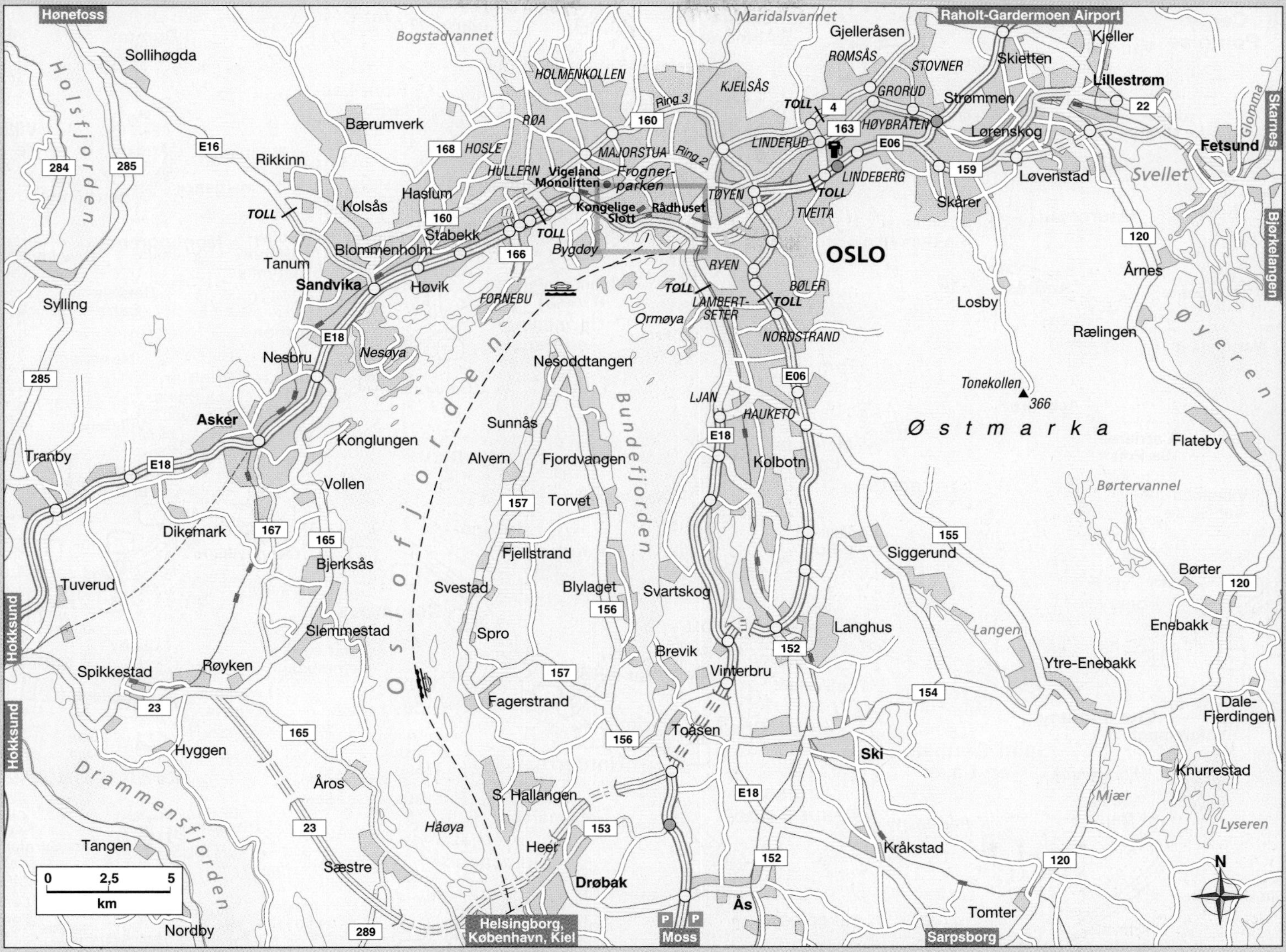
Hønefoss
Raholt-Gardermoen Airport
Maridalsvannet
Bogstadvannet
Sollihøgda
Holsfjorden
Gjelleråsen
RØMSÅS
STOVNER
Skjetten
Kjeller
Lillestrøm
HOLMENKOLLEN
KJELSÅS
GRORUD
Strømmen
Ring 3
TOLL
4
163
HØYBRÅTEN
Lørenskog
22
Skarnes
Glomma
Fetsund
Bærumverk
RØA
160
E16
168
HOSLE
MAJORSTUA
Ring 2
LINDERUD
E06
Rikkinn
284
285
HULLERN
Vigeland Monolitten
Frogner-parken
LINDEBERG
159
Løvenstad
Svellet
Kolsås
Haslum
Kongelige Slott
Rådhuset
TØYEN
TOLL
Skårer
TVEITA
Bjørkelangen
160
Stabekk
TOLL
Blommenholm
166
Bygdøy
OSLO
120
Tanum
RYEN
Årnes
Sandvika
Høvik
FORNEBU
TOLL
BØLER
Sylling
LAMBERT-SETER
TOLL
Losby
Ormøya
NORDSTRAND
Rælingen
Øyeren
Nesbru
E18
Nesøya
Nesoddtangen
285
E06
Tonekollen
366
LJAN
Bundefjorden
HAUKETO
Asker
Sunnås
Østmarka
Flateby
Tranby
E18
Konglungen
Alvern
Fjordvangen
E18
Kolbotn
Vollen
Børtervannel
157
Torvet
Oslofjorden
Dikemark
167
165
155
Siggerund
Bjerksås
Fjellstrand
Børter
Tuverud
Svestad
Blylaget
Svartskog
120
156
Hokksund
Slemmestad
Spro
Langhus
Langen
Enebakk
Brevik
152
Spikkestad
Røyken
157
Vinterbru
Ytre-Enebakk
Fagerstrand
154
23
Dale-Fjerdingen
165
Toåsen
156
Hokksund
Hyggen
Ski
Drammensfjorden
Knurrestad
Åros
E18
S. Hallangen
Mjær
Håøya
153
Lyseren
23
Tangen
Heer
Kråkstad
0 2,5 5 km
Sæstre
152
120
Drøbak
N
Ås
Tomter
Nordby
289
Helsingborg, København, Kiel
Moss
Sarpsborg

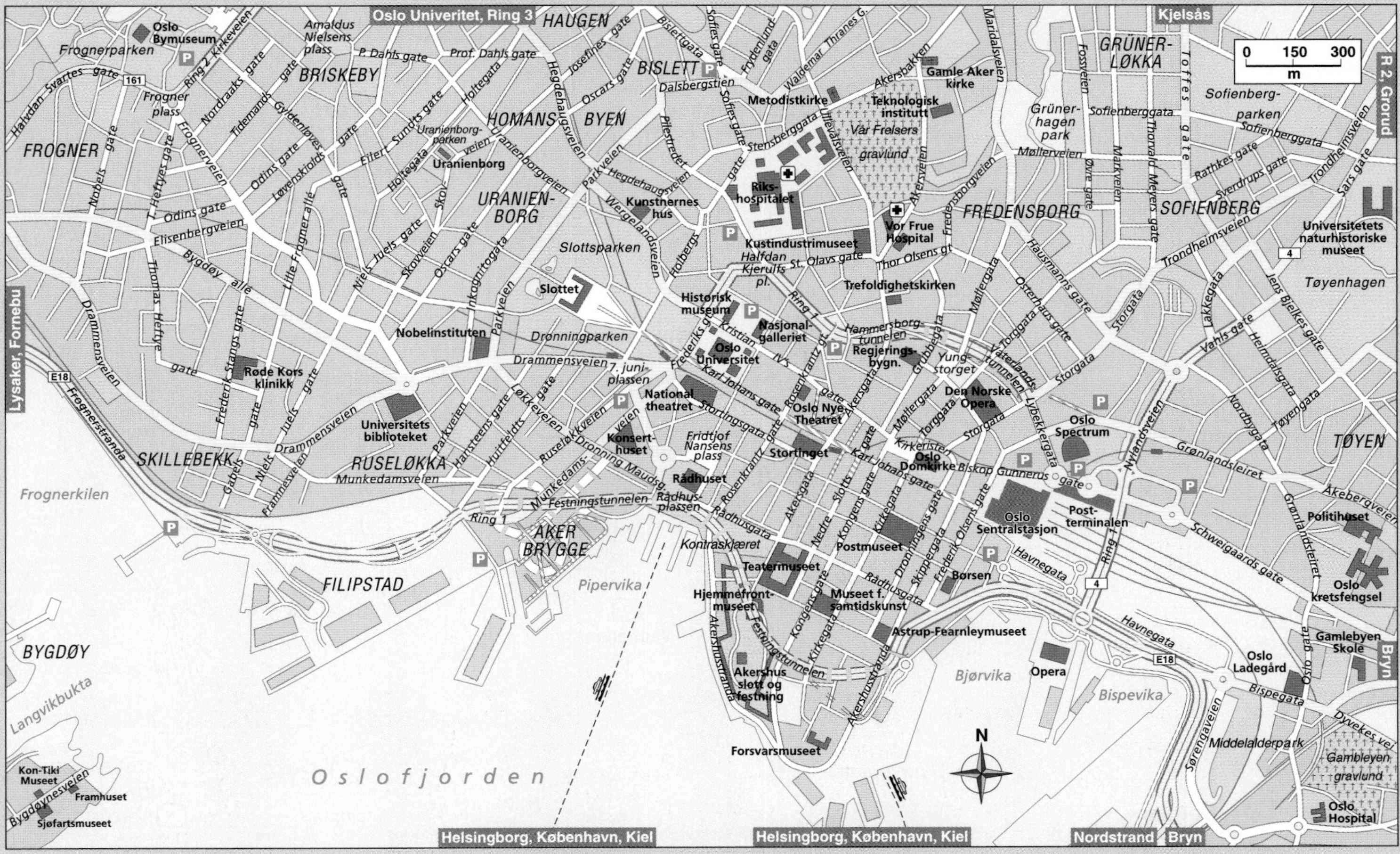
Oslo Univeritet, Ring 3
Kjelsås
Oslo Bymuseum
Amaldus Nielsens plass
HAUGEN
Frognerparken
P. Dahls gate
Prof. Dahls gate
BISLETT
GRÜNER-LØKKA
0 150 300 m
R 2, Grorud
BRISKEBY
Gamle Aker kirke
Frogner plass
Metodistkirke
Teknologisk institutt
Sofienberg-parken
FROGNER
HOMANSBYEN
Vår Frelsers gravlund
Grüner-hagen park
Uranienborg
Riks-hospitalet
URANIEN-BORG
Kunstnernes hus
FREDENSBORG
SOFIENBERG
Universitetets naturhistoriske museet
Slottsparken
Vor Frue Hospital
Kustindustrimuseet
Halfdan Kjerulfs pl.
Trefoldighetskirken
Tøyenhagen
Slottet
Historisk museum
Nasjonal-galleriet
Nobelinstituten
Dronningparken
Oslo Universitet
Regjerings-bygn.
Røde Kors klinikk
7. juni-plassen
National theatret
Oslo Nye Theatret
Den Norske Opera
Lysaker, Fornebu
Universitets biblioteket
Konsert-huset
Fridtjof Nansens plass
Stortinget
Oslo Spectrum
TØYEN
SKILLEBEKK
RUSELØKKA
Oslo Domkirke
Rådhuset
Frognerkilen
Rådhus-plassen
Festningstunnelen
Oslo Sentralstasjon
Post-terminalen
Politihuset
AKER BRYGGE
Ring 1
Kontraskjæret
Postmuseet
Teatermuseet
Børsen
FILIPSTAD
Pipervika
Hjemmefront-museet
Museet f. samtidskunst
Oslo kretsfengsel
Astrup-Fearnleymuseet
BYGDØY
Gamlebyen Skole
Bjørvika
Opera
Oslo Ladegård
Langvikbukta
Akershus slott og festning
Bispevika
Bryn
Middelalderpark
Forsvarsmuseet
N
Oslofjorden
Gamleyen gravlund
Kon-Tiki Museet
Framhuset
Sjøfartsmuseet
Oslo Hospital
Helsingborg, København, Kiel
Helsingborg, København, Kiel
Nordstrand
Bryn

Cergy-Pontoise
Vauréal
Rouen
Cergy
St-Ouen-l'Aumône
Pierrelaye
Taverny
Forêt Dom. de Montmorency
Domont
Beauvais
Neuville-s.-Oise
Jouy-le Moutier
Eragny
Beauchamp
Saint-Leu-la-Forêt
Vincourt
les Courlains
Le Plessis-Bouchard
St-Prix
Montlignon
Andilly
Margency
St-Brice-sous Forêt
F. Dom. de l'Hautil
Maurecourt
Conflans-Ste-Honorine
Seine
Herblay
Franconville
Ermont
Eaubonne
Soisy-Ss-Montmorency
Montmorency
Groslay
Meulan
Triel sur-Seine
Andrésy
Montigny-les-C.
Cormeilles-en-Parisis
Deuil-la-Barre
St-Gratien
Vernouillet
la Frette-sur-Seine
Montmagny
Forêt Dom. de St-Germain
Sannois
Enghien-les-Bains
Achères
Villetaneuse
Carrières-Ss-Poissy
Maisons-Laffitte
Argenteuil
Villennes-sur-Seine
Sartrouville
Villeneuve-la-Garenne
Le Mesnil-le-Roi
Bezons
Houilles
Gennevilliers
Mantes, Rouen
Poissy
TOLL
Colombes
Asnieres
Montesson
La Garenne-Colombes
Clichy
Le Vésinet
Carrières-s.-Seine
St-Ouen
Chambourcy
Levallois-Perret
Périphérique
Aigremont
Chatou
Courbevoie
Sacré Cœur
Saint Germain-en-Laye
Le Pecq
La Grande Arche
Fourqueux
Nanterre
LA DÉFENSE
Boulevard
WAGRAM
MONTMARTRE
Mareil-Marly
Croissy-sur-Seine
Rueil-Malmaison
Puteaux
Neuilly-s.-Seine
Gare St-Lazare
Gare du Nord
le Port-Marly
Arc de Triomphe
Élysée
TERNES
Opéra Garnier
Suresnes
CHAILLOT
Pl. de la Concorde
Louvre
MARAIS
l'Etang-la Ville
Bois de Boulogne
la Bretèche
Forêt Dom. de Marly-le-Roi
Bougival
Palais de Chaillot
Tour Eiffel
Champ de Mars
ST-GERMAIN DES PRÉS
Notre-Dame
St-Nom-la-Bretèche
Marly-le-Roi
Louveciennes
2008
Garches
Chavenay
Saint-Cloud
UNESCO
QUARTIER LATIN
Luxembourg
Noisy-le-Roi
Bailly
La Celle-St-Cloud
Vaucresson
Boulogne-Billancourt
GRENELLE
Jardin des Plantes
Villepreux
Gare Montparnasse
Tour
MONTPARNASSE
Rocquencourt
Parc des Expositions
Rennemoulin
Marnes-la-Coquette
Sèvres
Boulevard Périphérique
le Chesnay
Issy-les-Moulineaux
Vanves
Malakoff
Fontenay-le-Fleury
Les Clayes-s.-Bois
Château de Versailles
Ville-D'Avray
Montrouge
Gentilly
Meudon
Clamart
Versailles
Chaville
Arcueil
Bois-d'Arcy
Chatillon
Étang de St-Quentin
Pontchartrain
Viroflay
Vélizy-Villacoublay
Cachan
Fontenay-aux-Roses
Bagneux
St-Cyr-l'École
Le Plessis-Robinson
L'Hay-les-Roses
Sceaux
Bourg-la Reine
Montigny-le-Bretonneux
Buc
Jouy-en-Josas
Dreux
Guyancourt
Chatenay-Malabry
Voisins-le-Bretonneux
les Loges-en-Josas
Bièvres
Fresnes
Parc Nat. Rég. de Haute Vallée de Chevreuse
Toussus-le Noble
Antony
Verrières-le-Buisson
Rungis
Igny
St-Lambert
Magny-les-Hameaux
Châteaufort
Vauhallan
Massy
Wissous
la Brosse
Saclay
AÉROPORT DE PARIS-ORLY
Cressely
Villiers-le-Bâcle
Gif-sur-Yvette
Palaiseau
Paray-Vieille-Poste
Chevreuse
Orsay
Chilly-Mazarin
St-Rémy-les-Chevreuse
Villebon-s.-Y.
Champlan
Bures-s.-Y.
Le Mans, Orléans
Étampes
Fontainebleau

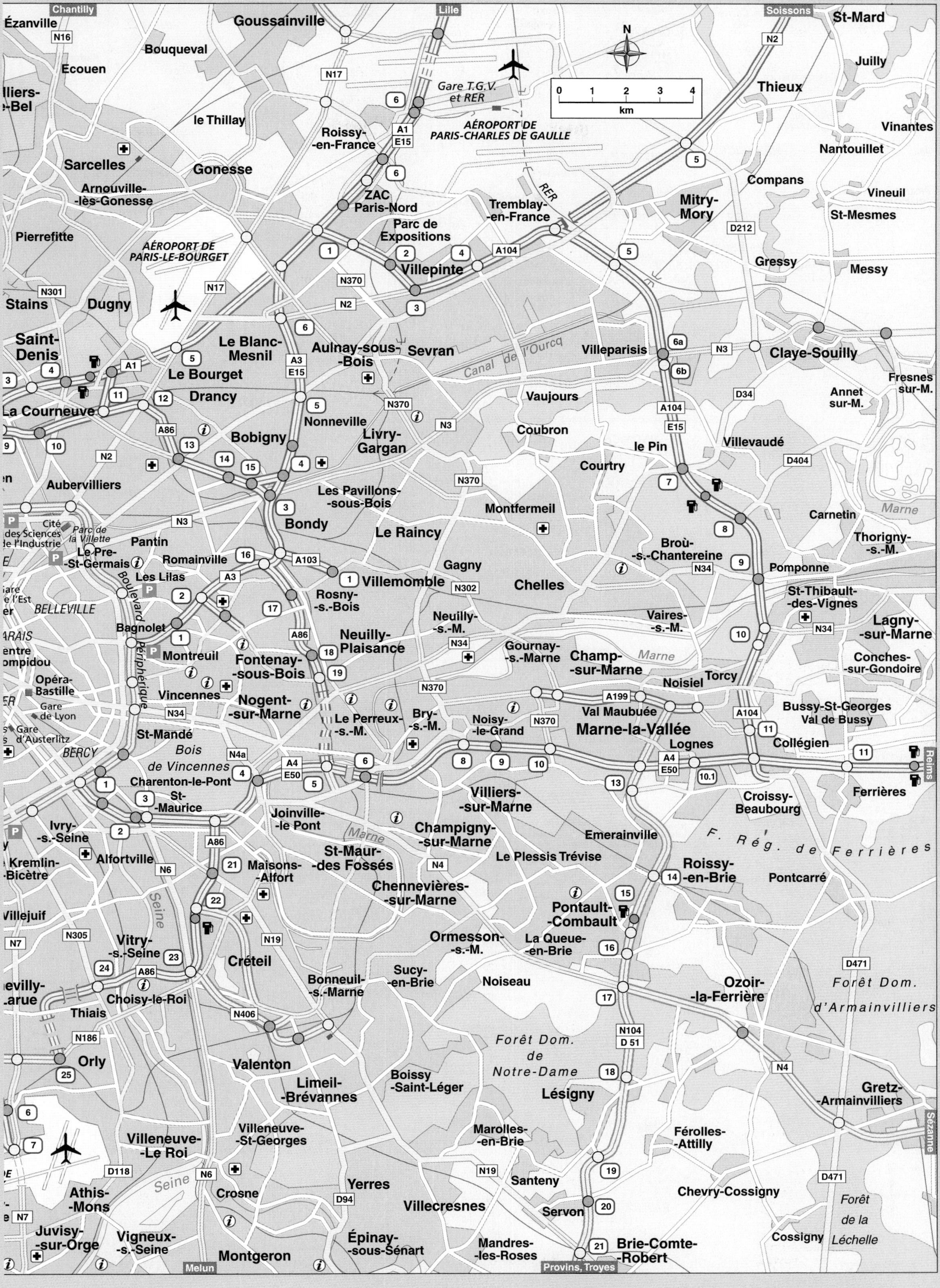
Chantilly
Lille
Soissons
Écouen
Goussainville
St-Mard
Bouqueval
Juilly
Gare T.G.V. et RER
AÉROPORT DE PARIS-CHARLES DE GAULLE
km
le Thillay
Roissy-en-France
Thieux
Vinantes
Nantouillet
Sarcelles
Gonesse
Arnouville-lès-Gonesse
Compans
Vineuil
ZAC Paris-Nord
Tremblay-en-France
RER
Mitry-Mory
St-Mesmes
Pierrefitte
Parc de Expositions
AÉROPORT DE PARIS-LE-BOURGET
Villepinte
Gressy
Messy
Stains
Dugny
Saint-Denis
Le Blanc-Mesnil
Aulnay-sous-Bois
Sevran
Canal de l'Ourcq
Villeparisis
Claye-Souilly
Fresnes sur-M.
Le Bourget
Drancy
Vaujours
Annet sur-M.
La Courneuve
Nonneville
Livry-Gargan
Coubron
Bobigny
le Pin
Villevaudé
Courtry
Aubervilliers
Les Pavillons-sous-Bois
Montfermeil
Carnetin
Marne
Bondy
Le Raincy
Cité des Sciences de l'Industrie
Parc de la Villette
Pantin
Broû-s.-Chantereine
Thorigny-s.-M.
Le Pre-St-Germais
Romainville
Gagny
Pomponne
Les Lilas
Villemomble
Chelles
St-Thibault-des-Vignes
BELLEVILLE
Rosny-s.-Bois
Neuilly-s.-M.
Vaires-s.-M.
Lagny-sur-Marne
Bagnolet
Boulevard Périphérique
Neuilly-Plaisance
Montreuil
Fontenay-sous-Bois
Gournay-s.-Marne
Champ-sur-Marne
Marne
Conches-sur-Gondoire
Opéra-Bastille
Torcy
Noisiel
Vincennes
Nogent-sur-Marne
Le Perreux-s.-M.
Bry-s.-M.
Noisy-le-Grand
Val Maubuée
Marne-la-Vallée
Bussy-St-Georges
Val de Bussy
Gare de Lyon
Gare d'Austerlitz
St-Mandé
Bois de Vincennes
Lognes
Collégien
BERCY
Reims
Charenton-le-Pont
St-Maurice
Villiers-sur-Marne
Croissy-Beaubourg
Ferrières
Ivry-s.-Seine
Joinville-le Pont
Marne
Champigny-sur-Marne
Emerainville
F. Rég. de Ferrières
Kremlin-Bicêtre
Alfortville
Maisons-Alfort
St-Maur-des Fossés
Le Plessis Trévise
Roissy-en-Brie
Pontcarré
Chennevières-sur-Marne
Villejuif
Seine
Pontault-Combault
Vitry-s.-Seine
Créteil
Ormesson-s.-M.
La Queue-en-Brie
Bonneuil-s.-Marne
Sucy-en-Brie
Noiseau
Ozoir-la-Ferrière
Forêt Dom. d'Armainvilliers
Choisy-le-Roi
Thiais
Orly
Valenton
Forêt Dom. de Notre-Dame
Limeil-Brévannes
Boissy-Saint-Léger
Lésigny
Gretz-Armainvilliers
Sézanne
Villeneuve-St-Georges
Marolles-en-Brie
Férolles-Attilly
Villeneuve-Le Roi
Santeny
Chevry-Cossigny
Seine
Athis-Mons
Crosne
Yerres
Villecresnes
Servon
Forêt de la Léchelle
Juvisy-sur-Orge
Vigneux-s.-Seine
Montgeron
Épinay-sous-Sénart
Mandres-les-Roses
Brie-Comte-Robert
Cossigny
Melun
Provins, Troyes

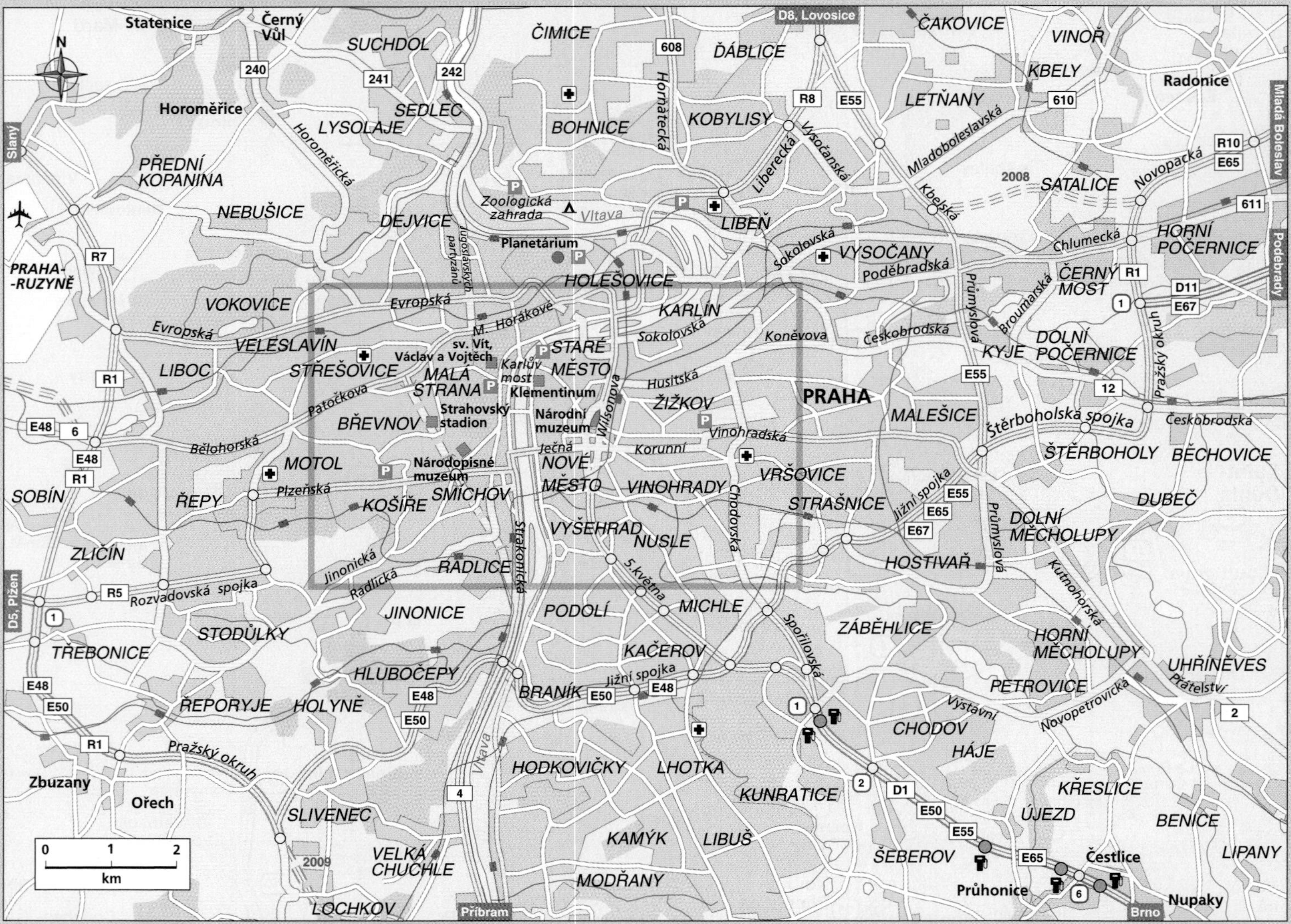
Statenice
Černý Vůl
SUCHDOL
ČIMICE
D8, Lovosice
ČAKOVICE
VINOŘ
608
ĎÁBLICE
KBELY
Radonice
240
241
242
Horoměřice
SEDLEC
LYSOLAJE
BOHNICE
KOBYLISY
R8
E55
LETŇANY
610
Mladá Boleslav
Slaný
Horoměřická
Hornátecká
Liberecká
Vysočanská
Mladoboleslavská
R10
E65
PŘEDNÍ KOPANINA
2008
SATALICE
Novopacká
NEBUŠICE
Zoologická zahrada
Vltava
LIBEŇ
Kbelská
611
DEJVICE
Jugoslávských partyzánů
Planetárium
Sokolovská
VYSOČANY
Chlumecká
HORNÍ POČERNICE
R7
Poděbradská
Podebrady
PRAHA-RUZYNĚ
HOLEŠOVICE
ČERNÝ MOST
R1
VOKOVICE
Evropská
KARLÍN
Průmyslová
Broumarská
D11
E67
Evropská
M. Horákové
Sokolovská
Konĕvova
Českobrodská
VELESLAVÍN
sv. Vít, Václav a Vojtěch
STARÉ MĚSTO
DOLNÍ POČERNICE
KYJE
R1
LIBOC
STŘEŠOVICE
Karlův most
MALÁ STRANA
Husitská
E55
Pražský okruh
Klementinum
PRAHA
12
Patočkova
Wilsonova
ŽIŽKOV
MALEŠICE
Strahovský stadion
Štěrboholská spojka
E48
6
BŘEVNOV
Národní muzeum
Vinohradská
Českobrodská
Bělohorská
Ječná
Korunní
ŠTĚRBOHOLY
BĚCHOVICE
E48
MOTOL
Národopisné muzeum
NOVÉ MĚSTO
VRŠOVICE
R1
Plzeňská
Jižní spojka
E55
SOBÍN
ŘEPY
SMÍCHOV
VINOHRADY
Chodovská
STRAŠNICE
DUBEČ
KOŠÍŘE
E65
VYŠEHRAD
E67
DOLNÍ MĚCHOLUPY
NUSLE
ZLIČÍN
Průmyslová
Jinonická
RADLICE
HOSTIVAŘ
Radlická
Strakonická
Kutnohorská
R5
5.května
D5, Plzeň
Rozvadovská spojka
MICHLE
1
JINONICE
PODOLÍ
Spořilovská
ZÁBĚHLICE
HORNÍ MĚCHOLUPY
STODŮLKY
TŘEBONICE
KAČEROV
Jižní spojka
UHŘÍNĚVES
HLUBOČEPY
E48
Přátelství
BRANÍK
E50
E48
PETROVICE
E48
E48
ŘEPORYJE
HOLYNĚ
E50
Výstavní
1
E50
R1
CHODOV
Novopetrovická
2
Pražský okruh
HÁJE
Vltava
HODKOVIČKY
LHOTKA
Zbuzany
4
2
D1
KŘESLICE
Ořech
KUNRATICE
SLIVENEC
E50
ÚJEZD
BENICE
0
1
2
km
E55
KAMÝK
LIBUŠ
VELKÁ CHUCHLE
ŠEBEROV
E65
Čestlice
LIPANY
2009
MODŘANY
Průhonice
6
Nupaky
LOCHKOV
Příbram
Brno

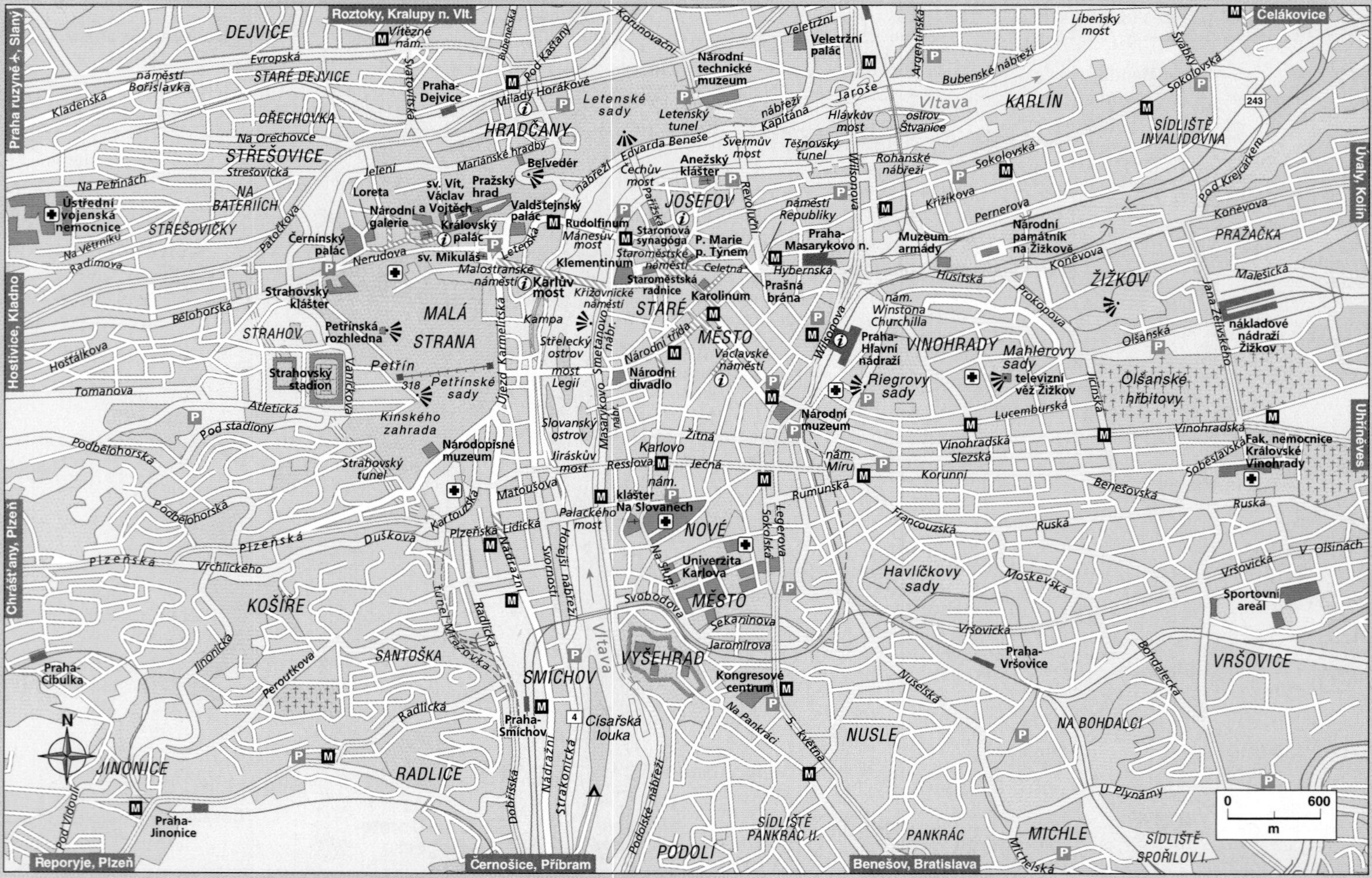
Roztoky, Kralupy n. Vlt.
Čelákovice
DEJVICE
Vítězné nám.
Veletržní palác
Libeňský most
Evropská
náměstí Bořislavka
STARÉ DEJVICE
Národní technické muzeum
Bubenské nábřeží
Praha-Dejvice
Milady Horákové
Argentinská
Praha ruzyně, Slaný
Kladenská
Letenské sady
Vltava
KARLÍN
ÓŘECHOVKA
Letenský tunel
nábřeží Kapitána Jaroše
ostrov Štvanice
Hlávkův most
SÍDLIŠTĚ INVALIDOVNA
Na Ořechovce
HRADČANY
Mariánské hradby
Edvarda Beneše
Svermův most
Těšnovský tunel
STŘEŠOVICE
Střešovická
Jelení
Belvedér
Čechův most
Anežský klášter
Rohanské nábřeží
Sokolovská
Úvaly, Kolín
Na Petřinách
NA BATERIÍCH
Loreta
sv. Vít, Václav a Vojtěch
Pražský hrad
JOSEFOV
Revoluční
Křižíkova
Pod Krejcárkem
Ústřední vojenská nemocnice
STŘEŠOVIČKY
Valdštejnský palác
Rudolfinum
náměstí Republiky
Pernerova
Koněvova
Národní památník na Žižkově
Černínský palác
Královský palác
Mánesův most
Staronová synagóga
P. Marie p. Týnem
Masarykovo n.
Muzeum armády
PRAŽAČKA
Radimova
Nerudova
sv. Mikuláš
Klementinum
Staroměstské náměstí
Celetná
Hybernská
Husitská
Malostranské náměstí
Karlův most
Staroměstská radnice
Prašná brána
Hostivice, Kladno
Strahovský klášter
Bělohorská
MALÁ STRANA
Křižovnické náměstí
Karolinum
ŽIŽKOV
Malešická
nám. Winstona Churchilla
Prokopova
nákladové nádraží Žižkov
Jana Želivského
STRAHOV
Petřínská rozhledna
Kampa
STARÉ
Olšanská
Praha-Hlavní nádraží
Střelecký ostrov
Národní třída
MĚSTO
VINOHRADY
Mahlerovy sady
Hošťálkova
Václavské náměstí
Petřín
Riegrovy sady
televizní věž Žižkov
Olšanské hřbitovy
Strahovský stadion
Petřínské sady
Národní divadlo
most Legií
Tomanova
Újezd
Karmelitská
Smetanovo nábř.
Atletická
Kinského zahrada
Národní muzeum
Lucemburská
Pod stadiony
Slovanský ostrov
Žitná
Vinohradská
Vinohradská
Fak. nemocnice Královské Vinohrady
Podbělohorská
Národopisné muzeum
Jiráskův most
Karlovo nám.
Ječná
nám. Míru
Slezská
Korunní
Soběslavská
Uhříněves
Strahovský tunel
Resslova
Matoušova
klášter Na Slovanech
Rumunská
Benešovská
Ruská
Podbělohorská
Kartouzská
Palackého most
NOVÉ
Francouzská
Ruská
Plzeňská
Lidická
Nádražní
Svornosti
Hořejší nábřeží
Plzeňská
Duškova
Univerzita Karlova
V Olšinách
Vrchlického
Na Slupi
Havlíčkovy sady
Moskevská
Vršovická
Chrášťany, Plzeň
Sportovní areál
KOŠÍŘE
tunel Mrázovka
Radlická
Svobodova
MĚSTO
Sekaninova
Vršovická
Praha-Cibulka
SANTOŠKA
Jaromírova
Praha-Vršovice
VRŠOVICE
Bohdalecká
Vltava
VYŠEHRAD
SMÍCHOV
Kongresové centrum
Nuselská
Peroutkova
Jinonická
Radlická
Praha-Smíchov
4
Císařská louka
Na Pankráci
5. května
NA BOHDALCI
JINONICE
NUSLE
RADLICE
U Plynárny
0
600
m
Pod Vidoulí
Praha-Jinonice
Dobříšská
Strakonická
Podolské nábřeží
SÍDLIŠTĚ PANKRÁC II.
PANKRÁC
MICHLE
SÍDLIŠTĚ SPOŘILOV I.
Michelská
PODOLÍ
Reporyje, Plzeň
Černošice, Příbram
Benešov, Bratislava

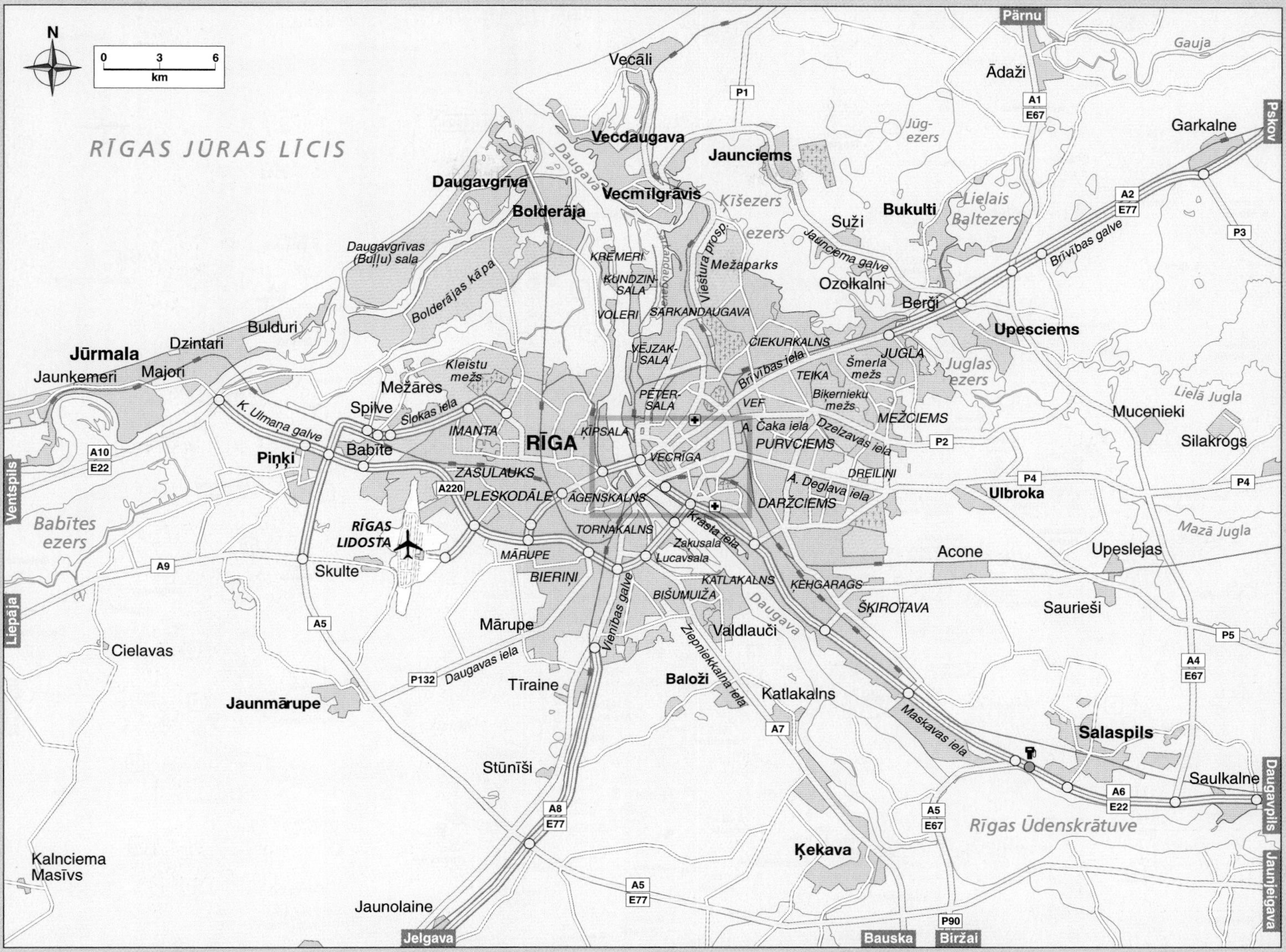
N
0 3 6
km
RĪGAS JŪRAS LĪCIS
Pärnu
Gauja
Vecāķi
Ādaži
P1
A1
E67
Pskov
Jūg-ezers
Garkalne
Vecdaugava
Jaunciems
Daugavgrīva
Vecmīlgrāvis
Ķīšezers
Bolderāja
Bukulti
Lielais Baltezers
Suži
A2
E77
P3
Daugavgrīvas (Buļļu) sala
Jaunciema gatve
Brīvības gatve
Bolderājas kāpa
KREMERI
Mežaparks
Ozolkalni
KUNDZIŅSALA
Berģi
VOLERI
SARKANDAUGAVA
Upesciems
Bulduri
ČIEKURKALNS
Jūrmala
Dzintari
JUGLA
VEJZAKSALA
TEIKA
Šmerla mežs
Juglas ezers
Jaunķemeri
Majori
Kleistu mežs
Mežāres
PĒTERSALA
Bikernieku mežs
Lielā Jugla
Spilve
VEF
MEŽCIEMS
Mucenieki
K. Ulmaņa gatve
Slokas iela
A. Čaka iela
Dzelzavas iela
IMANTA
KĪPSALA
PURVCIEMS
Silakrogs
A10
E22
RĪGA
P2
Piņķi
Babīte
VECRĪGA
DREILINI
ZASULAUKS
P4
P4
Ventspils
A220
PLESKODĀLE
ĀGENSKALNS
A. Deglava iela
Ulbroka
DARŽCIEMS
Babītes ezers
RĪGAS LIDOSTA
TORNAKALNS
Krasta iela
Mazā Jugla
Zakusala
Acone
Upeslejas
A9
Skulte
MĀRUPE
Lucavsala
BIERIŅI
KATLAKALNS
ĶENGARAGS
BIŠUMUIŽA
Daugava
Liepāja
ŠĶIROTAVA
Saurieši
Mārupe
Valdlauči
A5
Vienības gatve
P5
Cielavas
Ziepniekkalna iela
A4
E67
P132
Daugavas iela
Tīraine
Baloži
Jaunmārupe
Katlakalns
Maskavas iela
Salaspils
A7
Stūnīši
Saulkalne
A6
E22
Daugavpils
A8
E77
A5
E67
Rīgas Ūdenskrātuve
Ķekava
Kalnciema Masīvs
Jaunjelgava
A5
E77
Jaunolaine
P90
Jelgava
Bauska
Biržai

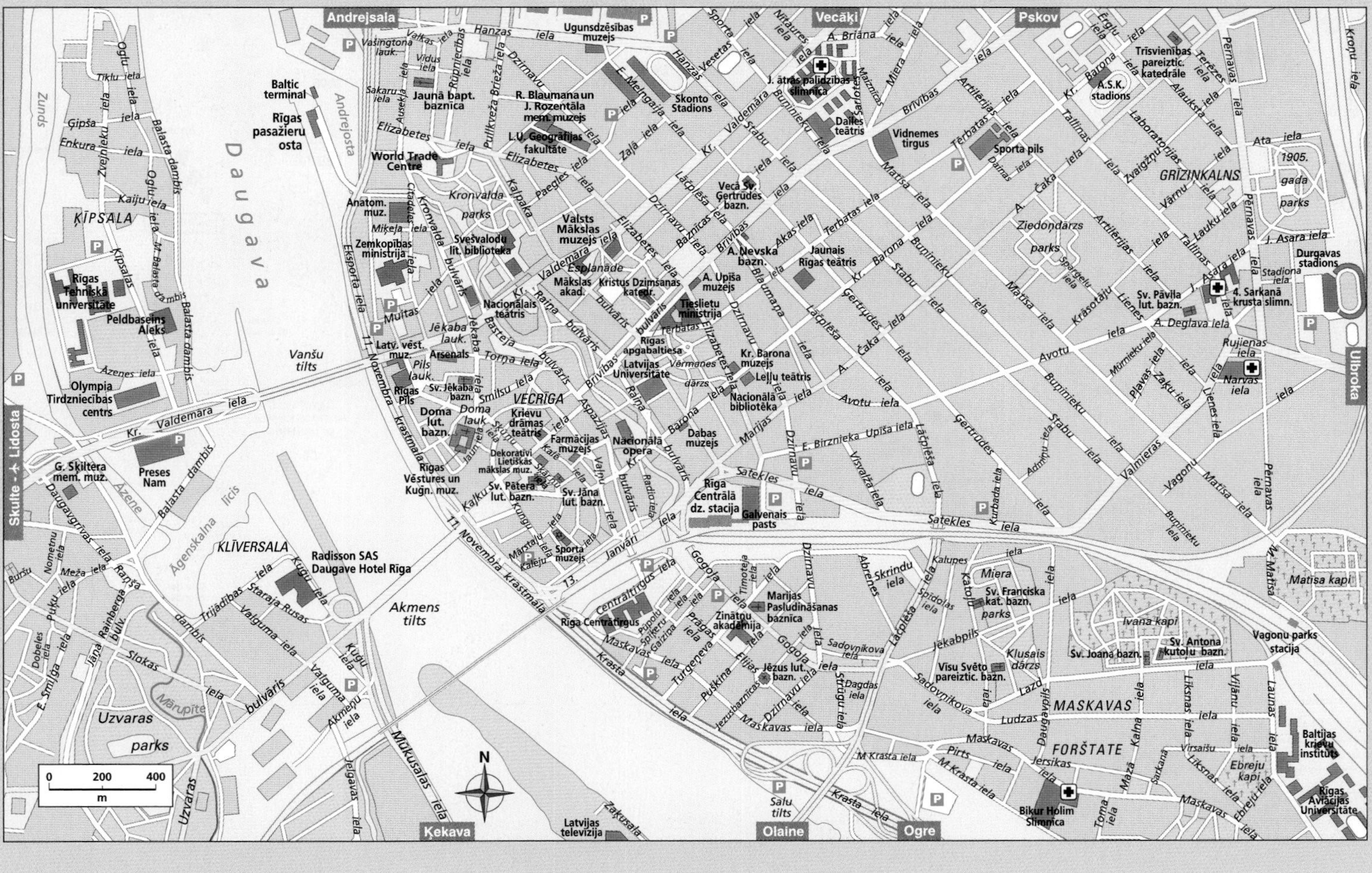
Andrejsala
Vecāķi
Pskov
Hanzas iela
Ugunsdzēsības muzejs
Baltic terminal
Rīgas pasažieru osta
Andrejosta
Jaunā bapt. baznīca
R. Blaumaņa un J. Rozentāla mem. muzejs
Skonto Stadions
J. ātrās palīdzības slimnīca
Dailes teātris
Trīsvienības pareiztic. katedrāle
A.S.K. stadions
L.U. Ģeogrāfijas fakultāte
World Trade Centre
Vidnemes tirgus
Sporta pils
Ķīpsala
Daugava
Kronvalda parks
Anatom. muz.
Valsts Mākslas muzejs
Vecā Sv. Ģertrūdes bazn.
GRĪZIŅKALNS
1905. gada parks
Zemkopības ministrija
Svešvalodu lit. biblioteka
Esplanāde
A. Ņevska bazn.
Jaunais Rīgas teātris
Ziedondārzs parks
Rīgas Tehniskā universitāte
Mākslas akad.
Kristus Dzimšanas katedr.
A. Upīša muzejs
Tieslietu ministrija
Daugavas stadions
Peldbaseins Aleks
Nacionālais teātris
Sv. Pāvila lut. bazn.
4. Sarkanā krusta slimn.
Latv. vēst. muz.
Arsenals
Rīgas apgabaltiesa
Latvijas Universitāte
Kr. Barona muzejs
Leļļu teātris
Vanšu tilts
Olympia Tirdzniecības centrs
Rīgas Pils
VECRĪGA
Nacionālā bibliotēka
Narvas iela
Ulbroka
Doma lut. bazn.
Krievu drāmas teātris
Farmācijas muzejs
Nacionālā opera
Dabas muzejs
Skulte - Lidosta
G. Skiltera mem. muz.
Preses Nams
Dekorativi Lietiskās mākslas muz.
Rīgas Vēstures un Kuģn. muz.
Sv. Pētera lut. bazn.
Sv. Jāņa lut. bazn.
Rīga Centrālā dz. stacija
Galvenais pasts
KLĪVERSALA
Radisson SAS Daugave Hotel Rīga
Āgenskalna līcis
Sporta muzejs
Akmens tilts
Centrāltirgus
Rīga Centrāltirgus
Marijas Pasludināšanas baznīca
Zinātņu akadēmija
Sv. Franciska kat. bazn.
Miera parks
Matīsa kapi
Ivana kapi
Sv. Jāņa bazn.
Sv. Antona kutoļu bazn.
Vagonu parks stacija
Jēzus lut. bazn.
Klusais dārzs
Visu Svēto pareiztic. bazn.
MASKAVAS FORŠTATE
Uzvaras parks
Mārupīte
0 200 400
m
N
Baltijas krievu institūts
Rīgas Aviācijas Universitāte
Bikur Holim Slimnīca
Salu tilts
Latvijas televīzija
Ķekava
Olaine
Ogre

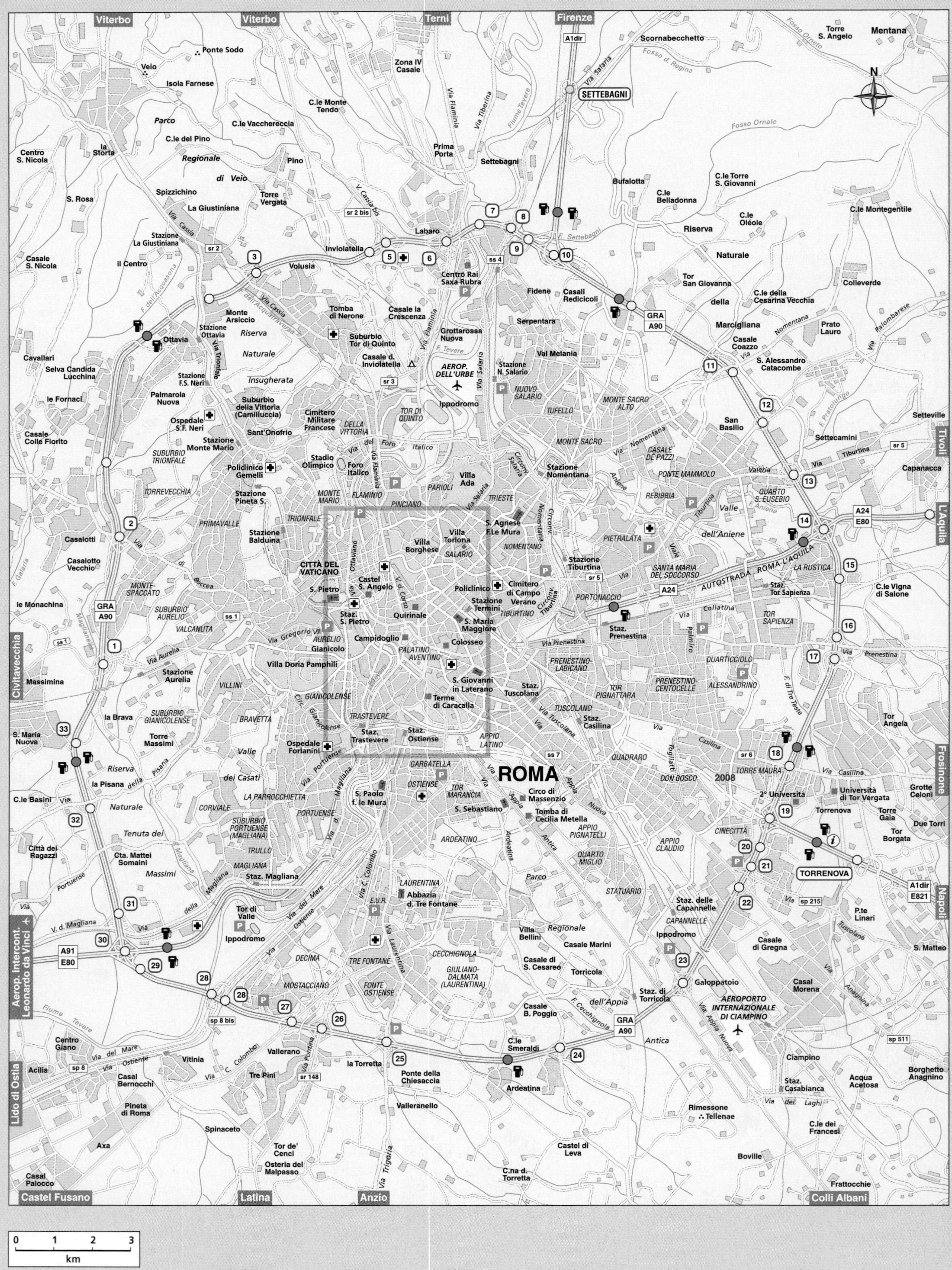
Viterbo
Viterbo
Terni
Firenze
A1dir
Scornabecchetto
Torre S. Angelo
Mentana
Ponte Sodo
Veio
Isola Farnese
Zona IV Casale
Via Salaria
SETTEBAGNI
C.le Monte Tendo
Via Flaminia
Via Tiberina
Fiume Tevere
Fosso Ornale
Parco
C.le Vacchereccia
C.le del Pino
Regionale
di Veio
la Storta
Centro S. Nicola
Prima Porta
Settebagni
Pino
Bufalotta
C.le Torre S. Giovanni
S. Rosa
Spizzichino
La Giustiniana
Torre Vergata
C.le Belladonna
C.le Montegentile
sr 2 bis
C.le Oléole
Riserva
Labaro
Inviolatella
Volusia
Stazione La Giustiniana
sr 2
sr 4
Casale S. Nicola
il Centro
Naturale
Centro Rai Saxa Rubra
Fidene
Casali Redicicoli
Tor San Giovanna
della
C.le della Cesarina Vecchia
Colleverde
Monte Arsiccio
Tomba di Nerone
Casale la Crescenza
Serpentara
GRA
A90
Marcigliana
Prato Lauro
Stazione Ottavia
Ottavia
Riserva
Suburbio Tor di Quinto
Grottarossa Nuova
Casale Coazzo
Via Nomentana
Via Palombarese
Cavallari
Naturale
Casale d. Inviolatella
Val Melania
S. Alessandro Catacombe
Selva Candida Lucchina
Stazione F.S. Neri
Insugherata
sr 3
AEROP. DELL'URBE
Stazione N. Salario
NUOVO SALARIO
le Fornaci
Palmarola Nuova
Suburbio della Vittoria (Camilluccia)
Ippodromo
TOR DI QUINTO
TUFELLO
MONTE SACRO ALTO
Ospedale S.F. Neri
Cimitero Militare Francese
DELLA VITTORIA
San Basilio
Settecamini
Setteville
Casale Colle Fiorito
Sant'Onofrio
Stazione Monte Mario
MONTE SACRO
CASAL DE' PAZZI
Tivoli
SUBURBIO TRIONFALE
Via del Foro Italico
Via Flaminia
Via Tiburtina
sr 5
Policlinico Gemelli
Stadio Olimpico
Foro Italico
Villa Ada
Stazione Nomentana
PONTE MAMMOLO
Valeria
Capanacca
TORREVECCHIA
Stazione Pineta S.
MONTE MARIO
FLAMINIO
PARIOLI
TRIESTE
REBIBBIA
QUARTO S. EUSEBIO
Valle
PINCIANO
TRIONFALE
A24
E80
PRIMAVALLE
Stazione Balduina
Villa Torlonia
S. Agnese F.Le Mura
Villa Borghese
SALARIO
NOMENTANO
PIETRALATA
dell'Aniene
L'Aquila
Casalotti
Casalotto Vecchio
CITTÀ DEL VATICANO
Stazione Tiburtina
SANTA MARIA DEL SOCCORSO
AUTOSTRADA ROMA-L'AQUILA
LA RUSTICA
C.le Vigna di Salone
MONTE-SPACCATO
Castel S. Angelo
S. Pietro
Policlinico
Cimitero di Campo Verano
Stazione Termini
Staz. Tor Sapienza
le Monachina
SUBURBIO AURELIO
Staz. S. Pietro
Quirinale
S. Maria Maggiore
PORTONACCIO
TIBURTINO
TOR SAPIENZA
VALCANUTA
ss 1
Campidoglio
Colosseo
Staz. Prenestina
AURELIO
Gianicolo
PALATINO
AVENTINO
Via Prenestina
Via Aurelia
Stazione Aurelia
Villa Doria Pamphili
PRENESTINO-LABICANO
QUARTICCIOLO
Civitavecchia
Massimina
VILLINI
GIANICOLENSE
S. Giovanni in Laterano
Terme di Caracalla
Staz. Tuscolana
TOR PIGNATTARA
PRENESTINO-CENTOCELLE
ALESSANDRINO
la Brava
SUBURBIO GIANICOLENSE
BRAVETTA
TRASTEVERE
TUSCOLANO
Staz. Casilina
Tor Angela
S. Maria Nuova
Torre Massimi
Ospedale Forlanini
Staz. Trastevere
Staz. Ostiense
APPIO LATINO
Via Casilina
Frosinone
Riserva
la Pisana
Valle
dei Casati
GARBATELLA
ss 7
QUADRARO
sr 6
TORRE MAURA
ROMA
DON BOSCO
2008
Università di Tor Vergata
Grotte Celoni
C.le Basini
LA PARROCCHIETTA
S. Paolo f. le Mura
OSTIENSE
TOR MARANCIA
Circo di Massenzio
2° Università
Naturale
CORVIALE
PORTUENSE
S. Sebastiano
Tomba di Cecilia Metella
Torrenova
Torre Gaia
Tenuta dei
SUBURBIO PORTUENSE (MAGLIANA)
APPIO PIGNATELLI
CINECITTÀ
Due Torri
Città dei Ragazzi
Cta. Mattei Somaini
TRULLO
ARDEATINO
APPIO CLAUDIO
Tor Borgata
MAGLIANA
QUARTO MIGLIO
TORRENOVA
Massimi
Staz. Magliana
Parco
Via Appia Antica
Via Ardeatina
LAURENTINA
STATUARIO
A1dir
E821
Abbazia d. Tre Fontane
Staz. delle Capannelle
sp 215
Napoli
Tor di Valle
E.U.R.
P.te Linari
V. d. Magliana
Ippodromo
Villa Bellini
Regionale
CAPANNELLE
Ippodromo
Aerop. Intercont. Leonardo da Vinci
A91
E80
DECIMA
TRE FONTANE
CECCHIGNOLA
Casale Marini
Casale di Gregna
S. Matteo
GIULIANO-DALMATA (LAURENTINA)
Casale di S. Cesareo
Torricola
MOSTACCIANO
FONTE OSTIENSE
Galoppatoio
Casal Morena
dell'Appia
Staz. di Torricola
AEROPORTO INTERNAZIONALE DI CIAMPINO
Fiume Tevere
sp 8 bis
Casale B. Poggio
GRA
A90
Antica
Centro Giano
Vallerano
C.le Smeraldi
sp 511
Via del Mare
sp 8
Vitinia
la Torretta
Ponte della Chiesaccia
Ciampino
Acilia
Casal Bernocchi
Tre Pini
sr 148
Ardeatina
Borghetto Anagnino
Acqua Acetosa
Staz. Casabianca
Lido di Ostia
Pineta di Roma
Valleranello
Rimessone
Tellenae
C.le dei Francesi
Spinaceto
Axa
Tor de' Cenci
Castel di Leva
Osteria del Malpasso
Boville
Casal Palocco
C.na d. Torretta
Frattocchie
Castel Fusano
Latina
Anzio
Colli Albani
0 1 2 3
km

M.te Mario
Foro Italico
Flaminio
Pinciano
Parioli
Policlinico Umberto I
Tiburtino
Tuscolano
Ardeatino
Fiera di Roma - EUR
Tor di Valle
EUR
Aerop. Leonardo da Vinci
Corviale
Aurelio
Primavalle
Città Giudiziaria
Cristo Re
Museo Africano d. Zoologia
Galleria Naz. d'Arte Moderna
Museo Naz. di Villa Giulia
Villa Borghese
Tempio di Esculapio
Galleria e Museo Borghese
SALARIO
Villa Albani
MACRO
Villa Ruffo
Pincio
Galoppatoio
Villa Medici
Porta Pinciana
LUDOVISI
SALLUSTIANO
CASTRO PRETORIO
Porta Pia
PRATI
CAMPO MARZIO
Musei Vaticani
CITTÀ DEL VATICANO
Castel S. Angelo
Palazzo di Giustizia
Mausoleo di Augusto
Ara Pacis
Trinità dei Monti
Palazzo Boncompagni
Palazzo Barberini (Gall. Naz. Arte Antica)
Museo Naz. Romano
Terme di Diocleziano
Basilica di S. Pietro
Piazza S. Pietro
COLONNA
Montecitorio
Fontana di Trevi
TREVI
Quirinale
Palazzo del Quirinale
Stazione Termini "Giovanni Paolo II"
PONTE
Pantheon
Palazzo Madama
Palazzo del Viminale
S. Maria Maggiore
PIGNA
REGOLA
Palazzo Farnese
Chiesa del Gesù
Vittoriano
Torre d. Milizie
S. ANGELO
MONTI
ESQUILINO
Esquilino
Villa Farnesina
Villa Lante
Pal. Corsini (Gall. Naz.)
Gianicolo
Teatro di Marcello
Capitolino
Musei Capitolini
Foro Romano
Domus Aurea
Terme di Traiano
ISOLA TIBERINA
CAMPITELLI
Palatino
Colosseo
Arco di Costantino
S. Clemente
TRASTEVERE
S. Maria in Cosmedin
Circo Massimo
Celio
S. Giovanni in Laterano
RIPA
Aventino
F.A.O.
CELIO
Villa Sciarra
Porta Metronia
Terme di Caracalla
TESTACCIO
Piramide di Caio Cestio
Cimitero Protestante
SAN SABA
Porta Latina
Porta S. Sebastiano
Staz. Roma Ostia
Staz. Ostiense
Air Terminal
Staz. Trastevere
GIANICOLENSE
Ospedale S. Camillo
Ospedale Spallanzani
Ospedale Forlanini
Ex Magazzini Generali
Scalo Merci San Paolo
APPIO LATINO
Domine Quo Vadis?
GARBATELLA
0 200 400 600 m

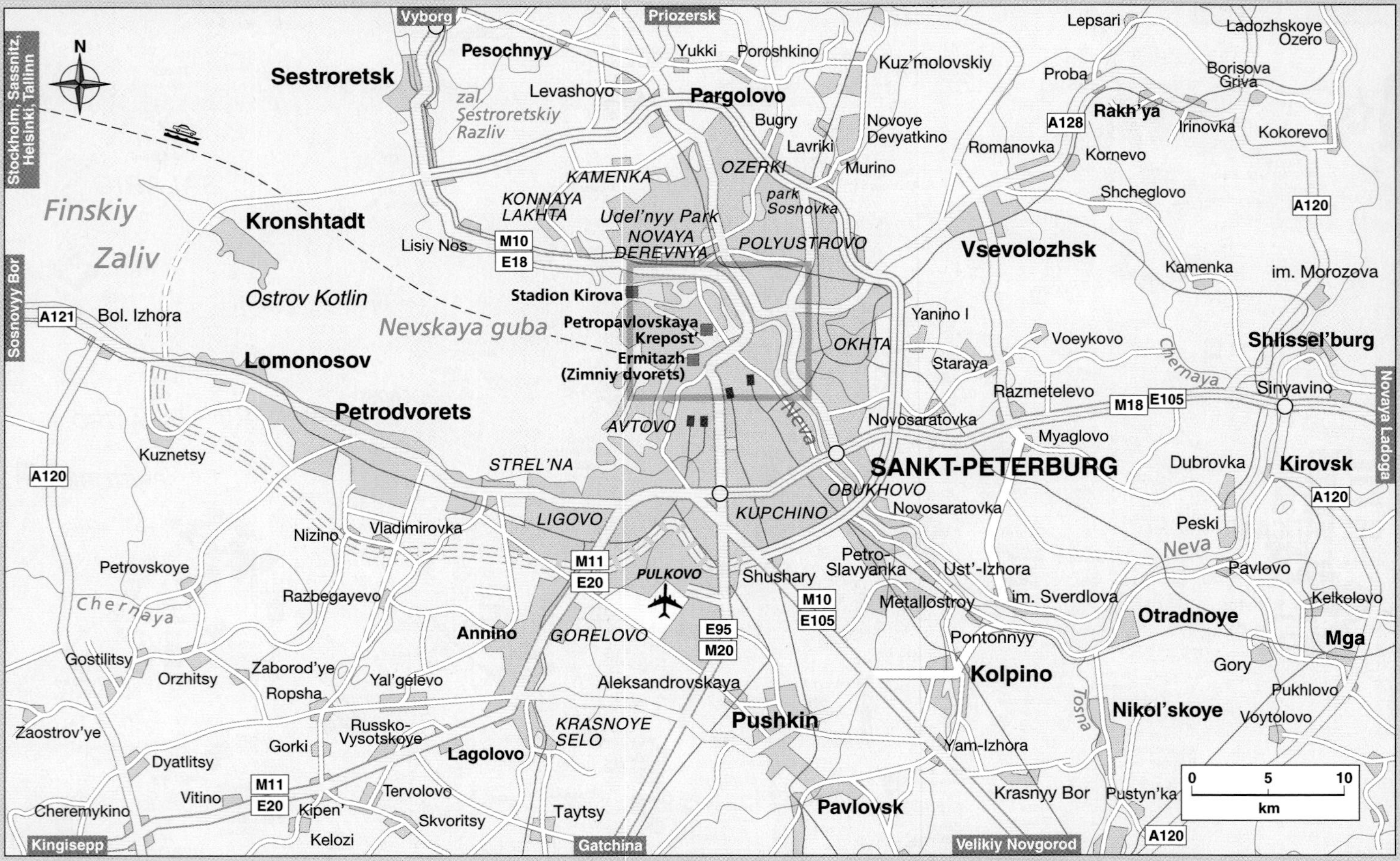
Vyborg
Priozersk
Stockholm, Sassnitz, Helsinki, Tallinn
N
Sestroretsk
Pesochnyy
Yukki
Poroshkino
Kuz'molovskiy
Lepsari
Ladozhskoye Ozero
Proba
Borisova Griva
zal. Sestroretskiy Razliv
Levashovo
Pargolovo
Bugry
Novoye Devyatkino
Lavriki
A128
Rakh'ya
Irinovka
Kokorevo
Romanovka
Kornevo
Murino
KAMENKA
OZERKI
Shcheglovo
park Sosnovka
A120
Finskiy Zaliv
Kronshtadt
KONNAYA LAKHTA
Udel'nyy Park
NOVAYA DEREVNYA
POLYUSTROVO
Vsevolozhsk
Lisiy Nos
M10
E18
Kamenka
im. Morozova
Sosnovyy Bor
Ostrov Kotlin
Stadion Kirova
A121
Bol. Izhora
Nevskaya guba
Petropavlovskaya Krepost'
Yanino I
Ermitazh (Zimniy dvorets)
OKHTA
Voeykovo
Shlissel'burg
Lomonosov
Staraya
Chernaya
Razmetelevo
Sinyavino
Novaya Ladoga
Petrodvorets
M18
E105
AVTOVO
Neva
Novosaratovka
Myaglovo
Kuznetsy
SANKT-PETERBURG
Dubrovka
Kirovsk
STREL'NA
A120
OBUKHOVO
Novosaratovka
LIGOVO
KUPCHINO
Peski
Nizino
Vladimirovka
Petro-Slavyanka
Ust'-Izhora
Pavlovo
Petrovskoye
M11
E20
PULKOVO
Shushary
Chernaya
Razbegayevo
M10
E105
Metallostroy
im. Sverdlova
Kelkolovo
Otradnoye
Annino
GORELOVO
E95
M20
Pontonnyy
Mga
Gostilitsy
Orzhitsy
Zaborod'ye
Ropsha
Yal'gelevo
Aleksandrovskaya
Kolpino
Gory
Pukhlovo
Tosna
Nikol'skoye
Voytolovo
Zaostrov'ye
Russko-Vysotskoye
KRASNOYE SELO
Pushkin
Gorki
Lagolovo
Yam-Izhora
Dyatlitsy
M11
E20
Vitino
Tervolovo
Krasnyy Bor
Pustyn'ka
0
5
10
km
Cheremykino
Kipen'
Skvoritsy
Taytsy
Pavlovsk
Kelozi
Kingisepp
Gatchina
Velikiy Novgorod
A120

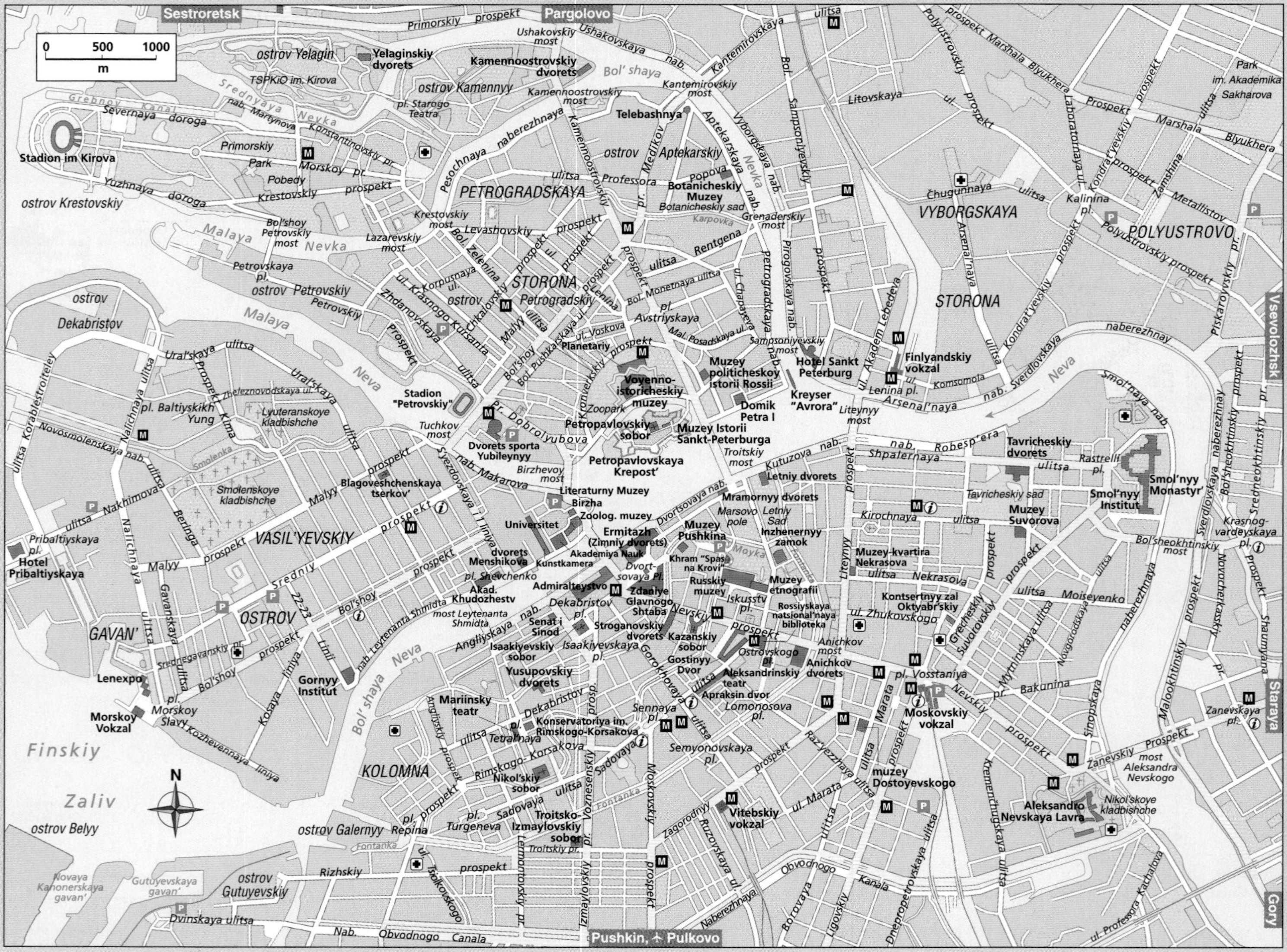
Sestroretsk
Pargolovo
0
500
1000
m
ostrov Yelagin
Yelaginskiy dvorets
Kamennoostrovskiy dvorets
ostrov Kamennyy
TSPKiO im. Kirova
Stadion im Kirova
Primorskiy Park Pobedy
ostrov Krestovskiy
Telebashnya
ostrov Aptekarskiy
Botanicheskiy Muzey
PETROGRADSKAYA
STORONA
Petrogradskiy
ostrov Petrovskiy
ostrov Dekabristov
Malaya Neva
Stadion "Petrovskiy"
Planetariy
Voyenno-istoricheskiy muzey
Zoopark
Petropavlovskiy sobor
Petropavlovskaya Krepost'
Dvorets sporta Yubileynyy
Muzey Istorii Sankt-Peterburga
Muzey politicheskoy istorii Rossii
Domik Petra I
Kreyser "Avrora"
Hotel Sankt Peterburg
Finlyandskiy vokzal
VYBORGSKAYA
STORONA
POLYUSTROVO
Park im. Akademika Sakharova
Tavricheskiy dvorets
Smol'nyy Monastyr
Smol'nyy Institut
Letniy dvorets
Mramornyy dvorets
Letniy Sad
Inzhenernyy zamok
Muzey Suvorova
Tavricheskiy sad
Blagoveshchenskaya tserkov'
Smolenskoye kladbishche
Lyuteranskoye kladbishche
Literaturny Muzey
Birzha
Zoolog. muzey
Universitet
Kunstkamera
Ermitazh (Zimniy dvorets)
Akademiya Nauk
Muzey Pushkina
Khram "Spas na Krovi"
Russkiy muzey
Muzey etnografii
Muzey-kvartira Nekrasova
Kontsertnyy zal Oktyabr'skiy
Rossiyskaya natsional'naya biblioteka
Menshikova dvorets
Akad. Khudozhestv
Admiralteystvo
Zdaniye Glavnogo Shtaba
Senat i Sinod
Stroganovskiy dvorets
Kazanskiy sobor
Gostinyy Dvor
Isaakiyevskiy sobor
Yusupovskiy dvorets
Aleksandrinskiy teatr
Apraksin dvor
Anichkov dvorets
Hotel Pribaltiyskaya
VASIL'YEVSKIY
OSTROV
GAVAN'
Lenexpo
Morskoy Vokzal
Gornyy Institut
Mariinskiy teatr
Konservatoriya im. Rimskogo-Korsakova
KOLOMNA
Nikol'skiy sobor
Troitsko-Izmaylovskiy sobor
Vitebskiy vokzal
muzey Dostoyevskogo
Moskovskiy vokzal
Aleksandro Nevskaya Lavra
Nikol'skoye kladbishche
Finskiy Zaliv
N
ostrov Belyy
ostrov Galernyy
ostrov Gutuyevskiy
Novaya Kanonerskaya gavan'
Gutuyevskaya gavan'
Nevskiy prospekt
Neva
Bol'shaya Neva
Fontanka
Moyka
Obvodnogo Canala
Vsevolozhsk
Staraya
Gory
Pushkin, Pulkovo

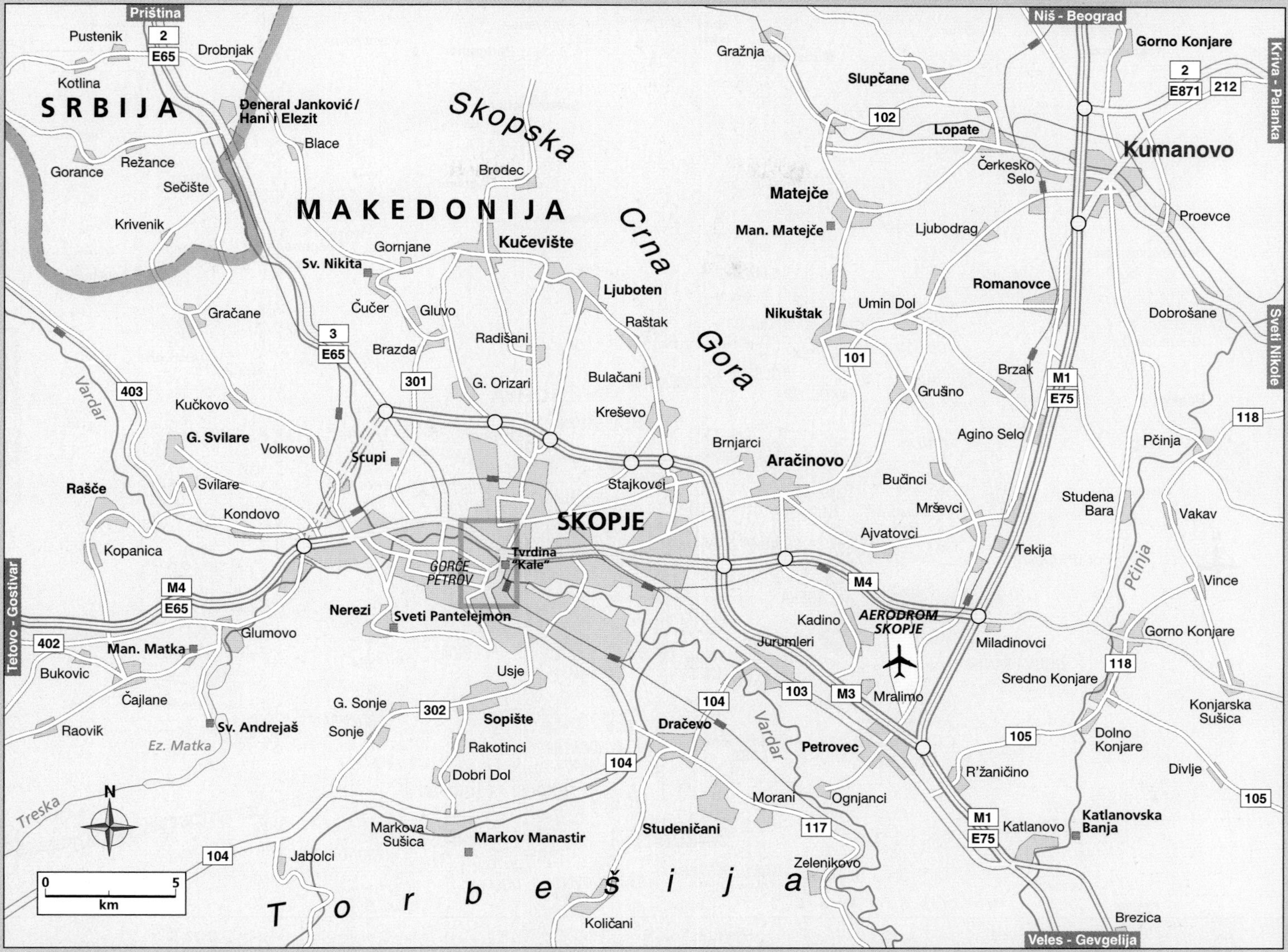
Priština
Niš - Beograd
Kriva - Palanka
Sveti Nikole
Tetovo - Gostivar
Veles - Gevgelija
SRBIJA
MAKEDONIJA
Skopska Crna Gora
Torbešija
Pustenik
Drobnjak
Kotlina
Đeneral Janković/ Hani i Elezit
Blace
Gorance
Režance
Sečište
Krivenik
Brodec
Gornjane
Kučevište
Sv. Nikita
Čučer
Gluvo
Ljuboten
Raštak
Gračane
Radišani
Brazda
G. Orizari
Bulačani
Kreševo
Kučkovo
G. Svilare
Volkovo
Scupi
Rašče
Svilare
Kondovo
Stajkovci
SKOPJE
Kopanica
GORČE PETROV
Tvrdina "Kale"
Nerezi
Sveti Pantelejmon
Man. Matka
Glumovo
Bukovic
Čajlane
Usje
Raovik
Sv. Andrejaš
Ez. Matka
G. Sonje
Sonje
Sopište
Rakotinci
Dobri Dol
Dračevo
Treska
Markova Sušica
Markov Manastir
Studeničani
Jabolci
Zelenikovo
Količani
Gražnja
Slupčane
Lopate
Gorno Konjare
Kumanovo
Čerkesko Selo
Matejče
Man. Matejče
Ljubodrag
Proevce
Romanovce
Nikuštak
Umin Dol
Dobrošane
Brzak
Grušno
Agino Selo
Pčinja
Brnjarci
Aračinovo
Bučinci
Studena Bara
Mrševci
Vakav
Ajvatovci
Tekija
Vince
AERODROM SKOPJE
Kadino
Jurumleri
Miladinovci
Gorno Konjare
Sredno Konjare
Mralino
Konjarska Sušica
Petrovec
Dolno Konjare
R'žaničino
Divlje
Morani
Ognjanci
Katlanovo
Katlanovska Banja
Brezica
Vardar
2
E65
3
E65
403
301
M4
E65
402
302
104
104
104
117
102
101
M1
E75
2
E871
212
118
M4
103
M3
118
105
105
M1
E75
N
0
5
km

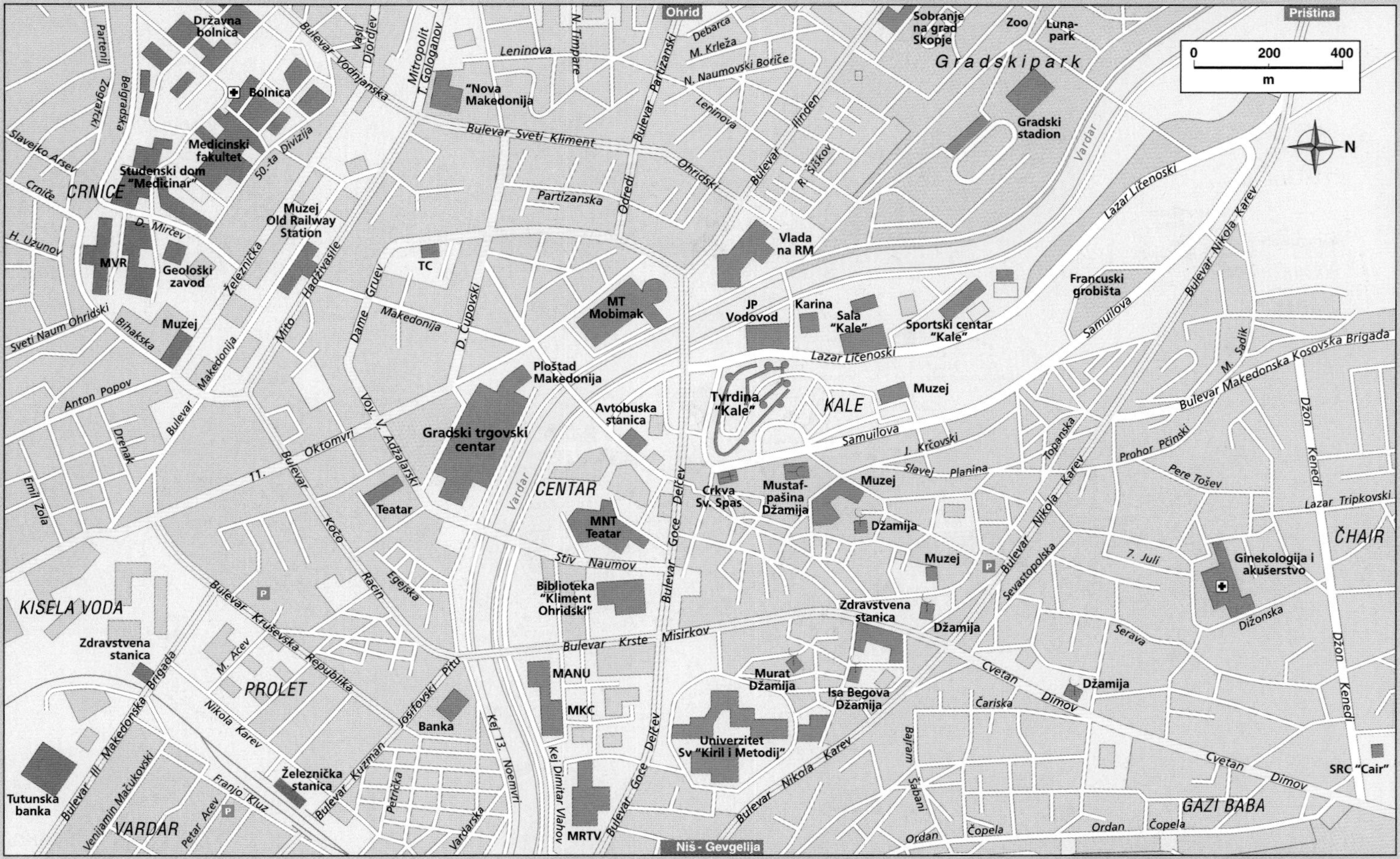
Ohrid
Priština
Niš - Gevgelija
Državna bolnica
Bolnica
Medicinski fakultet
Studenski dom "Medicinar"
CRNICE
MVR
Geološki zavod
Muzej Old Railway Station
Muzej
TC
"Nova Makedonija"
MT Mobimak
Ploštad Makedonija
Gradski trgovski centar
Avtobuska stanica
Teatar
CENTAR
MNT Teatar
Biblioteka "Kliment Ohridski"
KISELA VODA
Zdravstvena stanica
PROLET
Banka
MANU
MKC
Univerzitet Sv "Kiril i Metodij"
Železnička stanica
Tutunska banka
VARDAR
MRTV
Sobranje na grad Skopje
Zoo
Luna-park
Gradski park
Gradski stadion
Vlada na RM
JP Vodovod
Karina
Sala "Kale"
Sportski centar "Kale"
Francuski grobišta
Tvrdina "Kale"
KALE
Muzej
Crkva Sv. Spas
Mustaf-pašina Džamija
Muzej
Džamija
Muzej
Zdravstvena stanica
Džamija
Murat Džamija
Isa Begova Džamija
Džamija
Ginekologija i akušerstvo
ČHAIR
GAZI BABA
SRC "Cair"
Partenij
Zografski
Belgradska
Slavejko Arsov
Crniče
H. Uzunov
D. Mirčev
50.ta Divizija
Bulevar Vodnjanska
Vasil Đjordjev
Mitropolit T. Gologanov
Leninova
N. Timpare
Bulevar Sveti Kliment Ohridski
Bulevar Partizanski
Debarca
M. Krleža
N. Naumovski Boriče
Leninova
Bulevar Ilinden
R. Šiškov
Partizanska
Odredi
Železnička
Hadživasile
Mito
Dame Gruev
Makedonija
D. Čupovski
Sveti Naum Ohridski
Bihakska
Anton Popov
Bulevar Makedonija
Drenak
Emil Zola
11. Oktomvri
Voj. V. Adžalarski
Bulevar Koco Racin
Egejska
Stiv Naumov
Bulevar Goce Delčev
Bulevar Krste Misirkov
Bulevar Kruševska Republika
M. Acev
Nikola Karev
Bulevar III. Makedonska Brigada
Venijamin Mačukovski
Franjo Kluz
Petar Acev
Bulevar Kuzman
Josifovski Pitu
Petrička
Vardarska
Kej 13. Noemvri
Kej Dimitar Vlahov
Bulevar Goce Delčev
Lazar Ličenoski
Samuilova
Lazar Ličenoski
Samuilova
Bulevar Nikola Karev
Bulevar Makedonska Kosovska Brigada
M. Sadik
J. Krčovski
Slavej Planina
Topanska
Nikola Karev
Prohor Pčinski
Pere Tošev
Lazar Tripkovski
Džon Kenedi
7. Juli
Bulevar Nikola Karev
Sevastopolska
Serava
Dižonska
Cvetan Dimov
Čariska
Bajram Šabani
Ordan Čopela
Vardar
0
200
400
m
N

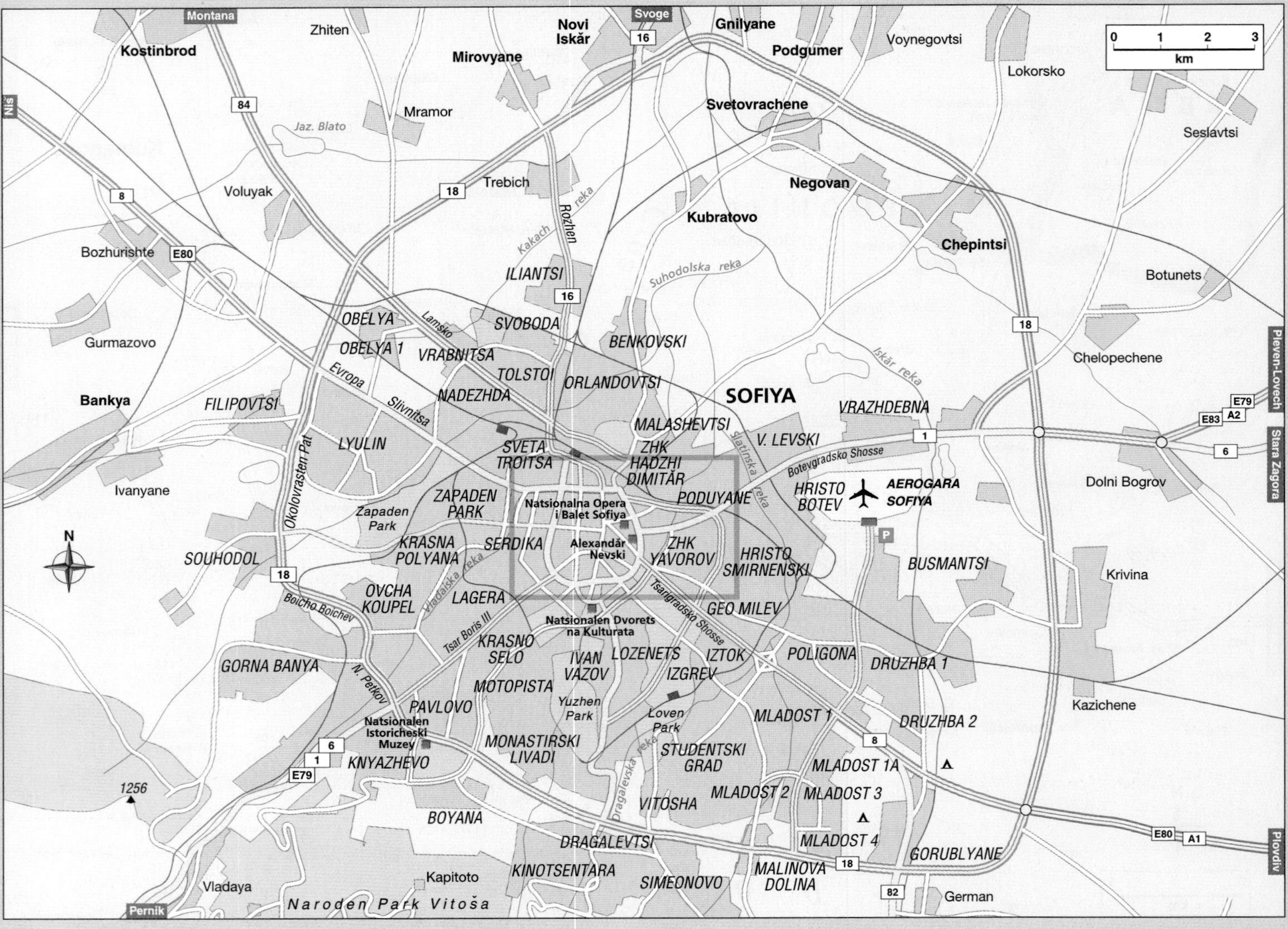
Montana
Svoge
Nis
Pernik
Pleven-Lovech
Stara Zagora
Plovdiv
0 1 2 3
km
Zhiten
Kostinbrod
Novi Iskăr
Mirovyane
Gnilyane
Podgumer
Voynegovtsi
Lokorsko
Mramor
Jaz. Blato
Svetovrachene
Seslavtsi
Voluyak
Trebich
Negovan
Kubratovo
Bozhurishte
Chepintsi
Rozhen
Kakach reka
Suhodolska reka
Botunets
ILIANTSI
OBELYA
Lamsko
SVOBODA
BENKOVSKI
Gurmazovo
OBELYA 1
VRABNITSA
Iskăr reka
Chelopechene
Evropa
TOLSTOI
ORLANDOVTSI
Bankya
FILIPOVTSI
Slivnitsa
NADEZHDA
SOFIYA
VRAZHDEBNA
MALASHEVTSI
LYULIN
SVETA TROITSA
ZHK HADZHI DIMITĂR
V. LEVSKI
Botevgradsko Shosse
Dolni Bogrov
Ivanyane
ZAPADEN PARK
Natsionalna Opera i Balet Sofiya
PODUYANE
HRISTO BOTEV
AEROGARA SOFIYA
Zapaden Park
Okolovrasten Pat
Slatinska reka
KRASNA POLYANA
SERDIKA
Aleksandăr Nevski
ZHK YAVOROV
HRISTO SMIRNENSKI
BUSMANTSI
Krivina
SOUHODOL
Vladaiska reka
OVCHA KOUPEL
LAGERA
Tsarigradsko Shosse
GEO MILEV
Boicho Boichev
Natsionalen Dvorets na Kulturata
Tsar Boris III
KRASNO SELO
IVAN VAZOV
LOZENETS
IZTOK
POLIGONA
DRUZHBA 1
GORNA BANYA
N. Patkov
IZGREV
MOTOPISTA
Kazichene
PAVLOVO
Yuzhen Park
Loven Park
MLADOST 1
DRUZHBA 2
Natsionalen Istoricheski Muzey
MONASTIRSKI LIVADI
STUDENTSKI GRAD
KNYAZHEVO
Dragalevska reka
MLADOST 1A
1256
MLADOST 2
MLADOST 3
VITOSHA
BOYANA
DRAGALEVTSI
MLADOST 4
GORUBLYANE
KINOTSENTARA
MALINOVA DOLINA
Kapitoto
SIMEONOVO
Vladaya
German
Naroden Park Vitoša
84
8
18
16
E80
E79
E83
A2
A1
6
1
82

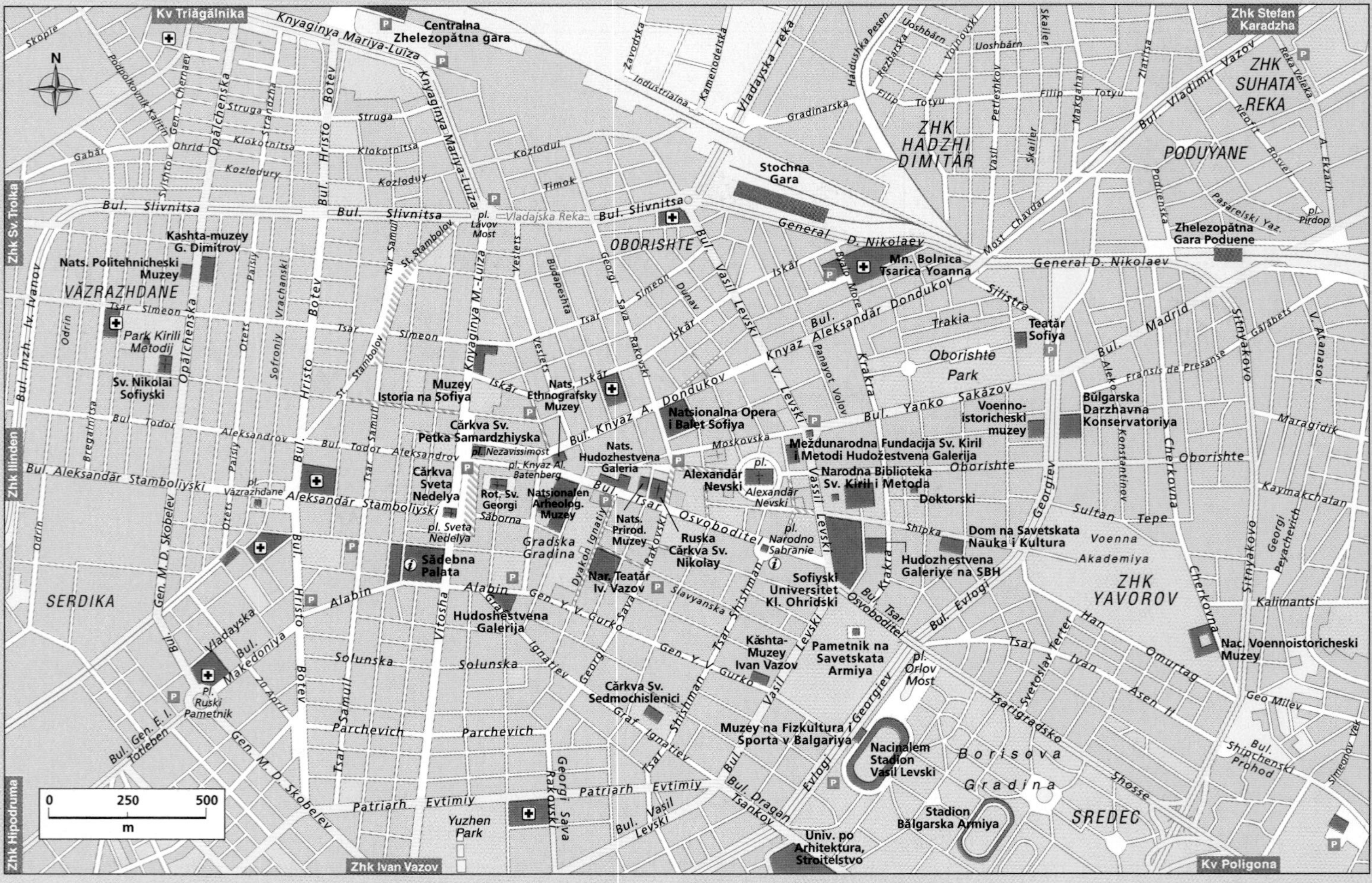
Kv Triăgălnika
Zhk Stefan Karadzha
Zhk Sv. Troika
Zhk Ilinden
Zhk Hipodruma
Zhk Ivan Vazov
Kv Poligona
Centralna Zhelezopătna gara
Knyaginya Mariya-Luiza
Skopie
Podpolkovnik Kalitin
Struga
Ohrid
Klokotnitsa
Kozloduy
Gabăr
Opălchenska
Hristo Botev
Zavodska
Industrialna
Kamenodelska
Vladayska reka
Haidushka Pesen
Rezbarska
Voinishki
Uoshbărn
Skaliter
Filip Totyu
Gradinarska
ZHK HADZHI DIMITĂR
Vasil Petleshkov
Bul. Vladimir Vazov
ZHK SUHATA REKA
PODUYANE
Stochna Gara
Timok
Bul. Slivnitsa
pl. Lavov Most
Vladajska Reka
OBORISHTE
General D. Nikolaev
Zhelezopătna Gara Poduene
Kashta-muzey G. Dimitrov
Nats. Politehnicheski Muzey
VĂZRAZHDANE
Tsar Simeon
Mn. Bolnica Tsarica Yoanna
Most Chavdar
Bul. Knyaz Aleksandăr Dondukov
Silistra
Trakia
Teatăr Sofiya
Park Kirili Metodij
Oborishte Park
Bul. Madrid
Sv. Nikolai Sofiyski
Muzey Istoria na Sofiya
Nats. Ethnografsky Muzey
Natsionalna Opera i Balet Sofiya
Bul. Yanko Sakăzov
Voenno-istoricheski muzey
Bălgarska Darzhavna Konservatoriya
Cărkva Sv. Petka Samardzhiyska
Nats. Hudozhestvena Galeria
Meždunarodna Fundacija Sv. Kiril i Metodi Hudoźestvena Galerija
Bul. Aleksandăr Stamboliyski
Cărkva Sveta Nedelya
Rot. Sv. Georgi Săborna
Natsionalen Arheolog. Muzey
Aleksandăr Nevski
Narodna Biblioteka Sv. Kiril i Metoda
Doktorski
Nats. Prirod. Muzey
Ruska Cărkva Sv. Nikolay
pl. Narodno Sabranie
Dom na Savetskata Nauka i Kultura
Sădebna Palata
Nar. Teatăr Iv. Vazov
Sofiyski Universitet Kl. Ohridski
Hudozhestvena Galeriye na SBH
SERDIKA
Alabin
Hudoshestvena Galerija
Gen. Y. V. Gurko
ZHK YAVOROV
Nac. Voennoistoricheski Muzey
Kăshta-Muzey Ivan Vazov
Pametnik na Savetskata Armiya
pl. Orlov Most
pl. Ruski Pametnik
Bul. Makedoniya
Solunska
Cărkva Sv. Sedmochislenici
Muzey na Fizkultura i Sporta v Balgariya
Nacinalem Stadion Vasil Levski
Borisova Gradina
Parchevich
Patriarh Evtimiy
Stadion Bălgarska Armiya
SREDEC
Yuzhen Park
Univ. po Arhitektura, Stroitelstvo
Bul. Dragan Tsankov
Tsarigradsko Shosse
0 250 500
m

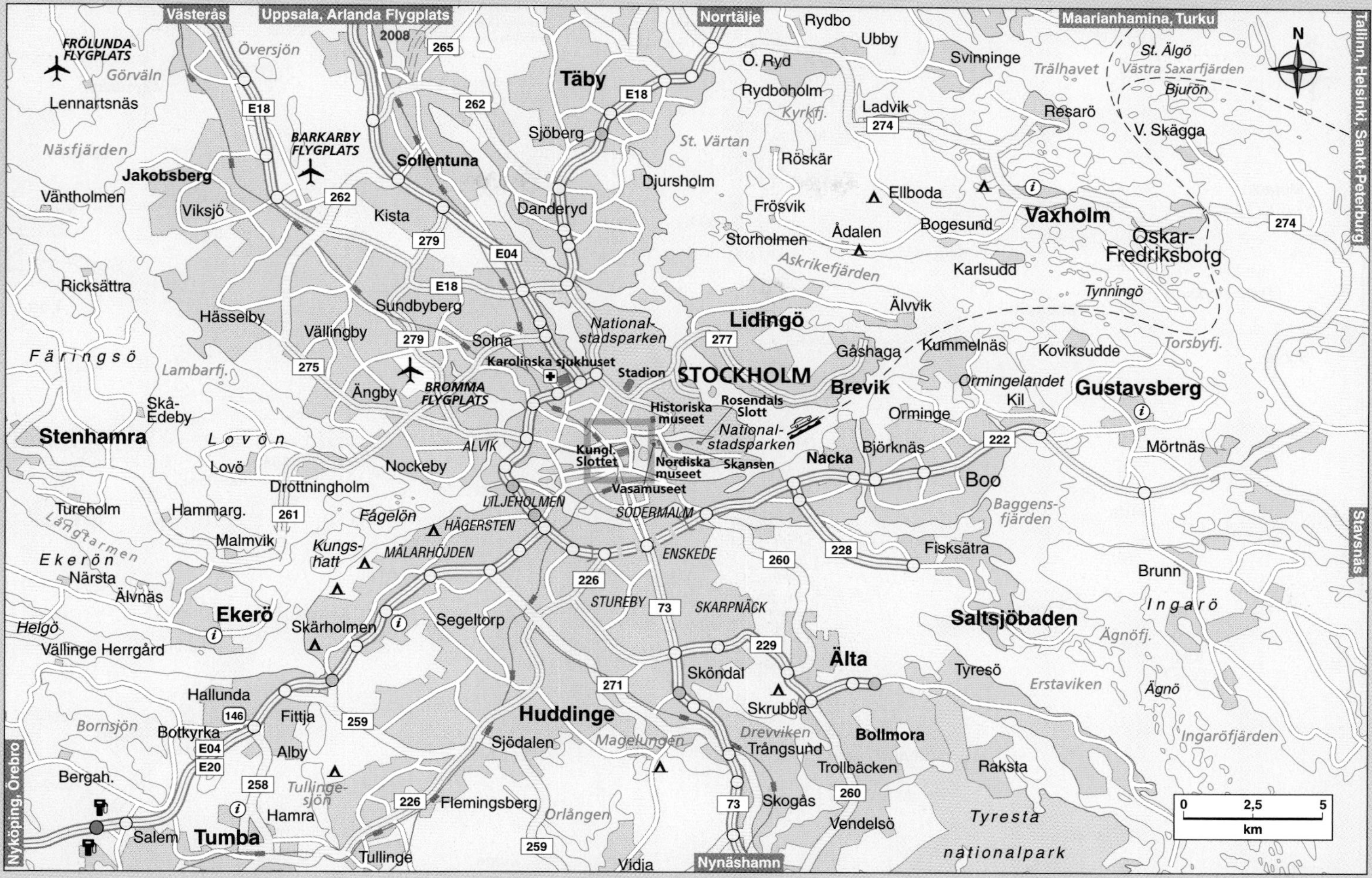
Västerås
Uppsala, Arlanda Flygplats
Norrtälje
Maarianhamina, Turku
Tallinn, Helsinki, Sankt-Peterburg
Stavsnäs
Nynäshamn
Nyköping, Örebro
FRÖLUNDA FLYGPLATS
Görväln
Lennartsnäs
Översjön
Näsfjärden
Jakobsberg
Vänthomen
Viksjö
BARKARBY FLYGPLATS
Sollentuna
Kista
Täby
Sjöberg
Danderyd
Djursholm
St. Värtan
Rydbo
Ubby
Ö. Ryd
Rydboholm
Kyrkfj.
Röskär
Frösvik
Storholmen
Ådalen
Ellboda
Ladvik
Svinninge
Trälhavet
Resarö
St. Älgö
Västra Saxarfjärden
Bjurön
V. Skägga
Vaxholm
Oskar-Fredriksborg
Bogesund
Karlsudd
Tynningö
Askrikefjärden
Älvvik
Ricksättra
Hässelby
Vällingby
Sundbyberg
Solna
Nationalstadsparken
Lidingö
Gåshaga
Kummelnäs
Koviksudde
Torsbyfj.
Färingsö
Lambarfj.
Karolinska sjukhuset
Stadion
STOCKHOLM
Brevik
Ormingelandet
Kil
Gustavsberg
Ängby
BROMMA FLYGPLATS
Skå-Edeby
Stenhamra
Lovön
Lovö
ALVIK
Historiska museet
Rosendals Slott
Nationalstadsparken
Kungl. Slottet
Nordiska museet
Skansen
Vasamuseet
Orminge
Nacka
Björknäs
Boo
Mörtnäs
Nockeby
Drottningholm
Tureholm
Hammarg.
Fågelön
LILJEHOLMEN
SÖDERMALM
Baggensfjärden
Långtarmen
Malmvik
Ekerön
Närsta
Älvnäs
Kungshatt
HÄGERSTEN
MÄLARHÖJDEN
ENSKEDE
Fisksätra
Brunn
Ekerö
Skärholmen
Segeltorp
STUREBY
SKARPNÄCK
Saltsjöbaden
Ingarö
Helgö
Vällinge Herrgård
Ängöfj.
Hallunda
Sköndal
Älta
Tyresö
Erstaviken
Ägnö
Huddinge
Skrubba
Fittja
Bornsjön
Botkyrka
Alby
Sjödalen
Magelungen
Drevviken
Trångsund
Bollmora
Ingaröfjärden
Bergah.
Tullingesjön
Trollbäcken
Raksta
Hamra
Flemingsberg
Skogås
Tyresta nationalpark
Salem
Tumba
Orlången
Vendelsö
Tullinge
Vidja
2008
E18
E04
E20
73
146
222
226
228
229
258
259
260
261
262
265
271
274
275
277
279
0 2,5 5 km

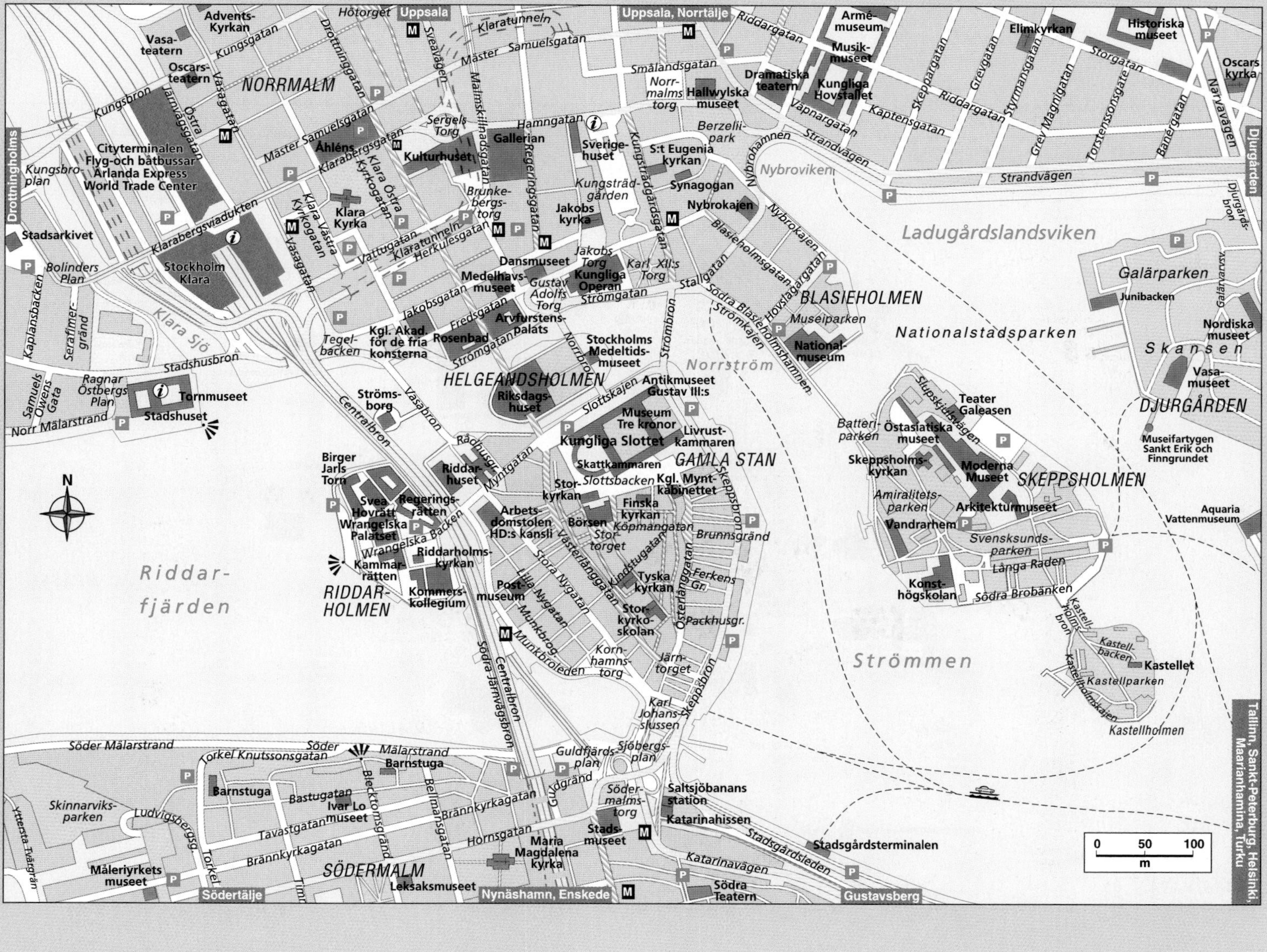
Hötorget
Uppsala
Uppsala, Norrtälje
Adventskyrkan
Vasateatern
Oscarsteatern
Kungsgatan
Drottninggatan
Sveavägen
Klaratunneln
Mäster Samuelsgatan
Riddargatan
Armémuseum
Musikmuseet
Historiska museet
Elimkyrkan
Storgatan
Oscars kyrka
NORRMALM
Östra Järnvägsgatan
Vasagatan
Smålandsgatan
Norrmalmstorg
Hallwylska museet
Dramatiska teatern
Kungliga Hovstallet
Skeppargatan
Grevgatan
Styrmansgatan
Narvavägen
Kaptensgatan
Grev Magnigatan
Torstenssonsgatan
Banérgatan
Kungsbron
Cityterminalen Flyg-och båtbussar Arlanda Express World Trade Center
Åhléns
Klarabergsgatan
Klara Östra Kyrkogatan
Kulturhuset
Sergels Torg
Hamngatan
Gallerian
Regeringsgatan
Malmskillnadsgatan
Sverigehuset
Kungsträdgårdsgatan
S:t Eugenia kyrkan
Berzelii park
Nybrohamnen
Strandvägen
Nybroviken
Djurgården
Djurgårdsbron
Kungsbroplan
Kungsträdgården
Synagogan
Nybrokajen
Drottningholms
Stadsarkivet
Klarabergsviadukten
Klara Västra Kyrkogatan
Klara Kyrka
Brunkebergstorg
Jakobs kyrka
Ladugårdslandsviken
Bolinders Plan
Stockholm Klara
Vattugatan
Klaratunneln
Herkulesgatan
Dansmuseet
Jakobs Torg
Karl XII:s Torg
Blasieholmsgatan
Galärparken
Junibacken
Kaplansbacken
Serafimergränd
Medelhavsmuseet
Gustav Adolfs Torg
Kungliga Operan
Strömgatan
Stallgatan
Södra Blasieholmshamnen
Hovslagargatan
BLASIEHOLMEN
Museiparken
Nationalstadsparken
Nordiska museet
Skansen
Klara Sjö
Tegelbacken
Jakobsgatan
Fredsgatan
Kgl. Akad. för de fria konsterna
Rosenbad
Arvfurstens palats
Norrbro
Stockholms Medeltidsmuseet
Strömbron
Nationalmuseum
Stadshusbron
Norrström
Vasamuseet
DJURGÅRDEN
Samuels Owens Gata
Ragnar Östbergs Plan
Tornmuseet
Stadshuset
Norr Mälarstrand
Strömsborg
Centralbron
Vasabron
HELGEANDSHOLMEN
Riksdagshuset
Antikmuseet Gustav III:s
Slottskajen
Museum Tre kronor
Livrustkammaren
Kungliga Slottet
GAMLA STAN
Batteriparken
Östasiatiska museet
Slupskjulsvägen
Teater Galeasen
Skeppsholmskyrkan
Moderna Museet
SKEPPSHOLMEN
Museifartygen Sankt Erik och Finngrundet
Birger Jarls Torn
Rådhusgr.
Myntgatan
Riddarhuset
Skattkammaren
Slottsbacken
Kgl. Myntkabinettet
Storkyrkan
Skeppsbron
Amiralitetsparken
Arkitekturmuseet
Aquaria Vattenmuseum
Svea Hovrätt
Regeringsrätten
Wrangelska Palatset
Arbetsdomstolen HD:s kansli
Finska kyrkan
Börsen
Köpmangatan
Stortorget
Brunnsgränd
Vandrarhem
Svensksundsparken
Wrangelska Backen
Riddarholmskyrkan
Västerlånggatan
Stora Nygatan
Kindstugatan
Ferkens Gr.
Långa Raden
Kammarrätten
Riddarfjärden
RIDDARHOLMEN
Kommerskollegium
Postmuseum
Lilla Nygatan
Tyska kyrkan
Österlånggatan
Konsthögskolan
Södra Brobänken
Kastellholmsbron
Storkyrkoskolan
Packhusgr.
Munkbrog.
Munkbroleden
Kornhamnstorg
Järntorget
Skeppsbron
Kastellbacken
Kastellet
Kastellparken
Kastellholmskajen
Strömmen
Södra Järnvägsbron
Centralbron
Karl Johansslussen
Kastellholmen
Söder Mälarstrand
Torkel Knutssonsgatan
Barnstuga
Guldfjärdsplan
Sjöbergsplan
Tallinn, Sankt-Peterburg, Helsinki, Maarianhamina, Turku
Skinnarviksparken
Barnstuga
Bastugatan
Ivar Lo museet
Blecktornsgränd
Bellmansgatan
Brännkyrkagatan
Gradgränd
Södermalmstorg
Saltsjöbanans station
Katarinahissen
Ludvigsbergsg.
Tavastgatan
Hornsgatan
Stadsmuseet
Stadsgårdsleden
Ytterste Tvärgränd
Torkel
Brännkyrkagatan
Maria Magdalena kyrka
Stadsgårdsterminalen
Katarinavägen
Målerlyrkets museet
SÖDERMALM
Leksaksmuseet
Timmermansgatan
Södra Teatern
Södertälje
Nynäshamn, Enskede
Gustavsberg
0 50 100 m

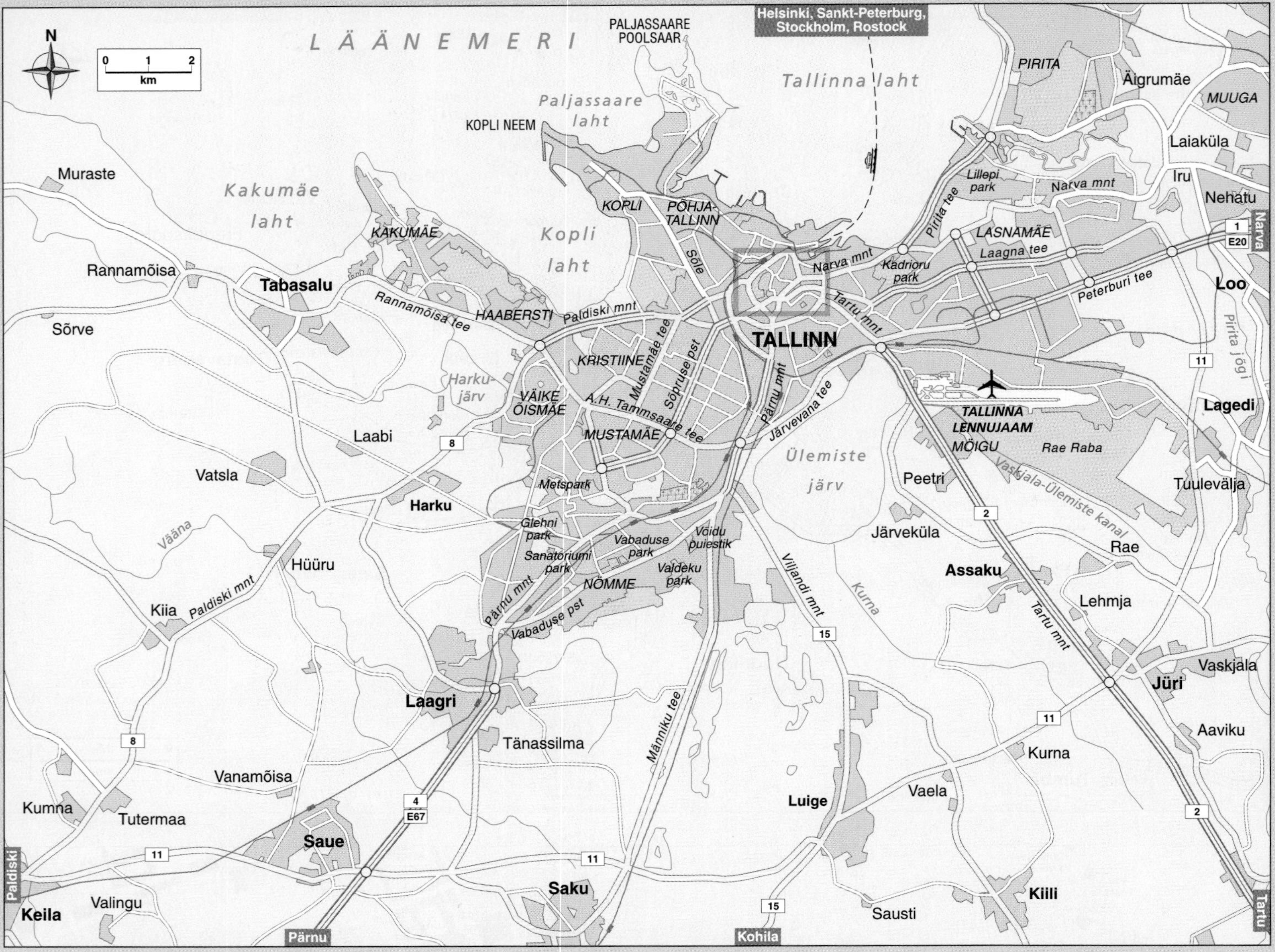
LÄÄNEMERI
Tallinna laht
Kopli laht
Kakumäe laht
Paljassaare laht
Helsinki, Sankt-Peterburg, Stockholm, Rostock
TALLINN
TALLINNA LENNUJAAM
Ülemiste järv
Tabasalu
Harku
Laagri
Saue
Saku
Keila
Jüri
Assaku
Loo
Lagedi
Kiili
Luige
Paldiski
Pärnu
Kohila
Tartu
Narva

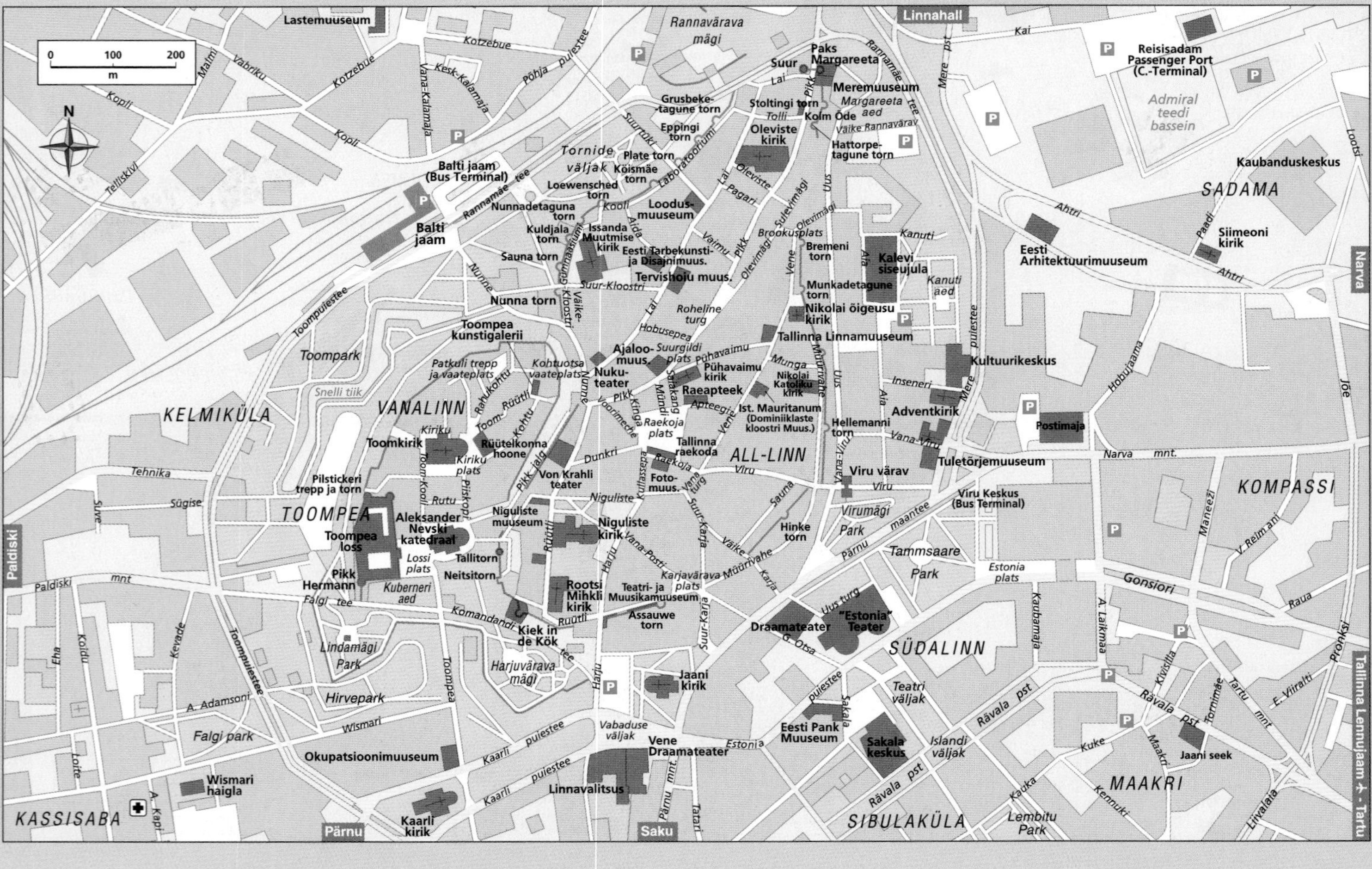
VANALINN
TOOMPEA
ALL-LINN
KELMIKÜLA
SADAMA
KOMPASSI
SÜDALINN
MAAKRI
SIBULAKÜLA
KASSISABA
Balti jaam (Bus Terminal)
Reisisadam Passenger Port (C.-Terminal)
Toompea loss
Aleksander Nevski katedraal
Toomkirik
Oleviste kirik
Niguliste kirik
Raeapteek
Viru värav
Viru Keskus (Bus Terminal)
"Estonia" Teater
Kiek in de Kök
Linnahall
Paldiski
Pärnu
Saku
Narva
Tallinna Lennujaam - Tartu

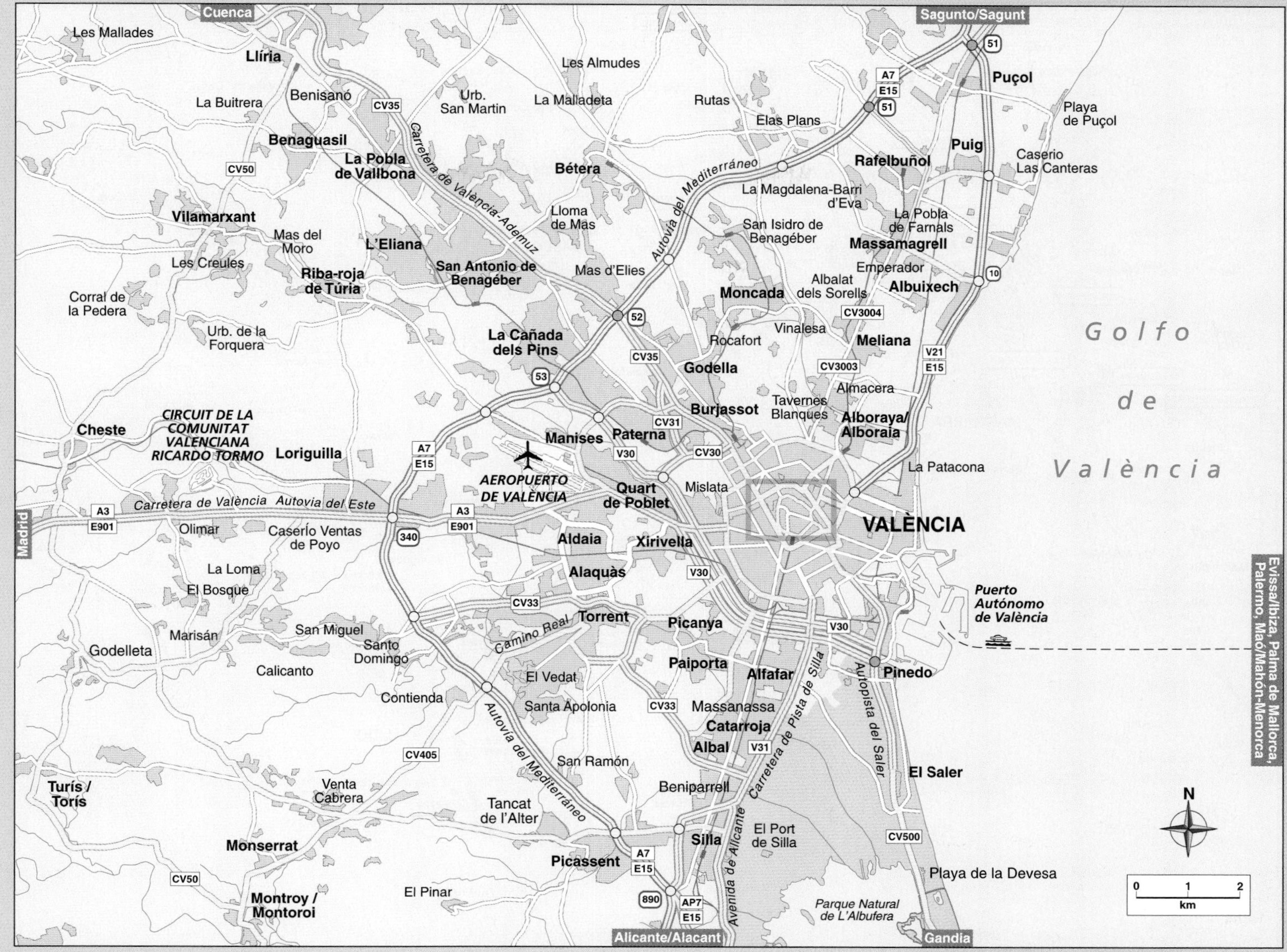
Cuenca
Sagunto/Sagunt
Les Mallades
Llíria
Les Almudes
Puçol
La Buitrera
Benisanó
Urb. San Martin
La Malladeta
Rutas
Playa de Puçol
Elas Plans
Benaguasil
La Pobla de Vallbona
Carretera de València-Ademuz
Bétera
Autovía del Mediterráneo
Rafelbuñol
Puig
Caserio Las Canteras
La Magdalena-Barri d'Eva
Vilamarxant
Mas del Moro
L'Eliana
Lloma de Mas
San Isidro de Benagéber
La Pobla de Farnals
Massamagrell
Les Creules
Riba-roja de Túria
San Antonio de Benagéber
Mas d'Elies
Emperador
Albuixech
Corral de la Pedera
Moncada
Albalat dels Sorells
Urb. de la Forquera
La Cañada dels Pins
Vinalesa
Rocafort
Meliana
Golfo de València
Godella
Almacera
Cheste
CIRCUIT DE LA COMUNITAT VALENCIANA RICARDO TORMO
Loriguilla
Manises
Paterna
Burjassot
Tavernes Blanques
Alboraya/ Alboraia
AEROPUERTO DE VALÈNCIA
Quart de Poblet
Mislata
La Patacona
Carretera de València
Autovia del Este
Madrid
Olimar
Caserío Ventas de Poyo
VALÈNCIA
Aldaia
Xirivella
La Loma
Alaquàs
El Bosque
Eivissa/Ibiza, Palma de Mallorca, Palermo, Maó/Mahón-Menorca
Puerto Autónomo de València
Marisán
San Miguel
Torrent
Picanya
Camino Real
Godelleta
Santo Domingo
Calicanto
El Vedat
Paiporta
Alfafar
Pinedo
Contienda
Santa Apolonia
Massanassa
Catarroja
Autopista del Saler
Carretera de Pista de Silla
Albal
San Ramón
Turís / Torís
Venta Cabrera
Beniparrell
El Saler
Tancat de l'Alter
Monserrat
El Port de Silla
Silla
Picassent
Avenida de Alicante
Playa de la Devesa
El Pinar
Montroy / Montoroi
Parque Natural de L'Albufera
Alicante/Alacant
Gandia
N
km

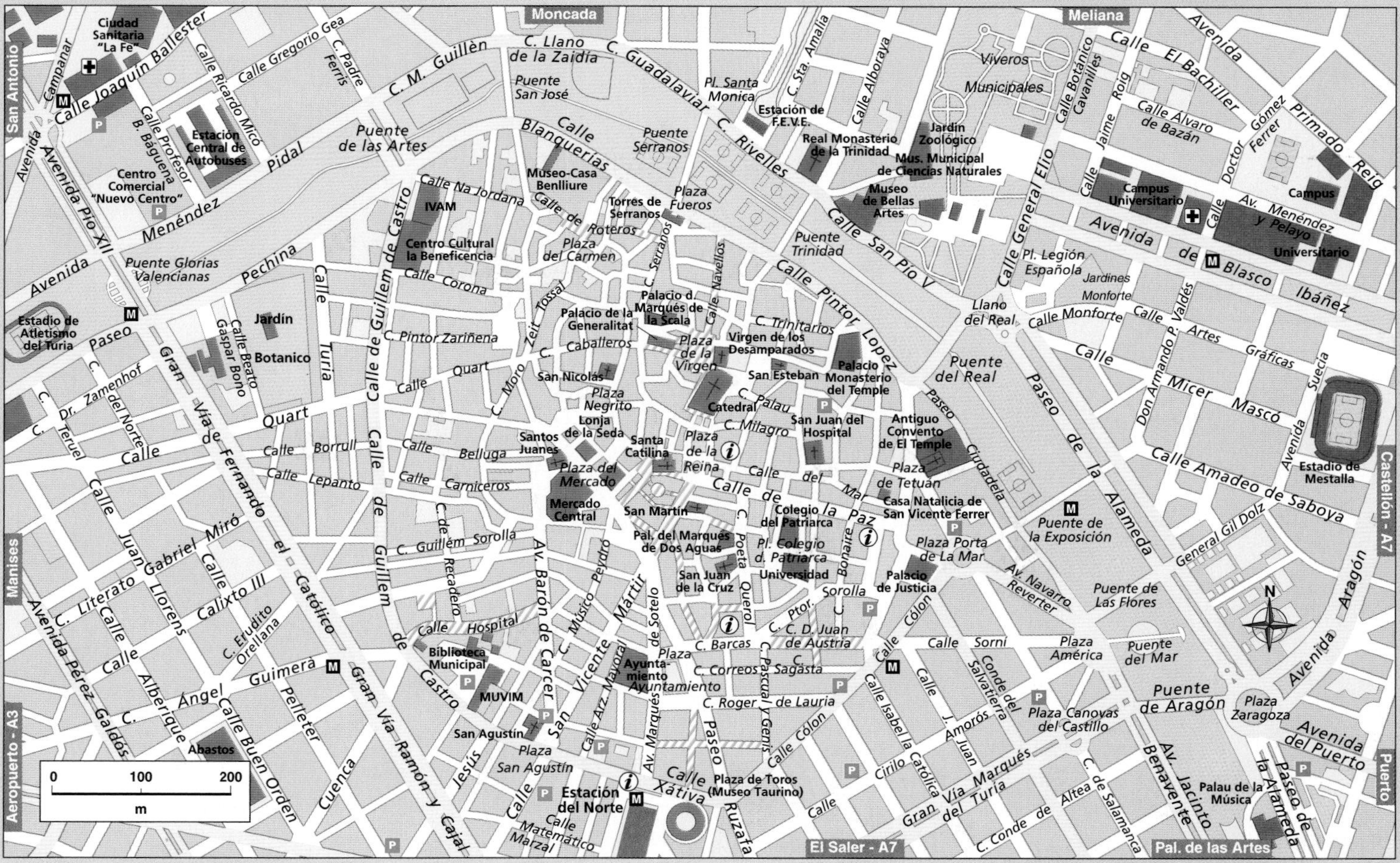
Moncada
Meliana
Ciudad Sanitaria "La Fe"
San Antonio
Calle Joaquín Ballester
Calle Gregorio Gea
C. Padre Ferris
C. M. Guillén
C. Llano de la Zaidia
C. Guadalaviar
Pl. Santa Mónica
C. Sta. Amalia
Calle Alboraya
Viveros Municipales
Calle El Bachiller
Avenida Primado Reig
Puente San José
Calle Ricardo Micó
Estación Central de Autobuses
Puente de las Artes
Calle Blanquerías
Puente Serranos
C. Rivelles
Estación de F.E.V.E.
Real Monasterio de la Trinidad
Jardín Zoológico
Mus. Municipal de Ciencias Naturales
Calle Álvaro de Bazán
Doctor Gómez Ferrer
Campus
Centro Comercial "Nuevo Centro"
Menéndez Pidal
Museo-Casa Benlliure
IVAM
Calle Na Jordana
Torres de Serranos
Plaza Fueros
Museo de Bellas Artes
Campus Universitario
Av. Menéndez y Pelayo
Universitario
Avenida Pío XII
Centro Cultural la Beneficencia
Plaza del Carmen
Puente Trinidad
Calle San Pío V
Pl. Legión Española
Avenida de Blasco Ibáñez
Puente Glorias Valencianas
Pechina
Calle Corona
Palacio d. Marqués de la Scala
Jardines Monforte
Calle Monforte
Estadio de Atletismo del Turia
Jardín Botanico
Calle Turia
Calle de Guillem de Castro
C. Pintor Zariñena
Palacio de la Generalitat
Caballeros
Plaza de la Virgen
Virgen de los Desamparados
Calle Pintor López
Llano del Real
Puente del Real
Artes Gráficas
Paseo
Calle Beato Gaspar Bono
Calle Quart
San Nicolás
San Esteban
Palacio Monasterio del Temple
Calle Micer Mascó
Gran Vía de Fernando el Católico
Plaza Negrito
Catedral
C. Milagro
San Juan del Hospital
Antiguo Convento de El Temple
Paseo de la Alameda
Lonja de la Seda
Santos Juanes
Santa Catalina
Plaza de la Reina
Calle Borrull
Calle Belluga
Plaza del Mercado
Calle de la Paz
Plaza de Tetuán
Ciudadela
Calle Amadeo de Saboya
Estadio de Mestalla
Calle Lepanto
Calle Carniceros
Mercado Central
San Martín
Colegio del Patriarca
Casa Natalicia de San Vicente Ferrer
Puente de la Exposición
General Gil Dolz
Castellón - A7
Calle Juan Llorens
Gabriel Miró
Calixto III
C. Guillem Sorolla
Pal. del Marqués de Dos Aguas
Pl. Colegio d. Patriarca
Plaza Porta de La Mar
Av. Navarro Reverter
Manises
Avenida Pérez Galdós
C. Literato
C. Erudito Orellana
Calle Hospital
San Juan de la Cruz
Universidad
Palacio de Justicia
Puente de Las Flores
Avenida Aragón
Calle Alberique
C. Ángel Guimerá
Biblioteca Municipal
Av. Barón de Cárcer
San Vicente Mártir
Plaza del Ayuntamiento
Ayuntamiento
C. Barcas
C. D. Juan de Austria
Calle Sorní
Conde de Salvatierra
Plaza América
Puente del Mar
MUVIM
C. Correos
Sagasta
C. Roger de Lauria
Plaza Canovas del Castillo
Puente de Aragón
Plaza Zaragoza
Avenida del Puerto
Aeropuerto - A3
Abastos
Calle Buen Orden
Pelleter
San Agustín
Plaza San Agustín
Gran Vía Ramón y Cajal
Calle Jesús
Estación del Norte
Calle Xàtiva
Plaza de Toros (Museo Taurino)
Calle Colón
Calle Isabel la Católica
Cirilo Amorós
Gran Vía Marqués del Turia
Av. Jacinto Benavente
Palau de la Música
Paseo de la Alameda
Puerto
Calle Matemático Marzal
Calle Ruzafa
El Saler - A7
C. Conde de Altea
C. de Salamanca
Pal. de las Artes
N
m

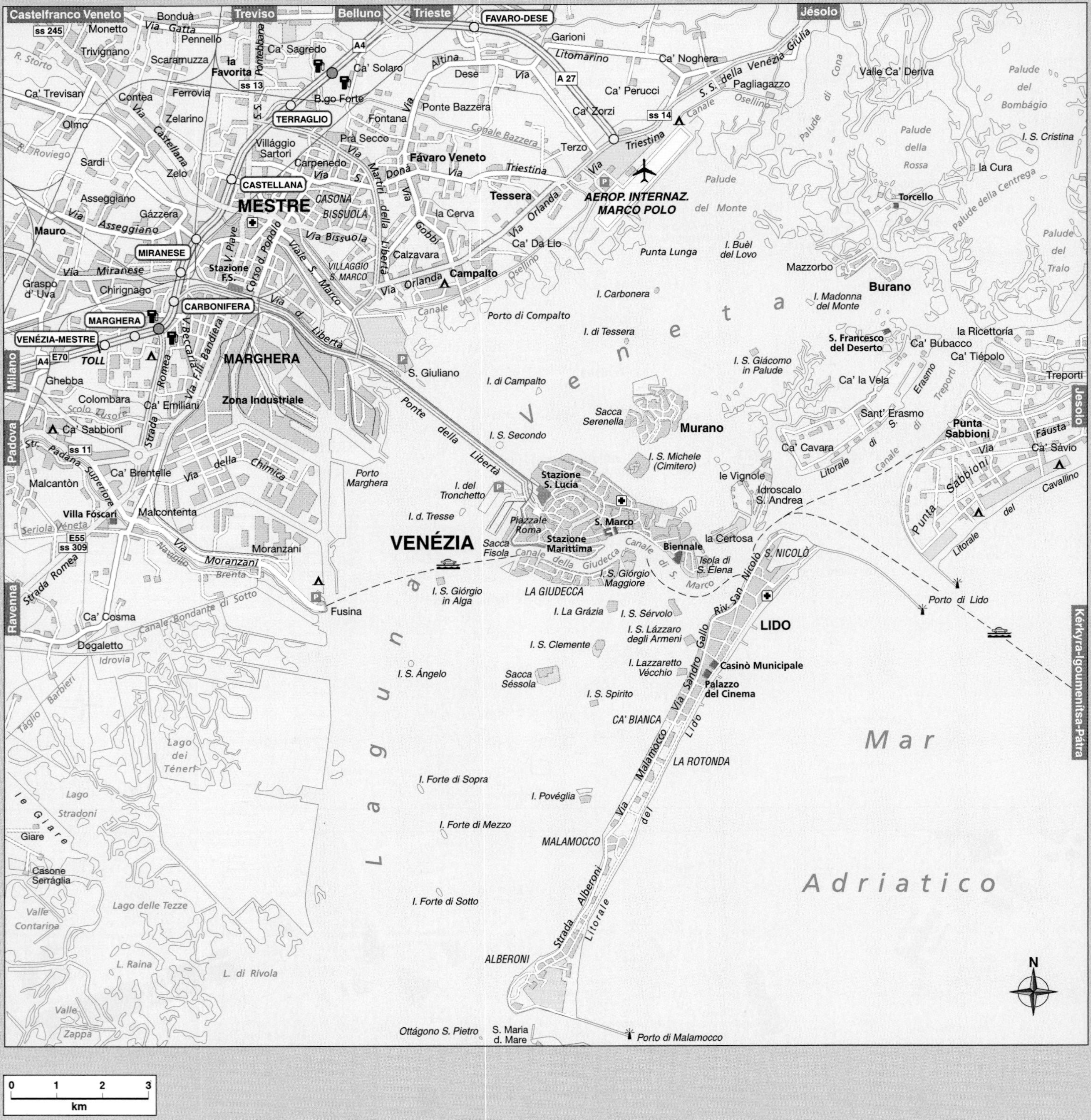
Castelfranco Veneto
Treviso
Belluno
Trieste
Jésolo
FAVARO-DESE
ss 245
Bonduà
Monetto
Via Gatta
Pennello
Garioni
Litomarino
Ca' Noghera
R. Storto
Trivignano
Scaramuzza
la Favorita
Ca' Sagredo
A4
Ca' Solaro
Altina
Dese
Via
A 27
S. S. della Venezia Giulia
Pagliagazzo
Valle Ca' Deriva
Palude del Bombágio
Ca' Trevisan
Contea
Ferrovia
ss 13
B.go Forte
Ca' Perucci
Osellino
Via Castellana
Zelarino
S. S. Pontebbana
TERRAGLIO
Fontana
Ponte Bazzera
Ca' Zorzi
ss 14
Canale
Olmo
Villággio Sartori
Prà Secco
Canale Bazzera
Terzo
Triestina
Palude della Rossa
I. S. Cristina
R. Roviego
Sardi
Carpenedo
Via S. Donà
Fávaro Veneto
Via Triestina
la Cura
Zelo
CASTELLANA
Via Martiri della Libertà
Via Orlanda
Palude
Asseggiano
CASONA
BISSUOLA
Tessera
AEROP. INTERNAZ. MARCO POLO
Torcello
Palude della Centrega
Gàzzera
MESTRE
la Cerva
del Monte
Via Asseggiano
Via Gobbi
Mauro
Via Bissuola
Ca' Da Lio
Palude del Tralo
MIRANESE
V. Piave
Corso d. Popolo
Viale S. Marco
Calzavara
Punta Lunga
I. Buèl del Lovo
Mazzorbo
Via Miranese
Stazione F.S.
VILLAGGIO S. MARCO
Campalto
Graspo d' Uva
Chirignago
Via Orlanda
Osellino
I. Carbonera
I. Madonna del Monte
Burano
CARBONIFERA
Via d. Libertà
Canale
MARGHERA
Porto di Compalto
V. Beccaria
Via F.lli Bandiera
I. di Tessera
S. Francesco del Deserto
la Ricettoria
VENÉZIA-MESTRE
Ca' Bubacco
Ca' Tiépolo
A4
E70
TOLL
MARGHERA
I. S. Giácomo in Palude
Ghebba
S. Giuliano
I. di Campalto
Ca' la Vela
Erasmo
Treporti
Milano
Strada Romea
Colombara
Ca' Emiliani
Zona Industriale
Scolo Lusore
Sacca Serenella
Sant' Erasmo
Jesolo
Ca' Sabbioni
Murano
Punta Sabbioni
Fáusta
Padova
Str. Padana Superiore
ss 11
Ponte della Libertà
I. S. Secondo
Ca' Cavara
Via
Ca' Sàvio
Ca' Brentelle
Via della Chimica
I. S. Michele (Cimitero)
le Vignole
Litorale di S. Erasmo
Canale di Treporti
Malcantòn
Porto Marghera
Stazione S. Lucia
I. del Tronchetto
Idroscalo S. Andrea
Punta Sabbioni
Cavallino
Villa Fòscari
Malcontenta
I. d. Tresse
S. Marco
Litorale del
Seriola Véneta
Piazzale Roma
E55
ss 309
Via Moranzani
Naviglio Brenta
Moranzani
VENÉZIA
Sacca Fisola
Stazione Marittima
Canale della Giudecca
Biennale
la Certosa
S. NICOLÒ
Canale di S. Marco
Isola di S. Elena
I. S. Giórgio Maggiore
Strada Romea
Ravenna
I. S. Giórgio in Alga
LA GIUDECCA
Porto di Lido
Fusina
Riv. San Nicolò
Ca' Cosma
Canale Bondante di Sotto
I. La Grázia
I. S. Sérvolo
LIDO
Kérkyra-Igoumenitsa-Pátra
I. S. Lázzaro degli Armeni
Dogaletto
I. S. Clemente
Idrovia
I. Lazzaretto Vécchio
Casinò Municipale
I. S. Ángelo
Sacca Séssola
Palazzo del Cinema
Taglio Barbieri
I. S. Spirito
Via Sandro Gallo
CA' BIANCA
Laguna Veneta
Lago dei Téneri
Mar Adriatico
Via Malamocco
Lido
LA ROTONDA
I. Forte di Sopra
Lago Stradoni
I. Povéglia
le Giare
Giare
I. Forte di Mezzo
Via del
MALAMOCCO
Casone Serráglia
Valle Contarina
Lago delle Tezze
I. Forte di Sotto
Strada Alberoni
Litorale
ALBERONI
L. Raina
L. di Rivola
N
Valle
Zappa
Ottágono S. Pietro
S. Maria d. Mare
Porto di Malamocco
0
1
2
3
km

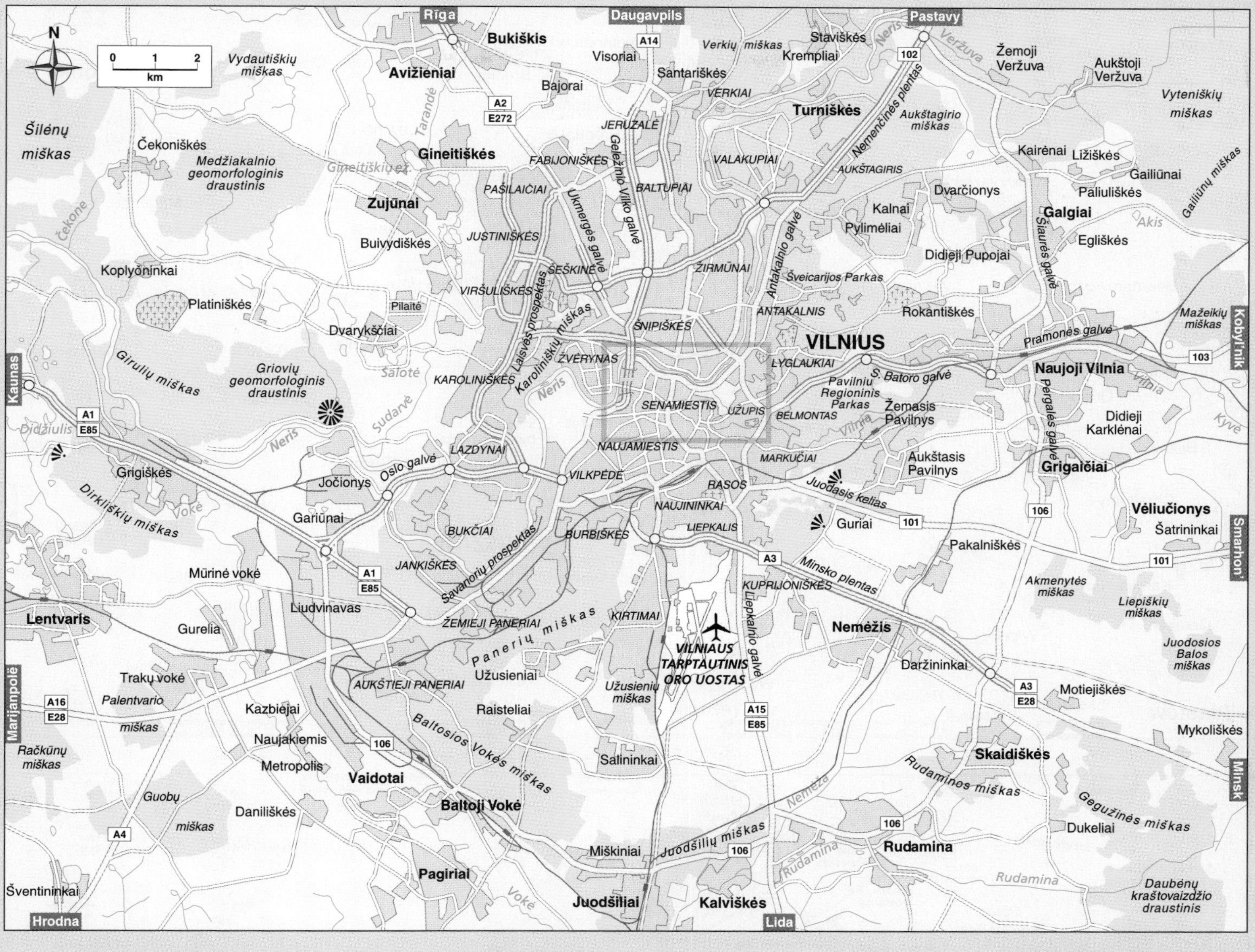
Rīga
Daugavpils
Pastavy
Kaunas
Kobyl'nik
Smarhon'
Minsk
Marijanpolė
Hrodna
Lida
N
0 1 2
km
VILNIUS
Bukiškis
Avižieniai
Visoriai
Bajorai
Santariškės
VERKIAI
Verkių miškas
Staviškės
Kremliai
Žemoji Veržuva
Aukštoji Veržuva
Vyteniškių miškas
Vydautiškių miškas
Šilėnų miškas
Čekoniškės
Medžiakalnio geomorfologinis draustinis
Gineitiškės
Gineitiškių ež.
JERUZALĖ
FABIJONIŠKĖS
PAŠILAIČIAI
BALTUPIAI
VALAKUPIAI
Turniškės
Aukštagirio miškas
AUKŠTAGIRIS
Kairėnai
Ližiškės
Gailiūnai
Paliuliškės
Gailiūnų miškas
Zujūnai
Buivydiškės
JUSTINIŠKĖS
ŠEŠKINĖ
VIRŠULIŠKĖS
ŽIRMŪNAI
Kalnai
Pylimėliai
Dvarčionys
Galgiai
Egliškės
Didieji Pupojai
Koplyčininkai
Platiniškės
Pilaitė
Dvarykščiai
ŠNIPIŠKĖS
ANTAKALNIS
Šveicarijos Parkas
Rokantiškės
Mažeikių miškas
Girulių miškas
Griovių geomorfologinis draustinis
Salotė
KAROLINIŠKĖS
ŽVĖRYNAS
LYGLAUKIAI
Pramonės galvė
Naujoji Vilnia
S. Batoro galvė
Pavilniu Regioninis Parkas
Žemasis Pavilnys
Didieji Karklėnai
SENAMIESTIS
UŽUPIS
BELMONTAS
Didžiulis
Neris
Sudarvė
LAZDYNAI
NAUJAMIESTIS
MARKUČIAI
Aukštasis Pavilnys
Grigaičiai
Grigiškės
Oslo galvė
Jočionys
VILKPĖDĖ
RASOS
Juodasis kelias
Dirkliškių miškas
Gariūnai
NAUJININKAI
BUKČIAI
BURBIŠKĖS
LIEPKALIS
Guriai
Vėliučionys
Šatrininkai
Pakalniškės
JANKIŠKĖS
Savanorių prospektas
Minsko plentas
KUPRIJONIŠKĖS
Akmenytės miškas
Liepiškių miškas
Mūrinė vokė
Liudvinavas
Lentvaris
Gurelia
ŽEMIEJI PANERIAI
Panerių miškas
KIRTIMAI
VILNIAUS TARPTAUTINIS ORO UOSTAS
Liepkalnio galvė
Nemėžis
Juodosios Balos miškas
Trakų vokė
Palentvario miškas
AUKŠTIEJI PANERIAI
Užusieniai
Užusienių miškas
Daržininkai
Motiejiškės
Kazbiejai
Raisteliai
Mykoliškės
Račkūnų miškas
Naujakiemis
Metropolis
Baltosios Vokės miškas
Salininkai
Skaidiškės
Vaidotai
Rudaminos miškas
Guobų miškas
Daniliškės
Baltoji Vokė
Gegužinės miškas
Dukeliai
Miškiniai
Juodšilių miškas
Rudamina
Šventininkai
Pagiriai
Juodšiliai
Kalviškės
Daubėnų kraštovaizdžio draustinis
A1
E85
A2
E272
A3
E28
A4
A14
A15
A16
101
102
103
106

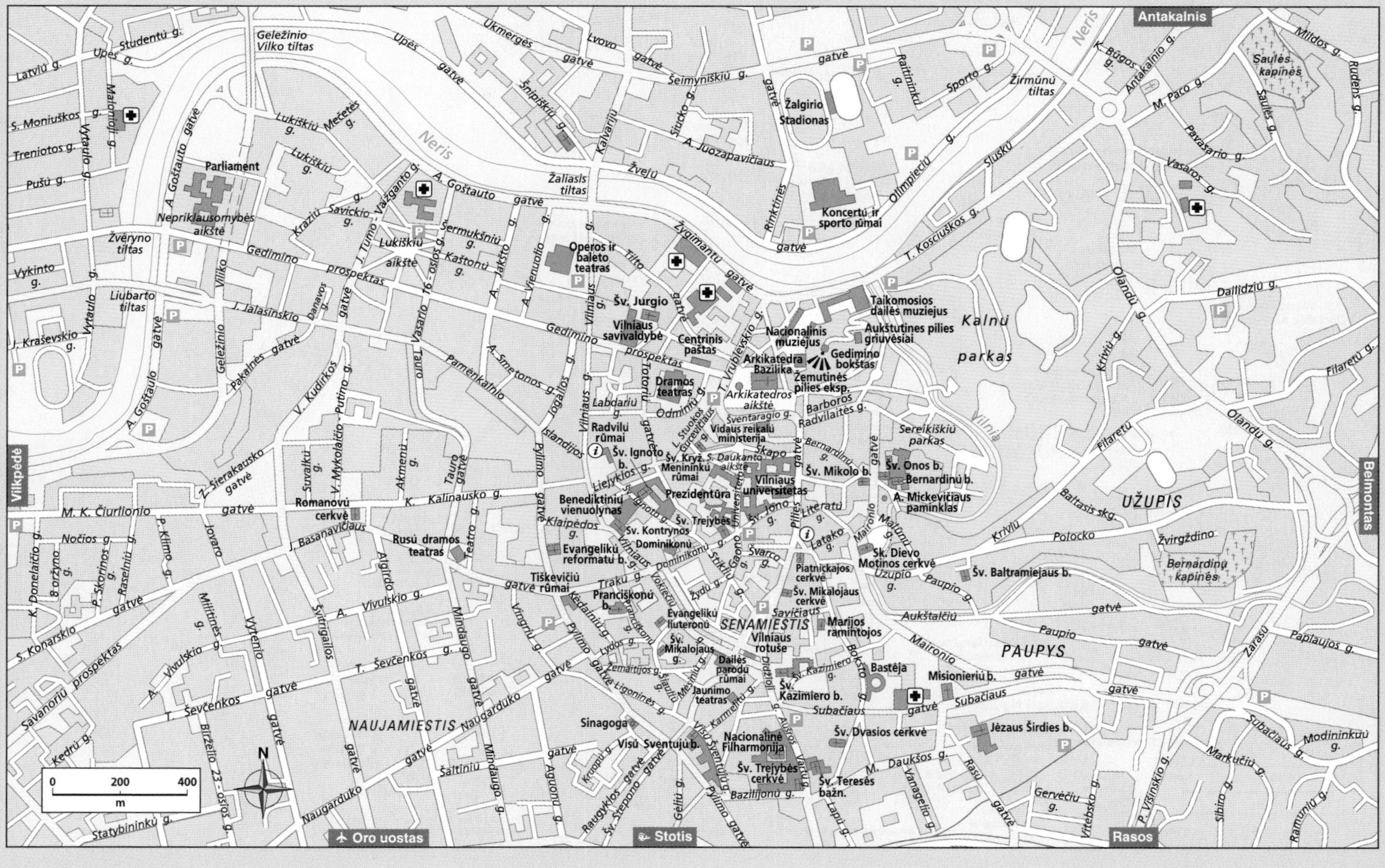
Antakalnis
Vilkpėdė
Belmontas
Oro uostas
Stotis
Rasos
N
0 200 400
m
Geležinio Vilko tiltas
Studentų g.
Latvių g.
Upės g.
Ukmergės gatvė
Lvovo gatvė
Šeimyniškių g.
Žalgirio Stadionas
Rinktinės g.
Sporto g.
Žirmūnų tiltas
Mildos g.
Saulės kapinės
S. Moniuškos g.
Treniotos g.
Pušų g.
Vytauto g.
Lukiškių g.
Mečetės g.
Neris
Kalvarijų g.
Šnipiškių g.
A. Juozapavičiaus g.
Olimpiečių g.
Slucko g.
Antakalnio g.
M. Paco g.
Saulės g.
Pavasario g.
Vasaros g.
Parliament
A. Goštauto gatvė
Nepriklausomybės aikštė
Žvėryno tiltas
Gedimino prospektas
Žaliasis tiltas
Žvejų g.
Koncertų ir sporto rūmai
T. Kosciuškos g.
Vykinto g.
Liubarto tiltas
Operos ir baleto teatras
Lukiškių aikštė
Šermukšnių g.
Kaštonų g.
Vienuolio g.
Jakšto g.
Žygimanto g.
Šv. Jurgio
Vilniaus savivaldybė
Centrinis paštas
Nacionalinis muziejus
Taikomosios dailės muziejus
Aukštutinės pilies griuvėsiai
Gedimino bokštas
Arkikatedra Bazilika
Žemutinės pilies eksp.
Kalnų parkas
Dailidžių g.
J. Jasinskio g.
J. Kraševskio g.
Pakalnės gatvė
A. Goštauto g.
Vasario 16-osios g.
Tauro g.
Pamėnkalnio g.
A. Smetonos g.
Jogailos g.
Dramos teatras
Labdarių g.
Arkikatedros aikštė
Barboros Radvilaitės g.
Odminių g.
Vidaus reikalų ministerija
Šventaragio g.
Radvilų rūmai
Šv. Ignoto b.
Šv. Kryž. b.
Mokslų Menininkų rūmai
Šv. Mykolo b.
Šv. Onos b.
Bernardinų b.
Serelkiškių parkas
Vilnia
Filaretų g.
Olandų g.
Z. Sierakausko gatvė
V. Kudirkos g.
V. Mykolaičio-Putino g.
Akmenų g.
M. K. Čiurlionio gatvė
K. Kalinausko g.
Romanovų cerkvė
Benediktinių vienuolynas
Prezidentūra
Vilniaus universitetas
Šv. Jonų b.
A. Mickevičiaus paminklas
UŽUPIS
Baltasis skg.
Krivių g.
Polocko g.
Žvirgždino g.
Bernardinų kapinės
K. Donelaičio g.
Naugarduko g.
J. Basanavičiaus g.
Rusų dramos teatras
Šv. Kontrynos
Dominikonų b.
Šv. Trejybės
Literatų
Maironio g.
Latako g.
Sk. Dievo Motinos cerkvė
Užupio g.
Šv. Baltramiejaus b.
Paupio g.
Tiškevičių rūmai
Evangelikų reformatų b.
Pranciškonų b.
Traku g.
Vokiečių g.
Piatnickajos cerkvė
Šv. Mikalojaus cerkvė
Aukštaičių gatvė
Vivulskio g.
Šv. Savičiaus
Marijos ramintojos
Evangelikų liuteronų
SENAMIESTIS
Vilniaus rotušė
PAUPYS
Paupio g.
Paplaujos g.
Zarasų g.
Savanorių prospektas
Vytenio gatvė
T. Ševčenkos gatvė
Šv. Mikalojaus
Dailės parodų rūmai
Šv. Kazimiero b.
Bastėja
Misionierių b.
Subačiaus gatvė
Jaunimo teatras
Naugarduko gatvė
NAUJAMIESTIS
Sinagoga
Visų Šventųjų b.
Nacionalinė Filharmonija
Šv. Dvasios cerkvė
Jėzaus Širdies b.
Mindaugo g.
Šaltinių g.
Šv. Trejybės cerkvė
Šv. Teresės bažn.
M. Daukšos g.
Modinlinkų g.
Markučių g.
Vingrių g.
Pylimo gatvė
Kedrų g.
Birželio 23-iosios g.
Statybininkų g.
Bazilijonų g.
Gėlių g.
Visų Šventųjų g.
Aguonų g.
Rūdninkų g.
Sodų g.
Vilniaus g.
Vilniaus g.
Rasų g.
Vitebsko g.
Gervėčių g.
P. Višinskio g.
Sibiro g.
Ramunių g.
Subačiaus g.

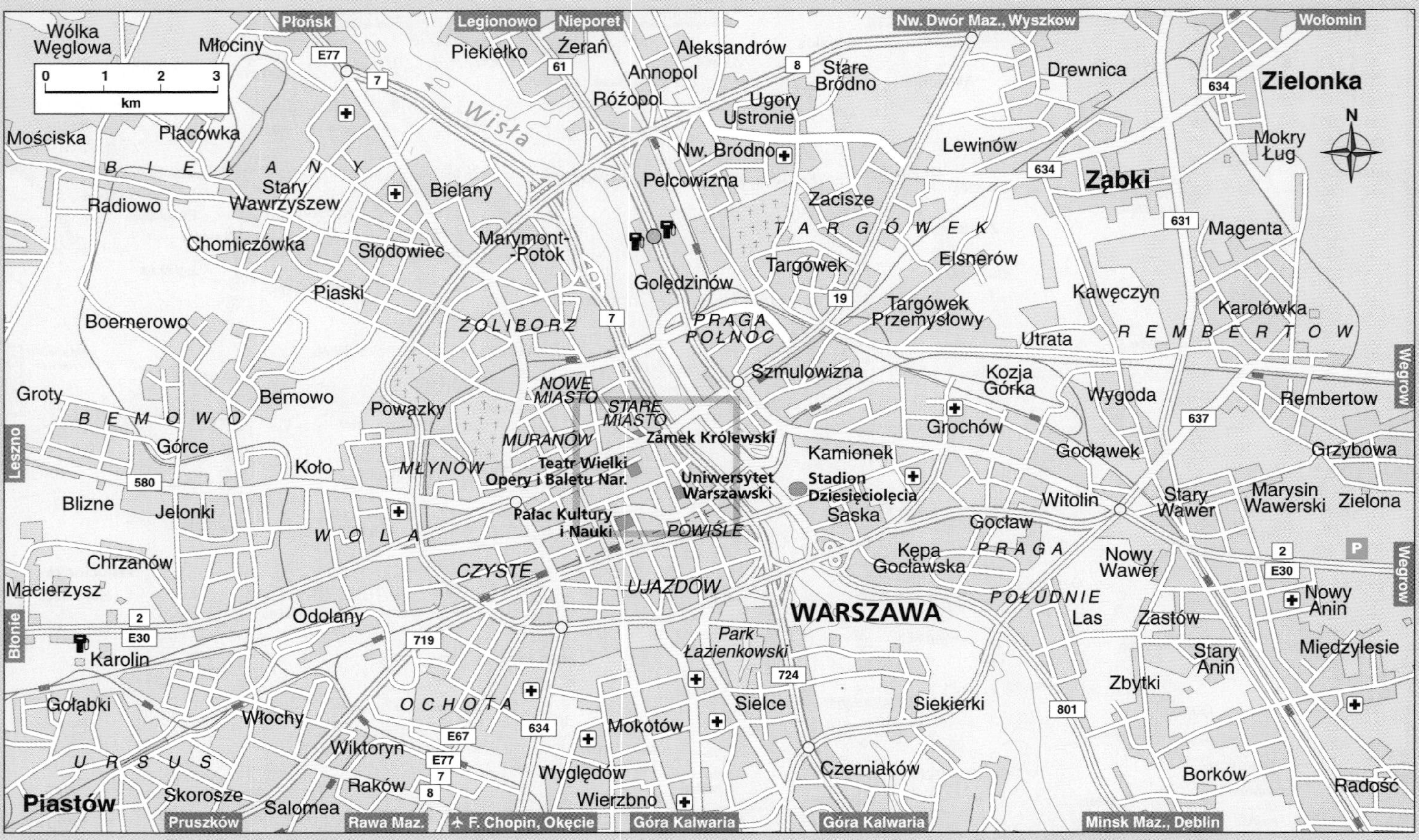

Płońsk
Legionowo
Nieporet
Nw. Dwór Maz., Wyszkow
Wołomin
Wólka Węglowa
Młociny
Piekiełko
Żerań
Aleksandrów
Annopol
Stare Bródno
Drewnica
Zielonka
km
Różopol
Ugory
Ustronie
Wisła
Mościska
Placówka
Nw. Bródno
Lewinów
Mokry Ług
BIELANY
Stary Wawrzyszew
Bielany
Pelcowizna
Zacisze
Ząbki
Radiowo
TARGÓWEK
Magenta
Chomiczówka
Słodowiec
Marymont-Potok
Elsnerów
Targówek
Piaski
Golędzinów
Kawęczyn
Boernerowo
ŻOLIBORZ
PRAGA POŁNOC
Targówek Przemysłowy
Karolówka
Utrata
REMBERTOW
Szmulowizna
Wegrow
Groty
Bemowo
NOWE MIASTO
Powązki
Kozja Górka
Wygoda
Rembertow
BEMOWO
STARE MIASTO
Grochów
Górce
MURANÓW
Zamek Królewski
Kamionek
Gocławek
Grzybowa
Leszno
Koło
MŁYNÓW
Teatr Wielki Opery i Baletu Nar.
Uniwersytet Warszawski
Stadion Dziesięciolecia
Blizne
Jelonki
Pałac Kultury i Nauki
Saska
Witolin
Stary Wawer
Marysin Wawerski
Zielona
WOLA
POWIŚLE
Gocław
Chrzanów
CZYSTE
Kępa Gocławska
PRAGA
Nowy Wawer
Macierzysz
UJAZDÓW
POŁUDNIE
Nowy Anin
Odolany
WARSZAWA
Las
Zastów
Błonie
Karolin
Park Łazienkowski
Stary Anin
Międzylesie
Gołąbki
OCHOTA
Sielce
Siekierki
Zbytki
Włochy
Mokotów
Wiktoryn
URSUS
Czerniaków
Borków
Radość
Raków
Wygledów
Piastów
Skorosze
Salomea
Wierzbno
Pruszków
Rawa Maz.
F. Chopin, Okęcie
Góra Kalwaria
Góra Kalwaria
Minsk Maz., Deblin
E77
E30
E67
580
719
634
724
801
637
631

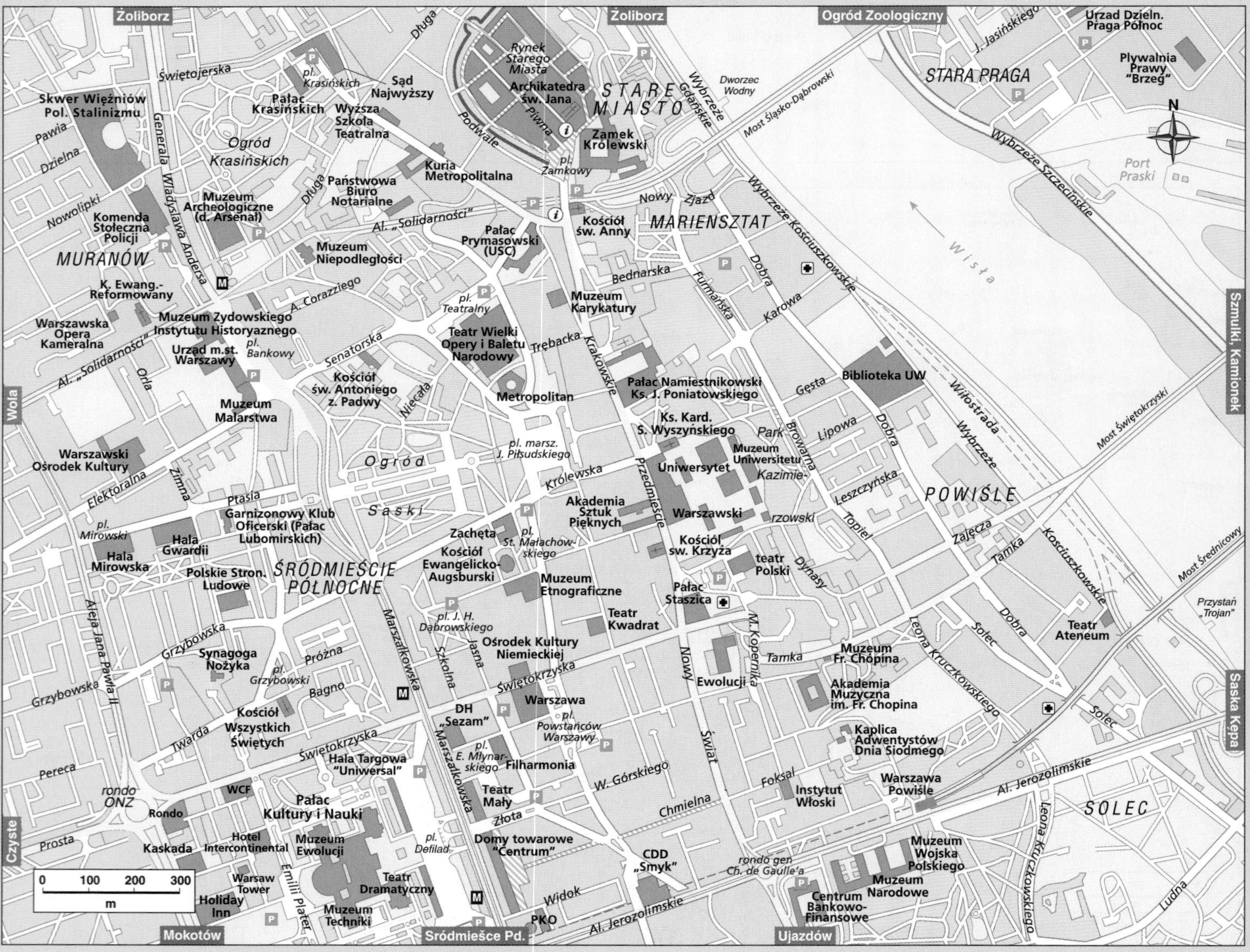

Żoliborz
Żoliborz
Ogród Zoologiczny
Urzad Dzieln. Praga Północ
Długa
Rynek Starego Miasta
Świętojerska
pl. Krasińskich
Sąd Najwyższy
Archikatedra św. Jana
STARE MIASTO
Dworzec Wodny
Wybrzeże Gdańskie
Most Śląsko-Dąbrowski
STARA PRAGA
Plywalnia Prawy "Brzeg"
Skwer Więźniów Pol. Stalinizmu
Pałac Krasińskich
Wyższa Szkoła Teatralna
Piwna
Zamek Królewski
Pawia
Ogród Krasińskich
Podwale
pl. Zamkowy
Port Praski
Dzielna
Kuria Metropolitalna
Wybrzeże Szczecińskie
Państwowa Biuro Notarialne
Nowy Zjazd
Muzeum Archeologiczne (d. Arsenał)
Nowolipki
Komenda Stołeczna Policji
Al. „Solidarności"
Pałac Prymasowski (USC)
Kościół św. Anny
MARIENSZTAT
Wisła
Muzeum Niepodległości
MURANÓW
Bednarska
K. Ewang.-Reformowany
A. Corazziego
Muzeum Karykatury
Dobra
Furmańska
Muzeum Żydowskiego Instytutu Historyaznego
pl. Teatralny
Karowa
Warszawska Opera Kameralna
Szmulki, Kamionek
Urzad m.st. Warszawy
pl. Bankowy
Teatr Wielki Opery i Baletu Narodowy
Trębacka
Senatorska
Al. „Solidarności"
Orla
Kościół św. Antoniego z. Padwy
Krakowskie
Pałac Namiestnikowski Ks. J. Poniatowskiego
Biblioteka UW
Gęsta
Wola
Muzeum Malarstwa
Niecała
Metropolitan
Ks. Kard. S. Wyszyńskiego
Wisłostrada
Lipowa
Most Świętokrzyski
pl. marsz. J. Piłsudskiego
Park
Muzeum Uniwersytetu
Browarna
Warszawski Ośrodek Kultury
Ogród
Uniwersytet
Kazimie-
Elektoralna
Królewska
Leszczyńska
POWIŚLE
Zimna
Ptasia
Akademia Sztuk Pięknych
Saski
Garnizonowy Klub Oficerski (Pałac Lubomirskich)
Warszawski
pl. Mirowski
Zachęta
pl. St. Małachowskiego
Kościół św. Krzyża
Tamka
Hala Gwardii
Hala Mirowska
Kościół Ewangelicko-Augsburski
teatr Polski
Dynasy
ŚRÓDMIEŚCIE PÓŁNOCNE
Polskie Stron. Ludowe
Muzeum Etnograficzne
Pałac Staszica
Most Średnicowy
Aleja Jana Pawła II
pl. J. H. Dąbrowskiego
Teatr Kwadrat
Przystań "Trojan"
Marszałkowska
Szkolna
Jasna
Ośrodek Kultury Niemieckiej
Nowy Świat
M. Kopernika
Solec
Teatr Ateneum
Grzybowska
Synagoga Nożyka
Próżna
Tamka
Muzeum Fr. Chopina
Leona Kruczkowskiego
pl. Grzybowski
Świętokrzyska
Ewolucji
Akademia Muzyczna im. Fr. Chopina
Grzybowska
Bagno
Warszawa
Kościół Wszystkich Świętych
DH "Sezam"
pl. Powstańców Warszawy
Saska Kępa
Twarda
Kaplica Adwentystów Dnia Siodmego
Świętokrzyska
Hala Targowa "Uniwersal"
pl. E. Młynarskiego
Filharmonia
Foksal
Pereca
rondo ONZ
WCF
Instytut Włoski
Warszawa Powiśle
Al. Jerozolimskie
Pałac Kultury i Nauki
Teatr Mały
W. Górskiego
Chmielna
SOLEC
Czyste
Rondo
Złota
Prosta
Hotel Intercontinental
Muzeum Ewolucji
pl. Defilad
Domy towarowe "Centrum"
Muzeum Wojska Polskiego
Kaskada
CDD „Smyk"
rondo gen Ch. de Gaulle'a
Teatr Dramatyczny
Muzeum Narodowe
Ludna
Warsaw Tower
Emilii Plater
Holiday Inn
Muzeum Techniki
Widok
Centrum Bankowo-Finansowe
Al. Jerozolimskie
PKO
m
Mokotów
Śródmieście Pd.
Ujazdów

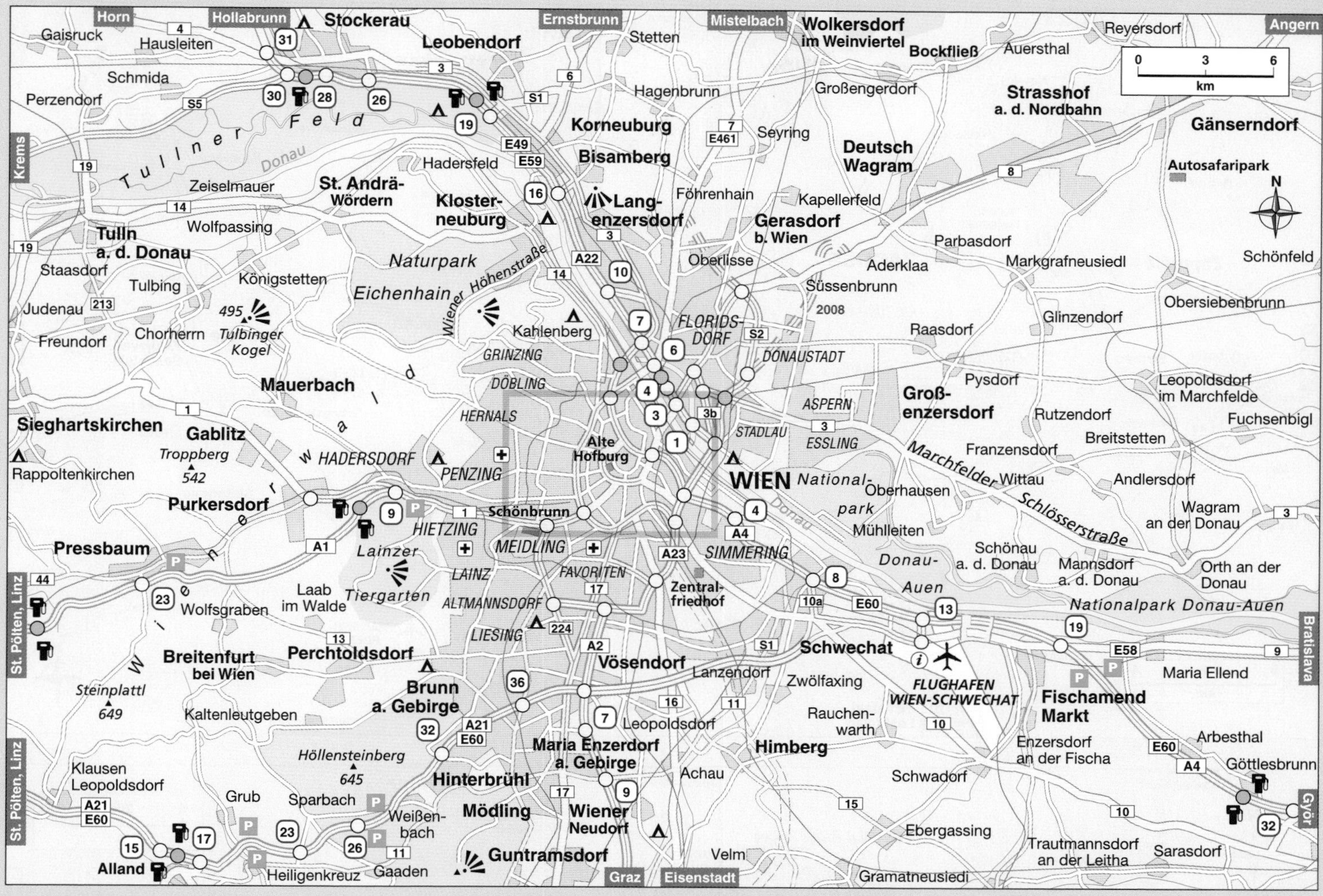

Horn
Hollabrunn
Stockerau
Ernstbrunn
Mistelbach
Wolkersdorf im Weinviertel
Angern
Gaisruck
Hausleiten
Leobendorf
Stetten
Bockfließ
Auersthal
Reyersdorf
Schmida
Perzendorf
Hagenbrunn
Großengerdorf
Strasshof a. d. Nordbahn
Tullner Feld
Donau
Korneuburg
Seyring
Deutsch Wagram
Gänserndorf
Krems
Hadersfeld
Bisamberg
Autosafaripark
Zeiselmauer
St. Andrä-Wördern
Kloster-neuburg
Lang-enzersdorf
Föhrenhain
Kapellerfeld
Gerasdorf b. Wien
Tulln a. d. Donau
Wolfpassing
Parbasdorf
Staasdorf
Naturpark
Oberlisse
Aderklaa
Markgrafneusiedl
Schönfeld
Königstetten
Eichenhain
Wiener Höhenstraße
Tulbing
Süssenbrunn
2008
Judenau
495
Tulbinger Kogel
Kahlenberg
Floridsdorf
Raasdorf
Glinzendorf
Obersiebenbrunn
Freundorf
Chorherrn
Grinzing
Donaustadt
Döbling
Pysdorf
Leopoldsdorf im Marchfelde
Mauerbach
Groß-enzersdorf
Hernals
Aspern
Rutzendorf
Fuchsenbigl
Sieghartskirchen
Gablitz
Essling
Stadlau
Breitstetten
Troppberg 542
Hadersdorf
Penzing
Alte Hofburg
Franzensdorf
Rappoltenkirchen
WIEN
National-park
Oberhausen
Wittau
Andlersdorf
Purkersdorf
Marchfelder Schlösserstraße
Wagram an der Donau
Mühlleiten
Schönbrunn
Hietzing
Meidling
Pressbaum
Lainzer Tiergarten
Lainz
Favoriten
Simmering
Schönau a. d. Donau
Mannsdorf a. d. Donau
Orth an der Donau
Donau-Auen
Laab im Walde
Wolfsgraben
Altmannsdorf
Zentral-friedhof
Nationalpark Donau-Auen
Liesing
Bratislava
Wienerwald
Perchtoldsdorf
Schwechat
Breitenfurt bei Wien
Vösendorf
Lanzendorf
Flughafen Wien-Schwechat
Zwölfaxing
Maria Ellend
Steinplattl 649
Brunn a. Gebirge
Fischamend Markt
Kaltenleutgeben
Leopoldsdorf
Rauchen-warth
St. Pölten, Linz
Arbesthal
Klausen Leopoldsdorf
Höllensteinberg 645
Maria Enzerdorf a. Gebirge
Himberg
Enzersdorf an der Fischa
Göttlesbrunn
Hinterbrühl
Achau
Grub
Sparbach
Schwadorf
Győr
Mödling
Weißen-bach
Wiener Neudorf
Ebergassing
Alland
Trautmannsdorf an der Leitha
Sarasdorf
Guntramsdorf
Heiligenkreuz
Gaaden
Velm
Graz
Eisenstadt
Gramatneusiedl
km
0 3 6

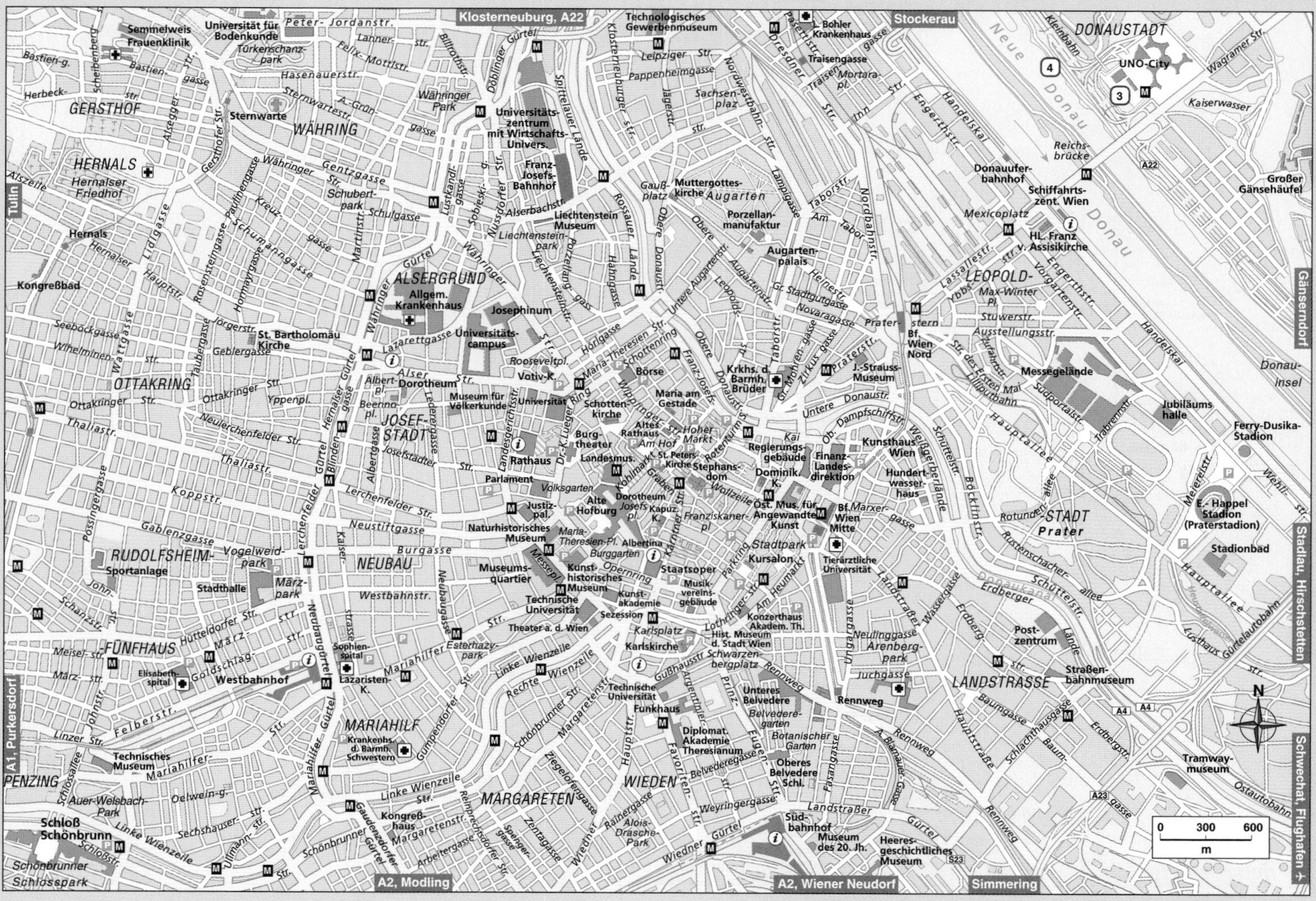

Klosterneuburg, A22
Stockerau
Technologisches Gewerbemuseum
Semmelweis Frauenklinik
Universität für Bodenkultur
Türkenschanz-park
Gersthof
Sternwarte
Währing
Währinger Park
Universitäts-zentrum mit Wirtschafts-Univers.
Franz-Josefs-Bahnhof
Hernals
Hernalser Friedhof
Tulln
Liechtenstein Museum
Muttergottes-kirche
Augarten
Porzellan-manufaktur
Augarten-palais
Donaustadt
UNO-City
Kaiserwasser
Neue Donau
Reichs-brücke
Donauufer-bahnhof
Schiffahrts-zent. Wien
Mexicoplatz
Hl. Franz v. Assisikirche
Großer Gänsehäufel
Kongreßbad
Alsergrund
Allgem. Krankenhaus
Josephinum
Universitäts-campus
St. Bartholomäus Kirche
Leopoldstadt
Bf Wien Nord
Praterstern
Gänserndorf
Ottakring
Votiv-K.
Dorotheum
Museum für Völkerkunde
Universität
Börse
Maria am Gestade
Krkhs. d. Barmh. Brüder
J.-Strauss-Museum
Messegelände
Jubiläums halle
Donau-insel
Ferry-Dusika-Stadion
Josefstadt
Schotten-kirche
Burg-theater
Rathaus
Landesmus.
Parlament
Regierungs-gebäude
Finanz-Landes-direktion
Kunsthaus Wien
Hundert-wasser-haus
St. Peters-Kirche
Stephans-dom
Dominik.-K.
Alte Hofburg
Justiz-pal.
Dorotheum
Öst. Mus. für Angewandte Kunst
Bf Wien Mitte
Stadt Prater
E.-Happel Stadion (Praterstadion)
Naturhistorisches Museum
Albertina
Stadtpark
Kursalon
Tierärztliche Universität
Stadionbad
Rudolfsheim
Sportanlage
Neubau
Museums-quartier
Kunst-historisches Museum
Staatsoper
Musik-vereins-gebäude
Stadthalle
Technische Universität
Kunst-akademie
Sezession
Konzerthaus
Akadem. Th.
Theater a. d. Wien
Karlskirche
Hist. Museum d. Stadt Wien
Schwarzen-bergplatz
Post-zentrum
Fünfhaus
Sophien-spital
Lazaristen-K.
Elisabeth-spital
Westbahnhof
Unteres Belvedere
Straßen-bahnmuseum
Landstrasse
Rennweg
Technische Universität
Funkhaus
Mariahilf
Krankenhs. d. Barmh. Schwestern
Diplomat. Akademie Theresianum
Botanischer Garten
Oberes Belvedere Schl.
Technisches Museum
Tramway-museum
Penzing
Wieden
Margareten
Auer-Welsbach-Park
Kongreß-haus
Alois-Drasche-Park
Süd-bahnhof
Museum des 20. Jh.
Heeres-geschichtliches Museum
Schloß Schönbrunn
Schönbrunner Schlosspark
A1, Purkersdorf
A2, Modling
A2, Wiener Neudorf
Simmering
Stadlau, Hirschstetten
Schwechat, Flughafen
m
0 300 600

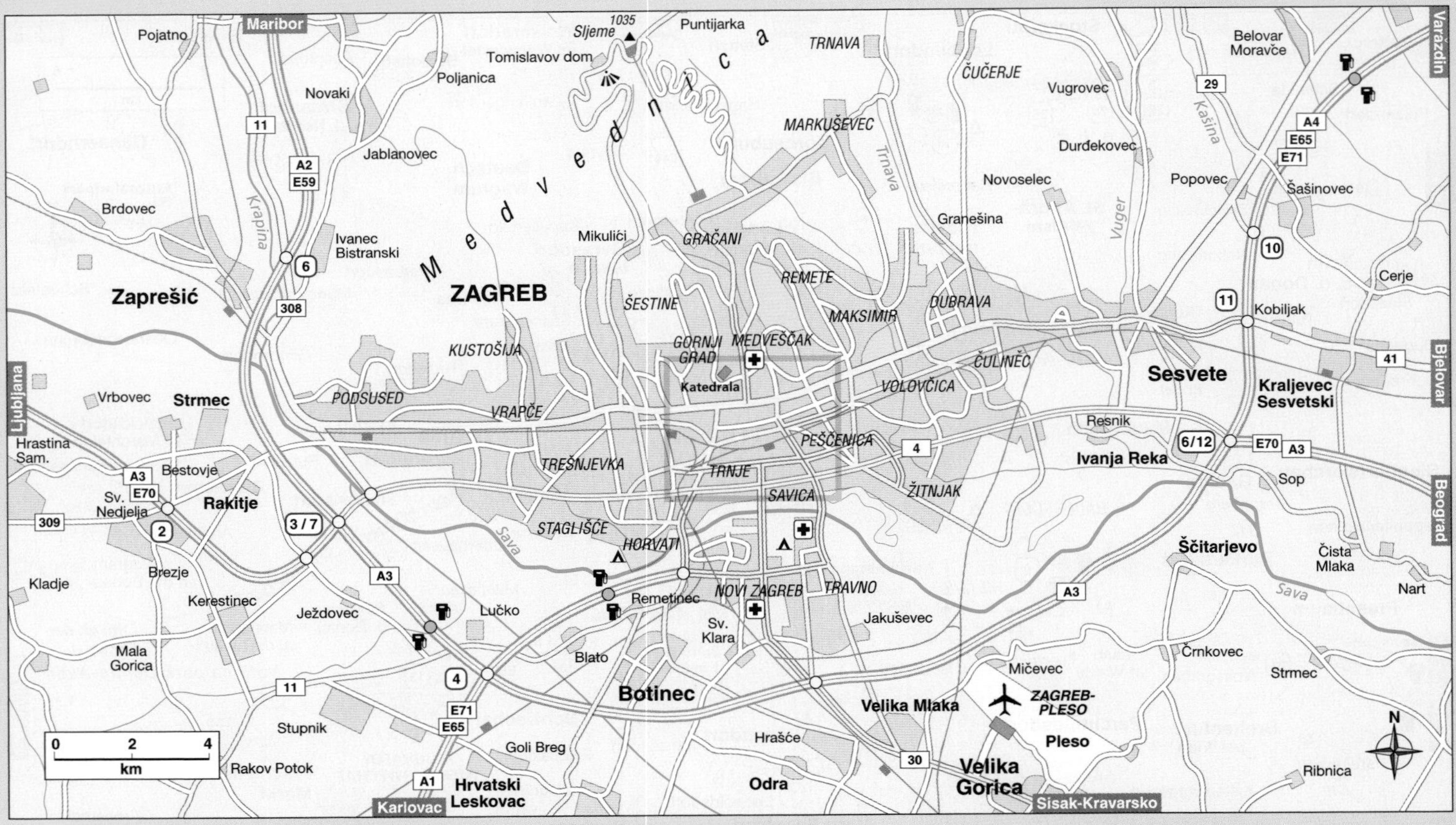

Maribor
Pojatno
Sljeme
1035
Puntijarka
Tomislavov dom
Poljanica
Novaki
TRNAVA
ČUČERJE
Vugrovec
Belovar
Moravče
Varaždin
Medvednica
11
A2
E59
Jablanovec
MARKUŠEVEC
Trnava
Kašina
Đurđekovec
29
A4
E65
E71
Novoselec
Popovec
Šašinovec
Brdovec
Krapina
Granešina
Vuger
Ivanec
Bistranski
Mikulići
GRAČANI
10
6
REMETE
Cerje
Zaprešić
ZAGREB
ŠESTINE
MAKSIMIR
DUBRAVA
11
Kobiljak
308
GORNJI GRAD
MEDVEŠČAK
KUSTOŠIJA
ČULINEČ
41
Bjelovar
Ljubljana
Vrbovec
Strmec
PODSUSED
Katedrala
VOLOVČICA
Sesvete
Kraljevec Sesvetski
VRAPČE
Resnik
Hrastina Sam.
PEŠČENICA
4
6/12
E70
A3
Ivanja Reka
A3
Bestovje
TREŠNJEVKA
TRNJE
Sop
Sv. Nedjelja
E70
Rakitje
SAVICA
ŽITNJAK
Beograd
309
2
3/7
Sava
STAGLIŠĆE
HORVATI
Ščitarjevo
Čista Mlaka
Kladje
Brezje
A3
Remetinec
NOVI ZAGREB
TRAVNO
A3
Sava
Nart
Kerestinec
Ježdovec
Lučko
Sv. Klara
Jakuševec
Mala Gorica
Blato
Mičevec
Črnkovec
4
11
Botinec
ZAGREB-PLESO
Strmec
Stupnik
E71
E65
Velika Mlaka
0 2 4
km
Goli Breg
Hrašće
Pleso
N
Rakov Potok
30
Velika Gorica
Ribnica
A1
Hrvatski Leskovac
Odra
Karlovac
Sisak-Kravarsko

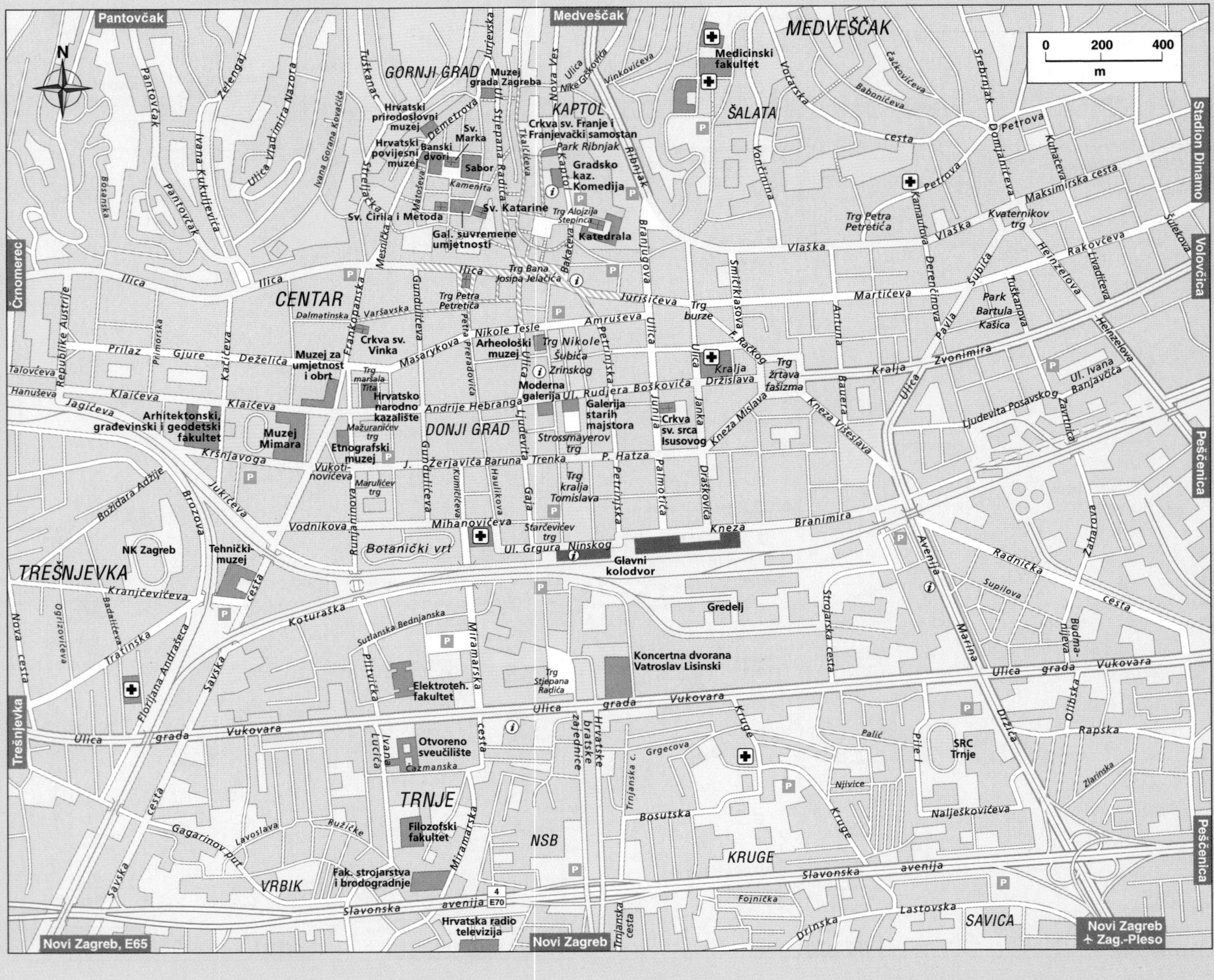

Pantovčak
Medveščak
MEDVEŠČAK
0 200 400
m
N
Zelengaj
Pantovčak
Ivana Kukuljevića
Ulica Vladimira Nazora
Ivana Gorana Kovačića
Tuškanac
Jurjevska
Nova Ves
Ulica Nike Grškovića
Vinkovićeva
Medicinski fakultet
Voćarska
Babonićeva
Čačkovićeva
Srebrnjak
GORNJI GRAD
Muzej grada Zagreba
Hrvatski prirodoslovni muzej
Demetrova
Sv. Marka
Hrvatski povijesni muzej
Banski dvori
Sabor
KAPTOL
Crkva sv. Franje i Franjevački samostan
Park Ribnjak
Gradsko kaz. Komedija
ŠALATA
Petrova
Kuhačeva
Vončinina
cesta
Domjanićeva
Petrova
Ul. Stjepana Radića
Tkalčićeva
Kaptol
Ribnjak
Kamenita
Matoševa
Strossmayerovo šetalište
Pantovčak
Bosanska
Sv. Katarine
Sv. Ćirila i Metoda
Trg Alojzija Stepinca
Katedrala
Gal. suvremene umjetnosti
Branjugova
Vlaška
Trg Petra Petrića
Kamaufova
Kvaternikov trg
Maksimirska cesta
Rakovčeva
Šubićeva
Heinzelova
Livadićeva
Šulekova
Črnomerec
Mesnička
Ilica
Trg Bana Josipa Jelačića
Bakačeva
Ilica
CENTAR
Frankopanska
Gundulićeva
Trg Petra Preradovića
Varšavska
Jurišićeva
Trg burze
Smičiklasova
Martićeva
Park Bartula Kašića
Tuškanova
Dalmatinska
Petra Preradovića
Nikole Tesle
Amruševa
Antuna
Derenčinova
Pavla
Republike Austrije
Primorska
Prilaz
Gjure
Deželića
Kačićeva
Muzej za umjetnost i obrt
Crkva sv. Vinka
Masarykova
Arheološki muzej
Trg Nikole Šubića Zrinskog
Petrinjska
Ulica
Kralja Držislava
F. Račkog
Trg žrtava fašizma
Bauera
Kralja
Zvonimira
Ulica
Heinzelova
Talovčeva
Hanuševa
Klaićeva
Trg maršala Tita
Hrvatsko narodno kazalište
Moderna galerija
Ul. Rudjera Boškovića
Galerija starih majstora
Junija
Janka
Kneza Mislava
Kneza Višeslava
Ul. Ivana Banjavčića
Ljudevita Posavskog
Zavrtnica
Jagićeva
Klaićeva
Arhitektonski, građevinski i geodetski fakultet
Muzej Mimara
Mažuranićev trg
Etnografski muzej
Andrije Hebranga
DONJI GRAD
Ljudevita
Crkva sv. srca Isusovog
Strossmayerov trg
Kršnjavoga
Vukotinovićeva
J. Žerjavića
Baruna Trenka
P. Hatza
Palmotićeva
Draškovića
Peščenica
Božidara Adžije
Brozova
Jukićeva
Marulićev trg
Gundulićeva
Kumičićeva
Hauliková
Gaja
Trg kralja Tomislava
Petrinjska
Runjaninova
Vodnikova
Mihanovićeva
Starčevićev trg
Kneza
Branimira
Zagrebačka
Radnička
Tehnički muzej
NK Zagreb
Botanički vrt
Ul. Grgura Ninskog
Glavni kolodvor
TREŠNJEVKA
Kranjčevićeva
Supilova
cesta
Badalićeva
Ogrizovićeva
Gredelj
Avenija
Budmanijeva
Koturaška
Sutlanska
Bednjanska
Miramarska
Strojarska cesta
Tratinska
Nova cesta
Savska
Florijana Andrašeca
Plitvička
Elektroteh. fakultet
Trg Stjepana Radića
Koncertna dvorana Vatroslav Lisinski
Marina
Držića
Ulica
grada
Vukovara
Oltilska
Trešnjevka
Ulica
grada
Vukovara
Ulica
grada
Vukovara
Lučića
Ivana
Otvoreno sveučilište
Čazmanska
cesta
Hrvatske bratske zajednice
Kruge
Grgecova
Palić
Pile I
SRC Trnje
Rapska
Zlarinska
TRNJE
Trnjanska c.
Njivice
Bosutska
Nalješkovićeva
Gagarinov put
Lavoslava
Ružička
Filozofski fakultet
Miramarska
NSB
Kruge
KRUGE
Pešćenica
Savska
VRBIK
Fak. strojarstva i brodogradnje
Slavonska
avenija
4
E70
Slavonska
avenija
Fojnička
Lastovska
Drinska
SAVICA
Hrvatska radio televizija
Trnjanska cesta
Novi Zagreb, E65
Novi Zagreb
Novi Zagreb
Zag.-Pleso
Stadion Dinamo
Volovčica
Peščenica

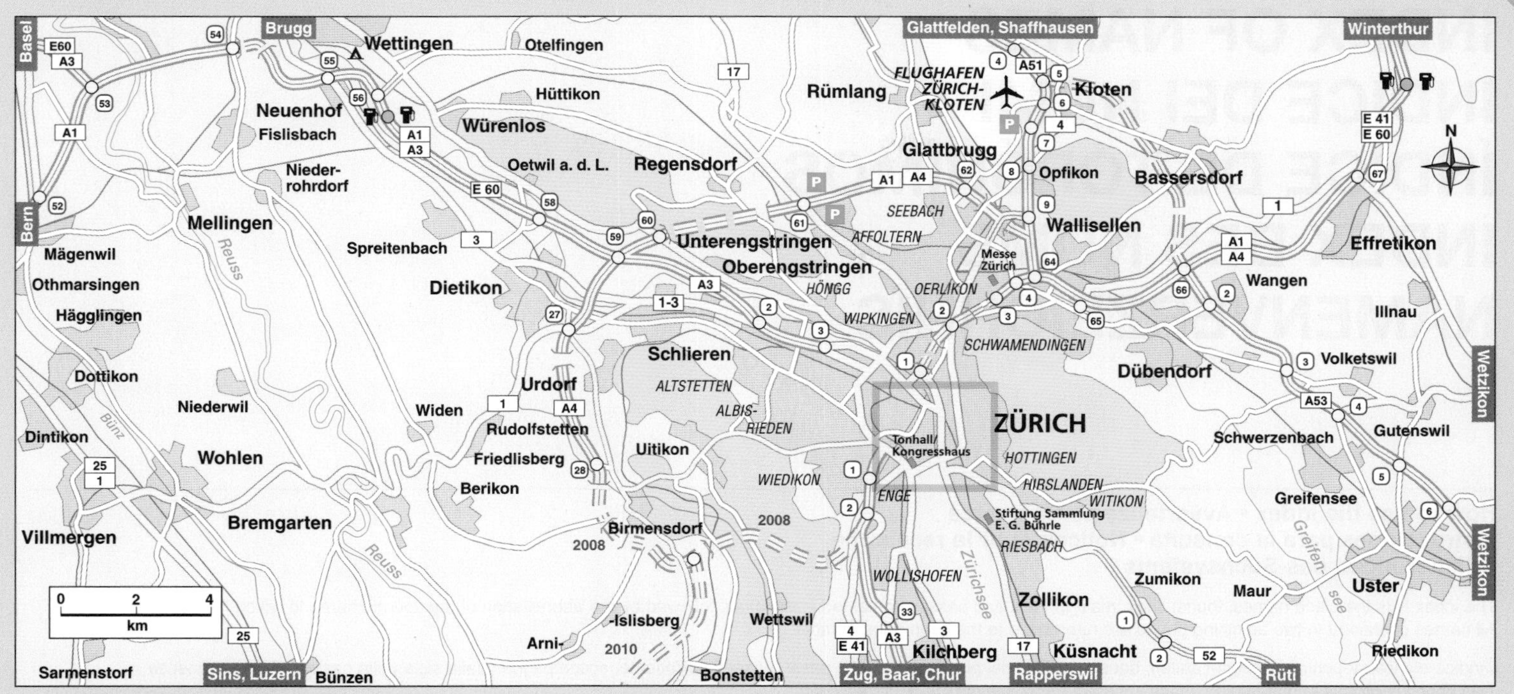
Basel
Brugg
Wettingen
Otelfingen
Glattfelden, Shaffhausen
Winterthur
FLUGHAFEN ZÜRICH-KLOTEN
Rümlang
Kloten
Neuenhof
Fislisbach
Hüttikon
Würenlos
Oetwil a. d. L.
Regensdorf
Glattbrugg
Opfikon
Bassersdorf
Nieder-rohrdorf
Mellingen
Spreitenbach
Unterengstringen
Oberengstringen
Wallisellen
Effretikon
Mägenwil
Othmarsingen
Hägglingen
Dietikon
SEEBACH
AFFOLTERN
HÖNGG
OERLIKON
WIPKINGEN
Messe Zürich
Wangen
Illnau
Schlieren
SCHWAMENDINGEN
Dübendorf
Volketswil
Dottikon
Niederwil
Urdorf
ALTSTETTEN
Widen
ALBIS-RIEDEN
ZÜRICH
Tonhall/Kongresshaus
Schwerzenbach
Gutenswil
Dintikon
Rudolfstetten
Friedlisberg
Uitikon
HOTTINGEN
HIRSLANDEN
WITIKON
Wohlen
Berikon
WIEDIKON
ENGE
Greifensee
Villmergen
Bremgarten
Birmensdorf
2008
Stiftung Sammlung E. G. Bührle
RIESBACH
Reuss
Zürichsee
WOLLISHOFEN
Zumikon
Maur
Uster
Zollikon
-Islisberg
Arni-
2010
Wettswil
Kilchberg
Küsnacht
Riedikon
Sarmenstorf
Sins, Luzern
Bünzen
Bonstetten
Zug, Baar, Chur
Rapperswil
Rüti
Bern
Wetzikon
km
0 2 4

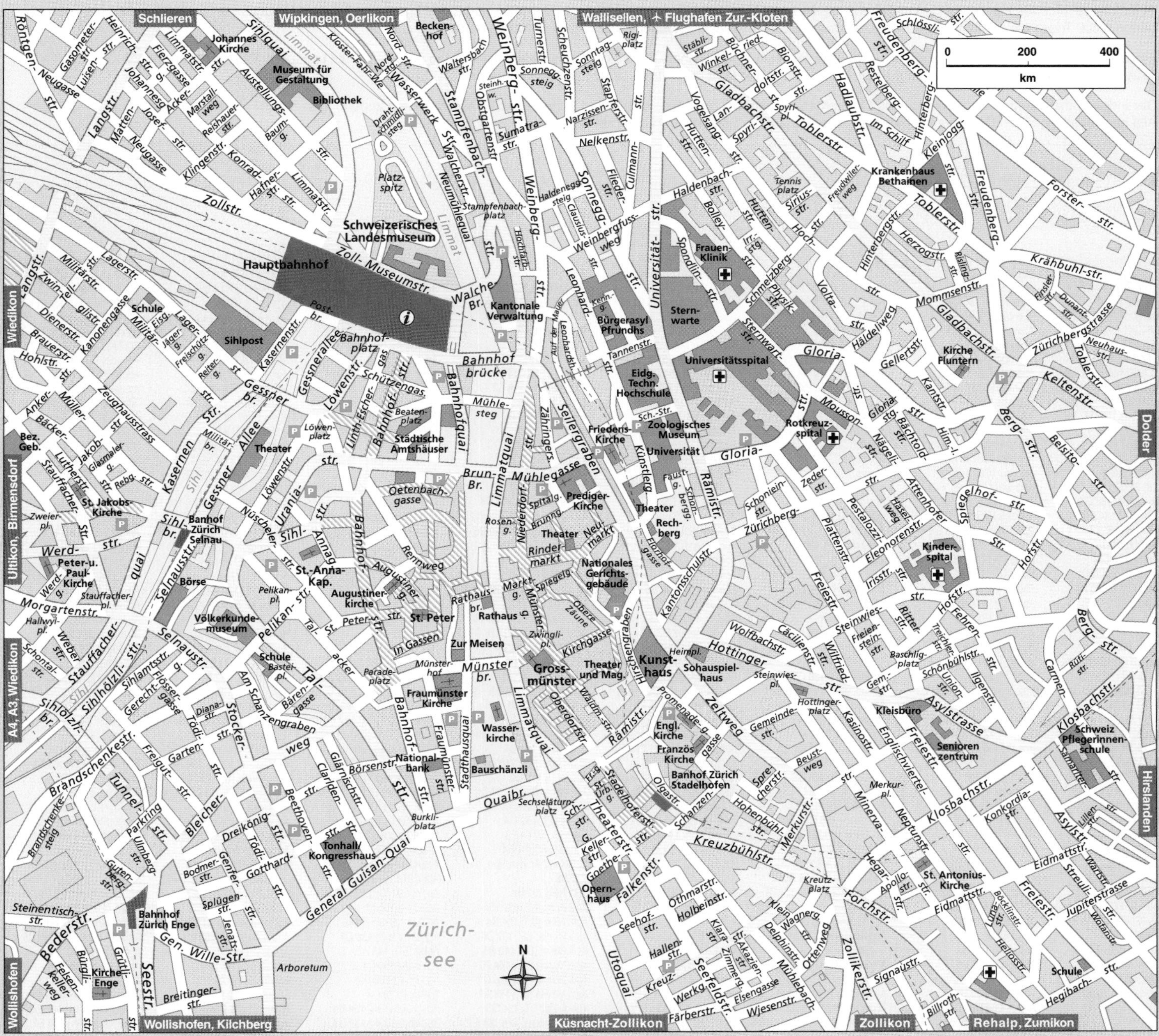
Schlieren
Wipkingen, Oerlikon
Wallisellen, Flughafen Zur.-Kloten
0 200 400
km
Johannes Kirche
Museum für Gestaltung
Bibliothek
Platzspitz
Schweizerisches Landesmuseum
Hauptbahnhof
Krankenhaus Bethanien
Frauen-Klinik
Sternwarte
Kantonale Verwaltung
Bürgerasyl Pfrundhs
Sihlpost
Schule
Bahnhofplatz
Bahnhofbrücke
Eidg. Techn. Hochschule
Universitätsspital
Kirche Fluntern
Zoologisches Museum
Universität
Rotkreuzspital
Theater
Städtische Amtshäuser
Friedens-Kirche
Prediger-Kirche
Rechberg
St. Jakobs-Kirche
Bahnhof Zürich Selnau
Nationales Gerichtsgebäude
Kinderspital
Peter-u.-Paul-Kirche
Börse
St.-Anna-Kap.
Augustinerkirche
St. Peter
Rathaus
Völkerkundemuseum
Zur Meisen
Kunsthaus
Sohauspielhaus
Grossmünster
Theater und Mag.
Fraumünster Kirche
Kleisbüro
Senioren zentrum
Schweiz Pflegerinnenschule
Wasserkirche
Engl. Kirche
Französ. Kirche
Bahnhof Zürich Stadelhofen
National-bank
Bauschänzli
Tonhall/Kongresshaus
St. Antonius-Kirche
Opernhaus
Bahnhof Zürich Enge
Zürichsee
Arboretum
Kirche Enge
Schule
Wiedikon
Uitikon, Birmensdorf
A4, A3, Wiedikon
Wollishofen
Dolder
Hirslanden
Wollishofen, Kilchberg
Küsnacht-Zollikon
Zollikon
Rehalp, Zumikon

INDEX OF NAMES
INDICE DEI NOMI
ÍNDICE DE TOPÓNIMOS
INDEX DES NOMS
NAMENVERZEICHNIS

How to use the index • Avvertenze per la ricerca
Instrucciones para la consulta • Notices pour la recherche
Erläuterungen des Suchsystems

The index lists the place names, tourist sites, main tunnels and passes contained in the atlas, followed by the abbreviation of the country name to which they belong. All names contained in two adjoining pages are referenced to the even page number.

L'indice elenca i toponimi dei centri abitati, dei siti turistici, dei principali tunnel e passi presenti nell'atlante, accompagnati dalla sigla della nazione di appartenenza. Tutti i nomi contenuti in due pagine affiancate sono riferiti alla pagina di numero pari.

El índice presenta los topónimos de localidades, lugares turísticos, principales túneles y puertos de montaña que figuran en el atlas, seguidos de la sigla que indica el País de pertenencia. Todos los nombres contenidos en dos páginas juntas éstan referidos a la página de número par.

L'index récense les noms des localités, sites touristiques, principales tunnels et cols contenus dans l'atlas, suivis par le sigle qui indique le Pays d'appartenance. Tous les noms contenus dans deux pages l'une à côté de l'autre sont rapportés à la page avec nombre pair.

Der Index enthält die im Atlas vorhandenen Ortsnamen, Sehenswürdigkeiten, wichtigsten Tunnels und Pässe, von dem zugehörigen Staatskennzeichen gefolgt. Alle in zwei anliegenden Seiten enthaltenen Namen sind auf die Seite mit gerader Zahl bezogen.

A

23 August [RO] 148 G1
Å [N] 192 C5
Aabenraa [DK] 156 C4
Aabybro [DK] 160 D3
Aachen [D] 30 F4
Aakirkeby [DK] 158 E4
Aalborg [DK] 160 D3
Aalburg [NL] 16 D6
Aalen [D] 60 B2
Aalestrup [DK] 160 D4
Aalsmane [LV] 198 F4
Aalsmeer [NL] 16 D4
Aalst (Alost) [B] 28 H2
Aalten [NL] 16 G6
Aalter [B] 28 G2
Äänekoski [FIN] 186 G3
Aapajärvi [FIN] 194 D6
Aarau [CH] 58 E5
Aarberg [CH] 58 D5
Aarburg [CH] 58 E5
Aareavaraa [S] 194 B6
Aareschlucht [CH] 70 F1
Aarlen (Arlon) [B] 44 E2
Aars [DK] 160 D4
Aarschot [B] 30 D4
Aarup [DK] 156 D3
Aavasaksa [FIN] 194 B8
Aba [H] 76 B2
Åbacka [S] 190 F3
Abades [E] 88 F4
Abadín [E] 78 E2
Abadíno [E] 82 H4
Abádszalók [H] 64 F6
A Baña [E] 78 B2
Abanades [E] 90 B5
Abanilla [E] 104 C2
Abano Terme [I] 110 G1
Abarán [E] 104 C2
Abárzuza [E] 84 A4
Abaújszántó [H] 64 G4
Abbadia [I] 114 G4
Abbadia San Salvatore [I] 114 G2
Abbasanta [I] 118 C4
Abbekås [S] 158 C3
Abbeville [F] 28 D4
Abbeydorney [IRL] 4 B3
Abbeyfeale [IRL] 4 C3
Abbeyleix [IRL] 4 E3
Abbiategrasso [I] 70 F5
Abborrträsk [S] 190 H3
Abdürrahim [TR] 130 H3
Abejar [E] 90 B2
Abela [P] 94 C2
Abéliéra [F] 108 E3
Abelnes [N] 164 C5
Abelvær [N] 190 C4
Abenberg [D] 46 G5
Abengibre [E] 98 C5
Abenójar [E] 96 D4
Abensberg [D] 60 E2
Aberaeron [GB] 10 B6
Aberchirder [GB] 6 F5
Aberdare [GB] 12 F2
Aberdeen [GB] 6 F6
Aberfeldy [GB] 8 E1
Abergavenny [GB] 12 F2
Abergele [GB] 10 C4
Aberlour [GB] 6 E5
Abersee [A] 60 H5
Abersoch [GB] 10 B4
Aberspier [D] 32 H5
Aberystwyth [GB] 10 B6
Abetone [I] 110 E4
Abide [TR] 130 H5
Abide [TR] 152 G2
Abiego [E] 90 G3
Abild [DK] 156 B4
Abild [S] 162 B4
Abingdon [GB] 12 H3
Abington [GB] 8 D4
Abisko [S] 192 F4
Abiúl [P] 86 D2
Abja-Paluoja [EST] 198 E3
Abla [E] 102 F4
Ablanitsa [BG] 148 B4
Ablis [F] 42 E4
Åbo [S] 190 C6
Åbo / Turku [FIN] 176 D4
Åboland [S] 166 C5
Abondance [F] 70 C2
Abony [H] 76 E2
Åbosjö [S] 190 G6
Aboyne [GB] 6 F6
Abrantes [P] 86 D4
Abraur [S] 190 G2
Abreschviller [F] 44 G5
Abric d'Ermites [E] 92 A6
Abriès [F] 70 C6
Abrigo de la Peña del Escrito [E] 98 C3
Abriola [I] 120 H4
Absdorf [A] 62 E4
Abtei [A] 74 B3
Abtenau [A] 60 H6
Abtsgmünd [D] 60 B2
Abtshagen [D] 20 D3
Åby [N] 164 G3
Åby [S] 162 C4
Åby [S] 168 B5
Abyarowshchyna [BY] 38 F2
Åbyn [S] 196 B4
A Cañiza [E] 78 C5
Acate [I] 126 F5
Accadia [I] 120 G2
Acceglio [I] 108 E2
Accettura [I] 120 H4
Acciaroli [I] 120 F5
Accous [F] 84 D4
Accumoli [I] 116 B3
Acedera [E] 96 B3
Acedo [E] 82 H6
Acehuche [E] 86 G4
Acerenza [I] 120 H3
Acerno [I] 120 F3
Acerra [I] 120 E3
Aceuchal [E] 94 G2
Acey, Abbaye d'– [F] 58 A4
Acharnés [GR] 134 C6
Achenkirch [A] 60 E6
Achensee [A] 60 E6
Achenwald [A] 60 E6
Achern [D] 58 F1
Acheux-en-Amiénois [F] 28 E4
Achílleio [GR] 132 G2
Achilleum [TR] 130 H5
Achim [D] 18 E5
Achinós [GR] 130 C3
Achladochóri [GR] 130 B2
Achladókampos [GR] 136 E2
Achleiten [A] 62 B4
Achnasheen [GB] 6 D4
Achtrup [D] 156 B4
Aci Castello [I] 126 G3
Aci Catena [I] 126 G3
Acinipo [E] 102 A4
Acıpayam [TR] 152 G6
Acireale [I] 126 G3
Aci Trezza [I] 126 G3
Acksi [S] 172 G3
A Coruña / La Coruña [E] 78 C2
Acqua Doria [F] 114 A5
Acquafredda, Castello di– [I] 118 C7
Acqualagna [I] 112 B6
Acquanegra sul Chiese [I] 110 E1
Acquapendente [I] 114 G3
Acquaro [I] 124 D6
Acquasanta Terme [I] 116 C3
Acquasparta [I] 116 A3
Acquaviva delle Fonti [I] 122 D3
Acquedolci [I] 126 F2
Acqui Terme [I] 108 H2
Acri [I] 124 D4
Acropolis Iberica [E] 90 F5
Ács [H] 64 A6
Acsa [H] 64 D5
Acsád [H] 74 F1
Ada [SRB] 76 E5
Adaköy [TR] 154 D2
Adalsbruk [N] 172 C3
Ådalsvollen [N] 190 C6
Adámas [GR] 138 D4
Adamclisi [RO] 204 E5
Adamuz [E] 96 C6
Adanero [E] 88 E3
Adapazari (Sakarya) [TR] 150 H3
Adare [IRL] 4 C3
Adaševci [SRB] 142 E2
Adelberg [D] 60 B2
Adelboden [CH] 70 D2
Adelebsen [D] 32 F4
Adelfia [I] 122 E3
Adelsheim [D] 46 D5
Adelsö [S] 168 D3
Adelsried [D] 60 C3
Ademuz [E] 98 D2
Adenau [D] 30 G6
Adjud [RO] 204 E4
Admont [A] 62 C6
Ådneram [N] 164 C3
Adolfsström [S] 190 F2
Adony [H] 76 C2
Adorf [D] 48 C3
Adra [E] 102 F5
Adradas [E] 90 B4
Adrall [E] 92 D1
Adramittium Thebe [TR] 152 C1
Adrano [I] 126 F3
Ádria [I] 110 G2
Adrigole [IRL] 4 B5
A. Drosiní [GR] 130 F2
Adutiškis [LT] 200 H4
Aegviidu [EST] 198 E1
Aerinó [GR] 132 H2
Ærøskøbing [DK] 156 D4
Aerzen [D] 32 F3
Aesoo [EST] 198 E2
A Estrada [E] 78 C3
Aetópetra [GR] 132 C1
Aetós [GR] 128 E4
Aetós [GR] 132 D5
Äetsä [FIN] 176 E2
Afaía [GR] 136 G1
Afántou [GR] 154 D4
Åfarnes [N] 180 E3
Afife [P] 78 A6
Afiónas [GR] 132 A2
Aflenz Kurort [A] 62 D6
A Fonsagrada [E] 78 F3
Afoss [N] 164 G3
Africo [I] 124 D7
Afritz [A] 72 H3
Afşar [TR] 152 H4
Afsluitdijk [NL] 16 E2
Áfysos [GR] 134 A3
Áfytos [GR] 130 B6
Aga [N] 170 C4
Ağaçbeylı [TR] 152 G3
Ağaçlı [TR] 150 E2
Agaete [E] 100 C6
Agalás [GR] 136 A2
Agalatovo [RUS] 178 H4
Ág. Anárgyroi [GR] 132 G2
Ág. Antónios [GR] 130 B5
Ág. Athanásios [GR] 128 H4
Agay [F] 108 E5
Agazzano [I] 110 C2
Ág. Charálampos [GR] 130 F3
Agde [F] 106 E5
Ag. Dimítrios [GR] 132 F4
Ág. Dionýsios [GR] 128 G6
Ag. Dionysíou, Moní– [GR] 130 D5
Agen [F] 66 E5
Agéranos [GR] 136 E5
Agerbæk [DK] 156 B2
Ag. Fotiá [GR] 140 G5
Ág. Geórgios [GR] 132 F4
Agger [DK] 160 B4
Aggersund [DK] 160 D4
Ággíus [I] 118 D2
Aggsbach-Dorf [A] 62 D4
Aggsbach-Markt [A] 62 D4
Aggstein [A] 62 D4
Aggtelek [H] 64 E3
Aghadoe [IRL] 4 B4
Aghleam / An Eachléim [IRL] 2 B3
Agiá [GR] 132 H1
Agía Ánna [GR] 132 H5
Agía Ánna [GR] 134 B4
Agía Efimía [GR] 132 C6
Agía Galíni [GR] 140 D5
Agìa Marina [CY] 154 F5
Agía Marína [GR] 136 G1
Agia Marína [GR] 154 A1
Agía Nápa [CY] 154 G5
Agía Paraskeví [GR] 134 G2
Agia Pelagía [GR] 136 F6
Agiásmata [GR] 134 G4
Agiásos [GR] 134 H2
Ágía Triáda [GR] 128 H5
Agía Triáda [GR] 132 D4
Ágía Triáda [GR] 136 C1
Ágía Varvára [GR] 140 E5
Ág. Ioánnis [GR] 132 H6
Ág. Ioánnis [GR] 154 A3
Agiófyllo [GR] 132 E1
Ágioi Déka [GR] 140 E5
Agiókampos [GR] 132 H4
Agiókampos [GR] 132 H1
Ágio Pnévma [GR] 130 C3
Ágios Amvrósios (Esentepe) [CY] 154 G5
Ágios Andréas [GR] 136 E3
Ágios Apóstoloi [GR] 136 F5
Agios Athanásios [GR] 128 F4
Agios Dimítrios [GR] 128 G6
Ágios Dimítrios [GR] 136 F4
Ágios Efstrátios [GR] 134 E1
Ágios Germanos [GR] 128 E4
Ágios Górdis [GR] 132 B2
Agios Konstantínos [GR] 132 H4
Agios Konstantínos [GR] 152 C5
Ágios Kýrikos [GR] 138 G1
Ágios Léon [GR] 136 A2
Ágios Márkos [GR] 128 H3
Ágios Matthaíos [GR] 132 B2
Ágios Mýron [GR] 140 E5
Ágios Nikítas [GR] 132 C4
Ágios Nikólaos [GR] 132 C2
Ágios Nikólaos [GR] 132 D4
Ágios Nikólaos [GR] 136 E4
Ágios Nikólaos [GR] 136 G2
Ágios Nikólaos [GR] 140 F4
Ágios Pétros [GR] 132 C5
Ágios Pétros [GR] 136 E3
Ágios Theodoros (Çayırova) [CY] 154 G5
Agios Vlásios [GR] 132 E4
Agira [I] 126 F3
Ag. Kyriakí [GR] 138 H1
Ağla [TR] 154 E1
Aglasterhausen [D] 46 C5
Ag. Lávra [GR] 136 D1
Ăglen [BG] 148 A3
Aglen [N] 190 C4
Agliano [I] 108 H2
Agliate [I] 70 G4
Ag. Loukás [GR] 134 C5
Ag. Marína [GR] 132 G4
Ag. Marína [GR] 134 C5
Ág. Marína [GR] 140 G3
Agnánta [GR] 132 D2
Agnanteró [GR] 132 F2
Agnäs [S] 190 H6
Ág. Nikólaos [GR] 130 C6
Agnita [RO] 204 D4
Agno [CH] 70 F3
Agnone [I] 116 E6
Agnone Bagni [I] 126 G4
Agnóntas [GR] 134 B3
Agoitz / Aoiz [E] 84 C4
Agolada [E] 78 C3
Agoncillo [E] 82 H6
Agon-Coutainville [F] 26 D3
Agordo [I] 72 E4
Ágosegyháza [H] 76 D3
Agost [E] 104 D2
Ag. Panteleïmonas [GR] 128 F4
Ag. Pelagía [GR] 140 E4
Ag. Pétros [GR] 128 G4
Ág. Pródromos [GR] 130 B5
Agramón [E] 104 B1
Agramunt [E] 92 C3
Ágras [GR] 128 F4
Agreda [E] 84 A6
Agreliá [GR] 132 F1
Agriá [GR] 132 H2
Agrigento [I] 126 D4
Agriliá [GR] 132 E5
Agrínio [GR] 132 E5
Agriovótano [GR] 134 B3
Agropoli [I] 120 F4
Ag. Roúmeli [GR] 140 C5
Ag. Stéfanos [GR] 138 E2
Ág. Theódoroi [GR] 132 H3
Ag. Theódoroi [GR] 136 F1
Ag. Thomás [GR] 140 E5
Ag. Triáda [GR] 134 C6
Ag. Triáda [GR] 140 D5
Agua, Cueva del– [E] 102 F2
Agua Amarga [E] 102 H5
Aguadulce [E] 102 G5
A Guarda / La Guardia [E] 78 A5
A Guarda / La Guardia [E] 96 G2
Aguasmestas [E] 78 G3
Aguas Nuevas [E] 98 B5
Aguda [P] 80 B4
A Gudiña [E] 78 D6
Agudo [E] 96 C3
Águeda [P] 80 B5
Agüero [E] 84 C5
Aguiar [P] 94 D2
Aguiar da Beira [P] 80 D5
Águila, Cuevas del– [E] 88 C5
Aguilafuente [E] 88 F3
Aguilar de Campoo [E] 82 D4
Aguilar de la Frontera [E] 102 C2
Aguilar del Alfambra [E] 98 E1
Águilas [E] 104 B4
Agüimes [E] 100 C6
Agulo [E] 100 B5
Agurain / Salvatierra [E] 82 H5
Aguzadera [E] 100 H3
Ağva / Yeşilçay [TR] 150 G2
Aha [D] 58 F3
Ahascragh [IRL] 2 D5
Ahat [TR] 152 G3
Ahaus [D] 16 G5
Åheim [N] 180 C4
Aheloy [BG] 148 F4
Ahigal [E] 88 A5
Ahıthisar [TR] 152 H3
Ahja [EST] 198 F3
Ahjärvi [FIN] 188 F6
Ahkiolahti [FIN] 188 C1
Ahlainen [FIN] 176 C1
Ahlbeck [D] 20 E3
Ahlbeck [D] 20 E4
Ahlen [D] 32 C3
Ahlerstedt [D] 18 E4
Ahlhorn [D] 18 C6
Ahmetbey [TR] 150 C2
Ahmetbeyler [TR] 152 C2
Ahmetçe [TR] 134 H1
Ahmetler [TR] 152 F3
Ahmetli [TR] 152 D3
Ahmoo [FIN] 176 G4
Ahmovaara [FIN] 188 F1
Ahnsen [D] 32 G2
Ahokylä [FIN] 196 E5
Ahola [FIN] 186 D2
Ahola [FIN] 196 F2
Ahonkylä [FIN] 186 C3
Ahrensbök [D] 18 G3
Ahrensburg [D] 18 G4
Ahrhütte [D] 30 G6
Ahrweiler [D] 30 G5
Ähtäri / Etseri [FIN] 186 E4
Ahtärinranta [FIN] 186 E3
Ähtävä / Esse [FIN] 196 C6
Åhus [S] 158 D2
Ahvela [FIN] 196 F3
Ahveninen [FIN] 186 E5
Ahveninen [FIN] 186 G2
Ahvensalmi [FIN] 188 E4
Ahvenselkä [FIN] 194 E7
Ahverinen [FIN] 188 F2

Aianí [GR] 128 F6
Aibar [E] 84 C4
Aich [D] 60 F3
Aicha [D] 60 H3
Aichach [D] 60 D3
Aichstetten [D] 60 B5
Aidenbach [D] 60 G3
Aidone [I] 126 F4
Aigen [A] 62 B3
Aigiáli [GR] 138 G3
Aigialoúsa (Yenierenköy) [CY] 154 G4
Aígina [GR] 136 G2
Aigínio [GR] 128 G5
Aígio [GR] 132 F6
Aigle [CH] 70 C2
Aiglsbach [D] 60 E3
Aignay-le-Duc [F] 56 G2
Aigósthena [GR] 134 B6
Aigre [F] 54 D6
Aigrefeuille-d'Aunis [F] 54 C5
Aigrefeuille-sur-Maine [F] 54 C2
Aiguablava [E] 92 G3
Aiguebelle [F] 70 B4
Aiguebelle [F] 108 D6
Aigueperse [F] 68 D1
Aigues-Mortes [F] 106 F4
Aigues-Vives [F] 106 C4
Aiguevives [F] 54 G2
Aiguilles [F] 70 B6
Aiguillon [F] 66 E5
Aigurande [F] 54 H5
Äijäjoki [FIN] 194 B5
Äijälä [FIN] 186 G3
Ailefroide [F] 70 B6
Aillant-sur-Tholon [F] 56 E1
Aime [F] 70 B4
Ainaži [LV] 198 D4
Ainet [A] 72 F2
Ainhoa [F] 84 C2
Ainsa [E] 84 E6
Airaines [F] 28 D4
Airan [F] 26 F4
Airasca [I] 70 D6
Aire [F] 28 E3
Aire-sur-l'Adour [F] 84 E2
Aire-sur-la-Lys [F] 28 E3
Airolo [CH] 70 F2
Airvault [F] 54 E3
Aisey-sur-Armançon [F] 56 F2
Aisey-sur-Seine [F] 56 G2
Aïssey [F] 58 B5
Aistaig [D] 58 G2
Aisými [GR] 130 G3
Aiterhofen [D] 60 G2
Aitolikó [GR] 132 E5
Aitrach [D] 60 B4
Aitrang [D] 60 C5
Aittojärvi [FIN] 196 E6
Aittolahti [FIN] 188 F4
Aittoperä [FIN] 196 D5
Aittovaara [FIN] 196 F3
Aiud [RO] 204 C4
Äivo / Oivu [FIN] 196 C6
Aix-en-Othe [F] 42 H6
Aix-en-Provence [F] 108 B4
Aixe-sur-Vienne [F] 66 G1
Aix-les-Bains [F] 68 H3
Aizanoi [TR] 152 G2
Aizenay [F] 54 B3
Aizkraukle [LV] 198 E5
Aizpute [LV] 198 B5
Ajaccio [F] 114 A5
Ajaur [S] 190 H4
Ajaureforsen [S] 190 F3
Ajdovščina [SLO] 74 A5
Ajka [H] 74 H2
Ajnovce [SRB] 146 D5
Ajo [E] 82 F3
Ajos [FIN] 196 C3
Akáki [CY] 154 F5
Akalan [TR] 150 D2
Akalen [TR] 152 G6
Akanthoú (Tatlısu) [CY] 154 G5
Akarca [TR] 152 G3
Äkäsjokisuu [FIN] 194 B6
Äkäslompolo [FIN] 194 C6
Akasztó [H] 76 C3
Akbaş [TR] 152 C1
Akbaş [TR] 152 G5
Akbük [TR] 152 D6
Akçakavak [TR] 154 E2
Akçakese [TR] 150 F2
Akçaköy [TR] 152 E5
Akçaköy [TR] 152 H5
Akçaova [TR] 150 G2
Akçaova [TR] 152 E6
Akçay [TR] 152 C1
Akçay [TR] 154 G2
Akdere [TR] 152 G5
Akdoğan (Lysi) [CY] 154 G5
Aken [D] 34 C4
Åker [S] 162 C3
Åkersberga [S] 168 E2
Åkersjön [S] 190 D6
Åkers styckerbruk [S] 168 C3
Akharım [TR] 152 H3
Akhisar [TR] 152 D3
Akhtopol [BG] 148 G5
Akine [TR] 154 F4
Akkarfjord [N] 194 B2
Akkavare [S] 190 H3
Akkaya [TR] 150 H5
Akkent [TR] 152 G4
Akköprü [TR] 154 E1
Akköy [TR] 152 D6
Akköy [TR] 152 F4
Akland [N] 164 F4
Akli [H] 76 A2
Akmeşe [TR] 150 G3
Akmyane [LT] 198 C6
Aknīste [LV] 198 F6
Akonlahti [FIN] 196 G5
Akonpohja [FIN] 188 F5
Akoúmia [GR] 140 D5
Akpınar [TR] 150 H5
Åkra [N] 170 B5
Akrai [I] 126 G5
Akraifia [GR] 134 B5
Akraífnio [GR] 134 B5
Akranes [IS] 192 A2
Akrapol [TR] 152 C2
Åkre [N] 182 C6
Åkrehamn [N] 164 A2
Akrogiáli [GR] 130 C4
Akropótamos [GR] 130 C4
Akrōtíri [CY] 154 F6
Akrotíri [GR] 138 F5
Akrovoúni [GR] 130 D3
Aksakal [TR] 150 D5
Aksakovo [BG] 148 F2
Akşar [TR] 152 G6
Aksaz [TR] 150 C4
Aksaz [TR] 152 F2
Aksaz Kaplica [TR] 152 F4
Aksdal [N] 164 A1
Aksla [N] 180 C6
Aktsyabrski [BY] 202 C6
Åkullsjön [S] 196 A5
Akureyri [IS] 192 C2
Akyaka [TR] 154 F4
Akyazı [TR] 150 H3
Akyazı [TR] 154 G3
Ål [N] 170 F3
Ala [I] 72 C5
Ala [S] 168 G5
Alaattin [TR] 152 G5
Alabanda [TR] 152 E6
Alabodarna [S] 156 H2
Alacadağ [TR] 154 H2
Alacant / Alicante [E] 104 E2
Alacat [TR] 150 E5
Alaçatı [TR] 134 H5
Alà dei Sardi [I] 118 D3
Ala di Stura [I] 70 C5
Aladzha Manastir [BG] 148 G2
Alaejos [E] 88 D2
Alagna-Valsésia [I] 70 E3
A Lagoa / Campo Lameiro [E] 78 B4
Alagón [E] 86 H4
Alagón [E] 90 E3
Alahärmä [FIN] 186 C2
Ala-Honkajoki [FIN] 186 C6
Alajärvi [FIN] 186 D2
Alajärvi [FIN] 196 F3
Alajoki [FIN] 194 D5
Alajoki [FIN] 196 D5
Alakylä [FIN] 194 C7
Alakylä [FIN] 196 D3
Alalampi [RUS] 188 H4
Ala-Livo [FIN] 196 E3
Alamaa [FIN] 186 F2
Alameda [E] 102 C3
Alamedilla [E] 102 F3
Alanäs [S] 190 E5
Alancık [TR] 152 C1
Åland [S] 168 D1
Alandroal [P] 94 E1
Ålandsbro [S] 184 F4
Alange [E] 94 H2
Alanís [E] 94 H4
Alanta [LT] 200 G4
Alapitkä [FIN] 188 C1
Alaquàs [E] 98 E4
Alaraz [E] 88 D4
Alarcón [E] 98 B3
Alaşehir [TR] 152 E4
Ålåsen [S] 190 E6
Alássio [I] 108 G4
Alastaro [FIN] 176 E3
Ala-Temmes [FIN] 196 D4
Alatoz [E] 98 C5
Alatri [I] 116 C6
Alatskivi [EST] 198 F2
Alattu [RUS] 188 H4
Ala-Valli [FIN] 186 C4
Alavattnet [S] 190 E5
Alaveteli / Nedervetil [FIN] 196 C6
Ala-Vieksi [FIN] 196 F5
Alavieska [FIN] 196 C5
Ala-Vuokki [FIN] 196 F4
Alavus [FIN] 186 D4
Alba [I] 108 G2
Alba Adriatica [I] 116 D3
Albacete [E] 98 B5
Albaching [D] 60 F4
Albacken [S] 184 D3
Alba de Tormes [E] 88 C3
Ålbæk [DK] 160 E2
Alba Fucens [I] 116 C5
Albaida [E] 98 E6
Albaina [E] 82 G5
Alba Iulia [RO] 204 C4
Albaladejo [E] 96 G5
Albalate de Cinca [E] 90 G4
Albalate del Arzobispo [E] 90 E5
Albalate de las Nogueras [E] 98 B1
Albalate de Zorita [E] 98 A1
Alban [F] 106 C3
Albánchez [E] 102 H4
Albanella [I] 120 F4
Albano di Lucania [I] 120 H4
Albano Laziale [I] 116 A6
Albaredo d'Adige [I] 110 F1
Albarella [I] 110 H2
Albares [E] 88 H6
Albarracín [E] 98 D1
Albarracín, Cuevas de- [E] 98 D1
Albatana [E] 104 C1
Albena [BG] 148 G2
Albenga [I] 108 G4
Albens [F] 70 A3
Albentosa [E] 98 E3
Alberga [S] 168 B3
Albergaria-a-Velha [P] 80 B5
Alberic [E] 98 E5
Albernoa [P] 94 D3
Albero Alto [E] 90 F3
Alberobello [I] 122 E3
Alberoni [I] 110 H1
Albersdorf [D] 18 E2
Albert [F] 28 E4
Albertacce [I] 114 B3
Albertirsa [H] 76 D1
Albertville [F] 70 B3
Albeşti [RO] 148 G1
Albi [F] 106 B2
Albier Montrond [F] 70 B5
Albignasego [I] 110 G1
Albinea [I] 110 E3
Albissola Marina [I] 108 H3
Albo [F] 114 C2
Albocácer / Albocàsser [E] 98 G2
Albocàsser / Albocácer [E] 98 G2
Alböke [S] 162 G4
Alboraia / Alboraya [E] 98 E4
Alboraya / Alboraia [E] 98 E4
Alborea [E] 98 C4
Albox [E] 102 H4
Albrechtice nad Vltavou [CZ] 48 F6
Albrechtsburg [A] 62 D4
Albudeite [E] 104 C3
Albufeira [P] 94 C5
Albujón [E] 104 C4
Albuñol [E] 102 E5
Albuñuelas [E] 102 D4
Alburquerque [E] 86 F5
Alby [S] 162 G6
Alby [S] 184 C4
Alcácer do Sal [P] 94 C1
Alcáçovas [P] 94 D2
Alcadozo [E] 98 B6
Alcafores [P] 86 G3
Alcaide [E] 102 H3
Alcalá de Chivert / Alcalá de Xivert [E] 98 G2
Alcalá de Guadaira [E] 94 G6
Alcalá de Henares [E] 88 G6
Alcalá de la Selva [E] 98 E2
Alcalá del Júcar [E] 98 C5
Alcalá de los Gazules [E] 100 G4
Alcalá del Río [E] 94 G6
Alcalá del Valle [E] 102 A3
Alcalá de Xivert / Alcalá de Chivert [E] 98 G2
Alcalá la Real [E] 102 D3
Álcamo [I] 126 C2
Alcanar [E] 92 A6
Alcanede [P] 86 C4
Alcanena [P] 86 C4
Alcañices [E] 80 G4
Alcañiz [E] 90 F6
Alcántara [E] 86 G4
Alcantara, Gole d'- [I] 124 A8
Alcantarilla [E] 104 C3
Alcantud [E] 90 B6
Alcaracejos [E] 96 C5
Alcaraz [E] 96 H6
Alcaria Ruiva [P] 94 D4
Alcarràs [E] 90 H5
Alçaşehir [TR] 152 G1
Alcaudete [E] 102 D2
Alcaudete de la Jara [E] 96 D1
Alcázar de San Juan [E] 96 G3
Alçitepe [TR] 130 H5
Alcobaça [P] 86 C3
Alcoba de los Montes [E] 96 D3
Alcobendas [E] 88 F5
Alcobertas [P] 86 C3
Alcocèber / Alcossebre [E] 98 G3
Alcocer [E] 90 A6
Alcochete [P] 86 B5
Alcoentre [P] 86 B4
Alcofra [P] 80 C5
Alcoi / Alcoy [E] 104 E1
Alcolea [E] 102 F5
Alcolea del Pinar [E] 90 B4
Alcolea del Río [E] 94 H5
Alconchel [E] 94 F2
Alcora / l'Alcora [E] 98 F3
Alcorcón [E] 88 F6
Alcorisa [E] 90 F6
Alcossebre / Alcocèber [E] 98 G3
Alcoutim [P] 94 D5
Alcover [E] 92 C4
Alcoy / Alcoi [E] 104 E1
Alcubierre [E] 90 F3
Alcubilla de Avellaneda [E] 88 H2
Alcubillas [E] 96 G5
Alcublas [E] 98 E3
Alcúdia [E] 104 F4
Alcudia de Guadix [E] 102 F4
Alcuéscar [E] 86 H6
Alda [E] 82 H5
Aldeacentenera [E] 96 B1
Aldeadávila de la Ribera [E] 80 F5
Aldea del Cano [E] 86 H6
Aldea del Fresno [E] 88 E5
Aldea del Rey [E] 96 E5
Aldea de Trujillo [E] 96 B1
Aldealpozo [E] 90 C3
Aldeanueva de Ebro [E] 84 A5
Aldeaquemada [E] 96 F6
Aldeatejada [E] 88 C3
Aldeavieja [E] 88 E4
Aldeburgh [GB] 14 G3
Aldeia da Ponte [P] 86 G2
Aldeia do Bispo [P] 86 G2
Aldeias das Neves [E] 94 C4
Aldenhoven [D] 30 F4
Aldernäset [S] 190 F5
Aldershot [GB] 14 D4
Aldinci [MK] 128 E1
Aldtsier [NL] 16 F2
Åled [S] 162 B5
Aledo [E] 104 B3
Alegranza [E] 100 E5
Alekovo [BG] 148 C3
Alekovo [BG] 148 E1
Aleksandrovac [SRB] 146 C1
Aleksandrovo [BG] 148 B3
Aleksandrów [PL] 38 A3
Aleksandrów [PL] 38 B6
Aleksandrów [PL] 52 F2
Aleksandrów Kujawski [PL] 36 F1
Aleksandrów Łódzki [PL] 36 G4
Aleksin [RUS] 202 F4
Aleksinac [SRB] 146 D3
Ålem [S] 162 G4
Alemdağ [TR] 150 F2
Ålen [N] 182 C3
Alençon [F] 26 F6
Alenquer [P] 86 B4
Aléria [F] 114 C4
Aléria [F] 114 C4
Alès [F] 106 F3
Áles [I] 118 C5
Aleşd [RO] 204 B4
Alessandria [I] 70 F6
Alessandria del Carretto [I] 122 D6
Alessándria della Rocca [I] 126 D3
Ålesund [N] 180 C3
Alexándreia [GR] 128 G4
Alexandria [RO] 148 B1
Alexandria Troas [TR] 130 H6
Alexandroúpoli [GR] 130 G3
Alf [D] 44 G2
Alfafar [E] 98 E5
Alfaites [P] 86 G2
Alfajarín [E] 90 E4
Alfambra [E] 98 E1
Alfambras [P] 94 B4
Alfândenga da Fé [P] 80 F4
Alfano [I] 120 G5
Alfarela de Jales [P] 80 E4
Alfaro [E] 84 B5
Alfarràs [E] 90 H4
Alfas [E] 104 F2
Alfatar [BG] 148 E1
Alfedena [I] 116 D6
Alfeizerão [P] 86 B3
Alfeld [D] 32 F3
Alfeld [D] 46 H5
Alfena [P] 80 C4
Alfés [E] 90 H5
Alfonsine [I] 110 G3
Alford [GB] 6 F6
Alforja [E] 92 B4
Alfoten [N] 180 C5
Alfoz [E] 78 E2
Alfreton [GB] 10 F5
Alfstad [N] 170 G5
Alfta [S] 174 D2
Algaida [E] 104 E5
Algajola [F] 114 B3
Algar [E] 100 G4
Algar [E] 104 H5
Algarås [S] 166 F4
Ålgård [N] 164 B5
Ålgård [N] 164 B3
Algarinejo [E] 102 D3
Algarra [E] 98 D3
Algatocín [E] 100 H4
Algeciras [E] 100 G5
Algemesí [E] 98 E5
Älgered [S] 184 E5
Alghero [I] 118 B3
Älghult [S] 162 F4
Alginet [E] 98 E5
Algodonales [E] 100 H3
Algodor [P] 94 D4
Algora [E] 90 A5
Algoso [P] 80 F4
Älgsjö [S] 190 G5
Alguazas [E] 104 C3
Algutsrum [S] 162 G5
Algyő [H] 76 E4
Alhama de Almería [E] 102 G5
Alhama de Aragón [E] 90 C4
Alhama de Granada [E] 102 D4
Alhama de Murcia [E] 104 B3
Alhambra [E] 96 G5
Alhamillo [E] 96 C4
Alhaurín de la Torre [E] 102 B5
Alhaurín el Grande [E] 102 B4
Alhojärvi [FIN] 186 F5
Ålholm Slot [DK] 20 B1
Ålhus [N] 180 C6
Alía [E] 96 C2
Ália [I] 126 D3
Aliaga [E] 98 F1
Aliağa [TR] 152 C3
Alíartos [GR] 134 A5
Alibeyli [TR] 152 D3
Alibunar [SRB] 142 H2
Alibunar [SRB] 204 B5
Aliç [TR] 150 B3
Alicante / Alacant [E] 104 E2
Alicudi Porto [I] 124 A5
Åliden [S] 196 A4
Alife [I] 120 E2
Alifuatpaşa [TR] 150 G3
Alija del Infantado [E] 80 H3
Alijó [P] 80 E4
Alíkampos [GR] 140 C4
Alikanás [GR] 136 A2
Alil Abasi [MK] 128 G1
Alimena [I] 126 E3
Alinci [MK] 128 E3
Alinda [TR] 152 E6
Alingsås [S] 162 B1
Alino [BG] 146 F5
Alinyá [E] 92 D2
Aliseda [E] 86 G5
Alistráti [GR] 130 C3
Ali Terme [I] 124 B7
Alivéri [GR] 134 C5
Aljaraque [E] 94 E5
Aljezur [P] 94 B4
Aljinovići [SRB] 146 A3
Aljubarrota [P] 86 C3
Aljucén [E] 86 G6
Aljustrel [P] 94 C3
Alkmaar [NL] 16 D3
Alkotz [E] 84 B3
Alkoven [A] 62 B4
Alkpınar [TR] 150 C2
Alksniupiai [LT] 200 F4
Alkvettern [S] 166 G2
Állai [I] 118 C5
Allaines [F] 42 E5
Allainville [F] 42 E4
Allan [F] 68 F6
Allanche [F] 68 C3
Alland [A] 62 E5
Allariz [E] 78 C5
Allauch [F] 108 B5
Alleen [N] 164 C5
Alleghe [I] 72 E4
Allejaur [S] 190 G3
Allemont [F] 68 H5
Allenbach [D] 44 G2
Allentsteig [A] 62 D3
Allepuz [E] 98 E1
Aller-Heiligen [D] 58 F1
Allersberg [D] 46 G6
Allershausen [D] 60 E3
Allerum [S] 156 H1
Alleuze, Château d'- [F] 68 C4
Allevard [F] 70 A4
Allgunnen [S] 162 F4
Allihies [IRL] 4 A5
Allingåbro [DK] 160 E5
Allinge [DK] 158 E4
Allo [E] 84 A4
Alloa [GB] 8 E3
Ållolukta [S] 192 G6
Allonnes [F] 42 E5
Allonnes [F] 54 E2
Allonö [S] 168 B5
Allos [F] 108 D3
Alloue [F] 54 E5
Ållsjön [S] 184 E2
Allstedt [D] 34 B5
Almacelles [E] 90 H4
Almada [P] 86 B5
Almadén [E] 96 C4
Almadén de la Plata [E] 94 G5
Almadenes, Cañón de los- [E] 104 B2
Almadenejos [E] 96 D4
Almadrones [E] 90 A5
Almagreira [P] 100 E4
Almagro [E] 96 F4
Almancil [P] 94 C5
Almandoz [E] 84 B3
Almansa [E] 98 D6
Almanza [E] 82 C4
Almaraz [E] 88 B6
Almargen [E] 102 B3
Almarza [E] 90 B2
Almås [N] 182 C2
Almásfüzitő [H] 64 B6
Almassora / Almazora [E] 98 F3
Almazán [E] 90 B3
Almazora / Almassora [E] 98 F3
Almedina [E] 96 G5
Almeida [P] 80 E6
Almeida de Sayago [E] 80 G5
Almeirim [P] 86 C4
Almelo [NL] 16 G4
Almenar [E] 90 H4
Almenara [E] 98 F4
Almenara [E] 102 B1
Almenara de Tormes [E] 80 G6
Almenar de Soria [E] 90 C3
Almendinilla [E] 102 D3
Almendra [P] 80 E5
Almendral [E] 94 G2
Almendralejo [E] 94 G2
Almenno S. Salvatore [I] 70 H4
Almere [NL] 16 E4
Almería [E] 102 G5
Almerimar [E] 102 F6
Almesåkra [S] 162 D2
Älmestad [S] 162 C1
Älmhult [S] 162 D5
Almodôvar [P] 94 C4
Almodóvar del Campo [E] 96 E4
Almodóvar del Pinar [E] 98 C3
Almodóvar del Río [E] 102 B1
Almogía [E] 102 C4
Almograve [P] 94 B3
Almoharín [E] 86 H6
Almonaster la Real [E] 94 F4
Almonte [E] 94 F6
Almoradí [E] 104 D3
Almoraima [E] 100 G5
Almorox [E] 88 E6
Almourol [P] 86 D4
Almsele [S] 190 F5
Älmsta-Väddö [S] 168 E1
Almudévar [E] 90 F3
Almuñécar [E] 102 D5
Almunge [S] 168 D1
Almuradiel [E] 96 F5
Almvik [S] 162 G2
Almyró [GR] 136 D4
Almyropótamos [GR] 134 D5
Almyrós [GR] 132 H3
Alness [GB] 6 E4
Alnwick [GB] 8 G5
Aloja [LV] 198 E4
Alol' [RUS] 198 H5
Alónnisos [GR] 134 C3
Álora [E] 102 B4
Alosno [E] 94 E5
Alost (Aalst) [B] 28 H2
Alozaina [E] 102 B4
Alp [E] 92 E2
Alpalhão [P] 86 E4
Alpbach [A] 60 E6
Alpedrinha [P] 86 F3
Alpe du Grand Serre [F] 68 H5
Alpen [D] 30 G2
Alpengarten [D] 60 D6
Alpera [E] 98 C5
Alphen-aan den Rijn [NL] 16 D5
Alpiarça [P] 86 C4
Alpirsbach [D] 58 F2
Alportel [P] 94 C5
Alpua [FIN] 196 D5
Alpuente [E] 98 D3
Alpullu [TR] 150 B2
Alqueva [P] 94 E3
Alquézar [E] 90 G3
Als [DK] 160 E4
Alsager [GB] 10 D5
Alsasua / Altsasu [E] 82 H5
Alsen [S] 182 G1
Alsenz [D] 46 B4
Alsfeld [D] 46 D1
Ålshult [S] 162 D5
Alsleben [D] 34 B4
Alsø [DK] 160 F6
Alsóőrs [H] 76 A2
Alsótold [H] 64 D5
Alsózsolca [H] 64 F5
Ålstad [N] 192 D5
Ålstad [S] 158 C3
Alstahaug [N] 190 D2
Alstätte [D] 16 G5
Alsterbro [S] 162 F4
Alstermo [S] 162 F4
Alston [GB] 8 F6
Alsunga [LV] 198 B5
Alsvåg [N] 192 D3
Alsvik [N] 192 D6
Alta [N] 194 B3
Altafulla [E] 92 C5
Altamira, Cuevas de- [E] 82 E3
Altamura [I] 122 D3
Altarejos [E] 98 B2
Altaussee [A] 62 A6
Altavilla Silentina [I] 120 F4
Altdahn [D] 44 H4
Altdorf [CH] 58 F6
Altdorf [D] 46 G5
Alt Duvenstedt [D] 18 F2
Altea [E] 104 F2
Altedo [I] 110 F3
Alteidet [N] 192 H1
Altena [D] 32 C5
Altenahr [D] 30 G5
Altenau [D] 32 G4
Altenberg [D] 48 E2
Altenberge [D] 16 H5
Altenberger Dom [D] 30 H4
Altenburg [A] 62 D3
Altenburg [D] 34 C6
Altenfelden [A] 62 B3
Altenglan [D] 44 H3
Altenhundem [D] 32 C5
Altenkirchen [D] 20 D1
Altenkirchen [D] 32 C6
Altenklingen [CH] 58 G4
Altenmarkt [A] 62 C6
Altenmarkt [A] 72 H1
Altenmarkt [D] 60 F5
Altenstadt [D] 60 B4
Altenstadt [D] 60 D5
Altensteig [D] 58 G1
Altentreptow [D] 20 D4
Altenwalde [D] 18 D3
Alter do Chão [P] 86 E5
Alteren [N] 190 E2
Althegnenberg [D] 60 D4
Altheim [A] 60 H4
Althofen [A] 74 B2
Altı [TR] 154 B1
Altimir [BG] 146 G3
Altınoluk [TR] 152 B1
Altınova [TR] 150 F3
Altınova [TR] 152 B2
Altıntaş [TR] 152 H2
Altınyayla [TR] 154 G1
Altipiani di Arcinazzo [I] 116 B6
Altkirch [F] 58 D4
Altlandsberg [D] 34 E2
Altmörbitz [D] 34 C6
Altmünster [A] 62 A5
Altnaharra [GB] 6 E3
Alto de los Leones de Castilla [E] 88 F4
Altomonte [I] 124 D3
Alton [GB] 14 D4
Altopascio [I] 110 E5
Altorricón [E] 90 H4
Altötting [D] 60 G4
Altrier [L] 44 F2
Alt Ruppin [D] 20 C6
Altsasu / Alsasua [E] 82 H5
Alt Schadow [D] 34 F3
Altshausen [D] 58 H3
Altstätten [CH] 58 H5
Alttajärvi [S] 192 G5
Altuna [S] 168 C1
Altura [E] 98 E3
Altwarp [D] 20 E4
Altwindeck [D] 58 F1
Alūksne [LV] 198 F4
Ålum [DK] 160 D5
Ålund [S] 196 A4
Alunda [S] 168 D1
Aluokta [S] 192 F6
Alupka [UA] 204 H4
Aluste [EST] 198 E2
Alvaiázere [P] 86 D3
Alvajärvi [FIN] 186 F1
Alvalade [P] 94 C3
Älvan [S] 166 H5
Älvängen [S] 160 H1
Alvastra [S] 166 G6
Alvdal [N] 182 B5
Älvdalen [S] 172 F2
Alvechurch [GB] 12 H1
Alverca do Ribatejo [P] 86 B5
Alversund [N] 170 B3
Alvesta [S] 162 D4
Alvestad [N] 164 A2
Älvhem [S] 160 H1
Alvignac [F] 66 G4
Ålvik [N] 170 C4
Alvik [S] 172 G4
Alvik [S] 196 B3
Älviken [S] 190 E6
Alvito [I] 116 C6
Alvito [P] 94 D2
Älvkarleby [S] 174 E4
Alvor [P] 94 B5
Älvros [S] 182 E6
Älvros [S] 182 G5
Älvsbacka [S] 166 F2
Älvsbyn [S] 196 A3
Älvsered [S] 162 B4
Älvsund [S] 184 E5
Ålvundeid [N] 180 F3
Alyekshytsy [BY] 24 G5
Alykí [GR] 130 E4
Alykí [GR] 130 E4
Alykí [GR] 138 E3
Alytus [LT] 24 G2
Alzenau [D] 46 D3
Alzey [D] 46 B4
Alzira [E] 98 E5
Alzon [F] 106 E3
Alzonne [F] 106 B4
Åmådalen [S] 172 G2
Amadora [P] 86 B5
Åmål [S] 166 D4
Amalfi [I] 120 E4
Amaliáda [GR] 136 C2
Amaliápoli [GR] 132 H3
Ámalo [GR] 138 G1
Amance [F] 58 B3
Amancey [F] 58 B5
Amandola [I] 116 C2
Amantea [I] 124 D5
Amantia [AL] 128 B5
Amarante [P] 80 C4
Amárantos [GR] 132 F3
Amărăştii de Sus [RO] 146 G2
Amareleja [P] 94 E3
Amári [GR] 140 D5
Amárynthos [GR] 134 C5
Amatrice [I] 116 C3
Amay [B] 30 E5
Ambarès [F] 66 D3
Ambazac [F] 54 G6
Amberg [D] 46 H5
Ambérieu-en-Bugey [F] 68 G2
Ambert [F] 68 D3
Ambiörnarp [S] 162 B3
Ambjörby [S] 172 E4
Ambla [EST] 198 E1
Amble [GB] 8 G5
Ambleside [GB] 10 D2
Amboise [F] 54 G2
Ämbra [EST] 198 E2
Ambrières [F] 26 E5
Åmdal [N] 164 D5
Ameixial [P] 94 C4
Amel [B] 30 F6
Amélia [I] 116 A3
Amélie-les-Bains [F] 92 F2
Amelinghausen [D] 18 F5
Amendolara [I] 122 D6
Amer [E] 92 F3
A Merca [E] 78 C5
Amerongen [NL] 16 E5
Amersfoort [NL] 16 E5
Amersham [GB] 14 E3
Amesbury [GB] 12 G4
A Mezquita [E] 78 E6
Amfiáreio [GR] 134 C5
Amfíkleia [GR] 132 G4
Amfilochía [GR] 132 D4
Amfípoli [GR] 130 C4
Ámfissa [GR] 132 G5
Amiens [F] 28 E5
Åmilden [S] 190 H4
Åminne [S] 168 G4
Amiternum [I] 116 C4
Amlach [LT] 72 F3
Åmli [N] 164 E3
Åmli [N] 164 E4
Amlwch [GB] 10 B3
Ammanford [GB] 12 E2
Ämmänsaari [FIN] 196 F4
Ammarnäs [S] 190 F2
Åmmeberg [S] 166 G4
Ammersricht [D] 48 B5
Ammóchostos (Gazimağusa) [CY] 154 G5
Ammótopos [GR] 132 D3
Ammoudára [GR] 140 E4
Ammoudára [GR] 140 F5
Åmnes [N] 164 F2
Amorbach [D] 46 D4
Amòreira, Acueducto de- [P] 86 E6
Amorgós [GR] 138 G4
Amorosi [I] 120 E2
Åmot [N] 164 E1
Åmot [N] 164 G1
Åmot [N] 170 G4
Åmot [N] 170 H3
Åmot [N] 172 C2
Åmot [S] 174 D3
Åmotfors [S] 166 D1
Åmotsdal [N] 164 E1
Amou [F] 84 D2
Ampelákia [GR] 132 G1
Ampelikó [GR] 134 H2
Ampelónas [GR] 132 G1
Ampezzo [I] 72 F4
Ampfing [D] 60 F4
Amphion [F] 70 B2

Amplepuis [F] 68 F2
Amposta [E] 92 A6
Ampudia [E] 82 C6
Ampuero [E] 82 F3
Ampuis [F] 68 F3
Ampus [F] 108 D4
Amriswil [CH] 58 H4
Am See [A] 72 C2
Amsele [S] 190 H5
Amsteg [CH] 70 F1
Amsterdam [NL] 16 D4
Amstetten [A] 62 C4
Amtoft [DK] 160 C4
Amurrio [E] 82 G4
Amvrosía [GR] 130 F2
Amygdaleónas [GR] 130 D3
Amygdaliá [GR] 132 G5
Amýkles [GR] 136 E4
Amýntaio [GR] 128 F4
Amzacea [RO] 148 G1
Anadia [P] 80 B6
Anáfi [GR] 138 F5
Anafonítria [GR] 136 A2
Anagni [I] 116 B6
Anáktora Néstoros [GR] 136 C4
Análipsi [GR] 138 H4
Anamourion [TR] 154 F4
Anamur [TR] 154 F4
Anan'ïv [UA] 204 G2
Anárgyroi [GR] 128 E5
Anarráchi [GR] 128 E5
Anascaul [IRL] 4 B4
Ånäset [S] 196 A5
Åna-Sira [N] 164 B5
Anastazewo [PL] 36 E2
Änätinpää [FIN] 196 G4
Anatolí [GR] 132 G1
Anatolikó [GR] 128 F5
Anávra [GR] 132 F3
Anávra [GR] 132 G3
Anávyssos [GR] 136 H1
Anaya [E] 88 F4
An Cabhán / Cavan [IRL] 2 E4
Anc. Batterie [F] 108 D2
Ance [LV] 198 C4
Ancenis [F] 40 G6
Ancerville [F] 44 C5
An Charraig / Carrick [IRL] 2 D2
An Cheathrú Rua / Carraroe [IRL] 2 B5
An Chloich Mhór / Cloghmore [IRL] 2 B3
Anchuras [E] 96 D2
An Clochán Liath / Dunglow [IRL] 2 E2
An Coireán / Waterville [IRL] 4 A4
Ancona [I] 112 C6
Ancy-le-Franc [F] 56 F2
Anda [N] 180 C5
An Daingean / Dingle [IRL] 4 A3
Andalo [I] 72 C4
Åndalsnes [N] 180 E3
Andåsen [S] 182 G5
Andau [A] 62 G6
Ändebol [S] 168 B4
Andebu [N] 164 H3
Andechs [D] 60 D5
Andelot [F] 44 D6
Andenes [N] 192 E2
Andenne [B] 30 D5
Andermatt [CH] 70 F1
Andernach [D] 30 H6
Andernos-les-Bains [F] 66 B3
Andersfors [S] 196 A5
Anderslöv [S] 158 C3
Anderstorp [S] 162 C3
Andijk [NL] 16 E3
Andilla [E] 98 E3
Andız [TR] 150 G6
Andocs [H] 76 A3
Andolsheim [F] 58 E3
Andornaktálya [H] 64 E5
Andorno Micca [I] 70 E4
Andorra [E] 90 F6
Andorra la Vella [AND] 84 H6
Andover [GB] 12 H4
Andrade, Castelo de- [E] 78 D2
Andraitx [E] 104 D5
Andravída [GR] 136 B1
Andreapol' [RUS] 202 D3
Andrespol [PL] 36 G4
Andretta [I] 120 G3
Andrézieux-Bouthéon [F] 68 E3
Ándria [I] 122 C2
Andriake [TR] 154 H3
Andrijevica [MNE] 146 A5
Andrítsaina [GR] 136 D3
Ándros [GR] 134 E6
Androússa [GR] 136 D4
Andrychów [PL] 50 G4
Andselv [N] 192 F3
Andújar [E] 102 D1
Anduze [F] 106 F3
An Eachléim / Aghleam [IRL] 2 B3
Ånebjør [N] 164 D3
Åneby [N] 172 B5
Aneby [S] 162 E2
Ånes [N] 180 F1
Anet [F] 42 E3
An Fhairche / Clonbur [IRL] 2 C4
Anfo [I] 72 B5
Anga [S] 168 G4
Änge [S] 182 G1
Ånge [S] 184 C4
Ånge [S] 190 G2
Ängebo [S] 184 D6
Angeja [P] 80 B5
Ängelholm [S] 156 H1
Angeli [FIN] 194 C4
Angelókastro [GR] 132 E5
Angelókastro [GR] 136 F2
Angelsberg [S] 168 B1
Ängelsfors [S] 174 D4
Angelstad [S] 162 C5
Angenstein [CH] 58 E4
Anger [A] 74 E1
Angermünde [D] 20 E6
Angern [A] 62 G4
Angers [F] 40 H6
Ängersjö [S] 182 G6
Ängersjö [S] 184 H1
Angerville [F] 42 E5
Ängesan [S] 194 B8
Ängesbyn [S] 196 B3
Anghelo Ruiu, Necropoli- [I] 118 B3
Anghiari [I] 110 G6
Angiari [I] 110 F1
Anglès [E] 92 F3
Angles-sur-l'Anglin [F] 54 F4
Anglet [F] 84 C2
Anglona [LV] 198 G6
Anglure [F] 44 A5
Ango, Manoir d'- [F] 28 C4
Angoulême [F] 66 E1
Angra do Heroísmo [P] 100 D3
Ångskär [S] 174 F4
Ängsö [S] 168 C2
Angueira [P] 80 G4
Angüés [E] 90 G3
Anguiano [E] 90 B1
Anguillara Sabazia [I] 114 H5
Anguillara Veneta [I] 110 G2
Angulo [E] 82 G4
Angvika [N] 180 F2
Anholt [DK] 160 G5
Aniane [F] 106 E4
Aniche [F] 28 F4
Anina [RO] 204 B5
Anıtkaya [TR] 152 H2
Anjala [FIN] 178 C3
Anjalankoski [FIN] 178 C3
Anjos [P] 100 E3
Anjum [NL] 16 F1
Ankaran [SLO] 72 H6
Ankarede [S] 190 E4
Ankarsrum [S] 162 G2
Ankarvattnet [S] 190 E4
Ankenesstrand [N] 192 E4
Anklam [D] 20 D4
Ankum [D] 32 D1
Anlezy [F] 56 E4
Ånn [S] 182 E2
Anna [EST] 198 E2
Annaberg [A] 60 H6
Annaberg [A] 62 D5
Annaberg-Buchholz [D] 48 D2
Annadalsvagen [N] 190 D3
Annalong [NIR] 2 G4
Annan [GB] 8 E5
Anna Paulowna [NL] 16 D3
An Nás / Naas [IRL] 2 F6
Anneberg [S] 160 H2
Anneberg [S] 162 E2
Annecy [F] 70 B3
Annefors [S] 174 D2
Annelund [S] 162 B1
Annemasse [F] 70 B2
Annenheim [A] 74 A3
Annerstad [S] 162 C5
Annestown [IRL] 4 E5
Annonay [F] 68 F4
Annopol [PL] 52 D1
Annot [F] 108 D3
Annoux [F] 56 F2
Annweiler [D] 46 B5
Anógeia [GR] 140 E4
Anoixi [GR] 132 E1
Áno Kalentíni [GR] 132 D3
Áno Kastrítsi [GR] 132 F6
Áno Merá [GR] 138 E2
Anópoli [GR] 140 C5
Áno Sagkri [GR] 138 F3
Áno Sýros [GR] 138 D2
Anould [F] 58 D2
Añover de Tajo [E] 96 F1
Áno Viánnos [GR] 140 F5
Áno Vrontoú [GR] 130 C2
Anquela del Ducado [E] 90 B5
An Rinn / Ringville [IRL] 4 E5
Ans [DK] 160 D6
Ansager [DK] 156 B2
Ansarve [S] 168 F5
Ansbach [D] 46 F5
Anse [F] 68 F2
Ansedónia [I] 114 F4
Anserall [E] 92 D1
Anseremme [B] 30 D6
Ansfelden [A] 62 B4
Ansião [P] 86 D2
Ansó [E] 84 D4
An Spidéal / Spiddal [IRL] 2 B5
Anstad [N] 180 F5
Anstey [GB] 10 F6
Anstruther [GB] 8 F3
Ansvar [S] 194 B8
Antagnod [I] 70 D3
Antanarav [LT] 200 G4
Antandros [TR] 134 H1
Antas [P] 80 D5
Antas, Tempio di- [I] 118 B6
Antas de Ulla [E] 78 D3
Antegnate [I] 70 H5
Anten [S] 160 H1
Antequera [E] 102 C4
Anterselva / Antholz [I] 72 E2
Antey St. André [I] 70 D3
Anthéor [F] 108 E5
Anthí [GR] 130 B3
Antholz / Anterselva [I] 72 E2
Anthótopos [GR] 132 G3
Antibes [F] 108 E5
Antigonea [AL] 128 C6
Antigua [E] 100 E6
Antigua Bilbilis [E] 90 D4
Antigüedad [E] 88 G1
Antíkýra [GR] 132 H5
Antimáchia [GR] 154 B2
An Tinbhear Mór / Arklow [IRL] 4 G4
Antíparos [GR] 138 E3
Antírrio [GR] 132 F5
Ántissa [GR] 134 G2
Ántissa [GR] 134 G2
Antjärn [S] 184 F4
Antnäs [S] 196 B3
Anton [BG] 148 A4
Antonin [PL] 36 E5
Antoniów [PL] 52 D1
Antonovo [BG] 148 D3
Antopal' [BY] 38 H2
Antraigues [F] 68 E5
Antrain [F] 26 D5
Antrim [NIR] 2 G3
Antrodoco [I] 116 B4
Antsla [EST] 198 F3
Anttila [FIN] 196 F5
Anttis [S] 194 B7
Anttola [FIN] 188 D6
Anttola [FIN] 188 F5
Antwerpen (Anvers) [B] 30 C3
An Uaimh / Navan [IRL] 2 F5
Anundshögen [S] 168 C2
Anvers (Antwerpen) [B] 30 C3
Anvin [F] 28 E3
Anykščiai [LT] 200 G4
Anzi [I] 120 H4
Anzio [I] 120 A1
Aoiz / Agoitz [E] 84 C4
Aosta / Aoste [I] 70 D4
Aoste / Aosta [I] 70 D4
Apaj [H] 76 C2
Apamea [TR] 150 E4
Åpåsdal [N] 164 D5
Apátfalva [H] 76 F4
Apatin [MNE] 204 A5
Apatin [SRB] 76 C6
Apchon [F] 68 B3
Ape [LV] 198 F4
Apécchio [I] 110 H6
Apeírathos [GR] 138 F3
Apeldoorn [NL] 16 F5
Apen [D] 18 C5
Apensen [D] 18 F4
Aperlai [TR] 154 H3
Aphrodisias [TR] 152 F5
Apice [I] 120 F2
Apinac [F] 68 E3
Aplared [S] 162 B2
A Pobra de Brollón / Puebla del Brollón [E] 78 D4
A Pobra de Navia [E] 78 E4
A Pobra de Trives [E] 78 D5
Apoíkia [GR] 134 E6
Apolakkiá [GR] 154 C4
Apolda [D] 34 B6
Apollo Aléo, Tempio di- [I] 124 F4
Apóllon [GR] 138 F3
Apollonia [AL] 128 A4
Apollonía [GR] 130 B4
Apollonía [GR] 138 D3
Apollonía [GR] 138 D4
Apollonia [TR] 150 E4
Apollonia [TR] 152 D2
Apollonia [TR] 154 G3
A Pontenova [E] 78 E2
Apostolove [UA] 204 F3
Apothicairerie, Grotte de l'- [F] 40 C5
Äppelbo [S] 172 F4
Appelhülsen [D] 16 H6
Appenweier [D] 44 H6
Appenzell [CH] 58 H5
Appiano / Eppan [I] 72 D3
Appingedam [NL] 16 H2
Appleby-in-Westmorland [GB] 10 E1
Apremont, Gorges d'- [F] 42 F5
Aprica [I] 72 B4
Apricena [I] 116 G6
Aprigliano [I] 124 D4
Aprilia [I] 116 A6
Aprilovo [BG] 148 D3
Apróhomok [H] 64 G4
Ápsalos [GR] 128 F4
Apt [F] 108 B3
Áptera [GR] 140 C4
Aquila [CH] 70 G2
Aquileia [I] 72 G5
Aquilonia [I] 120 G3
Aquino [I] 120 C1
Ar [S] 168 G3
Arabba [I] 72 E3
Araburg [A] 62 E5
Araceli [E] 102 C3
Aracena [E] 94 F4
Aráchova [GR] 132 F4
Aráchova [GR] 132 G5
Aračinovo [MK] 146 D6
Arad [RO] 76 G4
Aradíppou [CY] 154 G5
Aragona [I] 126 D4
Aragonese, Castello- [I] 124 F4
Arahal [E] 100 H2
Arakapás [CY] 154 F6
Åraksbø [N] 164 D3
Åram [N] 180 C4
Aramits [F] 84 D3
Araña, Cueva de la- [E] 98 D5
Aranda de Duero [E] 88 G2
Arandjelovac [SRB] 146 B1
Arandjelovac [SRB] 204 B6
Aranjuez [E] 96 G1
Arantzazu [E] 82 H5
Aras de Alpuente [E] 98 D3
Áratos [GR] 130 F2
Aravaca [E] 88 F5
Aravissós [GR] 128 G4
Arazede [P] 80 B6
Arbanasi [BG] 148 C3
Arbatax [I] 118 E5
Arbesbach [A] 62 C3
Arbetera [E] 90 B6
Arboga [S] 168 B3
Arbois [F] 58 A5
Arbon [CH] 58 H5
Arboréa [I] 118 B5
Arbrå [S] 174 D2
Arbroath [GB] 8 F2
Arbúcies [E] 92 F3
Árbus [I] 118 B6
Arc, Pont d'- [F] 106 G2
Arcachon [F] 66 B3
Arcas [E] 98 B2
Arc de Berà [E] 92 C5
Arce [I] 120 C1
Arcen [NL] 30 F3
Arc-en-Barrois [F] 56 H2
Arcévia [I] 116 B1
Archánes [GR] 140 E5
Archángelos [GR] 132 D3
Archángelos [GR] 154 D4
Archar [BG] 146 F2
Archena [E] 104 C2
Arches [F] 58 C2
Archiac [F] 66 D1
Archidona [E] 102 C3
Archivel [E] 104 A2
Arcidosso [I] 114 G2
Arcille [I] 114 F3
Arcinazzo Romano [I] 116 B5
Arcis-sur-Aube [F] 44 B5
Arco [I] 72 C5
Arco de Baúlhe [P] 80 D3
Arconville [F] 42 F2
Arcos de Jalón [E] 90 B4
Arcos de la Frontera [E] 100 G3
Arcos de la Sierra [E] 98 C1
Arcos de Valdevez [P] 78 B6
Ardagh [IRL] 4 C3
Årdal [N] 180 C6
Ardala [S] 166 E6
Årdala [S] 168 C4
Ardales [E] 102 B4
Årdalsosen [N] 164 B2
Årdalstangen [N] 170 E2
Ardara [IRL] 2 E2
Ardea [I] 116 A6
Ardee [IRL] 2 F5
Arden [DK] 160 D4
Ardenicës [AL] 128 B4
Ardentes [F] 54 H4
Ardez [CH] 72 B2
Ardfert [IRL] 4 B3
Ardfinnan [IRL] 4 D4
Ardglass [NIR] 2 G4
Ardino [BG] 130 E1
Ardisa [E] 84 C6
Ardon [F] 58 A6
Ardore [I] 124 D7
Ardres [F] 14 G6
Ardrossan [GB] 8 C3
Åre [S] 182 E1
Areas [E] 78 B5
Areatza [E] 82 G4
Årebrot [N] 180 B5
Arêches-Beaufort [F] 70 B3
Arèhava [BY] 38 G4
Arenals del Sol / Los Arenales del Sol [E] 104 D3
Arenas [E] 82 D2
Arenas del Rey [E] 102 D4
Arenas de San Pedro [E] 88 D5
Arendal [N] 164 F5
Arendonk [B] 30 D3
Arendsee [D] 20 A6
Arene / Arrankudiaga [E] 82 G4
Arenenberg [CH] 58 G4
Areños [E] 82 D3
Arenys de Mar [E] 92 F4
Arenzano [I] 108 H3
Areópoli [GR] 136 E5
Ares [E] 78 D2
Arès [F] 66 B3
Ares del Maestrat / Ares del Maestre [E] 98 F2
Ares del Maestre / Ares del Maestrat [E] 98 F2
Aréthousa [GR] 130 C4
Aretí [GR] 130 B4
Aretxabaleta [E] 82 H4
Arevalillo [E] 88 C4
Arévalo [E] 88 E3
Arezzo [I] 114 G1
Arfará [GR] 136 D3
Årfora [N] 190 C4
Argalastí [GR] 134 A3
Argállon [E] 96 B5
Argamasilla de Alba [E] 96 G4
Argamasilla de Calatrava [E] 96 E5
Argancy [F] 44 F4
Arganda del Rey [E] 88 G6
Arganil [P] 86 E2
Argási [GR] 136 B2
Argegno [I] 70 G3
Argelès-Gazost [F] 84 E4
Argelès-Plage [F] 92 G1
Argelès-sur-Mer [F] 92 G1
Argenta [I] 110 G3
Argentan [F] 26 F5
Argentat [F] 66 H3
Argentella [F] 114 A3
Argentera [I] 108 E2
Argentiera [I] 118 B3
Argentière [F] 70 C3
Argenton-Château [F] 54 D2
Argenton-sur-Creuse [F] 54 G4
Argentré [F] 26 E6
Argent-sur-Sauldre [F] 56 C2
Argés [E] 96 F2
Arginónta [GR] 154 A2
Argithéa [GR] 132 E3
Argomariz [E] 82 H5
Árgos [GR] 136 E2
Árgos Orestikó [GR] 128 E5
Argostóli [GR] 132 C6
Arguedas [E] 84 B5
Arguineguín [E] 100 C6
Arguís [E] 84 D6
Arguisuelas [E] 98 C3
Argy [F] 54 G3
Argyrádes [GR] 132 B3
Argyroúpoli [GR] 140 C5
Arhéa Olimbía [GR] 136 C2
Århus [DK] 156 D1
Ariano Irpino [I] 120 F2
Ariano nel Polésine [I] 110 H2
Aridaía [GR] 128 F3
Arif [TR] 154 H2
Arilje [SRB] 146 A3
Arinagour [GB] 6 A6
Ariño [E] 90 E5
Arinthod [F] 56 H6
Ariogala [LT] 200 F5
Aristoménis [GR] 136 D4
Aritzo [I] 118 D5
Ariza [E] 90 C4
Årjäng [S] 166 D2
Arjeplog [S] 190 G2
Arjona [E] 102 D1
Arjonilla [E] 102 D1
Arkádi [GR] 140 D4
Arkadia [PL] 36 H3
Arkalochóri [GR] 140 E5
Arkása [GR] 140 H3
Arkesíni [GR] 138 F4
Arkítsa [GR] 132 H4
Arklow / An Tinbhear Mór [IRL] 4 G4
Arkösund [S] 168 C5
Arkutino [BG] 148 F5
Ärla [S] 168 C3
Arlanc [F] 68 D3
Arlberg Tunnel [A] 72 B1
Arlempdes [F] 68 D5
Arlena di Castro [I] 114 G4
Arles [F] 106 G4
Arles-sur-Tech [F] 92 F2
Arló [H] 64 E4
Arlon (Aarlen) [B] 44 E2
Arlöv [S] 156 H3
Armadale [GB] 6 B5
Armagh [NIR] 2 F4
Armação de Pera [P] 94 B5
Arméni [GR] 132 G2
Armenioí [GR] 136 C3
Armenistís [GR] 138 G1
Arménoi [GR] 140 D5
Armentières [F] 28 F3
Armilla [E] 102 E4
Armiñón [E] 82 G5
Armólia [GR] 134 G5
Armoy [NIR] 2 G2
Armuña de Tajuña [E] 88 H6
Armutcuk [TR] 152 C1
Armutlu [TR] 150 C5
Armutlu [TR] 150 E4
Armutlu [TR] 152 D4
Armyansk [UA] 204 H3
Árna [GR] 136 E4
Arna [N] 170 B4
Arnac [F] 66 E4
Arnac-Pompadur [F] 66 G2
Arnafjord [N] 170 C2
Arnage [F] 42 B5
Arnager [DK] 158 E4
Arnaía [GR] 130 C5
Arnäs [S] 166 F5
Arnäs [S] 184 G2
Arnavutköy [TR] 150 E2
Arnavutköy [TR] 150 E4
Arnay-le-Duc [F] 56 F4
Arnborg [DK] 156 B1
Arneberg [N] 172 B3
Arneburg [D] 34 C1
Arnedillo [E] 90 C1
Arnedo [E] 84 A5
Arnes [E] 90 G6
Årnes [N] 172 C5
Årnes [N] 190 B5
Årnes [N] 190 C4
Arnhem [NL] 16 F5
Árnissa [GR] 128 F4
Arnoldstein [A] 72 H3
Arnön [S] 174 E1
Arnsberg [D] 32 C4
Arnsburg [D] 46 D2
Arnschwang [D] 48 D6
Arnstadt [D] 46 G1
Arnstein [D] 46 E3
Arnuera [E] 82 F3
Aroanía [GR] 136 D1
Aroche [E] 94 F4
Ároktő [H] 64 F5
Arola [FIN] 194 D3
Arolla [CH] 70 D3
Arolsen [D] 32 E5
Arona [I] 70 F4
Aronkylä [FIN] 186 B4
Åros [N] 164 H1
Arosa [CH] 70 H1
Årosjåkk [S] 192 F5
Årøsund [DK] 156 C3
Arouca [P] 80 C5
Arøysund [N] 164 H3
Arpacık [TR] 154 F2
Arpajon [F] 42 F4
Árpás [H] 62 H6
Arpela [FIN] 196 C2
Arquà Petrarca [I] 110 G1
Arquata del Tronto [I] 116 C3
Arquata Scrivia [I] 110 B2
Arquillinos [E] 102 F1
Arrabal / Oia [E] 78 A5
Arracourt [F] 44 F5
Arraiolos [P] 86 D6
Arrakoski [FIN] 176 H1
Arrankorpi [FIN] 176 H3
Arrankudiaga / Arene [E] 82 G4
Arrans [F] 56 F2
Arras [F] 28 F4
Arrasate o Mondragón [E] 82 H4
Arrate [E] 82 H4
Årre [DK] 156 B2
Arreau [F] 84 F4
Arrecife [E] 100 E6
Arrens-Marsous [F] 84 E4
Arrentela [P] 86 B5
Arriate [E] 102 A4
Arriaundi [E] 82 H4
Arriba Fóssil [P] 86 A5
Arrifana [P] 94 B4
Arriondas [E] 82 C2
Arroba de los Montes [E] 96 D3
Arromanches-les-Bains [F] 26 F3
Arronches [P] 86 F5
Arròs [E] 84 G5
Arròs [F] 84 G5
Arroyo de la Luz [E] 86 G5
Arroyo de la Miel-Benalmádena Costa [E] 102 B5
Arroyo de San Serván [E] 94 G2
Arruda dos Vinhos [P] 86 B4
Årsandøy [N] 190 C4
Ars-en-Ré [F] 54 B4
Arsen'yevo [RUS] 202 F4
Arsiè [I] 72 D5
Arsiero [I] 72 D5
Arslankaya [TR] 152 H1
Årslev [DK] 156 D3
Årsnes [N] 180 D4
Arsoli [I] 116 B5
Ars-sur-Moselle [F] 44 E4
Årsunda [S] 174 E4
Arsvågen [N] 164 A2
Arsy [F] 28 E6
Artà [E] 104 F5
Árta [GR] 132 D3
Artà, Coves d'- [E] 104 F5
Artajona [E] 84 B4
Artana [E] 98 F3
Ártánd [H] 76 H2
Arta Terme [I] 72 G3
Arteixo [E] 78 C2
Artemare [F] 68 H3
Artemisía [GR] 136 D4
Artemísio [GR] 134 A3
Artemónas [GR] 138 D3
Artena [I] 116 B6
Artenay [F] 42 E5
Artern [D] 34 A5
Artesa de Segre [E] 92 C3
Artesa de Segre / Montargull [E] 92 C2
Arth [CH] 58 F6
Arth [D] 60 F3
Arthous, Ancient Prieure d'- [F] 84 C2
Arthurstown [IRL] 4 E5
Arties [E] 84 G5
Artix [F] 84 E3
Artjärvi / Artsjö [FIN] 178 B3
Artotína [GR] 132 F4
Artouste-Fabrèges [F] 84 E4
Årtrik [S] 184 E2
Artsjö / Artjärvi [FIN] 178 B3
Artsyz [UA] 204 F4
A Rúa [E] 78 E5
Arucas [E] 100 C6
Arudy [F] 84 D3
Arundel [GB] 14 D5
Arva [E] 94 H6
Årvåg [N] 180 G1
Arvagh [IRL] 2 E4
Arversund [S] 182 G2
Árvi [GR] 140 F5
Arvidsjaur [S] 190 H3
Arvieux [F] 70 B6
Årvik [N] 180 C4
Arvika [S] 166 D2
Årviksand [N] 192 G1
Arvila [EST] 198 F1
Arville [F] 42 C5
Arykanda [TR] 154 H2
Arzachena [I] 118 E2
Arzacq-Arraziguet [F] 84 E2
Aržano [HR] 144 B2
Arzberg [D] 48 C3
Arze-Arce / Uriz [E] 84 C4
Arzignano [I] 72 D6
Arzl [A] 72 C1
Arzúa [E] 78 C3
As [B] 30 E4
Aš [CZ] 48 C3
Ås [N] 166 B2
Ås [N] 182 D2
Ås [S] 182 G2
Aså [DK] 160 E3
Åsa [N] 170 H5
Åsa [S] 160 H3
Asa [S] 162 E4
Aşağıçobanisa [TR] 152 D3
Aşağıgörle [TR] 152 F5
Aşağıinova [TR] 150 C5
Åsan [N] 190 C5
Åsäng [S] 184 E4
Ašanja [SRB] 142 G2
Åsarna [S] 182 G4
Asarum [S] 158 E1
Åsbro [S] 166 H4
Asby [S] 162 E2
Ascain [F] 84 C2
Ascea [I] 120 F5
Ascha [D] 60 G2
Aschach [A] 62 B4
Aschaffenburg [D] 46 D3
Aschau [A] 72 E1
Aschau [D] 60 F5
Aschbach Markt [A] 62 C5
Ascheberg [D] 16 H6
Ascheberg [D] 18 G2
Aschendorf [D] 16 H3
Aschersleben [D] 34 B4
Asciano [I] 114 G1
Ascó [E] 90 H6
Asco [F] 114 B3
Áscoli Piceno [I] 116 C3
Ascoli Satriano [I] 120 G2
Ascona [CH] 70 F3
Ascou Pailhères [F] 106 B5
Ase [N] 192 E3
Åsebyn [S] 166 D3
Åseda [S] 162 E4
Åsele [S] 190 G5
Åseli [N] 192 D6
Asemankylä [FIN] 188 C5
Asemanseutu [FIN] 186 D3
Åsen [N] 190 C6
Åsen [S] 172 F2
Åsen [S] 184 C4
Asendorf [D] 18 E6
Asenovgrad [BG] 148 B6
Asenovo [BG] 148 B2
Åsensbruk [S] 166 D4
Åseral [N] 164 D4
Åserund [N] 166 C1
Asfáka [GR] 132 C1
Asfeld [F] 44 B2
Åsgårdstrand [N] 164 H2
Asha (Pasaköy) [CY] 154 G5
Ashbourne [GB] 10 E5
Ashbourne [IRL] 2 F6
Åsheim [N] 182 C6
Ashford [GB] 14 F5
Ashington [GB] 8 G5
Ashmyany [BY] 200 H6
Ashton-under-Lyne [GB] 10 E4
Asiago [I] 72 D5
Asikkala [FIN] 178 A2
Asila [FIN] 188 D5
Asíni [GR] 136 F2
Asipovitsy [BY] 202 C5
Ask [N] 170 B3
Ask [N] 170 H5
Ask [S] 158 C2
Aska [FIN] 194 D6
Askainen / Villnäs [FIN] 176 D4
Askaniia-Nova [RUS] 204 H3
Askanija Nova [UA] 204 H3
Askeaton [IRL] 4 C3
Askeby [DK] 156 G4
Asker [N] 164 H1
Askersund [S] 166 G4
Askeryd [S] 162 E2
Askim [N] 166 C2
Askim [S] 160 G2
Askland [N] 164 E3
Asklepiyon [TR] 152 C2
Asklipieío [GR] 154 B2
Asklipieío [GR] 154 B2
Askola [FIN] 178 B4
Äsköping [S] 168 B3
Askós [GR] 130 B4
Askum [S] 166 B5
Askvoll [N] 170 B1
Askýfou [GR] 140 C5
Aslanapa [TR] 152 G1
Aslestad [N] 164 E2
Åsli [N] 170 G4
Åsljunga [S] 162 B6
Åsmansbo [S] 172 H5
Asmunti [FIN] 196 E2
Asnæs [DK] 156 F2
Åsnes [N] 172 D4
As Nogais [E] 78 E4
Ásola [I] 110 E1
Asolo [I] 72 E5
Asopía [GR] 134 B5
Asopós [GR] 136 F4
Asoru, Nuraghe- [I] 118 D7
Ásos [GR] 132 C5
Ásotthalom [H] 76 D4
Aspa [S] 168 C4
Aspang Markt [A] 62 E6
Asparuhovo [BG] 148 E4
Asparukovo [BG] 148 F3
Aspås [S] 182 G2
Aspe [E] 104 D2
Aspeå [S] 184 F1
Aspet [F] 84 G4
Aspnes [N] 190 D5
Aspö [S] 168 C2
As Pontes de García Rodríguez / Puentes de García Rodríguez [E] 78 D2
Aspres-sur-Buëch [F] 108 C2
Asprópyrgos [GR] 134 B6
Asprovalta [GR] 130 C4
Aspsele [S] 190 G6
Assamalla [EST] 198 F1
Assel [D] 18 E4
Assé-le-Boisne [F] 26 F6
Assemini [I] 118 C7
Assen [NL] 16 G3
Assens [DK] 156 D3
Assens [DK] 160 E5
Asserbo [DK] 156 G1
Assergi [I] 116 C4
Asseria [HR] 112 G5
Assessos [TR] 152 D6
Ássiros [GR] 128 H4
Assisi [I] 116 A2
Assling [D] 60 F5
Assmannshausen [D] 46 B3
Assoro [I] 126 F3
Assos [TR] 134 H1
Åsta [N] 172 C3
Astaffort [F] 66 E6
Astakós [GR] 132 D5
Åstan [N] 180 H1

Åstan [N] 180 H1
Asten [A] 62 B4
Asten [NL] 30 F3
Asti [I] 70 E6
Astira [TR] 152 C1
Astorga [E] 78 G6
Åstorp [S] 156 H1
Åstrand [S] 172 E5
Astravyets [BY] 200 H5
Ástros [GR] 136 E3
Astrup [DK] 160 D4
Astryna [BY] 24 G3
Astudillo [E] 82 D6
Astura, Torre- [I] 120 B1
Astypálaia [GR] 138 H4
Asvyeya [BY] 198 G6
Ászár [H] 64 A6
Aszód [H] 64 D6
Aszófő [H] 76 A2
Atalaia [P] 86 B5
Atalánti [GR] 132 H4
Atanneus [TR] 152 C2
Atapuerca [E] 82 E6
Atarfe [E] 102 E4
Atašiene [LV] 198 F5
Atburgazi [TR] 152 D6
Atça [TR] 152 E5
Ateca [E] 90 C4
Atella [I] 120 G3
Atessa [I] 116 E5
Ath [B] 28 G3
Athboy [IRL] 2 E5
Athea [IRL] 4 C3
Athenry [IRL] 2 C5
Athéras [GR] 132 C6
Athiénou [CY] 154 G5
Athína [GR] 134 C6
Athleague [IRL] 2 D5
Athlone / Baile Átha Luain [IRL] 2 D5
Athy [IRL] 4 F3
Atienza [E] 90 A4
Atina [I] 116 C6
Atkár [H] 64 E6
Atnbrua [N] 180 H6
Atnosen [N] 182 B6
Atouguia de Baleia [P] 86 B3
A Toxa [E] 78 B4
Åtran [S] 162 B4
Åträsk [S] 190 H5
Atri [I] 116 D3
Atripalda [I] 120 F3
Áttali [GR] 134 C4
Attel [D] 60 F4
Attendorn [D] 32 C5
Attersee [A] 60 H5
Attigny [F] 44 C2
Attleborough [GB] 14 G2
Attmar [S] 184 E5
Attnang-Puchheim [A] 62 A5
Attre [B] 28 G3
Attrup [DK] 160 D3
Åtvidaberg [S] 168 B6
Atzara [I] 118 D5
Atzendorf [D] 34 B4
Atzeneta del Maestrat [E] 98 F3
Au [A] 62 D6
Au [D] 60 E3
Aub [D] 46 E4
Aubagne [F] 108 B5
Aubange [B] 44 E3
Aubenas [F] 68 E6
Aubérive [F] 44 C3
Auberive [F] 56 H2
Aubeterre-sur-Dronne [F] 66 E2
Aubiet [F] 84 G3
Aubigny [F] 54 B3
Aubigny-les-Pothées [F] 28 H6
Aubigny-sur-Nère [F] 56 C2
Auboué [F] 44 E4
Aubrac [F] 68 C5
Aubusson [F] 68 B1
Auce [LV] 198 C6
Aucelon [F] 68 G6
Auch [F] 84 G2
Auchinleck [GB] 8 D4
Auchterarder [GB] 8 E2
Auchtermuchty [GB] 8 E2
Audelange [F] 56 H4
Audenarde (Oudenaarde) [B] 28 G2
Audenge [F] 66 C3
Auderville [F] 26 D1
Audeux [F] 58 B4
Audierne [F] 40 A3
Audincourt [F] 58 C4
Audlem [GB] 10 D5
Audnedal [N] 164 D5
Audressein [F] 84 G5
Audru [EST] 198 D3
Audun-le-Roman [F] 44 E3
Aue [D] 48 D2
Auen [A] 72 E1
Auen [CH] 72 E1
Auer / Ora [I] 72 D4
Auerbach [D] 46 H4
Auerbach [D] 48 C2
Auerbacher Schloss [D] 46 C4
Auffach [A] 60 F6
Augher [NIR] 2 F3
Aughnacloy [NIR] 2 F3
Aughrim [IRL] 4 G4
Augsburg [D] 60 D3
Augusta [I] 126 G4
Augustenborg [DK] 156 C4
Augustów [PL] 24 E3
Augustusburg [D] 48 D1
Aukra [N] 180 D2
Aukštadvaris [LT] 24 G1
Auktsjaur [S] 190 H3
Auletta [I] 120 G4
Aulla [I] 110 C4
Aullène [F] 114 B5
Aulnay [F] 54 D5
Aulstad [N] 170 H2
Ault [F] 28 C4
Aulus-les-Bains [F] 84 H5
Auly [RUS] 204 G1
Auma [D] 48 B2
Aumale [F] 28 D5
Aumetz [F] 44 E3
Aumont-Aubrac [F] 68 C5
Aunay-sur-Odon [F] 26 E4
Auneau [F] 42 E4
Aunet [N] 182 D2
Aunet [N] 190 C5
Aunet [N] 190 D4
Auneuil [F] 28 D6
Aunfoss [N] 190 D4
Auning [DK] 160 E5
Aups [F] 108 D4
Aurach [A] 60 F6
Aurach [D] 46 F5
Auray [F] 40 D4
Aurdal [N] 170 G3
Aure [N] 180 G1
Aurejärvi [FIN] 186 D5
Aurich [D] 18 B4
Aurignac [F] 84 G4
Aurillac [F] 68 B4
Auriol [F] 108 B5
Auris-en-Oisans [F] 70 A5
Auritz / Burguete [E] 84 C3
Aurlandsvangen [N] 170 D2
Auron [F] 108 E3
Auronzo di Cadore [I] 72 F3
Aursjøhytta [N] 180 F4
Aursmoen [N] 166 C1
Aursnes [N] 180 D3
Ausa Corno [I] 72 G5
Ausejo [E] 84 A5
Ausentum [I] 122 G6
Aussernbrünst [D] 60 H3
Austad [N] 164 C6
Austad [N] 164 D3
Austanå [N] 164 E3
Austborg [N] 190 D5
Austbygda [N] 170 F5
Austefjord [N] 180 C4
Austmarka [N] 172 D5
Austnes [N] 180 D3
Austpollen [N] 192 E4
Austrumdal [N] 164 B4
Auterive [F] 84 H4
Authon [F] 108 D3
Authon-du-Perche [F] 42 C5
Autio [S] 194 B7
Autol [E] 84 A5
Autti [FIN] 194 E8
Auttoinen [FIN] 176 H2
Autun [F] 56 F4
Auve [F] 44 C4
Auvers-s-Oise [F] 42 F3
Auvila [FIN] 188 E6
Auvillers-les-Forges [F] 28 H5
Auxerre [F] 56 E2
Auxi-le-Château [F] 28 D4
Auxonne [F] 56 H4
Auxy [F] 56 F4
Auzances [F] 56 B6
Auzon [F] 68 D3
Avå [FIN] 176 C4
Ava [S] 184 H1
Avafors [S] 196 B2
Availles-Limouzine [F] 54 F5
Aval, Falaise d'- [F] 26 G2
Avala [SRB] 142 G3
Avaldsnes [N] 164 A2
Avallon [F] 56 E3
Ávas [GR] 130 G3
Avaträsk [S] 190 F5
Avaviken [S] 190 G3
Avcılar [TR] 150 E3
Avdímou [CY] 154 F6
Ávdira [GR] 130 E3
Ávdira [GR] 130 E3
Åvedal [N] 164 B5
A Veiga [E] 78 E6
Aveiras de Cima [P] 86 C4
Aveiro [P] 80 B5
Avelengo / Hafling [I] 72 D3
Avellino [I] 120 F3
Aven Armand [F] 106 E2
Avenches [CH] 58 C6
Aven de Marzal [F] 106 G2
Aven d'Orgnac [F] 106 G2
Avène [F] 106 D3
Averbode [B] 30 D3
Aversa [I] 120 D3
Avesnes-le-Comte [F] 28 E4
Avesnes-sur-Helpe [F] 28 G4
Avesta [S] 174 D5
Avetrana [I] 122 F4
Avezzano [I] 116 C5
Avgerinós [GR] 128 E6
Avía [GR] 136 D4
Aviano [I] 72 F5
Aviemore [GB] 6 E5
Avigliana [I] 70 D5
Avigliano [I] 120 G3
Avigna [I] 72 D3
Avignon [F] 106 G3
Ávila [E] 88 E4
Avilés [E] 78 H3
Avinurme [EST] 198 F2
Avinyó [E] 92 E3
Avio [I] 72 C5
Avión [E] 78 C4
Avis [P] 86 D5
Avlákia [GR] 152 C5
Avlémonas [GR] 136 F6
Avlí [GR] 130 D3
Avliótes [GR] 132 A2
Avlóna [GR] 134 C5
Avlonári [GR] 134 C5
Avlum [DK] 160 C6
Avola [I] 126 G5
Avonmouth [GB] 12 F3
Avord [F] 56 C4
Avoriaz [F] 70 C2
Avradsberg [S] 172 F5
Avramov [BG] 148 E4
Avranches [F] 26 D4
Avril [F] 44 E3
Avşar [TR] 152 D6
Avtovac [BIH] 144 D3
Axat [F] 106 B5
Axel [NL] 28 H1
Axioúpoli [GR] 128 G3
Ax-les-Thermes [F] 106 A6
Axmarby [S] 174 E3
Axminster [GB] 12 F4
Axós [GR] 140 E4
Axvall [S] 166 F5
Ay [F] 44 B3
Ayagalip [TR] 130 G5
Ayamonte [E] 94 D5
Ayas [I] 70 D3
Aydın [TR] 152 D5
Aydıncık [TR] 130 G5
Aydıncık [TR] 154 F4
Ayerbe [E] 84 D6
Aykırıkçı [TR] 152 H2
Aylesbury [GB] 14 D3
Ayllón [E] 88 H3
Aylsham [GB] 14 G2
Ayna [E] 98 B6
Ayoó de Vidriales [E] 80 H3
Ayora [E] 98 D5
Ayr [GB] 8 C4
Ayrancı [TR] 152 G2
Ayrancılar [TR] 152 C4
Ay. Seryios (Yenibogaziçi) [CY] 154 G5
Äyskoski [FIN] 186 H2
Äystö [FIN] 186 B4
Aytos [BG] 148 F4
Ayvacık [TR] 134 H1
Ayvalık [TR] 152 B2
Ayvatlar [TR] 152 C2
Azaila [E] 90 F5
Azambuja [P] 86 C4
Azannes-et-Soumazannes [F] 44 D3
Azanúy [E] 90 H3
Azaruja [P] 86 D6
Azath [TR] 150 B2
Azay-le-Ferron [F] 54 G3
Azay-le-Rideau [F] 54 F2
Azeitão [P] 86 B6
Azervadinha [P] 86 C5
Azinheira dos Barros [P] 94 C2
Azıtepe [TR] 152 E4
Aziziye [TR] 150 C1
Aznalcóllar [E] 94 G5
Azpeitia [E] 82 H4
Azuaga [E] 96 A5
Azuara [E] 90 E5
Azuel [E] 96 D5
Azul, Cueva- [E] 104 E6
Azuqueca de Henares [E] 88 G5
Azur [F] 66 A6
Azyory [BY] 24 G4
Azzano Decimo [I] 72 F5
Azzurra, Grotta- [I] 120 D4
Azzurra, Grotta- [I] 120 F5

B

Baad [A] 60 B6
Baal [D] 30 F4
Baamonde [E] 78 D3
Baar [D] 60 D3
Baarle Nassau [NL] 30 D2
Baarn [NL] 16 E4
Babadag [RO] 204 F5
Babadağ [TR] 152 F5
Babaeski [TR] 150 B2
Babaköy [TR] 152 D2
Babek [BG] 148 B5
Babenhausen [D] 46 D3
Babenhausen [D] 60 C4
Babiak [PL] 22 G3
Babiak [PL] 36 F3
Babica [PL] 52 D4
Babice [PL] 50 G4
Băbiciu [RO] 148 A1
Babięta [PL] 24 B4
Babigoszcz [PL] 20 F4
Babimost [PL] 36 A3
Babin Potok [HR] 112 G3
Babjen [AL] 128 C3
BabnoPolje [SLO] 74 B6
Babócsa [H] 74 G5
Bábolna [H] 64 A6
Babriškes [LT] 24 G2
Babruysk [BY] 202 C5
Babušnica [SRB] 146 E4
Babylon [CZ] 48 D5
Babylón [CZ] 62 E2
Bač [MK] 128 E4
Bač [SLO] 74 A6
Bač [SRB] 142 E1
Bača [SLO] 72 H4
Bacău [RO] 204 D4
Baccarat [F] 44 F6
Baceno [I] 70 F2
Bacharach [D] 46 B3
Bachkovo [BG] 148 B6
Bachkovski Manastir [BG] 148 B6
Bachórz [PL] 52 E4
Bačina [SRB] 146 C3
Backåkra [S] 158 D3
Bačka Palanka [MNE] 204 A5
Bačka Palanka [SRB] 142 F1
Bäckaskog [S] 158 D1
Bačka Topola [MNE] 204 A5
Bačka Topola [SRB] 76 D5
Backe [S] 190 F6
Bäckebo [S] 162 F4
Bäckefors [S] 166 D4
Backen [S] 184 D4
Backen [S] 184 E4
Bäckhammar [S] 166 F3
Bački Breg [SRB] 76 C5
Bački Petrovac [SRB] 142 F1
Bački Sokolac [SRB] 76 D5
Backnang [D] 46 D6
Bačko Gradište [SRB] 142 G1
Bačko Novo Selo [SRB] 142 E1
Bačko Petrovo Selo [SRB] 76 E6
Bąćkowice [PL] 52 C1
Bacoli [I] 120 D3
Bacova mahala [BG] 148 B3
Bacqueville-en-Caux [F] 28 B4
Bácsalmás [H] 76 D5
Bácsbokod [H] 76 C5
Bácsborsód [H] 76 C5
Baczyna [PL] 34 H1
Bad Abbach [D] 60 F2
Badacsonytomaj [H] 74 H3
Bad Aibling [D] 60 F5
Badajoz [E] 86 F6
Badalona [E] 92 E4
Badalucco [I] 108 G4
Bad Aussee [A] 62 A6
Bad Bederkesa [D] 18 D4
Bad Bentheim [D] 16 H5
Bad Bergzabern [D] 46 B5
Bad Berka [D] 46 H1
Bad Berleburg [D] 32 D5
Bad Berneck [D] 46 H3
Bad Bertrich [D] 44 G1
Bad Bevensen [D] 18 G5
Bad Bibra [D] 34 B5
Bad Blankenburg [D] 46 H2
Bad Brambach [D] 48 C3
Bad Bramstedt [D] 18 F3
Bad Breisig [D] 30 H5
Bad Brückenau [D] 46 E2
Bad Buchau [D] 60 A4
Badderen [N] 192 H2
Bad Deutsch-Altenburg [A] 62 G5
Bad Doberan [D] 20 B3
Bad Driburg [D] 32 E4
Bad Düben [D] 34 D4
Bad Dürkheim [D] 46 B4
Bad Dürrenberg [D] 34 C5
Bad Dürrheim [D] 58 F3
Bad Elster [D] 48 C3
Bademli [TR] 134 G1
Bademli [TR] 152 C3
Bademli [TR] 152 E5
Bad Ems [D] 46 B2
Baden [A] 62 F5
Baden [CH] 58 F4
Baden-Baden [D] 58 F1
Bad Endorf [D] 60 F5
Badenweiler [D] 58 E3
Baderna [HR] 112 D2
Bädeshte [BG] 148 C5
Bad Essen [D] 32 D2
Bad Frankenhausen [D] 34 A5
Bad Freienwalde [D] 34 F1
Bad Friedrichshall [D] 46 D5
Bad Gandersheim [D] 32 G3
Badgastein [A] 72 G2
Bad Gleichenberg [A] 74 E3
Bad Godesberg [D] 30 H5
Bad Goisern [A] 60 H6
Bad Gottleuba [D] 48 F1
Bad Grund [D] 32 G4
Bad Hall [A] 62 B5
Bad Harzburg [D] 32 H3
Bad Herrenalb [D] 58 F1
Bad Hersfeld [D] 32 F6
Bad Hofgastein [A] 72 G1
Bad Homburg [D] 46 C2
Bad Honnef [D] 30 H5
Bad Hönnigen [D] 30 H5
Badia Gran [E] 104 E5
Badia Polésine [I] 110 F2
Badia Tedalda [I] 110 G6
Bad Iburg [D] 32 D2
Bad Ischl [A] 60 H5
Bad Karlshafen [D] 32 F4
Bad Kissingen [D] 46 E3
Bad Kleinen [D] 20 A4
Bad Kleinkirchheim [A] 72 H3
Bad König [D] 46 D4
Bad Königshofen [D] 46 F2
Bad Kösen [D] 34 B6
Bądkowo [PL] 36 F2
Bad Kreuznach [D] 46 B3
Bad Krozingen [D] 58 E3
Bad Laasphe [D] 32 D6
Bad Langensalza [D] 32 H6
Bad Lauchstädt [D] 34 B5
Bad Lausick [D] 34 D6
Bad Lauterberg [D] 32 G4
Bad Leonfelden [A] 62 B3
Bad Liebenstein [D] 46 F1
Bad Liebenwerda [D] 34 E5
Bad Liebenzell [D] 58 G1
Bad Lippspringe [D] 32 E3
Badljevina [HR] 142 C1
Bad Marienberg [D] 46 B1
Bad Meinberg [D] 32 E3
Bad Mergentheim [D] 46 E5
Bad Mitterndorf [A] 62 B6
Bad Münder [D] 32 F2
Bad Münster Ebernburg [D] 46 B3
Bad Münstereifel [D] 30 G5
Bad Muskau [D] 34 G5
Bad Nauheim [D] 46 C2
Bad Nenndorf [D] 32 F2
Bad Neuenahr [D] 30 G5
Bad Neustadt [D] 46 F2
Bad Oeynhausen [D] 32 E2
Badolato [I] 124 E6
Badolato Marina [I] 124 E6
Bad Oldesloe [D] 18 G3
Badonviller [F] 44 F6
Bad Orb [D] 46 D2
Badovinci [SRB] 142 F2
Badow [D] 18 H4
Bad Peterstal [D] 58 F2
Bad Pirawarth [A] 62 F4
Bad Pyrmont [D] 32 E3
Bad Radkersburg [A] 74 E3
Bad Ragaz [CH] 58 H6
Bad Reichenhall [D] 60 G5
Bad Rippoldsau [D] 58 F2
Bad Rothenfelde [D] 32 D2
Bad Saarow-Pieskow [D] 34 F3
Bad Sachsa [D] 32 G4
Bad Säckingen [D] 58 E4
Bad Salzdetfurth [D] 32 G3
Bad Salzuflen [D] 32 E3
Bad Salzungen [D] 46 F1
Bad Schallerbach [A] 62 B4
Bad Schandau [D] 48 F1
Bad Schmiedeberg [D] 34 D4
Bad Schönau [A] 74 F1
Bad Schönborn [D] 46 C5
Bad Schussenried [D] 60 B4
Bad Schwalbach [D] 46 B2
Bad Schwartau [D] 18 G3
Bad Segeberg [D] 18 G3
Bad Sooden-Allendorf [D] 32 F5
Bad St. Leonhard [A] 74 C2
Bad Sülze [D] 20 C3
Bad Tatzmannsdorf [A] 74 F1
Bad Tennstedt [D] 32 H5
Bad Tölz [D] 60 E5
Badu Andria [I] 118 E3
Badules [E] 90 D5
Bad Urach [D] 58 H2
Bad Vöslau [A] 62 F5
Bad Waldsee [D] 60 B4
Bad Wiessee [D] 60 E5
Bad-Wildungen [D] 32 E5
Bad Wilsnack [D] 20 B6
Bad Wimpfen [D] 46 D5
Bad Windsheim [D] 46 F5
Bad Wörishofen [D] 60 C4
Bad Wurzach [D] 60 B5
Bad Zwischenahn [D] 18 C5
Bække [DK] 156 B2
Bækmarksbro [DK] 160 B5
Baelen [B] 30 F5
Baells [E] 90 H3
Baelo Claudia [E] 100 G5
Baena [E] 102 D2
Bæverfjord [N] 180 F2
Baeza [E] 102 F2
Bagà [E] 92 E2
Bagamér [H] 64 H6
Bağarası [TR] 152 D5
Bägarin [BG] 148 D6
Bågede [S] 190 E5
Bagenalstown / Muine Bheag [IRL] 4 F4
Bagenkop [DK] 18 H1
Baggård [S] 190 H6
Bagh a Chaisteil / Castlebay [GB] 6 A5
Bagheria [I] 126 D2
Bagn [N] 170 G3
Bagnacavallo [I] 110 G4
Bagnara Calabra [I] 124 C7
Bagnères-de-Bigorre [F] 84 F4
Bagnères-de-Luchon [F] 84 F5
Bagni Contursi [I] 120 F4
Bagni del Másino [I] 70 H3
Bagni di Bormio [I] 72 B3
Bagni di Craveggia [I] 70 F3
Bagni di Lucca [I] 110 E5
Bagni di Rabbi [I] 72 C3
Bagni di Salomone [I] 72 E2
Bagni di Vinadio [I] 108 E3
Bagno a Ripoli [I] 110 F5
Bagno di Romagna [I] 110 G5
Bagnoles-de-l'Orne [F] 26 F5
Bagnoli di Sopra [I] 110 G1
Bagnolo Mella [I] 72 B6
Bagnolo Piemonte [I] 108 F1
Bagnolo San Vito [I] 110 E2
Bagnols-en-Forêt [F] 108 D5
Bagnols-les-Bains [F] 68 D6
Bagnols-sur-Cèze [F] 106 G3
Bagnone [I] 110 D4
Bagnoregio [I] 114 H3
Bagno Vignoni [I] 114 G2
Bagny [PL] 24 E4
Bågø [DK] 156 C3
Bagod [H] 74 F3
Bagolino [I] 72 B5
Bagrationovsk [RUS] 22 H2
Bagsund [N] 190 C5
Báguena [E] 90 D5
Bagunte [P] 80 B3
Bağyaka [TR] 154 D1
Bağyurdu [TR] 152 D4
Bağyüzü [TR] 152 C2
Bahabón de Esgueva [E] 88 G2
Baharlar [TR] 152 B1
Bahçecik [TR] 150 G3
Bahçeköy [TR] 150 B4
Bahçeköy [TR] 150 D2
Bahillo [E] 82 D5
Baia delle Zagare [I] 116 H6
Báia Domízia [I] 120 D2
Baia Mare [RO] 204 C3
Baiano [I] 120 E3
Baião [P] 80 C4
Báia Sardinia [I] 118 E2
Baiersbronn [D] 58 F2
Baigneux-les-Juifs [F] 56 G3
Baile an Sceilg / Ballinskelligs [IRL] 4 A4
Baile Átha Cliath / Dublin [IRL] 2 F6
Baile Átha Luain / Athlone [IRL] 2 D5
Băile Felix [RO] 76 H2
Bailén [E] 102 E1
Băileşti [RO] 146 F2
Băile Tuşnad [RO] 204 D4
Bailieborough [IRL] 2 F4
Bailleul [F] 26 H2
Bailleul [F] 28 F2
Bain-de-Bretagne [F] 40 F5
Bains-les-Bains [F] 58 C2
Baio [E] 78 B2
Baiona [E] 78 A5
Bais [F] 26 E6
Baisogala [LT] 200 F4
Baix [F] 68 F5
Baixas [F] 92 G1
Baja [H] 76 C4
Bajánsenye [H] 74 F3
Bajč [SK] 64 B5
Bajina Bašta [SRB] 142 F4
Bajmok [SRB] 76 D5
Bajna [H] 64 B6
Bajram Curri [AL] 146 A6
Bajša [SRB] 76 D6
Bajzë [AL] 144 E4
Bak [H] 74 G3
Bakacak [TR] 150 C5
Bakar [HR] 112 E1
Bakewell [GB] 10 E5
Bakhchysarai [UA] 204 H4
Bakhmach [UA] 202 E6
Bakio [E] 82 G3
Bakırköy [TR] 150 E3
Bakka [N] 164 F1
Bakke [N] 164 F4
Bakke [N] 166 C4
Bakkejord [N] 192 F2
Bakken [N] 182 C1
Bakko [N] 170 F5
Baklan [TR] 152 G4
Bakonszeg [H] 76 G1
Bakonybél [H] 74 H2
Bakonycsernye [H] 76 A1
Bakonygyepes [H] 74 H2
Bakonyjákó [H] 74 H2
Bakonypeterd [H] 76 A1
Bakonysárkány [H] 76 A1
Bakonyszombathely [H] 76 A1
Bakovac [HR] 112 F3
Baks [H] 76 E3
Baksa [H] 76 A5
Baksjöliden [S] 190 G5
Baktakék [H] 64 F4
Baktalórántháza [H] 64 H5
Baktsjaur [S] 190 H3
Bakum [D] 18 C6
Bäl [S] 168 G4
Bala [GB] 10 C5
Balaban [TR] 150 C1
Balabancık [TR] 150 B4
Balaguer [E] 92 B3
Balanegra [E] 102 F5
Bălăneşti [RO] 148 A1
Balassagyarmat [H] 64 C5
Balástya [H] 76 E4
Balat [TR] 152 D6
Balatonakali [H] 74 H2
Balatonalmádi [H] 76 A2
Balatonbereny [H] 74 G3
Balatonboglár [H] 74 H3
Balatonederics [H] 74 H3
Balatonföldvár [H] 76 A3
Balatonfüred [H] 76 A2
Balatonfűzfő [H] 76 A2
Balatongyörök [H] 74 G3
Balatonkenese [H] 76 A2
Balatonkeresztúr [H] 74 H3
Balatonlelle [H] 74 H3
Balatonszemes [H] 76 A3
Balazote [E] 98 B5
Balbigny [F] 68 E2
Balboa [E] 78 E4
Balbriggan [IRL] 2 F5
Bålby [S] 166 G3
Balchik [BG] 148 G2
Balcılar [TR] 150 B5
Balcon de Europa [E] 102 D5
Baldenstein [CH] 70 H1
Balderschwang [D] 60 B6
Baldock [GB] 14 E3
Baldone [LV] 198 E5
Bale [HR] 112 D2
Baleines, Phare des- [F] 54 B4
Baleira [E] 78 E3
Baleizão [P] 94 D3
Balestrand [N] 170 C1
Balestrate [I] 126 C2
Balewo [PL] 22 F4
Bälgviken [S] 168 B3
Balice [PL] 50 H3
Balıkesir [TR] 152 D1
Balıklıova [TR] 152 B4
Balıköy [TR] 152 F1
Bälinge [S] 158 C1
Bälinge [S] 162 B1
Bälinge [S] 168 D1
Balingen [D] 58 G2
Balinţ [RO] 76 H5
Balio Chitarra [I] 126 B2
Baljvine [BIH] 142 B3
Balkanec [BG] 148 B4
Balkanski [BG] 148 D2
Balkány [H] 64 H5
Balkıca [TR] 152 G6
Balla [IRL] 2 C4
Ballaban [AL] 128 C5
Ballachulish [GB] 6 C6
Ballaghaderreen [IRL] 2 D4
Ballangen [N] 192 E4
Ballantrae [GB] 8 C4
Ballao [I] 118 D6
Ballater [GB] 6 E6
Ballebro [DK] 156 C4
Bällefors [S] 166 F5
Ballen [DK] 156 E2
Ballenstedt [D] 34 A4
Balleroy [F] 26 E3
Ballerup [DK] 156 G2
Ballı [TR] 150 B3
Ballina [IRL] 2 C3
Ballina [IRL] 2 C6
Ballinafad [IRL] 2 D4
Ballinagh [IRL] 2 E4
Ballinahinch [NIR] 2 G4
Ballinakill [IRL] 4 E3
Ballinamore [IRL] 2 E4
Ballinascarty [IRL] 4 C5
Ballinasloe [IRL] 2 D5
Ballindine [IRL] 2 C4
Ballindooly Castle [IRL] 2 C5
Ballingarry [IRL] 4 C3
Ballingarry [IRL] 4 E4
Ballinhassig [IRL] 4 C5
Ballinrobe [IRL] 2 C4
Ballinskellligs / Baile an Sceilg [IRL] 4 A4
Ballinspittle [IRL] 4 C5
Ballintober, Abbey- [IRL] 2 C4
Ballintra [IRL] 2 E3
Ballio Zaffarana [I] 126 B2
Ballivor [IRL] 2 E5
Ballobar [E] 90 G4
Ballon [F] 42 B4
Ballon [IRL] 4 F4
Ballsh [AL] 128 B5
Ballshi [AL] 128 B4
Ballstad [N] 192 C4
Ballum [DK] 156 B3
Ballybay [IRL] 2 F4
Ballybofey [IRL] 2 E2
Ballybunion [IRL] 2 B6
Ballycanew [IRL] 4 F4
Ballycastle [IRL] 2 C3
Ballycastle [NIR] 2 G2
Ballyclare [NIR] 2 G3
Ballyconneely [IRL] 2 B4
Ballycotton [IRL] 4 D5
Ballycumber [IRL] 2 D5
Ballydehob [IRL] 4 B5
Ballydesmond [IRL] 4 C4
Ballyduff [IRL] 4 B3
Ballyduff [IRL] 4 D4
Ballyemund [IRL] 4 F4
Ballyfarnan [IRL] 2 D4
Ballygawley [NIR] 2 F3
Ballyglass [IRL] 2 C4
Ballygowan [NIR] 2 G4
Ballyhaunis [IRL] 2 C4
Ballyheige [IRL] 4 B3
Ballyhillin [IRL] 2 F1
Ballyjamesduff [IRL] 2 E4
Ballykeeran [IRL] 2 D5
Ballylanders [IRL] 4 D4
Ballylongford [IRL] 2 B6
Ballylynan [IRL] 4 F3
Ballymacoda [IRL] 4 D5
Ballymahon [IRL] 2 D5
Ballymena [NIR] 2 G3
Ballymoe [IRL] 2 D4
Ballymoney [NIR] 2 G2
Ballymore [IRL] 2 E5
Ballymore Eustace [IRL] 2 F6
Ballymote [IRL] 2 D3
Ballyragget [IRL] 4 E3
Ballyronan [NIR] 2 G3
Ballyroon [IRL] 4 B5
Ballysadare [IRL] 2 D3
Ballyshannon [IRL] 2 E3
Ballyvaughan [IRL] 2 C5
Ballywalter [NIR] 2 H4
Balmaseda [E] 82 G4
Balmazújváros [H] 64 G6
Balme [I] 70 C5
Balmúccia [I] 70 E3
Balogunyom [H] 74 F2
Balş [RO] 146 G1
Balsareny [E] 92 D3
Balsfjord [N] 192 F2
Balsicas [E] 104 C4
Balsorano [I] 116 C6
Bålsta [S] 168 D2
Balsthal [CH] 58 E5
Balta [UA] 204 E2
Baltaköy [TR] 152 E5
Baltanás [E] 88 F1
Baltar [E] 78 C6
Bălţi [MD] 204 E3
Baltimore [IRL] 4 B5
Baltinava [LV] 198 G5
Baltinglass [IRL] 4 F3
Baltiysk [RUS] 22 G1
Baltoji Vokė [LT] 24 H1
Baltrum [D] 18 B3
Balugães [P] 78 A6
Balvan [BG] 148 C3
Balvany [SK] 64 A5
Balvi [LV] 198 G4
Balya [TR] 152 D1
Balzers [FL] 58 H6
Bamberg [D] 46 G4
Bamble [N] 164 G3
Bana [H] 64 A6
Banafjäl [S] 184 G2
Banagher [IRL] 2 D6
Banarli [TR] 150 C3
Banatski Karlovac [SRB] 142 H2
Banatsko Aranđelovo [SRB] 76 E5
Banatsko Karadjordjevo [SRB] 76 F6
Banatsko Novo Selo [SRB] 142 H2
Banaz [TR] 152 G3
Banbridge [NIR] 2 G4
Banbury [GB] 14 D2
Banchory [GB] 6 F6
Bandakslí [N] 164 E2
Bande [E] 78 C5
Bandholm [DK] 156 F5
Bandırma [TR] 150 D4
Bandol [F] 108 B5
Bandon [IRL] 4 C5
Băneasa [RO] 148 C1

Banff [GB] 6 F5
Bångnäs [S] 190 E4
Bangor [F] 40 C5
Bangor [GB] 10 B4
Bangor [NIR] 2 H3
Bangor Erris [IRL] 2 C3
Bangsbo [DK] 160 E3
Bánhalma [H] 76 F1
Banica [BG] 146 G3
Banie [PL] 20 F6
Banie Mazurskie [PL] 24 D2
Baniska [BG] 148 C2
Banja [SRB] 144 E2
Banja [SRB] 146 B4
Banja Koviljača [SRB] 142 E3
Banjaloka [SLO] 112 F1
Banja Luka [BIH] 142 C3
Banjani [SRB] 146 A1
Banjska [SRB] 146 C4
Bánk [H] 64 H6
Banka [SK] 64 A3
Bankeryd [S] 162 D2
Bankháza [H] 76 C2
Bankya [BG] 146 F5
Bannalec [F] 40 C3
Banne [F] 106 F2
Bannesdorf [D] 20 A2
Bañolas / Banyoles [E] 92 F3
Banon [F] 108 C3
Baños de Alicún de las Torres [E] 102 F3
Baños de Cerrato [E] 88 F1
Baños de la Encina [E] 96 E6
Baños de Montemayor [E] 88 B4
Baños de Panticosa [E] 84 E5
Baños de Rio Tobia [E] 82 G6
Bánov [CZ] 62 H2
Bánovce nad Bebravou [SK] 64 B3
Banovići [BIH] 142 D3
Bánréve [H] 64 E4
Bansin [D] 20 E3
Banská Bystrica [SK] 64 C3
Banská Štiavnica [SK] 64 C3
Banské [SK] 64 G2
Bansko [BG] 130 B1
Bansko [MK] 128 H2
Banteer [IRL] 4 C4
Bantheville [F] 44 D3
Ban. Topola [SRB] 76 F6
Bantry [IRL] 4 B5
Bantry House [IRL] 4 B5
Banya [BG] 148 B5
Banya [BG] 148 D4
Banya [BG] 148 F4
Banyalbufar [E] 104 D4
Banyeres de Mariola [E] 104 D1
Banyoles / Bañolas [E] 92 F3
Banyuls-sur-Mer [F] 92 G2
Banz [D] 46 G3
Bapaume [F] 28 F4
Bar [MNE] 144 E5
Bara [RO] 76 H5
Baradla [H] 64 E3
Barajas [E] 88 G5
Barajas de Melo [E] 96 H1
Barakaldo [E] 82 G3
Baralla [E] 78 E4
Baranavichy [BY] 202 B6
Baránd [H] 76 G1
Baranowo [PL] 24 C5
Baranów Sandomierski [PL] 52 D2
Baraona [E] 90 B4
Baraqueville [F] 68 A6
Bårared [S] 162 B5
Barásoain [E] 84 B4
Barbadillo de Herreros [E] 90 A1
Barban [HR] 112 D2
Barbarano Vicentino [I] 72 D6
Barbaros [TR] 150 C3
Barba-Rossahöhle [D] 32 H5
Barbaste [F] 66 E5
Barbastro [E] 90 G3
Barbat [HR] 112 F3
Barbate [E] 100 F5
Bārbele [LV] 198 E6
Barberino Val d'Elsa [I] 110 F6
Barbezieux-St-Hilaire [F] 66 E2
Barbing [D] 60 F2
Barbizon [F] 42 F5
Barbotan-les-Thermes [F] 66 D6
Barby [D] 34 C3
Bärbyborg [S] 162 G6
Bârca [RO] 146 G2
Bárcabo [E] 84 E6
Barca de Alva [P] 80 E5
Barcarrota [E] 94 F2
Barcellona-Pozzo di Gotto [I] 124 B7
Barcelona [E] 92 E4
Barcelonnette [F] 108 E2
Barcelos [P] 80 C3
Bárcena de Pie de Concha [E] 82 E3
Barchfeld [D] 46 F1
Barchon [B] 30 E5
Barciany [PL] 24 B3
Barcin [PL] 36 E1
Barcino [PL] 22 B3
Bárcis [I] 72 F4
Barcones [E] 90 A4
Barcs [H] 74 H5
Barczewo [PL] 22 H4
Bardakçi [TR] 152 E2
Bardejov [SK] 52 D6
Bardejovské Kúpele [SK] 52 C5
Bardi [I] 110 C3
Bardo [PL] 50 C2
Bardolino [I] 72 C6
Bardonécchia [I] 70 B5
Bardovo [RUS] 198 H5
Bardowick [D] 18 G5
Bardufoss [N] 192 F3
Bärenalm [A] 62 B6
Barenburg [D] 32 E1
Barendrecht [NL] 16 C5
Barentin [F] 26 H3
Barenton [F] 26 E5
Bärfendal [S] 166 C5
Barfleur [F] 26 E2
Barga [I] 110 D4
Bargas [E] 96 F1
Barge [I] 108 F2
Bargteheide [D] 18 G4
Bari [I] 122 E2
Barič [SRB] 142 G3
Båring [DK] 156 D3
Bari Sardo [I] 118 E5
Barisciano [I] 116 C4
Bariyevo [BG] 148 B4
Barjac [F] 106 G2
Barjas [E] 78 E5
Barjols [F] 108 C4
Barkåker [N] 164 H2
Barkald [N] 182 C5
Barkarö [S] 168 B2
Barkava [LV] 198 F5
Barkowo [PL] 22 C4
Bârlad [RO] 204 E4
Bar-le-Duc [F] 44 D5
Barles [F] 108 D3
Barletta [I] 122 C2
Barlinek [PL] 20 G6
Barlingbo [S] 168 G4
Barmash [AL] 128 D6
Barmouth [GB] 10 B5
Barmstedt [D] 18 F3
Barnard Castle [GB] 10 F2
Bärnau [D] 48 C4
Barneberg [D] 34 A3
Barneveld [NL] 16 E5
Barneville-Carteret [F] 26 D2
Barnewitz [D] 34 D2
Barnówko [PL] 34 G1
Barnsley [GB] 10 F4
Barnstaple [GB] 12 E3
Barnstorf [D] 18 D6
Barntrup [D] 32 E3
Baroña, Castro de- [E] 78 B3
Barovo [MK] 128 F2
Barquilla de Pinares [E] 88 C5
Barr [F] 44 G6
Barracas [E] 98 E3
Barraco [E] 88 E5
Barrafranca [I] 126 E4
Barranco do Velho [P] 94 C5
Barrancos [P] 94 F3
Barrax [E] 98 B5
Barre-des-Cévennes [F] 106 E2
Barreiro [P] 86 B5
Barreiros / San Cosme [E] 78 F2
Barrême [F] 108 D3
Barrosa [E] 100 F4
Barrow-in-Furness [GB] 10 D2
Barruecopardo [E] 80 F5
Barruera [E] 84 F6
Barry [F] 106 G2
Barry [GB] 12 F3
Barryporeen [IRL] 4 D4
Barsanovo [RUS] 198 H5
Barsele [S] 190 G4
Barsinghausen [D] 32 F2
Barssel [D] 18 C5
Barstyciai [LT] 200 D3
Bar-sur-Aube [F] 44 C6
Bar-sur-Seine [F] 44 B6
Barsviken [S] 184 F4
Barth [D] 20 C2
Barton-upon-Humber [GB] 10 G4
Bartoszyce [PL] 22 H2
Barúmini [I] 118 C6
Barussa, Nuraghe- [I] 118 B7
Baruth [D] 34 E3
Barvaux-sur-Ourthe [B] 30 E5
Barver [D] 32 E1
Bårvik [N] 194 A2
Barwice [PL] 22 A4
Barysaw [BY] 202 C5
Baryshevo [RUS] 178 G3
Bărzina [BG] 146 G3
Barzio [I] 70 G3
Bas [E] 92 F2
Bås [N] 164 E4
Bašaid [SRB] 76 F6
Başalan [TR] 152 F5
Basauri [E] 82 G4
Basconcillos del Tozo [E] 82 E5
Basdahl [D] 18 E4
Basel [CH] 58 E4
Baselga di Pinè [I] 72 D4
Båsheim [N] 170 G5
Bashtanka [UA] 202 F8
Basi [LV] 198 B5
Basildon [GB] 14 F4
Basilice [I] 120 F2
Båsinge [S] 174 D6
Basingstoke [GB] 14 D4
Baška [HR] 112 F2
Baška Voda [HR] 144 B2
Baške Ostarije [HR] 112 G4
Bäsksjö [S] 190 F4
Başlamış [TR] 152 D2
Başmakçı [TR] 152 H4
Bäsna [S] 172 H4
Bassacutena [I] 118 D2
Bassano del Grappa [I] 72 D5
Bassenheim [D] 30 H6
Bassevuovdde [N] 194 C4
Bassoues [F] 84 F2
Bassum [D] 18 D6
Båstad [N] 166 C2
Båstad [S] 162 B6
Bastelica [F] 114 B4
Bastenaken (Bastogne) [B] 44 E1
Baştepe [TR] 152 H3
Bastfallet [S] 174 E5
Bastia [F] 114 C3
Bastia [I] 116 A2
Bastnäs [S] 166 E1
Bastogne (Bastenaken) [B] 44 E1
Bastuträsk [S] 190 H4
Bastuträsk [S] 190 H5
Batajnica [SRB] 142 G2
Batak [BG] 148 A6
Batakiai [LT] 200 E5
Batalha [P] 86 C3
Batanovtsi [BG] 146 F5
Batăr [RO] 76 H3
Bátaszék [H] 76 C4
Baté [H] 76 A4
Batea [E] 90 G6
Batelov [CZ] 48 H6
Batetskiy [RUS] 202 B2
Bath [GB] 12 G3
Batin [BG] 148 C2
Batina [HR] 76 C5
Batlava [SRB] 146 C4
Bátmonostor [H] 76 C5
Båtmuseum [N] 180 C4
Batnfjordsøra [N] 180 E2
Batočina [SRB] 146 C2
Bátonyterenye [H] 64 D5
Batorz [PL] 52 E1
Bátovce [SK] 64 B4
Batrina [HR] 142 C2
Båtsfjord [N] 194 E1
Båtsjaur [S] 190 G2
Battaglia Terme [I] 110 G1
Battenberg [D] 32 D6
Battice [B] 30 E5
Battipáglia [I] 120 F4
Battle [GB] 14 F5
Battonya [H] 76 G4
Batultsi [BG] 146 G4
Baturyn [UA] 202 E6
Bátya [H] 76 C4
Batyk [H] 74 G2
Batz-sur-Mer [F] 40 D6
Baud [F] 26 A6
Baugé [F] 42 A6
Baugy [F] 56 C3
Baume, Cirque de- [F] 56 H5
Baume, Grotte de la- [F] 58 B4
Baume-les-Dames [F] 58 B4
Baume-Les Messieurs, Abbeye de- [F] 56 H5
Baumholder [D] 44 H3
Baunei [I] 118 E5
Bauska [LV] 198 D6
Bautzen [D] 34 F6
Bavanište [SRB] 142 H2
Bavay [F] 28 G4
Baveno [I] 70 F3
Bavorov [CZ] 48 F6
Bawtry [GB] 10 F4
Bayard [F] 70 A4
Baydakovo [RUS] 198 H6
Bayerisch Eisenstein [D] 48 D6
Bayeux [F] 26 E3
Bayındır [TR] 150 F4
Bayındır [TR] 152 D4
Bayır [TR] 152 E6
Bayırköy [TR] 150 B5
Bayırköy [TR] 150 F4
Baykal [BG] 148 A2
Bayon [F] 44 E6
Bayonne [F] 84 C2
Bayrakçi Mağarasi [TR] 152 D5
Bayramdere [TR] 150 E4
Bayramiç [TR] 152 B1
Bayramşah [TR] 152 G1
Bayreuth [D] 46 H4
Bayrischzell [D] 60 F5
Baza [E] 102 G3
Bazas [F] 66 D4
Bazenheid [CH] 58 G5
Bazoches-sur-Hoëne [F] 26 G5
Bazolles [F] 56 E4
Baztan / Elizondo [E] 82 H4
Bazzano [I] 110 F3
Beaconsfield [GB] 14 D4
Béal an Mhuirthead / Belmullet [IRL] 2 B2
Beariz [E] 78 C4
Beas [E] 94 F5
Beasain [E] 84 A3
Beas de Segura [E] 102 G1
Beateberg [S] 166 F5
Beaucaire [F] 106 G4
Beaufort [IRL] 4 B4
Beaufort-en-Vallée [F] 54 E1
Beaufort-sur-Doron [F] 70 B3
Beaugency [F] 42 D6
Beaujeu [F] 68 F1
Beaulieu-sur-Dordogne [F] 66 H4
Beaulieu-sur-Mer [F] 108 F4
Beaumaris [GB] 10 B4
Beaumes de Venise [F] 106 H3
Beaumesnil [F] 26 H4
Beaumetz [F] 28 E4
Beaumont [B] 28 H4
Beaumont [F] 26 D1
Beaumont [F] 66 F4
Beaumont-de-Lomagne [F] 84 H2
Beaumont-le-Roger [F] 26 H4
Beaumont-sur-Sarthe [F] 26 F6
Beaune [F] 56 G4
Beaune-la-Rolande [F] 42 F6
Beaupréau [F] 54 C2
Beauraing [B] 30 D6
Beauregard, Manoir de- [F] 54 H2
Beaurepaire [F] 68 G4
Beaurepaire-en-Bresse [F] 56 H5
Beausite [F] 44 D4
Beauvais [F] 28 D6
Beauvallon [F] 108 D5
Beauvène [F] 68 E5
Beauvezer [F] 108 D3
Beauville [F] 66 F5
Beauvoir-sur-Mer [F] 54 B2
Beauvoir-sur-Niort [F] 54 D5
Beba Veche [RO] 76 E5
Bebenhausen [D] 58 G2
Bebra [D] 32 F6
Bebrene [LV] 198 F6
Bebrovo [BG] 148 D4
Beccles [GB] 14 H2
Becedas [E] 88 C4
Bečej [SRB] 76 E6
Bečej [SRB] 204 A5
Becerreá [E] 78 E4
Bécherel [F] 26 C5
Bechet [RO] 146 G2
Bechhofen [D] 46 F6
Bechyně [CZ] 48 F6
Becicherecu Mic [RO] 76 G5
Becilla de Valderaduey [E] 82 B5
Beçin Kalesi [TR] 154 C1
Beciu [RO] 148 A2
Beckenried [CH] 58 F6
Beckum [D] 32 C4
Beckum [D] 32 D3
Beclean [RO] 204 C4
Bécon-les-Granits [F] 40 G6
Bečov nad Teplou [CZ] 48 D3
Becsehely [H] 74 G4
Becske [H] 64 D5
Bédarieux [F] 106 D4
Bedburg [D] 30 G4
Beddingestrand [S] 158 C3
Bédée [F] 26 C5
Bedemler [TR] 152 C4
Beden [BG] 130 D1
Bedenac [F] 66 D2
Bedenica [HR] 74 F5
Bedford [GB] 14 E3
Będgoszcz [PL] 20 F5
Będków [PL] 36 H5
Bedlington [GB] 8 G5
Bednarka [PL] 52 D5
Bédole [I] 72 B4
Bedonia [I] 110 C3
Bedous [F] 84 D4
Bedsted [DK] 160 B4
Bedworth [GB] 14 D1
Będzin [PL] 50 G3
Będzino [PL] 20 H3
Beek [NL] 30 E4
Beekbergen [NL] 16 F5
Beek en Donk [NL] 30 E2
Beelitz [D] 34 D3
Beenz [D] 20 D5
Beerfelden [D] 46 D4
Beersel [B] 30 C4
Beeskow [D] 34 F3
Beesten [D] 32 C1
Befreiungshalle [D] 60 E2
Bégard [F] 26 A4
Beglezh [BG] 148 A3
Beg-Meil [F] 40 B3
Begndal [N] 170 G4
Begnecourt [F] 58 B2
Begonte [E] 78 D3
Begov Han [BIH] 142 D3
Begunitsy [RUS] 178 G6
Begur [E] 92 G3
Behramkale [TR] 134 H1
Behramlı [TR] 130 H5
Behringersmühle [D] 46 G4
Beilen [NL] 16 G3
Beilngries [D] 46 H6
Beinwil [CH] 58 E5
Beith [GB] 8 D3
Beitostølen [N] 170 F2
Beitstad [N] 190 C5
Beiuş [RO] 204 B4
Beja [P] 94 D3
Béjar [E] 88 B4
Bejís [E] 98 E3
Bekçiler [TR] 154 G1
Békés [H] 76 G3
Békéscsaba [H] 76 G3
Békésszentandrás [H] 76 F2
Bekilli [TR] 152 G4
Bekken [N] 172 D1
Bélâbre [F] 54 G4
Bela Crkva [SRB] 204 B5
Bel-Air [F] 26 C6
Bel-Air [F] 54 F5
Bel-Aire [F] 26 C6
Belalcázar [E] 96 C4
Bělá nad Radbuzou [CZ] 48 C5
Bela Palanka [SRB] 146 E4
Bélapátfalva [H] 64 E5
Bělá pod Bezdězem [CZ] 48 G2
Bělá pod Pradědem [CZ] 50 D3
Belava [LV] 198 F5
Belbaşı [TR] 154 H2
Belcaire [F] 106 A5
Bełchatów [PL] 36 G5
Belchin [BG] 146 G5
Belchite [E] 90 E5
Belčišta [MK] 128 D3
Belcoo [NIR] 2 E3
Belecke [D] 32 D4
Beled [H] 74 G1
Belej [HR] 112 E3
Belence [TR] 152 H3
Belene [BG] 148 B2
Bélesta [F] 106 B5
Belev [RUS] 202 F4
Belevi [TR] 152 D5
Belevren [BG] 148 F5
Belfast [NIR] 2 G3
Belfir [RO] 76 H3
Belfort [F] 58 C4
Belgern [D] 34 D5
Belgirate [I] 70 F4
Belgodère [F] 114 B3
Belgooly [IRL] 4 C5
Beli [HR] 112 E2
Belianes [E] 92 C3
Belianska Jaskyňa [SK] 52 B6
Belica [BG] 148 D1
Belica [HR] 74 F4
Belica [MK] 128 D2
Belica [MK] 128 E2
Beli Iskăr [BG] 146 G5
Belikij Novgorod [RUS] 202 C2
Belıklıçeşme [TR] 150 C5
Beli Manastir [HR] 76 B6
Belimel [BG] 146 F3
Belin-Béliet [F] 66 C4
Belinchón [E] 96 H1
Belinţ [RO] 76 H5
Belišće [HR] 76 B6
Belitsa [BG] 146 G6
Beljakovci [MK] 146 D6
Beljina [SRB] 142 G3
Belkavak [TR] 152 H1
Bella [I] 120 G3
Bellac [F] 54 F5
Bellaghy [NIR] 2 G3
Bellágio [I] 70 G3
Bellaguarda [E] 90 H5
Bellamont [D] 60 B4
Bellamonte [I] 72 D4
Bellano [I] 70 G3
Bellante [I] 116 D3
Bellapaïs (Beylerbeyi) [CY] 154 G5
Bellária [I] 110 H4
Bellcaire d'Urgell [E] 92 C3
Belleek [NIR] 2 E3
Bellegarde [F] 42 F6
Bellegarde [F] 106 G4
Bellegarde-en-Marche [F] 68 B1
Bellegarde-sur-Valserine [F] 70 A2
Belle-Isle-en-Terre [F] 40 D2
Bellême [F] 26 G6
Bellenaves [F] 56 D6
Bellencombre [F] 28 C5
Bellengreville [F] 28 C4
Bellevesvre [F] 56 H5
Belleville [F] 68 F2
Belleville-sur-Vie [F] 54 B2
Belley [F] 68 H3
Bellinge [DK] 156 D3
Bellinzona [CH] 70 G3
Bell-lloc d'Urgell [E] 90 H4
Bello [E] 90 D5
Bellö [S] 162 E2
Bellpuig [E] 92 C3
Belluno [I] 72 E4
Bellver, Castell de- [E] 104 E5
Bellver de Cerdanya [E] 92 E2
Bellvik [S] 190 F5
Belmez [E] 96 B5
Belmez de la Moraleda [E] 102 F2
Belmonte [E] 78 G3
Belmonte [E] 96 H3
Belmonte [P] 86 F2
Belmont-sur-Rance [F] 106 D3
Belmullet / Béal an Mhuirthead [IRL] 2 B2
Belœil [B] 28 G3
Belogradchik [BG] 146 E3
Belokamensk [UA] 204 H4
Beloljin [SRB] 146 C4
Belopolci [BG] 130 G1
Belo Pole [BG] 146 F2
Belo Polje [SRB] 146 B5
Belopol'ye [UA] 202 F6
Belorado [E] 82 F6
Bělotín [CZ] 50 E5
Belovec [BG] 148 D2
Belovo [BG] 148 A6
Belozem [BG] 148 B5
Belpasso [I] 126 G3
Belsen [D] 18 F6
Belsk Duży [PL] 38 B4
Beltinci [SLO] 74 F3
Belturbet [IRL] 2 E4
Beluša [SK] 64 B2
Belušić [SRB] 146 C2
Belvedere Campomoro [F] 114 A5
Belvedere du Cirque [F] 108 E2
Belvedere Marittimo [I] 124 C3
Belvedere Ostrense [I] 112 C6
Belver [P] 86 E4
Belvès [F] 66 F4
Belvis de la Jara [E] 96 D1
Belyy [RUS] 202 D3
Belz [F] 40 C4
Belz [UA] 52 H2
Bełżec [PL] 52 G2
Belzig [D] 34 D3
Bełżyce [PL] 38 D6
Bembibre [E] 78 F5
Bembirre [E] 78 C2
Bemposta [P] 80 F5
Bemposta [P] 86 D4
Benabarre [E] 90 H3
Benalmádena [E] 102 B5
Benalup [E] 100 G5
Benamaurel [E] 102 G3
Benaojón [E] 100 H4
Benasque [E] 84 F5
Benassal [E] 98 F2
Benassay [F] 54 E4
Benátky nad Jezerou [CZ] 48 G3
Benavente [E] 82 A5
Benavente [P] 86 C5
Benavila [P] 86 D5
Benavites [E] 78 G6
Bencık [TR] 154 C1
Bene [LV] 198 D6
Benedikt [SLO] 74 E3
Benediktbeuern [D] 60 D5
Benediktiner-Abtei [D] 60 F4
Beneixama / Benejama [E] 104 D1
Benejama / Beneixama [E] 104 D1
Benešov [CZ] 48 G4
Benešov [CZ] 62 C3
Benešov nad Ploučnicí [CZ] 48 F2
Benestad [S] 158 D3
Benetutti [I] 118 D4
Benévent l'Abbaye [F] 54 G6
Benevento [I] 120 F2
Benfeld [F] 58 E2
Bengtsfors [S] 166 D4
Beničanci [HR] 76 B6
Benicarló [E] 98 H2
Benicasim / Benicàssim [E] 98 G3
Benicàssim / Benicasim [E] 98 G3
Benidorm [E] 104 E2
Beniel [E] 104 C3
Benifaió [E] 98 E5
Benifallet [E] 90 G6
Benifassá, Monestir de- [E] 98 G2
Beniganín [E] 98 E6
Benilloba [E] 104 E1
Benimarfull [E] 104 E1
Benissa [E] 104 F2
Benkovac [HR] 112 G5
Benkovski [BG] 148 F2
Benneckenstein [D] 32 H4
Bennstedt [D] 34 B5
Bénodet [F] 40 B3
Benòs [E] 84 F5
Benòs [F] 84 F5
Benquerencia de la Serena [E] 96 B4
Benrath [D] 30 G4
Bensafrim [P] 94 B5
Bensberg [D] 30 H4
Bensersiel [D] 18 C3
Bensheim [D] 46 C4
Bensjö [S] 184 C3
Benzú [MA] 100 G6
Beočin [SRB] 142 F2
Beograd [SRB] 142 G2
Beograd [SRB] 204 B6
Bera / Vera de Bidasoa [E] 84 B2
Berane [MNE] 146 A5
Beranúy [E] 84 F6
Berat [AL] 128 B4
Beratón [E] 90 C3
Berbenno di Valtellina [I] 70 H3
Berberana [E] 82 G4
Bercedo [E] 82 F4
Bercel [H] 64 D5
Berceto [I] 110 D3
Berchem [L] 44 F3
Berching [D] 46 G6
Berchtesgaden [D] 60 G6
Bercinos del Real Camino [E] 82 C5
Berck-Plage [F] 28 D3
Berdalen [N] 164 D2
Berducedo [E] 78 F3
Berducido [E] 78 B4
Berdún [E] 84 C5
Berdychiv [UA] 202 C8
Berechiu [RO] 76 H3
Berehomet [UA] 204 D3
Berehove [UA] 204 B3
Berek [H] 76 F2
Berek [HR] 74 G6
Berest [PL] 52 C5
Berestowitsa [BY] 202 A6
Berettyószentmárton [H] 76 G1
Berettyóújfalu [H] 76 G1
Berezan' [UA] 202 E7
Berezhany [UA] 202 B8
Berezivka [UA] 204 F3
Berezna [UA] 202 D6
Berg [CH] 58 F4
Berg [D] 46 H2
Berg [D] 60 D5
Berg [N] 166 C3
Berg [N] 172 D5
Berg [N] 180 C6
Berg [N] 190 C3
Berg [S] 162 D4
Berg [S] 166 D4
Berga [D] 32 H5
Berga [E] 92 E2
Berga [S] 162 F4
Bergama [TR] 152 C2
Bergamo [I] 70 H4
Bergara [E] 82 H4
Berg bei Neamarkt [D] 46 H5
Bergby [S] 174 E3
Bergdala [S] 162 E5
Berge [N] 164 E1
Berge [S] 182 F1
Bergedorf [D] 18 G4
Bergeforsen [S] 184 E4
Bergen [D] 18 F6
Bergen [D] 18 H6
Bergen [D] 20 D2
Bergen [D] 44 F3
Bergen [D] 48 C3
Bergen [N] 170 B4
Bergen [NL] 16 D3
Bergen (Mons) [B] 28 G4
Bergen aan Zee [NL] 16 D3
Bergen op Zoom [NL] 16 C6
Berger [N] 164 H2
Bergerac [F] 66 E4
Berget [N] 190 E2
Bergfors [S] 192 G4
Bergheim [D] 30 G4
Berghem [S] 160 H3
Bergisch Gladbach [D] 30 H4
Bergkvara [S] 162 F6
Bergland [S] 190 F4
Berglern [D] 60 E3
Berglia [N] 190 D5
Bergliden [S] 196 A4
Berg-Neustadt [D] 32 C5
Bergö [FIN] 186 A3
Bergondo [E] 78 D2
Bergsäter [S] 190 F4
Bergshamra [S] 168 E2
Bergsjö [S] 166 F3
Bergsjö [S] 184 E6
Bergsjøstøl [N] 170 F4
Berg slussar [S] 166 H5
Bergsmoen [N] 190 C5
Bergstad [FIN] 176 G5
Bergstrøm [N] 166 C3
Bergues [F] 14 H6
Bergum [NL] 16 F2
Bergün [CH] 70 H2
Bergunda [S] 162 D5
Bergundhaugen [N] 172 B2
Bergvik [S] 174 E2
Berhida [H] 76 B2
Beringel [P] 94 D3
Beringen [B] 30 E3
Berini [RO] 76 G6
Bérisal [CH] 70 E2
Berja [E] 102 F5
Berkåk [N] 180 H3
Berkenthin [D] 18 G4
Berkesz [H] 64 H4
Berkheim [D] 60 B4
Berkhof [D] 32 F1
Berkovići [BIH] 144 C3
Berkovitsa [BG] 146 F3
Berkvigen [S] 190 G2
Berlanga [E] 94 H4
Berlanga de Duero [E] 90 A3
Berlevåg [N] 194 E1
Berlin [D] 34 E2
Berlingen [CH] 58 G4
Bermeo [E] 82 H3
Bermillo de Sayago [E] 80 G5
Bern [CH] 58 D6
Bernalda [I] 122 D4
Bernartice [CZ] 48 F5
Bernati [LV] 198 B6
Bernau [D] 34 E2
Bernau [D] 60 F5
Bernaville [F] 28 E4
Bernay [F] 26 G4
Bernburg [D] 34 B4
Berndorf [A] 62 E5
Berne [D] 18 D5
Bernedo [E] 82 H6
Bernek [A] 72 C1
Bernhardsthal [A] 62 G3
Bernkastel-Kues [D] 44 G2
Bernsdorf [D] 34 F5
Bernstein [A] 74 F1
Bernués [E] 84 D5
Beromünster [CH] 58 F5
Beronovo [BG] 148 E4
Beroun [CZ] 48 F4
Berovo [MK] 128 H1
Berre-l'Etang [F] 106 H5
Berrien [F] 40 C2
Berriozar [E] 84 B4
Berrocal [E] 94 F5
Berrocalejo [E] 88 C6
Berroquejo [E] 100 F4
Bersenbrück [D] 32 D1
Beršići [SRB] 146 B2
Bertinoro [I] 110 G4
Bertrix [B] 44 D2
Berwang [A] 60 C6
Berwick-upon-Tweed [GB] 8 F4
Beryslav [UA] 204 G3
Berzaune [LV] 198 F5
Berzeme [F] 68 E6
Berzence [H] 74 G4
Berzosa [E] 88 H2
Besalú [E] 92 F2
Besançon [F] 58 B5
Besande [E] 82 C3
Besenyőtelek [H] 64 E6
Besenyszög [H] 76 E1
Beşevler [TR] 150 G4
Beşevlet [TR] 150 G3
Besigheim [D] 46 D6
Běšiny [CZ] 48 D6
Beška [SRB] 142 G2
Bessan [F] 106 E4
Bessans [F] 70 C5
Bessay-sur-Allier [F] 56 D5
Besse-en-Chandesse [F] 68 C3
Besse-sur-Issole [F] 108 C5
Bessheim [N] 170 F1
Bessines-sur-Gartempe [F] 54 G6
Best [NL] 30 E2
Bestida [P] 80 B5
Bestorp [S] 168 A6
Beszowa [PL] 52 C2
Betancuria [E] 100 E6
Betanzos [E] 78 D2
Betelu [E] 84 B3
Bétera [E] 98 E4
Beteta [E] 90 B6
Bétharram, Grottes de- [F] 84 E4
Bethesda [GB] 10 B4
Béthune [F] 28 E3
Betliar [SK] 64 E3
Betna [N] 180 F2
Betsele [S] 190 G5
Bettenburg [D] 46 F3
Bettna [S] 168 C4

Bettola [I] 110 C2
Bettyhill [GB] 6 E2
Betws-y-Coed [GB] 10 C4
Betz [F] 42 G3
Betzdorf [D] 32 C6
Betzigau [D] 60 C5
Beuel [D] 30 H5
Beuil [F] 108 E3
Beulich [D] 44 H1
Beuron [D] 58 G3
Beuzeville [F] 26 G3
Bevagna [I] 116 A2
Bévercé-Malmedy [B] 30 F5
Beverley [GB] 10 G4
Beverstedt [D] 18 D4
Beverungen [D] 32 F4
Beverwijk [NL] 16 D4
Bevtoft [DK] 156 C3
Bewdley [GB] 12 G1
Bex [CH] 70 C2
Bexhill [GB] 14 E6
Beyağaç [TR] 152 F6
Beyarmudu (Pergamos) [CY] 154 G5
Beyazköy [TR] 150 C2
Beycayırı [TR] 150 B5
Beyce Sultan [TR] 152 G4
Beydağı [TR] 152 E4
Beydilli [TR] 152 H3
Beyel [TR] 152 E1
Beykög [TR] 152 H6
Beykoz [TR] 150 E2
Beylerbeyi (Bellapaïs) [CY] 154 G5
Beynac-et-Cazenac [F] 66 F4
Beynat [F] 66 H3
Beyobaşı [TR] 154 E1
Bezau [A] 60 B6
Bezdan [SRB] 76 C5
Bezden [BG] 146 F4
Bezděz [CZ] 48 G2
Bezdonys [LT] 200 G5
Bezhetë-Makaj [AL] 146 A6
Bezhetsk [RUS] 202 E2
Béziers [F] 106 D4
Béznar [E] 102 E4
Bezzecca [I] 72 C5
B. Hornberg [D] 46 D5
Biała [PL] 50 D3
Białaczów [PL] 38 A5
Biała Piska [PL] 24 D4
Biała Podlaska [PL] 38 F3
Biała Rawska [PL] 38 A4
Białawy Wielkie [PL] 36 C5
Białobrzegi [PL] 38 B4
Białogard [PL] 20 H3
Białogóra [PL] 22 D1
Białowieża [PL] 38 G1
Biały Bór [PL] 22 B4
Białystok [PL] 24 E5
Biancavilla [I] 126 G3
Bianco [I] 124 D7
Biar [E] 104 D1
Biarritz [F] 84 C2
Bias [F] 66 B5
Biasca [CH] 70 G2
Biasteri / Laguardia [E] 82 G6
Biatigala [LT] 200 E4
Biatorbágy [H] 76 C1
Biabktad [N] 194 C2
Bibbiena [I] 110 G6
Bibbiona [I] 114 E1
Biberach [D] 58 F2
Biberach an der Riss [D] 60 B4
Biberwier [A] 60 D6
Bibione [I] 72 G6
Bibury [GB] 12 H3
Bič [SLO] 74 C5
Bicaj [AL] 128 C1
Bicaz [RO] 204 D4
Bicester [GB] 14 D3
Bichl [D] 60 D5
Bicos [P] 94 C3
Bicske [H] 76 B1
Bidache [F] 84 C2
Bidalite [S] 162 F6
Bidart [F] 84 C2
Biddinghuizen [NL] 16 F4
Biddulph [GB] 10 E5
Bideford [GB] 12 D3
Bidjovagge [N] 192 H2
Bidovce [SK] 64 G3
Bidziny [PL] 52 D1
Bie [S] 168 B4
Bieber [D] 46 D3
Biebersdorf [D] 34 F4
Biecz [PL] 52 C4
Biedenkopf [D] 32 D6
Biegen [D] 34 F3
Biegen [D] 34 F3
Biejkvasslia [N] 190 D2
Biel [E] 84 C5
Biel / Bienne [CH] 58 D5
Bielany Wrocł. [PL] 50 C1
Bielawa [PL] 50 C2
Bielawy [PL] 36 G3
Bielczyny [PL] 22 E5
Bielefeld [D] 32 D3
Bielino [PL] 38 C1
Biella [I] 70 E4
Bielmonte [I] 70 E4
Bielopolje [HR] 112 H3
Bielowy [PL] 52 D4
Bielsa [E] 84 E5
Bielsa, Tunnel de- [E/F] 84 E5
Bielsk [PL] 36 H2
Bielsko-Biała [PL] 50 G4
Bielsk Podlaski [PL] 38 F1
Biely Kameň [SK] 62 G4
Bienenbüttel [D] 18 G5
Bieniów [PL] 34 H4
Bienne / Biel [CH] 58 D5
Bienvenida [E] 94 G3
Bienvenida [E] 96 D4
Bierberchren [D] 46 E5
Bierdzany [PL] 50 E2
Biermé [F] 40 H5
Bierre-Lès-Semur [F] 56 F3
Bierutów [PL] 36 D6
Bierzwnik [PL] 20 G6
Biescas [E] 84 D5
Biesenthal [D] 34 E1
Biesiekierz [PL] 20 H3
Bieskkenjárga [N] 194 C4
Bietigheim [D] 46 D6
Bieżuń [PL] 22 G6
Biga [TR] 150 C5
Bigadiç [TR] 152 D2
Bigastro [E] 104 D3
Biggar [GB] 8 E4
Biggleswade [GB] 14 E3
Bignasco [CH] 70 F2
Bigor [MNE] 144 E4
Bihać [BIH] 112 H3
Biharia [RO] 76 H2
Biharkeresztes [H] 76 H2
Biharnagybajom [H] 76 G1
Bijambarska Pećina [BIH] 142 D4
Bijeljani [BIH] 144 D3
Bijeljina [BIH] 142 E3
Bijelo Brdo [HR] 142 E1
Bijelo Polje [MNE] 146 A4
Bikava [LV] 198 G5
Bikovo [SRB] 76 D5
Bílá [CZ] 50 F5
Bila Tserkva [UA] 202 D8
Bilbao / Bilbo [E] 82 G4
Bilbo / Bilbao [E] 82 G4
Bileća [BIH] 144 D3
Bilecik [TR] 150 G4
Biled [RO] 76 G5
Bílenec [CZ] 48 E3
Biłgoraj [PL] 52 F2
Bilhorod Dnistrovs'kyi [UA] 204 F4
Bílina [CZ] 48 E2
Bilisht [AL] 128 D5
Biljanovac [SRB] 146 B3
Bilje [HR] 76 C6
Bilka [BG] 148 F3
Billdal [S] 160 G2
Billerbeck [D] 16 H6
Billericay [GB] 14 F4
Billesholm [S] 156 H1
Billingen [N] 180 E5
Billingsfors [S] 166 D4
Billom [F] 68 D2
Billsta [S] 184 G2
Billum [DK] 156 A2
Billund [DK] 156 C2
Bilopillia [UA] 202 E7
Bilousivka [UA] 202 E7
Bílovec [CZ] 50 E4
Bilska [LV] 198 F4
Bilsko [PL] 52 B4
Bilto [N] 192 H2
Bíňa [SK] 64 B5
Binas [F] 42 D6
Binasco [I] 70 G5
Binche [B] 28 H4
Bindslev [DK] 160 E2
Binéfar [E] 90 G4
Bingen [D] 46 B3
Bingen [N] 170 G6
Binghöhle [D] 46 G4
Bingsjö [S] 174 C3
Bingsta [S] 182 G3
Binibeca Vell [E] 104 H5
Binic [F] 26 B4
Binkos [BG] 148 D4
Bin Tepeler [TR] 152 E3
Binz [D] 20 D2
Binzen [D] 58 E4
Bioče [MNE] 144 E4
Biograd [HR] 112 G5
Bionaz [I] 70 D3
Bioska [SRB] 144 F1
Bircza [PL] 52 E4
Birgi [TR] 152 E4
Birgittelyst [DK] 160 D5
Biri [N] 172 B3
Birini [EST] 198 E2
Birini [LV] 198 E4
Biristrand [N] 172 B3
Birkala / Pirkkala [FIN] 176 F1
Birkeland [N] 164 C5
Birkeland [N] 164 E5
Birkenfeld [D] 44 G3
Birkenfeld [D] 46 E4
Birkenhead [GB] 10 D4
Birkenwerder [D] 34 E2
Birkerød [DK] 156 G2
Birkfeld [A] 74 E1
Birksdal [N] 180 D6
Birmingham [GB] 10 E6
Birnau [D] 58 H4
Biron, Château de- [F] 66 F4
Birr [IRL] 2 D6
Birstein [D] 46 D2
Birštonas [LT] 24 F1
Biržai [LT] 198 E6
Birżebbuga [M] 126 C6
Birži [LV] 198 F6
Birzuli [LV] 198 F4
Bisaccia [I] 120 G3
Bisacquino [I] 126 C3
Biscarrosse [F] 66 B4
Biscarrosse-Plage [F] 66 B4
Bisceglie [I] 122 D2
Bischoffen [D] 46 C1
Bischofsgrün [D] 46 H3
Bischofsheim [D] 46 E2
Bischofshofen [A] 72 G2
Bischofswerda [D] 34 F6
Biscoitos [P] 100 D3
Bisserci [BG] 148 D1
Bishop Auckland [GB] 10 F2
Bishop's Castle [GB] 10 C6
Bishop's Cleeve [GB] 12 G2
Bishop's Stortford [GB] 14 F3
Bisignano [I] 124 D4
Bisko [HR] 144 A2
Biskupice Oławskie [PL] 50 D1
Biskupice Radłowskico [PL] 52 C3
Biskupiec [PL] 22 F5
Biskupiec [PL] 22 H4
Biskupin [PL] 36 D1
Bisław [PL] 22 D5
Bislev [DK] 160 D4
Bismark [D] 34 B1
Bismo [N] 180 F5
Bispgården [S] 184 D3
Bispingen [D] 18 F5
Bistrec [BG] 148 E5
Bistreț [RO] 146 F2
Bistrica [MNE] 144 E3
Bistrica [SRB] 146 A3
Bistrica ob S. [SLO] 74 D5
Bistrița [RO] 204 C4
Bistritsa [BG] 146 F5
Bisztynek [PL] 22 H3
Bitburg [D] 44 F2
Bitche [F] 44 G4
Bitetto [I] 122 D3
Bithia [I] 118 C8
Bitola [MK] 128 E3
Bitonto [I] 122 D2
Bítov [CZ] 62 E2
Bitterfeld [D] 34 C4
Bitterstad [N] 192 D4
Bitti [I] 118 D4
Bıvıkali [TR] 150 C3
Bivio [CH] 70 H2
Bivio Manganaro [I] 126 D2
Bivona [I] 126 D3
Biyıklı [TR] 152 D5
Bizovac [HR] 76 B6
Bjåen [N] 164 D1
Bjala Cherkva [BG] 148 C3
Bjalizvor [BG] 148 C5
Bjår [N] 164 F1
Bjarisino [BY] 202 C5
Bjärklunda [S] 166 E6
Bjärnå / Perniö [FIN] 176 F5
Bjärnum [S] 158 D1
Bjärred [S] 156 H2
Bjärtrå [S] 184 F3
Bjästa [S] 184 G2
Bjelland [N] 164 D5
Bjelovar [HR] 74 G5
Bjerga [N] 164 C1
Bjergby [DK] 160 C5
Bjerkreim [N] 164 B4
Bjerkvik [N] 192 E4
Bjerre [DK] 156 D2
Bjerregård [DK] 156 A1
Bjerringbro [DK] 160 D5
Bjoenstrand [N] 164 B1
Bjølstad [N] 180 G6
Bjoneroa [N] 170 H4
Bjonevika [N] 170 H4
Bjørånes [N] 172 C1
Björbo [S] 172 G5
Bjordal [N] 164 C4
Bjordal [N] 170 B2
Bjørgo [N] 170 G3
Björka [S] 172 G3
Bjørkåsen [N] 192 F3
Björkberg [S] 172 H1
Björkberg [S] 190 G4
Bjørke [N] 180 D4
Bjørkedal [N] 180 C4
Björkefors [S] 162 F1
Bjørkelangen [N] 166 C1
Bjørkflåta [N] 170 F4
Björkfors [S] 190 E3
Björkhöjden [S] 184 D2
Björkliden [S] 192 F4
Björklinge [S] 168 D1
Bjørknes [N] 172 C6
Björkö [FIN] 176 C5
Björkö [S] 162 E3
Björkö [S] 168 F1
Björköby [FIN] 186 A2
Björksele [S] 190 G4
Björksjön [S] 184 F2
Björkvattnet [S] 190 D5
Björkvik [S] 168 B4
Bjørlia [N] 190 C4
Björna [S] 184 G1
Björneborg [S] 166 G3
Björneborg / Pori [FIN] 176 D1
Bjørnestad [N] 164 C4
Bjørnevasshytta [N] 164 D2
Bjørnevatn [N] 194 E3
Björnhult [S] 162 G3
Björnlunda [S] 168 C4
Björnrike [S] 182 F4
Björnsholm [S] 162 G1
Björnsjö [S] 184 G1
Bjørnstad [N] 190 D4
Björsäter [S] 166 F5
Björsäter [S] 168 B6
Bjørsvik [N] 170 B3
Bjuråker [S] 184 D6
Bjurberget [S] 172 E4
Bjurfors [S] 196 A5
Bjurholm [S] 156 H1
Bjurholm [S] 190 H6
Bjuröklubb [S] 196 B5
Bjurön [S] 174 G5
Bjursås [S] 172 H4
Bjurselet [S] 190 H4
Bjurträsk [S] 190 H4
Bjuv [S] 156 H1
Blace [SRB] 146 C3
Blachownia [PL] 50 F2
Blackburn [GB] 10 E3
Blacklion [IRL] 2 E3
Blackpool [GB] 10 D3
Blackstad [S] 162 G2
Blackwater [IRL] 4 F5
Bladåker [S] 168 E1
Blaenau Ffestiniog [GB] 10 B4
Blagaj [BIH] 144 C2
Blagaj Japra [BIH] 142 A2
Blagoevgrad [BG] 146 F6
Blagoevo [BG] 148 D2
Blagoveštenje, Manastir- [SRB] 146 B2
Blagovica [SLO] 74 C4
Blåhøj [DK] 156 B1
Blaiken [S] 190 F4
Blaikliden [S] 190 F4
Blain [F] 40 F5
Blair Atholl [GB] 8 E1
Blairgowrie [GB] 8 E2
Blaisy-Bas [F] 56 G3
Blaj [RO] 204 C4
Blajan [F] 84 G4
Błąkały [PL] 24 D2
Blakstad [N] 164 E5
Blâmont [F] 44 F6
Blanca [E] 104 C2
Blandford Forum [GB] 12 G4
Blanes [E] 92 F4
Blangy-sur-Bresle [F] 28 D4
Blanických Rytířů, Jeskyně- [CZ] 50 C5
Blankaholm [S] 162 G2
Blankenberge [B] 28 G1
Blankenburg [D] 32 H4
Blankenfelde [D] 34 E2
Blankenhain [D] 46 H1
Blankenheim [D] 30 G6
Blanquefort [F] 66 C3
Blansko [CZ] 50 C6
Blanzac [F] 66 E2
Blarney [IRL] 4 C5
Blarney Castle [IRL] 4 C5
Blascosancho [E] 88 E4
Błaszki [PL] 36 F5
Blatná [CZ] 48 E5
Blatnica [BIH] 142 C3
Blatnica [SK] 64 C2
Blatnice pod Sv. Antonínkem [CZ] 62 H2
Blato [HR] 144 A3
Blato [HR] 144 A2
Blattniksele [S] 190 G3
Blaubeuren [D] 60 B3
Blaufelden [D] 46 E5
Blaustein [D] 60 B3
Blåvand [DK] 156 A2
Blåvik [S] 162 E1
Blaye [F] 66 C2
Błażowa [PL] 52 E4
Blazquez [E] 96 B5
Bleckåsen [S] 182 F1
Bleckede [D] 18 G5
Blecksnäs [FIN] 186 A3
Bled [SLO] 74 B4
Bleiburg [A] 74 C3
Bleicherode [D] 32 G5
Bleik [N] 192 E3
Bleisfjord [N] 192 F4
Blendija [SRB] 146 D3
Bléneau [F] 56 D2
Blentarp [S] 158 C3
Blera [I] 114 H4
Blérancourt [F] 28 F6
Bléré [F] 54 G2
Blériot-Plage [F] 14 G6
Bleskestad [N] 164 C1
Blesle [F] 68 C3
Blessington [IRL] 2 F6
Bletterans [F] 56 H5
Blévy [F] 26 H5
Blexen [D] 18 D4
Bliesbruck-Reinheim, Parc Archéol. de- [F] 44 G4
Blieskastel [D] 44 G4
Bligny-sur-Ouche [F] 56 G4
Blikstorp [S] 166 F6
Blinisht [AL] 128 B1
Blinja [HR] 142 A1
Blintrop [D] 32 C5
Bliznaci [BG] 148 E2
Bliznak [BG] 148 F3
Bliznak [BG] 148 F3
Blizne [PL] 52 E4
Błogoszów [PL] 52 A2
Blois [F] 54 H1
Blokhus [DK] 160 D3
Blokzijl [NL] 16 F3
Blombacka [S] 166 F2
Blomberg [D] 32 E3
Blomsholms-Skeppet [S] 166 C4
Blomstermåla [S] 162 G4
Blönduós [IS] 192 B2
Błonie [PL] 36 C6
Błonie [PL] 38 B3
Błonie [PL] 38 F3
Bloška Polica [SLO] 74 B6
Blötberget [S] 172 H5
Błotnica [PL] 20 G3
Błotnica [PL] 38 B6
Błotno [PL] 20 F4
Blovice [CZ] 48 E5
Bludenz [A] 72 A1
Bludov [CZ] 50 C4
Blumberg [D] 58 F3
Blyth [GB] 8 G5
Bø [N] 164 F2
Bø [N] 164 G2
Bø [N] 170 B3
Bø [N] 170 B1
Bø [N] 192 D4
Bø [N] 192 E2
Bo [S] 166 H4
Boadilla del Monte [E] 88 F5
Boal [E] 78 F2
Boalt [S] 162 D6
Boário Terme [I] 72 B5
Bóbbio [I] 110 C2
Bobbio Pellice [I] 70 C6
Boberg [S] 184 C2
Bobice [PL] 52 E4
Bobin [PL] 52 B3
Bobingen [D] 60 D4
Bobitz [D] 20 A4
Böblingen [D] 58 G1
Bobolice [PL] 22 B3
Boboshevo [BG] 146 F6
Bobovdol [BG] 146 F5
Bobr [BY] 202 C5
Bobrová [CZ] 50 B5
Bobrovytsia [UA] 202 D7
Bobrowice [PL] 34 H4
Bobrowniki [PL] 24 F5
Bobrowniki [PL] 36 F1
Bobrynets' [UA] 204 G2
Bočac [BIH] 142 B3
Boca de Huergano [E] 82 C3
Bocairent [E] 104 E1
Boceguillas [E] 88 G3
Böçen [TR] 150 F5
Bochnia [PL] 52 B4
Bocholt [B] 30 E3
Bocholt [D] 16 G6
Bochov [CZ] 48 D3
Bochum [D] 30 H3
Bocigas [E] 88 E3
Bockara [S] 162 F3
Bockel [D] 18 E5
Bockenem [D] 32 G3
Boćki [PL] 38 E1
Böcksholm [S] 162 E4
Böckstein [A] 72 G2
Bockum Hövel [D] 32 C3
Bocognano [F] 114 B4
Boconád [H] 64 E6
Bócsa [H] 76 D3
Bocsig [RO] 76 H4
Böda [S] 162 H3
Boda [S] 166 E2
Boda [S] 172 H3
Boda [S] 184 E3
Bodaczów [PL] 52 F1
Bodafors [S] 162 D3
Boda glasbruk [S] 162 F5
Bodarsjön [S] 182 G6
Bodegraven [NL] 16 D5
Boden [S] 196 B3
Bodenmais [D] 48 D6
Bodenteich [D] 18 G6
Bodenwerder [D] 32 F3
Bodenwöhr [D] 48 C6
Bodjani [SRB] 142 E1
Bodman [D] 58 G4
Bodmin [GB] 12 C4
Bodø [N] 192 D6
Bodom [N] 190 C5
Bodrogkeresztúr [H] 64 G4
Bodrum [TR] 154 B2
Bodsjö [S] 182 H3
Bodsjöedet [S] 182 E1
Bodzanów [PL] 36 H2
Bodzanowice [PL] 50 F1
Bodzentyn [PL] 52 C1
Boëge [F] 70 B2
Boën [F] 68 E2
Bogács [H] 64 F5
Bøgard [N] 192 D3
Bogarra [E] 98 A6
Bogatić [SRB] 142 F2
Bogatovo [RUS] 22 G2
Bogatynia [PL] 48 G1
Boğaz (Bogázi) [CY] 154 G5
Boğazcık [TR] 154 G2
Bogázi (Boğaz) [CY] 154 G5
Boğaziçi [TR] 152 D5
Boğazköy [TR] 150 F4
Bogda [RO] 76 H5
Bogdana [RO] 148 B2
Bogdanci [MK] 128 G3
Bogdaniec [PL] 34 H2
Bogë [AL] 146 A6
Boge [S] 168 G4
Bogen [D] 60 G2
Bogen [N] 192 D5
Bogen [N] 192 E4
Bogen [S] 172 D6
Bogense [DK] 156 D2
Bogetići [MNE] 144 E4
Bogge [N] 180 F3
Böglosa [S] 168 C2
Bognanco [I] 70 E3
Bognes [N] 192 E4
Bognor Regis [GB] 14 D5
Bogojevo [SRB] 142 E1
Bogojevo [SRB] 146 D4
Bogoria [PL] 52 C2
Bogorodica [MK] 128 G3
Bogovina [SRB] 146 D2
Bogovinska Pećina [SRB] 146 D2
Bograngen [S] 172 E4
Boguchwałów [PL] 50 E3
Bogumiłowice [PL] 36 G6
Boguszów-Gorce [PL] 50 B2
Bogutovačka Banja [SRB] 146 B3
Bohain-en-Vermandois [F] 28 F5
Bohal [F] 26 B6
Bohdalov [CZ] 50 A5
Boheeshil [IRL] 4 B4
Bohinjska Bela [SLO] 74 B4
Bohinjska Bistrica [SLO] 74 A4
Böhmenkirch [D] 60 B2
Bohmte [D] 32 D2
Bohonal [E] 96 D2
Bohonal de Ibor [E] 88 B6
Böhönye [H] 74 H4
Bohula [MK] 128 F3
Boialvo [P] 80 B6
Boichinovtsi [BG] 146 F3
Bois-du-Four [F] 68 B6
Boitzenburg [D] 20 D5
Bóixols [E] 92 C2
Boizenburg [D] 18 G5
Böja [S] 166 F5
Bojano [I] 120 E1
Bojanów [PL] 52 D2
Bojanowo [PL] 36 C4
Bøjden [DK] 156 D4
Bojkovice [CZ] 62 H2
Bojnica [BG] 146 E2
Bojnice [SK] 64 B3
Bojnik [SRB] 146 D4
Bojtiken [S] 190 E3
Bokel [D] 18 F3
Bökemåla [S] 162 E6
Bökenäs [S] 166 C6
Bokinić [HR] 112 E3
Böklund [D] 18 F1
Bokod [H] 64 B6
Bokod [H] 64 B6
Bököny [H] 64 H5
Bokros [H] 76 E3
Boksitogorsk [RUS] 202 D1
Boksjok [N] 194 D2
Bol [HR] 144 A2
Bolaños de Calatrava [E] 96 F4
Bolayır [TR] 150 B4
Bolbec [F] 26 H3
Bolca [I] 72 C6
Bölcek [TR] 152 C2
Boldekow [D] 20 D4
Boldogasszonyfa [H] 76 A4
Boldva [H] 64 F4
Bøle [N] 190 B5
Böle [S] 182 G1
Bolekhiv [UA] 52 H6
Bolemin [PL] 34 H2
Bolesławiec [PL] 36 A6
Bolesławiec [PL] 36 E6
Bolesławów [PL] 50 C3
Boleszkowice [PL] 34 G2
Bolfiar [P] 80 B5
Bolfoss [N] 166 C1
Bolgatovo [RUS] 198 H5
Bolgheri [I] 114 E1
Bolhrad [UA] 204 E4
Boliden [S] 196 A4
Bolimów [PL] 38 A3
Bolinglanna / Buaile an Ghleanna [IRL] 2 B3
Boljanići [MNE] 144 E2
Boljevac [SRB] 146 D2
Boljevac [SRB] 204 B6
Boljun [HR] 112 E1
Bolkesjø [N] 164 G1
Bolkhov [RUS] 202 F4
Bolków [PL] 50 B1
Bollebygd [S] 162 B2
Bollène [F] 106 G2
Böllerkirche [D] 46 B3
Bollerup [S] 158 D3
Bollnäs [S] 174 D2
Bollstabruk [S] 184 F3
Bollullos de la Mitación [E] 94 G6
Bollullos Par del Condado [E] 94 F6
Bologna [I] 110 F3
Bologne [F] 44 C6
Bolótana [I] 118 C4
Bolsena [I] 114 H3
Bol'shakovo [RUS] 200 D5
Bol'shaya Izhora [RUS] 178 G5
Bol'shaya Yashchera [RUS] 198 H1
Bol'shie Sabicy [RUS] 198 H2
Bol'shiye Kolpany [RUS] 178 H6
Bol'shoye Zagor'e [RUS] 198 H3
Bol'shoy Sabsk [RUS] 198 G1
Bolstad [S] 166 D5
Bolstadøyri [N] 170 C3
Bolstaholm [FIN] 176 A5
Bolsward [NL] 16 E2
Bolszewo [PL] 22 D2
Boltaña [E] 84 E5
Boltenhagen [D] 18 H3
Boltigen [CH] 70 D1
Bolton [GB] 10 E4
Bolungarvík [IS] 192 A1
Bóly [H] 76 B5
Bolyarovo [BG] 148 E5
Bolyartsi [BG] 148 B6
Bolzano / Bozen [I] 72 D3
Bomarken [S] 166 C3
Bomarsund [FIN] 176 B5
Bomarzo [I] 114 H4
Bombarral [P] 86 B4
Bominago [I] 116 C4
Bom Jesus do Monte [P] 80 C3
Bomsund [S] 184 C2
Bonaduz [CH] 70 H1
Bonaguil, Château de- [F] 66 F5
Bonanza [E] 100 F3
Boñar [E] 82 C3
Bonar Bridge [GB] 6 E4
Bonares [E] 94 F6
Bonäs [S] 166 E2
Bonäs [S] 172 G3
Bonäset [S] 182 F1
Bonåsjøen [N] 192 D5
Bonassola [I] 110 C4
Bonaval [E] 88 G4
Bończa [PL] 38 B4
Bondal [N] 164 F1
Bondemon [S] 166 C4
Bondeno [I] 110 F2
Bondstorp [S] 162 C2
Bonefro [I] 116 F6
Bonete [E] 98 C6
Bonhamn [S] 184 G3
Bonhomme, Col du- [F] 58 D2
Bonifacio [F] 114 B6
Bonifati Marina [I] 124 C4
Bonilla [E] 98 B1
Bönitz [D] 34 E5
Bonlieu [F] 70 A1
Bonn [D] 30 G5
Bonnat [F] 54 H5
Bonndorf [D] 58 F4
Bønnerup Strand [DK] 160 F5
Bonnesvalyn [F] 42 H3
Bonnétable [F] 42 C5
Bonneuil-Matours [F] 54 F4
Bonneval [F] 42 D5
Bonneval-sur-Arc [F] 70 C4
Bonneville [F] 70 B2
Bonnières [F] 42 E3
Bonnieux [F] 106 H4
Bonnigheim [D] 46 D6
Bonny-sur-Loire [F] 56 D2
Bono [I] 118 D4
Bonorva [I] 118 C4
Bonport, Abbaye de- [F] 28 B6
Bonyhád [H] 76 B4
Boom [B] 30 C3
Boos [D] 30 G6
Boos [D] 60 B4
Boos [F] 28 C5
Booth of Toft [GB] 6 H3
Bootle [GB] 10 D4
Bopfingen [D] 60 C2
Boppard [D] 44 H1
Bor [CZ] 48 D4
Bor [RUS] 198 H2
Bor [S] 162 D4
Bor [SRB] 146 D2
Bor [SRB] 204 C6
Borås [N] 164 F4
Borås [S] 162 B2
Borba [P] 86 E6
Borbona [I] 116 B4
Borchen [D] 32 E4
Borci [BIH] 144 C2
Borculo [NL] 16 G5
Bordány [H] 76 E4
Bordeaux [F] 66 C3
Bordeira [P] 94 A4
Bordères [F] 84 F4
Bordesholm [D] 18 F2
Bordighera [I] 108 F4
Bording [DK] 160 C6
Bore [I] 110 C2
Boreci [SLO] 74 E3
Borek Wielkopolski [PL] 36 D4
Borello [I] 110 G5
Borensberg [S] 166 H5
Borg [N] 192 C4
Borgå / Porvoo [FIN] 178 B4
Borgafjäll [S] 190 E4
Borgarnes [IS] 192 A2
Borgeby [S] 156 H2
Borgen [N] 164 E3
Borgentreich [D] 32 E4
Börger [D] 18 B5
Borger [NL] 16 G3
Börgermoor [D] 18 B5
Borggård [S] 166 H5
Borghamn [S] 166 G6
Borghetto di Borbera [I] 110 B2
Borgholm [S] 162 G4
Borgholzhausen [D] 32 D2
Borghorst [D] 16 H5
Børglumkloster [DK] 160 D3
Borgo Callea [I] 126 D3
Borgoforte [I] 110 E2
Borgomanero [I] 70 F4
Borgond [H] 76 B2
Borgonovo Val Tidone [I] 70 G6
Borgorose [I] 116 B5
Borgo San Dalmazzo [I] 108 F3
Borgo San Lorenzo [I] 110 F5
Borgosésia [I] 70 E4
Borgo Ticino [I] 70 F4
Borgo Tossignano [I] 110 F4
Borgo Val di Taro [I] 110 C3
Borgo Valsugana [I] 72 D4
Borgo Vercelli [I] 70 F5
Borgsjö [S] 184 D4
Borgsjö [S] 190 G5
Borgstena [S] 162 B1
Borgund [N] 170 E2
Borgund [N] 180 B4
Borgvattnet [S] 184 C1
Borgvik [S] 166 E3
Borielsbyn [S] 196 B2
Borima [BG] 148 B4
Borino [BG] 130 D1
Borislavtsi [BG] 130 G1
Borisoglebskiy [RUS] 194 F3
Borisovo [RUS] 178 G3
Borja [E] 90 D3
Borken [D] 16 G6
Borken [D] 32 E6
Borkenes [N] 192 E3
Borki [RUS] 198 G3
Børkop [DK] 156 C2
Borków [PL] 52 B1
Borkum [D] 16 G1
Borlänge [S] 172 H4
Borlaug [N] 170 E2
Børlia [N] 182 B3
Borlu [TR] 152 E3
Bormes-les-Mimosas [F] 108 D6
Bórmio [I] 72 B3
Borna [D] 34 C6
Borneiro, Castro de- [E] 78 B2
Borne Sulinowo [PL] 22 B5
Bornhöved [D] 18 G3
Börnicke [D] 34 D1
Bornlitz [D] 18 F6
Bornos [E] 100 G3
Bornova [TR] 152 C4
Borodianka [UA] 202 D7
Borodinskoye [RUS] 178 F2
Boronów [PL] 50 F2
Borová Lada [CZ] 62 A2
Borovan [BG] 146 G3
Borovany [CZ] 62 C2
Borovets [BG] 146 G5
Borovica [BG] 146 E3
Borovichi [RUS] 198 H3
Borovik [RUS] 198 G3
Borovo [BG] 148 C2

Borovo [HR] 142 E1
Borovoy [RUS] 196 H4
Borovtsi [BG] 146 F3
Borów [PL] 52 D1
Borowa [PL] 36 D6
Borrby [S] 158 D3
Borre [DK] 156 G4
Borre [N] 164 H2
Borreby [DK] 156 F3
Borredà [E] 92 E2
Borremose [DK] 160 D4
Borriana / Burriana [E] 98 F3
Börringe [S] 158 C3
Borriol [E] 98 F3
Borris [DK] 156 B1
Borris [IRL] 4 F4
Borris-in-Ossory [IRL] 2 D6
Borrisokane [IRL] 2 D6
Borrisoleigh [IRL] 4 E3
Börrum [S] 168 C6
Borş [RO] 76 H2
Børş [RO] 204 B4
Børsa [N] 182 B1
Borşa [RO] 204 C3
Børselv [N] 194 C2
Borsfa [H] 74 F4
Borsh [AL] 132 B1
Borsodiánka [H] 64 F6
Borsodnádasd [H] 64 E4
Börstil [S] 174 G5
Bortholoma [D] 60 B2
Bort-les-Orgues [F] 68 B3
Börtnan [S] 182 F3
Bortnen [N] 180 B5
Borup [DK] 156 G3
Borynia [UA] 52 F6
Boryslav [UA] 52 G5
Boryspil' [UA] 202 D7
Borzechowo [PL] 22 D4
Borzone, Abbazia di- [I] 110 B3
Borzysław [PL] 22 B3
Bosa [I] 118 B4
Bosanci [HR] 112 G1
Bosanska Bojna [BIH] 112 H2
Bosanska Dubica [BIH] 142 B2
Bosanska Gradiška [BIH] 142 C2
Bosanska Kostajnica [BIH] 142 B2
Bosanska Krupa [BIH] 142 A2
Bosanska Rača [BIH] 142 F2
Bosanski Brod [BIH] 142 D2
Bosanski Novi [HR] 142 A2
Bosanski Petrovac [BIH] 142 A3
Bosanski Šamac [BIH] 142 D2
Bosansko Grahovo [BIH] 142 A4
Bošany [SK] 64 B3
Bősárkány [H] 62 G6
Bosc-Mesnil [F] 28 C5
Bosco Chiesanuova [I] 72 C5
Bösel [D] 18 C5
Bosgouet [F] 26 H3
Bosilegrad [SRB] 146 E5
Bosiljevo [HR] 112 G1
Bosjökloster [S] 158 C2
Bosjön [S] 166 F1
Boskoop [NL] 16 D5
Boskovice [CZ] 50 C5
Bosna Klanac [BIH] 142 D4
Bošnjace [SRB] 146 D4
Bošnjaci [HR] 142 E2
Bosruck Tunnel [A] 62 B6
Bössbo [S] 172 F2
Bossbøen [N] 164 E1
Bossea [I] 108 G3
Bossòst [E] 84 F5
Bostandere [TR] 150 C5
Boštanj [SLO] 74 D5
Böste [S] 158 C3
Boston [GB] 10 G6
Bostrak [N] 164 F3
Bosut [SRB] 142 F2
Bőszénfa [H] 76 A4
Boteå [S] 184 F2
Botevgrad [BG] 146 G4
Botevo [BG] 148 F2
Boticas [P] 80 E3
Botinec [HR] 74 E6
Botnen [N] 180 C4
Botngård [N] 190 B6
Bótoa [E] 86 F6
Bötom / Karijoki [FIN] 186 B4
Botoroaga [RO] 148 C1
Botorrita [E] 90 E4
Botoşani [RO] 204 D3
Botricello [I] 124 E5
Botsmark [S] 196 A5
Böttberg [D] 60 E5
Botten [S] 166 D3
Bottheim [N] 180 G5
Bottidda [I] 118 D4
Bottnaryd [S] 162 C2
Bottrop [D] 30 G3
Botun [MK] 128 D3
Botunets [BG] 146 G4
Bouaye [F] 54 B1
Bouchair [F] 28 E5
Bouconville-sur-Madt [F] 44 E5
Boudry [CH] 58 C6
Bouesse [F] 54 H4
Bouges-le-Château [F] 54 H3
Bouguenais [F] 54 B1
Bouillon [B] 44 D2
Bouilly [F] 44 A6
Boulay-Moselle [F] 44 F4
Bouligny [F] 44 E3
Boulogne-sur-Gesse [F] 84 G3
Boulogne-sur-Mer [F] 14 G6
Bouloire [F] 42 C5
Boumois, Château de- [F] 54 E2
Bouniagues [F] 66 E4
Bourbon-Lancy [F] 56 E5
Bourbon-l'Archambault [F] 56 D5
Bourbonne-les-Bains [F] 58 B2
Bourbourg [F] 14 H6
Bourbriac [F] 26 A4
Bourdeaux [F] 68 F6
Bourdeilles [F] 66 F2
Bourg [F] 66 D3
Bourg-Achard [F] 26 H3
Bourganeuf [F] 54 H6
Bourg-Argental [F] 68 F4
Bourg-de-Péage [F] 68 F5
Bourg-en-Bresse [F] 68 G2
Bourges [F] 56 C3
Bourg-et-Comin [F] 44 A2
Bourg-Lastic [F] 68 B2
Bourg-Madame [F] 92 E1
Bourgneuf-en-Retz [F] 54 B2
Bourgogne [F] 44 B3
Bourgoin-Jallieu [F] 68 G3
Bourg-St-Andéol [F] 106 G2
Bourg-St-Maurice [F] 70 C4
Bourgtheroulde-Infreville [F] 26 H4
Bourgueil [F] 54 E2
Bourideys [F] 66 C5
Bourmont [F] 58 B2
Bourne [GB] 10 G6
Bournemouth [GB] 12 G5
Bourneville [F] 26 H3
Bournezeau [F] 54 C3
Boussac [F] 56 B5
Boussens [F] 84 G4
Bouvignes [B] 30 D5
Bouvron [F] 40 F6
Bouxwiller [F] 44 G5
Bouzonville [F] 44 F3
Bova [I] 124 C8
Bovalino [I] 124 D7
Bovallstrand [S] 166 C5
Bova Marina [I] 124 C8
Bovan [SRB] 146 D3
Bovec [SLO] 72 H4
Bóveda [E] 78 D4
Bovegno [I] 72 B5
Bovense [DK] 156 E3
Bøverbru [N] 172 B4
Bøverdal [N] 180 F6
Boves [I] 108 F3
Bović [HR] 112 H1
Bovik [FIN] 176 A5
Bovino [I] 120 G2
Bovolenta [I] 110 G1
Bovolone [I] 110 F1
Bovrup [DK] 156 C4
Boxberg [D] 46 E5
Boxholm [S] 166 G6
Boxmeer [NL] 16 F6
Boxtel [NL] 30 E2
Boyalı [TR] 152 E3
Boyalıca [TR] 150 F4
Boyalica [TR] 152 F1
Boyalık [TR] 150 E2
Boyle [IRL] 2 D4
Bøylefoss [N] 164 F4
Bøyum [N] 170 D1
Božaj [MNE] 144 E4
Bozalan [TR] 152 F4
Bozan [TR] 152 H4
Božava [HR] 112 F5
Bozburun [TR] 154 D2
Bozcaada [TR] 130 H6
Bozcaatlı [TR] 152 F3
Bozdağ [TR] 152 E4
Bozdoğan [TR] 152 E5
Bozel [F] 70 B4
Bozen / Bolzano [I] 72 D3
Bozhane [TR] 150 F2
Bozhenci [BG] 148 C4
Bozhurishte [BG] 146 F4
Božica [SRB] 146 E5
Boží Dar [CZ] 48 D3
Bozkurt [TR] 152 G5
Bozkuş [TR] 152 G3
Bozkuş [TR] 152 G3
Bozlar [TR] 150 C4
Bozolan [TR] 152 C4
Bozouls [F] 68 B5
Bozouls, Trou de- [F] 68 B5
Bozüyük [TR] 150 G5
Bozveliisko [BG] 148 F3
Bozyaka [TR] 154 F1
Bozyazı [TR] 154 F4
Bózzolo [I] 110 E1
Bra [B] 30 E6
Bra [I] 108 G2
Brå [N] 182 B1
Braås [S] 162 E4
Brabecke [D] 32 D5
Brabova [RO] 146 F1
Bracciano [I] 114 H5
Brachlewo [PL] 22 E4
Bracieux [F] 54 H2
Bracigovo [BG] 148 A6
Bräcke [S] 182 H3
Brackenheim [D] 46 C6
Brackley [GB] 14 D3
Bracknell [GB] 14 D4
Brackwede [D] 32 D3
Brad [RO] 204 C4
Bradford [GB] 10 E3
Bradina [BIH] 144 C1
Bradvari [BG] 148 E1
Brae [GB] 6 G3
Brædstrup [DK] 156 C1
Braemar [GB] 6 E6
Braga [P] 80 C3
Bragança [P] 80 F3
Brahestad / Raahe [FIN] 196 C4
Brahetrolleborg [DK] 156 D4
Brail [CH] 72 B2
Brăila [RO] 204 E5
Braine [F] 44 A2
Braine-le-Comte [B] 28 H3
Braintree [GB] 14 F3
Brake [D] 18 D4
Brakel [B] 28 G3
Brakel [D] 32 E4
Bräkne-Hoby [S] 158 F1
Brålanda [S] 166 D5
Bram [F] 106 B4
Bramberg [A] 72 F1
Bramberg [CH] 72 F1
Brämhult [S] 162 B2
Bramming [DK] 156 B2
Brampton [GB] 8 E5
Bramsche [D] 32 D2
Branč [SK] 62 H3
Branč [SK] 64 A4
Branca [I] 116 B1
Brancaleone Marina [I] 124 D8
Brancion [F] 56 G6
Brancoli, Pieve di- [I] 110 D5
Brâncoveni [RO] 148 A1
Brand [A] 72 A1
Brandal [N] 180 C3
Brändåsen [S] 182 E5
Brändbo [S] 184 D5
Brandbu [N] 170 H4
Brande [DK] 156 C1
Bränden [S] 182 F6
Brandenberg [A] 60 E6
Brandenburg [D] 34 D2
Brand-Erbisdorf [D] 48 E1
Brandhof [A] 62 D6
Brandis [D] 34 E4
Brändö [FIN] 176 C5
Brandomil [E] 78 B2
Brandon [F] 56 F6
Brandon [GB] 8 F6
Brandstorp [S] 162 D1
Brandval [N] 172 D5
Brandvoll [N] 192 F3
Brandýsek [CZ] 48 F3
Brandýs n Labem [CZ] 48 G3
Branica [BG] 148 D6
Braniewo [PL] 22 F2
Branik [SLO] 72 H5
Branišovice [CZ] 62 F2
Branitz, Schloss- [D] 34 F4
Brankovice [CZ] 50 D6
Brännåker [S] 190 F4
Brännberg [S] 196 A3
Branne [F] 66 D3
Brannenburg [D] 60 F5
Brañosera [E] 82 D4
Brańsk [PL] 38 E1
Brantôme [F] 66 F2
Branzi [I] 70 H3
Bras-d'Asse [F] 108 C3
Braskereidfoss [N] 172 D4
Braslaw [BY] 200 H4
Braşov [RO] 204 D5
Brassac [F] 106 C3
Brassac-Jumeaux [F] 68 D3
Brasschaat [B] 30 D2
Bras-sur-Meuse [F] 44 D3
Brastad [S] 166 C5
Břasy [CZ] 48 E4
Brąszewice [PL] 36 F5
Brataj [AL] 128 B6
Bråte [N] 166 C1
Bratislava [SK] 62 G4
Bratków Dolny [PL] 36 F4
Bratovoeşti [RO] 146 G1
Brattabø [N] 170 C4
Brattåker [S] 190 F4
Brattbäcken [S] 190 F5
Bratten [S] 190 G5
Brattfors [S] 166 F2
Brattingsborg [DK] 156 E2
Brattjær [N] 190 B5
Brattli [N] 192 F3
Brattsele [S] 190 F6
Brattset [N] 180 G2
Brattvåg [N] 180 D3
Bratunac [BIH] 142 F4
Bråtveit [N] 164 C1
Bratya Daskolovi [BG] 148 C5
Braubach [D] 46 B2
Braunau [A] 60 G4
Braunfels [D] 46 C2
Braunlage [D] 32 H4
Braunschweig [D] 32 H2
Braus, Col de- [F] 108 F4
Bravone [F] 114 C4
Bray / Bré [IRL] 4 G3
Bray-sur-Seine [F] 42 G5
Bray-sur-Somme [F] 28 E5
Brazatortas [E] 96 D5
Brbinj [HR] 112 F5
Brčko [BIH] 142 E2
Brdjani [SRB] 146 B2
Bré / Bray [IRL] 4 G3
Brebina [RO] 148 B1
Brécey [F] 26 D4
Brechin [GB] 8 F2
Brecht [B] 30 D2
Břeclav [CZ] 62 G3
Brecon [GB] 12 F2
Brécy [F] 56 C3
Bred [S] 168 C2
Breda [NL] 16 D6
Bredaryd [S] 162 C4
Bredbyn [S] 184 F1
Breddin [D] 20 B6
Bredebro [DK] 156 B4
Bredelar [D] 32 E4
Bredevad [DK] 156 B4
Bredland [N] 164 D4
Bredsel [S] 196 A3
Bredsjö [S] 166 G1
Bredsjön [S] 184 E4
Bredstedt [D] 18 E1
Bredsten [DK] 156 C2
Bree [B] 30 E3
Breg [SLO] 74 D5
Bregana [HR] 74 E5
Breganze [I] 72 D5
Bregare [BG] 148 A2
Bregenz [A] 60 B6
Bregovo [BG] 146 E1
Bréhal [F] 26 D4
Brehna [D] 34 C5
Breidablik [N] 180 E5
Breidvik [N] 192 D6
Breil-sur-Roya [F] 108 F4
Brein [N] 180 C5
Breióborg [N] 164 C1
Breisach [D] 58 E3
Breisen [D] 34 D1
Breisjøberget [N] 172 D4
Breistein [N] 170 B3
Breitachklamm [D] 60 B6
Breite [CH] 58 F5
Breitenbrunn [D] 60 C4
Breitengussbach Hallstadt [D] 46 G4
Breitenhees [D] 18 G6
Breitungen [D] 46 F1
Breivik [N] 194 A2
Breivikbotn [N] 194 A2
Breivikeidet [N] 192 G2
Brekke [N] 170 B2
Brekken [N] 182 D3
Brekkhus [N] 170 C3
Brekkvassely [N] 190 D4
Brekovica [BIH] 112 H3
Brekstad [N] 190 B6
Bremen [D] 18 D5
Bremerhaven [D] 18 D4
Bremervörde [D] 18 E4
Bremke [D] 32 D5
Bremke [D] 32 D5
Bremnes [N] 192 D3
Bremsnes [N] 180 E2
Breń [PL] 20 H6
Brenes [E] 94 H6
Brenica [BG] 148 A3
Brenna [N] 182 D5
Brenna [N] 190 D3
Brennero, Passo del- / Brenner Pass [A/I] 72 D2
Brenner Pass / Brennero, Passo del- [A/I] 72 D2
Brennfjell [N] 192 G2
Brennsvik [N] 194 B2
Breno [I] 72 B5
Brénod [F] 68 H2
Brentwood [GB] 14 F4
Brenzone [I] 72 C5
Brescello [I] 110 E2
Bréscia [I] 72 B6
Bresdon [F] 54 D6
Breskens [NL] 28 G1
Bresles [F] 28 D6
Breslovec [BG] 148 B3
Bresnica [SRB] 146 B2
Bressanone / Brixen [I] 72 D3
Bressuire [F] 54 D3
Brest [BG] 148 A2
Brest [BY] 38 F3
Brest [F] 40 B2
Brestova [HR] 112 E2
Brestovac [HR] 142 C1
Brestovac [SRB] 146 D2
Brestovac [SRB] 146 D4
Brestovačka Banja [SRB] 146 D2
Brestovăţ [RO] 76 H5
Brestovik [SRB] 142 H3
Breteau [F] 56 D2
Bretenoux [F] 66 H4
Bretesche, Château de la- [F] 40 E5
Breteuil [F] 26 H5
Breteuil [F] 28 D5
Brétignolles-sur-Mer [F] 54 B3
Bretten [D] 46 C6
Breuberg [D] 46 D4
Breuil-Cervínia [I] 70 D3
Breukelen Ut [NL] 16 D5
Breuna [D] 32 E4
Brevens Bruk [S] 166 H4
Brevik [N] 164 G3
Brevik [S] 166 G5
Brevik [S] 168 E3
Breza [BIH] 142 D4
Breza [SK] 50 G5
Brezičani [BIH] 142 B2
Brežice [SLO] 74 D5
Brežiški Grad [SLO] 74 D5
Breznica [BG] 130 C1
Breznica [HR] 74 F5
Breznica Đak. [HR] 142 D1
Březnice [CZ] 48 E5
Breznik [BG] 146 F5
Brezno [SK] 64 D3
Brézolles [F] 26 H5
Brezová [SK] 62 H3
Brezovica [SK] 52 C6
Brezovica [SLO] 74 B5
Brezovica [SRB] 146 C6
Brezovo [BG] 148 B5
Brezovo Polje [BIH] 142 E2
Brezovo Polje [HR] 142 A2
Briançon [F] 70 B6
Briare [F] 56 D2
Briatico [I] 124 C6
Bribir [HR] 112 H5
Bribirske Mostine [HR] 112 H5
Briceni [MD] 204 D2
Bricquebec [F] 26 D2
Bridgend [GB] 12 E3
Bridgnorth [GB] 10 D6
Bridgwater [GB] 12 F4
Bridlington [GB] 10 G3
Bridport [GB] 12 F5
Brie-Comte-Robert [F] 42 G4
Brielle [NL] 16 C5
Brienne-le-Château [F] 44 B5
Brienz [CH] 70 E1
Brienza [I] 120 G4
Brieskow-Finkenheerd [D] 34 G3
Brieves [E] 78 G3
Briey [F] 44 E3
Brig [CH] 70 E2
Brigg [GB] 10 G4
Brighouse [GB] 10 E4
Brighton [GB] 14 E5
Brignogan-Plage [F] 40 B1
Brignoles [F] 108 C5
Brignoud [F] 68 H4
Brihuega [E] 88 H5
Brijesta [HR] 144 B3
Brilon [D] 32 D4
Brimnes [N] 170 D4
Brinay [F] 56 B3
Brinches [P] 94 E3
Bríndisi [I] 122 G4
Brinje [HR] 112 F2
Brinkum [D] 18 D5
Brinon [F] 56 E3
Brintbodarna [S] 172 F4
Briones [E] 82 G6
Brione Verzasca [CH] 70 F2
Brionne [F] 26 H4
Brioude [F] 68 D3
Brioux-sur-Boutonne [F] 54 D5
Briouze [F] 26 F5
Brisighella [I] 110 G4
Brissac-Quincé [F] 54 D1
Brissago [CH] 70 F3
Bristol [GB] 12 G3
Bristvica [HR] 116 H1
Brive-la-Gaillarde [F] 66 G3
Briviesca [E] 82 F5
Brixen / Bressanone [I] 72 D3
Brixham [GB] 12 E5
Brixlegg [A] 60 E6
Brka [BIH] 142 E2
Brnaze [HR] 144 A1
Brněnec [CZ] 50 C5
Brno [CZ] 50 C6
Bro [S] 168 D2
Bro [S] 168 G4
Broadford [IRL] 2 C6
Broadstairs [GB] 14 G5
Broager [DK] 156 C4
Brobacken [S] 194 B7
Broby [S] 158 D1
Broby [S] 168 B4
Broćanac [HR] 112 G2
Brocēni [LV] 198 C5
Brock [D] 32 C2
Bröckel [D] 32 G2
Brockenhurst [GB] 12 G5
Brockhöfe [D] 18 G6
Brod [BIH] 144 D2
Brod [SRB] 128 D1
Brodarevo [SRB] 146 A4
Brodarica [HR] 112 H6
Broddbo [S] 168 B1
Broddebo [S] 162 F1
Brode [SLO] 74 B5
Brodenbach [D] 44 H1
Broderup [DK] 156 B4
Brodestorf [D] 20 B3
Brodica [SRB] 146 D1
Brodick [GB] 8 C3
Brod na Kupi [HR] 112 F1
Brodnica [PL] 22 F5
Brodowe Łąka [PL] 24 B5
Brody [PL] 34 G4
Brody [PL] 34 H3
Brody [PL] 38 C6
Broglie [F] 26 G4
Brohl [D] 30 H6
Brojce [PL] 20 G3
Brok [PL] 38 C1
Brokind [S] 168 A6
Brolo [I] 124 B6
Bromarv [FIN] 176 E6
Brome [D] 32 H2
Bromma [N] 170 G4
Brommat [F] 68 B5
Bromölla [S] 158 E1
Brömsebro [S] 158 G1
Bromsgrove [GB] 12 H1
Bron [F] 68 G3
Brønderslev [DK] 160 E3
Broni [I] 70 G6
Bronice [PL] 34 G4
Bronikowo [PL] 20 H5
Bronisławów [PL] 36 H5
Bronken [N] 172 C4
Bronkow [D] 34 F4
Bronnbach [D] 46 E4
Brønnøysund [N] 190 C3
Brøns [DK] 156 B3
Bronte [I] 126 F3
Broons [F] 26 B5
Brørup [DK] 156 B2
Brösarp [S] 158 D2
Brossac [F] 66 E2
Brossasco [I] 108 F2
Brøstrud [N] 170 F4
Brötjemark [S] 162 D1
Broto [E] 84 E5
Brottby [S] 168 E2
Brøttem [N] 182 B2
Brotterode [D] 46 F1
Brøttum [N] 172 B3
Brou [F] 42 D5
Brouage [F] 54 C5
Brough [GB] 10 E2
Broughshane [NIR] 2 G3
Broughton in Furness [GB] 10 D2
Brouis, Col de- [F] 108 F4
Broumov [CZ] 50 B2
Brouvelieures [F] 58 C2
Brouwershaven [NL] 16 B5
Brovary [UA] 202 D7
Brovst [DK] 160 D3
Brownhills [GB] 10 E6
Brozas [E] 86 G4
Brseč [HR] 112 E2
Brtnice [CZ] 50 A6
Brua [N] 182 C5
Bruchhausen-Vilsen [D] 18 E6
Bruchhauser Steine [D] 32 D5
Bruchsal [D] 46 C5
Bruck [A] 72 F2
Brück [D] 34 D3
Bruck [D] 48 C6
Bruck an der Grossglocknerstrasse [A] 72 G1
Bruck an der Leitha [A] 62 G5
Bruck an der Mur [A] 74 D1
Brückl [A] 74 C3
Brudzeń Duży [PL] 36 G2
Brudzewo [PL] 36 A3
Brüel [D] 20 A4
Bruère-Allichamps [F] 56 C4
Bruff [IRL] 4 D4
Bruflat [N] 170 G3
Bruges (Brugge) [B] 28 G1
Brugg [CH] 58 F4
Brugge (Bruges) [B] 28 G1
Brugnato [I] 110 C4
Bruhagen [N] 180 E2
Brühl [D] 30 G4
Brújula, Puerto de la- [E] 82 F6
Bruksvallarna [S] 182 E3
Brûlon [F] 42 A5
Brumath [F] 44 H5
Brummen [NL] 16 F5
Brumov Bylnice [CZ] 64 A2
Brumunddal [N] 172 B3
Brunau [D] 34 B1
Bruneck / Brunico [I] 72 E2
Brunehamel [F] 28 H5
Brunete [E] 88 F5
Brunflo [S] 182 H2
Brunheda [P] 80 E4
Brunico / Bruneck [I] 72 E2
Bruniquel [F] 66 G6
Brunkeberg [N] 164 E2
Brunlund [DK] 156 C4
Brunna [S] 168 D1
Brunnby [S] 160 H6
Brunnen [CH] 58 F6
Brunnsberg [S] 172 F2
Brunsbüttel [D] 18 E3
Brunskog [S] 166 E2
Brunssum [NL] 30 F4
Bruntál [CZ] 50 D4
Bruravik [N] 170 D4
Brus [SRB] 146 C3
Brusand [N] 164 A4
Brušane [HR] 112 G4
Brusarci [BG] 146 F2
Brusasco [I] 70 E5
Brúsio [CH] 72 B4
Bruška [HR] 112 H5
Brusnichnoye [RUS] 178 E2
Brusník [SK] 64 D4
Brussel / Bruxelles [B] 30 C4
Brüssow [D] 20 E5
Brusy [PL] 22 C4
Bruvno [HR] 112 H4
Bruvoll [N] 172 C4
Bruxelles / Brussel [B] 30 C4
Bruyères [F] 58 C2
Bruzaholm [S] 162 E2
Bruzzano Zeffirio [I] 124 D8
Brvenik [SRB] 146 B3
Brwinów [PL] 38 B3
Bryansk [RUS] 202 E5
Brydal [N] 182 C5
Bryggja [N] 180 B5
Bryne [N] 164 A3
Bryrup [DK] 156 C1
Brza Palanka [SRB] 146 E1
Brzeće [SRB] 146 C4
Brzeg [PL] 50 D1
Brzeg Dolny [PL] 36 C6
Brześć Kujawski [PL] 36 F2
Brzesko [PL] 52 B4
Brzeszcze [PL] 50 G4
Brzezie [PL] 22 B4
Brzezie [PL] 36 E4
Brzeziny [PL] 36 E5
Brzeziny [PL] 36 H4
Brzeźnica [PL] 50 H4
Brzeźnica [PL] 52 D3
Brzeżno [PL] 36 D3
Brzostek [PL] 52 D4
Brzoza [PL] 22 D6
Brzóza [PL] 38 C4
Brzozie Lubawskie [PL] 22 F5
Brzozów [PL] 52 E4
Bua [S] 160 H3
Buaile an Ghleanna / Bolinglanna [IRL] 2 B3
Buavåg [N] 164 A1
Buberget [S] 190 H5
Bubiai [LT] 200 E4
Bubry [F] 40 D3
Buca [TR] 152 C4
Buçaco [P] 80 B6
Bučany [SK] 62 H4
Buccheri [I] 126 F4
Bucchianico [I] 116 D4
Buchach [UA] 204 C2
Bucheben [LT] 72 G2
Büchen [D] 18 G4
Buchen [D] 46 D4
Buchenwald [D] 34 A6
Buchholz [D] 18 F5
Buchin Prohod [BG] 146 F4
Buchloe [D] 60 C4
Buchlov [CZ] 62 G2
Büchold [D] 46 E3
Buchs [CH] 58 H6
Buchy [F] 28 C5
Bučin [MK] 128 E3
Bucine [I] 110 F6
Bučište [MK] 128 F1
Bučje [SRB] 144 E2
Bučje [SRB] 146 D2
Bückeburg [D] 32 E2
Bücken [D] 18 E6
Buckfastleigh [GB] 12 E5
Buckie [GB] 6 F5
Buckingham [GB] 14 D3
Buckow [D] 34 F2
Bückwitz [D] 34 D1
Bučovice [CZ] 50 C6
Bucquoy [F] 28 E4
Bucsa [H] 76 F1
Bucureşti [RO] 204 D5
Buczek [PL] 36 G5
Buczyna [PL] 52 F3
Bud [N] 180 E2
Buda [I] 110 G3
Budakeszi [H] 64 C6
Budakovo [MK] 128 E3
Budal [N] 182 B3
Budaörs [H] 64 C6
Budapest [H] 64 C6
Búðardalur [IS] 192 A2
Buddusò [I] 118 D3
Bude [GB] 12 D4
Budeč [CZ] 62 D2
Budeşti [RO] 204 E5
Budilovo [RUS] 198 G2
Budimci [HR] 142 D1
Budimić Japra [BIH] 142 A2
Budimir [HR] 144 A2
Büdingen [D] 46 D2
Budiščina [HR] 74 E5
Budišov nad Budišovkou [CZ] 50 D4
Budjevo [SRB] 146 A4
Budkovce [SK] 64 H3
Budmirici [MK] 128 F3
Budogoshch [RUS] 202 C1
Budomierz [PL] 52 G3
Budoni [I] 118 E3
Budowo [PL] 22 C2
Budoželja [SRB] 146 B3
Budrio [I] 110 F3
Budrovci [HR] 142 D1
Budry [PL] 24 C2
Budva [MNE] 144 D4
Budyně nad Ohří [CZ] 48 F3
Budziszewice [PL] 36 H4
Budzyń [PL] 36 C1
Bue [N] 164 B4
Bue Marino, Grotta del- [I] 118 E4
Bueña [E] 90 D6
Buen Amor, Castillo- [E] 80 H6
Buenavista del Norte [E] 100 B5
Buendia [E] 88 H6
Bufón de Arenillas [E] 82 D2
Bugac [H] 76 D3
Buğdayli [TR] 150 D5
Bugdorf [D] 32 G3
Bugeat [F] 66 H2
Buggerru [I] 118 B6
Bugojno [BIH] 142 C4
Bugøyfjord [N] 194 E3
Bugøynes [N] 194 E2
Bugyi [H] 76 C2
Bühl [D] 58 F1
Buhuşi [RO] 204 D4
Builth Wells [GB] 12 F1
Buis-les-Baronnies [F] 108 B2
Buitenpost [NL] 16 F2
Buitrago [E] 88 G4
Buj [H] 64 G4
Bujalance [E] 102 D1
Bujanovac [SRB] 146 D5
Bujaraloz [E] 90 F4
Buje [HR] 112 D1
Bujoru [RO] 148 C2
Bük [H] 74 F1
Buk [PL] 20 E5
Buk [PL] 36 C3
Bükkábrány [H] 64 F5
Bükkösd [H] 76 A5
Bukonys [LT] 200 F5
Bukovi [SRB] 146 A2
Bukovice [CZ] 50 C4
Bukovo, Manastir- [SRB] 146 E1
Bukowiec [PL] 36 B3
Bukowina Tatrzańska [PL] 52 B6
Bukowo Morskie [PL] 22 A2
Bukowsko [PL] 52 E5
Buksnes [N] 192 E3
Bukta [N] 190 B6
Buktamo [N] 192 F3
Bülach [CH] 58 F4
Bulat-Pestivien [F] 40 D2
Buldan [TR] 152 F4
Bŭlgarene [BG] 148 B4
Bŭlgarene [BG] 148 B3
Bŭlgarevo [BG] 148 G2
Bŭlgarovo [BG] 148 F4
Bŭlgarska Polyana [BG] 150 A1
Bŭlgarski Izvor [BG] 148 A4
Bulgnéville [F] 58 B2
Bulinac [HR] 74 G6
Bulinovac [SRB] 146 D3
Bulken [N] 170 C3
Bulkowo [PL] 36 H2
Bullarby [S] 166 C4
Bullas [E] 104 B2
Bulle [CH] 70 C1
Bullendorf [A] 62 F3
Bullmark [S] 196 A5
Bulqizë [AL] 128 C2
Bülstringen [D] 34 B2
Bultei [I] 118 D4
Buna [BIH] 144 C2
Bunclody [IRL] 4 F4
Buncrana [IRL] 2 F2
Bunde [D] 16 H2
Bünde [D] 32 E2

Bundoran [IRL] 2 D3
Bungay [GB] 14 G2
Bunge [S] 168 G3
Bunić [HR] 112 G3
Bunkris [S] 172 F2
Bunleix [F] 68 B2
Bunmahon [IRL] 4 E5
Bun na Abhna / Bunnahowen [IRL] 2 B3
Bunnahowen / Bun na Abhna [IRL] 2 B3
Bunnyconnellan [IRL] 2 C3
Buñol [E] 98 E4
Bunratty [IRL] 2 C6
Bunratty Castle [IRL] 2 C6
Buonalbergo [I] 120 F2
Buonconvento [I] 114 G2
Buonfornello [I] 126 D2
Buonvicino [I] 124 C3
Buoux, Fort de- [F] 108 B3
Bur [DK] 160 B5
Burano [I] 72 F6
Burbach [D] 32 C6
Burcei [I] 118 D7
Bureå [S] 190 G3
Bureå [S] 196 A4
Burela [E] 78 E2
Büren [CH] 58 D5
Büren [D] 32 D4
Burfjord [N] 192 H1
Burford [GB] 12 H3
Burg [D] 18 E3
Burg [D] 18 H2
Burg [D] 34 C3
Burg [D] 34 F4
Burgas [BG] 148 F4
Burgau [A] 74 E2
Burgau [D] 60 C3
Burgau [P] 94 B5
Burgbernheim [D] 46 F5
Burgdorf [CH] 58 E5
Burgdorf [D] 32 G2
Burgebrach [D] 46 F4
Bürgel [D] 34 B6
Bürgeln [D] 58 E4
Burgelu / Elburgo [E] 102 B4
Burghaun [D] 46 E1
Burghausen [D] 60 G4
Burg Hessenstein [D] 32 E5
Burgh-Haamstede [NL] 16 B5
Búrgio [I] 126 C3
Burgistein [CH] 58 D6
Burgjoss [D] 46 E3
Burg Klam [A] 62 C4
Burgkunstadt [D] 46 G3
Burglengenfeld [D] 48 B6
Burg Metternich [D] 44 G1
Burgoberbach [D] 46 F5
Burgos [E] 82 E6
Burgsinn [D] 46 E3
Burg Stargard [D] 20 D5
Burgsvik [S] 168 G6
Burguete / Auritz [E] 84 C3
Burguillos [E] 94 G5
Burguillos del Cerro [E] 94 G3
Burhan [TR] 150 F5
Burhaniye [TR] 152 C2
Burharkent [TR] 152 F5
Burie [F] 54 D6
Burila Mare [RO] 146 E1
Burjassot [E] 98 E4
Burlada [E] 84 B4
Burladingen [D] 58 G2
Burlo [D] 16 G6
Burnham-on-Crouch [GB] 14 F4
Burnham-on-Sea [GB] 12 F3
Burnley [GB] 10 E3
Burón [E] 82 C3
Buron, Château de- [F] 68 D3
Buronzo [I] 70 E4
Burravoe [GB] 6 H3
Burrel [AL] 128 B2
Burriana / Borriana [E] 98 F3
Burs [S] 168 G4
Burs [S] 168 G5
Bursa [TR] 150 F4
Burseryd [S] 162 B3
Bürstadt [D] 46 C4
Burtenbach [D] 60 C3
Burton upon Trent [GB] 10 E6
Burträsk [S] 196 A5
Burvik [S] 196 B5
Burwell [GB] 14 F2
Bury [GB] 10 E4
Buryn' [UA] 202 E6
Bury St Edmunds [GB] 14 F3
Burzenin [PL] 36 F5
Burziya [BG] 146 F3
Busalla [I] 110 B3
Busana [I] 110 D4
Busca [I] 108 F2
Busdorf [D] 18 F1
Buseto Palizzolo [I] 126 B2
Buševec [HR] 74 E6
Bushat [AL] 128 A1
Bushmills [NIR] 2 G2
Bushtricë [AL] 128 C1
Bus'k [UA] 202 B8
Busko-Zdrój [PL] 52 B2
Buśno [PL] 38 G6
Busot [E] 104 E2
Busovača [BIH] 142 D4
Bussang [F] 58 D3
Bussang, Col de- [F] 58 D3
Busseto [I] 110 D2
Bussolengo [I] 72 C6
Bussoleno [I] 70 C5
Bussum [NL] 16 E4
Bustnes [N] 190 E2
Busto Arsízio [I] 70 F4
Busto Garolfo [I] 70 F4
Büsum [D] 18 E2
Butan [BG] 146 G2
Butenky [UA] 202 F7
Butera [I] 126 E4
Bütgenbach [B] 30 F5
Buthrotum [AL] 132 B2
Butler's Bridge [IRL] 2 E4
Butrint [AL] 132 B2
Butryny [PL] 22 H4
Butsyn [UA] 38 H5
Buttapietra [I] 110 F1
Buttelstedt [D] 34 A6
Buttevant [IRL] 4 C4
Buttingsrud [N] 170 H4
Buttlar [D] 46 E1
Buttle [S] 168 G5
Buttstädt [D] 34 B6
Butzbach [D] 46 C2
Bützow [D] 20 B3
Buvarp [N] 190 C5
Buvika [N] 182 B1
Buxtehude [D] 18 F4
Buxton [GB] 10 E5
Buxu, Cueva del- [E] 82 C2
Buxy [F] 56 F5
Büyükada [TR] 150 F3
Büyükaturak [TR] 152 H2
Büyükbelen [TR] 152 D3
Büyükçekmece [TR] 150 E3
Büyükkaraağaç [TR] 154 E2
Büyükkarıştıran [TR] 150 C2
Büyükkonak [TR] 152 G6
Büyükkonuk (Komi Kebir) [CY] 154 G4
Büyükorhan [TR] 150 F5
Büyüksöğle [TR] 154 H2
Büyükyenice [TR] 152 C2
Büyükyoncalı [TR] 150 D2
Buz [AL] 128 B5
Buzançais [F] 54 G3
Buzancy [F] 44 D3
Buzău [RO] 204 E5
Buzescu [RO] 148 B1
Buzet [HR] 112 D1
Buziaş [RO] 76 H6
Buzyakovtsi [BG] 146 G5
By [S] 166 E1
By [S] 174 D5
Byahoml' [BY] 202 B4
Byala [BG] 148 C2
Byala [BG] 148 F3
Byala Slatina [BG] 146 G3
Byal Izvor [BG] 130 E1
Byalynichy [BY] 202 C5
Byaroza [BY] 202 A6
Byarozawka [BY] 202 A5
Byarum [S] 162 D2
Byberget [S] 182 H4
Bybjerg [DK] 156 F2
Bychawa [PL] 38 E6
Byczki [PL] 36 H4
Byczyna [PL] 36 E6
Bydgoszcz [PL] 22 D6
Bye [S] 184 B2
Bye [S] 184 F4
Byenyakoni [BY] 200 G6
Byershty [BY] 24 G3
Bygdeå [S] 196 A5
Bygdeträsk [S] 196 A5
Bygdin [N] 170 F2
Bygdsiljum [S] 196 A5
Bygland [N] 164 D4
Byglandsfjord [N] 164 D4
Bygstad [N] 170 B1
Bykle [N] 164 D2
Byllis [AL] 128 B5
Byrkjedal [N] 164 B3
Byrkjelo [N] 180 D5
Byrknes [N] 170 A2
Byrness [GB] 8 F5
Byrum [DK] 160 F3
Byrum [S] 162 H3
Byšice [CZ] 48 G3
Byske [S] 196 A4
Bystré [CZ] 50 B5
Bystrianska Jaskyňa [SK] 64 D2
Bystřice [CZ] 48 G4
Bystřice nad Pernštejnem [CZ] 50 B5
Bystřice pod Hostýnem [CZ] 50 D6
Bystřička [CZ] 50 E5
Bystrzyca Kłodzka [PL] 50 C3
Byszki [PL] 22 B5
Byszyno [PL] 20 H4
Bytča [SK] 50 F6
Bytnica [PL] 34 H3
Bytom [PL] 50 F3
Bytom Odrzański [PL] 36 A4
Bytonia [PL] 22 D4
Bytów [PL] 22 C3
Byvattnet [S] 184 F1
Byxelkrok [S] 162 H3
Bzenec [CZ] 62 G2
Bzovík [SK] 64 C4

C

Caaveiro, Monasterio de- [E] 78 D2
Cabação [P] 86 D5
Cabaço [E] 86 D3
Cabaj-Čápor [SK] 64 A4
Cabañaquinta [E] 78 H4
Cabañas [E] 78 D2
Cabanes [E] 98 G3
Čabar [HR] 74 C6
Cabeço de Vide [P] 86 E5
Cabertarar [TR] 152 F4
Cabeza del Buey [E] 96 C4
Cabezamesada [E] 96 G2
Cabezarados [E] 96 E4
Cabezarrubias del Puerto [E] 96 E5
Cabezas Rubias [E] 94 E4
Cabezo de Torres [E] 104 C3
Cabezón de la Sal [E] 82 E3
Cabezuela del Valle [E] 88 B5
Cabo de Gata [E] 102 G6
Cabo de Palos [E] 104 D4
Cabourg [F] 26 F3
Cabra [E] 102 C2
Cabra del Santo Cristo [E] 102 F2
Cabranes [E] 82 C2
Cábras [I] 118 B5
Cabreiros [E] 78 D2
Cabrela [P] 86 C6
Cabrera [E] 104 E6
Cabrerets [F] 66 G5
Cabrillas [E] 88 B3
Cacabelos [E] 78 F5
Čačak [SRB] 146 B2
Čačak [SRB] 204 B6
Cáccamo [I] 126 D2
Cacemes [P] 86 A5
Cáceres [E] 86 H5
Cachopo [P] 94 D5
Čachtice [SK] 62 H3
Čačini [HR] 76 A6
Cadaqués [E] 92 G2
Cadaval [P] 86 B4
Cadavedo [E] 78 G2
Čađavica [BIH] 142 B3
Čađavica [HR] 76 A6
Čadca [SK] 50 F5
Cadelbosco di Sopra [I] 110 E2
Cadenábbia [I] 70 G3
Cadenberge [D] 18 E3
Cadenet [F] 106 H4
Cadeuil [F] 54 C6
Cadí, Túnel del- [E] 92 E2
Cádiar [E] 102 E5
Cadillac [F] 66 D4
Cadipietra [I] 72 E2
Cádiz [E] 100 F4
Cadrete [E] 90 E4
Caen [F] 26 F3
Caernarfon [GB] 10 B4
Caerphilly [GB] 12 F3
Ćafasan [MK] 128 C3
Çağış [TR] 152 D1
Cagli [I] 112 B6
Cágliari [I] 118 C7
Çağman [TR] 154 H3
Cagnano Varano [I] 116 G6
Cagnes-sur-Mer [F] 108 E4
Caherdaniel / Cathair Dónall [IRL] 4 A4
Cahermurphy [IRL] 2 B6
Cahersiveen [IRL] 4 A4
Cahir [IRL] 4 D4
Cahors [F] 66 G5
Cahul [MD] 204 E4
Caiazzo [I] 120 E2
Cairnryan [GB] 8 C5
Cairo Montenotte [I] 108 G3
Cais do Pico [P] 100 C3
Caister-on-Sea [GB] 14 H2
Caivano [I] 120 E3
Cajarc [F] 66 G5
Čajetina [SRB] 146 A3
Čajniče [BIH] 144 E2
Čakajovce [SK] 64 A4
Çakallar [TR] 152 C1
Çakılı [TR] 150 C2
Çakır [TR] 150 C5
Çakırbeyli [TR] 152 E5
Çakırlı [TR] 150 C4
Çakmak [TR] 154 E1
Čakovec [HR] 74 F4
Çal [TR] 152 G4
Cal [TR] 152 H2
Cala [E] 94 G4
Cala Blanca [E] 104 G4
Cala Blava [E] 104 E5
Calabor [E] 80 F3
Calabritto [I] 120 F3
Calaceite [E] 90 G6
Calacuccia [F] 114 B3
Cala d'Oliva [I] 118 B2
Cala d'Or [E] 104 F6
Calaf [E] 92 D3
Calafat [E] 92 B5
Calafat [RO] 146 F2
Calafell [E] 92 D5
Cala Galdana [E] 104 G4
Cala Gonone [I] 118 E4
Calahonda-Chaparral [E] 102 B5
Calahonda-Chaparral [E] 102 E5
Calahorra [E] 84 A5
Calais [F] 14 G6
Cala Liberotto [I] 118 E4
Cala Mesquida [E] 104 F5
Cala Millor [E] 104 F5
Calamocha [E] 90 D5
Calamonte [E] 94 H2
Cala Moreia-Cala Morlanda [E] 104 F5
Cala Morell [E] 104 G4
Calañas [E] 94 F5
Calanda [E] 90 F6
Calangiánus [I] 118 D3
Cala'n Porter [E] 104 H5
Cala Pi [E] 104 E5
Călăraşi [MD] 204 E3
Călăraşi [RO] 204 E5
Cala Ratjada [E] 104 F5
cala Sa Calobra [E] 104 E4
Cala Santanyí [E] 104 E6
Calascibetta [I] 126 E3
Calasetta [I] 118 B7
Calasparra [E] 104 B2
Calatafimi [I] 126 B2
Calatañazor [E] 90 B3
Cala Tarida [E] 104 B5
Calatayud [E] 90 D4
Calatorao [E] 90 D4
Calatrava, Convento de- [E] 96 E5
Calatrava la Vieja [E] 96 F4
Calau [D] 34 F4
Cala Vadella [E] 104 B5
Calbe [D] 34 B4
Çalca [TR] 152 H3
Caldarola [I] 116 C2
Caldas da Rainha [P] 86 B3
Caldas de Monchique [E] 94 B4
Caldas de Reis [E] 78 B3
Caldas de Vizela [P] 80 C3
Caldelas [P] 78 B6
Caldes de Boí [E] 84 F6
Caldes de Malavella [E] 92 F3
Caldes de Montbui [E] 92 E4
Caldes d'Estrac [E] 92 F4
Caldirola [I] 110 B2
Calella [E] 92 F4
Calella de Palafrugell [E] 92 G3
Calenzana [F] 114 B3
Calera y Chozas [E] 88 C6
Caleruega [E] 88 H2
Cales de Mallorca [E] 104 F5
Calheta [P] 100 A3
Calheta [P] 100 C3
Calheta de Nesquim [P] 100 C3
Çali [TR] 150 F5
Càlig [E] 92 A6
Calignac [F] 66 E5
Çalıklı [TR] 152 F3
Călimăneşti [RO] 204 C5
Calimera [I] 122 G5
Calitri [I] 120 G3
Calizzano [I] 108 G3
Callac [F] 40 D2
Callan [IRL] 4 E4
Callander [GB] 8 D2
Callington [GB] 12 D4
Callosa d'en Sarrià [E] 104 E2
Callosa de Segura [E] 104 D3
Čalma [SRB] 142 F2
Călmăţuiu [RO] 148 B2
Calne [GB] 12 G3
Calolziocorte [I] 70 G4
Calonge [E] 92 G3
Calp / Calpe [E] 104 F2
Calpe / Calp [E] 104 F2
Çalpınar [TR] 154 H1
Caltabellotta [I] 126 C3
Caltagirone [I] 126 F4
Caltanissetta [I] 126 E3
Caltavuturo [I] 126 E2
Çaltepe [TR] 152 H5
Çalti [TR] 150 H4
Çaltılıbük [TR] 150 E5
Caltra [IRL] 2 D5
Călugăreni [RO] 148 C1
Caluso [I] 70 D5
Calvello [I] 120 H4
Calvi [F] 114 A3
Calvià [E] 104 D5
Calvörde [D] 34 B2
Calw [D] 58 G1
Calzadilla de la Cueza [E] 82 C5
Camacha [P] 100 B3
Camaiore [I] 110 D5
Camaldoli [I] 110 G5
Camaldoli, Eremo di- [I] 110 G5
Çamaltı [TR] 152 C4
Camarena de la Sierra [E] 98 E2
Camarès [F] 106 D3
Camaret-sur-Mer [F] 40 B2
Camarillas [E] 98 E1
Camariñas [E] 78 B2
Camarzana de Tera [E] 80 H3
Camas [E] 94 G6
Cambados [E] 78 B4
Cambeo [E] 78 C5
Camberg [D] 46 C2
Camberley [GB] 14 D4
Cambo-les-Bains [F] 84 C2
Camborne [GB] 12 C5
Cambrai [F] 28 F4
Cambre [E] 78 C2
Cambremer [F] 26 G4
Cambridge [GB] 14 F3
Cambrils [E] 92 C5
Camburg [D] 34 B6
Çamdere [TR] 152 G3
Camelford [GB] 12 C4
Çameli [TR] 154 F1
Camenca [MD] 204 E2
Camerino [I] 116 B2
Çamiçi [TR] 152 D6
Camigliatello [I] 124 D4
Camin [D] 18 H4
Caminha [P] 78 A5
Caminomorisco [E] 88 A4
Camínreal [E] 90 D6
Çamkonak [TR] 150 G2
Çamköy [TR] 154 C1
Çamlıbel (Mýrtou) [CY] 154 F5
Çamlık [TR] 152 F2
Çamlıpınar [TR] 154 F4
Cammarata [I] 126 D3
Camogli [I] 110 B3
Camp [IRL] 4 B3
Campagna [I] 120 F4
Campagnático [I] 114 F2
Campan [F] 84 F4
Campana [I] 124 E4
Campanario [E] 96 B3
Campanas / Kanpaneta [E] 84 B4
Campanet, Coves de- [E] 104 E4
Campaspero [E] 88 F2
Campbeltown [GB] 2 H2
Câmpeni [RO] 204 C4
Câmpia Turzii [RO] 204 C4
Campi Bisenzio [I] 110 E5
Campiglia Marittima [I] 114 E2
Campiglia Soana [I] 70 D4
Campillo de Altobuey [E] 98 C3
Campillo de Arenas [E] 102 E3
Campillo de Llerena [E] 96 A4
Campillos [E] 102 B3
Câmpina [RO] 204 D5
Campione d'Italia [I] 70 G3
Campisábalos [E] 88 H4
Campi Salentina [I] 122 G4
Campo [E] 84 F6
Campo [P] 94 E2
Campobasso [I] 120 E1
Campobecerros [E] 78 D6
Campobello di Licata [I] 126 E4
Campobello di Mazara [I] 126 B3
Campocologno [CH] 72 B4
Campo Coy [E] 104 B3
Campodarsego [I] 72 E6
Campo de Caso / Caso [E] 82 C2
Campo de Criptana [E] 96 G3
Campofelice di Fitalia [I] 126 D2
Campofilone [I] 116 D2
Campofiorito [I] 126 C3
Campoformido [I] 72 G5
Campogalliano [I] 110 E3
Campohermoso [E] 102 G5
Campo Lameiro / A Lagoa [E] 78 B4
Campo Ligure [I] 108 H2
Campo Maior [P] 86 F6
Campomanes [E] 78 H4
Campomarino [I] 116 F5
Campomarino [I] 122 F5
Camponaraya [E] 78 F5
Campora San Giovanni [I] 124 D5
Campo Real [E] 88 G6
Camporeale [I] 126 C2
Camporrobles [E] 98 D3
Campos [E] 104 E5
Camposampiero [I] 72 E6
Camposanto [I] 110 F2
Campotejar [E] 102 E3
Campo Túres / Sand in Taufers [I] 72 E2
Camprodón [E] 92 F2
Câmpulung [RO] 204 D5
Câmpulung Moldovenesc [RO] 204 D3
Çamsu [TR] 152 G2
Çamyayla [TR] 152 F6
Çamyuva [TR] 152 G2
Çan [TR] 150 C5
Cañada de Benatanduz [E] 98 F1
Cañadajuncosa [E] 98 B3
Cañaíca del Calar [E] 102 H2
Čanak [HR] 112 G3
Çanakçı [TR] 152 F1
Çanakkale [TR] 150 B5
Canale [I] 108 G1
Canales de Molina [E] 90 C5
Canal S. Bovo [I] 72 E4
Canaples [F] 28 E4
Canas de Senhorim [P] 80 C6
Cañaveral [E] 86 H4
Cañaveral de León [E] 94 G4
Cañaveras [E] 98 B1
Canazei [I] 72 E3
Cancale [F] 26 C4
Cancon [F] 66 E4
Candamo [E] 78 G3
Candamo, Cueva de- [E] 78 H3
Candanchú [E] 84 D4
Çandarlı [TR] 150 G3
Çandarlı [TR] 152 C3
Candás [E] 78 H3
Candasnos [E] 90 G4
Candé [F] 40 G6
Candela [I] 120 G2
Candelario [E] 88 B4
Candeleda [E] 88 C5
Candia Lomellina [I] 70 F5
Çandır [TR] 154 E2
Canelli [I] 108 H2
Canelobre, Cueva de- [E] 104 E2
Canero [E] 78 G2
Canet [F] 106 E4
Canet de Mar [E] 92 F4
Cañete [E] 98 C2
Cañete la Real [E] 102 B3
Canet-Plage [F] 92 G1
Canfranc [E] 84 D4
Cangas [E] 78 B4
Cangas [E] 78 E2
Cangas del Narcea [E] 78 F3
Cangas de Onís [E] 82 C2
Canha [P] 86 C5
Caniçada [P] 80 D3
Canicatti [I] 126 D4
Canicattini Bagni [I] 126 G5
Caniço [P] 100 A3
Caniles [E] 102 G4
Canillas del Aceituno [E] 102 C4
Canino [I] 114 G4
Cañizal [E] 88 D2
Cañizares [E] 90 B6
Canjáyar [E] 102 F5
Cannai [I] 118 B7
Cannara [I] 116 A2
Canne [I] 120 H2
Cánnero Riviera [I] 70 F3
Cannes [F] 108 E5
Canneto [I] 114 E1
Canneto sull'Óglio [I] 110 D1
Cannich [GB] 6 D5
Cannigione [I] 118 E2
Cannóbio [I] 70 F3
Cannock [GB] 10 E6
Canolo [I] 124 D7
Canosa di Púglia [I] 120 H2
Canossa [I] 110 D3
Canossa, Castello di- [I] 110 D3
Can Pastilla [E] 104 E5
Can Picafort [E] 104 F4
Cansano [I] 116 D5
Cantalapiedra [E] 88 D3
Cantalejo [E] 88 F3
Cantalpino [E] 88 D3
Cantanhede [P] 80 B6
Cantavieja [E] 98 F2
Čantavir [SRB] 76 D5
Canterbury [GB] 14 F5
Cantillana [E] 94 H5
Cantoral de la Peña [E] 82 D4
Cantoria [E] 102 H4
Cantù [I] 70 G4
Canvey Island [GB] 14 F4
Cany-Barville [F] 26 H2
Canyet de Mar [E] 92 G4
Canyon [N] 194 B3
Caoria [I] 72 D4
Cáorle [I] 72 F6
Caorso [I] 70 H6
Capaccio [I] 120 F4
Capaci [I] 126 C1
Capalbio [I] 114 F4
Capannoli [I] 110 E6
Caparde [BIH] 142 E3
Caparra, Ruinas de- [E] 88 B5
Caparroso [E] 84 B5
Capbreton [F] 66 A6
Cap-d'Ail [F] 108 F4
Capdella [E] 84 G6
Capdenac-Gare [F] 66 H5
Cap d'en Font [E] 104 H5
Capdepera [E] 104 F5
Capelas [P] 100 E2
Capellades [E] 92 D4
Capendu [F] 106 C5
Capens [F] 84 H4
Capestang [F] 106 D4
Capestrano [I] 116 C4
Cap Ferret [F] 66 B3
Capinha [P] 86 F2
Capistrello [I] 116 C5
Capizzi [I] 126 F2
Čapljina [BIH] 144 C3
Capmany [E] 92 G2
Capo Cavallo [F] 114 A3
Capodimonte [I] 114 G3
Capo di Ponte [I] 72 B4
Capodiponte [I] 110 D4
Capo d'Orlando [I] 124 B6
Capoferrato [I] 118 E7
Capolíveri [I] 114 E3
Capo Rizzuto [I] 124 F5
Caposile [I] 72 F6
Capoterra [I] 118 C7
Cappamore [IRL] 4 D3
Cappenberg [D] 32 C4
Cappoquin [IRL] 4 D5
Capracotta [I] 116 D6
Caprária [I] 114 D2
Capranica [I] 114 H4
Capri [I] 120 D4
Capriati a Volturno [I] 120 D1
Capriccioli [I] 118 E2
Captieux [F] 66 D5
Capua [I] 120 D2
Capurso [I] 122 E3
Čara [HR] 144 A3
Caracal [RO] 148 A1
Caracenilla [E] 98 B2
Caracovo [BG] 148 B5
Caracuel de Calatrava [E] 96 E4
Caraglio [I] 108 F2
Čarakovo [BIH] 142 B2
Caraman [F] 106 B3
Caramulo [P] 80 C6
Caranga [E] 78 G4
Caransebeş [RO] 204 B5
Carantec [F] 40 C1
Car Asen [BG] 148 D3
Carassai [I] 116 C2
Caraula [RO] 146 F1
Caravaca [E] 104 B2
Caravaggio [I] 70 H5
Carbajales de Alba [E] 80 H4
Carbajo [E] 86 F4
Carballo [E] 78 C2
Carbon-Blanc [F] 66 D3
Carboneras [E] 102 H5
Carboneras de Guadazaón [E] 98 C3
Carbonero el Mayor [E] 88 F3
Carbónia [I] 118 B7
Carbonin / Schluderbach [I] 72 E3
Carbonne [F] 84 H4
Carcaboso [E] 88 A5
Carcabuey [E] 102 C3
Carcaixent [E] 98 E5
Carcans [F] 66 C2
Carcans-Plage [F] 66 B2
Carcar [E] 84 A5
Carcare [I] 108 H3
Carcassonne [F] 106 B4
Carcastillo [E] 84 B5
Carcavelo [P] 86 A5
Carcelén [E] 98 C5
Carceri, Eremo delle- [I] 116 A2
Carcès [F] 108 C5
Carcoforo [I] 70 E3
Çardak [TR] 150 B5
Çardak [TR] 152 G3
Çardak [TR] 152 G5
Çardaklı [TR] 152 F6
Cardedeu [E] 92 E4
Cardejón [E] 90 C3
Cardelleda de Valdeorras [E] 78 E5
Cardeña [E] 96 D6
Cardenete [E] 98 C3
Cardiff [GB] 12 F3
Cardigan [GB] 4 H6
Cardito [I] 120 D1
Cardona [E] 92 D3
Carei [RO] 204 B3
Carene [TR] 152 C3
Carennac [F] 66 H4
Carentan [F] 26 E3
Carevac [BIH] 142 B4
Carev Dvor [MK] 128 D3
Carezza al Lago / Karersee [I] 72 D3
Cargèse [F] 114 A4
Carhaix-Plouguer [F] 40 C2
Caria [P] 86 F2
Cariati [I] 124 E4
Caričin Grad [SRB] 146 D4
Caričino [BG] 148 G2
Carignan [F] 44 D2
Carignano [I] 70 D6
Çarıklar [TR] 154 F4
Cariñena [E] 90 D4
Cariño [E] 78 E1
Carinola [I] 120 D2
Carlantino [I] 120 F1
Carlentini [I] 126 G4
Carlet [E] 98 E5
Carling [F] 44 F4
Carlingford [IRL] 2 G4
Carlisle [GB] 8 E6
Carloforte [I] 118 B7
Carlow [D] 18 H4
Carlow / Ceatharlach [IRL] 4 F4
Carlton [GB] 10 F4
Carmagnola [I] 70 D6
Carmarthen [GB] 12 E2
Carmaux [F] 106 C2
Cármenes [E] 78 H4
Carmona [E] 94 H6
Carnac [F] 40 D5
Carndonagh [IRL] 2 F1
Carnew [IRL] 4 F4
Carnia [I] 72 G4
Carnlough [NIR] 2 G3
Carnota [E] 78 B3
Carnoustie [GB] 8 F2
Caro [F] 26 B6
Carolei [I] 124 D4
Carolinensiel [D] 18 C3
Carona [I] 70 H3
Caronía [I] 126 F2
Carosino [I] 122 F4
Carpaneto Piacentino [I] 110 C2
Carpegna [I] 110 H5
Carpenédolo [I] 72 B6
Carpentras [F] 106 H3
Carpi [I] 110 E2
Carpignano Sesia [I] 70 E4
Carpineti [I] 110 E3
Carpineto Romano [I] 116 B6
Cărpiniş [RO] 76 F5
Carpino [I] 116 G6
Carpinone [I] 120 E1
Carpio [E] 88 D2
Carquefou [F] 40 F6
Carqueiranne [F] 108 C6
Carraig Airt / Carrickart [IRL] 2 F1
Carral [E] 78 C2
Carranza / Karrantza [E] 82 F3
Carrapateira [P] 94 A4
Carrara [I] 110 D4
Carraroe / An Cheathrú Rua [IRL] 2 B5
Carrascalejo [E] 96 C1
Carrascosa del Campo [E] 98 A2
Carrazeda de Ansiães [P] 80 E4
Carrazedo [P] 80 E3
Carrbridge [GB] 6 E5
Carregado [P] 86 B4
Carregal do Sal [P] 80 C6
Carrega Ligure [I] 110 B3
Carregueiro [P] 94 C3
Carrick / An Charraig [IRL] 2 D2
Carrickart / Carraig Airt [IRL] 2 F1
Carrickfergus [NIR] 2 G3
Carrickmacross [IRL] 2 F4
Carrick-on-Shannon [IRL] 2 D4
Carrick-on-Suir [IRL] 4 E4
Carriço [P] 86 C2
Carrigaline [IRL] 4 C5
Carrigallen [IRL] 2 E4
Carriganimmy [IRL] 4 C4
Carrigans [IRL] 2 F2
Carrión de Calatrava [E] 96 F4
Carrión de los Condes [E] 82 C5
Carrizo [E] 78 G5
Carrizosas [E] 96 G5
Carro [F] 106 G5
Carros [F] 108 E4
Carrouges [F] 26 F5
Carrowkeel [IRL] 2 F2
Carrù [I] 108 G2
Carryduff [NIR] 2 G4
Carry-le-Rouet [F] 106 H5
Çarshovë [AL] 128 C6
Carsoli [I] 116 B5
Carsulae [I] 116 A3
Cartagena [E] 104 C4
Cártama [E] 102 B4
Cartaxo [P] 86 C4
Cartaya [E] 94 E5
Cartelle [E] 78 C5
Carteret [F] 26 D2
Cartoixa de Porta Coeli [E] 98 E4
Cartoixa d'Escaldei [E] 90 H6
Cartuja de Aula Dei [E] 90 E3

Carviçais [P] 80 F5
Carvin [F] 28 F3
Carvoeiro [P] 94 B5
Carwitz [D] 20 D5
Casabermeja [E] 102 C4
Casabona [I] 124 E4
Casa Branca [P] 86 D5
Casa Branca [P] 94 C2
Casa Branca [P] 94 D1
Casacalenda [I] 116 E6
Casáccia [CH] 70 H2
Casalabate [I] 122 G4
Casalarreina [E] 82 G6
Casalbordino [I] 116 E5
Casal Borsetti [I] 110 H3
Casalbuono [I] 120 G5
Casalciprano [I] 116 E6
Casale [I] 126 B2
Casalecchio di Reno [I] 110 F3
Casale Monferrato [I] 70 E5
Casalmaggiore [I] 110 D2
Casalpusterlengo [I] 70 H6
Casal Velino [I] 120 F5
Casamáina [I] 116 C4
Casamari, Abbazia di– [I] 116 C6
Casamássima [I] 122 E3
Casamicciola Terme [I] 120 D3
Casamozza [F] 114 C3
Casarabonela [E] 102 B4
Casarano [I] 122 G5
Casar de Cáceres [E] 86 H5
Casar de las Hurdes [E] 88 A4
Casares [E] 100 H5
Casares, Cueva de los– [E] 90 B5
Casariche [E] 102 B3
Casarubios del Monte [E] 88 F6
Casas Cueva [E] 102 F3
Casas de Benítez [E] 98 B4
Casas de Don Pedro [E] 96 C3
Casas de Fernando Alonso [E] 98 B4
Casas de Jorós [E] 100 D6
Casas de Juan Núñez [E] 98 C5
Casas del Puerto [E] 104 C2
Casas de Reina [E] 94 H4
Casas–Ibáñez [E] 98 C4
Casatejada [E] 88 B6
Cascais [P] 86 A5
Cascante [E] 84 B6
Cascia [I] 116 B3
Casciana Terme [I] 110 E6
Cáscina [I] 110 D5
Căscioarele [RO] 148 D1
Casekow [D] 20 E5
Caselle [I] 70 D5
Caserta [I] 120 E2
Cashel [IRL] 4 D4
Cashel, Rock of– [IRL] 4 D4
Casillas del Ángel [E] 100 E6
Casina [I] 110 E3
Casinina [I] 110 H5
Casino di Terra [I] 114 E1
Casinos [E] 98 E4
Čáslav [CZ] 48 H4
Caso / Campo de Caso [E] 82 C2
Casola Valsenio [I] 110 G4
Casoli [I] 116 D5
Casoria [I] 120 E3
Caspe [E] 90 F5
Cassà de la Selva [E] 92 F3
Cassagnes–Bégonhès [F] 68 B6
Cassano allo Ionio [I] 122 C6
Cassano d'Adda [I] 70 G5
Cassano delle Murge [I] 122 D3
Cassel [F] 28 E2
Cassibile [I] 126 G5
Cassine [I] 108 H2
Cassino [I] 120 D1
Cassis [F] 108 B5
Cassuéjouls [F] 68 B5
Castagneto Carducci [I] 114 E1
Castalla [E] 104 D2
Castañar de Ibor [E] 96 C1
Castanet–Tolosan [F] 106 A3
Castanheira de Pera [P] 86 E2
Castasegna [CH] 70 H2
Casteau [B] 28 H3
Casteggio [I] 70 G6
Castejón de Monegros [E] 90 F4
Castejón de Sos [E] 84 F5
Castejón de Valdejasa [E] 90 E3
Castel Bolognese [I] 110 G4
Castelbouc [F] 68 C6
Castelbuono [I] 126 E2
Casteldelfino [I] 108 E2
Castel del Piano [I] 114 G2
Castel del Rio [I] 110 F4
Castel di Iudica [I] 126 F3
Castel di Sangro [I] 116 D6
Castel di Tora [I] 116 B4
Castel Doria, Terme di– [I] 118 D3
Castelejo [P] 94 A5
Castelfidardo [I] 116 C1
Castelfiorentino [I] 110 E6
Castelflorite [E] 90 G4
Castelfranco Emilia [I] 110 F3
Castelfranco in Miscano [I] 120 F2
Castelfranco Véneto [I] 72 E6
Castel Goffredo [I] 110 E1
Casteljaloux [F] 66 D5
Castellabate [I] 120 F5
Castellammare del Golfo [I] 126 C2
Castellammare di Stábia [I] 120 E3
Castellamonte [I] 70 D5
Castellana, Grotte di– [I] 122 E3
Castellana Grotte [I] 122 E3
Castellana Sícula [I] 126 E3
Castellane [F] 108 D4
Castellaneta [I] 122 E4
Castellar [E] 102 F1
Castellar de la Frontera [E] 100 G5
Castellar de la Muela [E] 90 C5
Castellar de Santiago [E] 96 F5
Castell'Arquato [I] 110 C2
Castell'Azzara [I] 114 G3
Castellazzo Bormida [I] 108 H2
Castelldans [E] 90 H5
Castell d'aro [E] 92 G3
Castell de Cabres [E] 98 G1
Castelldefels [E] 92 D5
Castell de Ferro [E] 102 E5
Castell de Mur / Cellers [E] 92 C2
Castelleone [I] 70 H5
Castelletto d'Orba [I] 110 A2
Castellfollit de la Roca [E] 92 F2
Castellina in Chianti [I] 110 F6
Castelló de la Plana / Castellón de la Plana [E] 98 F3
Castelló de la Ribera [E] 98 E6
Castelló d'Empúries [E] 92 G2
Castellón de la Plana / Castelló de la Plana [E] 98 F3
Castellote [E] 90 F6
Castello Tesino [I] 72 D4
Castellterçol [E] 92 E3
Castellúccio dei Sáuri [I] 120 G2
Castelluccio Sup. [I] 120 H5
Castelluzzo [I] 126 B2
Castelmagno [I] 108 F2
Castelmassa [I] 110 F2
Castelmauro [I] 116 E6
Castelmoron [F] 66 E5
Castelnau [F] 66 H4
Castelnaudary [F] 106 B4
Castelnau–de–Médoc [F] 66 C2
Castelnau–de–Montmiral [F] 106 B2
Castelnau d'Estretefonds [F] 84 H2
Castelnau–Magnoac [F] 84 F3
Castelnau–Montratier [F] 66 F5
Castelnovo ne' Monti [I] 110 D3
Castelnuovo Berardenga [I] 114 G1
Castelnuovo Berardenga [I] 114 G1
Castelnuovo della Dáunia [I] 120 F1
Castelnuovo di Garfagnana [I] 110 D4
Castelnuovo di Porto [I] 116 A5
Castelnuovo di Val di Cecina [I] 114 F1
Castelnuovo Don Bosco [I] 70 E6
Castelnuovo Monterotaro [I] 116 F6
Castelnuovo Scrívia [I] 70 F6
Castelo [P] 86 D2
Castelo Branco [P] 80 F5
Castelo Branco [P] 86 F3
Castelo Branco [P] 100 C3
Castelo de Paiva [P] 80 C4
Castelo de Vide [P] 86 F4
Castelo do Neiva [P] 78 A6
Castel Porziano [I] 114 H6
Castelraimondo [I] 116 B2
Castel San Giovanni [I] 70 G6
Castel San Lorenzo [I] 120 F4
Castel San Pietro Terme [I] 110 F4
Castelsaraceno [I] 120 H5
Castelsardo [I] 118 C2
Castelsarrasin [F] 66 F6
Castelseprio [I] 70 F4
Castelserás [E] 90 F6
Casteltérmini [I] 126 D3
Castelvecchio Subequo [I] 116 C5
Castelverde [I] 70 H6
Castelvetere in Val Fortore [I] 120 F1
Castelvetrano [I] 126 B3
Castel Volturno [I] 120 D2
Castenaso [I] 110 F3
Castets [F] 66 B5
Castiádas [I] 118 D7
Castigliole d'Orcia [I] 114 G2
Castiglioncello [I] 110 D6
Castiglione dei Pepoli [I] 110 F4
Castiglione del Lago [I] 114 H2
Castiglione della Pescáia [I] 114 E3
Càstiglione delle Stiviere [I] 72 B6
Castiglione Messer Marino [I] 116 E6
Castiglione Olona [I] 70 F4
Castiglion Fibocchi [I] 110 G6
Castiglion Fiorentino [I] 114 H1
Castilblanco [E] 96 C2
Castilblanco de los Arroyos [E] 94 G5
Castillejo de Martín Viejo [E] 86 H2
Castilliscar [E] 84 C5
Castillo de Locubín [E] 102 D3
Castillo de Matajudíos [E] 82 D5
Castillo de Tajarja [E] 102 D4
Castillo de Villamalefa [E] 98 F3
Castillon–la–Bataille [F] 66 D3
Castillonnès [F] 66 E4
Castillo Pasiega las Chimenas, Cuevas el– [E] 82 E3
Castione della Presolana [I] 72 A5
Castlebar [IRL] 2 C4
Castlebay / Bagh a Chaisteil [GB] 6 A5
Castlebellingham [IRL] 2 F5
Castleblayney [IRL] 2 F4
Castlebridge [IRL] 4 F5
Castlecomer [IRL] 4 E3
Castledermot [IRL] 4 F3
Castle Douglas [GB] 8 D5
Castleisland [IRL] 4 B4
Castlemaine [IRL] 4 B4
Castlemartyr [IRL] 4 D5
Castleplunkett [IRL] 2 D4
Castlepollard [IRL] 2 E5
Castlerea [IRL] 2 D4
Castletown [GBM] 10 B2
Castletownbere [IRL] 4 B5
Castletown House [IRL] 2 F6
Castletownroche [IRL] 4 D4
Castletownshend [IRL] 4 B5
Castlewellan [NIR] 2 G4
Castrejón [E] 88 D2
Castres [F] 106 B3
Castricum [NL] 16 D3
Castries [F] 106 F4
Castril [E] 102 G3
Castrillo de Don Juan [E] 88 G2
Castrillo de la Reina [E] 88 H2
Castrillón [E] 78 F3
Castro [I] 114 G3
Castro / Dozón [E] 78 C4
Castrobarto [E] 82 F4
Castrocalbón [E] 80 H3
Castro Caldelas [E] 78 D5
Castrocaro Terme [I] 110 G4
Castrocontrigo [E] 78 F6
Castro da Cola [P] 94 C4
Castro Daire [P] 80 C5
Castro dei Volsci [I] 120 C1
Castro del Río [E] 102 C2
Castro de Rei [E] 78 E3
Castrojeriz [E] 82 D6
Castro Marim [P] 94 D5
Castromil [E] 78 E6
Castromonte [E] 88 E1
Castronuevo [E] 88 D1
Castronuño [E] 88 D2
Castropol [E] 78 F2
Castrop–Rauxal [D] 30 H3
Castroreale [I] 124 B7
Castro–Urdiales [E] 82 G3
Castroverde [E] 78 E3
Castro Verde [P] 94 C4
Castroverde de Cerrato [E] 88 F2
Castrovillari [I] 122 C6
Castuera [E] 96 B4
Cataéggio [I] 70 H3
Çatalca [TR] 150 D2
Çatallar [TR] 154 H2
Catane [RO] 146 F2
Catània [I] 126 G3
Catanzaro [I] 124 E5
Catanzaro Marina [I] 124 E5
Catarroja [E] 98 E5
Catenanuova [I] 126 F3
Cateraggio [F] 114 C4
Cathair Dónall / Caherdaniel [IRL] 4 A4
Catoira [E] 78 B3
Catterick [GB] 10 F2
Cattolica [I] 112 B5
Cattolica Eraclea [I] 126 C3
Catus [F] 66 G5
Caudebec–en–Caux [F] 26 H3
Caudete [E] 104 D1
Caudeval [F] 106 B5
Caudry [F] 28 F4
Caulonia [I] 124 D7
Caulonia [I] 124 E6
Caumont [F] 26 E3
Caumont [F] 84 G4
Caunes–Minervois [F] 106 C4
Cauro [F] 114 B5
Căuşani [MD] 204 F3
Caussade [F] 66 G6
Cauterets [F] 84 E4
Cauville [F] 26 G2
Cava [E] 92 B6
Cava de' Tirreni [I] 120 E3
Cava d'Ispica [I] 126 F5
Cavaglià [I] 70 E5
Cavaillon [F] 106 H4
Cavalaire–sur–Mer [F] 108 D6
Cavalese [I] 72 D4
Cavalière [F] 108 D6
Cavallino [I] 72 F6
Cavallino [I] 122 G5
Cavalls, Cova dels– [E] 98 G2
Cavan / An Cabhán [IRL] 2 E4
Cavárzere [I] 110 G2
Çavdarhisar [TR] 152 G2
Çavdır [TR] 152 H6
Cave del Predil [I] 72 H4
Cavi [I] 110 B3
Caviaga [I] 70 H5
Cavo [I] 114 E2
Cavour [I] 70 C6
Cavriglia [I] 110 F6
Cavtat [HR] 144 C4
Çayağzi [TR] 150 F2
Çaybaşı [TR] 152 D4
Çayçinge [TR] 152 F2
Çayhisar [TR] 154 E1
Çayırova (Ágios Theodoros) [CY] 154 G5
Caylus [F] 66 G6
Cayrols [F] 68 A4
Çayyaka [TR] 150 F5
Cazalegas [E] 88 D6
Cazalla de la Sierra [E] 94 H5
Cazals [F] 66 F4
Cazaubon [F] 66 D6
Cazeneuve, Château de– [F] 66 D4
Cazères [F] 84 G4
Cazin [BIH] 112 H2
Čazma [HR] 74 F6
Cazorla [E] 102 F2
Cea [E] 78 C4
Cea [E] 82 C5
Ceatharlach / Carlow [IRL] 4 F4
Cebolla [E] 96 E1
Čebovce [SK] 64 C4
Cebreiro [E] 78 E4
Cebreros [E] 88 E5
Cebrones del Rio [E] 78 G6
Ceccano [I] 120 C1
Cece [H] 76 B3
Čečejovce [SK] 64 F3
Čechtice [CZ] 48 G5
Čechtín [CZ] 50 A6
Cécina [I] 114 E1
Ceclavín [E] 86 G4
Cecos [E] 78 F4
Cedeira [E] 78 D1
Cedillo [E] 86 F4
Cedros [P] 100 C2
Cedynia [PL] 34 F1
Cee [E] 78 B2
Cefalù [I] 126 E2
Cegléd [H] 76 D2
Céglie Messápica [I] 122 F4
Cegrane [MK] 128 D1
Cehegín [E] 104 B2
Ceillac [F] 108 E2
Ceira [P] 86 D2
Čejč [CZ] 62 G2
Čekiške [LT] 200 F5
Ceków Kolonia [PL] 36 E4
Čelákovice [CZ] 48 G3
Celano [I] 116 C5
Celanova [E] 78 C5
Čelarevo [SRB] 142 F1
Celaru [RO] 146 G1
Celbowo [PL] 22 D1
Celbridge [IRL] 2 F6
Čelebić [BIH] 142 B4
Celerina [CH] 70 H2
Čelić [BIH] 142 E3
Celico [I] 124 D4
Čelinac [BIH] 142 C3
Celjahavi [BY] 202 B6
Celje [SLO] 74 D4
Cella [E] 90 D6
Celldömölk [H] 74 G1
Celle [D] 32 G1
Celle di Bulgheria [I] 120 G5
Celle Ligure [I] 108 H3
Cellers / Castell de Mur [E] 92 C2
Celles [B] 28 G3
Celles–sur–Belle [F] 54 D4
Čelopeci [MK] 128 D2
Celorico da Beira [P] 80 D6
Celorico de Basto [P] 80 D4
Celsoy [F] 58 A3
Çeltek [TR] 152 H5
Çeltikköy [TR] 150 B4
Čemerno [BIH] 144 D2
Cemke [TR] 150 F2
Cenad [RO] 76 F4
Cencenighe [I] 72 E4
Cenei [RO] 76 F6
Ceneköy [TR] 150 C3
Cenicentos [E] 88 E5
Cenicero [E] 82 G6
Cenizzate [E] 98 C4
Čenta [SRB] 142 G2
Centallo [I] 108 F2
Centelles [E] 92 E3
Cento [I] 110 F3
Centuri [F] 114 C2
Centúripe [I] 126 F3
Cepagatti [I] 116 D4
Çepan [AL] 128 C5
Čepin [HR] 142 D1
Cepos [P] 86 E2
Čepovan [SLO] 72 H5
Ceprano [I] 120 C1
Čer [MK] 128 D2
Ćeralije [HR] 74 H6
Cerami [I] 126 F2
Ceranów [PL] 38 D2
Ceraso [I] 120 F5
Cerbère [F] 92 G2
Cercal [P] 86 B4
Cercal [P] 94 B3
Cerceda [E] 78 C2
Cerceda [E] 88 F5
Cercedilla [E] 88 F4
Cerchiara di Calábria [I] 122 D6
Cerda [I] 126 D2
Cerdedo [E] 78 C4
Cerdeira [P] 86 G2
Cerdon [F] 56 C2
Cerea [I] 110 F1
Cerecinos de Campos [E] 82 B6
Cered [H] 64 E4
Cereixo [E] 78 B2
Ceremosnja [SRB] 146 D1
Ceres [I] 70 D5
Ceresole Reale [I] 70 C4
Céret [F] 92 F2
Cerfontaine [B] 28 H4
Ceriale [I] 108 G3
Cerignola [I] 120 H2
Cérilly [F] 56 C5
Čerín [SK] 64 C3
Cerisiers [F] 42 H6
Cerizay [F] 54 D3
Çerkezköy [TR] 150 D2
Cerknica [SLO] 74 B6
Cerkno [SLO] 74 B5
Cerkovitsa [BG] 148 B2
Cerkvenjak [SLO] 74 E3
Cerkwica [PL] 20 G3
Çermë [AL] 128 B3
Cermei [RO] 76 H3
Cerna [HR] 142 E2
Cernache do Bom Jardim [P] 86 D3
Černá Hora [CZ] 50 C5
Cernavodă [RO] 204 E5
Černá v Pošumaví [CZ] 62 B3
Cernay [F] 58 D3
Cernégula [E] 82 E5
Černičevo [BG] 148 B5
Cerniébaud [F] 58 B6
Cernik [HR] 142 C1
Cernóbbio [I] 70 G4
Černookovo [BG] 148 G1
Černošín [CZ] 48 D4
Černovice [CZ] 48 G6
Černuc [CZ] 48 F3
Cerósimo [I] 122 C5
Cerovačke Špilje [HR] 112 H4
Cerovica [BIH] 144 C3
Çërravë [AL] 128 D4
Cerreto [I] 116 B5
Čerrik [AL] 128 B4
Cerro de los Angeles [E] 88 F6
Cerro de los Santos [E] 98 C6
Cerro Muriano [E] 96 C6
Certaldo [I] 110 E6
Cervatos [E] 82 E4
Cervatos de la Cueza [E] 82 C5
Červená [CZ] 48 F5
Červená Lhota [CZ] 48 G6
Červená–Řečice [CZ] 48 H5
Červená Skala [SK] 64 E2
Červená Voda [CZ] 50 C4
Červený Hrádek [CZ] 48 E2
Červený Hrádek [CZ] 48 F5
Červený Kameň [SK] 62 G4
Červený Kameň [SK] 64 A2
Červený Kláštor [SK] 52 B5
Červený Kostelec [CZ] 50 B2
Cervera [E] 92 C3
Cervera de la Cañada [E] 90 C4
Cervera del Llano [E] 98 B3
Cervera del Río Alhama [E] 84 A6
Cervera de Pisuerga [E] 82 D4
Cerveteri [I] 114 H5
Cérvia [I] 110 H4
Cervignano del Friuli [I] 72 G5
Cervinara [I] 120 E3
Cervione [F] 114 C4
Cervo [E] 78 E1
Cervo [I] 108 G4
Cesana Torinese [I] 70 B6
Cesarica [HR] 112 F3
Cesarò [I] 126 F2
Cesarzowice [PL] 36 C6
Cesena [I] 110 H4
Cesenático [I] 110 H4
Ceserhát–Surány [H] 64 D5
Cēsis [LV] 198 E4
Česká Bělá [CZ] 50 A5
Česká Kamenice [CZ] 48 F2
Česká Lípa [CZ] 48 G2
Česká Skalice [CZ] 50 B3
Česká Třebová [CZ] 50 B4
České Budějovice [CZ] 62 C2
České Libchavy [CZ] 50 B4
České Velenice [CZ] 62 C3
Český Brod [CZ] 48 G4
Český Krumlov [CZ] 62 B2
Český Šternberk [CZ] 48 G4
Český Těšín [CZ] 50 F5
Çeşme [TR] 134 H5
Çeşmealti [TR] 152 C4
Cespedosa [E] 88 C4
Cessalto [I] 72 F5
Cessenon–sur–Orb [F] 106 D4
Čestimensko [BG] 148 E1
Čestobrodica [SRB] 146 A2
Cestona / Zestoa [E] 84 A2
Cesvaine [LV] 198 F5
Cetate [RO] 146 F1
Çetibeli [TR] 154 D1
Cetinje [MNE] 144 E4
Cetóbriga [P] 86 B6
Cetona [I] 114 G2
Cetraro [I] 124 C4
Ceuta [E] 100 G6
Ceutí [E] 104 C3
Ceva [I] 108 G3
Cevico Navero [E] 88 F1
Čevo [MNE] 144 E4
Cewków [PL] 52 F3
Ceylan [TR] 154 G2
Ceyrat [F] 68 C2
Ceyzériat [F] 68 G2
Chaalis, Abbaye de– [F] 42 G3
Chabanais [F] 54 F6
Chabeuil [F] 68 F5
Chablis [F] 56 E2
Chabreloche [F] 68 D2
Chabris [F] 54 H3
Chachersk [BY] 202 D5
Chagny [F] 56 G5
Chailland [F] 26 E6
Chaillé–les–Marais [F] 54 C4
Chailley–Turny [F] 42 H6
Chailluz, Fort de– [F] 58 B4
Chairóneia [GR] 132 H5
Chalabre [F] 106 B5
Chalais [F] 66 E2
Chalamont [F] 68 G2
Chalampé [F] 58 E3
Chalandrítsa [GR] 132 F6
Chálki [GR] 132 G2
Chálki [GR] 154 C4
Chalkiádes [GR] 132 G2
Chalkída [GR] 134 B5
Chalkidóna [GR] 128 G4
Challans [F] 54 B2
Challes–les–Eaux [F] 70 A4
Chalonnes–sur–Loire [F] 54 D1
Châlons–en–Champagne [F] 44 B4
Chalon–sur–Saône [F] 56 G5
Chalupy [PL] 36 H6
Châlus [F] 66 G2
Chalusset, Château de– [F] 66 G1
Cham [CH] 58 F5
Cham [D] 48 C6
Chamberet [F] 66 H2
Chambéry [F] 68 H3
Chambilly [F] 56 E6
Chambley–Bussières [F] 44 E4
Chambon–sur–Lac [F] 68 C2
Chambon–sur–Voueize [F] 56 B6
Chambord [F] 54 H2
Chambord, Parc de– [F] 54 H2
Chamelet [F] 68 F2
Chameregg [D] 48 C6
Chammünster [D] 48 C6
Chamonix–Mont–Blanc [F] 70 C3
Champagnac–le–Vieux [F] 68 D3
Champagne–Mouton [F] 54 E5
Champagnole [F] 58 B6
Champaubert [F] 44 A4
Champdeniers [F] 54 D4
Champ du Bataille, Château du– [F] 26 H4
Champ du Feu [F] 58 D2
Champeix [F] 68 C3
Champéry [CH] 70 C2
Champex [CH] 70 C3
Champier [F] 68 G4
Champigné [F] 40 H6
Champigny–sur–Veude [F] 54 F2
Champillon [F] 44 B3
Champlan [F] 42 F4
Champlitte [F] 58 A3
Champlon [B] 30 E6
Champoluc [I] 70 D3
Champorcher [I] 70 D4
Champrond–en–Gâtine [F] 26 H6
Champtoceaux [F] 40 F6
Champvent [CH] 58 C6
Chamrousse [F] 68 H5
Chamusca [P] 86 C4
Chanaleilles [F] 68 D5
Chanas [F] 68 F4
Chandrinós [GR] 136 C4
Chaniá [GR] 140 C4
Chaniótis [GR] 130 C6
Channel Tunnel / La Manche, Tunnel sous– [F/GB] 14 G5
Chantada [E] 78 D4
Chantelle [F] 56 D6
Chantemerle [F] 70 B6
Chantilly [F] 42 G3
Chantonnay [F] 54 C3
Chão de Codes [P] 86 D4
Chaource [F] 44 B6
Chapelle–Royale [F] 42 D5
Chárakas [GR] 140 E5
Charavgí [GR] 128 F5
Charavines [F] 68 G4
Charbonnières–les–Bains [F] 68 F3
Charbowo [PL] 36 D2
Chard [GB] 12 F4
Charenton–du–Cher [F] 56 C4
Charité, Abbaye de la– [F] 58 B4
Charleroi [B] 30 C5
Charlestown [IRL] 2 D4
Charleville / Rath Luirc [IRL] 4 C4
Charleville–Mézières [F] 44 C2
Charlieu [F] 68 E1
Charlottenberg [S] 166 D1
Charly [F] 42 H3
Charly [F] 56 C4
Charmes [F] 44 E6
Charnawchytsy [BY] 38 G2
Charneca [P] 86 A5
Charny [F] 56 D1
Charnyany [BY] 38 G3
Charolles [F] 56 F6
Chârost [F] 56 B3
Charpentry [F] 44 D3
Charrières [CH] 70 C1
Charron [F] 54 C4
Charroux [F] 54 E5
Chartres [F] 42 E4
Charvarica [BG] 146 F6
Charzykowy [PL] 22 C4
Chassant [F] 42 D4
Chasseneuil–s.–Bonnieure [F] 54 E6
Chasse sur Rhone [F] 68 F3
Chassigny [F] 56 H3
Château–Arnoux [F] 108 C3
Châteaubourg [F] 26 D6
Châteaubriant [F] 40 F5
Château–Chinon [F] 56 E4
Château d'Oex [CH] 70 D1
Château–du–Loir [F] 42 B6
Châteaudun [F] 42 D5
Châteaugiron [F] 26 C6
Château–Gontier [F] 40 H5
Château–Landon [F] 42 F5
Château–la–Vallière [F] 42 B6
Château–l'Évêque [F] 66 F3
Châteaulin [F] 40 B2
Châteaumeillant [F] 56 B5
Châteauneuf [F] 66 E1
Châteauneuf–de–Randon [F] 68 D5
Châteauneuf–du–Faou [F] 40 C3
Châteauneuf–du–Pape [F] 106 G3
Châteauneuf–en–Thymerais [F] 26 H6
Châteauneuf–sur–Cher [F] 56 C4
Châteauneuf–sur–Sarthe [F] 40 H6
Châteauponsac [F] 54 G5
Château–Porcien [F] 28 H6
Château–Queyras [F] 70 B6
Château–Regnault [F] 44 C1
Châteaurenard [F] 42 G6
Château–Renault [F] 54 G1
Châteauroux [F] 54 H4
Château–Salins [F] 44 F5
Château–Thierry [F] 42 H3
Châteauvillain [F] 56 G2
Châtel [F] 70 C2
Châtelaillon–Plage [F] 54 C5
Châtelet [B] 30 C5
Châtelguyon [F] 68 C2
Châtellerault [F] 54 F3
Châtel–Montagne [F] 68 E1
Châtel–St–Denis [CH] 70 C1
Châtelus–Malvaleix [F] 54 H5
Châtenois [F] 44 E6
Chatham [GB] 14 F4
Châtillon [I] 70 D4
Châtillon–Coligny [F] 56 D1
Châtillon–en–Bazois [F] 56 E4
Châtillon–en–Diois [F] 68 G6
Châtillon–sur–Chalaronne [F] 68 G2
Châtillon–sur–Indre [F] 54 G3
Châtillon–sur–Loire [F] 56 D2
Châtillon–sur–Marne [F] 44 A3
Châtillon–sur–Seine [F] 56 G2
Châtre, Église de– [F] 54 D6
Chatteris [GB] 14 F2
Chaudes–Aigues [F] 68 C5
Chauffailles [F] 68 F1
Chaufour–lès–Bonnières [F] 42 E3
Chaumergy [F] 56 H5
Chaumont [F] 56 H1
Chaumont–sur–Aire [F] 44 D4
Chaumont–sur–Loire [F] 54 G2
Chaunay [F] 54 E5
Chauny [F] 28 F6
Chaussin [F] 56 H5
Chauvigny [F] 54 F4
Chaux–Neuve [F] 58 B6
Chavaleč [CZ] 50 B2
Chavdar [BG] 130 D1
Chaves [P] 80 E3
Chavusy [BY] 202 D5
Chayki [RUS] 198 H6
Chazelles–sur–Lyon [F] 68 F3
Cheb [CZ] 48 C3
Chęciny [PL] 52 B1
Cheddar [GB] 12 F3
Chef–Boutonne [F] 54 D5
Cheglevici [RO] 76 F5
Cheimarros [GR] 130 B3
Chekhov [RUS] 202 F3
Chekhovo [RUS] 22 H2
Cheles [E] 94 F2
Chełm [PL] 38 F6
Chełmek [PL] 50 G3
Chełmno [PL] 22 D5
Chelmsford [GB] 14 F4
Chełmża [PL] 22 E6
Chelst [PL] 36 B1
Cheltenham [GB] 12 G2
Chelva [E] 98 D3
Chémery–sur–Bar [F] 44 C2
Chemillé [F] 54 D2
Chemin [F] 56 H5
Chemnitz [D] 48 D1
Chenaux [CH] 58 C6
Chêne–Pignier [F] 54 F6
Chénérailles [F] 56 B6
Chenonceaux [F] 54 G2
Chepelare [BG] 130 E1
Chepstow [GB] 12 G3
Chera [E] 98 D4
Cherasco [I] 108 G2
Cherbourg [F] 26 D2
Cheremykino [RUS] 178 G5
Cherepovo [BG] 148 D6
Cherkasovo [RUS] 178 F3
Cherkasy [UA] 202 E8
Chern [RUS] 202 F4
Cherna Mesta [BG] 146 G6
Chernevo [RUS] 198 G2
Cherniakhiv [UA] 202 C7
Chernihiv [UA] 202 D6
Cherni rid [BG] 130 G1
Chernivtsi [UA] 204 D3
Chernomorets [BG] 148 F4
Chernyakhovsk [RUS] 24 C1
Chéroy [F] 42 G5
Cherskaya [RUS] 198 G4
Chérso [GR] 128 H3
Cherveix–Cubas [F] 66 G3
Chervena Voda [BG] 148 D2
Cherven Bryag [BG] 148 A3
Cherves–Richemont [F] 54 D6
Chervonohrad [UA] 52 H2
Chervyen' [BY] 202 C5
Cherykaw [BY] 202 D5
Cheste [E] 98 E4
Chester [GB] 10 D4
Chesterfield [GB] 10 F5
Chester–le–Street [GB] 8 F6
Chevagnes [F] 56 D5
Chevanceaux [F] 66 D2
Chevenez [CH] 58 D4
Chevilly, Château de– [F] 42 E6
Chevreuse [F] 42 F4

Chézal-Benoît [F] 56 B4
Chialamberto [I] 70 D5
Chiampo [I] 72 D6
Chianca, Dolmen di- [I] 122 D2
Chianciano Terme [I] 114 G2
Chiaramonti [I] 118 C3
Chiaramonti Gulfi [I] 126 F5
Chiaravalle [I] 112 C6
Chiaravalle [I] 112 C6
Chiaravalle Centrale [I] 124 D6
Chiaravalle della Colomba [I] 110 D2
Chiari [I] 70 H5
Chiaromonte [I] 122 C5
Chiasso [CH] 70 G4
Chiavari [I] 110 B3
Chiavenna [I] 70 G2
Chichester [GB] 14 D5
Chiclana de la Frontera [E] 100 F4
Chiclana de Segura [E] 102 G1
Chieming [D] 60 F5
Chieri [I] 70 D6
Chiesa [I] 110 G3
Chiesa in Valmalenco [I] 70 H3
Chiessi [I] 114 D2
Chieti [I] 116 D4
Chigny [F] 28 G5
Chiliadoú [GR] 134 C4
Chiliandaríou, Moní- [GR] 130 D5
Chiliomódi [GR] 136 F1
Chillarón de Cuenca [E] 98 B2
Chillon [CH] 70 C2
Chillón [E] 96 C4
Chimay [B] 28 H5
Chinadievo [UA] 204 B3
Chinchilla de Monte-Aragón [E] 98 C5
Chinchón [E] 96 G1
Chinon [F] 54 F2
Chióggia [I] 110 H1
Chíos [GR] 134 G4
Chipiona [E] 100 F3
Chippenham [GB] 12 G3
Chipping Norton [GB] 12 H2
Chipping Sodbury [GB] 12 G3
Chiprana [E] 90 F5
Chiprovtsi [BG] 146 F3
Chiren [BG] 146 G3
Chirivel [E] 102 H3
Chirpan [BG] 148 C5
Chisa [F] 114 B5
Chişinău [MD] 204 E3
Chişineu Criş [RO] 76 G3
Chiusa / Klausen [I] 72 D3
Chiusa di Pesio [I] 108 F3
Chiusaforte [I] 72 G4
Chiusa Sclàfani [I] 126 C3
Chiusi [I] 114 H2
Chiva [E] 98 E4
Chivasso [I] 70 D5
Chkalove [RUS] 204 H3
Chkalovo [PL] 24 D3
Chkalovo [RUS] 24 D1
Chlebowo [PL] 34 G3
Chlemoútsi [GR] 136 B1
Chlewice [PL] 50 H2
Chlewiska [PL] 38 B6
Chlewo [PL] 36 F4
Chlmec [SK] 64 H3
Chlumec nad Cidlinou [CZ] 48 H3
Chlum u Třeboně [CZ] 62 C2
Chmielnik [PL] 52 B2
Chmielno [PL] 36 A6
Chobienia [PL] 36 B5
Chobienice [PL] 36 B3
Choceň [CZ] 50 B4
Choceń [PL] 36 F2
Chochołów [PL] 50 H5
Chocianów [PL] 36 B5
Chociwel [PL] 20 G5
Choczewo [PL] 22 D1
Chodecz [PL] 36 F2
Chodel [PL] 38 D6
Chodos / Xodos [E] 98 F2
Chodov [CZ] 48 D3
Chodová Planá [CZ] 48 D4
Chodzież [PL] 22 B6
Chojna [PL] 20 F6
Chojnice [PL] 22 C4
Chojnów [PL] 36 B6
Cholet [F] 54 D2
Chomakovtsi [BG] 146 G3
Chomęciska Małe [PL] 52 F1
Chomutov [CZ] 48 E2
Chop [UA] 204 B3
Chóra [GR] 136 C4
Chorbadzhiysko [BG] 130 F2
Choreftó [GR] 134 A2
Chorges [F] 108 D2
Chorio [I] 124 C8
Choristí [GR] 130 D3
Chorley [GB] 10 D3
Chornobyl [UA] 202 D7
Chornomors'ke [UA] 204 G4
Choroszcz [PL] 24 E5
Chorro, Garganta del- [E] 102 B4
Chorros, Cueva de los- [E] 96 H6
Chorros del Mundo [E] 96 H6
Chortkiv [UA] 204 D2
Chorzele [PL] 22 H5
Chorzów [PL] 50 G3
Chorzyna [PL] 36 F5
Choszczno [PL] 20 G6
Chotěboř [CZ] 50 A5
Chotětín [CZ] 48 E4
Choumnikó [GR] 130 C3
Chouto [P] 86 D4
Chouvigny, Gorges de- [F] 56 C6
Choye [F] 58 A4
Chozoviótissa [GR] 138 G3
Chrast [CZ] 50 B4
Chrastava [CZ] 48 G1
Chrepiski Manastir [BG] 146 G4
Christchurch [GB] 12 G5
Christianoúpoli [GR] 136 C3
Christiansfeld [DK] 156 C3
Christinehof [S] 158 D2
Christkindl [A] 62 B5
Christós [GR] 138 G1
Chrudim [CZ] 50 A4
Chrýsafa [GR] 136 E4
Chrysochóri [GR] 130 E3
Chrysoskalítissa [GR] 140 B5
Chrysoúpoli [GR] 130 E3
Chrząchówek [PL] 38 D5
Chrzan [PL] 36 D3
Chrzanów [PL] 50 G3
Chudenice [CZ] 48 D5
Chudniv [UA] 202 C8
Chudoba [PL] 50 E1
Chudomir [BG] 148 D3
Chudovo [RUS] 202 C1
Chulkovo [RUS] 178 E3
Chupa [RUS] 196 H1
Chuprene [BG] 146 E3
Chur [CH] 70 H1
Church Stretton [GB] 10 D6
Churchtown [IRL] 4 E5
Churchtown [IRL] 4 F5
Churek [BG] 146 G4
Chvagnes-en-Paillers [F] 54 C2
Chvylevo [RUS] 202 C1
Chwaszczyno [PL] 22 D2
Chyhyryn [UA] 202 E8
Chyňava [CZ] 48 F4
Chýnov [CZ] 48 G5
Chýnovská Jeskyně [CZ] 48 G5
Chyžne [PL] 50 H5
Cianciana [I] 126 D3
Ciasna [PL] 50 F2
Ciążeń [PL] 36 E3
Cibakháza [H] 76 E2
Ciborro [P] 86 D6
Ciboure [F] 84 B2
Cicciano [I] 120 E3
Cicerone, Tomba di- [I] 120 C2
Ćićevac [SRB] 146 C3
Čičevci [BIH] 142 F4
Čičevo [BIH] 144 C2
Cichy [PL] 24 D3
Čičil [BG] 146 E2
Čiciuk [SRB] 146 C3
Ciclopi, Isole dei- [I] 126 G3
Čičmany [SK] 64 B2
Cide [TR] 204 H6
Cidones [E] 90 B2
Ciechanów [PL] 38 B1
Ciechanowiec [PL] 38 D1
Ciechocinek [PL] 36 F1
Ciemnik [PL] 20 G5
Ciempozuelos [E] 96 G1
Ciepielów [PL] 38 C5
Cieplice Śląskie-Zdrój [PL] 50 A1
Čierny Balog [SK] 64 D3
Cierp-Gaud [F] 84 F4
Cieśle [PL] 36 H2
Cieszanów [PL] 52 F3
Cieszyn [PL] 36 D5
Cieszyn [PL] 50 F4
Cieszyno [PL] 20 H5
Cieza [E] 104 C2
Ciężkowice [PL] 52 C4
Çiftlikköy [TR] 150 F3
Cifuentes [E] 90 A5
Cifuentes [E] 90 A5
Cigales [E] 88 E1
Cigánd [H] 64 H4
Cigliano [I] 70 E5
Cihangazi [TR] 150 G5
Cilipi [HR] 144 D4
Cill Airne / Killarney [IRL] 4 B4
Cillas [E] 90 C5
Cill Chainnigh / Kilkenny [IRL] 4 E4
Cill Charthaigh / Kilcar [IRL] 2 D2
Cill Chiaráin / Kilkieran [IRL] 2 B4
Cilleros [E] 86 G3
Cimadevilla [E] 78 B3
Cimburk [CZ] 50 C5
Cimburk [CZ] 62 G2
Cimino, Monte- [I] 114 H4
Cimitero Militare Britannico [I] 120 D1
Cimochy [PL] 24 E3
Cimoláis [I] 72 F4
Cîmpeni [RO] 204 C4
Çınarcık [TR] 150 F3
Cinco Casas [E] 96 G4
Cindere [TR] 152 F4
Çine [TR] 152 E6
Činěves [CZ] 48 H3
Ciney [B] 30 D5
Cinfães [P] 80 C4
Cingoli [I] 116 C1
Cinigiano [I] 114 F2
Cínisi [I] 126 C1
Cínovec [CZ] 48 E2
Cinquefrondi [I] 124 D6
Cintegabelle [F] 84 H4
Cintei [RO] 76 H4
Cintruénigo [E] 84 A6
Ciółkowo [PL] 36 H2
Circo de Barrosa [E] 84 E5
Cirella [I] 124 C3
Cirencester [GB] 12 G3
Cirey [F] 44 G6
Ciria [E] 90 C3
Ciriè [I] 70 D5
Čirkovicy [RUS] 178 G6
Cirò [I] 124 F4
Cirò Marina [I] 124 F4
Ciron [F] 54 G4
Çırpı [TR] 152 D4
Ciruli [LV] 198 C4
Cisa, Passo della- [I] 110 C3
Cisna [PL] 52 E6
Cisnădie [RO] 204 C5
Cisneros [E] 82 C5
Cista Provo [HR] 144 B2
Cista Velika [HR] 144 A2
Cisterna di Latina [I] 116 B6
Cisternino [I] 122 F3
Cistierna [E] 82 C4
Ciszyca [PL] 38 C3
Citak [TR] 152 E2
Cîteaux, Abbaye de- [F] 56 G4
Çitlik [TR] 154 D1
Čitluk [BIH] 144 C2
Cittadella [I] 72 D6
Città della Pieve [I] 114 H2
Città del Vaticano [V] 116 A5
Città di Castello [I] 114 H1
Cittaducale [I] 116 B4
Cittanova [I] 124 D7
Città Sant'Angelo [I] 116 D4
Ciudad Iberica [E] 90 C4
Ciudad Real [E] 96 E4
Ciudad Rodrigo [E] 86 H2
Ciudad Romana [E] 94 G4
Ciumeghiu [RO] 76 H3
Ciutadella de Menorca [E] 104 G4
Civica [E] 90 A5
Cividale del Friuli [I] 72 G5
Çivili [TR] 150 E5
Civita [I] 114 H3
Cívita Castellana [I] 116 A4
Civitanova Marche [I] 116 C1
Civitavécchia [I] 114 G5
Civitella del Tronto [I] 116 C3
Civitella di Romagna [I] 110 G5
Civitella in Val di Chiana [I] 114 G1
Civitella Paganico [I] 114 F2
Civitella Roveto [I] 116 C5
Civray [F] 54 E5
Civrieux-d'Azergues [F] 68 F2
Çivril [TR] 152 G4
Clacton-on-Sea [GB] 14 G4
Clairvaux-les-Lacs [F] 70 A1
Clamecy [F] 56 E3
Clamerey [F] 56 F3
Clamouse, Grotte de- [F] 106 E3
Clane [IRL] 2 F6
Clara [IRL] 2 D5
Clarecastle [IRL] 2 C6
Claremorris [IRL] 2 C4
Clarinbridge [IRL] 2 C5
Claros [TR] 152 C5
Clashmore [IRL] 4 D5
Classe [F] 54 D3
Claudy [NIR] 2 F2
Clausholm [DK] 160 E5
Clausthal-Zellerfeld [D] 32 G4
Claviere [I] 70 B6
Cleanovu [RO] 146 F1
Clécy [F] 26 F4
Cleethorpes [GB] 10 G4
Clefmont [F] 58 A2
Clefs [F] 42 B6
Clelles [F] 68 G5
Clementino, Porto- [I] 114 G4
Cléon-d'Andran [F] 68 F6
Clères [F] 28 C5
Clermont [F] 28 E6
Clermont-de-Beauregarde [F] 66 F3
Clermont-en-Argonne [F] 44 D4
Clermont-Ferrand [F] 68 C2
Clermont-l'Hérault [F] 106 E4
Clerval [F] 58 C4
Clervaux [L] 44 F1
Cléry [F] 42 E6
Cles [I] 72 C3
Clevedon [GB] 12 F3
Clifden [IRL] 2 B4
Cliffoney [IRL] 2 D3
Clisson [F] 54 C2
Clitheroe [GB] 10 E3
Clitunno, Fonti del- [I] 116 B3
Clitunno, Tempio del- [I] 116 B3
Clogan [IRL] 2 D6
Clogh [IRL] 4 F3
Clogheen [IRL] 4 D4
Cloghmore / An Chloich Mhór [IRL] 2 B3
Clohars-Carnoët [F] 40 C4
Clonakilty [IRL] 4 C5
Clonalis House [IRL] 2 D4
Clonard [IRL] 2 E5
Clonaslee [IRL] 2 D6
Clonbur / An Fhairche [IRL] 2 C4
Clondalkin [IRL] 2 F6
Clones [IRL] 2 E4
Clonfert [IRL] 2 D5
Clonmacnoise [IRL] 2 D5
Clonmany [IRL] 2 F1
Clonmel / Cluain Meala [IRL] 4 E4
Clonmellon [IRL] 2 E5
Clonroche [IRL] 4 F4
Cloonbannin [IRL] 4 C4
Cloonkeen [IRL] 4 B4
Cloonlara [IRL] 4 D3
Cloppenburg [D] 18 C6
Clough [NIR] 2 G4
Cloughjordan [IRL] 2 D6
Cloyes-sur-le-Loir [F] 42 D5
Cloyne [IRL] 4 D5
Cluain Meala / Clonmel [IRL] 4 E4
Cluina [E] 88 H2
Cluj Napoca [RO] 204 C4
Clun [GB] 10 C6
Cluny [F] 56 F6
Cluses [F] 70 B2
Clusone [I] 72 A5
Ćmielów [PL] 52 D1
Cmolas [PL] 52 D3
Cnocán na Líne / Knocknalina [IRL] 2 C2
Coachford [IRL] 4 C5
Coalville [GB] 10 E6
Coaña [E] 78 F2
Çobanısa [TR] 154 H1
Çobanlar [TR] 152 D2
Cobh [IRL] 4 D5
Coburg [D] 46 G3
Coca [E] 88 E3
Coceges del Monte [E] 88 F2
Cocentaina [E] 104 E1
Cochem [D] 44 G1
Cockermouth [GB] 8 D6
Code [LV] 198 D6
Codigoro [I] 110 G2
Codogno [I] 70 H6
Codos [E] 90 D4
Codróipo [I] 72 G5
Coesfeld [D] 16 H6
Coevorden [NL] 16 G4
Coflans [F] 70 B4
Cofrentes [E] 98 D5
Coghinas [I] 118 D3
Cognac [F] 54 D6
Cogne [I] 70 D4
Cogolin [F] 108 D5
Cogollos [E] 82 E6
Cogolludo [E] 88 H4
Cogul, Cova del- [E] 90 H5
Cohiniac [F] 26 A4
Coimbra [P] 86 D2
Coín [E] 102 B4
Coina [P] 86 B6
Coirós [E] 78 D2
Čoka [SRB] 76 E5
Colares [P] 86 A5
Cölbe [D] 32 D6
Colbitz [D] 34 B2
Colcerasa [I] 116 B1
Colchester [GB] 14 F3
Colditz [D] 34 D6
Coldstream [GB] 8 F4
Colembert [F] 14 G6
Colera [E] 92 G2
Coleraine [NIR] 2 G2
Colfiorito [I] 116 B2
Colfosco [I] 72 E3
Colico [I] 70 G3
Coligny [F] 56 H6
Colindres [E] 82 F3
Colintraive [GB] 8 C2
Collado Villalba [E] 88 F5
Coll de Nargó [E] 92 D2
Collécchio [I] 110 D2
Colledimezzo [I] 116 E5
Colle di Val d'Elsa [I] 114 F1
Colleferro [I] 116 B6
Collegno [I] 70 D5
Colle Isarco / Gossensass [I] 72 D2
Collesalvetti [I] 110 D6
Colle Sannita [I] 120 F2
Collesano [I] 126 E2
Colletorto [I] 116 F6
Colliano [I] 120 G3
Collinée [F] 26 B5
Cóllio [I] 72 B5
Collioure [F] 92 G2
Collodi [I] 110 E5
Collonges [F] 70 A2
Collonges-la-Rouge [F] 66 G3
Collooney [IRL] 2 D3
Colmar [F] 58 D3
Colmars [F] 108 D3
Colmenar [E] 102 C4
Colmenar de Oreja [E] 96 G1
Colmenar Viejo [E] 88 F5
Cologna Vèneta [I] 110 F1
Cologne [F] 84 G2
Cololgno al Serio [I] 70 H5
Colombey-les-Belles [F] 44 E5
Colombey-les-Deux-Églises [F] 44 C6
Colomiers [F] 84 H3
Colònia de Sant Jordi [E] 104 E6
Colonia Selladores [E] 96 E6
Colorno [I] 110 D2
Colosimi [I] 124 D5
Colunga [E] 82 C2
Colwyn Bay [GB] 10 C4
Comácchio [I] 110 H3
Comana [RO] 148 D1
Comana [RO] 148 G1
Comănești [RO] 204 D4
Comano Terme [I] 72 C4
Coma-ruga [E] 92 C5
Combarro [E] 78 B4
Combeaufontaine [F] 58 B3
Comber [NIR] 2 G4
Combourg [F] 26 C5
Combronde [F] 68 C1
Comburg [D] 46 E6
Comeglians [I] 72 G3
Comelico Superiore [I] 72 F3
Comillas [E] 82 E3
Cómiso [I] 126 F5
Comloşu Mare [RO] 76 F5
Commentry [F] 56 C6
Commequiers [F] 54 B2
Commercy [F] 44 D5
Como [I] 70 G4
Cómpeta [E] 102 D4
Compiègne [F] 28 E6
Comporta [P] 94 C1
Comps-sur-Artuby [F] 108 D4
Comrat [MD] 204 E4
Comunanza [I] 116 C2
Conca [I] 114 B5
Concarneau [F] 40 B3
Concesio [I] 72 B5
Conches-en-Ouche [F] 26 H4
Concordia Sagittaria [I] 72 F5
Condat [F] 68 C3
Condé-en-Brie [F] 42 H3
Condeixa-a-Nova [P] 86 D2
Condé-sur-Noireau [F] 26 E4
Condino [I] 72 B5
Condofuri [I] 124 C8
Condofuri Marina [I] 124 C8
Condom [F] 66 E6
Condove [I] 70 C5
Condrieu [F] 68 F3
Conegliano [I] 72 E5
Conflans en Jarnisy [F] 44 E4
Conflans-sur-Lanterne [F] 58 B3
Confolens [F] 54 F6
Cong [IRL] 2 C4
Congleton [GB] 10 E5
Congosto de Valdavia [E] 82 D4
Congresbury [GB] 12 F3
Conil de la Frontera [E] 100 F5
Conímbriga [P] 86 D2
Coningsby [GB] 10 G5
Conlie [F] 42 B5
Conna [IRL] 4 D5
Connantre [F] 44 B4
Connerré [F] 42 C5
Čonoplja [SRB] 76 D5
Conques [F] 68 B5
Conquista [E] 96 D5
Conquista de la Sierra [E] 96 B2
Conquista del Guadiana [E] 94 G2
Conselice [I] 110 G3
Conselve [I] 110 G1
Consett [GB] 8 F6
Constanța [RO] 204 F5
Constantí [E] 92 C5
Constantina [E] 96 A6
Constantine [F] 44 E3
Consuegra [E] 96 F3
Consuma [I] 110 F5
Contarina [I] 110 H2
Contay [F] 28 E4
Contea [I] 110 F5
Conțești [RO] 148 C2
Contigliano [I] 116 B4
Contis-Plage [F] 66 B5
Contres [F] 54 H2
Contrexéville [F] 58 B2
Controne [I] 120 F4
Contursi Terme [I] 120 F4
Conty [F] 28 D5
Conversano [I] 122 E3
Conwy [GB] 10 C4
Cookstown [NIR] 2 F3
Coole [IRL] 2 E5
Cooraclare [IRL] 2 B6
Cootehill [IRL] 2 F4
Cope [E] 104 B4
Copertino [I] 122 G5
Çöpköy [TR] 150 B3
Copparo [I] 110 G2
Coppenbrügge [D] 32 F3
Corabia [RO] 148 A2
Corato [I] 122 D2
Coray [F] 40 C3
Corbalán [E] 98 E2
Corbeil-Essonnes [F] 42 F4
Corbeny [F] 28 G6
Corbera d'Ebre [E] 90 G6
Corbie [F] 28 E5
Corbigny [F] 56 E3
Corbridge [GB] 8 F6
Corby [GB] 14 E2
Corcaigh / Cork [IRL] 4 C5
Corciano [I] 114 H2
Corcieux [F] 58 D2
Corcomroe Abbey [IRL] 2 C5
Corconne [F] 106 F3
Corconte [E] 82 E4
Corcubión [E] 78 B2
Cordenons [I] 72 F5
Cordes [F] 106 B2
Córdoba [E] 102 C1
Cordobilla de Lácara [E] 86 G6
Corella [E] 84 A6
Cori [I] 116 B6
Coria [E] 86 H3
Coria del Río [E] 94 G6
Coriano [I] 110 H5
Corigliano Calabro [I] 124 E3
Corinaldo [I] 112 C6
Coripe [E] 100 H3
Cork / Corcaigh [IRL] 4 C5
Corlățel [RO] 146 E1
Corlay [F] 26 A4
Corleone [I] 126 C2
Corleto Perticara [I] 120 H4
Çorlu [TR] 150 C3
Cormainville [F] 42 E5
Cormeilles [F] 26 G3
Cormery [F] 54 G2
Cornau [D] 18 D6
Cornellana [E] 78 G3
Córniglio [I] 110 D3
Cornimont [F] 58 D3
Cornuda la Valle [I] 72 E5
Cornudella de Montsant [E] 90 H6
Cornus [I] 118 B5
Corofin [IRL] 2 C6
Corovodë [AL] 128 C5
Corps [F] 68 H6
Corral de Almaguer [E] 96 G2
Corralejo [E] 100 E6
Corrales [E] 80 H5
Corral Rubio [E] 98 C6
Corre [F] 58 B3
Corréggio [I] 110 E2
Corridonia [I] 116 C2
Corsano [I] 122 G6
Corseul [F] 26 C4
Corte [F] 114 B4
Corte Brugnatella [I] 110 C2
Corte Figueira [P] 94 C4
Cortegada [E] 78 C5
Cortegana [E] 94 F4
Cortemaggiore [I] 70 H6
Cortemilia [I] 108 G2
Cortes [E] 90 D3
Cortes de la Frontera [E] 100 H4
Cortes de Pallás [E] 98 D5
Cortes de Peleas [E] 94 G2
Corte Zorrinha [P] 94 C4
Cortijos de Abajo [E] 96 E3
Cortina d'Ampezzo [I] 72 E3
Cortona [I] 114 H1
Coruche [P] 86 C5
Coruña del Conde [E] 88 H2
Corvara in Badia [I] 72 E3
Corvera [E] 104 C3
Corvey [D] 32 F4
Corwen [GB] 10 C5
Cosa [E] 90 D6
Cosa [I] 114 F4
Cosenza [I] 124 D4
Cosne-Cours-sur-Loire [F] 56 D3
Cosne d'Allier [F] 56 C5
Coşoveni [RO] 146 G1
Coşoveni [RO] 146 G1
Cospeito [E] 78 E3
Cossato [I] 70 E4
Cossé-le-Vivien [F] 40 G5
Cossonay [CH] 70 B1
Costa da Caparica [P] 86 A5
Costa de los Pins [E] 104 F5
Costa Nova do Prado [P] 80 B5
Costești [RO] 204 D5
Costigliole Saluzzo [I] 108 F2
Coswig [D] 34 C4
Coswig [D] 34 E6
Cote [E] 100 H3
Cotignac [F] 108 C5
Cotronei [I] 124 E5
Cottbus [D] 34 F4
Couches [F] 56 F5
Couço [P] 86 D5
Coucy-le-Château-Auffrique [F] 28 F6
Coudray-Montbault, Château de- [F] 54 D2
Couflenz [F] 84 G5
Cougnac, Grottes de- [F] 66 G4
Couhé [F] 54 E5
Couilly [F] 42 G3
Couiza [F] 106 B5
Coulanges-la-Vineuse [F] 56 E2
Coulmier-le-Sec [F] 56 G2
Coulommiers [F] 42 G4
Coulon [F] 54 D4
Coulonges [F] 54 D4
Coupar Angus [GB] 8 E2
Couptrain [F] 26 F5
Courboyer, Manoir de- [F] 26 G6
Courceau [F] 56 G3
Courchevel [F] 70 B4
Cour-Cheverny [F] 54 H2
Courçon [F] 54 C4
Cour-et-Buis [F] 68 G4
Courgains [F] 26 F6
Courmayeur [I] 70 C3
Courpière [F] 68 D2
Courriere [B] 30 D5
Coursan [F] 106 D5
Courseulles-sur-Mer [F] 26 F3
Cours-la-Ville [F] 68 F2
Courson-les-Carrières [F] 56 E2
Courtacon [F] 42 H4
Courtanvaux, Château de- [F] 42 C6
Courteilles [F] 26 G4
Courtelevant [F] 58 D4
Courtenay [F] 42 G6
Courtmacsherry [IRL] 4 C5
Courtomer [F] 26 G5
Courtown Harbour [IRL] 4 G4
Courtrai (Kortrijk) [B] 28 G2
Courville [F] 26 H6
Coutances [F] 26 D3
Couterne [F] 26 E5
Coutevroult [F] 42 G4
Coutras [F] 66 D3
Couvet [CH] 58 C6
Couvin [B] 28 H5
Covadonga [E] 82 C2
Covadonga [E] 82 C2
Covaleda [E] 90 B2
Covarrubias [E] 88 H1
Covarrubias [E] 90 B3
Covăsinț [RO] 76 H4
Covci [RO] 146 F2
Coventry [GB] 14 D2
Covide [P] 78 B6
Covilhã [P] 86 F2
Cowes [GB] 12 H5
Cox [F] 84 H2
Cózar [E] 96 G5
Cozes [F] 54 C6
Cozia, Mănăstirea- [RO] 204 C5
Cozzano [F] 114 B5
Craco [I] 122 D4
Craigavon [NIR] 2 G4
Crail [GB] 8 F3
Crailsheim [D] 46 E6
Craiova [RO] 76 H3
Craiova [RO] 146 G1
Crângeni [RO] 148 B1
Crângu [RO] 148 B2
Crans [CH] 70 D2
Craon [F] 40 G5
Craponne-sur-Arzon [F] 68 D3
Crato [P] 86 E5
Craughwell [IRL] 2 C5
Crawley [GB] 14 E5
Crea, Santuario di- [I] 70 E6
Crêches-sur-Saône [F] 68 F1
Crécy [F] 42 G4
Crécy-en-Ponthieu [F] 28 D3
Crécy-sur-Serre [F] 28 G6
Crediton [GB] 12 E4
Creevagh [IRL] 2 C3
Creglingen [D] 46 E5
Creil [F] 42 G2
Crema [I] 70 H5
Cremaste [TR] 150 B5
Crémieu [F] 68 G3
Cremona [I] 110 D1
Črenšovci [SLO] 74 F3
Créon [F] 66 D3
Crepaja [SRB] 142 G2
Crépy-en-Valois [F] 42 G3
Cres [HR] 112 E2
Crésantignes [F] 44 A6
Crescentino [I] 70 E5
Crespin [F] 28 G4
Crespino [I] 110 G2
Cressensac [F] 66 G3
Cresslough [IRL] 2 E1
Crest [F] 68 F6
Cresta [CH] 70 H2
Creussen [D] 46 H4
Creutzwald [F] 44 F4
Creuzburg [D] 32 G6
Crevalcore [I] 110 F3
Crevecœur-en-Auge [F] 26 G4
Crevecoeur [F] 28 D5
Crevillent / Crevillente [E] 104 D2
Crevillente / Crevillent [E] 104 D2
Crevoladossola [I] 70 E3
Crewe [GB] 10 D5
Crewkerne [GB] 12 F4
Criação Velha [P] 100 C3
Crianlarich [GB] 8 D2
Cricklade [GB] 12 H3
Crieff [GB] 8 E2
Crikvenica [HR] 112 F2
Crillon [F] 28 D5
Crimmitschau [D] 48 C1
Črišnjeva [HR] 112 F2
Crispiano [I] 122 E4
Crissolo [I] 108 F2
Cristo, Monasterio del- [E] 78 G3
Cristo del Espíritu-Santo [E] 96 E3
Crivitz [D] 20 A4
Crkvice [BIH] 142 D4
Crkvina [BIH] 142 D2
Crkvina Prolaz [MNE] 144 E3
Crmljan [SRB] 146 B5
Črmošnjice [SLO] 74 C6
Črna [SLO] 74 C4
Crna Bara [SRB] 76 E5
Crna Trava [SRB] 146 E4
Crnča [SRB] 142 F4
Crni Lug [BIH] 142 B4
Crni Vrh [SLO] 74 B5
Črnkovci [HR] 76 B6
Crnokliště [SRB] 146 E3
Črnomelj [SLO] 74 D6
Crocq [F] 68 B1
Crodo [I] 70 F2
Croithlí / Crolly [IRL] 2 E2
Croix Haute, Col de la- [F] 68 G6
Crolly / Croithlí [IRL] 2 E2
Cro-Magnon [F] 66 F3
Cromarty [GB] 6 E4
Cromer [GB] 14 G1
Crook [GB] 10 F1
Crookedwood [IRL] 2 E5
Crookhaven [IRL] 4 B5
Crookstown [IRL] 4 C5
Croom [IRL] 4 D3
Cropalati [I] 124 E4
Cropani [I] 124 E5
Crosia [I] 124 E4
Crossakeel [IRL] 2 E5
Crosshaven [IRL] 4 D5
Crossmaglen [NIR] 2 F4
Crossmolina [IRL] 2 C3
Crotone [I] 124 F5
Crowborough [GB] 14 E5
Croydon [GB] 14 E4
Crozant [F] 54 G5
Crozon [F] 40 B2
Cruas [F] 68 F6
Cruceni [RO] 142 H1
Cruces [E] 78 C3
Crucoli [I] 124 F4
Crumlin [NIR] 2 G3
Cruseilles [F] 70 B2
Crusheen [IRL] 2 C6
Cruzy [F] 56 F2
Cruzy [F] 106 D4
Crvenka [MNE] 204 A5
Crvenka [SRB] 76 D6
Csabacsüd [H] 76 F3
Csákánydoroszló [H] 74 F2
Csákvár [H] 76 B1
Csanádapáca [H] 76 F3
Csanádpalota [H] 76 F4
Csanytelek [H] 76 E3
Csapod [H] 62 G6
Csárdaszállás [H] 76 F2
Császártöltés [H] 76 C4
Csávoly [H] 76 C4

Csépa [H] 76 E3
Cserebökény [H] 76 E3
Cserepes [H] 64 G6
Cserkeszőlő [H] 76 E2
Csernely [H] 64 E4
Csesznek [H] 76 A1
Csobád [H] 64 F4
Csókakői Varrom [H] 76 B1
Csökmő [H] 76 G2
Csokonyavisonta [H] 74 H5
Csongrád [H] 76 E3
Csopak [H] 76 A2
Csór [H] 76 B2
Csorna [H] 62 G6
Csorvás [H] 76 F3
Csót [H] 74 H1
Csurgó [H] 74 G4
Cuadros [E] 78 H5
Cualedro [E] 78 D6
Cuba [P] 94 D2
Cubel [E] 90 C5
Cubells [E] 92 C3
Cubo de Bureba [E] 82 F5
Çubukdağı [TR] 152 F5
Çubuklu [TR] 154 F1
Cudillero [E] 78 G3
Cuéllar [E] 88 F2
Cuenca [E] 98 B2
Cuers [F] 108 C5
Cuerva [E] 96 E2
Cuesta Blanca de Arriba [E] 104 C4
Cuevas del Almanzora [E] 102 H4
Cuevas del Becerro [E] 102 B4
Cuevas de San Clemente [E] 88 H1
Cuevas de San Marcos [E] 102 C3
Cúglieri [I] 118 C4
Cugnon-sur-Semois [B] 44 D2
Cuhom [F] 28 E3
Cuijk [NL] 16 E6
Cuillé [F] 40 G4
Cuiseaux [F] 56 H6
Cuisery [F] 56 G6
Cujmir [RO] 146 E1
Çukurhisar [TR] 150 H5
Çukurköi [TR] 150 B2
Çukurköy [TR] 152 G5
Çukurören [TR] 152 G2
Culaccio [I] 110 D4
Culan [F] 56 B5
Culdaff [IRL] 2 F1
Culemborg [NL] 16 E5
Cúllar [E] 102 G3
Cullen [GB] 6 F5
Cullera [E] 98 F5
Cullompton [GB] 12 E4
Culoz [F] 68 H3
Cuma [I] 120 D3
Cumbernauld [GB] 8 D3
Cumbres de S. Bartolomé [E] 94 F4
Cumbres Mayores [E] 94 F4
Čumić [SRB] 146 B2
Cumnock [GB] 8 D4
Cunault [F] 54 E2
Cúneo [I] 108 F3
Čuništa [BIH] 142 D4
Čunski [HR] 112 E3
Cuntis [E] 78 B3
Cuorgnè [I] 70 D5
Cupar [GB] 8 F2
Cupello [I] 116 E5
Cupra Marittima [I] 116 D2
Cupramontana [I] 116 B1
Ćuprija [SRB] 146 C2
Cura, Santuari de- [E] 104 E5
Cura Nuova [I] 114 E2
Curel [F] 108 C3
Curia [P] 80 B6
Ćurlovac [HR] 74 G5
Curon Venosta / Graun im Vinschgau [I] 72 B2
Curraghmore [IRL] 4 E5
Curtatone [I] 110 E1
Curtea de Argeş [RO] 204 D5
Curtici [RO] 76 G4
Curtis [E] 78 D2
Čurug [SRB] 142 G1
Cusset [F] 68 D1
Custines [F] 44 E5
Custonaci [I] 126 B2
Cutigliano [I] 110 E4
Cutro [I] 124 F5
Cutting [F] 44 F5
Çüvenlı [TR] 150 C2
Cuveşdia [RO] 76 H5
Cuvilly [F] 28 E6
Cuxhaven [D] 18 D3
Cuzzola [I] 118 E3
Cvikov [CZ] 48 G2
Cwmbran [GB] 12 F2
Cybinka [PL] 34 G3
Cyców [PL] 38 F5
Cytonium [TR] 152 C2
Czacz [PL] 36 C3
Czajków [PL] 36 E5
Czaplinek [PL] 22 A5
Czarna [PL] 38 D4
Czarna Białostocka [PL] 24 F5
Czarna Białostocka [PL] 24 F5
Czarna Dąbrówka [PL] 22 C2
Czarna Górna [PL] 52 F5
Czarna Woda [PL] 22 D4
Czarne [PL] 22 B4
Czarnków [PL] 36 C1
Czarnożyły [PL] 36 F6
Czarny Dunajec [PL] 50 H5
Czastary [PL] 36 E6
Czchów [PL] 52 B4
Czechowice-Dziedzice [PL] 50 G4
Czeladź [PL] 50 G3
Czemierniki [PL] 38 E4
Czempiń [PL] 36 C3
Czeremcha [PL] 38 F2
Czerniejewo [PL] 36 D2
Czernikowo [PL] 36 F1
Czernin [PL] 22 E4
Czersk [PL] 22 D4
Czersk [PL] 38 C3
Czerwieńsk [PL] 34 H4
Czerwionka-Leszczyny [PL] 50 F3
Czerwony-Dwór [PL] 24 D3
Częstochowa [PL] 50 G1
Człopa [PL] 20 H6
Człuchów [PL] 22 C4
Czorsztyn [PL] 52 B5
Czudec [PL] 52 D4
Czyżew-Osada [PL] 38 D1

D

Daaden [D] 32 C6
Dabarska Spilja [BIH] 142 B3
Dabas [H] 76 C2
Dabern [D] 34 E4
Dąbie [PL] 20 F5
Dąbie [PL] 36 F3
Dabilja [MK] 128 G2
Dąbki [PL] 22 A2
Dąbki [PL] 36 C5
Dabo [F] 44 G5
Dabo, Roch. de- [F] 44 G5
Dăbovan [BG] 148 A2
Dăbovo [BG] 148 C4
Dąbrowa [PL] 36 E1
Dąbrowa [PL] 36 F4
Dąbrowa [PL] 38 E2
Dąbrowa [PL] 50 E2
Dąbrowa Białostocka [PL] 24 F4
Dąbrowa Górnicza [PL] 50 G3
Dąbrowa Tarnowska [PL] 52 C3
Dąbrówca Warszawska [PL] 38 C5
Dąbrówka [PL] 52 E2
Dąbrówka Kościelna [PL] 24 E6
Dąbrówka Leśna [PL] 36 C2
Dąbrówka Wielkopolska [PL] 36 A3
Dąbrówno [PL] 22 G5
Dăbuleni [RO] 146 G2
Dachau [D] 60 E4
Dachnów [PL] 52 F3
Dachsteinhöhlen [A] 62 A6
Dačice [CZ] 62 D2
Dad [H] 64 B6
Dadağlı [TR] 152 F4
Dädesjö [S] 162 E4
Dáfnes [GR] 132 F6
Dáfni [GR] 130 D5
Dáfni [GR] 130 F6
Dafní [GR] 134 B6
Dáfni [GR] 136 D2
Dafnónas [GR] 130 E2
Dafnotí [GR] 132 D2
Dağakça [TR] 150 F5
Dagali [N] 170 F4
Dagardı [TR] 152 F1
Dagda [LV] 198 G6
Dagebüll [D] 156 B5
Dağkızılca [TR] 152 D4
Dahlem [D] 30 F6
Dahlen [D] 34 D5
Dahlenburg [D] 18 G5
Dahme [D] 18 H2
Dahme [D] 34 E4
Dahmen [D] 20 C4
Dahn [D] 44 H4
Dähre [D] 32 H1
Daia [RO] 148 C1
Daikanvik [S] 190 F4
Daimiel [E] 96 F4
Daimoniá [GR] 136 F5
Daingean [IRL] 2 E6
Đakovica / Gjakove [SRB] 146 B6
Đakovo [HR] 142 D1
Daksti [LV] 198 E4
Dal [N] 170 F6
Dal [N] 172 C5
Dala [S] 166 F6
Dalaas [A] 72 B1
Dala-Floda [S] 172 G4
Dala-Husby [S] 174 D5
Dala-Järna [S] 172 G4
Dalama [TR] 152 E5
Dalaman [TR] 154 E2
Dalarö [S] 168 E3
Dalbeattie [GB] 8 D5
Dalberg [D] 44 H2
Dalby [DK] 156 G3
Dalby [S] 158 C3
Dalbyn [S] 172 H3
Dale [GB] 12 D1
Dale [N] 164 E3
Dale [N] 170 B3
Dale [N] 170 B1
Dale [N] 180 C4
Dalen [N] 164 E2
Dalen [N] 180 F3
Daleszyce [PL] 52 C1
Dalfors [S] 172 H2
Dalhem [S] 162 F1
Dalhem [S] 168 G4
Dalholen [N] 180 H5
Dalías [E] 102 F5
Daliowa [PL] 52 D5
Dalj [HR] 142 E1
Daljani [BIH] 144 C1
Dalkeith [GB] 8 E3
Dalkey [IRL] 2 F6
Dalmine [I] 70 H4
Dalmose [DK] 156 F3
Daløy [N] 170 A2
Dalry [GB] 8 C3
Dalsbruk / Taalintehdas [FIN] 176 E6
Dalselv [N] 190 E2
Dalseter [N] 170 G1
Dalseter [N] 180 H4
Dalsjöfors [S] 162 B2
Dalskog [S] 166 D4
Dals Långed [S] 166 D4
Dals Rostock [S] 166 D4
Dalstein [F] 44 F3
Daluis, Gorges de- [F] 108 E3
Dalum [S] 162 C1
Dalvík [IS] 192 C2
Daly [CY] 154 G5
Dalyan [TR] 130 H6
Dalyan [TR] 154 E2
Damási [GR] 132 F1
Damaskiniá [GR] 128 E5
Damasławek [PL] 36 D1
Damba [N] 180 B5
Dambaslar [TR] 150 C3
Dambeck [D] 20 C5
Dammartin-en-Goële [F] 42 G3
Damme [B] 28 G1
Damme [D] 32 D1
Dammen [N] 164 G2
Dammendorf [D] 34 G3
Damno [PL] 22 C2
Damp 2000 [D] 18 F1
Damparis [F] 56 H4
Dampierre [F] 42 F4
Dampierre [F] 58 A5
Dampierre-sur-Boutonne [F] 54 D5
Dampierre-sur-Salon [F] 58 A4
Damville [F] 26 H5
Damvillers [F] 44 D3
D. Andrijevci [HR] 142 D2
Dăneasa [RO] 148 A1
Daneţi [RO] 146 G2
Dångebo [S] 162 E5
Dangé-St-Romain [F] 54 F3
Danilov [RUS] 202 F1
Danilovgrad [MNE] 144 E4
Danişment [TR] 150 D5
Daniszyn [PL] 36 D5
Danków [PL] 34 H1
Dannäs [S] 162 C4
Dannemarie [F] 58 D4
Dannenberg [D] 18 H5
Dannenwalde [D] 20 D6
Dannike [S] 162 B2
Dánszentmiklós [H] 76 D2
Daon [F] 40 H5
Daoulas [F] 40 B2
Darabani [RO] 204 D3
Darány [H] 74 H5
Darbėnai [LT] 200 D4
Darbu [N] 164 G1
Darda [HR] 76 C6
Dardesheim [D] 32 H3
Dardhë [AL] 128 D5
Darfo [I] 72 B5
Dargilan, Grotte de- [F] 106 E2
Dargun [D] 20 C3
Darıca [TR] 150 D5
Darıca [TR] 150 F3
Darıçayırı [TR] 150 H2
Dariveren [TR] 152 G6
Därligen [CH] 70 E1
Darlington [GB] 10 F2
Darłówko [PL] 22 A2
Darłowo [PL] 22 A2
Darmstadt [D] 46 C3
Darney [F] 58 B2
Darnius [E] 92 G2
Daroca [E] 90 D5
Darque [P] 78 A6
Darro [E] 102 E3
Dartford [GB] 14 E4
Dartmouth [GB] 12 E5
Dartsel [S] 190 H3
Daruvar [HR] 74 G6
Darvas [H] 76 G2
Darwen [GB] 10 E3
Dasburg [D] 44 F1
Dashkavichy [BY] 24 H6
Dašice [CZ] 50 B4
Dasing [D] 60 D3
Daskalovo [BG] 146 F5
Dasochóri [GR] 130 E3
Dassel [D] 32 F4
Dassow [D] 18 H3
Dasswang [D] 46 H6
Daszyna [PL] 36 G3
Datça [TR] 154 C2
Datteln [D] 30 H2
Daugai [LT] 24 G2
Daugård [DK] 156 C2
Daugavpils [LV] 200 H3
Dauguli [LV] 198 E4
Daun [D] 30 G6
Dautphetal [D] 32 D6
Daventry [GB] 14 D2
Daviá [GR] 136 D2
Davik [N] 180 B5
Daviot [GB] 6 D5
Davle [CZ] 48 F4
Dávleia [GR] 132 H5
Davlós (Kaplıca) [CY] 154 G4
Davos [CH] 72 A2
Davutlar [TR] 152 D5
Dawlish [GB] 12 E5
Dax [F] 66 B6
Dazkırı [TR] 152 H4
D. Bukovińa [SRB] 142 F4
Ddrinci [BG] 148 F2
Deal [GB] 14 G5
Deão [P] 78 A6
Deauville [F] 26 G3
Debar [MK] 128 C2
Debeburnu [TR] 152 D2
Debelets [BG] 148 C3
Dębe Wielkie [PL] 38 C3
Dębica [PL] 52 D3
Dębina [PL] 50 E3
Dęblin [PL] 38 D5
Debnevo [BG] 148 B4
Dębnica Kaszubska [PL] 22 B2
Dębno [PL] 34 G1
Dębno [PL] 52 B4
Dębno [PL] 52 B5
Debovo [BG] 148 B2
Dębowo [PL] 24 E4
Debrc [SRB] 142 F3
Debrecen [H] 64 G6
Debrznica [PL] 34 H3
Debrzno [PL] 22 C5
Debür [BG] 148 C6
Dęby [PL] 24 C5
Dečani [SRB] 146 B5
Decazeville [F] 68 A5
Dechtice [SK] 62 H3
Decimomannu [I] 118 C7
Děčín [CZ] 48 F2
Decines [F] 68 G3
Decize [F] 56 D4
De Cocksdorp [NL] 16 D2
Dedaj [AL] 144 E4
Dedebağı [TR] 152 G6
Dedelow [D] 20 E5
Dedemsvaart [NL] 16 G4
Dédestapolcsány [H] 64 E4
Dedinci [BG] 148 D3
Dedino [MK] 128 G2
Dedovichi [RUS] 202 B2
Defile de L'Ecluse [F] 70 A2
Dég [H] 76 B3
Degaña [E] 78 F4
Degeberga [S] 158 D2
Degerby [FIN] 168 G1
Degerby [FIN] 176 G5
Degerfors [S] 166 G3
Degerhamn [S] 162 G6
Degerndorf [D] 60 F5
Degernes [N] 166 C3
Deggendorf [D] 60 G2
Değirmenalanı [TR] 152 F6
Değirmendere [TR] 150 G3
Değirmendere [TR] 152 C5
Değirmenyan [TR] 154 D2
Değirmisaz [TR] 152 F1
Dego [N] 194 D1
De Haan [B] 28 F1
Dehesa de Campoamor [E] 104 D3
Deià / Deyá [E] 104 E4
Deidesheim [D] 46 B5
Deifontes [E] 102 E3
Deining [D] 46 H6
Deinze [B] 28 G2
Deizisau [D] 58 H1
Dej [RO] 204 C4
Deje [S] 166 F2
Dekéleia [CY] 154 G5
De Koog [NL] 16 D2
De Kooy [NL] 16 D2
Dekov [BG] 148 B2
Delary [S] 162 C5
Delbrück [D] 32 D3
Delčevo [MK] 128 G1
Delden [NL] 16 G5
Delebäck [S] 166 F4
Delégyháza [H] 76 C1
Deleitosa [E] 96 C1
Đelekovec [HR] 74 G4
Delémont [CH] 58 D5
Delfoí [GR] 132 G5
Delfoí [GR] 132 G5
Delft [NL] 16 C5
Delfzijl [NL] 16 H2
Délia [I] 126 E4
Delianuova [I] 124 C7
Deliatyn [UA] 204 C3
Deliblato [SRB] 142 H2
Deliceto [I] 120 G2
Deliler [TR] 152 E3
Delitzsch [D] 34 C5
Dellach [A] 72 G3
Delle [F] 58 D4
Delme [F] 44 F5
Delmenhorst [D] 18 D5
Delnice [HR] 112 F1
Delouze-Rosières [F] 44 D5
Delsbo [S] 184 D6
Delvin [IRL] 2 E5
Delvina [AL] 132 B1
Delvináki [GR] 132 C1
Demandice [SK] 64 C4
Demänová [SK] 64 D2
Demänovská Jaskyňa Slobody [SK] 64 D2
Demecser [H] 64 H4
Demidov [RUS] 202 C4
Demigny [F] 56 G5
Demirci [TR] 150 F5
Demirci [TR] 152 E2
Demirhanlı [TR] 150 B2
Demir Kapija [MK] 128 G2
Demirköy [TR] 150 C1
Demirköy [TR] 150 G5
Demirören [TR] 152 G3
Demirtaş [TR] 150 F4
Demjansk [RUS] 202 C2
Demmin [D] 20 C3
Demoiselles, Grotte des- [F] 106 E3
Demonte [I] 108 F3
Demre [TR] 154 H3
Demyansk [RUS] 202 C2
Denain [F] 28 G4
Den Andel [NL] 16 G1
Denbigh [GB] 10 C4
Den Burg [NL] 16 D2
Dendermonde (Termonde) [B] 28 H2
Denekamp [NL] 16 G4
Đeneral Jankovič [SRB] 146 C6
Den Haag [NL] 16 C5
Den Helder [NL] 16 D2
Dénia [E] 104 F1
Denizgören [TR] 150 B5
Denizkent [TR] 150 C5
Denizköy [TR] 150 H2
Denizler [TR] 152 G4
Denizli [TR] 152 G5
Denkendorf [D] 60 E2
Denkingen [D] 58 H3
Den Oever [NL] 16 E2
Denzlingen [D] 58 E3
De Panne [B] 28 F1
Derbent [TR] 152 E4
Derby [GB] 10 E5
Derebağ [TR] 152 E6
Derecske [H] 76 G1
Dereham [GB] 14 G2
Dereköy [TR] 150 C1
Dereköy [TR] 152 E4
Dereköy [TR] 152 F2
Dereköy [TR] 152 G6
Dereköy [TR] 152 H5
Dereli [TR] 150 E6
Dereli [TR] 150 H4
Deringaj [HR] 112 H4
Dermantsi [BG] 148 A3
Dermbach [D] 46 F1
Dermulo [I] 72 C4
Derneburg [D] 32 G3
Deronje [SRB] 142 E1
Derreada [P] 94 B3
Derry (Londonderry) [NIR] 2 F2
Deruta [I] 116 A2
Derval [F] 40 F5
Dervéni [GR] 132 G6
Derventa [BIH] 142 D2
Dervishka mogila [BG] 150 A1
Descartes [F] 54 F3
Desenzano del Garda [I] 72 B6
Deset [N] 172 C2
Destína [GR] 132 G5
Desimirovac [SRB] 146 C2
Desio [I] 70 G4
Deskáti [GR] 132 F1
Deskle [SLO] 72 H5
Desmond's Castle [IRL] 4 D3
Desná [CZ] 48 H2
Dešov [CZ] 62 E2
Despeñaperros [E] 96 F6
Despotovac [SRB] 146 C2
Despotovo [SRB] 142 F1
Dessau [D] 34 C4
Deštné [CZ] 50 B3
Destriana [E] 78 G6
Destrnik [SLO] 74 E4
Désulo [I] 118 D5
Desvres [F] 28 D2
Deszk [H] 76 E4
Deta [RO] 204 B5
Detk [H] 64 E5
Detkovo [RUS] 198 G2
Detmold [D] 32 E3
Dětřichov nad Bystřicí [CZ] 50 D4
Dettelbach [D] 46 F4
Dettifoss [IS] 192 C2
Detva [SK] 64 D3
Deurne [NL] 30 F2
Deutschkreutz [A] 62 F6
Deutschlandsberg [A] 74 D3
Deutsch-Wagram [A] 62 F4
Deva [E] 82 H4
Deva [RO] 204 C5
Dévaványa [H] 76 F2
Devčići [HR] 112 F3
Devecikonağı [TR] 150 E5
Devecser [H] 74 H2
Devene [BG] 146 G3
Deventer [NL] 16 F5
Deveselu [RO] 148 A1
Devetaki [BG] 148 B3
Devic [MK] 128 E2
Devin [BG] 130 D1
Devizes [GB] 12 G3
Devnya [BG] 148 F3
Dewsbury [GB] 10 F4
Deyá / Deià [E] 104 E4
Deza [E] 90 C4
Dezzo [I] 72 B4
Dhërmi [AL] 128 B6
Diafáni [GR] 140 H2
Diagučiai [LT] 200 G4
Diakoftó [GR] 132 G6
Dialampí [GR] 130 F3
Diamante [I] 124 C3
Dianalund [DK] 156 F3
Diano Marina [I] 108 G4
Diarviailiai [LT] 200 F4
Diásello [GR] 132 F1
Diatlovo [BY] 202 A6
Diavatá [GR] 128 H4
Dicomano [I] 110 F5
Didcot [GB] 14 D3
Didesti [RO] 148 B1
Dídyma [GR] 136 F2
Didymóteicho [GR] 130 H1
Die [F] 68 G6
Dieburg [D] 46 C3
Diedorf [D] 32 G5
Diego Alvaro [E] 88 D4
Diekirch [L] 44 F2
Diemelstadt [D] 32 E4
Dienne [F] 68 B4
Dienten [A] 72 G1
Diepholz [D] 32 D1
Dieppe [F] 28 C4
Dierdorf [D] 46 B1
Dieren [NL] 16 F5
Dierhagen [D] 20 C2
Diesdorf [D] 32 H1
Diessen [D] 60 D5
Diest [B] 30 D4
Dietenheim [D] 60 B4
Dietfurt [D] 46 H6
Dietikon [CH] 58 F5
Dietmannsdorf [A] 74 D3
Dietmannsried [D] 60 C5
Dieue-sur-Meuse [F] 44 D4
Dieulefit [F] 68 F6
Dieulouard [F] 44 E5
Dieuze [F] 44 F5
Dieveniškės [LT] 200 G6
Diever [NL] 16 G3
Diez [D] 46 B2
Differdange [L] 44 E3
Digerberget [S] 182 G4
Digermulen [N] 192 D4
Digernes [N] 180 D3
Dignac [F] 66 E2
Dignano [I] 72 G4
Digne-les-Bains [F] 108 D3
Digny [F] 26 H6
Digoin [F] 56 E5
Dijon [F] 56 G4
Dikaia [GR] 150 A2
Dikanäs [S] 190 F4
Dikance [SRB] 128 C1
Dikili [TR] 152 C3
Dikli [LV] 198 E4
Diksmuide [B] 28 F2
Diktaío Ántro [GR] 140 F5
Diktýnaion [GR] 140 B4
Dílesi [GR] 134 C5
Dillenberg [D] 32 D6
Dillingen [D] 44 F3
Dillingen [D] 60 C3
Dílos [GR] 138 E2
Dilwyn [GB] 12 G1
Dímaina [GR] 136 F2
Dimaro [I] 72 C4
Dímitra [GR] 132 G1
Dimitrovgrad [BG] 148 C6
Dimitrovgrad [SRB] 146 E4
Dimmelsvik [N] 170 B5
Dimovo [BG] 146 E2
Dinami [I] 124 D6
Dinan [F] 26 C5
Dinant [B] 30 D6
Dinar [TR] 152 H4
Dinard [F] 26 C4
Dingelstädt [D] 32 G5
Dingle [S] 166 C5
Dingle / An Daingean [IRL] 4 A3
Dingli [M] 126 C6
Dingolfing [D] 60 F3
Dingwall [GB] 6 D4
Dinkelsbühl [D] 46 F6
Dinklage [D] 18 C6
Dinozé [F] 58 C2
Dinslaken [D] 30 G2
Dio [S] 162 D5
Díon [GR] 128 G6
Diosgyör [H] 64 F4
Dipkarpaz (Rizokárpasox) [CY] 154 H4
Dipótamos [GR] 130 D2
Dippoldiswalde [D] 48 E1
Dirgenler [TR] 154 H3
Dirnaich [D] 60 F3
Disenå [N] 172 C5
Disentis / Mustér [CH] 70 G1
Disneyland [F] 42 G3
Dispílí [GR] 128 E5
Diss [GB] 14 G2
Dístomo [GR] 132 H5
Dístrato [GR] 128 D6
Ditzingen [D] 58 G1
Diva Slatina [BG] 146 F3
Divci [SRB] 146 A1
Divčibare [SRB] 146 A2
Dívčí Hrady [CZ] 62 F2
Dives-sur-Mer [F] 26 F3
Divič [SRB] 142 E3
Divínski Hrad [SK] 64 D4
Divjakë [AL] 128 A4
Divonne-les-Bains [F] 70 B2
Dívri [GR] 132 G4
Divuša [HR] 142 A2
Dixence [CH] 70 D3
Dizy-le-Gros [F] 28 G6
Djäkneböle [S] 190 H6
Djala [SRB] 76 E4
Djauvik [S] 168 F5
Djupfest [N] 190 B6
Djupfors [S] 190 F3
Djúpivogur [IS] 192 C3
Djupsjö [S] 182 F1
Djupvik [N] 192 G2
Djura [S] 172 H4
Djurakovac [SRB] 146 B5
Djuramåla [DK] 162 E6
Djurås [S] 172 H4
D. Kronovo [SLO] 74 D5
Dłoń [PL] 36 C4
Dlouhá Loučka [CZ] 50 D4
Długie [PL] 36 A1
Długołęka [PL] 36 D6
Długosiodło [PL] 38 C1
Dmitriyev-L'govckiy [RUS] 202 F5
Dmitrov [RUS] 202 F2
Dmitrovsk-Orlovskiy [RUS] 202 F5
Dniprodzerzhyns'k [UA] 204 G1
Dnipropetrovs'k [UA] 204 H1
Dnipropudne [UA] 204 H2
Dno [RUS] 202 B2
Dobanovci [SRB] 142 G2
Dobapuszta [H] 76 E1
Dobbiaco / Toblach [I] 72 E3
Dobbrikow [D] 34 D3
Dobczyce [PL] 52 A4
Dobel [D] 58 G1
Dobele [LV] 198 D5
Döbeln [D] 34 D6
Doberlug Kirchhain [D] 34 E4
Döbern [D] 34 G5
Dobersberg [A] 62 D2
Dobiegniew [PL] 20 H6
Doboj [BIH] 142 D3
Doboz [H] 76 G3
Dobra [PL] 20 G4
Dobra [PL] 36 F4
Dobra [PL] 52 B4
Dobra [RO] 146 F1
Dobra Gora [MNE] 144 D4
Dobrá Niva [SK] 64 C3
Dobřany [CZ] 48 D5
Dobrčane [SRB] 146 D5
Dobrcz [PL] 22 D5
Dobre [PL] 38 C2
Dobre Miasto [PL] 22 G3
Döbriach [A] 72 H3
Dobrich [BG] 148 F2
Dobřichovice [CZ] 48 F4
Dobri Do [SRB] 146 C4
Dobri dol [BG] 146 F2
Dobrin [BG] 148 F1
Dobrinishte [BG] 130 B1
Dobrinja [BIH] 142 B3
Dobříš [CZ] 48 F4
Dobrits [BG] 148 E5
Dobrna [SLO] 74 D4
Dobrodan [BG] 148 B4
Dobrodzień [PL] 50 F2
Döbrököz [H] 76 B4
Dobromani [BIH] 144 C3
Dobromierz [PL] 50 B1
Dobromierz [PL] 50 H1
Dobromirka [BG] 148 C3
Dobromirtsi [BG] 130 F2
Dobromyl' [UA] 52 F5
Dobro Polje [BIH] 144 D2
Dobroselica [SRB] 146 A3
Dobrošinci [MK] 128 G2
Dobrosloveni [RO] 148 A1
Dobrosołowo [PL] 36 E3
Dobrosyn [UA] 52 H3
Dobroszyce [PL] 36 D6
Dobroteşti [RO] 148 B1
Dobrotitsa [BG] 148 F1
Dobrovelychkivka [UA] 204 F2
Dobrovnik [SLO] 74 F3
Dobrovodsky Hrad [SK] 62 H3
Dobrovol'sk [RUS] 24 D1
Dobrš [CZ] 48 E6
Dobruchi [RUS] 198 G2
Dobrun [BIH] 144 E1
Dobrush [BY] 202 D6
Dobrush [UA] 202 D6
Dobruška [CZ] 50 B3
Dobrzany [PL] 20 G5
Dobrzejewice [PL] 22 E6
Dobrzeń Wielki [PL] 50 E2
Dobrzyca [PL] 36 D4
Dobrzyń nad Wisłą [PL] 36 G2
Dobšinská l'Adová Jaskyňa [SK] 64 E2
Dóc [H] 76 E4
Dochamps [B] 30 E6
Dockasberg [S] 196 B2
Docksta [S] 184 F2
Doclea [MNE] 144 E4
Dödafallet [S] 184 D3
Döderhult [S] 162 G3
Dodóni [GR] 132 D2
Dodši [HR] 142 A1
Dodurga [TR] 150 G5
Doe Castle [IRL] 2 E1
Doesburg [NL] 16 F5
Doetinchem [NL] 16 F5
Doganbey [TR] 152 C6
Doğanbey [TR] 152 C5
Doganović [SRB] 146 C6
Döge [H] 64 H4
Döğer [TR] 152 H1
Dogliani [I] 108 G2
Dogueno [P] 94 C4
Dohňany [SK] 50 E6
Doiber [A] 74 E2
Dojč [SK] 62 G3
Dojeviće [SRB] 146 B4
Dojrenci [BG] 148 B3
Dokka [N] 170 H3
Dokkas [S] 192 H6
Dokkedal [DK] 160 E4
Dokkum [NL] 16 F2
Doksy [CZ] 48 G2
Doktorce [PL] 24 E6
Dolac [SRB] 146 B5
Dólar [E] 102 F4
Dolceácqua [I] 108 F4
Dol-de-Bretagne [F] 26 C4
Dole [F] 56 H4
Dølemo [N] 164 E4
Dolenci [MK] 128 D3
Dolenja Vas [SLO] 74 C6
Dolga Vas [SLO] 74 F3
Dolgellau [GB] 10 B5
Dolgorukovo [RUS] 202 G2
Dolhobyczów [PL] 52 H2
Doli [HR] 144 C3
Dolianá [GR] 132 C1
Dolianova [I] 118 D6
Dolice [PL] 20 G6
Dolíchi [GR] 128 G6
Dolina [SLO] 74 B6
Doljani [HR] 112 H4
Doljani [MNE] 144 E4
Doljevac [SRB] 146 D4
Döllach [A] 72 G2
Döllbach [D] 46 E2
Dolle [D] 34 B2
Døllii [N] 180 H4
Döllstädt [D] 32 H6
Dolmen de Dombate [E] 78 B2
Dolna Banya [BG] 146 G5
Dolna Dikanya [BG] 146 F5
Dolna Grupa [PL] 22 E5
Dolná Krupá [SK] 62 H4
Dolna Mahala [BG] 148 B5

Dolna Mitropolia [BG] 148 B3
Dolna Mitropoliya [BG] 148 A3
Dolná Strehová [SK] 64 D4
Dolni Chiflik [BG] 148 F3
Dolni Cibăr [BG] 146 F2
Dolni Dŭbnik [BG] 148 A3
Dolní Dvořiště [CZ] 62 C3
Dolní Kounice [CZ] 62 F2
Dolní Krupá [CZ] 48 G2
Dolni Lom [BG] 146 E3
Dolní Ročov [CZ] 48 E3
Dolno Dupeni [MK] 128 E4
Dolno Kamartsi [BG] 146 G4
Dolno Kosovrasti [MK] 128 C2
Dolno Levski [BG] 148 A5
Dolno Novkovo [BG] 148 D3
Dolno Tserovene [BG] 146 F3
Dolno Ujno [BG] 146 E5
Dolný Kubín [SK] 50 G6
Dolo [I] 110 H1
Dolores [E] 104 D3
Doloscy [RUS] 198 H6
Dolovo [SRB] 142 H2
Dolsk [PL] 36 C4
Dołubowo [PL] 38 E1
Dolyna [UA] 52 H6
Dolyns'ka [UA] 202 F8
Dolzhicy [RUS] 198 H2
Dołżyca [PL] 52 E6
Dom [A] 74 B2
Domaháza [H] 64 E4
Domaj-Has [AL] 146 B6
Domaniç [TR] 150 G5
Domanovići [BIH] 144 C3
Domašov [CZ] 50 D3
Domaszowice [PL] 50 E1
Domažlice [CZ] 48 D5
Dombas [N] 180 G5
Dombasle [F] 44 F5
Dombegyház [H] 76 G4
Dombóvár [H] 76 B4
Dombrád [H] 64 H4
Dombrot-le-Sec [F] 58 B2
Domburg [NL] 16 B6
Doméniko [GR] 132 F1
Domèvre-en-Haye [F] 44 E5
Domfront [F] 26 E5
Domingão [P] 86 D4
Dömitz [D] 18 H5
Domme [F] 66 G4
Dommitzsch [D] 34 D4
Domnitsa [GR] 132 F4
Domnovo [RUS] 22 H2
Domodedovo [RUS] 202 F3
Domodóssola [I] 70 E3
Domokós [GR] 132 G3
Domousnice [CZ] 48 G3
Dompaire [F] 58 C2
Dompierre [F] 56 E5
Dompierre-du-Chemin [F] 26 D5
Dompierre-sur-Besbre [F] 56 E5
Dompierre-sur-Mer [F] 54 C4
Domrémy-la-Pucelle [F] 44 D6
Dömsöd [H] 76 C2
Domurcali [TR] 150 B1
Dómus de Maria [I] 118 C8
Domusnóvas [I] 118 B6
Domžale [SLO] 74 C5
Donado [E] 80 G3
Donaghadee [NIR] 2 H3
Donaghmore [IRL] 4 E3
Doña Mencía [E] 102 C2
Donaueschingen [D] 58 F3
Donaustauf [D] 60 F2
Donauwörth [D] 60 D2
Don Benito [E] 96 B3
Doncaster [GB] 10 F4
Dondurma [TR] 150 B5
Donegal / Dún na nGall [IRL] 2 E2
Donja Brela [HR] 144 B2
Donja Brezna [MNE] 144 D3
Donja Bukovica [MNE] 144 E3
Donja Kamenica [SRB] 146 A1
Donja Kamenica [SRB] 146 E3
Donja Ljubata [SRB] 146 E5
Donja Šatornja [SRB] 146 B2
Donja Suvaja [HR] 112 H4
Donja-Vrijeska [HR] 74 G6
Donje Ljupče [SRB] 146 C5
Donje Petrčane [HR] 112 F5
Donji Koričani [BIH] 142 C3
Donji Krcin [SRB] 146 C3
Donji Lapac [HR] 112 H4
Donji Lipovik [MK] 128 G2
Donji Miholjac [HR] 76 B6
Donji Milanovac [SRB] 146 D1
Donji Stajevac [SRB] 146 E5
Donji Vakuf [BIH] 142 C4
Donji Zemunik [HR] 112 G5
Don Juan, Cueva de- [E] 98 D5
Donnalucata [I] 126 F5
Donnersbach [A] 62 B6
Donnersbachwald [A] 74 B1
Donostia-San Sebastián [E] 84 B2
Donovaly [SK] 64 C2
Dontilly [F] 42 G5
Donzenac [F] 66 G3
Donzère [F] 68 F6
Donzy [F] 56 D3
Doohooma / Dumha Thuama [IRL] 2 B3
Doonbeg [IRL] 2 B6
Doonloughan [IRL] 2 B4
Doorn [NL] 16 E5
Doornik (Tournai) [B] 28 G3
Dörarp [S] 162 C4
Dorchester [GB] 12 F5
Dordives [F] 42 G5
Dordrecht [NL] 16 D5
Dorëz [AL] 128 C3
Dorfen [D] 60 F4
Dorfmark [D] 18 F6
Dorgali [I] 118 E4
Doria, Castello- [I] 110 A3
Dório [GR] 136 D3
Dorkáda [GR] 130 B4
Dorking [GB] 14 E5
Dorkovo [BG] 148 A6
Dormagen [D] 30 G4
Dormánd [H] 64 E6
Dormans [F] 44 A3
Dornas [F] 68 E5
Dornauberg [A] 72 E2
Dornava [SLO] 74 E4
Dornbirn [A] 60 B6
Dornburg [D] 34 B6
Dorndorf [D] 46 F1
Dornes [F] 56 D5
Dorno [I] 70 F5
Dornoch [GB] 6 E4
Dornstetten [D] 58 G2
Dornum [D] 18 B3
Dorog [H] 64 C6
Dorogobuzh [RUS] 202 D4
Dorohoi [RO] 204 D3
Dorohucza [PL] 38 F6
Dorokhovo [RUS] 202 E3
Dorotea [S] 190 F5
Dörpen [D] 16 H3
Dörpstedt [D] 18 E2
Dorsten [D] 30 H2
Dortan [F] 68 H1
Dortmund [D] 32 C4
Dörtyol (Prastio) [CY] 154 G5
Dorum [D] 18 D3
Dörverden [D] 18 E6
Dörzbach [D] 46 E5
Dosbarrios [E] 96 G2
Döşeme [TR] 154 C3
Dos Hermanas [E] 94 G6
Dospat [BG] 130 D1
Dos Torres [E] 96 C5
Døstrup [DK] 156 B3
Dotnuva [LT] 200 F4
Douai [F] 28 F4
Douamont, Fort du- [F] 44 D3
Douarnenez [F] 40 B3
Douchy [F] 42 G6
Doucier [F] 58 A6
Doudeville [F] 26 H2
Doué-la-Fontaine [F] 54 E2
Douglas [GB] 8 D4
Douglas [GBM] 10 B2
Doulaincourt [F] 44 D6
Doulevant-le-Château [F] 44 C6
Doullens [F] 28 E4
Dourdan [F] 42 F4
Dourgne [F] 106 B4
Doussard [F] 70 B3
Douvaine [F] 70 B2
Douzy [F] 44 D2
Dover [GB] 14 G5
Dovre [N] 180 G5
Downham Market [GB] 14 F2
Downings [IRL] 2 E1
Downpatrick [NIR] 2 G4
Dowra [IRL] 2 E3
Dowsk [BY] 202 D5
Doxáto [GR] 130 D3
Dozón / Castro [E] 78 C4
Dozulé [F] 26 G3
Drabiv [UA] 202 E7
Drac, Coves del- [E] 104 F5
Dračevo [MK] 128 E1
Drachenfels [D] 30 H5
Drachenwand [A] 60 H5
Drachselsried [D] 48 D6
Drachten [NL] 16 F2
Drag [N] 190 C4
Drag Ájluokta [N] 192 E5
Dragalevtsi [BG] 146 F5
Drăgănești de Vede [RO] 148 B1
Drăgănești-Olt [RO] 148 A1
Drăgănești-Vlașca [RO] 148 C1
Dragaš [SRB] 146 B6
Drăgășani [RO] 204 D5
Dragatuš [SLO] 112 G1
Dragichevo [BG] 146 F5
Draginje [SRB] 146 A1
Draginovo [BG] 148 A6
Dragocvet [SRB] 146 C2
Dragoevo [MK] 128 F1
Dragoman [BG] 146 F4
Dragomir [BG] 148 A5
Dragomirovo [BG] 146 F5
Dragomirovo [BG] 148 B2
Dragomirovo [BG] 148 C3
Dragon, Caverne du- [F] 44 B2
Dragør [DK] 156 H3
Dragotina [HR] 142 A1
Dragov Doll [MK] 128 E2
Dragovishtitsa [BG] 146 E5
Dragsfjärd [FIN] 176 E5
Dragsholm Slot [DK] 156 F2
Draguignan [F] 108 D5
Drahanovice [CZ] 50 C5
Drahonice [CZ] 48 F6
Drahovce [SK] 62 H3
Draka [BG] 148 E5
Drakčići [SRB] 146 B3
Drakšenić [BIH] 142 B2
Dráma [GR] 130 D3
Dramče [MK] 146 E6
Drammen [N] 164 H1
Drangedal [N] 164 F3
Drängsered [S] 162 B4
Drängsmark [S] 196 A4
Drânic [RO] 146 G1
Dransfeld [D] 32 F4
Dranske [D] 20 D1
Drasenhofen [A] 62 F3
Drava Fok [H] 74 H5
Drávaszabolcs [H] 76 B6
Dravískos [GR] 130 C3
Dravograd [SLO] 74 C3
Drawno [PL] 20 H6
Drawsko Pomorskie [PL] 20 H5
Drążdżewo [PL] 24 B6
Draženov [CZ] 48 D5
Drażniew [PL] 38 E2
Drebkau [D] 34 F4
Drégelypalánk [H] 64 C5
Drei [D] 46 G1
Dreilingen [D] 18 G6
Dren [MK] 128 F3
Dren [SRB] 146 B4
Drenchia [I] 72 H4
Drenovac [SRB] 146 D5
Drenovci [HR] 142 E2
Drenovets [BG] 146 F2
Drensteinfurt [D] 32 C3
Drépano [GR] 128 F5
Dresden [D] 34 E6
Dretyń [PL] 22 B3
Dreux [F] 42 E3
Drevsjø [N] 182 D6
Drewitz [D] 34 C3
Drewitz [D] 34 E2
Drezdenko [PL] 36 B1
Drežnica [HR] 112 F2
Dreznik-Grad [HR] 112 G2
Driebergen [NL] 16 E5
Drienovo [SK] 64 C4
Driffield [GB] 10 G3
Drimoleague [IRL] 4 B5
Drina Kanjon [BIH] 142 E4
Drinjača [BIH] 142 E4
Drinovci [BIH] 144 B2
Driny [SK] 62 G4
Drionville [F] 28 E2
Driva [N] 180 H4
Drivstua [N] 180 H4
Drizë [AL] 128 C4
Drlače [SRB] 142 F4
Drnholec [CZ] 62 F2
Drniš [HR] 142 A5
Drnovo [SLO] 74 D6
Drøbak [N] 166 B2
Drobeta-Turnu Severin [RO] 204 C6
Drobin [PL] 36 H1
Drochtersen [D] 18 E3
Drogheda / Droichead Átha [IRL] 2 F5
Drohiczyn [PL] 38 E2
Drohobych [UA] 52 G5
Droichead Átha / Drogheda [IRL] 2 F5
Droichead Nua / Newbridge [IRL] 2 E6
Droitwich [GB] 12 G1
Drołtowice [PL] 36 D5
Dromahair [IRL] 2 D3
Dromcolliher [IRL] 4 C4
Dromore [NIR] 2 G4
Dromore West [IRL] 2 D3
Dronero [I] 108 F2
Dronninglund [DK] 160 E3
Dronten [NL] 16 F4
Dropla [BG] 148 G2
Drosáto [GR] 128 H3
Drosbacken [S] 182 E6
Drosendorf Stadt [A] 62 E2
Drosiá [GR] 134 B5
Drosopigí [GR] 128 E4
Drosopigí [GR] 132 D3
Drosselbjerg [DK] 156 E3
Drottninghaug [N] 180 D4
Droúseia [CY] 154 F6
Drozdowo [PL] 22 B2
Drugan [BG] 146 F5
Drumconrath [IRL] 2 F5
Drumevo [BG] 148 E3
Drumkeeran [IRL] 2 D3
Drumlish [IRL] 2 E4
Drummore [GB] 8 C5
Drumnadrochit [GB] 6 D5
Drumshanbo [IRL] 2 D4
Drumsna [IRL] 2 D4
Drusenheim [F] 44 H5
Druskininkai [LT] 24 F3
Drusti [LV] 198 F4
Druten [NL] 16 E5
Družetic [SRB] 146 A1
Druzhba [BG] 148 G3
Druzhba [RUS] 24 B2
Druzhnaja Gorka [RUS] 198 H1
Drvar [BIH] 142 A3
Drvenik [HR] 144 B3
Dryanovo [BG] 148 C4
Drygały [PL] 24 D4
Drymós [GR] 128 H4
Dryópi [GR] 136 F2
Dryopída [GR] 138 C2
Dryós [GR] 138 E3
Drzewce [PL] 36 F3
Drzewiany [PL] 22 B3
Drzewica [PL] 38 B5
D. Stupnica [HR] 142 A2
Duagh [IRL] 4 C3
Duas Igrejas [P] 80 G4
Dub [SRB] 146 A2
Dubá [CZ] 48 G2
Dubac [HR] 144 C4
Dubăsari [MD] 204 E3
Dubechne [UA] 38 H4
Duben [D] 34 E4
Dubí [CZ] 48 E2
Dubica [HR] 142 B2
Dubienka [PL] 38 G6
Dubin [PL] 36 D5
Dubinino [RUS] 178 F2
Dubliany [UA] 52 G5
Dublin / Baile Átha Cliath [IRL] 2 F6
Dubna [RUS] 202 E2
Dub nad Moravou [CZ] 50 D5
Dubňany [CZ] 62 G2
Dubnica nad Váhom [SK] 64 A2
Dŭbnitsa [BG] 130 C1
Dubno [UA] 202 B8
Dubovsko [BIH] 112 H3
Dubrava [BIH] 142 C3
Dubrava [HR] 74 F5
Dubrava [HR] 74 G4
Dubrava [RUS] 24 D2
Dubrave [BIH] 142 E2
Dubravica [BIH] 142 C4
Dubravka [HR] 144 D4
Dubrovka [RUS] 198 H5
Dubrovnik [HR] 144 C4
Dubrovno [RUS] 198 H3
Dubrovytsia [UA] 202 B7
Dubrowna [BY] 202 C4
Ducey [F] 26 D4
Duchcov [CZ] 48 E2
Ducherow [D] 20 E4
Duclair [F] 26 H3
Dudar [H] 76 A1
Dudelange [L] 44 E3
Düdenköy [TR] 154 H2
Duderstadt [D] 32 G4
Dudeștii Vechi [RO] 76 F5
Dudince [SK] 64 C4
Düdingen [CH] 58 D6
Dudley [GB] 10 D6
Due Carrare [I] 110 G1
Dueñas [E] 88 F1
Duesund [N] 170 B2
Dueville [I] 72 D6
Dufftown [GB] 6 F5
Duga Poljana [SRB] 146 B4
Duga Resa [HR] 112 G1
Duge Njive [HR] 144 B2
Dugi Rat [HR] 144 A2
Duğla [TR] 152 C2
Dugopolje [HR] 144 A2
Dugo Selo [HR] 74 F6
Duhnen [D] 18 D3
Duingen [D] 32 F3
Duingt [F] 70 B3
Duino [I] 72 H5
Duisburg [D] 30 G3
Duka [H] 74 G2
Dukat [AL] 128 A6
Dukat [SRB] 146 E5
Dukhovshchina [RUS] 202 D4
Dukla [PL] 52 D5
Dukovany [CZ] 62 F2
Dūkštas [LT] 200 H4
Dukštos [LT] 200 G5
Dŭlbok Izvor [BG] 148 C6
Duleek [IRL] 2 F5
Dŭlgopol [BG] 148 F3
Dülken [D] 30 F3
Dülmen [D] 16 H6
Dulnain Bridge [GB] 6 E5
Dulovka [RUS] 198 G4
Dulovo [BG] 148 E1
Dulpetorpet [N] 172 D4
Dumača [SRB] 142 F3
Dumakömlöd [H] 76 C3
Dumanlı [TR] 152 G4
Dumbarton [GB] 8 D3
Dumbrăveni [RO] 148 F1
Dumfries [GB] 8 D5
Dumha Thuama / Doohooma [IRL] 2 B3
Dumlupınar [TR] 152 H2
Dümpelfeld [D] 30 G6
Dun [F] 44 D3
Duna [N] 190 C4
Dunaengus [IRL] 2 B5
Dunaff [IRL] 2 F1
Dunaföldvár [H] 76 C3
Dunaharaszti [H] 76 C1
Dunaïvtsi [UA] 204 D2
Dunajská Streda [SK] 62 H5
Dunakeszi [H] 64 C6
Dunakiliti [H] 62 G5
Dunany [IRL] 2 F5
Dunapataj [H] 76 C3
Dunas de São Jacinto [P] 80 B5
Dunaszeg [H] 62 H5
Dunaszekcső [H] 76 C5
Dunaszentbenedek [H] 76 C3
Dunasziget [H] 62 G5
Dunatetétlen [H] 76 C3
Dunaújváros [H] 76 C2
Dunavecse [H] 76 C2
Dunavtsi [BG] 146 E2
Dunbar [GB] 8 F3
Dunbeath [GB] 6 F3
Dunblane [GB] 8 E2
Dunboy Castle [IRL] 4 A5
Dunboyne [IRL] 2 F6
Dunbrody Abbey [IRL] 4 E5
Duncormick [IRL] 4 F5
Dundaga [LV] 198 C4
Dundalk / Dún Dealgan [IRL] 2 F4
Dún Dealgan / Dundalk [IRL] 2 F4
Dundee [GB] 8 F2
Dunderland [N] 190 E2
Dunfanaghy [IRL] 2 E1
Dunfermline [GB] 8 E3
Dungannon [NIR] 2 F3
Dungarvan [IRL] 4 E5
Dungiven [NIR] 2 F2
Dunglow / An Clochán Liath [IRL] 2 E2
Dungourney [IRL] 4 D5
Dunje [MK] 128 F3
Dunjica [MK] 128 G2
Dunker [S] 168 C3
Dunkerque [F] 14 H6
Dunkerque Ouest [F] 14 H6
Dunkineely [IRL] 2 D2
Duńkowice [PL] 52 F3
Dún Laoghaire [IRL] 2 F6
Dunlavin [IRL] 4 F3
Dunleer [IRL] 2 F5
Dun-le-Palestel [F] 54 H5
Dunloe, Gap of- [IRL] 4 B4
Dunloy [NIR] 2 G2
Dunmanway [IRL] 4 C5
Dunmore [IRL] 2 C4
Dunmore Caves [IRL] 4 E4
Dunmore East [IRL] 4 E5
Dunmurry [NIR] 2 G3
Dún na nGall / Donegal [IRL] 2 E2
Dunoon [GB] 8 C3
Duns [GB] 8 F4
Dunshaughlin [IRL] 2 F5
Dunstable [GB] 14 E3
Dun-sur-Auron [F] 56 C4
Dunure [GB] 8 C4
Dunvegan [GB] 6 B4
Duoddar Sion [N] 194 B2
Dupnitsa [BG] 146 F6
Duquesa, Castillo de la- [E] 100 H5
Durabeyler [TR] 152 E1
Durach [BG] 148 E2
Duran [BG] 148 E2
Durance [F] 66 D5
Durango [E] 82 H4
Durankulak [BG] 148 G1
Duras [F] 66 E4
Durasıllı [TR] 152 E3
Durban-Corbières [F] 106 C5
Durbe [LV] 198 B6
Durbuy [B] 30 E5
Dúrcal [E] 102 E4
Đurđenovac [HR] 142 D1
Đurđevac [HR] 74 G5
Đurđevića Tara [MNE] 144 E2
Đurđevik [BIH] 142 E3
Đurđevi Stupovi [SRB] 146 B4
Düren [D] 30 G4
Durham [GB] 8 F6
Durhasan [TR] 152 F3
Durlas / Thurles [IRL] 4 E3
Durness [GB] 6 D2
Dürnkrut [A] 62 G4
Dürnstein [A] 62 D4
Durnstein [A] 74 B2
Durón [E] 90 A5
Durrës [AL] 128 A3
Durrow [IRL] 4 E3
Durrow Abbey [IRL] 2 E5
Durrus [IRL] 4 B5
Dursunbey [TR] 152 E1
Durtal [F] 42 A6
Duruelo de la Sierra [E] 90 A2
Dusetos [LT] 200 G4
Dŭskotna [BG] 148 E3
Dusnok [H] 76 C4
Dusocin [PL] 22 E5
Düsseldorf [D] 30 G3
Duszniki [PL] 36 B2
Duszniki-Zdrój [PL] 50 B3
Dutluca [TR] 150 F6
Dutluca [TR] 152 G5
Dutovlje [SLO] 72 H5
Duved [S] 182 E1
Düvertepe [TR] 152 E2
Düzağac [TR] 152 H2
Duztarla [TR] 152 C2
Dvärsätt [S] 182 G2
Dve Mogili [BG] 148 C2
Dvor [HR] 142 A2
Dvor [SLO] 74 C6
Dvorce [CZ] 50 D4
Dvory nad Žitavou [SK] 64 B5
Dvůr Králové nad Labem [CZ] 50 A3
Dwingeloo [NL] 16 G3
Dyat'kovo [RUS] 202 E5
Dyatlitsy [RUS] 178 G5
Dybäck [S] 158 C3
Dyblin [PL] 36 G2
Dyce [GB] 6 F6
Dyck [D] 30 G4
Dygowo [PL] 20 H3
Dylewo [PL] 24 C5
Dymchurch [GB] 14 F5
Dymniki [BY] 38 G2
Dynów [PL] 52 E4
Dyranut [N] 170 E4
Dyrnes [N] 180 F1
Dyrráchio [GR] 136 D3
Dysbodarna [S] 172 F3
Dýstos [GR] 134 C5
Dyulino [BG] 148 F3
Dyuni [BG] 148 F4
Dyvik [S] 168 E3
Džepišta [MK] 128 C2
Dzhankoi [UA] 204 H3
Dzhebel [BG] 130 F1
Dzhurovo [BG] 146 G4
Dzhuryn [UA] 204 E2
Dziadkowice [PL] 38 E2
Dziadowa Kłoda [PL] 36 D6
Działdowo [PL] 22 G5
Działoszyce [PL] 52 B3
Działoszyn [PL] 36 F6
Dziemiany [PL] 22 C3
Dzierzgoń [PL] 22 F4
Dzierzki [PL] 22 H4
Dzierżoniów [PL] 50 C2
Dzietrzychowo [PL] 24 B2
Džigolj [SRB] 146 D3
Dzivin [BY] 38 H3
Dziwnów [PL] 20 F3
Dziwnówek [PL] 20 F3
Džul'unica [BG] 148 C3
Džumajlija [MK] 128 F1
Dźwierzuty [PL] 22 H4
Dźwirzyno [PL] 20 G3
Dzyarechyn [BY] 24 H5
Dzyarzhynsk [BY] 202 B5

E

Easingwold [GB] 10 F3
Easky [IRL] 2 D3
Eastbourne [GB] 14 E6
East Grinstead [GB] 14 E5
East Kilbride [GB] 8 D3
Eastleigh [GB] 12 H5
Eaux-Bonnes [F] 84 D4
Eaux-Chaudes [F] 84 D4
Eauze [F] 66 D6
Ebberup [DK] 156 D3
Ebbo / Epoo [FIN] 178 B4
Ebbw Vale [GB] 12 F2
Ebecik [TR] 152 F5
Ebeleben [D] 32 H5
Ebelsbach [D] 46 F3
Ebeltoft [DK] 156 F1
Ebeltoft Færge [DK] 156 E1
Eben [A] 60 E6
Ebenfurth [A] 62 F5
Eben im Pongau [A] 72 H1
Ebensee [A] 62 A5
Eberbach [D] 46 B3
Eberbach [D] 46 D5
Eberdingen [D] 46 C6
Ebergötzen [D] 32 G4
Ebermannstadt [D] 46 G4
Ebern [D] 46 G3
Eberndorf [A] 74 C3
Ebersbach [D] 48 G1
Ebersberg [D] 60 E4
Eberschwang [A] 60 H4
Ebersdorf [D] 18 E4
Ebersdorf [D] 60 H3
Eberstein [A] 74 C3
Eberstein [D] 58 F1
Eberswalde [D] 34 F1
Ebes [H] 64 G6
Ebeylı [TR] 150 G4
Ebingen [D] 58 G3
Éboli [I] 120 F4
Ebrach [D] 46 F4
Ebreichsdorf [A] 62 F5
Ebreuil [F] 56 C6
Ebstorf [D] 18 G6
Eceabat [TR] 130 H5
Echallens [CH] 70 C1
Echallon [F] 68 H2
Echarri / Etxarri [E] 84 A3
Échevennoz [I] 70 D3
Echínos [GR] 130 E2
Échourgnac [F] 66 E3
Echternach [L] 44 F2
Écija [E] 102 B2
Eck [A] 62 A6
Ečka [SRB] 142 G1
Eckartsau [A] 62 F5
Eckartsberga [D] 34 B6
Eckernförde [D] 18 F1
Eckerö [FIN] 176 A5
Eckersholm [S] 162 D2
Eckwarden [D] 18 D4
Ecole Valentine [F] 58 B4
Ecommoy [F] 42 B5
Ecouis [F] 28 C6
Ecoust-St-Mein [F] 28 F4
Ecsegfalva [H] 76 F2
Ecthe [D] 32 G4
Ecueillé [F] 54 G3
Ecury [F] 44 B4
Ed [S] 166 C4
Ed[S] 184 E2
Eda [S] 166 D1
Eda glasbruk [S] 166 D1
Edam [NL] 16 E4
Edane [S] 166 E2
Eddelak [D] 18 E3
Ede [NL] 16 E5
Ede [S] 182 H1
Edebäck [S] 172 F6
Edebo [S] 168 E1
Edeby [S] 168 E1
Edefors [S] 184 C1
Edefors [S] 196 A2
Edelény [H] 64 F4
Edenbridge [GB] 14 E5
Edenderry [IRL] 2 E6
Edenkoben [D] 46 B5
Edersee [D] 32 E5
Édessa [GR] 128 F4
Edevik [S] 190 D5
Edewecht [D] 18 C5
Edgeworthstown [IRL] 2 E5
Edhem [S] 166 F6
Edinburgh [GB] 8 E3
Edincik [TR] 150 D4
Edineț [MD] 204 D3
Edirne [TR] 150 A2
Edland [N] 164 D1
Ēdole [LV] 198 B5
Édolo [I] 72 B4
Édon [F] 66 E2
Edremit [TR] 152 C1
Edsbro [S] 168 E1
Edsbruk [S] 162 G1
Edsbyn [S] 174 C2
Edsele [S] 184 D1
Edsleskog [S] 166 D4
Edsta [S] 184 E6
Edsvalla [S] 166 E2
Eeklo [B] 28 G1
Eelde [NL] 16 G2
Een [NL] 16 G2
Efendiköprüsü [TR] 152 G2
Eferding [A] 62 B4
Effeløt [N] 164 G2
Efkarpía [GR] 128 H3
Eforie [RO] 204 F5
Efpálio [GR] 132 F5
Efýra [GR] 136 C2
Éfyras [GR] 132 D3
Egebæk [DK] 156 B3
Egeln [D] 34 B3
Egense [DK] 160 E4
Eger [H] 64 E5
Egerlövő [H] 64 F5
Egernsund [DK] 156 C4
Egersund [N] 164 B4
Egervár [H] 74 G2
Egesheim [D] 58 G3
Egeskov [DK] 156 D4
Egestorf [D] 18 F5
Egg [A] 60 B6
Egg [A] 72 D2
Egg [CH] 72 D2
Eggedal [N] 170 G5
Eggenburg [A] 62 E3
Eggenfelden [D] 60 G3
Eggesin [D] 20 E4
Eggjaseteren [N] 190 D5
Egglham [D] 60 G3
Eggum [N] 192 C4
Eghezée [B] 30 D5
Egiertowo [PL] 22 D3
Egilsstaðir [IS] 192 C3
Egletons [F] 68 A3
Eglinton [NIR] 2 F2
Egmond aan Zee [NL] 16 D3
Egna / Neumarkt [I] 72 D4
Egremont [GB] 8 D6
Egsdorf [D] 34 E3
Egtved [DK] 156 C2
Eguzon [F] 54 G5
Egyek [H] 64 F6
Ehingen [D] 60 B3
Ehnen [L] 44 F3
Ehra-Lessien [D] 32 H2
Ehrenburg [A] 60 C6
Ehrenburg [D] 18 D6
Ehrenhausen [A] 74 D3
Ehrwald [A] 60 D6
Eiane [N] 164 B3
Eibar [E] 82 H4
Eibenstock [D] 48 C2
Eibergen [NL] 16 G5
Eibiswald [A] 74 D3
Eich [D] 46 C4
Eichendorf [D] 60 G3
Eichstätt [D] 60 D2
Eid [N] 190 B5
Eida [N] 164 B4
Eidanger [N] 164 G3
Eide [N] 164 B4
Eide [N] 164 C3
Eide [N] 170 B1
Eide [N] 180 E2
Eide [N] 190 D5
Eidem [N] 190 C3
Eidet [N] 180 H1
Eidfjord [N] 170 D4
Eiði [FR] 160 B1
Eidiet [N] 180 C6
Eidsborg [N] 164 E2
Eidsbugarden [N] 170 F1
Eidsbygda [N] 180 E3
Eidsdal [N] 180 E4
Eidsfoss [N] 164 G2
Eidskog [N] 172 D6
Eidslandet [N] 170 B3
Eidsøra [N] 180 F3
Eidstod [N] 164 E2
Eidsund [N] 164 B2
Eidsvåg [N] 180 F3
Eidsvoll [N] 172 C5
Eidsvoll verk [N] 172 C5
Eifa [D] 32 D6
Eigenrieden [D] 32 G5
Eik [N] 164 B2
Eikefjord [N] 180 B6
Eikelandsosen [N] 170 B4
Eiken [N] 164 C4
Eikenes [N] 180 B6
Eiksund [N] 180 C4
Eilenburg [D] 34 D5
Eilsleben [D] 34 A3
Eimisjärvi [FIN] 188 G3
Eina [N] 172 B4
Einastrand [N] 172 B4
Einavoll [N] 172 B4
Einbeck [D] 32 F3
Eindhoven [NL] 30 E2
Einsiedeln [CH] 58 G6
Einzinger Boden [A] 72 F1
Eisenach [D] 32 G6
Eisenbach [D] 46 D1
Eisenback [D] 58 F3
Eisenberg [D] 34 B6
Eisenerz [A] 62 C6
Eisenhüttenstadt [D] 34 G3
Eisenkappel [A] 74 C4
Eisenstadt [A] 62 F5
Eisensteinhöhle [A] 62 E5
Eisfeld [D] 46 G2
Eisgarn [A] 62 D2
Eišiškės [LT] 24 H2
Eislingen [D] 60 B2
Eisriesenwelt [A] 60 H6
Eitorf [D] 30 H5
Eivindvik [N] 170 B2
Eivissa / Ibiza [E] 104 C5
Ejby [DK] 156 D3
Ejea de los Caballeros [E] 84 C6
Ejheden [S] 172 H2
Ejstrupholm [DK] 156 C1
Ejulve [E] 90 E6
Ek [S] 166 F5
Ekáli [GR] 134 C6
Ekeby [S] 156 H2
Ekeby [S] 166 G6
Ekeby [S] 168 D3
Ekebyholm [S] 168 E2
Ekedal [S] 174 E6
Ekedalen [S] 166 F6
Ekenäs [S] 166 E4
Ekenäs / Tammisaari [FIN] 176 F6
Ekenässjön [S] 162 E3
Ekerö [S] 168 D3
Ekinhisar [TR] 152 H3

Ekinli [TR] 150 H3
Ekkerøy [N] 194 E2
Ekolsund [S] 168 D2
Ekornavallen [S] 166 F6
Ekorrbäcken [S] 194 B7
Ekorrträsk [S] 190 H5
Ekshärad [S] 172 F5
Eksingedal [N] 170 C3
Eksjö [S] 162 E2
Ekträsk [S] 190 H5
Ekzarh Antimovo [BG] 148 E4
Elaía [GR] 136 F4
Elaiochória [GR] 130 B5
Elaiónas [GR] 132 G5
El Alamo [E] 88 F6
El Alcornocal [E] 96 B5
El Altet [E] 104 D2
Elämäjärvi [FIN] 196 D6
Elanets' [UA] 204 F2
Elantxobe [E] 82 H3
Elassóna [GR] 132 F1
El Astillero [E] 82 F3
Eláteia [GR] 132 H4
Eláti [GR] 128 F6
Eláti [GR] 132 E2
Elatoú [GR] 132 F5
El Ballestero [E] 96 H5
El Barco de Ávila [E] 88 C5
El Barraco [E] 88 E5
Elbasan [AL] 128 B3
El Berrón [E] 78 H3
Elbeuf [F] 26 H4
Elbigenalp [A] 72 B1
Elbingerode [D] 32 H4
Elbląg [PL] 22 F3
El Bodón [E] 86 H2
El Bonillo [E] 96 H5
El Bosque [E] 100 H4
Elburg [NL] 16 F4
Elburgo / Burgelu [E] 102 B4
El Burgo de Ebro [E] 90 E4
El Burgo de Osma [E] 90 A3
El Burgo Ranero [E] 82 B5
El Cabaco [E] 88 B4
el Campello [E] 104 E2
El Canal [E] 104 C6
El Cañavate [E] 98 B3
El Carpio [E] 102 C1
El Carpio de Tajo [E] 96 E1
El Casar de Talamanca [E] 88 G5
El Castillo de las Guardas [E] 94 G5
El Castor [E] 100 H3
El Centenillo [E] 96 E6
El Cerro de Andévalo [E] 94 F4
Elche / Elx [E] 104 D2
Elche de la Sierra [E] 104 B1
Elçili [TR] 150 B2
El Coronil [E] 100 H3
El Cotillo [E] 100 E6
El Cubo de Don Sancho [E] 80 F6
El Cubo de Tierra del Vino [E] 80 H5
El Cuervo [E] 100 G3
El'cy [RUS] 202 D3
Elda [E] 104 D2
Eldalsosen [N] 170 C1
Eldena [D] 20 A5
Eldforsen [S] 172 G5
Eldrehaug [N] 170 E2
Elefsína [GR] 134 B6
Eleftherés [GR] 134 B6
Elefthério [GR] 132 G2
Eleftherochóri [GR] 128 E6
Eleftheroúpoli [GR] 130 D3
Eleja [LV] 198 D6
El Ejido [E] 102 F5
Elek [H] 76 G3
Elena [BG] 148 C4
Elenite [BG] 148 F4
Eleousa [GR] 154 D4
El Escorial [E] 88 F5
El Espinar [E] 88 E4
el Fondó dels Frares [E] 104 D2
Elgå [N] 182 D5
El Gargantón [E] 96 E3
El Garrobo [E] 94 G5
Elgg [CH] 58 G5
Elgin [GB] 6 E5
El Grado [E] 90 G3
El Grau [E] 98 F4
el Grau / Grao [E] 98 F6
Elgsnes [N] 192 E3
El Guijo [E] 96 C5
Eliaröd [S] 158 D2
Elimäki [FIN] 178 C3
Eling [S] 166 E6
Elin Pelin [BG] 146 G5
Elisenvaara [RUS] 188 H5
Eliseyna [BG] 146 G4
Elizondo [E] 84 C3
Elizondo / Baztan [E] 82 H4
Ełk [PL] 24 D4
Elkeland [N] 164 C5
Elkhovo [BG] 148 E5
Ellan [S] 174 G5
Elle [N] 164 B3
Ellenberg [D] 46 E6
Ellesmere [GB] 10 D5
Elling [DK] 160 E2
Ellinge [S] 158 C2
Ellingen [D] 46 G6
Ellmau [A] 60 F6
Ellon [GB] 6 G6
Ellös [S] 166 C6
Ellrich [D] 32 H4
Ellwangen [D] 46 E6
Elm [CH] 58 G6
Elmacık [TR] 150 B1
El Madroño [E] 94 F5
Elmalı [TR] 154 H2
El Masnou [E] 92 E4
El Médano [E] 100 B5
Elmen [A] 60 C6
El Minguillo [E] 96 G4
El Molar [E] 88 G5
El Molinillo [E] 96 E2
El Moral [E] 102 H2
Elmpt [D] 30 F3
Elmshorn [D] 18 F3
Elmstein [D] 46 B5
Elne [F] 92 G1
Elnesvågen [N] 180 E2
Elo / Monreal [E] 84 B4
Eloro [I] 126 G5
Elorz / Noain [E] 84 B4
Élos [GR] 140 B5
Előszállás [H] 76 C3
Eloúnta [GR] 140 F4
el Palmar [E] 98 F5
El Palmar de Troya [E] 100 G3
El Palmeral [E] 104 D2
El Palo [E] 102 C4
El Pardo [E] 88 F5
El Paular [E] 88 F4
El Pedernoso [E] 96 H3
El Pedroso [E] 94 H5
El Perelló [E] 92 B5
El Perelló [E] 98 F5
Elphin [IRL] 2 D4
El Pinar [E] 100 A5
El Piñero [E] 80 H5
el Pinós / Pinoso [E] 104 D2
El Pito [E] 78 G3
el Pla de Santa Maria [E] 92 C4
El Pobo de Dueñas [E] 90 C6
el Pont de Suert [E] 84 F6
el Port / Sóller [E] 104 E4
el Port de la Selva [E] 92 G2
El Portil [E] 94 E6
el Prat de Llobregat [E] 92 E5
El Priorato [E] 102 A1
El Puente del Arzobispo [E] 96 D1
El Puerto de Santa Maria [E] 100 F4
El Ramonete [E] 104 B4
El Real de la Jara [E] 94 G4
El Real de San Vicente [E] 88 D6
El Recuenco [E] 90 B6
El Retiro [E] 102 B5
El Robledo [E] 96 E3
El Rocío [E] 94 F6
El Rompido [E] 94 E6
El Ronquillo [E] 94 G5
El Royo [E] 90 B2
El Rubio [E] 102 B2
El Sabinar [E] 102 H2
El Saler [E] 98 E5
El Salobral [E] 98 B5
El Saucejo [E] 102 B3
Elsdorf [D] 30 G4
El Serrat [AND] 84 H6
Elsfleth [D] 18 D5
Elšica [BG] 148 A5
Elst [NL] 16 E5
Elsten [D] 18 C6
Elster [D] 34 D4
Elsterberg [D] 48 C2
Elsterwerda [D] 34 E5
El Tejar [E] 102 C3
Elten [D] 16 F6
El Tiemblo [E] 88 E5
Eltmann [D] 46 F3
El Toboso [E] 96 G3
El Tormillo [E] 90 G3
El Torno [E] 88 B5
El Torno [E] 100 G4
Eltravåg [N] 164 A1
El Tumbalejo [E] 94 F5
Eltville [D] 46 B3
Eltz [D] 44 H1
Elva [EST] 198 F3
Elvas [P] 86 F6
Elvbrua [N] 182 D6
Elvdal [N] 172 D1
Elven, Tour d'– [F] 40 D4
El Vendrell [E] 92 D5
Elverum [N] 172 C3
Elverum [N] 192 F3
Elvestad [N] 166 B2
El Villar de Arnedo [E] 84 A5
Elvira [E] 102 E3
Elviria [E] 102 B5
El Viso [E] 96 C5
El Viso del Alcor [E] 94 H6
Elvran [N] 182 C1
Elx / Elche [E] 104 D2
Ely [GB] 14 F2
Élyros [GR] 140 B5
Elzach [D] 58 F2
Elze [D] 32 F3
Emberménil [F] 44 F5
Embrun [F] 108 D2
Embute [LV] 198 C6
Emden [D] 16 H2
Emecik [TR] 154 C2
Emese [TR] 150 C5
Emet [TR] 152 F1
Emiralem [TR] 152 C3
Emlichheim [D] 16 G4
Emmaboda [S] 162 F5
Emmaljunga [S] 162 C6
Emmaste [EST] 198 C2
Emmeloord [NL] 16 F3
Emmen [NL] 16 G3
Emmendingen [D] 58 E3
Emmerich [D] 16 F6
Emmingen–Liptingen [D] 58 G3
Emőd [H] 64 F5
Emona [BG] 148 G4
Émpa [CY] 154 F6
Empesós [GR] 132 E3
Empfingen [D] 58 G2
Empoli [I] 110 E5
Émponas [GR] 154 D4
Emporeiós [GR] 134 G5
Emporeiós [GR] 154 A2
Emporeiós [GR] 154 B3
Empúriabrava [E] 92 G2
Empúries [E] 92 G3
Emsdetten [D] 16 H5
Emsfors [S] 162 G4
Emskirchen [D] 46 F5
Emstek [D] 18 C6
Emting–hausen [D] 18 D6
Emyvale [IRL] 2 F4
Enafors [S] 182 E2
Enäjärvi [FIN] 178 C3
Enånger [S] 174 E1
Enare / Inari [FIN] 194 D4
Enarsvedjan [S] 182 G1
Encamp [AND] 84 H6
Encarnación, Sant. de la– [E] 98 B6
Encinas de Abajo [E] 88 C3
Encinasola [E] 94 F3
Encinedo [E] 78 F6
Enciso [E] 90 C2
Encs [H] 64 F4
Endelave By [DK] 156 D2
Enden [N] 180 H6
Endingen [D] 58 E2
Endrefalva [H] 64 D4
Endrinal [E] 88 C4
Endrőd [H] 76 F2
Enebakk [N] 166 C1
Enese [H] 62 H6
Enevo [BG] 148 E2
Enez [TR] 130 H3
Enfesta / Pontecesures [E] 78 B3
Enfield [IRL] 2 E6
Engelberg [CH] 70 F1
Engelhartszell [A] 62 A3
Engelia [N] 170 H4
Engeln [D] 18 D6
Engelskirchen [D] 30 H4
Engelsviken [N] 166 B3
Engen [D] 58 G3
Enger [D] 32 D2
Enger [N] 170 H4
Engerdal [N] 182 D6
Engerneset [N] 172 D1
Engesland [N] 164 E4
Engesvang [DK] 160 C6
Enghien [B] 28 H3
Engi [CH] 58 G6
Engjane [N] 180 F2
England [D] 18 E1
Englefontaine [F] 28 G4
Engstingen [D] 58 H2
Énguera [E] 98 E6
Enguídanos [E] 98 C3
Engure [LV] 198 D5
Enkhuizen [NL] 16 E3
Enklinge [FIN] 176 B5
Enköping [S] 168 C2
Enmo [N] 182 B3
Enna [I] 126 E3
Ennezat [F] 68 D2
Ennis / Inis [IRL] 2 C6
Enniscorthy [IRL] 4 F4
Enniscrone [IRL] 2 C3
Enniskean [IRL] 4 C5
Enniskillen [NIR] 2 E3
Ennistymon [IRL] 2 B5
Enns [A] 62 C4
Eno [FIN] 188 G2
Enokunta [FIN] 186 E6
Enonkoski [FIN] 188 E4
Enonkylä [FIN] 196 E5
Enonteki / Enontekiö [FIN] 194 B5
Enontekiö / Enonteki [FIN] 194 B5
Enschede [NL] 16 G5
Ensisheim [F] 58 D3
Entlebuch [CH] 58 E6
Entradas [P] 94 D3
Entraigues [F] 54 H3
Entranis–sur–Nohain [F] 56 D3
Entraygues–sur–Truyère [F] 68 B5
Entre Ambos–os–Rios [P] 80 C4
Entrevaux [F] 108 E4
Entrèves [I] 70 C3
Entrimo [E] 78 C6
Entroncamento [P] 86 D4
Enviken [S] 174 C4
En Xoroi, Cova d'– [E] 104 H5
Enying [H] 76 B2
Eoux [F] 84 G4
Epannes [F] 54 D4
Epanomí [GR] 128 H5
Epe [D] 16 G5
Epe [NL] 16 F4
Épernay [F] 44 B3
Epernon [F] 42 E4
Ephesos [TR] 152 D5
Epídavros, Arhéa– [GR] 136 F2
Épila [E] 90 D4
Épinal [F] 58 C2
Epiry [F] 56 E3
Episcopía [I] 120 H5
Episkopí [CY] 154 F6
Episkopí [GR] 140 C4
Epitálio [GR] 136 C2
Epleny [H] 76 A2
Epône [F] 42 E3
Epoo / Ebbo [FIN] 178 B4
Eppan / Appiano [I] 72 D3
Eppenstein [A] 74 C2
Eppingen [D] 46 C5
Eptachóri [GR] 128 D6
Eptálofos [GR] 132 G5
Epuisay [F] 42 C5
Eraclea [I] 72 F6
Eraclea [I] 122 D5
Eraclea Mare [I] 72 F6
Eraclea Minoa [I] 126 C4
Eräjärvi [FIN] 176 G1
Eräslahti [FIN] 186 F6
Erateiní [GR] 132 G5
Erátyra [GR] 128 E5
Erba [I] 70 G4
Erbach [D] 46 D4
Erbach [D] 60 B3
Erbalunga [F] 114 C2
Erbè [I] 110 F1
Erbendorf [D] 48 B4
Ercolano [I] 120 E3
Ercsi [H] 76 C2
Érd [H] 76 C1
Erdal [N] 180 C6
Erdek [TR] 150 D4
Erdevik [SRB] 142 F2
Erding [D] 60 E4
Erdőhorváti [H] 64 G4
Erdut [HR] 142 E1
Eremitage [D] 46 H4
Erenköy (Kókkina) [CY] 154 F5
Eresós [GR] 134 G2
Erétria [GR] 134 C5
Erfde [D] 18 E2
Erfjord [N] 164 B2
Erftstadt [D] 30 G5
Erfurt [D] 32 H6
Ergama [TR] 152 D1
Ergili [TR] 150 D5
Ērgli [LV] 198 E5
Ergoldsbach [D] 60 F3
Erice [I] 126 B2
Erice [TR] 152 G3
Ericeira [P] 86 A4
Ericek [TR] 150 F4
Erikli [TR] 150 B4
Eriksberg [S] 168 B4
Eriksberg [S] 184 C2
Eriksberg [S] 190 F4
Erikslund [S] 184 D4
Eriksmåla [S] 162 E5
Erikstad [S] 166 D5
Eringsboda [S] 162 E6
Erka [N] 180 F5
Erkelenz [D] 30 F4
Erla [E] 84 C6
Erlangen [D] 46 G4
Erlenbach [D] 46 D4
Erlsbach [A] 72 E2
Ermelo [NL] 16 E4
Ermenonville [F] 42 G3
Ermesinde [P] 80 C4
Ermidas–Aldeia [P] 94 C3
Ermióni [GR] 136 F3
Ermitage, Grotte de l'– [F] 56 H4
Ermoúpoli [GR] 138 D2
Ermsleben [D] 34 B4
Erndtebrück [D] 32 D6
Ernée [F] 26 D6
Ernerwald [CH] 70 E2
Ernestinovo [HR] 142 E1
Ernstbrunn [A] 62 F3
Erp [D] 30 G5
Erquy [F] 26 B4
Erratzu [E] 84 C3
Errenteria / Rentería [E] 84 B2
Erro [E] 84 C3
Erronkari / Roncal [E] 84 C4
Ersekë [AL] 128 D5
Ersmark [S] 196 A6
Ersnäs [S] 196 B3
Erstein [F] 44 H6
Ertuğrul [TR] 152 D1
Ervasti [FIN] 196 E3
Ervedal [E] 86 D5
Ervedosa [P] 80 D4
Ervenik [HR] 112 H5
Ervidel [P] 94 D3
Ervik [N] 180 B4
Ervy–le–Châtel [F] 44 A6
Erwitte [D] 32 D4
Erxleben [D] 34 B3
Erythrés [GR] 134 B6
Erzsébet [H] 76 B5
Eržvilkas [LT] 200 E5
Esa / Yesa [E] 84 C4
Esatçe [TR] 130 H3
Esatlar [TR] 152 G1
Esbjerg [DK] 156 A2
Esblada [E] 92 C4
Esbo / Espoo [FIN] 176 G5
Escairón [E] 78 D4
Escalada [E] 82 E4
Escalaplano [I] 118 D6
Escalona [E] 84 E5
Escalona [E] 88 E6
Escalonilla [E] 96 E1
Escandón, Puerto de– [E] 98 E2
Escariche [E] 88 G6
Escároz / Ezkaroze [E] 84 C4
Escatrón [E] 90 F5
Eschede [D] 32 G1
Eschenbach [D] 46 H4
Eschenburg–Eibelshausen [D] 32 D6
Eschenlohe [D] 60 D6
Escherndorf [D] 46 F4
Eschershausen [D] 32 F3
Esch–sur–Alzette [L] 44 E3
Esch–sur–Sûre [L] 44 E2
Eschwege [D] 32 G5
Eschweiler [D] 30 F4
Escipions, Torre dels– [E] 92 C5
Escombreras [E] 104 C4
Escornalbou [E] 90 H6
Escos [F] 84 D2
Es Cubells [E] 104 C5
Escucha [E] 90 E6
Escúllar [E] 102 F4
Eşen [TR] 154 F3
Esence [TR] 150 E4
Esenköy [TR] 150 H4
Esens [D] 18 C3
Esentepe (Ágios Amvrósios) [CY] 154 G5
Esenyurt [TR] 150 E3
es Figueral [E] 104 C5
Esgos [E] 78 D5
Esguevillas de Esgueva [E] 88 F1
Eskelhem [S] 168 F4
Eskiçine [TR] 152 E6
Eskifjördur [IS] 192 D3
Eski Gediz [TR] 152 G2
Eskihisar [TR] 152 E6
Eskilstuna [S] 168 B3
Eskin [TR] 152 F3
Eskişehir [TR] 150 H5
Eskiyüregil [TR] 150 G5
Eskola [FIN] 196 C5
Eslared [S] 162 C5
Eslarn [D] 48 C5
Eslohe [D] 32 D5
Eslöv [S] 158 C2
Esmared [S] 162 B5
Eşme [TR] 152 F4
Es Mercadal [E] 104 H4
Esmoritz [P] 80 B4
Esnandes [F] 54 C4
Esnouvenaux [F] 56 H1
Espa [N] 172 C4
Espadilla [E] 98 F3
Espalion [F] 68 B5
Esparreguera [E] 92 D4
Espås [N] 182 B1
Espe [S] 170 C4
Espedal [N] 170 G1
Espejo [E] 102 C2
Espeland [N] 164 B4
Espeland [N] 170 B4
Espelette [F] 84 C2
Espeli [N] 164 D4
Espelkamp [D] 32 E2
Espera [E] 100 G3
Esperia [I] 120 C1
Espezel [F] 106 B5
Espiel [E] 96 C5
Espinama [E] 82 D3
Espinheiro, Convento de– [P] 94 D1
Espinho [P] 80 B4
Espinilla [E] 82 E4
Espinosa de los Monteros [E] 82 F4
Espírito Santo [P] 94 D4
Esplantas [F] 68 D5
Esponellà [E] 92 F2
Espoo / Esbo [FIN] 176 G5
Esporles [E] 104 E4
Es Port d'Alcúdia [E] 104 F4
es Port d'Andraitx [E] 104 D5
Esposende [P] 78 A6
Espot [E] 84 G6
Espot Esquí [E] 92 E2
Esprels [F] 58 C4
Esse / Ähtävä [FIN] 196 C6
Essen [D] 18 C6
Essen [D] 30 H3
Essenbach [D] 60 F3
Essertaux [F] 28 D5
Esslingen [D] 58 H1
Essoyes [F] 56 G1
Essuilles [F] 28 D6
Essunga [S] 166 D6
Estada [E] 90 G3
Estagel [F] 106 C6
Estaing [F] 68 B5
Estaires [F] 28 F3
Estang [F] 66 D6
Estanyol [E] 104 E5
Estarreja [P] 80 B5
Estavayer–le–Lac [CH] 58 C6
Este [I] 110 G1
Estela [P] 80 B3
Estella / Lizarra [E] 84 A4
Estellenchs [E] 104 D5
Estepa [E] 102 B3
Estepar [E] 82 E6
Estepona [E] 100 H5
Esteras, Cuesta de– [E] 90 B4
Esternay [F] 42 H4
Esterri d'Àneu [E] 84 G5
Esterwegen [D] 18 C5
Estíbaliz, Santuario de– [E] 82 H5
Estissac [F] 44 A6
Estói [P] 94 C5
Estoril [P] 86 A5
Estrées–St–Denis [F] 28 E6
Estremera [E] 96 H1
Estremoz [P] 86 E6
Esztergom [H] 64 C5
Etables–sur–Mer [F] 26 B4
Etagnac [F] 54 F6
Étain [F] 44 E3
Étalans [F] 58 B5
Etalle [B] 44 E2
Étampes [F] 42 F4
Étang–sur–Arroux [F] 56 F4
Etaples [F] 28 D3
Ete [H] 64 A6
Eteläinen [FIN] 176 G2
Etili [TR] 150 B5
Etne [N] 164 B1
Etoges [F] 44 A4
Éton [F] 44 D3
Etréaupont [F] 28 G5
Etrepagny [F] 28 C6
Etretat [F] 26 G2
Etropole [BG] 146 G4
Etseri / Ähtäri [FIN] 186 E4
Ettelbruck [L] 44 F2
Ettenheim [D] 58 E2
Ettlingen [D] 46 B6
Etxarri / Echarri [E] 84 A3
Eu [F] 28 C4
Eudorf [D] 46 D1
Euerhausen [D] 46 E4
Eugénie–les–Bains [F] 66 C6
Eulate [E] 82 H5
Eumeneia [TR] 152 H3
Eunate [E] 84 B4
Eupen [B] 30 F5
Eura [FIN] 176 D2
Euraåminne / Eurajoki [FIN] 176 C2
Eurajoki / Euraåminne [FIN] 176 C2
Euratsfeld [A] 62 C5
Eurialo, Castello– [I] 126 G5
Euromos [TR] 152 D6
Europa–Brücke [A] 72 D1
Europoort [NL] 16 C5
Euskirchen [D] 30 G5
Eussenhausen [D] 46 F2
Eutin [D] 18 G3
Eutzsch [D] 34 D4
Eväjärvi [FIN] 186 F6
Evangelísmos [GR] 132 G1
Evanger [N] 170 C3
Evaux–les–Bains [F] 56 B6
Evciler [TR] 152 B1
Evciler [TR] 152 H4
Evciler [TR] 154 F4
Évdilos [GR] 138 G1
Evendorf [D] 18 F5
Evenstad [N] 172 C2
Everöd [S] 158 D2
Everswinkel [D] 32 C3
Evertsberg [S] 172 F3
Evesham [GB] 12 H2
Evian [F] 70 C2
Evijärvi [FIN] 186 D1
Evinochóri [GR] 132 E5
Evisa [F] 114 A4
Evitskog [FIN] 176 G5
Evje [N] 164 D4
Evolène [CH] 70 D3
Évora [P] 94 D1
Évora Monte [P] 86 D6
Evran [F] 26 C5
Evrensekiz [TR] 150 C2
Evreux [F] 42 D2
Evron [F] 26 E6
Evry [F] 42 F4
Évzonoi [GR] 128 G3
Exaplátanos [GR] 128 F3
Éxarchos [GR] 132 H5
Excideuil [F] 66 G2
Exeter [GB] 12 E4
Exmes [F] 26 G5
Exmouth [GB] 12 E5
Exochí [GR] 128 G5
Exochí [GR] 130 C2
Exómvourgo [GR] 138 E2
Externsteine [D] 32 E3
Extertal [D] 32 E3
Extremoz [P] 78 B5
Eydehavn [N] 164 F5
Eyemouth [GB] 8 F4
Eyguières [F] 106 H4
Eygurande [F] 68 B2
Eylie [F] 84 G5
Eymet [F] 66 E4
Eymoutiers [F] 66 H2
Eyrarbakki [IS] 192 A3
Ézaro [E] 78 B2
Ezcaray [E] 82 F6
Ezere [LV] 198 C6
Ezermuiža [LV] 198 C4
Ezernieki [LV] 198 G6
Ezernijeki [LV] 198 D6
Ezine [TR] 130 H6
Ezkaroze / Escároz [E] 84 C4

F

Faaborg [DK] 156 D4
Faak [A] 74 A3
Fabara, Mausoleo de– [E] 90 G5
Fabbrico [I] 110 E2
Fåberg [N] 172 B2
Fabero [E] 78 F4
Fábiánsebestyén [H] 76 F3
Fabriano [I] 116 B1
Facheca [E] 104 E1
Fačkov [SK] 64 B2
Facture [F] 66 C3
Fadd [H] 76 C4
Faenza [I] 110 G4
Faeto [I] 120 F2
Fafe [P] 80 C3
Făgăraş [RO] 204 D4
Fågelfors [S] 162 F4
Fågelsjö [S] 182 G6
Fågelsundet [S] 174 F4
Fågelvik [S] 162 G1
Fageole, Col de la– [F] 68 C4
Fagerås [S] 166 E2
Fagerhaugen [N] 180 H3
Fagerheim Fjellstue [N] 170 E4
Fagerhult [S] 162 D1
Fagerhult [S] 162 F4
Fagerhult [S] 166 C5
Fagernes [N] 170 G3
Fagernes [N] 192 F2
Fagersanna [S] 166 F5
Fagersta [S] 168 A1
Fagerstrand [N] 166 B1
Fagervika [N] 190 D1
Fäggeby [S] 174 D5
Faglåvik [S] 162 B1
Fagnano Castello [I] 124 D4
Fagurhólsmyri [IS] 192 B3
Faial [P] 100 A3
Fai della Paganella [I] 72 C4
Faido [CH] 70 F2
Fains le Sources [F] 44 D4
Faistós [GR] 140 E5
Fajã do Ouvidor [P] 100 C3
Fajã dos Cubres [P] 100 C3
Faja Grande [P] 100 B3
Fakenham [GB] 14 G1
Fåker [S] 182 G3
Fakija [BG] 148 E5
Fakse [DK] 156 G4
Fakse Ladeplads [DK] 156 G4
Falaise [F] 26 F4
Falásarna [GR] 140 B4
Falatádos [GR] 138 E2
Falcade [I] 72 E4
Falconara, Castello di– [I] 126 E4
Falconara Marittima [I] 112 C6
Falcone [I] 124 A7
Falcsut [H] 76 B1
Faldsled [DK] 156 D4
Falerii Novi [I] 114 H4
Falerna [I] 124 D5
Falerna Marina [I] 124 D5
Falerum [S] 162 G1
Falileevo [RUS] 178 F6
Faliráki [GR] 154 D3
Falkenberg [D] 34 E5
Falkenberg [D] 60 G3
Falkenberg [S] 160 H4
Falkenstein [A] 62 F3
Falkenstein [A] 62 F3
Falkenstein [D] 34 A4
Falkenstein [D] 44 F1
Falkenstein [D] 48 C6
Falkenstein [D] 48 C2
Falkenstein, Château de– [F] 44 H5
Falkirk [GB] 8 E3
Falköping [S] 166 E6
Fałków [PL] 38 A6
Falla [S] 168 A5
Fållen [S] 162 D5
Fallersleben [D] 32 H2
Fallet [N] 172 C5
Fallet [N] 180 H5
Fällfors [S] 196 A4
Fallingbostel [D] 18 F6
Falmouth [GB] 12 C5
Falset [E] 90 H6
Falsterbo [S] 156 H3
Fălticeni [RO] 204 D3
Falträsk [S] 190 G4
Faludden [S] 168 G6
Falun [S] 174 C4
Faluszíget [H] 76 G2
Fámjin [FR] 160 A3
Fana [N] 170 B4
Fanano [I] 110 E4
Fanári [GR] 130 F3
Fanári [GR] 132 F2
Fanbyn [S] 184 D4
Fáncs [H] 76 B3
Fanefjord [DK] 156 G5
Fångåmon [S] 182 F2
Fanjeaux [F] 106 B4
Fannrem [N] 180 H1
Fano [I] 112 C5
Fanós [GR] 128 G3
Făntânele [RO] 148 B2
Fanthyttan [S] 166 H2
Farad [H] 62 G6
Fara Novarese [I] 70 F4
Fårbo [S] 162 G3
Farcheville, Château de– [F] 42 F5
Farébersviller [F] 44 G4
Fareham [GB] 12 H5
Fårevejle [DK] 156 F2
Farfa, Abbazia di– [I] 116 A4
Färgaryd [S] 162 B4
Färgelanda [S] 166 C5
Färila [S] 184 C6
Faringdon [GB] 12 H3
Faringe [S] 168 E1
Färingtofta [S] 158 C1
Farini [I] 110 C2
Färjestaden [S] 162 G5
Farkadóna [GR] 132 F2
Farkasgyepü [H] 74 H2
Farkaždin [SRB] 142 G1
Farlete [E] 90 F4
Fârliug [RO] 76 H6
Färlöv [S] 158 D1
Färna [S] 168 B2
Färnäs [S] 172 G3
Farnese [I] 114 G3
Farnham [GB] 14 D4
Faro [P] 94 C6
Fårö [S] 168 H3
Fårösund [S] 168 H3
Farranfore [IRL] 4 B4
Farre [DK] 160 D6
Fársala [GR] 132 G3
Farsø [DK] 160 D4
Farstad [N] 180 E2
Farstorp [S] 158 D1
Farsund [N] 164 C5
Farum [DK] 156 G2
Fårvang [DK] 160 D6
Fasanerie, Schloss– [D] 46 E2
Fasano [I] 122 E3
Fåset [N] 182 B4
Fasgar [E] 78 G5
Fasovka [UA] 202 D7
Faster [DK] 156 B1
Fasterholt [DK] 156 C1
Fastov [UA] 202 D7
Fatezh [RUS] 202 F5
Fátima [E] 100 H4
Fátima [P] 86 C3
Fatjas [S] 190 H1
Fatnica [BIH] 144 D3
Fättjaur [S] 190 E3
Faucille, Col de la– [F] 70 B1
Faucogney–et–la–Mer [F] 58 C3
Faulbach [D] 46 D4
Faulensee [CH] 70 E1
Faulquemont [F] 44 F4

Fausa [N] 180 D4
Fauske [N] 192 D6
Fauville [F] 26 H2
Fåvang [N] 170 H1
Favara [E] 98 E5
Favara [I] 126 D4
Faverges [F] 70 B3
Faverney [F] 58 B3
Favignana [I] 126 A2
Favone [F] 114 B5
Favorite [D] 46 B6
Favrholt [DK] 160 C6
Fawley [GB] 12 H5
Fayence [F] 108 D4
Fayet [F] 106 D3
Fayl-Billot [F] 58 A3
Fayón [E] 90 G5
Fay-sur-Lignon [F] 68 E5
Fazendas de Almeirim [P] 86 C4
Feakle [IRL] 2 C6
Fécamp [F] 26 G2
Feda [N] 164 C5
Fedje [N] 170 A2
Feengrotten [D] 46 H2
Fefor [N] 170 G1
Fegen [S] 162 B4
Feggeklit [DK] 160 C4
Fegyvernek [H] 76 F1
Fehrbellin [D] 34 D1
Fehring [A] 74 E2
Feigumfoss [N] 170 E1
Feios [N] 170 D2
Feiring [N] 172 C4
Feistritz [A] 74 E2
Feitos [P] 78 A6
Feketić [SRB] 76 D6
Felanitx [E] 104 F5
Felben [A] 72 F1
Felber-tauern Tunnel [A] 72 F2
Feld [A] 72 H3
Feldafing [D] 60 D5
Feldbach [A] 74 E2
Feldballe [DK] 160 E6
Feldberg [D] 20 D5
Feldberg [D] 58 F3
Feldkirch [A] 58 H5
Feldkirchen [A] 74 B3
Feldkirchen [D] 60 E5
Feldsted [DK] 156 C4
Felechosa [E] 82 B3
Feletto [I] 70 D5
Felgueiras [P] 80 C3
Felgyö [H] 76 E3
Félix [E] 104 B4
Felixstowe [GB] 14 G3
Felizzano [I] 70 E6
Fellbach [D] 58 H1
Fellern [A] 72 F1
Felletin [F] 68 B1
Fellingsbro [S] 168 A3
Felnac [RO] 76 G4
Felonica [I] 110 F2
Felsengarten [D] 46 G3
Felsőleperd [H] 76 B4
Felsőnyárád [H] 64 F4
Felsőszentiván [H] 76 C4
Felsőtárkány [H] 64 E5
Felsőzsolca [H] 64 F4
Feltre [I] 72 E5
Femsjö [S] 162 B4
Femundsenden [N] 182 D6
Fenagh [IRL] 2 E4
Fenais da Ajuda [P] 100 E3
Fene [E] 78 D2
Fenékpuszta [H] 74 G3
Fener [I] 72 E5
Fenestrelle [I] 70 C5
Fénétrange [F] 44 G5
Feneu [F] 40 H6
Fénis [I] 70 D4
Fenit [IRL] 4 B3
Fenstad [N] 172 C5
Fer a Cheval, Cirque du- [F] 58 A5
Feragen [N] 182 D4
Féraklos [GR] 154 D4
Ferbane [IRL] 2 D5
Ferdinandshof [D] 20 E4
Fére [GR] 132 H2
Fère, Château de- [F] 44 A3
Fère-Champenoise [F] 44 B4
Fère-en-Tardenois [F] 44 A3
Ferentino [I] 116 B6
Ferento [I] 114 H3
Féres [GR] 130 H3
Ferez [E] 104 B1
Feria [E] 94 G3
Feričanci [HR] 142 D1
Ferizli [TR] 150 H2
Ferla [I] 126 G5
Ferlach [A] 74 B3
Ferleiten [A] 72 G1
Fermignano [I] 110 H6
Fermo [I] 116 C2
Fermoselle [E] 80 G5
Fermoy [IRL] 4 D4
Fernancaballero [E] 96 E4
Fernán Núñez [E] 102 C2
Ferns [IRL] 4 F4
Fernstein [A] 60 C6
Ferovac [HR] 142 C1
Ferrandina [I] 122 D4
Ferrara [I] 110 G2
Ferreira [E] 78 E2
Ferreira do Alentejo [P] 94 D3
Ferreira do Zêzere [P] 86 D3
Ferreries [E] 104 G4
Ferreruela de Huerva [E] 90 D5
Ferrette [F] 58 D4
Ferriere [I] 110 C3
Ferrières [F] 42 G6
Ferrières-sur-Sichon [F] 68 D2
Ferring [DK] 160 B5
Ferrol [E] 78 D1
Fertöd [H] 62 G6
Fertőrákos [H] 62 F6
Fertőszentmiklós [H] 62 G6
Festenburg [A] 74 E1
Festøy [N] 180 D4
Festung Königstein [D] 48 F1
Festvåg [N] 192 D5
Fethard [IRL] 4 E4
Fethard [IRL] 4 F5
Fethiye [TR] 154 F2
Fetsund [N] 166 C1
Feu, Roche du- [F] 40 B3
Feucht [D] 46 G5
Feuchtwangen [D] 46 F6
Feurs [F] 68 E2
Fevik [N] 164 E5
Fiamignano [I] 116 B4
Fiastra, Abbadia di- [I] 116 C2
Fibiş [RO] 76 G5
Fíchti [GR] 136 E2
Ficulle [I] 114 H3
Fidenza [I] 110 D2
Fidje [N] 164 E4
Fieberbrunn [A] 60 F6
Fiegler [A] 74 B2
Fier [AL] 128 A4
Fier, Gorges du- [F] 70 A3
Fiera di Primiero [I] 72 E4
Fierzë [AL] 146 A6
Fiesch [CH] 70 E2
Fieschi, Basilica dei- [I] 110 B3
Fiésole [I] 110 F5
Fiesso Umbertiano [I] 110 G2
Figáleia [GR] 136 D3
Figari [F] 114 B6
Figeac [F] 66 H5
Figeholm [S] 162 G3
Figgjo [N] 164 B3
Figline Valdarno [I] 110 F6
Figueira da Foz [P] 80 A6
Figueira de Castelo Rodrigo [P] 80 E6
Figueiró dos Vinhos [P] 86 D3
Figueras / Figueres [E] 92 G2
Figueres / Figueras [E] 92 G2
Fiholm [S] 168 C3
Fiksdal [N] 180 D3
Filadélfi [GR] 130 B4
Filadélfia [I] 124 D6
Filaga [I] 126 D3
Fil'akovo [SK] 64 D4
Filatova Gora [RUS] 198 G3
Filevo [BG] 148 C6
Filey [GB] 10 G3
Filia [GR] 134 G2
Filiaşi [RO] 204 C6
Filiátes [GR] 132 C2
Filiatrá [GR] 136 C3
Filipovci [BG] 146 E4
Filipów [PL] 24 D3
Filippiáda [GR] 132 D3
Filippoi [GR] 130 D3
Filipstad [S] 166 F2
Filisur [CH] 70 H2
Filitosa [F] 114 A5
Fillan [N] 190 A6
Fillýra [GR] 130 G2
Filótas [GR] 128 F4
Filóti [GR] 138 F3
Filottrano [I] 116 C1
Filskov [DK] 156 B2
Filyriá [GR] 128 G4
Filzmoos [A] 72 H1
Finale Emilia [I] 110 F2
Finale Ligure [I] 108 H3
Fiñana [E] 102 F4
Finby / Särkisalo [FIN] 176 E5
Finderup [DK] 156 B1
Finestrat [E] 104 E2
Fingerboda [S] 166 H2
Finike [TR] 154 H3
Finiq [AL] 132 B1
Finisterre / Fisterra [E] 78 A2
Finja [S] 158 C1
Finnäs [S] 190 H4
Finnbo [S] 174 C4
Finnböle [S] 174 E5
Finnea [IRL] 2 E5
Finneby [S] 182 H5
Finneid [N] 192 D6
Finnentrop [D] 32 C5
Finnerödja [S] 166 G4
Finnlia [N] 164 G2
Finnøy [N] 192 D5
Finnsnes [N] 192 F3
Finnstad [N] 182 C5
Finntorp [S] 166 D3
Finnvelta [N] 172 D5
Finow [D] 34 E1
Finsand [N] 170 H4
Finsjö [S] 162 G4
Finspång [S] 168 A5
Finsta [S] 168 E2
Finsterwalde [D] 34 E5
Finström [FIN] 176 A5
Fionnay [CH] 70 D3
Fionnphort [GB] 8 B1
Fiorenzuola d'Arda [I] 110 C2
Firá / Thíra [GR] 138 F5
Firbis Castle [IRL] 2 C3
Firenze [I] 110 F5
Firenzuola [I] 110 F4
Firkeel [IRL] 4 A5
Firlej [PL] 38 E4
Firminy [F] 68 E3
Fiscal [E] 84 E5
Fischamend [A] 62 F5
Fischbach [D] 44 H2
Fischbach [D] 44 H4
Fischbeck [D] 32 F3
Fischbeck [D] 34 C2
Fischen [D] 60 B6
Fischerbócsa [H] 76 D3
Fishguard [GB] 4 H6
Fisíni [GR] 130 F6
Fiska [N] 180 C4
Fiskárdo [GR] 132 C5
Fiskebäckskil [S] 166 C6
Fiskebøl [N] 192 D4
Fiskevollen [N] 182 C5
Fiskö [FIN] 176 C4
Fiskøl [N] 164 F2
Fismes [F] 44 A3
Fiss [LT] 72 C1
Fiss [LT] 72 C1
Fisterra / Finisterre [E] 78 A2
Fıstıklı [TR] 150 E4
Fitero [E] 84 A6
Fitjar [N] 170 A5
Fiuggi [I] 116 B6
Fiumefreddo Bruzio [I] 124 D4
Fiumefreddo di Sicilia [I] 124 B8
Fiumicino [I] 114 H6
Fivemiletown [NIR] 2 F3
Fivizzano [I] 110 D4
Fjæra [N] 170 C5
Fjærland [N] 170 D1
Fjäl [S] 182 H2
Fjälkinge [S] 158 D2
Fjällåsen [S] 192 G5
Fjällbacka [S] 166 C5
Fjällgården [S] 182 G4
Fjällnäs [S] 182 D4
Fjällnäs [S] 190 G3
Fjaltring [DK] 160 B5
Fjand Gårde [DK] 160 B5
Fjärås [S] 160 H3
Fjärdhundra [S] 168 C2
Fjell [N] 170 A4
Fjellbu [N] 192 F4
Fjellerup [DK] 160 E5
Fjellheim [N] 170 F3
Fjellsrud [N] 166 C1
Fjelstrup [DK] 156 C3
Fjenneslev [DK] 156 F3
Fjerestad [N] 170 C2
Fjerritslev [DK] 160 D3
Fjon [N] 170 B2
Fjone [N] 164 E3
Fjordgård [N] 192 F2
Fjugesta [S] 166 G3
Flå [N] 170 G4
Flaçà [E] 92 G3
Fladdabister [GB] 6 G4
Fladungen [D] 46 F2
Flagy [F] 58 B3
Flaine [F] 70 C3
Flaka [FIN] 168 G1
Flakaberg [S] 194 A8
Flakaträsk [S] 190 F3
Flakk [N] 182 B1
Flakkstadvågen [N] 192 E3
Flåm [N] 170 D3
Flampouräri [GR] 132 D1
Flaran [F] 66 E6
Flärke [S] 184 G1
Flatabø [N] 170 C4
Flateby [N] 166 C1
Flateland [N] 164 D2
Flateland [N] 164 E4
Flåten [N] 192 G1
Flåtestøa [N] 172 C2
Flatmark [N] 180 F4
Flatøydegard [N] 170 G3
Flatråker [N] 170 B5
Flätsbo [S] 174 C3
Flått [N] 190 C4
Flattnitz [A] 74 B2
Flauenskjold [DK] 160 E3
Flaugeac [F] 66 E4
Flavigny-sur-Moselle [F] 44 E5
Fléchin [F] 28 E3
Flecken-berg [D] 32 D5
Fleckenstein, Château de- [F] 44 H4
Fleetwood [GB] 10 D3
Flehingen [D] 46 C6
Flekke [N] 170 B1
Flekkefjord [N] 164 C5
Flemma [N] 180 F2
Flen [S] 168 C4
Flensburg [D] 156 C5
Flerahopp [S] 162 F5
Flers [F] 26 E4
Flesberg [N] 164 G1
Flesje [N] 170 C2
Flesland [N] 170 A4
Flesnes [N] 192 E3
Fleurance [F] 84 G2
Fleuré [F] 54 F4
Fleurier [CH] 58 C6
Fleurus [B] 30 C5
Fleury [F] 28 C6
Flims [CH] 70 G1
Flims Waldhaus [CH] 70 G1
Flins [F] 42 F3
Flirsch [A] 72 B1
Flisa [N] 172 D4
Flisbrua [N] 172 D4
Flisby [S] 162 E2
Fliseryd [S] 162 G4
Flix [E] 90 H5
Flize [F] 44 C2
Floby [S] 162 C1
Floda [S] 160 H2
Floda [S] 172 H5
Floda [S] 190 H5
Flögåsen [S] 172 F2
Flogned [S] 166 D1
Flogny-la-Chapelle [F] 56 F1
Flöha [D] 48 D1
Flon [S] 182 E4
Flor [S] 182 H5
Florac [F] 68 D6
Florange [F] 44 E3
Florennes [B] 30 C5
Florenville [B] 44 D2
Floreşti [MD] 204 E3
Florídia [I] 126 G5
Flórina [GR] 128 E4
Flornes [N] 182 C1
Florø [N] 180 B5
Florstadt [D] 46 D2
Florvåg [N] 170 A3
Flostrand [N] 190 D2
Flötningen [S] 182 D6
Fluberg [N] 170 H3
Flüelen [CH] 58 F6
Fluglafjørður [FR] 160 B1
Flühli [CH] 58 E6
Flumeri [I] 120 F2
Flumet [F] 70 B3
Fluminimaggiore [I] 118 B6
Flums [CH] 58 H6
Fluren [S] 174 D1
Flymen [S] 162 F6
Flyn [S] 184 D1
Flystveit [N] 164 D4
Flytåsen [S] 174 C2
Fnideq [MA] 100 G6
Foça [TR] 152 B4
Foča-Srbinje [BIH] 144 D2
Fockbek [D] 18 F2
Focşani [RO] 204 E4
Födele [GR] 140 E4
Foeni [RO] 76 F6
Fogdö [S] 168 C3
Foggia [I] 120 G1
Föglö [FIN] 168 H1
Fohnsdorf [A] 74 C2
Foiano di Chiana [I] 114 G1
Foinikoúntas [GR] 136 D4
Foix [F] 84 H5
Fojnica [BIH] 142 C4
Fojnica [BIH] 144 D2
Fokstugu [N] 180 G5
Földeák [H] 76 F4
Foldereid [N] 190 C4
Földes [H] 76 G1
Foldingbro [DK] 156 B3
Folégandros [GR] 138 E4
Folelli [F] 114 C3
Folgaria [I] 72 C5
Folgarida [I] 72 C4
Folgoso [E] 78 E4
Foliá [GR] 130 D4
Foligno [I] 116 A2
Folkärna [S] 174 D5
Folkestad [N] 180 C4
Folkestone [GB] 14 F5
Folladal [N] 190 C5
Follafoss [N] 190 C5
Folldal [N] 180 H5
Follina [I] 72 E5
Föllinge [S] 190 E6
Follónica [I] 114 E2
Folmava [CZ] 48 D5
Fölsbyn [S] 166 D2
Folwarki [PL] 36 G6
Folyás [H] 64 G5
Fompedraza [E] 88 F2
Fondamente [F] 106 D3
Fondi [I] 120 C1
Fondo [I] 72 C3
Fönebo [S] 184 E6
Fonfría [E] 80 G4
Fonfría [E] 90 D5
Fonni [I] 118 D5
Fonseca, Castillo de- [E] 88 E3
Fontainebleau [F] 42 G5
Fontaine-de-Vaucluse [F] 106 H3
Fontaine-Française [F] 56 H3
Fontaine Guérard, Abbaye de- [F] 28 C6
Fontaine Henry, Château de- [F] 26 F3
Fontaine-le-Dun [F] 26 H2
Fontaine-sur-Coole [F] 44 B4
Fontanars dels Alforins [E] 98 D6
Fontanella [A] 72 A1
Fontanellato [I] 110 D2
Fontanelle [I] 72 F5
Fontanosas [E] 96 D4
Fonte Avellana, Monastero di- [I] 116 B1
Fontecha [E] 82 G5
Fonte Colombo, Convento di- [I] 116 B4
Fontedias [E] 78 C3
Fontenay, Abbaye de- [F] 56 F2
Fontenay-le-Comte [F] 54 C4
Fontenay-Trésigny [F] 42 G4
Fontevraud-l'Abbaye [F] 54 E2
Fontfroide, Abbaye de- [F] 106 C5
Fontgombault [F] 54 G4
Fontinha [P] 86 C2
Fontioso [E] 88 G1
Fontiveros [E] 88 D3
Font-Romeu [F] 92 E1
Fontstown [IRL] 4 F3
Fontvieille [F] 106 G4
Fonyód [H] 74 H3
Fonzaso [I] 72 E5
Fóppolo [I] 70 H3
Föra [S] 162 G4
Forbach [D] 58 F1
Forbach [F] 44 G4
Forbes, Castle- [IRL] 2 D4
Forcall [E] 98 F1
Forcalquier [F] 108 C3
Forcarei [E] 78 C4
Forchach [A] 60 C6
Forchheim [D] 46 G4
Forchtenstein [A] 62 F6
Ford [GB] 8 C2
Førde [N] 164 B1
Førde [N] 180 C6
Fordingbridge [GB] 12 G4
Fordongianus [I] 118 C5
Forenza [I] 120 H3
Forfar [GB] 8 F2
Forges-les-Eaux [F] 28 C5
Forino [I] 120 E3
Forio [I] 120 D3
Førland [N] 164 C5
Forlì [I] 110 G4
Forlì del Sánnio [I] 116 D6
Forlimpopoli [I] 110 G4
Formazza [I] 70 F2
Formazza [I] 70 F2
Formby [GB] 10 D3
Formerie [F] 28 D5
Formia [I] 120 C2
Formigine [I] 110 E3
Formiguères [F] 92 E1
Formofoss [N] 190 C5
Fornace [I] 114 G3
Fornaci di Barga [I] 110 D4
Fornalutx [E] 104 E4
Fornelli [I] 118 B2
Fornells [E] 104 H4
Forni Avoltri [I] 72 F3
Forni di Sopra [I] 72 F4
Forni di Sotto [I] 72 F4
Forno Alpi Graie [I] 70 C5
Forno di Zoldo [I] 72 E4
Fornos de Algodres [P] 80 D6
Fornovo di Taro [I] 110 D3
Foros do Arrão [P] 86 D5
Forøy [N] 190 D1
Forráskút [H] 76 E4
Forres [GB] 6 E5
Fors [S] 166 D6
Fors [S] 174 D5
Fors [S] 184 G1
Forsa [N] 192 E4
Forsbacka [S] 174 E4
Forsby / Koskenkylä [FIN] 178 B4
Forserum [S] 162 D2
Forset [N] 170 H2
Forshaga [S] 166 F2
Forsheda [S] 162 C4
Forshem [S] 166 E5
Förslöv [S] 162 B6
Forsmark [S] 174 F5
Forsmo [S] 184 E2
Forsnacken [S] 190 F3
Forsnäs [S] 190 G3
Forsnäs [S] 190 G2
Forsnes [N] 180 F1
Forsøl [N] 194 B2
Forssa [FIN] 176 F3
Forst [D] 34 G4
Forstinning [D] 60 E4
Forsvik [S] 166 G5
Fort Augustus [GB] 6 D5
Forte dei Marmi [I] 110 D5
Forte di Bibbiona [I] 114 E1
Forth [D] 46 G5
Fort-Mahon-Plage [F] 28 D3
Fortrose [GB] 6 E4
Fortun [N] 170 E1
Fortuna [E] 104 C2
Fortuneswell [GB] 12 F5
Fort William [GB] 6 C6
Forvik [N] 190 D3
Fos [F] 84 F5
Fösked [S] 166 F2
Foskros [S] 182 E5
Foskvallen [S] 182 E6
Fosnavåg [N] 180 C4
Fosnes [N] 190 C4
Fossano [I] 108 G2
Fossanova, Abbazia di- [I] 120 C1
Fossbakken [N] 192 F3
Fossby [N] 166 C3
Fossen [N] 180 D6
Fosser [N] 166 C1
Fosses [B] 30 C5
Fossland [N] 190 C5
Fossombrone [I] 112 B6
Fos-sur-Mer [F] 106 G5
Foteiná [GR] 128 G5
Foucarmont [F] 28 C4
Fouesnant [F] 40 B3
Fougères [F] 26 D5
Fougerolles [F] 58 C3
Foulain [F] 56 H2
Foulum [DK] 160 D5
Fouras [F] 54 C5
Fourcès [F] 66 D6
Fourfourás [GR] 140 D5
Foúrka [GR] 128 D6
Fourmies [F] 28 G5
Fourná [GR] 132 F3
Fourneaux [F] 54 H6
Fournels [F] 68 C5
Fournés [GR] 140 C4
Foúrnoi [GR] 138 H1
Fourquet [F] 66 F6
Fours [F] 56 E4
Foústani [GR] 128 G3
Fowey [GB] 12 C5
Foxford [IRL] 2 C3
Foynes [IRL] 4 C3
Foz [E] 78 E2
Foz do Arelho [P] 86 B3
Foz Giraldo [P] 86 E3
Frabosa Soprana [I] 108 G3
Frącki [PL] 24 E3
Fraga [E] 90 G5
Fragkísta [GR] 132 E4
Fragkokástello [GR] 140 C5
Fraize [F] 58 D2
Framley [DK] 156 D1
Framlingham [GB] 14 G3
Frammersbach [D] 46 D3
Främmestad [S] 166 D6
Framnäs [S] 190 H1
Frampol [PL] 52 F2
Framzelle [F] 14 G6
Francardo [F] 114 B3
Francavilla al Mare [I] 116 D4
Francavilla di Sicilia [I] 124 A8
Francavilla Fontana [I] 122 F4
Francelos [P] 80 B4
Francofonte [I] 126 G4
Frändefors [S] 166 D5
Franeker [NL] 16 F2
Frangy [F] 70 A2
Frankenberg [D] 32 E5
Frankenberg [D] 48 D1
Frankenburg [A] 60 H4
Frankenmarkt [A] 60 H5
Frankenthal [D] 46 B4
Frankfurt (Oder) [D] 34 G3
Frankfurt am Main [D] 46 C3
Frankrike [S] 190 D6
Frånsta [S] 184 D4
Františkovy Lázně [CZ] 48 C3
Franzburg [D] 20 C3
Frasassi, Grotte di- [I] 116 B1
Frascati [I] 116 A6
Frasdorf [D] 60 F5
Fraserburgh [GB] 6 G5
Frashër [AL] 128 C5
Frasne [F] 58 B6
Frasno, Puerto de- [E] 90 D4
Frassino [I] 108 F2
Frassinoro [I] 110 E4
Frasso [I] 120 E2
Fratel [P] 86 E4
Fratte Polesine [I] 110 G2
Frauenau [D] 60 H2
Frauenberg [D] 46 D1
Frauenburg [A] 74 B2
Frauenfeld [CH] 58 G4
Frauenkirch [CH] 72 A2
Frauenkirchen [A] 62 G5
Frauenstein [A] 62 B5
Frauenstein [D] 48 E1
Frauschereck [A] 60 H4
Frayssinet [F] 66 G4
Frechen [D] 30 G4
Frechilla [E] 82 C6
Freckenhorst [D] 32 C3
Fredensborg [DK] 156 G2
Fredericia [DK] 156 C2
Frederiks [DK] 160 C5
Frederiksberg [DK] 156 F3
Frederikshavn [DK] 160 E3
Frederikssund [DK] 156 G2
Frederiksværk [DK] 156 G2
Frednowy [PL] 22 F4
Fredrika [S] 190 G5
Fredriksberg [S] 172 G5
Fredrikshamn / Hamina [FIN] 178 D3
Fredrikstad [N] 166 B3
Fredriksten [N] 166 C3
Freest [D] 20 E3
Fregenal de la Sierra [E] 94 G3
Fregene [I] 114 H5
Frei [N] 180 F2
Freiberg [D] 48 E1
Freiburg [D] 18 E3
Freiburg im Breisgau [D] 58 E3
Freienesteinau [D] 46 D2
Freihung [D] 48 B5
Freila [E] 102 F3
Freilassing [D] 60 G5
Freising [D] 60 E3
Freistadt [A] 62 C3
Freital [D] 48 E1
Freixedas [P] 80 E6
Freixianda [P] 86 D3
Freixo de Espada à Cinta [P] 80 F5
Frejev [DK] 160 D4
Frejlev [DK] 20 B1
Fréjus [F] 108 D5
Fréjus, Tunnel de- [F/I] 70 B5
Frenchpark [IRL] 2 D4
Frenštát pod Radhoštěm [CZ] 50 E5
Freren [D] 32 C1
Freshford [IRL] 4 E4
Fresnay-sur-Sarthe [F] 26 F6
Fresnes [F] 28 F4
Fresnes [F] 58 B3
Fresnes-en-Woëvre [F] 44 E4
Fresno Alhándiga [E] 88 C4
Fresno de la Ribera [E] 88 D1
Fresno de Sayago [E] 80 G4
Fresno de Sayago [E] 80 G5
Fresvik [N] 170 D2
Fréteval [F] 42 D6
Fretigney-et-Velloreille [F] 58 B4
Fretzdorf [D] 20 C6
Freudenberg [D] 32 C6
Freudenberg [D] 46 D4
Freudenstadt [D] 58 F2
Freundsberg [A] 72 E1
Frévent [F] 28 E3
Freyburg [D] 34 B5
Freyenstein [D] 20 B5
Freyming Merlebach [F] 44 F4
Freystadt [D] 46 G6
Freyung [D] 60 H2
Frías [E] 82 F5
Fribourg [CH] 58 D6
Frick [CH] 58 E4
Fridafors [S] 162 D6
Fridingen [D] 58 G3
Friedberg [A] 74 E1
Friedberg [D] 46 C2
Friedberg [D] 60 D3
Friedburg [A] 60 H5
Friedeburg [D] 18 C4
Friedersdorf [D] 34 F3
Friedewald [D] 32 F6
Friedland [D] 20 D4
Friedland [D] 32 F5
Friedland [D] 34 F3
Friedrichroda [D] 46 F1
Friedrichshafen [D] 58 H4
Friedrichskoog [D] 18 E3
Friedrichsort [D] 18 G2
Friedrichstadt [D] 18 E2
Friedrichswalde [D] 20 D6
Friedstein [A] 62 B6
Friesach [A] 74 B2
Friesack [D] 34 D1
Friesenheim [D] 58 E2
Friesoythe [D] 18 C5
Frifelt [DK] 156 B3
Friggesund [S] 184 D6
Frihetsli [N] 192 G3
Frillesås [S] 160 H3
Frinkenberg [A] 72 E1
Frinnaryd [S] 162 E1
Friol [E] 78 D3
Fristad [S] 162 B2
Fritsla [S] 162 B2
Fritzlar [D] 32 E5
Fröderyd [S] 162 E3
Frödinge [S] 162 F2
Frohburg [D] 34 C6
Frohnleiten [A] 74 D1
Froissy [F] 28 D5
Fröjel [S] 168 F5
Frombork [PL] 22 F2
Frome [GB] 12 G4
Fromental [F] 26 F5
Fromentine [F] 54 A2
Frómista [E] 82 D5
Fromy [F] 44 D2
Fronsac [F] 84 F4
Fronteira [P] 86 E5
Frontenhausen [D] 60 F3
Frontera [E] 100 A5
Frontignan [F] 106 E4
Frontignon [F] 84 H2
Fronton [F] 84 H2
Fröseke [S] 162 F4
Frosinone [I] 116 C6
Fröskog [S] 166 D4
Frösö [S] 182 G2
Frosolone [I] 120 E1
Frossay [F] 40 E6
Frosta [N] 190 B6
Frostavallen [S] 158 C2
Frösthult [S] 168 C2
Frøstrup [DK] 160 C3
Frösunda [S] 168 E2
Frövi [S] 166 H2
Frøyrak [N] 164 D4
Fruges [F] 28 E3
Frutigen [CH] 70 D1
Fry [GR] 140 G3
Frýdek-Místek [CZ] 50 F5
Frýdlant [CZ] 48 G1
Frýdlant nad Ostravicí [CZ] 50 F5
Frýdštejn [CZ] 48 H2
Frygnowo [PL] 22 G5
Frymburk [CZ] 62 B3
Fryšták [CZ] 50 D6
Frysztak [PL] 52 D4
Fteri [GR] 132 F6
Ftterë [AL] 128 B6
Fuans [F] 58 C5
Fubine [I] 70 E6
Fucécchio [I] 110 E5
Fuencalderas [E] 84 C5
Fuencaliente [E] 96 D5
Fuencaliente de la Palma [E] 100 A4
Fuencaliente de Lucio [E] 82 E4
Fuencarral [E] 88 F5
Fuendejalón [E] 90 D3
Fuendetodos [E] 90 E4
Fuengirola [E] 102 B5
Fuenlabrada [E] 88 F6
Fuenlabrada de los Montes [E] 96 C3
Fuenmayor [E] 82 G6
Fuensalida [E] 96 E1
Fuensanta [E] 104 C3
Fuente Álamo [E] 98 C6
Fuente Álamo de Murcia [E] 104 C4
Fuentealbilla [E] 98 C4
Fuentecén [E] 88 G2
Fuente Dé [E] 82 D3
Fuente de Cantos [E] 94 G3
Fuente del Arco [E] 94 H4
Fuente del Maestre [E] 94 G3
Fuente del Obispo [E] 102 E2
Fuente de Pedro Naharro [E] 96 H2
Fuente de Santa Cruz [E] 88 E3
Fuente el Fresno [E] 96 F3
Fuente el Sauz [E] 88 G5
Fuente el Sol [E] 88 D3
Fuenteguinaldo [E] 86 H2
Fuentelapeña [E] 88 D2
Fuentelcésped [E] 88 G2
Fuentelespino de Haro [E] 96 H3
Fuentelespino de Moya [E] 98 D3
Fuentemilanos [E] 88 F4
Fuente Obejuna [E] 96 B5
Fuente Palmera [E] 102 B1
Fuentepinilla [E] 90 B3
Fuenterrabía / Hondarribia [E] 84 B2
Fuentes [E] 98 C2
Fuentesaúco [E] 80 H6
Fuentes de Andalucía [E] 102 A2
Fuentes de Ayódar [E] 98 F3
Fuentes de Ebro [E] 90 E4
Fuentes de Jiloca [E] 90 D4
Fuentes de León [E] 94 G4
Fuentes de Nava [E] 82 C6
Fuentes de Oñoro [E] 86 H2
Fuentes de Ropel [E] 82 A5
Fuentidueña de Tajo [E] 96 H1
Fuerte del Rey [E] 102 E2
Fügen [A] 72 E1
Fuglebjerg [DK] 156 F3
Fuglem [N] 182 C2

Fuhrberg [D] 32 G1
Fulda [D] 46 E2
Fulnek [CZ] 50 E5
Fülöpszállás [H] 76 C3
Fulpmes [A] 72 D1
Fulunäs [S] 172 E2
Fumay [F] 30 C6
Fumel [F] 66 F5
Funäsdalen [S] 182 E4
Funchal [P] 100 A3
Fundão [P] 86 F2
Fundres / Pfundres [I] 72 E2
Furadouro [P] 80 B4
Furculești [RO] 148 B2
Fure [N] 170 B1
Furnas [P] 100 E3
Furnes (Veurne) [B] 28 F1
Fürnitz [A] 72 H3
Fursest [N] 180 D4
Furset [N] 180 E2
Fürstenau [D] 32 C1
Fürstenberg [D] 20 D5
Fürstenfeld [A] 74 E2
Fürstenfeldbruck [D] 60 D4
Fürstenwalde [D] 34 F2
Fürstenwerder [D] 20 D5
Fürstenzell [D] 60 H3
Furta [H] 76 G2
Furtan [S] 166 E2
Fürth [D] 46 G5
Furth im Wald [D] 48 D6
Furtwangen [D] 58 F3
Furuby [S] 162 E4
Furudal [S] 172 H2
Furuflaten [N] 192 G2
Furusjö [S] 162 D1
Furusund [S] 168 F2
Furutangvik [N] 190 D4
Furuvik [S] 174 E4
Fusa [N] 170 B4
Fuscaldo [I] 124 D4
Fusch [A] 72 G1
Fushë Arrëz [AL] 128 B1
Fushë–Krujë [AL] 128 B2
Fushë–Kuqe [AL] 128 B2
Fushë Muhurr [AL] 128 C2
Fusio [CH] 70 F2
Füssen [D] 60 C6
Futog [SRB] 142 F1
Futrikelv [N] 192 F2
Füzesabony [H] 64 E5
Füzesgyarmat [H] 76 G2
Fuzeta [P] 94 D6
Fyláki [GR] 132 G3
Fylákio [GR] 130 H1
Fylakopi [GR] 138 D4
Fylí [GR] 134 B6
Fylí [GR] 134 C6
Fyllinge [S] 162 B5
Fynshav [DK] 156 D4
Fyresdal [N] 164 E3
Fyrkat [DK] 160 D5
Fyteíes [GR] 132 E4

G

Gaas [A] 74 F2
Gaasbeek [B] 28 H3
Gabarc [BG] 146 G3
Gabarret [F] 66 D6
Gabčíkovo [SK] 62 H5
Gabela [BIH] 144 C3
Gaber [BG] 146 F4
Gabicce Mare [I] 112 B5
Gąbin [PL] 36 H2
Gąbino [PL] 22 B2
Gaboš [HR] 142 E1
Gabrovica [BG] 146 G5
Gabrovka [SLO] 74 C5
Gabrovo [BG] 148 C4
Gać [PL] 24 D6
Gacé [F] 26 G5
Gacko [BIH] 144 D2
Gäda [S] 184 C5
Gäddede [S] 190 E5
Gäddeholm [S] 168 C2
Gadebusch [D] 18 H4
Gadna [H] 64 F4
Gádor [E] 102 G5
Gádoros [H] 76 F3
Gadžin Han [SRB] 146 D4
Gæidno [N] 194 D2
Gæidnovuoppe [N] 194 B4
Gaël [F] 26 B5
Găești [RO] 204 D5
Gaeta [I] 120 C2
Gaflenz [A] 62 C5
Gagarin [RUS] 202 E3
Gaggenau [D] 58 F1
Gagliano Castelferrato [I] 126 F3
Gagliano del Capo [I] 122 G6
Gagnef [S] 172 H4
Gahro [D] 34 E4
Gaildorf [D] 46 E6
Gaillac [F] 106 B2
Gaillimh / Galway [IRL] 2 C5
Gaillon [F] 28 C6
Gainsborough [GB] 10 F5
Gairloch [GB] 6 C4
Gairo [I] 118 E5
Gaj [HR] 142 B1
Gaj [SRB] 142 H2
Gajary [SK] 62 G4
Gajdobra [SRB] 142 F1
Gakovo [SRB] 76 C5
Gålå [N] 170 H1
Galåbodarna [S] 182 F3
Galan [F] 84 F4
Galanádo [GR] 138 F3
Galanito [N] 194 B4
Galanta [SK] 62 H4
Galapagar [E] 88 F5
Galashiels [GB] 8 E4
Galata [BG] 148 F3
Galatáki, Moní– [GR] 134 B4
Galatás [GR] 136 G2
Galați [RO] 204 E4
Galatia (Mehmetcik) [CY] 154 G4
Galati Marina [I] 124 B7
Galatina [I] 122 G5
Galátista [GR] 130 B5
Galatone [I] 122 G5
Galaxídi [GR] 132 G5
Galbally [IRL] 4 D4
Gålborget [S] 184 F1
Galdakao [E] 82 G4
Gáldar [E] 100 C6
Galeata [I] 110 G5
Galera [E] 102 G3
Galéria [F] 114 A3
Galgaguta [H] 64 D5
Galgagyörk [H] 64 D5
Galgamácsa [H] 64 D6
Galicea Mare [RO] 146 F1
Galinóporni (Kaleburnu) [CY] 154 H4
Galiny [PL] 22 H3
Galipsós [GR] 130 C4
Galissás [GR] 138 D2
Galisteo [E] 86 H4
Galižana [HR] 112 D2
Galizano [E] 82 F3
Gallarate [I] 70 F4
Gällared [S] 162 B4
Gallargues [F] 106 F4
Gallarus Oratory [IRL] 4 A3
Gallegos del Río [E] 80 G4
Gallegos de Solmirón [E] 88 C4
Gallenstein [A] 62 C6
Galliate [I] 70 F5
Gallípoli [I] 122 G5
Gällivare [S] 192 G6
Gallneukirchen [A] 62 B4
Gällö [S] 182 H3
Gällstad [S] 162 C2
Gallur [E] 90 D3
Galovo [BG] 146 G2
Gålsjö bruk [S] 184 F2
Galston [GB] 8 D3
Galtelli [I] 118 E4
Galten [DK] 156 D1
Galten [N] 182 D6
Gältjärn [S] 184 E4
Galtström [S] 184 F5
Galtür [A] 72 B2
Galveias [P] 86 D5
Gálvez [E] 96 E2
Gałwany [PL] 24 B3
Galway / Gaillimh [IRL] 2 C5
Galyatető [H] 64 E5
Gamaches [F] 28 C4
Gambara [I] 110 D1
Gambárie [I] 124 C7
Gambatesa [I] 120 F1
Gambolò [I] 70 F5
Gaming [A] 62 D5
Gamla Gränome [S] 168 D1
Gamla Uppsala [S] 168 D1
Gamleby [S] 162 G2
Gammalsälen [S] 172 F4
Gammel Estrup [DK] 160 E5
Gammel Skagen [DK] 160 E2
Gammelskolla [N] 172 B2
Gammelstaden [S] 196 B3
Gammertingen [D] 58 H3
Gams [CH] 58 H5
Gamvik [N] 194 D1
Gamzigrad [SRB] 146 D2
Gan [F] 84 E3
Ganacker [D] 60 G3
Ganagobie, Prieuré– [F] 108 C3
Gand (Gent) [B] 28 G2
Gandal [N] 164 B3
Gàndara [P] 86 E2
Ganderkesee [D] 18 D5
Gandesa [E] 90 G6
Gandia [E] 98 F6
Gandino [I] 70 H4
Gandrup [DK] 160 E4
Gandvik [N] 194 E2
Ganges [F] 106 E3
Gangi [I] 126 E3
Gângiova [RO] 146 G2
Gangkofen [D] 60 G3
Gannat [F] 68 D1
Gänserndorf [A] 62 F4
Gap [F] 108 D2
Gaperhult [S] 166 E4
Gara [H] 76 C5
Garaballa [E] 98 D3
Garabonc [H] 74 G3
Garafía [E] 100 A4
Garaguso [I] 122 C4
Gara Khitrino [BG] 148 E2
Garani [BY] 202 B5
Garavac [BIH] 142 D2
Garbagna [I] 110 B2
Garbno [PL] 24 B3
Garbów [PL] 38 D5
Garbsen [D] 32 F2
Garching [D] 60 G4
Garcia [E] 90 H6
Garciaz [E] 96 B2
Garčin [HR] 142 D2
Gârcov [RO] 148 A2
Gard, Pont du– [F] 106 G3
Garda [I] 72 C6
Gardanne [F] 108 B5
Gårdby [S] 162 G5
Gardeja [PL] 22 E4
Gardelegen [D] 34 B2
Gardíki [GR] 132 F4
Garding [D] 18 E2
Gärdnäs [S] 190 E5
Gardone Riviera [I] 72 B5
Gardone Val Trómpia [I] 72 B5
Gárdony [H] 76 B2
Gårdsby [S] 162 E4
Gardsjöbäcken [S] 190 F3
Gårdskär [S] 174 F4
Gårdslösa [S] 162 G5
Gardstad [N] 190 C4
Gårdstånga [S] 158 C2
Garein [F] 66 C5
Gårelehöjden [S] 184 E1
Garen [N] 170 D4
Gares / Puente la Reina [E] 84 B4
Garešnica [HR] 74 G6
Garéssio [I] 108 G3
Gargaliánoi [GR] 136 C4
Gargas, Grotte de– [F] 84 F4
Gargaur [S] 190 G3
Gargellen [A] 72 A2
Gargilesse–Dampierre [F] 54 H5
Gargnano [I] 72 C5
Gargoles de Abajo [E] 90 A5
Gárgyán [H] 76 D4
Gargždai [LT] 200 D4
Gari [MK] 128 D2
Garibaldi, Tomba di– [I] 118 E2
Garípa [GR] 140 E5
Garkalne [LV] 198 D5
Garlasco [I] 70 F5
Garlin [F] 84 E2
Garlstorf [D] 18 F5
Garmisch Partenkirchen [D] 60 D6
Garmo [N] 180 F5
Garnisch Gardens [IRL] 4 B5
Garoza [LV] 198 D5
Garpenberg [S] 174 D5
Garraf [E] 92 D5
Garrafe de Torío [E] 78 H5
Garray [E] 90 B2
Garrel [D] 18 C5
Garristown [IRL] 2 F5
Garrotxa, Zona Volcànica de la– [E] 92 F2
Garrovillas [E] 86 G4
Garrucha [E] 102 H5
Gars am Kamp [A] 62 E3
Garsås [S] 172 G3
Garsnas [S] 158 D3
Gartland [N] 190 C5
Gartow [D] 20 A6
Gartringen [D] 58 G1
Gartz [D] 20 E5
Garvão [P] 94 C3
Garwolin [PL] 38 C4
Garz [D] 20 D2
Gåsborn [S] 166 G1
Gåsbue [N] 180 F4
Gaschurn [A] 72 B2
Gascueña [E] 98 B1
Gasen [A] 74 D1
Gaskeluokta [S] 190 F4
Gąski [PL] 24 D3
Gąsocin [PL] 38 B1
Gaspoltshofen [A] 62 A4
Gässåsen [S] 184 D5
Gasteiner Klamm [A] 72 G1
Gastes [F] 66 B4
Gastoúni [GR] 136 B2
Gasztony [H] 74 F2
Gata [N] 172 C4
Gata de Gorgos [E] 104 F1
Gatchina [RUS] 178 H6
Gatehouse of Fleet [GB] 8 D5
Gåtér [H] 76 E3
Gateshead [GB] 8 G6
Gátova [E] 98 E4
Gatta [I] 110 D3
Gattendorf [A] 62 G5
Gattinara [I] 70 E4
Gaubert [F] 42 E5
Gaucín [E] 100 H4
Gaukås [N] 164 E3
Gaulstad [N] 190 C5
Gaupne [N] 170 D1
Gaushach [D] 46 E3
Gausvik [N] 192 E4
Gautefall [N] 164 F3
Gautestad [N] 164 D4
Gauville [F] 26 G5
Gavaloú [GR] 132 E5
Gavardo [I] 72 B6
Gavarnie [F] 84 E5
Gavarnie, Cirque de– [F] 84 E5
Gávavencsellő [H] 64 G4
Gaverina Terme [I] 70 H4
Gavi [I] 110 A2
Gavião [P] 86 E4
Gavirate [I] 70 F4
Gävle [S] 174 E4
Gavnø Slot [DK] 156 F4
Gavoi [I] 118 D4
Gavorrano [I] 114 F2
Gavray [F] 26 D4
Gavrilov- Yam [RUS] 202 F1
Gávrio [GR] 134 E6
Gávros [GR] 128 E5
Gavry [RUS] 198 G5
Gåvsta [S] 168 D1
Gävunda [S] 172 G4
Gäxsjö [S] 190 E6
Gaziköy [TR] 150 C4
Gazimağusa (Ammóchostos) [CY] 154 G5
Gazoldo degli Ippoliti [I] 110 E1
Gázoros [GR] 130 C3
Gbelce [SK] 64 B5
Gdańsk [PL] 22 E2
Gdov [RUS] 202 A2
Gdów [PL] 52 B4
Gdynia [PL] 22 E2
Gea de Albarracín [E] 98 D1
Geashill [IRL] 2 E6
Geaune [F] 84 E2
Gebesee [D] 32 H6
Geblar [D] 46 F1
Gebze [TR] 150 F3
Geçitkale (Lefkónikon) [CY] 154 G5
Geçkinli [TR] 150 B2
Gedem [D] 46 D2
Gedesby [DK] 20 B1
Gedinne [B] 44 D1
Gediz [TR] 152 G2
Gedser [DK] 20 B1
Gedsted [DK] 160 D4
Gedved [DK] 156 D1
Geel [B] 30 D3
Geertruidenberg [NL] 16 D6
Geeste [D] 16 H4
Geesthacht [D] 18 G4
Gefell [D] 48 B2
Gefrees [D] 46 H3
Gefýra [GR] 128 H4
Gefýria [GR] 132 F3
Gehren [D] 46 G2
Geijersholm [S] 172 F6
Geilenkirchen [D] 30 F4
Geilo [N] 170 E4
Geiranger [N] 180 E4
Geisa [D] 46 E1
Geiselhöring [D] 60 F2
Geiselwind [D] 46 F4
Geisenfeld [D] 60 E3
Geisenhausen [D] 60 F3
Geisingen [D] 58 G3
Geislingen [D] 60 B3
Geisnes [N] 190 C4
Geithain [D] 34 D6
Geithus [N] 170 G6
Gela [I] 126 E5
Geldern [D] 30 G2
Geldrop [NL] 30 E2
Geleen [NL] 30 F4
Gelej [H] 64 F5
Gelembe [TR] 152 D2
Gelgaudiškis [LT] 200 E5
Gelibolu [TR] 150 B5
Gelibolu [TR] 154 D1
Gelida [E] 92 D4
Gelnhausen [D] 46 D3
Gelnica [SK] 64 F2
Gelsa [E] 90 F4
Gelsenkirchen [D] 30 H3
Gelting [D] 156 C5
Gelu [RO] 76 G5
Gembloux [B] 30 D5
Gémenos [F] 108 B5
Gemerská Poloma [SK] 64 E3
Gemerská Ves [SK] 64 E3
Gemert [NL] 30 F2
Gemikonaği (Karavostasi) [CY] 154 F5
Gemiş [TR] 152 H5
Gemlik [TR] 150 F4
Gemmenich [B] 30 F4
Gemona del Friuli [I] 72 G4
Gémozac [F] 54 C6
Gemünd [D] 30 F5
Gemünden [D] 32 E6
Gemünden [D] 44 H2
Gemünden [D] 46 E3
Genappe [B] 30 C4
Génave [E] 96 G6
Genazzano [I] 116 B5
Gençay [F] 54 E4
Gencsapáti [H] 74 F1
Génelard [F] 56 F5
General Inzovo [BG] 148 D5
Generalski Stol [HR] 112 G1
General Toshevo [BG] 148 F1
Generli [TR] 150 C3
Genevad [S] 162 B5
Genève [CH] 70 B2
Gengenbach [D] 58 F2
Genillé [F] 54 G3
Genk [B] 30 E4
Genlis [F] 56 H4
Gennádio [GR] 154 D4
Genna Maria, Nuraghe– [I] 118 C6
Gennep [NL] 16 F6
Gennes [F] 54 E2
Génolhac [F] 68 D6
Génova [I] 110 B3
Genshagen [D] 34 E3
Gent (Gand) [B] 28 G2
Genthin [D] 34 C2
Gentioux [F] 68 A2
Genzano di Lucánia [I] 120 H3
Genzano di Roma [I] 116 A6
Georgianoí [GR] 128 G5
Georgioúpoli [GR] 140 C4
Georgi Traykov [BG] 148 F3
Georgsheil [D] 18 B4
Geotermia, Museo della– [I] 114 F1
Gera [D] 48 C1
Geraardsbergen [B] 28 H3
Gerabronn [D] 46 E5
Gerace [I] 124 D7
Gerakarou [GR] 130 B4
Gérakas [GR] 136 F4
Geráki [GR] 136 E4
Gerakiní [GR] 130 B5
Gérardmer [F] 58 D2
Geras [A] 62 E3
Gerasdorf bei Wien [A] 62 F4
Gerbéviller [F] 44 F6
Gerbstedt [D] 34 B4
Gérce [H] 74 G2
Gerchsheim [D] 46 E4
Geremeas [I] 118 D7
Gerena [E] 94 G5
Gerês [P] 78 B6
Geretsried [D] 60 E5
Gérgal [E] 102 G4
Gerince [TR] 154 C2
Gerlos [A] 72 E1
Germaringen [D] 60 C5
Germasogela [CY] 154 F6
Germay [F] 44 D6
Germencik [TR] 152 D5
Germering [D] 60 C4
Germering [D] 60 D4
Germersheim [D] 46 B5
Germigny–des–Pres [F] 42 F6
Gernika–Lumo [E] 82 H4
Gernrode [D] 34 A4
Gernsbach [D] 58 F1
Gernsheim [D] 46 C4
Gerola Alta [I] 70 H3
Gerolímenas [GR] 136 E5
Gerolstein [D] 30 G6
Gerolzhofen [D] 46 F4
Gerona / Girona [E] 92 F3
Geroskípou [CY] 154 F6
Gerovo [HR] 112 F1
Gerri de la Sal [E] 92 C1
Gersfeld [D] 46 E2
Gersthofen [D] 60 D3
Gerswalde [D] 20 D6
Gesäter [S] 166 C4
Gesäuse [A] 62 C6
Gescher [D] 16 G6
Geseke [D] 32 D4
Gespunsart [F] 44 C2
Gestelnburg [CH] 70 E2
Gesualdo [I] 120 F3
Gesunda [S] 172 G3
Geta [FIN] 176 A5
Getafe [E] 88 F6
Getaria [E] 84 A2
Gettlinge [S] 162 G6
Gettorf [D] 18 F2
Getxo [E] 82 G3
Gévezé [F] 26 C5
Gevgelija [MK] 128 G3
Gevigney–et–Mercey [F] 58 B3
Gevrey–Chambertin [F] 56 G4
Gevsjön [S] 182 E1
Gex [F] 70 B2
Gey [D] 30 F5
Geyikli [TR] 130 H6
Geyre [TR] 152 F5
Geysir [IS] 192 B3
Geyve [TR] 150 G3
Geziq [AL] 128 B1
Göhl [A] 62 D3
Ghedi [I] 72 B6
Gheorghieni [RO] 204 D4
Ghilarza [I] 118 C4
Ghimpaţi [RO] 148 C1
Ghisonaccia [F] 114 C4
Ghisoni [F] 114 B4
Giáltra [GR] 132 H4
Giannitsá [GR] 128 G4
Giannoúli [GR] 130 H2
Giardinetto [I] 120 G2
Giardini–Naxos [I] 124 B8
Giarmata [RO] 76 G5
Giarratana [I] 126 F5
Giarre [I] 124 A8
Giat [F] 68 B2
Giba [I] 118 B7
Gibellina [I] 126 B2
Gibellina, Ruderi di– [I] 126 C2
Gibilmanna, Santuario di– [I] 126 E2
Gibostad [N] 192 F2
Gibraleón [E] 94 E5
Gibraltar [GBZ] 100 G5
Gic [H] 74 H1
Gidböle [S] 184 G1
Gideå [S] 184 G1
Gideåkroken [S] 190 G5
Gidle [PL] 50 G1
Gieboldehausen [D] 32 G4
Giedraičiai [LT] 200 G5
Gielas [S] 190 E3
Gielniów [PL] 38 A5
Gien [F] 56 C2
Giengedal [N] 180 C5
Giengen [D] 60 C3
Giens [F] 108 C6
Giera [RO] 142 H1
Gierałtowice [PL] 50 G4
Gieselwerder [D] 32 F4
Giessen [D] 46 C1
Gieten [NL] 16 G3
Giethoorn [NL] 16 F3
Gietrzwałd [PL] 22 G4
Giffoni [I] 120 F3
Gifhorn [D] 32 H2
Gigen [BG] 148 A2
Giglio Porto [I] 114 E4
Gignac [F] 106 E4
Gijón / Xixón [E] 82 B1
Giksi [LV] 198 E4
Gilford [NIR] 2 G4
Gilja [N] 164 B3
Gilleleje [DK] 156 G1
Gillhov [S] 182 G4
Gills [GB] 6 F2
Gillstad [S] 166 E5
Gilserberg [D] 32 E6
Gilze [NL] 30 D2
Gimat [F] 84 G2
Gimdalen [S] 184 C3
Gimel–les–Cascades [F] 66 H3
Gimenells, Castell de– [E] 90 G4
Gimmestad [N] 180 C5
Gimo [S] 174 F5
Gimont [F] 84 G3
Ginci [BG] 146 F4
Gingst [D] 20 D2
Ginosa [I] 122 D4
Ginzling [A] 72 E2
Ginzo de Limia / Xinzo de Limia [E] 78 C6
Gióes [P] 94 D4
Gióia del Colle [I] 122 E3
Gióia Táuro [I] 124 C6
Gioiosa Marea [I] 124 A7
Giornico [CH] 70 G2
Giove Anxur, Tempio di– [I] 120 C2
Giovinazzo [I] 122 D2
Giraltovce [SK] 52 D6
Girgantai [LT] 24 E2
Girifalco [I] 124 D5
Girne (Kerýneia) [CY] 154 G5
Girolata [F] 114 A3
Giromagny [F] 58 C3
Girona / Gerona [E] 92 F3
Gironella [E] 92 E2
Girvan [GB] 8 C4
Gisholt [N] 164 F3
Gislaved [S] 162 C3
Gislev [DK] 156 E3
Gisors [F] 28 C6
Gisselås [S] 190 E6
Gisselfeld [DK] 156 F3
Gissi [I] 116 E5
Gisslarbo [S] 168 B2
Gistaín [E] 84 F5
Gistel [B] 28 F1
Gistrup [DK] 160 E4
Gittun [S] 190 G2
Giugliano In Campania [I] 120 D3
Giuliano di Roma [I] 120 C1
Giulianova [I] 116 D3
Giulvăz [RO] 76 G6
Giurgița [RO] 146 G2
Giurgiu [RO] 148 C1
Give [DK] 156 C2
Givet [F] 30 D6
Givors [F] 68 F3
Givry [B] 28 H4
Givry [F] 56 E3
Givry [F] 56 G5
Givry–en–Argonne [F] 44 C4
Giżałki [PL] 36 E3
Gizdavac [HR] 144 A1
Gizeux [F] 54 F2
Giżycko [PL] 24 C3
Gizzeria [I] 124 D5
Gjakove / Đakovica [SRB] 146 B6
Gjelten [N] 182 B5
Gjemnes [N] 180 F2
Gjerbës [AL] 128 C5
Gjerde [N] 180 D6
Gjermundshamn [N] 170 B5
Gjern [DK] 160 D6
Gjerrild [DK] 160 F5
Gjerstad [N] 164 F4
Gjersvik [N] 190 D4
Gjesvær [N] 194 C1
Gjeving [N] 164 F4
Gjinar [AL] 128 C3
Gjirokastër [AL] 128 C6
Gjølme [N] 180 H1
Gjøra [N] 180 G3
Gjóv [FR] 160 B1
Gjøvik [N] 172 B3
Gjøvik [N] 192 E3
G. Konjare [MK] 128 F1
Gkoritsá [GR] 136 E4
Gkoúra [GR] 136 D1
Gla [GR] 134 A5
Gladbeck [D] 30 H2
Gladenbach [D] 32 D6
Gladhammar [S] 162 G2
Gladstad [N] 190 C3
Glamoč [BIH] 142 B4
Glämos [N] 182 C3
Glamsbjerg [DK] 156 D3
Glandorf [D] 32 D2
Glanmire [IRL] 4 C5
Glanworth [IRL] 4 D4
Glarus [CH] 58 G6
Glasgow [GB] 8 D3
Glashütte [D] 48 E1
Glashütten [A] 74 C3
Glastonbury [GB] 12 F4
Glauchau [D] 48 C1
Glava [BG] 148 A3
Glava [S] 166 D2
Glavan [BG] 148 D5
Glavanovtsi [BG] 146 E4
Glavičice [BIH] 142 E3
Glavinitsa [BG] 148 E1
Glavnik [SRB] 146 C4
Gleann Cholm Cille / Glencolumbkille [IRL] 2 D2
Gleann na Muaidhe / Glenamoy [IRL] 2 C3
Głębock [PL] 22 G2
Glebychevo [RUS] 178 F3
Gleichen [D] 46 G1
Gleina [D] 48 C1
Gleinalm Tunnel [A] 74 D1
Gleisdorf [A] 74 E2
Glenamaddy [IRL] 2 D4
Glenamoy / Gleann na Muaidhe [IRL] 2 C3
Glencoe [GB] 6 C6
Glencolumbkille / Gleann Cholm Cille [IRL] 2 D2
Glendalough [IRL] 4 G3
Glenealy [IRL] 4 G4
Glengarriff [IRL] 4 B5
Glénic [F] 54 H5
Glenmore [IRL] 4 E4
Glenrothes [GB] 8 E3
Glenties [IRL] 2 E2
Glenville [IRL] 4 D5
Glesne [N] 170 G5
Gletsch [CH] 70 F2
Gletscher Garten [D] 60 G5
Glewitz [D] 20 C3
Glimåkra [S] 158 D1
Glimmingehus [S] 158 D3
Glin [IRL] 4 C3
Glina [HR] 112 H1
Glinka [PL] 50 G5
Glinojeck [PL] 38 A1
Glinsce / Glinsk [IRL] 2 B4
Glinsk / Glinsce [IRL] 2 B4
G. Lisina [SRB] 146 E5
Glissjöberg [S] 182 G5
Glitterheim [N] 180 F6
Gliwice [PL] 50 F3
Gllavë [AL] 128 B5
Globitsy [RUS] 178 F5
Globočica [SRB] 146 C6
Głodowa [PL] 22 B3
Gloggnitz [A] 62 E6
Głogoczów [PL] 50 H4
Glogovac [HR] 74 G5
Głogów [PL] 36 B5
Głogówek [PL] 50 E3
Głogów Małopolski [PL] 52 E3
Glomfjord [N] 190 E1
Glommen [S] 160 H4
Glommersträsk [S] 190 H4
Glömminge [S] 162 G5
Glorup [DK] 156 E4
Glóssa [GR] 134 B3
Glössbo [S] 174 E2
Glossop [GB] 10 E4
Glostrup [DK] 156 G2
Glöte [S] 182 F5
Gloucester [GB] 12 G2
Głowaczów [PL] 38 C4
Główczyce [PL] 22 C2
Glowe [D] 20 D2
Glöwen [D] 20 B6
Głowno [PL] 36 H4
Gložan [SRB] 142 F1
Glozhene [BG] 146 G2
Glozhene [BG] 148 A4
Glozhenski Manastir [BG] 148 A4
Głubczyce [PL] 50 E3
Głuchołazy [PL] 50 D3
Głuchów [PL] 36 F4
Głuchów [PL] 36 H4
Głuchowo [PL] 36 C3
Glücksburg [D] 156 C4
Glückstadt [D] 18 E3
Gluda [LV] 198 D5
Glumsø [DK] 156 F3
Glušci [SRB] 142 F2
Głuszyca [PL] 50 B2
Glýfa [GR] 132 H3
Glyfáda [GR] 132 F5
Glyfáda [GR] 136 G1
Glykí [GR] 132 C3
Glyngøre [DK] 160 C4
Gmünd [A] 62 C3
Gmünd [A] 72 H2
Gmund [D] 60 E5
Gmunden [A] 62 A5
Gnarp [S] 184 E5
Gnarrenburg [D] 18 E4
Gnas [A] 74 E3
Gnesau [A] 74 B3
Gnesta [S] 168 D4
Gneux [F] 44 B3
Gniechowice [PL] 50 C1
Gniew [PL] 22 E4
Gniewkowo [PL] 36 E1
Gniezno [PL] 36 D2
Gnisvärd [S] 168 F4
Gnjilane [SRB] 146 D5
Gnocchetta [I] 110 H2
Gnoien [D] 20 C3
Gnojnice [BIH] 144 C2
Gnosjö [S] 162 C3
Göbel [TR] 150 D5
Göçbeyli [TR] 152 C2
Göçek [TR] 154 F2
Goch [D] 16 F6
Göd [H] 64 C6
Godafoss [IS] 192 C2
Godalming [GB] 14 D5
Godby [FIN] 176 A5
Godech [BG] 146 F4
Godegard [S] 166 H5
Godelheim [D] 32 F4
Gödenroth [D] 44 H1
Goderville [F] 26 G2
Godętowo [PL] 22 D2
Godkowo [PL] 22 G3
Gödöllő [H] 64 D6
Godovič [SLO] 74 B5
Godowa [PL] 52 D4
Godøynes [N] 192 D6
Gödre [H] 76 A4
Godziesze Wielkie [PL] 36 E5
Godziszewo [PL] 22 E3
Goes [NL] 16 B6
Góglio [I] 70 E2
Gogolin [PL] 50 E2
Gógolo [I] 72 C3
Göhren [D] 20 E2
Goirle [NL] 30 E2
Góis [P] 86 E2
Góito [I] 110 E1
Goizueta [E] 84 B3
Gojani i Madh [AL] 128 B1
Gojsaliči [BIH] 142 E4
Gökçedağ [TR] 152 F1
Gökçek [TR] 152 H4
Gökçen [TR] 152 D4
Gökçeören [TR] 152 E3
Gokels [D] 18 F2
Gökova [TR] 154 D1
Gökpınar [TR] 154 H1
Göksholm [S] 166 H3
Göktepe [TR] 150 H3
Göktepe [TR] 152 F6
Gol [N] 170 G4
Gola [HR] 74 G4
Gołąb [PL] 38 D5
Gołańcz [PL] 36 D1
Gölbent [TR] 154 F3
Gölby [FIN] 176 A5
Golchen [D] 20 D4
Gölcük [TR] 150 C4
Gölcük [TR] 150 G3
Gölcük [TR] 152 D2
Gölcük [TR] 152 E4

Golçük [TR] 154 E1
Golčův Jeníkov [CZ] 48 H4
Golczewo [PL] 20 F4
Gołdap [PL] 24 D2
Goldbach [D] 46 D3
Goldberg [D] 20 B4
Goldelund [D] 156 B5
Golden [IRL] 4 D4
Goldenstedt [D] 18 D6
Gölecik [TR] 150 D4
Goleen [IRL] 4 B5
Golegã [P] 86 D4
Goleim [AL] 128 B6
Golema Crcorija [MK] 146 E6
Golemo Selo [SRB] 146 D5
Goleniów [PL] 20 F5
Goleniowy [PL] 50 H2
Golfe-Juan [F] 108 E5
Golfo Aranci [I] 118 E2
Golfo di Sogno [F] 114 B6
Gölhisar [TR] 152 G6
Golina [PL] 36 E3
Goliševa [LV] 198 G5
Golizyno [RUS] 202 F3
Goljam Dervent [BG] 150 B1
Goljamo Belovo [BG] 148 A6
Goljamo Kamenjane [BG] 130 G2
Goljan Man. [BG] 148 D5
Gollden [N] 194 B4
Göllersdörf [A] 62 E3
Gollhofen [D] 46 F4
Golling [A] 60 G6
Gölmarmara [TR] 152 D3
Golmayo [E] 90 B3
Golnice [PL] 36 A5
Golnik [SLO] 74 B4
Golodskoye [RUS] 202 F4
Gölova [TR] 154 H1
Gölpazarı [TR] 150 H4
Golpejas [E] 80 G6
Golspie [GB] 6 E4
Golssen [D] 34 E4
Göltarla [TR] 154 H2
Golub Dobrzyń [PL] 22 E6
Golubovci [MNE] 144 E4
Gołuchów [PL] 36 E4
Golvesh [BG] 148 F1
Gölyaka [TR] 150 D5
Golyalo Krushevo [BG] 148 E5
Golyam porovec [BG] 148 E2
Gölyazi [TR] 150 E5
Gołymin-Ośrodek [PL] 38 B1
Golzow [D] 34 D3
Gómara [E] 90 C3
Gombasecká Jaskyňa [SK] 64 E3
Gombe [TR] 154 G2
Gombo [I] 110 D5
Gömeç [TR] 152 B2
Gomes Aires [P] 94 C4
Gommern [D] 34 B3
Gomunice [PL] 36 G6
Gönc [H] 64 G3
Goncelin [F] 70 A4
Gondomar [P] 80 C4
Gondrecourt [F] 44 D5
Gondrin [F] 66 D6
Gönen [TR] 150 D5
Goni, Nuraghe- [I] 118 D6
Goniá [GR] 140 B4
Goniądz [PL] 24 E4
Gónnoi [GR] 132 G1
Gonnosfanádiga [I] 118 C6
Gönyű [H] 64 A6
Gonzaga [I] 110 E2
Gooik [B] 28 H3
Goole [GB] 10 F4
Goor [NL] 16 G5
Göpfritz [A] 62 D3
Goppenstein [CH] 70 E2
Göppingen [D] 60 B2
Góra [PL] 36 C5
Góra [PL] 36 H2
Góra Kalwaria [PL] 38 C3
Goransko [MNE] 144 D3
Góra Puławska [PL] 38 D5
Góra Świętej Anny [PL] 50 E3
Goražde [BIH] 144 E1
Gorbachevo [RUS] 202 F4
Gördalen [S] 172 E1
Gordaliza del Pino [E] 82 B5
Gordes [F] 106 H3
Gördes [TR] 152 E3
Goren Chiflik [BG] 148 F3
Gorenja Vas [SLO] 74 B5
Goresbridge [IRL] 4 F4
Gorey [IRL] 4 F4
Görgeteg [H] 74 H5
Gorgier [CH] 58 C6
Gorgonzola [I] 70 G5
Gorica [BG] 148 F4
Gorica [BIH] 144 B2
Gorica [HR] 112 F4
Gorica [SLO] 74 D4
Gorica Jamnička [HR] 74 E6
Goričan [HR] 74 F4
Goricë [AL] 128 D4
Gorinchem [NL] 16 D5
Gorino Veneto [I] 110 H3
Goritsy [RUS] 202 E2
Göritz [D] 20 E5
Gorízia [I] 72 H5
Gorjão [P] 86 D4
Gørlev [DK] 156 F3
Gorlice [PL] 52 C5
Görlitz [D] 34 G6
Gormanston Castle [IRL] 2 F5
Gormund [CH] 58 F5
Gorna Beshovica [BG] 146 G3
Gorna Cerovene [BG] 146 F3
Gorna Dikanja [BG] 146 F5
Gorna Kremena [BG] 146 G3
Gorna Mitropoliya [BG] 148 A3
Gorna Oryakhovitsa [BG] 148 C3
Gorna Studena [BG] 148 C3
Gornij [HR] 112 H4
Gorni Tsibur [BG] 146 F2
Gornja Grabovica [BIH] 144 C2
Gornjak, Manastir- [SRB] 146 C1
Gornja Klina [SRB] 146 B5
Gornja Ploča [HR] 112 G4
Gornja Radgona [SLO] 74 E3
Gornja Sabanta [SRB] 146 C2
Gornja Toponica [SRB] 146 D3
Gornja Tuzla [BIH] 142 E3
Gornja Vrijeska [HR] 74 G6
Gornji Lapac [HR] 112 H4
Gornji Milanovac [SRB] 146 B2
Gornji Podgradci [BIH] 142 B2
Gornji Ravno [BIH] 144 B1
Górno [PL] 52 C1
Gorno Alexandrovo [BG] 148 E4
Gorno Novo Selo [BG] 148 C5
Gorno Yabălkovo [BG] 148 E5
Gorobinci [MK] 128 F1
Gorodets [RUS] 198 H2
Gorodno [RUS] 198 H3
Górowo Iławeckie [PL] 22 G2
Gorredijk [NL] 16 F2
Gorron [F] 26 E5
Gørslev [DK] 156 G3
Gort [IRL] 2 C5
Górtys [GR] 136 D2
Górtys [GR] 140 E5
Görükle [TR] 150 E4
Gorv [N] 180 B5
Görvik [S] 184 C1
Gorzanów [PL] 50 C3
Görzke [D] 34 C3
Gorzkowice [PL] 36 G6
Gorzków-Osada [PL] 38 F6
Górzna [PL] 22 B5
Górzno [PL] 22 F6
Górzno [PL] 36 E4
Gorzów Śląski [PL] 50 F1
Gorzów Wielkopolski [PL] 34 H2
Górzyca [PL] 34 G2
Gorzyce [PL] 52 D2
Gorzyń [PL] 36 B2
Goržžam [N] 194 D3
Gosaldo [I] 72 E4
Gosau [A] 60 H6
Göschenen [CH] 70 F1
Gościno [PL] 20 G3
Gosdorf [A] 74 E3
Goslar [D] 32 G3
Goślice [PL] 36 H2
Gósol [E] 92 D2
Gospari [LV] 198 F6
Gospić [HR] 112 G4
Gosport [GB] 12 H5
Gossau [CH] 58 H5
Gosselies [B] 30 C5
Gossensass / Colle Isarco [I] 72 D2
Gössl [A] 62 B6
Gössweinstein [D] 46 G4
Gosticy [RUS] 198 G1
Gostilicy [RUS] 178 G5
Gostivar [MK] 128 D1
Gostków [PL] 36 F4
Göstling [A] 62 C5
Gostomia [PL] 22 A6
Gostun [SRB] 146 A4
Gostycyn [PL] 22 C5
Gostyń [PL] 36 C4
Gostynin [PL] 36 G2
Goszcz [PL] 36 D5
Goszczanowo [PL] 36 A2
Göteborg [S] 160 G2
Götene [S] 166 E5
Gotenica [SLO] 74 C6
Gotha [D] 32 H6
Gothem [S] 168 G4
Götlunda [S] 168 A3
Gotse Delchev [BG] 130 C1
Gottböle [FIN] 186 A4
Gottby [FIN] 176 A5
Gotthard Tunnel [CH] 70 F2
Göttingen [D] 32 F4
Gottne [S] 184 G1
Gottolengo [I] 110 D1
Gottröra [S] 168 E2
Göttweig [A] 62 D4
Götzis [A] 58 H5
Gouarec [F] 26 A5
Gouda [NL] 16 D5
Goules, Col des- [F] 68 C2
Goulven [F] 40 B1
Gouménissa [GR] 128 G3
Goumois [CH] 58 C5
Gourdon [F] 66 G4
Gourin [F] 40 C3
Gournay-en-Bray [F] 28 C5
Goúrnes [GR] 140 E4
Gourniá [GR] 140 G5
Gourville [F] 54 D6
Gout-Rossignol [F] 66 E2
Gouveia [P] 80 D6
Goúves [GR] 140 F4
Gouvets [F] 26 E4
Gouviá [GR] 132 B2
Gouzon [F] 56 B6
Govedartsi [BG] 146 G6
Govedjari [HR] 144 B3
Gøvstdal [N] 170 F5
Goworowo [PL] 24 C6
Gowran [IRL] 4 F4
Göynükbelen [TR] 150 F5
Gózd [PL] 38 C5
Gozdnica [PL] 34 H5
Gózd – Zaszosie [PL] 52 B1
Gözler [TR] 152 G4
Graal-Müritz [D] 20 B2
Grab [BIH] 144 D4
Grab [PL] 36 D4
Grabarka [PL] 38 E2
Grabaț [RO] 76 F5
Graberje [HR] 142 A1
Gråbo [S] 160 H2
Gråborg [S] 162 G5
Grabovac [SRB] 146 C1
Grabow [D] 20 A5
Grabów [PL] 36 F3
Grabowiec [PL] 52 G1
Grabówka [PL] 24 F5
Grabów nad Prosną [PL] 36 E5
Grabownica Starzeńska [PL] 52 E4
Grabowskie [PL] 24 D5
Gračac [HR] 112 H4
Gračanica [BIH] 142 D3
Gračanica [SRB] 142 E4
Gračanica [SRB] 146 C5
Graçay [F] 54 H3
Grächen [CH] 70 E2
Gračišće [HR] 112 D2
Gradac [BIH] 144 C3
Gradac [HR] 144 B3
Gradac [MNE] 144 E2
Gradac [MNE] 144 E4
Gradac, Manastir- [SRB] 146 B3
Gradačac [BIH] 142 D2
Graddis [N] 190 F1
Gräddö [S] 168 F2
Gradec [BG] 146 E2
Gradec Prokupski [HR] 112 H1
Gradefes [E] 82 C4
Graderas, Cueva de las- [E] 90 E6
Gradešnika [MK] 128 F3
Gradets [BG] 148 D4
Gradignan [F] 66 C3
Gradin [SLO] 112 D1
Gradina [HR] 112 F3
Gradina [SRB] 146 E4
Gradinarovo [BG] 148 E3
Gradisca d'Isonzo [I] 72 H5
Gradishte [BG] 148 B3
Gradište [HR] 142 E2
Gradište [SRB] 146 E3
Gradki [PL] 22 H3
Grado [E] 78 G3
Grado [I] 72 G6
Gradówek [PL] 34 H6
Gradsko [MK] 128 F2
Græsted [DK] 156 G1
Grafenau [D] 60 H2
Gräfenberg [D] 46 G4
Grafenegg [A] 62 E4
Gräfenhainichen [D] 34 C4
Grafenwöhr [D] 48 B4
Grafenwörth [A] 62 E4
Grafing [D] 60 E4
Grafrath [D] 60 D4
Gräfsnäs [S] 160 H1
Graglia, Santuário di- [I] 70 E4
Gragnano [I] 120 E3
Gråhaugen [N] 180 G2
Grahovo [MNE] 144 D4
Grahovo [SLO] 74 B6
Graiguenamanagh [IRL] 4 F4
Grainetière, Abbaye de la- [F] 54 C3
Graja, Cueva de la- [E] 102 E2
Grajewo [PL] 24 D4
Gralhos [P] 80 D3
Gralla [A] 74 D3
Grallagh [IRL] 2 D4
Gram [DK] 156 B3
Gramada [BG] 146 E2
Gramat [F] 66 G4
Gramatikovo [BG] 148 F5
Grambow [D] 20 E5
Grametten [A] 62 D2
Gramkow [D] 20 A3
Grammatikó [GR] 132 G3
Gramméni Oxyá [GR] 132 F4
Gramméno [GR] 132 C2
Grammichele [I] 126 F4
Gramsh [AL] 128 C4
Gram Slot [DK] 156 B3
Gramzda [LV] 198 B6
Gramzow [D] 20 D6
Gramzow [D] 20 E5
Gran [N] 172 B4
Granåbron [S] 172 F5
Granada [E] 102 E4
Granadilla de Abona [E] 100 B5
Granard [IRL] 2 E4
Granarolo dell'Emilia [I] 110 F3
Granåsen [S] 190 F5
Granátula de Calatrava [E] 96 F4
Granberget [S] 190 F5
Granboda [FIN] 176 B6
Grancey-le-Château [F] 56 G3
Grandas de Salime [E] 78 F3
Grandcamp-Maisy [F] 26 E2
Grand-Champ [F] 26 A6
Grand Chartreuse, Couvent de la- [F] 68 H4
Grande-Fougeray [F] 40 F5
Grandjouan [F] 40 F5
Grândola [P] 94 C2
Grandpré [F] 44 C3
Grandrieu [F] 68 D5
Grand Roc [F] 66 F3
Grand-Rozoy [F] 42 H3
Grandson [CH] 58 C6
Grand-St-Bernard, Col du- [CH/I] 70 C3
Grand-St-Bernard, Tunnel du- [CH/I] 70 C3
Grandvilliers [F] 28 D5
Grañén [E] 90 F3
Grangärde [S] 172 H5
Grange [IRL] 2 D3
Grange-Bleneau, Château de la- [F] 42 G4
Grange-le-Bocage [F] 42 H5
Grängesberg [S] 172 H6
Granges-sur-Vologne [F] 58 D2
Grängsjö [S] 184 E5
Granhult [S] 192 H6
Graninge [S] 184 E2
Granitola Torretta [I] 126 B3
Granitz, Jagdschloss- [D] 20 E2
Granja [P] 80 B4
Granja [P] 94 E3
Granja de Moreruela [E] 80 H4
Granja de Torrehermosa [E] 96 B5
Grankulla / Kauniainen [FIN] 176 H5
Grankullavik [S] 162 H3
Gränna [S] 162 D1
Grannäs [S] 190 F3
Granne [PL] 38 E2
Grannes [N] 190 E3
Gränningen [S] 184 C2
Granollers [E] 92 E4
Granowo [PL] 36 C3
Gransee [D] 20 D6
Gränsgård [S] 190 G3
Gransherad [N] 164 F1
Gransjö [S] 196 A2
Gränsjön [S] 166 D2
Gran Tarajal [E] 100 E6
Grantham [GB] 10 F6
Grantown-on-Spey [GB] 6 E5
Granträsk [S] 190 G5
Granvik [S] 166 G5
Granvika [N] 182 C5
Granville [F] 26 D4
Granvin [N] 170 C3
Granvollen [N] 172 B4
Grao / el Grau [E] 98 F6
Grasbakken [N] 194 E2
Gräsberg [S] 172 H5
Graševo [BG] 148 A6
Grašišče [SLO] 72 H6
Gräsmark [S] 166 E1
Gräsmyr [S] 190 H6
Gräso [S] 174 F5
Grassac [F] 66 F1
Grassano [I] 122 C4
Grassau [D] 60 F5
Grasse [F] 108 E4
Gråssjön [S] 184 C3
Gråsten [DK] 156 C4
Grästorp [S] 166 D6
Gratangen [N] 192 F4
Grätanliden [S] 190 F4
Gratkorn [A] 74 D2
Gratträsk [S] 190 H3
Graulhet [F] 106 B3
Graun im Vinschgau / Curon Venosta [I] 72 B2
Graus [E] 90 H3
Grava [S] 166 E2
Grávalos [E] 84 A5
Gravberget [N] 172 D3
Gravdal [N] 164 B4
Gravdal [N] 192 C4
Grave [NL] 16 E6
Gravedona [I] 70 G3
Gravelines [F] 14 H6
Gravellona Toce [I] 70 F3
Gravens [DK] 156 C2
Gravesend [GB] 14 F4
Gravhaug [N] 180 C5
Graviá [GR] 132 G4
Gravina in Púglia [I] 122 D3
Gravítsa [GR] 132 E3
Gravmark [S] 196 A5
Gravoúna [GR] 130 E3
Gray [F] 58 A4
Grayan-et-Hôpital [F] 54 B6
Graz [A] 74 D2
Grazalema [E] 100 H4
Gražiškiai [LT] 24 E2
Grazzanise [I] 120 D2
Grazzano Visconti [I] 110 C2
Grčak [SRB] 146 C3
Grčarice [SLO] 74 C6
Grdelica [SRB] 146 D4
Greaca [RO] 148 D1
Greaker [N] 164 H2
Great Dunmow [GB] 14 F3
Great Malvern [GB] 12 G2
Great Torrington [GB] 12 D3
Great Yarmouth [GB] 14 H2
Grebbestad [S] 166 B4
Grebenhain [D] 46 D2
Grebenstein [D] 32 F5
Grębkowo [PL] 38 D3
Grębocin [PL] 22 E6
Greding [D] 46 G6
Greencastle [NIR] 2 G5
Greenock [GB] 8 D3
Greetsiel [D] 16 H1
Gregolímano [GR] 132 H4
Greifenburg [A] 72 G3
Greiffenberg [D] 20 E6
Greifswald [D] 20 D3
Greillenstein [A] 62 D3
Grein [A] 62 C4
Greiz [D] 48 C2
Grenaa [DK] 160 F5
Grenade [F] 66 C6
Grenade [F] 84 H2
Grenchen [CH] 58 D5
Grenctale [LV] 198 E6
Grenoble [F] 68 H4
Grense-Jakobselv [N] 194 F3
Grenzland-Turm [CZ] 48 C4
Gréolières [F] 108 E4
Gréoux-les-Bains [F] 108 C4
Gressoney-la-Trinité [I] 70 E3
Gressoney-St-Jean [I] 70 E4
Gresten [A] 62 D5
Gretna Green [GB] 8 E5
Grettstadt [D] 46 F3
Greussen [D] 32 H5
Greux [F] 44 D6
Grevbäck [S] 166 G6
Greve in Chianti [I] 110 F6
Greven [D] 32 C2
Grevená [GR] 128 E6
Grevenbroich [D] 30 G4
Grevenbrück [D] 32 C5
Grevenmacher [L] 44 F2
Grevesmühlen [D] 18 H3
Greve Strand [DK] 156 G3
Greyabbey [NIR] 2 H4
Greystones [IRL] 4 G3
Grez-en-Bouère [F] 40 H5
Grezzana [I] 72 C6
Grianan of Aileach [IRL] 2 F2
Gries-am-Brenner [A] 72 D2
Griesbach [D] 60 H3
Gries in Sellrain [A] 72 D1
Grieskirchen [A] 62 A4
Griffen [A] 74 C3
Grignan [F] 106 H2
Grignols [F] 66 D5
Grigoriopol [UA] 204 E3
Grillby [S] 168 C2
Grimaldi [I] 124 D5
Grimaud [F] 108 D5
Grimdalen [N] 164 E2
Grimma [D] 34 D6
Grimmen [D] 20 D3
Grimo [N] 170 C4
Grimsås [S] 162 C3
Grimsbu [N] 180 H5
Grimsby [GB] 10 G4
Grimsdalshytta [N] 180 H5
Grimslöv [S] 162 D5
Grímsstaðir [IS] 192 C2
Grimstad [N] 164 E5
Grindaheim [N] 170 F2
Grindal [N] 180 H2
Grindavík [IS] 192 A3
Grindelwald [CH] 70 E1
Grindjorda [N] 192 E4
Grindsted [DK] 156 B2
Grinkiškis [LT] 200 F4
Griñón [E] 88 F6
Grinzane Cavour [I] 108 G2
Gripenberg [S] 162 E1
Gripenberg [S] 162 E1
Grisignano di Zocco [I] 72 D6
Grisolles [F] 84 H2
Grisslehamn [S] 174 G6
Grisvåg [N] 180 F1
Grivitsa [BG] 148 B3
Grivy [RUS] 198 G4
Grizáno [GR] 132 F2
Grižkabūdis [LT] 200 E5
Grøa [N] 180 G3
Gröbers [D] 34 C5
Grobiņa [LV] 198 B6
Gröbming [A] 74 B1
Grocka [SRB] 142 H3
Gródek [PL] 24 F5
Gródek [PL] 38 G1
Gródek nad Dunajcem [PL] 52 C4
Gröditz [D] 34 E5
Gródki [PL] 52 F1
Grodków [PL] 50 D2
Grodno [PL] 50 B2
Grodzeń [PL] 36 G1
Grodziec [PL] 36 A6
Grodziec [PL] 50 F4
Grodzisk Mazowieki [PL] 38 B3
Grodzisk Wielkopolski [PL] 36 B3
Groenlo [NL] 16 G5
Groix [F] 40 C4
Grojdibodu [RO] 148 A2
Grójec [PL] 36 D3
Grójec [PL] 38 B4
Grömitz [D] 18 H3
Gromnik [PL] 52 C4
Gromo [I] 72 A4
Gromovo [RUS] 178 G2
Gromovo [RUS] 200 D5
Grøna [N] 180 F5
Gronau [D] 16 G5
Gronau [D] 32 F3
Grönbo [S] 196 A4
Grønbua [N] 180 F6
Grøndal [N] 180 B5
Grong [N] 190 C5
Grönhögen [S] 158 G1
Grønhøj [DK] 160 C5
Gröningen [D] 34 A3
Groningen [NL] 16 G2
Grønnes [N] 180 E3
Grönskåra [S] 162 F4
Grönsö [S] 168 C2
Gropen [S] 166 G3
Grósio [I] 72 B4
Grossarl [A] 72 G1
Grossbeeren [D] 34 E2
Grossbreitenbach [D] 46 G2
Grossburgwedel [D] 32 G2
Grossenbrode [D] 18 H2
Grossenhain [D] 34 E5
Grossenkneten [D] 18 C5
Grossenzersdorf [A] 62 F4
Grosseto [I] 114 F3
Gross-Gerau [D] 46 C3
Gross-Gerungs [A] 62 C3
Grossglobnitz [A] 62 D3
Grosshabersdorf [D] 46 F5
Grossharras [A] 62 F3
Grosshöchstetten [CH] 58 E6
Gross Mohrdorf [D] 20 C2
Gross Oesingen [D] 32 H1
Gross-Pertenschlag [A] 62 C4
Gross-Pertholz [A] 62 C3
Grosspetersdorf [A] 74 F2
Grossraming [A] 62 C5
Gross Räschen [D] 34 F5
Gross Schönebeck [D] 34 E1
Gross-Siegharts [A] 62 D3
Gross-Umstadt [D] 46 D3
Grosswoltersdorf [D] 20 C6
Grostenquin [F] 44 F4
Grosuplje [SLO] 74 C5
Grøtavær [N] 192 E3
Grötholen [S] 182 E6
Grotli [N] 180 E5
Grotnes [S] 170 C4
Grottaglie [I] 122 F4
Grottaminarda [I] 120 F2
Grottammare [I] 116 D2
Grotteria [I] 124 D7
Grouw [NL] 16 F2
Grova [N] 164 F3
Grövelsjön [S] 182 D5
Grovfjord [N] 192 E4
Grozd'ovo [BG] 148 F3
Grožnjan [HR] 112 D1
Gr. Strömkendorf [D] 20 A3
Grua [N] 172 B5
Grubben [N] 190 E3
Grube [D] 18 H2
Grubišno Polje [HR] 74 G6
Gruda [HR] 144 D4
Grude [BIH] 144 B2
Grude [S] 162 B1
Grudusk [PL] 22 H6
Grudziądz [PL] 22 E5
Gruemirë [AL] 144 E5
Gruia [RO] 146 E1
Gruibingen [D] 60 B3
Gruissan [F] 106 D5
Grumentum [I] 120 H5
Grums [S] 166 E3
Grünau [A] 62 B5
Grünberg [D] 46 D1
Grünburg [A] 62 B5
Grundfors [S] 190 E4
Grundforsen [S] 172 E2
Grundlsee [A] 62 A6
Grundsel [S] 190 H3
Grundsjö [S] 190 F4
Grundsjö [S] 190 F5
Grundsjön [S] 184 C5
Grundsund [S] 166 C6
Grundsunda [S] 184 H2
Grundtjärn [S] 184 E1
Grünenplan [D] 32 F3
Grungedal [N] 164 E1
Grünheide [D] 34 F2
Grünhof [D] 20 E4
Grünstadt [D] 46 B4
Grunwald [PL] 22 G5
Grupčin [MK] 128 D1
Grüsch [CH] 58 H6
Gruškovje [SLO] 74 E4
Gruvberget [S] 174 D3
Gruyères [CH] 70 C1
Gruža [SRB] 146 B2
Gruzdžiai [LT] 200 E3
Grybów [PL] 52 C5
Grycksbo [S] 172 H4
Gryfice [PL] 20 G4
Gryfino [PL] 20 F5
Gryfów Śląski [PL] 48 H1
Grykë [AL] 128 A4
Gryllefjord [N] 192 E2
Grymyr [N] 170 H5
Gryneion [TR] 152 C3
Gryt [S] 168 C4
Gryt [S] 168 C6
Grytgöl [S] 166 H4
Grythyttan [S] 166 G2
Grytsjö [S] 190 E4
Grytstorp [S] 166 H5
Gryzy [PL] 24 D3
Grzmiąca [PL] 22 A4
Grzybno [PL] 22 F5
Gschnitz [A] 72 D2
Gschöder [A] 62 D6
Gschwend [D] 46 E6
Gstaad [CH] 70 D2
Gstadt [D] 60 F5
Gsteig [CH] 70 D2
Guadahortuna [E] 102 E3
Guadajoz [E] 94 H6
Guadalajara [E] 88 G5
Guadalcanal [E] 94 H4
Guadalcázar [E] 102 B1
Guadalerzas [E] 96 F3
Guadalest [E] 104 E2
Guadalmez [E] 96 C4
Guadalmina [E] 102 A5
Guadalupe [E] 96 C2
Guadalupe, Monasterio de- [E] 96 C2
Guadalupe, Santuario de- [E] 102 F1
Guadamur [E] 96 E2
Guadarrama [E] 88 F5
Guadix [E] 102 F4
Guagno [F] 114 B4
Gualdo Cattáneo [I] 116 A2
Gualdo Tadino [I] 116 B2
Guarcino [I] 116 C6
Guarda [CH] 72 B2
Guarda [P] 86 G2
Guardamar del Segura [E] 104 D3
Guardavalle [I] 124 D6
Guardiagrele [I] 116 D5
Guardialfiera [I] 116 E6
Guardia Lombardi [I] 120 F3
Guardia Piemontese [I] 124 C4
Guardia Sanframondi [I] 120 E2
Guardias Viejas [E] 102 F5
Guardo [E] 82 C4
Guareña [E] 94 H2
Guarromán [E] 96 E6
Guasila [I] 118 C6
Guastalla [I] 110 E2
Guazzora [I] 70 F6
Gubanitsy [RUS] 178 G6
Gubbhägen [S] 190 E5
Gúbbio [I] 116 A1
Gubbmyran [S] 172 E2
Gubbträsk [S] 190 G4
Guben [D] 34 G4
Guber [BIH] 144 B1
Guberevac [SRB] 146 B2
Gubin [PL] 34 G4
Guča [SRB] 146 B2
Gücenoluk [TR] 152 H1
Gudavac [BIH] 142 A2
Guddal [N] 170 B1
Guderup [DK] 156 C4
Gudhjem [DK] 158 E4
Gudow [D] 18 G4
Gudvangen [N] 170 D2
Guebwiller [F] 58 D3
Güéjar Sierra [E] 102 E4
Guémené-Penfao [F] 40 F5
Guémené-sur-Scorff [F] 40 D3
Guenange [F] 44 F3
Guer [F] 26 B6
Guérande [F] 40 D6
Guéret [F] 54 H6
Guérigny [F] 56 D4
Guethary [F] 84 C2
Gueugnon [F] 56 E5
Güglingen [D] 46 C6
Guglionesi [I] 116 F5
Gugny [F] 24 E5
Guía de Isora [E] 100 B5
Guichen [F] 26 C6
Guidonia [I] 116 A5
Guíglia [I] 110 E3
Guignes [F] 42 G4
Guijuelo [E] 88 C4
Guildford [GB] 14 D4
Guillaumes [F] 108 E3
Guillena [E] 94 G5
Guillestre [F] 108 E2
Guils [E] 92 D1
Guilvinec [F] 40 B3
Güimar [E] 100 C5
Guimarães [P] 80 C3
Guimerà [E] 92 C3
Guimiliau [F] 40 C2
Guincho [P] 86 A5
Guînes [F] 14 G6
Guingamp [F] 26 A4
Guipry [F] 40 F4
Guísamo [E] 78 D2
Guisborough [GB] 10 G2
Guise [F] 28 G5
Guissény [F] 40 B1
Guissona [E] 92 C3
Guitalens [F] 106 B3
Guitiriz [E] 78 D2
Guîtres [F] 66 D3
Gujan-Mestras [F] 66 B3
Gükçeyazı [TR] 152 D1
Gulbene [LV] 198 F4
Guldborg [DK] 156 F5
Gülec [TR] 150 C5
Gulgofjorden [N] 194 D1
Gulla [N] 180 G2
Gullabo [S] 162 F6
Gullaskruv [S] 162 F4
Gullbrå [N] 170 C2
Gulleråsen [S] 172 H3
Gullfoss [IS] 192 B3
Gullhaug [N] 164 H2
Gullringen [S] 162 F2
Gullsby [S] 172 E6
Gullspång [S] 166 F4
Gullstein [N] 180 F1
Güllü [TR] 152 F4
Güllüce [TR] 150 E5
Güllük [TR] 154 C1
Gülpınar [TR] 134 G1
Gulsele [S] 190 F6
Gulsrud [N] 170 H5
Gulsvik [N] 170 G4
Gülübintsi [BG] 148 D5
Gülübovo [BG] 148 D5
Gulyantsi [BG] 148 B2
Gumboda [S] 196 A5
Gumhöjden [S] 166 F1
Gumiel de Hizán [E] 88 G2
Gumlösa [S] 158 D1
Gummersbach [D] 32 C5
Gumpoldskirchen [A] 62 F5
Gumtow [D] 20 B6
Gümüldür [TR] 152 C5
Gümüşpınar [TR] 150 D2
Gümüşsu [TR] 152 H4
Gümüşsuyu [TR] 150 D3
Gümüşyeni [TR] 150 G5
Gümzovo [BG] 146 E2
Gundelfingen [D] 60 C3
Gundelsheim [D] 46 D5
Güneşli [TR] 152 E2
Güney [TR] 152 F4
Güney [TR] 152 G5
Güneyköy [TR] 152 F2
Güngör (Koutsovéntis) [CY] 154 G5
Güngörmez [TR] 152 D1
Gunja [HR] 142 E2
Günlüce [TR] 152 F1
Gunnarn [S] 190 G4
Gunnarp [S] 162 B4
Gunnarsbyn [S] 196 B2
Gunnarskog [S] 166 D1
Gunnarskulla [FIN] 176 G5
Gunnarvattnet [S] 190 E5
Gunnebo [S] 162 G2
Gunnilbo [S] 168 B2
Gunten [CH] 70 E1
Güntersberge [D] 32 H4
Güntersblum [D] 46 C4
Guntersdorf [A] 62 E3
Guntertshausen [A] 60 G4
Guntín [E] 78 D3
Günzburg [D] 60 C3
Gunzenhausen [D] 46 F6
Gurçeşme [TR] 150 C5
Gurcz [PL] 22 E4

Güre [TR] 152 F3
Güre [TR] 152 H3
Güreci [TR] 150 B5
Gurgazu [F] 114 B6
Gurk [A] 74 B2
Gurkovo [BG] 148 C4
Gurlevo [RUS] 178 F6
Gürpinar [TR] 150 E3
Gurrea de Gállego [E] 90 F3
Gürsu [TR] 150 F4
Gurtnellen [CH] 70 F1
Gušće [HR] 142 B1
Gusev [RUS] 24 D1
Gusinje [MNE] 146 A5
Gusmar [AL] 128 B6
Gúspini [I] 118 C6
Gusselby [S] 166 H2
Güssing [A] 74 F2
Gusswerk [A] 62 D6
Gustavfors [S] 172 F5
Gustavs / Kustavi [FIN] 176 C4
Gustavsberg [S] 168 E3
Gustavsberg [S] 190 H4
Gustavsfors [S] 166 D3
Güstrow [D] 20 B4
Gusum [S] 168 B6
Gusvattnet [S] 190 E5
Guta [BY] 202 D6
Gutcher [GB] 6 H3
Gutenstein [A] 62 E5
Gütersloh [D] 32 D3
Gutštejn [CZ] 48 D4
Guttannen [CH] 70 F1
Guttormsgard [S] 170 F4
Gützkow [D] 20 D3
Güvercinlik [TR] 154 C1
Güzelbahçe [TR] 152 C4
Güzelpinar [TR] 152 G4
Güzelyalı (Vavylás) [CY] 154 F5
Güzelyurt (Mórfou) [CY] 154 F5
Guzet-Neige [F] 84 H5
Gvardeiskoye [RUS] 22 H2
Gvardeysk [RUS] 24 B1
Gvarv [N] 164 F2
Gvozd [HR] 112 H1
Gvozd [MNE] 144 E3
Gwatt [CH] 70 D1
Gwda Wielka [PL] 22 B4
Gy [F] 58 B4
Gya [N] 164 B4
Gyarmat [H] 74 H1
Gyermely [H] 64 B6
Gyl [N] 180 F2
Gylien [S] 194 B8
Gylling [DK] 156 D2
Gýmeš [SK] 64 B4
Gymnó [GR] 134 C5
Gyomaendrőd [H] 76 F2
Gyömrő [H] 76 D1
Gyöngyös [H] 64 E5
Gyöngyöspata [H] 64 D5
Gyönk [H] 76 B3
Győr [H] 62 H6
Gysinge [S] 174 E5
Gýtheio [GR] 136 E4
Gyttorp [S] 166 G2
Gyueshevo [BG] 146 E6
Gyula [H] 76 G3
Gyulaj [H] 76 B4
Gzy [PL] 38 B1

H

Häädemeeste [EST] 198 D3
Haag [A] 62 C4
Haag [D] 60 F4
Haag am Hausruck [A] 62 A4
Haaksbergen [NL] 16 G5
Haapajärvi [FIN] 196 D6
Haapajoki [FIN] 196 C4
Haapa-Kimola [FIN] 178 B3
Haapakylä [FIN] 186 G3
Haapala [FIN] 196 D3
Haapamäki [FIN] 186 E4
Haapamäki [FIN] 188 D3
Haapamäki [FIN] 188 D1
Haapamäki [FIN] 196 E6
Haapasalmi [FIN] 188 F4
Haapavesi [FIN] 196 D5
Haapsalu [EST] 198 D2
Haar [D] 60 E4
Haarajoki [FIN] 176 H4
Haarajoki [FIN] 186 H5
Haarala [FIN] 186 G2
Haaraoja [FIN] 196 D4
Haarby [DK] 156 D3
Haaren [D] 32 E4
Haarlem [NL] 16 D4
Haavisto [FIN] 186 F5
Habartice [CZ] 48 G1
Habas [F] 84 D2
Habay [B] 44 E2
Habernau [A] 62 B5
Hablingbo [S] 168 F5
Habo [S] 162 D2
Håbol [S] 166 D4
Habry [CZ] 48 H4
Håby [S] 166 C5
Hachdorf [D] 58 G2
Hachenburg [D] 46 B1
Hachmühlen [D] 32 F2
Hacıdanişment [TR] 150 B1
Hacısungur [TR] 150 B3
Hackås [S] 182 G3
Häckeberga [S] 158 C3
Hacketstown [IRL] 4 F4
Hacksjö [S] 190 G5
Häcksvik [S] 162 B3
Hadamar [D] 46 B2
Hädanberg [S] 184 F1
Haddington [GB] 8 F3
Haderslev [DK] 156 C3
Haderup [DK] 160 C5
Hadiach [UA] 202 F7
Hadım [TR] 152 G4
Hadleigh [GB] 14 G3
Hadmersleben [D] 34 B3
Hadrian's Wall [GB] 8 F5
Hadsten [DK] 160 D6
Hadsund [DK] 160 E4
Hadzhidimitrovo [BG] 148 C2
Hadzhidimovo [BG] 130 C2
Hadžići [BIH] 144 C1
Hægeland [N] 164 D5
Hærland [N] 166 C2
Hafling / Avelengo [I] 72 D3
Hafsmo [N] 180 G1
Haftorsbygget [S] 172 F1
Haga [N] 172 C5
Hagafoss [N] 170 F3
Hagby [S] 162 F5
Hagby [S] 168 D2
Hagebro [DK] 160 C5
Hagen [D] 18 D4
Hagen [D] 32 C4
Hagenberg [A] 62 C4
Hagenburg [D] 32 F2
Hagenow [D] 18 H5
Hageri [EST] 198 D2
Hagetmau [F] 84 E2
Hagfors [S] 172 F6
Häggås [S] 190 F5
Häggemåla [S] 162 G4
Häggenås [S] 182 H1
Häggsåsen [S] 182 G2
Häggsjöbränna [S] 182 E1
Häggsjömon [S] 190 G5
Häggsjövik [S] 190 E6
Haglebu [N] 170 G4
Hagondange [F] 44 E4
Haguenau [F] 44 H5
Håhellarhytta [N] 164 D3
Hahn [D] 18 C4
Hahnbach [D] 46 H5
Hahót [H] 74 G3
Haibach ob der Donau [A] 62 B4
Haid [A] 62 B4
Haiger [D] 32 D6
Haigerloch [D] 58 G2
Häijää [FIN] 176 E1
Hailsham [GB] 14 E6
Hailuoto / Karlö [FIN] 196 D4
Haina [D] 32 E6
Hainburg [A] 62 G4
Hainfeld [A] 62 E5
Hainichen [D] 48 D1
Hainsbach [D] 60 F2
Haithabu [D] 18 F1
Hajdúböszörmény [H] 64 G6
Hajdúdorog [H] 64 G5
Hajdúhadház [H] 64 H5
Hajdúnánás [H] 64 G5
Hajdúsámson [H] 64 H6
Hajdúszoboszló [H] 64 G6
Hajdúszovát [H] 76 G1
Hajdúvid [H] 64 G5
Hajerdin [BG] 146 G3
Hajnówka [PL] 38 F1
Hajós [H] 76 C4
Håkafot [S] 190 E5
Håkenby [N] 166 C3
Hakkas [S] 194 A7
Hakkenpää [FIN] 176 D4
Häkkilä [FIN] 186 F3
Häkkiskylä [FIN] 186 F5
Hakkstabben [N] 194 B2
Hakokylä [FIN] 196 F4
Håksberg [S] 172 H5
Hakuni [FIN] 186 C4
Håkvika [N] 192 E4
Halaç [TR] 154 H3
Hålaforsen [S] 184 E1
Halámky [CZ] 62 C2
Hala Sultan Tekkesi [CY] 154 G5
Halásztelek [H] 76 C1
Halberstadt [D] 34 A3
Hald [DK] 160 E5
Halden [N] 166 C3
Haldensee [A] 60 C6
Haldensleben [D] 34 B2
Halenkov [CZ] 50 E6
Halesworth [GB] 14 G3
Häle-Täng [S] 166 D5
Hälgö [S] 168 C4
Halhjem [N] 170 B4
Halič [SK] 64 D4
Halich [UA] 204 C2
Halifax [GB] 10 E4
Halikarnassos [TR] 154 B2
Halikko [FIN] 176 E4
Halitpaşa [TR] 152 D3
Haljala [EST] 198 E1
Halk [DK] 156 C3
Halkivaha [FIN] 176 E2
Halkosaari [FIN] 186 C3
Hälla [S] 190 F6
Hallabro [S] 162 E6
Hallaçli [TR] 150 D2
Hallandsfossen [N] 164 D3
Hallapuro [FIN] 186 E2
Hallaryd [S] 162 C6
Hällbacken [S] 190 F2
Hällbo [S] 174 D2
Halle [B] 28 H3
Halle [D] 32 D3
Halle [D] 34 C5
Hälleberga [S] 162 F5
Hällefors [S] 166 G2
Hälleforsnäs [S] 168 B3
Hallein [A] 60 G6
Hallen [S] 182 G2
Hallenberg [D] 32 D5
Hallerud [S] 166 G4
Hällesjö [S] 184 D3
Hällestad [S] 166 H5
Hällevadsholm [S] 166 C5
Hälleviksstrand [S] 166 C6
Halli [FIN] 186 F5
Hallignicourt [F] 44 C5
Hallila [FIN] 178 B3
Hallingby [N] 170 H5
Hällingsåfallet [S] 190 E5
Hall in Tirol [A] 72 D1
Hällnäs [S] 174 F4
Hällnäs [S] 190 G2
Hällnäs [S] 190 H5
Hällristningar [S] 166 C4
Hallsberg [S] 166 H4
Hallshuk [S] 168 G3
Hällsjö [S] 184 F2
Hällsta [S] 168 B3
Hallstahammar [S] 168 B2
Hallstatt [A] 62 A6
Hallstavik [S] 168 E1
Halltorp [S] 162 F6
Halluin [F] 28 F2
Hällvik [S] 190 G2
Hallviken [S] 190 E6
Halmstad [S] 162 B5
Halna [S] 166 F5
Halne [N] 170 E4
Halne Fjellstue [N] 170 E4
Hals [DK] 160 E4
Hals [N] 180 F2
Halsa [N] 180 F2
Hal'shany [BY] 200 H6
Hålsjö [S] 184 E6
Halsskov [DK] 156 E3
Halstead [GB] 14 F3
Halsteren [NL] 16 C6
Halsua [FIN] 186 E1
Haltdalen [N] 182 C3
Haltern [D] 30 H2
Haltwhistle [GB] 8 F5
Haluna [FIN] 188 D1
Halvarsgårdarna [S] 172 H5
Halver [D] 32 C5
Ham [F] 28 F5
Hamallaj [AL] 128 A2
Hamamdere [TR] 152 F3
Hamamköy [TR] 152 E5
Hamar [N] 172 C3
Hambergen [D] 18 D5
Hamburg [D] 18 F4
Hamburgsund [S] 166 B5
Hambye, Abbaye de- [F] 26 D4
Hamdibey [TR] 150 C6
Hamdorf [D] 18 F2
Hämeenkyrö / Tavastkyro [FIN] 176 E1
Hämeenlinna / Tavastehus [FIN] 176 G3
Hämeler Wald [D] 32 G2
Hameln [D] 32 F3
Hämelschenburg [D] 32 F3
Hamersleben [D] 34 A3
Hamidiye [TR] 150 B3
Hamidiye [TR] 150 D1
Hamilton [GB] 8 D3
Hamina / Fredrikshamn [FIN] 178 D3
Hamingberg [N] 194 F1
Hamitli [TR] 150 B2
Hamlagrøosen [N] 170 C3
Hamm [D] 32 C3
Hammar [S] 166 G4
Hammarland [FIN] 176 A5
Hammarn [S] 166 G2
Hammarnäs [S] 182 G2
Hammarstrand [S] 184 D2
Hammarvika [N] 190 A6
Hammaslahti [FIN] 188 F3
Hammel [DK] 160 D6
Hammelburg [D] 46 E3
Hammer [N] 182 C1
Hammer [N] 190 C5
Hammerbach [D] 46 D2
Hammerdal [S] 182 H1
Hammerfest [N] 194 B2
Hammerhøj [DK] 160 D5
Hammershus [DK] 158 E4
Hamminkeln [D] 16 G6
Hamnbukt [N] 194 C3
Hamnes [N] 192 G2
Hamoir [B] 30 E5
Hampetorp [S] 168 A3
Hampovica [HR] 74 G5
Hamra [S] 172 H1
Hamrångefjärden [S] 174 E3
Hamre [N] 164 E5
Hamre [S] 174 D1
Hamremoen [N] 170 G5
Hams, Coves dels- [E] 104 F5
Hamula [FIN] 186 G2
Hamula [FIN] 188 C2
Hamzabey [TR] 150 C2
Hamzali [MK] 128 H2
Hamzići [BIH] 144 C2
Han [MNE] 144 D4
Hån [S] 166 C2
Hanasand [N] 164 B2
Hanaskog [S] 158 D1
Hanau [D] 46 D3
Hançalar [TR] 152 G4
Hâncești [MD] 204 E3
Hancevichy [BY] 202 B6
Handegg [CH] 70 F1
Handeland [N] 164 C3
Handen [S] 168 E3
Handlová [SK] 64 B3
Handöl [S] 182 E2
Handsjö [S] 182 G4
Hanerau-Hademarschen [D] 18 E2
Hanestad [N] 182 C6
Hanftal [A] 62 F3
Hangaskylä [FIN] 186 B4
Hangö / Hanko [FIN] 176 E6
Hangvar [S] 168 G3
Hanhimaa [FIN] 194 C6
Han i Hotit [AL] 144 E4
Hank [NL] 16 D6
Hankamäki [FIN] 196 F6
Hankasalmi [FIN] 186 H4
Hanken [S] 166 G5
Hankensbüttel [D] 32 H1
Hanko / Hangö [FIN] 176 E6
Hanna [PL] 38 F4
Hannivirta [FIN] 188 E4
Hann-Münden [D] 32 F5
Hannover [D] 32 F2
Hannuit (Hannut) [B] 30 D4
Hannusranta [FIN] 196 F5
Hannut (Hannuit) [B] 30 D4
Hanoğlu [TR] 152 G3
Han Pijesak [BIH] 142 E4
Hanskühnenburg [D] 32 G4
Hansnes [N] 192 G1
Hanstedt [D] 18 F5
Hanstholm [DK] 160 C3
Han-sur-Lesse [B] 30 D6
Han-sur-Nied [F] 44 F4
Hantháza [H] 76 D2
Hanušovce [SK] 64 G2
Hanušovice [CZ] 50 C4
Haparanda [S] 196 C2
Häppälä [FIN] 186 H4
Hapträsk [S] 196 A2
Hara [EST] 198 D2
Härad [S] 168 C3
Haradok [BY] 202 C4
Harads [S] 196 A2
Häradsbäck [S] 162 D5
Haraneset [N] 190 C4
Haras du Pin [F] 26 F5
Harbergsdalen [S] 190 E4
Harbo [S] 174 E6
Harboøre [DK] 160 B4
Harburg [D] 18 F4
Harburg [D] 60 C2
Hardbakke [N] 170 A2
Hardegg [A] 62 E3
Hardegsen [D] 32 F4
Hardelot-Plage [F] 28 D2
Hardemo [S] 166 H3
Hardenberg [NL] 16 G4
Harderwijk [NL] 16 E4
Hardeshøj [DK] 156 C4
Hardheim [D] 46 D4
Hardom [FIN] 178 B4
Hareid [N] 180 C3
Haren [D] 16 H3
Haren [NL] 16 G2
Harestua [N] 172 B5
Harfleur [F] 26 G3
Harg [S] 174 G5
Hargla [EST] 198 F4
Hargnies [F] 30 D6
Hargshamn [S] 174 G5
Harhala [FIN] 176 G2
Haría [E] 100 E5
Harivaara [FIN] 188 F1
Härjänvatsa [FIN] 176 F5
Härjåsjön [S] 182 G6
Harjavalta [FIN] 176 D2
Harju [FIN] 196 E4
Harjula [FIN] 196 D3
Harjunmaa [FIN] 196 G6
Harjunsalmi [FIN] 186 F6
Harkány [H] 76 B5
Härkeberga [S] 168 C2
Härkmeri [FIN] 186 B5
Härkmyran [S] 194 A8
Harlec [BG] 146 G2
Harlech [GB] 10 B5
Hårlev [DK] 156 G3
Harlingen [NL] 16 E2
Harlösa [S] 158 C2
Harlow [GB] 14 E4
Harmancık [TR] 150 F6
Harmandallar [TR] 152 F3
Harmanec [SK] 64 C3
Harmånger [S] 184 E6
Harmanköy [TR] 150 H4
Härmänkylä [FIN] 196 F4
Härmänmäki [FIN] 196 F4
Harmelen [NL] 16 D5
Harndrup [DK] 156 D3
Härnösand [S] 184 F4
Haro [E] 82 G5
Harodz'ki [BY] 200 H6
Haroldswick [GB] 6 H3
Háromfa [H] 74 G5
Haroué [F] 44 E6
Harpefoss [N] 170 H1
Harpenden [GB] 14 E3
Harplinge [S] 162 B5
Harpstedt [D] 18 D6
Harrå [S] 192 G5
Harrachov [CZ] 48 H2
Harran [N] 190 D5
Harre [DK] 160 C4
Harrogate [GB] 10 F3
Harrsjöhöiden [S] 190 E5
Harrsjön [S] 190 E5
Harrström [FIN] 186 A3
Harsa [S] 174 D1
Härsängen [S] 166 D5
Harsefeld [D] 18 E4
Harsewinkel [D] 32 D3
Hârşova [RO] 204 E5
Harsprånget [S] 190 H1
Harstad [N] 192 E3
Harste [D] 32 F4
Harsum [D] 32 G2
Harsvik [N] 190 B5
Harta [H] 76 C3
Hartberg [A] 74 E1
Hartha [D] 34 D6
Hartland [GB] 12 D3
Hartlepool [GB] 10 G2
Hartmannshain [D] 46 D2
Hartola [FIN] 186 G6
Hårve [S] 184 C6
Harwich [GB] 14 G3
Harzgerode [D] 34 A4
Hasanağa [TR] 150 E5
Hasanbey [TR] 150 D5
Hasanpaşa [TR] 150 G5
Haselund [D] 18 E1
Haselünne [D] 18 B6
Håsjö [S] 184 D3
Hasköy [TR] 130 H3
Hasköy [TR] 150 B2
Hasköy [TR] 152 G3
Haslach [A] 62 B3
Haslach [D] 58 F2
Hasle [DK] 158 E4
Haslemoen [N] 172 D4
Haslemere [GB] 14 D5
Haslev [DK] 156 G3
Hasparren [F] 84 C2
Haspe [D] 30 H3
Hasseki [TR] 134 H4
Hassel [D] 18 E6
Hassela [S] 184 E5
Hasselfelde [D] 32 H4
Hasselfors [S] 166 G4
Hasselt [B] 30 E4
Hasselt [NL] 16 F4
Hassfurt [D] 46 F3
Hassi [FIN] 186 F6
Hasslach [D] 46 H3
Hassle [S] 166 F4
Hassleben [D] 20 D5
Hässleholm [S] 158 D1
Hästbo [S] 174 D5
Hästbo [S] 174 E4
Hastersboda [FIN] 168 H1
Hästholmen [S] 166 G6
Hastiere-Lavaux [B] 30 D6
Hastings [GB] 14 F6
Hästveda [S] 158 D1
Hasvik [N] 194 A2
Hatě [CZ] 62 E3
Haţeg [RO] 204 C5
Hatfield [GB] 14 E3
Hatfjelldal [N] 190 E3
Hatıplar [TR] 152 D3
Hatsola [FIN] 188 D5
Hattem [NL] 16 F4
Hattingen [D] 30 H3
Hattonchâtel [F] 44 E4
Hättorp [S] 166 F4
Hattstedt [D] 18 E1
Hattula [FIN] 176 G2
Hattuvaara [FIN] 188 H1
Hattuvaara [FIN] 196 G6
Hatulanmäki [FIN] 196 E5
Hatvan [H] 64 D6
Hatvik [N] 170 B4
Haug [N] 170 E1
Haugan [N] 190 B6
Haugastøl [N] 170 E4
Haugbøen [N] 180 F3
Hauge [N] 164 B5
Haugesund [N] 164 A1
Hauggrend [N] 164 E2
Haughom [N] 164 C4
Haugsdorf [A] 62 E3
Haugsten [N] 170 G1
Hauho [FIN] 176 G2
Haukå [N] 180 B5
Haukedal [N] 170 C1
Haukeland [N] 170 B4
Haukeligrend [N] 164 D1
Haukeliseter [N] 170 D5
Haukilahti [FIN] 196 G4
Haukipudas [FIN] 196 D3
Haukivuori [FIN] 188 C5
Hauklappi [FIN] 188 E6
Haule [NL] 16 G2
Haunersdorf [D] 60 G3
Haunia [FIN] 176 D1
Haurida [S] 162 D2
Hausach [D] 58 F2
Hausen [D] 30 H5
Hausen [D] 46 E3
Hausen [D] 60 C4
Häusern [D] 58 F4
Hausham [D] 60 E5
Hausjärvi [FIN] 176 H3
Häusling [A] 62 D4
Hausmannstatten [A] 74 D2
Hautajärvi [FIN] 194 F7
Haut-Asco [F] 114 B3
Haut-Barr, Château du- [F] 44 G5
Hautecombe, Abbaye de- [F] 68 H3
Hautefort, Château de- [F] 66 G3
Haute-Nendaz [CH] 70 D2
Hauterive, Abbaye de- [CH] 58 D6
Hauteville-Lompnes [F] 68 H2
Hauteville Plage [F] 26 D3
Haut Kœnigsbourg [F] 58 D2
Hautmont [F] 28 G4
Hauzenberg [D] 62 A3
Havaj [SK] 52 D6
Havant [GB] 14 D5
Håvberget [S] 172 G5
Havdhem [S] 168 G5
Håvedalen [S] 166 C4
Havelange [B] 30 D5
Havelberg [D] 34 C1
Haverdal [S] 162 B5
Haverfordwest [GB] 12 D1
Haverhill [GB] 14 F3
Häverö [S] 168 E1
Håverud [S] 166 D4
Havířov [CZ] 50 F4
Hävla [S] 168 B4
Havlíčkův Brod [CZ] 48 H5
Havnäs [S] 190 F5
Havnbjerg [DK] 156 C4
Havneby [DK] 156 A4
Havnebyen [DK] 156 F1
Havnsø [DK] 156 F2
Havøysund [N] 194 B1
Havraň [CZ] 48 E2
Havran [TR] 152 C1
Havsa [TR] 150 B2
Havstensund [S] 166 B4
Hawick [GB] 8 E4
Hayange [F] 44 E3
Hayle [GB] 12 B5
Haymana [TR] 152 H1
Hay-on-Wye [GB] 12 F2
Hayrabolu [TR] 150 B3
Hayriye [TR] 150 E4
Hayrıye [TR] 152 G5
Haywards Heath [GB] 14 E5
Hazebrouck [F] 28 E2
Hazlov [CZ] 48 C3
Hazmburk [CZ] 48 F3
Hcıkasım [TR] 150 B5
Headford [IRL] 2 C4
Heathfield [GB] 14 E5
Hebnes [N] 164 B2
Heby [S] 168 C1
Hechingen [D] 58 G2
Hecho [E] 84 D4
Hechtel [B] 30 E3
Hechthausen [D] 18 E4
Hed [S] 168 A2
Hedal [N] 170 G4
Hedared [S] 162 B2
Hédauville [F] 28 E4
Hedburg [D] 46 G3
Hedby [S] 172 H4
Hedbyn [S] 166 H1
Heddal [N] 164 F2
Hedderen [N] 164 D3
Hédé [F] 26 C5
Hede [S] 168 B1
Hedehusene [DK] 156 G2
Hedekas [S] 166 C5
Hedemora [S] 174 D5
Heden [FIN] 186 B5
Heden [S] 172 E1
Heden [S] 172 G2
Hedenäset [S] 194 B8
Hedensted [DK] 156 C2
Hedesunda [S] 174 E5
Hedeviken [S] 182 F4
Hee [DK] 160 B6
Heek [D] 16 H5
Heemstede [NL] 16 D4
Heerde [NL] 16 F4
Heerenveen [NL] 16 F3
Heerlen [NL] 30 F4
Heeze [NL] 30 E3
Hegerum [S] 162 G2
Heggenes [N] 170 G2
Heglibister [GB] 6 G4
Hegra [N] 182 C1
Hegyeshalom [H] 62 G5
Hegyhátsál [H] 74 F2
Hegykő [H] 62 G6
Heia [N] 190 C5
Heia [N] 192 F3
Heidal [N] 180 G6
Heide [D] 18 E2
Heideck [D] 46 G6
Heidelberg [D] 46 C5
Heiden [D] 16 G6
Heidenau [D] 48 E1
Heidenheim [D] 60 C2
Heidenreichstein [A] 62 D2
Heigrestad [N] 164 B4
Heikendorf [D] 18 G2
Heikkurila [FIN] 188 E5
Heiland [N] 164 F3
Heilbad Heiligenstadt [D] 32 G5
Heilbronn [D] 46 D5
Heilevong [N] 180 B6
Heiligenberg [D] 58 H4
Heiligenblut [A] 72 G2
Heiligenbösch-Kirche [D] 44 G2
Heiligenhafen [D] 18 H2
Heiligenkreuz [A] 62 E4
Heiligenkreuz [A] 62 E5
Heiligenkreuz [A] 74 F2
Heiligenroth [D] 46 B2
Heiligkreuztal [D] 58 H3
Heilsbronn [D] 46 F5
Heimaey [IS] 192 A3
Heimdal [N] 182 B1
Heimertingen [D] 60 B4
Heinämaa [FIN] 178 B3
Heinämäki [FIN] 186 H1
Heinävaara [FIN] 188 G2
Heinävesi [FIN] 188 E3
Heinersdorf [D] 34 F2
Heino [NL] 16 F4
Heinola [FIN] 178 B2
Heinoniemi [FIN] 188 F4
Heinrichsruh [D] 20 E4
Heinsberg [D] 30 F4
Heippes [F] 44 D4
Heiterwang [A] 60 C6
Heituinlahti [FIN] 178 D2
Hejde [S] 168 G5
Hejlsminde [DK] 156 C3
Hejnice [CZ] 48 H1
Hejnsvig [DK] 156 B2
Hekal [AL] 128 B5
Hekimdağ [TR] 150 H5
Hel [PL] 22 E2
Heldenberg [A] 62 E4
Heldrungen [D] 34 A5
Helechal [E] 96 B4
Helensburgh [GB] 8 D2
Helfenburk [CZ] 48 F6
Helfštýn [CZ] 50 D5
Helgen [N] 164 F3
Helgum [S] 184 E2
Hell [N] 182 C1
Hella [N] 170 D1
Helland [N] 180 G1
Helle [N] 164 C4
Helle [N] 164 F4
Helleland [N] 164 B4
Hellendoorn [NL] 16 G4
Helleristninger [N] 180 B5
Helleristninger [N] 194 B3
Hellesøy [N] 170 A3
Hellesylt [N] 180 D4
Hellevad [DK] 156 B4
Hellevik [N] 170 B1
Hellevoetsluis [NL] 16 C5
Helligskogen [N] 192 G3
Hellín [E] 104 B1
Hellinge [DK] 156 E5
Hellsö [FIN] 168 H1
Helmond [NL] 30 E2
Helmsdale [GB] 6 E3
Helmsley [GB] 10 F3
Helmstedt [D] 34 A3
Helnessund [N] 192 D5
Helsa [D] 32 F5
Helsingborg [S] 156 H1
Helsinge [DK] 156 G1
Helsingfors / Helsinki [FIN] 176 H5
Helsingør [DK] 156 H1
Helsinki / Helsingfors [FIN] 176 H5
Helstad [N] 190 D4
Helston [GB] 12 B5
Heltermaa [EST] 198 C2
Helvia Recina [I] 116 C1
Hemau [D] 46 H6
Hemel Hempstead [GB] 14 E3
Hemer [D] 32 C4
Hèming [F] 44 G5
Hemling [S] 190 G6
Hemmet [DK] 156 A1
Hemmingen [S] 190 H4
Hemmingsmark [S] 196 A4
Hemmoor [D] 18 E3
Hemnes [N] 166 C2
Hemse [S] 168 G5
Hemsedal [N] 170 F3
Hemslingen [D] 18 F5
Hen [N] 170 H5
Henån [S] 166 C6
Hencida [H] 76 H1
Hendaye [F] 84 B2
Hendek [TR] 150 H3
Hendrik Ido Ambacht [NL] 16 D5
Hengelo [NL] 16 G5
Hengersberg [D] 60 G2
Heniches'k [UA] 204 H3
Hénin Beaumont [F] 28 F3
Henley-on-Thames [GB] 14 D4
Hennan [S] 184 D5
Henneberg [D] 46 F2
Hennebont [F] 40 C4
Hennef [D] 30 H5
Hennerhöle [A] 60 H6
Henne Strand [DK] 156 A2
Hennezel [F] 58 B2
Henningsvær [N] 192 D4
Hénoville [F] 28 D3
Henrichemont [F] 56 C3
Henriksfjäll [S] 190 E4
Henryków [PL] 50 C2
Henstedt-Ulzburg [D] 18 F3
Hepoköngäs [FIN] 196 E4
Hepola [FIN] 196 C3
Heppenheim [D] 46 C4
Heraclea [MK] 128 E3
Herad [N] 164 C5
Herad [N] 170 F3
Heradsbygd [N] 172 C3
Herajoki [FIN] 188 F1
Herakleia [TR] 152 D6
Hera Lacinia, Tempio di- [I] 124 F5
Hérault, Gorges de l'- [F] 106 E3
Herbault [F] 54 G1
Herberstein [A] 74 E2
Herbertingen [D] 58 H3
Herbertstown [IRL] 4 D4
Herbesthal [B] 30 F5
Herbeumont [B] 44 D2
Herbignac [F] 40 E5
Herbolzheim [D] 58 E2
Herborn [D] 46 C1
Herbrechtingen [D] 60 C3
Herby [PL] 50 F2
Herceg Novi [MNE] 144 D4
Hercegovac [HR] 74 G6
Hercegovska Goleša [SRB] 144 E2
Hercegszántó [H] 76 C5
Herdal [N] 180 D4
Herdberg [D] 32 D4
Herdla [N] 170 A3
Herdoniae [I] 120 G2
Hereford [GB] 12 G2
Herefoss [N] 164 E4
Héreg [H] 64 B6
Hereke [TR] 150 F3
Herencia [E] 96 G3
Herend [H] 74 H2
Herentals [B] 30 D3
Herfølge [DK] 156 G3
Herford [D] 32 E2
Hergiswil [CH] 58 F6
Héricourt [F] 58 C4
Heringsdorf [D] 20 E3
Herisau [CH] 58 H5
Hérisson [F] 56 C5
Herl'any [SK] 64 G2
Herleshausen [D] 32 G6
Herlufsholm [DK] 156 F3
Hermagor [A] 72 G3
Hermannsburg [D] 18 F6
Hermanns-Denkmal [D] 32 E3
Heřmanovice [CZ] 50 D3
Hermansverk [N] 170 D2
Heřmanův Městec [CZ] 50 A4
Herment [F] 68 B2
Hermeskeil [D] 44 G3

Hermo [E] 78 F4
Hermsdorf [D] 48 B1
Hernani [E] 84 B2
Herne [D] 30 H3
Herne Bay [GB] 14 G5
Herning [DK] 160 C6
Hernstein [A] 62 E5
Heroldsberg [D] 46 G5
Herøya [N] 164 G3
Herøysund [N] 170 B5
Herräkra [S] 162 E4
Herräng [S] 174 G5
Herraskylä [FIN] 186 D4
Herre [N] 164 G3
Herrenberg [D] 58 G1
Herrenchiemsee [D] 60 F5
Herrera [E] 96 E4
Herrera [E] 102 B2
Herrera del Duque [E] 96 C3
Herrera de los Navarros [E] 90 D5
Herrera de Pisuerga [E] 82 D5
Herrería [E] 90 C5
Herreruela [E] 86 G5
Herrestad [S] 166 C5
Herrgotts Kirche [D] 46 E5
Herrljunga [S] 162 B1
Herrnburg [D] 18 G3
Herrnhut [D] 48 G1
Herröskatan [FIN] 168 G1
Herrsching [D] 60 D4
Herrskog [S] 184 F3
Herrvik [S] 168 G5
Hersbruck [D] 46 H5
Herselt [B] 30 D3
Hertford [GB] 14 E3
Hertník [SK] 52 C6
Hervás [E] 88 B5
Hervik [N] 164 B2
Herzberg [D] 20 B4
Herzberg [D] 32 G4
Herzberg [D] 34 D1
Herzberg [D] 34 E4
Herzberg [D] 46 E1
Herzfeld [D] 32 D4
Herzfelde [D] 34 F2
Herzlake [D] 18 B6
Herzogenaurach [D] 46 G5
Herzogenburg [A] 62 E4
Herzsprung [D] 20 C6
Hesdin [F] 28 D3
Hesel [D] 18 C4
Heskestad [N] 164 B4
Heskestad [N] 164 C5
Hesnæs [DK] 20 B1
Hessel [DK] 160 C4
Hesselagergård [DK] 156 E4
Hessich-Lichtenau [D] 32 F5
Hess Oldendorf [D] 32 F2
Hessvik [N] 170 C4
Hestad [N] 170 C1
Hestenesøyri [N] 180 C5
Hestra [S] 162 C3
Hestra [S] 162 E1
Hetin [SRB] 76 F6
Het Loo [NL] 16 F5
Hettange-Grande [F] 44 E3
Hettstedt [D] 34 B4
Hetvehely [H] 76 A5
Heustreu [D] 46 F2
Heverlee [B] 30 D4
Heves [H] 64 E6
Hévíz [H] 74 G3
Hevlin [CZ] 62 F3
Hexentanzplatz [D] 34 A4
Hexham [GB] 8 F6
Heyrieux [F] 68 G3
Heysham [GB] 10 D3
Hidas [H] 76 B4
Hidasnémeti [H] 64 G3
Hieflau [A] 62 C6
Hiendelaencina [E] 88 H4
Hierapolis [TR] 152 G5
Hiersac [F] 54 D6
Hietakylä [FIN] 188 C3
Hietanen [FIN] 188 C6
Hietaniemi [FIN] 194 F6
Hietaperä [FIN] 196 F5
High Cross [IRL] 4 F3
High Wycombe [GB] 14 D4
Higuera, Torre de la- [E] 100 F2
Higuera de la Serena [E] 96 B4
Higuera de Vargas [E] 94 F2
Higuera la Real [E] 94 F3
Higueruela [E] 98 C5
Hihnavaara [FIN] 194 E6
Hiirola [FIN] 188 C5
Hiitinen / Hitis [FIN] 176 E6
Híjar [E] 90 F5
Hilchenbach [D] 32 C5
Hildal [N] 170 C5
Hildburghausen [D] 46 G2
Hilden [D] 30 G4
Hilders [D] 46 E2
Hildesheim [D] 32 G3
Hildre [N] 180 D3
Hilertshausen [D] 60 E3
Hilkerode [D] 32 G4
Hilla [FIN] 176 G5
Hille [S] 174 E4
Hillegom [NL] 16 D4
Hillerød [DK] 156 G2
Hillerstorp [S] 162 C3
Hillesøy [N] 192 F2
Hillilä [FIN] 196 C5
Hillion [F] 26 B4
Hillsand [S] 190 E5
Hillsborough [NIR] 2 G4
Hillswick [GB] 6 G3
Hilltown [NIR] 2 G4
Hilmo [N] 182 C2
Hilpoltstein [D] 46 G6
Hilterfingen [CH] 70 E1
Hiltulanlahti [FIN] 188 C2
Hilvarenbeek [NL] 30 E2
Hilversum [NL] 16 E4
Himanka [FIN] 196 C5
Himankakylä [FIN] 196 C5
Himarë [AL] 128 B6
Himlštejn [CZ] 48 D3
Himmelkoron [D] 46 H3
Himmelpforten [D] 18 E4
Hinckley [GB] 10 E6
Hindås [S] 160 H2
Hindelang [D] 60 C6
Hinderburg [D] 34 C1
Hindsig [DK] 156 B2
Hinnerjoki [FIN] 176 D3
Hinnerup [DK] 160 D6
Hinneryd [S] 162 C5
Hinojal [E] 86 H4
Hinojos [E] 94 F6
Hinojosa del Duque [E] 96 C4
Hinojosa del Valle [E] 94 H3
Hinterbichl [A] 72 F2
Hinterrhein [CH] 70 G2
Hintersee [D] 20 E4
Hinterstoder [A] 62 B6
Hinterthal [A] 72 G1
Hintertux [A] 72 D1
Hinterweidenthal [D] 44 H4
Hinterzarten [D] 58 F3
Hío [E] 78 B4
Hırkalı [TR] 152 E3
Hirnsdorf [A] 74 E2
Hirnyk [UA] 52 H2
Hirrlingen [D] 58 G2
Hirschaid [D] 46 G4
Hirschau [D] 48 B5
Hirschberg [D] 48 B2
Hirschegg [A] 60 B6
Hirschhorn [D] 46 C5
Hirsch-Stein [D] 48 B3
Hirsilä [FIN] 186 E6
Hirsingue [F] 58 D4
Hirson [F] 28 G5
Hîrşova [RO] 204 E5
Hirtshals [DK] 160 E2
Hirvassalmi [FIN] 194 D5
Hirvasvaara [FIN] 194 E7
Hirvensalmi [FIN] 186 H6
Hirvihaara [FIN] 176 H4
Hirvijärvi [S] 194 B8
Hirvijoki [FIN] 186 D2
Hirvisalo [FIN] 178 B2
Hisarcık [TR] 152 F2
Hisardžik [SRB] 146 A3
Hisarlık [TR] 150 G4
Hisartepe Dascylium [TR] 150 E4
Histria [RO] 204 F5
Hita [E] 88 H5
Hitchin [GB] 14 E3
Hitiaş [RO] 76 H6
Hitis / Hiitinen [FIN] 176 E6
Hitovo [BG] 148 F1
Hittarp [S] 156 H1
Hitterdal [N] 182 D4
Hitzacker [D] 18 H5
Hiukkajoki [FIN] 188 F5
Hjallerup [DK] 160 E3
Hjällstad [S] 172 E4
Hjälmseryd [S] 162 D3
Hjältanstorp [S] 184 D4
Hjärnarp [DK] 162 B6
Hjartåsen [N] 190 E2
Hjärtum [S] 166 C6
Hjelle [N] 180 C5
Hjelle [N] 180 D5
Hjellestad [N] 170 A4
Hjelmeland [N] 164 B2
Hjelset [N] 180 E3
Hjerkinn [N] 180 G4
Hjerpsted [DK] 156 B4
Hjerting [DK] 156 A2
Hjo [S] 166 F6
Hjøllund [DK] 156 C1
Hjørring [DK] 160 E2
Hjorte [DK] 156 D3
Hjorted [S] 162 G2
Hjorteset [N] 180 C5
Hjortkvarn [S] 166 H4
Hjortsberga [S] 158 F1
Hjortsberga [S] 162 D4
Hjulsbro [S] 168 A6
Hjulsjö [S] 166 G2
Hlinsko [CZ] 50 B4
Hlobyne [UA] 202 F7
Hlohovec [SK] 62 H4
Hluboká nad Vltavou [CZ] 62 C2
Hlučín [CZ] 50 E4
Hluk [CZ] 62 H2
Hlukhiv [UA] 202 E6
Hlusk [BY] 202 C6
Hlybokaya [BY] 202 B4
Hlyniany [UA] 52 G4
Hniezdne [SK] 52 B6
Hnilec [SK] 64 E2
Hnúšťa [SK] 64 D3
Hobermayer-Hofen [A] 74 E2
Hobol [H] 76 A5
Hobro [DK] 160 D5
Hocalar [TR] 152 H3
Hoče [SLO] 74 D4
Hoces del Cabriel [E] 98 C4
Hoces del Duratón [E] 88 G3
Hoces del Riaza [E] 88 G2
Höchberg [D] 46 E4
Hochburg [A] 60 G4
Hochburg [D] 58 E2
Hochdonn [D] 18 E3
Hochdorf [CH] 58 F5
Höchenschwand [D] 58 F4
Hochfelden [F] 44 H5
Hochosterwitz [A] 74 B3
Hochspeyer [D] 46 B4
Höchst [D] 46 D4
Höchstadt [D] 46 G4
Höchstädt [D] 60 C3
Hochstatten [D] 46 B3
Höckendorf [D] 48 E1
Hockenheim [D] 46 C5
Hoczew [PL] 52 E5
Hodal [N] 182 C4
Hodalen [N] 182 C4
Hodejov [SK] 64 E4
Hodenhagen [D] 18 E6
Hodkovice nad Mohelkou [CZ] 48 G2
Hódmezővásárhely [H] 76 E4
Hodøl [N] 182 D4
Hodonín [CZ] 62 G2
Hodoš [SLO] 74 F3
Hodošan [HR] 74 F4
Hoedekenskerke [NL] 28 H1
Hoei (Huy) [B] 30 D5
Hoek van Holland [NL] 16 C5
Hoenzethen [D] 18 G6
Hof [D] 48 B3
Hof [D] 58 F1
Hofgeismar [D] 32 F4
Hofheim [D] 46 F3
Hofles [N] 190 C4
Höfn [IS] 192 C3
Hofors [S] 174 D4
Hofstad [N] 190 B5
Högakustenbron [S] 184 F3
Höganäs [S] 156 H1
Hogdal [S] 166 B4
Högé [S] 184 B2
Högerud [S] 166 E2
Högfors [S] 166 H1
Högfors / Karkkila [FIN] 176 G4
Höghult [S] 162 F2
Högklint [S] 168 F4
Höglunda [S] 184 D2
Högnabba [FIN] 186 D1
Högsäter [S] 166 D5
Högsby [S] 162 F4
Høgset [N] 180 E2
Högsjö [S] 184 F3
Høgstadgård [N] 192 G3
Hogstorp [S] 166 C5
Högvålen [S] 182 E5
Hőgyész [H] 76 B4
Hohenau [A] 62 G3
Hohenbachschlucht [A] 72 B1
Hohenberg [A] 62 E5
Hohenbrunn [D] 60 E4
Hohenburg [D] 46 H5
Hoheneck [D] 46 F5
Hohenems [A] 58 H5
Hohenfels [D] 46 B4
Hohenhewen [D] 58 G4
Hohenkirchen [D] 60 E4
Hohenlimburg [D] 32 C4
Hohenlinden [D] 60 F4
Hohenlockstedt [D] 18 F3
Hohenneuffen [D] 58 H2
Hohenpeissenberg [D] 60 D5
Hohenschwangau [D] 60 C6
Hohenstein [D] 46 B2
Hohensyburg [D] 32 C4
Hohentauern [A] 74 C1
Hohentwiel [D] 58 G4
Hohen Wehrda [D] 46 E1
Hohenwerfen [A] 60 G6
Hohenwestedt [D] 18 F2
Hohenzollern [D] 58 G2
Hohne [D] 32 G1
Hohneck [F] 58 D3
Hohrodberg [F] 58 D3
Hohwacht [D] 18 G2
Hoikhankylä [FIN] 186 H3
Hoilola [FIN] 188 H3
Hoisko [FIN] 186 D2
Højby [DK] 156 F2
Højer [DK] 156 B4
Højerup [DK] 156 G4
Højslev Stby [DK] 160 C5
Hojsova Stráž [CZ] 48 D6
Hok [S] 162 D3
Hökåsen [S] 168 B2
Hökhuvud [S] 174 F5
Hokka [FIN] 186 H5
Hokksund [N] 164 G1
Hökön [S] 162 D6
Hoks Herrgård [S] 162 D3
Hokusukoski [FIN] 186 E4
Hol [N] 170 F3
Hol [S] 162 B1
Holand [N] 190 D5
Hola Prystan' [UA] 204 G3
Holašovice [CZ] 62 B2
Holbæk [DK] 156 F2
Holbeach [GB] 10 G6
Holbøl [DK] 156 C4
Holckenhavn [DK] 156 E3
Holdorf [D] 32 D1
Hole [S] 172 F5
Holeby [DK] 20 A1
Holedeč [CZ] 48 E3
Holešov [CZ] 50 D6
Holíč [SK] 62 G3
Holice [CZ] 50 B4
Hölick [S] 174 E1
Holiseva [FIN] 186 F5
Holja [FIN] 176 G2
Höljes [S] 172 E3
Hollabrunn [A] 62 E3
Hollád [H] 74 G3
Høllen [N] 164 D6
Hollenbach [D] 60 D3
Hollenegg [A] 74 D3
Hollenstedt [D] 18 F4
Hollerath [D] 30 F5
Hollestein [A] 62 C5
Hollfeld [D] 46 G4
Hollingsholm [N] 180 E2
Hollola [FIN] 176 H2
Hollolan [FIN] 176 H2
Hollum [NL] 16 F1
Höllviken [S] 156 H3
Holm [DK] 156 C4
Holm [FIN] 196 B6
Holm [N] 166 B3
Holm [N] 190 C4
Holm [S] 184 D4
Hólmavík [IS] 192 B2
Holmec [SLO] 74 C3
Holmedal [S] 166 D2
Holmegil [N] 166 C3
Holmestrand [N] 164 H2
Holmfirth [GB] 10 E4
Holmfors [S] 190 G4
Holmfors [S] 196 A3
Holmön [S] 196 A6
Holmsjö [S] 162 F6
Holmsjö [S] 184 C3
Holmsjö [S] 190 G6
Holmsund [S] 196 A6
Holmsveden [S] 174 E3
Holmudden [S] 168 H3
Holm-Zhirkovskij [RUS] 202 D3
Holoby [UA] 202 B7
Holovanivs'k [UA] 204 F2
Holovne [UA] 38 G5
Holøydal [N] 182 C5
Holsætra [N] 170 H2
Holsbybrunn [S] 162 E3
Holsen [N] 170 C1
Holsljunge [S] 162 B3
Holstebro [DK] 160 B5
Holsted [DK] 156 B2
Holsworthy [GB] 12 D4
Holt [GB] 14 G1
Holt [N] 164 F4
Holt [N] 192 F3
Holten [NL] 16 G5
Holtet [N] 166 C4
Holtet [N] 172 D4
Holtsås [N] 164 F2
Holtsee [D] 18 F2
Holtslätten [N] 172 C4
Holwerd [NL] 16 F1
Holycross [IRL] 4 E4
Holyhead [GB] 10 B3
Holywell [GB] 10 C4
Holywood [NIR] 2 G3
Holzdorf [D] 34 D4
Holzgau [A] 72 B1
Holzkirchen [D] 60 E5
Holzleitensattel [A] 72 C1
Holzminden [D] 32 F3
Holzschlag [D] 58 F3
Homberg [D] 32 F6
Homberg [D] 46 D1
Homborsund [N] 164 E5
Hombukt [N] 192 H1
Homburg [D] 44 G4
Hommelstø [N] 190 D3
Hommelvik [N] 182 C1
Hommersåk [N] 164 B3
Homokszentgyörgy [H] 74 H5
Homps [F] 106 C4
Homyel' [BY] 202 D6
Honaz [TR] 152 G5
Hondarribia / Fuenterrabía [E] 84 B2
Hönebach [D] 32 F6
Hønefoss [N] 170 H5
Honfleur [F] 26 G3
Høng [DK] 156 F3
Honiton [GB] 12 F4
Honkajoki [FIN] 186 C5
Honkakoski [FIN] 186 B6
Honkola [FIN] 186 G3
Hønning [DK] 156 B3
Honningsvåg [N] 180 B4
Honningsvåg [N] 194 C1
Honrubia [E] 98 B3
Honrubia de la Cuesta [E] 88 G3
Hontalbilla [E] 88 F3
Hontoria de la Cantera [E] 82 E6
Hontoria del Pinar [E] 90 A2
Hoofddorp [NL] 16 D4
Hoogerheide [NL] 30 C2
Hoogeveen [NL] 16 G3
Hoogezand [NL] 16 G2
Hoogkarspel [NL] 16 E3
Hoogstraten [B] 30 D2
Hooksiel [D] 18 C3
Höör [S] 158 C2
Hoorn [NL] 16 E3
Hopfgarten [A] 60 F6
Hoplandsjøen [N] 170 A2
Hopovo, Manastir- [SRB] 142 F2
Hopperstad Stavkirke [N] 170 C2
Hopseldet [N] 194 D1
Hopsten [D] 32 C2
Hoptrup [DK] 156 C3
Hora-Sv-Šebestiána [CZ] 48 E2
Horažďovice [CZ] 48 E6
Horb [D] 58 G2
Horbelev [DK] 20 B1
Hörby [S] 158 C2
Horcajo de los Montes [E] 96 D3
Horcajo de Santiago [E] 96 H2
Horche [E] 88 H5
Horda [S] 162 D4
Hörda [S] 162 D4
Hordain [F] 28 F4
Hordalia [N] 170 C5
Horgen [CH] 58 F5
Horgevik [N] 164 E2
Horgoš [SRB] 76 E5
Horgoū [MNE] 204 A5
Horia [RO] 76 G4
Hořice [CZ] 50 A3
Horitschon [A] 62 F6
Hörja [S] 158 C1
Horjul [SLO] 74 B5
Hörken [S] 166 G1
Horki [BY] 202 D4
Hormogos [E] 88 E6
Horn [A] 62 E3
Horn [D] 32 E3
Horn [D] 58 G4
Horn [N] 170 H4
Horn [N] 190 D3
Horn [S] 162 F2
Hornachos [E] 94 H3
Hornachuelos [E] 96 B6
Horna Štubňa [SK] 64 C3
Hornbæk [DK] 156 G1
Hornberg [D] 46 D5
Hornberg [D] 58 F2
Hornburg [D] 32 H3
Horncastle [GB] 10 G5
Horndal [S] 174 D5
Hörne [D] 18 E3
Horne [DK] 156 D4
Horneburg [D] 18 F4
Hörnefors [S] 190 H6
Hornesund [N] 164 D5
Horní Benešov [CZ] 50 D4
Horní Cerekev [CZ] 48 H6
Horní Lideč [CZ] 50 E6
Horní Loděnice [CZ] 50 D4
Hornindal [N] 180 D5
Hørning [DK] 156 D1
Horní Planá [CZ] 62 B3
Horní Vltavice [CZ] 62 A2
Hornnes [N] 164 D4
Hornos [E] 102 G1
Hornos de Peal [E] 102 F2
Hornoy [F] 28 D5
Hornsea [GB] 10 G4
Hornslet [DK] 160 E6
Hornum [DK] 160 D4
Horný Tisovník [SK] 64 C4
Horodenka [UA] 204 D2
Horodło [PL] 38 G6
Horodnytsia [UA] 202 C7
Horodok [UA] 52 G4
Horodyshche [UA] 202 E8
Horokhiv [UA] 202 B8
Horonkylä [FIN] 186 B4
Hořovice [CZ] 48 E4
Horred [S] 160 H3
Hörröd [S] 158 D2
Horrskog [S] 174 E5
Horsens [DK] 156 D2
Horsham [GB] 14 E5
Hørsholm [DK] 156 G2
Horslunde [DK] 156 E4
Horsmanaho [FIN] 188 E2
Horšovský Týn [CZ] 48 D5
Horst [B] 30 D4
Horst [D] 18 G5
Horst [NL] 30 F3
Hörstel [D] 32 C2
Horstmar [D] 16 H5
Horsunlu [TR] 152 F5
Hort [H] 64 D6
Horta [P] 100 C3
Horten [N] 164 H2
Hortezuela [E] 90 A3
Hortigüela [E] 88 H1
Hortobágy [H] 64 G6
Hörup [D] 156 B5
Hørve [DK] 156 F2
Horven [N] 190 C4
Horw [CH] 58 F6
Hosby [DK] 156 D2
Hoscheid [L] 44 F2
Hosenfeld [D] 46 E2
Hoset [N] 192 D6
Hoshtevë Vithkuq [AL] 128 C6
Hosjö [S] 174 C4
Hoslemo [N] 164 D2
Hospental [CH] 70 F1
Hospice de France [F] 84 F5
Hospital [IRL] 4 D4
Hospital de Orbigo [E] 78 G6
Hossa [FIN] 196 F3
Hossegor [F] 66 A6
Hosszúpályi [H] 76 H1
Hosszú-Pereszteg [H] 74 G2
Hostalric [E] 92 F4
Hoštejn [CZ] 50 C4
Hostens [F] 66 C4
Hostěradice [CZ] 62 F2
Hostianské Nemce [SK] 64 C4
Hostinné [CZ] 50 A2
Hostomice [CZ] 48 F4
Hoston [N] 180 H2
Hostouň [CZ] 48 D5
Hostovice [SK] 52 E6
Hostýn [CZ] 50 D6
Hotagen [S] 190 E5
Hotarele [RO] 148 D1
Hoting [S] 190 F5
Hotton [B] 30 E6
Hötzelsdorf [A] 62 E3
Hou [DK] 160 E4
Houdain [F] 28 E3
Houdan [F] 42 E3
Houdelaincourt [F] 44 D5
Houeillès [F] 66 D5
Houffalize [B] 30 E6
Houlbjerg [DK] 160 D5
Houlgate [F] 26 F3
Hourtin [F] 66 C2
Hourtin-Plage [F] 66 C2
Houthalen [B] 30 E3
Houtsala [FIN] 176 C5
Houtskär / Houtskari [FIN] 176 C5
Houtskari / Houtskär [FIN] 176 C5
Hov [DK] 156 D1
Hov [N] 170 H3
Hov [S] 166 G6
Hova [S] 166 F4
Hovborg [DK] 156 B2
Hovda [N] 170 G3
Hovdala [S] 158 C1
Hovden [N] 164 D1
Hovden [N] 192 D3
Høve [DK] 156 F2
Hove [DK] 160 B5
Hove [N] 180 C6
Hövelhof [D] 32 E3
Hoven [DK] 156 B1
Hoverberg [S] 182 G3
Hovet [N] 170 E3
Hovi [FIN] 188 C2
Hovin [N] 164 F1
Hovin [N] 182 B2
Hovinsholm [N] 172 B4
Hovland [N] 164 B4
Hovland [N] 170 C4
Hovmantorp [S] 162 E5
Hovsta [S] 166 H3
Howard, Castle- [IRL] 4 G4
Howth [IRL] 2 F6
Höxter [D] 32 F4
Hoya [D] 18 E6
Hoya-Gonzalo [E] 98 C5
Høyanger [N] 170 C1
Høydalen [N] 164 F3
Høydalsmo [N] 164 E2
Høydalsseter [N] 180 E6
Hoyerswerda [D] 34 F5
Høyjord [N] 164 H2
Høylandet [N] 190 C4
Hoym [D] 34 B4
Hoyos [E] 86 G3
Hoyos del Espino [E] 88 C5
Höytiä [FIN] 186 F4
Hozha [BY] 24 F3
Hrabaw [RUS] 202 C6
Hrachovo [SK] 64 D3
Hrad Beckov [SK] 64 A3
Hradec Králové [CZ] 50 A3
Hradec nad Moravicí [CZ] 50 E4
Hradec nad Svitavou [CZ] 50 B5
Hrádek [CZ] 48 F2
Hrádek [CZ] 50 A3
Hrádek [CZ] 62 F3
Hrádek nad Nisou [CZ] 48 G1
Hradhoviště [CZ] 62 C2
Hradvz'k [UA] 202 F8
Hranice [CZ] 50 E5
Hranovnica [SK] 64 E2
Hrastik [SLO] 74 D5
Hrastovlje [SLO] 72 H6
Hrebenne [PL] 52 G3
Hredino [RUS] 198 H3
Hřensko [CZ] 48 F1
Hriňová [SK] 64 D3
Hrob [CZ] 48 E2
Hrochův Týnec [CZ] 50 B4
Hrodna [BY] 24 F4
Hronov [CZ] 50 B2
Hrotovice [CZ] 62 E2
Hrtkovci [SRB] 142 F2
Hrubieszów [PL] 52 G1
Hrubov [SK] 52 E6
Hrubý Rohozec [CZ] 48 H2
Hrud [PL] 38 F3
Hrušov [SK] 64 B4
Hrušovany [CZ] 62 F3
Hrvace [HR] 144 A1
Hrvatska Kostajnica [HR] 142 B2
Huaröd [S] 158 D2
Huarte [E] 84 B4
Huben [A] 72 C2
Huben [A] 72 F2
Hubenov [CZ] 48 E4
Hubertusburg [D] 34 D5
Hubertusstock, Jagdschloss- [D] 20 D6
Hucqueliers [F] 28 D3
Huda Luknja [SLO] 74 D4
Huddersfield [GB] 10 E4
Huddinge [S] 168 D3
Huddunge [S] 174 E6
Hudiksvall [S] 174 E1
Huedin [RO] 204 C4
Huélago [E] 102 F3
Huélamo [E] 98 C2
Huelgoat [F] 40 C2
Huelma [E] 102 E3
Huelva [E] 94 E6
Huércal de Almería [E] 102 G5
Huércal-Overa [E] 102 H4
Huerta del Rey [E] 88 H2
Huerta de Valdecarábanos [E] 96 G2
Huérteles [E] 90 C2
Huerto [E] 90 G3
Huesa [E] 102 F2
Huesca [E] 84 D6
Huéscar [E] 102 G3
Hueselgau [D] 32 G6
Huete [E] 98 A1
Huétor Tájar [E] 102 D3
Hüfingen [D] 58 F3
Hufthamar [N] 170 A4
Huhdasjärvi [FIN] 178 C2
Huhla [BG] 130 G1
Huhtala [FIN] 196 D2
Huhtapuhto [FIN] 196 D5
Huhti [FIN] 176 F2
Huhtilampi [FIN] 188 G3
Huhus [FIN] 188 G2
Huissinkylä [FIN] 186 C3
Huittinen [FIN] 176 E2
Huizen [NL] 16 D3
Huizen [NL] 16 E4
Huizingen [B] 28 H3
Hujakkala [FIN] 178 E3
Hukkala [FIN] 188 E2
Hukvaldy [CZ] 50 E5
Hulderbo [N] 180 G5
Hulín [CZ] 50 D6
Huljen [S] 184 E4
Hulle [N] 180 G1
Hullsjön [S] 184 D4
Hulsing [DK] 160 E2
Hulst [NL] 28 H1
Hult [S] 162 E2
Hult [S] 166 F3
Hultanäs [S] 162 E4
Hultsfred [S] 162 F3
Hultsjö [S] 162 D3
Hum [BIH] 144 D2
Hum [HR] 112 E1
Humada [E] 82 E5
Humanes [E] 88 H5
Humble [DK] 156 E5
Humenné [SK] 64 H2
Humla [S] 162 C1
Humlebæk [DK] 156 G2
Humlum [DK] 160 B5
Hümme [D] 32 F4
Hummelsta [S] 168 C2
Hummelvik [N] 192 H1
Humpolec [CZ] 48 H5
Humppi [FIN] 186 F2
Humppila [FIN] 176 F3
Humprecht [CZ] 48 H2
Hunaudaye, Château de- [F] 26 B4
Hundåla [N] 190 D2
Hunderdorf [D] 60 G2
Hundested [DK] 156 G2
Hundorp [N] 170 H1
Hunedoara [RO] 204 C5
Hünfeld [D] 46 E1
Hunge [S] 182 H3
Hungen [D] 46 D2
Hungerford [GB] 12 H3
Hunnebostrand [S] 166 B5
Hunspach [F] 46 B6
Hunstanton [GB] 10 H6
Huntingdon [GB] 14 E2
Huntly [GB] 6 F5
Huopanankoski [FIN] 186 F2
Hurbanovo [SK] 64 B5
Hurdal [N] 172 B4
Hurdal Verk [N] 172 C4
Hurez, Mănăstirea- [RO] 204 C5
Huriel [F] 56 C5
Hurissalo [FIN] 188 D6
Hurskaala [FIN] 188 C4
Hürsovo [BG] 148 E2
Hurtanmaa [FIN] 178 D2
Hurup [DK] 160 B4
Hurva [S] 158 C2
Hus [CZ] 62 B2
Husa [N] 170 B5
Husă [N] 182 F1
Husaby [S] 166 E5
Húsavík [IS] 192 C2
Husbondliden [S] 190 G4
Husby [DK] 160 B5
Husbygård [S] 168 C4
Husby Långhundra [S] 168 D2
Husby-Sjuhundra [S] 168 E2
Huşi [RO] 204 E3
Husinec [CZ] 62 B2
Huskvarna [S] 162 D2
Husnes [N] 170 B5
Husö [FIN] 176 C6
Hustopeče [CZ] 62 F2
Husum [D] 18 E1
Husum [S] 184 G2
Husvika [N] 190 D3
Huta [PL] 52 C5
Huta Zawadzka [PL] 38 A4
Hutovo [BIH] 144 C3
Hüttenberg [A] 74 C2
Hüttschlag [A] 72 G1
Huttwil [CH] 58 E5
Huutijärvi [FIN] 176 F1
Huwniki [PL] 52 F4
Huy (Hoei) [B] 30 D5
Hvalba [FR] 160 A3
Hvalpsund [DK] 160 C4
Hvalvík [FR] 160 B1
Hvam [N] 172 B6
Hvammstangi [IS] 192 B2
Hvar [HR] 144 A2
Hveragerði [IS] 192 A3
Hvidbjerg [DK] 160 B4
Hvide Sande [DK] 156 A1
Hvittingfoss [N] 164 G2
Hvolsvöllur [IS] 192 A3
Hvoznitsa [BY] 38 G4
Hybo [S] 184 D6
Hycklinge [S] 162 F2
Hyde [GB] 10 E4
Hyen [N] 180 C5
Hyères [F] 108 C6
Hyervyaty [BY] 200 H5
Hyggen [N] 164 H1
Hylestad [N] 164 D3
Hyllested Skovgårde [DK] 160 F6
Hyltebruk [S] 162 B4
Hynnekleiv [N] 164 E4
Hyry [FIN] 196 D3
Hyrynsalmi [FIN] 196 F4
Hyssna [S] 160 H2
Hythe [GB] 14 F5
Hyttegrend [N] 192 F3
Hytti [FIN] 178 E2
Hyvinge / Hyvinkää [FIN] 176 H4
Hyvinkää / Hyvinge [FIN] 176 H4
Hyypiö [FIN] 194 D7
Hyžne [PL] 52 E4

I

Ialissós [GR] 154 D3
Ianca [RO] 148 A2
Iaşi [RO] 204 E3
Íasmos [GR] 130 F2

Iasos [TR] 154 B1
Iátova [E] 98 E4
Ibañeta, Puerto de- [E/F] 84 C3
Ibarska Klisura [SRB] 146 B3
Ibbenbüren [D] 32 C2
Ibeas de Juarros [E] 82 E6
Ibestad [N] 192 E3
Ibi [E] 104 E1
Ibieca [E] 84 D6
Ibiza / Eivissa [E] 104 C5
Ibrány [H] 64 H4
İbrice [TR] 150 B3
İbrikbaba [TR] 150 B4
İbriktepe [TR] 130 H2
Ichenhausen [D] 60 C3
Ichtratzheim [F] 44 H6
İçikler [TR] 152 E3
Idaío Ántro [GR] 140 E5
Idala [S] 160 H3
Idanha-a-Nova [P] 86 F3
Idar-Oberstein [D] 44 H3
Idbacka [S] 190 F5
Idensalmi / Iisalmi [FIN] 196 E6
Idivuoma [S] 192 H4
Idjoš [SRB] 76 E5
Idom [DK] 160 B5
Idre [S] 182 E6
Idrija [SLO] 74 B5
Idritsa [RUS] 198 H5
Idro [I] 72 B5
Idstein [D] 46 C2
Idyma [TR] 154 D1
Iecava [LV] 198 D5
Ieper (Ypres) [B] 28 F2
Ierápetra [GR] 140 G5
Ierissós [GR] 130 C5
Ieropigí [GR] 128 D5
If, Château d'- [F] 106 H5
Ifaístia [GR] 130 F6
Ifjord [N] 194 D2
Igal [H] 76 A4
Igalo [MNE] 144 D4
Igate [LV] 198 E4
Igea Marina [I] 110 H5
Igelbäcken [S] 166 G5
Igelfors [S] 168 A4
Igerøy [N] 190 C3
Iggesund [S] 174 E1
Iglesias [I] 118 B6
Igliauka [LT] 24 F1
Igliczna [PL] 50 C3
Igls [A] 72 D1
Ignaberga [S] 158 D1
Ignalina [LT] 200 H4
Ignatpol [UA] 202 C7
İğneada [TR] 150 D1
Igołomia [PL] 52 B3
Igoumenítsa [GR] 132 C2
Igralište [BG] 128 H2
Igrane [HR] 144 B2
Igrejinha [P] 86 D6
Igriés [E] 84 D6
Igualada [E] 92 D4
Igualeja [E] 102 A4
Igüeña [E] 78 G5
Iharosberény [H] 74 G4
Ihlienworth [D] 18 E3
Ii [FIN] 196 D3
Iiıca [TR] 150 D5
Iisalmi / Idensalmi [FIN] 196 E6
Iisvesi [FIN] 186 H3
Iittala [FIN] 176 G2
Iitti [FIN] 178 B2
IJmuiden [NL] 16 D4
Ikalis / Kaalinen [FIN] 186 D6
Ikast [DK] 160 C6
Ikhala [RUS] 188 G6
Ikhtiman [BG] 146 G5
İkizköy [TR] 154 C1
Ikkala [FIN] 176 G4
Ikkeläjärvi [FIN] 186 C4
Ikornnes [N] 180 D4
Ilanz [CH] 70 G1
Iława [PL] 22 F4
Il Casalone [I] 114 G4
il Castagno [I] 110 E6
Ilchester [GB] 12 F4
Ildır [TR] 134 H4
Ildir [TR] 134 H4
Ileía [GR] 134 A4
Ilfracombe [GB] 12 E3
İlhan [TR] 150 D4
Ílhavo [P] 80 B5
Ilia [RO] 204 C5
Ilıcalı [TR] 152 E2
Ilidža [BIH] 144 D1
Ilijaš [BIH] 142 D4
Il'inskoye [RUS] 202 F2
Ilirska Bistrica [SLO] 74 B6
Ilkley [GB] 10 E3
Illano [E] 78 F3
Illar [E] 102 F5
Illa Ravena [E] 104 F5
Illby / Ilola [FIN] 178 B4
Illertissen [D] 60 B4
Illescas [E] 88 F6
Illichivs'k [UA] 204 F3
Illiers-Combray [F] 42 D5
Illingen [D] 46 C6
Illmitz [A] 62 G6
Illo [FIN] 176 E2
Íllora [E] 102 D3
Illschwang [D] 46 H5
Illueca [E] 90 D4
Ilmajoki [FIN] 186 C3
Il'me [RUS] 178 F1
Ilmenau [D] 46 G1
Ilminster [GB] 12 F4
Ilmoila [FIN] 176 G2
Ilok [HR] 142 F1
Ilola / Illby [FIN] 178 B4
Ilomants / Ilomantsi [FIN] 188 G2
Ilomantsi / Ilomants [FIN] 188 G2
Iłowa [PL] 34 H5
Iłowiec [PL] 22 A5
Il Pulo [I] 122 D2
Il Pulo [I] 122 D3
Ilsbo [S] 184 E6
Ilsenburg [D] 32 H3
Ilseng [N] 172 C3
Ilshofen [D] 46 E6
Ilskov [DK] 160 C6
Ilūkste [LV] 198 F6
Ilvesjoki [FIN] 186 C4
Ilyaslar [TR] 152 E1
İlyaslı [TR] 152 F3
Ilz [A] 74 E2
Iłża [PL] 38 C6
Imatra [FIN] 178 E1
İmecik [TR] 154 H1
Ímeros [GR] 130 F3
Imfors [S] 184 E1
Immenhausen [D] 32 F5
Immenstaad [D] 58 H4
Immenstadt [D] 60 B5
Immingham [GB] 10 G4
Imola [I] 110 G4
Imotski [HR] 144 B2
Imperia [I] 108 G4
Imphy [F] 56 D4
Impilakhti [RUS] 188 H5
Imrehegy [H] 76 D4
İmroz [TR] 130 G5
Imsenden [N] 172 B1
Imsland [N] 164 B1
Imst [A] 72 C1
Inari [FIN] 196 H6
Inari / Enare [FIN] 194 D4
Inay [TR] 152 G3
Inca [E] 104 E5
Inch [IRL] 4 B4
Inch [IRL] 4 B6
Inchigeelagh [IRL] 4 C5
Inciems [LV] 198 E4
İncik [TR] 150 H6
İnciraltı [TR] 152 C4
İncirköy [TR] 154 F2
İncirliova [TR] 152 D5
Incisa in Val d'Arno [I] 110 F6
Incisioni Rupestri, Parco Nazionale delle- [I] 72 B4
Indal [S] 184 E4
Independenta [RO] 148 F1
Inđija [SRB] 142 G2
Inđija [SRB] 204 A5
Indre Billefjord [N] 194 C2
Indre Brenna [N] 194 C2
Indura [BY] 24 F4
İnece [TR] 150 B2
İnecik [TR] 150 C3
İnegöl [TR] 150 F5
Ineu [RO] 76 H4
Infantado [P] 86 C5
Infiesto [E] 82 C2
Ingå / Inkoo [FIN] 176 G5
Ingdalen [N] 180 H1
Ingelheim [D] 46 B3
Ingelmunster [B] 28 G2
Ingelstad [S] 162 E5
Ingenes [S] 170 B5
Ingenio [E] 100 C6
Ingevallsbo [S] 172 H5
Ingolsbenning [S] 174 D5
Ingolsheim [F] 46 B6
Ingolstadt [D] 60 E2
Ingwiller [F] 44 G5
İnhisar [TR] 150 H4
Iniesta [E] 98 C4
Iniö [FIN] 176 C5
Inis / Ennis [IRL] 2 C6
Inishannon [IRL] 4 C5
Inke [H] 74 G4
Inkerilä [FIN] 178 C2
Inkilä [FIN] 178 D2
Inkoo / Ingå [FIN] 176 G5
Innala [FIN] 186 E5
Inndyr [N] 192 D6
Innerkrems [A] 72 H2
Innerleithen [GB] 8 E4
Innertkirchen [CH] 70 F1
Innervik [S] 190 G2
Innfjorden [N] 180 E3
Innhavet [N] 192 E5
Innichen / San Cándido [I] 72 E3
Inning [D] 60 D4
Innsbruck [A] 72 D1
Innset [N] 180 H3
Innset [N] 192 F3
Innvik [N] 180 D5
İnönü [TR] 150 H5
Inowłódz [PL] 38 A5
Inowrocław [PL] 36 E1
Ins [CH] 58 D5
Insch [GB] 6 F6
Insjön [S] 172 H4
Ińsko [PL] 20 G5
Însurăţei [RO] 204 E5
Intepe [TR] 130 H5
Interlaken [CH] 70 E1
Intra [I] 70 F3
Inturkė [LT] 200 G5
Inveraray [GB] 8 C2
Inverbervie [GB] 8 G1
Invergarry [GB] 6 D5
Invergordon [GB] 6 E4
Invermoriston [GB] 6 D5
Inverness [GB] 6 D5
Inverurie [GB] 6 F6
Inviken [S] 190 E5
Inzell [D] 60 G5
Ioánnina [GR] 132 D2
Ionia [GR] 128 H4
Íos [GR] 138 E4
Iphofen [D] 46 F4
İpsala [TR] 130 H3
Ipswich [GB] 14 G3
Iraío [GR] 132 H6
Iraío [GR] 136 E2
Iraío [GR] 152 C6
Irákleia [GR] 130 B3
Irákleia [GR] 132 G4
Irákleia [GR] 138 F4
Irákleio [GR] 140 E4
Iranzu [E] 84 A4
Irdning [A] 62 B6
Iregszemcse [H] 76 B3
Ireo [GR] 152 C6
Irgıllı [TR] 152 H4
Irig [SRB] 142 F2
Irixoa [E] 78 D2
Irnfritz [A] 62 D3
Irsina [I] 122 C3
Irun [E] 84 B2
Iruña / Pamplona [E] 84 B4
Irunberri / Lumbier [E] 84 C4
Irurita [E] 84 B3
Irurtzun [E] 84 B3
Irvine [GB] 8 C3
Irvinestown [NIR] 2 E3
Isaba / Izaba [E] 84 C4
İsabey [TR] 152 G4
Isaccea [RO] 204 E4
Ísafjörður [IS] 192 A1
Isane [N] 180 C5
Isaszeg [H] 64 D6
Isbister [GB] 6 G3
Íscar [E] 88 E2
Ischgl [A] 72 B2
Ischia [I] 120 D3
Isdes [F] 56 C2
Ise [N] 166 C3
Iselle [I] 70 E2
Iselsberg [A] 72 G2
Iseltwald [CH] 70 E1
Isenvad [DK] 156 C1
Iseo [I] 72 A5
Iserlohn [D] 32 C4
Isernia [I] 120 E1
Isfjorden [N] 180 E3
Ishakı [TR] 150 B4
Isigni-sur-Mer [F] 26 E3
Işıklar [TR] 152 E4
Isıklı [TR] 152 H3
İsili [I] 118 D6
İsinda [TR] 154 G3
İskele [TR] 152 E1
Iskele (Trikomon) [CY] 154 G5
Iskra [RUS] 178 F3
Iškuras [N] 194 C4
Isla [E] 82 F3
Isla Cristina [E] 94 D5
Isla Mayor [E] 100 G2
Islares [E] 82 G3
Ismaning [D] 60 E4
Ismantorp [S] 162 G5
Isnäs [FIN] 178 B4
Isnestoften [N] 192 H1
Iso-Äiniö [FIN] 176 H2
Iso-Evo [FIN] 176 H2
Isojoki / Storå [FIN] 186 B5
Isokyla [FIN] 186 C3
Isokyla [FIN] 188 C3
Isokylä [FIN] 194 E7
Isokylä [FIN] 196 D4
Isokyrö / Storkyro [FIN] 186 B2
Isola [F] 108 E3
Isola 2000 [F] 108 E3
Isola del Gran Sasso d'Italia [I] 116 C4
Isola della Scala [I] 110 F1
Ísola delle Femmine [I] 126 C1
Isola del Liri [I] 116 C6
Ísola di Capo Rizzuto [I] 124 F5
Isolahti [FIN] 186 G4
Isona [E] 92 C2
Isoperä [FIN] 176 E3
Isorella [I] 110 D1
Isosuo [FIN] 178 B1
Isperikh [BG] 148 E2
Íspica [I] 126 G5
Issa [RUS] 198 H5
Isseikka [FIN] 196 F6
Isselburg [D] 16 F6
Issigeac [F] 66 E4
Isso [E] 104 B1
Issogne [I] 70 D4
Issoire [F] 68 C3
Issoudun [F] 56 B4
Is-sur-Tille [F] 56 H3
İstanbul [TR] 150 E3
Istarske Toplice [HR] 112 D1
Istebna [PL] 50 F5
Istha [D] 32 E5
Isthmía [GR] 136 F1
Istiaía [GR] 134 A3
Istibanja [MK] 128 G1
Istomino [RUS] 202 D4
Istranca [TR] 150 D2
Istres [F] 106 G5
Ístria [RO] 204 F5
Istunmäki [FIN] 186 H3
Isturits et d'Oxocelhaya, Grottes d'- [F] 84 C2
Istuzu [TR] 154 E2
Isums [S] 168 G4
Itä-Aure [FIN] 186 D5
Itä-Karttula [FIN] 188 C2
Itäkylä [FIN] 186 D2
Italica [E] 94 G6
Itämen [FIN] 186 E4
Itanós [GR] 140 H4
Itéa [GR] 128 F6
Itéa [GR] 132 F2
Itéa [GR] 132 G5
Itháki [GR] 132 D5
Itieli [I] 116 A4
Itri [I] 120 C2
Ittiri [I] 118 C3
Itxassou [F] 84 C2
Itzehoe [D] 18 F3
Ivacevičy [BY] 202 B6
Ivád [H] 64 E5
Ivalo [FIN] 194 D4
Ivanava [BY] 202 B6
Ivančice [CZ] 62 F2
Ivančići [BIH] 142 D4
Ivančický Viadukt [CZ] 62 F2
Ivančna Gorica [SLO] 74 C5
Ivanec [HR] 74 E4
Ivangorod [RUS] 198 G1
Ivanić Grad [HR] 74 F6
Ivanjica [SRB] 146 B3
Ivanjska [BIH] 142 B2
Ivankiv [UA] 202 D7
Ivankovo [HR] 142 E1
Ivano-Frankivs'k [UA] 204 C2
Ivano-Frankove [UA] 52 G4
Ivanovice na Hané [CZ] 50 C6
Ivanovo [BG] 148 D6
Ivanovo [BG] 148 E3
Ivanovo Manastir [BG] 148 C2
Ivanska [HR] 74 G6
Ivanski [BG] 148 E3
Ivarrud [N] 190 E3
Ivaylovgrad [BG] 130 G1
Iveland [N] 164 D5
Ivetofta [S] 158 E1
Ívira [GR] 130 C3
Ivíron, Moní- [GR] 130 D5
Ivréa [I] 70 E4
İvrindi [TR] 152 C1
Ivry-la-Bataille [F] 42 E3
Ivybridge [GB] 12 D5
Iwaniska [PL] 52 C2
Iwla [PL] 52 D5
Iwonicz-Zdrój [PL] 52 D5
Iwye [BY] 202 A5
Ixiá [GR] 154 D3
Izaba / Isaba [E] 84 C4
Izačić [BIH] 112 H3
Izarra [E] 82 G4
Izbica Kujawska [PL] 36 F2
Izbiceni [RO] 148 A2
Izbicko [PL] 50 E2
Izborsk [RUS] 198 G3
Izcar [E] 102 C2
Izeda [P] 80 F4
Izegem [B] 28 G2
Izernore [F] 68 H2
Izgrev [BG] 148 G5
Izmaïl [UA] 204 F4
İzmir [TR] 152 C4
İzmit [TR] 150 G3
İzmit (Kocaeli) [TR] 150 G3
Iznájar [E] 102 C3
Iznalloz [E] 102 E3
İznik [TR] 150 G4
Izola [SLO] 72 H6
Izsák [H] 76 D3
Izvoarele [RO] 148 C1
Izvor [BG] 146 E2
Izvor [BG] 146 F5
Izvor [MK] 128 D2
Izvor [MK] 128 E2
Izvor [SRB] 146 D2
Izvoz [RUS] 198 H1

J

Jaakonvaara [FIN] 188 G1
Jaala [FIN] 178 C2
Jaalanka [FIN] 196 E4
Jääli [FIN] 196 D3
Jaama [EST] 198 G1
Jääskö [FIN] 194 C7
Jabkenice [CZ] 48 G3
Jablanac [HR] 112 F3
Jablanica [BIH] 144 C1
Jablonec nad Jizerou [CZ] 48 H2
Jablonec nad Nisou [CZ] 48 H2
Jablonica [SK] 62 H3
Jabłonka [PL] 50 H5
Jabłonna [PL] 36 B3
Jablonné nad Orlicí [CZ] 50 C4
Jablonné v Podještědí [CZ] 48 G2
Jabłonowo Pomorskie [PL] 22 E5
Jablunkov [CZ] 50 F5
Jabugo [E] 94 F4
Jabuka [BIH] 144 E1
Jabuka [MNE] 144 E3
Jabuka [SRB] 142 G2
Jabuka [SRB] 144 E2
Jabukovik [SRB] 146 E4
Jaca [E] 84 D5
Jáchymov [CZ] 48 D3
Jacinki [PL] 22 B3
Jacobsdorf [D] 34 F3
Jaczowice [PL] 50 D2
Jade [D] 18 C4
Jädraås [S] 174 D3
Jadranska Lešnica [SRB] 142 F3
Jadraque [E] 88 H5
Jægerspris [DK] 156 G2
Jaén [E] 102 E2
Jagare [BIH] 142 C3
Jagel [D] 18 F1
Jagenbach [A] 62 D3
Jagodina [SRB] 146 C2
Jagodina [SRB] 204 B6
Jagodje [SLO] 72 H6
Jagodnjak [HR] 76 B6
Jagodzin [PL] 34 H5
Jagsthausen [D] 46 D5
Jahnsfelde [D] 34 F2
Jajce [BIH] 142 C4
Ják [H] 74 F2
Jakabszállás [H] 76 D3
Jakalj [SRB] 146 A2
Jakkukylä [FIN] 196 D3
Jakkula [FIN] 186 B3
Jäkkvik [S] 190 F2
Jakobsbakken [N] 192 E6
Jakobstad / Pietarsaari [FIN] 196 B6
Jakokoski [FIN] 188 F2
Jakšić [HR] 142 C1
Jakub [CZ] 48 H4
Jakubany [SK] 52 C6
Jakubčovice nad Odrou [CZ] 50 E5
Jakuszyce [PL] 48 H1
Jalasjärvi [FIN] 186 C4
Jaligny-sur-Besbre [F] 56 D6
Jałówka [PL] 24 G6
Jamaja [EST] 198 C3
Jamena [SRB] 142 E2
Jämijärvi [FIN] 186 C6
Jäminkipohja [FIN] 186 E5
Jämjöslätt [S] 158 G1
Jammerdal [N] 172 D5
Jämsä [FIN] 186 F5
Jämsänkoski [FIN] 186 F5
Jämshög [S] 158 E1
Jämtön [S] 196 B2
Jamurda [LV] 198 E5
Janakkala [FIN] 176 G3
Janče [MK] 128 C2
Jandía Playa [E] 100 D6
Jänese [EST] 198 F1
Janja [BIH] 142 F3
Janjina [HR] 144 B3
Jankov [CZ] 48 G5
Janków [PL] 36 E4
Jännevirta [FIN] 188 D2
Jánoshalma [H] 76 D4
Jánosháza [H] 74 G2
Jánossomorja [H] 62 G5
Janovice nad Úhlavou [CZ] 48 D5
Janów [PL] 24 E4
Janów [PL] 38 A3
Janów [PL] 50 G2
Janowiec [PL] 38 D5
Janowiec Wielkopolski [PL] 36 D1
Janów Lubelski [PL] 52 E2
Janowo [PL] 22 H5
Janów Podlaski [PL] 38 F3
Janské Lazně [CZ] 50 A2
Jänsmässholmen [S] 190 D6
Januszewice [PL] 38 A5
Janville [F] 42 E5
Janvry [F] 42 F4
Janzé [F] 26 C6
Jäppilä [FIN] 188 C4
Jarafuel [E] 98 D5
Jaraicejo [E] 96 B1
Jaraíz de la Vera [E] 88 B5
Jarak [SRB] 142 F2
Järämä [S] 192 G4
Jarama, Circuito de- [E] 88 G5
Jarandilla de la Vera [E] 88 B5
Järbo [S] 174 D4
Jarcevo [RUS] 202 D4
Jarczew [PL] 38 D4
Jardin [F] 54 F2
Jard-sur-Mer [F] 54 B3
Jaren [N] 172 B4
Jaren [S] 166 C3
Jargeau [F] 42 F6
Järkastaka [S] 192 H4
Jarkovac [SRB] 142 H1
Järkvissle [S] 184 E3
Järlåsa [S] 168 C1
Jarmen [D] 20 D3
Jarmenil [F] 58 C2
Jarmina [HR] 142 E1
Järn [S] 166 D5
Järna [S] 168 D4
Jarnac [F] 54 D6
Jarnages [F] 54 H6
Järnäsklubb [S] 184 H1
Järnforsen [S] 162 F3
Jarny [F] 44 E4
Jarocin [PL] 36 D4
Jaroměř [CZ] 50 B3
Jaroměřice nad Rokytnou [CZ] 62 E2
Jaroslavl [RUS] 202 F1
Jarosław [PL] 52 F3
Jarosławiec [PL] 22 B2
Järpås [S] 166 E5
Järpen [S] 182 F2
Järrestad [S] 158 D3
Jarrío [E] 78 F2
Järsnäs [S] 162 D2
Jarszewko [PL] 20 F4
Järva-Jaani [EST] 198 E2
Järvakandi [EST] 198 E2
Järvelä [FIN] 176 H3
Järvenpää [FIN] 178 C1
Järvenpää [FIN] 188 D5
Järvenpää / Träskända [FIN] 176 H4
Järvikylä [FIN] 196 E5
Järvsjö [S] 190 F5
Järvsö [S] 174 D1
Järvtjärn [S] 196 A5
Jaša Tomić [SRB] 142 H1
Jasenak [HR] 112 F2
Jasenjani [BIH] 144 C2
Jasenkovo [BG] 148 E2
Jasenná [CZ] 50 E6
Jasenovac [HR] 142 B1
Jasenovets [BG] 148 D2
Jasenovo [MNE] 144 E3
Jasenovo [SRB] 146 A3
Jasień [PL] 22 C3
Jasień [PL] 34 G4
Jasienica [PL] 50 F4
Jasienica Rosielna [PL] 52 E4
Jasienie [PL] 50 E1
Jasika [SRB] 146 C3
Jasikovo [SRB] 146 D1
Jasionówka [PL] 24 E5
Jašiūnai [LT] 200 G6
Jaskinia Raj [PL] 52 B1
Jaskyňa Domica [SK] 64 E3
Jasło [PL] 52 D4
Jasná [SK] 64 D2
Jasna Góra [PL] 50 G2
Jasno [RUS] 198 H3
Jasov [SK] 64 F3
Jasovská Jaskyňa [SK] 64 F3
Jastarnia [PL] 22 E1
Jastrebarsko [HR] 74 D6
Jastrowie [PL] 22 B5
Jastrzębia [PL] 22 D1
Jastrzębia [PL] 38 C5
Jastrzębie-Zdrój [PL] 50 F4
Jäsund [N] 164 C6
Jászágó [H] 64 D6
Jászalsószentgyörgy [H] 76 E1
Jászapáti [H] 64 E6
Jászárokszállás [H] 64 E6
Jászberény [H] 64 D6
Jászfényszaru [H] 64 D6
Jászkarajenő [H] 76 E2
Jászkisér [H] 76 E1
Jászkóhalma [H] 64 E6
Jászladány [H] 76 E1
Jaszów [PL] 50 D2
Jászszentandrás [H] 64 E6
Jászszentlászló [H] 76 D3
Jásztelek [H] 64 E6
Jät [S] 162 E5
Játar [E] 102 G3
Jatko [FIN] 196 E3
Jatov [SK] 64 A5
Jättendal [S] 184 E6
Jaubrun [F] 68 C5
Jauge [F] 66 C3
Jaun [CH] 70 D1
Jaungulbene [LV] 198 F4
Jauniniumuiža [LV] 198 C6
Jaunjelgava [LV] 198 E5
Jaunpils [LV] 198 C5
Jauntsaras [E] 84 B3
Jaurakkajärvi [FIN] 196 E3
Jauranna [LV] 198 F4
Jaurplebalga [LV] 198 F4
Jausiers [F] 108 E2
Jåvall [N] 166 C2
Javarus [FIN] 194 D7
Jävenitz [D] 34 B2
Javerdat [F] 54 F6
Javier / Xabier [E] 84 C4
Javierre [E] 84 E5
Javoříčko [CZ] 50 C5
Javorník [CZ] 50 C3
Jävre [S] 196 B4
Javron [F] 26 F5
Jawor [PL] 36 B6
Jawor Solecki [PL] 38 C6
Jaworzno [PL] 50 G3
Jayena [E] 102 D4
Jažići [BIH] 144 D2
Jazvina-Puszta [H] 76 A3
Jeanménil [F] 44 F6
Jebel [RO] 76 G6
Jedburgh [GB] 8 F4
Jedeszki [PL] 24 E4
Jedlina-Zdrój [PL] 50 B2
Jedlińsk [PL] 38 B5
Jednorożec [PL] 24 B6
Jedovnice [CZ] 50 C6
Jędrzejów [PL] 52 B2
Jédula [E] 100 G3
Jedwabne [PL] 24 D5
Jedwabno [PL] 22 H5
Jeesiö [FIN] 194 D6
Jegłownik [PL] 22 F3
Jēkabpils [LV] 198 F5
Jektevik [N] 170 B5
Jektvik [N] 190 D1
Jelah [BIH] 142 D3
Jelcz-Laskowice [PL] 50 D1
Jelenia Góra [PL] 50 A1
Jeleniewo [PL] 24 E2
Jelenino [PL] 22 B4
Jeleśnia [PL] 50 G5
Jelgava [LV] 198 D5
Jelizarovo [RUS] 198 G3
Jelling [DK] 156 C2
Jełowa [PL] 50 E2
Jels [DK] 156 C3
Jelsa [HR] 144 A3
Jelsa [N] 164 B2
Jelšane [SLO] 112 E1
Jelšava [SK] 64 E3
Jelsi [I] 120 F1
Jemieliste [PL] 24 E2
Jemnice [CZ] 62 D2
Jena [D] 46 H1
Jenbach [A] 60 E6
Jeneč [CZ] 48 F3
Jenikowo [PL] 20 G4
Jennersdorf [A] 74 E2
Jensåsvoll [N] 182 D3
Jeppo / Jepua [FIN] 186 C1
Jepua / Jeppo [FIN] 186 C1
Jerez de la Frontera [E] 100 F3
Jerez del Marquesado [E] 102 F4
Jerez de los Caballeros [E] 94 F3
Jerggul Holmestrand [N] 194 C4
Jergucati [AL] 132 B1
Jérica [E] 98 E3
Jerichow [D] 34 C2
Jerka [PL] 36 C4
Jerónimos, Mon. de los- [E] 104 C3
Jerpoint Abbey [IRL] 4 E4
Jerslev [DK] 160 E3
Jerup [DK] 160 E2
Jerxheim [D] 32 H3
Jerzens [A] 72 C1
Jerzu [I] 118 E5
Jerzwałd [PL] 22 F4
Jesberg [D] 32 E6
Jesenice [CZ] 48 E3
Jesenice [HR] 144 A2
Jesenice [SLO] 74 B4
Jesenice [SLO] 74 E5
Jeseník [CZ] 50 D3
Jesenovac [BIH] 142 B3
Jesenské [SK] 64 E4
Jesi [I] 116 C1
Jesionowo [PL] 20 G6
Jésolo [I] 72 F6
Jessen [D] 34 D4
Jessheim [N] 172 C5
Jestřebí [CZ] 48 G2
Jettenh. [D] 32 G4
Jettingen-Scheppach [D] 60 C3
Jeumont [F] 28 H4
Jevenstedt [D] 18 F2
Jever [D] 18 C4
Jevíčko [CZ] 50 C5
Jevišovice [CZ] 62 E2
Jevnaker [N] 170 H5
Jezerane [HR] 112 G2
Jezero [BIH] 142 B3
Jezero [HR] 112 G2
Jezerski [BIH] 112 H2
Jezersko [SLO] 74 B4
Jezevo [HR] 74 E6
Jeżewo [PL] 36 H1
Jeziorany [PL] 22 H3
Jeżów [PL] 36 H4
Jeżowe [PL] 52 E2
J. F. Kennedy Memorial Forest Park [IRL] 4 F5
Jičín [CZ] 48 H3
Jieznas [LT] 24 G1
Jihlava [CZ] 48 H5
Jijona / Xixona [E] 104 E2
Jilava [RO] 140 D6
Jilemnice [CZ] 48 H2
Jílové u Prahy [CZ] 48 F4
Jiltjer [S] 190 F3
Jimbolia [RO] 76 F5
Jimena [E] 102 E2
Jimena de la Frontera [E] 100 H5
Jimramov [CZ] 50 B5
Jince [CZ] 48 F4
Jindřichov [CZ] 50 D3
Jindřichovice [CZ] 48 C3
Jindřichův Hradec [CZ] 48 G6
Jirkov [CZ] 48 E2
Jistebnice [CZ] 48 F5
Joachimsthal [D] 20 D6
Jobbágyi [H] 64 D5
Jochberg [A] 72 F1
Jock [S] 194 B8
Jódar [E] 102 F2
Jodoigne [B] 30 D4
Joensuu [FIN] 188 F2
Joesjö [S] 190 E3
Jõgeva [EST] 198 F2
Johannelund [S] 190 H5
Johanneshov [S] 168 G3
Johanngeorgenstadt [D] 48 D2
Johannisholm [S] 172 F3
Johansfors [S] 162 F5
John o' Groats [GB] 6 F3
Johnstone [GB] 8 D3
Johnstown [IRL] 4 E3
Jõhvi [EST] 198 F1
Joigny [F] 42 H6
Joinville [F] 44 C5
Jokela [FIN] 176 H4
Jokijärvi [FIN] 186 H2
Jokikylä [FIN] 186 D4
Jokikylä [FIN] 196 D6
Jokikylä [FIN] 196 D4
Jokikylä [FIN] 196 D5
Jokikylä [FIN] 196 F4
Jokimaa [FIN] 176 H3
Jokioinen / Jookis [FIN] 176 F3
Jokiperä [FIN] 186 B3
Jokipii [FIN] 186 C4
Jokivarsi [FIN] 186 D4
Jokkmokk [S] 190 H1
Jökulsarlon [IS] 192 C3
Jolanda di Savóia [I] 110 G2
Jomala [FIN] 176 A5
Jönåker [S] 168 C5
Jonas, Grottes de- [F] 68 C3
Jonasvollen [N] 182 D5
Jonava [LT] 200 F5
Joncy [F] 56 F5
Jondal [N] 170 C4
Joniny [PL] 52 C4
Joniškis [LT] 198 D6
Jonkeri [FIN] 196 G5
Jönköping [S] 162 D2
Jonsberg [S] 168 C5
Jonsrud [N] 172 C4
Jonzac [F] 66 D1
Jookis / Jokioinen [FIN] 176 F3
Jordanów [PL] 50 H5
Jordanów Śląski [PL] 50 C1
Jordbro [S] 168 E3
Jördenstorf [D] 20 C3
Jordet [N] 172 D2
Jorgastak [N] 194 C4
Jörgen-Berg [CH] 70 G1
Jörlanda [S] 160 G1
Jormua [FIN] 196 F5
Jormvattnet [S] 190 E4
Joroinen / Jorois [FIN] 188 D4
Jorois / Joroinen [FIN] 188 D4
Jørpeland [N] 164 B3
Jorquera [E] 98 C5
Jørstad [N] 190 C5
Jošan [HR] 112 H4
Jošanica [BIH] 144 D1
Jošanica, Manastir- [SRB] 146 C2

Jošanička Banja [SRB] 146 B3
Jošavka [BIH] 142 C3
Josefov [CZ] 50 B3
Jøsenfjorden [N] 164 C2
Joševa [SRB] 142 F3
Josipdol [HR] 112 G2
Josipovac [HR] 76 B6
Jössefors [S] 166 D2
Josselin [F] 26 B6
Jøssund [N] 190 C5
Jostedal [N] 180 D6
Jósvafő [H] 64 F3
Jouarre [F] 42 H4
Jõuga [EST] 198 F1
Jougne [F] 58 B6
Joukio [FIN] 188 F6
Joukokylä [FIN] 196 F3
Joure [NL] 16 F3
Journaankylä [FIN] 178 B4
Joutsa [FIN] 186 G6
Joutseno [FIN] 178 E2
Joutsijärvi [FIN] 194 E7
Jovan [S] 190 G4
Joviac [F] 68 F6
Jøvik [N] 192 G2
Jovsa [SK] 64 H2
Joyeuse [F] 68 E6
Józefów [PL] 38 C3
Józefów [PL] 38 D6
Józefów [PL] 52 F2
Józsa [H] 64 G6
Juankoski [FIN] 188 D1
Juan-les-Pins [F] 108 E5
Judaberg [N] 164 B2
Judenburg [A] 74 C2
Judinsalo [FIN] 186 G6
Juelsminde [DK] 156 D2
Jugendburg [D] 46 C1
Jugon-les-Lacs [F] 26 B5
Jugorje [SLO] 74 D6
Juhtimäki [FIN] 186 D6
Juillac [F] 66 G3
Juist [D] 16 H1
Jukkasjärvi [S] 192 G5
Juknaičiai [LT] 200 D5
Juktån [S] 190 G4
Jule [N] 190 D5
Jülich [D] 30 F4
Julierpass [CH] 70 H2
Julita [S] 168 B3
Jullouville [F] 26 D4
Jumièges [F] 26 H3
Jumilla [E] 104 C1
Juminen [FIN] 196 F6
Jumisko [FIN] 194 E8
Jumkersrott [D] 18 B3
Jumkil [S] 168 D1
Jung [S] 166 E6
Jungsund [FIN] 186 B2
Junibodsand [S] 184 F5
Juniville [F] 44 C3
Junnikkala [FIN] 178 E1
Junosuando [S] 194 B7
Junqueira [P] 80 E4
Junsele [S] 190 F6
Juntusranta [FIN] 196 F3
Juodupė [LT] 198 F6
Juojärvi [FIN] 188 E3
Juoksengi [S] 194 B8
Juokslahti [FIN] 186 F5
Juorkuna [FIN] 196 E4
Jupiter [RO] 148 G1
Jurbarkas [LT] 200 E5
Jurignac [F] 66 E1
Jurklošter [SLO] 74 D5
Jurków [PL] 52 B4
Jūrmala [LV] 198 D5
Jurmo [FIN] 176 C4
Jurmo [FIN] 176 D6
Jurovski Brod [HR] 74 D6
Jurowce [PL] 24 E5
Jurva [FIN] 186 B3
Jurvala [FIN] 178 D2
Jurvansalo [FIN] 186 G2
Jushkino [RUS] 198 G2
Jushkozero [RUS] 196 H3
Jussey [F] 58 B3
Juszkowy Gród [PL] 24 F6
Juta [H] 74 H4
Jüterbog [D] 34 D3
Jutis [S] 190 F2
Jutrosin [PL] 36 D5
Jutsajaura [S] 192 G6
Juujärvi [FIN] 194 E8
Juuka [FIN] 188 E1
Juupajoki [FIN] 186 E6
Juurikka [FIN] 188 G4
Juva [FIN] 176 D4
Juva [FIN] 188 D5
Juvanum [I] 116 D5
Juvigny-le-Tertre [F] 26 E4
Juvola [FIN] 188 E4
Juvre [DK] 156 B3
Juzennecourt [F] 44 C6
Južnyj [RUS] 22 H2
Jyderup [DK] 156 F2
Jylhä [FIN] 186 G1
Jyllinge [DK] 156 G2
Jyrkäntoski [FIN] 194 F8
Jyrkha [FIN] 196 F5
Jyväskylä [FIN] 186 G4

K

Kaalamo [RUS] 188 G4
Kaalasjärvi [S] 192 G5
Kaalinen / Ikalis [FIN] 186 D6
Kaamanen [FIN] 194 D4
Kaanaa [FIN] 186 E6
Kääntojärvi [S] 192 H5
Kaarela [FIN] 196 D3
Kaaresuvanto [FIN] 192 H4
Kaarina [FIN] 176 D4
Kaarma [EST] 198 C3
Käärmelahti [FIN] 188 F5
Kaarssen [D] 18 H5
Kaartilankoski [FIN] 188 E5
Kaatsheuvel [NL] 16 D6
Kaavi [FIN] 188 D2
Kaba [H] 76 G1
Kabakca [TR] 150 D2
Kabalar [TR] 152 G4
Kabaltepe [TR] 130 H5
Kabböle [FIN] 178 B4
Kåbdalis [S] 190 H2
Kabelvåg [N] 192 D4
Kabile [LV] 198 C5
Kableshkovo [BG] 148 F4
Kać [SRB] 142 F1
Kačanik [SRB] 146 C6
Kacelovo [BG] 148 D2
Kaceřov [CZ] 48 E4
Kachanovo [RUS] 198 G4
Kačikol [SRB] 146 C5
Kačina [CZ] 48 H4
Kácov [CZ] 48 G4
Kaczorów [PL] 50 B1
Kadaň [CZ] 48 E3
Kadarkút [H] 74 H4
Kadikalesi [TR] 152 D5
Kadıköy [TR] 150 B4
Kadıköy [TR] 152 F4
Kadıköy [TR] 154 G2
Kadłubówka [PL] 38 E1
Kadłub Turawski [PL] 50 E2
Kadrifakovo [MK] 128 F1
Kadyanda [TR] 154 F2
Kadzidło [PL] 24 C5
Käenkoski [FIN] 188 G1
Kåfjord [N] 194 C1
Kaga [S] 166 H5
Kåge [S] 196 A4
Kågeröd [S] 158 C2
Kagkádi [GR] 136 C1
Kaharlyk [UA] 202 D7
Kahla [D] 46 H1
Kaïáfas [GR] 136 C2
Kaïméni Chóra [GR] 136 G2
Käina [EST] 198 C2
Kainach bei Voitsberg [A] 74 D2
Kainasto [FIN] 186 B4
Kaindorf [A] 74 E2
Kainu [FIN] 186 D1
Kainulasjärvi [S] 194 B7
Kaipiainen [FIN] 178 C2
Kairahta [FIN] 186 G4
Kairala [FIN] 194 E7
Kairila [FIN] 176 D1
Kaisepakte [S] 192 F4
Kaiserbach [D] 46 D6
Kaisersesch [D] 30 G6
Kaiserslautern [D] 44 H3
Kaiser-Wilhelm-Koog [D] 18 E3
Kaisheim [D] 60 D2
Kaišiadoris [LT] 200 F5
Kaitainsalmi [FIN] 196 F5
Kaitsor [FIN] 186 B2
Kaivanto [FIN] 196 E4
Kaivomäki [FIN] 188 D5
Kajaani / Kajana [FIN] 196 E5
Kajana / Kajaani [FIN] 196 E5
Kajánújfalu [H] 76 E3
Kajetans-Brücke [A] 72 C2
Kajoo [FIN] 188 E1
Kájov [CZ] 62 B2
Kajraly [RUS] 194 F7
Kakanj [BIH] 142 D4
Kakarriq [AL] 128 A1
Kakavi [AL] 132 C1
Kakerbeck [D] 34 B1
Kakhovka [UA] 204 G3
Käkilahti [FIN] 196 E5
Kaklıc [TR] 152 C4
Kaklik [TR] 152 G5
Kaklik [TR] 152 G5
Kakmå [HR] 112 G5
Kąkolewnica Wschodnia [PL] 38 E2
Kakopetriá [CY] 154 F5
Kakóvatos [GR] 136 C3
Käkrina [EST] 198 F2
Kakslauttanen [FIN] 194 D5
Kaktyni [LV] 198 E5
Kakuåsen [S] 190 E6
Kakushöhle [D] 30 G5
Kál [H] 64 E6
Kälä [FIN] 186 H5
Kalaja [FIN] 196 D6
Kalajoki [FIN] 196 C5
Kalak [N] 194 D2
Kalakoski [FIN] 186 D4
Kalamáki [GR] 132 H2
Kalamáki [GR] 134 A2
Kalamariá [GR] 128 H4
Kalamáta [GR] 136 D4
Kalámi [GR] 140 C4
Kalamítsi [GR] 130 D6
Kálamos [GR] 134 C5
Kalamotí [GR] 134 G5
Kalampáki [GR] 130 D3
Kalampáki [GR] 132 E2
Kalanchak [RUS] 204 G3
Kalándra [GR] 130 B6
Kalá Nerá [GR] 132 H2
Kalanti [FIN] 176 C3
Kälarne [S] 184 D3
Kálathos [GR] 154 D4
Kalavárda [GR] 154 D3
Kalávryta [GR] 136 D1
Kalax [FIN] 186 A4
Kalbe [D] 34 B1
Kalce [SLO] 74 B5
Kalčevo [BG] 148 E5
Káld [H] 74 G2
Kaldfarnes [N] 192 E3
Kaldhusseter [N] 180 E4
Kale [TR] 152 D1
Kale [TR] 152 F6
Kale [TR] 154 H3
Kaleburnu (Galinóporni) [CY] 154 H4
Kalekovets [BG] 148 B5
Kaleköy [TR] 130 G5
Kalela [FIN] 176 D3
Kalenić, Manastir- [SRB] 146 C2
Kálergo [GR] 134 D5
Kalesija [BIH] 142 E3
Kalety [PL] 50 F2
Kalétzi [GR] 132 D2
Kalétzi [GR] 136 C1
Kaleva [FIN] 176 E4
Kalí [GR] 128 G4
Kaliánoi [GR] 136 E1
Kalidón [GR] 132 E5
Kaliningrad [RUS] 22 G1
Kalinkavichy [BY] 202 C6
Kalinovik [BIH] 144 D2
Kalinovka [RUS] 24 C1
Kalinovo [PL] 24 D3
Kalinovo [SK] 64 D4
Kalirráchi [GR] 128 E6
Kalisty [PL] 22 G3
Kalisz [PL] 36 E4
Kalisz Pomorski [PL] 20 H5
Kalivári [GR] 134 E6
Kalix [S] 196 C2
Kaljord [N] 192 D4
Kalkan [TR] 154 G3
Kalkar [D] 16 F6
Kalkgruber [DK] 160 C5
Kalkım [TR] 152 C1
Kalkkinen [FIN] 178 A2
Kall [D] 30 G5
Kall [S] 182 F1
Källa [S] 162 H4
Kallarat [AL] 128 B6
Kållarbo [S] 174 C5
Kallaste [EST] 198 F2
Kallbäck [FIN] 178 A4
Källberget [S] 182 F3
Källered [S] 160 H2
Kalli [EST] 198 D3
Kallimasiá [GR] 134 G5
Kallinge [S] 158 F1
Kallio [FIN] 186 D5
Kallio [FIN] 196 F5
Kalliojoki [FIN] 196 G4
Kallislahti [FIN] 188 E5
Kallithéa [GR] 128 G6
Kallithéa [GR] 130 C3
Kallithéa [GR] 130 C6
Kallithéa [GR] 136 D2
Kallithéa [GR] 154 D3
Kalliuskoski [FIN] 196 E4
Kallmünz [D] 48 B6
Källö [H] 64 D5
Kallön [S] 190 G3
Kalloní [GR] 134 G2
Kalloní [GR] 136 F2
Kállósemjén [H] 64 H5
Kallsedet [S] 190 D6
Kallträsk [FIN] 186 B5
Källunga [S] 162 B1
Kallunki [FIN] 194 F7
Kalmakattio [FIN] 194 C5
Kálmánháza [H] 64 G5
Kalmar [S] 162 G5
Kalmari [FIN] 186 F3
Kalná [CZ] 48 G4
Kalna [SRB] 146 E3
Kalná nad Hronom [SK] 64 B4
Kalnciems [LV] 198 D5
Kalnik [PL] 22 G3
Kalochóri [GR] 128 E5
Kaló Chorió [GR] 140 F5
Kalocsa [H] 76 C4
Kalofer [BG] 148 B5
Kalogriá [GR] 132 E6
Kaloí Liménes [GR] 140 E5
Kalókastro [GR] 130 B3
Kalonéri [GR] 128 E5
Kaló Nero [GR] 136 C3
Kalopanagiótis [CY] 154 F5
Kaloskopí [GR] 132 G4
Kalotina [BG] 146 F4
Kaloyan [BG] 148 F2
Kaloyanovo [BG] 148 B5
Kálóz [H] 76 B2
Kalpáki [GR] 132 C1
Kalpio [FIN] 196 E4
Kals [A] 72 F2
Kalsdorf [A] 74 D2
Kalsdorf [A] 74 E2
Kalsvik [S] 168 E3
Kaltanenai [LT] 200 G4
Kaltenkirchen [D] 18 F3
Kaltennordheim [D] 46 F2
Kaltinėnai [LT] 200 E4
Kaluga [RUS] 202 F4
Kalugerovo [BG] 148 A5
Kalundborg [DK] 156 E2
Kalush [UA] 204 C2
Kałuszyn [PL] 38 C3
Kalv [S] 162 B3
Kalvåg [N] 180 B5
Kalvarija [LT] 24 E2
Kalvatn [N] 180 D4
Kalvehave [DK] 156 G4
Kalven [N] 194 B1
Kälviä / Kelviå [FIN] 196 C6
Kälvik [S] 162 G2
Kalvitsa [FIN] 188 C5
Kalvola [FIN] 176 G2
Kalwang [A] 74 C1
Kalwaria Zebrzydowska [PL] 50 H4
Kalyazin [RUS] 202 F2
Kálymnos [GR] 154 A2
Kalynivka [UA] 202 C8
Kalývia [GR] 132 E4
Kám [H] 74 G2
Kamanski Vučiak [HR] 142 C1
Kamáres [GR] 138 D3
Kamáres [GR] 138 E3
Kamáres [GR] 140 E5
Kamariótissa [GR] 130 F4
Kamburovo [BG] 148 D3
Kamchiya [BG] 148 F3
Kámeiros [GR] 154 D4
Kámen [CZ] 48 G5
Kamen [D] 32 C4
Kamenari [MNE] 144 D4
Kaména Voúrla [GR] 132 H4
Kamen Bryag [BG] 148 G2
Kamengrad [BIH] 142 B2
Kamenica [MK] 146 E6
Kamenice nad Lipou [CZ] 48 G6
Kamenichý Hrad [SK] 52 C6
Kameničná [SK] 64 A5
Kamenka [RUS] 178 F3
Kamennogorsk [RUS] 178 F2
Kamenný Újezd [CZ] 62 C2
Kameno [BG] 148 F4
Kamenovo [BG] 148 D2
Kamensko [HR] 142 C1
Kamensko [HR] 144 B2
Kamenz [D] 34 F6
Kamëz [AL] 128 B2
Kamianets'-Podil's'kyi [UA] 204 D2
Kamianka [UA] 202 E8
Kamianka-Dniprovs'ka [UA] 204 H2
Kamičak [BIH] 142 B3
Kamień [PL] 52 E3
Kamienica [PL] 52 B5
Kamieniec Ząbkowicki [PL] 50 C2
Kamienka [SK] 52 B5
Kamień Krajeński [PL] 22 C5
Kamienna Góra [PL] 50 B2
Kamień Pomorski [PL] 20 F3
Kamieńsk [PL] 36 G6
Kamínia [GR] 130 F6
Kamínia [GR] 132 D1
Kamion [PL] 38 A2
Kammerstein [A] 74 C1
Kamnica [SLO] 74 C5
Kamnik [SLO] 74 C4
Kampánis [GR] 128 H4
Kampen [D] 156 A4
Kampen [NL] 16 F4
Kamperland [NL] 16 B6
Kampiá [GR] 134 G4
Kampinos [PL] 38 A3
Kamp Lintfort [D] 30 G3
Kampor [HR] 112 F3
Kámpos [GR] 132 F5
Kámpos [GR] 136 D4
Kámpos [GR] 138 H2
Kámpos [GR] 140 B4
Kamula [FIN] 196 E5
Kamyanyets [BY] 38 G2
Kamyanyuki [BY] 38 G2
Kamýk nad Vltavou [CZ] 48 F5
Kanal [SLO] 72 H5
Kanala [FIN] 186 E1
Kanála [GR] 138 C2
Kanália [GR] 132 H2
Kanalláki [GR] 132 C3
Kanatlarci [MK] 128 E3
Kańczuga [PL] 52 E3
Kandava [LV] 198 C5
Kandel [D] 46 B5
Kandern [D] 58 E4
Kandersteg [CH] 70 D2
Kandestederne [DK] 160 E2
Kandíla [GR] 136 E2
Kandira [TR] 150 G2
Kanepi [EST] 198 F3
Kanestraum [N] 180 F2
Kanfanar [HR] 112 D2
Kangas [FIN] 196 D5
Kangasaho [FIN] 186 E3
Kangasala [FIN] 176 F1
Kangashäkki [FIN] 186 G3
Kangaskylä [FIN] 186 F1
Kangaslampi [FIN] 188 D4
Kangasniemi [FIN] 186 H5
Kanin [PL] 22 B2
Kaninkola [FIN] 176 E4
Kaniv [UA] 202 E7
Kanižarica [SLO] 74 D6
Kanjiža [SRB] 76 E5
Kanjon Cetine [HR] 144 A2
Kanjon Ugar [BIH] 142 C3
Kankaanpää [FIN] 186 C6
Kankainen [FIN] 186 G4
Kankova [SLO] 74 E3
Kånna [S] 162 C5
Kannonkoski [FIN] 186 F2
Kannus [FIN] 196 C5
Kannuskoski [FIN] 178 D2
Kanpaneta / Campanas [E] 84 B4
Kansız [TR] 150 E5
Kanstad [N] 192 E4
Kantala [FIN] 188 C4
Kántanos [GR] 140 B5
Kanteemaa [FIN] 176 E3
Kántia [GR] 136 F2
Kantojoki [FIN] 194 F8
Kantokylä [FIN] 196 D5
Kantomaanpää [FIN] 194 C8
Kantornes [N] 192 F2
Kantorp [S] 168 B4
Kantti [FIN] 186 C5
Kanturk [IRL] 4 C4
Kányavár [H] 74 F3
Kaolinovo [BG] 148 E2
Kaona [SRB] 146 B3
Kaonik [BIH] 142 D4
Kaonik [SRB] 146 C3
Kąp [PL] 24 C3
Kapaklı [TR] 150 E4
Kapaklı [TR] 152 D3
Kapandríti [GR] 134 C5
Kåpas [LV] 198 C5
Kapčiamiestis [LT] 24 F3
Kapellskär [S] 162 G5
Kapfenberg [A] 74 D1
Kapıkaya [TR] 152 F2
Kapıkırı [TR] 152 D6
Kapinci [HR] 74 H6
Kapitan Andreevo [BG] 150 A2
Kaplica (Davlós) [CY] 154 G4
Kaplice [CZ] 62 C3
Kapolcs [H] 74 H2
Kápolna [H] 64 E5
Kaposfüred [H] 74 H4
Kaposvár [H] 76 A4
Kapp [N] 172 B4
Kappel [D] 44 H2
Kappel [D] 58 E2
Kappeln [D] 18 F1
Kappelshamn [S] 168 G3
Kappelskär [S] 168 F2
Kappl [A] 72 B1
Kaprun [A] 72 F1
Kapsáli [GR] 136 F6
Kápsas [GR] 136 E2
Kapušany [SK] 64 G2
Kapuvár [H] 62 G6
Karaağaç [TR] 150 G2
Karabayır [TR] 154 F1
Karabeylı [TR] 152 G3
Karabiga [TR] 150 C4
Karabörtlen [TR] 154 E1
Karaburun [TR] 134 H4
Karaburun [TR] 150 E2
Karacaali [TR] 150 F4
Karacabey [TR] 150 E5
Karacaköy [TR] 150 D2
Karacalar [TR] 152 D2
Karacalar [TR] 152 E2
Karaçalı [TR] 150 G2
Karaçam [TR] 152 D2
Karacaoğlan [TR] 150 B2
Karacaşehir [TR] 150 H5
Karacasu [TR] 152 F5
Karaçulha [TR] 154 F2
Karád [H] 76 A3
Karahallı [TR] 152 G4
Karahisar [TR] 152 F5
Karainebeyli [TR] 150 B5
Karaisen [BG] 148 C3
Karakadağ [TR] 150 C1
Karakagür [TR] 150 B3
Karakamza [TR] 150 B1
Karakaya [TR] 152 D6
Karakiani [GR] 136 G1
Karakoumi (Karakum) [CY] 154 G5
Karaköy [TR] 152 B1
Karaköy [TR] 152 D4
Karaköy [TR] 152 F4
Karakum (Karakoumi) [CY] 154 G5
Karakür [TR] 152 F2
Karakurt [TR] 152 D2
Karakuzu [TR] 152 C3
Karala [EST] 198 C3
Karalaks [N] 194 C3
Karali [RUS] 188 H3
Karalin [BY] 24 H5
Karamanci [BG] 148 C6
Karamandere [TR] 150 D2
Karamanlı [TR] 152 H6
Karamürsel [TR] 150 F3
Karamyshevo [RUS] 198 H3
Karancslapujtő [H] 64 D4
Karaova [TR] 154 C1
Karapazar [TR] 150 H5
Karapelit [BG] 148 F2
Karapürçek [TR] 150 H3
Karasjok [N] 194 C3
Karasu [TR] 150 H2
Karász [H] 76 B4
Karataş [TR] 152 E3
Karats [S] 190 G1
Karavás [GR] 136 F6
Karaveliler [TR] 152 C2
Karavelovo [BG] 148 E5
Káravos [GR] 134 C5
Karavostasi (Gemikonağı) [CY] 154 F5
Karavostasis [GR] 138 E4
Karavukovo [SRB] 142 E1
Karawanški Predor [A/SLO] 74 B4
Karayakuplu [TR] 150 G3
Karbasan [TR] 152 G4
Karbenning [S] 168 B1
Kårböle [S] 182 H6
Karby [DK] 160 C4
Karby [S] 168 E2
Karcag [H] 76 F1
Karczowiska [PL] 36 B5
Kardakáta [GR] 132 C6
Kardam [BG] 148 G1
Kardámaina [GR] 154 B2
Kardámyla [GR] 134 G4
Kardamýli [GR] 136 D4
Kardašova-Řečice [CZ] 48 G6
Kardítsa [GR] 132 F2
Kärdla [EST] 198 C2
Kardos [H] 76 F3
Kardoskút [H] 76 F4
Kåremo [S] 162 G5
Karersee / Carezza al Lago [I] 72 D3
Karesuando [S] 192 H4
Kärevere [EST] 198 F2
Kargalı [TR] 150 F2
Kargı [TR] 154 F2
Kargów [PL] 52 C2
Kargowa [PL] 36 B3
Karhujärvi [FIN] 194 E7
Karhukangas [FIN] 196 D5
Karhula [FIN] 178 C4
Kårhus [N] 164 B1
Karhusjärvi [FIN] 178 E2
Kari [FIN] 188 D1
Kariani [GR] 130 C4
Karigasniemi [FIN] 194 C3
Karijoki / Bötom [FIN] 186 B4
Karine [TR] 152 C6
Karinkanta [FIN] 196 D4
Karis / Karjaa [FIN] 176 F5
Karise [DK] 156 G3
Karítaina [GR] 136 D2
Karjaa / Karis [FIN] 176 F5
Karjala [FIN] 176 D3
Karjalohia [FIN] 176 F5
Kärjenkoski [FIN] 186 B5
Kärkäälä [FIN] 186 G3
Karkaloú [GR] 136 D2
Kärki [LV] 198 E4
Karkkila / Högfors [FIN] 176 G4
Karkku [FIN] 176 E1
Karklampi [FIN] 186 F6
Kärkölä [FIN] 176 F4
Kärkölä [FIN] 176 H3
Karksi-Nuia [EST] 198 E3
Karlby [FIN] 168 H1
Karleby / Kokkola [FIN] 196 C6
Karlevistenen [S] 162 G5
Karlewo [PL] 22 F6
Karl Gustav [S] 160 H3
Karlholmsbruk [S] 174 F4
Karlino [PL] 20 H3
Karlö / Hailuoto [FIN] 196 D4
Karlobag [HR] 112 F4
Karlovac [HR] 112 G1
Karlóvasi [GR] 152 C5
Karlova Studánka [CZ] 50 D4
Karlovo [BG] 148 B4
Karlovy Vary [CZ] 48 D3
Karłowice [PL] 50 D1
Karlsberg [D] 44 H2
Karlsberg [S] 162 D1
Karlsberg [S] 172 H1
Karlsborg [S] 166 G5
Karlsborg [S] 196 C3
Karlshamn [S] 158 E1
Karlshöfen [D] 18 E4
Karlskoga [S] 166 G3
Karlskrona [S] 158 F1
Karlslunde Strand [DK] 156 G3
Karlsrud [N] 170 F5
Karlsruhe [D] 46 B6
Karlstad [S] 166 F3
Karlstadt [D] 46 E3
Karlštejn [CZ] 48 F4
Karlštejn [CZ] 50 B5
Karlstift [A] 62 C3
Karlstorp [S] 162 E3
Karmas [S] 192 F6
Kärnä [FIN] 186 D2
Kärnä [FIN] 186 G2
Kärnåsens Hembygdsgärd [S] 166 F1
Karniszyn [PL] 22 G6
Karnobat [BG] 148 E4
Karojba [HR] 112 D1
Karousádes [GR] 132 A2
Karow [D] 20 B4
Karpacz [PL] 50 A2
Karpasolo [FIN] 188 F3
Kárpathos [GR] 140 H3
Karpenísi [GR] 132 F4
Karperó [GR] 132 E1
Karpuzlu [TR] 152 E6
Karrantza / Carranza [E] 82 F3
Kärrbackstrand [S] 172 E3
Kärrbö [S] 168 A1
Karrebæksminde [DK] 156 F4
Kärsämä [FIN] 196 D4
Kärsämäki [FIN] 196 D5
Kārsava [LV] 198 G5
Karsibór [PL] 20 E4
Karşıyaka [TR] 150 D4
Karsjö [S] 174 D1
Karstädt [D] 20 A5
Karst en Yesos [E] 102 H5
Kärstna [EST] 198 E3
Karstø [N] 164 A2
Karstula [FIN] 186 F3
Kartal [TR] 150 F3
Kartala [BG] 146 G6
Kartena [LT] 200 D4
Kartéri [GR] 132 C3
Karteros [GR] 140 E4
Karthaía [GR] 138 C2
Karttula [FIN] 186 H2
Kartuzy [PL] 22 D2
Karungi [S] 196 C2
Karunki [FIN] 196 C2
Karup [DK] 160 C5
Karuse [EST] 198 D2
Karvala [FIN] 186 D2
Kärväskylä [FIN] 186 G1
Kårvatn [N] 180 G3
Karvia [FIN] 186 C5
Karvik [N] 192 H2
Kårvikhamn [N] 192 F2
Karviná [CZ] 50 F4
Karvio [FIN] 188 E3
Karvounári [GR] 132 C3
Karwia [PL] 22 D1
Karwica [PL] 24 C4
Karyá [GR] 128 G6
Karyá [GR] 132 C4
Karyá [GR] 136 E2
Karyés [GR] 130 D5
Karyés [GR] 132 G3
Karyés [GR] 136 E3
Karyótissa [GR] 128 G4
Karyoúpoli [GR] 136 E5
Kárystos [GR] 134 D6
Kås [DK] 160 D3
Kaş [TR] 154 G3
Kasaba [TR] 154 G3
Kašalj [SRB] 146 B4
Kascyukovichy [BY] 202 D5
Kåseberga [S] 158 D3
Kasejovice [CZ] 48 E5
Kashin [RUS] 202 E2
Kashirskoye [RUS] 200 C5
Kašina [HR] 74 E5
Kasinka Wielka [PL] 52 B4
Kåskats [S] 190 H2
Kaski [FIN] 176 F5
Kaskii [FIN] 188 D5
Kaskinen / Kaskö [FIN] 186 A4
Kaskö / Kaskinen [FIN] 186 A4
Kas'kovo [RUS] 178 G5
Kaslania Pass [GR] 128 F5
Käsmu [EST] 198 E1
Kasnäs [FIN] 176 E6
Káspakas [GR] 130 F6
Kašperk [CZ] 48 E6
Kašperské Hory [CZ] 48 E6
Kaspichan [BG] 148 E3
Kassa [FIN] 194 B7
Kassándreia [GR] 130 B6
Kassari [EST] 198 C2
Kassel [D] 32 F5
Kassiópi [GR] 132 B2
Kassópi [GR] 132 C3
Kastabos [TR] 154 D2
Kastaniá [GR] 128 G5
Kastaniá [GR] 132 E2
Kastaniá [GR] 132 F3
Kastaniá [GR] 136 E4
Kastaniá [GR] 136 E1
Kastaniá [GR] 136 F5
Kastaniés [GR] 150 A2
Kastelholms [FIN] 176 B5
Kastellaun [D] 44 H2
Kastélli [GR] 140 B4
Kastélli [GR] 140 F5
Kaštel Stari [HR] 142 A5
Kaštel Žegarski [HR] 112 H5
Kasterlee [B] 30 D3
Kastl [D] 46 H5
Kastlösa [S] 162 G6
Kastneshamn [N] 192 E3
Kastorf [D] 18 G4
Kastoría [GR] 128 E5
Kastráki [GR] 132 E4
Kastre [EST] 198 F3
Kastri [GR] 140 C6
Kástro [GR] 134 A5
Kástro [GR] 134 B3
Kástro [GR] 136 B1
Kastrosykiá [GR] 132 C3
Kastrup [DK] 156 H3
Kaszaper [H] 76 F4
Katáfyto [GR] 130 C2
Katákolo [GR] 136 B2
Kataloinen [FIN] 176 H2
Kätänjoki [FIN] 186 D3
Katápola [GR] 138 G4
Katará Pass [GR] 132 D1
Katastári [GR] 136 A2
Kåtaviken [S] 190 E2
Katerbow [D] 20 C6
Kateríni [GR] 128 G5
Kateřinská [CZ] 50 C6
Katerloch [A] 74 D2
Katerma [FIN] 196 F5
Kätkasuvanto [FIN] 194 B6
Kätkesuando [S] 194 B6
Katlanovo [MK] 128 E1
Katlanovska Banja [MK] 128 F1
Katlenburg-Duhm [D] 32 G4
Káto Achaïa [GR] 132 E6
Káto Alepochóri [GR] 134 B6
Káto Aséa [GR] 136 D3
Katochí [GR] 132 E5
Káto Dolianá [GR] 136 E3
Káto Kleitoría [GR] 136 D1
Káto Makrinoú [GR] 132 E5
Káto Nevrokópi [GR] 130 C2
Káto Pýrgos [CY] 154 F5
Káto Samikó [GR] 136 C2
Káto Tithoréa [GR] 132 H5
Katoúna [GR] 132 D4
Káto Velitsés [GR] 136 C1
Káto Vérmio [GR] 128 F5
Katovice [CZ] 48 E6
Káto Vlasía [GR] 136 D1
Káto Vrontoú [GR] 130 C2
Katowice [PL] 50 G3
Káto Zákros [GR] 140 H5
Katrineberg [S] 174 D3
Katrineholm [S] 168 B4
Katschberg Tunnel [A] 72 H2
Kattavía [GR] 154 C5
Katthammarsvik [S] 168 G5
Kattilakoski [FIN] 186 D1
Kättilstad [S] 162 F1
Kattisavan [S] 190 G4
Kattlunds [S] 168 G6
Kattuvuoma [S] 192 G4
Katumäki [FIN] 188 C3
Katundi i Ri [AL] 128 A2
Katuntsi [BG] 130 B2
Katwijk aan Zee [NL] 16 C4
Katy [PL] 20 F4
Kąty [PL] 52 E2
Katyčiai [LT] 200 D5
Katymár [H] 76 C5
Kąty Wrocławskie [PL] 50 C1
Kaub [D] 46 B3
Kaufbeuren [D] 60 C5
Kaufering [D] 60 D4
Kaufungen [D] 32 F5
Kauhajärvi [FIN] 186 C5
Kauhajärvi [FIN] 186 D2
Kauhajoki [FIN] 186 B4
Kauhava [FIN] 186 C2
Kaukalampi [FIN] 176 H3
Kaukela [FIN] 176 H1
Kaukonen [FIN] 194 C6
Kauksi [EST] 198 F2
Kaukuri [FIN] 176 F5
Kaulbach [D] 44 H3
Kaunas [LT] 200 F5
Kaunata [LV] 198 G5

Kauniainen / Grankulla [FIN] 176 H5
Kaunos [TR] 154 E2
Kauns [A] 72 C1
Kaupanger [N] 170 D2
Kaurajärvi [FIN] 186 C2
Kauria [FIN] 178 D1
Kauša [LV] 198 F6
Kausala [FIN] 178 B3
Kaustby / Kaustinen [FIN] 196 C6
Kaustinen / Kaustby [FIN] 196 C6
Kautokeino [N] 194 B4
Kauttua [FIN] 176 D3
Káva [H] 76 D1
Kavacık [TR] 150 B3
Kavacık [TR] 152 E1
Kavacık [TR] 152 H5
Kavadarci [MK] 128 F2
Kavajë [AL] 128 A3
Kavak [TR] 150 B4
Kavakdere [TR] 150 C2
Kavakköy [TR] 152 E6
Kavaklı [TR] 130 H2
Kavaklı [TR] 150 B2
Kavaklı [TR] 150 E3
Kavaklıdere [TR] 152 E6
Kavála [GR] 130 D3
Kavarna [BG] 148 G2
Kavaröskaten [S] 174 G5
Kåvenvallen [S] 182 E4
Kävlinge [S] 158 C2
Kávos [GR] 132 B3
Kavoúsi [GR] 140 G5
Kavşit [TR] 152 E5
Kavýli [GR] 130 H1
Kaxholmen [S] 162 D2
Kayabaşı [TR] 154 G1
Kayaköy [TR] 152 D4
Kayaköy [TR] 154 F2
Kayalar [TR] 150 D6
Kayapa [TR] 150 B1
Kayapa [TR] 152 C1
Käyhtiönmaa [FIN] 176 D2
Kayı [TR] 150 C3
Käylä [FIN] 194 F8
Kaymakçı [TR] 152 E4
Kaymaz [TR] 150 G2
Kaynarca [TR] 150 G2
Käyrämö [FIN] 194 D7
Kayran [TR] 152 F5
Kaysersberg [F] 58 D2
Kazaklar [TR] 152 F4
Kazanci [BIH] 142 B4
Kažani [MK] 128 E3
Kazanka [UA] 204 G2
Kazanlŭk [BG] 148 C4
Kazárma [GR] 136 D4
Kazichene [BG] 146 G5
Kazimierza Wielka [PL] 52 B3
Kazimierz Biskupi [PL] 36 E3
Kazimierz Dolny [PL] 38 D5
Kâzımpaşa [TR] 150 G3
Kazincbarcika [H] 64 F4
Kazlu-Rūda [LT] 24 F1
Kaznějov [CZ] 48 E4
Kaz'yany [BY] 200 H4
Kcynia [PL] 22 C6
Kdyně [CZ] 48 D5
Kéa [GR] 138 C2
Keadue [IRL] 2 D4
Keady [NIR] 2 F4
Kebrene [TR] 152 B1
Kecel [H] 76 C4
Kecskemét [H] 76 D2
Kėdainiai [LT] 200 F5
Kédros [GR] 132 F3
Kędzierzyn-Koźle [PL] 50 E3
Keel [IRL] 2 B3
Keenagh [IRL] 2 D5
Kefalári [GR] 136 E1
Kéfalos [GR] 154 A3
Kefalóvryso [GR] 132 C1
Kefalóvryso [GR] 132 F1
Kefermarkt [A] 62 C4
Kefken [TR] 150 G2
Keflavík [IS] 192 A3
Kehidakustány [H] 74 G3
Kehl [D] 44 H6
Kehra [EST] 198 E1
Kehrig [D] 30 H6
Kehtna [EST] 198 E2
Keighley [GB] 10 E3
Keihärinkoski [FIN] 186 F2
Keihäskoski [FIN] 176 E3
Keikyä [FIN] 176 E2
Keila-Joa [EST] 198 D1
Keipene [LV] 198 E5
Keisala [FIN] 186 E2
Keitele [FIN] 186 G1
Keith [GB] 6 F5
Kekava [LV] 198 D5
Kékestető [H] 64 E5
Kelankyla [FIN] 196 E2
Kelberg [D] 30 G6
Kelbra [D] 32 H5
Këlcyrë [AL] 128 C6
Kelebia [H] 76 D4
Kelebija [SRB] 76 D5
Keletá [GR] 136 E5
Kelekçi [TR] 152 G6
Kelemér [H] 64 E4
Keler [TR] 152 C5
Keles [TR] 150 F5
Kelheim [D] 60 E2
Kell [D] 44 G3
Kélla [GR] 128 F4
Kellenberg [D] 30 F4
Kellenhusen [D] 18 H2
Kellerberg [D] 32 D5
Kellinghusen [D] 18 F3
Kelloselkä [FIN] 194 F7
Kells [IRL] 2 F5
Kells [IRL] 4 B4
Kelmė [LT] 200 E4
Kelottijärvi [FIN] 192 H4
Kelso [GB] 8 F4
Keltaniemi [FIN] 178 B2
Kelujärvi [FIN] 194 D6
Kelvä [FIN] 188 F1
Kelviä / Kälviä [FIN] 196 C6
Kemaliye [TR] 152 E3
Kemalpaşa [TR] 152 D4
Kemberg [D] 34 D4
Kemecse [H] 64 H4
Kemence [H] 64 C5
Kemenesmagasi [H] 74 G1
Kemer [TR] 150 C4
Kemer [TR] 152 F5
Kemer [TR] 154 F2
Kemerburgaz [TR] 150 E2
Kemerköy [TR] 154 G3
Kémes [H] 76 A5
Kemi [FIN] 196 C3
Kemihaara [FIN] 194 E5
Kemijärvi [FIN] 194 E7
Keminmaa [FIN] 196 C2
Kemiö / Kimito [FIN] 176 E5
Kemnath [D] 48 B4
Kemnitz [D] 20 D3
Kemnitz [D] 34 D3
Kempele [FIN] 196 D4
Kempen [D] 30 G3
Kempolovo [RUS] 178 G5
Kempten [D] 60 C5
Kendal [GB] 10 E2
Kenderes [H] 76 F1
Kendice [SK] 64 G2
Kengis [S] 194 B7
Kengyel [H] 76 E2
Kenmare [IRL] 4 B4
Kentrikó [GR] 128 H3
Kéntro [GR] 136 C1
Kenyeri [H] 74 G1
Kenzingen [D] 58 E2
Kepez [TR] 150 B5
Kępice [PL] 22 B3
Kepno [PL] 36 E6
Kepsut [TR] 152 D1
Kerameía [GR] 134 H2
Keramídi [GR] 132 H2
Keramítsa [GR] 132 C2
Keramos [TR] 154 C1
Keramotí [GR] 130 E3
Keräntöjärvi [S] 194 B6
Kerasiá [GR] 134 B4
Kerasochóri [GR] 132 E3
Kerasóna [GR] 132 D3
Keratéa [GR] 136 H1
Keratókampos [GR] 140 F5
Kerava / Kervo [FIN] 176 H4
Kerecsend [H] 64 E5
Kerekegyháza [H] 76 D2
Kerí [GR] 136 A2
Kerien [F] 26 A4
Kerimäki [FIN] 188 F5
Kerisalo [FIN] 188 D4
Kerjean, Château de- [F] 40 B1
Kerken [D] 30 G3
Kerkíni [GR] 128 H3
Kerkonkoski [FIN] 186 H3
Kerkrade [NL] 30 F4
Kérkyra [GR] 132 B2
Kerma [FIN] 188 E3
Kermen [BG] 148 D4
Kernascléden [F] 40 C3
Kerpen [D] 30 G4
Kerpiçlik [TR] 152 F2
Kërrabë [AL] 128 B3
Kersilö [FIN] 194 D6
Kerstimbo [S] 174 E5
Kerteminde [DK] 156 E3
Kertészsziget [H] 76 G2
Kertil [TR] 152 D2
Kervo / Kerava [FIN] 176 H4
Kerýneia (Girne) [CY] 154 G5
Kerzers [CH] 58 D6
Kesälahti [FIN] 188 G5
Keşan [TR] 150 B3
Kesarevo [BG] 148 D3
Kesasjärv [S] 194 B8
Kesh [NIR] 2 E3
Keskastel [F] 44 G5
Keskikylä [FIN] 196 D4
Keskinen [FIN] 196 F4
Kesselfall [A] 72 F1
Kesselsdorf [D] 34 E6
Kesten'ga [RUS] 196 H2
Kesteren [NL] 16 E5
Kesti [FIN] 186 B4
Kestilä [FIN] 196 E5
Keswick [GB] 8 E6
Keszthely [H] 74 G3
Kétegyháza [H] 76 G3
Ketenovo [MK] 146 E6
Ketomella [FIN] 194 B5
Kętrzyn [PL] 24 C3
Kétsoproni [H] 76 F3
Kettering [GB] 14 E2
Kettilsby [S] 166 D3
Kettwig [D] 30 G3
Kęty [PL] 50 G4
Ketzin [D] 34 D2
Keula [D] 32 G5
Keuruu [FIN] 186 F4
Keväjärvi [FIN] 194 E4
Kevelaer [D] 30 F2
Kevo [FIN] 194 D3
Kežmarok [SK] 52 B6
Khaapalampi [RUS] 188 H5
Khadzilioni [BY] 24 H3
Kharava [BY] 38 H1
Kharmanli [BG] 148 D6
Khaskovo [BG] 148 C6
Kherson [UA] 204 G3
Khisariya [BG] 148 B5
Khiytola [RUS] 178 G1
Khlebarovo [BG] 148 D2
Khmel'nyts'kyi [UA] 202 C8
Khmil'nyk [UA] 202 C8
Khodoriv [UA] 204 C2
Kholm [RUS] 202 C3
Kholm-Zhirkovskiy [RUS] 202 D3
Khorol [UA] 202 F7
Khotyn [UA] 204 D2
Khoyniki [BY] 202 D6
Khust [UA] 204 C3
Khvoynaya [RUS] 202 D1
Khyriv [UA] 52 F5
Kiáto [GR] 132 H6
Kiaunoriai [LT] 200 E4
Kibæk [DK] 156 B1
Kiberg [N] 194 F2
Kiburi [LV] 198 B6
Kibyra [TR] 152 G6
Kičevo [MK] 128 D2
Kichenitsa [BG] 148 D2
Kichevo [BG] 148 F2
Kidałowice [PL] 52 F3
Kidderminster [GB] 12 G1
Kidlington [GB] 14 D3
Kidričevo [SLO] 74 E4
Kidsgrove [GB] 10 E5
Kidwelly [GB] 12 E2
Kiefersfelden [D] 60 F6
Kiel [D] 18 G2
Kielajoki [FIN] 194 D4
Kielce [PL] 52 B1
Kienberg [A] 72 F2
Kienberg [CH] 58 E5
Kiental [CH] 70 E1
Kierinki [FIN] 194 C7
Kiernozia [PL] 36 H3
Kiesilä [FIN] 178 D1
Kietävälä [FIN] 188 E6
Kietrz [PL] 50 E4
Kiezmark [PL] 22 E3
Kifisiá [GR] 134 C6
Kifjord [N] 194 D1
Kihelkonna [EST] 198 C3
Kihniö [FIN] 186 D5
Kiihtelysvaara [FIN] 188 G3
Kiikala [FIN] 176 F4
Kiikka [FIN] 176 E2
Kiikoinen [FIN] 176 E1
Kiiminki [FIN] 196 D3
Kiiskilä [FIN] 196 D6
Kiistala [FIN] 194 C6
Kije [PL] 52 B2
Kijevo [BIH] 144 D1
Kijevo [HR] 142 A4
Kijevo [SRB] 146 B5
Kijmajärvi [FIN] 176 E2
Kikerino [RUS] 178 G6
Kikinda [MNE] 204 B5
Kikinda [SRB] 76 F5
Kikół [PL] 36 G1
Kikut [N] 170 E4
Kil [N] 164 F4
Kil [S] 166 E2
Kil [S] 166 H3
Kila [GR] 128 F5
Kila [S] 166 E3
Kila [S] 168 B1
Kilafors [S] 174 D2
Kılavuzlar [TR] 152 H6
Kilbaha [IRL] 2 A6
Kilbeggan [IRL] 2 E5
Kilberry [IRL] 2 F5
Kilboghamn [N] 190 D2
Kilcar / Cill Charthaigh [IRL] 2 D2
Kilcock [IRL] 2 F6
Kilcolman Castle [IRL] 4 C4
Kilconnell [IRL] 2 D5
Kilcoole [IRL] 4 G3
Kilcooley Abbey [IRL] 4 E4
Kilcormac [IRL] 2 D6
Kilcullen [IRL] 2 E6
Kilcurry [IRL] 2 F4
Kildare [IRL] 2 E6
Kilderss [NIR] 2 F3
Kildorrery [IRL] 4 D4
Kilebygd [N] 164 G3
Kilen [N] 164 F2
Kilfenora [IRL] 2 B5
Kilfinnane [IRL] 4 D4
Kilgarvan [IRL] 4 B4
Kilifarevo [BG] 148 C4
Kilingi-Nõmme [EST] 198 E3
Kilitbahir [TR] 130 H5
Kilkee [IRL] 2 B6
Kilkeel [NIR] 2 G4
Kilkenny / Cill Chainnigh [IRL] 4 E4
Kilkieran / Cill Chiaráin [IRL] 2 B4
Kilkinkylä [FIN] 188 C6
Kilkinlea [IRL] 4 C3
Kilkís [GR] 128 H3
Kill [IRL] 4 E5
Killadysert [IRL] 2 B6
Killala [IRL] 2 C3
Killaloe [IRL] 2 C6
Killarney / Cill Airne [IRL] 4 B4
Killashandra [IRL] 2 E4
Killashee [IRL] 2 D5
Killeberg [S] 162 C6
Killeigh [IRL] 2 E6
Killenaule [IRL] 4 E4
Killimer [IRL] 2 B6
Killimor [IRL] 2 D5
Killin [GB] 8 D2
Killinge [S] 192 G5
Killinkoski [FIN] 186 D4
Killorglin [IRL] 4 B4
Killybegs [IRL] 2 D2
Killyleagh [NIR] 2 G4
Kilmacduagh Cathedral [IRL] 2 C5
Kilmacrenan [IRL] 2 E2
Kilmacthomas [IRL] 4 E5
Kilmaganny [IRL] 4 E4
Kilmaine [IRL] 2 C4
Kilmallock [IRL] 4 D4
Kilmanahan [IRL] 4 E4
Kilmarnock [GB] 8 D3
Kilmartin [GB] 8 C2
Kilmeaden [IRL] 4 E5
Kilmeage [IRL] 2 E6
Kilmeedy [IRL] 4 C4
Kilmelford [GB] 8 C2
Kilmichael [IRL] 4 C5
Kilmore Quay [IRL] 4 F5
Kilnaleck [IRL] 2 E4
Kilpisjärvi [FIN] 192 G3
Kilpola [FIN] 188 D5
Kilrush [IRL] 2 B6
Kilshannig [IRL] 4 B3
Kilsmo [S] 166 H4
Kilsyth [GB] 8 D3
Kiltealy [IRL] 4 F4
Kilternan [IRL] 4 G3
Kiltimagh [IRL] 2 C4
Kilvakkala [FIN] 186 D6
Kilvo [S] 196 A1
Kilwinning [GB] 8 C3
Kilyos [TR] 150 E2
Kimási [GR] 134 B4
Kimasozero [RUS] 196 H4
Kiminki [FIN] 186 E2
Kimito / Kemiö [FIN] 176 E5
Kimle [H] 62 H5
Kimméria [GR] 130 E2
Kimola [FIN] 178 B2
Kímolos [GR] 138 D4
Kimonkylä [FIN] 178 B3
Kimovaara [RUS] 196 H5
Kimry [RUS] 202 E2
Kincardine [GB] 8 E3
Kindberg [A] 62 D6
Kindelbrück [D] 32 H5
Kinding [D] 46 G6
Kindsjön [S] 172 E4
Kinéta [GR] 134 B6
Kingisepp [RUS] 198 G1
Kingsbridge [GB] 12 D5
Kingscourt [IRL] 2 F5
King's Lynn [GB] 14 F1
Kingston upon Hull [GB] 10 G4
Kington [GB] 12 F1
Kınık [TR] 150 F5
Kınık [TR] 152 C2
Kınık [TR] 154 F3
Kınık [TR] 154 G1
Kınıkyeri [TR] 152 G6
Kinlochbervie [GB] 6 D2
Kinlochewe [GB] 6 C4
Kinlochleven [GB] 6 C6
Kinlough [IRL] 2 D3
Kinna [S] 162 B3
Kinnadoohy [IRL] 2 B4
Kinnarp [S] 162 C1
Kinnbäck [S] 196 B4
Kinnegad [IRL] 2 E5
Kinni [FIN] 178 C1
Kinnitty [IRL] 2 D6
Kinnula [FIN] 186 F1
Kinnuranlahti [FIN] 188 C1
Kinrooi [B] 30 E3
Kinross [GB] 8 E2
Kinsale [IRL] 4 C5
Kinsarvik [N] 170 C4
Kintai [LT] 200 D4
Kintaus [FIN] 186 F4
Kinvarra [IRL] 2 C5
Kióni [GR] 132 D5
Kiónia [GR] 138 E2
Kipen' [RUS] 178 G5
Kipi [EST] 198 C3
Kipilahti [FIN] 178 B4
Kipina [FIN] 196 E3
Kipoureío [GR] 132 E1
Kirakkaköngäs [FIN] 194 D4
Kiralan [TR] 152 G4
Királyegyháza [H] 76 A5
Kıranköy [TR] 152 F3
Kirawsk [BY] 202 C5
Kiraz [TR] 152 E4
Kirazlı [TR] 150 B5
Kirbla [EST] 198 D2
Kircasalih [TR] 150 B2
Kirchbach [A] 72 G3
Kirchbach [A] 74 E2
Kirchberg [A] 60 F6
Kirchberg [D] 44 H2
Kirchberg [D] 46 E5
Kirchberg an der Pielach [A] 62 D5
Kirchbichl [A] 60 F6
Kirchdorf [D] 20 A3
Kirchdorf [D] 32 E1
Kirchdorf an der Krems [A] 62 B5
Kirchen [D] 18 C3
Kirchenlamitz [D] 48 B3
Kirchen-tellinsfurt [D] 58 H2
Kirchenthumbach [D] 46 H4
Kirchhain [D] 32 E6
Kirchheim [D] 32 F6
Kirchheimbolanden [D] 46 B4
Kirchheim unter Teck [D] 58 H1
Kirchhm i.l. [A] 60 H4
Kirchlauter [D] 46 F3
Kirchlinteln [D] 18 E6
Kirchschlag [A] 62 F6
Kirchseeon [D] 60 E4
Kirchundem [D] 32 C5
Kirchzell [D] 46 D4
Kircubbin [NIR] 2 H4
Kireç [TR] 152 E1
Kirikküla [EST] 198 D1
Kırıklar [TR] 152 C1
Kiriou, Roche de- [F] 40 D2
Kiriši [RUS] 202 C1
Kirjaluokta [S] 192 F5
Kir'jamo [RUS] 178 E6
Kırkağaç [TR] 152 D2
Kirkby Lonsdale [GB] 10 E2
Kirkcaldy [GB] 8 E3
Kirkcudbright [GB] 8 D5
Kirkeby [N] 182 D1
Kirkehamn [N] 164 B5
Kirke Hvalsø [DK] 156 F3
Kirkenær [N] 172 D4
Kirkenes [N] 194 E3
Kirkholt [DK] 160 E3
Kírki [GR] 130 G3
Kirkjubæjarklaustur [IS] 192 B3
Kirkjubøur [FR] 160 B2
Kirkkolati [RUS] 188 H4
Kirkkonummi / Kyrkslätt [FIN] 176 G5
Kırklareli [TR] 150 B1
Kirkonkylä [FIN] 176 E4
Kırkpınar [TR] 152 H6
Kirkvollen [N] 182 D2
Kirkwall [GB] 6 G2
Kirn [D] 44 H2
Kirov [RUS] 202 E4
Kirovohrad [UA] 202 E8
Kirovsk [RUS] 202 B1
Kirovskoye [RUS] 178 G3
Kirriemuir [GB] 8 F2
Kirtorf [D] 46 D1
Kiruna [S] 192 G5
Kisa [S] 162 F1
Kisbér [H] 64 A6
Kisdobsza [H] 74 H5
Kiseljak [BIH] 144 C1
Kishartyán [H] 64 D5
Kisielice [PL] 22 F4
Kisielnica [PL] 24 D5
Kisko [FIN] 176 F5
Kisköre [H] 64 F6
Kiskőrös [H] 76 D3
Kiskundorozsma [H] 76 E4
Kiskunfélegyháza [H] 76 E3
Kiskunhalas [H] 76 D4
Kiskunlacháza [H] 76 C2
Kiskunmajsa [H] 76 D4
Kişla [TR] 152 F3
Kisláng [H] 76 B2
Kisslegg [D] 60 B5
Kisszállás [H] 76 D4
Kist [D] 46 E4
Kistanje [HR] 112 H5
Kistelek [H] 76 E4
Kisterenye [H] 64 D5
Kisújszállás [H] 76 F1
Kisvárda [H] 64 H4
Kiszkowo [PL] 36 D2
Kiszombor [H] 76 F4
Kitajaur [S] 190 H2
Kitee [FIN] 188 G4
Kiten [BG] 148 F5
Kítion [CY] 154 G5
Kitkiöjärvi [S] 194 B6
Kitkiöjoki [S] 194 B6
Kítros [GR] 128 G5
Kitsi [FIN] 196 H6
Kittelfjäll [S] 190 E4
Kittendorf [D] 20 C4
Kittilä [FIN] 194 C6
Kittsee [A] 62 G5
Kitula [FIN] 176 F4
Kitula [FIN] 186 G5
Kitzbühel [A] 60 F6
Kitzingen [D] 46 F4
Kitzloch-Klamm [A] 72 G1
Kiukainen [FIN] 176 D2
Kiurujärvi [FIN] 194 E6
Kiuruvesi [FIN] 196 E6
Kiutaköngäs [FIN] 194 F8
Kivadár [H] 74 H5
Kivéri [GR] 136 E2
Kivesjärvi [FIN] 196 E4
Kiviapaja [FIN] 188 E5
Kivijärvi [FIN] 186 F2
Kivik [S] 158 D3
Kivikangas [FIN] 186 E1
Kivilahti [FIN] 188 G1
Kivilompolo [FIN] 194 B5
Kivilompolo [FIN] 194 C8
Kivioja [FIN] 194 C8
Kiviõli [EST] 198 F1
Kivisalmi [FIN] 186 H3
Kivisuo [FIN] 186 G5
Kivivaara [FIN] 196 G5
Kivi-Vigala [EST] 198 D2
Kivotós [GR] 128 E6
Kıyıkışlacık [TR] 154 C1
Kıyıköy [TR] 150 D1
Kızılca [TR] 152 G6
Kızılcabölük [TR] 152 F5
Kızılcasöğüt [TR] 152 G3
Kızılinler [TR] 150 H5
Kızılkoltuk [TR] 152 F2
Kızılören [TR] 152 H3
Kızılyaka [TR] 154 D1
Kjeeringvika [N] 192 E4
Kjelda [N] 190 C4
Kjeldebotn [N] 192 E4
Kjelfossen [N] 170 D2
Kjellerup [DK] 160 D6
Kjellmyra [N] 172 D4
Kjernmoen [N] 172 D3
Kjerrengvoll [N] 182 C3
Kjerret [N] 166 D1
Kjerringvåg [N] 190 A6
Kjerringvik [N] 190 C6
Kjerstad [N] 180 D3
Kjøllefjord [N] 194 D1
Kjølsdal [N] 180 C5
Kjøpsvik [N] 192 E4
Kjøra [N] 180 H1
Kjulo / Köyliö [FIN] 176 D2
K. Kamila [GR] 130 B3
Klacka-Lerberg [S] 166 G2
Kläckeberga [S] 162 G5
Kladanj [BIH] 142 E4
Kladnica [SRB] 146 A3
Kladnice [HR] 142 A5
Kladno [CZ] 48 F3
Kladovo [SRB] 204 C6
Kladruby [CZ] 48 D4
Klæbu [N] 182 B1
Klaffer [A] 62 B3
Klagenfurt [A] 74 B3
Klaipėda [LT] 200 D4
Klakegg [N] 180 D6
Klaksvík [FR] 160 B1
Klamila [FIN] 178 D3
Klana [HR] 112 E1
Klanac [HR] 112 G3
Klanjec [HR] 74 E5
Klanxbüll [D] 156 B4
Kläpen [N] 192 E3
Kläppen [S] 190 G3
Klarabro [S] 172 E4
Klärke [S] 184 E3
Klarup [DK] 160 E4
Klašnice [BIH] 142 C2
Klässbol [S] 166 E2
Klášterec nad Ohří [CZ] 48 D3
Klášter Teplá [CZ] 48 D4
Kláštor pod Znievom [SK] 64 C2
Klatovy [CZ] 48 D5
Klaukkala [FIN] 176 G4
Klaus an der Pyhrnbahn [A] 62 B5
Klausdorf [D] 20 D2
Klausdorf [D] 34 E3
Klausen / Chiusa [I] 72 D3
Klazienaveen [NL] 16 H3
Klazomenai [TR] 152 C4
Kłębowiec [PL] 22 A5
Klecko [PL] 36 D2
Kleczew [PL] 36 E3
Klein Glödniz [A] 74 B3
Kleinhau [D] 30 F5
Kleinhaugsdorf [A] 62 E3
Klein Vielen [D] 20 C5
Kleinzell [A] 62 E5
Kleisoúra [GR] 132 D3
Kleive [N] 180 E3
Kleivegrend [N] 164 E2
Kleivstua [N] 170 H5
Klejniki [PL] 24 F6
Klemensker [DK] 158 E4
Klement [A] 62 F3
Klempenow [D] 20 D4
Klempicz [PL] 36 C1
Klenčí pod čerchovem [CZ] 48 D5
Klenike [SRB] 146 D5
Klenjë [AL] 128 C2
Klenovica [HR] 112 F2
Kleppe [N] 164 A3
Kleppestø [N] 170 A3
Klerken [B] 28 F2
Kleśno [PL] 36 A1
Kleszczele [PL] 38 F2
Kletnya [RUS] 202 E5
Kleve [D] 16 F6
Klevshult [S] 162 D3
Klezeno [RUS] 198 G4
Klichaw [RUS] 202 C5
Kliczków [PL] 34 H5
Klietz [D] 34 C1
Klimátia [GR] 132 C2
Kliment [BG] 148 E2
Klimontów [PL] 52 B3
Klimontów [PL] 52 D2
Klimovo [RUS] 178 F3
Klimpfjäll [S] 190 E4
Klin [RUS] 202 E2
Klina [SRB] 146 B5
Klinča Sela [HR] 74 E6
Klingenbach [A] 62 F6
Klingenmunster [D] 46 B5
Klingenthal [D] 48 C3
Klink [D] 20 C5
Klintehamn [S] 168 F5
Klintfors [S] 196 A4
Klintholm [DK] 156 G4
Klintsy [RUS] 202 D5
Kliplev [DK] 156 C4
Klippan [S] 158 C1
Klippen [S] 190 E3
Klippen [S] 190 G5
Klippinge [DK] 156 G3
Klírou [CY] 154 G5
Klis [HR] 144 A2
Klisino [PL] 50 E3
Klisura [BG] 148 A4
Klisura [SRB] 146 E5
Klisura Sutjeske [BIH] 144 D2
Klitmøller [DK] 160 C3
Klixbüll [D] 156 B4
Kljajićevo [SRB] 76 D6
Ključ [BIH] 142 B3
Klobouky u Brna [CZ] 62 G2
Kłobuck [PL] 50 F1
Kłobuczyn [PL] 36 B5
Klobuk [BIH] 144 B2
Klockestrand [S] 184 F3
Kłoczew [PL] 38 D4
Kłodawa [PL] 34 H1
Kłodawa [PL] 36 F3
Kłodzko [PL] 50 C3
Kløfta [N] 172 B5
Klokkarvik [N] 170 A4
Klokkervik [N] 194 C2
Klokočevac [SRB] 146 D1
Klokočevci [HR] 76 B6
Klokotnica [BIH] 142 D3
Klooster [NL] 16 G4
Klos [AL] 128 B2
Klos [AL] 128 B1
Kloštar Ivanić [HR] 74 F6
Kloštar Podravski [HR] 74 G5
Kloster [S] 174 D5
Kloster Arnstein [D] 46 B2
Kloster Chorin [D] 34 F1
Klosterkirche in Altenmarkt [D] 60 G3
Klösterle [A] 72 B1
Klosterneuburg [A] 62 F4
Klosterruiner [N] 180 B4
Klosters [CH] 72 A2
Kloster Schäftlarn [D] 60 E5
Kloster Zella [D] 32 G5
Kloster Zinna [D] 34 D3
Kloten [S] 166 H1
Klötze [D] 34 A1
Klöverträsk [S] 196 B3
Kløvimoen [N] 190 D3
Klövsjö [S] 182 G4
Kl. Plasten [D] 20 C4
Kluczbork [PL] 50 E1
Klucze [PL] 50 G3
Kluczewsko [PL] 50 H1
Kluis [D] 20 D2
Kluki [PL] 22 C1
Kluki [PL] 36 G5
Klukowa Huta [PL] 22 D3
Klupe [BIH] 142 C3
Klusy [PL] 24 D4
Klutsiön [S] 182 E5
Klütz [D] 18 H3
Klyastsitsy [BY] 198 H6
Knaben [N] 164 C4
Knäm [S] 166 B4
Knapphus [N] 164 B1
Knäred [S] 162 B5
Knaresborough [GB] 10 F3
Knarvik [N] 170 B3
Knäsjö [S] 190 G6
Knätten [S] 182 G5
Knebel [DK] 160 E6
Knetzgau [D] 46 F3
Kneža [SLO] 72 H4
Knežak [SLO] 74 B6
Kneževi Vinogradi [HR] 76 C6
Kneževo [HR] 76 B5
Knezha [BG] 146 G3
Knežica [BIH] 142 B2
Knić [SRB] 146 B2
Knídi [GR] 128 F6
Knidos [TR] 154 B3
Kniebis [D] 58 F2
Knighton [GB] 10 C6
Knights Town [IRL] 4 A4
Knin [HR] 142 A4
Knislinge [S] 158 D1
Knittelfeld [A] 74 C2
Knivsta [S] 168 D2
Knjaževac [SRB] 146 E3
Knock [IRL] 2 C4
Knockcroghery [IRL] 2 D5
Knocknalina / Cnocán na Líne [IRL] 2 B2
Knocktopher [IRL] 4 E4
Knokke-Heist [B] 28 G1
Knosós [GR] 140 E4
Knottingley [GB] 10 F4
Knudshoved [DK] 156 E3
Knurów [PL] 50 F3
Knurowiec [PL] 38 C1
Knutby [S] 168 E1
Knutsford [GB] 10 D4
Knyazevo [RUS] 198 H5
Knyazhevo [BG] 148 E4
Knyazhicy [RUS] 198 G3
Knyszyn [PL] 24 E5
Kobarid [SLO] 72 H4
Kobbelveid [N] 192 E5
Kobeliaky [UA] 202 F7
København [DK] 156 H2
Koberg [S] 166 D6
Kobeřice [CZ] 50 E4
Kobiele Wlk. [PL] 36 H6
Kobilyane [BG] 130 F1
Kobišnica [SRB] 146 E1
Koblenz [D] 30 H6
Kobryn [BY] 38 G2
Kobułty [PL] 24 B4
Kobylany [PL] 38 F3
Kobylin [PL] 36 D4
Kobyłka [PL] 38 C2
Kobyl'nik [BY] 200 H5
Kocaali [TR] 150 B4
Kocaali [TR] 150 H2
Kocabaş [TR] 152 G5
Kocaburgaz [TR] 150 D4
Kocaçeşme [TR] 150 B4
Kocaeli (İzmit) [TR] 150 G3
Kocakaymaz [TR] 150 G2
Kočani [MK] 128 G1
Kocapınar [TR] 150 D5
Koçarlı [TR] 152 D5
Kocbeře [CZ] 50 A2
Koceljevo [SRB] 146 A1
Kočerin [BIH] 144 B2
Kočevje [SLO] 74 C6
Kočevska Reka [SLO] 74 C6
Kochel [D] 60 D5
Kocherinovo [BG] 146 F6
Kocherov [UA] 202 D7
Kochmar [BG] 148 F2
Kock [PL] 38 E4
Kocs [H] 64 B6
Kocsér [H] 76 E2
Kocsola [H] 76 B4
Kócsújfalu [H] 64 F6
Koczała [PL] 22 B4
Kodal [N] 164 H3
Koden' [PL] 38 F3
Kodersdorf [D] 34 G6
Kodesjärvi [FIN] 186 B5
Kodrąb [PL] 36 H6
Koetschette [L] 44 E2
Kofçaz [TR] 150 B1
Köflach [A] 74 D2
Kögbo [S] 174 E4
Køge [DK] 156 G3
Kogila [MK] 128 E3
Kogula [EST] 198 C3
Kohfidisch [A] 74 F2
Kohila [EST] 198 D2
Kohtla-Järve [EST] 198 F1
Koigi [EST] 198 E2
Koijärvi [FIN] 176 F3
Koikkala [FIN] 188 D5

Koiláda [GR] 136 F3
Koilovtsi [BG] 148 B3
Kõima [EST] 198 D2
Köinge [S] 162 B4
Koirakoski [FIN] 196 F6
Koisjärvi [FIN] 176 G4
Koíta [GR] 136 E5
Koivu [FIN] 194 C8
Koivulahti / Kvevlax [FIN] 186 B2
Koivumäki [FIN] 188 E3
Kojetín [CZ] 50 D6
Kökar [FIN] 168 H1
Kokava nad Rimavicou [SK] 64 D3
Kokemäki / Kumo [FIN] 176 D2
Kokin Brod [SRB] 146 A3
Kokkála [GR] 136 E5
Kokkário [GR] 152 C5
Kokkila [FIN] 176 E5
Kókkina (Erenköy) [CY] 154 F5
Kokkino Neró [GR] 132 H1
Kokkola / Karleby [FIN] 196 C6
Kokkolahti [FIN] 188 F4
Koklë [AL] 128 C4
Koklioí [GR] 132 C1
Koknese [LV] 198 E5
Kokonvaara [FIN] 188 E2
Kokorevo [RUS] 198 H3
Kokořín [CZ] 48 G3
Koksijde-Bad [B] 28 F1
Kola [BIH] 142 B3
Köla [S] 166 D1
Kołacz [PL] 20 H4
Kołacze [PL] 38 F5
Koláka [GR] 134 A5
Koláre [SK] 64 C5
Kolari [FIN] 194 B7
Kolari [SRB] 142 H3
Kolárovo [SK] 64 A5
Kolåsen [S] 190 D6
Kolašin [MNE] 144 E3
Kolbäck [S] 168 B2
Kołbacz [PL] 20 F5
Kołbaskowo [PL] 20 F5
Kolbenshån [S] 182 E4
Kolbermoor [D] 60 F5
Kołbiel [PL] 38 C3
Kolbotn [N] 166 B1
Kolbudy Górne [PL] 22 D3
Kolbuszowa [PL] 52 D3
Kolby [DK] 156 E2
Kolby Kås [DK] 156 E2
Kołczewo [PL] 20 F3
Kołczygłowy [PL] 22 C3
Koldby [DK] 160 B4
Kolding [DK] 156 C3
Koleczkowo [PL] 22 D2
Koler [S] 196 A3
Kölesd [H] 76 B4
Kolešino [MK] 128 H2
Kolga-Jaani [EST] 198 E2
Kolho [FIN] 186 E5
Koli [FIN] 188 F1
Kolín [CZ] 48 H4
Kolin [PL] 20 G5
Kolind [DK] 160 E6
Kolindrós [GR] 128 G5
Kolinec [CZ] 48 E6
Kölingared [S] 162 C1
Köljala [EST] 198 C3
Kolka [LV] 198 C4
Kolkonpää [FIN] 188 E5
Kolkontaipale [FIN] 188 D4
Kolky [UA] 202 B7
Kölleda [D] 34 A5
Kollerud [S] 172 E5
Kollínes [GR] 136 E3
Kollund [DK] 156 C4
Kolm-Saigurn [A] 72 G2
Köln [D] 30 G4
Kolnica [PL] 50 D2
Kolno [PL] 24 C5
Kolo [BIH] 144 B1
Koło [PL] 36 F3
Kołobrzeg [PL] 20 G3
Kolodruby [UA] 52 H5
Kolokolovo [RUS] 198 G2
Kolokot [SRB] 146 C6
Kolomyia [UA] 204 C3
Kolonia Korytnica [PL] 38 D4
Kolonjë [AL] 128 B4
Kolonowskie [PL] 50 F2
Kolophon [TR] 152 C5
Kolossai [TR] 152 G5
Kolossi [CY] 154 F6
Koloveč [CZ] 48 D5
Kolpino [RUS] 202 B1
Kolsätter [S] 182 G5
Kölsillre [S] 182 H4
Kolsjön [S] 184 D5
Kolsva [S] 168 B2
Kolta [SK] 64 B5
Kolu [FIN] 186 E3
Kolunič [BIH] 142 A3
Koluszki [PL] 36 H4
Kolut [SRB] 76 C5
Koluvere [EST] 198 D2
Kolvereid [N] 190 C4
Kolymvári [GR] 140 B4
Komádi [H] 76 G2
Komagvær [N] 194 F2
Koman [AL] 128 B1
Komańcza [PL] 52 E5
Kómara [GR] 130 H1
Komarevo [BG] 148 A2
Komárno [SK] 64 B5
Komarno [UA] 52 G4
Komárom [H] 64 A6
Komar Prolaz [BIH] 142 C4
Koma tou Yialou (Kumyalı) [CY] 154 G4
Komenda [SLO] 74 C4
Kómi [GR] 134 G5
Kómi [GR] 138 E1
Komi Kebir (Büyükkonuk) [CY] 154 G4
Komin [HR] 74 F5
Komirić [SRB] 142 F3
Kómito [GR] 134 D6
Komiža [HR] 116 H2
Komjáti [H] 64 F3
Kömlő [H] 64 E6
Komló [H] 76 B4
Komméno [GR] 132 D3
Kommerniemi [FIN] 188 E5
Kommunary [RUS] 178 G2
Komnes [N] 164 G2
Komniná [GR] 128 F5
Komniná [GR] 130 E2
Komninádes [GR] 128 D5
Komorane [SRB] 146 C5
Komorowo [PL] 36 C5
Komorzno [PL] 36 E6
Komossa [FIN] 186 C2
Komotiní [GR] 130 F2
Kömpöc [H] 76 E4
Kompolje [HR] 112 G3
Kompóti [GR] 132 D3
Komsomol'sk [RUS] 22 H1
Komsomol'skoye [RUS] 178 F2
Komula [FIN] 196 F5
Komunari [BG] 148 F3
Kömürköy [TR] 150 C2
Konak [SRB] 142 H1
Konakpınar [TR] 152 D1
Konarevo [SRB] 146 B3
Konarzyny [PL] 22 C4
Končanica [HR] 74 G6
Konče [MK] 128 G2
Konchansko-Suvorovskoye [RUS] 202 D1
Kondolovo [BG] 148 F5
Kondorfa [H] 74 F2
Kondoros [H] 76 F3
Kondrić [HR] 142 D1
Koněpruské Jeskyně [CZ] 48 F4
Køng [DK] 156 F4
Konga [S] 162 E6
Köngas [FIN] 194 C6
Köngäs [FIN] 194 D6
Kongasmäki [FIN] 196 E4
Kongensgruve [N] 164 G1
Kongensvollen [N] 190 A6
Kongerslev [DK] 160 E4
Kong Humbles Grav [DK] 156 E5
Konginkangas [FIN] 186 G3
Kongsberg [N] 164 G1
Kongselva [N] 192 D4
Kongsfjord [N] 194 E1
Kongshavn [N] 164 F5
Kongsmoen [N] 190 D4
Kongsnes [N] 170 C2
Kongsvinger [N] 172 D5
Konice [CZ] 50 C5
Koniecpol [PL] 50 H2
Konieczna [PL] 52 D5
König-Otto-Höhle [D] 46 H5
Königsbrück [D] 34 F6
Königsbrunn [D] 60 D4
Königsee [D] 46 G2
Königsfeld [D] 58 F3
Königshofen [D] 46 E4
Königslutter [D] 32 H2
Königssee [D] 60 G6
Königsstuhl [D] 20 D2
Königstein [D] 46 C2
Königstein [D] 48 F1
Königswartha [D] 34 F5
Königswiesen [A] 62 C4
Königswinter [D] 30 H5
Königs-Wusterhausen [D] 34 E3
Konin [PL] 36 E3
Koniščina [HR] 74 E5
Koniskós [GR] 132 F1
Konispol [AL] 132 B2
Kónitsa [GR] 128 D6
Köniz [CH] 58 D6
Konjevići [BIH] 142 E4
Konjic [BIH] 144 C1
Konjsko [BIH] 144 D4
Könnern [D] 34 B4
Konnerud [N] 164 H1
Konnevesi [FIN] 186 G3
Könni [FIN] 186 C3
Könnu [EST] 198 E1
Konopiště [CZ] 48 G4
Konopiste [MK] 128 F3
Konotop [PL] 20 H5
Konotop [PL] 36 B4
Końskie [PL] 38 A6
Konsko [MK] 128 G3
Konsmo [N] 164 D5
Konstancin-Jeziorna [PL] 38 B3
Konstantynów [PL] 38 E3
Konstantynów Łodzki [PL] 36 G4
Konstanz [D] 58 G4
Konteenperä [FIN] 194 E8
Kontiainen [FIN] 186 D2
Kontiás [GR] 130 F6
Kontinjoki [FIN] 196 F5
Kontiolahti [FIN] 188 F2
Kontiomäki [FIN] 196 F4
Kontiovaara [FIN] 188 G1
Kontiovaara [FIN] 188 G1
Kontkala [FIN] 188 F3
Kontokáli [GR] 132 B2
Kontopoúli [GR] 130 F6
Konttajärvi [FIN] 194 C7
Konush [BG] 148 C6
Konyavo [BG] 146 F5
Konyshevka [RUS] 202 F6
Konz [D] 44 F2
Koonga [EST] 198 D2
Köörtilä [FIN] 186 B6
Koosa [EST] 198 F2
Koparnes [N] 180 C4
Kópasker [IS] 192 C2
Köpenick [D] 34 E2
Koper [SLO] 72 H6
Köpernitz [D] 20 C6
Kopervik [N] 164 A2
Kópháza [H] 62 F6
Kopidlno [CZ] 48 H3
Köping [S] 168 B2
Köpingsvik [S] 162 G4
Kopisto [FIN] 196 C5
Koplik [AL] 144 E5
Köpmanholmen [S] 184 G2
Köpmannebro [S] 166 D4
Koporin, Manastir- [SRB] 146 C1
Kopor'ye [RUS] 178 F5
Koppang [N] 172 C1
Koppangen [N] 192 G2
Kopparberg [S] 166 H1
Kopperå [N] 182 D1
Kopperby [D] 18 F1
Koppom [S] 166 D2
Koprivets [BG] 148 C3
Koprivlen [BG] 130 C2
Koprivnica [HR] 74 G5
Koprivnica [SRB] 146 E2
Kopřivnice [CZ] 50 E5
Koprivshtitsa [BG] 148 A5
Köprübaşı [TR] 152 E3
Köprübaşı [TR] 152 F5
Köprühisar [TR] 150 G4
Köprüören [TR] 152 G1
Koprzywnica [PL] 52 D2
Kopsa [FIN] 196 D4
Kõpu [EST] 198 E3
Korbach [D] 32 E5
Korbevac [SRB] 146 D5
Korbielów [PL] 50 G5
Korbu [MD] 204 E2
Korcë [AL] 128 D5
Korčula [HR] 144 B3
Korczew [PL] 38 E2
Korczyców [PL] 34 G3
Korczyna [PL] 52 D4
Korenica [HR] 112 H3
Korenita [SRB] 142 F3
Korentovaara [FIN] 188 H1
Korespohja [FIN] 186 G5
Körez [TR] 152 F3
Korfantów [PL] 50 D2
Körfez [TR] 150 G3
Kórfos [GR] 136 F2
Korgen [N] 190 D2
Korgene [LV] 198 D4
Koria [FIN] 178 C3
Korinós [GR] 128 G5
Korinth [DK] 156 D4
Kórinthos [GR] 136 F1
Kórinthos, Arhéa- [GR] 136 F1
Korisós [GR] 128 E5
Korissía [GR] 138 C2
Korita [BIH] 144 D3
Korita [HR] 144 C4
Koritata [BG] 130 E2
Koritë [AL] 128 C5
Koriten [BG] 148 F1
Koríthi [GR] 136 A1
Korkea [FIN] 196 G5
Korkeakangas [FIN] 188 G4
Korlátka [SK] 62 H3
Körmend [H] 74 F2
Kormu [FIN] 176 G3
Korne [PL] 22 C3
Korneuburg [A] 62 F4
Kornevo [RUS] 22 G2
Kórnik [PL] 36 C3
Kornsjø [N] 166 C4
Kornwestheim [D] 58 H1
Kőrnye [H] 64 B6
Koromačno [HR] 112 E2
Koróni [GR] 136 D4
Kóronos [GR] 138 F3
Koronoúda [GR] 128 H3
Koronowo [PL] 22 D5
Korop [UA] 202 E6
Koropí [GR] 136 H1
Körösladány [H] 76 G2
Köröstarcsa [H] 76 G2
Korosten' [UA] 202 C7
Korostyshiv [UA] 202 D7
Korpavár [H] 74 G4
Korpi [FIN] 196 C6
Korpijärvi [FIN] 188 C6
Korpikå [S] 196 B2
Korpilahti [FIN] 186 G5
Korpilombolo [S] 194 B7
Korpo / Korppoo [FIN] 176 C5
Korpoström [FIN] 176 C5
Korppinen [FIN] 186 G1
Korppoo / Korpo [FIN] 176 C5
Korrigans [F] 40 D6
Korrö [S] 162 E5
Korsåsen [S] 172 H2
Korsberga [S] 162 E3
Korsberga [S] 166 F6
Korsen [N] 190 C5
Korsholm [S] 158 C2
Korsholm / Mustasaari [FIN] 186 B2
Korskrogen [S] 184 C6
Korsmo [N] 172 C5
Korsnäs [FIN] 186 A3
Korsø [DK] 160 C3
Korsør [DK] 156 E3
Korsun'-Shevchenkivs'kyi [UA] 202 E8
Korsveien [N] 182 B2
Korsvoll [N] 180 F1
Korsze [PL] 24 B3
Körteke [TR] 152 F6
Kortekylä [FIN] 186 E2
Korten [BG] 148 D4
Kortenberg [B] 30 C4
Kortesjärvi [FIN] 186 C1
Kortevaara [FIN] 196 G5
Kórthi [GR] 138 D1
Kortrijk (Courtrai) [B] 28 G2
Korucu [TR] 152 C2
Koruköy [TR] 150 C1
Koruköy [TR] 150 B4
Korup [DK] 156 D3
Korušce [HR] 142 A5
Korva [S] 194 B8
Korvala [FIN] 194 D7
Korvaluoma [FIN] 186 C5
Korvenkylä [FIN] 196 D5
Korvensuu [FIN] 176 D4
Koryčany [CZ] 62 G2
Korycin [PL] 24 E4
Korydallós [GR] 132 E1
Koryfási [GR] 136 C4
Korytnica-Kúpele [SK] 64 C2
Korytno [RUS] 198 G2
Korzeniste [PL] 24 D5
Korzenna [PL] 52 C5
Korzunovo [RUS] 194 F3
Korzybie [PL] 22 B2
Kos [GR] 154 B2
Kosanica [MNE] 144 E2
Košarovce [SK] 52 D6
Kościan [PL] 36 C3
Kościelec [PL] 36 F3
Kościerzyna [PL] 22 D3
Kose [EST] 198 E1
Kösedere [TR] 134 G1
Kosel [MK] 128 D3
Koserow [D] 20 E3
Košetice [CZ] 48 G5
Košice [SK] 64 G3
Kosik [RUS] 202 E5
Kosinë [AL] 128 C6
Kosjerić [SRB] 146 A2
Kösk [TR] 152 E5
Koška [HR] 142 D1
Koskeby [FIN] 186 B2
Koskela [FIN] 186 D2
Koskenkorva [FIN] 186 C3
Koskenkylä [FIN] 188 C2
Koskenkylä / Forsby [FIN] 178 B4
Koskenniska [FIN] 194 C4
Koskenpää [FIN] 186 F5
Koski [FIN] 176 E4
Koski [FIN] 176 H2
Koskimäki [FIN] 186 B3
Kóskina [GR] 134 D5
Koskolovo [RUS] 178 F6
Koškovce [SK] 52 E6
Koskue [FIN] 186 C4
Koskullskulle [S] 192 G6
Kosmás [GR] 136 E3
Kósmio [GR] 130 F2
Kosmo [N] 192 D6
Kosmonosy [CZ] 48 G3
Kosola [FIN] 186 C2
Kosovo Polje [SRB] 146 C5
Kosovska Mitrovica [SRB] 146 C4
Kosów Lacki [PL] 38 D2
Kössen [A] 60 F5
Kost [CZ] 48 H2
Kósta [GR] 136 F3
Kosta [S] 162 E5
Kostanjevac [HR] 74 D6
Kostanjevica [SLO] 74 D5
Kosta Perchevo [BG] 146 E2
Kostelec [CZ] 48 H6
Kostelec nad Černými [CZ] 48 G4
Kostelec nad Labem [CZ] 48 G3
Kostelec nad Orlicí [CZ] 50 B3
Kostelec na Hané [CZ] 50 C5
Kostenets [BG] 146 G5
Kosti [BG] 148 G5
Kostinbrod [BG] 146 F4
Kostojevići [SRB] 146 A2
Kostomłoty [PL] 36 C6
Kostomuksha [RUS] 196 G4
Kostopil' [UA] 202 B7
Kóstos [GR] 138 E3
Kostów [PL] 36 E6
Kostrzyń [PL] 34 G2
Kostrzyn [PL] 36 D2
Kosturino [MK] 128 G2
Košumberk [CZ] 50 B4
Košutovo [SRB] 146 B4
Koszalin [PL] 20 H3
Koszęcin [PL] 50 F2
Kőszeg [H] 74 F1
Kosztowo [PL] 22 C6
Koszuty [PL] 36 D3
Koszyce [PL] 52 B3
Kótaj [H] 64 H4
Kotala [FIN] 186 E4
Kótas [GR] 128 E4
Kotë [AL] 128 B5
Kotel [BG] 148 D4
Kötelec [H] 76 E1
Köthen [D] 34 C4
Kotila [FIN] 196 F4
Kotka [FIN] 178 C4
Kotlarnia [PL] 50 F3
Kotlice [PL] 52 G1
Kotlin [PL] 36 D4
Kotly [RUS] 178 F6
Kotola [FIN] 194 F7
Kotor [MNE] 144 D4
Kotorsko [BIH] 142 D2
Kotor Varoš [BIH] 142 C3
Kotovs'k [UA] 204 E3
Kotowice [PL] 50 G2
Kótronas [GR] 136 E5
Kötschach-Mauthen [A] 72 G3
Kotten [NL] 16 G6
Köttkulla [S] 162 C2
Kotvala [FIN] 186 F1
Kötzting [D] 48 D6
Koufália [GR] 128 G4
Koufós [GR] 130 C6
Kouhi [FIN] 186 H5
Koúklia [CY] 154 F6
Koukounariés [GR] 134 B3
Koúmanis [GR] 136 C2
Koúndouros [GR] 138 C2
Koúrenta [GR] 132 C2
Kourion [CY] 154 F6
Kournás [GR] 140 C5
Kouroúta [GR] 136 B2
Koutsó [GR] 130 E3
Koutsóchero [GR] 132 G2
Koutsourás [GR] 140 G5
Koutsovéntis (Güngör) [CY] 154 G5
Kouvola [FIN] 178 C3
Kovačevac [SRB] 146 B1
Kovachevica [BG] 130 C1
Kovachevtsi [BG] 146 F5
Kovachica [BG] 146 F2
Kovačica [SRB] 142 G2
Kovačica [SRB] 204 B5
Kovarce [SK] 64 A4
Kovarskas [LT] 200 G4
Kovel' [UA] 202 A7
Kovero [FIN] 188 G2
Kovin [SRB] 142 H2
Kovland [S] 184 E4
Kövra [S] 182 G3
Kowal [PL] 36 G2
Kowale Oleckie [PL] 24 D3
Kowalewo Pomorskie [PL] 22 E6
Kowary [PL] 50 A2
Köyceğiz [TR] 154 E1
Köyliö / Kjulo [FIN] 176 D2
Köysivaara [FIN] 194 D5
Koyunhis [TR] 150 F4
Koyunköy [TR] 150 G4
Koyunoba [TR] 152 F2
Kozağaci [TR] 154 G1
Kozak [TR] 152 C2
Kozan [TR] 150 G4
Kozáni [GR] 128 F5
Kozarac [BIH] 142 B2
Kozarac [HR] 76 B6
Kozar Belene [BG] 148 B3
Kozel [CZ] 48 E5
Kozel'sk [RUS] 202 F4
Koziatyn [UA] 202 C8
Kozica [HR] 144 B2
Koziebrody [PL] 36 H1
Koziegłowy [PL] 50 G2
Kozienice [PL] 38 C4
Kozí Hrádek [CZ] 48 G5
Kozina [SLO] 74 A6
Kozine [LV] 198 G4
Kozjak [MK] 128 D3
Kozlar [TR] 152 G6
Kozloduĭ [BG] 146 G2
Kozlov Bereg [RUS] 198 G2
Kozłowo [PL] 22 G5
Kozluk [BIH] 142 E3
Kozly [CZ] 48 E2
Kozly [RUS] 198 G4
Koźmin [PL] 36 D4
Kozojedy [CZ] 48 E4
Kozolupy [CZ] 48 D4
Kozpınar [TR] 150 G5
Kożuchów [PL] 36 A4
Kozy [PL] 50 G4
Kozyürük [TR] 150 B3
Krääkkiö [FIN] 176 F2
Krabbesholm [DK] 160 C5
Krabi [EST] 198 F4
Kräckelbäcken [S] 172 G2
Kraddsele [S] 190 F3
Kraftverk Harsprånget [S] 190 H1
Krąg [PL] 22 B3
Kragelund [DK] 160 E3
Kragenæs [DK] 156 F4
Kragerø [N] 164 F4
Kragujevac [SRB] 146 C2
Kragujevac [SRB] 204 B6
Krahës [AL] 128 B5
Kraište [BG] 146 G6
Krajenka [PL] 22 B5
Krajišnik [SRB] 142 H1
Krajn [AL] 128 B1
Krajna [SLO] 74 E3
Krajná Pol'ana [SK] 52 D5
Krajnik Gorny [PL] 20 E6
Krakača [BIH] 112 H2
Kråkan [S] 184 H1
Kråkeland [N] 164 C4
Krakės [LT] 200 F4
Krakhella [N] 170 B1
Kråklingbo [S] 168 G5
Kråklivollen [N] 182 C2
Kråkmo [N] 192 E5
Krakol'ye [RUS] 178 E6
Krakovec [UA] 202 A8
Krakovets' [UA] 52 F3
Kraków [PL] 50 H4
Krakow am See [D] 20 B4
Kråksmåla [S] 162 F4
Králíky [CZ] 50 C4
Kraljeva Sutjesca [BIH] 142 D4
Kraljevica [HR] 112 E2
Kraljevo [SRB] 146 B3
Kral'ovany [SK] 50 G6
Král'ov Brod [SK] 64 A5
Královec [CZ] 50 B2
Kralovice [CZ] 48 E4
Král'Ovský Chlmec [SK] 64 H3
Kralupy nad Vltavou [CZ] 48 F3
Kramfors [S] 184 F3
Kramolin [BG] 148 B3
Krampenes [N] 194 E2
Kramsach [A] 60 E6
Kråmvik [N] 164 E1
Kramvik [N] 194 F2
Kraneá [GR] 132 E2
Kranenburg [D] 16 F6
Kranevo [BG] 148 G2
Krångede [S] 184 D2
Krani [MK] 128 D4
Kraniá [GR] 132 E1
Kraniá Elassónas [GR] 132 F1
Kranichfeld [D] 46 G1
Kranídi [GR] 136 F3
Kranj [SLO] 74 B4
Kranjska Gora [SLO] 72 H3
Krapina [HR] 74 E5
Krapinske Toplice [HR] 74 E5
Krapkowice [PL] 50 E2
Krapperup [S] 156 G1
Krasen [BG] 148 F1
Krasiczyn [PL] 52 F4
Krasikovshchina [RUS] 198 G3
Krāslava [LV] 198 G6
Kraslice [CZ] 48 C3
Krásná Hora nad Vltavou [CZ] 48 F5
Krásna Hôrka [SK] 64 F3
Krásná Lípa [CZ] 48 G1
Krasnasyel'ski [BY] 24 G5
Krasnaya Hora [RUS] 202 D5
Krasne Folwarczne [PL] 24 E5
Kraśniczyn [PL] 38 F6
Kraśnik [PL] 52 E1
Krasnogorodsk [RUS] 198 G5
Krasnogorodskoye [RUS] 202 B3
Krasnogorsk [RUS] 202 F3
Krasnohryvka [UA] 202 D8
Krásno nad Kysucou [SK] 50 F5
Krasnoperekops'k [UA] 204 H3
Krasnopol [PL] 24 E3
Krasnopol'e [BY] 202 D5
Krasnopol'e [UA] 202 F6
Krasnosel'e [RUS] 24 D2
Krasnosielc [PL] 24 B6
Krasnovo [BG] 148 A5
Krasnoye [RUS] 198 H5
Krasnoye Selo [RUS] 178 H5
Krasnoznamensk [RUS] 200 E5
Krasnye Prudy [RUS] 198 G4
Krasnyje Gory [RUS] 198 H1
Krasnystaw [PL] 38 F6
Krasnyy Bor [RUS] 24 B1
Krasnyy Kholm [RUS] 202 E1
Krasocin [PL] 52 A1
Krašov [CZ] 48 E4
Krastë [AL] 128 C2
Krasulje [BIH] 142 B3
Krasznokvajda [H] 64 F3
Krátigos [GR] 134 H2
Kratovo [MK] 146 E6
Kratovska Stena [SRB] 146 A2
Krauchenwies [D] 58 H3
Kraushöhle [A] 62 C6
Krautheim [D] 46 E5
Kravaře [CZ] 48 F2
Kravaře [CZ] 50 E4
Kravarsko [HR] 74 E6
Kravik [N] 170 F5
Kravnsø [DK] 156 A2
Kraymorie [BG] 148 F4
Kražiai [LT] 200 E4
Kreba-Neudorf [D] 34 G5
Krefeld [D] 30 G3
Kregme [DK] 156 G2
Kremastí [GR] 136 F4
Kremastí [GR] 154 D3
Kremenchuk [UA] 202 F8
Kremenets' [UA] 202 B8
Kremmen [D] 34 D1
Kremna [SRB] 144 E1
Kremnica [SK] 64 C3
Krems [A] 62 E4
Kremsmünster [A] 62 B5
Křemže [CZ] 62 B2
Krenkerup [DK] 20 B1
Křenov [CZ] 50 C5
Krępa [PL] 36 F4
Krepcha [BG] 148 D2
Krepoljin [SRB] 146 D1
Kresna [BG] 130 B1
Kréstena [GR] 136 C2
Kresttsy [RUS] 202 C2
Kretinga [LT] 200 D4
Kreuth [D] 60 E5
Kreuzenstein [A] 62 F4
Kreuzlingen [CH] 58 G4
Kreuztal [D] 32 C6
Kreva [BY] 200 H6
Kriakėnava [LT] 200 F4
Krichim [BG] 148 B6
Kričov [BY] 202 D5
Kriebstein [D] 34 D6
Krieglach [A] 62 D6
Kriezá [GR] 134 C5
Krikello [GR] 132 F4
Krimml [A] 72 E1
Krimmler Wasserfälle [A] 72 E1
Křinec [CZ] 48 H3
Kringla [N] 170 B2
Krinídes [GR] 130 D3
Kristall-Höhle [D] 46 C2
Kristalopig [GR] 128 E5
Kristberg [S] 166 H5
Kristdala [S] 162 G3
Kristianopel [S] 158 G1
Kristiansand [N] 164 D5
Kristianstad [S] 158 D2
Kristiansund [N] 180 F2
Kristiinankaupunki / Kristinestad [FIN] 186 A5
Kristineberg [S] 172 E1
Kristineberg [S] 190 G4
Kristinefors [S] 172 E5
Kristinehamn [S] 166 F3
Kristinehov [S] 158 D2
Kristinestad / Kristiinankaupunki [FIN] 186 A5
Kristoffervalen [N] 192 G1
Kristóni [GR] 128 H3
Kristvallabrunn [S] 162 F5
Kritinía [GR] 154 C4
Kritsá [GR] 140 F5
Kriva Feja [SRB] 146 E5
Krivaň [SK] 64 D3
Kriva Palanka [MK] 146 E6
Kriva reka [BG] 148 E2
Krivčevo [SLO] 74 C4
Krivelj [SRB] 146 D2
Krivi Dol [MK] 128 F1
Krivodol [BG] 146 F3
Krivogaštani [MK] 128 E3
Křivoklát [CZ] 48 E4
Krivolak [MK] 128 F2
Križ [HR] 74 F6
Křižanov [CZ] 50 B6
Križevci [HR] 74 F5
Krk [HR] 112 E2
Krka [SLO] 74 C5
Krklja [MK] 146 E6
Krnjača [SRB] 142 G2
Krnjak [HR] 112 G1
Krnjeuša [BIH] 142 A3
Krnov [CZ] 50 D4
Krobia [PL] 36 C4
Kroczyce [PL] 50 G2
Krøderen [N] 170 G5
Krogsbølle [DK] 156 D2
Krogsered [S] 162 B4
Krokan [N] 170 E6
Krokebol [N] 166 C1
Krokeés [GR] 136 E4
Krokek [S] 168 B5
Kroken [N] 190 E3
Kroken [N] 192 F2
Kroknes [N] 194 F2
Krokom [S] 182 G2
Krokowa [PL] 22 D1
Kroksjö [S] 190 G5
Kroksjö [S] 196 A5
Krokstad [S] 166 C5
Krokstadelva [N] 164 G1
Krokstadøra [N] 180 H1
Krokstorp [S] 162 G3
Kroksund [N] 166 C2
Kroktorp [S] 172 G5
Krokvåg [S] 184 D2
Krokvik [S] 192 G5
Krolevets' [UA] 202 E6
Królewiec [PL] 38 A6
Królowy Most [PL] 24 F5
Kroměříž [CZ] 50 D6
Kromerowo [PL] 22 H4
Krompachy [SK] 64 F2
Kromy [RUS] 202 F5
Kronach [D] 46 H3
Kronegg [A] 62 C4
Kronoby / Kruunupyy [FIN] 196 C6
Kronsgaard [D] 156 C5
Kronshtadt [RUS] 178 G4
Kropa [SLO] 74 B4
Kröpelin [D] 20 B3
Kropp [D] 18 F2
Kroppenstedt [D] 34 B3
Kropstädt [D] 34 D3
Krościenko [PL] 52 F5
Krościenko nad Dunajcem [PL] 52 B5
Krosna [LT] 24 F2
Krośniewice [PL] 36 G3
Krosno [PL] 22 F3
Krosno [PL] 52 D4
Krosno Odrzańskie [PL] 34 H3
Krossbu [N] 180 E6
Krossen [N] 164 D6
Krostiz [D] 34 C5
Krote [LV] 198 B6
Krotoszyn [PL] 36 D4
Krouna [CZ] 50 B4
Kršan [HR] 112 E2
Kršete [HR] 112 D1
Krško [SLO] 74 D5
Krstac [MNE] 144 D3
Krstac [MNE] 144 E5
Kručov [SK] 52 D6
Krucz [PL] 36 B1
Kruge [HR] 112 H3
Kruglovo [RUS] 22 G1
Kruiningen [NL] 28 H1
Kruisland [NL] 16 C6
Krujë [AL] 128 B2
Kruk [N] 170 G2
Krukowo [PL] 24 B5
Krumbach [A] 62 E6
Krumbach [D] 60 C4
Krumë [AL] 146 B6
Krummendorf [D] 20 B3
Krumovgrad [BG] 130 F1
Krumpendorf [A] 74 B3
Krün [D] 60 D6
Krupá [CZ] 48 E3
Krupac [BIH] 144 C2
Krupac [BIH] 144 D1
Krupaja [SRB] 146 C1
Krupa na Vrbasu [BIH] 142 B3
Krupanj [SRB] 142 F3
Krupe [PL] 38 F6
Krupina [SK] 64 C4
Krupište [MK] 128 F1
Krupnik [BG] 128 H1
Krupp [RUS] 198 G3
Kruså [DK] 156 C4
Kruščić [SRB] 76 D6
Krušedol, Manastir- [SRB] 142 F2
Kruševac [SRB] 146 C3
Kruševo [MK] 128 E2
Krusha [BG] 146 E4
Krushari [BG] 148 F1
Krushevets [BG] 148 F5
Krushovene [BG] 148 A2
Krushovica [BG] 146 G2
Kruszwica [PL] 36 E2
Kruszyna [PL] 50 G1
Krutcy [RUS] 198 H4
Krute [MNE] 128 A1
Krutneset [N] 190 E3

Kruunupyy / Kronoby [FIN] 196 C6
Kruusila [FIN] 176 F4
Krya [TR] 154 E2
Kryakusa [RUS] 198 G3
Krýa Vrýsi [GR] 128 G4
Kryekuq [AL] 128 A4
Krylbo [S] 174 D6
Kryle [DK] 160 B6
Krylovo [RUS] 24 C2
Krymne [UA] 38 H4
Krynica [PL] 52 C5
Krynica Morska [PL] 22 F2
Krynki [PL] 24 F5
Kryopigí [GR] 130 C6
Kryspinów [PL] 50 H4
Kryve Ozero [UA] 204 F2
Kryvyi Rih [UA] 204 G2
Krzęcin [PL] 20 G6
Krzeczów [PL] 36 F6
Krzelów [PL] 36 C5
Krzepice [PL] 50 F1
Krzeszów [PL] 50 B2
Krzeszów [PL] 52 E2
Krzeszowice [PL] 50 H3
Krzeszyce [PL] 34 G2
Krzynowłoga Mała [PL] 22 H6
Krzystkowice [PL] 34 H4
Krzywiń [PL] 36 C4
Krzyżewo [PL] 24 B6
Krzyż Wlkp. [PL] 36 B1
Ksar-es-Seghir [MA] 100 G6
Książ [PL] 50 B1
Książ Wielki [PL] 52 A2
Ktísmata [GR] 132 C1
Kubbe [S] 184 F1
Küblis [CH] 70 H1
Kubrat [BG] 148 D2
Kuç [AL] 128 B6
Kučevo [SRB] 146 D1
Kuchl [A] 60 G6
Kućište [MNE] 146 A5
Kucovë [AL] 128 B4
Küçükbahçe [TR] 134 H4
Küçükçekmece [TR] 150 E3
Küçükkuyu [TR] 134 H1
Kuddby [S] 168 B5
Kudever' [RUS] 198 H5
Kudirkos Naumiestis [LT] 24 E1
Kudowa-Zdrój [PL] 50 B3
Kufstein [A] 60 F6
Kuggeboda [S] 158 F1
Kuggerud [N] 172 C5
Kuha [FIN] 196 E2
Kuhanen [FIN] 188 D2
Kühlungsborn [D] 20 B3
Kuhmalahti [FIN] 176 G1
Kuhmo [FIN] 196 G5
Kuhmoinen [FIN] 176 H1
Kühsen [D] 18 G4
Kuhstedt [D] 18 E4
Kühtai [A] 72 C1
Kuimetsa [EST] 198 E2
Kuivajärvi [FIN] 196 G4
Kuivaniemi [FIN] 196 D3
Kuivanto [FIN] 178 B3
Kuivasjärvi [FIN] 186 C5
Kuivasmäki [FIN] 186 F4
Kuivastu [EST] 198 D3
Kukës [AL] 128 C1
Kukinia [PL] 20 H3
Kukko [FIN] 186 E3
Kukko [FIN] 186 E3
Kukkola [FIN] 176 G2
Kukkola [RUS] 176 G2
Kukkulankoski [FIN] 196 C2
Kuklin [PL] 22 H5
Kuks [CZ] 50 B3
Kukujevci [SRB] 142 F2
Kükür [TR] 154 F4
Kukurečani [MK] 128 E3
Kula [BG] 146 E2
Kula [BIH] 144 D1
Kula [SRB] 76 D6
Kulaklı [TR] 150 G2
Kulalar [TR] 152 E2
Kula Novinska [HR] 144 C3
Kulaši [BIH] 142 C3
Kulata [BG] 130 B2
Kuldīga [LV] 198 C5
Ku'le [RUS] 198 G3
Kulefall [S] 168 B6
Kuleli [TR] 150 B2
Kulennoinen [FIN] 188 F5
Kulen Vakuf [BIH] 112 H4
Kulhuse [DK] 156 G2
Kuliai [LT] 200 D4
Kullaa [FIN] 176 D1
Kulla Gunnarstorp [S] 156 H1
Kullen [S] 158 B1
Kullo / Kulloo [FIN] 178 A4
Kulloo / Kullo [FIN] 178 A4
Küllsted [D] 32 G5
Kulmain [D] 48 B4
Kulmbach [D] 46 H3
Kuloharju [FIN] 196 E2
Kultaranta [FIN] 176 D4
Kulvemäki [FIN] 196 F5
Kulykiv [UA] 52 H3
Kumafşarı [TR] 152 G6
Kumafşarı [TR] 152 G6
Kumane [SRB] 76 E6
Kumanica [SRB] 146 B3
Kumanovo [MK] 146 D6
Kumarlar [TR] 150 B5
Kumbağ [TR] 150 C3
Kümbet [TR] 150 H5
Kumburk [CZ] 48 H2
Kumburun [TR] 130 H6
Kumkale [TR] 130 H5
Kumköy [TR] 150 E2
Kumla [S] 166 H3
Kumlinge [FIN] 176 B5
Kummavuopio [S] 192 G3
Kummeren [N] 192 D6
Kumo / Kokemäki [FIN] 176 D2
Kumpuvaara [FIN] 196 E2
Kumreut [D] 60 H3
Kumrovec [HR] 74 E5
Kumuu [FIN] 196 G4
Kumyalı (Koma tou Yialou) [CY] 154 G4
Kunadacs [H] 76 D2
Kunágota [H] 76 G4
Kuncsorba [H] 76 F2
Kunda [EST] 198 F1
Kunes [N] 194 C2
Kunfehértó [H] 76 D4
Kungälv [S] 160 G1
Kungsängen [S] 168 D2
Kungsäter [S] 160 H3
Kungsbacka [S] 160 H3
Kungsberg [S] 174 D4
Kungsfors [S] 174 D4
Kungshållet [S] 168 C3
Kungshamn [S] 166 B5
Kungsör [S] 168 B3
Kunhegyes [H] 76 F1
Kunín [CZ] 50 E5
Kunmadaras [H] 76 F1
Kunovice [CZ] 62 H2
Kunow [D] 20 E6
Kunów [PL] 52 C1
Kunowo [PL] 36 C4
Kunpeszér [H] 76 C2
Kunrau [D] 34 A2
Kunštát [CZ] 50 C5
Kunszentmárton [H] 76 E3
Kunszentmiklós [H] 76 C2
Kunžak [CZ] 48 H6
Künzelsau [D] 46 E5
Kuohatti [FIN] 196 G5
Kuohenmaa [FIN] 176 F2
Kuohijoki [FIN] 176 G2
Kuoksu [S] 192 H5
Kuolayarvi [RUS] 194 F7
Kuolio [FIN] 196 F2
Kuona [FIN] 196 D6
Kuopio [FIN] 188 D2
Kuora [FIN] 188 G1
Kuortane [FIN] 186 D3
Kuosku [FIN] 194 E6
Kup [H] 74 H2
Kup [PL] 50 E2
Kupferberg [D] 46 H3
Kupferzell [D] 46 E5
Kupinovo [SRB] 142 G3
Kupirovo [HR] 112 H4
Kupiškis [LT] 200 G4
Kupjak [HR] 112 F1
Kupli [LV] 198 D5
Küplü [TR] 130 H2
Küplü [TR] 150 G4
Kuprava [LV] 198 G4
Kupres [BIH] 142 C4
Kurbinovo [MK] 128 D4
Kurbnesh [AL] 128 B1
Kurchatov [RUS] 202 F6
Kurd [H] 76 B4
Kürdzhali [BG] 130 F1
Kurejoki [FIN] 186 D2
Kuressaare [EST] 198 C3
Kurevere [EST] 198 C3
Kurgolovo [RUS] 178 E5
Kurianka [PL] 24 F4
Kurikka [FIN] 186 C4
Kurilo [BG] 146 F4
Kuřim [CZ] 50 B6
Kurjala [FIN] 188 D3
Kurjenkylä [FIN] 186 D4
Kurkela [FIN] 176 F5
Kurkiyeki [RUS] 188 G6
Kurkkio [FIN] 194 C6
Kurkkio [S] 192 H5
Kürnare [BG] 148 B4
Kürnüç [TR] 150 H4
Kurobası [TR] 134 G1
Kurola [FIN] 188 D4
Kurolanahti [FIN] 188 C2
Kurovitsy [RUS] 178 E6
Kurów [PL] 38 D5
Kurowice [PL] 36 H4
Kurozwęki [PL] 52 C2
Kurravaara [S] 192 G5
Kuršėnai [LT] 200 E4
Kursīši [LV] 198 C6
Kursu [FIN] 194 E7
Kuršumlija [SRB] 146 C4
Kuršumlijska Banja [SRB] 146 C4
Kurşunlu [TR] 150 D4
Kurşunlu [TR] 150 F4
Kurtbey [TR] 150 B3
Kurtköy [TR] 150 G3
Kurtköyü [TR] 150 H2
Kurtti [FIN] 196 F3
Kuru [FIN] 176 F1
Kuru [FIN] 186 D6
Kurudere [TR] 152 D4
Kurvinen [FIN] 196 F2
Kurzelów [PL] 50 H1
Kurzeszyn [PL] 38 A4
Kurzętnik [PL] 22 F5
Kuşadasi [TR] 152 D5
Kuşçayır [TR] 150 B6
Kuşcenneti [TR] 150 D5
Kusel [D] 44 H3
Kushalino [RUS] 202 E2
Kuside [MNE] 144 D3
Kusmark [S] 196 A4
Küssnacht [CH] 58 F6
Kustavi / Gustavs [FIN] 176 C4
Küstrin-Kietz [D] 34 G2
Kuşu [TR] 152 F2
Kut [HR] 142 A1
Kuta [MNE] 144 E3
Kütahya [TR] 152 G1
Kutemajärvi [FIN] 186 H5
Kutina [HR] 142 B1
Kutjevo [HR] 142 D1
Kutná Hora [CZ] 48 H4
Kutno [PL] 36 G3
Kuttanen [FIN] 194 B5
Kuttura [FIN] 194 D5
Kúty [SK] 62 G3
Kuukservaara [FIN] 188 H2
Kuuminainen [FIN] 176 C1
Kuurtola [FIN] 196 F3
Kuusaa [FIN] 186 G4
Kuusaa [FIN] 196 D5
Kuusajoki [FIN] 194 C6
Kuusalu [EST] 198 E1
Kuusamo [FIN] 194 F8
Kuusankoski [FIN] 178 C3
Kuusiniemi [RUS] 196 H3
Kuusjärvi [FIN] 188 E2
Kuusjoki [FIN] 176 F4
Kuuttila [FIN] 186 B2
Kuvaskangas [FIN] 186 B6
Kuvshinovo [RUS] 202 D2
Kuyubaşi [TR] 150 G4
Kuyucak [TR] 150 H5
Kuyucak [TR] 152 E5
Kuyvozi [RUS] 178 H3
Kuzemki [RUS] 202 E4
Kuzma [SLO] 74 E3
Kuzmin [SRB] 142 F2
Kuźmina [PL] 52 E5
Kuznechnoye [RUS] 178 G1
Kuznetsovo [RUS] 202 B1
Kuznetsovs'k [UA] 202 B7
Kuźnia Raciborska [PL] 50 E3
Kuźnica [PL] 24 F4
Kuzovo [RUS] 198 H3
Kuzuluk [TR] 150 H3
Kvačany [SK] 50 H6
Kvænangsbotn [N] 192 H2
Kværndrup [DK] 156 D4
Kvål [N] 182 B2
Kvalsund [N] 194 B2
Kvalsvik [N] 180 C3
Kvalvåg [N] 170 A5
Kvalvåg [N] 180 F2
Kvam [N] 180 H6
Kvam [N] 190 C5
Kvammen [N] 180 G2
Kvamsøy Gml. Kirke [N] 170 C2
Kvanndal [N] 170 C4
Kvanne [N] 180 F2
Kvantenburg [S] 166 D5
Kvarnåsen [S] 190 H4
Kvarnberg [S] 172 G2
Kvarnberget [S] 172 G5
Kvarsebo [S] 168 C5
Kvarstadseter [N] 172 B2
Kvås [N] 164 C5
Kvasilov [UA] 202 B7
Kvasowka [BY] 24 G4
Kveaunet [N] 190 D5
Kvėdarna [LT] 200 D4
Kveejdet [N] 190 D5
Kveina [N] 190 C4
Kvelde [N] 164 G3
Kvelia [N] 190 D5
Kvenvær [N] 190 A6
Kvernessetra [N] 172 C1
Kvetkai [LT] 198 E6
Kvevlax / Koivulahti [FIN] 186 B2
Kvicksund [S] 168 B2
Kvigno [N] 170 D2
Kvikkjokk [S] 190 G1
Kvikne [N] 182 B4
Kvilda [CZ] 48 E6
Kvilldal [N] 164 C1
Kville [S] 166 C5
Kvillsfors [S] 162 F3
Kvinesdal [N] 164 C5
Kvinlog [N] 164 C4
Kvisler [N] 172 D4
Kvissleby [S] 184 E5
Kvistgård [DK] 156 G2
Kvisvik [N] 180 F2
Kviteseid [N] 164 E2
Kvitnes [N] 180 F2
Kvitten [N] 182 D4
Kwiatkowice [PL] 36 G4
Kwidzyn [PL] 22 E4
Kwilcz [PL] 36 B2
Kybartai [LT] 24 E1
Kyburg [CH] 58 G5
Kycklingvattnet [S] 190 E5
Kyffhäuser -Denkmal [D] 34 A5
Kyïv [UA] 202 D7
Kyjov [CZ] 62 G2
Kyläinpää [FIN] 186 B3
Kylämä [FIN] 186 F6
Kylemore Abbey [IRL] 2 B4
Kyle of Lochalsh [GB] 6 C5
Kyliia [UA] 204 F4
Kyllaj [S] 168 G4
Kylland [N] 164 D4
Kyllburg [D] 44 F1
Kyllíni [GR] 136 B1
Kylmäkoski [FIN] 176 F2
Kylmälä [FIN] 196 E4
Kylmämäki [FIN] 186 H4
Kymbo [S] 162 C1
Kyme [TR] 152 C3
Kými [GR] 134 C4
Kýmina [GR] 128 H4
Kymönkoski [FIN] 186 G2
Kynšperk nad Ohří [CZ] 48 C3
Kypärajärvi [FIN] 188 E3
Kypäravaara [FIN] 196 F4
Kyparissía [GR] 136 C3
Kyriáki [GR] 132 H5
Kyritz [D] 20 B6
Kyrkhult [S] 162 D6
Kyrkjebygdi [N] 164 E3
Kyrksæterøra [N] 180 G1
Kyrkslätt / Kirkkonummi [FIN] 176 G5
Kyrkstad [S] 196 B5
Kyrksten [S] 166 G2
Kyrö [FIN] 176 E4
Kyrönlahti [FIN] 186 D6
Kyröskoski [FIN] 176 E1
Kyrping [N] 170 B6
Kyšice [CZ] 48 F3
Kysucké Nové Mesto [SK] 50 F6
Kytäjä [FIN] 176 G4
Kýthira [GR] 136 F6
Kýthnos [GR] 138 C2
Kytömäki [FIN] 196 F4
Kyustendil [BG] 146 E6
Kyyjärvi [FIN] 186 E2
Kyynämöinen [FIN] 186 F4
Kyzikos [TR] 150 D4
Kyznecovo [RUS] 202 B1

L

Laa an der Thaya [A] 62 F3
Laage [D] 20 B3
Laage Weitendorf [D] 20 B3
Laája [FIN] 196 F4
Laajoki [FIN] 176 D3
Laakajärvi [FIN] 196 F5
Laakirchen [A] 62 A5
La Alameda [E] 96 E5
La Alamedilla [E] 88 E4
La Alberca [E] 88 B4
La Alberca de Záncara [E] 98 A3
La Albuera [E] 94 G2
La Aldea del Obispo [E] 96 B1
La Algaba [E] 94 G6
La Almarcha [E] 98 B3
La Almolda [E] 90 F4
La Almudena [E] 104 B2
La Almunia de Doña Godina [E] 90 D4
Laamala [FIN] 188 E6
Laanila [FIN] 194 D5
La Antigua [E] 82 A5
La Antilla [E] 94 E6
Laarbruch [D] 30 F2
Laas [A] 72 G3
Laàs [F] 84 D3
Laasala [FIN] 186 E3
Laatzen [D] 32 F2
La Azohía [E] 104 C4
Labacolla [E] 78 C3
Labajos [E] 88 E4
la Balme [F] 68 G5
La Baña [E] 78 F6
La Bañeza [E] 78 G6
La Barca de la Florida [E] 100 G4
La Barrela [E] 78 D4
La Bassée [F] 28 F3
la Bastide [F] 108 D4
Labastide-d'Armagnac [F] 66 D6
La Bastide de-Sérou [F] 84 H5
Labastide-Murat [F] 66 G4
La Bastide-Puylaurent [F] 68 D6
Labastide-Rouairoux [F] 106 C4
La Bastie d'Urfé [F] 68 E2
La Bâtiaz [CH] 70 C2
La Bâtie-Neuve [F] 108 D2
La Baule [F] 40 E6
La Bazoche-Gouet [F] 42 D5
Låbbyn [S] 166 D3
Łabędzie [PL] 20 H4
la Bégude-de-Mazenc [F] 68 F6
La Belle Etoile [F] 44 A5
Labenne [F] 66 A6
La Bérarde [F] 70 A5
L'Aber-Wrac'h [F] 40 B1
La Bien Aparecida [E] 82 F3
Labin [HR] 112 E2
Labinot Fushë [AL] 128 C3
La Bisbal de Falset [E] 90 H5
la Bisbal d'Empordà [E] 92 G3
Łabiszyn [PL] 36 E1
Labjana [SRB] 146 C5
Lábod [H] 74 H4
Laboe [D] 18 G2
Laborel [F] 108 C2
Labouheyre [F] 66 B5
La Bourboule [F] 68 C2
La Bóveda de Toro [E] 88 D2
Łabowa [PL] 52 C5
Labrags [LV] 198 B5
Labraunda [TR] 152 E6
Labrède [F] 66 C3
La Bresse [F] 58 D3
La Brillanne [F] 108 C3
Labrit [F] 66 C5
Łabunie [PL] 52 G1
Läby [S] 174 F6
Laç [AL] 128 B2
Laç [AL] 128 B2
La Cabrera [E] 88 G4
La Caillere-St-Hilaire [F] 54 C3
La Cala del Moral [E] 102 B5
La Cala del Moral [E] 102 C5
La Calahorra [E] 102 F4
La Calera [E] 100 B5
La Caleta [E] 100 C6
La Caleta [E] 100 E5
La Caletta [I] 118 E3
Lacalm [F] 68 C5
La Calzada de Calatrava [E] 96 E5
La Calzada de Oropesa [E] 88 C6
La Campana [E] 102 A2
La Campana [E] 104 B4
La Cañada de Cañepla [E] 102 H3
La Cañada de Verich [E] 90 F6
Lacanau [F] 66 C2
Lacanau-Océan [F] 66 B2
La Canonica [F] 114 C3
La Canonja [E] 92 C5
La Canourgue [F] 68 C6
La Capelle [F] 28 G5
Lacapelle-Marival [F] 66 H4
La Capte [F] 108 C6
Laćarak [SRB] 142 F2
La Caridad [E] 78 F2
La Carlota [E] 102 B2
La Carolina [E] 96 E6
La Cartuja [E] 100 F3
Lacaune [F] 106 C3
La Cavalerie [F] 106 D3
Lacave [F] 66 G4
Lacco Ameno [I] 120 D3
Lacedonia [I] 120 G2
La Celle-Dunoise [F] 54 H5
Lăceni [RO] 148 B1
La Cerca [E] 82 F4
Láces [I] 72 C3
La Chaise-Dieu [F] 68 D3
La Chambre [F] 70 B4
Lachamp [F] 68 C5
Lachanás [GR] 130 B3
Lachaniá [GR] 154 D4
La Chapelle [F] 68 F1
La Chapelle-d'Angillon [F] 56 C3
la Chapelle-en-Valgaudemar [F] 70 A6
La Chapelle-en-Vercors [F] 68 G5
La Chapelle-Glain [F] 40 G5
la-Chapelle-Laurent [F] 68 C4
La Charité-sur-Loire [F] 56 D3
La Chartre-sur-le-Loir [F] 42 C6
La Châtaigneraie [F] 54 D3
La Châtre [F] 54 H5
La Chaux-de-Fonds [CH] 58 C5
Lachendorf [D] 32 G1
la-Chevignerie [F] 40 E6
la Chèze [F] 26 B5
Lachowo [PL] 24 D4
La Ciotat [F] 108 B5
La Ciudad Encantada [E] 98 C2
Łąck [PL] 36 G2
Läckeby [S] 162 G5
Läckö [S] 166 E5
La Clayette [F] 56 F6
la Clisse [F] 54 C6
La Clusaz [F] 70 B3
La Cluse [F] 68 H2
La Cluse-et-Mijoux [F] 58 B6
La Codosera [E] 86 F5
La Colle Noire [F] 108 E5
La Colle St. Michel [F] 108 D3
Lacona [I] 114 D3
La Concepción [E] 102 C4
Láconi [I] 118 D5
La Coquille [F] 66 G2
La Coronada [E] 96 B3
La Corrèze [F] 66 H3
La Corte [I] 118 B3
La Coruña / A Coruña [E] 78 C2
La Côte-St-André [F] 68 G4
Lacourt [F] 84 G5
La Courtine [F] 68 B2
la Couvertoirade [F] 106 E3
Lacq [F] 84 D3
La Croisière [F] 54 G5
La Croix Ferrée [F] 66 H1
La Croixille [F] 26 D6
La Croix-Valmer [F] 108 D6
La Cueva Santa [E] 98 E3
La Cumbre [E] 96 B1
La Cure [F] 70 B1
Lad [H] 74 H5
Ląd [PL] 36 E3
Ladapeyre [F] 54 H5
Ladbergen [D] 32 C2
Ladby [DK] 156 E3
Lądek-Zdrój [PL] 50 C3
Ládi [GR] 130 H1
Ladíspoli [I] 114 H5
Ladoeiro [P] 86 F3
Ladon [F] 42 F6
Ladoye, Cirque de- [F] 58 A6
Ladushkin [RUS] 22 G2
Ladyzhyn [UA] 204 E2
La Encinilla y El Rubio [E] 100 G3
Lærdalsøyri [N] 170 E2
Laerma [GR] 154 D4
La Espina [E] 78 G3
La Estrella [E] 96 D1
La Felipa [E] 98 C5
La Fère [F] 28 F6
la Ferrière [F] 42 C6
la Ferrière [F] 70 A4
La Ferrière-en-Parthenay [F] 54 E3
Laferté [F] 58 B3
La Ferté-Bernard [F] 42 C5
La-Ferté-Chevresis [F] 28 G5
La Ferté-Gaucher [F] 42 H4
la-Ferté-Loupière [F] 56 E1
La Ferté-Macé [F] 26 F5
La Ferté-Milon [F] 42 H3
La Ferté-sous-Jouarre [F] 42 H3
La Ferté-St-Aubin [F] 56 B1
La Ferté-Vidame [F] 26 H5
La-Feuille [F] 28 C5
Laffrey [F] 68 H5
Láfka [GR] 136 E1
La Flèche [F] 42 B6
La Florida [E] 78 G3
La Flotte [F] 54 B4
La Font de la Figuera [E] 98 D6
la Foresta, Convento- [I] 116 B4
Laforsen [S] 182 H6
Lafortunada [E] 84 E5
La Franca [E] 82 D2
Lafrançaise [F] 66 F6
La Fregeneda [E] 80 E5
La Fresneda [E] 90 F6
La Frua [I] 70 F2
La Fuente de San Esteban [E] 80 F6
Lăga [BG] 148 A4
La Gacilly [F] 40 E5
La Gallega [E] 88 H2
Lagan [S] 162 C4
Laganás [GR] 136 B2
Lagarde [F] 44 F5
La Garde-Freinet [F] 108 D5
La Garriga [E] 92 E4
La Garrovilla [E] 94 G1
Lage [D] 32 E3
Łagiewniki [PL] 50 C2
Laginá [GR] 130 B4
La Gineta [E] 98 B5
L'Agiot Élancourt [F] 42 F3
Lagkáda [GR] 134 G4
Lagkáda [GR] 136 E4
Lagkadás [GR] 130 B4
Lagkádia [GR] 136 D2
Lagkadíkia [GR] 130 B4
Lagnieu [F] 68 G2
Lagnö [S] 168 C6
Lagny [F] 42 G3
Lagoa [P] 94 B5
Lagoa [P] 100 E3
Lagodaž [BG] 146 F6
Lagonegro [I] 120 G5
Lagonísi [GR] 136 H1
Lágos [GR] 130 F3
Lagos [P] 94 B5
Lagosanto [I] 110 H3
Łagów [PL] 34 H3
Łagów [PL] 52 C1
Łagówek [PL] 34 H3
La Granada de Rio Tinto [E] 94 F4
La Granadella [E] 90 H5
La Grand-Combe [F] 106 F2
La Grande-Motte [F] 106 F4
La Granja [E] 88 F4
La Granjuela [E] 96 B5
Lagrasse [F] 106 C5
La Grave [F] 70 B5
Lägsta [S] 190 G6
La Guardia / A Guarda [E] 78 A5
La Guardia / A Guarda [E] 96 G2
Laguardia / Biasteri [E] 82 G6
La Guardia de Jaén [E] 102 E2
Laguarres [E] 90 H3
Laguarta [E] 84 E5
Laguépie [F] 66 H6
La Guerche-de-Bretagne [F] 40 G4
La Guerche-sur-l'Aubois [F] 56 D4
Laguiole [F] 68 B5
Laguna de Duero [E] 88 E2
Laguna del Marquesado [E] 98 C2
Laguna de Negrillos [E] 82 B5
Laguna de Santiago [E] 100 B5
Laguna Negra [E] 90 B2
Lagunas de Villafáfila [E] 82 A6
Lagýna [GR] 128 H4
La Haba [E] 96 B3
Lahane [F] 66 B5
la Haye [F] 28 C5
La Haye-du-Puits [F] 26 D2
Lahdenperä [FIN] 186 F2
La Hermida [E] 82 D3
Laheycourt [F] 44 C4
La Higuera [E] 98 C6
Lahinch [IRL] 2 B5
La Hinojosa [E] 98 B3
Lahishyn [UA] 202 B6
Lahnajärvi [S] 194 B7
Lahnalahti [FIN] 188 D4
Lahnasjävi [FIN] 196 F5
Lahnberg [A] 72 F2
Lahnsattel [A] 62 D5
Lahnstein [D] 30 H6
Laholm [S] 162 B5
Laholuoma [FIN] 186 C5
La Horra [E] 88 G2
Lahoysk [BY] 202 B5
La Hoz de la Vieja [E] 90 E6
Lahr [D] 58 E2
Lähteenkylä [FIN] 176 D2
Lahti [FIN] 176 C4
Lahti / Lahtis [FIN] 178 B2
Lahtis / Lahti [FIN] 178 B2
La Hutte [F] 26 F6
Laibgaliai [LT] 200 G3
Laichingen [D] 60 B3
Laifour, Roches de- [F] 44 C1
L'Aigle [F] 26 G5
La Iglesuela del Cid [E] 98 F2
Laignes [F] 56 F2
Laiguéglia [I] 108 G4
L'Aiguillon [F] 54 B4
Laihela / Laihia [FIN] 186 B3
Laihia / Laihela [FIN] 186 B3
Laikko [FIN] 188 F6
Laïliás [GR] 130 C2
Laimbach [A] 62 D4
Laimoluokta [S] 192 G4
Lainate [I] 70 G4
Lainbach [A] 62 C6
Lainijaur [S] 190 G4
Lainio [S] 192 H5
Lairg [GB] 6 E3
Laisbäck [S] 190 F4
La Isla [E] 82 C2
Laissac [F] 68 B6
Laïsta [GR] 132 D1
Laisvall [S] 190 F2
Laitikkala [FIN] 176 G2
Laitila [FIN] 176 D3
Laitineva [FIN] 196 D4
Laize-la-Ville [F] 26 F4
la-Jaille-Yvon [F] 40 H5
La Jana [E] 92 B6
Lajares [E] 100 E6
La Javie [F] 108 D3
Lajes [P] 100 D3
Lajes das Flores [P] 100 B4
Lajes do Pico [P] 100 C3
Lajkovac [SRB] 146 A1
La Jonchère-St-Maurice [F] 54 G6
la Jonquera [E] 92 G2
Lajoskomárom [H] 76 B3
Lajosmizse [H] 76 D2
Lak [H] 64 F4
Łaka [PL] 50 F4
Lakaluoma [FIN] 186 D3
Lakaniemi [FIN] 186 D2
Łaka Prudnicka [PL] 50 D3
Lakatnik [BG] 146 F4
Lakaträsk [S] 194 A8
Lakavica [MK] 128 G2
Lakfors [N] 190 D3
Lakhdenpokh'ya [RUS] 188 G6
Laki [MK] 128 G1
Lakitelek [H] 76 E3
Lákka [GR] 132 B3
Lakkí [GR] 154 A2
Lákkoi [GR] 140 C4
Lákkoma [GR] 130 G4
Lakkópetra [GR] 132 E6
Lakócsa [H] 74 H5
Lakolk [DK] 156 A3
Lakselv [N] 194 C3
Laktaši [BIH] 142 C2
La Lantejuela [E] 102 B2
Lalapaşa [TR] 150 B1
Lálas [GR] 136 C2
l'Albagés [E] 90 H5
L'Albi [E] 92 B4
l'Alcora / Alcora [E] 98 F3
L'Alcúdia [E] 98 E5
L'Alcúdia (Ilice) [E] 104 D2
L'Alcúdia de Crespins [E] 98 E6
L'Aldea [E] 92 B5
l'Alguenya [E] 104 D2
La Lima [I] 110 E4
Lalín [E] 78 C4
Lalinde [F] 66 F4
La Línea de la Concepción [E] 100 H5
Lalkovo [BG] 150 B1
Lalm [AL] 128 B3
Lalm [N] 180 G6
La Loupe [F] 26 H6
Lalouvesc [F] 68 F4
La Louvière [B] 28 H4
L'Alpe-d'Huez [F] 70 A5
Lalueza [E] 90 F3
La Luisiana [E] 102 B2
Lam [D] 48 D6
La Machine [F] 56 D4
La Maddalena [I] 118 E2
Lama dei Peligni [I] 116 D5
La Magdalena [E] 78 G5
La Malène [F] 68 C6
Lamalou-les-Bains [F] 106 D4
La Manche, Tunnel sous-/ Channel Tunnel [F/GB] 14 G5
La Manga del Mar Menor [E] 104 D4
Lamarche [F] 58 B2
Lamargelle [F] 56 G3
La Marina [E] 104 D3
Lamarosa [P] 86 C5
Lamarque [F] 66 C2
Lamas do Vouga [P] 80 B5
Lamastre [F] 68 F5
La Mata [E] 104 D3
La Matanza [E] 82 B5
La Maucarrière [F] 54 E3
Lambach [A] 62 B4
Lamballe [F] 26 B4
Lambesc [F] 106 H4
Lamborn [S] 174 C3
Lambrecht [D] 46 B5
Lamego [P] 80 D4
la-Melleraye-de-Bretagne [F] 40 F5
L'Ametlla de Mar [E] 92 B5
Lamezia Terme [I] 124 D5
Lamía [GR] 132 G4
Lammhult [S] 162 D4
Lammi [FIN] 176 H2
Lammi [FIN] 186 D1
Lamminkylä [FIN] 188 G3
Lamminkylä [FIN] 196 F4
Lamminkyulya [RUS] 188 F6
Lamminmaa [FIN] 186 C4
La Molina [E] 92 E2
La Mongie [F] 84 F4
La Mota [E] 102 D3
La Mothe-Achard [F] 54 B3
La-Mothe-St-Héray [F] 54 D4
Lamotte-Beuvron [F] 56 B2
La Motte-Chalancon [F] 108 B2
la Motte-du-Caire [F] 108 C2
Lamouroux, Grottes de- [F] 66 G3
Lampaanjärvi [FIN] 186 H1
Lampaul [F] 40 A1
Lampaul-Plouarzel [F] 40 A1
Lampedusa [I] 126 A6
Lámpeia [GR] 136 C1
Lampeland [N] 164 G1
Lamperila [FIN] 188 C2
Lampeter [GB] 10 B6
Lampinsaari [FIN] 196 D5

L'Ampolla [E] 92 B5
Lamporecchio [I] 110 E5
Lampi [FIN] 176 C1
Lamprechtshausen [A] 60 G5
Lamprechtsofenloch [A] 60 G6
Lämsänkylä [FIN] 196 F2
Lamsfeld [D] 34 F4
Lamstedt [D] 18 E4
La Mudarra [E] 88 E1
La Muela [E] 90 E4
La Mure [F] 68 H5
Lamure-sur-Azergues [F] 68 F2
La Murta [E] 98 E5
Lana [I] 72 C3
Lanaja [E] 90 F4
La Napoule-Plage [F] 108 E5
Lanark [GB] 8 D4
La Nava [E] 94 F4
La Nava de Ricomalillo [E] 96 D1
La Nava de Santiago [E] 86 G6
Lancaster [GB] 10 D2
Lanciano [I] 116 E5
Łańcut [PL] 52 E3
Landau [D] 46 B5
Landau [D] 60 G3
Landeck [A] 72 C1
Landedo [P] 80 F3
Landendorf [A] 62 F3
Landepéreuse [F] 26 G4
Landerneau [F] 40 B2
Landersfjorden [N] 194 D2
Landeryd [S] 162 B4
Landesbergen [D] 32 E1
Landete [E] 98 D3
Landévennec [F] 40 B2
Landivisiau [F] 40 C2
Landivy [F] 26 D5
Landkirchen [D] 18 H2
Landön [S] 182 G1
Landquart [CH] 58 H6
Landrecies [F] 28 G4
Landsberg [D] 34 C5
Landsberg [D] 60 D4
Landsbro [S] 162 E3
Landshut [D] 60 F3
Landshut, Ruine- [D] 44 G2
Landskrona [S] 156 H2
Landštejn [CZ] 62 D2
Landstuhl [D] 44 H3
Landudec [F] 40 B3
Landvetter [S] 160 H2
Lane [N] 170 C1
Lanersbach [A] 72 E1
Lanesborough [IRL] 2 D5
La Neuve-Lyre [F] 26 H5
La Neuveville [CH] 58 D5
Langa [DK] 160 D5
Långå [S] 182 F4
Langa de Duero [E] 88 H2
Långåminne [FIN] 186 B3
Langangen [N] 164 G3
Langballig [D] 156 C5
Långban [S] 166 G1
Långbo [S] 174 D2
Langdal [N] 180 E4
Langeac [F] 68 D4
Langeais [F] 54 F2
Langehauk [N] 170 F3
Langeid [N] 164 D3
Långe Jan [S] 158 G1
Längelmäki [FIN] 186 F6
Langelsheim [D] 32 G3
Långemåla [S] 162 G4
Langen [A] 72 B1
Langen [D] 18 D4
Langen [D] 46 C3
Langenargen [D] 58 H4
Långenäs [S] 166 E1
Langenau [D] 60 B3
Langenburg [D] 46 E5
Langenes [N] 192 D3
Längenfeld [A] 72 C2
Langenfeld [D] 30 G4
Langenhahn [D] 46 B1
Langenhorn [D] 156 B5
Langenisarhofen [D] 60 G3
Langenlois [A] 62 E4
Langennaundorf [D] 34 E5
Langenorla [D] 46 H1
Langenselbold [D] 46 D3
Langenthal [CH] 58 E5
Langenwang [A] 62 E6
Langenzenn [D] 46 F5
Langeoog [D] 18 B3
Langeskov [DK] 156 E3
Langesø [DK] 156 D3
Langesund [N] 164 G3
Langevåg [N] 164 A1
Langevåg [N] 180 C3
Langewiese [D] 32 D5
Langfjord [N] 192 H1
Langfjordnes [N] 194 D1
Långflon [S] 172 E3
Langhammars [S] 168 H3
Langhirano [I] 110 D3
Langholm [GB] 8 E5
Långjöby [S] 190 F4
Långlöt [S] 162 G5
Långnäs [FIN] 176 B5
Langnau im Emmental [CH] 58 E6
Langø [DK] 156 E5
Langogne [F] 68 D5
Langoiran [F] 66 D3
Langon [F] 66 D4
Langquaid [D] 60 F2
Langraiz Oka / Nanclares de la Oca [E] 82 G5
Langreo / Langréu [E] 78 H4
Langres [F] 56 H2
Langréu / Langreo [E] 78 H4
Långron [S] 184 H1
Långsel [S] 194 A8
Långsele [S] 184 E2
Långsele [S] 190 F5
Långserud [S] 166 D3
Långshyttan [S] 174 D5
Langstrand [N] 194 B2
Långträsk [S] 190 H4
Långträsk [S] 196 A3
Languidou, Chapelle de- [F] 40 B3
Langula [D] 32 G5
Långvattnet [S] 190 H4
Langviken [S] 196 A4
Långviksmon [S] 184 G1
Långvind [S] 174 E2
Langwarden [D] 18 D4
Langwedel [D] 18 E6
Langweid [D] 60 D3
Langweiler [D] 44 H3
Langwies [CH] 70 H1
Lanhelas [P] 78 A5
Lanjarón [E] 102 E5
Lankas [LV] 198 B5
Lankila [FIN] 178 D3
Länkipohja [FIN] 186 F6
Lankojärvi [FIN] 194 C7
Lankoori [FIN] 176 C2
Lankosi [FIN] 186 B6
Lanleff, Temple de- [F] 26 A3
Lanmeur [F] 40 C1
Lanna [S] 162 C3
Länna [S] 168 C3
Lannabruk [S] 166 G3
Lannavaara [S] 192 H4
Lannemezan [F] 84 F4
Lannevesi [FIN] 186 F3
Lannilis [F] 40 B1
Lannion [F] 40 D1
Lanobre [F] 68 B3
La Noguera [E] 98 D1
Lanouaille [F] 66 G2
Lansån [S] 194 B8
Lansikylä [FIN] 186 D3
Lansjärv [S] 194 A8
Lanškroun [CZ] 50 C4
Lanslebourg-Mont-Cenis [F] 70 C5
Lanšperk [CZ] 50 B4
Lantosque [F] 108 F4
Lanusei [I] 118 E5
Lanvollon [F] 26 A4
Lánycsók [H] 76 B5
Lanzá [E] 78 C2
Lanzendorf [A] 62 F5
Lanžhot [CZ] 62 G3
Lanzo d'Intelvi [I] 70 G3
Lanzo Torinese [I] 70 D5
Lao [EST] 198 D3
Laodikeia [TR] 152 G5
La Oliva [E] 84 B5
La Oliva [E] 100 E6
Laon [F] 28 G6
La Orotava [E] 100 B5
La Paca [E] 104 B3
La Pacaudière [F] 68 E1
Lápafő [H] 76 A4
Lapalisse [F] 56 D6
La Pallice [F] 54 B4
La Palma [E] 104 C4
La Palma del Condado [E] 94 F6
Lapalme [F] 106 D5
La Palud-sur-Verdon [F] 108 D4
la Panouse [F] 68 D5
Łapanów [PL] 52 B4
Lápas [GR] 132 E6
La Pelechaneta / Pelejaneta [E] 98 F3
La Peraleja [E] 98 B1
la Péruse [F] 54 E6
La Petite-Pierre [F] 44 G5
Lapeyrade [F] 66 D5
Lapinjärvi / Lappträsk [FIN] 178 B3
Lapinlahti [FIN] 188 C1
Lapinsaari [FIN] 186 C3
Lapistó [H] 76 E3
Lápithos (Lâpta) [CY] 154 F5
La Plagne [F] 70 B4
la Plaine-Sur-Mer [F] 40 E6
La Plaza / Teverga [E] 78 G4
Laplume [F] 66 E5
la Pobla de Lillet [E] 92 E2
La Pobla de Massaluca [E] 90 G6
la Pobla de Segur [E] 92 C1
la Pobla de Vallbona [E] 98 E4
La Pobla Llarga [E] 98 E6
la Pobla Tornesa [E] 98 G3
La Pola de Gordón [E] 78 H5
La Portera [E] 98 D4
Lapoutroie [F] 58 D2
Lapovo [SRB] 146 C2
Lappach / Lappago [I] 72 E2
Lappago / Lappach [I] 72 E2
Lappajärvi [FIN] 186 D2
Lappäjärvi [FIN] 194 B5
Läppe [S] 168 B3
Lappeenranta / Villmanstrand [FIN] 178 E2
Lappfjärd / Lapväärtti [FIN] 186 B5
Lappfors [FIN] 186 C1
Lappi [FIN] 176 D3
Lappo [FIN] 176 C5
Lappo / Lapua [FIN] 186 C2
Lappohja / Lappvik [FIN] 176 F6
Lappträsk [S] 196 C2
Lappträsk / Lapinjärvi [FIN] 178 B3
Lappvattnet [S] 196 A5
Lappvik / Lappohja [FIN] 176 F6
la Primaude [F] 68 B6
Lapseki [TR] 150 B5
Lâpta (Lápithos) [CY] 154 F5
Laptevo [RUS] 198 H5
Lapua / Lappo [FIN] 186 C2
La Puebla de Almoradiel [E] 96 G3
La Puebla de Castro [E] 90 H3
La Puebla de Cazalla [E] 102 A3
La Puebla de Híjar [E] 90 F5
La Puebla de los Infantes [E] 96 B6
La Puebla del Río [E] 94 G6
La Puebla de Montalbán [E] 96 E1
La Puebla de Valdavia [E] 82 D4
La Puebla de Valverde [E] 98 E2
La Pueblanueva [E] 96 E1
La Puerta del Segura [E] 102 G1
La Punt [CH] 72 A3
Lapušnik [MNE] 146 C5
Lapväärtti / Lappfjärd [FIN] 186 B5
Łapy [PL] 24 E6
Laqueuille [F] 68 C2
L'Aquila [I] 116 C4
La Rábita [E] 102 E5
Laracha [E] 78 C2
Laragh [IRL] 4 G3
Laragne-Montéglin [F] 108 C2
La Rambla [E] 102 C2
l'Arbre [F] 54 E6
L'Arbresle [F] 68 F2
Lärbro [S] 168 G4
Larceveau-Arros-Cibits [F] 84 C3
Larche [F] 66 G3
Larche [F] 108 E2
Lårdal [N] 164 E2
Lardaro [I] 72 C4
Larderello [I] 114 F1
Lardero [E] 82 G6
Lárdos [GR] 154 D4
Lardosa [P] 86 F3
Laredo [E] 82 F3
La Réole [F] 66 D4
La Restinga [E] 100 A5
Largentière [F] 68 E6
L'Argentière-la-Bessée [F] 70 B6
Largs [GB] 8 C3
La Rhune [E] 84 B2
Lariano [I] 116 B6
La Rinconada [E] 94 G6
Larino [I] 116 F6
Larionovo [RUS] 178 G2
Lárisa [GR] 132 G2
Larissa [TR] 152 C3
Larkollen [N] 166 B3
L'Armelliere [F] 106 G4
Larmor [F] 40 C4
Lárnaka [CY] 154 G5
Larne [NIR] 2 G3
La Robla [E] 78 H5
La Roca de la Sierra [E] 86 G6
la Roca del Vallès [E] 92 E4
la Roche [CH] 70 D1
La Roche-Bernard [F] 40 E5
La Roche-Chalais [F] 66 E2
la Roche-de-Rame [F] 70 B6
La Roche-Derrien [F] 26 A3
La Roche-en-Ardenne [B] 30 E6
La Rochefoucauld [F] 54 E6
La Rochelle [F] 54 C4
La Roche-Posay [F] 54 F3
La Roche-sur-Foron [F] 70 B2
La Roche-sur-Yon [F] 54 B3
La Rochette [F] 70 A4
Larochette [L] 44 F2
La Roda [E] 98 B4
La Roda de Andalucía [E] 102 B3
Laroquebrou [F] 68 A4
La Roquebrussanne [F] 108 C5
Laroque-des-Arcs [F] 66 G5
Laroque-d'Olmes [F] 106 A5
La Roque-Gageac [F] 66 G4
La Rösa [CH] 72 B3
La Rouche-Courbon [F] 54 C5
Larraga [E] 84 B4
Larrau [F] 84 D3
Larret [F] 58 A3
Larroque [F] 106 B2
Larsmo / Luoto [FIN] 196 C6
Larsnes [N] 180 C4
l'Artigue [F] 84 H5
La Rubia [E] 90 B2
Laruns [F] 84 D4
Larvik [N] 164 G3
Lárymna [GR] 134 B5
La Salceda [E] 88 F4
la Salles-les Alpes [F] 70 B6
La Salvetat [F] 66 H6
La Salvetat-sur-Agout [F] 106 C3
Läsänkoski [FIN] 188 C5
Las Anorias [E] 98 C6
Lasarte-Oria [E] 84 B2
La Sauceda [E] 100 G4
Las Bárdenas Reales [E] 84 B6
Las Batuecas [E] 88 B4
Låsby [DK] 160 D6
Las Cabezas de San Juan [E] 100 G3
Las Caldas de Besaya [E] 82 E3
Lascaux, Grotte de- [F] 66 G3
la Selve [F] 106 C2
la Sénia [E] 92 A6
Lasenice [CZ] 62 C2
La Señuela [E] 100 G2
La Serna Del Monte [E] 88 G4
la Seu d'Urgell [E] 92 D1
La Seyne [F] 108 C6
Las Fuentes [E] 98 C5
Las Huelgas [E] 82 E6
Łasin [PL] 22 E5
Łask [PL] 36 G5
Łaskarzew [PL] 38 C4
Laski [PL] 22 B3
Laski [PL] 36 E6
Łasko [PL] 20 H6
Laško [SLO] 74 D5
Laskowa [PL] 52 B4
Laskowice [PL] 22 D5
Laskowice [PL] 50 D3
Laslovo [HR] 142 E1
Las Marías [E] 102 F5
Las Médulas [E] 78 E5
Las Mesas [E] 96 H3
Las Navas de la Concepción [E] 96 B6
Las Navas del Marqués [E] 88 E5
Las Negras [E] 102 H5
La Solana [E] 96 G4
La Souche [F] 68 E6
La Souterraine [F] 54 G5
Lasovo [SRB] 146 D2
Las Palas [E] 104 C4
Las Palmas de Gran Canaria [E] 100 C6
Las Pedroñeras [E] 96 H3
La Spézia [I] 110 C4
Las Rozas [E] 88 F5
Lassan [D] 20 E3
Lassay [F] 26 E5
Lassemoen [N] 190 D4
Lassigny [F] 28 E6
Lastein [N] 164 B2
La Sterza [I] 110 E6
Las Torcas [E] 98 C2
Las Torres de Cotillas [E] 104 C3
Lastovo [HR] 144 A3
Lastra a Signa [I] 110 E5
Lastras de Cuéllar [E] 88 F3
Lastres [E] 82 C2
Låstringe [S] 168 D4
Lastrup [D] 18 C6
Lastuk [FIN] 188 D1
Lastulahti [FIN] 188 D1
Lastva [BIH] 144 D4
La Suze-sur-Sarthe [F] 42 B5
Lašva [BIH] 142 D4
Las Veguillas [E] 88 C3
Las Ventas con Peña Aguilera [E] 96 E2
Las Ventas de S. Julián [E] 88 C6
Łaszczów [PL] 52 G2
Łaszki [PL] 52 F3
la Tannière [F] 26 D5
Låtefossen [N] 170 C5
Latera [I] 114 G3
Laterza [I] 122 D4
Lathen [D] 16 H3
La Thuile [I] 70 C4
Latiano [I] 122 F4
Latikberg [S] 190 F5
Latina [I] 120 B1
Latinac [SRB] 146 D3
Latisana [I] 72 G5
Látky [SK] 64 D3
Lató [GR] 140 F5
Latorpsbruk [S] 166 H3
La Torre [E] 98 D4
la Torre Baixa [E] 98 D2
La Torre de Esteban Hambrán [E] 88 E6
La Torresaviñán [E] 90 A5
La Tour-du-Pin [F] 68 G3
La Tranche-sur-Mer [F] 54 B4
Latresne [F] 66 D3
La Trimouille [F] 54 G4
La Trinité [F] 40 D5
La Trinité-Porhoët [F] 26 B5
Latronico [I] 120 H5
Latronquière [F] 66 H4
Latte, Fort la- [F] 26 B4
Latteluokta [S] 192 G4
Lattuna [FIN] 194 E6
La Turbie [F] 108 F4
Latva [FIN] 196 D5
Latvalampi [FIN] 188 E3
Laubrières [F] 40 G5
Laucha [D] 34 B5
Lauchdorf [D] 60 C4
Lauchhammer [D] 34 E5
Laudal [N] 164 D5
Lauder [GB] 8 F4
Laudio / Llodio [E] 82 G4
Laudona [LV] 198 F5
Lauenau [D] 32 F2
Lauenbrück [D] 18 E5
Lauenburg [D] 18 G5
Lauenstein [D] 48 E2
Lauf [D] 46 G5
Laufen [CH] 58 D4
Laufen [D] 60 G5
Laufenburg [CH] 58 F4
Laufenburg (Baden) [D] 58 F4
Lauffen [D] 46 D6
Laugnac [F] 66 E5
Laugratte [F] 66 E4
Lauingen [D] 60 C3
Laujar de Andarax [E] 102 F5
Laukaa [FIN] 186 G4
Laukeland [N] 170 B1
Laukka [FIN] 196 D4
Laukkala [FIN] 186 G1
Lauksundskaret [N] 192 G1
Laukuluspa [S] 192 G5
Laukuva [LT] 200 E4
Laukvik [N] 192 F1
Laukvik [N] 194 B3
Laukvika [N] 192 D5
Launceston [GB] 12 D4
La Unión [E] 104 C4
Laupen [CH] 58 D6
Laupheim [D] 60 B4
Lauragh [IRL] 4 B5
Laureana di Borrello [I] 124 D6
Laurencetown [IRL] 2 D5
Laurenzana [I] 120 H4
Lauria [I] 120 H5
Laurière [F] 54 G6
Laurino [I] 120 G4
Lausanne [CH] 70 C1
Laussig [D] 34 D5
Lautaporras [FIN] 176 F3
Lautemburg [D] 30 F4
Lauter [S] 168 H3
Lauterbach [D] 46 E1
Lauterbourg [F] 46 B6
Lauterbrunnen [CH] 70 E1
Lautere [LV] 198 F5
Lauterecken [D] 44 H3
Lauterhofen [D] 46 H5
Lautrec [F] 106 B3
Lauvåsen [N] 182 B2
Lauvsjølia [N] 190 D5
Lauvsnes [N] 190 C5
Lauvstad [N] 180 C4
Lauvuskylä [FIN] 196 G5
Lauvvik [N] 164 B3
Lauwersoog [NL] 16 G1
Lauzerte [F] 66 F5
Lauzun [F] 66 E4
La Vácherie [F] 68 G5
Lavagna [I] 110 B3
Laval [F] 26 E6
la Vall d'Uixó [E] 98 F4
La Vallivana [E] 98 G2
Lavamünd [A] 74 C3
Lavangnes [N] 192 E3
Lávara [GR] 130 H2
Lavardac [F] 66 E5
Lavardin [F] 42 C6
Lavardin [F] 42 C6
Lavarone [I] 72 D5
Lavaur [F] 106 B3
La Vecilla [E] 82 B3
Lavelanet [F] 106 A5
Lavello [I] 120 H3
Lavelsloh [D] 32 E2
La Venta [E] 102 F4
La Verna [I] 110 G6
la Veurdre [F] 56 D4
Lavia [FIN] 176 E1
Laviano [I] 120 G3
Lavik [N] 170 B2
la Vila Joiosa / Villajoyosa [E] 104 E2
la Villa / Stern [I] 72 E3
Lavinio-Lido di Enea [I] 120 A1
La Virgen del Camino [E] 78 H5
Lavis [I] 72 C4
Lavit [F] 66 F6
Lavong [N] 190 D2
Lavos [P] 86 C2
La Voulte-sur-Rhône [F] 68 F5
Lavoûte-Chilhac [F] 68 D4
Lavoûte-Polignac, Château de- [F] 68 D4
Lavoûte-sur-Loire [F] 68 D4
Lavoye [F] 44 D4
Lavra [E] 80 B3
Lavre [P] 86 C6
Lávrio [GR] 136 H1
Lavry [RUS] 198 G4
Lavsjö [S] 190 F5
La Wantzenau [F] 44 H6
Ławszowa [PL] 34 H5
Laxå [S] 166 G4
Laxe [E] 78 B2
Laxne [S] 168 C3
Laxsjö [S] 190 E6
Laxsjön [S] 184 E3
Laxtjärn [S] 172 G5
Laxviken [S] 190 E6
La Yedra [E] 102 F2
La Yesa [E] 98 E3
Läyliäinen [FIN] 176 G4
La Yunta [E] 90 C5
Laza [E] 78 D6
Lazarevac [SRB] 146 B1
Lazarevac [SRB] 204 B6
Lazarevo [SRB] 142 G1
Lazdijai [LT] 24 F2
Laze [SLO] 74 C4
Lázi [H] 76 A1
Laži [LV] 198 C4
Laziale [I] 116 B5
Lazise [I] 72 C6
Łaziska Górne [PL] 50 F3
Lazisko [SK] 64 D2
Lazkao [E] 84 A3
Lázně Bělohrad [CZ] 50 A3
Lázně Kynžvart [CZ] 48 C4
Laz Stubički [HR] 74 E5
La Zubia [E] 102 E4
Łazy [PL] 22 A2
Leacanabuaile Stone Fort [IRL] 4 A4
Leamington Spa [GB] 14 D2
Leap [IRL] 4 B5
Leatherhead [GB] 14 E4
Łeba [PL] 22 C1
Lebach [D] 44 G3
Le Ballon [F] 26 D6
Lebane [SRB] 146 D4
Lebanza [E] 82 D3
Le Bar [F] 108 E4
Le Barp [F] 66 C4
Le Beausset [F] 108 C5
Lebedin [UA] 202 F7
Lébényiniklós [H] 62 H6
Lebesby [N] 194 D2
Le Biot [F] 70 C2
Le Blanc [F] 54 G4
Łebno [PL] 22 D2
Le Boréon [F] 108 F3
Łebork [PL] 22 C2
Le Boulou [F] 92 G1
Le Bourg d'Oisans [F] 68 H5
Le Bourget [F] 68 H3
le Bousquet-d'Orb [F] 106 D3
Le Bouveret [CH] 70 C2
Lebrija [E] 100 G3
Lebring [A] 74 D3
Le Bugue [F] 66 F3
Lebus [D] 34 G2
Lebyazh'e [RUS] 178 G5
Le Calanche [F] 114 A4
le Caloy [F] 66 C6
Le Cap-d'Agde [F] 106 E5
Le Cateau-Cambrésis [F] 28 G4
Le Catelet [F] 28 F5
Le Caylar [F] 106 E3
Lecce [I] 122 G4
Lecco [I] 70 G4
Lécera [E] 90 E5
Lech [A] 72 B1
Lechainá [GR] 136 B1
L'Echalp [F] 70 C6
le Chambon-sur-Lignon [F] 68 E4
Le Chateau-d'Oléron [F] 54 B5
Le Châtelard [F] 70 A3
Le Châtelet [F] 56 B4
Le Chesne [F] 44 C2
Le Cheylard [F] 68 E5
Lechlade on Thames [GB] 12 H3
Lechmühlen [D] 60 D4
Lechovice [CZ] 62 F2
Léchovo [GR] 128 E5
Lēči [LV] 198 B5
Leciñena [E] 90 F3
Leck [D] 156 B4
Le Conquet [F] 40 A2
Le Coteau [F] 68 E2
Le Creusot [F] 56 F5
Le Croisic [F] 40 D6
Le Crotoy [F] 28 D3
Lectoure [F] 66 E6
Łęczna [PL] 38 E5
Łęczyca [PL] 20 G5
Łęczyca [PL] 36 G3
Ledal [N] 180 G1
Ledaña [E] 98 C4
Ledbury [GB] 12 G2
Ledeč nad Sázavou [CZ] 48 H5
Ledena Pećina [MNE] 144 E2
Ledenika Peštera [BG] 146 F3
Ledesma [E] 80 G6
Ledge [D] 20 B6
Lédignan [F] 106 F3
Ledigos [E] 82 C5
Leding [S] 184 G1
Ledmozero [RUS] 196 H4
Lednica [SK] 50 E6
Lednica [SK] 50 E6
Lednice [CZ] 62 G3
Le Donjon [F] 56 E6
Le Dorat [F] 54 F5
Ledreborg [DK] 156 G3
Lędyczek [PL] 22 B5
Leeds [GB] 10 F3
Leek [GB] 10 E5
Leek [NL] 16 G2
Leenane [IRL] 2 B4
Leens [NL] 16 G2
Leer [D] 18 B4
Leerdam [NL] 16 D5
Leese [D] 32 E1
Leesi [EST] 198 E1
Leeuwarden [NL] 16 F2
Le Faou [F] 40 B2
Le Faouët [F] 40 C3
le Fayet [F] 70 C3
Lefka [BG] 150 A1
Léfka (Lefke) [CY] 154 F5
Lefkáda [GR] 132 D4
Lefkádia [GR] 128 F4
Lefkadíti [GR] 132 G5
Lefke (Léfka) [CY] 154 F5
Léfkes [GR] 138 E3
Lefkími [GR] 132 B3
Lefkógeia [GR] 130 C2
Lefkónikon (Geçitkale) [CY] 154 G5
Lefkoşa (Lefkosía) [CY] 154 G5
Lefkosía (Lefkoşa) [CY] 154 G5
Léfktra [GR] 134 A5
le Folgoet [F] 40 B1
Le Folgoët [F] 40 B1
Le Fossat [F] 84 H4
Le Freney [F] 70 B5
le Fuilet [F] 54 C1
Leganés [E] 88 F6
Le-Gault-St-Denis [F] 42 E5
Legbąd [PL] 22 D4
Legden [D] 16 H5
Legé [F] 54 B2
Legionowo [PL] 38 B2
Léglise [B] 44 E2
Legnago [I] 110 F1
Legnano [I] 70 F4
Legnica [PL] 36 B6
Legnickie Pole [PL] 36 B6
Legoland [DK] 156 B2
le Gouray [F] 26 B5
Łęgowo [PL] 22 E3
Legrad [HR] 74 G4
Le Grand-Bourg [F] 54 G6
Le Grand-Lucé [F] 42 C5
Le Grand-Pressigny [F] 54 F3
Le Grau-du-Roi [F] 106 F4
Legrená [GR] 136 H2
le Gressier [F] 66 B3
Leguatiano [E] 82 G4
Léguevin [F] 84 H3
Łęg Wygoda [PL] 52 C3
Le Havre [F] 26 G3
Lehelitz [D] 34 C5
Le-Hérie-La Vieville [F] 28 G5
Lehmäjoki [FIN] 186 C2
Lehmen [D] 30 H6
Lehmo [FIN] 188 F2
Lehnice [SK] 62 H5
Lehnin [D] 34 D3
Le Hohwald [F] 44 G6
Le Houga [F] 66 C6
Lehrberg [D] 46 F5
Lehre [D] 32 H2
Lehrte [D] 32 G2
Lehtimäki [FIN] 186 D3
Lehtmetsa [EST] 198 E1
Lehtola [FIN] 194 E7
Lehtomäki [FIN] 196 F5
Lehtovaara [FIN] 188 H2
Lehtovaara [FIN] 196 F5
Leianokládi [GR] 132 G4
Leibnitz [A] 74 D3
Leicester [GB] 10 F6
Leiden [NL] 16 D4
Leie [EST] 198 E3
Leiferde [D] 32 G2
Leighlinbridge [IRL] 4 F4
Leighton Buzzard [GB] 14 E3
Leikanger [N] 170 D2
Leikanger [N] 180 B4
Leinefelde [D] 32 G5
Leinelä [FIN] 176 H2
Leinesodden [N] 190 D2
Leini [I] 70 D5
Leipalingis [LT] 24 F3
Leipämäki [FIN] 188 E4
Leipheim [D] 60 C3
Leipojärvi [S] 192 H6
Leipsoí [GR] 138 H2
Leipzig [D] 34 C5
Leira [N] 170 G3
Leira [N] 180 F1
Leira [N] 190 D2
Leirbotn [N] 194 B3
Leirfall [N] 182 C1
Leirgulen [N] 180 B5
Leiria [P] 86 C3
Leiro [E] 78 C4
Leirosa [P] 86 C2
Leirpollskogen [N] 194 D2
Leirvik [FR] 160 B1
Leirvik [N] 170 B1
Leirvik [N] 170 B5
Leirvik [N] 192 F4
Leirvika [N] 190 D2
Leisi [EST] 198 C3
Leisnig [D] 34 D6
Leissigen [CH] 70 E1
Leitir Mealláin / Lettermullan [IRL] 2 B5
Leitzkau [D] 34 C3
Leivadia [CY] 154 G5
Leivadítis [GR] 130 E2
Leivonmäki [FIN] 186 G5
Lejasciems [LV] 198 F4
Lekáni [GR] 130 D2
Łękawa [PL] 36 G6
Lekeitio / Lequeitio [E] 82 H4
Lekenik [HR] 74 E6
Lekeryd [S] 162 D2
Lekhchevo [BG] 146 F3
Łęki Górne [PL] 52 C4
Leknes [N] 180 D4
Leknes [N] 192 C4
Łeknica [PL] 34 G5
Leksand [S] 172 H4
Leksberg [S] 166 F5
Leksvik [N] 190 B6
Lekunberri [E] 84 B3
Lekvattnet [S] 172 E5
Leland [N] 190 D2
Le Lauzet-Ubaye [F] 108 D2
Le Lavandou [F] 108 D6
L'Elefante [I] 118 C2
Lelice [PL] 36 H1
Le Liège [F] 54 G2
Le Lion-D'Angers [F] 40 H6
Lelkowo [PL] 22 G2
Lelle [EST] 198 E2
Le Locle [CH] 58 C5
Le Logis-du-Pin [F] 108 D4
Le Loroux-Bottereau [F] 54 C1
Le Louroux [F] 40 G6
Lelów [PL] 50 H2
Le Luc [F] 108 D5
Le Lude [F] 42 B6
Lelystad [NL] 16 E4
Lem [DK] 156 B1
Le Mans [F] 42 B5
Le Markstein [F] 58 D3
Le Mas-d'Azil [F] 84 H4
Le Mayet [F] 68 D1
Lembach [F] 44 H5
Lembeck [D] 16 G6
Lembeye [F] 84 E3
Lemele [NL] 16 G4
Le Merlerault [F] 26 G5
Le-Mesnil-Vigot [F] 26 D3
Lemesos (Limassol) [CY] 154 F6
Lemetinvaara [FIN] 196 F5
Lemförde [D] 32 D1
Lemgo [D] 32 E3
Lemi [FIN] 178 D2
Lemke [D] 32 F1
Lemland [FIN] 176 B6
Lemmenjoki [FIN] 194 D4
Lemmer [NL] 16 F3
Lemnhult [S] 162 E3
Le Monastier [F] 68 E5
Le Monêtier-les-Bains [F] 70 B5
Le Mont-Dore [F] 68 C2
Le Monteix [F] 56 C6
Le Montet [F] 56 D5
Le Mont-St-Michel [F] 26 D4
Le Mont-St-Michel [F] 26 D4
Le Moulin du Pali [F] 108 E4
le Mouret [CH] 58 D6
Lemovzha [RUS] 198 H1
Lempäälä [FIN] 176 F2

Lempdes [F] 68 C3
Lempdes [F] 68 D2
Lempyy [FIN] 188 C3
le Mulins [F] 68 E2
Le Muret [F] 66 C4
Le Muy [F] 108 D5
Lemvig [DK] 160 B5
Lena [N] 172 B4
Lenart V Slovenskih Goricah [SLO] 74 E3
Lencloître [F] 54 E3
Lencouacq [F] 66 C5
Lend [A] 72 G1
Lendava [SLO] 74 F3
Lendery [RUS] 196 H6
Lendinara [I] 110 G2
Lendum [DK] 160 E3
Lenes [N] 180 G1
Le Neubourg [F] 26 H4
Lengefeld [D] 46 H1
Lengerich [D] 32 C1
Lengerich [D] 32 C2
Lenggries [D] 60 E5
Lengnau [CH] 58 F4
Lengyeltóti [H] 74 H3
Lenhovda [S] 162 E4
Leni [I] 124 B5
Lenina [BY] 202 D6
Léning [F] 44 F4
Lenk [CH] 70 D2
Lenna [I] 70 H3
Lennartsfors [S] 166 C3
Lenningen [N] 170 G2
Lenno [I] 70 G3
Leno [I] 72 B6
Lenola [I] 120 C1
Lenora [CZ] 62 B2
Le Nouvion-en-Thiérache [F] 28 G5
Lenovo [BG] 148 B6
Lens [F] 28 F3
Lensahn [D] 18 H2
Lensvik [N] 180 H1
Léntas [GR] 140 E5
Lentföhrden [D] 18 F3
Lenti [H] 74 F3
Lentiira [FIN] 196 G4
Lenting [D] 60 E2
Lentini [I] 126 G4
Lentvaris [LT] 24 H1
Lenungen [S] 166 D2
Lenzburg [CH] 58 F5
Lenzen [D] 20 A6
Lenzerheide [CH] 70 H1
Lenzkirch [D] 58 F3
Leoben [A] 72 H2
Leoben [A] 74 D1
Leogang [A] 60 G6
Leominster [GB] 12 G1
León [E] 78 H5
Léon [F] 66 B5
Leonarisso (Ziyamet) [CY] 154 G4
Leonberg [D] 58 G1
Leonessa [I] 116 B3
Leonessa [I] 120 G2
Leonforte [I] 126 F3
Leonídio [GR] 136 F3
Leontári [GR] 136 D3
Leóntio [GR] 136 E2
Leontýnský Zámek [CZ] 48 E4
Leopoldsburg [B] 30 E3
Leopoldsdorf [A] 62 F4
Leopovina [HR] 74 F5
Le Palais [F] 40 C5
Le Palmyre [F] 54 B6
L'Epau, Abbaye de- [F] 42 B5
Lepe [E] 94 E5
Le-Péage-de-Roussillon [F] 68 F4
Lepenica [SRB] 146 D5
Lepenicë [AL] 128 B6
Lepenoú [GR] 132 E4
Le Perthus [F] 92 G2
Lepetane [MNE] 144 D4
Le Pin-au-Haras [F] 26 G5
l'Epine [F] 44 C4
Lepistönmäki [FIN] 186 D1
le Pleynet [F] 70 A5
Lepoglava [HR] 74 E4
Le Poiré-sur-Vie [F] 54 B3
Le Pont [F] 70 A3
Le Pont-de-Beauvoisin [F] 68 H4
Le Pont-de-Claix [F] 68 H5
le Pont-de-Montvert [F] 68 D6
Le Pontet [F] 66 D2
Leporano [I] 122 E4
Le Porge [F] 66 C3
Le Portel [F] 28 D2
Leposavić [SRB] 146 C4
Le Pouldu [F] 40 C4
Lépoura [GR] 134 C5
Le Pouzin [F] 68 F5
Leppäkoski [FIN] 186 G6
Leppälä [FIN] 178 E2
Leppälahti [FIN] 186 H1
Leppälahti [FIN] 188 F3
Leppämäki [FIN] 188 C3
Leppäselkä [FIN] 186 G2
Leppävesi [FIN] 186 G4
Leppävirta [FIN] 188 D3
Lépreo [GR] 136 C3
Lepsény [H] 76 B2
Leptokaryá [GR] 128 G6
Lëpushë [AL] 146 A5
Le Puy-en-Velay [F] 68 D4
Lequeitio / Lekeitio [E] 82 H4
Leques, Col des- [F] 108 D4
Le Quesnoy [F] 28 G4
Ler [N] 182 B2
Le Rabot [F] 56 B2
Lerbäck [S] 166 H4
Lercara Friddi [I] 126 D3
Lerchenborg [DK] 156 E2
Lerdala [S] 166 F5
Lerga [E] 84 B4
Lerici [I] 110 C4
Lérida / Lleida [E] 90 H4
Lerín [E] 84 A4
Lerma [E] 88 G1
Lerm-et-Musset [F] 66 D5
Lermoos [A] 60 D6
Lérni [GR] 136 E2
Le Rozier [F] 106 E2
Lerresfjord [N] 194 B2
Lerum [S] 160 H2
Le Russey [F] 58 C5
Lerwick [GB] 6 G4
Lés [E] 84 F5
Leş [RO] 76 H2
Lesa [I] 70 F4
Les Abrets [F] 68 H3
Les Adrets [F] 108 E5
Les Aix-d'Angillon [F] 56 C3
Lešak [SRB] 146 B4
Lesaka [E] 84 B3
les Aldudes [F] 84 C3
Les Andelys [F] 28 C6
Les Antiques [F] 106 G4
Les Arcs [F] 70 C4
Les Arcs [F] 108 D5
les Avants [CH] 70 C1
Les Avellanes [E] 92 B2
Les Baux-de-Provence [F] 106 G4
les Borges Blanques [E] 92 B3
Les Bouchoux [F] 70 A2
Les Boulay Lue [F] 44 F4
Les Cabannes [F] 84 H5
L'Escala [E] 92 G3
Les Calanques [F] 106 H5
Lescar [F] 84 E3
L'Escarène [F] 108 F4
Les Cases d'Alcanar [E] 92 A6
Lesce [SLO] 74 B4
Les Contamines-Montjoie [F] 70 C3
les Coves de Vinromà [E] 98 G2
Les Deux-Alpes [F] 70 A5
Les Diablerets [CH] 70 D2
Lesdins [F] 28 F5
Les Echarmeaux [F] 68 F1
Les Echelles [F] 68 H4
Le Sentier [CH] 70 B1
Les Epesses [F] 54 C2
Les Escaldes [AND] 84 H6
Les Essarts [F] 54 C3
Les Eyzies-de-Tayac [F] 66 F3
Les-Fins [F] 58 C5
Les Forges [F] 26 A5
Les Gets [F] 70 C2
Les Halles [F] 68 F3
Les Haudères [CH] 70 D3
Les Hayons [F] 28 C5
Les Herbiers [F] 54 C2
Les Houches [F] 70 C3
Lesichovo [BG] 148 A5
Lésina [I] 116 F6
Les Issambres [F] 108 D5
Lesja [N] 180 G5
Lesjärvi [FIN] 176 F3
Lesjaskog [N] 180 F4
Lesjaverk [N] 180 F4
Lesjöfors [S] 166 F1
Leskelä [FIN] 196 D5
Lesko [PL] 52 E5
Leskovac [SRB] 146 D4
Leskova Dolina [SLO] 74 B6
Leskovik [AL] 128 D6
Leskovo [BG] 148 F1
Les Laumes [F] 56 F3
Les Lecques [F] 108 B5
Les Menuires [F] 70 B4
Lesmont [F] 44 B5
Lésna [PL] 48 H1
Lesneven [F] 40 B1
Lešnica [PL] 50 E3
Lešnica [SRB] 142 F3
Leśniów Wielki [PL] 34 H4
Lesnovo [MK] 128 F1
Lesogorskiy [RUS] 178 F2
Lesparre-Médoc [F] 66 C2
Lesperon [F] 66 B5
Les Pieux [F] 26 D2
Les Planches-en-Montagne [F] 58 B6
les Planes d'Hostoles [E] 92 F3
l'Espluga de Francolí [E] 92 C4
Les Ponts-de-Cé [F] 40 H6
Lesquin [F] 28 F3
Les Riceys [F] 56 F1
Les Rosiers [F] 54 E1
les Rotes [E] 104 F1
Les Rousses [F] 70 B1
Les Sables-d'Olonne [F] 54 B3
Les Saisies [F] 70 B3
Les Salles [F] 68 E2
Lessay [F] 26 D3
Lessebo [S] 162 E5
Lessila [FIN] 176 D1
Lessines [B] 28 G3
Lestards [F] 66 H2
l'Estartit [E] 92 G3
Lestelle Bétharram [F] 84 E4
Les-Thilliers-en-Vexin [F] 28 C6
Lestijärvi [FIN] 196 D6
Les Trois-Epis [F] 58 D2
Les Trois-Moutiers [F] 54 E2
Lesum [D] 18 D5
Lesura [BG] 146 G3
les Useres / Useras [E] 98 F3
Les Vans [F] 68 E6
Leszno [PL] 36 C4
Leszno [PL] 38 B3
Leszno Górne [PL] 36 A5
Létavértes [H] 76 H1
Letchworth [GB] 14 E3
Le Teil [F] 68 F6
Le Teilleul [F] 26 E5
le Temple [F] 66 C3
Letenye [H] 74 F4
Le Thillot [F] 58 C3
Letkés [H] 64 C5
Letku [FIN] 176 F4
Letmathe [D] 32 C4
Letnitsa [BG] 148 B3
Letohrad [CZ] 50 B4
Letoon [TR] 154 F3
Le Touquet-Paris-Plage [F] 28 D3
Le Touvet [F] 68 H4
Letovice [CZ] 50 C5
Le Trayas [F] 108 E5
Le Tremblade [F] 54 B5
Le Tréport [F] 28 C4
Letreros, Cueva de los- [E] 102 H3
Letsbo [S] 184 D6
Letschin [D] 34 G2
Letterfrack [IRL] 2 B4
Letterkenny [IRL] 2 E2
Lettermullan / Leitir Mealláin [IRL] 2 B5
Letur [E] 104 A1
Letychiv [UA] 202 C8
Letzlingen [D] 34 B2
Leu [RO] 146 G1
Leucate [F] 106 D6
Leuchtenburg [D] 46 H1
Leuglay [F] 56 G2
Leuk [CH] 70 D2
Leukerbad [CH] 70 D2
Leun [D] 46 C1
Leuna [D] 34 C5
Leussow [D] 18 H5
Leutasch [A] 60 D6
Leutenberg [D] 46 H2
Leutkirch [D] 60 B5
Leutschach [A] 74 D3
Leuven (Louvain) [B] 30 D4
Leuze [B] 28 G3
Levajok [N] 194 C3
Le Val-André [F] 26 B4
Levan [AL] 128 A4
Levänen [FIN] 178 D1
Levanger [N] 190 C6
Levanto [FIN] 176 H3
Lévanto [I] 110 C4
Levanzo [I] 126 A2
Leväranta [FIN] 194 E7
Levashovo [RUS] 178 H4
Leväsjoki [FIN] 186 B6
Le Vast [F] 26 E2
Le Vaudreuil [F] 28 B6
Levdun [N] 194 B2
Leven [GB] 8 F3
Levens [F] 108 E4
Le Verdon [F] 54 B6
Leverkusen [D] 30 G4
Levern [D] 32 D2
Le Vernet [F] 108 D3
Levet [F] 56 C4
Levice [SK] 64 B4
Levico Terme [I] 72 D5
Levídi [GR] 136 D2
Levie [F] 114 B5
Levier [F] 58 B5
Le Vigan [F] 106 E3
Levoča [SK] 64 E2
Levroux [F] 54 H3
Levski [BG] 148 B3
Levunovo [BG] 130 B2
Lewes [GB] 14 E5
Lewin Brzeski [PL] 50 D2
Leyburn [GB] 10 F2
Leysin [CH] 70 C2
Leżajsk [PL] 52 E3
Ležáky [CZ] 50 B4
Lézardrieux [F] 26 A3
Lézat [F] 70 A1
Lezay [F] 54 E5
Lezhë [AL] 128 B1
Lézignan-Corbières [F] 106 C5
Lezoux [F] 68 D2
Lezuza [E] 98 A5
Lgota [PL] 50 G3
L'gov [RUS] 202 F6
L'hermitage-Lorge [F] 26 A5
L'Hospitalet de l'Infant [E] 92 B5
l'Hospitalet de Llobregat [E] 92 E4
l'Hospitalet-l'Andorre [F] 92 E1
Liapádes [GR] 132 B2
Liatorp [S] 162 D5
Libáň [CZ] 48 H3
Liběchov [CZ] 48 F3
Liberec [CZ] 48 G2
Libiąż [PL] 50 G3
Libochovice [CZ] 48 F3
Libohovë [AL] 132 C1
Libourne [F] 66 D3
Libramont [B] 44 D1
Librazhd [AL] 128 C3
Librilla [E] 104 C3
Libusza [PL] 52 C4
Licata [I] 126 E4
Licciana Nardi [I] 110 D4
Lich [D] 46 C2
Licháda [GR] 132 H4
Lichfield [GB] 10 E6
Lichnice [CZ] 48 H4
Lichtenau [A] 62 D3
Lichtenau [D] 32 E4
Lichtenberg [D] 46 H2
Lichtenberg [F] 44 H5
Lichtenfels [D] 32 E5
Lichtenfels [D] 46 G3
Lichtensteig [CH] 58 G5
Lichtenstein [CH] 70 H1
Lichtenstein [D] 48 C2
Lichtenstein [D] 58 H2
Lichtenvoorde [NL] 16 G5
Lickershamn [S] 168 G4
Lički Osik [HR] 112 G3
Ličko Lešće [HR] 112 G3
Licodia Eubea [I] 126 F4
Licques [F] 14 G6
Lid [S] 166 F1
Lida [BY] 202 A5
Liden [S] 162 E2
Liden [S] 184 E4
Liden [S] 190 F4
Liden [S] 196 A4
Lidhult [S] 162 C5
Lidice [CZ] 48 F3
Lidingö [S] 168 E3
Lidköping [S] 166 E5
Lido degli Estensi [I] 110 H3
Lido delle Nazioni [I] 110 H3
Lido di Camaiore [I] 110 D5
Lido di Castel Fusano [I] 114 H6
Lido di Fermo [I] 116 D2
Lido di Jésolo [I] 72 F6
Lido di Latina [I] 120 B1
Lido di Metaponto [I] 122 D4
Lido di Óstia [I] 114 H6
Lido di Pomposa [I] 110 H3
Lido di Rivoli [I] 120 H1
Lido di Scanzano [I] 122 D5
Lido di Spina [I] 110 H3
Lido di Torre Mileto [I] 116 G5
Lido di Venézia [I] 110 H1
Lidoríki [GR] 132 G5
Lido Silvana [I] 122 F4
Lidsjöberg [S] 190 E5
Lidzbark [PL] 22 G5
Lidzbark Warmiński [PL] 22 H3
Liebegg [CH] 58 F5
Liebenau [A] 62 C3
Liebenau [D] 32 E1
Liebenwalde [D] 34 E1
Lieberose [D] 34 F4
Liebling [RO] 76 G6
Liechtenstein Klamm [A] 72 G1
Liedakkala [FIN] 196 C2
Liedenpohja [FIN] 186 D4
Lieg [D] 44 H1
Liège (Luik) [B] 30 E5
Lieksa [FIN] 196 G6
Lielvārde [LV] 198 E5
Lienz [A] 72 F2
Liepāja [LV] 198 B6
Liepna [LV] 198 G4
Lier [B] 30 D3
Lier [N] 164 H1
Lierbyen [N] 164 H1
Liérganes [E] 82 F3
Liernais [F] 56 F4
Lierville [F] 42 F2
Liesa [E] 84 D6
Liesjärvi [FIN] 186 E4
Lieskau [D] 34 E5
Lieske [D] 34 G5
Liesniemi [FIN] 176 E5
Liesse [F] 28 G6
Liestal [CH] 58 E4
Lieto / Lundo [FIN] 176 E4
Liétor [E] 98 B6
Lieu-Restauré, Abbaye de- [F] 42 G3
Lieurey [F] 26 G4
Lievestuore [FIN] 186 G4
Lievikoski [FIN] 176 D2
Liezen [A] 62 B6
Liezere [LV] 198 F5
Lifford [IRL] 2 F2
Liffré [F] 26 C6
Liggavägen [S] 190 H1
Ligieri [LV] 198 E5
Lignano Pineta [I] 72 G6
Lignano Sabbiadoro [I] 72 G6
Ligneuville [B] 30 F6
Lignières [F] 56 B4
Ligny-en-Barrois [F] 44 D5
Ligourió [GR] 136 F2
Ligueil [F] 54 F3
Ligugé, Abbaye de- [F] 54 E4
Lihjamo [FIN] 186 F4
Lihme [DK] 160 C5
Lihula [EST] 198 D2
Liiansaari [FIN] 178 D1
Liinahamari [RUS] 194 F3
Liitsola [FIN] 176 E2
Liiva [EST] 198 C2
Lijärvi [FIN] 194 D3
Lijeva Rijeka [MNE] 144 E4
Likavský Hrad [SK] 64 C2
Likenäs [S] 172 E4
Likosoúra [GR] 136 D3
Liland [S] 184 F3
Lilaste [LV] 198 D5
Lild Strand [DK] 160 C3
L'Ile-Bouchard [F] 54 F2
L'Ile-Rousse [F] 114 B3
Lilienfeld [A] 62 D5
Liljendal [FIN] 178 B4
Lilla Edet [S] 166 D6
Lillåfors [S] 194 A8
Lillafüred [H] 64 F4
Lillaz [I] 70 D4
Lillbo [S] 174 D1
Lillby [FIN] 186 C1
Lille [DK] 156 G3
Lille [F] 28 F3
Lillebo [N] 182 D6
Lillebonne [F] 26 H3
Lillefjord [N] 194 B2
Lillehammer [N] 172 B2
Lillerød [DK] 156 G2
Lillers [F] 28 E3
Lillesand [N] 164 E5
Lillestrøm [N] 166 C1
Lille Værløse [DK] 156 G2
Lillhaga [S] 172 H1
Lillhärad [S] 168 B2
Lillhärdal [S] 182 G6
Lillholmsjö [S] 182 G1
Lillkågesträsk [S] 196 A4
Lillkyro / Vähäkyro [FIN] 186 B2
Lillo [E] 96 G2
Lillögda [S] 190 G5
Lillpite [S] 196 A3
Lillsele [S] 190 H5
Lillviken [S] 190 F2
Limáni Chersonísou [GR] 140 F4
Limanköy [TR] 150 D1
Limanowa [PL] 52 B5
Limassol (Lemesos) [CY] 154 F6
Limatola [I] 120 E2
Limavady [NIR] 2 F2
Limbaži [LV] 198 E4
Limbourg [B] 30 F5
Limburg [D] 46 B2
Limedsforsen [S] 172 F3
Limenária [GR] 130 E4
Liménas [GR] 134 C4
Liméni [GR] 136 E5
Limerick / Luimneach [IRL] 4 D3
Limhamn [S] 156 H3
Limingo / Liminka [FIN] 196 D4
Liminka / Limingo [FIN] 196 D4
Liminkakylä [FIN] 196 D5
Limín Litochórou [GR] 128 G6
Liminpuro [FIN] 196 E4
Limmared [S] 162 C2
Limna [UA] 52 F6
Limnae [TR] 130 H5
Límnes [GR] 136 F2
Límni [GR] 134 B4
Limniá [GR] 130 D3
Limnítsa [GR] 132 F5
Limoges [F] 66 G1
Limogne-en-Quercy [F] 66 G5
Limone Piemonte [I] 108 F3
Limonest [F] 68 F2
Limone sul Garda [I] 72 C5
Limosano [I] 116 E6
Limours [F] 42 F4
Limoux [F] 106 B5
Lin [AL] 128 D3
Lina älv [S] 192 G6
Linares [E] 102 E1
Linares de Mora [E] 98 F2
Linares de Riofrío [E] 88 B4
Linariá [GR] 134 D3
Lincoln [GB] 10 G5
Lind [DK] 156 B1
Lindärva [S] 166 E5
Lindås [N] 170 B3
Lindås [S] 162 F5
Lindau [D] 34 C3
Lindau [D] 60 B5
Lindaunis [D] 18 F1
Linddalen [S] 166 G4
Linde [DK] 160 B5
Lindefallet [S] 174 E2
Lindefjell [N] 164 C4
Lindelbrunn [D] 46 B5
Lindelse [DK] 156 E4
Linden [BG] 130 C2
Linden [D] 44 H4
Lindenberg [D] 34 E2
Lindenberg [D] 60 B5
Lindenfels [D] 46 C4
Lindenholz [CH] 58 E5
Linderbach [D] 32 H6
Linderhof [D] 60 D6
Lindern [D] 18 C6
Linderöd [S] 158 D2
Lindesberg [S] 166 H2
Lindesnäs [S] 172 G5
Lindkoski [FIN] 178 B3
Lindlia [N] 170 G4
Lindome [S] 160 H2
Líndos [GR] 154 D4
Lindoso [P] 78 B6
Lindow [D] 20 C6
Lindsås [N] 164 E4
Lindum [DK] 160 D5
Lindved [DK] 156 C2
Líně [CZ] 48 D4
Lingbo [S] 174 E3
Linge [N] 180 E4
Lingen [D] 16 H4
Linghed [S] 174 D4
Linghem [S] 168 A5
Linguaglossa [I] 124 A8
Linken [D] 20 E5
Linköping [S] 168 A5
Linkvarnen [S] 184 A5
Linna [FIN] 186 F3
Linnankylä [FIN] 186 D5
Linnanperä [FIN] 186 F1
Linnerud [N] 172 C3
Linneryd [S] 162 E5
Linnes [N] 172 E1
Linnés Hammarby [S] 168 D1
Linosa [I] 126 B5
Linova [BY] 38 H2
Linovo [RUS] 198 G4
Linsdal [S] 162 G5
Linsell [S] 182 F5
Linthal [CH] 58 G6
Lintzel [D] 18 F6
Linum [D] 34 D1
Linz [A] 62 B4
Linz [D] 30 H5
Liomseter [N] 170 G2
Lioni [I] 120 F3
Liópraso [GR] 132 F2
Lipa [BIH] 144 B1
Lípa [CZ] 50 E6
Lipa [PL] 52 E2
Lipany [SK] 52 C6
Lipar [SRB] 76 D6
Lípari [I] 124 B6
Lipcani [MD] 204 D3
Liperi [FIN] 188 F3
Liperonmäki [FIN] 188 C4
Lipiany [PL] 20 F6
Lipica [SLO] 72 H6
Lipik [HR] 142 B1
Lipinki Łużyckie [PL] 34 G5
Lipka [PL] 22 C5
Lipljan [SRB] 146 C5
Lipnica [BG] 146 G3
Lipnica [PL] 22 C3
Lipnica [PL] 22 E6
Lipnice nad Sázavou [CZ] 48 H5
Lipnik [PL] 52 D2
Lipník nad Bečvou [CZ] 50 D5
Lipno [PL] 36 G1
Lipno nad Vltavou [CZ] 62 B3
Lipova [CZ] 50 E6
Lipova [RO] 76 H4
Lipovac [HR] 142 E2
Lipová-Lázně [CZ] 50 D3
Lipovci [SLO] 74 F3
Lipovica [SRB] 146 D4
Lipovka [RUS] 24 C1
Lipovljani [HR] 142 B1
Lipovo Polje [HR] 112 G3
Lipowina [PL] 22 G2
Lipowo [PL] 22 G4
Lippborg [D] 32 D4
Lippstadt [D] 32 D4
Lipsheim [F] 44 H6
Lipsk [PL] 24 F4
Lipsko [PL] 38 C6
Lipsko [PL] 52 F2
Liptovská Osada [SK] 64 C2
Liptovská Teplička [SK] 64 E2
Liptovské Matiašovce [SK] 50 H6
Liptovský-Mikuláš [SK] 64 D2
Lipusz [PL] 22 C3
Lis [AL] 128 B2
Lisboa [P] 86 B5
Lisburn [NIR] 2 G4
Liscarroll [IRL] 4 C4
Lisdoonvarna [IRL] 2 B5
Lisec [MK] 128 D1
Liseleje [DK] 156 G1
Liselund [DK] 156 G4
Liselund [DK] 156 G4
Lisia Góra [PL] 52 C3
Lisieux [F] 26 G4
Lisinki [FIN] 194 C7
Liskeard [GB] 12 D4
Lisland [N] 164 E2
L'Isle [CH] 70 B1
Lisle [F] 66 F2
L'Isle-Adam [F] 42 F3
L'Isle-de-Noé [F] 84 F3
L'Isle-en-Dodon [F] 84 G3
l'Isle-Jourdain [F] 54 F5
L'Isle-Jourdain [F] 84 H3
Lisleset [N] 170 F4
L'Isle-sur-la-Sorgue [F] 106 H3
L'Isle-sur-le-Doubs [F] 58 C4
Lisle-sur-Tarn [F] 106 B2
Lisma [FIN] 194 C5
Lismore [IRL] 4 D5
Lišnja [BIH] 142 C2
Lison, Source du- [F] 58 B5
Lišov [CZ] 62 C2
Lisów [PL] 34 G2
Lisse [NL] 16 D4
Lissewege [B] 28 G1
Lisskogsbrändan [S] 172 F4
List [D] 156 A4
Lista [S] 168 B3
Lişteava [RO] 146 G2
Listerby [S] 158 F1
Lištica [BIH] 144 C2
Listowel [IRL] 4 C3
Lit [S] 182 H2
Litene [LV] 198 F4
Litér [H] 76 A2
Liternum [I] 120 D3
Lit-et-Mixe [F] 66 B5
Lithakiá [GR] 136 A2
Lithínes [GR] 140 G5
Lití [GR] 128 H4
Litice [CZ] 50 B4
Litija [SLO] 74 C5
Litke [H] 64 D4
Litmalahti [FIN] 188 D2
Litmaniemi [FIN] 188 D2
Litóchoro [GR] 128 G6
Litoměřice [CZ] 48 F2
Litomyšl [CZ] 50 B4
Litovel [CZ] 50 C5
Litslena [S] 168 C2
Littlehampton [GB] 14 D5
Littleport [GB] 14 F2
Litultovice [CZ] 50 D4
Litvínov [CZ] 48 E2
Liubar [UA] 202 C8
Liubech [UA] 202 D6
Liubeshiv [UA] 202 B7
Liuboml' [UA] 38 G5
Liukoniai [LT] 200 G5
Liusselsstugan [S] 190 H2
Livada de Bihor [RO] 76 H2
Livade [HR] 112 D1
Livadeiá [GR] 132 H5
Livaderó [GR] 130 D2
Livadhja [AL] 132 B1
Livádi [GR] 128 G6
Livádi [GR] 130 B5
Livádi [GR] 136 F6
Livádi [GR] 138 D3
Livádia [GR] 154 B3
Livadochóri [GR] 130 F6
Līvāni [LV] 198 F6
Livari [MNE] 144 E5
Livarot [F] 26 G4
Liverá [GR] 128 F5
Livera (Sadrazamköy) [CY] 154 F5
Livernon [F] 66 H5
Liverpool [GB] 10 D4
Livigno [I] 72 B3
Livingston [GB] 8 E3
Livno [BIH] 144 B1
Livo [FIN] 196 E3
Livold [SLO] 74 C6
Livorno [I] 110 D6
Livorno Ferraris [I] 70 E5
Livov [SK] 52 C6
Livron-sur-Drôme [F] 68 F5
Liw [PL] 38 D2
Lixa [P] 80 C4
Lixoúri [GR] 132 C6
Lizard [GB] 12 B5
Lizarra / Estella [E] 84 A4
Lizartza [E] 84 B3
Lizy [F] 42 G3
Lizzano [I] 122 F4
Lješane [SRB] 146 B5
Ljig [SRB] 146 B1
Ljørdalen [N] 172 E2
Ljosland [N] 164 D4
Ljuba [SRB] 142 F2
Ljuban' [BY] 202 C6
Ljuban' [RUS] 202 C1
Ljubanište [MK] 128 D4
Ljubenovo [BG] 148 D5
Ljubinje [BIH] 144 C3
Ljubljana [SLO] 74 B5
Ljubno [SLO] 74 B4
Ljubno [SLO] 74 C4
Ljubogošta [BIH] 144 D1
Ljubostinja, Manastir- [SRB] 146 C3
Ljubovija [MNE] 204 A6
Ljubovija [SRB] 142 F4
Ljubovo [BIH] 144 B4
Ljubuški [BIH] 144 B2
Ljubytino [RUS] 202 C1
Ljudinovo [RUS] 202 E4
Ljugarn [S] 168 G5
Ljungby [S] 162 C5
Ljungbyhed [S] 158 C1
Ljungbyholm [S] 162 F5
Ljungdalen [S] 182 E3
Ljunghusen [S] 156 H3
Ljungsarp [S] 162 C2
Ljungsbro [S] 166 H5
Ljungskile [S] 166 C6
Ljusdal [S] 184 D6
Ljusfallshammar [S] 166 H4
Ljusne [S] 174 E2
Ljustero [S] 168 E2
Ljustorp [S] 184 E4
Ljusträsk [S] 190 H3
Ljutići [MNE] 144 E2
Ljuti Dol [BG] 146 G4
Ljutomer [SLO] 74 E4
Llafranc [E] 92 G3
Llagostera [E] 92 F3
Llanberis [GB] 10 B4
Llançà [E] 92 G2
Llandeilo [GB] 12 E2
Llandovery [GB] 12 E1
Llandrindod Wells [GB] 10 C6
Llandudno [GB] 10 C4
Llanelli [GB] 12 E2
Llanes [E] 82 D2
Llangefni [GB] 10 B4
Llangollen [GB] 10 C5
Llangurig [GB] 10 C6
Llanidloes [GB] 10 C6
Llantwit Major [GB] 12 E3
Llanuwchllyn [GB] 10 C5
Llavorsí [E] 84 G6
Lleida / Lérida [E] 90 H4
Llera [E] 94 H3
Llerena [E] 94 H4
Lles de Cerdanya [E] 92 D1
Llíria [E] 98 E4
Llivia [F] 92 E1
Llodio / Laudio [E] 82 G4
Lloret de Mar [E] 92 F4
Lluc, Monestir de- [E] 104 E4
Llucena / Lucena del Cid [E] 98 F3
Llucmajor [E] 104 E5
Lnáře [CZ] 48 E5
Lniano [PL] 22 D5
Loano [I] 108 G3
Loarre, Cast. de- [E] 84 D6
Löbau [D] 34 G6
Lobenstein [D] 46 H2
Łobez [PL] 20 G4
Lobios [E] 78 C6
Löbnitz [D] 20 C2
Łobodno [PL] 50 G1
Lobón [E] 94 G2
Lobonäs [S] 172 H1
Loborika [HR] 112 D2
Lobosh [BG] 146 F5
Loburg [D] 34 C3
Łobżenica [PL] 22 C5
Locana [I] 70 D4
Locarno [CH] 70 F3
Loccum [D] 32 E2
Lochaline [GB] 6 B6
Loch Baghasdail / Lochboisdale [GB] 6 A4
Lochboisdale / Loch Baghasdail [GB] 6 A4
Lochearnhead [GB] 8 D2
Lochem [NL] 16 F5
Loches [F] 54 G3
Loch Garman / Wexford [IRL] 4 F5
Lochgilphead [GB] 8 C2
Lochinver [GB] 6 D3
Lochmaddy / Loch nam Madadh [GB] 6 A3
Loch nam Madadh / Lochmaddy [GB] 6 A3
Łochocin [PL] 36 G1

Łochów [PL] 38 C2
Lochranza [GB] 8 C3
Lochteå / Lohtaja [FIN] 196 C5
Lockenhaus [A] 74 F1
Lockerbie [GB] 8 E5
Löcknitz [D] 20 E5
Locmaria [F] 40 C5
Locmariaquer [F] 40 D5
Locminé [F] 26 A6
Locorotondo [I] 122 E3
Locquirec [F] 40 C1
Locri [I] 124 D7
Locri Epizefiri [I] 124 D7
Locronan [F] 40 B3
Loctudy [F] 40 B3
Löddeköpinge [S] 156 H2
Lodè [I] 118 E3
Lode [LV] 198 E4
Löderup [S] 158 D3
Lodève [F] 106 D3
Lodi [I] 70 G5
Løding [N] 192 D6
Lødingen [N] 192 E4
Lodonero [I] 116 B4
Lodosa [E] 84 A5
Lödöse [S] 160 H1
Łódź [PL] 36 G4
Loeches [E] 88 G6
Loen [N] 180 D5
Loev [BY] 202 D6
Løfallstrand [N] 170 B5
Lofer [A] 60 G6
Lofsdal [FIN] 176 D5
Lofsdalen [S] 182 F5
Lofta [S] 162 G1
Loftahammar [S] 162 G2
Lofthus [N] 170 C4
Log [SLO] 72 H4
Loga [D] 18 B4
Loga [N] 164 C5
Logarska Dolina [SLO] 74 C4
Logatec [SLO] 74 B5
Lögda [S] 190 G5
Lögdeå [S] 184 H1
Logkaníkos [GR] 136 D3
Lognvik [N] 164 E1
Logroño [E] 82 G6
Logrosán [E] 96 C2
Løgstør [DK] 160 D4
Løgumkloster [DK] 156 B4
Lohals [DK] 156 E4
Lohberg [D] 48 D6
Lohéac [F] 26 C6
Lohikoski [FIN] 188 E6
Lohiniva [FIN] 194 C7
Lohiranta [FIN] 194 F8
Lohja [FIN] 176 G5
Lohmen [D] 20 B4
Lohne [D] 18 C6
Löhne [D] 32 E2
Lohnsfeld [D] 46 B4
Lohr [D] 46 E3
Lohtaja / Lochteå [FIN] 196 C5
Loiano [I] 110 F4
Loimaa [FIN] 176 E3
Loimaankunta [FIN] 176 E3
Loire, Gorges de la- [F] 68 E5
Lóiri [I] 118 E3
Loisirs, Parc de- [F] 66 B3
Loitz [D] 20 D3
Loja [E] 102 D3
Lojanice [SRB] 142 F3
Lojsta [S] 168 G5
Lojt Kirkeby [DK] 156 C4
Loka Brunn [S] 166 G2
Lokakylä [FIN] 186 F2
Lokalahti [FIN] 176 C4
Lokca [SK] 50 G5
Loke [SLO] 74 C4
Løken [N] 166 C1
Lokeren [B] 28 H2
Loket [CZ] 48 D3
Lokhvytsia [UA] 202 E7
Lokka [FIN] 194 E6
Løkken [DK] 160 D3
Løkken Verk [N] 180 H2
Loknya [RUS] 202 C3
Lőkösháza [H] 76 G4
Lokot' [RUS] 202 E5
Lokuta [EST] 198 E2
Lokve [HR] 112 F1
Lokve [SLO] 72 H5
Lokve [SRB] 142 H2
l'Olleria [E] 98 E6
Lölling [A] 74 C2
Lom [BG] 146 F2
Lom [CZ] 48 E2
Lom [N] 180 F5
Lõmala [EST] 198 C3
Łomazy [PL] 38 F3
Lombez [F] 84 G3
Lombrives, Grotte de- [F] 84 H5
Lom Cherkovna [BG] 148 D3
Lomello [I] 70 F6
Lomen [N] 170 F2
Lomma [S] 156 H2
Lomme [F] 28 F3
Lommel [B] 30 E3
Lom nad Rimavicou [SK] 64 D3
Lomnice nad Lužnicí [CZ] 62 C2
Lomonosov [RUS] 178 G5
Lompolo [FIN] 194 C5
Lomsjö [S] 190 F5
Łomża [PL] 24 D5
Lonato [I] 72 B6
Lončari [BIH] 142 E2
Lončarica [HR] 74 G6
Londinières [F] 28 C4
London [GB] 14 E4
Londonderry (Derry) [NIR] 2 F2
Lonevåg [N] 170 B3
Longá [GR] 132 F1
Longarone [I] 72 E4
Longeau [F] 56 H2
Longeville les St. Avold [F] 44 F4
Longford [IRL] 2 E4
Longny-au-Perche [F] 26 G6
Longobucco [I] 124 E4
Longo Mel [P] 86 D4
Longpont [F] 42 H3
Longré [F] 54 D5
Longroiva [P] 80 E5
Longset [N] 190 D2
Longtown [GB] 8 E5
Longué [F] 54 E1
Longueau [F] 28 E5
Longuyon [F] 44 E3
Longwy [F] 44 E3
Lonigo [I] 110 F1
Lonin [N] 190 B5
Løningdalen [N] 170 B4
Löningen [D] 18 C6
Löningsberg [S] 182 H4
Łoniów [PL] 52 D2
Lono [N] 164 C1
Lönsboda [S] 162 D6
Lønsdal [N] 190 E1
Lønset [N] 180 E3
Lønset [N] 180 G3
Lons-le-Saunier [F] 56 H5
Lønstrup [DK] 160 D2
Looberghe [F] 14 H6
Looe [GB] 12 D5
Loon Plage [F] 14 H6
Loosdorf [A] 62 D4
Lopar [HR] 112 F3
Lopare [BIH] 142 E3
Lopatica [MK] 128 E3
Lopatovo [RUS] 198 H3
Lope [LV] 198 E6
Lopera [E] 102 D1
Łopiennik [PL] 38 F6
Lopotkovo [RUS] 202 F4
Loppi [FIN] 176 G3
Lopud [HR] 144 C4
Lopukhinka [RUS] 178 G5
Łopuszna [PL] 52 B5
Łopuszno [PL] 52 B1
Loqueffret [F] 40 C2
Lora del Río [E] 102 A1
Lorca [E] 104 B3
Lorcé [B] 30 E5
Lorch [D] 46 B3
Lorch [D] 60 B2
Lordosa [P] 80 C5
Loredo [E] 82 F3
Loreley [D] 46 B2
Lørenskog [N] 166 B1
Lorentzen [F] 44 G5
Loreo [I] 110 H2
Loreto [I] 116 C1
Loreto Aprutino [I] 116 D4
Lórév [H] 76 C2
Lorgues [F] 108 D5
Lorica [I] 124 E4
Lorient [F] 40 C4
Lőrinci [H] 64 D6
Loriol-sur-Drôme [F] 68 F5
Lorlanges [F] 68 C3
Lormes [F] 56 E3
Lormont [F] 66 D3
Loro Ciuffenna [I] 110 F6
Lorqui [E] 104 C3
Lörrach [D] 58 E4
Lorris [F] 42 F6
Lörsfeld [D] 30 G4
L'Orso [I] 118 E2
Lorup [D] 18 B5
Loryma [TR] 154 D3
Los [S] 172 H1
Losa, Nuraghe- [I] 118 C4
Los Abrigos [E] 100 B5
Los Alares [E] 96 D2
Los Alcázares [E] 104 C4
Los Arcos [E] 82 H6
Los Arcos [E] 94 F2
Losar de la Vera [E] 88 B5
Los Arenales del Sol / Arenals del Sol [E] 104 D3
Losau [D] 46 H3
Los Barrios [E] 100 G5
Los Caños de Meca [E] 100 F5
Los Corrales de Buelna [E] 82 E3
Loscos [E] 90 D5
Los Cristianos [E] 100 B5
Losenstein [A] 62 C5
Los Escullos [E] 102 H6
Losevo [RUS] 188 G6
Los Galachos [E] 90 E4
Los Gigantes [E] 100 B5
Losheim [D] 30 F6
Losheim [D] 44 G3
Los Hinojonos [E] 96 H3
Łosice [PL] 38 E3
Los Isidros [E] 98 D4
Loški Potok [SLO] 74 C6
Loški Potok [SLO] 74 C6
Los Llanos de Aridane [E] 100 A4
Los Mallos [E] 84 D5
Los Millares [E] 102 G5
Los Molares [E] 100 H2
Los Navalmorales [E] 96 D2
Los Navalucillos [E] 96 D2
Los Ojuelos [E] 102 A2
Los Olmos [E] 90 E6
Losomäki [FIN] 188 E1
Łososina Dolna [PL] 52 B4
Los Palacios y Villafranca [E] 100 G2
l'Ospedale [F] 114 B5
Lossa [D] 34 B5
Los Santos de Maimona [E] 94 G3
Los Sauces [E] 100 B4
Lossburg [D] 58 F2
Losse [F] 66 D5
Lossiemouth [GB] 6 F4
Lostwithiel [GB] 12 C4
Los Urrutias [E] 104 C4
Los Villares [E] 102 E2
Los Yébenes [E] 96 F2
Löt [S] 162 G4
Lote [N] 180 C5
Løten [N] 172 C3
Lotorp [S] 168 B5
Lotoshino [RUS] 202 E3
Lötschberg Tunnel [CH] 70 E2
Lotta [RUS] 194 E5
Lotte [D] 32 D2
Lottefors [S] 174 D2
Löttorp-Högby [S] 162 H4
Lotyn [PL] 22 B4
Lotzorai [I] 118 E5
Loubens-Lauragais [F] 106 A3
Loučná nad Desnou [CZ] 50 C4
Loudéac [F] 26 A5
Loudes [F] 68 D4
Loudun [F] 54 E3
Loué [F] 42 B5
Loue, Source de la- [F] 58 B5
Louejärvi [FIN] 194 C8
Loughborough [GB] 10 F6
Loughbrickland [NIR] 2 G4
Loughglinn [IRL] 2 D4
Loughmoe Castle [IRL] 4 E3
Loughrea [IRL] 2 C5
Louhans [F] 56 G5
Louisburgh [IRL] 2 B4
Loukás [GR] 136 E2
Loukhi [RUS] 196 H1
Loukísia [GR] 134 B5
Loukusa [FIN] 196 E2
Loulay [F] 54 D5
Loulé [P] 94 C5
Louny [CZ] 48 E3
Louppy-sur-Loison [F] 44 D3
Lourdes [E] 78 D2
Lourdes [F] 84 E4
Louredo [P] 80 D3
Lourenzá [E] 78 E2
Loures [P] 86 B5
Lourical [P] 86 D2
Lourinhã [P] 86 B4
Loúros [GR] 132 D3
Lourosa [P] 80 B4
Loury [F] 42 E6
Lousa [P] 86 B5
Lousã [P] 86 E2
Lousada [P] 80 C4
Louth [GB] 10 G5
Loutrá [GR] 132 E4
Loutrá [GR] 134 H2
Loutrá [GR] 136 D2
Loutrá [GR] 138 C2
Loutrá Aidipsoú [GR] 134 A4
Loutrá Aridaías [GR] 128 F3
Loutrá Eleftherón [GR] 130 D4
Loutrá Kaítsas [GR] 132 F3
Loutráki [GR] 132 D4
Loutráki [GR] 134 A6
Loutrá Kounoupéli (Yrmínis) [GR] 132 E6
Loutrá Kyllínis [GR] 136 B2
Loutrá Lagkadá [GR] 130 B4
Loutrá Smokóvou [GR] 132 F3
Loutrá Vólvis [GR] 130 B4
Loutrá Ypátis [GR] 132 G4
Loutró Elénis [GR] 136 F1
Loutrós [GR] 130 G3
Loútsa [GR] 134 C6
Louvain (Leuven) [B] 30 D4
Louvie-Juzon [F] 84 E4
Louviers [F] 28 B6
Louvigné-du-Desert [F] 26 D5
Lövånger [S] 196 B5
Lovasberény [H] 76 B1
Lövåsen [S] 174 D5
Lövåsen [S] 184 D2
Lovászi [H] 74 F3
Lövberg [S] 190 E4
Lövberga [S] 190 F6
Lovech [BG] 148 B3
Lovére [I] 72 A5
Lövestad [S] 158 D3
Loviisa / Lovisa [FIN] 178 B4
Løvik [N] 180 D2
Lovisa / Loviisa [FIN] 178 B4
Lovište [HR] 144 B3
Lövnäs [S] 172 F2
Lövnäs [S] 190 F4
Lövnäs [S] 190 G5
Lövnäs [S] 190 G2
Lövnäsvallen [S] 182 F6
Lövö [FIN] 176 B5
Lövő [H] 62 G6
Lovosice [CZ] 48 F2
Lovraeid [N] 164 B2
Lovran [HR] 112 E1
Lovrenc na Pohorju [SLO] 74 D3
Lovrin [RO] 76 F5
Lövsjö [S] 190 E4
Lövsjön [S] 172 G5
Lövstabruk [S] 174 F5
Lövstad [S] 168 B5
Lövstrand [S] 190 F5
Lövvik [S] 190 F5
Łowcza [PL] 38 F5
Löwenberg [D] 34 E1
Löwenfreigehege [D] 30 F4
Lowenstein [D] 32 E5
Lowestoft [GB] 14 H2
Łowicz [PL] 36 H3
Łowinek [PL] 22 D5
Łowyń [PL] 36 B2
Löytänä [FIN] 186 F1
Löytölä [FIN] 196 F4
Lož [SLO] 74 B6
Lozarevo [BG] 148 E4
Lozari [F] 114 B3
Lozen [BG] 148 A6
Lozen [BG] 148 D6
Lozenets [BG] 148 G5
Loznica [BG] 148 D3
Loznica [MNE] 204 A6
Loznica [SRB] 142 F3
Loznica [SRB] 146 B2
Lozova [UA] 204 H1
Lozovac [HR] 112 H6
Lozovik [SRB] 146 C1
Lozoya [E] 88 G4
Lozoyuela [E] 88 G4
Lozzo di Cadore [I] 72 F3
Luanco [E] 78 H3
Luarca [E] 78 G2
Lubaczów [PL] 52 F3
Lubań [PL] 34 H6
Lubāna [LV] 198 F5
Lubartów [PL] 38 E5
Lubasz [PL] 36 C1
Lubawa [PL] 22 F5
Lubawka [PL] 50 B2
Lübbecke [D] 32 E2
Lübben [D] 34 F4
Lübbenau [D] 34 F4
Lübbow [D] 18 H6
Lübeck [D] 18 G3
Lubenec [CZ] 48 E3
Lubenice [HR] 112 E3
Lubersac [F] 66 G2
Lubia [E] 90 B3
Łubianka [PL] 22 E6
Łubianka [PL] 34 H1
Lubiatowo [PL] 20 F6
Lubiąż [PL] 36 B6
Lubichowo [PL] 22 D4
Lubień [PL] 50 H5
Lubień Kujawski [PL] 36 G2
Lubieszyn [PL] 20 F5
Lubin [PL] 36 B5
Lubiń [PL] 36 C4
Lublin [PL] 38 E5
Lubliniec [PL] 50 F2
Lubmin [D] 20 D3
Łubnice [PL] 36 E6
Lubniewice [PL] 34 H2
Łubno [PL] 22 C3
Lubny [UA] 202 E7
Lubomino [PL] 22 G3
Luboń [PL] 36 C3
Luboniek [PL] 36 F3
Luboradz [PL] 36 B6
Luboszów [PL] 34 H5
Luboszyce [PL] 36 B5
L'ubotín [SK] 52 C6
Lubowidz [PL] 22 G6
Lubowitz [PL] 50 E3
Łubowo [PL] 22 A4
Łubowo [PL] 36 D2
Lubraniec [PL] 36 F2
Lubrín [E] 102 H5
Lubsko [PL] 34 G4
Lubsza [PL] 50 D1
Lübtheen [D] 18 H5
Lubuczewo [PL] 22 B2
Luby [PL] 22 D4
Lübz [D] 20 B5
Lucainena de las Torres [E] 102 G5
Lucan [IRL] 2 F6
Lucareţ [RO] 76 H5
Lucca [I] 110 D5
Luče [SLO] 74 C4
Lucena [E] 102 C3
Lucena del Cid / Llucena [E] 98 F3
Lucenay [F] 56 F4
Luc-en-Diois [F] 68 G6
Lučenec [SK] 64 D4
Lucera [I] 120 G1
Lüchow [D] 18 H6
Luciana [E] 96 E4
Lucignano [I] 114 G1
Lucija [SLO] 72 H6
Lucito [I] 116 E6
Luckau [D] 34 E4
Luckenwalde [D] 34 E3
Lucksta [S] 184 E5
Lückstedt [D] 34 B1
Luco dei Marsi [I] 116 C5
Luçon [F] 54 C3
Luc-sur-Mer [F] 26 F3
Lucus Feroniae [I] 116 A5
Ludanice [SK] 64 A3
Ludbreg [HR] 74 F4
Lüdenscheid [D] 32 C5
Lüderitz [D] 34 B2
Ludgo [S] 168 C4
Lüdinghausen [D] 16 H6
Ludlow [GB] 10 D6
Ludomy [PL] 36 C2
Ludoni [RUS] 198 H2
Ludów Polski [PL] 50 C1
Ludvika [S] 172 H5
Ludwigsburg [D] 46 D6
Ludwigshafen [D] 46 C4
Ludwigshafen [D] 58 G4
Ludwigslust [D] 20 A5
Ludwigsstadt [D] 46 H2
Ludwin [PL] 38 E5
Ludza [LV] 198 G5
Luesia [E] 84 C5
Lug [BIH] 144 C3
Lug [HR] 76 C6
Luga [RUS] 198 H2
Lugagnano Val d'Arda [I] 110 C2
Lugano [CH] 70 G3
Lügde [D] 32 E3
Luggau [A] 72 G1
Lugnås [S] 166 F5
Lugo [E] 78 E3
Lugo [I] 110 G4
Lugoj [RO] 204 B5
Lugones [E] 78 H3
Luhačovice [CZ] 62 H2
Luhalahti [FIN] 186 D6
Luhanka [FIN] 186 G6
Luhtanen [FIN] 178 C1
Luhtapohja [FIN] 188 G2
Luhtikylä [FIN] 178 A3
Luidja [EST] 198 C2
Luigny [F] 42 D5
Luik (Liège) [B] 30 E5
Luikonlahti [FIN] 188 E2
Luimneach / Limerick [IRL] 4 D3
Luino [I] 70 F3
Luisenburg [D] 48 B4
Luka [SRB] 146 D1
Lukač [HR] 74 H5
Lukanja [SLO] 74 D4
Lukare [SRB] 146 C5
Lukavac [BIH] 142 D3
Lüki [BG] 148 B6
Lukiv [UA] 38 H5
Łukom [PL] 36 E3
Lukov [CZ] 50 E6
Lukovë [AL] 132 B1
Lukovica [SLO] 74 C4
Lukovit [BG] 148 A3
Lukovo [HR] 112 F3
Lukovo [MK] 128 C3
Lukovo [SRB] 146 C4
Lukovo [SRB] 146 D2
Lukovo Šugarje [HR] 112 G4
Łuków [PL] 38 D3
Lukšić [HR] 142 A5
Lukta [PL] 22 G4
Luktvatnet [N] 190 D2
Luleå [S] 196 B3
Lüleburgaz [TR] 150 C2
Lumbarda [HR] 144 B3
Lumbier / Irunberri [E] 84 C4
Lumbrales [E] 80 F6
Lumbrein [CH] 70 G1
Lumbres [F] 28 E2
Lumby [DK] 156 D3
Lumezzane [I] 72 B5
Lumijoki [FIN] 196 D4
Lumivaara [RUS] 188 G5
Lumivaara [RUS] 188 G6
Lummelundagrottorna [S] 168 G4
Lummen [B] 30 E4
Lummenlunda [S] 168 G4
Lumparland [FIN] 176 B5
Lumsås [DK] 156 F2
Lumsheden [S] 174 D4
Lun [HR] 112 F3
Luna [E] 84 C6
Lunas [F] 106 D3
Lund [DK] 156 C1
Lund [S] 158 C2
Lunda [S] 168 D2
Lundamo [N] 182 B2
Lunde [N] 164 F2
Lunde [N] 180 D5
Lunde [N] 180 D6
Lunde [S] 184 F3
Lundeborg [DK] 156 E4
Lunden [D] 18 E2
Lunden [N] 164 F3
Lunderseter [N] 172 D5
Lunderskov [DK] 156 C3
Lundo / Lieto [FIN] 176 E4
Lundsjön [S] 182 G1
Lüneburg [D] 18 G5
Lunel [F] 106 F4
Lünen [D] 32 C4
Lunéville [F] 44 F5
Lungern [CH] 70 E1
Lungro [I] 120 H6
Lungsjön [S] 184 D1
Lungsund [S] 166 F2
Lungvik [S] 184 F3
Luninyets [BY] 202 B6
Lunkkaus [FIN] 194 E6
Lunkuva [LT] 198 D6
Lunna [BY] 24 G4
Lünne [D] 16 H4
Lunteren [NL] 16 E5
Lunz [A] 62 D5
Luode [FIN] 186 D5
Luogosanto [I] 118 D2
Luopa [FIN] 186 C4
Luopioinen [FIN] 176 G1
Luostari [RUS] 194 F3
Luosto [FIN] 194 D7
Luoto / Larsmo [FIN] 196 C6
Luotola [FIN] 178 D2
Luotolahti [FIN] 178 D1
Lupara [I] 120 H2
Lupawa [PL] 22 C2
Lupeni [RO] 204 C5
Lupiac [F] 84 F2
Lupiana [E] 88 H5
Lupoglav [HR] 74 F6
Luque [E] 102 D2
Lura e Vjetër [AL] 128 C1
Lurcy-Lévis [F] 56 D4
Lure [F] 58 C3
Lureuil [F] 54 G4
Lurgan [NIR] 2 G4
Lurgrotte [A] 74 D2
Luri [F] 114 C2
Lušci Palanka [BIH] 142 A3
Lüsens [A] 72 D1
Lushnjë [AL] 128 B4
Lusi [FIN] 178 B2
Lusignan [F] 54 E4
Lusigny [F] 44 B6
Lusina [PL] 50 B1
Lusk [IRL] 2 F6
Lus-la-Croix-Haute [F] 68 G6
Luso [P] 80 B6
Luspa [FIN] 192 H4
Luspebryggan [S] 192 G6
Lussac-les-Châteaux [F] 54 F4
Lussac-les-Églises [F] 54 G5
Lussan [F] 106 G3
Lustenau [A] 58 H5
Luster [N] 170 E1
Łuszczów [PL] 38 E5
Lutago / Luttach [I] 72 E2
Lutcza [PL] 52 D4
Lutherstadt Eisleben [D] 34 B5
Lutherstadt Wittenberg [D] 34 D4
Lütjenburg [D] 18 G2
Lutnes [N] 172 E3
Lutojärvi [FIN] 188 F4
Lutol Suchy [PL] 36 A3
Lutomek [PL] 36 B2
Lutomiersk [PL] 36 G4
Luton [GB] 14 E3
Lutowo [PL] 22 C5
Lutrini [LV] 198 C5
Lutry [PL] 22 H3
Luts'k [UA] 202 B7
Lutta [FIN] 176 D2
Luttach / Lutago [I] 72 E2
Lutterworth [GB] 14 D2
Lututów [PL] 36 F5
Lützen [D] 34 C5
Lutzmannsburg [A] 74 F1
Lützow [D] 18 H4
Luukkola [FIN] 178 E1
Luukkonen [FIN] 188 E6
Luumäki [FIN] 178 D2
Luusalmi [RUS] 196 H3
Luusniemi [FIN] 188 C5
Luusua [FIN] 194 E8
Luvia [FIN] 176 C2
Lux [F] 56 G5
Luxembourg [L] 44 F3
Luxeuil-les-Bains [F] 58 C3
Luxey [F] 66 C5
Luz [P] 100 D2
Luzaide / Valcarlos [E] 84 C3
Lužani [HR] 142 C2
Luzarches [F] 42 F3
Luže [CZ] 50 B4
Luzeret [F] 54 G4
Luzern [CH] 58 F6
Luzhayka [RUS] 178 E2
Luzhki [RUS] 24 C2
Luzi Madhi [AL] 128 A3
Łuzki [PL] 38 E3
Luz-St-Sauveur [F] 84 E4
Luzy [F] 56 E5
Luzzara [I] 110 E2
Luzzi [I] 124 D4
L'viv [UA] 52 H4
Lvubertsy [RUS] 202 F3
Lwówek [PL] 36 B2
Lwówek Śląski [PL] 36 A6
Lyady [RUS] 198 G2
Lyamony [RUS] 198 G5
Lyaskelya [RUS] 188 H5
Lyaskovets [BG] 148 C3
Lyatno [BG] 148 E2
Lychen [D] 20 D5
Lyckeby [S] 158 F1
Lycksaberg [S] 190 G4
Lycksele [S] 190 G5
Lydd [GB] 14 F6
Lye [S] 168 G5
Lyel'chytsy [BY] 202 C6
Lyenin [BY] 202 B6
Lyepyel' [BY] 202 C4
Lygna [N] 172 B4
Lygre [N] 170 B5
Lykófos [GR] 130 H2
Lykorráchi [GR] 128 D6
Lyme Regis [GB] 12 F4
Lymington [GB] 12 H5
Lynderupgård [DK] 160 D5
Lyne [DK] 156 B2
Lyngby [DK] 156 G2
Lyngby [DK] 160 B4
Lyngdal [N] 164 C5
Lyngør [N] 164 F4
Lyngså [DK] 160 E3
Lyngseidet [N] 192 G2
Lyngvoll [N] 180 D5
Lynton [GB] 12 E3
Lyon [F] 68 F3
Lyons-la-Forêt [F] 28 C6
Lyozno [BY] 202 C4
Lypova Dolyna [UA] 202 E7
Lysá nad Labem [CZ] 48 G3
Łysa Polana [PL] 52 B6
Łyse [PL] 24 C5
Lysebotn [N] 164 C3
Lysekil [S] 166 C6
Lysi (Akdoğan) [CY] 154 G5
Lysianka [UA] 202 F7
Łysomice [PL] 22 E6
Lysøysund [N] 190 B5
Lyss [CH] 58 D5
Lysvik [S] 166 E1
Lytham St Anne's [GB] 10 D3
Lyuban' [RUS] 202 C1
Lyuben [BG] 148 B5
Lyubertsy [RUS] 202 F3
Lyubimets [BG] 148 D6
Lyubimets [RUS] 198 G2
Lyubytino [RUS] 202 C1
Lyudinovo [RUS] 202 E4
Lyulyakovo [BG] 148 E4

M

Maalahti / Malax [FIN] 186 B3
Maaninka [FIN] 188 C1
Maaninkavaara [FIN] 194 E8
Maanselkä [FIN] 196 F5
Maarianhamina / Mariehamn [FIN] 176 A5
Maarianvaara [FIN] 188 E2
Maarja [EST] 198 F2
Maasbree [NL] 30 F3
Maaseik [B] 30 F3
Maasland [NL] 16 C5
Maasmechelen [B] 30 E4
Maassluis [NL] 16 C5
Maastricht [NL] 30 E4
Maavesi [FIN] 188 D4
Mablethorpe [GB] 10 H5
Macael [E] 102 G4
Maçanet de Cabrenys [E] 92 F2
Maçanet de la Selva [E] 92 F4
Mação [P] 86 E4
Maccagno [I] 70 F3
Macclesfield [GB] 10 E4
Maceda [E] 78 D5
Macedo de Cavaleiros [P] 80 F4
Macelj [HR] 74 E4
Macerata [I] 116 C1
Macerata Féltria [I] 110 H5
Măceşu de Jos [RO] 146 G2
Machair Loiscthe / Rosepenna [IRL] 2 E1
Machault [F] 44 C3
Mâchecourt [F] 54 B2
Macherádo [GR] 136 A2
Machico [P] 100 A3
Machliny [PL] 22 A5
Machynlleth [GB] 10 B5
Maciejowice [PL] 38 C4
Macinaggio [F] 114 C2
Mackenrode [D] 32 G4
Mačkovci [SLO] 74 E3
Mačkovci [SLO] 74 E3
Macocha [CZ] 50 C6
Macomer [I] 118 C4
Mâcon [F] 68 G1
Macotera [E] 88 D3
Macroom [IRL] 4 C5
Macugnaga [I] 70 E3
Mád [H] 64 G4
Madalena [P] 100 C3
Madan [BG] 130 E1
Madängsholm [S] 162 C1
Madara [BG] 148 E3
Maddaloni [I] 120 E2
Made [NL] 16 D6
Madekoski [FIN] 196 D4
Maderuelo [E] 88 G3
Madésimo [I] 70 G2
Madieres [F] 106 E3
Madliena [LV] 198 E5
Madona [LV] 198 F5
Madonna dell'Acero [I] 110 E4
Madonna della Civita [I] 120 C2
Madonna della Neve [I] 116 B3
Madonna del Ponte [I] 112 C5
Madonna del Rosario [I] 126 C2
Madonna del Sasso [I] 70 E4
Madonna di Bracciano [I] 114 H5
Madonna di Campíglio [I] 72 C4
Madonna di Canneto [I] 116 E6
Madonna di Senales / Unserfrau [I] 72 C2
Madonna di Tirano [I] 72 B4
Madrid [E] 88 F5
Madridejos [E] 96 F3
Madrigal de las Altas Torres [E] 88 D3
Madrigal de la Vera [E] 88 C5
Madrigalejo [E] 96 B2
Madrigalejo del Monte [E] 88 G1
Mădrino [BG] 148 E4
Madroñera [E] 96 B2
Mäebe [EST] 198 C3
Maella [E] 90 G6
Mære [N] 190 C5
Maetzu [E] 82 H5
Mafra [P] 86 B4
Maga Circe, Grotta della- [I] 120 B2
Magallón [E] 90 D3
Magaluf [E] 104 D5
Magaña [E] 90 C2
Magasa [I] 72 B5
Magaz de Pisuerga [E] 88 F1
Magdalensberg [A] 74 B3
Magdbäcken [S] 184 G2
Magdeburg [D] 34 B3
Magellarë [AL] 128 C2
Magenta [I] 70 F5
Magerholm [N] 180 D3
Magescq [F] 66 B6
Maggia [CH] 70 F2
Maghera [NIR] 2 G3
Magherafelt [NIR] 2 G3
Magierowa Wola [PL] 38 C4
Magione [I] 114 H2
Magkanári [GR] 138 F4
Maglaj [BIH] 142 D3
Maglavit [RO] 146 F2
Maglehem [S] 158 D2
Magleнøj Strand [DK] 18 H1
Magliano dei Marsi [I] 116 C5
Magliano in Toscana [I] 114 F3
Magliano Sabina [I] 116 A4
Maglić [SRB] 146 B3
Máglie [I] 122 G5
Magnac-Laval [F] 54 G5
Magnesia [TR] 152 D5
Magneux Hte Rive [F] 68 E3
Magnières [F] 44 F6
Magnor [N] 166 D1
Magny-Cours [F] 56 D4
Magny-en-Vexin [F] 42 E2
Magny-Jobert [F] 58 C4
Maguelone [F] 106 E4
Maguiresbridge [NIR] 2 E3
Magura [BG] 146 E2
Magyarbánhegyes [H] 76 F4
Magyarboly [H] 76 B5
Magyarkeszi [H] 76 B3

Magyarmecske [H] 76 A5
Magyarszombatfa [H] 74 F3
Maheriv [UA] 52 G3
Mahide [E] 80 G3
Mahilyow [BY] 202 C5
Mahlow [D] 34 E2
Mahlsdorf [D] 34 B1
Mahlu [FIN] 186 F3
Mahmutlar [TR] 152 D4
Mahmutsevketpaşa [TR] 150 F2
Mahnala [FIN] 176 E1
Mahón / Maó [E] 104 H5
Mahora [E] 98 C4
Mahovo [HR] 74 F6
Maia [P] 80 B3
Maia [P] 100 E3
Maia [P] 100 E4
Maials [E] 90 H5
Maîche [F] 58 C5
Máida [I] 124 D5
Maidenhead [GB] 14 D4
Maidstone [GB] 14 F5
Maienfeld [CH] 58 H6
Maierato [I] 124 D6
Maijanen [FIN] 194 C7
Maillezais [F] 54 C4
Mailly-le-Camp [F] 44 B5
Mailly-le-Château [F] 56 E2
Mainburg [D] 60 E3
Mainhardt [D] 46 D6
Maintenon [F] 42 E4
Mainua [FIN] 196 E5
Mainz [D] 46 C3
Maiori [I] 120 E4
Maiori, Nuraghe- [I] 118 D2
Mair de Diu de Montgarri [E] 84 G5
Mairena del Alcor [E] 94 H6
Mairena del Aljarafe [E] 94 G6
Maisach [D] 60 D4
Maishofen [A] 72 F1
Maišiogala [LT] 200 G5
Maison-Neuve [F] 44 C6
Maissau [A] 62 E3
Máistir Gaoithe / Mastergeeby [IRL] 4 A4
Maja [HR] 142 A1
Majadahonda [E] 88 F5
Majadas [E] 86 H6
Majadas [E] 88 B6
Majaelrayo [E] 88 H4
Majavatn [N] 190 D4
Majdan [MK] 128 F3
Majdanek [PL] 38 E5
Majdan Królewski [PL] 52 D2
Majdanpek [SRB] 146 D1
Majdanpek [SRB] 204 B6
Majtum [S] 190 H2
Majur [SRB] 142 F2
Makarska [HR] 144 B2
Makaševičy [BY] 202 B6
Makedonski Brod [MK] 128 E2
Mäkela [FIN] 194 F8
Makhnovka [RUS] 198 H4
Mäkikylä [FIN] 186 F5
Mäkitalo [FIN] 194 C6
Mäkkilkylä [FIN] 186 E4
Makkola [FIN] 188 E4
Makljenovac [BIH] 142 D3
Makó [H] 76 F4
Makó-Rákos [H] 76 F4
Makov [SK] 50 F6
Maková Hora [CZ] 48 F5
Makoviš [SRB] 146 A2
Makovo [MK] 128 E3
Maków [PL] 50 H3
Mąkowarsko [PL] 22 C5
Maków Mazowiecki [PL] 38 B1
Maków Podhalański [PL] 50 H4
Makrakómi [GR] 132 F4
Makreš [MK] 146 D6
Mákri [GR] 130 G3
Mákri [GR] 136 E2
Makrochóri [GR] 128 G5
Makrýammos [GR] 130 E4
Makrygialós [GR] 140 G5
Makrynítsa [GR] 132 H2
Makryplágio [GR] 130 D2
Maksamaa / Maxmo [FIN] 186 B2
Maksatiha [RUS] 202 E2
Malå [S] 190 G4
Mala Bosna [SRB] 76 D5
Malacky [SK] 62 G4
Mala Domaša [SK] 64 G2
Maladzyechna [BY] 202 B5
Málaga [E] 102 C4
Malagón [E] 96 F3
Malahide [IRL] 2 F6
Málainn Mhóir / Malin More [IRL] 2 D2
Mała Karczma [PL] 22 E4
Mala Kladuša [BIH] 112 H2
Malăk Porovec [BG] 148 E2
Mala Krsna [SRB] 142 H3
Malalbergo [I] 110 F3
Malá Lehota [SK] 64 B3
Malamoneda [E] 96 E2
Malandríno [GR] 132 G5
Mälarhusen [S] 158 D3
Malaryta [BY] 38 G4
Mala Subotica [HR] 74 F4
Malaucène [F] 106 H3
Malax / Maalahti [FIN] 186 B3
Malaya Vishera [RUS] 202 C1
Malbork [PL] 22 E3
Malbouzon [F] 68 C5
Malbuisson [F] 58 B6
Malcésine [I] 72 C5
Malchin [D] 20 C4
Malchow [D] 20 C5
Malcocinado [E] 96 A5
Malcontenta [I] 110 H1
Malcov [SK] 52 C6
Maldegem [B] 28 G1
Maldon [GB] 14 F4
Małdyty [PL] 22 F4
Malé [I] 72 C4
Malechowo [PL] 22 B3
Máleme [GR] 140 B4
Malenovice [CZ] 50 D6
Malente-Gremsmühlen [D] 18 G2
Mälerås [S] 162 F4
Máles [GR] 140 F5
Malesco [I] 70 F3
Malesherbes [F] 42 F5
Malesína [GR] 134 B4
Malestroit [F] 26 B6
Maletto [I] 124 A8
Malexander [S] 162 E1
Malfourat, Mine de- [F] 66 E4
Malgovik [S] 190 F5
Malhadas [P] 80 G4
Malhao [P] 86 F2
Mália [GR] 140 F4
Malicorne [F] 42 B5
Mali Idjos [SRB] 76 D6
Malikovo [HR] 144 A1
Målilla [S] 162 F3
Mali Lošinj [HR] 112 E4
Malin [IRL] 2 F1
Malin [UA] 202 D7
Málinec [SK] 64 D3
Malines (Mechelen) [B] 30 C3
Malingsbo [S] 166 H1
Maliniec [PL] 36 E3
Malin More / Málainn Mhóir [IRL] 2 D2
Malinska [HR] 112 E2
Mali Prolog [HR] 144 B3
Maliq [AL] 128 D4
Mališevo / Malisheve [SRB] 146 B5
Malisheve / Mališevo [SRB] 146 B5
Maliskylä [FIN] 196 D5
Mali Štupelj [MNE] 146 B5
Malix [CH] 70 H1
Mali Zvornik [SRB] 142 E3
Maljevac [HR] 112 H2
Maljovica [BG] 146 G6
Malkara [TR] 150 B3
Małkinia Górna [PL] 38 D1
Malkkila [FIN] 188 E3
Malko Gradishte [BG] 148 D6
Malko Tŭrnovo [BG] 150 C1
Mal'kovo [RUS] 198 H5
Mallaig [GB] 6 B5
Mallersdorf [D] 60 F2
Málles Venosta / Mals im Vinschgau [I] 72 B2
Malling [DK] 156 D1
Mallnitz [A] 72 G2
Mallow [IRL] 4 C4
Malm [N] 190 C5
Malmbäck [S] 162 D2
Malmberget [S] 192 G6
Malmédy [B] 30 F5
Malmesbury [GB] 12 G3
Malmköping [S] 168 C3
Malmö [S] 156 H3
Malmslätt [S] 166 H5
Malo [I] 72 D5
Małogoszcz [PL] 52 B1
Maloja [CH] 70 H2
Malo-les-Bains [F] 14 H6
Malomirovo [BG] 148 E5
Malónas [GR] 154 D4
Malonno [I] 72 B4
Małopolski [PL] 52 A2
Malorad [BG] 146 G3
Małowidz [PL] 24 B5
Måløy [N] 180 B5
Maloyaroslavets [RUS] 202 F3
Malpartida de Cáceres [E] 86 G5
Malpartida de Plasencia [E] 88 B5
Malpica de Bergantiños [E] 78 C1
Malpica de Tajo [E] 96 E1
Mālpils [LV] 198 E5
Malsåker [S] 168 D3
Malšice [CZ] 48 G6
Mals im Vinschgau / Málles Venosta [I] 72 B2
Malsjö [S] 166 E3
Malsjöbodarna [S] 182 H4
Målsnes [N] 192 F2
Malta [A] 72 H2
Malta [LV] 198 G6
Maltat [F] 56 E5
Maltepe [TR] 150 C5
Maltepe [TR] 150 F3
Maltesholm [S] 158 D2
Malton [GB] 10 G3
Malu [RO] 146 G1
Malung [S] 172 F4
Malungen [N] 172 C4
Malungen [S] 184 E5
Malungsfors [S] 172 F4
Maluszyn [PL] 50 H1
Malva [E] 88 D1
Malveira [P] 86 B4
Malvik [N] 182 C1
Mályi [H] 64 F5
Mały Płock [PL] 24 D5
Malyye Rozhki [RUS] 198 G1
Mamaia [RO] 204 F5
Mamarrosa [P] 80 B6
Mamers [F] 26 G6
Mammola [I] 124 D7
Mamone [I] 118 E3
Mamonovo [RUS] 22 G2
Mám Trasna / Maumtrasna [IRL] 2 B4
Mamure Kalesi [TR] 154 F4
Mamyra [N] 190 B5
Mána [GR] 136 E1
Maña [SK] 64 B4
Manacor [E] 104 F5
Manamansalo [FIN] 196 E4
Manasija, Manastir- [SRB] 146 C2
Mancha Real [E] 102 E2
Manchester [GB] 10 E4
Manching [D] 60 E2
Manciano [I] 114 G3
Mancier [F] 66 D6
Mandal [N] 164 D6
Måndalen [N] 180 E3
Mándas [I] 118 D6
Mandelieu [F] 108 E5
Mandello del Lario [I] 70 G3
Mandelsloh [D] 32 F1
Manderscheid [D] 44 G1
Mandira [TR] 150 B2
Mándra [GR] 130 H2
Mándra [GR] 134 B6
Mandráki [GR] 154 B3
Mandrikó [GR] 154 C4
Manduria [I] 122 F4
Manerba del Garda [I] 72 B6
Manérbio [I] 72 A6
Manětín [CZ] 48 D4
Mánfa [H] 76 B5
Manfredónia [I] 120 H1
Mangalia [RO] 148 G1
Mangen [N] 166 C1
Manger [N] 170 A3
Mangfall Brücke [D] 60 E5
Mångsbodarna [S] 172 F3
Mangskog [S] 166 E1
Mangualde [P] 80 C6
Manguilla [E] 96 A4
Máni [GR] 130 H1
Maniago [I] 72 F4
Manisa [TR] 152 D3
Manita Peć [HR] 112 G4
Mank [A] 62 D5
Månkarbo [S] 174 E5
Mańki [PL] 22 G4
Manlleu [E] 92 E3
Mannheim [D] 46 C4
Mano [F] 66 C4
Manoláda [GR] 136 B1
Mañón [E] 78 E1
Manorhamilton [IRL] 2 D3
Manosque [F] 108 C4
Manresa [E] 92 D3
Månsåsen [S] 182 G2
Manschnow [D] 34 G2
Mansfeld [D] 34 B4
Mansfield [GB] 10 F5
Mansilla de las Mulas [E] 78 H6
Mansle [F] 54 E6
Manso [F] 114 A3
Mansoniemi [FIN] 186 C6
Mantamádos [GR] 134 H2
Manteigas [P] 86 F2
Mantes-la-Jolie [F] 42 E3
Mantila [FIN] 186 C4
Mantíneia [GR] 136 E2
Mäntlahti [FIN] 178 D4
Mantorp [S] 166 H6
Mantoúdi [GR] 134 B4
Mantova [I] 110 E1
Mäntsälä [FIN] 176 H3
Mänttä [FIN] 186 F5
Mäntyharju [FIN] 178 C1
Mäntyjärvi [FIN] 194 E8
Mäntylahti [FIN] 188 C1
Mäntyluoto [FIN] 176 C1
Manyas [TR] 150 D5
Manzanares [E] 96 F4
Manzanares el Real [E] 88 F5
Manzaneda [E] 78 E5
Manzanera [E] 98 E3
Manzanilla [E] 94 F6
Manzat [F] 68 C1
Maó / Mahón [E] 104 H5
Maqueda [E] 88 E6
Maranchón [E] 90 B5
Maranello [I] 110 E3
Marano di Napoli [I] 120 D3
Marano Lagunare [I] 72 G5
Marans [F] 54 C4
Maratea [I] 120 G5
Marateca [P] 86 B6
Marathiás [GR] 132 F5
Marathókampos [GR] 152 C6
Marathónas [GR] 134 C6
Marathópoli [GR] 136 C4
Maráthos [GR] 140 E4
Marathóvounos (Ulukışla) [CY] 154 G5
Maravillas, Cueva de las- [E] 94 F4
Marbach [D] 46 D6
Marbäck [S] 162 C2
Marbäck [S] 162 E2
Mårbacka [S] 166 E1
Mårbacken [S] 172 E5
Marbella [E] 102 B5
Marboz [F] 68 G1
Marburg [D] 32 D6
Marcali [H] 74 H3
Marčana [HR] 112 D2
Marceddí [I] 118 B5
Marcenais [F] 66 D3
March [GB] 14 F2
Marchaux [F] 58 B4
Marche-en-Famenne [B] 30 D6
Marchegg [A] 62 G4
Marchena [E] 102 A2
Marchenilla [E] 94 G6
Marcheprime [F] 66 C3
Marciac [F] 84 F3
Marciana Marina [I] 114 D2
Marcianise [I] 120 E3
Marcigny [F] 56 E6
Marcilla [E] 84 B5
Marcillac-Vallon [F] 68 B5
Marcillat-en-Combraille [F] 56 C6
Marcilly-le-Hayer [F] 42 H5
Marcinowice [PL] 50 C1
Marciszów [PL] 50 B1
Marckolsheim [F] 58 E2
Mardalsfoss [N] 180 F4
Mardie [F] 42 E6
Mårdsele [S] 190 H4
Mårdsjö [S] 184 C2
Mårdsund [S] 182 G2
Marebbe / St Vigil [I] 72 E3
Mare de Déu de la Balma [E] 98 G1
Mare de Déu del Toro [E] 104 H4
Mårem [N] 170 F5
Måren [N] 170 C2
Marennes [F] 54 B5
Marettimo [I] 126 A2
Mareuil [F] 54 C3
Mareuil [F] 66 F2
Marevo [RUS] 202 C2
Margarítes [GR] 140 D4
Margaríti [GR] 132 C3
Margate [GB] 14 G5
Margecany [SK] 64 F2
Margherita di Savoia [I] 120 H2
Margonin [PL] 22 B6
Marhaň [SK] 52 D6
Marhanets' [UA] 204 H2
Marhet [B] 44 E1
María [E] 102 H3
Maria Birnbaum [D] 60 D3
Maria de la Salut [E] 104 E5
Maria Dreierchen [A] 62 E3
Mariager [DK] 160 D5
Maria Laach [D] 30 H6
Maria Laach [D] 30 H6
Marialva [P] 80 E5
Maria Martenthal [D] 30 G6
Mariannelund [S] 162 F2
Marianopoli [I] 126 E3
Marianos [P] 86 C4
Mariánské Lázně [CZ] 48 D4
Máriapócs [H] 64 H5
Maria Saal [A] 74 B3
Mariastein [A] 60 F6
Maria Taferl [A] 62 D4
Maria Trost [A] 74 D2
Maria Wörth [A] 74 B3
Mariazell [A] 62 D5
Maribo [DK] 20 A1
Maribor [SLO] 74 E3
Marieby [S] 182 G2
Mariedal [S] 166 E5
Mariedamm [S] 166 H4
Mariefred [S] 168 C3
Mariehamn / Maarianhamina [FIN] 176 A5
Marieholm [S] 158 C2
Marieholm [S] 162 C3
Marielyst [DK] 20 B1
Mariëmont [B] 28 H4
Marienberg [D] 48 D2
Marienberg, Kloster- / Monte Maria, Abbazia di- [I] 72 B2
Marienborn [D] 34 A3
Marienburg [D] 44 G2
Marienheide [D] 32 C5
Marienstatt [D] 32 C6
Marienthal [D] 32 C6
Mariestad [S] 166 F5
Marieux [F] 28 E4
Marifjøra [N] 170 D1
Marignane [F] 106 H5
Marigny-le-Châtel [F] 44 A5
Marihn [D] 20 C4
Marija Bistrica [HR] 74 E5
Marijampolė [LT] 24 E1
Marikostinovo [BG] 130 B2
Marilles [B] 30 D4
Marín [E] 78 B4
Marina [EST] 198 E3
Marina [HR] 116 H1
Marina [I] 108 H3
Marina [I] 118 B6
Marina di Alberese [I] 114 F3
Marina di Amendolara [I] 122 D6
Marina di Árbus [I] 118 B6
Marina di Ardea [I] 116 A6
Marina di Camerota [I] 120 G5
Marina di Campo [I] 114 D3
Marina di Caronía [I] 126 F2
Marina di Carrara [I] 110 D4
Marina di Castagneto-Donorático [I] 114 E1
Marina di Chiéuti [I] 116 F5
Marina di Gáiro [I] 118 E6
Marina di Ginosa [I] 122 E4
Marina di Gioiosa Iónica [I] 124 D7
Marina di Grosseto [I] 114 F3
Marina di Léuca [I] 122 G6
Marina di Massa [I] 110 D4
Marina di Pietrasanta [I] 110 D5
Marina di Pisa [I] 110 D5
Marina di Ragusa [I] 126 F5
Marina di Ravenna [I] 110 H3
Marina di Schiavonea [I] 124 E3
Marina di Vasto [I] 116 E5
Mar'ina Horka [BY] 202 C5
Marinaleda [E] 102 B2
Marina Palmense [I] 116 D2
Marina Romea [I] 110 H3
Marine de Sisco [F] 114 C2
Marinella [I] 126 B3
Marineo [I] 126 D2
Marines [F] 42 F2
Maringues [F] 68 D2
Marinha Grande [P] 86 C3
Marinhais [P] 86 C5
Marinkainen [FIN] 196 C5
Mar'insko [RUS] 198 G2
Mariotto [I] 122 D3
Maristella [I] 118 B3
Maristova [N] 170 E2
Marjalija [E] 96 F2
Märjamaa [EST] 198 D2
Marjaniemi [FIN] 196 C4
Marjovaara [FIN] 188 G2
Markabygd [N] 190 C6
Markaryd [S] 162 C6
Markdorf [D] 58 H4
Marke [B] 28 G2
Market Deeping [GB] 14 E1
Market Drayton [GB] 10 D5
Market Harborough [GB] 14 E2
Markethill [NIR] 2 F4
Market Rasen [GB] 10 G5
Market Weighton [GB] 10 G4
Marki [PL] 38 B2
Markina-Xemein [E] 82 H4
Märkisch Buchholz [D] 34 E3
Markitta [S] 192 H6
Markkina [FIN] 192 H4
Markkleugast [D] 46 H3
Markneukirchen [D] 48 C3
Markop [N] 194 B2
Markópoulo [GR] 136 A1
Markópoulo [GR] 136 H1
Markovac [SRB] 146 C1
Markova Sušica [MK] 128 E1
Markovci pri Ptuju [SLO] 74 E4
Markov Manastir [MK] 128 E1
Markovo [BG] 148 E3
Markovo Kale [SRB] 146 D5
Markranstädt [D] 34 C5
Marksburg [D] 46 B2
Markt Bibart [D] 46 F4
Marktbreit [D] 46 E4
Markt Erlbach [D] 46 F5
Marktheidenfeld [D] 46 E4
Markt-Indersdorf [D] 60 E3
Marktjärn [S] 184 D4
Marktl [D] 60 G4
Marktoberdorf [D] 60 C5
Marktredwitz [D] 48 C4
Markt St Florian [A] 62 B4
Markt St Martin [A] 62 F6
Marktzeuln [D] 46 G3
Markušica [HR] 142 E1
Markušovce [SK] 64 F2
Markvarerc [CZ] 62 D2
Marl [D] 30 H2
Marlborough [GB] 12 H3
Marle [F] 28 G5
Marlenheim [F] 44 G6
Marlens [F] 70 B3
Marlow [D] 20 C3
Marma [S] 174 E4
Marmande [F] 66 E4
Marmara [TR] 150 C4
Marmaraereğlisi [TR] 150 D3
Marmári [GR] 134 D6
Marmaris [TR] 154 D2
Mármaro [GR] 134 G4
Marmelete [P] 94 B4
Marmolejo [E] 102 D1
Marmore, Cascata delle- [I] 116 A3
Marmoutier [F] 44 G5
Marmuri, Grotta su- [I] 118 D5
Marnay [F] 58 A4
Marne [D] 18 E3
Marnitz [D] 20 B5
Maróneia [GR] 130 F3
Maroslele [H] 76 E4
Maróstica [I] 72 D5
Marotta [I] 112 C6
Marpíssa [GR] 138 E3
Marquartstein [D] 60 F5
Marquion [F] 28 F4
Marquise [F] 14 G6
Marradi [I] 110 F5
Marrebæk [DK] 20 B1
Marrúbiu [I] 118 C5
Marsala [I] 126 B2
Mărşani [RO] 146 G2
Marsberg [D] 32 E4
Marschlins [CH] 58 H6
Marsciano [I] 116 A2
Marseillan [F] 106 E4
Marseillan-Plage [F] 106 E5
Marseille [F] 106 H5
Marseille-en-Beauvaisis [F] 28 D5
Marshavitsy [RUS] 198 H4
Marsico Nuovo [I] 120 G4
Marsico Vetere [I] 120 H4
Marsiliana [I] 114 F3
Marsjö [S] 168 A4
Marsliden [S] 190 E4
Märsta [S] 168 D2
Marstal [DK] 156 D4
Marstrand [S] 160 G1
Märsylä [FIN] 196 C5
Marta [I] 114 G3
Martano [I] 122 G5
Martel [F] 66 G4
Martelange [B] 44 E2
Mártély [H] 76 E4
Marten [BG] 148 D1
Martfű [H] 76 E2
Marthille [F] 44 F5
Marthon [F] 66 F1
Martigné-Ferchaud [F] 40 G5
Martigny [CH] 70 C2
Martigues [F] 106 H5
Martim Longo [P] 94 D4
Martin [SK] 64 C2
Martina / Martinsbruck [CH] 72 B2
Martina Franca [I] 122 E3
Martinci Čepinski [HR] 142 D1
Martín de la Jara [E] 102 B3
Martín de Yeltes [E] 88 B3
Martinet [E] 92 D1
Martinje [SLO] 74 E3
Martíno [GR] 134 B5
Martinsbruck / Martina [CH] 72 B2
Martinsicuro [I] 116 D3
Martinszell [D] 60 E3
Martinvast [F] 26 D2
Mártis [I] 118 C3
Martjanci [SLO] 74 E3
Martna [EST] 198 D2
Martock [GB] 12 F4
Martofte [DK] 156 E3
Martonvaara [FIN] 188 F1
Martonvásár [H] 76 C1
Martorell [E] 92 D4
Martos [E] 102 D2
Mårtsviken [S] 172 E3
Martti [FIN] 194 E6
Marttila [FIN] 176 E4
Maruflar [TR] 152 C3
Maruševec [HR] 74 E4
Marvão [P] 86 F5
Marvejols [F] 68 C5
Marvik [S] 164 B2
Marwałd [PL] 22 G5
Marxwalde [D] 34 F2
Marxzell [D] 46 B6
Marynin [PL] 38 F5
Maryport [GB] 8 D6
Marzabotto [I] 110 F4
Marzahna [D] 34 D3
Marzahne [D] 34 D2
Marzamemi [I] 126 G6
Marzocca [I] 112 C6
Măsca [RO] 76 H4
Maschen [D] 18 F5
Mas d'Azil, Grotte du- [F] 84 H4
Mas de Barberans [E] 92 A5
Mas de las Matas [E] 90 F6
Masegoso de Tajuña [E] 90 A5
Maser [I] 72 E5
Masevaux [F] 58 D3
Masfjordnes [N] 170 B2
Mashan [AL] 128 C4
Masi [N] 194 B4
Maside [E] 78 C4
Masi Torello [I] 110 G3
Maskjok [N] 194 D2
Masku [FIN] 176 D4
Maslarevo [BG] 148 C3
Maslenica [HR] 112 G4
Maslinica [HR] 116 H1
Maslovare [BIH] 142 C3
Maso [FIN] 186 G3
Maspalomas [E] 100 C6
Massa [I] 110 D4
Massa Fiscaglia [I] 110 G3
Massafra [I] 122 E4
Massa Lubrense [I] 120 E4
Massamagrell [E] 98 F4
Massa Marittima [I] 114 F2
Massat [F] 84 H5
Massay [F] 56 B3
Masseret [F] 66 G2
Masseube [F] 84 G3
Massiac [F] 68 C3
Mastaura [TR] 152 E5
Masterelv [N] 194 B2
Mastergeeby / Máistir Gaoithe [IRL] 4 A4
Masterud [N] 172 D5
Mas Thibert [F] 106 G4
Mastichári [GR] 154 B2
Mästocka [S] 162 B5
Masty [BY] 24 G4
Masugnsbyn [S] 192 H5
Maszewo [PL] 20 G5
Maszewo [PL] 34 G3
Matabuena [E] 88 G4
Mata de Alcántara [E] 86 G4
Mátala [GR] 140 D5
Matalascañas [E] 100 F2
Matalebreras [E] 84 A6
Matallana de Torío [E] 82 B5
Matallana de Toríos [E] 82 B3
Mataporquera [E] 82 E4
Matara [FIN] 188 E1
Matarágka [GR] 132 F2
Mataró [E] 92 E4
Mataruška Banja [SRB] 146 B3
Mätäsvaara [FIN] 196 G6
Matejče, Manastir- [MK] 146 D6
Matelica [I] 116 B2
Matera [I] 122 D4
Matersdalen [N] 170 B5
Mateševo [MNE] 144 E3
Matfors [S] 184 E5
Matha [F] 54 D5
Mathay [F] 58 C4
Mathildedal [FIN] 176 E5
Matignon [F] 26 B4
Matīši [LV] 198 E4
Matka, Manastir- [MK] 128 E1
Matkavaara [FIN] 196 F4
Matlock [GB] 10 E5
Matochina [BG] 150 A1
Matos [P] 94 D3
Matosinhos [P] 80 B4
Matour [F] 56 F6
Mátrafüred [H] 64 E5
Mátraháza [H] 64 E5
Mátraszentimre [H] 64 D5
Mátraterenye [H] 64 E5
Mátraverebély [H] 64 D5
Matre [N] 170 B5
Matre [N] 170 B2
Matrei am Brenner [A] 72 D1
Matrei in Osttirol [A] 72 F2
Matrosovo [RUS] 200 D5
Mattaur [S] 190 G2
Matteröd [S] 158 C1
Mattersburg [A] 62 F6
Mattighofen [A] 60 G4
Mattila [FIN] 188 E6
Mattilanmäki [FIN] 194 E7
Mattinata [I] 116 H6
Mattinen [FIN] 176 C4
Mattmar [S] 182 F2
Mattsee [A] 60 G5
Mättsund [S] 196 B3
Matulji [HR] 112 E1
Matyli [BY] 24 G3
Matzen [A] 60 E6
Matzen [A] 62 F4
Maubeuge [F] 28 G4
Maubourguet [F] 84 F3
Mauchline [GB] 8 D4
Mauerkirchen [A] 60 H4
Maukdal [N] 192 F3
Maula [FIN] 196 C2
Maulbronn [D] 46 C6
Mauléon [F] 54 D2
Mauléon-Licharre [F] 84 D3
Maulévrier [F] 54 D2
Maumtrasna / Mám Trasna [IRL] 2 B4
Maunujärvi [FIN] 194 C6
Maupas, Château de- [F] 56 C3
Maupertus-sur-Mer [F] 26 D2
Maura [N] 172 B5
Maurach [A] 60 E6
Maure [F] 26 B6
Mauriac [F] 68 B3
Maurnes [N] 192 D3
Mauron [F] 26 B6
Maurs [F] 66 H5
Maurstad [N] 180 B5
Maurvangen [N] 170 F1
Maury [F] 106 C6
Mautern [A] 74 C1
Mauterndorf [A] 72 H2
Mauth [D] 62 A2
Mauthausen [A] 62 C4
Mauvezin [F] 84 G2
Mauvoisin [CH] 70 D3
Mauzé-sur-le-Mignon [F] 54 C4
Mavréli [GR] 132 F1
Mavrochóri [GR] 128 E5
Mavrokklísi [GR] 130 H2
Mavroléfki [GR] 130 D3
Mavromáta [GR] 132 F3
Mavromáti [GR] 136 D3
Mavrothálassa [GR] 130 C3
Mavrovi Hanovi [MK] 128 D2
Mavrovo [MK] 128 D2
Mavrovoúni [GR] 132 G2
Mavrovoúni [GR] 136 E5
Maximiliana [E] 102 C4
Maximilians-Licharre [D] 46 H5
Maxmo / Maksamaa [FIN] 186 B2
Maybole [GB] 8 C4
Mayen [D] 30 H6
Mayenne [F] 26 E6
Mayet [F] 42 B6
Maynooth [IRL] 2 F6
Mayoralgo [E] 86 H5
Mayorga [E] 82 B5
Mayrhofen [A] 72 E1
Mäyry [FIN] 186 D3
Mazagón [E] 94 E6
Mazagran [F] 44 C3
Mazamet [F] 106 C4
Mazara del Vallo [I] 126 B3
Mazarrón [E] 104 B4
Mažeikiai [LT] 198 C6
Mazères [F] 106 A4
Mazerulles [F] 44 F5
Mázia [GR] 132 D2
Mazières-en-Gâtine [F] 54 D4
Maziköy [TR] 154 C2
Mazilmaja [LV] 198 B6
Mazirbe [LV] 198 C4
Mazotos [CY] 154 G6
Mazsalaca [LV] 198 E3
Mazurki [PL] 38 C4
Mazyr [BY] 202 C6
Mazzalve [LV] 198 E6
Mazzarino [I] 126 E4
Mazzaró [I] 124 B8
Mazzarrone [I] 126 F5
M. Bondone [I] 72 C4
Mchowo [PL] 22 H6
M. D. de la Salut [E] 92 F3
M. D. de Pinós [E] 92 D3
M. D. de Queralt [E] 92 D2
Mdzewo [PL] 22 G6
Mealhada [P] 80 B6
Méandre de Queuille [F] 68 C1
Meaux [F] 42 G3
Mechelen (Malines) [B] 30 C3
Mechernich [D] 30 G5
Mechka [BG] 148 C2
Mechowo [PL] 20 F4
Mecidiye [TR] 152 D3
Męcikał [PL] 22 C4
Meckenbeuren [D] 60 A5
Mecsér [H] 62 H5
Meda [P] 80 E5
Medak [HR] 112 G4
Mede [I] 70 F6
Medebach [D] 32 D5
Medelim [P] 86 F3
Medellín [E] 96 A3
Medelser Schlucht [CH] 70 G1
Medemblik [NL] 16 E3
Medena Selišta [BIH] 142 B4
Meden Rudnik [BG] 148 F4
Medenychi [UA] 52 H5
Medet [TR] 152 G6
Medetli [TR] 150 G4
Medevi [S] 166 G5
Medgidia [RO] 204 E5
Medgyesháza [H] 76 G3
Medhamn [S] 166 F3

Mediaş [RO] 204 C4
Medicina [I] 110 G3
Medina [H] 76 B4
Medina Azahara [E] 102 C1
Medinaceli [E] 90 B4
Medina del Campo [E] 88 E2
Medina de Pomar [E] 82 F4
Medina de Rioseco [E] 82 B6
Medina-Sidonia [E] 100 G4
Medininkai [LT] 200 G5
Medle [S] 196 A4
Médole [I] 110 E1
Médous, Grotte de- [F] 84 F4
Médousa [GR] 130 E2
Medovina [BG] 146 E2
Medskogen [S] 172 D4
Medstugan [S] 182 E1
Medugorje [BIH] 144 C2
Medulin [HR] 112 D3
Medvedja [SRB] 146 D4
Medved'ov [SK] 62 H5
Medvida [HR] 112 H5
Medvode [SLO] 74 B5
Medyka [PL] 52 F4
Medze [LV] 198 B6
Medzev [SK] 64 F3
Medzilaborce [SK] 52 E6
Medžitlija [MK] 128 E4
Meerane [D] 48 C1
Meerkerk [NL] 16 D5
Meersburg [D] 58 H4
Meeuwen [B] 30 E3
Mefjordvaer [N] 192 E2
Méga Chorió [GR] 132 F4
Méga Déreio [GR] 130 G2
Méga Doukáto [GR] 130 F3
Megáli Vólvi [GR] 130 B4
Megalochóri [GR] 132 F2
Megálo Chorió [GR] 154 B3
Megálo Livádi [GR] 138 C3
Megalópoli [GR] 136 D3
Mégara [GR] 134 B6
Megara Hyblaea [I] 126 G4
Méga Spílaio [GR] 132 G6
Megève [F] 70 B3
Megísti [GR] 154 G3
Megístis Lávras, Moní- [GR] 130 D5
Megorjelo [BIH] 144 C3
Meg. Panagía [GR] 130 C5
Megyaszó [H] 64 F4
Mehadia [RO] 204 C5
Mehamn [N] 194 D1
Mehikoorma [EST] 198 G3
Mehmetcik (Galatia) [CY] 154 G4
Mehov Krš [SRB] 146 B4
Mehring [D] 44 G2
Mehtäkylä [FIN] 196 C5
Mehun-sur-Yèvre [F] 56 B3
Meiåvollen [N] 182 C3
Meijel [NL] 30 F3
Meilen [CH] 58 F5
Meillant, Château de- [F] 56 C4
Meilleraye, Abbaye de- [F] 40 F5
Meina [I] 70 F4
Meine [D] 32 H2
Meinerzhagen [D] 32 C5
Meiningen [D] 46 F2
Meira [E] 78 E3
Meirāni [LV] 198 F5
Meiringen [CH] 70 E1
Meisenheim [D] 44 H3
Meisingset [N] 180 F2
Meissen [D] 34 E6
Meitingen [D] 60 D3
Męka [PL] 36 F5
Mekece [TR] 150 G4
Mekinje [SLO] 74 C4
Mekrijärvi [FIN] 188 H2
Meksa Šantić [SRB] 76 D5
Mel [I] 72 E4
Mélampes [GR] 140 D5
Melaniós [GR] 134 G4
Meláes [GR] 132 D3
Melbeck [D] 18 G5
Melbu [N] 192 D4
Meldal [N] 180 H2
Meldola [I] 110 G4
Meldorf [D] 18 E2
Melegnano [I] 70 G5
Melenci [SRB] 76 E6
Melene [TR] 152 B2
Melfi [I] 120 G3
Melgaço [P] 78 C5
Melgar de Arriba [E] 82 C5
Melgar de Fernamental [E] 82 D5
Melgarejo [E] 100 G3
Melholt [DK] 160 E3
Melhus [N] 180 F2
Melhus [N] 182 B1
Melide [E] 78 D3
Melides [P] 94 B2
Meligalás [GR] 136 D3
Melíki [GR] 128 G5
Melilli [I] 126 G4
Melisenda [I] 118 E6
Mélisey [F] 58 C3
Mélissa [GR] 130 E3
Melissáni [GR] 132 C6
Melíssi [GR] 132 E1
Melissópetra [GR] 128 D6
Melissourgós [GR] 130 B4
Melito di Porto Salvo [I] 124 C8
Melitopol' [UA] 204 H2
Melívoia [GR] 130 E2
Melk [A] 62 D4
Melksham [GB] 12 G3
Mellakoski [FIN] 194 C8
Mellansel [S] 184 F1
Mellansjö [S] 184 C5
Mellanström [S] 190 G3
Mellau [A] 60 B6
Mellby [S] 162 E3
Mellbystrand [S] 162 B5
Melle [D] 32 D2
Melle [F] 54 D5
Mellendorf [D] 32 F1
Mellerud [S] 166 D5
Mellieha [M] 126 C6
Mellilä [FIN] 176 E3
Mellin [D] 34 A1
Melloussa [MA] 100 G6
Mellrichstadt [D] 46 F2
Mellstaby [S] 158 G1
Melnica [SRB] 146 C1
Melnik [BG] 130 B2
Mělník [CZ] 48 F3
Mel'nikovo [RUS] 178 G2
Melrand [F] 26 A5
Melrose [GB] 8 F4
Melsomvik [N] 164 H3
Melsungen [D] 32 F5
Meltaus [FIN] 194 C7
Melton Mowbray [GB] 10 F6
Meltosjärvi [FIN] 194 C8
Melun [F] 42 G4
Melvich [GB] 6 E2
Mélykút [H] 76 D4
Melzo [I] 70 G5
Membrilla [E] 96 F4
Membrío [E] 86 F4
Memer [F] 66 H6
Mem Martins [P] 86 A5
Memmingen [D] 60 B4
Mémorial du Omaha Beach [F] 26 E3
Mena [UA] 202 E6
Menággio [I] 70 G3
Menai Bridge [GB] 10 B4
Menasalbas [E] 96 E2
Menat [F] 56 C6
Mencshely [H] 74 H2
Mendavia [E] 82 H6
Mende [F] 68 C6
Menden [D] 32 C4
Menderes [TR] 152 C4
Mendig [D] 30 H6
Mending [A] 62 C6
Mendrisio [CH] 70 G4
Ménéac [F] 26 B5
Menec [F] 40 D5
Menemen [TR] 152 C4
Menen [B] 28 F2
Menetés [GR] 140 H3
Ménez Hom [F] 40 B2
Menfi [I] 126 C3
Ménfőcsanak [H] 62 H6
Menga, Cueva de- [E] 102 C4
Mengamuñoz [E] 88 D4
Mengen [D] 58 H3
Mengeš [SLO] 74 C4
Mengíbar [E] 102 E1
Mengishevo [BG] 148 E3
Menídi [GR] 132 D3
Ménigoute [F] 54 E4
Ménina [GR] 132 C2
Menonen [FIN] 176 F3
Mens [F] 68 H6
Menstrup [DK] 156 F4
Menthon [F] 70 B3
Menton [F] 108 F4
Méntrida [E] 88 E6
Menyushi [RUS] 202 B2
Menz [D] 20 C6
Meppel [NL] 16 F3
Meppen [D] 16 H4
Mequinenza [E] 90 G5
Mequinenza, Castillo de- [E] 90 G5
Mer [F] 54 H1
Mera de Boixo [E] 78 D1
Meråker [N] 182 D1
Meran / Merano [I] 72 D3
Merano / Meran [I] 72 D3
Merate [I] 70 G4
Mercatale [I] 114 H1
Mercatino Conca [I] 110 H5
Mercato San Severino [I] 120 F3
Mercato Saraceno [I] 110 G5
Mercéz [SRB] 146 C4
Merdrignac [F] 26 B5
Méréville [F] 42 F5
Merges [H] 62 H6
Mergozzo [I] 70 F3
Méribel-les-Allues [F] 70 B4
Meriç [TR] 130 H2
Mérichas [GR] 138 C2
Merichleri [BG] 148 C5
Meriçler [TR] 152 D6
Mérida [E] 94 H2
Merijärvi [FIN] 196 C5
Merikarvia / Sastmola [FIN] 186 B6
Merimasku [FIN] 176 D4
Měřín [CZ] 50 A5
Mering [D] 60 D4
Merkendorf [D] 46 F6
Merkine [LT] 24 G2
Merklingen [D] 60 B3
Merlara [I] 110 F1
Merle, Tours de- [F] 66 H4
Merlevenez [F] 40 C4
Merligen [CH] 70 E1
Mern [DK] 156 G4
Mernye [H] 76 A4
Merošina [SRB] 146 D3
Merrahalsen [N] 170 G1
Mersch [D] 30 F4
Mersch [L] 44 F2
Merseburg [D] 34 C5
Mersinbeleni [TR] 152 D6
Mērsrags [LV] 198 C4
Merthyr Tydfil [GB] 12 F2
Mértola [P] 94 D4
Méru [F] 42 F2
Mervans [F] 56 G5
Merville [F] 28 E3
Méry [F] 44 A5
Meryemana [TR] 152 D5
Merzig [D] 44 F3
Mesagne [I] 122 F4
Mesão Frio [P] 80 D4
Mesariá [GR] 138 D1
Meschede [D] 32 D5
Meschers-sur-Gironde [F] 54 C6
Mešeišta [MK] 128 D3
Meseníkólas [GR] 132 F3
Meshchovsk [RUS] 202 E4
Mési [GR] 130 F3
Mesillas [E] 88 B5
Mesimvría [GR] 130 G3
Mesinge [DK] 156 E3
Meškasalis [LT] 24 G2
Mesklá [GR] 140 C4
Meslay [F] 40 H5
Mesnalien [N] 172 B2
Mesnil-Val [F] 28 C4
Mesocco [CH] 70 G2
Mesochóra [GR] 132 E2
Mesochóri [GR] 132 F1
Mesochóri [GR] 140 G2
Mésola [I] 110 H2
Mesolóngi [GR] 132 E5
Mesón do Vento [E] 78 C2
Mesopótamo [GR] 132 C3
Mespelbrunn [D] 46 D3
Messancy [B] 44 E2
Messas [F] 42 E6
Messdorf [D] 34 B1
Messelt [N] 172 C1
Messina [I] 124 B7
Messines de Baixo [P] 94 C5
Messíni [GR] 136 D4
Messkirch [D] 58 G3
Messlingen [S] 182 E3
Messtetten [D] 58 G3
Mesta [BG] 130 C1
Mestá [GR] 134 G5
Mestanza [E] 96 E5
Městec Králové [CZ] 48 H3
Mestervik [N] 192 F2
Mésti [GR] 130 G3
Mestilä [FIN] 176 D3
Mestlin [D] 20 B4
Město Albrechtice [CZ] 50 D3
Město Libavá [CZ] 50 D5
Mestre [I] 72 E6
Mesvres [F] 56 F5
Mesztegnyő [H] 74 H4
Metabief [F] 58 B6
Metagkítsi [GR] 130 C5
Metaljka [BIH] 144 E2
Metamórfosi [GR] 130 C5
Metanjac [MNE] 146 A4
Metapontium [I] 122 D4
Metaxádes [GR] 130 H1
Metaxás [GR] 128 F6
Metéora [GR] 132 E1
Méteren [F] 28 F2
Méthana [GR] 136 G2
Methóni [GR] 128 G5
Methóni [GR] 136 C4
Metković [HR] 144 C3
Metličina [BG] 148 F2
Metlika [SLO] 74 D6
Metnitz [A] 74 B2
Metóchi [GR] 132 E6
Metóchi [GR] 134 A3
Metsäkylä [FIN] 178 C3
Metsäkylä [FIN] 196 F3
Metsälä / Ömossa [FIN] 186 B5
Metsküla [EST] 198 C3
Métsovo [GR] 132 D1
Metten [D] 60 G2
Mettet [B] 30 C5
Mettingen [D] 32 C2
Mettlach [D] 44 F3
Mettmann [D] 30 G3
Metz [F] 44 E4
Metzervisse [F] 44 F3
Metzingen [D] 58 H2
Meulan [F] 42 F3
Meung-sur-Loire [F] 42 E6
Meuselwitz [D] 34 C6
Meux [B] 30 D5
Mexilhoeira Grande [P] 94 B5
Meximieux [F] 68 G2
Meyenburg [D] 20 B5
Meylan [F] 68 H4
Meymac [F] 68 B2
Meyrargues [F] 108 B4
Meyrueis [F] 106 E2
Meyzieu [F] 68 G3
Mézapos [GR] 136 E5
Mezdra [BG] 146 G4
Mèze [F] 106 E4
Mézel [F] 108 D3
Mężenin [PL] 24 D6
Mežica [SLO] 74 C4
Mézières [F] 54 F5
Mézières-en-Brenne [F] 54 G4
Mézilhac [F] 68 E5
Mézin [F] 66 D6
Mezőberény [H] 76 G3
Mezőcsát [H] 64 F5
Mezőfalva [H] 76 C2
Mezőhegyes [H] 76 F4
Mezőhék [H] 76 E2
Mezőkeresztes [H] 64 F5
Mezőkovácsháza [H] 76 F4
Mezőkövesd [H] 64 F5
Mezőlak [H] 74 H1
Mezőnyárád [H] 64 F5
Mezőörs [H] 64 A6
Mèzos [F] 66 B5
Mezősas [H] 76 G2
Mezőszilas [H] 76 B3
Mezőtúr [H] 76 F2
Mezquita de Jarque [E] 90 E6
Mezzojuso [I] 126 D2
Mezzolombardo [I] 72 C4
Mgarr [M] 126 C5
Miączyn [PL] 52 G1
Miami Platja [E] 90 H6
Mianowice [PL] 22 C2
Miasteczko Śląskie [PL] 50 F2
Miastko [PL] 22 B3
Miastkowo [PL] 24 C5
Michałkowo [PL] 24 B2
Michalovce [SK] 64 H2
Michałów [PL] 38 C6
Michałów [PL] 52 B2
Michałowo [PL] 24 F6
Michelдорf [A] 62 B5
Michelstadt [D] 46 D4
Michendorf [D] 34 D3
Michów [PL] 38 D5
Michurinskoye [RUS] 178 G3
Middelburg [NL] 16 B6
Middelfart [DK] 156 C3
Middelharnis [NL] 16 C5
Middelkerke-Bad [B] 28 F1
Middlesbrough [GB] 10 F2
Middlewich [GB] 10 D4
Midéa [GR] 136 F2
Midhurst [GB] 14 D5
Midleton [IRL] 4 D5
Midlum [D] 18 D3
Midsland [NL] 16 E1
Midsund [N] 180 D3
Midtgulen [N] 180 B5
Midtskogberget [N] 172 D2
Miechów [PL] 50 H3
Mieders [A] 72 D1
Miedes [E] 90 D4
Międzdroje [PL] 20 F3
Miedźno [PL] 50 G1
Międzybórz [PL] 36 D5
Międzybrodzie Bialskie [PL] 50 G4
Międzychód [PL] 36 B2
Międzygórze [PL] 50 C3
Międzylesie [PL] 50 C3
Międzyrzec Podlaski [PL] 38 E3
Międzyrzecz [PL] 36 A2
Miehikkälä [FIN] 178 D3
Miejsce Piastowe [PL] 52 D5
Miejska Górka [PL] 36 C5
Miélan [F] 84 F3
Mielec [PL] 52 D3
Mielno [PL] 20 H3
Mielno [PL] 34 G5
Mieluskylä [FIN] 196 D5
Mieraslompolo [FIN] 194 D3
Miercurea Ciuc [RO] 204 D4
Mieres [E] 78 H4
Mierkenis [S] 190 F1
Mieron [N] 194 B4
Mieroszów [PL] 50 B2
Miersig [RO] 76 H2
Mierzyno [PL] 22 D1
Miesbach [D] 60 E5
Mieścisko [PL] 36 D2
Mieste [D] 34 B2
Miesterhorst [D] 34 A2
Mieszkowice [PL] 34 G1
Mietoinen [FIN] 176 D4
Mieussy [F] 70 B2
Mifol [AL] 128 A5
Migennes [F] 42 H6
Migliacciaro [I] 114 C4
Migliarino [I] 110 D5
Migliarino [I] 110 G3
Migliónico [I] 122 D4
Mignano Monte Lungo [I] 120 D1
Migne [F] 54 G4
Miguel Esteban [E] 96 G3
Miguelturra [E] 96 E4
Mihăeşti [RO] 148 B1
Mihai Bravu [RO] 148 C1
Mihajlovac [SRB] 146 E1
Mihalgazi [TR] 150 H4
Mihályi [H] 62 G6
Mihla [D] 32 G6
Miiluranta [FIN] 196 E5
Mijares [E] 88 D5
Mijares [E] 98 D4
Mijas [E] 102 B5
Mijoux [F] 70 A1
Mikaelshulen [N] 164 G3
Mikalavas [LT] 24 G2
Mike [H] 74 H4
Mikhaylovo [BG] 146 G3
Mikkelbostad [N] 192 E3
Mikkeli / St Michel [FIN] 188 C6
Mikkelvika [N] 192 F1
Mikleuš [HR] 74 A6
Mikóháza [H] 64 G3
Mikolaivka [UA] 204 H4
Mikołajki [PL] 24 C4
Mikołajki Pomorskie [PL] 22 F4
Mikolin [PL] 50 D2
Mikołów [PL] 50 F3
Mikoszewo [PL] 22 E2
Mikre [BG] 148 A4
Mikrevo [BG] 130 B1
Mikró Chorió [GR] 132 F4
Mikró Déreio [GR] 130 G2
Mikrókampos [GR] 128 H4
Mikrópoli [GR] 130 C3
Mikrothíves [GR] 132 H3
Mikstat [PL] 36 E5
Mikulčice [CZ] 62 G3
Mikulov [CZ] 62 F3
Mikulovice [CZ] 50 D3
Mikulovice [CZ] 62 E2
Miłakowo [PL] 22 G3
Miland [N] 170 F5
Milano [I] 70 G5
Milano Marittima [I] 110 H4
Milanovac [HR] 76 A6
Milanówek [PL] 38 B3
Mílatos [GR] 140 F4
Milazzo [I] 124 B7
Mildenhall [GB] 14 F2
Milejczyce [PL] 38 F2
Milejewo [PL] 22 F3
Milena [I] 126 D3
Mileševa, Manastir- [SRB] 146 A3
Mileševo [SRB] 76 E6
Milet [TR] 152 D6
Miletići [HR] 112 G4
Mileto [I] 124 D6
Miletopolis [TR] 150 E4
Milevsko [CZ] 48 F5
Milford [IRL] 2 F2
Milford Haven [GB] 12 D2
Milharadas [P] 94 B4
Milići [BIH] 142 E4
Milicz [PL] 36 D5
Miliés [GR] 134 A2
Milín [CZ] 48 F5
Milína [GR] 134 A3
Milino [MK] 128 F1
Militello in Val di Catania [I] 126 F4
Miljevina [BIH] 144 D2
Millares [E] 98 E5
Millas [F] 92 F1
Millau [F] 106 D2
Millesimo [I] 108 G3
Millesvik [S] 166 E4
Millevaches [F] 68 B2
Millinge [DK] 156 D4
Millom [GB] 10 D2
Millstatt [A] 72 H3
Millstreet [IRL] 4 C4
Milltown [IRL] 4 B4
Milltown Malbay [IRL] 2 B6
Milmarcos [E] 90 C5
Milmersdorf [D] 20 D6
Milna [HR] 144 A2
Miločer [MNE] 144 D4
Miłocin [PL] 38 D5
Miłomłyn [PL] 22 G4
Milos [GR] 138 D4
Milosavci [BIH] 142 C2
Miloševa Kula [SRB] 146 D1
Miłosław [PL] 36 D3
Milovice u Hořic [CZ] 50 A3
Milow [D] 20 A5
Milówka [PL] 50 G5
Milreu [P] 94 C5
Milseburg [D] 46 E2
Milštejn [CZ] 48 G1
Miltach [D] 48 D6
Miltenberg [D] 46 D4
Milton Keynes [GB] 14 E3
Mimizan [F] 66 B4
Mimizan-Plage [F] 66 B4
Mimoň [CZ] 48 G2
Mina de São Domingos [P] 94 D4
Minas de Oro (Romanas) [E] 78 G3
Minas de Riotinto [E] 94 F5
Minateda, Cuevas de- [E] 104 B1
Minateda-Horca [E] 104 B1
Minaya [E] 98 B4
Minde [N] 164 C5
Mindelheim [D] 60 C4
Minden [D] 32 E2
Mindin [F] 40 E6
Mindszent [H] 76 E3
Minehead [GB] 12 E3
Mineo [I] 126 F4
Mineralni Bani [BG] 148 C6
Minerbio [I] 110 F3
Minervino di Lecce [I] 122 H5
Minervino Murge [I] 120 H2
Minervio [F] 114 C2
Minglanilla [E] 98 C4
Mingorria [E] 88 E4
Minićevo [SRB] 146 E3
Minne [S] 182 H5
Minnesund [N] 172 C4
Minnetler [TR] 152 D1
Miño [E] 78 D2
Mínoa [GR] 138 G4
Minot [F] 56 G2
Minsen [D] 18 C3
Minsk [BY] 202 B5
Mińsk Mazowiecki [PL] 38 C3
Minturnae [I] 120 D2
Minturno [I] 120 D2
Miočić [HR] 142 A5
Miočinovići [HR] 142 A1
Miokovićevo [HR] 74 H6
Mionica [SRB] 146 A1
Mira [E] 98 D3
Mira [I] 72 E6
Mira [P] 80 B6
Mirabel [E] 86 H4
Mirabella Imbáccari [I] 126 F4
Mirabello [I] 110 F2
Miradolo Terme [I] 70 G6
Mirador del Fito [E] 82 C2
Miraflores [E] 82 E6
Miraflores [E] 96 E4
Miraflores de la Sierra [E] 88 F4
Miramar [F] 108 E5
Miramare [I] 112 B5
Miramare, Castello di- [I] 72 H6
Miramas [F] 106 G4
Mirambeau [F] 66 D2
Miramont-de-Guyenne [F] 66 E4
Miranda [E] 84 B4
Miranda de Ebro [E] 82 G5
Miranda do Corvo [P] 86 D2
Miranda do Douro [P] 80 G4
Mirande [F] 84 F3
Mirandela [P] 80 E4
Mirándola [I] 110 F2
Mirano [I] 72 E6
Mirantes [E] 78 G5
Miravci [MK] 128 G2
Miravet [E] 90 H6
Mirebeau [F] 54 E3
Mirebeau [F] 56 H3
Mirecourt [F] 44 E6
Mirepoix [F] 106 B5
Mířkov [CZ] 48 D5
Mirna [SLO] 74 C5
Mirna Peč [SLO] 74 C5
Mirnice [HR] 144 A2
Miróbriga [P] 94 B2
Mirocin Średni [PL] 34 H4
Miroslav [CZ] 62 F2
Mirosławiec [PL] 20 H5
Mirošov [CZ] 48 E5
Mirovice [CZ] 48 F5
Mirovo [BG] 146 G5
Mirow [D] 20 C5
Mirów [PL] 50 G2
Mirsk [PL] 48 H1
Mirto [I] 124 E3
Mirueña [E] 88 D4
Mişca [RO] 76 H3
Misi [FIN] 194 D7
Mišićevo [SRB] 76 D5
Misilmeri [I] 126 D2
Miskolc [H] 64 F4
Miskolctapolca [H] 64 F5
Mislata [E] 98 E4
Mislinja [SLO] 74 D4
Missanello [I] 120 H5
Misso [EST] 198 F4
Mistelbach [A] 62 F3
Misten [N] 192 D5
Misterbianco [I] 126 G3
Misterhult [S] 162 G3
Mistretta [I] 126 F2
Misurina [I] 72 E3
Miszewo [PL] 22 D2
Mitchelstown [IRL] 4 D4
Mitchelstown Caves [IRL] 4 D4
Míthymna [GR] 134 G2
Mitrašinci [MK] 128 G1
Mitrópoli [GR] 132 F3
Mitrova Reka [SRB] 146 B4
Mitrovo [SRB] 146 C3
Mitseh [A] 74 C2
Mittådalen [S] 182 E3
Mittelberg [A] 60 B6
Mittelberg [A] 72 C2
Mittelberg [D] 60 C5
Mittelsaida [D] 48 E2
Mittelstenahe [D] 18 E4
Mittenwald [D] 60 D6
Mittenwalde [D] 20 D5
Mittenwalde [D] 34 E3
Mittersill [A] 72 F1
Mitterteich [D] 48 C4
Mittet [N] 180 E3
Mittewald [A] 72 F3
Mittweida [D] 34 D6
Mitwitz [D] 46 G3
Mizhiria [UA] 204 C3
Mizil [RO] 204 E5
Miziya [BG] 146 G2
Mjåland [N] 164 E4
Mjällby [S] 158 E2
Mjällom [S] 184 G3
Mjåvatn [N] 164 E4
Mjell [N] 170 C1
Mjöbäck [S] 162 B3
Mjölby [S] 166 H6
Mjølfjell [N] 170 D3
Mjölkbäcken [S] 190 E2
Mjönäs [S] 166 F1
Mjøndalen [N] 164 G1
Mjønes [N] 180 H1
Mjørlund [N] 172 B4
Mjösebo [S] 162 F4
Mjösjöby [S] 190 G6
M. Kalývia [GR] 132 F2
Mladá Boleslav [CZ] 48 G3
Mladá Vožice [CZ] 48 G5
Mladé Buky [CZ] 50 A2
Mladečská Jeskyně [CZ] 50 C5
Mladenovac [SRB] 146 B1
Mladenovac [SRB] 204 B6
Mlado Nagoričane [MK] 146 D6
Mlamolovo [BG] 146 F5
Mława [PL] 22 G6
Mleczno [PL] 36 B5
Mlekarevo [BG] 148 D5
Mlini [HR] 144 C4
Mlinište [BIH] 142 B4
Młodasko [PL] 36 B2
Młogoszyn [PL] 36 G3
Młynary [PL] 22 F3
Młynarze [PL] 24 C6
Mnich [CZ] 48 G6
Mnichovice [CZ] 48 G4
Mnichovo Hradiště [CZ] 48 G2
Mnichów [PL] 52 B2
Mniów [PL] 38 B6
Mníšek nad Hnilcom [SK] 64 F2
Mníšek pod Brdy [CZ] 48 F4
Mniszek [PL] 38 B5
Mo [N] 164 E2
Mo [N] 170 B2
Mo [N] 172 C4
Mo [N] 180 D4
Mo [S] 166 C4
Mo [S] 166 D3
Mo [S] 166 G3
Mo [S] 174 E2
Mo [S] 184 E2
Moan [N] 182 B5
Moaña [E] 78 B4
Moate [IRL] 2 D5
Moča [SK] 64 B5
Mocejón [E] 96 F1
Móchlos [GR] 140 G4
Mochós [GR] 140 F4
Mochowo [PL] 36 G1
Mochy [PL] 36 B4
Möckern [D] 34 C3
Mockfjärd [S] 172 H4
Möckmühl [D] 46 D5
Möckow [D] 20 D3
Moclín [E] 102 D3
Modane [F] 70 B5
Modave [B] 30 D5
Módena [I] 110 E3
Módi [GR] 132 H4
Módica [I] 126 F5
Modigliana [I] 110 G4
Modlęcin [PL] 34 H2
Modliborzyce [PL] 52 E1
Mödling [A] 62 F5
Modliszewko [PL] 36 D2
Modra [SK] 62 G4
Modra Špilja [HR] 116 H3
Modrava [CZ] 60 H2
Modriča [BIH] 142 D2
Modriště [MK] 128 E2
Modron [BIH] 142 D2
Modruš [HR] 112 G2
Modrý Kameň [SK] 64 C4
Modugno [I] 122 D2
Moeche, Castillo de- [E] 78 D1
Moelv [N] 172 B3
Moen [N] 192 F3
Moena [I] 72 D4
Moers [D] 30 G3
Moesgård [DK] 156 D1
Mofalla [S] 166 F6
Moffat [GB] 8 E4
Mofjell [N] 164 E4
Mogadouro [P] 80 F5
Mogán [E] 100 C6
Mogielnica [PL] 38 B4
Mogilica [BG] 130 E2
Mogilište [BG] 148 G2
Mogilno [PL] 36 E2
Móglia [I] 110 E2
Mogliano Veneto [I] 72 E6
Moglicë [AL] 128 C4
Mogno [CH] 70 F2
Mogno [CH] 70 F2
Mogón [E] 102 F2
Mogorella [I] 118 C5
Mogorić [HR] 112 G4
Mogoro [I] 118 C6
Moguer [E] 94 E6
Moha [H] 76 B1
Mohács [H] 76 B5
Mohärad [S] 162 C2
Moharras [E] 98 A4
Moheda [S] 162 D4
Mohelnice [CZ] 50 C4
Moher, Cliffs of- [IRL] 2 B5
Mohill [IRL] 2 E4
Möhkö [FIN] 188 H2
Moholm [S] 166 F5
Mohora [H] 64 D5
Mohyliv-Podil's'kyi [UA] 204 E2
Moi [N] 164 C4
Moià [E] 92 E3
Moikipää / Molpe [FIN] 186 A3
Moimenta da Beira [P] 80 D5
Mo-i-Rana [N] 190 E2
Moirans [F] 68 G4
Moirans-en-Montagne [F] 56 H6
Moíres [GR] 140 E5
Mõisaküla [EST] 198 E3
Moissac [F] 66 F6
Moita [P] 86 B5
Moita [P] 86 E3
Moixent [E] 98 D6
Mojácar [E] 102 H5
Mojados [E] 88 E2
Mojęcice [PL] 36 C6
Mojkovac [MNE] 144 E3
Mojonera [E] 102 F5
Mojstrana [SLO] 74 B4
Mokliště [MK] 128 F2
Mokobody [PL] 38 D3
Mokra Gora [SRB] 144 E1
Mokren [BG] 148 E4
Mokresh [BG] 146 F2
Mokrin [SRB] 76 F5
Mokronog [SLO] 74 D5
Mokrzyska [PL] 52 B4
Möksy [FIN] 186 E2
Mol [B] 30 D3
Mol [SRB] 76 E6
Mola [I] 72 A4
Mola di Bari [I] 122 E3
Moland [N] 164 E1
Moláoi [GR] 136 F4
Molare [I] 108 H2
Mold [GB] 10 C4
Moldava n. Bodvou [SK] 64 F3
Molde [N] 170 B2
Molde [N] 180 E3
Moldova Nouă [RO] 204 B6
Moldoviţa, Mănăstirea- [RO] 204 D3
Møldrup [DK] 160 D5
Moldusen [N] 172 D5
Moledo [P] 78 A5
Molenheide [B] 30 E3
Molens Van Kinderdijk [NL] 16 D5
Molėtai [LT] 200 G4
Molfetta [I] 122 D2
Moliden [S] 184 G2
Molières [F] 66 F6
Moliets-et-Maa [F] 66 A5
Molina de Aragón [E] 90 C5
Molina de Segura [E] 104 C3
Molinella [I] 110 G3
Molinicos [E] 102 H1
Molino de Villobas [E] 84 D5
Molinos [E] 90 E6
Molinos [E] 96 F3

Molinos de Duero [E] 90 B2
Molins de Rei [E] 92 E4
Moliterno [I] 120 H5
Molkom [S] 166 F2
Mollafeneri [TR] 150 F3
Mollas [AL] 128 B4
Mollas [AL] 128 D5
Möllbrücke [A] 72 G2
Mölle [S] 160 H6
Molledo [E] 82 E3
Möllenbeck [D] 20 D5
Mollerussa [E] 92 C3
Mollet del Vallès [E] 92 E4
Molliens [F] 28 D4
Mollina [E] 102 C3
Mölln [D] 18 G4
Mollösund [S] 160 G1
Mölltorp [S] 166 G5
Mölnbo [S] 168 D4
Mölndal [S] 160 G2
Mölnlycke [S] 160 H2
Mołodycz [PL] 52 F3
Mólos [GR] 132 G4
Moloskovitsy [RUS] 178 F6
Moloy [F] 56 G3
Molpe / Moikipää [FIN] 186 A3
Molsheim [F] 44 G6
Moltifao [I] 114 B3
Moltolieu [F] 106 B4
Molveno [I] 72 C4
Molvotitsy [RUS] 202 C2
Mombaroccio [I] 112 B5
Mombeltrán [E] 88 D5
Mombuey [E] 80 G3
Momchilgrad [BG] 130 F1
Momin Prohod [BG] 146 G5
Mommark [DK] 156 D4
Momo [I] 70 F4
Momrak [N] 164 E3
Monachil [E] 102 E4
Monaco [MC] 108 F4
Monaghan [IRL] 2 F4
Monäs [FIN] 186 B1
Monasterace Marina [I] 124 E6
Monasterboice [IRL] 2 F5
Monasterevin [IRL] 2 E6
Monasterio de Leyre [E] 84 C4
Monastir [I] 118 C6
Monastiráki [GR] 130 G3
Monastiráki [GR] 132 D4
Monbiel [CH] 72 A2
Moncalieri [I] 70 D6
Moncalvo [I] 70 E6
Monção [P] 78 B5
Moncarapacho [P] 94 C5
Moncayo [E] 90 C3
Mönchdorf [A] 62 C4
Mönchengladbach [D] 30 G3
Mönchhof [A] 62 G5
Mónchio d. Cortio [I] 110 D3
Monchique [P] 94 B4
Monclova [E] 102 B2
Moncofa [E] 98 F4
Moncontour [F] 26 B5
Moncoutant [F] 54 D3
Mondariz [E] 78 B5
Mondariz-Balneario [E] 78 B5
Mondatoríccio [I] 124 E4
Mondaye, Abbaye de- [F] 26 E3
Mondéjar [E] 88 G6
Mondello [I] 126 C1
Monđelos [SRB] 142 F2
Mondim de Basto [P] 80 D4
Mondolfo [I] 112 C6
Mondoñedo [E] 78 E2
Mondorf-les-Bains [L] 44 F3
Mondoubleau [F] 42 C5
Mondoví [I] 108 G3
Mondragone [I] 120 D2
Mondsee [A] 60 H5
Monéglia [I] 110 C4
Monegrillo [E] 90 F4
Monemvasía [GR] 136 F5
Monesi [I] 108 F3
Monesterio [E] 94 G4
Monestier-de-Clermont [F] 68 G5
Monêtier-Allemont [F] 108 C2
Moneygall [IRL] 2 D6
Moneymore [NIR] 2 F3
Monfalcone [I] 72 H5
Monfarracinos [E] 80 H5
Monfero [E] 78 D2
Monflanquin [F] 66 F5
Monforte [P] 86 E5
Monforte da Beira [P] 86 F4
Monforte de Lemos [E] 78 D4
Monghidoro [I] 110 F4
Mongstad [N] 170 A2
Monguelfo / Welsberg [I] 72 E3
Monheim [D] 30 G4
Monheim [D] 60 D2
Moní [CY] 154 G6
Moni Ap. Andreas [CY] 154 H4
Mönichkirchen [A] 62 E6
Moní Elónis [GR] 136 F3
Moni Panagias Eleousas [CY] 154 H4
Möniste [EST] 198 F4
Monistrol-d'Allier [F] 68 D4
Monistrol de Montserrat [E] 92 D4
Monistrol-sur-Loire [F] 68 E4
Monivea [IRL] 2 C5
Mońki [PL] 24 E5
Mönlas [D] 46 H5
Monmouth [GB] 12 G2
Monnai [F] 26 G4
Mönni [FIN] 188 F2
Monnickendam [NL] 16 D4
Monninkylä [FIN] 178 A4
Monodéndri [GR] 132 C1
Monódryo [GR] 134 C4
Monólithos [GR] 154 C4
Monopoli [I] 122 E3
Monor [H] 76 D1
Monóvar / Monòver [E] 104 D2
Monòver / Monóvar [E] 104 D2
Monpazier [F] 66 F4
Monplaisir [F] 42 C5
Monreal [E] 96 G2
Monreal / Elo [E] 84 B4
Monreal del Campo [E] 90 D6
Monreale [I] 126 C2
Monroy [E] 86 H5
Monroyo [E] 98 G1
Monrupino [I] 72 H6
Mons (Bergen) [B] 28 G4
Monsanto [P] 86 G3
Monsaraz [P] 94 E2
Monschau [D] 30 F5
Monségur [F] 66 D4
Monsélice [I] 110 G1
Mons En Baroeul [F] 28 F3
Monsheim [D] 46 B4
Mønsted [DK] 160 C5
Mönsterås [S] 162 G4
Monsummano Terme [I] 110 E5
Montabaur [D] 46 B2
Montagnac [F] 106 E4
Montagnana [I] 110 F1
Montagny [F] 68 E2
Montagut [E] 92 F2
Montaigu [F] 54 C2
Montaigu-de-Quercy [F] 66 F5
Montaigut [F] 56 C6
Montaigut-sur-Save [F] 84 H3
Montaione [I] 110 E6
Montalbán [E] 90 E6
Montalbán [E] 96 E2
Montalbano Elicona [I] 124 A7
Montalbano Jonico [I] 122 D5
Montalbo [E] 98 A2
Montalcino [I] 114 G2
Montaldo di Cosola [I] 110 B2
Montalegre [P] 78 C6
Montalieu [F] 68 G3
Montalivet-les-Bains [F] 66 C1
Montallegro [I] 126 C4
Montalto delle Marche [I] 116 C2
Montalto di Castro [I] 114 G4
Montalto Ligure [I] 108 G4
Montalto Uffugo [I] 124 D4
Montalvão [P] 86 E4
Montamarta [E] 80 H4
Montana [BG] 146 F3
Montana [CH] 70 D2
Montañana [E] 90 E4
Montánchez [E] 86 H6
Montanejos [E] 98 E3
Montaren [F] 106 G3
Montargil [P] 86 D5
Montargis [F] 42 F6
Montargull / Artesa de Segre [E] 92 C2
Montastruc la-Conseillère [F] 106 A3
Montauban [F] 26 C5
Montauban [F] 66 F6
Montauriol [F] 106 A3
Montbard [F] 56 F2
Montbazens [F] 66 H5
Montbazon [F] 54 F2
Montbéliard [F] 58 C4
Montbenoît [F] 58 C5
Montblanc [E] 92 C4
Mont-Blanc, Tunnel du- [F/I] 70 C3
Montbonnot [F] 68 H4
Montbrison [F] 68 E3
Montbron [F] 66 F1
Montbrun-les-Bains [F] 108 B3
Montceau-les-Mines [F] 56 F5
Montchanin [F] 56 F5
Montcornet [F] 28 G6
Montcuq [F] 66 F5
Mont-de-Marsan [F] 66 C6
Montdidier [F] 28 E5
Mont-Dol [F] 26 C4
Monte, Castel del- [I] 122 C2
Montealegre [E] 82 C6
Montealegre del Castillo [E] 98 C6
Monte Arabí, Cueva de- [E] 98 C6
Montebelluna [I] 72 E5
Montebourg [F] 26 D2
Montebruno [I] 110 B3
Monte-Carlo [MC] 108 F4
Montecassino, Abbazia di- [I] 120 D1
Montecatini-Terme [I] 110 E5
Montécchio [I] 112 B5
Montecchio Emilia [I] 110 D3
Montécchio Maggiore [I] 72 D6
Montech [F] 66 F6
Montechiaro, Castello di- [I] 126 D4
Monte Codi, Cant.- [I] 118 D6
Montecorice [I] 120 F5
Montecorvino Rovella [I] 120 F4
Monte da Pedra [P] 86 E4
Monte do Trigo [P] 94 E2
Montefalco [I] 116 A2
Montefalcone nel Sannio [I] 116 E6
Montefiascone [I] 114 H3
Montefiorentino, Convento di- [I] 110 H6
Montefiorino [I] 110 E4
Monteforte Irpino [I] 120 E3
Montefrío [E] 102 D3
Montegabbione [I] 114 H2
Montegiordano Marina [I] 122 D5
Montegiorgio [I] 116 C2
Monte Gordo [P] 94 D5
Montegrotto Terme [I] 110 G1
Montehermoso [E] 86 H3
Monteil [F] 68 F5
Monte Isola [I] 72 A5
Montejícar [E] 102 E3
Montelabbate [I] 112 B5
Montelaver [P] 86 B5
Montel-de-Gelat [F] 68 C1
Montélimar [F] 68 F6
Montella [I] 120 F3
Montellano [E] 100 H3
Montemaggiore Belsito [I] 126 D2
Monte Maria, Abbazia di- / Marienberg, Kloster- [I] 72 B2
Montemassi [I] 114 F2
Montemiccioli, Torre di- [I] 114 F1
Montemolín [E] 94 G4
Montemor-o-Novo [P] 86 C6
Montemor-o-Velho [P] 86 D2
Montemurlo [I] 110 E5
Montendre [F] 66 D2
Montenegro de Cameros [E] 90 B2
Montenero di Bisáccia [I] 116 E5
Monte Oliveto Maggiore, Abbazia di- [I] 114 G2
Montepulciano [I] 114 G2
Monterde [E] 90 C5
Montereale [I] 116 B4
Montereale Valcellina [I] 72 F4
Montereau [F] 56 C1
Montereau-Faut-Yonne [F] 42 G5
Monte Redondo [P] 86 C2
Monterenzio [I] 110 F4
Monteriggioni [I] 114 F1
Monteroda [D] 32 G5
Monteroni d'Arbia [I] 114 G1
Monteroni di Lecce [I] 122 G5
Monterosso al Mare [I] 110 C4
Monterosso Almo [I] 126 F5
Monterosso Grana [I] 108 F2
Monterotondo [I] 116 A5
Monterotondo Marittimo [I] 114 E1
Monterroso [E] 78 D4
Monterrubio de la Serena [E] 96 B4
Monterubbiano [I] 116 C2
Monte San Biagio [I] 120 C1
Montesano sulla Marcellana [I] 120 G5
Monte San Savino [I] 114 G1
Monte Sant'Angelo [I] 116 H6
Monte Santiago [E] 82 G4
Montesarchio [I] 120 E2
Montescaglioso [I] 122 D4
Montesclaros [E] 88 D6
Montese [I] 110 E4
Monte Senario, Convento- [I] 110 F5
Montesilvano Marina [I] 116 D4
Montesinos, Cueva de- [E] 96 G5
Montesquieu-Volvestre [F] 84 H4
Montesquiou [F] 84 F3
Montevarchi [I] 110 F6
Montevecchio [I] 118 B6
Monteverde [I] 120 G3
Monte Vergine, Santuario di- [I] 120 E3
Montevil [P] 94 C1
Montevil [P] 94 C1
Montfaucon-en-Velay [F] 68 E4
Montferrat [F] 108 D4
Montfort [F] 26 C6
Montfort [F] 84 G2
Montfort-en-Chalosse [F] 66 B6
Montfort l'Amaury [F] 42 E3
Mont Gargan [F] 66 H2
Montgat [E] 92 E4
Montgenèvre [F] 70 B6
Montgenèvre, Col de- [F/I] 70 B6
Montgeoffroy, Château de- [F] 40 H6
Montgesoye [F] 58 B5
Montgiscard [F] 106 A3
Montgrí, Castell de- [E] 92 G3
Montguyon [F] 66 D2
Monthermé [F] 44 C1
Monthey [CH] 70 C2
Monthois [F] 44 C3
Monthureux-sur-Saône [F] 58 B2
Monti [I] 118 D3
Monticelli Terme [I] 110 D3
Montichiari [I] 72 B6
Monticiano [I] 114 F2
Montiel [E] 96 G5
Montier-en-Der [F] 44 C5
Montignac [F] 66 G3
Montigny-le-Roi [F] 58 A2
Montigny-sur-Aube [F] 56 G2
Montijo [E] 94 G1
Montijo [P] 86 B5
Montilla [E] 102 C2
Montilleja [E] 98 C5
Monti-Sion, Santuari de- [E] 104 E5
Montivilliers [F] 26 G3
Montizón [E] 96 G6
Montlieu-la-Garde [F] 66 D2
Mont-Louis [F] 92 E1
Montluçon [F] 56 C5
Montluel [F] 68 G2
Montmajour, Abbaye de- [F] 106 G4
Montmarault [F] 56 C6
Montmédy [F] 44 D3
Montmélian [F] 70 A4
Montmeyan [F] 108 C4
Montmirail [F] 42 C5
Montmirail [F] 42 H4
Montmirey [F] 56 H4
Montmoreau-St-Cybard [F] 66 E2
Montmorillon [F] 54 F4
Montmort [F] 44 A4
Montoire-sur-le-Loir [F] 42 C6
Montoito [P] 94 E2
Montorio [E] 82 E5
Montorio al Vomano [I] 116 C3
Montoro [E] 102 D1
Montoy-Flanville [F] 44 F4
Montpellier [F] 106 E4
Montpellier-le-Vieux [F] 106 E2
Montpezat-de-Quercy [F] 66 G6
Montpon-Ménestérol [F] 66 E3
Montpont-en-Bresse [F] 56 G6
Mont-Ras [E] 92 G3
Montréal [F] 56 F3
Montréal [F] 66 D6
Montréal [F] 106 B4
Montredon-Labessonnie [F] 106 C3
Montréjeau [F] 84 F4
Montrésor [F] 54 G3
Montresta [I] 118 B4
Montret [F] 56 G5
Montreuil [F] 28 D3
Montreuil-aux-Lions [F] 42 H3
Montreuil-Bellay [F] 54 E2
Montreux [CH] 70 C1
Montrevault [F] 54 C1
Montrevel-en-Bresse [F] 68 G1
Montrichard [F] 54 G2
Montrøen [N] 182 C4
Montroi / Montroy [E] 98 E5
Mont-roig del Camp [E] 90 H6
Montrond-les-Bains [F] 68 E3
Montrose [GB] 8 F2
Montroy / Montroi [E] 98 E5
Montsalvy [F] 68 B5
Montsauche-les-Settons [F] 56 F3
Montségur [F] 106 A5
Montseny [E] 92 E3
Montserrat [E] 92 D4
Montsoreau [F] 54 E2
Mont-sous-Vaudrey [F] 56 H5
Monts-s-Guesnes [F] 54 E3
Mont-Ste-Odile [F] 44 G6
Montsûrs [F] 26 E6
Montuenga [E] 88 E3
Montuïri [E] 104 E5
Monturque [E] 102 C2
Monza [I] 70 G4
Monze [F] 106 C5
Monzón [E] 90 G3
Monzón de Campos [E] 82 D6
Monzuno [I] 110 F4
Moon-sur-Elle [F] 26 E3
Moordorf [D] 18 B4
Moosburg [D] 60 F3
Moosham [A] 72 H2
Moosinning [D] 60 E4
Moos in Passeier / Moso in Passiria [I] 72 D2
Mór [H] 76 B1
Mora [E] 96 F2
Mora [E] 96 F2
Mora [P] 86 D5
Mora [S] 172 G3
Mora [S] 174 C5
Mora, Puerto de la- [E] 102 E4
Morača, Manastir- [MNE] 144 E3
Móra d'Ebre [E] 90 H6
Mora de Rubielos [E] 98 E2
Moradillo de Roa [E] 88 G2
Morąg [PL] 22 G3
Mórahalom [H] 76 E4
Moraïtika [GR] 132 B2
Morakovo [MNE] 144 E3
Morakowo [PL] 36 D1
Móra la Nova [E] 90 H6
Moral de Calatrava [E] 96 F5
Moraleda de Zafayona [E] 102 D4
Moraleja [E] 86 G3
Morales del Vino [E] 80 H5
Morano Cálabro [I] 120 H6
Mora Stenar [S] 168 D2
Morasverdes [E] 88 B3
Moratalla [E] 104 B2
Morava [SLO] 74 C6
Moravče pri Gabrovki [SLO] 74 C5
Moravice [HR] 112 F1
Morávka [CZ] 50 F5
Moravská Třebová [CZ] 50 C4
Moravské Budějovice [CZ] 62 E2
Moravské Lieskové [SK] 62 H3
Moravský Beroun [CZ] 50 D4
Moravský Krumlov [CZ] 62 F2
Morawica [PL] 52 B2
Morbach [D] 44 G2
Mörbacka [S] 172 E4
Morbegno [I] 70 H3
Mörbisch [A] 62 F6
Mörbylånga [S] 162 G5
Morcenx [F] 66 B5
Morciano di Romagna [I] 112 B5
Morcone [I] 120 E2
Morcote [CH] 70 G3
Mordelles [F] 26 C6
Mordoğan [TR] 152 B4
Mordy [PL] 38 E3
Morecambe [GB] 10 D2
Moreda [E] 102 E3
Moreira [P] 80 B3
Morella [E] 98 G1
Morella la Vella [E] 98 G1
Moreno, Col de la- [F] 68 C2
Moreruela, Monasterio de- [E] 80 H4
Móres [I] 118 C3
Morestel [F] 68 G3
Moret-sur-Loing [F] 42 G5
Moretta [I] 108 F1
Moreuil [F] 28 E5
Morez [F] 70 B1
Mörfelden [D] 46 C3
Mórfi [GR] 132 C3
Mórfou (Güzelyurt) [CY] 154 F5
Morgantina [I] 126 F4
Morgat [F] 40 B2
Morgedal [N] 164 E2
Morges [CH] 70 B1
Morgex [I] 70 C3
Morgins [CH] 70 C2
Morgny [F] 28 C6
Morgongåva [S] 168 C1
Morhange [F] 44 F5
Mori [I] 72 C5
Moriani-Plage [F] 114 C3
Mórichida [H] 62 H6
Morigny Champigny [F] 42 F4
Morimondo, Abbazia di- [I] 70 F5
Moritzburg [D] 34 C6
Moritzburg [D] 34 E6
Moritzburg, Schloss- [D] 34 E6
Moriville [F] 44 F6
Morjärv [S] 196 B2
Mørk [N] 166 B2
Morkarla [S] 174 F6
Mørke [DK] 160 E6
Mørkøv [DK] 156 F2
Morkovice Slížany [CZ] 50 D6
Mörkret [S] 172 E1
Mørkveden [N] 192 C5
Morla [E] 78 F6
Morlaàs [F] 84 E3
Morlaix [F] 40 C2
Mörlunda [S] 162 F3
Mormanno [I] 120 H6
Mormant [F] 42 G4
Mornay-Berry [F] 56 D4
Mornese [I] 110 A2
Morón de Almazán [E] 90 B4
Morón de la Frontera [E] 100 H3
Morosaglia [F] 114 B3
Morović [SRB] 142 E2
Morøya [N] 192 D5
Morozzo [I] 108 G2
Morpeth [GB] 8 G5
Morra [I] 114 H1
Morral de Cabrafeixet [E] 92 B5
Mørriaunet [N] 190 B5
Morro del Jable [E] 100 D6
Mörrum [S] 158 E1
Mörsburg [CH] 58 G4
Morshyn [UA] 52 H6
Mörsil [S] 182 F2
Morskoga krog [S] 166 H2
Mörskom / Myrskylä [FIN] 178 B3
Morskoye [RUS] 200 D5
Morsum [D] 156 A4
Mørsvikbotn [N] 192 E5
Mortagne-au-Perche [F] 26 G5
Mortagne-sur-Sèvre [F] 54 C2
Mortágua [P] 80 B6
Mortain [F] 26 E5
Mortara [I] 70 F5
Mörtberg [S] 194 A8
Morteau [F] 58 C5
Mortegliano [I] 72 G5
Mörtfors [S] 162 G3
Mortier-Crolle, Château de- [F] 40 G5
Mortrée [F] 26 F5
Mörtschach [A] 72 G2
Morud [DK] 156 D3
Morup [S] 160 H4
Moryń [PL] 34 G1
Morzine [F] 70 C2
Morzycyn [PL] 20 F5
Mosal'sk [RUS] 202 E4
Mosås [S] 166 H3
Mosätt [S] 182 G5
Mosbach [D] 46 D5
Mosbekk [N] 166 D1
Mosby [N] 164 D5
Moščanci [SLO] 74 E3
Moscavide [P] 86 B5
Moščenica [HR] 142 A1
Moščenice [HR] 112 E2
Moščenička Draga [HR] 112 E2
Moschendorf [A] 74 F2
Moschopótamos [GR] 128 G5
Moscufo [I] 116 D4
Mosėdis [LT] 200 D3
Mosel [D] 48 C1
Moshult [S] 162 B4
Mosina [PL] 36 C3
Mosjö [S] 184 F2
Mosjøen [N] 190 D3
Moškanjci [SLO] 74 E4
Mosko [BIH] 144 D3
Moskog [N] 180 C6
Moskosel [S] 190 H3
Moskva [RUS] 202 F3
Moslavina [HR] 76 A6
Moso in Passiria / Moos in Passeier [I] 72 D2
Mosonmagyaróvár [H] 62 G5
Mosqueruela [E] 98 F2
Moss [D] 58 G4
Moss [N] 166 B2
Mossiberg [S] 172 F1
Mössingen [D] 58 G2
Most [CZ] 48 E2
Mosta [M] 126 C6
Mostar [BIH] 144 C2
Mosteiros [P] 100 E2
Mosterhamn [N] 170 A6
Mostesquiu [E] 92 E2
Mostki [PL] 52 C2
Most na Soči [SLO] 72 H4
Móstoles [E] 88 F6
Mostowo [PL] 22 A3
Mosty [PL] 38 F4
Mostys'ka [UA] 52 F4
Mosune [HR] 112 F2
Moszczanka [PL] 38 D4
Mota, Cast. de la- [E] 88 E2
Mota del Cuervo [E] 96 H3
Mota del Marqués [E] 88 D1
Motala [S] 166 G5
Motherwell [GB] 8 D3
Motilla del Palancar [E] 98 B3
Motjärnshyttan [S] 166 F1
Motko [RUS] 196 H6
Motovun [HR] 112 D1
Motricoux [F] 66 G6
Motril [E] 102 E5
Motta di Livenza [I] 72 F5
Motta Montecorvino [I] 120 F1
Motta Visconti [I] 70 F5
Motte-Glain, Château de la- [F] 40 G5
Móttola [I] 122 E4
Möttönen [FIN] 186 E2
Mou [DK] 160 E4
Mouchard [F] 58 A5
Moudon [CH] 70 C1
Moúdros [GR] 130 F6
Mougins [F] 108 E5
Mouhijärvi [FIN] 176 E1
Mouliherne [F] 54 E1
Moulins [F] 56 D5
Moulins-Engilbert [F] 56 E4
Moulins-la-Marche [F] 26 G5
Moulismes [F] 54 F5
Moult [F] 26 F4
Mountallen [IRL] 2 D4
Mount Bellew [IRL] 2 D5
Mount Charles [IRL] 2 E2
Mountmellick [IRL] 2 E6
Mountrath [IRL] 2 D6
Mountshannon [IRL] 2 C6
Moura [P] 94 E3
Mourão [P] 94 E2
Mouriés [GR] 128 H3
Mouros, Cast. dos- [P] 86 A5
Mourujärvi [FIN] 194 E8
Moustey [F] 66 C4
Moustiers-Ste-Marie [F] 108 D4
Mouthe [F] 58 B6
Mouthier [F] 58 B5
Mouthoumet [F] 106 C5
Moutier [CH] 58 D5
Moutier-d'Ahun [F] 54 H6
Moutiers [F] 54 B3
Moûtiers [F] 70 B4
Mouton-Rothschild [F] 66 C2
Moutoullás [CY] 154 F5
Moutsoúna [GR] 138 F3
Mouy [F] 28 D6
Mouzakaíoi [GR] 132 D2
Mouzáki [GR] 132 E2
Mouzáki [GR] 136 C2
Mouzon [F] 44 D2
Moville [IRL] 2 F2
Moy [NIR] 2 F3
Moyenvic [F] 44 F5
Moynalty [IRL] 2 F5
Moyne Abbey [IRL] 2 C3
Moyuela [E] 90 E5
Moyvore [IRL] 2 E5
Mozhaysk [RUS] 202 E3
Mozia [I] 126 B2
Mozirje [SLO] 74 C4
Mozyr' [RUS] 24 C2
Mpalí [GR] 140 D4
Mpampalió [GR] 132 E4
Mpampíni [GR] 132 D5
Mpatsí [GR] 134 E6
Mpenítses [GR] 132 B2
Mpórsio [GR] 136 C1
Mpoúkka [GR] 132 D4
Mprálos [GR] 132 G4
Mrągowo [PL] 24 B4
Mrakovica [BIH] 142 B2
Mramor [BIH] 144 C3
Mrazovac [BIH] 112 H2
Mrčajevci [SRB] 146 B2
Mrežičko [MK] 128 F3
Mrkonjić-Grad [BIH] 142 B3
Mrkopalj [HR] 112 F1
Mrocza [PL] 22 C5
Mroczeń [PL] 36 E6
Mrzeżyno [PL] 20 G3
Mrzygłód [PL] 52 E4
Mšeno [CZ] 48 G3
Mstislavl' [BY] 202 D5
Mstów [PL] 50 G1
Mszana Dolna [PL] 52 A5
Mszczonów [PL] 38 B4
Mt-Dauphin [F] 108 E1
Mt. Melleray Monastery [IRL] 4 D4
Mtsensk [RUS] 202 F4
Mt. St. Joseph Abbey [IRL] 2 D6
Muć [HR] 144 A1
Muccia [I] 116 B2
Much [D] 30 H4
Mücheln [D] 34 B5
Muchówka [PL] 52 B4
Muciélagos, Cava de los- [E] 102 H4
Mücka Mikow [D] 34 G5
Muckross [IRL] 4 B4
Muckross House [IRL] 4 B4
Mudanya [TR] 150 E4
Mudau [D] 46 D4
Mudela, Castillo de- [E] 96 F5
Müden [D] 18 F6
Mudiske [EST] 198 E2
Múdrets [BG] 148 D5
Muel [E] 90 E4
Muela de Cortes [E] 98 D5
Muelas del Pan [E] 80 G4
Muezerskiy [RUS] 196 H5
Muff [IRL] 2 F2
Muge [P] 86 C4
Mügeln [D] 34 D6
Muggendorf [D] 46 G4
Múggia [I] 72 H6
Mugiro [E] 84 B3
Muğla [TR] 154 D1
Müglizh [BG] 148 C4
Mugnano [I] 114 H2
Mugron [F] 66 C6
Mühlacker [D] 46 C6
Mühlbach [A] 72 G1
Mühlberg [D] 34 E5
Mühldorf [D] 60 F4
Mühlen [A] 74 C2
Mühlhausen [D] 32 G5
Mühlhausen [D] 46 H6
Mühlhausen [D] 60 B3
Muhola [FIN] 186 F1
Muhos [FIN] 196 D4
Muhovo [BG] 148 A5
Muine Bheag / Bagenalstown [IRL] 4 F4
Muiños [E] 78 C6
Muir of Ord [GB] 6 D5
Mujdžić [BIH] 142 B4
Mujejärvi [FIN] 196 G5
Mukacheve [UA] 204 B3
Mula [E] 104 B3
Mulazzo [I] 110 C4
Mulba [E] 94 H5
Mulegns [CH] 70 H2
Mülheim [D] 30 G3
Mülheim [D] 44 G2
Mulhouse [F] 58 D3
Muljava [SLO] 74 C5
Muljula [FIN] 188 G4
Müllheim [D] 58 E3
Mullinavat [IRL] 4 E4
Mullingar [IRL] 2 E5
Müllrose [D] 34 G3
Mullsjö [S] 162 C2
Mullyttan [S] 166 G3
Mulseryd [S] 162 C2
Multia [FIN] 186 F4
Multrå [S] 184 E2
Mumor [H] 74 F3
Muñana [E] 88 D4
Münchberg [D] 48 B3
Müncheberg [D] 34 F2
München [D] 60 E4
Münchhausen [D] 32 D6
Münchhausen [D] 34 E4
Mundaka [E] 82 H3
Munderkingen [D] 60 B4
Mundheim [N] 170 B4
Munera [E] 96 H5
Mungia [E] 82 G3
Muniaczkowice [PL] 52 B3
Muñico [E] 88 D4
Muniellos, Bosque de- [E] 78 F4
Muniesa [E] 90 E5
Munka-Ljungby [S] 156 H1
Munkebo [DK] 156 E3
Munkedal [S] 166 C5
Munkelven [N] 194 E3
Munkflohögen [S] 182 H1
Munkfors [S] 166 F1
Münnerstadt [D] 46 F3
Munsala [FIN] 186 C1
Münsingen [CH] 58 D6
Münsingen [D] 58 H2
Munsö [S] 168 D3
Münster [CH] 70 E2
Munster [D] 18 F6
Münster [D] 32 C3
Munster [F] 58 D3
Münstertal [D] 58 E3
Münzenberg [D] 46 C2
Münzkirchen [A] 62 A3
Muodoslompolo [S] 194 B6
Muonio [FIN] 194 B6
Muotkavaara [FIN] 194 C6
Muradiye [TR] 152 C3
Murakeresztúr [H] 74 G4
Muráň [SK] 64 E3
Murano [I] 72 E6
Muras [E] 78 E2
Murat [F] 68 C4
Muratdere [TR] 150 G5
Murati [EST] 198 F4
Muratlar [TR] 150 B6
Muratlar [TR] 152 F6
Muratlı [TR] 150 C3
Murato [F] 114 C3
Murat-sur-Vèbre [F] 106 D3
Murau [A] 74 B2
Muravera [I] 118 E6
Murazzano [I] 108 G2
Murça [P] 80 E4
Mürchevo [BG] 146 F3

Murchin [D] 20 E3
Murcia [E] 104 C3
Murciélagos, Cueva de los- [E] 102 C2
Murcielagos, Cueva de los- [E] 102 E5
Murczyn [PL] 36 E1
Mur-de-Barrez [F] 68 B4
Mur-de-Bretagne [F] 26 A5
Mureck [A] 74 E3
Mürefte [TR] 150 C4
Muret [F] 84 H3
Murga [H] 76 B4
Murgados [E] 78 D1
Murgaševo [MK] 128 E3
Murgia / Murguía [E] 82 G5
Murg-Kraftwerk [D] 58 F1
Murguía / Murgia [E] 82 G5
Muri [CH] 58 F5
Murias de Paredes [E] 78 G4
Murieta [E] 82 H6
Murighiol [RO] 204 F5
Murino [MNE] 146 A5
Muriquan [AL] 128 A1
Murjek [S] 196 A2
Murlo [I] 114 F2
Murnau [D] 60 D5
Muro [E] 104 E4
Muro [F] 114 B3
Muro de Alcoy / Muro del Comtat [E] 104 E1
Muro del Comtat / Muro de Alcoy [E] 104 E1
Murole [FIN] 186 E6
Muro Lucano [I] 120 G3
Murony [H] 76 G3
Muros [E] 78 B3
Murowana Goślina [PL] 36 C2
Mürren [CH] 70 E2
Murrhardt [D] 46 D6
Murrisk Abbey [IRL] 2 B4
Murru [EST] 198 D3
Murska Sobota [SLO] 74 E3
Mursko Središće [HR] 74 F4
Murta [RO] 146 G2
Murtas [E] 102 E5
Murten [CH] 58 D6
Murter [HR] 112 G6
Murtinheira [P] 80 A6
Murtolahti [FIN] 188 D1
Murtosa [P] 80 B5
Murtovaara [FIN] 196 F2
Murvica [HR] 112 G5
Mürzsteg [A] 62 D6
Mürzzuschlag [A] 62 E6
Musamaa [FIN] 186 C2
Musasău de Tinca [RO] 76 H2
Musetrene [N] 180 G6
Mussalo [FIN] 178 C4
Musselkanaal [NL] 16 H3
Mussidan [F] 66 E3
Mussomeli [I] 126 D3
Mussy [F] 56 G2
Mustafa Kemal Paşa [TR] 150 E5
Müstair [CH] 72 B3
Mustajärvi [FIN] 186 E5
Mustajõe [EST] 198 G1
Mustalahti [FIN] 186 F5
Mustasaari / Korsholm [FIN] 186 B2
Mustér / Disentis [CH] 70 G1
Mustikkaperä [FIN] 186 F2
Mustinmäki [FIN] 188 D3
Mustinsalo [FIN] 188 D3
Mustjala [EST] 198 C3
Mustla [EST] 198 E3
Mustola [FIN] 194 E4
Mustvee [EST] 198 F2
Muszaki [PL] 22 H5
Muszyna [PL] 52 C5
Muszynka [PL] 52 C5
Muta [SLO] 74 D3
Mutalahti [FIN] 188 H3
Mutanj [SRB] 146 B2
Mutilva [E] 84 B4
Mutlangen [D] 60 B2
Mutriku [E] 82 H4
Muttalip [TR] 150 H5
Mutterstadt [D] 46 B5
Muurame [FIN] 186 G5
Muurasjärvi [FIN] 196 D6
Muurikkala [FIN] 178 D3
Muurla [FIN] 176 F5
Muurola [FIN] 178 D3
Muurola [FIN] 194 C8
Muuruvesi [FIN] 188 D2
Muxía [E] 78 B2
Múzeum Oravskej Dediny [SK] 50 H6
Muzillac [F] 40 E5
Mužla [SK] 64 B5
Mužlja [SRB] 142 G1
Myakishevo [RUS] 198 H5
Mybotn [N] 192 E3
Myckelgensjö [S] 184 F1
Myczków [PL] 52 E5
Myggenäs [S] 160 G1
Myhinpää [FIN] 186 H3
Myjava [SK] 62 H3
Mykínes [GR] 136 E2
Myking [N] 170 F4
Myklebust [N] 180 B5
Myklebust [N] 180 D3
Myklestøyl [N] 164 D3
Mykolaïv [UA] 52 H5
Mykolaïv [UA] 204 G3
Mýkonos [GR] 138 E2
Myllyaho [FIN] 186 F1
Myllykoski [FIN] 178 C3
Myllykselä [FIN] 176 H2
Myllymaa [FIN] 176 E2
Myllymäki [FIN] 186 E4
Mýloi [GR] 136 E2
Mylopótamos [GR] 136 F6
Mylund [DK] 160 E3
Mynämäki [FIN] 176 D4
Myndos [TR] 154 B2
Myonnesos [TR] 152 C5
Myos [TR] 152 D6
Myra [TR] 154 H3
Myrane [N] 164 B4
Myrås [S] 190 G3
Myrdal [N] 170 D3
Myre [N] 192 D3
Myre [N] 192 E3
Myren [S] 172 E5
Myrhorod [UA] 202 F7
Mýrina [GR] 130 F6
Myrina [TR] 152 C3
Myrkky [FIN] 186 B4
Myrmoen [N] 182 D3
Myrnes [N] 192 H1
Myrnyi [UA] 204 G4
Myronivka [UA] 202 E8
Myrskylä / Mörskom [FIN] 178 B3
Myrtiés [GR] 154 A2
Mýrtos [GR] 140 F5
Mýrtou (Çamlıbel) [CY] 154 F5
Myrvika [N] 190 C4
Myrviken [S] 182 G3
Mysen [N] 166 C2
Myšenec [CZ] 48 F6
Myshall [IRL] 4 F4
Myshuryn Rih [UA] 202 F8
Myšlenice [PL] 50 H4
Myślibórz [PL] 34 G1
Myślice [PL] 22 F4
Mysłowice [PL] 50 G3
Mysovka [RUS] 200 D5
Mystegná [GR] 134 H2
Mystrás [GR] 136 E4
Mysubyttseter [N] 180 E5
Myszków [PL] 50 G2
Myszyniec [PL] 24 C5
Mýtikas [GR] 132 D5
Mytilíni [GR] 134 H2
Mytishchi [RUS] 202 F3
Mýtna [SK] 64 D3
Myto [BY] 24 H3
Mýto [CZ] 48 E4
Mzdowo [PL] 22 B3
Mzurki [PL] 36 G5

N

Nå [N] 170 C4
Naamijoki [FIN] 194 B7
Naantali / Nådend [FIN] 176 D4
Naarajärvi [FIN] 188 C4
Naarden [NL] 16 E4
Naarva [FIN] 188 G1
Nääs [S] 160 H2
Naas / An Nás [IRL] 2 F6
Nabaskoze / Navascués [E] 84 C4
Nabbelund [S] 162 H3
Nabburg [D] 48 C5
Náchod [CZ] 50 B3
Nacıvelioba [TR] 150 D5
Nacka [S] 168 E3
Nădab [RO] 76 G3
Nadarzyn [PL] 38 B3
Nadaš [RO] 76 H4
Naddvik [N] 170 E2
Nadela [E] 78 E3
Nådend / Naantali [FIN] 176 D4
Nădlac [RO] 76 F4
Nădlac [RO] 204 B5
Nadrin [B] 30 E6
Nádudvar [H] 76 G1
Nærbø [N] 164 A4
Næstved [DK] 156 F4
Näfels [CH] 58 G6
Náfpaktos [GR] 132 F5
Náfplio [GR] 136 F2
Naggen [S] 184 D5
Naglarby [S] 174 C5
Nagłowice [PL] 52 A2
Nagold [D] 58 G2
Nagu / Nauvo [FIN] 176 D5
Nagyatád [H] 74 H4
Nagybajom [H] 74 H4
Nagybaracska [H] 76 C5
Nagycenk [H] 62 F6
Nagycserkesz [H] 64 G5
Nagydorog [H] 76 B3
Nagyér [H] 76 F4
Nagyfüged [H] 64 E6
Nagygyanté [H] 76 G2
Nagygyimót [H] 74 H1
Nagyhalász [H] 64 H4
Nagyhegyes [H] 64 G6
Nagyhomok [H] 64 H4
Nagyigmánd [H] 64 A6
Nagyiván [H] 64 F6
Nagykálló [H] 64 H5
Nagykanizsa [H] 74 G4
Nagykáta [H] 76 D1
Nagykereki [H] 76 H1
Nagykölked [H] 74 F2
Nagykónyi [H] 76 B3
Nagykőrös [H] 76 D2
Nagylak [H] 76 F4
Nagylóc [H] 64 D5
Nagymágocs [H] 76 F3
Nagymaros [H] 64 C5
Nagyoroszi [H] 64 C5
Nagypuszta [H] 74 H4
Nagyrábé [H] 76 G1
Nagyszénás [H] 76 F3
Nagyvázsony [H] 74 H2
Naharros [E] 90 A4
Naharros [E] 98 B2
Nahe [D] 18 F3
Nahkiaisoja [FIN] 194 C8
Naila [D] 46 H3
Nailloux [F] 106 A4
Nailsworth [GB] 12 G3
Naipu [RO] 148 C1
Nairn [GB] 6 E5
Najac [F] 66 H6
Nájera [E] 82 G6
Näkkälä [FIN] 194 B5
Nakkesletta [N] 192 G1
Nakkila [FIN] 176 D2
Naklik [PL] 52 E2
Naklo [SLO] 74 B4
Nakło nad Notecią [PL] 22 C6
Nakovo [SRB] 76 F5
Nakskov [DK] 156 E5
Nälden [S] 182 G2
Nałęczów [PL] 38 D5
Nálepkovo [SK] 64 F2
Näljänkä [FIN] 196 F3
Nalkki [FIN] 196 E4
Nalzen [F] 106 A5
Nalžovké Hory [CZ] 48 E6
Nalžovské Hory [CZ] 48 E6
Nambroca [E] 96 F2
Namen (Namur) [B] 30 D5
Náměšť nad Oslavou [CZ] 50 B6
Námestovo [SK] 50 G5
Namlos [A] 60 C6
Namma [N] 172 D4
Nämpnäs [FIN] 186 A4
Namsos [N] 190 C5
Namsskogan [N] 190 D4
Namsvassgardån [N] 190 D4
Namur (Namen) [B] 30 D5
Namysłów [PL] 36 D6
Nanclares de la Oca / Langraiz Oka [E] 82 G5
Nancy [F] 44 E5
Nangis [F] 42 G4
Nannestad [N] 172 B5
Nans-les-Pins [F] 108 C5
Nant [F] 106 E3
Nantes [F] 40 F6
Nanteuil-le-Haudouin [F] 42 G3
Nantiat [F] 54 G6
Nantua [F] 68 H2
Nantwich [GB] 10 D5
Naours, Grottes de- [F] 28 E4
Náousa [GR] 128 F4
Náousa [GR] 138 E3
Näpagård [N] 170 F6
Napi [EST] 198 C2
Naples [TR] 150 C3
Nápoli [I] 120 E3
Na Pomezí [CZ] 50 C3
Naposenaho [FIN] 186 E2
När [S] 168 G5
Nåra [N] 170 A2
Narach [BY] 200 H5
Naraio, Castelo de- [E] 78 D2
Narberth [GB] 12 D1
Narbolía [I] 118 C5
Narbonne [F] 106 D5
Narbonne-Plage [F] 106 D5
Narbuvollen [N] 182 C4
Narcao [I] 118 B7
Nardis, Cascata di- [I] 72 C4
Nardò [I] 122 G5
Narechenski Bani [BG] 148 B6
Narew [PL] 24 F6
Narewka [PL] 24 F6
Närhilä [FIN] 186 G3
Narila [FIN] 188 D5
Narjordet [N] 182 C4
Narkaus [FIN] 194 D8
Narlıca [TR] 150 F4
Narni [I] 116 A4
Naro [I] 126 D4
Naro-Fominsk [RUS] 202 F3
Narol [PL] 52 G2
Narón [E] 78 D4
Närpes / Närpiö [FIN] 186 A4
Närpiö / Närpes [FIN] 186 A4
Narta [HR] 74 G6
Nartháki [GR] 132 G3
Nartkowo [PL] 20 G3
Nártuna [S] 168 E2
Naruska [FIN] 194 F6
Narva [EST] 198 G1
Narva [FIN] 176 F2
Närvä [FIN] 186 G6
Närvä [S] 192 H4
Narva-Jõesuu [EST] 198 G1
Närvijoki [FIN] 186 B3
Narvik [N] 192 E4
Näs [S] 162 D1
Näs [S] 166 G2
Näs [S] 168 F6
Näs [S] 172 G5
Naşa [TR] 152 F2
Näsåker [S] 184 E1
N. Åsarp [S] 162 C1
Năsăud [RO] 204 C3
Nasbinals [F] 68 C5
Näsby [S] 158 G1
Näsbyholm [S] 162 D3
Nascimiento del Río Cuervo [E] 98 C1
Näset [S] 184 D4
Näshulta [S] 168 B3
Našice [HR] 142 D1
Nasielsk [PL] 38 B2
Näsinge [S] 166 C4
Näsland [S] 190 H5
Násedlovice [CZ] 62 G2
Naso [I] 124 B6
Na Špičáku [CZ] 50 D3
Nassau [D] 46 B2
Nassereith [A] 72 C1
Nässja [S] 166 G5
Nässjö [S] 162 D2
Nässjö [S] 184 D1
Nässvallen [S] 182 F4
Nasswald [A] 62 E6
Nastan [BG] 130 D1
Nästansjö [S] 190 F4
Nastazin [PL] 20 G5
Nästeln [S] 182 G4
Nästi [FIN] 176 D3
Nastola [FIN] 178 B3
Näsum [S] 158 E1
Näsviken [S] 174 E1
Näsviken [S] 190 E6
Nata [CY] 154 F6
Natalinci [SRB] 146 B1
Nätra Fjällskog [S] 184 F2
Nattavaara [S] 196 A1
Nättraby [S] 158 F1
Nattvatn [N] 194 C3
Naturno / Naturns [I] 72 C3
Naturns / Naturno [I] 72 C3
Naucelle [F] 66 H6
Nauders [A] 72 B2
Nauen [D] 34 D2
Naujoji Akmenė [LT] 198 C6
Naul [IRL] 2 F5
Naumburg [D] 34 B6
Naumestis [LT] 200 F4
Naunhof [D] 34 D5
Nausta [S] 190 H2
Naustbukta [N] 190 C4
Naustdal [N] 180 C6
Nauste [N] 180 F3
Naustvika [N] 180 F4
Nautijaure [S] 190 H1
Nautsung [N] 170 B1
Nauvo / Nagu [FIN] 176 D5
Nava [E] 82 C2
Navacelles, Cirque de- [F] 106 E3
Navacerrada [E] 88 F4
Nava de la Asunción [E] 88 E3
Nava del Rey [E] 88 D3
Navahermosa [E] 96 E2
Navahrudak [BY] 202 B5
Navalagamella [E] 88 E5
Navalcán [E] 88 C6
Navalcarnero [E] 88 F6
Navaleno [E] 90 A2
Navalguijo [E] 88 C5
Navalmanzano [E] 88 F3
Navalmoral [E] 88 D5
Navalmoral de la Mata [E] 88 B6
Navalón [E] 98 D6
Navalperal de Pinares [E] 88 E5
Navalpino [E] 96 D3
Navalvillar de Ibor [E] 96 C1
Navalvillar de Pela [E] 96 B3
Navan / An Uaimh [IRL] 2 F5
Nåvårdalen [N] 182 B3
Navarredonda de Gredos [E] 88 C5
Navarrenx [F] 84 D3
Navarrés [E] 98 E5
Navarrete [E] 82 G6
Navàs [E] 92 E3
Navascués / Nabaskoze [E] 84 C4
Navas de Estena [E] 96 E2
Navas del Madroño [E] 86 G4
Navas del Rey [E] 88 E5
Navas de Oro [E] 88 E3
Navas de San Juan [E] 102 F1
Navata [E] 92 G2
Navatalgordo [E] 88 D5
Nävekvarn [S] 168 C5
Navelli [I] 116 C4
Navelsaker [N] 180 C5
Nave Redonda [P] 94 B4
Näverkärret [S] 166 H2
Naverstad [S] 166 C4
Naveta des Tudons [E] 104 G4
Navia [E] 78 F2
Navilly [F] 56 G5
Navit [N] 192 H2
Navlya [RUS] 202 E5
Navruz [TR] 150 C5
Naxås [S] 182 F1
Náxos [GR] 138 E3
Naxos [I] 124 B8
Nazaré [P] 86 C3
Nazifoaşa [TR] 150 G5
Nazilli [TR] 152 E5
Nazimovo [RUS] 198 H4
N. Bukovica [HR] 74 H6
N.-D. de Clausis [F] 108 E2
N.-D. de Kerdevot [F] 40 B3
N.-D. de la Salette [F] 68 H5
N.-D. de Lure [F] 108 C3
N.-D. de Miracles [F] 108 E4
N.-D.-du-Haut [F] 58 C3
N.-D. du Mai [F] 108 C6
Ndroq [AL] 128 B3
Néa Anchíalos [GR] 132 H3
Néa Artáki [GR] 134 B5
Néa Epídavros [GR] 136 F2
Néa Fókaia [GR] 130 B6
Néa Kallikráteia [GR] 130 B5
Néa Karváli [GR] 130 D3
Néa Kerdýllia [GR] 130 C4
Néa Koróni [GR] 136 D4
Neale [IRL] 2 C4
Néa Liosia [GR] 134 C6
Néa Mádytos [GR] 130 C4
Néa Mákri [GR] 134 C6
Néa Michanióna [GR] 128 H5
Néa Moní [GR] 134 G4
Néa Moudaniá [GR] 130 B5
Neamț, Mănăstirea- [RO] 204 D3
Neandria [TR] 130 H6
Néa Péramos [GR] 130 D3
Néa Péramos [GR] 134 B6
Néa Plágia [GR] 130 B5
Neápoli [GR] 128 E5
Neápoli [GR] 136 F5
Neápoli [GR] 140 F4
Neapolis [TR] 152 E5
Néa Poteídaia [GR] 130 B5
Néa Róda [GR] 130 C5
Néa Roúmata [GR] 140 B4
Néa Sánta [GR] 130 G2
Néa Stýra [GR] 134 D5
Neath [GB] 12 E2
Néa Tríglia [GR] 130 B5
Néa Výssa [GR] 130 H1
Néa Zíchni [GR] 130 C3
Nebiler [TR] 152 C2
Nebolchi [RUS] 202 C1
Nebra [D] 34 B5
Nechanice [CZ] 50 A3
Neckarelz [D] 46 D5
Neckargemünd [D] 46 C5
Neckargerach [D] 46 D5
Neckarsteinach [D] 46 C5
Neckarsulm [D] 46 D5
Neckenmarkt [A] 62 F6
Necşeşti [RO] 148 B1
Nečtiny [CZ] 48 D4
Neda [E] 78 D1
Nedansjö [S] 184 E4
Nedde [F] 66 H2
Neddemin [D] 20 D4
Neded [SK] 64 A5
Nedelišće [HR] 74 F4
Nederhögen [S] 182 G4
Nedervetil / Alaveteli [FIN] 196 C6
Neder Vindinge [DK] 156 F4
Nedre Eggedal [N] 170 G5
Nedre Gärdsjö [S] 172 H3
Nedre Soppero [S] 192 H4
Nedstrand [N] 164 B2
Nedvědice [CZ] 50 B5
Nędza [PL] 50 E3
Neede [NL] 16 G5
Neermoor [D] 18 B4
Neeroeteren [B] 30 E3
Nefyn [GB] 10 B4
Negorci [MK] 128 G3
Negoslavci [HR] 142 E1
Negotin [SRB] 146 E1
Negotin [SRB] 204 C6
Negotino [MK] 128 F2
Negovanovci [BG] 146 E2
Negrar [I] 72 C6
Negreira [E] 78 B3
Negren-Tino [CH] 70 G2
Négrondes [F] 66 F2
Negru Vodă [RO] 148 G1
Neheim-Hüsten [D] 32 C4
Nehoiu [RO] 204 D5
Neiden [N] 194 E3
Neitisuanto [S] 192 G5
Neittävä [FIN] 196 E4
Nejdek [CZ] 48 D3
Nekromanteío [GR] 132 C3
Neksø [DK] 158 E4
Nelas [P] 80 C6
Nelidovo [RUS] 202 D3
Nellim [FIN] 194 E4
Nellingen [D] 60 B3
Neltaa [FIN] 176 G4
Neman [RUS] 200 D5
Nembro [I] 70 H4
Neméa [GR] 136 E1
Neméa [GR] 136 E1
Nemenčinė [LT] 200 G5
Nemesnádudvar [H] 76 C4
Nemesszalók [H] 74 G1
Németkér [H] 76 C3
Nemila [BIH] 142 D4
Nemours [F] 42 G5
Nemrutkale [TR] 152 C3
Nemška Loka [SLO] 74 C6
Nemšová [SK] 64 A2
Nemti [H] 64 D5
Nemyriv [UA] 52 G3
Nenagh [IRL] 2 D6
Nendeln [FL] 58 H5
Neochóri [GR] 132 E5
Neochóri [GR] 132 F3
Neochóri [GR] 132 F2
Neochóri [GR] 134 A2
Neochóri [GR] 134 C5
Neochóri [GR] 136 B1
Néo Monastíri [GR] 132 G3
Néos Marmarás [GR] 130 C6
Nepi [I] 114 H4
Nepomuk [CZ] 48 E5
Neptun [RO] 148 G1
Nérac [F] 66 E5
Neratovice [CZ] 48 G3
Néré [F] 54 D5
Neresheim [D] 60 C2
Nereta [LV] 198 E6
Nereto [I] 116 D3
Neretva Kanjon [BIH] 144 C2
Nerezine [HR] 112 E3
Nerežišća [HR] 144 A2
Neringa-Nida [LT] 200 D5
Néris-les-Bains [F] 56 C6
Nerja [E] 102 D5
Nerja, Cueva de- [E] 102 D5
Nérondes [F] 56 C4
Nerpio [E] 102 H2
Nerpio, Cuevas de- [E] 102 H2
Nersingen [D] 60 B3
Nerskogen [N] 180 H3
Nerva [E] 94 F5
Nervesa della Battaglia [I] 72 E5
Nervi [I] 110 B3
Nerviano [I] 70 G4
Nes [N] 164 F2
Nes [N] 170 D1
Nes [N] 170 H4
Nes [N] 180 C6
Nes [NL] 16 F1
Nesactium [HR] 112 D2
Nesaseter [N] 190 D4
Nesbyen [N] 170 G4
Nesebŭr [BG] 148 F4
Neset [N] 190 E2
Nesflaten [N] 164 C1
Nesheim [N] 170 C3
Neskaupstaður [IS] 192 D3
Neslandsvatn [N] 164 F3
Nesle [F] 28 F5
Nesna [N] 190 D2
Nesoddtangen [N] 166 B1
Nespereira [P] 80 C3
Nesseby [N] 194 E2
Nesselwang [D] 60 C5
Nestáni [GR] 136 E2
Nestavoll [N] 180 H4
Nesterov [RUS] 24 D1
Nestório [GR] 128 D5
Nesttun [N] 170 B4
Nesvik [N] 164 B2
Neszmély [H] 64 B6
Netolice [CZ] 62 B2
Netretić [HR] 112 G1
Nettancourt [F] 44 C4
Netta Pierwsza [PL] 24 E4
Nettetal [D] 30 F3
Nettuno [I] 120 B1
Nettuno, Grotta di- [I] 118 B3
Neubeckum [D] 32 D3
Neuberg [A] 74 E1
Neuberg an der Mürz [A] 62 D6
Neubrandenburg [D] 20 D4
Neubukow [D] 20 A3
Neubulach [D] 58 G1
Neuburg [D] 60 D2
Neuburg [D] 60 H3
Neuchâtel [CH] 58 C5
Neu Darchau [D] 18 G5
Neudorf [D] 34 A4
Neudorf [D] 46 C5
Neudorf-Platendorf [D] 32 H2
Neuenburg [D] 18 C4
Neuenbürg [D] 46 C6
Neuenburg [D] 58 E3
Neuenhaus [D] 16 G4
Neuenkirchen [D] 18 F5
Neuenstein [D] 32 F6
Neuenstein [D] 46 D5
Neuenstein [D] 46 D5
Neuenwalde [D] 18 D3
Neuer Weg [D] 18 C4
Neufahrn [D] 60 F3
Neuf-Brisach [F] 58 E3
Neufchâteau [B] 44 D2
Neufchâteau [F] 44 D6
Neufchâtel-en-Bray [F] 28 C5
Neufchâtel-sur-Aisne [F] 44 B2
Neufeld [D] 18 E3
Neufelden [A] 62 B3
Neuffen [D] 58 H2
Neugersdorf [D] 48 G1
Neuhaus [D] 18 E3
Neuhaus [D] 18 H5
Neuhaus [D] 32 F4
Neuhaus [D] 46 G2
Neuhaus [D] 46 H4
Neuhaus [D] 60 H3
Neuhausen am Rheinfall [CH] 58 F4
Neuhof [D] 34 E3
Neuhofen an der Krems [A] 62 B4
Neuillé Port-Pierre [F] 54 F1
Neuilly-l'Évêque [F] 58 A3
Neuilly-St-Front [F] 42 H3
Neu-Isenburg [D] 46 C3
Neukalen [D] 20 C4
Neukirch [D] 34 F6
Neukirchen [A] 60 G4
Neukirchen [A] 72 F1
Neukirchen [D] 32 E6
Neukirchen [D] 156 B4
Neukloster [D] 20 A3
Neuland [D] 18 E3
Neulengbach [A] 62 E4
Neulingen [D] 46 C6
Neu Lübbenau [D] 34 F3
Neum [BIH] 144 C3
Neumarkt [A] 60 H5
Neumarkt [A] 74 B2
Neumarkt [D] 46 H5
Neumarkt / Egna [I] 72 D4
Neumarkt-St Veit [D] 60 F4
Neu-Moresnet [B] 30 F5
Neumorschen [D] 32 F6
Neu Mukran [D] 20 D2
Neumünster [D] 18 F3
Neunagelberg [A] 62 C3
Neunburg [D] 48 C5
Neung-sur-Beuvron [F] 56 B2
Neunkirchen [A] 62 E6
Neunkirchen [D] 44 G3
Neunkirchen-Seelscheid [D] 30 H4
Neuötting [D] 60 G4
Neupölla [A] 62 D3
Neuruppin [D] 20 C6
Neu Schrepkow [D] 20 B6
Neuschwanstein [D] 60 C6
Neusiedl am See [A] 62 G5
Neuss [D] 30 G3
Neustadt [D] 18 H3
Neustadt [D] 32 E6
Neustadt [D] 34 C1
Neustadt [D] 34 F6
Neustadt [D] 46 E3
Neustadt [D] 46 G2
Neustadt [D] 48 B1
Neustadt [D] 58 F3
Neustadt [D] 60 E2
Neustadt am Rübenberge [D] 32 F2
Neustadt an der Aisch [D] 46 F5
Neustadt an der Waldnaab [D] 48 C4
Neustadt an der Weinstrasse [D] 46 B5
Neustadt-Glewe [D] 20 A5
Neustift [A] 72 D1
Neustift / Novacella [I] 72 D2
Neustrelitz [D] 20 C5
Neu-Ulm [D] 60 B3
Neuvéglise [F] 68 C4
Neuves-Maisons [F] 44 E5
Neuvic [F] 66 E3
Neuvic [F] 68 B3
Neuville [F] 54 E3
Neuville [F] 68 F2
Neuville-aux-Bois [F] 42 E5
Neuvilly-en-Argonne [F] 44 D3
Neuvola [FIN] 186 H4
Neuvy [F] 54 H4
Neuvy-Bouin [F] 54 D3
Neuvy-sur-Barangeon [F] 56 C3
Neuwied [D] 30 H6
Neuzelle [D] 34 G3
Neveklov [CZ] 48 G4
Nevel' [RUS] 202 C3
Neverfjord [N] 194 B2
Nevers [F] 56 D4
Nevès [E] 92 D2
Nevesinje [BIH] 144 C2
Nevlunghavn [N] 164 G3
Nevossuo [FIN] 178 C3
New Alresford [GB] 12 H4
Newark-on-Trent [GB] 10 F5
Newbiggin-by-the-Sea [GB] 8 G5
Newbliss [IRL] 2 F4
Newbridge / Droichead Nua [IRL] 2 E6
Newburgh [GB] 8 E2
Newbury [GB] 12 H4
Newcastle [NIR] 2 G4
Newcastle Emlyn [GB] 10 A6
Newcastle-under-Lyme [GB] 10 E5
Newcastle upon Tyne [GB] 8 G6
Newcastle West [IRL] 4 C3
New Galloway [GB] 8 D5
Newgrange [IRL] 2 F5
Newhaven [GB] 14 E6
Newinn [IRL] 4 D4
Newmarket [GB] 14 F3
Newmarket [IRL] 4 C4
Newmarket-on-Fergus [IRL] 2 C6
Newport [GB] 10 D5
Newport [GB] 12 F3
Newport [GB] 12 H5
Newport [IRL] 2 C3
Newport [IRL] 4 D3
Newport-on-Tay [GB] 8 F2
Newport Pagnell [GB] 14 E3
New Quay [GB] 10 B6
Newquay [GB] 12 C4
New Romney [GB] 14 F5
New Ross / Ros Mhic Thriúin [IRL] 4 F4
Newry [NIR] 2 F4
Newton Abbot [GB] 12 E5
Newton Le Willows [GB] 10 D4
Newtonmore [GB] 6 D6
Newton Stewart [GB] 8 C5
Newtown [GB] 10 C6
Newtownabbey [NIR] 2 G3
Newtownards [NIR] 2 G3
Newtown Butler [NIR] 2 E4
Newtownhamilton [NIR] 2 F4
Newtownmountkennedy [IRL] 4 G3
Newtownstewart [NIR] 2 F3
Nexon [F] 66 G2
Nežilovo [MK] 128 E2
Niadinge [LT] 24 G2
Niana [I] 70 E4
Nianfors [S] 174 E1
Niaux, Grotte de- [F] 84 H5
Nibe [DK] 160 D4
Nicaj-Shalë [AL] 146 A6
Nicaj Shoshë [AL] 146 A6
Nicastro [I] 124 D5
Nice [F] 108 E4
Nickelsdorf [A] 62 G5
Nicknoret [S] 190 H4
Nicolosi [I] 126 G3
Nicopolis ad Istrum [BG] 148 C3
Nicosia [I] 126 F3
Nicotera [I] 124 C6
Nidda [D] 46 D2
Nidderau [D] 46 D2
Nideck, Château du- [F] 44 G6
Nideggen [D] 30 F5
Nidzica [PL] 22 G5
Niebla [E] 94 F5
Nieborow [PL] 36 H3
Niebüll [D] 156 B4
Nieby [D] 156 C5
Niechanowo [PL] 36 D2
Niechorze [PL] 20 G3
Niedalino [PL] 20 H3
Niederalben [D] 44 H3
Niederalteich [D] 60 G3
Niederau [A] 60 F6
Niederaula [D] 46 E1
Niederbronn-les-Bains [F] 44 H5
Niederelsungen [D] 32 E5
Niederkleen [D] 46 C2
Niederkrüchten [D] 30 F3
Niederndorf [A] 60 F6
Niederoderwitz [D] 48 G1
Nieder Stotzingen [D] 60 C3
Niederwinkling [D] 60 G2
Nieder-Wöllstadt [D] 46 C2
Niederwölz [A] 74 B2
Niedrzwica Duża [PL] 38 E6
Niedźwiedź [PL] 22 E5
Niemce [PL] 38 E5
Niemcza [PL] 50 C2
Niemegk [D] 34 D3
Niemica [PL] 22 A3

Niemijarvi [FIN] 188 H1
Niemis [S] 194 B8
Niemisel [S] 196 B2
Niemisjärvi [FIN] 186 H4
Niemiskylä [FIN] 196 G5
Niemodlin [PL] 50 D2
Nienburg [D] 32 F1
Nienhagen [D] 20 B3
Niepołomice [PL] 52 B4
Nieppe [F] 28 F3
Niepruszewo [PL] 36 C3
Nierstein [D] 46 C3
Niesky [D] 34 G5
Nieszawa [PL] 36 F1
Nietsak [S] 192 G6
Nieuil [F] 54 E6
Nieuweschans [NL] 16 H2
Nieuwpoort [B] 28 F1
Nigrán [E] 78 B5
Nigríta [GR] 130 B3
Nihattula [FIN] 176 G2
Niilivaara [FIN] 194 C6
Niinilahti [FIN] 186 G2
Niinimäki [FIN] 188 D3
Niinisalo [FIN] 186 C6
Niinivesi [FIN] 186 G2
Niirala [FIN] 188 G4
Niittumaa [FIN] 176 C2
Níjar [E] 102 G5
Nijemci [HR] 142 E2
Nijkerk [NL] 16 E5
Nijmegen [NL] 16 E6
Nijverdal [NL] 16 G4
Níkaia [GR] 132 G2
Nikaia [TR] 150 G4
Nikaranperä [FIN] 186 F3
Nikel' [RUS] 194 F3
Níki [GR] 128 E4
Nikiá [GR] 154 B3
Nikifóros [GR] 130 D3
Nikil [S] 166 H6
Nikísiani [GR] 130 D3
Nikitári [CY] 154 F5
Nikítas [GR] 130 C5
Nikkajärvi [FIN] 196 G5
Nikkala [S] 196 C2
Nikkaluokta [S] 192 F5
Nikkaroinen [FIN] 178 A1
Nikla [H] 74 H3
Nikolaevo [BG] 148 D4
Nikolaevskoye [RUS] 198 H2
Nikola Kozlevo [BG] 148 E2
Nikolayevo [RUS] 198 H2
Nikopol [BG] 148 B2
Nikopol' [UA] 204 H2
Nikópoli [GR] 132 D4
Nikšić [MNE] 144 E3
Nilivaara [S] 192 H6
Nilsiä [FIN] 188 D1
Nim [DK] 156 C1
Nîmes [F] 106 F3
Nin [HR] 112 G4
Ninfa [I] 116 B6
Ninove [B] 28 H3
Niort [F] 54 D4
Niquidetto [I] 70 D5
Niroú Kháni [GR] 140 E4
Niš [SRB] 146 D3
Nisa [P] 86 E4
Nisáki [GR] 132 B2
Niscemi [I] 126 F4
Niška Banja [SRB] 146 D3
Niskakoski [FIN] 194 E4
Niska-Pietilä [FIN] 178 F1
Nisko [PL] 52 E2
Nissafors [S] 162 C3
Nissi [EST] 198 D2
Nissilä [FIN] 196 E5
Nissoria [I] 126 F3
Nitaure [LV] 198 E5
Nitlax [FIN] 176 F6
Nitra [SK] 64 A4
Nitrianske Pravno [SK] 64 B2
Nitrianske Rudno [SK] 64 B3
Nitry [F] 56 F2
Nittedal [N] 172 B5
Nittenau [D] 48 C6
Nittendorf [D] 60 F2
Nittkvarn [S] 166 G1
Nivå [DK] 156 G2
Niva [FIN] 196 G4
Nivala [FIN] 196 D5
Nivelles [B] 28 H3
Niversac [F] 66 F3
Nixhöhle [A] 62 D5
Nizhyn [UA] 202 E7
Nižná [SK] 50 H6
Nižná Boca [SK] 64 D2
Nižná Polianka [SK] 52 D5
Nižná Slaná [SK] 64 E3
Nizy-le-Comte [F] 28 G6
Nizza Monferrato [I] 108 H2
Njavve [S] 190 G1
Njegoševo [SRB] 76 D6
Njetsavare [S] 190 H1
Njivice [HR] 112 E2
Njupeskärs Vattenfall [S] 172 E1
Njurandabommen [S] 184 E5
Njurunda [S] 184 E5
Njutånger [S] 174 E1
Noailles [F] 28 D6
Noain / Elorz [E] 84 B4
Noale [I] 72 E6
Noasca [I] 70 D4
Nöbbele [S] 162 E5
Nöbbelöv [S] 158 D2
Noceda [E] 78 F5
Nocera [I] 120 E3
Nocera Umbra [I] 116 B2
Noceto [I] 110 D2
Noci [I] 122 E3
Nocito [E] 84 D6
Nodeland [N] 164 D5
Nods [F] 58 B5
Noé [F] 84 H4
Noépoli [I] 122 C5
Noeux [F] 28 E3
Nofuentes [E] 82 F4
Nogale [LV] 198 C4
Nogales [E] 94 G2
Nogara [I] 110 F1
Nogaro [F] 84 F2
Nogarole Rocca [I] 110 E1
Nogent [F] 56 H2
Nogent-le-Roi [F] 42 E4
Nogent-le-Rotrou [F] 26 G6
Nogent-sur-Seine [F] 42 H5
Nogersund [S] 158 E2
Noginsk [RUS] 202 F3
Nogva [N] 180 D3
Noharre [E] 88 E3
Nohfelden [D] 44 G3
Noia Noya [E] 78 B3
Noidans-le-Ferroux [F] 58 B4
Noirétable [F] 68 E2
Noirmoutier-en-l'Ile [F] 54 A2
Noja [E] 82 F3
Nokia [FIN] 176 F1
Nokka [FIN] 186 H6
Nokkosmäenkulma [FIN] 186 B5
Nola [I] 120 E3
Nol Alafors [S] 160 H1
Nolay [F] 56 F4
Noli [I] 108 H3
Nomeny [F] 44 E5
Nomexy [F] 44 E6
Nömme [EST] 198 E2
Nonancourt [F] 26 H5
Nonant-le-Pin [F] 26 G5
Nonantola [I] 110 F3
Nonaspe [E] 90 G5
Nonnenhorn [D] 58 H4
Nonsfossen [N] 180 D6
Nontron [F] 66 F2
Nonza [F] 114 C2
Noordwijk aan Zee [NL] 16 C4
Noormarkku / Normark [FIN] 176 D1
Nopankylä [FIN] 186 B3
Noppikoski [S] 172 G2
Nor [N] 172 D5
Nor [N] 180 C5
Nor [S] 182 H3
Nora [I] 118 C7
Nora [S] 166 H2
Nora [S] 168 B6
Nørager [DK] 160 D4
Norberg [S] 168 B1
Norbi [EST] 198 C2
Norchia [I] 114 G4
Norcia [I] 116 B3
Nordagutu [N] 164 F2
Nordanå [S] 162 B6
Nordanå [S] 184 E3
Nordanåker [S] 184 D2
Nordanås [S] 190 F3
Nordanås [S] 190 G3
Nordanås [S] 190 G5
Nordanholen [S] 172 H4
Nordankäl [S] 184 D1
Nordanrå [S] 190 F4
Nordansjö [S] 190 F4
Nordausques [F] 14 H6
Nordberg [N] 180 F5
Nordborg [DK] 156 C4
Nordbottnen [S] 182 E2
Nordby [DK] 156 A3
Nordby [DK] 156 E1
Nordby [N] 166 B1
Nordby [N] 166 C2
Nordby [N] 172 C2
Norddeich [D] 16 H1
Nordeide [N] 170 C1
Norden [D] 16 H1
Norden [S] 190 H2
Nordenham [D] 18 D4
Norderåsen [S] 182 H1
Norderney [D] 16 H1
Norderö [S] 182 G2
Norderstedt [D] 18 F4
Nordeste [P] 100 E3
Nord Etnedal [N] 170 G2
Nordfjord [N] 194 E1
Nordfjordeid [N] 180 C5
Nordfold [N] 192 D5
Nordgulen [N] 170 B2
Nordhalben [D] 46 H2
Nordhallen [S] 182 E1
Nordhausen [D] 32 H5
Nordhella [N] 192 F2
Nordhorn [D] 16 H4
Nordingrå [S] 184 F3
Nordkapp [N] 194 C1
Nordkirchen [D] 32 C3
Nordkisa [N] 172 C5
Nordkjosbotn [N] 192 G3
Nord-Lenangen [N] 192 G2
Nordli [N] 190 D5
Nördlingen [D] 60 C2
Nordmaling [S] 184 H1
Nordmark [S] 166 F1
Nordmela [N] 192 E3
Nordøyvågen [N] 190 D2
Nordre Osen [N] 172 D2
Nordseter [N] 172 B2
Nordsinni [N] 170 H3
Nordsjö [S] 174 D1
Nordskjørin [N] 190 B5
Nordskov [DK] 156 E2
Nordvik [N] 180 G2
Nordvika [N] 180 F1
Nordwalde [D] 16 H5
Nore [S] 184 D6
Noresund [N] 170 G5
Norg [NL] 16 G2
Norheimsund [N] 170 C4
Nørholm [N] 164 E5
Norhyttan [S] 172 G5
Norinkylä [FIN] 186 B4
Norje [S] 158 E1
Norkino [RUS] 198 H5
Norma [I] 116 B6
Norn [S] 174 C5
Norra Finnskoga [S] 172 E3
Norrahammar [S] 162 D2
Norraker [S] 190 E5
Norrala [S] 174 E2
Norra Löten [S] 172 E3
Norra Mellby [S] 158 C1
Norra Råda [S] 166 F1
Norra Tresund [S] 190 F4
Norrback [FIN] 186 B3
Norrbäck [S] 190 G4
Norrberg [S] 190 F4
Norrboda [S] 172 H3
Norrboda [S] 174 G5
Norrby [S] 190 G4
Nørre Aaby [DK] 156 D3
Nørre Alslev [DK] 156 F5
Nørre Broby [DK] 156 D3
Nørre Lyndelse [DK] 156 D3
Nørre Nebel [DK] 156 A2
Nørre Snede [DK] 156 C1
Nørresundby [DK] 160 D3
Nørre Vejrup [DK] 156 B2
Nørre Vorupør [DK] 160 B4
Norrfjärden [S] 196 B3
Norrfors [S] 190 H6
Norrgravsjö [S] 190 G5
Norr Hede [S] 182 F4
Norrhult [S] 162 E4
Norriån [S] 194 A8
Norrköping [S] 168 B5
Norrmark / Noormarkku [FIN] 176 D1
Norrnäs [FIN] 186 A4
Norrskedika [S] 174 G5
Norrsunda [S] 168 D2
Norrsundet [S] 174 E3
Norrtälje [S] 168 E2
Norrtannflo [S] 184 E2
Norrvik [S] 196 A2
Nors [DK] 160 C3
Norsholm [S] 168 B5
Norsjö [S] 190 H4
Norsjövallen [S] 190 H4
Nörten-Hardenberg [D] 32 G4
Northallerton [GB] 10 F2
Northam [GB] 12 D3
Northampton [GB] 14 D2
North Berwick [GB] 8 F3
Northeim [D] 32 G4
North Ferriby [GB] 10 G4
Northleach [GB] 12 H2
North Walsham [GB] 14 G2
Northwich [GB] 10 D4
Nortorf [D] 18 F2
Nort-sur-Erdre [F] 40 F6
Norwich [GB] 14 G2
Nos [N] 164 F3
Nøsen [N] 170 F3
Nosivka [UA] 202 E7
Nossa Senhora da Conceição [P] 94 C2
Nossa Senhora da Serra [P] 80 F3
Nossa Senhora De Taúde [P] 80 C5
Nossa Senhora do Cabo [P] 86 A6
Nossebro [S] 166 D6
Nössemark [S] 166 C3
Nossen [D] 34 E6
Nótia [GR] 128 G3
Nötö [FIN] 176 D6
Noto [I] 126 G5
Noto Antica [I] 126 G5
Notodden [N] 164 F2
Notre-Dame de Consolation [F] 58 C5
Notre-Dame de-la-Roquette [F] 108 D5
Notre-Dame des Fontaines [F] 108 F3
Nottebäck [S] 162 E4
Nøtterøy [N] 164 H3
Nottingham [GB] 10 F5
Nottuln [D] 16 H6
Nouan-le-Fuzelier [F] 56 B2
Nouans-les-Fontaines [F] 54 G3
Nousu [FIN] 194 E7
Nouvaillé-Maupertuis [F] 54 E4
Nouvion [F] 28 D4
Nova [EST] 198 D2
Nova [H] 74 F3
Nová Baňa [SK] 64 B4
Nova Breznica [MK] 128 E1
Nová Bystrica [CZ] 62 D2
Nová Bystrica [SK] 50 G6
Novacella / Neustift [I] 72 D2
Novachene [BG] 146 G4
Novaci [MK] 128 E3
Nova Crnja [SRB] 76 F6
Novae Palesse [BY] 202 C6
Novafeltria [I] 110 H5
Nova Gorica [SLO] 72 H5
Nova Gradiška [HR] 142 C1
Novaja Kakhovka [UA] 204 G3
Novajidrány [H] 64 G4
Nova Kakhovka [RUS] 204 G3
Nova Kapela [HR] 142 C2
Nova Kasaba [BIH] 142 E4
Novakovo [BG] 148 C6
Nováky [SK] 64 B3
Novales [E] 90 F3
Novalesa, Abbazia di- [I] 70 C5
Nova Levante / Welschnofen [I] 72 D3
Novalja [HR] 112 F4
Nova Odesa [UA] 204 F3
Nová Paka [CZ] 48 H2
Nova Pazova [SRB] 142 G2
Nova Praha [UA] 202 F8
Novara [I] 70 F5
Novara di Sicilia [I] 124 A7
Nová Říšc [CZ] 48 H6
Nová Sedlica [SK] 52 F6
Novate Mezzola [I] 70 H3
Nova Topola [BIH] 142 C2
Nova Varoš [SRB] 146 A3
Novaya Zhizn' [RUS] 198 G2
Nova Zagora [BG] 148 D5
Nové Hrady [CZ] 62 C3
Novelda [E] 104 D2
Novellara [I] 110 E2
Nové Město nad Metují [CZ] 50 B3
Nové Mesto nad Váhom [SK] 64 A3
Nové Město na Moravě [CZ] 50 B5
Nové Město pod Smrkem [CZ] 48 H1
Nové Mitrovice [CZ] 48 E5
Noventa Vicentina [I] 110 G1
Novés [E] 88 E6
Noves [F] 106 G3
Nové Sady [SK] 64 A4
Nové Strašecí [CZ] 48 E3
Nové Zámky [SK] 64 B5
Novgorodka [RUS] 198 H4
Novgrad [BG] 148 C2
Novhorodka [UA] 202 F8
Novhorod-Siverskyi [UA] 202 E6
Novi Bečej [SRB] 76 E6
Novi di Módena [I] 110 E2
Novi Dojran [MK] 128 H3
Noviergas [E] 90 C3
Novi Grad [BIH] 142 D2
Novigrad [HR] 112 D1
Novigrad [HR] 112 G5
Novigrad Podravski [HR] 74 G5
Novi Han [BG] 146 G5
Novi Iskăr [BG] 146 F4
Novi Kazarci [SRB] 76 F5
Novi Kneževac [SRB] 76 E5
Novi Krichim [BG] 148 B6
Novi Ligure [I] 110 A2
Novi Marof [HR] 74 F5
Novion-Porcien [F] 28 H6
Novi Pazar [BG] 148 E2
Novi Pazar [SRB] 146 B4
Novi Sad [MNE] 204 A5
Novi Sad [SRB] 142 F1
Novi Senkovac [HR] 74 H6
Novi Travnik [BIH] 142 C4
Novi Vinodolski [HR] 112 F2
Novoarkhanhel's'k [UA] 202 E8
Novobobruysk [RUS] 24 B2
Novo Brdo [SRB] 146 C5
Novodugino [RUS] 202 E3
Novohrad-Volyns'kyi [UA] 202 C7
Novoiavorivs'ke [UA] 52 G3
Novo mesto [SLO] 74 D6
Novo Miloševo [SRB] 76 E6
Novomoskovs'k [UA] 204 H1
Novomyrhorod [UA] 202 E8
Novo Panicharovo [BG] 148 F5
Novorzhev [RUS] 198 H4
Novoselë [AL] 128 A5
Novoselets [BG] 148 D5
Novo Selo [BG] 146 E1
Novo Selo [BG] 146 G5
Novo Selo [BG] 148 B4
Novo Selo [BG] 148 D2
Novo Selo [MK] 128 H2
Novoseltsi [BG] 148 F5
Novosel'ye [RUS] 198 H3
Novosokol'niki [RUS] 202 C3
Novoukraïnka [UA] 52 H2
Novovolyns'k [UA] 52 H1
Novovorontsovka [UA] 204 G2
Novoye Jushkozero [RUS] 196 H3
Novozavidovskiy [RUS] 202 E2
Novo Zvečevo [HR] 142 C1
Novozybkov [RUS] 202 D6
Novska [HR] 142 B1
Nový Bohumín [CZ] 50 F4
Nový Bor [CZ] 48 G2
Nový Bydžov [CZ] 48 H3
Novy Bykhaw [BY] 202 C5
Nový Hrad [CZ] 50 C6
Novyi Buh [UA] 204 G2
Novyi Bykiv [UA] 202 E7
Nový Jičín [CZ] 50 E5
Nový Knín [CZ] 48 F4
Novyy Dvor [BY] 24 G3
Nowa Brzeźnica [PL] 36 G6
Nowa Cerekwia [PL] 50 E4
Nowa Dęba [PL] 52 D2
Nowa Karczma [PL] 22 D3
Nowa Karczma [PL] 22 F2
Nowa Ruda [PL] 50 C2
Nowa Sarzyna [PL] 52 E3
Nowa Słupia [PL] 52 C1
Nowa Sól [PL] 36 A4
Nowa Wieś [PL] 24 C6
Nowa Wieś Ełcka [PL] 24 D4
Nowa Wieś Lęborska [PL] 22 C2
Nowe [PL] 22 E4
Nowe Brzesko [PL] 52 B3
Nowe Czarnowo [PL] 20 F6
Nowe Miasteczko [PL] 36 A4
Nowe Miasto [PL] 38 B2
Nowe Miasto Lubawskie [PL] 22 F5
Nowe Miasto nad Pilicą [PL] 38 B5
Nowe Miasto nad Wartą [PL] 36 D3
Nowe Piekuty [PL] 38 E1
Nowe Polichno [PL] 34 H2
Nowe Skalmierzyce [PL] 36 E4
Nowe Warpno [PL] 20 E4
Nowica [PL] 22 F3
Nowogard [PL] 20 G4
Nowogród [PL] 24 C5
Nowogród Bobrzański [PL] 34 H4
Nowogród Bobrzański [PL] 34 H4
Nowogrodziec [PL] 34 H6
Nowosady [PL] 24 F6
Nowosielec [PL] 52 E2
Nowosiółki [PL] 52 H2
Nowowola [PL] 24 F4
Nowy Duninów [PL] 36 G2
Nowy Dwór [PL] 24 F4
Nowy Dwór Gdański [PL] 22 E3
Nowy Dwór Mazowiecki [PL] 38 B2
Nowy Korczyn [PL] 52 C3
Nowy Majdan [PL] 52 F2
Nowy Orzechów [PL] 38 F5
Nowy Sącz [PL] 52 C5
Nowy Staw [PL] 22 E3
Nowy Targ [PL] 52 A5
Nowy Tomyśl [PL] 36 B3
Nowy Wiśnicz [PL] 52 B4
Nowy Żmigród [PL] 52 D5
Noyant [F] 42 B6
Noyers [F] 56 F2
Noyers-sur-Jabron [F] 108 C3
Noyon [F] 28 F6
Nozay [F] 40 F5
Nozdrzec [PL] 52 E4
Nozeroy [F] 58 B6
Nožičko [BIH] 142 C2
N. Petrítsi [GR] 130 B2
N. Rubeža [MNE] 144 E3
N. Sandsjö [S] 162 E3
N. S. de Angosto [E] 82 G5
N. S. de Chilla [E] 88 C5
N. S. de Cortés [E] 96 H5
N. S. de Hontanares [E] 88 G3
N. S. de la Bienvenida [E] 90 B6
N. S. de la Cabeza [E] 102 G3
N. S. de la Estrella [E] 102 F1
N. S. del Remedio [E] 98 D4
N. S. del Valle [E] 82 C5
N. Selo [BIH] 142 D2
N. Senhora da Azinheira [P] 80 E3
N. Senhora d'Abadia [P] 78 B6
N. Senhora da Graça [P] 80 D3
N. Senhora dos Remédios [P] 80 D4
N. Señora de Irache [E] 84 A4
N. Skióni [GR] 130 C6
Nubledo [E] 78 H3
Nueil-les-Aubiers [F] 54 D2
Nueno [E] 84 D6
Nuestra Señora de Arcos [E] 96 E4
Nuestra Señora de la Antigua [E] 96 G5
Nuestra Señora de la Anunciada [E] 88 D1
Nuestra Señora de la Misericordia [E] 90 D3
Nuestra Señora de la Vega [E] 98 E2
Nuestra Señora del Rocío [E] 94 F6
Nuestra Señora del Yugo [E] 84 B5
Nuestra Señora de Monlora [E] 84 C6
Nuestra Señora de Piedra Albas [E] 94 D4
Nueva-Carteya [E] 102 C2
Nuévalos [E] 90 C4
Nuevo Baztán [E] 88 G6
Nufringen [D] 58 G1
Nuhören [TR] 152 H1
Nuijamaa [FIN] 178 E2
Nuits-St-Georges [F] 56 G4
Nules [E] 92 C4
Nules [E] 98 F4
Nulvi [I] 118 C3
Numana [I] 116 C1
Numancia [E] 90 B2
Nummela [FIN] 176 G4
Nummenkylä [FIN] 176 G3
Nummi [FIN] 176 F4
Nummijärvi [FIN] 186 C4
Nummikoski [FIN] 186 C5
Nuneaton [GB] 14 D1
Nunkirchen [D] 44 G3
Nunnanen [FIN] 194 C5
Nunnanlahti [FIN] 188 E1
Nuño Gómez [E] 88 D6
Nunsdorf [D] 34 E3
Nunspeet [NL] 16 F4
Nuoramoinen [FIN] 178 B1
Nuorgam [FIN] 194 D2
Nuoritta [FIN] 196 E3
Nuoro [I] 118 D4
Nupaky [CZ] 48 G4
Nur [PL] 38 D1
Nuragus [I] 118 C5
Nurallao [I] 118 D5
Nuraminis [I] 118 C6
Nuraxi, Nuraghe su- [I] 118 C6
Nürburg [D] 30 G6
Nürburgring [D] 30 G6
Núria, Santuari de- [E] 92 E2
Nurmaa [FIN] 178 C1
Nurmes [FIN] 196 G6
Nurmi [FIN] 176 F2
Nurmijärvi [FIN] 176 H4
Nurmijärvi [FIN] 196 G6
Nurmo [FIN] 186 C3
Nurmuiža [LV] 198 C5
Nürnberg [D] 46 G5
Nurri [I] 118 D6
Nürtingen [D] 58 H1
Nus [I] 70 D4
Nusnäs [S] 172 G3
Nusret [TR] 152 D1
Nuštar [HR] 142 E1
Nutheim [N] 164 F2
Nuttlar [D] 32 D5
Nuupas [FIN] 196 D2
Nuvsvåg [N] 192 H1
Nuvvus [FIN] 194 C3
N. Vånga [S] 166 E6
N. Vi [S] 162 E2
Nw. Ludzicko [PL] 20 H4
Nyåker [S] 190 H6
Nyárád [H] 74 H1
Nyárlörinc [H] 76 E3
Nyasvizh [BY] 202 B6
Nybergsund [N] 172 D2
Nyborg [DK] 156 E3
Nyborg [N] 190 D5
Nyborg [S] 196 C3
Nybro [S] 162 F5
Nyby [DK] 156 G4
Nyby [FIN] 186 A3
Nybyn [S] 184 A2
Nydala [S] 162 D3
Nydri [GR] 132 D4
Nye [S] 162 E3
Nyeharelaye [BY] 202 B5
Nyékládháza [H] 64 F5
Nyergesujfalu [H] 64 B6
Nygård [N] 170 C2
Nygård [N] 192 F4
Nygarden [N] 182 C6
Nyhammar [S] 172 H5
Nyhem [S] 184 C3
Nyhyttan [S] 166 G2
Nyírábrány [H] 64 H6
Nyíracsád [H] 64 H6
Nyíradony [H] 64 H5
Nyírbogát [H] 64 H5
Nyíregyháza [H] 64 H5
Nyírlugos [H] 64 H5
Nyírtelek [H] 64 G5
Nyírtura [H] 64 H5
Nykälä [FIN] 188 C4
Nykarleby / Uusikaarlepyy [FIN] 186 C1
Nyker [DK] 158 E4
Nykirke [N] 170 H3
Nykøbing [DK] 20 B1
Nykøbing [DK] 156 F2
Nykøbing [DK] 160 C4
Nyköping [S] 168 C5
Nykrogen [S] 168 B1
Nykroppa [S] 166 G2
Nykvarn [S] 168 D3
Nyland [S] 184 E4
Nyland [S] 184 F3
Nyland [S] 184 G1
Nylars [DK] 158 E4
Nyluspen [S] 190 F4
Nymburk [CZ] 48 G3
Nymfaía [GR] 130 F2
Nymindegab [DK] 156 A1
Nymo [N] 192 G1
Nynäshamn [S] 168 D4
Nyneset [N] 190 D5
Nyon [CH] 70 B1
Nyons [F] 106 H2
Nyrå [S] 184 E5
Nýrsko [CZ] 48 D6
Nyrud [N] 194 E4
Nysa [PL] 50 D2
Nysa [TR] 152 E5
Nysäter [S] 166 E3
Nyseter [N] 180 F5
Nyskoga [S] 172 E4
Nyskolla [N] 172 B2
Nyslott / Savonlinna [FIN] 188 E5
Nystad / Uusikaupunki [FIN] 176 C3
Nysted [DK] 20 B1
Nystova [N] 170 E2
Nytorp [S] 192 H6
Nytrøa [N] 182 B4
Nyúl [H] 62 H6
Nyvollen [N] 182 D1
Nyzhankovychi [UA] 52 F4
Nyzhnie Sirahozy [UA] 204 H2
Nyzhni Sirohozy [RUS] 204 H2

O

O, Château d'- [F] 26 F5
Oafae e Stillës [AL] 128 B3
Oafae Kemzës [AL] 128 B2
Oaivos [N] 194 B4
Oakham [GB] 10 F6
Oanes [N] 164 B3
Oban [GB] 8 C1
O Barco de Valdeorras [E] 78 E5
Őbarok [H] 64 B6
Obbekær [DK] 156 B3
Obbola [S] 196 A6
Obdach [A] 74 C2
Obedinenie [BG] 148 C3
Obejo [E] 96 C6
Obel [MK] 146 F6
Obeliai [LT] 200 G3
Oberammergau [D] 60 D6
Oberau [D] 60 D6
Oberaudorf [D] 60 F6
Oberdrauburg [A] 72 G3
Oberei [CH] 58 E6
Obergrafendorf [A] 62 D4
Obergünzburg [D] 60 C5
Obergurgl [A] 72 C2
Oberhaslach [F] 44 G6
Oberhausen [D] 30 G3
Oberhof [A] 74 B2
Oberhof [D] 46 G1
Oberhofen [CH] 70 E1
Oberjoch [D] 60 C6
Oberkirch [D] 58 F1
Oberkochen [D] 60 B2
Obermarchtal [D] 58 H3
Obermünchen [D] 60 F3
Obernai [F] 44 G6
Obernberg [A] 60 H4
Obernberg am Brenner [LT] 72 D2
Obernburg [D] 46 D4
Oberndorf [A] 60 G5
Oberndorf [D] 58 G2
Obernholz [D] 32 H1
Obernzell [D] 62 A3
Oberpullendorf [A] 74 F1
Oberried [CH] 70 E1
Oberriet [CH] 58 H5
Ober-Roden [D] 46 C3
Obersickte [D] 32 H3
Obersinn [D] 46 E3
Obersontheim [D] 46 E6
Oberstaufen [D] 60 B6
Oberstdorf [D] 60 B6
Oberstenfeld [D] 46 D6
Obersuhl [D] 32 F6
Obertauern [A] 72 H1
Obertraubling [D] 60 F2
Obertraun [A] 62 A6
Obervellach [A] 72 G2
Oberviechtach [D] 48 C5
Oberwald [CH] 70 F2
Oberwart [A] 74 F1
Oberwasser [D] 58 F2
Oberwesel [D] 46 B3
Oberwiesenthal [D] 48 D2
Oberwölzstadt [A] 74 B2
Oberzeiring [A] 74 C1
Óbidos [P] 86 B3
Obing [D] 60 F5
Objat [F] 66 G3
Objazda [PL] 22 B2
Ob. Kindberg [A] 62 D6
Öblarn [A] 62 B6
Obleševo [MK] 128 G1
Obljaj [HR] 112 H2
Obninsk [RUS] 202 F3
Obnova [BG] 148 B3
Ö. Bodane [S] 166 D4
Obodowo [PL] 22 C5
O Bolo [E] 78 E5
Oborishte [BG] 148 A5
Oborniki [PL] 36 C2
Oborniki Śląska [PL] 36 C6
Oborovo [HR] 74 F6
Obory [CZ] 48 F5
Obrenovac [SRB] 142 G3
Obrenovac [SRB] 204 B6
Obretenik [BG] 148 C2
Obrochishte [BG] 148 G2
Obrov [SLO] 74 B6
Obrovac [HR] 112 G5
Obrovac [HR] 144 A1
Obrovac [SRB] 142 F1
Obruchishte [BG] 148 D5
Obsteig [A] 72 C1
Obukhiv [UA] 202 D7
Obzor [BG] 148 F3
Ocaklar [TR] 150 D4
Ocaklı [TR] 150 B4
Ocaña [E] 96 G1
O Carballiño [E] 78 C4
Occhiobello [I] 110 G2
Ochagavía / Otsagi [E] 84 C4
Ochakiv [UA] 204 G3
Ochojec [PL] 50 F3
Ochozská Jesk. [CZ] 50 C6
Ochoz u Brna [CZ] 50 C6
Ochsattel [A] 62 E5
Ochsenburg [A] 62 E4
Ochsenfurt [D] 46 E4
Ochsenhausen [D] 60 B4
Ochtrup [D] 16 H5
Ociesęki [PL] 52 C2
Ockelbo [S] 174 E3
Ocksjön [S] 182 H4
Ocolna [RO] 146 G2
O Convento / Poio [E] 78 B4
O Corgo [E] 78 E3
Ócsa [H] 76 C1
Öcsöd [H] 76 E2
Ocypel [PL] 22 D4
Od [S] 162 B1
Odda [N] 170 C5
Odden [N] 172 C1
Odden [N] 192 G2
Odder [DK] 156 D1
Oddesund [DK] 160 B5
Ödeby [S] 166 H3
Odeceixe [P] 94 B4
Odeleite [P] 94 D5
Odelzhausen [D] 60 D4
Odemira [P] 94 B3
Ödemiş [TR] 152 E4
Odèn [E] 92 D2
Ödenäs [S] 162 B2
Odenbach [D] 44 H3
Odensbacken [S] 166 H3
Odense [DK] 156 D3
Odensjö [S] 162 C4
Odensvi [S] 162 F2
Odensvi [S] 168 B2
Oderberg [D] 34 F1
Oderljunga [S] 158 C1
Oderzo [I] 72 F5
Ödeshög [S] 166 G6
Odessa [UA] 204 F3
Ödestugu [S] 162 D2
Odivelas [P] 86 B5
Odivelas [P] 94 D2
Odnes [N] 170 H3
Odolanów [PL] 36 D5
Odoorn [NL] 16 G3
Odorheiu Secuiesc [RO] 204 D4

Odoyev [RUS] 202 F4
Odranci [SLO] 74 F3
Odry [CZ] 50 E5
Odrzywół [PL] 38 B5
Ødsted [DK] 156 C2
Odum [DK] 160 E6
Odžaci [SRB] 142 E1
Odžak [BIH] 142 D2
Odžak [MNE] 144 E2
Ödzemirci [TR] 152 H4
Odziena [LV] 198 E5
Oebisfelde [D] 34 A2
Oederan [D] 48 D1
Oeding [D] 16 G6
Oeijenbraak [B] 30 D3
Oelde [D] 32 D3
Oelsnitz [D] 48 C2
Oensinger Klus [CH] 58 E5
Oersberg [D] 18 F1
Oetmannshausen [D] 32 F5
Oëtre, Roche d'- [F] 26 F4
Oettingen [D] 46 F6
Oetz [A] 72 C1
Ófehértó [H] 64 H5
Offenbach [D] 46 C3
Offenburg [D] 44 H6
Offenheim [D] 46 B4
Offida [I] 116 C2
Ofir [P] 80 B3
Oforsen [S] 172 F6
Ofte [N] 164 E2
Ogenbargen [D] 18 C4
Oğlansini [TR] 154 F1
Ogliastro Cilento [I] 120 F4
Ognica [PL] 20 E6
Ognjanovo [BG] 130 C1
Ogre [LV] 198 E5
Ogrodzieniec [PL] 50 G2
Ogrosen [D] 34 F4
O Grove [E] 78 B4
Ogulin [HR] 112 G2
Ohat [H] 64 F6
Oheb [CZ] 50 A4
Ohlava [FIN] 196 D3
Ohordorf [D] 32 H1
Ohrdruf [D] 46 G1
Ohrid [MK] 128 D3
Öhringen [D] 46 D5
Ohtola [FIN] 186 D4
Óhuta [H] 64 G4
Oia [GR] 138 F5
Oiã [P] 80 B5
Oia / Arrabal [E] 78 A5
Oijärvi [FIN] 196 D3
Oikarainen [FIN] 194 D8
Oímbra [E] 78 D6
Oinasjärvi [FIN] 176 F4
O Incio [E] 78 E4
Oinoanda [TR] 154 G2
Oinói [GR] 134 B6
Oinoskylä [FIN] 186 F2
Oiron [F] 54 E3
Oirschot [NL] 30 E2
Oisemont [F] 28 D4
Oissel [F] 28 B6
Oisterwijk [NL] 16 D6
Oitti [FIN] 176 H3
Oítylo [GR] 136 E5
Oivu / Åivo [FIN] 196 C6
Öja [FIN] 196 C6
Öjaby [S] 162 D4
Ojakylä [FIN] 196 D5
Ojakylä [FIN] 196 E4
Ojala [FIN] 186 D2
Öjarn [S] 190 E6
Ojców [PL] 50 H3
Öje [S] 172 F3
Öjebyn [S] 196 B3
Ojén [E] 102 B5
Ojo Guareña [E] 82 F4
Ojós [E] 104 C2
Ojos Negros [E] 90 C6
Ojrzeń [PL] 38 A1
Öjung [S] 174 C1
Öjvasslan [S] 182 F6
Okalewo [PL] 22 F6
Okalewo [PL] 22 F6
Okány [H] 76 G2
Økdal [N] 182 B3
Okehampton [GB] 12 D4
Oker [D] 32 G3
Okhtyrka [UA] 202 F7
Okkelberg [N] 182 C1
Oklaj [HR] 112 H5
Oklubalı [TR] 150 H5
Okol [AL] 146 A6
Okonek [PL] 22 B5
Okonin [PL] 22 E5
Okopy [PL] 38 G5
Okoř [CZ] 48 F3
Okors [BG] 148 E2
Okrug [HR] 116 H1
Oksajärvi [S] 192 H5
Oksakoski [FIN] 186 E1
Oksava [FIN] 196 D6
Oksböl [DK] 156 A2
Oksdøl [N] 190 C5
Øksendalen [N] 170 H1
Øksendrup [DK] 156 E4
Øksfjord [N] 192 H1
Oksfjordhamn [N] 192 G1
Øksna [N] 172 C3
Øksnes [N] 192 D4
Okstad [N] 182 C2
Oktiabrs'ke [UA] 204 H4
Oktoniá [GR] 134 C4
Okučani [HR] 142 C1
Okulovka [RUS] 202 D2
Okuninka [PL] 38 F4
Ólafsfjörður [IS] 192 C2
Ólafsvík [IS] 192 A2
Ö. Lagnö [S] 168 E2
Olargues [F] 106 D4
Olaszfalu [H] 76 A2
Oława [PL] 50 D1
Olazagutia / Olazti [E] 82 H5
Olazti / Olazagutia [E] 82 H5
Olba [E] 98 E3
Olbasa [TR] 152 H6
Olbernhau [D] 48 E2
Ólbia [I] 118 E3
Olbięcin [PL] 52 E1
Oldcastle [IRL] 2 E5
Oldeberkoop [NL] 16 F3
Oldeide [N] 180 B5
Olden [N] 180 D5
Oldenburg [D] 18 C5
Oldenburg [D] 18 H2
Oldenzaal [NL] 16 G5
Olderdalen [N] 192 G2
Olderfjord [N] 194 C2
Oldervik [N] 192 G2
Oldham [GB] 10 E4
Oldmeldrum [GB] 6 F6
Old Mellifont Abbey [IRL] 2 F5
Oldřichovice [CZ] 50 F5
Oleby [S] 172 E5
Olecko [PL] 24 D3
Oléggio [I] 70 F4
Oleiros [E] 78 B3
Oleiros [E] 78 C2
Oleiros [P] 86 E3
Oleksandriia [UA] 202 F8
Oleksandrivka [UA] 202 E8
Oleksandrivka [UA] 204 G2
Olen [B] 30 D3
Ølen [N] 164 B1
Olèrdola [E] 92 D4
Olesa de Montserrat [E] 92 D4
Oleśnica [PL] 36 D6
Olešnice [CZ] 50 B5
Olesno [PL] 50 F1
Oleszno [PL] 50 H1
Oleszyce [PL] 52 F3
Oletta [F] 114 C3
Olette [F] 92 F1
Olevs'k [UA] 202 C7
Ølgod [DK] 156 B2
Olhain, Château Féodal d'- [F] 28 E3
Olhão [P] 94 C6
Ol'hopil' [UA] 204 E2
Oliana [E] 92 D2
Olia Speciosa [I] 118 D7
Olíena [I] 118 D4
Olingdal [S] 182 G6
Olingsjövallen [S] 182 G6
Olite [E] 84 B5
Oliva [E] 98 F6
Oliva de la Frontera [E] 94 F3
Oliva de Mérida [E] 94 H2
Olivadi [I] 124 D6
Olivares [E] 94 G6
Olivares de Júcar [E] 98 B3
Oliveira de Azeméis [P] 80 B5
Oliveira de Frades [P] 80 C5
Oliveira do Bairro [P] 80 B5
Oliveira do Hospital [P] 86 E2
Olivenza [E] 94 F2
Olivet [F] 42 E6
Olivone [CH] 70 G2
Ol'Ka [SK] 52 D6
Olkkala [FIN] 176 G4
Olkusz [PL] 50 G3
Ollerup [DK] 156 D4
Olliergues [F] 68 D2
Ollikkala [FIN] 178 C1
Ollila [FIN] 176 E4
Öllölä [FIN] 188 G3
Ölmbrotorp [S] 166 H3
Ölme [S] 166 F3
Olmedilla de Alarcón [E] 98 B3
Olmedillo de Roa [E] 88 G2
Olmedo [E] 88 E3
Olmedo [I] 118 B3
Olmeto [F] 114 B5
Ölmhult [S] 166 F2
Olmillos de Sasamón [E] 82 E5
Olocau del Rey [E] 98 F1
Olofsfors [S] 184 H1
Olofström [S] 158 E1
Olombrada [E] 88 F3
Olomouc [CZ] 50 D5
Olon / Oyon [E] 82 H6
Olonzac [F] 106 C4
Oloron-Ste-Marie [F] 84 D3
Olos Fthiotidos [GR] 132 G4
Olost [E] 92 E3
Olot [E] 92 F2
Olovo [BIH] 142 E4
Ołownik [PL] 24 C2
Olpe [D] 32 C5
Øls [DK] 160 D5
Olsätter [S] 166 F2
Olsberg [D] 32 D5
Olsborg [N] 192 F3
Olseröd [S] 158 D2
Ölserud [S] 166 E4
Ol'sha-Dolgaya [RUS] 202 D4
Olshammar [S] 166 G4
Olší [CZ] 50 B5
Ölsremma [S] 162 C2
Olst [NL] 16 F4
Ølstykke [DK] 156 G2
Olszowa Wola [PL] 38 B4
Olsztyn [PL] 22 H4
Olsztyn [PL] 50 G2
Olsztynek [PL] 22 G4
Olszyna [PL] 34 G4
Olszyna [PL] 34 H6
Oltedal [N] 164 B3
Olten [CH] 58 E5
Olteni [RO] 148 B1
Olteniţa [RO] 148 D1
Olteren [N] 192 G3
Oltre il Colle [I] 70 H4
Ölüdeniz [TR] 154 F2
Oluklu [TR] 150 H5
Olula del Río [E] 102 H4
Ölvega [E] 90 C3
Olvera [E] 102 A3
Olympía [GR] 136 C2
Olympiáda [GR] 130 C4
Ólympos [GR] 140 H2
Ólynthos [GR] 130 B5
Olza [PL] 50 E4
Oma, Bosque de- [E] 82 H4
Omagh [NIR] 2 F3
Omalí [GR] 128 E6
Omalós [GR] 140 C5
Oman [BG] 148 E5
Omarska [BIH] 142 B2
Ombygget Stavkirke [N] 170 D2
Omegna [I] 70 F3
Ömerköy [TR] 150 D5
Ömerli [TR] 150 F2
Omiš [HR] 144 A2
Omišalj [HR] 112 E2
Ommen [NL] 16 G4
Ommunddallen [N] 190 B5
Omodos [CY] 154 F6
Omoljica [SRB] 142 H2
Ömossa / Metsälä [FIN] 186 B5
Ömsjö [S] 184 E1
Omurtag [BG] 148 D3
Øn [N] 170 B1
Oña [E] 82 F5
Oñati [E] 82 H4
Onda [E] 98 F3
Ondara [E] 104 F1
Ondarroa [E] 82 H4
Ondić [HR] 112 H4
Ö Nësberg [S] 172 F5
Oneşti [RO] 204 D4
Onguera [E] 82 D2
Onil [E] 104 D1
Onkamo [FIN] 188 G3
Onkamo [FIN] 194 F7
Onkiniemi [FIN] 178 B1
Onnaing [F] 28 G4
Önneköp [S] 158 D2
Onoranza [I] 120 G1
Onsaker [N] 170 H4
Onsevig [DK] 156 E4
Ontiñena [E] 90 G4
Ontinyent [E] 98 E6
Ontojoki Porokylä [FIN] 196 F5
Ontur [E] 98 C6
Önusberg [S] 196 A3
Onuškis [LT] 24 G1
Onzonilla [E] 78 H6
Ooidonk [B] 28 G2
Oola [IRL] 4 D4
Oostburg [NL] 28 G1
Oostduinkerke [B] 28 F1
Oostende (Ostende) [B] 28 F1
Oosterbeek [NL] 16 F5
Oosterend [NL] 16 E1
Oosterhout [NL] 16 D6
Oosterwolde [NL] 16 G3
Oostmalle [B] 30 D3
Ootmarsum [NL] 16 G4
Opaka [BG] 148 D2
Opalenica [PL] 36 B3
Opařany [CZ] 48 F5
Oparić [SRB] 146 C3
Opatija [HR] 112 E1
Opatów [PL] 36 E6
Opatów [PL] 52 D1
Opatówek [PL] 36 E4
Opatowiec [PL] 52 B3
Opava [CZ] 50 E4
Ope [S] 182 G2
Opglabbek [B] 30 E4
Opi [I] 116 C6
O Pino [E] 78 C3
O Pino [E] 78 C3
Opinogóra Górna [PL] 38 B1
Opishnia [UA] 202 F7
Opladen [D] 30 G4
Oplenac, Manastir- [SRB] 146 B1
Opletnya [BG] 146 F4
Oploo [NL] 30 F2
Oplotnica [SLO] 74 D4
Opochka [RUS] 198 H5
Opočno [CZ] 50 B3
Opoczno [PL] 38 A5
Opole [PL] 50 E2
Opole Lubelskie [PL] 38 D6
Opol'ye [RUS] 178 F6
Oporów [PL] 36 G3
O Porriño [E] 78 B5
Opovo [SRB] 142 G2
Oppach [D] 34 G6
Oppaker [N] 172 C5
Oppdal [N] 180 H3
Oppdøl [N] 180 F3
Oppeby [S] 162 F1
Oppedal [N] 170 B2
Oppegård [N] 166 B1
Oppenau [D] 58 F2
Oppenheim [D] 46 C3
Oppheim [N] 170 C3
Opphus [N] 172 C2
Oppido Lucano [I] 120 H3
Oppido Mamertina [I] 124 C7
Oppidum d'Ensérune [F] 106 D4
Oppola [RUS] 188 G5
Opponitz [A] 62 C5
Oppsal [N] 164 B3
Opsa [BY] 200 H4
Ópusztaszer [H] 76 E4
Opuzen [HR] 144 B3
Orá [CY] 154 G6
Öra [S] 162 C1
Ora / Auer [I] 72 D4
Oradea [RO] 76 H2
Orahovac [SRB] 146 B6
Orahov Do [BIH] 144 C3
Orahovica [HR] 142 D1
Orahovlje [BIH] 144 B2
Oraison [F] 108 C3
Orajärvi [FIN] 194 C7
Orange [F] 106 G3
Orani [I] 118 D4
Oranienbaum [D] 34 C4
Oranienburg [D] 34 E1
Oranmore [IRL] 2 C5
Oraovica [SRB] 146 D4
Öras [N] 182 C2
Orašac [BIH] 112 H3
Orašac [MK] 146 D6
Orašac [SRB] 146 D4
Orasi [F] 114 B6
Orašje [BIH] 142 E2
Orăştie [RO] 204 C5
Oravainen / Oravais [FIN] 186 C2
Oravais / Oravainen [FIN] 186 C2
Öravan [S] 190 G5
Oravasaari [FIN] 186 G4
Oravi [FIN] 188 E4
Oravijoki [FIN] 196 E5
Oravikoski [FIN] 188 D3
Oravisalo [FIN] 188 F3
Oraviţa [RO] 204 B5
Oravská Lesná [SK] 50 G5
Oravská Polhora [SK] 50 G5
Oravský Podzámok [SK] 50 G6
Orba [E] 104 F1
Ørbæk [DK] 156 E3
Orbassano [I] 70 D6
Orbe [CH] 58 C6
Orbeasca [RO] 148 B1
Orbec [F] 26 G4
Orbetello [I] 114 F4
Orbey [F] 58 D2
Ørby [DK] 156 E1
Örbyhus [S] 174 F5
Örbyhus [S] 174 F5
Orca [P] 86 F3
Orcera [E] 102 G1
Orches [F] 54 F3
Orchies [F] 28 F3
Orchomenós [GR] 132 H5
Orchomenós [GR] 132 H5
Orchomenós [GR] 136 D2
Orcières [F] 70 A6
Orderud [N] 166 C2
Ordes [E] 78 C2
Ordino [AND] 84 H6
Orduña [E] 82 G4
Ore [S] 184 H1
Orebić [HR] 144 B3
Örebro [S] 166 H3
Öregrund [S] 174 G5
Orehova vas Rače [SLO] 74 E4
Orehoved [DK] 156 F4
Orehovica [BG] 148 A2
Orehovno [RUS] 198 H2
Oreiní [GR] 130 C3
Orel [RUS] 202 F5
Ören [TR] 152 C2
Ören [TR] 152 G2
Ören [TR] 154 C1
Ören [TR] 154 F2
Örencık [TR] 150 C6
Örencik [TR] 152 G1
Örenkaya [TR] 152 H3
Orense / Ourense [E] 78 C5
Oreoí [GR] 134 A3
Oresak [BG] 148 B4
Oreshari [BG] 130 G1
Orestiáda [GR] 130 H1
Öreström [S] 190 H5
Oresvika [N] 190 D2
Öreyd [S] 162 C3
Orgáni [GR] 130 G2
Organyà [E] 92 D2
Orgaz [E] 96 F2
Orgelet [F] 56 H6
Orgenvika [N] 170 G5
Orgeval [F] 42 F3
Orgjost [AL] 128 C1
Orgnac-l'Aven [F] 106 G2
Orgon [F] 106 H4
Orgosolo [I] 118 D4
Orgovány [H] 76 D3
Orhaneli [TR] 150 F5
Orhangazi [TR] 150 F4
Orhanıye [TR] 130 H3
Orhanlar [TR] 150 D5
Orhanlı [TR] 152 C4
Orhei [MD] 204 E3
Ør. Hvidbjerg [DK] 160 C4
Oria [E] 102 H4
Oria [I] 122 F4
Orihuela [E] 104 D3
Orihuela del Tremedal [E] 98 D1
Orikhiv [UA] 204 H2
Orikum [AL] 128 A6
Orikum [AL] 128 A6
Orimattila [FIN] 178 B3
Orio [E] 84 B2
Oriolo [I] 122 D5
Oripää [FIN] 176 E3
Orismala [FIN] 186 C3
Orissaare [EST] 198 C3
Oristano [I] 118 C5
Öriszentpéter [H] 74 F3
Orivesi [FIN] 186 E6
Orizare [BG] 148 F4
Ørjarvik [N] 180 E2
Ørje [N] 166 C2
Örjiva [E] 102 E5
Orkanger [N] 180 H1
Örkelljunga [S] 158 C1
Orkény [H] 76 D2
Orléans [F] 42 E6
Orlík nad Vltavou [CZ] 48 F5
Orlík nad Vltavou [CZ] 48 F5
Orlovat [SRB] 142 G1
Orly [F] 42 F4
Orly [RUS] 178 E6
Orlya [BY] 24 H4
Orlyak [BG] 148 F2
Orlyane [BG] 148 A3
Ormanlı [TR] 150 D2
Ormea [I] 108 G3
Ormemyr [N] 164 F1
Örménykút [H] 76 F2
Ormestad [N] 164 D6
Órmos [GR] 128 H5
Órmos [GR] 138 D1
Órmos Panagías [GR] 130 C5
Órmos Prínou [GR] 130 E4
Ormož [SLO] 74 E4
Ormsjö [S] 190 F5
Ormskirk [GB] 10 D4
Ornans [F] 58 B5
Ornäs [S] 174 C4
Ornavasso [I] 70 F3
Örnberg [FIN] 186 B2
Ornes [N] 190 D4
Orneta [PL] 22 G3
Ørnhøj [DK] 160 B6
Örnsköldsvik [S] 184 G2
Orolik [HR] 142 E1
Oron-la-Ville [CH] 70 C1
Oropa, Santuário d'- [I] 70 E4
Oropesa [E] 88 C6
Oropesa del Mar / Orpesa [E] 98 G3
Orošac [HR] 144 C4
Orosei [I] 118 E4
Orosháza [H] 76 F3
Oroso [E] 78 C3
Oroszlány [H] 64 B6
Oroszló [H] 76 B4
Ørpen [N] 170 G5
Orpesa / Oropesa del Mar [E] 98 G3
Orpington [GB] 14 E4
Orre [N] 164 A3
Orrefors [S] 162 F5
Orrfors [S] 194 B8
Orrliden [S] 172 E2
Orroli [I] 118 D6
Orrviken [S] 182 G2
Orsa [S] 172 G3
Orsala [S] 172 G5
Orsara di Púglia [I] 120 G2
Örsås [S] 162 B3
Orscholz [D] 44 F3
Örsebo [S] 162 E1
Örserum [S] 162 D1
Orsha [BY] 202 C4
Orsières [CH] 70 C3
Örsjö [S] 162 F5
Ørskog [N] 180 D3
Ørslev [DK] 156 G4
Örslösa [S] 166 E5
Ørsnes [N] 180 D3
Orsogna [I] 116 D5
Orsomarso [I] 120 H6
Orşova [RO] 204 C6
Orsoya [BG] 146 F2
Ørsta [N] 180 C4
Orsta [S] 168 A2
Ørsted [DK] 160 E5
Örsundsbro [S] 168 D2
Ort [A] 60 H4
Ortaca [TR] 150 B5
Ortaca [TR] 154 E2
Ortakent [TR] 154 B2
Ortaklar [TR] 152 D5
Ortaköy [TR] 150 H3
Ortaköy [TR] 152 E6
Orta Nova [I] 120 G2
Ortaoba [TR] 150 C5
Orta San Giúlio [I] 70 F4
Orte [I] 116 A4
Ortenberg [D] 46 D2
Ortenburg [D] 60 H3
Orth [A] 62 F4
Orthez [F] 84 D2
Orthovoúni [GR] 132 E1
Ortigueira [E] 78 E1
Ørting [DK] 156 D1
Ortisei / St Ulrich [I] 72 D3
Orţişoara [RO] 76 G5
Ortnevik [N] 170 C2
Orto [F] 114 B4
Örtomta [S] 168 B5
Ortona [I] 116 E4
Ortrand [D] 34 E5
Örträsk [S] 190 H5
Ortu [I] 118 C6
Ortueri [I] 118 C5
Öru [EST] 198 F3
Oruçoğlu [TR] 150 F2
Ørum [DK] 160 D5
Ørum [DK] 160 E5
Orume [I] 118 D4
Örup [S] 158 D3
Orval, Abbaye d'- [B] 44 D2
Orvalho [P] 86 E3
Ørvella [N] 164 F2
Orvieto [I] 114 H3
Örviken [S] 196 A4
Orvinio [I] 116 B5
Oryahovec [BG] 130 E1
Oryakhovo [BG] 146 G2
Ö. Ryd [S] 168 B5
Orzechowo [PL] 22 E6
Orzesze [PL] 50 F3
Orzhytsia [UA] 202 E7
Orzinuovi [I] 70 H5
Orzola [E] 100 E5
Orzysz [PL] 24 C4
Os [N] 182 C4
Os [S] 162 D4
Osa [N] 170 D3
Osby [S] 162 C6
Oschatz [D] 34 D5
Oschersleben [D] 34 B3
Óschiri [I] 118 D3
Ościłowo [PL] 38 A1
Ose [N] 164 D3
Øse [N] 192 F4
Osečina [SRB] 142 F3
Oseja de Sajambre [E] 82 C3
Osen [N] 190 B5
Osenets [BG] 148 D2
Osera de Ebro [E] 90 F4
Osidda [I] 118 D4
Osie [PL] 22 D4
Osieczna [PL] 22 D4
Osieczna [PL] 36 C4
Osiecznica [PL] 34 H3
Osiek [PL] 22 E4
Osiek [PL] 52 D2
Osijek [HR] 76 C6
Osikovitsa [BG] 146 G4
Ósilo [I] 118 C3
Osimo [I] 116 C1
Osinja [BIH] 142 C2
Osinów [PL] 34 F1
Osíou Louká, Moní- [GR] 132 H5
Osipaonica [SRB] 142 H3
Osjaków [PL] 36 F6
Osječenica [MNE] 144 D4
Oskal [N] 194 B4
Oskar [S] 162 F5
Oskar-Fredriksborg [S] 168 E3
Oskarshamn [S] 162 G3
Oskarström [S] 162 B5
Øskendalsøra [N] 180 F3
Oskowo [PL] 22 C2
Osl'any [SK] 64 B3
Osli [H] 62 G6
Oslo [N] 166 B1
Øsløs [DK] 160 C3
Osma [FIN] 194 D3
Osmancalı [TR] 152 C3
Osmaneli [TR] 150 G4
Osmankalfalar [TR] 152 H6
Osmanlar [TR] 152 C1
Osmanli [TR] 150 B2
Os'mino [RUS] 198 H1
Osmjany [BY] 202 A5
Ösmo [S] 168 D4
Osmoy-St-Valery [F] 28 C4
Osnabrück [D] 32 D2
Osnäs [FIN] 176 C4
Ošno Lubuskie [PL] 34 G2
Osoblaha [CZ] 50 D3
Osor [E] 92 F3
Osor [HR] 112 E3
Osorno la Mayor [E] 82 D5
Osowiec [PL] 24 E4
Osowo Lęborskie [PL] 22 C2
Osowo Leśne [PL] 22 D4
Osøyro [N] 170 B4
Os Peares [E] 78 D5
Ospedaletti [I] 108 F4
Ospitaletto [I] 72 A6
Oss [NL] 16 E6
Óssa [GR] 130 B4
Ossa de Montiel [E] 96 H5
Ossiach [A] 74 B3
Ossjøen [N] 170 E4
Östansjö [S] 166 G4
Östansjö [S] 182 G6
Östansjö [S] 190 G3
Östanvik [S] 172 H3
Oštarije [HR] 112 G2
Ostashkov [RUS] 202 D2
Ostaszewo [PL] 22 E3
Östavall [S] 184 C4
Ostbevern [D] 32 C3
Østbirk [DK] 156 C1
Østby [N] 172 E2
Osted [DK] 156 G3
Ostellato [I] 110 G3
Østenå [N] 164 F2
Ostende (Oostende) [B] 28 F1
Østerbo [N] 166 C3
Østerbø [N] 170 E3
Osterburg [D] 34 B1
Osterburken [D] 46 D5
Österbybruk [S] 174 F5
Østerby Havn [DK] 160 F3
Österbymo [S] 162 E2
Österede [S] 184 D3
Österfärnebo [S] 174 E5
Österforse [S] 184 E2
Östergraninge [S] 184 E3
Osterhever [D] 18 E2
Osterhofen [D] 60 G3
Osterholz-Scharmbeck [D] 18 D5
Øster Hurup [DK] 160 E4
Østerild [DK] 160 C3
Østerlars [DK] 158 E4
Österlövsta [S] 174 F5
Østermarie [DK] 158 E4
Östermark / Teuva [FIN] 186 B4
Ostermiething [A] 60 G4
Osterncappeln [D] 32 D2
Österneret [S] 190 F5
Österö [FIN] 186 B1
Osterode [D] 32 G4
Österreichisches Freilichtmuseum [A] 74 D2
Östersund [S] 182 G2
Östersundom [FIN] 176 H5
Østerud [N] 164 G1
Øster Ulslev [DK] 20 B1
Österunda [S] 168 C2
Östervåla [S] 174 E5
Östervallskog [S] 166 C2
Øster Vrå [DK] 160 E3
Ostfildern [D] 58 H1
Östfora [S] 168 C1
Östhammar [S] 174 G5
Ostheim [D] 46 F2
Osthofen [D] 46 B4
Ostia [I] 114 H6
Ostíglia [I] 110 F2
Ostiz [E] 84 B3
Ostland [D] 16 G1
Östloning [S] 184 E4
Östmark [S] 172 E5
Östnäs [S] 196 A6
Östomsjön [S] 172 E1
Ostra [I] 112 C6
Östraby [S] 158 C2
Ostrach [D] 58 H3
Östra Ed [S] 162 G1
Östra Frölunda [S] 162 B3
Östra Husby [S] 168 B5
Östra Kärne [S] 166 G2
Östra Luka [BIH] 142 B2
Ostrava [CZ] 50 E4
Östra Yttermark [FIN] 186 A4
Østre Kile [N] 164 E3
Oštrelj [BIH] 142 A3
Ostritz [D] 48 G1
Ostróda [PL] 22 G4
Ostrog, Manastir- [MNE] 144 E4
Ostroh [UA] 202 B8
Ostrołęka [PL] 24 C6
Ostromecko [PL] 22 D6
Ostroróg [PL] 36 B2
Ostros [MNE] 128 A1
Ostrov [CZ] 48 D3
Ostrov [RUS] 178 F2
Ostrov [RUS] 198 G3
Ostrovcy [RUS] 198 G2
Ostrov nad Oslavou [CZ] 50 B5
Ostrovo [BG] 148 D2
Ostrowice [PL] 20 H4
Ostrowiec [PL] 22 B3
Ostrowiec Świętokrzyski [PL] 52 C1
Ostrowite [PL] 22 D5
Ostrowite [PL] 36 E2
Ostrów Lubelski [PL] 38 E5
Ostrów Mazowiecka [PL] 38 D1
Ostrów Wielkopolski [PL] 36 E5
Ostrožac [BIH] 112 H3
Ostrožac [BIH] 144 C1
Ostrožany [PL] 38 E2
Ostrzeszów [PL] 36 E5
Ostuni [I] 122 F3
Ostvik [S] 196 A4
Østvika [N] 190 D4
Ostwald [F] 44 H6
Osuna [E] 102 B3
Oswestry [GB] 10 C5
Oświęcim [PL] 50 G4
Osztopán [H] 74 H4
Otalampi [FIN] 176 G4
Otanmäki [FIN] 196 E5
Otanów [PL] 20 F6
Otava [FIN] 188 C6
Otelec [RO] 76 F6
Otepää [EST] 198 F3
Oteren [N] 192 G2
Oterma [FIN] 196 E4
Otero de Bodas [E] 80 H3
Oteševo [MK] 128 D4
Otivar [E] 102 D5
Otley [GB] 10 F3
Otmuchów [PL] 50 D3
Otnes [N] 182 C6
Otočac [HR] 112 G3
Otočec [SLO] 74 D5
Otok [HR] 142 E2
Otok [SLO] 74 B6
Otoka [BIH] 142 A2
Otorowo [PL] 36 C2
Otradnoye [RUS] 178 G2
Otranto [I] 122 H5
Otrić [HR] 112 H4
Otrokovice [CZ] 50 D6
Otsa [EST] 198 F3
Otsagi / Ochagavía [E] 84 C4
Otta [N] 180 G6
Ottana [I] 118 D4
Ottaviano [I] 120 E3
Ottenby [S] 158 G1
Ottenschlag [A] 62 D4
Ottensheim [A] 62 B4
Ottenstein [A] 62 D3
Otterbach [D] 44 H3
Otterbäcken [S] 166 F4
Otterlo [NL] 16 E5
Otterndorf [D] 18 E3
Ottersberg [D] 18 E5
Otterup [DK] 156 D3
Öttevény [H] 62 H6
Ottnang [A] 62 A4
Ottobeuren [D] 60 C4
Ottobiano [I] 70 F5
Ottone [I] 110 B3
Ottsjö [S] 182 E2
Ottweiler [D] 44 G3
Ö. Tväråsel [S] 196 A3
Otwock [PL] 38 C3
Ouanne [F] 56 E2
Oucques [F] 42 D6
Oud Beijerland [NL] 16 C5
Ouddorp [NL] 16 B5
Oudenaarde (Audenarde) [B] 28 G2
Oude-Pekela [NL] 16 H2
Oudewater [NL] 16 D5
Oughterard [IRL] 2 C4
Ouistreham [F] 26 F3
Oulainen [FIN] 196 D5
Oullins [F] 68 F3
Oulu / Uleåborg [FIN] 196 D4
Oulunsalo [FIN] 196 D4
Oulx [I] 70 B5
Ounas [FIN] 196 E5
Oundle [GB] 14 E2
Oura [P] 80 E3
Ouranoúpoli [GR] 130 D5
Ourense / Orense [E] 78 C5
Ourique [P] 94 C4
Ourol [E] 78 E2
Ourscamps, Abbaye d'- [F] 28 F6
Oust [F] 84 G5
Outes [E] 78 B3
Outokumpu [FIN] 188 E2
Ouzouer-le-Marché [F] 42 D6
Ovabaşı [TR] 154 F4
Ovacık [TR] 152 E4
Ovacık [TR] 152 F4
Ovacık [TR] 154 H1

Ovada [I] 108 H2
Ovakent [TR] 152 E4
Ovanåker [S] 174 D2
Ovanmo [S] 184 D1
Ovansjö [S] 184 C4
Ovar [P] 80 B4
Ovčar Banja [SRB] 146 B2
Övedskloster [S] 158 C2
Ovelgönne [D] 18 F4
Ovenstädt [D] 32 E2
Överammer [S] 184 D2
Overåneset [N] 180 E4
Överäng [S] 190 D6
Overath [D] 30 H4
Överberg [S] 182 G5
Överbo [S] 174 C2
Overby [DK] 156 D2
Överby [S] 168 E3
Øverbygd [N] 192 F3
Överbyn [S] 172 E5
Overgård [DK] 160 E5
Överhogdal [S] 182 G5
Överhörnäs [S] 184 G2
Overijse [B] 30 C4
Överjeppo [FIN] 186 C1
Over Jerstal [DK] 156 C3
Överkalix [S] 194 B8
Överlännäs [S] 184 F2
Överlida [S] 162 B3
Övermark / Ylimarkku [FIN] 186 B4
Överö [FIN] 176 B5
Øverøye [N] 180 E3
Överrissjö [S] 190 G5
Överröda [S] 190 H5
Överselö [S] 168 C3
Övertänger [S] 174 C3
Overton [GB] 12 H4
Övertorneå [S] 194 B8
Övertorneå / Ylitornio [FIN] 194 B8
Överturingen [S] 182 H4
Överum [S] 162 G1
Oviedo [E] 78 H3
Ovindoli [I] 116 C5
Ovino [RUS] 202 C1
Övra [S] 190 F6
Övralid [S] 166 G5
Øvre Årdal [N] 170 E1
Övre Bäck [S] 196 B5
Øvre Dåsvatn [N] 164 D4
Øvre Espedal [N] 164 B3
Øvre Jervan [N] 182 C1
Øvre Moen [N] 164 C2
Øvre Rendal [N] 182 C6
Øvre Sirdal [N] 164 C3
Övre Soppero [S] 192 H4
Øvrestøl [N] 180 E4
Øvre Vats [N] 164 B1
Ovruch [UA] 202 C7
Øvstebø [N] 164 B3
Øvstedal [N] 180 E3
Ovtrup [DK] 156 A2
Owschlag [D] 18 F2
Öxabäck [S] 162 B3
Oxbakken [S] 168 C4
Oxberg [S] 172 G3
Oxelösund [S] 168 C5
Oxford [GB] 14 D3
Oxie [S] 156 H3
Oxsjön [S] 184 D4
Oxyá [GR] 132 E2
Oxýneia [GR] 132 E1
Øy [N] 164 E4
Oyace [I] 70 D3
Øyan [N] 182 D1
Øyangen [N] 180 H1
Øye [N] 170 F2
Øye [N] 180 D4
Øyenkilen [N] 166 B3
Øyer [N] 172 B2
Øyermoen [N] 172 D5
Øyestad [N] 164 E5
Øyfjell [N] 164 E2
Øylo [N] 170 F2
Øymark [N] 166 C2
Oyntdartfjørður [FR] 160 B1
Oyon / Olon [E] 82 H6
Oyonnax [F] 68 H2
Oyonnax [F] 68 H1
Oyrières [F] 58 A4
Øyslebø [N] 164 D5
Øystese [N] 170 C4
Oyten [D] 18 E5
Ozalj [HR] 74 D6
Ożarów [PL] 52 D1
Ożarów [PL] 52 D1
Ożarów Mazowiecki [PL] 38 B3
Ožbalt [SLO] 74 D3
Ózd [H] 64 E4
Ožď'any [SK] 64 D4
Özdere [TR] 152 C5
Ozegna [I] 70 D5
Ozerki [RUS] 178 F4
Ozernyy [RUS] 202 D3
Ozersk [RUS] 24 C2
Ozerskoye [RUS] 178 F2
Ozieri [I] 118 D3
Ozimek [PL] 50 E2
Ozora [H] 76 B3
Ozorków [PL] 36 G4
Ozren, Manastir– [BIH] 142 D3

P

Pääjärvi [FIN] 186 F3
Paakkila [FIN] 188 E2
Paakkola [FIN] 196 C2
Paanala [FIN] 186 G4
Paaso [FIN] 178 B1
Paatela [FIN] 188 D5
Paatinen [FIN] 176 D4
Paavola [FIN] 196 D4
Pabianice [PL] 36 G4
Pabiaržė [LT] 200 G5
Pabradė [LT] 200 G5
Pabuçlu [TR] 152 F3
Paceco [I] 126 B2
Pacentro [I] 116 D5
Pachiá Ámmos [GR] 140 G5
Pachino [I] 126 G6
Páchna [CY] 154 F6
Pachyammos [CY] 154 F5
Pácin [H] 64 H4
Paços de Ferreira [P] 80 C4
Pacov [CZ] 48 G5
Pacsa [H] 74 G3
Pacyna [PL] 36 H3
Pacy–sur–Eure [F] 42 E3
Paczków [PL] 50 C3
Pădarevo [BG] 148 E4
Padarosk [BY] 24 H6
Padasjoki [FIN] 176 H1
Padborg [DK] 156 C4
Padej [SRB] 76 E5
Paderborn [D] 32 E4
Paderne [P] 94 C5
Paderno Dugnano [I] 70 G4
Padiham [GB] 10 E3
Padina [SRB] 142 H2
Padinska Skela [SRB] 142 G2
Padirac, Gouffre de– [F] 66 H4
Padjene [HR] 112 H5
Padova [I] 110 G1
Padrenda [E] 78 C5
Padrógão Grande [P] 86 E3
Padrón [E] 78 B3
Padru [I] 118 E3
Padru Mannu [I] 118 C4
Padstow [GB] 12 C4
Padul [E] 102 E4
Padula [I] 120 G4
Padules [E] 102 F5
Paesana [I] 108 F2
Paestum [I] 120 F4
Paestum [I] 120 F4
Páfos [CY] 154 F6
Pag [HR] 112 F4
Pagani [I] 120 E3
Pagánico [I] 114 F2
Pagasaí [GR] 132 H2
Pagėgiai [LT] 200 D5
Pagnoz [F] 58 A5
Pagny–sur–Moselle [F] 44 E4
Páhi [H] 76 D3
Pahkakumpu [FIN] 194 E7
Pahkamäki [FIN] 186 G1
Pahranichny [BY] 24 G5
Pahtakuusikko [FIN] 194 D6
Paianía [GR] 134 C6
Paide [EST] 198 E2
Paignton [GB] 12 E5
Paijärvi [FIN] 178 D3
Pailhès [F] 84 H4
Paimbœuf [F] 40 E6
Paimio / Pemar [FIN] 176 E4
Paimpol [F] 26 A3
Paisievo [BG] 148 E2
Paisley [GB] 8 D3
Pajala [S] 194 B7
Pájara [E] 100 E6
Pajares, Puerto de– [E] 78 H4
Pajęczno [PL] 36 F6
Pajulahti [FIN] 188 C1
Pajulankylä [FIN] 188 C5
Pajuskylä [FIN] 186 H1
Pajuvaara [FIN] 196 F3
Pakość [PL] 36 E1
Pakosławice [PL] 50 D2
Pakoštane [HR] 112 G5
Pakosze [PL] 22 G3
Pakrac [HR] 142 B1
Pakruojis [LT] 200 F3
Paks [H] 76 C3
Palacios del Sil [E] 78 F4
Palacios de Sanabria [E] 80 G3
Paladru [F] 68 H4
Pala e Rughes, Nuraghe– [I] 118 D4
Palafrugell [E] 92 G3
Palagianello [I] 122 E4
Palagiano [I] 122 E4
Palagonia [I] 126 F4
Palaía Epídavros [GR] 136 F2
Palaiá Messíni [GR] 136 D3
Palaíkastro [GR] 140 H4
Palaiochóra [GR] 140 B5
Palaiochóri [GR] 130 C5
Palaiochóri [GR] 132 C3
Palaiochóri [GR] 132 E2
Palaiochóri [GR] 136 E3
Palaiokastrítsa [GR] 132 A2
Palaiomonastíri [GR] 132 E2
Palaiópoli [GR] 130 G4
Palaiópoli [GR] 138 D1
Palaiópyrgos [GR] 132 F2
Palaiópyrgos [GR] 132 F5
Paláiros [GR] 132 D4
Palaiseau [F] 42 F4
Palamás [GR] 132 F2
Palamós [E] 92 G3
Palamut [TR] 152 D3
Palancar, Monasterio del– [E] 86 H4
Päläng [S] 196 B3
Palanga [LT] 200 D4
Palas de Rei [E] 78 D3
Palatitsa [GR] 128 G5
Palatna [SRB] 146 C4
Palau [I] 118 E2
Palavas–les–Flots [F] 106 F4
Palazzo Adriano [I] 126 C3
Palazzolo Acréide [I] 126 G5
Palazzolo sull'Oglio [I] 70 H4
Palazzo San Gervasio [I] 120 H3
Paldiski [EST] 198 D1
Pale [BIH] 144 D1
Pāle [LV] 198 E4
Palena [I] 116 D5
Palencia [E] 82 C6
Paleócastro [GR] 130 B3
Palermo [AL] 128 B6
Palermo [I] 126 C2
Palestrina [I] 116 B5
Pálháza [H] 64 G3
Páli [H] 74 G1
Palić [SRB] 76 D5
Palikkala [FIN] 176 F3
Palín [SK] 64 H3
Palinuro [I] 120 G5
Paliouriá [GR] 132 E1
Palioúrion [GR] 130 C6
Paliseul [B] 44 D1
Paljakka [FIN] 178 C2
Paljakka [FIN] 196 F1
Paljakka [FIN] 196 F4
Pälkäne [FIN] 176 G2
Palkino [RUS] 198 G4
Palkisoja [FIN] 194 D5
Pallagório [I] 124 E4
Pallanza [I] 70 F3
Pallarés [E] 94 G4
Pallaruelo de Monegros [E] 90 F4
Pallas Grean [IRL] 4 D3
Pallestrina [I] 110 H1
Pallíni [GR] 134 C6
Palluau [F] 54 B2
Palma del Río [E] 102 B1
Palma de Mallorca [E] 104 E5
Palma di Montechiaro [I] 126 D4
Palmadula [I] 118 B3
Palma Nova [E] 104 D5
Palmanova [I] 72 G5
Pálmas Arboreá [I] 118 C5
Palmela [P] 86 B6
Palmi [I] 124 C7
Palo del Colle [I] 122 D2
Palohuornas [S] 192 H6
Páloi [GR] 154 B3
Palojärvi [FIN] 194 B5
Palojoensuu [FIN] 194 B5
Palokangas [FIN] 188 D3
Palokastër [AL] 128 C6
Palokka [FIN] 186 G4
Palokki [FIN] 188 E3
Palomäki [FIN] 196 F6
Palomares [E] 104 A5
Palomares del Campo [E] 98 A2
Palomas [E] 94 H2
Palombara Sabina [I] 116 B5
Palonurmi [FIN] 188 D1
Palos de la Frontera [E] 94 E6
Palota [SK] 52 E6
Pals [E] 92 G3
Pålsboda [S] 166 H4
Pålstrandudden [S] 196 A4
Pålsträsk [S] 196 A3
Paltamo [FIN] 196 F4
Paltanen [FIN] 186 H4
Pal'tsevo [RUS] 178 F3
Palumir [SRB] 146 B3
Palus [FIN] 176 D1
Paluzza [I] 72 G3
Palviainen [FIN] 188 D4
Pämark / Pomarkku [FIN] 176 D1
Pamhagen [A] 62 G6
Pamiątkowo [PL] 36 C2
Pamiers [F] 106 A4
Pamiętowo [PL] 22 C5
Pamma [EST] 198 C3
Pampaneira [E] 102 E5
Pamparato [I] 108 G3
Pampilhosa da Serra [P] 86 E2
Pamplona / Iruña [E] 84 B4
Pamporovo [BG] 130 E1
Pampow [D] 20 A4
Pamucak [TR] 152 D5
Pamukça [TR] 152 D1
Pamukçu [TR] 152 D1
Pamukkale [TR] 152 G5
Pamukova [TR] 150 G3
Pamukyazı [TR] 152 D5
Panagía [GR] 128 F6
Panagía [GR] 130 E4
Panagía [GR] 134 C5
Panagiá [GR] 140 F5
Panagia Aphendrika [CY] 154 H4
Panagia Chrysorrogiatissa [CY] 154 F6
Panagia tou Kykkou [CY] 154 F5
Panagyurishte [BG] 148 A5
Panaitólio [GR] 132 E5
Panajë [AL] 128 A5
Panasówka [PL] 52 F2
Panassac [F] 84 G3
Panayır [TR] 152 E2
Pancallo [I] 126 F3
Pancar [TR] 152 C4
Pančevo [SRB] 142 H2
Pančevo [SRB] 204 B6
Pancharevo [BG] 146 F5
Pancorbo, Garganta de– [E] 82 F5
Pancorvo [E] 82 F5
Pandėlys [LT] 198 E6
Pandino [I] 70 G5
Pandrup [DK] 160 D3
Panenský Týnec [CZ] 48 F3
Panes [E] 82 D3
Panevėžys [LT] 200 F4
Panicale [I] 114 H2
Paničkovo [BG] 148 C6
Paniza [E] 90 D4
Paniza, Puerto de– [E] 90 D5
Pankakoski [FIN] 196 G6
Pankala [FIN] 196 C5
Panker [D] 18 G2
Panki [PL] 50 F1
Pannohalma [H] 62 H6
Pannonhalma [H] 62 H6
Panoias [P] 80 D4
Páno Léfkara [CY] 154 G5
Páno Panagiá [CY] 154 F5
Páno Plátres [CY] 154 F6
Panormítis [GR] 154 C3
Pánormos [GR] 138 E1
Pánormos [GR] 140 D4
Pantaleo [I] 118 C7
Pantalica, Necropoli di– [I] 126 G4
Pantánassa [GR] 136 F5
Päntäne [FIN] 186 B4
Pantelej [MK] 128 G1
Pantelej, Manastir– [MK] 128 G1
Pantelleria [I] 126 A4
Pantón [E] 78 D4
Pantów [PL] 52 C1
Panxón [E] 78 B5
Páola [I] 124 D4
Pápa [H] 74 H1
Papadiánika [GR] 136 F5
Paparzyn [PL] 22 E5
Papasidero [I] 120 H6
Pápateszér [H] 74 H1
Pape [LV] 200 D3
Papenburg [D] 18 B5
Papile [LT] 198 C6
Papilys [LT] 198 E6
Paplin [PL] 38 D2
Papowo Biskupie [PL] 22 E5
Papozze [I] 110 G2
Pappenheim [D] 60 D2
Pápród [H] 76 A5
Paprotnia [PL] 38 E2
Parábita [I] 122 G5
Paraćin [SRB] 146 C2
Paraćin [SRB] 204 B6
Parád [H] 64 E5
Parada del Sil [E] 78 D5
Paradas [E] 100 H2
Paradeísi [GR] 154 D3
Parádeisia [GR] 136 D3
Parádeisos [GR] 130 E3
Paradela [E] 78 D4
Paradela [P] 78 C6
Paradies [D] 60 B6
Paradisgård [S] 166 F2
Paradyż [PL] 38 A5
Parainen / Pargas [FIN] 176 D5
Parakka [S] 192 H5
Parákoila [GR] 134 G2
Paralía [GR] 128 G5
Paralía [GR] 132 F6
Paralía [GR] 132 H6
Paralía [GR] 136 F4
Paralía Akrátas [GR] 132 G6
Paralía Iríon [GR] 136 F2
Paralía Kýmis [GR] 134 C4
Paralía Platánou [GR] 132 G6
Paralía Skotínas [GR] 128 H6
Paralímni [CY] 154 G5
Paralío Ástros [GR] 136 E3
Páramo del Sil [E] 78 F4
Paramythiá [GR] 132 C2
Paranésti [GR] 130 D2
Parantala [FIN] 186 F3
Parapótamos [GR] 132 C2
Parassapuszta [H] 64 C5
Parata, Tour de la– [F] 114 A5
Paravóla [GR] 132 E5
Paray–le–Monial [F] 56 E6
Parc de Chambord [F] 54 H1
Parcent [E] 104 F1
Parcé sur Sarthe [F] 42 A5
Parchim [D] 20 B5
Parc Ornithologique [F] 68 G2
Parczew [PL] 38 E4
Pardubice [CZ] 50 A4
Parechcha [BY] 24 G3
Paredes [E] 78 D5
Paredes [P] 80 C4
Paredes de Coura [P] 78 B5
Paredes de Nava [E] 82 C6
Paredes de Sigüenza [E] 90 A4
Parentis–en–Born [F] 66 B4
Paretón [E] 104 B4
Parey [D] 34 C2
Párga [GR] 132 C3
Pargas / Parainen [FIN] 176 D5
Pargny–sur–Saulx [F] 44 C4
Pargolovo [RUS] 178 H4
Parikkala [FIN] 188 F5
Paris [F] 42 F3
Parisot [F] 66 G6
Parje [SLO] 74 B6
Parkajoki [S] 194 B6
Parkano [FIN] 186 D5
Parkkila [FIN] 196 D5
Parkkima [FIN] 196 D6
Parknasilla [IRL] 4 B4
Parkumäki [FIN] 188 E5
Parla [E] 88 F6
Parlak [TR] 134 H4
Parłówko [PL] 20 F4
Parma [I] 110 D2
Parndorf [A] 62 G5
Pärnu [EST] 198 D3
Pärnu–Jaagupi [EST] 198 D2
Parola [FIN] 178 C2
Páros [GR] 138 E3
Paroveia [LT] 198 E6
Parpan [CH] 70 H1
Parsberg [D] 46 H6
Partakko [FIN] 194 D4
Partakoski [FIN] 178 D1
Partanna [I] 126 B3
Partenen [A] 72 B2
Parthenay [F] 54 D3
Parthéni [GR] 136 E2
Parthéni [GR] 154 A1
Partille [S] 160 H2
Partinello [F] 114 A3
Partinico [I] 126 C2
Partizani [SRB] 146 B1
Partizánske [SK] 64 B3
Partizanske Vode [SRB] 146 A3
Partry [IRL] 2 C4
Pårup [DK] 160 C6
Parychy [BY] 202 C6
Påryd [S] 162 F5
Pasaia [E] 84 B2
Pasaköy (Asha) [CY] 154 G5
Pasá Limáni [GR] 134 G5
Paşayiğit [TR] 150 B3
Paşcani [RO] 204 D3
Pas de la Casa [AND] 84 H6
Pasęęk [PL] 22 F3
Pas–en–Artois [F] 28 E4
Pasewalk [D] 20 E5
Pasi [FIN] 178 C2
Pasieczník [PL] 50 A1
Pasiene [LV] 198 G5
Pasjak [HR] 112 E1
Pasjane [SRB] 146 D5
Påskallavik [S] 162 G4
Pasmajärvi [FIN] 194 C7
Pašman [HR] 112 G5
Paspolo [TR] 150 C1
Passage East [IRL] 4 E5
Passage West [IRL] 4 D5
Passandra [TR] 152 B2
Passau [D] 60 H3
Passignano sul Trasimeno [I] 114 H2
Passow [D] 20 E6
Pasta Monte Granata [I] 116 G6
Pastavy [BY] 200 H4
Pastena, Grotte di– [I] 120 C1
Pastor [E] 78 C3
Pastoriza [E] 78 E2
Pastra [BG] 146 F6
Pastrana [E] 88 H6
Pāstrovo [BG] 148 C5
Pasvalys [LT] 198 E6
Pašvitinys [LT] 198 D6
Pasym [PL] 22 H4
Pásztó [H] 64 D5
Pasztowa Wola [PL] 38 C6
Patana [FIN] 186 D1
Patara [TR] 154 F3
Patavesi [FIN] 186 F6
Patay [F] 42 E5
Paterek [PL] 22 C6
Patergassen [A] 74 A3
Paterna [E] 98 E4
Paterna del Madera [E] 96 H6
Paterna de Rivera [E] 100 G4
Paternion [A] 72 H3
Paternò [I] 126 G3
Paternopoli [I] 120 F3
Patersdorf [D] 60 G2
Patio [RUS] 178 D3
Patiópoulo [GR] 132 E3
Patitíri [GR] 134 C3
Pátka [H] 76 B1
Patlangıç [TR] 154 G1
Pátmos [GR] 138 H2
Pątnów [PL] 36 F6
Pato [FIN] 176 D3
Patog [AL] 128 A2
Patos [AL] 128 B4
Patosi [AL] 128 B4
Pátra [GR] 132 F6
Patreksfjörður [IS] 192 A1
Patrickswell [IRL] 4 D3
Patrikka [FIN] 188 H2
Patsch [A] 72 D1
Pattada [I] 118 D3
Pattensen [D] 32 F2
Patterdale [GB] 10 D1
Patti [I] 124 A7
Pattijoki [FIN] 196 D4
Pătulele [RO] 146 E1
Páty [H] 64 C6
Pau [F] 84 E3
Pauillac [F] 66 C2
Paukarlahti [FIN] 188 D3
Paularo [I] 72 G3
Paulhaguet [F] 68 D4
Paulilatino [I] 118 C5
Paulinzella [D] 46 G1
Păuliş [RO] 76 H4
Paulström [S] 162 F3
Pauls–Kirche [D] 44 G2
Paulstown [IRL] 4 F4
Paulx [F] 54 B2
Paupys [LT] 200 E5
Pausa [D] 48 B2
Pausin [D] 34 D2
Pauträsk [S] 190 G4
Påvalsby [FIN] 176 E5
Pavel [BG] 148 C3
Pavel Banya [BG] 148 C5
Pavia [I] 70 G6
Pavia [P] 86 D5
Pavia, Certosa di– [I] 70 G5
Pavilly [F] 28 B5
Pavilosta [LV] 198 B5
Pávliani [GR] 132 G4
Pavlice [CZ] 62 E2
Pavlikeni [BG] 148 C3
Pávlos [GR] 134 A5
Pavlovsk [RUS] 178 H5
Pavullo nel Frignano [I] 110 E4
Pavy [RUS] 198 H3
Pawłowiczki [PL] 50 E3
Pawłowo [PL] 22 G5
Pawłowo [PL] 36 D1
Pawonków [PL] 50 F2
Paxoí [GR] 132 B3
Payerne [CH] 58 C6
Paymogo [E] 94 E4
Payrac [F] 66 G4
Pazardzhik [BG] 148 A6
Pazarić [BIH] 144 C1
Pazarköy [TR] 150 C6
Pazarköy [TR] 152 B1
Pazaryeri [TR] 150 G5
Pazin [HR] 112 D2
Pazo de Oca [E] 78 C3
Pchelino [RUS] 178 F3
Pchelnik [BG] 148 F3
Pcim [PL] 50 H4
Pčinja [MK] 128 E1
Peal de Becerro [E] 102 F2
Péaule [F] 40 E5
Péc / Peje [SRB] 146 B5
Pećane [HR] 112 H3
Peccioli [I] 110 E6
Pečenjevce [SRB] 146 D4
Pechenga [RUS] 194 F3
Pechina [E] 102 G5
Pech–Merle, Grotte du– [F] 66 G5
Pecica [RO] 76 G4
Pecineaga [RO] 148 G1
Peciu Nou [RO] 76 G6
Pecka [SRB] 142 F4
Peckelsheim [D] 32 E4
Pecorini a Mare [I] 124 A5
Pečory [RUS] 198 G3
Pec pod Sněžkou [CZ] 50 A2
Pécs [H] 76 B5
Pécsvárad [H] 76 B5
Pedagaggi [I] 126 G4
Pedaso [I] 116 D2
Pederobba [I] 72 E5
Pedersker [DK] 158 E4
Pedersöre / Pedersören k [FIN] 196 C6
Pedersören k / Pedersöre [FIN] 196 C6
Pédi [GR] 154 C3
Pedoulás [CY] 154 F5
Pedrafita do Cebreiro, Puerto– [E] 78 E4
Pedralba [E] 98 E4
Pedraza [E] 88 G3
Pedreguer [E] 104 F1
Pedreira [E] 78 D2
Pedrera [E] 96 F3
Pedrera [E] 102 B3
Pedrizas, Puerto de las– [E] 102 C4
Pedro Abad [E] 102 D1
Pedro Andrés [E] 102 H2
Pedro Bernardo [E] 88 D5
Pedroche [E] 96 C5
Pedrógão [P] 86 C2
Pedrógão [P] 94 E3
Pedro Martínez [E] 102 F3
Pedro Muñoz [E] 96 G3
Pedrosillo el Ralo [E] 80 H6
Peebles [GB] 8 E4
Peel [GBM] 10 B1
Peenemünde [D] 20 E3
Peera [FIN] 192 G3
Péfkos [GR] 128 D5
Péfkos [GR] 140 F5
Pega [P] 86 G2
Pegau [D] 34 C6
Pégeia [CY] 154 F6
Peggau [A] 74 D2
Pegli [I] 110 A3
Pegnitz [D] 46 H4
Pego [E] 104 F1
Pegões [P] 86 C6
Peguera [E] 104 D5
Peguerinos [E] 88 E5
Pehčevo [MK] 128 H1
Peheim [D] 18 C6
Pehlivanköy [TR] 150 B2
Peine [D] 32 G2
Peipohja [FIN] 176 D2
Peippu [FIN] 186 B6
Peïra–Cava [F] 108 F4
Peiraías [GR] 134 C6
Peiss [D] 60 E5
Peissenberg [D] 60 D5
Peiting [D] 60 D5
Peitz [D] 34 F4
Peje / Péc [SRB] 146 B5
Pejo [I] 72 C3
Pekkala [FIN] 194 D8
Pelagićevo [BIH] 142 E2
Pelasgía [GR] 132 H4
Pelatikovo [BG] 146 F6
Pełczyce [PL] 20 G6
Pełczyn [PL] 36 C5
Pelejaneta / La Pelechaneta [E] 98 F3
Pélekas [GR] 132 B2
Peleshi [RUS] 198 G2
Peletá [GR] 136 F4
Pelhřimov [CZ] 48 H5
Peliciego, Cueva de– [E] 104 C1
Peligros [E] 102 E4
Pelince [MK] 146 D6
Pelitözu [TR] 150 G4
Pelkosenniemi [FIN] 194 E7
Pélla [GR] 128 G4
Péllaro [I] 124 C7
Pellegrino Parmense [I] 110 C2
Pellegrue [F] 66 E4
Pellérd [H] 76 B5
Pellesmäki [FIN] 188 C2
Pellevoisin [F] 54 G3
Pellinge / Pellinki [FIN] 178 B5
Pellinki / Pellinge [FIN] 178 B5
Pello [FIN] 194 C7
Pello [S] 194 C7
Pellosniemi [FIN] 178 C1
Pelovo [BG] 148 A3
Pelplin [PL] 22 E4
Pelt [FIN] 194 B5
Peltosalmi [FIN] 196 E6
Pélussin [F] 68 F3
Pély [H] 64 E6
Pemaninos [TR] 150 D5
Pemar / Paimio [FIN] 176 E4
Pembroke [GB] 12 D2
Pembroke Dock [GB] 12 D2
Peñacerrada [E] 82 G5
Penacova [P] 86 E2
Peña Escrita, Cuevas de– [E] 96 D5
Peñafiel [E] 88 F2
Peñafiel [P] 80 C4
Peñaflor [E] 102 B1
Penaguiao [P] 80 D4
Peñalén [E] 90 B6
Peñalsordo [E] 96 C4
Penalva do Castelo [P] 80 D6
Penamacor [P] 86 G3
Peñaranda de Bracamonte [E] 88 D3
Peñaranda de Duero [E] 88 H2
Peñarroya, Castillo de– [E] 96 G4
Peñarroya de Tastavins [E] 98 G1
Peñarroya–Pueblonuevo [E] 96 B5
Penarth [GB] 12 F3
Peñascosa [E] 96 H6
Peñas de San Pedro [E] 98 B6
Peñausende [E] 80 H5
Penc [H] 64 C5
Pendik [TR] 150 F3
Pendine [GB] 12 D2
Pendus, Rocher des– [F] 68 B4
Penedono [P] 80 D5
Penela [P] 86 D2
Penestin [F] 40 E5
Peniche [P] 86 B3
Penicuik [GB] 8 E3
Penig [D] 48 D1
Peníscola / Peñíscola [E] 98 G2
Peñíscola / Peníscola [E] 98 G2
Penkum [D] 20 E5
Penmarch, Pointe de– [F] 40 B3
Pennabilli [I] 110 H5
Pennala [FIN] 178 B3
Penne [I] 116 D4
Penne [N] 164 B5
Penningby [S] 168 E2
Peno [RUS] 202 D3
Penrith [GB] 8 E6
Penryn [GB] 12 C5
Pensala [FIN] 186 C1
Pentagioí [GR] 132 F5
Pentálofo [GR] 128 E6
Pentálofo [GR] 132 E5
Pénte Vrýses [GR] 130 B4
Pentrez–Plage [F] 40 B2
Penzance [GB] 12 B5
Penzberg [D] 60 D5
Penzlin [D] 20 D5
Pepelow [D] 20 A3
Pępowo [PL] 36 C4
Peqin [AL] 128 B3
Pér [H] 62 H6
Perachóra [GR] 132 H6
Péra Chorion [CY] 154 G5
Perafita [P] 80 B3
Perä–Hyyppä [FIN] 186 C5
Peraía [GR] 128 H5
Perälä [FIN] 186 B4
Peraleda del Zaucejo [E] 96 B4
Peralejos [E] 98 E1
Peralejos de las Truchas [E] 90 C6
Perales del Alfambra [E] 98 E1
Perales de Tajuña [E] 88 G6
Peralta [E] 84 B5
Peralva [P] 94 D5
Pérama [GR] 132 D2
Pérama [GR] 140 D4
Peranka [FIN] 196 F3
Peränkylä [FIN] 176 C2
Peränne [FIN] 186 E4
Perä–Posio [FIN] 194 E8
Peräseinäjoki [FIN] 186 C4
Perast [MNE] 144 D4
Perchauer Sattel [A] 74 B2
Perchtoldsdorf [A] 62 F5
Percy [F] 26 D4
Perdasdefogu [I] 118 D6
Perdifumo [I] 120 F5
Perdigão [P] 86 E4
Pérdika [GR] 132 C3
Pérdika [GR] 132 D2
Pérdika [GR] 136 G2
Pereda de Ancares [E] 78 F4
Père de Montfort, Grotte du– [F] 54 C3
Peredo [P] 80 F4
Pereiaslav–Khmel'nyts'kyi [UA] 202 E7
Pereiro [P] 94 D5
Peremozhne [UA] 52 H5
Peremyshl' [RUS] 202 F4
Pereruela [E] 80 H5
Pereshchepyne [UA] 204 H1
Pereslavl'–Zalesskiy [RUS] 202 F2
Pereta [I] 114 F3
Peretu [RO] 148 B1
Perevolok [RUS] 198 G1
Perfugas [I] 118 C3
Perg [A] 62 C4
Pergamos (Beyarmudu) [CY] 154 G5
Pérgine Valsugana [I] 72 D4
Pergola [I] 112 B6
Perho [FIN] 186 E2
Periam [RO] 76 F5
Periana [E] 102 C4
Périers [F] 26 D3
Pérignác [F] 54 C6
Périgueux [F] 66 F3
Perii Broşteni [RO] 148 B1
Periš [SRB] 146 E3
Perisgrund [FIN] 186 A3

Perişoru [RO] 146 F1
Períssa [GR] 138 F5
Peristerá [GR] 130 B4
Peristeróna [CY] 154 F5
Perivóli [GR] 132 D1
Perjasica [HR] 112 G1
Perjen Tunnel [A] 72 C1
Perkáta [H] 76 C2
Perkpolder [NL] 28 H1
Perle [LV] 198 F5
Perleberg [D] 20 B6
Perles'e [RUS] 178 F6
Perlez [SRB] 142 G1
Perly [PL] 24 C2
Përmet [AL] 128 C6
Pernå / Pernaja [FIN] 178 B4
Pernaa [FIN] 186 C2
Pernacha de Cima [P] 86 D5
Pernaja / Pernå [FIN] 178 B4
Pernat [HR] 112 E2
Pernek [SK] 62 G4
Pernes [P] 86 C4
Pernes-les-Fontaines [F] 106 H3
Pernik [BG] 146 F5
Perniö / Bjärnå [FIN] 176 F5
Pernitz [A] 62 E5
Pernštejn [CZ] 50 B5
Pernu [FIN] 194 E8
Pérolles, Pont de- [CH] 58 D6
Peron [F] 70 A2
Péronne [F] 28 F5
Perosa Argentina [I] 70 C6
Pérouges [F] 68 G2
Perpignan [F] 92 G1
Perrero [I] 70 C6
Perros-Guirec [F] 40 D1
Persberg [S] 166 G2
Persenbeug [A] 62 D4
Pershagen [S] 168 D3
Perskogen [N] 192 G3
Persön [S] 196 B3
Perstorp [S] 158 C1
Perstorp [S] 184 H1
Perth [GB] 8 E2
Pertisau [A] 60 E6
Pertoča [SLO] 74 E3
Pertosa, Grotta di- [I] 120 G4
Pertoúli [GR] 132 E2
Perttaus [FIN] 194 C7
Pertteli [FIN] 176 F4
Pertuis [F] 108 B4
Pertunmaa [FIN] 178 B1
Pertusa [E] 90 G3
Peruc [CZ] 48 F3
Perúgia [I] 116 A2
Perunika [BG] 130 G1
Perushtica [BG] 148 B6
Perušić [HR] 112 G3
Péruwelz [B] 28 G3
Pervomais'k [UA] 204 F2
Pervomais'ke [UA] 204 H3
Pervomajskoye [RUS] 178 G3
Perwez [B] 30 D4
Pesac [RO] 76 F5
Pesadas de Burgos [E] 82 F5
Pesados [TR] 154 C1
Pesaguero [E] 82 D3
Pésaro [I] 112 B5
Pescaglia [I] 110 D5
Pescara [I] 116 D4
Pescasseroli [I] 116 C6
Péschici [I] 116 H5
Peschiera [I] 122 D4
Peschiera del Garda [I] 72 B6
Pescia [I] 110 E5
Pescina [I] 116 C5
Pescocostanzo [I] 116 D5
Pescolanciano [I] 116 D6
Pescopagano [I] 120 G3
Pescorocchiano [I] 116 B4
Peshkëpija [AL] 128 B5
Peshkopi [AL] 128 C2
Peshtera [BG] 148 A6
Pesio, Certosa di- [I] 108 F3
Peski [RUS] 178 F4
Pesmes [F] 56 H4
Pesnica pri Mariboru [SLO] 74 E3
Pesočani [MK] 128 D3
Pesochnyy [RUS] 178 H4
Peso da Régua [P] 80 D4
Pesoz [E] 78 F3
Pesquera del Duero [E] 88 F2
Pesqueza [E] 86 G4
Pessáni [GR] 130 G2
Pessin [D] 34 D2
Peštani [MK] 128 D4
Pestovo [RUS] 202 D1
Pešurići [BIH] 144 E1
Petäiskylä [FIN] 196 G5
Petäjäkylä [FIN] 186 G1
Petäjämäki [FIN] 188 C3
Petäjävesi [FIN] 186 F4
Petalídi [GR] 136 D4
Petaloúdes [GR] 154 D3
Pétange [L] 44 E3
Petehi [HR] 112 D2
Peteranec [HR] 74 G4
Peterborough [GB] 14 E2
Peterhead [GB] 6 G5
Peterlee [GB] 10 F1
Petersburg [A] 72 C1
Petersdorf [D] 18 H2
Petersdorf [D] 20 B3
Petersfield [GB] 14 D5
Petershagen [D] 32 E2
Petershagen [D] 34 F2
Petershausen [D] 60 E3
Pétervására [H] 64 E5
Pethelinós [GR] 130 C3
Pétifürdő [H] 76 B2
Petikträsk [S] 190 H4
Petilia Policastro [I] 124 E5
Petino [RUS] 24 B1
Petko Karavelov [BG] 148 C3
Petko Slaveykov [BG] 148 B4
Petkula [FIN] 194 D6
Petkus [D] 34 E3
Petlovac [HR] 76 B6
Petlovača [SRB] 142 F3
Petőháza [H] 62 G6
Petoúsi [GR] 132 C2
Petra [E] 104 E5
Pétra [GR] 128 G6
Pétra [GR] 134 G2
Petralia Soprana [I] 126 E3
Petrálona [GR] 130 B5
Petraná [GR] 128 F5
Petra tou Romiou [CY] 154 F6
Petrelë [AL] 128 B3
Petrella Tifernina [I] 116 E6
Petrelle [I] 114 H1
Petrer [E] 104 D2
Petreto-Bicchisano [F] 114 B5
Petrich [BG] 130 B2
Petrich [BG] 148 A5
Petrikov [BY] 202 C6
Petrila [RO] 204 C5
Petrina [SLO] 112 F1
Petrinja [HR] 142 A1
Petrodvorets [RUS] 178 G5
Petrohan [BG] 146 F4
Petrola [E] 98 C6
Petromäki [FIN] 188 D3
Petronell-Carnuntum [A] 62 G5
Petroşani [RO] 204 C5
Petrosino [I] 126 B3
Petrotá [GR] 150 A2
Petroússa [GR] 130 C2
Petrovac [MNE] 144 E5
Petrovac [SRB] 146 C1
Petrovac [SRB] 204 B6
Petrovaradin [SRB] 142 F1
Petrove [UA] 202 F8
Petrovice [CZ] 48 E6
Petrovice [CZ] 48 F5
Petrovići [BIH] 144 B2
Petrovo [BG] 130 B2
Petřvald [CZ] 50 E5
Petrykaw [RUS] 202 C6
Petrykivka [RUS] 204 G1
Petsákoi [GR] 132 F6
Petsikko [FIN] 194 D3
Pettenbach [A] 62 B5
Pettigo [NIR] 2 E3
Pettneu am A. [A] 72 B1
Peuerbach [A] 62 A4
Peura [FIN] 194 C8
Peurajärvi [FIN] 196 G5
Peurasuvanto [FIN] 194 D6
Pevensey [GB] 14 E6
Peveragno [I] 108 F3
Peypin [F] 108 B5
Peyragudes [F] 84 F5
Peyrat-le-Chateaux [F] 66 H1
Peyrehorade [F] 84 D2
Peyriac-Minervois [F] 106 C4
Peyrolles [F] 108 B4
Peyruis [F] 108 C3
Peyrusse-le-Roc [F] 66 H5
Pézenas [F] 106 E4
Pezinok [SK] 62 G4
Pezoúla [GR] 130 E3
Pezovo [MK] 146 D6
Pezuela de las Torres [E] 88 G6
Pfaffendorf [D] 46 G3
Pfaffenhofen [D] 60 E3
Pfaffen-hoffen [F] 44 H5
Pfäffikon [CH] 58 G5
Pfäffikon [CH] 58 G5
Pfafflar [A] 72 C1
Pfalzfeld [D] 44 H1
Pfalzgrafen Weller [D] 58 G2
Pfänder Tunnel [A] 60 B6
Pfarrkirchen [D] 60 G3
Pfatter [D] 60 F2
Pfeffenhausen [D] 60 F3
Pforzheim [D] 46 C6
Pfreimd [D] 48 C5
Pfronten [D] 60 C6
Pfullendorf [D] 58 H3
Pfullingen [D] 58 H2
Pfundres / Fundres [I] 72 E2
Pfunds [A] 72 C2
Pfungstadt [D] 46 C4
P. Gynaikókastro [GR] 128 H3
Phalsbourg [F] 44 G5
Phellos [TR] 154 G3
Philippeville [B] 30 C6
Philippsreut [D] 62 A2
Philippsthal [D] 32 F6
Phokaia [TR] 152 B3
Phönike [AL] 132 B1
Piacenza [I] 70 H6
Piádena [I] 110 D1
Piaggine [I] 120 G4
Piana [F] 114 A4
Piana Crixia [I] 108 H2
Piana degli Albanesi [I] 126 C2
Pian Castagna [I] 108 H2
Piancavallo [I] 72 F4
Pian d'Alma [I] 114 E2
Piàn di Scò [I] 110 F6
Pianella [I] 114 G1
Pianello Val Tidone [I] 110 C2
Pianiccia [I] 114 C4
Piani Resinelli [I] 70 G4
Pianoro [I] 110 F4
Pianotolli-Caldarello [F] 114 B6
Pias [P] 94 E2
Pias [P] 94 E3
Piasecznik [PL] 20 G5
Piaseczno [PL] 20 F6
Piaseczno [PL] 38 B3
Piaski [PL] 36 C4
Piaski [PL] 38 E6
Piastów [PL] 38 B3
Piaszczyna [PL] 22 C3
Piątek [PL] 36 G3
Piatra [RO] 148 B2
Piatra Neamţ [RO] 204 D4
Piazza al Serchio [I] 110 D4
Piazza Armerina [I] 126 E4
Piazza Brembana [I] 70 H4
Piazzatorre [I] 70 H3
Piazzola sul Brenta [I] 72 D6
Pićan [HR] 112 E2
Picassent [E] 98 E5
Picerno [I] 120 G4
Pichoux, Gorges de- [CH] 58 D5
Pickering [GB] 10 G3
Pico [I] 120 C1
Picquigny [F] 28 D4
Pidna [GR] 128 H5
Piechowice [PL] 48 H1
Piecki [PL] 24 C4
Piedade [P] 100 C3
Piedade, Ponta da- [P] 94 B5
Piedicavallo [I] 70 E4
Piedicroce [F] 114 C3
Piediluco [I] 116 B4
Piedimonte Etneo [I] 124 A8
Piedimonte Matese [I] 120 E2
Piedimulera [I] 70 E3
Piedra, Monasteiro de- [E] 90 C4
Piedrabuena [E] 86 F5
Piedrabuena [E] 96 E4
Piedrafita de Babia [E] 78 G4
Piedrahita [E] 88 C4
Piedralaves [E] 88 D5
Piedras Albas [E] 86 G4
Piekary Śląskie [PL] 50 F3
Piekło [PL] 22 E4
Pieksämäki [FIN] 188 C4
Pielavesi [FIN] 186 H1
Pieniężno [PL] 22 G3
Piennes [F] 44 E3
Pieńsk [PL] 34 G6
Pienza [I] 114 G2
Pierre-Buffière [F] 66 G2
Pierre-de-Bresse [F] 56 H5
Pierrefitte-Nestalas [F] 84 E4
Pierrefitte-sur-Aire [F] 44 D4
Pierrefonds [F] 42 G2
Pierrefort [F] 68 B4
Pierrefort, Château de- [F] 44 E5
Pierrelatte [F] 106 G2
Pierroton [F] 66 C3
Piertinjaure [S] 190 H1
Piesalankylä [FIN] 186 F4
Pieski [PL] 34 H2
Pieskowa Skala [PL] 50 H3
Piessling Urspr. [A] 62 B6
Piešťany [SK] 62 H3
Pieszyce [PL] 50 C2
Pietarsaari / Jakobstad [FIN] 196 B6
Pietra Bismantova [I] 110 D3
Pietragalla [I] 120 H3
Pietralba [F] 114 B3
Pietra Ligure [I] 108 G3
Pietralunga [I] 116 A1
Pietramelara [I] 120 D2
Pietraperzia [I] 126 E4
Pietrasanta [I] 110 D5
Pietravairano [I] 120 D2
Pietroşani [RO] 148 C2
Pietrowice [PL] 50 D3
Pietrzwałd [PL] 22 G4
Pieve di Bono [I] 72 B5
Pieve di Cadore [I] 72 F3
Pieve di Teco [I] 108 G4
Pievepelago [I] 110 E4
Pieve Santo Stéfano [I] 110 G6
Pievescola [I] 114 F1
Pieve S. Giacomo [I] 110 D1
Pigádi [GR] 132 H3
Pigés [GR] 132 E3
Pigí [GR] 132 F5
Píglio [I] 116 B6
Pigna [I] 108 F4
Pignola [I] 120 H4
Pihkainmäki [FIN] 188 C2
Pihkala [FIN] 196 D5
Pihlajalahti [FIN] 186 E5
Pihlajalahti [FIN] 188 E5
Pihlajavaara [FIN] 188 H1
Pihlajaveden as. [FIN] 186 E4
Pihlava [FIN] 176 C1
Pihtipudas [FIN] 186 F1
Piikkiö / Pikis [FIN] 176 E4
Piipola [FIN] 196 D5
Piippaharju [FIN] 186 H4
Piispa [FIN] 188 E1
Piispala [FIN] 186 F2
Pikalevo [RUS] 202 D1
Pikis / Piikkiö [FIN] 176 E4
Pikšas [LV] 198 D5
Pila [I] 70 D4
Pila [I] 110 H2
Piła [PL] 22 B6
Pilar de la Horadada [E] 104 D3
Pilar de la Mola [E] 104 C6
Pilas [E] 94 G6
Pilastri [I] 110 F2
Pilastro [I] 110 D3
Pilat, Dune de- [F] 66 B3
Pilat-Plage [F] 66 B3
Pileta, Cueva de la- [E] 100 H4
Pilgrimstad [S] 182 H3
Pilica [PL] 50 H2
Pílio [GR] 134 B4
Pilis [H] 76 D1
Piliscsaba [H] 64 C6
Pilisvörösvár [H] 64 C6
Piliuona [LT] 200 F5
Pilpala [FIN] 176 G4
Pilsrundāle [LV] 198 D6
Pilštanj [SLO] 74 D5
Piltene [LV] 198 B5
Pilträsk [S] 190 H3
Pilu [RO] 76 G3
Pilviškiai [LT] 24 E1
Pilzno [PL] 52 C4
Pina de Ebro [E] 90 F4
Piñar [E] 102 E3
Pinara [TR] 154 F2
Pinarejos [E] 88 F3
Pinarellu [F] 114 B5
Pınarhisar [TR] 150 C2
Pınarköy [TR] 154 C1
Pince [SLO] 74 F4
Pincehely [H] 76 B3
Pińczów [PL] 52 B2
Pindal, Cueva del- [E] 82 D2
Pineda de la Sierta [E] 90 A1
Pineda de Mar [E] 92 F4
Pinerolo [I] 70 C6
Pineto [I] 116 D3
Piney [F] 44 B5
Pinhal Novo [P] 86 B5
Pinhão [E] 80 D4
Pinhel [P] 80 E6
Pinkafeld [A] 74 E1
Pinneberg [D] 18 F4
Pino [E] 78 H4
Pino [F] 114 C2
Pino do Val [E] 78 B2
Pinofranqueado [E] 86 H3
Pinols [F] 68 D4
Piñor [E] 78 C4
Pinoso / el Pinós [E] 104 D2
Pinos Puente [E] 102 D3
Pinsk [BY] 202 B6
Pinsoro [E] 84 B6
Pintamo [FIN] 196 E3
Pinto [E] 88 F6
Pinzio [P] 80 E6
Pinzolo [I] 72 C4
Pióbbico [I] 110 H6
Piombino [I] 114 E2
Piona, Abbazia di- [I] 70 G3
Pionerskiy [RUS] 200 C5
Pionki [PL] 38 C5
Pionsat [F] 56 C6
Pióraco [I] 116 B2
Piorunkowice [PL] 50 D3
Piossasco [I] 70 D6
Piotrków [PL] 38 E6
Piotrkowice [PL] 36 C5
Piotrkowice [PL] 52 B2
Piotrków Kujawski [PL] 36 F2
Piotrków Trybunalski [PL] 36 H5
Piotrowice [PL] 38 C3
Piotrowo [PL] 36 C2
Piotta [CH] 70 F2
Piove di Sacco [I] 110 G1
Piovene-Rocchette [I] 72 D5
Pipriac [F] 40 F4
Piqeras [AL] 132 B1
Piqueras, Puerto de- [E] 90 B2
Piran [SLO] 72 H6
Piras [I] 118 E3
Pirčiupiai [LT] 24 H2
Pirdop [BG] 148 A4
Pirgovo [BG] 148 C2
Piriac-sur-Mer [F] 40 D5
Piriatin [UA] 202 E7
Pirin [BG] 130 B2
Pirkkala / Birkala [FIN] 176 F1
Pirlibey [TR] 152 E5
Pirltijärvi [FIN] 186 B6
Pirmasens [D] 44 H4
Pirna [D] 48 F1
Pirnesperä [FIN] 196 D5
Pirok [MK] 128 D1
Pirot [SRB] 146 E4
Pirou-Plage [F] 26 D3
Pirovac [HR] 112 G6
Pirtó [H] 76 D4
Pirttikoski [FIN] 176 F3
Pirttikylä / Pörtom [FIN] 186 B3
Pirttimäki [FIN] 186 H2
Pirttimäki [FIN] 196 F5
Pirttiniemi [FIN] 196 C6
Pisa [I] 110 D5
Pisa, Certosa di- [I] 110 D5
Pisanets [BG] 148 D2
Pisarovina [HR] 112 H1
Pişchia [RO] 76 G5
Pisciotta [I] 120 F5
Piscu Vechi [RO] 146 F2
Písek [CZ] 48 F6
Pishcha [UA] 38 G4
Pisodéri [GR] 128 E4
Pisogne [I] 72 B5
Písses [GR] 138 C2
Pissónas [GR] 134 C5
Pissos [F] 66 C4
Pissoúri [CY] 154 F6
Pisticci [I] 122 D4
Pistóia [I] 110 E5
Pisz [PL] 24 C4
Piszczac [PL] 38 F3
Pitäjänmäki [FIN] 196 D6
Piteå [S] 196 B3
Piteşti [RO] 204 D5
Pithiviers [F] 42 F5
Pitigliano [I] 114 G3
Pitkäjärvi [FIN] 176 F4
Pitkälahti [FIN] 188 C2
Pitlochry [GB] 8 E1
Pitomača [HR] 74 G5
Pitsiána [GR] 132 D3
Pitvaros [H] 76 F4
Pivka [SLO] 74 B6
Pivnica [HR] 74 H6
Pivski Manastir [MNE] 144 D3
Piwniczna [PL] 52 C5
Pizarra [E] 102 B4
Pizhma [RUS] 178 H6
Pizzighettone [I] 70 H6
Pizzo [I] 124 D6
Pizzoli [I] 116 C4
Pjatihatki [UA] 202 F8
Pjätteryd [S] 162 C5
Plabennec [F] 40 B1
Placis [LV] 198 E4
Plage de Pineto [F] 114 C3
Plagiá [GR] 128 H3
Plagiá [GR] 130 G2
Plaigne [F] 106 A4
Plaisance [F] 66 E4
Plaisance [F] 84 F2
Pláka [GR] 130 F6
Plakia [TR] 150 D4
Plakiás [GR] 140 D5
Plana [BIH] 144 D3
Planá [CZ] 48 D4
Planá nad Lužnicí [CZ] 48 G6
Plancios [I] 72 E3
Plancoët [F] 26 B4
Plandište [SRB] 142 H1
Plan d'Orgon [F] 106 H4
Plan-du-Lac [F] 70 C2
Plánice [CZ] 48 E5
Planina [SLO] 74 B5
Planina pri Sevnici [SLO] 74 D5
Planinica [SRB] 146 D2
Planjane [HR] 142 A5
Plankenburk [CZ] 50 C5
Plankenstein [A] 62 D5
Planoles [E] 92 E2
Plansee [A] 60 C6
Plasencia [E] 88 B5
Plasencia de Jalón [E] 90 E3
Plasencia del Monte [E] 84 D6
Plaški [HR] 112 G2
Plassen [N] 172 D2
Plassenburg [D] 46 H3
Plášťovce [SK] 64 C4
Plasy [CZ] 48 E4
Plataiés [GR] 134 B6
Platamona Lido [I] 118 C3
Platamónas [GR] 128 H6
Platamónas [GR] 130 D3
Platanákia [GR] 128 H2
Platanés [GR] 140 D4
Plataniá [GR] 134 B3
Platánia [GR] 136 C3
Plataniás [GR] 140 C4
Platanistós [GR] 134 D6
Plátanos [GR] 136 C2
Plátanos [GR] 136 E3
Plátanos [GR] 140 B4
Platariá [GR] 132 C2
Platerów [PL] 38 E2
Pláti [GR] 150 A2
Plati [I] 124 C7
Platiána [GR] 136 C2
Platičevo [SRB] 142 F2
Platja d'Aro [E] 92 G4
Platja des Canar [E] 104 C5
Plátsa [GR] 136 E4
Platta [CH] 70 G1
Plattling [D] 60 G3
Platygyáli [GR] 132 D5
Platýkampos [GR] 132 G2
Platýs Gialós [GR] 138 D3
Platys Gialós [GR] 138 E2
Platýstomo [GR] 132 F4
Plau [D] 20 B5
Plaue [D] 34 C2
Plauen [D] 48 C2
Plav [MNE] 146 A5
Plava [SRB] 146 B6
Plave [SLO] 72 H5
Plavecký Hrad [SK] 62 G3
Plavecký Mikuláš [SK] 62 G3
Plavinas [LV] 198 E5
Plavna [SRB] 146 E1
Pławna [PL] 36 A6
Playa Blanca [E] 100 E6
Playa de las Américas [E] 100 B5
Playa del Inglés [E] 100 C6
Playa de San Juán [E] 104 E2
Płazów [PL] 52 G2
Pleaux [F] 68 A3
Plech [D] 46 H4
Plecka Dąbrowa [PL] 36 G3
Pleinfeld [D] 46 G6
Plélan-le-Grand [F] 26 B6
Plémet [F] 26 B5
Pleniţa [RO] 146 F1
Plentzia [E] 82 G3
Plépi [GR] 136 G2
Pleshchanitsy [RUS] 202 B5
Plešivec [SK] 64 E3
Plesse [F] 40 F5
Plessenburg [D] 32 G4
Plessis-Bourré, Château du- [F] 40 H6
Plestin-les-Grèves [F] 40 C1
Pleszew [PL] 36 E4
Pleternica [HR] 142 C1
Plettenberg [D] 32 C5
Pleumartin [F] 54 F4
Pleven [BG] 148 A3
Pleyben [F] 40 C2
Pliego [E] 104 B3
Plikáti [GR] 128 D6
Plina Jezero [HR] 144 B3
Pliska [BG] 148 E2
Plitvice [HR] 112 G3
Plitvički Ljeskovac [HR] 112 G3
Pljevlja [MNE] 144 E2
Pllake [AL] 132 B1
Ploaghe [I] 118 C3
Ploča [SRB] 146 C3
Ploče [HR] 144 B3
Plochingen [D] 58 H1
Płochocin [PL] 38 B3
Płock [PL] 36 H2
Ploërmel [F] 26 B6
Ploieşti [RO] 204 D5
Plomári [GR] 134 H3
Plombières-les-Bains [F] 58 C3
Plomin [HR] 112 E2
Plön [D] 18 G2
Plonéour Lanvern [F] 40 B3
Płońsk [PL] 38 A2
Plopii Slăviteşti [RO] 148 B2
Płoskinia [PL] 22 G2
Plosky [BG] 130 B1
Płotno [PL] 20 G6
Płoty [PL] 20 G4
Plouaret [F] 40 D2
Plouay [F] 40 C4
Ploubalay [F] 26 C4
Ploudalmézeau [F] 40 B1
Plouescat [F] 40 B1
Plougasnou [F] 40 C1
Plougastel-Daoulas [F] 40 B2
Plougonven [F] 40 C2
Plouguenast [F] 26 B5
Plouguerneau [F] 40 B1
Plouha [F] 26 A4
Plouigneau [F] 40 C2
Ploumanac'h [F] 40 D1
Plounévez-Quintin [F] 40 D3
Plouray [F] 40 C3
Plovdiv [BG] 148 B6
Plozévet [F] 40 B3
Plungė [LT] 200 D4
Pluty [PL] 22 G2
Pluviers [F] 66 F1
Pluvigner [F] 40 D4
Plužine [BIH] 144 C2
Plužine [MNE] 144 D2
Płużnica [PL] 22 E5
Plymouth [GB] 12 D5
Płytnica [PL] 22 B5
Plýtra [GR] 136 F5
Plyussa [RUS] 198 H2
Plzeň [CZ] 48 E4
Pnevo [RUS] 198 G3
Pniewo [PL] 38 C2
Pniewy [PL] 36 B2
Pobedino [RUS] 200 E5
Pobes [E] 82 G5
Pobiedziska [PL] 36 D2
Pobierowo [PL] 20 F3
Pobikry [PL] 38 E1
Pobiti Kamŭni [BG] 148 F3
Poblado Celtico [E] 78 F2
Poblado Iberico [E] 90 H6
Poblado Iberico [E] 92 G3
Pobladura de la Sierra [E] 78 F5
Pobladura del Valle [E] 82 A5
Poblet [E] 92 C4
Pobra do Caramiñal / Puebla del Caramiñal [E] 78 B3
Počátky [CZ] 48 H6
Poceirão [P] 86 B6
Pochep [RUS] 202 E5
Pochinok [RUS] 202 D4
Pöchlarn [A] 62 D4
Pocinho [P] 80 E5
Počitelj [BIH] 144 C3
Pocking [D] 60 H4
Pocklington [GB] 10 G3
Poćkuny [PL] 24 F3
Poço do Inferno [P] 86 F2
Pocrnje [BIH] 144 C3
Pocsaj [H] 76 H1
Počuta [SRB] 146 A2
Poczesna [PL] 50 G2
Podari [RO] 146 G1
Podbanské [SK] 50 H6
Podberez'ye [RUS] 202 C2
Podbořany [CZ] 48 E3
Podborje [BIH] 144 B1
Podborov'ye [RUS] 198 G3
Podbožur [MNE] 144 D3
Podbrdo [SLO] 74 A4
Podbrezová [SK] 64 D3
Poddębice [PL] 36 F4
Poděbrady [CZ] 48 H3
Podelzig [D] 34 G2
Podem [BG] 148 A3
Podence [P] 80 F4
Podensac [F] 66 D4
Podersdorf am See [A] 62 G5
Podgaje [PL] 22 B5
Podgarić [HR] 74 F6
Podgora [HR] 144 B2
Podgorač [HR] 142 D1
Podgorac [SRB] 146 D2
Podgorica [MNE] 144 E4
Podgorie [AL] 128 D4
Podgornoye [RUS] 24 C1
Podgor'ye [RUS] 178 G3
Podgrad [SLO] 112 E1
Podgradec [AL] 128 D4
Podivín [CZ] 62 G3
Podklasztorze [PL] 36 H5
Podkoren [SLO] 72 H3
Podkova [BG] 130 F2
Podkrepa [BG] 148 C6
Podkriváň [SK] 64 D3
Podlehnik [SLO] 74 E4
Podljubelj [SLO] 74 B4
Podlugovi [BIH] 142 D4
Podnovlje [BIH] 142 D2
Podochóri [GR] 130 C4
Podogorá [GR] 132 E4
Podolesh'e [RUS] 198 G2
Podolínec [SK] 52 B6
Podol'sk [RUS] 202 F3
Podosoje [HR] 144 A1
Podrašnica [BIH] 142 B3
Podromanija [BIH] 144 D1
Podslon [BG] 148 D5
Podsreda [SLO] 74 D5
Podujevo [SRB] 146 C4
Podunavci [SRB] 146 B3
Podvinje [HR] 142 D2
Podvolovljek [SLO] 74 C4
Podwilcze [PL] 20 H4
Podwilk [PL] 50 H5
Poeldijk [NL] 16 C5
Poetto [I] 118 D7
Poggendorf [D] 20 D3
Poggibonsi [I] 110 E6
Póggio Renatico [I] 110 F3
Póggio Rusco [I] 110 F2
Pöggstall [A] 62 D4
Pogonianí [GR] 132 C1
Pogoritsa [BG] 148 D3
Pogórska Wola [PL] 52 C4
Pogórze [PL] 50 D3
Pogorzela [PL] 36 D4
Pogrodzie [PL] 22 F2
Pohja [FIN] 176 G1
Pohja / Pojo [FIN] 176 F5
Pohja-Lankila [FIN] 188 F6
Pohjankylä [FIN] 176 E5
Pohjansaha [FIN] 186 B6
Pohjaslahti [FIN] 186 E5
Pohjaslahti [FIN] 194 D8
Pohjoinen [FIN] 176 G2
Pohjoislahti [FIN] 186 F4
Pohjola [FIN] 178 B1
Pohorelá [SK] 64 E2
Pohořelice [CZ] 62 F2
Pohoskylä [FIN] 188 C5
Pohrebyshche [UA] 202 D8
Pohtola [FIN] 186 E6
Poiana Braşov [RO] 204 D5
Poiana Mare [RO] 146 F2
Poibrene [BG] 148 A5
Poijula [FIN] 196 E3
Poikelus [FIN] 186 D6
Poikko [FIN] 176 D4
Point [A] 62 C5
Pointe des Poulains [F] 40 C5
Point Sublime [F] 68 C6
Poio / O Convento [E] 78 B4
Poirino [I] 70 D6
Poissons [F] 44 D6
Poitiers [F] 54 E4
Poix [F] 28 D5
Poix-Terron [F] 44 C2
Pojate [SRB] 146 C2
Pojo / Pohja [FIN] 176 F5
Pókaszepetk [H] 74 G2
Pokka [FIN] 194 C5
Pokój [PL] 50 E1
Pokupsko [HR] 112 H1
Pol [E] 78 E3
Polača [HR] 142 A4
Polače [HR] 144 B3
Pola de Allande [E] 78 F3
Pola de Laviana [E] 82 B2
Pola de Lena [E] 78 H4
Pola de Siero [E] 78 H3
Pola de Somiedo [E] 78 G4
Połajewo [PL] 36 C1
Polán [E] 96 E2
Polanica-Zdrój [PL] 50 C3
Połaniec [PL] 52 C2
Polanów [PL] 22 B3
Polatsk [BY] 202 B4
Polcenigo [I] 72 F5
Półczno [PL] 22 C3
Połczyn-Zdrój [PL] 20 H4
Põlde [EST] 198 C3
Polémi [CY] 154 F6
Polena [BG] 128 H1
Polepy [CZ] 48 F2
Polesella [I] 110 G2
Polessk [RUS] 200 D5
Polfau [A] 62 C6
Polgár [H] 64 G5
Polgárdi [H] 76 B2
Poli [GR] 132 C5
Polianí [GR] 136 D3
Poliçan [AL] 128 C6
Poliçan [AL] 128 C5
Policastro Bussentino [I] 120 G5
Police [PL] 20 F5
Police nad Metují [CZ] 50 B2
Polička [CZ] 50 B5
Poličnik [HR] 112 G5
Policoro [I] 122 D5
Polida, Cova de na- [E] 104 H4
Polientes [E] 82 E4
Polignano [I] 110 E4
Polignano a Mare [I] 122 E3
Poligny [F] 58 A6
Polikrayshte [BG] 148 C3
Pólis [CY] 154 F5
Polistena [I] 124 D7
Polistilo [GR] 130 D3
Politiká [GR] 134 B4
Politikón [CY] 154 G5
Poljana [BG] 148 E5
Poljana [HR] 142 B1
Poljanak [HR] 112 G3
Poljčane [SLO] 74 D4
Polje [BIH] 142 D2
Poljica [HR] 144 A3
Poljice [BIH] 142 B4
Polkowice [PL] 36 B5
Pölläkkä [FIN] 186 H4
Pölläkkä [FIN] 188 E4
Pöllau [A] 74 E1
Polle [D] 32 F3
Pollença [E] 104 E4
Pollentia [E] 104 F4
Pollfoss [N] 180 E5
Polmak [N] 194 D2
Polná [CZ] 50 A5
Polo [FIN] 196 F2
Polomka [SK] 64 D2
Polop [E] 104 E2
Pološko [MK] 128 F3
Polska Cerekiew [PL] 50 E3
Polski Gradets [BG] 148 D5
Polski Trŭmbesh [BG] 148 C3
Polsko Kosovo [BG] 148 C3
Polso [FIN] 186 D1
Poltár [SK] 64 D4
Poltava [UA] 202 F7

Põltsamaa [EST] 198 E2
Põlva [EST] 198 F3
Polvela [FIN] 188 E1
Polvijärvi [FIN] 188 F2
Polyany [RUS] 178 F4
Polychnitos [GR] 134 G2
Polýgyros [GR] 130 B5
Polykárpi [GR] 128 F4
Polykástano [GR] 128 E5
Polýkastro [GR] 128 G3
Polymedium [TR] 134 G1
Polypótamo [GR] 128 E4
Polýrracho [GR] 128 F6
Polyrrinía [GR] 140 B4
Polzela [SLO] 74 C4
Pomar [E] 90 G4
Pomarance [I] 114 F1
Pomarico [I] 122 D4
Pomarkku / Påmark [FIN] 176 D1
Pomáz [H] 64 C6
Pombal [P] 86 D2
Pomellen [D] 20 E5
Pomézia [I] 116 A6
Pomigliano d'Arco [I] 120 E3
Pommersfelden [D] 46 G4
Pomorie [BG] 148 F4
Pomoy [F] 58 C3
Pompaples [CH] 70 B1
Pompei [I] 120 E3
Pompey [F] 44 E5
Pómpia [GR] 140 E5
Pompiano [I] 72 A6
Pomposa, Abbazia di– [I] 110 H2
Pomysk Wielki [PL] 22 C3
Poncin [F] 68 H2
Ponferrada [E] 78 F5
Poniatowa [PL] 38 D6
Poniec [PL] 36 C4
Ponikve [MK] 146 E6
Ponikve [SLO] 74 C5
Poniky [SK] 64 C3
Ponoarele [RO] 204 C5
Pons [F] 54 C6
Ponsa [FIN] 176 G1
Ponsacco [I] 110 E6
Pont [F] 56 H4
Pont [I] 70 C4
Ponta [P] 100 B3
Pontacq [F] 84 E3
Ponta Delgada [P] 100 E3
Pontailler–sur–Saône [F] 56 H4
Pontal [P] 94 B5
Pont–à–Mousson [F] 44 E4
Pontão [P] 86 D3
Pontarion [F] 54 H6
Pontarlier [F] 58 B6
Pontarso [I] 72 D4
Pontassieve [I] 110 F5
Pontaubault [F] 26 D4
Pont–Audemer [F] 26 G3
Pontaumur [F] 68 C2
Pont–Aven [F] 40 C3
Pont Canavese [I] 70 D4
Pont Cellier [F] 56 D5
Pontcharra [F] 70 A4
Pontchartrain [F] 42 E3
Pontchâteau [F] 40 E5
Pont–Croix [F] 40 B3
Pont–d'Ain [F] 68 G2
Pont–de–Briques [F] 28 D2
Pont–de–Dore [F] 68 D2
Pont–de–l'Arche [F] 28 B6
Pont del Diable [E] 92 C5
Pont–de–Roide [F] 58 C4
Pont–de–Salars [F] 68 B6
Pont–d'Espagne [F] 84 E4
Pont–de–Vaux [F] 56 G6
Ponte Arche [I] 72 C4
Ponteareas [E] 78 B5
Pontebba [I] 72 G3
Ponte–Caldelas [E] 78 B4
Ponteceno di Sopra [I] 110 C3
Ponteceso [E] 78 B2
Pontecesures / Enfesta [E] 78 B3
Pontechianale [I] 108 E2
Pontecorvo [I] 120 C1
Ponte da Barca [P] 78 B6
Pontedecimo [I] 110 B3
Ponte de Lima [P] 78 B6
Ponte della Venturina [I] 110 E4
Ponte dell'Olio [I] 110 C2
Pontedera [I] 110 E6
Ponte de Sôr [P] 86 D5
Pontedeume [E] 78 D2
Ponte di Legno [I] 72 B4
Ponte di Piave [I] 72 F5
Ponteland [GB] 8 F6
Pontelandolfo [I] 120 E2
Ponte–Leccia [F] 114 B3
Pontelongo [I] 110 G1
Ponte nelle Alpi [I] 72 E4
Pont–en–Royans [F] 68 G5
Ponte Nuovo [F] 114 B3
Pontenx–les–Forges [F] 66 B4
Ponte Oliveras [E] 78 B2
Ponte S. Pietro [I] 70 H4
Ponte Tresa [CH] 70 F3
Ponte Ulla [E] 78 C3
Pontevedra [E] 78 B4
Pontevico [I] 110 D1
Pontgibaud [F] 68 C2
Pontigny [F] 56 E1
Pontinia [I] 120 B1
Pontinvrea [I] 108 H3
Pontisméno [GR] 130 B3
Pontivy [F] 26 A5
Pont–l'Abbé [F] 40 B3
Pont–l'Evêque [F] 26 G3
Pontlevoy [F] 54 G2
Pontoise [F] 42 F3
Pontokómi [GR] 128 F5
Pontones [E] 102 G2
Pontoon [IRL] 2 C3
Pontorson [F] 26 D4
Pontpierre [L] 44 E3
Pont–Réan [F] 26 C6
Pontremoli [I] 110 C3
Pontresina [CH] 72 A3
Pontrieux [F] 26 A3
Ponts [E] 92 C3
Pont–Scorff [F] 40 C4
Pont–St–Esprit [F] 106 G2
Pont–St–Martin [I] 70 D4
Pont–St–Vincent [F] 44 E5
Pont–sur–Yonne [F] 42 G5
Pontvallain [F] 42 B6
Pontypool [GB] 12 F2
Pontypridd [GB] 12 F2
Ponza [I] 120 B3
Poole [GB] 12 G5
Pope [LV] 198 C4
Poperinge [B] 28 F2
Popilnya [UA] 202 D8
Popina [BG] 148 E1
Popintsi [BG] 148 A5
Popiołówka [PL] 24 E5
Popoli [I] 116 D5
Popovac [HR] 74 G6
Popovača [HR] 74 F6
Popovitsa [BG] 148 B6
Popovo [BG] 148 D3
Popovo [BG] 148 E5
Popovo [RUS] 178 F3
Popów [PL] 36 F6
Poppenhausen [D] 46 F3
Poppi [I] 110 G6
Poprad [SK] 64 E2
Popsko [BG] 130 G1
Populónia [I] 114 E2
Poraj [PL] 50 G2
Poranem [FIN] 186 E2
Porasa [FIN] 176 G1
Porazava [BY] 24 G6
Porcikeln [S] 196 A1
Porcuna [E] 102 D1
Porczyny [PL] 36 F4
Pordenone [I] 72 F5
Pordim [BG] 148 B3
Pordoi, Passo– [I] 72 E3
Poręba [PL] 50 G2
Poreč [HR] 112 D2
Porech'ye [RUS] 198 G1
Pori / Björneborg [FIN] 176 D1
Porjus [S] 190 H1
Porkala / Porkkala [FIN] 176 G5
Porkhov [RUS] 198 H3
Porkkala [FIN] 196 D5
Porkkala / Porkala [FIN] 176 G5
Pornainen [FIN] 178 A4
Pörnbach [D] 60 E3
Pornic [F] 54 B1
Pornichet [F] 40 E6
Pornóapáti [H] 74 F2
Poronin [PL] 52 A6
Póros [GR] 132 D6
Póros [GR] 132 D5
Póros [GR] 136 G2
Poroszló [H] 64 F6
Porozina [HR] 112 E2
Pórpi [GR] 130 F3
Porquerolles [F] 108 C6
Porraskoski [FIN] 176 H2
Porrentruy [CH] 58 D4
Porretta Terme [I] 110 E4
Porsgrunn [N] 164 G3
Pórszombat [H] 74 F3
Port a' Chlóidh / Portacloy [IRL] 2 C2
Portacloy / Port a' Chlóidh [IRL] 2 C2
Portadown [NIR] 2 G4
Portaferry [NIR] 2 H4
Portalegre [P] 86 E5
Portalrubio [E] 90 D6
Portariá [GR] 132 H2
Portarlington [IRL] 2 E6
Port Askaig [GB] 8 B2
Port Aventura [E] 92 C5
Portbail [F] 26 D2
Port–Barcarès [F] 92 G1
Portbou [E] 92 G2
Port–Camargue [F] 106 F4
Port–Cros [F] 108 D6
Port d'Adaia [E] 104 H4
Port–de–Bouc [F] 106 G5
Port de Pollença [E] 104 F4
Portel [P] 94 E2
Portela [P] 78 B5
Portela do Home [E] 78 B6
Port Ellen [GB] 2 H1
Portelo [P] 80 F3
Port–en–Bessin [F] 26 E3
Port Erin [GBM] 2 H5
Pórtes [GR] 136 G2
Portes les Valence [F] 68 F5
Pörtet [S] 166 E1
Port Eynon [GB] 12 E2
Portezuelo [E] 86 H4
Portglenone [NIR] 2 G3
Port–Grimaud [F] 108 D5
Porthcawl [GB] 12 E3
Porthmadog [GB] 10 B4
Porticcio [F] 114 A5
Portile de Fier [RO] 204 C6
Portilla de la Reina [E] 82 D3
Portillo [E] 88 E2
Portimão [P] 94 B5
Portimo [FIN] 194 D8
Portinatx [E] 104 C5
Portinho da Arrábida [P] 86 B6
Port–Joinville [F] 54 A2
Port Lairge / Waterford [IRL] 4 E5
Port–la–Nouvelle [F] 106 D5
Portlaoise [IRL] 2 E6
Port–Leucate [F] 106 D6
Port–Louis [F] 40 C4
Portman [E] 104 C4
Port–Manech [F] 40 C4
Portmarnock [IRL] 2 F6
Pörtmossen [FIN] 186 B3
Portnahaven [GB] 2 G1
Port–Navalo [F] 40 D5
Port Nis / Port of Ness [GB] 6 C2
Porto [E] 78 E6
Porto [F] 114 A4
Porto [I] 118 E3
Porto [P] 80 B4
Porto Alto [P] 86 B5
Porto Azzurro [I] 114 E3
Portobello [I] 118 D2
Portocelo [E] 78 E1
Porto Ceresio [I] 70 F3
Porto Cervo [I] 118 E2
Porto Cesareo [I] 122 G5
Pórto Chéli [GR] 136 F3
Porto Colom [E] 104 F5
Porto Corallo [I] 118 E6
Porto Corsini [I] 110 H3
Porto Covo [P] 94 B3
Porto Cristo [E] 104 F5
Porto d'Áscoli [I] 116 D3
Porto de Mós [P] 86 C3
Porto di Levante [I] 124 B6
Porto do Son [E] 78 B3
Porto Empedocle [I] 126 D4
Porto Ércole [I] 114 F4
Portoferráio [I] 114 D2
Portofino [I] 110 B3
Port of Ness / Port Nis [GB] 6 C2
Porto Garibaldi [I] 110 H3
Pórto Germenó [GR] 134 B6
Portogruaro [I] 72 F5
Porto Judeu [P] 100 D3
Pórto Kágio [GR] 136 E5
Pórto Karrás [GR] 130 C6
Porto Levante [I] 110 H2
Pörtom / Pirttikylä [FIN] 186 B3
Portomaggiore [I] 110 G3
Portomarín [E] 78 D4
Porto Moniz [P] 100 A3
Portomouro [E] 78 C3
Porto Novo [P] 86 B4
Portopalo di Capo Pássero [I] 126 G6
Porto–Pollo [F] 114 A5
Porto Potenza Picena [I] 116 C1
Portør [N] 164 F4
Pórto Ráfti [GR] 136 H1
Porto Recanati [I] 116 C1
Porto Rotondo [I] 118 E2
Portorož [SLO] 72 H6
Porto San Giorgio [I] 116 D2
Porto Sant'Elpidio [I] 116 D2
Porto Santoru [I] 118 E6
Porto Santo Stéfano [I] 114 F4
Portoscuso [I] 118 B7
Portos dos Fusos [P] 94 D5
Porto Tolle [I] 110 H2
Porto Tórres [I] 118 B3
Porto–Vecchio [F] 114 B6
Portovenere [I] 110 C4
Porto Viro [I] 110 H2
Portpatrick [GB] 8 B5
Portree [GB] 6 B4
Portroe [IRL] 2 C6
Portrush [NIR] 2 G2
Portsalon [IRL] 2 F1
Pörtschach [A] 74 B3
Portsmouth [GB] 12 H5
Port–Ste–Marie [F] 66 E5
Portstewart [NIR] 2 G2
Port–St–Louis–du–Rhône [F] 106 G5
Port–St–Marie, la Chartreuse de– [F] 68 C2
Port–sur–Saône [F] 58 B3
Port Talbot [GB] 12 E2
Portumna [IRL] 2 D6
Port–Vendres [F] 92 G2
Port William [GB] 8 C5
Porvola [FIN] 186 E6
Porvoo / Borgå [FIN] 178 B4
Porządzie [PL] 38 C1
Porzuna [E] 96 E3
Posada [E] 78 H3
Posada [E] 82 D2
Posada [I] 118 E3
Posada de Valdeón [E] 82 C3
Posadas [E] 102 B1
Posavski Podgajci [HR] 142 E2
Poschiavo [CH] 72 B3
Posedarje [HR] 112 G5
Poseídio [GR] 130 B6
Poseidonía [GR] 138 D2
Pósfa [H] 74 G1
Poshekhon'ye [RUS] 202 F1
Poshnjë [AL] 128 B4
Posio [FIN] 194 E8
Positano [I] 120 E4
Possagno [I] 72 E5
Pössneck [D] 46 H2
Posta [I] 116 B4
Postojna [SLO] 74 B6
Postojnska Jama [SLO] 74 B5
Postoloprty [CZ] 48 E3
Postomino [PL] 22 B2
Postuša [MK] 128 C2
Posušje [BIH] 144 B2
Poświętne [PL] 24 E6
Potamiá [GR] 130 E4
Potamiés [GR] 140 F4
Potamoí [GR] 130 D2
Potamós [GR] 136 F6
Potamós [GR] 140 A3
Potamoúla [GR] 132 E4
Potenštejn [CZ] 48 E5
Potenza [I] 120 H4
Potenza Picena [I] 116 C1
Potes [E] 82 D3
Potka [N] 192 G2
Potnjani [HR] 142 D1
Potoci [BIH] 144 C2
Potok [HR] 142 B1
Potok [PL] 52 D4
Pôtor [SK] 64 D4
Potsdam [D] 34 D2
Potštát [CZ] 50 D5
Pottenbrunn [A] 62 E4
Pottenstein [A] 62 E5
Pottenstein [D] 46 H4
Pöttmes [D] 60 D3
Potula [FIN] 176 H2
Potworów [PL] 38 B5
Pouancé [F] 40 G5
Pouèhonje–Volodarsk [RUS] 202 F1
Pougues–les–Eaux [F] 56 D4
Pouilly [F] 56 D3
Pouilly–en–Auxois [F] 56 F3
Pouilly–sous–Charlieu [F] 68 E1
Poúnta [GR] 138 E3
Pourtalet, Col du– [E/F] 84 D4
Poussay [F] 44 E6
Pouyastruc [F] 84 F3
Pouy–de–Touges [F] 84 G3
Pouzauges [F] 54 C3
Pouzihac [F] 106 G3
Považská Bystrica [SK] 64 B2
Považský Hrad [SK] 50 F6
Poviglio [I] 110 E2
Povlja [HR] 144 A2
Póvoa [P] 94 E3
Povoação [P] 100 E3
Póvoa de Lanhoso [P] 80 C3
Póvoa de Varzim [P] 80 B3
Powburn [GB] 8 F5
Powerscourt House [IRL] 4 G3
Powidz [PL] 36 E2
Powlalice [PL] 20 G4
Powodow [PL] 36 G4
Poyatos [E] 98 C1
Poyntzpass [NIR] 2 G4
Poyra [TR] 150 H5
Poyracık [TR] 152 C2
Poyralı [TR] 150 C2
Poyraz [TR] 152 E3
Poyrazdamları [TR] 152 E3
Poysdorf [A] 62 F3
Pöytyä [FIN] 176 E3
Poza de la Sal [E] 82 F5
Požane [HR] 112 D1
Požarevac [SRB] 204 B6
Pozazal, Puerto– [E] 82 E4
Pozedrze [PL] 24 C3
Požega [HR] 142 C1
Požega [SRB] 146 A2
Poženanje [SRB] 146 C6
Poznań [PL] 36 C2
Pozo Alcón [E] 102 F3
Pozoblanco [E] 96 C5
Pozo–Cañada [E] 98 B6
Pozohondo [E] 98 B6
Pózondon [E] 90 C6
Pozondón [E] 98 D1
Pozo Negro [E] 100 E6
Poźrzadło [PL] 34 H3
Pozuel de Ariza [E] 90 C4
Pozuelo [E] 98 B5
Pozuelo de Zarzón [E] 86 H3
Pozzallo [I] 126 F6
Pózzis [I] 72 G4
Pozzomaggiore [I] 118 C4
Pozzo S. Nicola [I] 118 B3
Pozzuoli [I] 120 D3
Prabuty [PL] 22 F4
Prača [BIH] 144 D1
Prachatice [CZ] 62 B2
Prácheň [CZ] 48 E6
Prácký Kopec [CZ] 62 F2
Pradell [E] 90 H6
Pradelle [F] 68 G6
Pradelles [F] 68 D5
Prádena [E] 88 G4
Prades [F] 92 F1
Pradillo [E] 90 B1
Pradła [PL] 50 H2
Prado del Rey [E] 100 H4
Pradoluengo [E] 82 F6
Præstø [DK] 156 G4
Pragersko [SLO] 74 D4
Prägraten [A] 72 F2
Praha [CZ] 48 F3
Prahecq [F] 54 D4
Prahovo [SRB] 146 E1
Praia a Mare [I] 120 G6
Praia da Barra [P] 80 B5
Praia da Tocha [P] 80 A6
Praia da Vieira [P] 86 C2
Praia da Vitória [P] 100 D3
Praia de Mira [P] 80 A5
Praia de Monte Clérigo [P] 94 B4
Praia de Santa Cruz [P] 86 B4
Praia do Norte [P] 100 C2
Praia Grande [P] 86 A5
Praiano [I] 120 E4
Praias–Sado [P] 86 B6
Prainha [P] 100 C3
Praisós [GR] 140 G5
Prakovce [SK] 64 F2
Prali [I] 70 C6
Pralognan–la–Vanoise [F] 70 B4
Prámanta [GR] 132 D2
Pranjani [SRB] 146 B2
Prapatnica [HR] 116 H1
Prasiá [GR] 132 E3
Prašice [SK] 64 A3
Prasiés [GR] 140 D4
Prastio (Dörtyol) [CY] 154 G5
Praszka [PL] 36 F6
Prat de Compte [E] 90 G6
Pratella [I] 120 D1
Prati di Tivo [I] 116 C4
Prato [I] 110 E5
Prats de Lluçanès [E] 92 E3
Prats–de–Mollo–la–Preste [F] 92 F2
Prauthoy [F] 56 H3
Pravdinsk [RUS] 22 H2
Pravets [BG] 146 G4
Pravia [E] 78 G3
Pravlov [CZ] 62 F2
Prebold [SLO] 74 D4
Préchac [F] 66 D4
Précy–sous–Thil [F] 56 F3
Precy sur Vrin [F] 42 G6
Predappio [I] 110 G4
Predazzo [I] 72 D4
Preddvor [SLO] 74 B4
Predeal [RO] 204 D5
Predejane [SRB] 146 E4
Predel [SLO] 72 H4
Predeşti [RO] 146 F1
Preding [A] 74 D3
Predlitz [A] 74 B2
Predoi / Prettau [I] 72 E2
Pré–en–Pail [F] 26 F5
Preetz [D] 18 G2
Pregarten [A] 62 C4
Preili [LV] 198 F6
Preitenštejn [CZ] 48 D4
Prekal [AL] 146 A6
Prekestol [N] 164 B3
Preko [HR] 112 G5
Prekonoška Pećina [SRB] 146 D3
Prelau [A] 72 F1
Prelog [HR] 74 F4
Prelon [BG] 148 B4
Přelouč [CZ] 48 H4
Prem [SLO] 74 B6
Premantura [HR] 112 D3
Prémery [F] 56 D3
Premià de Mar [E] 92 E4
Premnitz [D] 34 C2
Prenjas [AL] 128 C3
Prénouvellon [F] 42 D6
Prenzlau [D] 20 E5
Preobrazhenski Manastir [BG] 148 C3
Přerov [CZ] 50 D5
Prerow [D] 20 C2
Preselentsi [BG] 148 G2
Preševo [SRB] 146 D6
Presicce [I] 122 G6
Prešov [SK] 64 G2
Pressac [F] 54 F5
Pressath [D] 48 B4
Pressbaum [A] 62 E4
Pré St–Didier [I] 70 C3
Presteid [N] 192 E4
Prestfoss [N] 170 G5
Přeštice [CZ] 48 D5
Preston [GB] 10 D3
Prestwick [GB] 8 C4
Prettau / Predoi [I] 72 E2
Prettin [D] 34 D4
Pretul [A] 62 E6
Pretzsch [D] 34 D4
Preuilly–sur–Claise [F] 54 G3
Prevalje [SLO] 74 C3
Préveli, Moní– [GR] 140 D5
Préveranges [F] 56 B5
Préveza [GR] 132 D4
Prevršac [HR] 142 A1
Prezid [HR] 74 C6
Priaranza del Bierzo [E] 78 F5
Příběnice [CZ] 48 G5
Pribeta [SK] 64 B5
Priboj [BIH] 142 E3
Priboj [MNE] 144 E2
Priboj [SRB] 146 D5
Příbor [CZ] 50 E5
Príbovce [SK] 64 C2
Příbram [CZ] 48 F5
Přibyslav [CZ] 50 A5
Prichsenstadt [D] 46 F4
Pridvorci [BIH] 144 C2
Pridvorica [SRB] 146 B3
Priego [E] 90 B6
Priego de Córdoba [E] 102 D3
Priekulė [LT] 200 D4
Priekule [LV] 198 B6
Priekuli [LV] 198 E4
Prien [D] 60 F5
Prienai [LT] 24 F1
Priene [TR] 152 D6
Priero [I] 108 G3
Prievidza [SK] 64 B3
Prignano Cilento [I] 120 F5
Prigrevica [SRB] 76 C6
Prijeboj [HR] 112 G3
Prijedor [BIH] 142 B2
Prijepolje [SRB] 146 A3
Prikraj [HR] 74 F5
Prilep [MK] 128 E2
Prilike [SRB] 146 A3
Priluka [BIH] 144 B1
Přimda [CZ] 48 C4
Primel–Trégastel [F] 40 C1
Primišlje [HR] 112 G2
Primolano [I] 72 D5
Primorsk [RUS] 22 G1
Primorsk [RUS] 178 F4
Primorsko [BG] 148 F5
Primošten [HR] 116 H1
Primstal [D] 44 G3
Prínos [GR] 130 E4
Priolo Gargallo [I] 126 G4
Prioro [E] 82 C3
Priozersk [RUS] 178 G1
Pripek [BG] 130 F1
Prirechnyj [RUS] 194 F4
Prírodne Múzeum na Dukle [SK] 52 D5
Prisad [MK] 128 E2
Prisadets [BG] 150 A1
Priseltsi [BG] 148 F3
Prisoja [MNE] 146 A5
Prisoje [BIH] 144 B1
Prisovice [CZ] 48 G2
Prissac [F] 54 G4
Priština [SRB] 146 C5
Pritzerbe [D] 34 C2
Pritzier [D] 18 H5
Pritzwalk [D] 20 B5
Privas [F] 68 F5
Priverno [I] 120 C1
Privlaka [HR] 112 F4
Privlaka [HR] 142 E2
Prizren [SRB] 146 B6
Prizzi [I] 126 D3
Prnjavor [BIH] 142 C2
Prnjavor [SRB] 142 F3
Probištip [MK] 128 F1
Probstzella [D] 46 H2
Próchoma [GR] 128 H4
Prochowice [PL] 36 B6
Pródromos [CY] 154 F5
Pródromos [GR] 132 H5
Proença–a–Nova [P] 86 E3
Profilia [GR] 154 D4
Profítis [GR] 130 B4
Profondeville [B] 30 D5
Progled [BG] 130 E1
Prohor Pčinjski [SRB] 146 D6
Prokópi [GR] 134 B4
Prokuplje [SRB] 146 D4
Prolaz [BG] 148 D3
Prómachoi [GR] 128 F3
Promachónas [GR] 130 B2
Promna [PL] 38 B4
Promnik [PL] 52 B1
Pronsfeld [D] 30 F6
Propriano [F] 114 A5
Proseč [CZ] 50 B4
Prosenik [BG] 148 F4
Prosotsáni [GR] 130 C3
Prostějov [CZ] 50 C5
Prostki [PL] 24 D4
Prószków [PL] 50 E2
Proszowice [PL] 52 B3
Protarás [CY] 154 G5
Próti [GR] 130 C3
Protići [BIH] 142 B4
Protivanov [CZ] 50 C5
Protivín [CZ] 48 F6
Protokklísi [GR] 130 H2
Prötzel [D] 34 F2
Prouille [F] 106 B4
Prousós [GR] 132 E4
Provadiya [BG] 148 F3
Provins [F] 42 H5
Prozor–Rama [BIH] 144 C1
Pruchnik [PL] 52 F4
Prudhoe [GB] 8 F6
Prudnik [PL] 50 D3
Prügy [H] 64 G4
Průhonice [CZ] 48 F4
Prüm [D] 30 F6
Pruna [E] 102 A3
Prundu [RO] 148 D1
Prunet [F] 68 B4
Prunete [F] 114 C4
Prunet–et–Belpuig [F] 92 F1
Prunetta [I] 110 E5
Prunn [D] 60 E2
Prunn, Schlob– [D] 60 E2
Prusice [PL] 36 C5
Pruské [SK] 64 B2
Pruszcz [PL] 22 D5
Pruszcz Gdański [PL] 22 E3
Pruszków [PL] 38 B3
Prutting [D] 60 F5
Prüzen [D] 20 B4
Pruzhany [BY] 38 H1
Pruzhicy [RUS] 178 F6
Pruzhicy [RUS] 178 F6
Pryluky [UA] 202 E7
Prypyat' [UA] 202 D7
Przasnysz [PL] 22 H6
Przechlewo [PL] 22 C4
Przedbórz [PL] 36 H6
Przedecz [PL] 36 F3
Przełęk [PL] 50 D3
Przemków [PL] 36 A5
Przemocze [PL] 20 F5
Przemyśl [PL] 52 F4
Przemyśl [PL] 52 F4
Przesmyki [PL] 38 E2
Przewale [PL] 52 G2
Przewłoka [PL] 38 E4
Przeworsk [PL] 52 E3
Przewóz [PL] 34 G5
Przezmark [PL] 22 F4
Przeźmierowo [PL] 36 C2
Przodkowo [PL] 22 D2
Przybiernów [PL] 20 F4
Przybychowo [PL] 36 C1
Przygodzice [PL] 36 E5
Przyłęk [PL] 52 D3
Przylesie [PL] 50 D2
Przystajń [PL] 50 F1
Przysucha [PL] 38 B5
Przyszów [PL] 52 D2
Przyszowa [PL] 52 B5
Przytoczna [PL] 36 A2
Przytoczno [PL] 38 D4
Przytuły [PL] 24 D5
Przytyk [PL] 38 B5
Przywory [PL] 50 E2
Pšaca [MK] 146 E6
Psachná [GR] 134 B4
Psará [GR] 134 F4
Psarádes [GR] 128 D4
Psarshai [BY] 200 H6
Psáthi [GR] 138 D4
Psathópyrgos [GR] 132 F5
Psathotópi [GR] 132 D3
Pskov [RUS] 198 G3
Psychikó [GR] 132 G2
Psychró [GR] 140 F5
Pszczew [PL] 36 A2
Pszczyna [PL] 50 G4
Pszów [A] 60 H6
Pszów [PL] 50 F4
Pteléa [GR] 130 D2
Ptolemaïda [GR] 128 F5
Ptóo [GR] 134 B5
Ptuj [SLO] 74 E4
Ptujska Gora [SLO] 74 E4
Puchberg [A] 62 E5
Púchov [SK] 50 F6
Pučišća [HR] 144 A2
Puck [PL] 22 D1
Puçol [E] 98 F4
Pudasjärvi [FIN] 196 E3
Puebla de Alcocer [E] 96 C3
Puebla de Don Fadrique [E] 102 H2
Puebla de Don Rodrigo [E] 96 D3
Puebla de Guzmán [E] 94 E4
Puebla de la Calzada [E] 94 G1
Puebla de la Reina [E] 94 H2
Puebla del Brollón / A Pobra de Brollón [E] 78 D4
Puebla del Caramiñal / Pobra do Caramiñal [E] 78 B3
Puebla de Lillo [E] 82 C3
Puebla del Maestre [E] 94 H4
Puebla del Príncipe [E] 96 G6
Puebla de Obando [E] 86 G6
Puebla de Sanabria [E] 78 E6
Puebla de Vallés [E] 88 G4
Pueblica de Valverde [E] 80 H4
Pueblonuevo del Guadiana [E] 94 G1
Pueblonuevo del Guadiana [E] 94 G1
Puente Almuhey [E] 82 C4
Puente de Domingo Flórez [E] 78 E5
Puente de Génave [E] 96 G6
Puente de Montañana [E] 92 B2
Puente Genil [E] 102 C2
Puente la Reina / Gares [E] 84 B4
Puente la Reina de Jaca [E] 84 D5
Puentelarra [E] 82 G5
Puentenansa [E] 82 D3
Puente Romano [E] 86 G4
Puentes de García Rodríguez / As Pontes de García Rodríguez [E] 78 D2
Puente Viesgo [E] 82 E3
Puerta de Levante [E] 98 E5
Puerto Banús [E] 102 A5
Puerto Castilla [E] 88 C5
Puerto d. Carmen [E] 100 E6
Puerto de Béjar [E] 88 B4
Puerto de la Cruz [E] 100 B5
Puerto del Rosario [E] 100 E6
Puerto de Mazarrón [E] 104 C4
Puerto de Mogán [E] 100 C6
Puerto de Santa Cruz [E] 96 B2
Puerto de San Vicente [E] 96 C2
Puerto Lajas [E] 100 E6
Puerto Lápice [E] 96 F3
Puertollano [E] 96 E5
Puerto Lumbreras [E] 104 A4
Puerto Real [E] 100 F4
Puerto Rey [E] 104 A5
Puerto Rico [E] 100 C6
Puertoserrano [E] 100 H3
Pueyo, Monasterio de– [E] 90 G3
Puffendorf [D] 30 F4
Puget–sur–Argens [F] 108 D5
Puget–Théniers [F] 108 E4
Puget–Ville [F] 108 C5
Pugnochiuso [I] 116 H6
Puhja [EST] 198 F3
Puhos [FIN] 188 F4
Puhos [FIN] 196 E3
Puig [E] 98 F4
Puigcerdà [E] 92 E1
Puig–reig [E] 92 E3
Puise [EST] 198 D2
Puiseaux [F] 42 F5
Puivert [F] 106 B5
Pujjas [LV] 198 C6
Pukavik [S] 158 E1
Pukë [AL] 128 B1
Pukiš [BIH] 142 E3
Pukkila [FIN] 178 B3
Pula [HR] 112 D3
Pula [I] 118 C7
Puławy [PL] 38 D5
Pulborough [GB] 14 D5
Pulgar [E] 96 E2
Pulju [FIN] 194 C5
Pulkau [A] 62 E3
Pulkkila [FIN] 176 H2
Pulkkila [FIN] 196 D5
Pulkovo [RUS] 178 H5
Pulpí [E] 104 B4
Pulsa [FIN] 178 D2
Pulsnitz [D] 34 F6
Pulsujärvi [S] 192 G4
Pułtusk [PL] 38 B1
Pumpėnai [LT] 200 F4
Pumpula [FIN] 178 D2
Punat [HR] 112 F2
Punkaharju [FIN] 188 F5
Punkalaidun [FIN] 176 E2
Punta, Château de la– [F] 114 A4
Punta Ala [I] 114 E2
Punta de Moraira [E] 104 F2
Puntagorda [E] 100 A4
Punta Križa [HR] 112 E3

Punta Križa [HR] 112 E3

Punta Marina [I] 110 H4
Punta Prima [E] 104 H5
Puntas de Calnegre [E] 104 B4
Punta Umbría [E] 94 E6
Punxin [E] 78 C5
Puokio [FIN] 196 E4
Puolanka [FIN] 196 E4
Puoltikasvaara [S] 192 G5
Puottaure [S] 190 H2
Puralankylä [FIN] 186 F2
Purbach [A] 62 F5
Purchena [E] 102 G4
Pürgg [A] 62 B6
Purgstall [A] 62 D5
Purkersdorf [A] 62 E4
Purkjaur [S] 190 H1
Purmerend [NL] 16 D4
Purmojärvi [FIN] 186 D2
Pürnstein [A] 62 B3
Purnumukka [FIN] 194 D5
Purnuvaara [FIN] 196 F2
Purroy [E] 90 D4
Purroy de Solana [E] 90 H3
Purujärvi [FIN] 188 F5
Purullena [E] 102 F4
Pürvomay [BG] 148 C6
Puša [LV] 198 G6
Puščava [SLO] 74 D3
Pushkin [RUS] 178 H5
Pushkinskiye Gory [RUS] 198 H4
Püski [H] 62 G5
Puškino [RUS] 202 F3
Püspökladány [H] 76 G1
Pustevny [CZ] 50 E5
Pustków [PL] 52 D3
Pustoshka [RUS] 202 B3
Pusula [FIN] 176 G4
Puszcza [PL] 24 D2
Puszczykowo [PL] 36 C3
Pusztamérges [H] 76 D4
Pusztamiske [H] 74 H2
Pusztamonostor [H] 64 D6
Pusztaszemes [H] 76 A3
Putaja [FIN] 176 E1
Putanges-Pont-Ecrepin [F] 26 F5
Putbus [D] 20 D2
Putgarten [D] 20 D1
Putignano [I] 122 E3
Putignano, Grotta di- [I] 122 E3
Putikko [FIN] 188 F5
Putim [CZ] 48 F6
Putim [CZ] 48 F6
Putinci [SRB] 142 G2
Putineiu [RO] 148 B2
Putineiu [RO] 148 C1
Putkela [FIN] 188 H2
Putlitz [D] 20 B5
Putnok [H] 64 E4
Puttelange [F] 44 G4
Putten [NL] 16 E4
Puttgarden [D] 20 A2
Putyvl' [UA] 202 E6
Putzu Idu [I] 118 B5
Puumala [FIN] 188 E6
Puurmani [EST] 198 F2
Puvyalador [F] 92 E1
Puyguilhem [F] 66 F2
Puy-Guillaume [F] 68 D2
Puykkola [RUS] 188 G4
Puylaurens [F] 106 B3
Puy-l'Evêque [F] 66 F5
Puymorens, Col de- [F] 92 E1
Puzzittu, Nuraghe- [I] 118 E4
Pwllheli [GB] 10 B4
Pyaozerskiy [RUS] 196 G2
Pyaski [BY] 24 H5
Pyatchino [RUS] 178 F5
Pyatidorozhnoye [RUS] 22 G2
Pydhaitsi [UA] 204 C2
Pydnay [TR] 154 F3
Pyelishcha [BY] 38 G2
Pyhäjärvi [FIN] 196 E6
Pyhäjoki [FIN] 176 D3
Pyhäjoki [FIN] 196 C5
Pyhäkylä [FIN] 196 F3
Pyhältö [FIN] 178 D3
Pyhämaa [FIN] 176 C3
Pyhänsivu [FIN] 196 D4
Pyhäntä [FIN] 196 E5
Pyhäntaka [FIN] 178 B2
Pyhäranta [FIN] 176 C3
Pyhäsalmi [FIN] 196 E6
Pyhäselkä [FIN] 188 F3
Pyhtää / Pyttis [FIN] 178 C4
Pyla [CY] 154 G5
Pyla-sur-Mer [F] 66 B3
Pylés [GR] 140 H3
Pýli [GR] 128 D4
Pýli [GR] 132 E2
Pýli [GR] 134 B6
Pylí [GR] 154 B2
Pylkönmäki [FIN] 186 F3
Pýlos [GR] 136 C4
Pyntäinen [FIN] 186 B6
Pyöreinen [FIN] 188 C1
Pyörny [FIN] 186 B3
Pyramides [CH] 70 D2
Pyrgá [CY] 154 G5
Pyrgadíkia [GR] 130 C5
Pyrgáki [GR] 138 F3
Pyrgío [GR] 134 G5
Pýrgoi [GR] 128 F4
Pýrgos [GR] 128 H4
Pýrgos [GR] 136 C2
Pýrgos [GR] 138 H1
Pýrgos [GR] 140 E5
Pýrgos Gerakioú [GR] 136 E4
Pyrsógianni [GR] 128 D6
Pyrzyce [PL] 20 F6
Pyšely [CZ] 48 G4
Pyskowice [PL] 50 F3
Pytalovo [RUS] 198 G4
Pythagóreio [GR] 152 C6
Pyttis / Pyhtää [FIN] 178 C4
Pyyrinlahti [FIN] 186 G3
Pyzdry [PL] 36 D3

Q

Qiselay-et-Graciaux [F] 58 B4
Quadri [I] 116 D5
Quakenbrück [D] 18 C6
Qualitz [D] 20 B3
Quarona [I] 70 E4
Quarrata [I] 110 E5
Quarré-les-Tombes [F] 56 F3
Quarteira [P] 94 C5
Quartu Sant'Elena [I] 118 D7
Qudeschild [NL] 16 D2
Quebradas [P] 86 C4
Quedlinburg [D] 34 A4
Quelaines-St. Gault [F] 40 H5
Queluz [P] 86 B5
Quercamps [F] 28 E2
Quercianella [I] 110 D6
Querenca [P] 94 C5
Querfurt [D] 34 B5
Quéribus, Château de- [F] 106 C5
Quermanço [E] 92 G2
Quéroy, Grottes du- [F] 66 E1
Quesada [E] 102 F2
Questembert [F] 40 E5
Quettehou [F] 26 E2
Quiberon [F] 40 C5
Quickborn [D] 18 F4
Quillan [F] 106 B5
Quimper [F] 40 B3
Quimperlé [F] 40 C4
Quin Abbey [IRL] 2 C6
Quinéville [F] 26 E2
Quingey [F] 58 B5
Quinta da Bacalhôa [P] 86 B6
Quintana de la Serena [E] 96 B3
Quintana del Castillo [E] 78 G5
Quintana del Puente [E] 82 D6
Quintanaortuño [E] 82 E5
Quintanar de la Orden [E] 96 G3
Quintanar de la Sierra [E] 90 A2
Quintanar del Rey [E] 98 B4
Quintana Redonda [E] 90 B3
Quintanilha [P] 80 G4
Quintanilla de las Viñas [E] 88 H1
Quintanilla de Onésimo [E] 88 F2
Quintanilla-Sobresierra [E] 82 E5
Quintin [F] 26 A4
Quinto [E] 90 F4
Quiroga [E] 78 E5
Quirra, Castello di- [I] 118 E6
Quissac [F] 106 F3

R

Råå [S] 156 H2
Raab [A] 62 A4
Raabs an der Thaya [A] 62 D2
Raahe / Brahestad [FIN] 196 C4
Rääkkylä [FIN] 188 F3
Raalte [NL] 16 F4
Raanujärvi [FIN] 194 C7
Raattama [FIN] 194 C5
Rab [HR] 112 F3
Rabac [HR] 112 E2
Råbäck [S] 166 E5
Rabade [E] 78 E3
Rábade [E] 78 E3
Rábafüzes [H] 74 F2
Rábahidvég [H] 74 F2
Rabastens [F] 106 B2
Rabastens-de-Bigorre [F] 84 F3
Rabat [M] 126 C6
Rábatamasi [H] 62 G6
Rabbalshede [S] 166 C5
Rabča [SK] 50 G5
Rabí [CZ] 48 E6
Rábida, Monasterio de la- [E] 94 E6
Rabisha [BG] 146 E2
Rabka [PL] 50 H5
Rabrovo [BG] 146 E2
Rabštejn [CZ] 50 A4
Rabsztyn [PL] 50 H3
Råby-Rönö [S] 168 C4
Rača [SK] 62 G4
Rača [SRB] 146 C4
Rača [SRB] 146 C1
Rácalmás [H] 76 C2
Racalmuto [I] 126 D4
Racconigi [I] 108 G2
Rače [SLO] 74 E4
Ráches [GR] 132 H4
Raciąż [PL] 36 H1
Raciążek [PL] 36 F1
Racibórz [PL] 50 E4
Ráckeve [H] 76 C2
Racławice [PL] 52 B3
Rączki [PL] 22 G5
Raczki [PL] 24 E3
Råda [S] 172 F5
Radalj [SRB] 142 E3
Radanje [MK] 128 G1
Radanovići [MNE] 144 D4
Radashkovichy [BY] 202 B5
Rădăuţi [RO] 204 D3
Radawnica [PL] 22 B5
Radcliffe-on-Trent [GB] 10 F5
Raddusa [I] 126 F3
Rade [D] 18 F4
Råde [N] 166 B3
Radeberg [D] 34 F6
Radebeul [D] 34 E6
Radeburg [D] 34 E6
Radeče [SLO] 74 D5
Radęcin [PL] 20 H6
Radegast [D] 34 C4
Radehiv [UA] 202 B8
Radenci [SLO] 74 E3
Radenthein [A] 72 H3
Radevormwald [D] 30 H4
Radimlja [BIH] 144 C3
Radioteleskop Effelsberg [D] 30 G5
Radisne [UA] 204 H1
Radiviliv [UA] 202 B8
Radko Dimitrievo [BG] 148 E3
Radków [PL] 50 B2
Radlje ob Dravi [SLO] 74 D3
Radłów [PL] 50 F1
Radmirje [SLO] 74 C4
Radna [RO] 76 H4
Radnejaur [S] 190 G2
Radnevo [BG] 148 D5
Radnica [PL] 34 H3
Radnice [CZ] 48 E4
Radolfzell [D] 58 G4
Radom [PL] 38 C5
Rådom [S] 172 E5
Radomin [PL] 22 F6
Radomir [AL] 128 C1
Radomir [BG] 146 F5
Radomiru [RO] 146 G1
Radomsko [PL] 36 G6
Radomyshl' [UA] 202 D7
Radomyšl Wielki [PL] 52 C3
Radošina [SK] 64 A3
Radošovce [SK] 62 G3
Radostowo [PL] 22 H3
Radoszewice [PL] 36 F6
Radoszyce [PL] 38 A6
Radotín [CZ] 48 F4
Radovanu [RO] 146 F1
Radovašnica [SRB] 142 F3
Radovets [BG] 150 A1
Radovići [MNE] 144 D4
Radoviš [MK] 128 G2
Radovljica [SLO] 74 B4
Radowo Wielkie [PL] 20 G4
Radruz [PL] 52 G3
Radstadt [A] 72 H1
Radstock [GB] 12 G3
Radučić [HR] 112 H5
Raduczyce [PL] 36 F6
Radujevac [SRB] 146 E1
Radun' [BY] 24 H3
Radunci [BG] 148 C4
Raduša [MK] 146 C6
Radviliškis [LT] 200 F4
Radwanca [PL] 36 H4
Radymno [PL] 52 F4
Radzanów [PL] 22 G6
Radziądz [PL] 36 C5
Radziejów [PL] 36 F2
Radziłow [PL] 24 D5
Radziwie [PL] 36 G2
Radzovce [SK] 64 D4
Radzymin [PL] 38 B2
Radzyń Chełmiński [PL] 22 E5
Radzyń Podlaski [PL] 38 E4
Raec [MK] 128 F2
Ræhr [DK] 160 C3
Raesfeld [D] 16 G6
Raffadali [I] 126 D4
Rafína [GR] 134 C6
Rafsbotn [N] 194 B3
Raftsjöhöjden [S] 182 H1
Ragaciems [LV] 198 D5
Ragály [H] 64 E4
Ragama [E] 88 D3
Ragana [LV] 198 E5
Rågeleje [DK] 156 G1
Råglanda [S] 166 E3
Ragunda [S] 184 D2
Ragusa [I] 126 F5
Raguva [LT] 200 F4
Rahachow [BY] 202 C5
Raharney [IRL] 2 E5
Rahaugen [N] 166 C3
Rahden [D] 32 E2
Rahikka [FIN] 186 B4
Råholt [N] 172 C5
Raijala [FIN] 176 E2
Raimat [E] 90 H4
Rain [D] 60 D2
Raippaluoto / Replot [FIN] 186 A2
Raippo [FIN] 178 E2
Räisälä [FIN] 194 E7
Raisio / Reso [FIN] 176 D4
Raistakka [FIN] 194 E8
Raitaperä [FIN] 186 E3
Raival [F] 44 D4
Raivala [FIN] 186 C5
Raivala [FIN] 186 C6
Raja-Jooseppi [FIN] 194 E5
Rajäkoski [RUS] 194 E4
Rajamäki [FIN] 176 G4
Rajanovci [BG] 146 E2
Rajastrand [S] 190 E5
Rajë [AL] 146 A6
Rajec [SK] 64 B2
Rajecké Teplice [SK] 64 B2
Rajgród [PL] 24 E4
Rajić [HR] 142 B1
Rajka [H] 62 G5
Rajkova Pećina [SRB] 146 D1
Raka [SLO] 74 D5
Rakaka [H] 64 F3
Rakamaz [H] 64 G4
Rakek [SLO] 74 B5
Rakhiv [UA] 204 C3
Rakitna [SLO] 74 B5
Rakitnica [BG] 148 C5
Rakitovec [SLO] 112 D1
Rakitovo [BG] 148 A6
Rakke [EST] 198 F2
Rakkestad [N] 166 C2
Rákóczifalva [H] 76 E2
Rakoniewice [PL] 36 B3
Rakoš [SRB] 146 B5
Rakoszyce [PL] 36 C6
Rakova [SK] 50 F5
Rakovica [HR] 112 G2
Rakovitsa [BG] 146 E2
Rakovník [CZ] 48 E3
Rakovo [BG] 148 D4
Rakovski [BG] 148 B5
Rakovskovo [BG] 148 F3
Raków [PL] 52 C2
Raksi [H] 76 A4
Rakvere [EST] 198 F1
Ralja [SRB] 142 G3
Rälla [S] 162 G5
Ramacastañas [E] 88 D5
Ramacca [I] 126 F4
Rämälä [FIN] 188 D5
Ramales de la Victoria [E] 82 F3
Ramallosa [E] 78 B5
Ramallosa / Teo [E] 78 C3
Ramberg [N] 192 C4
Rambervillers [F] 44 F6
Rambin [D] 20 D2
Rambouillet [F] 42 E4
Rameshki [RUS] 202 E2
Ramfo [N] 180 G3
Ramirás [E] 78 C5
Ramkvilla [S] 162 E4
Ramljane [HR] 142 A5
Rämmen [S] 166 F1
Rammerskirchen [D] 30 G4
Ramnäs [S] 168 B2
Rämne [S] 166 C4
Râmnicu Sărat [RO] 204 E5
Râmnicu Vâlcea [RO] 204 D5
Ramnoús [GR] 134 C5
Ramosch [CH] 72 B2
Ramsau [A] 72 H1
Ramsberg [S] 166 H2
Ramsele [S] 184 D1
Ramsey [GBM] 8 C6
Ramsgate [GB] 14 G5
Rämshyttan [S] 172 H5
Ramsjö [S] 184 C5
Ramsli [N] 164 C4
Ramstein [D] 44 H3
Ramundberget [S] 182 D3
Ramvik [S] 184 F3
Ramygala [LT] 200 F4
Ramzova-Petrikov [CZ] 50 C3
Råna [N] 164 C5
Ranalt [A] 72 D2
Rånäs [S] 168 E2
Rancířov [CZ] 62 D2
Randaberg [N] 164 A3
Randalstown [NIR] 2 G3
Randamonys [LT] 24 G3
Randan [F] 68 D1
Randazzo [I] 124 A8
Rånddalen [S] 182 F5
Randegg [A] 62 C5
Randen [N] 180 G5
Randers [DK] 160 D5
Randijaur [S] 190 H1
Randín [E] 78 C6
Randos [GR] 128 D6
Randsjö [S] 182 F5
Randsverk [N] 180 G6
Råneå [S] 196 B2
Ranemsletta [N] 190 C5
Rânes [F] 26 F5
Ranft [CH] 58 F6
Rångedala [S] 162 B2
Rangendingen [D] 58 G2
Rangstrup [DK] 156 C3
Rani List [BG] 130 F1
Raniżów [PL] 52 D3
Rankinen [FIN] 196 D4
Rankweil [A] 58 H5
Rannankyla [FIN] 186 D4
Rannanmäki [FIN] 176 E3
Rannsundet [S] 182 E5
Ranntila [FIN] 194 C4
Ransäter [S] 166 F2
Ransby [S] 172 E4
Ranshofen [A] 60 G4
Ransta [S] 168 C2
Rantajärvi [S] 194 B8
Rantasalmi [FIN] 188 E4
Rantsila [FIN] 196 D4
Rantun [D] 156 A4
Ranua [FIN] 196 D2
Ranum [DK] 160 D4
Rånvassbotn [N] 192 E4
Ranzo [I] 108 G4
Raon-l'Etape [F] 44 F6
Ràossi [I] 72 C5
Rapallo [I] 110 B3
Räpina [EST] 198 G3
Rapla [EST] 198 D2
Rapolla [I] 120 G3
Raposa [P] 86 C5
Rapotice [CZ] 50 B6
Rappenloch-Schlucht [A] 60 B6
Rapperswil [CH] 58 G5
Rappottenstein [A] 62 D3
Rapsáni [GR] 132 G1
Raron [CH] 70 E2
Raša [HR] 112 E2
Räsälä [FIN] 188 D3
Rascafría [E] 88 F4
Raseiniai [LT] 200 E4
Råsele [S] 190 F5
Rašica [SLO] 74 C5
Rasimbegov [MK] 128 F3
Rasines [E] 82 F3
Rasivaara [FIN] 188 F3
Raška [SRB] 146 B4
Rasktinkylä [FIN] 196 G5
Raslavice [SK] 52 D6
Řásná [CZ] 48 H6
Rasony [BY] 198 H6
Rasovo [BG] 146 F2
Raspay [E] 104 C2
Rasquera [E] 90 H6
Rast [RO] 146 F2
Rästa [S] 166 H3
Rastatt [D] 46 B6
Råsted [DK] 160 D5
Rastede [D] 18 C5
Rastenfeld [A] 62 D3
Rasteš [MK] 128 D1
Rasti [FIN] 188 F4
Rastošnica [BIH] 142 E3
Rastovac [MNE] 144 D3
Rasueros [E] 88 D3
Rasy [PL] 36 G5
Raszków [PL] 36 D4
Rätan [S] 182 G4
Ratan [S] 196 A5
Rateče [SLO] 72 H3
Ratekau [D] 18 G3
Rathangen [IRL] 2 E6
Rathcoole [IRL] 2 F6
Rathcormack [IRL] 4 D5
Rathcroghan [IRL] 2 D4
Rathdrum [IRL] 4 G4
Rathenow [D] 34 C2
Rathfran Abbey [IRL] 2 C3
Rathfriland [NIR] 2 G4
Rathkeale [IRL] 4 C3
Rath Luirc / Charleville [IRL] 4 C4
Rathmelton [IRL] 2 F2
Rathmolyon [IRL] 2 F5
Rathmullan / Rathmullen [IRL] 2 F2
Rathmullen / Rathmullan [IRL] 2 F2
Rathnew [IRL] 4 G4
Rath of Mullamast [IRL] 4 F3
Rathvilty [IRL] 4 F4
Ratiboř [CZ] 50 E6
Ratingen [D] 30 G3
Ratipera [FIN] 186 E2
Ratková [SK] 64 E3
Ratkovo [SRB] 142 F1
Ratne [UA] 38 H4
Ratsichy [BY] 24 F4
Rattenberg [A] 60 E6
Ratten-Unterdorf [A] 74 E1
Rattersdorf [A] 74 F1
Rattosjärvi [FIN] 194 C7
Rättvik [S] 172 H3
Ratzeburg [D] 18 G4
Raubling [D] 60 F5
Raudaskylä [FIN] 196 D5
Raudeberg [N] 180 B4
Raudlia [N] 190 E2
Raufaröfn [IS] 192 C2
Raufoss [N] 172 B3
Rauha [FIN] 178 E1
Rauhala [FIN] 194 C6
Rauhaniemi [FIN] 188 E5
Raulach [F] 68 B4
Rauland Høyfjellshotell [N] 164 E1
Rauma / Raumo [FIN] 176 C2
Raumala [FIN] 176 E5
Raumo / Rauma [FIN] 176 C2
Raumünzach [D] 58 F1
Rauna [LV] 198 E4
Rauris [A] 72 G1
Raustå [N] 170 F5
Rautajärvi [FIN] 176 G1
Rautalampi [FIN] 186 H3
Rautaniemi [FIN] 176 E2
Rautas [S] 192 G5
Rautavaara [FIN] 196 F6
Rautila [FIN] 176 D4
Rautio [FIN] 196 C5
Rautjärvi [FIN] 178 F1
Rauvatn [N] 190 E2
Ravanica, Manastir- [SRB] 146 C2
Ravanička Pećina [SRB] 146 D2
Ravanusa [I] 126 E4
Rava-Rus'ka [UA] 52 G3
Ravattila [FIN] 178 E2
Ravazd [H] 62 H6
Ravča [HR] 144 B2
Ravda [BG] 148 F4
Ravel [F] 68 D2
Ravello [I] 120 E4
Rävemåla [S] 162 E5
Ravenglass [GB] 10 D2
Ravenna [I] 110 H4
Ravensbrück [D] 20 D5
Ravensburg [D] 46 C6
Ravensburg [D] 58 H4
Ravioskorpi [FIN] 178 B1
Rävmarken [S] 166 C4
Ravna Dubrava [SRB] 146 E4
Ravna Reka [SRB] 146 D2
Ravne [SLO] 74 C3
Ravnholt [DK] 156 E3
Ravno [BIH] 144 C3
Ravno Rašće [HR] 142 A1
Ravno Selo [SRB] 142 F1
Rawa Mazowiecka [PL] 38 A4
Rawicz [PL] 36 C5
Rayleigh [GB] 14 F4
Rayol [F] 108 D6
Räyrinki [FIN] 186 D1
Räyskälä [FIN] 176 G3
Rayvio [RUS] 188 G5
Razboj [BIH] 142 C2
Razbojna [SRB] 146 C3
Razbojna Dupka [MK] 128 E2
Razdol'e [UA] 204 H3
Razdol'ye [RUS] 178 G3
Razdrto [SLO] 74 B6
Razgrad [BG] 148 D2
Razhanka [BY] 24 H4
Ražica [BG] 148 F4
Razkrižje [SLO] 74 F4
Razlovci [MK] 128 G1
Razmetelevo [RUS] 178 H4
Ráztočno [SK] 64 B3
Reading [GB] 14 D4
Réalmont [F] 106 B3
Realp [CH] 70 F1
Reanaclogheen / Ré na gCloichín [IRL] 4 D5
Réau, Ancient Abbaye de la- [F] 54 F5
Réaup-Lisse [F] 66 D6
Reay [GB] 6 E2
Rebais [F] 42 H4
Rebolledo de la Torre [E] 82 D4
Reboly [RUS] 196 G5
Rebordelo [P] 80 E3
Rebrovo [BG] 146 F4
Rebŭrkovo [BG] 146 G4
Reç [AL] 128 C1
Recanati [I] 116 C1
Rečane [SRB] 146 C6
Recas [E] 96 F1
Recaş [RO] 76 H5
Recea [RO] 146 E1
Recey-sur-Ource [F] 56 G2
Rechnitz [A] 74 F1
Rechytsa [BY] 202 D6
Recke [D] 32 C2
Recklinghausen [D] 30 H2
Recoaro Terme [I] 72 C5
Recologne [F] 58 B4
Recópolis [E] 88 H6
Recsk [H] 64 E5
Recueda [E] 90 A3
Recz [PL] 20 G5
Ręczno [PL] 36 H6
Reda [PL] 22 D2
Redalen [N] 172 B3
Redcar [GB] 10 G2
Redditch [GB] 12 H1
Redea [RO] 148 A1
Redefin [D] 18 H5
Rédics [H] 74 F3
Redipuglia [I] 72 H5
Redon [F] 40 E5
Redondela [E] 78 B4
Redondo [P] 94 E1
Redruth [GB] 12 C5
Rędzikowo [PL] 22 B2
Rees [D] 16 F6
Reetz [D] 20 B5
Refnes [N] 192 E3
Reftele [S] 162 C4
Regalbuto [I] 126 F3
Regéc [H] 64 G4
Regen [D] 60 H2
Regensburg [D] 48 B6
Regenstauf [D] 48 B6
Reggello [I] 110 F6
Réggio di Calábria [I] 124 C7
Reggiolo [I] 110 E2
Réggio nell'Emilia [I] 110 E3
Reghin [RO] 204 C4
Regis-Breitingen [D] 34 C6
Regkínio [GR] 132 H4
Regna [S] 168 A4
Regonkylä [FIN] 186 C3
Reguengos de Monsaraz [P] 94 E2
Rehau [D] 48 B3
Rehborn [D] 44 H3
Rehden [D] 32 E1
Rehna [D] 18 H4
Reichéa [GR] 136 F4
Reichenau [D] 58 G4
Reichenau an der Rax [A] 62 E6
Reichenbach [D] 32 F5
Reichenbach [D] 34 G6
Reichenbach [D] 48 C2
Reichenberg [D] 34 F2
Reichertshausen [D] 60 E3
Reichertshofen [D] 60 E3
Reichstett [F] 44 H6
Reigate [GB] 14 E5
Reigersburg [A] 62 E2
Reignier [F] 70 B2
Reijola [FIN] 188 F3
Reila [FIN] 176 C3
Reillanne [F] 108 C3
Reims [F] 44 B3
Rein [A] 74 D2
Reinach [CH] 58 E4
Reinach [CH] 58 F5
Reinberg [D] 20 D3
Reine [N] 192 C5
Reinfeld [D] 18 G3
Reinhardshagen [D] 32 F4
Reinheim [D] 46 C3
Reinosa [E] 82 E4
Reinsfeld [D] 44 G2
Reinslisætra [N] 182 B5
Reinsvik [N] 180 F2
Reinsvoll [N] 172 B4
Reirat [N] 190 D4
Reisach [A] 72 G3
Reisbach [D] 60 G3
Reischach [D] 60 G4
Reischenhart [D] 60 F5
Reisjärvi [FIN] 196 D6
Reitan [N] 182 C3
Reit im Winkl [D] 60 F5
Reittiö [FIN] 188 D1
Reitzehain [D] 48 D2
Rejmyre [S] 168 B4
Rejowiec [PL] 38 F6
Rejowiec Fabryczny [PL] 38 F6
Rejštejn [CZ] 48 E6
Reka [HR] 74 F5
Reka [SLO] 74 A5
Rekeland [N] 164 B5
Reken [D] 16 G6
Rekijoki [FIN] 176 F4
Rekovac [SRB] 146 C2
Rekvik [N] 192 F2
Rel' [RUS] 198 G1
Rely [F] 28 E3
Remagen [D] 30 H5
Rémalard [F] 26 G6
Remels [D] 18 C4
Remeskylä [FIN] 196 E5
Remetea Mare [RO] 76 G5
Remich [L] 44 F3
Remígia, Cova- [E] 98 G2
Remiremont [F] 58 C3
Remmet [S] 182 G5
Remnes [N] 190 D2
Remolinos [E] 90 E3
Remouchamps [B] 30 E5
Remoulins [F] 106 G3
Remscheid [D] 30 H4
Remte [LV] 198 C5
Rémuzat [F] 108 B2
Rena [N] 172 C2
Ré na gCloichín / Reanaclogheen [IRL] 4 D5
Renaison [F] 68 E2
Renaix (Ronse) [B] 28 G3
Renålandet [S] 190 E6
Renbygda [N] 182 C3
Renceni [LV] 198 E4
Renchen [D] 58 F1
Renda [LV] 198 C5
Rendal [N] 180 G2
Rende [I] 124 D4
Rendsburg [D] 18 F2
Renfors [S] 190 H4
Rengsjö [S] 174 D2
Reni [UA] 204 E4
Renko [FIN] 176 G3
Renkum [NL] 16 E5
Rennebu [N] 180 H3
Rennerod [D] 46 B1
Rennertshofen [D] 60 D2
Rennes [F] 26 C6
Rennweg [A] 72 H2
Renon / Ritten [I] 72 D3
Rens [DK] 156 B4
Renså [N] 192 E4
Rentería / Errenteria [E] 84 B2
Rentína [GR] 130 C4
Rentína [GR] 132 F3
Rentjärn [S] 190 G4
Renträsk [S] 190 H3
Renvyle [IRL] 2 B4
Reolid [E] 96 H6
Répáshuta [H] 64 F5
Répcelak [H] 74 G1
Repino [RUS] 178 G4
Replot / Raippaluoto [FIN] 186 A2
Repo-Aslak [FIN] 194 D4
Repojoki [FIN] 194 C5
Reposaari [FIN] 176 C1
Reppen [N] 170 D1
République, Col de la- [F] 68 F4
Repvåg [N] 194 C2
Requena [E] 98 D4
Réquista [F] 106 C2
Rerik [D] 20 A3
Reşadiye [TR] 154 C2
Resana [I] 72 E6
Resanovci [BIH] 142 A4
Resavska Pećina [SRB] 146 D2
Resele [S] 184 E2
Resen [MK] 128 D3
Resende [E] 80 C4
Reshetylivka [UA] 202 F7
Reşiţa [RO] 204 B5
Reskjem [N] 164 F2
Resko [PL] 20 G4
Resmo [S] 162 G5
Resna [MNE] 144 D4
Reso / Raisio [FIN] 176 D4
Ressons [F] 28 E6
Reszel [PL] 24 B3
Retama [E] 96 D3
Retama, Garganta de- [E] 96 D3
Retamal de Llerena [E] 96 A4
Retamar [E] 102 G5
Retamosa [E] 96 C1
Retford [GB] 10 F5
Rethel [F] 44 C2
Rethem [D] 18 E6
Réthymno [GR] 140 D4
Retie [B] 30 D3
Retiers [F] 40 G4
Retortillo de Soria [E] 90 A3
Retournac [F] 68 E4
Rétság [H] 64 C5
Retuerta [E] 88 H1
Retuerta del Bullaque [E] 96 E2
Retuneri [FIN] 188 E2
Retz [A] 62 E3
Reuilly [F] 56 B3
Reus [E] 92 C5
Reusel [NL] 30 E3
Reuterstadt Stavenhagen [D] 20 C4
Reutlingen [D] 58 H2
Reutte [A] 60 C6
Revel [F] 106 B4
Révfülöp [H] 74 H3
Révigny-sur-Ornain [F] 44 C4
Revin [F] 44 C1
Revište [SK] 64 B3
Řevničov [CZ] 48 E3
Revò [I] 72 C3
Revonkylä [FIN] 188 G2
Revonlahti [FIN] 196 D4
Revsnes [N] 170 D2
Revsnes [N] 190 B5
Revsund [S] 182 H3
Revúca [SK] 64 E3
Rewal [PL] 20 F3
Rexbo [S] 172 H4
Rexnin [AL] 128 B6
Reykjalið [IS] 192 C2
Reykjavík [IS] 192 A3

Rey Moro, Cueva del- [E] 98 D6
Rēzekne [LV] 198 G5
Rezovo [BG] 148 G5
Rgotina [SRB] 146 E2
Rgotina [SRB] 204 C6
Rhade [D] 18 E5
Rhayader [GB] 10 C6
Rheda [D] 32 D3
Rhede [D] 16 G6
Rheinau [D] 44 H6
Rheinbach [D] 30 G5
Rheinberg [D] 30 G2
Rheinböllen [D] 44 H2
Rheindahlen [D] 30 F3
Rheine [D] 16 H5
Rheinfall [D] 58 F4
Rheinfelden [CH] 58 E4
Rheinfelden (Baden) [D] 58 E4
Rheinsberg [D] 20 C6
Rhein-Weser-Turm [D] 32 D5
Rheinzabern [D] 46 B5
Rhêmes N. D. [I] 70 C4
Rhenen [NL] 16 E5
Rhens [D] 30 H6
Rheydt [D] 30 G3
Rhinau [F] 58 E2
Rhinow [D] 34 C1
Rho [I] 70 G5
Rhoon [NL] 16 C5
Rhosneigr [GB] 10 B4
Rhyl [GB] 10 C4
Rhynern [D] 32 C4
Ría Formosa [P] 94 C6
Riaillé [F] 40 G6
Rialp [E] 84 G6
Riaño [E] 82 C3
Rians [F] 108 C4
Rianxo [E] 78 B3
Riaza [E] 88 G3
Ribabellosa [E] 82 G5
Ribadavia [E] 78 C5
Ribadelago [E] 78 E6
Ribadeo [E] 78 F2
Ribadesella [E] 82 C2
Ribaflecha [E] 90 C1
Ribaforada [E] 84 B6
Ribarci [SRB] 146 E5
Ribariće [SRB] 146 B4
Ribaritsa [BG] 148 A4
Riba-roja de Túria [E] 98 E4
Ribarska Banja [SRB] 146 D3
Ribas de Sil [E] 78 E5
Ribas do Miño, Monasterio de- [E] 78 D4
Ribčev Laz [SLO] 74 A4
Ribe [DK] 156 B3
Ribeauville [F] 58 D2
Ribécourt [F] 28 E6
Ribeira Brava [P] 100 A3
Ribeira de Pena [P] 80 D3
Ribeira Grande [P] 100 E3
Ribeirinha [P] 100 C3
Ribemont [F] 28 F5
Ribera [I] 126 C3
Ribérac [F] 66 E2
Ribera de Cardós [E] 84 G6
Ribera del Fresno [E] 94 H3
Ribes de Freser [E] 92 E2
Ribnica [BIH] 142 D3
Ribnica [SLO] 74 B6
Ribnica [SLO] 74 C6
Rîbniţa [MD] 204 E3
Ribnitz-Damgarten [D] 20 C2
Ribolla [I] 114 F2
Ricadi [I] 124 C6
Říčany [CZ] 48 G4
Riccia [I] 120 F1
Riccione [I] 112 B5
Richelieu [F] 54 F3
Richky [UA] 52 G3
Richmond [GB] 10 F2
Richtenberg [D] 20 C3
Rickarum [S] 158 D2
Rickling [D] 18 G3
Ricla [E] 90 D4
Ricse [H] 64 H4
Riddarhyttan [S] 166 H2
Ridderkerk [NL] 16 D5
Ridjica [SRB] 76 C5
Ridzewo [PL] 24 C3
Riebini [LV] 198 F6
Ried [A] 72 C1
Ried [A] 72 C2
Ried [CH] 72 C1
Riedbach [D] 46 E5
Riedenburg [D] 60 E2
Rieder [D] 60 C5
Riedern [D] 58 F4
Ried im Innkreis [A] 60 H4
Riedlingen [D] 58 H3
Riegel [D] 34 F5
Riegel [D] 58 E2
Riegersburg [A] 74 E2
Riego de Ambrós [E] 78 F5
Riekki [FIN] 196 F2
Riello [E] 78 G5
Rieneck [D] 46 E3
Riesa [D] 34 E5
Riesi [I] 126 E4
Riestedt [D] 34 B5
Rietavas [LT] 200 D4
Rietberg [D] 32 D3
Rieth [D] 20 E4
Rieti [I] 116 B4
Rietschen [D] 34 G5
Rieumes [F] 84 H3
Rieupeyroux [F] 66 H6
Rieussec [F] 106 C4
Rieux [F] 84 H4
Riez [F] 108 C4
Riezlern [A] 60 B6
Rīga [LV] 198 D5
Rígaio [GR] 132 G2
Rigáni [GR] 132 F5
Riglos [E] 84 D5
Rignac [F] 68 A5
Rignano Flaminio [I] 116 A4
Riihimäki [FIN] 176 G3
Riihivaara [FIN] 196 G5
Riihivalkama [FIN] 176 F3
Riiho [FIN] 186 E4
Riipi [FIN] 194 D6
Riispyy [FIN] 186 B5
Riistavesi [FIN] 188 D2
Rijeka [BIH] 142 D4
Rijeka [HR] 112 E1
Rijeka Crnojevića [MNE] 144 E4
Rijssen [NL] 16 G5
Říkonín [CZ] 50 B6
Riksgränsen [S] 192 F4
Rila [BG] 146 F6
Rilci [BG] 148 F2
Rillé [F] 54 F1
Rillo [E] 90 D6
Rilski Man. [BG] 146 F6
Rima [I] 70 E3
Rimaucourt [F] 44 D6
Rimavská Baňa [SK] 64 D3
Rimavská Sobota [SK] 64 E4
Rimbach [D] 60 G3
Rimbo [S] 168 E2
Rimella [I] 70 E3
Rimforsa [S] 162 F1
Rímini [I] 110 H5
Rimito / Rymättylä [FIN] 176 D5
Rimske Toplice [SLO] 74 D5
Rincón de la Victoria [E] 102 C5
Rincón de Soto [E] 84 A5
Rindal [N] 180 G2
Rindown Castle [IRL] 2 D5
Ringamåla [S] 162 E6
Ringarum [S] 168 B6
Ringaskiddy [IRL] 4 D5
Ringe [DK] 156 D3
Ringebu [N] 170 H1
Ringkøbing [DK] 160 B6
Ringnäs [S] 172 F2
Ringnes [N] 170 G5
Ringøy [N] 170 D4
Ringsheim [D] 58 E2
Ringstad [S] 168 B5
Ringsted [DK] 156 F3
Ringville / An Rinn [IRL] 4 E5
Ringwood [GB] 12 G5
Rinkilä [FIN] 188 E5
Rinna [S] 166 G6
Rinøya [N] 192 E4
Rinteln [D] 32 E2
Río [GR] 132 F5
Riobianco / Weissenbach [I] 72 D2
Río de Losa [E] 82 F4
Ríofrío [E] 78 G5
Riofrío de Llano [E] 90 A4
Riola Sardo [I] 118 B5
Riolobos [E] 86 H4
Río Lobos, Cañón del- [E] 88 H2
Riolo Terme [I] 110 G4
Riom [F] 68 C2
Riomaggiore [I] 110 C4
Rio Maior [P] 86 C4
Riomar [E] 92 B6
Rio Marina [I] 114 E2
Rio Mau [P] 80 B3
Riom-ès-Montagnes [F] 68 B3
Rion-des-Landes [F] 66 B5
Rionegro del Puente [E] 80 G3
Rionero in Vúlture [I] 120 G3
Riópar [E] 96 H6
Riós [E] 78 D6
Riosa [E] 78 H4
Rio Saliceto [I] 110 E2
Rioseco de Tapia [E] 78 G5
Rio Torto [P] 80 D6
Rioz [F] 58 B4
Ripač [BIH] 112 H3
Ripacandida [I] 120 G3
Ripanj [SRB] 142 G3
Riparbella [I] 114 E1
Ripatransone [I] 116 C2
Ripats [S] 192 G6
Ripky [UA] 202 D6
Ripley [GB] 10 E5
Ripoll [E] 92 E2
Ripon [GB] 10 F3
Riposto [I] 124 B8
Ripsa [S] 168 C4
Riquewihr [F] 58 D2
Risan [MNE] 144 D4
Risasvallen [S] 182 E4
Risbäck [S] 190 E4
Risberg [S] 172 F3
Riscle [F] 84 E2
Riseberga [S] 158 C1
Riseberga Kloster [S] 166 G3
Risede [S] 190 E5
Rish [BG] 148 E3
Risinge [S] 168 B5
Risliden [S] 190 H4
Risnes [N] 164 C4
Risnes [N] 170 B2
Rišňovce [SK] 64 A4
Risør [N] 164 F4
Risøyhamn [N] 192 E3
Rissa [N] 190 B6
Rissna [S] 182 H2
Risti [EST] 198 D2
Ristiina [FIN] 188 C6
Ristijärvi [FIN] 196 F4
Ristilä [FIN] 186 H4
Ristinge [DK] 156 E5
Ristinkylä [FIN] 188 E3
Ristna [EST] 198 C2
Ristovac [SRB] 146 D5
Risträsk [S] 190 G4
Risulahti [FIN] 188 D6
Risum-Lindholm [D] 156 B5
Risuperä [FIN] 186 E2
Ritíni [GR] 128 G5
Ritola [FIN] 186 D3
Ritsem [S] 192 F5
Ritten / Renon [I] 72 D3
Rittmanshausen [D] 32 G6
Riuttala [FIN] 176 D1
Riva-Bella [F] 26 F3
Riva dei Tarquini [I] 114 G4
Riva del Garda [I] 72 C5
Riva di Solto [I] 72 A5
Rivanazzano [I] 70 F6
Rivarolo Canavese [I] 70 D5
Rivarolo Mantovano [I] 110 E2
Riva Valdobbia [I] 70 E3
Rive-de-Gier [F] 68 F3
Rivello [I] 120 G5
Rivergaro [I] 110 C2
Rivesaltes [F] 92 G1
Rivinperä [FIN] 196 E5
Rivne [UA] 202 B7
Rivoli [I] 70 D5
Rizári [GR] 128 F4
Rízia [GR] 150 A2
Rizokárpasox (Dipkarpaz) [CY] 154 H4
Rízoma [GR] 132 E2
Rizómata [GR] 128 G5
Rizómylos [GR] 132 H2
Rizómylos [GR] 136 D4
Rjånes [N] 180 C4
Rjukan [N] 170 F6
Ro [I] 110 G2
Roa [E] 88 G2
Roa [N] 172 B5
Roald [N] 180 C3
Røan [N] 180 G2
Roana [I] 72 D5
Roanne [F] 68 E2
Roasjö [S] 162 B2
Roavvegieddi [N] 194 D3
Robăneştii de Jos [RO] 146 G1
Robbio [I] 70 F5
Röbel [D] 20 C5
Robella [I] 70 E5
Røberg [N] 182 B1
Robertingue [F] 14 G6
Robertsfors [S] 196 A5
Robleda [E] 86 H2
Robledillo de Gata [E] 86 H3
Robledo [E] 96 H5
Robledo de Chavela [E] 88 E5
Robledo del Buey [E] 96 D2
Robles de la Valcueva [E] 78 H5
Robliza de Cojos [E] 88 B3
Robres [E] 90 F3
Robres del Castillo [E] 90 C1
Robru [N] 170 F3
Rocamadour [F] 66 G4
Roccabianca [I] 110 D2
Roccadáspide [I] 120 F4
Rocca di Cambio [I] 116 C4
Rocca di Mezzo [I] 116 C4
Rocca di Neto [I] 124 F5
Rocca Imperiale [I] 122 D5
Roccalbegna [I] 114 G3
Roccalumera [I] 124 B8
Rocca Malatina, Sassi di- [I] 110 E4
Roccamonfina [I] 120 D2
Roccanova [I] 122 C5
Roccapalumba [I] 126 D2
Rocca Pia [I] 116 D5
Roccaraso [I] 116 D6
Rocca San Casciano [I] 110 G5
Rocca Sinibalda [I] 116 B4
Roccastrada [I] 114 F2
Rocca Vecchia [I] 122 H5
Roccaverano [I] 108 H2
Roccella Iónica [I] 124 D7
Roccelletta del Vescovo di Squillace [I] 124 E5
Rocche di Cusa [I] 126 B3
Rocchetta Bèlbo [I] 108 G2
Rocella Valdemonte [I] 124 A8
Rochdale [GB] 10 E4
Roche [E] 100 F4
Rochebloine, Château de- [F] 68 E5
Rochechouart [F] 54 F6
Rochecourbière, Grotte de- [F] 106 H2
Rochefort [B] 30 D6
Rochefort [F] 54 C5
Rochefort, Grotte de- [F] 40 H5
Rochefort-en-Terre [F] 40 E5
Rochefort-s-Nenon [F] 56 H4
Rochehaut [B] 44 D2
Rochemaure [F] 68 F6
Rocher, Château du- [F] 26 E6
Rocherolle, Château de la- [F] 54 G4
Rochers, Château des- [F] 26 D6
Rocheservière [F] 54 B2
Rochester [GB] 14 F4
Rochlitz [D] 34 D6
Rochsburg [D] 48 D1
Rociana del Condado [E] 94 F6
Rockcorry [IRL] 2 F4
Rockenhausen [D] 46 B4
Rockhammar [S] 166 H2
Rockneby [S] 162 G5
Rocroi [F] 28 H5
Rød [N] 166 B3
Róda [GR] 132 B1
Rødach [D] 46 G2
Roda de Eresma [E] 88 F4
Roda de Isábena [E] 84 F6
Rødal [N] 180 E4
Rodaljice [HR] 112 H5
Ródanas, Sant. de- [E] 90 D4
Rodange [L] 44 E3
Rodão, Portas de- [P] 86 E4
Rødberg [N] 170 F5
Rødby [DK] 20 A1
Rødby [S] 158 F1
Rødbyhavn [DK] 20 A1
Rødding [DK] 156 B3
Rødding [DK] 160 C5
Rödeby [S] 158 F1
Rodeiro [E] 78 C4
Rødekro [DK] 156 C4
Rodellar [E] 84 E6
Roden [NL] 16 G2
Rodenkirchen [D] 18 D4
Rodewald [D] 32 F1
Rodewisch [D] 48 C2
Rodez [F] 68 B6
Rodgau [D] 46 C3
Rødhus Klit [DK] 160 D3
Rodiá [GR] 132 G1
Rodi Gargánico [I] 116 G5
Roding [D] 48 C6
Rødkærsbro [DK] 160 D5
Rodolívos [GR] 130 C3
Rodópoli [GR] 128 H2
Ródos [GR] 154 D3
Rodovoye [RUS] 198 G4
Rodrigatos de la Obispalía [E] 78 G5
Rodrigo, Castelo- [P] 80 E6
Rødsjøen [N] 190 B6
Rødven [N] 180 E3
Rødvig [DK] 156 G4
Roela [EST] 198 F1
Roermond [NL] 30 F3
Roeselare (Roulers) [B] 28 F2
Roeulx [B] 28 H3
Roffiac [F] 68 C4
Roflaschlucht [CH] 70 G2
Röfors [S] 166 G4
Rofrano [I] 120 G5
Rogač [HR] 142 A6
Rogačica [SRB] 142 F4
Rogalice [PL] 50 D1
Rogalin [PL] 36 C3
Rogaška Slatina [SLO] 74 D4
Rogatec [SLO] 74 E4
Rogatica [BIH] 144 E1
Rogätz [D] 34 B2
Roggenburg [D] 60 C4
Rogil [P] 94 B4
Røgind [DK] 160 B6
Rögla [S] 158 C3
Rogliano [F] 114 C2
Rogliano [I] 124 D5
Rognac [F] 106 H5
Rognan [N] 192 D6
Rogne [N] 170 G2
Rognes [N] 182 B2
Rogovka [LV] 198 G5
Rogovo [RUS] 198 G4
Rogowo [PL] 36 D2
Rogozhinë [AL] 128 B3
Rogoznica [HR] 116 H1
Rogoźno [PL] 36 C2
Rogoźno [PL] 36 F5
Roguszyn [PL] 38 D2
Rohan [F] 26 A5
Rohatec [CZ] 62 G2
Rohatyn [UA] 204 C2
Rohožník [SK] 62 G4
Rohr [A] 72 E1
Rohrbach [A] 62 B3
Rohrbach-lès-Bitche [F] 44 G4
Rohrberg [D] 34 A1
Rohrenfels [D] 60 D3
Rohr i. Niederb. [D] 60 F2
Rohuküla [EST] 198 D2
Rohuneeme [EST] 198 D1
Roisel [F] 28 F5
Roja [LV] 198 C4
Rojales [E] 104 D3
Röjan [S] 182 G4
Rojão Grande [P] 80 C6
Röjdåfors [S] 172 E5
Rojiştea [RO] 146 G1
Rök [S] 166 G6
Röka [S] 190 G4
Röke [S] 158 C1
Rokiciny [PL] 36 H4
Rokietnica [PL] 52 F4
Rokiškis [LT] 200 G3
Rokity [PL] 22 C2
Rokkum [N] 180 F2
Roknäs [S] 196 A3
Rokua [FIN] 196 E4
Rokycany [CZ] 48 E4
Rokytnice [CZ] 50 B3
Rolandstorp [S] 190 E4
Rold [DK] 160 D4
Røldal [N] 170 C5
Rolfstorp [S] 160 H4
Rolle [CH] 70 B1
Rølvåg [N] 190 D2
Rolvsøy [N] 166 B3
Roma [I] 116 A5
Romagnano Sésia [I] 70 E4
Romakkajärvi [FIN] 194 C7
Romakloster [S] 168 G4
Roman [BG] 146 G3
Roman [RO] 204 D3
Romangordo [E] 88 B6
Romanija [BIH] 144 D1
Romanshorn [CH] 58 H4
Romans-sur-Isère [F] 68 F5
Romashiki [RUS] 178 G2
Rombas [F] 44 E4
Rom By [DK] 160 B5
Romena, Castello di- [I] 110 G5
Romena, Pieve di- [I] 110 G5
Romeral [E] 96 G2
Romfartuna [S] 168 B2
Romilly-sur-Seine [F] 44 A5
Romny [UA] 202 E7
Romont [CH] 70 C1
Romorantin-Lanthenay [F] 54 H2
Romppala [FIN] 188 F1
Romsey [GB] 12 H4
Romtemplom [H] 64 C6
Røn [N] 170 G2
Roncade [I] 72 E6
Roncadelle [I] 72 A6
Roncal / Erronkari [E] 84 C4
Roncegno [I] 72 D4
Roncesvalles [E] 84 C3
Ronchamp [F] 58 C3
Ronchi dei Legionari [I] 72 H5
Ronciglione [I] 114 H4
Ronco Canavese [I] 70 D4
Roncofreddo [I] 110 H5
Ronco Scrivia [I] 110 B3
Ronda [E] 102 A4
Rønde [DK] 160 E6
Ronehamn [S] 168 G5
Rong [N] 170 C3
Rõngu [EST] 198 F3
Ronkeli [FIN] 196 G5
Rönnäng [S] 160 G1
Rönnäs [FIN] 178 B4
Rønne [DK] 158 E4
Ronneburg [D] 48 C1
Ronneby [S] 158 F1
Rønnede [DK] 156 G4
Rönnigsåsen [S] 182 F4
Rönnliden [S] 190 H3
Rönnöfors [S] 190 D6
Rönnskär [S] 196 A4
Rönnynkylä [FIN] 186 F1
Rönö [S] 168 C5
Ronsberg [D] 60 C5
Ronse (Renaix) [B] 28 G3
Roodeschool [NL] 16 G1
Roonah Quay [IRL] 2 B3
Roosendaal [NL] 16 C6
Roosky [IRL] 2 D4
Ropa [PL] 52 C5
Ropaži [LV] 198 E5
Ropczyce [PL] 52 D3
Ropeid [N] 164 B1
Ropinsalmi [FIN] 192 H3
Ropotovo [MK] 128 E2
Ropsha [RUS] 178 E6
Ropsha [RUS] 178 G5
Roque, Pointe de la- [F] 26 G3
Roquebillière [F] 108 F4
Roquebrune-Cap-Martin [F] 108 F4
Roquefort [F] 66 C5
Roquefort-sur-Soulzon [F] 106 D3
Roquemaure [F] 106 G3
Roquesteron [F] 108 E4
Roquetaillade, Château de- [F] 66 D4
Roquetas de Mar [E] 102 F5
Roquetes [E] 92 A5
Rörbäcksnäs [S] 172 E3
Rore [BIH] 142 B4
Rörön [S] 182 G3
Røros [N] 182 C4
Rorschach [CH] 58 H5
Rörum [S] 158 D3
Rørvig [DK] 156 F2
Rørvik [N] 164 C5
Rørvik [N] 182 B1
Rørvik [N] 190 C4
Rörvik [S] 174 G6
Ros' [BY] 24 G5
Rosais [P] 100 C3
Rosala [FIN] 176 E6
Rosal de la Frontera [E] 94 E3
Rosa Marina [I] 122 F3
Rosans [F] 108 B2
Rosarno [I] 124 C6
Rosas / Roses [E] 92 G2
Rosbach [D] 46 C2
Rosche [D] 18 G6
Rościszewo [PL] 36 H1
Roscoff [F] 40 C1
Roscommon [IRL] 2 D5
Roscrea [IRL] 2 D6
Rosdorf [D] 32 F4
Rosegg [A] 74 B3
Roselle [I] 114 F2
Roselle Módica [I] 126 G6
Rosen [BG] 148 F4
Rosenberg [D] 46 E6
Rosenburg [A] 62 E3
Rosendal [N] 170 B5
Rosendal [S] 156 H1
Rosendal [S] 162 E1
Rosenheim [D] 60 F5
Rosenhof [A] 62 C3
Rosenholm [DK] 160 E6
Rosentorp [S] 172 H2
Rosepenna / Machair Loiscthe [IRL] 2 E1
Rosersberg [S] 168 D2
Roses / Rosas [E] 92 G2
Roseto Capo Spúlico [I] 122 D6
Roseto degli Abruzzi [I] 116 D3
Roseto Valfortore [I] 120 F2
Roshchino [RUS] 178 G4
Rosica [BG] 148 F1
Rosice [CZ] 50 B6
Rosignano-Marittimo [I] 110 D6
Rosignano Solvay [I] 114 E1
Rosino [BG] 148 B4
Roşiori [RO] 76 H1
Roşiori de Vede [RO] 148 B1
Roskilde [DK] 156 G2
Rosko [PL] 36 B1
Roskovec [AL] 128 B4
Roslags-Bro [S] 168 E1
Roslags-kulla [S] 168 E2
Roslavl' [RUS] 202 D5
Roslev [DK] 160 C4
Rosli [N] 180 G5
Rosmaninhal [P] 86 F4
Ros Mhic Thriúin / New Ross [IRL] 4 F4
Rosnowo [PL] 22 A3
Rosny sur Seine [F] 42 E3
Rosolina Mare [I] 110 H2
Rosolini [I] 126 G5
Rosoman [MK] 128 F2
Rosporden [F] 40 C3
Ross Abbey [IRL] 2 C4
Rossano [I] 124 E4
Rossas [P] 80 C5
Ross Carbery [IRL] 4 C5
Rosscor [NIR] 2 E3
Rosserk Abbey [IRL] 2 C3
Rosses Point [IRL] 2 D3
Rossfjord [N] 192 F2
Rosshaupten [D] 60 C5
Rossiglione [I] 108 H2
Rossio [P] 86 D4
Rossla [D] 34 A5
Rossland [N] 170 A3
Rosslare Harbour [IRL] 4 F5
Rosslau [D] 34 C4
Rosslea [NIR] 2 F4
Rossnes [N] 170 A3
Ross-on-Wye [GB] 12 G2
Rossosz [PL] 38 F4
Rossoszyca [PL] 36 F4
Røssvassbukt [N] 190 E3
Röstånga [S] 158 C2
Rostassac [F] 66 F5
Roštejn [CZ] 48 H6
Röster [S] 168 B6
Rostock [D] 20 B3
Rostov [RUS] 202 F2
Rostrenen [F] 40 D3
Rostrevor [NIR] 2 G4
Röström [S] 190 F5
Røstvollen [N] 182 D5
Rosvik [N] 192 D5
Rosyth [GB] 8 E3
Röszke [H] 76 E4
Roszki-Wodźki [PL] 24 E6
Rot [S] 172 F2
Rota [E] 100 F3
Rotberget [N] 172 D4
Roteberg [S] 168 C1
Rotemo [N] 164 D2
Rotenburg [D] 18 E5
Rotenburg [D] 32 F6
Rotenfels [D] 46 B3
Rotgülden [A] 72 H2
Roth [D] 46 G5
Rötha [D] 34 C6
Rothaus [D] 58 F4
Rothemühl [D] 20 E4
Rothenburg [D] 34 G5
Rothenburg, Ruine- [D] 46 G5
Rothenburg ob der Tauber [D] 46 E5
Rothéneuf [F] 26 C4
Rothenstein [D] 60 D2
Rotherham [GB] 10 F4
Rothes [GB] 6 E5
Rothesay [GB] 8 C3
Rotondella [I] 122 D5
Rótova [E] 98 E6
Rotsjö [S] 184 D3
Rott [D] 60 D5
Rott [D] 60 F5
Rottach [D] 60 E5
Rötteln [D] 58 E4
Rottenbach [D] 46 G2
Rottenbuch [D] 60 D5
Rottenburg [D] 58 G2
Rottenburg [D] 60 F3
Rottenmann [A] 62 B6
Rotterdam [NL] 16 C5
Rotthalmünster [D] 60 H4
Röttingen [D] 46 E5
Rottne [S] 162 E4
Rottneros [S] 166 E1
Rottweil [D] 58 G3
Rotvoll [N] 182 D2
Rötz [D] 48 C5
Roubaix [F] 28 F3
Rouchovany [CZ] 62 E2
Roudnice nad Labem [CZ] 48 F3
Rouen [F] 28 B5
Rouffach [F] 58 D3
Rouffignac, Grotte de- [F] 66 F3
Rougé [F] 40 F5
Rougemont [F] 58 C4
Rougemont [F] 58 D3
Rouillac [F] 54 D6
Roujan [F] 106 D4
Roukavichy [BY] 202 D5
Roulers (Roeselare) [B] 28 F2
Roundstone [IRL] 2 B4
Roundwood [IRL] 4 G3
Roússa [GR] 130 G2
Roussillon [F] 68 F4
Roussillon [F] 106 H4
Rouvres-en-Xaintois [F] 44 E6
Rovakka [S] 194 B7
Rovaniemi [FIN] 194 D8
Rovanjska [HR] 112 G4
Rovastinaho [FIN] 196 D2
Rovato [I] 72 A6
Roverbella [I] 110 E1
Rovereto [I] 72 C5
Rövershagen [D] 20 B3
Roverud [N] 172 D5
Roviés [GR] 134 B4
Rovigo [I] 110 G2
Rovinj [HR] 112 D2
Rovišće [HR] 74 F5
Rovjok [N] 192 G3
Rovte [SLO] 74 B5
Rów [PL] 20 F6
Rowy [PL] 22 B1
Rowy [PL] 36 F5
Royan [F] 54 B6
Royat [F] 68 C2
Royaumont, Abbaye de- [F] 42 F3
Roybon [F] 68 G4
Roye [F] 28 E5
Royère-de-Vassivière [F] 68 A1
Røyken [N] 164 H1
Röykkä [FIN] 176 G4
Røyrvik [N] 190 D4
Røyse [N] 170 H5
Røysheim [N] 180 F6
Royston [GB] 14 E3
Roza [BG] 148 D5
Rožaj [MNE] 146 B5
Różan [PL] 24 C6
Różanki [PL] 34 H1
Rožanstvo [SRB] 146 A3
Rozay-en-Brie [F] 42 G4
Rozdil [UA] 52 H5
Rozdory [RUS] 204 H1
Roženski Manastir [BG] 130 B2
Rožmberk nad Vltavou [CZ] 62 B3
Rožmitál pod Třemšínem [CZ] 48 E5
Rožňava [SK] 64 E3
Rožnov pod Radhoštěm [CZ] 50 E5
Rożnów [PL] 52 B4
Rozogi [PL] 24 C5
Rozoy [F] 28 G6
Rozprza [PL] 36 H5
Roztoky [CZ] 48 F3
Rožupe [LV] 198 F6
Rozvadov [CZ] 48 C4
Rozzano [I] 70 G5
Rrëshen [AL] 128 B1
Rtanj [SRB] 146 D2
Ru [E] 78 D3
Ruba [LV] 198 C6
Rubbestadneset [N] 170 A5
Rubena [E] 82 E6
Rubielos de Mora [E] 98 E2
Rubiera [I] 110 E3
Rucava [LV] 200 D3
Ruciane-Nida [PL] 24 C4
Rud [N] 164 H1
Rud [N] 170 G4
Rud [N] 170 H5
Rud [S] 166 F3
Ruda [PL] 24 D4
Ruda [S] 162 F4
Ruda Maleniecka [PL] 38 A6
Rudare [SRB] 146 C4
Rudawica [PL] 34 H5
Rudawka [PL] 24 F3
Ruda Wolińska [PL] 38 D3
Rudelsburg [D] 34 B6
Rudenica [SRB] 146 C3
Rüdersdorf [D] 34 F2
Rüdesheim [D] 46 B3
Rūdiškės [LT] 24 H1
Rudka [PL] 38 E1
Rudka [PL] 38 G5
Rudkøbing [DK] 156 E4
Rudky [UA] 52 G4
Rudna [PL] 22 C5
Rudna [PL] 36 B5
Rudna Glava [SRB] 146 D1
Rudnica [MNE] 144 E2
Rudnica [SRB] 146 B4
Rudnik [BG] 148 F3
Rudnik [PL] 50 E3
Rudnik [PL] 52 E2
Rudnik [SRB] 146 B2
Rudnik [SRB] 146 B5
Rudniki [PL] 50 F1
Rudnik Szlachecki-Kol. [PL] 38 D6
Rudno [PL] 22 E4
Rudno [PL] 38 E4
Rudno [SLO] 74 B4
Rudnya [RUS] 202 C4
Rudo [BIH] 144 E1
Rudolphstein [D] 46 H2
Rudolstadt [D] 46 H1
Rudozem [BG] 130 E1
Rudsgrendi [N] 164 F1
Rudsjön [S] 190 F6
Rudskoga [S] 166 G4
Ruds-Vedby [DK] 156 F3
Rudy [PL] 50 F3
Rudy-Rysie [PL] 52 B3
Rudzāti [LV] 198 F5
Rue [F] 28 D3
Rueda [E] 88 E2
Rueda, Monasterio de- [E] 90 F5
Rueda de Jalón [E] 90 D3
Ruelle-sur-Touvre [F] 66 E1
Ruen [BG] 148 F4
Ruffano [I] 122 G6
Ruffec [F] 54 E5
Ruffieux [F] 68 H3
Rugāji [LV] 198 G5
Rugby [GB] 14 D2
Rugeley [GB] 10 E6
Rugldalen [N] 182 C3
Rugles [F] 26 H5
Rugvica [HR] 74 F6
Ruha [FIN] 186 C3
Ruhala [FIN] 186 E5
Ruhällen [S] 168 C1
Rühen [D] 32 H2
Ruhland [D] 34 F5
Ruhmannsfelden [D] 60 G2
Ruhpolding [D] 60 G5
Ruidera [E] 96 G4
Ruínas [I] 118 C5
Ruinas de Castrotorafe [E] 80 H4
Ruinas Romanas [E] 96 D1
Ruínas Romanas [P] 94 D2
Rūjiena [LV] 198 E3
Rujište [SRB] 146 D2

Rujište [SRB] 146 D2
Ruju, Nuraghe- [I] 118 D3
Ruka [FIN] 194 F8
Rukke [S] 170 F4
Rullbo [S] 182 H6
Rülzheim [D] 46 B5
Rum [H] 74 G2
Ruma [SRB] 142 F2
Ruma [SRB] 204 A6
Rumboci [BIH] 144 B1
Rumburk [CZ] 48 G1
Rumelifeneri [TR] 150 E2
Rumia [PL] 22 D2
Rumigny [F] 28 H5
Rumilly [F] 70 A3
Rummen [B] 30 D4
Rummukkala [FIN] 188 E3
Rumo [FIN] 196 F5
Rumont [F] 44 D4
Rumpani [LV] 198 F4
Runcorn [GB] 10 D4
Runde [N] 180 C3
Rundfloen [N] 172 E3
Rundvik [S] 184 H1
Runni [FIN] 196 E6
Runović [HR] 144 B2
Ruokojärvi [FIN] 194 C7
Ruokojärvi [S] 194 B8
Ruokolahti [FIN] 178 E1
Ruokto [S] 192 F6
Ruona [FIN] 186 D3
Ruopsa [FIN] 194 E7
Ruorasmäki [FIN] 186 H6
Ruotaanmäki [FIN] 196 E6
Ruoti [I] 120 G3
Ruøtsinkylä Svenskby [FIN] 178 C3
Ruotsinpyhtää Strömfors [FIN] 178 C4
Ruovesi [FIN] 186 E5
Rupa [HR] 112 E1
Rupea [RO] 204 D4
Rupt [F] 58 C3
Rus [E] 102 F1
Rusalka [BG] 148 G2
Rusanivka [UA] 202 F7
Rúscio [I] 116 B3
Rusdal [N] 164 B4
Ruse [BG] 148 C2
Ruše [SLO] 74 D4
Rusele [S] 190 G4
Ruševo [HR] 142 D1
Rusfors [S] 190 G4
Rush [IRL] 2 F6
Rushden [GB] 14 E2
Rusiec [PL] 36 F5
Rusinowo [PL] 20 G4
Rusinowo [PL] 22 A6
Rusjasi [MK] 128 D2
Ruskeala [RUS] 188 G4
Ruski Krstur [SRB] 76 D6
Ruskila [FIN] 188 D2
Rusksele [S] 190 G4
Rusktråsk [S] 190 G4
Rusnė [LT] 200 D5
Rusokastro [BG] 148 F4
Rüsselsheim [D] 46 C3
Russi [I] 110 G4
Russliseter [N] 180 G6
Rust [A] 62 F5
Rust [D] 58 E2
Rustad [N] 172 B5
Rustefjelbma [N] 194 D2
Rusvekk [N] 172 D4
Ruswil [CH] 58 E6
Ruszów [PL] 34 H5
Rutalahti [FIN] 186 G5
Rute [E] 102 C3
Rutenbrock [D] 16 H3
Rüthen [D] 32 D4
Ruthin [GB] 10 C4
Rüthnick [D] 34 D1
Rüti [CH] 58 G6
Rüti [CH] 58 G5
Rutigliano [I] 122 E3
Rutka-Tartak [PL] 24 E2
Rutki-Kossaki [PL] 24 D6
Rutledal [N] 170 B2
Rutvik [S] 196 B3
Ruukki [FIN] 196 D4
Ruunaa [FIN] 196 G6
Ruurlo [NL] 16 F5
Ruutana [FIN] 176 F1
Ruuvaoja [FIN] 194 E6
Ruvallen [S] 182 E3
Ruvanaho [FIN] 194 F7
Ruvasiahtio [FIN] 188 F2
Ruvo di Púglia [I] 122 D2
Ruwer [D] 44 G2
Ruza [RUS] 202 E3
Ruzhany [BY] 24 H6
Ruzhintsi [BG] 146 E3
Ruzhyn [UA] 202 D8
Růžkovy Lhotice [CZ] 48 G5
Ružomberok [SK] 64 C2
Rvíziana [GR] 132 D3
Ry [DK] 156 D1
Ryå [DK] 160 D3
Ryabovo [RUS] 178 F4
Ryakhovo [BG] 148 D1
Ryákia [GR] 128 G5
Rybachiy [RUS] 200 C5
Rybarzowice [PL] 50 G5
Rybinsk [RUS] 202 F1
Rybnica [PL] 50 A1
Rybnik [PL] 50 F4
Rybník [SK] 64 E3
Rybno [PL] 22 G5
Ryboły [PL] 24 F6
Rychliki [PL] 22 F3
Rychmburk [CZ] 50 B4
Rychnov nad Kněžnou [CZ] 50 B3
Rychnowo [PL] 22 G4
Rychtal [PL] 36 E6
Rychwał [PL] 36 E3
Ryczywół [PL] 38 C4
Ryd [S] 162 D6
Rydaholm [S] 162 D4
Ryde [GB] 12 H5
Rydet [S] 160 G3
Rydland [N] 182 B6
Rydsnäs [S] 162 E2
Rydułtowy [PL] 50 F4
Rydzyna [PL] 36 C4
Rye [GB] 14 F5
Ryen [N] 164 E5
Ryfoss [N] 170 F2
Rygge [N] 166 B2
Rygozy [RUS] 198 H5
Ryhälä [FIN] 188 E5
Ryhäntä [FIN] 196 F4
Rykene [N] 164 E5
Ryki [PL] 38 D4
Ryl'sk [RUS] 202 F6
Rymań [PL] 20 G3
Rymanów [PL] 52 D5
Rýmařov [CZ] 50 D4
Rymättylä / Rimito [FIN] 176 D5
Rýmnio [GR] 128 F6
Ryn [PL] 24 C3
Rynarzewo [PL] 22 D6
Ryomgård [DK] 160 E5
Rypefjord [N] 194 B2
Rypin [PL] 22 F6
Ryslinge [DK] 156 D3
Ryssby [S] 162 D4
Rysum [D] 16 H2
Rytel [PL] 22 C4
Rytinki [FIN] 196 E2
Rytkynkylä [FIN] 196 D5
Rytro [PL] 52 B5
Ryuttyu [RUS] 188 H4
Rýzmberk [CZ] 48 D5
Rząśnik [PL] 38 C1
Rzecin [PL] 36 B1
Rzeczenica [PL] 22 B4
Rzeczyca [PL] 38 A5
Rzęgnowo [PL] 22 H6
Rzemień [PL] 52 D3
Rzepin [PL] 34 G3
Rzesznikowo [PL] 20 G4
Rzeszów [PL] 52 E3
Rzewnowo [PL] 20 F3
Rzgów [PL] 36 G4
Rzhev [RUS] 202 D3
Rzhishchiv [UA] 202 E7

S

Sääksjärvi [FIN] 186 D2
Sääksmäki [FIN] 176 F2
Saal [D] 60 F2
Saalbach [A] 72 F1
Saalburg [D] 46 C2
Saales [F] 44 G6
Saalfeld [D] 46 H2
Saalfelden [A] 60 G6
Saamatti [FIN] 176 F5
Saananmaja [FIN] 192 G3
Saanen [CH] 70 D1
Saaramaa [FIN] 178 D3
Saarbrücken [D] 44 G4
Saarburg [D] 44 F3
Sääre [EST] 198 C4
Saare [EST] 198 F2
Saarela [FIN] 186 G1
Saarenkylä [FIN] 194 D8
Saarenmaa [FIN] 176 D2
Saaresmäki [FIN] 196 E5
Saari [FIN] 188 F5
Saarijärvi [FIN] 186 F3
Saarikoski [FIN] 192 H3
Saarinen [FIN] 196 F4
Saario [FIN] 188 G3
Saarivaara [FIN] 188 G3
Saarivaara [FIN] 196 G4
Saarlouis [D] 44 F3
Saas Almagell [CH] 70 E3
Saas-Fee [CH] 70 E3
Saas Grund [CH] 70 E3
Sääskijärvi [FIN] 196 E2
Sääskjärvi [FIN] 178 B3
Sababurg [D] 32 F4
Šabac [MNE] 204 A6
Šabac [SRB] 142 F2
Sabadell [E] 92 E4
Sabaro [E] 82 C4
Sabáudia [I] 120 B2
Sabbioneta [I] 110 E2
Sabbucina [I] 126 E3
Sabile [LV] 198 C5
Sabiñánigo [E] 84 D5
Sabinarde Calatañazor [E] 90 A2
Sabinosa [E] 100 A5
Sabinov [SK] 52 C6
Sabiote [E] 102 F2
Sables-d'Or-les-Pins [F] 26 B4
Sablé-sur-Sarthe [F] 42 A5
Såbole [S] 182 F1
Saborsko [HR] 112 G2
Sabres [F] 66 C5
Sabrosa [P] 80 D4
Sabugal [P] 86 G2
Sabuncu [TR] 150 H6
Saby [S] 160 D3
Šaca [SK] 64 G3
Săcălaz [RO] 76 G5
Sacavém [P] 86 B5
Sacecorbo [E] 90 B5
Sacedón [E] 88 H6
Saceruela [E] 96 D4
Sacile [I] 72 F5
Sacra di San Michele [I] 70 C5
Sada [E] 78 D2
Sádaba [E] 84 B5
Sadala [EST] 198 F2
Sadikkiri [TR] 152 H1
Sadikov Bunar [SRB] 146 E4
Sadina [BG] 148 D2
Sadki [PL] 22 C6
Sadova [RO] 146 G2
Sadovets [BG] 148 A3
Sadovo [BG] 148 B6
Sadovo [BG] 148 F3
Sądów [PL] 34 G3
Sadowne [PL] 38 C2
Sadrazamköy (Livera) [CY] 154 F5
S. Adriano [I] 110 G4
Sadská [CZ] 48 G3
Sädvaluspen [S] 190 F2
Sæbø [N] 170 D4
Sæbø [N] 180 D4
Sæbøvik [N] 170 B5
Sæby [DK] 160 E3
Sæd [DK] 156 B4
Sădinenie [BG] 148 B5
Sădinenie [BG] 148 C5
Saelices [E] 96 H2
Sælvig [DK] 156 E2
Saepinum [I] 120 E1
Saerbeck [D] 32 C2
Sætra [N] 192 E2
Sætre [N] 164 H2
Sætre [N] 172 C2
Saeul [L] 44 E2
Sævareid [N] 170 B4
Sævråsvåg [N] 170 B3
Safa [TR] 150 G5
Safara [P] 94 E3
Safary-Park [A] 62 F4
Säffle [S] 166 E3
Saffron Walden [GB] 14 F3
Safonovo [RUS] 202 D4
Şag [RO] 76 G6
Sagard [D] 20 D2
S'Agaró [E] 92 G4
S. Agata di Esaro [I] 124 C3
Saggrenda [N] 164 G2
Sagiáda [GR] 132 B2
Sågmyra [S] 172 H4
Sagone [F] 114 A4
Sagres [P] 94 A5
Şagu [RO] 76 G5
Sagu / Sauvo [FIN] 176 E5
Sagunt / Sagunto [E] 98 F4
Sagunto / Sagunt [E] 98 F4
Sagvåg [N] 170 A5
Ságvár [H] 76 A3
Sahagún [E] 82 C5
Sahalahti [FIN] 176 G1
Sahankylä [FIN] 186 C4
Sahavaara [S] 194 B7
Sahilköy [TR] 150 F2
Şahin [TR] 150 B3
Şahinburgaz [TR] 150 D4
Sahrajärvi [FIN] 186 F4
Šahy [SK] 64 C5
Saignelégier [CH] 58 D5
Saija [FIN] 194 E7
Saikari [FIN] 186 H3
Saillagouse [F] 92 E1
Saillans [F] 68 G6
Sailly Flibeaucourt [F] 28 D4
Säimen [FIN] 188 F4
Sains [F] 28 G5
Saint Albain [F] 56 G6
Sainte-Lucie-de-Tallano [F] 114 B5
Sainte-Marie-Siché [F] 114 B5
Saintes [F] 54 C6
Saintfield [NIR] 2 G4
Saint-Ghislain [B] 28 G4
Saint Hilaire de la Côte [F] 68 G4
Saint-Jacques [I] 70 D3
Sairinen [FIN] 176 D4
Saissac [F] 106 B4
Saittarova [S] 192 H6
Saivomuotka [S] 194 B5
Sajaniemi [FIN] 176 G3
Sajenek [PL] 24 E3
Šajkaš [SRB] 142 G1
Sajószentpéter [H] 64 F4
Sakar [TR] 150 H4
Sakaravaara [FIN] 196 F4
Sakarya (Adapazari) [TR] 150 H3
Šakiai [LT] 200 E5
Säkinmäki [FIN] 186 H3
Sakıremer [TR] 152 D6
Sakızlık [TR] 150 G5
Sakowczyk [PL] 52 E5
Sakskøbing [DK] 156 F5
Saky [UA] 204 H4
Säkylä [FIN] 176 D3
Sala [S] 168 C1
Šal'a [SK] 64 A4
Salaberg [A] 62 C5
Salacgrīva [LV] 198 D4
Sala Consilina [I] 120 G4
Saladamm [S] 168 C1
Salahmi [FIN] 196 E5
Salamajärvi [FIN] 186 E1
Salamanca [E] 80 H6
Salamína [GR] 134 B6
Salamis [CY] 154 G5
Salantai [LT] 200 D4
Salaóra [GR] 132 D4
Salar [E] 102 D4
Sălard [RO] 76 H1
Salardú [E] 84 G5
Salas [E] 78 G3
Salaš [SRB] 146 E2
Salas de los Infantes [E] 88 H1
Salaspils [LV] 198 E5
Salau [F] 84 G5
Salbohed [S] 168 B1
Salbris [F] 56 B2
Salcia [RO] 146 E1
Šalčininkai [LT] 200 G6
Salcombe [GB] 12 D5
Sălcuța [RO] 146 F1
Saldaña [E] 82 C5
Salduba [E] 90 E3
Saldus [LV] 198 C5
Sale [I] 70 F6
Saleby [S] 166 E5
Salem [D] 58 H4
Salema [P] 94 A5
Salemi [I] 126 B2
Sälen [S] 172 E2
Salernes [F] 108 D4
Salerno [I] 120 F4
Salers [F] 68 B4
S. Alessio Siculo [I] 124 B8
Saletta [I] 70 C5
Salgótarján [H] 64 D4
Šalgovík [SK] 64 G2
Salhus [N] 170 B3
Sali [HR] 112 F5
Salice [F] 114 B4
Salice Terme [I] 70 F6
Salies-de-Béarn [F] 84 D2
Salies-du-Salat [F] 84 G4
Salignac-Eyvigues [F] 66 G4
Salihli [TR] 152 E4
Salihorsk [BY] 202 B6
Salinas [E] 78 H3
Salinas [E] 104 D2
Salinas de Pinilla [E] 96 H5
Salinas de Pisuerga [E] 82 D4
Salin-de-Giraud [F] 106 G5
Saline di Volterra [I] 114 F1
Sälinkää [FIN] 176 H3
Salins-les-Bains [F] 58 B5
Salir [P] 94 C5
Salisbury [GB] 12 G4
Salka [SK] 64 C5
Salla [FIN] 194 E7
Sallanches [F] 70 B3
Sallent de Gállego [E] 84 D4
Sälleryd [S] 158 G1
Salles-Curan [F] 106 D2
Salles-s.-l'Hers [F] 106 A4
Sallinge [S] 166 H2
Sallmunds [S] 168 G6
Salme [EST] 198 C3
Salmenkylä [FIN] 186 E4
Salmenniemi [FIN] 186 F2
Salmerón [E] 90 A6
Salmi [FIN] 186 D3
Salmi [S] 194 B7
Salmivaara [FIN] 194 E7
Sal'miyarvi [RUS] 194 F3
Salmoral [E] 88 D4
Salo [FIN] 176 E4
Salò [I] 72 B6
Salobreña [E] 102 D5
Saločiai [LT] 198 E6
Salon [F] 44 B5
Salona [HR] 144 A2
Salon-de-Provence [F] 106 H4
Salonta [RO] 76 H3
Salorino [E] 86 F5
Salou [E] 92 C5
Salovci [SLO] 74 F3
Salsåker [S] 184 F3
Salsbruket [N] 190 C4
Salse di Nirano [I] 110 E3
Salses-le-Château [F] 106 C6
Salsnes [N] 190 C4
Salsomaggiore Terme [I] 110 D2
Salsta [S] 168 D1
Salt [E] 92 F3
Saltash [GB] 12 D5
Saltbæk [DK] 156 E2
Saltoluokta [S] 192 F6
Saltrød [N] 164 F5
Saltsjöbaden [S] 168 E3
Saltum [DK] 160 D3
Saltvik [FIN] 176 B5
Saltvik [S] 162 G3
Saluböle [S] 184 H1
Saluzzo [I] 108 F2
Salvacañete [E] 98 D2
Salvada [P] 94 D3
Salvagnac [F] 106 B2
Salvarola, Terme di- [I] 110 E3
Salvaterra de Magos [P] 86 C5
Salvaterra de Miño [E] 78 B5
Salvatierra [E] 96 E5
Salvatierra / Agurain [E] 82 H5
Salvatierra de los Barros [E] 94 G2
Salviac [F] 66 G4
Salzburg [A] 60 G5
Salzburg [D] 46 F2
Salzgitter-Bad [D] 32 G3
Salzgitter-Lebenstedt [D] 32 G3
Salzhausen [D] 18 F5
Salzkotten [D] 32 D4
Salzwedel [D] 18 H6
Salzweg [D] 60 H3
Sama de Langreo [E] 78 H4
Samadet [F] 66 C6
Samadet [F] 84 E2
Samailli [TR] 152 E5
Samandıra [TR] 150 F3
Samarína [GR] 128 D6
Samassi [I] 118 C6
Samatan [F] 84 G3
Sambiase [I] 124 D5
Sambir [UA] 52 G5
Sambuca di Sicília [I] 126 C3
Sambucheto [I] 116 B3
Sambuci [I] 116 B5
Sambucina, Abbazia della- [I] 124 D4
Samedan [CH] 72 A3
Samer [F] 28 D2
Sámi [GR] 132 C6
Samitier [E] 84 E6
Şamlı [TR] 150 D6
Sammakkovaara [FIN] 188 E2
Sammatti [FIN] 186 D4
Sammi [FIN] 186 B6
Samnaun [CH] 72 B2
Samo [I] 124 C7
Samobor [HR] 74 E6
Samoëns [F] 70 C3
Samoklęski [PL] 38 E5
Samokov [BG] 146 G5
Samokov [MK] 128 D2
Samolva [RUS] 198 G3
Samoranovo [BG] 146 F6
Šamorín [SK] 62 G5
Samos [E] 78 E4
Sámos [GR] 152 C5
Samoš [SRB] 142 H1
Samos, Monasterio de- [E] 78 E4
Samostan Pleterje [SLO] 74 D6
Samothráki [GR] 130 F4
Samovodene [BG] 148 C3
Sampatikí [GR] 136 F3
Samper [E] 84 E6
Samper de Calanda [E] 90 F5
Sampéyre [I] 108 F2
Sampo [RUS] 198 G1
Samtens [D] 20 D2
Samugheo [I] 118 C5
Saná [GR] 130 B5
Sanad [SRB] 76 E5
San Adrián [E] 84 A5
San Agustín [E] 98 C3
San Agustín [E] 100 C6
San Andrés [E] 78 D1
San Anton Leitza [E] 84 B3
Sanary-sur-Mer [F] 108 C6
San Asensio [E] 82 G6
Sanat Eufemia [E] 82 D4
Sanaüja [E] 92 C3
San Bartolomé de las Abiertas [E] 96 D1
San Bartolomé de la Torre [E] 94 E5
San Bartolomeo in Galdo [I] 120 F1
San Benedetto dei Marsi [I] 116 C5
San Benedetto del Tronto [I] 116 D2
San Benedetto in Alpe [I] 110 G5
San Benedetto Po [I] 110 E2
San Benito [E] 96 D5
San Bernardino [CH] 70 G2
San Bernardino, Tunnel del- [CH] 70 G2
San Biagio di Callalta [I] 72 F6
San Biágio Plátani [I] 126 D3
San Bonifácio [I] 72 C6
San Bruzio [I] 114 F3
San Calogero [I] 126 C3
San Cándido / Innichen [I] 72 E3
San Carlos del Valle [E] 96 G5
San Casciano dei Bagni [I] 114 G2
San Casciano in Val di Pesa [I] 110 F6
San Cataldo [I] 122 G4
San Cataldo [I] 126 E3
Sancergues [F] 56 D3
Sancerre [F] 56 D3
Sancey-le-Grand [F] 58 C5
Sanchidrián [E] 88 E4
San Chírico Raparo [I] 120 H5
San Cipirello [I] 126 C2
San Claudio al Chienti [I] 116 C1
San Clemente [E] 98 A4
San Clemente a Casuria [I] 116 D4
San Clemente al Vomano [I] 116 D3
San Clodio, Monasterio de- [E] 78 C4
Sancoins [F] 56 D4
San Cosme / Barreiros [E] 78 F2
San Cristóbal de la Laguna [E] 100 C5
San Cristóbal de la Vega [E] 88 E3
Sancti Petri [E] 100 F4
Sancti-Spíritus [E] 88 A3
Sancti-Spíritus [E] 96 C3
Sancti Spiritus, Convent del- [E] 98 F4
Sancy-sur-Nied [F] 44 F4
Sand [N] 164 B1
Sand [N] 172 C4
Sånda [N] 164 E4
Sanda [N] 164 F2
Sanda [S] 174 G6
San Damiano d'Asti [I] 70 E6
Sandane [N] 180 C5
San Daniele del Friuli [I] 72 G4
San Daniele Po [I] 110 D2
Sandanski [BG] 130 B2
Sandared [S] 162 B2
Sandarne [S] 174 E2
Sandau [D] 34 C1
Sandaucourt [F] 44 E6
Sandbach [GB] 10 D5
Sande [D] 18 C4
Sande [N] 164 H2
Sande [N] 170 C1
Sandefjord [N] 164 H3
Sandeid [N] 164 B1
Sandem [N] 166 C2
San Demetrio Corone [I] 124 D4
Sanden [N] 164 F2
Sander [N] 172 C5
Sandhem [S] 162 C1
Sandias [E] 78 C5
Sandıklı [TR] 152 H3
Sand in Taufers / Campo Túres [I] 72 E2
Sandizell [D] 60 D3
Sandl [A] 62 C3
Sandla [EST] 198 C3
Sandnäset [S] 184 D4
Sandnes [N] 164 B3
Sandnes [N] 164 F3
Sandnes [N] 194 D2
Sandness [GB] 6 G3
Sandnessjøen [N] 190 D2
Sando [E] 80 G6
Sandö Bro [S] 184 F3
Sandomierz [PL] 52 D2
San Dónaci [I] 122 G4
San Donà di Piave [I] 72 F6
San Donato Milanese [I] 70 G5
Sandøreng [N] 190 E3
Sándorfalva [H] 76 E4
Sandown [GB] 12 H5
S. Andrea [I] 72 C6
S. Andrea [I] 120 D2
S. Andrea Apostolo dello Iónio [I] 124 E6
S. Andrés del Rabanedo [E] 78 H5
Sandrigo [I] 72 D6
Šandrovac [HR] 74 G5
Sandsbraten [N] 170 G5
Sandsjö [S] 172 G1
Sandsjö [S] 190 G5
Sandsjön [S] 166 F1
Sandslån [S] 184 F3
Sandsletta [N] 192 D4
Sandsøy [N] 192 E3
Sandstad [N] 172 D4
Sandstad [N] 190 A6
Sandstedt [D] 18 D4
Sandur [FR] 160 A2
Sandvatn [N] 164 C4
Sandve [N] 164 A2
Sandvig [DK] 158 E4
Sandvik [S] 162 G4
Sandvika [N] 164 H1
Sandvika [N] 190 C6
Sandvika [N] 190 D2
Sandvikal [N] 164 C5
Sandviken [S] 174 E4
Sandvikvåg [N] 170 A5
Sandwich [GB] 14 G5
San Emiliano [E] 78 G4
San Esteban [E] 84 B3
San Esteban de Gormaz [E] 88 H3
San Fele [I] 120 G3
San Felice Circeo [I] 120 B2
San Felice in Balsignano [I] 122 D2
San Felice sul Panaro [I] 110 F2
San Ferdinando di Púglia [I] 120 H2
San Fernando [E] 100 F4
San Francisco [E] 82 B6
San Fratello [I] 126 F2
San Fruttuoso [I] 110 B3
Sånga [S] 184 F2
San Galgano, Abbazia di- [I] 114 F2
Sangarcía [E] 88 E4
San Gavino Monreale [I] 118 C6
Sangazi [TR] 150 F3
San Gemini [I] 116 A3
San Gemini Fonte [I] 116 A3
Sangerhausen [D] 34 B5
San Germano [I] 70 E5
San Gimignano [I] 110 E6
San Ginesio [I] 116 C2
Sanginkylä [FIN] 196 E4
San Giorgio [I] 118 D6
San Giorgio di Livenza [I] 72 F6
San Giórgio di Nogaro [I] 72 G5
San Giorgio Iónico [I] 122 F4
San Giovanni, Grotta- [I] 122 F4
San Giovanni, Grotta di- [I] 118 B6
San Giovanni al Mavone [I] 116 C4
San Giovanni a Piro [I] 120 G5
San Giovanni di Sínis [I] 118 B5
San Giovanni in Croce [I] 110 D2
San Giovanni in Fiore [I] 124 E4
San Giovanni in Persiceto [I] 110 F3
San Giovanni in Venere [I] 116 E4
San Giovanni Lupatoto [I] 72 C6
San Giovanni Rotondo [I] 116 G6
San Giovanni Suergiu [I] 118 B7
San Giovanni Valdarno [I] 110 F6
San Giovenale [I] 114 H4
Sangis [S] 196 C2
San Giuliano Terme [I] 110 D5
San Giuseppe Jato [I] 126 C2
San Giustino [I] 110 G6
San Giusto [I] 116 B2
Sangla [EST] 198 F3
San Godenzo [I] 110 F5
Sangonera la Verde [E] 104 C3
Sangüesa / Zangoza [E] 84 C5
Sanguinet [F] 66 B4
Sáni [GR] 130 B6
San Ignacio de Loiola [E] 82 H4
Sanitz [D] 20 C3
San Javier [E] 104 D4
San José [E] 102 G6
San José / Sant Josep [E] 104 C5
San José del Valle [E] 100 G4
San Juan de Alicante / Sant Joan d'Alacant [E] 104 E2
San Juan del Olmo [E] 88 D4
San Juan de los Terreros [E] 104 B4
San Juan del Puerto [E] 94 E6
San Juan de Muskiz [E] 82 G3
San Juan de Ortega [E] 82 F6
Sankovo [RUS] 202 E1
Sankt Andrä [A] 62 G5
Sankt Gertraud / Santa Gertrude [I] 72 C3
Sankt Kathrein am Hauenstein [A] 62 E6
Sankt Leonhard [A] 72 C2
Sankt Leonhard in P. / San Leonardo in Passiria [I] 72 D2
Sankt Magdalena / Santa Maddalena Vallalta [I] 72 E2
Sankt Margareten [A] 74 B3
Sankt Martin [A] 60 G6
Sankt-Michaelisdonn [D] 18 E3
Sankt-Peterburg [RUS] 178 H4
Sankt Valentin auf der Haide / San Valentino alla Muta [I] 72 B2
San Lazzaro di Savena [I] 110 F3
San Leo [I] 110 H5
San Leonardo [I] 120 H1
San Leonardo, Monasterio de- [E] 88 C3
San Leonardo de Yagüe [E] 90 A2
San Leonardo in Passiria / Sankt Leonhard in P. [I] 72 D2
San Lorenzo [I] 124 C8
San Lorenzo de Calatrava [E] 96 E5
San Lorenzo de El Escorial [E] 88 F5
San Lorenzo de la Parrilla [E] 98 B2
San Lorenzo in Campo [I] 112 B6
San Lorenzo Nuovo [I] 114 G3
San Luca [I] 124 C7
Sanlúcar de Barrameda [E] 100 F3
Sanlúcar la Mayor [E] 94 G6
San Lúcido [I] 124 D4
Sanluri [I] 118 C6
San Marcello Pistoiese [I] 110 E4
San Marco Argentano [I] 124 D4
San Marco dei Cavoti [I] 120 F2
San Marco in Lamis [I] 116 G6
San Marino [RSM] 110 H5
Sânmartin [RO] 76 H2
San Martín de la Vega [E] 88 F6
San Martín del Pedroso [E] 80 G4
San Martín del Rey Aurelio / Sotrondio [E] 78 H4
San Martín de Pusa [E] 96 E1
San Martín de Unx [E] 84 B5
San Martín de Valdeiglesias [E] 88 E5
San Martino Buon Albergo [I] 72 C6
San Martino dei Colli [I] 114 H2
San Martino della Battaglia [I] 72 C6
San Martino delle Scale [I] 126 C2
San Martino di Castrozza [I] 72 E4
San Martino di Lupari [I] 72 E6
San Mateo de Gállego [E] 90 E3
San Mauro Castelverde [I] 126 E2
San Michele all'Ádige [I] 72 C4
San Michele di Plaianu [I] 118 C3
San Michele Salentino [I] 122 F4
San Miguel de Bernúy [E] 88 G3
San Miguel de las Dueñas [E] 78 F5
San Miguel de Salinas [E] 104 D3
San Millan [E] 82 F5
San Millán de la Cogolla [E] 82 G6
San Miniato [I] 110 E6
Sänna [EST] 198 F3
Sånna [S] 166 G4
Sånna [S] 166 G4
Sånna [S] 184 B5
Sånna [S] 174 E1
S. Anna di Alfaedo [I] 72 C5
Sannazzaro de' Burgondi [I] 70 F6
Sannenmöser [CH] 70 D1
Sannicandro di Bari [I] 122 D3
Sannicandro Gargánico [I] 116 G6

San Nicolás de Tolentino [E] 100 C6
Sânnicolau Mare [RO] 76 F5
San Nicolò [I] 110 G3
San Nicolò di Trullas [I] 118 C4
San Nicolò Gerrei [I] 118 D6
Sannidal [N] 164 F3
Sanniki [PL] 36 H3
Sanok [PL] 52 E5
San Pancrazio Salentino [I] 122 F4
San Paolo [I] 118 E3
San Paolo di Civitate [I] 116 F6
San Paolo di Peltuino [I] 116 C4
San Pedro [E] 82 C2
San Pedro [E] 98 B5
San Pedro de Alcántara [E] 102 A5
San Pedro de Arlanza [E] 88 H1
San Pedro de la Nave [E] 80 H4
San Pedro del Arroyo [E] 88 D4
San Pedro del Pinatar [E] 104 D4
San Pedro de Mérida [E] 94 H2
San Pelayo [E] 88 G1
San Pellegrino in Alpe [I] 110 D4
San Pellegrino Terme [I] 70 H4
San Piero a Sieve [I] 110 F5
San Pietro, Badia di– [I] 112 D6
San Pietro di Simbranos [I] 118 C3
San Pietro di Sorres [I] 118 C3
San Pietro in Casale [I] 110 F3
San Pietro in Valle [I] 116 B3
San Pietro Vernotico [I] 122 G4
San Polo d'Enza [I] 110 D3
San Priamo [I] 118 D7
San Prospero [I] 110 F2
Sanquhar [GB] 8 D4
San Quírico d'Orcia [I] 114 G2
San Rafael [E] 88 F4
San Rafael del Río [E] 92 A6
Sanremo [I] 108 F4
San Roman de Cameros [E] 90 B1
San Roque [E] 78 C2
San Roque [E] 100 G5
San Roque de Riomera [E] 82 F3
San Rufo [I] 120 G4
San Sadurniño [E] 78 D1
San Salvatore Monferrato [I] 70 F6
San Salvo [I] 116 E5
San Sebastián de la Gomera [E] 100 B5
San Sebastiano Curone [I] 110 B2
Sansepolcro [I] 110 G6
San Servando, Castillo de– [E] 96 F2
San Severino Marche [I] 116 B2
San Severo [I] 116 F6
San Sicario [I] 70 B5
Sanski Most [BIH] 142 B3
San Sosti [I] 124 D3
Santa, Cova– [E] 104 C5
Santa Amalia [E] 96 A2
Santa Ana de Cambas [P] 94 D4
Santa Bàrbara [E] 92 A5
Santa Bárbara [E] 94 E4
Santa Bárbara [P] 100 D3
Santacara [E] 84 B5
Santa Caterina di Pittinuri [I] 118 B4
Santa Caterina Valfurva [I] 72 B3
Santa Caterina Villarmosa [I] 126 E3
Santa Cesarea Terme [I] 122 H5
Santa Clara-a-Velha [P] 94 B4
Santa Coloma [AND] 84 H6
Santa Coloma de Farners [E] 92 F3
Santa Coloma de Queralt [E] 92 C4
Santa Colomba de Somoza [E] 78 F5
Santa Comba [E] 78 B2
Santa Comba Dão [P] 80 C6
Santa Comba de Rossas [P] 80 F4
Santa Cristina / St Christina [I] 72 D3
Santa Cristina d'Aro [E] 92 G3
Santa Croce Camerina [I] 126 F5
Santa Croce di Magliano [I] 116 F6
Santa Croce d. Sannio [I] 120 E1
Santa Croce sull'Arno [I] 110 E5
Santa Cruz [P] 100 A3
Santa Cruz da Graciosa [P] 100 D2
Santa Cruz das Flores [P] 100 C4
Santa Cruz de Campezo / Santi Kurutze Kanpezu [E] 82 H6
Santa Cruz de la Palma [E] 100 B4
Santa Cruz de la Serós [E] 84 D5
Santa Cruz de la Sierra [E] 96 B2
Santa Cruz de la Zarza [E] 96 G2
Santa Cruz del Retamar [E] 88 E6
Santa Cruz de Moya [E] 98 D3
Santa Cruz de Mudela [E] 96 F5
Santa Cruz de Tenerife [E] 100 C5
Santadi [I] 118 C7
Santa Domenica Vittoria [I] 124 A8
Santa Elena [E] 96 F6
Santaella [E] 102 B2
Santa Eufemia [E] 96 C4
Santa Eulalia [E] 78 H3
Santa Eulalia [E] 98 D1
Santa Eulália [P] 86 F6
Santa Eulalia del Río / Santa Eulària des Riu [E] 104 C5
Santa Eulalia de Oscos [E] 78 F3
Santa Eulària des Riu / Santa Eulalia del Río [E] 104 C5
Santa Fé [E] 102 E4
Santafiora [I] 114 G2
Sant'Agata dè Goti [I] 120 E2
Sant'Ágata di Militello [I] 126 F2
Sant'Agata di Púglia [I] 120 G2
Santa Gertrude / Sankt Gertraud [I] 72 C3
Sant'Agostino [I] 110 F3
Sant Agustí de Lluçanes [E] 92 E2
Santa Iria [P] 94 E3
Santa Justa [P] 86 D6
Sant'Alberto di Butrio [I] 110 B2
Santa Luce [I] 110 D6
Santa Lucía [E] 100 C6
Santa Lucia del Mela [I] 124 B7
Santa Luzia [P] 78 A6
Santa Luzia [P] 94 C3
Santa Maddalena Vallalta / Sankt Magdalena [I] 72 E2
Santa Magdalena de Polpis [E] 98 G2
Santa Margalida [E] 104 E5
Santa Margarida de Montbui [E] 92 D4
Santa Margarida do Sado [P] 94 C2
Santa Margherita [I] 118 C7
Santa Margherita di Bélice [I] 126 C3
Santa Margherita Lígure [I] 110 B3
Santa María [E] 104 E5
Santa Maria a Pié di Chienti [I] 116 C1
Santa Maria Arabona [I] 116 D4
Santa Maria Cápua Vetere [I] 120 E2
Santa Maria da Feira [P] 80 B4
Santa Maria d'Anglona [I] 122 D5
Santa María de Cayón [E] 82 F3
Santa María de Huerta [E] 90 B4
Santa Maria dei Lattani [I] 120 D2
Santa María de las Hoyas [E] 90 A2
Santa María del Campo [E] 82 E6
Santa María del Páramo [E] 78 G6
Santa María de Nieva [E] 102 H4
Santa Maria di Bressanoro [I] 70 H5
Santa Maria di Corte, Abbazia di– [I] 118 C4
Santa Maria di Portonovo [I] 112 D6
Santa Maria di Propezzano [I] 116 D3
Santa Maria di Rambona [I] 116 C2
Santa Maria di Ronzano [I] 116 C4
Santa Maria di Siponto [I] 120 H1
Santa Maria in Valle Porclaneta [I] 116 C5
Santa María la Real de Nieva [E] 88 E3
Santa Maria Maggiore [I] 70 F3
Santa Maria Mayor [P] 80 C4
Santa María Navarrese [I] 118 E5
Santa Maria Nuova [I] 116 C1
Santa Marinella [I] 114 G5
Santa Marta [E] 94 G2
Santa Marta [E] 98 B4
Santa Marta [P] 94 D4
Santa Marta de Tormes [E] 88 C3
Santana [P] 100 A3
Sântana [RO] 76 G4
Santana da Serra [P] 94 C4
Santana do Mato [P] 86 C5
Santander [E] 82 F3
Sant'Andrea [I] 122 H5
Sant'Andrea Bagni [I] 110 D2
Sant'Andrea di Conza [I] 120 G3
Sant'Andrea Frius [I] 118 D6
Sant'Ángelo in Vado [I] 110 H6
Sant'Angelo Lodigiano [I] 70 G5
Santa Ninfa [I] 126 B2
Sant'Anna, Santuario di– [I] 108 E3
Sant'Anna Arresi [I] 118 B7
Sant'Antimo, Abbazia di– [I] 114 G2
Sant'Antine, Nuraghe– [I] 118 C4
Sant'Antíoco [I] 118 B7
Sant Antoni de Portmany [E] 104 C5
Sant'António di Gallura [I] 118 D2
Santanyí [E] 104 E6
Santa Olalla [E] 88 E6
Santa Olalla del Cala [E] 94 G4
Santa Pau [E] 92 F2
Santa Pola [E] 104 D3
Sant'Apollinare in Classe [I] 110 H4
Santa Ponça [E] 104 D5
Sant'Arcangelo [I] 122 C5
Santarcángelo di Romagna [I] 110 H5
Santarém [P] 86 C4
Santa Restituta [I] 114 H3
Santa Sabina, Nuraghe– [I] 118 C4
Santa Severa [F] 114 C2
Santa Severa [I] 114 G5
Santas Martas [E] 78 H6
Santa Sofia [I] 110 G5
Santa Susanna [E] 92 F4
Santa Tegra, Monte de– [E] 78 A5
Santa Teresa di Riva [I] 124 B8
Santa Teresa Gallura [I] 118 D2
Santa Uxía de Ribeira [E] 78 B3
Santa Vitória [P] 94 D3
Sant Boi de Llobregat [E] 92 D4
Sant Carles de la Ràpita [E] 92 A6
Sant Celoni [E] 92 F4
Sant Cugat Sesgarrigues [E] 92 D4
Santed [E] 90 D5
Sant'Elia a Pianisti [I] 120 F1
Sant'Elia Fiumerapido [I] 120 D1
San Telmo [E] 94 F4
Santena [I] 70 D6
San Teodoro [I] 118 E3
Santéramo in Colle [I] 122 D3
Santervás de Campos [E] 82 C5
Santes Creus [E] 92 C4
Sant'Eufémia Lamézia [I] 124 D5
Sant'Eutizio, Abbazia di– [I] 116 B3
Sant Feliu de Codines [E] 92 E4
Sant Feliu de Guíxols [E] 92 G4
Sant Feliu de Llobregat [E] 92 E4
Sant Ferran de Ses Roquetes [E] 104 C6
Sant Francesc de Formentera [E] 104 C6
Sant Grau [E] 92 F4
Santhià [I] 70 E5
Sant Hilari Sacalm [E] 92 F3
Sant Hipòlit de Voltregà [E] 92 E3
Santiago [P] 80 F5
Santiago, Cuevas de– [E] 94 H4
Santiago de Alcántara [E] 86 F4
Santiago de Calatrava [E] 102 D2
Santiago de Compostela [E] 78 C3
Santiago de la Espada [E] 102 G2
Santiago de la Ribera [E] 104 D4
Santiago del Campo [E] 86 H5
Santiago do Cacém [P] 94 B2
Santiago do Escoural [P] 94 D1
Santibáñez [E] 82 D4
Santibáñez de Ayllón [E] 88 H3
Santibáñez de la Sierra [E] 88 B4
Santibáñez de Vidriales [E] 80 H3
Santibañez Zarzaguda [E] 82 E5
Santi Kurutze Kanpezu / Santa Cruz de Campezo [E] 82 H6
Santillana del Mar [E] 82 E3
Santimamiñe [E] 82 H4
Santiponce [E] 94 G6
Santissima Trinitá di Saccargia [I] 118 C3
Santisteban del Puerto [E] 102 F1
Sant Joan d'Alacant / San Juan de Alicante [E] 104 E2
Sant Joan de les Abadesses [E] 92 E2
Sant Joan de Llabritja [E] 104 C5
Sant Joan de Vilatorrada [E] 92 D3
Sant Josep, Gruta de– [E] 98 F4
Sant Josep / San José [E] 104 C5
Sant Juliá de Lória [AND] 84 H6
Sant Llorenç de Morunys [E] 92 D2
Sant Lluís [E] 104 H5
Sant Martí Sarroca [E] 92 D4
Sant Mateu [E] 98 G2
Sant Miquel de Balansat [E] 104 C5
Santo Aleixo [P] 86 E6
Santo Aleixo da Restauração [P] 94 F3
Santo Amador [P] 94 E3
Santo André [P] 94 B2
Santo Domingo [E] 96 C6
Santo Domingo de la Calzada [E] 82 G6
Santo Domingo de Silos [E] 88 H1
Santo Estevão [P] 86 G2
Santo Estevo [E] 78 D5
Santo Estevo, Monasterio de– [E] 78 D5
Santok [PL] 34 H1
S. Antolín [E] 82 D2
Santomera [E] 104 C3
Santoméri [GR] 136 C1
Santoña [E] 82 F3
S. Antoni de Calonge [E] 92 G3
S. Antonio di Santadi [I] 118 B5
Santo Stefano [I] 118 D7
Santo Stefano Belbo [I] 108 H2
Santo Stéfano di Cadore [I] 72 F3
Santo Stefano di Camastra [I] 126 F2
Santo Stéfano Quisquina [I] 126 D3
Santo Stino di Livenza [I] 72 F5
Santo Tirso [P] 80 C3
Santo Tomé [E] 102 F2
Santo Tomé del Puerto [E] 88 G3
Santovenia [E] 82 A6
Santovenia de Pisuerga [E] 88 E1
Sant Pau de Seguries [E] 92 F2
Sant Pere de Rodes [E] 92 G2
Sant Pere Pescador [E] 92 G3
Sant Pol de Mar [E] 92 F4
Sant Quirze de Besora [E] 92 E2
Sant Quirze de Colera [E] 92 G2
Sant Rafel [E] 104 C5
Sant Sadurní d'Anoia [E] 92 D4
Sant Salvador [E] 104 F5
Sant Tomàs [E] 104 G4
Santu Lussúrgiu [I] 118 C4
Santurce / Santurtzi [E] 82 G3
Santurtzi / Santurce [E] 82 G3
Sant Vicenç de Castellet [E] 92 D3
Sant Vicent del Raspeig / San Vicente del Raspeig [E] 104 E2
Sant Vicent de sa Cala [E] 104 C5
San Urbez, Santuario de– [E] 84 D6
San Valentino alla Muta / Sankt Valentin auf der Haide [I] 72 B2
San Venanzo [I] 114 H3
San Vicente de Alcántara [E] 86 F5
San Vicente de la Barquera [E] 82 E3
San Vicente del Raspeig / Sant Vicent del Raspeig [E] 104 E2
San Vincenzo [I] 114 E2
San Vincenzo, Abbazia di– [I] 116 D6
San Vito [I] 118 D6
San Vito al Tagliamento [I] 72 F5
San Vito Chietino [I] 116 E4
San Vito dei Normanni [I] 122 F4
San Vito di Cadore [I] 72 E3
San Vito lo Capo [I] 126 B1
San Vito Romano [I] 116 B5
San Vittore delle Chiuse [I] 116 B1
Sanxay [F] 54 E4
Sanxenxo [E] 78 B4
Sanza [I] 120 G5
Sanzay [F] 54 D2
São Barnabé [P] 94 C4
São Bartolomeu [E] 94 D4
São Bartolomeu da Serra [E] 94 C2
São Bartolomeu de Messines [P] 94 C5
São Brás de Alportel [P] 94 C5
São Cristóvão [P] 94 D1
São Domingos [P] 94 C3
São Francisco da Serra [P] 94 C2
São Gregório [P] 78 C5
São Jacinto [P] 80 B5
São Jacinto, Dunas de–[P] 80 B5
São João [P] 100 C3
São João da Madeira [P] 80 B4
São João da Pesqueira [P] 80 E5
São João da Serra [P] 80 C5
São João dos Caldeireiros [P] 94 D4
São Luis [P] 94 B3
São Manços [P] 94 E2
São Marcos [P] 80 B6
São Marcos da Ataboeira [P] 94 D4
São Marcos da Serra [P] 94 C4
São Martinho [P] 86 E2
São Martinho das Amoreiras [P] 94 C4
São Martinho do Porto [P] 86 B3
São Mateus [P] 100 C3
São Mateus da Calheta [P] 100 D3
São Matias [P] 94 D3
São Miguel de Acha [P] 86 F3
São Miguel de Machede [P] 94 E1
São Miguel do Pinheiro [P] 94 D4
São Pedro [P] 86 E2
São Pedro da Cadeira [P] 86 B4
São Pedro de Balsemão [P] 80 D4
São Pedro de Muel [P] 86 C2
São Pedro de Solis [P] 94 D4
São Pedro do Sul [P] 80 C5
Saorge [F] 108 F4
São Romão [P] 86 C6
São Romão [P] 94 C2
São Teotónio [P] 94 B4
Saou [F] 68 F6
São Vicente [P] 100 A3
São Vicente da Beira [P] 86 F3
Sapakpınar [TR] 150 G3
Sapanca [TR] 150 G3
Sapareva Banya [BG] 146 F6
Sapernoye [RUS] 178 G2
Sápes [GR] 130 G3
Şaphane [TR] 152 F2
Säpilä [FIN] 176 D2
Šapjane [HR] 112 E1
sa Pobla [E] 104 E4
Sapotskin [BY] 24 F3
Sappada [I] 72 F3
Sappee [FIN] 176 G2
Sappee [FIN] 176 H1
Sappemeer [NL] 16 G2
Sappen [N] 192 G2
Sappisaasi [S] 192 H5
Sappu [FIN] 188 E3
Sapri [I] 120 G5
Saqués [E] 84 D5
Saraby [N] 194 B2
Sarafovo [BG] 148 F4
Säräisniemi [FIN] 196 E4
Sarajevo [BIH] 144 D1
Sarakíniko [GR] 134 B4
Sarakinoí [GR] 128 F4
Saralog [RUS] 198 H1
Saramon [F] 84 G3
Sáránd [H] 76 H1
Saranda [AL] 132 B1
Saransko [BG] 148 E5
Sarantsi [BG] 146 G4
Sarata [UA] 204 F4
Saray [TR] 150 D2
Saraycık [TR] 152 E3
Sarayköy [TR] 152 F5
Šarbanovac [SRB] 146 D2
Sarbia [PL] 36 C1
Sarbinowo [PL] 20 H3
Sarbinowo [PL] 34 G2
Sárbogárd [H] 76 B3
Sarby [PL] 50 D2
Sarceda [E] 82 E3
Sárdara [I] 118 C6
Sardara, Terme di– [I] 118 C6
Sardes [TR] 152 E4
Sardínia [GR] 132 E4
Sardoal [P] 86 D4
S'Arenal [E] 104 E5
S'Arenal d'en Castell [E] 104 H4
Šarengrad [HR] 142 E1
Sarentino / Sarnthein [I] 72 D3
Sărenz [BG] 148 F1
Sarga, Cova de la– [E] 104 E1
Sargans [CH] 58 H6
Sári [H] 76 C2
Sarıbeyler [TR] 152 D2
Sarıcakaya [TR] 150 H4
Sari d'Orcino [F] 114 A4
Sarıgöl [TR] 152 F4
Sarıkaya [TR] 152 E4
Sariköy [TR] 150 C5
Sarılar [TR] 150 C3
Sariñena [E] 90 G4
Šarišský Hrad [SK] 64 F2
Sarısu [TR] 150 G3
Sariyer [TR] 150 E2
Sarkad [H] 76 G3
Sarkadkeresztúr [H] 76 G3
Sárkeresztúr [H] 76 B2
Särkijärvi [FIN] 196 E4
Särkilahti [FIN] 186 G6
Särkilahti [FIN] 188 F6
Särkimo [FIN] 186 B2
Särkisalmi [FIN] 188 F5
Särkisalo [FIN] 186 G3
Särkisalo / Finby [FIN] 176 E5
Šarkovo [BG] 150 B1
Şarköy [TR] 150 C4
Sarlat-la-Canéda [F] 66 G4
Sarmizegetuza [RO] 204 C5
Särna [S] 172 E1
Sarnaki [PL] 38 E2
Sarnano [I] 116 C2
Sarnate [LV] 198 B5
Sarnen [CH] 58 F6
Sarnes [E] 82 C2
Sárnico [I] 72 A5
Sărnino [BG] 148 G1
Sarno [I] 120 E3
Sarnow [D] 20 D4
Sarnowa [PL] 36 C5
Sarnówek [PL] 38 C6
Sarnthein / Sarentino [I] 72 D3
Sarny [UA] 202 B7
Särö [S] 160 G3
Saronída [GR] 136 H1
Saronno [I] 70 G4
Sárospatak [H] 64 G4
Šarovce [SK] 64 B5
Sarpsborg [N] 166 B3
Sarracín [E] 82 E6
Sarral [E] 92 C4
Sarralbe [F] 44 G4
Sarrebourg [F] 44 G5
Sarreguemines [F] 44 G4
Sárrétudvari [H] 76 G1
Sarre-Union [F] 44 G5
Sarria [E] 78 E4
Sarrión [E] 98 E2
Sarroch [I] 118 C7
Sarron [F] 84 E2
Sarsıla İskele [TR] 154 E2
Sársina [I] 110 G5
Sarstedt [D] 32 G2
Sárszentlőrinc [H] 76 B3
Sarteano [I] 114 G2
Sartène [F] 114 B5
Sárti [GR] 130 D6
Sartilly [F] 26 D4
Sartmustafa [TR] 152 E4
Saruhanli [TR] 152 D3
Sárvár [H] 74 G2
Sarvela [FIN] 186 C5
Sarvijoki [FIN] 186 B3
Sarvikumpu [FIN] 188 E3
Sarvinki [FIN] 188 G2
Sarvisvaara [S] 194 A8
Sărvsjön [S] 182 F4
Sarzana [I] 110 C4
Sarzeau [F] 40 D5
Sarzedas [P] 86 E3
Sasa [MK] 146 E6
Sa Savina [E] 104 C6
Sásd [H] 76 A4
Šašov [SK] 64 C3
Sassari [I] 118 C3
Sassello [I] 108 H3
Sassenage [F] 68 H4
Sassenberg [D] 32 D3
Sassenheim [NL] 16 D4
Sassnitz [D] 20 D2
Sassocorvaro [I] 110 H5
Sassoferrato [I] 116 B1
Sassofortino [I] 114 F2
Sasso Marconi [I] 110 F4
Sassonero [I] 110 F4
Sassuolo [I] 110 E3
Šaštin- Stráže [SK] 62 G3
Sastmola / Merikarvia [FIN] 186 B6
Såtåhaugvoll [N] 182 C3
Sataniv [UA] 202 B8
Sátão [P] 80 D5
Satchinez [RO] 76 G5
Sätenäs [S] 166 D5
Säter [S] 166 F5
Säter [S] 174 C5
Sätila [S] 160 H2
Satırlar [TR] 152 D3
Sätofta [S] 158 C2
Sátoraljaújhely [H] 64 G3
Satovcha [BG] 130 C1
Satow [D] 20 B3
Sätra brunn [S] 168 B1
Sátres [GR] 130 E2
Satrup [D] 18 F1
Sattajärvi [S] 194 B7
Sattanen [FIN] 194 D6
Sattendorf [A] 74 A3
Satter [S] 192 H6
Satu Mare [RO] 204 C3
Saturn [RO] 148 G1
Saturnia [I] 114 G3
Saturnia, Terme di– [I] 114 G3
Saucats [F] 66 C4
Saucliéres [F] 106 E3
Sauda [N] 164 C1
Sauðárkrókur [IS] 192 B2
Saudasjøen [N] 164 C1
Saudron [F] 44 D5
Saue [EST] 198 D1
Saue [EST] 198 D1
Sauerbrunn [A] 74 C2
Sauerlach [D] 60 E5
Saugos [LT] 200 D4
Saugues [F] 68 D4
Saujon [F] 54 C6
Saukkola [FIN] 176 G4
Saukonkyla [FIN] 186 D2
Sauland [N] 164 F1
Saulgau [D] 58 H3
Saulieu [F] 56 F3
Saulkrasti [LV] 198 D4
Sault [F] 108 B3
Sault-de-Navailles [F] 84 D2
Saulvaux [F] 44 D5
Saulx [F] 58 B3
Saulxures [F] 58 C3
Saumur [F] 54 E2
Saunajärvi [FIN] 196 G5
Saunakylä [FIN] 186 C5
Saunalahti [FIN] 188 C3
Saunavaara [FIN] 194 E7
Saus [N] 190 D3
Sausheim [F] 58 D3
Sauvagnat [F] 68 B2
Sauve [F] 106 F3
Sauveterre-de-Béarn [F] 84 D2
Sauveterre-de-Guyenne [F] 66 D4
Sauviant-sur-Vige [F] 54 G6
Sauvo / Sagu [FIN] 176 E5
Sauxillanges [F] 68 D3
Sauze d'Oulx [I] 70 C5
Sauzet [F] 66 F5
Sauzé-Vaussais [F] 54 E5
Sauzon [F] 40 C5
Sava [BG] 148 F3
Sava [I] 122 F4
Sävar [S] 196 A6
Sävast [S] 196 B3
Savaştepe [TR] 152 D2
Savci [SLO] 74 E4
Säve [S] 160 G2
Savelletri [I] 122 F3
Savelli [I] 124 E4
Savenaho [FIN] 186 G5
Savenay [F] 40 E6
Saverdun [F] 84 H4
Saverne [F] 44 G5
Savero [FIN] 178 C3
Savi [FIN] 176 E1
Säviä [FIN] 186 H1
Savigliano [I] 108 F2
Savignac-les-Eglises [F] 66 F3
Savignano Irpino [I] 120 F2
Savignano sul Rubicone [I] 110 H5
Savigny-sur-Braye [F] 42 C5
Savijärvi [FIN] 196 G5
Savikoski [FIN] 176 F2
Savikylä [FIN] 196 F6
Savines-le-Lac [F] 108 D2
Savine Vode [SRB] 146 B5
Saviniemi [FIN] 176 F3
Savino Selo [SRB] 142 F1
Saviore dell'Adamello [I] 72 B4
Savitaipale [FIN] 178 D2
Sävja [S] 168 D2
Šavnik [MNE] 144 E3
Savognin [CH] 70 H2
Sávoly [H] 74 G3
Savona [I] 108 H3
Savonlinna / Nyslott [FIN] 188 E5
Savonranta [FIN] 188 F4
Sävsjö [S] 162 D3
Sävsjön [S] 166 G1
Sävsjöström [S] 162 E4
Savudrija [HR] 72 H6
Savukoski [FIN] 194 E6
Sax [E] 104 D2
Saxdalen [S] 172 H5
Saxnäs [S] 190 E4
Saxtorpsskogen [S] 156 H2
Saxvallen [S] 182 E1
Säynätsalo [FIN] 186 G5
Säyneinen [FIN] 188 D1
Sázava [CZ] 48 G4
Sazonovo [RUS] 202 D1
S. Baudelio, Ermita de– [E] 90 A3
S. Benito de la Contienda [E] 94 F2
S. Biágio [I] 110 G3
Scaër [F] 40 C3
Scafa [I] 116 D4
Scalasaig [GB] 8 B2
Scalea [I] 120 H6
Scaletta Zanclea [I] 124 B7
Scälevik [N] 164 D6
Scalloway [GB] 6 G4
Scandiano [I] 110 E3
Scanno [I] 116 D5
Scansano [I] 114 F3
Scanzano Jónico [I] 122 D5
Scarborough [GB] 10 G3
Scardovari [I] 110 H2
Scarinish [GB] 6 A6
S. Carlo [I] 126 C3
Scarperia [I] 110 F5
Scarriff [IRL] 2 C6
Šćepan Polje [MNE] 144 D2
Scepsis [TR] 152 B1
Schaan [FL] 58 H6
Schachendorf [A] 74 F1
Schackenborg [DK] 156 B4
Schackendorf [D] 18 G3
Schaffhausen [CH] 58 G4
Schafstädt [D] 34 B5
Schäftlarn [D] 60 E5
Schagen [NL] 16 D3
Schalkholz [D] 18 E2
Schallaburg [A] 62 D4
Schallstadt [D] 58 E3
Schangnau [CH] 58 E6
Schaprode [D] 20 D2
Scharbeutz [D] 18 G3
Schärding [A] 60 H3
Scharfeneck [A] 62 F5
Scharnitz [A] 60 D6
Scharnstein [A] 62 B5
Schaumberg [A] 62 B4
Scheer [D] 58 H3
Scheessel [D] 18 E5
Schéggia [I] 116 A1
Scheibbs [A] 62 D5
Scheifling [A] 74 B2
Scheinfeld [D] 46 F4
Schellenberger Eishöhle [D] 60 G5
Schemmerhofen [D] 60 B4
Schenefeld [D] 18 F3
Scherfede [D] 32 E4
Schermbeck [D] 30 G2
Scherneck [D] 60 D3
Schesslitz [D] 46 G3
Scheveningen [NL] 16 C5
Scheyern [D] 60 E3
Schieder [D] 32 E3
Schierling [D] 60 F2
Schiermonnikoog [NL] 16 G1
Schiers [CH] 58 H6
Schifferstadt [D] 46 B5
Schilde [B] 30 D3
Schilpário [I] 72 B4
Schiltach [D] 58 F2
Schio [I] 72 D5
Schirets' [UA] 52 H4
Schirmeck [F] 44 G6
Schirnding [D] 48 C3
Schitu [RO] 148 C1
Schkeuditz [D] 34 C5
Schladen [D] 32 H3
Schladming [A] 72 H1
Schläg [A] 62 B3
Schlaining [A] 74 F1
Schlaiten [LT] 72 F2

Schlaitz [D] 34 C4
Schlanders / Silandro [I] 72 C3
Schlangenbad [D] 46 B3
Schleching [D] 60 F5
Schleiden [D] 30 F5
Schleiz [D] 48 B2
Schleswig [D] 18 F1
Schleusingen [D] 46 G2
Schlieben [D] 34 E4
Schlierbach [A] 62 B5
Schliersee [D] 60 E5
Schlitz [D] 20 C4
Schlitz [D] 46 E1
Schellerten [D] 32 G3
Schloss [D] 46 C5
Schlosshof [A] 62 G4
Schlosspark [F] 44 H5
Schlotheim [D] 32 H5
Schluchsee [D] 58 F3
Schlüchtern [D] 46 E2
Schluderbach / Carbonin [I] 72 E3
Schluderns / Sluderno [I] 72 C3
Schlüssberg [A] 62 B4
Schlüsselfeld [D] 46 F4
Schlutup [D] 18 H3
Schmalkalden [D] 46 F1
Schmallenberg [D] 32 D5
Schmidmühlen [D] 48 B6
Schmilka [D] 48 F1
Schmölln [D] 20 E5
Schmölln [D] 48 C1
Schnackenburg [D] 20 A6
Schnaittenbach [D] 48 B5
Schneeberg [D] 48 D2
Schneverdingen [D] 18 F5
Schober Pass [A] 74 C1
Schöder [A] 74 B2
Schöllkrippen [D] 46 D3
Schönau [D] 58 E3
Schönbach [A] 62 D4
Schönbeck [D] 20 D4
Schönberg [A] 72 D1
Schönberg [D] 18 G2
Schönberg [D] 18 H3
Schönberg [D] 48 C3
Schönberg [D] 60 H2
Schönbergerstrand [D] 18 G2
Schönborn [A] 62 E4
Schönebeck [D] 20 B6
Schönebeck [D] 34 B3
Schönecken [D] 44 F1
Schongau [D] 60 D5
Schönhagen [D] 18 G1
Schöningen [D] 32 H3
Schönleiten [D] 60 D3
Schönmünzach [D] 58 F1
Schöntal [D] 46 D5
Schönthal [D] 48 C5
Schönwald [D] 58 F3
Schönwalde [D] 18 H2
Schönwalde [D] 34 E2
Schoondijke [NL] 28 G1
Schoonebeek [NL] 16 G4
Schoonhoven [NL] 16 D5
Schoonoord [NL] 16 G3
Schopfheim [D] 58 E4
Schopfloch [D] 46 F6
Schöppenstedt [D] 32 H3
Schoppernau [A] 60 B6
Schöppingen [D] 16 H5
Schorndorf [D] 60 B2
Schotten [D] 46 D2
Schramberg [D] 58 F2
Schrems [A] 62 D3
Schriesheim [D] 46 C4
Schrobenhausen [D] 60 D3
Schröcken [A] 72 B1
Schruns [A] 72 A1
Schull [IRL] 4 B5
Schüpfheim [CH] 58 E6
Schuttertal [D] 58 E2
Schüttorf [D] 16 H5
Schwaan [D] 20 B3
Schwabach [D] 46 G5
Schwabhausen [D] 46 G1
Schwabhausen [D] 60 D4
Schwäbisch Gmünd [D] 60 B2
Schwäbisch Hall [D] 46 E6
Schwabmünchen [D] 60 C4
Schwaförden [D] 18 D6
Schwaigern [D] 46 D5
Schwalenberg [D] 32 E3
Schwalmstadt–Treysa [D] 32 E6
Schwalmstadt–Ziegenhain [D] 32 E6
Schwanbeck [D] 20 D4
Schwanden [CH] 58 G6
Schwandorf [D] 48 B5
Schwanebeck [D] 34 A3
Schwanenstadt [A] 62 A5
Schwanewede [D] 18 D5
Schwaney [D] 32 E4
Schwarmstedt [D] 32 F1
Schwarzach [A] 72 G1
Schwarzburg [D] 46 G2
Schwarzenau [A] 62 D3
Schwarzenbach [D] 48 B3
Schwarzenbek [D] 18 G4
Schwarzenberg [D] 48 D2
Schwarzenfeld [D] 48 B5
Schwarzenfels [D] 46 E2
Schwarze Pumpe [D] 34 F5
Schwarzsee [CH] 70 D1
Schwaz [A] 72 E1
Schwechat [A] 62 F4
Schweden–Stein [D] 34 C5
Schwedt [D] 20 E6
Schwegenheim [D] 46 B5
Schweich [D] 44 G2
Schweinfurt [D] 46 F3
Schweitenkirchen [D] 60 E3
Schwelm [D] 30 H3
Schwenningen [D] 58 F3
Schwerin [D] 20 A4
Schwerte [D] 32 C4
Schwetzingen [D] 46 C5
Schwittersdorf [D] 34 B4
Schwuelper [D] 32 G2
Schwyz [CH] 58 F6
Sciacca [I] 126 C3
Sciara del Fuoco [I] 124 C5
Scicli [I] 126 F5
Scilla [I] 124 C7
Ścinawa [PL] 36 B5
Scoglitti [I] 126 F5
S. Colombano al Lambro [I] 70 G6
Scopello [I] 70 E4
Scopello [I] 126 B1
Scordía [I] 126 F4
Scorzè [I] 72 E6
Scotch Corner [GB] 10 F2
Scourie [GB] 6 D2
Scrabster [GB] 6 F2
Scrignac [F] 40 C2
Scritto [I] 116 A1
Scunthorpe [GB] 10 G4
Scuol [CH] 72 B2
Scupi [MK] 128 E1
S. Damiano Macra [I] 108 F2
S. Doménico [I] 70 E2
Seaford [GB] 14 E6
Seaham [GB] 8 G6
Seara [E] 78 E5
Seatoller [GB] 10 D1
Seaton [GB] 12 F4
Sebbersund [DK] 160 D4
Sebečevo [SRB] 146 B4
Sebeş [RO] 204 C5
Sebezh [RUS] 198 H5
Sebnitz [D] 48 F1
Seč [CZ] 48 E5
Seč [CZ] 50 A4
Sećanj [SRB] 142 H1
Secemin [PL] 50 H2
Séchault [F] 44 C3
Seckau [A] 74 C1
Seclin [F] 28 F3
Secondigny [F] 54 D3
Sečovce [SK] 64 G3
Sečovlje [SLO] 112 D1
Seda [LT] 200 D3
Sedan [F] 44 D2
Sedbergh [GB] 10 E2
Sedelsberg [D] 18 C5
Sedemte Prestola, Manastir– [BG] 146 F4
Séderon [F] 108 B2
Sédico [I] 72 E4
Sédilo [I] 118 C4
Sédini [I] 118 C3
Sedlčany [CZ] 48 F5
Sedlec [CZ] 48 H4
Sedlec–Prčice [CZ] 48 G5
Sedlice [CZ] 48 E5
Sedrun [CH] 70 F1
Šeduva [LT] 200 F4
Sędziszów [PL] 52 D3
See [A] 72 B1
Seebach [A] 74 B2
Seeboden [A] 72 H2
Seebruck [D] 60 F5
Seefeld in Tyrol [A] 72 D1
Seehausen [D] 20 A6
Seehausen [D] 34 B3
Seehausen [D] 34 D4
Seehof [A] 62 D5
Seekirchen [A] 60 G5
Seelbach [D] 58 E2
Seeling–stadt [D] 48 C1
Seelisberg Tunnel [CH] 58 F6
Seelow [D] 34 F2
Seem [DK] 156 B3
Seeon [D] 60 F5
Seeon [D] 60 F5
Seerhausen [D] 34 E5
Sées [F] 26 F5
Seesen [D] 32 G3
Seeshaupt [D] 60 D5
Seethal [A] 74 B2
Seewalchen [A] 60 H5
Seewiesen [A] 62 D6
Seferihisar [TR] 152 C5
Sefrivatnet [N] 190 D3
Segalstad [N] 170 H2
Segarcea [RO] 146 G1
Segård [N] 172 B3
Segelvik [N] 192 G1
Segerstad [S] 162 G6
Segesd [H] 74 G4
Segesta [I] 126 B2
Seget [HR] 116 H1
Seggau [A] 74 D3
Seglinge [FIN] 176 B5
Segmon [S] 166 E3
Segni [I] 116 B6
Segóbriga [E] 96 H2
Segonzac [F] 54 D6
Segorbe [E] 98 E3
Segovia [E] 88 F4
Segré [F] 40 G5
Seğucak [TR] 150 E5
Ségur [F] 68 B6
Segura [E] 102 G1
Segura [P] 86 G4
Segura de León [E] 94 G4
Segura de los Baños [E] 90 E6
Segurilla [E] 88 D6
Şehirlioğlu [TR] 152 F3
Sehnde [D] 32 G2
Şehvarmaz [TR] 150 G3
Seia [P] 86 F2
Seiches–sur–le–Loir [F] 40 H6
Seifhennersdorf [D] 48 G1
Seilhac [F] 66 H3
Seilleraye, Château de la– [F] 40 F6
Seim [N] 170 B3
Seinäjoki [FIN] 186 C3
Seira [E] 84 F6
Seis / Siusi [I] 72 D3
Seissan [F] 84 G3
Seitenstetten Markt [A] 62 C5
Seixal [P] 86 B5
Seixo [P] 80 C5
Sejerby [DK] 156 E2
Sejny [PL] 24 E3
Sejs [DK] 156 C1
Seki [TR] 154 G2
Sela [N] 190 B5
Seland [N] 164 E5
Selanovtsi [BG] 146 G2
Selänpää [FIN] 178 C2
Selargius [I] 118 D7
Selb [D] 48 C3
Selbitz [D] 46 H3
Selbu [N] 182 C2
Selby [GB] 10 F4
Selca [SLO] 74 B4
Selce [HR] 112 F2
Selchow [D] 34 F3
Selçuk [TR] 152 D5
Selde [DK] 160 C4
Selendi [TR] 152 D3
Selendi [TR] 152 F3
Selenicë [AL] 128 B5
Selent [D] 18 G2
Sélestat [F] 58 E2
Selet [S] 196 A4
Seleuş [RO] 76 H4
Seleuš [SRB] 142 H2
Selevac [SRB] 146 B1
Selfjorden [N] 192 C4
Selfoss [IS] 192 A3
Selgua [E] 90 G3
Séli [GR] 128 F5
Selianítika [GR] 132 F6
Seligenstadt [D] 46 D3
Selimağa [TR] 152 E1
Selimiye [TR] 152 D6
Selínia [GR] 136 G1
Selinunte [I] 126 B3
Selishtë [AL] 128 C2
Selishte [BG] 146 F6
Selište [SRB] 146 D2
Selitë [AL] 128 B4
Selizharovo [RUS] 202 D3
Selje [N] 180 B4
Seljestad [N] 170 C5
Seljord [N] 164 F2
Selkie [FIN] 188 G2
Selkirk [GB] 8 E4
Selkisaray [TR] 152 H2
Selkopp [N] 194 B2
Sella [E] 104 E2
Sella di Corno [I] 116 B4
Sellasía [GR] 136 E3
Selles [F] 54 H2
Sellía [GR] 140 D5
Sellières [F] 56 H5
Sellin [D] 20 E2
Sellye [H] 76 A5
Selm [D] 32 C3
Šelmberk [CZ] 48 G5
Selmsdorf [D] 18 H3
Selnes [N] 190 B5
Selnica [SLO] 74 D3
Selongey [F] 56 H3
Selonnet [F] 108 D2
S. Elpidio a Mare [I] 116 C2
Selsälandet [S] 184 D2
Selseng [N] 170 D1
Selsingen [D] 18 E4
Selsjön [S] 184 E2
Selsø Slot [DK] 156 G2
Selsverket [N] 180 G5
Seltjärn [S] 184 F1
Seltz [F] 46 B6
Selva di Cadore [I] 72 E3
Selva di Val Gardena / Wolkenstein in Gröden [I] 72 E3
Selvik [N] 180 B6
Selvino [I] 70 H4
Šember [CZ] 48 G4
Semblana [P] 94 C4
Semeljci [HR] 142 D1
Semeyskoye [RUS] 178 F5
Semily [CZ] 48 H2
Semizovac [BIH] 144 D1
Semmering [A] 62 E6
Semmering Pass [A] 62 E6
Sempas [SLO] 72 H5
Sempeter [SLO] 72 H5
Šempeter v savinjski dolini [SLO] 74 C4
Semur–en–Auxois [F] 56 F3
Seňa [SK] 64 G3
Sena de Luna [E] 78 G4
Sénas [F] 106 H4
Şencöy [TR] 150 F3
Sencur [SLO] 74 B4
Senden [D] 16 H6
Sendenhorst [D] 32 C3
Sendim [P] 80 G5
Senec [SK] 62 H4
Seneffe [B] 28 H3
Senez [F] 108 D4
Senftenberg [D] 34 F5
Senica [SK] 62 G3
Senigállia [I] 112 C6
Senise [I] 122 C5
Senj [HR] 112 F2
Senlis [F] 42 G3
Sennecey–le–Grand [F] 56 G5
Sennelager [D] 32 E3
Sennestadt [D] 32 D3
Sennewitz [D] 34 C5
Sennik [BG] 148 B4
Sénnori [I] 118 C3
Senohrad [SK] 64 C4
Senoji Varena [LT] 24 G2
Senokos [BG] 148 G2
Senonches [F] 26 H6
Senoncourt [F] 58 B3
Senones [F] 44 G6
Senorbì [I] 118 D6
Señorío de Bértiz [E] 84 B3
Senovo [BG] 148 D2
Senovo [SLO] 74 D5
Senožaty [CZ] 48 H5
Senožeče [SLO] 74 B6
Sens [F] 42 G6
Sens–de–Bretagne [F] 26 D5
Senseruth [B] 44 D2
Senta [MNE] 204 A5
Senta [SRB] 76 E5
Senterada [E] 84 G6
Šentilj [SLO] 74 D3
Šentjanž [SLO] 74 D5
Šentjur [SLO] 74 D4
Šentvid pri Zavodnju [SLO] 74 C4
Senum [N] 164 D4
Sepekov [CZ] 48 F5
Sepino [I] 120 E1
Sępólno Krajeńskie [PL] 22 C5
Sępopol [PL] 22 H2
Şepreuş [RO] 76 H3
Septemvri [BG] 148 A6
Septemvriyci [BG] 146 F3
Sept–Saulx [F] 44 B3
Sepúlveda [E] 88 G3
Sequeros [E] 88 B4
Serain [F] 28 F5
Seraincourt [F] 28 H6
Seraing [B] 30 E5
Seraserli [TR] 152 H4
Seravezza [I] 110 D5
Serceören [TR] 150 E5
Serebryanskiy [RUS] 198 H2
Sered' [SK] 62 H4
Seredka [RUS] 198 G3
Seregélyes [H] 76 B2
Seregno [I] 70 G4
Sérent [F] 26 B6
Serfaus [A] 72 C2
Sergen [TR] 150 C1
Sergiyev Posad [RUS] 202 F2
Serhat [TR] 152 B1
Seriaji [LT] 24 F2
Seriate [I] 70 H4
Sérifos [GR] 138 D3
Serinhisar [TR] 152 G5
Serino [I] 120 F3
Sermaize–les–Bains [F] 44 C4
Sermenin [MK] 128 G3
Sermide [I] 110 F2
Sermoneta [I] 120 B1
Serock [PL] 38 B2
Seroczyn [PL] 38 D3
Seroick Jezioro Zegrzyńskie [PL] 38 B2
Serón [E] 102 G4
Serón de Nágima [E] 90 C3
Seròs [E] 90 G5
Serpa [P] 94 E3
Serpins [P] 86 E2
Serpukhov [RUS] 202 F3
Serra [E] 98 E4
Serracapriola [I] 116 F6
Serrada [E] 88 E2
Serra de Agua [P] 100 A3
Serra de' Conti [I] 112 C6
Serradifalco [I] 126 D3
Serradilla [E] 88 A6
Serramazzoni [I] 110 E3
Serra Nova [E] 104 F5
Serrant, Château de– [F] 40 G6
Serra Orrios [I] 118 E4
Serra San Bruno [I] 124 D6
Serra San Quirico [I] 116 B1
Serrastretta [I] 124 D5
Serravalle [CH] 70 G2
Serravalle Pistoiese [I] 110 E5
Serrenti [I] 118 C6
Serres [F] 108 C2
Sérres [GR] 130 C3
Serreta [P] 100 D3
Serri [I] 118 D6
Serrières [F] 68 F4
Sersale [I] 124 E5
Sertã [P] 86 E3
Sertolovo [RUS] 178 H4
Sertolovo [RUS] 178 H4
Seruci, Nuraghe– [I] 118 B7
Sérvia [GR] 128 F6
Servian [F] 106 D4
Servianá [GR] 132 D2
Servigliano [I] 116 C2
Serwy [PL] 24 E3
Sesa [E] 90 F3
Seseña Nuevo [E] 96 G1
Sesimbra [P] 86 B6
Seskinore [NIR] 2 F3
Sésklo [GR] 132 H2
Sesma [E] 82 H6
Sessa Aurunca [I] 120 D2
Sessvatn [N] 164 D1
Šestani [MNE] 144 E5
Šestanovac [HR] 144 B2
Sestao [E] 82 G3
Sesto / Sexten [I] 72 F3
Sesto al Reghena [I] 72 F5
Sesto Calende [I] 70 F4
Sesto Fiorentino [I] 110 F5
Sestola [I] 110 E4
Sesto S. Giovanni [I] 70 G5
Sestriere [I] 70 C5
Sestri Levante [I] 110 B4
Sestroretsk [RUS] 178 G4
Sestu [I] 118 C7
Sesué [E] 84 F5
Sesvete [HR] 74 E5
Séta [GR] 134 C4
Šeta [LT] 200 F4
Setcases [E] 92 F2
Sète [F] 106 E4
Seter [N] 182 D5
Seter [N] 190 B6
Setermoen [N] 192 F3
Setihovo [BIH] 144 E1
Setpsindiği [TR] 150 A1
Setså [N] 192 D6
Settebagni [I] 116 A5
Settimo Torinese [I] 70 D5
Settle [GB] 10 E3
Setúbal [P] 86 B6
Seui [I] 118 D5
Seulo [I] 118 D5
Seurre [F] 56 G4
Sevar [BG] 148 D1
Sevaster [AL] 128 B5
Sevastopol' [UA] 204 H4
Sevast'yanovo [RUS] 178 G1
Sevel [DK] 160 C5
Sevenoaks [GB] 14 E5
Sever [P] 80 C5
Sévérac–le–Château [F] 68 C6
Severin [D] 20 B4
Severin [HR] 74 G5
Ševětín [CZ] 62 C2
Sevettijärvi [FIN] 194 E3
Sevilla [E] 94 G6
Sevilleja de la Jara [E] 96 D2
Şevketiye [TR] 150 B5
Şevketiye [TR] 150 D5
Sevlievo [BG] 148 B4
Sevnica [SLO] 74 D5
Sevojno [SRB] 146 A2
Sevrier [F] 70 B3
Sevsk [RUS] 202 E5
Sexdrega [S] 162 B2
Sexten / Sesto [I] 72 F3
Seyches [F] 66 E4
Seyda [D] 34 D4
Seydiköy [TR] 152 C4
Seyðisfjörður [IS] 192 D3
Seyitömer [TR] 150 G6
Seymen [TR] 150 D3
Seyne [F] 108 D2
Seynod [F] 70 A3
Seyssel [F] 68 H2
Seysses [F] 84 H3
Şeytan Sofrasi [TR] 134 H2
Sežana [SLO] 72 H6
Sézanne [F] 44 A4
Sezimovo Ústí [CZ] 48 G5
Sezze [I] 120 B1
S. Fågelås [S] 166 F6
Sfáka [GR] 140 G5
Sfakiá [GR] 140 C5
Sfântu Gheorghe [RO] 204 D4
S. Felices de los Gallegos [E] 80 F6
Sforzacosta [I] 116 C2
S. Geraldo [P] 86 D6
S. Ginés de la Jara, Monasterio de– [E] 104 C4
S. Giorgio della Richinvelda [I] 72 F5
S. Giorgio d. Sannio [I] 120 F2
S. Giovanni Bianco [I] 70 H4
S. Giusta [I] 118 C5
S. Gregòrio [I] 118 D7
S. Gregorio Magno [I] 120 G4
S. Gusmé [I] 114 G1
Shabla [BG] 148 G2
Shaftesbury [GB] 12 G4
Shahovskaja [RUS] 202 E3
Shakhovskaya [RUS] 202 E3
Shanagolden [IRL] 4 C3
Shanklin [GB] 12 H5
Shannon [IRL] 2 C6
Shannonbridge [IRL] 2 D5
Sharashova [BY] 38 G1
Sharnevo [BG] 148 D5
Shatalovo [RUS] 202 D4
Shatsk [BY] 202 B5
Shats'k [UA] 38 G4
Shchors [UA] 202 D6
Shchors'k [UA] 204 F2
Shchuchin [BY] 24 H4
Shchuchyn [BY] 202 A6
's Heerenberg [NL] 16 F6
Sheerness [GB] 14 F4
Sheffield [GB] 10 F4
Shefford [GB] 14 E3
Shëmbill [AL] 128 B3
Shëngjergj [AL] 128 B3
Shëngjergj [AL] 146 A6
Shëngjin [AL] 128 A1
Shënmëri [AL] 146 B6
Shepetivka [UA] 202 C8
Shepton Mallet [GB] 12 F4
Sherborne [GB] 12 F4
Shercock [IRL] 2 F4
Sheringham [GB] 14 G1
's-Hertogen-Bosch [NL] 16 E6
Shetaj [AL] 128 A2
Shijak [AL] 128 A3
Shiki [RUS] 198 H4
Shilkovci [BG] 148 C4
Shillelagh [IRL] 4 F4
Shimsk [RUS] 202 C2
Shinrone [IRL] 2 D6
Shipchenski Manastir [BG] 148 C4
Shipchenski Prokhad [BG] 148 C4
Shipka [BG] 148 C4
Shipkovo [BG] 148 B4
Shiroka Lŭka [BG] 130 D1
Shirokë [AL] 128 A1
Shirokoye [RUS] 22 H2
Shivatsevo [BG] 148 D4
Shkalle [AL] 132 B2
Shklow [BY] 202 C5
Shkodër [AL] 128 A1
Shkorpilovtsi [BG] 148 F3
Shmoylovo [RUS] 198 H3
Shoshan [AL] 146 A6
Shostka [UA] 202 E6
Shpola [UA] 202 E8
Shranamanragh Bridge [IRL] 2 B3
Shrewsbury [GB] 10 D5
Shrule [IRL] 2 C4
Shtëpëz [AL] 128 C6
Shtërmen [AL] 128 B4
Shumen [BG] 148 E3
Shumsk [UA] 202 B8
Shyroke [UA] 204 G2
Shyshchytsy [BY] 202 B6
Siána [GR] 154 C4
Sianów [PL] 22 A3
Siare [EST] 198 D3
Siátista [GR] 128 E6
Šiauliai [LT] 200 D4
Sibabravas [LT] 200 F4
Sibari [I] 122 D6
Sibbhult [S] 158 D1
Sibbo / Sipoo [FIN] 176 H4
Šibenik [HR] 112 H6
Sibilla, Ruderi di– [I] 120 C1
Sibinj [HR] 142 D2
Sibiu [RO] 204 C5
Sibo [S] 174 D2
Sićevo [SRB] 146 D3
Sicignano degli Alburni [I] 120 G4
Siculiana [I] 126 D4
Šid [MNE] 204 A5
Šid [SRB] 142 E2
Sidári [GR] 132 A2
Siddeburen [NL] 16 H2
Sideby / Siipyy [FIN] 186 A5
Sidensjö [S] 184 F2
Siderno [I] 124 D7
Sidertjärn [S] 172 G1
Sidiró [GR] 130 G2
Sidirókastro [GR] 130 B3
Sidirónero [GR] 130 D2
Sidmouth [GB] 12 E4
Sidra [PL] 24 F4
Sidra [PL] 24 F4
Sidyma [TR] 154 F3
Sidzina [PL] 50 D2
Siebe [N] 194 B4
Siebenberg [D] 30 G6
Siecq [F] 54 D6
Siedlce [PL] 38 D3
Siedlinghausen [D] 32 D5
Siedlisko [PL] 22 A6
Siedlisko [PL] 36 A4
Siegburg [D] 30 H5
Siegen [D] 32 C6
Siegenburg [D] 60 E2
Sieggraben [A] 62 F6
Siegsdorf [D] 60 G5
Siekierki [PL] 34 F1
Siekkinen [FIN] 196 E2
Sielec [PL] 38 F6
Sielpia Wlk [PL] 38 A6
Siemiany [PL] 22 F4
Siemiatycze [PL] 38 E2
Siena [I] 114 F1
Sieniawa [PL] 52 F3
Sieniawka [PL] 48 G1
Sieniec [PL] 36 F6
Siennica [PL] 38 C3
Siennica Różana [PL] 38 F6
Sienno [PL] 38 C6
Sieppijärvi [FIN] 194 C7
Sieradz [PL] 36 F5
Sieraków [PL] 36 B2
Sieraków [PL] 50 F2
Sierakowice [PL] 22 D2
Sierck–les–Bains [F] 44 F3
Sierentz [F] 58 D4
Sierning [A] 62 B5
Sierpc [PL] 36 G1
Sierra Bermeja [E] 100 H4
Sierra de Fuentes [E] 86 H5
Sierra de Luna [E] 84 C6
Sierra de Yeguas [E] 102 B3
Sierra Nevada [E] 102 E4
Sierre [CH] 70 D2
Siete Aguas [E] 98 D4
Sievi [FIN] 196 D5
Siewierz [PL] 50 G2
Sifferbo [S] 172 H4
Siğacik [TR] 152 C5
Sigean [F] 106 D5
Sigena, Monasterio de– [E] 90 G4
Siggjarvåg [N] 170 A5
Sighetu Marmaţiei [RO] 204 C3
Sighişoara [RO] 204 D4
Siglufjörður [IS] 192 B2
Sigmaringen [D] 58 H3
Signes [F] 108 C5
Signy–l'Abbaye [F] 28 H6
Sígri [GR] 134 G2
Sigtuna [S] 168 D2
Sigüeiro [E] 78 C3
Sigüenza [E] 90 A4
Sigües [E] 84 C4
Sigulda [LV] 198 E5
Sihtuuna [FIN] 194 C8
Siikainen [FIN] 186 B6
Siikajoki [FIN] 196 D4
Siikakoski [FIN] 188 E5
Siikala [FIN] 176 G4
Siilinjärvi [FIN] 188 C2
Siipyy / Sideby [FIN] 186 A5
Siivikko [FIN] 196 E3
Sijarinska Banja [SRB] 146 D5
Sikeå [S] 196 A5
Sikfors [S] 196 A3
Síkinos [GR] 138 E4
Siklós [H] 76 B5
Sikopokh'ya [RUS] 188 H5
Sikórz [PL] 36 G2
Sikovuono [FIN] 194 D4
Siksjö [S] 190 F5
Siksjön [S] 190 H3
Sil [S] 190 F6
Šilale [LT] 200 D4
Silandro / Schlanders [I] 72 C3
Silánus [I] 118 C4
Silbaš [SRB] 142 F1
Silberstedt [D] 18 F1
Şile [TR] 150 F2
Siles [E] 102 H1
Şilindia [RO] 76 H4
Silíqua [I] 118 C7
Silivri [TR] 150 D3
Siljan [N] 164 G3
Siljansnäs [S] 172 G4
Silkås [S] 182 H1
Silkeborg [DK] 160 D6
Silla [E] 98 E5
Silla de Felipe II [E] 88 F5
Sillamäe [EST] 198 F1
Sillans–la–Cascade [F] 108 C4
Silleda [E] 78 C3
Sillé–le–Guillaume [F] 26 F6
Sillerud [S] 166 D3
Sillian [A] 72 F3
Sillre [S] 184 E3
Silnica [PL] 50 H1
Silno [PL] 22 C4
Šilo [HR] 112 F2
Sils [E] 92 F3
Silsand [N] 192 F3
Sils–Maria [CH] 70 H2
Siltakylä Broby [FIN] 178 C4
Siltala [FIN] 196 E5
Šilutė [LT] 200 D5
Šiluva [LT] 200 E4
Silva [E] 78 C2
Silvacane [F] 106 H4
Silvaplana [CH] 70 H2
Silvares [P] 86 F2
Silvenski Bani [BG] 148 D4
Silverdalen [S] 162 F3
Silvermines [IRL] 4 D3
Silves [P] 94 B5
Silvi Marina [I] 116 D4
Silz [A] 72 C1
Simagino [RUS] 178 G4
Simagino [RUS] 178 G4
Simanala [FIN] 188 E4
Simancas [E] 88 E2
Şimand [RO] 76 G4
Simaság [H] 74 G1
Simav [TR] 152 F2
Simaxis [I] 118 C5
Simbach [D] 60 G4
Simbach [D] 60 G3
Simena [TR] 154 H3
Simeonovgrad [BG] 148 D6
Simferopol' [UA] 204 H4
Simići [BIH] 142 E4
Simitli [BG] 128 H1
Šimkaičiai [LT] 200 E5
Simlångsdalen [S] 162 B5
Şimleu Silvaniei [RO] 204 C4
Simmelkaer [DK] 160 C6
Simmerath [D] 30 F5
Simmerberg [D] 60 B5
Simmern [D] 44 H2
Simnas [LT] 24 F2
Simo [FIN] 196 D3
Símonos Pétras, Moní– [GR] 130 D5
Simonstorp [S] 168 B4
Simontornya [H] 76 B3
Simorre [F] 84 G3
Simpele [FIN] 188 F6
Simplon Dorf [CH] 70 E2
Simplonpass [CH] 70 E2
Simrishamn [S] 158 D3
Simuna [EST] 198 F2
Šimuni [HR] 112 F4
Sinaia [RO] 204 D5
Sinalunga [I] 114 G2
Sinanaj [AL] 128 B5
Sinanoğlu [TR] 150 H2
Sinarcas [E] 98 D3
Sincanlı [TR] 152 H2
Sıncansarnıç [TR] 150 E5
Sindal [DK] 160 E2
Sindelfingen [D] 58 G1
Sindi [EST] 198 D3
Sındırgı [TR] 152 E2
Sinekçi [TR] 150 C5
Sinekli [TR] 150 D2
Sinemorets [BG] 148 G5
Sines [P] 94 B2
Sinettä [FIN] 194 C7
Sineu [E] 104 E5
Sinevo [RUS] 178 G2
Singen [D] 58 G4
Singerin [A] 62 E5
Singsås [N] 182 B2
Singusdal [N] 164 F3
Sinilähde [FIN] 178 B2
Siniscola [I] 118 E4
Sinj [HR] 144 A1
Sinnai [I] 118 D7
Sinnes [N] 164 C3
Sinópoli [I] 124 C7
Sinsen [A] 72 B1
Sinsen [CH] 72 B1
Sinsheim [D] 46 C5
Sintea Mare [RO] 76 H3
Sintra [P] 86 A5
Sintsi [FIN] 188 F3
Sinuessa [I] 120 D2
Sinyaya Nikola [RUS] 198 G4
Sinzig [D] 30 H5
Siófok [H] 76 A2
Sion [CH] 70 D2
Sion [CZ] 48 H4
Sion [F] 44 E6
Siorac–en–Périgord [F] 66 F4
Sipahi [TR] 150 B3
Šipči [SRB] 146 B4
Sipiren [FIN] 196 F4
Šipkovica [MK] 128 G1
Sipoo / Sibbo [FIN] 176 H4
Šipovo [BIH] 142 B4
Sippola [FIN] 178 C3
Sira [N] 164 C4

Sirač [HR] 142 C1
Siracusa [I] 126 G5
Siret [RO] 204 D3
Sirevåg [N] 164 B4
Şiria [RO] 76 H4
Sirig [SRB] 142 F1
Sirishtnik [BG] 146 F5
Širitovci [HR] 112 H5
Sirkka [FIN] 194 C6
Sirkön [S] 162 D5
Sirma [N] 194 D2
Sirmione [I] 72 B6
Sirnach [CH] 58 G5
Sirok [H] 64 E5
Široké [SK] 64 F2
Široki Brijeg [BIH] 144 B2
Sirolo [I] 116 C1
Siruela [E] 96 C3
Širvintos [LT] 200 G5
Sisak [HR] 142 A1
Sisamón [E] 90 C4
Sisante [E] 98 B4
Sisättö [FIN] 186 D6
Sisbacka [FIN] 186 C1
S. Isidoro del Campo [E] 94 G6
Šišljavič [HR] 112 H1
Sissa [I] 110 D2
Sissach [CH] 58 E4
Sissonne [F] 28 G6
Şiştarovăţ [RO] 76 H5
Sisteron [F] 108 C3
Sistiana [I] 72 H5
Sistranda [N] 190 A6
Sit. Anna [S] 168 C6
Sitasjaurestugorna [S] 192 F5
Siteía [GR] 140 G4
Sitges [E] 92 D5
Sitno [HR] 142 A5
Sitovo [BG] 148 E1
Sitrama de Tera [E] 80 H3
Sittard [NL] 30 F4
Sitten [D] 34 D6
Sittensen [D] 18 E5
Sittersdorf [A] 74 C3
Sittingbourne [GB] 14 F5
Sitzendorf [A] 62 E3
Siuntiol / Sjundea [FIN] 176 G5
Siurua [FIN] 196 D3
Siusi / Seis [I] 72 D3
Sivac [SRB] 76 D6
Sivakka [FIN] 196 F5
Sivakka [FIN] 196 G5
Sivakkavaara [FIN] 188 E2
Sivaslı [TR] 152 G3
Siverskiy [RUS] 178 H6
Síviri [GR] 130 B6
Sivriler [TR] 150 C1
Sivry-sur-Meuse [F] 44 D3
Six-Fours-les-Plages [F] 108 C6
Sixmilebridge [IRL] 2 C6
Sizun [F] 40 B2
Sjenica [SRB] 146 A4
S. Jeroni, Monestir de- [E] 98 E6
Sjisjka [S] 192 G5
Sjoa [N] 180 G6
Sjøåsen [N] 190 C5
Sjöberg [S] 190 F3
Sjöbo [S] 158 C3
Sjøholt [N] 180 D3
Sjøli [N] 172 C1
Sjørring [DK] 160 C4
Sjørup [DK] 160 C5
Sjötofta [S] 162 B3
Sjötorp [S] 166 F4
Sjoutnäset [S] 190 E5
Sjøvegan [N] 192 F3
Sjövik [S] 160 H1
S. Juan, Castillo de- [E] 104 B4
S. Juan de la Peña [E] 84 D5
Sjundea / Siuntiol [FIN] 176 G5
Sjursjok [N] 194 D2
Sjursvika [N] 192 E3
Sjusjøen [N] 172 B2
Skabland [N] 172 B4
Skåbu [N] 170 G1
Skadovs'k [UA] 204 G3
Skælskør [DK] 156 F3
Skærbæk [DK] 156 B3
Skafidia [GR] 136 B2
Skaftafell [IS] 192 B3
Skaftung [FIN] 186 A5
Skagaströnd [IS] 192 B2
Skage [N] 190 C5
Skagen [DK] 160 F2
Skaidi [N] 194 B2
Skaistkalne [LV] 198 E6
Skakavac [HR] 112 H1
Skála [GR] 134 A4
Skála [GR] 134 G2
Skála [GR] 136 A1
Skála [GR] 136 E4
Skála [GR] 138 H2
Skała [PL] 50 H3
Skalabiňa [SK] 64 C2
Skála Eresoú [GR] 134 G2
Skála Kalliráchis [GR] 130 E4
Skålan [S] 182 G4
Skála Oropoú [GR] 134 C5
Skala-Podil'ska [UA] 204 D2
Skálavík [FR] 160 B2
Skalbmierz [PL] 52 B3
Skaldö [FIN] 176 F6
Skalica [SK] 62 G3
Skalité [SK] 50 F5
Skalitsa [BG] 148 D5
Skallelv [N] 194 F2
Skälleröd [S] 166 B4
Skällerud [S] 166 D4
Skallerup Kit [DK] 160 E2
Skallskog [S] 172 G4
Skalmodal [S] 190 E3
Skalmsiö [S] 184 F1
Skalochóri [GR] 128 E5
Skalotí [GR] 130 D2
Skalotí [GR] 140 C5
Skals [DK] 160 D5
Skålsjön [S] 174 D3
Skalstugan [S] 182 E1
Skammestein [N] 170 G2
Skän [S] 184 D5
Skandáli [GR] 130 F6
Skanderborg [DK] 156 D1
Skånes Fagerhult [S] 162 C6
Skåne-Tranås [S] 158 D3
Skånevik [N] 170 B6
Skåningbukt [N] 192 G1
Skänninge [S] 166 H6
Skanör [S] 156 H3
Skansbachen [S] 172 G5
Skansen [N] 190 C6
Skansholm [S] 190 F4
Skansnäs [S] 190 F3
Skåpafors [S] 166 D4
Skępe [PL] 34 H3
Skar [N] 170 D2
Skara [S] 166 E5
Skäran [S] 196 A5
Skarberget [N] 192 E4
Skärblacka [S] 168 A5
Skarda [S] 190 G5
Skåre [S] 166 E2
Skåret [N] 172 E1
Skärhamn [S] 160 G1
Skarhult [S] 158 C2
Skarínou [CY] 154 G6
Skarjenfossen [N] 164 D2
Skärlöv [S] 162 G6
Skarmunken [N] 192 G2
Skarnes [N] 172 C5
Skarpengland [N] 164 D5
Skärplinge [S] 174 F4
Skarsfjord [N] 192 F1
Skarstein [N] 192 E3
Skarszewy [PL] 22 D3
Skårup [DK] 156 E4
Skärvången [S] 190 E6
Skarvberg-Tunnelen [N] 194 C2
Skarveberg [N] 194 B2
Skarvsjö [S] 190 F4
Skaryszew [PL] 38 C5
Skarżynek [PL] 38 B1
Skarżysko-Kamienna [PL] 38 B6
Skasberget [N] 172 D4
Skata [FIN] 176 E6
Skattungbyn [S] 172 G2
Skatval [N] 182 C1
Skaudvilė [LT] 200 E4
Skave [DK] 160 C5
Skavik [N] 194 B2
Skawina [PL] 50 H4
Skeda udde [S] 166 H6
Skedevi [S] 168 B4
Skedshult [S] 162 G1
Skedsmokorset [N] 172 B6
Skee [S] 166 C4
Skegness [GB] 10 H5
Skehobruk [S] 168 E1
Skei [N] 180 D6
Skei [N] 180 G2
Skeie [N] 164 C5
Skela [SRB] 142 G3
Skelani [BIH] 142 F4
Skelde [DK] 156 C4
Skellefteå [S] 196 A4
Skelleftehamn [S] 196 A4
Skelleftestrand [S] 196 A4
Skelmersdale [GB] 10 D4
Skender Vakuf [BIH] 142 C3
Skene [S] 162 B3
Skenshyttan [S] 172 H5
Skepastó [GR] 130 B4
Skępe [PL] 36 G1
Skeppshult [S] 162 C4
Skeppsmyra [S] 168 F1
Skeppsvik [S] 196 A6
Skerping [DK] 160 D3
Skerries [IRL] 2 F6
Ski [N] 166 B1
Skiáthos [GR] 134 B3
Skibbereen [IRL] 4 B5
Skibbild [DK] 160 C6
Skibby [DK] 156 G2
Skibniew-Podawce [PL] 38 D2
Skibotn [N] 192 G2
Skidal' [BY] 24 G4
Skien [N] 164 G3
Skierbieszów [PL] 52 G1
Skierniewice [PL] 36 H4
Skiippagurra [N] 194 D2
Skille [N] 190 D3
Skillingarid [S] 162 D3
Skillingaryd [S] 162 D3
Skillinge [S] 158 D3
Skillingmark [S] 166 D1
Skiniás [GR] 140 F5
Skinnarbu [N] 164 E1
Skinnerup [DK] 160 C3
Skinnskatteberg [S] 168 A1
Skiønne [N] 170 F5
Skipnes [N] 180 G1
Skipton [GB] 10 E3
Skiptvet [N] 166 B2
Skirö [S] 162 E3
Skivarp [S] 158 C3
Skive [DK] 160 C5
Skiveren [DK] 160 E2
Skivjane [SRB] 146 B5
Skjærhalden [N] 166 B3
Skjånes [N] 194 D1
Skjåvika [N] 190 D3
Skjeberg [N] 166 B3
Skjeggedal [N] 164 E4
Skjelbreid [N] 190 D5
Skjelstad [N] 190 C5
Skjelten [N] 180 D3
Skjelvik [N] 194 C2
Skjern [DK] 156 B1
Skjervefossen [N] 170 C3
Skjervøy [N] 192 G1
Skjold [N] 164 B1
Skjoldastraumen [N] 164 B1
Skjolden [N] 170 E1
Skjønhaug [N] 166 C2
Skjøtningberg [N] 194 D1
Sklithro [GR] 132 H2
Skoby [S] 168 D1
Skočivir [MK] 128 F3
Škocjanske Jame [SLO] 74 B6
Skoczów [PL] 50 F4
Skodje [N] 180 D3
Skødstrup [DK] 160 E6
Škofije [SLO] 72 H6
Škofja Loka [SLO] 74 B4
Škofljica [SLO] 74 C5
Skog [S] 174 E3
Skógafoss [IS] 192 B3
Skoganvarre [N] 194 C3
Skogar [IS] 192 B3
Skogen [S] 166 D3
Skoger [N] 164 H2
Skogfoss [N] 194 E3
Skoghall [S] 166 E3
Skogli [N] 170 F4
Skogly [N] 194 E3
Skogn [N] 190 C6
Skogså [S] 196 B2
Skogsby [S] 162 G5
Skogstad [N] 170 F2
Skogstorp [S] 160 H4
Skogstorp [S] 168 B3
Skogvatnet [N] 192 F4
Skoki [PL] 36 D2
Skokloster [S] 168 D2
Skole [UA] 52 G6
Skollenborg [N] 164 G2
Sköllersta [S] 166 H3
Skomdal [N] 164 E3
Skomielna Biała [PL] 50 H5
Skomlin [PL] 36 F6
Skönberga [S] 168 B5
Skópelos [GR] 134 B3
Skópelos [GR] 134 H2
Skopí [GR] 140 G4
Skopiá [GR] 132 G3
Skopje [MK] 128 E1
Skopós [GR] 128 E4
Skopun [FR] 160 A2
Skor [N] 164 B2
Skórcz [PL] 22 E4
Skórka [PL] 22 B6
Skoroszów [PL] 36 D5
Skorovatn [N] 190 D4
Skorped [S] 184 F2
Skørping [DK] 160 D4
Skörstorp [S] 162 C1
Skórzec [PL] 38 D3
Skotnes [N] 190 C4
Skotnoye [RUS] 178 H4
Skotoússa [GR] 130 B3
Skotträsk [S] 190 G4
Skotselv [N] 164 G1
Skotterud [N] 166 D1
Skoulikariá [GR] 132 E3
Skoúra [GR] 136 E4
Skoútari [GR] 130 B3
Skovballe [DK] 156 D4
Skovby [DK] 156 D4
Skövde [S] 166 F6
Skra [GR] 128 G3
Skrad [HR] 112 F1
Skradin [HR] 112 H6
Skradinski Buk [HR] 112 H6
Skråmestø [N] 170 A3
Skravena [BG] 146 G4
Skrea [S] 160 H4
Skrede [N] 180 C5
Skreia [N] 172 B4
Skrīveri [LV] 198 E5
Skröven [S] 194 A8
Skrunda [LV] 198 C5
Skucku [S] 182 G3
Skudeneshavn [N] 164 A2
Skulsk [PL] 36 E2
Skulte [LV] 198 D4
Skultorp [S] 166 F6
Skultuna [S] 168 B2
Skuodas [LT] 198 B6
Skurugata [S] 162 E2
Skurup [S] 158 C3
Škušava [LV] 198 G5
Skute [N] 170 H4
Skuteč [CZ] 50 B4
Skutskär [S] 174 E4
Skutvik [N] 192 D5
Skvyra [UA] 202 D8
Skwierzyna [PL] 34 H2
Skýcov [SK] 64 B3
Skýdra [GR] 128 G4
Skylloura (Yılmazköy) [CY] 154 F5
Skýros [GR] 134 D3
Skyttmon [S] 184 C1
Skyttorp [S] 168 D1
Sládkovičovo [SK] 62 H4
Śladów [PL] 38 A2
Slagavallen [S] 182 E5
Slagelse [DK] 156 F3
Slagnäs [S] 190 G3
Slane [IRL] 2 F5
Slangerup [DK] 156 G2
Slănic Moldova [RO] 204 D4
Slano [HR] 144 C3
Slantsy [RUS] 198 G1
Slaný [CZ] 48 F3
Šlapanice [CZ] 48 F3
Slåstad [N] 172 C5
Slatina [HR] 74 H6
Slatina [MNE] 144 E3
Slatina [RO] 204 D6
Slatina [SRB] 142 F3
Slatina [SRB] 146 B2
Slatina [SRB] 146 E1
Slatiňany [CZ] 50 A4
Slatino [MK] 146 C6
Slatinski Drenovac [HR] 74 H6
Slättåkra [S] 162 B5
Slättberg [S] 172 G3
Slättberg [S] 194 A8
Slåttevik [N] 164 A2
Slätthog [S] 162 D4
Slattum [N] 172 B6
Slåttvik [N] 190 D4
Slavětín [CZ] 50 C5
Slavhostice [CZ] 48 H3
Slavičin [CZ] 64 A2
Slavín [CZ] 48 G2
Slavkovichi [RUS] 198 H3
Slavkov u Brna (Austerlitz) [CZ] 50 C6
Slavonice [CZ] 62 D2
Slavonski Brod [HR] 142 D2
Slavotin [BG] 146 F3
Slavsk [RUS] 200 D5
Slavuta [UA] 202 B8
Slavutych [UA] 202 D6
Slavyanovo [BG] 148 B3
Sława [PL] 36 B4
Sławatycze [PL] 38 F4
Slawharad [BY] 202 D5
Sławków [PL] 50 G3
Sławno [PL] 22 B2
Sławoborze [PL] 20 H4
Sleaford [GB] 10 G6
Sleme [SLO] 74 C4
Slemmestad [N] 164 H1
Slepač Most [MNE] 146 A4
Slepčević [SRB] 142 F3
Ślesin [PL] 22 C6
Ślesin [PL] 36 E3
Sleszów [PL] 50 C1
Sletta [N] 194 A2
Slettafoss [N] 180 F4
Slette [N] 180 E5
Slettestrand [DK] 160 D3
Slettmo [N] 192 F2
Sliač [SK] 64 C3
Sliedrecht [NL] 16 D5
Sliema [M] 126 C6
Sligeach / Sligo [IRL] 2 D3
Sligo / Sligeach [IRL] 2 D3
Slinde [N] 170 D2
Slipra [N] 190 C6
Slite [S] 168 G4
Sliven [BG] 148 D4
Slivnica [SLO] 74 D4
Slivnitsa [BG] 146 F4
Slivno [HR] 144 B2
Slivo Pole [BG] 148 D1
Slivovo [SRB] 146 C5
Śliwa [PL] 22 F4
Śliwice [PL] 22 D4
Slobozia [RO] 148 C2
Slobozia Mândra [RO] 148 B2
Słomniki [PL] 52 A3
Slonim [BY] 202 A6
Słonowice [PL] 20 G4
Słońsk [PL] 34 G2
Sloten [NL] 16 F3
Slottsbron [S] 166 E3
Slough [GB] 14 E4
Sloup [CZ] 50 C5
Sloupsko - Šošuvské Jeskyně [CZ] 50 C5
Slovac [SRB] 146 A1
Slovenj Gradec [SLO] 74 D4
Slovenska Bistrica [SLO] 74 D4
Slovenská L'upča [SK] 64 C3
Slovenske Konjice [SLO] 74 D4
Slovenské Nové Mesto [SK] 64 G3
Slovinci [HR] 142 B1
Słubice [PL] 34 G3
Słubice [PL] 36 H2
Sluderno / Schluderns [I] 72 C3
Sluis [NL] 16 C6
Sluis [NL] 28 G1
Slŭnchev Bryag [BG] 148 F4
Slunj [HR] 112 G2
Słupca [PL] 36 E3
Słupia [PL] 52 C3
Słupiec [PL] 50 C2
Słupno [PL] 36 H2
Słupsk [PL] 22 B2
Slutsk [BY] 202 B6
Służewo [PL] 36 F1
Småge [N] 180 D2
Smålandsstenar [S] 162 C4
Smalåsen [N] 190 D4
Smalininkai [LT] 200 E5
Smârdioasa [RO] 148 C2
Smarhon' [BY] 200 H5
S. Maria della Versa [I] 70 G6
S. Maria in Calanca [CH] 70 G2
S. Marina Salina [I] 124 B5
Šmarje [SLO] 72 H6
Šmarje [SLO] 74 D4
S. Martino in Pensilis [I] 116 F6
Šmartno [SLO] 74 C5
Šmartno [SLO] 74 D4
S. Mauro Forte [I] 122 C4
S. M. de Naranco [E] 78 H3
Smedås [N] 182 C4
Smedbyn [S] 166 E3
Smědeč [CZ] 62 B2
Smederevo [SRB] 142 H3
Smederevo [SRB] 204 B6
Smederevska-Palanka [SRB] 146 C1
Smedjebacken [S] 172 H5
Smedjeviken [S] 182 E1
Smedstorp [S] 158 D3
Smęgorzów [PL] 52 C3
Smeland [N] 164 E3
Smelror [N] 194 F2
S. Michele di Ganzaria [I] 126 F4
Smidary [CZ] 48 H3
Śmigiel [PL] 36 C4
S. Miguel [E] 84 B3
S. Miguel de Escalada [E] 78 H6
S. Miguel del Arroyo [E] 88 F2
S. Miguel de las Victorias [E] 90 B6
Smila [UA] 202 E8
Smilde [NL] 16 G3
Smiljan [BG] 130 E1
Śmiłowo [PL] 22 B6
Smiltene [LV] 198 F4
Smínthi [GR] 130 E2
Smirnenski [BG] 146 F3
Smögen [S] 166 B5
Smogulec [PL] 22 C6
Smokvica [MK] 128 G3
Smołdzino [PL] 22 C1
Smoleń [PL] 50 H3
Smolensk [RUS] 202 D4
Smolevitschi [BY] 202 B5
Smolnica [PL] 34 G1
Smolník [SK] 64 F3
Smolyan [BG] 130 E1
Smolyanovtsi [BG] 146 F3
Smørfjord [N] 194 C2
Smørhamn [N] 180 B5
Smuka [SLO] 74 C6
Smyadovo [BG] 148 E3
Smygehamn [S] 158 C3
Snappertuna [FIN] 176 F5
Snaptun [DK] 156 D2
Snartemo [N] 164 C5
Snarup [DK] 156 D4
Snåsa [N] 190 C5
Snausen [N] 180 H1
Snavlunda [S] 166 G4
Snedsted [DK] 160 C4
Sneek [NL] 16 F2
Sneem [IRL] 4 B4
Snefjord [N] 194 B2
Snerta [N] 182 D6
Snesudden [S] 196 A2
Snězné [CZ] 50 B5
S. Nicola da Crissa [I] 124 D6
S. Nicolás del Puerto [E] 96 A5
Snihurivka [UA] 204 G3
Snilldal [N] 180 H1
Snina [SK] 64 H2
Snjatyn [UA] 204 D3
Šnjegotina Gornja [BIH] 142 C3
Snogebæk [DK] 158 E4
Snössvallen [S] 182 F6
Snöstorp [S] 162 B5
S. Ny [S] 166 E3
Soajo [P] 78 B6
Soanlakhti [RUS] 188 H4
Soave [I] 72 C6
Söbbön [S] 166 C4
Sober [E] 78 D5
Soběslav [CZ] 48 G6
Sobibór [PL] 38 G5
Sobieszewo [PL] 22 E2
Sobieszów [PL] 50 A1
Sobki [PL] 36 G5
Sobków [PL] 52 B2
Sobotín [CZ] 50 C4
Sobotište [SK] 62 H3
Sobotka [CZ] 48 H2
Sobótka [PL] 50 C1
Sobowidz [PL] 22 E3
Sobra [HR] 144 C3
Sobrado [E] 78 D3
Sobrado dos Monxes [E] 78 D3
Sobral da Adiça [P] 94 E3
Sobral de Monte Agraço [P] 86 B4
Sobran [TR] 150 H5
Sobrance [SK] 64 H2
Sobreira Formosa [P] 86 E3
Søby [DK] 156 D4
Soča [SLO] 72 H4
Sočanica [SRB] 146 C4
Sočerga [SLO] 112 D1
Sochaczew [PL] 38 A3
Sochaux [F] 58 C4
Sochocin [PL] 38 A2
Sochós [GR] 130 B4
Socodor [RO] 76 G3
Socovos [E] 104 B2
Socuéllamos [E] 96 H4
Sodankylä [FIN] 194 D6
Söderåkra [S] 162 F6
Söderala [S] 174 E2
Söderås [S] 172 H3
Söderbärke [S] 168 A1
Söderboda [S] 174 G5
Söderby [FIN] 178 C4
Söderby-Karl [S] 168 E1
Söderfors [S] 174 E5
Söderhamn [S] 174 E2
Söderköping [S] 168 B5
Södertälje [S] 168 D3
Söderudden [FIN] 186 A2
Södra Vallgrund [FIN] 186 A2
Södra Vi [S] 162 F2
Sodražica [SLO] 74 C6
Sødring [DK] 160 E5
Soest [D] 32 D4
Soest [NL] 16 E5
Soestdijk [NL] 16 E5
Sofádes [GR] 132 F3
Sofiero [S] 156 H1
Sofiïvka [UA] 202 F8
Sofikó [GR] 136 F1
Sofiya [BG] 146 F5
Sofó [GR] 132 G2
Sögel [D] 18 B6
Sogge bru [N] 180 E3
Sogliano al Rubicone [I] 110 H5
Sogndal [N] 170 D1
Sogndalstrand [N] 164 B5
Søgne [N] 164 D6
Sogn Folkemuseum [N] 170 D2
Sogn Gions [CH] 70 G1
Söğüdlüdere [TR] 154 F2
Soğukpınar [TR] 150 F5
Soğuksu [TR] 150 H2
Söğüt [TR] 150 H4
Söğüt [TR] 154 D2
Söğüt [TR] 154 G1
Söğütalan [TR] 150 E5
Söğütyaylası [TR] 152 H1
Sohren [D] 44 H2
Soidinkumpu [FIN] 194 F8
Soidinvaara [FIN] 196 F5
Soignies [B] 28 H3
Soini [FIN] 186 E3
Soissons [F] 42 H2
Sokal' [UA] 52 H2
Söke [TR] 152 D5
Soklot [FIN] 186 B1
Sokna [N] 170 H5
Soknedal [N] 182 B2
Soko Banja [SRB] 146 D3
Sokolac [BIH] 112 H3
Sokolac [BIH] 142 E4
Sokolany [PL] 24 F4
Sokółka [PL] 24 F5
Sokolniki [PL] 36 E5
Sokolov [CZ] 48 C3
Sokolovo [BG] 148 B4
Sokolovo [BG] 148 G2
Sokołów Małopolski [PL] 52 E3
Sokołów Podlaski [PL] 38 D2
Sokoły [PL] 24 E6
Sokovaara [FIN] 188 G1
Sol [SK] 64 G2
Sola [N] 164 A3
Solana de los Barros [E] 94 G2
Solana del Pino [E] 96 E5
Solánas [I] 118 D7
Solares [E] 82 F3
Solarolo [I] 110 G4
Solbacken [S] 168 E3
Solberg [N] 164 G2
Solberg [S] 190 G6
Solberga [S] 162 E2
Solbjerg [DK] 160 C4
Solbjerg [DK] 160 E4
Solčava [SLO] 74 C4
Solda / Sulden [I] 72 C3
Sölden [A] 72 C2
Soldeu [AND] 84 H6
Solec Kujawski [PL] 22 D6
Solec nad Wisłą [PL] 38 D6
Solec-Zdrój [PL] 52 C3
Solem [N] 190 C5
Solenzara [F] 114 B5
Solera del Gabaldón [E] 98 C3
Solesmes [F] 28 G4
Solesmes, Abbaye de- [F] 42 A5
Solevåg [N] 180 D3
Solf / Sulva [FIN] 186 B2
Solfonn [N] 170 C5
Solheim [N] 170 B2
Solignac [F] 66 G1
Solihull [GB] 12 H1
Solin [HR] 144 A2
Solingen [D] 30 H4
Solivella [E] 92 C4
Söll [A] 60 F6
Sollana [E] 98 E5
Sollebrunn [S] 162 B1
Sollefteå [S] 184 E2
Sollenau [A] 62 F5
Sollentuna [S] 168 D3
Soller [D] 30 G5
Sóller [E] 104 E4
Sóller / el Port [E] 104 E4
Søllerød [DK] 156 G2
Sollerön [S] 172 G3
Søllested [DK] 156 E5
Sollia [N] 182 B6
Solliden [S] 162 G5
Solliès-Pont [F] 108 C5
Sollihøgda [N] 170 H6
Solmaz [TR] 152 F6
Solmyra [S] 168 B2
Solna [S] 168 D3
Solnechnogorsk [RUS] 202 E3
Solnhofen [D] 60 D2
Solnice [CZ] 50 B3
Solojärvi [FIN] 194 D4
Solonka [UA] 202 A8
Solosancho [E] 88 D4
Sološnica [SK] 62 G4
Solothurn [CH] 58 D5
Solovi [RUS] 198 G3
Solovychi [UA] 38 H6
Sölöz [TR] 150 F4
Solrød Strand [DK] 156 G3
Solsa [S] 168 D4
Sølsnes [N] 180 E3
Solsona [E] 92 D2
Solsvik [N] 170 A3
Solt [H] 76 C3
Soltau [D] 18 F6
Sol'tsy [RUS] 202 C2
Soltvadkert [H] 76 D3
Solum [N] 170 G5
Solunto [I] 126 D2
Solutré, Roche de- [F] 56 F6
Solvang [N] 180 H5
Sölvesborg [S] 158 E1
Solvik [S] 166 D3
Solvorn [N] 170 D1
Soma [TR] 152 D2
Sømådal [N] 182 D5
Somaglia [I] 70 H6
Sømåseter [N] 182 D5
Sombernon [F] 56 G3
Sombor [MNE] 204 A5
Sombor [SRB] 76 C6
Someren [NL] 30 E3
Somerniemi [FIN] 176 F4
Somero [FIN] 176 F4
Somino [RUS] 202 D1
Sommariva del Bosco [I] 108 G2
Sommarset [N] 192 D5
Sommatino [I] 126 E4
Sommen [S] 162 E1
Sommepy-Tahure [F] 44 C3
Sömmerda [D] 34 A6
Sommerfeld [D] 34 D1
Sommersted [DK] 156 C3
Sommery [F] 28 C5
Sommesous [F] 44 B4
Sommières [F] 106 F3
Somo [E] 82 F3
Somogyacsa [H] 76 A3
Somogyapáti [H] 74 H5
Somogyjad [H] 74 H4
Somogyszob [H] 74 G4
Somogytarnóca [H] 74 H5
Somogyvár [H] 74 H3
Somosierra [E] 88 G4
Somosierra, Puerto de- [E] 88 G4
Somovit [BG] 148 B2
Sompolno [PL] 36 F2
Somport, Túnel de- [E/F] 84 D4
Sompuis [F] 44 B5
Sompujärvi [FIN] 196 D2
Somvik [S] 162 E1
Son [N] 166 B2
Son Bou [E] 104 H4
Sonceboz [CH] 58 D5
Soncillo [E] 82 E4
Soncino [I] 70 H5
Sóndalo [I] 72 B3
Sondby [FIN] 178 B4
Søndeled [N] 164 F4
Sønder Balling [DK] 160 C5
Sønderborg [DK] 156 C4
Sønderby [DK] 156 C4
Sønderby [DK] 156 F4
Sønderby [DK] 160 B6
Sønder Dråby [DK] 160 C4
Sønder Felding [DK] 156 B1
Sønderho [DK] 156 A3
Sønder Omme [DK] 156 B1
Sondershausen [D] 32 H5
Søndersø [DK] 156 D3
Søndervig [DK] 160 B6
Søndervika [N] 182 D4
Sondrio [I] 70 H3
Söndrum [S] 162 B5
Sonekulla [S] 158 E1
Songe [N] 164 F4
Songesand [N] 164 B3
Sonkaja [FIN] 188 G2
Sonkajärvi [FIN] 196 E6
Sonneberg [D] 46 G2
Sonntagberg [A] 62 C5
Sonogno [CH] 70 F2
Sonsbeck [D] 30 G2
Sonseca [E] 96 F2
Sonta [SRB] 76 C6
Sonthofen [D] 60 B6
Sontra [D] 32 F6
Son Xoriguer [E] 104 G4
Söörmarkku [FIN] 176 D1
Sopeira [E] 84 F6
Sopela [E] 82 G3
Sophienhöhle [D] 46 H4
Sople [PL] 52 F3
Sopoćani [SRB] 146 B4
Sopoćani, Manastir- [SRB] 146 B4
Soponya [H] 76 B2
Šoporňa [SK] 64 A4
Sopot [BG] 148 B4
Sopot [MK] 146 D6
Sopot [PL] 22 E2
Sopot [SRB] 146 B1
Sopotnica [MK] 128 D3
Sopparjok [N] 194 C3
Sopron [H] 62 F6
Sora [I] 116 C6
Soragna [I] 110 D2
Söråker [S] 184 F4
Sorano [I] 114 G3
Sorbas [E] 102 H5
Sorbie [GB] 8 C5
Sørbø [N] 164 B2
Sörbo [S] 166 C5
Sørbotn [N] 192 F2
Sörbygden [S] 184 D3
Sørbymagle [DK] 156 F3
Sørdal [N] 190 E1
Sore [F] 66 C4
Sóréd [H] 76 B1
Søre Herefoss [N] 164 E5
Soreide [N] 170 C2
Søre Moen [N] 190 C6
Sørenget [N] 190 C5
Soresina [I] 70 H5
Sörfjärden [S] 184 E5
Sør-Flatanger [N] 190 B5
Sörforsa [S] 174 E1
Sórgono [I] 118 D5
Sorgues [F] 106 G3
Sörgutvik [N] 190 C4
Sørhella [N] 180 G4
Soria [E] 90 B3
Soriano Calabro [I] 124 D6
Soriano nel Cimino [I] 114 H4
Sorica [SLO] 74 B4
Sorihuela del Guadalimar [E] 102 G1
Sorita [E] 98 G1
Sørkjosen [N] 192 G2

Sorkun [TR] 152 H3
Sorkwity [PL] 24 B4
Sörmjöle [S] 190 H6
Sørmo [N] 192 F3
Sorø [DK] 156 F3
Soroca [MD] 204 E2
Soroní [GR] 154 D3
Sorpe [E] 84 G5
Sørreisa [N] 192 F3
Sorrento [I] 120 E4
Sorsakoski [FIN] 188 D3
Sorsele [S] 190 G3
Sörsjön [S] 172 E2
Sorso [I] 118 C3
Sort [E] 84 G6
Sortavala [RUS] 188 H5
Sortino [I] 126 G4
Sörtjärn [S] 182 G4
Sortland [N] 192 D3
Sør-Tverrfjord [N] 192 H1
Sørumsand [N] 166 C1
Sorunda [S] 168 D4
Sörup [D] 156 C5
Sørup [DK] 160 D4
Sørvær [N] 194 A2
Sørværøy [N] 192 C5
Sørvågen [N] 192 C5
Sørvágur [FR] 160 A1
Sörvattnet [S] 182 E5
Sørvik [N] 190 B6
Sørvik [N] 192 E3
Sörviken [S] 184 D1
Sørvollen [N] 182 C5
Sösdala [S] 158 C2
Sos del Rey Católico [E] 84 C5
Soses [E] 90 H5
Sošice [HR] 74 D6
Sośnica [PL] 50 G2
Sośnica [PL] 22 A5
Sośnicowice [PL] 50 F3
Sosnicy [RUS] 198 H1
Sosnivka [UA] 52 H2
Sosnove [UA] 202 B7
Sosnovo [RUS] 178 G3
Sosnovo [RUS] 198 H1
Sosnovskoye [RUS] 178 E2
Sosnovyy [RUS] 196 H1
Sosnovyy Bor [RUS] 178 F5
Sosnowica [PL] 38 F5
Sosnowiec [PL] 50 G3
Sospel [F] 108 F4
Sossano [I] 110 F1
Šoštanj [SLO] 74 D4
Sóstis [GR] 130 F2
Søstrefoss [N] 180 D4
Sostrup [DK] 160 F5
Sot [SRB] 142 F2
Sotaseter [N] 180 E5
Soteska [SLO] 74 C6
Søtholmen [N] 166 C4
Sotillo de la Adrada [E] 88 E5
Sotillo de las Palomas [E] 88 D6
Sotin [HR] 142 E1
Sotkamo [FIN] 196 F5
Sotkuma [FIN] 188 F2
Sotobañado y Priorato [E] 82 D5
Soto del Barco [E] 78 H3
Soto de los Infantes [E] 78 G3
Soto del Real [E] 88 F5
Sotos [E] 98 C2
Sotresgudo [E] 82 D5
Sotrondio / San Martín del Rey Aurelio [E] 78 H4
Sotta [F] 114 B6
Sotteville les Rouen [F] 28 B5
Sottomarina [I] 110 H1
Sottrum [D] 18 E5
Sottunga [FIN] 176 B5
Soutélamos [E] 96 H4
Soual [F] 106 B3
Soúda [GR] 140 C4
Souesmes [F] 56 C2
Soufflenheim [F] 46 B6
Souflí [GR] 130 H2
Soúgia [GR] 140 B5
Souillac [F] 66 G4
Souilly [F] 44 D4
Soulac-sur-Mere [F] 54 B6
Soulaines-Dhuys [F] 44 C6
Soulópoulo [GR] 132 C2
Soultz [F] 44 H5
Soultz [F] 58 D3
Soumoulou [F] 84 E3
Soúnio [GR] 130 E2
Soúnio [GR] 136 H2
Souppes-sur-Lolng [F] 42 G5
Sourdeval [F] 26 E4
Sourdon [F] 28 E5
Soure [P] 86 D2
Sournia [F] 92 F1
Sourotí [GR] 130 B5
Soúrpi [GR] 132 H3
Sousceyrac [F] 66 H4
Sousel [P] 86 E6
Soustons [F] 66 A6
Soutelo [E] 78 C4
Southampton [GB] 12 H5
Southend-on-Sea [GB] 14 F4
South Molton [GB] 12 E4
Southport [GB] 10 D3
South Shields [GB] 8 G6
Southwold [GB] 14 H3
Soutomaior, Cast. de- [E] 78 B4
Souvála [GR] 136 G1
Souvigny [F] 56 D5
Søvang [DK] 156 B4
Søvassli [N] 180 H1
Sovata [RO] 204 D4
Sövdeborg [S] 158 C3
Söve [TR] 150 D5
Sover [I] 72 D4
Soverato [I] 124 E6
Soveria Mannelli [I] 124 D5
Sövestad [S] 158 D3
Sovetsk [RUS] 200 D5
Sovetskiy [RUS] 178 F3
Søvik [N] 180 D3
Sovinec [CZ] 50 D4
Sovjan [AL] 128 D4
Sowia Góra [PL] 36 B2
Sowiniec [PL] 20 G6
Soyen [D] 60 F4
Søyland [N] 164 A4
Sozaro [TR] 150 C1
Sozopol [BG] 148 F4
Spa [B] 30 E5
Spacco della Regina [I] 114 F4
Spaichingen [D] 58 G3
Spakenburg [NL] 16 E4
Spalding [GB] 10 G6
Spálené Poříčí [CZ] 48 E5
Spalt [D] 46 G6
Spanchevci [BG] 146 F3
S. Pancrázio [I] 72 C3
Spandau [D] 34 E2
Spånga [S] 168 C3
Spangenberg [D] 32 F5
Spangereid [N] 164 C6
Spannberg [A] 62 F4
Španovica [HR] 142 C1
S. Pantaleón de Losa [E] 82 F4
Sparanise [I] 120 D2
Spare [LV] 198 C5
Sparreholm [S] 168 C4
Sparresholm [DK] 156 F4
Spárta [GR] 134 B6
Spartà [I] 124 B7
Spárti [GR] 136 E4
Spárto [GR] 132 D4
Spas [AL] 146 B6
Spasovo [BG] 148 G1
Spasskaya Polist' [RUS] 202 C1
Spáta [GR] 134 C6
Spatharaíoi [GR] 138 H1
Spean Bridge [GB] 6 C6
Specke [S] 166 D2
S. Pedro [P] 94 E2
S. Pedro de Cardeña [E] 82 E6
S. Pedro de Teverga [E] 78 G4
Speinshart [D] 48 B4
Spekedalssetra [N] 182 C5
Spello [I] 116 A2
Spenge [D] 32 D2
Spennymoor [GB] 10 F1
Spenshult [S] 162 B4
Spentrup [DK] 160 E5
Sperchеiáda [GR] 132 F4
S. Pere de Ribes [E] 92 D4
Sperlonga [I] 120 C2
Spétses [GR] 136 F3
Speyer [D] 46 C5
Spezzano Albanese [I] 124 D3
Spicino [RUS] 198 G2
Spickendorf [D] 34 C5
Spiddal / An Spidéal [IRL] 2 B5
Spiegelau [D] 60 H2
Spiekeroog [D] 18 C3
Spielbg [D] 46 F5
Spielfeld [A] 74 D3
S. Pietro al Natisone [I] 72 H4
Spiez [CH] 70 E1
Spijkenisse [NL] 16 C5
Spílaia Diroú [GR] 136 E5
Spíli [GR] 140 D5
Spilimbergo [I] 72 F4
Spilja Hrustovača [BIH] 142 B3
Spillum [N] 190 C5
Spina, Necropoli di- [I] 110 G3
Spinalógka [GR] 140 F4
Spinazzola [I] 120 H3
Spincourt [F] 44 E3
Spind [N] 164 C5
Špindlerův-Mlýn [CZ] 50 A2
Spineta Nuova [I] 120 F4
Špionica Donja [BIH] 142 D3
Špišić Bukovica [HR] 74 G5
Spiss [A] 72 B2
Spišská Belá [SK] 52 B6
Spišská Nová Ves [SK] 64 E2
Spišské Podhradie [SK] 64 F2
Spišský Hrad [SK] 64 F2
Spišský Štvrtok [SK] 64 E2
Spital am Pyhrn [A] 62 B6
Spittal an der Drau [A] 72 H3
Spitz [A] 62 D4
Spjærøy [N] 166 B3
Spjald [DK] 160 B6
Spjelkavik [N] 180 D3
Spjutsund [FIN] 178 B4
Split [HR] 144 A2
Splügen [CH] 70 G2
Spodnja Idrija [SLO] 74 B5
Spodsbjerg [DK] 156 E4
Špogi [LV] 198 F6
Spohle [D] 18 C4
Spoleto [I] 116 B3
Spoltore [I] 116 D4
Spotorno [I] 108 H3
Spøttrup [DK] 160 C4
Sprakensehl [D] 32 H1
Spręcowo [PL] 22 G4
Spreenhagen [D] 34 F3
Spremberg [D] 34 F5
Spresiano [I] 72 E5
Springe [D] 32 F2
Sproge [S] 168 F5
Spy [B] 30 D5
Spychowo [PL] 24 C4
Spydeberg [N] 166 B2
Spytkowice [PL] 50 H5
Squillace [I] 124 E6
Squinzano [I] 122 G4
Srahmore [IRL] 2 C3
Srb [HR] 112 H4
Srbac [BIH] 142 C2
Srbica [SRB] 146 C5
Srbobran [MNE] 204 A5
Srbobran [SRB] 76 E6
Srdevići [BIH] 144 B1
Srdiečko [SK] 64 D2
Srebărna [BG] 148 E1
Srebrenica [BIH] 142 F4
Srebrenik [BIH] 142 D3
Sredets [BG] 148 C5
Sredets [BG] 148 F5
Središče ob Dravi [SLO] 74 F4
Sredishte [BG] 148 F1
Srednje [BIH] 142 D4
Srednogortsi [BG] 130 E1
Sredno Gradishte [BG] 148 C5
Sredogriv [BG] 146 E3
Srem [PL] 36 C3
Sremska Kamenica [SRB] 142 F1
Sremska Mitrovica [MNE] 204 A6
Sremska Mitrovica [SRB] 142 F2
Sremska Rača [SRB] 142 F2
Sremski Karlovci [SRB] 142 F2
Sribne [UA] 202 E7
Srní [CZ] 62 A2
Środa Śląska [PL] 36 C6
Środa Wielkopolska [PL] 36 D3
Srokowo [PL] 24 C3
S. Roque do P. [P] 100 C3
Srpci [MK] 128 E3
Srp. Itebej [SRB] 76 F6
Srpska Crnja [SRB] 76 F6
Srpski Miletić [SRB] 76 C6
S. Salvador de Leyre [E] 84 C4
S. Silvestre de Guzmán [E] 94 E5
S. Stefano d'Aveto [I] 110 C3
Sta [S] 182 E1
Staaken [D] 34 E2
Sta. Ana, Monasterio de- [E] 104 D2
Staatz [A] 62 F3
Stabbestad [N] 164 F4
Stabbursnes [N] 194 C2
Stabekk [N] 166 B1
Sta. Casilda [E] 82 F5
Stachy [CZ] 48 E6
Sta. Coloma [AND] 84 H6
Sta. Coloma de G. [E] 92 E4
Sta. Cristina de Lena [E] 78 H4
Stade [D] 18 E4
Stadl a. d. Mur [A] 74 B2
Stadra [S] 166 G2
Stadskanaal [NL] 16 H3
Stadt Allendorf [D] 32 E6
Stadthagen [D] 32 F2
Stadtilm [D] 46 G1
Stadtkyll [D] 30 F6
Stadtlauringen [D] 46 F3
Stadtlohn [D] 16 G5
Stadtoldendorf [D] 32 F3
Stadtroda [D] 48 B1
Stadtsteinach [D] 46 H3
St Aegyd [A] 62 D5
Sta. Elena [E] 84 E5
Sta. Espina, Monasterio de- [E] 88 E1
Stäfa [CH] 58 G5
Staffanstorp [DK] 158 C3
Staffarda, Abbazia di- [I] 108 F2
Staffelstein [D] 46 G3
Stafford [GB] 10 E5
St-Affrique [F] 106 D3
Stágeira [GR] 130 C4
St-Agnant [F] 54 C5
St-Agrève [F] 68 E5
Stahle [D] 32 F3
Stai [N] 172 C1
Staicele [LV] 198 E4
St-Aignan [F] 40 G5
St-Aignan [F] 54 H2
Staigue Fort [IRL] 4 B4
Stainach [A] 62 B6
Staines [GB] 14 E4
Stainsland [N] 164 D4
Stainville [F] 44 D5
Stainz [A] 74 D2
Stakčín [SK] 64 H2
Stakenjokk [S] 190 E4
Stakkvik [N] 192 G1
Stalać [SRB] 146 C3
St-Alban [F] 68 C5
St Albans [GB] 14 E3
Stalden [CH] 70 E2
Stalheim [N] 170 D3
Stalheims-Kleivene Museum [N] 170 C3
Stalída [GR] 140 F4
Stall [A] 72 G2
Stallarholmen [S] 168 C3
Stallberg [D] 20 E4
Ställberg [S] 166 G1
Ställdalen [S] 166 G1
Stalon [S] 190 F4
Stalowa Wola [PL] 52 E2
St-Amand-en-Puisaye [F] 56 D2
St-Amand-les-Eaux [F] 28 G3
St-Amand-Longpré [F] 42 C6
St-Amand-Montrond [F] 56 C4
St-Amans [F] 68 C5
St-Amant-Roche-Savine [F] 68 D3
Sta. Maria da Real [E] 78 C4
Sta. Maria de Conxo [E] 78 C3
Sta. María de la Vega [E] 88 D2
Sta. María de Lebeña [E] 82 D3
Sta. Maria de Melque [E] 96 E2
Sta. Maria de Mezonzo [E] 78 D3
Sta. Maria la Real [E] 82 D4
Sta. Maria la Real [E] 84 A6
Stambolovo [BG] 148 C3
St-Ambroix [F] 106 F2
Sta. M. de Bellpuig de les Avellanes [E] 92 B2
St-Amé [F] 58 C3
Stameriena [LV] 198 F4
Stamford [GB] 14 E1
Stamná [GR] 132 E5
St-Amour [F] 56 H6
Stampfen [A] 72 G2
Stams [A] 72 C1
Stamsund [N] 192 D4
St Andrä [A] 74 C3
St-André [F] 42 D3
St Andreasberg [D] 32 G4
St-André-de-Cubzac [F] 66 D3
St-André-les-Alpes [F] 108 D3
St Andrews [GB] 8 F2
Stånga [S] 168 G5
Stange [N] 172 C4
Stangerum [DK] 160 E5
Stanghelle [N] 170 B3
Staniewice [PL] 22 B2
Stanišić [SRB] 76 C5
Stanisławów [PL] 38 C3
Štanjel [SLO] 72 H5
Stanjevci [MK] 128 F1
Staňkov [CZ] 48 D5
St Annaparochie [NL] 16 F2
Stanós [GR] 130 C4
Stans [CH] 58 F6
Stansstad [CH] 58 F6
St-Anthème [F] 68 E3
St-Antoine [F] 68 G4
St.-Antoine, Chapelle- [F] 84 D3
St Anton [A] 72 B1
St-Antonin-Noble-Val [F] 66 G6
St. Antonino [F] 114 B3
Stany [PL] 52 D2
Stanzach [A] 60 C6
St-Août [F] 54 H4
Stapar [SRB] 76 C6
Staphorst [NL] 16 F3
Stapnes [N] 164 B4
Stąporków [PL] 38 B6
Stara [PL] 36 H6
Stara Bystrica [SK] 50 G6
Stara Cerlev [SLO] 74 C6
Starachowice [PL] 38 B6
Stara Gradiška [HR] 142 C2
Stara Krašnica [PL] 50 B1
Stará L'ubovňa [SK] 52 C6
Stara Moravica [SRB] 76 D5
Stara Novalja [HR] 112 F3
Stara Pazova [SRB] 142 G2
Stara Reka [BG] 148 D4
Stará Turá [SK] 62 H3
Stará Voda [CZ] 48 C4
Staravolya [BY] 38 G1
Stara Wrona [PL] 38 B2
Staraya Russa [RUS] 202 C2
Staraya Toropa [RUS] 202 C3
Stara Zagora [BG] 148 C5
Starcevo [BG] 130 E2
Stare Czarnowo [PL] 20 F5
Stare Dębno [PL] 20 H4
Staré Hory [SK] 64 C2
Stare Jeżewo [PL] 24 E5
Staré Město [CZ] 50 C3
Staré Město [CZ] 50 C4
Staré Město [CZ] 62 H2
Stare Osieczno [PL] 20 H6
Stargard-Szczeciński [PL] 20 F5
Stårheim [N] 180 C5
Stari Bar [MNE] 144 E5
Stari Dojran [MK] 128 H3
Starigrad [HR] 112 F3
Stari Grad [HR] 144 A2
Stari Gradac [HR] 74 G5
Starigrad Paklenica [HR] 112 G4
Stari Mikanovci [HR] 142 D1
Stari Slankamen [SRB] 142 G2
Staritsa [RUS] 202 E3
Starjak [HR] 74 E6
Starkov [CZ] 50 B5
Starnberg [D] 60 D4
Starod [SLO] 112 E1
Starodub [RUS] 202 E5
Starogard [PL] 20 G4
Starogard Gdański [PL] 22 E3
Starokostiantyniv [UA] 202 C8
Staromieście [PL] 50 H2
Staro Nagoričane, Manastir- [MK] 146 D6
Staro Oryakhovo [BG] 148 F3
Staropol'ye [RUS] 198 G1
Starosel [BG] 148 B5
Staroselci [BG] 148 A3
Staro selo [BG] 148 A4
Staro Selo [BG] 148 D1
Starożreby [PL] 36 H2
Starup [DK] 156 B2
Starup [DK] 156 C3
Starý Bernštejn [CZ] 48 G2
Stary Borek [PL] 52 E4
Starychi [UA] 52 G3
Stary Dzierzgoń [PL] 22 F4
Stary Gózd [PL] 38 B5
Starý Hrozenkov [CZ] 64 A2
Staryi Sambir [UA] 52 F5
Stary Plzenec [CZ] 48 E5
Stary Sącz [PL] 52 B5
Starý Smokovec [SK] 52 B6
Stary Szelków [PL] 38 B1
Starý Vestec [CZ] 48 G3
Stary Wieś [PL] 38 E6
Staryya Darohi [BY] 202 C6
Starzyny [PL] 50 H2
St-Astier [F] 66 F3
Staszów [PL] 52 C2
Stat. Angístis [GR] 130 C3
Stathelle [N] 164 G3
Statland [N] 190 C5
Statte [I] 122 E4
St-Aubane [F] 108 E4
St-Auban-sur-l'Ouvèze [F] 108 B2
St-Aubin-d'Aubigné [F] 26 C5
St-Aubin-du-Cormier [F] 26 D5
St-Aubin-sur-Mer [F] 26 F3
St.-Augustin, Château de- [F] 56 D4
St-Aulaye [F] 66 E2
Staume [N] 180 C5
Staupitz [D] 34 E5
St Austell [GB] 12 C5
Stava [S] 162 D1
Stavang [N] 180 B6
Stavanger [N] 164 B3
Stavaträsk [S] 196 A4
Stave [N] 192 E3
Staveley [GB] 10 F5
Stavelot [B] 30 E5
Stavenisse [NL] 16 C6
Staveren [NL] 16 E3
Stavern [D] 16 H3
Stavern [N] 164 G3
Stavertsi [BG] 148 A3
Stavkirke [N] 164 F2
Stavkirke [N] 170 E1
St-Avold [F] 44 F4
Stavre [S] 182 H3
Stavreviken [S] 184 E4
Stavrochóri [GR] 140 G5
Stavrodrómi [GR] 136 D2
Stavrós [GR] 128 G4
Stavrós [GR] 130 C4
Stavrós [GR] 132 C5
Stavrós [GR] 132 G3
Stavrós [GR] 134 B4
Stavrós [GR] 134 C6
Stavrós [GR] 140 C4
Stavrós tis Psókas [CY] 154 F5
Stavroúpoli [GR] 130 E2
Stavsjø [N] 172 B3
Stavsnäs [S] 168 E3
Stawiguda [PL] 22 G4
Stawiski [PL] 24 D5
Stawiszyn [PL] 36 E4
St-Aygulf [F] 108 D5
St-Bard [F] 68 B1
St. Barthèlemy [CH] 70 C1
St.-Barthélemy [F] 26 E4
St. Bartholomä [D] 60 G6
St-Béat [F] 84 F5
St-Beauzély [F] 106 D2
St-Benin [F] 56 D4
St-Benoît-du-Sault [F] 54 G5
St-Benoît-sur-Loire [F] 42 F6
St-Bertrand-de-Comminges [F] 84 F4
St.-Blaise [F] 106 G5
St Blasien [D] 58 F4
St-Blin [F] 44 D6
St-Bonnet-de-Joux [F] 56 F6
St-Bonnet-en-Champsaur [F] 68 H6
St-Bonnet-le-Château [F] 68 E3
St-Brevin-les-Pins [F] 40 E6
St-Brice-en-Coglès [F] 26 D5
St-Brieuc [F] 26 B4
St-Calais [F] 42 C5
St-Cast-le-Guildo [F] 26 B4
St-Céré [F] 66 H4
St-Cergue [CH] 70 B1
St-Cernin [F] 68 B4
St-Chamas [F] 106 H4
St-Chamond [F] 68 F3
St-Chély-d'Apcher [F] 68 C5
St-Chély-d'Aubrac [F] 68 B5
St-Chinian [F] 106 D4
St Christina / Santa Cristina [I] 72 D3
St Christoph [A] 72 B1
St. Christophe-en-Oisans [F] 70 A5
St-Ciers-sur-Gironde [F] 66 D2
St-Cirq-Lapopie [F] 66 G5
St.-Clair [F] 26 F3
St-Clar [F] 66 E6
St-Claud [F] 54 E6
St-Claude [F] 70 A1
St Clears [GB] 12 D2
St-Clément [F] 44 F6
St-Clément-sur-Durance [F] 108 E2
St-Côme-d'Olt [F] 68 B5
St.-Cosme-en-Vairais [F] 26 G6
St-Cyprien [F] 66 F4
St-Cyprien-Plage [F] 92 G1
St. David's [GB] 12 D1
St-Denis [F] 42 F3
St-Denis-d'Oléron [F] 54 B5
St-Denis d'Orques [F] 42 A5
St-Didier-en-Velay [F] 68 E4
St-Dié [F] 58 D2
St-Dizier [F] 44 C5
St-Donat-sur-l'Herbasse [F] 68 F4
St. Doulagh's Church [IRL] 2 F6
Steane [N] 164 E2
Ste-Anne-d'Auray [F] 26 A6
Ste-Anne-la-Palud [F] 40 B2
Ste.-Barbe [F] 40 C3
Stechelberg [CH] 70 E2
Štěchovice [CZ] 48 F4
Steckborn [CH] 58 G4
Ste-Croix [CH] 58 C6
Ste-Croix-Volvestre [F] 84 G4
Steeg [A] 72 B1
Steenbergen [NL] 16 C6
Ste.-Engrâce [F] 84 D4
Ste-Enimie [F] 68 C6
Steenvoorde [F] 28 E2
Steenwijk [NL] 16 F3
Stefáni [GR] 132 D3
Štefanikova Mohyla [SK] 62 H3
Stefaniná [GR] 130 C4
Stefanovo [BG] 148 F2
Ste-Foy-la-Grande [F] 66 E3
Stegaros [N] 170 E5
Ste-Gauburge-Ste-Colombe [F] 26 G5
Stege [DK] 156 G4
Stegeborg [S] 168 B5
Stegersbach [A] 74 E2
Stegna [PL] 22 E2
St-Egrève [F] 68 H4
Ste-Hélène [F] 66 C3
Ste-Hermine [F] 54 C3
Stehnovo [RUS] 198 H4
Steigen [N] 192 D5
Steilwände [D] 60 B5
Stein [A] 62 D4
Stein [D] 46 G5
Stein [N] 170 H5
Stein [N] 190 B5
Steinaberg bru [N] 170 C5
Steinach [A] 72 D2
Stein am Rhein [CH] 58 G4
Steinau [D] 46 E2
Steinbach [D] 46 H2
Steinberg [A] 74 F1
Steinberg [D] 156 C5
Steinberg am Rofan [A] 60 E6
Steine [N] 170 B2
Steinestø [N] 170 B3
Steinfeld [A] 72 G3
Steinfeld [D] 30 G5
Steinfeld [D] 32 D1
Steinfurt [D] 16 H5
Steingaden [D] 60 D5
Steinhagen [D] 20 C3
Steinhausen [D] 60 B4
Steinheim [D] 32 E3
Steinhorst [D] 32 G1
Steinibach [CH] 58 G6
Steinkjer [N] 190 C5
Steinløysa [N] 180 E2
Stein Pass [A/D] 60 G6
Steinsåsen [N] 182 D4
Steinsberg [D] 46 C5
Steinsburg [D] 46 F2
Steinsdal [N] 190 B6
Steinshøle [N] 170 F5
Steinsholt [N] 164 G2
Steinsøynes [N] 180 F1
Steinsvik [N] 180 C4
Ste.- Jalle [F] 108 B2
Steknica [PL] 22 C1
Ste-Livrade-sur-Lot [F] 66 E5
Stellendam [NL] 16 C5
St-Eloy-les-Mines [F] 56 C6
Ste-Marie-aux-Mines [F] 58 D2
Ste-Marie-de-Campan [F] 84 F4
Ste-Marie-du-Mont [F] 26 E2
Ste-Maure-de-Touraine [F] 54 F3
Ste-Maxime [F] 108 D5
Ste-Menehould [F] 44 C4
Ste-Mère-Eglise [F] 26 E2
St-Emilion [F] 66 D3
Sten [S] 162 D1
Stenay [F] 44 D3
Stenbjerg [DK] 160 B4
Stenbo [S] 162 G3
Stendal [D] 34 C2
Stende [LV] 198 C5
Steneby [S] 166 D4
Stengelsrud [N] 164 G1
St Englmar [D] 60 G2
Stenhammar [S] 168 B4
Stenhamra [S] 168 D3
Steni [GR] 134 C4
Steninge [S] 160 H5
Steninge [S] 168 D2
Stenlille [DK] 156 F3
Stenløse [DK] 156 G2
Stennäs [S] 190 G6
Stenó [GR] 136 E2
Stenoma [GR] 132 F4
Stensele [S] 190 F4
Stensjö [S] 162 G3
Stensjön [S] 162 E2
Stenstorp [S] 166 F6
Stensträsk [S] 190 H4
Stenstrup [DK] 156 D4
Stensund [S] 190 G2
Stensund [S] 190 G3
Stensunda [S] 168 E1
Stenträsk [S] 190 H2
Stenudden [S] 190 G2
Stenungsund [S] 160 G1
Steornabhagh / Stornoway [GB] 6 C2
Stepanci [MK] 128 E2
Stepnica [PL] 20 F4
Stepojevac [SRB] 146 B1
Sterdyń-Osada [PL] 38 D2
Sterehushche [UA] 204 G3
Sterlawki Wielkie [PL] 24 C3
Stern, Manastir- [BIH] 142 C2
Stern / la Villa [I] 72 E3
Stérna [GR] 130 D2
Sternberg [D] 20 B4
Šternberk [CZ] 48 H6
Šternberk [CZ] 50 D5
Stérnes [GR] 140 C4
Stérnia [GR] 138 E1
Sterringi [N] 180 F5
Sterzing / Vipiteno [I] 72 D2
Ste-Sévère [F] 56 B5
Stes-Maries-de-la-Mer [F] 106 F5
St. Estèphe [F] 66 C2
Ste-Suzanne [F] 42 A4
Stęszew [PL] 36 C3
Štětí [CZ] 48 F2
St-Étienne [F] 68 E3
St-Étienne [F] 108 C3
St-Étienne-de-Baïgorry [F] 84 C3
St-Étienne-de-St-Geoirs [F] 68 G4
St-Etienne-de-Tinée [F] 108 E3
Ste-Tulle [F] 108 C4
Stevenage [GB] 14 E3
Stevrek [BG] 148 D3
Stewarton [GB] 8 D3
Steyerberg [D] 32 E1
Steyersberg [A] 62 E6
Steyr [A] 62 B5
Steyr-Durchbruch [A] 62 B5
Stezherovo [BG] 148 B2
St-Fargeau [F] 56 D2
St.-Fiacre [F] 40 C3
St-Firmin [F] 68 H6
St-Florent [F] 40 G6
St-Florent [F] 56 B3
St-Florent [F] 114 C3
St.-Florent-des-Bois [F] 54 C3
St-Florentin [F] 42 H6
St. Florian [A] 60 H4
St-Flour [F] 68 C4
St-Fort-sur-Gironde [F] 66 D1
St.-Fort-sur-le-Né [F] 66 D1
St-Fulgent [F] 54 C2
St Gallen [A] 62 C6
St Gallen [CH] 58 H5
St Gallenkirch [A] 72 B1
St-Galmier [F] 68 E3
St. Gangolf [D] 44 F3
St-Gaudens [F] 84 G4
St-Gaultier [F] 54 G4
St-Geniez-d'Olt [F] 68 B6
St-Genis-de-Saintonge [F] 66 D1
St-Genix-sur-Guiers [F] 68 H3
St. George [CH] 70 B1
St Georgen [A] 60 H5
St Georgen [A] 74 C2
St Georgen [D] 58 F3
St-Georges [F] 40 G6
St-Georges-de-Didonne [F] 54 C6
St. Georges-on-Couzan [F] 68 E2
St-Geours-de-Maremne [F] 66 B6
St-Germain [F] 42 F3
St-Germain [F] 66 G2
St-Germain-de-Calberte [F] 106 F2
St-Germain-de-Joux [F] 68 H2
St-Germain-des-Fossés [F] 56 D6
St-Germain-des-Vaux [F] 26 D1
St-Germain-du-Bois [F] 56 G5
St-Germain-du-Plain [F] 56 G5
St-Germain-Laval [F] 68 E2
St-Germain-Lembron [F] 68 C3
St-Germain-l'Herm [F] 68 D3
St-Germain-Plage [F] 26 D3
St-Germer-de-Fly [F] 28 D6
St-Gervais [F] 106 D3
St-Gervais-d'Auvergne [F] 68 C1
St-Gervais-les-Bains [F] 70 C3
St-Géry [F] 66 G5
St-Gildas-des-Bois [F] 40 E5
St Gilgen [A] 60 H5
St-Gilles [F] 106 G4
St-Gilles-Croix-de-Vie [F] 54 B2
St-Gilles-Pligeaux [F] 26 A4
St-Gingolph [CH] 70 C2
St-Girons [F] 84 G5
St-Girons-en-Marensin [F] 66 B5
St-Girons-Plage [F] 66 A5
St Goar [D] 46 B2
St Goarshausen [D] 46 B2
St-Gobain [F] 28 F6
St-Gorgon-Main [F] 58 B5
St-Guénolé [F] 40 B3
St-Guilhem-le-Desert [F] 106 E3
St Helens [GB] 10 D4
St Helier [GBJ] 26 C3
St. Hilaire Cottes [F] 28 E3
St-Hilaire-de-Villefranche [F] 54 C5
St-Hilaire-du-Harcouët [F] 26 D5
St-Hippolyte [F] 58 C5
St-Hippolyte-du-Fort [F] 106 F3
St. Höga [S] 160 G1
St-Honoré les-Bains [F] 56 E4
St-Hubert [B] 44 D1
Stia [I] 110 G5
Sticciano Scalo [I] 114 F2
Stiefern [A] 62 E3
Stiens [NL] 16 F2
Stift Zwettl [A] 62 D3
Stigen [N] 172 E2
Stigen [S] 166 D5
Stigfoss [N] 180 E3
Stigliano [I] 122 C4
Stigliano, Bagni di- [I] 114 H5
Stignano [I] 124 D7
Stigsjö [S] 184 F4
Stigtomta [S] 168 C4

Stiklestad [N] 190 C6
Stilla [N] 194 B3
Stilo [I] 124 D6
St-Imier [CH] 58 D5
Stimlje [SRB] 146 C5
St Ingbert [D] 44 G4
Stintino [I] 118 B2
Štip [MK] 128 F1
Stirling [GB] 8 E3
Štirovača [HR] 112 F3
Štítary [CZ] 62 E2
Štítnik [SK] 64 E3
Štíty [CZ] 50 C4
St Ives [GB] 12 B5
St Ives [GB] 14 F2
Stixenstein [A] 62 E6
St-Jacut [F] 26 C4
St. Jakob [A] 72 F2
St Jakob im Rosental [A] 74 B3
St-James [F] 26 D5
Stjärnsund [S] 166 G4
Stjärnsund [S] 174 D5
St. Jaume d'Enveja [E] 92 B6
St-Jean-Brévelay [F] 26 A6
St-Jean-Cap-Ferrat [F] 108 F4
St-Jean-d'Angély [F] 54 D5
St-Jean-de-Bournay [F] 68 G3
St-Jean-de-Losne [F] 56 H4
St-Jean-de-Luz [F] 84 B2
St-Jean-de-Maurienne [F] 70 B5
St-Jean-de-Monts [F] 54 A2
St-Jean-du-Bruel [F] 106 E3
St-Jean-du-Gard [F] 106 F2
St-Jean-du-Liget, Chapelle- [F] 54 G3
St-Jean-en-Royans [F] 68 G5
St-Jean-le-Thomas [F] 26 D4
St-Jean-Pied-de-Port [F] 84 C3
St. Jeans-d'Arves [F] 70 B5
St-Jeoire [F] 70 B2
St. Joan de Penyagolosa [E] 98 F2
St Johann am Tauern [A] 74 C1
St Johann im Pongau [A] 72 G1
St Johann in Tirol [A] 60 F6
St Johnstown [IRL] 2 F2
Stjørdal [N] 182 C1
St.-Jores [F] 26 D3
St-Jorioz [F] 70 B3
St-Jory [F] 84 H3
St-Jouan-de-l'Isle [F] 26 B5
St-Jouin-de-Marnes [F] 54 E3
St-Juéry [F] 106 C2
St-Julien [F] 56 H6
St-Julien [F] 84 G4
St-Julien-Chapteuil [F] 68 E4
St-Julien-de-Vouvantes [F] 40 G5
St. Julien-du-Verdon [F] 108 D4
St-Julien-en-Beauchêne [F] 68 G6
St.-Julien-en-Born [F] 66 B5
St-Julien-en-Genevois [F] 70 B2
St-Julien-l'Ars [F] 54 F4
St-Junien [F] 54 F6
St Just [GB] 12 B5
St-Just-en-Chaussée [F] 28 E6
St-Just-en-Chevalet [F] 68 E2
St-Justin [F] 66 D5
St. Kanzian [A] 74 C3
St Lambrecht [A] 74 B2
St-Lary-Soulan [F] 84 F5
St-Laurent [F] 26 E3
St-Laurent [F] 66 G1
St.-Laurent-de-la-Cabrerisse [F] 106 C5
St.-Laurent-de-la-Salanque [F] 92 G1
St-Laurent-des-Autels [F] 54 C1
St.-Laurent-en-Gâtines [F] 54 G1
St-Laurent-en-Grandvaux [F] 70 B1
St-Laurent-les-Bains [F] 68 D6
St-Laurent-Médoc [F] 66 C2
St-Leger [F] 56 F4
St.-Léon, Chapelle- [F] 44 G5
St-Léonard-de-Noblat [F] 66 H1
St Leonhard [A] 62 D4
St-Leu-d'Esserent [F] 42 F2
St-Lizier [F] 84 G4
St-Lô [F] 26 E3
St Lorenzen [A] 72 F3
St-Louis [F] 58 E4
St-Loup-sur-Semouse [F] 58 C3
St-Luc [CH] 70 D2
St-Lunaire [F] 26 C4
St-Lys [F] 84 H3
St-Macaire [F] 66 D4
St-Maclou [F] 26 G3
St-Maixent-l'Ecole [F] 54 D4
St. Malm [S] 168 B4
St-Malo [F] 26 C4
St-Mamest [F] 66 F3
St. Marcel [F] 70 B4
St-Marcellin [F] 68 G4
St. Marcellin-en-Forez [F] 68 E3
St. Marein [A] 74 E2
St Margaret's Hope [GB] 6 G2
St. Märgen [D] 58 F3
St. Maria [D] 46 E6
St. Maria zu den Engeln [CH] 58 G5
St-Mars-la-Jaille [F] 40 G6
St. Martin [A] 62 C3
St. Martin [F] 40 E5
St-Martin-d'Auxigny [F] 56 C3
St-Martín-de-Crau [F] 106 G4
St-Martin-de-Londres [F] 106 E3
St. Martin-d'Entraunes [F] 108 E3
St-Martin-de-Ré [F] 54 B4
St.-Martin-du-Canigou [F] 92 F1
St-Martin-Lestra [F] 68 F3
St-Martin-l'Heureux [F] 44 C3
St. Martin Tennengebirge [A] 60 H6
St-Martin-Vésubie [F] 108 F3
St-Martory [F] 84 G4
St-Mathieu [F] 66 F1
St-Mathieu, Pointe de- [F] 40 A2
St-Mathieu-de-Tréviers [F] 106 E3
St-Maurice [CH] 70 C2
St-Maurice-la-Clouère [F] 54 E4
St. Maurice la Sotterraine [F] 54 G5
St-Maurice-Navacelles [F] 106 E3
St Maurice-sur-Moselle [F] 58 C3
St Mawes [GB] 12 C5
St-Maximin-la-Ste-Baume [F] 108 C5
St-Méen [F] 26 B5
St. Meinrad [CH] 58 G5
St. Mellösa [S] 166 H3
St Michael [A] 74 C1
St Michael [A] 74 F2
St Michael i. Lungau [A] 72 H2
St Michel / Mikkeli [FIN] 188 C6
St.-Michel-de Cuxa [F] 92 F1
St-Michel-de-Maurienne [F] 70 B5
St. Michel de Rieufret [F] 66 C4
St-Michel-en-Grève [F] 40 D1
St-Michel-en-l'Herm [F] 54 C4
St-Michel-Mont-Mercure [F] 54 C3
St-Mihiel [F] 44 D4
St. Miquel del Fai [E] 92 E3
St-Morand [F] 58 D4
St Moritz [CH] 70 H2
St-Nazaire [F] 40 E6
St. Nazaire les Eymes [F] 68 H4
St-Nectaire [F] 68 C2
St Neots [GB] 14 E2
St.-Nicodème [F] 26 A5
St-Nicolas [F] 40 E5
St.-Nicolas (St-Niklaas) [B] 28 H2
St Nicolas-de-Port [F] 44 E5
St-Nicolas-de-Redon [F] 40 E5
St-Nicolas-du-Pélem [F] 26 A4
St-Niklaas (St.-Nicolas) [B] 28 H2
St Niklaus [CH] 70 E2
St Nikolai [A] 74 B1
Støa [N] 172 E2
Stobeč [HR] 144 A2
Stobi [MK] 128 F2
Stoby [S] 158 D1
Stocka [S] 184 E6
Stockach [D] 58 G4
Stockaryd [S] 162 D3
Stockbridge [GB] 12 H4
Stockelsdorf [D] 18 G3
Stockenboy [A] 72 H3
Stockerau [A] 62 F4
Stockheim [D] 46 G3
Stockholm [S] 168 D3
Stockport [GB] 10 E4
Stocksbo [S] 174 C1
Stocksbo [S] 174 D4
Stockton on Tees [GB] 10 F2
Stoczek Klasztorny [PL] 22 H3
Stoczek Łukowski [PL] 38 D3
Stod [CZ] 48 D5
Stod [N] 190 C5
Stöde [S] 184 D4
Stødi [N] 190 E1
St Oedenrode [NL] 30 E2
Stojan Mikhaylovski [BG] 148 E2
Stojmirovo [MK] 128 H1
Stoke-on-Trent [GB] 10 E5
Stokite [BG] 148 B4
Stokkasjøen [N] 190 D3
Stokke [N] 164 H3
Stokkemarke [DK] 156 F5
Stokkland [N] 164 F2
Stokkvågen [N] 190 D2
Stokmarknes [N] 192 D4
Štoky [CZ] 48 H5
Stola [S] 166 E5
Stolac [BIH] 144 C3
Stolberg [D] 30 F4
Stolbovo [RUS] 198 G5
Stolbzy [BY] 202 B5
Stolin [BY] 202 B7
Stollberg [D] 48 C2
Stollberg [D] 48 D2
Stöllet [S] 172 E5
Stolno [PL] 22 E5
St Olof [S] 158 D3
Stolpe [D] 20 E6
Stolpe [D] 34 E2
Stolpen [D] 34 F6
Stołpie [PL] 38 F5
Stolzenau [D] 32 E1
St-Omer [F] 28 E2
Stómio [GR] 132 G1
Stömne [S] 166 E2
Stomorska [HR] 142 A6
Ston [HR] 144 C3
Stonařov [CZ] 48 H6
Stone [GB] 10 E5
Stonehaven [GB] 8 G1
Stongfjorden [N] 180 B6
Stonglandseidet [N] 192 E3
Stønjyumfoss [N] 170 E2
Stopanja [SRB] 146 C3
Stopnica [PL] 52 C2
Storå [S] 166 H2
Storå / Isojoki [FIN] 186 B5
Stora Blåsjön [S] 190 E4
Storås [N] 180 H2
Stora Sjöfallet [S] 192 F5
Storbäck [S] 190 F4
Storborgaren [S] 190 G6
Storby [FIN] 174 H5
Stord [N] 170 B5
Stordal [N] 180 D4
Stordalen [S] 192 F4
Storebro [S] 162 F2
Storebru [N] 180 B6
Store Darum [DK] 156 B3
Storehaug [N] 170 C1
Store Heddinge [DK] 156 G3
Storekorsnes [N] 194 B2
Storelv [N] 194 A2
Storelvavoll [N] 182 D3
Store Merløse [DK] 156 F3
Store Molvik [N] 194 D1
Støren [N] 182 B2
Storestandal [N] 180 D4
Storestølen [N] 170 E3
Stor-Evdal [N] 172 C1
Storfjellseter [N] 182 B6
Storfjord [N] 192 G3
Storfors [S] 166 G2
Storforshei [N] 190 E2
Storfossen [N] 194 C4
Storhögen [S] 182 H2
Storholmsjö [S] 190 E6
Storjola [S] 190 E4
Storjord [N] 190 E1
Storjord [N] 190 E1
Storjorda [N] 190 E1
Storkow [D] 34 F3
Storkyro / Isokyrö [FIN] 186 B2
Storlægda [N] 182 C5
Storli [N] 180 G3
Storlien [S] 182 D2
Stormi [FIN] 176 E2
Stornara [I] 120 G2
Stornaset [S] 190 F5
Stornes [N] 192 G2
Stornorrfors [S] 190 H6
Stornoway / Steornabhagh [GB] 6 C2
Storo [I] 72 B5
Storoddan [N] 180 G1
Storsätern [S] 182 D5
Storsävarträsk [S] 190 H5
Storseterfossen [N] 180 E4
Storsjö [S] 182 E3
Storslett [N] 192 G2
Størstein [N] 192 G1
Storsteinnes [N] 192 F3
Storsund [S] 196 A3
Stortinden [N] 194 B2
Storuman [S] 190 F4
Storvallen [S] 182 D2
Storvik [S] 174 D4
Storvika [N] 190 B5
Storvollen [N] 180 H4
Storvorde [DK] 160 E4
Storvorde [DK] 160 E4
Storvreta [S] 168 D1
Stössen [D] 34 B6
St Oswald [A] 62 C3
St. Oswald [A] 74 D3
St.-Oswald [F] 44 F3
Stotel [D] 18 D4
Sto. Toribio de Liébana [E] 82 D3
Stotternheim [D] 32 H6
St. Ottilien [D] 60 D4
Stouby [DK] 156 C2
St-Ouen [F] 28 D4
Stourbridge [GB] 10 D6
Stournaraïika [GR] 132 E2
Støvring [DK] 160 D4
Støvringgård [DK] 160 E5
Stowbtsy [BY] 202 B5
Stowmarket [GB] 14 G3
Stow-on-the-Wold [GB] 12 H2
Stozher [BG] 148 F2
St-Palais [F] 84 D3
St-Palais-sur-Mer [F] 54 B6
St. Pankraz [A] 62 B5
St-Pardoux-la-Rivière [F] 66 F2
St Paul [A] 74 C3
St-Paul [F] 108 E2
St-Paul [F] 108 E4
St-Paul-Cap-de-Joux [F] 106 B3
St-Paul-de-Fenouillet [F] 106 C6
St-Paulien [F] 68 D4
St-Paul-lès-Dax [F] 66 B6
St-Pé [F] 84 E4
St-Péray [F] 68 F5
St-Père [F] 56 E3
St-Père-en-Retz [F] 40 E6
St. Peter [A] 74 B3
St. Peter [CH] 70 H1
St Peter-Ording [D] 18 D2
St Peter Port [GBG] 26 C2
St-Péver [F] 26 A4
St-Philbert [F] 54 B2
St-Pierre-d'Albigny [F] 70 A4
St-Pierre-de-Chartreuse [F] 68 H4
St-Pierre-de-Chignac [F] 66 F3
St. Pierre d'Extravache [F] 70 C5
St-Pierre-d'Oléron [F] 54 B5
St-Pierre-Église [F] 26 E2
St-Pierre-en Port [F] 26 H2
St-Pierre-le-Moûtier [F] 56 D4
St-Pierre-Quiberon [F] 40 C5
St-Pierre-sur-Dives [F] 26 F4
St-Pois [F] 26 E4
St-Pol-de-Léon [F] 40 C1
St-Pol-sur-Ternoise [F] 28 E3
St Pölten [A] 62 E4
St-Pons-de-Thomieres [F] 106 C4
St-Porchaire [F] 54 C5
St-Pourçain sur-Sioule [F] 56 D6
St. Priest [F] 68 G3
St-Privat [F] 68 A3
St-Quay-Portrieux [F] 26 B4
St.-Quen-en-Belin [F] 42 B5
St-Quentin [F] 28 F5
St. Quirin [D] 48 C4
Strå [I] 110 G1
Straach [D] 34 D3
Strabane [NIR] 2 F2
Strachówka [PL] 38 C2
Stracia [I] 124 C8
Stracin [MK] 146 D6
Strådalen [S] 182 E5
Stradalovo [BG] 146 F6
Stradbally [IRL] 4 B3
Stradbally [IRL] 4 F3
Stradella [I] 70 G6
Stradone [IRL] 2 E4
Strádov [CZ] 50 A4
Straduny [PL] 24 D3
Straelen [D] 30 F3
Strakonice [CZ] 48 E6
Straldzha [BG] 148 E4
Stralki [BY] 198 G6
Strålsnäs [S] 166 H6
Stralsund [D] 20 D2
St-Rambert [F] 68 E3
St-Rambert-d'Albon [F] 68 F4
St-Rambert-en-Bugey [F] 68 G2
Stramnes [N] 170 B3
Strand [N] 172 C2
Strand [N] 192 D3
Strand [S] 190 E6
Stranda [N] 180 D4
Stranda [N] 194 C2
Strandby [DK] 160 C4
Strandby [DK] 160 E2
Strandcally Castle [IRL] 4 D5
Strande [D] 18 G2
Strandebarm [N] 170 B4
Strandhill [IRL] 2 D3
Strandlykkja [N] 172 C4
Strangford [NIR] 2 G4
Strängnäs [S] 168 C3
Strängsered [S] 162 C2
Strångsjö [S] 168 B4
Strání [CZ] 62 H2
Stranice [SLO] 74 D4
Stranorlar [IRL] 2 E2
Stránov [CZ] 48 G3
Stranraer [GB] 8 C5
St-Raphaël [F] 108 D5
Strasbourg [F] 44 H6
Strasburg [D] 20 E5
Straševina [MNE] 144 E3
Stråsjö [S] 174 D1
Strassburg [A] 74 B2
Strassengel [A] 74 D2
Strassfurt [D] 34 B4
Strasswalchen [A] 60 H5
Stratford-upon-Avon [GB] 12 H2
Strathaven [GB] 8 D3
Stratinska [BIH] 142 B2
Stratinska [BIH] 142 B2
Stratóni [GR] 130 C4
Stratoníki [GR] 130 C4
Strátos [GR] 132 E5
Straubenhardt [D] 46 C6
Straubing [D] 60 G2
Straum [N] 190 D2
Straume [N] 164 E1
Straume [N] 164 F3
Straume [N] 170 A4
Straumen [N] 180 F1
Straumen [N] 190 C4
Straumen [N] 190 C6
Straumen [N] 190 D2
Straumen [N] 192 D6
Straumfjorden [N] 192 D5
Straumsjøen [N] 192 D3
Straumsnes [N] 192 D4
Straumsnes [N] 192 E2
Straupitz [D] 34 F4
Strausberg [D] 34 F2
Straussfurt [D] 32 H5
Stravaj [AL] 128 C4
Straža [SRB] 146 D2
Strazh [RUS] 202 D5
Stražica [BG] 148 D3
Strážky [SK] 52 B6
Strážnice [CZ] 62 G2
Strážný [CZ] 62 A2
Strážske [SK] 64 H2
Štrba [SK] 64 E2
Štrbské Pleso [SK] 52 A6
Street [GB] 12 F4
Strehaia [RO] 204 C6
Strehla [D] 34 E5
Streitberg [D] 46 G4
Strękowa Góra [PL] 24 E5
Strelcha [BG] 148 A5
Strelci [BG] 148 B5
Střeliště [CZ] 50 A6
Strel'na [RUS] 178 H5
Strem [A] 74 F2
St-Rémy-de-Provence [F] 106 G4
St-Renan [F] 40 B2
Strenči [LV] 198 E4
Strendene [N] 190 D3
Strengberg [A] 62 C4
Stresa [I] 70 F3
S. Tresund [S] 190 F4
Streufdorf [D] 46 F2
St.-Révérien [F] 56 E3
Strezimirovci [SRB] 146 E4
Strezovce [SRB] 146 D6
Strib [DK] 156 C2
Stříbro [CZ] 48 D4
Štrigova [HR] 74 F4
Strilky [UA] 52 F5
Strimasund [S] 190 E2
St-Riquier [F] 28 D4
Strittjomvare [S] 190 G3
Strittmat [D] 58 E4
Striževac [SRB] 146 E4
Strmica [HR] 142 A4
Strmilov [CZ] 48 H6
Strobl [A] 60 H5
Strøby Egede [DK] 156 G3
Stroevo [BG] 148 B5
Strofyliá [GR] 134 B4
Ströhem [D] 32 E1
Strokestown [IRL] 2 D4
Strøm [N] 190 A6
Ström [S] 166 D2
Strömåker [S] 190 F5
St.-Roman, Abbaye de- [F] 106 G3
Strömbacka [S] 184 E6
Stromberg [D] 46 B3
Strómboli [I] 124 C5
St-Rome-de-Tarn [F] 106 D2
Strömfors [S] 196 A4
Strömholm [S] 190 G3
Strømmen [N] 166 B1
Strömmen [S] 182 E5
Stromness [GB] 6 F2
Strompdalen [N] 190 D4
Strömsbruk [S] 184 E6
Stromsfors [S] 168 B5
Strömsholm [S] 168 B2
Strömsillret [S] 172 E1
Strömsnäs [S] 184 D2
Strömsnäsbruk [S] 162 C5
Strømsood [N] 170 G4
Strömsrum [S] 162 G4
Strömstad [S] 166 B4
Strömsund [S] 190 E6
Strömsund [S] 190 F3
Strond [N] 164 E3
Strongoli [I] 124 F4
Stronie Śląskie [PL] 50 C3
Stroove [IRL] 2 F2
Stropkov [SK] 52 D6
Stroppo [I] 108 E2
Stroud [GB] 12 G3
Strovles [GR] 140 B5
Stróża [PL] 50 H4
Str. Pole [PL] 22 F3
Strub Pass [A] 60 G6
Strücklingen [D] 18 C5
Struer [DK] 160 B5
Struga [MK] 128 D3
Strugi-Krasnyye [RUS] 198 H2
Strugovo [MK] 128 E3
Struha [BY] 24 G4
Struhařov [CZ] 48 G4
Struino [BG] 148 E2
Strumica [MK] 128 G2
Strumień [PL] 50 F4
Strupina [PL] 36 C5
Stružec [HR] 142 B1
Stryama [BG] 148 B5
Strycksele [S] 190 H5
Stryi [UA] 204 C2
Stryj [UA] 52 H5
Stryjów [PL] 52 F1
Stryków [PL] 36 G4
Strymonikó [GR] 130 B3
Stryn [N] 180 D5
Strzałkowo [PL] 36 E3
Strzegocin [PL] 38 B2
Strzegom [PL] 50 B1
Strzegowo [PL] 38 A1
Strzelce [PL] 34 H1
Strzelce [PL] 36 G3
Strzelce Krajeńskie [PL] 36 A1
Strzelce Małe [PL] 36 H6
Strzelce Opolskie [PL] 50 E2
Strzelin [PL] 50 C2
Strzelno [PL] 36 E2
Strzyżów [PL] 38 G6
Strzyżów [PL] 52 D4
St.-Sabin, Chapelle- [F] 66 D5
St-Saëns [F] 28 C5
St. Salvator [A] 74 B2
St.-Samson-la-Poterie [F] 28 D5
St-Satur [F] 56 D3
St-Saturnin-lès-Apt [F] 108 B3
St-Saulge [F] 56 E4
St-Sauvant [F] 54 E4
St-Sauveur-en-Puisaye [F] 56 D2
St-Sauveur-le-Vicomte [F] 26 D2
St-Sauveur-sur-Tinée [F] 108 E3
St-Savin [F] 66 D2
St-Savin-sur-Gartempe [F] 54 F4
St-Seine-l'Abbaye [F] 56 G3
St-Sernin-sur-Rance [F] 106 C3
St-Sever [F] 26 E4
St-Sever [F] 66 C6
St. Slatnik [HR] 142 C2
St-Sulpice [F] 106 B3
St. Sulpice-les-Feuilles [F] 54 G5
St. Sundby [S] 168 B3
St. Susanna [E] 92 D3
St-Symphorien [F] 66 C4
St-Symphorien-de-Lay [F] 68 E2
St-Symphorien-d'Ozon [F] 68 F3
St-Symphorien-sur-Coise [F] 68 F3
St-Thégonnec [F] 40 C2
St-Thiébault [F] 58 A2
St-Trivier-de-Courtes [F] 56 G6
St.-Trond (St.-Truiden) [B] 30 D4
St-Tropez [F] 108 D5
St.-Truiden (St.-Trond) [B] 30 D4
Stubalj [HR] 142 B1
Stubbekøbing [DK] 156 G5
Stubbergård [DK] 160 C5
Stuben [A] 72 B1
Štubik [SRB] 146 E1
Stubline [SRB] 142 G3
Studánky [CZ] 62 B3
Studena [BG] 146 F5
Studená [CZ] 48 H6
Studenec [CZ] 48 H2
Studenica [SRB] 146 B3
Studénka [CZ] 50 E5
Studenzen [A] 74 E2
Studina [RO] 148 A2
Studzienice [PL] 22 C3
Studzienki [PL] 22 C6
Stugudal [N] 182 D3
Stugufläten [N] 180 F4
Stugun [S] 184 C2
Stuguvollmoen [N] 182 D3
Stühlingen [D] 58 F4
Stuibenfall [A] 72 C1
Stukenbrock [D] 32 E3
Stülpe [D] 34 E3
St.-Ulrich, Château- [F] 58 D2
St Ulrich / Ortisei [I] 72 D3
Stupari [BIH] 142 E3
Stupava [SK] 62 G4
Stupinigi [I] 70 D6
Stupnik [HR] 74 E6
Stuposiany [PL] 52 F6
Sturehov [S] 168 D3
Štúrovo [SK] 64 B5
St-Ursanne [CH] 58 D4
Stuttgart [D] 58 H1
St-Vaast-la-Hougue [F] 26 E2
St Valentin [A] 62 C4
St-Valery-en-Caux [F] 26 H2
St-Valery-sur-Somme [F] 28 D4
St-Vallier-de-Thiey [F] 108 E4
St-Vallier-sur-Rhône [F] 68 F4
St-Vaury [F] 54 H5
St. Veit [A] 72 F2
St Veit [A] 74 B3
St-Véran [F] 108 E1
St Vigil / Marebbe [I] 72 E3
St-Vincent [I] 70 D4
St-Vincent, Grotte de- [F] 108 D3
St-Vincent-de-Tyrosse [F] 66 A6
St. Vincent-du-Lorouër [F] 42 C6
St-Vincent-les-Forts [F] 108 D2
St Vith [B] 30 F6
St-Vivien-de-Médoc [F] 66 C1
St-Wandrille [F] 26 H3
St Wendel [D] 44 G3
St Wolfgang [A] 60 H5
St-Yan [F] 56 E6
Stykkishólmur [IS] 192 A2
Stylída [GR] 132 G4
Stymfalía [GR] 136 E1
St-Yorre [F] 68 D1
Stýpsi [GR] 134 G2
Stýra [GR] 134 D5
Styri [N] 172 C5
St-Yrieix-la-Perche [F] 66 G2
Styrnäs [S] 184 F2
Styrsö [S] 160 G2
Suadiye [TR] 150 G3
Suances [E] 82 E3
Suaredda [I] 118 E3
Subačius [LT] 200 F4
Subaşi [TR] 150 D2
Subaşı [TR] 152 D5
Subate [LV] 198 F6
Subbiano [I] 110 G6
Suben [A] 60 H4
Subiaco [I] 116 B5
Subkowy [PL] 22 E3
Subotica [MNE] 204 A5
Subotica [SRB] 76 D5
Subotište [SRB] 142 G2
Sučany [SK] 64 C2
Suceava [RO] 204 D3
Suceviţa, Mănăstirea- [RO] 204 D3
Sucha [PL] 48 H1
Sucha Beskidzka [PL] 50 H4
Suchá Hora [SK] 50 H6
Suchań [PL] 20 G5
Suchdol nad Lužnicí [CZ] 62 C2
Suchedniów [PL] 38 B6
Suchorze [PL] 22 B3
Suchowola [PL] 24 E4
Suchożebry [PL] 38 D3
Süchteln [D] 30 G3
Sucina [E] 104 C3
Sućuraj [HR] 144 B3
Sudbø [N] 164 E1
Sudbury [GB] 14 F3
Suddesjaur [S] 190 H2
Süden [D] 18 E1
Süderbrarup [D] 18 F1
Süderende [D] 156 A4
Süderlügum [D] 156 B4
Sudok [S] 196 A2
Sudova Vyshnia [UA] 52 G4
Sudzha [UA] 202 F6
Sueca [E] 98 E5
Suelli [I] 118 D6
Sugères [F] 68 D3
Süğütlü [TR] 150 H2
Suhindol [BG] 148 B3
Suhinichi [RUS] 202 E4
Suhl [D] 46 G2
Suho Polje [BIH] 142 E3
Suhopolje [HR] 74 H6
Šuica [BIH] 144 B1
Suijavaara [S] 194 B5
Suikka [FIN] 178 E1
Suinula [FIN] 176 F1
Suinula [FIN] 186 F5
Suio, Terme di- [I] 120 D2
Suippes [F] 44 C3
Sukeva [FIN] 196 E5
Sukhinichi [RUS] 202 E4
Sukošan [HR] 112 G5
Söksöd [H] 76 C4
Sukovo [SRB] 146 E4
Sul [N] 190 C6
Šula [MNE] 144 E2
Sulâmo [N] 182 D1
Suldal [N] 164 C1
Suldalseid [N] 164 C1
Suldalsosen [N] 164 C1
Sulden / Solda [I] 72 C3
Suldrup [DK] 160 D4
Sulechów [PL] 36 A3
Sulęcin [PL] 34 H2
Sulęczyno [PL] 22 C3
Sulejów [PL] 36 H5
Sulejówek [PL] 38 C3
Sulesund [N] 180 C3
Süleymaniye [TR] 150 B3
Süleymanlı [TR] 152 D3
Sulina [RO] 204 F4
Sulingen [D] 32 E1
Suliszewo [PL] 20 G6
Sulitjelma [N] 192 E6
Sulkava [FIN] 188 E5
Sulkava [FIN] 196 E6
Sulkavanjärvi [FIN] 186 G1
Sulkavankylä [FIN] 186 D4
Sułkowice [PL] 50 H4
Süller [TR] 152 E2
Süller [TR] 152 G4
Sully [F] 56 F4
Sully-sur-Loire [F] 56 C1
Sulmierzyce [PL] 36 D5
Sulmierzyce [PL] 36 G6
Sulmona [I] 116 D5
Süloğlu [TR] 150 B1
Sul'Ovské Skaly [SK] 50 F6
Sułów [PL] 36 D5
Sultançayırı [TR] 150 D5
Sultanhisar [TR] 152 E5
Sultanica [TR] 130 H4
Sultanköy [TR] 130 H2
Sultanköy [TR] 150 D3
Sülümenli [TR] 152 G4
Sulva / Solf [FIN] 186 B2
Sulviken [S] 190 D6
Sülysáp [H] 76 D1
Sulz [D] 58 G2
Sulzbach [A] 74 E3
Sulzbach [D] 46 D6
Sulzbach [D] 46 E6
Sulzbach-Rosenberg [D] 46 H5
Sumacarcer [E] 98 E5
Sumartin [HR] 144 A2
Sumba [FR] 160 A3
Sümeg [H] 74 G2
Sumer [BG] 146 F3
Sumiainen [FIN] 186 G3
Sumiswald [CH] 58 E6
Summa [FIN] 178 C3
Šumperk [CZ] 50 C4
Sumsa [FIN] 196 G4
Šumvald [CZ] 50 D4
Sumy [UA] 202 F6
Sund [FIN] 176 B5
Sund [N] 192 D3
Sund [S] 166 C3
Sund [S] 184 C5
Sundborn [S] 174 C4
Sundbyberg [S] 168 D3
Sundbyholm [S] 168 C3
Sunde [N] 170 B5
Sunde [N] 180 C6
Sunde [N] 190 A6
Sundebru [N] 164 F4
Sunderland [GB] 8 G6
Sundern [D] 32 C5
Sundet [S] 190 D6
Sundhultsbrunn [S] 162 E1
Sundklakk [N] 192 D4
Sundnäs [S] 190 G2
Sundö [S] 190 H5
Sundre [S] 168 F6
Sunds [DK] 160 C6
Sundsbø [N] 180 D3
Sundsli [N] 164 E3
Sundsøre [DK] 160 C4
Sundsvall [S] 184 E4
Sundsvoll [N] 190 C3
Sundvollen [N] 170 H5
Sungurlare [BG] 148 E4
Suni [I] 118 C4
Sunja [HR] 142 B1
Sunnanå [S] 182 G6
Sunnansjö [S] 172 G5

Sunnansjö [S] 184 D4
Sunnaryd [S] 162 C4
Sunndal [N] 170 C5
Sunndalsøra [N] 180 F3
Sunne [S] 166 E1
Sunnemo [S] 166 F1
Sunnersta [S] 168 D2
Suntaži [LV] 198 E5
Suodenniemi [FIN] 176 E1
Suojoki [FIN] 186 B5
Suokonmäki [FIN] 186 D3
Suolahti [FIN] 186 G3
Suolovuobme [N] 194 B3
Suomenlinna / Sveaborg [FIN] 176 H5
Suomenniemi [FIN] 178 D1
Suomijärvi [FIN] 186 C5
Suomusjärvi [FIN] 176 F4
Suonenjoki [FIN] 188 C3
Suontaka [FIN] 176 D3
Suontee [FIN] 188 C3
Suopelto [FIN] 176 H1
Suorva [S] 192 F5
Šuoššjávri [N] 194 B4
Suotuperä [FIN] 196 D5
Suovanlahti [FIN] 186 G2
Superga [I] 70 D5
Supetar [HR] 144 A2
Supino [I] 116 B6
Supraśl [PL] 24 F5
Surahammar [S] 168 B2
Šurany [SK] 64 B5
Suraż [PL] 24 E6
Surazh [BY] 202 C4
Surazh [RUS] 202 D5
Surbo [I] 122 G4
Surčin [SRB] 142 G2
Surduk [SRB] 142 G2
Surdulica [SRB] 146 E5
Surgères [F] 54 C5
Súria [E] 92 D3
Šurice [SK] 64 E4
Surju [EST] 198 E3
Šurlane [SRB] 146 D6
Surnadalsöra [N] 180 G2
Sŭrnitsa [BG] 130 C1
Sursee [CH] 58 E5
Surtainville [F] 26 D2
Surte [S] 160 H2
Survilliers [F] 42 G3
Susa [I] 70 C5
Šušara [SRB] 142 H2
Susch [CH] 72 B2
Suscinio, Château de– [F] 40 D5
Susek [SRB] 142 F1
Suševo [MK] 128 G2
Sushitsa [BG] 148 C3
Sušice [CZ] 48 E6
Suso y Yuso, Monasterios de– [E] 82 G6
Süssen [D] 60 B2
Susurluk [TR] 150 D5
Susz [PL] 22 F4
Sutivan [HR] 144 A2
Sutjeska [SRB] 142 H1
Sütlaç [TR] 152 H4
Sutomore [MNE] 144 E5
Sutri [I] 114 H4
Sutrieu [F] 68 H2
Sutton Coldfield [GB] 10 E6
Süttorf [D] 18 G6
Suure–Jaani [EST] 198 E2
Suurejõe [EST] 198 E2
Suuremõisa [EST] 198 C2
Suurlahti [FIN] 178 D1
Suurmäki [FIN] 188 E3
Suva Reka [SRB] 146 C6
Suvekas [LT] 200 G3
Suvereto [I] 114 E2
Suvorove [UA] 204 F4
Suvorovo [BG] 148 F2
Suvorovo [RUS] 202 E3
Suwałki [PL] 24 E3
Suystamo [RUS] 188 H4
Suzzara [I] 110 E2
Svabensverk [S] 174 C3
Svalöv [S] 158 C2
Svalyava [UA] 204 C3
Svanabyn [S] 190 F5
Svaneholm [S] 158 C3
Svanehölm [S] 166 H6
Svaneke [DK] 158 E4
Svanesund [S] 166 C6
Svängsta [S] 158 E1
Svaningen [S] 190 E5
Sv. Anna [CZ] 50 A5
Svannäs [S] 190 G2
Svanskog [S] 166 D3
Svanvik [N] 194 F3
Svappavaara [S] 192 G5
Svarar [FIN] 186 B3
Svärdsjo [S] 174 D4
Svarstad [N] 164 G2
Svartå [S] 166 G3
Svärta [S] 168 C4
Svartå Mustio [FIN] 176 F5
Svartberget [S] 194 B8
Svartbyn [S] 194 B8
Svarte [S] 158 C3
Svärtinge [S] 168 B5
Svartisdalen [N] 190 E2
Svartlå [S] 196 A2
Svartnäs [S] 174 D3
Svartnäs [S] 190 H4
Svartnes [N] 192 D6
Svartnes [N] 194 F2
Svarttjärn [S] 190 F3
Svartvik [S] 184 E5
Svatá Hora [CZ] 48 F5
Svatá Kateřina [CZ] 48 C5
Svategjel [N] 170 E2
Svätý Anton [SK] 64 C4
Svätý Jur [SK] 62 G4
Svatý Mikuláš [CZ] 50 B4
Svätý Peter [SK] 64 B5
Sv. Barbora [CZ] 48 G6
Sveaborg / Suomenlinna [FIN] 176 H5
Svedala [S] 158 C3
Svedasai [LT] 200 G4
Svedje [S] 184 E5
Svedje [S] 184 G1
Svedje [S] 190 E5
Sveg [S] 182 G5
Sveindal [N] 164 D4
Sveio [N] 164 A1
Švėkšna [LT] 200 D4
Svelgen [N] 180 B5
Svellingen [N] 190 A6
Svelvik [N] 164 H2
Svenarum [S] 162 D3
Švenčionėliaj [LT] 200 H4
Švenčionys [LT] 200 H5
Svendborg [DK] 156 E4
Svenes [N] 164 E4
Svenkerud [N] 170 G3
Svenljunga [S] 162 B3
Svennevad [S] 166 H4
Svensby [N] 192 G2
Svenskby [FIN] 176 F5
Svensköp [S] 158 D2
Svenstavik [S] 182 G3
Svenstorp [S] 158 C2
Svenstrup [DK] 160 D4
Sveom [N] 180 G5
Švermov [CZ] 48 F3
S. Vero Milis [I] 118 C5
Sveta Petka [SRB] 146 D2
Sveti Andrejaš [MK] 128 E1
Sveti Ivan Žabno [HR] 74 F5
Sveti Jovan Bigorski [MK] 128 C2
Sveti Konstantin [BG] 148 A6
Sveti Naum [AL] 128 D4
Sveti Nikita [MK] 146 C6
Sveti Nikole [MK] 128 F1
Sveti Pantelejmon [MK] 128 E1
Sveti Rok [HR] 112 G4
Sveti Stefan [MNE] 144 E5
Světlá nad Sázavou [CZ] 48 H5
Svetlen [BG] 148 D3
Svetlice [SK] 52 E6
Svetlina [BG] 148 D5
Svetlina [BG] 148 E5
Svetlogorsk [RUS] 200 C5
Svetlyy [RUS] 24 B2
Svetlyy [RUS] 194 E4
Svetogorsk [RUS] 178 F2
Svetozar Miletic [SRB] 76 C5
Svetvinčenat [HR] 112 D2
Svežen [BG] 148 B5
Svib [HR] 144 B2
S. Vicente de la Cabeza [E] 80 G4
Svidník [SK] 52 D5
Švihov [CZ] 48 D5
Svilajnac [SRB] 146 C1
Svilengrad [BG] 150 A2
Svilojevo [SRB] 76 C6
Svinesund [S] 166 C3
Svinesundbrö [N/S] 166 B3
Svingstad [N] 170 H3
Svingvoll [N] 170 H2
Svinhult [S] 162 E2
Svinná [SK] 64 B3
Svinndal [N] 166 B2
Svinninge [DK] 156 F2
Svir [BY] 200 H5
Svishtov [BG] 148 C2
Svislach [BY] 24 G5
Svitavy [CZ] 50 B4
Svitlovods'k [UA] 202 F8
Sv. Juraj [HR] 112 F2
Sv. Jurij [SLO] 74 E3
Sv. Martin [HR] 74 F4
Sv. Nikola [MNE] 128 A1
Svoboda [BG] 148 F1
Svoboda [RUS] 24 C2
Svobodnoye [RUS] 178 F2
Svode [BG] 146 G4
Svodín [SK] 64 B5
Svodje [SRB] 146 E4
Svoge [BG] 146 F4
Svolvær [N] 192 D4
Svorkmo [N] 180 H2
Svormuseet [N] 180 D5
Svratka [CZ] 50 B5
Svrčinovec [SK] 50 F5
Svrljig [SRB] 146 D3
Svullrya [N] 172 D5
Sv. Vid [HR] 112 F2
Svyetlahorsk [BY] 202 C6
Swaffham [GB] 14 G2
Swalmen [NL] 30 F3
Swanage [GB] 12 G5
Swanlinbar [IRL] 2 E4
Swansea [GB] 12 E2
Swarożyn [PL] 22 E3
Swarzędz [PL] 36 C2
Swarzewo [PL] 22 D1
Świdnica [PL] 34 H4
Świdnica [PL] 50 B1
Świdnik [PL] 38 E5
Świdwin [PL] 20 H4
Świebodzice [PL] 50 B1
Świebodzin [PL] 36 A3
Świecie [PL] 22 D5
Świecko [PL] 34 G3
Świeradów–Zdrój [PL] 48 H1
Świerczów [PL] 50 E1
Świerki [PL] 50 B2
Świerzawa [PL] 50 B1
Świerzno [PL] 20 F3
Święta [PL] 20 F4
Święta Anna [PL] 50 G1
Święta Lipka [PL] 24 B3
Święte [PL] 36 E3
Świętno [PL] 36 B4
Swindon [GB] 12 H3
Swinford [IRL] 2 C4
Świnoujście [PL] 20 E3
Swords [IRL] 2 F6
Swornegacie [PL] 22 C4
Swory [PL] 38 E3
Sybaris–Copia [I] 124 D3
Sychevka [RUS] 202 E3
Syców [PL] 36 D6
Sydanmää [FIN] 176 D2
Sykaminéa [GR] 134 G2
Sykäräinen [FIN] 196 D6
Syke [D] 18 D6
Sykéa [GR] 136 F4
Sykéa [GR] 140 G5
Sykiá [GR] 130 D6
Sykiá [GR] 132 F1
Sykióna [GR] 136 E1
Sykkylven [N] 180 D4
Sykoúri [GR] 132 G1
Sylling [N] 164 H1
Sylte [N] 180 E2
Symbister [GB] 6 H4
Sými [GR] 154 C3
Synsiö [FIN] 186 H5
Syötekylä [FIN] 196 E2
Sypnievo [PL] 22 C5
Sypniewo [PL] 24 C6
Syrau [D] 48 C2
Syrävaara [FIN] 196 G5
Sysmä [FIN] 178 A1
Sysslebäck [S] 172 E4
Syston [GB] 10 F6
Syväjärvi [FIN] 194 D7
Syvänniemi [FIN] 188 C2
Syvärinpää [FIN] 196 F6
Syvde [N] 180 C4
Sývota [GR] 132 C2
Syvsten [DK] 160 E3
Syyspohja [FIN] 178 E1
Szabadegyháza [H] 76 B2
Szabadszállás [H] 76 C3
Szabolcsbáka [H] 64 H4
Szada [H] 64 D6
Szadek [PL] 36 F4
Szakály [H] 76 B4
Szakcs [H] 76 B3
Szakmár [H] 76 C3
Szalánta [H] 76 B5
Szalkszentmárton [H] 76 C2
Szalonna [H] 64 F3
Szamocin [PL] 22 B6
Szamotuły [PL] 36 C2
Szandaszőlős [H] 76 E2
Szank [H] 76 D3
Szany [H] 74 G1
Szápár [H] 76 A1
Szarvas [H] 76 F2
Szarvasi Arboretum [H] 76 F2
Szarvaskő [H] 64 E5
Szászvár [H] 76 B4
Százhalombatta [H] 76 C1
Szczaniec [PL] 36 A3
Szczawne [PL] 52 E5
Szczawnica [PL] 52 B5
Szczebrzeszyn [PL] 52 F1
Szczecin [PL] 20 F5
Szczecinek [PL] 22 B4
Szczekociny [PL] 50 H2
Szczerców [PL] 36 G5
Szczucin [PL] 52 C3
Szczuczyn [PL] 24 D4
Szczurowa [PL] 52 B3
Szczyrk [PL] 50 G5
Szczytna [PL] 50 B3
Szczytno [PL] 24 B4
Szécsény [H] 64 D5
Szederkény [H] 76 B5
Szedres [H] 76 B4
Szeged [H] 76 E4
Szeghalom [H] 76 G2
Szegvár [H] 76 E3
Székely [H] 64 H4
Székesfehérvár [H] 76 B2
Székkutas [H] 76 F3
Szekszárd [H] 76 C4
Szemere [H] 64 F3
Szendehely [H] 64 C5
Szendrő [H] 64 F4
Szendrölád [H] 64 F4
Szentendre [H] 64 C6
Szentes [H] 76 E3
Szentlászló [H] 74 G3
Szentliszló [H] 76 A5
Szentlőrinc [H] 76 A5
Szenyér [H] 74 H4
Szephalom [H] 64 G3
Szerencs [H] 64 G4
Szestno [PL] 24 B3
Szetlew [PL] 36 E3
Szigetszentmiklós [H] 76 C1
Szigetvár [H] 76 A5
Szigliget [H] 74 H3
Szikszó [H] 64 F4
Szil [H] 62 G6
Szilvágy [H] 74 F3
Szilvásvárad [H] 64 E4
Szirák [H] 64 D5
Szittyóúrbő [H] 76 C2
Szklarska Poręba [PL] 48 H1
Szklary [PL] 52 E4
Szklary Górne [PL] 36 B5
Szlichtyngowa [PL] 36 B4
Szob [H] 64 C5
Szolnok [H] 76 E2
Szombathely [H] 74 F2
Szonowice [PL] 50 E3
Szőny [H] 64 B6
Szpetal Górny [PL] 36 G2
Szprotawa [PL] 34 H5
Szreńsk [PL] 22 G6
Szropy [PL] 22 F3
Sztabin [PL] 24 E4
Sztum [PL] 22 E4
Sztutowo [PL] 22 F2
Sztynort [PL] 24 C3
Szubin [PL] 22 C6
Szűcs [H] 64 E5
Szulmierz [PL] 22 H6
Szumirad [PL] 50 E1
Szumowo [PL] 24 D6
Szurdokpüspöki [H] 64 D5
Szwecja [PL] 22 B5
Szydłów [PL] 36 G5
Szydłów [PL] 52 C2
Szydłowiec [PL] 38 B6
Szydłowo [PL] 22 B6
Szymbark [PL] 22 F4
Szypliszki [PL] 24 E2

T

Taalintehdas / Dalsbruk [FIN] 176 E6
Taastrup [DK] 156 G2
Taavetti [FIN] 178 D2
Tab [H] 76 A3
Tabaja [BIH] 144 C3
Tábara [E] 80 H4
Taberg [S] 162 D2
Tabernas [E] 102 G5
Tabiano Bagni [I] 110 D2
Taboada [E] 78 D4
Tábor [CZ] 48 G5
Tábua [P] 86 E2
Tabuaço [P] 80 D5
Tabuenca [E] 90 D3
Täby [S] 168 D2
Tachov [CZ] 48 C4
Tackåsen [S] 172 H2
Tadcaster [GB] 10 F3
Tädene [S] 166 E5
Tafalla [E] 84 B4
Tafira [E] 100 C6
Tafjord [N] 180 E4
Tăfteă [S] 184 G2
Tagaranna [EST] 198 C3
Tagenac [F] 68 C4
Taggia [I] 108 G4
Taghmon [IRL] 4 F5
Tagliacozzo [I] 116 B5
Táglio di Po [I] 110 H2
Tahal [E] 102 G4
Tahitótfalu [H] 64 C6
Tahivilla [E] 100 G5
Tahtacı [TR] 152 C2
Tahtaköprü [TR] 150 G5
Tai di Cadore [I] 72 F4
Tailfingen [D] 58 G2
Taillebois [F] 26 F4
Taimoniemi [FIN] 186 G2
Tain [GB] 6 E4
Taininiemi [FIN] 196 D2
Tain–l'Hermitage [F] 68 F4
Taipadas [P] 86 C5
Taipale [FIN] 176 E1
Taipale [FIN] 186 F3
Taipale [FIN] 186 H2
Taipaleenharju [FIN] 196 E3
Taipaleenkyla [FIN] 186 D4
Taipalsaari [FIN] 178 D2
Tairbeart / Tarbert [GB] 6 B3
Taivalkoski [FIN] 196 F3
Taivalmaa [FIN] 186 C4
Taivassalo / Tövsala [FIN] 176 C4
Taizé [F] 56 F6
Tajada, Cuevas de la– [E] 98 D2
Tajcy [RUS] 178 H5
Tajo de las Figuras, Cueva del– [E] 100 G5
Takácsi [H] 74 H1
Takamaa [FIN] 176 F1
Takene [S] 166 F3
Takmak [TR] 152 F3
Talachyn [BY] 202 C5
Talalaïvka [UA] 202 F6
Talamone [I] 114 F3
Tál ar Groaz [F] 40 B2
Talarrubias [E] 96 C3
Talaván [E] 86 H4
Talavera de la Reina [E] 88 D6
Talavera la Real [E] 94 G1
Talaveruela [E] 88 C5
Talayuela [E] 88 B6
Talayuelas [E] 98 D3
Talcy [F] 42 D6
Tali [EST] 198 E3
Táliga [E] 94 F2
Talinen [S] 194 B7
Talla [I] 110 G6
Tallaght [IRL] 2 F6
Tallaki [RUS] 24 B1
Tallard [F] 108 D2
Tällas [S] 190 G3
Tallåsen [S] 172 D3
Tallåsen [S] 184 D6
Tällberg [S] 172 H3
Tallhed [S] 172 G2
Tallinn [EST] 198 D1
Talloires [F] 70 B3
Tallow [IRL] 4 D5
Tallsjö [S] 190 G5
Tallträsk [S] 190 G5
Talluskylä [FIN] 186 H2
Tallvik [S] 194 B8
Tállya [H] 64 G4
Talmont [F] 54 C6
Talmont–St–Hilaire [F] 54 B3
Talpaki [RUS] 24 B1
Talsi [LV] 198 C5
Talty [PL] 24 C4
Talvik [N] 192 H1
Tamajón [E] 88 H4
Tamames [E] 88 B3
Tamanes [N] 194 D2
Tamarë [AL] 144 F4
Tamarino [BG] 148 E5
Tamarit [E] 92 C5
Tamarite de Litera [E] 90 H4
Tamási [H] 76 B3
Tambohuse [DK] 160 C4
Taminaschlucht [CH] 58 H6
Tamis [TR] 134 G1
Tammela [FIN] 176 F3
Tammensiel [D] 18 E1
Tammerfors / Tampere [FIN] 176 F1
Tammijärvi [FIN] 186 G5
Tammilahti [FIN] 186 G5
Tammisaari / Ekenäs [FIN] 176 F6
Tamnič [SRB] 146 E2
Tampere / Tammerfors [FIN] 176 F1
Tamsalu [EST] 198 E1
Tamsweg [A] 72 H2
Tämta [S] 162 B1
Tamworth [GB] 10 E6
Tanabru [N] 194 D2
Tanágra [GR] 134 B5
Tananger [N] 164 A3
Tancarville [F] 26 G3
Tanda [SRB] 146 D1
Tandö [S] 172 F3
Tandragee [NIR] 2 G4
Tandsbyn [S] 182 G3
Tandsjöborg [S] 172 G1
Tänga [S] 156 H1
Tångaberg [S] 160 H3
Tangen [N] 166 B3
Tangen [N] 166 C1
Tangen [N] 172 C4
Tangen [N] 192 F3
Tanger [AFR] 100 F6
Tangerhütte [D] 34 B2
Tangermünde [D] 34 C2
Tanhua [FIN] 194 E6
Taninges [F] 70 B2
Tankolampi [FIN] 186 G3
Tanlay [F] 56 F2
Tann [D] 46 F1
Tannåker [S] 162 C4
Tännäs [S] 182 E4
Tänndalen [S] 182 D4
Tanne [D] 32 H4
Tannenhof [D] 20 C5
Tännforsen [S] 182 E1
Tannheim [A] 60 C6
Tannila [FIN] 196 D3
Tånno [S] 162 D4
Tanowo [PL] 20 F5
Tanttila [FIN] 176 H2
Tanum [N] 164 G3
Tanum [S] 166 C4
Tanumshede [S] 166 C4
Tanus [F] 106 C2
Tanvald [CZ] 48 H2
Taormina [I] 124 B8
Tapa [EST] 198 E1
Tapanivaara [FIN] 196 F4
Tapfheim [D] 60 C2
Tapia de Casariego [E] 78 F2
Tapionkylä [FIN] 194 C7
Tápiószecső [H] 76 D1
Tápiószele [H] 76 D1
Tápiószentmárton [H] 76 D1
Tápiószölös [H] 76 D1
Tapojärvi [FIN] 194 B6
Tapolca [H] 74 H3
Tapolcafő [H] 74 H1
Taponas [F] 68 F2
Tapperøje [DK] 156 G4
Taps [DK] 156 C3
Tapsony [H] 74 G4
Tapsony [H] 76 C1
Tara [IRL] 2 F5
Taraguilla [E] 100 G5
Tarajalejo [E] 100 D6
Tara Kanjon [MNE] 144 E3
Tara Kanjon [MNE] 144 E2
Taraklı [TR] 150 H4
Taramundi [E] 78 F2
Tarancón [E] 96 H2
Táranto [I] 122 E4
Tarare [F] 68 F2
Tarascon [F] 106 G4
Tarascon–sur–Ariège [F] 84 H5
Tarasp [CH] 72 B2
Tarazona [E] 84 A6
Tarazona de la Mancha [E] 98 B4
Tårbæk [DK] 156 H2
Tarbert [GB] 8 C3
Tarbert [IRL] 2 B6
Tarbert / Tairbeart [GB] 6 B3
Tarbes [F] 84 F3
Tarcento [I] 72 G4
Tarčin [BIH] 144 C1
Tarczyn [PL] 38 B4
Tardets–Sorholus [F] 84 D3
Tardienta [E] 90 F3
Tärendö [S] 194 B7
Tărgovişte [RO] 204 D5
Târgu Frumos [RO] 204 D3
Târgu Jiu [RO] 204 C5
Târgu Lăpuş [RO] 204 C3
Târgu Mureş [RO] 204 C4
Târgu Neamţ [RO] 204 D3
Târgu Secuiesc [RO] 204 D4
Tarhos [H] 76 G3
Tarhos [H] 76 G3
Tarifa [E] 100 G6
Tarján [H] 64 B6
Tarło [PL] 38 E5
Tarm [DK] 156 B1
Tarmstedt [D] 18 E5
Tärna [S] 168 C1
Tärnaby [S] 190 E3
Tarnala [FIN] 188 G5
Tarnaleleszz [H] 64 E5
Tarnaméra [H] 64 E6
Tärnamo [S] 190 E3
Tarnaörs [H] 64 E6
Tarnaszentmiklós [H] 64 E6
Târnăveni [RO] 204 C4
Tarnawa Duża [PL] 52 F1
Tarnawatka [PL] 52 G2
Tarnawka [PL] 52 E1
Tärnet [N] 194 F3
Tarnobrzeg [PL] 52 D2
Tarnogród [PL] 52 F2
Tárnok [H] 76 C1
Tarnos [F] 66 A6
Tărnova [RO] 76 H4
Tărnovci [BG] 148 D1
Tarnów [PL] 34 G1
Tarnów [PL] 38 C4
Tarnów [PL] 52 C4
Tarnów Jez. [PL] 36 B4
Tarnowo Podgórne [PL] 36 C2
Tarnowskie Góry [PL] 50 F3
Tärnsjö [S] 174 E5
Tärnvik [N] 192 D5
Tarouca [P] 80 D5
Tarp [D] 18 F1
Tarquinia [I] 114 G4
Tarquínia [I] 114 G4
Tarquinia Lido [I] 114 G4
Tarragona [E] 92 C5
Tärrajur [S] 190 H2
Tarrasa / Terrassa [E] 92 E4
Tàrrega [E] 92 C3
Tårs [DK] 156 E4
Tårs [DK] 160 E3
Tarsia [I] 124 D3
Tartas [F] 66 B6
Tartu [EST] 198 F3
Tårup [DK] 156 E3
Tarutino [UA] 204 F4
Tarvainen [FIN] 176 D4
Tarvasjoki [FIN] 176 E4
Tarvisio [I] 72 H3
Tarvola [FIN] 186 D2
Tasapää [FIN] 188 G4
Taşbükü [TR] 154 D2
Täsch [CH] 70 E3
Täsjö [S] 190 F5
Taşköy [TR] 152 F3
Taşkule [TR] 152 C3
Taşlıca [TR] 154 D3
Tasovice [CZ] 62 F3
Tassjö [S] 162 B6
Tata [H] 64 B6
Tatabánya [H] 64 B6
Tataháza [H] 76 D4
Tatarbunary [UA] 204 F4
Tatárszentgyörgy [H] 76 D2
Tatlısu (Akanthoú) [CY] 154 G5
Tatranská Kotlina [SK] 52 B6
Tatranská Lomnica [SK] 52 B6
Tau [N] 164 B3
Taubenlochschlucht [CH] 58 D5
Tauberbischofsheim [D] 46 E4
Taucha [D] 34 C5
Tauerntunnel [A] 72 G2
Tauern Tunnel [A] 72 H1
Taufers / Tubre [I] 72 B3
Taufkirchen [A] 60 H4
Taufkirchen [D] 60 F4
Taujėnai [LT] 200 G4
Taüll [E] 84 G6
Taunton [GB] 12 F4
Taunusstein [D] 46 B3
Tauplitz [A] 62 B6
Taurage [LT] 200 E5
Taurasi [I] 120 F3
Taurianova [I] 124 C7
Taurine, Terme– [I] 114 G5
Taurisano [I] 122 G6
Taurkains [LV] 198 E5
Tauros [GR] 134 C6
Tauste [E] 90 E3
Tauves [F] 68 B2
Tavaklı [TR] 134 G1
Tavannes [CH] 58 D5
Tavarnelle Val di Pesa [I] 110 F6
Tavas [TR] 152 G5
Tavascan [E] 84 G6
Tavastehus / Hämeenlinna [FIN] 176 G3
Tavastila [FIN] 178 C3
Tavastkenka [FIN] 196 E5
Tavastkyro / Hämeenkyrö [FIN] 176 E1
Tavaux [F] 56 H4
Tavelsjö [S] 190 H5
Taverna [I] 124 E5
Tavernelle [I] 114 H2
Tavernes [F] 108 C4
Tavernes de la Valldigna [E] 98 E6
Taviano [I] 122 G6
Tavira [P] 94 D5
Tavistock [GB] 12 D4
Tavna, Manastir– [BIH] 142 E3
Tavole Palatine [I] 122 D4
Tavşancil [TR] 150 F3
Tavşanlı [TR] 152 G1
Täxan [S] 190 F6
Taxenbach [A] 72 G1
Taxiarchón, Moní– [GR] 138 D3
Tayfur [TR] 150 B5
Taytan [TR] 152 E3
Täzha [BG] 148 E4
Tázlár [H] 76 D3
Tazones [E] 82 C1
Tczew [PL] 22 E3
Tczów [PL] 38 C5
Teano [I] 120 D2
Tearce [MK] 146 C6
Teascu [RO] 146 G1
Techendorf [A] 72 G3
Teck [D] 58 H2
Tecklenburg [D] 32 C2
Tecuci [RO] 204 E4
Teerijärvi / Terjärv [FIN] 196 C6
Teféli [GR] 140 E5
Tefenni [TR] 152 H6
Tegéa [GR] 136 E3
Tegelen [NL] 30 F3
Tegelträsk [S] 190 G6
Tegernsee [D] 60 E5
Teggiano [I] 120 G4
Téglás [H] 64 H5
Teglaszin [H] 74 F2
Teglio [I] 72 A4
Teguise [E] 100 E6
Tehi [FIN] 176 H1
Teichel [D] 46 H1
Teichiussa [TR] 152 D6
Teignmouth [GB] 12 E5
Teillay [F] 40 F5
Teillet [F] 106 C3
Teisendorf [D] 60 G5
Teisko [FIN] 186 E6
Teixeiro [E] 78 D2
Tejeda [E] 100 C6
Tejn [DK] 158 E4
Teke [TR] 150 F2
Tekeriš [SRB] 142 F3
Tekin [TR] 152 H4
Tekirdağ [TR] 150 C3
Tekmen [TR] 154 F4
Tekovské Lužany [SK] 64 B5
Telana [I] 118 E5
Telavåg [N] 170 A4
Telč [CZ] 48 H6
Teldau [D] 18 G5
Telde [E] 100 C6
Teleborg [S] 162 E5
Telekháza [H] 64 F6
Telese Terme [I] 120 E2
Telford [GB] 10 D6
Telfs [A] 72 C1
Telgte [D] 32 C3
Telheiro [P] 94 B3
Telish [BG] 148 A3
Teljo [FIN] 196 G5
Tellingstedt [D] 18 E2
Tellskap [CH] 58 F6
Telmessos [TR] 154 F2
Telšiai [LT] 200 E4
Telti [I] 118 D3
Tembleque [E] 96 G2
Temelín [CZ] 48 F6
Temerin [SRB] 142 F1
Temerin [SRB] 204 A5
Temmes [FIN] 196 D4
Temnata Dupka [BG] 146 F4
Témpi [GR] 132 G1
Témpio Pausánia [I] 118 D3
Templemore [IRL] 4 E3
Templetouhy [IRL] 4 E3
Templin [D] 20 D6
Templom [H] 64 C5
Temse [B] 30 C3
Temska [SRB] 146 E3
Tenala / Tenhola [FIN] 176 F5
Tenby [GB] 12 D2
Tence [F] 68 E4
Tenda, Colle di– / Tende, Col de– [F/I] 108 F3
Tende [F] 108 F3
Tende, Col de– / Tenda, Colle di– [F/I] 108 F3
Tendilla [E] 88 H6
Tenebrón [E] 88 A3
Tenero [CH] 70 F3
Tenevo [BG] 148 E5
Tenhola / Tenala [FIN] 176 F5
Tenhult [S] 162 D2
Tenja [HR] 142 E1
Tenk [H] 64 E6
Tennänget [S] 172 F3
Tennevol [N] 192 F3
Tenterden [GB] 14 F5
Tentudia, Mon. de– [E] 94 G4
Teo / Ramallosa [E] 78 C3
Teofipol' [UA] 202 B8
Teolo [I] 110 G1
Teos [TR] 152 C5
Teovo [MK] 128 E2
Tepasto [FIN] 194 C6
Tepecik [TR] 150 E5
Tepecik [TR] 150 F5
Tepecik [TR] 150 F3
Tepecik [TR] 152 G1
Tepeköy [TR] 152 E4
Tepelenë [AL] 128 B6
Tepeören [TR] 150 F3
Teplá [CZ] 48 D4
Teplice [CZ] 48 E2
Teplice nad Metují [CZ] 50 B2
Tepsa [FIN] 194 C6
Téramo [I] 116 C3
Ter Apel [NL] 16 H3
Teratyn [PL] 38 G6
Terchová [SK] 50 G6
Terebiń [PL] 52 G1
Terebišće [RUS] 198 G3
Terebovlia [UA] 202 B8
Teremia Mare [RO] 76 F5
Terena [P] 94 E2
Teresa de Confrentes [E] 98 D5
Teresin [PL] 38 A3
Teresin [PL] 38 G6
Terespol [PL] 38 F3
Terezín [CZ] 48 F2
Terezino Polje [HR] 74 H5
Tergnier [F] 28 F6
Terjärv / Teerijärvi [FIN] 196 C6
Terkoz [TR] 150 E2
Terland [N] 164 B4
Terlizzi [I] 122 D2
Termal [TR] 150 F3
Termas de Monfortinho [P] 86 G3
Terme di Lurisia [I] 108 F3
Terme di Valdieri [I] 108 F3
Terme Luigiane [I] 124 C4
Termes–d'Armagnac [F] 84 F2
Terme S. Lucia [I] 116 C2
Terme Vigliatore [I] 124 A7

Términi Imerese [I] 126 D2
Terminillo [I] 116 B4
Terminón [E] 82 E5
Térmoli [I] 116 F5
Termolovo [RUS] 178 G3
Termonde (Dendermonde) [B] 28 H2
Termonfeckin [IRL] 2 F5
Ternberg [A] 62 B5
Terndrup [DK] 160 E4
Terneuzen [NL] 28 H1
Terni [I] 116 A3
Ternitz [A] 62 E6
Ternopil' [UA] 202 B8
Térovo [GR] 132 D2
Terpan [AL] 128 B5
Terpezita [RO] 146 F1
Terpilitsy [RUS] 178 G6
Terpní [GR] 130 B3
Terracina [I] 120 C2
Terradillos de los Templarios [E] 82 C5
Terråk [N] 190 D4
Terralba [I] 118 C5
Terra Mala [I] 118 D7
Terra Mitica [E] 104 E2
Terranova di Pollino [I] 122 C6
Terrassa / Tarrasa [E] 92 E4
Terrasson-la-Villedieu [F] 66 G3
Terrateig [E] 98 E6
Terrazos [E] 82 F5
Terriente [E] 98 D2
Terskanperä [FIN] 196 D5
Tersløse [DK] 156 F3
Tertenía [I] 118 E6
Teruel [E] 98 E2
Tervahauta [FIN] 176 E1
Tervakoski [FIN] 176 G3
Tervel [BG] 148 F1
Tervo [FIN] 186 H2
Tervola [FIN] 196 C2
Tervuren [B] 30 C4
Terz [A] 62 D5
Terzaga [E] 90 C6
Tesárske Mlyňany [SK] 64 B4
Tesejerague [E] 100 D6
Těškovice [CZ] 50 E4
Teslić [BIH] 142 C3
Teslui [RO] 146 G1
Tessenberg [A] 72 F3
Tesseosen [N] 180 G6
Tessin [D] 20 C3
Tessy-sur-Vire [F] 26 E4
Tét [H] 62 H6
Tetbury [GB] 12 G3
Teterow [D] 20 C4
Teteven [BG] 148 A4
Tetovo [BG] 148 D2
Tetovo [MK] 128 D1
Tetrálofo [GR] 128 F5
Tettnang [D] 58 H4
Teuchrania [TR] 152 C3
Teufelshöhle [D] 46 H4
Teufen [CH] 58 H5
Teulada [E] 104 F2
Teulada [I] 118 C7
Teupitz [D] 34 E3
Teurnia [A] 72 H3
Teuro [FIN] 176 F3
Teuva / Östermark [FIN] 186 B4
Tevaniemi [FIN] 186 D6
Tevel [H] 76 B4
Teverga / La Plaza [E] 78 G4
Tevfikiye [TR] 130 H5
Tewkesbury [GB] 12 G2
Tewli [BY] 38 G2
Texeiro [E] 78 E3
Texing [A] 62 D5
Teysset [F] 66 E5
Thal [A] 72 F3
Thale [D] 34 A4
Thalfang [D] 44 G2
Thalheim [D] 48 D2
Thalmässing [D] 46 G6
Thalwil [CH] 58 F5
Thame [GB] 14 D3
Thann [F] 58 D3
Thannhausen [D] 60 C3
Tharandt [D] 48 E1
Tharigné-sur-Dué [F] 42 C5
Thárros [I] 118 B5
Tharsis [E] 94 E5
Thásos [GR] 130 E4
Thatcham [GB] 12 H4
Thaumiers [F] 56 C4
Theessen [D] 34 C3
Them [DK] 156 C1
Themar [D] 46 F2
Thénezay [F] 54 E3
Thenon [F] 66 F3
Theológos [GR] 130 E4
Theológos [GR] 134 A4
Théoule [F] 108 E5
Thera [TR] 154 E2
Thermá [GR] 130 G4
Thérma [GR] 138 G1
Thérmi [GR] 130 B4
Thermí [GR] 134 H2
Thermisía [GR] 136 G2
Thérmo [GR] 132 F5
Thermopýles [GR] 132 G4
Thermopýles [GR] 132 G4
Thernberg [A] 62 E6
Thérouanne [F] 28 E2
Thespiés [GR] 134 A5
Thesprotia [GR] 132 C2
Thessaloníki [GR] 128 H4
Thetford [GB] 14 G2
The Turoe Stone [IRL] 2 C5
Theuley [F] 58 B3
Theux [B] 30 E5
Thevet-St-Julien [F] 56 B4
Theze [F] 84 E3
Thiaucourt-Regniéville [F] 44 E4
Thiberville [F] 26 G4
Thiélbemont-Farémont [F] 44 C5
Thiendorf [D] 34 E5
Thiene [I] 72 D5
Thiers [F] 68 D2
Thiersee [A] 60 F6
Thiersheim [D] 48 C3
Thiesi [I] 118 C3
Thiessow [D] 20 E2
Thingvellir [IS] 192 A3
Thionville [F] 44 E3
Thíra [GR] 138 F5
Thíra / Firá [GR] 138 F5
Thirette [F] 68 H1
Thirsk [GB] 10 F3
Thisted [DK] 160 C4
Thísvi [GR] 132 H5
Thíva [GR] 134 B5
Thivars [F] 42 D4
Thiviers [F] 66 F2
Thizy [F] 68 F2
Tho, Pieve del- [I] 110 G4
Thoard [F] 108 D3
Thoissey [F] 68 G1
Tholey [D] 44 G3
Tholó [GR] 136 C3
Thomasberg [A] 62 E6
Thomas Street [IRL] 2 D5
Thomastown [IRL] 4 E4
Thônes [F] 70 B3
Thonon-les-Bains [F] 70 B2
Thorens-Glières, Château de- [F] 70 B3
Thorigné-en-Charnie [F] 42 A5
Thorikó [GR] 136 H1
Thörl [A] 62 D6
Thornbury [GB] 12 G3
Thorney [GB] 14 F2
Thornhill [GB] 8 D4
Thoronet, Abbaye du- [F] 108 D5
Thors [F] 44 C6
Thórshöfn [IS] 192 C2
Thouarcé [F] 54 D2
Thouars [F] 54 E2
Thouría [GR] 136 D4
Thoúrio [GR] 130 H1
Thueyts [F] 68 E5
Thuin [B] 28 H4
Thuir [F] 92 G1
Thum [D] 48 D2
Thun [CH] 70 D1
Thuret [F] 68 D2
Thürkow [D] 20 C4
Thurles / Durlas [IRL] 4 E3
Thurnau [D] 46 H3
Thurn Pass [A] 72 F1
Thurso [GB] 6 F2
Thury-Harcourt [F] 26 F4
Thusis [CH] 70 H1
Thyborøn [DK] 160 B4
Thymariá [GR] 130 H3
Thymianá [GR] 134 G5
Thyregod [DK] 156 C1
Tiana [I] 118 D5
Tibaes [P] 80 C3
Tibarrié [F] 106 C3
Tibava [SK] 64 H2
Tiberio, Grotta di- [I] 120 C2
Tibro [S] 166 F5
Ticha [BG] 148 D3
Tidaholm [S] 166 F6
Tidan [S] 166 F5
Tidersrum [S] 162 F1
Tidö [S] 168 B2
Tiefenbronn [D] 58 G1
Tiefencastel [CH] 70 H2
Tiefensee [D] 34 F2
Tiel [NL] 16 E5
Tielt [B] 28 G2
Tiemassaari [FIN] 188 D4
Tienen (Tirlemont) [B] 30 D4
Tiengen [D] 58 F4
Tiercé [F] 40 H6
Tierga [E] 90 D3
Tiermas [E] 88 H3
Tierp [S] 174 F5
Tieva [FIN] 194 C6
Tigănași [RO] 146 E1
Tighina [MD] 204 F3
Tigkáki [GR] 154 B2
Tignes [F] 70 C4
Tihany [H] 76 A2
Tihilä [FIN] 196 E5
Tihusniemi [FIN] 188 D4
Tiironkyla [FIN] 186 F2
Tiistenjoki [FIN] 186 D3
Tijarafe [E] 100 A4
Tíjola [E] 102 G4
Tikhvin [RUS] 202 C1
Tikkakoski [FIN] 186 G4
Tikkala [FIN] 186 F5
Tikkala [FIN] 188 G3
Tilberga [S] 168 C2
Tilburg [NL] 30 E2
Tilbury [GB] 14 F4
Til-Châtel [F] 56 H3
Tilloy Lès Mofflaines [F] 28 F4
Tiltagals [LV] 198 F5
Tilži [LV] 198 G5
Timahoe [IRL] 4 F3
Time [N] 164 A3
Tími [CY] 154 F6
Timiryazevo [RUS] 200 D5
Timişoara [RO] 76 G5
Timişoara [RO] 204 B5
Timmel [D] 18 B4
Timmele [S] 162 C2
Timmendorfer Strand [D] 18 H3
Timmernabben [S] 162 G4
Timmersdala [S] 166 F5
Timmervik [S] 166 D5
Timoleague [IRL] 4 C5
Timoniemi [FIN] 196 G5
Timovaara [FIN] 188 E1
Timrå [S] 184 E4
Timsfors [S] 162 C6
Tinahely [IRL] 4 F4
Tinajo [E] 100 E5
Tinca [RO] 76 H3
Tinchebray [F] 26 E4
Tindaya [E] 100 E6
Tineo [E] 78 G3
Tingelstad [N] 170 H4
Tinglev [DK] 156 B4
Tingnes [N] 172 B3
Tingsryd [S] 162 E5
Tingstad [S] 168 B5
Tingstäde [S] 168 G4
Tingvoll [N] 180 F2
Tinnoset [N] 164 F1
Tínos [GR] 138 E2
Tiñosillos [E] 88 E4
Tintern Abbey [IRL] 4 F5
Tintigni [B] 44 E2
Tinuži [LV] 198 E5
Tiobraid Arann / Tipperary [IRL] 4 D4
Tione di Trento [I] 72 C4
Tipasoja [FIN] 196 F5
Tipperary / Tiobraid Arann [IRL] 4 D4
Tiranë [AL] 128 B3
Tirano [I] 72 B4
Tiraspol [MD] 204 F3
Tire [TR] 152 D5
Tirgo [E] 82 G6
Tiriolo [I] 124 E5
Tirlemont (Tienen) [B] 30 D4
Tirmo [FIN] 178 B4
Tirol / Tirolo [I] 72 C3
Tirolo / Tirol [I] 72 C3
Tirrénia [I] 110 D6
Tirschenreuth [D] 48 C4
Tirstrup [DK] 160 E6
Tirýntha [GR] 136 F2
Tišća [BIH] 142 E4
Tiscar-Don Pedro [E] 102 F2
Tishevica [BG] 146 G3
Tishino [RUS] 22 H2
Tismana, Mănăstirea- [RO] 204 C5
Tisno [HR] 112 G6
Tišnov [CZ] 50 B6
Tisovec [SK] 64 D3
Tistrup [DK] 156 B2
Tisvilde [DK] 156 G1
Tiszaalpár [H] 76 E3
Tiszabábolna [H] 64 F6
Tiszabüra [H] 76 F1
Tiszacsege [H] 64 F6
Tiszacsermely [H] 64 H4
Tiszadob [H] 64 G5
Tiszaföldvár [H] 76 E2
Tiszafüred [H] 64 F6
Tiszajenő [H] 76 E2
Tiszakécske [H] 76 E2
Tiszalök [H] 64 G5
Tiszalúc [H] 64 F5
Tiszanána [H] 64 F6
Tiszaörs [H] 64 F6
Tiszaroff [H] 76 E1
Tiszasüly [H] 76 E1
Tiszaszőlős [H] 64 F6
Tiszatelek [H] 64 H4
Tiszaújváros [H] 64 F5
Tiszavasvári [H] 64 G5
Titaguas [E] 98 D3
Titel [SRB] 142 G1
Titisee [D] 58 F3
Tito [I] 120 G4
Tito Bustillo, Cueva de- [E] 82 C2
Titova Spilja [BIH] 142 A3
Titov Veles [MK] 128 F1
Titran [N] 190 A6
Tittling [D] 60 H3
Tittmoning [D] 60 G4
Titz [D] 30 F4
Tiuccia [F] 114 A4
Tiukka / Tjöck [FIN] 186 B4
Tiurajärvi [FIN] 194 C6
Tivat [MNE] 144 D4
Tived [S] 166 G4
Tiverton [GB] 12 E4
Tivoli [I] 116 B5
Tizzano [F] 114 A6
Tjæreborg [DK] 156 B2
Tjällmo [S] 166 H5
Tjalme [S] 192 G4
Tjåmotis [S] 190 G1
Tjautjas [S] 192 G6
Tjeldnes [N] 192 E4
Tjele [DK] 160 D5
Tjelle [N] 180 F3
Tjentište [BIH] 144 D2
Tjöck / Tiukka [FIN] 186 B4
Tjolöholm [S] 160 H3
Tjøme [N] 164 H3
Tjong [N] 190 D1
Tjønnefoss [N] 164 E3
Tjørhom [N] 164 C3
Tjørnhom [N] 164 C5
Tjørnuvik [FR] 160 A1
Tjøtta [N] 190 D3
Tjugum [N] 170 C1
Tjultrask [S] 190 F2
Tjuvkil [S] 160 G1
Tkon [HR] 112 G5
Tlachene [BG] 146 G3
Tleń [PL] 22 D4
Tlmače [SK] 64 B4
Tlos [TR] 154 G2
Tłuchowo [PL] 36 G1
Tlumačov [CZ] 50 D6
Tłuszcz [PL] 38 C2
Tobarra [E] 98 B6
Tobercurry [IRL] 2 D3
Tobermory [GB] 6 B6
Tobias [A] 62 D5
Toblach / Dobbiaco [I] 72 E3
Tocha [P] 80 A6
Tocina [E] 94 H5
Töcksfors [S] 166 C2
Todal [N] 180 G2
Todalen [N] 180 G3
Todi [I] 116 A3
Todorići [BIH] 142 B4
Tødsø [DK] 160 C4
Todtmoos [D] 58 E4
Todtnau [D] 58 E3
Tõdva [EST] 198 D1
Toftbyn [S] 174 C4
Tofte [N] 164 H2
Tofterup [DK] 156 B2
Tofteryd [S] 162 D3
Tofteseter [N] 170 H1
Toftesetra [N] 180 G5
Toftir [FR] 160 B2
Toftlund [DK] 156 B3
Togher [IRL] 2 D5
Tóház [H] 76 B3
Tohmajärvi [FIN] 188 G3
Toholampi [FIN] 196 C6
Tohvri [EST] 198 E3
Toichío [GR] 128 E5
Toijala [FIN] 176 F2
Toijola [FIN] 188 D6
Toikkala [FIN] 178 C2
Toikkala [FIN] 178 D2
Toirano, Grotte di- [I] 108 G3
Toitz [D] 20 C3
Toivakka [FIN] 186 G5
Toivola [FIN] 178 C1
Töjby [FIN] 186 A4
Tojšići [BIH] 142 E3
Tokačka [BG] 130 F2
Tokagjelet [N] 170 B4
Tokaj [H] 64 G4
Tokarnia [PL] 50 H4
Tokarnia [PL] 52 B2
Tokary [PL] 36 F4
Tokary [PL] 38 F2
Tokmak [UA] 204 H2
Tokod [H] 64 B6
Toksovo [RUS] 178 H4
Tolcsva [H] 64 G4
Toledo [E] 96 F1
Tolentino [I] 116 C2
Tolfa [I] 114 G4
Tolfta [S] 174 F5
Tolg [S] 162 E4
Tolga [N] 182 C4
Tolkis / Tolkkinen [FIN] 178 B4
Tolkkinen / Tolkis [FIN] 178 B4
Tolkmicko [PL] 22 F2
Tollarp [S] 158 D2
Tølløse [DK] 156 F3
Tolmachevo [RUS] 198 H1
Tolmezzo [I] 72 G4
Tolmin [SLO] 72 H4
Tolna [H] 76 C4
Tolne [DK] 160 E2
Toló [GR] 136 F2
Tolob [GB] 6 G4
Tolonen [FIN] 194 D5
Tolosa [E] 84 B3
Tolosa [P] 86 E4
Tolosenmäki [FIN] 188 G4
Tolox [E] 102 B4
Tolve [I] 120 H4
Tomar [P] 86 D3
Tomaševac [SRB] 142 G1
Tomaševo [MNE] 146 A4
Tomášikovo [SK] 62 H5
Tomaszów Lubelski [PL] 52 G2
Tomaszów Mazowiecki [PL] 36 H5
Tomatin [GB] 6 E5
Tombebœuf [F] 66 E4
Tomelilla [S] 158 D3
Tomelloso [E] 96 G4
Tomerdingen [D] 60 B3
Tomintoul [GB] 6 E5
Tomislavgrad [BIH] 144 B1
Tømmernes [N] 192 E5
Tommerup [DK] 156 D3
Tømmervåg [N] 180 F2
Tommola [FIN] 178 C1
Tompa [H] 76 D4
Tømra [N] 182 C2
Tomrefjord [N] 180 D3
Tomter [N] 166 B2
Tona [E] 92 E3
Tonara [I] 118 D5
Tonbridge [GB] 14 E5
Tondela [P] 80 C6
Tønder [DK] 156 B4
Tongeren (Tongres) [B] 30 E4
Tongres (Tongeren) [B] 30 E4
Tongue [GB] 6 E2
Tonnay-Boutonne [F] 54 C5
Tonnay-Charente [F] 54 C5
Tonneins [F] 66 E5
Tonnerre [F] 56 F2
Tonnes [N] 190 D1
Tönning [D] 18 E2
Tonquédec, Château de- [F] 40 D1
Tønsberg [N] 164 H3
Tonstad [N] 164 C4
Toomyvara [IRL] 2 D6
Toourmakeady / Tuar Mhic Éadaigh [IRL] 2 C4
Topares [E] 102 H3
Topchii [BG] 148 D2
Töpchin [D] 34 E3
Topczewo [PL] 24 E6
Topli Dol [SRB] 146 E3
Toplița [RO] 204 D4
Toplou [GR] 140 G4
Topo [P] 100 C3
Topola [SRB] 146 B1
Topola [SRB] 204 B6
Topolčani [MK] 128 E3
Topoľčany [SK] 64 B3
Topoľčiansky Hrad [SK] 64 A3
Topólia [GR] 140 B4
Topolnica [SRB] 146 D1
Topolovățu Mare [RO] 76 H5
Topolovec [BG] 146 F2
Topolovgrad [BG] 150 A1
Topolovica [HR] 74 G6
Topolovo [BG] 148 B6
Toporu [RO] 148 C1
Topusko [HR] 112 H1
Toques [E] 78 D3
Torà [E] 92 D3
Toral de los Vados [E] 78 F5
Torbalı [TR] 152 D4
Tørberget [N] 172 D2
Torbole [I] 72 C5
Torcello [I] 72 F6
Tordera [E] 92 F4
Tordesillas [E] 88 E2
Tordesilos [E] 90 C6
Töre [S] 196 B2
Töreboda [S] 166 F5
Toreby [DK] 20 A1
Torekov [S] 160 H6
Torelló [E] 92 E3
Toreno [E] 78 F5
Toresund [S] 168 C3
Torf [A] 74 B2
Torfyanovka [RUS] 178 E3
Torgåsmon [S] 172 F3
Torgau [D] 34 D5
Torgelow [D] 20 E4
Torgiano [I] 116 A2
Torhamn [S] 158 G1
Torhout [B] 28 F2
Tori [EST] 198 E3
Torigni-sur-Vire [F] 26 E3
Torija [E] 88 H5
Toril [E] 98 D2
Torino [I] 70 D5
Torino di Sangro [I] 116 E5
Torino di Sangro Marina [I] 116 E5
Torís / Turís [E] 98 E5
Torla [E] 84 E5
Torma [EST] 198 F2
Tormac [RO] 76 H6
Törmäkylä [FIN] 196 E4
Törmänki [FIN] 194 C7
Tormänmäki [FIN] 196 E4
Tormos [E] 84 D6
Tornal'a [SK] 64 E4
Tornavacas [E] 88 B5
Tornby [DK] 160 E2
Torneå / Tornio [FIN] 196 C2
Tørnes [N] 164 F3
Tørnes [N] 180 E2
Torneträsk [S] 192 G4
Tornio / Torneå [FIN] 196 C2
Tornioniemi [FIN] 188 E4
Tornjoš [SRB] 76 E5
Toro [E] 88 D1
Törökszentmiklós [H] 76 E2
Toróni [GR] 130 C6
Torony [H] 74 F2
Toropec [RUS] 202 C3
Toropets [RUS] 202 C3
Toros [BG] 148 A4
Toros de Guisando [E] 88 E5
Torp [FIN] 174 H5
Torp [S] 166 C5
Torpa [S] 162 C5
Torpa Stenhus [S] 162 B2
Torpo [N] 170 F3
Torpoint [GB] 12 D5
Torpsbruk [S] 162 D4
Torpshammar [S] 184 D4
Torquay [GB] 12 E5
Torquemada [E] 82 D6
Torralba [E] 90 B4
Torralba [E] 96 F4
Torralba de el Burgo [E] 90 A3
Torralba de Oropesa [E] 88 C6
Torrão [P] 94 D2
Torre [E] 102 D5
Torre Annunziata [I] 120 E3
Torre Beretti [I] 70 F6
Torreblanca [E] 98 G3
Torrecaballeros [E] 88 F4
Torrecampo [E] 96 D5
Torre Canne [I] 122 F3
Torrechiara, Castello di- [I] 110 D3
Torrecilla [E] 98 C1
Torrecilla de la Orden [E] 88 D2
Torrecilla del Pinar [E] 90 B5
Torrecillas de la Tiesa [E] 96 B1
Torreciudad, Santuario de- [E] 90 H3
Torre de D. Chama [P] 80 F3
Torre de Juan Abad [E] 96 G5
Torre del Bierzo [E] 78 F5
Torre del Compte [E] 102 E2
Torre del Greco [I] 120 E3
Torre del Lago Puccini [I] 110 D5
Torre dell'Impiso [I] 126 B1
Torre del Mar [E] 102 C5
Torredembarra [E] 92 C5
Torre de Moncorvo [P] 80 E5
Torre de' Pàsseri [I] 116 D4
Torre de Sta. María [E] 86 H6
Torredonjimeno [E] 102 D2
Torre Faro [I] 124 C7
Torrefarrera [E] 90 H4
Torregamones [E] 80 G4
Torre Grande [I] 118 B5
Torreguadiaro [E] 100 H5
Torreiglesias [E] 88 F3
Torreira [P] 80 B5
Torrejoncillo [E] 86 H4
Torrejón de Ardoz [E] 88 G6
Torrejón de la Calzada [E] 88 F6
Torrejón del Rey [E] 88 G5
Torrejón el Rubio [E] 88 A6
Torrelaguna [E] 88 G4
Torrelapaja [E] 90 C3
Torrelavega [E] 82 E3
Torrelobatón [E] 88 E1
Torrelodones [E] 88 F5
Torremaggiore [I] 116 F6
Torremejía [E] 94 H2
Torre Melissa [I] 124 F4
Torremocha [E] 86 H6
Torremocha de Jiloca [E] 98 D1
Torremocha del Pinar [E] 90 B5
Torremolinos [E] 102 B5
Torremormojón [E] 82 C6
Torrenostra [E] 98 G3
Torrent [E] 98 E5
Torrente de Cinca [E] 90 G5
Torrenueva [E] 96 F5
Torrenueva [E] 102 E5
Torre Orsaia [I] 120 G5
Torre-Pacheco [E] 104 C4
Torre Pellice [I] 70 C6
Torreperogil [E] 102 F2
Torrequemada [E] 86 H5
Torre Santa Susanna [I] 122 F4
Torres Cabrera [E] 102 C1
Torre S. Gennaro [I] 122 G4
Torres Novas [P] 86 C4
Torre S. Sabina [I] 122 F3
Torres Vedras [P] 86 B4
Torretta [I] 124 F4
Torrette di Fano [I] 112 C6
Torre Vã [P] 94 C3
Torrevieja [E] 104 D3
Torrflonäs [S] 184 C5
Torricella [I] 122 F5
Torri del Benaco [I] 72 C6
Torríglia [I] 110 B3
Torrijas [E] 98 E3
Torrijos [E] 96 E1
Tørring [DK] 156 C2
Tørring [N] 190 C5
Torrita di Siena [I] 114 G2
Torroella de Montgrí [E] 92 G3
Torrox [E] 102 D5
Torrubia [E] 96 D5
Torsåker [S] 168 D4
Torsåker [S] 174 D4
Torsängen [S] 166 E5
Torsås [S] 162 F6
Torsborg [S] 182 F3
Torsburgen [S] 168 G5
Torsby [S] 166 E1
Torsby [S] 172 E5
Torshälla [S] 168 B3
Tórshavn [FR] 160 B2
Torslanda [S] 160 G2
Torsminde [DK] 160 B5
Törtel [H] 76 E2
Tortinmäki [FIN] 176 E4
Tórtola de Henares [E] 88 H5
Tórtoles de Esgueva [E] 88 G2
Tortolì [I] 118 E5
Tortona [I] 110 B2
Tortora [I] 120 H6
Tortoreto [I] 116 D3
Tortoreto Lido [I] 116 D3
Tortorici [I] 126 F2
Tortosa [E] 92 A5
Tortosendo [P] 86 F2
Toruń [PL] 22 E6
Torup [S] 158 C3
Torup [S] 162 B4
Torup Strand [DK] 160 C3
Tõrva [EST] 198 E3
Tor Vaiánica [I] 116 A6
Torvikbukt [N] 180 F2
Tørvikbygd [N] 170 C4
Torvinen [FIN] 194 D7
Torvsjö [S] 190 F5
Torvund [N] 170 B1
Torzhok [RUS] 202 E2
Torzym [PL] 34 H3
Tosbotn [N] 190 D3
Toscolano Maderno [I] 72 B5
Tösens [A] 72 C2
Toses, Collado de- [E] 92 E2
Tosno [RUS] 202 B1
Toso [N] 170 H5
Tossa de Mar [E] 92 F4
Tossåsen [S] 182 G3
Tossavanlahti [FIN] 186 G1
Tösse [S] 166 D4
Tostedt [D] 18 F5
Tosterup [S] 158 D3
Tószeg [H] 76 E2
Toszek [PL] 50 F3
Totana [E] 104 B3
Totebo [S] 162 F2
Tôtes [F] 28 B5
Tótkomlós [H] 76 F4
Tøtlandsvik [N] 164 C2
Totleben [BG] 148 B3
Totnes [GB] 12 E5
Tøttdal [N] 190 C5
Tottijärvi [FIN] 176 F2
Tótvázsony [H] 74 H2
Toucy [F] 56 E2
Touffou [F] 54 F4
Toul [F] 44 E5
Toulon [F] 108 C6
Toulon sur Allier [F] 56 D5
Toulon-sur-Arroux [F] 56 F5
Toulouse [F] 84 H3
Tourcoing [F] 28 F3
Tourmalet, Col du- [F] 84 E4
Tournai (Doornik) [B] 28 G3
Tournan [F] 42 G4
Tournay [F] 84 F4
Tournon [F] 68 F5
Tournon-d'Agenais [F] 66 F5
Tournon-St-Martin [F] 54 G4
Tournus [F] 56 G6
Tourny [F] 28 C6
Tours [F] 54 F2
Tourves [F] 108 C5
Toury [F] 42 E5
Toutes Aures, Col de- [F] 108 D4
Touvois [F] 54 B2
Toužim [CZ] 48 D3
Tovačov [CZ] 50 D5
Tovarnik [HR] 142 E2
Tøvik [N] 180 E2
Tövsala / Taivassalo [FIN] 176 C4
Tovste [UA] 204 D2
Towcester [GB] 14 D2
Töysä [FIN] 186 D3
Trabada [E] 78 F2
Trabadelo [E] 78 E5
Trabanca [E] 80 G5
Trabazos [E] 80 G4
Traben-Trarbach [D] 44 G2
Trabia [I] 126 D2
Trabotivište [MK] 128 H1
Trabuc, Grottes de- [F] 106 F3
Tracheiá [GR] 136 F2
Trachíli [GR] 134 C5
Tracino [I] 126 A5
Trädet [S] 162 C1
Trælleborg [DK] 156 F3
Trafaria [P] 86 A5
Trafoi [I] 72 B3
Tragacete [E] 98 C1
Traian [RO] 148 B2
Traiguera [E] 92 A6
Traisen [A] 62 D5
Traiskirchen [A] 62 F5
Traismauer [A] 62 E4
Trajano [E] 100 G3
Trakai [LT] 24 H1
Trakošćan [HR] 74 E4
Tralee / Trá Lí [IRL] 4 B3
Trá Lí / Tralee [IRL] 4 B3
Tralleis [TR] 152 E5
Tramaríglio [I] 118 B3
Tramelan [CH] 58 D5
Tramonti di Sopra [I] 72 F4
Tramore [IRL] 4 E5
Tranås [S] 162 E1
Tranby [N] 164 H1
Tranco [E] 102 G1
Trancoso [P] 80 D6
Tranderup [DK] 156 D4
Tranekær [DK] 156 E4
Tranekær Slot [DK] 156 E4
Tranemo [S] 162 C3
Trångmon [S] 190 E4
Trängslet [S] 172 F2
Trångsviken [S] 182 G2
Tranhult [S] 162 C3
Trani [I] 122 D2
Trankil [S] 166 C3
Tranóvalto [GR] 128 F6
Tranøya [N] 192 E4
Transtrand [S] 172 F3
Tranum Strand [DK] 160 D3
Tranvik [S] 168 E3
Trápani [I] 126 B2
Trapishte [BG] 148 D3
Trappe d'Aiguebelle, Monastère de la- [F] 68 F6
Trappes [F] 42 F4
Traryd [S] 162 C5
Träskända / Järvenpää [FIN] 176 H4
Träskvik [FIN] 186 B5
Träslövsläge [S] 160 H4
Trasmiras [E] 78 D6
Trassem [D] 44 F3
Trăstenik [BG] 148 A3
Trate [SLO] 74 E3
Tratzberg [A] 60 E6
Traun [A] 62 B4
Traunkirchen [A] 62 A5
Traunreut [D] 60 G5
Traunstein [D] 60 G5
Trautenfels [A] 62 B6
Trautmannsdorf [A] 62 F5
Travemünde [D] 18 H3
Travers [CH] 58 C6
Travnik [BIH] 142 C4
Travo [F] 114 B5
Travo [I] 110 C2
Trazo [E] 78 C2
Trbovlje [SLO] 74 C5
Tréban [F] 56 D5
Trebatsch [D] 34 F3
Trebbin [D] 34 E3
Třebechovice pod Orebem [CZ] 50 B3
Třebenice [CZ] 48 F2
Trébeurden [F] 40 D1
Třebíč [CZ] 50 A6
Trebija [SLO] 74 B5
Trebinje [BIH] 144 D3
Trebisacce [I] 122 D6
Trebišov [SK] 64 G3
Trebnje [SLO] 74 C5
Třeboň [CZ] 62 C2
Tréboul [F] 40 B3
Třebovice [CZ] 50 B4
Trebujena [E] 100 F3
Trecastagni [I] 126 G3
Trecate [I] 70 F5
Trecenta [I] 110 F2
Trecesson, Château de- [F] 26 B6
Treffurt [D] 32 G5
Tregaron [GB] 10 B6
Trégastel [F] 40 D1
Tregnago [I] 72 C6
Tréguier [F] 26 A3
Trehörna [S] 162 E1
Treia [D] 18 E1
Treibach [A] 74 B3
Treignac [F] 66 H2
Treillieres [F] 40 F6

Treis [D] 44 H1
Trekanten [S] 162 F5
Trelde [DK] 156 C2
Trelleborg [S] 158 C3
Tremês [P] 86 C4
Tremestieri [I] 124 B7
Tremezzo [I] 70 G3
Tremisht [AL] 128 C6
Třemošná [CZ] 48 E4
Tremp [E] 92 C2
Trenčianska Turná [SK] 64 A2
Trenčianske Bohuslavice [SK] 64 A3
Trenčianske Teplice [SK] 64 B2
Trenčín [SK] 64 A2
Trend [DK] 160 C4
Trendelburg [D] 32 F4
Trengereid [N] 170 B4
Trent [CH] 70 C3
Trenta [SLO] 72 H4
Trento [I] 72 C4
Treppeln [D] 34 G3
Trept [F] 68 G3
Tres Cantos [E] 88 F5
Trescore Balneario [I] 70 H4
Tresenda [I] 72 B4
Tresfjord [N] 180 E3
Tresigallo [I] 110 G2
Treski [EST] 198 G3
Treskog [S] 166 D1
Treskovec, Manastir- [MK] 128 E2
Tresnuràghes [I] 118 B4
Trespaderne [E] 82 F5
Třešť [CZ] 48 H6
Tresta [GB] 6 H3
Tresta Rzadowa [PL] 36 H5
Trets [F] 108 B5
Tretten [N] 170 H2
Treuchtlingen [D] 60 D2
Treuenbrietzen [D] 34 D3
Treungen [N] 164 E3
Trevélez [E] 102 E4
Tréveray [F] 44 D5
Trevi [I] 116 B3
Treviglio [I] 70 H5
Trevignano Romano [I] 114 H4
Treviño [E] 82 G5
Treviso [I] 72 E6
Trévoux [F] 68 F2
Trezelles [F] 56 D6
Trezzano sul Naviglio [I] 70 G5
Trezzo sull'Adda [I] 70 G4
Trgovište [SRB] 146 E5
Trhomné [CZ] 48 D4
Trhová Kamenice [CZ] 50 A4
Trhové Sviny [CZ] 62 C2
Trhovište [SK] 64 H3
Triacastela [E] 78 E4
Triaize [F] 54 C4
Triánta [GR] 154 D3
Triaucourt-en-Argonne [F] 44 D4
Tribanj Kruščica [HR] 112 G4
Triberg [D] 58 F3
Tribsees [D] 20 C3
Tricárico [I] 120 H4
Tricase [I] 122 G6
Tricesimo [I] 72 G4
Trichiana [I] 72 E4
Trie [F] 84 F3
Trieben [A] 62 C6
Trier [D] 44 F2
Trieste [I] 72 H6
Trifels [D] 46 B5
Trignac [F] 40 E6
Trígono [GR] 128 E4
Trigueros [E] 94 F5
Tríkala [GR] 128 G4
Tríkala [GR] 132 F2
Tríkala [GR] 136 E1
Trikéri [GR] 134 A3
Trikomon (Iskele) [CY] 154 G5
Trilj [HR] 144 A1
Trillevallen [S] 182 F2
Trillo [E] 90 A5
Trílofo [GR] 132 G3
Trim [IRL] 2 F5
Trimburg [D] 46 E3
Trindade [P] 80 E4
Trindade [P] 94 D3
Třinec [CZ] 50 F5
Trinidad [E] 84 A4
Trinità d'Agultu e Vignola [I] 118 D2
Trinitápoli [I] 120 H2
Trinité, Ermitage de la- [F] 114 B6
Trino [I] 70 E5
Triollo [E] 82 D4
Triora [I] 108 F4
Trípoli [GR] 136 E2
Triponzo [I] 116 B3
Tripótama [GR] 136 D1
Triptis [D] 48 B1
Trisanna-Brücke [A] 72 B1
Trisulti, Abbazia di- [I] 116 C6
Trittau [D] 18 G4
Trittenheim [D] 44 G2
Trivento [I] 116 E6
Trnava [CZ] 50 B6
Trnava [SK] 62 H4
Trnovec nad Váhom [SK] 64 A4
Trnovo [BIH] 144 D1
Trnovo ob Soci [SLO] 72 H4
Troarn [F] 26 F3
Trocnov [CZ] 62 C2
Trödje [S] 174 E3
Troense [DK] 156 E4
Trofa [P] 80 B5
Trofaiach [A] 74 C1
Trofimovo [RUS] 198 H4
Trofors [N] 190 D3
Trogir [HR] 116 H1
Troia [I] 120 G2
Tróia [P] 86 B6
Troina [I] 126 F3
Troisdorf [D] 30 H5
Trois Fontaines, Abbaye des- [F] 44 C5
Trois-Ponts [B] 30 E5
Troïts'ke [UA] 204 F3
Troizína [GR] 136 G2
Trojane [SLO] 74 C4
Trøjborg [DK] 156 B4
Trolla [N] 182 B1
Trollböle [FIN] 176 F6
Trolleholm [S] 158 C2
Trolle Ljungby [S] 158 D2
Trollenäs [S] 158 C2
Trollhättan [S] 166 D6
Trollkyrkja [N] 180 E2
Trollvik [N] 192 G2
Tromello [I] 70 F5
Tromøy [N] 164 F5
Tromsø [N] 192 F2
Tromvik [N] 192 F2
Tronco [P] 80 E3
Trondheim [N] 182 B1
Trones [N] 190 E1
Trönninge [S] 162 A4
Trönninge [S] 162 B5
Tronvik [N] 190 B6
Trôo [F] 42 C6
Troódos [CY] 154 F6
Troon [GB] 8 C3
Tropea [I] 124 C6
Tropfstein-Höhle [A] 74 C3
Tropojë [AL] 146 B5
Trosa [S] 168 D4
Troškūnai [LT] 200 G4
Trosky [CZ] 48 H2
Trössing [A] 74 E3
Trossingen [D] 58 G3
Tröstau [D] 48 B3
Trostberg [D] 60 F4
Trosterud [N] 166 C2
Trostianets' [UA] 202 F7
Trostianets' [UA] 204 E2
Trouville [F] 26 G3
Trowbridge [GB] 12 G3
Troyan [BG] 148 B4
Troyanovo [BG] 148 E4
Troyanski Manastir [BG] 148 B4
Troyanska Pateka [BG] 148 B4
Trøyen [N] 182 B2
Troyes [F] 44 B6
Troyon [F] 44 D4
Trpanj [HR] 144 B3
Trpinja [HR] 142 E1
Tršić [SRB] 142 F3
Trstená [SK] 50 H6
Trstena [SRB] 146 D5
Trstenik [SRB] 146 C3
Trsteno [HR] 144 C3
Trstín [SK] 62 H3
Trubchevsk [RUS] 202 E5
Trubia [E] 78 H3
Truchas [E] 78 F6
Truchtersheim [F] 44 H5
Trud [BG] 148 B5
Trujillo [E] 96 B1
Trulben [D] 44 H4
Trün [BG] 146 E4
Trun [CH] 70 G1
Trun [F] 26 F4
Truro [GB] 12 C5
Truskavets' [UA] 52 G5
Trustrup [DK] 160 E6
Trutnov [CZ] 50 B2
Trutnowy [PL] 22 E3
Truva [TR] 130 H5
Tryavna [BG] 148 C4
Trydal [N] 164 D2
Tryde [S] 158 D3
Tryggelev [DK] 156 E5
Tryggestad [N] 180 D4
Tryńcza [PL] 52 E3
Trýpi [GR] 136 E4
Trypití [GR] 130 C5
Trysa [TR] 154 H3
Tryserum [S] 162 G1
Tryšiai [LT] 200 E3
Trysil Innbygda [N] 172 D2
Tryszczyn [PL] 22 D5
Trzcianka [PL] 22 A6
Trzciel [PL] 36 B3
Trzcinna [PL] 34 H1
Trzcińsko Zdrój [PL] 20 F6
Trzebiatów [PL] 20 G3
Trzebiel [PL] 34 G5
Trzebież [PL] 20 F4
Trzebina [PL] 50 D3
Trzebinia [PL] 50 G3
Trzebnica [PL] 36 C6
Trzebów [PL] 34 H2
Trzemeszno [PL] 36 E2
Trzepnica [PL] 36 H6
Trzepowo [PL] 22 D3
Trzešcianka [PL] 24 F6
Tržič [SLO] 74 B4
Trzin [SLO] 74 C5
Tržišče [SLO] 74 D5
Tsagkaráda [GR] 134 A2
Tsamandás [GR] 132 C1
Tsampíka, Moní- [GR] 154 D4
Tsangário [GR] 132 C3
Tsapel'ka [RUS] 198 H3
Tsarevets [BG] 148 C2
Tsarevo [BG] 148 G5
Tsarítsani [GR] 132 G1
Tschernitz [D] 34 G5
Tschierv [CH] 72 B3
Tsenovo [BG] 148 C2
Tsiurupyns'k [UA] 204 G3
Tsotíli [GR] 128 E6
Tsoútsouros [GR] 140 F5
Tsvelodubovo [RUS] 178 G3
Tua [N] 190 C5
Tua [P] 80 E4
Tuaim / Tuam [IRL] 2 C4
Tuam / Tuaim [IRL] 2 C4
Tuar Mhic Éadaigh / Toourmakeady [IRL] 2 C4
Tubilla del Agua [E] 82 E5
Tübingen [D] 58 G2
Tubre / Taufers [I] 72 B3
Tučepi [HR] 144 B2
Tuchan [F] 106 C5
Tüchen [D] 20 B6
Tuchola [PL] 22 D4
Tuchomie [PL] 22 C3
Tuchów [PL] 52 C4
Tuckur [FIN] 186 B2
Tuczno [PL] 20 H6
Tuddal [N] 164 F1
Tudela [E] 84 B6
Tudela de Duero [E] 88 E2
Tudu [EST] 198 F1
Tudulinna [EST] 198 F2
Tuffé [F] 42 C5
Tufjord [N] 194 B1
Tuhkakylä [FIN] 196 F5
Tuhkala [RUS] 196 G2
Tui [E] 78 B5
Tuin [MK] 128 D2
Tuineje [E] 100 E6
Tuiskula [FIN] 186 C3
Tuixén [E] 92 D2
Tūja [LV] 198 D4
Tukums [LV] 198 D5
Tulare [SRB] 146 D5
Tuławki [PL] 22 H3
Tulca [RO] 76 H3
Tulcea [RO] 204 F5
Tul'chyn [UA] 204 E2
Tulešice [CZ] 62 F2
Tuliszków [PL] 36 E3
Tulla [IRL] 2 C6
Tullamore [IRL] 2 E6
Tulle [F] 66 H3
Tullebolle [DK] 156 E4
Tulleråsen [S] 182 G1
Tullgarn [S] 168 D4
Tullinge [S] 168 D3
Tullins [F] 68 G4
Tulln [A] 62 E4
Tullow [IRL] 4 F4
Tułowice [PL] 50 D2
Tulppio [FIN] 194 F6
Tulsk [IRL] 2 D4
Tum [PL] 36 G3
Tumba [S] 168 D3
Tummsjøen [N] 190 D4
Tumulus de Gavrinis [F] 40 D5
Tun [S] 166 D5
Tuna [S] 162 F3
Tunaberg [S] 168 C5
Tuna Hästberg [S] 172 H5
Tunbridge Wells [GB] 14 E5
Tunbyn [S] 184 E5
Tunçbilek [TR] 150 G6
Tune [DK] 156 G3
Tunge [S] 160 H1
Tungelsta [S] 168 E4
Tungozero [RUS] 196 G2
Tunhovd [N] 170 F4
Tunnerstad [S] 162 D1
Tunnsjørørvika [N] 190 D4
Tunø By [DK] 156 D1
Tuntsa [FIN] 194 F6
Tunvågen [S] 182 G3
Tuohikotti [FIN] 178 C2
Tuohittu [FIN] 176 F5
Tuomioja [FIN] 196 D4
Tuonj [HR] 112 G2
Tuorila [FIN] 186 B6
Tuornoel, Château de- [F] 68 C2
Tupadły [PL] 36 E2
Tupitsyno [RUS] 198 G2
Tuplice [PL] 34 G4
Tuppurinmäki [FIN] 188 D3
Tura [H] 64 D6
Turaj [AL] 128 C1
Turalići [BIH] 142 E4
Turan [TR] 150 F4
Turanlı [TR] 152 C2
Turany [SK] 50 G6
Tūras [TR] 150 G2
Turawa [PL] 50 E2
Turba [EST] 198 D2
Turbe [BIH] 142 C4
Turčianske Teplice [SK] 64 C2
Turckheim [F] 58 D3
Turda [RO] 204 C4
Turégano [E] 88 F3
Turek [PL] 36 F4
Turenki [FIN] 176 G3
Turenne [F] 66 G3
Turgeliai [LT] 200 G6
Türgovishte [BG] 148 D3
Turgut [TR] 152 E6
Turgutbey [TR] 150 C2
Turgutlu [TR] 152 D4
Turgutreis [TR] 154 B2
Turhala [FIN] 196 E6
Türi [EST] 198 E2
Turi [I] 122 E3
Turiis'k [UA] 38 H5
Turís / Torís [E] 98 E5
Turjaci [HR] 144 A1
Turjak [SLO] 74 C5
Turka [PL] 38 G5
Turka [UA] 52 F6
Türkeli [TR] 150 C4
Túrkeve [H] 76 F2
Türkheim [D] 60 C4
Türkmen [TR] 152 C3
Turkovići [BIH] 144 D1
Turku / Åbo [FIN] 176 D4
Turleque [E] 96 F2
Turlough [IRL] 2 C4
Turmantas [LT] 200 H4
Turňa nad Bodvou [SK] 64 F3
Turnberry [GB] 8 C4
Turnhout [B] 30 D3
Türnitz [A] 62 D5
Turnov [CZ] 48 H2
Turnu Măgurele [RO] 148 B2
Turo [FIN] 194 D4
Turobin [PL] 52 F1
Túrony [H] 76 B5
Turośl [PL] 24 C5
Turów [PL] 38 E4
Turrach [A] 74 A2
Turre [E] 102 H5
Turriff [GB] 6 F5
Turtagrø [N] 170 E1
Turtel [MK] 128 G1
Turunç [TR] 154 D2
Turunçova [TR] 154 H3
Turzovka [SK] 50 F5
Tusa [I] 126 E2
Tusby / Tuusula [FIN] 176 H4
Tuscánia [I] 114 G4
Tušilovic [HR] 112 G1
Tuskö [S] 174 G5
Tustervatnet [N] 190 D3
Tuszów Narodowy [PL] 52 D2
Tuszyn [PL] 36 G5
Tuszyny [PL] 22 D5
Tutajev [RUS] 202 F1
Tutayev [RUS] 202 F1
Tutin [SRB] 146 B4
Tutjunniemi [FIN] 188 F3
Tutrakan [BG] 148 D1
Tutting [D] 60 H4
Tuttlingen [D] 58 G3
Tútugi [E] 102 G3
Tutzing [D] 60 D5
Tützpatz [D] 20 D4
Tuukkala [FIN] 186 H6
Tuukkala [FIN] 188 C6
Tuulos [FIN] 176 G2
Tuupovaara [FIN] 188 G3
Tuuruniemi [FIN] 194 D4
Tuusjärvi [FIN] 188 D2
Tuuski [FIN] 178 C4
Tuusniemi [FIN] 188 E2
Tuusula / Tusby [FIN] 176 H4
Tuv [N] 170 F3
Tuvas [FIN] 186 B4
Tuzi [MNE] 144 E4
Tuzla [BIH] 142 E3
Tuzla [TR] 134 G1
Tuzla [TR] 150 F3
Tuzlata [BG] 148 G2
Tuzsér [H] 64 H4
Tvååker [S] 160 H4
Tväråbäck [S] 190 H5
Tvärålund [S] 190 H5
Tvärminne [FIN] 176 F6
Tvärskog [S] 162 F5
Tvärud [S] 166 D1
Tvede [DK] 160 E5
Tvedestrand [N] 164 F4
Tveit [N] 164 B2
Tveita [N] 170 B4
Tveitsund [N] 164 E3
Tver' [RUS] 202 E2
Tverai [LT] 200 D4
Tverrå [N] 164 C3
Tverrå [N] 190 E2
Tverrelvmo [N] 192 G3
Tversted [DK] 160 E2
Tvinde [N] 170 C3
Tvindehaugen [N] 170 F1
Tving [S] 158 F1
Tvis [DK] 160 C5
Tvøroyri [FR] 160 A3
Tvrdošovce [SK] 64 A5
Tv-Torony [H] 74 G3
Tvŭrditsa [BG] 148 D4
Twann-Schlucht [CH] 58 D5
Twardogóra [PL] 36 D5
Tweng [A] 72 H1
Twimberg [A] 74 C2
Twist [D] 16 H4
Twistringen [D] 18 D6
Tworków [PL] 50 E4
Tworóg [PL] 50 F2
Tyamsha [RUS] 198 G3
Tychowo [PL] 22 A4
Tychy [PL] 50 G3
Tyczyn [PL] 52 E4
Tyfjord [N] 194 D1
Tyfors [S] 172 G5
Tyholland [NIR] 2 F4
Tyin [N] 170 F2
Tyinosen [N] 170 E2
Tykocin [PL] 24 E5
Tylawa [PL] 52 D5
Tylisos [GR] 140 E4
Tylldal [N] 182 B5
Tylösand [S] 162 B5
Tylstrup [DK] 160 E3
Tymbark [PL] 52 B4
Tymfristós [GR] 132 F4
Tympáki [GR] 140 D5
Tyndaris [I] 124 A7
Tynderö [S] 184 F4
Tyndrum [GB] 8 D2
Týnec nad Labem [CZ] 48 H4
Tynemouth [GB] 8 G6
Tyngsjö [S] 172 F5
Tyniec [PL] 50 H4
Týniště nad Orlicí [CZ] 50 B3
Tynkä [FIN] 196 C5
Týn nad Vltavou [CZ] 48 F6
Tynnelsö [S] 168 C3
Tynset [N] 182 B4
Tyresö [S] 168 E3
Tyringe [S] 158 C1
Tyrislöt [S] 168 C6
Tyristrand [N] 170 H5
Tyrjänsaari [FIN] 188 G1
Tyrnävä [FIN] 196 D4
Týrnavos [GR] 132 G1
Tyrós [GR] 136 F3
Týřov [CZ] 48 E4
Tyrrellspass [IRL] 2 E5
Tyry [FIN] 186 F6
Tysdal [N] 164 B2
Tysken [N] 172 D4
Tysse [N] 170 B1
Tysse [N] 170 B4
Tyssebotn [N] 170 B3
Tyssedal [N] 170 C5
Tystberga [S] 168 C4
Tyszki-Nadbory [PL] 24 D6
Tytuvėnai [LT] 200 E4
Tyulenovo [BG] 148 G2
Tyvsen [DK] 156 B4
Tywyn [GB] 10 B5
Tzermiádo [GR] 140 F5
Tzummarum [NL] 16 F2

U

Ub [SRB] 146 A1
Úbeda [E] 102 F2
Ubergsmoen [N] 164 F4
Überhamn [D] 18 E5
Überlingen [D] 58 G4
Ubli [HR] 144 A3
Ubrique [E] 100 H4
Uçarı [TR] 154 F4
Uccellina, Torre dell-' [I] 114 F3
Ucero [E] 90 A2
Uchanie [PL] 38 G6
Uchorowo [PL] 36 C2
Uchte [D] 32 E1
Uckange [F] 44 E3
Uckfield [GB] 14 E5
Uclés [E] 96 H2
Uçmakdere [TR] 150 C3
Üçpınar [TR] 152 D3
Ucria [I] 124 A7
Udavské [SK] 64 H2
Udbina [HR] 112 H4
Udbyhøj [DK] 160 E5
Udbyhøj Vasehuse [DK] 160 E5
Uddeholm [S] 166 F1
Uddel [NL] 16 F4
Uddel [NL] 16 F4
Udden [S] 166 D5
Uddevalla [S] 166 C5
Uddheden [S] 166 E1
Uden [NL] 16 E6
Udine [I] 72 G5
Údlice [CZ] 48 E2
Udorpie [PL] 22 C3
Udovo [MK] 128 G2
Ūdrupij [LV] 198 F4
Udvar [H] 76 B5
Ueckermünde [D] 20 E4
Ueffeln [D] 32 C1
Uelsen [D] 16 G4
Uelzen [D] 18 G6
Uetersen [D] 18 F4
Uetze [D] 32 G2
Uffenheim [D] 46 F5
Uga [E] 100 E6
Ugāle [LV] 198 C5
Ugao [SRB] 146 A4
Ugao-Miraballes [E] 82 G4
Ugento [I] 122 G6
Ugerløse [DK] 156 F3
Uggdal [N] 170 B5
Uggerby [DK] 160 E2
Uggersjev [DK] 156 D3
Ugglarps havsbad [S] 160 H4
Ugíjar [E] 102 F5
Ugine [F] 70 B3
Uglich [RUS] 202 F1
Ugljan [HR] 112 F5
Ugljane [HR] 144 A2
Ugny-sur-Meuse [F] 44 D5
Ugrinovci [SRB] 146 B2
Ugŭrchin [BG] 148 A4
Uğurluca [TR] 152 G2
Uğurlutepe [TR] 130 G5
Uherčice [CZ] 62 E2
Uherse Mineralne [PL] 52 E5
Uherské Hradiště [CZ] 62 H2
Uherský Brod [CZ] 62 H2
Uherský Ostroh [CZ] 62 H2
Uhlířské Janovice [CZ] 48 G4
Uhniv [UA] 52 G2
Uhříněves [CZ] 48 G4
Uhrovec [SK] 64 B3
Uhrovský Hrad [SK] 64 B3
Uhrsleben [D] 34 B3
Uhyst [D] 34 G5
Uig [GB] 6 B4
Úihartyán [H] 76 D2
Uimaharju [FIN] 188 G1
Uimila [FIN] 178 B2
Úitelep [H] 76 B3
Uithoorn [NL] 16 D4
Uithuizen [NL] 16 G1
Ujazd [PL] 36 H5
Ujazd [PL] 50 E3
Ujazd [PL] 52 C2
Újfehértó [H] 64 H5
Újiráz [H] 76 G2
Újkígyós [H] 76 G3
Újléta [H] 64 H6
Ujma Duża [PL] 36 F2
Újmajor [H] 74 H1
Újpetre [H] 76 B5
Ujście [PL] 22 B6
Újszász [H] 76 E1
Ujué [E] 84 B5
Ukk [H] 74 G2
Ukkola [FIN] 188 F1
Ukmergė [LT] 200 G5
Ükmez [TR] 152 C5
Ukonvaara [FIN] 188 E1
Ukri [LV] 198 D6
Ukta [PL] 24 C4
Ula [BY] 202 C4
Ula [TR] 154 D1
Ul'anka [SK] 64 C3
Ulan Majorat [PL] 38 E4
Ulanów [PL] 52 E2
Ulaş [TR] 150 C2
Ulbjerg [DK] 160 D5
Ulcinj [MNE] 144 E5
Uldum [DK] 156 C2
Uleåborg / Oulu [FIN] 196 D4
Ulefoss [N] 164 F2
Uleila del Campo [E] 102 H4
Ulëzë [AL] 128 B2
Ulfborg [DK] 160 B5
Ulgardereköyü [TR] 150 B5
Ulhówek [PL] 52 G2
Úlibice [CZ] 48 H3
Ulinia [PL] 22 C1
Ulivar [RO] 76 F6
Uljanik [HR] 142 B1
Uljma [SRB] 142 H2
Ullånger [S] 184 F3
Ullapool [GB] 6 D3
Ullared [S] 162 B4
Ullatti [S] 192 H6
Ullava [FIN] 196 C6
Ulldecona [E] 92 A6
Ulldemolins [E] 90 H5
Ullene [S] 166 E6
Ullerslev [DK] 156 E3
Ullervad [S] 166 F5
Üllés [H] 76 E4
Ullisjaur [S] 190 F4
Üllő [H] 76 D1
Ulm [D] 60 B3
Ulme [P] 86 D4
Ulmen [D] 44 G1
Ulmeni [RO] 148 D1
Ulnes [N] 170 G2
Ulog [BIH] 144 D2
Ulpiana [SRB] 146 C5
Ulpia Traiana [RO] 204 C5
Ulricehamn [S] 162 C2
Ulrika [S] 162 E1
Ulriksfors [S] 190 E6
Ulsberg [N] 180 H3
Ulsrud [N] 166 C1
Ulsted [DK] 160 E4
Ulsteinvik [N] 180 C4
Ulstrup [DK] 156 E2
Ulstrup [DK] 160 D5
Uluabat [TR] 150 E5
Ulubey [TR] 152 G3
Ulüçayır [TR] 150 H5
Uludağ [TR] 150 F5
Ulukışla (Marathóvounos) [CY] 154 G5
Uluköy [TR] 150 H6
Ulvåila [N] 172 D3
Ulvåsa [S] 166 H5
Ulverston [GB] 10 D2
Ulvesbüll [D] 18 E1
Ulvestad [N] 170 D1
Ulvik [N] 170 D3
Ulvika [N] 192 E4
Ulvila / Ulvsby [FIN] 176 D2
Ulvsby / Ulvila [FIN] 176 D2
Ulvsjön [S] 172 G1
Ulvsvåg [N] 192 E4
Umag [HR] 112 D1
Uman' [UA] 202 D8
Umasjö [S] 190 E2
Umbertide [I] 116 A1
Umbukta [N] 190 E2
Umčari [SRB] 142 H3
Umeå [S] 196 A6
Umfors [S] 190 E2
Umgransele [S] 190 G4
Umhausen [A] 72 C1
Umka [SRB] 142 G3
Umkirch [D] 58 E3
Umurbey [TR] 150 B5
Umurbey [TR] 150 F4
Umurlu [TR] 152 E5
Uña [E] 98 C2
Unaja [FIN] 176 C3
Unari [FIN] 194 D7
Unbyn [S] 196 B3
Uncastillo [E] 84 C5
Undenäs [S] 166 G5
Undersåker [S] 182 F2
Undva [EST] 198 C3
Uněšov [CZ] 48 D4
Ungheni [MD] 204 E3
Unhošť [CZ] 48 F3
Unichowo [PL] 22 C3
Uničov [CZ] 50 C4
Uniejów [PL] 36 F4
Unirea [RO] 146 F1
Unisław [PL] 22 D6
Unna [D] 32 C4
Unnaryd [S] 162 C4
Unserfrau / Madonna di Senales [I] 72 C2
Unset [N] 182 C5
Unsholtet [N] 182 C3
Untamala [FIN] 186 C2
Unterach [A] 60 H5
Unterbergen [A] 74 E1
Unterlüss [D] 18 G6
Unterradlberg [A] 62 E4
Unterschächen [CH] 70 G1
Unter-Schleissheim [D] 60 E4
Unteruhldingen [D] 58 H4
Unterwasser [CH] 58 H5
Unterweissenbach [A] 62 C4
Unterwössen [D] 60 F5
Untorp [S] 172 G2
Uors [CH] 70 G1
Úpice [CZ] 50 B2
Upiłka [PL] 22 C4
Upper Largo [GB] 8 F3
Upphärad [S] 166 D6
Upplands Väsby [S] 168 D2
Uppsala [S] 168 D1
Uppsete [N] 170 D3
Upyna [LT] 200 E4
Urachi, Nuraghe s'- [I] 118 C5
Uraiújfalu [H] 74 G1
Úras [I] 118 C6
Ura Vajgurore [AL] 128 B4
Urbánia [I] 110 H6
Urbeis [F] 58 D2
Úrbel del Castillo [E] 82 E5
Urbino [I] 112 B6
Urbise [F] 56 E6
Urbø [S] 164 E1
Urçay [F] 56 C5
Urda [E] 96 F3
Urdaibai [E] 82 H3
Urdos [F] 84 D4
Uriage-les-Bains [F] 68 H5
Uriz / Arze-Arce [E] 84 C4
Urjala [FIN] 176 F2
Urjalankylä [FIN] 176 F2
Urk [NL] 16 E3
Úrkút [H] 74 H2
Urla [TR] 152 C4
Urlingford [IRL] 4 E3
Urnäsch [CH] 58 H5
Urnes [N] 170 D1
Uroševac [SRB] 146 C6
Urpila [FIN] 186 F1
Urroz [E] 84 B4
Urshult [S] 162 E5
Ursus [PL] 38 B3
Urtimjaur [S] 196 A1
Ürünlü [TR] 150 B2
Ururi [I] 116 F6
Ury [F] 42 F5
Urzędów [PL] 38 D6
Urzelina [P] 100 C3
Urziceni [RO] 204 E5
Urzicuța [RO] 146 F2
Urzulei [I] 118 E5
Usagre [E] 94 H3
Uşak [TR] 152 G3
Ušće [SRB] 146 B3
Uście Gorlickie [PL] 52 C5
Usedom [D] 20 E4
Usellus [I] 118 C5
Useras / les Useres [E] 98 F3
Ushakovo [RUS] 22 G2
Uši [MK] 128 F2
Ušinci [BG] 148 D2
Usingen [D] 46 C2
Uskali [FIN] 188 G3
Uskedal [N] 170 B5
Uski [FIN] 178 D3
Uskopolie [BIH] 144 B1
Usküdar [TR] 150 E3
Usküp [TR] 150 C1
Uskūpdere [TR] 150 C1
Uslar [D] 32 F4
Usma [LV] 198 C5
Usmate Velate [I] 70 G4
Úsov [CZ] 50 C4
Uspen'ye [RUS] 202 B3
Ussé [F] 54 F2
Usseglio [I] 70 C5
Ussel [F] 68 B2
Ussel [I] 70 D4
Usseln [D] 32 D5
Usson-du-Poitou [F] 54 F5
Usson-en-Forez [F] 68 E3
Usson-les-Bains [F] 106 B6
Ustaoset [N] 170 E4
Ustaritz [F] 84 C2
Úštěk [CZ] 48 F2
Uster [CH] 58 G5
Ústí [CZ] 50 E6
Ustibar [BIH] 144 E2
Ústí nad Labem [CZ] 48 F2
Ústí nad Orlicí [CZ] 50 B4
Ustiprača [BIH] 144 E1
Ustje [RUS] 198 H1
Ustjuzhna [RUS] 202 E1
Ustka [PL] 22 B2
Ust'-Luga [RUS] 178 E6
Ustrem [BG] 150 A1
Ustroń [PL] 50 F5
Ustronie Morskie [PL] 20 H3
Ustrzyki Dolne [PL] 52 F5
Ustrzyki Górne [PL] 52 F6
Ustyluh [UA] 38 G6
Ustyuzhna [RUS] 202 E1
Ususău [RO] 76 H5
Usvaty [RUS] 202 C4
Usvyaty [RUS] 202 C4
Utajärvi [FIN] 196 E4
Utåker [N] 170 B5
Utansjö [S] 184 F3
Utbjoa [N] 164 B1
Utebo [E] 90 E3
Utena [LT] 200 G4
Utersum [D] 156 A5
Uthlede [D] 18 D4
Utiel [E] 98 D4
Utne [N] 170 C4
Utrecht [NL] 16 D5
Utrera [E] 100 G2
Utrillas [E] 90 E6
Utrine [SRB] 76 E5
Utsjö [S] 172 F4
Utsjoki [FIN] 194 D3
Utstein [N] 164 A2
Uttendorf [A] 60 G4
Uttendorf [A] 72 F1
Uttermossa [FIN] 186 B5
Uttersberg [S] 168 A2
Utti [FIN] 178 C3
Utting [D] 60 D4
Uttoxeter [GB] 10 E5
Utula [FIN] 178 E1
Utvalnäs [S] 174 E4
Utvängstorp [S] 162 C1
Utvik [N] 180 D5
Utvorda [N] 190 C4
Uukuniemen Kk. [FIN] 188 G5
Uukuniemi [FIN] 188 G5
Uurainen [FIN] 186 F4
Uuro [FIN] 186 B5
Uuro [FIN] 188 F2
Uusijoki [FIN] 194 E5

Uusikaarlepyy / Nykarleby [FIN] 186 C1
Uusikartano [FIN] 176 D3
Uusikaupunki / Nystad [FIN] 176 C3
Uusikylä [FIN] 178 B3
Uusi-Värtsilä [FIN] 188 G3
Uutela [FIN] 194 D6
Uva [FIN] 196 F4
Uvac [BIH] 144 E1
Úvaly [CZ] 48 G4
Uvanå [S] 172 F5
Uvarovka [RUS] 202 E3
Uvdal [N] 170 F4
Uvernet-Fours [F] 108 D2
Uyeasound [GB] 6 H3
Uzdowo [PL] 22 G5
Uzel [F] 26 A5
Uzerche [F] 66 G2
Uzès [F] 106 G3
Uzeste [F] 66 D4
Uzhorod [UA] 204 B3
Užice [SRB] 146 A2
Uzlovoye [RUS] 200 E5
Uzhots'kyi, Pereval- [UA] 52 F6
Užpaliai [LT] 200 G4
Üzümlü [TR] 154 F2
Uzunköprü [TR] 150 B3
Uzunkuyu [TR] 152 B4
Uzunpinar [TR] 152 G4
Uzuntarla [TR] 150 G3
Užventis [LT] 200 E4

V

Vä [N] 164 E1
Vä [S] 158 D2
Vaajakoski [FIN] 186 G4
Vaajasalmi [FIN] 186 H3
Vääkiö [FIN] 196 F3
Vääksy [FIN] 178 A2
Vaala [FIN] 196 E4
Vaalajärvi [FIN] 194 D6
Vaalimaa [FIN] 178 D3
Vaaljoki [FIN] 176 D3
Vaarakylä [FIN] 196 F5
Vaaraniva [FIN] 196 F3
Väärinmaja [FIN] 186 E5
Vaas [F] 42 B6
Vaasa / Vasa [FIN] 186 B2
Vaassen [NL] 16 F4
Väätäiskylä [FIN] 186 E3
Vabalninkas [LT] 200 F3
Vabres-l'Abbayeo [F] 106 D3
Vác [H] 64 C5
Vacha [D] 46 F1
Váchartyán [H] 64 C6
Väckelsång [S] 162 E5
Vad [S] 168 A1
Vădastra [RO] 148 A2
Vadépuszta [H] 76 A3
Väderstad [S] 166 G6
Vadheim [N] 170 C1
Vadili (Vatili) [CY] 154 G5
Vadna [H] 64 F4
Vado Ligure [I] 108 H3
Vadsø [N] 194 E2
Vadstena [S] 166 G5
Vaduz [FL] 58 H6
Væggerløse [DK] 20 B1
Vafaíka [GR] 130 E3
Vafiochóri [GR] 128 G3
Vág [H] 74 G1
Våga [N] 164 A2
Vågåmo [N] 180 G5
Vagan [BIH] 142 B4
Våge [N] 164 A1
Våge [N] 164 C6
Våge [N] 170 B5
Vage [N] 180 E3
Vågen [N] 190 A6
Vägeva [EST] 198 F2
Vaggeryd [S] 162 D3
Vaggsvik [N] 192 F3
Vágia [GR] 134 B5
Vagiónia [GR] 140 E5
Vaglio Basilicata [I] 120 H4
Vagnhärad [S] 168 D4
Vagos [P] 80 B5
Vågsbygd [N] 164 D6
Vågsele [S] 190 G5
Vågsjöfors [S] 172 E5
Vågslid [N] 164 D1
Vágur [FR] 160 A3
Vähäkyro / Lillkyro [FIN] 186 B2
Vahanka [FIN] 186 E3
Vahastu [EST] 198 E2
Vaheri [FIN] 186 G5
Vaï [GR] 140 H4
Vaiano [I] 110 F5
Vaiges [F] 40 H5
Vaiguva [LT] 200 E4
Vaihingen [D] 46 C6
Väike-Maarja [EST] 198 F1
Väike Rakke [EST] 198 F3
Vailly [F] 56 C2
Vainikkala [FIN] 178 E2
Vainupea [EST] 198 E1
Vainutas [LT] 200 D5
Vaison-la-Romaine [F] 106 H3
Vaite [F] 58 A3
Vajmat [S] 190 H2
Vajnede [LV] 198 C6
Vajont [I] 72 F4
Vajszló [H] 76 A5
Vajza [AL] 128 B5
Vakarel [BG] 146 G5
Vakern [S] 172 F5
Vakiflar [TR] 150 C2
Vaksdal [N] 170 B3
Vaksevo [BG] 146 F6
Vakumonë [AL] 128 B3
Vålådalen [S] 182 E2
Valajanaapa [FIN] 196 D2
Valajaskoski [FIN] 194 D8
Valandovo [MK] 128 G2
Valanhamn [N] 192 G1
Valareña [E] 84 B6
Valaská Belá [SK] 64 B2
Valašská Polanka [CZ] 50 E6
Valašské Klobouky [CZ] 50 E6
Valašské Meziříčí [CZ] 50 E5
Valbella [CH] 70 H1
Valberg [F] 108 E3
Vålberg [S] 166 E3
Valbiska [HR] 112 E2
Valbo [S] 174 E4
Valbondione [I] 72 A4
Valbonë [AL] 146 A5
Valbonnais [F] 68 H5
Vâlcani [RO] 76 F5
Valcarlos / Luzaide [E] 84 C3
Val-Claret [F] 70 C4
Valcum [H] 74 G3
Valdagno [I] 72 D6
Valdahon [F] 58 B5
Valdaj [RUS] 202 D2
Valdalen [N] 182 D5
Valday [RUS] 202 D2
Valdeazores [E] 96 D2
Valdecaballeros [E] 96 C2
Valdecabras [E] 98 C2
Valdecarros [E] 88 C3
Valdedios [E] 82 C2
Valdeganga [E] 98 C5
Valdeinfierno [E] 96 B5
Valdelacas de Tajo [E] 96 C1
Val del Charco del Agua Amarga, Cueva de la- [E] 90 F6
Valdeltormo [E] 90 G6
Valdemadera [E] 84 A6
Valdemärpils [LV] 198 C4
Valdemarsvik [S] 168 C6
Valdemorillo [E] 88 F5
Valdemoro [E] 88 F6
Valdemoro Sierra [E] 98 C2
Valdenoceda [E] 82 F4
Valdepeñas [E] 96 F5
Valdepeñas de Jaén [E] 102 E3
Valdepolo [E] 82 C4
Valderas [E] 82 B5
Valderice [I] 126 B2
Valderoure [F] 108 D4
Valderöy [N] 180 C3
Valderrobres [E] 98 G1
Valdesalor [E] 86 H5
Val d'Esquières [F] 108 D5
Valdeverdeja [E] 96 C1
Valdieri [I] 108 F3
Val d'Isère [F] 70 C4
Val-d'Izé [F] 26 D6
Valdobbiádene [I] 72 E5
Valdoviño [E] 78 D1
Valdštejn [CZ] 48 H2
Valdunquillo [E] 82 B6
Valea lui Mihai [RO] 204 B3
Valea Rea [RO] 148 F1
Valebø [N] 164 F2
Valečov [CZ] 48 G2
Vale da Rosa [P] 94 C5
Vale de Açor [P] 94 D3
Vale de Cambra [P] 80 C5
Vale de Lobos [P] 94 C5
Vale de Santarém [P] 86 C4
Vale do Arco [P] 86 D4
Vale do Côa, Parque Arqueológico do- [P] 80 E5
Vale do Poço [P] 94 D4
Vålega [P] 80 B5
Väleggio sul Míncio [I] 110 E1
Valen [N] 170 B5
Valença do Minho [P] 78 B5
Valençay [F] 54 H3
Valence [F] 66 E6
Valence [F] 66 F6
Valence [F] 68 F5
Valence d'Albigeois [F] 106 C2
Valence-sur-Baïse [F] 66 D6
València [E] 98 E4
Valencia de Alcántara [E] 86 F5
Valencia de Don Juan [E] 82 B5
Valencia de las Torres [E] 94 H3
Valencia del Ventoso [E] 94 G3
Valencia de Mombuey [E] 94 F3
Valenciennes [F] 28 G4
Văleni [RO] 148 B1
Vălenii de Munte [RO] 204 D5
Valensole [F] 108 C4
Valentano [I] 114 G3
Valentigney [F] 58 C4
Valenza [I] 70 F6
Våler [N] 166 B2
Våler [N] 172 D4
Valeria [E] 98 B3
Vales Mortos [P] 94 E4
Valevåg [N] 170 B6
Valfábbrica [I] 116 A2
Valga [EST] 198 F4
Valgeristi [EST] 198 D2
Valgrisenche [I] 70 C4
Valguarnera Caropepe [I] 126 F3
Välijoki [FIN] 178 D2
Välijoki [FIN] 194 D8
Valimítika [GR] 132 G6
Välivaara [FIN] 196 G6
Valjevo [SRB] 146 A1
Valjevo [SRB] 204 A6
Valjimena [E] 88 C4
Valjok [N] 194 C3
Valka [LV] 198 F4
Valkeajärvi [FIN] 186 E4
Valkeakoski [FIN] 176 F2
Valkeala [FIN] 178 C2
Valkeavaara [FIN] 188 G4
Valkenburg [NL] 30 F4
Valkenswaard [NL] 30 E3
Valkiamäki [FIN] 188 E6
Valkininkai [LT] 24 H2
Valko / Valkom [FIN] 178 B4
Valkom / Valko [FIN] 178 B4
Valla [S] 182 F1
Valla [S] 184 D3
Vallada [E] 78 F4
Valladolid [E] 88 E2
Vallåkra [S] 156 H2
Vallargärdet [S] 166 F2
Vallata [I] 120 F3
Vallbona de les Monges [E] 92 C4
Valldal [N] 180 E4
Valldemossa [E] 104 E4
Valle [LV] 198 E6
Valle [N] 164 D2
Valle de Abdalajís [E] 102 B4
Valle de Cabuérniga [E] 82 E3
Valle dei Templi [I] 126 D4
Valle de la Serena [E] 96 A3
Valle de los Caidos [E] 88 F5
Valle de Matamoros [E] 94 F3
Valledoria [I] 118 C2
Vallehermoso [E] 100 B5
Vallelunga Pratameno [I] 126 D3
Vallen [S] 184 D1
Vallentuna [S] 168 E2
Valleraugue [F] 106 E2
Vallet [F] 54 C2
Valletta [M] 126 C6
Vallfogona de Ripollès [E] 92 E2
Vallheim [N] 190 D4
Vallivana [E] 98 G2
Vallo di Lucania [I] 120 F5
Valloire [F] 70 B5
Valloires, Abbaye de- [F] 28 D3
Vallombrosa [I] 110 F5
Vallon-en-Sully [F] 56 C5
Vallon-Pont-d'Arc [F] 68 E6
Vallorbe [CH] 58 B6
Vallorcine [F] 70 C3
Valløuise [F] 70 B6
Valls [E] 92 C4
Vallsbo [S] 174 D3
Vallset [N] 172 C4
Vallsta [S] 174 D1
Vallter 2000 [E] 92 E2
Vallvik [S] 174 E2
Valmadrid [E] 90 E4
Valmiera [LV] 198 E4
Valmigère [F] 106 C5
Valmojado [E] 88 E6
Valmontone [I] 116 B6
Valmorel [F] 70 B4
Val Moutier [CH] 58 D5
Valö [S] 174 F5
Valognes [F] 26 D2
Valongo [P] 80 C4
Valoria la Buena [E] 88 F1
Valøya [N] 190 C5
Valozhyn [BY] 200 H6
Valpaços [P] 80 E3
Valpelline [I] 70 D3
Valporquero de Torío [E] 78 H5
Valpovo [HR] 76 B6
Valras-Plage [F] 106 D5
Valréas [F] 106 H2
Vals [CH] 70 G2
Valsamónero [GR] 140 E5
Valsavaranche [I] 70 C4
Valsebo [S] 166 C3
Valset [N] 190 B6
Valsinni [I] 122 D5
Valsjöbyn [S] 190 E5
Valsjön [S] 184 D5
Valskog [S] 168 B3
Vals-les-Bains [F] 68 E6
Valsøybotn [N] 180 G2
Välsta [S] 184 E6
Val-Suzon [F] 56 G3
Valtesíniko [GR] 136 D2
Val Thorens [F] 70 B5
Valtiendas [E] 88 G3
Valtierra [E] 84 B5
Valtimo [FIN] 196 F5
Valtola [FIN] 178 C2
Váltos [GR] 130 H1
Valtournenche [I] 70 D3
Valvanera, Monasterio de- [E] 90 B1
Valverde [E] 100 A5
Valverde, Santuario di- [I] 118 B3
Valverde de Cervera [E] 84 A6
Valverde de Júcar [E] 98 B3
Valverde del Camino [E] 94 F5
Valverde de Leganés [E] 94 F2
Valverde del Fresno [E] 86 G3
Valzul [LT] 72 B2
Vama Veche [RO] 148 G1
Vamberk [CZ] 50 B3
Vamdrup [DK] 156 C3
Våmhus [S] 172 G3
Vamlingbo [S] 168 F6
Vammala [FIN] 176 E2
Vámos [GR] 140 C4
Vámosmikola [H] 64 C5
Vámospércs [H] 64 H6
Vámosszabadi [H] 62 H6
Vampula [FIN] 176 E3
V. Ämtervik [S] 166 E2
Vamvakoú [GR] 132 G2
Vanås [S] 158 D1
Vana-Vigala [EST] 198 D2
Vanda / Vantaa [FIN] 176 H5
Vandel [DK] 156 C2
Vandellós [E] 90 H6
Vandenesse [F] 56 E4
Vandoies / Vintl [I] 72 E2
Vändra [EST] 198 E2
Vandžegala [LT] 200 F5
Väne [LV] 198 C5
Vanebu [N] 164 G2
Vänersborg [S] 166 D5
Väne-Ryr [S] 166 D6
Vaneskoski [FIN] 186 C6
Vånga [S] 158 D1
Vangaži [LV] 198 E5
Vängel [S] 190 F6
Vangsnes [N] 170 D2
Vanha-Kihlanki [S] 194 B6
Vanhakylä [FIN] 186 B5
Vanhamäki [FIN] 188 C5
Vänjaurbäck [S] 190 G5
Vänjaurträsk [S] 190 G5
Vânju Mare [RO] 146 E1
Vankiva [S] 158 D1
Vännacka [S] 166 D2
Vännäs [S] 190 H6
Vännäsberget [S] 194 B8
Vännäsby [S] 190 H6
Vannes [F] 40 D5
Vansbro [S] 172 G4
Vanse [N] 164 C5
Vansjö [S] 168 B1
Vänsjö [S] 182 H6
Vanstad [S] 158 D3
Vantaa / Vanda [FIN] 176 H5
Vanttauskoski [FIN] 194 D8
Vanvik [N] 164 C1
Vanvikan [N] 190 B6
Vanyarc [H] 64 D5
Vaplan [S] 182 G2
Vara [S] 166 E6
Varabla [EST] 198 D3
Varades [F] 40 G6
Varages [F] 108 C4
Varaklāni [LV] 198 F5
Varaldsøy [S] 170 B5
Varallo [I] 70 E4
Varanava [BY] 200 G6
Varangerbotn [N] 194 E2
Varano de' Melegari [I] 110 D3
Varaždin [HR] 74 F4
Varaždinske Toplice [HR] 74 F4
Varazze [I] 108 H3
Varberg [S] 160 H4
Varbola [EST] 198 D2
Vărbovo [BG] 148 D6
Varbyane [BG] 148 E2
Varces [F] 68 H5
Várda [GR] 136 B1
Varde [DK] 156 B2
Vardim [BG] 148 C2
Vardiste [BIH] 144 E1
Vårdö [FIN] 176 B5
Vardø [N] 194 F2
Várdomb [H] 76 C4
Vårdsberg [S] 168 A5
Varduva [LT] 200 D3
Varekil [S] 166 C6
Varel [D] 18 C4
Varellaíoi [GR] 134 D5
Varena [LT] 24 G2
Varengeville-sur-Mer [F] 28 C4
Varenna [I] 70 G3
Varennes-en-Argonne [F] 44 D3
Varennes-sur-Allier [F] 56 D6
Vareš [BIH] 142 D4
Varese [I] 70 F4
Varese Ligure [I] 110 C3
Vårgårda [S] 162 B1
Vargön [S] 166 D5
Vargträsk [S] 190 G5
Varhaug [N] 164 A4
Vårhus [N] 182 C3
Vári [GR] 138 D2
Variaş [RO] 76 G5
Varilhes [F] 84 H5
Varín [SK] 50 F6
Våring [S] 166 F5
Váris [GR] 128 F6
Varjakka [FIN] 196 D4
Varjisträsk [S] 190 H2
Varkaus [FIN] 188 D4
Várkiza [GR] 136 H1
Varland [N] 164 F1
Värmdö [S] 168 E3
Värmlandsbro [S] 166 E3
Varmo [I] 72 G5
Värmskog [S] 166 E2
Varna [BG] 148 F3
Varna [SRB] 142 F3
Varna (Vahrn) [I] 72 D2
Värnamo [S] 162 D4
Varnany [BY] 200 H5
Varnhem [S] 166 F5
Varniai [LT] 200 E4
Varnja [EST] 198 F2
Varnsdorf [CZ] 48 G1
Varntresk [N] 190 E3
Väröbacka [S] 160 H3
Városerdö [H] 76 G3
Városföld [H] 76 D3
Varoška Rijeka [BIH] 112 H2
Városlöd [H] 74 H2
Varovnik [BG] 148 F5
Varp [S] 166 C4
Varpaisjärvi [FIN] 196 F6
Várpalota [H] 76 B2
Varpanen [FIN] 178 C1
Varparanta [FIN] 188 E4
Varparanta [FIN] 188 F2
Varpsjö [S] 190 F5
Värriö [FIN] 194 E6
Vars [F] 108 E2
Vârşand [RO] 76 G3
Varsås [S] 166 F6
Varshko [RUS] 178 G3
Varsi [I] 110 C3
Varsseveld [NL] 16 F6
Vartdal [N] 180 C4
Vartemyagi [RUS] 178 H4
Vartius [FIN] 196 G4
Vârtoapele [RO] 148 B1
Vârtopu [RO] 146 F1
Värtsilä [FIN] 188 G3
Varv [S] 166 H5
Varvara [BG] 148 A6
Varvara [BG] 148 G5
Varvára [GR] 130 C4
Varzi [I] 110 B2
Varzy [F] 56 E3
Vasa / Vaasa [FIN] 186 B2
Vasalemma [EST] 198 D1
Vasankari [FIN] 196 C5
Vasarapera [FIN] 194 F8
Vasarás [GR] 136 E3
Vasbotna [N] 190 C5
Väse [S] 166 F3
Vasiláki [GR] 136 C2
Vasilevo [BG] 148 G2
Vasil'evskoye [RUS] 198 H4
Vasiliká [GR] 130 B5
Vasiliká [GR] 134 B3
Vasiliká [GR] 134 G2
Vasilikí [GR] 132 C5
Vasilikó [GR] 134 B5
Vasilikós [GR] 136 B2
Vasilishki [BY] 24 H3
Vasilitsi [GR] 136 D5
Vasil Levski [BG] 148 D5
Vaškai [LT] 198 D6
Vaskelovo [RUS] 178 H3
Vaskio [FIN] 176 E4
Vaskivesi [FIN] 186 D5
Vasknarva [EST] 198 G2
Vaskút [H] 76 C5
Vasles [F] 54 E4
Vaslui [RO] 204 E4
Vassbø [N] 164 B4
Vassbotten [S] 166 C4
Vassenden [N] 170 G1
Vassenden [N] 180 C6
Vässes [GR] 136 D3
Vassli [N] 180 G1
Vassmolösa [S] 162 F5
Vassnäs [S] 182 E1
Vasstrand [N] 192 F2
Vassurány [H] 74 F1
Vassy [F] 26 E4
Västan [S] 184 E5
Västansfors [S] 168 A1
Västansjö [S] 184 F3
Västansjö [S] 190 E3
Västansjö [S] 190 F4
Västansjön [S] 184 E5
Västbacka [S] 172 G1
Västbacken [S] 182 F1
Västeräker [S] 168 D2
Väster-Arådalen [S] 182 F3
Västerås [S] 168 B2
Västerby [S] 168 D4
Västerfärnebo [S] 168 B1
Västergärn [S] 168 F5
Västerhaninge [S] 168 E3
Västerhus [S] 184 G2
Västermyckeläng [S] 172 F2
Västermyrriset [S] 190 G5
Västerrottna [S] 166 E1
Västersel [S] 184 G2
Västervik [S] 162 G2
Vastila [FIN] 178 C3
Västillä [FIN] 186 F6
Västland [S] 174 F5
Vasto [I] 116 E5
Västra Frölunda [S] 160 G2
Västra Yttermark [FIN] 186 A4
Västrum [S] 162 G2
Vasvár [H] 74 G2
Vasylivka [UA] 204 H2
Vasyl'kiv [UA] 202 D7
Vasyl'kivka [UA] 204 F3
Vát [H] 74 G1
Vatan [F] 54 H3
Vaterá [GR] 134 G3
Váthi [GR] 128 H3
Vathiý [GR] 134 B5
Vathý [GR] 138 H4
Vathý [GR] 152 C6
Vathýlakkos [GR] 128 F5
Vathýlakkos [GR] 130 D2
Vathýpetro [GR] 140 E5
Vatili (Vadili) [CY] 154 G5
Vatne [N] 164 B3
Vatne [N] 164 D4
Vatne [N] 180 C4
Vatne [N] 180 D3
Vatnstraum [N] 164 E5
Vatólakkos [GR] 128 E6
Vatopedíou, Moní- [GR] 130 D5
Vatoúsa [GR] 134 G2
Vatra Dornei [RO] 204 D3
Vatta [H] 64 F5
Vättershus [S] 162 D1
Vattjom [S] 184 E4
Vattlång [S] 184 E6
Vattnäs [S] 172 G3
Vatvet [N] 166 C3
Vau [P] 94 B5
Vaucelles, Abbaye de- [F] 28 F4
Vauclaix [F] 56 E3
Vaucluse [F] 58 C5
Vaucouleurs [F] 44 D5
Vaudoy en Brie [F] 42 G4
Vau i Dejës [AL] 128 B1
Vauldalen [N] 182 D3
Vauvenargues [F] 108 B4
Vauvert [F] 106 F4
Vauville [F] 26 D1
Vauvillers [F] 58 B3
Vaux-Le Vicomte [F] 42 G4
Vavylás (Güzelyalı) [CY] 154 F5
Vawkavysk [BY] 24 G5
Vaxholm [S] 168 E3
Växjö [S] 162 E4
Växtorp [S] 162 B6
Vayrac [F] 66 H4
Vaysal [TR] 150 B1
Važecká Jaskyňa [SK] 64 D2
V. Bodarna [S] 160 H1
Vean [N] 180 G1
Vebbestrup [DK] 160 D4
Veberöd [S] 158 C3
Veblungsnes [N] 180 E3
Vebomark [S] 196 A5
Vecbebri [LV] 198 E5
Večelkov [SK] 64 E4
Vechta [D] 18 C6
Vecilla de Valderaduey [E] 82 C4
Vecinos [E] 88 B3
Veckholm [S] 168 D2
Vecpiebalga [LV] 198 F5
Vecsés [H] 76 C1
Vecumnieki [LV] 198 E5
Vedavågen [N] 164 A2
Vedbæk [DK] 156 G2
Veddelev [DK] 156 G2
Veddige [S] 160 H3
Vedea [RO] 148 C2
Vedelago [I] 72 E5
Vedersø Klit [DK] 160 B5
Vedevåg [S] 166 H2
Vedjeön [S] 190 E5
Vedum [S] 166 E6
Veendam [NL] 16 H2
Veenendaal [NL] 16 E5
Veere [NL] 16 B6
Vegacervera [E] 78 H5
Vega de Espinareda [E] 78 F4
Vega de los Árboles [E] 96 G4
Vegadeo [E] 78 F2
Vega de Pas [E] 82 F3
Vega de Valcarce [E] 78 E4
Vegårshei [N] 164 F4
Vegas de Coria [E] 88 B4
Vegas del Condado [E] 78 H5
Vegger [DK] 160 D4
Veggli [N] 170 F5
Veghel [NL] 16 E6
Veglie [I] 122 G5
Vegset [N] 190 C5
Vegusdal [N] 164 E4
Vehkajärvi [FIN] 176 G1
Vehkalah [FIN] 178 B1
Vehkaperä [FIN] 186 E3
Vehmaa [FIN] 176 D4
Vehmaa [FIN] 188 D5
Vehmasmäki [FIN] 188 C3
Vehmersalmi [FIN] 188 D2
Vehniä [FIN] 186 G4
Vehu [FIN] 186 E3
Vehuvarpee [FIN] 186 C6
Veidnesklubben [N] 194 C2
Veikkola [FIN] 176 G5
Veinge [S] 162 B5
Veio [I] 114 H5
Veiros [P] 86 E6
Veisiejai [LT] 24 F3
Veitshöchheim [D] 46 E4
Veivirženai [LT] 200 D4
Vejano [I] 114 H4
Vejby [DK] 156 G1
Vejbystrand [S] 162 B6
Vejen [DK] 156 B2
Vejer de la Frontera [E] 100 F5
Vejers Strand [DK] 156 A2
Vejinac [BIH] 112 H2
Vejle [DK] 156 C2
Vejprty [CZ] 48 D2
Vekilski [BG] 148 F2
Velada [E] 88 D6
Velagići [BIH] 142 B3
Vela Luka [HR] 144 A3
Velanídia [GR] 136 F5
Velas [P] 100 C3
Velbert [D] 30 H3
Velburg [D] 46 H6
Velbuzhdki Pateka (Velbuzhdki Prolaz) [BG/MK] 146 E6
Velbuzhdki Prolaz (Velbuzhdki Pateka) [BG/MK] 146 E6
Velchevo [BG] 148 B4
Velden [A] 74 B3
Velden [D] 46 H4
Velden [D] 60 F4
Veldhoven [NL] 30 E2
Velebit [SRB] 76 E5
Velefique [E] 102 G4
Velehrad [CZ] 62 G2
Velēna [LV] 198 F4
Velence [H] 76 B2
Velenje [SLO] 74 D4
Velešín [CZ] 62 C2
Velešta [MK] 128 D3
Velestíno [GR] 132 H2
Vélez-Blanco [E] 102 H3
Vélez-Málaga [E] 102 C5
Vélez-Rubio [E] 102 H3
Velgošti [MK] 128 D3
Vel. Grđevac [HR] 74 G6
Velhartice [CZ] 48 E6
Vel. Horozhanka [UA] 52 H4
Veličani [BIH] 144 C3
Velika [HR] 142 C1
Velika Brusnica [BIH] 142 D2
Velika Dapčevica [HR] 74 G6
Velika Drenova [SRB] 146 C3
Velika Gorica [HR] 74 E6
Velika Kladuša [HR] 112 H2
Velika Kopanica [HR] 142 D2
Velika Kruša [SRB] 146 B6
Velika Plana [SRB] 146 C1
Velika Remeta, Manastir- [SRB] 142 F2
Velika Slatina [SRB] 146 C5
Velike Lašče [SLO] 74 C5
Veliki Preslav [BG] 148 E3
Veliki Šiljegovac [SRB] 146 D3
Veliki Tabor [HR] 74 D5
Velikiye Luki [RUS] 202 C3
Veliki Zdenci [HR] 74 G6
Veliko Orašje [SRB] 146 C1
Veliko Tŭrnovo [BG] 148 C3
Veli Lošinj [HR] 112 E4
Velimlje [MNE] 144 D3
Velingrad [BG] 148 A6
Velipojë [AL] 128 A1
Veliternë [AL] 128 D4
Velizh [RUS] 202 C4
Veljun [HR] 112 G2
Velká Bíteš [CZ] 50 B6
Velká Hleďsebe [CZ] 48 C4
Velká nad Veličkou [CZ] 62 H2
Velké Bílovice [CZ] 62 G3
Velké Brezno [CZ] 48 F2
Velké Heraltice [CZ] 50 D4
Velké Kapušany [SK] 64 H3
Velké Karlovice [CZ] 50 E6
Vel'ké Leváre [SK] 62 G3
Velké Losiny [CZ] 50 C4
Velké Meziříčí [CZ] 50 B6
Velké Němčice [CZ] 62 F2
Velké Opatovice [CZ] 50 C5
Vel'ké Raškovce [SK] 64 H3
Vel'ke Ripňany [SK] 64 A3
Vel'ké Uherce [SK] 64 B3
Velkua [FIN] 176 D4
Velkuanmaa [FIN] 176 D5
Velký Beranov [CZ] 50 A5
Velký Bor [CZ] 48 E5
Velký Folkmar [SK] 64 F2
Vel'ký Krtíš [SK] 64 D4
Vel'ký Meder [SK] 62 H5
Vel'ký Šariš [SK] 64 G2
Velký Újezd [CZ] 50 D5
Velle [N] 180 D4
Velleclaire [F] 58 B4
Velleia [I] 110 C2
Velles [F] 54 H4
Velletri [I] 116 A6
Vellinge [S] 156 H3
Vel. Ljubin [UA] 52 G4
Velp [NL] 16 F5
Velpke [D] 32 H2
Velta [N] 172 D4
Vel. Trnovac [SRB] 146 D5
Veltrusy [CZ] 48 F3
Veluće [SRB] 146 C3
Velušina [MK] 128 E4
Velvary [CZ] 48 F3
Velventós [GR] 128 F5
Vel'ye [RUS] 198 H4
Velyka Lepetykha [UA] 204 G2
Velyki Mosty [UA] 52 H3
Velykyi Bereznyi [UA] 204 B2
Vemb [DK] 160 B5
Vemdalen [S] 182 F4
Vemhån [S] 182 G5
Vemmelv [DK] 156 F3
Vemmenæs [DK] 156 E4
Ven [N] 164 B3
Vena [S] 162 F3
Venabu [N] 170 H1
Venaco [F] 114 B4
Venafro [I] 120 D1
Venäjä [FIN] 176 F3
Venaria Reale [I] 70 D5
Venåsen [N] 180 H6
Venčane [SRB] 146 B1
Vence [F] 108 E4
Venda Nova [P] 80 D3
Vendargues [F] 106 F4
Vendas de Galizes [P] 86 E2
Vendas Novas [P] 86 C6
Vendays-Montalivet [F] 66 C1
Vendel [S] 174 F5
Vendelsö [S] 168 E3
Vendeuvre [F] 44 B6
Vendinha [E] 94 E2
Vendôme [F] 42 D6
Vendranges [F] 68 E2
Veneheitto [FIN] 196 E4
Veneskoski [FIN] 186 C3
Venets [BG] 148 C5
Venets [BG] 148 E4
Venets [BG] 148 E2
Venevere [EST] 198 F2
Venézia [I] 72 E6
Venialbo [E] 80 H5
Venjan [S] 172 F3
Venlo [NL] 30 F3
Venn [N] 182 B2
Vénna [GR] 130 F3
Vennesla [N] 164 D5
Vennesund [N] 190 C4
Venngarn [S] 168 D2
Venosa [I] 120 H3
Venoy [F] 56 E2
Venray [NL] 30 F2
Vent [A] 72 C2
Venta de Arraco [E] 84 D4
Venta de Baños [E] 88 F1
Venta del Moro [E] 98 D4
Venta de los Santos [E] 96 G6
Venta del Pobre [E] 102 H5
Ventadour, Château de- [F] 68 A3
Venta el Alto [E] 94 G5
Venta Nueva [E] 78 F4
Ventas de Huelma [E] 102 D4
Ventas de Zefarraya [E] 102 C4
Ventė [LT] 200 D5
Ventimíglia [I] 108 F4
Ventiseri [F] 114 B5
Ventnor [GB] 12 H5
Vento, Grotta del- [I] 110 D5
Ventosa de Pisuerga [E] 82 D5
Ventspils [LV] 198 B4
Venus [RO] 148 G1
Venzone [I] 72 G4
Vepsä [FIN] 196 D4

Vera [E] 102 H5
Vera [N] 190 C6
Vera de Bidasoa / Bera [E] 84 B2
Vera de Moncayo [E] 90 D3
Verba [UA] 38 H6
Verbania [I] 70 F3
Verberie [F] 42 G2
Verbicaro [I] 120 H6
Verbier [CH] 70 D3
Vercelli [I] 70 E5
Verch. Syn'ovydne [UA] 52 G6
Verdalsøra [N] 190 C6
Verdelles, Château de- [F] 42 A5
Verden [D] 18 E6
Verdenberg [CH] 58 H6
Verdens Ende [N] 164 H3
Verdikoússa [GR] 132 F1
Verdun [F] 44 D4
Verea [E] 78 C5
Vereja [RUS] 202 E3
Veresegyház [H] 64 C6
Vereya [RUS] 202 E3
Verfeil [F] 106 A3
Vergato [I] 110 F4
Vergeletto [CH] 70 F2
Verghia [F] 114 A5
Vergi [EST] 198 E1
Vérgi [GR] 130 B3
Vergiate [I] 70 F4
Vergína [GR] 128 G5
Vergt [F] 66 F3
Verh. Osel'ki [RUS] 178 H4
Verín [E] 78 D6
Verinsko [BG] 146 G5
Verket [N] 164 H2
Verkhn'odniprovs'k [UA] 204 G1
Verl [D] 32 D3
Verma [N] 180 F4
Vermafoss [N] 180 F4
Vermenton [F] 56 E2
Vermeş [RO] 76 H6
Vermiglio [I] 72 C4
Vermosh [AL] 146 A5
Vermuntila [FIN] 176 C3
Vernazza [I] 110 C4
Vern-D'anjou [F] 40 G6
Vernet [F] 84 H3
Vernet-les-Bains [F] 92 F1
Verneuil-sur-Avre [F] 26 H5
Verningen [N] 164 G3
Vernio [I] 110 F5
Vernon [F] 42 E2
Vernoux-en-Gâtine [F] 54 D3
Verny [F] 44 E4
Verőce [H] 64 C5
Véroia [GR] 128 G5
Verolanuova [I] 72 A6
Veroli [I] 116 C6
Verona [I] 72 C6
Verpelét [H] 64 E5
Verrabotn [N] 190 B6
Verrès [I] 70 D4
Verrières-de-Joux [F] 58 B6
Versailles [F] 42 F3
Verseg [H] 64 D6
Versmold [D] 32 D3
Versoix [CH] 70 B2
Versols-et-Lapeyre [F] 106 D3
Vertaala [FIN] 186 G4
Verteillac [F] 66 E2
Vertop [AL] 128 B5
Vertou [F] 54 C1
Vertus [F] 44 B4
Verucchio [I] 110 H5
Veruela, Monasterio de- [E] 90 D3
Verum [S] 162 C6
Verviers [B] 30 E5
Vervins [F] 28 G5
Vervnäs [S] 172 E2
Verwood [GB] 12 G5
Verzej [SLO] 74 E3
Verzuolo [I] 108 F2
Verzy [F] 44 B3
Vesala [FIN] 196 F2
Vesamäki [FIN] 186 H2
Vesanka [FIN] 186 G4
Vesanto [FIN] 186 G2
Vescovato [F] 114 C3
Vescovato [I] 110 D1
Vése [H] 74 G4
Veselec [BG] 148 E2
Veselie [BG] 148 F5
Veselí nad Lužnicí [CZ] 48 G6
Veselí nad Moravou [CZ] 62 H2
Veselinovo [BG] 148 E3
Veselynove [UA] 204 F3
Veshchevo [RUS] 178 F3
Veshtica [BG] 146 E2
Vesivehmaa [FIN] 178 A2
Veskoniemi [FIN] 194 D4
Vesnovo [RUS] 24 D1
Vesoul [F] 58 B3
Véssa [GR] 134 G5
Vessingebro [S] 160 H4
Vestbjerg [DK] 160 E3
Vestby [N] 166 B2
Vestbygd [N] 164 B5
Vester Åby [DK] 156 D4
Vesterby [DK] 156 D2
Vesterby [DK] 156 F4
Vester Egense [DK] 156 D2
Vester Egesborg [DK] 156 F4
Vesterli [N] 192 D6
Vesterø Havn [DK] 160 F3
Veste Rosenberg [D] 46 H3
Vestervig [DK] 160 B4
Vestfossen [N] 164 G1
Vestmanna [FR] 160 A1
Vestmarka [N] 166 D1
Vestnes [N] 180 E3
Vestone [I] 72 B5
Vestpollen [N] 192 D4
Vestre Jakobselv [N] 194 E2
Ves'yegonsk [RUS] 202 E1
Veszprém [H] 76 A2
Veszprémvarsány [H] 76 A1
Vésztő [H] 76 G2
Veteli / Vetil [FIN] 186 D1
Vetil / Veteli [FIN] 186 D1
Vetlanda [S] 162 E3
Vetlefjorden [N] 170 D1
Vetovo [BG] 148 D2
Vetovo [HR] 142 C1
Vetralla [I] 114 H4
Vetren [BG] 148 C4
Vetren [BG] 148 F4
Vetrino [BG] 148 F2
Vetriolo Terme [I] 72 D4
Větrný Jeníkov [CZ] 48 H5
Vetschau [D] 34 F4
Vettasjärvi [S] 192 H6
Vetti [N] 170 E1
Vettisfossen [N] 170 E1
Vetulónia [I] 114 F2
Vetunica [MK] 146 E6
Veules-les-Roses [F] 26 H2
Veulettes-sur-Mer [F] 26 H2
Veurne (Furnes) [B] 28 F1
Vevang [N] 180 E2
Vevey [CH] 70 C1
Vévi [GR] 128 E4
Vevring [N] 180 B6
Veynes [F] 108 C2
Veyrier [F] 70 B3
Vezdemarbán [E] 88 D1
Vézelay [F] 56 E3
Vézelise [F] 44 E6
Vézénobres [F] 106 F3
Vezin le Coquet [F] 26 C6
Vezirhan [TR] 150 G4
Vezzano [I] 72 C4
Vezzolano, Abbazia di- [I] 70 E6
V. Gafsele [S] 190 F5
V. Husby [S] 168 B5
Viadana [I] 110 E2
Viaduct du Millau [F] 106 D2
Viais [F] 54 B2
Vial. Berestavica [BY] 24 G5
Via Mala [CH] 70 H2
Viana [E] 82 H6
Viana de Duero [E] 90 B3
Viana do Alentejo [P] 94 D2
Viana do Bolo [E] 78 E6
Viana do Castelo [P] 78 A6
Vianden [L] 44 F2
Viane [F] 106 C3
Vianen [NL] 16 D5
Vianne [F] 66 E5
Vianos [E] 96 H6
Viaréggio [I] 110 D5
Vias [F] 106 E4
Viator [E] 102 G5
Viborg [DK] 160 D5
Vibo Valentia [I] 124 D6
Vibraye [F] 42 C5
Viby [DK] 156 G3
Viby [S] 166 G4
Vic [E] 92 E3
Vič [SLO] 74 C3
Viča [SRB] 146 B3
Vicarello [I] 114 H4
Vicchio [I] 110 F5
Vicdessos [F] 84 H5
Vicedo [E] 78 E1
Vic-en-Bigorre [F] 84 F3
Vicenza [I] 72 D6
Vic-Fezensac [F] 84 F2
Vichtis / Vihti [FIN] 176 G4
Vichy [F] 68 D1
Vickan [S] 160 G3
Vic-le-Comte [F] 68 D2
Vico [E] 84 A5
Vico [F] 114 A4
Vico del Gargano [I] 116 H6
Vico Equense [I] 120 E4
Vicoforte, Santuario di- [I] 108 G3
Vicovaro [I] 116 B5
Vic-sur-Aisne [F] 28 F6
Vic-sur-Cère [F] 68 B4
Victoire, Abbaye de la- [F] 42 G3
Victoria [M] 126 C5
Vidaga [LV] 198 F4
Vidago [P] 80 E3
Vidamlya [BY] 38 G2
Viðareiði [FR] 160 B1
Vidauban [F] 108 D5
Viddal [N] 180 D4
Viddalba [I] 118 D2
Vide [P] 86 F2
Videbæk [DK] 156 B1
Videle [RO] 204 D6
Videseter [N] 180 E5
Vidhas [AL] 128 B3
Vidigueira [P] 94 D2
Vidin [BG] 146 E2
Vidlin [GB] 6 H3
Vidnava [CZ] 50 D3
Vidsel [S] 196 A3
Vidzy [BY] 200 H4
Viechtach [D] 48 D6
Vieira [P] 86 C2
Vieja, Cueva de la- [E] 98 D5
Vieki [FIN] 196 G6
Viekšniai [LT] 198 C6
Vielikie Lazy [UA] 204 B3
Viella [E] 84 G5
Viella, Túnel de- [E] 84 F5
Vielsalm [B] 30 E6
Vienenburg [D] 32 H3
Vienne [F] 68 F3
Vieremä [FIN] 196 E6
Viernheim [D] 46 C4
Viersen [D] 30 G3
Vieru [RO] 148 C2
Vierumäki [FIN] 178 B2
Vierville [F] 26 E3
Vierzehnheiligen [D] 46 G3
Vierzon [F] 56 B3
Viesimo [FIN] 188 G3
Viešintos [LT] 200 G4
Viesīte [LV] 198 E6
Viesites [LV] 198 E6
Vieste [I] 116 H6
Vietas [S] 192 F5
Vietri di Potenza [I] 120 G4
Vietri sul Mare [I] 120 E4
Vieux-Boucau-les-Bains [F] 66 A6
Vievis [LT] 200 G5
Vif [F] 68 H5
Vig [DK] 156 F2
Vigeland [N] 164 C6
Vigévano [I] 70 F5
Vigge [S] 182 G3
Viggianello [I] 120 H6
Viggiano [I] 120 H5
Vígla [GR] 132 D3
Vígľ'aš [SK] 64 C3
Vigmostad [N] 164 D5
Vignale Monferrato [I] 70 E6
Vignanello [I] 114 H4
Vigneulles [F] 44 E4
Vignola [I] 110 E3
Vignola Mare [I] 118 D2
Vignory [F] 44 C6
Vigo [E] 78 B4
Vigo di Fassa [I] 72 D3
Vigrestad [N] 164 A4
Viguera [E] 90 B1
Vihantasalmi [FIN] 178 C1
Vihanti [FIN] 196 D4
Vihasjärvi [FIN] 176 G1
Vihiers [F] 54 D2
Vihren [BG] 130 B1
Vihtari [FIN] 188 E3
Vihtasuo [FIN] 196 G6
Vihti / Vichtis [FIN] 176 G4
Vihtijärvi [FIN] 176 G4
Vihtiläjärvi [FIN] 186 C6
Viiala [FIN] 176 F2
Viiksimo [FIN] 196 G4
Viinijärvi [FIN] 188 E2
Viinikoski [FIN] 196 E3
Viinistu [EST] 178 B6
Viisarimäki [FIN] 186 G5
Viitaila [FIN] 176 H2
Viitajärvi [FIN] 186 F2
Viitaniemi [FIN] 188 D1
Viitasaari [FIN] 186 G2
Viitavaara [FIN] 196 F4
Viitna [EST] 198 E1
Viivikonnä [EST] 198 F1
Vijciems [LV] 198 F4
Vijenac [MNE] 144 E2
Vík [IS] 192 B3
Vik [N] 164 E5
Vik [N] 180 C4
Vik [N] 180 G1
Vik [N] 190 C3
Vik [S] 158 D3
Vik [S] 168 D2
Vika [N] 164 D3
Vika [S] 172 G3
Vika [S] 174 C4
Vikajärvi [FIN] 194 D7
Vikan [N] 180 F1
Vikane [N] 166 B3
Vikanes [N] 170 B3
Vikarbyn [S] 172 H3
Vikby [FIN] 186 B2
Vike [N] 180 F3
Vikebukt [N] 180 E3
Vikedal [N] 164 B1
Viken [S] 156 H1
Viken [S] 182 H4
Viken [S] 190 D4
Viker [N] 170 H4
Viker [S] 166 G2
Vikersund [N] 170 G5
Vikeså [N] 164 B4
Vikmanshyttan [S] 174 C5
Vikoč [BIH] 144 E2
Vikran [N] 192 F2
Viksjö [S] 184 E3
Viksøyri [N] 170 C2
Vikštejn [CZ] 50 E4
Viktring [A] 74 B3
Vikvallen [S] 190 H3
Vikvarvet [N] 182 C2
Vila Baleira [P] 100 B3
Viladamat [E] 92 G3
Viladecans [E] 92 E4
Vila de Rei [P] 86 D3
Vila do Bispo [P] 94 A5
Vila do Conde [P] 80 B3
Vila do Porto [P] 100 E4
Vilafamés [E] 98 F3
Vila Fernando [P] 86 G2
Vila Flor [P] 80 E4
Vilafranca de Bonany [E] 104 E5
Vilafranca del Maestrat / Villafranca del Cid [E] 98 F2
Vilafranca del Penedès [E] 92 D4
Vila Franca de Xira [P] 86 B5
Vila Franca do Campo [P] 100 E3
Vila Fresca de Azeitão [P] 86 B6
Vilagarcía de Arousa [E] 78 B3
Viļaka [LV] 198 G4
Vilaller [E] 84 F6
Vila Mea [P] 80 E3
Vilameán [E] 78 B5
Vilamor [E] 84 G6
Vilamoura [P] 94 C5
Viļāni [LV] 198 F5
Vilanova d'Alcolea [E] 98 G3
Vilanova de Arousa [E] 78 B3
Vila Nova de Cerveira [P] 78 A5
Vila Nova de Famalicão [P] 80 C3
Vila Nova de Foz Côa [P] 80 E5
Vila Nova de Gaia [P] 80 B4
Vilanova de la Barca [E] 90 H4
Vila Nova de Milfontes [P] 94 B3
Vila Nova de Ourém [P] 86 D3
Vila Nova de Paiva [P] 80 D5
Vila Nova de S. André [P] 94 B2
Vila Nova de São Bento [P] 94 E3
Vila Nova do Corvo [P] 100 C3
Vilanova i la Geltrú [E] 92 D5
Vila Pouca de Aguiar [P] 80 D3
Vila Praia de Âncora [P] 78 A5
Vilarandelo [P] 80 E3
Vilar de Barrio [E] 78 D5
Vilardevós [E] 78 D6
Vila Real [P] 80 D4
Vila Real de Santo António [P] 94 D5
Vilar Formoso [P] 86 H2
Vila-rodona [E] 92 C4
Vilarouco [P] 80 E5
Vilars, Cova dels- [E] 90 H4
Vila-seca [E] 92 C5
Vilassar de Mar [E] 92 E4
Vila Velha de Ródão [P] 86 E4
Vila Verde [P] 78 B6
Vila Verde [P] 80 F3
Vila Verde da Raia [P] 80 E3
Vila Verde de Ficalho [P] 94 E3
Vila Viçosa [P] 86 E6
Vilches [E] 102 F1
Vildbjerg [DK] 160 C6
Vilémov [CZ] 48 H4
Vilhelmina [S] 190 F5
Vília [GR] 134 B6
Vilinska Jama [HR] 74 D6
Viljakkala [FIN] 186 D6
Viljandi [EST] 198 E3
Viljolahti [FIN] 188 E4
Vilkaviškis [LT] 24 E1
Vilkija [LT] 200 F5
Villa Adriana [I] 116 B5
Villaba del Rey [E] 98 B1
Villa Bartolomea [I] 110 F2
Villablanca [E] 94 D5
Villablino [E] 78 G4
Villabona [E] 84 B2
Villacañas [E] 96 G2
Villa Cancellieri [I] 126 F5
Villacarrillo [E] 102 F1
Villa Castelli [I] 122 F4
Villacastín [E] 88 E4
Villach [A] 72 H3
Villacidro [I] 118 C6
Villada [E] 82 C5
Villadangos del Páramo [E] 78 G6
Villa del Prado [E] 88 E6
Villa del Río [E] 102 D1
Villa de Ves [E] 98 D5
Villadiego [E] 82 E5
Villadoro [I] 126 E3
Villadossola [I] 70 E3
Villaeles de Valdavia [E] 82 D5
Villaescusa de Haro [E] 96 H3
Villa Estense [I] 110 G2
Villa Formosa [E] 86 E5
Villafranca del Bierzo [E] 78 F5
Villafranca del Cid / Vilafranca del Maestrat [E] 98 F2
Villafranca de los Barros [E] 94 G3
Villafranca de los Caballeros [E] 96 G3
Villafranca di Verona [I] 110 E1
Villafranca Montes de Oca [E] 82 F6
Villafranca Piemonte [I] 70 D6
Villafranca Tirrena [I] 124 B7
Villafrati [I] 126 D2
Villafrechós [E] 82 B6
Villafruela [E] 88 G1
Villafuerte [E] 88 F2
Villagarcia de la Torre [E] 94 H3
Village, Roche aux- [F] 44 C1
Villaggio Apulo [I] 122 E3
Villaggio Mancuso [I] 124 E5
Villagonzalo Pedernales [E] 82 E6
Villagordo [E] 102 E2
Villagrains [F] 66 C4
Villagrande Strisaili [I] 118 E5
Villaharta [E] 96 C6
Villahermosa [E] 96 G5
Villahoz [E] 88 G1
Villaines la Gonais [F] 42 C5
Villaines-la-Juhel [F] 26 F6
Villajos, Ermita de- [E] 96 G3
Villajoyosa / la Vila Joiosa [E] 104 E2
Villala [FIN] 188 F4
Villalba Alta [E] 78 E2
Villalba de Duero [E] 88 G2
Villalba de Guardo [E] 82 C4
Villalba del Alcor [E] 94 F6
Villalba de la Sierra [E] 98 C2
Villalba de los Alcores [E] 88 E1
Villalba de los Barros [E] 94 G2
Villalcázar de Sirga [E] 82 D5
Villalgordo del Marquesado [E] 98 A3
Villa Literno [I] 120 D3
Villalón de Campos [E] 82 C6
Villalpando [E] 82 B6
Villalpardo [E] 98 C4
Villaluenga [E] 96 F1
Villamalea [E] 98 C4
Villamañán [E] 78 H6
Villamanín [E] 78 H5
Villamanrique [E] 96 G6
Villamanrique de la Condesa [E] 94 F6
Villamar [I] 118 C6
Villamartín [E] 100 G3
Villamartín de Campos [E] 82 C6
Villamartín de Don Sancho [E] 82 C4
Villamassargia [I] 118 B7
Villamayor [E] 80 H6
Villamayor de Santiago [E] 96 H2
Villamediana de Iregua [E] 82 H6
Villamesías [E] 96 B2
Villa Minozzo [I] 110 D3
Villamuelas [E] 96 F2
Villandraut [F] 66 D4
Villandry [F] 54 F2
Villanova [I] 122 F3
Villanova d'Asti [I] 70 D6
Villanova Monteleone [I] 118 B3
Villanova Tulo [I] 118 D5
Villanúa [E] 84 D5
Villanubla [E] 88 E1
Villanueva de Alcardete [E] 96 H3
Villanueva de Algaidas [E] 102 C3
Villanueva de Argaño [E] 82 E5
Villanueva de Cameros [E] 90 B1
Villanueva de Cañedo [E] 80 H6
Villanueva de Córdoba [E] 96 C5
Villanueva de Gállego [E] 90 E3
Villanueva de Huerva [E] 90 E4
Villanueva del Aceral [E] 88 E3
Villanueva de la Fuente [E] 96 H5
Villanueva de la Jara [E] 98 B4
Villanueva de la Reina [E] 102 E1
Villanueva del Arzobispo [E] 102 G1
Villanueva de las Cruces [E] 94 E5
Villanueva de la Serena [E] 96 B3
Villanueva de la Sierra [E] 86 H3
Villanueva de las Torres [E] 102 F3
Villanueva de la Vera [E] 88 C5
Villanueva del Campo [E] 82 B6
Villanueva del Duque [E] 96 C5
Villanueva del Fresno [E] 94 F2
Villanueva de los Castillejos [E] 94 E5
Villanueva de los Infantes [E] 96 G5
Villanueva del Rey [E] 96 B5
Villanueva del Río Segura [E] 104 C2
Villanueva del Río y Minas [E] 94 H5
Villanueva del Trabuco [E] 102 C4
Villanueva de San Carlos [E] 104 H5
Villanueva de Sigena [E] 90 G4
Villanueva de Tapia [E] 102 C3
Villanuño de Valdavia [E] 82 D5
Villány [H] 76 B5
Villa Opicina [I] 72 H6
Villapalacios [E] 96 H6
Villapiana Scalo [I] 122 D6
Villaplana [I] 122 D6
Villa Potenza [I] 116 C1
Villapriolo [I] 126 E3
Villaputzu [I] 118 E6
Villaquejida [E] 82 B5
Villaquilambre [E] 78 H5
Villarcayo [E] 82 F4
Villard-de-Lans [F] 68 G5
Villardebelle [F] 106 B5
Villar de Cantos [E] 98 B3
Villar de Ciervo [E] 80 E6
Villardeciervos [E] 80 G3
Villar de Domingo García [E] 98 B1
Villardefrades [E] 88 D1
Villar del Arzobispo [E] 98 E3
Villar del Pedroso [E] 96 C1
Villar del Pozo [E] 98 B5
Villar del Rey [E] 86 F6
Villar de Olalla [E] 98 B2
Villar de Peralonso [E] 80 G6
Villar de Rena [E] 96 B3
Villar de Río [E] 90 C2
Villarejo de Fuentes [E] 96 H2
Villarejo de Salvanés [E] 96 G1
Villares de la Reina [E] 80 H6
Villares del Saz [E] 98 B2
Villargordo del Cabriel [E] 98 C4
Villaricos [E] 104 A5
Villarino [E] 80 F5
Villariño de Conso [E] 78 D6
Villarluengo [E] 98 F1
Villarmayor [E] 80 G6
Villa Romana del Casale [I] 126 E4
Villarosa [I] 126 E3
Villar Perosa [I] 70 C6
Villarquemado [E] 98 D1
Villarramiel [E] 82 C6
Villarreal de San Carlos [E] 88 A6
Villarreal – la Vila Reial [E] 98 F3
Villarrobledo [E] 96 H4
Villarroga de los Pinares [E] 98 F1
Villarroja [E] 84 A5
Villarroya de la Sierra [E] 90 C4
Villarrubia de los Ojos [E] 96 F3
Villars [CH] 70 C2
Villars-les-Dombes [F] 68 G2
Villars-sur-Var [F] 108 E4
Villarta [E] 98 C4
Villarta de los Montes [E] 96 D3
Villarta de San Juan [E] 96 F3
Villarubia de Santiago [E] 96 G1
Villasadino [E] 82 D5
Villasalto [I] 118 D6
Villasana de Mena [E] 82 F4
Villa San Giovanni [I] 124 C7
Villa Santa Maria [I] 116 D5
Villasante [E] 82 F4
Villa Santina [I] 72 G4
Villaseco de los Gamitos [E] 80 G6
Villaseco de los Reyes [E] 80 G5
Villasequilla [E] 96 F2
Villasimíus [I] 118 D7
Villa S. Lucia degli Abruzzi [I] 116 D4
Villasor [I] 118 C6
Villasrubias [E] 86 H3
Villastar [E] 98 D2
Villatobas [E] 96 G2
Villatoro [E] 82 E6
Villatoya [E] 98 C4
Villava [E] 84 B4
Villavelayo [E] 90 A1
Villaverde del Río [E] 94 H5
Villaverde de Trucios [E] 82 G3
Villaviciosa [E] 82 C2
Villaviciosa [E] 96 C6
Villavieja [E] 80 F6
Villa Vomano [I] 116 C3
Villé [F] 58 D2
Villebois-Lavalette [F] 66 E2
Ville-Devant-Chaumont [F] 44 D3
Villedieu-les-Poêles [F] 26 D4
Villédomain [F] 54 G3
Ville-en-Tardenois [F] 44 B3
Villefagnan [F] 54 E5
Villefontaine [F] 68 G3
Villefort [F] 68 D6
Villefranche [F] 108 F4
Villefranche-d'Albigeois [F] 106 C2
Villefranche-de-Conflent [F] 92 F1
Villefranche-de-Lauragais [F] 106 A4
Villefranche-de-Lonchat [F] 66 E3
Villefranche-de-Panat [F] 106 D2
Villefranche-de-Rouergue [F] 66 H5
Villefranche-du-Périgord [F] 66 F4
Villefranche-sur-Cher [F] 54 H2
Villefranche-sur-Saône [F] 68 F2
Villegats [F] 54 E5
Villel [E] 98 D2
Villemur [F] 106 A2
Villena [E] 104 D1
Villenauxe-la-Grande [F] 42 H5
Villeneuve [F] 66 H5
Villeneuve [F] 106 G3
Villeneuve d'Ascq [F] 28 F3
Villeneuve-de-Berg [F] 68 E6
Villeneuve-de-Marsan [F] 66 C6
Villeneuve-l'Archevêque [F] 42 H6
Villeneuve-Loubet [F] 108 E4
Villeneuve-sur-Allier [F] 56 D5
Villeneuve-sur-Lot [F] 66 E5
Villeneuve-sur-Yonne [F] 42 G6
Villerbon [F] 42 D6
Villeréal [F] 66 F4
Villeromaine [F] 42 D6
Villers [B] 30 C5
Villers [F] 26 G3
Villers-Bocage [F] 26 E3
Villers-Bretonneux [F] 28 E5
Villers-Cotterêts [F] 42 H3
Villersexel [F] 58 C4
Villers-le-Lac [F] 58 C5
Villerville [F] 26 G3
Villeseque [F] 66 G5
Ville-sur-Illon [F] 58 C2
Villetta Barrea [I] 116 D6
Villiers-St-Georges [F] 42 H4
Villingen [D] 58 F3
Villingsberg [S] 166 G3
Villmanstrand / Lappeenranta [FIN] 178 E2
Villnäs / Askainen [FIN] 176 D4
Villoldo [E] 82 C5
Villon [F] 56 F2
Villorba [I] 72 E5
Villoria [E] 88 D3
Villoslada de Cameros [E] 90 B1
Villstad [S] 162 C3
Villvattnet [S] 190 H5
Vilmajor [H] 76 F3
Vilmány [H] 64 G3
Vilnius [LT] 200 G5
Vilobacka [FIN] 186 C1
Vilovo [SRB] 142 G1
Vilppula [FIN] 186 E5
Vils [DK] 160 C4
Vilsbiburg [D] 60 F3
Vilseck [D] 46 H5
Vilshofen [D] 60 H3
Vilshult [S] 162 D6
Vilsund [DK] 160 C4
Vilunai [LT] 24 G1
Vilusi [MNE] 144 D3
Viluste [EST] 198 F3
Vilyeyka [BY] 202 B5
Vimianzo [E] 78 B2
Vimieiro [P] 86 D6
Vimioso [P] 80 G4
Vimmerby [S] 162 F2
Vimoutiers [F] 26 G4
Vimpeli [FIN] 186 D2
Vimperk [CZ] 62 A2
Vina [SRB] 146 D4
Vinac [BIH] 142 C4
Vinádio [I] 108 E3
Vinaixa [E] 92 C4
Vinaròs [E] 92 A6
Vinarsko [BG] 148 F4
Vinay [F] 68 G4
Vinça [F] 92 F1
Vinchiaturo [I] 120 E1
Vinci [I] 110 E5
Vindbyholt [DK] 156 G4
Vindelgransele [S] 190 G4
Vindeln [S] 190 H5
Vinderslev [DK] 160 D6
Vinderup [DK] 160 C5
Vindsvik [N] 164 C2
Vinebre [E] 90 H6
Vinga [RO] 76 G5
Vinga [RO] 76 H4
Vingåker [S] 168 B4
Vingelen [N] 182 C4
Vingnes [N] 172 B2
Vingrau [F] 106 C6
Vingrom [N] 170 H2
Vingstad [N] 192 G3
Vinhais [P] 80 F3
Vinica [BG] 148 E3
Vinica [MK] 128 G1
Vinica [SK] 64 C4
Vinica [SLO] 112 G1
Viničani [MK] 128 F2
Viniegra de Abajo [E] 90 B1
Vinishte [BG] 146 F3
Vinjani [HR] 144 B2
Vinje [N] 164 E1
Vinje [N] 170 C3
Vinjeøra [N] 180 G2
Vinkovci [HR] 142 E1
Vinliden [S] 190 G5
Vinnytsia [UA] 202 C8
Vinon-sur-Verdon [F] 108 C4
Vinslöv [S] 158 D1
Vinsnes [N] 164 E3
Vinsternes [N] 180 F1
Vinstra [N] 170 H1
Vintgar [SLO] 74 B4
Vintjärn [S] 174 D3
Vintl / Vandoies [I] 72 E2
Vintrosa [S] 166 G3
Viñuela de Sayago [E] 80 G5
Viñuelas [E] 88 G5
Vinuesa [E] 90 B2
Vinzelberg [D] 34 B2
Violès [F] 106 H3
Viozene [I] 108 G3
Vipava [SLO] 74 A5
Vipiteno / Sterzing [I] 72 D2
Vira [HR] 144 A2
Virányos [H] 64 G4
Virdois / Virrat [FIN] 186 D4
Vire [F] 26 E4
Viré [F] 56 G6
Vire Court [F] 40 B3
Vireda [S] 162 D1
Vireši [LV] 198 F4
Virestad [S] 162 D5
Virgen [A] 72 F2
Virgen de Criptana [E] 96 G3
Virgen de la Cabeza [E] 96 E6
Virgen de la Cabeza [E] 98 B4
Virgen de la Cabeza [E] 102 G2
Virgen de la Montaña [E] 86 H5
Virgen de la Muela [E] 96 G2
Virgen de la Peña [E] 90 H3
Virgen de la Peña [E] 94 E4
Virgen del Castillo [E] 88 F3
Virginia [IRL] 2 E5
Viriat [F] 68 G1
Virieu [F] 68 G4
Virieu-le-Grand [F] 68 H3
Virje [HR] 74 G5
Virkby / Virkkala [FIN] 176 G5
Virkkala / Virkby [FIN] 176 G5
Virkkula [FIN] 194 F8
Virklund [DK] 156 C1
Virmaanpää [FIN] 186 H3
Virmaila [FIN] 176 H1
Virmutjoki [FIN] 178 E1
Virojoki [FIN] 178 D3
Virolahti [FIN] 178 D3
Vironvay [F] 28 C6
Virovitica [HR] 74 H5
Virpazar [MNE] 144 E5
Virrat / Virdois [FIN] 186 D4
Virsbo [S] 168 B1
Virsbo bruk [S] 168 B1
Virserum [S] 162 F3
Virtaniemi [RUS] 194 E4
Virtasalmi [FIN] 188 D4
Virton [B] 44 E2
Virtsu [EST] 198 D3

Virttaa [FIN] 176 E3
Virvoru [RO] 146 F1
Vis [HR] 116 H2
Visaginas [LT] 200 H4
Visbek [D] 18 C6
Visby [DK] 156 B4
Visby [S] 168 G4
Visé [B] 30 E4
Višegrad [BIH] 144 E1
Visegrád [H] 64 C5
Viseu [P] 80 C6
Vishaj [AL] 128 B3
Vishnyeva [BY] 200 H6
Vishovgrad [BG] 148 C3
Vishtytis [LT] 24 D2
Visiedo [E] 90 D6
Vişina Veche [RO] 148 A2
Visingsborg [S] 162 D1
Viskafors [S] 162 B2
Viskinge [DK] 156 F2
Viškovci [HR] 142 D1
Viškovo [HR] 112 E1
Visland [N] 164 C4
Vislanda [S] 162 D5
Višnja Gora [SLO] 74 C5
Visočka Ržana [SRB] 146 E4
Viso del Marqués [E] 96 F5
Visoka [SRB] 146 A3
Visoki Dečani, Manastir- [SRB] 146 B5
Visoko [BIH] 142 D4
Visoko [SLO] 74 B4
Visp [CH] 70 E2
Vissefjärda [S] 162 F5
Visselhövede [D] 18 E6
Visseltofta [S] 162 C6
Vissenbjerg [DK] 156 D3
Visso [I] 116 B2
Vistdal [N] 180 F3
Vistheden [S] 196 A3
Vistino [RUS] 178 F5
Visuvesi [FIN] 186 E5
Visz [H] 74 H3
Visz [H] 76 A3
Vitalahti [FIN] 186 G5
Vitănești [RO] 148 C1
Vitanovac [SRB] 146 B3
Vitberget [S] 190 H2
Vitemölla [S] 158 D2
Viterbo [I] 114 H4
Viterbo, Bagni di- [I] 114 H4
Vithkuq [AL] 128 C5
Vitigudino [E] 80 F6
Vitina [BIH] 144 B2
Vitina [SRB] 146 C6
Vitis [A] 62 D3
Vítkov [CZ] 50 E4
Vitkovo [SRB] 146 C3
Vitolište [MK] 128 F3
Vitomirica [SRB] 146 B5
Vitoria-Gasteiz [E] 82 G5
Vitré [F] 26 D6
Vitry-le-François [F] 44 C5
Vitsand [S] 172 E5
Vitskøl Kloster [DK] 160 D4
Vitsyebsk [BY] 202 C4
Vittangi [S] 192 H5
Vittarp [DK] 156 A2
Vittaryd [S] 162 C4
Vitteaux [F] 56 G3
Vittel [F] 58 B2
Vittinge [S] 168 C1
Vittjärn [S] 172 D5
Vittjärv [S] 196 B3
Vittória [I] 126 F5
Vittoriosa [M] 126 C6
Vittório Véneto [I] 72 E5
Vitträsk [S] 194 A8
Vittsjö [S] 162 C6
Vittskövle [S] 158 D2
Vitvattnet [S] 196 C2
Vitzenburg [D] 34 B5
Vitznau [CH] 58 F6
Viù [I] 70 D5
Viuhkola [FIN] 178 D2
Vivario [F] 114 B4
Viveiro [E] 78 E1
Vivel del Río Martín [E] 90 E6
Viver [E] 98 E3
Viverols [F] 68 E3
Viverone [I] 70 E5
Viveros [E] 96 H5
Vivier, Château du- [F] 42 G4
Viviers [F] 68 F6
Vivonne [F] 54 E4
Vivungi [S] 192 H5
Vixía Herbeira [E] 78 D1
Vize [TR] 150 C2
Vizica [BG] 148 F5
Vizille [F] 68 H5
Vižinada [HR] 112 D1
Vizovice [CZ] 50 E6
Vizsoly [H] 64 G4
Vizzavona [F] 114 B4
Vizzini [I] 126 F4
Vjazy [RUS] 178 E3
Vjetrenica [BIH] 144 C3
Vlaardingen [NL] 16 C5
Vlacháva [GR] 132 E1
Vlacherná [GR] 132 D3
Vlachiótis [GR] 136 E4
Vlachokerasiá [GR] 136 E3
Vlachovo Březí [CZ] 48 E6
Vladičin Han [SRB] 146 D5
Vlădila [RO] 148 A1
Vladimir [MNE] 128 A1
Vladimirescu [RO] 76 G4
Vladimirovac [SRB] 142 H2
Vladimirovka [RUS] 178 H2
Vladimirovo [BG] 146 F3
Vladimirovo [BG] 148 F2
Vladimirskiy [RUS] 198 H3
Vlagtweed [NL] 16 H3
Vlahovo [BG] 130 E1
Vlaković [HR] 142 A1
V. Laole [SRB] 146 C1
Vlas [BG] 148 F4
Vlasenica [BIH] 142 E4
Vlašim [CZ] 48 G5
Vlaşin [RO] 148 C1
Vlasina Okruglica [SRB] 146 E5
Vlasotince [SRB] 146 D4
Vlieland [NL] 16 E1
Vlissingen [NL] 16 B6
Vlkava [CZ] 48 G3
Vlkolinec [SK] 64 C2
Vllahinë [AL] 128 B5
Vlochós [GR] 132 F2
Vlorë [AL] 128 A5
Vlotho [D] 32 E2
Vlychó [GR] 132 D5
V. Nedelja [SLO] 74 E4
Voćin [HR] 74 H6
Vöcklabruck [A] 62 A5
Voden [BG] 150 B1
Vodice [HR] 112 H6
Vodice [SLO] 74 B4
Vodinci [HR] 142 E1
Voditsa [BG] 148 D3
Vodňany [CZ] 48 F6
Vodnjan [HR] 112 D2
Vodskov [DK] 160 E3
Voergård [DK] 160 E3
Voerså [DK] 160 E3
Vogatsikó [GR] 128 E5
Vogelsdorf [D] 34 F2
Voghera [I] 70 F6
Vognillan [N] 180 H3
Vogogna [I] 70 E3
Vogorno [CH] 70 F3
Vogorno [CH] 70 G2
Vogošća [BIH] 144 D1
Vohburg [D] 60 E2
Vohenstrauss [D] 48 C5
Võhma [EST] 198 C3
Võhma [EST] 198 E2
Vöhringen [D] 60 B4
Void [F] 44 D5
Voikoski [FIN] 178 C2
Voiluoto [FIN] 176 C3
Voïnka [UA] 204 H3
Voiron [F] 68 H4
Voise [F] 42 E4
Võiske [EST] 198 D3
Voitsberg [A] 74 D2
Voix [F] 108 C3
Vojakkala [FIN] 176 G3
Vojany [SK] 64 H3
Vojčice [SK] 64 G3
Vojens [DK] 156 C3
Vojlovica [SRB] 142 H2
Vojmån [S] 190 F4
Vojnić [HR] 112 H1
Vojnik [SLO] 74 D4
Vojtanov [CZ] 48 C3
Vojtjajaure [S] 190 E3
Voknavolok [RUS] 196 G3
Voláda [GR] 140 H2
Vólakas [GR] 130 C2
Volary [CZ] 62 B2
Volda [N] 180 C4
Voldby [DK] 160 F5
Volders [A] 72 D1
Volendam [NL] 16 E4
Volfštejn [CZ] 48 D4
Volgosovo [RUS] 198 G2
Volimes [GR] 136 A2
Volissós [GR] 134 G4
Volkach [D] 46 F4
Völkermarkt [A] 74 C3
Volkhov [RUS] 202 C1
Völklingen [D] 44 G4
Volkmarsen [D] 32 E5
Volkovija [MK] 128 D2
Vollenhove [NL] 16 F3
Volmsjö [S] 190 G5
Volochys'k [UA] 202 B8
Volodarka [UA] 202 D8
Volodymyr-Volyns'kyi [UA] 38 H6
Volokolamsk [RUS] 202 E3
Voloma [RUS] 196 H5
Vólos [GR] 132 H2
Voloshovo [RUS] 198 H2
Volosovo [RUS] 178 G6
Volovo [BG] 148 C2
Volpiano [I] 70 D5
Volterra [I] 114 F1
Volterraio [I] 114 E2
Voltri [I] 110 A3
Voltti [FIN] 186 C2
Volturara Appula [I] 120 F1
Volvic [F] 68 C2
Volyně [CZ] 48 E6
Vonêche [B] 30 D6
Vonesha voda [BG] 148 C4
Vónitsa [GR] 132 D4
Võnnu [EST] 198 F3
Vönöck [H] 74 G1
Voorschoten [NL] 16 C4
Voorst [NL] 16 F5
Vopnafjörður [IS] 192 C2
Vörå / Vöyri [FIN] 186 B2
Vorau [A] 74 E1
Vorbasse [DK] 156 B2
Vorbourg [CH] 58 D4
Vorchdorf [A] 62 B5
Vörden [D] 32 D1
Vordernberg [A] 62 C6
Vorderriss [D] 60 D6
Vordingborg [DK] 156 F4
Vorë [AL] 128 B3
Voreinó [GR] 128 F3
Voreppe [F] 68 H4
Vorey [F] 68 E4
Vøringsfossen [N] 170 D4
Vormsele [S] 190 G4
Vormstad [N] 180 H2
Vormsund [N] 172 C5
Voroneț, Mănăstirea- [RO] 204 D3
Voronkova Niva [RUS] 198 H4
Vorontsovo [RUS] 198 H4
Vorsfelde [D] 32 H2
Võru [EST] 198 F3
Voruća [BIH] 142 D3
Voskopojë [AL] 128 C5
Voss [N] 170 C3
Vossijatskoje [UA] 204 G2
Votice [CZ] 48 G5
Votonósi [GR] 132 D1
Vouillé [F] 54 E4
Voukoliés [GR] 140 B4
Voúla [GR] 136 G1
Vouliagméni [GR] 136 G1
Voulpaix [F] 28 G5
Voúlpi [GR] 132 E3
Voulx [F] 42 G5
Vourkári [GR] 138 C2
Vourvouroú [GR] 130 C5
Voutás [GR] 134 A4
Vouvant [F] 54 C3
Vouvray [F] 54 G2
Vouzela [P] 80 C5
Vouziers [F] 44 C3
Voves [F] 42 E5
Vovoúsa [GR] 132 D1
Vowpa [BY] 24 G5
Voxna [S] 174 C2
Voxtorp [S] 162 D4
Vöylä [FIN] 194 D4
Voynica [BG] 146 E2
Voynitsa [RUS] 196 G3
Voynovo [BG] 148 F1
Vöyri / Vörå [FIN] 186 B2
Voz [HR] 112 F2
Vozarci [MK] 128 F2
Voznesens'k [UA] 204 F2
Vozrozhdenie [RUS] 178 F2
Vrå [DK] 160 E3
Vrå [S] 162 C5
Vrabinec [CZ] 48 F2
Vráble [SK] 64 B4
Vraćevšnica [SRB] 146 B2
Vrachnaíika [GR] 132 F6
Vrådal [N] 164 E2
Vråliosen [N] 164 E2
Vrams Gunnarstorp [S] 156 H1
Vrana [HR] 112 E3
Vrana [HR] 112 G5
Vranduk [BIH] 142 D4
Vranilovci [BG] 148 C4
Vranino [BG] 148 G2
Vranisht [AL] 146 B6
Vranja [HR] 112 E1
Vranjak [HR] 112 F3
Vranje [SRB] 146 D5
Vranjina [MNE] 144 E4
Vranjska Banja [SRB] 146 D5
Vranov nad Dyjí [CZ] 62 E2
Vranov nad Topl'ou [SK] 64 G2
Vransko [SLO] 74 C4
Vrapčići [BIH] 144 C2
Vrapčište [MK] 128 D1
Vrástama [GR] 130 C5
Vratarnica [SRB] 146 E2
Vratkovići [BIH] 144 D3
Vrátna [SK] 50 G6
Vratna, Manastir- [SRB] 146 E1
Vratnica [MK] 146 C6
Vratno [HR] 74 E4
Vratsa [BG] 146 G3
Vravróna [GR] 134 C6
Vražogrnac [SRB] 146 E2
Vrba [SLO] 74 B4
Vrbanja [BIH] 142 C3
Vrbanja [HR] 142 E2
Vrbanje [MNE] 144 D4
Vrbas [MNE] 204 A5
Vrbas [SRB] 76 D6
Vrbaška [BIH] 142 C2
Vrbnica [SRB] 146 B6
Vrbnik [HR] 112 F2
Vrbno pod Pradědem [CZ] 50 D3
Vrboska [HR] 144 A2
Vrbovce [SK] 62 H3
Vrbové [SK] 62 H3
Vrbovec [HR] 74 F5
Vrbovsko [HR] 112 F1
Vrchlabí [CZ] 50 A2
Vrčice [SLO] 74 D6
Vrčin [SRB] 142 G3
Vrdnik [SRB] 142 F2
Vreden [D] 16 G5
Vrees [D] 18 C5
Vrelo [HR] 112 G3
Vrelo Bune [BIH] 144 C2
Vrena [S] 168 C4
Vreoci [SRB] 146 B1
Vresovo [BG] 148 E4
Vresse [B] 44 D1
Vreta Kloster [S] 166 H5
Vretstorp [S] 166 G4
Vrgorac [HR] 144 B2
Vrhnika [SLO] 74 B5
Vrhpolje [BIH] 142 B3
Vriezenveen [NL] 16 G4
Vrigny [F] 44 B3
Vrigstad [S] 162 D3
Vrilisia [GR] 134 C6
Vrilissia [GR] 132 G3
Vrin [CH] 70 G1
Vrlika [HR] 142 A4
Vrnjačka Banja [SRB] 146 C3
Vron [F] 28 D3
Vrontádos [GR] 134 G4
Vrontoú [GR] 128 G6
Vroomshoop [NL] 16 G4
Vrosína [GR] 132 C2
Vrouchás [GR] 140 F4
Vroutek [CZ] 48 E3
Vroville [F] 44 E6
Vrpolje [HR] 112 H6
Vrpolje [HR] 142 D1
Vršac [SRB] 204 B5
Vršani [BIH] 142 E2
Vrsar [HR] 112 D2
Vrtoče [BIH] 142 A3
Vrtojba [SLO] 72 H5
Vrútky [SK] 50 F6
Vrŭv [BG] 146 E1
Vry [F] 44 F4
Vrýses [GR] 140 C4
Vrysoúla [GR] 132 C3
Vrýtaina [GR] 132 H3
Vsetín [CZ] 50 E6
V. Sjulsmark [S] 196 A5
V. Torsås [S] 162 D5
V. Trebeljevo [SLO] 74 C5
V. Trgovišce [HR] 74 E5
Vučitrn [SRB] 146 C5
Vučjavas [SLO] 74 E3
Vučkovci [BIH] 142 D2
Vuckovica [SRB] 146 B2
Vue [F] 54 B1
Vufflens, Château de- [CH] 70 B1
Vught [NL] 16 E6
Vŭglevtsi [BG] 148 C4
Vujanovo [SRB] 146 D4
Vuka [HR] 142 D1
Vukojevica [HR] 142 D1
Vukovar [HR] 142 E1
Vukovec [HR] 74 F5
Vulcănești [MD] 204 E4
Vülchedrum [BG] 146 F2
Vŭlchidol [BG] 148 F2
Vulci [I] 114 G4
Vuobmaved [FIN] 194 C4
Vuojalahti [FIN] 186 H5
Vuojärvi [FIN] 194 D7
Vuokatti [FIN] 196 F5
Vuolenkoski [FIN] 178 B2
Vuolijoki [FIN] 196 E5
Vuolle [FIN] 196 C5
Vuollerim [S] 196 A2
Vuonislahti [FIN] 188 F1
Vuorenkylä [FIN] 186 G6
Vuorenmaa [FIN] 176 E3
Vuorenmaa [FIN] 188 D5
Vuorijärvi [FIN] 186 C5
Vuorilahti [FIN] 186 F2
Vuoriniemi [FIN] 188 F5
Vuostimojärvi [FIN] 194 E7
Vuotner [S] 190 H3
Vuotsino [FIN] 194 E7
Vuotso [FIN] 194 D5
Vuottas [S] 194 A8
Vuottolahti [FIN] 196 E5
Vŭrbitsa [BG] 148 E3
Vŭrshets [BG] 146 F3
Vyalikaryta [BY] 38 G3
Vyartsilya [RUS] 188 G3
Vyaz'ma [RUS] 202 E3
Vybor [RUS] 198 H4
Vyborg [RUS] 178 F3
Vyerkhnyadzvinsk [BY] 202 B4
Vyhonochy [RUS] 202 E5
Vynnyky [UA] 52 H4
Vynohradiv [UA] 204 C3
Vyra [RUS] 178 H6
Vyritsa [RUS] 178 H6
Vyróneia [GR] 130 B2
Vyshgorodok [RUS] 198 G4
Vyshhorod [UA] 202 D7
Vyshniy Volochek [RUS] 202 D2
Vyškov [CZ] 50 C6
Vyskytná [CZ] 48 H5
Vyšná Revúca [SK] 64 C2
Vysock [RUS] 178 E3
Vysoká [CZ] 48 H4
Vysoká u Příbr. [CZ] 48 E5
Vysokaye [BY] 38 F2
Vysoké Mýto [CZ] 50 B4
Vysokoe [RUS] 24 C1
Vysokoye [RUS] 198 G2
Vysoký Chlumec [CZ] 48 F5
Vysoký Hrádek [CZ] 62 C2
Vyšší Brod [CZ] 62 B3
Vyssineá [GR] 128 E5
Vytína [GR] 136 D2

W

Waabs [D] 18 F1
Waalwijk [NL] 16 D6
Wabern [D] 32 E5
Wąbrzeźno [PL] 22 E5
Wachenroth [D] 46 F4
Wąchock [PL] 38 B6
Wachow [D] 34 D2
Wächtersbach [D] 46 D2
Wachtum [D] 18 C6
Wackersdorf [D] 48 C5
Wadebridge [GB] 12 C4
Wädenswil [CH] 58 F5
Wadlew [PL] 36 G5
Wadowice [PL] 50 G4
Wagenfeld [D] 32 E1
Wageningen [NL] 16 E5
Waging [D] 60 G5
Wagrain [A] 72 G1
Wągrowiec [PL] 36 D1
Wahlwies [D] 58 G4
Wahrenholz [D] 32 H1
Waiblingen [D] 58 H1
Waidhaus [D] 48 C5
Waidhofen an der Thaya [A] 62 D3
Waidhofen an der Ybbs [A] 62 C5
Waidring [A] 60 F6
Waischenfeld [D] 46 G4
Wakefield [GB] 10 F4
Walbeck [D] 34 A2
Wałbrzych [PL] 50 B2
Walchensee [D] 60 D6
Walchsee [A] 60 F5
Walcourt [B] 28 H4
Wałcz [PL] 22 A5
Wald [A] 72 E1
Wald [CH] 58 G5
Wald-angelloch [D] 46 C5
Waldbröl [D] 32 C6
Waldburg [D] 60 B5
Waldeck [D] 32 E5
Waldenbuch [D] 58 H1
Waldenburg [D] 46 D6
Waldenburg [D] 48 C1
Waldfischbach [D] 44 H4
Waldhausen [D] 46 D5
Waldheim [D] 34 D6
Waldkirch [D] 58 E3
Waldkirchen [D] 62 A3
Waldkraiburg [D] 60 F4
Waldmünchen [D] 48 C5
Waldowice [PL] 34 H2
Waldsassen [D] 48 C4
Waldshut [D] 58 F4
Waldweiler [D] 44 G3
Walenstadt [CH] 58 H6
Walhalla [D] 48 C6
Wallasey [GB] 10 D4
Walldorf [D] 46 C5
Walldürn [D] 46 D4
Wallenfels [D] 46 H3
Wallern [A] 62 G6
Wallersdorf [D] 60 G3
Wallerstein [D] 60 C2
Wallfahrtskirche [D] 60 C2
Wallingford [GB] 14 D3
Wallsbüll [D] 156 B4
Wals [A] 60 G5
Walsall [GB] 10 E6
Walsrode [D] 18 E6
Waltrop [D] 30 H2
Waltsberg [A] 74 E3
Wambach [D] 32 E6
Wambierzyce [PL] 50 B2
Wanderup [D] 18 E1
Wandlitz [D] 34 E1
Wanfried [D] 32 G5
Wangen [D] 60 B5
Wangenbourg [F] 44 G6
Wangerooge [D] 18 C3
Wangersen [D] 18 E4
Wängi [CH] 58 G5
Wankendorf [D] 18 G2
Wantage [GB] 12 H3
Wanzleben [D] 34 B3
Warburg [D] 32 E4
Wardenburg [D] 18 C5
Ware [GB] 14 E3
Waregem [B] 28 G2
Wareham [GB] 12 G5
Waremme [B] 30 E4
Waren [D] 20 C4
Warendorf [D] 32 D3
Warin [D] 20 A4
Warka [PL] 38 C4
Warlubie [PL] 22 E4
Warmbad Villach [A] 72 H3
Warmensteinach [D] 84 B4
Warminster [GB] 12 G4
Warmsen [D] 32 E2
Warnemünde [D] 20 B3
Warner Bros Park [E] 88 F6
Warnice [PL] 20 F5
Warnice [PL] 34 G1
Warnsveld [NL] 16 F5
Warrenpoint [NIR] 2 G4
Warrington [GB] 10 D4
Warstein [D] 32 D4
Warszawa [PL] 38 B3
Warszkowo [PL] 22 B2
Warta [PL] 36 F4
Warta Bolesławiecka [PL] 36 A6
Wartburg [D] 32 G6
Wartensee [CH] 58 F5
Wartenstein [A] 62 E6
Warth [A] 72 B1
Wartha [D] 32 G6
Warwick [GB] 12 H2
Washington [GB] 8 G6
Wasigenstein, Château de- [F] 44 H4
Wasilków [PL] 24 E5
Wąsosz [PL] 24 D4
Wąsosz [PL] 36 C5
Wasselonne [F] 44 G6
Wassen [CH] 70 F1
Wassenaar [NL] 16 C4
Wassenberg [D] 30 F4
Wasseralfingen [D] 60 C2
Wasserbillig [L] 44 F2
Wasserburg [D] 60 F4
Wasserfall Groppenstn. [A] 72 G2
Wasserkuppe [D] 46 E2
Wasserleonberg [A] 72 H3
Wasserschloss [D] 32 C3
Wasserschloss [D] 34 D4
Wassertrüdingen [D] 46 F6
Wassy [F] 44 C5
Wastl am Wald [A] 62 D5
Wasungen [D] 46 F1
Waterford / Port Lairge [IRL] 4 E5
Watergrasshill [IRL] 4 D5
Waterloo [B] 30 C4
Waterlooville [GB] 12 H5
Waterville / An Coireán [IRL] 4 A4
Watford [GB] 14 E4
Watten [F] 14 H6
Wattens [A] 72 D1
Watton [GB] 14 G2
Wattwil [CH] 58 G5
Watzelsdorf [A] 62 E3
Waulsort [B] 30 D6
Waver (Wavre) [B] 30 D4
Wavre (Waver) [B] 30 D4
Waxenberg [A] 62 B3
Waxweiler [D] 44 F1
Ważne Młyny [PL] 36 G6
Wda [PL] 22 D4
Wdzydze Kiszewskie [PL] 22 D3
Węchadłów [PL] 52 B2
Wechselburg [D] 34 D6
Weddelsborg [DK] 156 C3
Wedel [D] 18 F4
Wedemark [D] 32 F1
Weener [D] 18 B5
Weert [NL] 30 E3
Weesen [CH] 58 G6
Weeze [D] 30 F2
Wegberg [D] 30 F3
Wegeleben [D] 34 A4
Wegenstedt [D] 34 B2
Weggis [CH] 58 F6
Węgliniec [PL] 34 H6
Węgorzewo [PL] 24 C2
Węgorzyno [PL] 20 G5
Węgrów [PL] 38 D2
Węgrzynice [PL] 34 H3
Wegscheid [D] 62 A3
Wehr [D] 30 H6
Wehr [D] 58 E4
Weichselboden [A] 62 D6
Weichshofen [D] 60 F3
Weida [D] 48 C1
Weiden [D] 48 C4
Weidenberg [D] 46 H4
Weidensees [D] 46 H4
Weidenstetten [D] 60 B3
Weigetschlag [A] 62 B3
Weikersheim [D] 46 E5
Weil [D] 58 G1
Weilar [D] 46 F1
Weilburg [D] 46 C2
Weilheim [D] 60 D5
Weilmünster [D] 46 C2
Weimar [D] 32 D6
Weimar [D] 34 A6
Weinfelden [CH] 58 G4
Weingarten [D] 60 B5
Weinheim [D] 46 C4
Weinsberg [D] 46 D5
Weintor [D] 46 B5
Weirenstein [A] 72 F2
Weismain [D] 46 G3
Weissbriach [A] 72 G3
Weissenbach [A] 60 C6
Weissenbach [A] 72 H3
Weissenbach / Riobianco [I] 72 D2
Weissenberg [D] 34 G6
Weissenburg [D] 46 G6
Weissenegg [A] 74 D2
Weissenfels [D] 34 C6
Weissenhorn [D] 60 B3
Weissenkirchen [A] 62 D4
Weissensee [D] 32 H5
Weissenstadt [D] 48 B3
Weissenstein [D] 46 G4
Weisskirchen [A] 74 C2
Weisstannen [CH] 58 H6
Weisswasser [D] 34 G5
Weitensfeld [A] 74 B3
Weitersfelden [A] 62 C3
Weitra [A] 62 C3
Weiz [A] 74 D2
Wejherowo [PL] 22 D2
Welden [D] 60 C3
Wełdkowo [PL] 22 A3
Well [NL] 30 F2
Wellaune [D] 34 D5
Welle [D] 18 F5
Wellin [B] 30 D6
Wellingborough [GB] 14 E2
Wellington [GB] 12 F4
Wells [GB] 12 F4
Wells-next-the-Sea [GB] 14 G1
Wels [A] 62 B4
Welsberg / Monguelfo [I] 72 E3
Welschnofen / Nova Levante [I] 72 D3
Welshpool [GB] 10 C5
Weltenburg [D] 60 E2
Welwyn Garden City [GB] 14 E3
Welzheim [D] 60 B2
Wemding [D] 60 D2
Wemperhaardt [L] 30 F6
Wenddorf [D] 34 B2
Wendlingen [D] 58 H1
Wenecja [PL] 36 D1
Wengen [CH] 70 E1
Wennigsen [D] 32 F2
Wenns [A] 72 C1
Wépion [B] 30 D5
Weppersdorf [A] 62 F6
Werben [D] 34 C1
Werbomont [B] 30 E5
Werdau [D] 48 C2
Werder [D] 34 D2
Werdohl [D] 32 C5
Werfen [A] 60 G6
Werl [D] 32 C4
Werlte [D] 18 B6
Wermelskirchen [D] 30 H4
Wernberg [D] 48 C5
Werne [D] 32 C4
Werneck [D] 46 E3
Werneuchen [D] 34 F2
Wernigerode [D] 32 H4
Wertach [D] 60 C5
Wertheim [D] 46 D4
Werther [D] 32 D3
Wertingen [D] 60 C3
Wesel [D] 30 G2
Wesenberg [D] 20 C5
Wesendorf [D] 32 H1
Wesoła [PL] 52 C3
Wesselburen [D] 18 E2
Wesseling [D] 30 G4
Wessobrunn [D] 60 D5
West Bridgford [GB] 10 F5
West Bromwich [GB] 10 E6
Westbury [GB] 12 G4
Westende-Bad [B] 28 F1
Westendorf [A] 60 F6
Westenholz [D] 18 F6
Westensee [D] 18 F2
Westerhever [D] 18 D2
Westerholt [D] 18 B3
Westerland [D] 156 A4
Westerlo [B] 30 D3
Westerstede [D] 18 C4
Westkapelle [NL] 16 B6
Weston-super-Mare [GB] 12 F3
Westport [IRL] 2 C4
West Sandwick [GB] 6 H3
West-Terschelling [NL] 16 E1
Wetherby [GB] 10 F3
Wetlina [PL] 52 E6
Wetter [D] 30 H3
Wetter [D] 32 D6
Wetteren [B] 28 H2
Wettringen [D] 16 H5
Wetzikon [CH] 58 G5
Wetzlar [D] 46 C1
Wexford / Loch Garman [IRL] 4 F5
Weyer [A] 74 D1
Weyerburg [A] 72 F1
Weyer-Markt [A] 62 C5
Weyhausen [D] 32 G1
Weymouth [GB] 12 F5
Weyregg [A] 60 H5
Whitby [GB] 10 G2
Whitchurch [GB] 10 D5
Whitegate [IRL] 4 D5
Whitehead [NIR] 2 H3
Whithorn [GB] 8 C5
Whiting Bay [GB] 8 C3
Whitley Bay [GB] 8 G6
Whitstable [GB] 14 F5
Wiartel [PL] 24 C4
Wiązownica [PL] 52 F3
Wiblingen [D] 60 B3
Wicie [PL] 22 A2
Wicimice [PL] 20 G4
Wick [GB] 6 F3
Wickham Market [GB] 14 G3
Wicklow [IRL] 4 G4
Wicko [PL] 22 C1
Widawa [PL] 36 C6
Widawa [PL] 36 F5
Widdern [D] 46 D5
Widnes [GB] 10 D4
Widoma [PL] 52 A3
Widuchowa [PL] 20 E6
Więcbork [PL] 22 C5
Wiechowice [PL] 50 E4
Wiedenbrück [D] 32 D3
Wiefelstede [D] 18 C5
Wiehe [D] 34 B5
Wiehler Tropfsteinhöle [D] 30 H4
Wiek [D] 20 D1
Większyce [PL] 50 E3
Wielbark [PL] 22 H5
Wiele [PL] 22 D4
Wieleń [PL] 36 B1
Wielgie [PL] 36 F5
Wielgie [PL] 38 C6
Wielichowo [PL] 36 B3
Wieliczka [PL] 52 A4
Wieliczki [PL] 24 D3
Wielka Piaśnica [PL] 22 D1
Wielogłowy [PL] 52 B5
Wielogóra [PL] 38 C5
Wielowieś [PL] 50 F2
Wieluń [PL] 36 F6
Wien [A] 62 F4
Wiener Neustadt [A] 62 F5
Wienhausen [D] 32 G1
Wieniawa [PL] 38 B5
Wiepke [D] 34 B2
Wierden [NL] 16 G4
Wieruszów [PL] 36 E6
Wierzbica [PL] 38 B5
Wierzbice [PL] 50 C1
Wierzbowo [PL] 22 G5
Wierzchowo [PL] 22 B4
Wierzchucin Krolewski [PL] 22 C5
Wierzchucino [PL] 22 D1
Wies [D] 60 D5
Wiesau [D] 48 C4
Wiesbaden [D] 46 B3
Wiesberg [A] 72 B1
Wieselburg [A] 62 D4
Wiesen [CH] 70 H1
Wiesenburg [D] 34 C3
Wiesentheid [D] 46 F4
Wieskirche [D] 60 D5
Wiesloch [D] 46 C5
Wiesmath [A] 62 F6
Wiesmoor [D] 18 C4
Wietze [D] 32 G1
Wietzendorf [D] 18 F6
Wigan [GB] 10 D4
Wigston [GB] 10 F6
Wigton [GB] 8 E6
Wigtown [GB] 8 C5
Wijhe [NL] 16 F4
Wikingerburg [D] 44 F2
Wil [CH] 58 G5
Wilanów [PL] 38 B3
Wilczków [PL] 36 C6
Wilczkowo [PL] 22 G3
Wilczyska [PL] 52 C5
Wildalpen [A] 62 C6
Wildbad [D] 58 G1
Wildberg [D] 58 G1
Wildeck [D] 46 D6
Wildenburg [D] 44 G2

Wildenburg [D] 46 D4
Wildenrath [D] 30 F4
Wildenstein [CH] 58 E4
Wildenstein [D] 58 G3
Wildenstein Wasserfall [A] 74 C3
Wildeshausen [D] 18 D6
Wildhaus [CH] 58 H5
Wildkirchli [CH] 58 H5
Wildon [A] 74 D3
Wilfersdorf [A] 62 F3
Wilga [PL] 38 C4
Wilhelmsburg [A] 62 D5
Wilhelmsh [D] 32 F5
Wilhelmshaven [D] 18 C4
Wilhelmsthal [D] 32 F5
Wilhering [A] 62 B4
Wilków [PL] 38 B4
Wilków [PL] 50 H2
Wilkowo [PL] 34 H3
Willebroek [B] 30 C3
Willemstad [NL] 16 C6
Willingen [D] 32 D5
Willisau [CH] 58 E5
Willsbach [D] 46 D6
Wilnsdorf [D] 32 C6
Wilsin [NL] 16 D4
Wilster [D] 18 E3
Wilsum [D] 16 G4
Wilton [GB] 12 G4
Wiltz [L] 44 E2
Wimborne Minster [GB] 12 G5
Wimereux [F] 14 G6
Wincanton [GB] 12 G4
Winchester [GB] 12 H4
Windeck [D] 32 C6
Windermere [GB] 10 D2
Windisch [D] 48 C4
Windischgarsten [A] 62 B6
Windsbach [D] 46 G5
Wingen-sur-Moder [F] 44 G5
Winklern [A] 72 G2
Winnenden [D] 58 H1
Winnica [PL] 38 B2
Winnigstedt [D] 32 H3
Winnweiler [D] 46 B4
Winschoten [NL] 16 H2
Winsen [D] 18 G5
Winsen [D] 32 G1
Wińsko [PL] 36 C5
Winsum [NL] 16 G2
Winterberg [D] 32 D5
Winterfeld [D] 34 B1
Wintermoor [D] 18 F5
Winterstein [D] 32 G6
Winterswijk [NL] 16 G5
Winterthur [CH] 58 G4
Wipperfürth [D] 30 H4
Wippra [D] 34 A4
Wiry [PL] 50 C1
Wisbech [GB] 14 F2
Wischhafen [D] 18 E3
Wiselka [PL] 20 F3
Wiskitki [PL] 38 A3
Wisła [PL] 50 F5
Wiślica [PL] 52 B3
Wismar [D] 20 A3
Wiśniewo Ełckie [PL] 24 D4
Wiśniowa [PL] 52 A4
Wiśniowa [PL] 52 D4
Wissant [F] 14 G6
Wissembourg [F] 46 B6
Wissen [D] 32 C6
Wisznice [PL] 38 F4
Witham [GB] 14 F4
Withernsea [GB] 10 H4
Witków [PL] 52 H2
Witkowice [PL] 50 G1
Witkowo [PL] 36 E2
Witney [GB] 12 H3
Witnica [PL] 34 G1
Witnica [PL] 34 G2
Witostowice [PL] 50 C2
Witowo [PL] 36 F2
Wittdün [D] 18 D1
Witten [D] 30 H3
Wittenberge [D] 20 A6
Wittenborn [D] 18 G3
Wittenburg [D] 18 H4
Wittgenstein [D] 46 B4
Wittichenau [D] 34 F5
Wittingen [D] 32 H1
Wittislingen [D] 60 C3
Wittlich [D] 44 G2
Wittmund [D] 18 C4
Wittstock [D] 20 C5
Witzenhausen [D] 32 F5
Wiżajny [PL] 24 E2
Wizna [PL] 24 D5
Władysławowo [PL] 22 D1
Wleń [PL] 50 A1
Włocławek [PL] 36 G2
Włodawa [PL] 38 F4
Włoszczowa [PL] 50 H1
Włoszczowice [PL] 52 B2
Wodzisław [PL] 52 B2
Wodzisław Śląski [PL] 50 F4
Woerden [NL] 16 D5
Woerth [F] 44 H5
Woesten [B] 28 F2
Wohlen [CH] 58 F5
Wohra [D] 32 E6
Woijtowice [PL] 50 D2
Wojcieszków [PL] 38 D4
Wojcieszów [PL] 50 B1
Wójcin [PL] 36 E2
Wojnicz [PL] 52 C4
Wojsławice [PL] 38 F6
Wojtokiemie [PL] 24 E2
Woking [GB] 14 D4
Wola Idzikowska [PL] 38 F6
Wola Klasztorna [PL] 38 D5
Wola Obszańska [PL] 52 F2
Wola Rakowa [PL] 36 G4
Wola Uhruska [PL] 38 G5
Wola Wierzbowska [PL] 22 H6
Wolbórz [PL] 36 H5
Wolbrom [PL] 50 H3
Wołczyn [PL] 50 E1
Woldegk [D] 20 D5
Wolenice [PL] 36 D4
Wolfach [D] 58 F2
Wolfegg [D] 60 B5
Wolfen [D] 34 C4
Wolfenbüttel [D] 32 H3
Wolfhagen [D] 32 E5
Wolframs-Eschenbach [D] 46 F6
Wolfratshausen [D] 60 E5
Wolfsberg [A] 74 C3
Wolfsburg [D] 32 H2
Wolfstein [D] 44 H3
Wolgast [D] 20 E3
Wolhusen [CH] 58 E6
Wolibórz [PL] 50 C2
Wolica [PL] 52 B2
Wolin [PL] 20 F4
Wolin [PL] 20 F3
Wólka [PL] 52 A1
Wólka Dobryńska [PL] 38 F3
Wólka Łabuńska [PL] 52 G2
Wolkenstein [D] 48 D2
Wolkenstein in Gröden / Selva di Val Gardena [I] 72 E3
Wolkersdorf [A] 62 F4
Wollenberg [D] 34 F1
Wöllersdorf [A] 62 E5
Wollin [D] 34 C3
Wolmirstedt [D] 34 B3
Wolnzach [D] 60 E3
Wołomin [PL] 38 C2
Wołosate [PL] 52 F6
Wołow [PL] 36 C5
Wolsingham [GB] 10 F1
Wolsztyn [PL] 36 B3
Wolvega [NL] 16 F3
Wolverhampton [GB] 10 D6
Woodbridge [GB] 14 G3
Woodford [IRL] 2 C6
Wooler [GB] 8 F4
Wootton Bassett [GB] 12 G3
Worb [CH] 58 D6
Worbis [D] 32 G5
Worcester [GB] 12 G2
Worden-Sankt Andra [A] 62 F4
Wörgl [A] 60 F6
Workington [GB] 8 D6
Worksop [GB] 10 F5
Workum [NL] 16 E2
Wörlitz [D] 34 C4
Wormerveer [NL] 16 D4
Wormhout [F] 14 H6
Worms [D] 46 C4
Wörnitz [D] 46 F5
Worpswede [D] 18 E5
Wörrstadt [D] 46 B3
Wörth [A] 72 G1
Wörth [D] 46 B6
Wörth [D] 46 D4
Wörth [D] 60 F2
Wörth [D] 60 F3
Worthing [GB] 14 D5
Wozławki [PL] 22 H3
Woźniki [PL] 50 G2
Wożuczyn [PL] 52 G2
Wragby [GB] 10 G5
Wręczyca Wielka [PL] 50 F1
Wredenhagen [D] 20 C5
Wrexham [GB] 10 D5
Wriezen [D] 34 F2
Wróblew [PL] 36 F5
Wroblewo [PL] 36 B2
Wrocki [PL] 22 F5
Wrocław [PL] 36 C6
Wroniniec [PL] 36 B4
Wronki [PL] 24 D3
Wronki [PL] 36 B2
Wrząca Wielka [PL] 36 F3
Września [PL] 36 D3
Wschowa [PL] 36 B4
Wulfen [D] 30 H2
Wulkau [D] 34 C1
Wullersdorf [A] 62 E3
Wullowitz [A] 62 C3
Wünnenberg [D] 32 D4
Wunsiedel [D] 48 B3
Wunstorf [D] 32 F2
Wuppertal [D] 30 H3
Würgau [D] 46 G4
Wurmlinger Kapelle [D] 58 G2
Wurzbach [D] 46 H2
Würzbrunnen [CH] 58 E6
Würzburg [D] 46 E4
Wurzen [D] 34 D5
Wust [D] 34 C2
Wusterhausen [D] 34 D1
Wüstermarke [D] 34 E4
Wustrow [D] 20 C2
Wustrow [D] 20 C5
Wuustwezel [B] 30 D2
Wybcz [PL] 22 D6
Wydminy [PL] 24 D3
Wygoda [PL] 52 D4
Wyk [D] 156 A5
Wymondham [GB] 14 G2
Wyrzysk [PL] 22 C6
Wyśmierzyce [PL] 38 B4
Wysoka [PL] 22 B6
Wysokie [PL] 52 F1
Wysokie Mazowieckie [PL] 24 D6
Wysowa [PL] 52 C5
Wyszanów [PL] 36 E5
Wyszki [PL] 24 E6
Wyszków [PL] 38 C2
Wyszogród [PL] 38 A2
Wyszyna [PL] 36 F3

X

Xàbia [E] 104 F1
Xàbia / Jávea [E] 104 F1
Xabier / Javier [E] 84 C4
Xanten [D] 30 G2
Xánthi [GR] 130 E2
Xanthos [TR] 154 F3
Xàtiva [E] 98 E6
Xeraco [E] 98 F6
Xeresa [E] 98 E6
Xert [E] 98 G2
Xerta [E] 92 A5
Xertigny [F] 58 C2
Xesta, Puerto de la- [E] 78 E2
Xhoffraix [B] 30 F5
Xilopároiko [GR] 132 E2
Xinzo de Limia / Ginzo de Limia [E] 78 C6
Xirokámpi [GR] 136 E4
Xirókampos [GR] 154 A2
Xivert, Castell de- [E] 98 G3
Xixón / Gijón [E] 83 B2
Xixona / Jijona [E] 104 E2
Xodos / Chodos [E] 98 F2
Xove [E] 78 E1
Xubia [E] 78 D1
Xunqueira de Ambia [E] 78 D5
Xunqueira de Espadanedo [E] 78 D5
Xylaganí [GR] 130 F3
Xylofagou [CY] 154 G5
Xylókastro [GR] 132 H6
Xylópoli [GR] 130 B3
Xyniás [GR] 132 G3
Xynó Neró [GR] 128 E4

Y

Yablanitsa [BG] 148 A4
Yablanovo [BG] 148 D3
Yablonovka [RUS] 178 H2
Yacimiento de Botorrita [E] 90 E4
Yacimientos de Icnitas [E] 90 C2
Yağcılar [TR] 152 E1
Yağcılı [TR] 152 D2
Yağlılar [TR] 152 C1
Yagoda [BG] 148 C5
Yahotyn [UA] 202 E7
Yaiza [E] 100 E6
Yakimovo [BG] 146 F2
Yakkima [RUS] 188 G4
Yakoruda [BG] 146 G6
Yalakdere [TR] 150 F3
Yalıkavak [TR] 154 B1
Yalıköy [TR] 150 D2
Yalova [TR] 150 F3
Yalta [UA] 204 H4
Yaman [TR] 152 G4
Yambol [BG] 148 E5
Yamm [RUS] 198 G2
Yampil' [UA] 202 B8
Yampil' [UA] 202 E6
Yampil' [UA] 204 E2
Yancıklar [TR] 150 C2
Yanguas [E] 90 C2
Yanjukalns [LV] 198 F5
Yantarnyy [RUS] 22 G1
Yaraş [TR] 154 D1
Yarbasan [TR] 152 F2
Yarema [BG] 146 F5
Yarımca [TR] 150 G3
Yariş [TR] 152 G1
Yarm [GB] 10 F2
Yarmolyntsi [UA] 204 D2
Yarmouth [GB] 12 H5
Yartsevo [RUS] 202 D4
Yasen [BG] 148 A3
Yasna Polyana [BG] 148 F5
Yassıören [TR] 150 E2
Yassiören [TR] 152 F1
Yatağan [TR] 152 E6
Yavorets [BG] 148 B4
Yavoriv [UA] 52 G3
Yaylabayır [TR] 152 E2
Yayladamı [TR] 152 C2
Yaylaköy [TR] 152 H6
Yazhelbitsy [RUS] 202 C2
Yazıkent [TR] 152 E5
Yazıköy [TR] 154 B3
Yazıköy [TR] 152 H5
Yazır [TR] 152 G6
Yazır [TR] 154 H2
Yazırköy [TR] 152 F5
Ybbs an der Donau [A] 62 D4
Ybbsitz [A] 62 C5
Ychoux [F] 66 B4
Yderby [DK] 156 F1
Ýdra [GR] 136 G3
Ydrefors [S] 162 F2
Yecla [E] 104 D1
Yecla de Yeltes [E] 80 F6
Yeleğen [TR] 152 F4
Yelizavetino [RUS] 178 G6
Yel'na [RUS] 202 D4
Yel'nya [RUS] 202 D4
Yelo [E] 90 B4
Yel'tsy [RUS] 202 D3
Yelverton [GB] 12 D5
Yemel'yanovka [RUS] 196 G5
Yemikaraağac [TR] 150 E4
Yemişendere [TR] 152 F6
Yemişli [TR] 152 F2
Yenibogaziçi (Ay. Seryios) [CY] 154 G5
Yenice [TR] 130 H3
Yenice [TR] 150 C1
Yenice [TR] 150 C5
Yenice [TR] 150 D4
Yenice [TR] 152 F5
Yenice [TR] 152 H2
Yenicekent [TR] 152 F4
Yeniçiftlik [TR] 150 D3
Yenicöy [TR] 152 D3
Yenidoğan [TR] 152 D5
Yenierenköy (Aigialoúsa) [CY] 154 G4
Yenifoça [TR] 152 C3
Yeni Karpuzlu [TR] 130 H3
Yeniköy [TR] 130 H6
Yeniköy [TR] 150 C3
Yenikoy [TR] 150 D6
Yeniköy [TR] 150 E2
Yeniköy [TR] 150 F6
Yeniköy [TR] 150 F4
Yeniköy [TR] 150 G3
Yeniköy [TR] 152 E3
Yeniköy [TR] 152 F2
Yeniköy [TR] 154 G3
Yenipazar [TR] 150 H4
Yenipazar [TR] 152 E5
Yenişakran [TR] 152 C3
Yenisarıbey [TR] 150 D5
Yenişehir [TR] 150 G4
Yenişehir [TR] 152 F3
Yenişehir [TR] 152 F3
Yenne [F] 68 H3
Yeovil [GB] 12 F4
Yerkesik [TR] 154 D1
Yershi [RUS] 202 E4
Yerville [F] 26 H3
Yesa / Esa [E] 84 C4
Yeşilçay / Ağva [TR] 150 G2
Yeşilköy [TR] 150 E3
Yesilköy [TR] 152 F2
Yesılköy [TR] 154 G3
Yeşiller [TR] 150 F5
Yeşilova [TR] 150 D5
Yeşilova [TR] 152 H5
Yeşilvadi [TR] 150 F2
Yeşilyurt [TR] 152 F4
Yeşilyurt [TR] 154 D1
Yeşilyuva [TR] 152 G5
Yeste [E] 102 H1
Yevpatoria [UA] 204 H4
Yezyaryshcha [BY] 202 C4
Yiğitler [TR] 152 B1
Yılmazköy (Skylloura) [CY] 154 F5
Yılmazlı [TR] 154 G1
Ylakiai [LT] 198 C6
Ylä-Kuona [FIN] 188 F4
Ylämaa [FIN] 178 E3
Ylämylly [FIN] 188 F2
Yläne [FIN] 176 D3
Ylihärmä [FIN] 186 C2
Yli-Ii [FIN] 196 D3
Yli-Kärppä [FIN] 196 D2
Ylikiiminki [FIN] 196 D4
Ylikiä [FIN] 176 D5
Ylikylä [FIN] 186 B4
Ylikylä [FIN] 186 C2
Ylikylä [FIN] 186 E1
Yli-Lesti [FIN] 186 E1
Yli-Ii [FIN] 196 D3
Ylimarkku / Övermark [FIN] 186 B4
Yli-Nampa [FIN] 194 D7
Yli-Olhava [FIN] 196 D3
Ylistaro [FIN] 186 C3
Ylitornio / Övertorneå [FIN] 194 B8
Ylivieska [FIN] 196 D5
Yläsjärvi [FIN] 194 C6
Ylöjärvi [FIN] 176 F1
Ylönkylä [FIN] 176 E5
Yngsjö [S] 158 D2
Yoğuntas [TR] 150 B1
Yolağzı [TR] 130 H4
Yolüstü [TR] 152 F5
Yordankino [BG] 146 G4
York [GB] 10 F3
Youghal [IRL] 4 D5
Ypéria [GR] 132 G2
Yport [F] 26 G2
Yppäri [FIN] 196 C5
Ypres (Ieper) [B] 28 F2
Ýpso [GR] 132 B2
Ypsoús [GR] 136 D2
Yquem, Château- [F] 66 D4
Yrittäperä [FIN] 196 E3
Yrkje [N] 164 B2
Yrouerre [F] 56 F2
Yset [N] 182 B4
Yssandon, Puy d'- [F] 66 G3
Yssingeaux [F] 68 E4
Ystad [S] 158 D3
Ystebrød [N] 164 B4
Ytre Arna [N] 170 B3
Ytre Enebakk [N] 166 B1
Ytre Kjæs [N] 194 C2
Ytre Snillfjord [N] 180 G1
Ytterån [S] 182 G2
Ytterås [N] 182 C1
Ytterätrask [S] 196 A5
Ytterberg [S] 182 G5
Ytterboda [S] 172 H4
Ytterby [S] 160 G1
Ytterhogdal [S] 182 H5
Ytterjeppo [FIN] 186 C1
Yttermalung [S] 172 F4
Ytterselö [S] 168 C3
Ytterturingen [S] 182 H4
Yttervik [S] 190 E3
Yukarıkızılca [TR] 152 D4
Yukhavichy [BY] 198 H6
Yukhnov [RUS] 202 E4
Yuminda [EST] 198 E1
Yuncos [E] 96 F1
Yundola [BG] 146 G6
Yunquera [E] 102 B4
Yunquera de Henares [E] 88 H5
Yuntdağ [TR] 152 C3
Yunuseli [TR] 150 F4
Yuratsishki [BY] 200 H6
Yüreğil [TR] 152 E2
Yürücekler [TR] 150 F5
Yuste, Monasterio de- [E] 88 B5
Yusufça [TR] 152 G6
Yuvacık [TR] 154 D2
Yuzhnoukrains'k [UA] 204 F2
Yverdon-les-Bains [CH] 58 C6
Yvetot [F] 26 H3
Yvoir [B] 30 D5
Yvoire [F] 70 B2
Yxnerum [S] 168 B6

Z

Zaandam [NL] 16 D4
Zabalats' [BY] 24 H3
Žabalj [SRB] 142 G1
Zăbalt [RO] 76 H5
Zabar [H] 64 E4
Žabari [SRB] 146 C1
Żabice [PL] 36 B5
Zabierzów [PL] 50 H3
Zabki [PL] 38 B3
Ząbkowice Śląskie [PL] 50 C2
Zablaće [HR] 112 H6
Žabljak [MNE] 144 E2
Zabłudów [PL] 24 F6
Žabno [PL] 52 C3
Zabok [HR] 74 E5
Zabolottia [UA] 38 G4
Zabór [PL] 36 A4
Zăbrani [RO] 76 H5
Zábřeh [CZ] 50 C4
Zabrodzie [PL] 38 C2
Zabrze [PL] 50 F3
Zabrzeż [PL] 52 B5
Zabzun [AL] 128 C3
Zacháro [GR] 136 C3
Zachloroú [GR] 132 G6
Zadar [HR] 112 G5
Zadni Chodov [CZ] 48 C4
Zadvarje [HR] 144 A2
Zadzyezhzha [BY] 198 H6
Zafferana Etnea [I] 126 G3
Zafirovo [BG] 148 E1
Zafra [E] 94 G3
Žaga [SLO] 72 H4
Żagań [PL] 34 H5
Žagare [LT] 198 D6
Zagkliveri [GR] 130 B4
Zaglav [HR] 112 F5
Zaglavak [SRB] 146 A2
Zagorá [GR] 132 H2
Zagorje [HR] 112 G1
Zagorje [SLO] 74 C5
Zagórów [PL] 36 E3
Zagórz [PL] 52 E5
Zagórzany [PL] 52 C4
Zagoska [RUS] 198 H3
Zagreb [HR] 74 E6
Žagubica [SRB] 146 D1
Zagvozd [HR] 144 B2
Zagwiździe [PL] 50 E1
Zagyvapálfalva [H] 64 D5
Zahara [E] 100 H3
Zahara de los Atunes [E] 100 G5
Zahinos [E] 94 F3
Zahna [D] 34 D4
Zahody [RUS] 198 G3
Záhoří [CZ] 48 F6
Záhorská Ves [SK] 62 G4
Zahrádky [CZ] 48 G2
Zaiceva [LV] 198 G4
Zaidin [E] 90 G4
Zaisenhausen [D] 46 C5
Zajas [MK] 128 D2
Zaječar [SRB] 146 E2
Zaječar [SRB] 204 C6
Zákas [GR] 128 E6
Zakliczyn [PL] 52 C4
Zaklików [PL] 52 E1
Zakopane [PL] 50 H6
Zakroczym [PL] 38 B2
Zakrós [GR] 140 H5
Zakrós [GR] 140 H5
Zakrzewo [PL] 36 F1
Zakrzówek [PL] 38 C5
Zákupy [CZ] 48 G2
Zákynthos [GR] 136 B2
Zalaapáti [H] 74 G3
Zalabaksa [H] 74 F3
Zalabér [H] 74 G2
Zalaegerszeg [H] 74 G3
Zalakaros [H] 74 G3
Zalakomár [H] 74 G4
Zalakusáni [H] 74 G3
Zalalövő [H] 74 F3
Zalamea de la Serena [E] 96 B4
Zalamea la Real [E] 94 F5
Zalaszabar [H] 74 G3
Zalaszántó [H] 74 G3
Zalaszentbalázs [H] 74 G3
Zalaszentgrót [H] 74 G2
Zalău [RO] 204 C4
Žalec [SLO] 74 D4
Zalewo [PL] 22 F4
Załęże [PL] 22 H5
Zalishchyky [UA] 204 D2
Zalivnoye [RUS] 200 D5
Zalla [E] 82 G4
Zaltbommel [NL] 16 E6
Załuski [PL] 38 A2
Załuż [PL] 52 E5
Zalužnica [HR] 112 G3
Zamárdi [H] 76 A3
Zamarte [PL] 22 C4
Žamberk [CZ] 50 B4
Zambrana [E] 82 G5
Zambrów [PL] 24 D6
Zambujal [P] 86 B6
Zambujeira do Mar [P] 94 B4
Zamora [E] 80 H5
Zamość [PL] 24 C6
Zamość [PL] 24 C6
Zamość [PL] 52 F1
Zamostne [PL] 22 D2
Zandhoven [B] 30 D3
Zandvoort [NL] 16 D4
Zangoza / Sangüesa [E] 84 C5
Zaniemyśl [PL] 36 D3
Zánka [H] 74 H3
Zan'kovo [RUS] 198 G4
Zante [LV] 198 C5
Zaorejas [E] 90 B5
Zaostrog [HR] 144 B3
Zaostrov'ye [RUS] 178 H2
Zaozernoye [RUS] 24 C2
Zapadnaja Dvina [RUS] 202 D3
Zapadnaya Dvina [RUS] 202 C3
Zapałów [PL] 52 F3
Zapfendorf [D] 46 G3
Zaplyus'ye [RUS] 198 H2
Zapole [PL] 36 F5
Zapolyarnyy [RUS] 194 F3
Zapol'ye [RUS] 198 H2
Zaporizhzhia [UA] 204 H2
Zaporozhskoye [RUS] 178 H3
Záppeio [GR] 132 G2
Zapponeta [I] 120 H1
Zaprešić [HR] 74 E5
Zaprudy [BY] 38 H2
Zapyškis [LT] 200 F5
Zapytiv [UA] 52 H3
Zaragoza [E] 90 E4
Zárakes [GR] 134 D5
Zărand [RO] 76 H4
Zarańsko [PL] 20 H5
Zarasai [LT] 200 H4
Zarautz [E] 84 A2
Zarcilla de los Ramons [E] 104 B3
Zaręby-Warchoły [PL] 38 D1
Zarech'e [RUS] 198 H4
Zarechnyy [RUS] 196 G4
Zarenthien [D] 18 H6
Żarki [PL] 50 G2
Zárkos [GR] 132 F2
Zărnești [RO] 204 D5
Žarnovica [SK] 64 B3
Żarnów [PL] 38 A6
Żarnowiec [PL] 50 H2
Zarós [GR] 140 E5
Žarošice [CZ] 62 G2
Żarów [PL] 50 B1
Zarrentin [D] 18 H4
Żarska Wieś [PL] 34 H6
Zarszyn [PL] 52 E5
Żary [PL] 34 H5
Zarza-Capilla [E] 96 C4
Zarza de Alange [E] 94 H2
Zarzadilla de Totana [E] 104 B3
Zarza la Mayor [E] 86 G4
Zarzecze [PL] 38 D5
Zarzecze [PL] 52 E2
Zás [E] 78 B2
Zasa [LV] 198 F6
Zasieki [PL] 34 G4
Žatec [CZ] 48 E3
Zatom [PL] 20 H6
Zator [PL] 50 G4
Zaube [LV] 198 E5
Zauchwitz [D] 34 D3
Zavala [BIH] 144 C3
Zavet [BG] 148 D2
Zavidovići [BIH] 142 D3
Zavlaka [SRB] 142 F3
Zavoya [BG] 130 F2
Zavrc [SLO] 74 E4
Zawada [PL] 36 A4
Zawada [PL] 50 E2
Zawady [PL] 50 F1
Zawadzkie [PL] 50 F2
Zawichost [PL] 52 D1
Zawidów [PL] 48 G1
Zawiercie [PL] 50 G2
Zawoja [PL] 50 H5
Zawonia [PL] 36 D5
Zawroty [PL] 22 G4
Zayan'e [RUS] 198 G2
Zayan'ye [RUS] 198 G2
Zaytsevo [RUS] 178 F2
Žažina [HR] 142 A1
Zázriva [SK] 50 G6
Zbąszyń [PL] 36 B3
Zbąszynek [PL] 36 A3
Zblewo [PL] 22 D4
Zboj [SK] 52 F6
Zbojno [PL] 22 F6
Zborište [BIH] 112 H2
Zborov [SK] 52 D5
Zborowice [PL] 52 C4
Zbrachlin [PL] 22 D5
Zbraslav [CZ] 48 F4
Zbraslavice [CZ] 48 H4
Zbrašovske Aragonitové Jeskyně [CZ] 50 D5
Zbucz [PL] 38 F1
Zbuczyn Poduchowny [PL] 38 D3
Zdala [HR] 74 G5
Žďár [CZ] 48 E3
Žďár nad Sázavou [CZ] 50 B5
Zdenci [HR] 76 A6
Zdenska Vas [SLO] 74 C5
Zdiby [CZ] 48 F3
Zdice [CZ] 48 F4
Ždírec nad Doubrava [CZ] 50 A5
Zdounky [CZ] 50 D6
Zdunje [MK] 128 D1
Zduńska Wola [PL] 36 F5
Zduny [PL] 36 D5
Zduny [PL] 36 H3
Zdziechowice [PL] 52 E1
Zdzieszowice [PL] 50 E3
Žebrák [CZ] 48 E4
Zebreira [P] 86 G4
Zebrzydowa [PL] 34 H6
Zeddiani [I] 118 C5
Žednik [SRB] 76 D5
Zeebrugge [B] 28 G1
Zeewolde [NL] 16 E4
Zefyría [GR] 138 D4
Żegiestów-Zdrój [PL] 52 C5
Zehdenick [D] 20 D6
Zeil [D] 60 B5
Zeist [NL] 16 E5
Zeitz [D] 34 C6
Żelazna [PL] 22 D1
Żelazna Góra [PL] 22 G2
Żelechów [PL] 38 D4
Zelená Hora [CZ] 48 E5
Zelena morava [BG] 148 D3
Zelenika [MNE] 144 D4
Zelenogorsk [RUS] 178 G4
Zelenogradsk [RUS] 200 C5
Želetava [CZ] 50 A6
Železná [CZ] 48 C5
Železná Ruda [CZ] 48 D6
Železnik [SRB] 142 G3
Železniki [SLO] 74 B4
Železný Brod [CZ] 48 H2
Zelhem [NL] 16 F5
Želiezovce [SK] 64 B5
Želin [SLO] 74 A5
Zelina [HR] 74 F5
Zélio [GR] 132 H4
Želiv [CZ] 48 H5
Zelizna [PL] 38 E4
Żelkowo [PL] 22 C2
Zell [A] 62 A4
Zell [D] 44 G2
Zell [D] 58 E4
Zella [D] 32 G5
Zella-Mehlis [D] 46 G2
Zell am See [A] 72 F1
Zell am Ziller [A] 72 E1
Želnava [CZ] 62 B2
Zelów [PL] 36 G5
Zeltini [LV] 198 F4
Zeltweg [A] 74 C2
Želva [LT] 200 G5
Zelwa [PL] 24 F3
Zelzate [B] 28 H1
Žemaičiu Naumiestis [LT] 200 D5
Žemberovce [SK] 64 C4
Zemblak [AL] 128 D4
Zeme [I] 70 F5
Zemen [BG] 146 F5
Zemite [LV] 198 C5
Zemmer [D] 44 G2
Zemplinske Jastrabie [SK] 64 H3
Zemplíriská Teplica [SK] 64 G3
Zemun [SRB] 142 G2
Zenica [BIH] 142 D4
Žepa [BIH] 142 E4
Zepče [BIH] 142 D3
Zerbst [D] 34 C3
Żerczyce [PL] 38 E2
Zerevna [BG] 148 D4
Zerf [D] 44 F3
Zeri [I] 110 C3
Zerind [RO] 76 G3
Zermatt [CH] 70 D3
Zernez [CH] 72 B2
Zernien [D] 18 H6
Żerniki [PL] 36 C6
Zerqan [AL] 128 C2
Zestoa / Cestona [E] 84 A2
Žetale [SLO] 74 E4
Zetel [D] 18 C4
Zeulenroda [D] 48 B2
Zeven [D] 18 E5
Zevenaar [NL] 16 F5
Zevenergen [NL] 16 C6
Zevgaráki [GR] 132 E5
Zeybekçayırı [TR] 150 C6
Zeytinbaği [TR] 150 E3
Zeytindağ [TR] 152 C3
Zeytinli [TR] 152 C1
Zgierz [PL] 36 G4
Zg. Jezersko [SLO] 74 B4
Zgniłocha [PL] 22 H4
Zgórsko [PL] 52 C3
Zgorzelec [PL] 34 G6
Zg. Polskava [SLO] 74 D4
Zg. Polskava [SLO] 74 D4
Zhabinka [BY] 38 G2
Zhaludok [BY] 24 H4
Zhashkiv [UA] 202 D8
Zhedricy [RUS] 198 H4
Zhelezna [BG] 146 F3
Zheleznitsa [BG] 146 F5
Zheleznodorozhnyj [RUS] 24 B2
Zheleznogorsk [RUS] 202 F5
Zheleznya [RUS] 202 F4
Zhilentsi [BG] 146 E6
Zhitnica [BG] 148 B5
Zhitom i Madh [AL] 128 B5
Zhitosvyat [BG] 148 E4
Zhlobin [BY] 202 C6
Zhmerynka [UA] 202 C8
Zhodzina [BY] 202 C5
Zhoř [CZ] 48 D5
Zhovkva [UA] 52 H3
Zhovten' [UA] 204 F3
Zhovtneve [UA] 52 H1
Zhuprany [BY] 200 H6
Zhvtkavichy [BY] 202 C6
Zhydachiv [UA] 52 H5
Zhytomyr [UA] 202 C7
Žiar nad Hronom [SK] 64 C3
Zicavo [F] 114 B5
Zickhusen [D] 20 A4
Zidani Most [SLO] 74 D5
Ziddorf [D] 20 C4
Židlochovice [CZ] 62 F2
Ziębice [PL] 50 C2
Ziegenrück [D] 46 H2
Zieleniec Duży [PL] 24 B5
Zielona Chocina [PL] 22 C4
Zielona Góra [PL] 34 H4
Zielonczyn [PL] 20 F4

Zielonka [PL] 38 B3
Zieluń [PL] 22 G6
Ziemupe [LV] 198 B5
Zierenberg [D] 32 E5
Zierikzee [NL] 16 B6
Ziersdorf [A] 62 E3
Zierzow [D] 20 A5
Ziesar [D] 34 C3
Ziethen [D] 20 D4
Žiežmariai [LT] 200 F5
Žīguri [LV] 198 G4
Zijpe [NL] 16 C6
Žilina [SK] 50 F6
Ziliz [H] 64 F4
Zilupe [LV] 198 G5
Zimandu Nou [RO] 76 G4
Zimna Woda [PL] 22 H5
Zimnicea [RO] 148 C2
Zimnitsa [BG] 148 E4
Zinal [CH] 70 D3
Zingst [D] 20 C2
Zinnowitz [D] 20 E3
Zinnwald-Georgenfeld [D] 48 E2
Zinzulusa, Grotta- [I] 122 H5
Zipári [GR] 154 B2
Zirc [H] 76 A2
Zirchow [D] 20 E4
Žiri [SLO] 74 B5
Zirl [A] 72 D1
Zíros [GR] 140 G5
Žirovnice [CZ] 48 G6
Zistersdorf [A] 62 F3
Žitište [SRB] 142 G1
Žitkovac [SRB] 146 D3
Žitni Potok [SRB] 146 D4
Žitomislići [BIH] 144 C2
Žitoradja [SRB] 146 D4
Zítsa [GR] 132 C2
Zittau [D] 48 G1
Živaja [HR] 142 B1
Živinice [BIH] 142 E3
Živogošće [HR] 144 B2
Ziyamet (Leonarisso) [CY] 154 G4
Zizers [CH] 70 H1
Zlata [SRB] 146 D4
Zlatá Baňa [SK] 64 G2
Zlatá Koruna [CZ] 62 B2
Zlatar [BG] 148 E3
Zlatar Bistrica [HR] 74 E5
Zlatarevo [BG] 128 H2
Zlatari [SRB] 146 C3
Zlaté Hory [CZ] 50 D3
Zlaté Klasy [SK] 62 H4
Zlaté Moravce [SK] 64 B4
Zlatitsa [BG] 148 A4
Zlati voyvoda [BG] 148 D4
Zlatná na Ostrove [SK] 64 A5
Zlatna Panega [BG] 148 A4
Zlatni Pyasŭtsi [BG] 148 G2
Zlatograd [BG] 130 E2
Žleby [CZ] 48 H4
Zliechov [SK] 64 B2
Zlín [CZ] 50 D6
Žljebovi [BIH] 142 E4
Złocieniec [PL] 20 H5
Złoczew [PL] 36 F5
Zlogoš [BG] 146 E5
Zlonice [CZ] 48 F3
Zlot [SRB] 146 D2
Złotniki Kujawskie [PL] 36 E1
Złotoryja [PL] 36 B6
Złotów [PL] 22 B5
Zlotska Pećina [SRB] 146 D2
Złoty Stok [PL] 50 C3
Žlutice [CZ] 48 D3
Zlynka [RUS] 202 D6
Zmajevac [HR] 76 C5
Zmievka [RUS] 202 F5
Żmigród [PL] 36 C5
Žminj [HR] 112 D2
Zmiyevka [RUS] 202 F5
Zmysłowo [PL] 36 C4
Znamenka [RUS] 198 G3
Znamensk [RUS] 24 B1
Znamianka [UA] 202 F8
Zniev [SK] 64 B2
Żnin [PL] 36 D1
Znojmo [CZ] 62 E3
Zoetermeer [NL] 16 C5
Zoeterwoude [NL] 16 C5
Zofingen [CH] 58 E5
Zogaj [AL] 146 B6
Zolder [B] 30 E4
Żółkiewka-Osada [PL] 38 E6
Zölkow [D] 20 B4
Zollchow [D] 20 E5
Zolotonosha [UA] 202 E7
Żółtki [PL] 24 E5
Zomba [H] 76 B4
Zonhoven [B] 30 E4
Zóni [GR] 130 G1
Zonza [F] 114 B5
Zoo Svatý Kopeček [CZ] 50 D5
Zörbig [D] 34 C4
Zorge [D] 32 H4
Zorita [E] 96 B2
Zorneding [D] 60 E4
Zornitsa [BG] 148 E5
Żory [PL] 50 F4
Zossen [D] 34 E3
Zoutkamp [NL] 16 G2
Zoutleeuw [B] 30 D4
Zoúzouli [GR] 128 D6
Zovka [RUS] 198 G2
Zreče [SLO] 74 D4
Zrenjanin [SRB] 142 G1
Zrenjanin [SRB] 204 B5
Zrinski Topolovac [HR] 74 F5
Zrmanja [HR] 112 H5
Zrnovci [MK] 128 G1
Zruč nad Sázavou [CZ] 48 G4
Zrze [SRB] 146 B6
Zsadány [H] 76 G2
Zsámbék [H] 64 C6
Zsana [H] 76 D4
Zschopau [D] 48 D2
Zuani [F] 114 C4
Zuberec [SK] 50 H6
Zubin Potok [SRB] 146 B4
Zubiri [E] 84 B3
Zubné [SK] 52 E6
Zubříč [CZ] 50 E5
Zubrzyca Górna [PL] 50 H5
Zubtsov [RUS] 202 E3
Zudar [D] 20 D2
Zuera [E] 90 E3
Zug [CH] 58 F5
Zuidhorn [NL] 16 G2
Zuidlaren [NL] 16 G2
Zújar [E] 102 F3
Żukow [PL] 38 F4
Żukowo [PL] 22 D2
Žulová [CZ] 50 C3
Zülpich [D] 30 G5
Zumaia / Zumaya [E] 84 A2
Zumarraga [E] 82 H4
Zumaya / Zumaia [E] 84 A2
Žumberk [CZ] 62 C3
Zundert [NL] 30 D2
Zuoz [CH] 72 A3
Žur [SRB] 146 B6
Żurawica [PL] 52 F4
Zürich [CH] 58 F5
Żuromin [PL] 22 G6
Żurrieq [M] 126 C6
Zürs [A] 72 B1
Zurzach [CH] 58 F4
Zusmarshausen [D] 60 C3
Züsow [D] 20 A3
Züssow [D] 20 D3
Žuta Lokva [HR] 112 F2
Zutphen [NL] 16 F5
Zuyevo [RUS] 202 C1
Žužemberk [SLO] 74 C5
Zvarisht [AL] 128 C4
Zvečka [SRB] 142 G3
Zvenimir [BG] 148 E1
Zvenyhorodka [UA] 202 E8
Zverevo [RUS] 178 F3
Zvěřínek [CZ] 48 F5
Zvezdel [BG] 130 F1
Zvezdets [BG] 148 F5
Zvíkov [CZ] 48 F5
Zvolen [SK] 64 C3
Zvonce [SRB] 146 E4
Zvornik [BIH] 142 E3
Zweibrücken [D] 44 G4
Zweisimmen [CH] 70 D1
Zwettl [A] 62 D3
Zwettl an der Rodl [A] 62 B3
Zwickau [D] 48 C2
Zwiefalten [D] 58 H3
Zwierzno [PL] 22 F3
Zwierzyniec [PL] 52 F2
Zwiesel [D] 60 H2
Zwijndrecht [NL] 16 D5
Zwingenberg [D] 46 D5
Zwoleń [PL] 38 C5
Zwolle [NL] 16 F4
Żychlin [PL] 36 G3
Życiny [PL] 52 C2
Żydowo [PL] 36 D2
Zyel'va [BY] 24 H5
Zýgi [CY] 154 G6
Żyrardów [PL] 38 A3
Żywiec [PL] 50 G5
Żywocice [PL] 50 E3

9th edition November 2007

Original edition printed 1996

Published by ISTITUTO GEOGRAFICO DE AGOSTINI, Novara and Automobile Association Developments Limited whose registered office is Fanum House, Basing View, Basingstoke, Hampshire RG21 4EA, UK. Registered number 1878835.

ISBN-13: 978 0 7495 5451 4 (flexibound)
ISBN-10: 0 7495 5451 7
ISBN-13: 978 0 7495 5450 7 (wire bound)
ISBN-10: 0 7495 5450 9

A CIP catalogue record for this book is available from The British Library.

Printed in Italy by Canale & C. S.P.A., Torino on paper from EMAS (Eco Management and Audit Scheme) registered paper mills.
Paper: 90gsm Presto Silk.

ROAD DISTANCES
DISTANZE STRADALI
DISTANCIAS KILOMÉTRICAS
DISTANCES ROUTIÈRES
STRASSENENTFERNUNGEN

Frankfurt am Main-Ljubljana = 804 km

Amsterdam	Athina	Barcelona	Belfast	Beograd	Berlin	Bern	Birmingham	Bordeaux	Bratislava	Brussel/Bruxelles	Bucureşti	Budapest	Dublin	Edinburgh	Frankfurt am Main	Genève	Göteborg	Hamburg	Helsinki/Helsingfors	İstanbul	København	Köln	Kyïv	Lisboa	Ljubljana	London	Luxembourg	
2760																												
1557	2520																											
1312	3520	2265																										
1718	1044	1981	2816																									
655	2288	1863	1868	1247																								
838	1971	944	1725	1363	922																							
738	3285	1691	582	2244	1295	1152																						
1091	3049	552	1815	2007	1634	852	1241																					
1225	1618	1866	2324	577	671	938	1750	1879																				
206	2568	1355	1148	1673	763	637	574	883	1181																			
2181	1106	2597	3279	619	1646	1893	2706	2613	977	2136																		
1398	1429	1897	2497	388	864	1111	1923	2053	194	1353	788																	
1088	3455	2041	164	2594	1644	1502	358	1585	2101	925	3057	2274																
1190	3557	2143	305	2695	1746	1603	460	1686	2203	1026	3159	2376	468															
445	2323	1323	1545	1281	565	423	971	1150	788	400	1744	961	1321	1422														
908	2372	778	1683	1331	1072	165	1109	687	1088	706	1946	1261	1457	1561	573													
1178	3131	2479	2412	2090	823	1637	1839	2185	1514	1307	2490	1708	2187	2290	1214	1787												
463	2602	1763	1696	1561	294	910	1123	1470	985	591	1961	1178	1471	1574	487	1059	728											
2580	3590	3788	3792	2641	1959	2847	3220	3551	2208	2687	2483	2252	3567	3670	2489	2996	982	2192										
2649	1092	2913	3748	935	2179	2294	3175	2929	1509	2605	681	1320	3522	3626	2213	2261	3022	2493	3164									
920	2873	2220	2153	1832	564	1378	1580	1927	1255	1048	2231	1449	1928	2031	955	1528	269	469	1123	2764								
265	2506	1342	1352	1464	575	585	778	1062	972	208	1928	1145	1126	1230	192	735	1141	425	2500	2396	882							
2016	1994	3093	3228	1322	1398	2190	2655	2988	1251	2123	888	1123	3003	3106	1884	2340	2211	1681	1595	1569	1952	1935						
2296	3787	1237	3019	3188	2838	2150	2446	1202	3090	2095	3804	3103	2793	2897	2355	1989	3397	2681	4764	4119	3138	2273	4199					
1241	1572	1455	2294	530	999	836	1721	1471	435	1153	1146	443	2069	2173	804	803	1916	1203	2623	1462	1656	987	1565	2661				
533	2910	1486	766	2039	1090	947	193	1030	1546	370	2502	1719	541	645	766	905	1634	918	3015	2970	1375	574	2450	2243	1537			
386	2355	1149	1355	1469	762	431	782	946	1010	213	1965	1183	1129	1233	240	500	1326	610	2687	2401	1066	188	2081	2159	956	582		
1800	3145	614	2523	2573	2343	1535	1950	706	2458	1599	3189	2489	2298	2402	1859	1374	2901	2185	4268	3505	2642	1778	3684	619	2046	1750	1662	
868	3415	1821	461	2374	1425	1282	138	1365	1881	705	2837	2054	310	339	1101	1240	1969	1253	3350	3305	1710	909	2785	2578	1872	323	911	20
1236	2567	505	2003	1526	1541	623	1429	654	1419	1034	2141	1441	1778	1881	1003	422	2158	1442	3467	2457	1899	1025	2564	1711	999	1230	832	10
1077	1218	977	1963	1026	1033	350	1390	985	919	876	1642	942	1737	1841	662	317	1833	1120	2959	1958	1574	823	2064	2182	499	1190	669	15
1742	2448	2878	2955	1513	1124	1938	2381	2714	1178	1850	1341	1125	2729	2833	1620	2088	1938	1408	1183	2023	1678	1662	557	3927	1593	2181	1817	34
2449	2864	3584	3661	2084	1830	2644	3088	3420	1885	2556	1758	1831	3435	3539	2326	2794	2643	2114	1116	2440	2385	2368	871	4364	2300	2888	2523	41
827	1990	1370	1880	949	585	442	1297	1278	466	739	1421	639	1655	1759	390	591	1502	789	2511	1880	1242	573	1718	2576	435	1107	521	19
1859	597	1555	2746	1483	1693	1132	2173	1704	1376	1658	2099	1399	2521	2624	1444	1085	2586	1874	3563	2415	2327	1606	2521	2761	956	1973	1476	21
1490	3443	2790	2723	2402	1134	1949	2150	2497	1826	1618	2801	2019	2498	2601	1525	2098	315	1039	1030	3333	580	1446	2522	3710	2248	1950	1636	32
525	2465	1039	1248	1800	1068	592	659	583	1340	324	2295	1513	1023	1126	604	529	1626	910	2993	2732	1367	502	2428	1796	1287	475	407	13
2094	4028	1076	2818	2986	2637	1948	2244	1000	2889	1893	3602	2902	2592	2696	2153	1788	3196	2480	4563	3918	2936	2072	3997	300	2459	2044	1956	5
891	1946	1709	2045	904	341	769	1471	1601	328	902	1304	522	1820	1923	510	919	1186	657	2178	1836	927	693	1389	2814	664	1272	731	23
1618	2807	2825	2830	1766	996	1885	2257	2590	1333	1725	1676	1378	2604	2708	1527	2035	1760	1230	962	2357	1501	1537	1029	3803	1748	2057	1724	33
1658	1190	1354	2545	1282	1493	932	1972	1503	1175	1457	1898	1198	2320	2423	1243	884	2386	1673	3363	2214	2126	1405	2321	2560	755	1772	1275	19
2180	3190	3388	3393	2241	1558	2447	2819	3152	1809	2288	2084	1853	3167	3271	2089	2597	2284	1793	387	2765	2063	2099	1196	4365	2223	2619	2286	38
1727	1121	1990	2826	303	1389	1372	2252	2007	707	1682	824	539	2600	2704	1290	1339	2402	1644	2791	1113	2143	1474	1601	3196	539	2052	1478	25
2277	3998	998	3000	2957	2838	1919	2427	1183	2842	2076	3573	2873	2775	2878	2299	1759	3378	2662	4763	3889	3119	2255	4068	403	2430	2227	2128	5
2139	654	2402	3237	424	1668	1783	2664	2418	998	2094	598	809	3012	3115	1702	1750	2512	1982	3061	781	2253	1885	1485	3608	951	2464	1890	29
2095	735	2358	3193	380	1624	1739	2620	2375	954	2050	372	765	2968	3071	1658	1707	2468	1938	2854	555	2209	1841	1259	3564	907	2420	1846	29
1534	3488	2835	2768	2446	1175	1993	2195	2541	1870	1663	2846	2064	2543	2646	1570	2143	481	1084	505	3378	624	1497	2566	3755	2293	1995	1681	32
1920	3105	3127	3132	2063	1298	2187	2559	2892	1631	2027	1973	1675	2907	3011	1829	2337	2062	1533	90	2654	1803	1839	1326	4105	2046	2359	2026	36
2333	454	2597	3432	619	1862	1978	2858	2613	1193	2288	656	1004	3207	3310	1896	1945	2707	2177	3139	642	2447	2080	1543	3802	1145	2658	2085	31
2103	735	2366	3201	606	1765	1748	2628	2383	1083	2058	886	915	2976	3163	1666	1715	2778	2020	3167	1069	2518	1849	1773	3572	915	2428	1854	29
3071	4692	4371	4304	3743	2715	3529	3731	4078	3311	3199	3586	3355	4114	4182	3106	3679	1949	2620	1360	4267	2160	3033	2698	5291	3829	3531	3217	47
1897	3363	363	2603	2322	2202	1283	2030	803	2206	1695	2937	2237	2378	2482	1663	1123	2819	2103	4128	3253	2560	1686	3433	894	1795	1830	1492	3
1636	2550	2776	2849	1509	1018	1836	2275	2608	1077	1744	1384	1121	2623	2727	1518	1986	1733	1203	1142	2066	1474	1555	738	3821	1492	2075	1715	33
1202	2097	2342	2414	1056	584	1402	1841	2174	643	1309	1240	668	2189	2293	1084	1552	1397	868	1566	1922	1138	1121	815	3387	1057	1641	1281	28
1148	1664	1789	2246	622	629	861	1673	1802	66	1103	1022	240	2021	2125	711	1010	1473	943	2246	1554	1214	895	1319	3016	378	1473	933	23
1326	1435	1586	2424	394	988	968	1852	1603	417	1281	1009	347	2199	2302	889	936	2001	1243	2604	1325	1741	1073	1470	2793	135	1647	1074	21

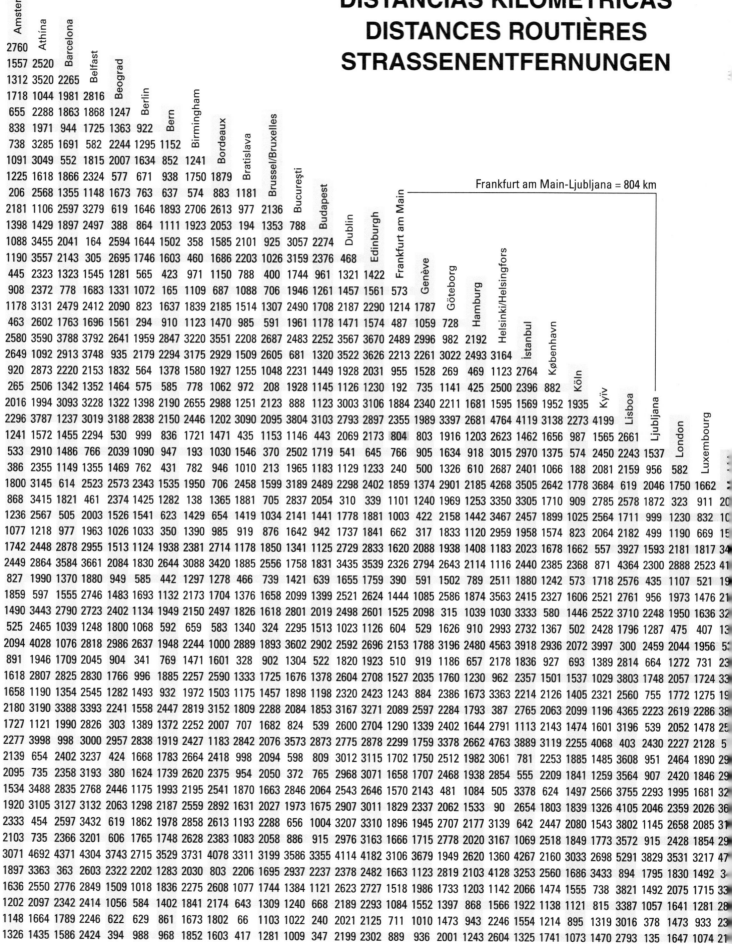